June 5–8, 2010
Cambridge, MA, USA

Association for Computing Machinery

Advancing Computing as a Science & Profession

STOC'10

Proceedings of the 2010 ACM International Symposium on Theory of Computing

Sponsored by:

ACM SIGACT

Supported by:

Microsoft Research, Google, NEC, & IBM

Association for
Computing Machinery

Advancing Computing as a Science & Profession

The Association for Computing Machinery
2 Penn Plaza, Suite 701
New York, New York 10121-0701

Notice to Past Authors of ACM-Published Articles
ACM intends to create a complete electronic archive of all articles and/or other material previously published by ACM. If you have written a work that has been previously published by ACM in any journal or conference proceedings prior to 1978, or any SIG Newsletter at any time, and you do NOT want this work to appear in the ACM Digital Library, please inform permissions@acm.org, stating the title of the work, the author(s), and where and when published.

ISBN: 978-1-60558-817-9

Additional copies may be ordered prepaid from:

ACM Order Department
PO Box 30777
New York, NY 10087-0777, USA

Phone: 1-800-342-6626 (USA and Canada)
+1-212-626-0500 (Global)
Fax: +1-212-944-1318
E-mail: acmhelp@acm.org
Hours of Operation: 8:30 am – 4:30 pm ET

ACM Order Number 508100

Printed in the USA

Foreword

The papers in this volume were presented at the 42nd ACM Symposium on Theory of Computing (STOC), held June 6-8, 2010 in Cambridge, Massachusetts, and sponsored by the ACM Special Interest Group on Algorithms and Computation Theory (SIGACT).

The papers at the Symposium were selected by the program committee from among 279 submissions. The committee's initial discussions were carried out electronically, and final decisions were made in a physical meeting of the committee on the Caltech campus on February 1–2. Following a merge of two papers with similar results and methods, the number of papers in the symposium stands at 78. All submissions received careful consideration, but they were not refereed in a formal sense. In addition, due to the page limit, many accepted papers appear in these Proceedings only in abbreviated form. Authors are encouraged to submit full versions of their papers for publication in journals.

The committee selected two papers for a Best Paper Award: "QIP=PSPACE," by Rahul Jain, Zhengfeng Ji, Sarvagya Upadhyay and John Watrous, and "An Improved LP-based Approximation for Steiner Tree," by Jaroslaw Byrka, Fabrizio Grandoni, Thomas Rothvoß and Laura Sanità. The committee selected "Augmenting Undirected Node-Connectivity by One" by László A. Végh for the Danny Lewin Best Student Paper Award.

The committee invited three leading researchers to present tutorials on the day preceding STOC. Ravindran Kannan spoke on "Spectral Methods for Matrices and Tensors," Michel Talagrand spoke on "Are Many Small Sets Explicitly Small?," and Andrea Montanari spoke on "Message Passing Algorithms: a Success Looking for Theoreticians." A paper associated with each tutorial is included in these Proceedings.

The 10th Knuth Prize was awarded to David S. Johnson for seminal contributions to the theoretical and experimental analysis of combinatorial algorithms. He presented the Knuth Prize Lecture on the afternoon of June 7.

The organization of STOC depends on the efforts of many people. I thank, above all, the members of the program committee, whose work was thorough and thoughtful at every step of the way. Thanks also to the external reviewers, without whose expert advice we could not have done our job properly. Most of the reviewers' names are listed in these Proceedings. The work of the committee was facilitated by Shai Halevi's conference software, and I am grateful to Shai for responding with alacrity to my questions. For their assistance with many items large and small thanks are due also to Richard Ladner and Lance Fortnow (the former and current SIGACT chairs), to the members of the local arrangements committee, and to Lisa Tolles of Sheridan Printing. Last but not least, thanks to my secretary Maria Lopez, who organized the PC meeting.

Theoretical Computer Science is a remarkable entwinement of current mathematical thought with computational questions, both foundational and applied. Some of the excitement of the field is, I think, evident in these Proceedings, as it also was in many excellent submissions which we could not include here.

Leonard J. Schulman
California Institute of Technology
STOC 2010 Program Chair

Table of Contents

Session 4B

Session Chair: Parikshit Gopalan *(Microsoft Research)*

Session 5A

Session Chair: Constantinos Daskalakis *(Massachusetts Institute of Technology)*

Session 5B

Session Chair: Leonard J. Schulman *(Caltech)*

Session 6A

Session Chair: Piotr Indyk *(Massachusetts Institute of Technology)*

Session 6B

Session Chair: Constantinos Daskalakis *(Massachusetts Institute of Technology)*

Session 7A

Session Chair: Valentine Kabanets *(Simon Fraser University)*

Session 7B

Session Chair: Parikshit Gopalan *(Microsoft Research)*

Session 8A

Session Chair: Ken Clarkson *(IBM Almaden Research)*

Session 8B

Session Chair: Oded Regev *(Tel Aviv)*

STOC 2010 Conference Organization

SIGACT Chair: Lance Fortnow *(Northwestern)*

Conference Chair: Michael Mitzenmacher *(Harvard)*

Program Chair: Leonard J. Schulman *(Caltech)*

Local Arrangements Committee:
Christian Borgs *(Microsoft Research)*
Jennifer Chayes *(Microsoft Research)*
Henry Cohn *(Microsoft Research)*
Erik Demaine *(Massachusetts Institute of Technology)*
Yael Tauman Kalai *(Microsoft Research)*
Paul Oka *(Microsoft Research)*

Program Committee:
Timothy Chan *(University of Waterloo)*
Ken Clarkson *(IBM Almaden Research)*
Constantinos Daskalakis *(Massachusetts Institute of Technology)*
Irit Dinur *(Weizmann Inst.)*
Faith Ellen *(University of Toronto)*
Alan Frieze *(Carnegie Mellon University)*
Parikshit Gopalan *(Microsoft Research)*
Piotr Indyk *(Massachusetts Institute of Technology)*
Valentine Kabanets *(Simon Fraser University)*
Yael Tauman Kalai *(Microsoft Research)*
Howard Karloff *(ATT Labs — Research)*
Robert Kleinberg *(Cornell)*
Assaf Naor *(NYU)*
Noam Nisan *(Hebrew University)*
Chris Peikert *(Georgia Tech)*
Jaikumar Radhakrishnan *(Tata Inst.)*
Oded Regev *(Tel Aviv)*
Alexander Russell *(University of Connecticut)*
Leonard J. Schulman, **chair** *(Caltech)*
Aravind Srinivasan *(University of Maryland)*
Santosh Vempala *(Georgia Tech)*
Andrew Yao *(Tsinghua)*

STOC 2010 External Reviewers

Ittai Abraham
Dimitris Achlioptas
Yehuda Afek
Peyman Afshani
Manindra Agrawal
Dorit Aharonov
Nir Ailon
Noga Alon
Alexandr Andoni
Spyros Angelopoulos
Spyridon Antonakopoulos
Aaron Archer
Sanjeev Arora
V Arvind
James Aspnes
Hagit Attiya
Per Austrin
Yossi Azar
Moshe Babaioff
Antar Bandyopadhyay
Nikhil Bansal
Yair Bartal
Alexander Barvinok
Mohsen Bayati
Paul Beame
Mikhail Belkin
Avraham Ben-Aroya
Michael Ben-Or
Petra Berenbrink
V Bhaskar
Avrim Blum
Liad Blumrosen
Hans Bodlaender
Andrej Bogdanov
Mikolaj Bojanczyk
Allan Borodin
Glencora Borradaile
Zvika Brakerski
Mark Braverman
Niv Buchbinder
Andrei Bulatov
Jin-Yi Cai
Gruia Calinescu
Emmanuel Candes
Moses Charikar
Arkadev Chattopadhyay
Bernard Chazelle
Chandra Chekuri
Chao Chen
Victor Chen
Xi Chen
Joseph Cheriyan
Steve Chien
Eden Chlamtac
Bogdan Chlebus
Maria Chudnovsky
Henry Cohn
Amin Coja-Oghlan
Thomas Colcombet
Richard Cole
Matthew Cook
Gerard Cornuejols
Nadia Creignou
Mary Cryan
Artur Czumaj
Xiaotie Deng
Nikhil Devanur
Alex Dimakis
Ajit Diwan
Shahar Dobzinski
Yevgeniy Dodis
Martin Dyer
Jeff Edmonds
Klim Efremenko
Edith Elkind
Ioannis Emiris
Jittat Fakcharoenphol
Uri Feige
Amos Fiat
Lance Fortnow
Nikolaos Fountoulakis
Pierre Fraigniaud
Oliver Friedmann
Eli Gafni
David Gamarnik
Juan A. Garay
Jim Geelen
Yoav Giora
Clint Givens
Ashish Goel
Gagan Goel
Michel Goemans
Leslie Ann Goldberg
Shafi Goldwasser
Michael Goodrich
Prasant Gopal
Manoj Gopalkrishnan
Navin Goyal
Ben Green
Elena Grigorescu
Sudipto Guha
Jiong Guo
Anupam Gupta
Venkatesan Guruswami
Vassos Hadzilacos
Nir Halman
Sariel Har-Peled
Prahladh Harsha
Jason Hartline
Avinatan Hassidim
Ishay Haviv
Tom Hayes
Elad Hazan
Iftach Ilan Heitner
Maurice Herlihy
Lisa Higham
Thore Husfeldt
Sandra Irani
Yuval Ishai
Pino Italiano
Kamal Jain
Rahul Jain
Svante Janson
Mark Jerrum
Ramesh Johari
David Johnson
Sham Kakade
Adam Kalai
Satyen Kale
Ravi Kannan
Haim Kaplan
Sanjiv Kapoor
Anna Karlin
Dmitriy Katz
Jonathan Katz
Tali Kaufman
Neeraj Kayal
Jon Kelner
Jonathan Kelner
David Kempe
Rohit Khandekar
Sanjeev Khanna
Subhash Khot
Guy Kindler
Valerie King
Philip Klein
Jon Kleinberg
Jochen Koenemann
Marcin Kozik
Robert Krauthgamer
Michael Krivelevich
Hari Krovi
Fabian Kuhn
Michael Langberg
Massimo Lauria
Ron Lavi
James Lee
Jon Lee
Lap-Kei Lee
Troy Lee
Daniel Lehmann
Asaf Levin
Lionel Levine
Xin Li
Leonid Libkin
Katrina Ligett
Yehuda Lindell
Christof Loeding
Daniel Lokshtanov
Shachar Lovett
Nancy Lynch
Vadim Lyubashevsky
Bin Ma
Konstantin Makarychev
Yury Makarychev
Sebastian Maneth

Yishay Mansour
Fabio Martinelli
Claire Mathieu
Jiri Matousek
Kevin Matulef
Marios Mavronicolas
Colin McDiarmid
Andrew McGregor
Frank McSherry
Manor Mendel
Daniele Micciancio
Peter bro Miltersen
Vahab Mirrokni
Joe Mitchell
Michael Mitzenmacher
Ankur Moitra
Michael Molloy
Ravi Montenegro
Cristopher Moore
Herve Moulin
Ian Munro
S Muthukrishnan
Steven Myers
Asaf Nachmias
Serban Nacu
Viswanath Nagarajan
Satyadev Nandakumar
Moni Naor
Hari Narayanan
Ofer Neiman
Jaroslav Nesetril
Calvin Newport
Van Nguyen
Kobbi Nissim
Sergey Norin
Yahav Nussbaum
Zeev Nutov
Krzyzstof Onak
Rotem Oshman
Rafail Ostrovsky
Mallesh Pai
Gopal Pandurangan
Rina Panigrahy
Gyula Pap
Luis Miguel Pardo
Rafael Pass
Mihai Patrascu
Ramamohan Paturi
David Peleg
Yuval Peres
Toniann Pitassi
Maria Gradinariu Potop-Butucaru
Manoj Prabhakaran
Yuval Rabani
Tal Rabin
Charles Rackoff
Harald Raecke
Prasad Raghavendra
Sergio Rajsbaum
Dana Randall
Sofya Raskhodnikova
R. Ravi
Saurabh Ray
Ran Raz
John Reif
Omer Reingold
Rennato Renner
Robert Rettinger
Adi Rosen
Alon Rosen
Aaron Roth
Guy Rothblum
Eric Ruppert
Amin Saberi
Barna Saha
Jared Saia
Michael Saks
Alex Samorodnitsky
Rahul Santhanam
Soumojit Sarkar
Atish Das Sarma
Anand Sarwate
Eli Ban Sasson
Saket Saurabh
Nitin Saxena
Christian Schaffner
Michael Schapira
Gideon Schechtman
Christian Scheideler
Russell Schwarz
Gil Segev
Pranab Sen
Sandeep Sen
Rocco Servidio
C. Seshadhri
Devavrat Shah
Ronen Shaltiel
Yogeshwer Sharma
Amin Shokrollahi
Igor Shparlinski
Amir Shplika
Tasos Sidiropoulos
Somnath Sikdar
Alistair Sinclair
Mohit Singh
Allan Sly
Adam Smith
Anthony Man-Cho So
Milind Sohoni
David Soloveichik
Daniel Spielman
Srikanth Srinivasan
Anand Srivastav
Nikhil Srivastava
Angelika Steger
Bernard von Stengel
David Steurer
Lakshminarayanan Subramanian
Mario Szegedy
Amnon Ta-Shma
Kunal Talwar
Siamak Tazari
Shanghua Teng
Moshe Tennenholtz
Prasad Tetali
Jayram Thathachar
Robin Thomas
Dimitrios Thilikos
Corentin Travers
Michael Trick
Christopher Umans
Eli Upfal
Salil Vadhan
Yevgeniy Vahlis
Vinod Vaikuntanathan
Leslie Valiant
Serguei Vassilvitskii
Juan Vera
Elad Verbin
Frank Verstraete
Eric Vigoda
Nisheeth Vishnoi
Sundar Vishwanathan
Jan Vondrak
John Watrous
Klaus Weihrauch
Oren Weimann
Ryan Williams
David Wilson
Philipp Woelfel
Ronald de Wolf
David Woodruff
Amir Yehudayoff
Sergey Yekhanin
Neal Young
Michele Zito
David Zuckerman
Uri Zwick

STOC 2010 Sponsor & Supporters

Sponsor: SIGACT

Platinum Supporter: Microsoft® Research

Gold Supporter: Google™

Silver Supporter: NEC

Friends: IBM®

Spectral Methods for Matrices and Tensors

Ravindran Kannan
Microsoft Research Labs., India *

ABSTRACT

While Spectral Methods have long been used for Principal Component Analysis, this survey focusses on work over the last 15 years with three salient features: (i) Spectral methods are useful not only for numerical problems, but also discrete optimization problems (Constraint Optimization Problems - CSP's) like the max. cut problem and similar mathematical considerations underlie both areas. (ii) Spectral methods can be extended to tensors. The theory and algorithms for tensors are not as simple/clean as for matrices, but the survey describes methods for low-rank approximation which extend to tensors. These tensor approximations help us solve Max-r-CSP's for $r > 2$ as well as numerical tensor problems. (iii) Sampling on the fly plays a prominent role in these methods. A primary result is that for any matrix, a random submatrix of rows/columns picked with probabilities proportional to the squared lengths (of rows/columns), yields estimates of the singular values as well as an approximation to the whole matrix.

Categories and Subject Descriptors

F.2.1 [**Computations on Matrices**]; G.3 [**Probabilistic Algorithms**]

General Terms

Algorithms

1. INTRODUCTION

Spectral methods have been widely used in many areas for Numerical problems under the name Principal Component Analysis. The algorithmic use of spectral methods for discrete problems is perhaps more recent. The first point of this survey is to suggest that similar mathematical considerations motivate both discrete and numerical applications.

*196/36 Second Main
Sadashivanagar, Bangalore 560080, India
kannan@microsoft.com

STOC'10, June 5–8, 2010, Cambridge, Massachusetts, USA.

Our second point is the extension of algorithms to tensors. Linear Algebra is unique in that it has beautiful theory which also translates to efficient as well as optimal algorithms. Tensors admit no such comparable theory or algorithms; indeed, some impossibility or hardness results are known for tensors. This is not our focus. Instead, we want to see what is algorithmically possible with tensors, of course, having to be less ambitious than for matrices. [But we seek provable error bounds.] The second purpose of this survey, then, is to present methods for matrices which extend to naturally to tensors. Two methods surveyed here - the Cut Norm introduced in section 2 and Length-Squared sampling procedure introduced in section 5 both have this flavor.

The third main point of the survey is faster randomized algorithms for large matrices (based on sampling) than traditional numerical algorithms; here length-squared sampling provides a starting point. Besides improving running time through sampling, one operates in a model where the massive matrices cannot be stored in Random Access Memory, but must be read and sampled on the fly. Several newer sampling procedures are also covered in section 7. Many open questions remain both in regard to algorithms and computational applications. We will list them in the text, but, here we mention two generic challenges to highlight possible directions for research.

Challenge 1: Find the spectrum of the web graph. The web graph (of hypertext links, for example) is a large "naturally occurring" graph. It is directed and so the adjacency matrix is not symmetric. The question is to find the singular values approximately. We will see that the randomized algorithms in the survey could be useful for this. But the provable upper bounds on sample size are too large. Can smaller sample sizes suffice ? We want a certificate on the error bound and confidence (probability of correctness) of the spectrum (say at least of the largest several hundred singular values) as computed for the particular matrix. [In a sense, this is seeking to make a Monte-Carlo algorithm into a Las Vegas one.] The motivation for the particular question is: there is much research on statistical properties of the web graph. But most, pertain to "local properties" - degree distribution (which is local in that we find the degree of one vertex at a time), local communities (in a neighborhood of one vertex), etc. The top singular value is a measure of "global" correlation. Further, the important notion of pagerank [BP98] as well as Kleinberg's HITS algorithm [Kle99] of course have links to the spectrum of the graph.

Challenge II Better provable Algorithms for Tensors

The second challenge is: while the methods here make a beginning in dealing with tensors much research remains to be done on algorithms for tensors. We seek better methods for maximizing (approximately) cubic and higher order forms (especially when there are unusually good solutions) and finding low-rank approximations to tensors faster.

Some notation For a matrix A, the Frobenius norm $||A||_F$ is the square root of the sum of the squares of its entries. The spectral norm $||A||_2$ is $\max_{x:|x|=1}|Ax|$. The abbreviation u.a.r stands for "uniformly at random". ϵ will be a positive error parameter. The material in sections 4 onwards (which may be read more or less independently of the earlier sections) is covered in greater detail in the monograph [KV08]. Spectral Graph Partitioning (starting with Fiedler's work [Fie75]) and many other important topics which are well covered elsewhere are not dealt with here.

2. APPROXIMATION OF MATRICES IN CUT-NORM, APPLICATIONS

Instead of the traditional low-rank approximations to matrices, we start with a form more suited to discrete applications. For an $m \times n$ matrix, a "rectangle" will mean one of the 2^{m+n} sets of the form (a subset of rows) $\times$ (a subset of columns). A "cut matrix" is an $m \times n$ matrix with all its entries in some rectangle equal and all entries outside this rectangle being zero; it is special rank 1 matrix. Our approximation to a matrix is by a sum of cut matrices. These approximations have the following desirable properties:

1. It is very easy to show they exist.
2. They can be found (and this in non-trivial) in polynomial, in fact in constant time (implicitly) with uniform random sample of $O(1)$ entries from the matrix.
3. Using this, one can solve the maximum cut problem to additive error $\epsilon n^2 M$ on n node graphs with maximum edge weight M. [This also extends to all MAX-2-CSP's.]
4. Both the existence as well as the algorithmic version (in constant time) can be extended to tensors and using this, one can approximately solve MAX-r-SAT for fixed r and other problems.

This is all described in this section. The main caveat for these methods is the error of $\epsilon n^2 M$. There are many applications where this is not good enough. In the discrete optimization setting (say as in Max Cut), if $M=1$, the max cut needs to be $\Omega(n^2)$ or equivalently, the graph needs to be dense for this error to be useful. Of course, many interesting problems are not dense. A similar situation holds for PCA as well. Section 4 describes a more amenable error bound for both these areas and how to achieve it using non-uniform sampling and thus address application issues.

A, B will stand for $m \times n$ matrices. If S is a subset of rows and T a subset of columns, then, we let

$$A(S,T) = \sum_{i\in S, j\in T} A_{ij}.$$

Define the "cut norm" of $||A||_\Box$ by

$$||A||_\Box = \mathrm{MAX}_{S,T}|A(S,T)|.$$

LEMMA 1. *Assume $|A_{ij}| \leq 1$. There exist $1/\epsilon^2$ cut matrices whose sum B approximates A in the sense*

$$||A-B||_\Box \leq \epsilon mn.$$

Proof: If $||A||_\Box \leq \epsilon mn$, we can take $B=0$. Otherwise, there is some S,T such that $|A(S,T)| \geq \epsilon mn$. Our first cut matrix in B has $A(S,T)/|S||T|$ in each entry of $S\times T$ and zero elsewhere. This subtracts from each $A_{ij}, i\in S, j\in T$, their average and it is easy to show that then $\sum_{i\in S,j\in T} A_{ij}^2$ decreases by at least $\epsilon^2 mn$ and so does $||A||_F^2$. Since $||\cdot||_F \geq 0$, the process must terminate in at most $1/\epsilon^2$ steps proving the Lemma.

An immediate question is whether such a B can be found in polynomial time. An affirmative answer was given by Frieze and Kannan [FK99] and indeed, they proved that it can be found in "constant time" in a sense to made clear later.

THEOREM 1. *[FK99] For A with $|A_{ij}| \leq 1$ and any fixed $\epsilon > 0$, we can find in polynomial time a matrix B which is the sum of $4/\epsilon^2$ cut matrices and satisfies $||A-B||_\Box \leq \epsilon mn$. In fact, given the entries of A in just a u.a.r. rectangle of size $O^*(1/\epsilon^4)\times O^*(1/\epsilon^4)$, we can find an implicit description of B.*

From the proof of the Lemma (1), we see that it suffices to determine if the cut norm of A is at most ϵmn and if not, find an S,T with $|A(S,T)| \geq \epsilon mn$. The exact problem is NP-hard. However, for the theorem an approximate version suffices: find the maximum value of $|A(S,T)|$ to within additive error ϵmn. [Really $\frac{\epsilon}{2}mn$, but redefine ϵ to avoid putting /2 etc.] Reduces to two problems: Max $A(S,T)$ and Max $-A(S,T)$. We describe the ideas behind a polynomial time algorithm for Max$A(S,T)$ which we may call

The Maximum Rectangle Problem:

- **S gives T**

  If we know the maximizing S, the T to go with it is just the columns of A whose sum in the S rows is positive.

- **Estimate Column sums in S rows**

  Pick a subset W of $s = O(1/\epsilon^2)$ rows u.a.r. The sum of each column in the S rows can be estimated (to additive error ϵmn) by $\frac{m}{s}\times$ sum in the $W\cap S$ rows.

- **Exhaustive Enumeration**

  Don't know S or $S\cap W$. But, we can try each subset $\tilde{W}$ of W (there are only 2^s of them) as a candidate $S\cap W$. For each, find the set of columns- T - whose sum in the $\tilde{W}$ rows is positive.

- **Choose best candidate**

  For each candidate T: Let S' be the rows with positive sum in the T columns. Take max $A(S',T)$ among all candidate T.

The Exhaustive enumeration step is inspired by an idea of Arora, Karger and Karpinski [AKK95]. Why does this algorithm work? We supply only a brief intuition. In the estimating column sums step, if we had the correct $S\cap W$, the only columns on which we could be wrong about the sign of the column sum in the S rows are ones where the column sum is close to 0. But these do not contribute much to $A(S,T)$ anyway. So, one of our candidate T in step 4 is correct in the sense that $A(S,T)$ is high for the true S. The last step finds the best T among the candidates; we didn't need the true (unknown) S; the best S for each T is just the S'.

How do we make this all constant time ? The idea is simple : Pick a u.a.r subset $\hat{S}$ of $\hat{s} = O^*(1/\epsilon^4)$ rows and a u.a.r. subset $\hat{T}$ of $\hat{s}$ columns at the outset. In the above algorithm, instead of finding $A(S',T)$ for each of the $2^{(1/\epsilon^2)}$ candidate T 's, estimate this quantity by $\frac{mn}{\hat{s}^2}A(S'\cap\hat{S}, T\cap\hat{T})$, for which we only need to know the entries of A in $\hat{S}\times\hat{T}$. One can show using Höffding-Azuma inequality that the estimate is within additive error at most $O(\epsilon mn)$ with high probability. [The failure probability is at most $e^{-\hat{s}/\epsilon^2} = e^{-1/\epsilon^2}$ for each candidate; so by the union bound, whp, there is no failure for any candidate.] Hence the best candidate is found with asserted error whp.

The approximation B has many algorithmic uses. First consider the Maximum cut problem in an undirected graph. The problem can obviously be written as (with $A=$ the $n\times n$ adjacency matrix of the graph)

$$\text{MAX}_{x\in\{0,1\}^n} \quad x^T A(1-x),$$

where x is a column vector and 1 is the vector of all 1's. We obviously have

$$\left|x^T A(1-x) \;-\; x^T B(1-x)\right| \le ||A-B||_\square.$$

Here, we see why the cut norm is defined the way it is; it is the most natural norm for ensuring that for 0-1 vectors x, y, $x^T Ay \approx x^T By$. [It is close to a more traditional "operator norm" - namely, it is easy to show that $||A||_\square$ is always within a factor of 4 of $\text{MAX}_{|x|_\infty=|y|_\infty=1} x^T Ay$.] So to get the maximum cut within additive error ϵn^2, it suffices to solve

$$\text{MAX}_{x\in\{0,1\}^n} x^T B(1-x).$$

Since B has constant (depending only on ϵ, not on n) rank, $x^T B(1-x)$ is determined by a constant number of variables, namely the components of x along the space spanned rows/columns of B. Thus, we have reduced the n variable problem to one with a constant number of variables. While there are many technical difficulties in solving the problem with B, conceptually, it is simple to argue that it can be solved in time exponential in the rank of B alone by enumeration: Put a fine enough grid in the row/column space of B. The number of grid points is exponential only in the dimension of the space. For each grid point, the value of $x^T B(1-x)$ is determined. It only remains to know which grid points correspond to 0-1 x 's. This is an integer program; but its relaxation Linear Program turns out to suffice for the error we seek.

Indeed, the attractive feature of this line is that these arguments can be extended in a straight forward manner to solve all dense MAX-2-CSP problems in polynomial time in a unified manner. Moreover, this also extends to approximating tensors in cut norm and that helps us solve all dense MAX-r-CSP problems for any fixed arity r. [Recall: In a MAX-r-CSP problem, one is given a list of m Boolean functions - $f_1, f_2, \ldots f_m$, each a function of only r of the variables. We have to find a truth setting of all variables which satisfies as many of the m functions as possible. MAX-r-SAT where each function is the disjunction of r literals is a central example.] Indeed, one gets:

THEOREM 2. *[FK99][AE02] Any MAX-r-CSP problem on n variables, where r is fixed, can be solved to additive error ϵn^r in constant time for fixed $\epsilon > 0$. [The running time depends exponentially on $O^*(1/\epsilon^2)$.]*

For $r=2$, the area of Property Testing [GGR98] proved the first such results by combinatorial means, often by exploiting the structure of particular problems. A flavor of the combinatorial difficulties is seen from the first problem so attacked - max.cut. by DelaVega [dlV96]: Akin to the Estimating columns sums and Exhaustive Enumeration steps of our algorithm for maximizing $A(S,T)$, the property testing algorithms do the following for max.cut: clearly in a max cut $(S,\bar{S})$, every vertex in S has more edges to $\bar{S}$ than to S. If we just picked a u.a.r. subset W, then try out all possible subsets $\tilde{W}$ of W as candidate $S\cap W$, we could classify each vertex by whether it has higher degree into $\tilde{W}$ or $W\setminus\tilde{W}$ and hope these would be respectively $\bar{S}$ and S vertices. But this does not work and indeed, the property testing based max cut algorithms work hard to fix this. In our setting, S, T are subsets of different sets and so are "decoupled" and this is what makes these steps work so simply here.

For general $r>2$, Andersson and Engebretsen [AE02] have given a purely combinatorial appraoch independently to prove theorem (2) too. Our approach to proving the theorem is based on an extension of cut matrices and norm to tensors which we describe in the next section.

Another application of the cut norm and approximation is to a version of the Szémeredi Regularity Lemma for graphs. For a graph $G(V,E)$ with edge weights, we denote by A_G the (weighted) adjacency matrix. For two graphs, G, G', on the same set of n vertices, we define a distance between them by $d_\square(G,G') = \frac{1}{n^2}\max_{S,T\subseteq V}|A_G(S,T) - A_{G'}(S,T)|$.

From Lemma 1, the following Lemma which is often called the Weak Regularity Lemma can be proved:

LEMMA 2. *[FK99] The vertex set of a graph $G(V,E)$ with all edge weights equal to 1 can be partitioned into $2^{O(1/\epsilon^2)}$ subsets $V_1, V_2, \ldots$ so that the graph G' in which for each edge (i,j), with say, $i\in V_r, j\in V_s$, has weight = (number of edges between V_r and V_s)/$|V_r||V_s|$ has $d_\square(G,G')\le\epsilon$*

Note that G' intuitively behaves like a random graph with edge probabilities given by edge weights in that the number of edges between subsets of vertices would be close to the expected numbers. A constructive version of the Szémeredi Regularity Lemma was shown in [ARH$^+$]. A simpler spectral algorithm is developed in [FK999].

There is an abstract (and improved) version of this lemma due to Tulsiani, Trevisan and Vadhan [TTV09] from which they are not only able to derive this result, but several others, like the Dense Model theorem of Green, Tao and Ziegler [GT08]. A recent result of Bansal and Williams [BW09] makes progress on the classical problem of complexity of Boolean Matrix multiplication; they use Lemma 2. We will describe in the next section an application of weak regularity to graph limits.

3. APPROXIMATION OF TENSORS IN CUT NORM AND APPLICATIONS

Recall that a r−tensor is an r dimensional array A with entries $A_{ijkl\ldots}$. A "rectangle" is a set of entries of the form $S_1 \times S_2 \times \ldots S_r$, where S_t is a subset of the t th index. [For $r = 2$, S_1 is a subset of rows and S_2 a subset of columns.] $A(S_1, S_2, \ldots S_r)$ is the sum of A 's entries in the rectangle $S_1 \times S_2 \times \ldots S_r$. We define the cut norm $||A||_\square$ exactly as for matrices - it is the maximum over all rectangles of $|A(S_1, S_2, \ldots S_r)|$. A cut tensor has the same entry in some rectangle and is zero elsewhere. Lemma 1 carries over with exactly the same simple proof as for matrices.

LEMMA 3. *[FK99] For a r−tensor A with $n_1 \times n_2 \times \ldots n_r$ entries, each at most 1 in absolute value, there exist $1/\epsilon^2$ cut tensors whose sum B approximates A in the sense*

$$||A - B||_\square \leq \epsilon n_1 n_2 \ldots n_r.$$

Interestingly, the constructive version also carries over with one extra twist. The idea for solving the maximum rectangle problem is:

- Want $S_1, S_2, \ldots S_r$ so that $A(S_1, S_2, \ldots, S_r)$ is max.
- If we knew the maximizing $S_1, S_2, \ldots S_{r-1}$, then the maximizing S_r consists of the i with $A(S_1, S_2, \ldots, S_{r-1}, i) > 0$.
- We can estimate this by taking random subsets $W_1, W_2, \ldots W_{r-1}$, trying out all subsets $\tilde{W}_1, \tilde{W}_2, \ldots \tilde{W}_{r-1}$ of the respective W_t as candidate $S_t \cap W_t$.
- This gives us many candidate S_r. How do we find the best one ? This needs the extra twist: define a $r-1$ tensor $\tilde{A}$ by

$$\tilde{A}_{i_1 i_2 \ldots i_{r-1}} = \sum_{i \in S_r} A_{i_1 i_2 \ldots i_{r-1} i}.$$

  Now recursively solve the maximum rectangle problem for the $r-1$ tensor. Then choose the S_r with best answer.

The above arguments can be used to show: for a MAX-r-CSP formula $F(x_1, x_2, \ldots, x_n)$ if we pick a u.a.r. subset Q with $|Q| = q = \text{poly}(1/\epsilon)$ variables and solve the "induced" MAX-r-CSP problem F^Q on the picked variables (the induced problem contains only those clauses all of whose literals are the picked variables or their negations), then we have whp:

$$\left| \frac{n^r}{q^r} \text{MAX}(F^Q) - \text{MAX}(F) \right| \leq \epsilon n^r,$$

where Max(F) denotes the maximum number of functions in F which can be simultaneously satisfied. [$\frac{n^r}{q^r}$ is a natural scaling factor. Note that this is interesting only when the answer to the whole problem is at least $\Omega(n^r)$. This holds for "dense" problems where there are $\Omega(n^r)$ clauses.] The question arises: what is the best poly($1/\epsilon$) in this result? Alon, delaVega, Karpinski and Kannan [ADKK02] prove $O^*(1/\epsilon^4)$ suffices.

THEOREM 3. *[ADKK02] Suppose $F(x_1, x_2, \ldots, x_n)$ is a MAX-r-CSP formula. If Q is u.a.r. subset of $q = O^*(1/\epsilon^4)$ of the n variables, then, for F^Q, the induced formula on Q, we have with probability at least 99/100,*

$$\left| MAX(F) - \frac{n^r}{q^r} MAX(F^Q) \right| \leq \epsilon n^r.$$

There are two parts to the theorem: first asserts that $\frac{n^r}{q^r}\text{MAX}(F^Q) \geq \text{MAX}(F) - \epsilon n^r$. This is simple: if one just takes the truth assignment to $\{x_1, x_2, \ldots, x_n\}$ which attains MAX(F), then usual facts about sampling can be used to prove that the SAME assignment to the sampled variables satisfies (whp) at least $\frac{q^r}{n^r}\text{MAX}(F) - \epsilon q^r$ of the clauses of F^Q. The other part is the non-trivial one - the reason is we have to rule out ANY assignment to the sampled variables from satisfying too many clauses. Indeed, this raises a basic question:
When can we say for a maximization problem that a sampled induced sub-problem gives a good estimate of the answer to the whole problem ?
The non-trivial part is: show that for small problem (the induced one on the sample), no solution gives an unduly high value. [Traditional sampling arguments tackle the other part easily.] A situation with a simple answer is bounded Linear Programming: it is easy to see that if a system of linear inequalities $Ax \leq b; 0 \leq x_i \leq 1$ in n variables has a solution, then, for a random subset Q of the n variables, the induced problem (slightly relaxed) has a solution too: $A^Q x^Q \leq \frac{q}{n} b + \delta; 0 \leq x_i \leq 1$ for $i \in Q$ where A^Q consists of the columns of A corresponding to the Q variables. But the converse is also true here using LP duality: if $Ax \leq b$ has no solution with $0 \leq x_i \leq 1$, then duality tells us that there is one combination of the inequalities which has no solution; this is equivalent to the existence of a $u \geq 0$ such that $\sum_j (u^T A)_j^- > u^T b$. Now for this u, we can show by traditional sampling that we have: $\sum_{j \in Q} (u^T A)_j^- > \frac{q}{n}(u^T b) - \delta$ demonstrating that there is no solution to a slight tightening of the sampled LP. This simple result for LP is used as part of the proof of Theorem 3.

Another result of a similar flavor about induced subproblems also goes into the proof of Theorem 3 and is worth mentioning independently here. Suppose A is a large $n \times n$ (note: it is square) matrix. If we pick a random subset Q of $[n]$ and look at the induced submatrix A^Q of A on $Q \times Q$, how does the cut norm of A^Q relate to the cut norm of A? It is easy to see that $||A^Q||_\square \geq \frac{q^2}{n^2}||A||_\square - \delta$, where δ is small, since, we could take the subsets S, T of $[n]$ which maximize $|A(S, T)|$ and argue by traditional Statistics that $|A(S \cap Q, T \cap Q)| \geq \frac{q^2}{n^2}|A(S, T)| - \delta$. The theorem below by Rudelson and Vershynin asserts a converse which is harder to prove. It is an improvement of a theorem in [ADKK02] and is proved using some Functional Analysis techniques.

THEOREM 4. *[RV07] Let $\epsilon > 0$ and suppose A is an $n \times n$ matrix with $||A||_F \in O(n)$; $||A||_\square \in O(\epsilon n^2)$; $|A_{ij}| \leq O(1/\epsilon)$. Then if Q is a u.a.r. subset of $\{1, 2, \ldots, n\}$ with $|Q| = q \in \Omega(1/\epsilon^2)$ and A^Q is the $q \times q$ submatrix of A with entries from $Q \times Q$, then*

$$E||A^Q||_\square = O(\epsilon q^2).$$

Open Question [ADKK02] actually proved such a result for r− tensors for any fixed r; but their proof required $q \in \Omega^*(1/\epsilon^4)$. Does a result as above with $O(1/\epsilon^2)$ hold for r− tensors ? The issue is that the techniques from Functional

Analysis are no more available for $r > 2$. (cf. also the next open question on approximating the cut norm has this flavor.)

It is not difficult to show that the problem of finding the cut-norm is MAX-SNP hard by a reduction from Max-Cut. Interestingly, using a deep result from Mathematics called Grothendik inequality, Alon and Naor [AN06] were able to show:

THEOREM 5. *[AN06] The cut norm of matrices can be approximated to within a factor of 1.782 in polynomial time.*

Their approach is: the cut norm problem can be reduced to the following problem:

$$\text{MAX} \sum_{i,j} A_{ij} x_i y_j \text{ subject to } x_i, y_j \in \{-1, +1\}.$$

This Integer Program has a standard Semi-Definite Programming relaxation, where the ± 1 variables x_i, y_j are replaced by vector variables u_i, v_j, required to be of length 1:

$$\text{MAX} \sum_{i,j} A_{ij} (u_i \cdot v_j) \text{ subject to } |u_i| = |v_j| = 1.$$

The theorem of Grothendik proves that the optimal value of the SDP is at most a factor of 1.782 times the optimal value of the integer program This automatically yields a constant factor approximation to the value of the integer program. But, finding a rounding procedure to achieve this was both non-trivial and first developed in [AN06].

Open Problem Develop $O(1)$ factor for cut norms of r-tensors. Note that the natural Semi Definite Program for $r = 2$ does not extend to $r = 3$.

In the last section, we saw the weak-regularity Lemma and a notion of distance between two graphs. Borgs, Chayes, Lovász, Sós, Szegedy and Vesztergombi [BCL$^+$06] defined other interesting notions of graph distances and graph limits. They generalize the notion of graph distances to graphs with different numbers of vertices. While the definition in Lemma 2 viewed the vertex sets of the two graphs having a fixed 1-1 mapping (labeled vertices), this is no more possible and relabeling of each vertex set as well as mapping one to the other have to be allowed. We do not give the precise definitions here. Suppose we do the partition of the vertex set as in Lemma 2. Then we could represent each V_r by a compound vertex and put an edge between compound vertices r, s of weight equal to (number of edges between V_r and $V_s)/|V_r||V_s|$. Then the Lemma is really saying that the compressed graph and the original are close in some metric. [This intuition needs to be formalized into a definition of distance between graphs.] They then use Theorem 3 to show:

THEOREM 6. *[BCL$^+$06] Let G be a simple graph and $\epsilon, \delta > 0$. Then the induced sub-graph of G on a random subset of $2^{1/\delta\epsilon^2}$ nodes is ϵ close to G with probability at least $1 - \delta$.*

They use this theorem in their extensive work on Graph Limits. Their notions facilitate the understanding of very large graphs which can be viewed as limits; but also can be approximated in the above sense by smaller graphs (with something akin to "compound vertices".) This raises the following somewhat loosely phrased:

Open Question Can we define a notion of limits for matrices and more generally $r-$ tensors and apply these to derive theorems similar to [BCL$^+$06] ?

4. NON-UNIFORM SAMPLING

Clearly, uniform sampling of rows/columns will not solve all problems. Indeed, if we have a matrix with just one non-zero row and all other rows were just 0's and we draw uniform sample of rows, we are likely to see only zeros and miss the all-important row. Less trivial examples are when only a small number of rows contain significantly higher absolute value entries than others. From the last sections, we can show that u.a.r. samples yield an approximation B to the given matrix A with error in cut norm of at most ϵmnM, where M is the max absolute value of an entry of A. It can also be shown that with poly$(1/\epsilon)$ u.a.r. samples, we can make $||A - B||_2 \leq \epsilon\sqrt{mn}M$, the point being (briefly) $||A - B||_\square = x^T(A - B)y$, where $|x| = \sqrt{m}$ and $|y| = \sqrt{n}$, so the $||A - B||_2$ error is $1/\sqrt{mn}$ times the $||A - B||_\square$ error. But this amount of error is not suitable for many applications.

A more useful error bound is given in Lemma (4), for not only matrices, but also tensors. Completely analogous to the matrix case, we make the following definitions: For an $r-$tensor A, and r vectors $w, x, y, z, \ldots$, $A(w, x, y, z, \ldots)$ is defined as $\sum_{i,j,k,l,\ldots} A_{i,j,k,l,\ldots} w_i x_j y_k z_l \ldots$. [It is analogous to the quadratic form $x^T Ay = \sum_{i,j} A_{ij} x_i y_j$ for matrices.] The Frobenius norm of A, denoted $||A||_F$ is again the square root of the sum of squares of the entries. The "spectral norm" of A denoted $||A||_2$ is the maximum over all unit length vectors $w, x, y, z, \ldots$ of $A(w, x, y, z, \ldots)$. A rank-1 $r-$ tensor is the outer product of r vectors, denoted $w \otimes x \otimes y \otimes z \ldots$ whose $i, j, k, l, \ldots$th entry is $w_i x_j y_k z_l \ldots$. We say that a tensor has rank at most k if it can be expressed as the sum of k rank-1 tensors.

LEMMA 4. *[dlVKKV05] For any A, $\epsilon > 0$, there exist a tensor B of rank at most $1/\epsilon^2$ such that*

$$||A - B||_2 \leq \epsilon ||A||_F. \tag{1}$$

The simple proof of the Lemma will be given shortly. A polynomial time sampling based algorithm is also available for producing such an approximation, but the algorithm given by delaVega, Karpinski, Kannan and Vempala[dlVKKV05] is non-trivial.

THEOREM 7. *[dlVKKV05] For any $A, \epsilon > 0$, we can find a tensor B of rank at most $4/\epsilon^2$ in time $(n/\epsilon)^{O(1/\epsilon^4)}$ such that with probability at least 3/4 we have*

$$||A - B||_2 \leq \epsilon ||A||_F.$$

For matrices, traditional singular value decomposition gives us a polynomial time algorithm, but, we will see a sampling-based algorithm which in essence can be made constant time after 2 passes through the matrix. In the case of tensors, no previous polynomial time algorithm was known at all. Before giving the proofs/algorithms, we will motivate the error bound of $||A - B||_2 \leq \epsilon ||A||_F$ of (1) by three application areas.

The first motivating area is Principal Component Analysis (PCA). Here, one often assumes that the top "few" singular values dominate. (In fact, that is in the first place one of the two justifications for making a low rank approximation. The other possible motivation for making a low-rank approximation is "de-noising" - where one assumes that the top few singular value components are the real data and the others are possibly noise- for example in Latent Semantic Indexing [DFLD88].)

PCA Assumption: The data consists of an $m \times n$ matrix A. The top k singular values $\sigma_1, \sigma_2, \ldots \sigma_k$ contain $1 - \epsilon$ of the "spectrum", where $k << m, n$. More precisely,

$$[\textbf{Strong-PCA}]\sigma_1^2 + \sigma_2^2 + \ldots + \sigma_k^2 \geq (1-\epsilon)||A||_F^2.$$

We need only a weaker version of this:

$$[\textbf{Weak-PCA}]\sigma_1^2 + \sigma_2^2 + \ldots + \sigma_k^2 \geq \Omega(||A||_F^2).$$

Under this assumption, (1) translates to a *"relative error ϵ"*.

A second area is Discrete Optimization. As we saw, the max-cut problem can be solved to additive error $\epsilon n^2 M$ for $n-$ node graphs where the edge weights are all at most M. This however is relative error ϵ only in case the total of all edge weights is $\Omega(n^2 M)$; if $M \leq 1$, this requires the graph to be dense. This raises the question:

Can we solve non-dense max cut problem to *relative error* ϵ ? In general, these problems are NP-hard. But an important special case, it turns out can be solved in polynomial time - namely when the edge weights satisfy the triangle inequality, as was shown using other methods[dlVK01]. A unified polynomial time algorithm using Theorem 7 for this problem and other weighted versions of MAX-2-CSP problems is developed in [dlVKKV05]. [In fact, they do this with a weaker condition than triangle inequality for all MAX-2-CSP problems.]

A third area is tensors. Many algorithms are known and used in practice for finding low-rank approximations to tensors [Kru89]. But as remarked earlier, neither the theory nor the algorithms are anywhere as nice as for matrices. There are solid reasons - NP-hardness [Has90], [HhL09] and non-uniqueness/existence. But beyond all this, is a basic question - what is it that we can find provably in polynomial time ? Theorem (7) seems to be a first step. The algorithm for Theorem (7) (which we will outline soon) is quite different from other known heuristics and draws on new uses of sampling in a vein somewhat similar to the maximum rectangle problem. Also, it turns out that the error bound in (1) suffices to tackle MAX-r-CSP problems where the weights satisfy a natural generalization of the triangle inequality to higher dimensions. Unweighted dense MAX-r-CSP's are a special case of this.

Proof of Lemma (4): If $||A||_2 \leq \epsilon||A||_F$, then we are done. If not, there are $w, x, y, z, \ldots$, all of length 1 such that $A(w, x, y, z, \ldots) \geq \epsilon||A||_F$. Now consider the $r-$dimensional array

$$B = A - (A(w, x, y, z, \ldots)w \otimes x \otimes y \otimes z \ldots\ldots$$

[This is of course basically a rank-1 update.] It is easy to see that $||B||_F^2 = ||A||_F^2 - (A(w, x, y, z, \ldots)^2)$. We may repeat on B and clearly this process will only go on for at most $1/\epsilon^2$ steps.

From the proof of the lemma, it is clear that again, the basic algorithmic question is to find a $w, x, y, z, \ldots$ all of unit length, maximizing $A(w, x, y, z, \ldots)$ to within additive error $\epsilon||A||_F$. We will present the algorithm for tensors later. First, we will tackle matrices by sampling.

5. SAMPLING IN LARGE MATRICES

Numerical Analysis gives us sophisticated polynomial time algorithms for many matrix problems to do with spectral analysis. Here, the focus is on using sampling to solve very large matrix problems approximately. First, we look at matrix multiplication. The product of two matrices A, B can be written as

$$AB = \sum_i A_i B^i,$$

where A_i (B^i respectively) is the i column of A (row of B, respectively). An immediate thought is to estimate the sum from a random sample of i 's. Consider a random sample of s i 's picked in i.i.d. trials. Let $p_1, p_2, \ldots p_n$ be the probabilities of picking $1, 2, \ldots n$ respectively in each trial. If $i_1, i_2, \ldots, i_s$ are the samples, then

$$X = \frac{1}{s}\sum_{t=1}^{s} \frac{1}{p_{i_t}} A_{i_t} B^{i_t}$$

is easily seen to be an unbiased estimator of AB. [I.e., $EX = AB$ entry-wise.] We would like to measure the variance, but this quantity depends on which entry we are talking about. Here, we make a simple-minded, important decision - lets look at the sum of variances of all the entries of X. This quantity, which we denote $\textbf{Var}X$ is seen to satisfy:

$$\textbf{Var}X \leq \frac{1}{s}\sum_{i=1}^{n} \frac{1}{p_i}|A_i|^2|B^i|^2.$$

A case of much interest is when $B = A^T$, when this simplifies to

$$\frac{1}{s}\sum_{i=1}^{n} \frac{1}{p_i}|A_i|^4.$$

By Calculus, one can see that this is minimized when the p_i are proportional to $|A_i|^2$. [Indeed it is not hard to show that these p_i are the minimizer of the actual variance, not just the upper bound here.] This leads to the following probability distribution for sampling the columns of a matrix which turns out to have many nice properties:

Length Squared Sampling : Pick a column with probability proportional to sum of squares of its entries.

Length squared sampling was first introduced by Frieze, Kannan and Vempala [FKV98]. Its applications to clustering were studied by Drineas, Frieze, Kannan, Vempala and Vinay [DFK+04]. The application to matrix multiplication is from [DK01]. See also [DKM06a].

[FKV98] proves that if we draw a sample of columns according to the length squared distribution and do an SVD on the sampled columns, this gives an low-rank approximation to A with provable error bounds. We state this below (without proof).

Algorithm: Fast-SVD

1. Sample s columns of A from the squared length distribution to form a matrix C.
2. Find $u^{(1)}, \ldots, u^{(k)}$, the top k left singular vectors of C.
3. Output $\sum_{t=1}^{k} u^{(t)} {u^{(t)}}^T A$ as a rank-k approximation to A.

The matrix $\sum_{t=1}^{k} u^{(t)} {u^{(t)}}^T A$ is really just the "projection" of A on the space spanned by the $u^{(t)}$ and so the theorem below says that A projected to the top singular space of C

(instead of the usual singular space of A) is a good low-rank approximation to A. [A_k is the best rank k approximation given by SVD.]

THEOREM 8. *[FKV98],[FKV04] The rank-k matrix found by Algorithm Fast-SVD (call it $\tilde{A}$) satisfies:*

$$\mathbf{E}\left(\|A-\tilde{A}\|_F^2\right) \leq \|A-A_k\|_F^2 + 2\sqrt{\frac{k}{s}}\|A\|_F^2$$

$$\mathbf{E}\left(\|A-\tilde{A}\|_2^2\right) \leq \|A-A_k\|_2 + \frac{2}{\sqrt{s}}\|A\|_F^2.$$

In fact the kind of error bound in the theorem is optimal in terms of the number of rows sampled; this was shown in [BY03].

[FKV98] and [FKV04] in fact apply the sampling once more - to pick a sample of rows of C according to the length-squared distribution. Then, it turns out that fining the SVD of the constant-sized matrix (with the sampled rows of C) suffices to give us a low-rank approximation to A. But the proof of this is more complicated. The reason is that from the sampled rows of C, one gets the right singular vectors of C, but only approximately. The error turns out to be bounded by $\epsilon||C||_F$. [It would be better if the error bound was relative, in terms of the singular values themselves. But length-squared sampling does not give this.] Then for the "low" singular values of C (less than $\epsilon||C||_F$), the approximation is no good. So, one has to throw out these low ones (these are in a sense "near-singularities") See [DKM06b] for a detailed explanation of the method and some improvements.

An improvement of the error bound, still using length-squared sampling was achieved using sophisticated techniques from the field of Probability in Banach spaces by Rudelson and Vershynin. Their result stated below picks a sample of s rows from A, where s is almost linear in a quantity r, they call the numerical rank of A; $r = ||A||_F^2/||A||_2^2$. [Recall the PCA assumptions; under even the weak PCA assumption, r is $O(1)$.] Their error bound is also better in that it involves $||A||_2$, rather than $||A||_F$.

THEOREM 9. *[RV07] Suppose A is an $m \times n$ matrix with numerical rank $r = ||A||_F^2/||A||_2^2$. Let $\epsilon, \delta \in (0,1)$ and $s \in \Omega^*(r/\epsilon^4\delta)$. Let B be a set of s rows of A picked in s i.i.d. trials, each according to length-squared and let $u^{(1)},\dots,u^{(k)}$ be the top k right singular vectors of B. Then, $\tilde{A} = A\sum_{t=1}^k u^{(t)}u^{(t)^T}$ satisfies the following with probability at least $1-2e^{-c/\delta}$:*

$$||A-\tilde{A}||_2 \leq \sigma_{k+1}(A) + \epsilon||A||_2.$$

Note also that this is a high probability (with exponential tails) rather than just in expectation.

In another application of length-squared sampling, [SV09] shows that if we run an iterative equation solver for an overdetermined system of equations with a Kaczmarz iteration (where one uses a violated equation to modify the current solution) with the added twist that the violated equation is picked according to the length squared distribution, then one gets a guaranteed rate of convergence; the reader is referred to the paper for details.

Length-squared sampling can also be used for tensors and is the basic ingredient in the proof of theorem 7; recall that we needed an algorithm to find for a tensor A, the maximum value of $A(w,x,y,z,\dots)$ to within $\epsilon||A||_F$. The idea behind the algorithm for this is to imitate the steps of the algorithm for the maximum rectangle problem:

1. If we knew the optimizing $x,y,z,\dots$, then the optimizing w is easy to find: it is just the vector $A(\cdot,x,y,z,\dots)$ (whose i th component is $A(e_i,x,y,z,\dots)$) scaled to length 1.
2. Now, $A(e_i,x,y,z,\dots) = \sum_{j,k,l,\dots} A_{i,j,k,l,\dots}x_jy_kz_l\dots$. The sum can be estimated by having just a few terms. But, an important question is: how do we make sure the variance is not too high, since the entries can have disparate values ?
3. Length squared sampling works ! [Stated here without proof.]

Achlioptas and McSherry [AM07] developed a different randomized algorithm for low-rank approximations of matrices - they sample individual entries independently and show using Random Matrix theory that with those on hand, we can get a good approximation to the matrix in spectral norm. Their results also have a bearing on "Compressed Sensing" in that they are able to infer something about the whole matrix from a random sample of entries.

6. CUR: AN INTERPOLATIVE LOW-RANK APPROXIMATION

We found in the last section an implicit low-rank approximation to A; implicit because, the actual approximation needed us to multiply A by the vectors $u^{(t)}$. In this section, we wish to describe an algorithm to get an explicit approximation of any matrix A given just a sample of rows and a sample of columns of A. Clearly if the sample is picked according to the uniform distribution, this attempt would fail in general. We will see that again the length squared distribution comes to our rescue; indeed, we will show that if the samples are picked according to the length squared or approximate length squared distributions, we can get an approximation for A. Again, this will hold for an arbitrary matrix A.

First suppose A is a $m \times n$ matrix and R (R for rows) is a $s \times n$ matrix constructed by picking s rows of A in i.i.d. samples, each according to approximate length-squared distribution. Similarly, let C (for columns) be a $m \times s$ matrix consisting of columns picked according to the length squared distribution on the columns. The motivating question for this section is: Can we get an approximation to A given just C, R ? An affirmative answer is given in the theorem below first proved by Drineas and Kannan. Here, one does not need the sampling probabilities to be exactly proportional to length squared; it suffices to have the probability of drawing column i to be at least its length squared / (c.$||A||_F^2$), where c is a constant. We call this approximate length squared sampling.

THEOREM 10. *[DK03], [DKM06c] Suppose C (respectively R) consists of a sample of $s \geq \Omega^*(k/\epsilon^4)$ columns (respectively rows) of A drawn in s i.i.d. trials, each according to (approximate) length squared probabilities. Then, from C and R, we can find a $s \times s$ matrix U so that*

$$E||A-CUR||_F \leq ||A-A_k||_F + \epsilon||A||_F$$
$$E||A-CUR||_2 \leq ||A-A_k||_2 + \epsilon||A||_F.$$

Open Problem Improve the dependence of $1/\epsilon^4$ in the theorem.

The approximation of A by the product CUR is reminiscent of the usual PCA approximation based on taking the leading k terms of the SVD decomposition. There, instead of C, R, we would have orthonormal matrices consisting of the leading singular vectors and instead of U, the diagonal matrix of singular values. The PCA decomposition of course gives the best rank-k approximation, whereas what the Theorem shows for CUR is only that its error is bounded in terms of the best error we can achieve. There are two main advantages of CUR over PCA:

1. CUR can be computed faster from A and also we only need to make two passes over A which can be assumed to be stored on external memory.

2. CUR preserves the sparsity of A - namely C, R are columns and rows of A itself. (U is a small matrix since typically s is much smaller than m, n). So any further matrix vector products Ax can be approximately computed as $C(U(Rx))$ quickly.

3. It is an interpolative approximation : unlike SVD, where the singular vectors are linear combinations of A's columns/rows, here C, R are actual columns/rows of A. An application illustrates the point. In doing, say, PCA on a "patient-gene" matrix in a Biological application (with entry i, j giving the gene expression of gene j for patient i), one gets a result which says that "these few linear combinations of genes/patients are important in explaining the data", where the linear combinations may involve negative weights as well as positive ones. Instead in CUR, we get a collection of individual genes/patients explaining the data, arguably providing better intuition. See for example [PMJ$^+$07] for this kind of application.

The CUR approximation has been extended to tensors as well by Mahoney, Maggioni and Drinesa [MMD]. There are many improvements and applications of CUR - see [MD09]. An important modification is given by Sun Xi, Zhang and Falustos [SXZF07]. They make the observation that the length squared sampling used in the original CUR algorithm may result in a lot of duplicates. They remove duplicates and reweight the unique columns/rows remaining by the square root of the number of copies. They show that with this new reweighting, one gets good approximations. More importantly, they have done empirical studies with Datamining applications to show the effectiveness in terms of space and time with the new approximation.

We also briefly describe an application of CUR to Recommendation Systems by Drineas, Kerneidis and Raghavan [DKR02]. The central object in a Recommendation System is the customer-preference matrix whose (i, j) th entry is the preference of customer i for product j. The basic question is: given a small sample of entries from the matrix (collected customer-product data) how does one make good recommendations to other customers. The idea of using CUR in [DKR02] is a departure from what we have discussed so far. So far, we had (somewhere) the whole matrix and used sampling to infer its properties, it being too large to deal with in full. Here, even collecting the matrix is expensive; we wish to infer its missing entries from the sample we know. But note that the techniques of this survey do apply to this "reverse engineering" problem. Indeed, [DKR02] prove that under some assumptions, we can make good recommendations with just a handful of customers' complete preferences (some complete rows) and all customer preferences for a handful of products (columns). Much care has to be taken, since the sampling cannot be assumed to be according to Length-squared.

The above raises a more general question. Can we bring costs of accurate data collection into our measures of efficiency ? We loosely formulate a candidate problem on these lines:

Open Question Suppose we wish to solve a large Linear Program : $\max c \cdot x$ subject to $Ax \le b$. But suppose we have to collect each piece of data - each A_{ij} costs c/ϵ^2 to get with accuracy $\pm\epsilon$. Find an efficient method for data collection + solution to within error $\pm\delta$, where the cost is the weighted sum of the data collection cost plus the running time.

7. RELATIVE ERROR APPROXIMATION

If A_k is the best rank k approximation (from SVD), then a natural way to measure error of any rank k approximation is relative to the "residue" of the spectrum, namely relative to $||A - A_k||_F$. So, we say a rank k approximation B makes relative error ϵ if

$$||A - B||_F \le (1 + \epsilon)||A - A_k||_F.$$

From simple examples, it is easy to see that length-squared sampling does not do this in general.

For multiplicative $(1+\epsilon)$-approximation, Har-Peled [HP05] gave a linear time algorithm that requires $O(\log n)$ passes over the input matrix. Deshpande and Vempala [DV06] improved this to $O(k)$ passes using volume sampling. Both these algorithms use adaptive sampling of [DRVW06] as a subroutine. Drineas, Mahoney and Muthukrishnan [DMM06] gave a different algorithm, where the sampling probabilities are computed using SVD, that achieves the same approximation ratio but takes more time because of the initial computation of SVD. Finally, Sarlös [Sar06] gave a linear time 2-pass algorithm for multiplicative $(1 + \epsilon)$-approximation that uses a small number of linear combinations of all the rows instead of a subsample; his algorithm which we call isotropic random projection is described below.

First, volume sampling is a generalization of length-squared sampling. We pick subsets of k rows instead picking rows one by one. The probability that we pick a subset S is proportional to the volume of the k-simplex $\Delta(S)$ spanned by these k rows along with the origin. The raw method will give us a factor $(k + 1)$ approximation (in expectation). Incidentally, it also proves that any matrix has k rows whose span contains a such an approximation. Moreover, this bound is tight, i.e., there exist matrices for which no k rows can give a better approximation.

LEMMA 5. *[DV06] Let S be a random subset of k rows of a given matrix A chosen with probability*

$$P_S = \frac{Vol(\Delta(S))^2}{\sum_{T:|T|=k} Vol(\Delta(T))^2}.$$

Let $\tilde{A}$ be the projection of A to the span of S and let $\tilde{A}_k$ be the best rank k approximation to $\tilde{A}$. Then,

$$\mathbf{E}\left(||A - \tilde{A}_k||_F^2\right) \le (k + 1)||A - A_k||_F^2.$$

More work is needed to convert this to a relative error ϵ approximation (which we do not describe here.)

Isotropic random projection also gives relative error approximations to the optimal rank-k matrix with roughly the same time complexity. Moreover, it makes only *two* passes over the input data.

The idea behind the algorithm can be understood by going back to the matrix multiplication algorithm described in section 5. There to multiply two matrices A, B, we picked random columns of A and rows of B and thus derived an estimate for AB from these samples. The error bound derived was additive and this is unavoidable. Suppose that we first project the rows of A randomly to a low-dimensional subspace, i.e., compute AR where R is random and $n \times k$, and similarly project the columns of B, then we can use the estimate $ARR^T B$. For low-rank approximation, the idea extends naturally: first project the rows of A using a random matrix R, then project A to the span of the columns of AR (which is low dimensional), and finally find the best rank k approximation of this projection. The algorithm is:

1. Let $l = Ck/\epsilon$ and R be a random $n \times l$ matrix; compute $B = AR$.
2. Project A to the span of the columns of B to get $\tilde{A}$.
3. Output $\tilde{A}_k$, the best rank-k approximation to $\tilde{A}$.

THEOREM 11. *[Sar06] Let A be an $m \times n$ real matrix with M nonzeros. Let $0 < \epsilon < 1$ and R be an $n \times l$ random matrix with i.i.d. Bernoulli entries with mean zero and $l \geq Ck/\epsilon$ where C is a universal constant. Then with probability at least 3/4,*

$$\|A - \tilde{A}_k\|_F \leq (1+\epsilon)\|A - A_k\|_F$$

and $\tilde{A}_k$ can be computed in two passes over the data in $O(Ml + (m+n)l^2)$ time using $O((m+n)r^2)$ space.

8. APPLICATIONS TO CLUSTERING, MIXTURES

Spectral methods are widely used for clustering and partitioning problems. Not many worst-case results have been proved; there are exceptions for special classes of graphs like planer graphs [ST07]. In general, spectral methods have been proven to work correctly with high probability under some assumptions on the generative model of the data. One class of such problems is the Planted Problems, where we are given a random graph modified by a "planted part" and the objective is to find the planted part. We describe an instance of this.

Consider a graph G which is the union of a purely random graph $G_{n,1/2}$ and an unknown clique on vertex set P, where $p = |P|$ is given. The problem is to recover P. If $p \geq c(n \log n)^{1/2}$ then with high probability, it is easy to recover P as the p vertices of largest degree. Alon, Krivelevich and Sudakov [AKS98], using spectral analysis, were able to improve this to $p = \Omega(n^{1/2})$.

Let A_G denote the adjacency matrix of G. The spectral approach of [AKS98] essentially maximizes $x^T Ax$ over vectors x with $|x| = 1$, expecting that the optimal solution is close to u, defined by $u_i = p^{-1/2}1_{i\in P}$, (u is the scaled characteristic vector of P) so that we may recover P from the optimal solution.

Frieze and Kannan [FK08] define a natural 3-dimensional array A related to the given graph : A_{ijk} will be ± 1 depending on whether the parity of the number of edges among the vertices i, j, k is odd or even respectively. They show that as long as $p \in O(n^{1/3}(\log n)^4)$, the maximum of the cubic form $\sum_{i,j,k} A_{ijk}x_i x_j x_k$ as the vector x varies over the unit ball is attained close to u, so that if we can find this maximum, then we can recover the clique. However, unlike the case of the quadratic form, where the maximization was an eignevalue computation which is well-known to be doable in polynomial time, there are in general no known polynomial time algorithms for maximizing cubic forms. So, the existential result does not automatically lead to an algorithm and this is left as an open question.

Open Question Suppose a $n \times n \times n$ array A is constructed as above from $G_{n,1/2}$ plus a planted clique of size $p \in \Omega(n^{1/3}(\log n)^c)$. Then can we maximize the function $\sum_{i,j,k} A_{ijk}x_i x_j x_k$, $|x| \leq 1$, even within $O(1)$ factors in polynomial time ?

Brubaker and Vempala [BV09] have generalized this to r tensors, where they show that maximizing over an r tensor whose entries are the parity of the number of edges in r cliques can find hidden cliques of size $n^{1/r}$. The computational question of approximately maximizing the r–ary forms is open.

Another class of models is in a sense also planted - there is a hidden partition which dictates probabilities. For example, McSherry [McS01] (following earlier papers) considers a model in which n objects are divided into k clusters $(k << n)T_1, T_2, \ldots T_k$. There is a number $p_{rs} \in [0,1]$ which is the probability of each edge between a vertex in T_r and one in T_s. Edges are chosen independently and we are given the resulting random graph on n vertices. Our job is to find the partition and p_{rs} of the generating model. This can be summarized as: we are given a 0-1 matrix A and are to find EA, where the expectation is entry-wise. [McS01] shows that under some technical conditions, spectral methods will yield the answer. Here is a quick idea of the method and its use of the deep results from the theory of random matrices. The matrix $A - \mathbf{E}\,A$ has random independent entries each with mean 0. The following celebrated theorem was first stated qualitatively by the physicist Wigner and proved by Füredi and Komlos[FK81]. See also [Vu05].

THEOREM 12. *Suppose A is a symmetric random matrix with independent (above-diagonal) entries each with standard deviation at most ν and bounded in absolute value by 1. Then, with high probability, the largest eigenvalue of $A - \mathbf{E}\,A$ is at most $c\nu\sqrt{n}$.*

The strength of this Theorem is seen from the fact that each row of $A - \mathbf{E}\,A$ is of length $O(\nu\sqrt{n})$, so the Theorem asserts that the top eigenvalue amounts only to the length of a constant number of rows; i.e., there is almost no correlation among the rows (since the top eigenvalue $= \max_{|x|=1} \|(A - \mathbf{E}\,A)x\|$ and hence the higher the correlation of the rows in some direction x, the higher its value). Thus one gets whp an upper bound on the spectral norm of $A - EA$:

$$\|A - \mathbf{E}\,A\| \leq c\nu\sqrt{n}.$$

Now, we can (approximately) find EA by doing SVD on A with the help of the following simple lemma.

LEMMA 6. *[AM07] Suppose A, B are $m \times n$ matrices with rank(B) $= k$. If $\hat{A}$ is the best rank k approximation to A, then*

$$\|\hat{A} - B\|_F^2 \leq 5k\|A - B\|^2.$$

While these ideas are clean, it turns out that they only help cluster "most" points correctly. The others are corrected in a messy "clean-up" phase. There has been progress on clustering in generative models: [AFKM01],[DHKS05],[DHKM07]. But the messiness of the clean-up phase haunts the field and raises the following:

Open Problem Clean up the clean-up phase of clustering algorithms for generative models (or dispense with it).

Another well-studied clustering problem has to do with learning mixtures of Gaussians and other probability densities. We only describe the part of this area which has to do with spectral algorithms. A provable connection to spectral method was struck by Vempala and Wang [VW04]. They proved an elegant result that given samples from a mixture of k spherical Gaussians, the $k-$ dimensional SVD subspace of the matrix whose rows are the samples contains all the centers. With the space of centers in hand, one can project to that subspace and learn in it. Extensions of this were given in [KSV08] and [AM05]. Two interesting variants of PCA have been proposed recently by Brubaker and Vempala - isotropic PCA [BV08] and robust PCA [Bru09] which tackle Gaussian mixture learning problems not amenable to standard PCA.

While we do not go into the subject of Spectral Partitioning of graphs, we briefly mention that there are many ways to partition nodes given edge weights which are to be treated as pairwise similarities between vertices. A well-used method is to normalize first each row sum to be 1, then find the second largest eignevalue and corresponding eigenvector of the the stochastic matrix. Then we partition the vertex set into 2 subsets: those with coordinate in the second eigenvector and those with low coordinates. The cut-off can be chosen. This algorithm and its variations are widely used [SM00]. Not many proofs of error bounds are known though. [ST07] prove bounds for planer graphs. [KVV04] prove that if one repeats this partitioning procedure on the subgraphs, then we can ensure that the graph is ultimately split into parts of high conductance with not too much edge weight "wasted" between different parts. [KM08] prove better bounds for planer graphs.

Acknowledgements I am grateful to Alan Frieze and Santosh Vempala for their collaboration on work reported here and to Santosh also for his comments on the manuscript. Thanks to all my coauthors.

9. REFERENCES

[ADKK02] N. Alon, W.F. DeLaVega, R. Kannan, and M. Karpinski, *Random sub-problems of max-snp problems*, 34th STOC (2002), 668–677.

[AE02] G. Andersson and L. Engebretsen, *Property testers for dense constraint satisfaction programs on finite domains*, Random Structures Algorithms **21** (2002), 14Ű32.

[AFKM01] Y. Azar, A. Fiat, A. Karlin, and F. McSherry, *Spectral analysis of data*, Proc. of STOC, 2001, pp. 619–626.

[AKK95] S. Arora, D. Karger, and M. Karpinski, *Polynomial time approximation schemes for dense instances of np-hard problems*, 27th STOC (1995), 284–293.

[AKS98] N. Alon, M. Krivelevich, and B. Sudakov, *Finding a large hidden clique in a random graph*, Random Structures and Algorithms **13** (1998), 457–466.

[AM05] D. Achlioptas and F. McSherry, *On spectral learning of mixtures of distributions*, Proc. of COLT, 2005.

[AM07] ______, *Fast computation of low-rank matrix approximations*, J. ACM **54** (2007), no. 2.

[AN06] N. Alon and A. Naor, *Approximating the cut-norm via grothendieck's inequality*, SIAM J. Comput. **35(4)** (2006), 787–803.

[ARH+] N. Alon, R.A.Duke, H.Lefmann, V.Rödl, and R.Yuster, *The algorithmic aspects of the regularity lemma*, Journal of Algorithms **16**.

[BCL+06] C. Borgs, J. Chayes, L. Lovász, V. Sós, B. Szegedy, and K. Vesztergombi, *Graph limits and parameter testing*, STOC, 2006.

[BP98] S. Brin and L. Page, *The anatomy of a large-scale hypertextual web search engine*, Proc. 7th international conference on World Wide Web (WWW), 1998, p. 107Ű117.

[Bru09] S. C. Brubaker, *Robust pca and clustering on noisy mixtures*, Proc. of SODA, 2009.

[BV09] C. Brubaker and S. Vempala, *Random Tensors and Planted Cliques*, Proc. of APPROX-RANDOM, 2009. 406-415.

[BV08] S. C. Brubaker and S. Vempala, *Isotropic pca and affine-invariant clustering*, Building Bridges Between Mathematics and Computer Science (M. Grötschel and G. Katona, eds.), Bolyai Society Mathematical Studies, vol. 19, 2008.

[BW09] N. Bansal and R. Williams, *Regularity lemmas and combinatorial algorithms*, Proc. IEEE 50 th FOCS, 2009, pp. 745–755.

[BY03] Z. Bar-Yossef, *Sampling lower bounds via information theory*, Proc. of STOC, 2003, pp. 335–344.

[DFK+04] P. Drineas, A. Frieze, R. Kannan, S. Vempala, and V. Vinay, *Clustering large graphs via the singular value decomposition*, Machine Learning **56** (2004), 9–33.

[DFLD88] S.T. Dumais, G.W. Furnas, T.K. Landauer, and S. Deerwester, *Using latent semantic analysis to improve information retrieval*, Proc. of CHI, 1988, pp. 281–285.

[DHKM07] A. Dasgupta, J. Hopcroft, R. Kannan, and P. Mitra, *Spectral clustering with limited independence*, Proc. of SODA, 2007, pp. 1036–1045.

[DHKS05] A. Dasgupta, J. Hopcroft, J. Kleinberg, and M. Sandler, *On learning mixtures of heavy-tailed distributions*, FOCS, 2005.

[DK01] P. Drineas and R. Kannan, *Fast monte-carlo algorithms for approximate matrix multiplication*, FOCS, 2001, pp. 452–459.

[DK03] ______, *Pass efficient algorithms for approximating large matrices*, SODA '03, 2003, pp. 223–232.

[DKM06a] P. Drineas, R. Kannan, and M. Mahoney, *Fast monte carlo algorithms for matrices i:*

Approximating matrix multiplication, SIAM J. on Computing **36** (2006), 132–157.

[DKM06b] ———, *Fast monte carlo algorithms for matrices ii: Computing a low-rank approximation to a matrix*, SIAM J. on Computing **36** (2006), 158–183.

[DKM06c] ———, *Fast monte carlo algorithms for matrices iii: Computing a compressed approximate matrix decomposition*, SIAM J. on Computing **36** (2006), 184–206.

[DKR02] P. Drineas, I. Kerenidis, and P. Raghavan, *Competitive Recommendation Systems*, Proceedings of the 34th Annual ACM Symposium on Theory of Computing (2002), 82–90.

[dlV96] W. Fernandez de-la Vega, *MAX-CUT has a Randomized Approximation Scheme in Dense Graphs*, Random Structures and Algorithms **8** (1996), 187–199.

[dlVK01] W. Fernandez de la Vega and C. Kenyon, *A randomized approximation scheme for metric max-cut*, J. Computer and System Sciences **63** (2001), 531–541.

[dlVKKV05] W. Fernandez de la Vega, M. Karpinski, R. Kannan, and S. Vempala, *Tensor decomposition and approximation schemes for constraint satisfaction problems*, STOC '05, 2005, pp. 747–754.

[DMM06] P. Drineas, M. W. Mahoney, and S. Muthukrishnan, *Subspace sampling and relative error matrix approximation: column-based methods*, Proc. of APPROX-RANDOM, 2006, pp. 316–326.

[DRVW06] A. Deshpande, L. Rademacher, S. Vempala, and G. Wang, *Matrix approximation and projective clustering via volume sampling*, Theory of Computing **2** (2006), no. 1, 225–247.

[DV06] A. Deshpande and S. Vempala, *Adaptive sampling and fast low-rank matrix approximation*, APPROX-RANDOM, 2006, pp. 292–303.

[Fie75] M. Fiedler, *A property of eigenvectors of nonnegative symmetric matrices and its application to graph theory*, Czech. Math. J. **25** (1975), 619–637.

[FK81] Z. Füredi and J. Komlós, *The eigenvalues of random symmetric matrices*, Combinatorica **1** (1981), no. 3, 233–241.

[FK99] A. Frieze and R. Kannan, *Quick approximation to matrices and applications*, Combinatorica **19** (1999), no. 2, 175–200.

[FK08] ———, *A new approach to the planted clique problem*, Proc. of FST & TCS, 2008.

[FK999] *A simple algorithm for constructing szemerédi's regularity partition*, Electronic journal of combinatorics **6** (1999).

[FKV98] Á. Frieze, R. Kannan, and S. Vempala, *Fast monte-carlo algorithms for finding low-rank approximations*, Proc. of FOCS, 1998, pp. 370–378.

[FKV04] A. Frieze, R. Kannan, and S. Vempala, *Fast monte-carlo algorithms for finding low-rank approximations*, J. ACM **51** (2004), no. 6, 1025–1041.

[GGR98] O. Goldreich, S. Goldwasser, and D. Ron, *Property testing and its connection to learning and approximation*, Journal of the ACM **5** (1998), no. 4, 653–750.

[GT08] B. Green and T. Tao, *The primes contain arbitrarily long arithmetic progressions*, Annals of Mathematics **167** (2008), 481Ű547.

[Has90] J. Hastad, *Tensor rank is np-complete*, J. Algorithms **11** (1990), 644–654.

[HhL09] C. Hillar and Lek heng Lim, *Most tensor problems are np hard*, The Computing Research Repository (2009).

[HP05] Har-Peled, *Low-rank matrix approximation in linear-time*, http://valis.cs.uiuc.edu/ sariel/papers/05/lrank/, 2005.

[Kle99] J. Kleinberg, *Authoritative sources in a hyperlinked environment*, Journal of the ACM **46** (1999).

[KM08] I. Koutis and G. L. Miller, *Graph partitioning into isolated, high conductance clusters: Theory, computation and applications to preconditioning*, Proc. of SPAA, 2008.

[Kru89] J. B. Kruskal, *Rank, decomposition, and uniqueness for 3-way and n-way arrays*, Multiway Data Analysis, R. Coppi and S. Bolasco, eds. NorthŰHolland, Amsterdam, 1989, p. 7Ű18.

[KSV08] R. Kannan, H. Salmasian, and S. Vempala, *The spectral method for general mixture models*, SIAM Journal on Computing **38** (2008), no. 3, 1141–1156.

[KV08] R. Kannan and S. Vempala, *Spectral algorithms*, Foundations and Trends in Theoretical Computer science **4:3-4** (2008).

[KVV04] R. Kannan, S. Vempala, and A. Vetta, *On clusterings: Good, bad and spectral*, J. ACM **51** (2004), no. 3, 497–515.

[McS01] F. McSherry, *Spectral partitioning of random graphs*, FOCS, 2001, pp. 529–537.

[MD09] M. W. Mahoney and P. Drineas, *Cur matrix decompositions for improved data analysis*, Proceedings of the National Academy of Sciences, vol. 106(3), 2009, pp. 697–702.

[MMD] M. W. Mahoney, M. Maggioni, and P. Drineas, *Tensor-cur decompositions for tensor-based data*, SIAM Journal on Matrix Analysis and Applications **30(2)**.

[PMJ+07] P. Paschou, M. W. Mahoney, A. Javed, J. Kidd, A. Pakstis, S. Gu, K. Kidd, and P. Drineas, *Intra- and inter-population genotype reconstruction from tagging snps*, Genome Research **17(1)** (2007), 96–107.

[RV07] M. Rudelson and R. Vershynin, *Sampling from large matrices: An approach through geometric functional analysis*, Journal of the ACM **54** (2007), no. 4.

[Sar06] T. Sarlós, *Improved approximation algorithms for large matrices via random projections*, FOCS, 2006, pp. 143–152.

[SM00] J. Shi and J. Malik, *Normalized cuts and image segmentation*, IEEE Transactions on Pattern Analysis and Machine Intelligence **22** (2000), no. 8, 888–905.

[ST07] D. A. Spielman and S. Teng, *Spectral partitioning works: Planar graphs and finite element meshes*, Linear Algebra and its Applications **421** (2007), no. 2-3, 284 – 305.

[SV09] T. Strohmer and R. Vershynin, *A randomized kaczmarz algorithm with exponential convergence*, Journal of Fourier Analysis and Applications **15** (2009), 262–278.

[SXZF07] J. Sun, Y. Xie, H. Zhang, and Christos Faloutsos, *Less is more: Compact matrix decomposition for large sparse graphs*, SIAM Conference on Date Mining, 2007, pp. 26–28.

[TTV09] L. Trevisan, M. Tulsiani, and Salil Vadhan, *Regularity boosting and efficiently simulating every high-entropy distribution*, Proc. of 24th IEEE Conference on Computational Complexity, 2009.

[Vu05] V. H. Vu, *Spectral norm of random matrices*, Proc. of STOC, 2005, pp. 423–430.

[VW04] S. Vempala and G. Wang, *A spectral algorithm for learning mixtures of distributions*, Journal of Computer and System Sciences **68** (2004), no. 4, 841–860.

Are Many Small Sets Explicitly Small?

Michel Talagrand
Université Pierre et Marie Curie
Equipe d'Analyse
Institut de Mathématiques, UMR 7586-CNRS
Boîte 186 - 4, Place Jussieu - 75252 PARIS CEDEX 05
spinglass@talagrand.net

ABSTRACT

We discuss various aspects of a conjecture that spans Analysis, Probability and Combinatorics. We find it interesting enough to offer a \$1000 prize for a solution of any of the main problems.

Categories and Subject Descriptors

G.3 [**Mathematics of Computing**]: Probability and Statistics; G.2 [**Mathematics of Computing**]: Discrete Mathematics; G.m [**Mathematics of Computing**]: Miscellaneous

General Terms

Theory

1. WHAT THIS IS ALL ABOUT

A central issue in mathematics and computer science is to gain understanding of subsets of spaces with many dimensions. Our natural intuition fails miserably at this. A fundamental fact is:

If a subset A of a space with many dimensions is "large", then "most" of the points of the space are "close to" A. (1.1)

This is the underlying philosophy of the theory of concentration of measure, one of the truly great ideas of Analysis and Probability. In (1.1), "large" and "most" will mean with respect to some probability measure. There is much more room on how to define "close to", and some new tentative definitions will be presented below. A very nice introduction to the fundamental theory of concentration of measure can be found in [3]. The most useful results are "dimension-free", in the sense that the provide inequalities that do not involve the dimension of the underlying space (which is the ultimate goal for not having to worry about large dimension). This is in particular the case for the Gaussian concentration of measure (see [3]) or the "convex-distance inequality" of [7] (see also [3]).

If the conjectures we propose turn out to be true, we will apparently learn something fundamentally new about the complexity of sets of large measure in the product of many spaces. On the other hand, to disprove these conjecture would possibly require genuinely new examples of "large sets". It therefore seems to be worthwhile to either prove or disprove them. For the reader in a hurry to cash a check, the main conjectures of the paper are Conjecture 2.1 and its "discrete version", Conjecture 7.1. The most extravagant and transformational result would be a positive solution of Problem 10.3. Our goal is to explain these conjectures with the proper background, and then to attempt to find their "proper formulation". Along the way, we will use the unique opportunity presented by this paper to mention three other of our favorite problems in Probability, all with a strong combinatorial flavor.

STOC'10, June 5–8, 2010, Cambridge, Massachusetts, USA

2. THE CONVEXITY CONJECTURE

Consider a subset A of $\mathbb{R}^M$. How many operations are required to build the convex hull of A from A? Of course the exact answer should depend on what exactly we call "operation", but Caratheodory's theorem asserts that any point in the convex hull of A is in the convex hull of a subset B of A such that $\mathrm{card} B = M + 1$ (and this cannot be improved) so we should expect that the number of operations is of order M, and that this cannot really be improved.

Suppose now that, in some sense, A is "large", and that, rather than wanting to construct all the convex hull of A, we only try to construct "a proportion of it". Do we really need a number of operations that grows with M? First, how do we tell that a set is "large"?

Probably the most natural measure on $\mathbb{R}^M$ is the canonical Gaussian measure $\gamma = \gamma_M$, i.e. the law of a sequence $(g_i)_{i \le M}$ of i.i.d. standard Gaussian r.v.s.

To simplify the discussion, let us assume that the set A is balanced, (or, if one prefers, is symmetric and star-shaped) i.e.

$$x \in A\ ,\ |\lambda| \le 1 \Rightarrow \lambda x \in A. \tag{2.1}$$

CONJECTURE 2.1. *There exists $\varepsilon > 0$ and an integer q with the following property. For any M, and any compact balanced set $A \subset \mathbb{R}^M$ with $\gamma(A) \ge 1 - \varepsilon$, we can find a convex compact set*

$$B \subset \underbrace{A + \cdots + A}_{q \text{ times}} \tag{2.2}$$

with $\gamma(B) \geq 1/2$, where of course the right hand side is the set of sums $x_1 + \cdots + x_q$ for $x_1, \ldots, x_q$ in A.

The word "compact" and the choice of the constant 1/2 are completely unimportant.

For large M the measure γ is basically concentrated on the sphere of radius $\sqrt{N}$, and this can be used to (easily) show that one obtains an equivalent conjecture if one replaces in Conjecture 2.1 the Gaussian measure γ by the uniform measure on the unit sphere. The same comment applies to Conjecture 3.3 below.

If this conjecture were true this would mean that q operations suffice to build a large convex set from any large set, *irrespective* of the dimension of the underlying space.

Wouldn't this be fundamental? The conjecture is discussed at length in the paper [5], but has attracted no attention. The present work is a renewed attempt to popularize this and related questions.

What support do we have for Conjecture 2.1? The truth is very little. The author tried to disprove it. He proved in [5] that $q = 2$ does not work, even if we replace $A + A$ by $L(A + A)$ for an arbitrarily large constant L. Whether $q = 3$ works is apparently open. We encourage the reader to spend a little time on this question. It is rather instructive to write a few natural examples of sets A for which one knows that $\gamma(A) > 9/10$ and to look at $A + A + A$. It turns out that this set is really huge in all the examples we could think of. Of course, the true obstacle is there: we have very little intuition of what really is a set of large measure in a high-dimensional space. A positive or negative solution of Conjecture 2.1 certainly qualifies for the \$1000 prize. It seems that if the conjecture is wrong, there is a chance that a counter-example to it would be a rather new kind of set and would be quite instructive. The same comments apply to the main conjectures in the rest of the paper.

3. GAUSSIAN PROCESSES

Certain early results of the author on Gaussian processes motivate the formulation of some of our conjectures, and the present section reviews these results. The reader who is not interested in either Gaussian or empirical processes can jump directly to Section 7, where the basic conjectures 7.1 and 7.2 are formulated in terms of very simple objects.

From the abstract point of view we use, a (centered) Gaussian process is a family $(X_t)_{t \in T}$ of jointly Gaussian r.v.s and the quantity of fundamental importance is $\mathsf{E} \sup_{t \in T} X_t$. It is discussed in detail in the first pages of [8], which contains a rather complete account of the author's ideas on stochastic processes, and let us simply say here that this is the natural measure of the "size" of the process. This processes induces a canonical distance d on the index set T, given by

$$d(s,t)^2 = \mathsf{E}(X_s - X_t)^2.$$

It turns out that, within a multiplicative factor, the quantity $\mathsf{E} \sup_{t \in T} X_t$ can be computed as a "functional of the geometry of the metric space (T, d)", i.e.

$$\frac{1}{L} \gamma_2(T,d) \leq \mathsf{E} \sup_{t \in T} X_t \leq L \gamma_2(T,d) \tag{3.1}$$

where L is a number and the quantity $\gamma_2(T,d)$ depends only on the geometry of the metric space (T,d). (Its exact definition is not important here and is explained at length in [8].) Thus (3.1) transforms a probabilistic problem (evaluating $\mathsf{E} \sup_{t \in T} X_t$) into a geometric problem (evaluating $\gamma_2(T,d)$). It is important to fully understand the nature of this result: it performs no magic. It is very difficult to estimate $\gamma_2(T,d)$ when the combinatorics of the space (T,d) are complicated. The meaning of (3.1) is simply that there is **no other way** to estimate $\mathsf{E} \sup_{t \in T} X_t$ than to estimate $\gamma_2(T,d)$.

At this point we make a half-column digression to mention that there remains a nice unsolved problem concerning the computation of $\gamma_2(T,d)$ in a rather explicit and concrete case. The author has proposed the following "the Ultimate Matching Conjecture" ([8], p. 110) that would (do a lot more than) nicely interpolate between the Ajtai-Komlòs-Tusnàdy matching theorem and the Leighton-Shor grid matching theorem.

CONJECTURE 3.1. *There exists a number L with the following property. Consider $\alpha_1 > 0$ and $\alpha_2 > 0$ with $1/\alpha_1 + 1/\alpha_2 = 1/2$. Then, given two independent i.i.d. samples $(X_i^1, X_i^2)_{i \leq N}$ and $(Y_i^1, Y_i^2)_{i \leq N}$ uniform in the unit square, with probability that goes to 1 as $N \to \infty$ there exists a one to one map π on $1, \ldots, N$ such that for $j = 1, 2$ we have*

$$\sum_{1 \leq i \leq N} \exp\left(\sqrt{\frac{N}{\log N}} \frac{|X_i^j - Y_{\pi(i)}^j|^{\alpha_j}}{L}\right) \leq 2.$$

The case $\alpha_1 = \alpha_2 = 4$ is of special interest. If it where true, with probability close to 1 we would find a matching π that satisfies, for some universal constant L^* both

$$\max_{i,j} |X_i^j - Y_{\pi(i)}^j| \leq L^* \frac{(\log N)^{3/4}}{N^{1/2}}$$

as in the Leighton-Shor grid matching theorem and

$$\sum_{i \leq N} |X_i^j - Y_{\pi(i)}^j| \leq L^* (\log N)^{1/2} N^{1/2}$$

as in the Ajtai-Komlòs-Tusnàdy matching theorem. Conjecture 3.1 (at least in certain crucial cases) essentially boils down to controlling $\gamma_2(T,d)$ where T is a certain class of functions on the unit square (which is defined through a control of the partial derivatives) and where d is the natural distance induced by $L_2([0,1]^2)$, see [8].

After this parenthesis, we go back to Gaussian processes. An essentially equivalent way to look at these is, given M, to consider the canonical process $(X_t)_{t \in \mathbb{R}^M}$ where the basic probability space is $(\mathbb{R}^M, \gamma)$ (recalling that γ is the canonical Gaussian measure) and where for $\boldsymbol{x} \in \mathbb{R}^M$ we have

$$X_t(\boldsymbol{x}) = \boldsymbol{t} \cdot \boldsymbol{x}, \tag{3.2}$$

the dot product of $\boldsymbol{t}$ and $\boldsymbol{x}$. In that case the canonical distance induced by the process is the Euclidean distance on $\mathbb{R}^M$.

Consider a convex balanced subset T of $\mathbb{R}^M$. Let us define

$$U = \mathsf{E} \sup_{t \in T} X_t = \int \sup_{t \in T} X_t(\boldsymbol{x}) d\gamma(\boldsymbol{x}), \tag{3.3}$$

where the process X_t is as in (3.2). (So, one might say that U measures the size of T with respect to the canonical Gaussian process.) Since $\sup_{t \in T} X_t \geq 0$ because T is balanced, it follows from Markov's inequality that for any number $v \geq 1$ one has

$$\gamma\left(\left\{\sup_{t \in T} X_t \geq vU\right\}\right) \leq \frac{1}{v}. \tag{3.4}$$

On the other hand, it is proved in [8] as a (non trivial) consequence of (3.1) that the following holds true.

PROPOSITION 3.2. *There exists a number L such that, (whatever the value of M and the choice of the set T) one can find a sequence $(H_k)_{k\geq 1}$ of half-spaces of $\mathbb{R}^M$ such that, with the notation* (3.3),

$$\left\{\sup_{t\in T} X_t \geq LU\right\} \subset \bigcup_k H_k \tag{3.5}$$

$$\sum_{k\geq 1} \gamma(H_k) \leq \frac{1}{2}. \tag{3.6}$$

Of course a half-space is simply a set of the type $\{x;\ t\cdot x \geq 1\}$ for some $t \in \mathbb{R}^M$. What this means is that not only the set $\{\sup_{t\in T} X_t \geq LU\}$ in (3.5) has a small measure for γ (which we know from (3.4)), but we have a kind of *explicit witness* of this, this set is covered by a union of simple sets (half-spaces) such that the *sum* of their measures is $\leq 1/2$. (Of course, the choice of the number $1/2$ is pretty arbitrary.) The information (3.5) is, in a sense, less fundamental than (3.1), but, on the other hand, it is still very much non trivial.

Only simple arguments about Gaussian measures are required to show from (3.5) that one can reformulate Conjecture 2.1 as follows.

CONJECTURE 3.3. *There exists an integer q with the following property. Given any integer M and any balanced set $A \subset \mathbb{R}^M$ with $\gamma(A) \geq 1 - 1/q$, there exists a sequence (H_k) of half-spaces of $\mathbb{R}^M$ such that*

$$x \notin \underbrace{A + \cdots + A}_{q \text{ times}} \Rightarrow x \in \bigcup_{k\geq 1} H_k$$

and

$$\sum_{k\geq 1} \gamma(H_k) \leq \frac{1}{2}.$$

We are not saying that the proper way to approach this conjecture is to look for a magic wand that would produce the half-spaces H_k. The point of the formulation of Conjecture 3.3 is to motivate further statements.

4. EMPIRICAL PROCESSES

Having proved (3.1) one would certainly like to find similar results for other classes of stochastic processes (a question that is explored in depth in [8]). Empirical processes constitute an important such class. They are certainly related to computer science, in particular in their rôle in dimension-reduction theorems as in [4]. The basic setting is as follows. Consider a sequence of i.i.d. uniformly distributed r.v.s Y_i in $[0, 1]$ and $\mathcal{F}$ a (finite) class of (Borel) functions. We assume for simplicity that $\int_0^1 f(x)dx = 0$ for each $f \in \mathcal{F}$. For $f \in \mathcal{F}$, consider the r.v.

$$X_f = \frac{1}{\sqrt{N}} \sum_{i\leq N} f(Y_i). \tag{4.1}$$

The problem is to estimate the size of the r.v.

$$\sup_{\mathcal{F}} X_f = \sup_{f\in\mathcal{F}} \frac{1}{\sqrt{N}} \sum_{i\leq N} f(Y_i), \tag{4.2}$$

say to bound its expectation. Given f, the central limit theorem shows that for large N the r.v. X_f is nearly Gaussian. Thus, a natural way to control the process $(X_f)_{f\in\mathcal{F}}$ is because it is close to a Gaussian process (that we understand through (3.1)). There is however a fundamentally different reason why the r.v. (4.2) can be small: it is because the larger r.v.

$$\sup_{f\in\mathcal{F}} \frac{1}{\sqrt{N}} \sum_{i\leq N} |f(Y_i)| \tag{4.3}$$

is already small. (In contrast, in the near-Gaussian case, one expects that there will be a lot of cancellation between terms and that this contributes in an essential way to the smallness of the sum.)

It can be shown in a precise way that the two previous methods are the *only* two ways to control the sup of the process $(X_f)_{f\in\mathcal{F}}$ [6]. Since the near-Gaussian case is well understood, the question is to understand the case (4.3), or, equivalently (since $N^{-1/2}$ is a normalization factor), to understand the quantity

$$\mathsf{E} \sup_{f\in\mathcal{F}} \sum_{i\leq N} f(Y_i), \tag{4.4}$$

where $\mathcal{F}$ consists of functions $f \geq 0$. Ideally we would like to be able to compute (4.4) as a function of the "geometry" of $\mathcal{F}$; but it is at present very unclear what would be the proper way to look at $\mathcal{F}$. Then the natural thought is that, if one cannot prove anything as satisfactory as (3.1), one should be less ambitious and try for something of the nature of (3.5). Another natural though is that, instead of (4.4), one should probably think first about a more basic problem of the same nature. We keep in mind that we are trying to prove inequalities, and that to do this there is no loss to replace continuous structures by ("suitably fine") discrete structures. Let us divide the interval $[0, 1]$ into M ($\gg N$) consecutive small intervals, and let us assume that each function of $\mathcal{F}$ is constant in these small intervals. Choosing the r.v.s $(Y_i)_{i\leq N}$ is pretty much the same (at least modulo a poissonization argument) as selecting each small interval with probability $p = N/M$.

5. SELECTOR PROCESSES

The previous considerations bring us naturally to *selector processes.* In a selector process we consider a finite set S and i.i.d. r.v.s $(\delta_i)_{i\in S}$ with $\mathsf{P}(\delta_i = 1) = p$ and $\mathsf{P}(\delta_i = 0) = 1 - p$. (The name arises from the fact that this process allows one to choose (= select) a random subset of size $\simeq p\text{card}S$ of S). Consider a class $\mathcal{F}$ of non negative functions on S or, equivalently, a class T of sequences $t = (t_i)_{i\in S}$ with $t_i \geq 0$. We are interested in the quantity

$$\mathsf{E}(T) := \mathsf{E} \sup_{t\in T} \sum_{i\in S} t_i\delta_i. \tag{5.1}$$

The situation of interest is where

$$\mathsf{E} \sup_{t\in T} \sum_{i\in S} t_i\delta_i \gg p \sup_{t\in T} \sum_{i\leq N} t_i = \sup_{t\in T} \mathsf{E} \sum_{i\in S} t_i\delta_i. \tag{5.2}$$

Before we pursue the discussion, let us explain the notation we will use throughout the paper. Let us denote by $\mu = \mu_p = \mu_{p,S}$ the law of the sequence $(\delta_i)_{i\in S}$. It is a product measure on $\{0,1\}^S$. It is convenient to think of points in

$\{0,1\}^S$ as subsets of S. We will denote by I, J, X, Y subsets of S, while A and B will denote subsets of $\{0,1\}^S$. Thus we have

$$\mathsf{E}(T) = \mathsf{E}\sup_{t\in T}\sum_{i\in S} t_i\delta_i = \mathsf{E}_p\sup_{t\in T}\sum_{i\in X} t_i.$$

The notation in the right-hand side means that we take expectation when $X \subset S$ is seen as a random element of the probability space $(\{0,1\}^S, \mu_p)$, and this is the notation we will use throughout the rest of the paper.

The problem of evaluating the quantity (5.2) has been partially solved in the very special case where T consists of sequences t with $t_i \in \{0,1\}$. This is explained in [9], a paper quite related to the present work. To introduce notation appropriate to that case, for a subset A of $\{0,1\}^S$ we define

$$\mathsf{E}_p(A) = \mathsf{E}_p\sup_{J\in A}\operatorname{card}(J\cap X), \tag{5.3}$$

which is simply the quantity $\mathsf{E}(T)$ of (5.1) for $T = \{\mathbf{1}_J\ ;\ J \in A\}$.

We will now make a one page digression to introduce the reader to some of the author's favorite obsessions about stochastic processes. We hope that the reader will find these questions beautiful and challenging. Our failure to solve them is a direct motivation for the less ambitious conjectures that are described in the present paper.

A first method to control the quantity (5.3) is through the obvious bound

$$\mathsf{E}_p(A) \le \max_{J\in A}\operatorname{card}J. \tag{5.4}$$

A second method is as follows.

LEMMA 5.1. *Assume that for a certain number $M \ge 1$ we have*

$$\sum_{J\in A}\left(\frac{p\operatorname{card}J}{M}\right)^M \le 1. \tag{5.5}$$

Then $\mathsf{E}_p(A) \le LM$, where L is a universal constant.

Proof. We use the "union bound" to write for any integer k

$$\mathsf{P}\Big(\sup_{J\in A}\operatorname{card}(J\cap X)\ge k\Big) \le \sum_{J\in A}\mathsf{P}(\operatorname{card}(J\cap X)\ge k).$$

Now

$$\mathsf{P}(\operatorname{card}(J\cap X)\ge k) \le \binom{\operatorname{card}J}{k}p^k \le \left(\frac{Cp\operatorname{card}J}{k}\right)^k,$$

using the elementary estimate

$$\left(\frac{m}{Ck}\right)^k \le \binom{m}{k} \le \left(\frac{Cm}{k}\right)^k, \tag{5.6}$$

where C is a universal constant. Now, by (5.5) we have $p\operatorname{card}J \le M$ for $J \in A$, so that for $k \ge 2CM$ we get, using simply that $k \ge M$ in the last inequality,

$$\left(\frac{Cp\operatorname{card}J}{k}\right)^k \le \left(\frac{p\operatorname{card}J}{2M}\right)^k \le 2^{-k}\left(\frac{p\operatorname{card}J}{M}\right)^M,$$

and combining these estimates with (5.5) that

$$\mathsf{P}\Big(\sup_{J\in A}\operatorname{card}(J\cap X)\ge k\Big) \le 2^{-k},$$

from which the result follows easily, using that since $M \ge 1$, the smallest integer $k \ge 2CM$ satisfies $k \le 3CM$. $\square$

Having found two genuinely different methods to bound $\mathsf{E}_p(A)$ we can use *mixtures* of them. This method is based on the observation that

$$\operatorname{card}(X\cap(I_1\cup I_2)) \le \operatorname{card}(X\cap I_1) + \operatorname{card}(X\cap I_2).$$

Therefore, if we consider $A_1, A_2 \subset \{0,1\}^S$ such that

$$\forall I \in A\ ,\ \exists I_1 \in A_1\ ,\ I_2 \in A_2\ ,\ I \subset I_1 \cup I_2, \tag{5.7}$$

we have $\mathsf{E}_p(A) \le \mathsf{E}_p(A_1) + \mathsf{E}_p(A_2)$. We can then apply the bound (5.3) to A_1 and the bound of Lemma 5.1 to A_2. More formally, let us define $\Psi(A)$ as the infimum of the numbers $M \ge 1$ for which we can find classes A_1 and A_2 such that (5.7) holds as well as

$$\max_{J\in A_1}\operatorname{card}J \le M\ ;\quad \sum_{J\in A_2}\left(\frac{p\operatorname{card}J}{M}\right)^M \le 1.$$

We have just shown that

$$\mathsf{E}_p(A) \le 2\Psi(A). \tag{5.8}$$

The natural question is whether the previous method is in full generality the best possible to bound $\mathsf{E}_p(A)$, i.e. whether the previous inequality can be reversed. Since $M \ge 1$ this can be true only when $\mathsf{E}_p(A) \ge 1$. (The case where $\mathsf{E}_p(A) \le 1$, such as when A consists of one single set that contains one single point is uninteresting.)

CONJECTURE 5.2. *There exists a universal constant L such that if $\mathsf{E}_p(A) \ge 1$ then $\Psi(A) \le L\mathsf{E}_p(A)$.*

The following statement is a more explicit form of the same conjecture.

CONJECTURE 5.3. *There exists a universal constant L with the following property. Consider any set S and any $p > 0$. Then for any $A \subset \{0,1\}^S$ with $\mathsf{E}_p(A) \ge 1$ we can find $B \subset \{0,1\}^S$ with the following properties, where $M = L\mathsf{E}_p(A)$:*

$$\forall I \in A\ ,\ \exists J \in B,\ \operatorname{card}(I\setminus J) \le M. \tag{5.9}$$

$$\sum_{J\in B}\left(\frac{p\operatorname{card}J}{M}\right)^M \le 1. \tag{5.10}$$

The difficulty in proving Conjecture 5.3 is that we are given A and we have to find B, which needs not be a subset of A. Moreover, nobody painted red the elements of B to help us find them.

In the same spirit as Conjecture 5.3 (and motivating it) is the problem of understanding the supremum of Bernoulli processes, that is the quantities $b(T) = \mathsf{E}\sup_{t\in T}|\sum_{i\in S}\varepsilon_i t_i|$, where now the ε_i are i.i.d random signs and T is a set of sequences on S. We do not assume here that $t_i \ge 0$. (The absolute values around the sum do not make the problem fundamentally different from the similar problem without these absolute values that we considered in the Gaussian case.) There are two immediate bounds for this quantity. The first one is through the trivial relation $b(T) \le \sup_{t\in T}|t_i|$, and the second is through a (elementary) comparison theorem with the Gaussian case, the inequality

$$b(T) \le \sqrt{2/\pi}\,\mathsf{E}\sup_{t\in T}\Big|\sum_{i\in S} g_i t_i\Big|,$$

where now the r.v.s g_i are independent standard Gaussian (so that in principle we understand the right-hand side using (3.1)). The author calls the problem of determining whether these two methods, and their mixtures as in the case of Conjecture 5.3, are really the only way to bound $b(T)$ the **Bernoulli problem**. The formal statement is as follows.

CONJECTURE 5.4. *(***The Bernoulli Conjecture***) There exists a universal constant L such that given any finite set S and any set T of sequences indexed by S, we can find two sets of sequences T_1 and T_2 which satisfy the following three properties:*

$$\forall t \in T_1 \ , \ \sum_{i\in S} |t_i| \le Lb(T)$$

$$\mathsf{E} \sup_{t\in T_2} \Big|\sum_{i\in S} g_i t_i\Big| \le Lb(T)$$

$$T \subset T_1 + T_2 = \{t_1 + t_2 \ , \ t_1 \in T_1, t_2 \in T_2\}. \tag{5.11}$$

The author has devoted a significant part of his life to the study of this question and offers a \$5000 prize for its solution. Amazingly enough, the program of constructing a decomposition such as in (5.11) can be carried out in many situations, as is detailed in [8].

We go back to the main story. It would be very interesting to be able to estimate in complete generality the quantity (5.1) as a function of the "geometry of T", by proving something in the spirit of Conjectures 5.3 and 5.4. This seems hopeless unless one first gives a positive solution to these conjectures, so it is apparently a very difficult project. Therefore, we should try first to look for weaker results. For this we will be guided by Proposition 3.2.

In order to distinguish conveniently between subsets of S and subsets of $\{0,1\}^S$, we will call a subset of $\{0,1\}^S$ a **class**.

We will say that a class $A \subset \{0,1\}^S$ is an *up-class* if

$$X \in A, Y \supset X \Rightarrow Y \in A.$$

We note that if A is an up-class, the map $p \mapsto \mu_p(A)$ is non-decreasing. We will say that a class $A \subset \{0,1\}^S$ is a *down-class* if

$$X \in A, Y \subset X \Rightarrow Y \in A.$$

If A is an up-class, its complement is a down-class, and conversely.

Given a subset I of S we consider the class

$$H_I = \{J \subset S; \ I \subset J\} \tag{5.12}$$

so that H_I is an up-class and

$$\mu_p(H_I) = p^{\operatorname{card} I}. \tag{5.13}$$

The notation H_I is motivated by the fact that these classes somewhat correspond to the half-spaces of Section 3. They are canonical, which motivates the following definition.

DEFINITION 5.5. *A class $A \subset \{0,1\}^S$ is p-small if there exists a family $\mathcal{I}$ of subsets of S such that*

$$A \subset \bigcup_{I\in\mathcal{I}} H_I \tag{5.14}$$

and

$$\sum_{I\in\mathcal{I}} \mu_p(H_I) = \sum_{I\in\mathcal{I}} p^{\operatorname{card} I} \le \frac{1}{2}. \tag{5.15}$$

Of course, the choice of the value $1/2$ is rather arbitrary. The idea of this definition is (again) that the sets H_I provide *explicit simple witnesses* that $\mu_p(A) \le 1/2$. It is particularly well adapted to the case where A is an up-class. Many natural classes are up-classes, such as in (5.17) below, and there is little hope to understand the structure of general classes unless we first understand that of up-classes.

Let us point out the following obvious fact.

LEMMA 5.6. *If A is p-small and $p' < p$ then A is p'-small.*

CONJECTURE 5.7. *There exists a number L with the following property. Consider any $0 < p < 1$, any set S and any set T of sequences $(t_i)_{i\in S}$ with $t_i \ge 0$. Let*

$$\mathsf{E}_p(T) = \mathsf{E}_p \sup_{t\in T} \sum_{i\in X} t_i := \int \sup_{t\in T} \sum_{i\in X} t_i d\mu_p(X). \tag{5.16}$$

Then the class

$$\Big\{X; \ \sup_{t\in T} \sum_{i\in X} t_i \ge L\mathsf{E}_p(T)\Big\} \tag{5.17}$$

is p-small.

A positive answer would give a version of Proposition 3.2 for selector processes. The practical-minded reader will ask what use would such a result have, and might not share the author's feeling that it would provide fundamental information. In some sense it is a result of the same nature than (3.1). It would show that if you are given a selector process, and would like to prove that, within a multiplicative factor that is a universal constant, the quantity $\mathsf{E}_p(T)$ (defined in (5.1)) satisfies $\mathsf{E}_p(T) \le M$ for a certain number M, there is in the end **no other way** than to find the witnesses that the set $\{X; \ \sup_{t\in T}\sum_{i\in X} t_i \ge LM\}$ is small.

One must realize that in Conjecture 5.7, the problem is for $p \le 1/2$. For $p \ge 1/2$, we leave it as a teaser the fact that the class (5.17) is empty for $L = 4$. (It could be easier to figure this out after reading Lemma 7.5 below.) Also, one feels that what matters is the case where p is sufficiently small, but we cannot quite prove it, and this will be discussed in the last section of the paper.

PROPOSITION 5.8. *With the notation of Conjecture 5.7, given a number $V > 0$, if we request that there exists a number $L(V)$ depending on V only such that the class*

$$\Big\{X; \ \sup_{t\in T} \sum_{i\in X} t_i \ge L(V)\mathsf{E}_p(T)\Big\} \tag{5.18}$$

is (Vp)-small for any $0 < p < 1$, any set S and any set T of sequences $(t_i)_{i\in S}$ with $t_i \ge 0$, the resulting conjecture is equivalent to Conjecture 5.7.

Proof. Assuming Conjecture 5.7 and given $V > 0$, let us prove that the class (5.18) is (Vp)-small if the number $L(V)$ is large enough. Using Lemma 5.6 we can assume that $V \ge 1$. Consider an integer $n > V$. It suffices to consider the case where $2np < 1$ for otherwise, as shown in Lemma 7.5 below, the class (5.18) is empty if $L(V)$ has been chosen large enough. Then, setting $p' = 1 - (1-p)^{2n}$ one proves that

$$\mathsf{E}_{p'} \sup_{t\in T} \sum_{i\in X} t_i \le 2n\mathsf{E}_p(T).$$

(We leave the proof inequality as a teaser for the reader who really wishes to penetrate this material. A hint can be found in Lemma 7.4 below.) It then follows from Conjecture 5.7 (used for p' rather than p) that the class (5.18) is p'-small if $L(V) = 2Ln$ where L is the constant of Conjecture 5.7. Now, since $2np < 1$ we have $(1-p)^{2n} \leq \exp(-2np) \leq 1 - np$ so that $p' \geq np \geq Vp$. □

In Proposition 11.2 below we will show that Conjecture 5.7 holds when T consists of a collection of sequences with disjoint support. However the case where T consists of a single constant sequence is already of interest, and we give the argument right away to ensure that the reader does not miss this important computation (which was already implicitly performed in the proof of Lemma 5.1).

LEMMA 5.9. *There exists a universal constant L_1 such that for each set $J \subset S$ the class $A = \{X \subset S;\ \mathrm{card} X \cap J \geq L_1 p \,\mathrm{card} J\}$ is p-small.*

Proof. Consider the smallest integer k with $k \geq L_1 p \,\mathrm{card} J$, and

$$\mathcal{I} = \{I \subset J;\ \mathrm{card} I = k\}$$

so that, if $m = \mathrm{card} J$, using (5.6)

$$\sum_{I \in \mathcal{I}} p^{\mathrm{card} I} = p^k \binom{m}{k} \leq \left(\frac{Cmp}{k}\right)^k. \tag{5.19}$$

Thus, if $L_1 \geq 2C$, then $k \geq 2Cpm$ and the quantity (5.19) is $\leq 2^k \leq 1/2$. On the other hand,

$$\mathrm{card}(X \cap J) \geq L_1 pm \Rightarrow \mathrm{card}(X \cap J) \geq k \Rightarrow \exists I \in \mathcal{I}, I \subset X,$$

so $\mathcal{I}$ witnesses that A is p-small. □

6. WEAKLY SMALL CLASSES

One problem when studying p-small classes is that one really wonders what kind of magic wand should be used to produce the family $\mathcal{I}$. The purpose of the present section is to introduce a related notion with which it might be easier to work. For two subsets I, Y of S, let us write

$$\begin{cases} \psi(I,Y) = 1 & \text{if } I \subset Y \text{ (i.e. } Y \in H_I), \\ \psi(I,Y) = 0 & \text{otherwise.} \end{cases} \tag{6.1}$$

DEFINITION 6.1. *We say that a class $A \subset \{0,1\}^S$ is weakly p-small if there exists a probability measure θ on $\{0,1\}^S$ such that*

$$A \subset \{\Psi \geq 1\} \tag{6.2}$$

where

$$\Psi(Y) = \frac{1}{2} \int p^{-\mathrm{card} I} \psi(I,Y) d\theta(I). \tag{6.3}$$

Of course, a probability measure on $\{0,1\}^S$ is simply a system of weights β_I for $I \subset S$, with $\beta_I \geq 0$ and $\sum_{I \subset S} \beta_I = 1$.

Since $\int \psi(I,Y) d\mu_p(Y) = \mu_p(H_I) = p^{\mathrm{card} I}$ Fubini Theorem implies that $\int \Psi(Y) d\mu_p(Y) = 1/2$. Thus when A is weakly p-small we have a concrete witness that A is small: the "somewhat simple" function Ψ is ≥ 1 on A, and of integral $\leq 1/2$. This function is somewhat simple because it is a convex combination of the simple functions $\psi(I,\cdot)$.

PROPOSITION 6.2. *If a class is p-small, it is weakly p-small.*

Proof. Consider a class $A \subset \{0,1\}^S$ and a family $\mathcal{I}$ of subsets of S that satisfies (5.14) and (5.15). Consider a probability measure θ on $\{0,1\}^S$ such that $\theta(\{I\}) \geq 2p^{\mathrm{card} I}$ for each $I \in \mathcal{I}$. Such a probability measure exists by (5.15), and $\Psi(Y) \geq 1$ for $Y \in H_I$ as seen from (6.3) by restricting the integral to $\mathcal{I}$. □

CONJECTURE 6.3. *There exist a number L such that every weakly p-small class is (p/L)-small.*

This seems to be a very nice problem of combinatorics. It sets aside the main theme of this paper (which is to try to discover some new structure of general up-classes) and in that sense it is not related to the main conjectures of the present work. It focuses on the issue of pulling the rabbit (i.e. the family $\mathcal{I}$) out of the hat. The reader is invited to analyze first the cases where θ is uniform over subsets of S with a given cardinality, or uniform over a class of disjoint subsets of S with the same cardinality to understand what seems to be going on.

The case where θ is carried by the sets of cardinality 1 is not difficult to settle, but is not completely trivial. It follows in particular from Theorem 11.1 below, but a simpler argument is as follow. Assume without loss of generality that $S = \{1, \ldots, N\}$ and that the sequence $a_i = \theta(\{i\})$ is non-increasing. For $k \geq 1$ define $n_k = \lfloor k/p \rfloor$. Consider that class $\mathcal{I} = \cup_{k \geq 1} \mathcal{I}_k$, where $\mathcal{I}_k$ consists of the subsets of $\{1, \ldots, n_k\}$ of cardinality k. Then if $X \subset S$ is not a subset of $\cup_{I \in \mathcal{I}} H_I$, the k-th element m_k of X is $> n_k$, and $\sum_{i \in X} a_i \leq \sum_k a_{n_k+1} \leq p \sum_i a_i \leq p$. Consequently if $\sum_{i \in X} a_i > p$ then $X \subset \cup_{I \in \mathcal{I}} H_I$, where $\sum_{I \in \mathcal{I}} (p/L)^{\mathrm{card} I} \leq 1/2$ if L is a large enough constant.

We could not yet decide the case where θ is carried by the sets of cardinality 2, and even the following subcase: Assume that S is the disjoint union of two subsets S_1 and S_2. Consider a probability measure θ^* on $S_1 \times S_2$, and the image θ of θ^* under the map $(i,j) \in S_1 \times S_2 \mapsto \{i,j\} \subset S$. To understand the depth of the problem, the reader might give a try to the case where S_1 and S_2 are disjoint unions of q sets $S_{1,1}, \ldots, S_{1,q}$ and $S_{2,1}, \ldots, S_{2,q}$ respectively and where θ is uniform over $\cup_{j \leq q} S_{1,j} \times S_{2,j}$.

There exists also some natural situations suggested by the theory of random graphs (and the paper [2]) that are not obvious to analyze. Consider for example the case where S is the set consisting of the$N(N-1)/2$ edges of a complete graph with N elements, so that a subset X of S is a graph, and consider the case where θ is uniform over the sets of k-cliques. (A k-clique is a complete subgraph on a subset of k vertices.) It is probable that many such situations should be analyzed before one forms enough intuition to decide Conjecture 6.3 one way or the other.

CONJECTURE 6.4. *There exists a number L such that with the notations of Conjecture 5.7 the class* (5.17) *is weakly p-small.*

In view of Proposition 6.2 this is weaker than Conjecture 5.7. Should Conjecture 6.3, have a positive answer, Proposition 5.8 shows that these conjectures would be equivalent, but of course it could happen that Conjecture 5.7 is true but Conjecture 6.3 is false.

As in Proposition 5.8 one can show that one gets the same conjecture if one requests that the class (5.17) is, say, $2p$-small.

The definition of weakly small classes is motivated by the following.

PROPOSITION 6.5. *Consider a class $A \subset \{0,1\}^S$. Then the following are equivalent.*

a) The class A is not weakly p-small.

b) There exists a probability measure ν on A such that

$$\forall I \subset S, \quad \nu(H_I) < 2p^{\mathrm{card} I}. \tag{6.4}$$

Proof. Let us assume b), so that, recalling the notation (6.1), we have

$$\int \psi(I,Y)d\nu(Y) = \nu(H_I) < 2p^{\mathrm{card} I}. \tag{6.5}$$

Considering a probability measure θ on $\{0,1\}^S$, by (6.3), (6.5) and Fubini Theorem we have

$$\int \Psi(Y)d\nu(Y) < 1,$$

so that since $\nu(A) = 1$ we have $A \not\subset \{\Psi \geq 1\}$. Thus A is not weakly p-small. Therefore b) $\Rightarrow$ a).

Conversely, let us assume that A is not weakly p-small. This implies that any convex combination of functions of the type $(1/2)p^{-\mathrm{card} I}\psi(I,\cdot)$ takes a value < 1 on A. The Hahn-Banach theorem then shows that A carries a probability measure ν for which the integral of any of these functions is < 1, which means that (6.4) holds. □

DEFINITION 6.6. *We say that a probability measure ν on $\{0,1\}^S$ is δ-spread if it satisfies*

$$\forall I \subset S, \quad \nu(H_I) \leq \delta^{\mathrm{card} I}. \tag{6.6}$$

In Definition 6.6 we have removed the factor 2 that occurs in (6.4). This factor is inappropriate for tensorization and is inelegant. The cost of doing this is that one cannot use Proposition 6.5 to characterize exactly weakly p-small classes by saying that they do not carry a p-spread measure. However we have the following, which is almost as nice, since the loss of a factor 2 is totally irrelevant here.

PROPOSITION 6.7. *Consider a class $A \subset \{0,1\}^S$. Then*

a) If the class A is not weakly p-small it carries a $2p$-spread probability measure.

b) If the class A carries a δ-spread probability measure it is not weakly δ-small.

Proof. We use Proposition 6.5 and we notice that $2p^{\mathrm{card} I} \leq (2p)^{\mathrm{card} I}$ when $\mathrm{card} I > 0$. □

In that spirit, we will show that Conjecture 6.4 can be reformulated as follows.

CONJECTURE 6.8. *There exists a number L with the following property. Consider any number $0 < p < 1$, any set S, any class $A \subset \{0,1\}^S$. Assume that for $J \in A$ we are given a sequence $t^J = (t_i^J)_{i\in S}$ with $t_i^J \geq 0$ and $\sum_{i\in J} t_i^J \geq 1$. Then if there exists a p-spread probability measure ν with $\nu(A) = 1$ we have (with the notation (5.16))*

$$\mathsf{E}_p \sup_{J\in A} \sum_{i\in X} t_i^J \geq \frac{1}{L}. \tag{6.7}$$

The point is that we only have $\sup_{J\in A} \mathsf{E}_p \sum_{i\in X} t_i^J \geq p$, so that (6.7) is a non-trivial statement.

The reformulation of Conjecture 5.7 as Conjecture 6.8 brings forward its true nature: it would be a new kind of lower bound on selector processes. In the last section of the paper we will prove a few results supporting Conjecture 6.8, in particular Corollary 11.4. This Corollary implies (but this is in fact already proved in [9]) that in the case of special interest when $\mathrm{card} J = n$ is a given integer for all $J \in A$, and where $t_i^J = 1/n$ for $i \in J$, then (6.7) holds. In other words,

$$\mathsf{E}_p(A) = \mathsf{E}_p \sup_{J\in A} \mathrm{card}(X \cap J) \geq n/L. \tag{6.8}$$

Proof that Conjecture 6.4 implies Conjecture 6.8. We set $T = \{t^J \,;\, J \in A\}$, so that for any $X \subset S$ we have

$$\sup_{J\in A} \sum_{i\in X} t_i^J = \sup_{t\in T} \sum_{i\in X} t_i,$$

and consequently

$$\mathsf{E}_p(T) = \mathsf{E}_p \sup_{t\in T} \sum_{i\in X} t_i = \mathsf{E}_p \sup_{J\in A} \sum_{i\in X} t_i^J.$$

We notice that since $\sum_{i\in J} t_i^J \geq 1$ we have

$$A \subset \Big\{X \,;\, \sup_{J\in A} \sum_{i\in X} t_i^J \geq 1\Big\} = \Big\{X \,;\, \sup_{t\in T} \sum_{i\in X} t_i \geq 1\Big\}.$$

Since A carries a p-spread probability measure, A is not p-small by Proposition 6.7 b) and if Conjecture 6.4 holds true the class A cannot be contained in the class (5.17) i.e. $L\mathsf{E}_p(T) > 1$, which is (6.7). □

Proof that Conjecture 6.8 implies Conjecture 6.4. We may assume that $p \leq 1/2$. Consider a set T of sequences $(t_i)_{i\in S}$ with $t_i \geq 0$ and, defining $\mathsf{E}_p(T)$ as in (5.16), consider a number V to be determined later and the class

$$A = \Big\{J \,;\, \sup_{t\in T} \sum_{i\in J} t_i \geq V\mathsf{E}_{2p}(T)\Big\}.$$

By definition of A

$$\forall J \in A\,,\ \exists (u_i^J)_{i\in S} \in T\,,\ \sum_{i\in J} u_i^J \geq V\mathsf{E}_{2p}(T). \tag{6.9}$$

Consider $J \in A$ and define $t^J = (t_i^J)_{i\in S}$ by $t_i^J = u_i^J$ if $i \in J$ and $t_i = 0$ otherwise. Thus for any $X \subset S$ we have

$$\sup_T \sum_{i\in X} t_i \geq \sum_{i\in X} u_i^J \geq \sum_{i\in X} t_i^J$$

and hence in particular

$$\mathsf{E}_{2p} \sup_T \sum_{i\in X} t_i \geq \mathsf{E}_{2p} \sup_{J\in A} \sum_{i\in X} t_i^J. \tag{6.10}$$

Assume for contradiction that there exists a $2p$-spread probability measure ν on A. Then, using (6.7) (for $2p$ rather than p), (6.9) and homogeneity, we get

$$\mathsf{E}_{2p} \sup_{J\in A} \sum_{i\in X} t_i^J \geq \frac{V\mathsf{E}_{2p}(T)}{L},$$

and combining with (6.10) :

$$\mathsf{E}_{2p}(T) = \mathsf{E}_{2p} \sup_T \sum_{i \in X} t_i \geq \frac{V \mathsf{E}_{2p}(T)}{L}.$$

If e.g $V = 2L$, this is impossible, so that A cannot carry a $(2p)$-spread probability measure, and by Proposition 6.7 it is p-small. □

One intrinsic difficulty in this circle of questions is that it is hard to analyze δ-spread probability measures.

We first study a fundamental example. Let $M = \text{card}S$, and consider the probability measure ν on $\{0,1\}^S$ that gives mass $1/M$ to each subset J of S of cardinality 1. Then ν is δ-spread for $\delta = 1/M$. To see this we note that $\nu(H_I) = 0$ unless $\text{card}I = 1$, and that when $\text{card}I = 1$ we have $\nu(H_I) = \delta$.

On the other hand, ν is supported by the up-class

$$A = \{X;\ \text{card}X \geq 1\}$$

and $\mu_p(A) = 1-(1-p)^M$. This is almost 1 for large M so A is not small for μ_p; but condition (6.6) is stable by tensorization; that is, if ν_1 on $\{0,1\}^{S_1}$ and ν_2 on $\{0,1\}^{S_2}$ satisfy this conditions so does $\nu_1 \otimes \nu_2$ on $\{0,1\}^{S_1} \times \{0,1\}^{S_2} = \{0,1\}^{S_1 \cup S_2}$ (here we assume that $S_1 \cap S_2 = \varnothing$). Thus, tensorization r times gives a measure ν that satisfies (6.6), but is supported by an up-class A with $\mu_p(A) = (1-(1-p)^M)^r$. For r large, $\mu_p(A)$ is as small as one wishes while A carries a δ-spread probability measure so is not weakly δ-small.

This example seem to have been brought to light in [1] (and I learned it through Noga Alon). Let us give two generalizations of it. In the first generalization we fix $k \leq M = \text{card}S$, and ν gives mass $\binom{M}{k}^{-1}$ to each subset J of S of cardinality k. Then $\nu(H_I) = 0$ if $\text{card}I > k$ while if $\text{card}I = n \leq k$ we have

$$\nu(H_I) = \frac{\binom{M-n}{k-n}}{\binom{M}{k}} = \frac{k(k-1)\cdots(k-n+1)}{M(M-1)\cdots(M-n+1)} \leq \left(\frac{k}{M}\right)^n.$$

In the second generalization, ν gives mass $1/N$ to each subset of a collection of N disjoint subsets of S of cardinality k. Then ν is δ-spread for $\delta = N^{-1/k}$.

To construct more complicated examples one can remark that the class of δ-spread positive measures is closed under the following two operations. Consider for $j = 1, 2$ a probability measure ν_j that lives on $\{0,1\}^{S_j}$ and is δ-spread, where S_1 and S_2 are disjoint sets. Then, as already pointed out, $\nu_1 \otimes \nu_2$ is δ-spread. Also, if Δ_j is the probability measure on $\{0,1\}^{S_j}$ that is concentrated at $\varnothing$, and if $\nu_1' = \nu_1 \otimes \Delta_2$ and $\nu_2' = \nu_2 \otimes \Delta_1$, then any probability measure $\nu \leq \nu_1' + \nu_2'$ is δ-spread. These claims are very simple to check. Iteration of these operations yields complicated examples, but we will show latter that none of these can be of help to disprove the main conjecture (Conjecture 7.8) of the next section.

Let us give a last example to demonstrate further the kind of complication that can arise in the structure of δ-spread measures. We consider three integers M, r and s. Consider a set S which is the disjoint union of r sets $S_1, \ldots, S_r$ of cardinality M, and

$$A = \{I \subset S\ ;\ \forall j \leq r, \text{card}(I \cap S_j) = 1\}.$$

Thus $\text{card}A = M^r$. Let us consider a set S', disjoint from S, of cardinality sM^r, and a map $\varphi : A \to \{0,1\}^{S'}$ such that the sets $\varphi(I)$ for $I \in A$ are each of cardinality s and form a partition of S'. Finally let

$$B = \{J \subset S \cup S'\ ;\ J \cap S \in A, J \cap S' = \varphi(J \cap S)\}.$$

Then it is quite straightforward to see that the uniform probability ν on B is δ-spread for $\delta = M^{-r/(r+s)}$.

7. POSITIVITY AND MORE DARING CONJECTURES

Consider a set T of sequences $t = (t_i)_{i \in S}$ and for $X \subset S$ define

$$\varphi(X) = \sup_{t \in T} \sum_{i \in X} t_i. \tag{7.1}$$

When $t_i \geq 0$ for every t in T, it is then clear that

$$\varphi(X \cup Y) \leq \varphi(X) + \varphi(Y). \tag{7.2}$$

Given an integer q and a class $A \subset \{0,1\}^S$, let us define

$$A^{(q)} = \{Y \subset S;\ \forall X_1, \ldots, X_q \in A,\ Y \not\subset X_1 \cup \cdots \cup X_q\}.$$

In words $A^{(q)}$ is the class of subsets of S that cannot be covered by q sets in A. It is an up-class. It follows from (7.2) that if

$$A = \{\varphi < a\}$$

then

$$\{\varphi \geq qa\} \subset A^{(q)}.$$

Now if $a = b\mathsf{E}_p\varphi$ $(= b\int \varphi(X) d\mu_p(X))$ we have $\mu_p(A) \geq 1 - 1/b$.

One should wonder whether Conjecture 5.7 would not follow from the more general fact that $A^{(q)}$ is p-small whenever $\mu_q(A)$ is not small.

CONJECTURE 7.1. *There exists a number q with the following property. For each $0 < p < 1$ and each class A we have*

$$\mu_p(A) \geq 1 - \frac{1}{q} \Rightarrow A^{(q)} \text{ is } p\text{-small.} \tag{7.3}$$

Let us observe that even when q is very large, it is not true that $\mu_p(A^{(q)})$ is very small. This is shown by the trivial example $A = \{\emptyset\}$, where for each q we have $A^{(q)} = A^c$.

One has the following weaker version of conjecture 7.1.

CONJECTURE 7.2. *Same as above, but requiring only*

$$\mu_p(A) \geq 1 - \frac{1}{q} \Rightarrow A^{(q)} \text{ is weakly } p\text{-small.} \tag{7.4}$$

Proving or disproving these conjectures qualifies for the prize, but this is not the case for any of the subsequent riskier conjectures.

The most obvious construction to disprove Conjecture 7.2 would be to consider a class $B \subset \{0,1\}^S$ that carries a p-spread measure and to define

$$A = \left\{I \subset S\ ;\ \forall J \in B, \text{card}(I \cap J) < \frac{1}{q}\text{card}J\right\},$$

so that $B \cap A^{(q)} = \emptyset$. But (6.8) implies that this construction fails to contradict (7.3) because $\mu_p(A)$ is very small.

One might think of Conjecture 7.1 as a discrete version of Conjecture 2.1. The parallel between these conditions is more obvious when Conjecture 2.1 is reformulated as Conjecture 3.3. (This is of course how we invented Conjecture 7.1.)

As was the case in Section 4 we get the same conjecture if in the conclusion we require, say, A to be $(p/2)$-small (provided we are permitted to change the value of q).

The crucial phenomenon in the present circle of ideas is that when $\mu_p(A) \geq 1/2$, the class $A^{(2)}$ seems to be extremely small. At least this appears to be the case on all the examples we know. It is this phenomenon that must be analyzed.

Much of the rest of the paper is devoted to the effort of trying to find "the proper formulation" of Conjecture 7.2. This will lead us through a series of more and more daring conjectures, and it is quite fascinating that none of them seems easy to disprove. It is equally fascinating that none of the subsequent ways to look at the problem that we will explore seems to bring us any closer to a positive solution.

Given a number $0 < \alpha < 1$, and a subset J of S let us define the probability $\theta_{J,\alpha}$ by

$$\theta_{J,\alpha}(\{I\}) = \alpha^{\mathrm{card}(J\cap I)}(1-\alpha)^{\mathrm{card}(J\setminus I)}.$$

Thus $\theta_{J,\alpha}$ is a product measure. When $i \notin J$ the factor of $\theta_{J,\alpha}$ of rank i is concentrated at 0, and when $i \in J$ it gives mass α to 1 and $1-\alpha$ to 0. An alternate way to look at this object is to observe that if we define $A_J = \{I \subset J\ ;\ I \in A\}$, then $\theta_{J,\alpha}(A) = \mu_{J,\alpha}(A_J)$, where $\mu_{J,\alpha}$ is defined as μ_p but for J instead of S and α instead of p.

CONJECTURE 7.3. *There exists a number $0 < \alpha < 1$ with the following property. Consider $0 < p < 1$ and an up-class $A \subset \{0,1\}^S$. Then the class*

$$\{J \subset S\ ;\ \theta_{J,\alpha}(A) > \mu_p(A)\}$$

is weakly αp-small.

We did not check it, but it seems virtually certain as in Proposition 5.8 that we get the same conjecture if we replace the condition "weakly αp-small" by the stronger condition "weakly p-small ".

Conjecture 7.3 is in the spirit of (1.1). One can think of the class $\{J \subset S\ ;\ \theta_{J,\alpha}(A) \leq \mu_p(A)\}$ as a kind of neighborhood of A, and the meaning of Conjecture 7.3 is that this neighborhood comprises "most of the points."

The main idea underlying Conjecture 7.3 is that it could be easier to prove a statement that does not involve the (somewhat mysterious) operation $(X, Y) \mapsto X \cup Y$. Let us note that the smaller α, the weaker is Conjecture 7.3.

Our next goal is to prove that Conjecture 7.3 implies Conjecture 7.2. We start by some simple observations.

For a class $A \subset \{0,1\}^S$ and an integer q we denote by $A_{(q)}$ the complement of $A^{(q)}$ i.e.

$$A_{(q)} = \{Y;\ \exists X_1,\dots,X_q \in A,\ Y \subset X_1 \cup \cdots \cup X_q\}. \quad (7.5)$$

We observe that this is a down-class. We also observe that if $A^{\sim}$ is the smallest down-class that contains A, i.e.

$$A^{\sim} = \{X \subset S\ ;\ \exists Y \in A,\ X \subset Y\}$$

then $A_{(q)} = A^{\sim}_{(q)}$. Thus, when proving any statement to the effect that $A_{(q)}$ is not small when one controls $\mu_p(A)$ from below, we can always assume that A is a down-class.

We note the formula

$$A^{(q_2)}_{(q_1)} = A^{(q_1 q_2)}. \quad (7.6)$$

LEMMA 7.4. *We have*

$$\mu_\beta(A_{(q)}) \geq \mu_\alpha(A)^q \quad (7.7)$$

for $\beta = 1-(1-\alpha)^q$.

Proof. The map $\varphi : (X_1,\dots,X_q) \mapsto X_1 \cup \cdots \cup X_q$ sends $\mu_\alpha^{\otimes q}$ to μ_β, so that since $A_{(q)} \supset \varphi(A \times \cdots \times A)$ we have

$$\begin{aligned}\mu_\beta(A_{(q)}) &\geq \mu_\beta(\varphi(A\times\cdots\times A))\\ &= \mu_\alpha^{\otimes q}(\varphi^{-1}(\varphi(A\times\cdots\times A)))\\ &\geq \mu_\alpha^{\otimes q}(A\times\cdots\times A) = \mu_\alpha(A)^q.\end{aligned}$$

□

LEMMA 7.5. *Given $0 < \alpha < 1$ there exists a number q_1 with the following property. If a down-class $A \subset \{0,1\}^S$ satisfies $\mu_\alpha(A) \geq 1 - 1/q_1$, then $A^{(q_1)} = \varnothing$.*

Proof. Consider q large enough so that $(1-\alpha)^q < 1/2$. Thus $\beta = 1-(1-\alpha)^q > 1/2$ and $\mu_\beta(A^{(q)}) \geq \mu_\alpha(A)^q$ by (7.7). Consider q_2 large enough so that $(1-1/q_2)^q \geq 1/2$. Hence if $\mu_\alpha(A) \geq 1-1/q_2$ we have $\mu_\beta(A^{(q)}) \geq 1/2$. Using (7.6) it therefore suffices to show that $A^{(2)} = \varnothing$ if A is a down-class and if $\mu_\beta(A) > 1/2$ for some $\beta \geq 1/2$. (One then use this for $A^{(q)}$ rather than A and one takes $q_1 = 2q_2$.) But then $\mu_{1/2}(A) \geq \mu_\beta(A) > 1/2$, and if A' is the image of A under the transformation that changes a subset X of S into its complement, then $\mu_{1/2}(A') = \mu_{1/2}(A) > 1/2$, so that $A \cap A' \neq \varnothing$. Thus there exists X and X' in A with $S = X \cup X'$ and therefore $A^{(2)} = \varnothing$. □

PROPOSITION 7.6. *Under Conjecture 7.3 the following is true. There exists a number q_1 such that for each $A \subset \{0,1\}^S$ we have*

$$\mu_p(A) \geq 1 - \frac{1}{q_1} \Rightarrow A^{(q_1)} \text{ is weakly } \alpha p\text{–small.}$$

Proof. As previously observed we can assume that A is a down-class. We consider q_1 as in Lemma 7.5. Using this lemma for J rather than S yields

$$\theta_{J,\alpha}(A) > \mu_p(A) \Rightarrow \theta_{J,\alpha}(A) \geq 1 - \frac{1}{q_1} \Rightarrow J \in A^{(q_1)}$$

and consequently

$$A^{(q_1)} \subset \{J\ ;\ \theta_{J,\alpha}(A) < \mu_p(A)\},$$

so that $A^{(q_1)}$ is weakly αp-small by Conjecture 7.3. □

Proof that Conjecture 7.3 implies Conjecture 7.2. From Lemma 7.5 we can assume $p < \alpha/2$. Let $p' = p/\alpha < 1/2$. Consider q_2 large enough that

$$p' < 1/2 \Rightarrow p'' := 1-(1-\alpha p')^{q_2} \geq p'.$$

Consider a down-class $A \subset \{0,1\}^S$. Using first that $p'' \geq p'$ and that $A_{(q_2)}$ is a down-class, and then Lemma 7.4 for $\alpha p' = p$ instead of α and q_2 instead of q we get

$$\mu_{p'}(A_{(q_2)}) \geq \mu_{p''}(A_{(q_2)}) \geq \mu_p(A)^{q_2}.$$

Thus, by Proposition 7.6, used for p' instead of p and $A_{(q_2)}$ instead of A, we have, since $\alpha p' = p$,

$$\begin{aligned}&\mu_p(A) \geq \left(1-\frac{1}{q_1}\right)^{1/q_2} \Rightarrow \mu_{p'}(A_{(q_2)}) \geq 1 - \frac{1}{q_1}\\ &\Rightarrow A^{(q_1)}_{(q_2)} = A^{(q_1 q_2)} \text{ is weakly } \alpha p\text{–small.}\end{aligned}$$

Thus Conjecture 7.2 holds for q large enough that $q \geq q_1 q_2$ and $1 - 1/q \geq (1 - 1/q_2)^{q_2}$. $\square$

We turn to a more refined version of Conjecture 7.3, that is "stable by tensorization".

DEFINITION 7.7. *Given two probability measures μ and μ' on $\{0,1\}^S$ we say that μ* dominates *μ' if for each up-class $A \subset \{0,1\}^S$ we have*

$$\mu(A) \geq \mu'(A).$$

Given a probability measure ν on $\{0,1\}^S$, we define a probability measure $W_\alpha(\nu)$ on $\{0,1\}^S$ by

$$W_\alpha(\nu)(A) = \int \theta_{J,\alpha}(A) d\nu(J). \tag{7.8}$$

CONJECTURE 7.8. *There exists a number $0 < \alpha < 1$ with the following property. Consider $0 < p < 1$ and a αp-spread probability measure ν on $\{0,1\}^S$ i.e. such that*

$$\nu(H_I) \leq (\alpha p)^{\operatorname{card} I} \tag{7.9}$$

for each subset I of S. Then the probability measure μ_p dominates the probability measure $W_\alpha(\nu)$, i.e for each up-class A it holds that

$$W_\alpha(\nu)(A) = \int \theta_{J,\alpha}(A) d\nu(J) \leq \mu_p(A).$$

This formulation is motivated by the fact that a statement of this type might be amenable to a proof by induction on the number of coordinates. We could not discover a suitable "induction hypothesis", but of course we checked that none of the measures ν constructed at the end of Section 4 disproves Conjecture 7.8. This follows from Theorem 11.10 below.

Proof that Conjecture 7.8 implies Conjecture 7.3. We assume that Conjecture 7.8 is true, and we consider an up-class $A \subset \{0,1\}^S$. Let us assume that the class

$$B = \{J \subset S\, ;\, \theta_{J,\alpha/2}(A) > \mu_p(A)\}$$

is not weakly $(\alpha p/2)$-small. By Proposition 6.5 we can find an αp-spread probability ν with $\nu(B) = 1$. Then for J in B we have

$$\theta_{J,\alpha}(A) \geq \theta_{J,\alpha/2}(A) > \mu_p(A).$$

Integrating this inequality in J with respect to ν shows that $W_\alpha(\nu)(A) > \mu_p(A)$. Thus μ_p does not dominate $W_\alpha(\nu)$, a contradiction that proves Conjecture 7.3 for $\alpha/2$ rather than α. $\square$

It seems potentially useful to point out a reformulation of Definition 7.7

DEFINITION 7.9. *Given two probability measures μ and μ' on $\{0,1\}^S$ we say that μ can be* pushed downwards *to μ' if there exists a probability measure λ on $\{0,1\}^S \times \{0,1\}^S$ such that its first marginal is μ, its second marginal is μ', and λ is supported by the set*

$$\{(X,Y);\ X \supset Y\}.$$

This is related to the very important idea of "mass transportation".

PROPOSITION 7.10. *The probability measure μ dominates the probability measure μ' if and only if the measure μ can be pushed downwards to the measure μ'.*

Proof. We prove only the easy part, the converse uses the Hahn-Banach theorem and is more delicate. Consider the probability measure λ as in Definition 7.9 and an up-class A. Then

$$\begin{aligned} \mu'(A) &= \lambda(\{(X,Y);\ Y \in A\}) \\ &= \lambda(\{(X,Y);\ Y \in A,\ X \supset Y\}) \\ &\leq \lambda(\{(X,Y);\ X \in A\}) = \mu(A) \end{aligned}$$

since $Y \in A,\ X \supset Y \Rightarrow X \in A$. $\square$

The point of mentioning this is that the probability measure λ of Definition 7.7 could be a useful object to consider.

Next we state a kind of "dual" formulation of Conjecture 7.8. The main idea is to now think of the quantity $\theta_{J,\alpha}(A)$ as a function of J. We recall the notation (6.1), and to lighten notation we write

$$h(I,J) = (\alpha p)^{-\operatorname{card} I} \psi(I,J) \tag{7.10}$$

if $I \neq \emptyset$ and $h(\emptyset, J) = 1$.

CONJECTURE 7.11. *There exists a number $0 < \alpha < 1$ with the following property. For any up-class A there exists a probability measure η on $\{0,1\}^S$ such that for any $J \subset S$ we have*

$$\theta_{J,\alpha}(A) \leq \mu_p(A) \int h(I,J) d\eta(I). \tag{7.11}$$

The present statement is related to Conjecture 6.4, and in some sense we have come a full circle since this no longer uses the idea of δ-spread measures.

Proof that Conjecture 7.11 implies Conjecture 7.8. If a probability measure μ is αp-spread, i.e. satisfies (7.9), then, using (7.8) in the first line and (7.11) in the second we have, for any up-class A

$$\begin{aligned} W_\alpha(\nu)(A) &= \int \theta_{J,\alpha}(A) d\nu(J) \\ &\leq \mu_p(A) \int \Big(\int h(I,J) d\eta(I) \Big) d\nu(J) \\ &= \mu_p(A) \int \Big(\int h(I,J) d\nu(J) \Big) d\eta(I) \\ &\leq \mu_p(A) \end{aligned}$$

since $\int h(I,J) d\nu(J) \leq 1$ by (7.9) and η is a probability. Thus μ_p dominates $W_\alpha(\nu)$, and this completes the proof. $\square$

Proof that Conjecture 7.8 implies Conjecture 7.11. Consider an up-class A, so that by Conjecture 7.8, for each αp-spread probability measure ν on $\{0,1\}^S$,

$$\int \theta_{\alpha,J}(A) d\nu(J) = W_\alpha(\nu)(A) \leq \mu_p(A).$$

Let us assume for contradiction that we cannot find a probability η as in (7.11). Consider the class $\mathcal{C}$ of functions g on $\{0,1\}^S$ for which there exists a probability measure η on $\{0,1\}^S$ such that

$$\forall J \subset S,\quad g(J) \leq \mu_p(A) \int h(I,J) d\eta(I).$$

Then $\mathcal{C}$ is a convex set, and since we assume that we cannot find η as in (7.11) we have $J \mapsto \theta_{\alpha,J}(A) \notin \mathcal{C}$. In fact, we can even find $\varepsilon > 0$ such that $\mathcal{C} \cap \mathcal{B}_\varepsilon = \varnothing$, where

$$\mathcal{B}_\varepsilon = \{f\ ;\ \forall J \subset S\ ,\ |\theta_{\alpha,J}(A) - f(J)| \leq \varepsilon\}.$$

This follows from an obvious compactness argument. The Hahn-Banach theorem implies that there exists a linear functional ν on the space of functions on $\{0,1\}^S$ separating the convex sets $\mathcal{C}$ and $\mathcal{B}_\varepsilon$, in the sense that

$$\sup_{g\in\mathcal{C}} \nu(g) := \beta < \inf_{g\in\mathcal{B}_\varepsilon} \nu(g). \tag{7.12}$$

Since $g \in \mathcal{C}$ and $g' \leq g$ imply $g' \in \mathcal{C}$, it follows that ν is positive, so it is a positive measure. Since $\mathcal{C}$ contains the constant function g given by $g(J) = \mu_p(A)$ for all $J \subset S$ (as is seen by taking $\eta(\{\emptyset\}) = 1$) we have $\beta > 0$, so we can as well by homogeneity assume that in (7.12) we have $\beta = \mu_p(A)$. Since for each $I \subset S$ the function $g(\cdot) = \mu_p(A)h(I,\cdot)$ is in $\mathcal{C}$, it follows from (7.12) that

$$\forall I \subset S,\ \ \nu(h(I,\cdot)) \leq 1$$

i.e.

$$\forall I \subset S,\ \ \nu(H_I) \leq (\alpha p)^{\mathrm{card} I}. \tag{7.13}$$

In particular if we take $I = \emptyset$ we see that ν has a mass at most one. Adding the appropriate mass at $\emptyset$ we turn ν into a probability measure without changing $\nu(H_I)$ for $I \neq \emptyset$, so (7.13) means that ν is (αp)-spread. Also by (7.12) we have $\beta = \mu_p(A) < \inf_{g\in\mathcal{B}_\varepsilon} \nu(g)$, and using this for the function $g : J \mapsto \theta_{\alpha,J}(A)$ yields, using (7.9) again

$$\beta = \mu_p(A) < \nu(g) = \int \theta_{\alpha,J}(A) d\nu(J) = W_\alpha(\nu)(A).$$

It follows that μ_p does not dominate $W_\alpha(\nu)$, a contradiction that finishes the proof. □

When studying Conjecture 7.11 we face the same problem as in Conjecture 6.4. What is the magic method that will produce the probability measure η? Of course one cannot help feeling that Conjecture 7.11 is too strong to be possibly true. Yet, inspection of simple cases shows that possibly something deep is going on. We will explain how to construct the probability η in the case where $A = \{X \subset S;\ X \neq \emptyset\}$. This amounts to find coefficients $\beta_I \geq 0$ such that (setting $N = \mathrm{card} S$ and recalling the notation (7.10)), the following holds true:

$$\sum_{I\subset S} \beta_I \leq \mu_p(A) = 1-(1-p)^N \tag{7.14}$$

and

$$\forall X \subset S,\ \ W^*_\alpha(A)(X) = 1-(1-\alpha)^{\mathrm{card} X} \leq \sum_{I\subset X} \beta_I h(I,X). \tag{7.15}$$

Although the construction is a posteriori simple, it is connected with deeper ideas that will be explained in Section 9. Assuming without loss of generality that α is small enough that $1-\alpha \geq \exp(-2\alpha)$, and using the fact that by concavity for all y and all s we have

$$1-e^{-y} \leq 1-e^{-s}+e^{-s}(y-s) = 1-(1+s)e^{-s}+e^{-s}y, \tag{7.16}$$

we see that for every s

$$\begin{aligned} W^*_\alpha(A)(X) &= 1-(1-\alpha)^{\mathrm{card} X} \leq 1-\exp(-2\alpha \mathrm{card} X) \\ &\leq 1-(1+s)e^{-s}+2\alpha e^{-s}\mathrm{card} X. \end{aligned}$$

Since $\mathrm{card} X = \alpha p \sum_{i\in S} h(\{i\},X)$ we see that (7.15) holds for $\beta_\emptyset = 1-(1+s)e^{-s}$, $\beta_{\{i\}} = 2\alpha^2 p e^{-s}$ for $i \in S$ and $\beta_I = \emptyset$ if $\mathrm{card} I \geq 2$. Thus

$$\sum_{I\subset S} \beta_I = 1-(1+s)e^{-s}+2\alpha^2 pNe^{-s},$$

and the optimal choice $s = 2\alpha^2 N$ gives

$$\sum_{I\subset S} \beta_I \leq 1-\exp(-2\alpha^2 pN) \leq 1-(1-p)^N$$

if $\alpha \leq 1/2$.

8. THE KAHN-KALAI CONJECTURE

Conjecture 8.1. *[2] There exists a universal constant L such that for all $0 < p < 1$, if $A \subset \{0,1\}^S$ is an up-class that satisfies $\mu_p(A) \leq 1/2$, then A is p'-small for $p' = p/(L \log \mathrm{card} S)$.*

Given the class A, the quantity of interest is the "threshold" $p = p_A$ defined by $\mu_p(A) = 1/2$. A positive solution to Conjecture 8.1 would mean that to compute p_A (within a logarithmic factor) there is no other way than to compute $p^*_A = \sup\{p\ ;\ A \text{ is } p\text{-small}\}$. This is very much in the spirit of (3.1) and Conjecture 5.7.

Conjecture 8.1 is discussed at length in [2]. Of course we have the following weaker version:

Conjecture 8.2. *As above, requiring only A to be weakly p'-small.*

Although this is difficult to explain, we feel that these conjectures are closely related to those of the previous sections, mainly in the sense that probably it requires a really new idea about up-classes to disprove them. Here are related questions .

Conjecture 8.3. *There exists a universal constant L with the following property. Consider a class $B \subset \{0,1\}^S$ and assume that for some integer m we have* $\mathrm{card} I = m$ *whenever $I \in B$. Assume that B carries a δ-spread measure ν and let $A = \{J \subset S, \exists I \in B, I \subset J\}$. Then if $p \geq L\delta \log(m+1)$ we have $\mu_p(A) \geq 1/2$.*

A more precise version of Conjecture 8.3 is as follows.

Conjecture 8.4. *There exists a universal constant L with the following property. Consider a class $B \subset \{0,1\}^S$ and assume that for some integer m we have* $\mathrm{card} I = m$ *whenever $I \in B$. Assume that B carries a δ-spread measure ν. Then for $p \geq \delta$ we have*

$$\mathsf{E}_p(B) = \mathsf{E}_p \sup_{I\in B} \mathrm{card}(X\cap I) \geq m(1-L\exp(-p/L\delta)) .$$

To see that this is stronger than (8.3) one simply observe that if A is as in the statement of that conjecture, then $\mu_p(A) \geq 1/2$ whenever $\mathsf{E}(B) \geq m-1/2$.

We formulate next a common generalization to both Conjecture 8.2 and the conjectures of the previous sections. We recall the notation (7.8).

Conjecture 8.5. *There exists a universal constant L with the following property. Consider $0 < p < 1/2$ and $\delta > 0$. Then if ν is a δ-spread measure on $\{0,1\}^S$, and if*

$$\alpha \leq 1-(1-p)^{\frac{1}{L\delta}} \tag{8.1}$$

then μ_p dominates $W_\alpha(\nu)$.

This conjecture is "dimension-independent", in the sense that the cardinality of S is irrelevant. The case $\delta = p$ recovers Conjecture 7.8.

Proof that Conjecture 8.5 implies Conjecture 8.2. Consider an up-class A and a δ-spread probability ν with $\nu(A) = 1$. Then under (8.1) μ_p dominates $W_\alpha(\nu)$, so that in particular $W_\alpha(\nu)(A) \le \mu_p(A)$. Therefore by (7.8) (and since $\nu(A) = 1$) we can find $J \in A$ with $\theta_{J,\alpha}(A) \le \mu_p(A)$. Since A is an up-class, for J in A we have $A \supset \{X ; X \supset J\}$. Thus we have, letting $M = \mathrm{card} S$,

$$\theta_{J,\alpha}(A) \ge \theta_{J,\alpha}(\{X; X \supset J\}) = \alpha^{\mathrm{card} J} \ge \alpha^M$$

and therefore

$$\mu_p(A) \ge \alpha^M. \tag{8.2}$$

Since $1 - p \le \exp(-p)$ if we set $\delta = p/2L \log M$ (where L is the constant of (8.1)) it holds that

$$(1-p)^{1/L\delta} \le \exp(-2\log M) \le \frac{1}{M^2}.$$

Therefore (8.1) is satisfied for $\alpha = 1 - 1/M^2$, so that (8.2) yields

$$\mu_p(A) \ge \left(1 - \frac{1}{M^2}\right)^M \ge \frac{1}{2}$$

for $M \ge 3$. Thus for $M \ge 3$, if $\mu_p(A) < 1/2$, we cannot find ν as above and A must be weakly δ-small. □

In Conjecture 8.5 the value of α can be very close to 1 (as in the previous proof) so this conjecture could be much riskier than the previous ones. It is of interest to test it on the case where, if $M = \mathrm{card} S$, ν gives mass $1/M$ to each set $I \subset S$ with $\mathrm{card} I = 1$, so that ν is $(1/M)$-spread, and (8.1) allows values of α as large as $1 - (1-p)^{M/L}$. To check that μ_p dominates $W_\alpha(\nu)$ one shows with a little work that the critical case is that of the class $A = \{I \subset S ; I \ne \emptyset\}$. It satisfies $\mu_p(A) = 1 - (1-p)^M$ and indeed $\mu_p(A) \ge W_\alpha(\nu)(A) = \alpha$ if $L \ge 1$.

9. MULTIPLICATIVE VERSION

CONJECTURE 9.1. *There exists a number $\alpha > 0$ with the following property. For each number $0 < p < 1/2$, each αp-spread measure ν and each up-class A we have (assuming $A \ne \{0,1\}^S$)*

$$-\int \log(1 - \theta_X(A)) d\nu(X) \le \log(1 - \mu_p(A)). \tag{9.1}$$

Here $\theta_X(A) = \theta_{X,\alpha}(A)$ is as in Conjecture 7.3. The value of α is kept implicit to lighten notation. As we will soon see, this conjecture is stronger than Conjecture 7.8. One can similarly formulate a conjecture stronger than Conjecture 8.5 by asking that (9.1) holds under (8.1).

Passing to complements, (9.1) means that for any down-class A one should have

$$\mu_p(A) \le \prod_X \theta_X(A)^{\nu(\{X\})}, \tag{9.2}$$

a "multiplicative" inequality.

Let us start with an example. Consider a subset $I \subset S$, and let $n = \mathrm{card} I$. Let $A = \{X \subset S; \ I \not\subset X\}$ so $\mu_p(A) = 1 - p^n$. It is clear that $\theta_X(A) = 1$ if $I \not\subset X$, and $\theta_X(A) = 1 - \alpha^n$ if $I \subset X$. Thus (9.2) holds for this class A provided

$$1 - p^n \le (1-\alpha^n)^{\nu(\{X; X \supset I\})} = (1 - \alpha^n)^{\nu(H_I)}.$$

This essentially requires that $\nu(H_I) \le (p/\alpha)^n = (p/\alpha)^{\mathrm{card} I}$. The meaning of Conjecture 9.1 is that this obviously necessary requirement is basically the only requirement for (9.2) to hold for general classes.

Throughout the rest of this section we denote by $\mathcal{D}(S)$ the class of measures ν on $\{0,1\}^S$ that satisfy (9.2) for every down-class $A \subset \{0,1\}^S$. (The dependence on α and p is kept implicit). We will show that the class $\mathcal{D}(S)$ enjoy remarkable stability properties, which seems to indicate that (9.1) is the "correct" conjecture.

THEOREM 9.2. *a) If $\mathrm{card} S = 1$ and $\nu(\{1\}) \le p$, then $\nu \in \mathcal{D}(S)$ (provided $1 - \alpha \ge 1/e$.)*

b) More generally, if α is small enough and if $\nu(\emptyset) \ge 1 - p^{\mathrm{card} S}$, then $\nu \in \mathcal{D}(S)$.

c) If S is the disjoint union $S = S_1 \cup S_2$, and if $\nu_1 \in \mathcal{D}(S_1)$, $\nu_2 \in \mathcal{D}(S_2)$ then $\nu_1 \otimes \nu_2 \in \mathcal{D}(S)$.

d) More generally, assume that S is a disjoint union $S = S_1 \cup S_2$, consider $\nu_1 \in \mathcal{D}(S_1)$ and for $X \in S_1$ consider $\nu_X \in \mathcal{D}(S_2)$. Consider the measure ν on $\{0,1\}^{S_1 \times S_2}$ given by

$$\nu(A) = \int \nu_X(\{Y; \ (X,Y) \in A\}) d\nu_1(X)$$

where $X \subset S_1$, $Y \subset S_2$. Then $\nu \in \mathcal{D}(S)$.

e) Assume that S is a disjoint union $S = S_1 \cup S_2$, and denote by Δ_j the probability on $\{0,1\}^{S_j}$ that is concentrated at $\emptyset$. Consider $\nu_1 \in \mathcal{D}(S_1)$ and $\nu_2 \in \mathcal{D}(S_2)$. Then any probability ν that satisfies $\nu \le \nu_1 \otimes \Delta_2 + \Delta_1 \otimes \nu_2$ belongs to $\mathcal{D}(S)$.

In Theorem 11.11 in the last section of the present paper, we will prove a more specialized result: If $k/N \le p$, the uniform probability ν on the sets $I \subset S$ with $\mathrm{card} I = k$ belongs to $\mathcal{D}(S)$.

A consequence of Theorem 9.2 is that, if there exists a αp-spread probability measure that does not satisfy (9.2), it cannot be constructed from simpler pieces using any of the operations of Theorem 9.2.

COROLLARY 9.3. *Conjecture 9.1 implies Conjecture 7.8.*

Proof. First, we observe that by the inequality $x \le -\log(1-x)$, under (9.1) we have

$$\int \theta_X(A) d\nu(X) \le \log(1 - \mu_p(A)). \tag{9.3}$$

Next, Theorem 9.2 implies that if ν satisfies (7.2), so do its powers $\nu^{\otimes n}$ (when we identify $(\{0,1\}^S)^n$ with $\{0,1\}^{S'}$ where $\mathrm{card} S' = n \mathrm{card} S$) so that, using (9.3) for $\nu^{\otimes n}$ and A^n,

$$\left(\int \theta_X(A) d\nu(X)\right)^n \le \log(1 - \mu_p(A)^n)$$

for all n, and thus

$$\int \theta_X(A)d\nu(X) \leq \mu_p(A)$$

whenever A is an up-class. □

Proof of Theorem 9.2. We find it convenient to use the formulation (9.2).

To prove a), we note that when card$S = 1$, the only non-trivial case to consider is $A = \{\varnothing\}$, in which case (9.2) reduces to

$$1 - p \leq (1-\alpha)^{\nu(\{1\})},$$

which holds for $\alpha \leq 1 - 1/e$ and $\nu(\{1\}) = p$.

To prove b) we observe that $\theta_X(A)$ decreases as X increases, so that it suffices to prove that $\mu_p(A) \leq \theta_S(A)^a$ for $a = p^{\mathrm{card}S}$. Given $\mu_p(A)$, what is the smallest possible value of $\theta_S(A)$? The density of θ_S with respect to μ_p at I depends only on card$I$, and increases with card$I$. It should then be clear that if $A_k = \{I \subset S;\ \ \mathrm{card}I \leq k\}$ then

$$\mu_p(A) \geq \mu_p(A_k) \Rightarrow \theta_S(A) \geq \theta_S(A_k)$$

and the whole matter is reduced to a struggle with the tails of the Binomial law, which is left to the interested reader.

To prove c), we consider a down-class $A \subset \{0,1\}^{S_1 \cup S_2}$. For $I \subset S_1$ we write

$$A_I = \{J \subset S_2;\ \ I \cup J \subset A\} \tag{9.4}$$

and for $J \subset S_2$ we write

$$A_J = \{I \subset S_1;\ \ I \cup J \in A\}. \tag{9.5}$$

Since $\nu_1 \in \mathcal{D}(S_1)$, for each $J \subset S_2$ we have, lightening notation by writing $\nu_{1,X}$ rather than $\nu_1(\{X\})$,

$$\eta_1(A_J) \leq \prod_{X \subset S_1} \theta_X(A_J)^{\nu_{1,X}},$$

where η_1 denotes the projection of μ_p on $\{0,1\}^{S_1}$. Using Fubini's theorem and Hölder's inequality we get

$$\mu_p(A) = \int \eta_1(A_J)d\eta_2(J) \leq \int \prod_{X \subset S_1} \theta_X(A_J)^{\nu_{1,X}} d\eta_2(J)$$
$$\leq \prod_{X \subset S_1} \left(\int \theta_X(A_J)d\eta_2(J)\right)^{\nu_{1,X}}, \tag{9.6}$$

where of course η_2 is the projection of μ_p on $\{0,1\}^{S_2}$.

Using Fubini's theorem again yields

$$\int \theta_X(A_J)d\eta_2(J) = \theta_X \otimes \eta_2(A) = \int \eta_2(A_I)d\theta_X(I). \tag{9.7}$$

Since $\nu_2 \in \mathcal{D}(S_2)$, writing $\nu_{2,X}$ rather than $\nu_2(\{X\})$ we get

$$\eta_2(A_I) \leq \prod_{Y \subset S_2} \theta_Y(A_I)^{\nu_{2,Y}} \tag{9.8}$$

so that, using Hölder's inequality again,

$$\int \eta_2(A_I)d\theta_X(I) \leq \prod_{Y \subset S_2} \left(\int \theta_Y(A_I)d\theta_X(I)\right)^{\nu_{2,Y}} \tag{9.9}$$
$$= \prod_{Y \subset S_2} \theta_{X \cup Y}(A)^{\nu_{2,Y}}$$

and combining (9.6) to (9.9) finally yields,

$$\mu_p(A) \leq \prod_{X \subset S_1, Y \subset S_2} \theta_{X \cup Y}(A)^{\nu_{1,X}\nu_{2,Y}}, \tag{9.10}$$

the required inequality.

To prove d), we simply replace (9.8) by

$$\eta_2(A_I) \leq \prod_{Y \subset S_2} \theta_Y(A_I)^{\nu_{X,Y}}$$

(where $\nu_{X,Y} = \nu_X(\{Y\})$). We proceed as above, and instead of (9.10) we get

$$\mu_p(A) \leq \prod_{X \subset S_1, Y \subset S_2} \theta_{X \cup Y}(A)^{\nu_{1,X}\nu_{X,Y}},$$

the required inequality.

To prove e), consider a down-class $A \subset \{0,1\}^S$ and its projections A_1 and A_2 on $\{0,1\}^{S_1}$ and $\{0,1\}^{S_2}$ respectively. Then we have, keeping the notation $\nu_{1,X}$ and $\nu_{2,Y}$,

$$\begin{aligned}\mu_p(A) &\leq \eta_1(A_1)\eta_2(A_2)\\ &\leq \prod_{X \subset S_1} \theta_X(A_1)^{\nu_{1,X}} \prod_{Y \subset S_2} \theta_Y(A_2)^{\nu_{2,Y}}\\ &= \prod_{X \subset S_1} \theta_X(A)^{\nu_{1,X}} \prod_{Y \subset S_2} \theta_Y(A)^{\nu_{2,Y}},\end{aligned}$$

where η_1 and η_2 are as before. This latter quantity is at most $\prod_{Z \subset S} \theta_Z(A)^{\nu(\{Z\})}$. This is because when $\nu(\{Z\}) \neq 0$ we have either $Z \subset S_1$ and $\nu(\{Z\}) \leq \nu_1(\{Z\}) = \nu_{1,Z}$ or else $Z \subset S_2$ and $\nu(\{Z\}) \leq \nu_2(\{Z\}) = \nu_{2,Z}$. □

Theorem 9.2 allows one to control measures ν that are built in a certain way out of two simpler pieces. It must be pointed out that one can simply construct measures ν that are in no natural way "made from simpler pieces". For example consider a group $\mathcal{G}$ of permutations of S and the image ν of its Haar measure under the action of $\mathcal{G}$ on a given subset of S. But how do we analyze this situation, and in which direction should one look??

10. BLOCKS

Suppose we want to disprove Conjecture 9.1. Then we have to construct both the αp-spread probability measure ν and the up-class A that witness the failure of (9.2).

As we have shown in Theorem 9.2 it is not possible to construct ν by simply combining the basic examples we know. In this section we prove a "dual result": the construction of the class A itself must be fairly complicated.

A natural approach to construct complicated up-classes is by recursively combining simpler classes. Probably the simplest such method is to consider two up-classes "on disjoint blocks" and then to take either their intersection or their reunion. In particular, our previous example $A = \{X;\ \ \forall i \leq m,\ \ X \cap S_i \neq \varnothing\}$ where $(S_i)_{i \leq m}$ are disjoint subsets of S is of this type.

The main result of this section is that if we start with the classes $A = \{S\}$ and iterate these operations as many times as we wish the resulting class satisfies (a lot more than) Conjecture 9.1.

If we want to control a class of sets with stability properties as above, it soon turns out that it does not suffice to control these sets through their measure μ_p, but that one must also control them for *all* product measures. A more subtle fact (that seems to be deeply related with the "multiplicative form" of Conjecture 9.1) is that it is very fruitful to perform an appropriate change of scale. Given $\boldsymbol{t} = (t_i)_{i\in S}$ we denote by $\zeta_{\boldsymbol{t}}$ the product measure on $\{0,1\}^S$ such that on the i-th factor the weight of 1 is $1-e^{-t_i}$ (and the weight of zero is e^{-t_i}). For a subset I of S we define $t_I = \prod_{i\in I} t_i$. We say that a function $\mathcal{P}(\boldsymbol{t})$ is a *polynomial* if

$$\mathcal{P}(\boldsymbol{t}) = \sum_{I\subset S} \beta_I t_I$$

where $\beta_I \geq 0$, $\beta_\varnothing = 0$. In particular a polynomial is a non-decreasing function of each of its variables.

DEFINITION 10.1. *Given $\gamma > 0$, we say that a up-class $A \subset \{0,1\}^S$ belongs to $\mathcal{C}_\gamma$ if the following occurs. Given any $\boldsymbol{q} \in (\mathbb{R}^+)^S$, there exists a polynomial $\mathcal{P}$ (depending on $\boldsymbol{q}$) with the following properties:*

$$\forall \boldsymbol{t}, \quad -\log(1-\zeta_{\boldsymbol{t}}(A)) \leq \mathcal{P}(\boldsymbol{t}) \qquad (10.1)$$

$$\mathcal{P}(\gamma \boldsymbol{q}) \leq -\gamma\log(1-\zeta_{\boldsymbol{q}}(A)). \qquad (10.2)$$

The notation keeps the set S implicit. Since we have assumed that a polynomial does not have a constant term, we have $\mathcal{P}(\gamma\boldsymbol{t}) \leq \gamma\mathcal{P}(\boldsymbol{t})$ for $\gamma \leq 1$; this makes it obvious that the collection $\mathcal{C}_\gamma$ increases as γ decreases.

Here is a first example.

PROPOSITION 10.2. *The set $A = \{X \subset S\ ;\ \ X \neq \varnothing\}$ belongs to class $\mathcal{C}_1$.*

Proof. We have $\zeta_{\boldsymbol{t}}(A) = 1 - \prod_{i\in S} e^{-t_i}$, so

$$-\log(1-\zeta_{\boldsymbol{t}}(A)) = \sum_{i\in S} t_i$$

and we see that $\mathcal{P}(\boldsymbol{t}) = \sum_{i\in S} t_i$ works independently of $\boldsymbol{q}$. □

We will prove that if γ is small enough, the collection $\mathcal{C}_\gamma$ has some nice stability properties, and we will prove that a class in $\mathcal{C}_\gamma$ satisfy a lot more than Conjecture 9.1. We hope that there exists $\gamma > 0$ such that any up-class A belongs to $\mathcal{C}_\gamma$, but since this might *really* be asking for too much, we will state this as a problem rather than a conjecture.

PROBLEM 10.3. *Is it true that there is a universal constant γ such that each up-class belongs to $\mathcal{C}_\gamma$?*

A positive solution would have sweeping consequences, since in particular it would prove Conjecture 8.5, as we show now.

THEOREM 10.4. *If an up-class A belongs to $\mathcal{C}_\gamma$, and if*

$$\alpha \leq 1-(1-p)^{\gamma/\delta}, \qquad (10.3)$$

then for each δ-spread measure ν on $\{0,1\}^S$ we have

$$-\int \log(1-\theta_{X,\alpha}(A))d\nu(X) \leq -\gamma\log(1-\mu_p(A)) \quad (10.4)$$

and

$$\int \theta_{X,\alpha}(A)d\nu(X) \leq \mu_p(A). \qquad (10.5)$$

If (10.5) holds for each up-class A then μ_p dominates $W_\alpha(\nu)$, and this shows that a positive solution of Problem 10.3 implies Conjecture 8.5.

Proof. Consider q with $p = 1-e^{-q}$, and $\boldsymbol{q} = (q_i)_{i\in S}$ with $q_i = q$ for each $i \in S$. By hypothesis we can find a polynomial $\mathcal{P}$ with

$$\forall \boldsymbol{t}, \quad -\log(1-\zeta_{\boldsymbol{t}}(A)) \leq \mathcal{P}(\boldsymbol{t}) \qquad (10.6)$$

$$\mathcal{P}(\gamma\boldsymbol{q}) \leq -\gamma\log(1-\zeta_{\boldsymbol{q}}(A)) = -\gamma\log(1-\mu_p(A)). \quad (10.7)$$

Consider the number t such that $1-e^{-t} = \alpha$. Consider $X \subset S$, and the sequence $\boldsymbol{t} = (t_i)_{i\in S}$ given by $t_i = 0$ if $i \notin X$ and $t_i = t$ if $i \in X$. Then

$$\zeta_{\boldsymbol{t}}(A) = \theta_{X,\alpha}(A). \qquad (10.8)$$

Writing $\mathcal{P}(\boldsymbol{t}) = \sum_{I\subset S}\beta_I t_I$, we see from (10.6) and (10.8) that

$$-\log(1-\theta_{X,\alpha}(A)) \ \leq\ \sum_{I\subset X}\beta_I t^{\operatorname{card} I}, \qquad (10.9)$$

so that for any probability measure ν we have

$$-\int \log(1-\theta_{X,\alpha}(A))d\nu(X) \leq \sum_I \beta_I t^{\operatorname{card} I}\nu(\{X;\ \ X\supset I\})$$

and if ν is δ-spread, when $t\delta \leq \gamma q$ we get

$$-\int \log(1-\theta_{X,\alpha}(A))d\nu(X) \leq \sum_I \beta_I (t\delta)^{\operatorname{card} I} \leq \mathcal{P}(\gamma\boldsymbol{q}). \qquad (10.10)$$

Combining with (10.6) shows that the condition $t\delta \leq \gamma q$ implies (10.4). But $t\delta \leq \gamma q$ means exactly $\alpha \leq 1-(1-p)^{\gamma/\delta}$.

It remains only to prove (10.5). For this, using (10.6) we write that by (7.16) for any s we have

$$\zeta_{\boldsymbol{t}}(A) \leq 1-e^{-\mathcal{P}(\boldsymbol{t})} \leq 1-(1+s)e^{-s} + e^{-s}\mathcal{P}(\boldsymbol{t}),$$

so that using (10.8), as in (10.10) we obtain

$$\int \theta_{X,\alpha}(A)d\nu(X) \leq 1-(1+s)e^{-s} + e^{-s}\mathcal{P}(\gamma\boldsymbol{q}).$$

We then chose $s = \mathcal{P}(\gamma\boldsymbol{q})$ and we use (10.7) to see that (since $\gamma \leq 1$)

$$1-\exp(-\mathcal{P}(\gamma\boldsymbol{q})) \leq 1-(1-\mu_p(A))^\gamma \leq \mu_p(A). \qquad \square$$

Now we describe the fundamental stability property of the class $\mathcal{C}_\gamma$. Consider a partition $S = \bigcup_{i\leq n} S_i$ of S. Given up-classes $A_i \subset \{0,1\}^{S_i}$ for $i \leq n$ and an up-class $A \subset \{0,1\}^n$ we define the up-class

$$A[A_1,\ldots,A_n] = \{X \subset S;\ \ \{i \leq n;\ \ X\cap S_i \in A_i\} \in A\}.$$

PROPOSITION 10.5. *If all the classes $A, A_1, \ldots, A_n$ belong to $\mathcal{C}_\gamma$ so does $A[A_1,\ldots,A_n]$.*

Proof. For $i \leq n$ and $\boldsymbol{t}_i \in (\mathbb{R}^+)^{S_i}$, let

$$F_i(\boldsymbol{t}_i) = -\log(1-\zeta_{\boldsymbol{t}_i}(A_i)).$$

Consider $\boldsymbol{q} \in (\mathbb{R}^+)^S$, and let $\boldsymbol{q}_i$ be its projection on $(\mathbb{R}^+)^{S_i}$. Since $A_i \in \mathcal{C}_\gamma$ we can find a polynomial $\mathcal{P}_i$ with

$$\forall \boldsymbol{t}_i \in (\mathbb{R}^+)^S\ ,\ F_i(\boldsymbol{t}_i) \ \leq\ \mathcal{P}_i(\boldsymbol{t}_i) \qquad (10.11)$$

$$\mathcal{P}_i(\gamma\boldsymbol{q}_i) \ \leq\ \gamma F_i(\boldsymbol{q}_i). \qquad (10.12)$$

For $\boldsymbol{u} \in (\mathbb{R}^+)^n$, let us consider

$$F_0(\boldsymbol{u}) = -\log(1 - \zeta_{\boldsymbol{u}}(A)).$$

Let $r_i = F_i(\boldsymbol{q}_i)$ and $\boldsymbol{r} = (r_i)_{i \le n}$. Since $A \in \mathcal{C}_\gamma$, there exists a polynomial $\mathcal{P}_0$ such that

$$\forall \boldsymbol{u} \in (\mathbb{R}^+)^n,\ F_0(\boldsymbol{u}) \le \mathcal{P}_0(\boldsymbol{u}) \tag{10.13}$$

$$\mathcal{P}_0(\gamma \boldsymbol{r}) \le \gamma F_0(\boldsymbol{r}). \tag{10.14}$$

The magic formula is that for $\boldsymbol{t} \in \mathbb{R}^{+S}$,

$$F(\boldsymbol{t}) := -\log(1 - \zeta_{\boldsymbol{t}}(A[A_1, \dots, A_n])) = F_0(\boldsymbol{u}) \tag{10.15}$$

where for $i \le n$, $u_i = F_i(\boldsymbol{t}_i)$, $\boldsymbol{u} = (u_i)_{i \le n}$ and when $\boldsymbol{t}_i$ is the projection of $\boldsymbol{t}$ on $(\mathbb{R}^+)^{S_i}$. This is a consequence of the fact that the image measure of $\zeta_{\boldsymbol{t}}$ under the map

$$X \mapsto (\mathbf{1}_{A_1}(X \cap S_1), \dots, \mathbf{1}_{A_n}(X \cap S_n))$$

is the measure $\zeta_{\boldsymbol{u}}$, so that $\zeta_{\boldsymbol{u}}(A) = \zeta_{\boldsymbol{t}}(A[A_1, \dots, A_n])$.

Let us define

$$\mathcal{P}(\boldsymbol{t}) = \mathcal{P}_0(\boldsymbol{v})$$

where $\boldsymbol{v} = (v_i)$, $v_i = \mathcal{P}_i(\boldsymbol{t}_i)$. This is a polynomial. Combining (10.15) with (10.11) and (10.13) we get

$$\begin{aligned}\forall \boldsymbol{t}\ ,\ F(\boldsymbol{t}) &= F_0(F_1(\boldsymbol{t}_1), \dots, F_n(\boldsymbol{t}_n)) \\ &\le \mathcal{P}_0(\mathcal{P}_1(\boldsymbol{t}_1), \dots, \mathcal{P}_n(\boldsymbol{t}_n)) = \mathcal{P}(\boldsymbol{t}).\end{aligned}$$

Combining (10.12), (10.14) and (10.15) we obtain

$$\begin{aligned}\mathcal{P}(\gamma \boldsymbol{q}) &= \mathcal{P}_0(\mathcal{P}_1(\gamma \boldsymbol{q}_1), \dots, \mathcal{P}_n(\gamma \boldsymbol{q}_n)) \\ &\le \mathcal{P}_0(\gamma F_1(\boldsymbol{q}_1), \dots, \gamma F_n(\boldsymbol{q}_n)) \\ &= \mathcal{P}_0(\gamma r_1, \dots, \gamma r_n) \\ &\le \gamma F_0(r_1, \dots, r_n) \\ &= \gamma F_0(F_1(\boldsymbol{q}_1), \dots, F_n(\boldsymbol{q}_n)) = \gamma F(\boldsymbol{q}). \quad \square\end{aligned}$$

The true difficulty is to prove that any class at all other than the classes of Proposition 10.2 belongs to $\mathcal{C}_\gamma$.

THEOREM 10.6. *There exists $\gamma > 0$ such that for each S the class $A = \{S\}$ belongs to the class $\mathcal{C}_\gamma$.*

Combining Propositions 10.2 et 10.5 with Theorem 10.6 we see that starting with the classes of Theorem 10.6, and iterating the operations "union on disjoint blocks" and "intersection on disjoint blocks" we can create only classes in $\mathcal{C}_\gamma$.

We define the function

$$F(u, v) = -\log(e^{-u} + e^{-v} - e^{-u-v})$$

for $u, v \ge 0$.

To prove Theorem 10.6 it suffices using Proposition 10.5 to consider the case where card$S = 2$, in which case Theorem 10.6 is equivalent to the following.

THEOREM 10.7. *There exists a number $\gamma > 0$ with the following property. Given $u_0, v_0 \ge 0$, we can find $a, b, c \ge 0$ such that*

$$\forall u, v\ ,\ F(u, v) \le au + bv + cuv \tag{10.16}$$

$$au_0 + bv_0 + \gamma c u_0 v_0 \le F(u_0, v_0). \tag{10.17}$$

It would be nice to know what is the best (= largest) value of γ for which Theorem 10.6 holds, and in particular whether it holds for $\gamma = 1$. Our present argument does not allow this.

In order to prove Theorem 10.6 we have to gain some understanding of which triples a, b, c satisfy (10.16). Fixing v, we observe that

$$\frac{\partial}{\partial u} F(u, v) = \frac{e^{-u}(1 - e^{-v})}{e^{-u} + e^{-v} - e^{-u-v}} \le 1 - e^{-v}.$$

Thus, since $F(0, v) = 0$, if $1 - e^{-v} \le a + cv$, then (10.16) holds for each u, and we need only be concerned with the case $a + cv \le 1 - e^{-v}$. Assuming that this occurs for certain values of v, these form an interval $[v_1, v_2]$. Consider $v_1 \le v \le v_2$. Setting $w = a + cv$, in order for (10.16) to hold we need that

$$\max_u (F(u, v) - uw) \le bv. \tag{10.18}$$

The maximum in the right-hand side is obtained for $\partial F / \partial u(u, v) = w$, i.e.

$$e^{-u} = \frac{we^{-v}}{(1 - w)(1 - e^{-v})}, \tag{10.19}$$

and after a few lines of algebra this maximum is found to be

$$\begin{aligned}\max_u (F(u, v) - uw) = f(v) &:= (1 - w)\log(1 - w) \\ &+ v(1 - w) + w \log w - w \log(1 - e^{-v}).\end{aligned} \tag{10.20}$$

This function is defined on the interval $[v_1, v_2]$. If $v = v_j$ for $j = 1$ or $j = 2$ one has $w = 1 - e^{-v_j}$ so one sees from (10.20) that $f(v_1) = f(v_2) = 0$. Also, from (10.20) we get (recalling that $w = a + cv$)

$$\begin{aligned}f'(v) &= 1 - \frac{w}{1 - e^{-v}} \\ &+ c(\log w - \log(1 - w) - v - \log(1 - e^{-v})) \\ &= 1 - \frac{w}{1 - e^{-v}} + c\left(\log \frac{we^{-v}}{(1 - w)(1 - e^{-v})}\right).\end{aligned}$$

The last term is ≤ 0 by (10.19), so that

$$f'(v) \le 1 - w = 1 - (a + cv). \tag{10.21}$$

LEMMA 10.8. *If*

$$(1 - a - b)^2 \le c(1 - a)v_1 \tag{10.22}$$

then (10.16) *holds.*

Proof. We have to prove (10.18) i.e. that $f(v) \le bv$ for $v_1 \le v \le v_2$. We have $f(v_1) = 0$, and (10.21) yields $f'(v) \le b$ if $1 - (a + cv) \le b$, i.e. $v \ge (1 - b - a)/c$. Thus it suffices to show that $f(v) \le bv$ for $v \le (1 - b - a)/c$. But since $f(v_1) = 0$ and since $f'(v) \le 1 - a$ by (10.21) we have

$$f(v) \le (1 - a)(v - v_1).$$

Now

$$(1 - a)(v - v_1) \le bv$$

since this inequality is equivalent to $(1 - a - b)v \le (1 - a)v_1$ and using (10.22) and since $v \le (1 - b - a)/c$. $\square$

Proof of Theorem 8.7. Without loss of generality we assume that $v_0 \ge u_0$, and we set $t = v_0 - u_0$. Since log(1+

$x) \leq x$ we have

$$\begin{aligned} F(u_0, v_0) &= -\log(e^{-u_0} + e^{-u_0-t} - e^{-2u_0-t}) \\ &= u_0 - \log(1 + e^{-t}(1 - e^{-u_0})) \\ &\geq u_0 - e^{-t}(1 - e^{-u_0}). \end{aligned}$$

Instead of (10.17) we will achieve the better inequality

$$a u_0 + b v_0 + \gamma c u_0 v_0 \leq u_0 - e^{-t}(1 - e^{-u_0}). \tag{10.23}$$

The proof totally lacks of glory. We produce the values of a, b, c by pure fiat depending on the values of u_0 and t, and we check in each case that (10.22) and (10.23) hold.

Case 1: $t \geq u_0$. If $b = 0$, $c = e^{-s}$, $a = 1 - (1+s)e^{-s}$ for a certain number s, then (10.16) is automatic by (7.16), and

$$a u_0 + b v_0 + \gamma c u_0 v_0 = (1 - (1+s)e^{-s})u_0 + \gamma e^{-s} u_0 v_0$$

is minimum for $s = \gamma v_0$, and this minimum has value $u_0(1 - e^{-\gamma v_0})$. And if $\gamma \leq 1/2$ we have

$$u_0(1 - e^{-\gamma v_0}) \leq u_0 - e^{-t}(1 - e^{-u_0})$$

because $1 - e^{-u_0} \leq u_0$ and $t = v_0 - u_0 \geq v_0/2 \geq \gamma v_0$ since $2u_0 \leq u_0 + t = v_0$. Thus (10.23) holds in this case.

Case 2: $t \leq u_0 \leq 4$. In that case, $u_0 \leq 4$ and $v_0 \leq 2u_0$. For a certain number L we have $e^{-u_0} \geq 1 - u_0 + u_0^2/L$ and

$$u_0 - e^{-t}(1 - e^{-u_0}) \geq u_0 - e^{-t}(u_0 - \frac{u_0^2}{L}) \geq \frac{e^{-4}u_0^2}{L} \geq \frac{e^{-4}u_0 v_0}{2L}.$$

Thus (assuming $\gamma \leq e^{-4}/2L$) we simply take $a = b = 0$, $c = 1$ to obtain (10.23) and we note that $1 - e^{-v} \leq a + cv = v$, so that (10.16) holds automatically.

Case 3: $t \leq u_0$, $u_0 \geq 4$. We chose

$$c = \frac{1}{2\gamma}\frac{e^{-t}}{u_0 v_0}\ ;\ b = \frac{e^{-t}}{4\max(1,t)}\ ;\ a + b = 1 - \frac{2e^{-t}}{u_0}.$$

We then have

$$a u_0 + b v_0 = (a+b)u_0 + tb \leq u_0 - 2e^{-t} + \frac{e^{-t}}{4},$$

and consequently

$$a u_0 + b v_0 + \gamma c u_0 v_0 \leq u_0 - e^{-t},$$

so it is obvious that (10.23) holds. To prove (10.16), we check that if γ is small enough then (10.22) holds, and since $1 - a \geq b$ it suffices to show that $(1 - a - b)^2 \leq b c v_1$, i.e.

$$\frac{4e^{-2t}}{u_0^2} \leq \frac{e^{-2t}}{8\gamma u_0 v_0 \max(1,t)} v_1. \tag{10.24}$$

Since v_1 satisfies $a + c v_1 = 1 - e^{-v_1}$, we have

$$e^{-v_1} \leq 1 - a = b + \frac{2e^{-t}}{u_0} \leq \frac{3}{4}e^{-t}$$

since $u_0 \geq 4$, and therefore $v_1 \geq \max(1,t)/L_1$. Since $v_0 = u_0 + t \leq 2u_0$, this implies (10.24) when $\gamma = 1/(64L_1)$. □

PROBLEM 10.9. *Does there exist $\gamma > 0$ such that all the classes*

$$A = \{X \subset S;\quad \text{card}X \geq k\}$$

belong to $\mathcal{C}_\gamma$?

11. MISCELLANEOUS PROOFS

To lighten notations, we write μ rather that μ_p.

THEOREM 11.1. *There exists a universal constant L_0 with the following property. Consider any set S, any numbers $t_i \geq 0$, $i \in S$, and any $0 < p < 1/2$. Then for $u \geq L_0$ we can find a family $\mathcal{I}$ of subsets of S with the following properties:*

$$\sum_{i \in X} t_i \geq L_0 u p \sum_{i \in S} t_i \Rightarrow \exists I \in \mathcal{I},\ I \subset X \tag{11.1}$$

$$\sum_{I \in \mathcal{I}} p^{\text{card} I} \leq 4\mu_p\left(\left\{X;\ \sum_{i \in X} t_i \geq pu \sum_{i \in S} t_i\right\}\right). \tag{11.2}$$

In particular, taking $u = \max(8, L_0)$ this proves Conjecture 5.7 in the case where T is reduced to a single point, but in fact it does a little bit more, and yields the following (very weak) support of Conjecture 5.7.

PROPOSITION 11.2. *Conjecture 5.7 holds when T consists of elements with disjoint support.*

Proof. Let us enumerate the elements of T as $t^1, \ldots, t^k$, let $U = \mathsf{E}_p \sup_{t \in T} \sum_{i \in X} t_i$ and let

$$A_k = \left\{X;\ \sum_{i \in X} t_i^k \geq L_0 U\right\}.$$

Thus

$$\mu\left(\bigcup_{k \leq k_0} A_k\right) \leq \mu\left(\sup_{t \in T}\sum_{i \in X} t_i \geq L_0 U\right) \leq \frac{1}{L_0}.$$

Since the classes A_k are independent for μ_p (because the sequences $\boldsymbol{t}^k$ have disjoint supports) we have

$$\mu\left(\bigcup_{k \leq k_0} A_k\right) = 1 - \prod_{k \leq k_0}(1 - \mu(A_k))$$

so that

$$\prod_{k \leq k_0}(1 - \mu(A_k)) \geq 1 - \frac{1}{L_0}.$$

Assuming without loss of generality that L_0 is large enough, we get

$$\sum_{k \leq k_0} -\log(1 - \mu(A_k)) \leq -\log\left(1 - \frac{1}{L_0}\right) \leq \frac{1}{8}$$

and since $x \leq -\log(1-x)$ we have

$$\sum_{k \leq k_0} \mu(A_k) \leq \frac{1}{8}.$$

Now, for each k, we have $U \geq U_k := p\sum_{i \in S} t_i^k$. We use Theorem 11.1 with $u = L_0 U/U_k \geq L_0$ to see that if

$$B_k = \left\{X;\ \sum_{i \in X} t_i^k \geq L_0^2 U\right\},$$

then we can find a family $\mathcal{I}_k$ of subsets of S with $B_k \subset \bigcup_{I \in \mathcal{I}_k} H_I$ and $\sum_{I \in \mathcal{I}_k} p^{\text{card} I} \leq 4\mu(A_k)$. The family $\mathcal{I} = \bigcup_k \mathcal{I}_k$ satisfies

$$\left\{X;\ \sup_{t \in T}\sum_{i \in X} t_i \geq L_0^2 U\right\} = \bigcup_k B_k \subset \bigcup_{I \in \mathcal{I}} H_I$$

and $\sum_{I\in\mathcal{I}} p^{\mathrm{card} I} \le 1/2$. □

Proof of Theorem 11.1. We set

$$U = p\sum_{i\in S} t_i \tag{11.3}$$

and given $u \ge 2$ we consider

$$B = \left\{X;\ \sum_{i\in X} t_i \ge uU\right\} \tag{11.4}$$

so that

$$\mu(B) \le \frac{1}{u}. \tag{11.5}$$

We consider a number $w \ge u$ to be specified later and

$$A = \left\{X;\ \sum_{i\in X} t_i \ge 8wU\right\}. \tag{11.6}$$

Consider

$$S_0 = \{i \in S;\ t_i \ge uU\},$$

and the family $\mathcal{I}_0$ consisting of the sets $I \subset S_0$ with $\mathrm{card} I = 1$. Thus

$$X \cap S_0 \ne \varnothing \Rightarrow \exists I \in \mathcal{I}_0,\ I \subset X \tag{11.7}$$

$$\sum_{I\in\mathcal{I}_0} p^{\mathrm{card} I} = p\,\mathrm{card}\mathcal{I}_0 = p\,\mathrm{card} S_0. \tag{11.8}$$

We have

$$X \cap S_0 \ne \varnothing \Rightarrow \left\{\sum_{i\in X} t_i \ge uU\right\} \Rightarrow X \in B$$

so, if $M_0 = \mathrm{card} S_0$,

$$1 - (1-p)^{M_0} \le \mu(B) \le \frac{1}{u}$$

and

$$e^{-pM_0} \ge (1-p)^{M_0} \ge 1 - \mu(B),$$

so that, since $u \ge 2$ and therefore $\mu(B) \le 1/2$,

$$pM_0 \le -\log(1-\mu(B)) \le 2\mu(B)$$

and (11.8) implies

$$\sum_{I\in\mathcal{I}_0} p^{\mathrm{card} I} \le 2\mu(B). \tag{11.9}$$

Consider

$$A' = \left\{X;\ X\cap S_0 = \varnothing,\ \sum_{i\in X} t_i \ge 8wU\right\}.$$

We have controlled $A\setminus A'$ through (11.7) and (11.9) and we turn to the control of A'.

For $k \ge 0$, we set

$$J_k = \{i \in S;\ 4^{-k-1}uU \le t_i < 4^{-k}uU\} \tag{11.10}$$

and $M_k = \mathrm{card} J_k$. Given $X \in A'$ we set $n_k = \mathrm{card}(J_k \cap X)$. Let

$$W_1 = \{k \ge 0;\ n_k \le wpM_k\}.$$

Thus

$$\begin{aligned}\sum_{k\in W_1} uU4^{-k}n_k &\le wp\sum_k uU4^{-k}M_k\\ &\le 4wp\sum_k\sum_{i\in J_k} t_i \le 4wU. \end{aligned} \tag{11.11}$$

Let

$$W_2 = \left\{k \ge 0;\ n_k \le 2^k\frac{w}{u}\right\}$$

so that

$$\sum_{k\in W_2} uU4^{-k}n_k \le 2wU. \tag{11.12}$$

Let $W = \{k \ge 0;\ k \notin W_1 \cap W_2\}$. Since $X \in A'$ we have

$$\begin{aligned}8wU &\le \sum_{i\notin S_0, i\in X} t_i \le \sum_{k\ge 0} 4^{-k}uU\,\mathrm{card}(X\cap J_k)\\ &\le \sum_{k\ge 0} uU4^{-k}n_k\end{aligned}$$

and we deduce from (11.11) and (11.9) that

$$\sum_{k\in W} uU4^{-k}n_k \ge 2wU$$

i.e.

$$\sum_{k\in W} 4^{-k}n_k \ge 2\frac{w}{u}. \tag{11.13}$$

For a set W of integers and $\boldsymbol{n} = (n_k)_{k\in W}$ let us define

$$A_{W,\boldsymbol{n}} = \{X \subset S;\ \forall k\in W,\ \mathrm{card}(X\cap J_k) = n_k\}.$$

We have shown that

$$A' \subset \bigcup_{W,\boldsymbol{n}} A_{W,\boldsymbol{n}},$$

where the union is over all choices of W and of $\boldsymbol{n}$ such that (11.13) holds together with

$$n_k > 2^k\frac{w}{u}\ \ ;\ \ n_k > wpM_k \tag{11.14}$$

To control the classes $A_{W,\boldsymbol{n}}$, we will now compare them with the classes

$$B_{W,\boldsymbol{n}} = \left\{X \subset S;\ \forall k\in W,\ \mathrm{card}(X\cap J_k) \ge \frac{2u}{w}n_k\right\}.$$

First we note that by (11.13) for X in B we have

$$\sum_{k\in W} 4^{-k}\mathrm{card}(X\cap J_k) \ge 4$$

so that by (11.10)

$$\sum_{i\in X} t_i \ge uU$$

and thus

$$B_{W,\boldsymbol{n}} \subset B. \tag{11.15}$$

We have

$$\mu(B_{W,\boldsymbol{n}}) = \prod_{k\in W} T(k) \tag{11.16}$$

where

$$T(k) = \mu(\{X \subset S;\ \mathrm{card}(X\cap J_k) \ge m_k\})$$

and where m_k is the smallest integer $\geq 2un_k/w$. Thus

$$T(k) \geq p^{m_k}(1-p)^{M_k-m_k}\binom{M_k}{m_k}.$$

We first show that in this bound the factor $(1-p)^{M_k-m_k}$ is not dangerous. Since $u \geq 2$, by (11.14) we have $m_k \geq 2un_k/w \geq 4pM_k$ and thus

$$(1-p)^{M_k} \geq \left(\frac{1}{L}\right)^{m_k}.$$

Here, as well as in the rest of the paper, L denotes a number, that need not be the same at each occurrence, while $L_0, L_1, \cdots$ denote specific constants. Thus, from (5.6) we get

$$T(k) \geq \left(\frac{pM_k}{Lm_k}\right)^{m_k}$$

and from (11.15) and (11.16) that

$$\prod_{k\in W}\left(\frac{pM_k}{L_1 m_k}\right)^{m_k} \leq \mu(B). \tag{11.17}$$

Consider now the class $\mathcal{I}_{W,\boldsymbol{n}}$ of subsets I of S that satisfy $I \subset \bigcup_{k\in W} J_k$ and $\operatorname{card}(I\cap J_k) = n_k$ for $k \in W$. Then, obviously,

$$\forall X \in A_{W,\boldsymbol{n}},\ \exists I \in \mathcal{I}_{W,\boldsymbol{n}},\ I \subset X. \tag{11.18}$$

On the other hand

$$\begin{aligned}\sum_{I\in\mathcal{I}_{W,\boldsymbol{n}}} p^{\operatorname{card} I} &= \prod_{k\in W} p^{n_k}\binom{M_k}{n_k} \\ &\leq \prod_{k\in W}\left(\frac{L_2 pM_k}{n_k}\right)^{n_k}\end{aligned} \tag{11.19}$$

using (5.6) again. The idea is now to use (11.17) to control the sum of the quantities (11.19) over all choices of W and $\boldsymbol{n}$ when $w = 8L_1L_2u$ (it is here that we fix w). Since m_k is the smallest integer $\geq 2un_k/w > 2^{k+1} \geq 2$, we have $m_k \leq 4un_k/w$, so $n_k \geq wm_k/4u \geq 2L_1L_2um_k$. Therefore

$$\frac{L_2pM_k}{n_k} \leq \frac{pM_k}{2L_1m_k},$$

and

$$\left(\frac{L_2pM_k}{n_k}\right)^{n_k} \leq 2^{-n_k}\left(\frac{pM_k}{L_1m_k}\right)^{n_k}.$$

Using the second part of (11.14) we have $pM_k \leq n_k/w \leq m_k/2u \leq L_1m_k$ and since $n_k \geq 2L_1L_2m_k \geq m_k$, we have

$$\left(\frac{L_2pM_k}{n_k}\right)^{n_k} \leq 2^{-n_k}\left(\frac{pM_k}{L_1m_k}\right)^{n_k} \leq 2^{-n_k}\left(\frac{pM_k}{L_1m_k}\right)^{m_k}.$$

Thus combining (11.17) and (11.19) we get

$$\sum_{I\in\mathcal{I}_{W,\boldsymbol{n}}} p^{\operatorname{card} I} \leq \left(\frac{1}{2}\right)^{\sum_{k\in W} n_k}\mu(B)$$

and it suffices to show that if we sum over all choices of W and n_k the coefficients $(1/2)^{\sum_{k\in W} n_k}$ the result is ≤ 2. This sum is at most

$$\prod_{k\geq 0}\Bigl(1+\sum_{n_k>2^k w/u} 2^{-n_k}\Bigr).$$

Now, whenever $w/u \geq 4$, we have

$$\sum_{n_k>2^k w/u} 2^{-n_k} \leq 2^{-2^{k+2}}$$

and $\prod_{k\geq 0}(1+2^{-2^{k+2}}) \leq 2$. □

Our next result also provides (much deeper) support for Conjecture 5.7.

THEOREM 11.3. *There exists a number q with the following property. Consider a set S that is a disjoint union $S = \bigcup_{1\leq k\leq k_0} S_k$, and $A \subset \{0,1\}^S$ such that*

$$\forall J \in A,\ \operatorname{card}(J\cap S_k) = 2^k. \tag{11.20}$$

Assume that there exists a p-spread probability measure ν with $\nu(A) = 1$. Then given any class $B \subset \{0,1\}^S$ with $\mu(B) \geq 1-1/q$, we can find $J^1,\ldots,J^q$ in B and $J \in A$ such that

$$\forall k \leq k_0,\ \operatorname{card}((J\setminus(J^1\cup\cdots\cup J^q))\cap S_k) \leq 2^{k-1}. \tag{11.21}$$

The following consequence should be compared to Conjecture 6.8

COROLLARY 11.4. *There exists a number L with the following property. Consider any set S that is a disjoint union $S = \bigcup_{1\leq k\leq k_0} S_k$, and consider a class T of sequences $\boldsymbol{t} = (t_i)_{i\in S}$ with $t_i \geq 0$. Assume that for each $\boldsymbol{t} \in T$ and each k, we have $\operatorname{card}\{i \in S_k;\ t_i \neq 0\} = 2^k$, and that for $i,j \in S_k$, if $t_i \neq 0$, $t_j \neq 0$ then $t_i = t_j$. (That is, each sequence $(t_i)_{i\in S_k}$ takes only two possible values, one of which is 0). Assume there is a probability measure ν on T such that*

$$\forall I \subset S,\ \nu(\{\boldsymbol{t};\ i \in I \Rightarrow t_i > 0\}) \leq p^{\operatorname{card} I}. \tag{11.22}$$

Then

$$\mathsf{E}_p \sup_{t\in T}\sum_{i\in X} t_i \geq \frac{1}{L}\inf_{t\in T}\sum_{i\in S} t_i. \tag{11.23}$$

Proof. Given $\boldsymbol{t} \in T$ let

$$J_{\boldsymbol{t}} = \{i \in S; t_i \neq 0\}.$$

Let $A \subset \{0,1\}^S$ be the class of the sets $J_{\boldsymbol{t}}$ as $\boldsymbol{t}$ varies in T and let ν' be the image of ν under the map $\boldsymbol{t} \mapsto J_{\boldsymbol{t}}$. By construction $\nu'(A) = 1$ and by (11.22) ν' is p-spread.

Let us now set

$$U = \mathsf{E}_p \sup_{t\in T}\sum_{i\in X} t_i$$

and consider the class

$$B = \Bigl\{X\ ;\ \sup_{t\in T}\sum_{i\in X} t_i \leq qU\Bigr\},$$

so that by Markov inequality we have $\mu(B) \geq 1-1/q$. We then apply Theorem 11.3 to find a set $J = J_{\boldsymbol{t}} \in A$ and sets $J^1,\ldots,J^q \in B$ such that if $J' = J^1\cup\cdots\cup J^q$ we have

$$\forall k \leq k_0\ ,\ \operatorname{card}(J_{\boldsymbol{t}}\setminus J') \leq 2^{k-1}.$$

Since in each set S_k the sequence $\boldsymbol{t}$ takes only two values, say 0 and a_k, we have

$$\sum_{i\in S_k\cap(J_{\boldsymbol{t}}\cap J')} t_i = a_k\operatorname{card}(J_{\boldsymbol{t}}\cap J') \geq a_k2^{k-1} = \frac{1}{2}\sum_{i\in S_k} t_i.$$

By summation over k we see that

$$\sum_{i \in J'} t_i \geq \frac{1}{2} \sum_i t_i.$$

Consequently since $J' = J^1 \cup \ldots \cup J^q$, then for some $\ell \leq q$ we have

$$\sum_{i \in J^\ell} t_i \geq \frac{1}{q} \sum_{i \in J'} t_i \geq \frac{1}{2q} \inf_{t \in T} \sum_{i \in S} t_i$$

and since $J^\ell \in B$ the definition of B shows that $\sum_{i \in J^\ell} t_i \leq qU$, so that

$$U = \mathsf{E}_p \sup_{t \in T} \sum_{i \in X} t_i \geq \frac{1}{2q^2} \inf_{t \in T} \sum_{i \in S} t_i,$$

which completes the proof. □

The proof of Theorem 11.3 elaborates on one idea of [9] . It combines isoperimetry with the second moment method. One version of the second moment method is the observation that for a r.v. $Z \geq 0$ we have

$$\mathsf{P}(Z > 0) \geq \frac{(\mathsf{E}Z)^2}{\mathsf{E}(Z^2)}. \tag{11.24}$$

This will used as follows. Suppose that to each $J \in A$ we associate a set $G_J \subset \{0,1\}^S$ and for $X \subset S$ let

$$Z(X) = \nu(\{J;\ X \in G_J\}).$$

Then the following holds true.

$$\{Z > 0\} \subset \bigcup_{J \in A} G_J \tag{11.25}$$

$$\begin{aligned} \mathsf{E}_p Z &= \int \nu(\{J;\ X \in G_J\}) d\mu(X) \\ &= \int \mu(G_J) d\nu(J) \end{aligned}$$

$$\begin{aligned} \mathsf{E}_p Z^2 &= \int \nu(\{J;\ X \in G_J\})^2 d\mu(X) \\ &= \int \nu^{\otimes 2}(\{(J,J');\ X \in G_J \cap G_{J'}\}) d\mu(X) \\ &= \int \mu(G_J \cap G_{J'}) d\nu(J) d\nu(J'). \end{aligned}$$

Thus, combining (11.24) and (11.25)

$$\mu\left(\bigcup_{J \in A} G_J\right) \geq \frac{\left(\int \mu(G_J) d\nu(J)\right)^2}{\int \mu(G_J \cap G_{J'}) d\nu(J) d\nu(J')}. \tag{11.26}$$

To make this relation useful we need lower bounds on the denominator. Let us assume that for some subset S' of S we have

$$\forall J \in A, \qquad \mathrm{card} J \cap S' = m \tag{11.27}$$

$$\forall J \in A \qquad G_J \subset H_{J \cap S'}. \tag{11.28}$$

Then $\mathrm{card}(J \cap S') \cup (J' \cap S')) = 2m - \mathrm{card}(J \cap J' \cap S)$ so that

$$\begin{aligned} \mu(G_J \cap G_{J'}) &\leq \mu(H_{J \cap S'} \cap H_{J' \cap S'}) \\ &= p^{2m - \mathrm{card}(J \cap J' \cap S)}. \end{aligned}$$

Thinking of J as fixed, we have

$$\begin{aligned} \mu(G_J \cap G_{J'}) > p^{2m-k+1} &\Rightarrow \mathrm{card}(J \cap J' \cap S) \geq k \\ &\Rightarrow \exists I \subset J,\ \mathrm{card} I = k,\ J' \supset I \end{aligned}$$

and thus

$$\begin{aligned} \nu(\{J';\ \mu(G_J \cap G_{J'}) \geq p^{2m-k+1}\}) &\leq \sum_{I \subset J, \mathrm{card} I = k} \nu(H_I) \\ &\leq \binom{m}{k} p^k \end{aligned}$$

because $\nu(H_I) \leq p^{\mathrm{card} I}$ since ν is p-spread. It follows that

$$\int \mu(G_J \cap G_{J'}) d\nu(J') \leq p^{2m} \sum_k \binom{m}{k} = 2^m p^{2m}.$$

So we have proved the following.

Lemma 11.5. *Under* (11.27) *and* (11.28) *and if ν is p-spread we have*

$$\mu\left(\bigcup_{J \in A} G_J\right) \geq 2^{-m} p^{-2m} \left(\int \mu(G_J) d\nu(J)\right)^2. \tag{11.29}$$

We are now going to formulate the main step of the proof of Theorem 11.3. For this it helps to think of $\{0,1\}^S$ as the product of the spaces $\{0,1\}^{S_\ell}$, $\ell = 1, \ldots, k_0$. We denote by μ_ℓ the measure μ_{p,S_ℓ}.

Proposition 11.6. *For $\ell = 1, \ldots, k_0$ we can find classes $C_\ell \subset \{0,1\}^{S_1} \times \cdots \times \{0,1\}^{S_\ell}$ with the following properties*

$$\mu_1(C_1) \geq \frac{1}{16} = 2^{-4} \tag{11.30}$$

$$\forall \ell < k_0,\ \forall J \in C_\ell,$$

$$\mu_{\ell+1}(\{Y \in \{0,1\}^{S_{\ell+1}};\ J \cup Y \in C_{\ell+1}\}) \geq 2^{-2^{\ell+3}} \tag{11.31}$$

$$C_{k_0} = \{Y \subset S;\ \exists J \in A,\ J \subset Y\}. \tag{11.32}$$

Proof. We define C_{k_0} by (11.32) and by decreasing induction the classes C_ℓ as the largest such that (11.31) holds. Therefore,

$$\forall \ell < k_0,\ \forall J \notin C_\ell,$$

$$\mu_{\ell+1}(\{Y \in \{0,1\}^{S_{\ell+1}};\ J \cup Y \in C_{\ell+1}\}) < 2^{-2^{\ell+3}}. \tag{11.33}$$

The issue is then to prove (11.30). We proceed by contradiction, assuming that $\mu_1(C_1) < 1/16$. Let

$$C_1' = C_1 \times \{0,1\}^{S_2} \times \cdots \times \{0,1\}^{S_{k_0}}$$

and for all $J \in A$ let

$$G_J^1 = C_1' \cap H_{J \cap S_1}.$$

We can use (11.29) with $m = 2$ because $\mathrm{card}(J \cap S_1) = 2$ so that

$$\begin{aligned} \frac{1}{16} > \mu_1(C_1) &= \mu(C_1') \geq \mu(\bigcup_{J \in A} G_J^1) \\ &\geq \frac{1}{4} p^{-4} \left(\int \mu(G_J^1) d\nu(J)\right)^2 \end{aligned}$$

and thus

$$\int \mu(G_J^1) d\nu(J) \leq \frac{p^2}{2}.$$

Since $\mu_1(H_{J\cap S_1}) = p^2$, if we set

$$D_1 = \{0,1\}^S \setminus C_1' = \{X \subset S;\ X \cap S_1 \notin C_1\}$$

we then have proved that

$$\int \mu(D_1 \cap H_{J\cap S_1}) d\nu(J) \geq \frac{p^2}{2}. \tag{11.34}$$

For $J \in A$ consider now the classes

$$D_1 \cap H_{J\cap(S_1\cup S_2)}.$$

Since $\mathrm{card} J \cap S_2 = 2^2 = 4$ for $J \in A$, and since the fact that $X \in D_1$ or not is determined by the set $X \cap S_1$ we have

$$\mu(D_1 \cap H_{J\cap(S_1\cup S_2)}) = p^4 \mu(D_1 \cap H_{J\cap S_1})$$

and by (11.34) we have

$$\int \mu(D_1 \cap H_{J\cap(S_1\cup S_2)}) d\nu(J) \geq \frac{p^6}{2}. \tag{11.35}$$

Consider the class

$$D_1' = \{X \subset S;\ X \cap S_1 \notin C_1,\ X \cap (S_1 \cup S_2) \in C_2\}.$$

Using (11.33) for $\ell = 1$ and Fubini Theorem, we see that

$$\mu(D_1') \leq 2^{-16}.$$

Consider the classes

$$G_J^2 = D_1' \cap H_{J\cap(S_1\cup S_2)}$$

so that we can use (11.29) with $m = 6$ to get

$$2^{-16} \geq \mu(D_1') \geq \mu\left(\bigcup G_J^2\right) \geq 2^{-6}p^{-12}\left(\int \mu(G_J^2)d\nu(J)\right)^2$$

and thus

$$\int \mu(G_J^2) d\nu(J) \leq \frac{1}{2^4}p^6. \tag{11.36}$$

Let $D_2 = D_1 \setminus D_1'$. Comparison of (11.36) and (11.35) yields

$$\int \mu(D_2 \cap H_{J\cap(S_1\cup S_2)}) d\nu(J) \geq \frac{p^6}{4},$$

while

$$D_2 = \{X \subset S;\ X \cap S_1 \notin C_1,\ X \cap (S_1 \cup S_2) \notin C_2\}.$$

Proceeding in this manner we show by induction on $\ell \leq k_0$ that

$$\int \mu(D_\ell \cap H_{J\cap(S_1\cup S_2 \cup\cdots\cup S_\ell)}) d\nu(J) \geq \frac{p^{2^{\ell+1}-2}}{2^\ell} \tag{11.37}$$

where

$$D_\ell = \{X \subset S;\ X \cap S_1 \notin C_1, \ldots, X \cap (S_1 \cup \cdots \cup S_\ell) \notin C_\ell\}.$$

But for $\ell = k_0$ this is a contradiction because $D_{k_0} \cap C_{k_0} = \emptyset$ while for $J \in A$ we have $H_J \subset C_{k_0}$ by definition of C_{k_0}, so that $\mu(D_{k_0} \cap H_J) = 0$ and the integrand in (11.37) is 0. □

LEMMA 11.7. *Consider numbers b_ℓ, $\ell = 1, \ldots, k_0$ with $b_\ell < 1$. Consider a class $B \subset \{0,1\}^S$ with $\mu(B) \geq 1 - \prod_{1\leq \ell \leq k_0}(1 - b_\ell)$. Then we can find classes $B_\ell \subset \{0,1\}^{S_1} \times \cdots \times \{0,1\}^{S_\ell}$ with $B = B_{k_0}$ and*

$$\mu(B_1) \geq b_1 \tag{11.38}$$

$$\forall \ell < k_0,\ \forall J \in B_\ell,$$
$$\mu_{\ell+1}(\{Y \in \{0,1\}^{S_{\ell+1}};\ J \cup Y \in B_{\ell+1}\}) \geq b_{\ell+1}. \tag{11.39}$$

Proof. Starting with $B_{k_0} = B$ we construct the classes B_ℓ by decreasing induction over ℓ, these classes being as large as possible such that (11.39) holds. Denoting by μ_ℓ' the measure $\mu_1 \otimes \cdots \otimes \mu_\ell$ on $\{0,1\}^{S_1} \times \cdots \times \{0,1\}^{S_\ell}$, we see by Fubini theorem that

$$b_{\ell+1}(1 - \mu_\ell'(B_\ell)) + \mu_\ell'(B_\ell) \geq \mu_{\ell+1}'(B_{\ell+1})$$

so that

$$(1 - b_{\ell+1})(1 - \mu_\ell'(B_\ell)) \leq 1 - \mu_{\ell+1}'(B_{\ell+1})$$

and by induction

$$1 - \mu_\ell'(B_\ell) \leq \frac{1}{\prod_{\ell+1\leq \ell' \leq k_0}(1 - b_{\ell'})}(1 - \mu(B))$$

which implies (11.38) when $\ell = 1$. □

The other key ingredient in the proof of Theorem 11.3 is the following "isoperimetric" result [7]. We mention here only the form we need.

LEMMA 11.8. *Consider two integers q and n. Then for any classes $A_1 \ldots, A_q \subset \{0,1\}^S$ we have*

$$\begin{aligned}\mu(\{X \subset S;\ \forall I^1 \in A_1, \ldots, I^q \in A_q,\\ \mathrm{card}(X \setminus (I^1 \cup \cdots \cup I^q)) \geq n\})\\ \leq \frac{1}{\mu(A_1)\cdots\mu(A_q)}\frac{1}{q^n}.\end{aligned} \tag{11.40}$$

Proof of Theorem 11.3. Let $q = 2^{2^6}$, and for $\ell \geq 1$ let $b_\ell = 2^{-2^\ell/q}$ so that for $\ell \geq 1$ we have

$$\left(\frac{1}{b_\ell}\right)^q \frac{1}{q^{2^\ell - 1}} < 2^{-2^{\ell+4}}. \tag{11.41}$$

Let $b = 1 - \prod_{\ell\geq 1}(1 - b_\ell) < 1$. We will prove that if $B \subset \{0,1\}^S$ satisfies $\mu(B) > b$, we find $J^1, \ldots, J^q$ in B as in (11.21). We consider the classes B_ℓ constructed from B in Lemma 11.7 and the classes C_ℓ constructed from A in Proposition 11.6. In the first step we use Lemma 11.8 with S_1 instead of S and $A_1, \ldots, A_q = B_1$, $n = 1$ together with the fact that $\mu_1(C_1) \geq 2^{-6}$ to find sets $I_1^1, \ldots, I_1^q \subset S_1$, $I_1^1, \ldots, I_1^q \in B_1$ and $X_1 \subset S_1$, $X_1 \in C_1$ with

$$\mathrm{card}(X_1 \setminus (I_1^1 \cup \cdots \cup I_1^q)) \leq 1.$$

In the second step we find sets $I_2^1, \ldots, I_2^q \subset S_2$, $I_1^\ell \cup I_2^\ell \in B_\ell$ for $\ell \leq q$, and $X_2 \subset S_2$, $X_1 \cup X_2 \in C_2$ with

$$\mathrm{card}(X_2 \setminus (I_2^1 \cup \cdots \cup I_2^q)) \leq 2 = 2^{2-1}.$$

This is possible by using Lemma 11.8 with S_2 instead of S and $n = 2$, because conditions (11.31) and (11.39) ensure that there are sufficiently many choices of I_2^ℓ, X_2^ℓ. We then continue in this manner. □

Our next result is a simple argument showing that to prove Conjecture 6.4 it suffices to prove it for arbitrary small values of p. We find it rather symptomatic that we do *not* know how to prove the corresponding result for Conjecture 5.7. This is because it is so difficult to work with p-small classes.

THEOREM 11.9. *Assume that there is a sequence $p_n \to 0$ and a number q with the following property. Given any n, any set S, any class $A \subset \{0,1\}^S$ with $\mu_{p_n}(A) \geq 1 - 1/q$, then $A^{(q)}$ is weakly p_n-small.*

Then for each $0 < p < 1$ and each $A \subset \{0,1\}^S$ with $\mu_p(A) \geq 1 - 1/q$, $A^{(q)}$ is weakly p-small.

Proof. Consider an integer r, and the map $\varphi : (\{0,1\}^S)^r \to \{0,1\}^S$ given by

$$\varphi(J_1, \ldots, J_r) = \bigcup_{\ell \leq r} J_\ell.$$

It is easy to see that if, keeping the dependence in n implicit, we define p' by

$$1 - p' = (1 - p_n)^r,$$

for any class $A \subset \{0,1\}^S$ we have

$$\mu_{p_n}(\varphi^{-1}(A)) = \mu_{p'}(A).$$

Assuming that $\mu_{p'}(A) \geq 1 - 1/q$, and setting $A' = \varphi^{-1}(A)$, we see that by hypothesis $A'^{(q)}$ is weakly p_n-small.

We recall that for two subsets I, Y of S, we define

$$\psi(I,Y) = 1 \text{ if } I \subset Y \text{ and } \psi(I,Y) = 0 \text{ otherwise.}$$

The fact that $A'^{(q)}$ is weakly p_n-small means that there is a probability measure θ' on $(\{0,1\}^S)^r$ such that, whenever $(Y_1, \ldots, Y_r) \in A'^{(q)}$ we have

$$\frac{1}{2} \int \prod_{\ell \leq r} (p_n^{-\mathrm{card} I_\ell} \psi(I_\ell, Y_\ell) d\theta((I_1, \ldots, I_r)) \geq 1. \quad (11.42)$$

Consider $Z \in A^{(q)}$ and

$$W(Z) = \Big\{ (Y_1, \ldots, Y_r) \in (\{0,1\}^S)^r; \; Z = \bigcup_{\ell \leq r} Y_\ell, \; Y_1, \ldots, Y_r \text{ are disjoint} \Big\}.$$

Thus, if $i \in Z$, and $(Y_1, \ldots, Y_r) \in W(Z)$, there is a unique $\ell \leq r$ with $i \in Y_\ell$. In this manner there is a canonical bijection between $W(Z)$ and $\{0, \ldots, r\}^Z$. The crucial observation is that for $Z \in A^{(q)}$ and any $I_1, \ldots, I_r$ we have

$$\mathrm{Av} \prod_{\ell \leq r} p_n^{-\mathrm{card} I_\ell} \psi(I_\ell, Y_\ell) \leq (p_n r)^{-\mathrm{card} I} \psi(I, Z), \quad (11.43)$$

where $I = \bigcup_{\ell \leq r} I_\ell$, and where Av denotes the average over all elements $(Y_1, \ldots, Y_r)$ of $W(Z)$. This is seen by first observing that the left hand side of (11.43) is zero unless $I_1, \ldots, I_r$ are disjoint, and then that

$$\mathrm{Av} \prod_{\ell \leq r} \psi(I_\ell, Y_\ell) = r^{-\mathrm{card} I} \psi(I, Z).$$

It then follows from (11.42) that if θ is the image measure of θ' under the map $(I_1, \ldots, I_r) \to \bigcup_{\ell \leq r} I_\ell$ then

$$\forall Z \in A^{(q)}, \; \frac{1}{2} \int (p_n r)^{-\mathrm{card} I} \psi(I, Z) d\theta(I) \geq 1.$$

Thus $A^{(q)}$ is $p_n r$-small.

Now take $n \to \infty$ and $r = r_n$ such that $p_n r \to -\log(1-p)$, so $p' = 1 - (1 - p_n)^{r_n} \to p$, and we have proved that if $A \subset \{0,1\}^S$ satisfies $\mu_p(A) \geq 1 - 1/q$, then $A^{(q)}$ is $-\log(1-p)$-weakly small and since $p < -\log(1-p)$ it is also p-weakly small. □

We now turn to a general principle that implies roughly that Conjecture 7.8 is true "when there are a lot of symmetries". We assume that ν is the uniform probability on a class B of subsets of S. Each set in B has the same cardinality m. Moreover there is a group Ξ of permutations of S with the following properties:

$$I \in B, \quad \sigma \in \Xi \Rightarrow \sigma(I) \in B. \quad (11.44)$$

$$\text{If } I = \{x_1, \ldots, x_m\} \in B, \; J = \{y_1, \ldots, y_m\} \in B, \; \exists \sigma \in \Xi, \; \forall i \leq m, \; \sigma(x_i) = y_i. \quad (11.45)$$

To give a non-trivial example, consider the case where S is the collection of all subsets of cardinality k of the set $\{1, \ldots, mk\}$ and where B consists of the partitions of the set $\{1, \ldots, mk\}$ into m sets of k elements. The previous conditions hold when Ξ is the group canonically induced on S by the group of permutations of $\{1, \ldots, mk\}$.

THEOREM 11.10. *There exists a number α with the following property. Whenever the probability ν as above is p-spread, then $\mu = \mu_p$ dominates $W_\alpha(\nu)$.*

Proof. The group Ξ acts on $\{0,1\}^S$. We say that a subset of $\{0,1\}^S$ is Ξ-invariant if it is invariant under this action.

We want to show that

$$W_\alpha(\nu)(A) \leq \mu(A) \quad (11.46)$$

for each up-class A. Since both $W_\alpha(\nu)$ and μ are invariant under the action of Ξ, taking average over this action it suffices to show that

$$\int f dW_\alpha(\nu) \leq \int f d\mu$$

for each monotone Ξ-invariant function f. Considering the classes $\{f \geq a\}$ we see that it suffices to prove (11.46) when A is an up-class Ξ-invariant.

For $k \leq m$ consider the classes

$$B_k = \{J \subset S; \; \mathrm{card} J = k, \exists I \in B, \; J \subset I\},$$

and define

$$k_0 = \inf\{k; \; A \cap B_k\} \neq \emptyset.$$

Then, for $I \in B$ and $J \in A, J \subset I$ we have $\mathrm{card} J \geq k_0$, so that

$$\theta_{\alpha,I}(A) \leq \sum_{k \geq k_0} \alpha^k (1-\alpha)^{m-k} \binom{m}{k},$$

and

$$W_\alpha(\nu)(A) = \int \theta_{\alpha,I}(A) d\nu(I) \leq \sum_{k \geq k_0} \alpha^k (1-\alpha)^{m-k} \binom{m}{k}.$$

Let us define

$$A_k = \{J \subset S; \; \exists I \in B, \mathrm{card}(J \cap I) \geq k\},$$

Then from (11.45) we see that since A is Ξ-invariant we have $A \supset A_{k_0}$.

Thus to prove (11.46) it suffices to prove that

$$b_{k_0} := \sum_{k \geq k_0} \alpha^k (1-\alpha)^{m-k} \binom{m}{k} \leq a_{k_0} := \mu(A_{k_0}). \quad (11.47)$$

It suffices to prove (11.47) when $k_0 \geq 1$, since when $k_0 = 0$ both left and right-hand sides are equal to 1. Also, for $k_0 \geq 1$,

$$b_{k_0} \leq b_1 = 1 - (1-\alpha)^m. \quad (11.48)$$

A first essential observation is that since we assume that ν is p-spread, we have by (11.29) (used for $G_I = H_I$) that

$$a_m = \mu(A_m) \geq 2^{-m}. \quad (11.49)$$

For any m we have $1-(1-\alpha)^m \leq 2^{-m}$ for α small enough (depending on m) so that in this case we have

$$b_{k_0} \leq b_1 = 1-(1-\alpha)^m \leq 2^{-m} \leq a_m \leq a_{k_0},$$

and (11.47) can be obtained for the small values of m simply by taking α small. Thus the issue is the case where m is large enough. We will prove that there is a number L_1 such that

$$L_1 k \leq m \Rightarrow a_k \geq 1 - \exp(-m/L_1). \quad (11.50)$$

First we show that this implies (11.46). The standard estimates on the tail of the binomial law imply that we can assume α small enough that

$$\sum_{m \geq k \geq m/L_1} \alpha^k (1-\alpha)^{m-k} \binom{m}{k} \leq 2^{-m}.$$

Then for $L_1 k_0 \geq m$ we have

$$b_{k_0} \leq 2^{-m} \leq a_m \leq a_{k_0}.$$

On the other hand, if $L_1 k_0 \leq m$ we have

$$b_{k_0} \leq 1-(1-\alpha)^m \leq 1 - \exp\left(-\frac{m}{L_1}\right) \leq a_{k_0}$$

using (11.50) and provided that $1-\alpha \geq \exp(-1/L_1)$. Thus, to complete the proof it remains only to check (11.50). This will follow from (11.29) and Lemma 11.8. Consider the class

$$C = \left\{ I \subset S;\ \forall J \in B,\ \mathrm{card}(I \cap J) < \frac{m}{32} \right\},$$

so that

$$A_m \subset \left\{ X \subset S;\ \forall I^1, \ldots, I^{16} \in C, \right.$$
$$\left. \mathrm{card}(X \setminus (I^1 \cup \cdots \cup I^{16})) \geq \frac{m}{2} \right\}$$

and by (11.49) and (11.40) we have

$$2^{-m} \leq \mu(A_m) \leq \frac{1}{\mu(C)^{16}} \frac{1}{16^{m/2}}$$

and thus $\mu(C) \leq 2^{-m/16}$. Now, $C^c \subset A_k$ for $32k \leq m$, and thus, for $32k \leq m$ we have $a_k \geq 1 - 2^{-m/16}$. □

It would be nice if one could prove that the probability measures of Theorem 11.9 satisfy (9.1). We do not know how to do this, but we at least we know how to handle the following special case.

THEOREM 11.11. *If α is small enough the following occurs. Consider a set S with $\mathrm{card} S = N$, and consider $k \leq N/2$. Then for each up-class A the uniform probability on the subsets of S of cardinality k satisfies (9.1) when $k/N \leq p$.*

We deduce this result from the following.

PROPOSITION 11.12. *If α is small enough the following occurs. Let $p = k/N$, $p' \leq (k-1)/(N-1)$. Denote by μ^i the product measure on $\{0,1\}^N$ such that on the factor of rank i, the weight of 1 is α, and that the weight of 1 is p' on the other factors. Then for each down-class $A \subset \{0,1\}^N$ we have*

$$\mu_p(A) \leq \left(\prod_{i \leq N} \mu^i(A) \right)^{1/N}. \quad (11.51)$$

Proof of Theorem 11.11. Let us denote by μ^{ij} the product measure on $\{0,1\}^N$ such that for the factor of rank i or j, the weight of 1 is α, and is $p'' = (k-2)/(N-2)$ for all the other factors. Then, using Fubini theorem and Proposition 11.12 for $N-1$ and $k-1$ rather than N and k we get for each i that

$$\mu^i(A) \leq \left(\prod_{j \neq i} \mu^{ij}(A) \right)^{1/(N-1)}$$

so that by (11.51)

$$\mu_p(A) \leq \left(\prod_{j \neq i} \mu^{ij}(A) \right)^{1/N(N-1)}$$

and iteration of this process yields (9.2). □

Proof of Proposition 11.12. Let μ_t^i be the product measure on $\{0,1\}^N$ such that on the factor of rank i the weight of 1 is $\alpha(t) = t\alpha + (1-t)p$ while on the other factors it is $p(t) = tp' + (1-t)p$. Let

$$\varphi(t) = \log \prod_{i \leq N} \mu_t^i(A)$$

so that

$$\exp \varphi(1) = \prod_{i \leq N} \mu^i(A) \quad ; \quad \exp \varphi(0) = \mu_p(A)^N$$

and it suffices to prove that $\varphi'(t) \geq 0$. Let $S = \{1, \ldots, N\}$ and for $j \in S$ let

$$A_j = \{X \subset S \setminus \{j\};\ X \in A,\ X \cup \{j\} \notin A\}.$$

Let $\mu_{j,t}^i$ be the projection of μ_t^i on $\{0,1\}^{S \setminus \{j\}}$. Then the (totally elementary) Russo-Margulis formula states that

$$\begin{aligned} -\frac{d}{dt}\mu_t^i(A) &= \frac{d}{dt}\alpha(t)\mu_{i,t}^i(A_i) + \frac{d}{dt}p(t)\sum_{j \neq i} \mu_{j,t}^i(A_j) \\ &= (\alpha - p)\mu_{i,t}^i(A_i) + (p'-p)\sum_{j \neq i} \mu_{j,t}^i(A_j) \end{aligned}$$

and thus (exchanging i and j in the double sum)

$$-\varphi'(t) = \sum_{i \leq N} \left((\alpha - p)\frac{\mu_{i,t}^i(A_i)}{\mu_t^i(A)} + (p'-p)\sum_{j \neq i} \frac{\mu_{i,t}^j(A_i)}{\mu_t^j(A)} \right). \quad (11.52)$$

We have to show that the right-hand side is ≤ 0. The basic reason is that

$$p' - p = \frac{k-1}{N-1} - \frac{k}{N} = -\frac{N-k}{N(N-1)} \leq -\frac{1}{2(N-1)}$$

so that $N-1$ terms with this coefficient easily outweigh a term with coefficient $\alpha - p \leq \alpha$. To check the details, let us fix $i \neq j$, let

$$B = \{X \subset S \setminus \{i,j\};\quad X \in A\}$$

and let μ_t be the projection of μ_t^i on $\{0,1\}^{S\setminus\{i,j\}}$, which is also the projection of μ_t^j on the same space. (It is the product measure that gives weight $p(t)$ to 1 in each factor). Then, since A is a down-class, we have

$$\mu_t^i(A) \leq \mu_t(B)$$

and also

$$\mu_t^i(A) \geq (1-\alpha(t))(1-p(t))\mu_t(B) \geq \frac{1}{4}\mu_t(B).$$

The same inequalities hold for $\mu_t^j(A)$, and thus $\mu_t^j(A) \leq 4\mu_t^i(A)$. Thus, to show that the right-hand side of (11.52) is ≤ 0 it suffices to show that for each i we have

$$4\alpha\mu_{i,t}^i(A_i) \leq \frac{1}{2(N-1)}\sum_{j\neq i}\mu_{i,t}^j(A_i). \tag{11.53}$$

If we make explicit the contribution of the factor of rank j, we see that for certain numbers $a_j \geq b_j$ we have

$$\begin{aligned}\mu_{i,t}^j(A_i) &= \alpha(t)a_j + (1-\alpha(t))b_j\\ \mu_{i,t}^i(A_i) &= p(t)a_j + (1-p(t))b_j\end{aligned}$$

and since $1/2 \geq \alpha(t) \geq p(t)$ we have $\mu_{i,t}^j(A_i) \geq \mu_{i,t}^i(A_i)$. Thus (11.53) holds if $\alpha = 1/8$. □

12. REFERENCES

[1] Michael Ben-Or and Nathan Linial. Collective coin flipping. In *Randomness and Computations*, pages 91–115. Academic Press, 1990.

[2] Jeff Kahn and Gil Kalai. Thresholds and expectation thresholds. *Combin. Probab. Comput.*, 16(3):495–502, 2007.

[3] Michel Ledoux. *The concentration of measure phenomenon*, volume 89 of *Mathematical surveys and monographs*. American Mathematical Society, Providence, R.I., 2001.

[4] Shahar Mendelson, Alain Pajor, and Nicole Tomczak-Jaegermann. Reconstruction and subgaussian operators in asymptotic geometric analysis. *Geom. Funct. Anal.*, 17(4):1248–1282, 2007.

[5] M. Talagrand. Are all sets of positive measure essentially convex? In *Geometric aspects of functional analysis (Israel, 1992–1994)*, volume 77 of *Oper. Theory Adv. Appl.*, pages 295–310. Birkhäuser, Basel, 1995.

[6] Michel Talagrand. Donsker classes and random geometry. *Ann. Probab.*, 15(4):1327–1338, 1987.

[7] Michel Talagrand. Concentration of measure and isoperimetric inequalities in product spaces. *Inst. Hautes Études Sci. Publ. Math.*, (81):73–205, 1995.

[8] Michel Talagrand. *The Generic Chaining*. Springer Monographs in Mathematics. Springer-Verlag, Berlin, 2005. Upper and lower bounds of stochastic processes.

[9] Michel Talagrand. Selector processes on classes of sets. *Probab. Theory Related Fields*, 135(4):471–486, 2006.

Message Passing Algorithms:
A Success Looking for Theoreticians

Andrea Montanari
Dept. of Electrical Engineering and Dept. of Statistics
Stanford University
montanari@stanford.edu

Abstract

Message passing algorithms have emerged as a powerful heuristic for addressing hard problems in a variety of applied fields. Interesting and successful examples can be found in domain as diverse as coding and communications, signal processing, artificial intelligence, game theory, high-dimensional statistics.

At least four reasons can be found for this success:

1. They are widely applicable whenever the underlying problem has a `local' structure with respect to a suitable graph;

2. They are easy to implement and have linear or next-to-linear complexity (within coding they are widely implemented in hardware);

4. They often subsume existing heuristics as special cases;

5. On some random instance distributions which are important in practice, they can be analyzed precisely and tuned to achieve near-optimal performances.

Each of these five points can be argued through examples. It would be highly desirable to make sense of them (of any subset of them) in a consistent theory.

Categories & Subject Descriptors: F.2.2 Nonnumerical Algorithms and Problems, Computations on discrete structures

General Terms: Algorithms, Theory

STOC'10, June 5–8, 2010, Cambridge, Massachusetts, USA.
ACM 978-1-4503-0050-6/10/06.

Perfect Matchings in $O(n \log n)$ Time in Regular Bipartite Graphs

Ashish Goel[*]
Departments of Management Science and Engineering and (by courtesy) Computer Science, Stanford University, Stanford, CA, USA
ashishg@stanford.edu

Michael Kapralov[†]
Institute for Computational and Mathematical Engineering, Stanford University, Stanford, CA, USA
kapralov@stanford.edu

Sanjeev Khanna[‡]
Department of Computer and Information Science, University of Pennsylvania, Philadelphia, PA, USA
sanjeev@cis.upenn.edu

ABSTRACT

In this paper we consider the well-studied problem of finding a perfect matching in a d-regular bipartite graph on $2n$ nodes with $m = nd$ edges. The best-known algorithm for general bipartite graphs (due to Hopcroft and Karp) takes time $O(m\sqrt{n})$. In regular bipartite graphs, however, a matching is known to be computable in $O(m)$ time (due to Cole, Ost, and Schirra). In a recent line of work by Goel, Kapralov, and Khanna the $O(m)$ time bound was improved first to $\tilde{O}\left(\min\{m, n^{2.5}/d\}\right)$ and then to $\tilde{O}\left(\min\{m, n^2/d\}\right)$.

In this paper, we give a randomized algorithm that finds a perfect matching in a d-regular graph and runs in $O(n \log n)$ time (both in expectation and with high probability). The algorithm performs an appropriately truncated *alternating random walk* to successively find augmenting paths. Our algorithm may be viewed as using adaptive uniform sampling, and is thus able to bypass the limitations of (non-adaptive) uniform sampling established in earlier work. Our techniques also give an algorithm that successively finds a matching in the support of a doubly stochastic matrix in expected time $O(n \log^2 n)$, with $O(m)$ pre-processing time; this gives a simple $O(m + mn \log^2 n)$ time algorithm for finding the Birkhoff-von Neumann decomposition of a doubly stochastic matrix.

We show that randomization is crucial for obtaining $o(nd)$ time algorithms by establishing an $\Omega(nd)$ lower bound for deterministic algorithms. We also show that there does not exist a randomized algorithm that finds a matching in a regular bipartite multigraph and takes $o(n \log n)$ time with high probability.

[*]Research supported in part by NSF award IIS-0904325.

[†]Research supported by a Stanford Graduate Fellowship

[‡]Supported in part by NSF Awards CCF-0635084 and IIS-0904314.

STOC'10, June 5–8, 2010, Cambridge, Massachusetts, USA.

Categories and Subject Descriptors

F.0 [**Theory of Computation**]: General

General Terms

Algorithms, Theory

Keywords

graph algorithms, matchings, bipartite regular graphs, Birkhoff-von Neumann decomposition

1. INTRODUCTION

A bipartite graph $G = (P, Q, E)$ with vertex set $P \cup Q$ and edge set $E \subseteq P \times Q$ is said to be d-regular if every vertex has the same degree d. We use $m = nd$ to denote the number of edges in G and n to represent the number of vertices in P (as a consequence of regularity, P and Q have the same size). Regular bipartite graphs have been studied extensively, in particular in the context of expander constructions, scheduling, routing in switch fabrics, and task-assignment [13, 1, 6].

A regular bipartite graph of degree d can be decomposed into exactly d perfect matchings, a fact that is an easy consequence of Hall's theorem [3] and is closely related to the Birkhoff-von Neumann decomposition of a doubly stochastic matrix [2, 15]. Finding a matching in a regular bipartite graph is a well-studied problem, starting with the algorithm of König in 1916 [12], which is now known to run in time $O(mn)$. The well-known bipartite matching algorithm of Hopcroft and Karp [11] can be used to obtain a running time of $O(m\sqrt{n})$. In graphs where d is a power of 2, the following elegant idea, due to Gabow and Kariv [8], leads to an algorithm with $O(m)$ running time. First, compute an Euler tour of the graph (in time $O(m)$) and then follow this tour in an arbitrary direction. Exactly half the edges will go from left to right; these form a regular bipartite graph of degree $d/2$. The total running time $T(m)$ thus follows the recurrence $T(m) = O(m) + T(m/2)$ which yields $T(m) = O(m)$. Extending this idea to the general case proved quite hard, and after a series of improvements (e.g. by Cole and Hopcroft [5], and then by Schrijver [14] to $O(md)$), Cole, Ost, and Schirra [6] gave an $O(m)$ algorithm for the case of general d. Their main interest was in edge coloring of general bipartite graphs, where finding perfect matchings in regular bipartite graphs is an important subroutine.

Recently, Goel, Kapralov, and Khanna [10], gave a sampling-based algorithm that computes a perfect matching in d-regular bipartite graphs in $O(\min\{m, \frac{n^{2.5}\log n}{d}\})$ expected time, an expression that is bounded by $\tilde{O}(n^{1.75})$. The algorithm of [10] uses uniform sampling to reduce the number of edges in the input graph while preserving a perfect matching, and then runs the Hopcroft-Karp algorithm on the sampled graph. The authors of [10] also gave a lower bound of $\tilde{\Omega}\left(\min\{nd, \frac{n^2}{d}\}\right)$ on the running time of an algorithm that uses non-adaptive uniform sampling to reduce the number of edges in the graph as the first step. This lower bound was matched in [9], where the authors use a two stage sampling scheme and a specialized analysis of the runtime of the Hopcroft-Karp algorithm on the sampled graph to obtain a runtime of $\tilde{O}\left(\min\{nd, \frac{n^2}{d}\}\right)$.

For sub-linear (in m) running time algorithms, the exact data model is important. In this paper, as well as in the sub-linear running time algorithms mentioned above, we assume that the graph is presented in the adjacency array format, i.e., for each vertex, its d neighbors are stored in an array. This is the most natural input data structure for our problem. Our algorithms will not make any ordering assumptions within an adjacency array.

Given a partial matching in an undirected graph, an *augmenting path* is a path which starts and ends at an unmatched vertex, and alternately contains edges that are outside and inside the partial matching. Many of the algorithms mentioned above work by repeatedly finding augmenting paths.

1.1 Our Results and Techniques

Our main result is the following theorem.

THEOREM 1. *There exists a randomized algorithm for finding a perfect matching in a d-regular bipartite graph $G = (P, Q, E)$ given in adjacency array representation, and takes time $O(n \log n)$ time both in expectation as well as with high probability.*

The algorithm is very simple: the matching is constructed by performing one augmentation at a time, and new augmenting paths are found by performing an *alternating random walk* with respect to the current matching. The alternating random walk on G, defined in Section 2, can be viewed as a random walk on a modified graph that encodes the current matching. The random walk approach may still be viewed as repeatedly drawing a uniform sample from the adjacency array of some vertex v; however this vertex v is now chosen adaptively, thus allowing us to bypass the $\tilde{\Omega}\left(\min\{nd, \frac{n^2}{d}\}\right)$ lower bound on non-adaptive uniform sampling established in [10]. Somewhat surprisingly, we show that the total time taken by these random augmentations can be bounded by $O(n \log n)$ in expectation, only slightly worse than the $\Omega(n)$ time needed to simply output a perfect matching. The proof involves analyzing the hitting time of the sink node in the random walk. We also establish that randomization is crucial to obtaining an $o(nd)$ time algorithm.

THEOREM 2. *For any $1 \leq d < n/12$, there exists a family of d-regular graphs on which any deterministic algorithm for finding a perfect matching requires $\Omega(nd)$ time.*

We also give a lower bound on the running time of any randomized algorithm for finding a perfect matching in d-regular bipartite multigraphs, even with edge multiplicities bounded above by $d/2$:

THEOREM 3. *Let A be any randomized algorithm that finds a matching in a d-regular bipartite multigraph with n nodes and edge multiplicities bounded above by $d/2$. Then there exists a family of graphs for which A probes at least $(\gamma/64)n \ln n$ locations in the input adjacency arrays with probability at least $n^{-\gamma}$.*

We note that the algorithm of Theorem 1 takes $O(n \log n)$ time with high probability on multigraphs with edge multiplicities less than $d/2$ and hence, the lower and upper bounds are tight in this particular case. It is also interesting to contrast Theorem 3 with the result of [16], which shows that sampling a constant number of edges incident to every vertex of a *complete* bipartite graph yields a subgraph that contains a perfect matching with high probability, i.e. the sampling complexity is $O(n)$ even if a high probability result is desired. The lower bound on the randomized algorithm is not as comprehensive as the deterministic lower bound: it holds only for very specific values of d (specifically, $d = \Theta(n)$), it bounds the "with high probability"-running time as opposed to the expected running time, and it works for multi-graphs. Obtaining tight upper and lower bounds for the entire range of parameters and for expected running time remains an interesting open problem.

Our techniques also extend to the problem of finding a perfect matching in the support of a doubly-stochastic matrix, as well as to efficiently compute the Birkhoff-von-Neumann decomposition of a doubly stochastic matrix.

THEOREM 4. *Given an $n \times n$ doubly-stochastic matrix M with m non-zero entries, one can find a perfect matching in the support of M in $O(n \log^2 n)$ expected time with $O(m)$ preprocessing time.*

In many applications of Birkhoff von Neumann decompositions (e.g. routing in network switches [4]), we need to find one perfect matching in a single iteration, and then update the weights of the matched edges. In such applications, each iteration can be implemented in $O(n \log^2 n)$ time (after initial $O(m)$ preprocessing time), improving upon the previous best known bound of $O(mb)$ where b is the bit precision.

COROLLARY 5. *For any $k \geq 1$, there exists an $O(m + kn \log^2 n)$ expected time algorithm for finding k distinct matchings (if they exist) in the Birkhoff-von-Neumann decomposition of an $n \times n$ doubly stochastic matrix with m non-zero entries.*

Finally, we note that an application of Yao's min-max theorem (see, for instance, [13]) to Theorem 1 immediately yields the following corollary:

COROLLARY 6. *For any distribution on regular bipartite graphs with $2n$ nodes, there exists a deterministic algorithm that runs in average time $O(n \log n)$ on graphs drawn from this distribution.*

A similar corollary also follows for doubly stochastic matrices.

1.2 Organization

Section 2 gives the $O(n \log n)$ time algorithm to find a perfect matching, and establishes Theorem 1. Building on the ideas developed in Section 2, we present in Section 3.1 algorithms for finding matchings in doubly-stochastic matrices, and computing a Birkhoff-von-Neumann decomposition, establishing Theorem 4 and Corollary 5. In Section 4, we present an $\Omega(nd)$ lower bound for any deterministic algorithm that finds a perfect matching in a d-regular graph. Finally, in Section 5 we present an $\Omega(n \log n)$ lower bound for any algorithm that finds a matching in a regular bipartite multigraph with high probability.

2. MATCHINGS IN d-REGULAR BIPARTITE GRAPHS

2.1 The Basic Algorithm

Let $G = (P, Q, E)$ denote the input d-regular graph and let M be a partial matching in G. We first describe the *alternating random walk* on G with respect to M. We assume that the algorithm has access to the function SAMPLE-OUT-EDGE that takes a vertex $u \in P$ and returns a uniformly random unmatched edge going out of u. The implementation and runtime of SAMPLE-OUT-EDGE depend on the representation of the graph. It is assumed in Theorem 1 and in this section that the graph G does not have parallel edges and is represented in adjacency array format, in which case SAMPLE-OUT-EDGE can be implemented to run in expected constant time. In Theorem 4, however, a preprocessing step will be required to convert the matrix to an augmented binary search tree, in which case SAMPLE-OUT-EDGE can be implemented to run in $O(\log n)$ time.

The alternating random walk starts at a uniformly random unmatched vertex $u_0 \in P$ and proceeds as follows:

1. Set v :=SAMPLE-OUT-EDGE(u_j);

2. If v is matched, set $u_{j+1} := M(v)$, otherwise terminate.

Note that an augmenting path with respect to M can be obtained from the sequence of steps taken by the alternating random walk by removing possible loops.

We now state a basic version of our algorithm:

Algorithm 1

Input: A d-regular bipartite graph $G = (P, Q, E)$ in adjacency array format.

Output: A perfect matching of G.

1. Set $j := 0$, $M_0 := \emptyset$.

2. Run the alternating random walk starting from a random unmatched vertex in P until it hits an unmatched vertex in Q.

3. Denote the augmenting path obtained by removing possible loops from the sequence of steps taken by the walk by p. Set $M_{j+1} := M_j \Delta p$.

4. Set $j := j + 1$ and go to step 2.

We prove in the next section that this algorithm takes $O(n \log n)$ time in expectation. The high probability result is obtained in section 2.3 by performing appropriately truncated random walks in step 2 instead of a single untruncated walk.

2.2 Expected Running Time Analysis

The core of our analysis is the following lemma, which bounds the time that it takes an alternating random walk in G with respect to a partial matching M that leaves $2k$ vertices unmatched to reach an unmatched vertex.

LEMMA 7. *Let $G = (P, Q, E)$ be a d-regular bipartite graph and let M be a partial matching that leaves $2k$ vertices unmatched. Then the expected number of steps before the alternating random walk in G reaches an unmatched vertex is at most $1 + n/k$.*

PROOF. It will be convenient to use the auxiliary notion of a *matching graph* $H(G, M)$ which will allow us to view alternating random walks in G with respect to M as random walks in $H(G, M)$ starting from a special source node s and hitting a special sink node t. We then get the result by bounding the hitting time from s to t in $H(G, M)$.

The matching graph corresponding to the matching M is defined to be the directed graph H obtained by transforming G as follows:

1. Orient edges of G from P to Q;

2. Contract each pair $(u, v) \in M$ into a supernode;

3. Add a vertex s connected by d parallel edges to each unmatched node in P, directed out of s;

4. Add a vertex t connected by d parallel edges to each unmatched node in Q, directed into t.

We now state some properties of the graph H. The graph H has $n + k + 2$ nodes and $n(d-1) + k(2d+1)$ edges. Note that for every vertex $v \in H$, $v \neq s, t$ the in-degree of v is equal to its out-degree. The out-degree of s equals dk, as is the in-degree of t. Finally, a random walk in H starting from s reaches t with probability 1, and, most importantly, such a walk corresponds to an alternating random walk in G with respect to M.

We now prove that the expected time that it takes a random walk in $H(G)$ starting from s to reach t is at most $1 + n/k$.

For a vertex $i \in V(H)$, we denote its out-degree by $\deg(i)$. Also, let $\mathbf{P}$ denote the transition matrix of the random walk, that is:

$$\mathbf{P}_{ij} = \begin{cases} 1/\deg(i) & \text{when } (i,j) \in E(H) \\ 0 & \text{otherwise.} \end{cases}$$

Denote the vector of out-degrees by $\deg(\cdot)$, the standard basis vector corresponding to a vertex j by e_j. Note that in fact the out-degree of the nodes of H can only assume 4 values: (1) the starting vertex s has $\deg(s) = dk$, (2) all unmatched nodes u have $\deg(u) = d$, (3) all supernodes v have $\deg(v) = d - 1$, and (4) $\deg(t) = 0$.

We assume wlog that all vertices are reachable from s since those that are not do not influence the runtime of the algorithm. It then follows that t is reachable from any vertex of H in at most $n+3$ steps, i.e. $||(\mathbf{P}^T)^{n+4}||_\infty < 1$, so $(\mathbf{I}-\mathbf{P}^T)^{-1}$ exists. The expected number of visits to a vertex $j \in V(H)$ during the random walk is given by

$$e_j^T \left[\sum_{k\geq 0}(\mathbf{P}^T)^k\right] e_s = e_j^T \left[\mathbf{I}-\mathbf{P}^T\right]^{-1} e_s. \quad (1)$$

Hence, the expected number of steps before reaching t is

$$\sum_{j\in V(H), j\neq s,t} e_j^T \left[\mathbf{I}-\mathbf{P}^T\right]^{-1} e_s.$$

Note that for all $j \neq t$ we have

$$e_j^T \left[\sum_{k\geq 0}(\mathbf{P}^T)^k\right] e_t = e_j^T e_t + e_j^T \left[\sum_{k\geq 0}(\mathbf{P}^T)^k\right] \mathbf{P}^T e_t = 0 \quad (2)$$

since $e_i^T \mathbf{P}^T e_t = \mathbf{P}_{ti} = 0$ for all i.

Hence, we can rewrite (1) as

$$\begin{aligned} e_j^T \left[\sum_{k\geq 0}(\mathbf{P}^T)^k\right] e_s &= e_j^T \left[\sum_{k\geq 0}(\mathbf{P}^T)^k\right] (e_s - e_t) \\ &= e_j^T \left[\mathbf{I}-\mathbf{P}^T\right]^{-1} (e_s - e_t). \end{aligned} \quad (3)$$

However, we have that

$$(\mathbf{I}-\mathbf{P}^T)^{-1}(e_s - e_t) = \frac{\deg(\cdot)}{dk}. \quad (4)$$

To verify equation (4), we calculate

$$(\mathbf{I}-\mathbf{P}^T)\frac{\deg(\cdot)}{dk} = \frac{\deg(\cdot)}{dk} - \mathbf{P}^T\frac{\deg(\cdot)}{dk} = e_s - e_t,$$

which follows from the following case analysis:

Case (1): $j \neq s,t$ Then

$$\begin{aligned} e_j^T \mathbf{P}^T \deg(\cdot) &= \sum_l \mathbf{P}_{lj}\deg(l) \\ &= \sum_{l\in V(H):(l,j)\in E(H)} \frac{1}{\deg(l)}\deg(l) = \deg(j) \end{aligned}$$

since the in-degree of every $j \in V(H), j \neq s,t$, is equal to its out-degree.

Case (2): $j = s$ Then

$$e_s^T \mathbf{P}^T \deg(\cdot) = \sum_l \mathbf{P}_{ls}\deg(l) = 0.$$

Case (3): $j = t$ Then

$$\begin{aligned} e_t^T \mathbf{P}^T \deg(\cdot) &= \sum_l \mathbf{P}_{lt}\deg(l) \\ &= \sum_{l\in V(H):(l,t)\in E(H)} \frac{1}{\deg(l)}\deg(l) = dk \end{aligned}$$

since the in-degree of t is dk.

Hence, the contribution from vertex j is

$$e_j^T \left[\mathbf{I}-\mathbf{P}^T\right]^{-1} (e_s - e_t) = \frac{\deg(j)}{dk},$$

so the expected number of steps before the random walk reaches t is at most

$$\sum_{j\in V(H), j\neq s,t} \frac{\deg(j)}{dk} \leq \frac{(n-k)+2k}{k} = 1 + \frac{n}{k}.$$

□

We can now prove

THEOREM 8. *Algorithm 1 finds a matching in a d-regular bipartite graph $G = (P, Q, E)$ in expected time $O(n \log n)$.*

PROOF. By Lemma 7 it takes at most $1 + n/(n-j)$ expected time to find an augmenting path with respect to partial matching M_j. Hence, the expected runtime of the algorithm is bounded by

$$\sum_{j=0}^{n-1} 1 + n/(n-j) = n + nH_n = O(n \log n),$$

where $H(n) := 1+1/2+1/3+\ldots+1/n$ is the n-th Harmonic number. □

2.3 Truncated Random Walks and High Probability Analysis

We now show how Algorithm 1 can be modified by introducing truncated random walks to obtain a running time of $O(n \log n)$ whp.

Algorithm 2

Input: A d-regular bipartite graph $G = (P, Q, E)$ in adjacency array format.

Output: A perfect matching of G.

1. Set $j := 0$, $M_0 := \emptyset$.
2. Repeatedly run alternating random walks for $2\left(1 + \frac{n}{n-j}\right)$ steps until a successful run is obtained.
3. Denote the augmenting path obtained by removing possible loops from the sequence of steps taken by the walk by p. Set $M_{j+1} := M_j \Delta p$.
4. Set $j := j + 1$ and go to step 2.

We now analyze the running time of our algorithm, and prove Theorem 1.

Proof of Theorem 1:

We now show that Algorithm 2 takes time $O(n \log n)$ whp. First note that by Lemma 7 and Markov's inequality, a truncated alternating random walk in step 2 succeeds with probability at least 1/2. Let X_j denote the time taken by the j-th augmentation. Let Y_j be independent exponentially distributed with mean $\mu_j := \frac{b_j}{\ln 2}$. Note that

$$\mathbf{Pr}[X_j \geq qb_j] \leq 2^{-q} = \exp\left[-\frac{qb_j \ln 2}{b_j}\right] = \mathbf{Pr}[Y_j \geq qb_j]$$

for all $q > 1$, so

$$\mathbf{Pr}[X_j \geq x] \leq \mathbf{Pr}[Y_j \geq x] \quad (5)$$

for all $x > b_j$. We now prove that $Y := \sum_{0\leq j\leq n-1} Y_j \leq cn\log n$ w.h.p. for a suitably large positive constant c. Denote $\mu := \mathbf{E}[Y]$. By Markov's inequality, for any $t, \delta > 0$

$$\mathbf{Pr}[Y \geq (1+\delta)\mu] \leq \frac{\mathbf{E}[e^{tY}]}{e^{t(1+\delta)\mu}}.$$

Also, for any j, and for $t < 1/\mu_j$, we have

$$\mathbf{E}[e^{tY_j}] = \frac{1}{\mu_j}\int_0^\infty e^{tx}e^{-x/\mu_j}dx = \frac{1}{1-t\mu_j}.$$

The two expressions above, along with the fact that the Y_j's are independent, combine to give:

$$\mathbf{Pr}[Y \geq (1+\delta)\mu] \leq \frac{e^{-t(1+\delta)\mu}}{\prod_{j=0}^{n-1}(1-t\mu_j)}. \quad (6)$$

Observe that μ_{n-1} is the largest of the μ_j's. Assume that $t = \frac{1}{2\mu_{n-1}}$, which implies that $(1-t\mu_j) \geq e^{-t\mu_j \ln 4}$. Plugging this into equation 6, we get:

$$\mathbf{Pr}[Y \geq (1+\delta)\mu] \leq e^{-(1+\delta-\ln 4)\mu/(2\mu_{n-1})}. \quad (7)$$

Further observe that $\mu = 2n/\ln 2 + (\mu_{n-1} - 2/\ln 2)H(n) \geq \mu_{n-1}H(n)$, where $H(n) := 1 + 1/2 + 1/3 + \ldots + 1/n$ is the n-th Harmonic number. Since $H(n) \geq \ln n$, we get our high probability result:

$$\mathbf{Pr}[Y \geq (1+\delta)\mu] \leq n^{-(1+\delta-\ln 4)/2}. \quad (8)$$

Since $\mu = O(n \log n)$, this completes the proof of Theorem 1. □

3. MATCHINGS IN DOUBLY-STOCHASTIC MATRICES AND REGULAR BIPARTITE MULTIGRAPHS

3.1 Doubly-Stochastic Matrices

We now apply techniques of the previous section to the problem of finding a perfect matching in the support of an $n \times n$ doubly stochastic matrix $\mathbf{M}$ with m non-zero entries. A doubly-stochastic matrix can be viewed as a regular graph, possibly with parallel edges, and we can thus use the same algorithm and analysis as above, provided that SAMPLE-OUT-EDGE can be implemented efficiently. We start by describing a simple data structure for implementing SAMPLE-OUT-EDGE. For each vertex v, we store all the outgoing edges from v in a balanced binary search tree, augmented so that each node in the search tree also stores the weight of all the edges in its subtree. Since inserts into, deletes from, and random samples from this augmented tree all take time $O(\log n)$ [7], we obtain a running time of $O(n \log^2 n)$ for finding a matching in the support of a doubly stochastic matrix.

Superficially, it might seem that initializing the balanced binary search trees for each vertex takes total time $\Theta(m \log n)$. However, note that there is no natural ordering on the outgoing edges from a vertex, and we can simply superimpose the initial balanced search tree for a vertex on the adjacency array for that vertex, assuming that the underlying keys are in accordance with the (arbitrary) order in which the edges occur in the adjacency array.

The complete Birkhoff-von Neumann decomposition can be computed by subtracting an appropriately weighted matching matrix from $\mathbf{M}$ every time a matching is found, thus decreasing the number of nonzero entries of $\mathbf{M}$. Note that the augmented binary search tree can be maintained in $O(\log n)$ time per deletion. This yields the algorithm claimed in Corollary 5.

3.2 Regular Bipartite Multigraphs

For regular bipartite multigraphs with edge multiplicities at most $d/2$, Algorithm 2 still takes time at most $O(n \log n)$ with high probability, since SAMPLE-OUT-EDGE can be implemented by sampling the adjacency list of the appropriate vertex in G until we find an unmatched edge. Each sample succeeds with probability at least $1/2$ since the matched edge can have multiplicity at most $d/2$. Here, we assume that an edge with multiplicity k occurs k times in the adjacency arrays of its endpoints.

We also note that our algorithm can be implemented to run in $O(n \log n)$ time without any assumptions on multiplicities if the data layout is as follows. For each vertex we have an adjacency array with edges of multiplicity k appearing as contiguous blocks of length k. Also, each element in the adjacency array is augmented with the index of the beginning of the block corresponding to its edge and the index of the end of the block. Assuming this data layout, SAMPLE-OUT-EDGE can be implemented in $O(1)$ expected time regardless of edge multiplicities: it is sufficient to sample locations outside the block corresponding to the currently matched edge.

It remains to note that when the size of the support of the set of edges, which we denote by m_s, is small, then the data representation used in finding a matching in a doubly-stochastic matrix can be used to find a matching in time $O(m_s + n \log^2 n)$. It is interesting to compare this runtime to the result of [6]. The runtime of their matching algorithm is stated as $O(m + n \log^3 d) = O(m)$, but it is easy to see that it can be implemented to run in $O(m_s + n \log^3 d)$ time.

REMARK 9. *Our algorithm can be used to obtain a simple algorithm for edge-coloring bipartite graphs with maximum degree d in time $O(m \log n)$ (slightly worse than the best known $O(m \log d)$ dependence obtained in [6]). In the first step one reduces the problem to that on a regular graph with $O(m)$ edges as described in [6]. The lists of neighbors of every vertex of the graph can then be arranged in a data structure that supports sampling and deletion in $O(1)$ amortized time. It remains to find matchings repeatedly, taking $O(n \log n)$ time per matching. This takes $O(nd \log n) = O(m \log n)$ time overall.*

4. AN $\Omega(nd)$ LOWER BOUND FOR DETERMINISTIC ALGORITHMS

In this section, we will prove Theorem 2. We will show that for any positive integer d, any deterministic algorithm to find a perfect matching in a d-regular bipartite graph requires $\Omega(nd)$ probes, even in the adjacency array representation, where the ordering of edges in an array is decided by an adversary. Specifically, for any positive integer d, we construct a family $\mathcal{G}(d)$ of simple d-regular bipartite graphs with $O(d)$ vertices each that we refer to as *canonical* graphs. A canonical bipartite graph $G(P \cup \{t\}, Q \cup \{s\}, E) \in \mathcal{G}(d)$ is defined as follows. The vertex set $P = P_1 \cup P_2$ and $Q = Q_1 \cup Q_2$ where $|P_i| = |Q_i| = 3d$ for $i \in \{1, 2\}$. The vertex s is connected to an arbitrary set of d distinct vertices in P_1 while the vertex t is connected to an arbitrary set of d distinct vertices in Q_2. In addition, G contains a matching M' of size d that connects a subset $Q_1' \subseteq Q_1$ to a subset $P_2' \subseteq P_2$, where $|Q_1'| = |P_2'| = d$. The remaining edges in E connect vertices in P_i to Q_i for $i \in \{1, 2\}$ so as to satisfy the property that the degree of each vertex in G is exactly d. It suffices to show an $\Omega(d^2)$ lower bound for graphs drawn from $\mathcal{G}(d)$ since we can take $\Theta(n/d)$ disjoint copies of canonical graphs to create a d-regular graph on n vertices.

Overview: Let $\mathcal{D}$ be a deterministic algorithm for finding a perfect matching in graphs drawn from $\mathcal{G}(d)$. We will analyze a game between the algorithm $\mathcal{D}$ and an adaptive adversary $\mathcal{A}$ whose goal is to maximize the number of edges that $\mathcal{D}$ needs to examine in order to find a perfect matching. In order to find a perfect matching, the algorithm $\mathcal{D}$ must find an edge in M', since s must be matched to a vertex in P_1, and thus in turn, some vertex in Q_1 must be matched to a vertex in P_2. We will show that the adversary $\mathcal{A}$ can always force $\mathcal{D}$ to examine $\Omega(d^2)$ edges in G before revealing an edge in M'. The specific graph $G \in \mathcal{G}(d)$ presented to the algorithm depends on the queries made by the algorithm $\mathcal{D}$. The adversary adaptively answers these queries while maintaining at all times the invariant that the partially revealed graph is a subgraph of some graph $G \in \mathcal{G}(d)$. The cost of the algorithm is the number of edge locations probed by it before $\mathcal{A}$ reveals an edge in M' to $\mathcal{D}$.

In what follows, we assume that the adversary reveals s, t and the partition of remaining vertices into P_i, Q_i for $1 \leq i \leq 2$, along with all edges from s to P_1 and all edges from t to Q_2, to the deterministic algorithm $\mathcal{D}$ at the beginning. The algorithm pays no cost for this step.

Queries: Whenever the algorithm $\mathcal{D}$ probes a new location in the adjacency array of some vertex $u \in P \cup Q$, we will equivalently view $\mathcal{D}$ as making a query $\mathcal{Q}(u)$ to the adversary $\mathcal{A}$, in response to which the adversary outputs a vertex v that had not been yet revealed as being adjacent to u.

Subgraphs consistent with canonical graphs: Given a bipartite graph $G'(P \cup \{t\}, Q \cup \{s\}, E')$, we say that a vertex $u \in P \cup Q$ is *free* if its degree in G' is strictly smaller than d. We now identify sufficient conditions for a partially revealed graph to be a subgraph of some canonical graph in $\mathcal{G}(d)$.

LEMMA 10. *Let $G_r(P \cup \{t\}, Q \cup \{s\}, E_r)$ be any simple bipartite graph such that*

(a) the vertex s is connected to d distinct vertices in P_1 and the vertex t is connected to d distinct vertices in Q_2,

(b) all other edges in G_r connect a vertex in P_i to a vertex in Q_i for some $i \in \{1, 2\}$,

(c) degree of each vertex in G_r is at most d, and

(d) at least $\frac{5d}{2}$ vertices each in both Q_1 and P_2 have degree strictly less than $\frac{d}{5}$.

Then for any pair u, v of free vertices such that $u \in P_i$ and $v \in Q_i$ for some $i \in \{1, 2\}$, and $(u, v) \notin E_r$, there exists a canonical graph $G(P \cup \{t\}, Q \cup \{s\}, E) \in \mathcal{G}(d)$ such that that $E_r \cup (u, v) \subseteq E$.

PROOF. Let $G'(P \cup \{t\}, Q \cup \{s\}, E')$ be the graph obtained by adding edge (u, v) to G_r, that is, $E' = E_r \cup \{(u, v)\}$. Since u and v are free vertices, all vertex degrees in G' remain bounded by d. We now show how G' can be extended to a d-regular canonical graph.

We first add to G' a perfect matching M' of size d connecting an arbitrary set of d *free* vertices in Q_1 to an arbitrary set of d *free* vertices in P_2. This is feasible since G' has at least $\frac{5d}{2}$ free vertices each in both Q_1 and P_2. In the resulting graph, since the total degree of all vertices in P_i is same as the total degree of all vertices in Q_i, we can repeatedly pair together a vertex of degree less than d in P_i with a vertex of degree less than d in Q_i until degree of each vertex becomes exactly d, for $i \in \{1, 2\}$. Let E'' be the set of edges added to $G' \cup M'$ in this manner, and let G'' be the final graph. The graph G'' satisfies all properties of a canonical graph in the family $\mathcal{G}(d)$ except that it may not be a simple graph. We next transform G'' into a simple d-regular graph by suitably modifying edges in E''.

Given any graph $H(V_H, E_H)$, we define

$$\Phi(H) = \sum_{(x,y) \in V_H \times V_H} \max\{0, \eta(x, y) - 1\},$$

where $\eta(x, y)$ denotes the number of times the edge (x, y) appears in H. Note that $\Phi(H) = 0$ iff H is a simple graph. Consider any edge (u, v) that has multiplicity more than one in G''. It must be that $(u, v) \in E''$ since G' is a simple graph. Assume w.l.o.g. that $u \in P_1$ and $v \in Q_1$. Let $X \subset P_1$ and $Y \subset Q_1$ respectively denote the set of vertices adjacent to v and u in G''. Using condition (d) on the graph G_r, we know that

$$|E'' \cap (P_1 \times Q_1)| \geq \left(\frac{5d}{2}\right)\left(\frac{4d}{5} + 1\right) - (d + 1) > 2d^2.$$

Since $|X| < d$ and $|Y| < d$, it follows that there must exist an edge $(u', v') \in E'' \cap (P_1 \times Q_1)$ such that $u' \notin X$ and $v' \notin Y$. We can thus replace edges $\{(u, v), (u', v')\}$ in E'' with edges $\{(u, v'), (u', v)\}$ without violating the d-regularity condition. It is easy to verify that the exchange reduces $\Phi(G'')$ by at least one, and that all edges involved in the exchange belong to the set E''. We can thus repeat this process until the graph G'' becomes simple, and hence a member of the family $\mathcal{G}(d)$. □

Adversary strategy: For each vertex $u \in P \cup \{t\}, Q \cup \{s\}$, the adversary $\mathcal{A}$ maintains a list $N(u)$ of vertices adjacent to u that have been so far revealed to the algorithm $\mathcal{D}$. Wlog we can assume that the algorithm $\mathcal{D}$ never queries a vertex u for which $|N(u)| = d$. At any step of the game, we denote by G_r the graph formed by the edges revealed thus far. We say the game is in *evasive* mode if the graph G_r satisfies the condition (a) through (d) of Lemma 10, and is in *non-evasive* mode otherwise. Note that the game always starts in the evasive mode, and then switches to non-evasive mode.

When the game is in the evasive mode, in response to a query $\mathcal{Q}(u)$ by $\mathcal{D}$ for some free vertex $u \in P_i$ $(i \in \{1, 2\})$, $\mathcal{A}$ returns an arbitrary free vertex $v \in Q_i$ such that $v \notin N(u)$. The adversary then adds v to $N(u)$ and u to $N(v)$. Similarly, when $\mathcal{D}$ asks a query $\mathcal{Q}(u)$ for some free vertex $u \in Q_i$ $(i \in \{1, 2\})$, $\mathcal{A}$ returns an arbitrary free vertex $v \in P_i$ such that $v \notin N(u)$. It then adds v to $N(u)$ and u to $N(v)$ as above.

As the game transitions from evasive to non-evasive mode, Lemma 10 ensures existence of a canonical graph $G \in \mathcal{G}(d)$ that contains the graph revealed by the adversary thus far as a subgraph. The adversary answers all subsequent queries by $\mathcal{D}$ in a manner that is consistent with the edges of G. The lemma below shows that the simple adversary strategy above forces $\Omega(d^2)$ queries before the evasive mode terminates.

LEMMA 11. *The algorithm makes $\Omega(d^2)$ queries before the game enters non-evasive mode.*

PROOF. The adversary strategy ensures that conditions (a) through (c) in Lemma 10 are maintained at all times as long as the game is in the evasive mode. So we consider the first time that condition (d) is violated. Since each query answered by the adversary in the evasive mode contributes 1 to the degree of exactly one vertex in $Q_1 \cup P_2$, $\mathcal{A}$ always answers at least $\Omega(d^2)$ queries before the number of vertices with degree less than $\frac{d}{5}$ falls below $\frac{5d}{2}$ in either Q_1 or P_2. The lemma follows. □

Since A can not discover an edge in M' until the game enters the non-evasive mode, we obtain the desired lower bound of $\Omega(d^2)$.

5. AN $\Omega(n \log n)$ HIGH PROBABILITY LOWER BOUND

In this section we prove the lower bound on the running time of a randomized algorithm for finding a matching in a regular bipartite multigraph stated in Theorem 3. We first reiterate that even though the algorithm obtained in section 2 is stated for simple graphs, the same runtime analysis applies for multigraphs as long as edge multiplicities are bounded above by $d/2$. The restriction on maximum edge multiplicity is necessary to ensure that SAMPLE-OUT-EDGE takes $O(1)$ time in expectation. In this section we show that every algorithm that finds a matching in a d-regular multigraph (even with edge multiplicities bounded above by $d/2$) probes at least $(\gamma/64)n \ln n$ locations in the input adjacency arrays with probability at least $n^{-\gamma}$ (on some fixed family of distributions). The lower bound instances use $d = \Theta(n)$.

We first introduce the following problem, which we will refer to as BIPARTITE-DISCOVERY(d).

DEFINITION 12. *(BIPARTITE-DISCOVERY(d))*
Let $G = (P, Q, E)$ be a bipartite multigraph with $|P| = 4d$ and $|Q| = d$. The set of edges $E(G)$ is constructed as follows. For each $u \in Q$ choose d neighbors in P uniformly at random with replacement. A node $u^* \in Q$ is then marked as special, and edges incident to the special node are referred to as special. The graph G is presented in adjacency array format with edges appearing in random order in adjacency lists. When an algorithm A queries a neighbor of a vertex $u \in Q$ or $v \in P$, an incident edge is returned uniformly at random among the yet undiscovered edges. The location of the edge in the adjacency arrays of both endpoints is revealed to A, i.e. it is no longer considered undiscovered when any of its endpoints is queried. The algorithm is not allowed to query the special node directly.

Algorithm A solves BIPARTITE-DISCOVERY(d) if it finds an edge incident to the special node. The cost of A is defined as the number of queries that it makes before discovering an edge to the special node.

We show the following:

LEMMA 13. *Any algorithm that solves BIPARTITE-DISCOVERY(d) makes at least $(\gamma/2)d \ln d$ queries with probability at least $d^{-\gamma}$ for any $\gamma > 0$.*

PROOF. Suppose that the algorithm has discovered J edges of G. Then the probability of the next query not yielding a special edge is at least $\frac{d^2-d-J}{d^2-J}$, independent of the actual set of edges of G that have already been discovered. Hence, the probability of not discovering a special edge after $J < d^2/3$ queries is at least

$$\prod_{j=0}^{J} \frac{d^2 - d - j}{d^2 - j} \geq \prod_{j=0}^{J} \frac{2d^2/3 - d}{2d^2/3} \geq e^{-2J/d}$$

for sufficiently large d. Hence, we have that the probability of not finding a special edge after $(\gamma/2)d \ln d$ queries is at least $d^{-\gamma}$. □

We now give a reduction from BIPARTITE-DISCOVERY(d) to the problem of finding a matching in a regular bipartite multigraph with edge multiplicities bounded by $d/2$:

Proof of Theorem 3:
Let A be an algorithm that finds a matching in a regular bipartite multigraph with edge multiplicities bounded above by $d/2$ and makes fewer than $(\gamma/64)n \ln n$ queries with probability at least $1 - n^{-\gamma}$ on every such graph. We will give an algorithm A' that solves BIPARTITE-DISCOVERY(d) and makes fewer than $(\gamma/2)d \ln d$ queries with probability strictly larger than $1 - d^{-\gamma}$.

Consider an instance $G = (P, Q, E)$ of BIPARTITE-DISCOVERY(d). Algorithm A' first checks if the degrees of all nodes in P are smaller than $d/2$. If there exists a node with degree strictly larger than $d/2$, A' queries all edges of all vertices in P and thus finds a special edge in at most $2d^2$ queries. Note that since the expected degree of vertices in P is $d/4$, the probability of this happening is at most e^{-d} for sufficiently large d by an application of the Chernoff bound with a union bound over vertices of P.

Now suppose that degrees of all nodes in P are at most $d/2$. A' adds a set of $3d$ vertices Q' to the Q side of the partition of G and connects nodes in Q' to nodes in P to ensure that the degree of every vertex in P and Q' is exactly d (it can be shown using an argument similar to the one in the proof of Lemma 10 that this can be done without introducing double edges). Denote the resulting regular multigraph by $G^+ = (P, Q \cup Q', E \cup E')$. Note that G^+ has $4d$ vertices in each part, and one vertex in the Q part of the bipartition is marked special together with its d adjacent edges. Now A' constructs the final graph by putting together two copies of G^+. In particular, we denote by G^- a mirrored copy of G^+, i.e. $G^- = (Q \cup Q', P, E \cup E')$, and finally denote by G^* the graph obtained by taking the union of G^+ and G^-, removing the two special nodes and identifying special edges in G^+ with special edges in G^-. Note that any matching in G^* contains a special edge, so algorithm A necessarily finds a special edge. Note that a query to an adjacency list in G^+ or G^- can be answered by doing at most one query on G. The number of vertices in each bipartition of G^* is $8d - 1$ and the degree of each node is d.

By assumption, algorithm A does not make more than $(\gamma'/64)n \ln n$ queries with probability at least $1 - n^{-\gamma'}$ for any $\gamma' > 0$. Setting $n = 8d - 1$ and $\gamma' = 2\gamma$, we get that A does not need more than $(2\gamma/64)8d \ln(8d) \leq (\gamma/2)d \ln d$ queries with probability at least $1 - (8d-1)^{-2\gamma} \geq 1 - d^{-2\gamma}$ for sufficiently large d. Hence, we conclude that A' probes at most $(\gamma/2)d \ln d$ locations with probability at least $1 - d^{-2\gamma} + e^{-d} > 1 - d^{-\gamma}$, contradicting Lemma 13. □

6. REFERENCES

[1] G. Aggarwal, R. Motwani, D. Shah, and A. Zhu. Switch scheduling via randomized edge coloring. *FOCS*, 2003.

[2] G. Birkhoff. Tres observaciones sobre el algebra lineal. *Univ. Nac. Tucumán Rev. Ser. A*, 5:147–151, 1946.

[3] B. Bollobas. *Modern graph theory.* Springer, 1998.

[4] C. Chang, D. Lee, and Y. Jou. Load balanced birkhoff-von neumann switches, part i: one-stage buffering. *Computer Communications*, 25(6):611–622, 2002.

[5] R. Cole and J. Hopcroft. On edge coloring bipartite graphs. *SIAM J. Comput.*, 11(3):540–546, 1982.

[6] R. Cole, K. Ost, and S. Schirra. Edge-coloring bipartite multigraphs in $O(E \log D)$ time. *Combinatorica*, 21(1):5–12, 2001.

[7] T. H. Cormen, C. E. Leiserson, and R. L. Rivest. *Introduction to Algorithms (3rd Ed).* MIT Press, 2009.

[8] H. Gabow and O. Kariv. Algorithms for edge coloring bipartite graphs and multigraphs. *SIAM J. Comput.*, 11(1):117–129, 1982.

[9] A. Goel, M. Kapralov, and S. Khanna. Perfect matchings in $\tilde{O}(n^{1.5})$ time in regular bipartite graphs. *http://arxiv.org/abs/0902.1617v2*, 2009.

[10] A. Goel, M. Kapralov, and S. Khanna. Perfect matchings via uniform sampling in regular bipartite graphs. *Proceedings of the twentieth annual ACM-SIAM symposium on Discrete algorithms*, pages 11–17, 2009.

[11] J. Hopcroft and R. Karp. An $n^{\frac{5}{2}}$ algorithm for maximum matchings in bipartite graphs. *SIAM J. Comput.*, 2(4):225–231, 1973.

[12] D. König. Uber graphen und ihre anwendung auf determinententheorie und mengenlehre. *Math. Annalen*, 77:453–465, 1916.

[13] R. Motwani and P. Raghavan. *Randomized Algorithms.* Cambridge University Press, 1995.

[14] A. Schrijver. Bipartite edge coloring in $O(\Delta m)$ time. *SIAM J. on Comput.*, 28:841–846, 1999.

[15] J. von Neumann. A certain zero-sum two-person game equivalent to the optimal assignment problem. *Contributions to the optimal assignment problem to the Theory of Games*, 2:5–12, 1953.

[16] D. W. Walkup. Matchings in random regular bipartite graphs. *Discrete Math*, 31:59–64, 1980.

Extensions and Limits to Vertex Sparsification

F. Thomson Leighton
Massachusetts Institute of Technology and
Akamai Technologies, Inc.
Cambridge, MA 02139
ftl@math.mit.edu

Ankur Moitra*
Massachusetts Institute of Technology
Cambridge, MA 02139
moitra@mit.edu

ABSTRACT

Suppose we are given a graph $G = (V, E)$ and a set of terminals $K \subset V$. We consider the problem of constructing a graph $H = (K, E_H)$ that approximately preserves the congestion of every multicommodity flow with endpoints supported in K. We refer to such a graph as a *flow sparsifier*. We prove that there exist flow sparsifiers that simultaneously preserve the congestion of all multicommodity flows within an $O(\log k/\log\log k)$-factor where $|K| = k$. This bound improves to $O(1)$ if G excludes any fixed minor. This is a strengthening of previous results, which consider the problem of finding a graph $H = (K, E_H)$ (a *cut sparsifier*) that approximately preserves the value of minimum cuts separating any partition of the terminals. Indirectly our result also allows us to give a construction for better quality cut sparsifiers (and flow sparsifiers). Thereby, we immediately improve all approximation ratios derived using vertex sparsification in [14].

We also prove an $\Omega(\log\log k)$ lower bound for how well a flow sparsifier can simultaneously approximate the congestion of every multicommodity flow in the original graph. The proof of this theorem relies on a technique (which we refer to as *oblivious dual certifcates*) for proving super-constant congestion lower bounds against many multicommodity flows at once. Our result implies that approximation algorithms for multicommodity flow-type problems designed by a black box reduction to a "uniform" case on k nodes (see [14] for examples) must incur a super-constant cost in the approximation ratio.

Categories and Subject Descriptors

G.2.2 [**Discrete Mathematics**]: Graph Theory—*graph algorithms, network problems*

*This research was supported in part by a Fannie and John Hertz Foundation Fellowship. Part of this work was done while the author was an intern at Microsoft Research New England.

STOC'10, June 5–8, 2010, Cambridge, Massachusetts, USA.

General Terms

Algorithms, Theory

Keywords

multicommodity flow, oblivious reductions

1. INTRODUCTION

Suppose we are given an n-node graph $G = (V, E)$ and a set of terminals $K \subset V$. We consider the problem of constructing a graph $H = (K, E_H)$ on just the terminal set K that approximately preserves the congestion of every multicommodity flow with endpoints supported in K. We refer to such a graph as a *flow sparsifier*.

1.1 Background

The notion of exactly representing or approximately preserving certain combinatorial properties of a graph G on a simpler graph is ubiquitous in combinatorial optimization, and has many applications in theoretical computer science (since such representations are often used to design faster and/or better approximation algorithms). For example, Mader's theorem implies that if we are only interested in the pair-wise minimum cuts between terminals - i.e. for all $a, b \in K$, the minimum cut separating a and b in G - then there is a capacitated graph $H = (K, E_H)$ that preserves all such cuts *exactly*. Additionally, elegant generalizations of Mader's theorem are given in [7], and these results are applied to some problems in network design which require subgraph solutions to be simple, or are subject to degree constraints.

Benczúr and Karger [3] proved that there is a capacitated graph $H = (V, E_H)$ on $O(n \log n)$ edges that approximates *all cuts* in $G = (V, E)$ to within a $1 + \epsilon$ factor, and gave a construction for such graphs that runs in nearly linear time. These results are now a common pre-processing step used to speed up the run-time of many algorithms and approximation algorithms (e.g. [3], [13]). Additionally, Chew [8] introduced the notion of a spanner - a sparse graph that approximates the shortest path distances in the original graph - and gave applications to motion planning in the plane. Related notions of spanners have long been studied in access control, property testing and data structures (see [4]). Spielman and Teng [16] gave a nearly-linear time algorithm for constructing weighted graphs on a nearly-linear number of edges that approximately preserve the Laplacian. These results are improved in [15] and in [2], and approximately preserving the Laplacian is an important step in devising nearly-linear time algorithms for solving diagonally dominant systems of linear equations [16].

Moitra [14] considered the problem of constructing a graph $H = (K, E_H)$ that approximately preserves the values of minimum cuts separating *any* partition of the terminals. We refer to such a graph as a *cut sparsifier*. Approximation algorithms can be run on H as a proxy for the original graph, thereby yielding the first $poly(\log k)$-approximation algorithms (or competitive ratios) for cut and flow problems such as l-multicut, requirement cut, various linear arrangement problems and Steiner oblivious routing. These results give approximation guarantees (or competitive ratios) that are independent of the size of the underlying graph, and only depend poly-logarithmically on the number of "interesting" nodes.

1.2 Our Results

In this paper we strengthen the results in [14] by finding a graph $H = (K, E_H)$ (that we call a flow sparsifier) that approximately preserves the congestion of every multicommodity flows with endpoints supported in K (rather than just requiring the value of minimum cuts separating any partition of the terminals to be preserved). Flow sparsifiers can be obtained from cut sparsifiers, with some degradation in quality corresponding to how well multicommodity flows are approximated by sparsest cuts. Here we consider flow sparsification directly, and are able to achieve the same quality guarantee for this stronger condition on flows as the previous work achieved for the weaker condition on just cuts.

1.2.1 The Quality of a Flow Sparsifier

Throughout this paper, we will consider only demand vectors whose endpoints are supported in the set K.

Given a graph $G = (V, E)$ and a set of terminals $K \subset V$, we say that a graph $H = (K, E_H)$ is a *flow sparsifier* if every demand vector that is feasible in G is also feasible in H. Then we define the *quality* of a flow sparsifier H as the worst-case ratio of the congestion of a flow in G to the congestion of the flow in H. So the quality of a flow sparsifier represents how well H approximates G as a flow network. In Section 3, we prove:

THEOREM 1. *For any capacitated graph $G = (V, E)$ and any set $K \subset V$ of size k, there is an $O(\frac{\log k}{\log \log k})$-quality flow sparsifier $H = (K, E_H)$. If G excludes a fixed minor, then there is an $O(1)$-quality flow sparsifier.*

In Section 2.2 we demonstrate that this notion of a flow sparsifier is stronger than the notion of a cut sparsifier in [14]. Following the method in [14], we prove this existential result by analyzing a zero-sum game. We note that in [14], the question of bounding the game value is transformed to a question about the integrality gap of the linear program [6] for the 0-extension problem. Yet only ℓ_1-metrics arise as metric costs in analyzing this game. But by allowing more expressive metric spaces, we are able to encode a game that attempts to preserve the congestion of multicommodity flows, which allows us to prove stronger results.

From this, we can directly improve the competitive ratio of Steiner oblivious routing by an $O(\log k)$ factor over previous results. With further effort, this result also allows us to write a stronger linear program for the problem of actually constructing a good flow sparsifier. Consequently, we can simplify the approximate separation oracles in [14] and give a construction for better quality flow sparsifiers:

THEOREM 2. *For any capacitated graph $G = (V, E)$ and any set $K \subset V$ of size k, there is a polynomial (in n and k) time algorithm to construct an $O(\frac{\log^2 k}{\log \log k})$-quality flow sparsifier $H = (K, E_H)$.*

The quality of these flow sparsifiers improves upon the quality of the cut sparsifiers in previous results by a factor of $\tilde{O}(\log^{1.5} k)$. Thereby, we can immediately improve the approximation ratios given in [14] for requirement-cut, l-multicut, and generalizations of min-cut linear arrangement and minimum linear arrangement by a factor of $\tilde{O}(\log^{1.5} k)$. Independently, Gupta, Nagarajan, and Ravi [10] have given an approximation algorithm for requirement cut that is also independent of the size of the graph, and improves upon the approximation algorithm implied by this paper.

1.2.2 Limits to Flow Sparsification

As we have noted above, many combinatorial properties of a graph G can be represented exactly or approximated within a constant factor on a smaller graph. In Section 6 we prove that the congestion of each multicommodity flow (with endpoints supported in K) is a rare example of a combinatorial property that *cannot* be approximated within a constant factor on a smaller graph. In particular, our main result is:

THEOREM 3. *For infinitely many values of k, there is a graph $G = (V, E)$ and a set $K \subset V$ of size k for which any flow sparsifier has quality at least $\Omega(\log \log k)$*

The proof of this theorem relies on a technique (which we refer to as *oblivious dual certifcates* and we introduce in Section 5) for proving super-constant congestion lower bounds against many multicommodity flows at once. To prove that no flow sparsifier of quality better than $\Omega(\log \log k)$ exists, we use oblivious dual certificates to refute many candidate flow sparsifiers at once. Specifically, these certificates constrain how the neighborhood of a terminal in a good flow sparsifier can grow, and we piece these local constraints together to derive a global contradiction.

Despite the long list of results on multicommodity flows, sparsest cut, and discrete metric spaces, no super-constant lower bound on the quality of a flow sparsifier was known prior to this work. We consider this a fundamental and natural question in the study of multicommodity flows. Our result implies that approximation algorithms for multicommodity flow-type problems designed by a black box reduction to a "uniform" case on k nodes (see [14] for examples) must incur a super-constant cost in the approximation ratio.

1.3 Network Coding

Here we briefly describe a somewhat surprising connection of this work to network coding theory. In this paper, we prove that there are $O(\frac{\log k}{\log \log k})$-quality flow sparsifiers. And in fact, these flow sparsifiers are generated as a convex combination of 0-extensions. Any such flow sparsifier preserves not only the multicommodity flow rate, but also the network coding rate (see [11] or [1] for a definition):

THEOREM 4. *Any flow sparsifier generated as a convex combination of 0-extensions that has quality ν also preserves* *the rates of all network coding problems with endpoints supported in K to within a ν-factor.*

In general undirected graphs, we do not know if the network coding rate equals the multicommodity flow rate, yet for the existential results on flow sparsifiers that we present here, we automatically preserve the network coding rate at least as well as the multicommodity flow rate. We defer the proof of this theorem, and the implications for network coding to the full version of our paper.

2. MAXIMUM CONCURRENT FLOW

An instance of the maximum concurrent flow problem consists of an undirected graph $G = (V, E)$, a subset $K \subset V$ of terminals, a capacity function $c : E \rightarrow \Re^+$ that assigns a non-negative capacity to each edge, and a set of demands $\{(s_i, t_i, f_i)\}$ where $s_i, t_i \in K$ and f_i is a non-negative demand. The maximum concurrent flow question asks, given such an instance, what is the largest fraction of the demand that can be simultaneously satisfied? This problem can be formulated as a polynomial-sized linear program, and hence can be solved in polynomial time. However, a more natural formulation of the maximum concurrent flow problem can be written using an exponential number of variables:

For any $a, b \in V$ let $P_{a,b}$ be the set of all (simple) paths from a to b in G. Then the maximum concurrent flow problem and the corresponding dual can be written as :

$$\begin{aligned} \max\ & \lambda \\ \text{s.t.}\ & \\ & \textstyle\sum_{P \in P_{s_i,t_i}} x(P) \geq \lambda f_i \\ & \textstyle\sum_{P \ni e} x(P) \leq c(e) \\ & x(P) \geq 0 \end{aligned}$$

$$\begin{aligned} \min\ & \textstyle\sum_e d(e)c(e) \\ \text{s.t.}\ & \\ & \forall_{P \in P_{s_i,t_i}} \textstyle\sum_{e \in P} d(e) \geq D(s_i, t_i) \\ & \textstyle\sum_i D(s_i, t_i) f_i \geq 1 \\ & d(e) \geq 0, D(s_i, t_i) \geq 0 \end{aligned}$$

For a maximum concurrent flow problem, let λ^* denote the optimum. Let $|K| = k$. Then for a given set of demands $\{s_i, t_i, f_i\}$, we associate a vector $\vec{f} \in \Re^{\binom{k}{2}}$ in which each coordinate corresponds to a pair $(x, y) \in \binom{K}{2}$ and the value $\vec{f}_{x,y}$ is defined as the demand f_i for the terminal pair $s_i = x, t_i = y$.

DEFINITION 1. $cong_G(\vec{f}) = \frac{1}{\lambda^*}$

Or equivalently $cong_G(\vec{f})$ is the minimum C s.t. $\vec{f}$ can be routed in G and the total flow on any edge is at most C times the capacity of the edge.

Throughout we will use the notation that graphs G_1, G_2 (on the same node set) are "summed" by taking the union of their edge set (and allowing parallel edges).

2.1 Flow Sparsifiers

DEFINITION 2. *$H = (K, E_H)$ is a flow sparsifier if for all $\vec{f} \in \Re^{\binom{k}{2}}$, $cong_H(\vec{f}) \leq cong_G(\vec{f})$*

So a vertex sparisifer is a "better" flow network than the original graph, in the sense that all demands (with endpoints supported in K) that are routable in G (with congestion at most 1) can also be routed in H.

DEFINITION 3. *The quality of a flow sparsifier H is*

$$\max_{\vec{f} \in \Re^{\binom{k}{2}}} \frac{cong_G(\vec{f})}{cong_H(\vec{f})}$$

We also make a simple, but very useful observation that if we are given $H = (K, E_H)$ such that H is a flow sparsifier for $G = (V, E)$, then there is a well-defined notion of the hardest flow (feasible in H) to route in G. So we can express the quality of H as a single maximum concurrent flow problem:

DEFINITION 4. *Let $H = (K, E_H)$ be a capacitated graph. Then let $\vec{H} \in \Re^{\binom{k}{2}}$ be the demand vector in which each coordinate (which corresponds to a pair $a, b \in K$) is set to $c_H(a, b)$ - i.e. the capacity of the edge $(a, b) \in E_H$ (if it exists, and is zero if not).*

CLAIM 1. *If $H = (K, E_H)$ is a flow sparsifier for $G = (V, E)$, $K \subset V$, then the quality of H (as a flow sparsifier) is $cong_G(\vec{H})$.*

So this allows us to restate our main theorem as:

THEOREM 3. *For infinitely many values of k, there is a graph $G = (V, E)$, $K \subset V$ of size k for which any flow sparsifier $H = (K, E_H)$ has $cong_G(\vec{H}) = \Omega(\log \log k)$*

2.2 Flow Sparsifiers are also Cut Sparsifiers

Here we prove that this notion of a flow sparsifier is stronger than the notion of a cut sparsifier in [14]: Suppose we are given an undirected, capacitated graph $G = (V, E)$ and a set $K \subset V$ of size k. Let $h : 2^V \rightarrow \Re^+$ denote the cut function of G. We define the function $h_K : 2^K \rightarrow \Re^+$ which we refer to as the terminal cut function on K:

$$h_K(A) = \min_{U \subset V \text{ s.t. } U \cap K = A} h(U)$$

The combinatorial interpretation of the terminal cut function is that $h_K(A)$ is just the minimum edge cut separating A from $K - A$ in G. Note that A is required to be a subset of K.

In particular, we prove that if G' is an α-quality flow sparsifier then G' is also an α-quality cut sparsifier - i.e. if h' is the cut function of G', then $h_K(A) \leq h'(A) \leq \alpha h_K(A)$ for all $A \subset K$. So the existential and constructive results that we present here are a strengthening of previous results. So suppose that G' is an α-quality flow sparsifier:

CLAIM 2. *For all $A \subset K$: $h_K(A) \leq h'(A)$*

PROOF. Suppose for some $A \subset K$: $h_K(A) > h'(A)$. Then the min-cut max-flow theorem implies that there is a flow $\vec{r}$ feasible in G such that the total demand crossing the (demand) cut $(A, K - A)$ is exactly $h_K(A)$. But this flow $\vec{r}$ cannot be feasible in G' because the cut $(A, K - A)$ has capacity $h'(A)$ in G' which is strictly smaller than the demand crossing the cut. So this implies $cong_G(\vec{r}) \leq 1 < cong_{G'}(\vec{r})$ which is a contradiction. □

CLAIM 3. *For all $A \subset K$: $h'(A) \leq \alpha h_K(A)$*

PROOF. Consider the flow $\vec{G'}$. This flow is feasible in G' - i.e. $cong_{G'}(\vec{G'}) = 1$. Now suppose that there is a cut $A \subset K$ such that $h'(A) > \alpha h_K(A)$. Choose the set $U \subset V$, $U \cap K = A$ such that $h(U) = h_K(A)$. The capacity crossing the cut $(U, V-U)$ is $h_K(A)$ but the total demand crossing the cut is $h'(A)$ so

$$cong_G(\vec{G'}) \geq \frac{h'(A)}{h_K(A)} > \alpha$$

and $cong_G(\vec{G'}) > \alpha cong_{G'}(\vec{G'})$ which is a contradiction. □

3. GOOD FLOW SPARSIFIERS EXIST

We prove that there exist flow sparsifiers that preserve the congestion of all multicommodity flows within an $O(\frac{\log k}{\log \log k})$-factor, and this bound improves to $O(1)$ if G excludes any fixed minor. This is a strengthening of previous results, which only guarantee that the value of minimum cuts separating any partition of the terminals is preserved. We prove this through a zero-sum game between an extension player and a congestion player. This game is similar to the one introduced in [14], but because the game will be played over the space of multicommodity flows we will need a more intricate argument.

3.1 0-Extensions

We give some preliminary definitions, before introducing the 0-extension problem, originally formulated by Karzanov [12]:

DEFINITION 5. *$f : V \rightarrow K$ is a 0-extension if for all $a \in K$, $f(a) = a$.*

DEFINITION 6. *Given a graph $G = (V, E)$ and a set $K \subset V$, and a 0-extension f, $G_f = (K, E_f)$ is a capacitated graph in which for all $a, b \in K$, the capacity of edge $(a, b) \in E_f$ is*

$$c_f(a,b) = \sum_{(u,v)\in E \ s.t. \ f(u)=a, f(v)=b} c(a,b)$$

So a 0-extension f is a clustering of the nodes in V into sets, with the property that each set contains exactly one terminal. And G_f results from collapsing each cluster corresponding to a terminal and preserving all edges joining distinct clusters.

CLAIM 4. *For any 0-extension f, and for any demand vector $\vec{d} \in \Re^{\binom{k}{2}}$, $cong_{G_f}(\vec{d}) \leq cong_G(\vec{d})$*

Roughly, contracting an edge can only make routing easier. The goal of the 0-extension problem is to find a 0-extension f that minimizes $\sum_{(u,v)\in E} c(u,v)D(f(u), f(v))$ over all such functions. Karzanov gave a (semi)metric relaxation of the 0-extension problem [12]:

$$\begin{array}{ll} \min & \sum_{(u,v)\in E} c(u,v)\delta(u,v) \\ \text{s.t.} & \\ & \delta \text{ is a semi-metric} \\ & \forall_{t,t'\in K} \delta(t,t') = D(t,t'). \end{array}$$

Let OPT^* denote the value of an optimal solution to the above linear programming relaxation of the 0-extension problem. Also let OPT denote the value of an optimal solution to the 0-extension problem. Clearly $OPT^* \leq OPT$. Calinescu, Karloff and Rabani [6] were the first to give bounds on the integrality gap of this linear program for general graphs, and proved an $O(\log k)$ bound. We will make use of an improved bound due to Fakcharoenphol, Harrelson, Rao and Talwar:

THEOREM 5. *[9] $OPT \leq O(\frac{\log k}{\log \log k})OPT^*$*

We will use the above theorem to show that, existentially, there is a graph H that that is an $O(\frac{\log k}{\log \log k})$-quality flow sparsifier. In fact, this graph will be a convex combination of 0-extensions graphs G_f of G.

We will also use a theorem due to Calinescu, Karloff and Rabani which gives a $O(1)$ bound when G excludes a fixed minor:

THEOREM 6. *[6] Suppose that G excludes $K_{r,r}$ as a minor. Then $OPT \leq O(r^2)OPT^*$*

3.2 A Zero-Sum Game

We can define the unit congestion polytope P_G with respect to G as:

$$P_G = \{\vec{f} \in \Re^{\binom{k}{2}} | cong_G(\vec{f}) \leq 1\}$$

We will also be interested in the boundary

$$S_G = \{\vec{f} \in \Re^{\binom{k}{2}} | cong_G(\vec{f}) = 1\}$$

DEFINITION 7. *We will call a metric space d on K realizable in G if there is some extension of d to V so that $\sum_{(u,v)\in E} c(u,v)d(u,v) \leq 1$.*

The set D_G of realizable metric spaces is clearly convex.

CLAIM 5. *The number of vertices in the polytope D_G is finite.*

PROOF. To prove this claim, consider the polytope P_G. This polytope can be realized as the projection of a higher dimensional polytope (that actually finds the realization of each multicommodity flow, and uses flow-conservation constraints as opposed to an explicit decomposition into flow paths). This higher dimensional polytope has a (polynomial in n, k) number of constraints, and hence a finite number of vertices and this implies that the projected polytope P_G also has a finite number of vertices. Each distinct facet of P_G contains a distinct subset of the vertices of P_G, and hence the number of facets of P_G is also finite. The facets of P_G are exactly the polar duals to the vertices of D_G, and this implies the claim. □

Given an undirected, capacitated graph $G = (V, E)$ and a set $K \subset V$ of terminals, an extension player (P1) and a cut player (P2) play the following zero-sum game that we will refer to as the extension-congestion game:

The extension player (P1) chooses a 0-extension f
The congestion player (P2) chooses a vertex $d_{\vec{r}}$ of D_G

We write $d_{\vec{r}}$ for a vertex of D_G because we will use $\vec{r}$ to denote a vertex of P_G that the half-space perpendicular to $d_{\vec{r}}$ contains. Equivalently, $\vec{r}$ is a multicommodity flow that is feasible in G and for which $\sum_{(a,b)} \vec{r}_{a,b} d_{\vec{r}}(a,b) = 1$.

Given a strategy f for P1 and a strategy $d_{\vec{r}}$ for P2, P2 wins

$$\begin{aligned} M(f, d_{\vec{r}}) &= \sum_{u,v\in K} d_{\vec{r}}(u,v)c_f(u,v) \\ &= \sum_{(a,b)\in E} d_{\vec{r}}(f(a), f(b))c(a,b) \end{aligned}$$

where $c_f : K \times K \rightarrow \Re^+$ is the capacity function for G_f.

The advantage of restricting the congestion player's strategies to be vertices of D_G is that the joint strategy space of the game is finite, so we can apply the standard Min-Max Theorem for finite strategy space games, rather than more general Min-Max Theorems for arbitrary convex spaces that are not necessarily characterized as the convex hull of a finite number of points.

DEFINITION 8. *Let ν denote the game value of the extension-congestion game*

LEMMA 1. $\nu \leq O(\frac{\log k}{\log \log k})$

PROOF. Using von Neumann's Min-Max Theorem, we can bound the game value by bounding the cost of P1's best response to any fixed, randomized strategy for P2. So consider any randomized strategy μ for P2. μ is just a probability distribution on vertices of D_G. We can define a semi-metric on V: $\delta(a,b) = \sum_{d_{\vec{r}}} \mu(d_{\vec{r}}) d_{\vec{r}}(a,b)$. Note that

$$\begin{aligned}\sum_{(a,b)\in E} \delta(a,b)c(a,b) &= \sum_{(a,b)\in E} \sum_{d_{\vec{r}}} \mu(d_{\vec{r}}) d_{\vec{r}}(a,b) c(a,b) \\ &= \sum_{d_{\vec{r}}} \mu(d_{\vec{r}}) \sum_{(a,b)\in E} d_{\vec{r}}(a,b)c(a,b) \\ &= \sum_{d_{\vec{r}}} \mu(d_{\vec{r}}) = 1\end{aligned}$$

Then using the theorem due to Fakcharoenphol, Harrelson, Rao and Talwar [9], there exists a 0-extension f such that

$$\sum_{(u,v)\in E} c(u,v)\delta(f(u),f(v)) \leq O(\frac{\log k}{\log \log k})$$

Then suppose P1 plays such a strategy f:

$$\begin{aligned}E_{d_{\vec{r}} \leftarrow \mu}[M(f,d_{\vec{r}})] &= \sum_{d_{\vec{r}}} \mu(d_{\vec{r}}) \sum_{(a,b)\in E} d_{\vec{r}}(f(a),f(b))c(a,b) \\ &= \sum_{(a,b)\in E} c(a,b) \sum_{d_{\vec{r}}} \mu(d_{\vec{r}}) d_{\vec{r}}(f(a),f(b)) \\ &= \sum_{(a,b)\in E} c(a,b)\delta(f(a),f(b)) \\ &= O(\frac{\log k}{\log \log k})\end{aligned}$$

□

Note also that we can replace the application of the theorem due to [9] in the zero-sum game above, and use instead the theorem due to [6]. And in the case in which G excludes $K_{r,r}$ as a minor, this gives us an improved bound of $\nu \leq O(r^2)$ on the game value.

THEOREM 1. *For any capacitated graph $G = (V, E)$ and any set $K \subset V$ of size k, there is an $O(\frac{\log k}{\log \log k})$-quality flow sparsifier $H = (K, E_H)$. And if G excludes $K_{r,r}$ as a minor, then this bound improves to $O(r^2)$.*

PROOF. We can again apply von Neumann's Min-Max Theorem, and get that there exists a distribution γ on 0-extensions such that $E_{f\leftarrow\gamma}[M(f,d_{\vec{r}})] = \nu$ for all $d_{\vec{r}} \in D_G$. Then let

$$H = \sum_{f\in supp(\gamma)} \gamma(f) G_f$$

Let $d_{\vec{r}} \in D_G$ be arbitrary. Then

$$\begin{aligned}E_{f\leftarrow\gamma}[M(f,d_{\vec{r}})] &= \sum_f \gamma(f) \sum_{(a,b)\in E} d_{\vec{r}}(f(a),f(b))c(a,b) \\ &= \sum_f \gamma(f) \sum_{u,v\in K} d_{\vec{r}}(u,v)c_f(a,b) \\ &= \sum_{u,v\in K} d_{\vec{r}}(u,v) \sum_f \gamma(f)c_f(a,b) \\ &= \sum_{u,v\in K} d_{\vec{r}}(u,v)c'(u,v)\end{aligned}$$

So for all $d_{\vec{r}} \in D_G$, we have that $\sum_{u,v\in K} d_{\vec{r}}(u,v)c'(u,v) \leq \nu$ And using strong duality (and the dual for maximum concurrent flow given in Section 2):

$$cong_G(\vec{H}) = \sup_{d_{\vec{r}}\in D_G} \sum_{u,v\in K} d_{\vec{r}}(u,v)c'(u,v) \leq \nu$$

□

In fact, these flow sparsifiers are generated as a convex combination of 0-extension graphs G_f. As we noted earlier, this theorem can be immediately applied to the reduction in [14] to get an improved competitive ratio of Steiner oblivious routing:

COROLLARY 1. *There is an $O(\frac{\log^2 k}{\log \log k})$-competitive Steiner oblivious routing scheme.*

Informally, this improvement comes from considering the question of finding an H that embeds with low-congestion into G directly, rather than constructing an H that approximates the terminal cut function and then relying on bounds on the max-flow min-cut ratio for maximum concurrent flow problems. This improves upon the previous bound by an $O(\log k)$ factor.

4. IMPROVED CONSTRUCTIONS

Here we give algorithms to construct $O(\frac{\log^2 k}{\log \log k})$-quality flow sparsifiers in general graphs. The quality of these flow sparsifiers improves upon the quality of the cut sparsifiers constructed in [14] by a factor of $\tilde{O}(\log^{1.5} k)$. We accomplish this by leveraging the improved existential result in Section 3 to write a stronger linear program for the problem of constructing a good quality flow sparsifier, and from this we can simplify the approximate separation oracles needed.

THEOREM 2. *For any capacitated graph $G = (V, E)$ and any set $K \subset V$ of size k, there is a polynomial (in n and k) time algorithm to construct an $O(\frac{\log^2 k}{\log \log k})$-quality flow sparsifier $H = (K, E_H)$.*

We defer the proof of this theorem to the full version of our paper.

5. OBLIVIOUS DUAL CERTIFICATES

Here we introduce the notion of oblivious dual certificates, which we use to prove super-constant congestion lower bounds against many multicommodity flows at once. We give a concrete example to illustrate the applications of such certificates in proving lower bounds on the quality of flow sparsifiers.

DEFINITION 9. *For a 0-extension f and $a \in K$, $f^{-1}(a) = \{u \in V | f(u) = a\}$ and $size(a) = |f^{-1}(a)|$*

So the size of a terminal $a \in K$ is just the number of vertices in V that are mapped to a by the 0-extension f.

We let $G = (V, E)$ be a constant degree expander on n nodes and choose *any* k terminals where $k = \frac{n}{\sqrt{\log^* n}}$. We need to prove that for every graph $G' = \sum_f \gamma(f) G_f$, the minimum congestion embedding of G' into G is super-constant. Strong duality implies that for any graph G', there is a dual certificate (i.e. a metric space) that provides a lower bound on the congestion of embedding G' into G, and this certificate actually achieves the optimum congestion. Optimal dual certificates for different flows can look quite different, and we can't hope to solve a linear program to find an optimal dual certificate for every possible G' in the space of our proof!

Instead, we give a single sub-optimal dual certificate that proves every $G' = \sum_f \gamma(f) G_f$ (that does not have too much total capacity) requires super-constant congestion (at least $\Omega(\sqrt{\log^* k})$) in order to embed into G. We refer to such a certificate, informally, as an oblivious dual certificate. Such a certificate provides a super-constant lower bound for the quality of many flow sparsifiers at once.

LEMMA 2. *There is a fixed metric space d such that for all 0-extensions f, either d certifies that G_f requires congestion at least $\Omega(\sqrt{\log^* k})$ in order to embed in G or G_f has at least $\frac{n}{10}$ edges.*

Why does this lemma imply what we are after? In general, given two demands $\vec{f_1}$ and $\vec{f_2}$ (on just the terminal set), if we have a lower bound of C for the congestion of embedding each $\vec{f_i}$ into G this does not imply a lower bound of C for the congestion of embedding a convex combination of $\vec{f_1}$ and $\vec{f_2}$ into G. The function $cong_G()$ is sub-additive. But if the metric spaces that certify a lower bound of C for $\vec{f_1}$ and $\vec{f_2}$ respectively, are the same then this metric space also certifies a lower bound of C for any convex combination of $\vec{f_1}$ and $\vec{f_2}$. This is easy to see from the dual (given in Section 2) to the maximum concurrent flow problem, because any metric space d certifies that the congestion of embedding $\vec{f}$ into G is at least

$$\frac{\sum_{a,b \in K} \vec{f}^{a,b} d(a,b)}{\sum_{(u,v) \in E} c(u,v) d(u,v)}$$

and this is a linear function in the demand vector $\vec{f}$.

In fact, the oblivious dual certificate that yields the above lemma is particularly simple: Choose d to be the shortest path metric (on G) resulting from placing a unit of distance on every edge in G.

Roughly, we will prove the above lemma by assuming that the metric space d does not certify that G_f requires congestion at least $\Omega(\sqrt{\log^* k})$ in order to embed in G. This will constrain how the neighborhood of any terminal in G_f can grow, and we will piece these local constraints together to demonstrate that an appropriately rooted breadth-first search tree cannot grow too quickly, and thus G_f contains too many edges.

PROOF. We prove this through contradiction. Suppose there is a 0-extension f for which there are at most $\frac{n}{10}$ total edges (counted with multiplicity) in G_f, and the cost of the oblivious dual certificate against G_f is at most $O(\sqrt{\log^* k})$. Given such a 0-extension f we will construct a breadth-first search tree in G_f. First, we decide how to root such a breadth first search tree. We first prove that there is a terminal $a \in K$ of size at least $\frac{3n}{4}$. This will be the root of our breadth-first search tree:

CLAIM 6. *If G_f has at most $\frac{n}{10}$ edges (counted with multiplicity), then there is a terminal $a \in K$ of size at least $\frac{3n}{4}$*

PROOF. We prove this by contradiction: assume that there is no terminal a of size at least $\frac{3n}{4}$. We know that $\sum_a \text{size}(a) = n$ because any 0-extension f is a clustering of all $|V| = n$ nodes in G. And in particular, there is at most one terminal a of size strictly greater than $\frac{n}{2}$. And the size of any such terminal is at most $\frac{3n}{4}$, so this implies that

$$\sum_{a \text{ s.t. } \text{size}(a) \leq \frac{n}{2}} \text{size}(a) \geq \frac{n}{4}$$

And G is an expander (that expands up to subsets of size $\frac{n}{2}$) so we know that each subset $f^{-1}(a)$ for a s.t. $\text{size}(a) \leq \frac{n}{2}$ has at least $\text{size}(a)$ incident edges. So if we count up the number of edges in G_f, there must then be at least $\frac{n}{8}$ edges (because by adding up all the incident edges to any set a of size at most $\frac{n}{2}$ we have at most double counted edges). This is a contradiction, because we have assumed that G_f has at most $\frac{n}{10}$ edges counted with multiplicity $\square$

So there is a terminal a of size at least $\frac{3n}{4}$, and of course such a terminal is unique. So we construct the breadth-first search tree (starting at the root a) in the graph G_f. Let this tree be T_a. Each node in T_a is a terminal. We assume that the constraint

$$\frac{\sum_{(a,b) \in E_f} c_f(a,b) d(a,b)}{\sum_{(u,v) \in E} c(u,v) d(u,v)} = O(\sqrt{\log^* k})$$

is satisfied and from this we will give a recurrence for how quickly T_a can grow at each depth depending on the number of terminals at earlier depths.

Let E_f^i be the edges of T_a that join levels i and $i+1$. By assumption (and because $E_f^i \subset E_f$):

$$\frac{\sum_{(a,b) \in E_f^i} c_f(a,b) d(a,b)}{\sum_{(u,v) \in E} c(u,v) d(u,v)} \leq O(\sqrt{\log^* k})$$

And from this, we will prove that there are at least $L = O(\sqrt{\log^* k})$ levels in the breath-first search tree T_a before T_a reaches at least $\frac{k}{2}$ terminals.

CLAIM 7. *If all nodes in G have at most constant degree then for any node $u \in V$, and any natural number p, for any set $A \subset V$ of p distinct nodes (not containing u),*

$$\sum_{a \in A} d(u,a) \geq \Omega(p \log p)$$

We can immediately apply this claim, to show that T_a cannot grow too quickly, otherwise there will be some level i where just the edges connecting level i to level $i+1$ provide a large value for the oblivious dual certificate already. So suppose that there are r terminals on level i of T_a. For each terminal i_q in this set $\{i_1, i_2, ...i_r\} \subset K$ let d_{i_q} be the number of distinct terminals in level $i+1$ that i_q is adjacent to (in G_f). Using the above claim:

$$\sum_{(a,b)\in E_f^i} c_f(a,b)d(a,b) \geq \Omega(\sum_{i_q} d_{i_q} \log d_{i_q})$$

So because G_f does not have too large a cost against the oblivious dual certificate (and $\sum_{(u,v)\in E} c(u,v)d(u,v) = \Theta(n)$) this implies that $\sum_{i_q} d_{i_q} \log d_{i_q} = O(n\sqrt{\log^* k}) = O(k \log^* k)$. If we fix $\sum_{i_1} d_{i_q} = D_i$, then $\sum_{i_q} d_{i_q} \log d_{i_q}$ is minimized for $d_{i_q} = \frac{D_i}{r}$. So this implies that

$$D_i \log \frac{D_i}{r} = O(k \log^* k)$$

Note that the number of terminals at level $i+1$ is at most D_i. Let $m_1, m_2, ...$ be the number of terminals at level $1, 2, ...$ respectively. Then we get the constraint $m_{i+1} \log \frac{m_{i+1}}{m_i} = O(k \log^* k)$. This constraint implies that the number of terminals at a given level is maximized by making the number of terminals on every earlier level as large as possible subject to the constraint. We can compute the recurrence:

$$m_1 = 1,\ m_2 = O(k\frac{\log^* k}{\log k}),\ m_3 = O(k\frac{\log^* k}{\log\log k}),$$

$$m_4 = O(k\frac{\log^* k}{\log\log\log k}),\ ...\ m_i = O(k\frac{\log^* k}{\log^{(i)} k})$$

where $\log^{(i)} k$ is the iterated logarithm. So in order to reach at least $\frac{k}{2}$ nodes, $L = \Omega(\log^* k)$.

But if after $L = \Omega(\log^* k)$ levels, the breadth-first search tree T_a has reached at most $\frac{k}{2}$ terminals, then we can give a lower bound on the number of edges in G_f using the expansion properties of G: Consider level i, and let $A_i \subset K$ be the set of terminals that have not yet been reached by the breadth-first search tree in the first i levels. So $|A_i| \geq \frac{k}{2}$ for all $i \leq L$. So this implies that $size(A_i) \geq \frac{k}{2}$, where the size of a subset of terminals is defined to be the sum of the sizes of each terminal in the set. Because $a \notin A_i$, and the size of a is at least $\frac{3n}{4}$, this implies that $size(A_i) \leq \frac{n}{4}$. So the set $f^{-1}(A_i)$ expands, and is incident to at least $size(A_i) \geq \frac{k}{2}$ edges. Because the tree T_a is a breadth-first search tree, each edge with exactly one endpoint in $f^{-1}(A_i)$ must join level i to level $i+1$ in the breadth-first search tree. So if we sum the number of edges with exactly one endpoint in $f^{-1}(A_i)$ over all $i \leq L$, we have counted each edge in G_f at most once, and we have counted at least $\frac{kL}{2} = \omega(n)$ edges. And this is not possible, because there are at most $\Theta(n)$ edges in G_f.

We can leverage this lemma to prove an $\Omega(\sqrt{\log^* k})$ lower bound on the quality of flow sparsifiers for G, provided that these flow sparsifiers are generated as a convex combination of 0-extension graphs, but this is not the result we are after.

The proof of our main theorem will follow the same pattern as outlined above: We will choose an oblivious dual certificate that is (roughly) a shortest path metric of an expander. This oblivious dual certificate will constrain how the neighborhood of a terminal in a good flow sparsifier can grow. We can then piece together these local constraints to get a global contradiction. Of course here we were able to use a natural notion of how quickly the neighborhood of a terminal grows, because we computed the breadth-first search tree and interpreted the oblivious dual certificate as a constraint on each level in the tree. Yet when we place no restriction on how a flow sparsifier is generated, we will require a more intricate notion of "how a neighborhood grows" that will revolve around how much flow can be sent to neighbors on only short paths, using local paths.

6. LIMITS TO FLOW SPARSIFICATION

Here we give a graph $G = (V, E)$ and a subset $K \subset V$ of size k for which every flow sparsifier H has quality $\Omega(\log\log k)$. This lower bound is unrestricted, and makes *no* assumptions on how H is generated.

6.1 The Graph G

Here we define the graph $G = (V, E)$, and highlight the properties of G that will be used in proving an $\Omega(\log\log k)$ lower bound using this graph. G is generated from another graph $G' = (K, E(G'))$. Set $x = \log^{1/3} n$ and let $k = \frac{n}{x}$. We choose $G' = (K, E(G'))$ to be an x-regular graph that has

$$girth(G') \geq \Omega(\frac{\log k}{\log x}) = \Omega(\frac{\log n}{\log\log n})$$

For each node $u \in G'$, we denote the set of neighbors of u in G' as $\Gamma(u)$. Additionally, order this set arbitrarily (for each node u), and let $\Gamma^i(u)$ be the ith neighbor of u in G'. This labeling scheme need not be consistent, and node u can label a neighbor v as the ith neighbor ($v = \Gamma^i(u)$) but v labels u as the jth neighbor ($u = \Gamma^j(v)$).

We construct $G = (V, E)$ from G': For each terminal $u \in G'$, construct a path $P_u = u, u_1, u_2, ...u_x$ in G. And for each edge $(u, v) \in G'$, suppose that $v = \Gamma^i(u), u = \Gamma^j(v)$, add an edge in G connecting u_i and v_j. See Figure 1*a*.

CLAIM 8. *Any matching M in G' can be routed in G - i.e. $cong_G(\vec{M}) \leq 1$*

DEFINITION 10. *Let C_G be the total capacity in G and let $\Delta(G)$ be the maximum degree of G. Also let C_H be the total capacity in H.*

DEFINITION 11. *Let $dist_G(u,v)$ and $dist_{G'}(u,v)$ be the natural shortest path distances on G, G' respectively*

We will need a number of properties of G in order to prove an $\Omega(\log\log k)$ lower bound:

1. $C_G \leq 2n$
2. $\Delta(G) = 3$
3. $\forall_{u,v\in K} dist_G(u,v) \geq dist_{G'}(u,v)$
4. $girth(G) \geq girth(G')$

6.2 Girth and Capacity Surgery

Let $H = (K, E(H))$ be an arbitrary flow sparsifier. We will argue that if all matchings M in G' can be routed in H with congestion at most 1, then $cong_G(\vec{H}) = \Omega(\log\log k)$. We do not assume anything structurally about H, so there are many different ways in which the demand $\vec{H}$ can result in super-constant congestion. We will need a complex argument to handle this, and ultimately we will reduce computing a lower bound on $cong_G(\vec{H})$ to a more structured embedding question about cut-width.

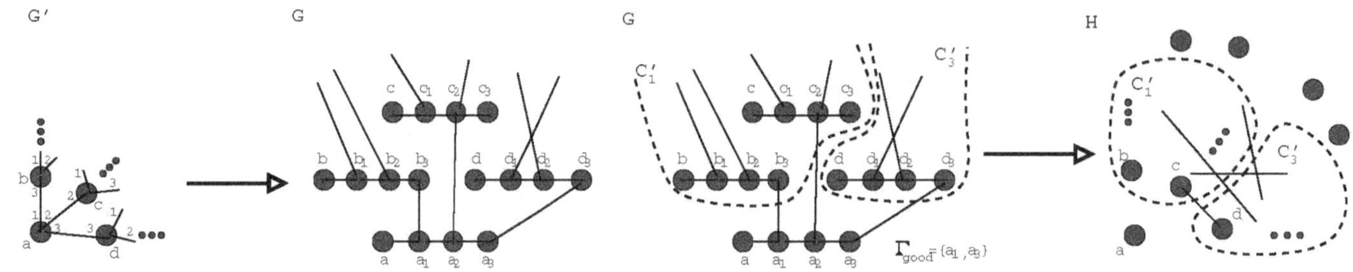

Figure 1: a. Constructing the graph $G = (V, E)$ from an x-regular, high-girth expander $G' = (K, E(G'))$ b. Constructing the partition $\{C'_i\}$ of terminals at distance at most D

Assume $c_1 > 32 \times c_2$ and $c_2 > 24$

Given H, we fix the optimal embedding of H into G. This is a min-congestion routing of $\vec{H}$ in G. Each edge $(u, v) \in E(H)$ is mapped to a flow in G from u to v of value $c_H(u, v)$. We can decompose such a flow from u to v in G into paths. We refer to such a decomposition as a path decomposition, and we assume that this decomposition uses only simple paths.

DEFINITION 12. *We call an edge $(u,v) \in E(H)$ girth-routed if at least $\frac{c_H(u,v)}{2}$ flow (of the $c_H(u, v)$ total flow) from u to v is routed using paths (in G) of length at least $\frac{girth(G')}{4}$.*

DEFINITION 13. *Let $H' = (K, E(H'))$ be the graph defined by deleting all girth-routed edges in H. Let C_{gr} be the total capacity of girth-routed edges in H - i.e. the total capacity deleted from H to obtain H'.*

If H $O(1)$-approximates the congestion of all multicommodity flows in G, then the total capacity in H must be $O(k)$. This is true because each node $u \in K$ has degree 1 in G, and so if the total capacity in H is $\omega(k)$ then there is a node $u \in K$ which is incident to $\omega(1)$ total units of capacity, and even just routing the demands in $\vec{H}$ incident to u would incur $\omega(1)$ congestion in G.

Given this, we know that if H $O(1)$-approximates the congestion of all multicommodity flows in G, then on average edges (u, v) in G' must be able to route a unit flow from u to v using constant length paths. Otherwise we could construct a matching M in which all edges need super-constant length paths to route a unit flow in H, and this flow would not be feasible in H because there would be $\Omega(k)$ pairs each using $\omega(1)$ units of capacity - but H has only $O(k)$ total capacity.

We need to formalize this notion, that edges in G' must on average use short paths (and in fact a stronger condition, that edges in G' must also not route flow in H that reaches nodes that are too far away according to the shortest path metric in G'). So we set $D = \log^{2/3} n$.

DEFINITION 14. *We call a path P connecting u and v (in H or H') good if P is length $< \frac{1}{c_2} \log \log n$ and reaches no terminal a for which either $dist_{G'}(u, a)$ or $dist_{G'}(v, a) \geq D$.*

We call an edge $(u, v) \in E(G')$ good if u can send at least $\frac{1}{2}$ unit of flow to v using only good paths in H', and otherwise we call edge (u, v) bad.

Note that the definition of a good edge is with respect to flows in H', not H. We need this for a technical reason.

Case 1

Suppose that $C_H \geq \frac{k}{c_1} \log \log n$

Then there is a node $u \in K$ that has at least $\frac{2}{c_1} \log \log n$ total capacity incident in H. And because v is degree one in G, this implies that $cong_G(\vec{H}) \geq \frac{2}{c_1} \log \log n$ so we can conclude that $C_H \leq \frac{k}{c_1} \log \log n$.

Case 2

Suppose that $C_{gr} \geq \frac{k}{\log^{1/3} n}$.

Then, in the optimal embedding of H into G there is at least $\frac{C_{gr}}{2} \geq \frac{k}{2 \log^{1/3} n}$ total capacity that uses paths of length at least $\frac{girth(G')}{4} = \Omega(\frac{\log n}{\log \log n})$. So the total capacity used in routing H into G is at least $\Omega(\frac{n \log^{1/3} n}{\log \log n})$. And $C_G \leq 2n$ so this implies that $cong_G(\vec{H}) \geq \Omega(\frac{\log^{1/3} n}{\log \log n})$. So we can conclude that $C_{gr} \leq \frac{k}{\log^{1/3} n}$

6.3 Matchings that are Difficult to Route

We will use the following elementary lemma to simplify the case analysis:

LEMMA 3. *Let G' be an x-regular graph on k terminals. Let $F \subset E(G')$, s.t. $|F| \geq ckx$. Then there is a matching $M \subset F$ s.t. $|M| \geq \frac{c}{2}k$*

PROOF. Let M be a maximal matching using only edges in F. Then let A be the set of terminals that are matched in M, and let B be the remaining terminals. No edge in F can have both endpoints in B, because otherwise M would not be maximal. So all edges in F are adjacent to a terminal in A. Because G' is x-regular, the number of edges in $E(G')$ adjacent to some terminal in A is at most $|A|x$, and this must be at least the size of F. So $|A|x \geq ckx$ In particular, $|A| \geq ck$, and every terminal in A is matched in M so there are at least $\frac{c}{2}k$ edges in M. □

Case 3

Suppose that there are at least $\frac{kx}{4}$ bad edges (in G'). We let F be the set of bad edges in G'. $|F| \geq \frac{kx}{4}$. We can use the above lemma to find a matching $M \subset F$ so that $|M| = \frac{k}{8}$. M is a matching, so $\vec{M}$ is routable with congestion at most 1 in G, and so must also be routable with congestion at most 1 in H.

For each edge $(u, v) \in M$, set $y_{u,v} = 1$. Then using Case 2, $C_{gr} \leq \frac{k}{\log^{1/3} n} = o(k)$. Deleting any edge $(a, b) \in E(H)$ of capacity $c_H(a, b)$ affects at most $c_H(a, b)$ units of flow in the routing of $\vec{M}$ in H because $\vec{M}$ can be routed in H with congestion at most 1. So we can set $y'_{u,v}$ as the amount of flow remaining using the same routing scheme for $\vec{M}$ in H' as for $\vec{M}$ in H, just deleting paths that traverse some girth-routed edge in H (which is deleted in order to obtain H').

$|M| = \frac{k}{8}$ and so $\sum_{u,v} y_{u,v} = \frac{k}{8}$. Because $C_{gr} \leq o(k)$, $\sum_{u,v} y'_{u,v} = \frac{k}{8} - o(k)$. Let $\vec{f}'(M)$ be the flow in H' that satisfies $y'_{u,v}$ that results from deleting all flow paths that traversed a girth-routed edge in H. Each edge $(u,v) \in M$ is bad, so if we decompose $\vec{f}'(M)$ into paths, then for any $(u,v) \in M$ at most $\frac{1}{2}$ unit of flow is carried by good paths. So the total flow carried by bad paths is at least

$$\sum_{u,v} y'_{u,v} - \frac{1}{2}|M| \geq \frac{k}{8} - o(k) - \frac{1}{2}|M| = \frac{k}{16} - o(k)$$

So there must be $\frac{k}{16}$ total units of flow on bad paths in H', and in particular there must be at least $\frac{k}{32}$ total units of flow on either paths of length at least $\frac{1}{c_2}\log\log n$ or at least $\frac{k}{32}$ total units of flow on paths that reach nodes a that are at least distance D from one of the two endpoints u or v of the flow. We consider these two sub-cases separately:

Case 3a

Suppose that there are $\frac{k}{32}$ total units of flow on paths in H' of length at least $\frac{1}{c_2}\log\log n$. Notice that the total capacity in H', $C_{H'}$ is at most the total capacity in H, C_H (because H' resulted from H by deleting girth-routed edges). And the total capacity in H' is at least $\frac{k}{32 \times c_2}\log\log n$. But then

$$C_{H'} \geq \frac{k}{32 \times c_2}\log\log n > \frac{k}{c_1}\log\log n \geq C_H$$

using Case 1, and we have a contradiction

Case 3b

Suppose that there are $\frac{k}{32}$ total units of flow on paths in H' that reach a node a that is distance at least D from one of the two endpoints u or v of the path.

Consider any such path, $P_{u,v}$ in H' that is carrying λ units of flow from $y'_{u,v}$. Suppose that a is the first node such that $dist_{G'}(u,a) \geq D$ or $dist_{G'}(v,a) \geq D$. Assume without loss of generality that $dist_{G'}(u,a) \geq D$. Construct a demand vector $\vec{r} \in \Re^{\binom{k}{2}}$ as follows: For each such path $P_{u,v}$, increment the demand $\vec{r}_{u,a}$ by λ.

So for each flow path carrying λ units of flow, we have added λ demand to some coordinate in $\vec{r}$.

CLAIM 9. *$\vec{r}$ is routable in H with congestion at most* 1

PROOF. We constructed $\vec{r}$ demands based on a flow $\vec{f}'(M)$ of congestion at most 1 in H', and the same routing scheme for $\vec{f}'(M)$ that achieved congestion at most 1 in H' also achieves congestion at most 1 in H. We then constructed demands by deleting segments of the flow paths - i.e. in the above example we preserved only the sub-path of $P_{u,v}$ from u to a and deleted the rest of the path. This flow resulting from deleting sub-paths still has congestion 1 in H and also satisfies the demands $\vec{r}$. □

Notice that for every path carrying λ flow we have added a demand equal to this flow value λ between two nodes $u, a \in K$ which are distance at least D apart in G' - i.e. $dist_{G'}(u,a) \geq D$.

Consider the minimum congestion embedding of the demand vector $\vec{r}$ into G. We can construct an oblivious dual certificate that certifies $\vec{r}$ has large congestion in G: for each edge in G, place a unit of distance on this edge.

The total distance × capacity units used is $C_G \leq 2n$. And we note that $dist_G(u,v) \geq dist_{G'}(u,v)$ for all $u, v \in K$ from the claim Section 6.1. So $\sum_{u,v} \vec{r}_{u,v} dist_G(u,v) \geq \frac{k}{32}D$.

This implies $cong_G(\vec{H}) \geq cong_G(\vec{r}) \geq \frac{\Omega(k)D}{2n} = \Omega(\log^{1/3} n)$. So we can conclude using Case 3a and 3b that there are at most $\frac{kx}{4}$ bad edges in G'.

6.4 Cut-Width

So we can remove all bad edges in G' from consideration, and there are at least $\frac{kx}{4}$ good edges remaining. This implies that there is a terminal $a \in G'$ that is incident to at least $\frac{x}{2}$ good edges. Consider such a terminal a.

Let $\Gamma_{good}(a)$ be the set of neighbors u of a for which the edge $(u,a) \in E(G')$ is good. We can define the induced path P_{good} as the path on just Γ_{good} in the order in which these nodes are labeled according to Γ. For each terminal b adjacent to a in G', we define a component C_j (assuming $b = \Gamma^j(a)$) that consists of all terminals that are distance at most D according to G' from terminal a and are in the depth-first search sub-tree (of G') rooted at terminal b. For each terminal b adjacent to a s.t. the edge (a,b) is bad, if $b = \Gamma^j(a)$ then choose the closest terminal c on the path P_a for which the edge (c,a) is good, and break ties arbitrarily. For each node $c \in \Gamma_{good}$, consider the set of terminals d that chose c, and set $C'_i = \cup_{d \text{ chooses } c} C_j$ if $\Gamma^i(u) = c$ and $\Gamma^j(u) = d$, and by definition any good terminal on the path P_a chooses itself.

So C'_i forms a partition of the set of terminals that are distance at most D (since $girth(G') >> D$) from terminal a in G', and for each component C'_i there is a terminal $c \in C'_i$ that is adjacent to a in G' and for which (a,c) is a good edge.

We construct a graph B in which we add a node for a, and a node i for each component C'_i. For each edge in H' from a node C'_i to a node in C'_j, we add an edge in B of the same capacity connecting the node i to the node j (and we allow parallel edges). See Figure 1*b*.

Intuitively, in B we allow routing within C'_i for free. But because each node i in B contains a terminal c which is a neighbor of a and for which (a,c) is a good edge, terminal a must be able to send at least $\frac{1}{2}$ units of flow from a to terminal c in H' using paths that do not reach any other node distance more than D from terminal a (according to $dist_{G'}$) and using only paths of length at most $\frac{1}{c_2}\log\log n$. Because in B we allow routing within C'_i for free, and have only removed nodes that are too far from a to be on any good path, in the graph B we must be able to send at least $\frac{1}{2}$ units of flow of flow from a to i using paths of length at most $\frac{1}{c_2}\log\log n$.

So consider the path P_{good} defined on $\{a\} \cup \Gamma_{good}(a)$ in which nodes in Γ_{good} are visited according to the order defined by $\Gamma(a)$. We will prove a lower bound on the minimum cut-width embedding of B into P_{good}. This will imply a cut-width lower bound on embedding B into P_a, and because every edge in H' routes at least $\frac{1}{2}$ of its capacity through paths of length at most $\frac{girth(G')}{4}$ (and consequently every edge in B connecting a node i to a node j must traverse the sub-path $a_i, a_{i+1}, ...a_j$ in P_a), and so this implies a lower bound on the congestion of embedding H' into G. So consider an interval I of P_{good}:

DEFINITION 15. *Given a set of flows out of a, we define the average path length as the sum over all flow paths P (in a path decomposition of the flow) of the weight of flow on the path times the length of the path:* $v(P) \times length(P)$.

Note that the average path length of a flow is independent of the particular choice of the path decomposition of the flow, provided every path in the path decomposition is simple.

DEFINITION 16. *We define the minimum cost-routing into an interval I as the minimum average path length of any flow (in B) that sends exactly* $\frac{1}{2}$ *unit of flow in total to the terminals in interval I.*

DEFINITION 17. *An interval I has the* (C, E) *property if the total capacity (of B) crossing I - i.e. has one endpoint to the left and one endpoint to the right of I - is at least C and if the minimum cost routing to I is at least E.*

Suppose that interval I has the (C, E)-property. Split I into I_1, I_2, I_3, three contiguous intervals. If there is total capacity at least $\frac{1}{6}$ in B crossing I_1 but not I, then I_1 has the $(C + \frac{1}{6}, E)$ property (because the minimum cost routing to I_1 is at least the minimum cost routing to I). Similarly, if there is at least $\frac{1}{6}$ capacity in B crossing I_3 but not I, then I_3 has the $(C + \frac{1}{6}, E)$ property.

Otherwise, there is at most $\frac{1}{6}$ total capacity entering I_2 from the left of I_1, and at most $\frac{1}{6}$ total capacity entering I_2 from the right of I_3. So consider the minimum cost routing to I_2. There must be at least $\frac{1}{2} - \frac{1}{6} - \frac{1}{6} = \frac{1}{6}$ total flow that enters I_2 from I_1 or I_3. So given the minimum cost routing to I_2 of cost α, we can stop paths that enter I_2 from I_1 or I_3 short, and reduce the cost of the routing by at least $\frac{1}{6}$. This would give a routing into I of cost $\alpha - \frac{1}{6}$, but the minimum cost routing into I is at least E, so $\alpha \geq E + \frac{1}{6}$. So either I_1 or I_3 has the $(C + \frac{1}{6}, E)$ property or I_2 has the $(C, E + \frac{1}{6})$ property.

So this implies that if we continue for $\log_3 \frac{x}{2}$ levels of this recursion (and there are in fact $\frac{x}{2}$ nodes in the path P_{good}), then we find an interval I that has the (C, E) property and $C + E \geq \frac{\log_3 \frac{x}{2}}{6}$ and so either C or E must be $\geq \frac{\log_3 \frac{x}{2}}{12}$.

If $C \geq \frac{\log_3 \frac{x}{2}}{12}$, then the cut-width of embedding B into the path P_{good} is at least C, which implies that at least C total capacity in H' has one endpoint in C'_i and one endpoint in C'_j, and the interval I in P_a is contained between the image of C'_i in P_a and the image of C'_j in P_a. Because this capacity is in H', and at least $\frac{1}{2}$ of this capacity is routing using the natural path in G and traverses the interval I, and in this case the congestion of embedding H' into G (using the fixed routing of H' into G - note that H' was defined based on the optimal embedding of H into G) is at least $\frac{C}{2} = \Omega(\log \log n)$.

If $E \geq \frac{\log_3 \frac{x}{2}}{12}$, then there is a node $u \in I$ for which the minimum cost routing to c is at least $\frac{\log_3 \frac{x}{2}}{12} > \frac{\log \log n}{c_2}$, but then the edge (a, u) would not be good. I is an interval in P_{good} and this yields a contradiction.

THEOREM 3. *For infinitely many values of k, there is a graph* $G = (V, E)$ *and a set* $K \subset V$ *of size k for which any flow sparsifier has quality at least* $\Omega(\log \log k)$

7. ACKNOWLEDGMENTS

We would like to thank Howard Karloff for many helpful discussions.

8. REFERENCES

[1] M. Adler, N. Harvey, K. Jain, R. Kleinberg, and A. R. Lehman. On the capacity of information networks. *Symposium on Discrete Algorithms*, pages 320–329, 1990.

[2] J. Batson, D. Spielman, and N. Srivastava. Twice-ramanujan sparsifiers. *Symposium on Theory of Computing*, pages 255–262, 2009.

[3] A. Benczúr and D. Karger. Approximating s-t minimum cuts in $\tilde{O}(n^2)$ time. *Symposium on Theory of Computing*, pages 47–55, 1996.

[4] A. Bhattacharyya, E. Grigorescu, K. M. Jung, S. Raskhodnikova, and D. Woodruff. Transitive-closure spanners. *Symposium on Discrete Algorithms*, pages 932–941, 2009.

[5] D. Bienstock, E. Brickell, and C. Monma. On the structure of minimum-weight k-connected spanning networks. *SIAM Journal on Discrete Mathematics*, pages 320–329, 1990.

[6] G. Calinescu, H. Karloff, and Y. Rabani. Approximation algorithms for the 0-extension problem. *Symposium on Discrete Algorithms*, pages 8–16, 2001.

[7] Y. H. Chan, W. S. Fung, L. C. Lau, and C. K. Yung. Degree bounded network design with metric costs. *Foundations of Computer Science*, pages 125–134, 2008.

[8] L. P. Chew. There is a planar graph almost as good as the complete graph. *Symposium on Computational Geometry*, pages 169–177, 1986.

[9] J. Fakcharoenphol, C. Harrelson, S. Rao, and K. Talwar. An improved approximation algorithm for the 0-extension problem. *Symposium on Discrete Algorithms*, pages 257–265, 2003.

[10] A. Gupta, V. Nagarajan, and R. Ravi. Improved approximation algorithm for requirement cut. *submitted*, 2009.

[11] N. Harvey, R. Kleinberg, and A. R. Lehman. On the capacity of information networks. *IEEE Transactions on Information Theory*, pages 251–260, 2006.

[12] A. Karzanov. Minimum 0-extensions of graph metrics. *European Journal of Combinatorics*, pages 71–101, 1998.

[13] R. Khandekar, S. Rao, and U. Vazirani. Graph partitioning using single commodity flows. *Journal of the ACM*, 2009.

[14] A. Moitra. Approximation algorithms for multicommodity-type problems with guarantees independent of the graph size. *Foundations of Computer Science*, pages 3–12, 2009.

[15] D. Spielman and N. Srivastava. Graph sparsification by effective resistances. *Symposium on Theory of Computing*, pages 563–568, 2008.

[16] D. Spielman and S. H. Teng. Nearly-linear time algorithms for graph partitioning, sparsification and solving linear systems. *Symposium on Theory of Computing*, pages 81–90, 2004.

Subgraph Sparsification and Nearly Optimal Ultrasparsifiers

Alexandra Kolla*
School of Mathematics
Institute for Advanced Study
Princeton, NJ 08540
akolla@math.ias.edu

Yury Makarychev
Toyota Technological Institute at Chicago
Chicago, IL 60637
yury@ttic.edu

Amin Saberi†
Management Science and Engineering Department
Stanford University
Stanford, CA 94305
saberi@stanford.edu

Shang-Hua Teng‡
Dept of Computer Science
University of Southern California
Los Angeles, CA 90089
shanghua@usc.edu

ABSTRACT

We consider a variation of the spectral sparsification problem where we are required to keep a subgraph of the original graph. Formally, given a union of two weighted graphs G and W and an integer k, we are asked to find a k-edge weighted graph W_k such that $G + W_k$ is a good spectral sparsifer of $G + W$. We will refer to this problem as the subgraph (spectral) sparsification. We present a nontrivial condition on G and W such that a good sparsifier exists and give a polynomial-time algorithm to find the sparsifer.

As an application of our technique, we show that for each positive integer k, every n-vertex weighted graph has an $(n - 1 + k)$-edge spectral sparsifier with relative condition number at most $\frac{n}{k} \log n\, \tilde{O}(\log\log n)$ where $\tilde{O}()$ hides lower order terms. Our bound nearly settles a question left open by Spielman and Teng about ultrasparsifiers.

We also present another application of our technique to spectral optimization in which the goal is to maximize the algebraic connectivity of a graph (e.g. turn it into an expander) with a limited number of edges.

Categories and Subject Descriptors

F.2 [**Theory of Computation**]: Analysis of Algorithms

*Research supported by NSF grant CCF-0832797.

†Research supported by AHPCRC and NSF

‡Research supported by NSF grant CCF-0635102.

STOC'10, June 5–8, 2010, Cambridge, Massachusetts, USA.

General Terms

Algorithms, Theory

Keywords

Graph sparsification, ultrasparsifiers, graph Laplacian, approximation algorithm

1. INTRODUCTION

Sparsification is an important technique for designing efficient graph algorithms, especially for dense graphs. Informally, a graph $\tilde{G}$ is a sparsifer of G if they are similar in a particular measure (which is important to the application that one has in mind), and that $\tilde{G}$ has linear or nearly linear number of edges. Various notions of graph approximation and sparsification have been considered in the literature. For example, Chew's [6] spanners (for shortest path planning) have the property that the distance between every pair of vertices in $\tilde{G}$ is approximately the same as in G. Benczur and Karger's [4] cut-sparsifiers (for cuts and flows) have the property that the weight of the boundary of every set of vertices is approximately the same in G as in $\tilde{G}$.

In this paper, we will mainly be interested in the spectral notion of graph similarity introduced by Spielman and Teng [18], [20]: we say that a weighted undirected graph H is a κ-approximation of another G if for all $x \in \mathbf{R}^V$,

$$x^T \mathcal{L}_G x \le x^T \mathcal{L}_{\tilde{G}} x \le \kappa x^T \mathcal{L}_G x \qquad (1)$$

where for a weighted undirected graph G, $\mathcal{L}_G$ is the *Laplacian matrix* of G defined as the following: For each i, $\mathcal{L}_G(i,i)$ is equal to the sum of weights of all edges incident to vertex i and for $i \ne j$, $\mathcal{L}_G(i,j) = -w_{i,j}$, where $w_{i,j}$ is the weight on edge (i,j).

In [18, 20], the following spectral sparsification problem is considered. Given a weighted graph $G = (V, E, w)$, an integer $\tilde{m} \le |E|$, and $\kappa \ge 1$, find a graph $\tilde{G} = \{V, \tilde{E}, \tilde{w}\}$ such that $|\tilde{E}| \le \tilde{m}$ and $\tilde{G}$ is a κ-approximation of G. We will refer to this problem and its corresponding optimization problem as the SPECTRAL SPARSIFICATION. Spielman and Teng showed that every weighted graph has a nearly linear-sized spectral sparsifier and gave a nearly linear-time algorithm for computing such a sparsifier. Recently, Batson, Spielman, and Srivastava [3] gave a beautiful, polynomial-time construction to produce a linear-sized spectral sparsifier.

In this paper, we introduce a variation of the spectral sparsification problem which we will refer to as the SUBGRAPH SPARSIFICATION. In our version, we are given two weighted graphs G and W, an integer k and $\kappa \geq 1$. The goal is to find a k-edge weighted graph W_k such that $(G+W_k)$ is a κ-approximation of $(G+W)$. The challenge in the new version of the sparsification problem is that we have to respect part of the graph, i.e., G, and only modify part of graph given in W.

As the main technical contribution of the paper, we give a nontrivial condition about G and W such that a good sparsifier exists. Our proof critically uses the intuition of Batson, Spielman, and Srivastava [3], that uses potential functions that guide an incremental process for selecting the edges of the sparisifier. We will refer to that as as the *BSS process*. We have enhanced their approach with new understanding about subspace sparsification and spectral approximation.

Our challenge, at high level, is the following. The BSS process uses two carefully chosen barriers (see Section 2) so that at each step, all eigenvalues can be kept far enough from these barriers. They have $\Theta(n)$ edges to select. So they consider the entire n-dimensional space and have step size $\Theta(1/n)$ on these barriers.

On the other hand, we can only add k edges, where k can be arbitrarily smaller than n. The addition of each edge can only increase smallest eigenvalue to the second smallest eigenvalue. Therefore the addition of k edges can only improve the subspace defined by the k smallest eigenvalue. Now, the critical part of the argument is that to build a good sparsifier, we need to ensure that the addition of the edges does not increase the high spectra by too much. So in our incremental process, we need to keep track of two subspaces, a fixed one defined by the k smallest eigenvalues and a floating one defined by the higher spectra.

We developed an analysis for performing spectral analysis in the projection of a sequence of two subspaces, which might be interesting on its own right. Our analysis also provide a nice example for using majorization.

Our ability to conduct sparsification on a subgraph enables us to obtain improved results for a few problems on spectral optimization. The first application that we consider is the problem of finding ultrasparsifiers as defined in Spielman and Teng [18]. For parameters $\kappa \geq 1$ and $k \geq 1$, a weighted undirected graph U is a (κ, k)-*ultrasparsifier* of another graph G, if U has at most $n-1+k$ edges, and G is a κ-approximation of U. Ultrasparsifiers are essential in the application of the preconditioning techniques for solving linear systems [18, 20]. It has been shown in [18] that every weighted undirected graph G has a $(\frac{n}{k}\log^{O(1)} n, k)$ ultrasparsifiers, for any k.

As an application of our subgraph sparsification technique, we will show that for every positive integer k, every n-vertex weighted graph has a $(\frac{n}{k}\log n\,\tilde{O}(\log\log n), k)$-ultrasparsifier. Our bound almost settles the previous question about ultrasparsifiers left open by Spielman and Teng.

At high level, our solution to ultrasparsification is quite simple, once we have our subgraph sparsification result. Given a weighted graph$G$, we first construct a low-stretch spanning tree [2, 7, 1] T of G. We then apply an elegant result of Spielman and Woo [21] which states that the sum of the relative condition numbers of $\mathcal{L}_G$ and $\mathcal{L}_T$ is equal to the total stretch to embed G onto T. We will also use Spielman–Woo's tail distribution bound on the number of relative eigenvalues of $\mathcal{L}_G$ and $\mathcal{L}_T$ that are larger than a given parameter.

Algorithmically, we start with the best available [1] low-stretch spanning tree T of G whose total stretch is $n\log n\,\tilde{O}(\log\log n)$. We then consider the subgraph sparsification problem defined by T and $W = \frac{k}{n\log n\tilde{O}(\log\log n)}G$. We apply the structure theorem of Spielman and Woo [21] to show that (T, W) satisfy our condition for subgraph sparsification and apply our result to show that there exists a k-edge weighted graph W_k whose edges are in W such that $T+W_k$ is a spectral approximation of $T+W$. It is then not hard to prove that $T+W_k$ is an a $(\frac{n}{k}\log n\,\tilde{O}(\log\log n), k)$-ultrasparsifier.

As another application of our technique on subgraph sparsification, we consider the following spectral optimization problem studied in [5]: Given a graph G and a parameter k, we are asked to find k edges amongst a set of candidate edges to add to G so as to maximize its algebraic connectivity. Algebraic connectivity has emerged as an important parameter for measuring the robustness and stability of a network and is an essential factor in the performance of various search, routing and information diffusion algorithms.

The spectral optimization considered in this paper is known to be NP-hard [15] and no approximation guarantee for it was known prior to our work. We give an SDP-based approximation algorithm for the problem. Our techniques for subgraph sparsification enable us to develop a novel *rounding* scheme in order to find a combinatorial solution. Since the integrality gap of the SDP is unbounded, our analysis involves adding a separate upper bound, which is roughly the k-th largest eigenvalue of the Laplacian of G to approximate the optimum solution.

2. PRELIMINARIES

Matrix Notation and Definitions. We write $A \succeq 0$ to denote that symmetric matrix A is positive semidefinite; similarly, we write $A \succeq B$ to denote that matrix $A-B$ is positive semidefinite.

We denote the (non-normalized) Laplacian matrix of a graph G by $\mathcal{L}_G$. Recall that $\mathcal{L}_G$ is the matrix with $\mathcal{L}_G(i,i)$ equal to the sum of weights of all edges incident to vertex i, and $\mathcal{L}_G(i,j) = -w_{ij}$ where w_{ij} is the weight of the edge (i,j). For brevity, we write $G_1 \preceq G_2$ to denote $\mathcal{L}_{G_1} \preceq \mathcal{L}_{G_2}$.

For an $n\times n$ matrix A, let $\lambda_{\min}(A) \equiv \lambda_1(A) \leq \lambda_2(A) \leq \cdots \leq \lambda_n(A) \equiv \lambda_{\max}(A)$ be the set of eigenvalues in the increasing order.

We denote the column space of a matrix A (which is equal to the image or range of the corresponding linear operator) by $\operatorname{Im} A$. We denote the kernel or nullspace of A by $\ker A$. Let $A^\dagger$ be the pseudoinverse of A. If A is symmetric, $A^\dagger$ is also symmetric and $AA^\dagger = A^\dagger A = P_{\operatorname{Im}(A)}$, where $P_{\operatorname{Im}(A)}$ is the orthogonal projection on $\operatorname{Im}(A)$. Let $A \bullet B \equiv \operatorname{tr} A^T B$ be the Frobenius product of matrices A and B. We define the *condition number* of a non-singular matrix A as $\kappa = \|A\|\|A^{-1}\|$, which is equal to $\lambda_{\max}(A)/\lambda_{\min}(A)$ if A is a positive definite matrix. For positive definite matrices A and B with $\operatorname{Im} A = \operatorname{Im} B$, we define the relative condition number as

$$\kappa(A,B) = \max_{x \notin \ker B} \frac{x^T A x}{x^T B x} \cdot \max_{x \notin \ker A} \frac{x^T B x}{x^T A x}.$$

Ultrasparsifiers. We say that a graph is k–ultrasparse if it has at most $n-1+k$ edges. We note that a spanning tree is 0–ultrasparse. A *(κ, k)-ultrasparsifier* of a graph $G = (V, E, w)$ is a k–ultrasparse subgraph of G such that $U \preceq G \preceq \kappa \cdot U$ [18].

3. MATRIX SPARSIFIERS

In this section, we prove an analog of the sparsification theorem of Batson, Spielman, and Srivastava [3].

DEFINITION 3.1 (GRAPH PATCH). *Let G be a (weighted) graph. A graph W on the vertices of G is a (k, T, λ^*)-patch for G if the following properties hold*[1],

1. $\lambda_{k+1}(\mathcal{L}_G \mathcal{L}_{G+W}^\dagger) \equiv \lambda_{k+1}((\mathcal{L}_{G+W}^\dagger)^{1/2} \mathcal{L}_G (\mathcal{L}_{G+W}^\dagger)^{1/2}) \geq \lambda^*$;
2. $\mathrm{tr}(\mathcal{L}_W \mathcal{L}_{G+W}^\dagger) \leq T$.

We prove that for every patch, there exists a "patch sparsifier" supported on $O(k)$ edges. Specifically, we prove the following theorem.

CLAIM 3.2. *Let $W = (V, E_W, \{w_e\}_{e \in E_W})$ be a (k, T, λ^*)-patch for G with edge weights w_e and $N \geq 8k$. Then there is a weighted graph $W_k = (V, E_{W_k}, \{\tilde{w}_e\}_{e \in E_{W_k}})$ with edge weights $\tilde{w}_e$ such that*

1. *W_k has at most N edges; $E_{W_k} \subseteq E_W$.*
2. *$c_1 \min(N/T, 1)\lambda^* \mathcal{L}_{G+W} \preceq \mathcal{L}_{G+W_k} \preceq c_2 \mathcal{L}_{G+W}$, for some absolute constants c_1 and c_2.*
3. *$\sum_{e \in E_{W_k}} \tilde{w}_k \leq \min(1, N/T) \sum_{e \in E_W} w_e$.*

We say that W_k is a patch sparsifier of W with respect to G.

The claim will follow immediately from the following theorem, which is is of independent interest. We will also show another (related) application of this theorem in Section 5.

THEOREM 3.3. *Suppose we are given a positive definite $n \times n$ matrix X and a sequence of matrices $Y_i = v_i v_i^T$ ($i = 1, \ldots, m$) with*

$$X + \sum_{i=1}^m Y_i = M^*,$$

and $\lambda_{\max}(M^*) \leq 1$. Additionally, suppose each matrix Y_i has cost $cost_i \geq 0$ and $\sum_{i=1}^m cost_i = 1$. Let $\lambda^* = \lambda_{k+1}(X)$, and $T = \lceil \mathrm{tr}(M^* - X) \rceil$. Then for every $N > 8k$ there exists a set of weights w_i with $|\{w_i : w_i \neq 0\}| = N$ such that the matrix $M = X + \sum_{i=1}^m w_i Y_i$ satisfies,

$$c_1 \min(N/T, 1) \cdot \lambda^* \cdot \lambda_{\min}(M^*) \leq \lambda_{\min}(M) \leq \lambda_{\max}(M) \leq c_2,$$

where c_1 and c_2 are some absolute constants, and

$$\sum_{i=1}^m w_i cost_i \leq \min(1, N/T).$$

[1] $\lambda_{k+1}(\mathcal{L}_G \mathcal{L}_{G+W}^\dagger) = \lambda_{k+1}((\mathcal{L}_{G+W}^\dagger)^{1/2} \mathcal{L}_G (\mathcal{L}_{G+W}^\dagger)^{1/2})$ since $\lambda_i(AB) = \lambda_i(BA)$ for every two square matrices A and B

Proof Overview. Our proof closely follows the approach of Batson, Spielman, and Srivastava [3]. We construct matrix M in N steps; at each step we choose an index i and weight w_i and add $w_i Y_i$ to the sum $X + \sum_{i=1}^m w_i Y_i$. Recall that Batson, Spielman, and Srivastava define two "barriers" l and u and maintain the property that all eigenvalues of M lie between l and u. At each step, they increase l and u and update matrix M so that this property still holds. Finally, the ratio between u and l becomes very close to 1, which means that $\lambda_{\min}(M)$ is very close to $\lambda_{\max}(M)$. During this process, they keep track not only of the smallest and largest eigenvalues of M but of all n eigenvalues to avoid accumulation of eigenvalues in neighborhoods of l and u. To this end, they define two potential functions, the lower potential function $\Phi_l(M) = \sum_{i=1}^n \frac{1}{\lambda_i(M) - l}$ and the upper potential function $\Phi^u(M) = \sum_{i=1}^n \frac{1}{u - \lambda_i(M)}$, and then ensure that $\Phi_l(M)$ and $\Phi^u(M)$ do not increase over time. That guarantees that all eigenvalues of M stay far away from l and u.

In our proof, however, we cannot keep an eye on all eigenvalues. After each step, only one eigenvalue increases, and thus we need $\theta(n)$ steps to increase all eigenvalues participating in the definition of $\Phi_l(M)$. But our goal is to "patch" X in roughly k steps. So we focus our attention only on k smallest and T largest eigenvalues.

Let S be the eigenspace of X corresponding to k smallest eigenvalues, and P_S be the projection onto S. We define the lower potential function as follows,

$$\Phi_l(A) = \mathrm{tr}(P_S(A - lI)P_S)^\dagger = \sum_{i=1}^k \frac{1}{\lambda_i(A|_S) - l},$$

where $A|_S$ denotes the restriction of A to the space S ($A|_S$ is a $k \times k$ matrix). Note that the space S is fixed, and the eigenvector corresponding to the smallest eigenvalue will not necessarily lie in S after a few steps. We want to ensure that after N steps,

$$\sum_{i=1}^m w_i Y_i|_S \succeq c \min(N/T, 1) \sum_{i=1}^m Y_i|_S = c \min(N/T, 1)(M^* - X)|_S,$$

or in other words, $\lambda_{\min}((Z(\sum_{i=1}^m w_i Y_i)Z)|_S) \geq c \min(N/T, 1)$, where $Z = ((P_S(M^* - X)P_S)^\dagger)^{1/2}$. To this end, we show how to update M and l so that $\Phi_l(Z(\sum_{i=1}^m w_i Y_i)Z)$ does not increase, and l equals $c \min(N/T, 1)$ after N steps. It remains to lower bound $\lambda_{\min}(M)$ in the entire space. We know that all eigenvalues of X (and therefore, of M) in $S^\perp$ are at least λ^*. We show that that together with an upper bound on $\lambda_{\max}(M)$ implies that $\lambda_{\min}(M) \geq c_1 \min(N/T, 1) \cdot \lambda^* \lambda_{\min}(M^*)$ (the product of the lower bounds on $\lambda_{\min}$ in spaces S and $S^\perp$ divided by the upper bound on $\lambda_{\max}$).

Similarly, we amend the definition of the upper potential function. Since we need to bound $\lambda_{\max}$ in the entire space, we cannot restrict $\Phi^u(M)$ to a fixed subspace. For a matrix A, we consider the eigenspace of A corresponding to its largest T eigenvalues. Denote it by $L_A(A)$; denote the projection onto $L(A)$ by $P_{L(A)}$. Then

$$\Phi^u(A) = \mathrm{tr}(P_{L(A)}(uI - A)^{-1}P_{L(A)}) = \mathrm{tr}(P_{L(A)}(uI - A)P_{L(A)})^\dagger = \sum_{i=n-T+1}^N \frac{1}{u - \lambda_i(A)}.$$

Note that both definitions of $\Phi^u(A)$ — in terms of regular inverse and in terms of pseudoinverse — are equivalent since $L(A)$ is an invariant subspace of A. However, $\Phi_l(A)$ is not equal to $\text{tr}(P_S(A-lI)^{-1}P_S)$ in general since S is not necessarily an invariant subspace of A.

Our algorithm and analysis are similar to those of Batson, Spielman, and Srivastava [3]. However, several complications arise because we are controlling eigenvalues in different subspaces and, moreover, one of these subspaces, $L(A)$, is not fixed.

Let us summarize the proof. We construct the matrix M iteratively in N steps. Let $A^{(q)}$ be the matrix and $w_i^{(q)}$ be the weights after q steps. We define an auxiliary matrix $B^{(q)}$ as $Z(A^{(q)}-X)Z$. We have,

$$A^{(q)} = X + \sum_i w_i^{(q)} Y_i;$$

$$B^{(q)} = \sum_i w_i^{(q)} Z Y_i Z = Z(A^{(q)} - X)Z.$$

We will ensure that the following properties hold after each step (for some values of constants l_0, δ_L, u_0, δ_U, ϵ_L, ϵ_U, which we will specify later).

1. $\Phi_{l_0}(B^{(0)}) \le \epsilon_L$ and $\Phi^{u_0}(A^{(0)}) \le \epsilon_U$.

2. Each matrix $A^{(q)}$ and $B^{(q)}$ is obtained by a rank-one update of the previous one:

$$A^{(q+1)} = A^{(q)} + tY_i,$$
$$B^{(q+1)} = B^{(q)} + tZY_iZ$$

   for some i.

3. Lower and upper potentials do not increase. Namely, for every $q = 0, 1, \ldots, N$,

$$\Phi^{u_0+(q+1)\delta_U}(A^{(q+1)}) \le \Phi^{u_0+q\delta_U}(A^{(q)}) \le \epsilon_U \text{ and}$$
$$\Phi_{l+(q+1)\delta_L}(B^{(q+1)}) \le \Phi_{l_0+q\delta_L}(B^{(q)}) \le \epsilon_L.$$

4. At each step q, $\lambda_{\min}(B^{(q)}|_S) > l \equiv l_0 + q\delta_L$ and $\lambda_{\max}(A^{(q)}) < u \equiv u_0 + q\delta_U$. In particular, this condition ensures that all terms in the definitions of upper and lower potentials are positive.

5. At each step q, the total cost is at at most $q/\max(N,T)$: $\sum w_i^{(q)} cost_i \le q/\max(N,T)$.

We present the complete proof in Sections 3.2 and 3.3. In Section 3.2, we first find conditions under which we can update $A^{(q)}$ and u (Lemma 3.10), and $B^{(q)}$ and l (Lemma 3.11). Then we show that both conditions can be simultaneously satisfied (Lemma 3.12). In Section 3.1, we prove several theorems that we need later to deal with a non-fixed subspace $L(A)$. Finally, in Section 3.3, we combine all pieces of the proof together.

3.1 Some Basic Facts about Matrices

3.1.1 Sherman–Morrison Formula

We use the Sherman–Morrison Formula, which describes the behavior of the inverse of a matrix under rank-one updates. We first state the formula for regular inverse [8], and then we show that a similar expression holds for the pseudoinverse.

LEMMA 3.4 (SHERMAN–MORRISON FORMULA). *If A is a nonsingular $n \times n$ matrix and $Y = vv^T$ is a rank-one update, then*

$$(A+Y)^{-1} = A^{-1} - \frac{A^{-1}YA^{-1}}{1 + A^{-1} \bullet Y}$$

LEMMA 3.5. *If A is a symmetric (possibly singular) $n \times n$ matrix, $Y = vv^T$ is a rank-one update, then*

$$(A + PYP)^{\dagger} = A^{\dagger} - \frac{A^{\dagger} Y A^{\dagger}}{1 + A^{\dagger} \bullet Y},$$

where P is the orthogonal projection on $\text{Im}(A)$.

PROOF. Let $\bar{v} = Pv$ and $\bar{Y} = PYP = \bar{v}\bar{v}^T$. Note that $A^{\dagger}YA^{\dagger} = A^{\dagger}\bar{Y}A^{\dagger}$, since $PA^{\dagger} = P$, and

$$A^{\dagger} \bullet \bar{Y} = \text{tr}\, A^{\dagger}\bar{Y} = \text{tr}\, A^{\dagger}(PYP) = \text{tr}(PA^{\dagger}P)Y = A^{\dagger} \bullet Y.$$

We need to verify that

$$(A+\bar{Y})\left(A^{\dagger} - \frac{A^{\dagger}\bar{Y}A^{\dagger}}{1+A^{\dagger}\bullet\bar{Y}}\right) = \left(A^{\dagger} - \frac{A^{\dagger}\bar{Y}A^{\dagger}}{1+A^{\dagger}\bullet\bar{Y}}\right)(A+\bar{Y}) = P.$$

Since A is a symmetric matrix, $AA^{\dagger} = A^{\dagger}A = P$. Since $P^2 = P$, $P\bar{Y}P = \bar{Y}$ and $\bar{Y}A^{\dagger}\bar{Y} = \bar{v}\bar{v}^T A \bar{v}\bar{v}^T = \bar{v}(A \bullet \bar{Y})\bar{v}^T = (A \bullet \bar{Y})\bar{Y}$. We calculate,

$$\begin{aligned}
(A+\bar{Y})\left(A^{\dagger} - \frac{A^{\dagger}\bar{Y}A^{\dagger}}{1+A^{\dagger}\bullet\bar{Y}}\right) &= \\
AA^{\dagger} + \bar{Y}A^{\dagger} &- \frac{\bar{P}(YA^{\dagger} + \bar{Y}A^{\dagger}\bar{Y}A^{\dagger})}{1+A^{\dagger}\bullet\bar{Y}} \\
&= P + \bar{Y}A^{\dagger} - \frac{(1+A^{\dagger}\bullet\bar{Y})\bar{Y}A^{\dagger}}{1+A^{\dagger}\bullet\bar{Y}} \\
&= P + \bar{Y}A^{\dagger} - \bar{Y}A^{\dagger} = P.
\end{aligned}$$

Similarly, $(A^{\dagger} - \frac{A^{\dagger}\bar{Y}A^{\dagger}}{1+A^{\dagger}\bullet\bar{Y}})(A+\bar{Y}) = P$. □

3.1.2 Majorization

LEMMA 3.6 (MAJORIZATION). *For every positive semidefinite matrix A, every projection matrix P, and every $r \in \{1,\ldots,n\}$*

$$\sum_{i=n-r+1}^{n} \lambda_i(A) \ge \sum_{i=n-r+1}^{n} \lambda_i(PAP). \tag{2}$$

In particular, $\lambda_{\max}(A) \ge \lambda_{\max}(PAP)$.

PROOF. Let $e_1,\ldots,e_n$ be an orthonormal eigenbasis of A so that e_i has eigenvalue $\lambda_i(A)$. Similarly, let $\tilde{e}_1,\ldots,\tilde{e}_n$ be an orthonormal eigenbasis of PAP so that $\tilde{e}_i$ has eigenvalue $\lambda_i(PAP)$. Write

$$\tilde{e}_i = \sum_{j=1}^{n} \langle e_j, \tilde{e}_i \rangle e_j.$$

Note that if $\lambda_i(PAP) \neq 0$ then $\tilde{e}_i \in \text{Im}(PAP) \subseteq \text{Im}(P)$ and $P\tilde{e}_i = \tilde{e}_i$. Then

$$\lambda_i(PAP) = \tilde{e}_i^T PAP\tilde{e}_i = \tilde{e}_i A \tilde{e}_i = \sum_{j=1}^{n} \langle e_j, \tilde{e}_i\rangle^2 \lambda_j(A).$$

If $\lambda_i(PAP) = 0$ then trivially

$$\lambda_i(PAP) = 0 \le \sum_{j=1}^{n} \langle e_j, \tilde{e}_i\rangle^2 \lambda_j(A).$$

Therefore,

$$\sum_{i=n-r+1}^{n} \lambda_i(PAP) \leq \sum_{i=n-r+1}^{n} \sum_{j=1}^{n} \langle e_j, \tilde{e}_i \rangle^2 \lambda_j(A)$$
$$= \sum_{j=1}^{n} \left(\sum_{i=n-r+1}^{n} \langle e_j, \tilde{e}_i \rangle^2 \right) \lambda_j(A).$$

That is, $\sum_{i=n-r+1}^{n} \lambda_j(PAP)$ is at most the sum of $\lambda_j(A)$ with weights $\sum_{i=n-r+1}^{n} \langle e_j, \tilde{e}_i \rangle^2$. The total weight of all $\lambda_1(A), \ldots, \lambda_n(A)$ is r:

$$\sum_{i=n-r+1}^{n} \underbrace{\sum_{j=1}^{n} \langle e_j, \tilde{e}_i \rangle^2}_{\|\tilde{e}_i\|^2} = \sum_{i=n-r+1}^{n} \|\tilde{e}_i\|^2 = r.$$

The weight of each $\lambda_j(A)$ in the sum is at most 1:

$$\sum_{i=n-r+1}^{n} \langle e_j, \tilde{e}_i \rangle^2 \leq \sum_{i=1}^{n} \langle e_j, \tilde{e}_i \rangle^2 = 1.$$

Therefore, the sum does not exceed the sum of the r largest eigenvalues $\sum_{i=n-r+1}^{n} \lambda_r(A)$. □

COROLLARY 3.7. *For every positive semidefinite matrix A, every projection matrix P and $u > \lambda_{\max}(A)$, the following inequality holds.*

$$\Phi^u(PAP) = \sum_{i=n-T+1}^{n} \frac{1}{u - \lambda_i(PAP)}$$
$$\leq \sum_{i=n-T+1}^{n} \frac{1}{u - \lambda_i(A)} = \Phi^u(A)$$

PROOF. The statement follows from the Karamata Majorization Inequality. The inequality claims that for every two non-increasing sequences that satisfy (2) and for every increasing convex function f,

$$\sum_{i=n-k+1}^{n} f(\lambda_i(A)) \geq \sum_{i=n-k+1}^{n} f(\lambda_i(PAP)).$$

Plugging in $f(x) = \frac{1}{u-x}$ (defined on $(0, u)$), we obtain the desired inequality. □

LEMMA 3.8. *Let A be a positive semidefinite matrix such that $A \preceq I_n$. Assume $\mathrm{Tr}(A) \leq r \in \mathbb{N}$. Then for every positive semidefinite matrix M, $A \bullet M \leq \sum_{i=N-r+1}^{N} \lambda_i(M)$.*

PROOF. By von Neumann's inequality [14],

$$A \bullet M = \mathrm{tr}(AM) \leq \sum_{i=1}^{n} \lambda_i(A)\lambda_i(M).$$

Since $\sum_{i=1}^{n} \lambda_i(A) \leq r$ and all $\lambda_i(A) \leq 1$, we can easily see that the above product achieves its maximum when the largest r eigenvalues of A are 1 and the rest are 0. In this case, we have,

$$A \bullet M \leq \sum_{i=1}^{n} \lambda_i(A)\lambda_i(M) = \sum_{i=n-r+1}^{n} \lambda_i(M).$$

□

As a corollary we get the following result.

COROLLARY 3.9. *Let X, M^* and T be as in Theorem 3.3. Then for any positive semidefinite matrix U, we have $U \bullet (M^* - X) \leq \sum_{i=n-T+1}^{n} \lambda_i(U)$.*

3.2 Barrier Shifts

In this section, we analyze how we can update matrices $A^{(q)}$ and $B^{(q)}$, and increment barriers l and r so that the upper and lower potentials do not increase. Let us think of $\Phi^u(A)$ as a function of an n^2 dimensional vector (consisting of entries of A). Then in the first approximation $\Phi^{u+\delta_U}(A + tY) \approx \Phi^{u+\delta_U}(A) + tY \bullet U$, where U is the gradient of $\Phi^{u+\delta_U}$ at A (U is an $n \times n$ matrix). Thus the potential function does not increase, $\Phi^{u+\delta_U}(A + tY) \leq \Phi^u(A)$, roughly when $tY \bullet \frac{U}{\Phi^u(A) - \Phi^{u+\delta_U}(A)} \leq 1$.

Similarly, $\Phi_{l+\delta_L}(B + tY) \leq \Phi_l(B)$, roughly when $tY \bullet \frac{L}{\Phi_{l+\delta_L}(B) - \Phi_l(B)} \geq 1$, where L is the gradient of $\Phi_{l+\delta_L}$ at B.

Following [3], we make these statements precise (we need to take into account lower order terms). We define matrices U_A and L_B,

$$U_A = \frac{((u + \delta_U)I - A)^{-2}}{\Phi^u(A) - \Phi^{u+\delta_U}(A)} + ((u + \delta_U)I - A)^{-1};$$
$$L_B = \frac{(P_S(B - (l + \delta_L)I)P_S)^{\dagger 2}}{\Phi_{l+\delta_L}(B) - \Phi_l(B)} - (P_S(B - (l + \delta_L)I)P_S)^{\dagger}$$

LEMMA 3.10 (UPPER BARRIER SHIFT). *Suppose $\lambda_{max}(A) < u$ and $Y = vv^T$ is a rank-one update. If $U_A \bullet Y \leq \frac{1}{t}$ then $\Phi^{u+\delta_U}(A + tY) \leq \Phi^u(A)$ and $\lambda_{\max}(A + tY) < u + \delta_U$.*

PROOF. Let $u' = u + \delta_U$ and $P = F_{L(A+tY)}$. By the Sherman–Morrison formula (Lemma 3.4), we can write the updated potential as:

$$\Phi^{u+\delta_U}(A + tY) = \mathrm{tr}\, P(u'I - A - tY)^{-1} P$$
$$= \mathrm{tr}\, P \left((u'I - A)^{-1} + \frac{t(u'I - A)^{-1} Y (u'I - A)^{-1}}{1 - t(u'I - A)^{-1} \bullet Y} \right) P$$
$$= \mathrm{tr}\, P(u'I - A)^{-1} P + \mathrm{tr} \frac{tP(u'I - A)^{-1} Y (u'I - A)^{-1} P}{1 - t(u'I - A)^{-1} \bullet Y}$$
$$\leq \Phi^{u+\delta_U}(PAP) + \frac{t(u'I - A)^{-2} \bullet Y}{1 - t(u'I - A)^{-1} \bullet Y}$$
$$\leq \Phi^{u+\delta_U}(A) + \frac{t(u'I - A)^{-2} \bullet Y}{1 - t(u'I - A)^{-1} \bullet Y}$$
$$= \Phi^u(A) - (\Phi^u(A) - \Phi^{u+\delta_U}(A)) + \frac{(u'I - A)^{-2} \bullet Y}{1/t - (u'I - A)^{-1} \bullet Y}.$$

Here, we used Corollary 3.7 for the inequality on line 4.

Substituting $U_A \bullet Y \leq 1/t$ gives $\Phi^{u+\delta_U}(A + tY) \leq \Phi^u(A)$. The statement about $\lambda_{\max}$ follows from continuity of eigenvalues. □

LEMMA 3.11 (LOWER BARRIER SHIFT). *Suppose $\lambda_{\min}(B|_S) > l + \delta_L$ and $Y = vv^T$ is a rank-one update. If $L_B \bullet Y \geq 1/t$ then $\Phi_{l+\delta_L}(B + tY) \leq \Phi_l(B)$ and $\lambda_{\min}((B + tY)|_S) > l + \delta_L$.*

PROOF. We proceed as in the proof for the upper potential. Let $l' = l + \delta_L$ and $P = P_S$. By the Sherman–Morrison formula for the pseudoinverse (Lemma 3.5), we have:

$$\Phi_{l+\delta_L}(B + tY)$$
$$= \mathrm{tr}(P(B + tY - l'I)P)^{\dagger} = \mathrm{tr}(P(B - l'I)P + tPYP)^{\dagger}$$
$$= \mathrm{tr}(P(B - l'I)P)^{\dagger} - \frac{t\,\mathrm{tr}((P(B - l'I)P)^{\dagger} Y (P(B - l'I)P)^{\dagger})}{1 + t(P(B - l'I)P)^{\dagger} \bullet Y}$$
$$= \Phi_l(B) + (\Phi_{l+\delta_L}(B) - \Phi_l(B)) - \frac{t(P(B - l'I)P)^{\dagger 2} \bullet Y}{1 + t(P(B - l'I)P)^{\dagger} \bullet Y}$$

Note that matrix U_A is positive semidefinite. Rearranging shows that $\Phi_{l+\delta_L}(B+Y) \le \Phi_l(B)$ when $L_A(\pi) \ge 1/t$. It is immediate that $\lambda_{\min}(P_S(A+t\pi\pi^T)P_S) > l+\delta_L$ since $\lambda_{\min}(P_SAP_S) > l+\delta_L$. □

Now we prove that we can choose Y_i and t so that conditions of both lemmas are satisfied.

LEMMA 3.12. *(Both Barriers) If $\Phi^u(A) \le \epsilon_U$ and $\Phi_l(B) \le \epsilon_L$ and $\epsilon_U, \epsilon_L, \delta_U, \delta_L$ satisfy*

$$0 \le \frac{1}{\delta_U} + \epsilon_U + \max(N,T) \le \frac{1}{\delta_L} - \epsilon_L,$$

and X, Y_i, $cost_i$, Z, T and N as in Theorem 3.3, M^*-X is non-singular on S, then there exists i and positive t for which

$$L_B \bullet (ZY_iZ) \ge 1/t \ge U_A \bullet Y_i, \text{ and} \tag{3}$$

$$cost_i \cdot t \le 1/\max(N,T). \tag{4}$$

We will use the following lemma

LEMMA 3.13. $\sum_{i=1}^m U_A \bullet Y_i \le \frac{1}{\delta_U} + \epsilon_U$ *and* $\sum_{i=1}^m L_B \bullet (ZY_iZ) \ge \frac{1}{\delta_L} - \epsilon_L$.

PROOF. 1. We use Corollary 3.9 to bound the Frobenius product of Y_i with each of the two summands in the definition of U_A (note that they are positive semidefinite), we get $\sum_{i=1}^m U_A \bullet Y_i$ equals

$$\begin{aligned}
U_A \bullet \sum_{i=1}^m Y_i &= U_A \bullet (M^*-X) \\
&= \frac{((u+\delta_U)I-A)^{-2}}{\Phi^u(A)-\Phi^{u+\delta_U}(A)} \bullet (M^*-X) \\
&\quad + ((u+\delta_U)I-A)^{-1} \bullet (M^*-X) \\
&\le \sum_{i=n-T+1}^{n} \lambda_i\left(\frac{((u+\delta_U)I-A)^{-2}}{\Phi^u(A)-\Phi^{u+\delta_U}(A)}\right) \\
&\quad + \sum_{i=n-T+1}^{n} \lambda_i\left(((u+\delta_U)I-A)^{-1}\right) \\
&= \frac{\sum_{i=n-T+1}^{n} \frac{1}{(u+\delta_U-\lambda_i(A))^2}}{\Phi^u(A)-\Phi^{u+\delta_U}(A)} \\
&\quad + \sum_{i=n-T+1}^{n} \frac{1}{(u+\delta_U)-\lambda_i(A)}
\end{aligned}$$

Note that the first term is at most $1/\delta_U$, since

$$\begin{aligned}
\sum_{i=n-T+1}^{n} &\frac{1}{(u+\delta_U-\lambda_i(A))^2} \\
&\le \sum_{i=n-T+1}^{n} \frac{1}{(u-\lambda_i(A))(u+\delta_U-\lambda_i(A))} \\
&= \frac{1}{\delta_U}\sum_{i=n-T+1}^{n}\left(\frac{1}{u-\lambda_i(A)} - \frac{1}{(u+\delta_U)-\lambda_i(A)}\right) \\
&= \frac{\Phi^u(A)-\Phi^{u+\delta_U}(A)}{\delta_U}
\end{aligned}$$

and the second term equals $\Phi^{u+\delta_U}(A)$. Thus $\sum_{i=1}^m U_A \bullet Y_i \le \epsilon_U + 1/\delta_U$.

For the second part, let P be the projection on $\mathrm{Im}(M^*-X)$. Since (M^*-X) is non-singular on S, $PP_S = P_S$. We have,

$$\begin{aligned}
\sum_{i=1}^m L_B \bullet ZY_iZ &= L_B \bullet \sum_{i=1}^m ZY_iZ \\
&= L_B \bullet Z(M^*-X)Z = L_B \bullet P \\
&= \mathrm{tr}\left(\frac{(P_S(B-(l+\delta_L)I)P_S)^{\dagger 2}}{\Phi_{l+\delta_L}(B)-\Phi_l(B)} - (P_S(B-(l+\delta_L)I)P_S)^{\dagger}\right) \\
&= \frac{\sum_{i=1}^k (\lambda_i(B|_S)-(l+\delta_L))^{-2}}{\Phi_{l+\delta_L}(B)-\Phi_l(B)} - \sum_{i=1}^k \frac{1}{\lambda_i(B|_S)-(l+\delta_L)} \\
&\ge 1/\delta_L - \epsilon_L,
\end{aligned}$$

where the last line follows from Claim 3.6 in [3]. □

PROOF OF LEMMA 3.12. For the previous lemma, we get:

$$\begin{aligned}
\sum_{i=1}^m (U_A \bullet Y_i + \max(N,T)cost_i) &\le \frac{1}{\delta_U} + \epsilon_U + \max(N,T) \\
&\le L_B \bullet (ZY_iZ).
\end{aligned}$$

Thus for some i, $U_A \bullet Y_i + \max(N,T)cost_i \le L_B \bullet (ZY_iZ)$. Letting $t = (L_B \bullet (ZY_iZ))^{-1}$, we satisfy (3) and (4). □

3.3 Proof of Theorem 3.3

Now we are ready to prove Theorem 3.3. We assume that M^*-X is non-singular on S (which we can ensure by an arbitrary small perturbation).

We start with $A^{(0)} = X$, $B^{(0)} = 0$ and all weights $w_i^{(0)} = 0$. We define parameters as follows,

$$\begin{aligned}
\delta_L &= 1/(2\max(N,T)), & \epsilon_L &= 1/(4\delta_L), & l_0 &= -4k\delta_L, \\
\delta_U &= 4\delta_L, & \epsilon_U &= 1/(4\delta_L), & u_0 &= 4T\delta_L + 1,
\end{aligned}$$

so as to satisfy conditions of Lemma 3.12,

$$\Phi^u(A^{(0)}) = \Phi^u(X) = \sum_{i=1}^T \frac{1}{u_0 - \lambda_{n+1-i}(X)} \le T/(u_0-1) = \epsilon_U,$$

$$\Phi_l(B^{(0)}) = \sum_{i=1}^k \frac{1}{0-l_0} = -k/l_0 = \epsilon_L,$$

$$1/\delta_U + \epsilon_U + \max(N,T) = \frac{3}{2}\max(N,T) = 1/\delta_L - \epsilon_L.$$

Then we iteratively apply Lemma 3.12. At iteration q, we find an index i and a positive t such that $L_{B^{(q)}}(ZY_iZ) \ge 1/t \ge U_{A^{(q)}}(Y_i)$, $cost_i \cdot t \le 1/\max(N,T)$, and increment the weight of matrix Y_i by t: $w_i^{(q+1)} = w_i^{(q)} + t$; update $l = l + \delta_L$ and $u = u + \delta_U$. The total cost increases by at most $1/\max(N,T)$. Finally, after N iterations we obtain matrices $A^{(N)}$ and $B^{(N)}$ with

$$\lambda_{\max}(A^{(N)}) \le u_0 + N\delta_U = 2(N+T)/\max(N,T) + 1 \equiv \theta_{\max}$$

$$\lambda_{\min}(B^{(N)}|_S) \ge l_0 + N\delta_L = (N/2-2k)/\max(N,T) \equiv \theta_{\min}.$$

Now consider an arbitrary unit vector v. Let $v = v_S + v_{S^\perp}$, where $v_S \in S$ and $v_{S^\perp} \perp S$. Since $B^{(N)} \succeq \theta_{\min}P_S$ and $v_S \in S$,

$v_S^T A^{(N)} v_S$

$$= v_S^T(X + (P_S(M^* - X)P_S)^{1/2} B^{(N)} (P_S(M^* - X)P_S)^{1/2}) v_S$$

$$\geq v_S^T(X + (P_S(M^* - X)P_S)^{1/2} \theta_{\min} P_S (P_S(M^* - X)P_S)^{1/2}) v_S$$

$$= \theta_{\min} v_S^T M^* v_S + (1 - \theta_{\min}) v_S^T X v_S \geq \theta_{\min} \lambda_{\min}(M^*) \|v_S\|^2.$$

On the other hand, $v_{S^\perp}^T A^{(N)} v_{S^\perp} \leq \theta_{\max} \|v_{S^\perp}\|$. Thus from the triangle inequality for the norm induced by $A^{(N)}$, we get

$$(v^T A^{(N)} v)^{1/2} \geq \theta_{\min}^{1/2} \lambda_{\min}(M)^{1/2} \|v_S\| - \theta_{\max}^{1/2} \|v_{S^\perp}\|$$

$$\geq \theta_{\min}^{1/2} \lambda_{\min}(M)^{1/2} - (\theta_{\max}^{1/2} + \theta_{\min}^{1/2} \lambda_{\min}(M)^{1/2}) \|v_{S^\perp}\|.$$

Since S is an eigenspace of X corresponding to k smallest eigenvalues,

$$(v^T A^{(N)} v)^{1/2} \geq (v^T X v)^{1/2} \geq (v_{S^\perp}^T X v_{S^\perp})^{1/2} \geq \lambda^{*1/2} \|v_{S^\perp}\|.$$

One of the two bounds above for $(v^T A^{(N)} v)^{1/2}$ increases and the other decreases as $\|v_{S^\perp}\|$ increases. They are equal when

$$\|v_{S^\perp}\| = \frac{\theta_{\min}^{1/2} \lambda_{\min}(M^*)^{1/2}}{\lambda^{*1/2} + \theta_{\max}^{1/2} + \theta_{\min}^{1/2} \lambda_{\min}(M^*)^{1/2}}.$$

Therefore,

$$(v^T A^{(N)} v)^{1/2} \geq \frac{\theta_{\min}^{1/2} \lambda^{*1/2} \lambda_{\min}(M^*)^{1/2}}{\lambda^{*1/2} + \theta_{\max}^{1/2} + \theta_{\min}^{1/2} \lambda_{\min}(M^*)^{1/2}}.$$

We conclude that $\lambda_{\min}(A^{(N)}) = \min_{v:\|v\|=1} v^T A^{(N)} v$ is at least

$$\frac{\theta_{\min} \lambda^* \lambda_{\min}(M^*)}{\left(\lambda^{*1/2} + \theta_{\max}^{1/2} + \theta_{\min}^{1/2} \lambda_{\min}(M^*)^{1/2}\right)^2}.$$

Plugging in the values of parameters, we get the statement of the theorem for $M = A^{(N)}$. The total cost is at most $N/\max(N,T) = \min(1, N/T)$. □

Finally, we prove Claim 3.2.

PROOF CLAIM 3.2. Let $V = \operatorname{Im}(\mathcal{L}_{G+W}) = \ker(\mathcal{L}_{G+W})^\perp$. Let $\mathcal{L}_e$ be the Laplacian of the edge e. Define

$$X = \left((\mathcal{L}_{G+W}^\dagger)^{1/2} \mathcal{L}_G (\mathcal{L}_{G+W}^\dagger)^{1/2}\right)\Big|_V,$$

$$Y_e = w_e \left((\mathcal{L}_{G+W}^\dagger)^{1/2} \mathcal{L}_e (\mathcal{L}_{G+W}^\dagger)^{1/2}\right)\Big|_V,$$

$$cost_e = w_e / \left(\sum\nolimits_{d \in E_W} w_d\right).$$

Since $\mathcal{L}_G + \sum_{e \in E_W}^m w_e \mathcal{L}_e = \mathcal{L}_{G+W}$, we have $X + \sum_{e \in E_W} Y_e = I$. By the definition of the (k, T, λ^*)-patch, $\operatorname{tr}(I - X) \leq T$ and $\lambda^* \leq \lambda^{k+1}(X)$. We apply Theorem 3.3 to matrices X, Y_e and $M^* = I$. We obtain a set of weights ρ_e — supported on at most N edges — such that

$$c_1 \min(N/T, 1) \cdot \lambda^* \leq \lambda_{\min}\left(X + \sum\nolimits_{e \in E_W} \rho_e Y_e\right)$$

$$\leq \lambda_{\max}\left(X + \sum\nolimits_{e \in E_W} \rho_e Y_e\right) \leq c_2,$$

Let $\tilde{w}_e = \rho_e w_e$. Weights $\tilde{w}_i$ define subgraph W_k with at most N edges. It follows that

$$c_1 \min(N/T, 1) \lambda^* \mathcal{L}_{G+W} \preceq \mathcal{L}_{G+W_k} \preceq c_2 \mathcal{L}_{G+W}.$$

The total weight of edges of W_k is

$$\sum_{e \in E_W} \rho_e w_e = (\sum_{e \in E_W} \rho_e cost_e) \sum_{d \in E_W} w_d \leq \min(1, N/T) \sum_{d \in E_W} w_d.$$

□

4. CONSTRUCTING NEARLY-OPTIMAL ULTRASPARSIFIERS

We now apply our subgraph sparsification to build ultrasparsifiers. Recall that a weighted graph U is a (κ, k)-ultrasparsifier of another graph G if $U \preceq G \preceq \kappa \cdot U$ and U has only $n - 1 + k$ edges, where n is the number of vertices in U and G. The main result of this section is the following theorem.

THEOREM 4.1. *For any integer $k > 0$, every graph has an $(\frac{n}{k} \log n \, \tilde{O}(\log \log n), k)$–ultrasparsifier.*

Our basic idea to build a good ultrasparsifier U is quite simple. Without loss of generality, we can assume that G is connected and has $O(n)$ edges. Otherwise given a graph G, we can first find a linear size sparsifier using [3], for each of its connected components, and build a good ultrasparsifier for each component. Because U is only k edges away from a tree, our construction starts with good tree T. As it will be much more clear below, the quality of a tree is measured by its *stretch*, as introduced by Alon, Karp, Peleg and West [2].

Suppose T is a spanning tree of $G = (V, E, w)$. For any edge $e \in E$, let $e_1, \cdots, e_k$ be the edges on the unique path in T connecting the endpoints of e. The *stretch* of e w.r.t. T is given by $\operatorname{st}_T(e) = w(e)(\sum_{i=1}^k \frac{1}{w(e_i)})$. The stretch of the graph G with respect to T is defined by $\operatorname{st}_T(G) = \sum_{e \in E} \operatorname{st}_T(e)$. Our construction will start with a spanning tree with the lowest possible stretch. By [1], we can in polynomial time grow a spanning tree T with

$$\operatorname{st}_T(G) = O(n \log n \log \log n (\log \log \log n)^3).$$

REMARK 4.2. *For the sake of simplicity of the presentation, we will show the construction of ultrasparsifiers with $\Theta(k)$ edges. We note that by choosing the appropriate constants, the number of edges can be made exactly k.*

Let $\kappa = c_1 \cdot \operatorname{st}_T(G)/k$ for a sufficiently large constant c_1. Our job is to choose $\Theta(k)$ more weighted edges $\tilde{W}$ and set $U = T + \tilde{W}$ such that $c_2 \cdot U \preceq G \preceq \kappa \cdot U$, for a constant c_2. To this end, let $W = (1/(c_3\kappa)) \cdot G$, for some constant c_3. Then, $G = c_3\kappa \cdot W \preceq c_3\kappa \cdot (W + T)$. Also, because $T \preceq G$, we have $T + W \preceq (1 + 1/(c_3\kappa))G \preceq c_4 \cdot G$, for a constant c_4. Therefore, if we can find a $\Theta(k)$–edge subgraph $\tilde{W}$ of W such that $T + \tilde{W} \preceq \Theta(1) \cdot (T + W)$, we can then build a $n - 1 + \Theta(k)$ edge graph $U = T + \tilde{W}$ satisfying $c_2 \cdot U \preceq G \preceq \kappa \cdot U$ (if we choose our constants c_i's carefully).

To apply our subgraph sparsification results to construct $\tilde{W}$, we use the following structure result of Spielman and Woo ([21]: Theorem 2.1 and Corollary 2.2).

LEMMA 4.3 (THEOREM 2.1 IN [21]).

1. *$Tr(\mathcal{L}_T^{\dagger\,1/2} \mathcal{L}_G \mathcal{L}_T^{\dagger\,1/2}) = st_T(G)$.*
2. *For every $t > 0$, the number of eigenvalues of $(\mathcal{L}_T^\dagger)^{1/2} \mathcal{L}_G (\mathcal{L}_T^\dagger)^{1/2}$ greater than t is at most $st_T(G)/t$.*

We now use Lemma 4.3 to prove the following lemma, from which Theorem 4.1 follows directly.

LEMMA 4.4. *W is a $(k, O(k), \Theta(1))$–patch for T.*

PROOF. Let $\lambda_i = \lambda_i((\mathcal{L}_{T+W}^{\dagger})^{1/2}\mathcal{L}_T(\mathcal{L}_{T+W}^{\dagger})^{1/2})$ be the i-th eigenvalue, and y_i be the corresponding eigenvector. Let $x_i = L_{T+W}^{1/2}y_i$. Then,

$$\lambda_i = \lambda_i((\mathcal{L}_{T+W}^{\dagger})^{1/2}\mathcal{L}_T(\mathcal{L}_{T+W}^{\dagger})^{1/2}) = \frac{x_i^T\mathcal{L}_Tx_i}{x_i^T\mathcal{L}_Tx_i + x_i^T\mathcal{L}_Wx_i}$$

$$= \frac{x_i^T\mathcal{L}_Tx_i}{x_i^T\mathcal{L}_Tx_i + x_i^T\mathcal{L}_Gx_i/(c_3\kappa)},$$

implying

$$\frac{x_i^T\mathcal{L}_Gx_i}{x_i^T\mathcal{L}_Tx_i} = \frac{1-\lambda_i}{\lambda_i}c_3\kappa = \left(\frac{1-\lambda_i}{\lambda_i}\right)c_3c_1\frac{\mathrm{st}_T(G)}{k} = \frac{\mathrm{st}_T(G)}{\frac{k}{c_1c_3}\frac{\lambda_i}{1-\lambda_i}}.$$

It follows from the definition of λ_i that $0 \le \lambda_i < 1$. Hence, $(1-\lambda_{i-1})/\lambda_{i-1} \ge (1-\lambda_i)/\lambda_i$. By Courant—Fischer theorem and the property 2 of Lemma 4.3, we have $k \le \frac{k}{c_1c_3}\frac{\lambda_{k+1}}{1-\lambda_{k+1}}$. Therefore, $\lambda_{k+1} \ge \frac{c_1c_3}{1+c_1c_3} = \Theta(1)$. We also have,

$$\mathrm{tr}\left((\mathcal{L}_{T+W}^{\dagger})^{1/2}\mathcal{L}_W(\mathcal{L}_{T+W}^{\dagger})^{1/2}\right) \le \mathrm{tr}\left((\mathcal{L}_T^{\dagger})^{1/2}\mathcal{L}_W(\mathcal{L}_T^{\dagger})^{1/2}\right)$$

$$= \frac{1}{c_3\kappa}\mathrm{tr}\left((\mathcal{L}_T^{\dagger})^{1/2}\mathcal{L}_G(\mathcal{L}_T^{\dagger})^{1/2}\right) \le \frac{k}{c_3c_1\mathrm{st}_T(G)}\mathrm{st}_T(G)$$

$$= \frac{k}{c_3c_1} = \Theta(k).$$

We proved that W is a $(k, O(k), \Theta(1))$-patch for T. □

It is easy to see that the parameters of the ultrasparsifiers we obtained are optimal, up to $\tilde{O}(\log n)$.

5. MAXIMIZING ALGEBRAIC CONNECTIVITY BY ADDING FEW EDGES

In this section, we present an approximation algorithm for the following problem: given a graph $G = (V, E_{base})$, a set of candidate edges E_{cand}, and a parameter k, add at most k candidate edges to G so as to maximize its algebraic connectivity. In other words, find a subset $E \subset E_{cand}$ that maximizes $\lambda_2(\mathcal{L}_{G+E})$. The problem was introduced by Ghosh and Boyd [5], who presented a heuristic for it. It is known that the problem is NP-hard [15]. But prior to this work, no approximation algorithm was known for it.

We use two upper bounds for the cost of the combinatorial solution in order to prove an approximation guarantee: one upper bound is the SDP value, λ_{SDP}, and the other is $\lambda_{k+2}(\mathcal{L}_G)$ (see Lemma 5.1). Note that neither of these two bounds are good approximations for the value of the optimum solution by themselves. For instance, if G consists of n isolated vertices, (V, E_{cand}) is an expander, and $k < n$, then the value of the combinatorial solution is 0 but $\lambda_{SDP} \sim k/n$. But the combination of these two bounds lead to a good upper bound for the optimum solution λ_{OPT}.

For clarity and simplicity of exposition, we assume here that (V, E_{base}) and (V, E_{cand}) are bounded degree graphs with the maximum degree Δ. Our algorithm uses a natural semidefinite relaxation that was also used by Ghosh and Boyd [5]. We introduce a variable w_e (the weight of the edge e) for each candidate edge $e \in E_{cand}$; add constraints that all edge weights are between 0 and 1, and the total weight is at most k. Then we require that $\lambda_2(\mathcal{L}_G + \sum_e w_e\mathcal{L}_e) \ge \lambda_{SDP}$ (where $\mathcal{L}_e$ is the Laplacian of the edge e). We do that by adding an SDP constraint $\mathcal{L}_G + \sum_e w_e\mathcal{L}_e \succeq \lambda_{SDP}P_{(1,\dots,1)^\perp}$, where $P_{(1,\dots,1)^\perp}$ is the projection on the space orthogonal to $(1,\dots,1)$. We get the following SDP relaxation.

$$\text{maximize: } \lambda_{SDP},$$
$$\text{subject to: } \mathcal{L}_G + \sum_{e\in E_{cand}} w_e\mathcal{L}_e \succeq \lambda_{SDP}\cdot P_{(1,\dots,1)^\perp},$$
$$\sum_{e\in E_{cand}} w_e \le k,$$
$$0 \le w_e \le 1 \text{ for every } e \in E_{cand}.$$

We solve the semidefinite program and obtain the solution $\{w_e\}_{e\in E_{cand}}$. The total weight of all edges is k, however, the number of edges involved, or the support of the solution could be significantly higher than k.

We use our algorithm to *sparsify* the SDP solution using Theorem 3.3. More precisely, we apply Theorem 3.3 with $X = \mathcal{L}_G/(4\Delta)$ and $Y_e = w_i\mathcal{L}_e/(4\Delta)$ restricted to the space $(1,\dots,1)^\perp$, $N = 8k$, $T = \mathrm{tr}(\sum_e w_e\mathcal{L}_e)/(4\Delta) \le k$ and $cost_i = w_i$ (we divide $\mathcal{L}_G$ and $\mathcal{L}_e$ by 4Δ to ensure that $\lambda_{\max}(X + \sum_e Y_i) \le 1$). We get a set of weights ρ_e supported on at most $8k$ edges s.t.

$$\frac{1}{4\Delta}\lambda_2(\mathcal{L}_G + \sum_e \rho_e w_e\mathcal{L}_e) = \lambda_{\min}(X + \sum_e \rho_e Y_e)$$

$$\ge c\lambda_{k+2}(X)\lambda_{\min}(X + \sum_e Y_e) \ge c\frac{1}{(4\Delta)^2}\lambda_{k+2}(\mathcal{L}_G)\lambda_{SDP}.$$

That is, we obtain a combinatorial weighted solution $\tilde{w}_e = \rho_i w_i$ whose value is at least $c\lambda_{k+2}(\mathcal{L}_G)\lambda_{SDP}/(4\Delta)$ (if $k + 2 > n$, the value is at least $c\lambda_{SDP}$). We next show that $\lambda_{SDP} \ge \lambda_{OPT}$ and $\lambda_{k+2}(G) \ge \lambda_{OPT}$. Therefore, the value of the solution is at least $c\lambda_{OPT}^2/\Delta$.

LEMMA 5.1. *The value of the optimal solution, λ_{OPT}, is at most $\lambda_{k+2}(\mathcal{L}_G)$.*

PROOF. Consider the optimal solution E. Let $\mathcal{L}_E$ be the Laplacian of the graph formed by E. Note that $\mathrm{rank}(\mathcal{L}_E) \le |E| \le k$, therefore, $\dim\ker\mathcal{L}_E \ge n - k$. Let S be the $k+1$-dimensional space spanned by the eigenvectors of $\mathcal{L}_G$ corresponding to $\lambda_2(\mathcal{L}_G), \dots, \lambda_{k+2}(\mathcal{L}_G)$. Since $\dim S + \dim\ker E > n$, spaces S and $\ker\mathcal{L}_E$ have a non-trivial intersection. Choose a unit vector $v \in \ker S \cap \mathcal{L}_E$. We have

$$v(\mathcal{L}_G + \mathcal{L}_E)v^T \le \lambda_{k+2}(\mathcal{L}_G) + 0 = \lambda_{k+2}(\mathcal{L}_G).$$

Also v is orthogonal to the vector $(1,\dots,1)^\perp$. Therefore,

$$\lambda_{OPT} = \lambda_2(\mathcal{L}_G + \mathcal{L}_E) \le \lambda_{k+2}(\mathcal{L}_G).$$

□

The edges in the support of $\tilde{w}_e$, $E = \{\tilde{w}_e : \tilde{w}_e \ne 0\}$, form a non-weighted combinatorial solution. Since $\lambda_{\max}(\mathcal{L}_X + \sum_e \tilde{w}_e\mathcal{L}_e) = O(\Delta)$, all weights $\tilde{w}_e$ are bounded by $O(\Delta)$, and thus the algebraic connectivity of $G + E$ is at least $c\lambda_{k+2}(\mathcal{L}_G)\lambda_{SDP}/\Delta^2$.

THEOREM 5.2. *There is a polynomial time approximation algorithm that finds a solution of value at least $c\lambda_{OPT}^2/\Delta$ supported on at most $8k$ edges with total weight at most k. If $k \ge n$ the algorithm finds a constant factor approximation.*

We present two corollaries for special instances of the problem.

Corollary 5.3. *If it is possible to make G an expander by adding k edges (and thus $\lambda_{OPT} \sim \Delta$), then the algorithm finds a constant factor approximation.*

Note that if the graph formed by candidate edges is an expander then the value of the following SDP solution $w_e = k/|E_{cand}|$ for each edge $e \in E_{cand}$ is $\Omega(k/n)$, thus $\lambda_{SDP} \geq ck/n$.

Corollary 5.4. *If the graph formed by candidate edges is an expander, then the approximation algorithm from Theorem 5.2 finds a solution of value at least $c\frac{k}{n\Delta}\lambda_{OPT}$.*

Remark 5.5. *It is possible to get rid of the dependence on Δ in Theorem 5.2 and Corollary 5.4 and obtain approximation guarantees of $c\min(\lambda_{OPT}, \lambda_{OPT}^2)$ and $\frac{ck}{n}\lambda_{OPT}$ respectively. We omit the details in this extended abstract.*

Acknowledgments

This research was conducted in part while the authors were visiting Microsoft Research New England (and the second author was a postdoctoral researcher at MSR-NE). We would like to thank Microsoft Research for their hospitality.

We are grateful to Dan Spielman for his insightful help in our work on ultrasparsifers.

6. REFERENCES

[1] I. Abraham, Y. Bartal, and O. Neiman. Nearly tight low stretch spanning trees. In *Proceedings of the 49th annual Symposium on Foundations of Computer Science,* pp. 781–790, 2008.

[2] N. Alon, R. Karp, D. Peleg, and D. West. A Graph-Theoretic Game and its Application to the k-Server Problem, In *SIAM J. Comput.* vol. 24-1, pp. 78–100, 1995.

[3] J. Batson, D. A. Spielman, and N. Srivastava. Twice-Ramanujan Sparsifiers. In *Proceedings of the 50th annual Symposium on Foundations of Computer Science,* pp. 255–262, 2009.

[4] A. A. Benczur and D. R. Karger. Approximating $s-t$ minimum cuts in $O(n^2)$ time. In *Proceedings of the 28th annual Symposium on the Theory of Computing* pp. 47–55, 1996.

[5] A. Ghosh and S. Boyd. Growing well–connected graphs. In *Proceedings of the 45th conference on Decision and Control,* 2006.

[6] P. Chew. There is a planar graph almost as good as the complete graph. In *Proceedings of the second annual symposium on Computational geometry,* pp. 169–177, ACM, 1986.

[7] M. Elkin, Y. Emek, D. A. Spielman and S. Teng. Lower-stretch spanning trees In *Proceedings of the 37th annual ACM symposium on Theory of Computing,* pp. 494–503, 2005.

[8] G. H. Golub and C. F. Van Loan. Matrix Computations, 3rd. Edition. The Johns Hopkins University Press, Baltimore, MD, 1996.

[9] A. Ghosh. Designing Well-Connected Networks, Ph.D. Dissertation, Stanford University, 2006.

[10] A. Ghosh, S. Boyd, and A. Saberi. Minimizing Effective Resistance of a Graph. In SIAM Review, problems and techniques section, 50(1):37-66, 2008.

[11] A. Lubotzky, R. Phillips, and P. Sarnak. Ramanujan graphs. In *Combinatorica,* 8(3):261–277, 1988.

[12] D. G. Luenberger. A Combined Penalty Function and Gradient Projection Method for Nonlinear Programming.

[13] G. A. Margulis. Explicit group theoretical constructions of combinatorial schemes and their application to the design of expanders and concentrators. In *Problems of Information Transmission,* 24(1):39–46, July 1988.

[14] L. Mirsky. A trace inequality of John von Neumann. *Monats. Math.* 79(4):303–306, 1975.

[15] D. Mosk–Aoyama. Maximum algebraic connectivity augmentation is NP-hard. *Operations Research Letters,* vol. 36(6), Nov. 2008, 677–679.

[16] D. A. Spielman. Personal Communication.

[17] D. A. Spielman and N. Srivastava. Graph sparsification by effective resistances. In *Proceedings of the 40th ACM Symposium on Theory of Computing,* pp. 563–568, 2008. Full version available at http://arXiv.org/abs/0803.0929.

[18] D. A. Spielman, and S. Teng. Nearly-linear time algorithms for graph partitioning, graph sparsification, and solving linear systems. In *Proceedings of the 36th annual ACM Symposium on Theory of Computing,* pp. 81–90, 2004.

[19] D. A. Spielman and S. Teng. Nearly-linear time algorithms for preconditioning and solving symmetric, diagonally dominant linear systems. CoRR, abs/cs/0607105, 2008. Available at http://www.arxiv.org/abs/cs.NA/0607105.

[20] D. A. Spielman and S. Teng. Spectral sparsification of graphs. CoRR, abs/0808.4134, 2008. Available at http://arxiv.org/abs/0808.4134.

[21] D. A. Spielman and J. O. Woo. A note on preconditioning with low stretch spanning trees. http://arxiv.org/abs/0903.2816.

How to Compress Interactive Communication

[Extended Abstract]*

Boaz Barak[†]
Princeton University
Princeton, NJ
boaz@cs.princeton.edu

Mark Braverman[‡]
Microsoft Research New England
Cambridge, MA
mbraverm@cs.toronto.edu

Xi Chen[§]
University of Southern California
Los Angeles, CA
csxichen@gmail.com

Anup Rao[¶]
University of Washington
Seattle, WA
anuprao@cs.washington.edu

ABSTRACT

We describe new ways to simulate 2-party communication protocols to get protocols with potentially smaller communication. We show that every communication protocol that communicates C bits and reveals I bits of information about the inputs to the participating parties can be simulated by a new protocol involving at most $\tilde{O}(\sqrt{CI})$ bits of communication. If the protocol reveals I bits of information about the inputs to an observer that watches the communication in the protocol, we show how to carry out the simulation with $\tilde{O}(I)$ bits of communication.

These results lead to a direct sum theorem for randomized communication complexity. Ignoring polylogarithmic factors, we show that for worst case computation, computing n copies of a function requires $\sqrt{n}$ times the communication required for computing one copy of the function. For average case complexity, given any distribution μ on inputs, computing n copies of the function on n inputs sampled independently according to μ requires $\sqrt{n}$ times the communication for computing one copy. If μ is a product distribution, computing n copies on n independent inputs sampled according to μ requires n times the communication required for computing the function. We also study the complexity of computing the sum (or parity) of n evaluations of f, and obtain results analogous to those above.

To the best of our knowledge, our results give the first compression schemes for general randomized protocols and the first direct sum results in the general setting. Previous results applied only when the protocols were restricted to running in a bounded number of rounds, where each message can be compressed in turn, and only applied when the parties are given independent inputs.

Categories and Subject Descriptors

F.2.2 [**Theory of Computation**]: Analysis of algorithms and problem complexity

General Terms

Theory

Keywords

Information theory, communication complexity, compression, direct sum.

*A preliminary full version of this paper is available on the ECCC and the authors' home pages.

†Supported by NSF grants CNS-0627526, CCF-0426582 and CCF-0832797, US-Israel BSF grant 2004288 and Packard and Sloan fellowships.

‡Part of the work done while visiting the Institute for Advanced Study, Princeton, NJ, supported by a Clay Mathematics Institute Liftoff Fellowship.

§Most of the work done while the author was a postdoc at Princeton University, NJ. Supported by NSF Grants CCF-0832797 and DMS-0635607.

¶Most of the work done while the author was a member at the Institute for Advanced Study, Princeton, NJ. Supported by NSF Grant CCF 0832797.

1. INTRODUCTION

In this work we address two questions: (1) Can we compress the communication of an interactive protocol so it is close to the information conveyed between the parties? (2) Is it harder to compute a function on n independent inputs than to compute it on a single input? In the context of communication complexity, the two questions are related, and our answer to the former will yield an answer to the latter.

Techniques for message compression, first considered by Shannon [Sha48], have had a big impact on computer science, especially with the rise of the Internet and data intensive applications. Today we know how to encode messages so that their length is essentially the same as the amount of information that they carry (see for example the text [CT91]). Can we get a similar savings in an interactive setting? A first attempt might be to simply compress each message of the interaction in turn. However, this compression involves at least 1 bit of communication for every message of the interaction, which can be much larger than the total information conveyed between the parties. In this paper, we show how to compress interactive communication protocols in a way that is independent of the number of rounds of communication, and in some settings, give compressed protocols with communication that has a near-linear dependence on the information conveyed in the original protocol.

The second question is one of the most basic questions of theoretical computer science, called the *direct sum* question, and is closely related to the *direct product* question. A direct product theorem in a particular computational model asserts that the probability of success of performing n independent computational tasks decreases in n. Famous examples of such theorems include Yao's XOR Lemma [Yao82] and Raz's Parallel Repetition Theorem [Raz95]. In the context of communication complexity, Shaltiel [Sha03] gave a direct product theorem for the discrepancy of a function, but it remains open to give such a theorem for the success probability of communication tasks. A recent progress on direct product for computing n copies of the disjointness function has been reported in [Kla10]. A direct sum theorem asserts that the amount of resources needed to perform n independent tasks grows with n. While the direct sum question for general models such as Boolean circuits has a long history (cf [Uhl74, Pau76, GF81]), no general results are known, and indeed they cannot be achieved by the standard reductions used in complexity theory, as a black-box reduction mapping a circuit C performing n tasks into a circuit C' performing a single task will necessarily make C' *larger* than C, rather than making it smaller. Indeed it is known that at least the most straightforward/optimistic formulation of a direct sum theorem for Boolean circuits is *false.*[1]

Nevertheless, direct sum theorems are known to hold in other computational models. For example, an optimal direct sum theorem is easy to prove for decision tree depth. A more interesting model is *communication complexity*, where this question was first raised by Karchmer, Raz, and Wigderson [KRW91] who conjectured a certain direct sum result for deterministic communication complexity of relations, and showed that it would imply that $\mathbf{P} \not\subseteq \mathbf{NC}^1$. Feder, Kushilevitz, Naor, and Nisan [FKNN91] gave a direct sum theorem for non-deterministic communication complexity, and deduced from it a somewhat weaker result for deterministic communication complexity— if a single copy of a function f requires C bits of communications, then n copies require $\Omega(\sqrt{C}n)$ bits. Feder et al also considered the direct sum question for *randomized* communication complexity (see also Open Problem 4.6 in [KN97]) and showed that the dependence of the communication on the error of the protocol for many copies can be better than that obtained by the naive protocol for many copies.

Chakrabarti et al [CSWY01] gave a direct sum theorem in the case that the communication involves one simultaneous round of communication, while Jain et al [JRS03] (improved upon by [HJMR07]) gave a direct sum theorem for the distributional complexity of bounded round randomized protocols when the inputs are assumed to be independent of each other. These results only apply when the number of rounds in the protocol is bounded to be much less than the total communication, and so give no guarantees in the standard model, with unbounded number of rounds.

All of the works mentioned above had a common outline that we follow in this work as well. They began by measuring the information that an observer learns about the inputs of the parties by watching the messages and public randomness of the protocol, a quantity that they called the *information cost* of the protocol. In our paper, we shall refer to this measure of information as the *external information cost* of the protocol, to contrast it with the *internal information cost* that we shall define later:

Definition 1. (External Information Cost) Given a distribution μ on inputs X, Y, and protocol π, denoting by $\pi(X,Y)$ the public randomness and messages exchanged during the protocol, the *external information cost* $\mathsf{IC}^{o}_{\mu}(\pi)$ is defined to be the mutual information between the inputs and $\pi(X,Y)$:

$$\mathsf{IC}^{o}_{\mu}(\pi) \stackrel{def}{=} I(XY;\pi(X,Y))$$

The external information cost is always smaller than the communication complexity, and if the inputs to the parties are independent of each other (i.e. X is independent of Y), an optimal direct sum theorem can be proved for this measure of complexity. This means that from a protocol computing n copies of f with communication C, one can obtain a protocol computing f with external information cost C/n, as long as the inputs to f are independent of each other. Thus the problem of proving direct sum theorems for independent inputs reduces to the problem of simulating a protocol τ with small external information cost with a protocol ρ that has small communication. That is, the direct sum question reduces to the problem of protocol compression. Previous works carried out the compression by compressing every message of the protocol individually, hence the dependency on the number of rounds. Our stronger method of compression allows us to get new direct sum theorems that are independent of the number of rounds of communication.

1.1 Our Results

In our work we work with two different measures of the information complexity of a communication protocol. The first is the external information cost, defined above. The second measure, which we call the internal information cost of the protocol, is the information that the *parties* in the protocol learn by watching the messages and public randomness of the protocol, that they did not already know. Formally,

Definition 2. (Internal Information Cost) Given a distribution μ on inputs X, Y, and protocol π, denoting by $\pi(X,Y)$ the public randomness and messages exchanged

[1]The example comes from fast matrix multiplication. By a counting argument, there exists an $n \times n$ matrix A over GF(2) such that the map $x \mapsto Ax$ requires a circuit of $\Omega(n^2/\log n)$ size. But the map $(x_1,\ldots,x_n) \mapsto (Ax_1,\ldots,Ax_n)$ is just the product of the matrices A and X (whose columns are $x_1,\ldots,x_n$) and hence can be carried out by a circuit of $O(n^{2.38}) \ll n \cdot (n^2/\log n)$. See Shaltiel's paper [Sha03] for more on this question.

during the protocol, the *internal information cost* $\mathsf{IC^i}_\mu(\pi)$ is defined to be

$$\mathsf{IC^i}_\mu(\pi) \stackrel{def}{=} I(X;\pi(X,Y)|Y) + I(Y;\pi(X,Y)|X).$$

Since each party knows her own input, the protocol can only reveal less information to her than to an independent observer. Thus the internal information cost is never larger than the external information cost. It can be shown that the internal information cost of a protocol is the same as the external information cost, if the inputs are independent of each other. However, in the case that the inputs are dependent, the internal information cost may be significantly smaller — for example, if μ is a distribution where $X = Y$ always, then the internal information cost is always 0, though the external information cost may be arbitrarily large. It is also easy to check that if π is deterministic, then the internal information cost is simply the sum of the entropies $\mathsf{IC^i}_\mu(\pi) = H(\pi(X,Y)|Y)+H(\pi(X,Y)|X)$, which is the same as $H(\pi(X,Y))$ if X, Y are independent.

The notion of internal information cost was used implicitly by Bar-Yossef et al [BYJKS04], and a direct sum theorem for this notion (using the techniques originating from Razborov [Raz92] and Raz [Raz95]) is implicit in their work. This direct sum theorem holds whether or not the inputs to the parties are independent of each other, unlike the analogous result for information cost. We can convert any protocol computing n copies of f with communication C into one that computes f with internal information cost C/n and communication complexity C.

Our most important contributions are two new *protocol compression* methods that reduce the communication of protocols in terms of their information cost. The first method can simulate a protocol of internal information cost I and communication complexity C using an expected number of $\tilde{O}(\sqrt{IC})$ communication bits. The second method can simulate a protocol of external information cost I with $\tilde{O}(I)$ communication. Note that in both cases the communication complexity of the simulation is *independent* of the number of rounds. Indeed, these are the first compression schemes that do true *protocol* compression, as opposed to compressing each round at a time, and are the first results that succeed for multi-round protocols even when the inputs are not independent.

As a result, we obtain the first non-trivial direct sum theorem for randomized communication complexity. Previous results applied in the special case that the communication is one way, or only in the distributional setting if the number of rounds are bounded and the inputs to the protocol are independent of each other. Loosely speaking, letting f^n be the function that outputs the concatenation of n invocations of f on independent inputs, and letting f^{+n} be the function that outputs the XOR of n such invocations, we show that (a) the randomized communication complexity of both f^n and f^{+n} is up to polylogarithmic factors $\sqrt{n}$ times the communication complexity of f, and (b) the distributional complexity of both f^n and f^{+n} over the distribution μ^n, where μ is a product distribution over individual input pairs, is n times the distributional complexity of f.[2]

[2]In both (a) and (b), there is a loss of a constant additive factor in the actual statement of the result for f^{+n}. This accounts for the fact that if, say, f is the XOR function itself then clearly there is no direct sum theorem. See Remark 1.

1.1.1 Compressing Communication Protocols

We give two new *protocol compression* algorithms, that take a protocol π whose information cost is small and transform it into a protocol τ of small *communication complexity*.[3] Below we denote the communication complexity of a protocol τ by $\mathsf{CC}(\tau)$.

THEOREM 1. *There is a universal constant c such that for every distribution μ, every protocol π, and every $\epsilon > 0$, there exists functions π_x, π_y, and a protocol τ such that $|\pi_x(X,\tau(X,Y)) - \pi(X,Y)| < \epsilon$,*

$$\Pr[\pi_x(X,\tau(X,Y)) \neq \pi_y(Y,\tau(X,Y))] < \epsilon$$

and

$$\mathsf{CC}(\tau) \le c\sqrt{\mathsf{CC}(\pi)\cdot \mathsf{IC^i}_\mu(\pi)}\frac{\log(\mathsf{CC}(\pi)/\epsilon)}{\epsilon}.$$

If the players want to obtain the results of running the protocol π, they can run τ instead and then use the functions π_x, π_y to reconstruct the effects of running π. The condition $|\pi_x(X,\tau(X,Y)) - \pi(X,Y)| < \epsilon$ ensures that the transcript of τ specifies a unique leaf in the protocol tree for π in such a way that this leaf is ϵ-close in statistical distance to the leaf sampled by π. The condition that $\Pr[\pi_x(X,\tau(X,Y)) \neq \pi_y(Y,\tau(X,Y))] < \epsilon$ guarantees that with high probability both players achieve a consensus on what the sampled leaf was. Thus, the triple τ, π_x, π_y specify a new protocol that is a compression of π.

Our second result gives a simulation for protocols with small external information cost:

THEOREM 2. *For every distribution μ, every protocol π, and every $\alpha > 0$, there exists functions π_x, π_y, and a protocol τ such that $|\pi_x(X,\tau(X,Y)) - \pi(X,Y)| < \alpha$,*

$$\Pr[\pi_x(X,\tau(X,Y)) \neq \pi_y(Y,\tau(X,Y))] < \alpha$$

and

$$\mathsf{CC}(\tau) \le O\left(\mathsf{IC^o}_\mu(\pi)\frac{\text{polylog}(\mathsf{CC}(\pi)/\alpha)}{\alpha^2}\right).$$

Our results can be viewed as a generalization of the traditional notion of string compression, a notion that applies only to the restricted case of deterministic one way protocols. In the above theorems, our compressed protocols may use public randomness that can be large (though still bounded in terms of the communication complexity of the original protocol). However, we note that by the results of Newman [New91], any protocol that achieves some functionality can be converted into another protocol that achieves the same functionality and uses few public random bits. Thus our compression schemes are useful even when public randomness is expensive.

1.1.2 Direct sum theorems

Given a function $f : \mathcal{X}\times\mathcal{Y}\to\mathcal{Z}$, we define the function $f^n : \mathcal{X}^n\times\mathcal{Y}^n\to\mathcal{Z}^n$ to be the concatenation of the evaluations:

$$f^n(x_1,\ldots,x_n,y_1,\ldots,y_n) \stackrel{def}{=} (f(x_1,y_1), f(x_2,y_2),\ldots,f(x_n,y_n)).$$

[3] We note that this is in the communication complexity model, and hence these algorithms are not necessarily computationally efficient. Even for single message compression, there are distributions with small entropy that cannot be efficiently compressed (e.g. pseudorandom distributions).

Denote by $R_\rho(f)$ the communication complexity of the best randomized public coin protocol for computing f that errs with probability at most ρ. In this paper we show:

THEOREM 3. (DIRECT SUM FOR RANDOMIZED COMMUNICATION COMPLEXITY) *For every $\alpha > 0$,*

$$\mathsf{R}_\rho(f^n) \cdot \log\left(\mathsf{R}_\rho(f^n)/\alpha\right) \geq \Omega\left(\mathsf{R}_{\rho+\alpha}(f)\alpha\sqrt{n}\right)$$

Theorem 3 is obtained using Yao's min-max principle from an analogous theorem for *distributional* communication complexity. For a distribution μ on the inputs $\mathcal{X} \times \mathcal{Y}$, we write $D^\mu_\rho(f)$ to denote the communication complexity of the best protocol (randomized or deterministic) that computes f with probability of error at most ρ when the inputs are sampled according to μ. We write μ^n to denote the distribution on n inputs, where each is sampled according to μ independently.

We first state the direct sum theorem for internal information cost that is implicit in the work of [BYJKS04].

THEOREM 4. *For every μ, f, ρ there exists a protocol τ computing f on inputs drawn from μ with probability of error at most ρ and communication at most $\mathsf{D}^{\mu^n}_\rho(f^n)$ such that $\mathsf{IC}^{\mathsf{i}}{}_\mu(\tau) \leq \frac{2D^{\mu^n}_\rho(f^n)}{n}$.*

Compressing protocol τ above using Theorem 1 reduces the communication of this protocol to $\tilde{O}\left(\sqrt{\mathsf{IC}^{\mathsf{i}}{}_\mu(\tau)\mathsf{D}^{\mu^n}_\rho(f^n)}\right) = \tilde{O}(\mathsf{D}^{\mu^n}_\rho(f^n)/\sqrt{n})$. Formally, we prove:

THEOREM 5. (DIRECT SUM FOR DISTRIBUTIONAL COMMUNICATION COMPLEXITY) *For every $\alpha > 0$,*

$$\mathsf{D}^{\mu^n}_\rho(f^n) \cdot \log\left(\mathsf{D}^{\mu^n}_\rho(f^n)/\alpha\right) \geq \Omega\left(\mathsf{D}^{\mu}_{\rho+\alpha}(f)\alpha\sqrt{n}\right)$$

The communication complexity bound of Theorem 5 only grows as the square root of the number of repetitions. However, in the case that the distribution on inputs is a product distribution, we use our stronger compression (Theorem 2) to obtain a direct sum theorem that is optimal up to logarithmic factor:

THEOREM 6. (DIRECT SUM FOR PRODUCT DISTRIBUTIONS) *If μ is a product distribution, then for every $\alpha > 0$*

$$\mathsf{D}^{\mu^n}_\rho(f^n) \cdot \operatorname{polylog}\left(\mathsf{D}^{\mu^n}_\rho(f^n)/\alpha\right) \geq \Omega\left(\mathsf{D}^{\mu}_{\rho+\alpha}(f)\alpha^2 n\right)$$

1.1.3 XOR Lemmas for communication complexity

When n is very large in terms of the other quantities, the above theorems can be superseded by trivial arguments, since f^n must require at least n bits of communication just to describe the output. Our next set of theorems show that almost the same bounds apply to the complexity of the XOR (or more generally sum modulo K) of n copies of f, where the trivial arguments do not hold. Assume that the output of the function f is in the group $\mathbb{Z}_K$ for some integer K, and define

$$f^{+n}(x_1, \ldots, x_n, y_1, \ldots, y_n) \stackrel{def}{=} \sum_{i=1}^{n} f(x_i, y_i).$$

We have the following results for the complexity of f^{+n}:

THEOREM 7. (XOR LEMMA FOR RANDOMIZED COMMUNICATION COMPLEXITY) *For every $\alpha > 0$,*

$$\mathsf{R}_\rho(f^{+n}) \cdot \log\left(\mathsf{R}_\rho(f^{+n})/\alpha\right) \geq \Omega\left((\mathsf{R}_{\rho+\alpha}(f) - 2\log K)\,\alpha\sqrt{n}\right)$$

THEOREM 8. (XOR LEMMA FOR DISTRIBUTIONAL COMMUNICATION COMPLEXITY) *For every $\alpha > 0$,*

$$\mathsf{D}^{\mu^n}_\rho(f^{+n}) \cdot \log\left(\mathsf{D}^{\mu^n}_\rho(f^{+n})/\alpha\right) \geq \Omega\left((\mathsf{D}^{\mu}_{\rho+\alpha}(f) - 2\log K)\,\alpha\sqrt{n}\right)$$

THEOREM 9. (XOR LEMMA FOR PRODUCT DISTRIBUTIONS) *If μ is a product distribution, then for every $\alpha > 0$,*

$$\mathsf{D}^{\mu^n}_\rho(f^{+n}) \cdot \operatorname{polylog}\left(\mathsf{D}^{\mu^n}_\rho(f^{+n})/\alpha\right) \geq \Omega\left((\mathsf{D}^{\mu}_{\rho+\alpha}(f) - 2\log K)\,\alpha n\right)$$

Remark 1. If $f : \mathbb{Z}_K \times \mathbb{Z}_K \to \mathbb{Z}_K$ is itself the sum function, then the communication complexity of f^{+n} does not grow at all, since there is a simple protocol to compute $\sum_i (x_i + y_i) = \sum_i x_i + \sum_j y_j$ using $2\log K$ bits. This suggests that some kind of additive loss (like the $2\log K$ term above) is necessary in the above theorems.

Guide to the rest of the paper: In this extended abstract, we only provide a high level outline of the proofs. The full proof appears in the full version (available on the ECCC and the authors' home pages). Section 2 contains an informal overview of the proof ideas, while Sections 5 and 6 contain proof sketches for our results for the non-product and product case respectively.

2. OUR TECHNIQUES

We now give an informal overview of our compression algorithms. Our direct sum results are obtained in Section 4 by combining these with the direct sum for information cost. Full description of the compression algorithms is given in Section 5 (for the general case) and 6 (for the product distribution case).

The goal of our compression algorithms is to take a protocol that uses large amounts of communication and conveys little information, and convert it into a protocol that makes better use of the communication to achieve better communication complexity. (Such algorithms need not be necessarily computationally efficient, see Footnote 3.)

Note that generic message compression can be fit into this context by considering a deterministic one-way protocol, where player X needs to send a message to player Y. In this classical setting it is well known that protocol compression (i.e. simple data compression) can be achieved. In principle, one could try to apply round-by-round message compression to compress entire protocols. This approach suffers from the following fatal flaw: individual messages may (and are even likely) to contain $\ll 1$ bits of information. The communication cost of ≥ 1 bit per round would thus be $\gg$ the internal information cost of the round. Thus any attempt to implement the compression on a round-by-round basis, as opposed to an entire-protocol basis may work when the number of rounds is bounded, but is doomed to fail in general.

An instructive example on conveying a subconstant amount of information that we will use later in this exposition is the following. Suppose that player X gets n independent random bits $x_1, \ldots, x_n$ and Y has no information about them. X then computes the majority $m = MAJ(x_1, \ldots, x_n)$ and sends it to Y. With a perfectly random prior, the bit m is perfectly balanced, and thus in total X conveys one bit of information to Y. Suppose that in the protocol Y only really cared about the value of x_5. How much information did X convey about the input x_5? By symmetry and independence of the inputs, X conveys $1/n$ bits of information about x_5. After the bit m (suppose $m = 1$) is received by Y, her estimate of $P[x_5 = 1]$ changes from $1/2$ to $1/2 + \Theta(1/\sqrt{n})$. The fact that changing the probability from $1/2$ to $1/2 + \epsilon$ only costs ϵ^2 bits of information is the cause for the apparent suboptimality of our general compression algorithm.

There are several challenges that need to be overcome to compress an arbitrary protocol. An interesting case to consider is a protocol where the players alternate sending each other messages, and each transmitted message is just a bit with internal information cost $\epsilon \ll 1$. In this case, we cannot afford to even transmit one bit to simulate each of the messages, since that would incur an overhead of $1/\epsilon$, which would be too large for our application. This barrier was one of the big stumbling blocks for earlier works, which is why their results applied only when the number of rounds in the protocols was forced to be small.

We give two methods to solve this problem. The first works for all distributions, achieving sub-optimal parameters, while the second works only for product distributions and achieves optimal parameters up to poly-logarithmic factors. In both solutions, the players simulate the original protocol π using shared randomness. The intuition is that if a message contains a small amount of information, then we do not need to communicate it, and can sample it using shared randomness instead.

It will be convenient to think of a protocol in terms of its protocol tree, after fixing the shared randomness (there may still be private randomness that is not fixed). This is a binary tree where every node v belongs to one of parties in the protocol, and specifies the probability of sending 1 or 0 as the next bit. We then define the tree of probabilities illustrated in Figure 1 as follows. For each node v_x of the protocol tree that is owned by the player X (i.e. it is her turn to speak), player X knows the "correct" probabilities $O_{v_x,x}(0)$ and $O_{v_x,x}(1)$ of the bit that she is about to send. Player Y does not know these probabilities, but she has estimates $O_{v_x,y}(0)$ and $O_{v_x,y}(1)$ for them based on her input Y (formally these estimates are simply the probability of seeing a 0 or 1 conditioned on the protocol reaching v_x and conditioned on y). In the case where the input distribution μ is a product distribution $\mu = \mu_x \times \mu_y$, the X player can also compute the estimates $O_{v_x,y}(0)$ and $O_{v_x,y}(1)$, since they are independent of the input y given the node v_x. The goal is to simulate the protocol according to the "correct" distributions.

2.1 Compression According to the Internal Information Cost

In our first compression protocol, the players use shared randomness to sample the bit at every node of the protocol tree for $\pi(x, y)$. In other words, for every prefix v of messages, each player samples the next bit of the interaction according to the best guess that they have for how this bit is distributed, even if the next bit is actually transmitted by the other player in the original protocol. The players do this using shared randomness, in a way that guarantees that if their guesses are close to the correct distribution, then the probability that they sample the same bit is high. More precisely, the players share a random number $\kappa_v \in [0, 1]$ for every node v in the tree, and each player guesses the next bit following v to be 1, if the player's estimated probability for the message being 1 is at least κ_v. Note that the player that owns v samples the next bit with the correct probability. It's not hard to see that the probability of getting inconsistent samples at the node v is at most

$$|O_{v,x} - O_{v,y}| \stackrel{def}{=} |O_{v,x}(0) - O_{v,y}(0)| + |O_{v,x}(1) - O_{v,y}(1)|.$$

Once they have each sampled from the possible interactions, we shall argue that there is a *correct leaf* in the protocol tree, whose distribution is exactly the same as the leaf in the original protocol. This is the leaf that is obtained by starting at the root and repeatedly taking the edge that was sampled by the owner of the node. We then show how the players can use hashing and binary search to communicate a poly-logarithmic number of bits with each other to resolve the inconsistencies in their samples and find this correct path with high probability. In this way, the final outcome will be statistically close to the distribution of the original protocol. An example run for this protocol is illustrated on Figure 2. The additional interaction cost scales according to the expected number of inconsistencies on the path to the correct leaf, which we show can be bounded by $\sqrt{I \cdot C}$, where I is the internal information cost and C is the communication cost of the original protocol.

Recall from the Majority example above that ϵ information can mean that $|O_{v,x} - O_{v,y}| \approx \sqrt{\epsilon}$. In fact, the "worst case" example for us is when in each round I/C information is conveyed, leading to a per-round error of $\sqrt{I/C}$ and a total expected number of mistakes of $\sqrt{I/C} \cdot C = \sqrt{I \cdot C}$.

2.2 Compression According to the External Information Cost

Our more efficient solution gives a protocol with communication complexity within polylogarithmic factors of the external information cost. It is illustrated on Figure 3. The idea in this case is to simulate chunks of the protocol that convey a constant amount of information each. If we can simulate a portion of the protocol that conveys a constant (or even 1/poly-log) amount of information using poly-logarithmic number of bits of communication, then we can simulate the entire protocol using $\tilde{O}(I)$ bits of communication.

The advantage the players have in the case that we are measuring information from the viewpoint of an observer is that for each node in the tree, the player who owns that node not only knows the correct distribution for the next bit, but also knows what the distribution that the observer has in mind is. They can use this shared knowledge to sample entire paths according to the distribution that is common knowledge at every step. In general, the distribution of the sampled path can deviate quite a bit from the correct distribution. However, we argue that if the information conveyed on a path is small (1/polylog bit), then the difference between the correct and the approximate probability is constant. After sampling the approximate bits for the appropriate number of steps so as to cover 1/polylog information, the players can communicate to estimate the correct probability with which this node was supposed to occur. The players can then either accept the sequence or

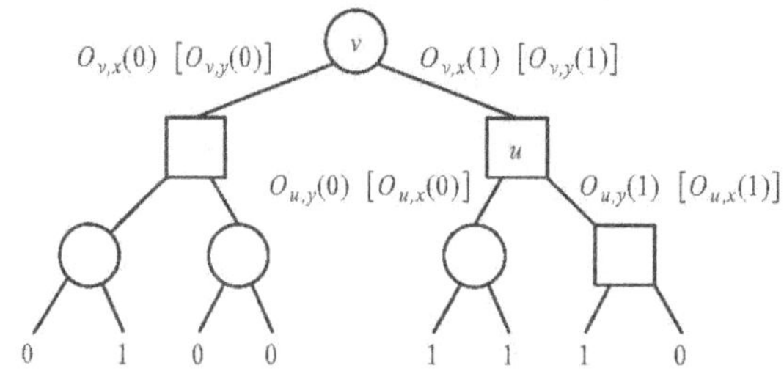

The round nodes are owned by X and the square nodes are owned by Y. On each edge the "correct" probability is indicated. The "approximate" probability that is estimated by the player who does not own the node is shown in the brackets.

Figure 1: An illustration of the protocol tree for π.

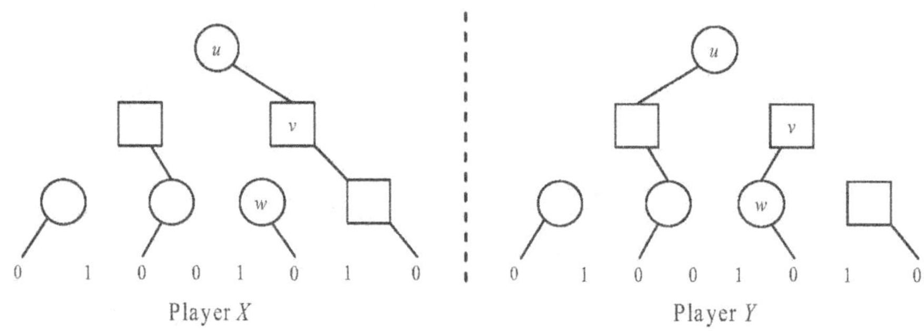

The circle nodes are owned by player X and the square nodes are owned by Y. The figure illustrates the states of the protocol trees after all the bits have been sampled. The players then proceed to resolve their disagreements. The disagreement at node u is resolved in favor of X since he owns the node. The protocol proceeds to node v where the disagreement is resolved in favor of Y. The final computation path in this case is $u - v - w$, the output is 0, and the total number of disagreements along the path is 2.

Figure 2: An illustration of the compression protocol for non-product distributions.

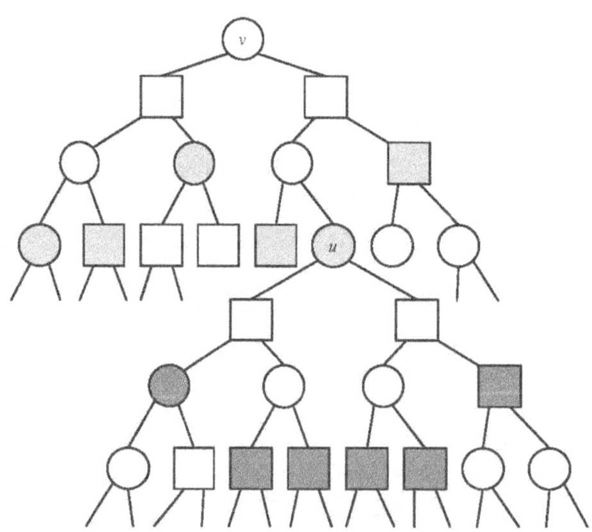

The gray layer represents the "frontier" of nodes where some fixed amount of information is conveyed in the original protocol, and which is simulated in one iteration of the compressed protocol. Once the players agree on a node u, they compute a new frontier, illustrated here by the black layer.

Figure 3: An illustration of the compression protocol for product distributions.

resample a new sequence in order to get a final sample that behaves in a way that is close to the distribution of the original protocol.

There are several technical challenges involved in getting this to work. The fact that the inputs of the players are independent is important for the players to decide how many messages the players should try to sample at once to get to the frontier where 1/ polylog bits of information have been revealed. When the players' inputs are dependent, they cannot estimate how many messages they should sample before the information cost becomes too high, and we are unable to make this approach work.

3. PRELIMINARIES

Notation. We reserve capital letters for random variables and distributions, calligraphic letters for sets, and small letters for elements of sets. Throughout this paper, we often use the notation $|b$ to denote conditioning on the event $B = b$. Thus $A|b$ is shorthand for $A|B = b$. Given a sequence of symbols $A = A_1, A_2, \dots, A_k$, we use $A_{\leq j}$ to denote the prefix of length j. We denote by $|A - B|$ the *statistical/total variation* distance between distributions A and B.

Entropy. We use $H(X) \stackrel{def}{=} \sum_x \Pr[X = x] \log(1/\Pr[X = x])$ to denote the *entropy* of a random variable X. The *conditional entropy* $H(X|Y)$ is defined to be $\mathbb{E}_{y \in_R Y}[H(X|Y = y)]$. Note that $H(AB) = H(A) + H(B|A)$. The *mutual information* between two random variables A, B, denoted $I(A;B)$ is defined to be the quantity $H(A) - H(A|B) = H(B) - H(B|A)$. The *conditional mutual information* $I(A;B|C)$ is $H(A|C) - H(A|BC)$. We observe that if C_1, C_2, D, B are random variables then $I(C_1C_2;B|D) = I(C_1;B|D) + I(C_2;B|C_1D)$. We will also use the following simple corollary:

PROPOSITION 1. (SUPER-ADDITIVITY OF MUTUAL INFORMATION) *Let C_1, C_2, D, B be random variables such that for every fixing of D, C_1 and C_2 are independent. Then*

$$I(C_1;B|D) + I(C_2;B|D) \quad \leq \quad I(C_1C_2;B|D).$$

Divergence. Another way to define distance between two distributions A, B is their *informational divergence*, denoted as $\mathbb{D}(A||B) \stackrel{def}{=} \sum_x A(x)\log(A(x)/B(x))$. For example, if B is the uniform distribution on $\{0,1\}^n$ then $\mathbb{D}(A||B) = n - H(A)$ (see below). It's well known that $\mathbb{D}(A||B) \geq |A - B|^2$. Some other easy to verify facts include

PROPOSITION 2. *Let A, B, C be random variables in the same probability space. For every a in the support of A and c in the support of C, let B_a denote $B|A = a$ and B_{ac} denote $B|A = a, C = c$. Then $I(A;B|C) = \mathbb{E}_{a,c \in_R A,C}[\mathbb{D}(B_{ac}||B_c)]$, and $\mathbb{E}_{a \in_R A}[|(B_a) - B|] \leq \sqrt{I(A;B)}$.*

Communication complexity. Let $\mathcal{X}, \mathcal{Y}$ denote the set of possible inputs to the two players, who we name P_x, P_y. In this paper[4], we view a *private coins protocol* for computing a function $f : \mathcal{X} \times \mathcal{Y} \to \mathbb{Z}_K$ as a binary tree with the following structure: (1) Each node is *owned* by P_x or by P_y, (2) For every $x \in \mathcal{X}$, each internal node v owned by P_x is associated with a distribution $O_{v,x}$ supported on the children of v. Similarly, for every $y \in \mathcal{Y}$, each internal node v owned by P_y is associated with a distribution $O_{v,y}$ supported on the children of v, (3) The leaves of the protocol are labeled by output values from $\mathbb{Z}_K$.

A public coin protocol is a distribution on private coins protocols, run by first using shared randomness to sample an index r and then running the corresponding private coin protocol π_r. Every private coin protocol is thus a public coin protocol. The protocol is called deterministic if all distributions labeling the nodes have support size 1. The *communication complexity* of a public coin protocol π, denoted $\mathsf{CC}(\pi)$, is the maximum depth of the protocol trees in the support of π.

Given a protocol π, $\pi(x, y)$ denotes the concatenation of the public randomness with all the messages that are sent during the execution of π. We call this the *transcript* of the protocol. We shall use the notation $\pi(x,y)_j$ to refer to the j'th transmitted bit in the protocol. We write $\pi(x,y)_{\leq j}$ to denote the concatenation of the public randomness in the protocol with the first j message bits that were transmitted in the protocol. Given a transcript, or a prefix of the transcript, v, we write $\mathsf{CC}(v)$ to denote the number of message bits in v (i.e. the length of the communication).

We often assume that every leaf in the protocol is at the same depth. We can do this since if some leaf is at depth less than the maximum, we can modify the protocol by adding dummy nodes which are always picked with probability 1, until all leaves are at the same depth. This does not change the communication complexity.

Communication Complexity notation. For a function $f : \mathcal{X} \times \mathcal{Y} \to \mathbb{Z}_K$, a distribution μ supported on $\mathcal{X} \times \mathcal{Y}$, and a parameter $\rho > 0$, $D^\mu_\rho(f)$ denotes the communication complexity of the cheapest deterministic protocol for computing f on inputs sampled according to μ with error ρ. $R_\rho(f)$ denotes the cost of the best randomized public coin protocol for computing f with error at most ρ on *every* input. We shall use the fact, first observed by Yao, that von-Neumman's Min-Max Theorem implies that $R_\rho(f) = \max_\mu D^\mu_\rho(f)$.

Finding differences in inputs. We use the following lemma of Feige et al. [FPRU94]:

LEMMA 1 ([FPRU94]). *There is a randomized public coin protocol τ with communication complexity $O(\log(k/\epsilon))$ such that on input two k-bit strings x, y, it outputs the first index $i \in [k]$ such that $x_i \neq y_i$ with probability at least $1 - \epsilon$, if such an i exists.*

A remark on the role of public and private randomness. We include the public randomness in the transcript, but not the private randomness. Making private randomness public can have a dramatic effect on the internal information cost of the protocol. Consider a protocol where one party sends a message of $x \oplus r$ where x is its input and r is random. If the randomness r is private then this message has zero internal information cost. If the randomness is public then the message completely reveals the input. This protocol may seem trivial since its communication complexity is larger than the input length, but in fact we will be dealing with exactly such protocols, as our goal will be to "compress" communication of protocols that have very large communication complexity, but very small internal information cost.

[4]The definitions we present here are equivalent to the classical definitions and are more convenient for our proofs.

4. PROOF OF THE DIRECT SUM THEOREMS

In this section, we prove our direct sum theorems. By Yao's minimax principle, for every function f, $R_\rho(f) = \max_\mu D^\mu_\rho(f)$. Thus Theorem 5 implies Theorem 3 and Theorem 8 implies Theorem 7. So we shall focus on proving Theorem 5, Theorem 6, and the XOR Lemmas (Theorem 8 and Theorem 9).

By Theorem 4, the main step to establish Theorem 5 is to give an efficient simulation of a protocol with small internal information cost by a protocol with small communication complexity. We shall use our two results on compression, that we restate here:

THEOREM 1 (RESTATED) There is a universal constant c such that for every distribution μ, every protocol π, and every $\epsilon > 0$, there exists functions π_x, π_y, and a protocol τ such that $|\pi_x(X, \tau(X,Y)) - \pi(X,Y)| < \epsilon$, $\Pr[\pi_x(X, \tau(X,Y)) \neq \pi_y(Y, \tau(X,Y))] < \epsilon$ and

$$\mathsf{CC}(\tau) \leq c\sqrt{\mathsf{CC}(\pi) \cdot \mathsf{IC}^i{}_\mu(\pi)} \frac{\log(\mathsf{CC}(\pi)/\epsilon)}{\epsilon} .$$

THEOREM 2 (RESTATED). For every distribution μ, every protocol π, and every $\alpha > 0$, there exists functions π_x, π_y, and a protocol τ such that $|\pi_x(X, \tau(X,Y)) - \pi(X,Y)| < \alpha$, $\Pr[\pi_x(X, \tau(X,Y)) \neq \pi_y(Y, \tau(X,Y))] < \alpha$ and

$$\mathsf{CC}(\tau) \leq O\left(\mathsf{IC}^o{}_\mu(\pi) \frac{\operatorname{polylog}(\mathsf{CC}(\pi)/\alpha)}{\alpha^2}\right) .$$

Proof of Theorem 3 from Theorem 1. Let π be any protocol computing f^n on inputs drawn from μ^n with probability of error less than ρ. Then by Theorem 4, there exists a protocol τ_1 computing f on inputs drawn from μ with error at most ρ with $\mathsf{CC}(\tau_1) \leq \mathsf{CC}(\pi)$ and $\mathsf{IC}^i{}_\mu(\tau_1) \leq 2\mathsf{CC}(\pi)/n$. Next, applying Theorem 1 to the protocol τ_1 gives that there must exist a protocol τ_2 computing f on inputs drawn from μ with error at most $\rho + \alpha$ and

$$\begin{aligned}\mathsf{CC}(\tau_2) &\leq O\left(\sqrt{\mathsf{CC}(\tau_1)\mathsf{IC}^i{}_\mu(\tau_1)}\log(\mathsf{CC}(\tau_1)/\alpha)/\alpha\right) \\ &= O\left(\sqrt{\mathsf{CC}(\pi)\mathsf{CC}(\pi)/n}\log(\mathsf{CC}(\pi)/\alpha)/\alpha\right) \\ &= O\left(\frac{\mathsf{CC}(\pi)\log(\mathsf{CC}(\pi)/\alpha)/\alpha}{\sqrt{n}}\right)\end{aligned}$$

This proves Theorem 5. □

Proof of Theorem 6 from Theorem 2. Let π be any protocol computing f^n on inputs drawn from μ^n with probability of error less than ρ. Then by Theorem 4, there exists a protocol τ_1 computing f on inputs drawn from μ with error at most ρ with $\mathsf{CC}(\tau_1) \leq \mathsf{CC}(\pi)$ and $\mathsf{IC}^i{}_\mu(\tau_1) \leq 2\mathsf{CC}(\pi)/n$. Since μ is a product distribution, we have that $\mathsf{IC}^o{}_\mu(\pi) = \mathsf{IC}^i{}_\mu(\pi)$. Next, applying Theorem 2 to the protocol τ_1 gives that there must exist a protocol τ_2 computing f on inputs drawn from μ with error at most $\rho + \alpha$ and

$$\begin{aligned}\mathsf{CC}(\tau_2) &\leq O\left(\mathsf{IC}^o{}_\mu(\tau_1)\operatorname{polylog}(\mathsf{CC}(\tau_1)/\alpha)/\alpha^2\right) \\ &= O\left(\frac{\mathsf{CC}(\pi)\operatorname{polylog}(\mathsf{CC}(\pi)/\alpha)}{n\alpha^2}\right)\end{aligned}$$

This proves Theorem 6. □

Proof of the XOR Lemma. The proof for Theorem 8 (XOR Lemma for distributional complexity) is very similar. First, we show an XOR-analogue of Theorem 4:

THEOREM 10. *For every distribution μ, there exists a protocol τ computing f with probability of error ρ over the distribution μ with $\mathsf{CC}(\tau) \leq \mathsf{D}^{\mu^n}_\rho(f^{+n}) + 2\log K$ such that if τ' is the protocol that is the same as τ but stops running after $\mathsf{D}^{\mu^n}_\rho(f^{+n})$ message bits have been sent, then $\mathsf{IC}^i{}_\mu(\tau') \leq \frac{2D^{\mu^n}_\rho(f^{n+})}{n}$.*

Now let π be any protocol computing f^{+n} on inputs drawn from μ^n with probability of error less than ρ. Then by Theorem 10, there exists a protocol τ_1 computing f on inputs drawn from μ with error at most ρ with $\mathsf{CC}(\tau_1) \leq \mathsf{CC}(\pi) + 2\log K$ and such that if τ_1' denotes the first $\mathsf{CC}(\pi)$ bits of the message part of the transcript, $\mathsf{IC}^i{}_\mu(\tau_1') \leq 2\mathsf{CC}(\pi)/n$. Next, applying Theorem 1 to the protocol τ_1' gives that there must exist a protocol τ_2' simulating τ_1' on inputs drawn from μ with error at most $\rho + \alpha$ and

$$\begin{aligned}\mathsf{CC}(\tau_2') &\leq O\left(\sqrt{\mathsf{CC}(\tau_1')\mathsf{IC}^i{}_\mu(\tau_1')}\log(\mathsf{CC}(\tau_1')/\alpha)/\alpha\right) \\ &= O\left(\sqrt{\mathsf{CC}(\pi)\mathsf{CC}(\pi)/n}\log(\mathsf{CC}(\pi)/\alpha)/\alpha\right) \\ &= O\left(\frac{\mathsf{CC}(\pi)\log(\mathsf{CC}(\pi)/\alpha)/\alpha}{\sqrt{n}}\right)\end{aligned}$$

Finally we get a protocol for computing f by first running τ_2' and then running the last $2\log K$ bits of π. Thus we must have that $O\left(\frac{\mathsf{CC}(\pi)\log(\mathsf{CC}(\pi)/\alpha)/\alpha}{\sqrt{n}}\right) + 2\log K \leq D^\mu_{\rho+\alpha}(f)$, as in the theorem. □

5. COMPRESSION ACCORDING TO THE INTERNAL INFORMATION COST

THEOREM 1 (RESTATED) There is a universal constant c such that for every distribution μ, every protocol π, and every $\epsilon > 0$, there exists functions π_x, π_y, and a protocol τ such that $|\pi_x(X, \tau(X,Y)) - \pi(X,Y)| < \epsilon$, $\Pr[\pi_x(X, \tau(X,Y)) \neq \pi_y(Y, \tau(X,Y))] < \epsilon$ and

$$\mathsf{CC}(\tau) \leq c\sqrt{\mathsf{CC}(\pi) \cdot \mathsf{IC}^i{}_\mu(\pi)} \frac{\log(\mathsf{CC}(\pi)/\epsilon)}{\epsilon} .$$

Proof sketch. Here is a high level sketch of the proof. Let μ be a distribution over $\mathcal{X} \times \mathcal{Y}$. Let π be a public coin protocol that does some computation using the inputs X, Y drawn according to μ. Our goal is to give a protocol τ that simulates π on μ such that[5]

$$\mathsf{CC}(\tau) = O\left(\sqrt{\mathsf{CC}(\pi) \cdot \mathsf{IC}^i{}_\mu(\pi)}\log(\mathsf{CC}(\pi))\right) .$$

For the sake of simplicity, here we assume that the protocol π has no public randomness. π then specifies a protocol tree which is a binary tree of depth $\mathsf{CC}(\pi)$ where every non-leaf node w is owned by one of the players, whose turn is to speak in this node. Each non leaf node has a "0 child" and a "1 child". For every such node w in the tree and every possible message $b \in \{0,1\}$, the X player gets input x and uses this to define $O_{w,x}(b)$ as the probability in π that conditioned on reaching the node w and the input being x, the next bit will be b. The Y player defines $O_{w,y}(b)$ analogously.

[5]We identify the communication complexity of the protocols π, τ with their expected communication under μ, as by adding a small error, the two can be related using an easy Markov argument.

Note that if w is owned by the X player, then $O_{w,x}(b)$ is exactly the correct probability with which b is transmitted in the real protocol.

For every such node w, the players use public randomness to sample a shared random number $\kappa_w \in [0,1]$ for every non-leaf node w in the tree. The X player uses these numbers to define the child $C_x(w)$ for every node w as follows: if $O_{w,x}(1) < \kappa_w$, $C_x(w)$ is set to the 0 child of w, and is set to the 1 child otherwise. The Y Player does the same using the values $O_{w,y}(1)$ (but the same κ_w) instead.

Now let $v_0, \ldots, v_{\mathsf{CC}(\pi)}$ be the correct path in the tree. This is the path where every subsequent node was sampled by the player that owned the previous node: for every i,

$$v_{i+1} = \begin{cases} C_x(v_i) & \text{if X player owns } v_i \\ C_y(v_i) & \text{if Y player owns } v_i \end{cases}$$

$v_{\mathsf{CC}(\pi)}$ has the same distribution as a leaf in π was supposed to have, and the goal of the players will be to identify $v_{\mathsf{CC}(\pi)}$ with small communication.

In order to do this, the X player will compute the sequence of nodes $v_0^x, \ldots, v_{\mathsf{CC}(\pi)}^x$ by setting $v_{i+1}^x = C_x(v_i^x)$. Similarly, the Y player computes the path $v_0^y, \ldots, v_{\mathsf{CC}(\pi)}^y$ by setting $v_{i+1}^y = C_y(v_i^y)$. Observe that if these two paths agree on the first k nodes, then they must be equal to the correct path upto the first k nodes.

So far, the parties have not communicated at all. Now the parties communicate to find the first index i for which $v_i^x \neq v_i^y$. If $v_{i-1} = v_{i-1}^x = v_{i-1}^y$ was owned by the X player, the parties reset the i'th node in their paths to v_i^x. Similarly, if v_{i-1} was owned by the Y player, the parties reset their i'th node to be v_i^y. In this way, they keep fixing their paths until they have computed the correct path.

Thus the communication complexity of the new protocol is bounded by the number of mistakes times the communication complexity of finding a single mistake. Every path in the tree is specified by a $\mathsf{CC}(\pi)$-bit string, and finding the first inconsistency reduces to the problem of finding the first difference in two $\mathsf{CC}(\pi)$-bit strings. A simple protocol of Feige et al [FPRU94] (based on hashing and binary search) gives a protocol for finding this first inconsistency, with communication only $O(\log \mathsf{CC}(\pi))$. We show that if we are at node v_i in the protocol and the next bit has ϵ information, then the probability that $\Pr[C_x(v_i) \neq C_y(v_i)] \leq \sqrt{\epsilon}$. Since the total internal information cost is $\mathsf{IC}^{\mathsf{i}}_{\mu}(\pi)$, we can use the Cauchy-Schwartz inequality to bound the expected number of mistakes by $\sqrt{\mathsf{CC}(\pi)\mathsf{IC}^{\mathsf{i}}_{\mu}(\pi)}$.

6. COMPRESSION ACCORDING TO THE EXTERNAL INFORMATION COST

In this section we demonstrate how to compress protocols according to the information learnt by an observer watching the protocol. We shall sketch the proof of Theorem 2.

THEOREM 2 (RESTATED). For every distribution μ, every protocol π, and every $\alpha > 0$, there exists functions π_x, π_y, and a protocol τ such that $|\pi_x(X, \tau(X,Y)) - \pi(X,Y)| < \alpha$, $\Pr[\pi_x(X,\tau(X,Y)) \neq \pi_y(Y,\tau(X,Y))] < \alpha$ and

$$\mathsf{CC}(\tau) \leq O\left(\mathsf{IC}^{\mathsf{o}}{}_{\mu}(\pi)\frac{\operatorname{polylog}(\mathsf{CC}(\pi)/\alpha)}{\alpha^2}\right).$$

Proof sketch of Theorem 2. Given a function f, distribution μ and protocol π, we want to come up with a protocol τ simulating π such that $\mathsf{CC}(\tau) = \tilde{O}(\mathsf{IC}^{\mathsf{o}}{}_{\mu}(\pi))$. We assume that π is a private coin protocol, in this proof sketch, for simplicity. For every non-leaf node w we denote by O_w the probability of transmitting a 1 at the node w conditioned on reaching that node (without taking into consideration the actual values of the inputs to the protocol). We shall write $O_{w,x}$, $O_{w,y}$ to denote this probability conditioned on a particular fixing of x or y, and conditioned on the event of reaching w during the run of the protocol. As a technical condition, we will assume that for every w, $O_{w,x}, O_{w,y} \in 1/2 \pm \beta$ for $\beta = 1/\operatorname{polylog}(\mathsf{CC}(\pi))$. This condition can be achieved for example by re-encoding π so that each party, instead of sending a bit b, sends $\operatorname{polylog}(\mathsf{CC}(\pi))$ random bits such that their majority is b.

For every node w owned by the X player, we define the *divergence at* w, denoted by D_w as $\mathbb{D}(O_{w,x}||O_w)$ where

$$\mathbb{D}(p||q) = p\log(p/q) + (1-p)\log((1-p)/(1-q))$$

equals the divergence (also known as the Kullback-Leibler divergence) between the p-biased coin and the q-biased coin. Given a node v, we define $\mathcal{B}_v$ to be the set of descendants w of v such that if we sum up $D_{w'}$ for all intermediate nodes w' on the path from v to w we get a total $< \beta$ but adding D_w makes the total at least β or w is a leaf. We define B_v to bo the distribution over $\mathcal{B}_v$ that is induced by following the probabilities $O_{w'}$ along the path. Note that this distribution is known to both parties. We define B_{vx} to be the distribution obtained by assigning the probability of an edge according to $O_{w,x}$ for nodes owned by the x player and O_w for nodes owned by the y player. Similarly we define the distribution B_{vy}.

The protocol proceeds as follows: (initially v is set to the root of the tree, t below is some large constant)

1. Both parties use their shared randomness to obtain a random element w according to the distribution B_v. (This involves first sampling a random leaf and then using binary search to find the first location in which the divergence surpasses β.)

2. The X player sends a bit a_1 that equals 1 with probability $\min\{1, B_{vx}(w)/(tB_v(w)\}$.

3. The Y player sends a bit a_2 that equals 1 with probability $\min\{1, B_{vy}(w)/(tB_v(w)\}$.

4. If $a_1 = a_2 = 1$ then they set $v = w$. If v is a leaf they end the protocol, otherwise to go back to Step 1.

To get a rough idea why this protocol makes sense, consider the case that all the nodes in $\mathcal{B}_v$ are two levels below v, with the first node (i.e., v) owned by the X player, and the node in the intermediate level owned by the Y player. For a node $w \in \mathcal{B}_v$, let $B_{vxy}(w)$ be the true probability of arriving at w, and let $\tilde{B}(w) = B_v(w)$ be the estimated probability. Fixing w, we write $B(w) = B_1B_2$ and $\tilde{B}(w) = \tilde{B}_1\tilde{B}_2$, where B_i denotes the true probability that step i is taken according to w, and $\tilde{B}_i$ denotes this probability as estimated by an observer who does not know x, y.

The probability that w is output at the end of Step 1 is $\tilde{B}_1\tilde{B}_2$. Now assume that the threshold t is set high enough so that we can assume that $tB_v(w) > B_{vx}(w), B_{vy}(y)$ with high probability. In this case the probability that w is accepted equals

$$\Pr[a_1 = 1]\Pr[a_2 = 1] = \left(\frac{B_1\tilde{B}_2}{t\tilde{B}_1\tilde{B}_2}\right)\left(\frac{\tilde{B}_1 B_2}{t\tilde{B}_1\tilde{B}_2}\right) = \frac{B_1 B_2}{t^2\tilde{B}_1\tilde{B}_2} \quad (1)$$

thus the total probability that w is output is $\tilde{B}_1\tilde{B}_2$ times (1) which is exactly its correct probability B_1B_2 divided by t^2, and hence we get a multiplicative overhead of t^2, but output the right distribution over w.

7. DISCUSSION AND OPEN PROBLEMS

The main problem that remains open is whether optimal, or near-optimal compression is possible for protocols in the general setting.

Open Problem: Is there a generic way to convert any two-party protocol π over a general distribution μ into a protocol that uses only $O(\mathsf{IC}^{\mathsf{i}}{}_{\mu}(\pi))$ bits of communication?

An affirmative answer would show that the communication complexity of f^n is $\Omega(n)$ times as high as the communication complexity of f. Curiously enough, it turns out [BR] that the converse is true as well, and the problem above is *complete* for randomized communication direct sum — one can show that if there is no such compression scheme, then there is a (partial) function U for which a direct sum theorem fails to hold.[6] In this function U, each player gets as input a protocol tree, as well as the probabilities for all the nodes he owns, and the output is simply the output of the protocol. Unfortunately, by design, information theoretic techniques seem to be powerless in proving lower bounds for U.

Acknowledgements

We thank Noga Alon, Emanuel Milman, Alex Samorodnitsky, Avi Wigderson and Amir Yehudayoff for useful discussions.

8. REFERENCES

[BR] M. Braverman and A. Rao. Work in progress.

[BYJKS04] Z. Bar-Yossef, T. S. Jayram, R. Kumar, and D. Sivakumar. An information statistics approach to data stream and communication complexity. *Journal of Computer and System Sciences*, 68(4):702–732, 2004.

[CSWY01] A. Chakrabarti, Y. Shi, A. Wirth, and A. Yao. Informational complexity and the direct sum problem for simultaneous message complexity. In B. Werner, editor, *Proceedings of the 42nd Annual IEEE Symposium on Foundations of Computer Science*, pages 270–278, Los Alamitos, CA, Oct. 14–17 2001. IEEE Computer Society.

[CT91] T. M. Cover and J. A. Thomas. *Elements of Information Theory.* Wiley series in telecommunications. J. Wiley and Sons, New York, 1991.

[6]In a partial function/promise problem the protocol only needs to compute the function if the pair of inputs comes from some subset. Our results in this paper for information measured according to the viewpoint of the players carry over to promise problems as well.

[FKNN91] T. Feder, E. Kushilevitz, M. Naor, and N. Nisan. Amortized communication complexity. *SIAM Journal on Computing*, 24(4):736–750, 1995. Prelim version by Feder, Kushilevitz, Naor FOCS 1991.

[FPRU94] U. Feige, D. Peleg, P. Raghavan, and E. Upfal. Computing with noisy information. *SIAM Journal on Computing*, 23(5):1001–1018, 1994.

[GF81] G. Galbiati and M. Fischer. On the complexity of 2-output boolean networks. *Theor. Comput. Sci.*, 16:177–185, 1981.

[HJMR07] P. Harsha, R. Jain, D. A. McAllester, and J. Radhakrishnan. The communication complexity of correlation. In *IEEE Conference on Computational Complexity*, pages 10–23. IEEE Computer Society, 2007.

[JRS03] R. Jain, J. Radhakrishnan, and P. Sen. A direct sum theorem in communication complexity via message compression. In J. C. M. Baeten, J. K. Lenstra, J. Parrow, and G. J. Woeginger, editors, *ICALP*, volume 2719 of *Lecture Notes in Computer Science*, pages 300–315. Springer, 2003.

[Kla10] H. Klauck. A strong direct product theorem for disjointness. In *STOC*, 2010.

[KN97] E. Kushilevitz and N. Nisan. *Communication complexity.* Cambridge University Press, Cambridge, 1997.

[KRW91] M. Karchmer, R. Raz, and A. Wigderson. Super-logarithmic depth lower bounds via the direct sum in communication complexity. *Computational Complexity*, 5(3/4):191–204, 1995. Prelim version CCC 1991.

[New91] I. Newman. Private vs. common random bits in communication complexity. *Information Processing Letters*, 39(2):67–71, 31 July 1991.

[Pau76] W. Paul. Realizing boolean functions on disjoint sets of variables. *Theor. Comput. Sci.*, 2:383–396, 1976.

[Raz92] Razborov. On the distributed complexity of disjointness. *TCS: Theoretical Computer Science*, 106, 1992.

[Raz95] R. Raz. A parallel repetition theorem. *SIAM Journal on Computing*, 27(3):763–803, June 1998. Prelim version in STOC '95.

[Sha48] C. E. Shannon. A mathematical theory of communication. *Bell System Technical Journal*, 27, 1948. Monograph B-1598.

[Sha03] R. Shaltiel. Towards proving strong direct product theorems. *Computational Complexity*, 12(1-2):1–22, 2003.

[Uhl74] D. Uhlig. On the synthesis of self-correcting schemes from functional elements with a small number of reliable elements. *Matematicheskie Zametki*, 15(6):937–944, 1974.

[Yao82] A. C.-C. Yao. Theory and applications of trapdoor functions (extended abstract). In *FOCS*, pages 80–91. IEEE, 1982.

A Strong Direct Product Theorem for Disjointness

[Extended Abstract] *

Hartmut Klauck
Centre for Quantum Technologies and
SPMS, Nanyang Technological University
Singapore
hklauck@gmail.com

ABSTRACT

A strong direct product theorem states that if we want to compute k independent instances of a function, using less than k times the resources needed for one instance, then the overall success probability will be exponentially small in k. We establish such a theorem for the randomized communication complexity of the Disjointness problem, i.e., with communication $const \cdot kn$ the success probability of solving k instances of size n can only be exponentially small in k. This solves an open problem of [KSW07, LSS08]. We also show that this bound even holds for AM-communication protocols with limited ambiguity.

The main result implies a new lower bound for Disjointness in a restricted 3-player NOF protocol, and optimal communication-space tradeoffs for Boolean matrix product.

Our main result follows from a solution to the dual of a linear programming problem, whose feasibility comes from a so-called Intersection Sampling Lemma that generalizes a result by Razborov [Raz92].

Categories and Subject Descriptors

F.1 [**Theory of Computation**]: Computation by Abstract Devices; F.2 [**Theory of Computation**]: Analysis of Algorithms and Problem Complexity

General Terms

Theory

Keywords

complexity theory, lower bounds, communication complexity, direct product theorems, disjointness problem, communication-space tradeoffs

*A full version of this paper is available at `http://arxiv.org/abs/0908.2940`

1. INTRODUCTION

1.1 Direct product theorems

One of the fundamental questions that can be asked in any model of computation is how well computing several instances of the same problem can be composed. Are significant savings possible when computing the same function f on k independent inputs? Or is it true that the optimal way to do this is to run the same algorithm independently k times?

This question can be asked for any measure of complexity and is usually referred to as the *direct sum problem*. In this paper we consider the model of randomized communication complexity. A protocol between players Alice and Bob is given k inputs $(x_1, y_1), \ldots, (x_k, y_k)$, and has to output the vector of k answers $f(x_1, y_1), \ldots, f(x_k, y_k)$. The question is how the protocol can optimally distribute its resources among the k input instances it needs to compute. In this setting we are not only concerned with the overall communication, but also with the achievable success probability. If the trivial way of computing f for k input instances by running the same protocol k times independently is really optimal, then we should expect the success probability σ to go down exponentially with k.

Such statements can come in two flavors. First, if every protocol with communication c has constant error probability when computing just *one* instance of f, then for computing k instances with communication c we expect σ to be exponentially small in k. If this is the case for a function f, we say that a *weak* direct product theorem holds for f. If this is the case for *all* functions, we say that a weak direct product theorem holds in general.

However, even if we allow our protocol to use communication kc we might expect σ to be exponentially small in k, unless the protocol could somehow correlate its computation on several instances for all possible choices of inputs. If such a statement is true we call it a *strong* direct product theorem (SDPT).

Strong direct product theorems are usually hard to prove and sometimes not even true. In particular Shaltiel [Sha01] exhibits a general setup in which strong direct product theorems cannot be expected, and in fact even direct sum theorems (in which we do not care about the success probability but only about the scaling of the complexity with k) do not hold. His main argument is that in the distributional complexity setting one can construct functions f for which there is a "hard core" of some size ϵ that cannot be ignored when allowing only error probability $\epsilon/3$ (making computing one instance hard), yet given k instances only roughly ϵk of them will be in the hard core, and we can re-allocate most of our resources to those. By construction f is trivial outside the hard core and we can easily solve the other instances. Altogether this approach uses roughly ϵk times the resources needed for one instance while having very small overall error. The main conclusion of this example should be that when proving direct sum type statements in the distributional setting one should expect to lose a factor of ϵ in the complexity bound.

An incomplete list of examples of "positive" results about DPT's are Nisan et al.'s [NRS94] strong direct product theorem for "decision forests", Parnafes et al.'s [PRW97] direct product theorem for "forests" of communication protocols, Shaltiel's strong direct product theorems for "fair" decision trees and for the discrepancy bound for communication complexity under the uniform distribution [Sha01], Lee et al.'s analogous result for arbitrary distributions [LSS08], Viola and Wigderson's extension to the multiparty case [VW08], Ambainis et al.'s SDPT for the quantum query complexity of symmetric functions [ASW09], Jain et al.'s SDPT for subdistribution bounds in communication complexity [JKN08], Ben-Aroya et al.'s SDPT for the quantum one-way communication complexity of the Index function [BRW08], Impagliazzo et al.'s DPT for uniform circuits [IJKW08] and several more. In a similar vein are "XOR"-lemmas like Yao's [Yao82]. "Direct Sum" results which state that k times the resources are needed without the success probability deterioration are also important in communication complexity, see [KN97, BBCR10].

In this paper we focus on the Disjointness problem in communication complexity. Suppose Alice has an n-bit input x and Bob has an n-bit input y. These x and y represent sets, and $\mathrm{DISJ}_n(x,y) = 1$ iff those sets are disjoint. Note that DISJ_n is the negation of $\mathrm{NDISJ}_n = \mathrm{OR}_n(x \wedge y)$, where $x \wedge y$ is the n-bit string obtained by bitwise AND-ing x and y. In many ways, NDISJ_n plays a central role in communication complexity. In particular, it is "NP complete" [BFS86] in the communication complexity world. The communication complexity of NDISJ_n has been well studied: e.g. it takes $\Theta(n)$ bits of communication classically [KS92, Raz92] and $\Theta(\sqrt{n})$ quantumly [AA03, Raz03].

For the case where Alice and Bob want to compute k instances of Disjointness, we establish a strong direct product theorem in Section 3:

> **SDPT for randomized communication complexity:**
> Every randomized protocol that computes $\mathrm{NDISJ}_n^{(k)}$ using $T \leq \beta k n$ bits of communication has worst-case success probability $\sigma = 2^{-\Omega(k)}$.

Note that the same result holds for DISJ_n by symmetry. Previously, Klauck et al. [KSW07] proved that the same success probability bound holds when the communication is $\beta k \sqrt{n}$ (but even in the quantum case). The same bound was obtained by Beame et al. [BPSW06] for randomized communication, and they give an SDPT for the *rectangle bound* under product distributions (under such distributions DISJ_n has complexity $\sqrt{n}$). The rectangle bound appears in the literature also under the name *corruption bound* [Yao83, K03, BPSW06]. Klauck [K04] also showed a weak DPT for the rectangle bound under *all* distributions, which implies that with communication βn the success probability goes down exponentially in k.

Our approach is as follows. First we massage the problem in a very similar manner as in [KSW07]. This leads to the problem of finding k elements in the intersection of two N bit strings. Since these can easily be verified, we can assume that the protocol either gives up or produces correct outputs. We are interested in the tradeoff between success probability and communication.

The next step is to formulate a linear program that corresponds to a relaxation of an integer program expressing a convex combination of partitions of the communication matrix with the desired acceptance probabilities. Similar programs have been considered before by Lovász [L90] and by Karchmer et al. [KKN95], but have rarely been used to bound randomized communication complexity. The program expresses that we can detect inputs x, y with intersection size k with "high" probability, while not accepting inputs with smaller intersection size at all, and, trivially but importantly, accepting the remaining inputs with probability at most 1. This extra constraint expresses the fact that we do not talk about covers of the communication matrix, but partitions. Unsurprisingly we prove the lower bound by exhibiting a solution to the dual.

To prove feasibility of the dual solution we provide what we call the intersection sampling lemma. This lemma is a generalization of Razborov's main lemma from [Raz92] and follows from it by a rather simple induction argument. The intersection sampling lemma states that (for suitable distributions) any rectangle that is large among the disjoint x, y is also large for inputs that have intersection size k. This is true for every k, losing a 2^k factor. Razborov's Lemma is essentially the same statement for $k = 1$.

1.2 Applications

1.2.1 Communication-Space Tradeoffs

Our main result has some applications to other problems. First, we consider communication-space tradeoffs. Research on communication-space tradeoffs has been initiated by Lam et al. [LTT92] in a restricted setting, and by Beame et al. [BTY94] in a general model of space-bounded communication complexity. In the setting of communication-space tradeoffs, players Alice and Bob are space bounded circuits, and we are interested in the communication cost when given particular space bounds.

We study the problems of *Boolean matrix-vector product* and *Boolean matrix product*. In the first problem there are an $N \times N$ matrix A (input to Alice) and a vector b of dimension N (input to Bob), and the goal is to compute the vector $c = Ab$, where $c_i = \vee_{j=1}^{n} (A[i,j] \wedge b_j)$. In the problem of matrix multiplication two input matrices have to be multiplied with the analogous Boolean product.

Time-space tradeoffs for Boolean matrix-vector multiplication have been analyzed in an average case scenario by Abrahamson [Abr90], whose results give a worst case lower bound of $TS = \Omega\left(N^{3/2}\right)$ for classical algorithms. He conjectured that a worst case lower bound of $TS = \Omega(N^2)$ holds, which was later confirmed in [KSW07].

Beame et al. [BTY94] gave tight lower bounds for communication-space tradeoffs for the matrix-vector product and matrix product over finite fields, but stated the complexity of Boolean matrix-vector multiplication as an open problem. Klauck [K04] generalized the results for finite fields to the quantum case, but also showed the following lower bounds for the Boolean product and randomized protocols: for matrix-vector product $CS^2 = \Omega(N^2)$, and for matrix-matrix product $CS^2 = \Omega(N^3)$. Using our direct product result we are now able to show that any randomized protocol for matrix-vector product satisfies $CS = \Omega(N^2)$, and for matrix-matrix product $CS = \Omega(N^3)$. These bounds match the trivial upper bounds.

1.2.2 Multiparty Communication

Consider the Nondisjointness problem in the 3 player number-on-the-forehead setting, i.e., Alice sees inputs y, z Bob sees x, z and Charlie sees x, y. They have to decide whether there is an index i such that $x_i = y_i = z_i = 1$. Lee and Shraibman [LS09] as well as Chattopadhyay and Ada [CA08] show that the randomized complexity of this problem is $\Omega(n^{1/4})$. Prior to these results larger bounds were shown for models in which the interaction between the players is restricted. In particular, in the model with one-way communication, Viola and Wigderson show a $\Omega(\sqrt{n})$ lower bound [VW07], and in the model, where Charlie sends a single message, followed by an arbitrary protocol between Alice and Bob, Beame et al. [BPSW06] show an $\Omega(n^{1/3})$ lower bound, which was later simplified by Ben-Aroya et al. [BRW08]. Using our main theorem we can show that the latter type of protocol actually needs communication $\Omega(\sqrt{n})$.

1.3 The Smooth Rectangle Bound

Our main result is proved by giving a solution to the dual of a linear program. While this program is tailor made for the problem at hand, this is a general approach described e.g. in [L90, KKN95].

In [L90] Lovász in describes such a LP-based lower bound method for randomized protocols, which can be seen to be equivalent to the rectangle bound (for a proof see [JK10]). Adding a seemingly trivial constraint to the LP described by Lovász in gives a more powerful lower bound method (via the dual), by using the fact that protocols *partition* the inputs into rectangles instead of covering them. The lower bound method is similar to the rectangle bound, but allows the use of negative weights for a small fraction of the 1-inputs. We refer to this enhanced LP-based lower bound method as the *smooth rectangle bound*, because it can be seen as a maximum of the rectangle bounds achievable by functions that are close to the function f we are interested in. The smooth rectangle bound is defined and explored in [JK10]. The linear program that we use to establish our main result also uses the partition property crucially, and in fact, Lemma 1 could not be established using the rectangle bound.

The smooth rectangle bound relates to the rectangle bound similar to the way the generalized discrepancy method (introduced by [S08, K07] and named so in [CA08]) relates to the standard discrepancy bound (both methods are lower bounds on quantum communication, and the generalized discrepancy is in fact equivalent to Linial and Shraibman's (approximate) γ_2-measure [LiS09]).

We can pinpoint the power of the smooth rectangle bound more closely by observing that it actually lower bounds unambiguous AM-protocols. Indeed our main result also holds for AM-protocols with ambiguity $2^{\epsilon k}$. Note that NDISJ$_n$ has very efficient nondeterministic protocols (and so does its k-fold), so the lower bound really comes from the partition constraints. In particular we show that any unambiguous AM-protocol for NDISJ$_n$ needs linear communication (while nondeterministic protocols need communication $O(\log n)$).

2. PRELIMINARIES

2.1 Some Definitions on Communication Complexity

The protocols we consider are in the standard two-player model [Yao79, KN97] unless stated otherwise. The randomized protocols we consider are public coin protocols. Success probability of a protocol is defined to be the probability over the coins to compute the correct output for a worst case input. Note that we require both players to agree on a common output.

A nondeterministic protocol for a Boolean function f is a cover of the 1-inputs in the communication matrix of f with 1-chromatic rectangles, its cost is the logarithm of the number of rectangles used. Alternatively, a nondeterministic protocol can be viewed as a proof system, in which a prover sends a proof to Alice, after which Alice and Bob verify the proof. In a valid protocol for all 1-inputs there exists a proof that is accepted, and for all 0-inputs all proofs are rejected. The cost is the amount of communication between Alice and Bob. A nondeterministic protocol with ambiguity t is a nondeterministic protocol in which each 1-input has no more than t different proofs. For $t = 1$ such protocols are called unambiguous.

Karchmer et al. [KNSW94] have shown that nondeterministic protocols with ambiguity t have complexity at least $\Omega(\sqrt{D(f)}/t)$. Also the rank lower bound holds for unambiguous protocols.

In the case that we want to compute a k-tuple of Boolean functions by a nondeterministic protocol, we assume that the prover wants to convince Alice and Bob of the fact that $f(x_i, y_i) = 1$ for as many i as possible. Such a protocol is correct, if for all $x_1, y_1, \ldots, x_k, y_k$ such that $f(x_i, x_i) = 1$ for all $i \in I \subseteq \{1, \ldots, k\}$ there is a proof such that Alice and Bob agree on output $o_1, \ldots, o_k$ with $o_i = 1 \iff i \in I$, while for no $i \notin I$ there exists a proof such that $o_i = 1$ will be an output. Note that in this definition we never require the prover to convince Alice and Bob of the fact that $f(x_i, y_i) = 0$ for any position i, so this is genuine one-sided nondeterminism for many-output problems.

In other words every nondeterministic protocol with ambiguity t is a collection of at most 2^c rectangles each labeled by an output sequence such that for each input $x_1, y_1, \ldots, x_k, y_k$ and each rectangle R with output $o_1, \ldots, o_k$ containing that input: $o_i \leq f(x_i, y_i)$ for all i, and there exists a rectangle containing the input where $o_i = f(x_i, y_i)$ for all i. Furthermore each input is contained in at most t such rectangles. The communication cost is then c.

An Arthur-Merlin communication protocol (first suggested in [BFS86]) with ambiguity t and communication c is a convex combination of a set of nondeterministic protocols P_i, each occurring with probability p_i. Each nondeterministic protocol is a collection of at most 2^c rectangles each labeled by an output sequence and each input is contained in at most t such rectangles per P_i. We require that for each input $x_1, y_1, \ldots, x_k, y_k$ with probability at least $1 - \epsilon$ the protocol P_i has $x_1, y_1, \ldots, x_k, y_k$ in some rectangle labeled

$f(x_1, y_1), \ldots, f(x_k, y_k)$, whereas with probability at most ϵ a P_i contains the input in a rectangle labeled with $o_j = 1$ while $f(x_j, y_j) = 0$ for some i. An AM-protocol with ambiguity 1 is called unambiguous (note that for different values of the public coin different proofs are allowed for the same input).

2.2 Communicating Circuits

In the standard model of communication complexity Alice and Bob are computationally unbounded entities, but we are also interested in what happens if they have bounded memory, i.e., they work with a bounded amount of storage. To this end we model Alice and Bob as communicating circuits. In short, these circuits place no restrictions on local gates, but require the number of bits stored locally to be bounded. Communication is the number of wires crossing between Alice and Bob's part of the circuit. We refer the reader to the full version of the paper for the definitions regarding the model of communicating circuits.

3. THE DIRECT PRODUCT THEOREM

In this section we formally state and prove our main result.

3.1 Massaging the Problem

In this section we bring the k-fold NDISJ$_n$ problem into anther form that will be easier to handle. More precisely, we will consider the following three problems. We freely identify strings $x \in \{0,1\}^n$ with the sets they are characteristic vectors of.

DEFINITION 1. *1. NDISJ$_n^{(k)}$ is the problem, given k pairs of strings x_i, y_i of length n each, to compute the k-tuple of function values of NDISJ$_n$ on these.*

2. SEARCH$_n^{(k)}$ is the problem, given k pairs of strings x_i, y_i of length n each, to find indices $j_1, \ldots, j_k$, such that x_i and y_i intersect in j_i. If x_i and y_i are disjoint, output 0 for position i.

3. SEARCH$_{\binom{N}{k}}$ is the problem, given two strings x, y of length N, to find k indices $j_1, \ldots, j_k$, such that x and y intersect in all j_i. If $|x \cap y| < k$ output 0.

We will prove that problem 3) is hard in the following subsections and state the result now.

LEMMA 1 (MAIN). *There are constants $0 < \alpha, \beta, \gamma \leq 1$ such that every randomized protocol with communication βN for the problem SEARCH$_{\binom{N}{k}}$ with $k \leq \gamma N$ has success probability at most $2^{-\alpha k}$.*

We now establish that the first two problems are also at least as hard as 3) by reductions very similar to the analogous reductions in [KSW07].

THEOREM 2 (SDPT FOR SEARCH). *There are constants $0 < \alpha', \beta \leq 1$ such that every randomized protocol with communication βkn for the problem SEARCH$_n^{(k)}$ has success probability at most $2^{-\alpha' k}$.*

PROOF. We show that a protocol for SEARCH$_n^{(k)}$ can be used to solve SEARCH$_{\binom{N}{K}}$ for $K = \alpha k/4$ and $N = kn$. Fix a protocol P for SEARCH$_n^{(k)}$ with success probability σ. Now consider the following protocol that acts on N-bit inputs x, y:

1. Apply a uniformly random permutation π to x and to y.
2. Run P on $\pi(x)$, $\pi(y)$.
3. If P makes at least $\alpha k/4$ outputs $\neq 0$, then output any $\alpha k/4$ of them (after undoing π).
4. Otherwise output 0.

This protocol P' uses the same communication as P. Note that P' will work correctly and solve SEARCH$_{\binom{N}{\alpha k/4}}$, whenever P makes no errors and at least $\alpha k/4$ positions i with $x_i = y_i = 1$ end up in different blocks after applying the permutation π (so that they can be produced as outputs by P), assuming that $\alpha k/4$ such positions exist.

The probability of at least $\alpha k/4$ positions i with $x_i = y_i = 1$ being in different blocks (assuming that so many exist) is at least

$$\frac{N}{N} \cdot \frac{N-n}{N-1} \cdots \frac{N - \alpha(k/4)n + 1}{N - \alpha(k/4) + 1} \geq (1 - \alpha/4)^{\alpha k/4}.$$

So the success probability of P' is at least $\sigma \cdot (1-\alpha/4)^{\alpha k/4}$ which defines α' via

$$2^{-\alpha K} = 2^{-\alpha \cdot (\alpha k/4)} \geq 2^{-\alpha' k} \cdot (1 - \alpha/4)^{\alpha k/4}.$$

This allows us to choose a constant $\alpha' > 0$, since $(1 - \alpha/4)^{\alpha/4} \geq 2^{-\alpha^2/8}$ for $0 \leq \alpha < 1$.

The above argument only works, if $\alpha k/4 \leq \gamma N \iff n \geq \alpha/(4\gamma)$. Since the right hand side involves only constants the opposite case can be covered by assuming $n = O(1)$, i.e., we now have to show that solving many size $O(1)$ instances is hard. But when the communication is less than $\epsilon k = \Theta(kn)$, it can easily be shown via an information theoretic argument, that it is impossible to solve SEARCH$_n^{(k)}$ with better success than $2^{-\Omega(k)}$: under the uniform distribution the players don't communicate enough to agree on a set of k outputs of sufficient entropy. □

THEOREM 3 (SDPT FOR NDISJ$_n$). *There are constants $0 < \alpha'', \beta'' \leq 1$ such that every randomized protocol for NDISJ$_n^{(k)}$ with $\beta'' kn$ communication has success probability $\sigma \leq 2^{-\alpha'' k}$.*

PROOF. A protocol P for NDISJ$_n^{(k)}$ with success probability σ and communication $C \leq \beta'' kn$ can be used to build a protocol P' for SEARCH$_n^{(k)}$ with slightly worse success probability:

1. Run P on the original inputs and remember which blocks are accepted.
2. Run simultaneously (at most k) binary searches on the accepted blocks for a limited number of steps that halve the search space. Stop after $s = 2\log(1/\beta'')$ such steps. Each iteration is computed by running P on the parts of the blocks that are known to contain a position j with $x_i(j) = y_i(j) = 1$, halving the remaining instance size each time.
3. Run the trivial protocol on each of the remaining parts of the instances to look for an intersection there (each remaining part has size $n/2^s$).

This new protocol P' uses communication $(s+1)C+kn/2^s = O(\beta'' \log(1/\beta'')kn)$. With probability at least σ^{s+1}, P succeeds in all iterations, in which case P' solves $\text{SEARCH}_n^{(k)}$.

So setting β'' such that $\beta \geq O(\beta'' \log(1/\beta''))$ and $\alpha'' = \alpha'/(s+1)$ we get the desired reduction. □

3.2 Our Approach

In order to establish Lemma 1 we need to use a new approach to prove lower bounds in communication complexity. To see this we discuss the main techniques available. The rectangle bound cannot be used to prove Lemma 1, because there exist large monochromatic rectangles for all possible outputs except rejection, since the problem has low nondeterministic complexity: simply guess k outputs and check. While large rectangles for the inputs that must be rejected need to have at least constant error due to Razborov's lower bound for the distributional complexity of DISJ_n [Raz92], simply considering those inputs cannot establish the error bound we seek. So the rectangle bounds appears to be unsuitable for our purpose. Note, however, that it might be possible to establish the strong direct product theorem for DISJ_n using the rectangle bound, but our approach via Lemma 1 cannot go this way.

Another main method for proving lower bounds for randomized communication complexity is the γ_2/generalized discrepancy method due to Linial and Shraibman/Sherstov [LiS09, S08] (and inspired by earlier work in [K07]). However, since these lower bounds work in the quantum setting, they cannot improve upon the tight quantum bounds in [KSW07].

Finally one could employ information theoretic techniques like in [BKKS04]. However, proving direct product statements with such methods seems to be difficult.

We show our main result using a technique based on linear programming. In the dual picture we still have to argue that all rectangles have certain properties, however, this time we allow positive and negative weights instead of a single hard distribution. This expresses the extra constraints given to us by the fact that a protocol partitions the communication matrix into rectangles instead of just covering it.

In the next subsections we first describe our linear program, then define a costly solution to the dual, and finally prove that this solution is feasible.

3.3 The Linear Program

In this section we provide a linear program, whose value gives a lower bound on the communication complexity of solving $\text{SEARCH}_{\binom{n}{k}}$ with success probability σ. This will be our tool to establish Lemma 1.

So consider any protocol for $\text{SEARCH}_{\binom{n}{k}}$ with success probability σ. We can assume that the protocol either rejects, or outputs $i_1, \ldots, i_k$. In the latter case we require that the inputs x, y do actually intersect on those positions, or the other way around, that wrong outputs of this form have probability 0. This we can assume, because Alice and Bob can simply check an output, before making it "official". The communication overhead is just two bits to agree on the output being correct. Furthermore in this case every message sequence has a fixed particular set of outputs that Alice and Bob agree on, i.e., for any rectangle R that corresponds to a leaf of the communication tree (for any value of the random coins) there are k different positions $i_1, \ldots, i_k$ such that all inputs $x, y \in R$ intersect on them, or the protocol rejects (they need not be unique though). Otherwise the protocol would declare a non-rejecting output that is not correct for some inputs (note that by definition Alice and Bob must agree on an output in each terminal rectangle in the communication tree).

We can change such a protocol to a protocol with binary output in which inputs with intersection size k are accepted with probability $\geq \sigma$, whereas all inputs with intersection size smaller than k are accepted with probability 0. Furthermore on all inputs acceptance happens with probability at most 1. This latter trivial constraint is important in our proof. The linear program is now as follows. We have real variables w_R for *all* rectangles $R \subseteq \{0,1\}^n \times \{0,1\}^n$.

$$\min \sum_R w_R \quad \text{s.t.} \tag{1}$$

$$\text{for all } x, y \text{ with } |x \cap y| < k: \sum_{R: x,y \in R} w_R = 0 \tag{2}$$

$$\text{for all } x, y \text{ with } |x \cap y| = k: \sum_{R: x,y \in R} w_R \geq \sigma \tag{3}$$

$$\text{for all } x, y \text{ with } |x \cap y| \geq k: \sum_{R: x,y \in R} w_R \leq 1 \tag{4}$$

$$w_R \geq 0 \tag{5}$$

Let P be a randomized protocol with communication c and success probability σ for the problem of accepting inputs x, y with $|x \cap y| = k$ while rejecting inputs x, y with $|x \cap y| < k$ with certainty (acceptance probability on the other inputs does not matter). P can be used to create a solution to the above program with cost 2^c: P is a convex combination of deterministic protocols $P_1, \ldots, P_m$ with probabilities $p_1, \ldots, p_m$, and each deterministic protocol P_i corresponds to a partition of the inputs into 2^c rectangles. We restrict our attention to the rectangles on which protocols P_i accept. The weight w_R of a rectangle R is the sum of the p_i over all P_i in which R occurs as an accepting rectangle. Then for all inputs x, y the value $\sum_{R:x,y \in R} w_R$ is simply the acceptance probability of the protocol P, and the solution is feasible with cost 2^c. Hence for any σ the logarithm of the optimal cost of the program yields a lower bound on the necessary communication.

Recall that above we have not only required that the protocol P accepts inputs x, y that intersect in exactly k positions with some probability $\geq \sigma$, but we have also that for each accepting message sequence (i.e., each accepting rectangle R) there is a set of positions $I \subseteq \{1, \ldots, n\}$, $|I| = k$ such that for all inputs $x, y \in R$ we have $I \subseteq x \cap y$. Denote by $\mathcal{R}_v$ the set of all rectangles R for which there is an $I \subseteq \{1, \ldots, n\}$, $|I| = k$ such that all $x, y \in R$ satisfy $I \subseteq x \cap y$. We can hence restrict the rectangles R to come from $\mathcal{R}_v$ in our LP. This also makes the constraints (2) superfluous.

We now take the dual of the program (with restricted rectangle set $\mathcal{R}_v$) and then show a lower bound by exhibiting a feasible solution of high cost.

The dual is

$$\max \sum_{x,y} \sigma\phi_{x,y} + \psi_{x,y} \quad \text{s.t.} \tag{6}$$

$$\phi_{x,y} \geq 0 \tag{7}$$

$$\psi_{x,y} \leq 0 \tag{8}$$

$$\text{if } |x \cap y| \neq k \text{ then } \phi_{x,y} = 0 \tag{9}$$

$$\text{for all } R \in \mathcal{R}_v : \sum_{x,y \in R} \phi_{x,y} + \psi_{x,y} \leq 1 \tag{10}$$

The program asks us to put weights on the inputs, where inputs x, y with intersection size k should receive positive weights, and some other inputs negative weights. The constraints demand that all rectangles in $\mathcal{R}_v$ either have small weight or contain enough negative weight to cancel most of the positive weight (we will discuss this approach further in Section 5). However, we can only afford an overall amount of negative weight which is much smaller than the overall positive weight (by a factor of σ), because otherwise the objective function becomes negative. Negative weights make it easier to satisfy the rectangle constraints (10), but deteriorate the cost function. Note that later on we will prove that all rectangles are either small, or the inequality in (10) can even be made negative. This is similar to the standard argument occurring with the usual rectangle bound: rectangles are either small, or they have large error. In the LP formulation both possibilities are rolled into one statement.

Intuitively the LP formulation states that it is hard to cover the inputs with intersection size k while keeping the partition constraints (4) satisfied. Note that the primal without (4), but keeping (2) has a very simple solution of cost $\exp(k \log n)$, even for $\sigma = 1$. The issue with that solution is that it corresponds to a nondeterministic protocol, but not to a randomized one.

3.4 The Solution

Having found a dual program which will allow us to prove a lower bound, we start by defining distributions on inputs with different intersection sizes in a similar way to [Raz92].

Definition 2. *For $I = \{i_1, \ldots, i_k\} \subseteq \{1, \ldots, n\}$ with $|I| = k$ denote by $S_{I,n}$ the set of inputs $x, y \in \{0,1\}^n \times \{0,1\}^n$ such that $x \cap y = \{i_1, \ldots, i_k\}$. Furthermore let $T_{k,n} = \cup_{I:|I|=k} S_{I,n}$ denote the set of all inputs with intersection size k.*

$\mu_{k,n,m}$ is a distribution on $\{0,1\}^n \times \{0,1\}^n$. All $x, y \notin T_{k,n}$ have probability 0. Inputs in $T_{k,n}$ that also satisfy $|x| = |y| = m$ are chosen uniformly, i.e., with probability

$$\frac{1}{\binom{n}{m}\binom{m}{k}\binom{n-m}{m-k}}.$$

An easy calculation shows

Lemma 4.

$$\mu_{2k,n+k,m+k}(x,y) = \frac{\binom{n}{k}}{\binom{n+k}{2k}} \cdot \mu_{k,n,m}(x',y'),$$

$$\mu_{k,n+k,m+k}(x,y) = \frac{1}{\binom{n+k}{k}} \cdot \mu_{0,n,m}(x',y'),$$

$$\mu_{k,n,m}(x,y) = \frac{1}{\binom{n}{k}} \cdot \mu_{0,n-k,m-k}(x',y'),$$

$$\mu_{k+1,n,m}(x,y) = \frac{n-k}{\binom{n}{k+1}} \cdot \mu_{1,n-k,m-k}(x',y'),$$

where $x'y'$ are inputs resulting from x, y, when k intersecting positions are removed.

The solution to the dual program is based on the following intuition. Since the problem is symmetric, we should assign weights uniformly for all inputs x, y with a given intersection size (and set size). Naturally we put a good amount of positive weight on the inputs in $T_{k,n}$, and these are the only inputs with positive weights. We do not need to put negative weights on inputs with smaller intersection sizes, since we already restricted the set of viable rectangles to $\mathcal{R}_v$, hence those inputs appear in no rectangle in the program. All we need to do is to find a set of inputs to assign negative weights to, in order to enforce the rectangle constraints (the overall negative weight we can distribute is σ times the overall positive weight, and we hope that the program stays feasible with a large objective function for σ exponentially small in k). It turns out the $2k$-intersection inputs work just fine. This is because the $2k$-intersection inputs end up in many more rectangles than their weight suggests compared to the k-intersection inputs.

So we define a solution as follows (the input length is set to $n + k$ in the remainder of the section):

- The positive weight inputs are in $T_{k,n+k}$. Their weight is defined as $\phi_{x,y} = 2^{\beta n}\mu_{k,n+k,m+k}(x,y)$.
- The negative weight inputs are in $T_{2k,n+k}$. Their weight is $\psi_{x,y} = -2^{\beta n}2^{-\alpha k}\mu_{2k,n+k,m+k}(x,y)$.
- For all other inputs $x, y : \phi_{x,y} = \psi_{x,y} = 0$.

$\beta, \alpha > 0$ are some constants that we choose later. We can right away compute the value of this solution, before checking its feasibility. If we set $\sigma = 2^{-\alpha k+1}$, then the value is

$$\begin{aligned} &\sum_{x,y} \sigma\phi_{x,y} + \psi_{x,y} \\ = &\sum_{x,y \in T_{k,n+k}} \sigma 2^{\beta n}\mu_{k,n+k,m+k}(x,y) \\ - &\sum_{x,y \in T_{2k,n+k}} 2^{\beta n}2^{-\alpha k}\mu_{2k,n+k,m+k}(x,y) \\ = &\; 2^{\beta n}2^{-\alpha k}, \end{aligned}$$

since both μ's are distributions. So for $\alpha k \leq (\beta/2)n$ we get a linear lower bound on the communication, and we will require $k \leq \gamma n/2$ for some $\gamma \leq \beta$ and set $\alpha = 1/2$. Hence, all that remains to establish Lemma 1 is showing feasibility of our solution for these parameters.

The "sign" constraints (7,8,9) are obviously satisfied, so the only thing we need to check are the rectangle constraints (10). The following lemma is the main ingredient of the proof.

Lemma 5 (Intersection Sampling Lemma). *There is a constant $\gamma > 0$, such that for each rectangle $R = A \times B \subseteq \{0,1\}^n \times \{0,1\}^n$ with $\mu_{0,n,m}(R) \geq 2^{-\gamma n}$ and all $k \leq \gamma n/2$ we have $\mu_{k,n,m}(R) \geq \mu_{0,n,m}(R)/2^{k+1}$.*

This lemma is a generalization of Razborov's main lemma in [Raz92], which is essentially the same statement for $k = 1$.

We shall give the proof in the next section, however, now it's time to show that our solution to the dual program is feasible.

So let us check the rectangle constraints. If R is a rectangle first suppose that $\mu_{k,n+k,m+k}(R) \leq 2^{-\beta n}$. In this case $\sum_{x,y \in R} \phi_{x,y} \leq \sum_{x,y \in R \cap T_{k,n+k}} 2^{\beta n} \mu_{k,n+k,m+k}(x,y) \leq 1$.

Hence we need only worry about large rectangles $R \in \mathcal{R}_v$. For each such R there is a set $I = \{i_1, \ldots, i_k\}$ of size k such that all inputs x, y in R intersect on I. If we remove those positions from the universe $\{1, \ldots, n+k\}$ (I is actually unique for all rectangles that contain inputs with positive weights at all) we can consider R as a rectangle R' in $\{0,1\}^n \times \{0,1\}^n$. Clearly $\mu_{0,n,m}(R') \geq \mu_{k,n+k,m+k}(R)$, since all inputs in $R \cap T_{k,n+k}$ have a corresponding input in $R' \cap T_{0,n}$, and for each x,y:$\mu_{0,n,m}(x,y) = \mu_{k,n+k,m+k} \cdot \binom{n+k}{k}$. So the intersection sampling lemma is applicable to R' as long as we set $\beta = \gamma$ and $k \leq \gamma n/2$. The lemma tells us that $\mu_{k,n,m}(R') \geq \mu_{0,n,m}(R')/2^{k+1}$.

Consequently,

$$\mu_{2k,n+k,m+k}(R) = \mu_{k,n,m}(R') \cdot \frac{\binom{n}{k}}{\binom{n+k}{2k}} \quad (11)$$

$$\geq \mu_{0,n,m}(R') \cdot \frac{\binom{n}{k}}{\binom{n+k}{2k} 2^{k+1}} \quad (12)$$

$$= \mu_{k,n+k,m+k}(R) \cdot \frac{\binom{n}{k}\binom{n+k}{k}}{\binom{n+k}{2k} 2^{k+1}} \quad (13)$$

$$\geq \mu_{k,n+k,m+k}(R) \cdot \Omega(2^k/\sqrt{k}), \quad (14)$$

where (11) and (13) follow from Lemma 4, (12) from Lemma 5, and (14) using Sterling approximation.

So, surprisingly, the intersection sampling lemma lets us conclude that R contains a lot more weight on $2k$-intersections inputs than on k-intersection inputs. Of course this is really a consequence of the fact that we forced the original protocol to be correct in its (non-rejecting) outputs, and hence the fact that every rectangle we consider has one set of k positions that all its inputs intersect in.

So

$$\sum_{x,y \in R} \phi_{x,y} + \psi_{x,y}$$

$$= \sum_{x,y \in R \cap T_{k,n+k}} 2^{\beta n} \mu_{k,n+k,m+k}(x,y) - \sum_{x,y \in R \cap T_{2k,n}} 2^{\beta n} \mu_{2k,n+k,m+k}(x,y) 2^{-\alpha k}$$

$$\leq 0.$$

The rectangle constraints are satisfied and our program is indeed feasible. We have the parameters $\beta = \gamma$, and $\sigma = 2^{-\alpha k+1}$, and $\alpha = 1/2$, as well as $k \leq \gamma n/2$. Overall our solution to the dual proves that no protocol with communication βn can solve SEARCH$_{\binom{n+k}{k}}$ with success better than σ, as long as $k \leq \gamma n/2$. By adjusting constants this proves Lemma 1.

3.5 The Intersection Sampling Lemma

In this section we prove Lemma 5 which we have used to establish the feasibility of the solution to the linear program exhibited in the previous section.

The base of the induction proof will be provided by Razborov's main lemma from [Raz92] restated as follows:

FACT 6. *There is a constant $\delta > 0$, such that for all $m \in \{n/4 - \delta n, \ldots, n/4\}$ and for every rectangle $R \subseteq \{0,1\}^n \times \{0,1\}^n$ with $\mu_{0,n,m}(R) \geq 2^{-\delta n}$ we have*

$$\mu_{1,n,m}(R) \geq \mu_{0,n,m}(R)/(3/2).$$

The factor 3/2 corresponds to error 2/5 in the original statement, but it can be seen easily, that any error $1/2 - \epsilon$ can be achieved in Razborov's proof by reducing the size of the rectangles considered suitably (i.e., by lowering the communication bound δn considered). Also Razborov fixes $m = n/4$, but slightly smaller sets can be accommodated in the proof.[1]

We prove the following statement by induction.

LEMMA 7. *There is a constant $\gamma > 0$, such that for $m = n/4$ and every rectangle $R = A \times B \subseteq \{0,1\}^n \times \{0,1\}^n$ with $\mu_{0,n,m}(R) \geq 2^{-\gamma n}$ and all $k \leq \gamma n/2$ we have*

$$\mu_{k,n,m}(R) \geq \mu_{0,n,m}(R)/2^k - k \cdot 2^{-\delta(n-k+1)}.$$

In fact we choose $\gamma = \delta/3$ (and assume $k \leq \gamma n/2$). Then the above statement implies Lemma 5 as stated in the previous subsection.

PROOF OF LEMMA 7. Clearly the base of the induction over k is true by Fact 6. So consider any rectangle R, such that $\mu_{0,n,m}(R) \geq 2^{-\gamma n}$ and assume $k \leq \gamma n/2$.

For all $I \subseteq \{1, \ldots, n\}$ with $|I| = k$ let's denote by R_I the rectangle that is the intersection of R with the rectangle that fixes $x_i = y_i = 1$ for all $i \in I$. Now $R \cap \{T_{k,n} \cup \cdots \cup T_{n,n}\} = \cup_{I:|I|=k} R_I$. Furthermore every input $x, y \in T_{k+1,n} \cap R$ lies in exactly $k+1$ rectangles R_I, while all inputs $x, y \in T_{k,n} \cap R$ lie in exactly one R_I. Hence

$$\mu_{k+1,n,m}(R) = \sum_{I:|I|=k} \mu_{k+1,n,m}(R_I)/(k+1).$$

Again we can reinterpret the R_I as rectangles R'_I in the set $\{0,1\}^{n-k} \times \{0,1\}^{n-k}$, because each R_I has all its inputs intersecting on the set I, so we only consider what happens on the other positions.

Note that $\mu_{0,n-k,m-k}(R'_I) = \mu_{k,n,m}(R_I) \cdot \binom{n}{k}$ by Lemma 4, so we can conclude that $\mu_{0,n-k,m-k}(R'_I)$ is large whenever $\mu_{k,n,m}(R_I)$ is.

Let $\mathcal{I} = \{I \subseteq \{1, \ldots, n\} : |I| = k \wedge \mu_{0,n-k,m-k}(R'_I) \leq 2^{-\delta(n-k)}\}$. Then

$$\sum_{I \in \mathcal{I}} \mu_{k,n,m}(R_I) \leq \sum_{I \in \mathcal{I}} \mu_{0,n-k,m-k}(R'_I) / \binom{n}{k} \leq 2^{-\delta(n-k)}. \quad (15)$$

[1]The proof needs to be adjusted in several ways. First of all, instead of mixing the distributions on intersection size 1 and 0 in the proportions 1/4 and 3/4 we need to mix them uniformly. Secondly, the constant 1/3 in the definition of x-bad can be replaced with a constant close to 1, and consequently the numbers in Claims 3 and 4 need to be adjusted. A bit more troublesome is allowing m to be slightly smaller than $n/4$, since this makes Fact 2 false, although it remains approximately true, tilting all other estimates by $1 + \delta$ factors.

Now

$$\mu_{k+1,n,m}(R)$$
$$= \sum_{I:|I|=k} \mu_{k+1,n,m}(R_I)/(k+1) \quad (16)$$
$$= \sum_{I:|I|=k} \mu_{1,n-k,m-k}(R'_I) \cdot \frac{n-k}{\binom{n}{k+1}\cdot(k+1)} \quad (17)$$
$$\geq \sum_{I:|I|=k\wedge I\notin\mathcal{I}} \mu_{1,n-k,m-k}(R'_I) \cdot \frac{n-k}{\binom{n}{k+1}\cdot(k+1)} \quad (18)$$
$$\geq \sum_{I:|I|=k\wedge I\notin\mathcal{I}} \mu_{0,n-k,m-k}(R'_I) \cdot \frac{(n-k)/(3/2)}{\binom{n}{k+1}\cdot(k+1)} \quad (19)$$
$$\geq \sum_{I:|I|=k\wedge I\notin\mathcal{I}} \mu_{k,n,m}(R_I) \cdot \frac{(n-k)\binom{n}{k}}{\binom{n}{k+1}\cdot(k+1)\cdot 2} \quad (20)$$
$$= \sum_{I:|I|=k\wedge I\notin\mathcal{I}} \mu_{k,n,m}(R_I) \cdot \frac{1}{2} \quad (21)$$
$$\geq \sum_{I:|I|=k} \mu_{k,n,m}(R_I) \cdot \frac{1}{2} - 2^{-\delta(n-k)} \quad (22)$$
$$\geq \sum_{I:|I|=k} \mu_{0,n,m}(R_I) \cdot \frac{1}{2^{k+1}} - (k+1)2^{-\delta(n-k)}. \quad (23)$$

(17), (20) are via Lemma 4, (19) uses Fact 6, (22) is from (15), and (23) uses the induction hypothesis. □

4. APPLICATIONS

4.1 Communication-Space Tradeoffs for Boolean Matrix Products

In this section we use the strong direct product result for the communication complexity of Disjointness Theorem 3 to prove tight communication-space tradeoffs.

THEOREM 8. *Every bounded-error protocol with communication C in which Alice and Bob have bounded space S and that computes the Boolean matrix-vector product, satisfies $CS = \Omega(N^2)$.*

THEOREM 9. *Every bounded-error protocol with communication C in which Alice and Bob have bounded space S and that computes the Boolean matrix product, satisfies $CS = \Omega(N^3)$.*

The proofs are given in the full version of the paper.

4.2 Multiparty

THEOREM 10. *In the model where Charlie sends one message, followed by an arbitrary interaction between Alice and Bob, the 3-party Disjointness problem has randomized complexity $\Omega(\sqrt{n})$.*

PROOF. This proof idea is due to [BRW08]. Let P be a protocol for the 3-party NDISJ$_n$ problem with $\epsilon\sqrt{n}$ communication and error 1/3.

We partition $\{1,\ldots,n\}$ into $\sqrt{n}$ blocks of size $\sqrt{n}$. Charlie's input z is restricted to contain 1's in one particular block, and 0's elsewhere. So in effect z chooses one of $\sqrt{n}$ instances of NDISJ$_{\sqrt{n}}$ problems given to Alice and Bob. Since Charlie's message does not depend on z, Alice and Bob may reuse it in $\sqrt{n}$ runs of P in order to determine, for all of the $\sqrt{n}$ possible z, the value of all of their NDISJ$_{\sqrt{n}}$ problems with overall communication ϵn. For each block the error probability is at most ϵ. The expected number of blocks where the protocol fails is at most $2\epsilon\sqrt{n}$ with probability at least 1/2 by the Markov inequality. So for every input x, y to Alice and Bob there is a message from Charlie which will make them give the wrong answer for at most $2\epsilon\sqrt{n}$ blocks with probability at least 1/2.

We may now simply replace Charlie's message by a uniformly random string which will deteriorate the probability of having at least $(1-2\epsilon)\sqrt{n}$ blocks correct to $2^{-\epsilon\sqrt{n}}\cdot 1/2$. We have found a 2 player protocol with communication ϵn and the mentioned success probability to compute $(1-2\epsilon)\sqrt{n}$ instances of Nondisjointness correctly. In [BRW08] a general argument is given that relates the success probability in this situation to the standard situation of an SDPT (in which success means all the outputs are correct). For small enough ϵ this contradicts our main result. The idea of such "threshold DPT"'s is further investigated in [U09]. □

5. THE LINEAR PROGRAMMING BOUND AND LIMITED AMBIGUITY

A major tool to prove randomized communication complexity bounds is the rectangle bound (see [K03, BPSW06]). The method was originally introduced by Yao [Yao83], and its most prominent, but by no means only use is in Razborov's Disjointness bound [Raz92]. Informally the rectangle bound states that all rectangles in the communication matrix are either small or have large error (under some hard distribution).

In [L90] Lovász describes the following LP to lower bound randomized communication complexity.

$$\min \sum_R w_R \qquad \text{s.t.} \quad (24)$$
$$\text{for } x,y \text{ with } f(x,y)=1: \sum_{R:x,y\in R} w_R \geq 1-\epsilon \quad (25)$$
$$\text{for } x,y \text{ with } f(x,y)=0: \sum_{R:x,y\in R} w_R \leq \epsilon \quad (26)$$
$$w_R \geq 0 \quad (27)$$

He takes the dual.

$$\max \sum_{x,y:f(x,y)=1} (1-\epsilon)\phi_{x,y}$$
$$+ \sum_{x,y:f(x,y)=0} \epsilon\phi_{x,y} \qquad \text{s.t.} \quad (28)$$
$$\text{for } x,y \text{ with } f(x,y)=1: \phi_{x,y} \geq 0 \quad (29)$$
$$\text{for } x,y \text{ with } f(x,y)=0: \phi_{x,y} \leq 0 \quad (30)$$
$$\text{for all } R: \sum_{x,y\in R} \phi_{x,y} \leq 1 \quad (31)$$

Note that here R ranges over all rectangles in the communication matrix. One can now prove a lower bound by exhibiting a solution to the dual. Let $\phi(x,y)$ describe such a solution.

The optimum of this program characterizes by the (one-sided) rectangle bound, as shown in [JK10].

Instead of proceeding like Lovász, who relaxes (31) (and obtains the spectral discrepancy bound, which can be exponentially smaller), we note the absence of the "trivial" constraint

$$\text{for all } x, y \text{ with } f(x,y) = 1 : \sum_{R:x,y \in R} w_R \leq 1. \qquad (32)$$

The primal Lovász LP augmented with (32) obviously also gives a lower bound on randomized communication. This method is the smooth rectangle bound described in [JK10].

Is the smooth rectangle bound really stronger than the standard one? Let us find out the strongest type of communication protocol that we can still lower bound. Consider unambiguous AM-protocols, i.e., convex combinations of partitions with bounded error, see Section 2. It is easy to see that the LP with constraint (32) lower bounds such protocols. Note that $N(\text{NDISJ}_n) = O(\log n)$, and hence also $AM(\text{NDISJ}_n) = O(\log n)$. However, we can show that unambiguous AM protocols for NDISJ_N need linear communication. To prove that the smooth rectangle bound is large for NDISJ_n we can restrict the set of rectangles to $\mathcal{R}_v = \{R : \exists i : x, y \in R \Rightarrow i \in x \cap y\}$. This is possible by the same argument as Theorem 3, using binary search for a limited number of iterations followed by a trivial protocol for the resulting small instance of Nondisjointness, to get a protocol for the problem of finding an i with $x_i = y_i = 1$. Again we can assume that we do not accept without having seen a witness i. We define a solution to the dual as follows:

- Inputs in $T_{0,n}$ have weight $\phi_{x,y} = -\infty$.
- Inputs in $T_{1,n}$ have weight $\phi_{x,y} = 2^{\beta n} \mu_{1,n,n/4}(x,y)$.
- Inputs in $T_{2,n}$ have weight $\psi_{x,y} = -2^{\beta n} \mu_{2,n,n/4}(x,y) \cdot 3/4$.
- All other inputs have weight 0.

Using these weights it is easy to show that any unambiguous AM-protocol for NDISJ_n needs communication $\Omega(n)$ (with Fact 6 being the main ingredient of the proof). It is known [KNSW94] that nondeterministic protocols with ambiguity t need communication $\sqrt{D(f)}/t$ for the deterministic complexity D, and the rank lower bound is also known to hold for unambiguous nondeterministic protocols. However, these methods do not allow errors, and the first bound cannot achieve linear lower bounds at all (the approximate rank cannot give better bounds than $\sqrt{n}$ either since it lower bounds quantum protocols [Raz03]).

We can also generalize our main result Theorem 3 in a similar fashion:

THEOREM 11. *Assume an AM-protocol with ambiguity $2^{\epsilon k}$ computes k instances of $NDISJ_n$. Then the success probability of the protocol (over the random bits) is at most $2^{\Omega(-k)}$ unless the communication is at least βkn.*

The proof of this statement is practically identical to the proof of Theorem 3. Going through the reductions in section 3 we see that they need only a constant repetition of the original protocol, and a polynomial increase in the ambiguity.

When we come to the search problem and the linear programming formulation note that we have to replace the right hand side of constraint (4) by $\leq 2^{\epsilon k}$. In the dual this increases the gap between ϕ's and ψ's in the objective function, but that gap is already exponentially large in k, so nothing in the construction really changes.

Note that this bound is quite tight, since with ambiguity $2^{O(k)}$ we can reduce the communication to any fraction of kn, and with ambiguity n^k the communication collapses to $O(k \log n)$ even without any error.

Acknowledgments

I thank Rahul Jain and Shengyu Zhang for insightful discussions. The idea of a "smooth" rectangle bound originated in discussion between us. Ronald de Wolf gave very helpful comments to an earlier version of this paper.

6. REFERENCES

[AA03] S. Aaronson and A. Ambainis. Quantum search of spatial regions. In *Proceedings of 44th IEEE FOCS*, pages 200–209, 2003. quant-ph/0303041.

[Abr90] K. Abrahamson. A time-space tradeoff for Boolean matrix multiplication. In *Proceedings of 31st IEEE FOCS*, pages 412–419, 1990.

[ASW09] Andris Ambainis, Robert Spalek, Ronald de Wolf. A New Quantum Lower Bound Method, with Applications to Direct Product Theorems and Time-Space Tradeoffs. In*Algorithmica*, 55(3): 422–461, 2009.

[BFS86] L. Babai, P. Frankl, and J. Simon. Complexity classes in communication complexity theory. In *Proceedings of 27th IEEE FOCS*, pages 337–347, 1986.

[BKKS04] Ziv Bar-Yossef, T. S. Jayram, Ravi Kumar, D. Sivakumar. An information statistics approach to data stream and communication complexity. In *J. Comput. Syst. Sci.*, 68(4): 702–772, 2004.

[BBCR10] Boaz Barak, Mark Braverman, Xi Chen, and Anup Rao. How to Compress Interactive Communication. In *STOC 2010.*

[BTY94] P. Beame, M. Tompa, and P. Yan. Communication-space tradeoffs for unrestricted protocols. *SIAM Journal on Computing*, 23(3):652–661, 1994.

[BPSW06] Paul Beame, Toniann Pitassi, Nathan Segerlind, Avi Wigderson. A Strong Direct Product Theorem for Corruption and the Multiparty Communication Complexity of Disjointness. In *Computational Complexity*, 15(4): 391–432, 2006.

[BRW08] Avraham Ben-Aroya, Oded Regev, Ronald de Wolf. A Hypercontractive Inequality for Matrix-Valued Functions with Applications to Quantum Computing and LDCs. In *FOCS 2008*, pages 477–486, 2008.

[CA08] A. Chattopadhyay, A. Ada. Multiparty Communication Complexity of Disjointness. ECCC Technical Report 15(002), 2008.

[IJKW08] R. Impagliazzo, R. Jaiswal, V. Kabanets, A. Wigderson. Uniform Direct Product Theorems: Simplified, Optimized, and Derandomized. In: *STOC 2008*, pages 579–588, 2008.

[JKN08] Rahul Jain, Hartmut Klauck, Ashwin Nayak. Direct product theorems for classical communication complexity via subdistribution bounds. In: *STOC 2008*, pages 599–608, 2008.

[JK10] Rahul Jain, Hartmut Klauck. The Partition Bound for Classical Communication Complexity and Query Complexity. To appear in *IEEE Conference on Computational Complexity 2010*. See arXiv:0910.4266.

[JKS03] T. S. Jayram, Ravi Kumar, D. Sivakumar. Two applications of information complexity. In *STOC 2003*, pages 673–682, 2003.

[KS92] B. Kalyanasundaram and G. Schnitger. The probabilistic communication complexity of set intersection. *SIAM Journal on Discrete Mathematics*, 5(4):545–557, 1992.

[KNSW94] Mauricio Karchmer, Ilan Newman, Michael E. Saks, Avi Wigderson. Non-Deterministic Communication Complexity with Few Witnesses. In *J. Comput. Syst. Sci.*, 49(2): 247–257, 1994.

[KKN95] Mauricio Karchmer, Eyal Kushilevitz, Noam Nisan. Fractional Covers and Communication Complexity. In *SIAM J. Discrete Math.*, 8(1): 76–92, 1995.

[K03] Hartmut Klauck. Rectangle Size Bounds and Threshold Covers in Communication Complexity. In: *IEEE Conference on Computational Complexity 2003*, pages 118–134, 2003.

[K04] Hartmut Klauck. Quantum and Classical Communication-Space Tradeoffs from Rectangle Bounds. In *FSTTCS 2004*, pages 384–395, 2004.

[K07] Hartmut Klauck. Lower Bounds for Quantum Communication Complexity. *SIAM J. Comput.*, 37(1): 20–46, 2007.

[KSW07] Hartmut Klauck, Robert Spalek, Ronald de Wolf. Quantum and Classical Strong Direct Product Theorems and Optimal Time-Space Tradeoffs. In *SIAM J. Comput.*, 36(5): 1472–1493, 2007.

[KN97] E. Kushilevitz and N. Nisan. *Communication Complexity.* Cambridge University Press, 1997.

[LTT92] T.W. Lam, P. Tiwari, and M. Tompa. Trade-offs between communication and space. *Journal of Computer and Systems Sciences*, 45(3):296–315, 1992. Earlier version in STOC'89.

[LSS08] Troy Lee, Adi Shraibman, Robert Spalek. A Direct Product Theorem for Discrepancy. *IEEE Conference on Computational Complexity*, pages 71–80, 2008.

[LS09] Troy Lee, Adi Shraibman. Disjointness is Hard in the Multiparty Number-on-the-Forehead Model. *Computational Complexity*, 18(2): 309–336, 2009.

[LiS09] Nati Linial, Adi Shraibman. Lower bounds in communication complexity based on factorization norms. *Random Struct. Algorithms*, 34(3), pages 368–394, 2009.

[L90] L. Lovász. Communication Complexity: A Survey. In *Paths, Flows, and VLSI Layout, edited by B. H. Korte*, Springer, 1990.

[NRS94] N. Nisan, S. Rudich, and M. Saks. Products and help bits in decision trees. In *Proceedings of 35th FOCS*, pages 318–329, 1994.

[NS94] N. Nisan and M. Szegedy. On the degree of Boolean functions as real polynomials. *Computational Complexity*, 4(4):301–313, 1994. Earlier version in STOC'92.

[PRW97] I. Parnafes, R. Raz, and A. Wigderson. Direct product results and the GCD problem, in old and new communication models. In *Proceedings of 29th ACM STOC*, pages 363–372, 1997.

[Raz92] A. Razborov. On the distributional complexity of disjointness. *Theoretical Computer Science*, 106(2):385–390, 1992.

[Raz03] A. Razborov. Quantum communication complexity of symmetric predicates. *Izvestiya of the Russian Academy of Science, mathematics*, 67(1):159–176, 2003. quant-ph/0204025.

[Sha01] R. Shaltiel. Towards proving strong direct product theorems. In *Proceedings of 16th IEEE Conference on Computational Complexity*, pages 107–119, 2001.

[S08] Alexander A. Sherstov. The pattern matrix method for lower bounds on quantum communication. *STOC 2008*, pages 85–94, 2008.

[U09] Falk Unger. A Probabilistic Inequality with Applications to Threshold Direct-product Theorems. *FOCS 2009*, 2009.

[VW07] E. Viola and A. Wigderson. One-way multi-party communication lower bound for pointer jumping with applications. In: *Proceedings of the 48th IEEE Symposium on Foundations of Computer Science*, 2007.

[VW08] Emanuele Viola, Avi Wigderson. Norms, XOR Lemmas, and Lower Bounds for Polynomials and Protocols. In *Theory of Computing* 4(1): 137–168, 2008.

[Yao79] A. C-C. Yao. Some Complexity Questions Related to Distributive Computing . In *Proceedings of STOC 1979*, pages 209–213, 1979.

[Yao82] A. C-C. Yao. Theory and applications of trapdoor functions. In *Proceedings of 23rd IEEE FOCS*, pages 80–91, 1982.

[Yao83] A. C-C. Yao. Lower Bounds by Probabilistic Arguments. *24th IEEE Symp. Foundations of Computer Science*, pp. 420–428, 1983.

Hardness Amplification in Proof Complexity

Paul Beame*
Computer Science & Engineering
University of Washington
Seattle, WA 98195-2350
beame@cs.washington.edu

Trinh Huynh*†
Computer Science & Engineering
University of Washington
Seattle, WA 98195-2350
trinh@cs.washington.edu

Toniann Pitassi‡
Computer Science
University of Toronto
Toronto, ON M5S 1A4
toni@cs.toronto.edu

ABSTRACT

We present a general method for converting any family of unsatisfiable CNF formulas that is hard for one of the simplest proof systems – tree resolution – into formulas that require large rank in very strong proof systems, including any proof system that manipulates polynomials of degree at most k (known as Th(k) proofs). These include high degree versions of Lovász-Schrijver and Cutting Planes proofs.

We introduce two very general families of these proof systems, denoted $T^{cc}(k)$ and $R^{cc}(k)$. The proof lines of $T^{cc}(k)$ are arbitrary Boolean functions, each of which can be evaluated by an efficient k-party randomized communication protocol. $T^{cc}(k)$ proofs include Th($k-1$) proofs as a special case. $R^{cc}(k)$ proofs generalize $T^{cc}(k)$ proofs and require only that each inference be checkable by a short k-party protocol.

For all $k \in O(\log \log n)$, our main results are as follows: First, any unsatisfiable CNF formula of high resolution rank can be efficiently transformed into another CNF formula requiring high rank in all $R^{cc}(k)$ systems, and exponential tree size in all $T^{cc}(k)$ systems. Secondly, there are strict rank hierarchies for all $R^{cc}(k)$ systems, and strict tree-size hierarchies for all $T^{cc}(k)$ systems. Finally, we apply our general method to give optimal integrality gaps for low rank $R^{cc}(2)$ proofs for MAX-2t-SAT, which imply optimal integrality gaps for low rank Cutting Planes and Th(1) proofs.

Categories and Subject Descriptors

F.0 [**Theory of Computation**]: General

General Terms

Theory

Keywords

Proof Complexity, Communication Complexity

*Research supported by NSF grant CCF-0830626

†Also known as Dang-Trinh Huynh-Ngoc

‡Research Supported by NSERC

STOC'10, June 5–8, 2010, Cambridge, Massachusetts, USA.

1. INTRODUCTION

Over the last decade or so there have been a large number of results proving lower bounds on the rank required to refute (or approximately optimize over) systems of constraints in a wide variety of semi-algebraic (a.k.a. polynomial threshold) proof systems. These include systems such as Lovász-Schrijver [25], Cutting Planes [14, 9], Positivstellensatz [15], Sherali-Adams [33], and Lasserre [23] proofs.

Highlights of this work include recent linear rank lower bounds for Lasserre proofs [30, 36] for many constraint optimization problems as well as rank lower bounds for semi-algebraic proof systems for other important optimization problems [7, 31, 13]. In addition to these rank lower bounds, there are a few superpolynomial lower bounds on the size of tree-like proofs in specific semi-algebraic proof systems [16, 15, 20]. Exciting and important as these results are, their proofs rely on delicate constructions of problem-specific local distributions on inputs that satisfy constraints based on the specific rules for each proof system. Furthermore, because there are few effective reductions for such proof systems, lower bounds for one problem usually do not translate to other problems.

A very different approach for proving lower bounds for semi-algebraic proofs was developed in [2], whereby the problems of lower-bounding the rank or tree-like proof size are reduced to a lower bound problem in communication complexity. This allows the results to be applicable to a much wider class of proof systems, called Th(k) proofs, which generalizes the semi-algebraic proof systems discussed above. In these systems, a proof consists of a sequence of lines, each of which is a multivariate polynomial inequality of degree at most k; the only requirement is that each line either expresses an input constraint or is a semantic consequence of a constant number (say two or three) of its predecessors. [2] showed that if an unsatisfiable CNF formula G has a small-rank (or small tree-like size) Th($k-1$) refutation then, over every partition of the variables of G for k parties, there is an efficient k-party randomized NOF protocol that outputs a falsified clause in G. Thus to lower bound the rank of Th($k-1$) proofs it suffices find an unsatisfiable family of CNF formulas with the property that the k-player NOF complexity of this underlying search problem (outputting a falsified clause) is hard.

Though this communication complexity approach was decoupled from the specifics of the proof system, the reduction given in [2] was very problem-specific and delicate. One source of the difficulty was that the clause search problem needs to be hard for randomized protocols to solve but is always easy nondeterministically, as the players can simply guess and verify a violated clause. Much of the delicacy of the argument was in carefully embedding a specific candidate function (set disjointness), which appeared to have these characteristics, into the search problem of an unsatisfiable CNF.

Indeed, using a long and involved argument, [2] showed the feasibility of this communication complexity approach by constructing a particular family of CNF formulas, $(k-1)$-fold Tseitin tautologies over $\Theta(\log n)$-degree LPS expander graphs, such that lower bounds on the k-party randomized NOF communication complexity of the k-party set disjointness function yield rank and tree-like size lower bounds for $\mathrm{Th}(k-1)$ refutations. The recent lower bounds of Lee and Shraibman [24] and Chattopadhyay and Ada [8] for the k-party randomized communication complexity of set disjointness thus yield unconditional rank bounds for $\mathrm{Th}(k)$ proofs. Unfortunately, though the set disjointness bounds apply for k up to $(1-o(1))\log\log n$, the details of the reduction in [2], which was claimed for each constant k, only apply for $k = O(\log\log\log n)$. Moreover, the method only applies to this one particular family of unsatisfiable formulas, and no other lower bounds for $\mathrm{Th}(k)$ proofs have been known by any other method.

In this paper for the first time we provide a simple and general method that produces unsatisfiable formulas requiring proofs of large rank and tree-like size in semi-algebraic proof systems. This applies to a broad range of systems including all of $\mathrm{Th}(k)$ for k up to $(1-o(1))\log\log n$. Our method allows one to take any unsatisfiable formula requiring large rank in a very simple proof system, resolution, and derive new formulas that require large rank and tree-like proof size in these very powerful semi-algebraic systems. In particular, this construction applies to all formulas of large resolution width [4] since resolution width is a lower bound on resolution rank. A simplified statement of our main result is the following.

THEOREM 1.1. *Let F be any family of polynomial-size 3-CNF formulas in m variables with resolution rank r. Then for any $\epsilon > 0$ and integer $1 \le k \le (1-\epsilon)\log\log n$, there is a family of polynomial-size CNF formulas $G = Lift_k(F)$ on $n = m^{O(k)}$ variables such that G requires $Th(k+1)$ refutations of rank $r^{\Omega(1)}/\log^{O(1)} n$ and tree-size $\exp(r^{\Omega(1)})$. In particular, if r is $m^{\Omega(1)}$ then G requires $Th(k+1)$ rank $n^{\Omega(1/k)}$, and tree-size $\exp(n^{\Omega(1/k)})$.*

Our lower bounds are much more general than this statement. In particular, our proof shows that the lifted formula requires large rank in any proof system in which the truth of each line in a proof can be verified by an efficient k-party randomized communication protocol; the above theorem follows by the reduction in [2]. Our lower bounds also apply to proof systems in which individual proof lines may not be efficiently verifiable but in which any falsifying assignment at an inferred line can be traced to one of its antecedents using an efficient k-party randomized communication protocol.

Our method is an example of a kind of hardness amplification that we term *hardness escalation*. The usual form of hardness amplification in circuit complexity is a method for amplifying the probability of error. That is, a complexity class C is fixed (or nearly fixed), and the goal is to go from a function that is weakly hard (e.g., any circuit in C that approximates f has non-negligible probability of error) to a function that is much harder (e.g., any circuit in a slightly smaller class than C that approximates f has error exponentially close to $1/2$). With hardness escalation, we start with an object, a function f (or in this case an unsatisfiable 3-CNF formula), that is hard for some complexity class (a proof system here), and we construct a related function g (or lifted formula in this case) that is nearly as hard for a larger complexity class (respectively, more powerful proof system).

Our proof uses intuition and ideas from the pattern matrix method developed by Sherstov [35] and from a related method developed earlier by Raz and McKenzie [29]. Both of these are hardness escalation methods for communication complexity. Each method begins with a computational problem that is hard for a weak complexity measure, either a relation R of large decision tree complexity ([29]), or a function f of large approximate polynomial degree ([35]), and extends the problem using a "pattern matrix" to produce a problem of large deterministic ([29]), or large randomized and quantum ([35]), two-party communication complexity.

We use the k-party generalizations of the pattern matrix method developed in [24, 8]. Starting with a function f on m variables, and a parameter k, these generalizations *lift* f to obtain another function $g = \mathrm{Lift}_k(f)$ on mk bit-strings. The transformation replaces each original variable e_i by a Boolean *selector function* Ψ on k bit-strings. As long as f is hard in the weak measure, g is hard in the k-player number-on-forehead (NOF) randomized communication complexity model (for a particular partition of the new variables).

A key obstacle when trying to apply the pattern matrix method to the proof complexity setting is that the approach only works with Boolean functions, and not with unsatisfiable CNF formulas. To overcome this obstacle, we associate a family of Boolean functions $\mathcal{Z}_F$ with every unsatisfiable CNF F and show that if the hardness assumption on F is satisfied then there is some function $f \in \mathcal{Z}$ that has large decision tree complexity. Furthermore, if there is an efficient communication protocol that outputs falsified clauses in $\mathrm{Lift}(F)$, then there is an efficient protocol for $\mathrm{Lift}(f)$ for any $f \in \mathcal{Z}$. In this way we are able to combine the hardness escalation ideas of [29, 35] to obtain our results. We can also prove a converse to our result, thus characterizing the $\mathrm{Th}(k)$ rank of our lifted formulas. That is, in addition to deriving lower bounds on the rank of proofs for $\mathrm{Lift}_k(F)$ in terms of the resolution rank r of F, we also show that the rank of $T^{cc}(2)$ proofs (and even resolution) proofs of $\mathrm{Lift}_k(F)$ is not much larger than r.

Using the above lower bounds, we prove new rank separation theorems for hierarchies of polynomial threshold proof systems. By considering $\mathrm{Lift}_k(F)$ for certain unsatisfiable CNF formulas F that require large rank resolution refutations but need only small rank Cutting Planes refutations, we obtain strong rank separations between the power of $T^{cc}(k+1)$ and $R^{cc}(k)$, between $\mathrm{Th}(k)$ and $\mathrm{Th}(k-1)$, and between $\mathrm{CP}(k)$ and $\mathrm{CP}(k-1)$ refutations where $\mathrm{CP}(k)$ is the natural generalization of Cutting Planes to degree k.

Finally, using Sherstov's strengthened degree-discrepancy lemma for 2-player communication complexity [35], we apply our techniques to prove optimal integrality gaps for a large family of optimization problems even after n^{ϵ} rounds of CP or $\mathrm{Th}(1)$.

Due to space limitations some proofs are omitted or only sketched. Details appear in the full paper.

Related Work on Hardness Escalation. Hardness escalation results have been obtained in models such as communication complexity [35], sub-exponential time complexity [17], and circuit depth ([19, 12, 29]). A similar concept called hardness condensing was introduced in [6].

There have been a few papers in proof complexity implicitly using the idea of hardness escalation. First, several papers use the fact that if a formula F requires large resolution width, then the *xorification* of F, obtained by replacing each variable by an xor of several variables (and then rewriting as a CNF), is hard with respect to resolution size. [26] show how to replace variables in a somewhat hard unsatisfiable formula by hard functions in order to prove hardness escalation theorems for restricted tree-like proof systems. Lastly, Schoenebeck [30] obtains rank lower bounds for Lasserre proofs based on resolution rank lower bounds for particular families of formulas.

2. PRELIMINARIES

For a CNF formula F, let clauses(F) denote the set of clauses of F and let $|F|$ denote $|\text{clauses}(F)|$. F is a t-CNF formula iff every clause contains at most t literals. For any function f on m bits and any function h on s bits, we denote by $f \circ h$ the following function on ms bits: $f \circ h := f(h(\cdots), \cdots, h(\cdots))$.

Let F be an unsatisfiable CNF formula over variables $x_1, \ldots, x_n$ consisting of m clauses. The canonical Boolean relation associated with F is the predicate $R_F(x, y)$, where x is a vector of length n, and y is a number, $1 \leq y \leq m$. $R_F(\alpha, \beta)$ is true if and only if α is a Boolean assignment and the clause C_β in F is falsified by α. Associated with a Boolean relation $R(x, y)$ is a search problem: given x, output a y such that $R(x, y)$ is satisfied. Given a Boolean relation $R(x, y)$, we call a function g a *subfunction* of R if $R(x, g(x))$ is satisfied for every x. In other words, g is a particular function that solves the search problem associated with R. For example, for the canonical Boolean relation R_F associated with an unsatisfiable CNF formula F, the search problem, F_{search} is the problem of finding a violated clause given a Boolean assignment to the variables of F. A function g is a subfunction of R_F if for any truth assignment α, $g(\alpha)$ returns a clause of F that is falsified by α.

We adopt the usual notion of Boolean decision tree for a Boolean function. For a relation R, a decision tree T computes the search problem associated with R if it computes some subfunction of R. The *decision tree complexity* of f, denoted $D(f)$, is the minimum height of all decision trees computing f.

Hard Search Problems. Given an unsatisfiable CNF formula F that is somewhat hard (the decision tree complexity of F_{search}, $D(F_{\text{search}})$, is superpolylogarithmic in the size of F), we want to identify a set $\mathcal{Z}$ of Boolean functions associated with F that witnesses the hardness of F. Specifically, we want $\mathcal{Z}$ to have the property that if $D(F_{\text{search}})$ is large then $\mathcal{Z}$ contains a function with large decision tree complexity. This alone would be straightforward. However, we also want $\mathcal{Z}$ to be constructable from algorithms computing F_{search}.

A natural choice for the collection of functions from F_{search} would be to define $f_S(\alpha) = 1$ for some $S \subseteq \text{clauses}(F)$ if and only if there is some clause in S that is falsified by α. One might hope to argue that one such f_S would have decision tree complexity close to that of F_{search}. The obvious way to try to show this would be to reason by reduction; however, it is not clear how to construct a decision tree for F_{search} from decision trees for such a collection of f_S since both $f_S(\alpha)$ and $f_{\overline{S}}(\alpha)$ may equal 1. Some sort of symmetry-breaking scheme is required and this scheme must satisfy the property that for $S \subset T$ we have $f_T(\alpha) = 1$ whenever $f_S(\alpha) = 1$.

We say that a set $\mathcal{Z}$ of Boolean functions over the set of variables of an unsatisfiable CNF formula F is a *consistent system of functions for F* iff $\mathcal{Z} = \{f_S \mid S \subseteq \text{clauses}(F)\}$ and for any input assignment α there exists a clause C in F falsified by α such that for any $f_S \in \mathcal{Z}$ we have that $f_S(\alpha) = 1$ if and only if $C \in S$.

PROPOSITION 2.1. *Given an unsatisfiable CNF formula F, any function f^* that is a subfunction of R_F (that is, it solves the search problem F_{search}) yields a consistent system $\mathcal{Z}_{f^*}$ of functions for F.*

PROOF. Use the clause $C = f^*(\alpha)$ and define $f_S(\alpha) = 1$ iff $C \in S$. □

The following proposition says that any consistent system of functions for F witnesses the hardness of F.

PROPOSITION 2.2. *For any unsatisfiable CNF formula F and any consistent system $\mathcal{Z}$ of functions for F, there exists a function $f_S \in \mathcal{Z}$ such that $D(F_{\text{search}}) \leq D(f_S)\lceil \log_2 |F| \rceil$.*

PROOF. Build a decision tree for F_{search} using binary search by querying the f_S for subsets $S \subseteq \text{clauses}(F)$ to narrow down the search. The requirement of consistency ensures that the path followed by binary search on input α yields the falsified clause C. To derive the tree for F_{search} replace each query of f_S by the optimal decision tree for f_S, yielding the claimed bound. □

Communication Complexity. Given a function (or relation) f, some number $k \geq 2$ of players, and a partition of the input of f for these players, we consider the *number-on-the-forehead (NOF)* communication model (cf.[22]), in which each player sees all inputs except the those in the block of the partition that is assigned to him, and the goal is compute f using a minimum of communication. Let $|\mathcal{P}|$ denote the maximum number of bits communicated in a communication protocol $\mathcal{P}$ and $\mathcal{P}(x)$ the output of the protocol on input x. A randomized protocol $\mathcal{P}$ is said to compute a function f with error at most ϵ if on any input x, with probability at least $1 - \epsilon$ (over the players' random coins c), $\mathcal{P}(x, c) = f(x)$.

If f is a search problem, the standard definition (e.g. [22]) of randomized communication complexity states that $\mathcal{P}$ computes f with error at most ϵ if and only if on any input x, for at least $1 - \epsilon$ fraction of the outcomes of random coins c, $\mathcal{P}(x, c) \in f(x)$. Among these good outcomes, the values $\mathcal{P}(x, c)$ may not be the same element in $f(x)$. However, for our construction, we require a stronger notion.

A randomized protocol $\mathcal{P}$ is said to *consistently compute* a relation f with error at most ϵ if there is a function f^* contained in f – that is, $f^*(x) \in f(x)$ for every x, such that $\mathcal{P}$ computes f^* with error at most ϵ.

Proof Systems and the Complexity of Clause Search. A wide variety of proof systems exist in the literature. In most of these proof systems, a proof or refutation can be expressed as a sequence of *lines*, each of which is either (a translation of) an input clause or follows from some previous lines via some sound *inference rule*. We call such proofs *standard proofs*. Similarly in a standard refutation system of an unsatisfiable formula f, a proof is again a asequence of lines, where the first line is f, the last line is the trivially false formula, and all other lines follow from some sound inference rule of the underlying proof system.

We associate a DAG $\mathcal{G} = (V, E)$ with every standard proof P, where V is the set of lines in P and $(u, v) \in E$ if line v is derived via some inference rule using line u. The *size* of P is the number of bits in P, which is lower-bounded by the number of lines in P. The *rank* of P is the length of the longest path in $\mathcal{G}$. We consider $\mathcal{G}$ to be a tree if every internal node has fanout one. (The axioms, which are not internal nodes, can be repeated.) If $\mathcal{G}$ is a tree, we say that P is *tree-like*. The *size complexity* and *rank complexity* of F in a standard proof system are the minimum size and minimum rank, respectively, of all proofs for F in that system. Similarly, we define *tree-like size complexity* as the minimum over all proofs are restricted to be tree-like.

Note that restricting a proof to be tree-like does not increase the rank of a proof because the same line can be re-derived multiple times without affecting the rank. Tree-like size, however, can be much larger than general size.

In the most well-studied proof systems, there is a set of derivation rules (which can be thought of as inference schemas) of the form $F_1, F_2, \ldots, F_t \vdash G$ and each derivation step in a proof must be an instantiation of one of these rules. One such basic system is *resolution*, which manipulates clauses. Its only rule is the *resolution rule*: the clause $(A \vee B)$ is derived from $(A \vee x)$ and $(B \vee \neg x)$, where A and B are arbitrary disjunctions of literals and x is a variable. A resolution refutation of an unsatisfiable CNF formula f is a sequence of clauses, ending with the empty clause, such that each clause is either a clause of f, or follows from two previously derived clauses via the resolution rule. The well-known connection showing that DPLL executions and tree-like resolution proofs are equivalent gives us the following proposition.

PROPOSITION 2.3. [11] *For any CNF formula F, the minimum rank of any resolution proof of F is equal to $D(F_{\text{search}})$.*

Another proof system is the *Cutting Planes* (CP) proof system which manipulates integer linear inequalities. A CP refutation is a sequence of inequalities, ending with $0 \geq 1$, such that all other inequalities are either axioms ($0 \leq x_i$, $x_i \leq 1$), translated input clauses (input clause $(\ell_1 \vee \cdots \vee \ell_t)$ is translated as $\ell'_1 + \cdots + \ell'_t \geq 1$ where $\ell' = x$ if $\ell = x$ and $\ell' = (1 - x)$ if $\ell = \neg x$) or follow from two previously derived inequalities via either addition

$$p_1 \geq 0, \ldots, p_t \geq 0 \ \vdash \ \sum_{i=1}^{t} \lambda_i p_i \geq 0,$$

where each p_i is a linear form, or division with rounding

$$\sum_i c a_i x_i \geq b \ \vdash \ \sum_i a_i x_i \geq \lceil b/c \rceil,$$

where a_i, b, c, and $\lambda_i \geq 0$ are integers. There is a natural extension of CP, denoted CP(k), in which the above CP proof rules are extended to include p_i that are degree k multivariate polynomials and the x_i are replaced by degree k monomials. Since the input clauses are linear there are two other rules that allow the creation of higher degree inequalities, namely $p \geq 0 \ \vdash \ x_i p \geq 0$ and $p \geq 0 \ \vdash \ p \geq x_i p$ for all polynomials p of degree at most $k - 1$ and variables x_i.

Other important well-studied proof systems are the Lovász-Schrijver proof systems (LS_0, LS, LS_+, and $\text{LS}_{+,\star}$) which manipulate polynomial inequalities of degree at most 2, and the Sherali-Adams and Lasserre proof systems which generalize the Lovász-Schrijver systems to higher degree.

Each of the above proof systems has a specific set of inference rule schemas, which allows them to have polynomial-time verifiers. We also consider more powerful *semantic proof systems* which restrict the form of the lines and the fan-in of the inferences but dispense with the requirement of a polynomial-time verifier and allow any semantically sound inference rule with a given fan-in. (Each line is a clause or follows via some semantic inference rule.) The fan-in must be restricted because the semantic rules are so strong.

For integer $k \geq 1$, we denote by $\text{Th}(k)$ the semantic proof system, introduced in [2], whose proofs have fan-in 2, lines consist of polynomial inequalities of degree at most k, and input clauses and axioms are represented as linear inequalities as in the definition of CP above.

The following proposition follows from Caratheodory's Theorem. It is not hard to show that one can extend these simulations by $\text{Th}(k)$ proofs to CP(k) and $LS^k_{+,\star}$.

PROPOSITION 2.4. *(1) Any CP proof of size (tree-like size) S and rank r can be converted to a* $\text{Th}(1)$ *proof of size (tree-like size) $O(S)$ and rank $O(r \log n)$. (2) Any* LS_0*, LS, or* LS_+ *proof of size (tree-like size) S and rank r can be converted to a* $\text{Th}(2)$ *proof of size (tree-like size) $O(S)$ and rank $O(r \log n)$.*

In this paper we also consider more general semantic proof systems than $\text{Th}(k)$, namely those for which the fan-in is bounded and the truth value of each line can be computed by a multiparty communication protocol.

For any $k, C \geq 1$, we denote by $T^{cc}(k, C)$ the semantic proof system of fan-in 2 in which each proof line is a Boolean function whose value, for every partition of the input variables into k groups, can be computed by a C-bit randomized k-party NOF communication protocol of error at most $1/3$. Both k and C may be integer functions of the input size of the formulas. In keeping with the usual notions of what constitutes efficient communication protocols, we use $T^{cc}(k)$ to denote the union of all $T^{cc}(k, C)$ over all C in $\log^{O(1)} n$.

Via standard boosting, we can replace the error $1/3$ in the above definition by ϵ at the cost of increasing C by an $O(\log 1/\epsilon)$ factor. So, without loss of generality, in defining $T^{cc}(k)$ we can assume that the error is at most $1/n^{\log^{\Omega(1)} n}$.

Note also that a semantic proof of rank r that satisfies the same conditions as a $T^{cc}(k, C)$ proof except that it has rules of fan-in at most $t \geq 2$ can be simulated by a $T^{cc}(k, 2Ct \log_2 t)$ proof of rank $r \log_2 t$ by replacing each inference by a binary tree of height $\log_2 t$ in which lines of internal nodes are conjunctions of their predecessors.

For polylogarithmic k, the following lemma shows that $\text{Th}(k)$ is a subclass of $T^{cc}(k + 1)$.

LEMMA 2.5. *For some constant $c > 0$, every* $\text{Th}(k)$ *refutation of a CNF formula on n variables is also a $T^{cc}(k + 1, ck^3 \log^2 n)$ proof.*

PROOF. By the well-known result of Muroga [27], linear threshold functions on n Boolean values only require coefficients of $O(n \log n)$ bits. Since a degree k threshold polynomial is a linear function on at most n^k monomials, it is equivalent to a degree k threshold polynomial with coefficients of $O(kn^k \log n)$ bits. As shown in [2], over any input partition there is a randomized $(k+1)$-party communication protocol of cost $O(k \log^2 s)$ and error $\leq 1/s^{\Omega(1)}$ to verify a degree k polynomial inequality with s-bit coefficients. $\square$

We also define another class of proofs based on k-party communication complexity that we will see is even more general than $T^{cc}(k, C)$. For any integer functions $k, C \geq 1$, we denote by $R^{cc}(k, C)$ the semantic proof system of arbitrary fan-in in which each proof line is a Boolean function such that the proof satisfies the following property: for every partition of the input variables into k groups, and every inference of B from $A_1, \ldots, A_s$ in the proof, there is a C-bit randomized k-party NOF communication protocol of error at most $1/3$ that computes a (partial) function $f_{A_1,\ldots,A_s \vdash B}$ from the inputs to the set $[s]$ such that on every input α, if B evaluates to false on input α then $A_{f_{A_1,\ldots,A_s \vdash B}(\alpha)}$ evaluates to false on input α. We write $R^{cc}(k)$ to denote the union of all $R^{cc}(k, C)$ over all C in $\log^{O(1)} n$.

Lemma 2.6. *Every $T^{cc}(k, C)$ proof is an $R^{cc}(k, C)$ proof.*

Proof. The inferences in the $T^{cc}(k, C)$ are all of fan-in at most 2 and hence derive each line B from some lines A_1 and A_2. To compute the function $f_{A_1,A_2 \vdash B}$ the players evaluate A_1 on input α using the protocol given by the $T^{cc}(k, C)$ proof. If that evaluates to false then they output 1; otherwise, they output 2. $\square$

We can sharpen this relationship further using a standard method for strengthening a proof system S by adding resolution rules over the lines of S [21]. Given a proof system S, we define related proof system $R(S)$ as follows: Lines of $R(S)$ are unordered disjunctions of lines of S and their negations. For every inference rule in S, $A_1, \ldots, A_t \vdash B$, there is the corresponding rule $(G \vee A_1), \ldots, (G \vee A_t) \vdash (G \vee B)$ where G is an arbitrary disjunction of lines of S and their negations. In addition there are extended resolution rules that allow the introduction of new disjuncts, $G \vdash (G \vee A_1 \vee \ldots \vee A_t)$, or cuts on lines of S, namely $(G \vee A), (H \vee \neg A) \vdash (G \vee H)$, where A is a line of S and G and H are arbitrary disjunctions of lines of S and their negations.

Lemma 2.7. *Every $R(T^{cc}(k, C))$ proof is an $R^{cc}(k, C)$ proof.*

Proof. For rules that correspond to rules of $T^{cc}(k, C)$ we apply the simple argument from Lemma 2.6 on the lines that are not common to all formulas. For the resolution rules, observe that the players only need to evaluate the line A to determine whether to select $(G \vee A)$ or $(H \vee \neg A)$. $\square$

In particular, this shows via Lemma 2.5 that $R^{cc}(k+1, ck^3 \log^2 n)$ proofs include the proof system $R(\mathrm{Th}(k))$ (suggested by Hirsch). It is not clear whether one can efficiently simulate $R(\mathrm{Th}(k))$ using $T^{cc}(k)$ proofs.

The following lemma, which is implicit in [2], gives the key relationships between $T^{cc}(k)$ and $R^{cc}(k)$ proofs and randomized communication protocols that consistently compute F_{search}.

Lemma 2.8. *Let $\epsilon > 0$ and F be an n-variable CNF formula.*

(i) If F has an $R^{cc}(k, C)$ refutation of rank r then, over any partition of the variables, there is an ϵ-error randomized k-party communication protocol $\mathcal{P}$ consistently computing F_{search} such that $|\mathcal{P}|$ is $O(Cr \log(r/\epsilon))$.

(ii) If F has a tree-like $T^{cc}(k, C)$ refutation of size S then, over any partition of the variables, there is an ϵ-error randomized k-party protocol $\mathcal{P}$ consistently computing F_{search} such that $|\mathcal{P}|$ is $O(C \log S \log \frac{\log S}{\epsilon})$.

Proof. First assume that we have a rank r refutation in $R^{cc}(k, C)$. On input α, the k players backtrack from the last derived inequality in the proof $(0 \geq 1)$ to find some clause that is falsified by α. When they are at a line B that follows from lines $A_1, \ldots, A_s$ in the proof, they run the protocol for $f_{A_1,\ldots,A_s \vdash B}$, implied by the $R^{cc}(k, C)$ definition for the inference at B, $O(\log(r/\epsilon))$ times and take the majority answer to reduce its error below ϵ/r. Then the players move to the line indicated by that answer. The probability that this protocol makes an error is at most the sum of all error probabilities on any path in the proof. Since the last line evaluates to false on input α, in the case that there is no error the players will return a fixed clause in the proof that is falsified by α, which implies that they consistently compute F_{search}.

For the second case of a size S tree-like refutation, there is some line in the refutation that is derived from between $S/3$ and $2S/3$ of the lines of the refutation tree. The players first evaluate that line with error at most $\epsilon/(2 \log_2 S)$ by repeating the protocol $O(\log(\log S/\epsilon))$ times. If the line evaluates to false then they continue within that subtree; otherwise, they remove the nodes of that subtree. This is done recursively until a falsified clause is found. The depth of recursion is at most $2 \log_2 S$. The rest is similar to the first case. $\square$

3. HARDNESS ESCALATION

The high level idea of our method of hardness escalation is to take a somewhat hard an unsatisfiable t-CNF formula F (one for which F_{search} requires a large height decision tree) over variables $e_1, \ldots, e_m$, and build a new CNF formula $G = \mathrm{Lift}(F)$ of size $m^{O(t)}$ by lifting F using some function ψ that encodes e_i using a larger collection of input bits. This lifting over CNF is adapted from previous work for Boolean functions, which we review next.

3.1 Lifting Decision Tree Complexity

Given $k, s > 0$ and a domain A, a function $\psi_k : \{0,1\}^s \times A^k \mapsto \{0,1\}$ is called a *selector* if there is some $h : A^k \mapsto [s]$ such that $\psi_k(x, y_1, \ldots, y_k) = x_{h(y_1,\ldots,y_k)}$ for every $x \in \{0,1\}^s$ and $y_i \in A$. Informally, ψ_k outputs a bit in x that is selected by the values of $y_1, \ldots, y_k$.

We consider two specific selector encodings ψ_k: the tensor selector $\psi^{\mathrm{T}}_{k,\ell}$ and the parity selector $\psi^{\oplus}_{k,a}$. For the tensor selector $\psi^{\mathrm{T}}_{k,\ell}(x, y)$, we have $s = \ell^k$ and $A = [\ell]$, and we think of $x \in \{0,1\}^s$ as indexed by A^k and hence $h(\cdot)$ is just the identity function on A^k. For the parity selector $\psi^{\oplus}_{k,a}(x, y)$, we have $s = 2^a$, $A = \{0,1\}^a$, and we think of x as indexed by a-bit arrays and $h(y_1, \ldots, y_k) = y_1 \oplus \cdots \oplus y_k$.

Given an initial function f over variables x, define g, the $(k+1)$-lifted version of f, to be the function $f \circ \psi_k$.

It is not hard to see that if the decision tree complexity of f is d, then for any $k \geq 2$, and over any partition of the variables into k groups, there is a k-party communication protocol computing g of cost approximately $d \cdot c$, where c is the cost of computing ψ_k. The k players just simulate the decision tree for f and the cost of computing any single variable in f encoded by ψ_k is c bits. If ψ_k is simple enough, and therefore c is negligible, then this cost is approximately equal to d. Ideally, we would like to argue that this is the best that the players can do. Intuitively, since we have encoded each input bit in f indirectly, the players need to communicate $\Omega(1)$ bits in order to be able to "learn" any single bit. If the decision tree complexity of f is large, we would hope that g has large communication complexity. Recent results in communication complexity show that we cannot do much better than the above trivial protocol, subject to some constraints on ψ_k.

We need the following approximation notion to bridge decision tree complexity and communication complexity. Given any $0 \leq \epsilon < 1$, the *ϵ-degree* of a real-valued function f, $\deg_\epsilon(f)$, is the smallest d for which there exists a multivariate real-valued polynomial p of degree d such that $||f - p||_\infty = \max_x |f(x) - p(x)| \leq \epsilon$. This notion of approximating a real-valued function is polynomially related to decision tree complexity.

PROPOSITION 3.1. [28, 1] *For every Boolean function f, $\deg_{5/6}(f) \leq D(f) \leq (4\deg_{5/6}(f))^6$.*

Finally we state the communication lower bounds for $g = f\circ\psi_k$. The following input partition is always assumed when the communication complexity of g is discussed: there are $k+1$ players and for each input $(x, y_1, \ldots, y_k)$ to each ψ_k, player 0 is assigned x, and each player i, for $1 \leq i \leq k$, is assigned y_i. Intuitively, the inputs $y_1, \ldots, y_k$ given to players 1 through k determine which bits of x are given to f. The next two results say that, when ψ_k is either $\psi^{\mathrm{T}}_{k,\ell}$ or $\psi^{\oplus}_{k,a}$, and the encoding ψ_k is over a large enough number of new variables, then the communication complexity of g is polynomial related to $D(f)$ (up to a factor depending only on k).

THEOREM 3.2. [8] *Let $f : \{0,1\}^m \mapsto \{0,1\}$ with 5/6-degree $d > 2$. If $\ell > \frac{2^{2^{k+1}}kem}{d}$ then any $(k+1)$-party communication protocol $\mathcal{P}$ computing $g = f \circ \psi^{\mathrm{T}}_{k,\ell}$ with error 1/3 must have $|\mathcal{P}| = \Omega(\frac{d}{2^k})$.*

THEOREM 3.3. [3] *Let $f : \{0,1\}^m \mapsto \{0,1\}$ with 5/6-degree $d > 2$. If $2^a > \frac{2^{2^{k+1}+2k}em}{d}$ then any $(k+1)$-party communication protocol $\mathcal{P}$ computing $g = f \circ \psi^{\oplus}_{k,a}$ with error 1/3 must have $|\mathcal{P}| = \Omega(\frac{d}{2^k})$.*

The first theorem uses the tensor selector while the second uses the parity selector. We will use both to prove lower bounds for $T^{cc}(k)$ and $R^{cc}(k)$ proof systems. The parity selector requires fewer bits to encode each variable, thus leading to stronger proof complexity lower bounds as a function of the number of variables (though it is no more efficient with respect to formula size). In contrast, the lifted CNF formula derived using the tensor selector is easier to refute by small degree threshold proofs, allowing us to prove rank separations for the hierarchies of $T^{cc}(k)$ and $R^{cc}(k)$ proof systems.

Overview of the Hardness Escalation Argument. Before giving the formal construction and proofs for the two selectors, we present a brief overview of our argument. Let F be any t-CNF over the variables $e_1, \ldots, e_m$. To lift F to obtain a harder unsatisfiable formula G, every variable e_i of F will be replaced by a set of variables V_i. The V_i variables be comprised of $k+1$ sets of variables: x, and $y_1, \ldots, y_k$. A selector function ψ_k will use the y variables to select one x variable to represent e_i. The clauses in G will state that the V_i variables represent a valid ψ-encoding, and that with respect to this encoding, F is true. By Lemma 2.8, we know that if G has low $T^{cc}(k)$ rank, then there is an efficient $(k+1)$-party protocol for solving the search problem associated with G, G_{search}. Thus to prove a $T^{cc}(k)$ rank lower bound for G, it suffices to prove that G_{search} is hard in the $(k+1)$-party NOF model.

Now any function associated with G is also a lifting of the corresponding function associated with F. In particular, $G_{\text{search}} = F_{\text{search}} \circ \psi_k$. The intuition for why it should be hard is similar to that of the lifting of Boolean functions: here G_{search} is a lifting of F_{search}, and the decision tree complexity of F_{search} is large. To prove this, assume for sake of contradiction that G_{search} is easy for $(k+1)$-party communication. Then the players can efficiently compute G_{search} over the variables V_i. This in turn means that given the variables V_i, they can efficiently compute $F_{\text{search}}(e_1, \ldots, e_m)$, where each $e_i = \psi_k(V_i)$. It follows that there exists a consistent system $\mathcal{Z}$ of functions for F such that for any function $f_S \in \mathcal{Z}$, the players can easily compute $f_S \circ \psi_k$. In other words, the lifting of any $f_S \in \mathcal{Z}$ is easy for k-party communication. It then follows that for appropriate choices of ψ_k, any function in $\mathcal{Z}$ has low decision tree complexity. Then by Proposition 2.2, we can conclude that the decision tree complexity of F_{search} is small, contradicting our assumption. We now proceed to the formal arguments for each of the selector functions.

3.2 Hardness using the Tensor Selector

Let F be any t-CNF over the variables $e_1, \ldots, e_m$. Given $k, \ell \geq 2$, $G = \mathrm{Lift}^{\mathrm{T}}_{k,\ell}(F)$ is a CNF formula defined over m sets of variables $V_1, \ldots, V_m$, where each V_i is further partitioned into two sets X_i of size ℓ^k and Y_i of size $k\ell$. Intuitively, every V_i is an encoding of e_i based on $\psi^{\mathrm{T}}_{k,\ell}$. Each X_i represents a k-dimensional tensor of size ℓ^k each of whose cells c is associated with a variable $x_{i,c} \in X_i$. Y_i, which is indexed as $\{y_{i,p,a} : 1 \leq p \leq k, 1 \leq a \leq \ell\}$, selects a unique cell c in this tensor as follows: For each $p \in [k]$, exactly one of the variables $y_{i,p,a}$ for $a \in [\ell]$ is true, and the value a_p such that y_{i,p,a_p} is true is the p-th coordinate of c. Every clause in F is then transformed into a set of clauses over these V_i. Formally, the clauses in G consist of:

- For $1 \leq i \leq m, 1 \leq j \leq k$, exactly one of $y_{i,p,1}, \ldots, y_{i,p,\ell}$ is 1:
  (I) $y_{i,p,1} \vee \cdots \vee y_{i,p,\ell}$
  (II) $(1 \leq a < a' \leq \ell)$: $\neg y_{i,p,a} \vee \neg y_{i,p,a'}$
- For every clause, say $\neg e_{i_1} \vee e_{i,2} \vee \cdots \vee e_{i_t}$, in F and for every t-tuple of cells $(c_1, \ldots, c_t)$, if Y_{i_1} selects c_1, Y_{i_2} selects c_2, etc., then $\neg x_{i_1,c_1} \vee x_{i_2,c_2} \cdots \vee x_{i_t,c_t}$ must be satisfied: this is translated into one clause of $tk+t$ literals. For example, if the coordinates of $c_1, \ldots, c_t$ are $(a^1_1, \ldots, a^1_k), \ldots, (a^t_1, \ldots, a^t_k)$, respectively, then the clause would be:
  (III) $\neg y_{i_1,1,a^1_1} \vee \cdots \vee \neg y_{i_1,k,a^1_k} \vee \cdots \vee \neg y_{i_t,1,a^t_1} \vee \cdots$
  $\vee \neg y_{i_t,k,a^t_k} \vee \neg x_{i_1,c_1} \vee x_{i_2,c_2} \vee \cdots \vee x_{i_t,c_t}$

The next proposition shows that as long as the clauses of F are not too large, then G is also not too large, and that G is unsatisfiable as long as F is.

PROPOSITION 3.4. *If F is a t-CNF over m variables, then $G = \mathrm{Lift}^{\mathrm{T}}_{k,\ell}(F)$ is a CNF formula of $|F|\ell^{tk} + O(mk\ell^2)$ clauses of size at most $\max\{tk+t, \ell\}$ over $n = m(\ell^k + k\ell)$ variables. Furthermore, if F is unsatisfiable, then so is G.*

We say that an assignment to $X_1, Y_1, \ldots, X_m, Y_m$ of G is a *valid encoding* of an assignment to variables $e_1, \ldots, e_m$ of F if all clauses (I) and (II) are satisfied and for every i, $x_{i,c} = e_i$ where c is selected by Y_i.

We fix the following input partition to $k+1$ players when discussing the communication complexity of G_{search}: player 0 is assigned all of the X_i's, and each player p, for $1 \leq p \leq k$, is assigned $\{y_{i,p,a} : 1 \leq i \leq m, 1 \leq a \leq \ell\}$.

The following lemma says that if G_{search} is easy in communication complexity, then there exists a consistent system $\mathcal{Z} = \{f_S : S \subseteq \text{clauses}(F)\}$ for F such that for every $f_S \in \mathcal{Z}$, computing $f_S \circ \psi^{\mathrm{T}}_{k,\ell}$ is also easy in communication complexity.

LEMMA 3.5. *Given any unsatisfiable t-CNF formula F and $G = \mathrm{Lift}^{\mathrm{T}}_{k,\ell}(F)$. Suppose that there is a $(k+1)$-party communication protocol $\mathcal{P}$ consistently computing G_{search} with error ϵ such that $|\mathcal{P}| \leq C$. Then there exists a consistent system $\mathcal{Z} = \{f_S : S \subseteq \text{clauses}(F)\}$ of functions for F such that for every S, there is a $(k+1)$-party communication protocol $\mathcal{P}_S$ consistently computing $f_S \circ \psi^{\mathrm{T}}_{k,\ell}$ with error ϵ such that $|\mathcal{P}_S| \leq C$.*

PROOF. For every input assignment α to F, we fix any input assignment α^{T} to G that is a valid encoding of α. Let g^* be the subfunction of G_{search} that is computed by $\mathcal{P}$.

We first observe that on any input assignment α and α^{T}, $g^*(\alpha^{\mathrm{T}})$ always outputs a type (III)-clause. This is because α^{T} is a valid encoding. This clause corresponds to a unique clause in F that is falsified by α. Thus g^* uniquely determines a subfunction f^* of F_{search}.

Given f^*, we define the consistent system $\mathcal{Z} = \mathcal{Z}_{f^*}$ for F using the construction in Proposition 2.1. For every $f_S \in \mathcal{Z}$, the protocol $\mathcal{P}_S$ for $f_S \circ \psi^{\mathrm{T}}_{k,\ell}$ is adapted from $\mathcal{P}$ in the straightforward way. □

The next theorem is our main result on the proof complexity of G which glues all the parts together.

THEOREM 3.6. *There are absolute constants $c, c' > 0$ such that the following holds. Let F be any t-CNF formula on m variables having resolution rank at least r and let $G = \mathrm{Lift}^{\mathrm{T}}_{k,\ell}(F)$ for $\ell \geq \frac{c2^{2^{k+1}} km}{(r/\log|F|)^{1/6}}$. Then for any C and $M = c'(r/\log_2|F|)^{1/6}/(C2^k)$,*

- *any $R^{cc}(k+1, C)$ refutation of G of rank R must have $R\log_2 R \geq M$, and*
- *any tree-like $T^{cc}(k+1, C)$ refutation of G of size S must have $\log S \log\log S \geq M$.*

PROOF. We will prove only the first part; the second part follows similarly. Let P be a $R^{cc}(k+1, C)$ refutation of G of rank R. Lemma 2.8, there exists a $(k+1)$-party protocol $\mathcal{P}$ consistently computing G_{search} of error $1/3$ such that $|\mathcal{P}|$ is $O(CR\log R)$.

Now on the one hand, by Lemma 3.5, there exists a consistent system $\mathcal{Z} = \{f_S : S \subseteq \text{clauses}(F)\}$ of functions for F such that for every S, there exists a $(k+1)$-party protocol $\mathcal{P}_S$ computing $f_S \circ \psi^{\mathrm{T}}_{k,\ell}$ of error $1/3$ such that $|\mathcal{P}_S|$ is $O(CR\log R)$.

On the other hand, by Proposition 2.3, the assumption on the resolution rank of F implies that $D(F_{\text{search}}) \geq r$. By Proposition 2.2, there exists a function $f_S \in \mathcal{Z}$ such that

$$D(f_S) \geq \frac{D(F_{\text{search}})}{\lceil \log_2|F| \rceil} = \frac{r}{\lceil \log_2|F| \rceil}.$$

By Proposition 3.1, we have $d = \deg_{5/6}(f_S) \geq (D(f_S))^{1/6}/4 \geq (\frac{r}{\log_2|F|})^{1/6}/4$.

Finally, by Theorem 3.2, we must have $CR\log R$ that is $\Omega(d/2^k)$ which is $\Omega((r/\log_2|F|)^{1/6}/2^k)$. □

We note that we have a somewhat matching upper bound on the rank complexity of G.

LEMMA 3.7. *Let F be a t-CNF formula on m variables having resolution rank r. Then for any $\ell \geq 1$, there is an $T^{cc}(2, \log_2(rk\ell))$ proof of $G = \mathrm{Lift}^{\mathrm{T}}_{k,\ell}(F)$ of rank at most $crk\log_2\ell$, where $c > 0$ is some absolute constant.*

PROOF SKETCH. The main idea is to first build a decision tree (over linear inequalities) for G_{search} using the decision tree for F_{search}, and then convert this decision tree to a $T^{cc}(2)$ refutation. For every e_i there is precisely one variable $x_{i,(a_1,\ldots,a_k)}$ whose value will replace that of e_i in evaluating G. This selection is determined by the one tuple for which all of $y_{i,1,a_1}, \ldots, y_{i,k,a_k}$ evaluate to 1. Whenever the decision tree for F_{search} queries a variable e_i, the decision tree for G_{search} does k binary searches to find this tuple. Then the query of e_i is replaced by a query to $x_{i,(a_1,\ldots,a_k)}$.

The second step is carried out by following the standard conversion of decision trees to proofs implicit in the equivalence in Proposition 2.3. The conversion produces a binary proof tree where each line can be viewed as a disjunction of two linear inequalities on at most $rk\ell$ variables which can be evaluated efficiently by a 2-party randomized protocol. □

The following corollary, which implies Theorem 1.1, follows easily from Theorem 3.6, Lemma 3.7, and Proposition 3.4.

COROLLARY 3.8. *Let t be some constant. Suppose that a family of polynomial-size t-CNF formulas F on m variables has resolution rank complexity $r = r(m)$. Then, for every constant $\epsilon > 0$ and $k \leq (1-\epsilon)\log\log n$, there is a family of CNF formulas $G = \mathrm{Lift}^{\mathrm{T}}_k(F)$ on $n = m^{O(k)}$ variables of size $n^{O(t)}$ such that*

- *G requires $R^{cc}(k+1)$ rank complexity $\Omega(r^{1/7})$;*
- *there is a $T^{cc}(2)$ refutation of G of rank $O(r\log n)$;*
- *G requires $T^{cc}(k+1)$ tree-size $\exp(\Omega(r^{1/7}))$.*

3.3 Hardness using the Parity Selector

Let F be any t-CNF over the variables $e_1, \ldots, e_m$. Given $k, a \geq 2$, $\mathrm{Lift}^{\oplus}_{k,a}(F)$ is a CNF defined over m sets of variables $V_1, \ldots, V_m$, where each V_i is further partitioned into two sets X_i and Y_i. The difference here with $\mathrm{Lift}^{\oplus}_{k,a}(F)$ is that every V_i is an encoding of e_i based on $\psi^{\oplus}_{k,a}$. That is, each X_i has 2^a variables that are indexed by a-bit vectors, each $Y_i = \{y_{i,p,b} : 1 \leq p \leq k, 1 \leq b \leq a\}$ has ka variables, and each Y_i selects a unique a-bit vector c with $c_b = \oplus_{p=1}^{k} y_{i,p,b}$, for $1 \leq b \leq a$. The clauses in $\mathrm{Lift}^{\oplus}_{k,a}(F)$ consist of:

(*) For every clause, say $e_{i_1} \vee \cdots \vee e_{i_t}$, in F and for every t-tuple of a-bit vectors $(c_1, \ldots, c_t)$, if Y_{i_1} selects c_1, Y_{i_2} selects c_2, etc., then $x_{i_1,c_1} \vee \cdots \vee x_{i_t,c_t}$ must be satisfied. For every clause and t-tuple, this is translated into $\leq 2^{tka}$ clauses of size $tka + t$ in the straightforward way. That is, there are $\leq 2^{ka}$ assignments to the bits in Y_{i_1} that make them select c_1, and similarly for Y_{i_2}, etc. There is one clause, similar to the clauses of type (III) in the tensor selector case, corresponding to each such assignment.

PROPOSITION 3.9. *If F is a t-CNF over m variables, then $G = \mathrm{Lift}^{\oplus}_{k,a}(F)$ is a CNF formula of at most $|F|2^{tka+ta}$ clauses of size at most $ka + t$ over $n = m(2^a + ka)$ variables. Furthermore, if F is unsatisfiable, then so is G.*

The rest of the proofs for this section are very similar to those in the last section. The first difference is that since $\psi^{\oplus}_{k,a}$ gives a more efficient encoding than $\psi^{\mathrm{T}}_{k,\ell}$, the blow-up in the number of variables of G is significantly reduced. The second difference is that, here, G has a small rank resolution refutation, as opposed to a $CC(2)$ refutation in the last section when the lifting was done using tensor-encoding. There, small rank resolution refutation was impossible because the final clauses were too large.

By using Theorem 3.3 for $\psi^{\oplus}_{k,a}$ in place of Theorem 3.2 we can replace the function $G = \mathrm{Lift}^{\mathrm{T}}_{k,\ell}(F)$ in Theorem 3.6 by $G = \mathrm{Lift}^{\oplus}_{k,a}(F)$ and obtain exactly the same conclusion provided that $2^a > (c2^{2^{k+1}+2k}m)/(r/\log|F|)^{1/6}$.

On the other hand, one can upper bound the rank complexity of $\mathrm{Lift}^{\oplus}_{k,a}(F)$ in terms of that of F, even in resolution.

LEMMA 3.10. *Let F be a t-CNF formula on m variables having resolution rank r. There is some absolute constant $c > 0$ such that for any $a \geq 1$, there is a resolution refutation of $G = \mathrm{Lift}^{\oplus}_{k,a}(F)$ of rank at most $crka$.*

COROLLARY 3.11. *Let t be some constant. Suppose that a family of polynomial size t-CNF formulas F on m variables has resolution rank complexity $r = r(m)$. Then, for every $\epsilon > 0$ and $k \leq (1-\epsilon)\log\log n$, there is a family of CNF formulas $G = \mathrm{Lift}^{\oplus}_{k}(F)$ on $n = m^{O(1)}$ variables of size $n^{O(tk)}$ such that*

- *G has $R^{cc}(k+1)$ rank complexity $\Omega(r^{1/7})$;*
- *there is a resolution refutation of G of rank $O(rk\log n)$;*
- *G requires $T^{cc}(k+1)$ tree-size $\exp(\Omega(r^{1/7}))$.*

4. PROOF SYSTEM HIERARCHIES

In this section we separate $R^{cc}(k)$ and $\mathrm{CP}(k)$ in terms of rank and separate $T^{cc}(k)$ and $\mathrm{CP}(k)$ in terms of tree-like size, thereby separating $R^{cc}(k+1)$ from $R^{cc}(k)$ and $T^{cc}(k+1)$ from $T^{cc}(k)$. In particular we show that if an unsatisfiable t-CNF formula F has a small rank CP proof, then $G = \mathrm{Lift}^{\mathrm{T}}_{k-1,\ell}(F)$ has a small rank $\mathrm{CP}(k)$ proof (that can be made small and tree-like). Moreover, if F requires large resolution rank, then with the right parameters, G has no small rank $R^{cc}(k)$ (or small tree-like $T^{cc}(k)$) proof. Thus G is a separating instance.

The pigeonhole principle is known to be hard for resolution but admits a small rank CP proof. Since we need the clauses of the input formula to be of constant size for the size of the formula $\mathrm{Lift}^{\mathrm{T}}_{k,\ell}(F)$ to be polynomial, we use the following generalization of the pigeonhole principle [4].

Let $\mathcal{G} = (U \cup V, E)$ be any bipartite graph, where U represents the pigeons and V the holes and associate a variable $0 \leq e_{(u,v)} \leq 1$ with each edge $(u,v) \in E$. $\mathcal{G}$–PHP consists of the following clauses, which have been translated to inequalities:

(P) for all $u \in U$: $\sum_{(u,v)\in E} e_{(u,v)} \geq 1$

(H) for all $u \neq u' \in U, v \in V$ s.t. $(u,v),(u',v) \in E$: $e_{(u,v)} + e_{(u',v)} \leq 1$

PROPOSITION 4.1. [4] *For every n, there is a bipartite graph $\mathcal{G} = (U \cup V, E)$, where $|U| = |V| + 1 = n$ and the degree of every vertex in U is ≤ 5, such that $\mathcal{G}$–PHP is a polynomial size 5-CNF on $m = 5n$ variables and requires resolution rank $\Omega(m)$.*

From this and Corollary 3.8, we immediately obtain a rank lower bound for a lifting of $\mathcal{G}$–PHP.

LEMMA 4.2. *There is a family of bipartite graphs $\mathcal{G}$ and a family of polynomial-size CNF formulas $\mathrm{Lift}^{\mathrm{T}}_{k-1}(\mathcal{G}\text{–PHP})$ on n variables that requires $R^{cc}(k)$ rank $n^{\Omega(1/k)}$ and $T^{cc}(k)$ tree-like refutation size $\exp(n^{\Omega(1/k)})$ for $k \leq (1-\epsilon)\log\log n$ and any constant $\epsilon > 0$.*

Our upper bound for the lifted versions of $\mathcal{G}$–PHP will be derived from the following CP rank upper bound for $\mathcal{G}$–PHP itself.

PROPOSITION 4.3. [5] *For any $\mathcal{G} = (U \cup V, E)$ with $|U| = |V| + 1$, $\mathcal{G}$–PHP has a CP refutation of rank $O(\log|U|)$.*

Before considering the lifted version of $\mathcal{G}$–PHP, we define some convenient $\mathrm{CP}(k)$ consequences for lifted formulas. Suppose that F has variables $e_1, \ldots, e_m$ and let $G = \mathrm{Lift}^{\mathrm{T}}_{k-1}(F)$. The variables in G are $x_{i,c}$ (each cell c is indexed by a tuple in $[\ell]^{k-1}$) and $y_{i,p,a}$, where $1 \leq i \leq m$, $1 \leq p \leq k-1$, and $1 \leq a \leq \ell$. For each variable e_i of F define a degree k polynomial

$$\mathbf{e_i} := \sum_{c=(a_1,\ldots,a_k)\in[\ell]^{k-1}} x_{i,c}\mathbf{y_{i,c}},$$

where $\mathbf{y_{i,c}} := y_{i,1,a_1} \cdot y_{i,2,a_2} \cdots y_{i,k-1,a_{k-1}}$ and then define the following forms:

(I') for all $1 \leq i \leq m$: $\sum_{c\in[\ell]^{k-1}} \mathbf{y_{i,c}} \geq 1$

(II') for all $1 \leq i \leq m$ and $c \neq c' \in [\ell]^{k-1}$: $\mathbf{y_{i,c}} + \mathbf{y_{i,c'}} \leq 1$

(III') for all clauses in F, say $\neg e_{i_1} \vee e_{i_2} \vee \cdots \vee e_{i_t}$, and for every t-tuple of cells $(c^1, \ldots, c^t)$,

$$\mathbf{y_{i_1,c^1}} x_{i_1,c^1} + \mathbf{y_{i_2,c^2}}(1 - x_{i_2,c^2}) + \cdots + \mathbf{y_{i_t,c^t}}(1 - x_{i_t,c^t}) \leq t - 1$$

LEMMA 4.4. *For any $k, \ell \geq 2$ and any CNF formulas F and $G = \mathrm{Lift}^{\mathrm{T}}_{k-1,\ell}(F)$, given the families of clauses (I), (II), and (III) in G, there are $\mathrm{CP}(k)$ derivations of rank k of all (I'), (II'), and (III') inequalities as well as $0 \leq \mathbf{y_{i,c}} \leq 1$ and $0 \leq \mathbf{e_i} \leq 1$.*

LEMMA 4.5. *For any $\mathcal{G} = (U \cup V, E)$ with $|U| = |V| + 1$ and the degree of every vertex in U is at most t, the formula $G = \mathrm{Lift}^{\mathrm{T}}_{k-1,\ell}(\mathcal{G}\text{–PHP})$ has a $\mathrm{CP}(k)$ refutation of rank $O(\log|U| + tk\log\ell)$, for any $k, \ell \geq 2$.*

PROOF SKETCH. For ease of notation, we denote the variables in $F = \mathcal{G}-\mathrm{PHP}$ by $e_1, \ldots, e_m$ where $m = |E|$. We apply Lemma 4.4 to obtain a rank k derivation of the inequalities (I'), (II'), (III') and $0 \le \mathsf{e}_i \le 1$ from the original inequalities for G. Given the inequalities (I'),(II'), and (III') we then show that for each (P)-type axiom $e_{i_1} + \ldots + e_{i_t} \ge 1$ (for some $t > 0$) in F, we can derive the corresponding inequality $\mathsf{e}_{i_1} + \ldots + \mathsf{e}_{i_t} \ge 1$ via a rank-$O(tk \log \ell)$ proof in CP(k). Given inequalities (I'),(II'), and (III'), we also show that for all (H) axioms $e_{i_1} + e_{i_2} \le 1$ in F, $\mathsf{e}_{i_1} + \mathsf{e}_{i_2} \le 1$ is derivable via a rank-$O(k \log \ell)$ proof in CP(k). Finally, we simulate the CP-refutation for F in Proposition 4.3 with each variable e_i replaced by the degree k polynomial e_i. □

We remark that the construction in Lemma 4.5 can be similarly applied to any unsatisfiable t-CNF formula F to show that if F has small rank CP proof, then $\mathrm{Lift}^{\mathrm{T}}_{k-1,\ell}(F)$ has a small rank CP(k) proof. Lemmas 4.2 and 4.5 together yield the following separations of our proof systems.

THEOREM 4.6. *For any $\epsilon > 0$ there is a family of unsatisfiable CNF formulas G on n variables that requires nearly polynomial rank $n^{\Omega(1/\log\log n)}$ in all $R^{cc}(k)$ systems and nearly exponential tree-like size $\exp(n^{\Omega(1/\log\log n)})$ in all $T^{cc}(k)$ systems, but has logarithmic rank and polynomial tree-like size in CP(k) systems, for any $k \le (1-\epsilon)\log\log n$.*

5. INTEGRALITY GAPS

The MAX-SAT problem is well studied in the theory of approximation algorithms and optimal inapproximability results are known under the assumption that $\mathsf{P} \neq \mathsf{NP}$. There are also unconditional inapproximability results known for a restricted class of algorithms that involve applying Cutting Planes or LS+ procedures to a relaxation of the standard integer program (e.g. [5, 30]). Here we use our lifting approach to derive optimal unconditional inapproximability results for small rank Th(1) proofs.

Given a CNF formula $G = \{C_1 \wedge \cdots \wedge C_m\}$ over variables $x_1, \ldots, x_n$, we can add a new set of variables $z_1, \ldots, z_m$, and define $C'_i = \neg z_i \vee C_i$. Let G' be $C'_1 \wedge \cdots \wedge C'_m$. If we convert these clauses into linear constraints and add Boolean constraints, we obtain a linear program L_G with objective function $\sum_i z_i$ that is a natural LP relation of the MAX-SAT problem for G.

There are $2^t\binom{n}{t}$ clauses over n variables that contain exactly t different variables. Let $\mathcal{N}^{t,n}_m$ be the probability distribution induced by choosing m of these clauses uniformly and independently.

Let F be a t-CNF formula. We consider $G = \mathrm{Lift}^{\mathrm{T}}_{1,2}(F)$ as described earlier, except that since we have set $k = 1$ and $\ell = 2$, the form of G can be considerably simplified. That is, the variables of G will consist of two bit-vectors, x and y, in which x will contain n blocks, each of size 2, y will be a vector of length n, where y_i indicates which of the two elements of block i will be chosen in x. Each clause of F is transformed into 2^t clauses in G, corresponding to each of the 2^t possible bits of x that could be chosen by y. Thus if F has m clauses, each of size t, G has $2^t m$ clauses, each of size $2t$, and F is unsatisfiable if and only if G is unsatisfiable. (There is no need for the clauses on the y_i-variables that were used in the case of larger ℓ.)

The following theorem, which is key to getting an integrality gap, is a quantitatively stronger version of Theorem 3.2, for the case $k = 1$ and $\ell = 2$.

THEOREM 5.1. *Let F be any t-CNF formula on n variables having resolution rank at least r, and let $G = \mathrm{Lift}^{\mathrm{T}}_{1,2}(F)$. Then any $R^{cc}(2, C)$ refutation of G of rank R must have $CR \log R \ge r^\delta$ for some constant $\delta > 0$.*

The proof of Theorem 5.1 relies on the following stronger version of Theorem 3.2 for the special case of 2 players due to Sherstov [35]. Theorem 3.2 requires that ℓ be large. The theorem below has much less dependence on the degree, and as a result it does not require ℓ to be large. However, this quantitatively stronger version is currently only known to hold for 2-player communication complexity.

THEOREM 5.2. [35] *Let f be a boolean function on n variables with sign-degree at least d (and hence 5/6-degree at least d). Then any 2-party communication protocol $\mathcal{P}$ computing $g = f \circ \psi^{\mathrm{T}}_{1,2}$ with error 1/3 must have $|\mathcal{P}| = \Omega(d)$.*

The proof of Theorem 5.1 is similar to that of Theorem 3.6, using Theorem 5.2 instead of Theorem 3.2, and is omitted.

We now see how the above theorem can be applied to derive an integrality gap for small rank Th(1) or Cutting Planes proofs.

COROLLARY 5.3. *Let $t \ge 3$ be an integer. There exists $\delta < 1$ such that for all $\epsilon > 0$ there is a $\Delta > 1$ such that for a randomly chosen F from $\mathcal{N}^{t,n}_{\Delta n}$, the integrality gap of any n^δ round Cutting Planes (or Th(1)) relaxation of L_G, the linear relaxation of the $2t$-CNF $G = \mathrm{Lift}^{\mathrm{T}}_{1,2}(F)$, is at least $1 - 1/2^{2t} + \epsilon$ with high probability.*

PROOF. Given ϵ, fix $\Delta \gg 2^t \ln 2/\epsilon'^2$, where $(1 - 1/2^t + \epsilon')(2^t/(2^t-1) - \epsilon) = 1$. A random assignment satisfies each of F's clauses with probability $1-1/2^t$, so the expected number of satisfied clauses of F is $(1-1/2^t)\Delta n$. For appropriate choice of Δ, the probability that a random assignment satisfies more than a $1 - 1/2^t + \epsilon'$ fraction of equations is less than 2^{-n} by Chernoff bounds. Thus with high probability, no assignment satisfies more than a $1 - 1/2^t + \epsilon'$ fraction of F's equations. By the construction of G from F, each clause of F has precisely 2^t corresponding clauses in G. It follows that with high probability, no assignment satisfies more than a $1 - 1/2^{2t} + \epsilon$ fraction of G's clauses.

On the other hand, since $t \ge 3$, any Resolution refutation of F requires linear rank [10, 4]. Thus by Theorem 5.1 even after Th(1) inference of rank n^δ (and in particular n^δ rounds of Cutting Planes), there is some non-integral assignment α to the $x_i's$ that satisfies all linear constraints corresponding to the clauses of G. Extend this assignment by setting all the z_i's to 1 and it follows that all constraints of L_G, are also satisfied. Thus we have a solution satisfying all equations that survives even after n^δ rounds. □

Note that since a random assignment on average satisfies a $1 - 1/2^{2t}$ fraction of clauses of any $2t$-CNF formula, this yields an optimal integrality gap for rank n^δ Th(1) inference for MAX-$2t$-SAT for any $t \ge 3$. Such a result was previously only known for the special case of Cutting Planes proofs [5] and the proof relied on the specific form of inference rather than the general sound inference allowed for Th(1) proofs.

6. DISCUSSION

We can obtain a similar integrality gap to that of Corollary 5.3 for any problem for which we can prove a decision tree lower bound. That is, take any optimization problem that can be expressed naturally as a t-CNF formula, and such that an integrality gap of $1-\gamma$ can be proven for decision trees. (Such a result is usually elementary to obtain.) Then by our lifting technique, we can show that any small $R^{cc}(2,C)$ refutation (including Cutting Planes and Th(1) proofs) for the lifted version has an integrality gap of $1-\gamma/2^t$. Our approach only works at present for proof systems that correspond to 2-player communication complexity. However, an extension of Theorem 5.2 to the multiparty setting (as was done with the qualitatively weaker Theorem 3.2 which was originally proven for the 2-player case [34]) would immediately yield integrality gaps for stronger matrix cut systems, such as LS+ and Lasserre.

Our work raises several other natural open questions. Our lower bounds apply for k up to $(1-o(1))\log\log n$. We conjecture that it should be possible to derive hardness escalation results that work when k is $\Omega(\log n)$. Can our methods be strengthened to obtain general (dag-like) size lower bounds? Such a result, even for $k=3$, would give the first unrestricted size lower bounds for Lovász-Schrijver proofs.

Finally, there are many general questions related to hardness escalation. What relationships are there between the various forms of hardness amplification, hardness escalation, hardness condensing, and hardness amplification? What other examples of hardness escalation can be shown, possibly given reasonable assumptions? It would be very interesting to obtain a hardness escalation result that lifts lower bounds for a circuit class where cryptography is not possible to a circuit class were cryptography is possible (e.g., lifting from DNF lower bounds to TC_0 lower bounds) as such a result would cross the "natural proof" barrier.

Acknowledgements

We thank Ran Raz and Rahul Santhanam for very helpful conversations. In particular we thank Rahul for suggesting the term *hardness escalation*.

7. REFERENCES

[1] R. Beals, H. Buhrman, R. Cleve, M. Mosca, and R. de Wolf. Quantum lower bounds by polynomials. *JACM*, 48(4):778–797, 2001.

[2] P. Beame, T. Pitassi, and N. Segerlind. Lower bounds for Lovász-Schrijver systems and beyond follow from multiparty communication complexity. *SIAM J. Comput.*, 37(3):845–869, 2007.

[3] P. Beame and D.-T. Huynh-Ngoc. Multiparty communication complexity and threshold circuit size of AC^0. In *50th IEEE FOCS*, 53–62, 2009.

[4] E. Ben-Sasson and A. Wigderson. Short proofs are narrow – resolution made simple. *JACM*, 48(2):149–169, 2001.

[5] J. Buresh-Oppenheim, N. Galesi, S. Hoory, A. Magen, and T. Pitassi. Rank bounds and integrality gaps for cutting planes procedures. In *44th IEEE FOCS*, 318–327, 2003.

[6] J. Buresh-Oppenheim and R. Santhanam. Making hard problems harder. TR06-03, ECCC, 2006.

[7] M. Charikar, K. Makarychev, and Y. Makarychev. Integrality gaps for Sherali-Adams relaxations. In *41st ACM STOC*, 283–292, 2009.

[8] A. Chattopadhyay and A. Ada. Multiparty communication complexity of disjointness. TR08-002, ECCC, 2008.

[9] V. Chvátal. Edmonds polytopes and a hierarchy of combinatorial problems. *Discrete Mathematics*, 4:305–337, 1973.

[10] V. Chvátal and Endre Szemerédi. Many hard examples for resolution. *JACM*, 35(4):759–768, 1988.

[11] M. Davis, G. Logemann, and D. Loveland. A machine program for theorem proving. *CACM*, 5:394–397, 1962.

[12] J. Edmonds, R. Impagliazzo, S. Rudich, and J. Sgall. Communication complexity towards lower bounds on circuit depth. *Computational Complexity*, 10:210–246, 2001.

[13] K. Georgiou, A. Magen, T. Pitassi, and I. Tourlakis. Integrality gaps of $2-o(1)$ for vertex cover SDPs in the Lovasz-Schrijver hierarchy. In *48th IEEE FOCS*, 702–712, 2007.

[14] R.E. Gomory. Outline of an algorithm for integer solutions to linear programs. *Bull. of the AMS*, 64:275–278, 1958.

[15] D. Grigoriev. Linear lower bound on degrees of Positivstellensatz calculus proofs for the parity. *TCS*, 259:613–622, 2001.

[16] D. Grigoriev, E. A. Hirsch, and D. V. Pasechnik. Complexity of semi-algebraic proofs. In *STACS* LNCS v. 2285, 419–430, 2002.

[17] R. Impagliazzo and R. Paturi. On the complexity of k-SAT. *JCSS*, 67:367–375, 2001.

[18] R. Impagliazzo, T. Pitassi, and A. Urquhart. Upper and lower bounds on tree-like cutting planes proofs. In *9th IEEE LICS*, 220–228, 1994.

[19] M. Karchmer, R. Raz, and A. Wigderson. Super-logarithmic depth lower bounds via direct sum in communication complexity. *Computational Complexity*, 5:191–204, 1995.

[20] A. Kojevnikov and A. Itsykson. Lower bounds of static Lovasz-Schrijver calculus proofs for Tseitin tautologies. In *33rd ICALP*, 323–334, 2006.

[21] J. Krajíček. Discretely ordered modules as a first-order extension of the cutting planes proof system. *JSL*, 63(4):1582–1596, 1998.

[22] E. Kushilevitz and N. Nisan. *Communication Complexity*. Cambridge University Press, 1997.

[23] J.B. Lasserre. An explicit SDP relaxation for nonlinear 0-1 programs. In *IPCO, LNCS v. 2081*, 293–303, 2001.

[24] T. Lee and A. Shraibman. Disjointness is hard in the multi-party number-on-the-forehead model. In *23rd IEEE CCC*, 81–91, 2008.

[25] L. Lovasz and A. Schrijver. Cones of matrices and set-functions and 0-1 optimization. *SIAM J. Optimization*, 1(2):166–190, 1991.

[26] A. Maciel and T. Pitassi. Lower bounds on constant-depth Frege proofs with mod connectives modulo a hardness conjecture. In *11th IEEE LICS*, 189–200, 2006.

[27] S. Muroga. *Threshold logic and its applications*. John Wiley & Sons, 1971.

[28] N. Nisan and M. Szegedy. On the degree of boolean functions as real polynomials. *Computational Complexity*, 4:301–314, 1994.

[29] R. Raz and P. McKenzie. Separation of the monotone NC hierarchy. *Combinatorica*, 19(3):403–435, 1999.

[30] G. Schoenebeck. Linear level Lasserre lower bounds for certain k-CSPs. In *49th IEEE FOCS*, 593–602, 2008.

[31] G. Schoenebeck, L. Trevisan, and M. Tulsiani. A linear round lower bound for Lovasz-Schrijver SDP relaxations of Vertex Cover. In *22nd IEEE CCC*, 205–216, 2007.

[32] N. Segerlind and T. Pitassi. Exponential lower bounds and integrality gaps for tree-like Lovasz-Schrijver procedures. In *ACM-SIAM SODA*, 355–364, 2009.

[33] A. Sherali and W. Adams. A hierarchy of relaxations between the continuous and convex hull representations for zero-one programming problems. *SIAM J. Disc. Math.*, 3:411–430, 1990.

[34] A. A. Sherstov. Separating AC^0 from depth-2 majority circuits. In *39th ACM STOC*, 294–301, 2007.

[35] A. A. Sherstov. The pattern matrix method for lower bounds on quantum communication. In *40th ACM STOC*, 85–94, 2008. Full version: *CoRR, abs/0906.4291*.

[36] M. Tulsiani. CSP gaps and reductions in the Lasserre hierarchy. In *41st ACM STOC*, 303–312, 2009.

Load Balancing and Orientability Thresholds for Random Hypergraphs

[Extended Abstract]

Pu Gao[*] [†]
Department of Combinatorics and Optimization
200 University Ave. W., University of Waterloo
N2L 3G1, Waterloo, Ontario, Canada
jane.p.gao@gmail.com

Nicholas C. Wormald[‡]
Department of Combinatorics and Optimization
200 University Ave. W., University of Waterloo
N2L 3G1, Waterloo, Ontario, Canada
nwormald@math.uwaterloo.ca

ABSTRACT

Let $h > w > 0$ be two fixed integers. Let H be a random hypergraph whose hyperedges are all of cardinality h. To *w-orient* a hyperedge, we assign exactly w of its vertices positive signs with respect to the hyperedge, and the rest negative. A (w,k)-orientation of H consists of a w-orientation of all hyperedges of H, such that each vertex receives at most k positive signs from its incident hyperedges. When k is large enough, we determine the threshold of the existence of a (w,k)-orientation of a random hypergraph. The (w,k)-orientation of hypergraphs is strongly related to a general version of the off-line load balancing problem. The graph case, when $h = 2$ and $w = 1$, was solved recently by Cain, Sanders and Wormald and independently by Fernholz and Ramachandran, thereby settling a conjecture made by Karp and Saks. Motivated by a problem of cuckoo hashing, the special hypergraph case with $w = k = 1$, was solved in three separate preprints dating from October 2009, by Frieze and Melsted, by Fountoulakis and Panagiotou, and by Dietzfelbinger, Goerdt, Mitzenmacher, Montanari, Pagh and Rink.

Categories and Subject Descriptors

G.2 [**DISCRETE MATHEMATICS**]: Graph Theory—*Hypergraphs*; G.3 [**PROBABILITY AND STATISTICS**]: Probabilistic algorithms (including Monte Carlo)

[*]Current affiliation: Max Planck Institut Informatik, 66123 Saarbrücken, Saarland, Germany

[†]The research reported in this paper forms part of this author's Ph.D. thesis "Generation and properties of random graphs and analysis of randomized algorithms" submitted to the University of Waterloo in 2009.

[‡]Research supported by the Canadian Research Chairs Program and NSERC

STOC'10, June 5–8, 2010, Cambridge, Massachusetts, USA.

General Terms

Algorithms, Theory

Keywords

load balancing, hypergraph orientation, cores, orientability thresholds

1. INTRODUCTION

In this paper we consider a generalisation to random hypergraphs of a commonly studied orientation problem on graphs. An *h-hypergraph* is a hypergraph whose hyperedges are of all of cardinality h. Let $h > w$ be two given positive integers. We consider $\mathcal{G}_{n,m,h}$, the probability space of the set of all h-hypergraphs on n vertices and m hyperedges with the uniform distribution. A hyperedge is said to be *w-oriented* if exactly w distinct vertices in it are marked with positive signs with respect to the hyperedge. The *indegree* of a vertex is the number of positive signs it receives. Let k be a positive integer. A (w,k)-orientation of an h-hypergraph is a w-orientation all hyperedges such that each vertex has indegree at most k. If such a (w,k)-orientation exists, we say the hypergraph is *(w,k)-orientable*; for $w = 1$ we simply say *k-orientable*. Of course, being able to determine the (w,k)-orientability of an h-hypergraph H for all k solves the optimisation problem of minimising the maximum indegree of a w-orientation of H. If a graph (i.e. the case $h = 2$) is $(1,k)$-oriented, we may orient each edge of the graph in the normal fashion towards its vertex of positive sign, and we say the graph is *k-oriented*.

Note that a sufficiently sparse hypergraph is easily (w,k)-orientable. On the other hand, a trivial requirement for (w,k)-orientability of an h-hypergraph with m edges is $m \le kn/w$, since any w-orientation has average indegree mw/n. In this paper, we show the existence and determine the value of a sharp threshold (defined more precisely in Section 2) at which a random h-hypergraph from $\mathcal{G}_{n,m,h}$ fails to be (w,k)-orientable, provided k is a sufficiently large constant. We show that the threshold is the same as the threshold at which a certain type of subhypergraph achieves a critical density. In the above, as elsewhere in this paper, the phrase "for k sufficiently large" means for k larger than some constant depending only on w and h.

1.1 Applications to load balancing, and some previous results

The hypergraph orientation problem is motivated by classical load balancing problems which have appeared in various guises in computer networking. A seminal result of Azar, Broder, Karlin and Upfal [2] is as follows. Throw n balls sequentially into n bins, with each ball put into the least full of $h \geq 2$ randomly chosen boxes. Then, with high probability, by the time all balls are allocated, no bin contains many more than $(\ln \ln n)/\ln h$ balls. If, instead, each ball is placed in a random bin, a much larger maximum value is likely to occur, approximately $\ln n/(\ln \ln n)$. This surprisingly simple method of reducing the maximum is widely used for load balancing. It has become known as the multiple-choice paradigm, the most common version being two-choice, when $h = 2$.

One application of load balancing occurs when work is spread among a group of computers, hard drives, CPUs, or other resources. In the on-line version, the jobs arrive sequentially and are assigned to separate machines. To save time, the load balancer decides which machine a job goes to after checking the current load of only a few (say h) machines. The goal is to minimise the maximum load of a machine. Mitzenmacher, Richa and Sitaraman [19] survey the history, applications and techniques relating to this. In particular, Berenbrink, Czumaj, Steger and Vőcking [2, 3] show an achieveable maximum load is $m/n + O(\log \log n)$ for m jobs and n machines when $h \geq 2$.

Another application of load balancing mentioned by Cain, Sanders and the second author [5] is the disk scheduling problem, in which any w out of h pieces of data are needed to reconstruct a logical data block. Individual pieces can be initially stored on different disks. Such an arrangement has advantageous fault tolerance features to guard against disk failures. It is also good for load balancing: when a request for a data block arrives, the scheduler can choose any w disks among the h relevant ones. See Sanders, Egner and Korst [20] for further references.

These load balancing problems correspond to the (w, k)-orientation problem for h-hypergraphs, with $w = 1$ in the case of the job scheduling problem. The machines (bins) are vertices and a job (ball) is an edge consisting of precisely the set of machines to which it can be allocated. A job is allocated to a machine by assigning a positive sign to that vertex. The maximum load is then equal to the maximum indegree of a vertex in the (w, k)-oriented hypergraph.

1.2 Off-line version

In the on-line versions, the edges of the hypergraph arrive one by one, but the off-line version, in which the edges are all exposed at the start, is also of interest. For instance, in the disk scheduling problem, the scheduler may be able to process a large number of requests together, to balance the load better. Of course, the on-line and off-line versions are the same if $h = 1$, i.e. there is no choice. For $h = 2$, the off-line version experiences an even better improvement than the on-line one. If $m < cn$ items are allocated to n bins, for c constant, the expected maximum load is bounded above by some constant c' depending on c.

To our knowledge, previous theoretical results concern only the case $w = 1$ (this also applies to on-line problem). For $w = 1$ it is well known that an optimal off-line solution, i.e. achieving minimum possible maximum load, can be found in polynomial time ($O(m^2)$) by solving a maximum flow problem. As explained in [5], it is desirable to achieve fast algorithms that are close to optimal with respect to the maximum load. There are linear time algorithms that achieve maximum load $O(m/n)$ [10, 16, 18].

A central role in solutions of the off-line orientation problem with $(w, h) = (1, 2)$ is played by the *k-core* of a graph, being the largest subgraph with minimum degree at least k. The sharp threshold for the k-orientability of the random graph $\mathcal{G}(n, m) = \mathcal{G}_{n,m,2}$ was found in [5], and simultaneously by Fernholz and Ramachandran [13]. These were proofs of a conjecture of Karp and Saks that this threshold coincides with the threshold at which the $(k + 1)$-core has average degree at most $2k$. (It is obvious that a graph cannot be k-oriented if it has a subgraph of average degree greater than $2k$.) In each case, the proof analysed a linear time algorithm that finds a k-orientation *asymptotically almost surely* (a.a.s.; i.e. with probability $1 - o(1)$ as $n \to \infty$) when the mean degree of the $(k + 1)$-core is slightly less than $2k$. In this sense, the algorithms are asymptotically optimal since the threshold for the algorithms succeeding coincides with the threshold for existence of a k-orientation. The proof in [13] was significantly simpler than the other, which was made possible because a different algorithm was employed. It used a trick of "splitting vertices" to postpone decisions and thereby reduced the number of variables to be considered.

Since the preparation of the original version of the present paper, three preprints appeared by Frieze and Melsted [11], Fountoulakis and Panagiotou [12], and by Dietzfelbinger, Goerdt, Mitzenmacher, Montanari, Pagh and Rink [9] which independently study the threshold of $(1, 1)$-orientability of $\mathcal{G}_{n,m,h}$, i.e. the case $w = k = 1$. This has applications to cuckoo hashing. However, there seems to be no easy way to extend the proofs in [9, 11, 12] to solve for the case $k > 1$, even when $w = 1$.

1.3 Our contribution

We solve the generalisation of the conjecture of Karp and Saks mentioned above, for fixed $h > w > 0$, provided k is sufficiently large. That is, we find the threshold of (w, k)-orientation of random h-hypergraphs in $\mathcal{G}_{n,m,h}$. The determination of this threshold helps to predict loads in the off-line w-out-of-h disk scheduling problem, where the randomness of the hypergraph is justified by the random intial allocation of file segments to disks. We believe furthermore that the characterisation of the threshold in terms of density of a type of core, and possibly our method of proof, will potentially help lead to fast algorithms for finding asymptotically optimal orientations.

Our approach has a significant difference from that used in the graph case when $(w, h) = (1, 2)$. The algorithm used in [13] does not seem to apply in the hypergraph case, at least, splitting vertices cannot be done without creating hyperedges of larger and larger size. The algorithm used by [5], on the other hand, generalises in an obvious way, but it is already very complicated to analyse in the graph case, and the extension of the analysis to the hypergraph case seems formidable. However, in common with both approaches, we first find what we call the $(w, k+1)$-core in the hypergraph, which is an analogue of the $(k + 1)$-core in graphs. We use the differential equation method to determine the size and density of this core. From here, we use the natural representation of the orientation problem in terms of flows. It is quite easy to generalise the network flow formulation from the case $h = 2$, $w = 1$ to the arbitrary case, giving a problem that can be solved in time $O(m^2)$ for $m = \Theta(n)$. Unlike the approaches for the graph case, we do not study an algorithm that solves the load balancing problem. Instead, we use the minimum cut characterisation of the maximum flow to show that a.a.s. the hypergraph can be (w, k)-oriented if and only if the density of its $(w, k+1)$-core is below a certain threshold. When the density of the $(w, k+1)$-core is above this threshold, it is trivially too dense to be (w, k)-oriented.

Even the case $w = 1$ of our result gives a significant generalisation of the known results. We prove that the threshold of the orientability coincides with the threshold at which certain type of density (in the case $w = 1$, this refers to the average degree divided by h) of the $(w, k+1)$-core is at most k, and also the threshold at which a certain type of induced subgraph (in the case $w = 1$, this refers to the standard induced subgraph) does not appear. For the graph case, our method provides a new proof (for sufficiently large k) of the Karp-Saks conjecture that we believe is simpler than the proofs of [5] and [13].

We give precise statements of our results, including definition of the $(w, k+1)$-core, in Section 2. In Section 3 we study the properties of the $(w, k+1)$-core. In Section 4, we formulate the appropriate network flow problem, determine a canonical minimum cut for a network corresponding to a non-(w, k)-orientable hypergraph, and give conditions under which such a minimum cut can exist. Finally, in Section 5, we show that for k is sufficiently large, such a cut a.a.s. does not exist when the density of the core is below a certain threshold. Proofs not given in this paper will be provided in a longer version [14].

2. MAIN RESULTS

Let $h > w > 0$ and $k \geq 2$ be given constants. For any h-hypergraph H, we examine whether a (w, k)-orientation exists. We call a vertex *light* if the degree of the vertex is at most k. For any light vertex v, we can give v the positive sign with respect to every hyperedge x that is incident to v (we call this *partially orienting* x towards to v), without violating the condition that each vertex has indegree at most k. Remove v from H, and for each hyperedge x incident to v, simply update x by removing v. Then the size of x decreases by 1, and it has one less vertex that needs to be given a positive sign. If a hyperedge becomes of size $h - w$, we can simply remove that hyperedge from the hypergraph. Repeating this until no light vertex exists, we call the remaining hypergraph $\widehat{H}$ the $(w, k+1)$-*core* of H. Every vertex in $\widehat{H}$ has degree at least $k+1$, and every hyperedge in $\widehat{H}$ of size $h - j$ requires a $(w - j)$-orientation in order to complete a w-orientation of the original hyperedge in H.

Instead of considering the probability space $\mathcal{G}_{\bar{n},\bar{m},h}$, we may consider $\mathcal{M}_{\bar{n},\bar{m},h}$, the probability space of random uniform multihypergraphs with $\bar{n}$ vertices and $\bar{m}$ hyperedges, such that each hyperedge x is of cardinality h, and each vertex in x is chosen independently, uniformly at random from $[\bar{n}]$. Actually $\mathcal{M}_{\bar{n},\bar{m},h}$ may be a more accurate model for the off-line load balancing problem in some applications, and as we shall see, results for the non-multiple edge case can be deduced from it. For a nonnegative integer vector $\mathbf{m} = (m_2, \ldots, m_h)$, we also define the probability space $\mathcal{M}_{n,\mathbf{m}}$, being the obvious generalisation of $\mathcal{M}_{n,m,h}$ to non-uniform multihypergraphs in which m_i is the number of hyperedges of size i.

All our asymptotic notation refers to $n \to \infty$. For clarity, we consider $H \in \mathcal{M}_{\bar{n},\bar{m},h}$. We use n, m_{h-j} and μ for the number of vertices, the number of hyperedges of size $h - j$ and the average degree of $\widehat{H}$. We parametrise the number $\bar{m}$ of edges in the hypergraphs under study by letting $\bar{\mu} = \bar{\mu}(n)$ denote $h\bar{m}/\bar{n}$, the average degree of $H \in \mathcal{M}_{\bar{n},\bar{m},h}$ (or of $H \in \mathcal{G}_{\bar{n},\bar{m},h}$).

Our first observation concerns the distribution of $\widehat{H}$ and its vertex degrees. Let $\text{Multi}(n, m, k+1)$ denote the multinomial distribution of n integers summing to m, restricted to each of the integers being at least $k+1$. We call this *truncated multinomial*.

PROPOSITION 2.1. *Let $h > w \geq 1$ be two fixed integers. Let $H \in \mathcal{M}_{\bar{n},\bar{m},h}$ and let $\widehat{H}$ be its $(w, k+1)$-core. Conditional on its number n of vertices and numbers m_{h-j} of hyperedges of size $h - j$ for $j = 0, \ldots, w-1$, the random hypergraph $\widehat{H}$ is distributed uniformly randomly on multihypergraphs with all vertices of degree at least $k+1$ and having the same parameters n and m_{h-j} for each j. Furthermore, the degree distribution of $\widehat{H}$ is the truncated multinomial distribution* $\text{Multi}(n, m, k+1)$ *where $m = \sum (h-j) m_{h-j}$.*

The following theorem shows that the size and the number of hyperedges of $\widehat{H}$ are highly concentrated around the solution of a system of differential equations. It covers any $h > w \geq 2$ for sufficiently large k. For special case $w = 1$, the concentration result was already known for all $k \geq 0$, for example in [5, Theorem 3]. The particular system of differential equations is given in the long version of the paper [14].

THEOREM 2.2. *Let $h > w \geq 2$ be two fixed integers. Assume $ck \leq \bar{\mu} := h\bar{m}/\bar{n}$ for some constant $c > 1$. Let $H \in \mathcal{M}_{\bar{n},\bar{m},h}$ and let $\widehat{H}$ be its $(w, k+1)$-core. Let n be the number of vertices and m_{h-j} the number of hyperedges of size $h - j$ of $\widehat{H}$. Then, provided k is sufficiently large, there are constants $\alpha > 0$ and $\beta_{h-j} > 0$, which are determined by the solution of a certain differential equation system that depends only on $\bar{\mu}$, k, w and h, for which a.a.s. $n \sim \alpha\bar{n}$ and $m_{h-j} \sim \beta_{h-j}\bar{n}$ for $0 \leq i \leq w-1$. The same conclusion (with the same constants) holds if $H \in \mathcal{G}_{\bar{n},\bar{m},h}$.*

The differential equation system is rather complicated so it is not included here.

Let $\mathcal{P}$ be a hypergraph property and let $\mathcal{M}_{n,m,h} \in \mathcal{P}$ denote the event that a random hypergraph from $\mathcal{M}_{n,m,h}$ has the property $\mathcal{P}$. Following [1, Section 10.1], we say that $\mathcal{P}$ has a *sharp threshold function* $f(n)$ if for any constant $\epsilon > 0$, $\mathbf{P}(\mathcal{M}_{n,m,h} \in \mathcal{P}) \to 1$ when $m \leq (1-\epsilon)f(n)$, and $\mathbf{P}(\mathcal{M}_{n,m,h} \in \mathcal{P}) \to 0$ when $m \geq (1+\epsilon)f(n)$.

Recall that n denotes the number of vertices and m_{h-j} denotes the number of hyperedges of size $h - j$ in $\widehat{H}$. Let $\kappa(\widehat{H})$ denote $\sum_{j=0}^{w-1}(w-j)m_{h-j}/n$. Then $\kappa(\widehat{H})$ defines a certain type of density of $\widehat{H}$. We say that a hypergraph H has *property* $\mathcal{T}$ if its $(w, k+1)$-core $\widehat{H}$ satisfies the condition that $\kappa(\widehat{H})$ is at most k. (Since w and k are fixed, we often drop them from the notation.) The following theorem, proved using Theorem 2.2, immediately gives the corollary that there is a sharp threshold function for the property $\mathcal{T}$.

THEOREM 2.3. *Let $H \in \mathcal{M}_{\bar{n},\bar{m},h}$. Let $\bar{\mu}$ be the average degree of H and let $\widehat{H}$ be the $(w, k+1)$-core of H. Then for all sufficiently k, there exists a strictly increasing function $c(\bar{\mu})$ of $\bar{\mu}$, such that for any fixed $c_2 > c_1 > 1$ and for any $c_1 k < \bar{\mu} < c_2 k$, a.a.s. $\kappa(\widehat{H}) \sim c(\bar{\mu})$.*

COROLLARY 2.4. *There exists a sharp threshold function $f(\bar{n})$ for the hypergraph property $\mathcal{T}$ in $\mathcal{M}_{\bar{n},\bar{m},h}$ provided k is sufficiently large.*

The function $c(\bar{\mu})$ in the theorem, and the threshold function in the corollary, are determined by the solution of the differential equation system referred to in Theorem 2.1.

We have defined a (w, k)-orientation of a uniform hypergraph in Section 1. We can similarly define a (w, k)-orientation of a non-uniform hypergraph G with sizes of hyperedges between $h - w + 1$ and h to be a simultaneous $(w - j)$-orientation of each hyperedge of size $h - j$ such that every vertex has indegree at most k. By counting the positive signs in orientations, we see that if property $\mathcal{T}$ fails, there is no (w, k)-orientation of $\widehat{H}$, and hence there is no (w, k)-orientation of H.

For a nonnegative integer vector $\mathbf{m} = (m_{h-w+1}, \ldots, m_h)$, let $\mathcal{M}(n, \mathbf{m}, k+1)$ denote $\mathcal{M}_{n,\mathbf{m}}$ restricted to multihypergraphs with minimum degree at least $k+1$. By Proposition 2.1, $\mathcal{M}(n, \mathbf{m}, k+1)$ has the distribution of the $(w, k+1)$-core of $H \in \mathcal{M}_{\bar{n},\bar{m},h}$ conditioned on the number of vertices being n and the number of hyperedges of each size being given by $\mathbf{m}$. To emphasise the difference, we will use G to denote a not-necessarily-uniform hypergraph in cases where we might use H for a uniform hypergraph.

Given a vertex set S, we say a hyperedge x is *partially contained in* S if $|x \cap S| \geq 2$.

DEFINITION 2.5. *Let $0 < \gamma < 1$. We say that a multihypergraph G has property $\mathcal{A}(\gamma)$ if for all $S \subset V(G)$ with $|S| < \gamma|V(G)|$ the number of hyperedges partially contained in S is strictly less than $k|S|/2w$.*

In the following theorem, $\mathbf{m} = \mathbf{m}(n)$ denotes an integer vector for each n.

THEOREM 2.6. *Let γ be any constant between 0 and 1. Then there exists a constant $N > 0$ depending only on γ, such that for all $k > N$ and any $\epsilon > 0$, if $\mathbf{m}(n)$ satisfies $\sum_{j=0}^{w-1}(w-j)m_{h-j}(n) \leq kn - \epsilon n$ for all n, then $G \in \mathcal{M}(n, \mathbf{m}(n), k+1)$ a.a.s. either has a (w, k)-orientation or does not have property $\mathcal{A}(\gamma)$.*

We show in the forthcoming Corollary 4.2 that for certain values of γ, a.a.s. $\widehat{H}$ has property $\mathcal{A}(\gamma)$ if $\bar{\mu}$ is constrained to be at most hk/w. We will combine this with Corollary 2.4 and Theorem 2.6 and a relation we will show between $\mathcal{M}_{\bar{n},\bar{m},h}$ and $\mathcal{G}_{\bar{n},\bar{m},h}$ (Lemma 3.1), to obtain the following.

COROLLARY 2.7. *Let $h > w > 0$ be two given integers and k be a sufficiently large constant. Let $f(\bar{n})$ be the threshold function of property $\mathcal{T}$ whose existence is asserted in Corollary 2.4. Then $f(\bar{n})$ is a sharp threshold for the (w, k)-orientability of $\mathcal{M}_{\bar{n},\bar{m},h}$ and $\mathcal{G}_{\bar{n},\bar{m},h}$.*

For any vertex set $S \subset V(H)$, define *the subgraph induced by S with parameter w* to be the subgraph of G on vertex set S whose set of hyperedges is $\{x' = x \cap S : x \in H,\ s.t.\ |x'| \geq h - w + 1\}$. Call this hypergraph H_S. Let $d(H_S)$ denote the degree sum of vertices in the hypergraph H_S and let $e(H_S)$ denote the number of hyperedges in H_S. From the above results we will obtain the following.

COROLLARY 2.8. *The following three graph properties have the same sharp threshold in $\mathcal{M}_{\bar{n},\bar{m},h}$ and in $\mathcal{G}_{\bar{n},\bar{m},h}$.*

(i) H is (w, k)-orientable.

(ii) H has property $\mathcal{T}$.

(iii) There exists no $H' \subset H$ as an induced subgraph with parameter w such that $d(H') - (h - w)e(H') > ks$.

The proofs of Proposition 2.1, Theorem 2.2, 2.3 and 2.6 will appear in [14].

3. ANALYSING THE SIZE AND DENSITY OF THE $(W, K+1)$-CORE

A model of generating random graphs via multigraphs, used by Bollobás and Frieze [4] and Chvatál [7], is described as follows. Let $\mathcal{P}_{\bar{n},\bar{m}}$ be the probability space of functions $g : [\bar{m}] \times [2] \to [\bar{n}]$ with the uniform distribution. Equivalently, $\mathcal{P}_{\bar{n},\bar{m}}$ can be described as the uniform probability space of allocations of $2\bar{m}$ balls into $\bar{n}$ bins. A probability space of random multigraphs can be obtained by taking $\{g(i,1), g(i,2)\}$ as an edge for each i. This model can easily be extended to generate non-uniform random multihypergraphs by letting $\mathbf{m} = (m_2, \ldots, m_h)$ and taking $\mathcal{P}_{\bar{n},\mathbf{m}} = \{g : \cup_{i=2}^{h}[m_i] \times [i] \to [\bar{n}]\}$. Let $\mathcal{M}_{\bar{n},\mathbf{m}}$ be the probability space of random multihypergraphs obtained by taking each $\{g(j,1), \ldots, g(j,i)\}$ as a hyperedge, where $j \in [m_i]$ and $2 \leq i \leq h$. (Loops and multiple edges are possible.) Note that $\mathcal{M}_{\bar{n},\mathbf{m}}$, where $\mathbf{m} = (m_2) = (\bar{m})$, is a random multigraph; it was shown in [7] that if this is conditioned on being simple (i.e. no loops and no multiple edges), it is equal to $\mathcal{G}_{\bar{n},\bar{m},2}$, and that the probability of a multigraph in $\mathcal{M}_{\bar{n},(\bar{m})}$ being simple is $\Omega(1)$ if $\bar{m} = O(\bar{n})$. This result is easily extended to the following result, using the same method of proof.

LEMMA 3.1. *Assume $h \geq 2$ is a fixed integer and $\mathbf{m} = (m_2, \ldots, m_h)$ is a non-negative integer vector. Assume further that $\sum_{i=2}^{h} m_i = O(\bar{n})$. Then the probability that a multihypergraph in $\mathcal{M}_{\bar{n},\mathbf{m}}$ is simple is $\Omega(1)$.*

Cain and the second author [6] recently introduced a new model to analyse the k-core of a random (multi)graph or (multi)hypergraph, including its size and degree distribution. This model is called the *pairing-allocation* model. A generalisation of this, the *partition-allocation* model, is defined below. We will use this model to prove Theorem 2.6 and to analyse a randomized algorithm called the RanCore algorithm, defined later in this section, which outputs the $(w, k+1)$-core of a given h-hypergraph.

Given $h \geq 2$, n, $\mathbf{m} = (m_2, \ldots, m_h)$, $\mathbf{L} = (l_2, \ldots, l_h)$ and a nonnegative integer k such that $D - \ell \geq kn$, where $D = \sum_{i=2}^{h} i m_i$ and $\ell = \sum_{i=2}^{h} l_i$, let V be a set of n bins, and $\mathbf{M}$ a collection of pairwise disjoint sets $\{M_1, \ldots, M_h\}$, where M_i is a set of $i m_i$ balls partitioned into parts, each of size i, for all $2 \leq i \leq h$. Let Q be an additional bin aside from V. It may assist the reader to know that Q 'represents' all the hyperedge incidences at vertices of degree less than k, and l_i is the number of these incidences in edges of size i.

The *partition-allocation* model $\mathcal{P}(V, \mathbf{M}, \mathbf{L}, k)$ is the uniform probability space whose elements are the allocations of balls to bins defined as follows. Let $\mathcal{C} = \{c_2, \dots, c_h\}$ be a set of colours. Colour the balls in M_i with c_i. (The role of the colours is only to denote the size of the part a ball lies in.) Then allocate the D balls uniformly at random (u.a.r.) into the bins in $V \cup \{Q\}$, such that the following constraints are satisfied:

(i) Q contains exactly ℓ balls;

(ii) each bin in V contains at least k balls;

(iii) for any $2 \le i \le h$, the number of balls with colour c_i that are contained in Q is l_i.

We call Q the *light* bin and all bins in V *heavy*. To assist with the analysis in some situations, we consider the following algorithm which clearly generates a probability space equivalent to $\mathcal{P}(V, \mathbf{M}, \mathbf{L}, k)$. We call this alternative the *allocation-partition* algorithm since it allocates before partitioning the balls. First, allocate D balls randomly into bins $\{Q\} \cup V$ with the restriction that Q contains exactly ℓ balls and each bin in V contains at least k balls. Then colour the balls u.a.r. with the following constraints:

(i) exactly im_i balls are coloured with c_i;

(ii) for each $i = 2, \dots, h$, the number of balls with colour c_i contained in Q is exactly l_i.

Finally, take u.a.r. a partition of the balls such that for each $i = 2, \dots, h$, all balls with colour c_i are partitioned into parts of size i.

To prove Theorem 2.2, we will convert the problem to a question about $\mathcal{P}(V, \mathbf{M}, \mathbf{L}, k+1)$, in particular the $(w, k+1)$-core of the hypergraph induced in the obvious way by the bins containing at least $k+1$ balls.

A deletion algorithm producing the k-core of a random multigraph was analysed in [6]. The differential equation method [22] was used to analyse the size and the number of hyperedges of the final k-core. The degree distribution of the k-core was shown to be a truncated multinomial. We now extend this deletion algorithm to find the $(w, k+1)$-core of H in $\mathcal{M}_{\tilde{n},\tilde{m},h}$ and $\mathcal{G}_{\tilde{n},\tilde{m},h}$, analysing it using the partition-allocation model. We also prove Proposition 2.1 by considering the allocation-partition algorithm which generates $\mathcal{P}(V, \mathbf{M}, \mathbf{0}, k+1)$.

The deletion algorithm referred to above is the following, and is expressed in the setting of representing multihypergraphs using bins for vertices, where each hyperedge x is a set $h(x)$ of $|x|$ balls. Initially let LV be the set of all light vertices/bins, and let $\overline{LV} = V(H) \setminus LV$ be the set of heavy vertices. A *light* ball is any ball contained in LV.

RanCore Algorithm to derive the $(w, k+1)$-core
Input: an h-hypergraph H. Set $t := 0$.
  While neither LV nor $\overline{LV}$ is empty,
    t:=t+1;
    Remove all empty bins;
    U.a.r. choose a light ball v, let x be the hyperedge that contains v, and let u be the vertex/bin that contains v;
    If $|x| \ge h - w + 2$, update x with $x \setminus \{u\}$, otherwise, remove this hyperedge x from the current hypergraph. If any vertex/bin $u \in \overline{LV}$ becomes light, move u to LV together with all balls in it;
  If LV is empty, ouput the remaining hypergraph, otherwise, output the empty graph.

The output is clearly the $(w, k+1)$-core of the input hypergraph H.

Theorems 2.2 and 2.3 are proved in [14] by analysing the RanCore algorithm and the differential equations that result. These equations can be numerically solved when the values of h, w, k and μ are given. Table 3 gives the results of some computations, where h, w and k are given, $\widetilde{\mu}$ is the average degree of the hypergraph at the threshold for $\mathcal{T}$ given in Corollary 2.4, and $\widehat{\mu}$ is the corresponding average degree of its core $\widehat{H}$. By Corollary 2.7, discussed in the next section, $\widetilde{\mu}$ is also our main target, the threshold for orientability. Note that $\widehat{\mu}$ must be at least hk/w by the definition of property $\mathcal{T}$, and that it follows from the trivial upper bound of the orientability threshold given in the introduction part that $\widetilde{\mu}$ is at most hk/w.

h	w	k	$\widetilde{\mu}$	$\widehat{\mu}$
3	2	4	5.485	6.65086
3	2	10	14.766	15.5872
3	2	40	59.991	60.0773
10	2	4	19.99999	20.0003

Table 1: Some numerical computation results

4. THE (W, K)-ORIENTABILITY OF THE $(W, K+1)$-CORE

In this section we prove Corollary 2.8 assuming Theorem 2.6, and study the basic network flow formulation of the problem that is used in the next section to prove Theorem 2.6.

The proof of the following lemma is provided in [14].

LEMMA 4.1. *Let $H \in \mathcal{M}_{\tilde{n},\tilde{m},h}$ and let $\widehat{H}$ be the $(w, k+1)$-core of H. Let c_1 be a constant that can depend on k, with the constraint that $2 \le c_1 < h^2e^2\bar{\mu}$. Let $0 < \gamma = \varphi(k, c_1) = (c_1/h^2e^2\bar{\mu})^2$. Then a.a.s. for all $S \subset V(\widehat{H})$ with $|S| < \gamma n$, the number of hyperedges partially contained in S is less than $c_1|S|$.*

We next show that for any fixed $0 < \gamma < 1$, $\widehat{H}$ a.a.s. has property $\mathcal{A}(\gamma)$, defined in Definition 2.5.

COROLLARY 4.2. *Assume that $H \in \mathcal{M}_{\tilde{n},\tilde{m},h}$ with $\tilde{m} \le hk/w$, and that $\widehat{H}$ is the $(w, k+1)$-core of H. Let $\gamma = e^{-4}h^{-6}/4$. Then provided $k \ge 4w$, a.a.s. either $\widehat{H}$ is empty or $\widehat{H}$ has property $\mathcal{A}(\gamma)$.*

Proof. Apply Lemma 4.1 with $c_1 = k/2w$. Clearly $c_1 < ch^2e^2k$, and $c_1 \ge 2$ provided $k \ge 4w$. Then $\gamma \le \phi(k, c_1)$. By Definition 2.5, $\widehat{H}$ a.a.s. has property $\mathcal{A}(\gamma)$. ∎

Proof of Corollary 2.7 Let $\widehat{H}$ be the $(k+1)$-core of the random multihypergraph $H \in \mathcal{M}_{\tilde{n},\tilde{m},h}$. Let $\epsilon > 0$ be any constant. By Theorem 2.3, there exists a constant $\delta > 0$, such that a.a.s. if $\tilde{m} \le f(\tilde{m}) - \epsilon\tilde{n}$, then $\sum_{j=0}^{w-1}(w-j)m_{h-j} \le kn - \delta n$. By Theorem 2.6 and Corollary 4.2, there exists a constant N depending only on h and w such that provided $k > N$, $\widehat{H}$ a.a.s. has a (w, k)-orientation. On the other hand, if $\bar{m} \geq f(\bar{m}) + \epsilon\bar{n}$, then a.a.s. $\sum_{j=0}^{w-1}(w-j)m_{h-j} \geq kn + \delta n$, and hence clearly $\widehat{H}$ is not (w,k)-orientable. Therefore $f(\bar{n})$ is a sharp threshold function for the (w,k)-orientation of $\mathcal{M}_{\bar{n},\bar{m},h}$. By Lemma 3.1, $f(\bar{n})$ is also a sharp threshold function for the (w,k)-orientation of $\mathcal{G}_{\bar{n},\bar{m},h}$. ∎

Let G be a non-uniform multihypergraph with the sizes of its hyperedges between $h-w+1$ to h. In the rest of the paper, we will use the following notations. Let $E_{h-j} = \{x \in E(G) : |x| = h-j\}$. For any given $S \subset [n]$, let $m_{h-j,i}(S) := |\{x \in E_{h-j} : |x \cap S| = i\}|$ for any $0 \leq i \leq h-j$. When the context is clear we may drop S from the notation. Let $\overline{S}$ denote the set $[n] \setminus S$ and let $d(S)$ denote the sum of degrees of vertices in S.

Recall the definition of induced subgraph with parameter w above the statement of Corollary 2.8 in Section 2. The following Lemma generalises Hakimi's theorem [15, Theorem 4] for graphs, and is proved in [14] using network flows and the max-flow min-cut theorem in a fashion similar to that used for numerous combinatorial problems (see [8, 21] for examples). A similar network flow setting was used in [20, Section 3.3] to study the load balancing problem with $w=1$ and $h=2$.

LEMMA 4.3. *A multihypergraph G with sizes of hyperedges between $h-w+1$ and h has a (w,k)-orientation if and only if*

$$d(H_S) - (h-w)e(H_S) \leq k|S|, \quad \text{for all } S \subset V(G).$$

The following corollary is immediate.

COROLLARY 4.4. *A hypergraph $H \in \mathcal{G}_{\bar{n},\bar{m},h}$ has a (w,k)-orientation if and only if for any $S \subset V(H)$,*

$$d(H_S) - (h-w)e(H_S) \leq k|S|.$$

Proof of Corollary 2.8. This follows directly from Corollary 2.7 and Corollary 4.4. ∎

For any vertex set S, define

$$\partial^*(S) = d(S) - \sum_{j=0}^{w-1} \sum_{i=w-j+1}^{h-j} (i-(w-j))m_{h-j,i}, \qquad (1)$$

which measures a type of expansion in the hypergraph. For each hyperedge x of size $h-j$ which intersects S with i vertices, its contribution to $\partial^*(S)$ is $w-j \geq 0$ if $i \geq w-j+1$ and $i \geq 0$ otherwise. Therefore $\partial^*(S) \geq 0$ for any S. The following lemma characterises the existence of the (w,k)-orientation of G in terms of $\partial^*(S)$. (For the proof, see [14].)

LEMMA 4.5. *The following two graph properties of a multihypergraph G with sizes of hyperedges between $h-w+1$ and h are equivalent.*

(i) $\quad d(H_S) - (h-w)e(H_S) \leq k|S|, \quad$ *for all* $S \subset V(G)$;

(ii) $\quad \partial^*(S) \geq k|S| + \left(\sum_{j=0}^{w-1}(w-j)m_{h-j}\right) - kn,$

for all $S \subset V(G)$.

It follows from Lemma 4.3 and Lemma 4.5 that G is (w,k)-orientable if and only if Lemma 4.5 (ii) holds.

For any $S \subset V(G)$, let

$$q_{h-j}(S) = \sum_{i=1}^{h-j} i m_{h-j,i}, \quad \eta(S) = \sum_{j=0}^{w-1}\sum_{i=1}^{h-j-1} m_{h-j,i}. \qquad (2)$$

In other words, $q_{h-j}(S)$ denotes the contribution to $d(S)$ from hyperedges of size $h-j$ and $\eta(S)$ denotes the number of hyperedges which intersect both S and $\overline{S}$. When the context is clear, we may use q_{h-j} and η instead to simplify the notation.

Recall that given a vertex set S, a hyperedge x is partially contained in S if $|x \cap S| \geq 2$. Let $\rho(S)$ denote the number of hyperedges partially contained in S and let $\nu(S)$ denote the number of hyperedges intersecting S.

The following lemma, proved in [14], shows that, instead of checking Lemma 4.5 (ii), we can check that certain other events do not occur.

LEMMA 4.6. *Suppose that for some $S \subset V(G)$,*

$$\partial^*(S) < k|S| + \left(\sum_{j=0}^{w-1}(w-j)m_{h-j}\right) - kn. \qquad (3)$$

Then all of the following hold:

(i) $\quad \rho(\overline{S}) > k|\overline{S}|/w$;

(ii) $\quad \nu(S) < k|S|$;

(iii) $\quad (h-w)\rho(S) > d(S) - k|S|$;

(iv) $\quad$ *If, in addition,* $\displaystyle\sum_{j=0}^{w-1} \frac{w-j}{h-j} q_{h-j}(S) \geq (1-\delta)k|S|$

for some $\delta > 0$, then $\eta(S) < h^2\delta k|S|$.

5. PROOF OF THEOREM 2.6

Recall from Section 2 that $\mathcal{M}(n, \mathbf{m}, k+1)$ is $\mathcal{M}_{n,\mathbf{m}}$, which is a random multihypergraph with given edge sizes, restricted to multihypergraphs with minimum degree at least $k+1$. In this section we discuss the only remaining proof, that of Theorem 2.6. This theorem relates the orientability of $\mathcal{M}(n, \mathbf{m}, k+1)$ to a kind of density. Recall that this probability space was important because, by Proposition 2.1, it gives the distribution of the $(w, k+1)$-core $\widehat{H}$ of $H \in \mathcal{M}_{\bar{n},\bar{m},h}$ conditioned on the values of n, the number of vertices and m_{h-j}, the number of hyperedges of size $h-j$ for each j, in the core.

It is clear, that given values of n and $\mathbf{m}$, the probability space of random multihypergraphs generated by $\mathcal{P}([n], \mathbf{M}, \mathbf{0}, k+1)$, with $|M_{h-j}| = (h-j)m_{h-j}$ $(h = 0, \ldots, w-1)$, is equivalent to $\mathcal{M}(n, \mathbf{m}, k+1)$. So we may, and do, make use of the partition-allocation model for proving results about $\mathcal{M}(n, \mathbf{m}, k+1)$. For the full proof of Theorem 2.6 we refer to [14]. An outline is as follows.

In this setting, $\epsilon > 0$ and $k \geq 2$ are fixed. Let G be a random multihypergraph from the probability space $\mathcal{M}(n, \mathbf{m}, k+1)$. Without loss of generality, we may assume that $\epsilon < \frac{1}{2}$ since ϵ may be taken arbitrarily small. By the hypothesis of Theorem 2.6, we consider only $\mathbf{m}$ such that $\sum_{j=0}^{w-1}(w-j)m_{h-j} \leq kn - \epsilon n$. We may also assume that $\sum_{j=0}^{w-1}(w-j)m_{h-j} \geq kn - 2\epsilon n$ since otherwise, by Theorem 2.3, we can simply add a set of random hyperedges so that the assumption holds. This is valid because (w,k)-orientability is a decreasing property (i.e. it holds in all subgraphs of G whenever G has the property).

Let $q_{h-j}(S)$ and $\eta(S)$ be as defined in (2). The partition-allocation model gives a good foundation for proving that a.a.s. has certain properties concerning the distribution of vertex degrees and intersections of hyperedge sets with vertex sets. Using this and various other probabilistic tools, we show that

(a) the probability that $G \in \mathcal{M}(n, \mathbf{m}, k+1)$ has property $\mathcal{A}(\gamma)$ and contains some set S with $|S| < \gamma n$ for which both Lemma 4.6(ii) and (iii) holds is $o(1)$;

(b) there exists $\delta > 0$, such that when k is large enough, a.a.s. $\sum_{j=0}^{w-1} \frac{w-j}{h-j} q_{h-j} \geq (1-\delta)k|S|$, and the probability of $G \in \mathcal{M}(n, \mathbf{m}, k+1)$ containing some set S with $\gamma n \leq |S| \leq (1-\gamma)n$ and $\eta(S) < h^2 \delta k|S|$ is $o(1)$.

We also show the deterministic result that

(c) no multihypergraph G with property $\mathcal{A}(\gamma)$ contains any sets S with $|S| > (1-\gamma)n$ for which Lemma 4.6(i) holds.

It follows that the probability that G has property $\mathcal{A}(\gamma)$ and contains some set S for which all parts (i)–(iv) of Lemma 4.6 hold is $o(1)$. Then by Lemmas 4.5 and 4.6,

$$\mathbf{P}(G \in \mathcal{A}(\gamma) \wedge G \text{ is not } (w,k)\text{-orientable}) = o(1).$$

Finally, Lemma 3.1 shows that the result applies to random (simple) hypergraphs as well.

6. REFERENCES

[1] N. Alon and J. Spencer. *The probabilistic method.* Wiley-Interscience Series in Discrete Mathematics and Optimization. John Wiley & Sons, Inc., Hoboken, NJ. xviii+352 pp., third edition, 2008.

[2] Y. Azar, A. Z. Broder, A. R. Karlin, and E. Upfal. Balanced allocations. *SIAM J. Comput.*, 29(1):180–200, 1999.

[3] P. Berenbrink, A. Czumaj, A. Steger, and B. Vőcking. Balanced allocations: The heavily loaded case. *32th Annual ACM Symposium on Theory of Computing,* pages 745–754, 2000.

[4] Béla Bollobás and Alan M. Frieze. On matchings and hamiltonian cycles in random graphs. In *Random graphs '83 (Poznan', 1983)*, pages 23–46. North-Holland Math. Stud., 118, North-Holland, Amsterdam, 1985.

[5] J. Cain, P. Sanders, and N. Wormald. The random graph threshold for k-orientiability and a fast algorithm for optimal multiple-choice allocation. In *Proc. ACM-SIAM Symposium on Discrete Algorithms (SODA)*, pages 469–476, January 2007.

[6] J. Cain and N. Wormald. Encores on cores. *Electronic Journal of Combinatorics*, 13:RP 81, 2006.

[7] V. Chvátal. Almost all graphs with $1.44n$ edges are 3-colorable. *Random Structures Algorithms*, 2(1):11–28, 1991.

[8] William J. Cook, William H. Cunningham, William R. Pulleyblank, and Alexander Schrijver. *Combinatorial optimization. (English summary).* Wiley-Interscience Series in Discrete Mathematics and Optimization. A Wiley-Interscience Publication. John Wiley & Sons, Inc., New York, x+355 pp., 1998.

[9] M. Dietzfelbinger, A. Goerdt, M. Mitzenmacher, A. Montanari, R. Pagh and M. Rink. Tight Thresholds for Cuckoo Hashing via XORSAT. preprint available at `http://arxiv.org/abs/0912.0287`.

[10] M. Dietzfelbinger and F. Meyer auf der Heide. Simple, efficient shared memory simulations. In *5th ACM Symposium on Parallel Algorithms and Architectures, Velen, Germany, SIGACT and SIGARCH*, pages 110–119, June 30–July 2, 1993.

[11] A. Frieze and P. Melsted. Maximum Matchings in Random Bipartite Graphs and the Space Utilization of Cuckoo Hashtables.preprint available at `http://arxiv.org/abs/0910.5535`.

[12] N. Fountoulakis and K. Panagiotou.Sharp Load Thresholds for Cuckoo Hashing. preprint available at `http://arxiv.org/abs/0910.5147`.

[13] D. Fernholz and V. Ramachandran. The k-orientability thresholds for $G_{n,p}$. In *Proc. ACM-SIAM Symposium on Discrete Algorithms (SODA)*, pages 459–468 January 2007.

[14] P. Gao and N. Wormald. Orientability thresholds for random hypergraphs. 2010, preprint.

[15] S. L. Hakimi. On the degrees of the vertices of a directed graph. *J. Franklin Inst.*, 279:290–308, 1965.

[16] R. M. Karp, M. Luby, and F. Meyer auf der Heide. Efficient pram simulation on a distributed memory machine. In *24th ACM Symp. on Theory of Computing*, pages 318–326, May 1992.

[17] B.D. McKay and N.C. Wormald. Asymptotic enumeration by degree sequence of graphs with degrees $o(n^{1/2})$. *Combinatorica*, 11(4):369–382, 1991.

[18] F. Meyer auf der Heide, C. Scheideler, and V. Stemann. Exploiting storage redundancy to speed up randomized shared memory simulations. *Theoret. Comput. Sci.*, 162(2):245–281, August 1996.

[19] M. Mitzenmacher, A. Richa, and R. Sitaraman. The power of two random choices: a survey of techniques and results. In *Handbook of randomized computing*, volume I, II, pages 255–312. Comb. Optim., 9, Kluwer Acad. Publ., Dordrecht, 2001.

[20] P. Sanders, S. Egner, and J. Korst. Fast concurrent access to parallel disks. *Algorithmica*, 35(1):21–55, 2003.

[21] Alexander Schrijver. *Combinatorial optimization. Polyhedra and efficiency,* volume B. Algorithms and Combinatorics, 24, Springer-Verlag, Berlin, 2003. pp. i–xxxiv.

[22] N.C. Wormald. Differential equations for random processes and random graphs. *The Annals of Applied Probability*, 5(4):1217–1235, November 1995.

Combinatorial Approach to the Interpolation Method and Scaling Limits in Sparse Random Graphs

Mohsen Bayati
Stanford University
bayati@stanford.edu

David Gamarnik
MIT
gamarnik@mit.edu

Prasad Tetali*
Georgia Tech
tetali@math.gatech.edu

ABSTRACT

We establish the existence of free energy limits for several sparse random hypergraph models corresponding to certain combinatorial models on Erdös-Rényi graph $\mathbb{G}(N, c/N)$ and random r-regular graph $\mathbb{G}(N, r)$. For a variety of models, including independent sets, MAX-CUT, Coloring and K-SAT, we prove that the free energy both at a positive and zero temperature, appropriately rescaled, converges to a limit as the size of the underlying graph diverges to infinity. In the zero temperature case, this is interpreted as the existence of the scaling limit for the corresponding combinatorial optimization problem. For example, as a special case we prove that the size of a largest independent set in these graphs, normalized by the number of nodes converges to a limit w.h.p., thus resolving an open problem, (see Conjecture 2.20 in [Wor99], as well as [Ald],[BR],[JT08] and [AS03]).

Our approach is based on extending and simplifying the interpolation method of Guerra and Toninelli. Among other applications, this method was used to prove the existence of free energy limits for Viana-Bray and K-SAT models on Erdös-Rényi graphs. The case of zero temperature was treated by taking limits of positive temperature models. We provide instead a simpler combinatorial approach and work with the zero temperature case (optimization) directly both in the case of Erdös-Rényi graph $\mathbb{G}(N, c/N)$ and random regular graph $\mathbb{G}(N, r)$. In addition we establish the large deviations principle for the satisfiability property for constraint satisfaction problems such as Coloring, K-SAT and NAE-K-SAT. For example, let $p(c, q, N)$ and $p(r, q, N)$ denote, respectively, the probability that random graphs $\mathbb{G}(N, c/N)$ and $\mathbb{G}(N, r)$ are properly q-colorable. We prove the existence of limits of $N^{-1} \log p(c, q, N)$ and $N^{-1} \log p(r, q, N)$, as $N \to \infty$.

*Research supported in part by the NSF grants DMS-0701043 and CCR-0910584

STOC'10, June 5–8, 2010, Cambridge, Massachusetts, USA.

Categories and Subject Descriptors

G.3 [**Mathematics of Computing**]: Probability and Statistics

General Terms

Algorithms, Theory

Keywords

Constraint Satisfaction Problems, Partition Function, Random Graphs

1. INTRODUCTION

Consider two random graph models on nodes $[N] \triangleq \{1, \dots, N\}$, the Erdös-Rényi graph $\mathbb{G}(N, c/N)$ and the random r-regular graph $\mathbb{G}(N, r)$. The first model is obtained by adding each edge of the $N(N-1)/2$ possible edges randomly independently with probability c/N, where $c > 0$ is a constant (does not grow with N). The second is a graph chosen uniformly at random from the space of all r-regular graphs on N nodes, where the integer r is a fixed constant. Consider the size $|\mathcal{I}_N|$ of a largest independent set $\mathcal{I}_N \subset [N]$ in $\mathbb{G}(N, c/N)$ or $\mathbb{G}(N, r)$. It is straightforward to see that $|\mathcal{I}_N|$ grows linearly with N. It was conjectured in several papers including Conjecture 2.20 in [Wor99], [GNS06], [BR], as well as [JT08] and [AS03] that $|\mathcal{I}_N|/N$ converges in probability as $N \to \infty$. The fact that the actual value of $|\mathcal{I}_N|$ concentrates around its mean follows from a standard Azuma-type inequality. However, a real challenge is to show that the expected value of $|\mathcal{I}_N|$ normalized by N does not fluctuate around different values, for large N.

This conjecture is in fact just one of a family of similar conjectures. Consider, for example, the random MAX-K-SAT problem - the problem of finding the largest number of satisfiable clauses of size K in a uniformly random instance of a K-SAT problem on N variables with cN clauses. This problem can be viewed as an optimization problem over a sparse random *hypergraph*. A straightforward argument shows that at least $1 - 2^{-K}$ fraction of the clauses can be satisfied with high probability (w.h.p.). It was conjectured in [CGHS04] that the proportion of the largest number of satisfiable clauses has a limit w.h.p. as $N \to \infty$. As a third example, consider the problem of partial q-coloring of a graph: finding a q-coloring of nodes which maximizes the total number of properly colored edges. It is natural to conjecture again that value of this maximum has a scaling limit w.h.p. (though we are not aware of any papers explicitly stating this conjecture).

Recently a powerful rigorous statistical physics method was introduced by Guerra and Toninelli [GT02] and further developed by Franz and Leone [FL03], Franz, Leone and Toninelli [FLT03], Panchenko and Talagrand [PT04], and Montanari [Mon05]. The method is based on an ingenious interpolation between a random hypergraph (spin glass) model on N nodes on the one hand, and a disjoint union of random hypergraph models on N_1 and N_2 nodes, on the other hand, where $N = N_1 + N_2$. Using this method it is possible to show for certain random hypergraph models that when one considers the expected log-partition function, the derivative of the interpolation function has a definite sign at *every value* of the interpolation parameter. As a result the expected log-partition function of the N-node model is larger (or smaller depending on the details of the model) than the sum of the corresponding expected log-partition functions on N_1 and N_2-node models. This super(sub)-additivity property is used to argue the existence of the (thermodynamic) limit of the expected log-partition function scaled by N. From this the existence of the scaling limits for the ground states (optimization problems described above) is also shown by taking a limit as positive temperature approaches zero temperature. In [FL03], the method was used to prove the scaling limit of log-partition functions corresponding to random K-SAT model for even K (and the so-called Viana-Bray models with random symmetric Hamiltonian functions.) The case of odd K was also later resolved using the same method [FM].

Results and technical contributions. The goal of the present work is to simplify and extend the applicability of the Guerra-Toninelli interpolation method, and we do this in several important ways.

First, we extend the interpolation method to a variety of models on Erdös-Rényi graphs not considered before. Specifically, we consider independent set, MAX-CUT, Ising model, graph coloring (henceforth referred to as Coloring), K-SAT and Not-All-Equal K-SAT (NAE-K-SAT) models. The coloring model, in particular, is of special interest as it becomes the first non-binary model to which interpolation method is applied.

Second, we provide a simpler and a more combinatorial interpolation scheme as well as analysis. Moreover, we treat the zero temperature case (optimization problem) directly and separately from the case of the log-partition function, and again the analysis turns out to be substantially simpler. As a result, we prove the existence of the limit of the appropriately rescaled value of the optimization problems in these models, including independent set problem, thus resolving an open problem earlier stated.

Third, we extend the above results to the case of random regular graphs (and hypergraph ensembles, depending on the model). The case of random regular graphs has been considered before by Franz, Leone and Toninelli [FLT03] for the K-SAT and Viana-Bray models with even number of variables per clause, and Montanari [Mon05] in the context of bounds on the performance of certain *low density parity check* (LDPC) codes. In fact, both papers consider general degree distribution models. The second of these papers introduces a multi-phase interpolation scheme. In this paper we consider a modification of the interpolation scheme used in [FLT03] and apply it to the same six models we are focusing in the case of Erdös-Rényi graph.

Finally, we prove the large deviation principle for the satisfiability property for Coloring, K-SAT and NAE-K-SAT models on Erdös-Rényi graph in the following sense. A well known satisfiability conjecture [Fri99] states that for each of these models there exists a (model dependent) critical value c^* such that for every $\epsilon > 0$, when the number of edges (or clauses for a SAT-type problem) is at most $(c^* - \epsilon)N$, the model is colorable (satisfiable) w.h.p. and when it is at least $(c^* + \epsilon)N$, it is not colorable (not satisfiable) w.h.p. as $N \to \infty$. Friedgut came close to proving this conjecture by showing that these models exhibit sharp phase transition: there exists a sequence c_N^* such that for every ϵ, the model is colorable (satisfiable) w.h.p. as $N \to \infty$ when the number of edges (clauses) is at most $(c_N^* - \epsilon)N$ and is not colorable (satisfiable) w.h.p. when the number of edges (clauses) is at least $(c_N^* + \epsilon)N$. It is also reasonable to conjecture, and indeed was shown for the case $K = 2$, that not only the satisfiability conjecture is valid, but, moreover, the probability of satisfiability $p(c, N)$ decays to zero exponentially fast when $c > c^*$.

In this paper we show that for these three models, namely Coloring, K-SAT and NAE-K-SAT, the limit $r(c) \triangleq \lim_{N\to\infty} N^{-1} \log p(c, N)$ exists for every c. Namely, while we do not prove the satisfiability conjecture and exponential rate of convergence to zero of the satisfiability probability above the critical threshold, we do prove that if the convergence to zero occurs exponentially fast, it does so at a well-defined rate. Assuming the validity of the satisfiability conjecture and the exponential rate of decay to zero above c^*, our result implies that $r(c) = 0$ when $c < c^*$ and $r(c) < 0$ when $c > c^*$. Moreover, our results would imply the satisfiability conjecture, if one could strengthen Friedgut's result as follows: for every $\epsilon > 0$, $p(c_N^* + \epsilon, N)$ converges to zero exponentially fast, where c_N^* is the same sequence as in Friedgut's theorem.

Organization of the paper. The remainder of the paper is organized as follows. In the following section we introduce the sparse random (Erdös-Rényi) and random regular (hyper)-graphs and introduce various combinatorial models of interest. Our main results are stated in Section 3. The proof for the case of Erdös-Rényi graphs is presented in Section 4. In the interest of space, the proofs random regular graphs are presented in the Appendix. In the Appendix, we also state and prove a simple modification of a classical super-additivity theorem - if a sequence is nearly super-additive, it has a limit after an appropriate normalization.

Notations. We close this section with a few notational conventions. $\mathbb{R}(\mathbb{R}_+)$ denotes the set of (non-negative) real values and $\mathbb{Z}(\mathbb{Z}_+)$ denotes the set of (non-negative) integer values. As before, $[N]$ denotes the set of integers $\{1, \ldots, N\}$. Throughout the paper, we treat $[N]$ as a set of nodes, and we consider splitting this into two sets of nodes, namely $[N_1] = \{1, \ldots, N_1\}$ and $\{N_1 + 1, \ldots, N\}$. For symmetry, with some abuse of notation, it is convenient to denote the second set by $[N_2]$ where $N_2 = N - N_1$. $\text{Bi}(N, \theta)$ denotes binomial distribution with N trials and success probability θ. $\text{Pois}(c)$ denotes a Poisson distribution with parameter c. A sequence of random variables X_N is said to converge to a random variable X with high probability (w.h.p.) if for every $\epsilon > 0$, $\lim_{N\to\infty} \mathbb{P}(|X_N - X| > \epsilon) = 0$. This is the usual convergence in probability.

2. SPARSE RANDOM HYPERGRAPHS

Given a set of nodes $[N]$, and a positive integer K, a directed hyperedge is any ordered set of nodes $(i_1, \dots, i_K) \in [N]^K$. An undirected hyperedge is an unordered set of K not necessarily distinct nodes $i_1, \dots, i_K \in [N]$. A directed (undirected) K-uniform hypergraph on the node set $[N]$ is a pair $([N], E)$, where E is any set of directed (undirected) K-hyperedges $E = \{e_1, \dots, e_{|E|}\}$. A hypergraph is called simple if the nodes within each hyperedge $e_m, 1 \le m \le |E|$ are distinct and all the hyperedges are distinct. A (directed or undirected) hypergraph is called r-regular if each node $i \in [N]$ appears in exactly r hyperedges. The necessary condition for such a hypergraph to exist is $Nr/K \in \mathbb{Z}_+$. A degree $\Delta_i = \Delta_i(\mathbb{G})$ of a node i is the number of hyperedges containing i. A matching is a set of hyperedges such that each node belongs to exactly one edge. In this paper we use the terms hypergraph and graph (hyperedge and edge) interchangeably.

In order to address a variety of random models in a unified way, we introduce two random directed hypergraph models, namely Erdös-Rényi model $\mathbb{G}(N, M), M \in \mathbb{Z}_+$ and random regular graph model $\mathbb{G}(N, r), r \in \mathbb{Z}_+$. These two graph models, each consisting of N nodes, are described as follows. The first model $\mathbb{G}(N, M)$ is obtained by selecting M directed hyperedges uniformly at random with replacement from the space of all $[N]^K$ hyperedges. A variant of this is a *simple* Erdös-Rényi graph also denoted for convenience by $\mathbb{G}(N, M)$, which is obtained by selecting M edges uniformly at random without replacement from the set of all undirected hyperedges each consisting of *distinct* K nodes. In this paper we will consider exclusively the case when $M = \lceil cN \rceil$ and c is a positive constant (does not grow with N). In this case the probability distribution of the degree of a typical node is $\text{Pois}(cK) + O(1/N)$. For this reason we will also call it a *sparse* random Erdös-Rényi graph.

The second model $\mathbb{G}(N, r)$ is defined to be an r-regular directed K-uniform hypergraph generated uniformly at random from the space of all such graphs. We assume $Nr/K \in \mathbb{Z}_+$, so that the set of such graphs is non-empty. A simple (directed or undirected) version of $\mathbb{G}(N, r)$ is defined similarly. In this paper we consider exclusively the case when r is a constant (as a function of N) and we call $\mathbb{G}(N, r)$ a *sparse* random regular graph.

From non-simple to simple graphs. While it is common to work with simple hypergraphs, for our purpose it is more convenient to establish results for directed non-simple hypergraphs first. It is well-known, however, that both $\mathbb{G}(N, M)$ and $\mathbb{G}(N, r)$ graphs are simple with probability which remains at least a constant as $N \to \infty$, as long as c, r, K are constants. Since we prove statements which hold w.h.p., our results have immediate ramification for simple Erdös-Rényi and regular graphs.

It will be useful to recall the so-called configuration method of constructing the random regular graph [Bol85], [Bol80], [Gal63]. To each node i associate r nodes denoted $j_1^i, \dots, j_r^i$. We obtain a new set of Nr nodes. Consider a matching $e_1, \dots, e_{Nr/K}$ generated uniformly at random on this set of nodes. From this set of edges we generate a graph on the original N nodes by projecting each of the edge to their representative. Namely an edge $(i_1, \dots, i_K)$ in the graph on N nodes is created iff there is an edge in this set of the form $(j_{k_1}^{i_1}, \dots, j_{k_K}^{i_K})$ for some $k_1, \dots, k_K \in [r]$. The resulting graph is random r-regular (not necessarily simple) graph, which we again denote by $\mathbb{G}(N, r)$. From now on when we talk about configuration graph, we have in mind the graph just described on Nr nodes. It is known [JŁR00] that with probability bounded away from zero as $N \to \infty$ the resulting graph is in fact simple.

Given a hypergraph $\mathbb{G} = ([N], E)$ we will consider a variety of combinatorial structures on $\mathbb{G}$, which can be defined in a unified way using the notion of a Markov Random Field (MRF). The MRF is a hypergraph $\mathbb{G}$ together with an alphabet $\chi = \{0, 1, \dots, q-1\}$, denoted by $[q^-]$, and a set of node and edge potentials $H_i, i \in [N], H_e, e \in E$. A node potential is a function $H_i : [q^-] \to \mathbb{R}$ and an edge potential is a function $H_e : [q^-]^K \to \{-\infty\} \cup \mathbb{R}$. Given a MRF $(\mathbb{G}, \chi, H_i, H_e, i \in [N], e \in E)$ and any $x \in [q^-]^N$, let

$$H(x) = \sum_{i \in [N]} H_i(x_i) + \sum_{e \in E} H_e(x_e), \qquad H(\mathbb{G}) = \sup_{x \in [q^-]^N} H(x),$$

where $x_e = (x_i, i \in e)$. Namely, $H(x)$ is the value associated with a chosen assignment x and H is the optimal value, or the groundstate in the statistical physics terminology. In many cases the node and edge potentials will be random functions generated i.i.d. (see examples below).

Associated with an MRF is the Gibbs probability measure $\mu_{\mathbb{G}}$ on the set of node values $[q]^N$ defined as follows. Fix a parameter $\lambda > 0$ consider the probability measure $\mu_{\mathbb{G}}(x) = \lambda^{H(x)}/Z_{\mathbb{G}}$ to every assignment $x \in [q]^N$, where $Z_{\mathbb{G}} = \sum_x \lambda^{H(x)}$ is the normalizing *partition function*. Observe that $\lim_{\lambda \to \infty} \log_\lambda Z_{\mathbb{G}} = H(\mathbb{G})$. Sometimes one considers $\lambda = \exp(1/T)$ where T is *temperature*. The case $T = 0$, namely $\lambda = \infty$ then corresponds to zero temperature, or equivalently the optimization. We distinguish this with a positive temperature case, namely $\lambda < \infty$.

We will consider in this paper a variety of MRF defined on sparse random graphs $\mathbb{G}(N, \lfloor cN \rfloor)$ and $\mathbb{G}(N, r)$. (In the statistical physics literature x_i are called spin values, and the corresponding MRF is called a *diluted spin glass model.*) We now describe some examples of concrete and well-known MRF and show that they fit the framework described above.

Independent set. $K = 2$ and $q = 2$. Define $H_i(1) = 1, H_i(0) = 0$ for all $i \in [N]$. Define $H_e(1,1) = -\infty, H_e(1,0) = H_e(0,1) = H_e(0,0) = 0$ for every edge $e = (i_1, i_2)$. Then for every vector $x \in \{0,1\}^N$ we have $H(x) = -\infty$ if there exists an edge $e_j = (i_1, i_2)$ such that $x_{i_1} = x_{i_2} = 1$ and $H(x) = |\{i : x_i = 1\}|$, otherwise. Equivalently, $H(x)$ takes finite value only on x corresponding to independent sets, and in this case it is the cardinality of the independent set. $H(\mathbb{G})$ is the cardinality of the largest independent set.

MAX-CUT. $K = 2$ and $q = 2$. Define $H_i(0) = H_i(1) = 0$. Define $H_e(1,1) = H_e(0,0) = 0, H_e(1,0) = H_e(0,1) = 1$. Every vector $x \in \{0,1\}^N$ partitions nodes into two subsets of nodes taking values 0 and 1 respectively. $H(x)$ is the number of edges between the two subsets. $H(\mathbb{G})$ is the largest such number, also called maximum cut size. The more general case of this model is q-coloring.

Anti-ferromagnetic Ising model. $K = 2$ and $q = 2$. Fix $\beta > 0, B \in \mathbb{R}$. Define $H_i(0) = -B, H_i(1) = B$. Define $H_e(1,1) = H_e(0,0) = -\beta, H_e(1,0) = H_e(0,1) = \beta$. It is more common to use alphabet $\{-1,1\}$ instead of $\{0,1\}$ for this model. We use the latter for consistency with the remaining models.

q-Coloring $K = 2$ and q is arbitrary. $H_i(x) = 0, \forall x \in [q^-]$ and $H_e(x,y) = 0$ if $x = y$ and $H_e(x,y) = 1$ otherwise. Therefore for every $x \in [q^-]^N, H(x)$ is the number of properly colored edges and $H(\mathbb{G})$ is the maximum number of properly colored edges.

Random K-SAT. $K \geq 2$ is arbitrary, $q = 2$. $H_i = 0$ for all $i \in [N]$. The edge potentials are defined as follows. For each edge $e \in E$ generate $a_e = (a_1, \ldots, a_K)$ uniformly at random from $\{0,1\}$, independently for all edges. For each edge e set $H_e(a_1, \ldots, a_K) = 0$ and $H_e(x) = 1$ for all other $x = (x_1, \ldots, x_K)$. Then for every $x \in \{0,1\}^N$, $H(x)$ is the number of satisfied clauses and $H(\mathbb{G})$ is the largest number of satisfiable clauses. Often this model is called (random) MAX-K-SAT model. We drop the MAX prefix in the notation.

NAE-K-SAT (Not-All-Equal-K-SAT). The setting is as above except now we set $H_e(a_1, \ldots, a_K) = H_e(1-a_1, \ldots, 1-a_K) = 0$ and $H_e(x) = 1$ for all other x for each e.

It is for the K-SAT and NAE-K-SAT models that considering directed as opposed to undirected hypergraphs is convenient, as for these models the order of nodes in edges matters. For the remaining models, however, this is not the case.

In several examples considered above we have had only two possible values for the edge potential H_e and one value for the node potential. Specifically, for the cases of Coloring, K-SAT and NAE-K-SAT problems, H_e took only values 0 and 1. It makes sense to call instances of such problems "satisfiable" if $H(\mathbb{G}) = |E|$, namely every edge potential takes value 1. In the combinatorial optimization terminology this corresponds to finding a proper coloring, a satisfying assignment and a NAE satisfying assignment, respectively. We let $p(N, M) = \mathbb{P}(H(\mathbb{G}(N, M)) = M)$ denote the probability of satisfiability when the underlying graph is Erdös-Rényi graph $\mathbb{G}(N, M)$. We also let $p(N, r) = \mathbb{P}(H(\mathbb{G}(N, r)) = rNK^{-1})$ denote the satisfiability probability for a random regular graph $\mathbb{G}(N, r)$.

3. MAIN RESULTS

We now state our main results. Our first set of results concerns Erdös-Rényi graph $\mathbb{G}(N, \lfloor cN \rfloor)$.

THEOREM 1. *For every $c > 0$, and for every one of the six models described in Section 2, there exists (model dependent) $H(c)$ such that*

$$\lim_{N\to\infty} N^{-1} H(\mathbb{G}(N, \lfloor cN \rfloor)) = H(c), \qquad (1)$$

w.h.p. Also for every $c > 0$ there exists $p(c)$ such that

$$\lim_{N\to\infty} N^{-1} \log p(N, \lfloor cN \rfloor) = p(c), \qquad (2)$$

w.h.p. for Coloring, K-SAT and NAE-K-SAT models. Moreover, $H(c)$ is continuous and non-decreasing function of c for all models except for independent set and Ising model. For independent set $H(c)$ is non-increasing. For Coloring, K-SAT and NAE-K-SAT, $p(c)$ is continuous and non-increasing in c.

As a corollary one obtains the following variant of the satisfiability conjecture.

COROLLARY 1. *For Coloring, K-SAT and NAE-K-SAT models there exists a critical value c_h^* such that $H(c) = c$ when $c < c_h^*$ and $H(c) < c$ when $c > c_h^*$. Similarly, there exists c_p^*, such that $p(c) = 0$ when $c < c_p^*$ and $p(c) < 0$ when $c > c_p^*$.*

Namely, there exists a threshold value c^* such that if the number of clauses is smaller than $c^* N$ there exists a *nearly* satisfiable assignment (assignment satisfying all but $o(N)$ clauses), and if the number of clauses is larger than $c^* N$, then every assignment violates linearly in N many clauses. The interpretation for Coloring is similar. The result above was established earlier by the second author for randomly generated linear programming problem, using local weak convergence and martingale techniques [Gam04]. It would be interesting to see if the same result is obtainable using the interpolation method.

Can one use Corollary 1 to prove the satisfiability conjecture in the precise sense? The answer would be affirmative, provided that a stronger version of Friedgut's result [Fri99] on the sharp thresholds for satisfiability properties holds.

CONJECTURE 1. *For the Coloring, K-SAT and NAE-K-SAT models there exists a sequence M_N^* and $\gamma > 0$, such that for every $\epsilon > 0$, $\lim_{N\to\infty} p(N, \lfloor (1-\epsilon) M_N^* \rfloor) = 1$ and $p(N, \lfloor (1+\epsilon) M_N^* \rfloor) = O(\exp(-\gamma N))$, for all N.*

In contrast, Friedgut's sharp phase transition result [Fri99] replaces the second part of this conjecture with (the weaker) $\lim_{N\to\infty} p(N, \lfloor (1+\epsilon) M_N^* \rfloor) = 0$. Thus, we conjecture that beyond the phase transition region M_N^*, not only is the model *not satisfiable* w.h.p., but in fact the probability of satisfiability converges to zero exponentially fast. Conjecture 1 together with Theorem 1 implies the satisfiability conjecture using a simple counting argument which we omit.

Let us now state our results for the existence of the scaling limit for the log-partition functions.

THEOREM 2. *For every $c > 0, \lambda \geq 1$, and for every one of the models described in Section 2, there exists (model dependent) $z(c)$ such that*

$$\lim_{N\to\infty} N^{-1} \log Z(\mathbb{G}(N, \lfloor cN \rfloor)) = z(c), \qquad (3)$$

w.h.p., where $z(c)$ is continuous non-decreasing functions of c for all models except for independent set and Ising model. For independent set $H(c)$ is non-increasing.

Remark: The case $\lambda = 1$ is actually uninteresting as it corresponds to no interactions between the nodes leading to $Z(\mathbb{G}) = \prod_{i\in[N]} \lambda^{\sum_{x\in[q^-]} H_i(x)}$. In this case the limit of $N^{-1} \log Z(\mathbb{G}(N, \lfloor cN \rfloor))$ exists trivially when node potentials H_i are i.i.d. For independent set, the proof holds for $\lambda < 1$ as well. But, unfortunately the proof technique based on interpolation method does not seem to extend to the case $\lambda < 1$ in the other models. For Ising model this corresponds to a ferromagnetic case and the existence of the limit was established in [DM] using a local analysis technique.

We now turn to our results on random regular graphs.

THEOREM 3. *For every $r \in \mathbb{Z}_+$, and for all of the models described in the previous section, there exists (model dependent) $H(r)$ such that $\lim_{N\to\infty, N\in r^{-1}K\mathbb{Z}_+} N^{-1} H(\mathbb{G}(N, r)) = H(r)$ w.h.p. Also for every $r \in \mathbb{Z}_+$ there exists $p(r)$ such that $\lim_{N\to\infty, N\in r^{-1}K\mathbb{Z}_+} N^{-1} \log p(N, r) = p(r)$ for K-SAT and NAE-K-SAT models.*

Note, that in the statement of the theorem we take limits along subsequence N such that NrK^{-1} is an integer, so that the resulting random hypergraph is well-defined. Unlike the case of Erdös-Rényi graph, we were unable to prove the existence of the large deviation rate $\lim N^{-1}\log p(N,r)$ as $N \to \infty$ and $N \in r^{-1}K\mathbb{Z}_+$, for the case of coloring on random regular graph. At the end of the proof of Theorem 3 we discuss challenges associated with obtaining such a result, which we still believe is true.

Finally, we state our results for the log-partition function limits for random regular graphs.

THEOREM 4. *For every $r \in \mathbb{Z}_+, \lambda \geq 1$, and for every one of the six models described in the previous section, there exists (model dependent) $z(r)$ such that w.h.p, we have*

$$\lim_{N\to\infty} N^{-1}\log Z(\mathbb{G}(N,r)) = z(r). \tag{4}$$

4. PROOFS: OPTIMIZATION PROBLEMS IN ERDÖS-RÉNYI GRAPHS

The following simple observation will be useful throughout the paper. Given two hypergraphs $\mathbb{G}_i = ([N], E_i)$, $i = 1,2$ on the same set of nodes $[N]$ for each one of the six models in Section 2

$$|H(\mathbb{G}_1) - H(\mathbb{G}_2)| = O(|E_1 \Delta E_2|). \tag{5}$$

This follows from the fact that adding (deleting) an edge to (from) a graph changes the value of H by at most 1 for all models except for the Ising model, where the constant is β.

Our main technical result leading to the proof of Theorem 1 is as follows.

THEOREM 5. *For every $1 \leq N_1, N_2 \leq N-1$ such that $N_1 + N_2 = N$, and all models*

$$\mathbb{E}[H(\mathbb{G}(N,\lfloor cN \rfloor))] \geq \mathbb{E}[H(\mathbb{G}(N_1,\mathcal{M}_1))] + \mathbb{E}[H(\mathbb{G}(N_2,\mathcal{M}_2))]. \tag{6}$$

For Coloring, K-SAT and NAE-K-SAT

$$\log p(N,\lfloor cN \rfloor) \geq \log p(N,\mathcal{M}_1) + \log p(N,\mathcal{M}_2). \tag{7}$$

Here $\mathcal{M}_j \overset{d}{\triangleq} \mathrm{Bi}(\lfloor cN \rfloor, N_j/N)$, $j = 1,2$.

Remark: The randomness underlying the probability $p(N,\mathcal{M}_j)$ is both with respect to the randomness in the graph generation and randomness of $\mathcal{M}_j$. Also in the theorem above, we do not assume independence of $\mathcal{M}_j, j = 1,2$. In other words, $p(N,\mathcal{M}_j) \triangleq \sum_{M\geq 0}\mathbb{P}(N_j,M)\mathbb{P}(\mathcal{M}_j = M)$.

Let us first show how this result implies Theorem 1.

PROOF OF THEOREM 1. Since $\mathcal{M}_j$ have binomial distribution, we have $\mathbb{E}[|\mathcal{M}_j - \lfloor cN_j \rfloor|] = O(\sqrt{N})$. This together with observation (5) and Theorem 5 implies

$$\mathbb{E}[H(\mathbb{G}(N,\lfloor cN \rfloor))] \geq \mathbb{E}[H(\mathbb{G}(N_1,\lfloor cN_1 \rfloor))] + \mathbb{E}[H(\mathbb{G}(N_2,\lfloor cN_2 \rfloor))] - O(\sqrt{N}).$$

Namely the sequence $\mathbb{E}[H(\mathbb{G}(N,\lfloor cN \rfloor))]$ is "nearly" superadditive, short of the $O(\sqrt{N})$ correction term. Now we use Proposition 3 in the Appendix for the case $\alpha = 1/2$ to conclude that the limit $\lim_{N\to\infty} N^{-1}\mathbb{E}[H(\mathbb{G}(N,\lfloor cN \rfloor))] \triangleq H(c)$ exists. Showing that, this also implies convergence of $H(\mathbb{G}(N,\lfloor cN \rfloor))/N$ to $H(c)$ w.h.p. can be done using standard concentration results [JLR00] and we skip the details. It remains to show that $H(c)$ is a non-decreasing continuous function for all models (except for independent set and Ising), and is non-increasing for independent set. For all models (except independent set and Ising), $\mathbb{E}[H(\mathbb{G}(N,M_1))]$ is at most $\mathbb{E}[H(\mathbb{G}(N,M_2))]$ when $M_1 \leq M_2$ - adding hyperedges can only increase the objective value. For independent set, the opposite $\mathbb{E}[H(\mathbb{G}(N,M_1))] \geq \mathbb{E}[H(\mathbb{G}(N,M_2))]$ holds. The continuity follows from (5) which implies

$$|\mathbb{E}[H(\mathbb{G}(N,M_1))] - \mathbb{E}[H(\mathbb{G}(N,M_2))]| = O(|M_1 - M_2|).$$

In fact, this implies Lipschitz continuity of $H(c)$. This concludes the proof of (1).

We now turn to the proof of (2). We first establish the following claim for the three models of interest (Coloring, K-SAT, NAE-K-SAT).

LEMMA 1. *For Coloring, K-SAT, NAE-K-SAT,*

$$\log p(N_j,\mathcal{M}_j) \geq \log p(N_j,\lfloor cN_j \rfloor) - O(\sqrt{N}), \quad j = 1,2. \tag{8}$$

Before proving Lemma 1, we state and prove the following useful property.

LEMMA 2. *There exist a constant $\omega > 0$, such that for Coloring, K-SAT, NAE-K-SAT with large enough N, and all $M = \Theta(N)$,*

$$\mathbb{P}(N, M+m) \geq \omega^m\,\mathbb{P}(N,M) \tag{9}$$

where $m = O(N)$ is a positive integer.

Remark: Lemma 2 requires $m = O(N)$, $M = \Theta(N)$, and $N \gg 1$ only for the Coloring.

PROOF. We first assume K-SAT or NAE-K-SAT models. Note that for these models there exists a constant $\omega > 0$ such that for *every* graph and potential realization $(\mathbb{G} = (V,E), H)$ such that the problem is satisfiable (namely $H(\mathbb{G}) = |E|$), if a randomly chosen hyperedge e is added with a potential chosen according to the model, then

$$\mathbb{P}(H(\mathbb{G}+e) = |E|+1) \geq \omega.$$

In other words, if the current graph is satisfiable, the new graph obtained by adding a hyperedge remains satisfiable with at least a constant probability. Indeed, for example for the case of K-SAT, if the instance is satisfiable and x is a satisfying assignment, the added edge remains consistent with x with probability at least $\omega \triangleq 1 - 1/2^K$. For the case of NAE-K-SAT it is $\omega = 1 - 1/2^{K-1}$. This observation implies that for every positive M, m,

$$\mathbb{P}[H(\mathbb{G}(N,M+m)) = M + m | H(\mathbb{G}(N,M)) = M] \geq \omega^m,$$

further implying the desired bound.

For the case of Coloring the proof is more involved. Given a constant $\delta > 0$ we call a graph $\mathbb{G}$ on N nodes δ-unusual if it is colorable and in every coloring assignment there exists a color class with size at least $(1-\delta)N$. Namely, for every x such that $H(x) = |E|$, there exists $k \in [q^-]$ such that the cardinality of the set $\{i \in [N] : x_i = k\}$ is at least $(1-\delta)N$. We claim that if $M = \Theta(N)$ then

$$\mathbb{P}(\mathbb{G}(N,M) \text{ is } \delta\text{-unusual}) \leq \alpha^N(\delta), \tag{10}$$

for some $\alpha(\delta)$ such that $\alpha(\delta) \to 0$ as $\delta \to 0$. The claim is shown using the first moment method - the expected number of graphs with such a property is at most $\alpha^N(\delta)$. Indeed, given a subset $C \subset [N]$ such that $|C| \geq (1-\delta)N$, the probability that the graph $\mathbb{G}(N,M)$ is has a proper coloring with all nodes in C having the same color is at most $(1-(1-\delta)^2)^{\Theta(N)}$, since we must have that no edge falls within the class C. There are at most $\binom{N}{\delta N} \approx \exp(H(\delta)N)$

choices for the subset C, where $H(\delta) = -\delta \log \delta - (1-\delta)\log(1-\delta)$ is the usual entropy function. It is easy to check that $\alpha(\delta) \triangleq \exp(H(\delta))(1-(1-\delta)^2)^{\Theta(1)}$ satisfies $\alpha(\delta) \stackrel{\delta \to 0}{\to} 0$ and the claim is established.

Now observe that if a graph $\mathbb{G} = (V, E)$ is colorable but not δ-unusual, then adding a random edge e we obtain $\mathbb{P}(H(\mathbb{G}+e) = |E|+1) \geq \delta(1-\delta) \triangleq \tilde{\omega}$. Namely, in this case the probability goes down by at most a constant factor. This observation implies that when $M = \Theta(N)$, we have

$$\begin{aligned}
&\mathbb{P}\big(H(\mathbb{G}(N, M+1) = M+1)\big) \geq \\
&\mathbb{P}\big(H(\mathbb{G}(N, M+1) = M+1) | \mathbb{G}(N, M) \text{ colorable \& not } \delta\text{-unusual}\big) \\
&\quad \times \mathbb{P}\big(\mathbb{G}(N, M) \text{ colorable \& not } \delta\text{-unusual}\big) \\
&\quad \geq \tilde{\omega}\mathbb{P}\big(\mathbb{G}(N, M) \text{ colorable \& not } \delta\text{-unusual}\big) \\
&\quad \geq \tilde{\omega}\mathbb{P}\big(\mathbb{G}(N, M) \text{ colorable}\big) - \tilde{\omega}\mathbb{P}\big(\mathbb{G}(N, M)\ \delta\text{-unusual}\big) \\
&\quad = \tilde{\omega}\mathbb{P}\big(H(\mathbb{G}(N, M) = M)\big) - \tilde{\omega}\alpha^N(\delta).
\end{aligned}$$

From this we obtain that if $M = \Theta(N)$, then

$$\begin{aligned}
&\mathbb{P}\big(H(\mathbb{G}(N, M+m) = M+m)\big) \\
&\qquad \geq \tilde{\omega}^m \mathbb{P}(H(\mathbb{G}(N, M) = M)) - \tilde{\omega}(1-\tilde{\omega})^{-1}\alpha^N(\delta)
\end{aligned}$$

Now observe that $\mathbb{P}\big(H(\mathbb{G}(N, M) = M)\big) \geq (1-1/q)^M$. Indeed split nodes into q equal groups. The likelihood that this creates a valid q-coloring is at least the claimed value. Now select δ small enough, so that $\alpha(\delta) < (\tilde{\omega}/2)(1-1/q)$. Then for this choice of δ, we have obtain $\mathbb{P}\big(H(\mathbb{G}(N, M+m) = M+m)\big) \geq (\tilde{\omega}/2)^m \mathbb{P}\big(H(\mathbb{G}(N, M) = M)\big)$ for all large enough N. □

Proof of Lemma 1. For m, M, N satisfying conditions of Lemma 2

$$\begin{aligned}
&\log \mathbb{P}\big(H(\mathbb{G}(N, M+m)) = M+m\big) \\
&\qquad \geq \log \mathbb{P}\big(H(\mathbb{G}(N, M)) = M\big) - m \log(1/\omega).
\end{aligned}$$

Now, suppose $\mathcal{M}_j \stackrel{d}{=} \text{Bi}(\lfloor cN \rfloor, N_j/N)$. Using the concavity of log

$$\begin{aligned}
&\log \mathbb{P}\big(H(\mathbb{G}(N_j, \mathcal{M}_j)) = \mathcal{M}_j\big) \\
&= \log\Big(\sum_{M=0}^{|N_j^2|} \mathbb{P}\big(H(\mathbb{G}(N_j, M)) = M\big)\mathbb{P}(\mathcal{M}_j = M)\Big) \\
&\geq \sum_{M=0}^{|N_j^2|} \log(\mathbb{P}\big(H(\mathbb{G}(N_j, M)) = M\big))\mathbb{P}(\mathcal{M}_j = M) \\
&\stackrel{(a)}{\geq} \sum_{M < d\lfloor cN_j \rfloor} \log(\mathbb{P}\big(H(\mathbb{G}(N_j, M)) = M\big))\mathbb{P}(\mathcal{M}_j = M) \\
&\qquad - O(\sqrt{N}).
\end{aligned}$$

Where (a) uses $\mathbb{P}\big(H(\mathbb{G}(N_j, M)) = M\big) \geq (1-1/q)^M$ and a standard tail inequality for a large enough constant d (e.g. $d = 10$). Now, for $M < \lfloor cN_j \rfloor$ we can use the trivial inequality

$$\mathbb{P}\Big(H(\mathbb{G}(N_j, M)) = M\Big) \geq \mathbb{P}\Big(H(\mathbb{G}(N_j, M)) = \lfloor cN_j \rfloor)\Big),$$

and for other M we use Lemma 2 and $\mathbb{E}[|\mathcal{M}_j - \lfloor cN_j \rfloor|] = O(\sqrt{N})$ to obtain (8). □

Lemma 1 in combination with Theorem 5 implies

$$\begin{aligned}
\log p(N, \lfloor cN \rfloor) \geq \log p(N_1, \lfloor cN_1 \rfloor) \\
+ \log p(N_2, \lfloor cN_2 \rfloor) - O(\sqrt{N}).
\end{aligned}$$

To complete the proof of (2), we use Proposition 3 from the Appendix with α again set to 1/2. Monotonicity of $p(c)$ is proven similarly as for $H(c)$. Lipschitz continuity of $p(c)$ is similar to $H(c)$ and using Lemma 2.

We now turn to the proof of Theorem 5 and in particular introduce the interpolation construction.

Proof of Theorem 5. We begin by constructing a sequence of graphs interpolating between $\mathbb{G}(N, \lfloor cN \rfloor)$ and a disjoint union of $\mathbb{G}(N_1, \mathcal{M}_1)$ and $\mathbb{G}(N_2, \lfloor cN \rfloor - \mathcal{M}_1)$. Given N, N_1, N_2 s.t. $N_1 + N_2 = N$ and any $0 \leq r \leq \lfloor cN \rfloor$, let $\mathbb{G}(N, \lfloor cN \rfloor, r)$ be the random graph on nodes $[N]$ obtained as follows. It contains precisely $\lfloor cN \rfloor$ hyperedges. The first r hyperedges $e_1, \ldots, e_r$ are selected u.a.r. from all the possible directed hyperedges (namely they are generated as hyperedges of $\mathbb{G}(N, \lfloor cN \rfloor)$. The remaining $\lfloor cN \rfloor - r$ hyperedges $e_{r+1}, \ldots, e_{\lfloor cN \rfloor}$ are generated as follows. For each $j = r+1, \ldots, \lfloor cN \rfloor$, with probability N_1/N, e_j is generated independently u.a.r. from all the possible hyperedges on nodes $[N_1]$, and with probability N_2/N, it is generated u.a.r. from all the possible hyperedges on nodes $[N_2](=\{N_1+1, \ldots, N\})$. The choice of node and edge potentials H_v, H_e is done exactly according to the corresponding model, as for the case of graphs $\mathbb{G}(N, \lfloor cN \rfloor)$. Observe that when $r = \lfloor cN \rfloor$, $\mathbb{G}(N, \lfloor cN \rfloor, r) = \mathbb{G}(N, \lfloor cN \rfloor)$, and when $r = 0$, $\mathbb{G}(N, \lfloor cN \rfloor, r)$ is a union of disjoint graphs $\mathbb{G}(N_1, \mathcal{M}_1), \mathbb{G}(N_2, \mathcal{M}_2)$, conditioned on $\mathcal{M}_1 + \mathcal{M}_2 = \lfloor cN \rfloor$, where $\mathcal{M}_j \stackrel{d}{=} \text{Bi}(\lfloor cN \rfloor, N_j/N)$.

Proposition 1. *For every* $r = 1, \ldots, \lfloor cN \rfloor$,

$$\mathbb{E}[H(\mathbb{G}(N, \lfloor cN \rfloor, r))] \geq \mathbb{E}[H(\mathbb{G}(N, \lfloor cN \rfloor, r-1))]$$

Also for Coloring, K-SAT and NAE-K-SAT models

$$\begin{aligned}
&\mathbb{P}\Big(H(\mathbb{G}(N, \lfloor cN \rfloor, r)) = \lfloor cN \rfloor\Big) \\
&\qquad \geq \mathbb{P}\Big(H(\mathbb{G}(N, \lfloor cN \rfloor, r-1)) = \lfloor cN \rfloor\Big)
\end{aligned}$$

Let us first show how Theorem 5 follows from this proposition. Observe that for a disjoint union of two graphs $\mathbb{G} = \mathbb{G}_1 + \mathbb{G}_2$, with $\mathbb{G} = (V, E), \mathbb{G}_1 = (V_1, E_1), \mathbb{G}_2 = (V_2, E_2)$, we always have $H(\mathbb{G}) = H(\mathbb{G}_1) + H(\mathbb{G}_2)$ and $\mathbb{P}\big(H(\mathbb{G}) = |E|\big) = \mathbb{P}\big(H(\mathbb{G}_1) = |E_1|\big)\mathbb{P}\big(H(\mathbb{G}_2) = |E_2|\big)$.

To prove (7), using Proposition 1 we have

$$\begin{aligned}
&\log \mathbb{P}(N, \lfloor cN \rfloor) \\
&\quad \geq \log\big[\sum_{k \geq 0} \mathbb{P}(\mathcal{M}_1 = k)\mathbb{P}(N_1, k)\mathbb{P}(N_2, \lfloor cN \rfloor - k)\big] \\
&\quad \geq \sum_{k \geq 0} \mathbb{P}(\mathcal{M}_1 = k) \log\big[\mathbb{P}(N_1, k)\mathbb{P}(N_2, \lfloor cN \rfloor - k)\big] \\
&\qquad = \log \mathbb{P}(N_1, \mathcal{M}_1) + \log \mathbb{P}(N_2, \mathcal{M}_2).
\end{aligned}$$

Proof of (6) is similar (and simpler). □

Proof of Proposition 1. Observe that $\mathbb{G}(N, \lfloor cN \rfloor, r-1)$ is obtained from $\mathbb{G}(N, \lfloor cN \rfloor, r)$ by deleting a hyperedge chosen u.a.r. independently from r hyperedges $e_1, \ldots, e_r$

and adding a hyperedge either to nodes $[N_1]$ or to $[N_2]$ with probabilities N_1/N and N_2/N respectively. Let $\mathbb{G}_0$ be the graph obtained after deleting but before adding a hyperedge. For the case of K-SAT and NAE-K-SAT (two models with random edge potentials), assume that $\mathbb{G}_0$ also encodes the underlying edge potentials of the instance. For the case of Coloring, K-SAT, NAE-K-SAT, note that the maximum value that H can achieve for the graph $\mathbb{G}_0$ is $\lfloor cN \rfloor - 1$ since exactly one hyperedge was deleted. We will establish a stronger result: conditional on *any* realization of the graph $\mathbb{G}_0$ (and random potentials), we claim that

$$\mathbb{E}[H(\mathbb{G}(N, \lfloor cN \rfloor, r))|\mathbb{G}_0] \geq \mathbb{E}[H(\mathbb{G}(N, \lfloor cN \rfloor, r-1))|\mathbb{G}_0]. \quad (11)$$

And

$$\mathbb{P}(H(\mathbb{G}(N, \lfloor cN \rfloor, r)) = \lfloor cN \rfloor | \mathbb{G}_0) \geq \mathbb{P}(H(\mathbb{G}_0(N, \lfloor cN \rfloor, r-1)) = \lfloor cN \rfloor | \mathbb{G}_0) \quad (12)$$

for Coloring, K-SAT, NAE-K-SAT. Proposition then follows immediately from these claims by averaging over $\mathbb{G}_0$. Observe that *conditional on any realization* $\mathbb{G}_0$, $\mathbb{G}(N, \lfloor cN \rfloor, r)$ is obtained from $\mathbb{G}_0$ by adding a hyperedge to $[N]$ u.a.r. That is the generation of this hyperedge is independent from the randomness of $\mathbb{G}_0$. Similarly, conditional on any realization $\mathbb{G}_0$, $\mathbb{G}(N, \lfloor cN \rfloor, r-1)$ is obtained from $\mathbb{G}_0$ by adding a hyperedge to $[N_1]$ or $[N_2]$ u.a.r. with probabilities N_1/N and N_2/N respectively.

We now prove properties (11) and (12) for each of the six models.

Independent sets. Let $O^* \subset [N]$ be the set of nodes which belong to *every* largest independent set in $\mathbb{G}_0$. Namely if $I \subset [N]$ is an i.s. such that $|I| = H(\mathbb{G}_0)$, then $O^* \subset I$. Then for every edge $e = (i, k)$, $H(\mathbb{G}_0 + e) = H(\mathbb{G}_0) - 1$ if $i, k \in O^*$ and $H(\mathbb{G}_0 + e) = H(\mathbb{G}_0)$ if either $i \notin O^*$ or $k \notin O^*$. Here $\mathbb{G}_0 + e$ denotes a graph obtained from $\mathbb{G}_0$ by adding e. When the edge e is generated u.a.r. from the all possible edges, we then obtain $\mathbb{E}[H(\mathbb{G}_0 + e)|\mathbb{G}_0] - H(\mathbb{G}_0) = -(\frac{|O^*|}{N})^2$. Therefore, $\mathbb{E}[H(\mathbb{G}(N, \lfloor cN \rfloor, r)|\mathbb{G}_0] - H(\mathbb{G}_0) = -(\frac{|O^*|}{N})^2$. By a similar argument

$$\begin{aligned}
&\mathbb{E}[H(\mathbb{G}(N, \lfloor cN \rfloor, r-1)|\mathbb{G}_0] - H(\mathbb{G}_0) \\
&= -\frac{N_1}{N}(\frac{|O^* \cap [N_1]|}{N_1})^2 - \frac{N_2}{N}(\frac{|O^* \cap [N_2]|}{N_2})^2 \\
&\leq -(\frac{N_1}{N}\frac{|O^* \cap [N_1]|}{N_1} + \frac{N_2}{N}\frac{|O^* \cap [N_2]|}{N_2})^2 \\
&= -(\frac{|O^*|}{N})^2 = \mathbb{E}[H(\mathbb{G}(N, \lfloor cN \rfloor, r)|\mathbb{G}_0] - H(\mathbb{G}_0),
\end{aligned}$$

and (11) is established.

MAX-CUT. Given $\mathbb{G}_0$, let $\mathcal{C}^* \subset \{0,1\}^{[N]}$ be the set of optimal solutions. Namely $H(x) = H(\mathbb{G}_0), \forall x \in \mathcal{C}^*$ and $H(x) < H(\mathbb{G}_0)$ otherwise. Introduce an equivalency relationship $\sim$ on $[N]$. Given $i, k \in [N]$, define $i \sim k$ if *for every* $x \in \mathcal{C}^*, x_i = x_k$. Namely, in every optimal cut, nodes i and k have the same value. Let $O_j^* \subset [N], 1 \leq j \leq J$ be the corresponding equivalency classes. Given any edge $e = (i, k)$, observe that $H(\mathbb{G}_0 + e) = H(\mathbb{G}_0)$ if $i \sim k$ and $H(\mathbb{G}_0 + e) = H(\mathbb{G}_0) + 1$ otherwise. Thus

$$\mathbb{E}[H(\mathbb{G}(N, \lfloor cN \rfloor, r)|\mathbb{G}_0] - H(\mathbb{G}_0) = 1 - \sum_{1 \leq j \leq J} (\frac{|O_j^*|}{N})^2,$$

and

$$\mathbb{E}[H(\mathbb{G}(N, \lfloor cN \rfloor, r-1)|\mathbb{G}_0] - H(\mathbb{G}_0) = 1 - \frac{N_1}{N} \sum_{1 \leq j \leq J} (\frac{|O_j^* \cap [N_1]|}{N_1})^2 - \frac{N_2}{N} \sum_{1 \leq j \leq J} (\frac{|O_j^* \cap [N_2]|}{N_2})^2.$$

Using $\frac{N_1}{N}(\frac{|O_j^* \cap [N_1]|}{N_1})^2 + \frac{N_2}{N}(\frac{|O_j^* \cap [N_2]|}{N_2})^2 \geq (\frac{|O_j^*|}{N})^2$ we obtain (11).

Ising. The proof is similar to the MAX-CUT problem but requires extra care and we leave that for the journal version.

Coloring. Let $\mathcal{C}^* \subset [q^-]^N$ be the set of optimal colorings. Namely $H(x) = H(\mathbb{G}_0), \forall x \in \mathcal{C}^*$. Given $i, k \in [N]$, define $i \sim k$ iff $x_i = x_k$ for every $x \in \mathcal{C}^*$. Namely, in every optimal coloring assignments, i and k receive the same color. Then for every edge e, $H(\mathbb{G}_0 + e) = H(\mathbb{G}_0) - 1$ if $i \sim k$ and $H(\mathbb{G}_0 + e) = H(\mathbb{G}_0)$ otherwise. The remainder of the proof of (11) is similar to the one for MAX-CUT.

Now let us show (12). Thus assume $\mathbb{G}_0$ is a colorable graph. Since it has $\lfloor cN \rfloor - 1$ edges it means $H(\mathbb{G}_0) = \lfloor cN \rfloor - 1$. Letting $O_j^* \subset [N], 1 \leq j \leq J$ denote the equivalence classes, we obtain that

$$\mathbb{P}\Big(H(\mathbb{G}(N, \lfloor cN \rfloor, r)) = \lfloor cN \rfloor \Big| \mathbb{G}_0\Big) = 1 - \sum_{1 \leq j \leq J} \Big(\frac{|O_j^*|}{N}\Big)^2.$$

Similarly,

$$\mathbb{P}\Big(H(\mathbb{G}(N, \lfloor cN \rfloor, r-1)) = \lfloor cN \rfloor \Big| \mathbb{G}_0\Big) = 1 - \frac{N_1}{N} \sum_{1 \leq j \leq J} \Big(\frac{|O_j^* \cap [N_1]|}{N_1}\Big)^2 - \frac{N_2}{N} \sum_{1 \leq j \leq J} \Big(\frac{|O_j^* \cap [N_2]|}{N_2}\Big)^2.$$

The relation (12) then again follows from convexity.

K-SAT. Let $\mathcal{C}^* \subset \{0,1\}^N$ be the set of optimal assignments. Define a node i (variable x_i) to be *frozen* if either $x_i = 0, \forall x \in \mathcal{C}^*$ or $x_i = 1, \forall x \in \mathcal{C}^*$. Namely, in every optimal assignment the value of i is always the same. Let O^* be the set of frozen variables. Let $e = (i_1, \ldots, k_K) \subset [N]$ be a hyperedge and let $H_e : \{0,1\}^K \to \{0,1\}$ be some corresponding edge potential. Namely, for some $y_1, \ldots, y_K \in \{0,1\}, H_e(x_{i_1}, \ldots, x_{i_k}) = 0$ if $x_{i_1} = y_1, \ldots, x_{i_K} = y_K$ and $H_e = 1$ otherwise. Consider adding e with H_e to the graph $\mathbb{G}_0$. Note that if $e \cap ([N] \backslash O^*) \neq \emptyset$ then $H(\mathbb{G}_0 + e) = H(\mathbb{G}_0) + 1$, as in this case at least one variable in e is non-frozen and can be adjusted to satisfy the clause. Otherwise, suppose $e \subset O^*$, and let $x_{i_1}^*, \ldots, x_{i_K}^* \in \{0,1\}$ be the corresponding frozen values of $i_1, \ldots, i_K$. Then $H(\mathbb{G}_0 + e) = H(\mathbb{G}_0)$ if $x_{i_1}^* = y_1, \ldots, x_{i_K}^* = y_K$, and $H(\mathbb{G}_0 + e) = H(\mathbb{G}_0) + 1$ otherwise. Moreover, for the random choice of H, the first event $H(\mathbb{G}_0 + e) = H(\mathbb{G}_0)$ occurs with probability $1/2^K$. We conclude that

$$\mathbb{E}\Big[H(\mathbb{G}(N, \lfloor cN \rfloor, r)\Big|\mathbb{G}_0\Big] - H(\mathbb{G}_0) = 1 - \frac{1}{2^K}\Big(\frac{|O^*|}{N}\Big)^K,$$

$$\mathbb{P}\Big(H(\mathbb{G}(N, \lfloor cN \rfloor, r)) = \lfloor cN \rfloor \Big| \mathbb{G}_0, H(\mathbb{G}_0) = \lfloor cN \rfloor - 1\Big) = 1 - \frac{1}{2^K}\Big(\frac{|O^*|}{N}\Big)^K.$$

Similarly,

$$\mathbb{E}[H(\mathbb{G}(N,\lfloor cN\rfloor,r)|\mathbb{G}_0,H_0]-H(\mathbb{G}_0)$$
$$=1-\frac{1}{2^K}\frac{N_1}{N}\Big(\frac{|O^*\cap[N_1]|}{N_1}\Big)^K-\frac{1}{2^K}\frac{N_2}{N}\Big(\frac{|O^*\cap[N_2]|}{N_2}\Big)^K,$$

and

$$\mathbb{P}\Big(H(\mathbb{G}(N,\lfloor cN\rfloor,r))=\lfloor cN\rfloor\Big|\mathbb{G}_0,H(\mathbb{G}_0)=\lfloor cN\rfloor-1\Big)$$
$$=1-\frac{1}{2^K}\frac{N_1}{N}\Big(\frac{|O^*\cap[N_1]|}{N_1}\Big)^K-\frac{1}{2^K}\frac{N_2}{N}\Big(\frac{|O^*\cap[N_2]|}{N_2}\Big)^K.$$

Using the convexity of the function x^K on $x\in[0,\infty)$, we obtain the result.

NAE-K-SAT. The proof is very similar. The estimate $1/2^K$ changes to $2/2^K$, but the rest of the proof is the same.

We have established (11) and (12). With this, the proof of Proposition 1 is complete. □

5. PROOFS: LOG-PARTITION FUNCTION IN ERDÖS-RÉNYI GRAPHS

The following property serves as an analogue of (5). Given two hypergraphs $\mathbb{G}_i=([N],E_i),\ i=1,2$ on the same set of nodes $[N]$ for each one of the six models and each finite λ

$$|\log Z(\mathbb{G}_1)-\log Z(\mathbb{G}_2)|=O(|E_1\Delta E_2|). \tag{13}$$

This follows from the fact that adding (deleting) an hyperedge to (from) a graph results in multiplying or dividing the partition function by at most λ for all models except for the Ising model, where the corresponding value is λ^β.

The analogue of Theorem 5 is the following result.

THEOREM 6. *For every $1\le N_1,N_2\le N-1$ such that $N_1+N_2=N$ and every $\lambda>1$*

$$\mathbb{E}[\log Z(\mathbb{G}(N,cN))]\ge\mathbb{E}[\log Z(\mathbb{G}(N_1,\mathcal{M}_1))]$$
$$+\mathbb{E}[\log Z(\mathbb{G}(N_2,\mathcal{M}_2))]$$

where $\mathcal{M}_j\overset{d}{=}\mathrm{Bi}(cN,N_j/N),\ j=1,2$.

As before, we do not assume independence of $\mathcal{M}_j,j=1,2$. Let us first show how this result implies Theorem 2.

PROOF PROOF OF THEOREM 2. Since $\mathcal{M}_j$ have binomial distribution, using observation (13) and Theorem 6 we obtain

$$\mathbb{E}[\log Z(\mathbb{G}(N,\lfloor cN\rfloor))]\ge\mathbb{E}[\log Z(\mathbb{G}(N_1,\lfloor cN_1\rfloor))]$$
$$+\mathbb{E}[Z(\mathbb{G}(N_2,\lfloor cN_2\rfloor))]-O(\sqrt{N}).$$

Now we use Proposition 3 in the Appendix for the case $\alpha=1/2$ to conclude that the limit

$$\lim_{N\to\infty}N^{-1}\mathbb{E}[\log Z(\mathbb{G}(N,\lfloor cN\rfloor))]\triangleq z(c)$$

exists. Showing that this also implies convergence of $N^{-1}\mathbb{E}[\log Z(\mathbb{G}(N,\lfloor cN\rfloor))]$ to $z(c)$ w.h.p. again can be done using standard concentration results [JLR00] by applying property (13) and we skip the details. The proof of continuity and monotonicity of $z(c)$ is similar to the one of $H(c)$. □

Thus it remains to prove Theorem 6.

PROOF OF THEOREM 6. Construct an interpolating graph $\mathbb{G}(N,\lfloor cN\rfloor,r),0\le r\le\lfloor cN\rfloor$ exactly as in the previous subsection. We now establish the following analogue of Proposition 1. □

PROPOSITION 2. *For every $r=1,\ldots,cN$,*

$$\mathbb{E}[\log Z(\mathbb{G}(N,cN,r))]\ge\mathbb{E}[\log Z(\mathbb{G}(N,cN,r-1))]. \tag{14}$$

Let us first show how Theorem 6 follows from this proposition. Observe that for disjoint union of two graphs $\mathbb{G}=\mathbb{G}_1+\mathbb{G}_2$, with $\mathbb{G}=(V,E),\mathbb{G}_1=(V_1,E_1),\mathbb{G}_2=(V_2,E_2)$, we always have $\log Z(\mathbb{G})=\log Z(\mathbb{G}_1)+\log Z(\mathbb{G}_2)$. Theorem 6 then follows from Proposition 2.

PROOF OF PROPOSITION 2. Recall that $\mathbb{G}(N,cN,r-1)$ is obtained from $\mathbb{G}(N,cN,r)$ by deleting a hyperedge chosen u.a.r. independently from r hyperedges $e_1,\ldots,e_r$ and adding a hyperedge e either to nodes $[N_1]$ or to $[N_2]$ with probabilities N_1/N and N_2/N respectively. Let as before $\mathbb{G}_0$ be the graph obtained after deleting but before adding a hyperedge, and let Z_0 and μ_0 be the corresponding partition function and Gibbs measure respectively. In the case of K-SAT and NAE-K-SAT models we assume that $\mathbb{G}_0$ encodes the realizations of the random potentials as well. We now show that conditional on any realization of the graph $\mathbb{G}_0$

$$\mathbb{E}[\log Z(\mathbb{G}(N,cN,r))|\mathbb{G}_0]\ge\mathbb{E}[\log Z(\mathbb{G}(N,cN,r-1))|\mathbb{G}_0]. \tag{15}$$

The proof of (15) is done on a case by case basis and it is very similar to the proof of (11).

Independent sets. We have

$$\mathbb{E}[\log Z(\mathbb{G}(N,cN,r))|\mathbb{G}_0]-\log Z_0$$
$$=\mathbb{E}[\log\frac{Z(\mathbb{G}(N,cN,r))}{Z_0}|\mathbb{G}_0]$$
$$=\mathbb{E}[\log\frac{\sum_I\lambda^{|I|}-\sum_I 1_{\{e\subset I\}}\lambda^{|I|}}{\sum_I\lambda^{|I|}}|\mathbb{G}_0]$$
$$=\mathbb{E}[\log(1-\mu_0(e\subset I_0))|\mathbb{G}_0],$$

where the sums $\sum_I$ are over independent sets only and I_0 denotes an independent set chosen randomly according to μ_0. Notice, that since we are conditioning on graph $\mathbb{G}_0$ the only randomness underlying the expectation operator is the randomness of the hyperedge e and the randomness of set I_0. Note that $\mu_0(e\subset I_0)<1$ since $\mu_0(e\not\subset I_0)\ge\mu_0(I_0=\emptyset)>0$. Using the expansion $\log(1-x)=-\sum_{m\ge1}x^m/m$

$$\mathbb{E}[\log Z(\mathbb{G}(N,cN,r))|\mathbb{G}_0]-\log Z_0$$
$$=-\mathbb{E}[\sum_{k=1}^\infty\frac{\mu_0(e\subset I_0)^k}{k}|\mathbb{G}_0]$$
$$=-\sum_{k=1}^\infty\frac{1}{k}\ \mathbb{E}[\sum_{I^1,\ldots,I^k}1_{\{e\subset\cap_{j=1}^kI^j\}}\frac{\lambda^{\sum_{j=1}^k|I^j|}}{Z_0^k}|\mathbb{G}_0]$$
$$=-\sum_{k=1}^\infty\frac{1}{k}\sum_{I^1,\ldots,I^k}\frac{\lambda^{\sum_{j=1}^k|I^j|}}{Z_0^k}\mathbb{E}[1_{\{e\subset\cap_{j=1}^kI^j\}}|\mathbb{G}_0]$$
$$=-\sum_{k=1}^\infty\frac{1}{k}\sum_{I^1,\ldots,I^k}\frac{\lambda^{\sum_{j=1}^k|I^j|}}{Z_0^k}\Big(\frac{|\cap_{j=1}^kI^j|}{N}\Big)^2,$$

where in the last equality we have used the fact that e is distributed u.a.r. Similar calculation for $\log Z(\mathbb{G}(N,cN,r-1))$ that is obtained by adding an hyperedge to $G_0\cap[N_1]$ with probability N_1/N or to $G_0\cap[N_2]$ with probability N_2/N

gives

$$\mathbb{E}[\log Z(\mathbb{G}(N,cN,r-1))|\mathbb{G}_0] - \log Z_0$$
$$= -\sum_{k=1}^{\infty}\frac{1}{k}\sum_{I^1,\ldots,I^k}\frac{\lambda^{\sum_{j=1}^k |I^j|}}{Z_0^k}[\frac{N_1}{N}(\frac{|\cap_{j=1}^k I^j\cap[N_1]|}{N_1})^2 + \frac{N_2}{N}(\frac{|\cap_{j=1}^k I^j\cap[N_2]|}{N_2})^2].$$

Again using the convexity of $f(x)=x^2$ we obtain

$$\mathbb{E}[\log Z(\mathbb{G}(N,cN,r))|\mathbb{G}_0] - \log Z_0 \geq \mathbb{E}[\log Z(\mathbb{G}(N,cN,r-1))|\mathbb{G}_0] - \log Z_0$$

and (15) is established.

MAX-CUT. Similarly to the case of independent sets, if $\mathbb{G}(N,cN,r)$ is obtained from $\mathbb{G}_0$ by adding an edge (i,j) where i,j are chosen uniformly at random, we have $\mathbb{E}[\log Z(\mathbb{G}(N,cN,r))|\mathbb{G}_0] - \log Z_0$

$$\begin{aligned} &= \mathbb{E}[\log\frac{Z(\mathbb{G}(N,cN,r))}{Z_0}|\mathbb{G}_0] \\ &= \mathbb{E}[\log\frac{\sum_x 1_{\{x_i=x_j\}}\lambda^{H(x)} + \lambda\sum_x 1_{\{x_i\neq x_j\}}\lambda^{H(x)}}{\sum_x\lambda^{H(x)}}|\mathbb{G}_0] \\ &= \log\lambda + \mathbb{E}[\log(1-(1-\frac{1}{\lambda})\mu_0(x_i=x_j))|\mathbb{G}_0].\end{aligned}$$

Since $\lambda>1$ we have $0<(1-\lambda^{-1})\mu_0(x_i=x_j)<1$ (this is where the condition $\lambda>1$ is used) implying $\mathbb{E}[\log Z(\mathbb{G}(N,cN,r))|\mathbb{G}_0] - \log Z_0 - \log\lambda$

$$\begin{aligned} &= -\mathbb{E}[\sum_{k=1}^{\infty}\frac{(1-\lambda^{-1})^k\mu_0(x_i=x_j)^k}{k}|\mathbb{G}_0] \\ &= -\sum_{k=1}^{\infty}\frac{(1-\lambda^{-1})^k}{k}\mathbb{E}[\sum_{x_1,\ldots,x_k}\frac{\lambda^{\sum_{\ell=1}^k H(x_\ell)}}{Z_0^k}1_{\{x_i^\ell=x_j^\ell,\forall\ell\}}|\mathbb{G}_0] \\ &= -\sum_{k=1}^{\infty}\frac{(1-\lambda^{-1})^k}{k}\sum_{x_1,\ldots,x_k}\frac{\lambda^{\sum_{\ell=1}^k H(x_\ell)}}{Z_0^k}\mathbb{E}[1_{\{x_i^\ell=x_j^\ell,\forall\ell\}}|\mathbb{G}_0].\end{aligned}$$

Now for every sequence of vectors $x_1,\ldots,x_k$ introduce equivalency classes on $[N]$. Given $i,k\in[N]$, say $i\sim k$ if $x_i^\ell = x_k^\ell, \forall\ell=1,\ldots,k$. Namely, in every one of the cuts defined by $x_\ell, \ell=1,\ldots,k$, the nodes i and k belong to the same group. Let $O_s, 1\leq s\leq J$ be the corresponding equivalency classes. For an edge $e=(i,j)$ generated u.a.r., observe that $\mathbb{E}\left[1_{\{x_i^\ell=x_j^\ell\forall\ell\}}|\mathbb{G}_0\right] = \sum_{s=1}^J\left(\frac{|O_s|}{N}\right)^2$. Thus

$$\mathbb{E}[\log Z(\mathbb{G}(N,cN,r))|\mathbb{G}_0] - \log Z_0 - \log\lambda = -\sum_{k=1}^{\infty}\frac{(1-\lambda^{-1})^k}{k}\sum_{x_1,\ldots,x_k}\frac{\lambda^{\sum_{\ell=1}^k H(\ell)}}{Z_0^k}\sum_{s=1}^J\left(\frac{|O_s|}{N}\right)^2,$$

and similarly,

$$\mathbb{E}[\log Z(\mathbb{G}(N,cN,r-1))|\mathbb{G}_0] - \log Z_0 - \log\lambda$$
$$= -\sum_{k=1}^{\infty}\frac{(1-\lambda^{-1})^k}{k}\sum_{x_1,\ldots,x_k}\frac{\lambda^{\sum_{\ell=1}^k H(\ell)}}{Z_0^k}\sum_{s=1}^J(\frac{N_1}{N}(\frac{|O_s\cap[N_1]|}{N_1})^2 + \frac{N_2}{N}(\frac{|O_s\cap[N_2]|}{N_2})^2).$$

Using the convexity of the function $f(x)=x^2$, we obtain (15).

Ising, Coloring, K-SAT and NAE-K-SAT. The proofs of the remaining cases are obtained similarly and is omitted. The condition $\lambda>1$ is used to assert positivity of $1-\lambda^{-1}$ in the logarithm expansion. □

Acknowledgements

Authors are grateful for the insightful discussions with Silvio Franz, Andrea Montanari, Lenka Zdeborová, Florant Krzakala, and especially thankful to anonymous referees for helpful technical comments and notation suggestions. Authors also thank Microsoft Research New England for the hospitality and the inspiring atmosphere, in which this work began.

6. REFERENCES

[Ald] D. Aldous, `http://www.stat.berkeley.edu/~aldous/Research/OP/index.html`

[AS03] D. Aldous and J. M. Steele, *The objective method: Probabilistic combinatorial optimization and local weak convergence*, Discrete Combinatorial Probability, H. Kesten Ed., Springer-Verlag, 2003.

[BGT09] M. Bayati, D. Gamarnik, and P. Tetali, *Combinatorial approach to the interpolation method and scaling limits in sparse random graphs*, arXiv:0912.2444, 2009.

[Bol80] B. Bollobás, *A probabilistic proof of an asymptotic formula for the number of regular graphs*, European J. Combinatorics **1** (1980), 311–316.

[Bol85] B. Bollobás, *Random graphs*, Academic Press, Inc., 1985.

[BR] B. Bollobás and O. Riordan, *Sparse graphs: metrics and random models*, http://arxiv.org/abs/0812.2656.

[CGHS04] D. Coppersmith, D. Gamarnik, M. Hajiaghayi, and G. Sorkin, *Random MAXSAT, random MAXCUT, and their phase transitions*, Random Structures and Algorithms **24** (2004), no. 4, 502–545.

[DM] A. Dembo and A. Montanari, *Ising models on locally tree-like graphs*, Ann. of Appl. Prob., To appear.

[FL03] S. Franz and M. Leone, *Replica bounds for optimization problems and diluted spin systems*, Journal of Statistical Physics **111** (2003), no. 3/4, 535–564.

[FLT03] S. Franz, M. Leone, and F. L. Toninelli, *Replica bounds for diluted non-Poissonian spin systems*, J. Phys. A: Math. Gen. **36** (2003), 10967 – 10985.

[FM] S. Franz and A. Montanari, *Private communication.*

[Fri99] E. Friedgut, *Sharp thresholds of graph properties, and the k-SAT problem*, J. Amer. Math. Soc. **4** (1999), 1017–1054.

[Gal63] R. G. Gallager, *Low density parity-check codes*, MIT Press, 1963.

[Gam04] D. Gamarnik, *Linear phase transition in random linear constraint satisfaction problems*,

Prob. Th. & Rel. Fields. **129** (2004), no. 3, 410–440.

[GNS06] D. Gamarnik, T. Nowicki, and G. Swirscsz, *Maximum weight independent sets and matchings in sparse random graphs. Exact results using the local weak convergence method,* Random Structures and Algorithms **28** (2006), no. 1, 76–106.

[GT02] F. Guerra and F.L. Toninelli, *The thermodynamic limit of diluted spin glass models,* Commun. Math. Phys. **230** (2002) no. 1, 71–79; also available at http://arxiv.org/abs/cond-mat/0204280

[JŁR00] S. Janson, T. Łuczak, and A. Rucinski, *Random graphs,* John Wiley and Sons, Inc., 2000.

[JT08] S. Janson and A. Thomason, *Dismantling sparse random graphs,* Combinatorics, Probability and Computing **17** (2008), 259 – 264.

[Mon05] A. Montanari, *Tight bounds for LDPC and LDGM codes under map decoding,* IEEE Transactions on Information Theory **51** (2005), no. 9, 3221–3246.

[PT04] D. Panchenko and M. Talagrand, *Bounds for diluted mean-fields spin glass models,* Probability Theory and Related Fields **130** (2004), 312–336.

[Wor99] N. Wormald, *Models of random regular graphs,* in J.D. Lamb and D.A. Preece, editors, Surveys in Combinatorics, volume 267 ed., pp. 239–298, Cambridge University Press, 1999.

Appendix

7. PROOFS: RANDOM REGULAR GRAPHS

Our result leading to the proof of Theorem 3 is as follows.

THEOREM 7. *For every N_1, N_2 such that $N = N_1 + N_2$ and $N_1 r/K, N_2 r/K$ are integers,*

$$\mathbb{E}[H(\mathbb{G}(N,r))] \geq \mathbb{E}[H(\mathbb{G}(N_1,r))] + \mathbb{E}[H(\mathbb{G}(N_2,r))] - O(N^{\frac{5}{6}}).$$

In the interest of space we omit proof of Theorem 7. This proof is described in the longer version of this paper [BGT09].

PROOF OF THEOREM 3. The existence of the limit

$$\lim_{N\to\infty, N\in r^{-1}K\mathbb{Z}_+} N^{-1}\mathbb{E}[H(\mathbb{G}(N,r))] = H(r)$$

follows immediately from Theorem 7 and Proposition 3 from the Appendix. Then the convergence w.h.p.

$$\lim_{N\to\infty, N\in r^{-1}K\mathbb{Z}_+} N^{-1}H(\mathbb{G}(N,r)) = H(r),$$

follows once again using standard concentration results [JŁR00].

The proof of the existence of the large deviations limit $\lim_{N\to\infty, N\in r^{-1}K\mathbb{Z}_+} N^{-1}\log p(N,r) = p(r)$ for K-SAT and NAE-K-SAT models uses the same interpolation process and the same proof as the one used in the case of Erdös-Rényi graph. □

The proof of Theorem 4 uses the same interpolation as the one above and the proof itself mimics the one for Theorem 2. For this reason, we omit the details.

8. MODIFIED SUPER-ADDITIVITY THEOREM

PROPOSITION 3. *Given $\alpha \in (0,1)$, suppose a non-negative sequence $a_N, N \geq 1$ satisfies*

$$a_N \geq a_{N_1} + a_{N_2} - O(N^\alpha). \tag{16}$$

for every N_1, N_2 s.t. $N = N_1 + N_2$. Then the limit $\lim_{N\to\infty}\frac{a_N}{N}$ exists.

PROOF. It is convenient to define $a_N = a_{\lfloor N \rfloor}$ for every real not necessarily integer value $N \geq 1$. It is then straightforward to check that the property (16) holds when extended to reals as well (thanks to the correction term $O(N^\alpha)$). Let

$$a^* = \limsup_{N\to\infty} \frac{a_N}{N}.$$

Fix $\epsilon > 0$ and find k such that $1/k < \epsilon \leq 1/(k-1)$. Find find $N_0 = N_0(\epsilon)$ such that $N_0^{-1}a_{N_0} \geq a^* - \epsilon$, $k^\alpha N_0^{\alpha-1} < \epsilon$. Clearly, such N_0 exists. Consider any $N \geq kN_0$. Find r such that $kN_0 2^r \leq N \leq kN_0 2^{r+1}$. Applying (16) iteratively with $N_1 = N_2 = N/2$ we obtain

$$\begin{aligned} a_N &\geq 2^r a_{\frac{N}{2^r}} - \sum_{0\leq l\leq r-1} O\Big(2^l(\frac{N}{2^l})^\alpha\Big) \\ &= 2^r a_{\frac{N}{2^r}} - O\Big(2^{(1-\alpha)r}N^\alpha\Big), \end{aligned}$$

Now let us find i such that $(k+i)N_0 \leq N/2^r \leq (k+i+1)N_0$. Note $i \leq k$. Again using (16) successively with N_0 for N_1 and $N/2^r, (N/2^r) - N_0, (N/2^r) - 2N_0, \ldots$ for N_2, we obtain

$$\begin{aligned} a_{\frac{N}{2^r}} &\geq (k+i)a_{N_0} - O\Big(k(\frac{N}{2^r})^\alpha\Big) \\ &\geq (k+i)a_{N_0} - O\Big(k(\frac{N}{2^r})^\alpha\Big). \end{aligned}$$

Combining, we obtain

$$\begin{aligned} a_N &\geq 2^r(k+i)a_{N_0} - O\Big(2^{(1-\alpha)r}N^\alpha\Big) - O\Big(k2^{r(1-\alpha)}N^\alpha\Big) \\ &= 2^r(k+i)a_{N_0} - O\Big(k2^{r(1-\alpha)}N^\alpha\Big). \end{aligned}$$

Then

$$\begin{aligned} \frac{a_N}{N} &\geq \frac{2^r(k+i)}{2^r(k+i+1)}\frac{a_{N_0}}{N_0} - O\Big(k2^{r(1-\alpha)}N^{\alpha-1}\Big) \\ &\geq (1 - \frac{1}{(k+i+1)})(a^* - \epsilon) - O\Big(k2^{r(1-\alpha)}N^{\alpha-1}\Big) \\ &\geq (1-\epsilon)(a^* - \epsilon) - O\Big(k2^{r(1-\alpha)}N^{\alpha-1}\Big), \end{aligned}$$

where $1/k < \epsilon$ is used in the last inequality. Now

$$k2^{r(1-\alpha)}N^{\alpha-1} \leq k2^{r(1-\alpha)}(k2^rN_0)^{\alpha-1} = k^\alpha N_0^{\alpha-1} < \epsilon,$$

again by the choice of N_0. We have obtained

$$\frac{a_N}{N} \geq (1-\epsilon)(a^* - \epsilon) - \epsilon,$$

for all $N \geq N_0 k$. Since ϵ was arbitrary the proof is complete. □

The Maximum Multiflow Problems with Bounded Fractionality

[Extended Abstract] *

Hiroshi Hirai†
Research Institute for Mathematical Sciences
Kyoto University
Kyoto 606-8502, Japan
hirai@kurims.kyoto-u.ac.jp

ABSTRACT

This paper addresses a fundamental issue in the multicommodity flow theory. For an undirected capacitated supply graph (G, c) having commodity graph H, the maximum multiflow problem is to maximize the total flow-value of multicommodity flows with respect to $(G, c; H)$. For a commodity graph H, the *fractionality* of H is the least positive integer k with property that there exists a $1/k$-integral optimal multiflow in the maximum multiflow problem for every integer-capacitated supply graph (G, c) having H as a commodity graph. If such a positive integer k does not exist, then the fractionality is defined to be $+\infty$. Around 1990, Karzanov raised the problem of classifying commodity graphs with *finite* fractionality, gave a necessary condition (*property P*) for the finiteness of fractionality, and conjectured that the property P is also sufficient.

Our main result affirmatively solves Karzanov's conjecture in algorithmic form: *If H has property P, then there exists a $1/24$-integral optimal multiflow in maximum multiflow problem for every integer-capacitated supply graph having H as a commodity graph, and there exists a strongly polynomial time algorithm to find it.*

Our proof is based on a special combinatorial duality relation involving a class of CAT(0) complexes, and on a fractional version of the splitting-off method for finding an optimal multiflow with a bounded denominator.

Categories and Subject Descriptors

G.2 [**Mathematics of Computing**]: DISCRETE MATHEMATICS

*A full version of this paper is available at [12]

†Supported by a Grant in Aid for Culture, Sports, Science and Technology of Japan.

General Terms

Algorithms

Keywords

multicommodity flows, metrics, polynomial time algorithms

1. INTRODUCTION

Let $G = (VG, EG)$ be an undirected graph with nonnegative edge capacity $c : EG \to \mathbf{R}_+$. Let $S \subseteq VG$ be a set of terminals. Let H be a simple undirected graph on S, called a *commodity graph.* A *multiflow* (*multicommodity flow*) f is a pair $(\mathcal{P}, \lambda)$ of a set $\mathcal{P}$ of paths connecting the ends of some edge of H and its nonnegative flow-value function $\lambda : \mathcal{P} \to \mathbf{R}_+$ satisfying capacity constraint $\sum_{P \in \mathcal{P}: e \in P} \lambda(P) \leq c(e)$ for $e \in EG$. The total flow-value $\|f\|$ is defined to be $\sum_{P \in \mathcal{P}} \lambda(P)$. The *maximum multiflow problem* with respect to $(G, c; H)$ is formulated as:

$$\text{Maximize } \|f\| \text{ over all multiflows } f \text{ for } (G, c; H). \quad (1.1)$$

This is a fundamental optimization problem in operations research.

Sometimes (1.1) has a special *combinatorial* solution, depending on the structure of commodity graph H. Suppose $H = K_2$ (one edge). Then problem (1.1) is the maximum flow problem. The max-flow min-cut theorem, due to Ford-Fulkerson [5], says that if c is integral, then there exists an integral maximum flow. Suppose $H = K_2 + K_2$ (a matching of size 2). Then problem (1.1) is the maximum 2-commodity flow problem. Hu [13] showed that there exists a *half-integral* maximum flow whenever c is integral. However, in 3-commodity flow problem, an analogous theorem does not hold. It is known that there is no positive integer k such that all integer-capacitated 3-commodity flow problems have a $1/k$-integral maximum flow.

Motivated by these facts, Karzanov [16] defined the *fractionality* $\mathrm{frac}(H)$ of a commodity graph H by the least positive integer k with the property that there exists a $1/k$-integral maximum flow in problem (1.1) for every integer-capacitated graph (G, c) having H as a commodity graph. If such a positive integer k does not exist, then $\mathrm{frac}(H)$ is defined to be $+\infty$. The above-described examples show $\mathrm{frac}(K_2) = 1$, $\mathrm{frac}(K_2 + K_2) = 2$, and $\mathrm{frac}(K_2 + K_2 + K_2) = +\infty$.

Karzanov [17] raised the following fundamental problem:

Classify the commodity graphs having finite fractionality.

By a deep analysis on the LP-dual to (1.1), Karzanov [16] showed that the following property (*property P*) is necessary for the finiteness of the fractionality: (P) for any triple A, B, C of pairwise intersecting maximal stable sets of H, we have $A \cap B = B \cap C = C \cap A$. See also [22, Section 73.3b]. Further he conjectured that property P is also *sufficient* for the finiteness of fractionality [17].

Our main contribution solves this conjecture in an algorithmic form:

THEOREM 1.1. *Suppose that a commodity graph H has property P. Then there exists a 1/12-integral optimal multiflow in maximum multiflow problem (1.1) for every Eulerian supply graph having H as a commodity graph, and there exists a strongly polynomial time algorithm to find it.*

This completes the classification of commodity graphs having finite fractionality. In particular we have $\mathrm{frac}(H) \in \{1, 2, 4, 6, 8, 12, 24, +\infty\}$. Still there is a gap from the stronger conjecture $\mathrm{frac}(H) \in \{1, 2, 4, +\infty\}$.

Overview. We consider (1.1) in a general weighted version. Instead of a commodity graph, we are given a nonnegative terminal weight $\mu : \binom{S}{2} \to \mathbf{R}_+$. Here a multiflow f is a pair $(\mathcal{P}, \lambda)$ of a set $\mathcal{P}$ of paths connecting distinct terminals in S and its nonnegative flow-value function $\lambda : \mathcal{P} \to \mathbf{R}_+$ satisfying the capacity constraint. The total flow-value $\|f\|_\mu$ is defined to be $\sum_{P \in \mathcal{P}} \mu(s_P, t_P)\lambda(P)$, where s_P and t_P denote the ends of P. The *μ-weighted maximum multiflow problem* is formulated as:

$$\text{Maximize } \|f\|_\mu \text{ over all multiflows } f \text{ for } (G, c; S). \qquad (1.2)$$

Problem (1.1) for commodity graph H is a special case of (1.2) for 0-1 valued weight μ_H defined by $\mu_H(s,t) = 1 \overset{\text{def}}{\iff} st \in EH$. Then the *fractionality* $\mathrm{frac}(\mu)$ of terminal weight μ is defined by a similar way. For a terminal weight μ, a polyhedron P_μ and its subset T_μ in $\mathbf{R}^S_+$ are defined by

$$\begin{aligned} P_\mu &= \{p \in \mathbf{R}^S_+ \mid p(s) + p(t) \geq \mu(s,t)\ (s,t \in S)\}, \\ T_\mu &= \text{the set of minimal elements of } P_\mu. \end{aligned}$$

This polyhedral set T_μ is called the *tight span*, introduced independently by Isbell [14] and Dress [4]. The dimension $\dim T_\mu$ is defined to be the largest dimension of faces of T_μ. Karzanov [19] and the author [9] established that the 2-dimensionality of T_μ is necessary for the finiteness of $\mathrm{frac}(\mu)$. Further, as is remarked in [9, Section 7], the property P of H is equivalent to the 2-dimensionality of the tight span of the corresponding 0-1 weight μ_H. We derive Theorem 1.1 from a constructive proof of the following general result.

THEOREM 1.2. *If $\dim T_\mu \leq 2$, then there exists a 1/12-integral optimal multiflow in the μ-weighted maximum multiflow problem (1.2) for every Eulerian supply graph.*

Our proof is based on a deep analysis on LP-dual to (1.2), initiated by Karzanov [16, 18, 19] and continued by the author [9, 11]. As is well-known, e.g., [20], the LP-dual to (1.2) is given as a linear optimization over metrics on VG:

$$\begin{array}{lll} \text{Minimize} & \displaystyle\sum_{e \in EG} c(e)d(e) & \qquad (1.3) \\ \text{subject to} & d\text{: metric on } VG, & \\ & d(s,t) \geq \mu(s,t) \quad (s,t \in S). & \end{array}$$

In [11], we established that if $\dim T_\mu \leq 2$, then weight μ is *embedded into* a CAT(0) complex $\mathcal{K}$ and LP-dual (1.3) is equivalent to a version of the *minimum 0-extension problem* on the graph of $\mathcal{K}$. Our proof is based on this special duality relation. Section 2 briefly summarizes this embedding into CAT(0) complexes and the combinatorial multiflow duality. Section 3 sketches the proof of the main result, which is based on a *fractional version of splitting-off method for finding an optimal multiflow with bounded denominator.* The prototype of this method was devised in [9] for a special case.

In closing, we shall remark that this type of a method for bounding the denominator of an optimal solution seems new in the area of combinatorial optimization or polyhedral combinatorics. In the design of approximation algorithms for NP-hard problems, an optimal solution of an LP-relaxation with small denominator often plays crucial roles. Let us mention some connection to such an area below.

Connection to 0-extension, multicut, and integer multiflow. The LP-dual (1.3) naturally arises as a relaxation of multicut or 0-extension problem. Suppose that μ is 0-1 valued weight corresponding to a commodity graph H. Then (1.3) is an LP-relaxation of the minimum multicut problem for $(G, c; H)$. Garg, Vazirani, and Yannakakis [7] gave an $O(\log k)$-approximation algorithm based on this relaxation, where $k = |EH|$. Suppose that μ is a metric. Then, by the nonnegativity of c, the inequality constraint in (1.3) becomes the equality constraint $d(s,t) = \mu(s,t)$ $(s,t \in S)$. This is a metric relaxation of the minimum 0-extension problem for $(G, c; \mu)$, originally considered by Karzanov [18]. Calinescu, Karloff, and Rabani [2] devised an $O(\log k)$-approximation algorithm based on this relaxation, where $k = |S|$. Of course, (1.1) is a natural LP-relaxation of the integer multiflow maximization problem. A design of a good approximation algorithm for integer multiflows is still a great challenge [8, 24].

We hope that our result and method would provide new idea and tools to the area of approximation algorithms.

2. MULTIFLOW COMBINATORIAL DUALITIES

Here we describe a combinatorial duality relation for μ-weighted maximum multiflow problem (1.2) by a folder complex. A *folder complex* (an *F-complex*) is a CAT(0) polygonal complex obtained by gluing Euclidean right-triangular cells, introduced and studied by Chepoi [3, Section 7]. We shall represent terminal weight μ as a *distance among subsets* (not necessarily points) in a metric space on an F-complex. For a metric d on a set S and two subsets $A, B \subseteq S$, the minimum distance $d(A, B)$ between A and B is defined by $\min\{d(p,q) \mid (p,q) \in A \times B\}$. We use the notion of *piecewise Euclidean cell complexes*; see [1] for a formal definition. The detail of this section is given by Section 2 in the full version [12].

Folder complexes. We consider a finite 2-dimensional piecewise Euclidean cell complex $\mathcal{K}$ by obtained by gluing squares and isosceles right triangles along edges of the same isometry type. More precisely, for some positive real δ, each

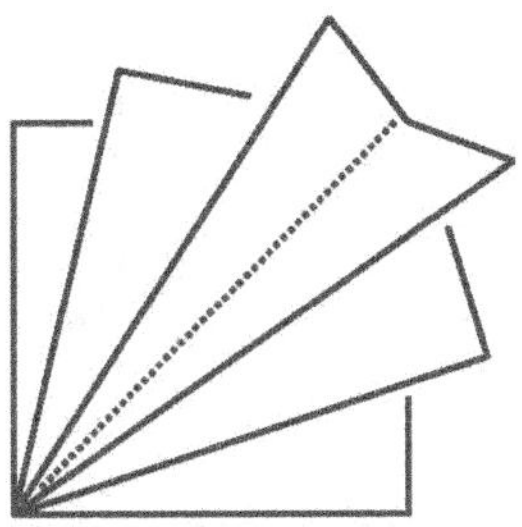

Figure 1: A folder

2-dimensional cell (2-cell) is isometric to

square $\{(x_1, x_2) \in \mathbf{R}^2 \mid 0 \leq x_1 \leq \delta,\ 0 \leq x_2 \leq \delta\}$ or
triangle $\{(x_1, x_2) \in \mathbf{R}^2 \mid 0 \leq x_1 \leq x_2 \leq \delta\}$

in the Euclidean plane. Also we suppose that each maximal 1-dimensional cell is isometric to segment $[0, \delta]$. A longer edge of a triangle is called a *hypotenuse*, and other edges are called *legs*; a maximal 1-cell is a leg. δ is called the *leg-length*. Therefore if two 2-cells share a common edge e, then e is either the hypotenuse of both of them or a leg of both of them. A *folder* of $\mathcal{K}$ is a square, or the union of all triangles sharing one common hypotenuse; see Figure 1. So $\mathcal{K}$ is obtained by gluing folders along legs. Then $\mathcal{K}$ is called a *folder complex* (an *F-complex*) [3, Section 7] if $\mathcal{K}$ is a CAT(0) space, i.e., is simply-connected and has nonpositive curvature; see [1]. This curvature condition can be characterized in a combinatorial way as follows. For each vertex p in $\mathcal{K}$, consider the boundary graph of the union of all folders containing p, and replace each hypotenuse by series of two legs. The resulting graph (*link graph*) Π_p has girth at least 8 if and only if the curvature at p is nonpositive. Therefore $\mathcal{K}$ is an F-complex if and only if $\mathcal{K}$ is simply connected and for each vertex p in $\mathcal{K}$ the link graph Π_p has girth at least 8

A subset R of $\mathcal{K}$ is called *normal* if it satisfies the following axiom: (1) R is a connected subcomplex of $\mathcal{K}$ with the property that if R contains a leg e, then every cell containing e belongs to R and (2) there are no two triangles σ and σ' sharing a leg and a right angle such that $(\sigma \cup \sigma') \cap R$ coincides with the union of the hypotenuses of σ and σ'.

Although $\mathcal{K}$ has the l_2-length metric by definition, we are mainly interested in the l_1-length metric. Note that each 2-cell has a natural l_1-metric so that the coordinate axes are parallel to legs. From this we can naturally define the l_1-length metric $d_{\mathcal{K}}$.

Let $\Gamma = \Gamma^{\mathcal{K}}$ be the (simple undirected) graph consisting of all legs of $\mathcal{K}$, called the *leg-graph*. Equivalently, Γ is the graph obtained by deleting all hypotenuses from the 1-skeleton graph of $\mathcal{K}$. The edge-length of Γ is given by δ uniformly. Let $d_{\Gamma,\delta}$ denote the shortest path metric on Γ with uniform edge-length δ. For two normal sets N and M, one can easily see $d_{\mathcal{K}}(N, M) = d_{\Gamma,\delta}(N \cap V\Gamma, M \cap V\Gamma)$.

An F-complex $\mathcal{K}$ is said to be *orientable* if its leg-graph Γ has an orientation the property that (1) in each square its diagonal edges have same direction (in the local coordinate), and (2) in each folder consisting of triangles, the hypotenuse joins a source and a sink.

F-complex realization and multiflow duality. For a terminal weight $\mu : \binom{S}{2} \to \mathbf{R}_+$ on terminal set S, an *F-complex realization* of μ is a pair $(\mathcal{K}; \{R_s\}_{s \in S})$ of an F-complex $\mathcal{K}$ and a family $\{R_s\}_{s \in S}$ of normal sets satisfying

$$\mu(s,t) = d_{\mathcal{K}}(R_s, R_t) \quad (s, t \in S).$$

Namely μ is realized by the distances among normal sets R_s.

THEOREM 2.1 ([11, THEOREM 4.5]). *For a rational distance μ on a finite set S, the following two conditions are equivalent:*

(1) $\dim T_\mu \leq 2$.

(2) μ has an F-complex realization.

It is known that a realization of μ is obtained by subdividing 2-dimensional polyhedral set T_μ into triangles and squares [9, 11]. Recall that for a commodity graph H, let μ_H denote the 0-1 valued terminal weight defined by $\mu_H(s,t) = 1 \overset{\text{def}}{\Longleftrightarrow} st \in EH$.

PROPOSITION 2.2. *For a commodity graph H with property P on terminal S, there is an F-complex realization of μ_H with size $O(|S|^2)$.*

See Sections 6 and 7 in the full version [12] for details. Here by the size we mean the number of maximal cells.

Suppose that a weight μ on terminal set S has an F-complex realization $(\mathcal{K}; \{R_s\}_{s \in S})$. Consider the μ problem (1.2) for $(G, c; S)$ and consider the following *discrete location problem* (a version of the minimum 0-extension problem) on the leg-graph Γ of $\mathcal{K}$:

$$\begin{array}{lll} \text{Minimize} & \displaystyle\sum_{xy \in EG} c(xy) d_{\Gamma,\delta}(\rho(x), \rho(y)) & (2.1) \\ \text{subject to} & \rho : VG \to V\Gamma, & \\ & \rho(s) \in R_s \cap V\Gamma \quad (s \in S). & \end{array}$$

Our previous paper established the following duality relation, extending a result in [18].

THEOREM 2.3 ([11, THEOREM 2.1]). *Suppose that $\mathcal{K}$ is orientable. Then the maximum value of the μ-problem (1.2) is equal to the minimum value of the discrete location problem (2.1).*

By subdivision we can always replace a nonorientable realization by orientable one; see Figure 2. So by an F-complex we mean orientable one.

Let μ be a weight on terminal set S, and let $(\mathcal{K}; \{R_s\}_{s \in S})$ be its (orientable) F-complex realization. Let (G, c) be a capacitated graph with terminal set S. The optimal value of (1.2) is denoted by $\mathrm{opt}(G, c)$. A map ρ feasible to the dual (2.1) is called a *potential*. For a potential ρ, a metric d^ρ on VG is defined by $d^\rho(x,y) := d(\rho(x), \rho(y))$ for $x, y \in VG$. For a potential ρ, the objective value of (2.1) is denoted by $c \cdot d^\rho$.

3. SPLITTING-OFF WITH POTENTIAL UPDATE

Our proof of the main theorem is based on a fractional version of splitting-off operation. Recall the splitting-off operation; see, e.g., [6, 15, 21]. For two edges $e = xy$ and $e' = yz$ incident to y, a triple (e, y, e') is called a *fork*. For a fork $\tau = (e, y, e')$, the *splitting-off* operation at τ is to decrease the capacity of edges e and e' by one, and add a new edge e^* joining y, z with unit capacity. A fork τ is said to *splittable* if the splitting-off operation at τ does not decrease the optimal value $\mathrm{opt}(G, c)$. The splitting-off is a powerful algorithmic method to prove the existence of an integral optimal multiflow in Eulerian instances. However we will face the situation that there is no splittable fork and no integral optimal multiflow. How can we prove the existence of a $1/k$-integral optimal multiflow for a positive integer k independent on the size of supply graph ? Our previous paper [10] devised a (prototype of) method to overcome this difficulty by a fractional splitting-off operation combining dual update. The detail of this section is given by Sections 3 and 4 in the full version [12].

Basic idea of the proof. Here we describe a basic idea of our proof. Suppose that we are given an instance of the problem $(G, c; S, \mu)$ and an F-complex realization $(\mathcal{K}; \{R_s\}_{s\in S})$ of μ with leg-length $\delta = 2$. Suppose further that (G, c) is Eulerian. In this extended abstract, for giving a clear explanation of the essential idea, we assume here that *μ is a metric.* Then we can always take an optimal multiflow with property that no flow passes through a terminal as an intermediate node, and hence it is unnecessary to consider splitting-off at terminals; there are subtle technical problems on splitting-off at terminals in the case where μ is not a metric (see the full version). Furthermore we can take a realization $\mathcal{K}$ such that each R_s is a single vertex; this is the ordinary metric embedding of μ into $\mathcal{K}$. So the problem (2.1) is (essentially) the minimum 0-extension problem on the graph Γ. We work on the 2-subdivision $\mathcal{K}^2$ instead of $\mathcal{K}$; see Figure 2. By using the standard method [6, p. 50], convert (G, c) so that each inner node has degree four; this is a technical requirement.

For an optimal potential ρ, partition the set of inner nodes in VG into three sets:

$$\begin{aligned} S_\rho &= \{x \mid \rho(x) \text{ is the midpoint of a folder in } \mathcal{K}\},\\ M_\rho &= \{x \mid \rho(x) \text{ is the midpoint of a leg in } \mathcal{K}\},\\ C_\rho &= \{x \mid \rho(x) \text{ is a vertex of } \mathcal{K}\}. \end{aligned}$$

The first key claim is the following:

PROPOSITION 3.1. *For an optimal potential ρ and an inner node y, if $y \in S_\rho$, then y has a splittable fork.*

See Section 3.3 in [12] for the proof. Therefore, if (G, c) is Eulerian and $M_\rho \cup C_\rho = \emptyset$, then there is an integral optimal multiflow. Based on this proposition, we consider the following proof scheme. We always keep (G, c) together with optimal potential ρ, denoted by $(G, c; \rho)$. We repeatedly update $(G, c; \rho) \to (G_1, c_1; \rho_1) \to \cdots \to (G_m, c_m : \rho_m)$ toward the goal where (i) $M_{\rho_m} \cup C_{\rho_m} = \emptyset$, (ii) (G_m, kc_m) is Eulerian for a positive integer k independent on the size of input, and (iii) an optimal multiflow for (G_{i-1}, c_{i-1}) can be recovered from an optimal multiflow for (G_i, c_i). Then set $(G, c) \leftarrow (G_m, kc_m)$. According to Proposition 3.1, there is an integral multiflow in (G, c). By reversing the procedure, we obtain a $1/k$-integral optimal multiflow for the original supply graph. This is our proof scheme.

Next we describe this update procedure, which is a fractional version of the splitting-off. For a fork $\tau = (e, y, e')$, consider the graph (G^τ, c) obtained from (G, c) by adding a new inner node y^τ and a new edge $e^\tau = yy^\tau$ and reconnecting e and e' to y^τ. The capacity of e^τ is defined by $c(e) + c(e')$. Then we can identify a multiflow for (G, c)

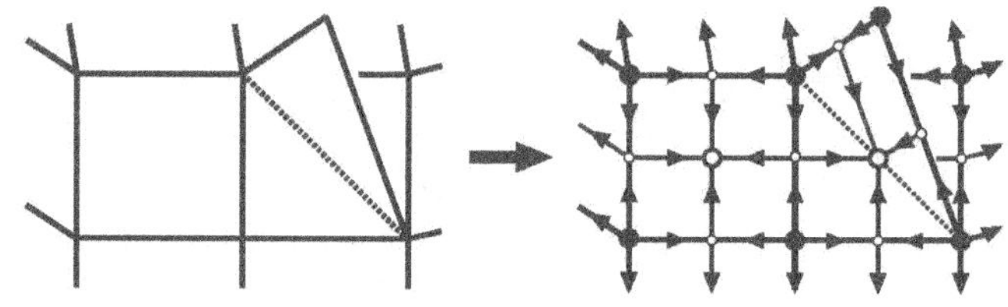

Figure 2: 2-subdivision with forward orientation

with a multiflow for (G^τ, c). So this does not change the problem. The *fractional splitting-off* operation at τ is to decrease $c(e^\tau)$ as much as possible keeping the optimal value invariant. The maximum possible value

$$\alpha(\tau) := \max\{0 \le \alpha \le c(e^\tau) \mid \mathrm{opt}(G^\tau, c - \alpha\chi_{e^\tau}) = \mathrm{opt}(G, c)\}$$

is called the *splitting capacity*. Let $c^\tau = c - \alpha(\tau)\chi_{e^\tau}$. Clearly if (G^τ, c^τ) has a $1/k$-integral optimal multiflow, then so does (G, c).

Suppose that we are given an optimal potential ρ for (G, c). Then ρ can also be extended to an optimum for (G^τ, c) by setting $\rho(y^\tau) := \rho(y)$. By the min-max relation (Theorem 2.3), $\alpha(\tau)$ can also be represented as

$$\alpha(\tau) = \min\left\{ \frac{c\cdot d^{\rho'} - c\cdot d^{\rho}}{d^{\rho'}(e^\tau)} \;\middle|\; \rho'\text{: potential with } d^{\rho'}(e^\tau) > 0 \right\}.$$

A potential ρ' attaining the minimum in RHS is called *critical*. Note that ρ' is optimal to the new graph (G^τ, c^τ). The *SPUP operation* at an unsplittable fork τ is to update $(G, c; \rho) \leftarrow (G^\tau, c^\tau; \rho')$ for a critical potential ρ' with respect to τ.

The second key claim is that we can always take a critical potential ρ' obtained by *moving ρ toward a desired direction.* To describe it, orient leg-graph Γ^2 of $\mathcal{K}^2$ so that each vertex in $\mathcal{K}$ is a source, and each midpoint of a folder in $\mathcal{K}$ is a sink, which is denoted by $\overrightarrow{\Gamma^2}$; see Figure 2. For a potential ρ, a potential ρ' is said to be a *forward neighbor* of ρ if for each node x with $\rho'(x) \neq \rho(x)$, there is an edge $\overrightarrow{pq}$ in $\overrightarrow{\Gamma^2}$ such that $(\rho(x), \rho'(x)) = (p, q)$, or there are two consecutive edges $\overrightarrow{pq}, \overrightarrow{qr}$ belonging to a common folder in $\overrightarrow{\Gamma^2}$ such that $(\rho(x), \rho'(x)) = (p, r)$.

PROPOSITION 3.2. *For a fork τ at an inner node y in C_ρ, there is a critical forward neighbor ρ' of ρ. In addition, if each node in $M_\rho \cup C_\rho$ has even degree, then $\alpha(\tau)$ is half- or 2/3-integral.*

The former part follows from an analysis of the adjacency of the feasible polyhedron of LP-dual (1.3); see [11, Section 4.1]. The latter part can be understood as follows. Compare S_ρ with $S_{\rho'}$. By definition of a forward neighbor, we have $S_\rho \subseteq S_{\rho'}$. So, in the numerator $c\cdot d^{\rho'} - c\cdot d^{\rho}$, terms by edges joining S_ρ cancel out. From this fact, even degree condition at $M_\rho \cup C_\rho$, and the bipartiteness of Γ^2, the numerator $c\cdot d^{\rho'} - c\cdot d^{\rho}$ is an even integer. Moreover, $d^{\rho'}(e^\tau)$ is one of $1, 2, 3, 4$ since both $\rho'(y)$ and $\rho'(y^\tau)$ belong to folders containing $\rho(y)$. For inner nodes in M_ρ, we have the following; see [12, Section 4.4].

PROPOSITION 3.3. *Suppose that each node in $M_\rho \cup C_\rho$ has even degree. For an (unsplittable) inner node y in M_ρ of degree four,*

(1) there is a forward neighbor ρ' of ρ such that ρ' is also optimal and $\rho'(y) \neq \rho(y)$ (thus $y \in S_{\rho'}$), or

(2) there are a fork τ at y and its critical forward neighbor ρ' of ρ such that $\alpha(\tau) = 1$ and $\{y, y^\tau\} \subseteq S_{\rho'}$.

According to two propositions, we repeatedly apply SPUP operations toward $M_\rho \cup C_\rho = \emptyset$ (Proposition 3.3 (1) can also be regarded as SPUP with $\alpha(\tau) = 0$). In the procedure, each node is moving into S_ρ. Here we emphasize that *even degree condition at S_ρ is unnecessary to keep $\alpha(\tau)$ half- or 2/3-integral.* A particular lucky situation is the case where both y and y^τ fall into S_ρ. Although edge e^τ may have very fractional capacity, it never contributes the denominator-increase of α in the subsequent SPUP procedure. This is an intuition behind our proof.

The whole proof is carried out as follows. We may assume that there is no splittable fork. Take an optimal potential ρ. Take a fork τ at inner node y in C_ρ. According to Proposition 3.2, apply SPUP operation $(G, c; \rho) \leftarrow (G^\tau, c^\tau; \rho')$ for a critical forward neighbor ρ' of ρ. Repeat it. Then C_ρ is nonincreasing. By appropriate choices of forks at C_ρ, we can make $(G, c; \rho)$ such that (i) $C_\rho = \emptyset$, (ii) $(G, 12c)$ is Eulerian, and (iii) each inner node in M_ρ has even degree in $(G, 6c)$; this is the most difficult part in the proof [12, Section 4]. Set $(G, c) \leftarrow (G, 6c)$. Again make (G, c) so that each inner node in M_ρ has degree four. Take an inner node y in M_ρ. According to Proposition 3.3, replace ρ by ρ' with property (1) or apply SPUP at a fork τ with property (2). Then M_ρ decreases. Further $(G, 2c)$ is Eulerian, and each inner node in M_ρ has even degree. Repeat it until M_ρ is empty. Then the resulting problem has a half-integral optimal multiflow, and thus the original problem has a 1/12-integral optimal multiflow. The proof is done.

Algorithmic discussion. Here we briefly discuss how to obtain a strongly polynomial time algorithm; see Section 7 in the full version [12] for details. Our proof is constructive. Each step searches all nodes and forks of required properties, and applies splitting-off or SPUP to decrease the number of nodes in question. Once the problem becomes trivial to have an integral optimum, we obtain a $1/k$-integral optimum for the original problem by reversing the operations. It uses oracles for computing an optimal potential, computing the splitting capacity, and computing a critical neighbor. Our analysis here supposes that *an F-complex realization is given and its size is fixed.* A feasible solution d in (1.3) is said to be *minimal* if there is no other feasible solution d' with $d' \leq d$. By adding dummy terminals (at most the number of vertices of a realization $\mathcal{K}$), we can establish one-to-one correspondence between potentials in (2.1) and minimal extreme solutions in (1.3) [11, Section 3.1]. Since LP (1.3) has the $\{0, 1, -1\}$-valued constraint matrix of $|VG|^3 \times |VG|^2$ size, we can find a minimal extreme optimal solution d^* in strongly polynomial time by the method of Tardos [23]. From d^*, we can recover an optimal potential ρ^*. Consider the splitting capacity α. Let $h(\alpha) := \mathrm{opt}(G^\tau, c - \alpha\chi_{e^\tau}) - \mathrm{opt}(G, c)$. Then $h(\alpha)$ is a monotone nonincreasing piecewise linear concave function. The gradient of h at α is given by $d^\rho(e^\tau)$ for an optimal potential ρ of $(G^\tau, c - \alpha\chi_{e^\tau})$. So the possible values of the gradients are $0, 1, 2, \ldots, \mathrm{diam}\,\Gamma$, where $\mathrm{diam}\,\Gamma$ denotes the diameter of Γ. Therefore we can determine α by solving (1.3) at most $\mathrm{diam}\,\Gamma$ time. Next consider a critical neighbor ρ' in Propositions 3.2 and 3.3 , Suppose that we are given an optimal potential ρ. Then d^ρ is an optimal minimal extreme solution, and $d^{\rho'}$ is necessarily a minimal extreme solution *adjacent to d^ρ*. Based on this fact, we can compute ρ' in strongly polynomial time.

By a technical requirement of our proof, we need to make the input supply graph have degree at most four. The reduction in [6, p. 50] replaces inner node x by $O((\deg x)^2)$ new inner nodes of degree four, where $\deg x$ denotes the degree of x. To get polynomial time algorithm, we need to decrease the degree before this reduction. This is naturally achieved by the splitting-off as a preprocessing. Let $n = |VG|$. As in [15, Section 4], by examining splitting-off for all forks (in $O(n^3)$ steps) we can make (G, c) have no splittable fork. This can be done in strongly polynomial time.

Now one can easily see that each inner node has degree $O(n^2)$; an inner node of sufficiently large degree always has a splittable fork. By the reduction, each node x is replaced by $O(n^4)$ nodes of degree four, and the supply graph has $O(n^5)$ nodes. Then we can apply our proof directly, and we obtain a strongly polynomial time algorithm to find a 1/12-integral optimal multiflow. Recall Proposition 2.2. In the case where μ comes from a commodity graph with property P, the assumption fixing the size of a realization is unnecessary. Thus we obtain the algorithmic part of Theorem 1.1.

4. REFERENCES

[1] M. R. Bridson and A. Haefliger, *Metric Spaces of Non-Positive Curvature*, Springer-Verlag, Berlin, 1999.

[2] G. Calinescu, H. Karloff, and Y. Rabani, Approximation algorithms for the 0-extension problem, *SIAM Journal on Computing* **34** (2004/05), 358–372.

[3] V. Chepoi, Graphs of some CAT(0) complexes, *Advances in Applied Mathematics* **24** (2000), 125–179.

[4] A. W. M. Dress, Trees, tight extensions of metric spaces, and the cohomological dimension of certain groups: a note on combinatorial properties of metric spaces, *Advances in Mathematics* **53** (1984), 321–402.

[5] L. R. Ford, Jr. and D. R. Fulkerson, *Flow in Networks*, Princeton University Press, Princeton, 1962.

[6] A. Frank, Packing paths, circuits, and cuts — a survey, in: *Paths, Flows, and VLSI-Layout* (B. Korte, L. Lovász, H. J. Prömel, A. Schrijver, eds.), Springer, Berlin, 1990, pp. 47–100.

[7] N. Garg, V. V. Vazirani, and M. Yannakakis, Approximate max-flow min-(multi)cut theorems and their applications, *SIAM Journal on Computing* **25** (1996), 235–251.

[8] V. Guruswami, S. Khanna, R. Rajaraman, B. Shepherd, and M. Yannakakis, Near-optimal hardness results and approximation algorithms for edge-disjoint paths and related problems, *Journal of Computers and System Sciences* **67** (2003), 473–496.

[9] H. Hirai, Tight extensions of distances and the dual fractionality of undirected multiflow problems, *Journal of Combinatorial Theory, Series B* **99** (2009), 843–868.

[10] H. Hirai, Bounded fractionality of the multiflow feasibility problem for demand graph $K_3 + K_3$ and

related maximization problems, RIMS-preprint 1645, (2008), available at `http://www.kurims.kyoto-u.ac.jp/preprint/file/RIMS1645.pdf`.

[11] H. Hirai, Folder complexes and multi ow combinatorial dualities, RIMS-preprint 1675, (2009), available at `http://www.kurims.kyoto-u.ac.jp/preprint/file/RIMS1675.pdf`.

[12] H. Hirai, The maximum multi ow problems with bounded fractionality, RIMS-preprint 1682, (2009), available at `http://www.kurims.kyoto-u.ac.jp/preprint/file/RIMS1682.pdf`.

[13] T. C. Hu, Multi-commodity network ows, *Operations Research* **11** (1963), 344–360.

[14] J. R. Isbell, Six theorems about injective metric spaces, *Commentarii Mathematici Helvetici* **39** (1964), 65–76.

[15] A. V. Karzanov, On a class of maximum multicommodity ow problems with integer optimal solutions, in: *Selected Topics in Discrete Mathematics* (A. K. Kelmans, ed.), American Mathematical Society Translations Series 2, Volume 158, American Mathematical Society, Providence, 1994, pp. 81–99.

[16] A. V. Karzanov, Polyhedra related to undirected multicommodity ows, *Linear Algebra and its Applications* **114/115** (1989), 293–328.

[17] A. V. Karzanov, Undirected multi ow problems and related topics – some recent developments and results, in: *Proceedings of the International Congress of Mathematician, Volume II*, Kyoto, Japan 1991, 1561–1571.

[18] A. V. Karzanov, Minimum 0-extensions of graph metrics, *European Journal of Combinatorics* **19** (1998), 71–101.

[19] A. V. Karzanov, Metrics with nite sets of primitive extensions, *Annals of Combinatorics* **2** (1998), 211–241.

[20] M. V. Lomonosov, Combinatorial approaches to multi ow problems, *Discrete Applied Mathematics* **11** (1985), 93 pp.

[21] L. Lovasz, vOn some connectivity properties of Eulerian graphs, *Acta Mathematica Academiae Scientiarum Hungaricae* **28** (1976), 129–138.

[22] A. Schrijver, *Combinatorial Optimization—Polyhedra and E ciency*, Springer-Verlag, Berlin, 2003.

[23] E. Tardos, A strongly polynomial algorithm to solve combinatorial linear programs, *Operations Research* **34** (1986), 250–256.

[24] V. V. Vazirani, *Approximation Algorithms,* Springer-Verlag, Berlin, 2001.

Faster Approximation Schemes for Fractional Multicommodity Flow Problems via Dynamic Graph Algorithms

[Extended Abstract] *

Aleksander Mądry[†]
Massachusetts Institute of Technology
Cambridge, MA 02139
madry@mit.edu

ABSTRACT

We combine the work of Garg and Könemann, and Fleischer with ideas from dynamic graph algorithms to obtain faster $(1-\varepsilon)$-approximation schemes for various versions of the multicommodity flow problem. In particular, if ε is moderately small and the size of every number used in the input instance is polynomially bounded, the running times of our algorithms match – up to poly-logarithmic factors and some provably optimal terms – the $\Omega(mn)$ *flow-decomposition barrier* for *single-commodity* flow.

Categories and Subject Descriptors

F.2 [**Theory of Computation**]: Analysis of Algorithms and Problem Complexity

General Terms

Algorithms, Theory

Keywords

Multicommodity flow problems, Dynamic graph algorithms

1. INTRODUCTION

Flow problems are one of the most fundamental problems in optimization; they have a long list of scientific and engineering applications — see e.g. Ahuja *et al.* [1]. Usually, an instance of such problem consists of a directed graph $G=(V,E,u)$ with capacities $u: E \rightarrow \mathbb{R}^+$ on the arcs, and a source-sink pair (s_1,t_1) (in case of single-commodity flow); or a set of k source-sink pairs $\{(s_i,t_i)\}_{1\leq i\leq k}$ (in case of multicommodity flow). The task is to find flows $(f_1,\ldots,f_k)$, where f_i is a flow of commodity i from s_i to t_i, that optimize some objective function while each flow satisfies node conservation constraints and the total flow $\sum_i f_i(e)$ of the commodities through any arc e is not exceeding its capacity $u(e)$. The simplest multicommodity flow problem is the *maximum multicommodity flow* problem – in this case the objective is to maximize the sum of the flows $\sum_i |f_i|$, where $|f_i|$ is the amount of commodity i routed from s_i to t_i. A generalization of this problem is the *maximum weighted multicommodity flow* problem in which additionally we are given weights $w_1,\ldots,w_k$ and we want to maximize the weighted sum of the flows $\sum_i w_i|f_i|$. Another popular variation of the multicommodity flow problem is the *maximum concurrent flow* problem. In this problem, we are given a set of k positive demands $d_1,\ldots,d_k$ and are asked to find a multicommodity flow that is feasible (i.e. obeys arc capacities) and routes λd_i units of commodity i between each source-sink pair (s_i,t_i) – the goal is to maximize the value of λ. If there is a cost function $c: E \rightarrow \mathbb{R}^+$ associated with arcs, where $c(e)$ is the price of routing one unit of flow through arc e, the *minimum cost concurrent flow* problem is to find a maximum concurrent flow whose total cost i.e. the sum of the costs incurred by the flow on each arc, is within some target budget B.

Although all the problems defined above can be solved optimally in polynomial time by formulating them as linear programs, in many applications it is more important to compute an approximate solution fast than to compute an optimal one. Therefore, much effort was put into obtaining efficient *fully polynomial-time approximation schemes* (FPTAS) for multicommodity flow problems. A fully polynomial-time approximation scheme for a maximization problem is an algorithm that, given an instance of the problem and an accuracy parameter $\varepsilon > 0$, computes, in time polynomial in the size of the input and $1/\varepsilon$, a solution that has objective value within a factor of $(1-\varepsilon)$ of the optimal one.

1.1 Previous work

Over the past two decades there has been a rich history of results providing FPTASes for multicommodity flow problems. Shahrokhi and Matula [31] presented the first combinatorial fully polynomial-time approximation scheme for the maximum concurrent flow problem with uniform arc capacities, and introduced the idea of using an exponential

[†]Supported by a Fulbright Science and Technology Award, by NSF contract CCF-0829878, and by ONR grant N00014-05-1-0148.

*The full version of this extended abstract is available as [22].

STOC'10, June 5–8, 2010, Cambridge, Massachusetts, USA.

length function to control arc congestion. Subsequently, a series of results [19, 21, 13, 15, 25, 32, 26, 18, 16] based on Langrangian relaxation and linear programming decomposition yielded algorithms that had significantly improved running time and could be applied to various versions of the multicommodity flow problem with arbitrary arc capacities. All the above algorithms compute an initial (infeasible) flow and then redistribute it from more congested paths to less congested ones by repeatedly solving an oracle subproblem of either minimum cost single-commodity flow [21, 13, 15, 26, 18, 16], or shortest path [31, 19, 25, 32].

In [33], Young deviated from this theme by presenting an *oblivious rounding* algorithm that avoids rerouting of the flow. Instead, it builds the solution from scratch. At each step it employs shortest path computations (with respect to exponential length function that models the congestion of the arcs) to augment the flow along suitable (i.e. relatively uncongested) paths. At the end, it obtains the final feasible solution by scaling down the flow by the maximum congestion it incurred on arcs. A similar approach was taken by Garg and Könemann [12]; however they managed to provide an elegant framework for solving multicommodity flow problems that yields a simple analysis of the correctness of the obtained algorithms. This allowed them to match and, in some cases, improve over the running time of the algorithms obtained via the redistribution methodology. Subsequently, Fleischer [11] used this framework to develop significantly faster algorithms for various multicommodity flow problems. In particular, for the maximum multicommodity flow problem she managed to obtain a running time of $\widetilde{O}(m^2\varepsilon^{-2})$ (where $\widetilde{O}(\cdot)$ notation hides poly-logarithmic factors) that is independent of the number of commodities. For the weighted version, she proposed an algorithm running in $\widetilde{O}(m^2\varepsilon^{-2}\min\{\log M, k\})$ time, where $\log M$ is the upper bound on the size of binary representation of every number used in the input instance. For the maximum (resp. minimum cost) concurrent flow problem her algorithm has a running time of $\widetilde{O}((m+k)m\varepsilon^{-2})$ (resp. $\widetilde{O}((m+k)m\varepsilon^{-2}\log M)$). Her results for both versions of the concurrent flow problem were later improved by Karakostas [17], who was able to reduce the term in the running time that depends on k from $\widetilde{O}(km\varepsilon^{-2})$ (resp. $\widetilde{O}(km\varepsilon^{-2}\log M)$) to $\widetilde{O}(kn\varepsilon^{-2})$. Interestingly, he also showed that if we want to obtain the $(1-\varepsilon)$-approximation of only the *value* of the maximum (resp. minimum cost) concurrent flow rate (without obtaining the actual flow) then this can be done in $\widetilde{O}(m^2\varepsilon^{-2})$ (resp. $\widetilde{O}(m^2\varepsilon^{-2}\log M)$) time.

All the above algorithms have quadratic dependence of their running times on $1/\varepsilon$. Klein and Young [20] give evidence that this quadratic dependence is inherent for *Dantzig-Wolfe-type* algorithms[1] — all the FPTASes mentioned so far are of this type. As it turns out, better dependence on $1/\varepsilon$ can be obtained. Bienstock and Iyengar [6] adapted the technique of Nesterov [23] to give an FPTAS that has $O(\frac{1}{\varepsilon \log 1/\varepsilon})$ dependence on $1/\varepsilon$. Very recently, Nesterov [24] obtained an approximation scheme where this dependence is just linear. However, both these algorithms repeatedly solve a convex quadratic program as their oracle subproblem. This causes their running time to have a worse dependence on parameters other than $1/\varepsilon$ compared to the algorithms described above – for example, the approximation scheme due to Nesterov has the running time of $\widetilde{O}(k^2m^2\varepsilon^{-1})$.

1.2 Our contribution

We build on the work of Garg and Könemann [12] and Fleischer [11] to obtain faster approximation schemes for various versions of multicommodity flow problems. At a high level — when the size of every number used in the input instance (e.g. capacities, weights, and costs on arcs) is polynomially bounded — our improvements break the bottlenecking term of $\Omega(m^2\varepsilon^{-2})$ that all the previous Dantzig-Wolfe-type algorithms suffer from, by substituting it with $\widetilde{O}(mn\varepsilon^{-2})$ term. Our result is based on two main ideas.

The first one stems from an observation that the shortest-path subproblems that algorithms following the framework of Garg-Könemann solve repeatably are closely related. Each successive subproblem corresponds to the same underlying graph – only the lengths of some of the arcs are increased. This suggests that treating each of these subproblems as an independent task – as it is the case in all the previous algorithms – is suboptimal. One might wonder, for example, whether it is possible to maintain a data structure that allows answering such a sequence of shortest-path queries more efficiently than just by computing everything from scratch in each iteration. Indeed, it turns out that this kind of questions were already studied extensively in the area of *dynamic graph algorithms* (see e.g. [10, 3, 7, 9, 27, 4, 8, 28, 30, 29, 5]). In particular, the data structure that we would like to maintain corresponds to the *decremental dynamic all-pair shortest path* problem. Unfortunately, if we are interested in solutions whose overall running time is within our intended bounds, then it seems there is no suitable existing result that can be used (see section 3 for details).

This lack of existing solution fitting our needs brings us to the second idea of the paper. We note that when we employ the Garg-Könemann framework to solve multicommodity flow problems, it is not necessary to compute the (approximately) shortest path for each shortest-path subproblem. All we really need is that the set of the suitable paths over which we are optimizing the length comes from a set that contains *all* the flowpaths of some *fixed* optimal solution to the multicommodity flow instance that we are solving. To exploit this fact, we introduce a random set of paths $\widehat{\mathcal{P}}$ (see Definition 5) – that can be seen as a sparsification of the set of all paths in G, and that with high probability has the above-mentioned property. Next, we combine the ideas from dynamic graph algorithms to design an efficient data structure that maintains all-pair shortest path distances with respect to the set $\widehat{\mathcal{P}}$. This data structure allows us to modify (in an almost generic manner) the existing algorithms for various multicommodity flow problems that are based on the Garg-Könemann framework and transform them into Monte-Carlo algorithms with improved running times.

The summary of our results and their comparison with the previous ones can be found in Figure 1. Note that there exist instances of concurrent flow problems (see Figure 2) for which any (approximately) optimal solution has representation size of $\Omega(kn)$. Therefore, in the setting where ε

[1] A *Dantzig-Wolfe-type* algorithm for a fractional packing problem – in which the goal is to find x in some polytope P that satisfies the set of packing inequalities $Ax \leq b$ – is an algorithm that accesses P only by queries of the form: "given a vector c, what is the $x \in P$ minimizing $c \cdot x$?".

Problem	Previous best	This paper
maximum multicommodity flow	$\widetilde{O}(m^2\varepsilon^{-2})$ [11]	$\widetilde{O}(mn\varepsilon^{-2})$
maximum weighted multicommodity flow	$\widetilde{O}(m^2\varepsilon^{-2}\min\{\log M, k\})$ [11]	$\widetilde{O}(mn\varepsilon^{-2}\log^2 M)$
maximum concurrent flow	$\widetilde{O}((m^2+kn)\varepsilon^{-2})$ [17] $\widetilde{O}(k^2m^2\varepsilon^{-1})$ [24]	$\widetilde{O}((m+k)n\varepsilon^{-2}\log M)$
minimum cost concurrent flow	$\widetilde{O}((m^2\log M + kn)\varepsilon^{-2})$ [17]	$\widetilde{O}((m+k)n\varepsilon^{-2}\log M)$

Figure 1: Comparison of $(1-\varepsilon)$-approximation schemes for multicommodity flow problems. $\widetilde{O}(\cdot)$ notation hides poly-logarithmic factors, m is the number of arcs, n is the number of vertices, k is the number of commodities, and $\log M$ is the upper bound on the size of binary representation of any number used in the input instance.

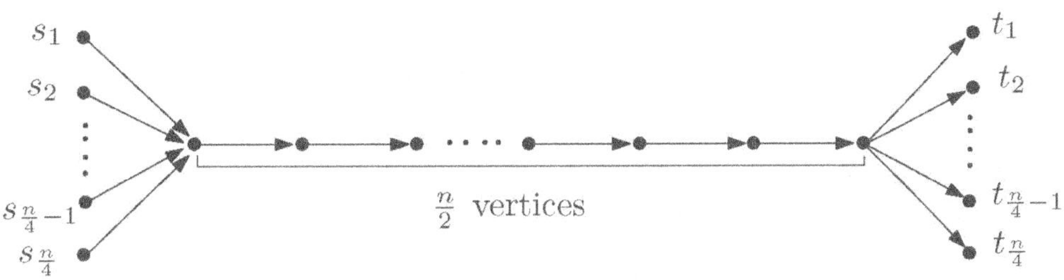

Figure 2: By choosing any set of $k \le n/16$ distinct (s_i, t_j) pairs as source-sink pairs for k commodities and setting all demands to 1, we obtain an instance of the maximum concurrent flow problem for which any $(1-\varepsilon)$-approximate solution has representation size $\Omega(kn)$ – each of $n/2-1$ arcs on the middle path has to have non-zero flow of all k commodities flowing through it.

is fixed or moderately small, say $1/\log^{O(1)} n$, and the size of every number used in the input instance is polynomially bounded, the corresponding $\widetilde{O}(kn)$ term in the running time of our algorithms for concurrent flow problems is optimal (up to poly-logarithmic factors). Interestingly, in this setting, the running time of all our algorithms matches – up to poly-logarithmic factor and modulo the nearly-optimal $\widetilde{O}(kn)$ term in case of concurrent flow problems – the $\Omega(mn)$ *flow-decomposition barrier* for *single-commodity* flows. Recall that in the case of the maximum single-commodity flow problem Goldberg and Rao [14] presented an algorithm that improves upon this barrier. Therefore, we find the question whether one can also achieve a similar improvement for the maximum multicommodity flow problem very intriguing.[2]

1.3 Notations and Definitions

Let $G = (V, E, u)$ be a *directed* graph with capacities $u: E \rightarrow \mathbb{R}^+$. In addition to capacities, we will often equip arcs of G with lengths given by some *length function* $l: E \rightarrow \mathbb{R}^+$. For any directed path p in G, by the *length of p with respect to l* we mean a quantity $l(p) := \sum_{e\in p} l(e)$. For any two vertices u and v of G, a u-v path is a directed path in G that starts at u and ends at v. We define *distance from u to v (with respect to l)* for $u, v \in V$ to be the length (with respect to l) of the shortest u-v path. We will omit the reference to the length function l whenever it is clear from the context which length function we are using.

For $1 \le i \le k$, we denote by $\mathcal{P}_i$ the set of all s_i-t_i paths in G, where $\{(s_i, t_i)\}_i$ is the set of k source-sink pairs of the instance of the multicommodity flow problem we are considering. Let $\mathcal{P} = \bigcup_{i=1}^k \mathcal{P}_i$. For a given subset $U \subseteq V$ of vertices, let $\mathcal{P}(U)$ be the set of all paths in $\mathcal{P}$ that pass through at least one vertex from U. Finally, for a given $j > 0$, let $\mathcal{P}(U, j)$ be the set of all the paths from $\mathcal{P}(U)$ that consist of at most j arcs.

1.4 Outline of the paper

We start with section 2 where we illustrate the Garg-Könemann framework [12] for the maximum multicommodity flow problem – we also outline the current best algorithm for this problem due to Fleischer [11]. Next, in section 3, we introduce the main ideas and tools behind our results – the connection between fast approximation schemes for multicommodity flow problems and dynamic graph algorithm for maintaining (approximately) shortest paths with respect to the sparsified set of paths. In particular, we formally define the set $\widehat{\mathcal{P}}$, and the $(\delta, M_{\max}, M_{\min}, \widehat{\mathcal{P}})$-ADSP data structure that we will be using for maintenance of the (approximately) shortest paths that we are interested in. We conclude in section 4 with showing how these concepts lead to a more efficient algorithm for the maximum multicommodity flow problem, and stating the results obtained for the weighted version of the problem as well as for the maximum concurrent flow problem and its generalization to the version with costs.

[2]Note that the only obvious lower bound for the running time of an algorithm solving the maximum multicommodity problem is $\Omega(m + \min\{k, n\}n)$. This bound can be established by constructing instances as in Figure 2, where each of $k \le n$ commodities corresponds to the source-sink pair (s_i, t_i) for $1 \le i \le k$, all the arcs outgoing from s_is have capacity of 1, and the rest of the arcs have capacity of k. Clearly, any (approximately optimal) solution to such instances has representation size of $\Omega(\min\{k, n\}n)$.

Input : Graph $G = (V, E)$, capacities $u(e)$, commodity pairs $\{(s_i, t_i)\}_i$, accuracy parameter $\varepsilon > 0$
Output: (Infeasible) flow f

Initialize $f \leftarrow \emptyset$, and $l(e) \leftarrow \gamma$ for all arcs $e \in E$, where $\gamma = (1+\varepsilon)/((1+\varepsilon)n)^{1/\varepsilon}$
while there is a path $p \in \mathcal{P}$ with $l(p) < 1$ **do**
  Select path p that is the shortest one (with respect to l) in $\mathcal{P}$
  Find the bottleneck capacity u of p
  (* $u \leftarrow \min_{e \in p} u(e)$ *)
  Augment the flow f by routing u units of flow along the path p
  foreach arc e in p **do** $l(e) \leftarrow l(e)(1 + \frac{\varepsilon u}{u(e)})$
end
return f

Figure 3: Garg-Könemann algorithm for finding maximum multicommodity flow

2. GARG-KÖNEMANN FRAMEWORK FOR SOLVING MULTICOMMODITY FLOW PROBLEMS

Our algorithms will follow the framework for solving multicommodity flow problems that was developed by Garg and Könemann [12] (see also [2] for a presentation of this framework from a slightly different perspective). For illustrative purposes, we focus only on the variation of the framework for the maximum multicommodity flow problem.

The starting point of this framework is the following path-based linear programming formulation of the maximum multicommodity problem:

$$\begin{aligned} \max \sum_{p \in \mathcal{P}} f_p & & \\ \text{s.t.} \sum_{p \ni e} f_p \leq u(e) & \qquad \forall e \in E, & (1) \\ f_p \geq 0 & \qquad \forall p \in \mathcal{P}. & \end{aligned}$$

Here f_p represents the flow on path $p \in \mathcal{P}$, and we recall that $\mathcal{P}$ is the set of all s_i-t_i paths in G, where $\{(s_i, t_i)\}_i$ is the set of k source-sink pairs of the instance of the maximum multicommodity flow problem we are considering. The dual of this linear program corresponds to assigning lengths $l(\cdot)$ to the arcs in such a way that length of every path in $\mathcal{P}$ is at least one and the total volume of the network i.e. $\sum_{e \in E} l(e)u(e)$ is minimized.

$$\begin{aligned} \min \sum_{e \in E} l(e)u(e) & & \\ \text{s.t.} \sum_{e \in p} l(e) \geq 1 & \qquad \forall p \in \mathcal{P}, & (2) \\ l(e) \geq 0 & \qquad \forall e \in E. & \end{aligned}$$

Intuitively, the total volume is an upper bound on the value of the maximum multicommodity flow, since when lengths $l(\cdot)$ constitute a feasible dual solution, routing one unit of flow between any source-sink pair uses up a volume of at least one.

To find a $(1-\varepsilon)$-approximate solution to the above linear program (1) and thus to obtain corresponding multicommodity flow, Garg and Könemann employ an algorithm presented in Figure 3. The algorithm maintains flow f, and a length function l. Initially, $f = 0$, and $l = \gamma$ i.e. there is no flow routed, and the length of each arc is γ, where $\gamma = (1+\varepsilon)/((1+\varepsilon)n)^{1/\varepsilon}$ is very small. Now, as long as there are paths in $\mathcal{P}$ having length smaller than one, the algorithm chooses the shortest path p among these paths and augments the flow f along it. The amount of flow routed over p is equal to the *bottleneck capacity* u of p i.e. u is the minimal capacity among all the capacities of the arcs of p. After augmenting the flow, we update the length function by multiplying the length $l(e)$ of each arc e of p by a factor of $(1 + \frac{\varepsilon u}{u(e)})$.

It is not hard to see that the final flow f produced by the above procedure may violate some of the arc capacities. Therefore, to obtain a feasible solution we need to scale the final flow f down by the maximum congestion f incurred on arcs. Since we only augment the flow along paths with length smaller than one and our length update rule ensures that the length of arcs is exponential in their congestion, we can conclude that this maximum congestion is not very large.

LEMMA 1 (SEE [12]). *The flow obtained by scaling the final flow f down by $\log_{1+\varepsilon} \frac{1+\varepsilon}{\gamma}$ is feasible.*

Moreover, the fact that we always augment the flow along the shortest path in $\mathcal{P}$ – which intuitively means that we aim at routing the flow through arcs that are relatively uncongested – allowed Garg and Könemann to bound the quality of the obtained solution.

LEMMA 2 (SEE [12]). *If f is the final flow computed then $\frac{|f|}{\log_{1+\varepsilon} \frac{1+\varepsilon}{\gamma}} \geq (1-2\varepsilon)OPT$, where OPT is the value of the optimal flow.*

The key ingredient in the proof of the above lemma is an observation – a simple consequence of weak duality between linear programs (1) and (2) – that for *any* length function l there is always a path p in $\mathcal{P}$ whose length with respect to l is at most $1/OPT$ fraction of the total volume of the graph G i.e. $l(p) \leq \frac{\sum_e l(e)u(e)}{OPT}$.

Now, to analyze the running time of the algorithm, we note that in each augmentation the length of the arc with bottleneck capacity increases by a factor of $(1+\varepsilon)$. Since no arc achieves a length bigger than $(1+\varepsilon)$, there can be at most $m\lfloor \log_{1+\varepsilon} \frac{1+\varepsilon}{\gamma} \rfloor = \tilde{O}(m\varepsilon^{-2})$ augmentations of the flow. To perform each such augmentation we have to find the shortest path in $\mathcal{P}$, this can be done in $\tilde{O}(km)$ time by running Dijkstra's algorithm from each possible source. This establishes the following theorem.

THEOREM 3 (SEE [12]). *For any $\varepsilon > 0$ one can compute $(1-2\varepsilon)$-approximation to maximum multicommodity flow problem in time $\tilde{O}(km^2\varepsilon^{-2})$.*

Subsequently, Fleischer [11] presented a more efficient version of the above algorithm. Her improvement is based on the realization that whenever we need the shortest path in the Garg-Könemann algorithm, it is sufficient to compute an $(1+\varepsilon)$-*approximately* shortest path. This allows for modification of the algorithm of Garg and Könemann to avoid solving the shortest-path problem for all the source-sink pairs each time the flow is augmented. Instead, we cycle through all commodities, keeping augmenting the flow along the shortest path corresponding to given commodity as long as the length of this path is at most $(1+\varepsilon)\widehat{\alpha}$ – where $\widehat{\alpha}$ is a lower bound estimate of the current length of the shortest path in $\mathcal{P}$ maintained by the algorithm – and moving on once it does not. To start, we set $\widehat{\alpha} = \gamma$ and we do not increase its value as long as we manage to augment the flow along some path in $\mathcal{P}$ of small enough length (i.e. at most $(1+\varepsilon)\widehat{\alpha}$). Once we are unable to find such a path i.e. our cycling through commodities made a full cycle, we set $\widehat{\alpha} \leftarrow (1+\varepsilon)\widehat{\alpha}$, and start cycling again unless $\widehat{\alpha}$ is already bigger than one – in which case we scale the obtained flow down to make it feasible and the algorithm terminates. The algorithm is presented in Figure 4. An important implementation detail is that when cycling through commodities, we group together source-sink pairs that share the same source. This allows us to take advantage of the fact that one execution of Dijkstra's algorithm computes simultaneously the shortest paths for all these pairs. To see why the above modifications reduce the number of shortest path computations needed, notice that each execution of Dijkstra's algorithm either results in flow augmentation, or causes us to move on in our cycling to the next group of commodities that was not yet examined. Note that our way of updating the value of $\widehat{\alpha}$ ensures that there is at most $\lfloor \log_{(1+\varepsilon)} \frac{1}{\gamma} \rfloor = O(\log m\varepsilon^{-2})$ full cycles through commodities. Also, the number of flow augmentation is still at most $m\lfloor \log_{1+\varepsilon} \frac{1+\varepsilon}{\gamma} \rfloor = \widetilde{O}(m\varepsilon^{-2})$. Therefore, we have at most $\widetilde{O}((m+\min\{k,n\})\varepsilon^{-2})$ executions of Dijkstra's algorithm – instead of $\widetilde{O}(km\varepsilon^{-2})$ executions in the original algorithm due to Garg and Könemann. Fleischer proves the following theorem.

```
Input  : Graph G = (V, E), capacities u(e), commodity
         pairs {(s_i, t_i)}_i, accuracy parameter ε > 0
Output: Flow f
Initialize f ← ∅, α̂ ← γ, and l(e) ← γ for all arcs e ∈ E,
where γ = (1 + ε)/((1 + ε)n)^{1/ε}
I(s) ← {i | s_i = s} for each s ∈ V
  (* grouping source-sink pairs sharing sources *)
while α̂ < 1 do
    foreach s ∈ V with I(s) ≠ ∅ do
        (* cycling through commodities *)
        Use Dijkstra's algorithm to find the shortest (with
        respect to l) path p in ∪_{i∈I(s)} P_i
        while l(p) < (1 + ε)α̂ do
            Find the bottleneck capacity u of p
            (* u ← min_{e∈p} u(e) *)
            Augment the flow f by routing u units of flow
            along the path p
            foreach arc e in p do l(e) ← l(e)(1 + εu/u(e))
            Use Dijkstra's algorithm to find the shortest
            (with respect to l) path p in ∪_{i∈I(s)} P_i
        end
    end
    α̂ ← (1 + ε)α̂        (* increase the value of α̂ *)
end
Scale f down by a factor of max_{e∈E} f(e)/u(e) and return
it
```

Figure 4: Fleischer's algorithm for solving maximum multicommodity flow

THEOREM 4 (SEE [11]). *For any $0.15 > \varepsilon > 0$ the algorithm in Figure 4 runs in time $\widetilde{O}(m^2\varepsilon^{-2})$, and returns a flow that has value at least $(1-4\varepsilon)OPT$.*

3. SOLVING MULTICOMMODITY FLOW PROBLEMS AND DYNAMIC GRAPH ALGORITHMS

As described in the previous section, the approximation scheme for the maximum multicommodity flow problem due to Garg and Könemann [12] finds a near-optimal solution by repeatedly solving the oracle subproblem of computing the shortest path in graph G with respect to some evolving length function l. (The same general approach is also used for the other variants of multicommodity flow problems.) As a consequence, the running time of the resulting approximation schemes is dominated by the time needed to solve these subproblems using Dijkstra's algorithm. By careful choice of the subproblems as well as better utilization of the computed answers, the number of these (single-source) shortest path computations was reduced considerably in subsequent improvements due to Fleischer [11] and Karakostas [17]. However, the reduced numbers are still $\Omega(m\varepsilon^{-2})$ which leads to a time complexity of $\Omega(m^2\varepsilon^{-2})$ for the corresponding algorithms.

The main observation behind the construction of our improved approximation schemes is that treating each of the oracle subproblems as an independent task (and thus using Dijkstra's algorithm each time), as the above-mentioned results do, is suboptimal. After all, each successive subproblem corresponds to the same underlying graph – only with lengths of some of the arcs increased. Therefore, one might hope to construct a data structure that solves such a sequence of subproblems more efficiently than by computing each time everything from scratch. More precisely, one might wonder whether there is an efficient data structure that maintains a directed graph G with lengths on arcs and supports operations of: increasing a length of some arc; answering shortest-path distance query; and returning shortest vertex-to-vertex path.

It turns out that the problem of designing such a data structure is already known in the literature as the *decremental dynamic all-pairs shortest path* problem and extensive work have been done on this and related problems (see e.g. [10, 3, 7, 9, 27, 4, 8, 28, 30, 29, 5]). However, if we are interested in solutions whose overall running time is within our intended bounds, the result that is closest to what we need is the one by Roditty and Zwick [28]. They show if G were *undirected* and had positive, *integer* lengths on edges, with maximum length being b, a $(1+\delta)$-approximate solution to the decremental dynamic all-pair shortest path problem can be implemented with total maintenance time of $\widetilde{O}(\frac{mnb}{\delta})$, $O(1)$ time needed to answer any vertex-to-vertex shortest-path distance query, and returning shortest vertex-to-vertex path in $O(n)$ time.[3] Unfortunately, in our applications the graph G is not only directed, but also the lengths of the arcs (when we scale them to make them integral) can be of order of $b = \Omega(n^{1/\varepsilon})$ with $\varepsilon < 0.15$. Therefore, the resulting run-

[3]Note that there can be as many as mb edge length increases in a sequence, thus this solution is faster than naïve solution that just computes all-pairs shortest-path after each edge-length increase, or one that just answers each of the queries using Dijkstra's algorithm.

ning time would be prohibitive. Further, the construction of Roditty and Zwick assumes that the sequence of operations to be handled is oblivious to the behavior of the data structure (e.g. to its randomized choices). This feature is a shortcoming from our point of view since in our setting the way the length function of the graph evolves depends directly on which shortest paths the data structure chose to output previously.

To circumvent this lack of suitable existing solutions, we realize that for our purposes it is sufficient to solve a simpler task than the decremental dynamic all-pairs shortest path problem in its full generality (i.e. in the directed setting, and allowing large lengths on arcs and adversarial requests). Namely, when we are using the Garg-Könemann framework to solve multicommodity flow problems, it is not necessary to compute for each subproblem the (approximately) shortest path among all the suitable paths in the set $\mathcal{P}$. As we will prove later, to establish satisfactory bounds on the quality of the final flow, it suffices that whenever we solve some shortest-path subproblem, the set of suitable paths over which we are optimizing the length comes from a set that contains *all* the flowpaths of some fixed optimal solution to the instance of the multicommodity flow problem that we are solving.

With this goal in mind, we define the following random subset $\widehat{\mathcal{P}}$ of paths in $\mathcal{P}$.[4] One may view $\widehat{\mathcal{P}}$ as a sparsification of the set $\mathcal{P}$.

DEFINITION 5. *For $j = 1, \ldots, \lceil \log n \rceil$, let S_j be a random set obtained by sampling each vertex of V with probability $p_j = \min\{\frac{10 \ln n}{2^j}, 1\}$. Define $\widehat{\mathcal{P}} := \bigcup_{j=1}^{\lceil \log n \rceil} \mathcal{P}(S_j, 2^j)$, where $\mathcal{P}(U, j')$ for a given $U \subseteq V$, and $j' > 0$ is the set of all paths in $\mathcal{P}$ that consist of at most j' arcs and pass through at least one vertex of U.*

It turns out that this sparsification $\widehat{\mathcal{P}}$ retains, with high probability, the key property that we need.

LEMMA 6. *For any fixed multicommodity flow solution $f = (f_1, \ldots, f_k)$, with high probability, all the flowpaths of f are contained in $\widehat{\mathcal{P}}$.*

PROOF. Let $p_1, \ldots p_q$ be the decomposition of the flow f into flowpaths. By definition, all p_i are contained in the set $\mathcal{P}$. Furthermore, by standard flow decomposition argument we know that $q \leq km \leq n^4$. Let us focus now on some particular path p_i. Let $1 \leq t \leq n$ be the number of arcs in this path, and let j^* be the smallest j for which $t \leq 2^j$. The probability that $p_i \in \mathcal{P}(S_{j^*}, 2^{j^*}) \subseteq \widehat{\mathcal{P}}$ is exactly the probability that at least one vertex from p is in S_{j^*}. Simple computation shows that the probability that none among $t+1$ vertices of p_i is in $\mathcal{P}(S_{j^*}, 2^{j^*})$ is at most

$$(1 - \frac{10 \ln n}{2^{j^*}})^{t+1} \leq e^{-\frac{10(t+1)\ln n}{2^{j^*}}} \leq e^{-5 \ln n} = n^{-5}.$$

Therefore, by union bounding over all $q \leq n^4$ paths p_i, we get that indeed $\{p_1, \ldots, p_q\} \subseteq \widehat{\mathcal{P}}$ with high probability. □

3.1 $(\delta, M_{\max}, M_{\min}, \mathcal{Q})$-ADSP data structure

Once we defined set $\widehat{\mathcal{P}}$, our goal is to devise an efficient way of maintaining the $(1+\delta)$-approximate shortest paths with respect to it. We start by formally defining our task.

[4]It is worth noting that a very similar set was used in [28] albeit with a slightly different motivation.

DEFINITION 7. *For any $\delta \geq 0$, $M_{\max} \geq 2M_{\min} > 0$ and a set of paths $\mathcal{Q} \subseteq \mathcal{P}$, let the δ-*approximate decremental *$(M_{\max}, M_{\min}, \mathcal{Q})$-*shortest path problem *($(\delta, M_{\max}, M_{\min}, \mathcal{Q})$-ADSP, for short) be a problem in which one maintains a directed graph G with a length function l on its arcs that supports four operations (sometimes we will refer to these operations as* requests*):*

- *Distance(u, v, β), for $u, v \in V$, and $\beta \in [M_{\min}, M_{\max}/2]$: let d^* be the length of the shortest (with respect to l) u-v path in $\mathcal{Q}$; if $d^* \leq 2\beta$ then the query returns a value d such that $d \leq d^* + \delta\beta$. If $d^* > 2\beta$, the query may return either d as above, or ∞;*
- *Increase(e, ω), for $e \in E$ and $\omega \geq 0$: increases the length $l(e)$ of the arc e by ω;*
- *Path(u, v, β), for $u, v \in V$, and $\beta \in [M_{\min}, M_{\max}/2]$: returns a u-v path of length at most Distance(u, v, β), as long as Distance$(u, v, \beta) \neq \infty$;*
- *SSrcDist(u, β) for $u \in V$, and $\beta \in [M_{\min}, M_{\max}/2]$: returns Distance$(u, v, \beta)$ for all $v \in V$.*

Intuitively, β is our guess on the interval $[\beta, 2\beta]$ in which the length of the shortest path we are interested in is. We say that β is *(u, v)-accurate* for given $(\delta, M_{\max}, M_{\min}, \mathcal{Q})$-ADSP data structure R and $u, v \in V$, if the length d^* of the shortest u-v path in $\mathcal{Q}$ is at least β and the data structure R returns a finite value in response to Distance(u, v, β) query. Note that if β is (u, v)-accurate then the $\delta\beta$-additive error guarantee on the distance estimation supplied by R in response to Distance(u, v, β) query implies a $(1+\delta)$ *multiplicative* error guarantee. Also, as long as d^* is at least $M_{\min}$ (this will be always the case in our applications), we can employ binary search to ask $O(\log \log M_{\max}/M_{\min})$ Distance$(u, v, \cdot)$ queries and either realize that d^* is bigger than $M_{\max}$, or find $0 \leq i \leq \lceil \log M_{\max}/2M_{\min} \rceil$ such that $\beta_i = \min\{2^i M_{\min}, M_{\max}/2\}$ is (u, v)-accurate.[5] Finally, it is worth emphasizing that we do not require that the paths returned in response to Path$(\cdot, \cdot, \cdot)$ queries are from $\mathcal{Q}$ – all we insist on is just that all the suitable paths from $\mathcal{Q}$ are considered when the path to be returned is chosen.

Using the ideas and tools from dynamic graph algorithms we can obtain an implementation of the $(\delta, M_{\max}, M_{\min}, \widehat{\mathcal{P}})$-ADSP data structure that is tailored to maintain the shortest paths from set $\widehat{\mathcal{P}}$ and whose performance is described in the following theorem. The proof of the theorem appears in the full version of the paper [22].

THEOREM 8. *For any $1 > \delta > 0$, $M_{\max} \geq 2M_{\min} > 0$, $(\delta, M_{\max}, M_{\min}, \widehat{\mathcal{P}})$-ADSP data structure can be maintained in total expected time $\widetilde{O}(mn \frac{\log M_{\max}/M_{\min}}{\delta})$ plus additional $O(1)$ per Increase$(\cdot, \cdot)$ request in the processed sequence. Each Distance$(\cdot, \cdot, \cdot)$ and Path$(\cdot, \cdot, \cdot)$ query can be answered in $\widetilde{O}(n)$ time, and each SSrcDist$(\cdot, \cdot)$ query in $\widetilde{O}(m)$ time.*

[5]The binary search chooses i in the middle of the current range of values in which the desired value of i may lie (initially this range is $[0, \lceil \log M_{\max}/2M_{\min} \rceil]$), and if the Distance$(u, v, \beta_i)$ query returns ∞ then the left half of the range (including the i queried) is dropped, otherwise the other half is dropped.

3.2 Solving the decremental dynamic all-pair shortest paths problem using an ADSP data structure

Interestingly, we can use the $(\delta, M_{\max}, M_{\min}, \widehat{\mathcal{P}})$-ADSP data structure construction from Theorem 8 to obtain a $(1+\varepsilon)$-approximate solution to the oblivious decremental dynamic all-pair shortest path problem in directed graphs with rational arc lengths, where obliviousness means that the sequence of requests that we process does not depend on the randomness used in the solution.

THEOREM 9. *For any $1 > \varepsilon > 0$, and $L \geq 1$ there exists a $(1+\varepsilon)$-approximate Monte Carlo solution to the oblivious decremental dynamic all-pair shortest paths problem on directed graphs where arc lengths are rational numbers between 1 and L, that has total maintenance cost of $\widetilde{O}(mn\frac{\log L}{\varepsilon})$ plus additional $O(1)$ per increase of the length of any arc, and answers shortest path queries for any vertex pair in $\widetilde{O}(n(\log\log_{(1+\varepsilon)} L)(\log\log L))$ time.*

Note that even when we allow lengths to be quite large (e.g. polynomial in n), the maintenance cost of our solution is still similar to the one that Roditty and Zwick achieved in [28] for undirected graphs with small integer lengths. Unfortunately, our distance query time is $\widetilde{O}(n)$ instead of the $O(1)$ time obtained in [28]. So, the gain that we get over a naïve solution for the problem is that we are able to answer ($(1+\varepsilon)$-approximately) shortest path queries for any vertex pair in $\widetilde{O}(n)$ time, as opposed to the $O(m + n\log n)$ time required by Dijkstra's algorithm. The proof of the theorem appears in the full version of the paper [22].

4. MAXIMUM MULTICOMMODITY FLOW

We proceed to develop a faster algorithm for the maximum multicommodity flow problem. As we indicated in the previous section, the basic idea behind our improvement is modification of Fleischer's algorithm (presented in Figure 4) to make it exploit the dependencies between the oracle subproblems. More precisely, instead of employing Dijkstra's algorithm each time, we answer the shortest-path questions by querying a $(\delta, M_{\max}, M_{\min}, \widehat{\mathcal{P}})$-ADSP data structure (as described in Theorem 8) that we maintain for appropriate choice of δ, $M_{\max}$, and $M_{\min}$, and where $\widehat{\mathcal{P}}$ is a sparsification of $\mathcal{P}$, as described in Definition 5. However, the straightforward implementation of this idea encounters some difficulties.

First, we have to justify the fact that while answering shortest-path queries we take into account mainly paths in $\widehat{\mathcal{P}}$, as opposed to the whole set $\mathcal{P}$. Second, an important feature of Dijkstra's algorithm that is exploited in Fleischer's approximation scheme, is the fact that whenever one computes the distance between a pair of vertices using this algorithm it simultaneously computes all single-source shortest-path distances. Unfortunately, in our case we cannot afford to replicate this approach; thus we need to circumvent this issue in a more careful manner. We address these problems below.

4.1 Existence of short paths in $\widehat{\mathcal{P}}$

As mentioned in section 2, the key ingredient used in the Garg-Könemann framework to bound the quality of the solution for the maximum multicommodity flow problem is the fact that for any length function l of G there is always a path p in $\mathcal{P}$ with length $l(p)$ being at most $\sum_e l(e)u(e)/OPT$. We prove now that with high probability the same property still holds when we consider only paths in $\widehat{\mathcal{P}}$.

LEMMA 10. *With high probability, for any length function l, there exists a path $p \in \widehat{\mathcal{P}}$ with $l(p) \leq \frac{\sum_e l(e)u(e)}{OPT}$, where OPT is the optimal value of the maximum multicommodity flow.*

PROOF. Let $f^* = (f_1^*, f_2^*, \ldots, f_k^*)$ be some optimal multicommodity flow with $\sum_i |f_i^*| = OPT$. By Lemma 6 we know that with high probability $\widehat{\mathcal{P}}$ contains all the flowpaths $p_1, \ldots, p_q$ of f^*. The fact that f^* has to obey the capacity constraints implies that $\sum_e l(e)u(e) \geq \sum_{j=1}^q l(p_j)f^*(p_j)$. But $OPT = \sum_i |f_i^*| = \sum_{j=1}^q f^*(p_j)$; an averaging argument shows that there exists a j^* such that $l(p_{j^*}) \leq \frac{\sum_e l(e)u(e)}{OPT}$ as desired. □

To get a slightly different perspective on the above statement, note that the only property of $\widehat{\mathcal{P}}$ we are using in the proof is that it contains (with high probability) all the flowpaths of some optimal solution. This means that if we consider a restriction LP' of the linear program (1) in which we set to zero all the variables f_p with $p \in \mathcal{P} \setminus \widehat{\mathcal{P}}$, then with high probability the optimum of this restricted linear program LP' is still equal to the original optimum i.e. OPT. Therefore, one may view the statement of the above lemma as a simple consequence of the weak duality between LP' and its dual linear program.

4.2 Randomized cycling through commodities

For a given value of $\widehat{\alpha}$, and some $(\delta, M_{\max}, M_{\min}, \widehat{\mathcal{P}})$-ADSP data structure R, we say that a source-sink pair (s,t) is *admissible for $\widehat{\alpha}$ (with respect to R)* if upon querying R with $\mathsf{Distance}(s,t,\widehat{\alpha})$ the obtained answer is at most $(1+2\delta)\widehat{\alpha}$. In other words, (s,t) is admissible for $\widehat{\alpha}$ if R's estimate of the distance from s to t in $\widehat{\mathcal{P}}$ is small enough that our algorithm could choose to augment the flow along this path – provided $\widehat{\alpha}$ was its current lower-bound estimate of the length of the shortest path in $\widehat{\mathcal{P}}$. Obviously, our algorithm is vitally interested in finding source-sink pairs that are admissible for its current value of $\widehat{\alpha}$ – these pairs are the ones that allow augmentation of the flow.

Unfortunately, given the set of all possible pairs $\{(s_i,t_i)\}_i$, and the data structure R, it is not clear at all which one among them (if any) are admissible for given $\widehat{\alpha}$. Note, however, that if we deem some source-sink pair (s,t) inadmissible for $\widehat{\alpha}$ (by querying R for the corresponding s-t distance) then, since our length function is always increasing, this pair will never become admissible for $\widehat{\alpha}$ again. This suggests the following natural approach for identification of admissible pairs for a given $\widehat{\alpha}$. We cycle through all the sink-source pairs and query R for the corresponding distance, we stick with one pair as long as it is admissible, and move on once it becomes inadmissible. Clearly, the moment we cycled through all pairs, we know that all the pairs are inadmissible for $\widehat{\alpha}$ with respect to the current length function l. The problem with this approach is that the resulting number of s-t distance queries is at least k and thus this would lead to the somewhat prohibitive bottleneck of $\widetilde{\Omega}(kn)$ in the running time (note that k can be $\Omega(n^2)$).

To alleviate this problem we note that a very similar issue arose in Fleischer's algorithm – she avoided the above bottleneck by grouping the source-sink pairs according to common sources and exploiting the fact that Dijkstra's algorithm computes all single-source shortest-path distances simultaneously. Therefore, one execution of Dijkstra's algorithm either finds an (analog of) admissible pair, or deems *all* the pairs sharing the same source inadmissible. Unfortunately, although our ADSP data structure allows single-source shortest-path distance queries, these queries require $\widetilde{O}(m)$ time and we cannot afford to use them to obtain s-t distances in the manner Fleischer did – this could cause $\Omega(m^2\varepsilon^{-2})$ worst-case running time. We therefore devise a different method of circumventing the bottleneck. To describe it, let us assume that we are given some vertex s, and a set $I(s)$ of source-sink pairs that have s as their common source and that have not yet been deemed inadmissible for our current value of $\widehat{\alpha}$. Our procedure samples $\lceil \log n \rceil$ source-sink pairs from $I(s)$ and checks whether any of them is admissible using the $\mathsf{Distance}(\cdot,\cdot,\cdot)$ query. If so, then we return the admissible pair found. Otherwise, i.e. if none of them was admissible, we use the $\mathsf{SSrcDist}(\cdot,\cdot)$ query to check which (if any) source-sink pairs in $I(s)$ are inadmissible, remove them from the set $I(s)$ and return an admissible pair (if any was found). We repeat the whole procedure – if $I(s)$ became empty, we proceed to the next possible source s – until we examine all source-sink pairs. The algorithm is summarized in Figure 6 – for convenience, we substituted for δ, $M_{\max}$, and $M_{\min}$ the actual values used in our algorithm. The intuition behind this procedure is that if all $\lceil \log n \rceil$ samples from $I(s)$ turned out to be inadmissible then with probability at least $(1-\frac{1}{n})$, at least half of the pairs in $I(s)$ is inadmissible, and therefore the $\mathsf{SSrcDist}(\cdot,\cdot)$ query will reduce the size of $I(s)$ by at least half. Therefore, as we will show later, the expected number of $\mathsf{SSrcDist}(\cdot,\cdot)$ queries is not too large.

4.3 Our algorithm

We present our algorithm for the maximum multicommodity flow problem in Figure 5. As we already noted, the basic idea behind it is making Fleischer's algorithm (presented in Figure 4) to answer distance queries using an $(\varepsilon/2, 1, \gamma, \widehat{\mathcal{P}})$-ADSP data structure (where $\widehat{\mathcal{P}}$ is constructed as in Definition 5). To implement this idea efficiently, we incorporated the randomized cycling through commodities described above. The following theorem is proved in the full version of the paper [22].

THEOREM 11. *For any $0.15 > \varepsilon > 0$, with high probability, the algorithm presented in Figure 5 finds a $(1-3\varepsilon)$-approximate solution to the maximum multicommodity flow problem in expected $\widetilde{O}(mn\varepsilon^{-2})$ time.*

4.4 Weighted maximum multicommodity flow

Recall that the weighted maximum multicommodity flow problem is a generalization of the maximum multicommodity problem in which each commodity i has a positive weight w_i associated with it and we want to find a solution $f = (f_1, \ldots, f_k)$ that maximizes $\sum_i w_i|f_i|$. By scaling, we may ensure that the minimum weight is one, and maximum weight has some value W. In the full version of the paper [22], we present a simple modification of our algorithm for the maximum multicommodity flow problem that can solve this generalization. We prove there the following statement.

Input : Graph $G = (V, E)$, capacities $u(e)$, commodity pairs $\{(s_i, t_i)\}_i$, accuracy parameter $\varepsilon > 0$
Output: Flow f
Initialize $f \leftarrow \emptyset$, $\widehat{\alpha} \leftarrow \gamma$, and $l(e) \leftarrow \gamma$ for all arcs $e \in E$, where $\gamma = (1+\varepsilon)/((1+\varepsilon)n)^{1/\theta}$, and $\theta = \varepsilon(1+\varepsilon)$
Sample sets $\{S_j\}_{j=1,\ldots,\lceil \log n \rceil}$ to indicate the set $\widehat{\mathcal{P}}$ (see Definition 5)
Initialize $(\varepsilon/2, 1, \gamma, \widehat{\mathcal{P}})$-ADSP data structure R as in Theorem 8
while $\widehat{\alpha} < 1$ **do**
  $I(s) \leftarrow \{i \mid s_i = s\}$ for each $s \in V$
    (* initializing pairs to be examined *)
  foreach $s \in V$ with $I(s) \neq \emptyset$ **do**
      (* cycling through commodities *)
    $\langle (s,t), I(s) \rangle \leftarrow$
    $\leftarrow$ Find_Admissible_Pair$(\varepsilon, R, \widehat{\alpha}, I(s))$
    while $I(v) \neq \emptyset$ **do**
      $p \leftarrow R.\mathsf{Path}(s, t, \widehat{\alpha})$
      Find the bottleneck capacity u of p
      (* $u \leftarrow \min_{e \in p} u(e)$ *)
      Augment the flow f by routing u units of flow along the path p
      foreach arc e in p **do** $R.\mathsf{Increase}(e, \frac{\varepsilon u l(e)}{u(e)})$;
      $l(e) \leftarrow l(e)(1 + \frac{\varepsilon u}{u(e)})$ $\langle (s,t), I(s) \rangle \leftarrow$
      Find_Admissible_Pair$(\varepsilon, R, \widehat{\alpha}, I(s))$
    end
  end
  $\widehat{\alpha} \leftarrow (1+\varepsilon/2)\widehat{\alpha}$ (* increase the value of $\widehat{\alpha}$ *)
end
Scale f down by a factor of $\max_{e \in E} f(e)/u(e)$ and return it

Figure 5: Improved algorithm for solving maximum multicommodity flow. Find_Admissible_Pair procedure is described in Figure 6.

Input : Accuracy parameter $\varepsilon > 0$, $(\varepsilon/2, 1, \gamma, \widehat{\mathcal{P}})$-ADSP data structure R, lower bound $\widehat{\alpha}$ on $\min_{p \in \widehat{\mathcal{P}}} l(p)$, and a set $I(s)$ of source-sink pairs that might be admissible for $\widehat{\alpha}$
Output: $\langle (s,t), I'(s) \rangle$, where $I'(s)$ is a subset of $I(s)$, and (s,t) is: an admissible pair for $\widehat{\alpha}$ if $I'(s) \neq \emptyset$; an arbitrary pair otherwise
for $i = 1, \ldots, \lceil \log n \rceil$ **do**
  Sample a random source-sink pair (s,t) from $I(s)$
  if $R.\mathit{Distance}(s, t, \widehat{\alpha}) \leq (1+\varepsilon)\widehat{\alpha}$ **then**
      (* checking admissibility for $\widehat{\alpha}$ *)
    return $\langle (s,t), I(s) \rangle$
  end
end
    (* No admissible pairs sampled *)
Use $R.\mathsf{SSrcDist}(s, \widehat{\alpha})$ to check admissibility for $\widehat{\alpha}$ of all the source-sink pairs in $I(s)$
Let $I'(s)$ be the subset of admissible pairs from $I(s)$
if $I'(s) \neq \emptyset$ **then**
  return $\langle (s,t), I'(s) \rangle$ where $(s,t) \in I'(s)$
else
  return $\langle (s,t), \emptyset \rangle$ where (s,t) is an arbitrary pair
end

Figure 6: Procedure Find_Admissible_Pair

Corollary 12. *For any $0.15 > \varepsilon > 0$, there exists a Monte Carlo algorithm that finds a $(1-3\varepsilon)$-approximate solution to weighted maximum multicommodity flow problem in expected $\widetilde{O}(mn\varepsilon^{-2}\log^2 W)$ time.*

4.5 Maximum concurrent flow

In the maximum concurrent flow problem, in addition to graph $G=(V,E)$ with capacities $u(\cdot)$ (we assume that $\min_e u(e)=1$, and let $U:=\max_e u(e)$), and k source-sink pairs (s_i,t_i), we also have a demand $d_i>0$ associated with each commodity i. The task is to find a feasible multicommodity flow routing λd_i units of each commodity i for maximum λ. The following theorem is proved in the full version of the paper [22].

Theorem 13. *For any $0.15 > \varepsilon > 0$, there exists a Monte Carlo algorithm that finds a $(1-4\varepsilon)$-approximate solution for maximum concurrent flow problem in expected time $\widetilde{O}((m+k)n\varepsilon^{-2}\log U)$.*

4.6 Minimum cost concurrent flow

As noted in [12] and [11], the approach for solving the maximum concurrent flow problem extends easily to the case of the minimum cost concurrent flow problem in which we additionally have a cost function $c(\cdot)$ on arcs (routing one unit of flow along arc e incurs a cost of $c(e)$), and we are interested in finding maximum concurrent flow whose total cost is within some target budget B. In fact, as pointed out in [11], this extension can be easily adapted to handle multiple budgets B_j corresponding to different cost functions c_j. In the full version of this paper [22] we outline a modification of our algorithm for the maximum concurrent flow problem that establishes the following corollary.

Corollary 14. *For any $0.15 > \varepsilon > 0$, there exists a Monte Carlo algorithm that finds a $(1-5\varepsilon)$-approximate solution for minimum cost concurrent flow problem in expected time $\widetilde{O}((m+k)n\varepsilon^{-2}\log(U+B))$.*

Acknowledgments

We are grateful to Michel Goemans, Debmalya Panigrahi, and anonymous reviewers for helpful comments. We also thank Lisa Fleischer, and David Shmoys for providing useful references.

5. REFERENCES

[1] R. K. Ahuja, T. L. Magnanti, and J. B. Orlin. *Network flows: theory, algorithms, and applications.* Prentice-Hall, Inc., Upper Saddle River, NJ, USA, 1993.

[2] S. Arora, E. Hazan, and S. Kale. The multiplicative weights update method: A meta-algorithm and applications. Available at http://www.cs.princeton.edu/~arora/pubs/MWsurvey.pdf.

[3] G. Ausiello, G. F. Italiano, A. M. Spaccamela, and U. Nanni. On-line computation of minimal and maximal length paths. *Theoretical Computer Science*, 95(2):245–261, 1992.

[4] S. Baswana, R. Hariharan, and S. Sen. Maintaining all-pairs approximate shortest paths under deletion of edges. In *Proceedings of the 14th Annual ACM-SIAM Symposium on Discrete Algorithms*, pages 394–403, Philadelphia, PA, USA, 2003. Society for Industrial and Applied Mathematics.

[5] S. Baswana, R. Hariharan, and S. Sen. Improved decremental algorithms for maintaining transitive closure and all-pairs shortest paths. *Journal of Algorithms*, 62(2):74–92, 2007.

[6] D. Bienstock and G. Iyengar. Solving fractional packing problems in $\widetilde{O}(1/\varepsilon)$ iterations. In *Proceedings of the 36th Annual ACM Symposium on Theory of Computing*, pages 146–155, New York, NY, USA, 2004. ACM.

[7] C. Demetrescu and G. F. Italiano. Fully dynamic transitive closure: breaking through the $o(n^2)$ barrier. In *Proceedings of the 41st Annual Symposium on Foundations of Computer Science*, page 381, Washington, DC, USA, 2000. IEEE Computer Society.

[8] C. Demetrescu and G. F. Italiano. A new approach to dynamic all pairs shortest paths. In *Proceedings of the 35th Annual ACM Symposium on Theory of Computing*, pages 159–166, New York, NY, USA, 2003. ACM.

[9] C. Demetrescu and G. F. Italiano. Fully dynamic all pairs shortest paths with real edge weights. *Journal of Computer and System Sciences*, 72(5):813–837, 2006.

[10] S. Even and Y. Shiloach. An on-line edge-deletion problem. *Journal of ACM*, 28(1):1–4, 1981.

[11] L. K. Fleischer. Approximating fractional multicommodity flow independent of the number of commodities. *SIAM Journal of Discrete Mathematics*, 13(4):505–520, 2000.

[12] N. Garg and J. Könemann. Faster and simpler algorithms for multicommodity flow and other fractional packing problems. In *Proceedings of the 39th Annual Symposium on Foundations of Computer Science*, pages 300–309, 1998.

[13] A. V. Goldberg. A natural randomization strategy for multicommodity flow and related algorithms. *Information Processing Letters*, 42(5):249–256, 1992.

[14] A. V. Goldberg and S. Rao. Beyond the flow decomposition barrier. *Journal of ACM*, 45(5):783–797, 1998.

[15] M. D. Grigoriadis and L. G. Khachiyan. Fast approximation schemes for convex programs with many blocks and coupling constraints. *SIAM Journal on Optimization*, 4(1):86–107, 1994.

[16] M. D. Grigoriadis and L. G. Khachiyan. Approximate minimum-cost multicommodity flows in $\widetilde{O}(\varepsilon^{-2}knm)$ time. *Mathematical Programming*, 75(3):477–482, 1996.

[17] G. Karakostas. Faster approximation schemes for fractional multicommodity flow problems. In *Proceedings of the 13th annual ACM-SIAM Symposium on Discrete Algorithms*, pages 166–173, Philadelphia, PA, USA, 2002. Society for Industrial and Applied Mathematics.

[18] D. Karger and S. Plotkin. Adding multiple cost constraints to combinatorial optimization problems, with applications to multicommodity flows. In *Proceedings of the 27th Annual ACM Symposium on Theory of Computing*, pages 18–25, New York, NY, USA, 1995. ACM.

[19] P. Klein, S. Plotkin, C. Stein, and E. Tardos. Faster approximation algorithms for the unit capacity concurrent flow problem with applications to routing and finding sparse cuts. *SIAM Journal on Computing*, 23(3):466–487, 1994.

[20] P. Klein and N. Young. On the number of iterations for dantzig-wolfe optimization and packing-covering approximation algorithms. In *In Proceedings of the 7th International IPCO Conference*, pages 320–327. Springer, 2002.

[21] T. Leighton, F. Makedon, S. Plotkin, C. Stein, E. Tardos, and S. Tragoudas. Fast approximation algorithms for multicommodity flow problems. *Journal of Computer and System Sciences*, 50(2):228–243, 1995.

[22] A. Madry. Faster approximation schemes for fractional multicommodity flow problems via dynamic graph algorithms. arXiv:1003.5907. Available at http://arxiv.org/abs/1003.5907

[23] Y. Nesterov. Smooth minimization of non-smooth functions. *Mathematical Programming*, 103(1):127–152, 2005.

[24] Y. Nesterov. Fast gradient methods for network flow problems. In *The 20th International Symposium of Mathematical Programming*, 2009.

[25] S. A. Plotkin, D. B. Shmoys, and E. Tardos. Fast approximation algorithms for fractional packing and covering problems. *Mathematics of Operations Research*, 20:257–301, 1995.

[26] T. Radzik. Fast deterministic approximation for the multicommodity flow problem. In *Proceedings of the 6th Annual ACM-SIAM Symposium on Discrete Algorithms*, pages 486–492, Philadelphia, PA, USA, 1995. Society for Industrial and Applied Mathematics.

[27] L. Roditty and U. Zwick. Improved dynamic reachability algorithms for directed graphs. In *Proceedings of the 43rd Symposium on Foundations of Computer Science*, page 679, Washington, DC, USA, 2002. IEEE Computer Society.

[28] L. Roditty and U. Zwick. Dynamic approximate all-pairs shortest paths in undirected graphs. In *Proceedings of the 45th Annual IEEE Symposium on Foundations of Computer Science*, pages 499–508, Washington, DC, USA, 2004. IEEE Computer Society.

[29] L. Roditty and U. Zwick. A fully dynamic reachability algorithm for directed graphs with an almost linear update time. In *Proceedings of the 36th Annual ACM Symposium on Theory of Computing*, pages 184–191, New York, NY, USA, 2004. ACM.

[30] L. Roditty and U. Zwick. On dynamic shortest paths problems. In *Proceedings of 12th Annual European Symposium on Algorithms*, pages 580–591, 2004.

[31] F. Shahrokhi and D. W. Matula. The maximum concurrent flow problem. *Journal of ACM*, 37(2):318–334, 1990.

[32] D. B. Shmoys. Cut problems and their application to divide-and-conquer. pages 192–235, 1997.

[33] N. E. Young. Randomized rounding without solving the linear program. In *Proceedings of the 6th Annual ACM-SIAM Symposium on Discrete Algorithms*, pages 170–178, Philadelphia, PA, USA, 1995. Society for Industrial and Applied Mathematics.

A Full Characterization of Quantum Advice

Scott Aaronson *
MIT

Andrew Drucker †
MIT

ABSTRACT

We prove the following surprising result: given any quantum state ρ on n qubits, there exists a local Hamiltonian H on poly (n) qubits (e.g., a sum of two-qubit interactions), such that any ground state of H can be used to simulate ρ on all quantum circuits of fixed polynomial size. In terms of complexity classes, this implies that $\mathsf{BQP/qpoly} \subseteq \mathsf{QMA/poly}$, which supersedes the previous result of Aaronson that $\mathsf{BQP/qpoly} \subseteq \mathsf{PP/poly}$. Indeed, we can exactly characterize quantum advice, as equivalent in power to *untrusted* quantum advice combined with trusted *classical* advice.

Proving our main result requires combining a large number of previous tools—including a result of Alon et al. on learning of real-valued concept classes, a result of Aaronson on the learnability of quantum states, and a result of Aharonov and Regev on 'QMA_+ super-verifiers'—and also creating some new ones. The main new tool is a so-called *majority-certificates lemma*, which is related to boosting in machine learning, and which seems likely to find independent applications. In its simplest version, this lemma says the following. Given any set S of Boolean functions on n variables, any function $f \in S$ can be expressed as the pointwise majority of $m = O(n)$ functions $f_1, \ldots, f_m \in S$, such that each f_i is the unique function in S compatible with $O(\log |S|)$ input/output constraints.

Categories and Subject Descriptors

F.1.3 [**Theory of Computation**]: Computation by Abstract Devices—*Complexity Measures and Classes*

*Email: aaronson@csail.mit.edu. MIT EECS, Cambridge, MA, USA. Based upon work supported by the National Science Foundation under Grant No. 0844626. Also supported by a DARPA YFA grant, a Sloan Fellowship, and the Keck Foundation.

†Email: adrucker@mit.edu. MIT EECS, Cambridge, MA, USA. Supported by a DARPA YFA grant. The author was supported during part of this work by an Akamai Presidential Graduate Fellowship.

General Terms

Theory

Keywords

quantum computation, learning, compression, advice, local Hamiltonians, nonuniform computation, boosting, Karp-Lipton Theorem

1. INTRODUCTION

> *How much classical information is needed to specify a quantum state on n qubits?*

This question has inspired a rich and varied set of responses, in part because it can be interpreted in many ways. If we want to specify a quantum state ρ *exactly*, then of course the answer is 'an infinite amount,' since amplitudes in quantum mechanics are continuous. A natural compromise is to try to specify ρ *approximately*, i.e., to give a description which yields a state $\widetilde{\rho}$ whose statistical behavior is close to that of ρ under every measurement. (This statement is captured by the requirement that ρ and $\widetilde{\rho}$ are close under the so-called *trace distance* metric.) But it is not hard to see that even for this task, we still need to use an exponential (in n) number of classical bits.

This fact can be viewed as a disappointment, but also as an opportunity, since it raises the prospect that we might be able to encode massive amounts of information in physically compact quantum states: for example, we might hope to store 2^n classical bits in n qubits. But an obvious practical requirement is that we be able to retrieve the information reliably, and this rules out the hope of significant 'quantum compression' of classical strings, as shown by a landmark result of Holevo [21] from 1973. Consider a sender Alice and a recipient Bob, with a one-way quantum channel between them. Then Holevo's Theorem says that, if Alice wants to encode an n-bit classical string x into an m-qubit quantum state ρ_x, in such a way that Bob can retrieve x (with probability 2/3, say) by measuring ρ_x, then Alice must take $m \geq n - O(1)$ (or $m \geq n/2 - O(1)$, if Alice and Bob share entanglement). In other words, for this communication task, quantum states offer essentially no advantage over classical strings. In 1999, Ambainis et al. [13] generalized Holevo's result as follows: even if Bob wants to learn only a *single bit* x_i of $x = x_1 \ldots x_n$ (for some $i \in [n]$ unknown to Alice), and is willing to destroy the state ρ_x in the process of learning that bit, Alice still needs to send $m = \Omega(n)$ qubits for Bob to succeed with high probability.

These results say that the exponential descriptive complexity of quantum states cannot be effectively harnessed for classical data storage, but they do not bound the number of practically meaningful 'degrees of freedom' in a quantum state used for purposes other than storing data. For example, a quantum state could be useful for computation, or it could be a physical system worthy of study in its own right. The question then becomes, what useful information *can* we give about an n-qubit state using a 'reasonable' number (say, $\operatorname{poly}(n)$) of classical bits?

One approach to this question is to identify special subclasses of quantum states for which a faithful approximation can be specified using only $\operatorname{poly}(n)$ bits. This has been done, for example, with matrix product states [30] and 'tree states' [1]. A second approach is to try to describe an *arbitrary* n-qubit state ρ concisely, in such a way that the state $\widetilde{\rho}$ recovered from the description is close to ρ with respect to some natural subclass of *measurements*. This has been done for specific classes like the 'pretty good measurements' of Hausladen and Wootters [20]. A more ambitious goal in this vein, explored by Aaronson in two previous works [2, 6] and continued in the present paper, is to give a description of an n-qubit state ρ which yields a state $\widetilde{\rho}$ that behaves approximately like ρ with respect to all (binary) measurements performable by quantum circuits of 'reasonable' size—say, of size at most n^c, for some fixed $c > 0$. Then if c is taken large enough, $\widetilde{\rho}$ is arguably 'just as good as' ρ for practical purposes.

Certainly we can achieve this goal using $2^{n^{c+O(1)}}$ bits: simply give approximations to the measurement statistics for every size-n^c circuit. However, the results of Holevo [21] and Ambainis et al. [13] suggest that a much more succinct description might be possible. This hope was realized by Aaronson [2], who gave a description scheme in which an n-qubit state can be specified using $\operatorname{poly}(n)$ classical bits. There is a significant catch in Aaronson's result, though: the encoder Alice and decoder Bob both need to invest exponential amounts of computation.

In a subsequent paper [6], Aaronson gave a closely-related result which significantly reduces the computational requirements: now Alice can generate her message in polynomial time (for fixed c). Also, while Bob cannot necessarily construct the state $\widetilde{\rho}$ efficiently on his own, if he is presented with such a state (by an untrusted prover, say), Bob can *verify* the state in polynomial time. The catch in this result is a weakened approximation guarantee: Bob cannot use $\widetilde{\rho}$ to predict the outcomes of *all* the measurements defined by size-n^c circuits, but only *most* of them (with respect to a samplable distribution used by Alice in the encoding process). Aaronson [2, 6] conjectured that the tradeoff between this result and the previous one revealed an inherent limit to quantum compression.

1.1 Our Quantum Information Result

The main result of this paper is that Aaronson's conjecture was false: one really can get the best of both worlds, and simulate an arbitrary quantum state ρ on all small circuits, using a different state $\widetilde{\rho}$ that is easy to recognize. Indeed, we can even take $\widetilde{\rho}$ to be the *ground state of a local Hamiltonian*: that is, the unique pure state $\widetilde{\rho} = |\psi\rangle\langle\psi|$ on $\operatorname{poly}(n)$ qubits that is compatible with $\operatorname{poly}(n)$ local constraints, each involving a constant number of qubits. In a sense, then, this paper completes a 'trilogy' of which [2, 6] were the first two installments.

Here is a formal statement of our result.

THEOREM 1. *Let $c, \varepsilon > 0$, and let ρ be any n-qubit quantum state. Then there exists a 2-local Hamiltonian H on $\operatorname{poly}(n, \frac{1}{\varepsilon})$ qubits with unique ground state $|\psi\rangle\langle\psi|$, and a transformation $C \longrightarrow C'$ of quantum circuits, computable in time $\operatorname{poly}(n, 1/\varepsilon)$ given H, such that the following holds: $|C'(|\psi\rangle\langle\psi|) - C(\rho)| \le \varepsilon$ for any measurement C definable by a quantum circuit of size n^c. (Here $C(\rho)$ is the probability that C accepts ρ.)*

In other words, the ground states of local Hamiltonians are 'universal quantum states' in a very non-obvious sense. For example, suppose you own a quantum software store, which sells quantum states ρ that can be fed as input to quantum computers. Then our result says that *ground states of local Hamiltonians are the only kind of state you ever need to stock.* What makes this surprising is that being a good piece of quantum software might entail satisfying an exponential number of constraints: for example, if ρ is supposed to help a customer's quantum computer Q evaluate some Boolean function $f : \{0,1\}^n \to \{0,1\}$, then $Q(\rho, x)$ should output $f(x)$ for *every* input $x \in \{0,1\}^n$. By contrast, any k-local Hamiltonian H can be described as a set of at most $\binom{n}{k} = O(n^k)$ constraints.

One can also interpret Theorem 1 as a statement about communication over quantum channels. Suppose Alice (who is computationally unbounded) has a classical description of an n-qubit state ρ. She would like to describe ρ to Bob (who is computationally bounded), at least well enough for Bob to be able to *simulate* ρ on all quantum circuits of some fixed polynomial size. However, Alice cannot just send ρ to Bob, since her quantum communication channel is noisy and there is a chance that ρ might get corrupted along the way. Nor can she send a faithful classical description of $|\psi\rangle$, since that would require an exponential number of bits. Our result provides an alternative: Alice can send a different quantum state σ, of $\operatorname{poly}(n)$ qubits, together with a $\operatorname{poly}(n)$-bit classical string x. Then, Bob can use x to *verify* that σ can be used to accurately simulate ρ on all small measurements.

We believe Theorem 1 makes a significant contribution to the study of the effective information content of quantum states. It does, however, leave open whether a quantum state of n qubits can be efficiently encoded *and* decoded in polynomial time, in a way that is 'good enough' to preserve the measurement statistics of measurements defined by circuits of fixed polynomial size. This remains an important problem for future work.

1.2 Impact on Quantum Complexity Theory

The questions addressed in this paper, and our results, are naturally phrased and proved in terms of complexity classes. In recent years, researchers have defined quantum complexity classes as a way to study the 'useful information' embodied in quantum states. One approach is to study the power of nonuniform *quantum advice*. The class $\mathsf{BQP/qpoly}$, defined by Nishimura and Yamakami [27], consists of all languages decidable in polynomial time by a quantum computer, with the help of a $\operatorname{poly}(n)$-qubit advice state that depends only on the input length n. This class is analogous to the classical class $\mathsf{P/poly}$. To understand the role of quantum information in determining the power of BQP/qpoly, a useful benchmark of comparison is the class BQP/poly of decision problems efficiently solvable by a quantum computer with poly (n) bits of *classical* advice. It is open whether BQP/qpoly = BQP/poly.

A second approach studies the power of quantum *proof systems*, by analogy with the classical class NP. Kitaev (unpublished, 1999) defined the complexity class now called QMA, for 'Quantum Merlin-Arthur'. This is the class of decision problems for which a 'yes' answer can be proved by exhibiting a *quantum witness state* (or *quantum proof*) $|\psi\rangle$, on poly (n) qubits, which is then checked by a skeptical polynomial-time quantum verifier. A natural benchmark class is QCMA (for 'Quantum Classical Merlin-Arthur'), defined by Aharonov and Naveh [9]. This is the class of decision problems for which a 'yes' answer can be checked by a *quantum* verifier who receives a *classical* witness. Here the natural open question is whether QMA = QCMA.

In this paper we prove a new upper bound on BQP/qpoly:

THEOREM 2. BQP/qpoly $\subseteq$ QMA/poly.

Previously Aaronson showed in [2] that BQP/qpoly $\subseteq$ PP/poly, and showed in [6] that BQP/qpoly is contained in the 'heuristic' class HeurQMA/poly; Theorem 2 supersedes both of these earlier results.

Theorem 2 says that one can always replace polynomial-size quantum advice by polynomial-size *classical* advice, together with a polynomial-size quantum *witness* (or equivalently, *untrusted* quantum advice). Indeed, we can *characterize* the class BQP/qpoly, as equal to the subclass of QMA/poly in which the quantum witness state $|\psi_n\rangle$ can only depend on the input length n.[1]

Using Theorem 2, we also obtain several other results for quantum complexity theory:

(1) Without loss of generality, every quantum advice state can be taken to be the ground state of some local Hamiltonian H. (This essentially follows by combining our BQP/qpoly $\subseteq$ QMA/poly result with the result of Kitaev that LOCAL HAMILTONIANS is QMA-complete.)

(2) It is open whether for every local Hamiltonian H on n qubits, there exists a quantum circuit of size poly (n) that prepares a ground state of H. It is easy to show that an affirmative answer would imply QMA = QCMA. As a consequence of Theorem 2, we can show that an affirmative answer would also imply BQP/qpoly = BQP/poly—thereby establishing a previously-unknown connection between quantum proofs and quantum advice.

(3) In the full version of this paper, we generalize Theorem 2 to show that QCMA/qpoly $\subseteq$ QMA/poly.

(4) In the full version, we also use our new characterization of BQP/qpoly to prove a quantum analogue of the Karp-Lipton Theorem [24]. Recall that the Karp-Lipton Theorem says that if NP $\subset$ P/poly, then the polynomial hierarchy collapses to the second level. Our 'Quantum Karp-Lipton Theorem' says that if NP $\subset$ BQP/qpoly (that is, NP-complete problems are efficiently solvable with the help of quantum advice), then $\Pi_2^{\mathsf{P}} \subseteq \mathsf{QMA}^{\mathsf{PromiseQMA}}$. As far as we know, this is the first nontrivial result to derive unlikely consequences from a hypothesis about quantum machines being able to solve NP-complete problems in polynomial time.

[1] We call this restricted class YQP/poly; in another notation it would be OQMA/poly∩coOQMA/poly (where the O stands for 'oblivious').

1.3 Proof Overview

We now give an overview of the proof Theorem 2, that BQP/qpoly $\subseteq$ QMA/poly. As we will explain, our proof rests on a new idea we call the 'majority-certificates' technique, which is not specifically quantum and which seems likely to find other applications.

We begin with a language $L \in$ BQP/qpoly and, for $n > 0$, a poly(n)-size quantum circuit $Q(x, \xi)$ that computes $L(x)$ with high probability when given the 'correct' advice state $\xi = \rho_n$ on poly (n) qubits. The challenge, then, is to force Merlin to supply a witness state ρ' that behaves like ρ_n on every input $x \in \{0,1\}^n$.

Every potential advice state ξ defines a function $f_\xi : \{0,1\}^n \to [0,1]$, by $f_\xi(x) := \Pr[Q(x,\xi) = 1]$. For each such ξ, let $\widehat{f}_\xi(x) := [f_\xi(x) \geq 1/2]$ be the Boolean function obtained by rounding f_ξ. As a simplification, suppose that Merlin is restricted to sending an advice state ξ for which $f_\xi(x) \notin (1/3, 2/3)$: that is, an advice state which renders a 'clear opinion' about every input x. (This simplification helps to explain the main ideas, but does not follow the actual proof.) Let S be the set of all Boolean functions $f : \{0,1\}^n \to \{0,1\}$ that are expressible as $\widehat{f}_\xi$ for some such advice state ξ. Then S includes the 'target function' $f^* := L_n$ (the restriction of L to inputs of length n), as well as a potentially-large number of other functions. However, we claim S is not *too* large: $|S| \leq 2^{\text{poly}(n)}$. This bound on the 'effective information content' of quantum states was derived previously by Aaronson [2, 6], building on the work of Ambainis et al. [13].

One might initially hope that, just by virtue of the size bound on S, we could find some set of poly(n) values

$$(x_1, f^*(x_1)), \ldots, (x_k, f^*(x_t))$$

which *isolate* f^* in S—that is, which differentiate f^* from all other members of S. In that case, the trusted classical advice could simply specify those values, as 'tests' for Arthur to perform on the quantum state sent by Merlin. Alas, this hope is unfounded in general. For consider the case where f^* is the identically-zero function, and S consists of f^* along with the 'point function' f_y (which equals 1 on y and 0 elsewhere), for all $y \in \{0,1\}^n$. Then f^* can only be isolated in S by specifying its value at *every* point!

Luckily, this counterexample leads us to a key observation. Although f is not isolatable in S by a small number of values, each point function f_y *can* be isolated (by its value at y), and moreover, f_y is quite 'close' to f. In fact, if we choose any three distinct strings x, y, z, then $f^* = \text{MAJ}(f_x, f_y, f_z)$. (Of course if f^* were the identically-zero function, it could be easily specified with classical advice! But f^* could have been any function in this example.)

This suggests a new, more indirect approach to our general problem: we try to express f as the pointwise majority vote

$$f^*(x) \equiv \text{MAJ}(f_1(x), \ldots, f_m(x)),$$

of a small number ($m = O(n)$, say) of *other* functions $f_1, \ldots, f_m$ in S, where each f_i is isolatable in S by specifying at most $k = O(\log|S|)$ of its values. Indeed, we will

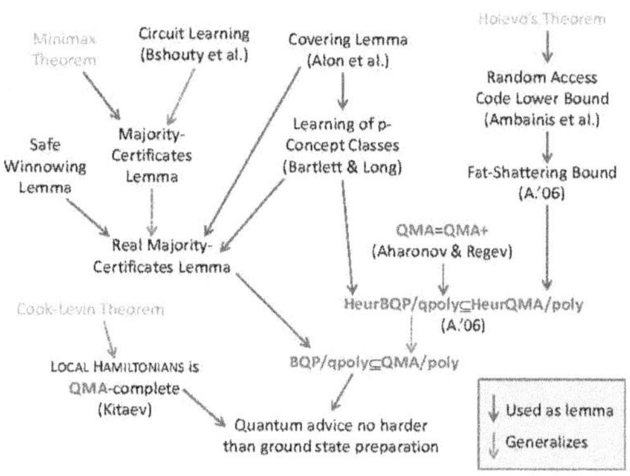

Figure 1: Dependency structure of our proof that quantum advice states can be expressed as ground states of local Hamiltonians.

show this can *always* be done. We call this key result the *majority-certificates lemma*; we will say more about its proof and its relation to earlier work in Section 1.4.

With this lemma in hand, we can solve our (artificially simplified) problem: in the QMA/poly protocol for L, we use certificates which isolate $f_1, \ldots, f_m \in S$ as above as the classical advice for Arthur. Arthur requests from Merlin each of the m states $\xi_1, \ldots, \xi_m$ such that $f_i = f_{\xi_i}$, and verifies that he receives appropriate states by checking them against the certificates. This involves multiple measurements of each ξ_i—and an immediate difficulty is that, since measurements are irreversible in quantum mechanics, the process of verifying the witness state might also destroy it. However, we get around this difficulty by appealing to a result of Aharonov and Regev [11]. This result essentially says that a QMA protocol in which Arthur is granted the (physically unrealistic) ability to perform 'non-destructive measurements' on his witness state, can be efficiently simulated by an ordinary QMA protocol.

To build intuition, we will begin (in Section 2) by proving the majority-certificates lemma for Boolean functions, as described above. However, to remove the artificial simplification we made and prove Theorem 2, we will need to generalize the lemma substantially, to a statement about possibly-infinite sets of real-valued functions $f : \{0,1\}^n \to [0,1]$. In the general version, the hypothesis that S is finite and not too large gets replaced by a more subtle assumption: namely, an upper bound on the so-called *fat-shattering dimension* of S. To prove our generalization, we use powerful results of Alon et al. [12] and Bartlett and Long [15] on the learnability of real-valued functions. We then use a bound on the fat-shattering dimension of real-valued functions defined by quantum states (from Aaronson [6], building on Ambainis et al. [13]). Figure 1 shows the overall dependency structure of the proof.

1.4 Majority-Certificates Lemma in Context

The majority-certificates lemma is closely related to the seminal notion of *boosting* [29] from computational learning theory. Boosting is a broad topic with a vast literature, but a common 'generic' form of the boosting problem is as follows: we want to learn some target function f^*, given sample data of the form $(x, f^*(x))$. We assume we have a *weak learning algorithm* $A^{f^*,\mathcal{D}}$, with the property that, for any probability distribution $\mathcal{D}$ over inputs x, with high probability A finds a hypothesis $f \in \mathcal{F}$ which predicts $f^*(x)$ 'reasonably well' when $x \sim \mathcal{D}$. The task is to 'boost' this weak learner into a *strong* learner B^{f^*}. The strong learner should output a collection of functions $f_1, \ldots, f_m \in \mathcal{F}$, such that a (possibly-weighted) majority vote over $f_1(x), \ldots, f_m(x)$ predicts $f^*(x)$ 'extremely well.' It turns out [29, 19] that this goal can be achieved in a very general setting.

Our majority-certificates lemma has strengths and weaknesses compared to boosting. Our assumptions are much milder than those of boosting: rather than needing a weak learner, we assume only that the hypothesis class S is 'not too large.' Also, we represent our target function f^* *exactly* by $\mathrm{MAJ}(f_1, \ldots, f_m)$, not just approximately. On the other hand, we do not give an efficient algorithm to *find* our majority-representation. Also, the f_i's are not 'explicitly given': we only give a way to *recognize* each f_i, under the assumption that the function purporting to be f_i is in fact drawn from the original hypothesis class.

The proof of our lemma also has similarities to boosting. As an analogue of a 'weak learner', we show that for every distribution $\mathcal{D}$, there exists a function $f \in S$ which agrees with the target function f^* on most $x \sim \mathcal{D}$, *and* which is isolatable in S by specifying $O(\log |S|)$ queries. Using the Minimax Theorem, we then nonconstructively 'boost' this fact into the desired majority-representation of f^*. We note that Nisan used the Minimax Theorem for boosting in a similar way, in his alternative proof of Impagliazzo's 'hard-core set theorem' (see [22]).

The majority-certificates lemma is also reminiscent of Bshouty et al.'s algorithm [16], for learning small circuits in the complexity class $\mathsf{ZPP}^{\mathsf{NP}}$. Our lemma lacks the algorithmic component of this earlier work, but unlike Bshouty et al., we do not require the functions being learned to come with any succinct labels (such as circuit descriptions).

1.5 Organization of the Paper

In Section 2, we prove the Boolean majority-certificates-lemma. In Section 3, we give our real-valued generalization of this lemma, and in Section 4 we use it to prove Theorem 2, and state some consequences for quantum complexity theory. Finally, Theorem 1 is proved in Section 4.3.

2. MAJORITY-CERTIFICATES LEMMA

A *Boolean concept class* is a family of sets $\{S_n\}_{n \geq 1}$, where each S_n consists of Boolean functions $f : \{0,1\}^n \to \{0,1\}$ on n variables. Abusing notation, we will often use S to refer directly to a set of Boolean functions on n variables, with the quantification over n being understood.

By a *certificate*, we mean a partial Boolean function $C : \{0,1\}^n \to \{0,1,*\}$. The *size* of C, denoted $|C|$, is the number of inputs x such that $C(x) \in \{0,1\}$. A Boolean function $f : \{0,1\}^n \to \{0,1\}$ is *consistent* with C if $f(x) = C(x)$ whenever $C(x) \in \{0,1\}$. Given a set S of Boolean functions and a certificate C, let $S[C]$ be the set of all functions $f \in S$ that are consistent with C. Say that a function $f \in S$ is *isolated in* S by the certificate C if $S[C] = \{f\}$.

We now prove a lemma that represents one of the main tools of this paper.

LEMMA 3 (MAJORITY-CERTIFICATES LEMMA). *Let S be a set of Boolean functions $f : \{0,1\}^n \to \{0,1\}$, and let $f^* \in S$. Then there exist $m = O(n)$ certificates $C_1, \ldots, C_m$,* *each of size $k = O(\log|S|)$, and functions $f_1, \ldots, f_m \in S$, such that*

(i) $S[C_i] = \{f_i\}$ *all* $i \in [m]$;

(ii) $\mathrm{MAJ}(f_1(x), \ldots, f_m(x)) = f^*(x)$ *for all* $x \in \{0,1\}^n$.

PROOF. Our proof of Lemma 3 relies on the following claim.

CLAIM 4. *Let $\mathcal{D}$ be any distribution over inputs $x \in \{0,1\}^n$. Then there exists a function $f \in S$ such that*

(i) f is isolatable in S by a certificate C of size $k = O(\log|S|)$;

(ii) $\Pr_{x\sim\mathcal{D}}[f(x) \neq f^*(x)] \leq \frac{1}{10}$.

Lemma 3 follows from Claim 4 by a boosting-type argument, as follows. Consider a two-player game where:

- Alice chooses a certificate C of size k that isolates some $f \in S$, and
- Bob simultaneously chooses an input $x \in \{0,1\}^n$.

Alice wins the game if $f(x) = f^*(x)$. Claim 4 tells us that for every mixed strategy of Bob (i.e., distribution $\mathcal{D}$ over inputs), there exists a pure strategy of Alice that succeeds with probability at least 0.9 against $\mathcal{D}$. Then by the Minimax Theorem, there exists a mixed strategy for Alice—that is, a probability distribution $\mathcal{C}$ over certificates—that allows her to win with probability at least 0.9 against *every* pure strategy of Bob. Now suppose we draw $C_1, \ldots, C_m$ independently from $\mathcal{C}$, isolating functions $f_1, \ldots, f_m$ in S. Fix an input $x \in \{0,1\}^n$; then by the success of Alice's strategy against x, and applying a Chernoff bound,

$$\Pr_{f_1,\ldots,f_m\sim\pi}[\mathrm{MAJ}(f_1(x), \ldots, f_m(x)) \neq f^*(x)] < \frac{1}{2^n},$$

provided we choose $m = O(n)$ suitably. But by the union bound, this means there must be a *fixed* choice of $C_1, \ldots, C_m$ such that $\mathrm{MAJ}(f_1, \ldots, f_m) \equiv f^*(x)$, where each f_i is isolated in S by C_i. This proves Lemma 3, modulo the Claim. □

PROOF OF CLAIM 4. By symmetry, we can assume without loss of generality that f^* is the identically-zero function. Given the mixed strategy $\mathcal{D}$ of Bob, we construct the certificate C as follows. Initially C is empty: that is, $C(x) = *$ for all $x \in \{0,1\}^n$. In the first stage, we draw $t = O(\log|S|)$ inputs $x_1, \ldots, x_t$ independently from $\mathcal{D}$. For any $f: \{0,1\}^n \to \{0,1\}$, let

$$w_f := \Pr_{x\sim\mathcal{D}}[f(x) = 1].$$

Now suppose f is such that $w_f > 0.1$. Then

$$\Pr_{x_1,\ldots,x_t\sim\mathcal{D}}[f(x_1) = 0 \wedge \cdots \wedge f(x_t) = 0] < 0.9^t \leq \frac{1}{|S|},$$

provided $t \geq \log_{10/9}|S|$. So by the union bound, there must be a *fixed* choice of $x_1, \ldots, x_t$ that kills off every $f \in S$ such that $w_f > 0.1$—that is, such that $f(x_1) = \cdots = f(x_t) = 0$ implies $w_f \leq 0.1$. Fix that $x_1, \ldots, x_t$, and set $C(x_i) := 0$ for all $i \in [t]$. In the second stage, our goal is just to isolate some *particular* function $f \in S[C]$. We do this recursively as follows. If $|S[C]| = 1$ then we are done. Otherwise, there exists an input x such that $f(x) = 0$ for some $f \in S[C]$ and $f(x) = 1$ for other $f \in S[C]$. If setting $C(x) := 0$ decreases $|S[C]|$ by at least a factor of 2, then set $C(x) := 0$; otherwise set $C(x) := 1$. Since $S[C]$ can halve in size at most $\log_2|S|$ times, this procedure terminates after at most $\log_2|S|$ steps with $|S[C]| = 1$. The end result is a certificate C of size $O(\log|S|)$, which isolates a function f in S for which $w_f \leq 1/10$. We have therefore found a pure strategy for Alice that fails with probability at most $1/10$ against $\mathcal{D}$, as desired. □

3. EXTENSION TO REAL FUNCTIONS

In this section, we extend the majority-certificates lemma from Boolean functions to real-valued functions $f: \{0,1\}^n \to [0,1]$. We will need this extension for the application to quantum advice in Section 4. In proving our extension we will have to confront several new difficulties. Firstly, the concept classes S that we want to consider can now contain a *continuum* of functions—so Lemma 3, which assumed that S was finite and constructed certificates of size $O(\log|S|)$, is not going to work. In Section 3.1, we review notions from computational learning theory, including fat-shattering dimension and ε-covers, which (combined with results of Alon et al. [12] and Bartlett and Long [15]) can be used to get around this difficulty. Secondly, it is no longer enough to isolate a function $f_i \in S$ that we are interested in; instead we will need to 'safely' isolate f_i, which roughly speaking means that (i) f_i is consistent with some certificate C, and (ii) any $f \in S$ that is even *approximately* consistent with C is close to f_i. In Section 3.2, we prove a 'safe winnowing lemma' that can be used for this purpose. Finally, in Section 3.3, we put the pieces together to prove a real-valued majority-certificates lemma.

3.1 Background from Learning Theory

A *p-concept class* S is a family of functions $f: \{0,1\}^n \to [0,1]$ (as usual, quantification over all n is understood). Given functions $f, g: \{0,1\}^n \to [0,1]$ and a subset of inputs $X \subseteq \{0,1\}^n$, we will be interested in three measures of the distance between f and g restricted to X:

$$\Delta_\infty(f,g)[X] := \max_{x\in X}|f(x) - g(x)|,$$

$$\Delta_1(f,g)[X] := \sum_{x\in X}|f(x) - g(x)|,$$

$$\Delta_2(f,g)[X] := \sqrt{\sum_{x\in X}(f(x) - g(x))^2}.$$

For convenience, we define $\Delta_\infty(f,g) := \Delta_\infty(f,g)[\{0,1\}^n]$, and similarly for $\Delta_1(f,g)$ and $\Delta_2(f,g)$. Also, given a distribution $\mathcal{D}$ over $\{0,1\}^n$, define

$$\Delta_1(f,g)\langle\mathcal{D}\rangle := \mathop{\mathrm{E}}_{x\sim\mathcal{D}}[|f(x) - g(x)|].$$

Finally we will need the notions of coverability and fat-shattering dimension.

DEFINITION 5 (COVERABILITY). *Let S be a p-concept class. The subset $C \subseteq S$ is an ε-cover for S if for all $f \in S$, there exists a $g \in C$ such that $\Delta_\infty(f,g) \leq \varepsilon$.*

DEFINITION 6 (FAT-SHATTERING DIMENSION). *Let S be a p-concept class and $\varepsilon > 0$ be a real number. We say the set $A \subseteq \{0,1\}^n$ is ε-shattered by S if there exists a function $r: A \to [0,1]$ such that for all $2^{|A|}$ Boolean functions*

$g : A \to \{0,1\}$, *there exists a p-concept* $f \in S$ *such that for all* $x \in A$, *we have* $f(x) \le r(x) - \varepsilon$ *whenever* $g(x) = 0$ *and* $f(x) \ge r(x) + \varepsilon$ *whenever* $g(x) = 1$. *Then the* ε-*fat-shattering dimension of* S, *or* $\text{fat}_\varepsilon(S)$, *is the size of the largest set* ε-*shattered by* S.

The following central result was shown by Alon et al. [12] (see also [23]).

THEOREM 7 ([12]). *Every p-concept class* S *has an* ε-*cover of size* $\exp\left[O\left((n + \log 1/\varepsilon)\,\text{fat}_{\varepsilon/4}(S)\right)\right]$.

Building on the work of Alon et al. [12], Bartlett and Long [15] then proved the following:

THEOREM 8 ([15]). *Let* S *be a p-concept class and* $\mathcal{D}$ *be a distribution over* $\{0,1\}^n$. *Fix an* $f : \{0,1\}^n \to [0,1]$ *(not necessarily in* S*) and an error parameter* $\alpha > 0$. *Suppose we form a set* $X \subseteq \{0,1\}^n$ *by choosing* m *inputs independently with replacement from* $\mathcal{D}$. *Then there exists a positive constant* K *such that, with probability at least* $1-\delta$ *over* X, *any hypothesis* $h \in S$ *that minimizes* $\Delta_1(h,f)[X]$ *also satisfies*

$$\Delta_1(h,f)\langle\mathcal{D}\rangle \le \alpha + \inf_{g \in S} \Delta_1(g,f)\langle\mathcal{D}\rangle,$$

provided $m \ge \frac{K}{\alpha^2}\left(\text{fat}_{\alpha/5}(S)\log^2\frac{1}{\alpha} + \log\frac{1}{\delta}\right)$.

Theorem 8 has the following corollary, which is similar to Corollary 2.4 of Aaronson [6], but more directly suited to our purposes here.

COROLLARY 9. *Let* S *be a p-concept class and* $\mathcal{D}$ *be a distribution over* $\{0,1\}^n$. *Fix an* $f \in S$ *and an error parameter* $\varepsilon > 0$. *Suppose we form a set* $X \subseteq \{0,1\}^n$ *by choosing* m *inputs independently with replacement from* $\mathcal{D}$. *Then there exists a positive constant* K *such that, with probability at least* $1-\delta$ *over* X, *any hypothesis* $h \in S$ *that satisfies* $\Delta_\infty(h,f)[X] \le \varepsilon$ *also satisfies* $\Delta_1(h,f)\langle\mathcal{D}\rangle \le 11\varepsilon$, *provided* $m \ge \frac{K}{\varepsilon^2}\left(\text{fat}_\varepsilon(S)\log^2\frac{1}{\varepsilon} + \log\frac{1}{\delta}\right)$.

PROOF. In the full version. □

3.2 Safe Winnowing Lemma

To prove the real-valued majority-certificates lemma, the first step is to prove a so-called 'safe winnowing lemma.' This lemma says intuitively that, given any set S of real-valued functions with a small ε-cover (or equivalently, with polynomially-bounded fat-shattering dimension), it is possible to find a set of $k = \text{poly}(n)$ constraints $|f(x_1) - a_1| \le \epsilon$, $\ldots$, $|f(x_k) - a_k| \le \epsilon$ that are *essentially* compatible with one and only one function $f \in S$. Here 'essentially' means that (i) any function that satisfies the constraints is close to f in L_∞-norm, and (ii) f itself not only satisfies the constraints, but does so with a 'margin to spare.'

LEMMA 10 (SAFE WINNOWING LEMMA). *Let* S *be a set of functions* $f : \{0,1\}^n \to [0,1]$. *Fix a function* $f^* \in S$ *and subset* $Y \subseteq \{0,1\}^n$. *For some parameter* $\varepsilon > 0$, *let* C *be a finite* ε-*cover for* S. *Then there exists an* $f \in S$, *as well as a subset* $Z \subseteq \{0,1\}^n$ *of size at most* $k = \log_2|C|$, *such that:*

(i) Every $g \in S$ *that satisfies* $\Delta_\infty(f,g)[Y \cup Z] \le \frac{\varepsilon}{5k}$ *also satisfies* $\Delta_\infty(f,g) \le 3\varepsilon$.

(ii) $\Delta_\infty(f,f^*)[Y] \le \varepsilon/5$.

PROOF. Let $\delta := \frac{\varepsilon}{5k}$. We construct (f,Z) by an iterative procedure. Initially let $S_0 := S$, let $f_0 := f^*$, and let $Z_0 := Y$. We will form new sets $S_1, S_2, \ldots$ by repeatedly adding constraints of the form $f(x) \le \alpha$ or $f(x) \ge \alpha$ for various x, α, maintaining the invariant that $f_t \in S_t$. At iteration t, suppose there exists a function $g \in S_{t-1}$ such that $\Delta_\infty(f_{t-1},g)[Y \cup Z_{t-1}] \le \delta$, but nevertheless

$$|f_{t-1}(z_t) - g(z_t)| > 3\varepsilon$$

for some input z_t. Then first set $Z_t := Z_{t-1} \cup \{z_t\}$ (i.e., add z_t into our set of inputs, if it is not already there). Let $v := \frac{1}{2}[f_{t-1}(z_t) + g(z_t)]$, let A be the set of all functions $h \in S_{t-1}$ such that $h(z_t) < v$, and let B be the set of all $h \in S_{t-1}$ such that $h(z_t) \ge v$. Also, for any given set M, let $M^\diamond := M \cap C$. Then clearly $\min\{|A^\diamond|, |B^\diamond|\} \le |S_{t-1}^\diamond|/2$. If $|A^\diamond| < |B^\diamond|$, then set $S_t := A$; otherwise set $S_t := B$. Then set $f_t := f_{t-1}$ if $f_{t-1} \in S_t$ and $f_t := g$ otherwise. Since $|S_t^\diamond|$ can halve at most $k = \log_2|C|$ times, it is clear that after $T \le k$ iterations we have $|S_T^\diamond| \le 1$. Set $f := f_T$ and $Z := Z_T$. Then by the triangle inequality,

$$\Delta_\infty(f,f^*)[Y] \le T\delta \le \frac{\varepsilon}{5},$$

and also

$$|f(z_t) - f_t(z_t)| \le (T-t)\delta < \frac{\varepsilon}{5}$$

for all $t \in [T]$. So suppose by contradiction that there still exists a function $g \in S_T$ such that $\Delta_\infty(f,g)[Y \cup Z] \le \delta$ but $|f(x) - g(x)| > 3\varepsilon$ for some x, and consider functions $p, q \in C$ in the cover such that $\Delta_\infty(f,p) \le \varepsilon$ and $\Delta_\infty(g,q) \le \varepsilon$. Then $p, q \in S_T^\diamond$ but $p \ne q$, which contradicts the fact that $|S_T^\diamond| \le 1$. Also notice that for all $g \in S$, if $\Delta_\infty(f,g)[Y \cup Z] \le \delta$ then $g \in S_T$. Thus $\Delta_\infty(f,g)[Y \cup Z] \le \delta$ implies $\Delta_\infty(f,g) \le 3\varepsilon$ as desired. □

Note that Lemma 10 is still interesting in the special case $Y = \varnothing$, in which case f^* is irrelevant, and the problem reduces to finding a Z such that every $g \in S$ that satisfies $\Delta_\infty(f,g)[Z] \le \frac{\varepsilon}{5k}$ also satisfies $\Delta_\infty(f,g) \le 3\varepsilon$.

3.3 Real-Valued Majority-Certificates Lemma

We are finally ready to generalize Lemma 3 to the case of real-valued functions.

LEMMA 11 (REAL MAJORITY-CERTIFICATES). *Let* S *be a p-concept class, let* $f^* \in S$, *and let* $\varepsilon > 0$. *Then for some* $m = O(n/\varepsilon^2)$, *there exist functions* $f_1, \ldots, f_m \in S$, *sets* $X_1, \ldots, X_m \subseteq \{0,1\}^n$ *each of size*

$$k = O\left(\left(n + \frac{\log^2\frac{1}{\varepsilon}}{\varepsilon^2}\right)\text{fat}_{\frac{\varepsilon}{48}}(S)\right),$$

and an $\alpha = \Omega\left(\frac{\varepsilon}{(n + \log 1/\varepsilon)\,\text{fat}_{\varepsilon/48}(S)}\right)$ *for which the following holds. All* $g_1, \ldots, g_m \in S$ *that satisfy* $\Delta_\infty(f_i,g_i)[X_i] \le \alpha$ *for* $i \in [m]$ *also satisfy* $\Delta_\infty(f^*,g) \le \varepsilon$, *where* $g(x) := \sum_{i=1}^m g_i(x)$.

PROOF. Let $\beta := \varepsilon/48$, let $t := C\left(n + \log\frac{1}{\beta}\right)\text{fat}_\beta(S)$ where C is a suitably large constant, and let $\alpha := 0.4\beta/t$. Also, let S_{fin} be a finite α-cover for S: that is, a finite subset $S_{\text{fin}} \subseteq S$ such that for all $f \in S$, there exists a $g \in S_{\text{fin}}$ such that $\Delta_\infty(f,g) \le \alpha$.[2] Given f and X, let $S[f,X]$

[2]We will need S_{fin} for the technical reason that the basic Minimax Theorem only works with finite strategy spaces.

be the set of all $g \in S$ such that $\Delta_\infty(f,g)[X] \le \alpha$. Now consider a two-player game where Alice chooses a function $f \in S_{\text{fin}}$ and a set $X \subseteq \{0,1\}^n$ of size k, and Bob simultaneously chooses an input $x \in \{0,1\}^n$. Alice's *penalty* in this game (the number she is trying to minimize) equals $\sup_{g \in S[f,X]} |f^*(x) - g(x)|$. We claim that there exists a mixed strategy for Alice—that is, a probability distribution $\mathcal{P}$ over (f,X) pairs—that gives her an expected penalty of at most $\varepsilon/2$ against every pure strategy of Bob. Let us see why the lemma follows from this claim. Fix an input $x \in \{0,1\}^n$, and suppose Alice draws $(f_1,X_1),\dots,(f_m,X_m)$ independently from $\mathcal{P}$. Then for all $i \in [m]$,

$$\mathop{\mathrm{E}}_{(f_i,X_i)\sim\mathcal{P}}\left[\sup_{g \in S[f,X]} |f^*(x) - g(x)|\right] \le \frac{\varepsilon}{2}.$$

Thus, letting $z_1,\dots,z_m$ be independent random variables in $[0,1]$, each with expectation at most $\varepsilon/2$, the expression

$$\Pr_{(f_i,X_i)\sim\mathcal{P}\forall i}\left[\begin{array}{c}\exists g_1 \in S[f_1,X_1],\dots,g_m \in S[f_m,X_m] \ : \\ \left|f^*(x) - \frac{g_1(x)+\cdots+g_m(x)}{m}\right| > \varepsilon\end{array}\right]$$

is at most $\Pr[z_1 + \cdots z_m > \varepsilon m]$ by the triangle inequality. This, in turn, is less than $2\exp\left(-2(\varepsilon m)^2/m\right) < 2^{-n}$ by Hoeffding's inequality, provided we choose $m = O\left(n/\varepsilon^2\right)$ suitably. By the union bound, this means that there must be a fixed choice of $f_1,\dots,f_m$ and $X_1,\dots,X_m$ such that

$$\left|f^*(x) - \frac{g_1(x)+\cdots+g_m(x)}{m}\right| \le \varepsilon$$

for all $g_1 \in S[f_1,X_1],\dots,g_m \in S[f_m,X_m]$ and all inputs $x \in \{0,1\}^n$ simultaneously, as desired. We now prove the claim. By the Minimax Theorem, our task is equivalent to the following: given any mixed strategy $\mathcal{D}$ of Bob, find a *pure* strategy of Alice that achieves a penalty of at most $\varepsilon/2$ against $\mathcal{D}$. In other words, given any distribution $\mathcal{D}$ over inputs $x \in \{0,1\}^n$, we want a fixed function $f \in S_{\text{fin}}$, and a set $X \subseteq \{0,1\}^n$ of size k, such that

$$\mathop{\mathrm{E}}_{x\sim\mathcal{D}}\left[\sup_{g \in S[f,X]} |f^*(x) - g(x)|\right] \le \frac{\varepsilon}{2}.$$

We construct this (f,X) pair as follows. In the first stage, we let Y be a set, of size at most

$$M := \frac{K}{\beta^2}\left(\text{fat}_\beta(S)\log^2\frac{1}{\beta} + \log\frac{1}{\delta}\right),$$

formed by choosing M inputs independently with replacement from $\mathcal{D}$. Here $\beta = \varepsilon/48$ as defined earlier, $\delta = 1/2$, and K is the constant from Corollary 9. Then by Corollary 9, with probability at least $1 - \delta = 1/2$ over the choice of Y, any $g \in S$ that satisfies $\Delta_\infty(f^*,g)[Y] \le \beta$ also satisfies $\Delta_1(f^*,g)\langle\mathcal{D}\rangle \le 11\beta$. So there must be a *fixed* choice of Y with that property. Fix that Y, and let S' be the set of all $g \in S$ such that $\Delta_\infty(f^*,g)[Y] \le \beta$. In the second stage, our goal is just to winnow S' down to a particular function f. More precisely, we want to find an $f \in S' \cap S_{\text{fin}}$, and a set $X \subseteq \{0,1\}^n$ containing Y, such that any $g \in S$ that satisfies $\Delta_\infty(f,g)[X] \le \alpha$ also satisfies $\Delta_\infty(f,g) \le 11\beta$. We find this (f,X) pair as follows. By Theorem 7, the class S' has a 4β-cover of size

$$N \le \exp\left[O\left(\left(n + \log\frac{1}{\beta}\right)\text{fat}_\beta(S)\right)\right].$$

Let $t := \log_2 N$. Then by Lemma 10, there exists a function $u \in S'$, as well as a subset $Z \subseteq \{0,1\}^n$ of size at most t, such that:

(i) $\Delta_\infty(u,f^*)[Y] \le 0.8\beta$.

(ii) Every $g \in S'$ that satisfies $\Delta_\infty(u,g)[Y \cup Z] \le \frac{0.8\beta}{t}$ also satisfies $\Delta_\infty(u,g) \le 12\beta$.

Let $X := Y \cup Z$, and observe that

$$\begin{aligned}|X| &= O\left(\frac{1}{\beta^2}\text{fat}_\beta(S)\log^2\frac{1}{\beta} + \left(n + \log\frac{1}{\beta}\right)\text{fat}_\beta(S)\right)\\ &= O\left(\left(n + \frac{\log^2 1/\varepsilon}{\varepsilon^2}\right)\text{fat}_{\varepsilon/48}(S)\right)\end{aligned}$$

as desired. Now let f be a function in S_{fin} such that $\Delta_\infty(f,u) \le \alpha$. Let us check that f has the properties we want. First,

$$\begin{aligned}\Delta_\infty(f^*,f)[Y] &\le \Delta_\infty(f^*,u)[Y] + \Delta_\infty(u,f)[Y]\\ &\le 0.8\beta + \alpha < 0.9\beta,\end{aligned}$$

hence $f \in S'$ as desired. Next, any $g \in S$ that satisfies $\Delta_\infty(f,g)[X] \le \alpha$ also satisfies

$$\Delta_\infty(f^*,g)[Y] \le \Delta_\infty(f^*,f)[Y] + \Delta_\infty(f,g)[Y] \le 0.9\beta + \alpha < \beta,$$

hence $g \in S'$, hence $\Delta_1(f^*,g)\langle\mathcal{D}\rangle \le 11\beta$. So any $g \in S$ that satisfies $\Delta_\infty(f,g)[X] \le \alpha$ satisfies

$$\Delta_\infty(u,g)[Z] \le \Delta_\infty(u,f)[Z] + \Delta_\infty(f,g)[Z] \le 2\alpha = \frac{0.8\beta}{t},$$

hence $\Delta_\infty(u,g) \le 12\beta$ (since such a g must belong to S'), hence

$$\Delta_\infty(f,g) \le \Delta_\infty(f,u) + \Delta_\infty(u,g) \le \alpha + 12\beta \le 13\beta.$$

To conclude,

$$\begin{aligned}&\mathop{\mathrm{E}}_{x\sim\mathcal{D}}\left[\sup_{g \in S[f,X]} |f^*(x) - g(x)|\right]\\ &\le \Delta_1(f^*,f)\langle\mathcal{D}\rangle + \sup_{g \in S[f,X]} \Delta_\infty(f,g)\\ &\le 11\beta + 13\beta = \frac{\varepsilon}{2}\end{aligned}$$

as desired. This proves the claim and hence the lemma. □

4. APPLICATION TO QUANTUM ADVICE

In this section, we use the real-valued majority-certificates lemma to prove Theorem 2.

4.1 Bestiary of Quantum Complexity Classes

Given a language $L \subseteq \{0,1\}^*$, let $L : \{0,1\}^* \to \{0,1\}$ be the characteristic function of L. We now give a formal definition of the class $\mathsf{BQP/qpoly}$.

DEFINITION 12. *A language L is in $\mathsf{BQP/qpoly}$ if there exists a poly-time quantum algorithm A and polynomial p such that for all n, there exists an advice state ρ_n on $p(n)$ qubits such that $A(x,\rho_n)$ outputs $L(x)$ with probability $\ge 2/3$ for all $x \in \{0,1\}^n$.*

Closely related to quantum advice are *quantum proofs.* We now recall the definition of QMA (Quantum Merlin-Arthur), a quantum version of NP.

DEFINITION 13. *A language L is in* QMA *if there exists a polynomial-time quantum algorithm A and polynomial p such that for all $x \in \{0,1\}^n$:*

(i) If $x \in L$ then there exists a witness ρ_x on $p(n)$ qubits such that $A(x, \rho_x)$ accepts with probability $\geq 2/3$.

(ii) If $x \notin L$ then $A(x, \rho)$ accepts with probability $\leq 1/3$ for all ρ.

We will actually need a generalization of QMA, which was called QMA_+ by Aharonov and Regev [10].[3]

DEFINITION 14. *A language L is in QMA_+ if there exists a polynomial-time algorithm A, which takes $x \in \{0,1\}^n$ as input and produces quantum circuits $C_{x,1}, \ldots, C_{x,m}$ and rational numbers $r_{x,1}, \ldots, r_{x,m}$ as output, as well as polynomials p, q such that for all $x \in \{0,1\}^n$:*

(i) If $x \in L$ then there exists a witness ρ_x on $p(n)$ qubits such that $|\Pr[C_{x,i}(\rho_x) \text{ accepts}] - r_{x,i}| \leq 1/q(n)$ for all $i \in [m]$.

(ii) If $x \notin L$ then for all ρ, there exists an $i \in [m]$ such that $|\Pr[C_{x,i}(\rho) \text{ accepts}] - r_{x,i}| > 5/q(n)$.

Aharonov and Regev [10] made the following extremely useful observation, which we prove in the full version for completeness.

THEOREM 15 ([11]). $\mathsf{QMA}_+ = \mathsf{QMA}$.

To state our results, it will be helpful to have the further notion of *untrusted advice*, which is like advice in that it depends only on the input length n, but like a witness in that it cannot be trusted. This notion has been studied before: Chakaravarthy and Roy [17] and Fortnow and Santhanam [18] defined the complexity class ONP ('Oblivious NP'), which is like NP except that the witness can depend only on the input length. Independently, Aaronson [6] defined the complexity class YP,[4] which is easily seen to equal ONP∩coONP. We will adopt the 'Y' notation in this paper, because it is much easier to write YQP/poly (for example) than OQMA/poly ∩ coOQMA/poly.

We now give a formal definition of YP, as well as a slight variant called YP*.

DEFINITION 16. *A language L is in* YP *if there exist polytime algorithms A, B and a polynomial p such that:*

(i) For all n, there exists an advice string $y_n \in \{0,1\}^{p(n)}$ such that $A(x, y_n) = 1$ for all $x \in \{0,1\}^n$.

(ii) If $A(x, y) = 1$, then $B(x, y) = L(x)$.

L is in YP* *if A ignores x, depending only on y.*

Clearly P ⊆ YP* ⊆ YP ⊆ P/poly ∩ NP ∩ coNP. Also, Aaronson [6] showed that ZPP ⊆ YP. We will be interested in the natural quantum analogues of YP and YP*:

[3]Aharonov and Regev actually defined QMA_+ in a slightly more general way. However, the definition below is all we need; note that all these classes turn out to equal QMA anyway.

[4]YP stands for 'Yoda Polynomial-Time,' a nomenclature that seems to make neither more nor less sense than 'Arthur-Merlin.'

DEFINITION 17. *A language L is in* YQP *if there exist polynomial-time quantum algorithms A, B and a polynomial p such that:*

(i) For all n, there exists an advice state ρ_n on $p(n)$ qubits such that $A(x, \rho_n)$ accepts with probability $\geq 2/3$ for all $x \in \{0,1\}^n$.

(ii) If $A(x, \rho)$ accepts with probability $\geq 1/3$, then $B(x, \rho)$ outputs $L(x)$ with probability $\geq 2/3$.

L is in YQP* *if A ignores x, depending only on ρ.*

Clearly BQP ⊆ YQP* ⊆ YQP ⊆ BQP/qpoly ∩ QMA ∩ coQMA. By direct analogy to QMA_+, we can define the following generalizations of YQP and YQP*:

DEFINITION 18. *A language L is in YQP_+ if there exists a polynomial-time algorithm A, which takes $x \in \{0,1\}^n$ as input and produces quantum circuits $C_{x,1}, \ldots, C_{x,m}$ and rational numbers $r_{x,1}, \ldots, r_{x,m}$ as output; a polynomial-time quantum algorithm B; and polynomials p, q such that:*

(i) For all n, there exists an advice state ρ_n on $p(n)$ qubits such that $|\Pr[C_{x,i}(\rho_n) \text{ accepts}] - r_{x,i}| \leq 1/q(n)$ for all $i \in [m]$ and $x \in \{0,1\}^n$.

(ii) If $|\Pr[C_{x,i}(\rho) \text{ accepts}] - r_{x,i}| \leq 5/q(n)$ for all $i \in [m]$, then $B(x, \rho)$ outputs $L(x)$ with probability $\geq 2/3$.

L is in YQP_+^* if moreover A ignores x.

Then we have the following counterpart to Theorem 15:

THEOREM 19. $\mathsf{YQP}_+ = \mathsf{YQP}$ *and* $\mathsf{YQP}_+^* = \mathsf{YQP}^*$.

PROOF. In the full version. □

4.2 Characterizing Quantum Advice

Fix a polynomial-size quantum circuit Q. For a given advice state ρ, let $f_\rho(x) := \Pr[Q \text{ accepts } x, \rho]$. Let S be the p-concept class consisting of f_ρ for all $p(n)$-qubit mixed states ρ. Then Aaronson [6] proved the following.

THEOREM 20 ([6]). $\mathrm{fat}_\gamma(S) = O(p(n)/\gamma^2)$.

We now prove the following characterization of BQP/qpoly, which immediately implies (and strengthens) Theorem 2:

THEOREM 21. BQP/qpoly = YQP/poly.

PROOF. One direction (YQP/poly ⊆ BQP/qpoly) is obvious, since untrusted quantum advice and trusted classical advice can both be simulated by trusted quantum advice. We prove that BQP/qpoly ⊆ YQP/poly. It suffices to show that BQP/qpoly ⊆ YQP_+/poly, since YQP = YQP_+ by Theorem 19. Let $L \in$ BQP/qpoly, let Q be a quantum algorithm that decides L with completeness and soundness errors $1/5$, and let $x \in \{0,1\}^n$ be the input. Also, let $f_\xi(z) := \Pr[Q(z, \xi) \text{ accepts}]$, where ξ is a $p(n)$-qubit quantum advice state for Q. Then by definition, there exists a 'true' advice state ρ_n such that

$$|f_{\rho_n}(z) - L(z)| \leq 0.2$$

for all $z \in \{0,1\}^n$. Let S be the p-concept class consisting of f_ξ for all $p(n)$-qubit mixed states ξ. Then Theorem 20 implies that $\mathrm{fat}_\gamma(S) = O(p(n)/\gamma^2)$ for all $\gamma > 0$. Set $\gamma := 1/480$. Then by Lemma 11, for some $m = O(n)$, there exist $p(n)$-qubit mixed states $\rho[1], \ldots, \rho[m]$, sets $X_1, \ldots, X_m \subseteq \{0,1\}^n$ each of size $k = O(n \cdot p(n))$, and an $\alpha = \Omega\left(\frac{1}{n \cdot p(n)}\right)$ for which the following holds:

(*) *All $p(n)$-qubit states $\sigma[1],\ldots,\sigma[m]$ that for $i\in[m]$ satisfy $\Delta_\infty(f_{\rho[i]},f_{\sigma[i]})[X_i]\leq 5\alpha$, satisfy $\Delta_\infty(f_{\rho_n},f_\sigma)\leq 0.1$ as well, where $\sigma:=\frac{1}{m}(\sigma[1]+\cdots+\sigma[m])$.*

Our $\mathsf{YQP}_+/\mathsf{poly}$ simulation is now the following. The classical /poly advice encodes the sets $X_1,\ldots,X_m$, as well as a rational approximation $r_{i,z}$ to $f_{\rho[i]}(z)$ for each $i\in[m]$ and $z\in X_i$. The untrusted quantum advice ρ'_n consists of m registers of $p(n)$ qubits each; in the honest case, ρ'_n is simply $\rho[1]\otimes\cdots\otimes\rho[m]$. Let $\sigma[i]$ be the ith register of ρ'_n. Then given the advice, the YQP_+ machine A outputs a circuit $C_{i,z}$ that runs $Q(z,\sigma[i])$ and outputs the result, for each $i\in[m]$ and $z\in X_i$. The machine B chooses $i\in[m]$ uniformly at random, then runs $Q(x,\sigma[i])$ and outputs the result. We are interested in the difference between $\Pr[C_{i,z}(\rho'_n)\text{ accepts}]$ and $r_{i,z}$. In the honest case,

$$\Pr\left[C_{i,z}(\rho'_n)\text{ accepts}\right]=\Pr[Q(z,\rho[i])\text{ accepts}]=f_{\rho[i]}(z)$$

for all i,z. Moreover, we can easily arrange each $r_{i,z}$ to be within α of $f_{\rho[i]}(z)$, by using $O(\log n)$ bits to specify each $r_{i,z}$. For the soundness case, suppose

$$\left|\Pr\left[C_{i,z}(\rho'_n)\text{ accepts}\right]-r_{i,z}\right|\leq 5\alpha$$

for all $i\in[m]$ and $z\in X_i$. Then by (*), we have $\Delta_\infty(f_{\rho_n},f_\sigma)\leq 0.1$. Notice that by linearity of expectation,

$$\Pr[B\text{ accepts}]=\mathop{\mathrm{E}}_{i\in[m]}[\Pr[Q(x,\sigma[i])\text{ accepts}]]=f_\sigma(x),$$

and that this holds regardless of what entanglement might be present among the m registers $\sigma[1],\ldots,\sigma[m]$. Hence

$$\begin{aligned}&|\Pr[B\text{ accepts}]-L(x)|\\&\leq|\Pr[B\text{ accepts}]-f_{\rho_n}(x)|+|f_{\rho_n}(x)-L(x)|\\&\leq 0.1+0.2\end{aligned}$$

which is less than 1/3, so $L\in\mathsf{YQP}_+/\mathsf{poly}=\mathsf{YQP}/\mathsf{poly}$. □

Theorem 21 actually yields the stronger result $\mathsf{BQP}/\mathsf{qpoly}\subseteq\mathsf{YQP}^*/\mathsf{poly}$, since the machine A had no dependence on the input x. We therefore have $\mathsf{BQP}/\mathsf{qpoly}=\mathsf{YQP}^*/\mathsf{poly}=\mathsf{YQP}/\mathsf{poly}$: the two definitions of YQP collapse in the presence of polynomial-size classical advice. Since we never needed the assumption that the BQP/qpoly machine computes a *language* (i.e., a total Boolean function), another strengthening we can easily observe is PromiseBQP/qpoly = PromiseYQP/poly.

4.3 The Complexity of Preparing Quantum Advice States

If we combine Theorem 21 with known QMA-completeness results, we can obtain a striking consequence for quantum complexity theory. Namely, *the preparation of quantum advice states can always be reduced to the preparation of ground states of local Hamiltonians*—despite the fact that quantum advice states involve an exponential number of constraints, while ground states of local Hamiltonians involve only a polynomial number. In particular, if ground states of local Hamiltonians can be prepared by polynomial-size circuits, then we have not only QMA = QCMA, but also BQP/qpoly = BQP/poly. The following theorem makes this connection precise.

THEOREM 22. *Let Q be a polynomial-size quantum circuit that takes an advice state ρ_n. Then there exists another polynomial-size quantum circuit Q' with the following property. For all n and $\varepsilon>0$, there exists a 2-local Hamiltonian H on $\mathrm{poly}(n,1/\varepsilon)$ qubits, such that for all ground states $|\phi\rangle$ of H and inputs $x\in\{0,1\}^n$,*

$$\left|\Pr\left[Q'\text{ accepts }x,|\phi\rangle\right]-\Pr[Q\text{ accepts }x,\rho_n]\right|\leq\varepsilon.$$

Furthermore, Q' can be efficiently generated given Q together with a description of H.

PROOF. Kempe, Kitaev, and Regev [25] proved that the 2-LOCAL HAMILTONIANS problem is QMA-complete. Furthermore, examining their proof, we find that it yields the following stronger result. Let V be a QMA verification procedure with completeness and soundness errors δ. Then there exists a 2-local Hamiltonian H, as well as a polynomial-time 'recovery procedure' R, such that if $|\phi\rangle$ is any ground state of H, then with $\Omega(1/\mathrm{poly}(n))$ probability, $R(|\phi\rangle)$ outputs a state $|\varphi\rangle$ such that $\Pr[V\text{ accepts }|\varphi\rangle]\geq 1-\delta$. To prove the stronger result: consider a ground state of H, which Kempe et al. show to be a *history state* of the form

$$|\phi\rangle=\frac{1}{\sqrt{T}}\sum_{t=1}^{T}|t\rangle|\phi_t\rangle.$$

Then R can simply measure the clock register $|t\rangle$, postselect on obtaining the outcome $t=1$, and then retrieve $|\varphi\rangle$ from the computation register $|\phi_1\rangle$. Now let Q be a polynomial-size quantum circuit that takes advice state ρ_n, and let (A,B) be the YQP/poly checking algorithm (with error parameter δ) from Theorem 21. Then by the above, there exists a 2-local Hamiltonian H on $\mathrm{poly}(n,1/\delta)$ qubits, as well as a polynomial-time algorithm R, such that

(i) If $|\phi\rangle$ is any ground state of H, then with at least $1-\delta$ probability, $R(|\phi\rangle)$ outputs a state $|\varphi\rangle$ such that $\Pr[A\text{ accepts }|\varphi\rangle]\geq 1-\delta$.

(ii) This $|\varphi\rangle$ satisfies $|B_\varphi(x)-Q_{\rho_n}(x)|\leq\delta$ for all $x\in\{0,1\}^n$, where $B_\varphi(x):=\Pr[B\text{ accepts }x,|\varphi\rangle]$ and

$$Q_{\rho_n}(x):=\Pr[Q\text{ accepts }x,\rho_n].$$

We can now combine R and B into a single algorithm Q', such that $\left|Q'_\phi(x)-Q_{\rho_n}(x)\right|\leq 2\delta$ for all $x\in\{0,1\}^n$. Setting $\delta:=\varepsilon/2$ then yields the corollary. □

Let us make two remarks about Theorem 22. First, as a 'free byproduct,' we get that

$$\left|\Pr\left[Q'\text{ accepts }x,|\phi\rangle\right]-\Pr[Q\text{ accepts }x,\rho_n]\right|\leq 2\varepsilon$$

for all $|\phi\rangle$ that are *ε-close* in trace distance to a ground state of H. Second, there is nothing special here about 2-LOCAL HAMILTONIANS. So far as we know, *all* existing QMA completeness reductions have the property we needed for Theorem 22: namely, the property that any ground state of the new instance can be transformed into a QMA witness for the original instance, with $\Omega(1/\mathrm{poly}(n))$ success probability. As one example, Aharonov et al. [8] showed that even finding the ground state energy of a nearest-neighbor Hamiltonian on the line is QMA-complete, provided the line is composed of qudits with $d\geq 12$. We can combine their result with Theorem 21 to show that for all $L\in\mathsf{BQP}/\mathsf{qpoly}$, there exists a nearest-neighbor qudit Hamiltonian H on the line, such that any ground state of H is a valid quantum advice state for L.

PROOF OF THEOREM 1. Fix $c, \varepsilon > 0$, and let ρ be the n-qubit state in Theorem 1. Let $Q(C, \xi)$ be an (efficiently constructible) polynomial-size quantum circuit that takes a description of a quantum measurement circuit C of size n^c, as well as a quantum state ξ of n qubits, and that outputs the measurement result $C(\xi)$.

Fix $\rho_n := \rho$. Let H be the 2-local Hamiltonian given by Theorem 22, with ground state $|\psi\rangle$, and let $Q'(C, \xi)$ be the circuit in that Theorem, efficiently derivable given Q and H. Then, if we define the measurement C' as $C'(\xi) := Q'(C, \xi)$, we have

$$\left|C'(|\psi\rangle\langle\psi|) - C(\rho)\right| = \left|Q'(C, |\psi\rangle\langle\psi|) - Q(C, \rho)\right| \leq \varepsilon.$$

□

5. OPEN PROBLEMS

One open problem is simply to find more applications of the majority-certificates lemma, which seems likely to have uses outside of quantum complexity theory. Also, can we improve the parameters of the majority-certificates lemma (the size of the certificates or the number $O(n)$ of certificates), or alternatively, show that the current parameters are essentially optimal? Can we prove the real-valued majority-certificates lemma with an error tolerance α that depends only on the desired accuracy ε of the final approximation, not on n or the fat-shattering dimension of S?

On the quantum complexity side, we mention several questions. First, in Theorem 22, is the polynomial blowup in the number of qubits unavoidable? Second, can we use the ideas in this paper to prove any upper bound on the class $\mathsf{QMA/qpoly}$ better than the $\mathsf{PSPACE/poly}$ upper bound shown by Aaronson [5]? Third, if $\mathsf{NP} \subset \mathsf{BQP/qpoly}$, then does $\mathsf{QMA}^{\mathsf{PromiseQMA}}$ contain not just Π_2^{P} but the entire polynomial hierarchy? Finally, is $\mathsf{BQP/qpoly} = \mathsf{BQP/poly}$?

6. ACKNOWLEDGMENTS

We thank Sanjeev Arora, Kai-Min Chung, Avinatan Hassidim, John Watrous, and Colin Zheng for helpful discussions, and the anonymous reviewers for their comments.

7. REFERENCES

[1] S. Aaronson. Multilinear formulas and skepticism of quantum computing. *STOC*, p. 118–127, 2004.

[2] S. Aaronson. Limitations of quantum advice and one-way communication. *Theory of Computing*, 1:1–28, 2005. quant-ph/0402095.

[3] S. Aaronson. Quantum computing, postselection, and probabilistic polynomial-time. *Proc. Roy. Soc. London*, A461(2063):3473–3482, 2005.

[4] S. Aaronson. Oracles are subtle but not malicious. *Complexity (CCC)*, p. 340–354, 2006.

[5] S. Aaronson. QMA/qpoly is contained in PSPACE/poly: de-Merlinizing quantum protocols. *Complexity (CCC)*, p. 261–273, 2006.

[6] S. Aaronson. The learnability of quantum states. *Proc. Roy. Soc. London*, 463(2088):3089–3114, 2007.

[7] S. Aaronson and G. Kuperberg. Quantum versus classical proofs and advice. *Theory of Computing*, 3(7):129–157, 2007.

[8] D. Aharonov, D. Gottesman, S. Irani, and J. Kempe. The power of quantum systems on a line. *Comm. Math. Phys.*, 287(1):41–65, 2009.

[9] D. Aharonov and T. Naveh. Quantum NP - a survey. quant-ph/0210077, 2002.

[10] D. Aharonov and O. Regev. A lattice problem in Quantum NP. *FOCS*, p. 210–219, 2003.

[11] D. Aharonov and O. Regev. Lattice problems in NP intersect coNP. *J. ACM*, 52(5):749–765, 2005.

[12] N. Alon, S. Ben-David, N. Cesa-Bianchi, and D. Haussler. Scale-sensitive dimensions, uniform convergence, and learnability. *J. ACM*, 44(4):615–631, 1997.

[13] A. Ambainis, A. Nayak, A. Ta-Shma, and U. V. Vazirani. Quantum dense coding and quantum finite automata. *J. ACM*, 49:496–511, 2002.

[14] L. Babai. Local expansion of vertex-transitive graphs and random generation in finite groups. *STOC*, p. 164–174, 1991.

[15] P. L. Bartlett and P. M. Long. Prediction, learning, uniform convergence, and scale-sensitive dimensions. *J. Comput. Sys. Sci.*, 56(2):174–190, 1998.

[16] N. H. Bshouty, R. Cleve, R. Gavaldà, S. Kannan, and C. Tamon. Oracles and queries that are sufficient for exact learning. *J. Comput. Sys. Sci.*, 52(3):421–433, 1996.

[17] V. Chakaravarthy and S. Roy. Oblivious symmetric alternation. *STACS*, p. 230–241, 2006.

[18] L. Fortnow and R. Santhanam. Fixed-polynomial size circuit bounds, 2006. ECCC TR06-157.

[19] Y. Freund and R. E. Schapire. A decision-theoretic generalization of on-line learning and an application to boosting. *J. Comput. Sys. Sci.*, 55(1):119–139, 1997.

[20] P. Hausladen and W. K. Wootters. A 'pretty good' measurement for distinguishing quantum states. *J. Modern Optics*, 41(12):2385–2390, 1994.

[21] A. S. Holevo. Some estimates of the information transmitted by quantum communication channels. *Problems of Information Transmission*, 9:177–183, 1973. English translation.

[22] R. Impagliazzo. Hard-core distributions for somewhat hard problems. *FOCS*, p. 538–545, 1995.

[23] S. Kakade and A. Tewari. Learning theory lecture notes, 2008. ttic.uchicago.edu/~tewari/LT_SP2008.html.

[24] R. M. Karp and R. J. Lipton. Turing machines that take advice. *Enseign. Math.*, 28:191–201, 1982.

[25] J. Kempe, A. Kitaev, and O. Regev. The complexity of the Local Hamiltonian problem. *SIAM J. Comput.*, 35(5):1070–1097, 2006.

[26] C. Marriott and J. Watrous. Quantum Arthur-Merlin games. *Computational Complexity*, 14(2):122–152, 2005.

[27] H. Nishimura and T. Yamakami. Polynomial time quantum computation with advice. *Inform. Proc. Lett.*, 90:195–204, 2003.

[28] R. Raz. Quantum information and the PCP theorem. *FOCS*, p. 459–468, 2005.

[29] R. E. Schapire. The strength of weak learnability. *Machine Learning*, 5(2):197–227, 1990.

[30] G. Vidal. Efficient classical simulation of slightly entangled quantum computations. *Phys. Rev. Lett.*, 91, 2003.

[31] J. Watrous. Succinct quantum proofs for properties of finite groups. *FOCS*, p. 537–546, 2000.

BQP and the Polynomial Hierarchy*

Scott Aaronson†
MIT

ABSTRACT

The relationship between BQP and PH has been an open problem since the earliest days of quantum computing. We present evidence that quantum computers can solve problems outside the entire polynomial hierarchy, by relating this question to topics in circuit complexity, pseudorandomness, and Fourier analysis.

First, we show that there exists an oracle relation problem (i.e., a problem with many valid outputs) that is solvable in BQP, but not in PH. This also yields a non-oracle relation problem that is solvable in quantum *logarithmic* time, but not in AC^0.

Second, we show that an oracle *decision* problem separating BQP from PH would follow from the *Generalized Linial-Nisan Conjecture*, which we formulate here and which is likely of independent interest. The original Linial-Nisan Conjecture (about pseudorandomness against constant-depth circuits) was recently proved by Braverman, after being open for twenty years.

Categories and Subject Descriptors

F.1.3 [**Theory of Computation**]: Computation by Abstract Devices—*Complexity Measures and Classes*

General Terms

Theory

Keywords

constant-depth circuits, Fourier analysis, Linial-Nisan Conjecture, quantum complexity classes

*We regret that, because of space limitations, we are unable to prove anything in this extended abstract. Readers interested in the proofs should stop reading now and go to www.scottaaronson.com/papers/bqpph.pdf.

†Based upon work supported by the National Science Foundation under Grant No. 0844020. Also supported by a DARPA YFA grant and the Keck Foundation.

1. INTRODUCTION

A central task of quantum computing theory is to understand how BQP—Bounded-Error Quantum Polynomial-Time, the class of all problems feasible for a quantum computer—fits in with classical complexity classes. In their original 1993 paper defining BQP, Bernstein and Vazirani [9] showed that $\mathsf{BPP} \subseteq \mathsf{BQP} \subseteq \mathsf{P}^{\#\mathsf{P}}$.[1] Informally, this says that quantum computers are at least as fast as classical probabilistic computers and no more than exponentially faster (indeed, they can be simulated using an oracle for counting). Bernstein and Vazirani also gave evidence that $\mathsf{BPP} \neq \mathsf{BQP}$, by exhibiting an oracle problem called RECURSIVE FOURIER SAMPLING that requires $n^{\Omega(\log n)}$ queries on a classical computer but only n queries on a quantum computer. The evidence for the power of quantum computers became dramatically stronger a year later, when Shor [23] (building on work of Simon [24]) showed that FACTORING and DISCRETE LOGARITHM are in BQP. On the other hand, Bennett et al. [8] gave oracle evidence that $\mathsf{NP} \not\subset \mathsf{BQP}$, and while no one regards such evidence as decisive, today it seems extremely unlikely that quantum computers can solve NP-complete problems in polynomial time. A vast body of research, continuing to the present, has sought to map out the detailed boundary between those NP problems that are feasible for quantum computers and those that are not.

However, there is a complementary question that—despite being universally recognized as one of the "grand challenges" of the field—has had essentially zero progress over the last sixteen years:

> *Is* BQP *in* NP*? More generally, is* BQP *contained anywhere in the polynomial hierarchy* $\mathsf{PH} = \mathsf{NP} \cup \mathsf{NP}^{\mathsf{NP}} \cup \mathsf{NP}^{\mathsf{NP}^{\mathsf{NP}}} \cup \cdots$ *?*

The "default" conjecture is presumably $\mathsf{BQP} \not\subset \mathsf{PH}$, since no one knows what a simulation of BQP in PH would look like. Before this work, however, there was no formal evidence for or against that conjecture. Almost all the problems for which we have quantum algorithms—including FACTORING and DISCRETE LOGARITHM—are easily seen to be in $\mathsf{NP} \cap \mathsf{coNP}$.[2] One notable exception is RECURSIVE FOURIER SAMPLING, the problem that Bernstein and Vazirani [9] originally used to construct an oracle A relative to which $\mathsf{BPP}^A \neq$

[1]The upper bound was later improved to $\mathsf{BQP} \subseteq \mathsf{PP}$ by Adleman, DeMarrais, and Huang [2].

[2]Here we exclude BQP-complete problems such as approximating the Jones polynomial [3], which, by the very fact of being BQP-complete, seem hard to interpret as "evidence" for $\mathsf{BQP} \not\subset \mathsf{PH}$.

BQP^A. One can show, without too much difficulty, that RECURSIVE FOURIER SAMPLING yields oracles A relative to which $\mathsf{BQP}^A \not\subset \mathsf{NP}^A$ and indeed $\mathsf{BQP}^A \not\subset \mathsf{MA}^A$. However, while it is reasonable to conjecture that RECURSIVE FOURIER SAMPLING (as an oracle problem) is not in PH, it is open even to show that this problem (or any other BQP oracle problem) is not in AM! Recall that AM = NP under plausible derandomization assumptions. Thus, until we solve the problem of constructing an oracle A such that $\mathsf{BQP}^A \not\subset \mathsf{AM}^A$, we cannot even claim to have oracle evidence (which is itself, of course, a weak form of evidence) that BQP $\not\subset$ NP.

Before going further, we should clarify that there are two questions here: whether BQP $\subseteq$ PH and whether PromiseBQP $\subseteq$ PromisePH. In the unrelativized world, it is entirely possible that quantum computers can solve promise problems outside the polynomial hierarchy, but that all *languages* in BQP are nevertheless in PH. However, for the specific purpose of constructing an oracle A such that $\mathsf{BQP}^A \not\subset \mathsf{PH}^A$, the two questions are equivalent, basically because one can "offload" a promise into the construction of the oracle A.

1.1 Motivation

There are at least four reasons why the BQP versus PH question is so interesting. At a basic level, it is both theoretically and practically important to understand what classical resources are needed to simulate quantum physics. For example, when a quantum system evolves to a given state, is there always a short classical proof that it does so? Can one estimate quantum amplitudes using approximate counting (which would imply $\mathsf{BQP} \subseteq \mathsf{BPP}^{\mathsf{NP}}$)? If something like this were true, then while the exponential speedup of Shor's factoring algorithm might stand, quantum computing would nevertheless seem much less different from classical computing than previously thought.

Second, if BQP $\not\subset$ PH, then many possibilities for new quantum algorithms might open up to us. One often hears the complaint that there are too few quantum algorithms, or that progress on quantum algorithms has slowed since the mid-1990s. In our opinion, the real issue here has nothing to do with quantum computing, and is simply that there are too few natural NP-intermediate problems for which there plausibly *could be* quantum algorithms! In other words, instead of focussing on GRAPH ISOMORPHISM and a small number of other NP-intermediate problems, it might be fruitful to look for quantum algorithms solving completely different types of problems—problems that are not necessarily even in PH. In this paper, we will see a new example of such a quantum algorithm, which solves a problem called FOURIER CHECKING.

Third, it is natural to ask whether the $\mathsf{P} \stackrel{?}{=} \mathsf{BQP}$ question is related to that *other* fundamental question of complexity theory, $\mathsf{P} \stackrel{?}{=} \mathsf{NP}$. More concretely, is it possible that quantum computers could provide exponential speedups even if P = NP? If BQP $\subseteq$ PH, then certainly the answer to that question is no (since $\mathsf{P} = \mathsf{NP} \Longrightarrow \mathsf{P} = \mathsf{PH}$). Therefore, if we want evidence that quantum computing could survive a collapse of P and NP, we must also seek evidence that BQP $\not\subset$ PH.

Fourth, a major challenge for quantum computing research is to *get better evidence that quantum computers cannot solve* NP*-complete problems in polynomial time.* As an example, could we show that if NP $\subseteq$ BQP, then the polynomial hierarchy collapses? At first glance, this seems like a wild hope; certainly we have no idea at present how to prove anything of the kind. However, notice that if BQP $\subseteq$ AM, then the desired implication would follow immediately! For in that case, coNP $\subseteq$ BQP, hence coNP $\subseteq$ AM, hence $\mathsf{PH} = \Sigma_2^{\mathsf{P}}$, where the last implication was shown by Boppana, Håstad, and Zachos [10].

1.2 Our Results

This paper presents the first formal evidence for the possibility that BQP $\not\subset$ PH. Perhaps more importantly, it places the relativized BQP versus PH question at the frontier of (classical) circuit lower bounds. The heart of the problem, we will find, is to extend Braverman's spectacular recent proof [11] of the Linial-Nisan Conjecture, in ways that would reveal a great deal of information about small-depth circuits independent of the implications for quantum computing.

We have two main contributions. First, we achieve an oracle separation between BQP and PH for the case of *relation problems*. A relation problem is simply a problem where the desired output is an n-bit string (rather than a single bit), and any string from some nonempty set S is acceptable. Relation problems arise often in theoretical computer science; one well-known example is finding a Nash equilibrium (shown to be PPAD-complete by Daskalakis et al. [13]). Within quantum computing, there is considerable precedent for studying relation problems as a warmup to the harder case of decision problems. For example, in 2004 Bar-Yossef, Jayram, and Kerenidis [4] gave a relation problem with quantum one-way communication complexity $O(\log n)$ and randomized one-way communication complexity $\Omega(\sqrt{n})$. It took several more years for Gavinsky et al. [15] to achieve the same separation for decision problems, and the proof was much more complicated.[3]

Formally, our result is as follows:

THEOREM 1. *There exists an oracle A relative to which $\mathsf{FBQP}^A \not\subset \mathsf{FBPP}^{\mathsf{PH}^A}$, where* FBQP *and* FBPP *are the relation versions of* BQP *and* BPP *respectively.*[4]

Interestingly, the oracle A in Theorem 1 can be taken to be a *random* oracle. By contrast, Aaronson and Ambainis [1] have shown that, under a plausible conjecture about influences in low-degree polynomials, one cannot separate the decision classes BQP and BPP by a random oracle without also separating P from $\mathsf{P}^{\#\mathsf{P}}$ in the unrelativized world. In other words, the use of relation problems (rather than decision problems) seems essential if one wants a random oracle separation.

Underlying Theorem 1 is a new lower bound against AC^0 circuits (constant-depth circuits composed of AND, OR, and NOT gates). The close connection between AC^0 and the polynomial hierarchy that we exploit is not new. In the early 1980s, Furst-Saxe-Sipser [14] and Yao [28] noticed that, if we have a PH machine M that computes (say) the PARITY

[3]Recently, Shepherd and Bremner [22] proposed a beautiful *sampling* problem that is solvable efficiently on a quantum computer but that they conjecture is hard classically. This provides yet another example where it seems easier to find evidence for the power of quantum computers once one moves away from decision problems.

[4]Confusingly, the F stands for "function"; we are simply following the standard naming convention for classes of relation problems (FP, FNP, etc).

of a 2^n-bit oracle string, then by simply reinterpreting the existential quantifiers of M as OR gates and the universal quantifiers as AND gates, we obtain an AC^0 circuit of size $2^{\text{poly}(n)}$ solving the same problem. It follows that, if we can prove a $2^{\omega(\text{polylog}\, n)}$ lower bound on the size of AC^0 circuits computing PARITY, we can construct an oracle A relative to which $\oplus\mathsf{P}^A \not\subset \mathsf{PH}^A$. The idea is the same for constructing an A relative to which $\mathcal{C}^A \not\subset \mathsf{PH}^A$, where $\mathcal{C}$ is any complexity class.

Indeed, the relation between PH and AC^0 is so direct that we get the following as a more-or-less immediate counterpart to Theorem 1:

THEOREM 2. *In the unrelativized world (with no oracle), there exists a relation problem solvable in* BQLOGTIME *but not in nonuniform* AC^0.

Here BQLOGTIME is the class of problems solvable by uniform logarithmic-*size* quantum circuits, with random access to the input string $x_1 \ldots x_n$. It should not be confused with the much larger class BQNC, of problems solvable by logarithmic-*depth* quantum circuits.

The relation problem that we use to separate BQP from PH, and BQLOGTIME from AC^0, is called FOURIER FISHING. The problem can be informally stated as follows. We are given oracle access to n Boolean functions $f_1, \ldots, f_n : \{0,1\}^n \to \{-1,1\}$, which we think of as chosen uniformly at random. The task is to output n strings, $z_1, \ldots, z_n \in \{0,1\}^n$, such that the corresponding squared Fourier coefficients $\widehat{f_1}(z_1)^2, \ldots, \widehat{f_n}(z_n)^2$ are "often much larger than average." Notice that if f_i is a random Boolean function, then each of its Fourier coefficients $\widehat{f_i}(z)$ follows a normal distribution—meaning that with overwhelming probability, a constant fraction of the Fourier coefficients will be a constant factor larger than the mean. Furthermore, it is straightforward to create a quantum algorithm that samples each z with probability proportional to $\widehat{f_i}(z)^2$, so that larger Fourier coefficients are more likely to be sampled than smaller ones.

On the other hand, computing any *specific* $\widehat{f_i}(z)$ is easily seen to be equivalent to summing 2^n bits. By well-known lower bounds on the size of AC^0 circuits computing the MAJORITY function (see Håstad [26] for example), it follows that, for any fixed z, computing $\widehat{f_i}(z)$ cannot be in PH as an oracle problem. Unfortunately, this does not directly imply any separation between BQP and PH, since the quantum algorithm does not compute $\widehat{f_i}(z)$ either: it just samples a z with probability proportional to $\widehat{f_i}(z)^2$. However, we will show that, if there exists a $\mathsf{BPP}^{\mathsf{PH}}$ machine M that even *approximately* simulates the behavior of the quantum algorithm, then one can solve MAJORITY by means of a *nondeterministic* reduction—which uses approximate counting to estimate $\Pr[M \text{ outputs } z]$, and adds a constant number of layers to the AC^0 circuit. The central difficulty is that, if M knew the specific z for which we were interested in estimating $\widehat{f_i}(z)$, then it could choose adversarially never to output that z. To solve this, we will show that we can "smuggle" a MAJORITY instance into the estimation of a *random* Fourier coefficient $\widehat{f_i}(z)$, in such a way that it is information-theoretically impossible for M to determine which z we care about.

Our second contribution is to define and study a new black-box decision problem, called FOURIER CHECKING. Informally, in this problem we are given oracle access to *two* Boolean functions $f, g : \{0,1\}^n \to \{-1,1\}$, and are promised that either

(i) f and g are both uniformly random, or

(ii) f is uniformly random, while g is extremely well correlated with f's Fourier transform over $\mathbb{Z}_2^n$ (which we call "forrelated").

The problem is to decide whether (i) or (ii) is the case.

It is not hard to show that FOURIER CHECKING is in BQP: basically, one can prepare a uniform superposition over all $x \in \{0,1\}^n$, then query f, apply a quantum Fourier transform, query g, and check whether one has recovered something close to the uniform superposition. On the other hand, being forrelated seems like an extremely "global" property of f and g: one that would not be apparent from querying *any* small number of $f(x)$ and $g(y)$ values. And thus, one might conjecture that FOURIER CHECKING (as an oracle problem) is not in PH.

In this paper, we adduce strong evidence for that conjecture. Specifically, we show that for every $k \leq 2^{n/4}$, the forrelated distribution over $\langle f, g \rangle$ pairs is $O\left(k^2/2^{n/2}\right)$*-almost k-wise independent*. By this we mean that, if one had $1/2$ prior probability that f and g were uniformly random, and $1/2$ prior probability that f and g were forrelated, then even conditioned on any k values of f and g, the posterior probability that f and g were forrelated would still be

$$\frac{1}{2} \pm O\left(\frac{k^2}{2^{n/2}}\right).$$

We conjecture that this almost k-wise independence property is enough, by itself, to imply that an oracle problem is not in PH. We call this the *Generalized Linial-Nisan Conjecture*.

Without the $\pm O\left(k^2/2^{n/2}\right)$ error term, our conjecture would be equivalent[5] to a famous conjecture in circuit complexity made by Linial and Nisan [18] in 1990. Their conjecture stated that *polylogarithmic independence fools* AC^0: in other words, every probability distribution over N-bit strings that is *uniform* on every small subset of bits, is indistinguishable from the truly uniform distribution by AC^0 circuits. When we began investigating this topic a year ago, even the original Linial-Nisan Conjecture was still open. Since then, Braverman [11] (building on earlier work by Bazzi [5] and Razborov [20]) has given a beautiful proof of that conjecture. In other words, to construct an oracle relative to which $\mathsf{BQP} \not\subset \mathsf{PH}$, it now suffices to generalize Braverman's Theorem from k-wise independent distributions to almost k-wise independent ones. We believe that this is by far the most promising approach to the BQP versus PH problem.

Alas, generalizing Braverman's proof is much harder than one might have hoped. To prove the original Linial-Nisan Conjecture, Braverman showed that every AC^0 function $f : \{0,1\}^n \to \{0,1\}$ can be well-approximated, in the L_1-norm, by *low-degree sandwiching polynomials*: real polynomials $p_\ell, p_u : \mathbb{R}^n \to \mathbb{R}$, of degree $O(\text{polylog}\, n)$, such that $p_\ell(x) \leq f(x) \leq p_u(x)$ for all $x \in \{0,1\}^n$. Since p_ℓ and p_u trivially have the same expectation on any k-wise independent

[5] Up to unimportant variations in the parameters

distribution that they have on the uniform distribution, one can show that f must have almost the same expectation as well. To generalize Braverman's result from k-wise independence to almost k-wise independence, we will show that it suffices to construct low-degree sandwiching polynomials that satisfy a certain additional condition. This new condition (which we call "low-fat") basically says that p_ℓ and p_u must be representable as linear combinations of *terms* (that is, products of x_i's and $(1-x_i)$'s), in such a way that the sum of the absolute values of the coefficients is bounded—thereby preventing "massive cancellations" between positive and negative terms. Unfortunately, while we know two techniques for approximating AC^0 functions by low-degree polynomials—that of Linial-Mansour-Nisan [17] and that of Razborov [19] and Smolensky [25]—neither technique provides anything like the control over coefficients that we need. To construct low-fat sandwiching polynomials, it seems necessary to reprove the LMN and Razborov-Smolensky theorems in a more "conservative," less "profligate" way. And such an advance seems likely to lead to breakthroughs in circuit complexity and computational learning theory having nothing to do with quantum computing.

Let us mention three further applications of FOURIER CHECKING:

First, if the Generalized Linial-Nisan Conjecture holds, then just like with FOURIER FISHING, we can "scale down by an exponential," to obtain a promise problem that is in $\mathsf{BQLOGTIME}$ but not in AC^0.

Second, without any assumptions, we can prove the new results that there exist oracles relative to which $\mathsf{BQP} \not\subset \mathsf{BPP_{path}}$ and $\mathsf{BQP} \not\subset \mathsf{SZK}$. We can also reprove all previous oracle separations between BQP and classical complexity classes in a unified fashion.

Third, independent of its applications to complexity classes, FOURIER CHECKING yields the largest gap between classical and quantum query complexity yet known. Its bounded-error randomized query complexity is $\Omega(N^{1/4})$ (and we conjecture $\Theta(\sqrt{N})$), while its quantum query complexity is only $O(1)$. Prior to this work, the best known gaps were of the form $N^{\Omega(1)}$ versus $O(\log N)$ (for Simon's and Shor's algorithms), or $\Theta(\log N)$ versus $O(1)$ (for the Bernstein-Vazirani problem).[6] Buhrman et al. [12] explicitly raised the open problem of finding a larger gap. We also get a *property* (namely, the property of being forrelated) that takes $N^{\Omega(1)}$ queries to test classically but only $O(1)$ queries to test quantumly.

1.3 In Defense of Oracles

This paper is concerned with finding oracles relative to which BQP outperforms classical complexity classes. As such, it is open to the usual objections: "But don't oracle results mislead us about the 'real' world? What about non-relativizing results like $\mathsf{IP} = \mathsf{PSPACE}$ [21]?"

In our view, it is most helpful to think of oracle separations, not as strange metamathematical claims, but as *lower bounds in a concrete computational model that is natural and well-motivated in its own right.* The model in question is *query complexity*, where the resource to be minimized is the number of accesses to a very long input string. When someone gives an oracle A relative to which $\mathcal{C}^A \not\subset \mathcal{D}^A$, what they really mean is simply that they have found a problem that $\mathcal{C}$ machines can solve using superpolynomially fewer queries than $\mathcal{D}$ machines. In other words, $\mathcal{C}$ has "cleared the first possible obstacle"—the query complexity obstacle—to having capabilities beyond those of $\mathcal{D}$. Of course, it could be (and sometimes is) that $\mathcal{C} \subseteq \mathcal{D}$ for other reasons, but if we do not *even* have a query complexity lower bound, then proving one is in some sense the obvious place to start.

Oracle separations have played a role in many of the central developments of both classical and quantum complexity theory. As mentioned earlier, proving query complexity lower bounds for PH machines is essentially equivalent to proving size lower bounds for AC^0 circuits—and indeed, the pioneering AC^0 lower bounds of the early 1980s were explicitly motivated by the goal of proving oracle separations for PH.[7] Within quantum computing, oracle results have played an even more decisive role: the first evidence for the power of quantum computers came from the oracle separations of Bernstein-Vazirani [9] and Simon [24], and Shor's algorithm [23] contains an oracle algorithm (for the PERIOD-FINDING problem) at its core.

Having said all that, if for some reason one still feels averse to the language of oracles, then (as mentioned before) one is free to scale everything down by an exponential, and to reinterpret a relativized separation between BQP and PH as an *un*relativized separation between $\mathsf{BQLOGTIME}$ and AC^0.

2. PRELIMINARIES

It will be convenient to consider Boolean functions of the form $f : \{0,1\}^n \to \{-1,1\}$. Throughout this paper, we let $N = 2^n$; we will often view the truth table of a Boolean function as an "input" of size N. Given a Boolean function $f : \{0,1\}^n \to \{-1,1\}$, the Fourier transform of f is defined as

$$\hat{f}(z) := \frac{1}{\sqrt{N}} \sum_{x \in \{0,1\}^n} (-1)^{x \cdot z} f(x).$$

Recall Parseval's identity:

$$\sum_{x \in \{0,1\}^n} f(x)^2 = \sum_{z \in \{0,1\}^n} \hat{f}(z)^2 = N.$$

2.1 Problems

We first define the FOURIER FISHING problem, in both "distributional" and "promise" versions. In the distributional version, we are given oracle access to n Boolean functions $f_1, \ldots, f_n : \{0,1\}^n \to \{-1,1\}$, which are chosen uniformly and independently at random. The task is to output n strings, $z_1, \ldots, z_n \in \{0,1\}^n$, at least 75% of which satisfy $\left|\hat{f}_i(z_i)\right| \geq 1$ and at least 25% of which satisfy $\left|\hat{f}_i(z_i)\right| \geq 2$. (Note that these thresholds are not arbitrary, but were carefully chosen to produce a separation between the quantum and classical models!)

We now want a version of FOURIER FISHING that removes the need to assume the f_i's are uniformly random, replacing

[6] De Beaudrap, Cleve, and Watrous [7] gave an $N^{\Omega(1)}$ versus $O(1)$ separation, but for a non-standard model of quantum query complexity where one gets to map $|x\rangle$ to $|\sigma(x)\rangle$ for a permutation σ (rather than $|x\rangle|y\rangle$ to $|x\rangle|y \oplus \sigma(x)\rangle$ as in the standard model).

[7] Yao's paper [28] was entitled "Separating the polynomial-time hierarchy by oracles"; the Furst-Saxe-Sipser paper [14] was entitled "Parity, circuits, and the polynomial time hierarchy."

it with a worst-case promise on the f_i's. Call an n-tuple $\langle f_1, \ldots, f_n \rangle$ of Boolean functions *good* if

$$\sum_{i=1}^{n} \sum_{z_i : |\widehat{f_i}(z_i)| \geq 1} \widehat{f_i}(z_i)^2 \geq 0.8Nn,$$

$$\sum_{i=1}^{n} \sum_{z_i : |\widehat{f_i}(z_i)| \geq 2} \widehat{f_i}(z_i)^2 \geq 0.26Nn.$$

(We will show in Lemma 6 that the vast majority of $\langle f_1, \ldots, f_n \rangle$ are good.) In PROMISE FOURIER FISHING, we are given oracle access to Boolean functions $f_1, \ldots, f_n : \{0,1\}^n \to \{-1,1\}$, which are promised to be good. The task, again, is to output strings $z_1, \ldots, z_n \in \{0,1\}^n$, at least 75% of which satisfy $\left|\widehat{f_i}(z_i)\right| \geq 1$ and at least 25% of which satisfy $\left|\widehat{f_i}(z_i)\right| \geq 2$.

Next we define a decision problem called FOURIER CHECKING. Here we are given oracle access to two Boolean functions $f, g : \{0,1\}^n \to \{-1,1\}$. We are promised that either

(i) $\langle f, g \rangle$ was drawn from the uniform distribution $\mathcal{U}$, which sets every $f(x)$ and $g(y)$ by a fair, independent coin toss.

(ii) $\langle f, g \rangle$ was drawn from the "forrelated" distribution $\mathcal{F}$, which is defined as follows. First choose a random real vector $v = (v_x)_{x \in \{0,1\}^n} \in \mathbb{R}^N$, by drawing each entry independently from a Gaussian distribution with mean 0 and variance 1. Then set $f(x) := \operatorname{sgn}(v_x)$ and $g(x) := \operatorname{sgn}(\widehat{v}_x)$ for all x. Here $\operatorname{sgn}(\alpha) := \alpha / |\alpha|$, and $\widehat{v}$ is the Fourier transform of v over $\mathbb{Z}_2^n$:

$$\widehat{v}_y := \frac{1}{\sqrt{N}} \sum_{x \in \{0,1\}^n} (-1)^{x \cdot y} v_x.$$

In other words, f and g *individually* are still uniformly random, but they are no longer independent: now g is extremely well correlated with the Fourier transform of f (hence "forrelated").

The problem is to accept if $\langle f, g \rangle$ was drawn from $\mathcal{F}$, and to reject if $\langle f, g \rangle$ was drawn from $\mathcal{U}$. Note that, since $\mathcal{F}$ and $\mathcal{U}$ overlap slightly, we can only hope to succeed with overwhelming probability over the choice of $\langle f, g \rangle$, not for every $\langle f, g \rangle$ pair.

We can also define a promise-problem version of FOURIER CHECKING. In PROMISE FOURIER CHECKING, we are promised that the quantity

$$p(f, g) := \frac{1}{N^3} \left(\sum_{x, y \in \{0,1\}^n} f(x) (-1)^{x \cdot y} g(y) \right)^2$$

is either at least 0.05 or at most 0.01. The problem is to accept in the former case and reject in the latter case.

2.2 Complexity Classes

See the Complexity Zoo[8] for the definitions of standard complexity classes, such as BQP, AM, and PH. When we write $\mathcal{C}^{\mathsf{PH}}$ (i.e., a complexity class $\mathcal{C}$ with an oracle for the polynomial hierarchy), we mean $\cup_{k \geq 1} \mathcal{C}^{\Sigma_k^{\mathsf{P}}}$.

We will consider not only decision problems, but also *relation problems* (also called *function problems*). In a relation problem, the output is not a single bit but a poly (n)-bit string y. There could be many valid y's for a given instance, and the algorithm's task is to output any one of them.

The definitions of FP and FNP (the relation versions of P and NP) are standard. We now define FBPP and FBQP, the relation versions of BPP and BQP.

DEFINITION 3. FBPP *is the class of relations* $R \subseteq \{0,1\}^* \times \{0,1\}^*$ *for which there exists a probabilistic polynomial-time algorithm* A *that, given any input* $x \in \{0,1\}^n$, *produces an output* y *such that* $\Pr[(x, y) \in R] = 1 - o(1)$, *where the probability is over* A*'s internal randomness. (In particular, this implies that for every* x, *there exists at least one* y *such that* $(x, y) \in R$.) FBQP *is defined the same way, except that* A *is a quantum algorithm rather than a classical one.*

An important point about FBPP and FBQP is that, as far as we know, these classes do not admit amplification. In other words, the value of an algorithm's success probability might actually matter, not just the fact that the probability is bounded above 1/2. This is why we adopt the convention that an algorithm "succeeds" if it outputs $(x, y) \in R$ with probability $1 - o(1)$. In practice, we will give oracle problems for which the FBQP algorithm succeeds with probability $1 - 1/\exp(n)$, while any $\mathsf{FBPP}^{\mathsf{PH}}$ algorithm succeeds with probability at most (say) 0.99. How far the constant in this separation can be improved is an open problem.

Another important point is that, while $\mathsf{BPP}^{\mathsf{PH}} = \mathsf{P}^{\mathsf{PH}}$ (which follows from $\mathsf{BPP} \subseteq \Sigma_2^{\mathsf{P}}$), the class $\mathsf{FBPP}^{\mathsf{PH}}$ is strictly larger than $\mathsf{FP}^{\mathsf{PH}}$. To see this, consider the relation problem where we are given n, and asked to output any string of Kolmogorov complexity at least n. Clearly this problem is in FBPP: just output a random $2n$-bit string. On the other hand, just as obviously the problem is not in $\mathsf{FP}^{\mathsf{PH}}$. This is why we need to construct an oracle A such that $\mathsf{FBQP}^A \not\subset \mathsf{FBPP}^{\mathsf{PH}^A}$: because constructing an oracle A such that $\mathsf{FBQP}^A \not\subset \mathsf{FP}^{\mathsf{PH}^A}$ is trivial and not even related to quantum computing.

We now discuss some "low-level" complexity classes. AC^0 is the class of problems solvable by a nonuniform family of AND/OR/NOT circuits, with depth $O(1)$, size poly (n), and unbounded fanin. When we say "AC^0 circuit," we mean a constant-depth circuit of AND/OR/NOT gates, not necessarily of polynomial size. Any such circuit can be made into a *formula* (i.e., a circuit of fanout 1) with only a polynomial increase in size. The circuit has *depth* d if it consists of d alternating layers of AND and OR gates (without loss of generality, the NOT gates can all be pushed to the bottom, and we do not count them towards the depth). For example, a DNF (Disjunctive Normal Form) formula is just an AC^0 circuit of depth 2.

We will also be interested in quantum *logarithmic* time, which can be defined naturally as follows:

DEFINITION 4. BQLOGTIME *is the class of languages* $L \subseteq \{0,1\}^*$ *that are decidable, with bounded error, by a* LOGTIME-*uniform family of quantum circuits* $\{C_n\}_n$ *such that each* C_n *has* $O(\log n)$ *gates, and can include gates that make random-access queries to the input string* $x = x_1 \ldots x_n$ *(i.e., that map* $|i\rangle |z\rangle$ *to* $|i\rangle |z \oplus x_i\rangle$ *for every* $i \in [n]$*).*

One other complexity class that arises in this paper, which is less well known than it should be, is $\mathsf{BPP}_{\mathsf{path}}$. Loosely speaking, $\mathsf{BPP}_{\mathsf{path}}$ can be defined as the class of problems that are solvable in probabilistic polynomial time, given the

[8] www.complexityzoo.com

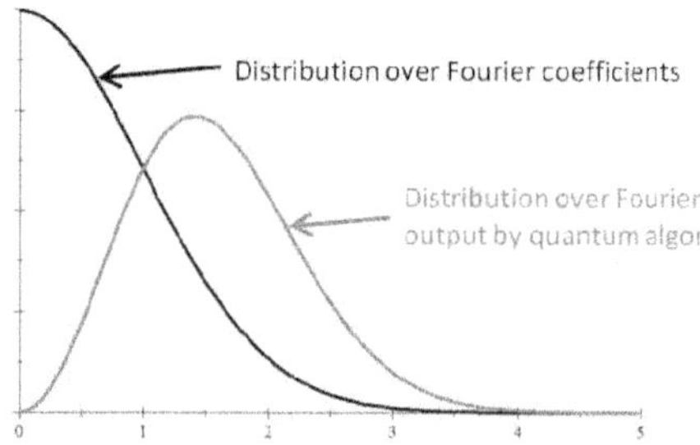

Figure 1: The Fourier coefficients of a random Boolean function follow a Gaussian distribution, with mean 0 and variance 1. However, larger Fourier coefficients are more likely to be observed by the quantum algorithm.

ability to "postselect" (that is, discard all runs of the computation that do not produce a desired result, even if such runs are the overwhelming majority).

3. QUANTUM ALGORITHMS

In this section, we show that FOURIER FISHING and FOURIER CHECKING both admit simple quantum algorithms.

3.1 Algorithm for Fourier Fishing

Here is a quantum algorithm, FF-ALG, that solves FOURIER FISHING with overwhelming probability in $O(n^2)$ time and n quantum queries (one to each f_i). For $i := 1$ to n, first prepare the state

$$\frac{1}{\sqrt{N}} \sum_{x \in \{0,1\}^n} f_i(x) |x\rangle,$$

then apply Hadamard gates to all n qubits, then measure in the computational basis and output the result as z_i.

Intuitively, FF-ALG samples the Fourier coefficients of each f_i under a distribution that is skewed towards larger coefficients; the algorithm's behavior is illustrated pictorially in Figure 1. Recall the definition of a "good" tuple $\langle f_1, \ldots, f_n \rangle$ from Section 2.1. Assuming $\langle f_1, \ldots, f_n \rangle$ is good, it is not hard to analyze FF-ALG's success probability.

LEMMA 5. *Assuming $\langle f_1, \ldots, f_n \rangle$ is good, FF-ALG succeeds with probability $1 - 1/\exp(n)$.*

We also have the following:

LEMMA 6. *$\langle f_1, \ldots, f_n \rangle$ is good with probability $1-1/\exp(n)$, if the f_i's are chosen uniformly at random.*

Combining Lemmas 5 and 6, we find that FF-ALG succeeds with probability $1-1/\exp(n)$, where the probability is over both $\langle f_1, \ldots, f_n \rangle$ and FF-ALG's internal randomness.

3.2 Algorithm for Fourier Checking

We now turn to FOURIER CHECKING, the problem of deciding whether two Boolean functions f, g are independent or forrelated. Here is a quantum algorithm, FC-ALG, that solves FOURIER CHECKING with constant error probability using $O(1)$ queries. First prepare a uniform superposition over all $x \in \{0,1\}^n$. Then query f in superposition, apply Hadamard gates to all n qubits, query g in superposition, and apply Hadamard gates to all n qubits again, to create the state

$$\frac{1}{N^{3/2}} \sum_{x,y,z \in \{0,1\}^n} f(x)(-1)^{x \cdot y} g(y)(-1)^{y \cdot z} |z\rangle.$$

Finally, measure in the computational basis, and "accept" if and only if the outcome $|0\rangle^{\otimes n}$ is observed. If needed, repeat the whole algorithm $O(1)$ times to boost the success probability.

It is clear that the probability of observing $|0\rangle^{\otimes n}$ (in a single run of FC-ALG) equals

$$p(f,g) := \frac{1}{N^3} \left(\sum_{x,y \in \{0,1\}^n} f(x)(-1)^{x \cdot y} g(y) \right)^2.$$

Recall that PROMISE FOURIER CHECKING was the problem of deciding whether $p(f,g) \geq 0.05$ or $p(f,g) \leq 0.01$, promised that one of these is the case. Thus, we immediately get a quantum algorithm to solve PROMISE FOURIER CHECKING, with constant error probability, using $O(1)$ queries to f and g.

For distributional FOURIER CHECKING, we also need the following theorem, which is proved in the full version.

THEOREM 7. *If $\langle f, g \rangle$ is drawn from the uniform distribution $\mathcal{U}$, then $\mathrm{E}_{\mathcal{U}}[p(f,g)] = \frac{1}{N}$. If $\langle f, g \rangle$ is drawn from the forrelated distribution $\mathcal{F}$, then $\mathrm{E}_{\mathcal{F}}[p(f,g)] > 0.07$.*

4. FOURIER FISHING LOWER BOUND

In Section 3.1, we gave a quantum algorithm for FOURIER FISHING that made only one query to each f_i. By contrast, it is not hard to show that any classical algorithm for FOURIER FISHING requires exponentially many queries to the f_i's—or in complexity terms, that FOURIER FISHING is not in FBPP. In this section, we give a much stronger result: that FOURIER FISHING is not even in $\mathsf{FBPP}^{\mathsf{PH}}$. This result does not rely on any unproved conjectures.

4.1 Constant-Depth Circuit Lower Bounds

Our starting point will be the following AC^0 lower bound, which can be found in the book of Håstad [26] for example.

THEOREM 8 ([26]). *Any depth-d circuit that accepts all n-bit strings of Hamming weight $n/2+1$, and rejects all strings of Hamming weight $n/2$, has size $\exp\left(\Omega\left(n^{1/(d-1)}\right)\right)$.*

We now give a corollary of Theorem 8, which (though simple) seems to be new, and might be of independent interest. Consider the following problem, which we call ε-BIAS DETECTION. We are given a string $y = y_1 \ldots y_m \in \{0,1\}^m$, and are promised that each bit y_i is 1 with independent probability p. The task is to decide whether $p = 1/2$ or $p = 1/2 + \varepsilon$.

COROLLARY 9. *Let $\mathcal{U}[\varepsilon]$ be the distribution over $\{0,1\}^m$ where each bit is 1 with independent probability $1/2+\varepsilon$. Then any depth-d circuit C such that*

$$\left| \Pr_{x \sim \mathcal{U}[\varepsilon]}[C(x)] - \Pr_{x \sim \mathcal{U}[0]}[C(x)] \right| = \Omega(1)$$

has size $\exp\left(\Omega\left(1/\varepsilon^{1/(d+2)}\right)\right)$.

Corollary 9 is proved in the full version. The proof proceeds exactly as one would expect: we start with an AC^0 circuit C for ε-BIAS DETECTION, and then use many copies of C, on different random subsets of the input bits, to get an AC^0 circuit that with high probability distinguishes all strings of Hamming weight $n/2+1$ from all strings of Hamming weight $n/2$.

4.2 Secretly Biased Fourier Coefficients

In this section, we state two lemmas indicating that one can *slightly* bias one of the Fourier coefficients of a random Boolean function $f:\{0,1\}^n \rightarrow \{-1,1\}$, and yet still have f be indistinguishable from a random Boolean function (so that, in particular, an adversary has no way of knowing which Fourier coefficient was biased). These lemmas will play a key role in our reduction from ε-BIAS DETECTION to FOURIER FISHING.

Fix a string $s \in \{0,1\}^n$. Let $\mathcal{A}[s]$ be the probability distribution over functions $f:\{0,1\}^n \rightarrow \{-1,1\}$ where each $f(x)$ is 1 with independent probability $\frac{1}{2}+(-1)^{s \cdot x}\frac{1}{2\sqrt{N}}$, and let $\mathcal{B}[s]$ be the distribution where each $f(x)$ is 1 with independent probability $\frac{1}{2}-(-1)^{s \cdot x}\frac{1}{2\sqrt{N}}$. Then let $\mathcal{D}[s]=\frac{1}{2}(\mathcal{A}[s]+\mathcal{B}[s])$ (that is, an equal mixture of $\mathcal{A}[s]$ and $\mathcal{B}[s]$).

Now consider the following game involving Alice and Bob, which closely models our problem. First, Alice chooses a string $s \in \{0,1\}^n$ uniformly at random. She then draws f according to $\mathcal{D}[s]$. She keeps s secret, but sends the truth table of f to Bob. After examining the entire truth table, Bob can output any string $z \in \{0,1\}^n$ such that $\left|\widehat{f}(z)\right| \geq \beta$. Bob's goal is to avoid outputting s. The following lemma says that, regardless of Bob's strategy, if β is sufficiently greater than 1, then Bob *must* output s with probability significantly greater than $1/N$.

LEMMA 10. *In the above game, we have*

$$\Pr[s=z] \geq \frac{e^{\beta}+e^{-\beta}}{2\sqrt{e}N},$$

where the probability is over s, f, and Bob's random choices.

Lemma 10 is proved in the full version. The intuition behind it is simple: f looks to Bob almost exactly like a random Boolean function. Let V_β be the set of all $s \in \{0,1\}^n$ such that $\left|\widehat{f}(s)\right| \geq \beta$. Then when Alice biases f, of course she significantly increases the probability that $s \in V_\beta$. But the biased Fourier coefficient $\widehat{f}(s)$ still gets "lost in the noise"—that is, it is information-theoretically impossible for Bob to tell s apart from the exponentially many *other* strings z that are in V_β just by chance. Therefore, the best Bob can do is basically just to output a random element of V_β. But since $|V_\beta| \ll N$, this strategy will cause Bob to output s with probability $\gg 1/N$.

Formalizing the above intuition involves a surprisingly simple Bayesian calculation. Basically, all we need to do is fix f together with Bob's output z (which we know belongs to V_β), and then calculate how likely f was to be drawn from $\mathcal{D}[z]$ rather than $\mathcal{D}[z']$ for some $z' \neq z$.

To see the connection to our problem, think of Bob as a putative AC^0 circuit for FOURIER FISHING, and Alice as an AC^0 reduction that uses Bob to solve ε-BIAS DETECTION. Bob might *try* not to cooperate, but by choosing s randomly, Alice can force even an adversarial Bob to give her useful information about the magnitude of $\widehat{f}(s)$.

Now let $\mathcal{D}=\mathrm{E}_s[\mathcal{D}[s]]$ (that is, an equal mixture of all the $\mathcal{D}[s]$'s). Then we prove in the full version that $\mathcal{D}$ is extremely close in variation distance to $\mathcal{U}$, the uniform distribution over all Boolean functions $f:\{0,1\}^n \rightarrow \{-1,1\}$.

LEMMA 11. $\|\mathcal{D}-\mathcal{U}\|=O(1/\sqrt{N})$.

An immediate corollary of Lemma 11 is that, if a FOURIER FISHING algorithm succeeds with probability p on $\langle f_1,\ldots,f_n\rangle$ drawn from $\mathcal{U}^n$, then it also succeeds with probability at least $p-\|\mathcal{D}^n-\mathcal{U}^n\| \geq p-O(n/\sqrt{N})$ on $\langle f_1,\ldots,f_n\rangle$ drawn from $\mathcal{D}^n$.

4.3 Putting It All Together

Using the results of Sections 4.1 and 4.2, we can give a lower bound on the constant-depth circuit complexity of FOURIER FISHING.

THEOREM 12. *Any depth-d circuit that solves the* FOURIER FISHING *problem, with probability at least* 0.99 *over $f_1,\ldots,f_n$ chosen uniformly at random, has size* $\exp\left(\Omega\left(N^{1/(2d+8)}\right)\right)$.

Combining Theorem 12 with standard diagonalization tricks, we can also give an oracle separation (in fact, a *random* oracle separation) between the complexity classes FBQP and $\mathsf{FBPP}^{\mathsf{PH}}$.

THEOREM 13. $\mathsf{FBQP}^A \not\subset \mathsf{FBPP}^{\mathsf{PH}^A}$ *with probability* 1 *for a random oracle A.*

If we "scale down by an exponential," then we can eliminate the need for the oracle A, and get a relation problem that is solvable in quantum *logarithmic* time but not in AC^0.

THEOREM 14. *There is a relation in* $\mathsf{BQLOGTIME} \setminus \mathsf{AC}^0$.

Theorems 12, 13, and 14 are proved in the full version.

5. FOURIER CHECKING LOWER BOUND

Section 4 settled the relativized BQP versus PH question, if we are willing to talk about relation problems. Ultimately, though, we also care about decision problems. So in this section we consider the FOURIER CHECKING problem, of deciding whether two Boolean functions f,g are independent or forrelated. In Section 3.2, we saw that FOURIER CHECKING has quantum query complexity $O(1)$. What is its classical query complexity?[9]

It is not hard to give a classical algorithm that solves FOURIER CHECKING using $O(\sqrt{N})=O(2^{n/2})$ queries. In the next section, we will show that FOURIER CHECKING has a property called *almost k-wise independence*, which immediately implies a lower bound of $\Omega(\sqrt[4]{N})=\Omega(2^{n/4})$ on its randomized query complexity[10] (as well as exponential lower bounds on its MA, $\mathsf{BPP_{path}}$, and SZK query complexities). Indeed, we conjecture that almost k-wise independence is enough to imply that FOURIER CHECKING is not in PH. We discuss the status of that conjecture in Section 6.

[9] So long as we consider the distributional version of FOURIER CHECKING, the deterministic and randomized query complexities are the same (by Yao's principle).

[10] With some more work, we believe that the randomized query complexity lower bound can be improved to $\Omega(\sqrt{N})$, though we have not pursued that here.

5.1 Almost k-Wise Independence

Let $X = x_1 \ldots x_N \in \{0,1\}^N$ be a string. Then a *literal* is an expression of the form x_i or $1 - x_i$, and a *k-term* is a product of k literals (each involving a different x_i), which is 1 if the literals all take on prescribed values and 0 otherwise. We can give an analogous definition for strings over the alphabet $\{-1,1\}$; we simply let the literals have the form $\frac{1 \pm x_i}{2}$.

Let $\mathcal{U}$ be the uniform distribution over N-bit strings. The following definition will play a major role in this work.

DEFINITION 15. *A distribution $\mathcal{D}$ over N-bit strings is ε-almost k-wise independent if for every k-term C,*

$$1 - \varepsilon \leq \frac{\Pr_{X \sim \mathcal{D}} [C(X)]}{\Pr_{X \sim \mathcal{U}} [C(X)]} \leq 1 + \varepsilon.$$

(Note that $\Pr_{X \sim \mathcal{U}} [C(X)]$ is just 2^{-k}.)

In other words, there should be no assignment to any k input bits, such that conditioning on that assignment gives us much information about whether X was drawn from $\mathcal{D}$ or $\mathcal{U}$.

Now let $\mathcal{F}$ be the forrelated distribution over pairs of Boolean functions $f, g : \{0,1\}^n \to \{-1,1\}$, where we first choose a vector $v = (v_x)_{x \in \{0,1\}^n} \in \mathbb{R}^N$ of independent $\mathcal{N}(0,1)$ Gaussians, then set $f(x) := \operatorname{sgn}(v_x)$ and $g(x) := \operatorname{sgn}(\widehat{v}_x)$ for all $x \in \{0,1\}^n$.

THEOREM 16. *$\mathcal{F}$ is $O(k^2/\sqrt{N})$-almost k-wise independent for all $k \leq \sqrt[4]{N}$.*

We prove Theorem 16 in the full version. To do so, we first compute the measure of the Gaussian distribution on an affine subspace of $\mathbb{R}^{2N}$ defined by $K + L$ equations of the form $v_{x_i} = a_i$ and $\widehat{v}_{y_j} = b_j$. This computation is somewhat involved, but is enormously aided by rotational invariance and other nice properties of the Gaussian distribution. We then perform a discretization step, to deal with the fact that the functions f and g are Boolean.

5.2 Oracle Separation Results

The following lemma says that *any* almost k-wise independent distribution is indistinguishable from the uniform distribution by $\mathsf{BPP_{path}}$ or SZK machines.

LEMMA 17. *Suppose a probability distribution $\mathcal{D}$ over oracle strings is $1/t(n)$-almost $\operatorname{poly}(n)$-wise independent, for some superpolynomial function t. Then no $\mathsf{BPP_{path}}$ machine or SZK protocol can distinguish $\mathcal{D}$ from the uniform distribution $\mathcal{U}$ with non-negligible bias.*

We can combine Theorem 16 and Lemma 17 with standard diagonalization tricks, to obtain an oracle relative to which $\mathsf{BQP} \not\subset \mathsf{BPP_{path}}$ and $\mathsf{BQP} \not\subset \mathsf{SZK}$.

THEOREM 18. *There exists an oracle A relative to which $\mathsf{BQP}^A \not\subset \mathsf{BPP}^A_{\mathsf{path}}$ and $\mathsf{BQP}^A \not\subset \mathsf{SZK}^A$.*

Since $\mathsf{BPP} \subseteq \mathsf{MA} \subseteq \mathsf{BPP_{path}}$, Theorem 18 supersedes the previous results that there exist oracles A relative to which $\mathsf{BPP}^A \neq \mathsf{BQP}^A$ [9] and $\mathsf{BQP}^A \not\subset \mathsf{MA}^A$ [27].

Lemma 17 and Theorem 18 are proved in the full version.

6. THE GENERALIZED LN CONJECTURE

In 1990, Linial and Nisan [18] conjectured that "polylogarithmic independence fools AC^0"—or loosely speaking, that every probability distribution $\mathcal{D}$ over n-bit strings that is uniform on all small subsets of bits, is *indistinguishable* from the uniform distribution by polynomial-size, constant-depth circuits. We now state a variant of the Linial-Nisan Conjecture, not with the best parameters but with weaker, easier-to-understand parameters that suffice for our application.

CONJECTURE 19 (LINIAL-NISAN OR LN CONJECTURE). *Let $\mathcal{D}$ be an $n^{\Omega(1)}$-wise independent distribution over $\{0,1\}^n$, and let $f : \{0,1\}^n \to \{0,1\}$ be computed by an AC^0 circuit of size $2^{n^{o(1)}}$ and depth $O(1)$. Then*

$$\left| \Pr_{x \sim \mathcal{D}} [f(x)] - \Pr_{x \sim \mathcal{U}} [f(x)] \right| = o(1).$$

After seventeen years of almost no progress, in 2007 Bazzi [5] finally proved the LN Conjecture for the special case of depth-2 circuits (also called DNF formulas). Bazzi's proof was about 50 pages, but it was dramatically simplified a year later, when Razborov [20] discovered a 3-page proof. Then in 2009, Braverman [11] gave a breakthrough proof of the full LN Conjecture.

THEOREM 20 (BRAVERMAN'S THEOREM [11]). *Let $f : \{0,1\}^n \to \{0,1\}$ be computed by an AC^0 circuit of size S and depth d, and let $\mathcal{D}$ be a $(\log \frac{S}{\varepsilon})^{7d^2}$-wise independent distribution over $\{0,1\}^n$. Then for all sufficiently large S,*

$$\left| \Pr_{x \sim \mathcal{D}} [f(x)] - \Pr_{x \sim \mathcal{U}} [f(x)] \right| \leq \varepsilon.$$

We conjecture a modest-seeming extension of Braverman's Theorem, which says (informally) that *almost* k-wise independent distributions fool AC^0 as well.

CONJECTURE 21 (GLN CONJECTURE). *Let $\mathcal{D}$ be a $1/n^{\Omega(1)}$-almost $n^{\Omega(1)}$-wise independent distribution over $\{0,1\}^n$, and let $f : \{0,1\}^n \to \{0,1\}$ be computed by an AC^0 circuit of size $2^{n^{o(1)}}$ and depth $O(1)$. Then*

$$\left| \Pr_{x \sim \mathcal{D}} [f(x)] - \Pr_{x \sim \mathcal{U}} [f(x)] \right| = o(1).$$

By the usual correspondence between AC^0 and PH, the GLN Conjecture immediately implies the following counterpart of Lemma 17:

> *Suppose a probability distribution $\mathcal{D}$ over oracle strings is $1/t(n)$-almost $\operatorname{poly}(n)$-wise independent, for some superpolynomial function t. Then no PH machine can distinguish $\mathcal{D}$ from the uniform distribution $\mathcal{U}$ with non-negligible bias.*

And thus we get the following implication:

THEOREM 22. *Assuming the GLN Conjecture, there exists an oracle A relative to which $\mathsf{BQP}^A \not\subset \mathsf{PH}^A$.*

The proof is the same as that of Theorem 18; the only difference is that the GLN Conjecture now plays the role of Lemma 17. Likewise:

THEOREM 23. *Assuming the GLN Conjecture for the special case of depth-2 circuits (i.e., DNF formulas), there exists an oracle A relative to which $\mathsf{BQP}^A \not\subset \mathsf{AM}^A$.*

As a side note, it is conceivable that one could prove $\Pr_{x\sim\mathcal{D}}[\varphi(x)] - \Pr_{x\sim\mathcal{U}}[\varphi(x)] = o(1)$ for every almost k-wise independent distribution $\mathcal{D}$ and small *CNF* formula φ, without getting the same result for DNF formulas (or vice versa). However, since BQP is closed under complement, even such an asymmetric result would imply an oracle A relative to which $\mathsf{BQP}^A \not\subset \mathsf{AM}^A$.

If the GLN Conjecture holds, then we can also "scale down by an exponential," to obtain an *unrelativized* decision problem that is solvable in BQLOGTIME but not in AC^0.

THEOREM 24. *Assuming the GLN Conjecture, there exists a promise problem in* $\mathsf{BQLOGTIME} \setminus \mathsf{AC}^0$.

6.1 Low-Fat Polynomials

Given that the GLN Conjecture would have such remarkable implications for quantum complexity theory, the question arises of how we can go about proving it. As we are indebted to Louay Bazzi for pointing out to us, the GLN Conjecture is *equivalent* to the following conjecture, about approximating AC^0 functions by low-degree polynomials.

CONJECTURE 25 (LOW-FAT SANDWICH CONJECTURE). *For every function* $f:\{0,1\}^n \to \{0,1\}$ *computable by an* AC^0 *circuit, there exist polynomials* $p_\ell, p_u : \mathbb{R}^n \to \mathbb{R}$ *of degree* $k = n^{o(1)}$ *that satisfy the following three conditions.*

(i) ***Sandwiching:*** $p_\ell(x) \le f(x) \le p_u(x)$ *for all* x.

(ii) L_1***-Approximation:*** $\mathrm{E}_{x\sim\mathcal{U}}[p_u(x) - p_\ell(x)] = o(1)$.

(iii) ***Low-Fat:*** $p_\ell(x)$ *and* $p_u(x)$ *can be written as linear combinations of terms,* $p_\ell(x) = \sum_C \alpha_C C(x)$ *and* $p_u(x) = \sum_C \beta_C C(x)$ *respectively, such that* $\sum_C |\alpha_C| 2^{-|C|} = n^{o(1)}$ *and* $\sum_C |\beta_C| 2^{-|C|} = n^{o(1)}$. *(Here a term is a product of literals of the form* x_i *and* $1 - x_i$*.)*

If we take out condition (iii), then Conjecture 25 becomes equivalent to the *original* LN Conjecture (see Bazzi [5] for a proof). And indeed, all progress so far on "Linial-Nisan problems" has crucially relied on this connection with polynomials. Bazzi [5] and Razborov [20] proved the depth-2 case of the LN Conjecture by constructing low-degree, approximating, sandwiching polynomials for every DNF, while Braverman [11] proved the full LN Conjecture by constructing such polynomials for every AC^0 circuit.[11] Given this history, proving Conjecture 25 would seem like the "obvious" approach to proving the GLN Conjecture.

It is easy to prove one direction of the equivalence: that to prove the GLN Conjecture, it suffices to construct low-fat sandwiching polynomials for every AC^0 circuit. The other direction—that the GLN Conjecture implies Conjecture 25, and hence, there is no loss of generality in working with polynomials instead of probability distributions—follows from a linear programming duality calculation.

7. DISCUSSION

We now take a step back, and use our results to address some conceptual questions about the relativized BQP versus PH question, the GLN Conjecture, and what makes them so difficult.

The first question is an obvious one. Complexity theorists have known for decades how to prove constant-depth circuit lower bounds, and how to use those lower bounds to give oracles A relative to which (for example) $\mathsf{PP}^A \not\subset \mathsf{PH}^A$ and $\oplus\mathsf{P}^A \not\subset \mathsf{PH}^A$. So why should it be so much harder to give an A relative to which $\mathsf{BQP}^A \not\subset \mathsf{PH}^A$? What makes this AC^0 lower bound different from all other AC^0 lower bounds?

The answer seems to be that, while we have powerful techniques for proving that a function f is not in AC^0, *all of those techniques, in one way or another, involve arguing that* f *is not approximated by a low-degree polynomial.* The Razborov-Smolensky technique [19, 25] argues this explicitly, while even the random restriction technique [14, 28, 26] argues it "implicitly," as shown by Linial, Mansour, and Nisan [17]. And this is a problem, if f is also computed by an efficient quantum algorithm. For Beals et al. [6] proved the following in 1998:

LEMMA 26 ([6]). *Suppose a quantum algorithm* Q *makes* T *queries to a Boolean input* $X \in \{0,1\}^N$. *Then* Q*'s acceptance probability is a real multilinear polynomial* $p(X)$, *of degree at most* $2T$.

In other words, if a function f is in BQP, then for that very reason, f *has* a low-degree approximating polynomial! As an example, we already saw that the following polynomial p, of degree 4, successfully distinguishes the forrelated distribution $\mathcal{F}$ from the uniform distribution $\mathcal{U}$:

$$p(f,g) := \frac{1}{N^3}\left(\sum_{x,y\in\{0,1\}^n} f(x)(-1)^{x\cdot y} g(y)\right)^2. \qquad (1)$$

Therefore, we cannot hope to prove a lower bound for FOURIER CHECKING, by any argument that would also imply that such a p cannot exist.

This brings us to a second question. If

(i) every known technique for proving $f \notin \mathsf{AC}^0$ involves showing that f is not approximated by a low-degree polynomial, but

(ii) every function f with low quantum query complexity *is* approximated by a low-degree polynomial,

does that mean there is no hope of solving the relativized BQP versus PH problem using polynomial-based techniques?

We believe the answer is no. The essential point here is that an AC^0 function can be approximated by different *kinds* of low-degree polynomials. Furthermore, to show that $f \notin \mathsf{AC}^0$, it suffices to show that f is not approximated by a low-degree polynomial in *any one* of these senses. For example, even though the PARITY function has degree 1 over the finite field $\mathbb{F}_2$, Razborov and Smolensky showed that over other fields (such as $\mathbb{F}_3$), any degree-$o(\sqrt{n})$ polynomial disagrees with PARITY on a large fraction of inputs—and that is enough to imply that PARITY$\notin \mathsf{AC}^0$. In other words, we simply need to find a *type* of polynomial approximation that works for AC^0 circuits, but does not work for FOURIER CHECKING. If true, Conjecture 25 (the Low-Fat Sandwich Conjecture) provides exactly such a type of approximation.

But this raises another question: what is the significance of the "low-fat" requirement in Conjecture 25? Why, of

[11] Strictly speaking, Braverman constructed approximating polynomials with slightly different (though still sufficient) properties. We know from Bazzi [5] that it must be possible to get sandwiching polynomials as well.

all things, do we want our approximating polynomial p to be expressible as a linear combination of terms, $p(x) = \sum_C \alpha_C C(x)$, such that $\sum_C |\alpha_C| 2^{-|C|} = n^{o(1)}$?

The answer takes us to the heart of what an oracle separation between BQP and PH would have to accomplish. Notice that, although the polynomial p from equation (1) solved the FOURIER CHECKING problem, it did so only by *cancelling massive numbers of positive and negative terms,* then representing the answer by the tiny residue left over. Not coincidentally, this sort of cancellation is a central feature of quantum algorithms. By contrast, we show that, if a polynomial p does *not* involve such massive cancellations, but is instead more "conservative" and "reasonable" (like the polynomials that arise from classical decision trees), then p cannot distinguish almost k-wise independent distributions from the uniform distribution, and therefore cannot solve FOURIER CHECKING. If Conjecture 25 holds, then every small-depth circuit can be approximated, not just by any low-degree polynomial, but by a "reasonable" low-degree polynomial—one with a bound on the coefficients that prevents massive cancellations. This would prove that FOURIER CHECKING has no small constant-depth circuits, and hence that there exists an oracle separating BQP from PH.

8. OPEN PROBLEMS

First, of course, prove the GLN Conjecture, or prove the existence of an oracle A relative to which $\mathsf{BQP}^A \not\subset \mathsf{PH}^A$ by some other means. A natural first step would be to prove the GLN Conjecture for the special case of DNFs: as shown in Theorem 23, this would imply an oracle A relative to which $\mathsf{BQP}^A \not\subset \mathsf{AM}^A$. We have offered a \$200 prize for the PH case and a \$100 prize for the AM case.[12]

Second, it would be of interest to prove the GLN Conjecture for classes of functions weaker than (or incomparable with) DNFs: for example, monotone DNFs, read-once formulas, and read-k-times formulas.

Third, can we give an example of a Boolean function $f : \{0,1\}^n \rightarrow \{-1,1\}$ that is well-approximated by a low-degree polynomial, but *not* by a low-degree low-fat polynomial?

Fourth, can we give an oracle relative to which $\mathsf{BQP} \not\subset \mathsf{IP}$?

Fifth, what else does the GLN Conjecture imply?

Sixth, how much can we say about the BQP versus PH question in the unrelativized world? As one concrete challenge, can we find a nontrivial way to "realize" the FOURIER CHECKING oracle (in other words, an explicit computational problem that is solvable using FOURIER CHECKING)?

Seventh, how far can the gap between the success probabilities of FBQP and $\mathsf{FBPP}^{\mathsf{PH}}$ algorithms be improved?

9. ACKNOWLEDGMENTS

I thank Louay Bazzi for reformulating the GLN Conjecture as the Low-Fat Sandwich Conjecture, Andy Drucker, Lance Fortnow, and Sasha Razborov for helpful discussions, and an anonymous reviewer for comments.

10. REFERENCES

[1] S. Aaronson and A. Ambainis. The need for structure in quantum speedups. arXiv:0911.0996, 2009.

[2] L. Adleman, J. DeMarrais, and M.-D. Huang. Quantum computability. *SIAM J. Comput.*, 26(5):1524–1540, 1997.

[3] D. Aharonov, V. Jones, and Z. Landau. A polynomial quantum algorithm for approximating the Jones polynomial. In *Proc. ACM STOC*, p. 427–436, 2006.

[4] Z. Bar-Yossef, T. S. Jayram, and I. Kerenidis. Exponential separation of quantum and classical one-way communication complexity. *SIAM J. Comput.*, 38(1):366–384, 2008.

[5] L. Bazzi. Polylogarithmic independence can fool DNF formulas. In *Proc. IEEE FOCS*, p. 63–73, 2007.

[6] R. Beals, H. Buhrman, R. Cleve, M. Mosca, and R. de Wolf. Quantum lower bounds by polynomials. *J. ACM*, 48(4):778–797, 2001.

[7] J. N. de Beaudrap, R. Cleve, and J. Watrous. Sharp quantum versus classical query complexity separations. *Algorithmica*, 34(4):449–461, 2002.

[8] C. Bennett, E. Bernstein, G. Brassard, and U. Vazirani. Strengths and weaknesses of quantum computing. *SIAM J. Comput.*, 26(5):1510–1523, 1997.

[9] E. Bernstein and U. Vazirani. Quantum complexity theory. *SIAM J. Comput.*, 26(5):1411–1473, 1997.

[10] R. B. Boppana, J. Håstad, and S. Zachos. Does co-NP have short interactive proofs? *Inf. Proc. Lett.*, 25:127–132, 1987.

[11] M. Braverman. Poly-logarithmic independence fools AC^0 circuits. In *Proc. IEEE Complexity*, p. 3–8, 2009.

[12] H. Buhrman, L. Fortnow, I. Newman, and H. Röhrig. Quantum property testing. *SIAM J. Comput.*, 37(5):1387–1400, 2008.

[13] C. Daskalakis, P. W. Goldberg, and C. H. Papadimitriou. The complexity of computing a Nash equilibrium. *Commun. ACM*, 52(2):89–97, 2009.

[14] M. Furst, J. B. Saxe, and M. Sipser. Parity, circuits, and the polynomial time hierarchy. *Math. Systems Theory*, 17:13–27, 1984.

[15] D. Gavinsky, J. Kempe, I. Kerenidis, R. Raz, and R. de Wolf. Exponential separation for one-way quantum communication complexity, with applications to cryptography. *SIAM J. Comput.*, 38(5):1695–1708, 2008.

[16] A. Klivans and D. van Melkebeek. Graph nonisomorphism has subexponential size proofs unless the polynomial-time hierarchy collapses. *SIAM J. Comput.*, 31:1501–1526, 2002.

[17] N. Linial, Y. Mansour, and N. Nisan. Constant depth circuits, Fourier transform, and learnability. *J. ACM*, 40(3):607–620, 1993.

[18] N. Linial and N. Nisan. Approximate inclusion-exclusion. *Combinatorica*, 10(4):349–365, 1990.

[19] A. A. Razborov. Lower bounds for the size of circuits of bounded depth with basis $\{\&, \oplus\}$. *Mathematicheskie Zametki*, 41(4):598–607, 1987.

[20] A. A. Razborov. A simple proof of Bazzi's theorem. *ACM Trans. Comput. Theory*, 1(1), 2009.

[21] A. Shamir. IP=PSPACE. *J. ACM*, 39(4):869–877, 1992.

[22] D. Shepherd and M. J. Bremner. Temporally unstructured quantum computation. *Proc. Roy. Soc. London*, A465(2105):1413–1439, 2009.

[23] P. W. Shor. Polynomial-time algorithms for prime factorization and discrete logarithms on a quantum computer. *SIAM J. Comput.*, 26(5):1484–1509, 1997.

[24] D. Simon. On the power of quantum computation. In *Proc. IEEE FOCS*, p. 116–123, 1994.

[25] R. Smolensky. Algebraic methods in the theory of lower bounds for Boolean circuit complexity. In *Proc. ACM STOC*, p. 77–82, 1987.

[26] J. Håstad. *Computational Limitations for Small Depth Circuits.* MIT Press, 1987.

[27] J. Watrous. Succinct quantum proofs for properties of finite groups. In *Proc. IEEE FOCS*, p. 537–546, 2000.

[28] A. C-C. Yao. Separating the polynomial-time hierarchy by oracles. In *Proc. IEEE FOCS*, p. 1–10, 1985.

[12] See http://scottaaronson.com/blog/?p=381

A Quantum Lovász Local Lemma

Andris Ambainis *
Faculty of Computing
University of Latvia
Riga, Latvia

Julia Kempe †
School of Computer Science
Tel Aviv University
Tel Aviv, Israel

Or Sattath
School of Computer Science
The Hebrew University and
Tel-Aviv University
Israel

ABSTRACT

The Lovász Local Lemma (LLL) is a powerful tool in probability theory to show the existence of combinatorial objects meeting a prescribed collection of "weakly dependent" criteria. We show that the LLL extends to a much more general geometric setting, where events are replaced with subspaces and probability is replaced with relative dimension, which allows to lower bound the dimension of the intersection of vector spaces under certain independence conditions.

Our result immediately applies to the k-QSAT problem: For instance we show that any collection of rank 1 projectors with the property that each qubit appears in at most $2^k/(e \cdot k)$ of them, has a joint satisfiable state.

We then apply our results to the recently studied model of random k-QSAT. Recent works have shown that the satisfiable region extends up to a density of 1 in the large k limit, where the density is the ratio of projectors to qubits. Using a hybrid approach building on work by Laumann et al. [27] we greatly extend the known satisfiable region for random k-QSAT to a density of $\Omega(2^k/k^2)$. Since our tool allows us to show the existence of joint satisfying states without the need to construct them, we are able to penetrate into regions where the satisfying states are conjectured to be entangled, avoiding the need to construct them, which has limited previous approaches to product states.

Primary Classification: F.m Theory of Computation $\hookrightarrow$ Miscellaneous

Additional Classifictation: F.2.2 Theory of Computation $\hookrightarrow$ Analysis of Algorithms and Problem Complexity $\hookrightarrow$ Nonnumerical Algorithms and Problems
General Terms: Theory
Keywords: Local Lemma, Probabilistic Method, Quantum Computation, Quanum SAT, Random Quantum SAT

1. INTRODUCTION AND RESULTS

In probability theory, if a number of events are all independent of one another, then there is a positive (possibly small) probability that none of the events will occur. The Lovász Local Lemma (presented in 1975 by Erdős and Lovász [16]) allows one to relax the independence condition slightly: As long as the events are "mostly" independent of one another and are not individually too likely, then there is still a positive probability that none of them occurs. In its simplest form it states

Theorem 1 ([16]). *Let $B_1, B_2, \ldots, B_n$ be events with $Pr(B_i) \leq p$ and such that each event is mutually independent of all but d of the others. If $p \cdot e \cdot (d+1) \leq 1$ then $Pr(\bigwedge_{i=1}^{n} \overline{B_i}) > 0$.*

The Lovász Local Lemma (LLL) is an extremely powerful tool in probability theory as it supplies a way of dealing with rare events and of showing that a certain event holds with positive probability. It has found an enormous range of applications (see, e.g., [3]), for instance to graph colorability [16], lower bounds on Ramsey numbers [38], geometry [31], and algorithms [37]. For many of these results there is no known proof which does not use the Local Lemma.

One notable application of the LLL is to determine conditions under which a k-CNF formula is *satisfiable*. If each clause of such a formula Φ involves a disjoint set of variables, then it is obvious that Φ is satisfiable. One way to see this is to observe that a *random assignment* violates a clause with probability $p = 2^{-k}$ and hence the probability that all m clauses are satisfied by a random assignment is $(1-p)^m > 0$. But what if some of the clauses share variables, i.e., if they are "weakly dependent"? This question is readily answered by using the LLL:

Corollary 2. *Let Φ be a k-SAT formula in CNF-form. If every variable appears in at most $2^k/(e \cdot k)$ clauses then Φ is satisfiable.*

This corollary follows from Thm. 1 by letting B_i be the event that the i-th clause is not satisfied for a random assignment, which happens with probability $p = 2^{-k}$, and noting that each clause depends only on the $d \leq (2^k/e) - k$ other clauses that share a variable with it. In particular this

*Supported by University of Latvia Research Grant ZB01-100, FP7 Marie Curie Grant PIRG02-GA-2007-224886 and ESF project 1DP/1.1.1.2.0/09/APIA/VIAA/044.
†Supported by the European Commission under the Integrated Project Qubit Applications (QAP) funded by the IST directorate as Contract Number 015848, by an Alon Fellowship of the Israeli Higher Council of Academic Research, by an Individual Research Grant of the Israeli Science Foundation, by a European Research Council (ERC) Starting Grant, by a Raymond and Beverly Sackler Career Development Chair and by the Wolfson Family Charitable Trust.

corollary gives a better understanding of SAT, the prototype NP-complete problem in classical complexity theory.

In the last decade enormous advances have been made in the area of *quantum complexity*, the theory of easy and hard problems for a quantum computer. In particular, a natural quantum analog of k-SAT, called k-QSAT, was introduced by Bravyi [9]: Instead of clauses we have projectors $\Pi_1, \ldots, \Pi_m$, each acting non-trivially on k qubits, and we have to decide if all of them can be satisfied jointly. More precisely, we ask if there is a state $|\Psi\rangle$ on all qubits such that $\Pi_i|\Psi\rangle = 0$ for all $1 \leq i \leq m$ (in physics language: we ask if the system is *frustration-free*). This problem[1] was shown to be QMA$_1$-complete for $k \geq 4$ [9] and as such has received considerable attention [29, 30, 6, 11, 28, 27, 10].

Note that the question is easy for a set of *"disjoint"* projectors: If no two projectors share any qubits, then clearly $|\Psi\rangle = |\Psi_1\rangle \otimes \cdots \otimes |\Psi_m\rangle$ is a satisfying state, where $|\Psi_i\rangle$ is such that $\Pi_i|\Psi_i\rangle = 0$, just like in the case of disjoint k-SAT. It is thus very natural to ask if there still is a joint satisfying state when the projectors are "weakly" dependent, i.e., share qubits only with a few other projectors. One might speculate that a *quantum* local lemma should provide the answer.

Motivated by this question we ask: Is there a quantum local lemma? What will take the role of notions like *probability space, probability, events, conditional probability* and *mutual independence*? What properties should they have? And can we prove an analogous statement to Cor. 2 for k-QSAT?

Our results.

We answer all these questions in the positive by first showing how to generalize the notions of probability and independence in a meaningful way applicable to the quantum setting and then by proving a quantum local lemma. We then show that it implies a statement analogous to Cor. 2 for k-QSAT with exactly the same parameters as in the classical case. As we describe later in this section, we then combine our results with recent advances in the study of random QSAT to substantially widen the satisfiable range and to provide greatly improved lower bounds on the conjectured threshold between the satisfiable and the unsatisfiable region.

Let us first focus on the conceptual step of finding the right notions of *probability* and *independence*. In the quantum setting we deal with vector spaces and the probability of a certain event to happen is determined by its dimension.

It is thus very natural to have the correspondence defined in Fig. 1 of classical and "quantum" notions, using the apparent similarity between events and linear spaces.

This definition by analogy brings us surprisingly far. It can be verified (see Lemma. 7) that many useful properties hold for R, like (i) $0 \leq \mathrm{R} \leq 1$, (ii) monotonicity: $A \subseteq B \Rightarrow \mathrm{R}(A) \leq \mathrm{R}(B)$, (iii) the chain rule, (iv) an "inclusion/exclusion" formula and (v) $\mathrm{R}(A) + \mathrm{R}(A^\perp) = 1$.

There are, however, two important differences between probability and relative dimension. One concerns the complement of events. For probabilities, the conditional version of property (v) holds: $\Pr(A|B) + \Pr(\overline{A}|B) = 1$. For R we can easily find counterexamples to the statement $\mathrm{R}(A|B) + \mathrm{R}(A^\perp|B) = 1$ (for instance two non-equal non-orthogonal lines A and B in a two-dimensional space, where $\mathrm{R}(A|B) + \mathrm{R}(A^\perp|B) = 0$). It is this property that is used in most proofs of the local lemma, and one of the difficulties in our proof of a quantum LLL (QLLL) is to circumvent its use. The second difference concerns our notion of *R-independence*. In probability theory, if A and B are independent, then so are $\overline{A}$ and B. Again, this is not true any more for R and easy counterexamples can be found (see Sec. 2). It is thus important to find the right formulation of a quantum local lemma concerning mutual independence of events. Keeping these caveats in mind and using our notion of relative dimension, we prove a general quantum LLL (see Sec. 3), which in its simplest form gives:

Theorem 3. *Let $X_1, X_2, \ldots, X_n$ be subspaces, where $R(X_i) \geq 1-p$ and such that each subspace is mutually R-independent of all but d of the others. If $p \cdot e \cdot (d+1) \leq 1$ then $R(\bigcap_{i=1}^n X_i) > 0$.*

Note that in contrast to the classical LLL in Thm. 1 which is stated in terms of the "bad" events B_i, here we are working with the "good" events. While in the classical case these two formulations are equivalent, this is no longer the case for our notion of R-independence.

An immediate application of our QLLL is to k-QSAT, where we are able to show the exact analogue of Cor. 2.

Corollary 4. *Let $\{\Pi_1, \ldots, \Pi_m\}$ be a k-QSAT instance where all projectors have rank 1. If every qubit appears in at most $2^k/(e \cdot k)$ projectors, then the instance is satisfiable.*

It follows by defining (with a slight abuse of notation) subspaces $X_i = \Pi_i^\perp$ of satisfying states for Π_i. Noticing that $\mathrm{R}(X_i) = 1 - 2^{-k}$ and that projectors are mutually R-independent whenever they do not share qubits, and observing that an equivalent formulation of the k-QSAT-problem is to decide whether $\dim(\bigcap_{i=1}^m \Pi_i^\perp) > 0$, Thm. 3 gives the desired result (see Secs. 2 and 3 for details and more applications to k-QSAT).

Random QSAT.

Over the past few decades a considerable amount of effort was dedicated to understanding the behavior of *random k-SAT formulas* [25, 33, 32]. Research in this area has witnessed a fruitful collaboration among computer scientists, physicists and mathematicians, and is motivated in part by an attempt to better understand the class NP, as well as some recent surprising applications to hardness of approximation (see, e.g., [17]).

The main focus in this area is an attempt to understand the *phase transition phenomenon* of random k-SAT, namely, the sharp transition from being satisfiable with high probability at low clause density to being unsatisfiable with high probability at high clause density. The existence of this phase transition at a critical density α_c was proven by Friedgut in 1999 [19];[2] however only in the $k = 2$ case its value is known exactly ($\alpha_c = 1$ [12, 20, 8]). A long line of works for $k = 3$ have narrowed it down to $3.52 \leq \alpha_c \leq 4.49$ [24, 21, 14] (with evidence that $\alpha_c \approx 4.267$ [33]), and in the large k limit it has been shown that $2^k \ln 2 - O(k) \leq \alpha_c \leq 2^k \ln 2$ [1].

---

[1]when defined with an appropriate promise gap for no-instances

[2]Actually, it is still not known whether the critical density converges for large n; see [19] for details on this technical (but nontrivial) issue.

Probability space Ω	$\longrightarrow$	Vector space V
Event $A \in \Omega$	$\longrightarrow$	Subspace $A \subseteq V$
Complement $\overline{A} = \Omega \setminus A$	$\longrightarrow$	Orthogonal subspace $A^{\perp}$
Probability $\Pr(A)$	$\longrightarrow$	Relative dimension $\mathrm{R}(A) := \frac{\dim A}{\dim V}$
Union and Disjunction $A \vee B, A \wedge B$	$\longrightarrow$	$A + B = \{a + b \mid a \in A, b \in B\}, A \cap B$
Conditioning $\Pr(A\|B) = \frac{\Pr(A \wedge B)}{\Pr(B)}$	$\longrightarrow$	$\mathrm{R}(A\|B) := \frac{\mathrm{R}(A \cap B)}{\mathrm{R}(B)} = \frac{\dim(A \cap B)}{\dim(B)}$
A, B independent $\Pr(A \wedge B) = \Pr(A) \cdot \Pr(B)$	$\longrightarrow$	A, B R-independent $\mathrm{R}(A \cap B) = \mathrm{R}(A) \cdot \mathrm{R}(B)$

Figure 1: Definition of correspondence between classical and quantum terminology

The quantum analogue of this question, namely understanding the behavior of random k-QSAT instances, has recently started attracting attention. As in the classical case, the motivation here comes from an attempt to understand QMA_1, the quantum analogue of NP (of which k-QSAT is a complete problem), as well as the possibility of applications to hardness of approximation, but also from the hope to obtain insight into phase transition effects in other quantum physical systems.

The definition of a random k-QSAT instance is similar to the one in the classical case. Fix some $\alpha > 0$. Then a random k-QSAT instance on n qubits of density α is obtained by repeating the following $m = \alpha n$ times: choose a random subset of k qubits and pick a random rank-1 projector on them. An equivalent way to describe this is to say that we choose a random k-uniform hypergraph from the ensemble $G_k(n, m)$, in which $m = \alpha n$ k-hyperedges are picked uniformly at random from the set of all possible k-hyperedges on n vertices (with repetitions) and then a random rank-1 projector is chosen for each hyperedge.

In a first work on the random k-QSAT model, Laumann et al. [28] fully characterize the $k = 2$ case and show a threshold at density $\alpha_c^q = 1/2$ using a transfer matrix approach introduced by Bravyi [9]. Curiously, the satisfying states in the satisfiable region are *product states*. They also establish the first lower and upper bounds on a possible (conjectured [10]) threshold. In a recent breakthrough Bravyi, Moore and Russell [10] have dramatically improved the upper bound to $0.574 \cdot 2^k$, *below* the large k limit of $\ln 2 \cdot 2^k \approx 0.69 \cdot 2^k$ for the classical threshold! In [27], the upper bound was further improved to $0.5 \cdot 2^k$, by using a refined argument.

Recently, Laumann et al. [27] have given substantially improved lower bounds, essentially showing the following.

Theorem 5. *[27] If there is a matching of projectors to qubits such that (i) each projector is matched to a qubit on which it acts nontrivially and (ii) no qubit is matched to more than one projector, then the k-QSAT instance is satisfiable.*

Such a matching exists with high probability for random instances of QSAT if the density is below some critical value $c(k)$ (hence $c(k) \leq \alpha_c^q$), with $c(3) \approx 0.92$ and $c(k) \to 1$ for large k.

There remained a distressingly large gap between the best rigorous lower (< 1) and upper ($0.5 \cdot 2^k$) bounds for a satisfiable / non-satisfiable threshold of random k-QSAT.

Using our quantum LLL we are able to dramatically improve the lower bound on such a threshold. To get a better intuition on the kind of bounds the quantum LLL can give in this setting, let us first look at a simple toy example: random k-QSAT instances picked according to the uniform distribution on *D-regular* k-hypergraphs $G_k(n, D)$ (so $m = Dn/k$ and their density is $\alpha = D/k$). It is easy to see that a matching as assumed in Thm. 5 only exists iff $k \geq D$, so this technique shows satisfiability only below density 1. Our Cor. 4, on the other hand, immediately implies that the instance is satisfiable as long the density $\alpha \leq 2^k/(e \cdot k^2)$. It is this order of magnitude that we manage to achieve also in the random k-QSAT model described above. We show

Theorem 6. *A random k-QSAT instance of density $\alpha \leq 2^k/(12 \cdot e \cdot k^2)$ is satisfiable with high probability for any $k \geq 1$. Hence $\alpha_c^q \geq 2^k/(12 \cdot e \cdot k^2)$.*

All previous lower bound proofs [28, 27] were based on constructing *tensor product states* which satisfy all constraints. The question whether there is a region which is satisfiable only by entangled states was raised in [10]. In fact it is conjectured [27] that $c(k)$ is the critical density above which entangled states would necessarily appear as satisfying states. To our knowledge no technique has allowed to deal with entangled satisfying states in this setting. Using the quantum LLL allows us to show the existence of a satisfying state without the need to generate it, and in particular the satisfying state need not be a product state (and probably is not). We conjecture that the improvement in our bound, which is roughly exponential in k, is due to this difference.

The main difficulty we encounter in the proof of Thm. 6 (see Sec. 4) is that even though the *average degree* in $G_k(n, m = \alpha n)$ is of the right order of magnitude ($\approx 2^k/k$) to apply the quantum LLL (Cor. 4), the maximum degree can deviate vastly from it (its expected size is roughly logarithmic in n), and hence prevent a direct application of the quantum LLL. The key insight is that we can split the graph into two parts, one essentially consisting of *high degree* vertices that deviate by too much from the average degree and the other part containing the remaining vertices. We then show that the first part obeys the matching conditions of Thm. 5 [27] and hence has a satisfying state, and the second part obeys the maximum degree requirements of the quantum LLL and is hence also satisfiable. The challenge is to "glue" these two satisfying solutions together. For this we need to make sure that each edge in the second part intersects the first part in at most one qubit (by adding all other edges to the first part, while carefully treating the resulting dependencies). We can then create a new $(k-1)$-local projector of rank 2 for each intersecting edge, which reflects the fact that one qubit of this edge is already "taken". This allows to effectively decouple the two parts.

Discussion and Open Problems.

We have shown a general quantum LLL. An obvious open

question is whether it has more applications for quantum information.

We call our generalization of the Lovász Local Lemma "quantum" in view of the applications we have given. However, stricto sensu there is nothing *quantum* in our version of the LLL; It is a statement about subspaces and the dimensions of their intersections. As such it seems to be very versatile and we hope that it will find a multitude of other applications, not only in quantum information, but also in geometry or linear algebra. More generally, our LLL holds for any set of objects with a valuation R and operations $\bigcap$ and $+$ that obey properties (i)-(iv) (see Lemma 7) and might be applicable even more generally. Since the LLL has so many applications, we hope that our "geometric" LLL becomes equally useful.

The standard proof of the classical LLL is *non-constructive* in the sense that it asserts the existence of an object that obeys a system of constraints with limited dependence, but does not yield an efficient procedure for *finding* an object with the desired property. In particular, it does not provide an efficient way to find the actual satisfying assignment in Cor. 2. A long line of research [5, 2, 34, 13, 39, 35] has culminated in a very recent breakthrough result by Moser [36] (see also [37]), who gave an *algorithmic* proof of the LLL that allows to efficiently *construct* the desired satisfying assignment (and more generally the object whose existence is asserted by the LLL [37]). Moser's algorithm itself is a rather simple random walk on assignments; an innovative information theoretic argument proves its correctness (see also [18]). This opens the exciting possibility to draw an analogy for a (possibly quantum) algorithm to construct the satisfying state in instances of QSAT which are known to be satisfiable via our QLLL, and we hope to explore this connection in future work.

Structure of the paper.

In Sec. 2 we study properties of relative dimension R and of R-independence, allowing us to prove a general QLLL in Sec. 3. Sec. 4 extends our results to the random k-QSAT model and presents our improved bound on the size of the satisfiable region.

2. PROPERTIES OF RELATIVE DIMENSION

Here we summarize and prove some of the properties of the *relative dimension R* and of *R-independence* as defined in Fig. 1, which will be useful in the proof of the quantum LLL in the next section.

Lemma 7. *For any subspaces $X, Y, Z, X_i \subseteq V$ the following hold*

(i) $0 \leq R(X) \leq 1$.

(ii) Monotonicity: $X \subseteq Y \rightarrow R(X) \leq R(Y)$.

(iii) Chain Rule: $R(\bigcap_{i=1}^n X_i|Y) = R(X_1|Y) \cdot R(X_2|X_1 \cap Y) \cdot R(X_3|X_1 \cap X_2 \cap Y) \cdot \ldots \cdot R(X_n|\bigcap_{i=1}^{n-1} X_i \cap Y)$.

(iv) Inclusion/Exclusion: $R(X) + R(Y) = R(X+Y) + R(X \cap Y)$.

(v) $R(X) + R(X^\perp) = 1$ *and* $R(X|Y) + R(X^\perp|Y) \leq 1$.

(vi) $R(X|Z) + R(Y|Z) - R(X \cap Y|Z) \leq 1$.

PROOF. Properties (i), (ii), (iii) and (v) follow trivially from the definition.

Property (iv) follows from $\dim(X) + \dim(Y) = \dim(X \cap Y) + \dim(X+Y)$, which is an easy to prove statement about vector spaces (see e.g. [26], Thm. 5.3).

Property (vi) follows from (ii) and (iv): Inclusion/exclusion (iv) gives $\mathrm{R}(X \cap Z) + \mathrm{R}(Y \cap Z) = \mathrm{R}(X \cap Z + Y \cap Z) + \mathrm{R}(X \cap Y \cap Z) \leq \mathrm{R}(Z) + \mathrm{R}(X \cap Y \cap Z)$, where the last inequality follows from the monotonicity property (ii) using $X \cap Z + Y \cap Z \subseteq Z$. Dividing by $\mathrm{R}(Z)$ gives the desired result. □

We also need to extend our definition of R-independence (Fig. 1) to the case of several subspaces, in analogy to the case of events.

Definition 8 (Mutual independence). *An event A (resp. subspace X) is mutually independent (resp. mutually R-independent) of a set of events (resp. subspaces) $\{Y_1, \ldots, Y_\ell\}$ if for all $S \subseteq [\ell]$, $\Pr(A|\bigwedge_{i\in S} Y_i) = \Pr(A)$ (resp. $R(X|\bigcap_{i\in S} Y_i) = R(X)$).*

Note that unlike in the case of probabilities, it is possible that two subspaces A and B are mutually R-independent but $\overline{A}$ and B are not mutually R-independent. One example for this are the following subspaces of $\mathbb{R}^4$: $A = \mathrm{span}\{(1,0,0,0), (0,1,0,0)\}$ and $B = \mathrm{span}\{(1,0,0,0),(0,1,1,0)\}$. We have $\mathrm{R}(A|B) = \mathrm{R}(A) = 1/2$ but $\mathrm{R}(A^\perp|B) = 0$ while $\mathrm{R}(A^\perp) = 1/2$.

Let us now relate the notion of mutual R-independence to the situation in k-QSAT instances. We first associate a subspace with a projector, in the natural way.

Definition 9 (Projectors and associated subspace). *A k-local projector on n-qubits is a projector of the form $\pi \otimes I_{n-k}$, where π is a projector on k qubits $q_1, \ldots, q_k$ and I_{n-k} is the identity on the remaining qubits. We say that Π acts on $q_1, \ldots, q_k$. For a projector Π, let its satisfying space be $X_{\Pi^\perp} := \ker \Pi = \{|\Psi\rangle \mid \Pi|\Psi\rangle = 0\}$. When there is no risk of confusion we denote $X_{\Pi^\perp}$ by $\Pi^\perp$ and its complement by Π.*

Recall that in statements like Cor. 4 we would like to say that two projectors are mutually R-independent if they do not share any qubits. This is indeed the case, as the following lemma shows.

Lemma 10. *Assume a projector Π does not share any qubits with projectors $\Pi_1, \ldots, \Pi_\ell$. Then $X_{\Pi^\perp}$ is mutually R-independent of $\{X_{\Pi_1^\perp}, \ldots, X_{\Pi_\ell^\perp}\}$.*

PROOF. Let us split the Hilbert space $\mathcal{H}$ of the entire system into $\mathcal{H} = \mathcal{H}_1 \otimes \mathcal{H}_2$, where $\mathcal{H}_1$ is the space which consists of the qubits Π acts on non-trivially (and $\Pi_1, \ldots, \Pi_\ell$ act as identity) and the remaining space $\mathcal{H}_2$. By assumption there are projectors π and $\pi_1, \ldots, \pi_\ell$ such that $\Pi = \pi \otimes I_{n-k}$ and $\Pi_i = I_k \otimes \pi_i$. For every $S \subseteq [\ell]$,

$$\begin{aligned}\mathrm{R}(\Pi|\bigcap_{i\in S}\Pi_i) &= \frac{\dim(\Pi \bigcap_{i\in S}\Pi_i)}{\dim(\bigcap_{i\in S}\Pi_i)} = \frac{\dim(\pi \otimes \bigcap_{i\in S}\pi_i)}{\dim(I \otimes \bigcap_{i\in S}\pi_i)} \\ &= \frac{\dim(\pi)\dim(\bigcap_{i\in S}\pi_i)}{\dim(\mathcal{H}_1)\dim(\bigcap_{i\in S}\pi_i)} = \mathrm{R}(\Pi).\end{aligned}$$

□

Remark: In exactly the same way one can show that Π is mutually R-independent of $\{\Pi_1^\perp, \ldots, \Pi_\ell^\perp\}$ and that both Π

and $\Pi^\perp$ are mutually R-independent of $\{\Pi_1, \ldots, \Pi_\ell\}$. Hence the property of not sharing qubits (or, for subspaces, having a certain tensor structure), which in particular implies mutual R-independence, is in some sense a stronger notion of independence than R-independence. To prove our quantum LLL we only require the weaker notion of R-independence, which potentially makes the quantum LLL more versatile and applicable in settings where there is no tensor structure.

3. THE QUANTUM LOCAL LEMMA

We begin by stating the classical general Lovász Local Lemma. To this end we need to be more precise about what we mean by "weak" dependence, introducing the notion of the *dependency graph* for both events and subspaces (see e.g. [3] for the case of events), where we use *relative dimension* R as in Fig. 1.

Definition 11 (Dependency graph for events/subspaces). *The directed graph $G = ([n], E)$ is a dependency graph for (i) the events $A_1, \ldots, A_n$ if for every $i \in [n]$, A_i is mutually independent of $\{A_j | (i,j) \notin E\}$,*
(ii) the subspaces $X_1, \ldots, X_n$ if for every $i \in [n]$, X_i is mutually R-independent of $\{X_j | (i,j) \notin E\}$.

With these notions in place we can state the general Lovász Local Lemma (sometimes also called the asymmetric LLL).

Theorem 12 ([16]). *Let $A_1, A_2, \ldots, A_n$ be events with dependency graph $G = ([n], E)$. If there exists $0 \leq y_1, \ldots, y_n < 1$, such that $Pr(A_i) \leq y_i \cdot \prod_{(i,j)\in E}(1 - y_j)$, then*

$$Pr(\bigwedge_{i=1}^{n} \overline{A_i}) \geq \prod_{i=1}^{n}(1 - y_i).$$

In particular, with positive probability no event A_i holds.

We prove a quantum generalization of this lemma with exactly the same parameters. As mentioned before, we have to modify the formulation of the LLL to account for the unusual way R-independence behaves under complement. We are now ready to state and prove our main result.

Theorem 13 (Quantum Lovász Local Lemma). *Let $X_1, X_2, \ldots, X_n$ be subspaces with dependency graph $G = ([n], E)$. If there exist $0 \leq y_1, \ldots, y_n < 1$, such that*

$$R(X_i) \geq 1 - y_i \prod_{j|(i,j)\in E} (1 - y_j), \qquad (1)$$

then $R(\bigcap_{i=1}^{n} X_i) \geq \prod_{i=1}^{n}(1 - y_i)$.

Note that when R is replaced by Pr and $\bigcap$ by $\bigwedge$ we recover the LLL Thm. 12. Our proof uses properties that hold both for Pr and R, in particular we also prove Thm. 12. One can say that we generalize the LLL to any notion of probability for which the properties (i)-(iv) of Lemma 7 hold (these are the only properties of R we need in the proof).

Proof of Theorem 13. We modify the proof in [3] in order to avoid using the property $\Pr(A|B) + \Pr(\overline{A}|B) = 1$ which does not hold for R. To show Thm. 13, it is sufficient to prove the following Lemma.

Lemma 14. *For any $S \subset [n]$, and every $i \in [n]$,*

$$R(X_i | \bigcap_{j\in S} X_j) \geq 1 - y_i.$$

Thm. 13 now follows from the chain rule (Lemma 7.iii):

$$\mathrm{R}(\bigcap_{i=1}^{n} X_i) = \mathrm{R}(X_1)\mathrm{R}(X_2|X_1)\mathrm{R}(X_3|X_1 \cap X_2)\ldots\mathrm{R}(X_n| \bigcap_{j=1}^{n-1} X_j)$$
$$\geq \prod_{i=1}^{n} (1 - y_i).$$

We prove the lemma by complete induction on the size of the set S. For the base case, if S is empty, we have

$$\mathrm{R}(X_i) \geq 1 - \left[y_i \prod_{j|(i,j)\in E} (1 - y_j) \right] \geq 1 - y_i.$$

Inductive step: To prove the statement for S we assume it is true for all sets of size $< |S|$. Fix i and define $D = S \cap \{j|(i,j) \in E\}$ and $I = S \backslash D$ (I and D are the independent and dependent part of S with respect to the ith element). Let $\mathcal{X}_I = \bigcap_{j\in I} X_j$ and $\mathcal{X}_D = \bigcap_{j\in D} X_j$. Then

$$1 - \mathrm{R}(X_i| \bigcap_{j\in S} X_j) = 1 - \mathrm{R}(X_i|\mathcal{X}_I \cap \mathcal{X}_D)$$
$$= 1 - \frac{\mathrm{R}(X_i \cap \mathcal{X}_D|\mathcal{X}_I)}{\mathrm{R}(\mathcal{X}_D|\mathcal{X}_I)} = \frac{\mathrm{R}(\mathcal{X}_D|\mathcal{X}_I) - \mathrm{R}(X_i \cap \mathcal{X}_D|\mathcal{X}_I)}{\mathrm{R}(\mathcal{X}_D|\mathcal{X}_I)}. \qquad (2)$$

To show the lemma we need to upper bound this expression by y_i. We first upper bound the numerator:

$$\mathrm{R}(\mathcal{X}_D|\mathcal{X}_I) - \mathrm{R}(X_i \cap \mathcal{X}_D|\mathcal{X}_I) \leq 1 - \mathrm{R}(X_i|\mathcal{X}_I)$$
$$= 1 - \mathrm{R}(X_i) \leq y_i \prod_{j|(i,j)\in E} (1 - y_j),$$

where for the first inequality we use Lemma 7.vi, then the fact that X_i and $\mathcal{X}_I$ are R-independent, and the assumption on $\mathrm{R}(X_i)$, Eq. (1) in Thm. 13.

Now, we lower bound the denominator of Eq. (2). Suppose $D = \{j_1, \ldots, j_{|D|}\}$, then $\mathrm{R}\left(\bigcap_{j\in D} X_j|\mathcal{X}_I\right)$ can be written as

$$\mathrm{R}\left(X_{j_1}|\mathcal{X}_I\right) \cdot \ldots \cdot \mathrm{R}\left(X_{j_{|D|}}|X_{j_1} \cap \ldots \cap X_{j_{|D|-1}} \cap \mathcal{X}_I\right)$$
$$\geq \prod_{j\in D} 1 - y_j \geq \prod_{j|(i,j)\in E} 1 - y_j.$$

The equality follows from the chain rule (Lemma 7.iii), the first inequality follows from the inductive assumption, and the second inequality follows from the fact that $D = \{j|(i,j) \in E\} \cap S \subseteq \{j|(i,j) \in E\}$, and that $y_j < 1$. □

For many applications we only need a simpler version of the quantum LLL, often called the symmetric version, which we have already stated in Thm. 3.

Proof of Theorem 3. Thm. 3 follows from Thm. 13 in the same way the symmetric LLL of Thm. 1 follows from the more general LLL of Thm. 12 [3]; we include it here for completeness: If $d = 0$ then $\mathrm{R}(\bigcap_{i=1}^{n} X_i) = \Pi_{i=1}^{n}\mathrm{R}(X_i) > 0$ by the chain rule (Lemma 7.iii) and mutual R-independence of all subspaces. For $d \geq 1$, by the assumption there is a dependency graph $G = ([n], E)$ for the subspaces $X_1, \ldots, X_n$ in which for each i; $|\{j|(i,j) \in E\}| \leq d$. Taking $y_i = 1/(d+$

1) (< 1) and using that for $d \geq 1$, $(1-\frac{1}{d+1})^d > \frac{1}{e}$ we get

$$\begin{aligned}\mathrm{R}(X_i) &\geq 1 - p \geq 1 - \frac{1}{e(d+1)} \\ &\geq 1 - \frac{1}{d+1}(1-\frac{1}{d+1})^d \geq 1 - y_i(1-y_i)^{|\{j|(i,j)\in E\}|},\end{aligned}$$

which is the necessary condition Eq. (1) in Thm. 13. Hence

$$\mathrm{R}(\bigcap_{i=1}^{n} X_i) \geq (1 - \frac{1}{d+1})^n > 0. \tag{3}$$

□

Note that Eq. (3) also allows us to give a lower bound on the dimension of the intersecting subspace, which might be useful for some applications.

We can now move to the implications of the QLLL for "sparse" instances of QSAT and prove Cor. 4. It is a special case of this slightly more general Corollary.

Corollary 15. *Let $\{\Pi_1, \dots, \Pi_m\}$ be a k-QSAT instance where all projectors have rank at most r. If every qubit appears in at most $D = 2^k/(e \cdot r \cdot k)$ projectors, then the instance is satisfiable.*

PROOF. By assumption, each projector shares qubits with at most $k(D-1)$ other projectors. As we have already shown in Lemma 10, each $\Pi_i^\perp$ is mutually R-independent from all but $d = k(D-1)$ of the other $\Pi_j^\perp$. With $p = r \cdot 2^{-k}$ we have $\mathrm{R}(\Pi_i^\perp) \geq 1 - p$. The corollary follows from Thm. 3 because $p \cdot e \cdot (d+1) \leq r \cdot 2^{-k} \cdot e(k(2^k/(e \cdot r \cdot k) - 1) + 1) \leq 1$. □

4. AN IMPROVED LOWER BOUND FOR RANDOM QSAT

This section is devoted to the proof of Thm. 6. As mentioned in the introduction, in *random k-QSAT* we study a distribution over instances of k-QSAT with fixed density, defined as follows.

Definition 16 (Random k-QSAT). *Random k-QSAT of density α is a distribution over instances $\{\Pi_1, \dots, \Pi_m\}$ on n qubits, where $m = \alpha n$, obtained as follows:*

1. *Construct a k-uniform hypergraph G with n vertices and m edges (the constraint hypergraph) by choosing m times, uniformly and with replacement, from the $\binom{n}{k}$ possible k-tuples of vertices.*

2. *For each edge i ($1 \leq i \leq m$) pick a k-qubit state $|v_i\rangle$ acting on the corresponding qubits uniformly from all such states (according to the Haar measure) and set $\Pi_i = |v_i\rangle\langle v_i| \otimes I_{n-k}$.*

Remark: ($G_k(n,m)$ **vs.** $G_k(n,p)$) The distribution on hypergraphs obtained in the first step is denoted by $G_k(n,m)$ and has been studied extensively (see, e.g., [7, 3]). A closely related model is the so called Erdös-Renyi $G_k(n,p)$ model, where each of the $\binom{n}{k}$ k-tuples is independently chosen to be an edge with probability p. For $p = m/\binom{n}{k}$ the expected number of edges in $G_k(n,p)$ is m and these two distributions are very close to each other. In most cases proving that a certain property holds in one implies that it holds in the other (see [7]). There seems to be no consensus whether to define the random k-SAT and k-QSAT models with respect to the distribution $G_k(n,m)$ or $G_k(n,p)$; for instance the upper bounds on the random k-QSAT threshold of [10] are shown in the $G_k(n,m)$ model, whereas the lower bounds [28, 27] are given in the $G_k(n,p)$ model. This, however, does not matter, as properties such as being satisfiable with high probability will always hold for both models.

As mentioned, for $\alpha = c \cdot 2^k/k^2$, even though a graph from $G_k(n,m)$ has average degree $D_{avg} = k\alpha = c \cdot 2^k/k$, and hence *on average* each qubit appears in $c \cdot 2^k/k$ projectors, we cannot apply the QLLL and its Cor. 4 directly: The degrees in $G_k(n,m)$ are distributed according to a Poisson distribution with mean D_{avg} and hence we expect to see some high degree vertices (in fact the expected maximum degree at constant density is expected to be roughly logarithmic in n [7]). The idea behind the proof of Thm. 6 is to single out the "high-degree" part $V_{\mathcal{H}}$ of the graph and to treat it separately. The key is to show (i) that the matching conditions of Laumann et al.'s Thm. 5 is fulfilled by $V_{\mathcal{H}}$ on one hand and (ii) to demonstrate how to "glue" the solution on $V_{\mathcal{H}}$ with the one provided by QLLL on the remaining graph.

We first show how to glue two solutions, which also clarifies the requirements for $\mathcal{H}$.

Lemma 17 (Gluing Lemma). *Let $\mathcal{P} = \{\Pi_1, \dots, \Pi_m\}$ be an instance of k-QSAT with rank-1 projectors. Assume that there is a subset of the qubits $V_{\mathcal{H}}$ and a partition of the projectors into two sets $\mathcal{H}$ and $\mathcal{L}$, where $\mathcal{H}$ (possibly empty) consists of all projectors that act only on qubits in $V_{\mathcal{H}}$, such that*

1. *The reduced instance given by $\mathcal{H}$ (restricted to qubits in $V_{\mathcal{H}}$) is satisfiable.*

2. *Each qubit $\notin V_{\mathcal{H}}$ appears in at most $2^k/(4 \cdot e \cdot k)$ projectors from $\mathcal{L}$.*

3. *Each projector in $\mathcal{L}$ has at most one qubit in $V_{\mathcal{H}}$.*

Then $\mathcal{P}$ is satisfiable.

PROOF. Let $|\Phi_{\mathcal{H}}\rangle$ be a satisfying state for $\mathcal{H}$ on the qubits $V_{\mathcal{H}}$ (if $\mathcal{H} = \emptyset$ this can be any state). To extend it to the whole instance, we need to deal with the projectors in $\mathcal{L}$ acting on a qubit from $V_{\mathcal{H}}$. Let $\mathcal{L} = \{\Pi_1, \dots, \Pi_\ell\}$. From $\mathcal{L}$ we construct a new "decoupled" instance $\mathcal{L}' = \{Q_1, \dots, Q_\ell\}$ of k-QSAT with projectors of rank at most 2 that have no qubits in $V_{\mathcal{H}}$. If $\Pi_i \in \mathcal{L}$ does not act on any qubit in $V_{\mathcal{H}}$, we set $Q_i := \Pi_i$. Otherwise, order the k qubits on which Π_i acts such that the first one is in $V_{\mathcal{H}}$. Π_i can be written as $\Pi_i = |v_i\rangle\langle v_i| \otimes I_{n-k}$, where $|v_i\rangle$ is a k-qubit state. We can decompose $|v_i\rangle = a_0|0\rangle \otimes |v_i^0\rangle + a_1|1\rangle \otimes |v_i^1\rangle$, where the first part of the tensor product is the qubit in $V_{\mathcal{H}}$ and $|v_i^1\rangle$ and $|v_i^2\rangle$ are $(k-1)$-qubit states on the remaining qubits. Define $Q_i = |v_i^1\rangle\langle v_i^1| + |v_i^2\rangle\langle v_i^2| \otimes I_{n-k+1}$. Call $V_{\mathcal{L}'}$ the set of qubits on which the projectors in $\mathcal{L}'$ act on. Note that by construction $V_{\mathcal{L}'}$ is disjoint from $V_{\mathcal{H}}$, and that $V_{\mathcal{H}} \cup V_{\mathcal{L}'}$ is the set of all qubits in $\mathcal{P}$; hence $\mathcal{H}$ and $\mathcal{L}'$ are "decoupled".

Claim 18. *Assume there is a satisfying state $|\Phi_{\mathcal{L}'}\rangle$ for $\mathcal{L}'$ on $V_{\mathcal{L}'}$. Then $|\Phi\rangle = |\Phi_{\mathcal{H}}\rangle \otimes |\Phi_{\mathcal{L}'}\rangle$ is a satisfying state for $\mathcal{P}$.*

PROOF. By construction, $|\Phi\rangle$ satisfies all the projectors from $\mathcal{H}$ and all projectors in $\mathcal{L}$ that do not have qubits in $V_{\mathcal{H}}$. To see that it also satisfies any projector Π_i from $\mathcal{L}$ with a qubit in $V_{\mathcal{H}}$, observe that $|\Phi_{\mathcal{L}'}\rangle$ is orthogonal to both $|v_i^1\rangle$ and $|v_i^2\rangle$. Hence no matter how $|\Phi_{\mathcal{L}'}\rangle$ is extended on the qubit of $V_{\mathcal{H}}$ in Π_i, the resulting state is orthogonal to $|v_i\rangle$. □

It remains to show that $\mathcal{L}'$ is satisfiable. This follows immediately from Cor. 15: we observe that each projector in $\mathcal{L}'$ can be viewed as a k-local projector of rank at most 4; and by the assumption each qubit in $V_{\mathcal{L}'}$ appears in at most $2^k/(4 \cdot e \cdot k)$ projectors of $\mathcal{L}'$. □

The Gluing Lemma 17 only depends on the underlying constraint hypergraph. We can hence give the construction of the "high degree" part of the instance purely in terms of hypergraphs, and will from now on associate subsets of edges with the corresponding subsets of projectors. Motivated by the Gluing Lemma, our goal is to separate a set of "high degree" vertices $V_{\mathcal{H}}$ (above a certain cut-off degree D) with induced edges $\mathcal{H}$ such that each edge outside $\mathcal{H}$ has at most one vertex in $V_{\mathcal{H}}$. We achieve this by starting with the high degree vertices and iteratively adding all those edges that intersect in more than one vertex.

Definition 19 (Construction of $V_{\mathcal{H}}$). *Let $G = G([n], E)$ be a k-uniform hypergraph and $D > 0$. Construct sets of vertices $V_0, V_1, \ldots \subseteq [n]$ and edges $E_1, E_2 \ldots \subseteq E$ iteratively in the following steps, starting with all sets empty:*

0) Let $V_0 = \{v \in V | \deg(v) > D\}$.

1) For all $e \in E \setminus E_0$, if e has 2 or more vertices in V_0, then add e to E_1, and add to V_1 all vertices in e not already in V_0.

⋮

i) For all $e \in E \setminus (E_0 \cup \ldots \cup E_{i-1})$, if e has 2 or more vertices in $\bigcup_{j=0}^{i-1} V_j$, add e to E_i, and add to V_i all the vertices in E_i which are not already in $\bigcup_{j=0}^{i-1} V_j$.

Stop at the first step s such that $E_s = \emptyset$.

Let $V_{\mathcal{H}} := \bigcup_{i=0}^{s} V_i$, $\mathcal{H} := \bigcup_{i=1}^{s} E_i$ and $\mathcal{L} := E \setminus \mathcal{H}$.

By construction all the V_i are disjoint and similarly for the E_i. The process of adding edges stops at some step s ($E_s = \emptyset$), because $E \setminus (E_0 \cup \ldots \cup E_{s-1})$ keeps shrinking until this happens. Note that $\mathcal{H}$ consists precisely of all those edges in E that have only vertices in $V_{\mathcal{H}}$ (i.e. $G(V_{\mathcal{H}}, \mathcal{H})$ is the hypergraph induced by G on $V_{\mathcal{H}}$).

To show that a random k-QSAT instance of density α is satisfiable with high probability, we only need to show that the construction of $V_{\mathcal{H}}$, $\mathcal{H}$ and $\mathcal{L}$ of Def. 19 fulfills the conditions of the Gluing Lemma 17 with high probability. We set $D = 2^k/(4 \cdot e \cdot k)$ in Def. 19, so that conditions 2. and 3. are fulfilled by construction. To finish the proof of Thm. 6 it thus suffices to show that the instance given by $\mathcal{H}$ on qubits in $V_{\mathcal{H}}$ is satisfiable. To show this we build on Laumann et al.'s Thm. 5.

Lemma 20. *For a random k-QSAT instance with density $\alpha < 2^k/(12 \cdot e \cdot k^2)$, the reduced instance $\mathcal{H}$ obtained in the construction of Def. 19 with $D = 2^k/(4 \cdot e \cdot k)$ fulfills the matching conditions of Thm. 5 with high probability.*

PROOF. The proof of this key lemma proceeds in two parts. The first one (Lemma 21) shows that *any* hypergraph induced by a *small enough* subset of vertices in a hypergraph from $G_k(n, \alpha n)$ fulfills the matching conditions. The second part (Lemma 22) then shows that $V_{\mathcal{H}}$ is indeed small enough with high probability.

Lemma 21 (Small subgraphs have a matching). *Let G be a random hypergraph distributed according to $G_k(n, \alpha n)$ and let $\gamma = (e(e^2 \cdot \alpha)^{1/(k-2)})^{-1}$. With high probability, for all $W \subset V$ with $|W| < \gamma n$, the induced hypergraph on W obeys the matching conditions of Thm. 5.*

PROOF. There is simple intuition why small sets obey the matching conditions - the density inside a small induced graph is much smaller than the density of G: For simplicity set $\alpha = 2^{k-1}$ and $\gamma = 1/(2 + 2\delta)$ for some $\delta > 0$. Imagine fixing $W \subset V$ of size γn and then picking the graph G according to $G_k(n, p)$ with $p = \alpha n / \binom{n}{k} \approx \frac{\alpha}{n^{k-1}} = (\frac{2}{n})^{k-1}$. The induced graph on W is distributed according to $G_k(\gamma n, p)$ and hence its density is $\alpha' = p \cdot \binom{\gamma n}{k}/\gamma n \approx p \cdot (\gamma n)^{k-1} = (1+\delta)^{-(k-1)} \ll 1$. At such low densities the matching conditions are fulfilled with high probability (see the remark below Thm. 5). We proceed to prove the somewhat stronger statement that the matching conditions hold for *all* small subsets.

Let us first examine the matching conditions. We can construct a bipartite graph $B(G)$, where on the left we put the edges of G and on the right the vertices of G. We connect each edge on the left with those vertices on the right that are contained in that edge. Then the matching conditions of Thm. 5 are equivalent to saying that there is a matching in $B(G)$ that covers all left vertices.

By Hall's theorem [22, 15], such a matching exists iff for all t, every subset of t edges on the left is connected to at least t vertices on the right. Hence, there is a "bad" subset $W \subset V$ with $|W| < \gamma n$ not obeying the matching conditions iff for some $t < \gamma n$ there is a subset of vertices of size $t-1$ that contains t edges. Let us compute the probability of such a bad event to happen.

First, fix a subset $S \subseteq V$ of size $t-1$ and let us compute the probability that it contains t edges. The probability that a random edge lands in S is at most $((t-1)/n)^k$. Since in $G_k(n, m)$ all m edges are picked independently, we get

$$\Pr[S \text{ contains } t \text{ edges}] \leq \binom{m}{t} \left(\frac{t-1}{n}\right)^{kt}.$$

By the union bound over all subsets S of size $t-1$ (there are $\binom{n}{t-1}$ of them) and all t we get the following bound

$$\begin{aligned}\Pr[\exists \text{"bad" W}] &\leq \sum_{t=1}^{\gamma n} \binom{n}{t-1} \binom{m}{t} \left(\frac{t-1}{n}\right)^{kt} \\ &\leq \sum_{t=1}^{\gamma n} \binom{n}{t} \binom{\alpha n}{t} \left(\frac{t}{n}\right)^{kt} \\ &\leq \left(\frac{ne}{t}\right)^{t} \left(\frac{\alpha n e}{t}\right)^{t} \left(\frac{t}{n}\right)^{kt} \\ &= \sum_{t=1}^{\gamma n} \left(e^2 \alpha \left(\frac{t}{n}\right)^{k-2}\right)^{t} =: \sum_{t=1}^{\gamma n} a_t.\end{aligned}$$

Note that the sum is clearly dominated by the first term ($t = 1$). More precisely we have

$$\begin{aligned}\forall 1 \leq t < \gamma n - 1 \quad \frac{a_{t+1}}{a_t} &= e^2 \alpha \left(\frac{t+1}{t}\right)^{(k-2)t} \left(\frac{t+1}{n}\right)^{k-2} \\ &\leq e^2 \alpha e^{k-2} \gamma^{k-2} =: r < 1,\end{aligned}$$

where for the last inequality we have used the bound on γ. Hence $\sum_{t=1}^{\gamma n} a_t \leq \sum_{t=1}^{\gamma n} a_1 r^{t-1} = \frac{1}{1-r} a_1$, and we get $\Pr[\exists \text{"bad" W}] \leq \frac{1}{1-r} \frac{e^2 \alpha}{n^{k-2}} \to 0$. □

Lemma 22 ($V_{\mathcal{H}}$ is small). *Let G be a hypergraph picked from $G_k(n, \alpha n)$ and let $V_{\mathcal{H}}$ be the set of vertices generated by the procedure in Definition 19 with $D = 2^k/(4 \cdot e \cdot k)$. Then for $k \geq 12$ and $\alpha k \leq D/3$, with high probability $|V_{\mathcal{H}}| \leq (\epsilon_0 + o(1))n$ for some ϵ_0 satisfying $\epsilon_0 < \gamma$ where γ is the constant from Lemma 21.*

Remark: As is standard in the model of random k-SAT and random k-QSAT, if we look at the large k limit we will always first take the limit $n \to \infty$ for fixed k and then $k \to \infty$. Hence we will always treat k (and D and α) as a constant in $O(\cdot)$ and $o(\cdot)$ terms.

PROOF. Throughout the proof we will set α to its maximum allowed value of $D/(3k)$. The statement of Lemma 22 for smaller α then follows by monotonicity.

For the proof of this lemma, we first replace $G_k(n, \alpha n)$ by a slightly different model of random hypergraphs $G'_k(n, \alpha' n)$. In $G'_k(n, \alpha' n)$, we first generate a random sequence of vertices of length $k\alpha' n$ with each vertex picked i.i.d. at random. We then divide the sequence into blocks of length k and, for each block that contains k different vertices, we create a hyperedge. (For blocks that contain the same vertex twice, we do nothing.)

The expected number of blocks containing the same vertex twice is $O(\binom{k}{2}\alpha') = O(1)$. Therefore, we can choose $\alpha' = \alpha + o(1)$ and, with high probability, we will get at least αn edges (and each of those edges will be uniformly random). This means that it suffices to prove the lemma for $G'_k(n, \alpha' n)$.

For this model, we will show that $|V_i|$ satisfies the following bounds:

Claim 23. *There is an $\epsilon_0 < \frac{\gamma}{2}$ and $\epsilon_i := 2^{-i}\epsilon_0$ such that for all $i : 0 \leq i \leq l$ with $l := \lceil \frac{3}{2} \log n \rceil$, with probability at least $1 - \frac{2^i}{n^2}$,*

$$|V_i| \leq \epsilon_i n. \tag{4}$$

This implies that V_l is empty with probability at least $1 - O(\frac{1}{\sqrt{n}})$. In this case, $|V_{\mathcal{H}}| = \sum_{i=0}^{l-1} |V_i|$. With probability at least $1 - \frac{2^{l+1}}{n^2} = 1 - O(\frac{1}{\sqrt{n}})$, (4) is true for all i. Then,

$$|V_{\mathcal{H}}| = \sum_{i=0}^{l-1} |V_i| \leq 2\epsilon_0 n < \gamma n,$$

which completes the proof of the lemma.

In what follows we will repeatedly use Azuma's inequality [4, 23, 3]:

Let $Y_0, \ldots, Y_n$ be a martingale, where $|Y_{i+1} - Y_i| \leq 1$ for all $0 \leq i < n$. For any $t > 0$,

$$\Pr(|X_n - X_0| \geq t) \leq \exp(-\frac{t^2}{2n}). \tag{5}$$

We now prove Claim 23, by induction on i. We start with the base case $i = 0$. Here, we will also bound R_0, the number of edges incident to V_0, and show

$$\Pr[R_0 \geq \epsilon_0 D n] \leq \frac{1}{2n^2}. \tag{6}$$

The $i = 0$ case.

Recall that $V_0 = \{v | \deg(v) \geq D\}$. By linearity of expectation, $E[|V_0|] = n\Pr(\deg(v) \geq D)$. The degree of a vertex is a sum of independent 0-1 valued random variables with expectation slightly less than $\alpha' k$. In the large n limit, this becomes a Poisson distribution with mean $\leq \alpha' k = D/3 + o(1)$. Using the tail bound for Poisson distributions (see, e.g., [3] Thm. A.1.15), we obtain $\Pr(\deg(v) \geq D) \leq (e^2/27)^{D/3}$. Note that for $k \geq 12$ we have $(\frac{e^2}{27})^{D/3} \leq \frac{5}{8}\epsilon_0$, where we set

$$\epsilon_0 = \frac{\alpha'}{12D^2 k} = \frac{D/(3k) + o(1)}{12D^2 k} \leq \frac{1}{12Dk^2} < \frac{\gamma}{2}.$$

Then, $E[|V_0|] \leq \frac{5}{8}\epsilon_0 n$.

To bound $E[R_0]$, observe that $R_0 \leq \sum_{v \in V_0} \deg(v)$ and hence

$$\begin{aligned} E[R_0] &\leq n\Pr(\deg(v) \geq D) \cdot E[\deg(v) | \deg(v) \geq D] \\ &\leq \frac{5}{8}\epsilon_0 n \cdot E[\deg(v) | \deg(v) \geq D] \leq \frac{5}{6}\epsilon_0 n D, \end{aligned}$$

where for the last inequality we have used $E[\deg(v) | \deg(v) \geq D] \leq \frac{4}{3}D$, which follows from the following simple fact:

Fact 24. *Let X be a random variable distributed according to a Poisson distribution with mean λ. Then for $k > 1$, $E[X | X \geq k\lambda] \leq (k+1)\lambda$.*

PROOF.

$$\begin{aligned} E[X | X \geq k\lambda] &= \frac{\sum_{j=k\lambda}^{\infty} j \cdot \Pr(X = j)}{\Pr(X \geq k\lambda)} \\ &= \frac{1}{\Pr(X \geq k\lambda)} \sum_{j=k\lambda}^{\infty} j e^{-\lambda} \frac{\lambda^j}{j!} = \frac{1}{\Pr(X \geq k\lambda)} \lambda \sum_{j=k\lambda}^{\infty} e^{-\lambda} \frac{\lambda^{j-1}}{(j-1)!} \\ &= \lambda \left(1 + \frac{\Pr(X = k\lambda - 1)}{\Pr(X \geq k\lambda)}\right) \leq \lambda \left(1 + \frac{\Pr(X = k\lambda - 1)}{\Pr(X = k\lambda)}\right) \\ &= \lambda \left(1 + \frac{k\lambda}{\lambda}\right) = (1 + k)\lambda. \end{aligned}$$

□

To prove (4) and (6), we use Azuma's inequality Eq. (5). Let $X_0, X_1, \ldots, X_{k\alpha' n}$ be the martingale defined in the following way. We pick the vertices of the sequence defining G at random one by one and let X_i be the expectation of $|V_0|$ (resp. R_0) when the first i vertices of the sequence are already chosen and the rest is still uniformly random. Picking one vertex in any particular way changes the size of $|V_0|$ by at most 1 and of R_0 by at most D (when the degree of a vertex crosses the threshold D to be in V_0). Therefore, for V_0, $|X_i - X_{i-1}| \leq 1$ ($|X_i - X_{i-1}| \leq D$ for the bound on R_0). For V_0, by Azuma's inequality

$$\Pr[||V_0| - E[|V_0|]| \geq t] = \Pr[|X_{k\alpha' n} - X_0| \geq t] \leq e^{-\frac{t^2}{2k\alpha' n}}.$$

To make this probability less than $1/n^2$, we chose

$$t = 2\sqrt{k\alpha'}\sqrt{n \ln n}.$$

Then, with probability at least $1 - \frac{1}{n^2}$, $|V_0| \leq E[|V_0|] + O(\sqrt{n \log n}) \leq \frac{5}{8}\epsilon_0 n + O(\sqrt{n \log n}) \leq \epsilon_0 n$, which gives bound (4). Similarly, to show bound (6) for R_0, we choose

$$t = 2D\sqrt{k\alpha'}\sqrt{n(\ln n + 1)}.$$

Then, we get that with probability at least $1 - \frac{1}{2n^2}$, $R_0 \leq E[R_0] + O(\sqrt{n \log n}) \leq \frac{5}{6}\epsilon_0 n D + O(\sqrt{n \log n}) \leq \epsilon_0 n D$.

The $i > 0$ case.

We will first *condition* on the event $\mathcal{F}$ that bound (6) holds and bounds (4) hold for all previous i. Moreover, we fix the following objects:

- The sets $V_0, \ldots, V_{i-1}$;
- The edges in $E_1, \ldots, E_{i-1}$;
- The degrees of all vertices $v \in V_0 \cup \ldots \cup V_{i-1}$;

Conditioning on $V_0, \ldots, V_{i-1}$ and their degrees is equivalent to fixing the number of times that each $v \in V_0 \cup \ldots \cup V_{i-1}$ appears in the sequence defining the graph G according to $G'_k(n, \alpha' n)$. Furthermore, conditioning on $E_1, \ldots, E_{i-1}$ means that we fix some blocks of the sequence to be equal to edges in $E_1, \ldots, E_{i-1}$. We can then remove those blocks from the sequence and adjust the degrees of the vertices that belong to those edges. Conditioning on $E_1, \ldots, E_{i-1}$ also means that we condition on the fact that there is no other block containing two vertices from $V_0 \cup \ldots \cup V_{i-2}$.

We now consider a random sequence of vertices satisfying those constraints. Let B be the total number of blocks (after removing $E_0, \ldots, E_{i-1}$) and call M_j the number of blocks that contain one element of V_j for $0 \leq j \leq i-1$. (The M_j are fixed since the V_j are fixed.) The sequence of vertices on the B blocks is uniformly random among all sequences with a fixed number of occurrences of elements in V_j (a total of M_j) and such that no two of them occur in the same block. Note that an edge from E_i must have at least one of its vertices in V_{i-1}. We have $M_0 + \ldots + M_{i-2}$ blocks containing one vertex from $V_0 \cup \ldots \cup V_{i-2}$ each. For each of those blocks, the probability that one of the M_{i-1} occurrences of $v \in V_{i-1}$ ends up in it is at most

$$(k-1)\frac{M_{i-1}}{kB - M_0 - \ldots - M_{i-2}}. \tag{7}$$

For any other block, the probability that two or more occurrences of $v \in V_{i-1}$ are in it is at most

$$\begin{aligned}
&\binom{k}{2}\frac{M_{i-1}(M_{i-1}-1)}{(kB - M_0 - \ldots - M_{i-2})(kB - M_0 - \ldots - M_{i-2} - 1)} \\
&\leq \binom{k}{2}\left(\frac{M_{i-1}}{kB - M_0 - \ldots - M_{i-2}}\right)^2. \qquad (8)
\end{aligned}$$

Observe that $E_{j+1} + M_j \leq DV_j$ for $j \geq 1$ since each vertex in V_j is incident to less than D edges. Moreover, $E_1 + M_0 \leq R_0$. Note that this implies that $kB - (M_0 + M_1 + \ldots + M_{i-2}) \geq k\alpha' n - k\left[R_0 + D(V_1 + \ldots + V_{i-2})\right]$. Recall that we are conditioning on the event $\mathcal{F}$ that the bounds in (4) and (6) hold, and hence we can further bound $kB - (M_0 + M_1 + \ldots + M_{i-2}) \geq k\alpha' n - k\left[\epsilon_0 n D + D(\epsilon_1 n + \ldots + \epsilon_{i-2} n)\right] \geq k\alpha' n - 2kD\epsilon_0 n$. For our choice of $\epsilon_0 \leq \frac{\alpha'}{12kD^2}$ we hence obtain

$$kB - (M_0 + \ldots + M_{i-2}) \geq \alpha' \frac{k}{2} n.$$

By combining (7) and (8), using the union bound for all relevant blocks, we get

$$\begin{aligned}
E[|E_i|] &\leq \left((k-1)\frac{M_0 + \ldots + M_{i-2}}{\alpha' \frac{k}{2} n} + \alpha' n \binom{k}{2}\frac{M_{i-1}}{(\alpha' \frac{k}{2} n)^2}\right) M_{i-1} \\
&\leq 2M_{i-1}\left(\frac{M_0 + \ldots + M_{i-1}}{\alpha' n}\right) \\
&\leq 2D^2 V_{i-1}\left(\frac{R_0/D + V_1 + \ldots + V_{i-1}}{\alpha' n}\right).
\end{aligned}$$

Since we are conditioning on the event $\mathcal{F}$ that (4) and (6) hold, we can bound R_0 and V_j and obtain

$$\begin{aligned}
E[|E_i|] &\leq 2D^2 V_{i-1}\left(\frac{\epsilon_0 n + \epsilon_1 n + \ldots + \epsilon_{i-1} n}{\alpha' n}\right) \\
&\leq 2D^2 V_{i-1}\frac{2\epsilon_0}{\alpha'} \leq \frac{V_{i-1}}{3k},
\end{aligned}$$

where we have substituted $\epsilon_0 = \frac{\alpha'}{12D^2 k}$. Together with the observation that $|V_i| \leq k|E_i|$ we have hence shown in our setting that

$$E[|V_i|] \leq V_{i-1}/3. \tag{9}$$

The large deviation bound (4) again follows from Azuma's inequality (5). We pick the sequence of kB vertices (after removing $E_0, \ldots, E_{i-1}$) vertex by vertex and let X_i to be the expectation of $|V_i|$ after picking the i first vertices of the sequence. Then, $X_0, X_1, \ldots, X_{kB}$ form a martingale and choosing one vertex of the sequence affects $|V_i|$ by at most k. Therefore, $|X_i - X_{i-1}| \leq k$ when bounding $|V_i|$. We now apply Azuma's inequality (5) with $t = 2k\sqrt{k\alpha' n(\ln n + 1)}$ and obtain, in our setting of fixed sets V_j, fixed degrees of their elements and fixed sets E_j for $0 \leq j \leq i-1$, and conditioning on the event $\mathcal{F}$,

$$\Pr(||V_i| - E[|V_i|]| \geq O(\sqrt{n \log n})) \leq \frac{1}{2n^2}.$$

Using Eq. (9), the induction hypothesis and the fact that we are conditioning on bound (4) to hold, we get that with probability at least $1 - \frac{1}{2n^2}$,

$$\begin{aligned}
|V_i| &\leq E[|V_i|] + O(\sqrt{n \log n}) \leq \frac{V_{i-1}}{3} + O(\sqrt{n \log n}) \\
&\leq \frac{\epsilon_{i-1} n}{3} + O(\sqrt{n \log n}) \leq \epsilon_i n.
\end{aligned}$$

Since this holds for all fixed sets V_j, fixed degrees of their elements and fixed sets E_j for $0 \leq j \leq i-1$, it also holds when we remove this conditioning (while still conditioning on the event $\mathcal{F}$). By the union bound, $\mathcal{F}$ does not hold with probability at most $\frac{2^i - \frac{1}{2}}{n^2}$. Hence, with probability at least $1 - \frac{2^i}{n^2}$, $V_i \leq \epsilon_i n$ and we have shown the bound in (4). □

This terminates the proof of Lemma 20 for all $k \geq 12$. For smaller values of k our bound of $\alpha \leq 2^k/(12 \cdot e \cdot k^2)$ is smaller than the bound obtained by Laumann et al. [27], and hence the Lemma also holds. Hence we have shown Thm. 6. □

Remark: Note that in the limit of large k our results can be tightened to give a bound of $\alpha \leq (D - O(\sqrt{D \log D}))/k = 2^k/(4 \cdot e \cdot k^2) - O(\sqrt{2^{k/2}}\sqrt{k})$ for the satisfiable region. The analysis essentially changes only for the bound on $E[|V_0|]$ in the beginning of the $i = 0$ base case, where we have to use the tail bound for the Poisson distribution for smaller deviations.

Acknowledgments

The authors would like to thank the Erwin Schrödinger International Institute in Vienna, where part of this work was done, for its hospitality. We thank Noga Alon, Chris Laumann and Oded Regev for valuable discussions.

5. REFERENCES

[1] D. Achlioptas and Y. Peres. The threshold for random k-sat is $2^k \ln 2 - O(k)$. *American Mathematical Society*, 17(4):947–974, 2004.

[2] N. Alon. A parallel algorithmic version of the local lemma. *Random Structures and Algorithms*, 2(4):367–378, 1991.

[3] N. Alon and J.H. Spencer. *The probabilistic method.* Wiley-Interscience, 2004.

[4] K. Azuma. Weighted sums of certain dependent random variables. *Tohoku Mathematical Journal*, 19(3):357–367, 1967.

[5] J. Beck. An algorithmic approach to the Lovász local lemma. *Random Structures and Algorithms*, 2(4):343–365, 1991.

[6] S. Beigi and P.W. Shor. On the complexity of computing Zero-Error and Holevo capacity of quantum channels. *Arxiv preprint arXiv:0709.2090*, 2007.

[7] B. Bollobás. *Random Graphs.* Cambridge University Press, 2nd edition, 2001.

[8] B. Bollobás, C. Borgs, J.T. Chayes, J.H. Kim, and D.B. Wilson. The scaling window of the 2-SAT transition. *Random Structures and Algorithms*, 18(3):201–256, 2001.

[9] S. Bravyi. Efficient algorithm for a quantum analogue of 2-SAT. *Arxiv preprint quant-ph/0602108*, 2006.

[10] S. Bravyi, C. Moore, and A. Russell. Bounds on the quantum satisfibility threshold. *Innovations in Computer Science*, pages 482–489, 2010.

[11] S. Bravyi and B. Terhal. Complexity of stoquastic frustration-free hamiltonians. *Arxiv preprint arXiv:0806.1746*, 2008.

[12] V. Chvátal and B. Reed. Mick gets some (the odds are on his side). In *Proceedings of the 33rd Annual Symposium on Foundations of Computer Science*, pages 620–627, 1992.

[13] A. Czumaj and C. Scheideler. Coloring non-uniform hypergraphs: A new algorithmic approach to the general Lovász local lemma. In *Proceedings of the 11th Symposium on Discrete Algorithms*, pages 30—39, 2000.

[14] J. Diaz, L. Kirousis, D. Mitsche, and X. Perez-Gimenez. A new upper bound for 3-sat. In *Proceedings of IARCS Annual Conference on Foundations of Software Technology and Theoretical Computer Science*, pages 163–174, 2008.

[15] R. Diestel. *Graph Theory (Graduate Texts in Mathematics).* Springer Heidelberg, 1997.

[16] P. Erdős and L. Lovász. Problems and results on 3-chromatic hypergraphs and some related questions. *Infinite and finite sets*, 2:609–627, 1975.

[17] U. Feige. Relations between average case complexity and approximation complexity. In *Proceedings of the 34th Annual ACM Symposium on Theory of Computing*, pages 534–543, 2002.

[18] L. Fortnow. A Kolmogorov Complexity Proof of the Lovász Local Lemma. `http://bit.ly/AsHlm`, 2009.

[19] E. Friedgut. Sharp thresholds of graph properties, and the k-Sat problem. *Journal of the American Mathematical Society*, 12(4):1017–1054, 1999.

[20] A. Goerdt. A threshold for unsatisfiability. In *Mathematical Foundations of Computer Science 1992*, pages 264–274. 1992.

[21] M.T. Hajiaghayi and G.B. Sorkin. The satisfiability threshold of random 3-SAT is at least 3.52. *Arxiv preprint math/0310193*, 2003.

[22] P. Hall. On representatives of subsets. *J. London Math. Soc*, 10(1):26–30, 1935.

[23] W. Hoeffding. Probability inequalities for sums of bounded random variables. *Journal of the American Statistical Association*, pages 13–30, 1963.

[24] A.C. Kaporis, L.M. Kirousis, and E. Lalas. Selecting complementary pairs of literals. *Electronic Notes in Discrete Mathematics*, 16:47–70, 2003.

[25] S. Kirkpatrick and B. Selman. Critical behavior in the satisfiability of random boolean expressions. *Science*, 264(5163):1297–1301, 1994.

[26] A.I. Kostrikin. *Linear algebra and geometry.* Taylor & Francis, 1997.

[27] C.R. Laumann, A.M. Läuchli, R. Moessner, A. Scardicchio, and S. L Sondhi. On product, generic and random generic quantum satisfiability. *Arxiv preprint arXiv:0910.2058*, 2009.

[28] C.R. Laumann, R. Moessner, A. Scardicchio, and S.L. Sondhi. Phase transitions and random quantum satisfiability. *Arxiv preprint arXiv:0903.1904*, 2009.

[29] Y.K. Liu. Consistency of local density matrices is QMA-Complete. In *Approximation, Randomization, and Combinatorial Optimization. Algorithms and Techniques*, pages 438–449. 2006.

[30] Y.K. Liu. The complexity of the consistency and n-representability problems for quantum states. *Arxiv preprint arXiv:0712.3041*, 2007.

[31] P. Mani-Levitska and J. Pach. Decomposition problems for multiple coverings with unit balls. *Manuscript*, 1987.

[32] M. Mézard, T. Mora, and R. Zecchina. Clustering of solutions in the random satisfiability problem. *Physical Review Letters*, 94(19):197205, 2005.

[33] M. Mezard, G. Parisi, and R. Zecchina. Analytic and algorithmic solution of random satisfiability problems. *Science*, 297(5582):812–815, 2002.

[34] M. Molloy and B. Reed. Further algorithmic aspects of the local lemma. In *Proceedings of the 30th Annual ACM Symposium on Theory of Computing*, pages 524—529, 1998.

[35] R.A. Moser. Derandomizing the Lovász local lemma more effectively. *Arxiv preprint arXiv:0807.2120*, 2008.

[36] R.A. Moser. A constructive proof of the Lovász Local Lemma. In *Proceedings of the 41th Annual ACM Symposium on Theory of Computing*, pages 343–350, 2009.

[37] R.A. Moser and G. Tardos. A constructive proof of the general Lovász Local Lemma. *Journal of the ACM*, 57(2):1–15, 2010.

[38] J. Spencer. Asymptotic lower bounds for Ramsey functions. *Discrete Math*, 20(1):69–76, 1977.

[39] A. Srinivasan. Improved algorithmic versions of the Lovász local lemma. In *Proceedings of the 19th Symposium on Discrete Algorithms*, pages 611–620, 2008.

Near-Optimal Extractors Against Quantum Storage

Anindya De*
Computer Science Division
University of California, Berkeley
USA
anindya@cs.berkeley.edu

Thomas Vidick†
Computer Science Division
University of California, Berkeley
USA
vidick@cs.berkeley.edu

ABSTRACT

We show that Trevisan's extractor and its variants [22, 19] are secure against bounded quantum storage adversaries. One instantiation gives the first such extractor to achieve an output length $\Theta(K - b)$, where K is the source's entropy and b the adversary's storage, together with a polylogarithmic seed length. Another instantiation achieves a logarithmic key length, with a slightly smaller output length $\Theta((K-b)/K^{\gamma})$ for any $\gamma > 0$. In contrast, the previous best construction [21] could only extract $(K/b)^{1/15}$ bits. Some of our constructions have the additional advantage that every bit of the output is a function of only a polylogarithmic number of bits from the source, which is crucial for some cryptographic applications.

Our argument is based on bounds for a generalization of quantum random access codes, which we call *quantum functional access codes*. This is crucial as it lets us avoid the local list-decoding algorithm central to the approach in [21], which was the source of the multiplicative overhead.

Categories and Subject Descriptors

F.0 [**Theory of Computation**]: General

General Terms

Theory

Keywords

Extractors, Bounded Quantum Storage, Random Access Codes

---

*Supported by the "Berkeley Fellowship for Graduate Study" and Luca Trevisan's US-Israel BSF grant 2006060.

†Supported by ARO grant W911NF-09-1-0440 and NSF grant CCF-0905626.

STOC'10, June 5–8, 2010, Cambridge, Massachusetts, USA.

1. INTRODUCTION

Randomness extractors are fundamental building blocks in pseudorandomness theory, with many applications to derandomization, error-correcting codes, and expanders, among others. They are also of central importance in cryptography, where they are often used to build key generation primitives. In this context, one usually has the notion of an adversary, a malicious observer who is trying to discover a bit of the honest player's output. A prominent model for adversaries is the bounded storage model, introduced by Maurer [16], in which the adversary is allowed to store a limited amount of information about the extractor's input.

Formally, we say that a function $\mathrm{Ext} : \{0,1\}^N \times \{0,1\}^t \to \{0,1\}^m$ is a (K, ε) strong extractor if for every distribution X with min-entropy at least K (X is called the *source*) and uniformly random Y (called the *seed*), the distribution $(Y, \mathrm{Ext}(X, Y))$ is within a statistical distance of at most ε from the uniform distribution. The extractor is said to be secure against b bits of storage if $Ext(X,Y)$ is ε-close to uniform even from the point of view of an adversary who has been allowed to store b bits of information about X, and has also later been revealed the seed Y.

Constructions of extractors are known that are almost-optimal in all parameters, even in the presence of the adversary (in fact, a result by Lu [15] shows that any (K, ε) strong extractor is essentially a $(K + b, \varepsilon)$ extractor secure against b bits of storage). Nevertheless, in a world in which no adversary can be trusted, König *et al.* [13] introduced the following interesting twist: what if the adversary is allowed *quantum* memory? In this setting, the fundamental difficulty that arises is a familiar one, with a long history: how much information can be encoded in a quantum state?

The fact that this question can admit very different answers depending on its precise formulation is reflected in the fact that some, but not all, classical extractor constructions are secure in the presence of a quantum adversary, as was demonstrated in [8]. While many constructions have been shown to be sound on a case-by-case basis [13, 14, 7, 21], all have parameters that are far from optimal either in terms of seed length or of output length.

Central to the proof of our result are bounds on a construct which we call quantum functional access codes (QFAC), and we introduce them next.

Quantum functional access codes.

Holevo [11] was the first to tackle the question of the information capacity of a quantum state, showing that one needs at least n qubits in order to encode n bits of information.

However, this bound only holds when it is required that the whole n bits be recoverable from the quantum storage. As such, it is generally not applicable in a cryptographic context, where typically even partial information is important. Instead of asking for the whole input $x \in \{0,1\}^n$ to be recoverable from its encoding $\Psi(x)$, Ambainis *et al.* [1] consider encodings in which it is only required that any bit of x can be recovered from $\Psi(x)$ with probability $1/2 + \varepsilon$ (over the measurement's randomness), and they call such encodings 'random access codes' (RACs). Note that, since the encoding is quantum, the recoverability of any one bit does not imply the recoverability of the whole string x, so that Holevo's bound does not apply. Nevertheless, Ambainis *et al.* showed that RACs require essentially $(1 - H(1/2 + \varepsilon))n$ qubits to encode n bits, where H is the binary entropy function, providing a linear lower bound for fixed ε. These bounds have proved instrumental in many results in information theory. In fact, as pointed out in [21], random access codes provide a way to construct one-bit extractors that are secure against quantum storage.

We push this question even further: what if, instead of asking that the encoding lets us recover any bit of the input, we asked that it lets us recover any one function of the input out of some fixed set of functions of the input? For example, we could ask about encodings that let us recover the XOR of any k bits of the input[1], but one can also consider more general settings.

One might ask about the relevance of such encodings, when we already know that there are strong linear lower bounds on RACs — surely, these will extend to any encoding which lets us recover more than any single bit of the input. The key point here is that, even though both Holevo's bound and the RAC lower bounds are linear in the input length when the success probability p is fixed, the two bounds scale very differently when one considers the dependence on p: while an improvement on Holevo's lower bound, due to Nayak and Salzman [17], scales as $n - \log 1/p$, the RAC bound scales as $(4\varepsilon^2/\ln 2)n$ for small $\varepsilon = 2p - 1$. So we are asking, how does the minimal length of the code scale with the success probability, depending on the set of functions that we are trying to recover?

Define a (n, b, ε) QFAC for a set of n-bit strings A and a set of functions $\mathcal{C}$ from A to $\{0,1\}$ as a b-qubit encoding of strings $x \in A$ such that, for any function $f \in \mathcal{C}$, one can recover $f(x)$ from the encoding of x with success probability $1/2 + \varepsilon$.[2] Intuitively, the more the set of functions $\mathcal{C}$ is error resilient (i.e., the more spread-out the images $(f(x))_{f\in\mathcal{C}} \in \{0,1\}^{|\mathcal{C}|}$), the stronger the lower bound should be on the length of the encoding. For example, using a simple reduction to known results we can show that any (n, b, ε) QFAC for the set $\mathcal{C} = \{f_y : x \mapsto x \cdot y \mod 2,\ y \in \{0,1\}^n\}$ must have length $b \geq n - \log 1/\varepsilon$. If one simply used the fact that any bit of x can be recovered from such a QFAC with probability $1/2 + \varepsilon$, the resulting bound would be the much weaker $O(\varepsilon^2 n)$.

We believe that QFACs constitute a primitive that should be of wide interest in studying the properties of quantum states from an information-theoretic point of view. In this paper, we demonstrate the relevance of this construct by showing how good bounds on some QFACs can be used to prove the security of an extractor against quantum storage with almost-optimal parameters. In fact, many previous constructions of extractors against quantum storage can be seen as implicitly proving bounds on QFACs. For example, the construction in [13] shows that any (n, b, ε) QFAC for a set of 2-universal hashing functions must have length $b \geq n - 2\log 1/2\varepsilon$.

Techniques.

In this section we give an overview of our proof technique, explaining the connection between extractors and QFACs in the context of Trevisan's general construction paradigm [22]. To describe this, let us first give a brief overview of the main steps that go into the proof of the construction by Ta-Shma [21].

The construction starts by encoding the weakly random source $x \sim X$ using a locally list-decodable code C [20]. This is followed by an application of the Nisan-Wigderson generator [18], interpreting $C(x)$ as the truth table of the "hard" function.

The proof of correctness for this construction, as the first part of ours, follows the general reconstruction framework of [22]. For the sake of contradiction, assume that there is a test T, which performs a measurement on the adversary's quantum encoding $\Psi(x)$ in order to distinguish the output from uniform with advantage ε. A Markov argument shows that for at least an $\varepsilon/2$ fraction of the samplings x from the source (call them bad samplings), T can distinguish the output (when the source is x) from uniform with success at least $\varepsilon/2$. Consider any such bad sampling x. A standard hybrid argument, along with properties of the Nisan-Wigderson generator, allows us to construct a circuit T' (using little non-uniformity about x) which predicts a random position of $C(x)$ with probability $\frac{1}{2} + \frac{\varepsilon}{m}$. Further, T' makes exactly one query to T.

At this stage, we have constructed a small circuit T', which uses the adversary's quantum information in order to predict the bits of $C(x)$ with some small success probability. The proof in [21] shows how from such a circuit, one can construct another circuit which predicts any position of x with probability 0.99 and queries T' at most $q = (m/\varepsilon)^c$ times ($c = 15$ for the code in [21]). This gives a random access code for x; however since it makes q measurements on the quantum state $\Psi(x)$, the no-cloning theorem forces us to see it as having a length of $q \cdot b$ qubits. The main drawback of this method is that the quantum state needs to be copied a large number of times in order to get a RAC – thus yielding a weaker bound on the output length than one might hope for.

Our proof departs fundamentally from the usual reconstruction paradigm at this point: instead of using a short RAC for $C(x)$ to construct a longer RAC for x, we give a direct analytical argument showing that any RAC for $C(x)$ must be long. Note that a RAC for $C(x)$ is simply a QFAC for the class of functions $f_i : x \mapsto C(x)_i$. Intuitively, such a QFAC cannot be short, even though its success probability $1/2 + \varepsilon/m$ is small. If the QFAC is classical (CFAC), this is easy to show: assume that there existed a short CFAC for this problem. One can just repeat the recovery procedure to get a string y that agrees with $C(x)$ at a fraction $1/2 + \varepsilon/m$ of positions, and then one can use the good list-decoding properties of C to argue that the CFAC essentially lets us

[1]Such codes were introduced in [2], where they are called XOR-QRACs

[2]A RAC is then simply a QFAC for the set of coordinate functions $f_i : x \mapsto x_i$.

recover the whole input x, and hence must be long. In the quantum setting, however, it is far from obvious if this is true, the primary difficulty being that we cannot repeat the recovery procedure, since it involves measuring a quantum state.

In order to overcome this difficulty, we directly prove a lower bound on the length of the QFAC derived from the code. This lets us derive a contradiction, proving that our extractor is safe against quantum storage. The idea for the lower bound consists in seeing any good QFAC as an adversary which uses small memory, and is able to predict codeword positions. Using the fact that list decodable codes can be interpreted as one-bit strong extractors, we can then use a a result by Koenig and Terhal [14] to show that such an adversary would imply a classical adversary with similar storage against a one-bit strong extractor, which we know does not exist. This leads to a contradiction, thus proving the lower bound.

Our results.

We show that any extractor based on Trevisan's construction paradigm and its variants [22, 19] is also safe against a bounded quantum storage adversary, with almost the same parameters as the classical construction. Rather than give the full technical result here (see Theorem 4.5), we discuss instantiations with two specific codes.

We first use a code from [9], which is obtained through the concatenation of the Reed-Solomon code and the Hadamard code. This lets us prove the following:

THEOREM 1.1. *For any constants $\gamma, c, c' > 0$, there is a polynomial-time computable function $Ext : \{0,1\}^N \times \{0,1\}^t \to \{0,1\}^m$, where $t = O(\log N)$ and $m = \Omega\left(\frac{K-b}{K^\gamma}\right)$, which is a (K, N^{-c}) extractor against b qubits of quantum storage, for any $K \geq N^{c'}$.*

We note that the construction in [21] uses the concatenation of a Reed-Muller code with the Hadamard code, the parameters of the Reed-Muller code being chosen so that one can do local list-decoding. In contrast, our analysis just needs a good list-decoding radius, but no local list-decoding property. Hence our result carries over to [21] and in particular implies that the construction in [21] has much better output length than the one shown in that paper, which was $\Omega((K/b)^{1/15})$.

This first construction does not have the desirable property of *local computability.* By using a different code, we can also show the following:

THEOREM 1.2. *For any constants $\alpha, c > 0$, there is a function $Ext : \{0,1\}^N \times \{0,1\}^t \to \{0,1\}^m$, where $t = O(\log^4 N)$ and $m = \Omega(\alpha N - b)$, which is a $(\alpha N, N^{-c})$ extractor against b qubits of quantum storage. Moreover, each bit output by the extractor is computable in* $\text{poly}\log N$ *time.*

Even though it has a slightly larger seed length (note however that its output length is the optimal $\Theta(\alpha N - b)$), a major advantage of this extractor is its simplicity: each bit of the output is simply the XOR of $O(\log N)$ bits of the source, chosen based on the seed. In particular, it is locally computable[3]. On the other hand, that construction is restricted to extracting from linear entropy rates. This is inevitable, as lower bounds by Viola [24] show that locally computable extractors cannot extract from sources with entropy less than $N^{0.99}$ using a polylogarithmic seed length.

[3]For this to hold, we also need to check that the bits to be XOR-ed can be chosen in poly-logarithmic time, which is the case in this construction.

The QFACs at the heart of this second construction are in fact the XOR-QRACs from [2]. A by-product of our proof is an improvement of the lower bound proved in that paper on the length of such codes (see Corollary 3.10).

A nice side feature of both these constructions, especially if one is interested in cryptographic applications, is that it is possible to achieve an arbitrary inverse polynomial statistical distance from the uniform distribution, while paying only a polylogarithmic cost in terms of output length and seed length (this will be apparent from the more detailed statement of Theorem 1.1 given in Section 4). This property was not known to hold for previous short seed extractor constructions against quantum storage.

Applications to cryptography.

Our results are of direct applicability to the following key expansion scenario. Alice and Bob share a small secret uniformly random key k. They would like to expand it into a longer key k' in order to securely communicate in presence of an adversary Eve. A public source of weak randomness R (assume that R has min-entropy at least K) is available to all parties. When the string R is broadcast, Eve is allowed to compute an arbitrary function Ψ which maps the input to a state on b qubits *i.e.*, $\Psi : \{0,1\}^{|R|} \to \mathbb{C}^{2^b \times 2^b}$ and store the result. However, once she stores $\Psi(R)$, her access to R is cut off. The goal is to come up with an efficient function Ext which can be used by Alice and Bob to compute the shared string $k' = Ext(R, k)$. The required security condition is that k' is close to being uniformly random to Eve, even given her knowledge of $\Psi(R)$. In fact, we would like k' to remain random even if k is later revealed to Eve (after $\Psi(R)$ is computed and access to R has been cut off).

For this application, it is important that Ext be *locally computable*, i.e. individual bits of the output should be a function of a polylogarithmic number of bits of the source R. Indeed, since we are putting a cap on the adversary's storage it would be unreasonable not to put a similar cap on the memory used by the honest parties Alice and Bob to compute bits of their shared key.

Our second construction has the property of being locally computable: every bit of the output is a function of polylogarithmically many bits from the source. While various constructions of classical locally computable extractors are already known [6, 15, 23, 5], ours are the first to be proved secure against quantum adversaries. This makes them particularly suitable for use in the context of bounded storage cryptography.

We note here that the results in this paper have recently been extended by Portmann, Renner, and the authors to show that Trevisan's extractor is secure in a broader context than that of the bounded-storage model [4]: they show security when one has a lower bound on the *conditional min-entropy* of the source, conditioned on the adversary's quantum information. This is a more general assumption since it is implied by the bounded storage assumption, but the converse is not true in general. Proving security in this setting is crucial in a cryptographic context, as it allows secure composability of the extractor with other cryptographic primitives.

Organization of the paper.

We start with some preliminaries in Section 2. In Section 3 we introduce quantum functional access codes and give bounds for some specific families of these codes. In Section 4 we describe our construction and state its parameters. Finally, the proof of security is given in Section 5.

2. NOTATION AND PRELIMINARIES

The following notations are used throughout the paper. For $x \in \{0,1\}^n$, x_i denotes the ith bit of x. Given two n-bit strings x, y, we let $\Delta(x,y)$ denote their relative Hamming distance, i.e. the fraction of positions at which they differ. $\mathcal{D}_b$ denotes the set of all density matrices on b qubits (complex 2^b-dimensional positive matrices with trace 1). In general, a measurement M is described by a list of positive operators M_a such that $\sum_a M_a^\dagger M_a = Id$. The probability that outcome a is observed when the measurement is performed on a density matrix ρ is then given by $\mathrm{Tr}(M_a \rho M_a^\dagger)$. All logarithms are taken in base 2. Throughout, H will denote the binary entropy function $H(x) = -x \log x - (1-x)\log(1-x)$ for $0 < x < 1$. We set the convention that $H(0) = H(1) = 0$.

Distributions.

The uniform distribution on $\{0,1\}^n$ is denoted by U_n. We will manipulate random variables that have both classical and quantum parts. In general, given two classical random variables X, Y, $X \circ Y$ is the same as the random variable (X, Y). Given two states ρ, σ, $\rho \circ \sigma$ is just $\rho \otimes \sigma$. Finally, given a classical random variable $X : \Omega \to \{0,1\}^n$ and a quantum variable $\rho : \Omega \to \mathcal{D}_b$, $X \circ \rho$ denotes the state $\mathbb{E}_{w \in \Omega}[|X(w)\rangle\langle X(w)| \otimes \rho(w)]$. The statistical distance between two distributions D_1 and D_2 (or, more generally, the trace distance when these distributions involve quantum components) is denoted by $\|D_1 - D_2\|$.

DEFINITION 2.1. *A (classical) distribution X is said to have min-entropy at least K (denoted $H_\infty(X) \geq K$) if $\forall x$, $Pr[X = x] \leq 2^{-K}$.*

Extractors.

We first give the the formal definition of a strong extractor.

DEFINITION 2.2. *$Ext : \{0,1\}^N \times \{0,1\}^t \to \{0,1\}^m$ is said to be a (K, ε) strong extractor if for every distribution X with min-entropy at least K, we have that $\|U_{m+t} - Ext(X, U_t) \circ U_t\| \leq \varepsilon$. Here both U_t's in the second expression correspond to the same sampling.*

X is usually called the source *(and N its length), while the extractor's second input is called the* seed *(of length t).*

We now extend this definition to that of a strong extractor secure against a bounded-storage quantum adversary.

DEFINITION 2.3. *$Ext : \{0,1\}^N \times \{0,1\}^t \to \{0,1\}^m$ is said to be a (K, ε) strong extractor against b qubits of quantum storage if for every map $\Psi : \{0,1\}^N \to \mathcal{D}_b$ and every distribution X such that $H_\infty(X) \geq K$*

$$\|U_m \circ \Psi(X) \circ U_t - Ext(X, U_t) \circ \Psi(X) \circ U_t\| \leq \varepsilon \qquad (1)$$

where both U_t's in the second expression correspond to the same sampling.

We note that condition (1) above is equivalent to requiring that for any collection of measurements $\{M^0_{u,y}, M^1_{u,y}\}$ on $\mathcal{D}_b$,

$$\Big|\mathbb{E}_{x \sim X, y \sim U_t}\Big[\mathrm{Tr}\Big(\mathbb{E}_{u \in \{0,1\}^m}\Big[M^1_{u,y}\Psi(x)(M^1_{u,y})^\dagger\Big]\Big) - \mathrm{Tr}\Big(M^1_{Ext(x,y),y}\Psi(x)(M^1_{Ext(x,y),y})^\dagger\Big)\Big]\Big| \leq \varepsilon$$

Quantum codes.

A (n, b) quantum encoding is a map $\Psi : \{0,1\}^n \to \mathcal{D}_b$. A fundamental theorem due to Holevo states that, for any fixed measurement M, the outcome of that measurement when performed on $\Psi(x)$ cannot contain more information about x than a classical string of b bits:

THEOREM 2.4. *[11] Let X be any distribution on $\{0,1\}^n$ and $\Psi(X) = \mathbb{E}_{x \in X}[\Psi(x)]$. For a particular measurement M, let Y_M denote the classical random variable resulting from applying the measurement on $\Psi(X)$. If $I(X : Y)$ denotes the mutual information of X and Y and $S(\Psi(X))$ denotes the von Neumann entropy of $\Psi(X)$, then $I(X : Y) \leq S(\Psi(X))$.*

Oracle circuits.

Our proofs of security will involve the construction of oracle circuits. If A is an oracle circuit, we denote by A^B the circuit that uses B as the oracle. Further, let C be an oracle machine which uses A as an oracle (denoted by C^A). Then it is understood that when C calls A, then A calls the appropriate oracle B. Thus $C^A \equiv C^{A^B}$. We will say that a circuit $C : \{0,1\}^{n+t} \to \{0,1\}$ computes a function f with t bits of advice if there is a string $a \in \{0,1\}^t$ such that for every $x \in \{0,1\}^n$, $C(x, a) = f(x)$.

We will use the following easy claim:

CLAIM 2.5. *Let B be any oracle such that oracle circuit A can be constructed using at most t_1 bits of advice and A queries B at most q_1 times. Again let C be an oracle circuit which queries A and C can be constructed using at most t_2 bits of advice. Further, C queries A at most q_2 times. Then C can be considered as an oracle circuit which queries B at most $q_1 q_2$ times and can be constructed using at most $t_1 + t_2$ bits of advice.*

3. QUANTUM FUNCTIONAL ACCESS CODES

Consider the following problem from the theory of error-correcting codes. Let $C : \{0,1\}^n \to \{0,1\}^m$ be a code which is (ε, L) list-decodable i.e. for any $x \in \{0,1\}^m$, there are at most L codewords y such that $\Delta(x,y) \leq \frac{1}{2} - \varepsilon$. Let $A = \{C(x) : x \in \{0,1\}^n\}$ be the set of all codewords, and consider $Enc : A \to \{0,1\}^b$, a probabilistic encoding such that for every $z \in A$, z_i can be recovered from $Enc(z)$ with probability $\frac{1}{2} + 2\varepsilon$, on average over the choice of $i \in [m]$. Given $Enc(z)$, by performing the recovery procedure for every index i, we obtain a string y which will agrees with z on at least a $\frac{1}{2} + \varepsilon$ fraction of the positions with high probability. But then the exact element z can be recovered using just an additional $\log |L|$ bits of advice (as per the list-decodability property of C). Hence, Enc can be seen as a high-probability encoding of any codeword, using only $b + \log |L|$ bits. However, the obvious information-theoretic bound shows that this must be at least $\log |C|$ bits, implying that $b \geq \log \frac{|C|}{|L|}$. This is much better than the bound $b \geq O(\varepsilon^2 \log |C| / \log n)$, for small ε, that one gets if there is no guarantee on the structure of the set C (see Theorem 3.2 in [21] for a proof).

To model this situation more precisely, note that the recovery procedure lets us recover any bit of $C(x)$ with non-trivial probability. As such, *Enc* can be seen as a probabilistic encoding of every $x \in \{0,1\}^n$ which lets us evaluate a class of functions $\mathcal{C} = \{g_i : x \mapsto C(x)_i,\ i \in [n]\}$. This is a generalization of the usual random access codes, introduced in [1], for which $\mathcal{C} = \mathcal{C}_1 = \{g_i : x \mapsto x_i,\ i \in [n]\}$.

It is natural to expect that lower bounds for this more demanding kind of random access code would be tighter than more general lower bounds, in a way that depends on the structure of $\mathcal{C}$. We introduce the following definition:

DEFINITION 3.1. *Let $A \subset \{0,1\}^n$, and $\mathcal{C} \subset \{f : A \to \{0,1\}\}$ a set of functions defined on A. For $\varepsilon \in (0, 1/2]$, a (n, b, ε) quantum functional access code, or QFAC, for $(A, \mathcal{C})$ is a map $\Psi : A \to \mathcal{D}_b$ such that, for every $f \in \mathcal{C}$, there is a measurement $M_f = \{M_f^0, M_f^1\}$ such that for every $x \in A$, $Tr(M_f^{f(x)} \Psi(x) (M_f^{f(x)})^\dagger) \geq 1/2 + \varepsilon$. If this first property only holds on average over the choice of f, then we'll say that Ψ is a (n, b, ε) QFAC* on average *for $(A, \mathcal{C})$.*

The discussion above shows a strong lower bound on the length of any *classical* functional access code for a set of functions $\mathcal{C} = \{g_i : x \mapsto C(x)_i,\ i \in [n]\}$ that is derived from a good list-decodable code C. However, the classical argument cannot be extended in a straightforward manner to the quantum case, as it is dependent upon performing successive measurements on the encoding. If the encoding is quantum, the first such measurement will destroy the state, and we will not be able to proceed further.

Nevertheless, for some specific cases, such bounds follow from previously known results. We start with the standard setting of random access codes, for which Theorem 4.1 in [1] implies the following (see also Theorem 3.2 in [21]):

LEMMA 3.2. *Let $A \subseteq \{0,1\}^n$ and $\varepsilon \in (0, 1/2]$ such that there exists a (n, b, ε) quantum functional access code for $(A, \mathcal{C}_1)$. Then $\log |A| \leq O\left(\frac{b \log n}{\varepsilon^2}\right)$.*[4]

Central to this work is the fact that functional access codes for larger classes of functions than the simple coordinate functions $\mathcal{C}_1$ enjoy much stronger lower bounds, with a weaker dependence on the success probability ε. König, Maurer and Renner [13] show the following:

THEOREM 3.3 ([13], THM. 12 AND COR. 13). *Let $\mathcal{C}$ be the set of all functions from $\{0,1\}^n$ to $\{0,1\}$. Then any (n, b, ε) QFAC on average for $(A, \mathcal{C})$ satisfies $\log |A| \leq b + 2 \log 1/2\varepsilon$. Moreover, the same bound holds if $\mathcal{C}$ is any family of two-universal hash functions, and the decoding procedure is only required to be correct on average over the choice of $x \in A$.*

[4]As noted in [21], the loss of a factor $\log n$ is inevitable. Note however that this can be removed in the case where $A = \{0,1\}^n$ by following the proof for quantum random access codes in [1].

There is an obvious connection between lower bounds on the length of QFACs and lower bounds on one-way quantum communication complexity, even though results in the latter setting usually do not focus on the error dependence as much as is needed for our applications. Nevertheless, the following bound easily follows from known results:

LEMMA 3.4. *Let $\mathcal{C} = \{g_y : x \mapsto x \cdot y \mod 2,\ y \in \{0,1\}^n\}$. If there exists a (n, b, ε) QFAC for $(A, \mathcal{C})$, then $\log |A| \leq b + 2 \log(1/2\varepsilon)$.*

PROOF. Note that any (n, b, ε) QFAC for $(A, \mathcal{C})$ implies a one-way quantum protocol for the communication problem in which Alice is given $x \in A$, Bob is given $y \in \{0,1\}^n$, and their goal is to output $x \cdot y \mod 2$. Using a reduction from [3], any such protocol communicating b qubits and succeeding with probability $1/2 + \varepsilon$ can be transformed into a protocol that sends any $x \in A$ to Bob, using b qubits, with success probability $4\varepsilon^2$. Theorem 1.1 in [17] then shows that $b \geq \log |A| - \log(1/4\varepsilon^2)$. □

Families of two-universal hash functions over $\{0,1\}^n$, as well as the Hadamard code, both have size $\Omega(2^n)$, which makes them unsuitable for our purposes. Indeed, in our applications to extractors we will use the seed to select a few random functions from the family $\mathcal{C}$ and apply them to the source in order to obtain the output. However, using any of the last two function families would require a seed of length linear in the source length, whereas we would like it to be poly-logarithmic.

Our main result relies on the fact, proved below, that there are no short QFACs for families of functions that are defined from list-decodable codes. This extends the discussion introducing this section to the case of quantum encodings, and in fact we will get essentially the same bound as stated there — even though, as we argued was necessary, the proof will be very different. It will be useful to consider *approximately* list-decodable codes, which we define as follows:

DEFINITION 3.5. *Let $\varepsilon, \delta > 0$ and $L \in \mathbb{N}$. A code $C : \{0,1\}^N \to \{0,1\}^{\overline{N}}$ is (ε, δ, L) approximately list-decodable if for every $x \in \{0,1\}^{\overline{N}}$, there exists at most L strings $\{y_i\}_{i=1}^L \in \{0,1\}^N$, such that for any string $z \in \{0,1\}^N$ satisfying $\Delta(x, C(z)) < 1/2 - \varepsilon$, $\exists i \in \{1, \ldots, L\}$ such that $\Delta(z, y_i) \leq \delta$. If C is $(\varepsilon, 0, L)$ approximately-list decodable then we simply say that C is (ε, L) list-decodable.*

PROPOSITION 3.6. *Let $\varepsilon, \delta > 0$ and $L \in \mathbb{N}$. Let $C : \{0,1\}^N \to \{0,1\}^{\overline{N}}$ be a $(\varepsilon/2, \delta, L)$ approximately list-decodable code, and $\mathcal{C} = \{f_i : x \mapsto C(x)_i,\ i \in [\overline{N}]\}$. Let $A \subseteq \{0,1\}^N$, and suppose that there exists a (N, b, ε) QFAC on average for $(A, \mathcal{C})$. Then*

$$\log |A| < H(\delta) N + b + \log L + O(\log 1/\varepsilon)$$

Moreover, this bound holds even when we only require the QFAC to have success probability $1/2 + \varepsilon$ on average over the choice of $x \in A$, instead of for all x.

The proof crucially relies on the result by König and Terhal [14] that strong one-bit extractors are automatically safe against quantum adversaries, in some range of parameters. It proceeds through the following three steps:

1. Show that any (ε, δ, L) approximately list-decodable code C defines a good 1-bit classical strong extractor.

2. Use Theorem III.1 from [14] to show that the previous extractor is automatically safe against quantum adversaries that are allowed a bounded amount of storage.

3. Conclude by showing how the security against quantum storage implies a lower bound on any QFAC on average for $(A, \mathcal{C})$.

We proceed with the details.

PROOF. Let $t = \log \overline{N}$ (assume it an integer for simplicity) and consider the following 1-bit extractor

$$\begin{aligned} E: \{0,1\}^N \times \{0,1\}^t &\to \{0,1\} \\ (x,y) &\mapsto C(x)_y \end{aligned}$$

The following claim proves item 1 above.

CLAIM 3.7. *$E : \{0,1\}^N \times \{0,1\}^t \to \{0,1\}$ as defined above is a (K,ε) strong extractor for any $K > H(\delta)N + \log L + \log \frac{2}{\varepsilon}$.*

PROOF. Assume for the sake of contradiction that E is not a (K,ε) strong extractor. Then there is a distribution D with min-entropy K, and a statistical test T such that the following holds.

$$|\mathop{\mathbb{P}}_{y\sim U_t, x\sim D}[T(y) = C(x)_y] - \frac{1}{2}| \geq \varepsilon$$

With a possible flip in the output of circuit T, we get a new test T' such that

$$\mathop{\mathbb{P}}_{y\sim U_t, x\sim D}[T'(y) = C(x)_y] \geq \frac{1}{2} + \varepsilon$$

By a Markov argument, there is a set $BAD \subseteq \{0,1\}^N$ such that for every $x \in BAD$,

$$\mathop{\mathbb{P}}_{y\sim U_t}[T'(y) = C(x)_y] \geq \frac{1}{2} + \frac{\varepsilon}{2}$$

and $\mathbb{P}_{x\sim D}[x \in BAD] \geq \varepsilon/2$. Evaluating T' on every possible $y \in \{0,1\}^t$ results in a string x' such that

$$\mathop{\mathbb{P}}_{y\in\{0,1\}^t}[x'_y = C(x)_y] \geq \frac{1}{2} + \frac{\varepsilon}{2} \tag{2}$$

We can now use the $(\varepsilon/2, \delta, L)$ list-decodability properties of C. For any x' satisfying (2) we can get a set of $k \leq L$ strings $x^1, \ldots, x^k$ such that at least one of them satisfies that

$$\mathop{\mathbb{P}}_{y\sim\mathcal{U}_N}[x^i_y = x_y] \geq 1 - \delta \tag{3}$$

Note that process of finding $x^1, \ldots, x^k$ need not be polynomial time, but we only require existence here; the important point is that the list of x^i is uniquely determined by x' (take the lexicographically smallest list satisfying the conditions in the fact). If $x^1, \ldots, x^k$ are known, then we require at most $\log L$ bits to specify $i \in [t]$ such that x^i satisfies (3). Once x^i is specified, we know that x must be among one of the at most $2^{H(\delta)N}$ possible N-bit strings which are δ-close to x. Hence we require an additional $H(\delta)N$ bits to fully specify x. Thus, the total amount of bits used to specify x is $\log L + H(\delta)N$, which in turn implies that the size of the set BAD is bounded by $L \cdot 2^{H(\delta)N}$.

To conclude the argument, observe that every element in BAD is sampled with probability at most 2^{-K} and hence $\mathbb{P}_{X\in D}[X \in BAD] \leq (L \cdot 2^{-K+H(\delta)N})$. However, this is a contradiction if

$$L \cdot 2^{-K+H(\delta)N} < \frac{\varepsilon}{2} \quad \text{i.e.} \quad K > H(\delta)N + \log L + \log\frac{2}{\varepsilon}$$

which gives the bound stated in the claim. □

Let $\eta > 0$ be an error parameter, $A \subseteq \{0,1\}^N$, and $\mathcal{U}_A$ the uniform distribution on A. Theorem III.1 in [14] implies that, as long as

$$\log|A| - b \geq K + \log 1/\eta, \tag{4}$$

the function E is automatically a $(\log|A|, 3\sqrt{\eta})$ extractor that is secure against b qubits of quantum storage (see Definition 2.3). This means that, for any collection of quantum states $\Psi(x) \in \mathcal{D}_b$, knowledge of y and $\Psi(x)$ cannot help distinguish $E(x,y)$ from a uniformly random bit with advantage more than $3\sqrt{\eta}$ (over the choice of x in A, and uniform y). In particular, we have that for any collection of measurements $\{M_y^0, M_y^1\}_{y\in\{0,1\}^t}$ on $\mathcal{D}_b$,

$$\mathbb{E}_{x\in A,\, y\in\{0,1\}^t}\left[\mathrm{Tr}(M_y^{C(x)_y}\Psi(x)(M_y^{C(x)_y})^\dagger)\right] \leq 1/2 + 3\sqrt{\eta}/2$$

By definition, any (N,b,ε) QFAC on average for $(A,\mathcal{C})$, even one that is only correct on average over the choice of x, contradicts this conclusion for $\eta = 4\varepsilon^2/9$. Hence our assumption (4) on the size of A must be contradicted, i.e. any such QFAC must be such that $\log|A| < K + b + \log 9/4\varepsilon^2$. Setting K to be the smallest possible value satisfying the condition in Claim 3.7, we get

$$\log|A| < H(\delta)N + b + \log L + O(\log 1/\varepsilon)$$

We describe two instantiations of this proposition, for specific families of codes. The first one, which will let us get an extractor with optimal seed length, is based on the following from [9]:

FACT 3.8. *For any $N \in \mathbb{N}$, $\varepsilon > 0$, there exists a polynomial-time computable code $C_R : \{0,1\}^N \to \{0,1\}^{\overline{N}}$, where $\overline{N} = O(N/\varepsilon^4)$, that is $(\varepsilon, O(1/\varepsilon^2))$ list-decodable.*

These codes lead to the following, the proof of which follows immediately from Proposition 3.6:

COROLLARY 3.9. *Let C_R be the code from Fact 3.8, and $\mathcal{C}_R = \{f_i : x \mapsto C(x)_i,\ i \in [\overline{N}]\}$. Then any (N,b,ε) QFAC on average for $(A, \mathcal{C}_R)$ is such that*

$$\log|A| < b + O(\log 1/\varepsilon)$$

Moreover, this bound holds even when we only require the QFAC to have success probability $1/2 + \varepsilon$ on average over the choice of $x \in A$.

Our second main construction uses a QFAC for the class $\mathcal{C}_k = \{g : x \mapsto \bigoplus_{j=1}^k x_{i_j},\ (i_1, \ldots, i_k) \in [n]\}$. QFACs for this class of functions were introduced in [2], where they are called XOR-QRACs. That paper shows a bound on the length of such codes using a generalization of the hypercontractive inequality to matrix-valued functions. We improve their result by showing the following:

COROLLARY 3.10. *Let k, N be integers, and $\varepsilon > 2k^2/2^N$. Let $A \subset \{0,1\}^N$. If there exists a (N,b,ε) QFAC on average for $(A, \mathcal{C}_k)$, then*

$$\log|A| < b + H\left(\frac{1}{k}\ln\frac{2}{\varepsilon}\right)N + O\left(\log\frac{1}{\varepsilon}\right)$$

Moreover, this bound holds even when we only require the QFAC to have success probability $1/2 + \varepsilon$ on average over the choice of $x \in A$.

By generalizing the proof of Theorem 7 in [2] (which is only stated for $A = \{0,1\}^N$ in that paper), we can get the bound $\log|A| \leq b + \left(1 - \frac{1}{2\ln 2}(2\varepsilon)^{2/k} + o_N(1)\right) N$ for all $k \geq \log\log N$. This would lead to an extractor construction which only works for sources with min-entropy γN for $\gamma > 0.28$, and our improvement on their bound gets rid of this constraint.

PROOF. The following lemma (for a reference, see [12], Lemma 42) shows that for any $\varepsilon > 2k^2/2^N$, the XOR code is $(\varepsilon, (1/k)\ln(2/\varepsilon), 4/\varepsilon^2)$ approximately list-decodable.

LEMMA 3.11. *For every $\varepsilon > 2k^2/2^N$ and $z' \in (\{0,1\}^N)^k$, there is a list of $t \leq 4/\varepsilon^2$ elements $x^1, \ldots, x^t \in \{0,1\}^N$ such that the following holds: for every $z \in \{0,1\}^N$ which satisfies*

$$\mathbb{P}_{\{y_1,\ldots,y_k\}\in\binom{N}{k}}[z'_{(y_1,\ldots,y_k)} = \oplus_{i=1}^k z_{y_i}] \geq \frac{1}{2} + \varepsilon$$

there is an $i \in [t]$ such that

$$\mathbb{P}_{y\sim\mathcal{U}_N}[x^i_y = z_y] \geq 1 - \delta$$

with $\delta = (1/k)\ln(2/\varepsilon)$.

Note that in [12] the lemma is proved for tuples instead of sets, and has a $t \leq 1/\varepsilon^2$. However, since most tuples are sets, it is straightforward to get the above version for sets. Plugging the list-decoding parameters from this lemma in the bound of Proposition 3.6 immediately gives the result. □

4. CONSTRUCTION OVERVIEW

Our construction follows the general paradigm introduced by Trevisan [22] and its subsequent adaptation against quantum storage by Ta-shma [21]. However, our proof technique differs from that of [21] in that it avoids constructing random access codes by copying the adversary's storage many times. Rather, we use the much stronger bounds on QFACs proved in Section 3. This is crucial in allowing us to prove an additive, rather than multiplicative, dependence of the output on the adversary's storage.

We first describe a few standard tools that are used in the construction, before giving it in detail. Its correctness will be proved in Section 5.

4.1 Preliminaries

DEFINITION 4.1. *A collection of subsets $S_1, \ldots, S_m \subset [t]$ is called a (t, n, m, ρ) weak design if for all i, $|S_i| = n$ and for all j, $\sum_{i<j} 2^{|S_i\cap S_j|} \leq \rho(m-1)$.*

The following theorem is due to Raz, Reingold and Vadhan [19].

THEOREM 4.2. *For every $m, t \in \mathbb{N}$ and $\rho \geq 2$, there is a (t, n, m, ρ) design which is computable in time $(mt)^{O(1)}$ with $t = O(\frac{n^2}{\log\rho})$.*

Note that the value of t blows up when ρ approaches 1. In order to keep t bounded even as ρ approaches 1, we can use a construction given in [19]. Even though the construction is computable in polynomial time, it does not meet many finer notions of efficiency which are of interest to us. Hartman and Raz [10] achieved similar parameters with a better efficiency:

THEOREM 4.3. *For every $m, t \in \mathbb{N}$ such that $m > n^{\log n}$ and $0 < \gamma < \frac{1}{2}$, there is a $(t, n, m, 1+\gamma)$ design such that $t = O(n^2\log\frac{1}{\gamma})$. Further, each individual set in the design can be output in time polynomial in t and n.*

For the purposes of this paper, let $t(n, \rho)$ denote the smallest value of t for which Theorems 4.2 or 4.3 guarantee the existence of a weak (t, n, m, ρ) design. Whether we use Theorem 4.2 or 4.3 depends on how small we want ρ to be.

Our last tool is the Nisan-Wigderson generator with respect to a function $f : \{0,1\}^n \to \{0,1\}$.

DEFINITION 4.4. *Let $S_1, \ldots, S_m$ be a (t, n, m, ρ) weak-design. Let $x \in \{0,1\}^{2^n}$. Then $NW^x : \{0,1\}^t \to \{0,1\}^m$ is defined as*

$$NW^x(y) = x_{y_{S_1}}, \ldots, x_{y_{S_m}}$$

Here x_{S_j} denotes the restriction of x to the indices in S_j.

4.2 Description of the construction

Let $C : \{0,1\}^N \to \{0,1\}^{\overline{N}}$ be a code with good (possibly approximate) list-decoding capabilities, and $(S_1, \ldots, S_m)$ be a $(t, \log\overline{N}, m, \rho)$ design as discussed above. Then the extractor is obtained by combining these two constructs in the following way:

$$\begin{aligned} Ext_C : \{0,1\}^N \times \{0,1\}^t &\to \{0,1\}^m \\ (x, y) &\mapsto NW^{C(x)}(y) \end{aligned}$$

4.3 Main theorem

Our main result is the following:

THEOREM 4.5. *Let $\delta, \varepsilon > 0$. Let $C : \{0,1\}^N \to \{0,1\}^{\overline{N}}$ be a $(\varepsilon/m, \delta, L)$ approximately list-decodable code, and $t = t(\log\overline{N}, \rho)$ such that there exists a $(t, \log\overline{N}, m, \rho)$ design for all large enough m. Then for any $K, b \in \mathbb{N}$ the function $Ext_C : \{0,1\}^N \times \{0,1\}^t \to \{0,1\}^m$ is a $(K, 2\varepsilon)$ extractor secure against b qubits of quantum storage, where*

$$m = \frac{K - b - t - H(\delta)N - \log L - \Omega(\log(1/\varepsilon) + \log N)}{1+\rho}$$

We give two instantiations of this result. The first one uses the codes from Fact 3.8, and lets us achieve optimal seed length. We obtain it by setting $\rho = K^{\gamma/2}$, for any $\gamma > 0$, and using the combinatorial designs guaranteed by Theorem 4.2:

COROLLARY 4.6. *Let $\gamma, c, c' > 0$ be any constants. Let C_R be the code obtained from Fact 3.8 by setting $\varepsilon = N^{-c}$. Then the function $Ext_{C_R} : \{0,1\}^N \times \{0,1\}^t \to \{0,1\}^m$, where $t = O(\log N)$ and $m = \Omega\left(\frac{K-b}{K^\gamma}\right)$, is a $(K, 2\varepsilon)$ extractor against b qubits of quantum storage for any $K \geq N^{c'}$.*

An inconvenient aspect of this construction, particularly relevant to cryptography, is that, even though the extractor is polynomial-time computable, it is not *locally computable*. Indeed, any bit of the output may require polynomial time to be computed, whereas one might wish for it to be computable in polylogarithmic time. We achieve such an extractor by taking $C = C_k : \{0,1\}^N \to \{0,1\}^{\binom{N}{k}}$ the XOR code $C_k(x)_{y_1,\ldots,y_k} = x_{y_1} \oplus \ldots \oplus x_{y_k}$. By using these codes together with the designs from Theorem 4.3, the bound from Corollary 3.10 gives the following:

COROLLARY 4.7. *Let $\alpha, \delta, c > 0$ be any constants. Then there is a $k = O(\log(m/\varepsilon)/\delta^2)$ such that the function $Ext_{C_k} : \{0,1\}^N \times \{0,1\}^t \to \{0,1\}^m$, where $t = O(\log^4 N)$ and $m = \frac{1}{2}((\alpha - 2\delta)N - b)$, is a $(\alpha N, N^{-c})$ extractor against b qubits of quantum storage.*

Note that this extractor is locally computable, and every individual bit of the output can be computed in polylogarithmic time, as the designs in Theorem 4.3 are locally computable. Note also that the extractor only works for linear entropy rates: as mentioned earlier, this is tight due to lower bounds by Viola [24] on the seed length required to extract from sources with polynomially small min-entropy using low complexity circuits.

5. PROOF OF SECURITY

We give the proof of security of our construction. The first steps of the proof follow the general reconstruction paradigm from [22], and we give them first.

5.1 Proofs in the reconstruction paradigm

We start with the following standard observation.

OBSERVATION 5.1. *In order to prove that $Ext : \{0,1\}^N \times \{0,1\}^t \to \{0,1\}^m$ is a $(K, 2\varepsilon)$ strong extractor against b qubits of storage, it suffices to prove that for any collection of measurements $\{M^1_{u,y}, M^0_{u,y}\}_{(u,y)\in\{0,1\}^{m+t}}$ on $\mathcal{D}_b$, and $\Psi : \{0,1\}^N \to \mathcal{D}_b$, there are at most $\varepsilon 2^K$ strings $x \in \{0,1\}^N$ such that*

$$\Big|\mathbb{E}_{y\in\{0,1\}^t}\Big[Tr\Big(\mathbb{E}_{u\in\{0,1\}^m}\Big[M^1_{u,y}\Psi(x)(M^1_{u,y})^\dagger\Big]\Big) - Tr\Big(M^1_{Ext(x,y),y}\Psi(x)(M^1_{Ext(x,y),y})^\dagger\Big)\Big]\Big| > \varepsilon \quad (5)$$

PROOF. Assume for contradiction that $Ext : \{0,1\}^N \times \{0,1\}^t \to \{0,1\}^m$ is not a $(K, 2\varepsilon)$ strong extractor against b qubits of quantum storage. By definition, there exist measurements $\{M^1_{u,y}, M^0_{u,y}\}_{(u,y)\in\{0,1\}^{m+t}}$ on b qubits such that

$$\Big|\mathbb{E}_{x\sim X, y\sim U_t}\Big[\mathrm{Tr}\Big(\mathbb{E}_{u\in\{0,1\}^m}\Big[M^1_{u,y}\Psi(x)(M^1_{u,y})^\dagger\Big]\Big) - \mathrm{Tr}\Big(M^1_{Ext(x,y),y}\Psi(x)(M^1_{Ext(x,y),y})^\dagger\Big)\Big]\Big| > 2\varepsilon$$

where X is the source's distribution. Since it has min-entropy at least K, it must be true that for at least $\varepsilon 2^K$ inputs x,

$$\Big|\mathbb{E}_{y\sim U_t}\Big[\mathrm{Tr}\Big(\mathbb{E}_{u\in\{0,1\}^m}\Big[M^1_{u,y}\Psi(x)(M^1_{u,y})^\dagger\Big]\Big) - \mathrm{Tr}\Big(M^1_{Ext(x,y),y}\Psi(x)(M^1_{Ext(x,y),y})^\dagger\Big)\Big]\Big| > \varepsilon$$

□

Fix a collection of measurements $\{M^1_{u,y}, M^0_{u,y}\}_{u,y\in\{0,1\}^{m+t}}$ on $\mathcal{D}_b$. The previous observation shows that, in order to show that Ext is a strong extractor, it suffices to bound the number of strings x such that (5) holds. For this, we use the reconstruction approach in [22]. For a fixed x, define $M_x : \{0,1\}^{m+t} \to \{0,1\}$ as the probabilistic procedure which, on input $(u,y) \in \{0,1\}^{m+t}$, outputs 1 with probability $\mathrm{Tr}(M^1_{u,y}\Psi(x)(M^1_{u,y})^\dagger)$, where $\Psi(x)$ is the state of the adversary's storage on x. For the most part our proofs will simply treat M_x as a probabilistic oracle. Moreover, all probabilities that we write involving M_x, or other oracle circuits making calls to M_x, will implicitly be taken over M_x's internal randomness.

The first step is to use the standard hybrid argument followed by Yao's distinguisher versus predictor lemma to get an oracle circuit T which queries M_x exactly once, and is such that T predicts $Ext(x,y)_i$ with some advantage over a random guess when y as well as the value of x on some related points are given as input. We skip the (by now, standard) argument and state the final result (see [22] for details).

LEMMA 5.2. *Let x, ε be such that (5) is satisfied, and $Ext(x,y)_i$ be the ith bit of the extractor's output on (x,y). Then using $m + \log m + 3$ bits of classical advice, we can construct an oracle circuit T which makes one query to M_x and is such that for some $1 \le i \le m$, T satisfies:*

$$Pr_{y\in U_t}\big[T^{M_x}(y, Ext(x,y)_1, \ldots, Ext(x,y)_{i-1}) = Ext(x,y)_i\big] \ge \frac{1}{2} + \frac{\varepsilon}{m} \quad (6)$$

Our next step is to construct a small circuit R_x which predicts the value of $C(x)$ at any position y with some non-negligible success probability, leading to the following technical lemma:

LEMMA 5.3. *Let x, ε be such that (5) is satisfied. Then using $m(1+\rho) + \log m + t + O(1)$ bits of classical advice, we can construct an oracle circuit R_x which makes one query to M_x and predicts $C(x)_z$ with probability $1/2 + \varepsilon/m$, on average over the choice of $z \in \{0,1\}^N$.*

PROOF. By Lemma 5.2, using $m+\log m+3$ bits of advice, we can get an oracle circuit T which makes exactly one query to M_x and for some $1 \le i \le m$ satisfies

$$\mathbb{P}_y[T^{M_x}(y, C(x)_{y_{S_1}}, \ldots, C(x)_{y_{S_{i-1}}}) = C(x)_{y_{S_i}}] \ge \frac{1}{2} + \frac{\varepsilon}{m}$$

Let us split y into two parts $z = y_{S_i}$ and $w = y_{[t]-S_i}$. Let y_{S_j} be denoted by $h_j(z,w)$. The above probability can then be rewritten as

$$\mathbb{P}_{z,w}\,[T^{M_x}(z, w, C(x)_{h_1(z,w)}, \ldots, C(x)_{h_{i-1}(z,w)}) = C(x)_z] \ge \frac{1}{2} + \frac{\varepsilon}{m}$$

By an averaging argument, we can fix a w (using at most t bits of advice) such that the above inequality holds with the probability taken over z. Let us hardwire all the possible values of $C(x)_{h_j(z,w)}$ (for the fixed value of w), as z varies over $\{0,1\}^N$ and j varies between 1 and $i-1$, into the circuit T. By the definition of a weak design, there are at most $(m-1)\rho$ bits that need to be hardwired. Let R_x be the circuit with all the hardwired values. R_x satisfies the following

$$\mathbb{P}_z[R_x^{M_x}(z) = C(x)_z] \ge \frac{1}{2} + \frac{\varepsilon}{m} \quad (7)$$

The total classical advice taken so far is $m + \log m + t + m\rho + O(1)$. □

5.2 Security against quantum storage from lower bounds on QFACs

Assume for contradiction that there is an adversary to Ext, which can distinguish its output from uniform given access to the seed y and some partial quantum information $\Psi(x) \in \mathcal{D}_b$ about the source. Such an adversary can be described by the mapping Ψ, together with a collection of measurements $\{M^1_{u,y}, M^0_{u,y}\}_{u,y\in\{0,1\}^{m+t}}$ on $\mathcal{D}_b$ describing the adversary's measurement on his quantum information $\Psi(x)$, when provided with the seed and the extractor's output[5].

For a fixed x, let $M_x : \{0,1\}^{m+t} \to \{0,1\}$ as in Section 5.1. By Observation 5.1, to prove that Ext is a $(K, 2\varepsilon)$ strong extractor secure against b qubits of quantum storage, it suffices to prove that there are at most $\varepsilon 2^K$ strings x such that (5) holds.

The key conceptual step in our proof is to observe that from the circuit R_x given by Lemma 5.3, we can construct a QFAC for the family $\mathcal{C} = \{f_i : x \mapsto C(x)_i, i \in [\overline{N}]\}$ of codeword positions, and the set A of all x satisfying (5). The strong lower bounds we proved in Section 3 then let us bound the size of the set A as a function of the adversary's storage and the list-decoding properties of C. The following claim makes this connection formal.

CLAIM 5.4. *Let $\eta > 0$ and $A \subseteq \{0,1\}^N$ be such that, for any $x \in A$, using only c bits of classical advice, we can construct a circuit R_x which has access to a b-qubit quantum state and is such that for a random y, it predicts $C(x)_y$ with probability $1/2 + \eta$. Then the cardinality of A is at most $s \cdot 2^c$, where s is the maximum size of a set B such that there exists a (N, b, η) QFAC for $(B, \mathcal{C})$.*

PROOF. The c advice bits partition the set A into 2^c sets A_s, for $s \in \{0,1\}^c$. Fix such a s and consider the set A_s. Since s has been fixed, all $x \in A_s$ have the same circuit R_x; only the b-qubit quantum state $\Psi(x)$ on which it operates depends on x. Hence there is a fixed set of measurements such that, for a random y, the measurement M_y on $\Psi(x)$ outputs $C(x)_y$ with probability $1/2 + \eta$. This means we have a (N, b, η) QFAC for $(A_s, \mathcal{C})$. Hence the size of A_s is bounded by the maximum size of any set for which such a code exists. This gives us the promised bound on A. □

To finish the proof of Theorem 4.5, note that by Proposition 3.6, any $(N, b, \varepsilon/m)$ QFAC for $(A, \mathcal{C})$ satisfies

$$\log|A| \leq b + H(\delta)\,N + \log L + O(\log m/\varepsilon)$$

Applying Claim 5.4 to the advice circuit promised by Lemma 5.3, we deduce that the number of strings x such that (5) holds is at most

$$2^{b+H(\delta)N+\log L+O(\log(m/\varepsilon))} \cdot 2^{m(1+\rho)+\log m+t+O(1)}$$

Using $\log(m) = O(\log N)$, this expression can be upper-bounded by

$$2^{b+H(\delta)N+m(1+\rho)+\log L+t+O(\log(1/\varepsilon)+\log N)}$$

[5]This describes the most general situation, as we can always assume that any measurement made by the adversary is done at the end of his recovery procedure.

Using the bound on m given in Theorem 4.5, we immediately get that this expression is upper-bounded by $\varepsilon 2^K$, finishing the proof of the theorem.

Acknowledgements.

We are grateful to Falk Unger and Umesh Vazirani for comments which helped us improve the presentation in this paper. The first author would like to thank Luca Trevisan for kindly sharing his understanding of extractors.

6. REFERENCES

[1] A. Ambainis, A. Nayak, A. Ta-shma, and U. V. Vazirani. Dense quantum coding and quantum finite automata. *Journal of the ACM*, 49(4):496–511, 2002. Preliminary version in *Proc. of STOC 1999.*

[2] A. Ben-Aroya, O. Regev, and R. de Wolf. A Hypercontractive Inequality for Matrix-Valued Functions with Applications to Quantum Computing and LDCs . In *Proceedings of the 49th IEEE Symposium on Foundations of Computer Science*, pages 477–486, 2008. Full version at arXiv:0705.3806.

[3] R. Cleve, W. v. Dam, M. Nielsen, and A. Tapp. Quantum entanglement and the communication complexity of the inner product function. In *QCQC '98: Selected papers from the First NASA International Conference on Quantum Computing and Quantum Communications*, pages 61–74, London, UK, 1998. Springer-Verlag.

[4] A. De, C. Portmann, R. Renner, and T. Vidick. Trevisan's extractor in the presence of quantum side information. Technical report arXiv:0912.5514, 2009.

[5] A. De and L. Trevisan. Extractors using hardness amplification. In Proc. of APPROX-RANDOM, pages 462–475, 2009.

[6] S. Dziembowski and U. Maurer. Optimal randomizer efficiency in the bounded-storage model. *Journal of Cryptology*, 17(1):5–26, 2004.

[7] S. Fehr and C. Schaffner. Randomness extraction via *delta* -biased masking in the presence of a quantum attacker. In R. Canetti, editor, *TCC*, volume 4948 of *Lecture Notes in Computer Science*, pages 465–481. Springer, 2008.

[8] D. Gavinsky, J. Kempe, I. Kerenidis, R. Raz, and R. de Wolf. Exponential separation for one-way quantum communication complexity, with applications to cryptography. *SIAM Journal of Computing*, 38(5):1695–1708, 2008. Preliminary version in *Proc. of STOC 2007.*

[9] V. Guruswami, J. Håstad, M. Sudan, and D. Zuckerman. Combinatorial bounds for list decoding. *IEEE Transactions on Information Theory*, 48(5):1021–1034, 2002.

[10] T. Hartman and R. Raz. On the distribution of the number of roots of polynomials and explicit weak designs. *Random Structures and Algorithms*, 23(3):235–263, 2003.

[11] A. Holevo. Information-theoretic aspects of quantum measurement. *Problems of Information Transmission*, 9(2):31–42, 1973.

[12] R. Impagliazzo, R. Jaiswal, and V. Kabanets. Approximately List-Decoding Direct Product Codes and Uniform Hardness Amplification. In *Proceedings*

of the 47th IEEE Symposium on Foundations of Computer Science, pages 187–196, 2006. Full version at `http://www1.cs.columbia.edu/~rjaiswal/`.

[13] R. König, U. Maurer, and R. Renner. On the power of quantum memory. *IEEE Transactions on Information Theory*, 51(7):2391–2401, 2005.

[14] R. König and B. Terhal. The bounded storage model in presence of a quantum adversary. *IEEE Transactions on Information Theory*, 54(2):749–762, 2008.

[15] C.-J. Lu. Encryption against storage-bounded adversaries from on-line strong extractors. *Journal of Cryptology*, 17(1):27–42, 2004.

[16] U. M. Maurer. Conditionally-perfect secrecy and a provably-secure randomized cipher. *Journal of Cryptology*, 5(1):53–66, 1992.

[17] A. Nayak and J. Salzman. Limits on the ability of quantum states to convey classical messages. *Journal of the ACM*, 53(1):184–206, 2006.

[18] N. Nisan and A. Wigderson. Hardness vs randomness. *Journal of Computer and System Sciences*, 49:149–167, 1994. Preliminary version in *Proc. of FOCS'88.*

[19] R. Raz, O. Reingold, and S. P. Vadhan. Extracting all the randomness and reducing the error in trevisan's extractors. *J. Comput. Syst. Sci.*, 65(1):97–128, 2002. Preliminary version in *Proc. of STOC 1999.*

[20] M. Sudan, L. Trevisan, and S. Vadhan. Pseudorandom generators without the XOR lemma. *Journal of Computer and System Sciences*, 62(2):236–266, 2001. Preliminary version in *STOC and CCC 1999.*

[21] A. Ta-shma. Short seed extractors against quantum storage. In *Proceedings of the 41st ACM Symposium on Theory of Computing*, pages 401–409, 2009.

[22] L. Trevisan. Extractors and pseudorandom generators. *Journal of the ACM*, 48(4):860–879, 2001.

[23] S. P. Vadhan. Constructing locally computable extractors and cryptosystems in the bounded-storage model. *Journal of Cryptology*, 17(1):43–77, 2004.

[24] E. Viola. The complexity of constructing pseudorandom generators from hard functions. *Computational Complexity*, 13(3-4):147–188, 2004.

Public-Key Cryptography from Different Assumptions

[Extended Abstract]

Benny Applebaum[*]
Weizmann Institute of Science
Rehovot, Israel
abenny@cs.technion.ac.il

Boaz Barak[†]
Princeton University,
Princeton, NJ, USA
boaz@cs.princeton.edu

Avi Wigderson[‡]
Institute for Advanced Study
Princeton, NJ, USA
avi@ias.edu

ABSTRACT

This paper attempts to broaden the foundations of public-key cryptography. We construct new public-key encryption schemes based on new hardness-on-average assumptions for natural *combinatorial* **NP**-hard optimization problems. We consider the following assumptions:

1. It is infeasible to solve a random set of sparse linear equations mod 2, of which a small fraction is noisy.
2. It is infeasible to distinguish between a random unbalanced bipartite graph, and such a graph in which we "plant" at random in the large side a set S with only $|S|/3$ neighbors.
3. There is a pseudorandom generator in $\mathbf{NC}^0$ where every output depends on a random constant-size subset of the inputs.

We obtain semantically secure public-key encryption schemes based on several combinations of these assumptions with different parameters. In particular we obtain public-key encryption from Assumption 1 on its own, yielding the first noisy-equations type public-key scheme in which the noise rate is higher than one over the square root of the number of equations. We also obtain public-key encryption based on a combination of Assumptions 2 and 3. These are arguably of more "combinatorial"/"private-key" nature than any assumptions used before for public-key cryptography. Our proof involves novel "search to decision" and "search to prediction" reductions for *sparse* noisy linear equations.

The strength of our assumptions raise new algorithmic and pseudorandomness questions (and new parameters for old ones). We give some evidence for these assumptions by studying their resistance to certain classes of natural algorithms, including semi-definite programs, $\mathbf{AC}^0$ circuits, low-degree polynomials, and cycle counting. We also relate our assumptions to other problems such as planted clique and learning juntas.

[*]Work done while at Princeton University. Supported by NSF grants CNS-0627526, CCF-0426582 and CCF-0832797.

[†]Supported by NSF grants CNS-0627526, CCF-0426582 and CCF-0832797, US-Israel BSF grant 2004288 and Packard and Sloan fellowships.

[‡]Supported by NSF Grant CCF-0832797.

STOC'10, June 5–8, 2010, Cambridge, Massachusetts, USA

Categories and Subject Descriptors

E.3 [**Data Encryption**]: Public key cryptosystems; F.2.2 [**Nonnumerical Algorithms and Problems**]: Computations on discrete structures

General Terms

Algorithms, Security, Theory

Keywords

3LIN, Densest Subgraph Problem, Expander Graphs, Learning Juntas, Learning Parity with Noise, NC0, Public Key Cryptography

1. INTRODUCTION

Public key encryption (PKE) is a central notion in cryptography, and many of the exciting cryptographic applications in theory and practice are based on it. But despite 30+ years of research, very few candidates for such encryptions are known, and these are based on a handful of computational problems of a very structured algebraic or geometric nature, from the areas of number theory, lattices, and error-correcting codes (e.g., [19, 52, 40, 3]). This leaves open the troublesome possibility that a new mathematical breakthrough could render them insecure.

In this aspect public-key cryptography ("cryptomania" in the language of Impagliazzo [29]) seems very different from *private key cryptography* ("minicrypt") where many different candidates exist, and can be based on seemingly much less structured combinatorial problems including natural average-case variants of **NP**-complete problems such as random 3-SAT [1], planted clique [32], and learning parity with noise [26, 11].[1] Thus a major goal of cryptography is to base public-

[1] Learning parity with noise (LPN), as well as the related mod p variant of "learning with errors" (LWE), have been used for public key cryptography as well [4, 51, 47]. However, the known public key schemes require noise levels much lower than those needed for private-key cryptography. In particular all of these schemes inherently require noise of magnitude $\varepsilon < 1/\sqrt{m}$, where m is the number of equations.

key encryption on assumptions that are weaker, or at least different, than those currently used.

A complete solution to this problem would be obtained by constructing public key encryption based solely on the existence of one-way functions. This is a longstanding open problem, and cannot be achieved via black-box reductions [30]. Short of that, we believe that major progress would be made by a construction of public key encryption based on a natural and well-studied average-case variant of an **NP**-complete problem. This paper is a step in this direction.

In this work we give constructions of a public key encryption based on different assumptions about the hardness of combinatorial problems (e.g., satisfying random local constraints and detecting graph expansion). The proposed systems are not as efficient as some known candidate constructions, and are based on assumptions that are not as well-studied as, say, the hardness of factoring. For this reason we initiate here a study of the algorithmic and pseudorandomness questions which arise, relate them to known results, and obtain some preliminary new ones.

The main advantage of the new schemes is the relatively general and unstructured nature of the new assumptions. These include a variant of the *planted densest subgraph* problem, a pseudorandom generator based on the expander-based one-way function of Goldreich [24] (a *private-key* primitive), and the 3LIN problem which can be seen as a sparse variant of the *learning parity with noise* problem with noise level much higher than those used before in public-key cryptography (in particular larger than $1/\sqrt{m}$, see Footnote 1). These seem qualitatively different than previous assumptions.

Structure of the paper.

Section 2 contain somewhat informal statements of our results and some discussion on their implications and relation to prior works. Section 3 contains a description of our scheme and a high level overview of the proofs of our main results. Section 4 contains formal statements of the main results as well as some proof outlines. A preliminary full version of this paper is available on the authors' home page.

2. OUR RESULTS AND RELATED WORK

2.1 New cryptosystems

We say that a bipartite graph G is an (m, n, d)*-graph*, if it has m vertices on one side (which we call the "top" side), n vertices on the other side (called the "bottom"), and every top vertex has degree d. Similarly, an (m, n, d)*-matrix* is an $m \times n$ matrix over GF(2), in which every row has d entries of value 1. Roughly speaking, we consider the following assumptions (see Section 4 for precise statements):

Assumption $\mathsf{dLIN}(m, \varepsilon)$ It is infeasible to recover x from $(A, Ax+e)$, where A is a random (m, n, d) matrix, x is chosen randomly from $\mathrm{GF}(2)^n$, and $e \in \mathrm{GF}(2)^m$ is chosen such that $e_i = 1$ with probability ε independently for every i.

Assumption $\mathsf{DUE}(m, q, d)$ (Decisional Unbalanced Expansion) It is infeasible to distinguish between: **(a)** a random (m, n, d)-graph and **(b)** a random (m, n, d) graph in which the edges going out of a random q-sized subset S of the top vertices are modified to ensure S will have only $q/3$ neighbors.

Assumption $\mathsf{DSF}(m, d)$ (Decisional Sparse Function) With high probability, the following d-local, $\mathbf{NC}^0$ mapping G of n to m bits is a pseudorandom generator: every output bit of $G(x_1, \ldots, x_n)$ is $\mathrm{MAJ}(x', x'', x''')$ where each of x', x'', x''' is the parity of $d/3$ random coordinate of x.

In all of the above, "infeasibility" and "pseudorandomness" are defined with respect to probabilistic polynomial time (PPT) algorithms with some constant success probability (e.g., 0.99). The parameters m, d, q, ε can be functions of n. We construct three public-key encryption schemes each based on a different combination of the above assumptions:

THEOREM 1. *For every constants $c > 0$ and function $m = m(n), d = d(n)$, if both Assumptions $\mathsf{DUE}(m, c\log n, d)$ and $\mathsf{DSF}(m, d)$ hold then there exists a semantically secure public key encryption.*

Both the DUE and DSF assumptions are arguably much more "combinatorial" and of a "private key" nature than any assumptions used before to construct public-key cryptography. DSF assumes that a variant of Goldreich's candidate one-way function is a pseudorandom generator— a strong assumption but still of a "private key" nature. DUE is closely related to the *densest subgraph problem*— a combinatorial optimization problem of independent interest [22, 34, 9, 7].

Indeed, we can look at an (m, n, d)-graph G as a d-uniform *hypergraph* H of n vertices and m hyperedges, where the i-th hyperedge of H contains the d neighbors of the i-th top-vertex of G. In this formulation, the DUE assumption is about the hardness of distinguishing hypergraphs that contain a somewhat *dense* sub-hypergraph — a set T of $q' = q/3$ vertices, such that the induced sub-hypergraph on T has at least q hyperedges— from graphs where the induced sub-hypergraph of every set of q' vertices (for q' up to roughly $n^{0.1}$ size or some other super-logarithmic bound) has only about q'/d edges. Thus DUE is equivalent to the problem of distinguishing between a random fairly sparse hypergraph ($m = O(n)$ hyperedges) and a random hypergraph with a planted somewhat *dense* (average degree larger than 1) small subgraph.[2]

Note that we use DUE with a planted set of size $O(\log n)$. While, generally speaking, making the set smaller doesn't necessarily make the problem easier, there is always a brute force attack of time $\binom{n}{q}$, and hence the scheme obtained can be at best secure against $t^{O(\log t)}$-time adversaries, where t is the running time of the honest parties. While ideally one would want at least sub-exponential security, we note that the best construction of public key encryption using (even idealized) one-way functions has security at most $O(t^2)$ [41, 10] and this is optimal for black-box methods [30, 8].

This seems to make a *qualitative* difference. Some evidence for this is the fact that for $\varepsilon < 1/\sqrt{m}$ LWE can be solved in **SZK** [25] and even (a suitable promise problem variant of) $\mathbf{NP} \cap \mathbf{coNP}$ [2], while in the worst-case these problems are **NP**-hard for sufficiently large noise [6, 20].

[2] Note however that there is a more "algebraic" view to DUE, since a set of q vertices with $< q$ neighbors will result in a linear relation of length at most q in the rows of the adjacency matrix. So, one can think of DUE also as a shortest codeword problem for the dual code of this matrix. However due to the imbalance, the dual code here has rate so close to 1 that it contains rather short codewords in any case (e.g., of length $m^{1/c}$).

THEOREM 2. *There is a constant c so that if Assumption* $\mathsf{3LIN}(cn^{1.4}, n^{-0.2}/c)$ *holds then there exists a semantically secure public key encryption.*

The 3LIN problem is a central and well studied constraint satisfaction problem. Furthermore, the above parameters seem to resist sub-exponential time algorithms (see Section 2.2.) It should be mentioned that other public key encryption schemes were based on solving (dense) random noisy equations mod 2 and mod p [4, 51, 47]. Still our assumption seems different from those due to the sparsity and the use of larger noise rate (see Footnote 1 and Section 2.3). Moreover, our assumption is based on the hardness of a *search* problem (i.e. find an x satisfying most equations) with parameters for which *refutation* variant of 3LIN (i.e. certify that no such x satisfying most equations exists) is harder than refuting a random 3SAT formula with $O(n^{1.4})$ clauses. Note that finding an efficient algorithm to refute random 3SAT formulas with $o(n^{1.5})$ clauses is a longstanding open problem. Random 3SAT is perhaps the prototypical example of a "combinatorial" average-case computational problem. Of course, this connection is not formal, only suggestive, and does not directly shed light on the strength of our assumption, as no reductions are known between the *search* and *refutation* versions of random noisy 3XOR.

THEOREM 3. *For every constants* d, c *and* $q = q(n)$, *there exists a constant* c' *such that if* $d\mathsf{LIN}(c'n \log n, 1/(c'q)))$ *and* $\mathsf{DUE}(cn, q, 2d)$ *hold then there exists a semantically secure public key encryption.*

Compared to Thm. 2, Thm. 3 allows us much more flexibility in the choice of parameters for 3LIN; specifically, we avoid the parameter range in which [21]'s non deterministic algorithm for the refutation variant of this problem works. This comes at the expense of using the additional, combinatorial assumption DUE.[3] Again, it seems (see Section 2.2) that the resulting schemes achieves sub-exponential security.

We stress that we do *not* claim that our cryptosystems are "better" or "more secure" than previous candidates for public key encryption. Indeed, the integer factoring problem underlying schemes such as [49] is probably the most well-studied average-case computational problem. Also, lattice based systems such as [3, 51, 47] have the important advantage of being based on *worst-case* problems such as gap shortest vector and shortest linearly independent vectors. Nevertheless we believe our constructions do suggest that problems with less algebraic or geometric structure may be useful for public key cryptography.

2.2 More about the assumptions

We now elaborate on the evidence that support our assumptions and on some of their additional applications. To test the validity of our assumptions, we show unconditionally that they do resist various concrete algorithms, as well as provide some reductions between these and other computational problems. While our primary motivation is to broaden the foundations for public key cryptography, we believe that the computational problems we use are natural and interesting in their own right.[4] They broaden the class of hardness-on-average and pseudorandomness problems studied in the past in both the algorithmic and cryptographic communities, and focus attention on parameters of significance for public-key encryption.

The dLIN *problem.*

We show that for the parameters we use, the noisy linear equation problem 3LIN *unconditionally* resists: (1) "Myopic" attacks that look at the entire matrix but only at some n^{δ} of the "noisy bits", or those that look at linear combinations of these "noisy bits". (2) Attacks that apply low-degree polynomials or $\mathbf{AC}^0$ circuits to the "noisy bits". (3) n^{δ} rounds of the Lasserre hierarchy [36] of semi-definite programs, for some constant $\delta > 0$. The first item follows similarly to the analysis of Mossel et al [43], the second item employs the results of Viola [55] and Braverman [15], and the third item is implied by Schoenebeck [53].

The last item is especially interesting as semidefinite programs seem to be the strongest algorithmic tool that is currently available to attack constraint satisfaction problems. Moreover, the Lasserre hierarchy is strictly stronger than other hierarchies for linear and semidefinite programs such as the Lovasz-Schrijver [39] hierarchies (LS, and LS+) and the Sherali-Adams [54] hierarchy [37].

We also obtain a new (average-case) reduction from the dLIN problem into its decisional version (where one needs to distinguish $(1-\varepsilon)$-satisfiable random equations from completely random ones that will be of course only $1/2 + o(1)$ satisfiable). A similar reduction (from search to decision) was presented in [11] for the non-sparse case, however their techniques do not hold in the sparse case which turns to be significantly more challenging. As the sparse case is an important variant of this problem (see [4, 5]), we believe that our reduction is of independent interest.

The DSF *problem.*

We show that the non-linear pseudorandom generator G of the DSF assumption resists some of the above attacks as well. Specifically, its output is n^{δ}-wise independent and fools $\mathbf{AC}^0$ circuits and linear tests over GF(2). In fact, we prove a more general result about the security of the following construction of [24]. For a sequence of m subsets of $[n]$, $S = S_1, \ldots, S_m$ of size $d = O(1)$ and a d-local predicate P, let $G_{S,P} : \{0,1\}^n \to \{0,1\}^m$ be the d-local mapping whose i-th output is obtained by applying the predicate P to the input string x restricted to the d indices of the set S_i. Goldreich [24] conjectured that when the mapping is length preserving (i.e., $m = n$), the function $G_{S,P}$ is one-way for a random choice of the collection S and essentially any non-trivial predicate P. This assumption was supported by both theoretical and practical evidence [24, 45, 17]. Recently, [14] showed that if the predicate P is biased towards a linear combination of two of its inputs, then the function becomes vulnerable when the output length m is sufficiently larger than the input length (i.e., $m > cn$ for a constant

[3] We note that known algorithms for DUE (i.e., counting small subgraphs) place some restrictions on the value of q for which $\mathsf{DUE}(cn, q, d)$ and we'll need $q \in [n^{\varepsilon}, \sqrt{n}]$ where ε is some constant depending on c. The actual range of parameters for which our result holds is somewhat broader.

[4] As an example, following this work, a variant of the DUE assumption was recently used by [7] (co-authored by the second author) to argue about the complexity of pricing financial derivatives. The DUE assumption also served as partial motivation for [9]'s recent work on the densest subgraph problem.

$c = c(d) > 1$). We complement this by giving a combinatorial condition on S and P under which the function $G_{S,P}$ is pseudorandom with respect to the above family of non-trivial distinguishers (i.e., n^δ-wise independent tests, $\mathbf{AC}^0$ circuits and linear tests over GF(2)) even when m is polynomially larger than n.[5] This suggests that the vulnerability discovered by [14] only holds for a "bad" choice of the predicate P. Our work also provides a new candidate for an $\mathbf{NC}^0$ pseudorandom generator with polynomial stretch (e.g., from n input bits to n^2 output bits). The existence of such a primitive is an important open question [18, 43, 5, 5] which is also motivated by the ability to achieve highly efficient secure multiparty computation [31]. The only prior candidate (surviving a similar class of non-trivial attacks) was due to [43].

The DUE *problem.*
We also show that the unbalanced expansion (DUE) problem resists "cycle counting" algorithms (a basic and surprisingly useful technique to identify dense subgraphs of a graph by counting the number of small cycles in the graph containing specific vertices [9]). In addition we show that variants of the DUE assumption are implied by variants of other problems such as small-set vertex expansion in general (not necessarily bipartite) graphs, and the planted clique problem in $G_{n,p}$ for small $p = p(n)$. Finally, we prove that our third cryptosystem, which is based on a combination of DUE and DSF implies that a k-junta (i.e., a function $g : \{0,1\}^n \to \{0,1\}$ which depends in at most k of its variables) cannot be PAC-learned in less than $n^{\Omega(k)}$ time. The junta learning problem [12, 13] is one of the most central open problems in computational learning theory.[6]

2.3 Prior works

The notion of "structure" in complexity assumptions is necessarily informal but we can still offer below some comparisons of our schemes with previous ones. We do not review all previous assumptions used for candidates for public key encryption; see the survey [57] and the web site [38] for more. It seems that currently those candidates that are considered secure can be classified as falling into two broad categories: schemes based on number theoretic or group theoretic problems such as factoring (e.g. [49, 52]) and discrete log in various groups (e.g. [19, 42, 35]) and schemes based on knapsack/lattices/error correcting codes (e.g., [40, 3, 4, 51, 47]).

Our *non-linear* scheme (based on DSF and DUE) seems genuinely different from all previous constructions we are aware of. Our *linear* scheme (based on solely on 3LIN or dLIN and DUE) has some similarities to coding/lattice-based schemes but there are some important differences, which we now discuss.

Of the coding/lattice based schemes, the McEliece [40] system seems to use more algebraic structure, in the sense that the underlying assumption is that decoding a "shuffled" Goppa code is as hard as decoding a random linear code. A similar observation applies to the Hidden Field Equations (HFE) scheme of Patarin [46] that implicitly assumes that a shuffled low degree univariate polynomial over $\mathrm{GF}(p^n)$ is indistinguishable from a random family of quadratic equations over $\mathrm{GF}(p)^n$.

More similar to ours are the schemes of Alekhnovich [4] and Regev [51]. Regev's scheme (and others such as [48, 47]) is based on the *Learning With Error* problem that is a mod p analog of the learning parity with noise problem. Specifically, like our 3LIN problem it is the task of recovering x from $(A, Ax + e)$ except A is a random (dense) $m \times n$ matrix in $\mathrm{GF}(p)$ for $p > m$, and each coordinate of e is distributed as a discrete Gaussian with standard deviation εp. However, as mentioned in Footnote 1, to make decryption work in all those schemes one needs to take $\varepsilon \ll 1/\sqrt{m}$ which seems to make a qualitative difference in the nature of the problem [25, 2]. Most similar to ours is Alekhnovich's scheme [4][7] that uses the (decisional variant) of the standard (dense) parity with noise problem. However, he too needed to use noise level of less than $1/\sqrt{m}$. While no analogous results to [25, 2] are known for the mod 2 case, it still seems as an important advantage that we are able to handle much higher noise levels (in some cases at the expense of using DUE as well).

3. OVERVIEW OF THE TECHNIQUES

To highlight some of our techniques let us sketch the proofs of Thms. 2 and 3. We define $\mathsf{SearchLIN}(d, m, \varepsilon)$ to be the problem of recovering x given a random d-sparse $m \times n$ matrix M and the vector $b = Mx + e$, where x is chosen at random in $\mathrm{GF}(2)^n$ and $e \in \mathrm{GF}(2)^m$ is chosen at random so that $e_i = 1$ with probability ε (we call e an ε-noise vector). Note that with extremely high probability this x to be recovered is unique. We let $\mathsf{Search3LIN}(m, \varepsilon) = \mathsf{SearchLIN}(3, m, \varepsilon)$.

PKE from $\mathsf{3LIN}(\Omega(n^{1.4}), O(n^{-0.2}))$.
The proof proceeds by a sequence of reductions, ending with showing that under our hardness assumption on the *search* problem, a related *prediction* problem is hard as well. This prediction problem gets essentially the same input, a matrix M and a vector $b = Mx + e$ *except its last bit*, and asks to predict that bit. In other words, given the value of $m - 1$ noisy (3-sparse) equations, we are asked to predict the value of another independent equation. A natural way to predict is to solve the search problem, and use the recovered solution x to evaluate the new equation (which will predict it correctly with probability $1 - \epsilon$). Our reduction shows that essentially this is the only way to go about prediction. If search is hard, so is prediction, even if all we ask for is a constant advantage (say 1/10) over guessing.

The twist is that the distribution of sparse matrices we use

[5]Roughly speaking, our condition requires S to be a good expander and P to satisfy a (stronger) variant of t-resiliency [16]. See full version for details.

[6]In addition, the DSF assumption on its own can be formulated as a "dual" version of the junta learning problem in which the target function is not local, but instead the data points given to the learner are "local". More formally, in terms of learning theory, in DSF the learner should learn a function f_x, represented by an n-bit vector x, which maps a d-size set $S \subseteq [m]$ to the value $P(x_S)$ for some known (randomly chosen) predicate P.

[7]Indeed, as observed by Ron Rivest and Madhu Sudan (personal communication), both our linear scheme and Alekhnovich's have a common generalization, where the public key is a matrix G whose dual subspace has a "planted" short vector, which serves as the private key. Similar structure occurs in many lattice-based cryptosystems such as [3, 50], where the public key is roughly a generating set for a lattice whose dual lattice has a planted short (in ℓ_2) basis.

The scheme $\mathcal{E}(\mathcal{D}, \varepsilon)$:

Public encryption key: A d-sparse matrix $M \in \mathrm{GF}(2)^{m \times n}$ sampled from distribution $\mathcal{D}$.

Private decryption key: A q-size subset $S \subseteq [m]$ for which: $m \in S$ and $\sum_{i \in S} M_i = 0^n$ where M_i is the i-th row of M.

Encryption: Randomly choose $x \xleftarrow{R} \mathcal{U}_n$ and a noise vector $e \in \{0,1\}^m$ whose entries are iid Bernoulli variables with mean ε. To encrypt 0, send the vector $b = Mx + e$. To encrypt 1, send the vector b with its last bit flipped.

Decryption: To decrypt $y \in \{0,1\}^m$ output the sum $\sum_{i \in S} y_i$. (Decryption errs with probability at most $q\varepsilon$.)

Figure 1: Our basic cryptosystem scheme, used in the proofs of Thms. 2 and 3. m, d, q, ε can depend on the security parameter n. The distribution $\mathcal{D}$ is over matrices with d 1's per row, in which the last row is a linear combination of $q-1$ other rows. We show that under certain assumptions the scheme can be instantiated to achieve constant privacy. This can be amplified to full-fledged security using [28].

in this reduction is special. Formally, for any distribution $\mathcal{D}$ on $(m, n, 3)$-matrices, define the following *prediction* problem Predict3LIN$(\mathcal{D}, \varepsilon)$: given M drawn from $\mathcal{D}$ and the first $m-1$ bits of $Mx+e$ where x, e as above, predict the m'th bit of $Mx+e$ with probability at least 3/5. We will reduce the search problem Search3LIN(m, ε) (where matrices are drawn uniformly) to the prediction problem Predict3LIN$(\mathcal{D}_0, \varepsilon)$, in which matrices are drawn from a special distribution $\mathcal{D}_0$.

Our cryptosystem.

Before explaining the reduction, let us explain how the prediction problem Predict3LIN$(\mathcal{D}_0, \varepsilon)$ can be turned into a public-key system. This system is also described in Figure 1. The distribution $\mathcal{D}_0$ has the property that if M is in the support of $\mathcal{D}_0$, then there is a linear relation involving M's last row and at most $q \ll 1/\varepsilon$ other rows. Moreover, it is possible to efficiently sample a random matrix M from $\mathcal{D}_0$ together with such a set S of rows involved in this linear relation. Since $q\varepsilon$ is small, if we add an ε-noise vector e to Mx, then with high probability no equation in S will be noisy, which means that given the value of $Mx+e$ on the coordinates in S, one can recover the value of Mx on the mth coordinate. Thus, the linear relation can serve as a sort of "trapdoor" for the Predict3LIN$(\mathcal{D}_0, \varepsilon)$ problem. One can turn this observation into a PKE by using relatively standard techniques such as hardness amplification [28].

Search to approximate search.

To get from Search3LIN(m, ε) to Predict3LIN$(\mathcal{D}_0, \varepsilon)$ we use a chain of three reductions through two intermediate problems. The first is an "approximate search" problem AppSearch3LIN(m, ε), which is the variant of Search3LIN in which the goal is relaxed to only recover a vector x' that is *close* to the true answer x in Hamming distance. We use error correcting properties of sparse equations to show that the two problems are equivalent up to constant loss in the parameters. In essence, we can use $O(n \lg n)$ more noisy equations to detect the "errors" in the approximate solution vector x' and correct them to recover x.

Search to prediction on the uniform distribution.

The next intermediate problem is Predict3LIN(m, ε) which is the problem Predict3LIN$(\mathcal{D}, \varepsilon)$ where $\mathcal{D}$ is the uniform distribution over $(m, n, 3)$-matrices - the *same* distribution on matrices used in Search3LIN(m, ε) and AppSearch3LIN(m, ε). We reduce AppSearch3LIN(m, ε) to Predict3LIN$(m+O(n), \varepsilon)$. A key observation used in the proof is that by adding two 3-sparse random equations that share a common variable, we get a random 4-sparse equation of the form $x_i + x_j + x_k + x_\ell = b$, and so given such an equation one can turn a predictor for $x_i + x_j + x_k$ into a predictor to x_ℓ. By carefully combining many pairs of equations it can be shown that at the end, we will get predictions for a large fraction of the variables, and that most of these predictions will be correct. Hence, together they form a good approximation for x.

Prediction on a different distribution.

The last step is a reduction between the two prediction problems Predict3LIN(m, ε) to Predict3LIN$(\mathcal{D}_0, \varepsilon)$ where $\mathcal{D}_0$ is the special distribution above. This step is composed of two stages. First we use the results of Feige, Kim, and Ofek [21] to argue that small linear relations involving the last row of M will exist in our setting of parameters with some (small) constant probability for the uniform distribution. Therefore the statistical distance between $\mathcal{D}_0$ (in which such a relation is sampled first) and the uniform distribution is bounded away from 1. We complete the proof by showing how to turn a good predictor for Predict3LIN$(\mathcal{D}, \varepsilon)$ into a good predictor A for Predict3LIN$(\mathcal{D}', \varepsilon)$ for every two distributions $\mathcal{D}, \mathcal{D}'$ over matrices with related parameters whose statistical (or computational!) distance is bounded away from 1. This differs from most proofs of this type, since we want the difference in prediction probability of the two predictors to be much smaller than the statistical (or computationsl) distance of the two distributions! For example, even if A perfectly solves Predict3LIN$(\mathcal{D}, \varepsilon)$ with no error, it might be a terrible predictor which errs with probability 1/2 when instances are generated according to $\mathcal{D}'$. Still, we show how to turn it into a useful predictor with respect to $\mathcal{D}'$ as well. The idea is to identify (via sampling) the instances on which A is likely to succeed and use it *only* for these cases. Then, we amplify the success probability by breaking a single instance of Predict3LIN to many smaller instances of the problem. These instances are rerandomized by relying on the symmetry and linearity of the 3-LIN constraints.

Thm. 3: PKE from DUE *and* dLIN.

The description above completes the reduction of Thm. 2. For Thm. 3, in which smaller values of m are used, such small linear relations between rows of M will *not* exist, and hence the distribution $\mathcal{D}_0$ as above will be statistically far from the uniform distribution on d-sparse matrices. Here our extra assumption DUE comes to the rescue, basically to prove that *computationally* its distance from uniform will be bounded away from 1. The next two paragraphs highlight the main ideas in that proof.

The use of DUE, as well as the extension to large sparsity

$d > 3$ introduce some additional difficulties that we need to overcome. In particular, for our cryptosystem we need DUE to hold even if one of the members of the planted shrinking set is revealed. Hence, to prove security we show that solving this variant of DUE assumption (denoted by DUE_1) implies a solution to the original DUE problem.

In particular, given a random (m, n, d) graph with a planted shrinking set, an algorithm for DUE_1 can be used to distinguish with some constant advantage between nodes that participate in the shrinking set to other nodes. This distinguisher allows us to "shave" many nodes of the large side of the graph while preserving the existence of a (smaller) shrinking set. The resulting graph will have m' top nodes and n bottom nodes where $m' < n$. (Recall that we started with $m > n$ top nodes.) For this case, we can detect the existence of a shrinking set by using Hall's theorem via a matching based algorithm. This leads directly to a solution for DUE. Note that this argument shows only that, under the DUE assumption, the distribution $\mathcal{D}_0$ is not completely computationally-far from the uniform distribution. Here again, we need to rely on the strong version of the reduction from $\mathsf{PredictLIN}(\mathcal{D}, \varepsilon)$ to $\mathsf{PredictLIN}(\mathcal{D}', \varepsilon)$.

Another difficulty arises from the use of a large sparsity $d > 3$, as in this case the combination of two equations with overlap of one variable does not lead to an equation of sparsity $d + 1$ as in the $d = 3$ case. We overcome this problem by employing a different reduction from PredictLIN to AppSearchLIN. Specifically, given an instance of AppSearchLIN with locality d, we combine pairs of equations with no overlap to obtain a $2d$-LIN instance. Then, we generate $(2d-2)$-LIN equations by combining pairs of equations with a common variable. This information, together with a prediction algorithm for $2d$-LIN can be used to obtain a 2-LIN equation. By repeating this process we obtain a random 2-LIN (or MAX-CUT) instance. Now we can employ one of the known algorithms (e.g.,the SDP of [23]) to obtain a solution that satisfies a large fraction of the constraints. Finally, we argue that since the 2-LIN instance is random the resulting assignment is close to the original assignment and therefore it is a valid solution for AppSearchLIN.

4. FORMAL STATEMENTS

4.1 Preliminaries

The SearchLIN problem. A matrix M is *d-sparse* if every row has exactly d nonzero elements. The distribution $\mathcal{T}_{p,n,d}$ chooses a d-sparse matrix by selecting any of the possible $\binom{n}{d}$ rows with probability p. The distribution $\mathcal{M}_{m,n,d}$ picks an $m \times n$ d-sparse matrix by choosing each row independently at random (with replacement) from all possible $\binom{n}{d}$ choices. We define $\mathsf{SearchLIN}(d, m, \varepsilon)$ to be the problem of recovering x from $(M, Mx + e)$ where $M \stackrel{R}{\leftarrow} \mathcal{M}_{m,n,d}$, $x \stackrel{R}{\leftarrow} \mathbb{F}_2^n$, and e is chosen at random such that $e_i = 1$ with probability ε. We say that $\mathsf{SearchLIN}(d, m, \varepsilon)$ is *intractable* if for every PPT algorithm A, and every sufficiently large n, the probability that A solves $\mathsf{SearchLIN}(d, m(n), \varepsilon(n))$ is smaller than 2/3.

Indistinguishability. A pair of distribution ensembles $\mathcal{X}_n, \mathcal{Y}_n$ are *ε-indistinguishable* if for every PPT algorithm C, we have $|\Pr[C(\mathcal{X}) = 1] - \Pr[C(\mathcal{Y}) = 1]| < \varepsilon$. An ensemble $\mathcal{X}_n$ is *ε-pseudorandom* if $\mathcal{X}_n$ is ε-indistinguishable from $\mathcal{U}_n$, the uniform distribution over n-bit strings.

Public-key encryption scheme. A *$(\alpha(n), \beta(n))$-secure public-key bit encryption scheme* is a triple (Gen, Enc, Dec) of PPT algorithms such that the algorithm Gen, on input 1^n produces a pair of private and public keys $(\mathsf{pk}, \mathsf{sk})$ and the scheme satisfy the following properties:

- $(1 - \alpha)$-*correctness*: For a random bit $b \stackrel{R}{\leftarrow} \{0, 1\}$ and a pair of random keys $(\mathsf{pk}, \mathsf{sk}) \stackrel{R}{\leftarrow} \mathsf{Gen}(1^n)$ we have: $\Pr[\mathsf{Dec}_{\mathsf{sk}}(\mathsf{Enc}_{\mathsf{pk}}(b)) = b] \geq 1 - \alpha$.
- β-*privacy*: The random variables $(\mathsf{pk}, \mathsf{Enc}_{\mathsf{pk}}(0))$ and $(\mathsf{pk}, \mathsf{Enc}_{\mathsf{pk}}(1))$ are $\beta(n)$-indistinguishable, where pk is chosen by $\mathsf{Gen}(1^n)$.

If α and β are constants that satisfy $\alpha < (1 - \sqrt{\beta})/2$, we say that the scheme is a *weak PKE*. It was shown in [28, Thm. 6] that a weak PKE can be converted into semantically secure PKE [27] which supports arbitrary (polynomially) long messages.

4.2 Properties of the scheme $\mathcal{E}(\mathcal{D}, \varepsilon)$

Two of our constructions are based on the general bit-encryption scheme which is described in Figure 1. Recall that the public key is matrix M, and the private-key is a short non-trivial linear dependency S among the rows of M which includes the last row. To encrypt the bit σ, one generates an m-bit vector b by perturbing a random vector in the image of M, and then XOR-s the last entry of b with the plaintext σ. The knowledge of the short linear-dependency S allows to decrypt the ciphertext b' by summing-up the bits that are indexed by the set S. The following lemma shows that decryption succeeds the noise rate ε is sufficiently small.

LEMMA 1. *For every pair (M, S) of public/private keys, and every plaintext $\sigma \in \{0, 1\}$, the decryption errs with probability at most $\alpha = \frac{1}{2} - \frac{1}{2}(1 - 2\cdot\varepsilon)^q < \varepsilon q$, where the probability is taken over the randomness of the encryption algorithm.*

To prove that the scheme is secure, it should be shown that it is hard to predict the last entry of the ciphertext b. Our main technical theorem shows that as long as M is chosen from a distribution which is not too far from $\mathcal{M}_{m,n,d}$ or $\mathcal{T}_{m/\binom{n}{d},n}$ the scheme is "somewhat" secure assuming that SearchLIN is intractable for related parameters. Formally,

THEOREM 4. *Let $0 < \delta < 1$ be a constant and d be either 3 or an even number larger than 3, and $m(n) = \Omega(n \lg n), \varepsilon = \varepsilon(n) \leq 0.01$ be functions. Let $\mathcal{D} = \{\mathcal{D}_n\}$ be a distribution ensemble which is $(1 - \delta)$-computationally indistinguishable from $\mathcal{M}_{m,n,d}$ or $\mathcal{T}_{m/\binom{n}{d},n}$. Then there exists a constant c which depends only in δ and d such that:*

1. *For $d = 3$: If $\mathsf{SearchLIN}(3, cm, \varepsilon)$ is intractable then the public-key encryption scheme $\mathcal{E}(\mathcal{D}, \varepsilon)$ is $(1 - \delta/2)$-private.*
2. *For $d > 3$: If $\mathsf{SearchLIN}(d/2, cm, \frac{1-\sqrt{1-2\varepsilon}}{2})$ is intractable then the public-key encryption scheme $\mathcal{E}(\mathcal{D}, \varepsilon)$ is $(1 - \delta/2)$-private.*[8]

[8]As a special case, the theorem essentially shows that for d-LIN, prediction is as hard as search. By combining this with Yao's theorem [56], one can show that the corresponding decision problem (distinguishing a random $(1-\varepsilon)$-satisfiable instance from a random one) is as hard as search as well (with some loss in the parameters).

PROOF. We will sketch the proof only for the (simpler) case of $d = 3$. As described in Section 3, we gradually reduce Search3LIN to the task of breaking $\mathcal{E}(\mathcal{D}, \varepsilon)$.

Step 1: From Search3LIN to AppSearch3LIN. Suppose that we have an algorithm A that solves AppSearch3LIN(m, ε); that is, given a random ε-satisfiable 3-LIN instance $(M, b = Mx + e)$ A outputs an assignment $\hat{x}$ which is 0.1-close to x. We show how to convert A into an algorithm that solves Search3LIN$(m+t, \varepsilon)$ with almost the same success probability, where $t \geq \Omega(n \ln n)$. Given an input $(M, b) \in \mathbb{F}_2^{(m+t)\times n} \times \mathbb{F}_2^{m+t}$, we invoke the approximation algorithm A on the first m rows of the input, and get an approximation $\hat{x}$ for x. Then, we use the information given by the last t rows of the input to correct the errors in $\hat{x}$ as follows. We will recover the i-th bit of x by letting each equation of the form $x_i + x_k + x_\ell = v$ to vote for the correct value of x_i. This vote is simply $\hat{x}_k + \hat{x}_\ell + v_s$, i.e., we compute the value of x_i assuming that v is not noisy and that the approximation for $\hat{x}_k$ and $\hat{x}_\ell$ is correct. Finally, we take the majority of all votes. To analyze the algorithm, we show that each index i is likely to participate in many equations and that w.h.p most of these equations will include only indices for which x and $\hat{x}$ agree, hence, we output x_i with probability at least $1 - o(1/n)$ and therefore (by a union bound) all the indices of x are recovered w.h.p.

Step 2: From AppSearch3LIN to Predict3LIN. Suppose that we have an algorithm A that solves Predict3LIN(m, ε). That is, given a random input $(M, b = Mx + e)$ the algorithm A predicts the value b_m without reading it. It will be convenient to parse the input as a tuple (M', b', v) where (M', b') is the first $m-1$ rows of (M, b) ("training set"), and $v = (i, j, k)$ is the support of the last row of M ("test triple"). We show how to use A to solve AppSearch3LIN$(m + t, \varepsilon)$ for $t = \Omega(n)$. Our reduction employs a subroutine B which transforms a random 3-LIN instance with t equations and noise ε into a random 4-LIN instance with $t/5$ equations and noise $\varepsilon' = 2\varepsilon(1 - \varepsilon)$ and the *same* planted solution. Given B we proceeds as follows.

We break the 3-LIN instance into two parts: the first m equations (M, b) and the remaining t equations (T, z) which are converted into a random 4-LIN instance (R, y) with $t/5$ equations via the subroutine B. Then, we invoke the predictor A for $t/5$ iterations, where the 3-LIN instance (T, z) is being used as the training set in all the iterations, and the test triple of the r-th iteration $v = (i, j, k)$ is randomly chosen from the support of the r-th 4-LIN equation $x_i + x_j + x_k + x_\ell = b$. We guess the value of the variable x_ℓ (which does not appear in v) by XOR-ing A's prediction bit with the LHS b of the 4-LIN equation. Our guess will be correct if the equation is not noisy and the prediction succeeds (or if both events do not happen simultaneously). It can be shown that, if A is a good predictor (e.g., succeeds with probability 0.99) then, with high probability, we will get good guesses for most indices (e.g., 0.9 fraction) and thus obtain a good approximation for x.

Finally, to implement the subroutine B we partition the 3-LIN equations into pairs that share a single variable x_i, and then combine each pair into a 4-LIN equation by simple addition. We make sure that the partition is oblivious to the other entries of the equations by first selecting a random representative from each equation, and then combining pairs that share a common representative. It is not hard to verify that such a strategy results in a random instance of 4-LIN system, and that, except with probability $\exp(-\Omega(t))$, we will get enough equations.

Step 3: Predicting over other distributions. Let $\mathcal{D}$ be a distribution ensemble over 3-sparse matrices which is $(1 - \delta)$-computationally close to $\mathcal{M}_{m,n}$ for some constant δ.[9] Suppose that $\mathcal{E}(\mathcal{D}, \varepsilon)$ is not $(1 - \delta/2)$-private. Hence, there exists a $(1 - \delta/4)$-predictor A for the problem Predict3LIN$(\mathcal{D}, \varepsilon)$ in which the the matrix $\binom{M}{v}$ of the Predict3LIN instance $(M, b = Mx + e, v)$ is chosen from $\mathcal{D}$ and x and e are chosen as before. We show that A can be converted into an 0.99-predictor B for Predict3LIN(m', ε) (over the the uniform distribution) where $m' = c(m-1)+1$ and the constant $c = c(\delta)$ depends only on δ.

Let $\frac{1}{2} < \alpha < \beta < 1 - \delta/4$ be constants, we call a pair (M, v) *good* (resp. *bad*) if A succeeds on an instance $(M, b = Mx+e, v)$ with probability larger than β (resp., smaller than α) over a random choice of x and ε-noisy e. A proper choice of α and β guarantees that: (1) a random pair selected from $\mathcal{M}_{m,n}$ will be good with some constant probability $\gamma > 0$ (by Markov and the closeness of $\mathcal{D}$); and (2) one can efficiently distinguish bad pairs from good pairs by estimating A's success probability (say, via Chernoff bound).

Let us now describe the algorithm B. Given an input (M, b, v) for Predict3LIN(m', ε) partition the matrix M (resp. the vector b) to c sub-matrices $M_1, \ldots, M_c$ (resp. vectors $b_1, \ldots, b_c$) each with $m - 1$ rows. Rerandomize the i-th instance as follows: choose a random $x_i \xleftarrow{R} \mathcal{U}_n$ and a random permutation π_i over $[n]$; Generate the triple $(T_i = \pi_i(M_i), a_i = b_i + T_i \cdot \pi_i(x_i), v_i = \pi(v))$, where we write $\pi(R)$ to denote the matrix R with columns permuted according to π. Note that each of the c instances we created is a random instance of Predict3LIN(m, ε) and, in addition, all the instances are independently distributed. Also, observe that given a good prediction σ_i for the i-th instance we can compute a good prediction for the original instance (M, v, x) by adding σ_i (over $\mathbb{F}_2$) to $\langle x_i, v\rangle$. Hence, we apply A to each instance, translate its answer into a prediction for (M, v, x) and output the majority over the predictions, ignoring the votes of the entries for which (T_i, v_i) are bad. Since $\frac{1}{2} < \alpha$ and $\gamma > 0$ are constants, a sufficiently large constant c decreases the error probability below 0.01. □

4.3 PKE based on 3LIN

We instantiate the scheme $\mathcal{E}(\mathcal{D}, \varepsilon)$ as follows. Let $H_{q,n}^{2,3}$ be the uniform distribution over matrices with n columns and q rows, where each row contains exactly 3 ones and each column contains either 0 or 2 ones. Consider the distribution $\mathcal{T}_{p,n,q}$ which is simply $\mathcal{T}_{p,n}$ conditioned on the event that the matrix T contains a submatrix of rows $H \in \text{support}(H_{q,n}^{2,3})$ that includes the last row of T. Since $H_{q,n}^{2,3}$ is efficiently samplable (via standard techniques), it is possible to sample a triple (M, H, S) where $M \xleftarrow{R} \mathcal{T}_{p,n,q}$, $H \xleftarrow{R} H_{q,n}^{2,3}$ and $M_S = H$ (i.e., S is a q-size subset of the rows of M which points to the submatrix H). We will use this distribution for our key-generation algorithm. First, we argue that the distribution $\mathcal{T}_{p,n,q}$ is not too far (in statistical distance) from $\mathcal{T}_{p,n}$.

LEMMA 2. *There exists a function $q = \Theta(n^{0.2})$ and a con-*

[9]The proof easily extends to the case where $\mathcal{D}$ is close to $\mathcal{T}_{p,n}$ for $p = m/\binom{n}{3}$.

stant $\delta < 1$ such that the distribution $\mathcal{T}_{p=n^{1.4}/\binom{n}{3},n}$ is $1-\delta$ statistically indistinguishable from $\mathcal{T}_{p,n,q}$.

The (omitted) proof relies on the results of Feige, Kim and Ofek [21]. We can now establish Thm. 2.

PROOF OF THM 2. Let p, $q(n)$ and δ be the parameters obtained from Lemma 2 and let $c = c(\delta)$ be the parameter obtained from Thm. 4. Suppose that $\mathsf{Search3LIN}(cn^{1.4}, \varepsilon)$ is intractable for $\varepsilon = kn^{-0.2}$ where k is a sufficiently small constant that will be determined later. By Lemma 2 and Thm. 4, we get that the scheme $\mathcal{E}$ instantiated with the distribution $\mathcal{T}_{p=n^{-1.6},n,q}$ and noise rate ε is $\beta = (1-\delta/2)$-private. Since β is bounded away from 1, and since the error α tends to zero with k (Lemma 1), a sufficiently small constant k will make the error α smaller than $(1-\sqrt{\beta})/2$. Hence, we obtain a weak PKE which can be converted to a semantically secure PKE via the transformation of [28]. □

4.4 PKE based on dLIN and DUE

In the previous section we constructed a PKE based on the intractability of $\mathsf{Search3LIN}(n^{1.4}, n^{-0.2})$, our goal in this section is to relax this assumption and replace it with the intractability of solving the SearchLIN problem with a smaller number of equations ($m = n \log n$), and larger noise rate (e.g., $\varepsilon = n^{-0.1}$). We do this at the expense of adding the DUE as an additional assumption.

The DUE problem. In the following we view a d-sparse matrix $M \in \mathbb{F}_2^{m\times n}$ as a bipartite graph $G = ((V_{\mathsf{Top}}, V_{\mathsf{Bot}}), E)$ with m "top" nodes (each node correspond to a row) and n "bottom" nodes (each node correspond to a column) where each top node has degree d. We call such a graph an (m, n, d) graph. Graphs chosen from $\mathcal{M}_{m,n,d}$ will be, with high probability, very good expanders. That is, we expect that small sets S of top vertices will have almost $d|S|$ neighbors. The distribution $\mathcal{F}^q_{n,m,d}$ is a perturbed version of $\mathcal{M}_{m,n,d}$ in which we plant a single q-size top subset S with a small ("shrinking") neighborhood. Formally, $\mathcal{F}^q_{m,n,d}$ is the result of the following random process: choose G from $\mathcal{M}_{n,m,d}$, choose at random subsets $S \subseteq V_{\mathsf{Top}}$ and $T \subseteq V_{\mathsf{Bot}}$ of sizes q and $q/3$ respectively, and choose a random graph $H \xleftarrow{R} \mathcal{M}_{q/3,q,d}$. Then replace all the $d|S|$ edges in G that are incident to S with the edges from H. In the DUE problem the goal is to distinguish between a random graph sampled from $\mathcal{M}_{n,m,d}$ to a graph sampled from $\mathcal{F}^q_{n,m,d}$. Let $m = m(n), d = d(n)$ and $q = q(n)$ be some functions of n. We say that $\mathsf{DUE}(m, q, d)$ is *δ-intractable* if the distribution ensembles $\mathcal{M}_{n,m(n),d(n)}$ and $\mathcal{F}^q_{n,m(n),d(n)}$ are δ computationally indistinguishable.

The key generation algorithm. Again, we rely on the general bit-encryption of Figure 1. Our key generation algorithm will be based on the DUE planted distribution. We will sample a pair of private/public-keys as follows. Let M be an d-sparse matrix chosen from $\mathcal{F}^q_{n,m(n),d}$ and let S be a shrinking set of size q. We say that a row i in S is degenerate if it is spanned by the other rows in S. Go over the rows of S in a random order, until a degenerate row i is found. (Such a row must exist as S is shrinking and therefore the column rank of the rows indexed by S is smaller than q.) Then, permute the i-th row of M with the last row, and set the public-key to be the permuted matrix M', and the private key to be the set S' which contains the last row of M' and the rows that span it, i.e., $\sum_{j\in S'} M'_j \pmod 2 = \mathbf{0}$.

Security. Let $\mathcal{K} = \mathcal{K}^q_{n,m,d}$ denote the distribution of the public key. Our goal now is to show that $\mathcal{K}$ is $(1-\delta)$ computationally close to the ensemble $\mathcal{M} = \mathcal{M}_{n,m,d}$ for some constant δ, and then apply Thm. 4. Recall that the intractability of DUE asserts that the above is true for the distribution $\mathcal{F} = \mathcal{F}^q_{n,m,d}$, and note that $\mathcal{F}$ can be written as a convex combination $\alpha\mathcal{K}+(1-\alpha)\overline{\mathcal{K}}$, where $\overline{\mathcal{K}}$ is essentially $\mathcal{F}$ conditioned on the last row being out of the planted shrinking set. In general, this does not necessarily means that a good distinguisher for $\mathcal{K}$, yields a good distinguisher for $\mathcal{F}$. Consider, for example, an algorithm that always output 1 on inputs from $\mathcal{K}$, but will output 0 on inputs from $\overline{\mathcal{K}}$. Such an algorithm can be a very good distinguisher for $\mathcal{K}$, and still be useless for $\mathcal{F}$ (say, if it outputs 1 on the uniform distribution with probability α). The crux of the lemma, is to show that in this case, we can distinguish $\mathcal{K}$ from $\overline{\mathcal{K}}$, and therefore can recover some information regarding the planted shrinking set. This information allows us to certify the "shrinkage" of a noticeable fraction of the graphs in $\mathcal{F}$, and so it leads to a distinguisher for $\mathcal{F}$.

THEOREM 5. *Suppose that $\mathsf{DUE}(cm, q, d)$ is $1/2000c^2$ intractable. Then $\mathcal{K}^q_{n,m,d}$ is $(1-\delta)$ computationally close to the ensemble $\mathcal{M}_{n,m,d}$ where $\delta = \delta(c)$ is a constant which depends only in the constant c.*

PROOF SKETCH. Let $\mathcal{K}_n = \mathcal{K}^q_{n,m,d}$, $\mathcal{F}_n = \mathcal{F}^q_{n,m,d}$ and $\mathcal{M}_n = \mathcal{M}_{n,m,d}$. Assume, towards a contradiction, that we have a δ-distinguisher A for $\mathcal{K}_n$ and $\mathcal{M}_n$ where $\delta = 1 - 1/500c^2$. We use A to break DUE as follows. Given a graph G, create the graph G_i in which the i-th row is permuted with the last row, and invoke A on all the G_i's for $i \in [m]$. Define a graph G' by keeping only the rows i of G for which $A(G_i)$ outputs "planted". If the number of remaining rows is larger than n/kc we output "random" where k is some fixed universal constant (e.g., 18). Otherwise, think of G' as a bipartite graph with (at most) n/kc left vertices with degree d and n right vertices, and check whether there exists a perfect matching that consists of all left nodes. If so output "random"; otherwise, output "planted".

We argue that when $G \xleftarrow{R} \mathcal{M}_n$ the above algorithm outputs "random" with probability $1 - o(1)$. Indeed, suppose that we outputted "planted". Then, G' has no matching that consists of all left vertices, and therefore, by Hall's theorem, G' has a shrinking left set. Since G' is a subgraph of G, it follows that G has a left set of vertices of size at most n/kc which shrinks. By standard calculations, a random graph $G \xleftarrow{R} \mathcal{M}_n$, will have such a set only with probability $o(1)$.

It is left to show that when $G \xleftarrow{R} \mathcal{F}_n$ the output is "planted" with some fixed constant probability (e.g., 1/20). To prove this we claim that for a typical graph $G \xleftarrow{R} \mathcal{K}_n$, we have that $A(G_i)$ outputs (1) "planted" for most rows i in the shrinking set, and (2) "random" for most rows i outside of the shrinking set. Assuming that the claim is true (with the appropriate parameters), we complete the argument by noting that if G satisfies (2) then G' has at most n/kc rows, and, in addition by (1), at least $q/2$ rows from the shrinking set appear in G'. Since the neighborhood of these rows is at most $q/3$, the graph G' has no perfect matching (by Hall's theorem), and the algorithm outputs "planted".

It is left to prove the claim. The first part of the claim follows (via Markov) from the fact that A, being a δ distinguisher, outputs "planted" with high probability over $G \xleftarrow{R}$

$\mathcal{K}_n$. The second part of the claim follows from DUE; as if (2) is violated $A(G_i)$ outputs "planted" with high probability over $G \xleftarrow{R} \mathcal{F}_n$ and a random $i \xleftarrow{R} [m]$, and since $A(H_i)$, where $H \xleftarrow{R} \mathcal{M}_n$ and $i \xleftarrow{R} [m]$, outputs "random" with high probability (by our assumption on A), we break DUE. □

COROLLARY 1 (THM. 3 RESTATED). *For every constants d, c and function $q = o(n)$, there exist constants a, b for which: if $\mathsf{DUE}(cn, q, 2d)$ is $1/2000c^2$ intractable as well as $\mathsf{SearchLIN}(d, an \log n, 1/(bq))$ is intractable then there exists a semantically secure PKE.*

PROOF. Suppose that the assumptions hold with parameters d, q, c and sufficiently large constant $a, b > 1$. By Thms. 4 and 5, the resulting scheme is β-private for some constant $0 < \beta < 1$ where β does not depend on the constant b. Hence, by taking b to be sufficiently large, we can reduce the decryption error $\alpha = \frac{1}{2} - \frac{1}{2}(1 - 2 \cdot \varepsilon)^q$ (see Lemma 1) below $(1 - \sqrt{\beta})/2$ and get a PKE. □

4.5 PKE based on DSF and DUE

For an (m, n, d) graph $G = ((V_{\mathsf{Top}}, V_{\mathsf{Bot}}), E)$, and a predicate $f : \{0,1\}^d \to \{0,1\}$, we define the function $G_f : \{0,1\}^n \to \{0,1\}^m$ obtained by mapping every $x \in \{0,1\}^n$ to $(f(x_{\Gamma(1)}), \ldots, f(x_{\Gamma(m)}))$, where $\Gamma(i)$ denotes the neighbors of the i-th "top" node. We prove that there exists a PKE under the assumption that **(1)** (*Decisional Sparse Function* DSF) There exists a function $f : \{0,1\}^d \to \{0,1\}$ for which the distribution $(G, G_f(U_n))$ is ε-indistinguishable from the distribution $(G, \mathcal{U}_m)$ where $G \xleftarrow{R} \mathcal{M}_{m,n,d}$; and **(2)** $\mathsf{DUE}(m, q, d)$ is ε intractable for some $q \in \Theta(\log n)$.

The cryptosystem. The cryptosystem is slightly different than the previous ones, and is inspired by Naor's commitment [44]. To generate a key choose a graph $G \xleftarrow{R} \mathcal{F}^q_{n,m,d}$ together with a q-size shrinking set S, as well as a random string $r \xleftarrow{R} \mathcal{U}_m$. The pair (G, r) is the public-key, while the private key consists of the shrinking set S, and the graph H which is the subgraph of G induced by the set S and its neighbors. To encrypt we choose a random $x \xleftarrow{R} \mathcal{U}_n$. To encrypt the bit 0 output $y = G_f(x)$; To encrypt the bit 1, output $y = G_f(x) + r \pmod 2$. To decrypt a ciphertext z, we output 0 if and only if z_S the restriction of z to the set S is in the image of H_f. (This verification can be implemented efficiently by trying all possible $2^{q/3} = \mathrm{poly}(n)$ preimages.) It is not hard to prove the following Lemma which establishes Theorem 1.

LEMMA 3. *(1) The scheme is errorless with respect to a fraction of $1 - 2^{-q/3}$ of the public-keys. (2) Under the assumptions above, the scheme is 4ε private.*

PROOF SKETCH. (1) Fix G, S and H and let $v = r_S$. We show that for all but $2^{-q/3}$ fraction of the v's the scheme is errorless. Indeed, a decryption error can happen only if there are two different preimages $w_0, w_1 \in \{0,1\}^{q/3}$ for which $H_f(w_0) = H_f(w_1) + v$. Hence, the probability of choosing a "bad" v is at most $2^{q/3} \cdot 2^{q/3}/2^q$. (2) Follows by a standard hybrid argument. □

Since our decryption algorithm looks at only $O(\log m)$ of the bits of an m-bit ciphertext, and since for most of the keys the scheme is errorless, we can show, via standard techniques [33], that there is no efficient algorithm to PAC learn $O(\log m)$-juntas under the same assumptions.

Acknowledgements.

We thank Noga Alon, Moses Charikar, Shafi Goldwasser, Thomas Holenstein, Ron Rivest, Madhu Sudan and Salil Vadhan for useful discussions. We also thank Aditya Bhaskara for sharing with us a copy of [9].

5. REFERENCES

[1] D. Achlioptas and A. Coja-Oghlan. Algorithmic barriers from phase transitions. In *FOCS*, pages 793–802, 2008.

[2] D. Aharonov and O. Regev. Lattice problems in NP intersect coNP. *J. ACM*, 52:749–765, 2005.

[3] M. Ajtai and C. Dwork. A public-key cryptosystem with worst-case/average-case equivalence. In *STOC*, pages 284–293, 1997.

[4] M. Alekhnovich. More on average case vs approximation complexity. In *FOCS*, pages 298–307, 2003.

[5] B. Applebaum, Y. Ishai, and E. Kushilevitz. Cryptography in NC^0. *SIAM J. Comput*, 36(4):845–888, 2006.

[6] S. Arora, L. Babai, J. Stern, and Z. Sweedyk. The hardness of approximate optima in lattices, codes, and systems of linear equations. *J. Comput. Syst. Sci.*, 54(2):317–331, 1997.

[7] S. Arora, B. Barak, M. Brunnermeier, and R. Ge. Computational complexity and information asymmetry in financial products. In *ICS*, 2010.

[8] B. Barak and M. Mahmoody-Ghidary. Merkle puzzles are optimal — an $O(n^2)$ attack on key exchange from a random oracle. In *Proceedings of CRYPTO '09*, 2009.

[9] A. Bhaskara, M. Charikar, E. Chlamtac, U. Feige, and A. Vijayaraghavan. Detecting high log-density — an $O(n^{1/4})$-approximation for densest k-subgraph. In *STOC*, 2010.

[10] E. Biham, Y. J. Goren, and Y. Ishai. Basing weak public-key cryptography on strong one-way functions. In *TCC*, volume 4948, pages 55–72, 2008.

[11] A. Blum, M. Furst, M. Kearns, and R. J. Lipton. Cryptographic primitives based on hard learning problems. In *CRYPTO*, pages 278–291, 1994.

[12] A. L. Blum. Relevant examples and relevant features: Thoughts from computational learning theory. AAAI Fall Symposium on Relevance, 1994.

[13] A. L. Blum and P. Langley. Selection of relevant features and examples in machine learning. *Artificial Intelligence*, 97(1-2):245–271, 1997.

[14] A. Bogdanov and Y. Qiao. On the security of goldreich's one-way function. In *APPROX-RANDOM*, pages 392–405, 2009.

[15] M. Braverman. Poly-logarithmic independence fools AC^0 circuits. In *CCC*, pages 3–8, 2009.

[16] Chor, Goldreich, Hastad, Freidmann, Rudich, and Smolensky. The bit extraction problem or t-resilient functions. In *FOCS*, 1985.

[17] J. Cook, O. Etesami, R. Miller, and L. Trevisan. Goldreich's one-way function candidate and myopic backtracking algorithms. In *TCC*, 2009.

[18] M. Cryan and P. B. Miltersen. On pseudorandom generators in NC^0. In *Proc. 26th MFCS*, 2001.

[19] W. Diffie and M. E. Hellman. New directions in cryptography. *IEEE Transactions on Information Theory*, 22(5):644–654, 1976.

[20] I. Dinur, G. Kindler, R. Raz, and S. Safra. Approximating cvp to within almost-polynomial factors is np-hard. *Combinatorica*, 23(2):205–243, 2003.

[21] U. Feige, J. H. Kim, and E. Ofek. Witnesses for non-satisfiability of dense random 3CNF formulas. In *FOCS*, pages 497–508, 2006.

[22] U. Feige, D. Peleg, and G. Kortsarz. The dense k-subgraph problem. *Algorithmica*, 29(3):410–421, 2001.

[23] Goemans and Williamson. Improved approximation algorithms for maximum cut and satisfiability problems using semidefinite programming. *J. ACM*, 42, 1995.

[24] O. Goldreich. Candidate one-way functions based on expander graphs. Technical Report TR00-090, Electronic Colloquium on Computational Complexity (ECCC), 2000.

[25] O. Goldreich and S. Goldwasser. On the limits of nonapproximability of lattice problems. *J. Comput. Syst. Sci.*, 60(3):540–563, 2000.

[26] O. Goldreich, H. Krawczyk, and M. Luby. On the existence of pseudorandom generators. *SIAM J. Comput*, 22:1163, 1993.

[27] S. Goldwasser and S. Micali. Probabilistic encryption. *J. Comput. Syst. Sci.*, 28(2):270–299, 1984.

[28] T. Holenstein and R. Renner. One-way secret-key agreement and applications to circuit polarization and immunization of public-key encryption. In *CRYPTO*, pages 478–493, 2005.

[29] R. Impagliazzo. A personal view of average-case complexity. In *Structure in Complexity Theory Conference*, pages 134–147, 1995.

[30] R. Impagliazzo and S. Rudich. Limits on the provable consequences of one-way permutations. In *STOC*, pages 44–61, 1989.

[31] Y. Ishai, E. Kushilevitz, R. Ostrovsky, and A. Sahai. Cryptography with constant computational overhead. In *STOC*, pages 433–442, 2008.

[32] A. Juels and M. Peinado. Hiding cliques for cryptographic security. *Designs, Codes and Cryptography*, 20(3):269–280, 2000.

[33] M. Kearns and L. Valiant. Cryptographic limitations on learning Boolean formulae and finite automata. *J. ACM*, 41(1):67–95, 1994.

[34] S. Khot. Ruling out PTAS for graph min-bisection, densest subgraph and bipartite clique. In *FOCS*, pages 136–145, 2004.

[35] N. Koblitz. Elliptic curve cryptosystems. *Mathematics of Computation*, 48:203–209, 1987.

[36] J. B. Lasserre. An explicit exact SDP relaxation for nonlinear 0-1 programs. In *IPCO: 8th Integer Programming and Combinatorial Optimization Conference*, 2001.

[37] M. Laurent. A comparison of the Sherali-Adams, Lovasz-Schrijver, and Lasserre relaxations for 0-1 programming. *MOR: Mathematics of Operations Research*, 28:470–496, 2003.

[38] H. Lipmaa. Cryptology pointers: Public key cryptography: Concrete systems, 1997. Web site, url: `http://www.adastral.ucl.ac.uk/~helger/crypto/link/public/concrete.php`.

[39] L. Lovász and A. Schrijver. Cones of matrices and set-functions and 0-1 optimization. *SIAM Journal on Optimization*, 1(2):166–190, 1991.

[40] R. J. McEliece. A public-key cryptosystem based on algebraic coding theory. *DSN Progress Report*, pages 42–44, 1978.

[41] R. Merkle. Secure communications over insecure channels. *Commun. ACM*, 21(4):294–299, 1978.

[42] V. S. Miller. Use of elliptic curves in cryptography. In *CRYPTO*, volume 218, pages 417–426, 1985.

[43] E. Mossel, A. Shpilka, and L. Trevisan. On epsilon-biased generators in NC^0. *Random Struct. Algorithms*, 29(1):56–81, 2006.

[44] M. Naor. Bit commitment using pseudorandomness. *J. Cryptology*, 4(2):151–158, 1991.

[45] S. K. Panjwani. An experimental evaluation of goldreich's one-way function. Technical report, IIT, Bombay, 2001.

[46] J. Patarin. Hidden fields equations (HFE) and isomorphisms of polynomials (IP): Two new families of asymmetric algorithms. In *EUROCRYPT*, pages 33–48, 1996.

[47] C. Peikert. Public-key cryptosystems from the worst-case shortest vector problem. In *STOC*, pages 333–342, 2009.

[48] C. Peikert, V. Vaikuntanathan, and B. Waters. A framework for efficient and composable oblivious transfer. In *CRYPTO*, pages 554–571, 2008.

[49] M. O. Rabin. Digitalized signatures and public-key functions as intractable as factorization. Technical Report MIT/LCS/TR-212, 1979.

[50] O. Regev. New lattice-based cryptographic constructions. *J. ACM*, 51(6):899–942, 2004.

[51] O. Regev. On lattices, learning with errors, random linear codes, and cryptography. In *STOC*, pages 84–93, 2005.

[52] R. L. Rivest, A. Shamir, and L. Adelman. A method for obtaining digital signatures and public-key cryptosystems. *Commun. ACM*, 21(2):120–126, 1978.

[53] G. Schoenebeck. Linear level Lasserre lower bounds for certain k-csps. In *FOCS*, pages 593–602, 2008.

[54] H. D. Sherali and W. P. Adams. A hierarchy of relaxation between the continuous and convex hull representations for zero-one programming problems. *SIAM J. Disc. Math.*, 3:411–430, 1990.

[55] E. Viola. The sum of d small-bias generators fools polynomials of degree d. In *CCC*, pages 124–127, 2008.

[56] A. C. C. Yao. Theory and applications of trapdoor functions. In *FOCS*, pages 80–91, 1982.

[57] H. Zhu. Survey of computational assumptions used in cryptography broken or not by Shor's algorithm. Master's thesis, School of Computer Science McGill University, 2001.

Oblivious RAMs without Cryptographic Assumptions

[Extended Abstract]

Miklós Ajtai
IBM Almaden Research Center
650 Harry Road
San Jose, CA 95120
ajtai@almaden.ibm.com

ABSTRACT

We show that oblivious on-line simulation with only polylogarithmic increase in the time and space requirements is possible on a probabilistic (coin flipping) RAM without using any cryptographic assumptions. The simulation will fail with a negligible probability. If n memory locations are used, then the probability of failure is at most $n^{-\log n}$. Pippenger and Fischer has shown in 1979, see [7], that a Turing machine with one-dimensional tapes, performing a computation of length n can be simulated on-line by an oblivious Turing machine with two dimensional tapes, in time $O(n \log n)$, where a Turing machine is oblivious if the movements of it heads as a function of time are independent of its input. For RAMs the notion of obliviousness was defined by Goldreich in 1987 in [2], and he proved a simulation theorem about it. A RAM is oblivious if the distribution of its memory access pattern, which memory cells are accessed at which time, is independent of the program running on the RAM, provided that the time used by the program is fixed. That is, an adversary watching the memory access will not know anything about the program running on the machine apart from its total time. Ostrovsky, improving Goldreich's theorem, has shown in 1990, see [4], [5], [3], that a RAM using n memory cells can a be simulated by an oblivious RAM with a random oracle (where the random bits can be accessed repeatedly) so that the increase of the space and time requirement is only about a factor of poly$(\log n)$ (Goldreich's factor was about $\exp[(\log n)^{1/2}]$). In both cases the oblivious RAM with a random oracle, can be replaced, by an oblivious probabilistic (coin-flipping) RAM, provided that we accept some unproven cryptographic assumptions, e.g., the existence of a one-way function. In this paper we show that simulation with an oblivious, coin-flipping RAM, with only a factor of poly$(\log n)$ increase in time and space requirements, is possible, even without any cryptographic assumptions.

STOC'10, June 5–8, 2010, Cambridge, Massachusetts, USA.

Categories and Subject Descriptors

F.1.3 [**Theory of Computation**]: Computation by Abstract Devices—*complexity measures and classes*; F.1.3 [**Theory of Computation**]: Analysis of Algorithms and Problem Complexity—*tradeoffs among complexity measures*

General Terms

Theory

1. INTRODUCTION

In the theorems of Goldreich and Ostrovsky, described in the Abstract, it is assumed that the oblivious RAM has a protected CPU, that is, a constant number of registers, so that, the accesses to these registers are not included into the memory access pattern, and so they are not available to the adversary. We show that the protected CPU is not needed for the present results, since a protected CPU can be simulated on a RAM, so that the time requirement is increasing only by a constant factor, and the space requirement by an additive constant. In fact we may even let the adversary know which instruction is executed at each time, and the results still remain the same. (Note however, that the theorems of Goldreich and Ostrovsky hold even for an adversary who can see the contents of all memory cells outside the protected CPU. There is no equivalent statement in the present result.)

Pippenger and Fischer has shown in 1979, see [7], that a Turing machine with one-dimensional tapes performing a computation of length n can be simulated on-line by an oblivious Turing machine with two dimensional tapes in time $O(n \log n)$, where a Turing machine is oblivious if the movements of its heads as a function of time are independent of its output. Obliviousness means in other words that if an adversary is watching an oblivious Turing machine but can see only the movements of the heads without seeing the contents of the cells of the tapes, then, apart from n, the total time of computation on the original machine, he will not gain any information about the input.

For RAM machines obliviousness was defined by Goldreich, see [2] or [3] as a natural extension of this concept as we will describe later. Theorems which can be considered as the analogue of the mentioned theorems for Turing machine were proved by Goldreich and then improved by Ostrovsky, see [2], [4], [5], [3]. To state these result we use the RAM model as defined in [1]. Suppose that each memory cell of the machine contains a $0, 1$ sequence of length q. For the definition of obliviousness we divide the total memory into the CPU and the main memory. The CPU contains a constant number of cells (their number is independent of q) that we will call registers and the remaining memory cells form the memory of the machine. The registers have the following roles, the results of the arithmetic operations always appear in a register, the instruction pointer is a register, the read instruction puts the content of a memory cell into a register etc. Apart from that, there may be a few registers for temporary storage.

The motivation of the definition of obliviousness is the assumption that there is an adversary who does not see at all what happens in the *CPU*, but when the machine accesses a memory cell to fetch its content to put it into a register or to store the content of a register in a memory cell, then the adversary will know which memory cell was accessed. That is, the adversary knows the access pattern of the memory cells but does not have any information about the accesses of registers and instructions performed on their contents. Since the total time spent on a program cannot be hidden efficiently, we assume that it is known to the adversary. Therefore, in the following discussion, we will assume that the total time spent by the program is fixed. This picture was partly motivated by the problem of software protection, where a physically protected *CPU* is a natural and useful assumption, see [2], [4], [5],[3].

The RAM is oblivious in a deterministic sense if the access pattern of the memory cells (outside the *CPU*) is independent of the program that is executed. To make an oblivious *RAM*, in this deterministic sense, one solution is the following. At each time when an access is needed, the *CPU* reads and rewrites the contents of all of the memory cells used by the program, and this way it hides the single actual operation. There is no more efficient solution in this deterministic sense. Goldreich proved however, see [2], [3], that if the RAM has access to a random oracle then a much more efficient solution is possible. Namely, we will say that a program is oblivious if the distribution of its memory access pattern is independent of the of the program that is executed. Therefore the adversary does not gain any information about the program apart from the time used by it. In Goldreich's solution the time for executing the program increases by a factor of $2^{\sqrt{2\log n \log\log n}}$, where the original program is using a RAM with n memory locations. (The oblivious simulation is on-line in the sense that the simulating program gets the input words and produces the output words in the same overall order than the original program.)

Ostrovsky has improved the efficiency of the simulation so that the time requirement of the oblivious simulation is increased only by a factor of $\text{poly}(\log n)$ and in fact if the time t required by the machine is smaller than n, by a factor of $\text{poly}(\log t)$, and the space requirement of the simulation is larger than the space requirement of the original program by the same $\min\{\text{poly}(\log n), \text{poly}(\log t)\}$ factor. See [4], [5], [3]. Ostrovsky's simulation is called the hierarchical algorithm because of the nature of the data structure used by the RAM. The hierarchical algorithm is also using a random oracle. For a more practical solution (in both cases) the random oracle may be substituted by a probabilistic (coin flipping) RAM, provided that we accept some unproven cryptographic assumption, in the case of Ostrovsky's theorem the existence of a one-way function. Note that a machine using a random oracle has the advantage compared to a coin flipping machine, that the random oracle remembers "for free" previous random steps, while a coin flipping machine, if it does not store this information, then it cannot recover it later. We also note that in the mentioned theorems the simulation can be performed with probability one.

Oblivious simulations are also of interest as a possible defense against so called "cache attacks", see Osvik, Shamir, and Tromer [6], and in general keeping computation more secure.

2. THE MAIN RESULT.

We show that oblivious on-line simulation with polylogarithmic increase in the time and space is possible on a probabilistic (coin flipping) RAM without using any cryptographic assumptions. The simulation will fail with a negligible probability. If n memory locations are used, then the probability of failure is at most $n^{-\log n}$. In case of failure the adversary will get some information about the input. The solution is an extension of Ostrovsky's hierarchical algorithm, some parts of the proofs remain unchanged, but there are also new difficulties leading to combinatorial problems. The most important change is that the randomization is done in different way, so that the machine is now able to recover efficiently the results of previously performed randomizations. This makes it possible to replace the random oracle by coin flipping.

Another improvement is that the assumption about the existence of a protected *CPU* can be dropped, we formulate the theorem directly on a RAM, that is, the adversary will also know which registers are accessed at each time, and which instruction has been executed. However for the proof we use the same protected *CPU* computational model as Goldreich and Ostrovsky and then show, that in a RAM, a protected *CPU* can be simulated.

Computational Model. We use a von Nuemann type random access machine, where data and program are not distinguished. For the definition for such a machine see e.g., in [1] the random access stored program (RASP) machines, in the modified form where the contents of the memory cells are not arbitrary integers, but integers in the interval $[0, 2^q - 1]$.

In order to present the main result concisely, without too many defintions, we restrict our attention to one specific RAM described in [1], with the mentioned modifications. However our results remain true for a very large class of machines including essentially every reasonable defintion for a RAM. Later we will discuss what is "reasonable" in more detail.

For each positive integer $q \geq 10$, $\mathcal{M}_q$ is a machine with 2^q memory cells each containing a sequence of 0, 1 bits of length q. These cells will be called $\texttt{cell}(0), \texttt{cell}(1), \ldots, \texttt{cell}(2^q-1)$. We will consider the sequences contained in the cells as the binary representations of natural numbers from the interval $[0, 2^q-1]$, so if we say that a cell contains the natural number i, we mean it contains its binary representation. (We may restrict the number of memory cells if needed, by simply saying that a particular program is using only the first m cells for some $m < 2^q$. Therefore our requirement that the machine has $2^q - 1$ memory cells, is not a real restriction). The state of the machine at each time is a function which assigns to each of memory cells its content.

$\mathcal{M}_q$ has γ_0 instructions. The names or encodings of these instructions are integers in $[0, 2^q - 1]$.

$\texttt{cell}(0)$ is called the accumulator of the machine and $\texttt{cell}(1)$

the instruction pointer. (The choice of these particular cells for the mentioned roles have no significance.)

The machine $\mathcal{M}_q$ has six types of instructions. (a) arithmetic operations, (b) an instruction to generate a random number, (c) instructions moving data between the memory cells, (d) control transfer instructions, which determine which instruction will be executed next, (e) input/output instructions, and (f) the halt instruction to terminate the execution of the program. We will define each of these types later in more detail.

The machine $\mathcal{M}_q$ is working in cycles, each cycle counts as one time unit. In each cycle it does the following. It checks the content of the instruction pointer. Its content is interpreted as an address, of a memory cell, say, number i. Then the machine executes the instruction whose name is in cell i. An instruction may have parameters (for the sake of simplicity we assume that each instruction has at most one parameter). A parameter typically is the address of a memory cell. The content of cell $i+1$ is considered as the parameter of the instruction in cell number i. The machine executes the instruction with the indicated parameter and then, if it is not a control transfer instruction, it increases the content of the instruction pointer by 2. If it is a control transfer instruction then the instruction defines the new content of the instruction pointer. We will say that *a memory cell or register is involved in an instruction* if its content is used by the machine to execute the instruction, or the result of the instruction is placed in it. We will use this concept by considering an adversary who wants to get some information about what the machine is doing, and at each instruction knows which memory cells/registers are involved in the instructions, but does not know their contents.

(a) The arithmetic instructions are $+, \times, -, \lfloor x/y \rfloor$, the constants $0, 1$, and $2^q - 1$. In case of the arithmetic operations of the form $f(x, y)$, at the time when the machine reads the instruction, which is in $\texttt{cell}(i)$, x must be in the accumulator, and y must be in the memory cell whose address is the parameter of the instruction, that is, y is in $\texttt{cell}(a)$ where a is the content of $\texttt{cell}(i+1)$. The result appears in the accumulator. In the case of the constants, the result of the instruction, that is, the constant, appears in the accumulator (and the value of the parameter is irrelevant).

(b) an instruction to generate a random number. A random integer from the interval $[0, 2^q - 1]$ appears in the accumulator, the value of the parameter is irrelevant.

(c) instructions moving data between the memory cells. Read instruction: if the value of the parameter is a, then the instruction puts the content of $\texttt{cell}(a)$ into the accumulator. Write instruction: if the value of the parameter is a, then the instruction puts the content of the accumulator into $\texttt{cell}(a)$.

(d) control transfer instructions, GOTO X instruction. If the value of the parameter is X then the content of the intruction pointer is changed into a. "IF $X = 0$ THEN GOTO Y" instruction. If the content of the accumulator is 0 then the content of the instruction pointer is changed into Y, where Y is the value of the parameter, otherwise the value of the instruction pointer is increased by 2. "IF $X > 0$ THEN GOTO Y" If the content of the accumulator is greater than 0, then the content of the instruction pointer is changed into Y, where Y is the value of the parameter, otherwise the value of the instruction pointer is increased by 2.

(e) input/output instructions. INPUT instruction. The input is written in the accumulator. OUTPUT instruction. The value of the accumulator is given as output. In both cases the value of the parameter is irrelevant.

(f) HALT instruction. Terminates the execution of the program.

The first few memory cells sometimes will be also called registers. (Intuitively this corresponds to the CPU of a computer.)

A state of the machine $\mathcal{M}_q$, as we have indicated earlier, is a function which assigns to each of it cells a possible content. A history of the machine $\mathcal{M}_q$ is a function defined on an inititial segment I of the natural numbers which assigns a state $S(t)$ to each $t \in I$ with the following property. Suppose that $t, t+1 \in I$ and in $S(t)$ the content of the instruction pointer is a. If a is the name of an instruction different of the input instruction and the random number generator instruction, then we get $S(t+1)$ from $S(t)$, by executing the instruction a with the values contained in the memory cells of $\mathcal{M}_q$ defined by $S(t)$. If a is the input or random number generator instruction then $S(t+1)$ must be a state that is obtained from $S(t)$ by executing instruction a with the values of the memory cells described in $S(t)$, and with a suitably chosen value of the input or the generated random number.

Before the machine starts to work, a program P_0 of constant length is placed in the memory. We will call this the starting program. We may think that this is a small program, whose role is to write in the memory a larger program P and data for P. When we will consider an adversary who wants to get some information about what the machine is doing, we will assume that P_0 is known to the adversary. Because of this, the exact way as P_0 gets into the machine is irrelevant.

We assume that a deterministic program P can run on the machine in the following way. (The assumption that P is deterministic is not essential, we make it only for the sake of simplicity.) Program P_0, the starting program, is already in the machine and asks for inputs. The first part of the input received by P_0 is the program P, (when we say program P, some data for the program may be included in it). P_0 writes the program P into the memory and then transfers the control to program P. While P is running it may ask for input and may also provide output. In this situation we will say that the program P_0 runs the program P. We assume that program P does not use all of the 2^q, q-bit words as possible outputs, say, P can use a q bit word in the output only if its last bit is 0. The remaining q-bit words will be called *exceptional words*, we will explain their roles later. (Actually only a single exceptional word will be needed.)

We will also consider cases when the starting program is not P_0 but another program P_1. P_1 will not run P in the sense described above, rather it will only simulate P in a sense that we will define later.

In the cases of both P_0 and P_1, we define the *history* of the machine $\mathcal{M}_q$, as the sequence of its states. The initial state of the machine $\mathcal{M}_q$ is the state when it starts to work. (E.g. it may contain the program P_0 or P_1 in its initial sate.) Further states of the machine are uniquely determined by its initial sate, by its inputs, and the results of the randomizations. A history of the machine $\mathcal{M}_q$ is a sequence H_t, $t = 0, 1, ...$, where H_t describes the state of the machine at time t, including whether it gives an output or gets an input and if yes what is its value. H_0 is the initial state of the machine. If in the initial state the machine contains the program P_i and later it gets the program P and a sequence a as input, where a is intended as input for P, then the corresponding history will be denoted by $\texttt{history}(P_i, P, a)$. $\texttt{history}(P_1, P, a)$ is a random variable, with respect to the random steps of P_1, whose distribution will be denoted by $\Lambda(P_1, P, a)$.

The *visible history* of the machine $\mathcal{M}_q$ is a sequence $\mathcal{V}_t$, $t = 0, 1, \ldots$, where $\mathcal{V}_t$ consists of the following information, encoded in some way.

(a) the name of the instruction that was executed at time t,

(b) the addresses of the memory cells that were involved in the instruction executed at time t, together with their roles in the instruction, and the name of the intruction.

(c) if an exceptional output was given by the machine at time t, then this fact.

$\Lambda'(P_1, P, a)$ will denote the distribution on the visible histories induced by $\Lambda(P_1, P, a)$. The expression "visible history" is motivated by the assumption that this is what an adversary can see form the operation of the machine.

The *input sequence* of a history H of the machine is a sequence $a_0, a_1, \ldots$ containing all of the inputs occurring in the history H in their order of occurrences. (The timing of the inputs is not included in this sequence.) The sequence $t_0, t_1, \ldots$, where t_i is the time when the machine gets input a_i, for $i = 0, 1, \ldots$ will be called the *input-time sequence* of history H. We define the analogue notions for output sequences as well. We get the input/output or *i/o sequence* of history H, by merging its input and output sequences in the order of their timing, and attaching to each element of the sequence an extra bit which tells whether the corresponding element represents an input or an output. We define *i/o-time sequence* of history H in a similar way, by merging the corresponding input-time an output-time sequences with the extra bits attached.

We will assume that each program P declares its *memory requirements*, that is, a natural number n with the property that P during its execution will use only the first n memory cells of $\mathcal{M}_q$. We assume that the number n is known to P_0, since it it is encoded in some way in the program P. (This is not an essential requirement it can be avoided in the same way as it is done in [4], [5] or [3], but for the sake of simplicity we leave this requirement in the formulation of our results.)

The *conceded history* of program P at input a will be a triplet $\langle n, T, \iota \rangle$, where (a) n is the memory requirement of P, (b) T is the total time used by $\mathcal{M}_q$, when executing P with input a from the start of P_0 till the machine halts, and (c) ι is the i/o-time sequence of $\texttt{history}(P_0, P, a)$. Intuitively, the conceded history is the part of the history, which cannot be hidden from the adversary, at least not without great loss of efficiency, and so we rather assume that the adversary already knows it. Therefore we may assume that the conceded history is fixed and consider the distribution of the visible history with the condition that the conceded history is what we fixed.

Assume now that we replace P_0 by another program P_1 which does not run P only it tries to simulate it in some way. In this case we also allow, that at an arbitrary time, P_1 *declares failure* by giving an exceptional output. (Intuitively this means that P_1 says that "I cannot continue the simulation in the required way". This may happen if the randomizations, performed by P_1, created an unlikely situation, where P_1 would need extra time to keep its data in working order, but this extra time would give information to an adversary about the program P or its input.) When failure is declared, $\mathcal{M}_q$ gives an exceptional output and then stops. Therefore the history and even the visible history of the machine will always show if failure was declared and at what time.

We will say that P_1 *is a correct simulating program*, if for all program P and for all input sequence a, $\texttt{history}(P_0, P, a)$ and $\texttt{history}(P_1, P, a)$ has the same input/output sequence with probability 1, with respect to the randomization done by P_1.

Consider now the situation when the input/output sequence of $\texttt{history}(P_1, P, a)$ may contain an exceptional output (that is, a declaration of failure). The maximal initial segment of the input/output sequence of $\texttt{history}(P_1, P, a)$ which does not contain a failure declaration will be called the *reliable i/o sequence of* $\texttt{history}(P_1, P, a)$.

The program P_1 *is a partially correct simulating program* if for all program P and for all input sequence a, the reliable i/o sequence of $\texttt{history}(P_1, P, a)$ is identical to an initial segment of the i/o sequence of $\texttt{history}(P_0, P, a)$ with probability 1, with respect to the randomization done by P_1.

Assume that $\varepsilon(n)$ is a function, so that for all natural number n, $\varepsilon(n)$ is a real in $[0, 1]$. We will say that *the program P_1 is an oblivious simulating program with an $\varepsilon(n)$ failure rate*, if the following conditions are satisfied:

(i) P_1 is a partially correct simulating program,

(ii) for all programs P and input sequences a, if $\mathcal{V}$ is a random visible history according to distribution $\Lambda'(P_1, P, a)$, then for each natural number t, the probability, that in $\mathcal{V}$ failure is declared at time t, is at most $\varepsilon(n)$, where n is the space requirement of P.

(iii) for each conceded history $\mathbf{h}$, there exists a distribution $\mathcal{D}_{\mathbf{h}}$ on the set of visible histories so that the following holds. For all program P and input sequence a, if $\mathbf{h}$ is the conceded history of $\texttt{history}(P_0, P, a)$, then the distribution $\mathcal{D}_{\mathbf{h}}$ is identical to the conditional distribution of $\Lambda'(P_1, P, a)$, with the condition that failure has not been declared. (That is, the distribution of the visible history of $\texttt{history}(P_1, P, a)$, with the condition that there is no failure, is uniquely determined by the conceded history.)

A simulating program as defined above, with high probability, will not give any information about P and a to the adversary, who knows only the visible history, in addition to what is already contained in the conceded history. Indeed, if the conceded history is fixed, then the distribution of the visible history is also fixed. So the adversary only sees a random value of a random variable whose distribution is known to him. Since the randomization is done by the coin flipping of $\mathcal{M}_q$, the result of it does not contain any additional information about P or a.

Suppose now that the total time in $\texttt{history}(P_0, P, a)$ is T. (T can be determined from the conceded history of $\texttt{history}(P_0, P, a)$.) Assume also that the total time required for the simulation is always at most T', that is, we have that in $\texttt{history}(P_1, P, a)$ there is always a halt instruction no later then time T'. We claim that under these circumstances if P_1 is an oblivious simulating program with failure rate $\varepsilon(n)$, and we choose the pair $\langle P, a \rangle$ at random, so that $\langle P, a \rangle = \langle P^{(i)}, a^{(i)} \rangle$ for $i = 0, 1$ with probabilities

$\frac{1}{2}$, where the conceded history of $\mathtt{history}(P_0, P^{(i)}, a^{(i)})$ is the same $\mathbf{h}$ for $i = 0, 1$, then an adversary, knowing the visible history of $\mathtt{history}(P_1, P, a)$, cannot decide whether $\langle P, a\rangle = \langle P^{(0)}, a^{(0)}\rangle$ or $\langle P, a\rangle = \langle P^{(1)}, a^{(1)}\rangle$ with a greater probability than $\frac{1}{2} + T'\varepsilon(n)$. Indeed, if S is a probabilistic strategy for the adversary, then we may consider the probability of its success both with the condition that there is a failure of the simulation, and with the condition that there is no failure. In the second case the conditional distribution of the visible history of $\mathtt{history}(P_1, P^{(i)}, a^{(i)})$ is $\mathcal{D}_{\mathbf{h}}$ for both $i = 0$ and $i = 1$. Because of the symmetry the probability that S gives the correct answer is exactly $\frac{1}{2}$. Therefore by Bayes' theorem, even if in the case of failure S always gives the correct answer, the probability of success for S, without any conditions, will be at most $(1 - T'\varepsilon(n))\frac{1}{2} + T'\varepsilon(n) \le \frac{1}{2}(1 + T'\varepsilon(n))$.

THEOREM 1. *There exists $c_1, c_2, c_3 > 0$, such that for all $q > 10$ there exists a program P_1 of length at most c_3 for the machine $\mathcal{M}_q$, so that for all sufficiently large q, P_1 is an oblivious simulating program with failure rate at most $n^{-\log n}$. Assume further that P is a program with input "a" so that the space requirement of $\mathtt{history}(P_0, P, a)$ is n, and its total time is t. Then the space requirement of $\mathtt{history}(P_1, P, a)$ is at most $n(\log n)^{c_1}$ and the total time of $\mathtt{history}(P_1, P, a)$ is at most $t(\log n)^{c_2}$.*

Sketch of the proof of Theorem 1. First we formulate Lemma 1 below, that will show that the existence of a protected CPU in the sense of [2], [4], [5], and [3] is not needed as an additional assumption, since such a protected CPU can be simulated in $\mathcal{M}_q$.

We have defined the history of $\mathcal{M}_q$ for the case, when at time 0 the program P_0 or P_1 is in the memory of the machine, and it runs or simulates another program P, which may also get some input a. Therefore, the history depended on three parameters P_i, P, and a. Below, we will need the notion of history in a simpler case, when at time 0 the machine contains a program Q, and while this program is running, there is no further input. The history and visible history for this case is defined in the same way as earlier. We need this notion when we will consider a time interval $[t_1, t_2]$ from a history $\mathtt{history}(P_i, P, a)$, with the property that there is no input in the interval $[t_1, t_2]$. The content of the memory of $\mathcal{M}_q$, at time t_1, can be viewed as a program Q which is running on the machine till time t_2. For discussing the program Q in itself only, we measure the time in a different way, that is, we say that Q starts at time 0 and works till time $t_2 - t_1$. The following general definition of a program is motivated by these considerations.

Definition 1. A program P is a sequence of natural numbers in the interval $[0, 2^q]$. When we say that the machine $\mathcal{M}_q$ starts to work with P in its memory, then we mean that P occupies an initial segment of the memory cells, and the contents of the remaining cells are 0s. If P is deterministic and in the time interval $[0, t]$ the program P does not ask for an input, then P uniquely determines the sequence of the states of $\mathcal{M}_q$ in this interval, which is called the history of the program P in the time interval $[0, t]$, and is denoted by $\mathtt{history}_{[0,t]}(P)$. The visible history in the same interval is the sequence whose ith element is the name of the instruction which is executed by P at time i, together with the memory cells involved in it. (The earlier defintion of "visible history" have had a larger number of parameters, so there is no danger that two notion of "visible history" could be confused.) $\mathtt{length}(P)$ will denote the length of the program P, that is, the number of elements of the sequence P.

2. $\mathtt{cont}_t^{(H)}(i)$ will denote the content of memory cell number i in history H at time t. If the choice of history is clear from the context we may omit the subscript $^{(H)}$. If P, Q are programs then $P \circ Q$ will denote their concatenation as sequences.

3. Suppose that P is a program, t, i, j are nonnegative integers $i \le j$. Then $\mathtt{state}(P, t, i, j)$ is a sequence of q bit words defined in the following way. Assume that $\mathcal{M}_q$ starts to work from the initial state P, and works till time t without asking for input. Then $\mathtt{state}(P, t, i, j)$ is the sequence $\mathtt{cont}_t(i), ..., \mathtt{cont}_t(j)$.

4. The set of memory cells $\mathtt{cell}(0), ..., \mathtt{cell}(i-1)$ will be denoted by $\mathtt{cellset}(i)$.

LEMMA 1. *There exists a $\beta > 0$, and for for all positive integers α there exists a $c_\alpha > 0$, such that for all $q > 10$ there exists a deterministic program P' for the machine $\mathcal{M}_q$ with $\mathtt{length}(P') = \beta$ so that the following holds. For all deterministic programs P with $\mathtt{length}(P) \le \alpha$ and for all positive integers t, statement (1) implies that both conditions (2) and conditions (3) are statisfied, where*

(1). if $\mathcal{M}_q$ starts to work from the initial state P, then $\mathcal{M}_q$ does not ask for any inputs, does not give any outputs, in the interval $[0, t]$, and all of the memory cells involved in the instructions during the time interval $[0, t]$ are in the set $\mathtt{cellset}(\alpha)$.

(2). $\mathtt{state}(P, t, 0, \alpha-1) = \mathtt{state}(P' \circ P, c_\alpha t, \beta, \beta+\alpha-1)$

(3). if H is the history of the machine $\mathcal{M}_q$ starting from the initial state $P' \circ P$, then the machine does not ask for any input during the time interval $[0, c_\alpha t]$ in history H, and the visible history of H in the interval $[0, c_\alpha t]$ does not depend on P.

Remark. 1. This lemma implies that a program P of constant size, whose execution involves only those memory cells where the program is residing at the start, can be run by another program efficiently in an oblivious way.

2. Using this lemma we will be able to accomplish the same task obliviously on a RAM, that can be accomplished by using a protected CPU, if our goal is to make the program oblivious. Note that in [2], [4], [5], [3] the protected CPU is used for other tasks as well. Namely, with the help of a protected CPU the contents of all other memory cells can be encrypted, and so the adversary can even see the (encrypted) contents of all of the memory cells outside the protected CPU, without gaining any meaningful knowledge about the input. In the present context however, when we consider the knowledge of the adversary in an information theoretic sense, without taking into account the limitation imposed by computation, such an encryption is not possible.

3. In the proof of this lemma to access the memory cells obliviously is not a problem, since at each step we may access all of them. The problematic instructions are the conditional instructions of the type "IF $X = 0$ THEN GOTO Y".

4. We assumed that both P and P' are deterministic. We will be able to use the lemma for probabilistic programs too in the following way. The randomizations will take place

at predetermined times and we will apply the lemma only for the time intervals between the randomizations. P will work as a deterministic program, separately in each of these intervals, and the previously chosen random values will be parts of the initial states of P in these intervals. We will use the same solutions for input/output instructions and instructions involving cells not in $\texttt{cellset}(\alpha)$. All of these instructions will be executed only at predetermined time and the lemma will be applied only to the time interval between them.

Now we return to the sketch of the proof of Theorem 1. We are following the idea of using Interactive Turing Machines, as described in [2], [4], [5], or [3], for the simulation. We present it in an essentially equivalent but formally somewhat different computational model. The reason why we use a different setup is to make it easier to express our present goals. We do not assume that the reader is familiar with the notion of Interactive Turing Machines.

Suppose that $\tilde{\gamma} > 0$ is a constant that we will choose later. P_1 will simulate the program P in the following way. We cut the memory of $\mathcal{M}_q$ into two parts. The first part consists of the set of the first $\tilde{\gamma}$ memory cells, which we will call the CPU (and later will play the role of a protected *CPU*). The second part consists of the remaining memory cells whose set will be called the memory module. This partition will be used in the following way. $\texttt{history}(P_0, P, a)$ is a sequence $H_0, H_1, ...$, where H_t is the state of the machine $\mathcal{M}_q$ at time t. P_1 will represent H_t with a data structure R_t stored in the memory module. During the simulation, when going from time t to time $t+1$, P_1 has to transform R_t into R_{t+1} on the average in poly$(\log n)$ time.

The change in the history $\texttt{history}(P_0, P, a)$ from H_t to H_{t+1} involves only the contents of a constant number of memory cells. Namely those memory cells which are involved in the execution of the instruction at time t. (This may include an input appearing in the accumulator.) Therefore P_1 will do the following. (a) Using the data structure R_t, it will determine the contents of the memory cells which are involved in the instructions at time t in $\texttt{history}(P_0, P, t)$, and copy them into the *CPU*. (b) In the *CPU* it will determine which memory cells are those whose content are changing from H_t to H_{t+1}, and what are those changes. Then (c) based on the results of the previous step it changes R_t into R_{t+1}.

The difficulty is that the representation R_t must be chosen in a way that all of these steps can be carried out obliviously in the sense of Theorem 1. Step (b) can be carried out by using Lemma 1. The computation done in the *CPU* with a constant number of registers, can be transformed into an oblivious computation using the lemma, if we allow that the number of registers is a larger constant. As we mentioned earlier all of the randomizations, input output instructions and accesses for memory cells outside the *CPU* will be done at predetermined times and we apply Lemma 1 only to the time intervals between them. Therefore the only problem is to represent the states of the machine in history $\texttt{history}(P_0, P_1, a)$ in a way that the necessary changes can be made obliviously.

Since the total memory requirement of $\texttt{history}(P_0, P_1, a)$ is n memory cells, the problem can be formulated in the following way. There are n variables $x_0, ..., x_{n-1}$ with initial values 0, whose values are sometimes changing. R_t has to represent somehow the current evaluation of these variables so that the change of the value of a variable can be carried out obliviously in poly$(\log n)$ time. Below we formulate this problem in a framework which makes its solution a special case of Theorem 1.

This special case of Theorem 1 formulated in Lemma 2 has the following form. It restricts the theorem to a single program P, and it also weakens the adversary. First we describe the program P which will be used in Lemma 2. Program P does the following. If an input arrives of the form $\langle a, v, 0\rangle$ then P puts the integer v into memory cell with address $a + k_0$, where k_0 is a fixed integer, and gives the output v. If an input arrives of the form $\langle a, v, 1\rangle$ then P reads the content of memory cell number $a + k_0$ and gives its value as output. (We assume that the initial content of each memory cell is 0)

If a is restricted to the interval $[0, n-1]$ then we can say that P is maintaining the values of the variables $x_0, ..., x_{n-1}$, with initial values 0, so that if an input of the type $\langle a, v, 0\rangle$ arrives a new value v is set for variable x_a, while an input $\langle a, v, 1\rangle$ is interpreted as a question of the present value of variable x_a and P responds according to this. (In the first case the output v has no function, and in the second case the input v has no function. They are included only to make the lengths of the outputs and inputs the same in the two cases. This way the two cases have identical conceded histories, and so an adversary knowing only this cannot tell, whether in a specific instance the value of a variable was set, or a question was asked about it.) The triplet $\langle a, v, \delta\rangle$, $\delta = 0, 1$ may be encoded in several actual input words. The actual encoding is irrelevant the only important point is that the number of input words which code $\langle a, v, \delta\rangle$ is always the same. Assume that the values v are always integers in the interval $[0, \wp]$. A program P which accomplishes the task described above, will be called a memory-maintenance program with n variables and with values in $[0, \wp]$. Suppose that $\wp < 2^q$ and $n < 2^q$, then the memory requirement of the memory maintenance program is $n + c$ memory cells, where c is a constant.

As we said earlier Lemma 2 is a special case of Theorem 1 in the sense that the adversary in the lemma will be weaker than in the theorem. In the description of this weaker adversary, for each natural number l, M_l will denote the set of all memory cells number i of $\mathcal{M}_q$ with $i \geq l$. We replace the notion visible history (in the definition of obliviousness) by the notion of k-visible history, where the k-visible history of $\mathcal{M}_q$ is the sequence $\mathcal{V}_t$, $t = 0, 1, ...$, where $\mathcal{V}_t$ consists of the following information encoded in some way.

(a) the name of the instruction that was executed at time t, provided that at least one of the memory cells involved in the instruction is in M_k.

(b) the addresses of those memory cells in M_k that were involved in the instruction executed at time t

(c) if an exceptional output was given by the machine at time t, then this fact

We define now the notion of an k-oblivious simulating program the same way as an oblivious simulating program, but we replace the notion of visible history everywhere with k-visible history. In particular $\mathcal{D}_O$ in properties (ii), (iii), and (iv) of the definition will be a distribution on k-visible histories, and in property (iv) we are speaking about the distribution of the k-visible history of $\texttt{history}(P_1, P, a)$.

In other words we have now an adversary who does not see what happens in the first k memory cells. We will use this in the case when k is a constant. The machine this way will work as if it had a protected CPU with k registers. (By Lemma 1, we will be able to simulate this situation so that an adversary even with the complete original powers, that has been defined for Theorem 1, will not get any additional information.)

LEMMA 2. *There exists a constant $\tilde{\gamma} > 0$ so that Theorem 1 holds if P is a memory maintenance program, and we require of P_1 that it must be only a $\tilde{\gamma}$-oblivious simulating program.*

Before we sketch the proof of Lemma 2 we give some simple definitions which will be useful both in the sketch and the final proof.

Definition We will assume that $n = 2^d$ is a power of 2. Part of the memory of the machine $\mathcal{M}_q$ (outside the protected cells) is partitioned into blocks of poly$(\log n)$ memory cells, each will be called a bucket. We have altogether $2n-1$ buckets. The set of buckets is partitioned into $d+1$ classes $\mathcal{B}_0, \mathcal{B}_1, ..., \mathcal{B}_d$ called buffers. Buffer $\mathcal{B}_i$ contains exactly 2^i buckets $\mathbf{b}_{i,0}, ..., \mathbf{b}_{i,2^i-1}$.

Definition 1. A tree T is partially ordered set with a largest element 1_T and with the property that for all $a, b \in T$ if $a, b \in T$ are incomparable then they do not have a common lower bound in T.

Definition We assume that d is a positive integer, $n = 2^d$, and T_n is a binary tree of depth d with $2n-1$ elements. The ith level of T will be denoted by $L_i^{(T_n)}$. We have that $|L_i^{(T_n)}| = 2^i$ for $i = 0, 1, ..., d$. We will omit the subscript $^{(T_n)}$ if its choice is clear from the context. Assume that $\tau \in T_n \backslash L_d$. The two successors of τ will be labelled by 0 and 1, and according to this denoted by $\tau^{(0)}$ and $\tau^{(1)}$. Suppose that $\delta = \langle \delta_0, ...\delta_{d-1} \rangle$ is a 0,1 sequence of length d. We associate with the sequence δ a branch of the tree $b_0, ..., b_d$ with the property that $b_0 = 1_{T_n}$ and $b_{i+1} = b_i^{(\delta_i)}$ for all $i = 0, 1, ..., d-1$. Clearly $b_i \in L_i$. We will use the notation $\texttt{branch}(\delta) = \{b_0, ..., b_{d-1}\}$, $\texttt{node}(\delta, i) = b_i$ and $\texttt{leaf}(\delta) = b_{d-1}$. $\mathbf{L}_j = \mathbf{L}_j^{(T_n)}$ will denote the set $\bigcup_{s \le j} L_s^{(T_n)}$. The ancestor unique of an element $\tau \in T_n$ will be denoted by τ°.

Sketch of the proof of Lemma 2. The program P_1 of the lemma will maintain the values of the variables almost the same way as the "hierarchical algorithm" given by Ostrovsky, see [4], [5], [3]. The main difference will be in the randomization. Because of that, we add extra steps to the hierarchical algorithm as explained below.

First we sketch the basic idea of Ostrovsky's hierarchical algorithm in the present context. We make some minor changes compared to the original formulation, however these do not affect the substance.

Assume that the algorithm $\mathcal{H}$, using a random oracle, wants to store and recall the values of the variables $x_0, ..., x_{n-1}$ in an oblivious way. (The new algorithm with coin flipping only, will be denoted by $\mathcal{Y}$.) For the sake of simplicity and without the loss of generality we assume that $n = 2^d$, where d is an integer.

We will use the buckets and buffers defined earlier. In the case of algorithm $\mathcal{H}$, a bucket will contain $O(\log n)$ memory cells. The buckets will contain information about the values of the variables in form of pairs $\langle a, v \rangle$, where $a \in [0, n-1]$, $v \in [0, \wp]$. These pairs are represented in a way that a pair occupies only a constant number of memory cells. A bucket can contain only one copy of a pair.

While $\mathcal{H}$ is working, at each time, and for each $a \in [0, n-1]$, there is exactly one pair of the form $\langle a, v \rangle$ which is contained in one of the buckets, and it is contained only in one bucket. If the pair $\langle a, v \rangle$ is contained in a bucket, at a time, then the value of the variable x_a at this time is v. Therefore the goal of algorithm $\mathcal{H}$ is to keep these pairs in places that can be found in poly$(\log n)$ time on the average in an oblivious way. Algorithm $\mathcal{H}$, using a random oracle, accomplishes this in the following way.

Algorithm $\mathcal{H}$ will get, through its inputs, either a request for the value of a variable, or a request for changing its value. These requests will be handled in a similar way, therefore we call each of them a request for an access for the variable. The time of algorithm $\mathcal{H}$ (after an initial setup) is partitioned into intervals $\mathbf{A}_1, \mathbf{B}_1, \mathbf{A}_2, \mathbf{B}_2, ..., \mathbf{A}_i, \mathbf{B}_i, ...$ which are coming in the given order. The ith request for an access of a variable will arrive at the beginning of interval $\mathbf{A}_i$ and $\mathcal{H}$ completes the necessary changes and gives the required output in this interval. Therefore we will call $\mathbf{A}_i$ an access interval. The length of the time interval $\mathbf{A}_i$ will be $O(\text{poly}(\log n))$, and it will be independent of i.

The intervals $\mathbf{B}_i$ are used for a random rearrangement of the pairs in the buckets. These intervals are called epochs in Ostrovsky's description of the hierarchical algorithm. Sometimes we will also call them bookkeeping intervals. The length of an epoch $\mathbf{B}_i$ will depend on i in a way that, for all $k = 1, 2, ...$ the total length of epochs $\mathbf{B}_1, ..., \mathbf{B}_k$ will not be greater than $k$poly$(\log n)$. We will achieve this by requiring that $|\mathbf{B}_i| \le \text{poly}(\log n) 2^{\mathbf{a}(i)}$, where $\mathbf{a}(i)$ is the largest integer so that $2^{\mathbf{a}(i)}$ is a divisor of both i and $n = 2^d$.

First we describe what happens in an interval $\mathbf{B}_i$. The algorithm $\mathcal{H}$ does not keep any other data then i and the pairs in the buckets. In epoch $\mathbf{B}_i$ the algorithm $\mathcal{H}$ reorganizes the contents of the buckets in the following way. $\mathcal{H}$ goes through all of the buckets in $\bigcup_{j \le \mathbf{a}(i)} \mathcal{B}_j$ in a predetermined order. For each pair $\langle a, v \rangle$ that $\mathcal{H}$ finds in any of these buckets it randomly chooses a new destination bucket, where they have to go, by the end of $\mathbf{B}_i$. The randomization is done by the random oracle by providing a value $h(a, i) \in \{0, 1, ..., 2^{\mathbf{a}(i)} - 1\}$ with uniform distribution. The meaning of the number $h(a, i)$ is that the pair $\langle a, v \rangle$ must get into bucket $\mathbf{b}_{\mathbf{a}(i), h(a,i)}$ of buffer $\mathcal{B}_{\mathbf{a}(i)}$ by the end of epoch $\mathbf{B}_i$. $\mathbf{b}_{\mathbf{a}(i), h(a,i)}$ will be called the destination bucket of the pair $\langle a, v \rangle$. It is important that the random hash value $h(a, i)$ depends only on a and i. At this time only the random choice of the destination bucket takes place, so that each of the destination buckets has uniform distribution on buffer $\mathcal{B}_{\mathbf{a}(i)}$ and all of these choices are mutually independent. $\mathcal{H}$ does not take out the pairs at this point from the buckets, it only attaches the random destination to each pair, some way.

Since the buckets contain only $O(\log n)$ memory cells, this choice of and recording of destinations can be done obliviously using poly$(\log n)$ time for each bucket that is altogether $2^{\mathbf{a}(i)}$poly$(\log n)$ time.

The next phase of the algorithm, whose details are not sketched here, takes each pair to its chosen destination. This is done by using several times, an oblivious sorting network e.g., Batcher's algorithm or AKS network. A possible way to do this is described in [4], [5], and a slightly different one in [3]. We will use this technique, with either of the two solutions, in the present proof without any essential changes. For our purposes, it is enough to know, that each pair gets into its chosen destination in a deterministic and oblivious way in time $2^{\mathbf{a}(i)}\text{poly}(\log n)$. This completes the description of $\mathcal{H}$ in the epoch $\mathbf{B}_i$.

We note here that with a small probability it may happen that too many pairs has the same destination bucket and, so there is not enough memory cells in the bucket to store all of the pairs sent there, We will say in such a case that the bucket is overfilled. In algorithm $\mathcal{H}$ this does not cause a serious problem, since if this happens, the whole randomization can be repeated and the additional expected time will be very small. However in the new algorithm $\mathcal{Y}$, using coin flipping only, this treatment of overfilling could leak information to the adversary. Therefore we will use in algorithm $\mathcal{Y}$ bigger buckets with size $O(\text{poly}(\log n))$, and will show that with high probability no buckets will be overfilled. (Since the randomization will be different this requirement will create major difficulties in the proof.) If a bucket is still overfilled then the algorithm $\mathcal{Y}$ will declare failure.

The described action of algorithm $\mathcal{H}$ in the epochs $\mathbf{B}_i$ has the result, that if a pair $\langle a, v\rangle$ is not moved during the intervals $\mathbf{A}_j$ then during the various epochs it travels through the buffers $\mathcal{B}_0, \mathcal{B}_1, ..., \mathcal{B}_d$ in this order and then it stays in $\mathcal{B}_d$. Motivated by this we may define the initial setup in a way that all of the pairs $\langle a, 0\rangle$, $a \in [0, n-1]$ are put in the buckets of $\mathcal{B}_d$ in a random way. The randomization can be accomplished in a similar way, that we have described above. Actually this initial setup can be avoided and the number of buffers and buckets can be increased gradually putting only pairs $\langle a, v\rangle$ into them where there was already a request for access for the value of x_a, see [4], [5]. For the sake of a picture with less complicating factors for the coin flipping algorithm that we will describe later, we allow an initial setup.

Now we describe the algorithm $\mathcal{H}$ in an access interval $\mathbf{A}_j$. At the beginning of this interval a request arrives concerning the value of the variable x_{a_j}. The algorithm $\mathcal{H}$ has to find a pair of the form $\langle a_j, x\rangle$ which must be in one of the $2n-1$ buckets. Since the time allowed for this step is only $\text{poly}(\log n)$, $\mathcal{H}$ cannot look in all of the buckets. It searches for the pair in the following way. $\mathcal{H}$ searches for the bucket containing $\langle a_j, x\rangle$ in the buffers $\mathcal{B}_0, ..., \mathcal{B}_d$ in this order. When it gets to buffer $\mathcal{B}_r$, for some fixed $r = 0, 1, ..., d$, $\mathcal{H}$ does the following. Knowing r and j, it finds the largest integer $i_r < j$ so that $\mathbf{a}(i_r) = r$. The importance of this integer i_r is that $\mathbf{B}_{i_r}$ was the last epoch, when the destination buckets were in buffer $\mathcal{B}_{\mathbf{a}(i_r)} = \mathcal{B}_r$. Therefore, if at the beginning of $\mathbf{B}_{i_r}$ the pair $\langle a_j, x\rangle$ was in a bucket in $\bigcup_{s\le r}\mathcal{B}_s$, then during $\mathbf{B}_{i_r}$ it got into a bucket in buffer $\mathcal{B}_r$, namely into bucket $\mathbf{b}_{r,h(a_j,i_r)}$. $\mathcal{H}$ using the random oracle determines $h(a_j, i_r)$ and checks whether the pair is really there. If $\mathcal{H}$ finds the pair it removes it and puts it into the single bucket $\mathbf{b}_{0,0}$ of buffer $\mathcal{B}_0$.

Even if $\mathcal{H}$ has found a pair $\langle a_j, x\rangle$ in one of the buffers, it repeats the same action for the remaining buffers pretending still looking for the pair $\langle a_j, x\rangle$ and pretending putting it into $\mathbf{b}_{0,0}$.

This action of $\mathcal{H}$ reveals for the adversary a bucket in each buffer $\mathcal{B}_r$ that is searched by $\mathcal{H}$. This bucket is $\mathbf{b}_{r,h(a_j,i_r)}$ in $\mathcal{B}_r$. For a fixed a_j and i_r, $h(a_j, i_r)$ has uniform distribution on $[0, 2^r-1]$. Therefore at this point the adversary gets the value of $h(a_j, i_r)$. At other times during the execution of the algorithm $\mathcal{H}$ the adversary will get other values $h(u, v)$ but never again with $u = a_j$, $v = i_r$. Therefore when the adversary gets the values of h, he will simply see the values of independent random variables with predetermined distribution. Consequently the adversary does not gain any information from the addresses of the buckets searched by $\mathcal{H}$. The search of the buckets and all of the other actions of $\mathcal{H}$ can be done in a way that the sequence of these buckets uniquely determine the memory access pattern of $\mathcal{H}$.

After all of the buffers have been searched in the described way, the pair $\langle a_j, x\rangle$ is in the bucket of $\mathcal{B}_0$. Changing x, if needed, and giving the appropriate output can be done obliviously in a deterministic way. This describes the action of $\mathcal{H}$ in an access interval $\mathbf{A}_j$.

Summarizing this process, in each access interval we bring the pair $\langle a, x\rangle$ to the buffer $\mathcal{B}_0$, where x_a is the variable to be accessed, and x is its current value. Later, during the epochs $\mathbf{B}_j$, the pair $\langle a, y\rangle$, where y is the new value of the variable x_a will go through the buffers $\mathcal{B}_0, \mathcal{B}_1, ...$ with a random choice of the bucket where it is located, until there will be a request again concerning x_a. The algorithm is oblivious, because the only memory accesses which are not known in advance are the accesses for the contents of the buckets $\mathbf{b}_{r,h(a_j,i_r)}$, $i = 1, 2, ...$, $r = 1, 2, ...d$ described above, and, as we have seen, this sequence has a predetermined distribution which is independent of the input.

Replacing the random oracle with coin flipping. We describe now an algorithm $\mathcal{Y}$, with coin flipping instead of using a random oracle, which essentially accomplishes the same thing as algorithm $\mathcal{H}$. Later we will modify algorithm $\mathcal{Y}$ because in the simple form presented here the probability of overfilling of a bucket may be too high. However this modified algorithm will differ from $\mathcal{Y}$ only in the choice of a parameter. The reason why the algorithm is working remains the same.

Suppose that $\mathcal{Y}'$ is the algorithm that we get from $\mathcal{H}$ by simply using coin flipping instead of a random oracle. The problem will be that algorithm $\mathcal{Y}'$ will not know what was the destination of the pair $\langle a_j, x\rangle$ when it was put into buffer $\mathcal{B}_{\mathbf{a}}(i) = \mathcal{B}_r$. To keep this information in the memory even for buffer $\mathcal{B}_1$ with only 2 buckets, would require keeping n bits of information in the memory so that they are available obliviously. This is a task almost as difficult as the original problem. Therefore algorithm $\mathcal{Y}'$ does not meet our requirements.

To overcome this difficulty our solution is the following. Instead of putting the pairs $\langle a, x\rangle$ directly into a bucket in the physical memory of $\mathcal{M}_q$, first we give them a symbolic address (may be also called a logical address) which will be a node of the binary tree T_n defined earlier. This symbolic address will depend only on a, and not on x, but it may change in each time interval $\mathbf{A}_i$ or $\mathbf{B}_i$, that is, it also depends on the time. The current symbolic address of an $a \in \{0, 1, ..., n-1\}$ will be denoted by $\mathtt{symb}(a)$. If $\mathtt{symb}(a) = \tau$, then the pair $\langle a, x\rangle$ is at node τ of the tree. This assignment of symbolic addresses will be done in a random way, as we will describe below, but using only $\text{poly}(\log n)$ random bits, which can be kept in the memory so that the symbolic addresses can be recalculated d-obliviously any time.

Recall that L_i has denoted the ith level of the tree as defined in the definition of T_n. Separately for each node τ of the tree in L_i, $i = 0, 1, ..., d$ we will select a random bucket $\mathbf{p}(\tau)$ in $\mathcal{B}_i$ with uniform distribution. The pair $\langle a, x\rangle$ with $\mathtt{symb}(a) = \tau$ will be stored in bucket $\mathbf{p}(\tau)$. So we may say that the physical address of $\langle a, x\rangle$ will be $\mathbf{p}(\tau)$, if $\mathtt{symb}(a) =$

τ. $\mathcal{Y}$ will select $\mathbf{p}(\tau)$ with uniform distribution on $\mathcal{B}_i$, if $\tau \in L_i$. These selections will be mutually independent, and also independent of the random selections of the symbolic addresses $\mathtt{symb}(a)$. $\mathbf{p}(\tau)$ will change during the execution of algorithm $\mathcal{Y}$ but only in the intervals $\mathbf{B}_i$. Since $\mathcal{Y}$ has to know which is the bucket $\mathbf{p}(\tau)$, when it has to find a pair $\langle a, x\rangle$ with $\mathtt{symb}(a) = \tau$, the address of $\mathbf{p}(\tau)$ in $\mathcal{M}_q$, that we will denote by $\bar{\mathbf{p}}(\tau)$, must be stored somewhere, and when needed recovered in an oblivious way. For all possible $\tau \in T_n$ storing $\bar{\mathbf{p}}(\tau)$ obliviously requires altogether storing about $O(n \log n)$ bits obliviously, just like in the original problem. Our solution will be, as we describe in more details below, that we will store the addresses $\bar{\mathbf{p}}(\tau)$ in the buckets, the same way as we store the data about the values of the variables x_a. More precisely we will store pairs $\langle \bar{\tau}, \bar{\mathbf{p}}(\tau)\rangle$, where the element τ of the tree will be represented by the integer $\bar{\tau}$, in some efficient way. To do that each node $\tau \in T_n$, $\tau \neq 1$ will have a symbolic address $\mathtt{symb}_T(\tau)$ which is an element of the tree with $\mathtt{symb}_T(\tau) > \tau$ and the pair $\langle \bar{\tau}, \bar{\mathbf{p}}(\tau)\rangle$ will be stored in the bucket $\mathbf{p}(\mathtt{symb}_T(\tau))$. The requirement $\mathtt{symb}_T(\tau) > \tau$ is very important. This will guarantee that as $\mathcal{Y}$ will go down on a branch B of the tree starting from the root, and looking into all buckets $\mathbf{p}(\sigma)$ with $\sigma \in B$, by the time $\mathcal{Y}$ reaches a $\tau \in B$ and needs to know what is $\bar{\mathbf{p}}(\tau)$ it already have seen it in a bucket $\mathbf{p}(\sigma)$ for some $\sigma > \tau$. We will describe below more precisely how this is done by $\mathcal{Y}$. Since $\mathbf{p}(1_{T_n}) = \mathbf{b}_{0,0}$, we do not need a symbolic address for 1_{T_n}.

The algorithm $\mathcal{Y}$ generates a random function χ which assigns to each integer $a \in [0, n-1]$ a 0,1 sequence $\chi(a)$ of length d. We require from the function χ that for any subset $A \subseteq [0, n-1]$ with $|A| \leq \mathrm{poly}(\log n)$ the random variables $\chi(a)$, $a \in A$ are mutually independent. Such a random function χ can be generated by selecting only $\mathrm{poly}(\log n)$ random bits. For example $\chi(a)$ can be the determined by the value of a random polynomial of degree $(\log n)^c$ over the finite field F_{2^d}. The coefficients are chosen uniformly from F_{2^d} and can be represented altogether by $(\log n)^{c+1}$ random bits. The value of the polynomial is an element of the field which over a fixed basis, can be interpreted as a 0,1 sequence of length d. Therefore the random function χ can be generated by $\mathrm{poly}(\log n)$ coin flipping during the setup, the algorithm $\mathcal{Y}$ will keep the results of these coinflips, and so it can recalculate $\chi(a)$ d-obliviously any time for each $a \in [0, n-1]$. It is very important that *the randomization of χ will be performed only once* and the same $\mathrm{poly}(\log n)$ random bits defining χ are used till $\mathcal{Y}$ halts.

Recall that a branch was assigned to each 0,1 sequence s of length d, and denoted by $\mathtt{branch}(s)$. Therefore by the randomization of χ we also assign a random branch $\mathtt{branch}(\chi(a))$ to each integer $a \in [0, n-1]$. For such an integer a, $\mathtt{symb}(a)$ *will be always in* $\mathtt{branch}(\chi(a))$.

$\mathtt{symb}(a)$ for $a \in [0, n-1]$ will be determined in the following way. At the beginning $\mathtt{symb}(a)$ is the leaf at the end of $\mathtt{branch}(\chi(a))$.

Suppose that in an interval $\mathbf{A}_j$ the input is $\langle a_j, v_j, \Psi_j\rangle$. Then for all $a \in [0, n-1]$, if $\mathtt{symb}(a) \in \mathtt{branch}(\chi(a_j))$ at the beginning of $\mathbf{A}_j$ then at the end of $\mathbf{A}_j$, $\mathtt{symb}(a)$ is changed into 1_{T_n}. The symbolic addresses of all of the other integers $a \in [0, n-1]$ remain unchanged.

In an epoch $\mathbf{B}_i$ the change is the following. If at the beginning of $\mathbf{B}_i$ we have $\tau = \mathtt{symb}(a) \in \bigcup_{s \geq \mathtt{a}(i)} L_s$ then $\mathtt{symb}(a)$ remains unchanged in $\mathbf{B}_i$. Otherwise, that is, if $\tau \in \bigcup_{s < \mathtt{a}(i)} L_s$, $\mathtt{symb}(a)$ is changed into the unique element of $\mathtt{branch}(\chi(a)) \cap L_{\mathtt{a}(i)}$. This completes the description of how the symbolic addresses are selected.

The selections of the buckets $\mathbf{p}(\tau)$. We have to assign to each node $\tau \in L_i$ a bucket $\mathbf{p}(\tau)$ in buffer $\mathcal{B}_i$ for $i = 0, 1, ..., d$. For each $\tau \in L_i$, $\mathbf{p}(\tau)$ will be chosen at random with uniform distribution from $\mathcal{B}_i$ and the choices will be mutually independent for $\tau \in L_i$, $i = 0, 1, ..., d$, moreover they will be also independent of the choice of the function χ. At the startup we make a random selection for $\mathbf{p}(\tau)$, for each $\tau \in T_n$, and update it only in the time intervals $\mathbf{B}_i$. In the access intervals $\mathbf{A}_i$ all physical addresses $\mathbf{p}(\tau)$ remain unchanged.

In the epoch $\mathbf{B}_i$ algorithm $\mathcal{Y}$ updates the assigned addresses only for the nodes in $\bigcup_{s \leq \mathtt{a}(i)} L_s$. $\mathcal{Y}$ randomizes a new bucket $\mathbf{p}(\tau)$ for each node $\tau \in L_s$ with uniform distribution on $\mathcal{B}_s$, for $s = 0, 1..., \mathtt{a}(i)$. As in the startup these randomization are mutually independent, and independent of all of the earlier randomizations. This completes the description of the selections of the buckets $\mathbf{p}(\tau)$. These randomizations are the analogues of the randomizations done by the hierarchical algorithm $\mathcal{H}$ in the interval $\mathbf{B}_i$ using the random oracle and will be used for the same purpose. In the present case however, the randomizations are done by coin flipping, so the algorithm $\mathcal{Y}$ have to remember the results in some way.

We describe now how the algorithm $\mathcal{Y}$ stores the results of the randomizations of the buckets $\mathbf{p}(\tau)$. The current $\bar{\mathbf{p}}(\tau)$, that is, the address of the bucket assigned to the node τ, will be stored in the form of a pair $\langle \bar{\tau}, \bar{\mathbf{p}}(\tau)\rangle$. Such a pair will be placed in a bucket in the same way as we do with the pairs $\langle a, v\rangle$ storing the values of variables. Therefore τ will have symbolic address $\mathtt{symb}_T(\tau) \in T_n$ and the pair $\langle \bar{\tau}, \bar{\mathbf{p}}(\tau)\rangle$ will be stored in the bucket assigned to $\mathtt{symb}_T(\tau)$, that is, in $\mathbf{p}(\mathtt{symb}_T(\tau))$.

There is however an important complication. Namely, for each $\tau \in T_n$ the algorithm $\mathcal{Y}$ can search the bucket $\mathbf{p}(\tau)$ only once, otherwise the obliviousness of the algorithm is lost. $\mathcal{Y}$ may search the same bucket as $\mathbf{p}(\sigma)$ for another node $\sigma \neq \tau$ of the tree, but in the role of $\mathbf{p}(\tau)$. The reason is that for the adversary a single search looks like searching in a randomly chosen bucket, while repeated searches in the same bucket may indicate e.g., repetition in the input. (This is the same situation as in [5] and [3].) The solution for $\mathcal{Y}$ will be that after it used the bucket $\mathbf{p}(\tau)$ once, it erases the pair $\langle \bar{\tau}, \bar{\mathbf{p}}(\tau)\rangle$. So the address of $\mathbf{t}(\tau)$ is simply not available till the next randomization of $\mathbf{p}(\tau)$, when $\mathcal{Y}$ creates a new pair $\langle \bar{\tau}, \bar{\mathbf{p}}(\tau)\rangle$.

Changes of the symbolic address of $\mathtt{symb}_T(\tau)$ *during the algorithm.* At the startup $\mathtt{symb}_T(\tau) = \tau^\circ$, where τ° is the unique ancestor of τ. This can be done only if $\tau \neq 1_T$, but for $\tau = 1_T$, $\mathbf{p}(\tau)$ is always $\mathbf{b}_{0,0}$, so $\mathcal{Y}$ does not have to store this information. Therefore, at the beginning, the pair $\langle \bar{\tau}, \bar{\mathbf{p}}(\tau)\rangle$ will be stored in the bucket assigned to the node τ°, that is, in $\mathbf{p}(\tau^\circ)$. When we randomize a new $\mathbf{p}(\tau)$ then the old pair $\langle \bar{\tau}, \bar{\mathbf{p}}(\tau)\rangle$ is erased from the memory.

In an access interval $\mathbf{A}_i$, with input $\langle a_i, v_i, \Psi_i\rangle$ the following happens. If $\mathtt{symb}_T(\tau) \in \mathtt{branch}(\chi(a_i))$ then $\mathtt{symb}_T(\tau)$ will change into 1_{T_n} at the end of $\mathbf{A}_i$, otherwise it remains unchanged.

We consider now the change of $\mathtt{symb}_T(\tau)$ in an epoch $\mathbf{B}_j$. If $\mathtt{symb}_T(\tau) \in \bigcup_{s \geq \mathtt{a}(i)} L_i$, then $\mathtt{symb}_T(\tau)$ remains unchanged in $\mathbf{B}_i$. Otherwise, at the end of $\mathbf{B}_i$ it changes into ρ, where

ρ is the smallest node in $\bigcup_{s\leq \mathbf{a}(i)} L_i$ which is larger than τ. This completes the definition of the symbolic address of $\mathtt{symb}_T(\tau)$.

This definition implies that in the access interval $\mathbf{A}_j$ with input $\langle a_j, v_j, \Psi_j\rangle$, the algorithm $\mathcal{Y}$ will be able to go down the branch $\chi(a_j)$ starting from 1_T and check for each node τ the bucket $\mathbf{p}(\tau)$. Indeed, as we have seen, the pair $\langle \bar{\tau}, \bar{\mathbf{p}}(\tau)\rangle$ is always contained in a bucket $\mathbf{p}(\rho)$, for some $\rho \geq \tau^\circ > \tau$, which is also on the branch, but comes earlier. Therefore when the algorithm $\mathcal{Y}$ goes down the branch $\mathtt{branch}(\chi(a))$, looking in the buckets assigned to the nodes, by the time it reaches the node τ it will know what is $\bar{\mathbf{p}}(\tau)$.

This completes the sketch of the coinflipping algorithm. The reason why it finds the pair $\langle a, v\rangle$ is the same as in the case of Ostrovsky's hierarchical algorithm. The reason why it will be oblivious is also the same. Namely once $\mathcal{Y}$ looks at a bucket $\mathbf{b}_{i,j}$, all of the symbolic addresses $\mathtt{symb}(a)$ and $\mathtt{symb}(\tau)$ whose value was $\mathbf{b}_{i,j}$ till now, are changed into 1_{T_n}. Therefore the bucket in the same role will not be used again by $\mathcal{Y}$. This implies that the buckets checked by $\mathcal{Y}$ are the values of independent random variables with previously fixed distributions. So the adversary does not gain any information from them. On the other hand if we fix the sequence of buckets that $\mathcal{Y}$ checks, then $\mathcal{Y}$ is oblivious in a deterministic sense, and therefore there is no other information available to the adversary than the bucket sequence.

Problems concerning the algorithm $\mathcal{Y}$. As we have remarked earlier overfilling a bucket if the algorithm is using an oracle is not a problem. For a detailed explanation see [4], [5] or [3]. The essential reason is that in case of an overfilling by $\mathcal{H}$ the randomization, which is a random hashing, can be repeated. $\mathcal{H}$ can be executed in a way that the fact that there is an overfilling gives only information about the randomization and not about the pairs $\langle a, v\rangle$ in the buckets.

This is not true for the algorithm $\mathcal{Y}$. The randomization of χ creates a new problem. This randomization cannot be repeated frequently, since such a repetition would involve relocating all of the pairs $\langle a, x\rangle$ into new bucket, so it would take at least $n \log n$ time. An overfilling may result, for example, from the event that for many of the arriving access requests $\langle a, v\rangle$, the set $\mathtt{branch}(\chi(a))$ is the same. Therefore, if χ is not re-randomized then repeating the other part of the randomization will not help. Consequently, to prove the theorem, we have to show that with a probability higher than $1 - n^{-\log n}$, no overfilling will occur.

To prove this, first we have to show that

(4). *for each fixed $\tau \in T_n$ the number of $a \in [0, n-1]$ with $\mathtt{symb}(a) = \tau$, will be at most* $\mathrm{poly}(\log n)$.

(We will show that this implies that for each fixed $\tau \in T_n$ we have $|\{\sigma \in T_n \mid \mathtt{symb}_T(\sigma) = \tau\}| \leq \mathrm{poly}(\log n)$). The randomization of the physical addresses $\mathbf{p}(\tau)$ does not cause a serious problem, it will only slightly increase the exponent in $\mathrm{poly}(\log n)$ in the upper bound.

For the proof of the upper bound (4) we have to modify the algorithm $\mathcal{Y}$. (The upper bound may hold for the original form of $\mathcal{Y}$ as well, but the proof breaks down.) The disadvantage of the presented form of the algorithm $\mathcal{Y}$ is that the expected number of pairs $\langle a, x\rangle$ in each bucket $\mathbf{b}_{i,j}$ is a constant. Moreover, if we fix χ, and consider only the other part of the randomization, then the expected number of pairs in each fixed bucket, will depend on the choice of the bucket. For some buckets, this expected number can be as high as about $\log n$. On the other hand, for the proof, at least with the technique that we will use, we need this expected number (for buckets which do not correspond to the leaves of the tree) to be as low as $(\log n)^{-c_1}$, for some constant $c_1 > 0$, that will be selected later. The reason is that during the algorithm when we move one pair $\langle a, v\rangle$ to the bucket $\mathbf{b}_{0,0}$ we will have to move others pairs $\langle a', v'\rangle$ as well where $\mathtt{symb}(a') \in \mathtt{branch}(\chi(a))$. This may lead to the situation that the evaluation pairs are moving faster, or in larger numbers, to the top of the tree then they are moving downward towards the leaves of the tree during the epochs $\mathbf{B}_i$. One possible solution for the problem could be, that after each access interval $\mathbf{A}_i$, we will have not one but $(\log n)^{c_1}$ epochs $\mathbf{B}_i$. Actually we will use an equivalent solution, instead of having many epochs after each access interval $\mathbf{A}_i$, we will have only one epoch $\mathbf{B}_i$ but in this epoch we move the symbolic addresses not from $\bigcup_{s>\mathbf{a}(i)} L_s$ into $L_{\mathbf{a}(i)}$, but from $\bigcup_{s>\kappa(i)} L_s$ into $L_{\kappa(i)}$, where $\kappa(i)$ is approximately $\mathbf{a}(i) + c_1 \log\log n$. This will have the same effect as the solution with many epochs. We will denote this modified version of the algorithm by $\mathcal{A}$.

In the detailed proof we define $\mathcal{A}$ in several stages. Namely first we look at only the movement of the symbolic adresses on the tree T_n during the algorithm without defining the physical adresses at all. The algorithm which works with the symbolic addresses only will be called $\mathcal{T}$. The advantage of this approach is that the problem of overfilling, which is the main combinatorial difficulty in the proof, can be formulated and solved already in this simplified framework. Naturally the introduction of physical addresses will create a new overfilling problem, since the physical addresses $\mathbf{p}(\tau)$ associated by different nodes τ of the tree can be accidentally the same. Since the choices of the buckets $\mathbf{p}(\tau)$ are completely random and independent, this will not cause a serious problem. This completes the sketch of the proof.

3. REFERENCES

[1] A. V. Aho, J. E. Hopcroft, and J. D. Ullman. *The Design and Analysis of Computer Algorithms.* Addison-Wesley Publishing Company, Reading, Massachusetts, 1974.

[2] O. Goldreich. Towards a theory of software protection and simulation by oblivious rams. In *STOC, Proceedings of the Nineteenth Annual ACM Symposium on Theory of Computing, 25-27 May 1987, New York City, NY, USA*, pages 182–194. ACM, 1987.

[3] O. Goldreich and R. Ostrovsky. Software protection and simulation on oblivious rams. *J. ACM*, 43(3):431–473, 1996.

[4] R. Ostrovsky. Efficient computation on oblivious rams. In *STOC, Proceedings of the Twenty Second Annual ACM Symposium on Theory of Computing, 14-16 May 1990, Baltimore, Maryland, USA*, pages 514–523. ACM, 1990.

[5] R. Ostrovsky. *Software Protection and Simulation on Oblivious RAM's.* PhD thesis, MIT, 1992.

[6] D. A. Osvik, A. Shamir, and E. Tromer. Cache attacks and countermeasures: The case of aes. In D. Pointcheval, editor, *CT-RSA*, volume 3860 of *Lecture Notes in Computer Science*, pages 1–20. Springer, 2006.

[7] N. Pippenger and M. J. Fischer. Relations among complexity measures. *J. ACM*, 26(2):361–381, 1979.

On the Round Complexity of Covert Computation

Vipul Goyal
Microsoft Research, India
vipul@microsoft.com

Abhishek Jain
UCLA
abhishek@cs.ucla.com

ABSTRACT

In STOC'05, von Ahn, Hopper and Langford introduced the notion of covert computation. In covert computation, a party runs a secure computation protocol over a covert (or steganographic) channel without knowing if the other parties are participating as well or not. At the end of the protocol, if all parties participated in the protocol and if the function output is "favorable" to all parties, then the output is revealed (along with the fact that everyone participated). All covert computation protocols known so far require a large polynomial number of rounds. In this work, we first study the question of the round complexity of covert computation and obtain the following results:

- There does not exist a constant round covert computation protocol with respect to black box simulation even for the case of two parties. (In comparison, such protocols are known even for the multi-party case if there is no covertness requirement.)
- By relying on the two slot non-black-box simulation technique of Pass (STOC'04) and techniques from cryptography in NC^0 (Applebaum et al, FOCS'04), we obtain a construction of a constant round covert multi-party computation protocol.

Put together, the above adds one more example to the growing list of tasks for which non-black-box simulation techniques (introduced in the work of Barak in FOCS'01) are necessary.

Finally, we study the problem of covert multi-party computation in the setting where the parties only have point to point (covert) communication channels. We observe that our covert computation protocol for the broadcast channel inherits, from the protocol of Pass, the property of secure composition in the *bounded concurrent setting*. Then, as an application of this protocol, somewhat surprisingly we show the existence of covert multi-party computation with point to point channels (assuming that the number of parties is a constant).

STOC'10, June 5–8, 2010, Cambridge, Massachusetts, USA.

Categories and Subject Descriptors

F.1.2 [**Theory of Computation**]: Interactive and reactive computation

General Terms

Theory

Keywords

Cryptography, covert computation, round complexity

1. INTRODUCTION

A conventional steganographic framework allows for encoding hidden messages within larger, seemingly innocent messages. This allows a group of parties to realize a "covert channel" on which they can meaningfully communicate without leaking even the existence of such a communication to "undesirable entities". The notion of *covert computation* was introduced by von Ahn et al [16] as a generalization of this framework. Covert computation allows a group of parties to securely perform arbitrary computation without leaking the existence of this computation to undesirable entities (some of whom may even be potential participants of this computation).

To understand the notion of covert computation, consider the example of secret handshake: a problem well studied in the security community (see [3] and the references therein). Consider the scenario where two CIA agents, both of whom possess some signed credentials, wish to converse with each other. However, none of them wishes to reveal the fact that he is a CIA agent unless the other one is a CIA agent as well. It seems that in such a setting, one can run a well known "ordinary" secure computation protocol [10, 17] which would output 1 if both of them are CIA agents and 0 otherwise. However, for this to work, one of the parties needs to come forward and ask the question: "shall we run a protocol to see if both of us are CIA agents?". This already reveals the information that this party is probably a CIA agent! Is it possible for the agents to run a secure computation protocol such that even the existence of the protocol execution is not known until and unless the credentials of both agents are verified and valid (and they both participated in the protocol)?

von Ahn et al [16] gave a construction for covert two-party computation satisfying a *game based* definition. Subsequent to this work, Chandran et al [8] proposed a cleaner simulation based definition of covert computation by strengthening the "standard" secure computation ideal world requirements.

Chandran et al [8] also proposed a construction of *covert multi-party computation* satisfying this definition assuming the existence of a (covert) communication channel shared among all participants (that is, a broadcast channel).

Very informally, the scenario of covert computation is as follows. There are various parties who carry out normal "innocent" conversations with each other. There might be parties which are interested in carrying out a protocol for a particular task. Such *participating* parties compute outgoing messages as per the protocol specifications and encode these messages in the innocent looking messages of the channel (using steganographic techniques). We refer to this as a "covert communication channel". Upon receipt of a message, a participating party runs the decoding procedure to get the next incoming message of the protocol. At the end of the protocol, if every party was participating and the output of the computation was "favorable"[1], the parties may learn the output and the fact that everyone participated. A covert computation protocol should satisfy the following security properties (in addition to those already satisfied by standard secure computation protocols): (1) No outsider can tell if the parties are running a protocol or just communicating normally, (2) Even if one party does not take part in the protocol, or the output of the computation is unfavorable, then the transcript of the conversation looks indistinguishable from "innocent looking" conversations *even to a party participating in the protocol*. It is the second property which makes the construction of covert computation protocols interesting and highly non-trivial.

It was shown in [16] that using standard steganographic techniques, the task of designing a covert computation protocol can be reduced to the task of designing an ordinary secure computation protocol where a message sent by a party looks indistinguishable from random to all other parties (and the outside world) until and unless the output is favorable to all parties (and all parties participated as opposed to simply sending messages drawn from the uniform distribution). von Ahn et al [16] discuss several applications of covert computation such as *dating* (where the existence of computation is revealed only if both parties are interested in each other) or bit agreement in general (to see if all the parties are like-minded), cheating in Internet games and so on.

The notion of covert computation is theoretically intriguing (independent of its applications). Covert computation can be seen to have the same relationship with ordinary secure computation as steganographic communication has with encrypted communication. Covert computation is an example of a protocol problem that is formulated by a strengthening of the ideal world security requirements (as opposed to specifications of a new real-world setting in which protocols providing ordinary ideal world security are desired). Covert computation comes with various fundamental technical challenges unrelated to the kind encountered before in the literature of secure computation. Standard techniques like **zero knowledge proofs inherently break down** in the setting of covert computation. This is because if a party is able to "verify" a proof given by another party, the fact that the other party is participating is immediately revealed.

There are a few natural questions that arise while considering the notion of covert computation. These issues were discussed in [16], and we briefly recall them here:

[1]In the secret handshake example above, this would amount to the credentials of both parties being valid

Synchronization. One question we may ask is "don't parties have to tell each other that they are interested in running a covert computation protocol for function f anyway?". This is not the case as discussed in [16]: As part of protocol specification, we could have information about how and when to initiate a particular protocol. This could be in the form of "If we wish to compute function f, then the protocol begins with the first message exchanged after 2 p.m.". If a party is interested in computing function f, then he starts hiding the protocol messages in the "ordinary looking" messages starting from 2 p.m. Of course, it could be the case that other parties are not interested, in which case some parties would be executing the protocol, while others would just be carrying on "normal" conversations. The protocol execution does not take place in this case, and knowledge about which parties intended to take part in the protocol is not revealed to anyone. (Instead, other parties will just observe ordinary-seeming conversations.)

MPC + Steganography = Covert MPC? Is it the case that by combining multi-party computation and steganography, we can obtain covert computation protocols? Again, as argued by [16], this is not the case: Recall that steganographically encoding all messages of a standard secure multi-party computation protocol would yield a protocol for which no outside observer can determine if the protocol for computing the function is being run or not. This however provides no guarantee whatsoever to the participants of the protocol itself. Covert computation must guarantee that the protocol execution remains hidden from participating parties.

We assume that all parties know a common circuit for the function f and further, they know the roles they will play in the protocol. We call a party a non-participating party if it does not play the required role during protocol execution. The parties also possess information about the synchronization of the protocol. Adversarial parties also know all such details.

1.1 Round Complexity of Covert Computation

Round complexity is a parameter of special importance in the setting of covert computation. In this setting, the issues of round complexity may relate to questions about *feasibility* of secure computation as opposed to just efficiency. This is because, a party may not be able to exchange hundreds of messages back and forth with another party without raising the suspicion that a computation is going on. In general, *the covert communication channel might restrict the number of messages which the parties are allowed to send.*

The protocols constructed in [16, 8] require a large polynomial number of rounds in the security parameter as well as the number of parties. In order to obtain more realistic protocols for covert computation, it is important to ask whether this is inherent.

1.2 Our Contributions

We first study the question of the round complexity of covert computation and obtain the following results:

1) There does not exist a constant round covert computation protocol with respect to black box simulation even for the case of two parties. (In comparison, such protocols are known even for the multi-party case if there is no covertness requirement.)

2) Next, we build upon on the two slot non-black-box simulation technique of Pass [14], and the techniques from Applebaum et al [1] to construct (based on standard assumptions) a "covert" encryption scheme with a constant depth circuit for the encryption function. Using these techniques, we obtain a construction of a constant round covert multiparty computation protocol.

Put together, the above adds one more example to the growing list of tasks for which non-black-box simulation techniques (introduced in the work of Barak [4]) are necessary.

Finally, we initiate the study of covert multiparty computation in the setting where the parties only have point to point covert communication channels. This setting is fundamentally different from the one where a covert broadcast channel is available. This is because now a party may not have an innocent reason to send the same message to multiple other parties. Doing such might immediately reveal that the party is trying to carry out a protocol. Thus, the known techniques of implementing broadcast using point-to-point channels inherently fail. At any stage in the protocol, a non-trivial agreement between more than two parties on the same message implies the loss of covertness.

Towards that end, we observe that our covert computation protocol for the broadcast channel inherits, from the protocol of Pass [14], the property of composition in the bounded concurrent setting. Then, as an application of this protocol, we provide the first construction of covert multiparty computation with point to point channels assuming that the number of parties is a constant.

1.3 Our Techniques

We now give a high-level overview of the techniques used in each of our results.

Impossibility of Constant-Round Covert Computation with Black Box Simulation. One of the key requirements for successful simulation in the setting of secure two-party computation is the following. The simulator must be able to extract the input of the adversary (and send it to the trusted party in the ideal world). Black-box simulators are restricted to do that by means of rewinding (i.e., by making extra oracle calls to the adversary). In particular, a black-box simulator may run multiple "threads of execution" with the adversary and finally output a single thread, called the "main-thread". Any other thread is referred to as a "look-ahead" thread. A black-box simulator "will fail" if: (a) the main thread is honestly executed (e.g., the adversary does not abort at any point during the main thread), but (b) the simulator obtains no "useful information" in *any* look-ahead thread. In order to prove our impossibility result, we will construct an adversary for which any black-box simulator "fails" (in the aforementioned sense) with noticeable probability.

Recall that in the setting of covert two-party computation, a party p_1 may either send a meaningful message (i.e., a message that encodes a protocol message) or a "non-participating" message (i.e., a message drawn uniformly from the broadcast channel). The covertness property requires that these two events must be indistinguishable to the other party p_2. In particular, for any secure covert computation protocol, the covertness property must hold even if p_1 and p_2 (as described above) are in fact the adversary and the simulator algorithms respectively. Then, the central idea to our impossibility result is the inability of any black-box simulator (say) $\mathcal{S}$ of a covert computation protocol to determine whether an adversarial party is participating in the main thread or not (at least until additional information can be extracted via rewinding). First, consider a simple adversarial party $\mathcal{A}$ who does not participate in the covert computation *at all* (i.e., sends messages drawn randomly from the communication channel). However, if $\mathcal{A}$ does not participate at all, at some point (after rewinding $\mathcal{A}$ a number of times), $\mathcal{S}$ must give up in trying to extract its input (and conclude that $\mathcal{A}$ is not participating).

Now, consider the case when $\mathcal{A}$ participates in each round of the covert computation protocol with some sufficiently low probability. In this case, the following could happen with non-negligible probability (if the protocol is constant round). $\mathcal{A}$ might participate honestly throughout in the "main thread"; however, $\mathcal{S}$ will not have any evidence of this fact (in keeping with the *covertness* property of the protocol). Further, when $\mathcal{S}$ rewinds $\mathcal{A}$ to create a number of "look-ahead" threads, $\mathcal{A}$ might not participate in any of them with noticeable probability. Thus, $\mathcal{S}$ might give up as in the first case and conclude that $\mathcal{A}$ is not participating at all (as opposed to running till it is able to extract the input).

We note that our proof only works for the constant round case. This is because if the number of the rounds in the protocol are non-constant, very roughly speaking, the simulator may have a large number of rewinding opportunities. As a result, the probability that the adversary doesn't participate in any of the look aheads (but participates in the entire main thread) may become negligible.

To summarize, since the simulator is unable to determine whether the adversary participated in the main thread or not (at least until one look-ahead thread is successful), it runs the risk of creating "too few" look ahead threads (such that the adversary does not participate in any of them) and then giving up in extraction. Roughly speaking, if the simulator is still successful, then it must be essentially "straight-line". Then, by using standard techniques, we can derive a contradiction based on this fact.

Constant-Round Covert Computation with Non Black Box Simulation. In many works, constant round multiparty computation protocols have been designed using techniques from Beaver et al [7]. The design of the protocol can be viewed as having two high level steps:

SEMI-HONEST PROTOCOL. The first step is to design a constant round protocol secure only against semi-honest adversaries. The basic idea is to have the parties run a secure computation protocol whose round complexity is linear in the depth of the circuit it evaluates (e.g., the semi-honest GMW protocol). Such a secure computation protocol is run to jointly generate a garbled circuit [17] for the desired (final) functionality. The parties can then evaluate this garbled circuit offline on their own later on. Note that the gate tables for all the gates in the garbled circuit are generated in *parallel*; then, if the circuit to generate any gate table has *constant* depth, the secure computation protocol will only have a *constant* number of rounds.

This is indeed the case in [7] since they simply use the XOR function as the encryption scheme to generate the gate tables. However, note that fresh keys must be used for each XOR operation. Then, to avoid blowing up the size of the keys exponentially, the parties now need to run a local preprocessing phase in which they expand their keys by application of a pseudorandom generator (PRG). However, the basic BMR technique breaks down in the covert setting. The high level reason can be understood as follows. The PRG evaluations in local preprocessing phase (in which the parties expand their keys) have to be later repeated at the time of garbled circuit evaluation. Then, the fact that the computation done in the preprocessing phase "conforms" to the computation done while evaluating the received garbled circuit leaks the fact that all parties are participating in the protocol (even if the output is not favorable). In summary, the XOR function coupled with the PRG evaluations does not preserve covertness of the parties.

To solve this problem, we construct a new covert encryption scheme[2] in NC^0 using techniques from Applebaum et al [1]. We then use this encryption scheme (instead of the XOR function as in [7]) to compute the gate tables. This allows us to remove the BMR local processing phase entirely.

Forgetting our goal of obtaining a covert computation protocol, consider the protocol in which we use such an encryption scheme in gate tables and use standard GMW for gate table generation. We believe this protocol is of independent interest since it also gives an arguably cleaner alternative to the Beaver et al [7] protocol (which in turn has been used widely in the study of round complexity of secure computation).

COMPILING WITH ZERO-KNOWLEDGE PROOFS. Next, we "compile" the above semi-honest secure protocol with constant round *simulation-sound*[3] zero knowledge proofs.

In order to adopt such an approach to our setting, we first note that zero knowledge proofs break down in the setting of covert computation since they are "verifiable". To this end, [8] introduced the notion of *zero knowledge proofs to garbled circuits*. Roughly speaking, a zero knowledge proof to garbled circuit is a protocol between two parties—a sender and a receiver—who share common input (x, L) while the sender additionally has a private input v. If the receiver can prove that $x \in L$ to a garbled circuit prepared by the sender, then it will receive a private value v, else it will receive a random value. Intuitively, this protocol can be seen as covert conditional oblivious transfer, where a value is sent from a sender to a receiver conditioned upon the fact that a given NP statement (for e.g., an assertion that a party behaved honestly "so far" in the protocol) is true. In this protocol, the sender does not learn whether or not the receiver was able to prove the statement correctly to the garbled circuit (hence preserving the covertness of the zero-knowledge prover).

Our impossibility result implies that non black-box techniques are necessary to construct such a gadget (henceforth referred to as ZKSend) in the constant-round setting. To this end, we use the non black-box simulation technique of Pass [14] (which in turn builds on the work of Barak [4]). We note that the protocol of Pass is a *simulation-sound* zero knowledge argument system.

We stress that a naive attempt to adopt the techniques of [14] in the construction of ZKSend of [8] does not work. The main difficulty is in proving the (stand-alone) soundness of the new construction. Complications arise in our setting because the construction of ZKSend in [8] crucially uses a *proof* system, while the protocol in [14] is an *argument* system. We refer the reader to section 5.1 for more details.

Finally, we note that zero-knowledge proofs to garbled circuits cannot be applied to achieve secure covert multi-party computation as "easily" as ordinary zero-knowledge proofs can be applied to achieve secure (ordinary) multi-party computation. This problem was also faced by Chandran et al [8] who introduced what one can call a "delayed verification" technique (where the usage of zero-knowledge protocols is deferred to the end of the protocol). Here we are able to adopt the techniques from [8] to our setting without major difficulties.

Covert Computation over Point-to-Point Channels. There exists a rich body of literature on designing secure computation protocols over point to point channels (see [12] and references therein). However, to our knowledge, a common theme in all these works is a party sending the same message to multiple (or all) other parties over the pairwise private channels. Unfortunately, such techniques are inherently bound to fail in our scenario. The key challenge in our setting is to design a protocol where the messages exchanged between a pair of parties look indistinguishable from random even given the messages exchanged between all other pairs of parties (till the point when it is clear that all the parties are participating and that the output is favorable).

The basic idea of our construction is as follows. As part of the protocol specifications, the n parties are grouped into $n/2$ pairs. Each pair of parties run a covert two-party computation protocol (say) Σ to emulate a *virtual party*. This leads to a total of $n/2$ virtual parties. These virtual parties are further grouped into $n/4$ pairs and each pair of virtual parties run Σ to emulate another virtual party. By applying this idea recursively, there would eventually be a single virtual party which has all the required inputs and thus computes the output. Very informally, even if a single (real) party behaves honestly in the protocol, the final single virtual party would be "honest" as well.

We model a virtual party in the form of a *reactive* functionality. In particular, we define a hierarchy of reactive functionalities where the functionality at level 0 has all the required inputs and can compute the output while each functionality at level $\log(n)$ defines the algorithm of a real party. Further, we show how a pair of virtual parties at some level can communicate with each other through parties at the level just "below". We now briefly outline some of the key challenges in realizing this construction.

Note that in the above construction, there would be multiple uncoordinated executions of the covert two-party computation protocol Σ. To this end, we will require Σ to be secure in the *bounded concurrent* setting. Fortunately, our constant-round covert computation protocol (over the broadcast channel) inherits, from the protocol of Pass [14], the property of composition in the bounded concurrent set-

[2]Intuitively, the encryption keys and the ciphertexts produced by a covert encryption scheme are indistinguishable from the uniform distribution.

[3]In order to ensure that the resultant protocol is constant-round (in the multi-party case), not only must the zero-knowledge proofs be constant-round, but they must also be executed in *parallel*. We note that in such a scenario, we run the risk of mauling attacks (for instance, an adversary who acts as the verifier in a "left" execution may be able to use this interaction in order to prove a statement in a "right" execution). The notion of simulation-soundness, introduced by Sahai [15], guarantees robustness against such attacks; therefore using simulation-sound zero knowledge proofs (instead of standard zero-knowledge) is crucial in the constant-round setting.

ting. Then, by making some necessary changes to this protocol, we can obtain a covert two-party computation protocol Σ for reactive functionalities in the bounded-concurrent setting. Further, note that the communication channel of the virtual parties (as described above) can, in general, be controlled by a man in the middle. We employ techniques from the work of Barak et al [5] to solve this problem.

We note, however, that our construction only works for a constant number of parties. This is because the computational overhead of our protocol is $O(k^{\log(n)}) \cdot |C|$ where k is the security parameter, n is the number of parties (and hence $\log(n)$ is the depth of the tree) and $|C|$ is the size of the circuit of the functionality. One approach to extend our construction to work for any polynomial number of parties would be to obtain a covert two-party computation protocol with *constant computational overhead* [11].

Due to lack of space, we omit the details of our construction from this extended abstract. We refer the reader to the full version of the paper for a detailed description.

2. PRELIMINARIES AND MODEL

Similar to [16], we note that it is enough to construct covert computation protocols only for the uniform channel which defines "innocent messages" as messages chosen uniformly at random (i.e., the parties are allowed to only send random messages). This is due to the following lemma:

LEMMA 1. *If Π covertly realizes the functionality f for the uniform channel, then there exists a protocol Σ^{Π} that covertly realizes f for any broadcast channel B.*

The intuition behind why this lemma is true is that once we construct a protocol where the messages of the parties look indistinguishable from random, we can use steganographic techniques to embed such messages into innocent conversations of any other channel. Upon decoding a given conversation for the channel, a party would only see a random looking message regardless of whether a message was embedded in the conversation or not. We refer the reader to [16] for a full proof of the above lemma.

A *covert functionality* F is a tuple of functions (f, g). Informally, f denotes the usual secure computation functionality whose output is the output of the protocol while g decides if the output of the computation is favorable or not. We extend the standard Ideal/Real world simulation paradigm in order to define secure covert multi-party computation [8].

IDEAL MODEL. In the ideal model there is a trusted party which computes the desired functionality $F = (f, g)$ based on the inputs and the participation data handed to it by the players. An execution in the ideal model proceeds as follows:

Inputs Each participating party P_i has input x_i. We represent the vector of inputs by $\vec{x}$.
Send inputs to trusted party Honest participating parties always send their inputs to the trusted party. Honest non-participating parties are assumed to send $\perp$ to the trusted party (jumping ahead, this corresponds to sending regular uniformly selected messages according to the broadcast channel in the real world). Corrupted parties, on the other hand, may decide to send modified values or $\perp$ to the trusted party. We do not differentiate between malicious participating parties and malicious non-participating parties.
Trusted party computes the result If any party sent $\perp$ as its input, the trusted party sets the output to be $\perp$. Otherwise, it sets the output to be $f(\vec{x})$ (resp. $\perp$) if $g(\vec{x}) = 1$ (rep. $g(\vec{x}) = 0$). If necessary, it generates and uses uniform random coins for the computation.
Trusted party sends results to adversary The trusted party sends the output to the adversary.
Trusted party sends results to honest players The adversary, depending on its view up to this point, prepares a (possibly empty) list of honest parties who should get the output. The trusted party sends the output to the parties in that list and sends $\perp$ to others.
Outputs An honest participating party always outputs the response it received from the trusted party. Non-participating parties and corrupted parties output $\perp$, by convention. The adversary outputs an arbitrary function of its entire view (which includes the view of all malicious parties) throughout the execution of the protocol.

Note that in standard MPC, it is implicitly assumed that every player is taking part in the protocol and that this information is public. In covert computation, however, if the result from the trusted party is $\perp$, the adversary cannot tell whether this is because some party did not participate (or if any honest party participated at all) or because the output was not favorable.

REAL MODEL. Honest participating parties follow all instructions of the prescribed protocol, while malicious parties are coordinated by a single adversary and may behave arbitrarily. Non-participating parties are assumed to draw messages uniformly from the broadcast channel. At the conclusion of the protocol, honest participating parties compute their output as prescribed by the protocol, while the non-participating parties and malicious parties output $\perp$. Without loss of generality, we assume the adversary outputs its entire view of the execution of the protocol.

We say that a covert multi party computation protocol is secure if the output distributions of the ideal wold and real world executions are (computationally) indistinguishable. We refer the reader to the full version for more details.

3. IMPOSSIBILITY OF CONSTANT ROUND COVERT COMPUTATION WITH BLACK BOX SIMULATION

In this section, we show the existence of a PPT computable covert two-party functionality for which there does not exist any constant-round covert computation protocol with respect to a black-box simulator. Our impossibility result rules out any expected polynomial time simulator which uses the adversarial algorithm as an oracle.

Let us first consider any two-party covert functionality F and assume that there exists a *constant*-round covert computation protocol Π that securely realizes F with respect to a black-box simulator. We first construct a real world adversary for Π and derive a lower bound on the probability p_{fail} with which every black-box simulator for Π gets full participation from the adversary in the "main thread" (where main thread is defined as the execution thread output by the simulator in its view), but fails to get any participation in all other threads of execution. In other words p_{fail} is the probability with which the simulator is essentially "straight-line". As we will show later in the proof, p_{fail} is noticeable (in the security parameter) if the functionality F is such that an adversary in a real world execution of Π can distinguish whether or not an honest party is participating in the protocol only with negligible probability. This is indeed true for several covert functionalities. In the second part of the proof, we give an example of such a functionality and finally derive a contradiction based on the fact (established in the first part) that the black-box simulator for any constant-round protocol for this functionality is "straight-line" with noticeable probability.

In this extended abstract, we only give a sketch of the main ideas used to derive the lower bound on the probability p_{fail} (as described above). We refer the reader to the full version of our paper for complete details.

Let F be any covert functionality for two parties (P_1, P_2). Let Π be any constant-round covert computation protocol that securely realizes F with respect to a black-box simulator. Without loss of generality, we assume that P_2 sends the first message in Π. Let $\{\mathcal{T}_k\}_k$ be a family of q-wise independent predicates, where $t \in \mathcal{T}_k$ maps $\{0,1\}^{\leq \text{poly}(\kappa)}$ to $\{0,1\}$ such that on any randomly chosen valid input β, t outputs 1 with probability $1/q^2$.[4] Here q is a parameter polynomial in the security parameter (to be determined later). Suppose that the adversary chooses a predicate t from the q-wise independent family $\mathcal{T}_k$. Now consider an execution between an adversary and the other party (which may be emulated by the simulator). We will say that a query β made by the other party (resp. simulator) to the adversary is $\mathsf{favorable}$ if t outputs 1 on β *as well as* on every prior query in that execution (resp. execution thread).

Adversary P_1^*. We first describe our adversary P_1^*. We assume that P_1^* has the required input and random tape as would an honest party. Then P_1^* works as follows. P_1^* first chooses a predicate t from the q-wise independent family $\mathcal{T}_k$. Now consider any round in the execution of Π. If the query from P_2 is $\mathsf{favorable}$, then P_1^* sends an honest reply (as it would if it were participating honestly in the protocol); otherwise it sends a message drawn from the uniform distribution[5].

Since the number of rounds in Π is a constant (say) c, it follows that P_1^* participates in Π with a noticeable probability $(= (1/q^2)^c)$. Let $\mathcal{S}$ be a black-box simulator for protocol Π. We now use a hybrid argument to derive a lower bound on the probability p_{fail}, defined as follows. Consider the view output by $\mathcal{S}$ at the end of its interaction with P_1^*. As mentioned earlier, we will refer to the thread of execution in this view as the "main thread". Then, informally speaking, p_{fail} is the probability that $\mathcal{S}$ finds full participation from P_1^* in the main thread (i.e., the predicate t chosen by P_1^* returns 1 on every query from $\mathcal{S}$ in the main thread), but fails to find any participation from P_1^* in any other execution thread (i.e., the predicate t chosen by P_1^* returns 0 on every query from $\mathcal{S}$ in any thread other than the main thread).

We now construct a series of hybrids $\mathcal{H}_i$, $i \in [0,3]$, where each hybrid represents the interaction between an adversarial P_1 (referred to as $\mathcal{A}$) with a strategy we define and the simulator $\mathcal{S}$. The adversary $\mathcal{A}$ in $\mathcal{H}_3$ is identical to P_1^*. In each hybrid, we define and analyze the winning probability of $\mathcal{A}$ such that p_{fail} is the probability with which $\mathcal{A}$ wins in $\mathcal{H}_3$.

Hybrid $\mathcal{H}_0$. In this experiment, $\mathcal{A}$ simply sends a message drawn from the uniform distribution on receiving any query from $\mathcal{S}$. Let q be the median of the number of queries that $\mathcal{S}$ makes. That is, with probability 1/2 (where probability is taken over all the coins of $\mathcal{S}$ and $\mathcal{A}$), $\mathcal{S}$ makes at most q queries. Note that $q = \text{poly}(\kappa)$. We say that $\mathcal{A}$ wins in this experiment if every query from $\mathcal{S}$ in the main thread (defined by the view output by $\mathcal{S}$) is $\mathsf{favorable}$, but every other query is *not* $\mathsf{favorable}$. Looking ahead, if $\mathcal{A}$ were to reply honestly on each $\mathsf{favorable}$ query (as it does in $\mathcal{H}_3$), then the winning probability of $\mathcal{A}$ would be identical to p_{fail}.

We analyze the winning probability of $\mathcal{A}$ over the choices of t for a fixed execution defined by a random tape of $\mathcal{S}$ and a random tape that $\mathcal{A}$ uses to draw messages from the uniform distribution. Consider the event that every query from $\mathcal{S}$ in the main thread is $\mathsf{favorable}$ (i.e., t outputs 1 on every simulator query in the main thread). Now consider the event that every query from $\mathcal{S}$ that is not in the main thread is not $\mathsf{favorable}$ (i.e., t outputs 0 on any query not in the main thread). We observe that these two events are independent conditioned on $\mathcal{S}$ making at most q queries (since in this case t essentially behaves as a random function and the queries made by $\mathcal{S}$ and its view in general are independent of the choice of t). Then, by a simple probability analysis, we show that $\Pr[\mathcal{A} \text{ wins}] \geq \frac{1}{2q^{2c}} \cdot (1 - \frac{1}{q})$, which is noticeable in the security parameter.

Hybrid $\mathcal{H}_1$. Same as $\mathcal{H}_0$ except the following. On receiving any $\mathsf{favorable}$ query β from $\mathcal{S}$, $\mathcal{A}$ checks if it had earlier received a $\mathsf{favorable}$ query $\beta' \neq \beta$ in a "different" thread (in the sequel, we will refer to this check as the *stopping condition*). If the check succeeds, then $\mathcal{A}$ stops the experiment and we say that $\mathcal{S}$ wins. Otherwise, the winning criterion for $\mathcal{A}$ in this experiment is defined exactly as in $\mathcal{H}_0$.

Intuitively, the only difference between $\mathcal{H}_0$ and $\mathcal{H}_1$ is that in $\mathcal{H}_1$, whenever $\mathcal{S}$ is successful in making a $\mathsf{favorable}$ query in more than one execution thread, $\mathcal{A}$ stops the experiment and declares $\mathcal{S}$ to be the winner. However, in this case, $\mathcal{S}$ would have won in $\mathcal{H}_0$ as well. Then, it can be shown that the winning probability of $\mathcal{A}$ in $\mathcal{H}_1$ is identical to that in $\mathcal{H}_0$.

Hybrid $\mathcal{H}_2$. Same as $\mathcal{H}_1$, except that on receiving any $\mathsf{favorable}$ query from $\mathcal{S}$, if the *stopping condition* is false, $\mathcal{A}$ sends an honest reply (as it would if it were participating honestly) to $\mathcal{S}$ (instead of sending a message drawn from the uniform distribution). However, if the *stopping condition* is true, it continues to stop the experiment as in $\mathcal{H}_1$. The winning criterion for $\mathcal{A}$ in this experiment is defined exactly as in $\mathcal{H}_1$.

The key property of the interaction between $\mathcal{A}$ and $\mathcal{S}$ in this experiment is that $\mathcal{A}$ participates honestly only in at most a single thread of execution (since $\mathcal{A}$ stops experiment just before this property stops being true). Now, in order to bound the winning probability of $\mathcal{A}$ from below, we consider an experiment where $\mathcal{A}$ "exposes" such a thread of its interaction (if it exists) to an external party P_1. More specifically, $\mathcal{A}$ forwards each $\mathsf{favorable}$ query in this thread to P_1 and then forwards back its response to $\mathcal{S}$. Now, note that if all the replies of P_1 were drawn from the uniform distribution, then this experiment is identical $\mathcal{H}_1$, otherwise if P_1 replied honestly to each query, then it is identical to

[4]Such a family can be easily constructed from a family of q-wise independent hash functions.

[5]Note that the check for a query being $\mathsf{favorable}$ implicitly ensures that P_1^* sends an honest reply only if it had not already stopped participating in the protocol in an earlier round.

$\mathcal{H}_2$. Let ϵ be the probability with which a PPT machine can distinguish between these two cases. Then, the winning probability of $\mathcal{A}$ in $\mathcal{H}_2$ must be at least $\frac{1}{2q^{2c}} \cdot (1 - \frac{1}{q}) - \epsilon$.

Looking ahead, the probability ϵ would be negligible for several functionalities in keeping with the covertness property of the protocol Π. Hence, the winning probability of $\mathcal{A}$ in this experiment would still be noticeable.

Hybrid $\mathcal{H}_3$. Same as $\mathcal{H}_2$ except that on receiving any favorable query from $\mathcal{S}$, $\mathcal{A}$ sends an honest reply (as it would if it were participating honestly) even if the *stopping condition* is true (as opposed to stopping the experiment). We observe that by definition, $\mathcal{A}$ in this experiment is identical to P_1^*. The winning criterion for $\mathcal{A}$ in this experiment is defined exactly as in $\mathcal{H}_2$.

Then, the winning probability of $\mathcal{A}$ in $\mathcal{H}_3$ is identical to that in $\mathcal{H}_2$; intuitively, this is because the only difference between $\mathcal{H}_2$ and $\mathcal{H}_3$ is that for some choices of the random tapes of $\mathcal{S}$ and $\mathcal{A}$, $\mathcal{A}$ might stop the experiment in $\mathcal{H}_2$ (and hence lose); however, note that for all these random tapes, $\mathcal{A}$ will lose in $\mathcal{H}_3$ as well. Hence, we have that $\mathsf{p}_{fail} = \Pr[\mathcal{A} \text{ wins}] \geq \frac{1}{2q^{2c}} \cdot (1 - \frac{1}{q}) - \epsilon$.

Completing the proof. In the second part of the proof, we give an example of a functionality for which the probability ϵ is negligible. Hence the probability with which the simulator is "essentially" straight line (that is, p_{fail}) is noticeable. Finally we show that for our functionality, this contradicts the security of the protocol Π.

4. COVERT COMPUTATION PRIMITIVES

In this section, we briefly describe the main primitives that we use in our construction (see full version for more details).

Covert Commitments [9]: In a covert commitment scheme, the messages of a party in the commitment phase look indistinguishable from random to the other party. The commitment scheme based on the Goldreich-Levin hard-core predicate is a covert bit commitment scheme that is perfectly binding. Let $x = x[1], \ldots, x[k]$ be any string. $Com(x)$ denotes a covert commitment to the bits $x[1], \ldots, x[k]$. Further, $Open(Com(x))$ denotes the decommitment to $Com(x)$ (which includes x along with the randomness used in computing $Com(x)$).

Covert 1-out-of-2 and 1-out-of-4 Oblivious Transfer [16, 8, 13]: In covert 1-out-of-2 and 1-out-of-4 oblivious transfer (OT) protocols, we require that messages of a party throughout the protocol look indistinguishable from random to the other party. Covert 1-out-of-2 OT is presented in [16], while a covert 1-out-of-4 OT is given in [8].

Covert Yao's Garbled Circuit [16, 17]: This is a version of garbled circuit [17] in which the garbled circuit *program* (which is simply a series of encrypted gate tables [17, 7]) can be evaluated in a "non-verifiable" manner.

Covert GMW protocol [8, 10]: This is the same as the standard (semi-honest) GMW protocol [10], except that (a) *covert* 1-out-of-4 OT is used, and (b) the final output share broadcast phase is excluded. That is, in covert GMW protocol, the parties initially finally hold the *shares of the output* (rather than the output itself). Note that zero-knowledge proofs are not used in this protocol (and thus the protocol by itself does not provide any guarantees against malicious adversaries).

Covert Encryption scheme in NC^0 [1]: In a covert encryption scheme, we require that the ciphertext be indistinguishable from random. Given a covert encryption scheme in NC^1 (which can be constructed using standard techniques), we use techniques from Applebaum et al [1] to construct a covert encryption scheme whose encryption function is in NC^0.

5. CONSTANT ROUND COVERT MULTIPARTY COMPUTATION

At a high level, our constant-round covert computation protocol can be seen as the result of a two step process: (a) First, construct a *constant*-round semi-honest covert computation protocol adopting techniques from the work of Beaver et al [7]. (b) Next, the semi-honest protocol is "compiled" with a gadget known as *zero knowledge proofs to garbled circuits* in order to guarantee security against malicious adversaries. In the subsection below, we first discuss the notion of zero-knowledge proof to garbled circuit as introduced by Chandran et al [8], and then give a constant-round construction for the same with some additional security properties (that are necessary when using this gadget in the constant-round setting). Later, we will use our construction of constant-round zero knowledge proof to garbled circuit in presenting our constant-round covert computation protocol.

5.1 Zero Knowledge Proofs to Garbled Circuits

Zero Knowledge proofs have been established as a basic building block for constructing multi-party computation protocols secure against active adversaries. However, in the setting of covert computation, this technique does *not* work because if one party "verifies" that another party is executing the protocol honestly, then covertness is immediately compromised. To this end, Chandran et al [8] introduced the notion of zero knowledge proofs to garbled circuits, where a party gives a proof of its honest behavior to a *garbled circuit* prepared by another party. More specifically, consider two parties (sender, receiver) who share a common input (x, L). The sender wishes to give the receiver a private value v, only if $x \in L$ and the receiver has a valid witness (for $x \in L$). Chandran et al [8] gave a protocol for this setting based on Blum's 3-round (public-coin) ZK proof for Graph Hamiltonicity. In their protocol, the parties first exchange the first two messages of Blum's protocol. Then the sender (verifier) prepares and sends a garbled circuit to the receiver (prover); this garbled circuit takes as input the last prover message and outputs v if the verification is successful, else it outputs a random value. Since Blum's protocol is a zero knowledge *proof* with soundness 1/2, if the theorem is false, there does not exist (with probability 1/2) a "correct" last prover message. [8] also show how to improve the soundness of this basic protocol.

As implied by the results in the previous section, non black-box techniques are necessary to construct such a gadget (henceforth referred to as ZKSend) in the constant-round setting. To this end, we use the non black-box simulation technique of Pass [14] (which in turn builds on the work of Barak [4]). Fortunately, in the zero knowledge protocol of Pass [14], except for the last message, the prover only sends commitments and the verifier only sends random strings. Then, using the same idea as above, we can modify Pass' protocol such that the receiver (prover) sends the last message to a garbled circuit prepared by the sender (verifier), and receives an output value depending upon whether or not the verification was successful.

However, this naive attempt fails since Pass' protocol is an *argument* system. In particular, even if the receiver (prover) was dishonest, a satisfying last message might exist which, very informally speaking, allows the dishonest receiver (prover) to get the sender's input value out of the garbled circuit (even though the receiver does not have such a message explicitly). Then, to be able to reduce the security of ZKSend in such a case to the soundness of Pass' protocol, it seems that the garbled circuit evaluation subprotocol would need to be able to support extraction of the inputs. However, as implied by the impossibility result in the previous section, very informally speaking, such a subprotocol cannot work in a constant number of rounds (using a black-box extractor).

To solve the above problem, we observe that such an extraction of the input will not be required by the simulator of our final covert computation protocol constructed using ZKSend as a building block. Instead, such an extraction would only be required to prove a separate lemma that reduces the following security property of ZKSend to the soundness of Pass' protocol: assuming that the statement is false, the view of a cheating receiver (prover) must be indistinguishable across the two cases where an honest sender (verifier) uses a fixed input value in the ZKSend execution in the first case and a random value as its input in the ZKSend execution in the second case. (Looking ahead, such a lemma would be used in the hybrid experiments to prove the indistinguishability of the simulated view from the view in the real protocol execution.) Hence, the extraction procedure is only required to work with a noticeable probability (as opposed to overwhelming probability). This is because of the following. Say we can extract the input to the garbled circuit (which is the last prover message in Pass' protocol) with a noticeable probability. Then we can use that message to violate the soundness of the protocol of Pass with a noticeable probability.

Using these ideas, we now describe our protocol $ZKSend_{ij}$, where P_i is the sender (verifier) and P_j is the receiver (prover). P_i and P_j share a common input (x_j, L_j). P_i additionally has a private input v. Let $\ell(\kappa)$ be the length parameter and $\mathcal{H}_\kappa$ be a family of collision resistant hash functions. Let cWI-UARG be the 5-round witness indistinguishable universal argument (WI-UARG) of Barak and Goldreich [6] instantiated with the commitment scheme *Com*. The protocol $ZKSend_{ij}$ proceeds in the following steps (see full version for more details).

Stage 1 (Setup): P_i sends $h \xleftarrow{R} \mathcal{H}_\kappa$ to P_j.

Stage 2 (Slot 1): P_j sends a covert commitment $c_1 = Com(0^\kappa)$ to P_i, who responds by sending the first challenge $r_1 \xleftarrow{R} \{0,1\}^{j\ell(\kappa)}$.

Stage 3 (Slot 2): P_j sends a covert commitment $c_2 = Com(0^\kappa)$ to P_i, who responds by sending the second challenge $r_2 \xleftarrow{R} \{0,1\}^{(n+1-j)\ell(\kappa)}$.

Stage 4 (Main Proof Body):
1. P_i and P_j exchange (only) the first 4 messages of a 5-round cWI-UARG where P_j proves the following statement: either $x_j \in L_j$ or there exists a decommitment to c_1 (resp. c_2) to a program Π such that Π takes as input c_1 (resp. c_2) and a string y of length $j\ell(\kappa) - \kappa$ (resp. $(n+1-j)\ell(\kappa) - \kappa$), and outputs r_1 (resp. r_2). Let m_{final} denote the final message of this cWI-UARG.
2. Let $k = \omega(\log(\kappa))$. P_j chooses k pairs of random shares of m_{final} and sends covert commitments to these shares to P_i.

Stage 5 (Challenge-Response): Now, P_i and P_j engage in a 2-round challenge-response protocol, where P_i randomly selects one share from each pair of random shares of m_{final} and P_j reveals the shares selected by P_i. Note that P_j does not send openings to the commitments, but simply the shares selected by P_i.

Stage 6 (Garbled Circuit): Finally, P_i sends a covert garbled circuit, $Gar[i \rightarrow j]$, with the following description:
1. It takes as input, decommitments to the the random shares of m_{final}. This input is provided by P_j. It then checks whether the decommitments to the shares are *correct*, each pair of shares are shares of the same string, and that correct shares were revealed in stage 5.
2. If either of the above checks fail, then it simply outputs a uniformly chosen random number. Otherwise, it runs the final step of the honest verifier algorithm V for cZK on m_{final}. If the output is accept, then it outputs v, else it outputs a uniformly chosen random number.
3. P_j executes covert 1-out-of-2 OT with P_i as necessary in order to evaluate the garbled circuit $Gar[i \rightarrow j]$ and obtain an output.

We prove the following four security properties of our ZKSend construct.

1. Consider a ZKSend execution between a sender (verifier) and a receiver (prover) who share a common input (x, L). The sender's input in the protocol is either a fixed value v or a random value. Then, we show that unless the receiver (prover) "knows a witness for $x \in L$", it cannot distinguish between the two cases where the sender (verifier) is using v in the first case and a random value as its input in the second case. As noted earlier, we prove this security property by reducing it to the soundness of Pass' protocol.

2. Next, we show that an adversarial sender (verifier) who is running a polynomially-bounded number of concurrent executions of ZKSend cannot distinguish whether it is "interacting" with honest receivers (provers) or the simulator. Our simulator relies on the simulator of Pass' protocol to "simulate" the ZKSend executions; as such, we prove this security property by reducing it to the zero knowledge property of Pass' protocol. We stress that even though our covert computation protocol (see Section 5) consists of only *parallel* executions of ZKSend, we consider the more general setting of *bounded-concurrency* as it proves to be useful in the construction of a covert computation protocol over *point-to-point* channels.

3. Now consider a polynomially-bounded number of concurrent executions of ZKSend between an adversary and the simulator, where the adversary is acting as the sender (verifier) in some "left" executions (which are being "simulated" by the simulator) and as the receiver (prover) in a "right" execution with a false theorem as the common input. Then, we show that any such adversary cannot distinguish whether the simulator uses a fixed input value v or a random value as its input in the "right" execution. We stress that we cannot reduce this security property into the simulation soundess of Pass' protocol for the following reasons. Such a proof would require us to construct an adversary who proves a false theorem in Pass' protocol, which in turn, requires rewinding our adversary in the "right" execution (to extract the last message of Pass' protocol). However in this case, very informally speaking, the simulator who is "simulating" the "left" executions, may also get rewound and hence no longer work. Solving this problem requires going into the details of the simulation soundness proof technique of Pass to prove this security property *directly*. In particular, we show that the two slot simulation technique of Pass is powerful enough to handle this scenario as well.

4. Finally, we show that our ZKSend protocol preserves the covertness of both the sender and the receiver. In particular, we show that messages of a sender (resp. receiver) are indistinguishable from random to a receiver (resp. sender).

5.2 Our Protocol

Let $P_1, \ldots, P_n$ be n parties that hold inputs $x_1, \ldots, x_n$ respectively. Let $F = (f, g)$ be a covert functionality that they wish to compute. F outputs $f(x_1, \ldots, x_n)$ if the function output is favorable to all parties, else it outputs $\perp$. Here $g(\cdot)$ is the function that determines whether the function output is favorable ($g(x_1, \ldots, x_n) = 1$) or not ($g(x_1, \ldots, x_n) = 0$). We now give the construction of a constant-round covert multi-party computation protocol that securely realizes F.

Overview. At a high level, our protocol consists of three main phases: (a) *Input Commitment phase*: In this phase, all parties commit to their inputs and randomness (note that we do not require coin flipping in our protocol) and run an "extract enable" phase with each other. Intuitively, the purpose of this phase is to enable the simulator to extract the input and randomness of malicious parties during the simulation. (b) *Garbled Circuit Generation phase*: In this phase, the parties run the covert version of the GMW protocol to jointly construct a covert garbled circuit that evaluates the appropriate function (that the parties wish to compute). Each party only obtains an individual share of the garbled circuit as the output of covert-GMW protocol. (c) *Output Exchange phase*: In this phase, parties exchange their garbled circuit shares with each other if and only if all the parties behaved honestly till the end of the previous phase. By incorporating some validity checks in this phase, we are able to ensure output correctness (without compromising covertness).

Intuitively, the garbled circuit generation phase can be viewed as a semi-honest covert computation protocol. Here we adopt techniques from [7] to ensure that the protocol is constant-round. Then, by adding the other two phases, we essentially "compile" the semi-honest protocol (with zero-knowledge proofs to garbled circuits, as will be evident from the description of each phase) to obtain security against active adversaries. In each phase, the key challenge is to ensure that the number of rounds are only a constant. For lack of space, below we only highlight the main ideas in our protocol.

Input Commitment phase. In the Input Commitment phase, all parties commit to their inputs and randomness and run an "extract enable" sub-phase. Intuitively, the purpose of the ExtractEnable sub-phase is to allow the simulator to extract the input and randomness (for the garbled circuit generation phase) of the malicious parties. We note that Chandran et al [8] used a challenge-response phase of linear round-complexity to enable black-box extraction. However, our impossibility result from the previous section rules out such an approach in the constant-round setting. To this end, we use our construction of zero-knowledge proof to garbled circuit (as described in the last subsection) to enable extraction, as described below.

The main idea of the ExtractEnable sub-phase is as follows. Let the value we would like to enable the simulator to extract be V_i for party P_i. Each party P_i executes the following sub-protocol with each party P_j, in *parallel*.

1) P_i picks a random string r and computes $y = f_{owp}(r)$, where f_{owp} is a one-way permutation. It sends y to P_j.
2) P_j and P_i now engage in an execution of $ZKSend_{ij}$, where P_i is the sender with input V_i and P_j is the receiver, on the following NP statement as the common input: "$\exists r$ such that $y = f_{owp}(r)$" (for a specific witness relation such that any witness for this NP statement contains such an r). Note that an honest P_j will not have a witness for this NP statement and is instructed to simply send random strings during the execution of $ZKSend_{ij}$.

Note that the malicious parties may deviate from the protocol specification (for example, by sending an incorrect garbled circuit inside ZKSend), which may result in the simulator failing to extract. Looking ahead, the later stages will force the output of *all* the parties to be $\perp$ in this case.

Garbled Circuit Generation phase. In this phase, the parties run an instance of the covert-GMW protocol (see section 4) to jointly construct a covert garbled circuit that evaluates the appropriate function, such that each party only obtains a single share of this garbled circuit. The key challenge in this phase is to use only a constant number of rounds.

In many works, constant round multi-party computation protocols have been designed using techniques from Beaver et al [7]. The basic idea is to have the parties run a secure computation protocol (like GMW) to jointly generate a garbled circuit (which they can evaluate on their own later on). To keep the protocol constant round, the encryption scheme used in [7] to generate the gate tables is the simple XOR function. Further, to avoid blowing up the size of the wire keys exponentially, the parties run a preprocessing phase locally in which (among other things) they expand their wire keys using a pseudorandom generator (PRG). Unfortunately, such a preprocessing phase fails in the setting of covert computation. This is because the PRG evaluations done locally by a party during garbled circuit generation will have to be performed again (locally) while evaluating the resulting garbled circuit. Thus, the fact that the computation done in the preprocessing phase "conforms" to the computation done while evaluating the received garbled circuit leaks the fact that all parties are participating in the protocol (even if the output is not favorable).

To solve this problem, we eliminate the preprocessing phase and move the required cryptographic operations (involved in generating the gate tables) into the circuit of the underlying secure computation protocol. However this presents the following problem. If we use GMW (or a similar protocol like covert-GMW) as the underlying secure computation protocol, the number of rounds required will be linear in the depth of the circuit (which generates a gate table) being evaluated. Thus, any cryptographic operations done by this circuit should be in NC^0 for our protocol to be constant rounds.

Towards that end, to still keep the secure computation protocol constant round, we construct an encryption scheme in NC^0 using techniques from Applebaum et al [1]. We would require that the encryption keys and the ciphertexts produced by such an encryption scheme are indistinguishable from the uniform distribution. We construct such an encryption scheme based on standard assumptions.[6][7] Forgetting our goal of obtaining a covert computation protocol, consider the protocol in which we use such an encryption scheme in gate tables and use standard GMW for gate table generation. We believe this protocol is of independent interest since it also gives a arguably cleaner alternative to the Beaver et al [7] protocol (which in turn has been used widely in the study of round complexity of secure computation).

Then, in this phase, the parties engage in an execution of the covert-GMW protocol that takes as input the shares of the wire keys (and other relevant information). The encryption scheme used in the construction of gate tables is the covert encryption scheme in NC^0. At the end of protocol, each party P_i will hold only a share GC_i of the garbled circuit GC and other necessary information required to evaluate GC (but not GC itself).

Output Exchange phase. In the previous two stages, no information about the output (or participation) was revealed to any party (even if they deviate arbitrarily from the protocol). In other words, the messages exchanged between the parties in the previous stages were "not valuable" for deducing any potentially unknown information. In this phase, the parties actually exchange valuable messages having information so as to be able to get the function output at the end. Specifically, the parties exchange their garbled circuit shares *conditioned* upon the fact that *every* party was honest till the end of the Garbled Circuit Generation phase. This is done using our ZKSend construct as described below.

If any party deviated from the protocol during the Input commitment or Garbled Circuit Generation phase, it could be potentially dangerous for P_i to give out its garbled circuit share (since then the garbled circuit is not guaranteed to be correctly constructed). Hence, P_i breaks its share GC_i further into n sub-shares $\{GC_i^j\}_{j=1}^n$ and transfers these sub-shares in *parallel* to other parties P_j using $ZKSend_{ij}$. In particular, in an execution of $ZKSend_{ij}$, the input of P_i is GC_i^j while P_j is supposed to prove an NP statement which asserts that P_j was "honest" in the protocol up to the end of the Garbled Circuit Generation phase.

If any of the $n-1$ parties was dishonest previously, it is guaranteed that at least one of those n sub-shares will be "lost" (since ZKSend will output a randomly selected value instead of the right sub-share to a dishonest party); in this case, GC is "lost" as well.

After all the executions of ZKSend are completed, P_i obtains $\{GC_1^i, \ldots, GC_n^i\}$. It then broadcasts $GC^i = \bigoplus_{j=1}^n GC_j^i$. Upon receiving GC^i for all i, all parties compute $GC = \bigoplus_{i=1}^n GC^i$.

This completes the description of the main ideas in our protocol. We note that apart from the above, our construction uses other (new and old) ideas to ensure correctness of the output, simulatability of the protocol etc. We refer the reader to the full version for more details.

[6]Applebaum et al [1] show that there do not exist any encryption schemes such that the decryption function is in NC^0. However, fortunately, for our purpose, we only require the encryption function to be in NC^0.

[7]The option of simply moving the pre-processing phase of [7] to the secure computation protocol circuit would require that circuit to evaluate a PRG. We however, note that a PRG with appropriate stretch exists in NC^0 based only on non-standard assumptions [2].

6. ACKNOWLEDGEMENTS

We thank Yuval Ishai for useful discussions. We also thank Chris Peikert for his extremely useful comments that helped us in improving the presentation of our results.

7. REFERENCES

[1] B. Applebaum, Y. Ishai, and E. Kushilevitz. Cryptography in nc^0. In *FOCS*, 2004.

[2] B. Applebaum, Y. Ishai, and E. Kushilevitz. On pseudorandom generators with linear stretch in nc^0. *Computational Complexity*, 2008.

[3] G. Ateniese, M. Blanton, and J. Kirsch. Secret handshakes with dynamic and fuzzy matchin. In *NDSS*, 2007.

[4] B. Barak. How to go beyond the black-box simulation barrier. In *FOCS*, 2001.

[5] B. Barak, R. Canetti, Y. Lindell, R. Pass, and T. Rabin. Secure computation without authentication. In *CRYPTO*, 2005.

[6] B. Barak and O. Goldreich. Universal arguments and their applications. In *CCC*, 2002.

[7] D. Beaver, S. Micali, and P. Rogaway. The round complexity of secure protocols (extended abstract). In *STOC*, 1990.

[8] N. Chandran, V. Goyal, R. Ostrovsky, and A. Sahai. Covert multi-party computation. In *FOCS*, 2007.

[9] O. Goldreich and L. A. Levin. A hard-core predicate for all one-way functions. In *STOC*, 1989.

[10] O. Goldreich, S. Micali, and A. Wigderson. How to play any mental game. In *STOC*, 1987.

[11] Y. Ishai, E. Kushilevitz, R. Ostrovsky, and A. Sahai. Cryptography with constant computational overhead. In *STOC*, 2008.

[12] J. Katz and C.-Y. Koo. Round-efficient secure computation in point-to-point networks. In *EUROCRYPT*, 2007.

[13] M. Naor and B. Pinkas. Efficient oblivious transfer protocols. In *SODA*, 2001.

[14] R. Pass. Bounded-concurrent secure multi-party computation with a dishonest majority. In *STOC*, 2004.

[15] A. Sahai. Non-malleable non-interactive zero knowledge and adaptive chosen-ciphertext security. In *FOCS*, 1999.

[16] L. von Ahn, N. Hopper, and J. Langford. Covert two-party computation. In *STOC*, 2005.

[17] A. C.-C. Yao. Protocols for secure computations. In *FOCS*, 1982.

Detecting High Log-Densities – an $O(n^{1/4})$ Approximation for Densest k-Subgraph

Aditya Bhaskara[*]
Princeton University
Princeton, NJ
bhaskara@cs.princeton.edu

Moses Charikar[†]
Princeton University
Princeton, NJ
moses@cs.princeton.edu

Eden Chlamtac[‡]
Weizmann Institute of Science
Rehovot, Israel
eden.chlamtac@weizmann.ac.il

Uriel Feige[§]
Weizmann Institute of Science
Rehovot, Israel
uriel.feige@weizmann.ac.il

Aravindan Vijayaraghavan[¶]
Princeton University
Princeton, NJ
aravindv@cs.princeton.edu

ABSTRACT

In the Densest k-Subgraph problem, given a graph G and a parameter k, one needs to find a subgraph of G induced on k vertices that contains the largest number of edges. There is a significant gap between the best known upper and lower bounds for this problem. It is NP-hard, and does not have a PTAS unless NP has subexponential time algorithms. On the other hand, the current best known algorithm of Feige, Kortsarz and Peleg [10], gives an approximation ratio of $n^{1/3-\varepsilon}$ for some fixed $\varepsilon > 0$ (later estimated at around $\varepsilon = 1/90$).

We present an algorithm that for every $\varepsilon > 0$ approximates the Densest k-Subgraph problem within a ratio of $n^{1/4+\varepsilon}$ in time $n^{O(1/\varepsilon)}$. If allowed to run for time $n^{O(\log n)}$, the algorithm achieves an approximation ratio of $O(n^{1/4})$. Our algorithm is inspired by studying an average-case version of the problem where the goal is to distinguish random graphs from random graphs with planted dense subgraphs – the approximation ratio we achieve for the general case matches the "distinguishing ratio" we obtain for this planted problem.

At a high level, our algorithms involve cleverly counting appropriately defined trees of constant size in G, and using these counts to identify the vertices of the dense subgraph. We say that a graph $G(V, E)$ has log-density α if its average degree is $\Theta(|V|^{\alpha})$. The algorithmic core of our result is a procedure to output a k subgraph of 'nontrivial' density whenever the log-density of the densest k-subgraph is larger than the log-density of the host graph.

We outline an extension to our approximation algorithm which achieves an $O(n^{1/4-\varepsilon})$-approximation in $O(2^{n^{O(\varepsilon)}})$ time. We also show that, for certain parameter ranges, eigenvalue and SDP based techniques can outperform our basic distinguishing algorithm for random instances (in polynomial time), though without improving upon the $O(n^{1/4})$ guarantee overall.

[*]supported by NSF awards MSPA-MCS 0528414, CCF 0832797, and AF 0916218.

[†]supported by NSF awards MSPA-MCS 0528414, CCF 0832797, and AF 0916218.

[‡]supported by a Sir Charles Clore Postdoctoral Fellowship.

[§]The author holds the Lawrence G. Horowitz Professorial Chair at the Weizmann Institute. Work supported in part by The Israel Science Foundation (grant No. 873/08).

[¶]supported by NSF awards MSPA-MCS 0528414, CCF 0832797, and AF 0916218.

STOC'10, June 5–8, 2010, Cambridge, Massachusetts, USA.

1. INTRODUCTION

In this paper, we study the Densest k-Subgraph (DkS) problem: Given a graph G and parameter k, find a subgraph of G on k vertices with maximum density (average degree). This problem may be seen as an optimization version of the classical NP-complete decision problem CLIQUE. The approximability of DkS is an important open problem and despite much work, there remains a significant gap between the currently best known upper and lower bounds.

In addition to being NP-hard (as seen by the connection to CLIQUE), the DkS problem has also been shown not to admit a PTAS under various complexity theoretic assumptions. Feige [9] has shown this assuming random 3-SAT formulas are hard to refute, while more recently this was shown by Khot [16] assuming that NP does not have randomized algorithms that run in sub-exponential time (i.e. that $NP \not\subseteq \cap_{\varepsilon>0} BPTIME(2^{n^{\varepsilon}})$).

The current best approximation ratio of $n^{1/3-\varepsilon}$ for some small $\varepsilon > 0$. was achieved by Feige, Kortsarz and Peleg [10]. Recently, and independently of our work, Goldstein and Langberg [15] have estimated this guarantee to be approximately $n^{0.32258}$, and present an algorithm for which they computed the approximation ratio to be roughly $n^{0.3159}$. Other known approximation algorithms have approximation guarantees that depend on the parameter k. The greedy heuristic of Asahiro et al. [5] obtains an $O(n/k)$ approximation. Linear and semidefinite programming (SDP) relaxations were studied by Srivastav and Wolf [18] and by Feige and Langberg [11], where the latter authors show how they can be used to get approximation ratios somewhat better than n/k. Feige and Seltser [12] show graphs for which the integrality gap of the natural SDP relaxation is $\Omega(n^{1/3})$, indicating that in the worst case, the approximation ratios achieved in [10] are better than those achievable by this SDP. When the input is a complete graph with edge weights that satisfy the triangle inequality, a simple greedy algorithm achieves an approximation ratio of 2 (though the analysis of this algorithm is apparently not easy, see [7]).

A related problem to DkS is the max density subgraph problem, where the aim is to find a subgraph H which maximizes the ratio of number of edges to number of vertices in H. It turns out that this can be solved in polynomial time [14]. Charikar et al. [8] recently showed an $O(n^{1/3})$ approximation to the maximization version of label cover. This problem is at least as difficult as DkS in the sense that there is an approximation preserving randomized reduction from DkS (see [8] for example) to it. No reduction in the opposite direction is known.

Our algorithm for DkS is inspired by studying an average-case version we call the 'Dense vs Random' question (see Section 3 for a precise definition). Here the aim is to distinguish random graphs from graphs containing a dense subgraphs, which can be viewed as the task of efficiently certifying that random graphs do not contain dense subgraphs. This distinguishing problem is similar in flavour to the well-studied planted clique problem (see [1]). Getting a better understanding of this planted question seems crucial for further progress on DkS.

Some recent papers have used the hypothesis that (bipartite versions of) the planted dense subgraph problem is computationally hard: Applebaum et al. [3] use this in the design of a new public key encryption scheme. More recently, Arora et al. [4] use this to demonstrate that evaluating certain financial derivatives is computationally hard. The use of such hardness assumptions provides additional motivation for the study of algorithms for these problems.

1.1 Our results

Our main result is a polynomial time $O(n^{1/4+\varepsilon})$ approximation algorithm for DkS, for any constant $\varepsilon > 0$. That is, given $\varepsilon > 0$, and a graph G with a k-subgraph of density d, our algorithm outputs a k-subgraph of density $\Omega\left(d/n^{1/4+\varepsilon}\right)$ in polynomial time. In particular, our techniques give an $O(n^{1/4})$-approximation algorithm running in $O(n^{\log n})$ time.

At a high level, our algorithms involve cleverly counting appropriately defined subgraphs of constant size in G, and use these counts to identify the vertices of the dense subgraph. A key notion which comes up in the analysis is the following:

DEFINITION 1.1. *The* log-density *of a graph $G(V, E)$ with average degree D is $\log_{|V|} D$. In other words, if a graph has log-density α, its average degree is $|V|^{\alpha}$.* [1]

We first consider the random setting – distinguishing between G drawn from $G(n, p)$, and G containing a k-subgraph H of certain density planted in it. In fact, we examine a few variants (i.e. in the second case each of G and H may or may not be random). For all these variants we show that if the log-density of G is α and that of H is β, with $\beta > \alpha$, we can solve the distinguishing problem in time $n^{O(1/(\beta-\alpha))}$.

Our main technical contribution is that a result of this nature can be proven for arbitrary graphs. Informally, our main result, which gives a *family* of algorithms, parametrized by a rational number r/s, can be stated as follows (see Theorem 4.5 for a more precise statement):

THEOREM 1.2. **(informal)** *Let $s > r > 0$ be relatively prime integers, let G be an undirected graph with maximum degree $D = n^{r/s}$, which contains a k-subgraph H with average degree d. Then there is an algorithm running in time $n^{O(r)}$ that finds a k-subgraph of average degree $\Omega(d/D^{(s-r)/s})$.*

Note that the log-density of H does not explicitly occur in the statement of the theorem. However, it turns out we can pre-process the graph, and restrict ourselves to the case $kD = n$ (see Appendix A.1), in which case $D^{(s-r)/s} = k^{r/s}$, thus the output subgraph has average degree $d/k^{r/s}$. So if the log-density of H is β (recall that G has log-density $\leq r/s$), the output graph has density $d/k^{r/s} = k^{\beta-r/s}$. Thus the difference in the log-densities also plays a role in the case of arbitrary graphs.

Also note that the theorem deals with the *maximum* degree in G, and not average degree (which defines the log-density). It turns out that this upper-bound on the log-density will suffice (and will be more useful in the analysis).

As we observed earlier, we give a family of algorithms parameterized by a rational number. Thus, given G and k, we pick r/s appropriately and appeal to the theorem. In some sense, this family of algorithms is a systematic generalization of the (somewhat ad hoc) algorithms of [10].

Finally, observe that theorem implies an approximation ratio of at most $D^{(s-r)/s} \leq n^{r(s-r)/s^2} \leq n^{1/4}$ for every choice of $s > r > 0$. As we mentioned, the statement above is informal. If we choose to restrict the running time to $O(n^{s_0})$ by limiting ourselves to $r < s \leq s_0$ (i.e. the bound on D will not be exact), we lose a factor n^{1/s_0} in the approximation. We refer to Section 4 for the details.

Outline of techniques. The distinguishing algorithm for the Dense vs Random problem is based on the fact that in $G(n, p)$, instances of any fixed constant size structure appear more often when the graph has a higher log-density. More precisely, given parameters r, s, we will define a (constant size) tree $T_{r,s}$ such that a fixed set of leaves can be completed to many instances of $T_{r,s}$ in a graph with log-density $> r/s$, whereas in a random graph with log-density $< r/s$ there will only be a negligible number of such instances. Thus, if the log-density of H is greater than r/s, finding a small set of vertices in H (and using them as leaves of $T_{r,s}$) can help reveal larger portions of a dense subgraph. Though our intuition comes from random graphs, the heart of the argument carries over to worst-case instances.

We use a linear programming relaxation to guide us in our search for the fixed vertices' assignment and obtain the dense subgraph. In order to extract consistent feasible solutions from the LP even under the assumptions that fixed vertices belong to H, the LP relaxation will have a recursive structure similar to the Lovász-Schrijver hierarchy [17]. Feasible solutions to this LP (when they exist) can be found in

[1]We will ignore low order terms when expressing the log-density. For example, graphs with constant average degree will be said to have log-density 0, and cliques will be said to have log-density 1.

time $n^{O(r)}$ (where the depth of the recursion will be roughly r), while the rest of the algorithm (given the LP solution) will take linear time. As we shall see, there is also a combinatorial variant of our algorithm, which, rather than relying on an LP solution, finds the appropriate set of leaves by exhaustive search (in time $n^{r+O(1)}$). While the analysis is essentially the same as for the LP variant, it is our hope that a mathematical programming approach will lead to further improvements in running time and approximation guarantee.

The approximation ratio we achieve for general instances of DkS matches the "distinguishing ratio" we are currently able to achieve for various random settings. This suggests the following concrete open problem which seems to be a barrier for obtaining an approximation ratio of $n^{1/4-\varepsilon}$ for DkS – distinguish between the following two distributions:

$\mathcal{D}_1$: graph G picked from $G(n, n^{-1/2})$, and
$\mathcal{D}_2$: graph G picked from $G(n, n^{-1/2})$ with the induced subgraph on $\sqrt{n}$ vertices replaced with $G(\sqrt{n}, n^{-(1/4+\varepsilon)})$.

In section 5.1 we will see that this distinguishing problem can be solved in time $2^{n^{O(\varepsilon)}}$, and moreover in arbitrary graphs we can approximate DkS to within an $n^{1/4-\varepsilon}$ factor in time $2^{n^{O(\varepsilon)}}$. These mildly exponential algorithms are interesting given the recent results of [4] and [3], which are based on the assumption that planted versions of DkS are hard.

In section 5.2, we show that in the random setting we can beat the log-density based algorithms for certain ranges of parameters. We use different techniques for different random models, some of which are very different from those used in sections 3 and 4. Interestingly, none of these techniques give a distinguishing ratio better than $n^{1/4}$ when $k = D = \sqrt{n}$.

1.2 Organization of paper

In Section 2, we introduce some notation, and describe simplifying assumptions which will be made in later sections (some of these were used in [10]). In Section 3, we consider two natural 'planted' versions of DkS, and present algorithms for these versions. The analysis there motivates our approximation algorithm for DkS, which will be presented in Section 4. In Section 5, we explore approaches to overcome the log-density barrier that limits our algorithms in Section 4. In Section 5.1 we give an $O(n^{1/4-\varepsilon})$ approximation algorithm for arbitrary graphs with run time $O(2^{n^{O(\varepsilon)}})$ time, and in Section 5.2, we show that in various random settings, we can obtain a $\sqrt{D}$-approximation (which is better than the log-density guarantee for $1 < D < \sqrt{n}$).

2. NOTATION AND SIMPLIFICATIONS

We now introduce some notation which will be used in the rest of the paper. Unless otherwise stated, $G(V, E)$ refers to an input graph on n vertices, and k refers to the size of the subgraph we are required to output. Also, H will denote the densest k-subgraph (breaking ties arbitrarily) in G, and d denotes the average degree of H. For $v \in V$, $\Gamma(v)$ denotes the set of neighbors of v, and for a set of vertices $S \subseteq V$, $\Gamma(S)$ denotes the set of all neighbors of vertices in S. Finally, for any number $x \in \mathbb{R}$, will use the notation $\text{fr}(x) = x - \lfloor x \rfloor$.

We will make the following simplifying assumptions in the remaining sections: (these are justified in Section A of the appendix)

1. There exists a D such that (a) the maximum degree of G is at most D, and (b) a greedy algorithm finds a k-subgraph of density $\max\{1, kD/n\}$ in G.
2. d is the minimum degree in H (rather than the average degree)
3. It suffices to find a subgraph of size *at most* k, rather than exactly k. In Section 4 we use 'k-subgraph' more loosely to mean a subgraph on at most k vertices.
4. When convenient, we may also take G (and hence H) to be bipartite.
5. The edges of the graph G are assumed to be unweighted, since we can bucket the edges into $O(\log n)$ levels according to the edge weights (which we assume are all positive), and output the densest of the k-subgraphs obtained by applying the algorithm to each of the graphs induced by the edges in a bucket. This incurs a loss of just $O(\log n)$ factor in the approximation.

In many places, we will ignore leading constant factors (for example, we may find a subgraph of size $2k$ instead of k). It will be clear that these do not seriously affect the approximation factor.

3. RANDOM GRAPH MODELS

An $f(n)$-approximation algorithm for Densest k-Subgraph must be able to distinguish between graphs where any k-subgraph has density at most c, and graphs with an $cf(n)$-dense k-subgraph planted in them. Random graphs are a natural class of graphs that do not contain dense k-subgraphs. Further, random graphs seem to present challenges for currently best known algorithms for DkS. Hence, it is instructive to see what parameters allow us to efficiently solve this distinguishing problem.

We consider three variants of the random distinguishing problem, in increasing order of difficulty. In the *Random Planted Model*, we would like to distinguish between two distributions:

$\mathcal{D}_1$: Graph G is picked from $G(n, p)$, with $p = n^{\alpha-1}$, $0 < \alpha < 1$.
$\mathcal{D}_2$: G is picked from $G(n, n^{\alpha-1})$ as before. A set S of k vertices is chosen arbitrarily, and the subgraph on S is replaced with a random graph H from $G(k, k^{\beta-1})$ on S.

A slightly harder variant is the *Dense in Random* problem, in which we would like to distinguish between G chosen from $\mathcal{D}_1$, as before, and G which is chosen similarly to $\mathcal{D}_2$, except that the planted subgraph H is now an *arbitrary* graph with average degree k^β (that is, log-density β). Here, the algorithm must be able to detect the second case with high probability regardless of the choice of H.

Finally, we consider the *Dense versus Random* problem, in which we would like to distinguish between $G \sim \mathcal{D}_1$, and an *arbitrary* graph G which contains a k-subgraph H of log-density β.

Observe that for $G \sim \mathcal{D}_1$, a k-subgraph would have expected average degree $kp = kn^{\alpha-1}$. Further, it can be shown that densest k-subgraph in G will have average degree $\max\{kn^{\alpha-1}, 1\}$, w.h.p. (up to a logarithmic factor). Thus if we can solve the distinguishing problem above, its 'distinguishing ratio' would be $\min_\beta(k^\beta/\max\{kn^{\alpha-1},1\})$, where β ranges over all values for which we can distinguish (for the corresponding values of k,α). If this is the case for all $\beta>\alpha$, then the distinguishing ratio is never more than

$$\begin{aligned}\frac{k^\alpha}{\max\{kn^{\alpha-1},1\}} &= \min\left\{\left(\frac{n}{k}\right)^{1-\alpha}, k^\alpha\right\}\\ &= n^{\alpha(1-\alpha)}\cdot\min\left\{\left(\frac{n^{1-\alpha}}{k}\right)^{1-\alpha}, \left(\frac{k}{n^{1-\alpha}}\right)^{\alpha}\right\}\\ &\le n^{\alpha(1-\alpha)}\\ &\le n^{1/4}.\end{aligned}$$

In this section we will only discuss the Random Planted Model and the Dense versus Random problem, while the intermediate Dense in Random problem is only examined in Section 5.2.

3.1 The random planted model

One easy way of distinguishing between the two distributions in the Random Planted Model involves looking at the highest degree vertices, or at the pairs of vertices with the largest intersection of neighborhoods. This approach, which is discussed in Section 5.2 is not only a distinguishing algorithm, but can also identify H in the case of $G\sim\mathcal{D}_2$. However, it is not robust, in the sense that we can easily avoid a detectable contribution to the degrees of vertices of H by resampling the edges between H and $G\setminus H$ with the appropriate probability.

Rather, we examine a different approach, which is to look for constant size subgraphs H' which act as 'witnesses'. If $G\sim\mathcal{D}_1$, we want that w.h.p. G will not have a subgraph isomorphic to H', while if $G\sim\mathcal{D}_2$, w.h.p. G should have such a subgraph. It turns out that whenever $\beta>\alpha$, such an H' can be exists, and thus we can solve the distinguishing problem.

Standard probabilistic analysis (cf. [2]) shows that if a graph has log-density greater than r/s (for fixed integers $0<r<s$) then it is expected to have constant size subgraphs in which the ratio of edges to vertices is $s/(s-r)$, and if the log-density is smaller than r/s, such subgraphs are not likely to exist (i.e., the occurrence of such subgraphs has a threshold behavior). Hence such subgraphs can serve as witnesses when $\alpha<r/s<\beta$.

Observe that in the approach outlined above, r/s is rational, and the size of the witnesses increases as r and s increase. This serves as intuition as to why the statement of Theorem 1.2 involves a rational number r/s, with the running time depending on the value of r.

3.2 Dense versus Random

The random planted model above, though interesting, does not seem to say much about the general DkS problem. In particular, for the Dense versus Random problem, simply looking for the occurrence of subgraphs need not work, because the planted graph could be very dense and yet not have the subgraph we are looking for.

To overcome this problem, we will use a different kind of witness, which will involve special constant-size trees, which we call *templates*. In a *template witness* based on a tree T, we fix a small set of vertices U in G, and count the number of trees isomorphic to T whose set of leaves is exactly U. The templates are chosen such that a random graph with log-density below a threshold will have a count at most polylogarithmic for *every* choice of U, while we will show by a counting argument that in any graph (or subgraph) with log-density above the same threshold, there exists a set of vertices U which coincide with the leaves of at least n^ε copies of T (for some constant $\varepsilon>0$). As noted in Section 2, we may assume *minimum* degree k^β in H as opposed to average degree (this will greatly simplify the counting argument).

As an example, suppose the log-density is $2/3$. In this case, the template T we consider is the tree $K_{1,3}$ (a claw with three leaves). For any triple of vertices U, we count the number of copies of T with U as the set of leaves – in this case this is precisely the number of common neighbors of the vertices in U. In this case, we show that if $G\sim\mathcal{D}_1$, with $\alpha\le 2/3$, *every* triple of vertices has at most $O(\log n)$ common neighbors. While in the dense case, with $\beta=2/3+\varepsilon$, there exists some triple with at least $k^{3\varepsilon}$ common neighbors. Since for ranges of parameters of interest $k^{3\varepsilon}=\omega(\log n)$, we have a distinguishing algorithm.

Let us now consider a log-density threshold of r/s (for some relatively prime integers $s>r>0$). The tree T we will associate with the corresponding template witness will be a caterpillar – a single path called the *backbone* from which other paths, called *hairs*, emerge. In our case, the hairs will all be of length 1. More formally,

DEFINITION 3.1. *An (r,s)-caterpillar is a tree constructed inductively as follows: Begin with a single vertex as the leftmost node in the backbone. For s steps, do the following: at step i, if the interval $[(i-1)r/s, ir/s]$ contains an integer, add a hair of length 1 to the rightmost vertex in the backbone; otherwise, add an edge to the backbone (increasing its length by 1).*

This inductive definition is also useful in deriving an upper bound on the number of (r,s)-caterpillars in $G(n,p)$ (for $p\le n^{r/s-1}$) with a fixed sequence of 'leaves' (end-points of the hairs) $v_0,v_1,\dots,v_r$. We do this by bounding the number of candidates for each internal (backbone) vertex, and showing that with high probability, this is at most $O(\log n)$. We begin by bounding the number of candidates for the rightmost backbone vertex in a *prefix* of the (r,s) caterpillar (as per the above inductive construction). For each $t=1,\dots,r$, let us write $S_{v_0,\dots,v_{\lfloor tr/s\rfloor}}(t)$ for the set of such candidates at step t (given the appropriate prefix of leaves). The following claim upper bounds the cardinality of these sets (with high probability). (Recall the notation $\mathrm{fr}(x)=x-\lfloor x\rfloor$.)

CLAIM 3.2. *Suppose G is drawn from $G(n,p)$, with $p\le n^{r/s-1}$. Then for every $1\le t\le s$, every sequence of vertices $U_i=v_0,\dots,v_{\lfloor tr/s\rfloor}$, and every vertex $v\in V\setminus U_i$, we have*

$$\Pr[v\in S_{v_0,\dots,v_{\lfloor tr/s\rfloor}}(t)]\le n^{\mathrm{fr}(tr/s)-1}(1+o(1)).$$

Intuitively, the claim follows from two simple observations: (a) For any set of vertices $S\subseteq V$ in $G(n,p)$, w.h.p. the neighborhood of S has cardinality at most $pn|S|$ (since the degree of every vertex is tightly concentrated around pn), and (b) for every vertex set S, the expected cardinality of its intersection with the neighborhood of any vertex v is at most $\mathbb{E}[|S\cap\Gamma(v)|]\le p|S|$. Applying these bounds inductively to the construction of the sets $S(t)$ when $p=n^{r/s-1}$ then implies $|S(t)|\le n^{\mathrm{fr}(tr/s)}$ for every t.

PROOF (SKETCH). In fact, it suffices to show equality for $p = n^{r/s-1}$ (since for sparser random graphs the probability can only be smaller). More precisely, for this value of p, we show:

$$\Pr[v \in S_{v_0,\ldots,v_{\lfloor tr/s \rfloor}}(t)] = n^{\mathrm{fr}(tr/s)-1}(1 \pm o(1)).$$

We prove the claim by induction. For $i = 1$, it follows by definition of $G(n,p)$: $\Pr[v \in S_{v_0}(1)] = p = n^{r/s-1}$. For $t > 1$, assume the claim holds for $t-1$. If the interval $[(t-1)r/s, tr/s]$ contains an integer (for $1 < t \le s$ it must be $\lceil (t-1)r/s \rceil$), then $S(t) = S(t-1) \cap \Gamma(v_{\lceil (t-1)r/s \rceil})$. Thus, by definition of $G(n,p)$ and the inductive hypothesis,

$$\begin{aligned}\Pr[v \in S_{v_0,\ldots,v_{\lfloor tr/s \rfloor}}(t)] &= p \cdot \Pr[v \in S_{v_0,\ldots,v_{\lfloor (t-1)r/s \rfloor}}(t-1)] \\ &= n^{r/s-1} n^{\mathrm{fr}((t-1)r/s)-1}(1+o(1)) \\ &= n^{\mathrm{fr}(tr/s)-1}(1 \pm o(1)).\end{aligned}$$

Otherwise, if the interval $[(t-1)r/s, tr/s]$ does not contain an integer, then $S(t) = \Gamma(S(t-1))$. In this case, by the inductive hypothesis, the cardinality of the set $|S(t-1)|$ is tightly concentrated around $n^{\mathrm{fr}((t-1)r/s)}$ (using Chernoff-Hoeffding bounds). If we condition on the choice of all $S(t')$ for $t' < t$, and $S(t-1)$ has (approximately) the above cardinality, then for every v not appearing in the previous sets, we have

$$\begin{aligned}&\Pr[v \in S_{v_0,\ldots,v_{\lfloor tr/s \rfloor}}(t)] \\ &= \Pr[\exists u \in S_{v_0,\ldots,v_{\lfloor tr/s \rfloor}}(t-1) : (u,v) \in E] \\ &= 1-(1-p)^{|S(t-1)|} \\ &= p|S(t-1)|(1-o(1)) \quad \text{since } p|S(t-1)| = o(1) \\ &= n^{r/s-1} n^{\mathrm{fr}((t-1)r/s)}(1 \pm o(1)) \\ &= n^{\mathrm{fr}(tr/s)-1}(1 \pm o(1)).\end{aligned}$$

Note that a more careful analysis need also bound the number of vertices participating in $S(t) \cap S(t')$ for all $t' < t$. Further, even in this case, tight concentration assumed above is only achieved when the expected size of the set is $n^{\Omega(1)}$. However, this is guaranteed by the inductive hypothesis, assuming r and s are relatively prime. □

Now by symmetry, the same bounds can be given when constructing the candidate sets in the opposite direction, from right to left (note the symmetry of the structure). Thus, once all the leaves are fixed, every candidate for an internal vertex can be described, for some $t \in [1, s-1]$, as the rightmost backbone vertex in the tth prefix, as well as the leftmost backbone vertex in the $(s-t)$th prefix starting from the right. By Claim 3.2, the probability of this event is at most

$$n^{\mathrm{fr}(tr/s)-1} n^{\mathrm{fr}((s-t)r/s)-1}(1+o(1)) = n^{-1}(1+o(1)).$$

Thus, since the (r,s)-caterpillar has $s-r$ internal vertices and $r+1$ leaves, it follows by standard probabilistic arguments that, for some universal constant $C > 0$, the probability that total number of caterpillars for any sequence of leaves exceeds $(\log n)^{s-r}$ is at most $(s-r)n^{r+1}n^{-C\log\log n}$, which is $o(1)$ for any constants r, s.

Now let us consider the number of (r,s)-caterpillars with a fixed set of leaves in a k-subgraph H with minimum degree at least $d = k^{(r+\varepsilon)/s}$. Ignoring low-order terms (which would account for repeated leaves), the number of (r,s)-caterpillars in H (double counting each caterpillar to account for constructing it inductively once from each direction) is at least kd^s (since it is a tree with s edges), whereas the number of possible sequences of leaves is at most k^{r+1}. Thus, the number of (r,s) caterpillars in H corresponding to the average sequence of $(r+1)$ H-vertices is at least $kd^s/k^{r+1} = k^{r+\varepsilon}/k^r = k^\varepsilon$. Note that the parameters for the high probability success of the dense-versus-random distinguishing algorithm are the same as for the random planted model, giving, as before, an distinguishing ratio of $\tilde{O}(n^{1/4})$ in the worst case.

4. AN LP BASED ALGORITHM FOR ARBITRARY GRAPHS

We now give a general algorithm for DkS inspired by the distinguishing algorithm in the Dense vs Random setting. For a graph G with maximum degree $D = n^{r/s}$, we will use the (r,s)-caterpillar template, and keep track of sets $S(t)$ as before. We then fix the leaves one by one, while maintaining suitable bounds on $S(t)$.

Let us start by describing the LP relaxation.[2] Taking into account the simplifications from Section 2, we define a hierarchy of LPs which is satisfied by a graph which contains a subgraph of size at most k with minimum degree at least d. This hierarchy is at most as strong as the Lovász-Schrijver LP hierarchy based on the usual LP relaxation (and is possibly weaker). Specifically, for all integers $t \ge 1$, we define $\mathbf{DkS\text{-}LP}_t(G,k,d)$ to be the set of n-dimensional vectors $(y_1, \ldots y_n)$ satisfying:

$$\sum_{i \in V} y_i \le k \quad \text{and} \tag{1}$$

$$\exists y_{ij} \ : \ i,j \in V \ \text{s.t.}$$

$$\forall i \in V \quad \sum_{j \in \Gamma(i)} y_{ij} \ge d y_i \tag{2}$$

$$\forall i,j \in V \quad y_{ij} = y_{ji} \tag{3}$$

$$\forall i,j \in V \quad 0 \le y_{ij} \le y_i \le 1 \tag{4}$$

if $t > 1$, $\forall i \in V$ s.t. $y_i \neq 0$, we have

$$\{y_{i1}/y_i, \ldots, y_{in}/y_i\} \in \mathbf{DkS\text{-}LP}_{t-1}(G,k,d) \tag{5}$$

Given an LP solution $\{y_i\}$, we write $\mathrm{LP}_{\{y_i\}}(S) = \sum_{i \in S} y_i$. When the solution is clear from context, we denote the same by $\mathrm{LP}(S)$. We call this the *LP-value* of S. When the level in the hierarchy will not be important, we will simply write DkS-LP instead of DkS-LP$_t$. A standard argument shows that a feasible solution to DkS-LP$_t(G,k,d)$ (along with all the recursively defined solutions implied by constraint (5)) can be found in time $n^{O(t)}$. For completeness, we outline this in Appendix B

Informally, we can think of the LP as giving a distribution over subsets of V, with y_i being the probability that i is in a subset. Similarly y_{ij} can be thought of as the probability that both i, j are 'picked'. We can now think of the solution $\{y_{ij}/y_i : 1 \le j \le n\}$ as a distribution over subsets, conditioned on the event that i is picked.

[2]The entire algorithm can be executed without solving an LP, by performing an exhaustive search for the best set of leaves, with running time comparable to that of solving the LP. We will elaborate on this later.

Algorithm outline.

The execution of the algorithm follows the construction of an (r, s)-caterpillar. We perform s steps, throughout maintaining a subset $S(t)$ of the vertices. For each t, we perform either a 'backbone step' or a 'hair step' (which we will describe shortly). In each of these steps, we will either find a dense subgraph, or extend an inductive argument that will give a lower bound on the ratio $\mathrm{LP}(S(t))/|S(t)|$. Finally, we show that if none of the steps finds a dense subgraph, then we reach a contradiction in the form of a violated LP constraint, namely $LP(S(s)) > |S(s)|$.

4.1 The Algorithm

Let us now describe the algorithm in detail. The algorithm will take two kinds of steps, *backbone* and *hair*, corresponding to the two types of caterpillar edges. While these steps differ in the updates they make, both use the same procedure to search locally for a dense subgraph starting with a current candidate-set. Let us now describe this procedure.

DkS-Local(S, k)

- Consider the bipartite subgraph induced on $S, \Gamma(S)$.
- For all $k' = 1, \ldots, k$, do the following:
  - Let $T_{k'}$ be the set of k' vertices in $\Gamma(S)$ with the highest degree (into S).
  - Take the $\min\{k', |S|\}$ vertices in S with the most neighbors in $T_{k'}$, and let $H_{k'}(S)$ be the bipartite subgraph induced on this set and $T_{k'}$.
- Output the subgraph $H_{k'}(S)$ with the largest average degree.

We will analyze separately the performance of this procedure in the context of a leaf-step and that of a hair-step. We begin by relating the performance of this procedure to an LP solution.

CLAIM 4.1. *Given a set of vertices* $S \subseteq V$, *and an LP solution* $\{y_i\} \in \mathrm{DkS\text{-}LP}(G, k, d)$, *let* $k' = \lceil \mathrm{LP}(\Gamma(S)) \rceil$. *Then* DkS-Local$(S, k)$ *outputs a subgraph with average degree at least*

$$\frac{1}{\max\{|S|, k'\}} \cdot \sum_{j \in \Gamma(S)} y_j |\Gamma(j) \cap S|.$$

PROOF. By constraint (1), $k' = \lceil \mathrm{LP}(\Gamma(S)) \rceil \leq k$. Thus in Procedure DkS-Local, the vertices in $T_{k'}$ must have at least $\sum_{j \in \Gamma(S)} y_j |\Gamma(j) \cap S|$ edges to S: indeed, the summation $\sum y_j |\Gamma(j) \cap S|$ can be achieved by taking $\sum_{j \in T_{k'}} 1 \cdot |\Gamma(j) \cap S|$ and moving some of the weight from vertices in $T_{k'}$ to lower-degree (w.r.t. S) vertices (and perhaps throwing some of the weight away). After choosing the $\min\{k', |S|\}$ vertices in S with highest degree, the remaining subgraph $H_{k'}(S)$ has average degree at least

$$\frac{\min\{k', |S|\}}{|S|} \cdot \frac{1}{k'} \cdot \sum_{j \in \Gamma(S)} y_j |\Gamma(j) \cap S|.$$

This proves the claim. □

The backbone step in the algorithm first performs DkS-Local on the current S, and then sets S to be $\Gamma(S)$. The following lemma gives a way to inductively maintain a lower bound on $\mathrm{LP}(S(t))/|S(t)|$ assuming DkS-Local does not find a sufficiently dense subgraph.

LEMMA 4.2. *Given* $S \subseteq V$, *and an LP solution* $\{y_i\}$ *for* DkS-LP(G, k, d): *for any* $\rho \geq 1$ *such that* $\mathrm{LP}(S)/|S| \geq \rho/d$, *either* DkS-Local$(S, k)$ *outputs a subgraph with average degree at least* ρ *or we have*

$$\mathrm{LP}(\Gamma(S)) \geq \frac{d\mathrm{LP}(S)}{\rho}.$$

PROOF. By the LP constraints (4) and (2), we have

$$\sum_{j \in \Gamma(S)} y_j |\Gamma(j) \cap S| \geq \sum_{j \in \Gamma(S)} \sum_{i \in \Gamma(j) \cap S} y_{ij} = \sum_{i \in S} \sum_{j \in \Gamma(i)} y_{ij} \geq d\mathrm{LP}(S).$$

By Claim 4.1, Dks-Local(S, k) outputs a subgraph with average degree $\geq d\mathrm{LP}(S)/\max\{|S|, k'\}$, where $k' = \mathrm{LP}(\Gamma(S))$ (note that we are ignoring some roundoff error which will be negligible in the context of the algorithm).

If $k' \leq |S|$, then we are done, since by our assumption, $d\mathrm{LP}(S)/|S| \geq \rho$. Now suppose $k' \geq |S|$. The output graph has average degree at least $d\mathrm{LP}(S)/k'$. If this is at least ρ, we are done. If not, $k' \geq d\mathrm{LP}(S)/\rho$, and since $k' = \mathrm{LP}(\Gamma(S))$, we get the desired result. □

Let us now consider a hair step. In this case, the algorithm performs DkS-Local on the current set, and then picks a vertex $j \in V$ to act as a "leaf". The new S is then set to equal $S \cap \Gamma(j)$. The following lemmas prove that either DkS-Local finds a sufficiently dense subgraph, or we can pick j so as to inductively maintain certain bounds. Let us first prove a simple averaging lemma.

LEMMA 4.3. *Let* x_j, $(1 \leq j \leq n)$ *be reals in* $[0, 1]$, *with* $\sum_j x_j \leq k$. *Let* P_j *and* Q_j *be some non-negative real numbers such that for some* $P, Q > 0$,

$$\sum_j x_j P_j \geq P, \text{ and } \sum_j x_j Q_j \leq Q. \qquad (6)$$

Then there exists a j *such that* $P_j \geq P/(2k)$ *and* $P_j/Q_j \geq P/(2Q)$.

PROOF. By our assumption $\sum_j x_j (P_j - \frac{P}{2k}) \geq P - \frac{P}{2} = \frac{P}{2}$. Thus from (6), it follows that there exists a j such that $x_j > 0$ and

$$P_j - \frac{P}{2k} \geq \frac{P}{2Q} \cdot Q_j.$$

This choice of j clearly satisfies the required properties. □

LEMMA 4.4. *Let* $S \subseteq V$, *and let* $\{y_i\} \in \mathrm{DkS\text{-}LP}(G, k, d)$ *be an LP solution (for which there exist corresponding* $\{y_{ij}\}$*). Then for any* $\rho \geq 1$, *either* DkS-Local(S, k) *outputs a* ρ*-dense subgraph, or there exists some vertex* $j \in G$, *such that* $y_j > 0$, *and*

$$\mathrm{LP}_{\{y_{ij}/y_j | i \in V\}}(S \cap \Gamma(j)) \geq \frac{d \cdot \mathrm{LP}_{\{y_i\}}(S)}{2k}, \text{ and}$$

$$\mathrm{LP}_{\{y_{ij}/y_j | i \in V\}}(S \cap \Gamma(j))/|S \cap \Gamma(j)| \geq \frac{d \cdot \mathrm{LP}_{\{y_i\}}(S)}{2\rho \cdot \max\{k, |S|\}}.$$

PROOF. By constraints (2) of the LP we have

$$\sum_{j\in\Gamma(S)} y_j LP_{\{y_{ij}/y_j|i\in V\}}(S\cap\Gamma(j)) = \sum_{j\in\Gamma(S)}\sum_{i\in\Gamma(j)\cap S} y_{ij}$$

$$= \sum_{i\in S}\sum_{j\in\Gamma(i)} y_{ij} \geq d\mathrm{LP}_{\{y_i\}}(S). \qquad (7)$$

From Claim 4.1, it follows that if the subgraph found by DkS-Local has average degree less than ρ, we must have $\rho > \sum_{j\in\Gamma(S)} y_j|\Gamma(j)\cap S|/\max\{|S|,k'\}$, or in other words

$$\sum_{j\in\Gamma(S)} y_j|\Gamma(j)\cap S| \leq \rho\max\{|S|,k'\} \leq \rho\max\{|S|,k\}. \quad (8)$$

Thus the lemma follows immediately from Lemma 4.3 and equations (7) and (8). □

We now formally describe the algorithm. It takes as input a graph G, a parameter k, and $\{y_i\}$, a solution to DkS-LP$_{r+2}(G,k,d)$. Throughout, a set $S\subseteq V$, and an LP solution $\{y_i\}$ are maintained.

DkS-Cat$_{r,s}(G,k,\{y_i\})$

- Let $S_0 = V$.
- For all $t = 1,\ldots,s$, do the following:
  - For $t>1$, let H_t be the output of Procedure DkS Local(S_{t-1},k).
  - If the interval $[(t-1)r/s, tr/s]$ contains an integer, perform a **hair step**:
    Choose some vertex j_t as in Lemma 4.4 (or for $t=1$, choose any j_1 such that $y_{j_1}>0$), and
    - Let $S_t = S_{t-1}\cap\Gamma(j_t)$.
    - Replace the LP solution $\{y_i\}$ with $\{y_{ij_t}/y_{j_t} \mid i\in V\}$.
  - Otherwise, perform a **backbone step**:
    Let $S_t = \Gamma(S_{t-1})$.
- Output the subgraph H_t with the highest average degree.

Note that since the "conditioning" step (replacing y_i's by y_{ij}/y_j) in the hair steps is only performed $r+1$ times, then by constraint (5), at every step of the algorithm $\{y_i\}$ satisfies DkS-LP(G,k,d).

A combinatorial algorithm.

Note that the only time the algorithm uses the LP values is in choosing the leaves. Thus, even in the absence of an LP solution, the algorithm can be run by trying all possible sequences of leaves (the analysis will still work by replacing the LP solution with the optimum $0-1$ solution). While this would take time $O(n^{r+1})$ as opposed to linear time (for the LP-based rounding algorithm), this is comparable to the time needed to solve the LP. An interesting open question is if it is possible to avoid the dependence on r, the number of leaves.

4.2 Performance guarantee

The analysis is quite straightforward. We follow the various steps, and each time apply Lemma 4.2 or Lemma 4.4, as appropriate. Our main result is the following:

THEOREM 4.5. *Let $s>r>0$ be relatively prime integers, let G be an undirected (bipartite) graph with maximum degree $\leq D = n^{r/s}$, let $\{y_i\}\in$ DkS-LP$_{r+1}(G,k,d)$, and define $\gamma=\max\{Dk/n,1\}$. Then if d' is the average degree of the subgraph found by* DkS-Cat$_{r,s}(G,k,\{y_i\})$, *we have*

$$\max\{d',\gamma\} = \Omega(d/D^{(s-r)/s}).$$

Note that when the log-density α of G is not rational, we can choose rational $\alpha\leq r/s\leq\alpha+\varepsilon$ for any small $\varepsilon>0$. We then still appeal to Theorem 4.5 as before, though the greedy algorithm might only return a subgraph of average degree $\gamma'>\gamma/n^{\varepsilon}$. Thus, the loss in the approximation ratio is at most n^{ε}. A fairly straightforward calculation shows that this implies a $O(n^{1/4+\varepsilon})$-approximation in $n^{O(1/\varepsilon)}$ time for all $\varepsilon>0$ (including $\varepsilon=1/\log n$).

Before going into the details of the proof, let us note the similarities between the algorithm and the random models discussed earlier. Recall that in the random case, the sets $S(t)$ (corresponding to S_t in the algorithm) had cardinality tightly concentrated around $n^{\mathrm{fr}(tr/s)}$. Similarly here, if we assume that $k=n/D(=D^{(s-r)/r})$, and that d (the density of the subgraph implied by the LP) is at least $\rho k^{r/s}$ (for some $\rho\geq 1$), then we show (see Corollary 4.7) that if until step t the algorithm has not found an $\Omega(\rho)$-dense subgraph, then the current candidate set satisfies

$$\frac{\mathrm{LP}(S_t)}{|S_t|} > \rho^{-\mathrm{fr}(tr/s)\cdot s/r}\left(\frac{k}{n}\right)^{\mathrm{fr}(tr/s)} = \left(\frac{1}{D}\right)^{\mathrm{fr}(tr/s)},$$

which will yield a contradiction at the final step (for $t=s$).

One difficulty is that we avoid making the assumption that $kD=n$ (which is possible, but would incur a $O(\sqrt{\log n})$ loss in the approximation guarantee). Instead, we use the fact that the greedy algorithm finds a k-subgraph with average degree $\gamma\geq\max\{1,Dk/n\}$. Specifically, we show that at step t of the algorithm, either a subgraph with average degree $\Omega(\rho)$ has already been found, or the greedy algorithm gives the desired approximation (i.e. $\gamma\geq\rho$), or we have the desired lower bounds on LP(S_t) and LP$(S_t)/|S_t|$.

Notation. In what follows, we let $\rho=d/(2D^{(s-r)/s})$ denote the desired average degree of the output subgraph (up to a constant factor). We also write $L_t=\lfloor tr/s\rfloor$. Note that the number of hair steps up to and including step t is precisely L_t+1.

We now state the main technical lemma.

LEMMA 4.6. *Let $s>r>0$ be relatively prime integers, let G be an undirected (bipartite) graph with maximum degree at most $D=n^{r/s}$, and let $\{y_i\}$ be a solution to* DkS-LP$_{r+1}(G,k,d)$. *Let $\gamma=\max\{Dk/n,1\}$. For $t=1,\ldots,s$, let d'_t be the average degree of the densest of the subgraphs found by* DkS-Cat$_{r,s}(G,k,\{y_i\})$ *up through step t. Then either*

$$\max\{d'_t,\gamma\}=\Omega(\rho),$$

or we have

$$\mathrm{LP}(S_t) \geq \frac{d^t}{2^{L_t}\rho^{t-L_t-1}k^{L_t}}, \text{ and}$$
$$\frac{\mathrm{LP}(S_t)}{|S_t|} \geq \frac{d^t}{2^{L_t}\gamma\rho^{t-1}D^{t-L_t}}. \qquad (9)$$

The following simple corollary immediately implies Theorem 4.5 (by contradiction) when we take $t=s$.

COROLLARY 4.7. *In the notation of Lemma 4.6, either* $\max\{d'_t, \gamma\} = \Omega(d/D^{(s-r)/s})$, *or we have*

$$\frac{\mathrm{LP}(S_t)}{|S_t|} \geq \frac{2^{t-\lfloor tr/s \rfloor}}{D^{\mathrm{fr}(tr/s)}}.$$

PROOF.

$$\begin{aligned}\frac{\mathrm{LP}(S_t)}{|S_t|} &\geq \frac{d^t}{2^{L_t}\gamma\rho^{t-1}D^{t-L_t}} && \text{By Lemma 4.6}\\ &> \frac{d^t}{2^{L_t}\rho^t D^{t-L_t}} && \rho > \gamma\\ &= \frac{d^t}{2^{L_t}D^{t-L_t}} \cdot \frac{(2D^{(s-r)/s})^t}{d^t} && \text{definition of } \rho\\ &= \frac{2^{t-L_t}}{D^{t-L_t-t(s-r)/s}} = \frac{2^{t-L_t}}{D^{tr/s-L_t}}\end{aligned}$$

□

Let us now proceed to the proof of Lemma 4.6.

PROOF OF LEMMA 4.6. We prove by induction that if the algorithm does not find any $\Omega(\rho)$ dense subgraph in steps 1 through t, the lower bounds (9) hold. Assume that $\rho > \gamma$ (≥ 1, since otherwise we are done).

For $t = 1$, the bounds hold trivially: Fix a node j_1 s.t. $y_{j_1} > 0$. Then $\mathrm{LP}_{\{y_{ij_1}/y_{j_1} | i \in V\}}(S_1) \geq d$ (by constraint (2)) and so $\mathrm{LP}(S_1)/|S_1| \geq d/|\Gamma(j_1)| \geq d/D (\geq d/(\gamma D))$, which is exactly what we need.

Now assume the lemma holds for some $1 \leq t \leq s-1$. We will show it for $t+1$, considering separately backbone and hair steps.

First, suppose $t+1$ is a backbone step. Then the interval $[tr/s, (t+1)r/s]$ does not contain an integer, i.e. we have $tr/s < L_t + (s-r)/s$. By Lemma 4.2, if $LP(S_t)/|S_t| \geq \rho/d$ then either Procedure DkS-Local(S_t, k) produces a ρ-dense subgraph, or we have $\mathrm{LP}(S_{t+1}) = \mathrm{LP}(\Gamma(S_t)) \geq d\mathrm{LP}(S_t)/\rho$. In that case, since $|S_{t+1}| = |\Gamma(S_t)| \leq D|S_t|$, the claim follows immediately from the inductive hypothesis. Thus it suffices to show that indeed $LP(S_t)/|S_t| \geq \rho/d$. This follows from Corollary 4.7, which gives

$$\frac{\mathrm{LP}(S_t)}{|S_t|} \geq \frac{2^{t-L_t}}{D^{tr/s-L_t}} > \frac{2^{t-L_t}}{D^{(s-r)/s}} = \frac{2^{t+1-L_t}\rho}{d}.$$

Now, on the other hand, suppose $t+1$ is a hair step. Then the interval $[tr/s, (t+1)r/s]$ does contain an integer, i.e. $tr/s \geq L_t + (s-r)/s$. Assuming Procedure DkS-Local(S_t, k) does not return a subgraph with average degree at least ρ, by Lemma 4.4, there is some choice of vertex j_{t+1} such that, denoting $y'_i = y_{ij_{t+1}}$ for all $i \in V$, the following inequalities hold simultaneously:

$$\begin{aligned}\mathrm{LP}_{\{y'_i\}}(S_{t+1}) &= \mathrm{LP}_{\{y'_i\}}(S_t \cap \Gamma(j_{t+1}))\\ &\geq \frac{d \cdot \mathrm{LP}_{\{y_i\}}(S_t)}{2k}, \qquad (10)\end{aligned}$$

$$\mathrm{LP}_{\{y'_i\}}(S_{t+1})/|S_{t+1}| \geq \frac{d \cdot \mathrm{LP}_{\{y_i\}}(S_t)}{2\rho \cdot \max\{k, |S_t|\}}. \qquad (11)$$

Thus, the lower bound we require for $\mathrm{LP}(S_{t+1})$ follows from (10) and the inductive hypothesis. If $|S_t| \geq k$, the bound on $\mathrm{LP}(S_{t+1})/|S_{t+1}|$ similarly follows from (11) and the inductive hypothesis. Thus, it remains to show the required bound when $|S_t| < k$. In that case, (11) gives

$$\begin{aligned}\mathrm{LP}(S_{t+1})/|S_{t+1}| &\frac{d\mathrm{LP}(S_t)}{2\rho k}\\ &\geq \frac{d^{t+1}}{2^{L_t+1}\rho^{t-L_t}k^{L_t+1}} && \text{inductive hypothesis}\\ &> \frac{d^{t+1}}{2^{L_t+1}\rho^t} \cdot \frac{\gamma^{L_t}}{k^{L_t+1}} && \text{since } \rho > \gamma\\ &\geq \frac{d^{t+1}}{2^{L_t+1}\rho^t} \cdot \frac{D^{L_t+1}}{\gamma n^{L_t+1}} && \text{since } \gamma \geq kD/n\\ &\geq \frac{d^{t+1}}{2^{L_t+1}\rho^t} \cdot \frac{D^{L_t+1}}{\gamma n^{(t+1)r/s}} && \text{since } \tfrac{tr}{s} \geq L_t + \tfrac{s-r}{s}\\ &\geq \frac{d^{t+1}}{2^{L_t+1}\rho^t} \cdot \frac{1}{\gamma D^{t+1-(L_t+1)}}. && \text{since } D \geq n^{r/s}\end{aligned}$$

Since $L_{t+1} = L_t + 1$, the bound follows. This concludes the proof. □

5. SUBSEQUENT WORK

We mention in brief, a couple of extensions towards improving upon the $O(n^{1/4})$ approximation algorithm presented above. In Section 5.1 we describe an algorithm which gives an approximation ratio strictly better than $n^{1/4}$ for arbitrary graphs in subexponential ($2^{n^{O(\varepsilon)}}$) time. The algorithm is a modification of the caterpillar based algorithm presented in Section 4.

In Section 5.2 we show that for $k > \sqrt{n}$ (though not for the crucial value of $k = \sqrt{n}$), we can improve upon the results of Section 3. Using, variously, eigenvalue techniques and SDPs, we obtain distinguishing algorithms which outperform the log-density gap for increasingly hard random planted models.

5.1 Improved approximation with 'mildly' exponential run time

We will now consider an extension of our approach to the case when the log-density of the subgraph H is (slightly) less than the log-density of the host graph (a crucial case if one wants to go beyond $n^{1/4}$-approximations). This is done at the expense of running time – we obtain a modification of our caterpillar-based algorithm, which yields an approximation ratio of $O(n^{(1-\varepsilon)/4})$ in time $2^{n^{O(\varepsilon)}}$. The main modification is that for each leaf, rather than picking an individual vertex, we will pick a cluster of roughly $O(n^{\varepsilon})$ vertices (which is responsible for the increased running time). The cluster will be used similarly to a single leaf vertex: rather than intersecting the current set with the neighborhood of a single vertex, we will intersect the current set with the neighborhood of the cluster (i.e. with the union of all neighborhoods of vertices in the cluster).

Motivation. We now outline why such a procedure could work (and why we *need* to look at sets of size roughly n^{ε}) by examining the random planted model. Let G be a random graph with log-density α, and let r/s denote a rational number roughly equal to $\alpha+\delta$ (for a small constant δ). Let us call an $(r+1)$-tuple of leaves 'special' if there is an (r, s) caterpillar 'supported' on it, in the sense of Section 3.2. Since $r/s > \rho$, most $(r+1)$-tuples of vertices are not special.

The crucial observation is the following: say we pick a set S of vertices, and ask how many $(r+1)$-tuples from S are special. This number turns out to be 'large' (polynomial as opposed to polylogarithmic in n) roughly iff $|S| > n^\delta$. Now suppose we had planted a random graph H on k vertices and log-density $\alpha - \varepsilon$ in G. Further suppose δ is such that $k^{\varepsilon+\delta} \ll n^\delta$ (when k is much smaller than n, this is achieved by setting δ to be a constant multiple of ε). By the above claim, sets in H of size $k^{\varepsilon+\delta}$ would have a 'large' number of special tuples (since $r/s =$ (log-density of H) $+ \varepsilon + \delta$). But this number, by choice is much smaller than n^δ, thus if there was no H planted, sets of size $k^{\varepsilon+\delta}$ would not have many special tuples! This gives a distinguishing algorithm which runs in time roughly $\binom{n}{k^{\varepsilon+\delta}}$.

Let us now state the result (for arbitrary graphs) formally. We refer the reader to [6] for details of the analysis.

THEOREM 5.1. *For every $\varepsilon > 0$, there is a randomized $O(2^{n^{6\varepsilon}})$-time algorithm which for every graph G with high probability finds a k-subgraph whose average degree is within $\tilde{O}(n^{(1-\varepsilon)/4})$ of the optimum.*

5.2 Beyond log-density in the planted model

Let us consider the *Dense in Random* question defined in Section 3 (slightly different from Dense versus Random). By the simplification from Section A.1, we will assume $kD = n$. We show that in the case $D < \sqrt{n}$, a simple SDP based approach gives a bound better than the log-density approach of Section 3.2.

Suppose $D = n^\rho$, with $\rho < 1/2$. By assumption, $k = n^{1-\rho}$. Suppose we are given a graph with a planted k-subgraph H of average degree d. In this case, a simple calculation shows that the second eigenvalue is at least d (the eigenvector has roughly $x_i = \frac{1}{\sqrt{k}}$ for $i \in H$, and $x_i = -\frac{\sqrt{k}}{n}$ for $i \notin H$). On the other hand, Füredi and Kómlos [13] show that a random graph with degree n^ρ has $\lambda_2 = O(n^{\rho/2})$, whp. Suppose we set $d = n^{\rho/2}$ (this is much smaller than k^ρ for $k > \sqrt{n}$), then the second eigenvalue can be used to distinguish between the two cases. Thus we can distinguish better in this parameter range. Details of these calculations can be found in the full version [6].

Improvements for Dense vs Random. Such an idea can also be used for the *Dense versus Random* question of Section 3.2. Here we consider a natural SDP relaxation for the densest k subgraph problem considered by [12], and show that this performs better than the algorithm presented earlier in the parameter range $k > \sqrt{n}$. The SDP is as follows

$$\max \sum_{(i,j)\in E(G)} X_{ij} \quad \text{subject to} \tag{12}$$
$$\sum_i X_{ii} = k \tag{13}$$
$$\sum_j X_{ij} = kX_{ii} \quad \text{for all } i \tag{14}$$
$$X_{ij} \le X_{ii} \quad \text{for all } i,j \tag{15}$$
$$X \succeq 0 \tag{16}$$

It is easy to see that this is a relaxation, and that there exists an SDP solution of value $|E(H)|$, where H is a k-subgraph. Let us now bound the SDP value for a random graph by exhibiting a dual solution.

Let us consider the dual. We have the variables t (eq. 13), y_i (eq. 14), z_{ij} (eq. 15). The dual is

$$\min\ kt \quad \text{subject to}$$
$$U - A \succeq 0$$
$$U_{ii} = t - ky_i - \sum_j z_{ij} \quad \text{for all } i$$
$$U_{ij} = y_i + z_{ij} \quad \text{for all } i,j$$

For a random graph, we note that $\frac{D}{n}J - A + \lambda_2 I \succeq 0$, where J is the all-ones matrix (it is easy to see this considering two cases: the all ones vector, and vectors orthogonal to it). Using this, we can prove the following (see [6] for details).

THEOREM 5.2. *For a random graph $G(n,p)$ of average degree D ($D = np$), with high probability the value of the SDP is at most $k(\sqrt{D} + k^2D/n)$.*

As stated earlier, the distinguishing guarantee in Theorem 5.2 is better than the log-density guarantee from Section 3.2 when $k > \sqrt{n}$.

6. REFERENCES

[1] N. Alon, M. Krivelevich, and B. Sudakov. Finding a large hidden clique in a random graph. pages 457–466, 1998.

[2] N. Alon and J. Spencer. *The Probabilistic Method.* Wiley Interscience, third edition, 2008.

[3] B. Applebaum, B. Barak, and A. Wigderson. Public key cryptography from different assumptions. Preliminary version as cryptology eprint report 2008/335 by Barak and Wigderson, 2008.

[4] S. Arora, B. Barak, M. Brunnermeier, and R. Ge. Computational complexity and information asymmetry in financial products. In *Proceedings of the First Symposium on Innovations in Computer Science (ICS)*, 2010.

[5] Y. Asahiro, R. Hassin, and K. Iwama. Complexity of finding dense subgraphs. *Discrete Appl. Math.*, 121(1-3):15–26, 2002.

[6] A. Bhaskara, M. Charikar, E. Chlamtac, U. Feige, and A. Vijayaraghavan. Detecting high log-densities – an $O(n^{1/4})$ approximation for densest k-subgraph. *CoRR*, abs/1001.2891, 2010.

[7] B. E. Birnbaum and K. J. Goldman. An improved analysis for a greedy remote-clique algorithm using factor-revealing LPs. *Algorithmica*, 1:42–59, 2009.

[8] M. Charikar, M. Hajiaghayi, and H. J. Karloff. Improved approximation algorithms for label cover problems. In *ESA*, volume 5757 of *Lecture Notes in Computer Science*, pages 23–34. Springer, 2009.

[9] U. Feige. Relations between average case complexity and approximation complexity. In *Proceedings of the 34th annual ACM Symposium on Theory of Computing (STOC'02)*, pages 534–543. ACM Press, 2002.

[10] U. Feige, G. Kortsarz, and D. Peleg. The dense k-subgraph problem. *Algorithmica*, 29(3):410–421, 2001.

[11] U. Feige and M. Langberg. Approximation algorithms for maximization problems arising in graph partitioning. *J. Algorithms*, 41(2):174–211, 2001.

[12] U. Feige and M. Seltser. On the densest k-subgraph problems. Technical Report CS97-16, Weizmann Institute of Science, Rehovot, Israel, 1997.

[13] Z. Füredi and J. Komlós. The eigenvalues of random symmetric matrices. *Combinatorica*, 1:233–241, 1981.

[14] G. Gallo, M. D. Grigoriadis, and R. E. Tarjan. A fast parametric maximum flow algorithm and applications. *SIAM J. Comput.*, 18(1):30–55, 1989.

[15] D. Goldstein and M. Langberg. The dense k subgraph problem. *CoRR*, abs/0912.5327, 2010.

[16] S. Khot. Ruling out PTAS for graph min-bisection, densest subgraph and bipartite clique. In *Proceedings of the 44th Annual IEEE Symposium on the Foundations of Computer Science (FOCS'04)*, pages 136–145, 2004.

[17] L. Lovász and A. Schrijver. Cones of matrices and set-functions and 0-1 optimization. *SIAM Journal on Optimization*, 1:166–190, 1991.

[18] A. Srivastav and K. Wolf. Finding dense subgraphs with semidefinite programming. In *Proceedings of the International Workshop on Approximation Algorithms for Combinatorial Optimization (APPROX)*, pages 181–191, 1998.

APPENDIX

A. SIMPLIFICATIONS

We present a few simplifying assumptions which can be made with a small loss in the approximation guarantee (at most a constant factor in most cases). We refer the reader to [6] for detailed proofs.

We begin with a greedy algorithm which allows us to bound the maximum degree in G, taken from [10] (Lemmas 3.2 and 3.3).

LEMMA A.1. *There exists a polynomial time algorithm which, given a graph G containing a k-subgraph with average degree d, outputs a k-subgraph H' and an $(n-k/2)$-subgraph G' s.t.*

1. *For some $D > 0$, G' has maximum degree $\le D$ and H' has average degree $\Omega(\max\{Dk/n, 1\})$.*
2. *Either G' contains a k-subgraph with average degree $\Omega(d)$, or H' has average degree $\Omega(d)$.*

PROOF. Let U be the set of $k/2$ vertices of highest degree in G (breaking ties arbitrarily), and let $D = \min_{u\in U} \deg(u)$. Let U' be the set of $k/2$ vertices of G of highest degree into U. Let H' be the graph induced on $U \cup U'$. Observe that H' has $\Omega(Dk^2/n)$ edges and average degree $\Omega(Dk/n)$ (it also has average degree at least 1, assuming G has at least $k/2$ edges).

Now let G' be the subgraph induced on $V \setminus U$ (note that by definition, G' has maximum degree $\le D$). Let H be the densest k-subgraph in G, and let α be the fraction of edges of H that are incident with vertices of U. If $\alpha \le 1/2$, then the $dk/2$ of the edges in H remain in G' (and thus G' still has a k-subgraph with average degree $\Omega(d)$. On the other hand, if $\alpha \ge 1/2$ then it is not hard to see that the H' must have average degree $\Omega(d)$. □

The next lemma is a simple observation that allows our algorithm to return a subgraph of size *at most* k (rather than exactly k). Essentially, if we have picked fewer than k vertices so far, we can remove the corresponding edges from G and repeat on the remaining graph.

LEMMA A.2. *Given an algorithm which, whenever a graph G contains a k-subgraph of average degree $\Omega(d)$ returns a k'-subgraph of average degree $\Omega(d')$, for some (arbitrary) $k' < k$, we can also find a (exactly) k-subgraph with average degree $\Omega(d')$ for such G.*

We now treat the assumption that G (and hence H) is bipartite:

LEMMA A.3. *Given an $f(n)$-approximation for DkS on bipartite n-vertex graphs, we can approximate DkS on arbitrary graphs within an $\Omega(f(2n))$-factor.*

Finally, we note that it suffices to consider minimum degree in H, rather than average degree (by standard pruning arguments, and Lemma A.2).

LEMMA A.4. *Approximation algorithms for DkS lose at most a constant factor by assuming the densest k-subgraph has minimum degree d as opposed to average degree.*

A.1 Bounding the product kD

Our manipulations are simpler if we assume that $kD \le n$. While we do not make this assumption in the main algorithm, it is often instructive to consider this case. In fact, we can make this assumption, at the cost of losing an $O(\sqrt{\log n})$ factor in the approximation guarantee. This is because if $D > n/k$, we take a random subgraph G' of G by keeping every edge with probability $n/(kD)$. It is easy to see using standard probabilistic arguments that the new average degree is n/k and the density of the k-subgraph of density d is also scaled proportionally.

B. SOLVING THE LP

We will show that the linear program DkS-LP$_t(G, k, d)$ can be solved in time $n^{O(t)}$ by giving an equivalent formulation with explicit constraints which has total size (number of variables and constraints) $n^{O(t)}$. We start by defining a homogenized version of the basic LP. We say that a vector $(y_1, \ldots, y_n, h)$ is a solution to $\textbf{DkS-hom}_t(G, k, d)$ if it satisfies:

$$\begin{aligned}
\sum_{i\in V} y_i \le kh, &\quad \text{and} \\
h \ge 0 & \\
\exists\{y_{ij} \mid i,j \in V\} &\quad \text{s.t.} \\
\forall i \in V &\quad \sum_{j\in\Gamma(i)} y_{ij} \ge d y_i \\
\forall i,j \in V &\quad y_{ij} = y_{ji} \\
\forall i,j \in V &\quad 0 \le y_{ij} \le y_i \le h \\
\text{if } t > 1,\ \forall i \in V &\quad \{y_{i1}, \ldots, y_{in}, y_i\} \in \textbf{DkS-hom}_{t-1}(G,k,d)
\end{aligned}$$

Note that the condition $(y_1, \ldots, y_n) \in$ DkS-LP$_t(G, k, d)$ is now equivalent to $(y_1, \ldots, y_n, 1) \in$ DkS-hom$_t(G, k, d)$. Moreover, the definition of DkS-hom$_t$ can be made fully explicit by expanding the recursively defined constraints, giving an explicit LP on $n^{t+O(1)}$ variables and $n^{t+O(1)}$ constraints, which can be solved in time $n^{O(t)}$ by standard techniques.

Approximation Schemes for Steiner Forest on Planar Graphs and Graphs of Bounded Treewidth*

MohammadHossein Bateni†
Department of Computer Science
Princeton University
Princeton, NJ, USA
mbateni@cs.princeton.edu

MohammadTaghi Hajiaghayi‡
AT&T Labs–Research
Florham Park, NJ, USA
hajiagha@research.att.com

Dániel Marx§
School of Computer Science
Tel Aviv University
Tel Aviv, Israel
dmarx@cs.bme.hu

ABSTRACT

We give the first *polynomial-time approximation scheme* (PTAS) for the *Steiner forest* problem on planar graphs and, more generally, on graphs of bounded genus. As a first step, we show how to build a *Steiner forest spanner* for such graphs. The crux of the process is a clustering procedure called *prize-collecting clustering* that breaks down the input instance into separate subinstances which are easier to handle; moreover, the terminals in different subinstances are far from each other. Each subinstance has a relatively inexpensive Steiner tree connecting all its terminals, and the subinstances can be solved (almost) separately. Another building block is a PTAS for *Steiner forest* on graphs of bounded treewidth. Surprisingly, *Steiner forest* is NP-hard even on graphs of treewidth 3. Therefore, our PTAS for bounded treewidth graphs needs a nontrivial combination of approximation arguments and dynamic programming on the tree decomposition. We further show that *Steiner forest* can be solved in polynomial time for series-parallel graphs (graphs of treewidth at most two) by a novel combination of dynamic programming and minimum cut computations, completing our thorough complexity study of *Steiner forest* in the range of bounded treewidth graphs, planar graphs, and bounded genus graphs.

*For the omitted proofs and further discussion, refer to the full version of the paper [6].

†The author was supported by NSF ITR grants CCF-0205594, CCF-0426582 and NSF CCF 0832797, NSF CAREER award CCF-0237113, MSPA-MCS award 0528414, NSF expeditions award 0832797, as well as a Gordon Wu fellowship.

‡He is also with the Department of Computer Science, University of Maryland, College Park, MD, USA.

§He is supported by ERC Advanced Grant DMMCA.

STOC'10, June 5–8, 2010, Cambridge, Massachusetts, USA.

Categories and Subject Descriptors

F.2.2 [**ANALYSIS OF ALGORITHMS AND PROBLEM COMPLEXITY**]: Nonnumerical Algorithms and Problems—*Computation on Discrete Structures*; G.1 [**NUMERICAL ANALYSIS**]; G.2 [**DISCRETE MATHEMATICS**]

General Terms

Algorithms, Design, Performance, Theory

1. INTRODUCTION

One of the most fundamental problems in combinatorial optimization and network design with both practical and theoretical significance is the Steiner forest problem, in which given a weighted graph $G = (V,E)$ and a set consisting of pairs of terminals, called *demands*, $\mathcal{D} = \{(s_1,t_1),(s_2,t_2),\ldots,(s_k,t_k)\}$, the goal is to find a minimum-cost forest F of G such that every pair of terminals in $\mathcal{D}$ is connected by a path in F. The first and the best approximation factor for this problem is 2 due to Agrawal, Klein and Ravi [1] (see also Goemans and Williamson [17]). The conference version of the Agrawal, Klein and Ravi [2] appeared in 1991, and there have been no improved approximation algorithms invented for Steiner forest. Recently Borradaile, Klein and Mathieu [11] obtain a Polynomial Time Approximation Scheme (PTAS) for Euclidean Steiner forest where the terminals are in the Euclidean plane. They pose obtaining a PTAS for Steiner forest in planar graphs, the natural generalization of Euclidean Steiner forest, as the main open problem. We note that in network design, planarity is a natural restriction, since in practical scenarios of physical networking, with cable or fiber embedded in the ground, crossings are rare or nonexistent. In this paper, we settle this open problem by obtaining a PTAS for planar graphs (and more generally, for bounded genus graphs) via a novel technique of *prize-collecting clustering* with potential use to obtain other PTASs in planar graphs.

The special case of the Steiner forest problem when all pairs have a common terminal is the classical Steiner tree problem, one of the first problems shown NP-hard by Karp [19]. The problem remains hard even on planar graphs [15]. In contrast to Steiner forest, a long sequence of papers give approximation factors better than 2 for this problem [29, 30, 7, 31, 25, 20, 18, 27]; the current best approximation ratio is 1.55 [27]. Since the problem is APX-hard in general graphs [8, 28], we do not expect to obtain a PTAS for this problem in general graphs. However, for the Euclidean Steiner tree problem, the classic works of Arora [5] and Mitchell [24] present a PTAS. Obtaining a PTAS for Steiner tree on planar graphs, the natural generalization of Euclidean Steiner tree, remained a major open problem since the conference version of Arora [4] in 1996. Only in 2007, Borradaile, Mathieu, and Klein [12] settle this problem with a nice technique of constructing *light spanners* for Seiner trees in planar graphs. In this paper, we also generalize this result to obtain light spanners for Steiner forests.

Most approximation schemes for planar graph problems use (implicitly or explicitly) the fact that the problem is easy to solve on bounded-treewidth graphs (in fact, Demaine et al. [13] provide a general method of reducing many optimization problems on planar graphs to bounded-treewidth graphs). In particular, a keystone blackbox in the algorithm of Borradaile et al. [12] for Steiner tree is the result that, for every fixed value of k, the problem is polynomial-time solvable on graphs having treewidth at most k. There is a vast literature on algorithms for bounded-treewidth graphs and in most cases polynomial-time (or even linear-time) solvability follows from the well-understood standard technique of dynamic programming on tree decompositions. However, for Steiner *forest,* the obvious way of using dynamic programming does not give a polynomial-time algorithm. The difficulty is that, unlike in Steiner tree, a solution of Steiner forest induces a partition on the set of terminals and a dynamic programming algorithm needs to keep track of exponentially many such partitions. In fact, this approach seems to fail even for series-parallel graphs (that have treewidth at most 2); the complexity of the problem for series-parallel graphs was stated as an open question by Richey and Parker [26] in 1986. We resolve this question by giving a polynomial-time algorithm for Steiner forest on series-parallel graphs. The main idea is that even though algorithms based on dynamic programming have to evaluate subproblems corresponding to exponentially many partitions, the function describing these exponentially many values turn out to be submodular and it can be represented in a compact way by the cut function of a directed graph. On the other hand, Steiner forest becomes NP-hard on graphs of treewidth at most 3 [16]. Thus perhaps this is the first example when the complexity of a natural problem changes as treewidth increases from 2 to 3. In light of this hardness result, we investigate the approximability of the problem on bounded-treewidth graphs and show that, for every fixed k, Steiner forest admits a PTAS on graphs of treewidth at most k. The main idea of the PTAS is that if the dynamic programming algorithm considers only an appropriately constructed polynomial-size subset of the set of all partitions, then this produces a solution close to the optimum. Very roughly, the partitions in this subset are constructed by choosing a set of center points and classifying the terminals according to the distance to the center points. Our PTAS for planar graphs (and more generally, for bounded genus graphs) uses this PTAS for bounded-treewidth graphs. This completes our thorough study of Steiner forest in the range of bounded treewidth graphs, planar graphs and bounded genus graphs.

1.1 Our results and techniques

Our main result in this paper is a PTAS for the planar Steiner forest problem.

THEOREM 1. *For any constant $\bar{\varepsilon} > 0$, there is a polynomial-time $(1+\bar{\varepsilon})$-approximation algorithm for the Steiner forest problem on planar graphs and, more generally, on graphs of bounded genus.*

To this end, we build a *Steiner forest spanner* for the input graph and the set of demands; this is done in two steps. Roughly speaking, a Steiner forest spanner is a subgraph of the given graph whose cost is no more than a constant factor times the cost of the optimal Steiner forest, and furthermore, it contains a nearly optimal Steiner forest. Denote by $\mathrm{OPT}_{\mathcal{D}}(G)$ the minimum cost of a Steiner forest of G satisfying (connecting) all the demands in $\mathcal{D}$. We sometimes use OPT instead of $\mathrm{OPT}_{\mathcal{D}}(G)$. A subgraph H of G is a *Steiner forest spanner* with respect to demand set $\mathcal{D}$ if it has the following two properties:

Spanning Property: There is a forest in H that connects all demands in $\mathcal{D}$ and has length at most $(1+\varepsilon)OPT_{\mathcal{D}}(G)$, namely, $\mathrm{OPT}_{\mathcal{D}}(H) \leq (1+\varepsilon)\mathrm{OPT}_{\mathcal{D}}(G)$.

Shortness Property: The total length of H is not more than $f(\varepsilon)\cdot OPT_{\mathcal{D}}(G)$.

THEOREM 2. *Given any fixed $\varepsilon > 0$, a bounded genus graph $G_{in}(V_{in},E_{in})$ and demand pairs $\mathcal{D}$, we can compute in polynomial time a Steiner forest spanner H for G_{in} with respect to demand set $\mathcal{D}$.*

The algorithm that we propose achieves this in time $O(n^2 \log n)$. The entire algorithm for Steiner forest runs in polynomial time but the exponent of the polynomial depends on ε and the genus of the input graph.

The proof of Theorem 2 heavily relies on a novel clustering method presented in Theorem 3 that allows us to (almost) separately build the spanners for smaller and far apart sets of demands. The rest of the spanner construction—done separately for each of the sets—uses ideas of Borradaile et al. [12], although there are still several technical differences. The clustering technique works for general graphs as opposed to the rest of the construction which requires the graphs to have bounded genus.

THEOREM 3. *Given an $\varepsilon > 0$, a graph $G_{in}(V_{in},E_{in})$, and a set $\mathcal{D}$ of pairs of vertices, we can compute in polynomial time a set of trees $\{T_1,\ldots,T_k\}$, and a partition of demands $\{\mathcal{D}_1,\ldots,\mathcal{D}_k\}$, with the following properties.*

1. *All the demands are covered, i.e., $\mathcal{D} = \bigcup_{i=1}^{k} \mathcal{D}_i$.*
2. *All the terminals in $\mathcal{D}_i$ are spanned by the tree T_i.*
3. *The sum of the costs of all the trees T_i is no more than $(\frac{4}{\varepsilon}+2)OPT_{\mathcal{D}}(G_{in})$.*
4. *The sum of the costs of minimum Steiner forests of all demand sets $\mathcal{D}_i$ is no more than $1+\varepsilon$ times the cost of a minimum Steiner forest of G_{in}; i.e., $\sum_i OPT_{\mathcal{D}_i}(G_{in}) \leq (1+\varepsilon)OPT_{\mathcal{D}}(G_{in})$.*

The last condition implies that (up to a small factor) it is possible to solve the demands $\mathcal{D}_i$ separately. Notice that this may lead to paying for portions of the solution more than once.

We will prove Theorem 3 in Section 3. Roughly speaking, the algorithm here first recognizes some connected components by running a 2-approximation Steiner forest algorithm. Clearly, this construction satisfies all but the last condition of the theorem. However, at this point, these connected components might not be sufficiently far from each other such that we can consider them separately. To fix this, we contract each connected component into a "super vertex" to which we assign a prize (potential) that is proportional to the sum of the edge weights of the corresponding component. Now we run an algorithm that we call *prize-collecting clustering*. The algorithm as well as some parts of its analysis bears similarities to a primal-dual method due to Agrawal, Klein and Ravi [2] and Goemans and Williamson [17]. Indeed our analysis strengthens these previous approaches by proving some local guarantees (instead of the global guarantee provided in these algorithms). In some sense, this clustering algorithm can also be seen as a generalization of an implicit clustering algorithm of Archer, Bateni, Hajiaghayi, and Karloff [3] who improve the best approximation factor for prize-collecting Steiner tree to $2-\varepsilon$, for some constant $\varepsilon > 0$. In this clustering, we consider a topological structure of the graph in which each edge is a curve connecting its endpoints whose length is equal to its weight. We color (portions of) edges by different colors each corresponding to a super vertex. These colors form a laminar family and the "depth" of each color is at most the prize given to its corresponding super vertex. Using this coloring scheme we further connect some of these super vertices to each other with a cost proportional to the sum of their prizes. At the end, we show that now we can consider these combined connected components as separate clusters and, roughly speaking, an optimum solution need not connect two different clusters because of the concept of depth. We believe the prize-collecting clustering presented in this paper might have applications for other problems (esp. to obtain PTASs).

To obtain a PTAS as promised in Theorem 1, we first construct a spanner Steiner forest based on Theorem 2. On this spanner, we utilize a technique due to Klein [21], and Demaine, Hajiaghayi and Mohar [13] that reduces the problem of obtaining a PTAS in a planar (and more generally, bounded genus) graph whose total edge weight is within a constant factor of the optimum solution to that of finding an optimal solution in a graph of bounded treewidth (see the proof of Theorem 1 in Section 4 for more details.) However, there are no known polynomial-time algorithms in the literature for Steiner forest on bounded-treewidth graphs, so we cannot plug in such an algorithm to complete our PTAS. Therefore, we need to investigate Steiner forest on bounded-treewidth graphs.

Resolving an open question of Richey and Parker [26] from 1986, we design a polynomial-time algorithm for Steiner forest on series-parallel graphs. Very recently, using completely different techniques, a polynomial-time algorithm was presented for the special case of outerplanar graphs [16].

THEOREM 4. *The Steiner forest problem can be solved in polynomial time for subgraphs of series-parallel graphs (i.e., graphs of treewidth at most 2).*

Surprisingly, it turns out that the problem becomes NP-hard on graphs of treewidth at most 3 [16]. In the full version [6] we give a (different) NP-hardness proof, that highlights how submodularity (and hence the approach of Theorem 4) breaks if treewidth is 3. There exist a few known problems that are polynomial-time solvable for trees but NP-hard for graphs of treewidth 2 [32, 22, 23, 26], but to our knowledge, this is the first natural example where there is a complexity difference between treewidth 2 and 3.

Not being able to solve Steiner forest optimally on bounded-treewidth graphs is not an unavoidable obstacle for obtaining a PTAS on planar graphs: the technique of Klein [21], and Demaine, Hajiaghayi and Mohar [13] can still be applied when we have a PTAS for graphs of bounded treewidth. In Section 5, we demonstrate such a PTAS:

THEOREM 5. *For every fixed $w \geq 1$ and $\varepsilon > 0$, there is a polynomial-time $(1+\varepsilon)$-approximation algorithm for Steiner Forest on graphs with treewidth at most w.*

Note that the exponent of the polynomial in Theorem 5 depends on both ε and w; it remains an interesting question for future research whether this dependence can be removed.

The main idea of the PTAS of Theorem 5 is to reduce the set of partitions considered in the dynamic programming algorithm to a polynomially bounded subset, in a way that an $(1+\varepsilon)$-approximate solution using only these partitions is guaranteed to exist. The implementation of this idea consists of three components. First, we have to define which partitions belong to the polynomially bounded subset. These partitions are defined by choosing a bounded number of center points and a radius for each center. A terminal is classified into a class of the partition based on which center points cover it. Second, we need an algorithm that finds the best solution using only the allowed subset of partitions. This can be done following the standard dynamic programming paradigm, but the technical details are somewhat tedious. Third, we have to argue that there is a $(1+\varepsilon)$-approximate solution using only the allowed partitions. We show this by proving that if there is a solution that uses partitions that are not allowed, then it can be modified, incurring only a small increase in the cost, such that it uses only allowed partitions. The main argument here is that for each partition appearing in the solution, we try to select suitable center points. If these center points do not generate the required partition, then this means that a terminal is misclassified, which is only possible if the terminal is close to a center point. In this case, we observe that two components of the solution are close to each other and we can join them with only a small increase in the cost. The crucial point of the proof is a delicate charging argument, making use of the structure of bounded-treewidth graphs, which shows that repeated applications of this step results in a total increase that is not too large.

2. BASIC DEFINITIONS

Let $G(V,E)$ be a graph. As is customary, let $\delta(V')$ denote the set of edges having one endpoint in a subset $V' \subseteq V$ of vertices. For a subset of vertices $V' \subseteq V$, the subgraph of G induced by V' is denoted by $G[V']$. With slight abuse of notation, we sometimes use the edge set to refer to the graph itself. Hence, the above-mentioned subgraph may also be referred to by $E[V']$ for simplicity. We denote the length of a shortest x-to-y path in G as $\text{dist}_G(x,y)$. For an edge set E, we denote by $\ell(E) := \sum_{e \in E} c_e$ the total length of edges in E.

A collection $\mathcal{S}$ is said to be *laminar* if and only if for any two sets $C_1, C_2 \in \mathcal{S}$, we have $C_1 \subseteq C_2$, $C_2 \subseteq C_1$, or $C_1 \cap C_2 = \emptyset$. Suppose $\mathcal{C}$ is a partition of a ground set V. Then, $\mathcal{C}(v)$ denotes for each $v \in V$ the set $C \in \mathcal{C}$ that contains v.

Given an edge $e = (u,v)$ in a graph G, the *contraction* of e in G denoted by G/e is the result of unifying vertices u and v in G, and removing all loops and multiple edges except the shortest edge. The contraction G/E' is defined as the result of iteratively contracting all the edges of E' in G, i.e., $G/E' := G/e_1/e_2/\ldots/e_k$ if $E' = \{e_1, e_2, \ldots, e_k\}$. Clearly, the planarity of G is preserved after the contraction. Similarly, contracting edges does not increase the cost of an optimal Steiner forest.

Finally we often use well-known concepts of *treewidth*, *nice tree-decomposition* and *2-cell embedding* in this paper. Due to lack of space, we refer the reader to the full version of the paper or standard graph theory texts such as [14] to see the exact definitions of these terms.

3. PRIZE-COLLECTING CLUSTERING

In this section, we describe an algorithm PC-CLUSTERING that is used to prove Theorem 3. The algorithm as well as its analysis bears similarities to the primal-dual method due to Agrawal, Klein and Ravi [1] and Goemans and Williamson [17]. It uses a technique that we call *prize-collecting clustering* and our analysis strengthens the previous approaches by proving some local guarantees (instead of the global guarantee provided in previous algorithms). We build a forest F_2 each of whose components correspond to one T_i sought in Theorem 3. Along the way, we also come up with a vector y satisfying the sets of constraints (1)-(3) below. During the process, we maintain a vector y satisfying all these constraints, and at the end, it will be true that all the constraints (2) hold with equality. The analysis takes advantage of the connection between F_2 and y.

We start with a 2-approximate[1] solution F^* satisfying all the demands in $\mathcal{D}$; the cost of F^* is at most 2OPT. The forest F^* consists of tree components T_i^*. In the following, we connect some of these components to make the trees T_i. It is easy to see that this construction guarantees the first two conditions of Theorem 3. We work on a graph $G(V,E)$ formed from G_{in} by contracting each tree component of F^*. A potential ϕ_v is associated with each vertex v of G, which is $\frac{1}{\varepsilon}$ times the cost of the tree component of F^* corresponding to v in case v is the contraction of a tree component, and zero

[1]Such a solution can be found via Goemans-Williamson's Steiner forest algorithm, for instance.

otherwise. We produce a solution to the following system of linear equations, where $y_{S,v}$ is defined for any $v \in S \subseteq V$, and c_e denotes the length of the edge e.

$$\sum_{S:e\in\delta(S)} \sum_{v\in S} y_{S,v} \leq c_e \qquad \forall e \in E, \qquad (1)$$

$$\sum_{S\ni v} y_{S,v} \leq \phi_v \qquad \forall v \in V, \qquad (2)$$

$$y_{S,v} \geq 0 \qquad \forall v \in S \subseteq V. \qquad (3)$$

These constraints are very similar to the dual LP for the *prize-collecting Steiner tree* problem when ϕ_v are thought of as penalty values corresponding to the vertices. In the standard linear program for the prize-collecting Steiner tree problem, there is a special *root* vertex to which all the terminals are to be connected. Then, no set containing the root appears in the formulation.

The solution is built up in two stages. First we perform an *unrooted growth* to find a forest F_1 and a corresponding y vector. In the second stage, we *prune* some of the edges of F_1 to get another forest F_2. Uncontracting the trees T_i^* turns F_2 into the Steiner trees T_i in the statement of Theorem 3. Below we describe the two phases of Algorithm 1 (PC-CLUSTERING).

Growth.

We begin with a zero vector y, and an empty set F_1. We maintain a partition $\mathcal{C}$ of vertices V into clusters; it initially consists of singleton sets. Each cluster is either *active* or *inactive*; the cluster $C \in \mathcal{C}$ is *active* if and only if $\sum_{C'\subseteq C}\sum_{v\in C'} y_{C',v} < \sum_{v\in C}\phi_v$. A vertex v is *live* if and only if $\sum_{C\ni v} y_{C,v} < \phi_v$. Equivalently, a cluster $C \in \mathcal{C}$ is active if and only if there is a live vertex $v \in C$. We simultaneously *grow* all the active clusters by η. In particular, if there are $\kappa(C) > 0$ live vertices in an active cluster C, we increase $y_{C,v}$ by $\eta/\kappa(C)$ for each live vertex $v \in C$. Hence, y_C defined as $\sum_{v\in C} y_{C,v}$ is increased by η for an active cluster C. We pick the largest value for η that does not violate any of the constraints in (1) or (2). Obviously, η is finite in each iteration because the values of these variables cannot be larger than $\sum_v \phi_v$. Hence, at least one such constraint goes tight after the growth step. If this happens for an edge constraint for $e = (u,v)$, then there are two clusters $C_u \ni u$ and $C_v \ni v$ in $\mathcal{C}$; at least one of the two is growing. We merge the two clusters into $C = C_u \cup C_v$ by adding the edge e to F_1, remove the old clusters and add the new one to $\mathcal{C}$. Nothing needs to be done if a constraint (2) becomes tight. The number of iterations is at most $2|V|$, because at each event either a vertex dies, or the size of $\mathcal{C}$ decreases.

We can think of the growth stage as a process that colors portions of the edges of the graph. This gives a better intuition to the algorithm, and makes several of the following lemmas intuitively simple. Consider a topological structure in which vertices of the graph are represented by points, and each edge is a curve connecting its endpoints whose length is equal to the weight of the edge. Suppose a cluster C is growing by an amount η. This is distributed among all the live vertices $v \in C$, where $y_{C,v}$ is increased by $\eta' := \eta/\kappa(C)$. As a result, we color by color v a connected portion with length η' of all the edges in $\delta(C)$. Finally, each edge e gets exactly $\sum_{C:e\in\delta(C)} y_{C,v}$ units of color v. We can perform a clean-up process, such that all the portions of color v are consecutive on an edge.[2] Hence, as a cluster expands, it colors its boundary by the amount of growth. At the time when two clusters merge, their colors barely touch each other. At each point in time, the colors associated with the vertices of a cluster form a connected region.

Pruning.

Let $\mathcal{S}$ contain every set that is a cluster at some point during the execution of the growth step. It can be easily observed that the clusters $\mathcal{S}$ are laminar and the maximal clusters are the clusters of $\mathcal{C}$. In addition, notice that $F_1[C]$ is connected for each $C \in \mathcal{S}$.

Let $\mathcal{B} \subseteq \mathcal{S}$ be the set of all such clusters that are tight, namely, for each $S \in \mathcal{B}$, we have $\sum_{S'\subseteq S}\sum_{v\in S'} y_{S',v} = \sum_{v\in S}\phi_v$. In the pruning stage, we iteratively remove some edges from F_1 to obtain F_2. More specifically, we first initialize F_2 with F_1. Then, as long as there is a cluster $S \in \mathcal{B}$ such that $F_2 \cap \delta(S) = \{e\}$, we remove the edge e from F_2.

A cluster C is called a *pruned cluster* if it is pruned in the second stage in which case, $\delta(C) \cap F_2 = \emptyset$. Hence, a pruned cluster cannot have non-empty and proper intersection with a connected component of F_2.

Algorithm 1 PC-CLUSTERING

Input: planar graph $G_{in}(V_{in}, E_{in})$, and set of demands $\mathcal{D}$.
Output: set of trees T_i with associated $\mathcal{D}_i$.

Use the algorithm of Goemans and Williamson [17] to find a 2-approximate Steiner forest F^* of $\mathcal{D}$, consisting of tree components $T_1^*, \ldots, T_k^*$.
Contract each tree T_i^* to build a new graph $G(V,E)$.
For any $v \in V$, let ϕ_v be $\frac{1}{\varepsilon}$ times the cost of the tree T_i^* corresponding to v, and zero if there is no such tree.
Let $F_1 \leftarrow \emptyset$.
Let $y_{S,v} \leftarrow 0$ for any $v \in S \subseteq V$.
Let $\mathcal{S} \leftarrow \mathcal{C} \leftarrow \{\{v\} : v \in V\}$.
while there is a live vertex **do**
  Let η be the largest possible value such that simultaneously increasing y_C by η for all active clusters C does not violate Constraints (1)-(3).
  Let $y_{C(v),v} \leftarrow y_{C(v),v} + \frac{\eta}{\kappa(C(v))}$ $\forall$ live vertices v.
  if $\exists e \in E$ that is tight and connects two clusters **then**
    Pick one such edge $e = (u,v)$.
    Let $F_1 \leftarrow F_1 \cup \{e\}$.
    Let $C \leftarrow \mathcal{C}(u) \cup \mathcal{C}(v)$.
    Let $\mathcal{C} \leftarrow \mathcal{C} \cup \{C\} \setminus \{\mathcal{C}(u), \mathcal{C}(v)\}$.
    Let $\mathcal{S} \leftarrow \mathcal{S} \cup \{C\}$.
Let $F_2 \leftarrow F_1$.
Let $\mathcal{B}$ be the set of all clusters $S \in \mathcal{S}$ such that $\sum_{v\in S} y_{S,v} = \sum_{v\in S}\phi_v$.
while $\exists S \in \mathcal{B}$ such that $F_2 \cap \delta(S) = \{e\}$ for an edge e **do**
  Let $F_2 \leftarrow F_2 \setminus \{e\}$.
Construct F from F_2 by uncontracting all trees T_i^*.
Let F consist of tree components T_i.
Output the set of trees $\{T_i\}$, along with $\mathcal{D}_i := \{(s,t) \in \mathcal{D} : s,t \in V(T_i)\}$.

We first bound the cost of the forest F_2. The following lemma is similar to the analysis of the algorithm in [17]. However, we do not have a primal LP to give a bound on the dual. Rather, the upper bound for the cost is the sum of all the potential values $\sum_v \phi_v$. In addition, we bound the cost of a forest F_2 that may have more than one connected component, whereas the prize-collecting Steiner tree algorithm of [17] finds a connected graph at the end.

LEMMA 6. *The cost of F_2 is at most $2\sum_{v\in V}\phi_v$.*

PROOF. The strategy is to prove that the cost of this forest is at most $2\sum_{v\in S\subseteq V} y_{S,v} \leq 2\sum_{v\in V}\phi_v$. The equality follows from Equation (2). Recall that the growth phase has several events corresponding to an edge or set constraint going tight. We first break

---

[2] We can do without the clean-up if we perform the coloring in a lazy manner. That is, we do not do the actual color assignment until the edge goes tight or the algorithm terminates. At this point, we go about putting colors on the edges, and we make sure the color corresponding to any pair (S,v) forms a consecutive portion of the edge. This property is not needed as part of our algorithm, though, and is merely for the sake of having a nice coloring which is of independent interest.

apart y variables by epoch. Let t_j be the time at which the jth event point occurs in the growth phase ($0 = t_0 \le t_1 \le t_2 \le \cdots$), so the jth epoch is the interval of time from t_{j-1} to t_j. For each cluster C, let $y_C^{(j)}$ be the amount by which $y_C := \sum_{v \in C} y_{C,v}$ grew during epoch j, which is $t_j - t_{j-1}$ if it was active during this epoch, and zero otherwise. Thus, $y_C = \sum_j y_C^{(j)}$. Because each edge e of F_2 was added at some point by the growth stage when its edge packing constraint (1) became tight, we can exactly apportion the cost c_e amongst the collection of clusters $\{C : e \in \delta(C)\}$ whose variables "pay for" the edge, and can divide this up further by epoch. In other words, $c_e = \sum_j \sum_{C:e \in \delta(C)} y_C^{(j)}$. We will now prove that the total edge cost from F_2 that is apportioned to epoch j is at most $2\sum_C y_C^{(j)}$. In other words, during each epoch, the total rate at which edges of F_2 are paid for by all active clusters is at most twice the number of active clusters. Summing over the epochs yields the desired conclusion.

We now analyze an arbitrary epoch j. Let C_j denote the set of clusters that existed during epoch j. Consider the graph F_2, and then collapse each cluster $C \in C_j$ into a supernode. Call the resulting graph H. Although the nodes of H are identified with clusters in C_j, we will continue to refer to them as clusters, in order to to avoid confusion with the nodes of the original graph. Some of the clusters are active and some may be inactive. Let us denote the active and inactive clusters in C_j by C_{act} and C_{dead}, respectively. The edges of F_2 that are being partially paid for during epoch j are exactly those edges of H that are incident to an active cluster, and the total amount of these edges that is paid off during epoch j is $(t_j - t_{j-1})\sum_{C \in C_{act}} \deg_H(C)$. Since every active cluster grows by exactly $t_j - t_{j-1}$ in epoch j, we have $\sum_C y_C^{(j)} \ge \sum_{C \in C_j} y_C^{(j)} = (t_j - t_{j-1})|C_{act}|$. Thus, it suffices to show that $\sum_{C \in C_{act}} \deg_H(C) \le 2|C_{act}|$.

First we must make some simple observations about H. Since F_2 is a subset of the edges in F_1, and each cluster represents a disjoint induced connected subtree of F_1, the contraction to H introduces no cycles. Thus, H is a forest. All the leaves of H must be alive, because otherwise the corresponding cluster C would be in $\mathcal{B}$ and hence would have been pruned away.

With this information about H, it is easy to bound $\sum_{C \in C_{act}} \deg_H(C)$. The total degree in H is at most $2(|C_{act}| + |C_{dead}|)$. Noticing that the degree of dead clusters is at least two, we get $\sum_{C \in C_{act}} \deg_H(C) \le 2(|C_{act}| + |C_{dead}|) - 2|C_{dead}| = 2|C_{act}|$ as desired. □

The following lemma gives a sufficient condition for two vertices that end up in the same component of F_2. This is a corollary of our pruning rule which has a major difference from other pruning rules. Unlike the previous work, we do not prune the entire subgraph; rather, we only remove some edges, increasing the number of connected components.

LEMMA 7. *Two vertices u and v of V are connected via F_2 if there exist sets S, S' both containing u, v such that $y_{S,v} > 0$ and $y_{S',u} > 0$.*

PROOF. The growth stage connects u and v since $y_{S,v} > 0$ and $u, v \in S$. Consider the path p connecting u and v in F_1. All the vertices of p are in S and S'. For the sake of reaching a contradiction, suppose some edges of p are pruned. Let e be the first edge being pruned on the path p. Thus, there must be a cluster $C \in \mathcal{B}$ cutting e; furthermore, $\delta(C) \cap p = \{e\}$, since e is the first edge pruned from p. The laminarity of the clusters $\mathcal{S}$ gives $C \subset S, S'$, since C contains exactly one endpoint of e. If C contains both or no endpoints of p, it cannot cut p at only one edge. Thus, C contains exactly one endpoint of p, say v. We then have $\sum_{C' \subseteq C} y_{C',v} = \phi_v$, because C is tight. However, as C is a *proper* subset of S, this contradicts with $y_{S,v} > 0$, proving the supposition is false. The case C contains u is symmetric. □

Consider a pair (v, S) with $y_{S,v} > 0$. If subgraph G' of G has an edge that goes through the cut $(S, \bar{S})$, at least a portion of length $y_{S,v}$ of G' is colored with the color v due to the set S. Thus, if G' cuts all the sets S for which $y_{S,v} > 0$, we can charge part of the length of G' to the potential of v. Later in Lemma 10, we are going to use potentials as a lower bound on the optimal solution. More formally, we say a graph $G'(V, E')$ *exhausts a color u* if and only if $E' \cap \delta(S) \neq \emptyset$ for any $S : y_{S,u} > 0$. The proof of the following corollary is omitted here, however, it is implicit in the proof of Lemma 10 below. We do not use this corollary explicitly. Nevertheless, it gives insight into the analysis below.

COROLLARY 8. *If a subgraph H of G connects two vertices u_1, u_2 from different components of F_2 (which are contracted versions of the components in the initial 2-approximate solution), then H exhausts the color corresponding to at least one of u_1 and u_2.*

We can relate the cost of a subgraph to the potential value of the colors it exhausts.

LEMMA 9. *Let L be the set of colors exhausted by subgraph G' of G. The cost of $G'(V, E')$ is at least $\sum_{v \in L} \phi_v$.*

This is quite intuitive. Recall that the y variables color the edges of the graph. Consider a segment on edges corresponding to cluster S with color v. At least one edge of G' *passes through* the cut $(S, \bar{S})$. Thus, a portion of the cost of G' can be charged to $y_{S,v}$. Hence, the total cost of the graph G' is at least as large as the total amount of colors paid for by L. Here is the formal proof.

PROOF. The cost of $G'(V, E)$ is

$$
\begin{aligned}
\sum_{e \in E'} c_e &\ge \sum_{e \in E'} \sum_{S: e \in \delta(S)} y_S \qquad \text{by (1)}\\
&= \sum_S |E' \cap \delta(S)| y_S\\
&\ge \sum_{S: E' \cap \delta(S) \neq \emptyset} y_S\\
&= \sum_{S: E' \cap \delta(S) \neq \emptyset} \sum_{v \in S} y_{S,v}\\
&= \sum_v \sum_{S \ni v: E' \cap \delta(S) \neq \emptyset} y_{S,v}\\
&\ge \sum_{v \in L} \sum_{S \ni v: E' \cap \delta(S) \neq \emptyset} y_{S,v}\\
&= \sum_{v \in L} \sum_{S \ni v} y_{S,v},
\end{aligned}
$$

because $y_{S,v} = 0$ if $v \in L$ and $E' \cap \delta(S) = \emptyset$,

$$
= \sum_{v \in L} \phi_v \qquad \text{by a tight version of (2).}
$$
□

Recall that the trees T_i^* of the 2-approximate solution F^* are contracted in F_2. Construct F from F_2 by uncontracting all these trees. Let F consist of tree components T_i. It is not difficult to verify that F is indeed a forest, but we do not need this condition since we can always remove cycles to find a forest. Define $\mathcal{D}_i := \{(s,t) \in \mathcal{D} : s, t \in V(T_i)\}$, and let OPT_i denote (the cost of) the optimal Steiner forest satisfying the demands $\mathcal{D}_i$.

LEMMA 10. *$\sum_i OPT_i \le (1+\varepsilon)OPT$.*

PROOF. If each tree component of OPT only satisfies demands from a single $\mathcal{D}_i$, we are done. Otherwise, we build a solution OPT' consisting of forests OPT'_i for each $\mathcal{D}_i$, such that $\sum_i \text{OPT}'_i \le (1+\varepsilon)\text{OPT}$. Then, $\text{OPT}_i \le \text{OPT}'_i$ finishes the argument. Instead of explicitly identifying the forests OPT'_i, we construct an *inexpensive* set of trees $\mathcal{T}$ where each $T \in \mathcal{T}$ is associated with a subset $D_T \subseteq \mathcal{D}$ of demands, such that

- $T \in \mathcal{T}$ connects all the demands in D_T,
- all the demands are satisfied, namely, $\cup_{T\in\mathcal{T}} D_T = \mathcal{D}$, and
- for each $T \in \mathcal{T}$, there exists a $\mathcal{D}_i$ where $D_T \subseteq \mathcal{D}_i$.

Then, each OPT'_i above is merely a collection of several trees in $\mathcal{T}$. We now describe how $\mathcal{T}$ is constructed. Start with the optimal solution OPT. Contract the trees T_i^* of the 2-approximate solution F^* to build a graph $\hat{\mathrm{OPT}}$. Initially, the set $D_{\hat{T}}$ associated with each connected component $\hat{T}$ of $\hat{\mathrm{OPT}}$ specifies the set of demands connected via $\hat{T}$; notice that the endpoints of any demand are both part of one super-node because F^* is feasible. If the color u corresponding to a component T_i^* is exhausted by $\hat{\mathrm{OPT}}$, add T_i^* to $\mathcal{T}$, and let $D_{T_i^*}$ be the set of demands satisfied via T_i^*. Then, for every component $\hat{T}_i$ of $\hat{\mathrm{OPT}}$, remove $\cup_{T\in\mathcal{T}} D_T$ from $D_{\hat{T}_i}$. Finally, construct the uncontracted version of all the components $\hat{T}_i$, and add them to $\mathcal{T}$.

The first condition above clearly holds by the construction. For the second condition, note that at the beginning all the demands are satisfied by the trees $\hat{T}_i$, and we only remove demands from $D_{\hat{T}_i}$ when they are satisfied elsewhere. The last condition is proved by contradiction. Suppose a tree $T \in \mathcal{T}$ satisfies demands from two different groups $\mathcal{D}_1$ and $\mathcal{D}_2$. Clearly, T cannot be one of the contracted trees T_i^*, since those trees only serve a subset of one $\mathcal{D}_i$. Hence, T must be a tree component of OPT. Let $u, v \in V$ be two vertices from different components of F_2 that are connected in T. Since u and v are not connected in F_2, Lemma 7 ensures that for at least one of these vertices, say u, we have $y_{S,u} = 0\ \forall S \ni u, v$. Thus, $y_{S,u} > 0$ implies $v \notin S$. As T connects u and v, this means T exhausts the color u. We reach a contradiction, because the demands corresponding to u are still in D_T.

Finally, we show that the cost of $\mathcal{T}$ is small. Recall that $\mathcal{T}$ consists of two kinds of trees: tree components of OPT as well as trees corresponding to exhausted colors of OPT. We claim the cost of the latter is at most εOPT. Let L be the set of exhausted colors of OPT. The cost of the corresponding trees is $\varepsilon \sum_{v\in L} \phi_v$ by definition of ϕ_v. Lemma 9, however, gives $\mathrm{OPT} \geq \sum_{v\in L} \phi_v$. Therefore, the total cost of $\mathcal{T}$ is at most $(1+\varepsilon)$OPT. □

Now, we are ready to prove the main theorem of this section.

PROOF OF THEOREM 3. The first condition of the lemma follows directly from our construction: we start with a solution, and never disconnect one of the tree components in the process. The construction immediately implies the second condition. By Lemma 6, the cost of F_2 is at most $2\sum_{v\in V} \phi_v \leq \frac{4}{\varepsilon}\mathrm{OPT}$. Thus, F costs no more than $(4/\varepsilon + 2)$OPT, giving the third condition. Finally, Lemma 10 establishes the last condition. □

4. PTAS FOR PLANAR STEINER FOREST

The full version of the paper [6] shows how to build a spanner for the input graph $G_{in}(V_{in}, E_{in})$ with respect to the demand set $\mathcal{D}$. From Theorem 3, we obtain a set of trees $\{T_1, \ldots, T_k\}$, associated with a partition of demands $\{\mathcal{D}_1, \ldots, \mathcal{D}_k\}$: tree T_i connects all the demands $\mathcal{D}_i$, and the total cost of trees T_i is in $O(\mathrm{OPT})$. The construction goes along the same lines as that of Borradaile et al. [12], yet there are certain differences, especially in the analysis. We separately build a graph H_i for each T_i, and finally let H be the union of all graphs H_i.

Having proved the spanner result, we can present our main PTAS for *Steiner forest* on planar graphs in this section. We first mention two main ingredients of the algorithm. We invoke the following result due to Demaine, Hajiaghayi and Mohar [13].

THEOREM 11 ([13]). *For a fixed genus g, and any integer $k \geq 2$, and for every graph G of Euler genus at most g, the edges of G can be partitioned into k sets such that contracting any one of the sets results in a graph of treewidth at most $O(g^2 k)$. Furthermore, such a partition can be found in $O(g^{5/2} n^{3/2} \log n)$ time.*

As a corollary, this holds for a planar graph (which has genus zero).

We can now prove the main theorem of this paper. Algorithm 2 (PSF-PTAS) shows the steps of the PTAS.

Algorithm 2 PSF-PTAS

Input: planar graph $G_{in}(V_{in}, E_{in})$, and set of demands $\mathcal{D}$.
Output: Steiner forest F satisfying $\mathcal{D}$.

Construct the Steiner forest spanner H.
Let $k \leftarrow 2f(\varepsilon)/\bar{\varepsilon}$.
Let $\varepsilon \leftarrow \min(1, \bar{\varepsilon}/6)$.
Using Theorem 11, partition the edges of H into $E_1, \ldots, E_k$.
Let $i^* \leftarrow \arg\min_i \ell(E_i)$.
Find a $(1+\varepsilon)$-approximate Steiner forest F^* of $\mathcal{D}$ in H/E_{i^*} via Theorem 5.
Output $F^* \cup E_{i^*}$.

PROOF OF THEOREM 1. Given are planar graph G_{in}, and the set of demand pairs $\mathcal{D}$. We build a Steiner forest spanner H using Theorem 2. For a suitable value of k whose precise value will be fixed below, we apply Theorem 11 to partition the edges of H into $E_1, E_2, \ldots, E_k$. Let E_{i^*} be the set having the least total length. The total length of edges in E_{i^*} is at most $\ell(H)/k$. Contracting E_{i^*} produces a graph H^* of treewidth $O(k)$.

Theorem 5 allows us to find a solution OPT^* corresponding to H^*. Adding the edges E_{i^*} clearly gives a solution for H whose value is at most $(1+\varepsilon)\mathrm{OPT}_{\mathcal{D}}(H) + \ell(H)/k$. Letting $\varepsilon = \min(1, \bar{\varepsilon}/6)$ and $k = 2f(\varepsilon)/\bar{\varepsilon}$ guarantees that the cost of this solution is

$$\begin{aligned} &\leq (1+\varepsilon)^2 \mathrm{OPT}_{\mathcal{D}}(G_{in}) + \ell(H)/k \\ &\leq (1+\varepsilon)^2 \mathrm{OPT}_{\mathcal{D}}(G_{in}) + \frac{\bar{\varepsilon}}{2}\mathrm{OPT}_{\mathcal{D}}(G_{in}) \\ &(1+\bar{\varepsilon})\mathrm{OPT}_{\mathcal{D}}(G_{in}). \quad \square \end{aligned}$$

The running time of all the algorithm except for the bounded-treewidth PTAS is bounded by $O(n^2 \log n)$. The parameter k above has a singly exponential dependence on ε. Yet, the running time of the current procedure for solving the bounded-treewidth instances is not bounded by a low-degree polynomial; rather, k and ε appear in the exponent in the polynomial. Were we able to improve the running time of this procedure, we would obtain a PTAS that runs in time $O(n^2 \log n)$.

4.1 Extension to bounded-genus graphs

We can generalize this result to the case of bounded-genus graphs. Theorem 3 does not assume any special structure for the input graph. To construct a spanner in this case, we use the generalized ideas of Borradaile et al. [10]. This process does not increase the Euler genus of the graph, since the resulting graph has a subset of original edges. Theorem 11 works for such graphs as well, and hence, as in Theorem 1, we can reduce the problem to a bounded-treewidth graph on which we apply Theorem 5.

THEOREM 12. *For any constant $\varepsilon > 0$, there is a polynomial-time $(1+\varepsilon)$-approximation algorithm for the graphs of Euler genus at most g.*

5. PTAS FOR GRAPHS OF BOUNDED TREEWIDTH

The purpose of this section is to sketch the proof of Theorem 5. For definitions concerning tree decompositions, we refer the reader to the full version [6]. We define a notion of group that will be crucial in the algorithm. A group is defined by a set S of center vertices, a set X of "interesting" vertices, and a maximum distance r; the *group* $\mathcal{G}_G(X, S, r)$ contains S and those vertices of X that are at distance at most r from some vertex in S.

LEMMA 13. *Let T be a Steiner tree of $X \subseteq V(G)$ with cost W. For every $\varepsilon > 0$, there is a set $S \subseteq X$ of $O(1+1/\varepsilon)$ vertices such that $X = \mathcal{G}_G(X, S, \varepsilon W)$.*

Let $\mathcal{B} = (B_i)_{i=1...n}$ be the bags of a rooted nice tree decomposition of width k. Let V_i be the set of vertices appearing in B_i or in a descendant of B_i. Let A_i be the set of *active vertices* at bag B_i: those vertices $v \in V_i$ for which there is a demand $\{v, w\} \in \mathcal{D}$ with $w \notin V_i$. Let $G_i := G[V_i]$. A Steiner forest F induces a partition $\pi_i(F)$ of A_i for every $i = 1, \ldots, n$: let two vertices of A_i be in the same class of $\pi_i(F)$ if and only if they are in the same component of F. Note that if F is restricted to G_i, then a component of F can be split into up to $k+1$ components, thus $\pi_i(F)$ is a coarser partition then the partition defined by the components of the restriction of F to G_i.

Let $\Pi = (\Pi_i)_{i=1...n}$ be a collection such that Π_i is a set of partitions of A_i. If $\pi_i(F) \in \Pi_i$ for every bag B_i, then we say that F *conforms* to Π. The following lemma gives an algorithm for finding a solution whose cost is minimum among the solutions conforming to a given Π. The proof follows the standard dynamic programming approach, but is quite tedious and technical, see the full version [6].

LEMMA 14. *For every fixed k, there is a polynomial time algorithm that, given a graph G with treewidth at most k and a collection Π, finds the minimum cost Steiner forest conforming to Π.*

Next we construct a polynomial-size collection Π such that there is a $(1+\varepsilon)$-approximate solution that conforms to Π. Putting together these two results, we get a PTAS for the Steiner forest problem on bounded treewidth graphs. Recall that the collection Π contains a set of partitions Π_i for each $i \in I$. Each partition in Π_i is defined by a sequence $((S_1, r_1), \ldots, (S_p, r_p))$ of at most $k+1$ pairs and a partition ρ of $\{1, \ldots, p\}$. The pair (S_j, r_j) consists of a set S_j of $O((k+1)(1+1/\varepsilon))$ vertices of G_i and a nonnegative integer r_j, which equals the distance between two vertices of G. There are at most $|V(G)|^{O((k+1)(1+1/\varepsilon))} \cdot |V(G)|^2$ possible pairs (S_j, r_j) and hence at most $|V(G)|^{O((k+1)^2(1+1/\varepsilon))}$ different sequences. The number of possible partitions ρ is $O(k^k)$. Thus if we construct Π_i by considering all possible sequences constructed from every possible choice of (S_j, r_j), the size of Π_i is polynomial in $|V(G)|$ for every fixed k and ε.

We construct the partition π corresponding to a particular sequence and ρ the following way. Each pair (S_j, r_j) can be used to define a group $R_j = \mathcal{G}_G(A_i, S_j, r_j)$ of A_i. Roughly speaking, for each class P of ρ, there is a corresponding class of π that contains the union of R_j for every $j \in P$. However, the actual definition is somewhat more complicated. We want π to be a partition, which means that the subsets of A_i corresponding to the different classes of ρ should be disjoint. In order to ensure disjointness, we define $R'_j := R_j \setminus \bigcup_{j'=1}^{j-1} R_{j'}$. The partition π of A_i is constructed as follows: for each class P of ρ, we let $\bigcup_{j \in P} R'_j$ be a class of π. Note that these classes are disjoint by construction. If these classes fully cover A_i, then we put the resulting partition π into Π_i; otherwise, the sequence does not define a partition. This finishes the construction of Π_i.

Before showing that there is a good approximate solution conforming to the collection Π defined above, we need a further definition. For two vertices u and v, we denote by $u < v$ the fact that the topmost bag containing u is a proper descendant of the topmost bag containing v. Note that each bag is the topmost bag of at most one vertex in a nice tree decomposition (recall that we can assume that the root bag contains only a single vertex). Thus if u and v appear in the same bag, then $u < v$ or $v < u$ holds, i.e., this relation defines an ordering of the vertices in a bag. We can extend this relation to connected subset of vertices: for two disjoint connected sets K_1, K_2, $K_1 < K_2$ means that K_2 has a vertex v such that $u < v$ for every vertex $u \in K_1$, in other words, $K_1 < K_2$ means that the topmost bag where vertices from K_1 appear is a proper descendant of the topmost bag where vertices from K_2 appear. If there is a bag containing vertices from both K_1 and K_2, then either $K_1 < K_2$ or $K_2 < K_1$ holds. The reason for this is that the bags containing vertices from $K_1 \cup K_2$ form a connected subtree of the tree decomposition, and if the topmost bag in this subtree contains vertex $v \in K_1 \cup K_2$, then $u < v$ for every other vertex u in $K_1 \cup K_2$.

LEMMA 15. *There is a $(1+k\varepsilon)$-approximate solution conforming to Π.*

PROOF. Let F be a minimum cost Steiner forest. We describe a procedure that adds further edges to F to transform it into a Steiner forest F' that conforms to Π and has cost at most $(1+k\varepsilon)\ell(F)$. We need a delicate charging argument to show that the total increase of the cost is at most $k\varepsilon \cdot \ell(F)$ during the procedure. In each step, we charge the increase of the cost to an ordered pair (K_1, K_2) of components of F. We are charging only to pairs (K_1, K_2) having the property that $K_1 < K_2$ and there is a bag containing vertices from both K_1 and K_2. Observe that if B_i is the topmost bag where vertices from K_1 appear, then these properties imply that a vertex of K_2 appears in this bag as well. Otherwise, if every bag containing vertices of K_2 appears above B_i, then there is no bag containing vertices from both K_1 and K_2; if every bag containing vertices from K_2 appears below B_i, then $K_1 < K_2$ is not possible. Thus a component K_1 can be the first component of at most k such pairs (K_1, K_2): since the components are disjoint, the topmost bag containing vertices from K_1 can intersect at most k other components. We will charge a cost increase of at most $\varepsilon \cdot \ell(K_1)$ on the pair (K_1, K_2), thus the total increase is at most $k\varepsilon \cdot \ell(F)$. It is a crucial point of the proof that we charge on (pairs of) components of the original solution F, even after several modification steps, when the components of F' can be larger than the original components of F. Actually, in the proof to follow, we will refer to three different types of components:

(a) Components of the current solution F'.

(b) Each component of F' contains one or more components of F.

(c) If a component of F is restricted to the subset V_i, then it can split into up to $k+1$ components.

To emphasize the different meanings, and be clear as well, we use the terms a-component, b-component, and c-component.

Initially, we set $F' := F$ and it will be always true that F' is a supergraph of F, thus F' defines a partition of the b-components of F. Suppose that there is a bag B_i such that the partition $\pi_i(F')$ of A_i induced by F' is not in Π_i. Let $K_1 < K_2 < \cdots < K_p$ be the b-components of F intersecting B_i, ordered by the relation $<$. Some of these b-components might be in the same a-component of F'; let ρ be the partition of $\{1, \ldots, p\}$ defined by F' on these b-components.

Let $A_{i,j}$ be the subset of A_i contained in K_j. The intersection of b-component K_j with V_i gives rise to at most $k+1$ c-components, each of cost at most $\ell(K_j)$. Thus by Lemma 13, there is a set $S_j \subseteq V(K_j)$ of at most $O((k+1)(1+1/\varepsilon))$ vertices such that $A_{i,j} = \mathcal{G}_{G_i}(A_{i,j}, S_j, r_j)$ for some $r_j \leq \varepsilon \cdot \ell(K_j)$. If the sequence (S_1, r_1), $\ldots$, (S_p, r_p) and the partition ρ give rise to the partition $\pi_i(F')$, then $\pi_i(F') \in \Pi_i$. Otherwise, let us investigate the reason why this sequence and ρ do not define the partition $\pi_i(F')$. Let R_j, R'_j be defined as in the definition of Π_i, i.e., $R_j = \mathcal{G}_G(A_i, S_j, r_j)$ and $R'_j := R_j \setminus \bigcup_{j'=1}^{j-1} R_{j'}$. It is clear that $A_{i,j} \subseteq R_j$. Therefore, every vertex of A_i is contained in some R_j and hence in some R'_j. Thus the sequence does define a partition π, but maybe a partition different from $\pi_i(F')$. Let $\rho(j)$ be the class of ρ containing j. If for every $1 \leq j \leq p$, every vertex of $A_{i,j}$ is contained in $\bigcup_{j' \in \rho(j)} R'_{j'}$, then π and $\pi_i(F')$ are the same. So suppose that some vertex $v \in A_{i,j}$ is not in $\bigcup_{j' \in \rho(j)} R'_{j'}$. As $v \in R_j$, this means that $v \in R_{j^*}$ for some $j^* < j$ and $j^* \notin \rho(j)$. The fact that $R_{j^*} = \mathcal{G}_{G_i}(A_i, S_{j^*}, r_{j^*})$ contains $v \in A_{i,j}$ means that there is a vertex $u \in S_{j^*}$ such that $d_{G_i}(u,v) \le r_{j^*} \le \varepsilon \cdot \ell(K_{j^*})$. Note that u is a vertex of b-component K_{j^*} (as $u \in S_{j^*}$ and by definition S_{j^*} is a subset of $V(K_{j^*})$) and v is a vertex of b-component K_j. We modify F' by adding a shortest path that connects u and v. Clearly, this increases the cost of F' by at most $\varepsilon \cdot \ell(K_{j^*})$, which we charge on the pair (K_{j^*}, K_j). Note that K_j and K_{j^*} both intersect the bag B_i and $K_{j^*} < K_j$, as required in the beginning of the proof. Furthermore, K_j and K_{j^*} are in the same a-component of F' after the modification, but not before. Thus we charge at most once on the pair (K_{j^*}, K_j).

Since the modification always extends F', the procedure described above terminates after a finite number of steps. At this point, every partition $\pi_i(F')$ belongs to the corresponding set Π_i, that is, the solution F' conforms to Π. □

6. ALGORITHM FOR SERIES-PARALLEL GRAPHS

A series-parallel graph can be built form elementary blocks using two operations: parallel connection and series connection. The algorithm of Theorem 4 uses dynamic programming on the construction of the series-parallel graph. For each subgraph arising in the construction, we find a minimum weight forest that connects some of the terminal pairs, connects a subset of the terminals to the "left exit point" of the subgraph, and connects the remaining terminals to the "right exit point" of the subgraph. The minimum weight depends on the subset of terminals connected to the left exit point, thus it seems that we need to determine exponentially many values (one for each subset). Fortunately, it turns out that the minimum weight is a submodular function of the subset. Furthermore, we show that this function can be represented by the cut function of a directed graph and this directed graph can be easily constructed if the directed graphs corresponding to the building blocks of the series-parallel subgraph are available. Thus, following the construction of the series-parallel graph, we can build all these directed graphs and determine the value of the optimum solution by the computation of a minimum cut.

Formally, a *series-parallel graph* $G(x,y)$ with distinguished vertices x,y is an undirected graph that can be constructed using the following rules:

- An edge xy is a series-parallel graph.
- If $G_1(x_1,y_1)$ and $G_2(x_2,y_2)$ are series-parallel graphs, then the graph $G(x,y)$ obtained by identifying x_1 with x_2 and y_1 with y_2 is a series-parallel graph with distinguished vertices $x := x_1 = x_2$ and $y := y_1 = y_2$ *(parallel connection).*
- If $G_1(x_1,y_1)$ and $G_2(x_2,y_2)$ are series-parallel graphs, then the graph $G(x,y)$ obtained by identifying y_1 with x_2 is a series-parallel graph with distinguished vertices $x := x_1$ and $y := y_2$ *(series connection).*

We prove Theorem 4 in this section by constructing a polynomial-time algorithm to solve *Steiner forest* on series-parallel graphs. It is well-known that the treewidth of a graph is at most 2 if and only if it is a subgraph of a series parallel graph [9]. Since setting the length of an edge to ∞ is essentially the same as deleting the edge, it follows that *Steiner forest* can be solved in polynomial time on graphs with treewidth at most 2.

Let $(G,\mathcal{D})$ be an instance of *Steiner forest* where G is series parallel. For $i = 1,\dots,m$, denote by $G_i(x_i,y_i)$ all the intermediary graphs appearing in the series-parallel construction of G. We assume that these graphs are ordered such that $G = G_m$ and if G_i is obtained from G_{j_1} and G_{j_2}, then $j_1, j_2 < i$. Let $\mathcal{D}_i \subseteq \mathcal{D}$ contain those pairs $\{u,v\}$ where both vertices are in $V(G_i)$. Let A_i be those vertices $v \in V(G_i)$ for which there exists a pair $\{v,u\} \in \mathcal{D}$ with $u \notin V(G_i)$ (note that $A_m = \emptyset$ and $\mathcal{D}_m = \mathcal{D}$). For every G_i, we define two integer values a_i, b_i and a function f_i:

- Let a_i be the minimum cost of a solution F of the instance $(G_i,\mathcal{D}_i)$ with the additional requirements that x_i and y_i are connected in F and every vertex in A_i is in the same component as x_i and y_i.
- Let G'_i be the graph obtained from G_i by identifying vertices x_i and y_i. Let b_i be the minimum cost of a solution F of the instance $(G'_i,\mathcal{D}_i)$ with the additional requirement that A_i is in the same component as $x_i = y_i$.
- For every $S \subseteq A_i$, let $f_i(S)$ be the minimum cost of a solution F of the instance $(G_i,\mathcal{D}_i)$ with the additional requirements that x_i and y_i are not connected, every $v \in S$ is in the same component as x_i, and every $v \in A_i \setminus S$ is in the same component as y_i. (If there is no such F, then $f_i(S) = \infty$.)

The main combinatorial property that allows us to solve the problem in polynomial time is that the functions f_i are submodular. We prove something stronger: the functions f_i can be represented in a compact way as the cut function of certain directed graphs.

If D is a directed graph with lengths on the edges and $X \subseteq V(D)$, then $\delta_D(X)$ denotes the total length of the edges leaving X. For $X,Y \subseteq V(D)$, we denote by $\lambda_D(A,B)$ the minimum length of a directed cut that separates A from B, i.e., the minimum of $\delta_D(X)$, taken over all $A \subseteq X \subseteq V(D) \setminus B$ (if $A \cap B \neq \emptyset$, then $\lambda_D(A,B)$ is defined to be ∞).

Definition 1. Let D_i be a directed graph with nonnegative edge lengths. Let s_i and t_i be two distinguished vertices and let A_i be a subset of vertices of D_i. We say that (D_i,s_i,t_i,A_i) *represents* f_i if $f_i(S) = \lambda_{D_i}(S \cup \{s_i\}, (A_i \setminus S) \cup \{t_i\})$ for every $S \subseteq A_i$. If s_i, t_i, A_i are clear from the context, then we simply say that D_i represents f_i.

A function f defined on the subsets of a ground set U is *submodular* if $f(X) + f(Y) \ge f(X \cap Y) + f(X \cup Y)$ holds for every $X,Y \subseteq U$. For example, it is well known that $\delta_G(X)$ is a submodular function on the subsets of $V(G)$. Submodularity is a powerful unifying concept of combinatorial optimization: classical results on flows, cuts, matchings, and matroids can be considered as consequences of submodularity. The following (quite standard) proposition shows that if a function can be represented in the sense of Definition 1, then the function is submodular. In the proof of Theorem 4, we show that every function f_i can be represented by a directed graph, thus it follows that every f_i is submodular. Although we do not use this observation directly in the paper, it explains in some sense why the problem is polynomial-time solvable.

PROPOSITION 16. *If a function $f_i : 2^{A_i} \to \mathbb{R}^+$ can be represented by (D_i,s_i,t_i,A_i) (in the sense of Definition 1), then f_i is submodular.*

PROOF OF THEOREM 4. We assume that in the given instance of *Steiner forest* each vertex appears only in at most one pair of $\mathcal{D}$. To achieve this, if a vertex v appears in $k > 1$ pairs, then we subdivide an arbitrary edge incident to v by $k-1$ new vertices such that each of the $k-1$ edges on the path formed by v and the new vertices has length 0. Replacing vertex v in a pair by any of the new vertices does not change the problem.

For every $i = 1,\dots,m$, we compute the values a_i, b_i, and a representation D_i of f_i. In the optimum solution F for the instance $(G_m,\mathcal{D})$, vertices x_m and y_m are either connected or not. Thus the cost of the optimum solutions is the minimum of a_m and $f_m(\emptyset)$ (recall that $A_m = \emptyset$). The value of $f_m(\emptyset)$ can be easily determined by computing the minimum cost s-t cut in D_m.

If G_i is a single edge e, then a_i and b_i are trivial to determine: a_i is the length of e and $b_i = 0$. The directed graph D_i representing f_i

can be obtained from G_i by renaming x_i to s_i, renaming y_i to t_i, and either removing the edge e (if $\mathcal{D}_i = \emptyset$) or replacing e with a directed edge $\overrightarrow{s_it_i}$ of length ∞ (if $\{u,v\} \in \mathcal{D}_i$).

If G_i is not a single edge, then it is constructed from some G_{j_1} and G_{j_2} either by series or parallel connection. Suppose that a_{j_p}, b_{j_p}, and D_{j_p} for $p = 1,2$ are already known. We show how to compute a_i, b_i, and D_i in this case.

Parallel connection. Suppose that G_i is obtained from G_{j_1} and G_{j_2} by parallel connection. It is easy to see that $a_i = \min\{a_{j_1} + b_{j_2}, b_{j_1} + a_{j_2}\}$ and $b_i = b_{j_1} + b_{j_2}$. To obtain D_i, we join D_{j_1} and D_{j_2} by identifying s_{j_1} with s_{j_2} (call it s_i) and by identifying t_{j_1} with t_{j_2} (call it t_i). Furthermore, for every $\{u,v\} \in \mathcal{D}_i \setminus \{\mathcal{D}_{j_1} \cup \mathcal{D}_{j_2}\}$, we add directed edges $\overrightarrow{uv}$ and $\overrightarrow{vu}$ with length ∞.

To see that D_i represents f_i, suppose that F is the subgraph that realizes the value $f_i(S)$ for some $S \subseteq A_i$. We have to show that there is an appropriate $X \subseteq V(D_i)$ certifying $\lambda_{D_i}(S \cup \{s\}, (A_i \setminus S) \cup \{t\}) \le \ell(F)$. The graph F is the edge disjoint union of two graphs $F_1 \subseteq G_{j_1}$ and $F_2 \subseteq G_{j_2}$. For $p = 1,2$, let $S^p \subseteq A_{j_p}$ be the set of those vertices that are connected to x_{j_p} in F_p, it is clear that F_p connects $A_{j_p} \setminus S^p$ to y_{j_p}. Since F_p does not connect x_i and y_i, we have that $\ell(F_p) \ge f_{j_p}(S^p)$. Since D_{j_p} represents f_{j_p}, there is a set X_p in D_{j_p} with $S^p \cup \{s_{j_p}\} \subseteq X_p \subseteq V(D_i) \setminus ((A_{j_p} \setminus S^p) \cup \{t_{j_p}\})$, and $\delta_{D_{j_p}}(X_p) = f_{j_p}(S^p)$. We show that $\delta_{D_i}(X_1 \cup X_2) = \delta_{D_{j_1}}(X_1) + \delta_{D_{j_2}}(X_2)$. Since D_i is obtained from joining D_{j_1} and D_{j_2}, the only thing that has to be verified is that the edges with infinite length added after the join cannot leave $X_1 \cup X_2$. Suppose that there is such an edge $\overrightarrow{uv}$, assume without loss of generality that $u \in X_1$ and $v \in V(D_{j_2}) \setminus X_2$. This means that $u \in S^1$ and $v \notin S^2$. Thus F connects u with x_i and v with y_i, implying that F does not connect u and v. However $\{u,v\} \in \mathcal{D}_i$, a contradiction. Therefore, for the set $X := X_1 \cup X_2$, we have

$$\begin{aligned}\delta_{D_i}(X) = \delta_{D_{j_1}}(X_1) + \delta_{D_{j_2}}(X_2) = f_{j_1}(S^1) + f_{j_2}(S^2)\\ \le \ell(F_1) + \ell(F_2) = \ell(F) = f_i(S),\end{aligned}$$

proving the existence of the required X.

Suppose now that for some $S \subseteq A_i$, there is a set X with $S \cup \{s_i\} \subseteq X \subseteq V(D_i) \setminus ((A_i \setminus S) \cup \{t_i\})$. We have to show that $\delta_{D_i}(X) \ge f_i(S)$. For $p = 1,2$, let $X_p = X \cap V(D_{j_p})$ and $S^p = A_{j_p} \cap X_p$. Since D_{j_p} represents f_{j_p}, we have that $\delta_{D_{j_p}}(X_p) \ge f_{j_p}(S^p)$. Let F_p be a subgraph of G_{j_p} realizing $f_{j_p}(S^p)$. Let $F = F_1 \cup F_2$; we show that $\ell(F) \ge f_i(A_i)$, since F satisfies all the requirements in the definition of $f_i(A_i)$. It is clear that F does not connect x_i and y_i. Consider a pair $\{u,v\} \in \mathcal{D}_i$. If $\{u,v\} \in \mathcal{D}_{j_p}$, then F connects u and v. Otherwise, let $\{u,v\} \in \mathcal{D}_i \setminus \{\mathcal{D}_{j_1} \cup \mathcal{D}_{j_2}\}$. Suppose that F does not connect u and v, without loss of generality, suppose that $u \in X_1$ and $v \notin X_2$. This means that there is an edge $\overrightarrow{uv}$ of length ∞ in D_i and $\delta_{D_i}(X) = \infty \ge f_i(S)$ follows. Thus we proved $\ell(F) \ge f_i(A_i)$ and we have

$$\begin{aligned}\delta_{D_i}(X) = \delta_{D_{j_1}}(X_1) + \delta_{D_{j_2}}(X_2) \ge f_{j_1}(S^1) + f_{j_2}(S^2)\\ = \ell(F_1) + \ell(F_2) = \ell(F) \ge f_i(S),\end{aligned}$$

what we had to show.

Series connection. Suppose that G_i is obtained from G_{j_1} and G_{j_2} by series connection and let $\mu := y_{j_1} = x_{j_2}$ be the middle vertex. It is easy to see that $a_i = a_{j_1} + a_{j_2}$ (vertex μ has to be connected to both x_i and y_i). To compute b_i, we argue as follows. Denote by $G^R_{j_2}$ the graph obtained from G_{j_2} by swapping the names of distinguished vertices x_{j_2} and y_{j_2}. Observe that the graph G'_i in the definition of b_i arises as the parallel connection of G_{j_1} and $G^R_{j_2}$. It is easy to see that $a^R_{j_2}$, $b^R_{j_2}$, and $f^R_{j_2}$ corresponding to $G^R_{j_2}$ can be defined as $a^R_{j_2} = a_{j_2}$, $b^R_{j_2} = b_{j_2}$, and $f^R_{j_2}(S) = f_{j_2}(A_{j_2} \setminus S)$. Furthermore, if D_{j_2} represents f_{j_2}, then the graph $D^R_{j_2}$ obtained from D_{j_2} by swapping the names of s_{j_2} and t_{j_2} represents $f^R_{j_2}$. Thus we have everything at our disposal to construct a directed graph D'_i that represents the function f'_i corresponding to the parallel connection of G_{j_1} and $G^R_{j_2}$. Now it is easy to see that $b_i = f'_i(A_i)$: graph G'_i is isomorphic to the parallel connection of G_{j_1} and $G^R_{j_2}$ and the definition of b_i requires that A_i is connected to $x_i = y_i$. The value of $f'_i(A_i)$ can be determined by a simple minimum cut computation in D'_i.

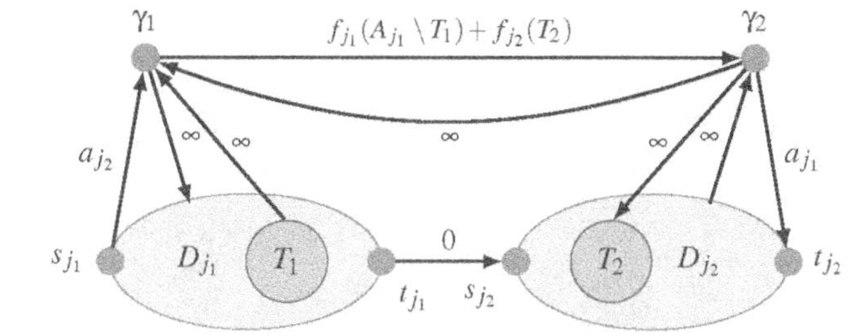

Figure 1: Construction of D_i in a series connection.

Let $T_1 \subseteq A_{j_1}$ contain those vertices v for which there exists a pair $\{v,u\} \in \mathcal{D}_i$ with $u \in A_{j_2}$ and let $T_2 \subseteq A_{j_2}$ contain those vertices v for which there exists a pair $\{v,u\} \in \mathcal{D}_i$ with $u \in A_{j_1}$. Observe that $A_i = (A_{j_1} \setminus T_1) \cup (A_{j_2} \setminus T_2)$ (here we are using the fact that each vertex is contained in at most one pair, thus a $v \in T_1$ cannot be part of any pair $\{v,u\}$ with $u \notin V(D_i)$). To construct D_i, we connect D_{j_1} and D_{j_2} with an edge $\overrightarrow{t_{j_1}s_{j_2}}$ of length 0 and set $s_i := s_{j_1}$ and $t_i := t_{j_2}$. Furthermore, we introduce two new vertices γ_1, γ_2 and add the following edges (see Figure 1):

- $\overrightarrow{s_{j_1}\gamma_1}$ with length a_{j_2},
- $\overrightarrow{\gamma_1\gamma_2}$ with length $f_{j_1}(A_{j_1} \setminus T_1) + f_{j_2}(T_2)$,
- $\overrightarrow{\gamma_2 t_{j_2}}$ with length a_{j_1},
- $\overrightarrow{\gamma_2\gamma_1}$ with length ∞,
- $\overrightarrow{\gamma_1 v}$ with length ∞ for every $v \in V(D_{j_1})$,
- $\overrightarrow{v\gamma_2}$ with length ∞ for every $v \in V(D_{j_2})$,
- $\overrightarrow{v\gamma_1}$ with length ∞ for every $v \in T_1$, and
- $\overrightarrow{\gamma_2 v}$ with length ∞ for every $v \in T_2$.

Suppose that F is the subgraph that realizes the value $f_i(S)$ for some $S \subseteq A_i$; we have to show that D_i has an appropriate cut with value $f_i(S)$. Subgraph F is the edge-disjoint union of subgraphs $F_1 \subseteq G_{j_1}$ and $F_2 \subseteq G_{j_2}$. We consider 3 cases: in subgraph F, vertex μ is either connected to neither x_{j_1} nor y_{j_2}, connected only to x_{j_1}, or connected only to y_{j_2}.

Case 1: μ is connected to neither x_{j_1} nor y_{j_2}. In this case, vertices of A_{j_1} are not connected to y_i and vertices of A_{j_2} are not connected to x_i, hence $S = A_i \cap A_{j_1} = A_{j_1} \setminus T_1$ is the only possibility. Furthermore, F connects both T_1 and T_2 to μ. It follows that $\ell(F) = \ell(F_1) + \ell(F_2) \ge f_{j_1}(A_{j_1} \setminus T_1) + f_{j_2}(T_2)$. Set $X = V(D_i) \cup \{\gamma_1\}$: now we have $\delta_{D_i}(X) = f_{j_1}(A_{j_1} \setminus T_1) + f_{j_2}(T_2) \le \ell(F)$, X contains $(A_{j_1} \setminus T_1) \cup \{s_i\}$, and is disjoint from $(A_{j_2} \setminus T_2) \cup \{t_i\}$.

Case 2: μ is connected only to x_i. This is only possible if $A_{j_1} \setminus T_1 \subseteq S$. Clearly, $\ell(F_1) \ge a_{j_1}$. Subgraph F_2 has to connect every vertex in $(S \cap A_{j_2}) \cup T_2$ to x_{j_2} and every vertex $A_i \setminus S = A_{j_2} \setminus (S \cup T_2)$ to y_{j_2}. Hence $\ell(F_2) \ge f_{j_2}((S \cap A_{j_2}) \cup T_2)$ and let $X_2 \subseteq V(D_{j_2})$ be the corresponding cut in D_{j_2}. Set $X := X_2 \cup V(D_{j_1}) \cup \{\gamma_1, \gamma_2\}$, we have $\delta_{D_i}(X) = f_{j_2}((S \cap A_{j_2}) \cup T_2) + a_{j_1} \le \ell(F_2) + a_{j_1} \le \ell(F)$ (note that no edge with infinite length leaves X since $T_2 \subseteq X_2$). As X contains S and contains none of the vertices in $A_i \setminus S$, we proved the existence of the required cut.

Case 3: μ is connected only to y_i. Similar to case 2.

Suppose now that for some $S \subseteq A_i$, there is a set $X \subseteq V(D_i)$ with $S \cup \{s_i\} \subseteq X \subseteq V(D_i) \setminus ((A_i \setminus S) \cup \{t_i\})$. We have to show that $\delta_{D_i}(X) \geq f_i(S)$. If $\delta_{D_i}(X) = \infty$, then there is nothing to show. In particular, because of the edge $\overrightarrow{\gamma_2\gamma_1}$, we are trivially done if $\gamma_2 \in X$ and $\gamma_1 \notin X$. Thus we have to consider only 3 cases depending which of γ_1, γ_2 are contained in X.

Case 1: $\gamma_1 \in X$, $\gamma_2 \notin X$. In this case, the edges having length ∞ ensure that $V(D_{j_1}) \subseteq X$ and $V(D_{j_2}) \cap X = \emptyset$, thus $\delta_{D_i}(X) = \ell(\overrightarrow{\gamma_1\gamma_2}) + \ell(\overrightarrow{t_{j_1}s_{j_2}}) = f_{j_1}(A_{j_1} \setminus T_1) + f_{j_2}(T_{j_2})$. We also have $S = A_{j_1} \setminus T_1$. Now it is easy to see that $f_i(S) \leq f_{j_1}(A_{j_1} \setminus T_1) + f_{j_2}(T_{j_2})$: taking the union of some F_1 realizing $f_{j_1}(A_{j_1} \setminus T_1)$ and some F_2 realizing $f_{j_2}(T_{j_2})$, we get a subset F realizing $f_i(S)$.

Case 2: $\gamma_1, \gamma_2 \in X$. The edges starting from γ_1 and having length ∞ ensure that $V(D_{j_1}) \subseteq X$. Furthermore, $\gamma_2 \in X$ ensures that $T_2 \subseteq X$. Let $X_2 := X \cap V(D_{j_2})$, we have $X_2 \cap A_{j_2} = T_2 \cup (S \cap A_{j_2})$, which implies $\delta_{D_{j_2}}(X_2) \geq f_{j_2}(T_2 \cup (S \cap A_{j_2}))$. Observe that $\delta_{D_i}(X) = a_{j_1} + \delta_{D_{j_2}}(X_2)$ (the term a_{j_1} comes from the edge $\overrightarrow{\gamma_2 t_i}$). Let F_1 be a subset of G_{j_1} realizing a_{j_1} and let F_2 be a subset of G_{j_2} realizing $f_{j_2}(T_2 \cup (S \cap A_{j_2}))$. Let $F := F_1 \cup F_2$, note that F connects vertices S with x_i, vertices $A_i \setminus S$ with y_i, and vertices in $T_1 \cup T_2$ with μ. Thus $f_i(S) \leq \ell(F) = a_{j_1} + f_{j_2}(T_2 \cup (S \cap A_{j_2})) = \delta_{D_i}(X)$, what we had to show.

Case 3: $\gamma_1, \gamma_2 \notin X$. Similar to Case 2. □

7. REFERENCES

[1] A. Agrawal, P. Klein, and R. Ravi. When trees collide: an approximation algorithm for the generalized Steiner problem on networks. *SIAM J. Comput.*, 24(3):440–456, 1995.

[2] A. Agrawal, P. N. Klein, and R. Ravi. When trees collide: An approximation algorithm for the generalized Steiner problem on networks. In *STOC*, pages 134–144, 1991.

[3] A. Archer, M. Bateni, M. Hajiaghayi, and H. Karloff. Improved approximation algorithms for prize-collecting Steiner tree and TSP. In *FOCS*, 2009.

[4] S. Arora. Polynomial time approximation schemes for Euclidean TSP and other geometric problems. In *FOCS*, page 2, 1996.

[5] S. Arora. Polynomial time approximation schemes for Euclidean traveling salesman and other geometric problems. *J. ACM*, 45(5):753–782, 1998.

[6] M. Bateni, M. Hajiaghayi, and D. Marx. Approximation schemes for Steiner forest on planar graphs and graphs of bounded treewidth. *CoRR*, abs/0911.5143, 2009.

[7] P. Berman and V. Ramaiyer. Improved approximations for the Steiner tree problem. In *SODA*, pages 325–334, 1992.

[8] M. Bern and P. Plassmann. The Steiner problem with edge lengths 1 and 2. *Information Processing Letters*, 32:171–176, 1989.

[9] H. L. Bodlaender. A partial k-arboretum of graphs with bounded treewidth. *Theoretical Computer Science*, 209(1-2):1–45, 1998.

[10] G. Borradaile, E. D. Demaine, and S. Tazari. Polynomial-time approximation schemes for subset-connectivity problems in bounded genus graphs. In *STACS*, pages 171–182, 2009.

[11] G. Borradaile, P. N. Klein, and C. Mathieu. A polynomial-time approximation scheme for Euclidean Steiner forest. In *FOCS*, pages 115–124, 2008.

[12] G. Borradaile, C. Mathieu, and P. N. Klein. A polynomial-time approximation scheme for Steiner tree in planar graphs. In *SODA*, pages 1285–1294, 2007.

[13] E. D. Demaine, M. Hajiaghayi, and B. Mohar. Approximation algorithms via contraction decomposition. In *SODA*, pages 278–287, 2007.

[14] R. Diestel. *Graph Theory (Graduate Texts in Mathematics)*. Springer, August 2005.

[15] M. R. Garey and D. S. Johnson. The rectilinear Steiner tree problem is NP-complete. *SIAM J. Appl. Math.*, 32(4):826–834, 1977.

[16] E. Gassner. The Steiner forest problem revisited. *J. Disc. Alg.*, In Press, Corrected Proof, 2009.

[17] M. X. Goemans and D. P. Williamson. A general approximation technique for constrained forest problems. *SIAM J. Comput.*, 24(2):296–317, 1995.

[18] S. Hougardy and H. J. Prömel. A 1.598 approximation algorithm for the Steiner problem in graphs. In *Proceedings of the tenth annual ACM-SIAM symposium on Discrete algorithms (SODA)*, pages 448–453, 1999.

[19] R. M. Karp. On the computational complexity of combinatorial problems. *Networks*, 5:45–68, 1975.

[20] M. Karpinski and A. Zelikovsky. New approximation algorithms for the Steiner tree problems. *J. Comb. Opt.*, 1(1):47–65, 1997.

[21] P. N. Klein. A linear-time approximation scheme for TSP in undirected planar graphs with edge-weights. *SIAM J. Comput.*, 37(6):1926–1952, 2008.

[22] D. Marx. NP-completeness of list coloring and precoloring extension on the edges of planar graphs. *J. Graph Theory*, 49(4):313–324, 2005.

[23] D. Marx. Complexity results for minimum sum edge coloring. *Discrete Applied Mathematics*, 157(5):1034–1045, 2009.

[24] J. S. B. Mitchell. Guillotine subdivisions approximate polygonal subdivisions: A simple polynomial-time approximation scheme for geometric TSP, k-MST, and related problems. *SIAM Journal on Computing*, 28(4):1298–1309, 1999.

[25] H. J. Prömel and A. Steger. RNC-approximation algorithms for the Steiner problem. In *Proceedings of the 14th Annual Symposium on Theoretical Aspects of Computer Science (STACS)*, pages 559–570, 1997.

[26] M. B. Richey and R. G. Parker. On multiple Steiner subgraph problems. *Networks*, 16(4):423–438, 1986.

[27] G. Robins and A. Zelikovsky. Tighter bounds for graph Steiner tree approximation. *SIAM J. Disc. Math.*, 19(1):122–134, 2005.

[28] M. Thimm. On the approximability of the Steiner tree problem. *Theor. Comput. Sci.*, 295(1-3):387–402, 2003.

[29] A. Zelikovsky. An 11/6-approximation for the Steiner problem on graphs. In *Fourth Czechoslovakian Symp. Combinatorics, Graphs, and Complexity (1990) in Annals of Discrete Mathematics*, volume 51, pages 351–354, 1992.

[30] A. Zelikovsky. An 11/6-approximation algorithm for the network Steiner problem. *Algorithmica*, 9(5):463–470, 1993.

[31] A. Zelikovsky. Better approximation bounds for the network and Euclidean Steiner tree problems. Technical report, University of Virginia, Charlottesville, VA, USA, 1996.

[32] X. Zhou and T. Nishizeki. The edge-disjoint paths problem is NP-complete for partial k-trees. In *Algorithms and computation (Taejon, 1998)*, pages 417–426. Springer, Berlin, 1998.

Optimal Homologous Cycles, Total Unimodularity, and Linear Programming

Tamal K. Dey
Department of Computer Science and Engineering
The Ohio State University
Columbus, OH 43210, USA.
tamaldey@cse.ohio-state.edu

Anil N. Hirani
Department of Computer Science
University of Illinois at Urbana-Champaign
Urbana, IL 61801, USA.
hirani@cs.illinois.edu

Bala Krishnamoorthy
Department of Mathematics
Washington State University
Pullman, WA 99164, USA.
bkrishna@math.wsu.edu

ABSTRACT

Given a simplicial complex with weights on its simplices, and a nontrivial cycle on it, we are interested in finding the cycle with minimal weight which is homologous to the given one. Assuming that the homology is defined with integer ($\mathbb{Z}$) coefficients, we show the following (Theorem 18):

> *For a finite simplicial complex K of dimension greater than p, the boundary matrix $[\partial_{p+1}]$ is totally unimodular if and only if $H_p(L, L_0)$ is torsion-free, for all pure subcomplexes L_0, L in K of dimensions p and $p+1$ respectively, where $L_0 \subset L$.*

Because of the total unimodularity of the boundary matrix, we can solve the optimization problem, which is inherently an integer programming problem, as a linear program and obtain an integer solution. Thus the problem of finding optimal cycles in a given homology class can be solved in polynomial time. This result is surprising in the backdrop of a recent result which says that the problem is NP-hard under $\mathbb{Z}_2$ coefficients which, being a *field*, is in general easier to deal with. Our result implies, among other things, that one can compute in polynomial time an optimal $(d-1)$-cycle in a given homology class for any triangulation of an orientable compact d-manifold or for any finite simplicial complex embedded in $\mathbb{R}^d$. Our optimization approach can also be used for various related problems, such as finding an optimal *chain* homologous to a given one when these are not cycles.

Categories and Subject Descriptors

F.2.2 [**Analysis of Algorithms and Problem Complexity**]: Nonnumerical Algorithms and Problems—*geometrical problems and computations, computations on discrete structures*; G.1.6 [**Numerical Analysis**]: Optimization—*integer programming, linear programming*

General Terms

Algorithms, Theory

Keywords

Computational topology, homology localization, simplicial complex, optimal chain

1. INTRODUCTION

Topological cycles in shapes embody their important features. As a result they find applications in scientific studies and engineering developments. A version of the problem that often appears in practice is that given a cycle in the shape, compute the shortest cycle in the same topological class (homologous). For example, one may generate a set of cycles from a simplicial complex using the persistence algorithm [10] and then ask for tightening them while maintaining their homology classes. For two dimensional surfaces, this problem and its relatives have been widely studied in recent years; see, for example, [2, 3, 5, 6, 8]. A natural question is to consider higher dimensional spaces which allow higher dimensional cycles such as closed surfaces within a three dimensional topological space. High dimensional applications arise, for example, in the modeling of sensor networks by Vietoris-Rips complexes of arbitrary dimension [7, 20]. Not surprisingly, these generalizations are hard to compute which is confirmed by a recent result of Chen and Freedman [4]. Notwithstanding this negative development, our result shows that optimal homologous cycles in any finite dimension are polynomial time computable for a large class of shapes if homology is defined with integer coefficients.

Let K be a simplicial complex. Informally, a p-cycle in K is a collection of p-simplices whose boundaries cancel mutually. One may assign a non-zero weight to each p-simplex in K which induces a weighted 1-norm for each p-cycle in K. For example, the weight of a p-simplex could be its volume. Given any p-cycle c in K, our problem is to compute a p-cycle c^* which has the minimal weighted 1-norm in the homology class of c. If some of the weights are zero the problem can still be posed and solved, except that one may not call it weighted 1-norm minimization. The homology classes are defined with respect to coefficients in an abelian group such as $\mathbb{Q}$, $\mathbb{R}$, $\mathbb{Z}$, $\mathbb{Z}_n$ etc. Often, the group $\mathbb{Z}_2$ is used mainly because of simplicity and intuitive geometric interpretations.

Chen and Freedman [4] show that under $\mathbb{Z}_2$ coefficients, computing an optimal p-cycle c^* is NP-hard for $p \geq 1$. Moreover, their result implies that various relaxations may still be NP-hard. For example, constant factor approximation of c^* is NP-hard. Even if the rank of the p-dimensional homology group is constant, computing c^* remains NP-hard for $p \geq 2$. The only settled positive case is a result of Chambers, Erickson, and Nayyeri [3] who show that computing optimal homologous loops for surfaces with constant genus is polynomial time solvable though they prove the problem is NP-hard if genus is not a constant.

The above negative results put a roadblock in computing optimal homologous cycles in high dimensions. Fortunately, our result shows that it is not so hopeless - if we switch to the coefficient group $\mathbb{Z}$ instead of $\mathbb{Z}_2$, the problem becomes polynomial time solvable for a fairly large class of spaces. This is a little surprising given that $\mathbb{Z}$ being not a *field* seems harder to deal with than $\mathbb{Z}_2$ in general. For example, $\mathbb{Z}_2$-valued chains form a vector space but $\mathbb{Z}$-valued chains do not.

The problem of computing an optimal homologous cycle (or more generally, chain) can be cast as a linear optimization problem. Consequently, the problem becomes polynomial time solvable if the homology group is defined over the reals. For then, the problem can be solved by linear programming. Indeed this is the approach taken by Tahbaz-Salehi and Jadbabaie [20]. However, in general the optimal cycle in that case may have fractional coefficients for its simplices, which may be awkward in certain applications. One advantage of using $\mathbb{Z}$ is that simplices appear with integral coefficients in the solution, a fact which aligns more with the geometric meaning of a cycle. On the other hand, the linear programming has to be replaced by integer programming in case of $\mathbb{Z}$. Then, it is not immediately clear if the optimization problem is polynomial time solvable.

Our main observation is that the optimization problem that we formulate can be solved by linear programming under certain conditions, although it is inherently an integer programming problem. It is known that a linear program provides an integer solution if and only if the constraint matrix has a property called *total unimodularity*. A matrix is totally unimodular if and only if each of its square submatrices has a determinant of 0, 1, or -1. We give a precise topological characterization of the complexes for which the constraint matrix is totally unimodular. For this class of complexes the optimal cycle can be computed in time polynomial in the number of simplices.

We can allow several variations to our problem because of our optimization based approach. For example we can probe into intermediate solutions; we can produce the chain that bounds the difference of the input and optimal cycles, and so forth. In fact we can also find an optimal chain homologous to a given one when the chains are not cycles. In other words we can leverage the flexibility of the optimization formulation by linking results from two apparently different fields, optimization theory and algebraic topology.

2. BACKGROUND

Since our result bridges the two very different fields of algebraic topology and optimization, we recall some relevant basic concepts and definitions from these two fields.

2.1 Basic definitions from algebraic topology

Let K be a finite simplicial complex of dimension greater than p. A p-chain with $\mathbb{Z}$ coefficients in K is a *formal sum* of a set of oriented p-simplices in K where the sum is defined by addition in $\mathbb{Z}$. Equivalently, it is an integer valued function on the oriented p-simplices, which changes sign when the orientation is reversed [14, page 37].

Two p-chains can be added by adding their values on corresponding p-simplices, resulting in a group $C_p(K)$ called the p-chain group of K. The *elementary chain basis* for $C_p(K)$ is the one consisting of integer valued functions that take the value 1 on a single oriented p-simplex, -1 on the oppositely oriented simplex, and 0 everywhere else. For an oriented p-simplex σ, we use σ to denote both the simplex and the corresponding elementary chain basis element. The group $C_p(K)$ is free and abelian. The boundary of an oriented p-simplex $\sigma = [v_0, \ldots, v_p]$ is given by

$$\partial_p \, \sigma = \sum_{i=0}^{p} (-1)^i [v_0, .., \widehat{v_i}, .., v_p] \,,$$

where $\widehat{v_i}$ denotes that the vertex v_i is to be deleted. This function on p-simplices extends uniquely [14, page 28] to the *boundary operator* which is a homomorphism:

$$\partial_p \colon C_p(K) \to C_{p-1}(K) \,.$$

Like a linear operator between vector spaces, a homomorphism between free abelian groups has a unique matrix representation with respect to a choice of bases [14, page 55]. The matrix form of ∂_p will be denoted $[\partial_p]$. Let $\{\sigma_i\}_{i=0}^{m-1}$ and $\{\tau_j\}_{j=0}^{n-1}$ be the sets of oriented $(p-1)$- and p-simplices respectively in K, ordered arbitrarily. Thus $\{\sigma_i\}$ and $\{\tau_j\}$ also represent the elementary chain bases for $C_{p-1}(K)$ and $C_p(K)$ respectively. With respect to such bases $[\partial_p]$ is an $m \times n$ matrix with entries 0, 1 or -1. The coefficients of $\partial_p \, \tau_j$ in the $C_{p-1}(K)$ basis become the column j (counting from 0) of $[\partial_p]$.

The kernel $\ker \partial_p$ is called the group of *p-cycles* and denoted $Z_p(K)$. The image $\operatorname{im} \partial_{p+1}$ forms the group of *p-boundaries* and denoted $B_p(K)$. Both $Z_p(K)$ and $B_p(K)$ are subgroups of $C_p(K)$. Since $\partial_p \circ \partial_{p+1} = 0$, we have that $B_p(K) \subseteq Z_p(K)$, that is, all p-boundaries are p-cycles though the converse is not necessarily true. The p dimensional homology group is the quotient group $H_p(K) = Z_p(K) / B_p(K)$. Two p-chains c and c' in K are *homologous* if $c = c' + \partial_{p+1} \, d$ for some $(p+1)$-chain d in K. In particular, if $c = \partial_{p+1} \, d$, we say c is homologous to zero. If a cycle c is not homologous to zero, we call it a *non-trivial cycle*.

For a finite simplicial complex K, the groups of chains $C_p(K)$, cycles $Z_p(K)$, and $H_p(K)$ are all finitely generated abelian groups. By the fundamental theorem of finitely generated abelian groups [14, page 24] any such group G can be written as a direct sum of two groups $G = F \oplus T$ where $F \cong (\mathbb{Z} \oplus \cdots \oplus \mathbb{Z})$ and $T \cong (\mathbb{Z}/t_1 \oplus \cdots \oplus \mathbb{Z}/t_k)$ with $t_i > 1$ and t_i dividing t_{i+1}. The subgroup T is called the *torsion* of G. If $T = 0$, we say G is *torsion-free*.

Let L_0 be a subcomplex of a simplicial complex L. The quotient group $C_p(L)/C_p(L_0)$ is called the group of *relative chains* of L modulo L_0 and is denoted $C_p(L, L_0)$. The boundary operator $\partial_p \colon C_p(L) \to C_{p-1}(L)$ and its restriction to L_0 induce a homomorphism

$$\partial_p^{(L,L_0)} \colon C_p(L, L_0) \to C_{p-1}(L, L_0) \,.$$

As before, we have $\partial_p^{(L,L_0)} \circ \partial_{p+1}^{(L,L_0)} = 0$. Writing $Z_p(L, L_0) = \ker \partial_p^{(L,L_0)}$ for *relative cycles* and $B_p(L, L_0) = \operatorname{im} \partial_{p+1}^{(L,L_0)}$ for *relative boundaries*, we obtain the *relative homology group*

$H_p(L, L_0) = Z_p(L, L_0)/B_p(L, L_0)$. Sometimes, to distinguish it from relative homology, the usual homology $H_p(L)$ is called the *absolute homology group* of L.

2.2 Total unimodularity and optimization

Recall that a matrix is *totally unimodular* (TU) if the determinant of each square submatrix is 0, 1, or −1. The significance of total unimodularity in our setting is due to the following result:

THEOREM 1. *[23] Let A be an $m \times n$ totally unimodular matrix and* $\mathbf{b}$ *an integral vector, i.e.,* $\mathbf{b} \in \mathbb{Z}^m$. *Then the polyhedron* $\mathcal{P} := \{\mathbf{x} \in \mathbb{R}^n \mid A\mathbf{x} = \mathbf{b},\ \mathbf{x} \geq \mathbf{0}\}$ *is integral meaning that $\mathcal{P}$ is the convex hull of the integral vectors contained in $\mathcal{P}$. In particular, the extreme points (vertices) of $\mathcal{P}$ are integral. Similarly the polyhedron* $\mathcal{Q} := \{\mathbf{x} \in \mathbb{R}^n \mid A\mathbf{x} \geq \mathbf{b}\}$ *is integral.*

The following corollary shows why the above result is significant for optimization problems. Consider an integral vector $\mathbf{b} \in \mathbb{Z}^m$ and a real vector of cost coefficients $\mathbf{f} \in \mathbb{R}^n$. Consider the *integer* linear program

$$\min \mathbf{f}^T\mathbf{x} \quad \text{subject to} \quad A\mathbf{x} = \mathbf{b},\ \mathbf{x} \geq \mathbf{0} \text{ and } \mathbf{x} \in \mathbb{Z}^n. \quad (1)$$

COROLLARY 2. *Let A be a totally unimodular matrix. Then the integer linear program (1) can be solved in time polynomial in the dimensions of A.*

PROOF. Relax the integer linear program (1) to a linear program by removing the integrality constraint $\mathbf{x} \in \mathbb{Z}^n$. Then an interior point method for solving linear programs will find a real solution $\mathbf{x}^*$ in polynomial time [15] if it exists, and indicates the unboundedness or infeasibility of the linear program otherwise. In fact, since the matrix A has entries 0, 1 or −1, one can solve the linear program in strongly polynomial time [21, 22]. That is, the number of arithmetic operations do not depend on $\mathbf{b}$ and $\mathbf{f}$ and solely depends on the dimension of A. One still needs to show that the solution $\mathbf{x}^*$ is integral.

If the solution is unique then it lies at a vertex of the polyhedron $\mathcal{P}$ and thus it will be integral because of Theorem 1. If the optimal solution set is a face of $\mathcal{P}$ which is not a vertex then an interior point method may at first find a non-integral solution. However, by [1, Corollary 2.2] the polyhedron $\mathcal{P}$ must have at least one vertex. Then, by [1, Theorem 2.8] if the optimal cost is finite, there exists a vertex of $\mathcal{P}$ where that optimal cost is achieved. Following the procedure described in [12], starting from the possibly non-integral solution obtained by an interior point method one can find such an integral optimal solution at a vertex in polynomial time. □

3. PROBLEM FORMULATION

Let K be a finite simplicial complex of dimension p or more. Given an integer valued p-chain $x = \sum_{i=0}^{m-1} x(\sigma_i)\,\sigma_i$ we use $\mathbf{x} \in \mathbb{Z}^m$ to denote the vector formed by the coefficients $x(\sigma_i)$. Thus $\mathbf{x}$ is the representation of the chain x in the elementary p-chain basis and we will use $\mathbf{x}$ and x interchangeably. For a vector $\mathbf{v} \in \mathbb{R}^m$ the *1-norm* (or ℓ^1-norm) $\|\mathbf{v}\|_1$ is defined to be $\sum_i |v_i|$. Let W be any real $m \times m$ diagonal matrix with diagonal entries w_i. Then the 1-norm of $W\mathbf{v}$, that is, $\|W\mathbf{v}\|_1$ is $\sum_i |w_i||v_i|$. (If W is a general $m \times m$ nonsingular matrix then $\|W\mathbf{v}\|_1$ is called the *weighted 1-norm* of $\mathbf{v}$.) The norm or weighted norm of an integral vector $\mathbf{v} \in \mathbb{Z}^m$ is defined by considering $\mathbf{v}$ to be in $\mathbb{R}^m$. We now state in words the problem of optimal homologous chains and later formalize it in (2):

> Given a p-chain $\mathbf{c}$ in K and a diagonal matrix W of appropriate dimension, the optimal homologous chain problem (OHCP) is to find a chain $\mathbf{c}^*$ which has the minimal 1-norm $\|W\mathbf{c}^*\|_1$ among all chains homologous to $\mathbf{c}$.

REMARK 3. *The natural case where simplices are weighted and the optimality of the chains is to be determined with respect to these weights, we may take W to be diagonal with w_i being the weight of simplex σ_i. In our formulation some of the weights can be 0. Notice that the signs of the simplex weights are ignored in our formulation since we only work with norms.*

REMARK 4. *In Section 1 we surveyed the computational topology literature on the problem of finding optimal homologous* cycles. *The flexibility of our formulation allows us to solve the more general, optimal homologous* chain *problem, with the cycle case being a special case requiring no modification in the equations, algorithm, or theorems.*

REMARK 5. *The choice of 1-norm is important. At first, it might seem easier to pose OHCP using 2-norm. Since then, when OHCP is formulated with only equality constraints as in (2), calculus can be used to pose the minimization as a stationary point problem, which can be solved as a linear system of equations. By using 1-norm instead of 2-norm, we have to solve a linear program (as we will show below) instead of a linear system. But in return, we are able to get integer valued solutions when the appropriate conditions are satisfied.*

The formulation of OHCP is the *weighted ℓ^1-optimization* of homologous chains. This is very general and allows for different types of optimality to be achieved by choosing different weight matrices. For example, assume that the simplicial complex K of dimension greater than p is embedded in $\mathbb{R}^d$, where $d \geq p + 1$. Let W be a diagonal matrix with the i-th diagonal entry being the Euclidean p-dimensional volume of a p-simplex. This specializes the problem to the *Euclidean ℓ^1-optimization* problem. The resulting optimal chain has the smallest p-dimensional volume amongst all chains homologous to the given one. If W is taken to be the identity matrix, with appropriate additional conditions to the above formulation, one can solve the *ℓ^0-optimization* problem. The resulting optimal solution has the smallest *number* of p-simplices amongst all chains homologous to $\mathbf{c}$, as we show in Section 3.2.

The central idea of this paper consists of the following steps: (i) write OHCP as an integer program involving 1-norm minimization, subject to linear constraints; (ii) convert the integer program into an integer *linear* program by converting the 1-norm cost function to a linear one using the standard technique of introducing some extra variables and constraints; (iii) find the conditions under which the constraint matrix of the integer linear program is totally unimodular; and (iv) for this class of problems, relax the integer linear program to a linear program by dropping the constraint that the variables be integral. The resulting optimal chain obtained by solving the linear program will be an integer valued chain homologous to the given chain.

3.1 Optimal homologous chains and linear programming

Now we formally pose OHCP as an optimization problem. After showing existence of solutions we reformulate the optimization problem as an integer linear program and eventually as a linear program.

Assume that the number of p- and $(p+1)$-simplices in K is m and n respectively and let W be a diagonal $m \times m$ matrix. Given an integer valued p-chain $\mathbf{c}$ the optimal homologous chain problem is to solve:

$$\boxed{\begin{aligned}&\min_{\mathbf{x},\mathbf{y}} \|W\,\mathbf{x}\|_1 \quad \text{such that}\\ &\qquad \mathbf{x} = \mathbf{c} + [\partial_{p+1}]\,\mathbf{y},\ \text{and}\ \mathbf{x} \in \mathbb{Z}^m,\ \mathbf{y} \in \mathbb{Z}^n\,.\end{aligned}} \tag{2}$$

In the problem formulation (2) we have given no indication of the algorithm that will be used to solve the problem. Before we develop the computational side, it is important to show that a solution to this problem always exists.

CLAIM 6. *For any given p-chain $\mathbf{c}$ and any matrix W, the solution to problem (2) exists.*

PROOF. Define the set

$$U_{\mathbf{c}} := \{\|W\,\mathbf{x}\|_1 \mid \mathbf{x} = \mathbf{c} + [\partial_{p+1}]\,\mathbf{y},\ \mathbf{x} \in \mathbb{Z}^m \text{ and } \mathbf{y} \in \mathbb{Z}^n\}\,.$$

We show that this set has a minimum which is contained in the set. Consider the subset $U'_{\mathbf{c}} \subseteq U_{\mathbf{c}}$ defined by

$$\begin{aligned}U'_{\mathbf{c}} = \{\|W\,\mathbf{x}\|_1 \mid \|W\,\mathbf{x}\|_1 \le \|W\,\mathbf{c}\|_1,\\ \mathbf{x} = \mathbf{c} + [\partial_{p+1}]\,\mathbf{y},\ \mathbf{x} \in \mathbb{Z}^m \text{ and } \mathbf{y} \in \mathbb{Z}^n\}\,.\end{aligned}$$

This set $U'_{\mathbf{c}}$ is finite since $\mathbf{x}$ is integral. Therefore, $\inf U_{\mathbf{c}} = \inf U'_{\mathbf{c}} = \min U'_{\mathbf{c}}$. □

In the rest of this paper we assume that W is a diagonal matrix obtained from *weights* on simplices as follows. Let w be a real-valued weight function on the oriented p-simplices of K and let W be the corresponding diagonal matrix (the i-th diagonal entry of W is $w(\sigma_i) = w_i$).

The resulting objective function $\|W\,\mathbf{x}\|_1 = \sum_i |w_i|\,|x_i|$ in (2) is not linear in x_i. It is however, piecewise-linear in these variables. As a result, (2) can be reformulated as an integer *linear* program in the following standard way [1, page 18]:

$$\begin{aligned}\min\ & \sum_i |w_i|\,(x_i^+ + x_i^-)\\ \text{subject to}\ & \mathbf{x}^+ - \mathbf{x}^- = \mathbf{c} + [\partial_{p+1}]\,\mathbf{y}\\ & \mathbf{x}^+,\, \mathbf{x}^- \ge \mathbf{0}\\ & \mathbf{x}^+,\, \mathbf{x}^- \in \mathbb{Z}^m,\ \mathbf{y} \in \mathbb{Z}^n\,.\end{aligned} \tag{3}$$

Comparing the above formulation to the standard form integer linear program in (1), note that the vector $\mathbf{x}$ in (1) corresponds to $[\mathbf{x}^+, \mathbf{x}^-, \mathbf{y}]^T$ in (3) above. Thus the minimization is over $\mathbf{x}^+$, $\mathbf{x}^-$ and $\mathbf{y}$, and the coefficients of x_i^+ and x_i^- in the objective function are $|w_i|$, but the coefficients corresponding to y_j are zero. The linear programming relaxation of this formulation just removes the constraints about the variables being integral. The resulting linear program is:

$$\begin{aligned}\min\ & \sum_i |w_i|\,(x_i^+ + x_i^-)\\ \text{subject to}\ & \mathbf{x}^+ - \mathbf{x}^- = \mathbf{c} + [\partial_{p+1}]\,\mathbf{y}\\ & \mathbf{x}^+,\, \mathbf{x}^- \ge \mathbf{0}\,.\end{aligned} \tag{4}$$

To use the result about standard form polyhedron in Theorem 1 we can eliminate the free (unrestricted in sign) variables $\mathbf{y}$ by replacing these by $\mathbf{y}^+ - \mathbf{y}^-$ and imposing the non-negativity constraints on the new variables [1, page 5]. The resulting linear program has the same objective function, and the equality constraints:

$$\mathbf{x}^+ - \mathbf{x}^- = \mathbf{c} + [\partial_{p+1}]\,(\mathbf{y}^+ - \mathbf{y}^-)\,, \tag{5}$$

and thus the equality constraint matrix is $\begin{bmatrix} I & -I & -B & B\end{bmatrix}$, where $B = [\partial_{p+1}]$. We now prove a result about the total unimodularity of this matrix.

LEMMA 7. *If $B = [\partial_{p+1}]$ is totally unimodular then so is the matrix $\begin{bmatrix} I & -I & -B & B\end{bmatrix}$.*

PROOF. The proof uses operations that preserve the total unimodularity of a matrix. These are listed in [15, page 280]. If B is totally unimodular then so is the matrix $\begin{bmatrix} -B & B\end{bmatrix}$ since scalar multiples of columns of B are being appended on the left to get this matrix. The full matrix in question can be obtained from this one by appending columns with a single ± 1 on the left, which proves the result. □

As a result of Corollary 2 and Lemma 7, we have the following *algorithmic* result.

THEOREM 8. *If the boundary matrix $[\partial_{p+1}]$ of a finite simplicial complex of dimension greater than p is totally unimodular, the optimal homologous chain problem (2) for p-chains can be solved in polynomial time.*

PROOF. We have seen above that a reformulation of OHCP (2), without the integrality constraints, leads to the linear program (4). By Lemma 7, the equality constraint matrix of this linear program is totally unimodular. Then by Corollary 2 the linear program (4) can be solved in polynomial time, while achieving an integral solution. □

REMARK 9. *One may wonder why Theorem 8 does not work when $\mathbb{Z}_2$-valued chains are considered instead of integer-valued chains. We could simulate $\mathbb{Z}_2$ arithmetic while using integers or reals by modifying (2) as follows:*

$$\begin{aligned}&\min_{\mathbf{x},\mathbf{y}} \|W\,\mathbf{x}\|_1 \quad \textit{such that} \quad \mathbf{x} + 2\,\mathbf{u} = \mathbf{c} + [\partial_{p+1}]\,\mathbf{y},\\ &\quad \textit{and} \quad \mathbf{x} \in \{0,1\}^m,\ \mathbf{u} \in \mathbb{Z}^m,\ \mathbf{y} \in \mathbb{Z}^n\,.\end{aligned} \tag{6}$$

The trouble is that the coefficient 2 of $\mathbf{u}$ destroys the total unimodularity of the constraint matrix in the linear programming relaxation of the above formulation, even when $[\partial_{p+1}]$ is totally unimodular. Thus we cannot solve the above integer program as a linear program and still get integer solutions.

REMARK 10. *We can associate weights with $(p+1)$-simplices while formulating the optimization problem (2). Then, we could minimize $\|W\mathbf{z}\|_1$ where $\mathbf{z} = [\mathbf{x}, \mathbf{y}]^T$. In that case, we obtain a p-chain c^* homologous to the given chain c and also a $(p+1)$-chain d whose boundary is $c^* - c$ and the weights of c^* and d together are the smallest. If the given cycle c is null homologous, the optimal y would be an optimal $(p+1)$-chain bounded by c.*

REMARK 11. *The simplex method and its variants search only the basic feasible solutions (vertices of the constraint polyhedron), while choosing ones that never make the objective function worse. Thus if the polyhedron is integral, one could stop the simplex method at any step before reaching optimality and still obtain an integer valued homologous chain whose norm is no worse than that of the given chain.*

3.2 Minimizing the number of simplices

The general weighted ℓ^1-optimization problem (2) can be specialized by choosing different weight matrices. One can also solve variations of the OHCP problem by adding other constraints which do not destroy the total unimodularity of the constraint matrix. We consider one such specialization here – that of finding a homologous chain with the smallest *number* of simplices.

If the matrix W is chosen to be the identity matrix, then one can solve the ℓ^0-optimization problem by solving a modified version of the ℓ^1-optimization problem (2). One just imposes the extra condition that every entry of $\mathbf{c}$ and $\mathbf{x}$ be in $\{-1, 0, 1\}$. With this choice of $W = I$ and with $\mathbf{c} \in \{-1, 0, 1\}^m$, the problem (2) becomes:

$$\min_{\mathbf{x},\mathbf{y}} \|\mathbf{x}\|_1 \quad \text{such that} \\ \mathbf{x} = \mathbf{c} + [\partial_{p+1}]\,\mathbf{y}, \text{ and } \mathbf{x} \in \{-1,0,1\}^m,\ \mathbf{y} \in \mathbb{Z}^n . \tag{7}$$

THEOREM 12. *For any given p-chain $\mathbf{c} \in \{-1, 0, 1\}^m$, a solution to problem (7) exists. Furthermore, amongst all $\mathbf{x}$ homologous to $\mathbf{c}$, the optimal homologous chain $\mathbf{x}^*$ has the smallest number of nonzero entries, that is, it is the ℓ^0-optimal homologous chain.*

PROOF. The proof of existence is identical to the proof of Claim 6. The condition that $\mathbf{c}$ takes values in -1, 0, 1 ensures that at least $\mathbf{x} = \mathbf{c}$ can be taken as the solution if no other homologous chain exists. For the ℓ^0-optimality, note that since the entries of the optimal solution $\mathbf{x}^*$ are constrained to be in $\{-1, 0, 1\}$, the 1-norm measures the number of nonzero entries. Thus the 1-norm optimal solution is also the one with the smallest number of non-zero entries. □

REMARK 13. *Note that even with the given chain $\mathbf{c}$ taking values in $\{-1, 0, 1\}$, without the extra constraint that $\mathbf{x} \in \{-1, 0, 1\}^m$ (rather than just $\mathbf{x} \in \mathbb{Z}^m$), the optimal 1-norm solution components may take values outside $\{-1, 0, 1\}$. For example, consider the simplicial complex K triangulating a cylinder which is shaped like an hourglass. Let c_1 and c_2 be the two boundary cycles of the hour glass so that $c_1 + c_2$ is not trivial. Let z be the smallest cycle around the middle of the hour glass which is homologous to each of c_1 and c_2. Since $c_1 + c_2 = 2z$, the optimal cycle homologous to $c_1 + c_2$ has values 2 or -2 for some edges even if c_1 and c_2 have values only in $\{-1, 0, 1\}$ for all edges. It may or may not be true that the number of nonzero entries is minimal in such an optimal solution. We have not proved it either way. But Theorem 12 provides a guarantee for computing ℓ^0-optimal solution when the additional constraints are placed on $\mathbf{x}$.*

The linear programming relaxation of problem (7) is

$$\begin{aligned} \min\ & \sum_i (x_i^+ + x_i^-) \\ \text{subject to}\ \ & \mathbf{x}^+ - \mathbf{x}^- = \mathbf{c} + [\partial_{p+1}]\,\mathbf{y} \\ & \mathbf{x}^+, \mathbf{x}^- \le \mathbf{1} \\ & \mathbf{x}^+, \mathbf{x}^- \ge \mathbf{0} . \end{aligned} \tag{8}$$

One can show the integrality of the feasible set polyhedron by using slack variables to convert the inequalities $\mathbf{x}^+ \le \mathbf{1}$ and $\mathbf{x}^- \le \mathbf{1}$ to equalities and then using the $\mathcal{P}$ form of the polyhedron from Theorem 1. Equivalently, all the constraints can be written as inequalities and the $\mathcal{Q}$ polyhedron can be used. For a change we choose the latter method here. Writing the constraints as inequalities, in matrix form the constraints are

$$\begin{bmatrix} -I & I & B & -B \\ I & -I & -B & B \\ -I & 0 & 0 & 0 \\ 0 & -I & 0 & 0 \\ I & 0 & 0 & 0 \\ 0 & I & 0 & 0 \\ 0 & 0 & I & 0 \\ 0 & 0 & 0 & I \end{bmatrix} \begin{bmatrix} \mathbf{x}^+ \\ \mathbf{x}^- \\ \mathbf{y}^+ \\ \mathbf{y}^- \end{bmatrix} \ge \begin{bmatrix} -\mathbf{c} \\ \mathbf{c} \\ -\mathbf{1} \\ -\mathbf{1} \\ \mathbf{0} \\ \mathbf{0} \\ \mathbf{0} \\ \mathbf{0} \end{bmatrix}, \tag{9}$$

where $B = [\partial_{p+1}]$. Then analogously to Lemma 7 and Theorem 8 the following are true.

LEMMA 14. *If $B = [\partial_{p+1}]$ is totally unimodular then so is the constraint matrix in (9).*

THEOREM 15. *If the boundary matrix $[\partial_{p+1}]$ of a finite simplicial complex of dimension greater than p is totally unimodular, then given a p-chain that takes values in $\{-1, 0, 1\}$, a homologous p-chain with the smallest number of non-zeros taking values in $\{-1, 0, 1\}$ can be found in polynomial time.*

In subsequent sections, we characterize the simplicial complexes for which the boundary matrix $[\partial_{p+1}]$ is totally unimodular. These are the main theoretical results of this paper, formalized as Theorems 16, 18, and 23.

4. MANIFOLDS

Our results in Section 5.1 are valid for *any* finite simplicial complex. But first we consider a simpler case – simplicial complexes that are triangulations of manifolds. We show that for finite triangulations of compact p-dimensional *orientable* manifolds, the top non-trivial boundary matrix $[\partial_p]$ is totally unimodular irrespective of the orientations of its simplices. We also give examples of non-orientable manifolds where total unimodularity does not hold. Further examination of why total unimodularity does not hold in these cases leads to our main results in Theorems 18.

4.1 Orientable manifolds

Let K be a finite simplicial complex that triangulates a $(p+1)$-dimensional compact orientable manifold M. As before, let $[\partial_{p+1}]$ be the matrix corresponding to $\partial_{p+1} : C_{p+1}(K) \to C_p(K)$ in the elementary chain bases.

THEOREM 16. *For a finite simplicial complex triangulating a $(p+1)$-dimensional compact orientable manifold, $[\partial_{p+1}]$ is totally unimodular irrespective of the orientations of the simplices.*

PROOF. First, we prove the theorem assuming that the $(p+1)$-dimensional simplices of K are oriented *consistently*. Then, we argue that the result still holds when orientations are arbitrary.

Consistent orientation of $(p+1)$-simplices means that they are oriented in such a way that for the $(p+1)$-chain c, which takes the value 1 on each oriented $(p+1)$-simplex in K, $\partial_{p+1} c$ is carried by the topological boundary ∂M of M. If M has no boundary then $\partial_{p+1} c$ is 0. It is known that consistent orientation of $(p+1)$-simplices always exists for a finite triangulation of a compact orientable manifold. Therefore, assume that the given triangulation has consistent orientation for the $(p+1)$-simplices. The orientation of the p- and lower dimensional simplices can be chosen arbitrarily.

Each p-face τ is the face of either one or two $(p+1)$-simplices (depending on whether τ is a boundary face or not). Thus the row of $[\partial_{p+1}]$ corresponding to τ contains one or two nonzeros. Such a nonzero entry is 1 if the orientation of τ agrees with that of the corresponding $(p+1)$-simplex and -1 if it does not.

Heller and Tompkins [13] gave a sufficient condition for the unimodularity of $\{-1,0,1\}$-matrices whose columns have no more than two nonzero entries. Such a matrix is TU if its rows can be divided into two partitions (one possibly empty) with the following condition. If two nonzeros in a column belong to the same partition, they must be of opposite signs, otherwise they must be in different row partitions. Consider $[\partial_{p+1}]^T$, the transpose of $[\partial_{p+1}]$. Each column of $[\partial_{p+1}]^T$ contains at most two nonzero entries, and if there are two then they are of opposite signs because of the consistent orientations of the $(p+1)$-dimensional simplices. In this case, the simple division of rows into two partitions with one containing all rows and the other empty works. Thus $[\partial_{p+1}]^T$ and hence $[\partial_{p+1}]$ is totally unimodular.

Now, reversing the orientation of a $(p+1)$-simplex means that the corresponding column of $[\partial_{p+1}]$ be multiplied by -1. This column operation preserves the total unimodularity of $[\partial_{p+1}]$. Since any arbitrary orientation of the $(p+1)$-simplices can be obtained by preserving or reversing their orientations in a consistent orientation, we have the result as claimed. □

As a result of the above theorem and Theorem 8 we have the following result.

COROLLARY 17. *For a finite simplicial complex triangulating a $(p+1)$-dimensional compact orientable manifold, the optimal homologous chain problem can be solved for p-dimensional chains in polynomial time.*

The result in Corollary 17 when specialized to $\mathbb{R}^{p+1}$ also appears in [19] though the reasoning is different.

4.2 Non-orientable manifolds

For non-orientable manifolds we give two examples which show that total unimodularity may not hold in this case. We also discuss the role of torsion in these examples in preparation for Theorem 18.

Our first example is the Möbius strip and the second one is the projective plane. Simplicial complexes for these two non-orientable surfaces are shown in Figure 1. The boundary matrices $[\partial_2]$ for these simplicial complexes are given in the Appendix in (11) and (12).

Let M be the Möbius strip. We consider its absolute homology $H_1(M)$ and its relative homology $H_1(M, \partial M)$ relative to its boundary. Consult [14, page 135] to see how the various homology groups are calculated using an exact sequence. We note that $H_1(M) \cong \mathbb{Z}$, that is, its H_1 group has no torsion. This can be seen by reducing the matrix (11) in the Appendix to Smith normal form (SNF). The SNF for the matrix consists of a 6×6 identity matrix on the top and a zero block below, which implies the absence of torsion.

Let K be the simplicial complex triangulating M. Consider a submatrix S of the matrix $[\partial_2]$ shown in Appendix as (11). This submatrix is formed by selecting the columns in the order 5, 4, 3, 2, 1, 0. From the matrix thus formed, select the rows 0, 3, 8, 9, 10, 2 in that order. This selection of rows and columns corresponds to all the triangles and the edges encountered as one goes from left to right in the Möbius triangulation shown in Figure 1. The resulting submatrix is :

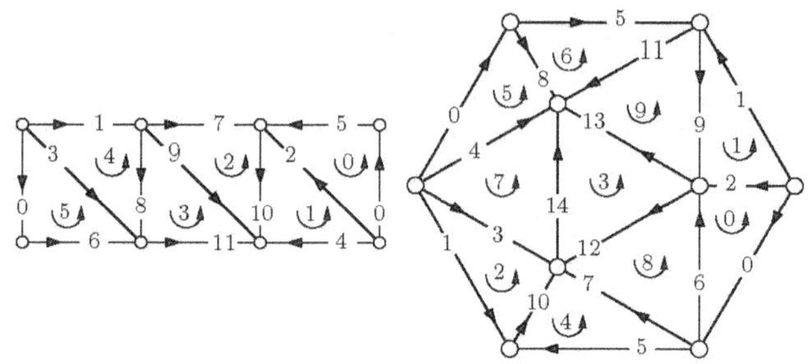

Figure 1: Triangulations of two non-orientable manifolds, shown as abstract simplicial complexes. The left figure shows a triangulation of the Möbius strip and the right one shows the projective plane. The numbers are the edge and triangles numbers. These correspond to the row and column numbers of the matrices (11) and (12).

$$S = \begin{bmatrix} 1 & 0 & 0 & 0 & 0 & 1 \\ -1 & 1 & 0 & 0 & 0 & 0 \\ 0 & -1 & 1 & 0 & 0 & 0 \\ 0 & 0 & -1 & 1 & 0 & 0 \\ 0 & 0 & 0 & -1 & 1 & 0 \\ 0 & 0 & 0 & 0 & 1 & -1 \end{bmatrix}$$

The determinant of this matrix is -2 and this shows that the boundary matrix is not totally unimodular. The SNF for this matrix, it turns out, *does* reveal the torsion. This matrix S is the relative boundary matrix $\partial_2^{(L,L_0)}$ where $L = K$ and L_0 are the edges in ∂M. The SNF has 1's along the diagonal and finally a 2. This is an example where there is no torsion in the absolute homology but some torsion in the relative homology and the boundary matrix is not totally unimodular. We formulate this condition precisely in Theorem 18.

The matrix $[\partial_2]$ given in Appendix as (12) for the projective plane triangulation is much larger. But it is easy to find a submatrix with determinant greater than 1. This can be done by finding the Möbius strip in the triangulation of the projective plane. For example if one traverses from top to bottom in the triangulation of the projective plane in Figure 1 the triangles encountered correspond to columns 6, 9, 3, 8, 4 of (12) and the edges correspond to rows 5, 11, 13, 12, 7. The corresponding submatrix is

$$S = \begin{bmatrix} -1 & 0 & 0 & 0 & -1 \\ -1 & 1 & 0 & 0 & 0 \\ 0 & -1 & 1 & 0 & 0 \\ 0 & 0 & -1 & 1 & 0 \\ 0 & 0 & 0 & -1 & 1 \end{bmatrix}$$

and its determinant is -2. Thus the boundary matrix (12) is not totally unimodular. Again, we observe that there is relative torsion in $H_1(L, L_0)$ for the subcomplexes corresponding to the selection of S from $[\partial_2]$. Here L consists of the triangles specified above, which form a Möbius strip in the projective plane. The subcomplex L_0 consists of the edges forming the boundary of this strip. This connection between submatrices and relative homology is examined in the next section.

5. SIMPLICIAL COMPLEXES

Now we consider the more general case of simplicial complexes. Our result in Theorem 18 characterizes the total unimodularity of boundary matrices for arbitrary simplicial complexes. Since we do not use any conditions about the geometric realization or embedding in $\mathbb{R}^n$ for the complex, the result is also valid for abstract simplicial complexes. As a corollary of the characterization we show that the OHCP can be solved in polynomial time as long as the input complex satisfies a torsion-related condition.

5.1 Total unimodularity and relative torsion

Let K be a finite simplicial complex of dimension greater than p. We will need to refer to its subcomplexes formed by the union of some of its simplices of a specific dimension. This is formalized in the definition below.

Definition 1. A *pure simplicial complex* of dimension p is a simplicial complex formed by a collection of p-simplices and their proper faces. Similarly, a *pure subcomplex* is a subcomplex that is a pure simplicial complex.

An example of a pure simplicial complex of dimension p is one that triangulates a p-dimensional manifold. Another example, relevant to our discussion, is a subcomplex formed by a collection of some p-simplices of a simplicial complex and their lower dimensional faces.

Let $L \subseteq K$ be a pure subcomplex of dimension $p+1$ and $L_0 \subset L$ be a pure subcomplex of dimension p. If $[\partial_{p+1}]$ is the matrix representing $\partial_{p+1} : C_{p+1}(K) \to C_p(K)$, then the matrix representing the relative boundary operator

$$\partial_{p+1}^{(L,L_0)} : C_{p+1}(L, L_0) \to C_p(L, L_0)\,,$$

is obtained by first *including* the columns of $[\partial_{p+1}]$ corresponding to $(p+1)$-simplices in L and then, from the submatrix so obtained, *excluding* the rows corresponding to the p-simplices in L_0 and any zero rows. The zero rows correspond to p-simplices that are not faces of any of the $(p+1)$-simplices of L.

As before, let $[\partial_{p+1}]$ be the matrix of ∂_{p+1} in the elementary chain bases for K. Then the following holds.

THEOREM 18. *$[\partial_{p+1}]$ is totally unimodular if and only if $H_p(L, L_0)$ is torsion-free, for all pure subcomplexes L_0, L of K of dimensions p and $p+1$ respectively, where $L_0 \subset L$.*

PROOF. ($\Rightarrow$) We show that if $H_p(L, L_0)$ has torsion for some L, L_0 then $[\partial_{p+1}]$ is not TU. Let $\left[\partial_{p+1}^{(L,L_0)}\right]$ be the corresponding relative boundary matrix. Bring $\left[\partial_{p+1}^{(L,L_0)}\right]$ to Smith normal form using the reduction algorithm [14][pages 55–57]. This is a block matrix

$$\begin{bmatrix} D & 0 \\ 0 & 0 \end{bmatrix}$$

where $D = \operatorname{diag}(d_1, \ldots, d_l)$ is a diagonal matrix and the block row or column of zero matrices shown above may be empty, depending on the dimension of the matrix. Recall that d_i are integers and $d_i \geq 1$. Moreover, since $H_p(L, L_0)$ has torsion, $d_k > 1$ for some $1 \leq k \leq l$. Thus the product $d_1 \ldots d_k$ is greater than 1. By a result of Smith [17] quoted in [15, page 50], this product is the greatest common divisor of the determinants of all $k \times k$ square submatrices of $\left[\partial_{p+1}^{(L,L_0)}\right]$. But this implies that some square submatrix of $\left[\partial_{p+1}^{(L,L_0)}\right]$, and hence of $[\partial_{p+1}]$, has determinant magnitude greater than 1. Thus $[\partial_{p+1}]$ is not totally unimodular.

($\Leftarrow$) Assume that $[\partial_{p+1}]$ is not totally unimodular. We will show that then there exist subcomplexes L_0 and L of dimensions p and $(p+1)$ respectively, with $L_0 \subset L$, such that $H_p(L, L_0)$ has torsion. Let S be a square submatrix of $[\partial_{p+1}]$ such that $|\det(S)| > 1$. Let L correspond to the columns of $[\partial_{p+1}]$ that are *included* in S and let B_L be the submatrix of $[\partial_{p+1}]$ formed by these columns. This submatrix B_L may contain zero rows. Those zero rows (if any) correspond to p-simplices that do not occur as a face of any of the $(p+1)$-simplices in L. In order to form S from B_L, these zero rows can first be safely discarded to form a submatrix B'_L. This is because $\det(S) \neq 0$ and so these zero rows cannot occur in S.

The rows in B'_L correspond to p-simplices that occur as a face of some $(p+1)$-simplex in L. Let L_0 correspond to rows of B'_L which are *excluded* to form S. Now S is the matrix representation of the relative boundary matrix $\partial_p^{(L,L_0)}$. Reduce S to Smith normal form. The normal form is a square diagonal matrix. Since the elementary row and column operations preserve determinant magnitude, the determinant of the resulting diagonal matrix has magnitude greater than 1. Thus at least one of the diagonal entries in the normal form is greater than 1. But then by [14, page 61] $H_p(L, L_0)$ has torsion. □

REMARK 19. *The characterization appears to be no easier to check than the definition of total unimodularity since it involves checking* every *L, L_0 pair. However, it is also no* harder *to check than total unimodularity. This leads to the following result of possible interest in computational topology and matroid theory.*

COROLLARY 20. *For a simplicial complex K of dimension greater than p, there is a polynomial time algorithm for answering the following question: Is $H_p(L, L_0)$ torsion-free for all subcomplexes L_0 and L of dimensions p and $(p+1)$ such that $L_0 \subset L$?*

PROOF. Seymour's decomposition theorem for totally unimodular matrices [16],[15, Theorem 19.6] yields a polynomial time algorithm for deciding if a matrix is totally unimodular or not [15, Theorem 20.3]. That algorithm applied on the boundary matrix $[\partial_{p+1}]$ proves the above assertion. □

REMARK 21. *Note that the naive algorithm for the above problem is clearly exponential. For every pair L, L_0 one can use a polynomial time algorithm to find the Smith normal form. But the number of L, L_0 pairs is exponential in the number of p and $(p+1)$-simplices of K.*

REMARK 22. *The same polynomial time algorithm answers the question : Does $H_p(L, L_0)$ has torsion for* some *pair L, L_0 ?*

5.2 A special case

In Section 4 we have seen the special case of compact orientable manifolds. We saw that the top dimensional boundary matrix of a finite triangulation of such a manifold is totally unimodular. Now we show another special case for which the boundary matrix is totally unimodular and hence OHCP is polynomial time solvable. This case occurs when we ask for optimal d-chains in a simplicial complex K which is embedded in $\mathbb{R}^{d+1}$. In particular, OHCP can be solved by linear programming for 2-chains in 3-complexes embedded in $\mathbb{R}^3$. This follows from the following result:

THEOREM 23. *Let K be a finite simplicial complex embedded in $\mathbb{R}^{d+1}$. Then, $H_d(L, L_0)$ is torsion-free for all pure subcomplexes L_0 and L of dimensions d and $d+1$ respectively, such that $L_0 \subset L$.*

PROOF. We consider the $(d+1)$-dimensional relative *cohomology group* $H^{d+1}(L, L_0)$ (See [14] for example). It follows from the Universal Coefficient Theorem for cohomology [14, Theorem 53.1] that

$$H^{d+1}(L, L_0) = \mathrm{Hom}(H_{d+1}(L, L_0), \mathbb{Z}) \oplus \mathrm{Ext}(H_d(L, L_0), \mathbb{Z})$$

where Hom is the group of all homomorphisms from $H_{d+1}(L, L_0)$ to $\mathbb{Z}$ and Ext is the group of all of extensions between $H_d(L, L_0)$ and $\mathbb{Z}$. These definitions can be found in [14, Chapter 5 and 7]. The main observation is that if $H_d(L, L_0)$ has torsion, $\mathrm{Ext}(H_d(L, L_0), \mathbb{Z})$ has torsion and hence $H^{d+1}(L, L_0)$ has torsion.

On the other hand, by Alexander Spanier duality [18, page 296]

$$H^{d+1}(L, L_0) = H_0(\mathbb{R}^{d+1} \setminus |L_0|, \mathbb{R}^{d+1} \setminus |L|)$$

where $|L|$ denotes the underlying space of L. Since 0-dimensional homology groups cannot have torsion, $H^{d+1}(L, L_0)$ cannot have torsion. We reach a contradiction. □

COROLLARY 24. *Given a d-chain c in a weighted finite simplicial complex embedded in $\mathbb{R}^{d+1}$, an optimal chain homologous to c can be computed by a linear program.*

PROOF. Follows from Theorem 23, Theorem 18, and Theorem 2. □

5.3 Total unimodularity and Möbius complexes

As a second special case, we provide a necessary condition for total unimodularity of the boundary matrix. We introduce the notion of higher dimensional generalizations of cylinder surface and Möbius strip. We also define matrices that characterize these complexes as relative boundary matrices. It is then easy to see that the presence of a Möbius subcomplex in the given complex implies that the boundary matrix can not be totally unimodular. Thus the absence of Möbius subcomplexes is a necessary condition for total unimodularity.

Definition 2. A $(p+1)$-dimensional *cycle complex* is a sequence $\sigma_0, \ldots, \sigma_{k-1}$ of $(p+1)$-simplices such that σ_i and σ_j have a common face if and only if $j = (i+1) \pmod{k}$ and that common face is a p-simplex. Such a cycle complex triangulates a $(p+1)$-manifold. We call it a $(p+1)$-dimensional *cylinder complex* if it is orientable and a $(p+1)$-dimensional *Möbius complex* if it is nonorientable.

Definition 3. A $k \times k$ matrix C is called a *k-cycle matrix (k-CM)* if either

(a) $k \geq 2$, $C_{ij} \in \{-1, 0, 1\}$, and C has the following form up to row and column permutations and scalings by -1:

$$C = \begin{bmatrix} 1 & 0 & 0 & \cdots & 0 & 0 & \alpha \\ 1 & 1 & 0 & \cdots & 0 & 0 & 0 \\ 0 & 1 & 1 & \cdots & 0 & 0 & 0 \\ \vdots & \vdots & \vdots & \ddots & \vdots & \vdots & \vdots \\ 0 & 0 & 0 & \cdots & 1 & 0 & 0 \\ 0 & 0 & 0 & \cdots & 1 & 1 & 0 \\ 0 & 0 & 0 & \cdots & 0 & 1 & 1 \end{bmatrix}, \ \alpha = \pm 1; \qquad (10)$$

or

(b) $k = 1$, and $C = \begin{bmatrix} 0 \end{bmatrix}$ or $C = \begin{bmatrix} 2 \end{bmatrix}$.

For $k \geq 2$, a k-CM with $\alpha = (-1)^k$ is termed a *cylinder cycle matrix* (k-CCM), while one with $\alpha = (-1)^{k+1}$ is termed a *Möbius cycle matrix* (k-MCM). For $k = 1$, $\begin{bmatrix} 0 \end{bmatrix}$ is the 1-CCM, and $\begin{bmatrix} 2 \end{bmatrix}$ is the 1-MCM. We will refer to the form shown in (10) as the *normal form* cycle matrix.

As an example, consider a Möbius strip K triangulated with k triangles shown in Figure 2, with $k \geq 5$. Let K_0 be the edge of the Möbius strip. In the figure, K_0 consists of the horizontal edges. Then the relative boundary matrix $\left[\partial_2^{(K,K_0)}\right]$ of the Möbius strip K modulo its edge K_0 is a k-MCM. The orientations of triangle τ_{k-1} and that of the terminal edge e_0 are opposite if k is even, but the orientations agree if k is odd, giving $\alpha = (-1)^{k+1}$. Note that in Section 4.2, the submatrix S of the boundary matrix of the Möbius strip was such a relative boundary matrix and it is an example of a 6-MCM. Another example in that section was the 5-MCM obtained from the boundary matrix of the projective plane.

Similarly, we observe a k-CCM as the relative boundary-2 matrix of a cylinder triangulated with k triangles, modulo the cylinder's edges. Reversing the orientation of an edge or a triangle results in scaling the corresponding row or column, respectively, of the boundary matrix by -1. These examples motivate the names "Möbius" and "cylinder" matrices – a cycle matrix can be interpreted as the relative boundary matrix of a Möbius or cylinder complex. So, we have the following result:

LEMMA 25. *Let K be a finite simplicial complex of dimension greater than p. The boundary matrix $[\partial_{p+1}]$ has no k-MCM for any $k \geq 2$ if and only if K does not have any $(p+1)$-dimensional Möbius complex as a subcomplex.*

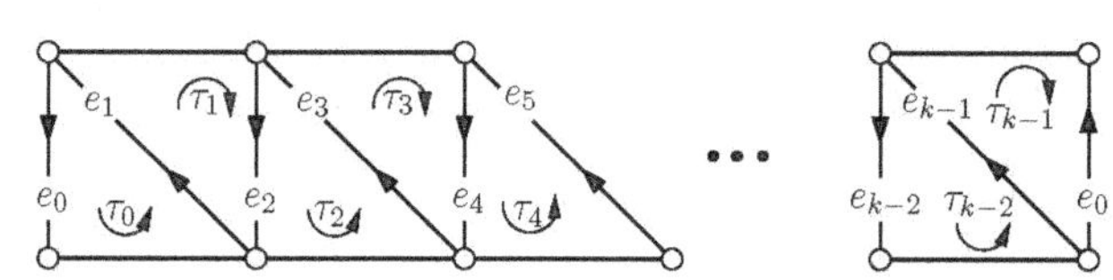

Figure 2: Triangulation of a Möbius strip with k triangles.

It is now easy to see that the absence of Möbius complexes is a necessary condition for total unimodularity. We first need the simple result that an MCM is not totally unimodular.

LEMMA 26. *Let C be a k-CM for any $k \geq 1$. Then $\det C = 0$ if it is a k-CCM, and $|\det C| = 2$ if it is a k-MCM.*

PROOF. If C is not in the normal form it can be brought into that form using a series of row and column exchanges, and scalings by -1. Note that these operations preserve the value of $|\det C|$. Now assume that C has been brought into the normal form and call that matrix C'. When $k \geq 2$, we expand along the first row of C' to get $\det C' = 1 + (-1)^{k+1}\alpha$, and the claim follows. The result holds trivially for the case of $k = 1$. □

THEOREM 27. *If the simplicial complex K of dimension greater than p has a Möbius subcomplex of dimension $p+1$ then $[\partial_{p+1}]$ is not totally unimodular.*

PROOF. If there is a Möbius subcomplex then by Lemma 25 an MCM appears as a submatrix of $[\partial_{p+1}]$. That MCM matrix is trivially the certificate for $[\partial_{p+1}]$ being not totally unimodular, since by Lemma 26, its determinant has magnitude 2. □

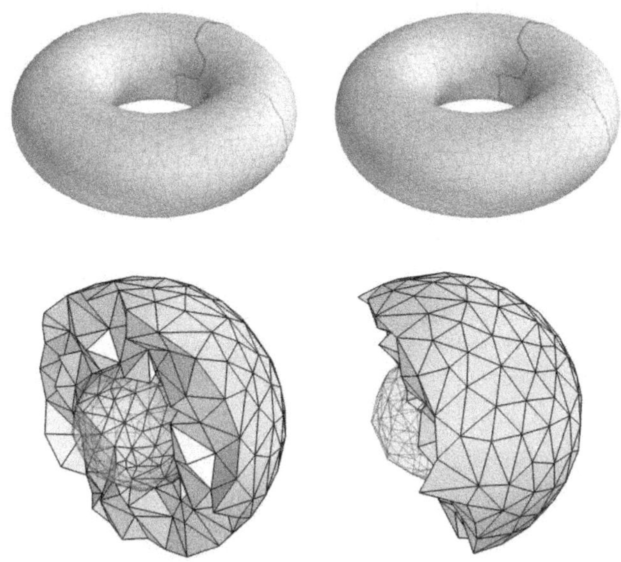

Figure 3: Some experimental results.

6. EXPERIMENTAL RESULTS

We have implemented our linear programming method to solve the optimal homologous chain problem. In Figure 3 we show some results of preliminary experiments.

The top row shows the computation of optimal homologous 1-chains on the simplicial complex representation of a torus. The longer chain in each torus figure is the initial chain and the tighter shorter chain is the optimal homologous chain computed by our algorithm. The bottom row shows the result of the computation of an optimal 2-chain on a simplicial complex of dimension 3. The complex is the tetrahedral triangulation of a solid annulus – a solid ball from which a smaller ball has been removed. Two cut-away views are shown. The outer surface of the sphere is the initial chain and the inner surface is computed as the optimal 2-chain.

7. DISCUSSION

Several questions crop up from our problem formulation and results. Instead of 1-norm $\|W\mathbf{x}\|_1$, we can consider minimizing $\sum_i w_i x_i$. In this case, the weights appear with signs and solutions may be unbounded. Nevertheless, our result in Theorem 8 remains valid. Of course, in this case we do not need to introduce x_i^+ and x_i^- since the objective function uses x_i rather than $|x_i|$. We may introduce more generalization in the OHCP formulation by considering a general matrix W instead of requiring it to be diagonal and then asking for minimizing $\|W\mathbf{x}\|_1$. We do not know if the corresponding optimization problem can be solved by a linear program. Can this optimization problem be solved in polynomial time for some interesting classes of complexes?

We showed that OHCP under $\mathbb{Z}$ coefficients can be solved by linear programs for a large class of topological spaces that have no relative torsion. This leaves a question for the cases when there is relative torsion. Is the problem NP-hard under such constraint? Taking the cue from our results, one can also ask the following question. Even though we know that the problem is NP-hard under $\mathbb{Z}_2$ coefficients, is it true that OHCP in this case is polynomial time solvable at least for simplicial complexes that have no relative torsions (considered under $\mathbb{Z}$)? The answer is negative since OHCP for surfaces in $\mathbb{R}^3$ is NP-hard under $\mathbb{Z}_2$ coefficients [3] even though they are known to be torsion-free.

Even if the input complex has relative torsion, the constraint polyhedron of the linear program may still have vertices with integer coordinates. In that case, the linear program may still give an integer solution for chains that steer the optimization path toward such a vertex. In fact, we have observed experimentally that, for some 2-complexes with relative torsion, the linear program finds the integer solution for some input chains. It would be nice to characterize the class of chains for which the linear program still provides a solution even if the input complex has relative torsion.

A related question that has also been investigated recently is the problem of computing an optimal homology basis from a given complex. Again, positive results have been found for low dimensional cases such as surfaces [11] and one dimensional homology for simplicial complexes [5, 9]. The result of Chen and Freedman [4] implies that even this problem is NP-hard for high dimensional cycles under $\mathbb{Z}_2$. What about $\mathbb{Z}$? As in OHCP, would we have any luck here?

Acknowledgments. We acknowledge the helpful discussions with Dan Burghela from OSU mathematics department. Tamal Dey acknowledges the support of NSF grants CCF-0830467 and CCF-0915996. The research of Anil Hirani is funded by NSF CAREER Award, Grant No. DMS-0645604. We acknowledge the opportunity provided by NSF via a New Directions Short Course at the Institute for Mathematics and its Applications (IMA) which initiated the present collaboration of the authors.

8. REFERENCES

[1] D. Bertsimas and J. N. Tsitsiklis. *Introduction to Linear Optimization*. Athena Scientific, Belmont, MA., 1997.

[2] E. W. Chambers, É. C. de Verdière, J. Erickson, F. Lazarus, and K. Whittlesey. Splitting (complicated) surfaces is hard. *Comput. Geom. Theory Appl.*, 41:94–110, 2008.

[3] E. W. Chambers, J. Erickson, and A. Nayyeri. Minimum cuts and shortest homologous cycles. In *25th Ann. Sympos. Comput. Geom.*, pages 377–385, 2009.

[4] C. Chen and D. Freedman. Hardness results for homology localization. In *ACM/SIAM Sympos. Discrete Algorithms*, 2010. to appear.

[5] C. Chen and D. Freedman. Measuring and computing natural generators for homology groups. *Computational Geometry*, 43(2):169 – 181, 2010. Special Issue on the 24th European Workshop on Computational Geometry (EuroCG'08).

[6] É. C. de Verdière and J. Erickson. Tightening non-simple paths and cycles on surfaces. In *Proc. 17th Ann. ACM-SIAM Sympos. Discrete Algorithms*, pages 192–201, 2006.

[7] V. de Silva and R. Ghrist. Homological sensor networks. *Notices of the American Mathematical Society*, 54(1):10–17, 2007.

[8] T. K. Dey, K. Li, J. Sun, and D. Cohen-Steiner. Computing geometry-aware handle and tunnel loops in 3d models. *ACM Trans. Graph.*, 27:1–9, 2008.

[9] T. K. Dey, J. Sun, and Y. Wang. Approximating loops in a shortest homology basis from point data. *arXiv:0909.5654v2[cs.CG]*, page Online, 2009.

[10] H. Edelsbrunner, D. Letscher, and A. Zomorodian. Topological persistence and simplification. *Discrete Comput. Geom.*, 28:511–533, 2002.

[11] J. Erickson and K. Whittlesey. Greedy optimal homotopy and homology generators. In *Proc. 16th Ann. ACM-SIAM Sympos. Discrete Algorithms*, pages 1038–1046, 2005.

[12] O. Güler, D. den Hertog, C. Roos, T. Terlaky, and T. Tsuchiya. Degeneracy in interior point methods for linear programming: a survey. *Annals of Operations Research*, 46-47(1):107–138, March 1993.

[13] I. Heller and C. B. Tompkins. An extension of a theorem of Dantzig's. In H. W. Kuhn and A. W. Tucker, editors, *Linear Inequalities and Related Systems*, Annals of Mathematics Studies, no. 38, pages 247–254. Princeton University Press, Princeton, N.J., 1956.

[14] J. R. Munkres. *Elements of Algebraic Topology*. Addison–Wesley Publishing Company, Menlo Park, 1984.

[15] A. Schrijver. *Theory of Linear and Integer Programming*. Wiley-Interscience Series in Discrete Mathematics. John Wiley & Sons Ltd., Chichester, 1986. A Wiley-Interscience Publication.

[16] P. D. Seymour. Decomposition of regular matroids. *J. Combin. Theory Ser. B*, 28(3):305–359, 1980.

[17] H. J. S. Smith. On systems of linear indeterminate equations and congruences. *Philosophical Transactions of the Royal Society of London*, 151:293–326, 1861.

[18] E. H. Spanier. *Algebraic Topology*. McGraw-Hill Book Co., New York, 1966.

[19] J. Sullivan. A crystalline approximation theorem for hypersurfaces. PhD thesis, Department of Mathematics, Princeton University, 1990.

[20] A. Tahbaz-Salehi and A. Jadbabaie. Distributed coverage verification algorithms in sensor networks without location information. *IEEE Transactions on Automatic Control*, forthcoming, 55(8), August 2010.

[21] E. Tardos. A strongly polynomial minimum cost circulation algorithm. *Combinatorica*, 5(3):247–255, September 1985.

[22] E. Tardos. A strongly polynomial algorithm to solve combinatorial linear programs. *Operataions Research*, 34(2):250–256, March 1986.

[23] A. F. Veinott, Jr. and G. B. Dantzig. Integral extreme points. *SIAM Review*, 10(3):371–372, 1968.

APPENDIX

A. BOUNDARY MATRICES FOR NON-ORIENTABLE SURFACES

The boundary matrices $[\partial_2]$ for the Möbius strip and projective plane triangulations shown in Figure 1 are given below. The row numbers are edge numbers and the column numbers are triangle numbers which are displayed in Figure 1.

$[\partial_2]$ for Möbius strip :

$$\begin{bmatrix} & 0: & 1: & 2: & 3: & 4: & 5: \\ \\ 0: & 1 & 0 & 0 & 0 & 0 & 1 \\ 1: & 0 & 0 & 0 & 0 & -1 & 0 \\ 2: & -1 & 1 & 0 & 0 & 0 & 0 \\ 3: & 0 & 0 & 0 & 0 & 1 & -1 \\ 4: & 0 & -1 & 0 & 0 & 0 & 0 \\ 5: & 1 & 0 & 0 & 0 & 0 & 0 \\ 6: & 0 & 0 & 0 & 0 & 0 & 1 \\ 7: & 0 & 0 & -1 & 0 & 0 & 0 \\ 8: & 0 & 0 & 0 & 1 & -1 & 0 \\ 9: & 0 & 0 & 1 & -1 & 0 & 0 \\ 10: & 0 & 1 & -1 & 0 & 0 & 0 \\ 11: & 0 & 0 & 0 & 1 & 0 & 0 \end{bmatrix} \quad (11)$$

$[\partial_2]$ for projective plane :

$$\begin{bmatrix} & 0: & 1: & 2: & 3: & 4: & 5: & 6: & 7: & 8: & 9: \\ \\ 0: & -1 & 0 & 0 & 0 & 0 & -1 & 0 & 0 & 0 & 0 \\ 1: & 0 & 1 & 1 & 0 & 0 & 0 & 0 & 0 & 0 & 0 \\ 2: & 1 & -1 & 0 & 0 & 0 & 0 & 0 & 0 & 0 & 0 \\ 3: & 0 & 0 & -1 & 0 & 0 & 0 & 0 & 1 & 0 & 0 \\ 4: & 0 & 0 & 0 & 0 & 0 & 1 & 0 & -1 & 0 & 0 \\ 5: & 0 & 0 & 0 & 0 & -1 & 0 & -1 & 0 & 0 & 0 \\ 6: & -1 & 0 & 0 & 0 & 0 & 0 & 0 & 0 & 1 & 0 \\ 7: & 0 & 0 & 0 & 0 & 1 & 0 & 0 & 0 & -1 & 0 \\ 8: & 0 & 0 & 0 & 0 & 0 & -1 & 1 & 0 & 0 & 0 \\ 9: & 0 & 1 & 0 & 0 & 0 & 0 & 0 & 0 & 0 & -1 \\ 10: & 0 & 0 & 1 & 0 & -1 & 0 & 0 & 0 & 0 & 0 \\ 11: & 0 & 0 & 0 & 0 & 0 & 0 & -1 & 0 & 0 & 1 \\ 12: & 0 & 0 & 0 & -1 & 0 & 0 & 0 & 0 & 1 & 0 \\ 13: & 0 & 0 & 0 & 1 & 0 & 0 & 0 & 0 & 0 & -1 \\ 14: & 0 & 0 & 0 & -1 & 0 & 0 & 0 & 1 & 0 & 0 \end{bmatrix} \quad (12)$$

Improving Exhaustive Search Implies Superpolynomial Lower Bounds

Ryan Williams*
IBM Almaden Research Center
650 Harry Road
San Jose, CA 95120
ryanwill@us.ibm.com

ABSTRACT

The P vs NP problem arose from the question of whether exhaustive search is necessary for problems with short verifiable solutions. We still do not know if even a slight algorithmic improvement over exhaustive search is universally possible for all NP problems, and to date no major consequences have been derived from the assumption that such an improvement exists.

We show that there are natural NP and BPP problems for which minor algorithmic improvements over the trivial deterministic simulation already entail lower bounds such as NEXP $\not\subseteq$ P/poly and LOGSPACE $\neq$ NP. These results are especially interesting given that similar improvements *have* been found for many other hard problems. Optimistically, one might hope our results suggest a new path to lower bounds; pessimistically, they show that carrying out the seemingly modest program of finding slightly better algorithms for all search problems may be extremely difficult (if not impossible).

We also prove unconditional superpolynomial time-space lower bounds for improving on exhaustive search: there is a problem verifiable with $k(n)$ length witnesses in $O(n^a)$ time (for some a and some function $k(n) \leq n$) that cannot be solved in $k(n)^c n^{a+o(1)}$ time and $k(n)^c n^{o(1)}$ space, *for every* $c \geq 1$. While such problems can always be solved by exhaustive search in $O(2^{k(n)} n^a)$ time and $O(k(n) + n^a)$ space, we can prove a *superpolynomial* lower bound in the parameter $k(n)$ when space usage is restricted.

*This work began while the author was a member of the Institute for Advanced Study in Princeton, New Jersey, supported by NSF Grant CCF-0832797 (Expeditions in Computing) and NSF Grant DMS-0835373 (Pseudorandomness). At IBM, the author is supported by the Josef Raviv Memorial Fellowship.

STOC'10, June 5–8, 2010, Cambridge, Massachusetts, USA.

Categories and Subject Descriptors

F.1.3 [**Computation by Abstract Devices**]: Complexity Measures and Classes

General Terms

Theory

Keywords

lower bounds, improved exponential algorithms, exact algorithms, time-space tradeoffs

1. INTRODUCTION

To what extent can we avoid exhaustive search for generic search problems? This is one of the many offshoots of the P versus NP problem and it is the central question addressed in the area of exact algorithms for NP-hard problems.The general message of this research has been that the trivial enumeration of all possible solutions *can* be quantitatively improved upon for many problems (and their number is increasing every year). This success leads one to wonder if *all* NP problems allow some modest improvement over brute-force search. More precisely, let $V(x, y)$ be a verifier that runs on witnesses y of length $|x|^c$ and takes $O(|x|^d)$ time. The runtime of exhaustive search for a witness is $O(2^{|x|^c}|x|^d)$. Can we always find a witness in $O(2^{.99|x|^c}|x|^d)$? What about $O(2^{|x|^c-\log^2|x|}|x|^{100d})$? Can we approximate the fraction of witnesses that V accepts in this time? If V uses only $s(n)$ space, can we find a witness in $O(2^{.99|x|^c}|x|^d)$ time and $O(|x|^{100c} + s(n))$ space? These questions are the focus of the present paper.

Here we offer the first concrete evidence that the above minor improvements will be difficult to achieve for some problems. We do not rule out the possibility of these improvements; rather, we demonstrate that they would already imply superpolynomial lower bounds in complexity theory. (Optimists might say we have given a new approach to proving class separations.) We show that the task of finding improved algorithms is connected naturally to the task of proving superpolynomial lower bounds. Regardless of one's complexity-theoretic worldview, our results show that one cannot believe simultaneously that "superpolynomial lower bounds are far beyond our current techniques" and "simple tricks should suffice for improved exponential algorithms."[1]

[1]This was Mihai Patrascu's eloquent way of putting it.

1.1 Main Results

1.1.1 Circuit Lower Bounds From CircuitSAT

Let CIRCUIT SAT be the problem of finding a satisfying assignment to a Boolean circuit (over AND, OR, NOT gates). The CIRCUIT SAT problem is often the first NP-complete problem introduced in textbooks. Due to its applications in hardware/software verification and automated reasoning, the problem has been extensively studied in many areas of computer science. (Although CNF satisfiability gets all the fanfare, most formulas obtained in practice start as Boolean circuits.) Clearly, for circuits with n input variables and $\text{poly}(n)$ gates, the problem can be solved in $2^n \cdot \text{poly}(n)$ time on any robust model of computation, and it is not known how to solve the problem even slightly faster.[2]

On a seemingly unrelated front, progress has been nearly nonexistent on proving superpolynomial circuit lower bounds for over a decade. It is known that the exponential-time version of Merlin-Arthur does not have polynomial size circuits [BFT98], but it is not known how to improve the lower bound to even $\mathsf{EXP}^{\mathsf{NP}}$, the class of problems solvable in exponential time with an NP oracle. Since it appears unlikely that NP does not have polynomial size circuits, this is indeed a frustrating state of affairs.

These two lines of research can be related to each other in a striking way:

THEOREM 1.1. *Suppose there is a superpolynomial $s(n)$ such that, for all k,* CIRCUIT SAT *on circuits with n input variables and n^k gates is solvable in $2^n poly(n^k)/s(n)$ time by a (co-non)deterministic algorithm. Then* $\mathsf{NEXP} \not\subseteq \mathsf{P}/poly$.

That is, practically any nontrivial improvement over exhaustive search for CIRCUIT SAT (or nontrivial proofs of circuit unsatisfiability) would already imply superpolynomial circuit lower bounds for nondeterministic exponential time. The best known deterministic algorithm for CNF satisfiability takes $2^{n-\Omega(n/\ln(m/n))}\text{poly}(m)$, where m is the number of clauses and n is the number of variables [DH08, CIP06]. For more complex circuits, the current state of the art is a randomized SAT algorithm for AC^0 circuits which runs in $2^{n-n^{1-o(1)}}$ time on circuits with $n^{1+o(1)}$ gates [CIP09]. Both time bounds are noticeably smaller than the hypothesis of Theorem 1.1.[3] Of course this does not mean that the hypothesis can be achieved, but it does seem possible at the present time.

One intuitive way of viewing Theorem 1.1 is that, if we could understand the structure of circuits well enough to solve their satisfiability problem faster, then this understanding could be translated into concrete lower bounds for those circuits. We can solidify this intuition in two ways, by extending Theorem 1.1 to restricted circuit classes, and by showing that even faster Circuit Satisfiability would lead to stronger lower bounds.

For example, if satisfiability of Boolean formulas on n variables and n^c connectives can be solved in $2^n \cdot \text{poly}(n^c)/s(n)$, then E^{NP} does not have (non-uniform) polynomial size formulas.[4] If satisfiability of $\mathsf{AC}^0[6]$ circuits (constant depth circuits with AND, OR, NOT, and MOD6 gates) on n variables and n^c gates can be solved in at most $2^{n/3} \cdot \text{poly}(n^c)/s(n)$ time, then E^{NP} does not have polysize $\mathsf{AC}^0[6]$ circuits.[5]

Interestingly, it does not take a much stronger assumption to get a nearly optimal circuit lower bound for E^{NP}, and consequently $\mathsf{EXP}^{\mathsf{NP}}$:

THEOREM 1.2. *If* CIRCUIT SAT *on n variables and m gates is in $O(2^{(1-\delta)n} poly(m))$ (co-non)deterministic time for some $\delta > 0$, then there is $\varepsilon > 0$ and a language in E^{NP} that does not have $2^{\varepsilon n}$ size circuits.*

That is, an algorithm for CIRCUIT SAT with running time comparable to the best known algorithms for k-CNF SAT would entail strong circuit lower bounds.[6]

One may be skeptical that these small improvements are possible for Circuit Satisfiability. Similar results can also be established for problems efficiently solvable with randomness. The *Circuit Acceptance Probability Problem* (CAPP) is to approximate (within $\pm 1/6$) the fraction of satisfying assignments of a given Boolean circuit on n variables and n^c gates for some c [KC99, KRC00, For01, Bar02, IKW02]. CAPP can be solved easily in $O(n^c)$ time with a randomized algorithm. It is known that CAPP is in polynomial time if and only if PromiseBPP $=$ P [For01], so the problem is "complete" in some sense. We show that essentially any nontrivial derandomization for CAPP implies superpolynomial circuit lower bounds.

THEOREM 1.3. *Suppose there is a superpolynomial $s(n)$ such that, for all c, there is an $O(2^n \cdot poly(n^c)/s(n))$ nondeterministic algorithm for CAPP on n variables and n^c gates. Then* $\mathsf{NEXP} \not\subseteq \mathsf{P}/poly$.

(A *nondeterministic approximation algorithm* for CAPP always has at least one accepting computation, and always outputs a good approximation when it enters an accept state.) The proof of Theorem 1.3 holds even if we replace CAPP with the problem of distinguishing between circuits which are unsatisfiable and circuits with at least 2^{n-1} satisfying assignments. We interpret Theorem 1.3 to say that *circuit lower bounds are much easier than derandomization*: any weak derandomization of CAPP would already yield a quite strong circuit lower bound.

Theorem 1.3 also implies "amplification" results:

THEOREM 1.4. *If CAPP has a nondeterministic $O(2^n \cdot poly(n)/s(n))$ time algorithm that succeeds on all inputs, then for all $\varepsilon > 0$, CAPP has a nondeterministic $O(2^{n^\varepsilon})$ time algorithm with n^ε advice that succeeds on infinitely many inputs.*

[2]We use the $\text{poly}(n)$ notation to denote $O(n^c)$ factors for a fixed $c > 0$ independent of n.

[3]AC^0 circuits have constant depth and are comprised of AND, OR, NOT gates, with unbounded fan-in for each gate.

[4]Recall E^{NP} is the class of languages recognized by algorithms running in $2^{O(n)}$ time that can query an NP oracle (with queries of $2^{O(n)}$ length). As far as we know, non-linear size circuit lower bounds are not known for this class. However an $n^{3-o(1)}$ lower bound on formula size follows from work of Hastad [Has98].

[5]The weaker exponent in the algorithm is due to the apparent weakness of $\mathsf{AC}^0[6]$ reductions. It is very possible this can be improved upon.

[6]This should be contrasted with the case of general CNF-SAT, where no algorithm of the kind required in Theorem 1.2 is known. Recent work with Patrascu indicates that the problem of finding such a CNF-SAT algorithm is also closely related to other problems in theoretical computer science [PW10].

THEOREM 1.5. *If CAPP on n variables and m gates has a nondeterministic $O(2^{(1-\delta)n} \cdot poly(m))$ time algorithm that succeeds on all inputs, then CAPP has a nondeterministic polynomial time algorithm with $O(\log n)$ advice that succeeds on infinitely many inputs.*

The prospects for achieving an improved CAPP algorithm seem to be good. A necessary first step towards proving results like BPP $\subseteq$ NSUBEXP is to find some non-trivial CAPP algorithm. (Note we do not necessarily have to build a pseudorandom generator to achieve the algorithm.) For CNF formulas of length n, Luby and Velikovic [LV96] have given a deterministic $n^{2^{O(\sqrt{\log\log n})}}$ algorithm for approximating the number of solutions. Note it was already known that NEXP $\neq$ MA iff NEXP $\not\subseteq$ P/poly [IKW02]. However it could still have been the case that NEXP $=$ MA and yet Circuit SAT and CAPP have slightly better algorithms. The above results show this conjunction is impossible.

1.1.2 Improved Algorithms Imply LOGSPACE $\neq$ NP *and Subexponential Algorithms*

One strength of the above results is that there is no space restriction needed for the improved algorithms: our hypotheses only require SAT algorithms running in $O(2^n/s(n))$ time and $O(2^n/s(n))$ space for sufficiently large $s(n)$. Next we show that if exhaustive search can be improved in a way that preserves the verifier's space bound, then very surprising consequences result.

Here we shall study problems with *limited nondeterminism*, which only need short witnesses (e.g., of poly$(\log n)$ length) although verification still takes polynomial time. In particular we look at the case where the amount of nondeterminism is *logarithmic* in n ("log-nondeterminism"), and hence exhaustive search is already in *polynomial time*. This case is of interest as there are many polynomial time problems which fall in this category, and for which researchers have tried to find faster algorithms than a canonical one. The 3SUM problem is a well-known example [GO95]; satisfiability of exponential size circuits is another.[7]

It is natural to think that it may be easier to universally improve on log-nondeterminism problems. After all, the search space is no longer exponential in the running time of the verifier — now they are both polynomials in n. From this perspective it appears more likely that a clever pruning of the search space can be done.

Consider a problem solvable with witnesses of $\log n$ length, $O(n^c)$ time, and poly$(\log n)$ space.[8] The obvious deterministic simulation runs in $O(n^{c+1})$ time and poly$(\log n)$ space. We show that any universal improvement in the runtime exponent can be amplified into an *arbitrary polynomial* speedup with nondeterministic algorithms. Such a speedup would have dramatic consequences.

THEOREM 1.6. *Suppose for all $c, d \geq 1$ that every problem Π solvable with $\log n$ nondeterministic bits, n^c time, and $(\log n)^d$ space can be solved by some deterministic algorithm in $O(n^{c+.99})$ time and $poly(\log n)^d$ space. Then every such Π can also be solved by some nondeterministic algorithm in $O(n^3)$ time.*

Of course, the .99 is not special, and can be substituted with any $\delta < 1$.

COROLLARY 1.1. *The hypothesis of Theorem 1.6 implies* LOGSPACE $\neq$ NP*; in fact,* SC $\neq$ NP*, where* SC *is the class of problems solvable in (simultaneous) polynomial time and polylogarithmic space.*

COROLLARY 1.2. *The hypothesis of Theorem 1.6 implies that the quantified Boolean formula problem has a proof system where every QBF of length n has proofs of $2^{\varepsilon n}$ length for all $\varepsilon > 0$.*

That is, either the exponent in the trivial algorithm is optimal for some constant c, or we separate complexity classes in a surprising way. Note if the trivial algorithm is optimal for $c = 1$, then SAT cannot be solved in subquadratic time and polylog space, a problem that remains open despite much effort.

Identifying an explicit natural problem in place of "every problem" in Theorem 1.6 is nontrivial. (We could always use a form of the "Bounded Halting Problem", but this is undesirable.) The proof of Theorem 1.6 uses a delicate inductive argument that makes it difficult to extend to lower bounds on a natural problem.

1.1.3 Unconditional Lower Bounds

We want to understand the extent to which the exponential part of exhaustive search (namely, the exponential runtime in the witness length) can be reduced, without affecting the runtime of verification. We can prove unconditional lower bounds for improving on exhaustive search in this manner, based on Theorem 1.6 and its consequences. We first state a superpolynomial lower bound in terms of the witness length. To our knowledge no similar lower bounds have been reported.

THEOREM 1.7. *There is a problem Π verifiable with $k(n)$-length witnesses in $O(n^a)$ time (for some constant a and some $k(n) \leq n$) that cannot be solved in $k(n)^c n^a \cdot poly(\log n)$ time and $k(n)^c \cdot (\log n)^c$ space,* for all c.

Note if we could "only" change the "some $k(n)$" to "all $k(n)$" then we would separate P from NP. The theorem does rule out certain (daffy, but until now possible) strategies for trying to show LOGSPACE $=$ NP. For example, it is not possible to transform an arbitrary $O(n^a)$ time verifier with witnesses of length k into an $O(n^{a+o(1)})$ time and $O(\text{poly}(\log n))$ space verifier with witnesses of length $10^{10} \log k$. The proof uses the framework of Theorem 1.6.

Extending this result to circuit satisfiability on general computational models is an interesting challenge. We manage to show a related lower bound for CIRCUIT SAT:

THEOREM 1.8. *For every $\varepsilon > 0$,* CIRCUIT SAT *on k variables and m gates cannot be solved in $k^{1-\varepsilon} m^{1+o(1)}$ time and $m^{o(1)}$ space.*

---

[7]In 3SUM, we are given a set A of n numbers and wish to find three numbers that sum to zero. The problem can be easily solved in $O(n^2)$, and it is a key bottleneck in the solution of many problems in geometry and data structures. Finding an $O(n^{1.99})$ algorithm is a major challenge.

[8]In place of poly$(\log n)$ space, one may substitute any constructible function $f(n)$ satisfying $\log n \leq f(n) \leq n^{o(1)}$ for the remaining results in this paper. We have chosen poly$(\log n)$ for concreteness.

This is already interesting, because we do not know how to prove that SAT is not in $O(n^{2-\varepsilon})$ time and $n^{o(1)}$ space on general models (the case where $k = m$).[9] It is known that SAT (and consequently, CIRCUIT SAT) cannot be solved in less than $n^{1.8}$ time and $n^{o(1)}$ space [Wil08b]. It is also known (in a precise sense) that current techniques will not allow us to extend this bound to n^2 [Wil10]. This limitation seems related to our inability to extend Theorem 1.8 to arbitrary polynomials in k.

1.1.4 A Nontrivial Simulation

In the full version of the paper, we report a baby step towards improving brute force search. We observe a nontrivial deterministic simulation of nondeterministic multitape Turing machines, inspired by a nontrivial derandomization of randomized multitape Turing machines of Van Melkebeek and Santhanam [vMS05].

THEOREM 1.9. *For every multitape Turing machine M running in time t that accesses a tape of nondeterministic bits, there is a $\delta > 0$ and a deterministic TM that simulates M in $O(2^{(1-\delta)t})$ time.*

A group led by Lipton [Lip09a] has recently proved related results. Our simulation is not yet enough to imply lower bounds, as the simulation runtime does not scale with the amount of nondeterminism.

1.2 An Overview of Our Techniques

Our basic approach is simple: we assume the opposite of the desired lower bound (i.e., that we have decent uniform algorithms and very good non-uniform circuits), and construct an efficient simulation of the hard class, so tight that any nontrivial CIRCUIT SAT or CAPP algorithm contradicts a time hierarchy. This idea can be traced back to the first paper on P/poly, by Karp and Lipton [KL80]. One of their many corollaries (credited to Meyer) is that $\mathsf{P} = \mathsf{NP}$ implies $\mathsf{EXP} \not\subseteq \mathsf{P/poly}$. To prove this, one shows that (1) $\mathsf{EXP} \subseteq \mathsf{P/poly}$ implies $\mathsf{EXP} = \Sigma_2\mathsf{P}$, and (2) $\mathsf{P} = \mathsf{NP}$ implies $\Sigma_2\mathsf{P} = \mathsf{P}$. Since $\mathsf{EXP} \neq \mathsf{P}$, it cannot be that both are true. Our results can be seen as extreme sharpenings of this basic result: to get circuit lower bounds for classes like NEXP, we may assume *far less* than $\mathsf{P} = \mathsf{NP}$.

To illustrate, let us sketch the result that faster circuit satisfiability implies NEXP circuit lower bounds. It is known that $\mathsf{NEXP} \subseteq \mathsf{P/poly}$ implies a simulation of $\mathsf{NTIME}[2^n]$ which guesses a polynomial size circuit encoding a witness, then runs an exponential time verifier [IKW02]. We observe that $\mathsf{NEXP} \subseteq \mathsf{P/poly}$ implies that *every* verifier for an NEXP language has small circuits that encode witnesses. Therefore we are free to construct any verifier we need to get a contradiction. We choose one that exploits efficient reductions from NP to SAT, translated up to NEXP. Using a small witness circuit, we can replace the exponential time verifier with a single call to CIRCUIT SAT on $n + O(\log n)$ variables and $\text{poly}(n)$ gates. It follows that an $O(2^n \cdot \text{poly}(n)/s(n))$ algorithm for CIRCUIT SAT implies $\mathsf{NTIME}[2^n] \subseteq \mathsf{NTIME}[2^n \cdot \text{poly}(n)/s(n)]$, a contradiction. For the lower bound that follows from approximating the solutions to a circuit, we use efficient *PCP of Proximity* verifiers of Ben-Sasson *et al.* [BGHSV05] in the CIRCUIT SAT instance.

[9] Here n is the total length of the input.

In order to prove that stronger improved algorithms yield stronger consequences such as $\mathsf{LOGSPACE} \neq \mathsf{NP}$, we use ideas from the existing time-space lower bounds for SAT, along with an inductive trick that (assuming a universal speedup over exhaustive search) lets us repeatedly reduce any exponent in the time bound of a complexity class until it becomes a fixed constant, leading to superpolynomial lower bounds. Further development of this trick produces unconditional lower bounds for bounded nondeterminism.

2. PRELIMINARIES

We assume the reader is familiar with basic concepts in complexity and algorithms. In the following paragraphs, we focus on a few particulars needed for this paper.

2.1 Notation and Background

We define $[n] := \{1, \ldots, n\}$. As usual, unless otherwise specified a function has domain $\mathbb{N}$ and co-domain $\mathbb{N}$, is assumed to be time (or space) constructible within the appropriate bounds, and is monotone nondecreasing. All logarithms are in base two. A circuit is Boolean (with AND, OR, NOT gates), unless indicated otherwise.

Computational Model and Complexity.

In almost all our results one may assume any deterministic computational model in which $O(\text{poly}(\log n))$ bits of information may be processed in a single step. This includes all flavors of Turing machines (including random access), random access machines with logarithmic size registers, and so on. (The main reason for this is given below.) We shall indicate clearly when this is not the case.

Fix a finite alphabet Σ. We usually assume $\Sigma = \{0, 1\}$. $\mathsf{NTIME}[t(n)]$ ($\mathsf{TIME}[t(n)]$) denote the classes of languages recognized in $O(t(n))$ time by a nondeterministic (deterministic) algorithm, respectively. $\mathsf{TISP}[t(n), s(n)]$ denotes those languages recognized by some algorithm that runs in both $O(t(n))$ time and $O(s(n))$ space. Recall $\mathsf{P} = \bigcup_{k\geq 1} \mathsf{TIME}[n^k]$ and $\mathsf{NP} = \bigcup_{k\geq 1} \mathsf{NTIME}[n^k]$. Steve's Class (abbreviated SC) is $\bigcup_{k\geq 1} \mathsf{DTISP}[n^k, (\log n)^k]$.

$i.o.-\mathcal{C}$ is the class of languages $L \subset \Sigma^*$ such that there is a language $L' \in \mathcal{C}$ where $L \cap \Sigma^n = L' \cap \Sigma^n$ holds for infinitely many n.

We say that L is a *unary language* if $L \subseteq \{1\}^*$. We use the following nondeterministic time hierarchy theorem.

THEOREM 2.1 ([ZAK83]). *Let t_1 and t_2 be time constructible functions such that $t_1(n+1) \leq o(t_2(n))$. There is a unary language in $\mathsf{NTIME}[t_2(n)]$ that is not in $\mathsf{NTIME}[t_1(n)]$.*

Inspecting our proofs, one observes that we do not need the full strength of Theorem 2.1 but merely that there is a unary language in $\mathsf{NTIME}[t_1(n) \log^c t_1(n))]$ that isn't in $\mathsf{NTIME}[t_1(n)]$, for some $c > 0$. This particular time hierarchy is model-independent because the class $\mathsf{NTIME}[n \cdot \text{poly}(\log n)]$ is very robust with respect to the computational model. This is a family of results due to Gurevich and Shelah [GS89]. For example, let $\mathsf{NTIME}_{RTM}[t(n)]$ be the languages recognized with nondeterministic $t(n)$ time random-access Turing machines, and let $\mathsf{NTIME}_{TM}[t(n)]$ denote the same class for multitape Turing machines.

THEOREM 2.2 (GUREVICH AND SHELAH [GS89]). $\bigcup_{c>0} \mathsf{NTIME}_{RTM}[n \log^c n] = \bigcup_{c>0} \mathsf{NTIME}_{TM}[n \log^c n]$.

The random-access Turing machine can be replaced by any model M which has programs of $O(1)$ size and processes $O(\text{poly}(\log n))$ bits of information in a single step. Let us sketch the proof of Theorem 2.2 under this generic requirement. The idea is that a multitape TM can simulate an M-computation running in time $O(n \cdot \text{poly}(\log n))$ by guessing a computation history and verifying the correctness of the history. More precisely, the length of such a history is $O(n \cdot \text{poly}(\log n))$ bits: we use $O(\text{poly}(\log n))$ bits for each step, giving a "snapshot" which describes the timestep, bits read and written, the memory locations of these bits, and the state or program counter during that step. These snapshots are guessed in temporal order: the ith snapshot corresponds to the ith step. In this ordering, a multitape TM can verify that, assuming that all the reads are correct, the program counter and writes are all correct. A multitape TM can (in $O(n \cdot \text{poly}(\log n))$ time) sort these snapshots in *spatial* order as well, ordering the snapshots primarily by the index of the register/cell being read in that time step, and using the temporal order as a secondary key. In this ordering, a multitape TM can verify that the reads are correct by verifying that the previous snapshot *wrote* the same information.

2.2 Related Work

Subexponential and Parameterized Complexity.

A theory of (sub)exponential time complexity for NP-hard problems has been developing. Much work has gone into extending reducibility notions to subexponential time algorithms (e.g., [IP01, IPZ01, CJ03, CG07, CIP06, Tra08]). The theory has found interesting evidence for the *exponential time hypothesis* (ETH) that 3-SAT is not in $2^{o(m)}$ time, where m is the number of clauses. If ETH is false, then many other problems have subexponential algorithms as well.

In parameterized complexity, one studies paired problems with an input and parameter k written in unary. It is often convenient to define a parameterized problem when the computational problem of interest is hard, but only for certain inputs whose difficulty can be measured by the parameter. For example, the LONGEST PATH problem is NP-complete, but if one wants to find a longest path in a graph with treewidth at most k, there is a $2^{O(k \log k)}\text{poly}(n)$ algorithm [FL89]. Parameterized complexity is inherently tied to the study of exact algorithms for NP. A problem is *fixed-parameter tractable* (FPT) when it has an algorithm with $f(k)n^c$ runtime for some function f and a universal c.

If a problem does not seem to be FPT, one tries to find evidence for this, using reducibility notions similar to NP-completeness. There is a hierarchy of problems, all technically solvable in polynomial time when the parameter k is constant, which do not seem to be FPT. (In fact many hierarchies have been proposed; cf. the text of Flum and Grohe [FG06].) The most basic is the W-hierarchy, where the lowest level is the class FPT of problems which are FPT. The next level $W[1]$ already contains problems which are not in FPT, assuming ETH [DF99, FG06]. There is a rough analogy between the W-hierarchy and the polynomial time hierarchy: in the W-hierarchy, $f(k)\log n$ bits are guessed in each alternation (instead of $\text{poly}(n)$), and the deterministic verifier only reads some $f(k)$ bits of the input. FPT equals the entire W-hierarchy if and only if Circuit SAT (with n variables and m gates) is in $2^{n/s(n)}\text{poly}(m)$ time for some unbounded $s(n)$ [ADR95]. (Note this runtime is much faster than those in our hypotheses.) Indeed, there is a sense in which the aforementioned subexponential time theory is isomorphic to questions in parameterized complexity [CG07].

Limited Nondeterminism.

Kintala and Fisher [KF77] initiated the study of classes with limited nondeterminism. Buss and Goldsmith [BG93] and Bloch, Buss, and Goldsmith [BBG98] considered classes with only logarithmic nondeterminism, as we study here. A related but more refined model (the guess-and-check model) was introduced by Cai and Chen [CC97]. Flum, Grohe, and Weyer [FGW06] gave a framework connecting limited nondeterminism with parameterized complexity.

Better Algorithms And Better Lower Bounds.

The idea that better algorithms can lead to better lower bounds is a recurring theme in theoretical computer science. Here we cite a few examples which seem to be most relevant to our work.

- Work of F. Zane and his co-authors [Zan98] in the late 90's alternated between finding faster SAT algorithms and proving new exponential lower bounds for depth-three circuits, both accomplished using new structure theorems for CNF formulas.
- In the DFA INTERSECTION problem, one is given k DFAs with at most n states each, and the task is to decide if all DFAs accept a common string. Karakostas, Lipton, and Viglas [KLV03] prove if DFA INTERSECTION is solvable in $n^{o(k)}$ time, then $\mathsf{NTIME}[n]$ is contained in $\mathsf{TIME}[2^{\varepsilon n}]$ for all $\varepsilon > 0$ and $\mathsf{LOGSPACE} \neq \mathsf{NP}$. However, observe that DFA INTERSECTION is PSPACE-complete [Koz77], while the problems we consider are either in BPP or NP, and we do not need to assume subexponential algorithms. Lipton has also advocated this type of approach for proving lower bounds in his popular blog [Lip09b].
- Impagliazzo, Kabanets, and Wigderson [IKW02] have shown that if CAPP is solvable in nondeterministic $2^{n^{o(1)}}$ time infinitely often, then $\mathsf{NEXP} \not\subseteq \mathsf{P/poly}$. Kabanets and Impagliazzo [KI04] showed that a nondeterministic $2^{n^{o(1)}}$ time algorithm for *Polynomial Identity Testing* implies that either $\mathsf{NEXP} \not\subseteq \mathsf{P/poly}$ or the Permanent does not have arithmetic circuits of polynomial size. Our results appear to be incomparable: while identity testing looks easier than the problems we study (even CAPP), our running time assumptions are much weaker and there is no "or" in our conclusion.

If improved algorithms of the kind needed in this paper exist, their discovery probably will not be hindered by the known barriers in complexity (but perhaps another unforseen one). The full version of the paper contains a brief discussion on this point.

3. CIRCUIT LOWER BOUNDS FROM IMPROVED ALGORITHMS

We start by proving consequences of better CIRCUIT SAT algorithms. The notion of "universal witness circuits" shall be useful. A language L has universal witness circuits if every correct verifier for L has circuits that encode a witness accepted by the verifier, on every input in L.

DEFINITION 3.1. *Let L be a language in* $\mathsf{NTIME}[t(n)]$. *A polynomial time algorithm V is a* verifier for L *if* $x \in L \iff (\exists y : |y| \le t(|x|))[V(x,y) = 1]$.

DEFINITION 3.2. *A language $L \in \mathsf{NTIME}[t(n)]$* has $S(n)$-size universal witness circuits *if* for all *polynomial time verifiers V for L, there is a k and an $O(S(n))$-size Boolean circuit family $\{C_n\}$ with the property:*

$x \in L \iff V(x, w(x)) = 1$, where $w(x)$ is the concatenation of the outputs of $C_\ell(\langle x, z\rangle)$ evaluated over all $z \in \{0,1\}^{\lceil \log_2 t(n)\rceil + 1}$ in lexicographical order, and $\ell \ge n$ is an integer of appropriate length.

The universal witness property may look strong, but all of NEXP has universal witness circuits of polynomial size, in the case that NEXP $\subseteq$ P/poly. The key to this observation is that if a language does not have such circuits, then *some* correct verifier for NEXP accepts witnesses that *cannot* be encoded with small circuits, infinitely often. This verifier can be used to test strings for high circuit complexity, which is enough to obtain pseudorandom generators, leading to a contradiction. The following can be easily obtained from work of Impagliazzo, Kabanets, and Wigderson [IKW02].

LEMMA 3.1 (FOLLOWS FROM [IKW02]). *If* NEXP *has polynomial size circuits, then every language in* NEXP *has universal witness circuits of polynomial size.*

We also need a strong completeness result for satisfiability.

THEOREM 3.1 ([TOU01, FLvMV05]). *There is a fixed d such that for every $L \in \mathsf{NTIME}[n]$, L reduces to 3SAT in $O(n(\log n)^d)$ time. Moreover there is an algorithm (with random access to its input) that, given an instance of L and an integer $i \in [cn(\log n)^d]$ in binary (for some c depending on L), outputs the ith clause of the resulting 3SAT formula in $O((\log n)^d)$ time.*

The value of d depends on the particular computational model chosen. For most models one can take d to be small, e.g. $d = 4$. Theorem 3.1 holds under any computational model that accesses up to $O(\text{poly}(\log n))$ bits per step. Most proofs of it essentially rely the fact that nondeterministic Turing machines can simulate most other nondeterministic models with polylog overhead, as well as the Hennie-Stearns two-tape simulation of multitape Turing machines (cf. [AB09], Section 1.7) which introduces another log overhead. The Hennie-Stearns simulation can be converted (with constant overhead) into a circuit [PF79], which can then be efficiently converted to 3-CNF using the Tseitin transformation [Tse68]. See Van Melkebeek ([vM07], Lemma 2.2) for an alternative proof based on sorting networks. By standard translation/padding arguments (substituting 2^n in place of n in the above), the theorem can be scaled up to exponential time bounds:

COROLLARY 3.1. *Every language L in $\mathsf{NTIME}[2^n]$ can be reduced to 3SAT instances of $c2^n \cdot n^4$ size. Moreover there is an algorithm that, given an instance of L and an integer $i \in [c2^n \cdot n^4]$ in binary, outputs the ith clause of the resulting 3SAT formula in $O(n^4)$ time.*

We are now ready to prove the main result of this section: a generic theorem relating the solvability of CIRCUIT SAT to lower bounds on universal witness circuits for NEXP.

THEOREM 3.2. *Let $c \ge 1$. Let $a(n)$ be a monotone increasing and unbounded function. Let $S(n)$ and $T(n)$ be functions such that*

- *$T(n)/(S(n) + n^8)^c \ge \Omega(n^4 \cdot a(n))$ and*
- *$n \le S(n) \le O(2^n/n \cdot 1/a(n))$.*

Suppose CIRCUIT SAT *on n variables and m gates can be solved in $O(2^n m^c/T(n))$ co-nondeterministic time. Then $\mathsf{NTIME}[2^n]$ does not have $S(n)$-size universal witness circuits.*

PROOF. Suppose $\mathsf{NTIME}[2^n]$ has $S(n)$ universal witness circuits. We show that a faster (co-non)deterministic algorithm for Circuit Satisfiability implies a contradiction to the nondeterministic time hierarchy.

Let $L \in \mathsf{NTIME}[2^n]$ be arbitrary. By Corollary 3.1, L can be reduced to 3SAT instances of $c2^n \cdot n^4$ size, for some c. Let $V(x, y)$ be a verifier for L that reduces x to a 3-CNF formula ϕ_x of $c2^n \cdot n^4$ size, substitutes the ith bit of y for the ith variable of ϕ_x, then returns 1 if and only if the resulting formula evaluates to 1.

Since L has universal witness circuits, it is the case that for all $x \in L$, there is some y of length at most $c2^n \cdot n^4$ such that $V(x,y) = 1$, and y can be encoded with a $S(|x|)$ size circuit. That is, for all x, there is a circuit C_y that takes inputs of length $\ell = \log(c2^{|x|}|x|^4)$ and has size at most $S(|x|)$, such that the witness y equals the concatenation of $C_y(z)$ over all $z \in \{0,1\}^\ell$ in lexicographical order.

Consider the following nondeterministic algorithm N for L. On input x, existentially guess the circuit C_y, using $O(S(|x|)\log S(|x|)) \le O(2^n/a(n))$ bits. Then construct a circuit D with ℓ input variables X, as follows. Given an integer $i \in [c2^n \cdot n^4]$, the ith clause of ϕ_x can be computed in $O(n^4)$ time (via Corollary 3.1). By the standard translation of algorithms into circuits, it follows that the ith clause can be computed with an $O(n^8)$ size circuit; call it E. Lead the input variables X of D into the inputs of E, whose $3n + O(\log n)$ output wires encode the Xth clause of ϕ_x. These output wires encode the indices of three variables in ϕ_x, along with three "negation bits" indicating 1 for variables which are negated, if any. For convenience, call the variable indices z_1, z_2, z_3. Evaluate $a_1 = C_y(z_1)$, $a_2 = C_y(z_2)$, and $a_3 = C_y(z_3)$. Letting b_1, b_2, b_3 be the negation bits of z_1, z_2, z_3 (respectively), output $\neg[(a_1 \oplus b_1) \vee (a_2 \oplus b_2) \vee (a_3 \oplus b_3)]$. That is, $D(X)$ outputs 1 if and only if the Xth clause is not satisfied, i.e., D is unsatisfiable if and only if C_y encodes a satisfying assignment for ϕ_x. The circuit D has $O(n^8 + S(|x|))$ size and ℓ inputs.

Finally, N calls a fast algorithm for circuit satisfiability on D, and *accepts* if and only if D is unsatisfiable. N runs in time $O(2^n/a(n) + 2^\ell \cdot (n^8 + S(n))^c/T(n))$, which is at most

$$\le O(2^n/a(n) + 2^n n^4 \cdot (n^8 + S(n))^c/T(n)).$$

By assumption on $T(n)$ and $S(n)$, this time bound is at most $O(2^n/a(n))$.

Recall that L was an arbitrary language from $\mathsf{NTIME}[2^n]$, so we now have

$$\mathsf{NTIME}[2^n] \subseteq \mathsf{NTIME}[2^n/a(n)].$$

Since $2^{n+1}/a(n+1) = o(2^n)$, we have a contradiction to the strong nondeterministic time hierarchy theorem [SFM78, Zak83]. □

It is now easy to show that faster Circuit Satisfiability implies $\mathsf{NEXP} \not\subseteq \mathsf{P}/\text{poly}$. We say that a function f is *super-polynomial in n* if for all k, $n^k = o(f(n))$.

REMINDER OF THEOREM 1.1 *Suppose there is a superpolynomial function $s(n)$ such that* CIRCUIT SAT *on circuits with n variables and n^k gates can be solved in $2^n \cdot poly(n^k)/s(n)$ time by a (co-non)deterministic algorithm, for all k. Then* $\mathsf{NEXP} \not\subseteq \mathsf{P}/poly$.

PROOF. Let $S(n) = n^k$ and $T(n) = s(n)$ in Theorem 3.2. Then a $2^n \cdot \text{poly}(n^k)/s(n)$ time algorithm for Circuit Satisfiability implies that $\mathsf{NTIME}[2^n]$ does not have n^k universal witness circuits. Since k can be arbitrary, $\mathsf{NTIME}[2^n]$ does not have polynomial size universal witness circuits, hence NEXP also does not. By the contrapositive of Lemma 3.1, we conclude that $\mathsf{NEXP} \not\subseteq \mathsf{P}/\text{poly}$. □

3.1 Extensions

It is also possible to extend Theorem 1.1 to larger circuit lower bounds, and to weaker problems such as FORMULA SAT, the problem of satisfying Boolean formulas. Unfortunately the derandomization results do not seem to apply to restricted circuit classes. Also, as far as we know, Lemma 3.1 does not extend to superpolynomial circuit sizes [Imp10], so we need another way to obtain universal witness circuits for NEXP. This can be accomplished with the following lemma:

LEMMA 3.2 (FOLKLORE). *Let $\mathcal{C}$ be any class of circuits. If E^{NP} has (non uniform) circuits of size $S(n)$ from class $\mathcal{C}$, then $\mathsf{NTIME}[2^n]$ has universal witness circuits of size $S(n)$ from class $\mathcal{C}$.*

PROOF. Let L be a language in $\mathsf{NTIME}[2^n]$. Let $V(x,y)$ be a nondeterministic verifier for L running in $d2^{|x|}$ time. Consider the following E^{NP} machine:

$N(x,i)$: *Binary search for the lexicographically smallest z such that $V(x,z)$ accepts, by querying:* given (x,y) where $|y| = d2^{|x|}$, is there $z \le y$ such that $V(x,z)$ accepts? *Then output the ith bit of z.*

Note the queries can be computed in NP, and N needs at most $d2^n$ queries to the oracle. Since every such N has size $S(n)$ circuits from class $\mathcal{C}$, $\mathsf{NTIME}[2^n]$ has $S(n)$-size universal witness circuits from $\mathcal{C}$. □

REMINDER OF THEOREM 1.2 *If* CIRCUIT SAT *on n variables and m gates is in $O(2^{(1-\delta)n}m^c)$ time for some $\delta > 0$ and $c \ge 1$, then there is $\varepsilon > 0$ and a language in E^{NP} that does not have $2^{\varepsilon n}$ size circuits.*

PROOF. Let $T(n) = 2^{\delta n}$ and $S(n) = 2^{\delta n/c}/n^5$. Note the constraints of Theorem 3.2 are satisfied, hence we have: *if Circuit SAT on n variables and m gates is in $O(2^{(1-\delta)n}m^c)$ time, then* NEXP *does not have $2^{\delta n/c}/n^5$-size universal witness circuits.* The result follows from Lemma 3.2 and setting $\varepsilon < \delta/c$. □

More extensions are given in the full version of the paper.

3.2 Circuit Lower Bounds From Very Weak Derandomization

We now turn to the *Circuit Acceptance Probability Problem* (CAPP): given a Boolean circuit C with n inputs and poly(n) gates, the goal is to compute an approximation to the number of assignments satisfying C, within an additive factor of $1/6$. More precisely, we wish to output a number v such that

$$\left| v - \frac{1}{2^n} \cdot \sum_{x \in \{0,1\}^n} C(x) \right| < 1/6.$$

CAPP has been studied extensively [KC99, KRC00, For01, Bar02, IKW02]. We prove:

REMINDER OF THEOREM 1.3 *If there is a nondeterministic algorithm for CAPP with $O(2^n \cdot poly(n)/s(n))$ running time (for any superpolynomial $s(n)$), then* $\mathsf{NEXP} \not\subseteq \mathsf{P}/poly$.

In the previous section, we saw that strong reductions to 3SAT imply an efficient NEXP verifier. The verifier universally tries all possible clauses in an exponentially long 3-CNF formula, and checks the values of three variables in each trial. This universal quantifier is replaced with a poly(n) size circuit which (on a variable assignment) checks the clause indexed by the input to the circuit. Our idea is to replace this universal quantifier with a random choice, so that instead of testing satisfiability of the circuit, it suffices to approximate the number of solutions. Naturally, this suggests the use of *probabilistically checkable proofs* (PCPs). We use the *PCPs of Proximity* of Ben-Sasson, Goldreich, Harsha, Sudan, and Vadhan, which imply PCPs for NEXP with nice properties.[10]

THEOREM 3.3 ([BGHSV05]). *Let $T : \mathbb{Z}^+ \to \mathbb{Z}^+$ be non-decreasing. Then for every $s > 0$ and every language $L \in \mathsf{NTIME}[T(n)]$ there exists a PCP verifier $V(x,y)$ with soundness s, perfect completeness, randomness complexity $r = \log_2 T(|x|) + O(\log\log T(|x|))$, query complexity $q = poly(\log T(|x|))$, and verification time $t = poly(|x|, \log T)$. More precisely:*

- *V has random access to x and y, uses at most r random bits in any execution, makes q queries to the candidate proof y. and runs in at most t steps.*
- *If $x \in L$ then there's a y of $T(|x|)poly(\log T(|x|))$ length such that* $\Pr[V(x,y)$ *accepts*$] = 1$.
- *If $x \notin L$ then for all y,* $\Pr[V(x,y)$ *accepts*$] \le s$.

We shall be interested in the case $T(n) = 2^n$. Then the above PCP verifier uses $n + O(\log n)$ bits of randomness, poly(n) verification time, and poly(n) query complexity.

PROOF OF THEOREM 1.3. The proof proceeds similarly to Theorem 1.1. We start by assuming $\mathsf{NEXP} \subseteq \mathsf{P}/\text{poly}$, so that all languages in NEXP have universal witness circuits. Let L be a language in $\mathsf{NTIME}[2^n] - \mathsf{NTIME}[2^n \cdot \text{poly}(n)/s(n)]$.

Let $V(x,y)$ be the PCP verifier of Theorem 3.3 for L where $T(n) = 2^n$ and $s = 1/2$. For some $k > 0$, V tosses $n + k\log n$ coins, queries the $O(2^n)$ length string y in $O(n^k)$ places, and runs in $O(n^k)$ time. Let $c > 0$ be such that the circuit complexity of any function encoding a $2^n n^k$-bit witness of V on inputs of length n is at most $n^c + c$.

We now describe an alternative nondeterministic algorithm N for L. On input x of length n, existentially guess a circuit C with $n^c + c$ size. Construct a circuit D that simulates V as follows. The circuit D has $n + k\log n$ input wires r, corresponding to the random bits of V. Once r is fixed, the verifier V runs in $O(n^k)$ time and queries y in $O(n^k)$

[10]Note that Or Meir has recently found a more combinatorial approach to these results, cf. [Mei09].

positions. By the standard translation of oracle machines to circuits, V can be simulated by a circuit of size $O(n^{2k})$ with *oracle gates* for the string y. These oracle gates each have $n+O(1)$ input wires and output the bit of y indexed by the input wires. Replace each oracle gate with a copy of C. The resulting circuit D has $O(n^{2k+c})$ size. Run the presumed nondeterministic algorithm for CAPP on the D, and *accept* if and only if the fraction returned is greater than 3/4.

Let y be the string obtained by evaluating C on all inputs in lexicographical order. By construction, $D(z) = 1$ if and only if $V(x, y)$ outputs 1 on the string of coin tosses z.

If there is a witness y for the input x, then there is a C of size $O(n^c)$ which encodes y. On such a C, the fraction of inputs accepted by D is 1. On the other hand, if there is no witness y for x, then certainly no circuit C encodes a witness for x, and hence on every circuit C, the fraction of inputs accepted by D is at most 1/2. Hence the algorithm N is correct.

Assuming CAPP can be solved in $2^n \cdot \text{poly}(n)/s(n)$ time for some superpolynomial $s(n)$, the time of the entire simulation is $2^n \cdot \text{poly}(n)/s(n)$. This contradicts the choice of L. □

The above proof can be generalized along the lines of Theorem 3.2 in a straightforward way. A completely analogous argument to Theorem 1.2 shows the following.

THEOREM 3.4. *If there is an $O(2^{(1-\delta)n}m^c)$ nondeterministic algorithm for CAPP on circuits of n variables and m gates, then* NEXP *does not have $2^{\varepsilon n}$-size universal witness circuits for some $\varepsilon > 0$. Consequently,* E^{NP} *does not have $2^{o(n)}$ size circuits.*

Impagliazzo, Kabanets, Wigderson [IKW02] showed partial converses to Theorem 1.3 and Theorem 3.4:

- If NEXP $\not\subseteq$ P/poly, then CAPP has a nondeterministic algorithm that works on infinitely many inputs in $O(2^{n^{\varepsilon}})$ time with n^{ε} advice, for every $\varepsilon > 0$.
- (Implicitly shown) If NTIME$[2^n]$ does not have $2^{o(n)}$-size universal witness circuits, then CAPP has a nondeterministic polytime algorithm that works on infinitely many inputs with $O(\log n)$ advice.[11]

Combining these results with Theorem 1.3 and Theorem 3.4, we have the following "amplifications" of CAPP algorithms:

REMINDER OF THEOREM 1.4 *If CAPP has a nondeterministic $O(2^n \cdot poly(n)/s(n))$ time algorithm that succeeds on all inputs, then for all $\varepsilon > 0$, CAPP (in fact, all of* MA*) has a nondeterministic $O(2^{n^{\varepsilon}})$ time algorithm with n^{ε} advice that succeeds on infinitely many inputs.*

[11] This follows because, if NTIME$[2^n]$ did not have such circuits, then there is an $\varepsilon > 0$ and a poly(2^n) time algorithm with n bits of advice that, on infinitely many inputs, nondeterministically generates a 2^n-bit truth table of a Boolean function f_n which has circuit complexity at least $2^{\varepsilon n}$ for sufficiently large n. (This is essentially the negation of what it means to have universal witness circuits: there is a verifier for some L which on infinitely many inputs $x_i \in L$, only accepts witnesses which *do not* have small circuits. Hard-coding these x_i as advice, we get that any witness accepted by the verifier on x_i has high circuit complexity.) But it is known (even from [KvM99]) that this assumption implies pseudorandom generators for polynomial size circuits, strong enough to prove MA $\subseteq$ *i.o.* $-$ NP$/O(\log n)$. Hence CAPP has the desired type of algorithm.

REMINDER OF THEOREM 1.5 *If CAPP on n variables and m gates has a nondeterministic $O(2^{(1-\delta)n} \cdot poly(m))$ time algorithm that succeeds on all inputs, then CAPP has a nondeterministic polynomial time algorithm with $O(\log n)$ advice that succeeds on infinitely many inputs.*

The above two results can also be viewed as gap theorems: if CAPP can't be solved infinitely often in NP with logarithmic advice, then CAPP can't be in $2^{.99n} \cdot \text{poly}(m)$ nondeterministic time.

Evidence for Derandomization of CAPP(?).

The hypothesis of Theorem 1.3 looks potentially provable to us. Van Melkebeek and Santhanam [vMS05] have shown that for every probabilistic k-tape Turing machine running in time t, there is a $\delta > 0$ such that the machine can be simulated deterministically in $O(2^{(1-\delta)t})$ time. Unfortunately this is not quite enough to achieve the circuit lower bound for NEXP. To do that, we would need (for example) that every probabilistic k-tape Turing machine with $b(n)$ bits of randomness running in time $t(n)$ can be simulated deterministically in $\text{poly}(t) \cdot 2^b/s(b)$ time, for a superpolynomial function s. In our desired application, $t(n)$ is a polynomial factor larger than $b(n)$.

4. FURTHER IMPROVEMENTS

In the full version of the paper, we show that improving the runtime of exhaustive search for problems with limited nondeterminism would have surprising consequences. Here we only have enough space to briefly summarize these results, which use tools from prior work on time-space lower bounds for satisfiability.

REMINDER OF THEOREM 1.6 *Suppose there is $\delta > 0$ such that for all $c, d \geq 1$, every problem Π solvable with $\log n$ nondeterministic bits, n^c time, and $(\log n)^d$ space can be solved by a deterministic algorithm in $O(n^{c+(1-\delta)})$ time and $poly(\log n)^d$ space. Then every such Π can also be solved with a nondeterministic algorithm in $O(n^3)$ time, i.e.,* SC $\subseteq$ NTIME$[n^3]$.

REMINDER OF COROLLARY 1.1 *The hypothesis of Theorem 1.6 implies* LOGSPACE $\neq$ NP.

PROOF. Assume LOGSPACE = NP. Then NTIME$[n] \subseteq$ TISP$[n^c, \log n]$ for some c. By padding, NTIME$[n^4]$ is in TISP$[n^{4c}, \log n]$. By Theorem 1.6, we have TISP$[n^{4c}, \log n] \subseteq$ NTIME$[n^3]$. This is a contradiction to the nondeterministic time hierarchy. □

REMINDER OF COROLLARY 1.2 *The hypothesis of Theorem 1.6 implies that the quantified Boolean formula problem has a proof system where every QBF of length n has proofs of $2^{\varepsilon n}$ length for all $\varepsilon > 0$.*

PROOF. Theorem 1.6 says for all k, TISP$[n^k, O(\log n)] \subseteq$ NTIME$[n^3]$. Let $\varepsilon > 0$, and let $f(n) = 2^{\varepsilon n/3}$. By padding, TISP$[f(n)^k, O(\log f(n))] \subseteq$ NTIME$[f(n)^3]$. That is, we have TISP$[2^{\varepsilon kn/3}, O(n)] \subseteq$ NTIME$[2^{\varepsilon n}]$. Since k can be arbitrarily large, it follows that SPACE$[O(n)] \subseteq$ NTIME$[2^{\varepsilon n}]$. A quantified Boolean formula of length n can be easily solved using $O(n)$ space. Therefore quantified Boolean formulas of length n can be recognized in $2^{\varepsilon n}$ time with a nondeterministic algorithm. The conclusion follows. □

These ideas also lead to an *unconditional* lower bound.

REMINDER OF THEOREM 1.7 *For some a and some $k(n) \leq n$, there is a problem Π solvable with $k(n)$ nondeterminism and $O(n^a)$ time that cannot be solved in $k(n)^c n^a \cdot poly(\log n)$ time and $k(n)^c \cdot poly(\log n)$ space,* for all constants c.

In fact, a stronger statement holds: either polynomial nondeterminism cannot be simulated in polytime, or we have strong time lower bounds on simulating log-nondeterminism with polylog space.

THEOREM 4.1. *Either $\mathsf{P} \neq \mathsf{NP}$, or there is a problem verifiable with $\log n$ size witnesses in $O(n^c)$ time and $poly(\log n)$ space that is* **not** *solvable in $O(n^{c+.99})$ time and $poly(\log n)$ space, for some $c \geq 1$.*

We cannot yet extend these lower bounds to problems like Circuit SAT on general computational models, due to the inefficiency of reductions from arbitrary languages to Circuit SAT. We could extend them to Circuit SAT on multitape Turing machines, but those lower bounds are easy: the opposite of the lower bound implies that Circuit Evaluation (the case where there are *no* input variables) is in $n \cdot \text{poly}(\log n)$ time and $\text{poly}(\log n)$ space, which is already known to be false. (In fact, on multitape Turing machines the set of palindromes requires nearly quadratic time in the polylog space setting.)

However we can extend the lower bound slightly to generic computational models, using the strong nondeterministic time hierarchy [Zak83] (Theorem 2.1).

THEOREM 4.2. *For all $\varepsilon > 0$,* CIRCUIT SAT *on circuits with k input gates and m total gates cannot be solved in $m^{1+o(1)}k^{1-\varepsilon}$ time and $m^{o(1)}$ space.*

Recall we do not know how to prove that SAT can't be solved in $O(N^{2-\varepsilon})$ time and $N^{o(1)}$ space on general models (the particular case where $k = m$).

5. CONCLUSION

We have seen that universal improvements over exhaustive search, even marginal ones, would have surprising consequences in complexity theory. This connection between improved exponential algorithms and superpolynomial lower bounds shows that two communities have been implicitly working towards similar goals. In the full version of the paper, more results along these lines are presented, along with a detailed discussion of interesting open problems.

Acknowledgments.

I am grateful to Russell Impagliazzo, Dick Lipton, Mihai Patrascu, Mohan Paturi, Ken Regan, and John Rogers for useful discussions on this work. Special thanks are due to V. Arvind, Andrew Drucker, and Rahul Santhanam for their valuable comments and corrections on a draft of this paper.

6. REFERENCES

[ADR95] K. Abrahamson, R. G. Downey, and M. R. Fellows. Fixed-parameter tractability and completeness IV: On completeness for W[P] and PSPACE analogs. *Annals of Pure and Applied Logic* 73:235–276, 1995.

[AB09] S. Arora and B. Barak. *Computational Complexity – a modern approach.* Cambridge University Press, 2009.

[BFNW93] L. Babai, L. Fortnow, N. Nisan, and A. Wigderson. BPP has subexponential simulations unless EXPTIME has publishable proofs. *Computational Complexity* 3:307–318, 1993.

[Bar02] B. Barak. A probabilistic-time hierarchy theorem for slightly non-uniform algorithms. In *Proc. of RANDOM*, 194–208, 2002.

[BGHSV05] E. Ben-Sasson, O. Goldreich, P. Harsha, M. Sudan, and S. Vadhan. Short PCPs verifiable in polylogarithmic time. In *Proc. IEEE Conf. on Computational Complexity*, 120–134, 2005.

[BBG98] S. Bloch, J. F. Buss, and J. Goldsmith. Sharply bounded alternation and quasilinear time. *Theory Comput. Syst.* 31(2):187–214, 1998.

[BFT98] H. Buhrman, L. Fortnow, and T. Thierauf. Nonrelativizing separations. In *Proc. IEEE Conf. on Computational Complexity*, 8–12, 1998.

[BG93] J. F. Buss and J. Goldsmith. Nondeterminism within P. *SIAM J. Computing* 22:560–572, 1993.

[CJ03] L. Cai and D. Juedes. On the existence of subexponential parameterized algorithms. *J. Comput. Syst. Sci.* 67(4):789–807, 2003.

[CC97] L. Cai and J. Chen. On the amount of nondeterminism and the power of verifying. *SIAM J. Computing* 26(3):733–750, 1997.

[CIP06] C. Calabro, R. Impagliazzo, and R. Paturi. A duality between clause width and clause density for SAT. In *Proc. IEEE Conf. on Computational Complexity*, 252–260, 2006.

[CIP09] C. Calabro, R. Impagliazzo, and R. Paturi. The complexity of satisfiability of small depth circuits. In *Proc. International Workshop on Parameterized and Exact Computation*, 2009.

[CG07] Y. Chen and M. Grohe. An isomorphism between subexponential and parameterized complexity theory. *SIAM J. Computing* 37:1228–1258, 2007.

[DH08] E. Dantsin and E. A. Hirsch. Worst-case upper bounds. In *Handbook of Satisfiability*, A. Biere, M. Heule, H. van Maaren and T. Walsh (eds.), 341–362, 2008.

[DF99] R. G. Downey and M. R. Fellows. *Parameterized complexity.* Springer-Verlag, 1999.

[FL89] M. R. Fellows and M. A. Langston. On search, decision and the efficiency of polynomial-time algorithms. In *Proc. ACM Symposium on Theory of Computing*, 501–512, 1989.

[FGW06] J. Flum, M. Grohe, and M. Weyer. Bounded fixed-parameter tractability and $\log^2 n$ nondeterministic bits. *J. Comput. Syst. Sci.* 72(1):34–71, 2006.

[FG06] J. Flum and M. Grohe. *Parameterized complexity theory.* Springer, 2006.

[For01] L. Fortnow. Comparing notions of full derandomization. In *Proc. IEEE Conf. on Computational Complexity*, 28–34, 2001.

[FLvMV05] L. Fortnow, R. Lipton, D. van Melkebeek, and A. Viglas. Time-space lower bounds for satisfiability. *JACM* 52(6):835–865, 2005.

[GO95] A. Gajentaan and M. H. Overmars. On a class of $O(n^2)$ problems in computational geometry. *Computational Geometry: Theory and Applications* 5(3):165–185, 1995.

[GS89] Y. Gurevich and S. Shelah. Nearly linear time. *Logic at Botik '89*, Springer-Verlag LNCS 363, 108–118, 1989.

[Har89] J. Hartmanis. Gödel, von Neumann, and the P?=NP problem. *Bulletin of the European Association for Theoretical Computer Science* 101–107, June 1989. See also: M. Sipser. The history and status of the P versus NP question. In *Proc. ACM Symposium on Theory of Computing*, 603–618, 1992.

[Has98] J. Hastad. The shrinkage exponent of De Morgan formulae is 2. *SIAM J. Computing*, 27:48–64, 1998.

[Imp10] R. Impagliazzo, personal communication.

[IKW02] R. Impagliazzo, V. Kabanets, and A. Wigderson. In search of an easy witness: exponential time versus probabilistic polynomial time. *J. Comput. Syst. Sci.* 65(4):672–694, 2002.

[IP01] R. Impagliazzo and R. Paturi. On the complexity of k-SAT. *J. Comput. Syst. Sci.* 62(2):367–375, 2001.

[IPZ01] R. Impagliazzo, R. Paturi, and F. Zane. Which problems have strongly exponential complexity? *J. Comput. Syst. Sci.* 63(4):512–530, 2001.

[KC99] V. Kabanets and J.-Y. Cai. Circuit minimization problem. In *Proc. ACM Symposium on Theory of Computing*, 73–79, 2000.

[KRC00] V. Kabanets, C. Rackoff, and S. A. Cook. Efficiently approximable real-valued functions. *Electronic Colloquium on Computational Complexity*, TR00-034, 2000.

[KI04] V. Kabanets and R. Impagliazzo. Derandomizing polynomial identity tests means proving circuit lower bounds. *Computational Complexity* 13(1-2):1–46, 2004.

[Kan84] R. Kannan. Towards separating nondeterminism from determinism. *Mathematical Systems Theory* 17(1):29–45, 1984.

[KLV03] G. Karakostas, R. J. Lipton, and A. Viglas. On the complexity of intersecting finite state automata and NL versus NP. *Theor. Comp. Sci.* 302(1-3):257–274, 2003.

[KL80] R. M. Karp and R. J. Lipton. Some connections between nonuniform and uniform complexity classes. In *Proc. ACM Symposium on Theory of Computing* 302–309, 1980.

[KF77] C. M. R. Kintala and P. C. Fisher. Computations with a restricted number of nondeterministic steps (Extended Abstract). In *Proc. ACM Symposium on Theory of Computing*, 178–185, 1977.

[KvM99] A. Klivans and D. van Melkebeek. Graph nonisomorphism has subexponential size proofs unless the polynomial-time hierarchy collapses. *SIAM J. Computing* 31(5):1501–1526, 2002.

[Koz77] D. Kozen. Lower bounds for natural proof systems. In *Proc. IEEE Symposium on Foundations of Computer Science*, 254–266, 1977.

[Lip09a] R. J. Lipton. *Simulation of nondeterministic machines.* Weblog post available at `http://rjlipton.wordpress.com/2009/05/11/simulation-of-nondeterministic-machines/`

[Lip09b] R. J. Lipton. *An approach to the P=NP question?* Weblog post available at `http://rjlipton.wordpress.com/2009/10/02/an-approach-to-the-pnp-question/`

[LV96] M. Luby and B. Velickovic. On deterministic approximation of DNF. *Algorithmica* 16(4/5):415–433, 1996.

[vMS05] D. van Melkebeek and R. Santhanam. Holographic proofs and derandomization. *SIAM J. Computing*, 35:59–90, 2005.

[vM07] D. van Melkebeek. A survey of lower bounds for satisfiability and related problems. *Foundations and Trends in Theoretical Computer Science* 2:197âĂŞ303, 2007.

[Mei09] O. Meir. Combinatorial PCPs with efficient verifiers. In *Proc. IEEE Symposium on Foundations of Computer Science*, 463–471, 2009.

[PW10] M. Patrascu and R. Williams. On the possibility of faster SAT algorithms. In *Proc. ACM-SIAM Symposium on Discrete Algorithms*, 2010.

[PF79] N. Pippenger and M. J. Fischer. Relations among complexity measures. *JACM* 26(2):361–381, 1979.

[SFM78] J. Seiferas, M. J. Fischer, and A. Meyer. Separating nondeterministic time complexity Classes. *JACM* 25:146–167, 1978.

[Tou01] I. Tourlakis. Time-space tradeoffs for SAT on nonuniform machines. *J. Comput. Syst. Sci.* 63(2):268–287, 2001.

[Tra08] P. Traxler. The time complexity of constraint satisfaction. In *Proc. International Workshop on Parameterized and Exact Computation*, 190–201, 2008.

[Tse68] G. Tseitin. On the complexity of derivation in propositional calculus. *Studies in Constr. Math. and Math. Logic*, 1968.

[Wil08b] R. Williams. Time-space lower bounds for counting NP solutions modulo integers. *Computational Complexity* 17(2):179–219, 2008.

[Wil10] R. Williams. Alternation-trading proofs, linear programming, and lower bounds. In *Proc. Symposium on Theoretical Aspects of Computer Science*, 2010.

[Zak83] S. Zak. A Turing machine hierarchy. *Theor. Comp. Sci.* 26:327–333, 1983.

[Zan98] F. Zane. *Circuits, CNFs, and satisfiability.* Ph.D. Thesis, University of California at San Diego, 1998.

On the Complexity of Circuit Satisfiability (Extended Abstract)

Ramamohan Paturi *
University of California, San Diego
paturi@cs.ucsd.edu

Pavel Pudlák†
Institute of Mathematics
Academy of Sciences of the Czech Republic
pudlak@math.cas.cz

ABSTRACT

In this paper, we are concerned with the exponential complexity of the *Circuit Satisfiability* (**CktSat**) problem and generally with the exponential complexity of **NP**-complete problems. Over the past 15 years or so, researchers have obtained a number of exponential-time algorithms with improved running times for exactly solving a variety of **NP**-complete problems. The improvements are typically in the form of better exponents compared to exhaustive search. Our goal is to develop techniques to prove specific lower bounds on the exponents under plausible complexity assumptions. We consider natural, though restricted, algorithmic paradigms and prove upper bounds on the success probability. Our approach has the advantage of clarifying the relative power of various algorithmic paradigms.

Our main technique is a a success probability amplification technique, called *the Exponential Amplification Lemma*, which shows that for any $f(n,m)$-size bounded probabilistic circuit family $\mathcal{A}$ that decides **CktSat** with success probability at least $2^{-\alpha n}$ for $\alpha < 1$ on inputs which are circuits of size m with n variables, there is another probabilistic circuit family $\mathcal{B}$ that decides **CktSat** with size roughly $f(\alpha n, f(n,m))$ and success probability about $2^{-\alpha^2 n} > 2^{-\alpha n}$. In contrast, the standard method for boosting success probability by repeated trials will improve it to $(1-(1-2^{-\alpha n})^t)$ ($\approx t2^{-\alpha n}$ for $t = O(2^{\alpha n})$) using circuits of size about $tf(n,m)$.

Using this lemma, we derive tight bounds on the exponent of the success probability for deciding the **CktSat** problem in a variety of probabilistic computational models under complexity assumptions. For example, we show that the success probability cannot be better than $2^{-n+o(n)}$ for deciding **CktSat** by probabilistic polynomial size circuits unless **CktSat** (thereby all of **NP**) for polynomial size instances can be decided by 2^{n^μ} size *deterministic* circuits for some $\mu < 1$, which is considered an unlikely event. As another example, we show that probabilistic quasilinear size circuits cannot achieve success probability better than $2^{-n+o(n)}$ unless **CktSat** (as well as **NP**) has $O(m^{O(\lg\lg m)})$ size deterministic circuits, which is very close to the statement $\mathbf{NP} \subseteq \mathbf{P/poly}$, an unlikely scenario.

Categories and Subject Descriptors

F.2.3 [**Theory of Computation**]: ANALYSIS OF ALGORITHMS AND PROBLEM COMPLEXITY—*Tradeoffs among Complexity Measures*

General Terms

Algorithms,Theory

Keywords

Circuit Satisfiability, **NP**-completeness

1. INTRODUCTION

It is well-known that all **NP**-complete problems are equivalent as far as polynomial-time solvability is concerned. However, much less is known about the exact complexity of these problems. If we assume $\mathbf{NP} \neq \mathbf{P}$ or other appropriate complexity statement, what can we say about the exact worst-case complexity of **NP**-complete problems? An important context for this question is the development of a series of exact exponential-time algorithms with improved run times for a number of problems including IndependentSet, k-SAT, and k-colorability. The series of improvements are typically in the form of better exponents compared to exhaustive search. However, exact worst-case complexity of these problems seem to differ considerably. These improvements prompt several complexity questions, chief among them is whether we can expect continued improvements in the exponent. Is there a limit beyond which one should not expect improvement? How do these limits differ for different problems? Can we explain the differing limits in terms of the structural properties of the problems? What are the likely exact complexities of various **NP**-complete problems? Are the likely complexities of various problems related?

The current state of the art in complexity theory is far from being able to resolve these questions, especially the

*This research is supported by NSF grant CCF-0947262 from the Division of Computing and Communication Foundations.

†Partially supported by the Institute for Theoretical Computer Science, Prague (project 1M0545 of MŠMT ČR), grant IAA100190902 of GA AV ČR and Institutional Research Plan No. AV0Z10190503.

STOC'10, June 5–8, 2010, Cambridge, Massachusetts, USA.

question of best exponents, even under reasonable complexity assumptions. We believe that it would be productive to approach these questions from the viewpoint of known algorithmic paradigms. Such an approach might be able to clarify the relative power of various algorithmic paradigms and might even be able to shed light on the best exponents in natural, though restricted, computational models under complexity assumptions. Furthermore, the study of the limitations of algorithmic paradigms might result in sharper versions of existing problems and suggest new directions of research. This paper presents an attempt in this direction and obtains nontrivial, interesting new results.

We propose to approach the randomized exact algorithms for **NP**-complete problems by studying the important subclass **OPP** of algorithms and its generalizations. **OPP** is the class of one-sided probabilistic polynomial-time algorithms. In contrast to the conventional complexity classes, **OPP** is a class of algorithms rather than a class of problems. This class captures a common design paradigm for randomized exact exponential-time algorithms: to repeat sufficiently many times a one-sided error probabilistic polynomial time algorithm that is correct with an exponentially small probability so that the overall algorithm finds a witness with constant probability. **OPP** includes Davis-Putnam-style backtracking algorithms developed in recent times to provide improved exponential-time upper bounds [4, 3, 33, 15, 14, 16, 12, 19, 18] for a variety of **NP**-hard problems. While the original versions of some of these algorithms are couched as exponential-time algorithms, one can observe from a formalization by Eppstein [17] that these algorithms can be converted into probabilistic polynomial-time algorithms whose success probability is the reciprocal of the best exponential-time bound. **OPP** also includes local search algorithms such as Schöning's [39]. **OPP** is interesting not just because of ubiquity, but because such algorithms are ideal from the point of view of space efficiency, parallelization, and speed-up by quantum computation. What are the limitations of such algorithms for deciding **NP**-complete problems? Could the best algorithms for canonical **NP**-complete problems such as **CktSat** (the problem of deciding whether a circuit is satisfiable) or k-SAT be in **OPP**?

In addition to **OPP**, there are several other important algorithmic paradigms for designing exact algorithms for **NP**-hard problems, for example, exponential-time divide-and-conquer [27, 37], inclusion-exclusion/Möbius inversion [25, 8, 6, 7], dynamic programming [20, 36], group algebra [26, 44], sieve algorithms [2, 31], and Voronoi cell computations [30]. However, we argue that **OPP** and its generalizations could serve as an excellent starting point for the study of exponential-time algorithms for **NP**-complete problems in general.

Consider the problem of k-colorability for $k \geq 3$. The best-known algorithm [8] for this problem applies the inclusion-exclusion principle to achieve an $\tilde{O}(2^n)$ algorithm where n in the number of vertices of the graph. This algorithm and the prior best-known algorithms [37, 16, 11, 9] do not belong to the class **OPP**. This raises a natural question whether we can expect an **OPP** algorithm for k-colorability whose success probability is at least 2^{-n}. Beyond this, can we expect **OPP**-style optimal algorithms for k-colorability? Does there exist any **OPP** algorithm for k-colorability whose success probability is at least c^{-n} where c is independent of k? Negative answers (or evidence to that effect) for these questions would provide convincing proof (or evidence) that exponential-time inclusion-exclusion and dynamic programming paradigms are strictly more powerful than that of **OPP**. On the other hand, results that would show k-colorability can be solved by an **OPP** algorithm with c^{-n} success probability would be exciting. Similar situation exists with respect to the Hamiltonian path problem where we know of no **OPP** algorithms that succeed with significantly better than $1/n!$ success probability whereas it is well-known that there are $O(n^2 2^n)$ algorithms [5, 25] based on exponential-time dynamic programming and inclusion-exclusion techniques. It seems that resolving the question, whether **OPP**-style optimal algorithms exist for k-colorability and Hamiltonian path, is related to a fundamental issue regarding the tradeoff between time and success probability which in turn might hold one of the keys (the others being **P** versus **NP** and derandomization) for the complexity theory of exact algorithms for **NP**-complete problems.

To study the exponents in the exact complexity of **NP**-complete problems, it is useful to parameterize **NP** problem instances with two parameters. Usually, **NP** problem instances are parameterized by the size of the input. However, for the purpose of capturing the exponential complexity, it is more natural to parameterize the instances in terms of an additional *complexity* parameter. For example, the **CktSat** problem instances are parameterized by n, the number of variables, and m, the length of the input, which is a description of a circuit. A graph problem such as k-colorability is parameterized by n, the number of vertices, and m, the length of the representation of the graph. These parameters are natural and robust with respect to the representation of the input. We assume that problems are presented together with a complexity parameter. It is also useful to endow the class **NP** with a canonical complexity parameter so we can state properties of **NP** in terms of the complexity parameter and the size of the input. Consider an **NP** predicate in the form $\exists x \Phi(y, x)$ where y is the input instance, x the witness, and Φ is a polynomial-time (in the length of y) computable predicate. We canonically parameterize **NP** problem instances by n, the length of the witness, as well as m, the length of the input. Focus on the length of the witness is natural when we consider exponential-time exact algorithms.

We use the notation $\mathbf{NP}(n, m)$ and $\mathbf{CktSat}(n, m)$ to be explicit about the parameterization. Complexity bounds are usually expressed as functions of both n and m. We would like to observe that any problem instance in $\mathbf{NP}(n, m)$ can be reduced to a $\mathbf{CktSat}(n, m')$ instance in time t preserving the witness length, where t and m' are polynomially bounded in m.

The results in the paper concern the more general class $\mathbf{OP}(T(n, m))$ of one-sided probabilistic algorithms that run in time $T(n, m)$ with success probability bounded by a small exponential function in n, independent of m. In addition to the case where $T(n, m)$ is polynomially bounded in m, we consider other natural cases. In fact, several of the branch-and-bound algorithms mentioned earlier run in quasilinear time where the success probability is inverse of the exponential run time. We will also consider more powerful models where the algorithm can check exponentially many candidates to find a witness. In particular, we consider the class $\mathbf{OP}(T(n, m))$ of algorithms for the following cases of $T(n, m)$:

- $T(n, m)$ is polynomially bounded in m,
- $T(n, m)$ is quasilinearly bounded in m (of the form $O(m \lg^k m)$ for some $k \geq 0$),
- $T(n, m)$ is subexponential in n and quasilinear in m, and
- $T(n, m)$ is a small exponential in n and quasilinear in m.

Our results include upper bounds on the success probability for deciding the **CktSat** problem in all of the models mentioned above subject to various complexity assumptions. These bounds are tight in the sense they achieve the best possible constant in the exponent. In particular, we show that the **CktSat** problem cannot be decided with success probability better than $2^{-n+o(n)}$ by **OPP** algorithms unless there are $m2^{O(n^{\mu} \lg^{1-\mu} m)}$ size *deterministic* circuits with $\mu < 1$ for deciding **CktSat**(n, m) (Theorem 4). The latter condition implies that **CktSat**(n, m) can be decided by deterministic circuits of size $2^{n^{\mu'}}$ for some $\mu' < 1$ if m is polynomially bounded in n, which is considered an unlikely event.

We will also prove similar upper bounds on the success probability for quasilinear probabilistic circuits. However, in this case, a much weaker assumption suffices. In particular, we show that the success probability cannot be better than $2^{-n+o(n)}$ in quasilinear probabilistic models unless **CktSat**(n, m) has $O(\text{poly}(m) n^{O(\lg \lg m)})$ deterministic size circuits. The latter statement is very close to the statement $\mathbf{NP} \in \mathbf{P/poly}$, which is an unlikely event.

We will further show that the success probability in the subexponential model cannot be better than $2^{-n+o(n)}$ unless **CktSat**(n, m) has $2^{o(n)}\text{poly}(m)$ deterministic circuits (Theorem 6). In particular, the latter condition violates **ETH**.

We will also show an optimal upper bound on the success probability for small exponential time models of the form $2^{\alpha n} m \lg^k m$ for $\alpha < 1$. We show that the success probability in this model cannot be better than $2^{-(1-\alpha-\varepsilon)n+o(n)}$ for any $\varepsilon > 0$ unless **CktSat**(n, m) has $2^{\beta n}\text{poly}(m)$ size deterministic circuits where $\beta = 1/(1 + \varepsilon/\alpha) < 1$. Although the latter statement is weaker, it still would be surprising if there is a constant factor reduction in the number of existential quantifiers for all of **NP**.

Our results essentially rule out any but exhaustive search algorithms for **CktSat** in the **OPP** and other models. We believe that our results are the first of their kind. We hope that these results would put a new emphasis on obtaining similar results for combinatorial problems such as k-colorability and Hamiltonian path as well as on the general problem of time-success probability tradeoffs.

In Section 1.1, we present some related prior work. In Section 1.2, we describe the key ideas underlying our results. We define basic concepts and complexity measures in Section 2. In Section 3, we present informal descriptions of the lemmas (Exponential Amplification Lemma and the hash-down lemma) followed by their proofs. Finally, in Section 3.3 we present our conditional upperbounds on the success probability for deciding **CktSat**.

1.1 Related Prior Work

While there is a large amount of literature on the topic of the satisfiability problem, we will focus in this section on previous research dealing with lower bounds on the exponential complexity of **CktSat** and related **NP**-complete problems.

Stearns and Hunt in their 1990 paper [40] considered the concept of *power index* to characterize the exponential complexities of basic **NP**-complete problems. Power index is defined to be the infimum of all θ for which the problem is in $\mathbf{DTIME}(2^{m^{\theta}})$ where m is the length of the input. They have hypothesized that the power index of the CNF Satisfiability problem is 1 (*Satisfiability Hypothesis*) and using this assumption they have shown that the power index of the Clique problem is $\frac{1}{2}$ (in terms of the number of edges in the graph). They get their results mainly by analyzing how reductions change input lengths. The less a reduction blows up the input size, the tighter the connection between the power indices of the problems.

While these results are interesting, they are more sensitive to how the input is represented. We feel that it is more natural to parameterize **NP** in terms of witness size as well as input size, since the obvious exhaustive search algorithm is strongly exponential in the witness size, but may only be weakly exponential (as in the case of the Clique problem) in the input size. More importantly, while [40] assumed the Satisfiability Hypothesis to obtain lower bounds on the power indices for other **NP**-complete problems, in this paper we provide a justification for their assumption by showing that an analogous power index (for the success probability) for a closely related problem, **CktSat**, is 1 in **OPP**-style models under complexity assumptions that are intimately related to the **P** versus **NP** question. Moreover, success probability is parameterized using the more natural and robust parameter, the witness length.

In an earlier paper, Schnorr [38] considered the problems in the classes **NQL**, the nondeterministic quasilinear time and **QL**, the deterministic quasilinear time, under quasilinear time reductions. He showed that the CNF Satisfiability problem (and thereby the **CktSat** problem) are complete for **NQL** under quasilinear time reductions. In fact, Stearns and Hunt cite this result to provide an indirect justification for the Satisfiability Hypothesis since the power index of the CNF Satisfiability problems is at least as large as the power index of any language in **NQL**. Schnorr in this paper comments that $\mathbf{P} \neq \mathbf{NP}$ implies $\mathbf{QL} \neq \mathbf{NQL}$ but the converse is not clear. Our Theorem 5 provides certain strengthening of the forward implication: the probabilistic version of **QL** cannot achieve better than $2^{-n+o(n)}$ success probability unless **NP** has almost polynomial size circuits.

More recently, Impagliazzo, Paturi and Zane [22] explored the question whether we can expect continued improvements in terms of better exponents for the exact complexity of problems such as k-SAT, k-colorability and IndependentSet and showed that the possibility of arbitrarily small exponents for various **NP**-complete problems is one and the same. In particular, they defined the notion of subexponential time reduction families (SERF) and showed that several search problems including k-SAT, IndependentSet, k-Set Cover, Clique, Vertex Cover and k-colorability are SERF-equivalent. They also showed that some of these problems such as k-SAT and k-colorability are SERF-complete for the class of **SNP** of search problems expressible by second order existential formulas whose first order part is universal. If any of these problems can be solved subexponentially (in terms of witness length), then every problem in **SNP** can be solved in subexponential time (in terms of witness length). The key to the equivalence is a lemma called the *Sparsification Lemma* which shows one can achieve witness size-preserving reductions among these problems in subexponential time.

In a subsequent paper [21], Impagliazzo and Paturi considered the exact complexity s_k of k-SAT where $s_k = \inf\{\varepsilon | \exists \text{ a } 2^{\varepsilon n} \text{ randomized algorithm for deciding } k\text{-SAT}\}$. Under the assumption $s_3 > 0$, called the *Exponential Time Hypothesis* (**ETH**), they showed that the sequence is increasing infinitely often as k increases. Even under **ETH**, it is an open question to prove a specific lower bound for s_3, that is, to prove $s_3 > c$ for some specific $c > 0$. It is also open whether $s_\infty = 1$ where $s_\infty = \lim_{k\to\infty} s_k$. More generally, it is an open question to prove optimal exponential lower bounds for any **NP**-complete problem under plausible complexity assumptions.

Adopting **ETH** as an axiom casts light on the complexity of many other problems. Marx [28, 29] used Sparsification Lemma to show that **ETH** implies that the complexity of database queries is determined by their treewidth. Very recently, Traxler [41] has shown that **ETH** implies $(k, 2)$-CSP has k^{cn} complexity where c is an absolute constant, thus ruling out the possibility (under **ETH**) of a c^n time algorithm where c is independent of k. In contrast, k-coloring, a very important case of $(k, 2)$-CSP, has long been known to have such a c^n algorithm for c independent of k, and very recently, the c has been improved to 2 [8].

There are a number of results that relate the complexity of **CktSat** in terms of the tractability of parameterized problems. Abrahamson, Downey and Fellows have shown that the existence of $2^{o(n)}\text{poly}(m)$ algorithms for **CktSat** problem for circuits of size m and n variables is equivalent to the problem of the tractability of the class of fixed parameter problems [1]. Other interesting results regarding the connection between the possibilities of somewhat improved algorithms for parameterized problems and subexponential time algorithms of the form $2^{o(n)}\text{poly}(m)$ for **CktSat** can be found in [13].

While the work of [22] and the subsequent results based on **ETH** as well as the results connecting the complexity of **CktSat** with fixed parameter tractability are interesting and represent progress, we still do not have specific lower bounds on the exponents even under **ETH** as the constants in results based on **ETH** (such as those in [41]) depend on the assumed constant s_3 in **ETH**. In contrast, our results do obtain a specific lower bound on the exponent of the success probability for **OPP** and other models under reasonable complexity assumptions. Interestingly, our work suggests the possibility that the question of specific lower bounds on the exponents is related to the questions of **P** versus **NP** and time-success probability tradeoff for **NP**-complete problems.

We would also like to mention the recent time-space lower bounds (see [43] for a survey): the Formula Satisfiability problem cannot be decided by a deterministic random-access machine that runs in time $m^{1.801}$ and space $m^{o(1)}$ where m is the input length. Unlike our results, these results do not depend on any complexity assumptions. On the other hand, our results deal with exponential time/probability and related algorithmic paradigms.

1.2 Key Ideas

Our key idea is a reduction which effects a simultaneous tradeoff between computational resources and problem instance parameters. Several basic conditions are needed to obtain such a tradeoff. One of them is to be able to parameterize the problem instances by two parameters, witness size and input size. Another is to be able to parameterize the computational models with two resources or complexity parameters (as functions of the instance parameters). For example, size and success probability are the computational resources for probabilistic circuit models. We then need a *non black-box* reduction technique where the computation itself (after hashing down) is the reduced instance. Identity of the space of instances and the space of computations seems to be crucially necessary for the reduction technique. The last condition distinguishes the **CktSat** problem from other satisfiability problems such as **CNFSAT**. Consider a probabilistic computation that checks the satisfiability of a CNF F. To represent the computation as a CNF F', either F' would have to be of exponentially large size or it would require an increase in the number of variables. In either case, it is not clear how to achieve the desired tradeoff between the complexity parameters and instance parameters when CNFs are the instances.

These basic ideas are brought together to obtain a simultaneous tradeoff between computational resources and between instance parameters to prove our key lemma, *the Exponential Amplification Lemma* (Lemma 2). The Exponential Amplification Lemma is a success probability amplification technique which shows that for any $f(n, m)$-size bounded probabilistic circuit family $\mathcal{A}$ that decides **CktSat** with success probability at least $2^{-\alpha n}$ on inputs which are circuits of size m with n variables, there is another probabilistic circuit family $\mathcal{B}$ that decides **CktSat** with size roughly $f(\alpha n, f(n, m))$ and success probability about $2^{-\alpha^2 n}$ which is greater than $2^{-\alpha n}$ for $\alpha < 1$. In contrast, the standard method for boosting success probability by repeated trials will improve it to $(1-(1-2^{-\alpha n})^t)$ ($\approx t2^{-\alpha n}$ for $t = O(2^{\alpha n})$) using circuits of size about $tf(n, m)$. Consider the following example that will make clear the advantage of the Exponential Amplification Lemma over the standard probability boosting technique. Let $f(n, m) = m^k$ for some $k \geq 0$. If **CktSat** for polynomial size circuits can be solved with $2^{-\alpha n}$ success probability by a probabilistic circuit family of size m^k, then the lemma guarantees a probabilistic circuit family of size about m^{2k} which solves **CktSat** for polynomial size circuits with success probability of about $2^{-\alpha^2 n}$. On the other hand, the standard boosting technique improves the success probability to $m^k 2^{-\alpha n}$ using the same resources. From this example, it is clear that the lemma provides an exponential advantage for $\alpha < 1$.

Elements of our technique are present in [21] where instances of CNF satisfiability are parameterized by the number of variables and the maximum width of the clauses and a subexponential time reduction was used to trade up the width for reducing the number of variables thereby obtaining relationships among the exponents. Traxler [41] also obtains a similar tradeoff between the size of the domain and the number of variables for constraint satisfaction problems. Whereas the techniques in [21, 41] only involve reductions among instances trading one parameter for another, our current technique for **CktSat** obtains simultaneous tradeoffs between algorithmic resources and instance parameters by effecting them in terms of each other.

2. CIRCUITS, CIRCUIT SATISFIABILITY, AND CIRCUIT FAMILIES

Let $\mathcal{C}$ denote the class of circuits with a single output over the standard, bounded fan-in basis AND, OR, and NOT. Each source node in the directed acyclic graph of a circuit C is either labeled by a variable or by a constant. Let $n = n(C)$ denote the number of variables of C, Let $\mathbf{size}(C)$ denote the count of gates in the circuit where each source node is counted as a gate. Encoding of a circuit contains two parts: the first part encodes the number of variables in unary notation and the second part is a standard encoding of the circuit as a binary string. For a circuit C, let $\mathbf{desc}(C)$ denote the encoding of the circuit and let $m(C) = |\mathbf{desc}(C)|$. $m(C)$ is at least $n(C)$ and is $O(\mathbf{size}(C)\lg(\mathbf{size}(C)))$.

In this paper, we are primarily concerned with **CktSat**, the *Circuit Satisfiability* problem: given an encoding of $C \in \mathcal{C}$, does there exist a $x \in \{0,1\}^{n(C)}$, that is, a setting of the variables of C, such that C with setting x outputs 1. In such a case, we say that the circuit C is *satisfiable*.

A *probabilistic circuit* is a circuit where each variable is further distinguished as an input variable or a random variable. For input variables y and random variables z, $C(y,z)$ denotes the output of the probabilistic circuit C. $C^y(z)$ denotes the *specialization* of the circuit when its first argument is fixed at the value y. Let $\mathbf{Pr}[C^y(z) = 1]$ denote the probability that the circuit C outputs 1 for the input y, where the random variables z of C take the values 0 or 1 with equal probability.

Input instances for the **CktSat** problem are encodings of circuits and are parameterized by the number of variables and the length of the encoding. In our constructions, we also deal with circuits with multiple outputs. Earlier notions and notation extend naturally to such circuits.

We consider probabilistic circuit families indexed by instance parameters as computational models. A family $\mathcal{F}$ of circuits is a collection $\{F_{n,m} | n, m \geq 1\}$ where $F_{n,m}$ is a probabilistic circuit whose inputs are encodings of circuits with n variables and of encoding length m. For $f : \mathbb{N} \times \mathbb{N} \to \mathbb{R}$, we say that a circuit family $\{F_{n,m}\}$ is f-bounded if $\mathbf{size}(F_{n,m}) \leq O(f(n,m))$. We say that a circuit family $\{F_{n,m}\}$ *decides* **CktSat** with *success probability* $p(n)$ if for all inputs which are encodings of circuits with n variables and of encoding length m, $F_{n,m}$ outputs 1 with probability at least $p(n)$ for all satisfiable circuits and otherwise outputs 0 with probability 1. In other words, $p(n) = \inf_{m,y} \mathbf{Pr}[F^y_{n,m}(z) = 1]$, where y is a length m string which is an encoding of a satisfiable circuit with n variables and z denotes the string of random variables of $F_{n,m}$.

Let $\mathcal{F}$ be a circuit family $\{F_{n,m}\}$ deciding **CktSat** with success probability $p(n)$. We define the (exponential) *complexity* of $\mathcal{F}$ for deciding **CktSat** for inputs which are circuits with n variables as

$$E_{\mathbf{CktSat}}(\mathcal{F}, n) = \lg(1/p(n))/n.$$

The idea is that $E_{\mathbf{CktSat}}(\mathcal{F}, n)$ captures the exponent c of the success probability $p(n)$ when expressed as $(2^{-n})^c$. The larger the exponent, the higher the complexity of $\mathcal{F}$. The complexity of $\mathcal{F}$ is defined as
$E_{\mathbf{CktSat}}(\mathcal{F}) = \limsup_{n\to\infty} E_{\mathbf{CktSat}}(\mathcal{F}, n)$.

We define the complexity $E_{\mathbf{CktSat}}(f)$ of deciding **CktSat** as the *best* exponent achievable by an f-bounded probabilistic circuit family. More precisely,

$$E_{\mathbf{CktSat}}(f) = \inf\{\varepsilon | \exists \text{ an } f\text{-bounded family } \mathcal{F} \text{ for deciding } \mathbf{CktSat} \text{ such that} E_{\mathbf{CktSat}}(\mathcal{F}) \leq \varepsilon\}.$$

We are interested in f-bounded circuit families where $f(n,m) = O(2^{\alpha(n)n} m^k \lg^l m)$ where $\alpha(n)$ is $0, o_n(1)$, or constant, $k \geq 1$, and $l \geq 0$. Such circuit families support computing paradigms where one can evaluate $2^{\alpha(n)n}$ witnesses to find a satisfying solution since a circuit of encoding length m can be evaluated at a given input by a circuit of size $m \lg^l m$ for some $l \geq 0$ [34, 35]. We use the notation $\tilde{O}(f)$ to suppress polylogarithmic factors in f.

3. COMPLEXITY OF CIRCUIT SATISFIABILITY

We know that $E_{\mathbf{CktSat}}(\mathbf{2^{o(n)}\tilde{O}(m)}) \leq E_{\mathbf{CktSat}}(\mathbf{m^k})$ $\leq E_{\mathbf{CktSat}}(\mathbf{\tilde{O}(m)}) \leq 1$. We also know that $E_{\mathbf{CktSat}}(\mathbf{2^{\alpha n}\tilde{O}(m)}) \leq 1-\alpha$. It is open whether any of these complexities can be lower bounded. In this paper, we prove $E_{\mathbf{CktSat}}(\mathbf{2^{o(n)}\tilde{O}(m)}) = E_{\mathbf{CktSat}}(\mathbf{m^k}) = E_{\mathbf{CktSat}}(\mathbf{\tilde{O}(m)}) = 1$ under complexity assumptions. We also prove that for any $\alpha < 1$ and $\varepsilon > 0$, $E_{\mathbf{CktSat}}(\mathbf{2^{\alpha n}\tilde{O}(m)}) \geq 1 - \alpha - \varepsilon$ under a certain complexity assumption.

Our results follow from a repeated application of the Exponential Amplification Lemma, which shows how to construct a probabilistic circuit family $\mathcal{G}$ for deciding **CktSat** with improved success probability $2^{-\alpha^2 n}$ from a given f-bounded circuit family $\mathcal{F}$ that decides **CktSat** with success probability $2^{-\alpha n}$. In the following, we provide an informal description of the proof of the lemma.

Let $F_{n,m}$ be a probabilistic circuit in the family $\mathcal{F}$ and let $F_{n,m}(y,z)$ denote the probabilistic computation of $F_{n,m}$ on an input y where z represents the random variables. Let y be the encoding of a circuit C with n variables and encoding length m. Since $F_{n,m}(y,z)$ decides the satisfiability of C with one-sided error, the specialization $F^y_{n,m}(z)$ and the circuit C are equivalent with respect to satisfiability. We will treat the computation $C' = F^y_{n,m}(z)$ as a **CktSat** problem instance. The size of C' is $m' = f(n,m)$ and it may have as many as $r = f(n,m)$ variables. The idea is to use the encoding of C' as input to the probabilistic circuit $F_{r,m'}$ from the family $\mathcal{F}$ to decide the satisfiability of C.

So far the transformation from C to C' does not represent any useful tradeoff between the instance parameters. To make progress, we need the following crucial observation. If C is satisfiable and if $\alpha < 1$, then the density of satisfying assignments in C' will be high, that is, at least $2^{-\alpha n}$. Using a technique of Valiant and Vazirani [42], we can hash down the circuit C' to obtain another circuit C'' with reduced number of variables, about αn, in such a way that C'' and C' are equivalent with respect to satisfiability and that the size of C'' is about the same as that of C' (up to polylogarithmic factors). Overall, we can constructively transform a circuit C with n variables and encoding length m to C'' with about αn variables and encoding length $m'' \approx f(n,m)$ (up to polylogarithmic factors). We will then input C'' to the probabilistic circuit $F_{\alpha n, m''}$ from the family $\mathcal{F}$ to achieve an improved success probability of about

$2^{-\alpha^2 n}$. The probabilistic circuit family $\mathcal{G}$ is designed to implement this amplification in such a way that $\mathcal{G}$ is g-bounded where $g(n,m) \approx f(\alpha n, \tilde{O}(f(n,m))$ (up to polylogarithmic factors).

In the next two subsections we state and prove the hash-down lemma and the Exponential Amplification Lemma. In the subsequent section, we state our results on the exponential complexity of **CktSat**.

3.1 Hash-Down Lemma

As is clear from the previous description, an important ingredient in the proof of the Exponential Amplification Lemma is the construction of a circuit **Sparse**(C), which equivalent to the circuit C with respect to satisfiability, but with fewer variables. This construction is closely related to that of the unique satisfiability construction of Valiant and Vazirani [42] and is captured in the following hash-down lemma, Lemma 1.

Let $C \in \mathcal{C}$ be a satisfiable circuit with n variables and let m denote its description length. Let $S^C \subseteq \{0,1\}^n$ be the nonempty set of satisfying assignments to the variables of C. Let $s = \lfloor \lg |S^C| \rfloor - 2$; we will assume that $s > 0$.

The intuition for the construction of **Sparse**(C) is as follows. If the set S^C is intersected with a random subcube of dimension $(n-s)$, we expect to get a nonempty intersection. Therefore, $(n-s)$ bits are sufficient to locate a satisfying assignment in the intersection. This intuition is operationalized by restricting C to inputs from a random coset of a random linear transformation from $\{0,1\}^n$ to $\{0,1\}^s$. Such a restriction turns out to be equivalent with respect to satisfiability since the random coset contains a satisfying assignment with sufficiently high probability. Moreover, members of the coset can be generated by a small-size circuit given their $(n-s)$-bit address in the coset. The details are provided below.

We follow the standard idea of using pairwise independent functions for hashing. However, rather than using random linear transformations we will use random Toeplitz matrices to achieve the desired pairwise independence. It requires only a linear number of bits to specify a random Toeplitz matrix over GF(2). Linear randomness together with fast GCD and convolution algorithms [10, 32] will only require a quasilinear computation to select a random coset and to address its members. While we can live with polynomial overhead for some of our theorems, quasilinear hashing is necessary when we work with quasilinear size circuit models.

Let n be fixed. Let $t = (t_{-n+1}, \cdots, t_{-1}, t_0, t_1, \cdots, t_{n-1}) \in \{0,1\}^{2n-1}$. We will denote by T_t the Toeplitz matrix determined by t, which is the matrix defined by $T_t(i,j) = t_{(j-i)}$ for $0 \le i,j \le n-1$. For a column vector $z \in \{0,1\}^n$, let $(T_t z)_s$ denote the column vector of the first s bits of $T_t z$, the product of the matrix T_t with the column vector z. For $t \in \{0,1\}^{2n-1}$ and $w \in \{0,1\}^s$, define the affine linear transformation $h_{t,w}(z) = (T_t z)_s + w$. It is well-known that $\{h_{t,w}\}$ is a pairwise independent family of functions from $\{0,1\}^n$ to $\{0,1\}^s$.

We would like to parameterize the cosets $H_{t,w} = \{z | h_{t,w}(z) = 0\}$. For $w \in \{0,1\}^s$ and $x \in \{0,1\}^{n-s}$ we will define the column vector $(w;x)$ to be the concatenation of w and x. For $w \in \{0,1\}^s$ and t such that T_t is invertible, we define $J_{t,w}(x) := T_t^{-1}(w;x)$ to obtain the needed parameterization of the coset $H_{t,w}$. When T_t is nonsingular, it is easy to see that $\mathbf{Image}(J_{t,w}) = H_{t,w}$. Indeed, if $z \in H_{t,w}$, then by definition $h_{t,w}(z) = (T_t z)_s + w = 0$. This implies that there exists an $x \in \{0,1\}^{n-s}$ such that $T_t z + (w;x) = 0$. Since we are working over GF(2) and since T_t is nonsingular, it follows that $z = T_t^{-1}(w;x) = J_{t,w}(x)$. Similarly, if $z \in \mathbf{Image}(J_{t,w})$, then $z \in H_{t,w}$.

The circuit $\mathbf{Sparse}^{t,w}(C)$ with $(n-s)$ variables is the composition of $J_{t,w}$ with C, *i.e.*, $\mathbf{Sparse}^{t,w}(C)(x) = C(J_{t,w}(x))$.

LEMMA 1. *C and $\mathbf{Sparse}^{t,w}(C)$ are equivalent with respect to satisfiability with probability at least 1/4. Furthermore, $\mathbf{Sparse}^{t,w}(C)$ can be constructed in size $\tilde{O}(m)$ and its description can be computed by a circuit of size $\tilde{O}(m)$ given* **desc**$(C), t$ *and* w.

PROOF. Our goal is to prove

$$\mathbf{Pr}_{t,w}[S^C \cap \mathbf{Image}(J_{t,w}) \neq \emptyset] \geq 1/4,$$

where we are assuming the uniform distribution on $t \in \{0,1\}^{2n-1}$ and $w \in \{0,1\}^s$. However, $\mathbf{Image}(J_{t,w}) = H_{t,w}$ if T_t is nonsingular. We will first argue that $\mathbf{Pr}_{t,w}[S^C \cap H_{t,w} \neq \emptyset] \geq 3/4$ assuming T_t is nonsingular. We then use the result of Kaltofen and Lobo [24] which states $\mathbf{Pr}[T_t \text{ is nonsingular}] \geq 1/2$ to conclude

$$\begin{aligned}&\mathbf{Pr}_{t,w}[S^C \cap \mathbf{Image}(J_{t,w}) \neq \emptyset]\\ &\geq \mathbf{Pr}_{t,w}[S^C \cap H_{t,w} \neq \emptyset] - \mathbf{Pr}[T_t \text{ is singular}] \geq 1/4\end{aligned}$$

For $z \in S^C$, let $q_{t,w}(z)$ denote the indicator function for the event $z \in H_{t,w}$, *i.e.*, $h_{t,w}(z) = 0$. Let $Q_{t,w} := \sum_{z \in S^C} q_{t,w}(z)$. We have $Q_{t,w} \neq 0$ iff $S^C \cap H_{t,w} \neq \emptyset$. We will upper bound the probability of the event $Q_{t,w} = 0$ using Chebyshev's inequality: $\mathbf{Pr}[Q_{t,w} = 0] \leq \frac{\mathbf{Var}[Q_{t,w}]}{(\mathbf{E}[Q_{t,w}])^2}$. Using the property of pairwise independence of the functions $h_{t,w}$, we get

$$\begin{aligned}\mathbf{Var}[Q_{t,w}] &= \mathbf{E}[Q_{t,w}^2] - \mathbf{E}[Q_{t,w}]^2\\ &= (|S^C|^2 - |S^C|)2^{-2s} + |S^C|2^{-s} - |S^C|^2 2^{-2s}\\ &= |S^C|(2^{-s} - 2^{-2s}).\end{aligned}$$

Hence

$$\begin{aligned}\frac{\mathbf{Var}[Q_{t,w}]}{\mathbf{E}[Q_{t,w}]^2} &= \frac{|S^C|(2^{-s} - 2^{-2s})}{|S^C|^2 2^{-2s}}\\ &= \frac{1 - 2^{-s}}{|S^C| 2^{-s}} \leq \frac{1 - 2^{-s}}{4} < 1/4.\end{aligned}$$

This completes the proof that C and $\mathbf{Sparse}^{t,w}(C)$ are equivalent with respect to satisfiability with probability at least 1/4..

Using fast GCD and convolution algorithms as well as the Gohberg-Semencul formula for the inverse of a Toeplitz matrix [10, 32], one can compute $J_{t,w}(x) = T_t^{-1}(w;x)$ with bit complexity $\tilde{O}(n)$. Since $m \geq n$, the circuit $\mathbf{Sparse}^{t,w}(C)$ can be constructed in $\tilde{O}(m)$ size. It is easy to check that the description of $\mathbf{Sparse}^{t,w}(C)$ can be computed by a circuit of size $\tilde{O}(m)$. $\square$

It should be noted that there are linear size circuit constructions [23] for pairwise independent hash functions which would improve upon the construction in Lemma 1 in terms of circuit size by eliminating the polylogarithmic factor. However, we still need a logarithmic factor for describing the circuit and as a result the improved construction would not make a significant difference as far as our results are concerned.

3.2 Exponential Amplification Lemma

LEMMA 2. **Exponential Amplification Lemma:** *Let $\mathcal{F}$ be an f-bounded family for some $f : \mathbb{N} \times \mathbb{N} \to \mathbb{R}$ such that $E_{\mathbf{CktSat}}(\mathcal{F}) < \delta$ for $0 < \delta < 1$. Assume $f(n, m) \geq m$ for all n. Then there exists a g-bounded circuit family $\mathcal{G}$ such that, for all sufficiently large n, $E_{\mathbf{CktSat}}(\mathcal{G}) < \delta^2$ where*

$$g(n, m) = O(f(\lceil \delta n \rceil + 5, \tilde{O}(f(n, m)))).$$

PROOF. Let $F_{n,m}$ be the probabilistic circuit from the family $\mathcal{F}$ that decides **CktSat** for circuits of description size m and n variables. $F_{n,m}$ itself has m input variables which encode the description of a circuit D of n variables. Also $F_{n,m}$ has r random variables y. By assumption $\mathbf{size}(F_{n,m}) = O(f(n, m))$, $r = O(f(n, m))$, and the success probability $p(n)$ of $F_{n,m}$ is greater than $2^{-\delta n}$ for all sufficiently large n.

Let $n' = \lceil \delta n \rceil + 5$ and $s = r - n'$. It follows that $p(n) > 2^{-n'}$. We will construct a g-bounded family $\mathcal{G}$ of probabilistic circuits that decides **CktSat** with success probability $p(r - s) = p(n')$ for circuits with n variables where $g(n, m) = O(f(n', \tilde{O}(f(n, m))))$. A key idea is, for a given circuit D, to view $F_{n,m}(\mathbf{desc}(D), y)$ as a (deterministic) boolean circuit $C(y) := F_{n,m}^{\mathbf{desc}(D)}(y)$ of r variables. When D is satisfiable, it follows that $C(y)$ has at least $2^{(r - \lceil \delta n \rceil)}$ solutions for all sufficiently large n. We apply the **Sparse**() function to C to obtain a circuit with n' variables which is equivalent to D with respect to satisfiability. We then apply the description of **Sparse**(C) as input to an appropriate circuit from the family $\mathcal{F}$ to improve success probability. The details of this construction are presented in the following algorithm and figures.

Circuit $G_{n,m}$ (see Figure 1):

Input: $\mathbf{desc}(D)$ of $D \in \mathcal{C}$ with n variables and description length m.
$C(y) := F_{n,m}^{\mathbf{desc}(D)}(y)$, the specialization of $F_{n,m}$ to the input $\mathbf{desc}(D)$.
If $r > n'$,
  Select random $t \in \{0, 1\}^{2r-1}$ and $w \in \{0, 1\}^s$.
  If T_t is invertible, compute the description of a circuit $J_{t,w}(x)$ that computes $T_t^{-1}(w; x)$ for $x \in \{0, 1\}^{n'}$.
  $\mathbf{Sparse}^{t,w}(C)(x) := C(J_{t,w}(x))$.
  $H(x) := \mathbf{Sparse}^{t,w}(C)(x)$ where $x \in \{0, 1\}^{n'}$. (see Figure 2)
else
  $H(x) = C(x)$ where $x \in \{0, 1\}^r$.
PrepCkt: Compute the description of the circuit H. Let $m' = |\mathbf{desc}(H)|$.
Apply $F_{n'',m'}$ to $\mathbf{desc}(H)$ where $n'' = n'$ if $r > n'$, otherwise $n'' = r$.
Output: $F_{n'',m'}(\mathbf{desc}(H))$.

We will first argue that D and H are equivalent with respect to satisfiability. It is clear that if D is unsatisfiable, H is unsatisfiable. If D is satisfiable, then it follows from Lemma 1 that $\mathbf{Sparse}^{t,w}(C)$ is satisfiable with probability at least 1/4. Since $n'' \leq \lceil \delta n \rceil + 5$, it follows $F_{n'',m'}$ outputs 1 on input $\mathbf{desc}(H)$ with probability at least $2^{-\delta n''}$, which implies that the success probability of $G_{n,m}$ is at least $2^{-\delta' \delta n - 6\delta' - 5}$ for some $\delta' < \delta$. It then follows that $E_{\mathbf{CktSat}}(\mathcal{G}, n) < \delta^2$ for all sufficiently large n.

We will now upper bound the size of $G_{n,m}$. By Lemma 1, $\mathbf{Sparse}^{t,w}(C)(x)$ can be described using at most $m' = \tilde{O}(f(n, m))$ bits and the description itself can be computed by a circuit of size $\tilde{O}(f(n, m)))$. It follows that the size of H is also bounded by $\tilde{O}(f(n, m))$ whether $r > n'$ or not.

Thus, the size of $G_{n,m}$ is upper bounded by

$$f(n'', m') + \tilde{O}(f(n, m)) \leq f(\lceil \delta n \rceil + 5, \tilde{O}(f(n, m))) + \tilde{O}(f(n, m))$$
$$\leq O(f(\lceil \delta n \rceil + 5, \tilde{O}(f(n, m)))) \text{ since } f(n, m) \geq m.$$

□

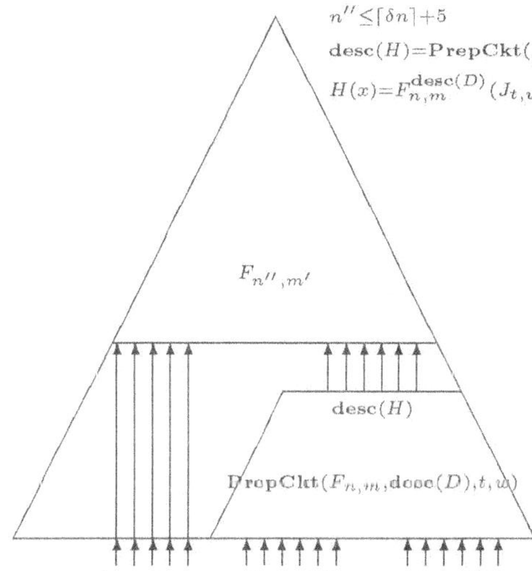

Figure 1: Circuit $G_{n,m}$

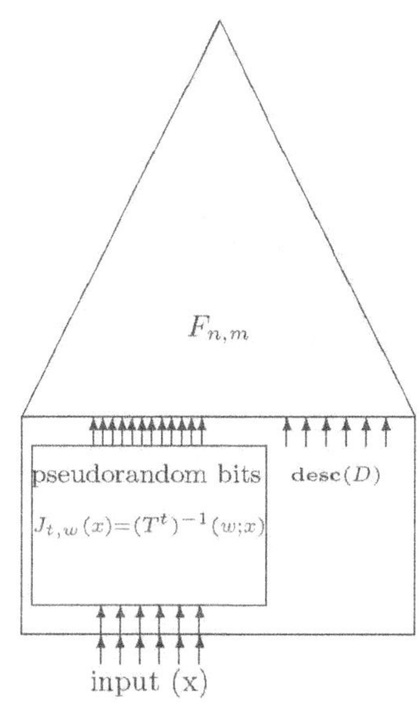

Figure 2: $H(x) = F_{n,m}^{\mathbf{desc}(D)}(J_{t,w}(x))$

We present the following lemma which states how to boost the success probability by repeated independent trails. The proof follows from standard arguments.

LEMMA 3. *If C is a probabilistic circuit of size M deciding* **CktSat** *with success probability $q > 0$ for a set of inputs, then there exists a deterministic circuit D of size $\tilde{O}(M^2)/q$ that decides* **CktSat** *on the same set of inputs. The same holds for any set in* **NP** *in place of* **CktSat**.

3.3 Results

In this section, we will show that for certain $f(n, m)$, any $f(n, m)$-bounded probabilistic circuit family deciding **CktSat** cannot succeed with probability better than $2^{-n+o(n)}$, based on the assumption that **CktSat** does not have small size deterministic circuits. The outline of our argument is as follows: we start with an $f(n, m)$-bounded probabilistic circuit family that decides **CktSat** with success probability $2^{-\delta n}$ for $\delta < 1$ and construct a deterministic circuit family for deciding **CktSat** by repeated application of the Exponential Amplification Lemma followed by an application of Lemma 3. The size of the resulting deterministic circuit family depends on $f(n, m)$. The smaller the f, the smaller the size of the deterministic circuit family.

In the following theorems we state the size of the resulting deterministic circuits for deciding **CktSat**(n, m). While our size bounds hold for any n and m, the implausibility of small size deterministic circuits for deciding **CktSat**(n, m) also depends on the relative size of m with respect to n. For example, the **CktSat** problem for circuits where the description length m is exponentially large in n (say, $m = 2^n$) is decidable by a *polynomially bounded* (say, $f(n, m) = \Omega(m^2 \lg m)$) deterministic circuit family since **CktSat**(n, m) can be decided by circuits of size $2^n \tilde{O}(m)$. In remarks following the theorems, we point out explicitly for what values of m (as a function of n) the existence of the resulting deterministic circuit family is considered implausible.

THEOREM 4. *For $k > 1$, either $E_{\mathbf{CktSat}}(\mathbf{m^k}) = 1$ or there exists a $\mu < 1$ such that* **CktSat**(n, m) *can be decided by deterministic circuits of size $m2^{O(n^\mu \lg^{1-\mu} m)}$.*

Remarks: Consider the second clause in the disjunction of the statement of the theorem: there exists a $\mu < 1$ such that **CktSat**(n, m) can be decided by deterministic circuits of size $m2^{O(n^\mu \lg^{1-\mu} m)}$. This statement implies that **CktSat**(n, m) can be decided by $O(2^{n^{\mu'}})$ size deterministic circuits for some $\mu' < 1$ for the case where m is bounded by a polynomial in n. It is currently believed that such circuits are unlikely to exist. Even when $m = 2^{o(n)}$, the statement implies that **CktSat** can be decided by deterministic circuits of size $2^{o(n)}$, which contradicts **ETH**.

Outline of the Proof: We assume that there exists a family $\mathcal{F}$ of probabilistic circuits of size $O(m^k)$ for some $k > 1$ achieving success probability $2^{-\delta n}$ for some $\delta < 1$. We apply the Exponential Amplification Lemma $d = \max(1, \lfloor (\lg \frac{n}{2 \lg m + O(\lg \lg m)})/(\lg(\frac{1}{\delta} + \lg k) \rfloor)$ times followed by an application of Lemma 3 to obtain a deterministic circuit family of size $m2^{O(n^\mu \lg^{1-\mu} m)}$ where $\mu = \frac{\lg k}{\lg(k/\delta)} < 1$ and the constant in the big O notation depends on k and δ.

THEOREM 5. *Either $E_{\mathbf{CktSat}}(\tilde{\mathbf{O}}(\mathbf{m})) = 1$ or* **CktSat**(n, m) *can be decided by deterministic circuits of size $O(\text{poly}(m) n^{O(\lg \lg m)})$.*

Remarks: The statement **CktSat**(n, m) can be decided by quasi-polynomial size deterministic circuits is very close to the statement $\mathbf{NP} \subseteq \mathbf{P/poly}$, which is considered unlikely. Theorem 5 is proved by applying the Exponential Amplification Lemma about $O(\lg n)$ times.

We will also get tight upper bounds on the success probability when $f(n, m)$ is quasilinear in m and subexponential or exponential in n.

THEOREM 6. *Either $E_{\mathbf{CktSat}}(\mathbf{2^{o(n)}\tilde{O}(m)}) = 1$ or* **CktSat**(n, m) *can be decided by deterministic circuits of size $2^{o(n)}\text{poly}(m)$.*

Remarks: Theorem 6 is proved by applying the Exponential Amplification Lemma $\omega_n(1)$ times. When we restrict m to be polynomial in n, the second clause in the statement of the theorem implies that **CktSat**(n, m) has subexponential size circuits, which contradicts **ETH**.

THEOREM 7. *For every $\alpha, \varepsilon > 0$, either $E_{\mathbf{CktSat}}(\mathbf{2^{\alpha n}\tilde{O}(m)}) \geq 1 - \alpha - \varepsilon$ or* **CktSat**(n, m) *can be decided by deterministic circuits of size $2^{n/(1+\varepsilon/\alpha)}\text{poly}(m)$.*

Remarks: In other words, if the success probability is better than $2^{-(1-\alpha)n+o(n)}$, the theorem implies that **CktSat**(n, m) can be decided by deterministic circuits of size $2^{cn}\text{poly}(m)$ where $c = 1/(1 + \frac{\varepsilon}{\alpha}) < 1$. We note that the standard success probability boosting technique (as opposed to the Exponential Amplification Lemma) would give deterministic circuits of size $2^{(1-\varepsilon)n}\text{poly}(m)$. It is easy to see that $c < (1 - \varepsilon)$ as long as $\alpha < 1$.

Acknowledgments: The authors would like to thank Boaz Barak, Chris Calabro, Russell Impagliazzo, Mike Saks, Salil Vadhan, Avi Wigderson, and Ryan Williams for helpful discussions. We would also like to thank the reviewers for valuable comments.

4. REFERENCES

[1] Karl R. Abrahamson, Rodney G. Downey, and Michael R. Fellows. Fixed-parameter tractability and completeness iv: On completeness for w[p] and pspace analogues. *Ann. Pure Appl. Logic*, 73(3):235–276, 1995.

[2] Miklós Ajtai, Ravi Kumar, and D. Sivakumar. A sieve algorithm for the shortest lattice vector problem. In *STOC '01*, 601–610, 2001.

[3] Richard Beigel. Finding maximum independent sets in sparse and general graphs. In *SODA '99*, 856–857, 1999.

[4] Richard Beigel and David Eppstein. 3-coloring in time $o(1.3446^n)$: A no-mis algorithm. In *FOCS '95*, 444–452, 1995.

[5] Richard Bellman. Dynamic programming treatment of the traveling salesman problem. *Journal of the ACM*, 9(1):61–63, 1962.

[6] Andreas Björklund, Thore Husfeldt, Petteri Kaski, and Mikko Koivisto. Fourier meets möbius: Fast subset convolution. In *STOC '07*, 67–74, 2007.

[7] Andreas Björklund, Thore Husfeldt, Petteri Kaski, and Mikko Koivisto. Computing the tutte polynomial in vertex-exponential time. In *FOCS '08*, 677–686, 2008.

[8] Andreas Björklund, Thore Husfeldt, and Mikko Koivisto. Set partitioning via inclusionŰexclusion. *SIAM Journal of Computing*, 39(2):546–563, 2009.

[9] Hans Bodlaender and Dieter Kratsch. An exact algorithm for graph coloring with polynomial memory. Technical Report UU-CS-2006-015, Utrecht University, 2006.

[10] Richard P. Brent, Fred G. Gustavson, and David Y. Y. Yun. Fast solution of toeplitz systems of equations and computation of padé approximants. *J. Algorithms*, 1(3):259–295, 1980.

[11] J. M. Byskov. *Exact Algorithms for Graph Colouring and Exact Satisfiability*. PhD thesis, Aarhus University, August 2005.

[12] Jesper Makholm Byskov. Algorithms for k-colouring and finding maximal independent sets. In *SODA '03*, 456–457, 2003.

[13] Jianer Chen, Xiuzhen Huang, Iyad A. Kanj, and Ge Xia. Strong computational lower bounds via parameterized complexity. *J. Comput. Syst. Sci.*, 72(8):1346–1367, 2006.

[14] Evgeny Dantsin, Andreas Goerdt, Edward A. Hirsch, Ravi Kannan, Jon Kleinberg, Christos Papadimitriou, Prabhakar Raghavan, and Uwe Schöning. A deterministic $(2 - 2/(k+1))^n$ algorithm for k-sat based on local search. *Theoretical Computer Science*, 289(1):69–83, 2002.

[15] David Eppstein. Improved algorithms for 3-coloring, 3-edge-coloring, and constraint satisfaction. In *SODA '01*, 329–337, 2001.

[16] David Eppstein. Small maximal independent sets and faster exact graph coloring. *Journal of Graph Algorithms and Applications*, 7:131–140, 2003.

[17] David Eppstein. Quasiconvex analysis of multivariate recurrence equations for backtracking algorithms. *ACM Trans. Algorithms*, 2(4):492–509, 2006.

[18] F. Fomin, F. Grandoni, and D. Kratsch. Measure and conquer : a simple $o(2^{0.288n})$ independent set algorithm. In *SODA '06*, 18–25, 2006.

[19] Jens Gramm, Edward A. Hirsch, Rolf Niedermeier, and Peter Rossmanith. Worst-case upper bounds for max-2-sat with an application to max-cut. *Discrete Applied Mathematics*, 130(2):139–155, 2003.

[20] Michael Held and Richard M. Karp. A dynamic programming approach to sequencing problems. In *Proceedings of the 1961 16th ACM national meeting*, 71.201–71.204, 1961.

[21] R. Impagliazzo and R. Paturi. The complexity of k-sat. *Journal of Computer and Systems Sciences*, 62(2):367–375, March 2001.

[22] R. Impagliazzo, R. Paturi, and F. Zane. Which problems have strongly exponential complexity? *Journal of Computer and System Sciences*, 63:512–530, 1998.

[23] Yuval Ishai, Eyal Kushilevitz, Rafail Ostrovsky, and Amit Sahai. Cryptography with constant computational overhead. In *STOC '08*, 433–442, 2008.

[24] E. Kaltofen and A. Lobo. On rank properties of toeplitz matrices over finite fields. In *ISSAC '96*, 241–249, 1996.

[25] Richard M. Karp. Dynamic programming meets the principle of inclusion and exclusion. *Operations Research Letters*, 1:49–51, April 1982.

[26] Ioannis Koutis. Faster algebraic algorithms for path and packing problems. In *ICALP '08*, 575–586, 2008.

[27] E. Lawler. A note on the complexity of the chromatic number problem. *Information Processing Letters*, 5(3):66–67, 1976.

[28] Dániel Marx. Can you beat treewidth? In *FOCS '07*, 169–179, 2007.

[29] Dániel Marx. On the optimality of planar and geometric approximation schemes. In *FOCS '07*, 338–348, 2007.

[30] Daniele Micciancio and Panagiotis Voulgaris. A deterministic single exponential time algorithm for most lattice problems based on voronoi cell computations. In *STOC '10*, 2010. To appear.

[31] Daniele Micciancio and Panagiotis Voulgaris. Faster exponential time algorithms for the shortest vector problem. In *SODA '10*, 1468–1480, 2010.

[32] Victor Pan. *Structured Matrices and Polynomials: Unified Superfast Algorithms*. Birkhäuser, 2001.

[33] R. Paturi, P. Pudlák, and F. Zane. Satisfiability coding lemma. *Chicago Journal of Theoretical Computer Science*, December 1999.

[34] Nicholas Pippenger. Fast simulation of combinational logic circuits without random-access storage. In *Fifteenth Allerton Conference* , 25–33, 1977.

[35] Nicholas Pippenger and Michael J. Fischer. Relations among complexity measures. *J. ACM*, 26(2):361–381, 1979.

[36] J. M. Robson. Algorithms for maximum independent sets. *Journal of Algorithms*, 7:425–440, September 1986.

[37] Michael E. Saks. Space efficient algorithms for np-hard sequencing and partition problems. manuscript, November 1998.

[38] Claus-Peter Schnorr. Satisfiability is quasilinear complete in nql. *J. ACM*, 25(1):136–145, 1978.

[39] U. Schöning. A probabilistic algorithm for k-sat and constraint satisfaction problems. In *FOCS '99*, 410–414, 1999.

[40] Richard Edwin Stearns and Harry B. Hunt. Power indices and easier hard problems. *Mathematical Systems Theory*, 23(4):209–225, 1990.

[41] Patrick Traxler. The time complexity of constraint satisfaction. In *2008 Dagstuhl Workshop on Moderately Exponential-time Algorithms*, 2008.

[42] L. Valiant and V. Vazirani. NP is as easy as detecting unique solutions. *Theoretical Computer Science*, 47:85–93, 1986.

[43] Dieter van Melkebeek. A survey of lower bounds for satisfiability and related problems. *Electronic Colloquium on Computational Complexity (ECCC)*, 14(099), 2007.

[44] Ryan Williams. Finding paths of length k in $O^*(2^k)$ time. *Information Processing Letters*, 109(6):315–318, 2009.

Satisfiability Allows No Nontrivial Sparsification Unless The Polynomial-Time Hierarchy Collapses

Holger Dell*
Humboldt University of Berlin, Germany
dell@informatik.hu-berlin.de

Dieter van Melkebeek†
University of Wisconsin-Madison, USA
dieter@cs.wisc.edu

ABSTRACT

Consider the following two-player communication process to decide a language L: The first player holds the entire input x but is polynomially bounded; the second player is computationally unbounded but does not know any part of x; their goal is to cooperatively decide whether x belongs to L at small cost, where the cost measure is the number of bits of communication from the first player to the second player.

For any integer $d \geq 3$ and positive real ϵ we show that if satisfiability for n-variable d-CNF formulas has a protocol of cost $O(n^{d-\epsilon})$ then coNP is in NP/poly, which implies that the polynomial-time hierarchy collapses to its third level. The result even holds when the first player is conondeterministic, and is tight as there exists a trivial protocol for $\epsilon = 0$. Under the hypothesis that coNP is not in NP/poly, our result implies tight lower bounds for parameters of interest in several areas, namely sparsification, kernelization in parameterized complexity, lossy compression, and probabilistically checkable proofs.

By reduction, similar results hold for other NP-complete problems. For the vertex cover problem on n-vertex d-uniform hypergraphs, the above statement holds for any integer $d \geq 2$. The case $d = 2$ implies that no NP-hard vertex deletion problem based on a graph property that is inherited by subgraphs can have kernels consisting of $O(k^{2-\epsilon})$ edges unless coNP is in NP/poly, where k denotes the size of the deletion set. Kernels consisting of $O(k^2)$ edges are known for several problems in the class, including vertex cover, feedback vertex set, and bounded-degree deletion.

Categories and Subject Descriptors

F.1.3 [**Computation by Abstract Devices**]: Complexity Measures and Classes—*Relations among complexity classes*

*Supported by the Deutsche Forschungsgemeinschaft within the research training group "Methods for Discrete Structures" (GRK 1408).

†Research mostly done while visiting the Humboldt University of Berlin. Partially supported by the Humboldt Foundation and by NSF award CCF-0728809.

STOC'10, June 5–8, 2010, Cambridge, Massachusetts, USA.

General Terms

Algorithms, Theory

1. INTRODUCTION

Satisfiability of Boolean formulas constitutes one of the most central problems in computer science. It has attracted a lot of applied and theoretical research because of its immediate relevance in areas like AI and verification and as the seminal NP-complete problem. Of particular interest is d-SAT, the satisfiability problem for d-CNF formulas, which is NP-complete for any integer $d \geq 3$ [15, 35, 31].

In this paper we investigate the complexity of d-SAT and other NP-complete problems in a communication setting that captures several transformations studied in the theory of computing. Assuming the polynomial-time hierarchy does not collapse, we show that a trivial communication protocol is essentially optimal for d-SAT. Under the same hypothesis the result implies tight lower bounds for parameters of interest in several areas. We first discuss those areas and then state our result for d-SAT.

Sparsification.

The satisfiability of d-CNF formulas chosen by uniformly at random picking m clauses out of all possible clauses on n variables seems to exhibit a phase transition as a function of the ratio m/n. We know that the probability of satisfiability jumps from almost zero to almost one when the ratio m/n crosses a very narrow region around $2^d \ln 2$, and the existence of a single threshold point is conjectured [25, 1, 2]. Experiments also suggest that known SAT solvers have the hardest time on randomly generated instances when the ratio m/n lies around the threshold, and in some cases rigorous analyses corroborate the experiments.

Nevertheless, from a complexity-theoretic perspective these results fall short of establishing sparse formulas as the hardest instances. This is because formulas that express problems like breaking random RSA instances exhibit a lot of structure and therefore have a negligible contribution to the uniform distribution. An interesting complexity-theoretic formalization would be a reduction from arbitrary formulas to formulas on the same number of variables that are sparse. Impagliazzo et al. [30] developed such reductions but they run in subexponential time. In polynomial time we can trivially reduce a d-CNF formula to one with $m = O(n^d)$ clauses. Since there are only $2^d \cdot \binom{n}{d} = O(n^d)$ distinct d-clauses on n variables, it suffices to remove duplicate clauses. Is there a polynomial-time reduction that maps a d-CNF formula on n variables to one on n variables and $m = O(n^{d-\epsilon})$ clauses for some positive constant ϵ?

Kernelization.

Parameterized complexity investigates the computational difficulty of problems as a function of the input size and an additional natural parameter, k, which often only takes small values in instances of practical interest. A good example – and one we will return to soon – is deciding whether a given graph has a vertex cover of size at most k. The holy grail in parameterized complexity are algorithms with running times of the form $O(f(k) \cdot s^c)$ on instances of size s and parameter k, where f denotes an arbitrary computable function and c a constant. Kernelization constitutes an important technique for realizing such running times: Reduce in time polynomial in s to an instance of size bounded by some computable function g of the parameter k only, and then run a brute-force algorithm on the reduced instance; the resulting algorithm has a running time of the form $O(s^c + f(k))$. In order to obtain good parameterized algorithms the functions f and g should not behave too badly, which justifies the quest for kernels of polynomial or smaller size $g(k)$.

The number of variables n forms a natural parameter for satisfiability. In the case of d-CNF formulas, n is effectively polynomially related to the size of the input, which makes the existence of kernels of polynomial size trivial. Nevertheless, the quest for a small kernel is a relaxation of the quest for sparsification in polynomial time. Eliminating duplicate clauses yields a kernel of bitlength $O(n^d \log n)$. Does satisfiability of n-variable d-CNF formulas have kernels of size $O(n^{d-\epsilon})$?

Lossy Compression.

Harnik and Naor [28] introduced a notion of compression with the goal of succinctly storing instances of computational problems for resolution in the future, where there may be more time and more computational power available. The compressed version need not be an instance of the original problem, and the original instance need not be recoverable from the compressed version. The only requirement is that the solution be preserved. In the case of decision problems this simply means the yes/no answer. In analogy to image compression one can think of the Harnik-Naor notion of compression as a "lossy compression", where the only aspect of the scenery that is guaranteed not to be lost is the solution to the problem.

Harnik and Naor applied their notion to languages in NP and showed the relevance to problems in cryptography when the compression is measured as a function of the bitlength of the underlying witnesses. In the case of satisfiability the latter coincides with the number of variables of the formula. This way lossy compression becomes a relaxation of the notion of kernelization – we now want a polynomial-time mapping reduction to *any* problem, rather than to the original problem, such that the reduced instances have small bitlength as a function of n. For d-CNF formulas bitlength $O(n^d)$ is trivially achievable – simply map to the characteristic vector that for each possible d-clause on n variables indicates whether it is present in the given formula. Can we lossily compress to instances of bitlength $O(n^{d-\epsilon})$?

Probabilistically Checkable Proofs.

A somewhat different question deals with the size of probabilistically checkable proofs (PCPs). A PCP for a language L is a randomized proof system in which the verifier only needs to read a constant number of bits of the proof in order to verify that a given input x belongs to L. Completeness requires that for every input x in L there exists a proof which the verifier accepts with probability one. Soundness requires that for any input x outside of L no proof can be accepted with probability above some constant threshold less than one. For satisfiability of Boolean formulas, Dinur [18] constructed PCPs of bitlength $O(s \cdot \text{poly} \log s)$, where s denotes the size of the formula. For d-CNF formulas on n variables, Dinur's construction yields PCPs of bitlength $O(n^d \cdot \text{poly} \log n)$. On the other hand, standard proofs only contain n bits. Do n-variable d-CNF formulas have PCPs of bitlength $O(n^{d-\epsilon})$?

Our Results for Satisfiability.

We give evidence that the answer to all four of the above questions is negative: If any answer is positive then coNP is in NP/poly. The latter is considered unlikely as it means the existence of a nonuniform polynomial-time proof system for tautologies, or equivalently, that coNP has polynomial-size nondeterministic circuits, and implies that the polynomial-time hierarchy collapses to its third level [40].

We obtain those statements as corollaries to a more general result, in which we consider the following communication process to decide a language L.

Definition 1 (Oracle Communication Protocol). *An* oracle communication protocol *for a language L is a communication protocol between two players. The first player is given the input x and has to run in time polynomial in the length of the input; the second player is computationally unbounded but is not given any part of x. At the end of the protocol the first player should be able to decide whether $x \in L$. The cost of the protocol is the number of bits of communication from the first player to the second player.*

We often refer to the second player as the oracle. Note that the bits sent by the oracle do not contribute towards the cost. By default the players in an oracle communication protocol are deterministic, but one can consider variants in which one or both players are randomized, nondeterministic, etc.

Satisfiability of n-variable d-CNF formulas has a trivial protocol of cost $O(n^d)$. The following result implies that there is no protocol of cost $O(n^{d-\epsilon})$ unless the polynomial-time hierarchy collapses. In fact, the result even holds when the first player is conondeterministic, i.e., when the first player can have multiple valid moves to choose from in any given step, possibly leading to different conclusions about the satisfiability of a given input formula φ, but such that (i) if φ is satisfiable then every valid execution comes to that conclusion, and (ii) if φ is not satisfiable then at least one valid execution comes to that conclusion.

Theorem 1. *Let $d \geq 3$ be an integer and ϵ a positive real. If* coNP $\not\subseteq$ NP/poly, *there is no protocol of cost $O(n^{d-\epsilon})$ to decide whether an n-variable d-CNF formula is satisfiable, even when the first player is conondeterministic.*

The corollaries about sparsification, kernelization, and lossy compression follow by considering deterministic single-round protocols in which the polynomial-time player acts as a mapping reduction, sends the reduced instance to the computationally unbounded player, and the latter answers this query as a membership oracle. The corollary about probabilistically checkable proofs follows by considering a similar single-round protocol in which the first player is conondeterministic. Note that Theorem 1 can handle more general reductions, in which multiple queries are made to the oracle over multiple rounds. The above corollaries can be strengthened correspondingly. In fact, Theorem 1 is even more general as it allows the oracle to play a more active role that goes beyond answering queries from the polynomial-time player.

Our Results for Other NP-Complete Problems.

By reducibility the lower bounds from Theorem 1 carry over to other parameterized NP-complete problems, where the tightness depends on how the reduction affects the parameterization. In fact, we derive Theorem 1 from a similar result for the vertex cover problem on d-uniform hypergraphs.

Theorem 2. *Let $d \geq 2$ be an integer and ϵ a positive real. If* coNP $\not\subseteq$ NP/poly, *there is no protocol of cost $O(n^{d-\epsilon})$ to decide whether a d-uniform hypergraph on n vertices has a vertex cover of at most k vertices, even when the first player is conondeterministic.*

The cases of Theorem 2 with $d \geq 3$ are equivalent to the corresponding cases of Theorem 1. Note, though, that Theorem 2 also holds for $d = 2$, i.e., for standard graphs.

Similar to Theorem 1, Theorem 2 can be interpreted in terms of (graph) sparsification, kernelization, lossy compression, and probabilistically checkable proofs. Regarding kernelization, Theorem 2 has an interesting implication for the vertex cover problem parameterized by the size of the vertex cover – one of the prime examples of a parameterized problem that is NP-hard but fixed-parameter tractable. Kernelizations for this problem have received considerable attention. For standard graphs S. Buss [11] came up with a kernelization avant la lettre. He observed that any vertex of degree larger than k must be contained in any vertex cover of size k, should it exist. This gives rise to a kernelization with $O(k^2)$ vertices and $O(k^2)$ edges. Subsequently, several researchers tried to reduce the size of the kernel. Various approaches based on matching, linear programming, and crown reductions (see [27] for a survey) led to kernels with $O(k)$ vertices, but the resulting kernels are all dense. It remains open to find kernels with $O(k^{2-\epsilon})$ edges. Since $k \leq n$, the case $d = 2$ of Theorem 2 implies that such kernels do not exist unless the polynomial-time hierarchy collapses.

In fact, a similar result holds for a wide class of problems known as vertex deletion problems. For a fixed graph property Π, the corresponding vertex deletion problem asks whether removing at most k vertices from a given graph G can yield a graph that satisfies Π. A host of well-studied specific problems can be cast as the vertex deletion problem corresponding to some graph property Π that is inherited by subgraphs. Examples besides the vertex cover problem include the feedback vertex set problem and the bounded-degree deletion problem (see Section 5 for the definitions of these problems and for more examples).

If only finitely many graphs satisfy Π or if all graphs satisfy Π, the vertex deletion problem is trivially decidable in polynomial time. For all other graph properties Π that are inherited by subgraphs, Lewis and Yannakakis [36] showed that the problem is NP-hard.[1] They did so by constructing a mapping reduction from the vertex cover problem. By improving their reduction such that it preserves the size of the deletion set up to a constant factor, we obtain the following result.

Theorem 3. *Let Π be a graph property that is inherited by subgraphs, and is satisfied by infinitely many but not all graphs. Let ϵ be a positive real. If* coNP $\not\subseteq$ NP/poly, *there is no protocol of cost $O(k^{2-\epsilon})$ for deciding whether a graph satisfying Π can be obtained from a given graph by removing at most k vertices, even when the first player is conondeterministic.*

Theorem 3 implies that problems like feedback vertex set and bounded-degree deletion do not have kernels consisting of $O(k^{2-\epsilon})$ edges unless the polynomial-time hierarchy collapses. For both problems the result is tight in the sense that kernels with $O(k^2)$ edges exist. For feedback vertex set we argue that Thomassé's recent kernel [39] does the job; for bounded-degree deletion a kernel with $O(k^2)$ edges was known to exist [21].

Techniques and Related Work.

At a high level our approach refines the framework developed by Bodlaender et al. [9] to show that certain parameterized NP-hard problems are unlikely to have kernels of polynomial size. Harnik and Naor [28] realized the connection between their notion of lossy compression and kernelization and PCPs for satisfiability of general Boolean formulas, and Fortnow and Santhanam [24] proved the connection with the hypothesis coNP $\not\subseteq$ NP/poly in the superpolynomial setting. Several authors subsequently applied the framework in that setting [14, 10, 19, 22, 32, 33].

We develop the first application of the framework in the polynomial setting, i.e., to problems that *do* have kernels of polynomial size, or more generally, oracle communication protocols of polynomial cost. Under the same hypothesis we show that problems like d-SAT and vertex cover do not have protocols of polynomial cost of degree less than the best known. In order to obtain these tight results, a crucial new ingredient is the use of high-density subsets of the integers without nontrivial arithmetic progressions of length three.

Our main result, Theorem 2, deals with the vertex cover problem on d-uniform hypergraphs, or equivalently, with the clique problem on such graphs, parameterized by the number of vertices. The proof consists of two steps.

Step 1. Assuming the clique problem on n-vertex d-uniform hypergraphs has a protocol of cost $O(n^c)$ for some constant $c < d$, some NP-complete language L has the following property: The problem OR(L) of deciding whether at least one of t given instances $x_1, x_2, \ldots, x_t$ is in L has a protocol of cost $O(t \log t)$ for instances where t is a sufficiently large polynomial in $s = \max_{1 \leq i \leq t} |x_i|$.

Step 2. Any language L with that property is in coNP/poly.

Combining the two steps we conclude that the hypothesis of Step 1 fails unless coNP $\subseteq$ NP/poly.

Since the clique problem on d-uniform hypergraphs is NP-complete for any integer $d \geq 2$, without loss of generality we

[1] In fact, Lewis and Yannakakis showed this to be the case even for graph properties that are inherited by *induced* subgraphs only.

can take L in Step 1 to be this language. In order to obtain a low-cost protocol for OR(L) it suffices to reduce the question whether at least one of t given graphs has a clique of a given size into a single instance of the clique problem on a d-uniform hypergraph with few vertices n, and then run the presumed protocol of cost $O(n^c)$ on the latter hypergraph.

As observed by Harnik and Naor [28], the disjoint union of the given hypergraphs provides such a reduction. However, the number of vertices is $n = s \cdot t$, so even for $c = 1$ the cost of the resulting protocol for OR(L) is $\omega(t \log t)$, which is too much for Step 2. As a critical piece in our proof, we present a reduction that works for an NP-hard subset of clique instances and only needs $n = s \cdot t^{1/d+o(1)}$ vertices. The cost of the resulting protocol for OR(L) then goes down to $O(n^c) = O\big((s \cdot t^{1/d+o(1)})^c\big)$, which is $O(t \log t)$ for sufficiently large polynomials $t(s)$ as $c < d$.

Our reduction hinges on a graph packing that is based on high-density subsets of the integers without nontrivial arithmetic progressions of length three. After we developed our construction, we have learned about other applications of those sets in the theory of computing, including three-party communication protocols [13], the asymptotically best known algorithm for matrix multiplication [16], the soundness analysis of graph tests for linearity [29], and lower bounds for property testing [4, 3, 8, 6, 5, 7]. The latter two applications as well as ours implicitly or explicitly rely on a connection due to Ruzsa and Szemerédi [37] between these subsets and dense three-partite graphs whose edges partition into triangles and that contain no other triangles. The graph packing we develop is most akin to a construction by Alon and Shapira [7] in the context of property testing. We refer to Section 4 for a more detailed discussion of the relationships.

Step 2 shows that whenever OR(L) has a cheap protocol, the complement of L has short witnesses that can be verified efficiently with the help of a polynomial-size advice string. We refer to Step 2 as the Complementary Witness Lemma. It involves a refined analysis and generalization of a result by Fortnow and Santhanam [24] that establishes the case where the protocol implements a mapping reduction to instances of bitlength bounded by some fixed polynomial in s. We analyze what happens for mapping reductions without the latter restriction. We also observe that the argument generalizes to our oracle communication protocol setting. Our applications of Theorem 1 only use oracle communication protocols that implement mapping or general reductions. However, the setting of oracle communication protocols is more natural and allows us to prove known results in a simpler way.

Organization.

We review some preliminaries in Section 2. Section 3 contains the proof of the main result (Theorem 2) following the two-step approach outlined above, and fleshes out the first step modulo the packing construction. We develop the latter in Section 4. Section 5 expands on the implications for satisfiability (Theorem 1 and its corollaries) and for vertex deletion problems (Theorem 3). We provide the intuition underlying our results and the most important formalities here, but refer to [17] for more discussion and omitted proofs.

2. PRELIMINARIES

The OR *of a language* L is the language OR(L) that consists of all tuples $(x_1, \ldots, x_t)$ for which there is an $i \in [t]$ with $x_i \in L$. A *mapping reduction*, or $\leq_m^p$*-reduction*, from L to L' is a polynomial-time mapping R from $\{0,1\}^*$ to $\{0,1\}^*$ such that $R(x) \in L'$ if and only if $x \in L$. A *kernelization* of a parameterized problem (L, k) consisting of a language L and a parameterization $k : \{0,1\}^* \to \mathbb{N}$ is a $\leq_m^p$-reduction from L to itself that maps instances with parameter k to instances of bitlength at most $g(k)$ for some function g independent of the input size.

A d-CNF formula on the variables $x_1, \ldots, x_n$ is a conjunction of clauses where a clause is a disjunction of exactly d literals, i.e., the variables x_i and their negations $\overline{x_i}$. We denote by d-SAT the problem of deciding whether a given d-CNF formula has at least one satisfying assignment, i.e., a truth assignment to its variables that makes the formula evaluate to true.

A hypergraph $G = (V(G), E(G))$ consists of a finite set $V(G)$ of vertices and a set $E(G)$ of subsets of $V(G)$, the (hyper)edges. A hypergraph is d-uniform if every edge has size exactly d. A *vertex cover of* G is a set $S \subseteq V(G)$ that contains at least one vertex from every edge of G, and d-VERTEX COVER is the problem of deciding whether, for a given d-uniform hypergraph G and integer k, there exists a vertex cover of G of size at most k. Similarly, a *clique of* G is a set $S \subseteq V(G)$ all of whose subsets of size d are edges of G, and d-CLIQUE is the problem of deciding whether, for given (G, k), there exists a clique of G of size at least k. The two problems are dual to each other, in the sense that $\overline{G}$, the d-uniform hypergraph obtained from G by flipping the presence of all edges of size d, has a clique of size k if and only if G has a vertex cover of size $n - k$. Note that this transformation preserves the number of vertices.

3. MAIN THEOREM

In this section we establish Theorem 2 – that d-VERTEX COVER has no oracle communication protocol of cost $O(n^{d-\epsilon})$ for any positive constant ϵ unless coNP $\subseteq$ NP/poly, where n represents the number of vertices of the d-uniform hypergraph. For ease of exposition we actually develop the equivalent result for d-CLIQUE rather than for d-VERTEX COVER. Theorem 2 then follows by hypergraph complementation.

We follow the two-step approach outlined in the introduction. In the first step we use a presumed low-cost protocol for d-CLIQUE to devise a low-cost protocol for the OR of some NP-complete language L. We do so by first translating the given instance of OR(L) into an equivalent instance of d-CLIQUE with few vertices, and then running the presumed low-cost protocol for d-CLIQUE on that instance.

The choice of the NP-complete language L does not matter. For convenience we pick it to be 3-SAT. Thus, given t 3-CNF formulas $\varphi_1, \ldots, \varphi_t$, we need to construct a d-uniform hypergraph G on few vertices n and an integer k such that at least one of the φ_i's is satisfiable if and only if G has a clique of size at least k. We first apply a standard translation of the t individual 3-SAT-instances $\varphi_1, \ldots, \varphi_t$, say of size s, into equivalent d-CLIQUE-instances consisting of d-uniform hypergraphs $G_1, \ldots, G_t$ on $3s$ vertices each, such that G_i has a clique of size s if and only if φ_i is satisfiable. All that is left then is to turn these t instances into a single instance of d-CLIQUE which is positive if and only if at least one of the t instances is. If we take G as the disjoint union of the G_i's, then G is a d-uniform hypergraph that has a clique of size s if and only if at least one of the G_i's has a clique of size s. However, this G contains $n = s \cdot t$ vertices, which is too many for our purposes. In order to do better, we need to pack the graphs G_i more tightly while maintaining the properties required of the reduction. The following almost-optimal packing of cliques is the critical ingredient in our construction and allows us to achieve the almost-optimal lower bounds given in Theorem 2.

Lemma 1 (Packing Lemma). *For any integers $s \geq d \geq 2$ and $t > 0$ there exists a d-uniform hypergraph P on $O(s \cdot \max(s, t^{1/d+o(1)}))$ vertices such that*

(i) the hyperedges of P partition into t cliques $K_1, \ldots, K_t$ on s vertices each, and

(ii) P contains no cliques on s vertices other than the K_i's.

Furthermore, for any fixed d, the hypergraph P and the K_i's can be constructed in time polynomial in s and t.

Condition (i) in Lemma 1 formalizes the notion of a packing. The part that P contains the t cliques K_i ensures the completeness of the reduction, i.e., that G has a clique of size s if at least one of the G_i's does. The part that the K_i's are edge-disjoint and condition (ii) guarantee the soundness of the reduction, i.e., that G has a clique of size s only if at least one of the G_i's does.

We defer the proof of Lemma 1 to Section 4. Using it as sketched above we obtain the following reduction.

Lemma 2. *For any integer $d \geq 2$, there is a $\leq^p_m$-reduction from* OR(3-SAT) *to d-*CLIQUE *that maps t-tuples of instances of bitlength s each to instances on $O(s \cdot \max(s, t^{1/d+o(1)}))$ vertices.*

Proof. Let $\varphi_1, \ldots, \varphi_t$ be the t instances of 3-SAT. Without loss of generality, assume that each formula has exactly s clauses, each consisting of a sequence of 3 literals. Let P and $K_1, \ldots, K_t$ be the hypergraphs provided by Lemma 1. Along the lines of the standard reduction from 3-SAT to 2-CLIQUE [31], we first translate the 3-CNF formulas φ_i into d-uniform hypergraphs G_i on the vertex sets $V(K_i) \times [3]$. For each i, we identify the elements of $V(K_i) \times [3]$ with (positions of) literals of φ_i: The first component selects a clause from φ_i and the second component selects a literal from the clause. We let G_i be the d-uniform hypergraph with as edges all subsets $e \subseteq V(K_i) \times [3]$ of size d such that no two elements of e correspond to the same clause φ_i or represent complementary literals. Note that each such e induces a satisfying assignment of the conjunction of the d clauses touched by e, and that G_i has a clique of size s if and only if φ_i is satisfiable.

Let G be the union of the G_i's, that is, the graph with $V(G) = \bigcup_{i \in [t]} V(G_i) \subseteq V(P) \times [3]$ and $E(G) = \bigcup_{i \in [t]} E(G_i)$. If φ_i has a satisfying assignment, then G_i has a clique of size s and so has G. For the other direction, let K be a clique of size s in G. The projection K' of K onto the first component is a clique of size s in P. By property (ii) of Lemma 1, $K' = K_i$ for some $i \in [t]$. Moreover, by property (i) of Lemma 1, the projections of $E(G_i)$ and $E(G_j)$ for $j \neq i$ are disjoint. It follows that K is a clique of size s in G_i, and therefore φ_i is satisfiable.

Thus, $(G, s) \in d$-CLIQUE if and only if $(\varphi_1, \ldots, \varphi_t) \in$ OR(3-SAT). Since G and s are computable in time polynomial in the bitlength of $(\varphi_1, \ldots, \varphi_t)$ and $|V(G)| \leq 3|V(P)| \leq O(s \cdot \max(s, t^{1/d+o(1)}))$, we have established the $\leq^p_m$-reductions claimed in Lemma 2. ∎

Lemma 2 represents the essence of the first step of the proof of Theorem 2 – obtaining a low-cost protocol for OR(3-SAT) out of a low-cost protocol for d-CLIQUE. The second step shows in general how to use a low-cost protocol for OR(L) to build a proof system with advice for $\overline{L}$. That step is captured in the following lemma.

Lemma 3 (Complementary Witness Lemma). *Let L be a language and $t : \mathbb{N} \rightarrow \mathbb{N} \setminus \{0\}$ be polynomially bounded such that the problem of deciding whether at least one out of $t(s)$ inputs of length at most s belongs to L has an oracle communication protocol of cost $O(t(s) \log t(s))$, where the first player can be conondeterministic. Then $L \in$* coNP/poly.

The proof and further discussion of Lemma 3 can be found in [17]. Theorem 2 follows by combining Lemma 2 with Lemma 3.

4. THE PACKING LEMMA

In this section we establish Lemma 1, which is a critical ingredient in the proof of Theorem 2. We first develop the construction for the case $d = 2$, i.e., for standard graphs, and then show how to generalize it to d-uniform hypergraphs for arbitrary $d \geq 2$. We also discuss the relationship of our construction to earlier ones.

Our Construction.

We need to construct a graph P on few vertices such that

(i) the edges of P partition into t cliques $K_1, \ldots, K_t$ on s vertices each, and

(ii) P contains no other cliques on s vertices.

We first focus on realizing condition (i) and then see how to modify the construction to also realize (ii).

We construct P as an s-partite graph and think of the s partitions as the columns of a two-dimensional array of vertices, say of size p by s. Each of the K_i's then contains exactly one vertex from each of the s columns. Condition (i) expresses that P is a packing of the K_i's. The trivial packing consists of the disjoint union and requires $p = t$ rows, resulting in $s \cdot t$ vertices in total. The trivial packing is wasteful because it leaves many of the potential edges unused. In an ideal packing each of the p^2 potential edges between two columns of the array are assigned to some K_i. This would only require a number of rows $p = \sqrt{t}$ and therefore $s \cdot \sqrt{t}$ vertices. We can realize such a tight packing by picking the vertex of K_i in column j as the value of j under a hash function h_i from a minimum 2-universal family. If p is a prime at least s, we can identify the rows as well as the columns with elements of $\mathbb{F}_p$ and use the family of linear functions over $\mathbb{F}_p$. More precisely, we construct P on the vertex set $V(P) = [s] \times \mathbb{F}_p$ as the union of the t cliques K_i on the vertex sets $V(K_i) = \{(j, h_i(j)) \mid j \in [s]\}$, where h_i is a linear function over $\mathbb{F}_p$ uniquely associated with K_i. See Figure 1a. Note that there are p^2 distinct linear functions h_i over $\mathbb{F}_p$, so we can accommodate that many cliques K_i. Moreover, since two points define a line, every edge of P is contained in exactly one of the K_i's. For arbitrary values of s and t,

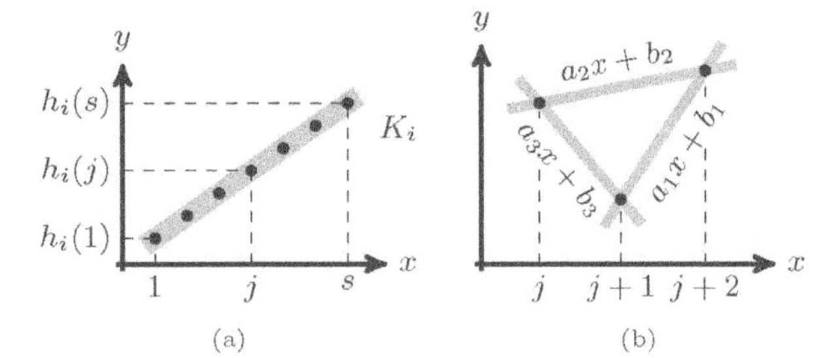

Figure 1: (a) The placement of one of the K_i's. (b) Triangle on three consecutive abscissae.

we can pick p to be the first prime $p \geq \max(s, \sqrt{t})$, resulting in a packing with $O(s \cdot \max(s, \sqrt{t}))$ vertices.

Note that this P is in fact a complete s-partite graph and therefore fails to satisfy condition (ii) miserably – *every* clique of size s that has one vertex from each column is present in P, which is many more than just the K_i's. In order to remedy that problem, let us analyze the cliques of size s in P more closely.

Let K denote a clique of size s in P. Each of the s columns of P has to contain exactly one vertex of K, i.e., there exists a function $h : [s] \to \mathbb{F}_p$ such that $V(K) = \{(j, h(j)) \mid j \in [s]\}$. We would like to ensure that K coincides with one of the cliques K_i, or equivalently, that the function h coincides with one of the linear functions h_i.

Consider three consecutive columns, j, $j+1$, and $j+2$, and the triangle that K induces between them – see Figure 1b, where each edge is labeled by the linear function h_i defining the clique K_i to which the edge belongs. We claim that the highest-order coefficients of those linear functions have to form an arithmetic progression. This follows by considering the two paths in Figure 1b that go from the vertex in column j to the one in column $j+2$. The direct path on top involves an increase in y-value of $2a_2$, whereas the indirect path on the bottom involves an increase in y of a_3 followed by an increase of a_1. Since both paths end up at the same point, we have that $2a_2 = a_1 + a_3$, or equivalently, that $a_3 - a_2 = a_2 - a_1$, or yet equivalently, that the sequence a_1, a_2, a_3 forms an arithmetic progression. If we restrict the highest-order coefficients of the linear functions to come from a subset $A \subseteq \mathbb{F}_p$ that contains no nontrivial arithmetic progressions of length three, the arithmetic progression a_1, a_2, a_3 has to be trivial, i.e., $a_1 = a_2 = a_3$. The latter implies that the three lines in Figure 1b coincide. As this implication holds for all choices of three consecutive columns, we conclude that all vertices of K lie on a single line defined by one of the h_i's, as we wanted.

Of course, the additional restriction on the highest-order coefficients means that we need to choose p larger. However, we only need to increase p slightly thanks to the existence of efficiently constructible subsets $A \subseteq \mathbb{F}_p$ of high density that contain no nontrivial arithmetic progressions of length three. For our purposes the following classical result from additive combinatorics suffices.

Lemma 4 (AP$_3$-Free Sets [38]). *For every positive integer p there exists a subset $A \subseteq \mathbb{Z}_p$ of size at least $p^{1-o(1)}$ which contains no nontrivial arithmetic progressions of length three. Furthermore, such a set A can be determined in time polynomial in p.*

The resulting graph P has $s \cdot p$ vertices where $p = O\big(\max(s, \sqrt{t}^{1+o(1)})\big)$.

This finishes the construction of the packing lemma for the case of standard graphs. The generalization to d-uniform hypergraphs follows by using polynomials of degree $d-1$ instead of linear functions over $\mathbb{F}_p$. Their use guarantees requirement (i) in Lemma 1. Regarding requirement (ii), the following proof shows that the case $d > 2$ reduces to the case $d = 2$. For arbitrary $d \geq 2$, we fulfill requirement (ii) by restricting the coefficient of degree $d-1$ to a set that contains no nontrivial arithmetic progressions of length three, namely the set $A \subseteq \mathbb{F}_p$ determined in Lemma 4.

Proof (of Lemma 1). Let p be the smallest prime such that $p \geq s$ and $|A| \cdot p^{d-1} \geq t$, where A denotes the set given by Lemma 4. We have that $p = O\big(\max(s, t^{1/d+o(1)})\big)$ and can compute p and the set A in time polynomial in s and t.

Let $V(P) = [s] \times \mathbb{F}_p$. We consider polynomials of degree at most $d-1$ over $\mathbb{F}_p$ whose coefficient of x^{d-1} belongs to A. Note that there are $|A| \cdot p^{d-1} \geq t$ such polynomials. For $i \in [t]$, let h_i denote the ith such polynomial in lexicographic order, and let K_i be the complete d-uniform hypergraph on vertex set $V(K_i) = \{(j, h_i(j)) \mid j \in [s]\}$. We define the d-uniform hypergraph P as the union of the t cliques K_i. The hypergraphs P and K_i can be constructed in time polynomial in s and t.

In order to argue property (i), it suffices to observe that every hyperedge of P is contained in at most one of the K_i's. This follows because the requirement that a given hyperedge of P belongs to K_i is equivalent to stipulating the value of h_i on d distinct values $j \in [s]$, which uniquely determines h_i as a polynomial of degree at most $d-1$ over $\mathbb{F}_p$, and therefore determines i.

In order to argue property (ii), we need to establish the following for any function $h : [s] \to \mathbb{F}_p$: If for every subset $D \subseteq [s]$ of size d there exists an $i \in [t]$ such that h and h_i agree on D, then there exists an $i \in [t]$ such that h and h_i agree on all of $[s]$. The property follows by applying the next claim to successive values of $j \in [s-d]$, where q_k denotes the polynomial h_i which the hypothesis gives for the subset $D = [j, j+d] \setminus \{k\}$.

Claim. For each $k \in [j, j+d]$, let q_k be a polynomial of degree at most $d-1$ such that the set of coefficients of degree $d-1$ of the q_k's contains no nontrivial arithmetic progression of length three. If for all $k, \ell \in [j, j+d]$, the polynomials q_k and q_ℓ agree on $[j, j+d] \setminus \{k, \ell\}$, then the polynomials q_k are all the same.

We prove the claim by induction on d. We already argued the base case $d = 2$, captured by Figure 1b, earlier in Section 4. For the inductive step, assume the claim holds for $d-1$ and let us prove it for d. Let $q_j, \ldots, q_{j+d}$ be polynomials as in the claim. For each $k \in [j, j+d-1]$, define q'_k as the difference quotient $\Delta_{j+d}(q_k)$, i.e., $q'_k : [j, j+d-1] \to \mathbb{F}_p$ such that $q'_k(x) = (q_k(x) - q_k(j+d))/(x - j - d)$ for $x \in [j, j+d-1]$. Note that q'_k is a polynomial of degree at most $d-2$ whose coefficient of degree $d-2$ equals the coefficient of q_k of degree x^{d-1}. Moreover, for $k, \ell \in [j, j+d-1]$, the polynomials q'_k and q'_ℓ agree on each $x \in [j, j+d-1] \setminus \{k, \ell\}$ because the polynomials q_k and q_ℓ agree on both x and $j+d$.

Thus, by the induction hypothesis, all polynomials q'_k are the same. By the definition of $q'_k = \Delta_{j+d}(q_k)$ and the fact that the polynomials q_k for $k \in [j, j+d-1]$ agree on $j+d$, this implies that the polynomials q_k for $k \in [j, j+d-1]$ are all the same, say q. All that remains to show is that the polynomial q_{j+d} also coincides with q. The latter follows because q_{j+d} is a polynomial of degree at most $d-1$ which agrees with the polynomial q of degree at most $d-1$ on all d points in $[j, j+d-1]$. ∎

Related Constructions.

After we developed our construction we learned about similar applications of high-density subsets of the integers without nontrivial arithmetic progressions of length three.

Back in 1976, Ruzsa and Szemerédi [37] constructed dense three-partite graphs whose edges partition into triangles and that contain no other triangles. Their construction corresponds to the case $(d, s) = (2, 3)$ of our Packing Lemma, and appears between any three consecutive columns of our construction for $d = 2$ and general s. Our geometric derivation of the arithmetic progression condition $2a_2 = a_1 + a_3$, as captured in Figure 1b, may be new; all the derivations we have found in the literature work by manipulating equations in a – to us – less intuitive way.

Different aspects of the Ruzsa-Szemerédi construction matter for the various applications we know of in the theory of computing. For their soundness analysis of graph tests for linearity, Håstad and Wigderson [29] use the interpretation that for each of the p points in the first column, the triangles involving that point span an induced matching of $p^{1-o(1)}$ edges between the other columns.

Another application area is the lower bounds for testing the graph property of being F-free, where F is some fixed graph. An ϵ-tester for this property accepts all graphs that are F-free, and rejects all graphs that are at least ϵ away from being F-free, i.e., from which at least ϵn^2 edges need to be removed to make it F-free [26]. A strategy for proving lower bounds on the number of queries of such a tester is to construct high-density graphs G with the following properties: (i) the edges of G partition into copies of F, and (ii) G contains few other copies of F so the total number of copies of F in G is significantly less than expected in a random graphs of the same density as G [3]. Qualitatively, (i) implies that G is far from being F-free, and (ii) implies that testers with few queries have a small probability of detecting a violation of F-freeness on input G. Alon and coauthors [3, 8, 6, 5, 7] constructed such graphs G for various F based on [37].

The requirements for our application are similar but not identical to the ones for property testing. On the one hand we only need to consider the cases where F is a clique; on the other hand the graphs G cannot contain *any* copy of F other than those in which the edges partition. Our actual construction is very similar to the one Alon and Shapira develop in [7]. Their construction would also work for our purposes. Our proof differs from theirs and makes the arithmetic progression condition more transparent. Our construction slightly improves[2] on theirs as we only restrict the highest-order coefficient to the set A, whereas they restrict all coefficients to that set.

[2]This allows us to relax the condition $q(\epsilon) = \max\{m : (f(m))^k \geq \epsilon\}$ in Lemma 4.1 of [7] to $q(\epsilon) = \max\{m : f(m) \geq \epsilon\}$.

5. CONSEQUENCES OF MAIN THEOREM

Our lower bound for oracle communication protocols for d-VERTEX COVER, Theorem 2, has two types of consequences. The first are similar lower bounds for other parameterized NP-complete problems, and follow from parameter-frugal reductions from d-VERTEX COVER to these problems. The second type involves lower bounds for parameters of interest in settings that are captured by our oracle communication model. In this section we first cover the consequences for satisfiability and then those for vertex deletion problems.

5.1 Satisfiability

Theorem 1, our tight oracle communication lower bound for d-SAT parameterized by the number of variables of the formula, immediately follows from Theorem 2 and the next lemma.

Lemma 5. *For every $d \geq 3$, there is a $\leq^p_m$-reduction from d-VERTEX COVER to d-SAT that maps d-uniform hypergraphs on n vertices to d-CNF formulas on $O(n)$ variables.*

The following corollary to Theorem 1 embodies the consequences for sparsification, kernelization, and lossy compression.

Corollary 1. *Let $d \geq 3$ be an integer. If coNP $\not\subseteq$ NP/poly, then there is no polynomial-time reduction from d-SAT to any problem that makes at most $O(n^b)$ queries and only queries strings of bitlength $O(n^c)$, where b and c are any nonnegative reals with $b + c < d$.*

In particular, under the hypothesis that coNP $\not\subseteq$ NP/poly, Corollary 1 implies that $\leq^p_m$-reductions cannot reduce the density of n-variable d-SAT instances to $O(n^c)$ clauses for any constant c below the trivial $c = d$. This is what the title of the paper refers to, and contrasts the situation at the subexponential-time level. The sparsification lemma of [30] gives a reduction which, on input an n-variable d-CNF formula and a rational $\epsilon > 0$, runs in time $2^{\epsilon n} \cdot \text{poly}(n)$ and makes $2^{\epsilon n}$ nonadaptive queries, each of which are d-CNF formulas with at most $f(d, \epsilon) \cdot n$ clauses. The best known bound on the sparsification constant $f(d, \epsilon)$ is $(d/\epsilon)^{3d}$ [12]. The sparsification lemma implies that sparse instances of d-SAT are hard under subexponential-time reductions while Corollary 1 suggests that such a result is impossible under $\leq^p_m$-reductions. Interpretations of Corollary 1 in terms of kernelization and lossy compression follow along the same lines.

Another consequence of Theorem 1 deals with the size of probabilistically checkable proofs for satisfiability. Recall that Dinur [18] constructed such PCPs of size $O(s \cdot \text{poly} \log s)$, where s denotes the bitlength of the formula. Based on a connection due to Harnik and Naor between PCPs and lossy compression [28], Fortnow and Santhanam [24] showed that satisfiability of Boolean formulas does not have PCPs of size bounded by a polynomial in the number of variables only, unless coNP $\subseteq$ NP/poly. Plugging in our lower bound for d-SAT into their argument shows that d-SAT does not have q-query PCPs of size $O(n^{d/q-\epsilon})$ unless coNP $\subseteq$ NP/poly. Since $q \geq 3$ this bound is not tight. Using a different argument and exploiting the fact that Theorem 1 also holds for conondeterministic protocols, we can close the gap between the upper and lower bound.

Corollary 2. *Let $d \geq 3$ be an integer and ϵ a positive real. If coNP $\not\subseteq$ NP/poly, then d-*SAT *does not have probabilistically checkable proofs of bitlength $O(n^{d-\epsilon})$ where n denotes the number of variables of the input formula.*

Proof. Suppose that d-SAT has PCPs of size $s = O(n^c)$ that make q nonadaptive queries, where c and q are constants. We claim that this implies a conondeterministic multi-valued mapping reduction from d-SAT to q-SAT that maps formulas on n variables to instances of bitlength $O(n^c \log n)$ in the following sense: There exists a nondeterministic polynomial-time Turing machine M which outputs a q-CNF formula on each computation path (where the formula may depend on the input and the computation path) such that (i) if the input is in d-SAT then every output is in q-SAT, and (ii) otherwise at least one output is not in q-SAT. For $c < d$, Theorem 1 then shows that coNP $\subseteq$ NP/poly.

All that remains is to argue the claim. For a given formula φ on n variables, introduce s new variables y, namely one for each bit position in a candidate PCP of size s. If the PCP system reads at most q bits of the proof, each condition the PCP system checks can be expressed efficiently as a q-CNF. By picking a condition according to the distribution of the PCP system and a clause of the corresponding q-CNF formula uniformly at random, we obtain a polynomial-time randomized procedure that produces a q-clause on the variables y with the property that if φ is satisfiable, then all q-clauses produced are simultaneously satisfiable, and otherwise less than a constant fraction $\rho < 1$ is. By averaging, the latter implies that for every collection of candidate PCPs of size s for an unsatisfiable input φ, there exists a produced q-clause that is violated by more than a fraction $1 - \rho$ of the collection. Since there are 2^s candidate PCPs of size s in total, this means that there is a set of $s/\log(1/\rho)$ produced q-clauses that cannot be satisfied by any PCP of size s. The reduction nondeterministically guesses $s/\log(1/\rho)$ many q-clauses that are produced by the PCP system on input φ, and outputs their conjunction. The conjunction has bitlength $O(n^c \log n)$, is always satisfiable if φ is, and is not satisfiable on at least one computation path otherwise. ∎

5.2 Vertex Cover and Deletion Problems

Theorem 2 yields applications for d-VERTEX COVER similar to Corollaries 1 and 2 for d-SAT, using the number of vertices n as the parameter. A more natural parameter for d-VERTEX COVER is the size k of the vertex cover. We now investigate the consequences of Theorem 2 for this parameterization, first for the case $d = 2$, i.e., for standard graphs, and then for d-uniform hypergraphs for general d.

Result for Standard Graphs.

We consider the following generalization of the vertex cover problem. Recall that a graph property is a predicate on graphs that is invariant under graph isomorphism.

Definition 2 (Vertex Deletion). *Fix a graph property* Π. *The problem* Π-VERTEX DELETION *is to decide, for a given graph G and integer k, whether there exists a subset S of at most k vertices such that $G \setminus S$ satisfies* Π.

We say that a graph property Π is inherited by subgraphs if whenever a graph G satisfies Π, every subgraph of G also satisfies Π. The following natural graph problems are special cases of Π-VERTEX DELETION for a graph property Π that is inherited by subgraphs.

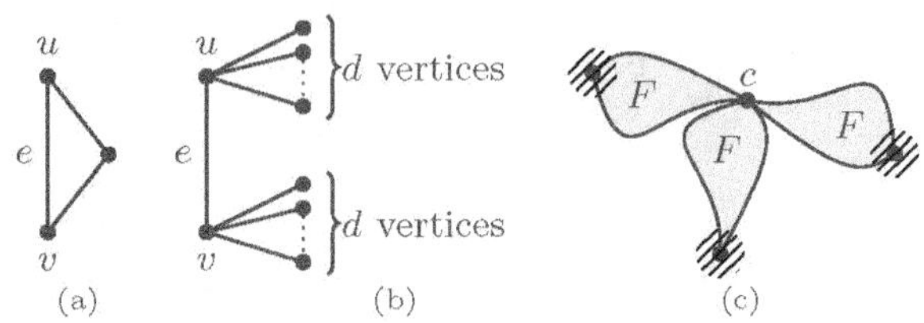

Figure 2: (a) and (b) Replacement of an edge $e = \{u, v\}$ in the transformation from G to G' in the proof of Lemma 6 for FEEDBACK VERTEX SET and BOUNDED-DEGREE DELETION, respectively. (c) Connected component C' that might remain after removing a vertex cover S of G from the naïve construction of G', centered around a vertex c that has degree 3 in G and does not belong to S.

- VERTEX COVER: Can we delete k vertices to destroy all edges?
- FEEDBACK VERTEX SET: Can we delete k vertices to destroy all cycles?
- BOUNDED-DEGREE DELETION: Can we delete k vertices to get a maximum degree of d?
- NON-PLANAR DELETION: Can we delete k vertices to make the graph planar?
- Can we delete k vertices to make the graph embeddable into some surface?
- Can we delete k vertices to make the graph exclude any fixed set of minors?

As mentioned in the introduction, if only finitely many graphs satisfy Π or if all graphs satisfy Π, Π-VERTEX DELETION is trivially decidable in polynomial time. For all other graph properties Π that are inherited by subgraphs, Theorem 3 implies that Π-VERTEX DELETION does not have kernels with $O(k^{2-\epsilon})$ edges unless coNP $\subseteq$ NP/poly.

We now prove Theorem 3 by constructing a $\leq_m^p$-reduction from VERTEX COVER to Π-VERTEX DELETION that blows up the size of the deletion set by no more than a constant factor. In order to develop some intuition, we first consider the standard reduction from VERTEX COVER to FEEDBACK VERTEX SET [31]. The reduction replaces every edge e of a VERTEX COVER-instance G by a cycle of length three using an additional new vertex, as depicted in Figure 2a. Let us denote the resulting graph by G'. Since every cycle in G' contains two vertices that are adjacent in G, every vertex cover of G hits every cycle of G' and therefore is a feedback vertex set of G'. Conversely, every feedback vertex set of G' contains a vertex of every triangle we created, and can therefore be turned into a vertex cover of G of at most the same size. Thus, G has a vertex cover of size k if and only if G' has a feedback vertex set of size k.

As another example, consider the case of BOUNDED-DEGREE DELETION. In the known reduction from VERTEX COVER to this problem [34], d new edges are attached to every vertex of G (see Figure 2b). Removing any vertex cover of G from G' reduces the maximum degree to d. Vice versa, any set that reduces the maximum degree in G' to d can be transformed into a vertex cover of G of at most the same size.

Next consider the more general case in which the minimal graphs that violate Π are connected. Generalizing the above two examples we obtain G' by replacing every edge of the VERTEX COVER-instance G by a copy of a fixed connected graph F violating Π. We refer to F as a "forbidden" graph since no graph satisfying Π can contain F as a subgraph. Thus, any deletion set in G' has to pick at least one vertex from every copy of F. Projecting the deletion set back onto the graph G yields a vertex cover of size no more than the deletion set. This way we can guarantee the soundness of the reduction – if G' has a deletion set of size at most k then G has a vertex cover of size at most k.

For the completeness of the reduction, we would like to ensure that removing a vertex cover S of G from G' leaves a graph $G' \setminus S$ satisfying Π. This is not automatically the case because $G' \setminus S$ may contain components of the form depicted in Figure 2c, where the bullets are vertices of G and the hashed vertices are part of the vertex cover S (and are therefore not part of $G' \setminus S$) but the center vertex is not. Such a component could contain a copy of F, in which case $G' \setminus S$ would not satisfy Π. However, by attaching the copies of F in an appropriate way we can make sure that the connected components of $G' \setminus S$ are all "simpler" than F. Picking F to be a "simplest" connected graph that violates Π then does the job as long as all minimal graphs violating Π are connected.

More generally, consider a graph F violating Π whose most complex connected component C is as simple as possible among all graphs violating Π. If F has no other connected component of the same complexity as C, then the above construction still works, using a copy of C to replace every edge in G and including a copy of $F \setminus C$ for every vertex of G.

In the most general case, where minimal graphs violating Π can have multiple components of the same complexity, we use a slightly different construction that involves multiple copies of G. The graph F now becomes a "simplest" graph for which the number of disjoint copies of F that satisfies Π is bounded. The reduction is no longer parameter preserving in general, but the parameter k' for G' is still linearly bounded by the parameter k for G. The latter ensures that the lower bound for Π-VERTEX DELETION is as strong as for VERTEX COVER modulo a constant factor.

The simplicity measure we use is the same as in [36] but the construction is a bit different. The construction in [36] blows up the parameter k' to $\Theta(nk)$. A straightforward modification reduces k' to $\Theta(k^2)$. We further reduce k' to $\Theta(k)$ using a matching argument.

Lemma 6. *Let Π be a graph property that is inherited by subgraphs, and is satisfied by infinitely many but not all graphs. There is a $\leq_m^p$-reduction from* VERTEX COVER *to* Π-VERTEX DELETION *that maps instances with parameter k to instances with parameter $O(k)$.*

The proof of Lemma 6 can be found in [17]. Theorem 3 then follows by combining Lemma 6 with Theorem 2.

Theorem 3 applies, among others, to FEEDBACK VERTEX SET, another problem whose kernelization has received considerable attention in parameterized complexity. Theorem 3 implies that FEEDBACK VERTEX SET does not have kernels consisting of $O(k^{2-\epsilon})$ edges unless coNP $\subseteq$ NP/poly. This result is tight – a kernel with $O(k^2)$ edges follows from recent work by Thomassé [39]. He constructs a kernel with at most $4k^2$ vertices and maximum degree at most $4k$. For such an instance to be positive, the number of edges can be no larger than $8k^2$. Indeed, suppose that S is a feedback vertex set of G of size at most k. Then the graph induced by $V(G) \setminus S$ is a forest and has at most $4k^2$ edges. All other edges of G are incident to a vertex of S. As the maximum degree is no larger than $4k$, at most $4k^2$ edges are incident to S. Summing up, G has at most $8k^2$ edges. Thus, if G has more than $8k^2$ edges, we can reduce to a trivial negative instance; otherwise, we reduce to G. This results in a kernel with $O(k^2)$ edges.

Extension to Hypergraphs.

We now turn to vertex cover and related problems on d-uniform hypergraphs. Since $k \leq n$, Theorem 2 implies that d-VERTEX COVER does not have kernels with $O(k^{d-\epsilon})$ edges unless coNP $\subseteq$ NP/poly. We point out that kernels with $O(k^d)$ edges exist for d-VERTEX COVER. This follows from a generalization of Buss' high-degree rule (see the introduction) and a folklore application of the sunflower lemma (see [23, chapter 9.1], for example). Recall that for a hypergraph G, a sunflower with heart $h \subseteq V(G)$ and p petals is a set of distinct edges whose pairwise intersection is exactly h. The kernelization proceeds by repeatedly picking a sunflower with at least $k+1$ petals, removing the involved edges, and adding the heart as a new edge to the graph. Note that in this process, edges of size less than d may be added to G. To get back a d-uniform graph, one can complete those edges with fresh vertices, which doesn't affect the number of edges nor the minimum size of a vertex cover. The process continues until no sunflower with $k+1$ petals exists, which is bound to happen as the number of edges decreases in every step. The sunflower lemma of Erdős and Rado [20] states that any d-uniform hypergraph with more than $d! \cdot k^d$ edges has a sunflower with $k+1$ petals. Thus, the hypergraph that remains at the end has at most $d \cdot d! \cdot k^d = O(k^d)$ edges, and has a vertex cover of size at most k if and only if the original hypergraph does.

Regarding extensions of Theorem 3 to d-uniform hypergraphs for $d > 2$, we cannot expect to rule out protocols of cost $O(k^{d-\epsilon})$ for all hypergraph properties Π that are inherited by subgraphs and for which the deletion problem is nontrivial. This is because the property Π could only depend on the primal graph underlying the hypergraph, for which protocols of cost $O(k^2)$ are known in some cases.

6. CONCLUSION

In this paper we introduced a model of communication that captures various settings of interest in the theory of computing. For NP-complete problems like d-SAT, d-VERTEX COVER, and d-CLIQUE we showed that trivial protocols are essentially optimal as function of the witness size, unless the polynomial-time hierarchy collapses. Under the hypothesis that the latter does not happen, the result implies tight lower bounds for parameters captured by the communication model, including the size of PCPs, and polynomial-time sparsification, kernelization, and lossy compression.

Acknowledgments

We would like to thank the following people for discussions, comments, pointers to the literature, and guidance: Matt Anderson, Albert Atserias, Kord Eickmeyer, Martin Grohe, Johan Håstad, Danny Hermelin, Daniel Lokshtanov, Moritz Müller, Saket Saurabh, Mathias Schacht, Asaf Shapira, Luca Trevisan, Chris Umans, Thomas Watson, Dalibor Zelený.

7. REFERENCES

[1] D. Achlioptas and C. Moore. Random k-SAT: two moments suffice to cross a sharp threshold. *SICOMP*, 36(3):740–762, 2007.

[2] D. Achlioptas and Y. Peres. The threshold for random k-SAT is $2^k \log 2 - O(k)$. *Journal of the AMS*, 17(4):947–973, 2004.

[3] N. Alon. Testing subgraphs in large graphs. *RSA*, 21(3–4):359–370, 2002.

[4] N. Alon, E. Fischer, M. Krivelevich, and M. Szegedy. Efficient testing of large graphs. *Combinatorica*, 20(4):451–476, 2000.

[5] N. Alon, T. Kaufman, M. Krivelevich, and D. Ron. Testing triangle-freeness in general graphs. *SIAM Journal on Discrete Mathematics*, 22(2):786–819, 2008.

[6] N. Alon and A. Shapira. Testing subgraphs in directed graphs. *JCSS*, 69(3):354–382, 2004.

[7] N. Alon and A. Shapira. Linear equations, arithmetic progressions and hypergraph property testing. *Theory of Computing*, 1(1):177–216, 2005.

[8] N. Alon and A. Shapira. A characterization of easily testable induced subgraphs. *Combinatorics, Probability and Computing*, 15(6):791–805, 2006.

[9] H. L. Bodlaender, R. G. Downey, M. R. Fellows, and D. Hermelin. On problems without polynomial kernels. *JCSS*, 75(8):423–434, 2009.

[10] H. L. Bodlaender, S. Thomassé, and A. Yeo. Kernel bounds for disjoint cycles and disjoint paths. In *ESA*, pages 635–646, 2009.

[11] J. F. Buss and J. Goldsmith. Nondeterminism within P. *SICOMP*, 22(3):560–572, 1993.

[12] C. Calabro, R. Impagliazzo, and R. Paturi. A duality between clause width and clause density for SAT. In *CCC*, pages 252–260, 2006.

[13] A. K. Chandra, M. L. Furst, and R. J. Lipton. Multi-party protocols. In *STOC*, pages 94–99, 1983.

[14] Y. Chen, J. Flum, and M. Müller. Lower bounds for kernelizations. *ECCC*, 14(137), 2007.

[15] S. A. Cook. The complexity of theorem-proving procedures. In *STOC*, pages 151–158, 1971.

[16] D. Coppersmith and S. Winograd. Matrix multiplication via arithmetic progressions. *Journal of Symbolic Computation*, 9(3):251–280, 1990.

[17] H. Dell and D. van Melkebeek. Satisfiability allows no nontrivial sparsification unless the polynomial-time hierarchy collapses. *ECCC*, 17(38), 2010.

[18] I. Dinur. The PCP theorem by gap amplification. *JACM*, 54(3):12, 2007.

[19] M. Dom, D. Lokshtanov, and S. Saurabh. Incompressibility through colors and IDs. In *ICALP*, pages 378–389, 2009.

[20] P. Erdős and R. Rado. Intersection theorems for systems of sets. *Journal of the London Mathematical Society*, 35:85–90, 1960.

[21] M. R. Fellows, J. Guo, H. Moser, and R. Niedermeier. A generalization of Nemhauser and Trotter's local optimization theorem. In *STACS*, pages 409–420, 2009.

[22] H. Fernau, F. V. Fomin, D. Lokshtanov, D. Raible, S. Saurabh, and Y. Villanger. Kernel(s) for problems with no kernel: On out-trees with many leaves. In *STACS*, pages 421–432, 2009.

[23] J. Flum and M. Grohe. *Parameterized Complexity Theory*. Springer, 2006.

[24] L. Fortnow and R. Santhanam. Infeasibility of instance compression and succinct PCPs for NP. In *STOC*, pages 133–142, 2008.

[25] E. Friedgut and J. Bourgain. Sharp thresholds of graph properties, and the k-SAT problem. *Journal of the AMS*, 12(4):1017–1054, 1999.

[26] O. Goldreich, S. Goldwasser, and D. Ron. Property testing and its connection to learning and approximation. *JACM*, 45(4):653–750, 1998.

[27] J. Guo and R. Niedermeier. Invitation to data reduction and problem kernelization. *SIGACT News*, 38(1):31–45, 2007.

[28] D. Harnik and M. Naor. On the compressibility of NP instances and cryptographic applications. In *FOCS*, pages 719–728, 2006.

[29] J. Håstad and A. Wigderson. Simple analysis of graph tests for linearity and PCP. *RSA*, 22(2):139–160, 2003.

[30] R. Impagliazzo, R. Paturi, and F. Zane. Which problems have strongly exponential complexity? *JCSS*, 63(4):512–530, 2001.

[31] R. M. Karp. Reducibility among combinatorial problems. *Complexity of computer computations*, 43:85–103, 1972.

[32] S. Kratsch and M. Wahlström. Preprocessing of min ones problems: A dichotomy. *Arxiv Preprint*, 2009.

[33] S. Kratsch and M. Wahlström. Two edge modification problems without polynomial kernels. In *IWPEC*, pages 264–275, 2009.

[34] M. S. Krishnamoorthy and N. Deo. Node-deletion NP-complete problems. *SICOMP*, 8(4):619–625, 1979.

[35] L. A. Levin. Universal search problems. *Problemy Peredachi Informatsii*, 9(3):265–266, 1973.

[36] J. M. Lewis and M. Yannakakis. The node-deletion problem for hereditary properties is NP-complete. *JCSS*, 20(2):219–230, 1980.

[37] I. Z. Ruzsa and E. Szemerédi. Triple systems with no six points carrying three triangles. In *Combinatorics, Vol. II*, volume 18 of *Colloquia Mathematica Societatis János Bolyai*, pages 939–945. North-Holland, 1978.

[38] R. Salem and D. C. Spencer. On sets of integers which contain no three terms in arithmetical progression. *Proceedings of the National Academy of Sciences, USA*, 28(12):561–563, 1942.

[39] S. Thomassé. A quadratic kernel for feedback vertex set. In *SODA*, pages 115–119, 2009.

[40] C.-K. Yap. Some consequences of non-uniform conditions on uniform classes. *TCS*, 26(3):287–300, 1983.

Recognizing Well-Parenthesized Expressions in the Streaming Model

Frédéric Magniez*
LRI, Univ. Paris-Sud, CNRS
F-91405 Orsay, France
magniez@lri.fr

Claire Mathieu†
Computer Science Dept.
Brown University
Providence RI 02912, U.S.A
claire@cs.brown.edu

Ashwin Nayak‡
C&O and IQC, U. Waterloo
and Perimeter Institute
Waterloo ON N2L 3G1, Canada
anayak@math.uwaterloo.ca

ABSTRACT

Motivated by a concrete problem and with the goal of understanding the relationship between the complexity of streaming algorithms and the computational complexity of formal languages, we investigate the problem DYCK(s) of checking matching parentheses, with s different types of parenthesis.

We present a one-pass randomized streaming algorithm for DYCK(2) with space $O(\sqrt{n \log n})$ bits, time per letter polylog(n), and one-sided error. We prove that this one-pass algorithm is optimal, up to a $\log n$ factor, even when two-sided error is allowed, and conjecture that a similar bound holds for any constant number of passes over the input.

Surprisingly, the space requirement shrinks drastically if we have access to the input stream *in reverse*. We present a two-pass randomized streaming algorithm for DYCK(2) with space $O((\log n)^2)$, time polylog(n) and one-sided error, where the second pass is in the reverse direction. Both algorithms can be extended to DYCK(s) since this problem is reducible to DYCK(2) for a suitable notion of reduction in the streaming model. Except for an extra $O(\sqrt{\log s})$ multiplicative overhead in the space required in the one-pass algorithm, the resource requirements are of the same order.

For the lower bound, we exhibit hard instances ASCENSION(m) of DYCK(2) with length $\Theta(mn)$. We embed these in what we call a "one-pass" communication problem with $2m$-players, where $m = \tilde{O}(n)$. To establish the hardness of ASCENSION(m), we prove a direct sum result by following the "information cost" approach, but with a few twists. Indeed, we play a subtle game between public and private coins for MOUNTAIN, which corresponds to a primitive instance ASCENSION(1). This mixture between public and private coins for MOUNTAIN results from a balancing act between the direct sum result and a combinatorial lower bound for MOUNTAIN.

*Supported in part by French ANR grants ANR-08-EMER-012 and ANR-07-SESU-013.

†Part of this work was funded by NSF grant CCF-0728816.

‡Work done in part while visiting the Center for Computational Intractability, Rutgers University and DIMACS, with support from NSF grants CCF-832797 and CCF 832787. Research also supported in part by NSERC Canada. Research at Perimeter Institute is supported in part by the Government of Canada through Industry Canada and by the Province of Ontario through MRI.

STOC'10, June 5–8, 2010, Cambridge, Massachusetts, USA.

Categories and Subject Descriptors

F.2.0 [**Theory of Computation**]: Analysis of Algorithms and Problem Complexity—*General*; E.4 [**Data**]: Coding and Information Theory

General Terms

Algorithms, Languages, Theory

Keywords

Streaming Algorithm, Communication Complexity, Parenthesis Expression, Linear Hashing, Information Cost

1. INTRODUCTION

The area of streaming algorithms has experienced tremendous growth over the last decade in many applications. Streaming algorithms sequentially scan the whole input piece by piece in one pass, or in a small number of passes (i.e., they do not have random access to the input), while using sublinear memory space, ideally polylogarithmic in the size of the input. The design of streaming algorithms is motivated by the explosion in the size of the data that algorithms are called upon to process in everyday real-time applications. Examples of such applications occur in bioinformatics for genome decoding, in Web databases for the search of documents, or in network monitoring. The analysis of Internet traffic [2], in which traffic logs are queried, was one of the first applications of this kind of algorithm. Few studies have been made in the context of formal languages, although these would have ramifications for massive data such as DNA sequences and large XML files. For instance, in the context of databases, properties decidable by streaming algorithm have been studied [21, 20], but only in the restricted case of deterministic and constant memory space algorithms.

Motivated by a concrete problem and with the goal of understanding the relationship between the complexity of streaming algorithms and the computational complexity of formal languages, we investigate the problem DYCK(s) of checking matching parentheses, with s different types of parenthesis. Regular languages are by definition decidable by deterministic streaming algorithms with constant space. The DYCK languages are some of the simplest context-free languages and yet already powerful. These languages play a central role in the theory of context-free languages, since every context-free language L can be mapped to a subset of DYCK(s) [8], for some s. In addition to its theoretical importance, the problem of checking matching parentheses is enountered frequently in database applications, for instance in verifying that an XML file is well-formed.

Deciding membership in DYCK(s) has already been addressed in the massive data setting, more precisely through property testing algorithms. An ε-property tester [5, 6, 11] for a language L accepts all strings of L and rejects all strings which are ε-far from strings in L, for the normalized Hamming distance. For every fixed $\varepsilon > 0$, DYCK(1) is ε-testable in constant time [1], whereas in general DYCK(s) are ε-testable in time $\tilde{O}(n^{2/3})$, with a lower bound of $\tilde{\Omega}(n^{1/11})$ [18]. In [10], a comparison between property testers and streaming algorithms has been made. Streaming algorithms have the advantage of access to the entire string, albeit not in a random access fashion.

With random access to the input, context-free languages are known to be recognizable in space $O((\log n)^2)$ [12]. In the special case of DYCK(s), logarithmic space is sufficient, as we may run through all possible heights, and check parentheses at the same height. This scheme does not seem to easily translate to streaming algorithms, even with a small number of passes over the input.

In the streaming model, DYCK(1) has a one-pass streaming algorithm with logarithmic space, using a height counter. Using a straightforward one-way communication complexity argument for EQUALITY, we can deduce that DYCK(2) requires linear space for deterministic one-pass streaming algorithms. A relaxation of DYCK(s) is IDENTITY(s) in the free group with s generators, where local simplifications $\overline{a}a = \epsilon$ are allowed in addition to $a\overline{a} = \epsilon$, for every type of parenthesis $(a, \overline{a})$. There is a logarithmic space algorithm for recognizing the language IDENTITY(s) [15] that can easily be massaged into a one-pass streaming algorithm with polylogarithmic space. Again, this algorithm does not extend to DYCK(s).

We show that DYCK(s) is reducible to DYCK(2), for a suitable notion of reduction in the streaming model, with a $\log s$ factor expansion in the input length. Our first algorithm is a one-pass randomized streaming algorithm for DYCK(2) with space $O(\sqrt{n \log n})$ bits and time polylog(n) (**Theorem 1**). If we had no space constraints the algorithm would be very simple: when we encounter an upstep (a or b), push it on a stack, when we encounter a downstep ($\overline{a}$ or $\overline{b}$), pop the top item from the stack and check that they match. However the stack may grow to linear size in this process. To avoid this growth, the basic strategy of our algorithm is to use a linear hash function to periodically (every $\sqrt{n/\log n}$ letters) compress stack information. As long as we compress only upsteps or only downsteps, all at different heights, we are able to detect mismatches with high probability. The algorithm has one-sided error; it accepts words that belong to the language with certainty. Although simple, we show that this appealing algorithm is nearly optimal in its space usage, even when two-sided error is allowed (**Corollary 1**).

We conjecture that our lower bound still holds if we read the stream several times, but always in the same direction. Surprisingly, the situation is drastically different if we can read the data stream *in reverse*. We present a second algorithm, a randomized two-pass streaming algorithm for DYCK(2) with $O((\log n)^2)$ space and time polylog(n), where the second pass is in the reverse direction (**Theorem 2**). This algorithm uses a hierarchical decomposition of the stream into blocks; whenever the algorithm reaches the end of a block, it compresses the information about subwords from within the block. This compression is what reduces the stack size from $\Theta(\sqrt{n \log n})$ down to $O(\log n)$, but prevents us from checking that certain matching pairs of parentheses are well-formed. However, given the profile of the word (i.e., the sequence of heights), we can pinpoint exactly the matching pairs that do not get checked. As it turns out, a pair that does not get checked when scanning the input left to right is necessarily checked when scanning in the reverse direction. Like the one-pass algorithm, this algorithm has only one-sided error, and always accepts words that belong to the language. We note that it is straightforward to extend the algorithms so that they recognize the language of substrings (which are subwords of consecutive letters) of DYCK(2).

As mentioned above, we also investigate the lower bound on the space required for any one-pass randomized streaming algorithm. Such a lower bound is by nature hard to prove because of the connection of the problem with IDENTITY(2). Moreover, proving a non-trivial lower bound based on two-party communication complexity is hopeless: the related communication problem automatically reduces to EQUALITY after local checks and simplifications by both players, leading to only an $\Omega(\log n)$ lower bound. Instead, we build hard instances ASCENSION(m) of DYCK(2) with length $\Theta(mn)$, that we embed in a "one-pass" communication problem with $2m$ players, where $m = \Theta(n)$. The constraint is that the length of each message in the protocol be less than size, a function of n. Our main result (**Theorem 4**) is that such a protocol requires $\mathsf{size} = \Omega(n)$, which proves that our one-pass algorithm is optimal for probability of error of order $1/n \log n$, and within an $O(\log n)$ factor of optimal for constant error (**Corollary 1**).

To establish the hardness of ASCENSION(m), we prove a *direct sum* result that captures its relationship to solving m instances of the intermediate problem MOUNTAIN, which involves only two players. We follow the "information cost" approach taken in [7, 19, 4, 14, 13], among other works before and since. We adapt this notion to suit both the nature of streaming algorithms and of our problem. The idea is to focus on the information about a part of the input contained in a part of the protocol transcript, given the remaining inputs.

Using this notion of information cost, we prove a direct sum result (**Lemma 3**). A remarkable device here is the use of an "easy" distribution for the information cost for protocols, that are correct with high probability in the worst case. The use of an easy distribution "collapses" ASCENSION(m) to an instance of MOUNTAIN, which may be planted in any one of the m coordinates. This technique was developed in [4], but comes with a few twists in our case. Indeed, we play a subtle game between public and private coins. Namely, in protocols for ASCENSION(m) only public coins are allowed for all players, whereas for MOUNTAIN one of the players, Bob, can also access private coins, while Alice, the other player, cannot. This mixture between public and private coins for MOUNTAIN arises from a balancing act between the direct sum result and our combinatorial lower bound for MOUNTAIN (**Theorem 3**). Namely, we are only able to prove the lower bound for MOUNTAIN when Alice only uses public coins, whereas the direct sum only holds, with our definition of information cost, when Bob has access to additional private coins.

We note that as a bonus, our lower bound provides a $\tilde{\Omega}(\sqrt{n})$ lower bound for the problem of checking priority queues in the one-pass streaming model, solving an open problem of [9].

2. DEFINITIONS AND PRELIMINARIES

DEFINITION 1 (DYCK). *Let s be a positive integer. Then* $\mathrm{DYCK}(s)$ *denotes the language over alphabet* $\Sigma = \{a_1, \overline{a}_1, \ldots, a_s, \overline{a}_s\}$ *defined recursively by:*

$$\mathrm{DYCK}(s) = \epsilon + \sum_{i \leq s} a_i \cdot \mathrm{DYCK}(s) \cdot \overline{a}_i \cdot \mathrm{DYCK}(s).$$

We also denote by $\mathrm{DYCK}(s)$ the problem of deciding whether a word $w \in \Sigma^*$ is in the language $\mathrm{DYCK}(s)$.

In streaming algorithms, a *pass* on an input $x \in \Sigma^n$ means that x is given as an *input stream* $x_1, x_2, \ldots, x_n$, which arrives sequentially, i.e., letter by letter in this order. For simplicity, we assume throughout this article that the length n of the input is always given to the algorithm in advance. Nonetheless, all our algorithms can be adapted to the case in which n is unknown until the end of a pass. See [16] for an introduction to streaming algorithms.

DEFINITION 2 (STREAMING ALGORITHM). *Fix an alphabet Σ. A k-pass* streaming algorithm $\boldsymbol{A}$ *with space $s(n)$ and time $t(n)$ is an algorithm such that for every input stream $x \in \Sigma^n$: (1) $\boldsymbol{A}$ performs k sequential passes on x; (2) $\boldsymbol{A}$ maintains a memory space of size $s(n)$ bits while reading x; (3) $\boldsymbol{A}$ has running time at most $t(n)$ per letter x_i; (4) $\boldsymbol{A}$ has preprocessing and postprocessing time $t(n)$.*
We say that $\boldsymbol{A}$ is bidirectional *if it is allowed to access to the input in the reverse order, after reaching the end of the input. Then the parameter k is the total number of passes in either direction.*

DEFINITION 3 (STREAMING REDUCTION). *Fix two alphabets Σ_1 and Σ_2. A problem P_1 is $f(n)$-streaming reducible to a problem P_2 with space $s(n)$ and time $t(n)$, if for every input $x \in \Sigma_1^n$, there exists $y = y_1 y_2 \ldots y_n$, with $y_i \in \Sigma_2^{f(n)}$, such that: (1) y_i can be computed deterministically from x_i using space $s(n)$ and time $t(n)$; (2) From a solution of P_2 with input y, a solution on P_1 with input x can be computed with space $s(n)$ and time $t(n)$.*

FACT 1. *Let P_1 be $f(n)$-streaming reducible to a problem P_2 with space $s_0(n)$ and time $t_0(n)$. Let $\boldsymbol{A}$ be a k-pass streaming algorithm for P_2 with space $s(n)$ and time $t(n)$. Then there is a k-pass streaming algorithm for P_1 with space $s(n \times f(n)) + s_0(n)$ and time $t(n \times f(n)) + t_0(n)$ with the same properties as $\boldsymbol{A}$ (deterministic/randomized, unidirectional/bidirectional).*

PROPOSITION 1. $\mathrm{DYCK}(s)$ *is $\lceil \log s \rceil$-streaming reducible to* $\mathrm{DYCK}(2)$ *with space and time* $\mathrm{O}(\log s)$.

PROOF. We encode a parenthesis a_i by a word of length $l = \lceil \log s \rceil$ with only parentheses of type a_1, a_2. We let $f(a_i)$ be the binary expansion of i over l bits where 0 is replaced by a_1 and 1 by a_2. Then $f(\overline{a}_i)$ is defined similarly, except that we write the binary expansion of i in the opposite order. Then $x_1 \ldots x_n$ is in $\mathrm{DYCK}(s)$ if and only $f(x_1) \ldots f(x_n)$ is in $\mathrm{DYCK}(2)$. □

Typically, such as in parsing XML files, the above reduction can be implemented with constant space and time. Indeed, given an upstate (*start-tag*) <w> (respectively, a downstep (*end-tag*) </w>), where w is an ASCII string denoting the type of parenthesis (*tag*), we can generate the above encoding of w into a_1, a_2 (respectively, into $\overline{a}_1, \overline{a}_2$), while reading w as a stream itself, i.e., character by character.

By Proposition 1, it is enough to design streaming algorithms for $\mathrm{DYCK}(2)$. That is the objective of the next section.

3. ALGORITHMS

From now on we consider $\mathrm{DYCK}(2)$ where the input is a stream of n letters $x_1 x_2 \ldots x_n$ in the alphabet $\Sigma = \{a, \overline{a}, b, \overline{b}\}$. We first introduce a few definitions. An *upstep* is a letter a or b, a *downstep* is a letter $\overline{a}$ or $\overline{b}$.

DEFINITION 4. *Let $x \in \Sigma^n$.*
The height *of x is* $\mathrm{height}(x) = |x|_a + |x|_b - |x|_{\overline{a}} - |x|_{\overline{b}}$.
For $1 \leq i < j \leq n$, (i, j) is a matching pair *for x if* $\mathrm{height}(x[1, i-1]) = \mathrm{height}(x[1, j])$ *and* $\mathrm{height}(x[1, k]) > \mathrm{height}(x[1, i-1])$ *for all $k \in \{i, \ldots, j-1\}$.*
The height of a matching pair (i, j) *is* $\mathrm{height}(x[1, i-1])$.
A matching pair (i, j) for x is well-formed, *if $(x[i], x[j])$ equals $(a, \overline{a})$ or $(b, \overline{b})$,* ill-formed *otherwise.*

It follows that any index i forms a matching pair with at most one other index, and that a matching pair consists of an upstep and a downstep. These definitions are extended to subsets $I \subseteq [1, n]$ of indices of letters of x. For instance, we say that I is a *matching set* for x, if $I = \cup\{i, j\}$, where the union is over a subset of the matching pairs (i, j) for x. To prove correctness of our algorithms, we use the following well-known characterization of $\mathrm{DYCK}(2)$.

FACT 2. *Let $x \in \Sigma^n$. Then $x \in \mathrm{DYCK}(2)$ if and only if:* $\mathrm{height}(x) = 0$, *the height of every prefix of x is nonnegative, and $[1, n]$ is a well-formed (matching) set for x.*

For ease of notation, we identify an increasing sequence $i_1 < i_2 < \cdots < i_m$ of indices with the corresponding subword $x_{i_1} x_{i_2} \ldots x_{i_m}$ of x. We also use this correspondence in reverse when the indices of the subword are clear from the context.

During the computation the algorithm implicitly keeps track of the height of the word read so far. Let p be a prime number such that $n^{1+c} \leq p < 2n^{1+c}$, for some fixed constant $c \geq 1$. We assume that the algorithm can access a random function $\mathrm{hash}(\cdot)$ that maps subwords v of x to integers in $[0, p-1]$, as follows: $\mathrm{hash}(x_{i_1} x_{i_2} \ldots x_{i_m}) = \sum_j \mathrm{hash}(x_{i_j})$, with

$$\mathrm{hash}(x_i) = \begin{cases} \alpha^{\mathrm{height}(x[1,i-1])} \bmod p & \text{if } x_i = a, \\ -\alpha^{\mathrm{height}(x[1,i])} \bmod p & \text{if } x_i = \overline{a}, \\ 0 & \text{otherwise,} \end{cases}$$

where α is a uniformly random integer in $[0, p-1]$. Note that the computation of $\mathrm{hash}(v)$ depends not just on v but also on the height of its letters *within* x.

Given x and v, the value of hash(v) is a polynomial in α of degree at most n. By the Schwartz-Zippel lemma, if it is not identically zero then, for a random α, the probability that hash(v) $= 0$ is at most $n/p \leq n^{-c}$. In particular:

FACT 3. *Let $x \in \Sigma^n$ and $v = x_{i_1}x_{i_2}\dots$ be a subword of x. If $v \in$ DYCK(2), then hash(v) $= 0$ for all α. If v has exactly one ill-formed matching pair at some height, then hash(v) $\neq 0$ with probability at least $1 - n^{-c}$, for a uniformly random integer $\alpha \in [0, p-1]$.*

For any letter x_i, we may compute hash(x_i) in time polylog n and space O($\log n$). Moreover, for any word v the value of hash(v) can be maintained with O($\log n$) space.

3.1 The one-pass algorithm

Algorithm 1 reads the stream in blocks of $\sqrt{n \log n}$ letters. It uses a stack data structure encoding the subword formed by the letters seen so far that belong to matching pairs that have not yet been checked.

Algorithm 1 One-pass algorithm

```
S ← empty stack
for i ← 1 to √(n/log n) do
    Algorithm 2 (S) {reads √(n log n) letters from stream}
end for
if S not empty, reject: "missing closing parenthesis"
return accept
```

For clarity, we describe an "off-line" version of **Algorithm 2** that executes once the entire block has been read. It can easily be converted to an "online" algorithm that takes polylog n time per letter.

Within a block, **Algorithm 2** first does the obvious checks with a straightforward stack-based algorithm—any upstep followed by a downstep must match and, once checked, can be discarded. The block is now reduced to a sequence w' of only downsteps followed by a sequence w'' of only upsteps. To look up needed information about the blocks that have previously been read, the algorithm accesses a stack. Each stack item is of the form (h, ℓ) *encoding* a subword v of the stream x, in the sense that $h =$ hash(v) and $\ell =$ height(v).

As the algorithm processes the letters in w', it incorporates them into the last stack item. More precisely, given a downstep x_j and given $(h, \ell) =$ (hash(v), height(v)), it can compute hash(vx_j) $= h +$ hash(x_j) and height(vx_j) $= \ell - 1$, thus encoding vx_j without explicit knowledge of v. Note that this relies on the linearity of the hash function.

Once the encoded subword v has height 0, to test whether it is well-formed, the algorithm checks whether hash(v) $= 0$. If this test succeeds, the entry of the stack encoding v can now be removed. Finally the subword w'' is processed in a straightforward manner by creating a new stack item. An example execution of the algorithm is shown in Appendix A.

For the analysis, we first start with the following observations about **Algorithm 1**.

FACT 4. *Let (h, ℓ) be a stack item encoding a subword v. Then $v = v_u v_d$, where v_u has only upsteps and v_d has only downsteps.*

Define a partial order between words by taking the transitive closure of $uv \prec ul\bar{l'}v$, where $l, l' \in \{a, b\}$, i.e., $w \prec x$ if w is a subword of x obtained by removing some (well-formed or not) matching pairs in x.

Algorithm 2 One-pass subroutine: reading one block

```
input: stack S
read w = next √(n log n) letters (or less if stream ends)
check that matching pairs in w are well-formed (else reject: "mismatch")
simplify w into w'w'', where w' has only downsteps and w'' has only upsteps
for i ← 1 to |w'| do
    pop (h, ℓ) from S (if empty, reject: "extra closing parenthesis")
    {(h, ℓ) encodes a v s.t. h = hash(v) and ℓ = height(v)}
    h ← h + hash(w'_i) and ℓ ← ℓ − 1
    push (h, ℓ) on S
    {(h, ℓ) now encodes vw'_i}
    if ℓ = 0 then
        check that h = 0 (else reject: "mismatch")
        pop and discard (h, ℓ)
    end if
end for
if w'' ≠ ε then push (hash(w''), |w''|) on S
{(hash(w''), |w''|) encodes w''}
output: stack S
```

FACT 5. *Consider S right after pushing the encoding of a subword ending with x_j. Let $v_1, v_2, \dots, v_m$ be the subwords encoded by the current stack (in bottom-up order). Then $v_1 v_2 \dots v_m \preceq x[1, j]$, height($v_i$) ≥ 0 for every i, and only v_m may have height 0. Moreover, if (h, ℓ) is a stack item encoding a subword v, then for every downstep $j \in v$ there is a unique upstep $i \in v$ such that (i, j) is a matching pair for x.*

Then, we conclude with the correctness of our algorithm.

THEOREM 1. ***Algorithm 1** is a one-pass randomized streaming algorithm for* DYCK(2) *with space O($\sqrt{n \log n}$) and time polylog(n). If the stream belongs to* DYCK(2) *then the algorithm accepts it with certainty; otherwise it rejects it with probability at least $1 - n^{-c}$.*

PROOF. Each stack element takes space O($\log n$) bits and each execution of Algorithm 2 adds at most one element to the stack. There are at most $\sqrt{n/\log n}$ stack items at any time, hence the space used is O($\sqrt{n \log n}$). The processing time is easy by inspection.

To prove correctness, first assume that $x \in$ DYCK(2). By Fact 2 the height of every prefix is non-negative, so the algorithm does not reject because of an extra closing parenthesis; and the height of x is 0, so the algorithm does not reject because of a missing closing parenthesis. For each block w, the matching pairs within w are all well-formed, so the algorithm does not reject them either. Finally, whenever the algorithm checks $h = 0$ for a stack item such that $\ell = 0$, by Fact 5 the corresponding subword v is a matching set for x and since $x \in$ DYCK(2), v is well-formed. Then by Fact 3, it passes the hash test in **Algorithm 2**. Therefore the algorithm is correct in this case.

Second, assume that $x \notin$ DYCK(2). By Fact 2, x fails to be in DYCK(2) for one of the following reasons. Either some prefix of x has negative height (too many closing parentheses): then the algorithm detects the problem when it tries to pop an item from an empty stack. Or, height$(x) > 0$: then the algorithm detects the problem at the very end when it sees that the stack is not empty. Or, there is at least one matching pair (i, j) where x is ill-formed: that is the only non trivial case. If i, j are within the same block, then the algorithm rejects during the internal checks within the block. Assume now that i and j are in different blocks. If the algorithm stops before getting to x_j, it does so after correctly rejecting the word. Assume it examines x_j. Then, since x_i is in a different block, x_j is in w', and thus is encoded and pushed on S. If the algorithm never checks the stack item whose subword v contains x_j, then the final stack is not empty and the algorithm rejects the word. Finally, assume that at some point the algorithm checks the stack item encoding v. By Fact 5, v also contains x_i. By Fact 4, this is the only ill-formed matching pair at that height, so by Fact 3, the probability that v fails the hash test in **Algorithm 2** is at least $1 - n^{-c}$, for a uniformly random choice of α. So the algorithm is correct with high probability. □

3.2 The bidirectional algorithm

The second algorithm uses a hierarchical decomposition of the stream x into nested blocks of 2^i letters for $i \leq k = \lceil \log n \rceil$. Up to padding we can assume that $n = 2^k$: we append to x the word $(a\overline{a})^i$ of suitable length (assuming that x is of even size, otherwise $x \notin$ DYCK(2)). We use $O(\log n)$ bits of memory to store, after the first pass, the number of letters padded. Thanks to this assumption, the algorithm uses the same hierarchical decomposition, whether we read the stream from left to right or from right to left. During the right to left pass, letters $\overline{a}, \overline{b}$ are interpreted as a, b, respectively (and vice-versa).

As before, we use a stack data structure in such a way that Fact 5 still holds. Each stack item is now of the form (h, ℓ, f) encoding a subword v of x, in the sense that $h = \text{hash}(v)$, $\ell = \text{height}(v)$, and in addition $f = \text{first}(v)$ is the index in x of the first letter in v.

Algorithm 3 Bi-directional algorithm

> $S \leftarrow$ empty stack
> **Algorithm 4** (k, S), reading stream from left to right { $k = \lceil \log n \rceil$ }
> if S is not empty, **reject:** "missing closing parenthesis"
> **Algorithm 4** (k, S), reading stream from right to left
> {Right to left, $\overline{a}, \overline{b}$ are interpreted as a, b (and vice-versa)}
> **return accept**

Algorithm 4 recursively decomposes x into nested blocks (Figure 2 in Appendix A). An *i-block* is a substring of the form $x[(q-1)2^i + 1, q2^i]$ for $1 \leq q \leq n/2^i$. The main difference between **Algorithm 4**(k, S) and **Algorithm 2**(S) is that whenever in a recursive call the algorithm reaches the end of the current block, it compresses *without checking* the stack items encoding subwords from within the block. This compression is what reduces the stack size from $\sqrt{n/\log n}$ down to $O(\log n)$, but now Fact 4 no longer holds. Since hash at a given height is commutative, we may lose information. For example compressing hash$(ba\overline{a})$ with hash$(b\overline{b}\overline{b})$ gives hash$(ba\overline{a}b\overline{b}\overline{b})$, which is equal to hash$(ba\overline{b}b\overline{a}\overline{b})$: one word is in DYCK(2), the other one is not, but after compressing we can no longer distinguish between them. The crux of the analysis is that such information loss cannot occur both when reading the stream from left to right and when reading it from right to left (Fact 6 below, and Figure 3 in Appendix A).

Algorithm 4 Block algorithm $(i$, stack $S)$ { reads i-block B_i, increases stack size by at most 1 }

```
if i ≥ 1 then
  {read two (i − 1)-blocks B and B′}
  Algorithm 4(i − 1, S)
  Algorithm 4(i − 1, S)
  if S has two items with first letters in B_i then
    {there are at most two such items, necessarily on top}
    pop (h2, ℓ2, f2) from S   {encodes v2}
    pop (h1, ℓ1, f1) from S   {encodes v1}
    push (h1 + h2, ℓ1 + ℓ2, f1) on S {encodes v1v2}
  end if
else
  read one letter y
  if y is a downstep then
    pop (h, ℓ, f) from S (if empty, reject: "extra closing
    parenthesis")
    {encodes some subword v}
    h ← h + hash(y) and ℓ ← ℓ − 1
    push (h, ℓ, f) on S { now encodes vy}
    if ℓ = 0 then
      check that h = 0 (if not, reject: "mismatch")
      pop and discard (h, ℓ, f)
    end if
  else
    push(hash(y), 1, first(y)) on S { encodes y}
  end if
end if
```

For the analysis, noting that Fact 5 remains valid for **Algorithm 3**, we derive the following invariant of **Algorithm 3** that is weaker than Fact 4.

FACT 6. *A stack item encoding a subword that starts with letter f is discarded exactly when the algorithm reads the letter f' such that (f, f') is a matching pair.*

We now state a simple observation from the definition of matching pairs.

FACT 7. *Let $v = uu'$ be a subword of x, and let $d \geq 0$. Then $u \times u'$ has at most one matching pair at height d.*

We conclude with the correctness of our algorithm.

THEOREM 2. ***Algorithm 3** is a bidirectional two-pass randomized streaming algorithm for* DYCK(2) *with space* $O((\log n)^2)$ *and time* polylog(n). *If the input belongs to* DYCK(2) *then the algorithm accepts it with certainty; otherwise it rejects it with probability at least $1 - n^{-c}$.*

PROOF. In terms of space requirements, each stack element takes space $O(\log n)$ and the stack has size at most $2k = 2\log n$, hence space $O((\log n)^2)$. The processing time is easy by inspection, while noticing by induction that each execution of **Algorithm 4** generates only one new stack item.

To analyze the algorithm, observe (using Fact 5) that as in the proof of Theorem 1 it is correct whenever $x \in$ DYCK(2). Now, assume that $x \notin$ DYCK(2) and apply Fact 2. If some prefix of x has negative height or if the final height of x is non-zero, then as in the proof of Theorem 1 the algorithm is correct.

Finally, consider the case when x has an ill-formed matching pair. Let i be minimum such that some i-block B_i contains an ill-formed matching pair (j, j'). By minimality, x_j and $x_{j'}$ are in different $(i-1)$-blocks B and B'. Let m be the minimum, over upsteps x_l of B, of height$(x[1, l-1])$. Let m' be the minimum, over downsteps x_l of B', of height$(x[1, l])$ (see Figure 3 in Appendix A).

Up to reversing left-to-right and right-to-left directions, we may assume that $m \geq m'$.

Immediately after reading B, since j is not yet matched, the stack necessarily contains an item encoding a word containing j; moreover, since all compressions in B involve items with first letter in B, the first letter f of that word is in B, hence starts at height $\geq m$. Since $m \geq m'$, the letter f' matching f is in B_i, and so, from Fact 6 by the end of reading B' that item has been discarded. Let (h, ℓ, f) be that discarded item, encoding a subword v.

Since the first letter f of v is in B, all of the letters of v are in $B \cup B'$. By Fact 5, v is a matching set, and, by Fact 7, its matching pairs in $B \times B'$ are all at different heights. So, at the height d of pair (i, i'), v only contains (j, j'), which is ill-formed, plus possibly some matching pairs coming from $B \times B$ or from $B' \times B'$, pairs that are all well-formed by minimality of i. Overall, at height d the word v has exactly one ill-formed matching pair, so by Fact 3, the probability that v passes the hash test of **Algorithm 4** is at most n^{-c}, for a uniformly random choice of α. So the algorithm is correct with probability $1 - n^{-c}$. □

4. LOWER BOUNDS

We define a family of hard instances for DYCK(2) as follows. For any word $Z \in \{a, b\}^n$, let $\overline{Z}$ be the matching word associated with Z. For positive integers m, n, consider the following instances of length $\Theta(mn)$:

$$\begin{aligned} w &= X_1 \overline{Y}_1 \overline{c}_1 c_1 Y_1 \; X_2 \overline{Y}_2 \overline{c}_2 c_2 Y_2 \; \ldots \\ &\quad \ldots \; X_m \overline{Y}_m \overline{c}_m c_m Y_m \; \overline{X}_m \; \ldots \; \overline{X}_2 \; \overline{X}_1, \end{aligned}$$

where for every i, $X_i \in \{0,1\}^n$, $Y_i = X_i[n - k_i + 2, n]$ for some $k_i \in \{1, 2, \ldots, n\}$, and $c_i \in \{a, b\}$. The word w is in DYCK(2) if and only if, for every i, $c_i = X_i[n - k_i + 1]$.

Intuitively, for $m = n/\log n$ recognizing w is difficult with space $o(n)$. After reading X_i, the streaming algorithm does not have enough space to store information about the bit at unknown index $(n - k_i + 1)$. When it reads c_i it is therefore unable to decide whether $c_i = X_i[n - k_i + 1]$. Moreover, after reading $\overline{Y}_m$ it does not have enough space to store information about all indices $k_1, k_2, \ldots, k_m$. When it reads $\overline{X}_m \ldots \overline{X}_2 \; \overline{X}_1$ it therefore misses out on its second chance to check whether $c_i = X_i[n - k_i + 1]$ for every i. The formal proof contains several subtleties and is executed in the language of communication complexity.

We define a communication problem ASCENSION(m) (Figure 5 in Appendix B) associated with the hard instances described above. For convenience, we replace suffixes by prefixes. Formally, in the problem ASCENSION(m) there are $2m$ players $A_1, A_2, \ldots, A_m$ and $B_1, B_2, \ldots, B_m$. Player A_i has $X_i \in \{0,1\}^n$, B_i has $k_i \in [n]$, a bit c_i and the prefix $X_i[1, k_i - 1]$ of X_i. Let $\mathbf{X} = (X_1, X_2, \ldots, X_m)$, $\mathbf{k} = (k_1, k_2, \ldots, k_m)$ and $\mathbf{c} = (c_1, c_2, \ldots, c_m)$. The goal is to compute $f_m(\mathbf{X}, \mathbf{k}, \mathbf{c}) = \bigvee_{i=1}^m f(X_i, k_i, c_i) = \bigvee_{i=1}^m (X_i[k_i] \oplus c_i)$, which is 0 if $X_i[k_i] = c_i$ for all i, and 1 otherwise.

Motivated by the streaming model, we require each message to have length at most size bits, where the parameter size is a function of m and n and corresponds to the space used in the streaming algorithm. We also require the communication between the $2m$ participants in a one-pass protocol to be in the following order:

Round 1

- For i from 1 to $m - 1$, player A_i sends message M_{A_i} to B_i, then B_i sends message M_{B_i} to A_{i+1};
- A_m sends message M_{A_m} to B_m;

Round 2

- B_m sends message M_{B_m} to A_m;
- For i from m down to 2, A_i sends message M'_{A_i} to A_{i-1};
- A_1 computes the output.

A streaming algorithm for DYCK(2) with space 'size' implies a communication protocol for ASCENSION(m) as described above. So a lower bound on size follows from a lower bound on the communication complexity of ASCENSION(m).

To establish the hardness of solving ASCENSION(m), we prove a *direct sum* result that captures its relationship to solving m instances of a "primitive" problem MOUNTAIN defined as follows. In the problem MOUNTAIN (Figure 4 in Appendix B), Alice has an n-bit string $X \in \{0,1\}^n$, and Bob has an integer $k \in [n]$, a bit c and the prefix $X[1, k-1]$ of X. The goal is to compute the Boolean function $f(X, k, c) = (X[k] \oplus c)$ which is 0 if $X[k] = c$, and 1 otherwise. In a one-pass protocol for MOUNTAIN, the communication occurs in the following order: Alice sends a message M_A to Bob, Bob sends a message M_B to Alice, then Alice outputs $f(X, k, c)$.

As mentioned in Section 1, we follow the "information cost" approach, a method that has been particularly successful in recent works on direct sum results.

The direct sum result is proven using the superadditivity of mutual information for inputs (k_i, c_i) picked independently from a carefully chosen distribution. In the defining information cost, we measure mutual information with respect to a distribution on which the MOUNTAIN function is the constant 0, eventhough we consider protocols for the problem that are correct with high probability in the worst case. The use of this easy distribution collapses the function ASCENSION(m) to an instance of MOUNTAIN in any chosen coordinate. We massage this technique into a form that is better suited to the streaming model and to proving lower bounds for the primitive function MOUNTAIN.

We finish by giving a combinatorial argument that protocols computing MOUNTAIN in the worst case necessarily reveal "a lot" of information even when its inputs are chosen according to the easy distribution.

4.1 Information cost

We measure the *information cost* of a one-pass public-coin randomized protocol P for ASCENSION(m) (of the form described in the previous section), with respect to some distribution ν on the inputs $(\mathbf{X}, \mathbf{k}, \mathbf{c})$, by $\mathrm{IC}_\nu(P) = \mathrm{I}(\mathbf{k}, \mathbf{c} : M_{B_m} | \mathbf{X}, R)$, where R denotes the public-coins of P. From this we define the *information cost* of the problem ASCENSION(m) itself with respect to a distribution ν and error parameter δ as follows: $\mathrm{IC}_\nu^{\mathrm{pub}}(\text{ASCENSION}(m), \delta) = \min(\mathrm{IC}_\nu(P))$, where the minimum is over one-pass public-coin randomized protocols P for the problem, with worst-case error at most δ. Note that the information cost implicitly depends on size, the length of each message.

For the problem MOUNTAIN we play a subtle game between public and private coins. We consider protocols in which Alice has access only to public coins R, whereas Bob additionally has access to some independent private coins R_B. We define $\mathrm{IC}_\nu(P) = \mathrm{I}(k, c : M_B|X, R)$, where R denotes only the public-coins of P. Further, we define $\mathrm{IC}_\nu^{\mathrm{mix}}(\text{MOUNTAIN}, \delta) = \min(\mathrm{IC}_\nu(P))$, where P ranges over "mixed" public and private coin randomized protocols with worst case error at most δ where Alice and Bob share public coins, and only Bob has access to extra private coins.

We also make use of a related measure of complexity for MOUNTAIN when P ranges over protocols where Alice's message is deterministic, and Bob has access to private coins R_B: $\mathsf{DIC}_\nu^{\mathrm{mix}}(\text{MOUNTAIN}, \mu, \delta) = \min(\mathrm{IC}_\nu(P))$, i.e., the minimum information cost with respect to ν, where P ranges over protocols for MOUNTAIN, in which Alice's message M_A is deterministic given her input X, while Bob may use his private coins R_B to generate his message. Further, the distributional error of P is at most δ when the inputs are chosen according to μ. Note that in general, and certainly in our application, ν and μ may be different, meaning that we measure the information cost of the protocol with respect to some distribution ν, while we measure its error under a potentially different distribution μ. For later use, we recall that the distributional error under μ is $\mathrm{Exp}_{(X,k,c)\sim\mu}(\Pr(P \text{ fails on } (X, k, c)))$, where the probability is over the private coins R_B of Bob.

We begin by relating the information cost for protocols in which Alice is deterministic to that of mixed randomized protocols.

LEMMA 1.

$$\mathsf{DIC}_\nu^{\mathrm{mix}}(\text{MOUNTAIN}, \mu, 2\delta) \leq 2 \times \mathrm{IC}_\nu^{\mathrm{mix}}(\text{MOUNTAIN}, \delta).$$

PROOF. Consider a randomized protocol P for MOUNTAIN with worst-case error at most δ such that $\mathrm{IC}_\nu^{\mathrm{mix}}(\text{MOUNTAIN}, \delta) = \mathrm{IC}_\nu(P)$. We further assume that Alice and Bob have uniformly distributed public coins R, and only Bob has extra private coins R_B. Then

$$\mathrm{IC}_\nu^{\mathrm{mix}}(\text{MOUNTAIN}, \delta) = \operatorname*{Exp}_r(\mathrm{I}(k, c : M_{B_m}|X, R = r)),$$

Since P has worst-case error at most δ, it has distributional error at most δ under μ:

$$\operatorname*{Exp}_r\Big(\operatorname*{Exp}_{(X,k,c)\sim\mu}(\Pr(P \text{ fails on } (X, k, c)|R = r))\Big) \leq \delta.$$

Therefore, by the Markov inequality, there is a set $\mathcal{R}$ with $\Pr(R \in \mathcal{R}) \geq \frac{1}{2}$ such that

$$\forall r \in \mathcal{R}, \quad \operatorname*{Exp}_{(X,k,c)\sim\mu}(\Pr(P \text{ fails on } (X, k, c)|R = r)) \leq 2\delta.$$

Now consider the information cost of P under the distribution ν over inputs. Let $\mathrm{U}(\mathcal{R})$ denote the uniform distribution on $\mathcal{R}$. We have

$$\operatorname*{Exp}_{r\sim\mathrm{U}(\mathcal{R})}(\mathrm{I}(k, c : M_{B_m}|X, R = r)) \leq 2\times\mathrm{IC}_\nu^{\mathrm{mix}}(\text{MOUNTAIN}, \delta),$$

since the event $\mathcal{R}$ has probability at least 1/2. Therefore, there exists an $r \in \mathcal{R}$ such that $\mathrm{I}(k, c : M_{B_m}|X, R = r) \leq 2\times\mathrm{IC}_\nu^{\mathrm{mix}}(\text{MOUNTAIN}, \delta)$. Let P_r be the protocol obtained by fixing the public coins used in P to r. Then Alice's message M_A is deterministic. By definition of $\mathcal{R}$, the protocol P_r has distributional error at most 2δ under μ, and $\mathrm{IC}_\nu(P) \leq 2 \times \mathrm{IC}_\nu^{\mathrm{mix}}(\text{MOUNTAIN}, \delta)$. □

4.2 Information cost of Mountain

As explained before, and formally proved in the next section, the information cost approach entails showing that the MOUNTAIN problem is "hard" even when we restrict our attention to an easy distribution. We prove such a result here.

Let μ be the distribution over inputs (X, k, c) in which X is a uniformly random n-bit string, k is a uniformly random integer in $[n]$ and c a uniformly random bit. This is a hard distribution for MOUNTAIN (as is implicit in [17, 3]). We consider the information cost of MOUNTAIN under the distribution μ_0 obtained by conditioning μ on the event that the function value is 0: $\mu_0(X, k, c) = \mu(X, k, c|X[k] = c)$.

LEMMA 2. *If* $\mathsf{size} \leq n/100$, *then*

$$\mathsf{DIC}_{\mu_0}^{\mathrm{mix}}(\text{MOUNTAIN}, \mu, 1/16n^2) = \Omega(\log n).$$

PROOF. Let P be a randomized protocol for MOUNTAIN, where Alice's message M_A is deterministic, with distributional error at most $1/16n^2$ under the distribution μ, such that $|M_A| \leq n/100$. We prove that $\mathrm{IC}_{\mu_0}(P) = \Omega(\log n)$. In the following, all expressions involving mutual information and entropy are with respect to the distribution μ_0.

By Markov inequality, there are at least 2^{n-1} strings U on which P fails with error at most $1/8n^2$ on average on input (U, k, c), where (k, c) are uniformly distributed. Let $S \subseteq \{0, 1\}^n$ of size at least 2^{n-1} be the set of such strings U. Then P has error probability less than $1/4n$ on input (U, k, c), for every (k, c).

Let α be a possible message M_A from Alice to Bob when her inputs range in S, and let $S_\alpha = \{U \in S : M_A(U) = \alpha\}$. For every string $V \in S_\alpha$, we bound from below the mutual information of k and M_B, the randomized message that Bob sends back to Alice, as k varies. For this we construct a set $I \subseteq [n]$ such that the message distributions $m_k = M_B(\alpha, V[1, k-1], k, V[k])$ for $k \in I$ are pairwise well-separated in ℓ_1 distance. This is in turn established by exhibiting, for each $k \in I$, a string $V_k \in S_\alpha$ such that $V_k[1, k-1] = V[1, k-1]$ and $V_k[k] \neq V[k]$. The details follow.

Associate with S_α its dictionary T, a 2-rank tree (a tree with either 1 or 2 children at any internal node), all whose nodes except the root are labeled by bits; the root has an empty label. Each string V in S_α is in one-to-one correspondence with a top-down path π in T from the root to one of its leaves, where the label of the $(i+1)$th node in π is $V[i]$. We identify $V \in S_\alpha$ with the path π in T, and refer to this path as V.

The tree T has $|S_\alpha|$ leaves, each at depth n. For a fixed $V \in S_\alpha$, let I be the set of integers k such that the $(k+1)$th node in path V has out-degree 2. By construction, for every $k \in I$ there exists another string, say, $V_k \in S_\alpha$ such that $V_k[1, k-1] = V[1, k-1]$ and $V_k[k] \neq V[k]$. Set $c_k = V[k]$ for every $k \in [n]$. Then the message distributions satisfy $M_B(\alpha, V[1, k-1], k, c_k) = M_B(\alpha, V_k[1, k-1], k, c_k)$, for all $k \in I$. Let $m_k = M_B(\alpha, V[1, k-1], k, c_k)$. Let $k, k' \in I$ be distinct indices such that $k < k'$. As $V_{k'}[1, k'-1] = V[1, k'-1]$, the message distribution $M_B(\alpha, V_{k'}[1, k-1], k, c_k)$ on input $(V_{k'}, k, c_k)$ equals m_k, and also $M_B(\alpha, V_{k'}[1, k'-1], k', c_{k'})$ on input $(V_{k'}, k', c_{k'})$ equals $m_{k'}$. However, $V_{k'}[k] = V[k] = c_k$, so the function evaluates to 0 on input $(V_{k'}, k, c_k)$, and $V_{k'}[k'] \neq V[k'] = c_{k'}$, so the function value is 1 on $(V_{k'}, k', c_{k'})$. The protocol P

computes its outputs from $m_k, V_{k'}$ and $m_{k'}, V_{k'}$, respectively, on these instances, and errs with probability at most $1/4n$.

We use the above property of the distributions $\{m_k\}$ to bound from below the mutual information of k in the message M_B, given V.

PROPOSITION 2.

$$\mathrm{I}(k : M_B | X = V) \geq \left(\frac{4|I| - n}{4n}\right) \log n - 2.$$

(We prove this below.)

Next, we observe from the properties of 2-rank trees that the number of strings $V \in S_\alpha$ for which $|I| = l$ is at most 2^l. The number of V for which $|I| \leq l - 2$ is therefore at most 2^{l-1}. Now fix $l = \log |S_\alpha|$, and note that the proportion of $V \in S_\alpha$ with $|I| \geq l - 1$ is at least $1/2$. Therefore $\mathrm{Exp}_{V \sim \mathrm{U}(S_\alpha)} |I| \geq \frac{l-1}{2}$.

We now concentrate on the messages α such that $\Pr_{X \text{ uniform}}(M_A(X) = \alpha | X \in S) \geq 2^{-n/10}$. Then $l = \log |S_\alpha| \geq n - 1 - n/10 = 0.9n - 1$, and by Proposition 2 for n large enough, $\mathrm{Exp}_{V \sim \mathrm{U}(S_\alpha)}(\mathrm{I}(k, c : M_B | X = V)) \geq \frac{1}{10} \log n - 2$.

Consider the set $\mathcal{A}$ of messages α which have probability at most $2^{-n/10}$ given $X \in S$. These messages occur with probability at most $2^{n/100} 2^{-n/10} = 2^{-9n/10}$, which is negligible. Therefore we conclude that $\mathrm{I}(k, c : M_B | X) = \Omega(\log n)$. □

PROOF PROOF OF PROPOSITION 2. Fix a string V, and the corresponding set of indices I. Suppose we are given as input a distribution $m = m_k$, for some $k \in I$. We recover k using the following procedure Π:

1. For each $k' \in I$, simulate the Alice's computation of the output in the protocol P, by setting $M_B = m$, the input distribution, and $X = V_{k'}$.
2. Let $(d_{k'})_{k' \in I}$ be the sequence of outputs Alice generates from the above simulation. Output the largest k' for which $d_{k'} = 1$. This is our guess for k.

On input m_k, the simulation of P above generates $d_k = 1$, and $d_{k'} = 0$ for $k' > k$, with probability at least $1 - 1/4n$ for any fixed $k' \geq k$. Therefore, the procedure outputs $k' = k$ with probablity at least $3/4$.

We now argue that the entropy of k is significantly reduced when given M_B, X, under the distribution μ_0 (i.e., when $c_k = X[k]$). This is equivalent to saying that the mutual information of k and M_B is high. When the inputs are picked according to the distribution μ_0, we have

$$\begin{aligned} \mathrm{I}(k, c : M_B | X = V) &= \mathrm{H}(k | X = V) - \mathrm{H}(k | M_B, X = V) \\ &= \log n - \mathrm{H}(k | M_B, X = V). \end{aligned}$$

We bound from above the conditional entropy $\mathrm{H}(k|M_B, X = V)$. We first separate the values of $k \notin I$ as follows. Let $p = |I|/n$, and define the Boolean random variable J as 1 iff $k \in I$. We have

$$\begin{aligned} &\mathrm{H}(k | M_B, X = V) \\ &= \mathrm{H}(kJ | M_B, X = V) \\ &= \mathrm{H}(J | M_B, X = V) + \mathrm{H}(k | M_B, X = V, J) \\ &= \mathrm{H}(p) + (1 - p)\mathrm{H}(k | M_B, X = V, k \notin I) \\ &\quad + p\,\mathrm{H}(k | M_B, X = V, k \in I) \\ &\leq 1 + (1 - p) \log n + \mathrm{H}(k | M_B, X = V, k \in I) \\ &\leq 1 + (1 - p) \log n + \mathrm{H}(k | K, X = V, k \in I), \end{aligned}$$

where K is the random variable computed by our finding procedure Π, and the final step follows from the Data Processing Inequality. For any fixed $k \in I$, given M_B the procedure Π computes $K = k$ with probability at least $3/4$. By the Fano Inequality, we have

$$\begin{aligned} \mathrm{H}(k | K, X = V, k \in I) &\leq \mathrm{H}\left(\frac{1}{4}\right) + \frac{1}{4} \log(|I| - 1) \\ &\leq 1 + \frac{1}{4} \log n. \end{aligned}$$

□

By combining Lemmas 1 and 2 we get

THEOREM 3.

$$\mathrm{IC}^{\mathrm{mix}}_{\mu_0}(\textsc{Mountain}, 1/32n^2) = \Omega(\log n).$$

4.3 Reduction from Ascension to Mountain

We now study the information cost of $\textsc{Ascension}(m)$ for the distribution μ_0^m over $(\{0,1\}^n \times [n] \times \{0,1\})^m$ for $\mathbf{X} = (X_1, X_2, \ldots, X_m)$, $\mathbf{k} = (k_1, k_2, \ldots, k_m)$ and $\mathbf{c} = (c_1, c_2, \ldots, c_m)$. We state a direct sum property that relates this cost to that of one instance of MOUNTAIN, and then conclude.

LEMMA 3.

$$\mathrm{IC}^{\mathrm{pub}}_{\mu_0^m}(\textsc{Ascension}(m), \delta) \geq m \times \mathrm{IC}^{\mathrm{mix}}_{\mu_0}(\textsc{Mountain}, \delta).$$

PROOF. Let P be a public-coin randomized protocol for $\textsc{Ascension}(m)$ with worst-case error δ such that $\mathrm{IC}_{\mu_0^m}(P) = \mathrm{IC}^{\mathrm{pub}}_{\mu_0^m}(\textsc{Ascension}(m), \delta)$.

From P, we construct the following protocol P'_j for MOUNTAIN, where $j \in [n]$. Let (X, k, c) be the input for MOUNTAIN.

1. Alice sets A_j's input X_j to its input X.
2. Bob sets B_j's input $(k_j, X_j[1, k_j - 1], c_j)$ to its input $(k, X[1, k - 1], c)$.
3. Alice and Bob generate, using public coins, (X_i, k_i, c_i) according to μ_0, independently for all $i < j$, and X_i uniformly independently for $i > j$.
4. Bob generates (k_i) uniformly independently for $i > j$, but using his private coins. Then Bob sets $c_i = X_i[k_i]$ for $i > j$ (so that (X_i, k_i, c_i) are distributed according to μ_0, independently for all $i > j$).
5. Alice and Bob run the protocol P by simulating the players $(A_i, B_i)_{i=1}^m$ as follows:
   (a) Alice runs P until she generates the message M_{A_j} from player A_j. She sends this message to Bob.
   (b) Bob continues running P until he generates the message M_{B_m} from player B_m. He sends this message to Alice.
   (c) Alice completes the rest of the protocol P until the end, and produces as output for P'_j, the output of player A_1 in P.

By definition of the distribution μ_0, we have $f(X_i, k_i, c_i) = 0$ for all $i \neq j$. So $f_m(\mathbf{X}, \mathbf{k}, \mathbf{c}) = f(X, k, c)$, and each protocol P'_j computes the function f, i.e., solves MOUNTAIN, with worst-case error δ.

We prove that $\mathrm{IC}_{\mu_0^m}(P) = \sum_j \mathrm{IC}_{\mu_0}(P'_j)$, which implies the result, since only Bob uses private coins in P'_j.

Let R denote the public coins used in the protocol P. By applying the chain rule to $\mathrm{IC}_{\mu_0^m}(P)$, we get

$$\begin{aligned} & \mathrm{IC}_{\mu_0^m}(P) \\ = & \ \mathrm{I}(\mathbf{k}, \mathbf{c} : M_{B_m} | \mathbf{X}, R) \\ = & \sum_j \mathrm{I}(k_j, c_j : M_{B_m} | \mathbf{X}, k_1, c_1, \ldots, k_{j-1}, c_{j-1}, R) \end{aligned}$$

Let $R_j = (R, (X_i)_{j \neq i}, (k_i, c_i)_{i<j})$. These are all the public random coins used in the protocol P'_j, and any further random coins $(k_i, c_i)_{i>j}$ are used only by Bob. Since for all j

$$\mathrm{IC}_{\mu_0}(P'_j) = \mathrm{I}(k_j, c_j : M_{B_m} | X_j, R_j),$$

which is the same as

$$\mathrm{I}(k_j, c_j : M_{B_m} | \mathbf{X}, k_1, c_1, \ldots, k_{j-1}, c_{j-1}, R),$$

the direct sum result follows. □

THEOREM 4. *Let P be a public-coin randomized protocol for* ASCENSION$(n/\log n)$ *with worst-case error probability* $1/32n^2$, *then* $\mathsf{size} = \Omega(n)$.

PROOF. Let $m = n/\log n$ and $\delta = 1/32n^2$, and let P be a public-coin randomized protocol for ASCENSION(m) with worst-case error probability δ. $\mathrm{IC}_{\mu_0^m}(P)$ is at most size, and by definition $\mathrm{IC}^{\mathrm{pub}}_{\mu_0^m}(\text{ASCENSION}(m), \delta)$ is less than or equal to $\mathrm{IC}_{\mu_0^m}(P)$. By Lemma 3, we have $\mathrm{IC}^{\mathrm{pub}}_{\mu_0^m}(\text{ASCENSION}(m), \delta) \geq m \times \mathrm{IC}^{\mathrm{mix}}_{\mu_0}(\text{MOUNTAIN}, \delta)$. By Theorem 3, we get $\mathrm{IC}^{\mathrm{mix}}_{\mu_0}(\text{MOUNTAIN}, \delta) = \Omega(\log n)$. Combining yields $\mathsf{size} = \Omega(m \log n) = \Omega(n)$. □

COROLLARY 1. *Every one-pass randomized streaming algorithm for* DYCK(2) *with (two-sided) error* $O(1/n' \log n')$ *uses* $\Omega(\sqrt{n' \log n'})$ *space, where n' is the input length.*

PROOF. Assume we have a one-pass randomized streaming algorithm for DYCK(2) with (two-sided) error $O(1/n' \log n')$ uses space size, where n' is the input length. Then, by the discussion at the beginning of Section 4, there is a public-coin randomized protocol for ASCENSION$(n/\log n)$ with $n = \Theta(\sqrt{n' \log n'})$ and with worst-case error probability $1/32n^2$. By Theorem 4, the messages have length $\Omega(n)$, and therefore, the streaming algorithm has space $\Omega(n) = \Omega(\sqrt{n' \log n'})$. □

Acknowledgements

For earlier discussions, F.M. would like to thank Michel de Rougemont, Miklos Santha, Umesh Vazirani, and especially Pranab Sen, who, among other things, noticed that the logarithmic space algorithm for IDENTITY(s) in [15] can be converted to a one-pass randomized streaming algorithm with logarithmic space. We would also like to thank an anonymous referee for pointing out a $\sqrt{\log n}$ factor improvement of our original one-pass algorithm.

5. REFERENCES

[1] N. Alon, M. Krivelich, I. Newman, and M. Szegedy. Regular languages are testable with a constant number of queries. *SIAM J. Comput.*, 30(6), 2000.

[2] N. Alon, Y. Matias, and M. Szegedy. The space complexity of approximating the frequency moments. *J. Comput. Syst. Sci*, 58(1):137–147, 1999.

[3] A. Ambainis, A. Nayak, A. Ta-Shma, and U. Vazirani. Dense quantum coding and quantum finite automata. *J. ACM*, 49(4):1–16, July 2002.

[4] Z. Bar-Yossef, T. S. Jayram, R. Kumar, and D. Sivakumar. An information statistics approach to data stream and communication complexity. *J. Comput. Syst. Sci*, 68(4):702–732, 2004.

[5] M. Blum and S. Kannan. Designing programs that check their work. *J. ACM*, 42(1):269–291, 1995.

[6] M. Blum, M. Luby, and R. Rubinfeld. Self-testing/correcting with applications to numerical problems. *J. Comput. Syst. Sci*, 47(3):549–595, 1993.

[7] A. Chakrabarti, Y. Shi, A. Wirth, and A. C.-C. Yao. Informational complexity and the direct sum problem for simultaneous message complexity. In *IEEE FOCS*, pages 270–278, 2001.

[8] N. Chomsky and M. Schotzenberger. Computer programming and formal languages. In P. Braffort and D. Hirschberg, editors, *The algebraic theory of context-free languages*, pages 118–161, 1963.

[9] M. Chu, S. Kannan, and A. McGregor. Checking and spot-checking the correctness of priority queues. In *ICALP*, pages 728–739, 2007.

[10] J. Feigenbaum, S. Kannan, M. Strauss, and M. Viswanathan. Testing and spot-checking of data streams. *Algorithmica*, 34(1):67–80, 2002.

[11] O. Goldreich, S. Goldwasser, and D. Ron. Property testing and its connection to learning and approximation. *J. ACM*, 45(4):653–750, 1998.

[12] J. Hopcroft and J. Ullman. *Formal Languages and Their Relation to Automata*. Addison-Wesley, 1969.

[13] R. Jain, J. Radhakrishnan, and P. Sen. A lower bound for the bounded round quantum communication complexity of Set Disjointness. In *IEEE FOCS*, pages 220–229, 2003.

[14] T. S. Jayram, R. Kumar, and D. Sivakumar. Two applications of information complexity. In *ACM STOC*, pages 673–682. ACM, 2003.

[15] R. Lipton and Y. Zalcstein. Word problems solvable in logspace. *J. ACM*, 24(3):522–526, 1977.

[16] S. Muthukrishnan. *Data Streams: Algorithms and Applications*. Now Publishers Inc., 2005.

[17] A. Nayak. Optimal lower bounds for quantum automata and random access codes. In *IEEE FOCS*, pages 369–376, 1999.

[18] M. Parnas, D. Ron, and R. Rubinfeld. Testing membership in parenthesis languages. *Random Struct. Algor.*, 22(1):98–138, 2003.

[19] M. Saks and X. Sun. Space lower bounds for distance approximation in the data stream model. In *ACM STOC*, pages 360–369, 2002.

[20] L. Segoufin and C. Sirangelo. Constant-memory validation of streaming XML documents against DTDs. In *ICDT*, pages 299–313, 2007.

[21] L. Segoufin and V. Vianu. Validating streaming XML documents. In *ACM PODS*, pages 53–64, 2002.

APPENDIX

A. EXAMPLE EXECUTIONS

Figure 1 shows an example of execution of our one-pass algorithm. Here there are eight blocks, and they are shown after the internal simplifications have already been done. The dotted vertical lines mark times at which the stack changes size, either starting a new stack item (for example, at time t_0) or discarding a stack item (for example, at time t_4). Note that blocks and stack items are staggered: the first item incorporates the first block and the downsteps of the second block, the second item incorporates the upsteps of the second block and the downsteps of the third block, etc. The bullets mark times when the algorithm checks and discards an item, if the hash value is 0. The horizontal lines go from the time when a stack item is created to the time when it is checked and discarded. For example, at time t_7 the algorithm checks and discards an item (h_m, ℓ_m) such that h_m incorporates the upsteps marked in bold on the figure, namely $x(t_1, t_2]$, and incorporates the downsteps marked in bold on the figure, namely $x(t_2, t_3]$, $x(t_4, t_5]$ and $x(t_6, t_7]$.

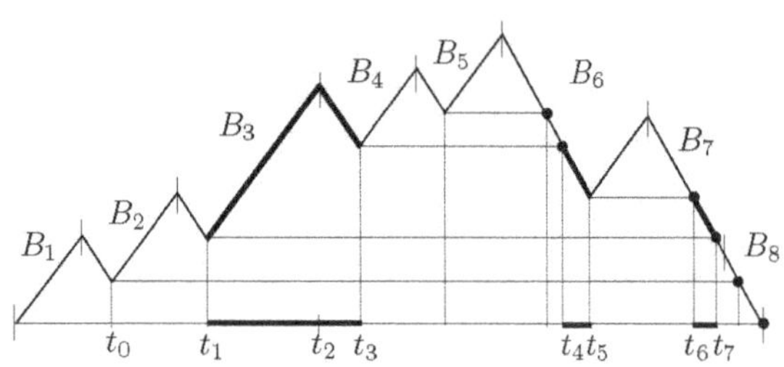

Figure 1: Example of execution of Algorithm 1

Figure 2 illustrates the logarithmic block decomposition of the input word into all the blocks that will be activated during one-pass. They are identical from the left-to-right pass and the right-to-left pass since thanks to padding the input length is a power of 2. At every instant, only one i-block is activated for each i.

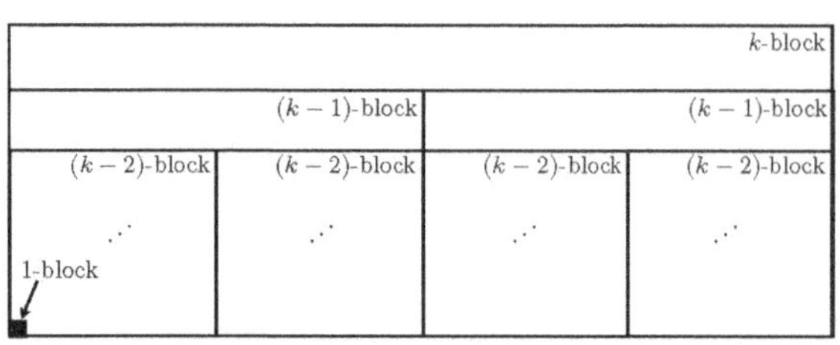

Figure 2: Decomposition in block-structure

Figure 3 gives an intuition of the proof of Fact 6. The bold-face lines represent matching pairs between the two $(i-1)$-blocks B, B' within the same i-block B_i. In the case of the figure, those pairs are checked during the left-to-right pass, since the minimum height m within the left $(i-1)$-block B is larger than the minimum height m' with the right $(i-1)$-block B' (during the right-to-left pass, they are compressed without any checks when B_i is processed).

B. FIGURES FOR HARD INSTANCES

Figure 4 presents an input stream with its division between players Alice and Bob. The horizontal axis represents the length of the stream seen so far, and the vertical axis represents the corresponding height. We introduce a potential mismatch denoted by letter c in Bob's input.

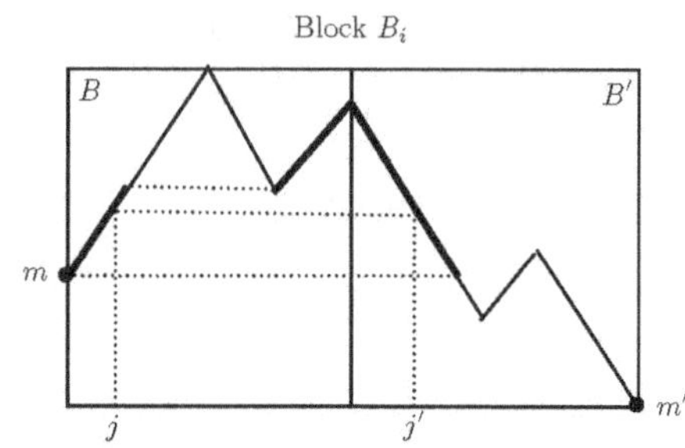

Figure 3: Illustration of Fact 6

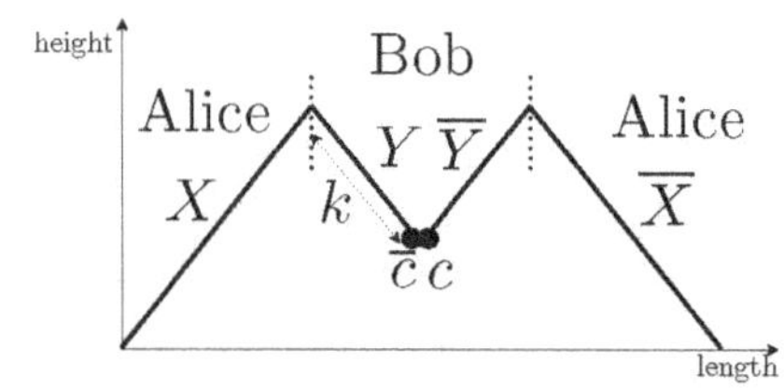

Figure 4: Problem Mountain: $\overline{Y}[1, k-1] = \overline{X}[1, k-1]$. The word is well-formed if and only if $c = \overline{X}[k]$.

Figure 5 presents the m-fold nesting of the above stream. The stream is now divided between $2m$ players. There are m potential mismatches, the ith one caused by the letter c_i in B_i's input.

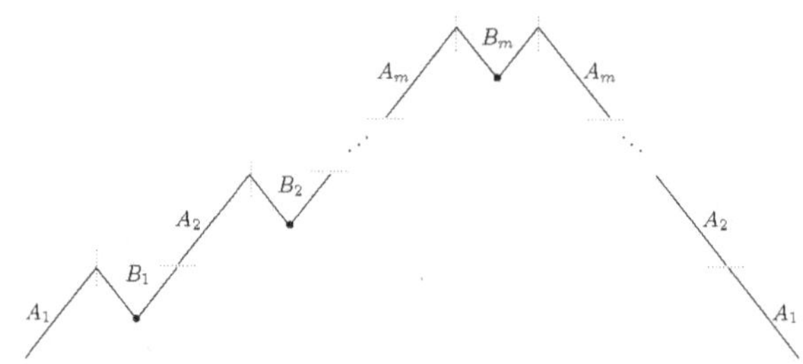

Figure 5: Problem Ascension(m): The word is well-formed if and only $c_i = \overline{X}_i[k_i]$, for all i.

Measuring Independence of Datasets

Vladimir Braverman*
UCLA
vova@cs.ucla.edu

Rafail Ostrovsky†
UCLA
rafail@cs.ucla.edu

ABSTRACT

Approximating pairwise, or k-wise, independence with sublinear memory is of considerable importance in the data stream model. In the streaming model the joint distribution is given by a stream of k-tuples, with the goal of testing correlations among the components measured over the entire stream. Indyk and McGregor (SODA 08) recently gave exciting new results for measuring pairwise independence in this model.

Statistical distance is one of the most fundamental metrics for measuring the similarity of two distributions, and it has been a metric of choice in many papers that discuss distribution closeness. For pairwise independence, the Indyk and McGregor methods provide $\log n$-approximation under statistical distance between the joint and product distributions in the streaming model. Indyk and McGregor leave, as their main open question, the problem of improving their $\log n$-approximation for the statistical distance metric.

In this paper we solve the main open problem posed by Indyk and McGregor for the statistical distance for pairwise independence and extend this result to any constant k. In particular, we present an algorithm that computes an (ϵ, δ)-approximation of the statistical distance between the joint and product distributions defined by a stream of k-tuples. Our algorithm requires $O\left(\left(\frac{1}{\epsilon}\log(\frac{nm}{\delta})\right)^{(30+k)^k}\right)$ memory and a single pass over the data stream.

Categories and Subject Descriptors

F.2 [**Theory of Computation**]: ANALYSIS OF ALGORITHMS AND PROBLEM COMPLEXITY

*Supported in part by NSF grants 0716835, 0716389, 0830803, 0916574.

†Supported in part by IBM Faculty Award, Xerox Innovation Group Award, the Okawa Foundation Award, Lockheed Martin, Intel, Teradata, NSF grants 0716835, 0716389, 0830803, 0916574, BSF grant and U.C. MICRO grant.

General Terms

Algorithms, Theory

Keywords

Data Streams, Randomized Algorithms, Dimension Reduction, Theory of Computation.

1. INTRODUCTION

Finding correlations between columns of a table is a fundamental problem in databases. Virtually all commercial databases construct query plans for queries that employ cross-dimensional predicates. The basic step is estimating "selectivity" (i.e., the number of rows that satisfy the predicate conditions) of the complex predicate. Without any prior knowledge, the typical solution is to compute selectivity of each column separately and use the multiplication as an estimate. Thus, optimizers make a "statistical independence assumption" which sometimes may not hold. Incorrect estimations may lead to suboptimal query plans and decrease performance significantly. Identifying correlations between database columns by measuring a level of independence between columns has a long history in the database research community (see, e.g., Poosala and Ioannidis [26]). For data warehouses, it is important to find correlated columns for correct schema construction, as Kimball and Caserta note in [23]. In practice, typical solutions for finding correlations between columns are either histograms (see e.g., [26]) or sampling (see e.g., Ilyas, Markl, Haas, Brown, Aboulnaga [19]). These methods have their natural disadvantages, i.e., they do not tolerate deletions and may require several passes over the data. When it comes to very large data volumes, it is critical to maintain sublinear in terms of memory solutions that do not require additional passes over the data and can tolerate incremental updates of the data, e.g., deletions.

For these purposes, a theoretical *data stream model* can be useful. For data warehouses, the "loading" phase of the ETL process (see e.g., Kimball and Caserta [23]) can be seen as a data stream. When reading a database table, the process can be considered as a stream of data tuples. Thus, the data stream model represents another setting where approximating pairwise or k-wise independence with sublinear memory is of considerable importance.

1.1 Precise Definition of the Problem

The natural way to model database tables in a streaming model is by considering a stream of tuples. In this paper we consider a stream of k-tuples $(i_1, \ldots, i_k)$ where $i_l \in [n]$. (For simplicity, we assume that elements of all columns are drawn from the same domain, even though our approach trivially extends to a general case of different domains.) As pointed out in [26, 19, 21], the natural way to define a joint distribution of two (or more) columns is given by the frequencies of all combinations of coordinates. Similarly, the distribution of each column is defined by the corresponding set of frequencies; the definition of a product distribution follows. Let us define these notions precisely.[1]

DEFINITION 1.1. *Let D be a stream of elements $p_1, \ldots, p_m$, where each stream element is a k-tuple $\mathbf{i} = (\mathbf{i}_1, \ldots, \mathbf{i}_k)$, where $\mathbf{i}_l \in [n]$. Here m is the size of stream D. A* frequency *of a tuple $\mathbf{i} \in [n]^k$ is defined as the number of times it appears in D: $f_\mathbf{i} = |\{j : p_j = \mathbf{i}\}|$. For $l \in [k]$, a l-th* margin frequency *of $t \in [n]$ is the number of times t appears as a l-th coordinate: $f_l(t) = \sum_{\mathbf{i} \in [n]^k, \mathbf{i}_l = t}^{n} f_\mathbf{i}$. A* joint distribution *is defined by a vector of probabilities $P_{joint}(\mathbf{i}) = \frac{f_\mathbf{i}}{m}, \mathbf{i} \in [n]^k$. A l-th* margin distribution *is defined by a vector of probabilities $P_l(t) = \frac{f_l(t)}{m}$, $t \in [n]$. A* product distribution *is defined as: $P_{product}(\mathbf{i}) = \prod_{l=1}^{k} P_l(\mathbf{i}_l), \mathbf{i} \in [n]^k$.*

Statistical distance is one of the most fundamental metrics for measuring the similarity of two distributions, and it has been a metric of choice in many papers that discuss distribution closeness (see e.g., [1, 2, 4, 6, 21, 28, 27]). Given two distributions over a discrete domain, the statistical distance is half of L_1 distance between the probability vectors.

DEFINITION 1.2. *Consider two distributions over a finite domain Ω given by two random variables V, U.* Statistical distance *$\Delta(V, U)$ is defined as:*

$$\Delta(V, U) = \frac{1}{2} \sum_{x \in \Omega} |P(V = x) - P(U = x)|.$$

In particular, one of the most common methods of measuring independence is computing statistical distance between product and joint distributions (see e.g., [4, 21]). This is precisely the way we define our problem:

DEFINITION 1.3. *An* Independence Problem *is the following: Given stream D of k-tuples, $(1 \pm \epsilon)$-approximate, with one pass over D, with small memory the statistical distance between joint and product distribution $\Delta(P_{joint}, P_{product})$.*

In the streaming model, Indyk and McGregor [21] recently gave exciting new results for measuring pairwise independence, i.e., for $k = 2$. To measure the independence, they consider two metrics: L_2 and L_1. Recall that the L_2 distance between two probability distributions is a L_2 distance of their probability vectors. In particular, the Independence Problem under the L_2 metric is defined as $\|P_{joint} - P_{product}\|_2$. For the L_2 metric and $k = 2$, Indyk and McGregor give an $(1 \pm \epsilon)$-approximation using polylogarithmic space. Recently Braverman, Chung, Liu, Mitzenmacher and Ostrovsky [8] generalized the L_2 results of [21] to any constant k.[2] However, it is well known that for probability distributions, statistical distance is a significantly more powerful metric then the L_2 metric. For instance, consider two distributions on $[2n]$, where the first distribution is uniform on $\{1, \ldots, n\}$ and the second is uniform on $\{n+1, \ldots, 2n\}$. In this case the statistical distance is 1 but the L_2 distance is $\sqrt{2/n} \to 0$. We refer a reader to a paper of Batu, Fortnow, Rubinfeld, Smith and White [5] for a further discussion.

For the statistical distance L_1 metric and $k = 2$, the Indyk and McGregor methods provide $\log n$-approximation with polylogarithmic memory. In addition to $\log n$-approximation, Indyk and McGregor give an $(1 \pm \epsilon)$-approximation that requires $\Omega(n)$ memory, and also give a method that requires two passes to solve a promise problem for a restricted range of parameters. Indyk and McGregor leave, as their main open question, the problem of improving their $\log n$-approximation for the statistical distance metric.

In this paper we solve the main open problem posed by Indyk and McGregor for the statistical distance for pairwise independence and extend this result to any constant k. In particular, we present an algorithm that computes an (ϵ, δ)-approximation of the statistical distance between the joint and product distributions defined by a stream of k-tuples. Our algorithm requires $O\left(\left(\frac{1}{\epsilon} \log(\frac{nm}{\delta})\right)^{(30+k)^k}\right)$ memory and a single pass over the data stream. Theorem 2.5 formally describes our main result. We stress that we omit from this version optimization of constants and poly-log factors (including exponents) in our constructions and analysis, which we leave for the journal version of this paper.

1.2 Implicit Tensors

It is convenient to present an alternative, equivalent formulation of the *Independence Problem* as well. We can consider the problem of approximating the sum of absolute values of a *tensor* M_{Ind}.

DEFINITION 1.4. *An s-dimensional* tensor *M is a s-dimensional array with indexes in the range $[n]$; that is, M has an entry for each $\mathbf{i} \in [n]^s$. We denote by $m_\mathbf{i}$ the $\mathbf{i}$-th entry of M for each $\mathbf{i} \in [n]^s$.*

DEFINITION 1.5. *Let M be a s-dimensional tensor with entries $m_\mathbf{i}, \mathbf{i} \in [n]^s$. An L_1-norm of M is a $|M| = \sum_{\mathbf{i} \in [n]^s} |m_\mathbf{i}|$.*

For example, a 1-dimensional tensor is an n-dimensional vector, a 2-dimensional tensor is an $n \times n$-matrix and so forth.

Many streaming problems address *explicitly* defined vectors (or matrices) where entries are equal to frequencies of corresponding stream elements. The Independence problem diverges from this setting; e.g., for pairwise independence, a pair (i, j) affects all entries in i-th row and j-th column of the product probability matrix. To reflect this important difference we consider the case where the entries of a tensor are defined *implicitly* by a data stream.

DEFINITION 1.6. *Let $\mathcal{D}$ be a collection of data streams of size m of elements from domain Ω. Let $\mathcal{F} : \mathcal{D} \times [n]^s \mapsto R$ be a fixed function. We say that s-dimensional tensor M with entries $m_\mathbf{i} = \mathcal{F}(D, \mathbf{i}), \mathbf{i} \in [n]^s$* is implicity defined *by $\mathcal{F}$, given D. We denote an implicitly defined tensor as $\mathcal{F}(D)$.*

[1] Here and henceforth, we use lowercase Latin characters for indexes. We use an italic font for integers and a boldface font for multidimensional indexes, e.g., $i \in [n]$ and $\mathbf{i} \in [n]^k$. For a multidimensional index, we use subscript to indicate its coordinate, e.g., $\mathbf{i}_1$ indicates the first coordinate of $\mathbf{i}$.

[2] It is worth pointing out that our methods in [8] are completely different and do not seem to apply to the L_1 problem.

DEFINITION 1.7. *Let $\mathcal{D}$ be a collection of data streams of size m of k-tuples from domain $[n]^k$. A k-wise* Independence Function $\mathcal{F}_{Ind} : \mathcal{D} \times [n]^k \mapsto R$ *is a function defined as $\mathcal{F}_{Ind}(D, \mathbf{i}) = m^k f_{\mathbf{i}} - \prod_{l=1}^{k} f_l(\mathbf{i}_l)$ for $\mathbf{i} \in [n]^k$. Here $f_{\mathbf{i}}$ is given by Definition 1.1.* Statistical distance tensor M_{Ind} *is a k-dimensional tensor implicitly defined by $\mathcal{F}_{Ind}$, i.e., $M_{Ind} = \mathcal{F}_{Ind}(D)$.*

The main objective of our paper is approximating $|M_{Ind}|$. In particular, this implies solving the Independence problem since $\Delta(P_{joint}, P_{product}) = \frac{1}{m^k}|M_{Ind}|$, and since $m = |D|$ can be computed precisely. We thus freely interchange the notions of the Independence Problem and computing $|M_{Ind}|$. In fact, our approach is applicable to any function $\mathcal{F}$ for which conditions of our main theorems are true.

1.3 Why Existing Methods for Estimating L_1 Do Not Work

Alon, Matias and Szegedy [3] initiated the study of computing norms of vectors defined by a data stream. In their setting vector entries are defined by frequencies of the corresponding elements in the stream. Their influential paper was followed by a sequence of results including, among many others, works by Bhuvanagiri, Ganguly, Kesh and Saha [7]; Charikar, Chen and Farach-Colton [14]; Cormode and Muthukrishnan [15, 16]; Feigenbaum, Kannan, Strauss and Viswanathan [17]; Ganguly and Cormode [18]; Indyk [20]; Indyk and Woodruff [22]; and Li [24] as well as work of authors [9, 10, 13].

There is an important difference between settings of [3] and the Independence problem. Indeed, while the entries of the independence tensor M_{Ind} are defined by frequencies of tuples, there is no linear dependence. As a result, the aforementioned algorithms are not directly applicable to the Independence problem.

To illustrate this point, consider the celebrated method of stable distributions by Indyk [20]. For L_1 norm, Indyk observed that a polylogarithmic (in terms of n and m) number of sketches of the form $\sum C_i v_i$ gives an $(1 \pm \epsilon)$-approximation of $|V|$, when C_i are independent random variables with Cauchy distribution. Let us discuss the applicability of this method to the problem of pairwise independence. A sketch $\sum_{\mathbf{i}} C_{\mathbf{i}} m_{\mathbf{i}}$, $\mathbf{i} \in [n]^2$, would solve this problem; unfortunately, it is not clear how to construct a sketch in this form. In particular, the probability matrix of the product distribution is given implicitly as two vectors of margin sketches. It is not hard to construct sketches for margin distributions; however, it is not at all clear how to obtain a sketch for product distribution without using a multiplication of margin sketches. On the other hand, if we do use a multiplication of margin sketches (this is the approach of Indyk and McGregor), the random variable that is associated with the tensor's elements is a product of independent Cauchy variables. Therefore, random variables for distinct entries are *not independent*, and thus typical arguments used for stable distribution methods do not work anymore. In fact, the main focus of the Indyk and McGregor analysis is to overcome this problem:

> *"Perhaps ironically, the biggest technical challenges that arise relate to ensuring that different components of our estimates are sufficiently independent."*

For pairwise independence, Indyk and McGregor use the product of two Cauchy variables, where one of them is "truncated." Using elegant observations, they show that such a sketch allows achieving $\log n$-approximation of the statistical distance. Unfortunately, it is not clear how the method of a Cauchy product can be improved at all, since the $\log n$ factor is a necessary component of their seemingly tight analysis.

1.4 A Description of Our Approach

As we discuss below, solving the Independence problem requires developing multiple new tools and using them jointly with known methods.

Dimension Reduction for Implicit Tensors. Our solution can be logically divided into three steps which are explained, informally, below.

First, we prove that given a *polylog*-approximation algorithm for k-dimensional tensors and an ϵ-approximation algorithm for a special type of $(k-1)$-dimensional tensors, it is possible to derive an ϵ-approximation algorithm on k-dimensional tensors, where the resulting algorithm increases memory bound by a factor $O((\frac{1}{\epsilon}\log\frac{nm}{\delta})^{O(1)})$. Thus, we can *trade* dimensionality and precision for memory. To illustrate this step, consider pairwise independence. There exist an ϵ-approximation algorithm on vectors [20] and a $\log n$-approximation algorithm on matrices [21]. We show that these algorithms can be used to obtain an ϵ-approximation algorithm on matrices. This informal idea is stated precisely as Dimension Reduction Theorem 2.1. This theorem is the main technical contribution of our paper; the majority of the paper is devoted to establishing its validity.

Second, given a *polylog*-approximation algorithm for k-dimensional tensors and an ϵ-approximation algorithm on vectors, we can derive an ϵ-approximation algorithm on k-dimensional tensors by applying the Dimension Reduction Theorem recursively k-times. The memory will be increased by a factor roughly $O((\frac{1}{\epsilon}\log\frac{nm}{\delta})^{(30+k)^k})$ which is $O((\frac{1}{\epsilon}\log\frac{nm}{\delta})^{O(1)})$ for constant k. This informal idea is stated precisely as Theorem 2.2.

Third, we show that the conditions for Theorem 2.2 hold for the Independence problem. These results are stated in Lemmas 2.4 and 2.3, and in fact are a generalization of results from [20, 21].

The rest of our discussion is devoted to a description of the main ideas behind the Dimension Reduction Theorem.

Hyperplanes and Absolute Vectors. Consider a matrix M; a very natural idea to approximate $|M|$ is by approximating a L_1 norm of a vector with entries equal to L_1 norms of rows of M. We generalize this idea to tensors by defining the following operators.

DEFINITION 1.8. *For any $s, t \geq 0$, we denote by $(,)$ a mapping from $[n]^s \times [n]^t$ to $[n]^{s+t}$ obtained by concatenation of coordinates. For instance, $((1, 2), 3)$ is a an element from $[n]^3$ with coordinates $1, 2, 3$ respectfully.*

DEFINITION 1.9. *Let M be a s-dimensional tensor with entries $m_{\mathbf{j}}, \mathbf{j} \in [n]^s$. For any $l \in [n]$, $Hyperplane(M, l)$ is a $(s-1)$-dimensional tensor with entries $m_{(l,\mathbf{i})}$ for $\mathbf{i} \in [n]^{s-1}$.*

For example, when $k = 2$, the l-th hyperplane of a matrix M is its l-th row.

DEFINITION 1.10. *An l-th hyperplane is* α-significant *if* $|Hyperplane(M,l)| \geq \alpha|M|$.

For example, when $k = 2$, the l-th row is α-significant[3] if the L_1-norm of the vector defined by the l-th row carries at least α-fraction of $|M|$.

DEFINITION 1.11. *For a s-dimensional tensor M, an $AbsoluteVector(M)$ is a vector of dimensionality n with entries $|Hyperplane(M,l)|, l \in [n]$. In particular, $|AbsoluteVector(M)| = |M|$.*

Projected Dimensions. To prove Dimension Reduction Theorem 2.1 we need to map s-dimensional tensors to $(s-1)$-dimensional tensors with a small distortion of L_1. We come up with the following mapping.

DEFINITION 1.12. *Let M be a s-dimensional tensor with entries $m_{\mathbf{i}}$, where $\mathbf{i} \in [n]^s$, and let $0 \leq t \leq s$. A* Suffix-Sum *tensor $T_t(M)$ is a $(s-t)$-dimensional tensor with entries (for each $\mathbf{i} \in [n]^{s-t}$):*

$$m'_{\mathbf{i}} = \sum_{\mathbf{j} \in [n]^t} m_{(\mathbf{j},\mathbf{i})}$$

Also, we define $T_0(M) = M$. In other words, the $\mathbf{i}$-th entry of $T_t(M)$ is obtained by summing all elements of M with the $(s-t)$-suffix equal to $\mathbf{i}$. In particular, $T_s(M)$ is a scalar that is equal to $\sum_{\mathbf{i} \in [n]^s} m_{\mathbf{i}}$.

For matrix M with entries $m_{i,j}$, the Suffix-Sum operator $T_1(M)$ defines a vector V with entries $v_j = \sum_i m_{i,j}$. In other words, all entries of M that belong to the same columns (i.e., have the same second coordinate, i.e., the same "suffix") are "summed-up" to generate a single entry of V. Note that the Suffix-Sum operator is different from the AbsoluteVector operator. In the latter case we sum up the absolute values that belong to the same hyperplane, i.e., have identical prefix; in the former case we sum up all elements (and not their absolute values) that have an identical suffix.

Clearly $|T_1(M)| \leq |M|$; however, it is possible in general that $|T_1(M)| \ll |M|$. The key observation is that in some cases $|T_1(M)| \sim |M|$ and thus we can use an approximation of $|T_1(M)|$ to approximate $|M|$. To illustrate this point, consider a matrix M with entries $m_{i,j}$ that contains a very "significant" row i (i.e., $\sum_j |m_{i,j}| \sim |M|$). The key observation is that in this case $|T_1(M)| \sim |M|$; thus, if there is a significant row, it can approximated using $|T_1(M)|$. The same idea is easily generalized: if a s-dimensional tensor M contains a $(1-\epsilon)$-significant hyperplane $Hyperplane(M,l)$, then $|T_1(M)|$ is an 2ϵ-approximation of $|Hyperplane(M,l)|$. We prove this statement in Fact 3.6.

Note that $T_1(M)$ is a $(s-1)$-dimensional tensor; if M is a matrix, then $T_1(M)$ is a vector for which we can apply methods from [20]. Thus, approximating $|T_1(M)|$ is potentially an easier problem.

[3]It is important to note that the notion of α-significant is *different* from the notion of α-major in our other paper in this STOC [12]. In particular, here, we compare an element with the entire sum, while in [12] we compare an element with the sum of all elements except of that element. Further, notice that α-significant ≤ 1, while α-major can be arbitrary large.

Certifying Tournaments. We have shown that $T_1(M)$ can be useful for approximating $|M|$. However, when can we rely on the value of $|T_1(M)|$? In particular, how can we distinguish between the cases when there is a heavy hyperplane (and thus $|T_1(M)|$ is a good approximation) and the case when there is no heavy hyperplane (and thus $|T_1(M)|$ does not contain reliable information)? The second key observation is that it can be done using "certifying tournaments." To illustrate this point, consider again the case $k = 2$, where M is a matrix. Split M into two random sub-matrices by sampling the rows w.p. $1/2$. If there is a heavy row, then with probability close to 1, one sub-matrix will have a significantly larger norm then the other. Recall that the method of [21] gives us a $\log n$-approximation. Thus, for very heavy rows, the *ratio* between approximations of norms obtained by the method from [21] will be large. On the other hand, we show that if there are no heavy rows, then such behavior is quite unlikely to be observed many times. Thus, there exists a way to distinguish between the first and the second cases for $(1 - \frac{\epsilon}{\log^2 n})$-significant rows.[4]

The method of certifying tournaments can be generalized to any $s \leq k$ as follows. Let M be a s-dimensional tensor with entries $m_{\mathbf{i}}$ for $\mathbf{i} \in [n]^s$. We "split" M into two "sampled" s-dimensional tensors M^0 and M^1 by randomly sampling the first coordinate. That is, M^1 has entries $m_{\mathbf{i}}H(\mathbf{i}_1)$ and M^0 has entries $m_{\mathbf{i}}(1 - H(\mathbf{i}_1))$, where $H : [n] \mapsto \{0,1\}$ is pairwise independent and uniform. If there exists a β-approximation algorithm for sampled tensors, and there exists an ϵ-approximation algorithm for Suffix-Sum, $|T_1(M^0)|$ and $|T_1(M^0)|$, then we can approximate L_1 norm of significant hyperplanes. Indeed, if there exists a significant hyperplane M_l of M, then the ratio between β-approximations of $|M^0|$ and $|M^1|$ will be large. If this is the case, the approximation of $T(M^{H(l)})$ is also an ϵ-approximation of $|M_l|$.

To summarize, our main technical Theorem 4.3 proves that it is possible to output a number U such that U is either an approximation of some hyperplane or 0. Further, if there exists a $(1 - \frac{\epsilon}{\beta^2})$-significant hyperplane, then with high probability, U is its approximation. We call such an algorithm an α-ThresholdMax algorithm, for $\alpha = O(\frac{\epsilon}{\beta^2})$.

Indirect Sampling. Many streaming algorithms compute statistics on *sampled* streams, which are random subsets of D defined by some randomness $\mathcal{H}$. In many cases, a sampled stream directly corresponds to a collection of sampled entries of a frequency vector. In contrast, subsets of D do not correspond directly to entries M_{Ind}. Thus, our algorithms employ *indirect* sampling, where randomness defines sampled entries of M_{Ind} rather then the entries of a data stream D. We define a Prefix-Zero operator.

DEFINITION 1.13. *Let M be a s-dimensional tensor with entries $m_{\mathbf{i}}, \mathbf{i} \in [n]^s$ and let $H_1, \ldots, H_t, t \leq s$ be hash functions $H_j : [n] \mapsto \{0,1\}$. A* Prefix-Zero *tensor $W(M, H_1, \ldots, H_t)$ a is a s-dimensional tensor with entries $m_{\mathbf{i}} \prod_{l=1}^{t} H_l(\mathbf{i}_l)$.*

Our algorithms work with tensors that are defined by com-

[4]It is worth noting that the idea of "split-and-compare" is not new. Group testing [16] exploits a similar approach. However, the methods from [16] require ϵ-approximation of L_1; in contrast, we use certifying tournaments to improve the approximation.

positions of $\mathcal{F}_{Ind}$, Prefix-Zero and Suffix-Sum. We thus extend the definition of implicitly defined tensors.

Definition 1.6. (Revised) *Let $\mathcal{D}$ be a collection of data streams of size m of elements from domain Ω and let $\mathfrak{H}$ be a collection of hash functions from $[n]$ to $\{0,1\}$. Let $\mathcal{F} : \mathcal{D} \times \mathfrak{H}^t \times [n]^s \mapsto R$ be a fixed function, for some $0 \le t \le s$. We say that a s-dimensional tensor M with entries $m_{\mathbf{i}} = \mathcal{F}(D, \mathcal{H}, \mathbf{i}), \mathbf{i} \in [n]^s$ is* implicitly defined *by $\mathcal{F}$, given $D \in \mathcal{D}$ and $\mathcal{H} \in \mathfrak{H}^t$. We denote an implicitly defined tensor as $\mathcal{F}(D, \mathcal{H})$.*

EXAMPLE 1.14. *Consider $k = 2$. Then $\mathcal{F}'(D, H) = W(\mathcal{F}_{Ind}(D), H)$ defines a matrix that represents a collection of rows sampled by a hash function $H : [n] \mapsto \{0,1\}$.*

Generalizing the Method of Indyk and Woodruff [22]. The ThresholdMax algorithm solves the problem that resembles the well-known problem of finding an element with maximal frequency, see, e.g., [14] and [15]. The celebrated method of Indyk and Woodruff [22] uses maximal entries to estimate L_p norms on vectors defined by frequencies. We apply the ideas of [22] to approximate $|AbsoluteVector(M)| = |M|$.

Unfortunately, the method of Indyk and Woodruff [22] is not directly applicable since some basic tools available for frequency vectors (such as L_2 norm approximation) cannot be used. We propose a different algorithm which is still in the same spirit as [22]. We prove Lemmas 5.5 and 5.3 which state that an existence of an α-ThresholdMax algorithm for an implicitly defined vector V implies an existence of an (ϵ, δ)-approximation algorithm for $|V|$, with memory increased by an additional factor of $\frac{1}{\alpha} poly(\frac{1}{\epsilon} \log \frac{nm}{\delta})$.

Other Technical Issues. There are several other technical issues that need to be resolved. We need to prove that the methods of Indyk [20] and Indyk and McGregor [21] are applicable for k-dimensional tensors that are obtained from M_{Ind} by applying Prefix-Zero and Suffix-Sum operators. We prove these claims in Lemmas 2.4 and 2.3. To prove our main theorems, certain properties of the operations on tensors should be established. We prove these in Section 3.

1.5 Related Work

Measuring pairwise independence between two or more random variables is a fundamental problem that touches many areas of computer science. The problems of efficiently testing pairwise, or k-wise, independence were recently considered by Alon, Andoni, Kaufman, Matulef, Rubinfeld and Xie [1]; Alon, Goldreich and Mansour [2]; Batu, Fortnow, Fischer, Kumar, Rubinfeld and White [4]; and Batu, Kumar and Rubinfeld [6]. These works address the problem of minimizing the number of samples needed to obtain sufficient approximation, when the joint distribution is accessible through a sampling procedure. Unlike the work in [1, 2, 4, 6], in the streaming model, the joint distribution is given by a stream of tuples.

2. MAIN THEOREMS

The proof of our result is based on three main steps which are summarized by the following theorems. The remainder of this paper is devoted to establishing these theorems.

THEOREM 2.1. ***Dimension Reduction for Implicit Tensors.*** *Let $s \ge 1$ and let M be a s-dimensional tensor with $poly(n,m)$-bounded entries that is defined by a function $\mathcal{F}$, i.e., $M = \mathcal{F}(D, \mathcal{H})$ where D is a data stream and $\mathcal{H}$ is a fixed randomness. Let $H : [n] \mapsto \{0,1\}$ be an arbitrary fixed hash function. Assume that*

1. *There exists an algorithm $\mathfrak{A}(D, \mathcal{H}, H, \delta)$ that, given D and an access to $\mathcal{H}$ and H, in one pass obtains $(\log^k(n), \delta)$-approximation of $|W(M, H)|$;*
2. *There exists an algorithm $\mathfrak{B}(D, \mathcal{H}, H, \epsilon, \delta)$ that, given D and an access to $\mathcal{H}$ and H, in one pass obtains an (ϵ, δ)-approximation of $|T_1(W(M, H))|$;*
3. *Both algorithm require memory $\nu(n, m, \epsilon, \delta) \le O((\frac{1}{\epsilon} \log \frac{nm}{\delta})^{(30+k)^s})$, beyond the memory required for H and $\mathcal{H}$.*

Then there exists an algorithm that, given an access to $\mathcal{H}$, in one pass obtains an (ϵ, δ)-approximation of $|M|$ using memory $(\frac{1}{\epsilon} \log \frac{nm}{\delta})^{(30+k)^{s+1}}$.

PROOF. Follows from Theorem 4.3, Lemma 5.5, Lemma 5.3 and elementary computations.

Indeed, the assumptions of Theorem 2 imply, by Theorem 4.3, an existence of a $\frac{\epsilon}{\log^{2k}(n)}$-ThresholdMax algorithm (see Definition 4.2) for restricted function $\mathcal{F}' = AbsoluteVector(\mathcal{F}(D, \mathcal{H}))$. The existence of a ThresholdMax algorithm implies, by Lemma 5.3, the existence of a Cover algorithm (see Definition 5.2) for $AbsoluteVector(\mathcal{F}(D, \mathcal{H}))$. The assumption that the entries of M are polynomially bounded and Fact 3.7 imply that the entries of $AbsoluteVector(\mathcal{F}(D, \mathcal{H}))$ are polynomially bounded as well. By Lemma 5.5, there exists an (ϵ, δ)-approximation algorithm for $|AbsoluteVector(\mathcal{F}(D, \mathcal{H}))|$ and $|AbsoluteVector(\mathcal{F}(D, \mathcal{H}))| = \sum_{i \in [n]} |Hyperplane(\mathcal{F}(D, \mathcal{H}), l)| = |M|$.

After substituting the parameters, the memory required is less than (for sufficiently large n) $\frac{1}{\epsilon^{30}} \log(\frac{1}{\delta}) \log^{2k+20}(nm) \nu(n, m, \frac{\epsilon^7}{\log^4(nm)}, \frac{\epsilon^{17}}{\log^{2k}(n) \log^8(mn)}) \le (\frac{1}{\epsilon} \log \frac{nm}{\delta})^{(30+k)^{s+1}}$. □

THEOREM 2.2. ***Approximation Theorem for Tensors*** *Let M be a k-dimensional tensor with entries bounded by $poly(n,m)$ and implicitly defined by a function $\mathcal{F}(D)$. Assume that*

1. *There exists an algorithm $\mathfrak{B}_s(D, H_1, \ldots, H_s)$ (for some $s < k$) that, given D and an access to fixed hash functions $H_1, \ldots, H_s$, in one pass obtains an (ϵ, δ)-approximation of $|T_s(W(M, H_1, \ldots, H_s))|$;*
2. *There exist algorithms $\mathfrak{A}_{s_1,s_2}(D, H_1, \ldots, H_{s_1})$ (for any $0 \le s_2 \le s_1 \le s$) that, given D and an access to H_is, in one pass obtain a $(\log^k(n), \delta)$-approximation of $|T_{s_2}(W(M, H_1, \ldots, H_{s_1}))|$;*
3. *All algorithms use memory bounded by $O((\frac{1}{\epsilon} \log \frac{nm}{\delta})^{20})$, beyond the memory required for H_is.*

Then there exists an algorithm that in one pass obtains an (ϵ, δ)-approximation of $|M|$ using memory $O((\frac{1}{\epsilon} \log \frac{nm}{\delta})^{(30+k)^k})$.

PROOF. Define $g(x) = (\frac{1}{\epsilon}\log\frac{nm}{\delta})^{(30+k)^{k-x}}$ First, we show that for any $s_1 \leq s$ there exists an algorithm $\mathfrak{B}_{s_1}(D, H_1, \ldots, H_{s_1})$ that gives an (ϵ,δ)-approximation of $|T_{s_1}(W(M, H_1, \ldots, H_{s_1}))|$ and uses memory at most $g(s_1)$.

We prove this fact by induction on s_1. For $s_1 = s$, the fact follows from the first assumption of Theorem 2.2 since $g(s) \geq (\frac{1}{\epsilon}\log\frac{nm}{\delta})^{20}$. For $s_1 < s$, denote $\mathcal{F}'(D, H_1, \ldots, H_{s_1}) = T_{s_1}(W(\mathcal{F}(D), H_1, \ldots, H_{s_1}))$. Denote $M' = \mathcal{F}'(D, H_1, \ldots, H_{s_1})$ and let H be an arbitrary hash function. By Corollary 3.4, $W(M', H) = W(\mathcal{F}'(D, H_1, \ldots, H_{s_1}), H) = W(T_{s_1}(W(\mathcal{F}(D), H_1, \ldots, H_{s_1}), H)$, i.e.,

$$W(M', H) = T_{s_1}(W(M, H_1, \ldots, H_{s_1}, H)). \quad (1)$$

Thus, and by the second assumption of the theorem, there exists an algorithm $\mathfrak{A}_{s_1,s_1+1}$ that in one pass obtains a $(\log^k(n), \delta)$-approximation of $|W(M', H)|$ using memory less than or equal to $g(s_1 + 1)$.

Also, by Corollary 3.5 and by (1):

$$T_1(W(M', H)) = T_{s_1+1}(W(M, H_1, \ldots, H_{s_1}, H)). \quad (2)$$

By induction, there exists an algorithm that gives an (ϵ,δ)-approximation of $|T_{s_1+1}(W(M, H_1, \ldots, H_{s'}, H))| = |T_1(W(M', H))|$ using memory $g(s_1 + 1)$.

M' is implicitly defined by a fixed function $\mathcal{F}'(D, H_1, \ldots, H_s)$. By Fact 3.7, M' entries are polynomially bounded. Thus, by (1) and (2), all assumptions of Theorem 2.1 are satisfied for M'. Therefore, there exists an algorithm that gives an ϵ-approximation of $|M'| = |T_{s_1}(W(M, H_1, \ldots, H_{s_1}))|$ using memory $g(s_1)$.

In particular, there exists an algorithm that for any H gives an ϵ-approximation of $|T_1(W(M, H))|$ using $g(1)$. Also, by the second assumption of the theorem, there exists an algorithm that gives a $\log^k(n)$-approximation of $|T_0(W(M, H))| = |W(M, H)|$. Thus, we can apply Theorem 2.1 for M and obtain an ϵ-approximation of $|M|$. The resulting memory usage will be $O((\frac{1}{\epsilon}\log\frac{nm}{\delta})^{(30+k)^k})$. □

We use the following lemmas (the proofs can be found in the full version of our paper [11]).

LEMMA 2.3. *There exists an algorithm $\mathfrak{B}_{k-1}$ that, given a data stream D and an access to hash functions $H_1, \ldots, H_{k-1}$, in one pass obtains an ϵ-approximation of $|T_{k-1}(W(M_{Ind}, H_1, \ldots, H_{k-1}))|$ using memory $O(\frac{1}{\epsilon^2}\log\frac{1}{\delta}\log\frac{nm}{\epsilon\delta})$.*

LEMMA 2.4. *There exists an algorithm $\mathfrak{A}_{s_1,s_2}$ (for any $0 \leq s_2 \leq s_1 \leq k$) that, given a data stream D and an access to hash functions $H_1, \ldots, H_{s_1}$, in one pass obtains a $\log^k n$-approximation of $|T_{s_2}(W(M_{Ind}, H_1, \ldots, H_{s_1}))|$ using memory $O(\log(nm)\log\frac{1}{\delta})$.*

THEOREM 2.5. ***Main Theorem*** *Let $k \geq 2$ be a constant, and let D be a stream of k-tuples from $[n]^k$. For any $0 < \epsilon < 1$, there exists an algorithm that makes a single pass over D and returns an (ϵ,δ)-approximation of the statistical distance between product and joint distribution (see Definition 1.1) using memory $O((\frac{1}{\epsilon}\log(\frac{nm}{\delta}))^{(30+k)^k})$.*

PROOF. By Lemma 2.3 and Lemma 2.4, the algorithms required by Theorem 2.2 exist for M_{Ind}. Also, by Fact 3.7, the entries of M_{Ind} are polynomially bounded. Thus all assumptions of Theorem 2.2 are true for M_{Ind}. Applying Theorem 2.2 to M_{Ind}, we obtain the main result. □

3. PROPERTIES OF TENSORS

We prove the following useful facts about Suffix-Sum and Prefix-Zero operations.

FACT 3.1. *Let M be a t-dimensional tensor and $0 \leq s \leq t$. Then*

$$W(T_s(M), H) = T_s(W(M, H_1 = \mathbf{1}, \ldots, H_s = \mathbf{1}, H)).$$

PROOF. Denote by $m_{\mathbf{w}}$ (for $\mathbf{w} \in [n]^t$) the $\mathbf{w}$-th entry of M. For any $\mathbf{i} \in [n]^{t-s}$, denote by $a_{\mathbf{i}}$ the entry of $T_s(M)$. By Definition 1.12:

$$a_i = \sum_{\mathbf{j}\in[n]^s} m_{(\mathbf{j},\mathbf{i})}.$$

Denote by $b_{\mathbf{i}}$ the entry of $W(T_s(M), H)$. By Definitions 1.12 and 1.13:

$$b_{\mathbf{i}} = H(\mathbf{i}_1)a_{\mathbf{i}} = \sum_{\mathbf{j}\in[n]^s} m_{(\mathbf{j},\mathbf{i})}H(\mathbf{i}_1).$$

Denote by $c_{\mathbf{i}}$ the $\mathbf{i}$-th entry of $T_s(W(M, H_1 = \mathbf{1}, \ldots, H_s = \mathbf{1}, H))$. By Definitions 1.12 and 1.13:

$$c_{\mathbf{i}} = \sum_{\mathbf{j}\in[n]^s} m_{(\mathbf{j},\mathbf{i})}H(\mathbf{i}_1).$$

Thus, for any $\mathbf{i}$, $b_{\mathbf{i}} = c_{\mathbf{i}}$ and the fact is correct. □

FACT 3.2. *Let M be a t-dimensional tensor and let $0 \leq s < t$. Then $T_1(T_s(M)) = T_{s+1}(M)$.*

PROOF. Denote by $m_{\mathbf{w}}$ (for $\mathbf{w} \in [n]^t$) the $\mathbf{w}$-th entry of M. For $\mathbf{j} \in [n]^{t-s}$ denote $b_{\mathbf{j}}$ to be an entry of $T_s(M)$. By Definition 1.12:

$$b_{\mathbf{j}} = \sum_{\mathbf{u}\in[n]^s} m_{(\mathbf{u},\mathbf{j})}.$$

For every $\mathbf{i} \in [n]^{t-s-1}$, denote by $c_{\mathbf{i}}$ the entry of $T_1(T_s(M))$. By Definition 1.12:

$$c_{\mathbf{i}} = \sum_{l\in[n]} b_{(l,\mathbf{i})} = \sum_{l\in[n]}\sum_{\mathbf{u}\in[n]^s} m_{(\mathbf{u},(l,\mathbf{i}))} =$$

$$\sum_{l\in[n]}\sum_{\mathbf{u}\in[n]^s} m_{((\mathbf{u},l),\mathbf{i})} = \sum_{\mathbf{v}\in[n]^{s+1}} m_{(\mathbf{v},\mathbf{i})}.$$

For any $\mathbf{i} \in [n]^{t-s-1}$ denote by $a_{\mathbf{i}}$ the entry of $T_{s+1}(M)$. By Definition 1.12:

$$a_{\mathbf{i}} = \sum_{\mathbf{v}\in[n]^{s+1}} m_{(\mathbf{v},\mathbf{i})}.$$

Thus, for any $\mathbf{i}$, $a_{\mathbf{i}} = c_{\mathbf{i}}$ and the fact is correct. □

FACT 3.3. *Let M be a t-dimensional tensor, let $s \leq t$ and let $H_1, \ldots, H_s$ and $G_1, \ldots, G_s$ be hash functions. Then*

$$W(M, H_1G_1, \ldots, H_sG_s) = W(W(M, H_1, \ldots, H_s), G_1, \ldots, G_s))$$

COROLLARY 3.4. *Let M be a t-dimensional tensor and let $0 \leq s < t$. Let $M' = T_s(W(M, H_1, \ldots, H_s))$. Then*

$$W(M', H) = T_s(W(M, H_1, \ldots, H_s, H)).$$

PROOF. Denote $M'' = W(M, H_1, \ldots, H_s)$. Then by Fact 3.1:

$$W(M', H) = W(T_s(M''), H) =$$

$$T_s(W(M'', G_1 = 1, \ldots, G_k = 1, H)).$$

Also by Fact 3.3:

$$W(M'', G_1, \ldots, G_s, H) =$$

$$W(W(M, H_1, \ldots, H_s, 1), G_1, \ldots, G_s, H) =$$

$$W(M, H_1, \ldots, H_s, H).$$

□

COROLLARY 3.5. *Let M be a t-dimensional tensor and let $0 \leq s < t$. Let $M' = T_s(W(M, H_1, \ldots, H_s))$. Then*

$$T_1(M', H)) = T_{s+1}(W(M, H_1, \ldots, H_s, H)).$$

PROOF. By Fact 3.2 and Corollary 3.4:

$$T_{s+1}(W(M, H_1, \ldots, H_s, H)) =$$

$$T_1(T_s(W(M, H_1, \ldots, H_s, H))) = T_1(W(M', H)).$$

□

FACT 3.6. *Let M be an arbitrary s-dimensional tensor, let M_l be $(1-\epsilon/2)$-significant hyperplane of M, $M_l = Hyperplane(M, l)$, and let $M' = T_1(M)$. Then $|M'|$ is an ϵ-approximation of $|M_l|$.*

PROOF. We have

$$|M'| = \sum_{i \in [n]^{s-1}} |\sum_{j \in [n]} m_{(j,i)}| \leq$$

$$\sum_{i \in [n]^{s-1}} \sum_{j \in [n]} |m_{(j,i)}| = |M| \leq \frac{1}{1-\epsilon/2}|M_l| \leq (1+\epsilon)|M_l|.$$

On the other hand,

$$|M'| = \sum_{i \in [n]^{s-1}} |\sum_{j \in [n]} m_{(j,i)}| \geq$$

$$\sum_{i \in [n]^{s-1}} (|m_{(l,i)}| - \sum_{j \in [n], j \neq l} |m_{(j,i)}|) = |M_l| - (|M| - |M_l|) =$$

$$\geq (2 - \frac{1}{1-\epsilon/2})|M_l| \geq (1-\epsilon)|M_l|.$$

□

FACT 3.7.

1. *Let M be a s-dimensional tensor with polynomially bounded (in n and m) entries for $s \leq k$. Let M' be a tensor obtained from M by an arbitrary composition of Prefix-Zero, AbsoluteVector, Hyperplane and Suffix-Sum operators. Then the entries of M' are polynomially bounded.*

2. *All entries of M_{Ind} are integers with absolute values bounded by $2m^k$ and thus claim 1 is true for M_{Ind}.*

PROOF. The first claim follows from the fact that the entries of M' are sums of disjoint subsets of M and that the number of entries in M is bounded by n^k. The second claim follows from Definition 1.7. □

4. CERTIFYING TOURNAMENTS

Recall that certifying tournaments allow us to distinguish the case when there exists an extremely significant hyperplane and where all hyper-planes are "light" in the implicit tensors. Furthermore, in case there is heavy hyperplane, certifying tournaments return a good approximation of the weight of the heavy hyperplane[5]. The algorithm is as follows:

ALGORITHM 4.1. *TensorTournament($D, \mathcal{H}, H, \epsilon$)*

1. *Repeat in parallel $O(\frac{\log \frac{1}{\delta}}{p})$ times where $p = 1 - \sqrt{1-\epsilon/2}$.*
   (a) *Generate 2-wise independent random hash function Z from $[n]$ to $\{0,1\}$ such that $Z(i) = 0$ w.p. 0.5. Denote $Z_1 = HZ$, $Z_0 = H(1-Z)$.*
   (b) *Compute in a single pass over D for $i = 0, 1$: $\mathfrak{t}_i = \mathfrak{A}(D, \mathcal{H}, Z_i, \epsilon, \delta')$, where $\delta' = \frac{p\epsilon}{4 \log \frac{1}{\delta}}$.*
   (c) *Simultaneously (in the same pass), compute $\mathfrak{l}_i = \mathfrak{B}(D, \mathcal{H}, Z_i, \delta')$.*
   (d) *Put $\mathfrak{u}_i = \max\{\frac{\mathfrak{l}_i}{\beta}, \mathfrak{t}_i, 0\}$, $i = 0, 1$.*
   (e) *Define $\lambda' = (1+\epsilon)\lambda$, where λ is the constant from Fact 4.4, $\lambda = (1 + \frac{2(1-\epsilon)^{1/4}}{1-(1-\epsilon)^{1/4}})$.*
   (f) *Compute*
   $$U' = \begin{cases} \mathfrak{u}_1, & \text{if } \mathfrak{u}_1 \geq \lambda' \beta^2 \mathfrak{u}_0, \\ \mathfrak{u}_0, & \text{if } \mathfrak{u}_0 \geq \lambda' \beta^2 \mathfrak{u}_1, \\ 0, & \text{otherwise.} \end{cases}$$
2. *Output U to be the minimum of all U's.*

DEFINITION 4.2. *Let $\mathcal{F}$ be a fixed function that defines implicit vectors, given a data stream and a fixed randomness and denote $V = \mathcal{F}(D, \mathcal{H})$ as a vector with entries v_i. For $\alpha > 0.5$, an α-*ThresholdMax *algorithm for restricted $\mathcal{F}$ is an algorithm that receives as an input a data stream D and an access to a randomness $\mathcal{H}$ and a random function $H : [n] \mapsto \{0,1\}$, and in one pass over D returns $U \geq 0$ such that w.p. at least $1-\delta$:*

1. *If $U > 0$ then U is an ϵ-approximation of $|v_i|$ for some i with $H(i) = 1$.*
2. *If [6] $|VH| > 0$ and there exists i such that $H(i) = 1$ and $|v_i| \geq (1-\alpha)|VH|$ then U is an ϵ-approximation of $|v_i|$.*

THEOREM 4.3. *Let H be a fixed hash function defined as above and let $\epsilon \leq 0.1$. Let M be a s-dimensional tensor implicitly defined by a fixed function $\mathcal{F}$, stream D and randomness $\mathcal{H}$, $M = \mathcal{F}(D, \mathcal{H})$. Assume that there exist two algorithms:*

[5]It is important to note that despite superficial similarities, this is different from *Hybrid-Major* algorithm in [12] since here we reduce $(\log n)$-approximation of L_1 norm to ϵ-approximation, while in *Hybrid-Major* we approximate all increasing functions with high accuracy using L_2 norm.

[6]Here and henceforth we denote by VH a vector with entries $v_i H(i)$, $i \in [n]$.

- *An algorithm $\mathfrak{A}(D,\mathcal{H},H,\delta)$ that in one pass obtains (β,δ)-approximation of $|W(M,H)|$ using memory $\mu_1(n,m,\epsilon,\delta)$;*

- *An algorithm $\mathfrak{B}(D,\mathcal{H},H,\epsilon,\delta)$ that in one pass over D obtains an (ϵ,δ)-approximation of $|T_1(W(M,H))|$ using memory $\mu_2(n,m,\epsilon,\delta)$;*

and let $\alpha = \frac{\epsilon}{64\beta^2}$. Then, the Algorithm TensorTournament$(D,\mathcal{H},H,\epsilon)$ is an α-ThresholdMax algorithm for restricted $\mathcal{F}'$ (see Definition 4.2), where $\mathcal{F}'(D,\mathcal{H}) = AbsoluteVector(\mathcal{F}(D,\mathcal{H}))$. The algorithm makes a single pass over D and uses memory $O(\frac{1}{\epsilon}\log\frac{1}{\delta}(\mu_1(n,m,\epsilon/3,\delta\epsilon/\log(1/\delta)) + \mu_2(n,m,\epsilon/3,\delta\epsilon/\log(1/\delta)) + \log nm)$.

PROOF.
Denote $M^t = W(M,Z_t)$ for $t = 0,1$. Let $M_i = Hyperplane(M,i)$ for $i \in [n]$ and let V' to be a vector with elements $|M_i|$. By Definition 1.11, $V' = \mathcal{F}'(D,\mathcal{H})$. Further, let V be a vector with entries $v_i = |M_i|H(i)$. We prove that the algorithm satisfies two conditions of Definition 4.2 for the ThresholdMax algorithm for V and H.

Proof of the first condition of Definition 4.2
We prove the following stronger statements which imply the first condition of Definition 4.2:

I. If there is no $(1-\epsilon)$-significant entry v_l then, w.p. at least $1-\frac{\delta}{3}$, $U = 0$.

II. If $|V| > 0$ and there is a $(1-\epsilon)$-significant entry v_l then, w.p. at least $1-\frac{\delta}{3}$, either $U = 0$ or U is a 3ϵ-approximation of $|v_l|$.

Proof of statement I
By definitions of $\mathfrak{B},\mathfrak{A}$, we have w.p. at least $1-8\delta'$ for $t = 0,1$: $\mathfrak{u}_t \geq \frac{\mathfrak{l}_t}{\beta} \geq \frac{|M^t|}{\beta^2}$; and $\mathfrak{t}_t \leq (1+\epsilon)|T_1(M^t,H)| \leq (1+\epsilon)|M^t|$; and $\frac{\mathfrak{l}_t}{\beta} \leq |M^t|$. Thus,

$$\frac{|M^t|}{\beta^2} \leq \mathfrak{u}_t \leq (1+\epsilon)|M^t|. \quad (3)$$

Following the terminology of Fact 4.4, we define $X = |M^1|$ and $Y = |M^0|$. We have the following relations:

$$|V| = \sum_i v_i = \sum_i H(i)|M_i| =$$

$$\sum_{i\in[n]} H(i) \sum_{\mathbf{j}'\in[n]^{s-1}} |m_{(i,\mathbf{j}')}| = |W(M,H)|,$$

$$X = |M^1| = \sum_{\mathbf{j}\in[n]^s} Z(\mathbf{j}_1)H(\mathbf{j}_1)|m_{\mathbf{j}}| =$$

$$\sum_{i\in[n]} Z(i)H(i) \sum_{\mathbf{j}'\in[n]^{s-1}} |m_{(i,\mathbf{j}')}| =$$

$$\sum_i Z(i)H(i)|M_i| = \sum_i Z(i)v_i,$$

and similarly

$$Y = |M^0| = \sum_i (1-Z(i))H(i)|M_i| = \\ = |V| - X = |V| - |M^1|. \quad (4)$$

By statement **I**, for all i, $v_i < (1-\epsilon)|V|$. Thus we can apply Fact 4.4. We have:

$$P((|M^0| \geq \lambda|M^1|) \cup (|M^1| \geq \lambda|M^0|)) =$$

$$P((X \geq \lambda Y) \cup (Y \geq \lambda X)) \leq \sqrt{1-\epsilon}.$$

Let Υ be the event $(\mathfrak{u}_0 \geq \lambda'\beta^2\mathfrak{u}_1) \cup (\mathfrak{u}_1 \geq \lambda'\beta^2\mathfrak{u}_0)$. Let Φ be the event that $\frac{|M^t|}{\beta^2} \leq \mathfrak{u}_t \leq (1+\epsilon)|M^t|$ for both values of t. We have $P(\Upsilon) \leq P(\Upsilon,\Phi) + P(\bar{\Phi})$. By (3), we have $P(\bar{\Phi}) \leq 8\delta'$. Also, events $\mathfrak{u}_0 \geq \lambda'\beta^2\mathfrak{u}_1$ and Φ imply that $|M^0| \geq \lambda|M^1|$; indeed:

$$|M^0| \geq \frac{\mathfrak{u}_0}{(1+\epsilon)} \geq \frac{\lambda'}{1+\epsilon}\beta^2\mathfrak{u}_1 \geq \lambda|M^1|.$$

Thus we have

$$P(\Upsilon,\Phi) \leq P((|M^0| \geq \lambda|M^1|) \cup (|M^1| \geq \lambda|M^0|)) \leq \sqrt{1-\epsilon}.$$

We summarize that if no $(1-\epsilon)$-significant v_i exists, then

$$P(U' \neq 0) \leq P(\Upsilon) \leq \sqrt{1-\epsilon} + O(\delta') \leq \sqrt{1-\epsilon/2}.$$

Recall that the number of repetitions is $O(\frac{1}{p}\log 1/\delta)$, where $p = 1-\sqrt{1-\epsilon/2}$. Thus $P(U \neq 0) \leq (1-p)^{\frac{1}{p}\log\frac{3}{\delta}} \leq \frac{\delta}{3}$.

Proof of statement II
Let v_l be a $(1-\epsilon)$-significant entry of V. Assume, w.l.o.g., that for one execution of the main cycle of the *Tournament* algorithm, $Z(l) = 0$. Statement **II** implies $|V| > 0$ which implies $v_l = |M_l|H(l) > 0$ which implies $(1-Z(l))H(l) = 1$. Thus, $|Hyperplane(M^0,l)| = |Hyperplane(W(M,(1-Z)H),l)| = |M_l| = v_l$. Therefore by (4), $|Hyperplane(M^0,l)| = v_l \geq (1-\epsilon)|V| \geq (1-\epsilon)|M^0|$, i.e., the l-th hyperplane of M^0 is $(1-\epsilon)$-significant. By Fact 3.6, $|T(M^0)|$ is an 2ϵ-approximation of $|M_l|$. By the assumptions of the theorem, $\mathfrak{B}$ returns an ϵ-approximation of $|T(M^0)|$. Thus, $\mathfrak{t}_0$ is a 3ϵ-approximation of $|M_l|$, w.p. at least $1-\delta'$, in which case

$$\mathfrak{u}_0 \geq \mathfrak{t}_0 \geq (1-3\epsilon)|M_l|.$$

Also, by the assumption of Theorem 4.3, w.p. at least $1-\delta'$, we have $\frac{\mathfrak{l}_0}{\beta} \leq |M^0|$. Thus

$$\mathfrak{u}_0 = \max\{\frac{\mathfrak{l}_0}{\beta},\mathfrak{t}_0,0\} \leq \max\{|M^0|,(1+3\epsilon)|M_l|\} \leq (1+3\epsilon)|M_l|.$$

On the other hand, w.p. at least $1-2\delta'$

$$\mathfrak{u}_1 = \max\{\frac{\mathfrak{l}_1}{\beta},\mathfrak{t}_1,0\} \leq \max\{|M^1|,(1+\epsilon)|M^1|\} = (1+\epsilon)|M^1|.$$

But since $Z_s(l) = 0$ we have by (4):

$$|M^1| \leq |V| - |Hyperplane(M^0,l)| = |V| - v_l \leq \frac{\epsilon}{1-\epsilon}|M_l|.$$

Combining all of the above computations, we conclude that w.p. at least $1-4\delta'$ (for sufficiently small ϵ, e.g., $\epsilon \leq 0.1$):

$$\mathfrak{u}_1 \leq (1+\epsilon)|M_1| \leq \frac{\epsilon(1+\epsilon)}{1-\epsilon}|M_l| \leq \frac{\epsilon(1+\epsilon)}{(1-\epsilon)(1-3\epsilon)}\mathfrak{u}_0 < \lambda'\mathfrak{u}_0.$$

Thus, U' is equal to either 0 or u_0 w.p. at least $1-4\delta'$. Recall simultaneously u_0 is a 3ϵ-approximation of $|M_l| = v_l$. The same inequality is true if $Z(l) = 1$. By union bound, w.p. at least $1 - \Omega(\frac{\log \frac{1}{\delta}}{p}\delta') = 1 - \Omega(\delta)$, U is either 0 or a 3ϵ-approximation of v_l.

Proof of the second condition of Definition 4.2

Finally, consider the case when v_l is a $(1-\alpha)$-significant entry of V. Consider the case when $Z(l) = 0$. Repeating the arguments from the proof of statement **II**, we have, w.p. at least $1-4\delta'$, u_0 is a 3ϵ-approximation of v_l and

$$u_1 \le (1+\epsilon)|M^1| \le (1+\epsilon)\frac{\alpha}{(1-\alpha)}v_l \le 4\alpha v_l.$$

Therefore,

$$u_0 \ge (1-3\epsilon)v_l \ge \frac{(1-3\epsilon)}{4\alpha}u_1 \ge \lambda'\beta^2 u_1.$$

Thus, w.p. $1-4\delta'$, $U' = u_0 = (1 \pm 3\epsilon)v_l$. The same is true when $Z(l) = 1$. Thus, U is a 3ϵ-approximation of v_l w.p. at least $1-\Omega(\delta)$.

Conclusion and memory analysis

Since both conditions of Definition 4.2 are met (substituting ϵ with $\epsilon/3$), we conclude that *TensorTournament* is an α-ThresholdMax algorithm for restricted $\mathcal{F}'$. Let us count the memory needed for a single iteration of the main cycle of the algorithm. To generate pairwise independent Z, we need $O(\log n)$ bits. In addition, we need $\mu_1 + \mu_2$ for the algorithms $\mathfrak{B}$ and $\mathfrak{A}$ and $O(\log nm)$ bits to keep the auxiliary variables. Thus, in total we need memory $O(\frac{1}{\epsilon}\log\frac{1}{\delta}(\mu_1(n,m,\epsilon/3,\delta\epsilon/\log(1/\delta)) + \mu_2(n,m,\epsilon/3,\delta\epsilon/\log(1/\delta)) + \log nm)$. Recall that we do not count memory required to store $\mathcal{H}$ and H. □

FACT 4.4. *Let V be a n-dimensional vector with non-negative entries $v_i \ge 0, i \in [n]$. Let Z be 2-wise independent random hash functions from $[n]$ to $\{0,1\}$, such that $P(Z(i)=1) = 0.5$. Let $X = \sum_i v_i Z(i)$, and $Y = L_1(V) - X$. If there exists $\epsilon > 0$ such that for all i $v_i < (1-\epsilon)L_1(V)$, then for $\lambda = \lambda(\epsilon) \ge 1 + \frac{2(1-\epsilon)^{1/4}}{1-(1-\epsilon)^{1/4}}$ we have*

$$P((X \ge \lambda Y) \cup (Y \ge \lambda X)) \le \sqrt{1-\epsilon}.$$

5. APPROXIMATING L_1 NORMS OF IMPLICIT VECTORS

DEFINITION 5.1. *Let V with $v_i \ge 0$ be a vector from R^n. A set $\mathcal{U}$ of positive numbers is an* ϵ-cover *of V if:*

1. *All elements of $\mathcal{U}$ are ϵ-approximations of distinct and positive coordinates from V (i.e., there is a one-to-one mapping ρ from the set $\mathcal{U}$ to a subset $S' \subseteq [n]$ such that for all $U \in \mathcal{U}$, U is an ϵ-approximation of $v_{\rho(U)}$.)*
2. *$\mathcal{U}$ contains ϵ-approximations of all ϵ-significant elements of V (i.e., for all v_i such that $v_i \ge \epsilon|V|$, it is true that $i \in S'$.)*

The size *of the cover is $|\mathcal{U}|$.*

DEFINITION 5.2. *Let $\mathcal{F}$ be a fixed function that implicitly defines vectors, given a data stream D and a fixed randomness $\mathcal{H}$. Denote $V = \mathcal{F}(D,\mathcal{H})$. A* Cover algorithm for restricted $\mathcal{F}$ *is an algorithm that receives as an input a data stream D, an access to a randomness $\mathcal{H}$ and a random function $H: [n] \mapsto \{0,1\}$ and an ϵ and δ. The algorithm makes a single pass over D and w.p. at least $1-\delta$, returns an ϵ-cover of vector with entries $v_i H(i)$.*

LEMMA 5.3. *Let $\mathcal{F}$ be a fixed function that implicitly defines vectors, given a data stream D and a fixed randomness $\mathcal{H}$. An existence of α-ThresholdMax algorithm for restricted $\mathcal{F}$ that uses memory $\mu(n,m,\epsilon,\delta)$ implies an existence of a Cover algorithm for restricted $\mathcal{F}$ for any ϵ. The Cover algorithm uses memory $O(\frac{1}{\epsilon^2\delta\alpha}(\mu(n,m,\epsilon,\delta^2\epsilon^2\alpha) + \log nm))$.*

PROOF. Denote by $\mathfrak{L}_\alpha(D,\mathcal{H},H,\epsilon,\delta)$ the existing α-ThresholdMax algorithm for restricted $\mathcal{F}$.

Using $\mathfrak{L}_\alpha$ we construct the following algorithm. Let $\epsilon' = \epsilon^2\delta/3$ and $\varrho = \lceil\frac{1}{\epsilon'\alpha}\rceil$. Let G be a pairwise independent random hash function from $[n]$ to $[\varrho]$ that is independent of $\mathcal{H}$ and H. For $s \in [\varrho]$, define function F_s as $F_s(i) = \mathbf{1}_{G(i)=s}$ and execute, in parallel for all s, $\mathfrak{L}_\alpha(D,\mathcal{H},HF_s,\epsilon,\delta/\varrho)$. Let U_s be the output of s-th ran of $\mathfrak{L}_\alpha$. The output of our new algorithm is a set of all strictly positive U_s. We show below that the output is indeed ϵ-cover of V with probability at least $1-\delta$.

Let $V = \mathcal{F}(D,\mathcal{H})$ be a vector with entries v_i and let V_s be a vector with entries $v_{s,i} = v(i)F_s(i)$. By the union bounds and by the definition of α-ThresholdMax algorithm, w.p. at least $1-\delta$, every positive U_s is an ϵ approximation of $|v_{i_s}|$ for some i_s with $H(i_s)F_s(i_s) = 1$. But this implies that U_s is an approximation of $|v_i|$ with $H(v_i) = 1$. Since G splits $[n]$ into disjoint subsets, the output of our algorithm corresponds to ϵ-approximations of absolute values of a set of distinct entries of V. I.e., the first condition of ϵ-cover is correct.

To show that the second condition is true as well, let S_ϵ be set of all is such that $|v_i H(i)| \ge \epsilon|VH| > 0$. Consider a fixed $i \in S_\epsilon$. Let $X_i = |VHF_{G(i)}| - |v_i| = \sum_{j\ne i}|v_j|H(j)F_{G(i)}(j) \ge 0$. By pairwise independence of G: $E(X_i) = \sum_{j\ne i}|v_j|H(j)P(G(j)=G(i)) \le \frac{|VH|}{\varrho}$.

Let Ψ_i be the event that $X_i > \frac{\epsilon}{\varrho\epsilon'}|VH|$; by Markov inequality $P(\Psi_l) \le \frac{\epsilon'}{\epsilon}$. Note that if Ψ_i does not happen, then $|VHF_{G(i)}| - |v_i| \le \frac{\epsilon}{\varrho\epsilon'}|VH| \le \frac{1}{\varrho\epsilon'}|v_i| \le \alpha|v_i|$, in which case $|v_i| \ge (1-\alpha)|VHF_{G(i)}|$. Let Γ_l be the event that $U_{G(i)}$ is not an ϵ-approximation of $|v_i|$. By the properties of algorithm $\mathfrak{L}_\alpha$, $P(\Gamma_i|\bar{\Psi}_i) \le \frac{\delta}{\varrho}$. Thus

$$P(\Gamma_i) \le P(\Gamma_i|\bar{\Psi}_i) + P(\Psi_i) \le \frac{\delta}{\varrho} + \frac{\epsilon'}{\epsilon}.$$

Finally, let $\Phi_{i,j}$ be the event where there is a collision between i and j. By pairwise independence of G, $P(\Phi_{i,j}) = \frac{1}{\varrho}$, and thus the probability of collisions for ϵ-significant entries is bounded by $\frac{1}{\epsilon^2\varrho}$. Thus, the probability that the output of the algorithm does not meet the second condition of ϵ-cover is bounded by $P((\cup_{i\in S_\epsilon}\Gamma_i)\cup(\cup_{i,j\in S_\epsilon}\Phi_{i,j})) \le \frac{\delta}{\varrho\epsilon} + \frac{\epsilon'}{\epsilon^2} + \frac{1}{\varrho\epsilon^2} \le \delta$. □

DEFINITION 5.4. *Let $\mathcal{F}$ be a fixed function that defines an implicit vector $V = \mathcal{F}(D,\mathcal{H})$, given D and a randomness $\mathcal{H}$, as in Definition 1.6. An algorithm that receives as an input a data stream D and an access to a randomness $\mathcal{H}$ and in one pass over D returns an (ϵ,δ)-approximation of $|\mathcal{F}(D,\mathcal{H})|$ is called an* (ϵ,δ)-approximation algorithm for $L_1(\mathcal{F})$.

Finally, we are ready to state our main lemma, which is a strict generalization of Indyk and Woodruff [22] (for the proof see our full version [11]):

LEMMA 5.5. *Let $\mathcal{F}$ be a fixed function that defines an implicit vector $V = \mathcal{F}(D, \mathcal{H})$, given D and a randomness $\mathcal{H}$. Assume that V has non-negative entries bounded by $poly(n, m)$. Then the existence of Cover algorithm $\mathfrak{Q}(D, \mathcal{H}, H, \epsilon, \delta)$ for restricted $\mathcal{F}$ (see Definition 5.2) that uses memory $\mu(n, m, \epsilon, \delta)$ implies an existence of an $(\epsilon, 2/3)$-approximation algorithm for $L_1(\mathcal{F})$ (Definition 5.4) that uses memory*

$$O\left(\frac{1}{\epsilon}\log(n)\mu(n, m, \frac{\epsilon^7}{\log^3(nm)}, \frac{\epsilon}{\log(nm)}) + \frac{1}{\epsilon^2}\log^2(nm)\right).$$

Acknowledgments

We thank Piotr Indyk for a helpful discussion.

6. REFERENCES

[1] N. Alon, A. Andoni, T. Kaufman, K. Matulef, R. Rubinfeld, N. Xie, "Testing k-wise and almost k-wise independence," *Proceedings of the ACM symposium on Theory of computing*, 2007, pp. 496-Ű505.

[2] N. Alon, O. Goldreich, Y. Mansour, "Almost k-wise independence versus k-wise independence," *Inform. Process. Lett.*, 88:107Ű110, 2003.

[3] N. Alon, Y. Matias, M.Szegedy, "The space complexity of approximating the frequency moments". *Proceedings of the twenty-eighth annual ACM symposium on Theory of computing*, pp.20-29, 1996.

[4] T. Batu, L. Fortnow, E. Fischer, R. Kumar, R. Rubinfeld, P. White, "Testing random variables for independence and identity," *FOCS*, 2001, pp. 442Ű-451.

[5] T. Batu , L. Fortnow , R. Rubinfeld , W. D. Smith , P. White, "Testing that distributions are close," *Proceedings of the 41st Annual Symposium on Foundations of Computer Science*, p.259, 2000.

[6] T. Batu, R. Kumar, R. Rubinfeld, "Sublinear algorithms for testing monotone and unimodal distributions," *In Proc. 36th Annual ACM Symposium on the Theory of Computing*, pp. 381-Ű390, 2004.

[7] L. Bhuvanagiri, S. Ganguly, D. Kesh, C. Saha, "Simpler algorithm for estimating frequency moments of data streams," *in ACM-SIAM Symposium on Discrete Algorithms*, 2006, pp. 708Ű-713.

[8] V. Braverman, K.-M. Chung, Z. Liu, M. Mitzenmacher, R. Ostrovsky, "AMS Without 4-Wise Independence on Product Domains," STACS 2010.

[9] V. Braverman, R. Ostrovsky, "Effective Computations on Sliding Windows," SIAM J. Comput. Volume 39, Issue 6, pp. 2113-2131 (2010).

[10] V. Braverman, R. Ostrovsky, "Smooth Histograms for Sliding Windows," In Proceedings of the 48th Annual IEEE Symposium on Foundations of Computer Science (October 21 - 23, 2007).

[11] V. Braverman, R. Ostrovsky, "Measuring Independence of Datasets," http://arxiv.org/abs/0903.0034.

[12] V.Braverman, R.Ostrovsky, "Zero-One Frequency Laws," STOC 2010.

[13] V. Braverman, R. Ostrovsky, C. Zaniolo, "Optimal sampling from sliding windows," In Proceedings of the Twenty-Eighth ACM SIGMOD-SIGACT-SIGART Symposium on Principles of Database Systems (Providence, Rhode Island, USA, June 29 - July 01, 2009).

[14] M. Charikar, K. Chen, M. Farach-Colton, "Finding frequent items in data streams," *Theoretical Computer Science*, v.312 n.1, p.3-15, 2004.

[15] G. Cormode and S. Muthukrishnan. "An Improved Data Stream Summary: The Count-Min Sketch and its Applications". J. Algorithms, 55(1):58Ű75, April 2005.

[16] G. Cormode, S. Muthukrishnan, "What's New: Finding Significant Differences in Network Data Streams," INFOCOM 2004.

[17] J. Feigenbaum, S. Kannan, M. Strauss, M. Viswanathan, "An Approximate L1-Difference Algorithm for Massive Data Streams," *Proceedings of the 40th Annual Symposium on Foundations of Computer Science*, p.501, 1999.

[18] S. Ganguly, G. Cormode, "On Estimating Frequency Moments of Data Streams," APPROX-RANDOM 2007.

[19] I. F. Ilyas, V. Markl , P. Haas, P. Brown, A. Aboulnaga, "CORDS: automatic discovery of correlations and soft functional dependencies," *SIGMOD 2004*.

[20] P. Indyk, "Stable distributions, pseudorandom generators, embeddings, and data stream computation," *J. ACM*, 53 (2006), pp. 307-Ű323.

[21] P. Indyk, A. McGregor, "Declaring Independence via the Sketching of Sketches," *ACM-SIAM Symposium on Discrete Algorithms*, 2008.

[22] P. Indyk, D. P. Woodruff, "Optimal approximations of the frequency moments of data streams," *in ACMSymposium on Theory of Computing*, 2005, pp. 202Ű-208.

[23] R. Kimball, Joe Caserta, "The Data Warehouse ETL Toolkit: Practical Techniques for Extracting, Cleanin," John Wiley & Sons, 2004.

[24] P. Li, "Estimators and tail bounds for dimension reduction in $l_\alpha, (0 \leq \alpha \leq 2)$ using stable random projections," SODA 2008.

[25] S. Muthukrishnan, "Data Streams: Algorithms And Applications," *Foundations and Trends in Theoretical Computer Science*, Volume 1, Issue 2.

[26] V. Poosala, Y. E. Ioannidis, "Selectivity Estimation Without the Attribute Value Independence Assumption," *Proceedings of the 23rd International Conference on Very Large Data Bases*, pp.486-495, 1997.

[27] R. Rubinfeld, R. A. Servedio, "Testing monotone high-dimensional distributions," *In Proc. 37th Annual ACM Symposium on the Theory of Computing*, pp. 147-156, 2005.

[28] A. Sahai, S. Vadhan, "Manipulating statistical difference," DIMACS Series in Discrete Mathematics and Theoretical Computer Science, vol. 43., pp. 251-270.

Zero-One Frequency Laws

Vladimir Braverman*
UCLA
vova@cs.ucla.edu

Rafail Ostrovsky†
UCLA
rafail@cs.ucla.edu

ABSTRACT

Data streams emerged as a critical model for multiple applications that handle vast amounts of data. One of the most influential and celebrated papers in streaming is the "AMS" paper on computing frequency moments by Alon, Matias and Szegedy. The main question left open (and explicitly asked) by AMS in 1996 is to give the precise characterization for which functions G on frequency vectors m_i $(1 \le i \le n)$ can $\sum_{i\in[n]} G(m_i)$ be approximated efficiently, where "efficiently" means by a single pass over data stream and poly-logarithmic memory. No such characterization was known despite a tremendous amount of research on frequency-based functions in streaming literature. In this paper we finally resolve the AMS main question and give a precise characterization (in fact, a zero-one law) for *all* monotonically increasing functions on frequencies that are zero at the origin.

That is, we consider all monotonic functions $G : R \mapsto R$ such that $G(0) = 0$ and G can be computed in poly-logarithmic time and space and ask, for which G in this class is there an $(1\pm\epsilon)$-approximation algorithm for computing $\sum_{i\in[n]} G(m_i)$ for any polylogarithmic ϵ? We give an algebraic characterization for all such G so that:

- For all functions G in our class that satisfy our algebraic condition, we provide a very general and constructive way to derive an efficient $(1\pm\epsilon)$-approximation algorithm for computing $\sum_{i\in[n]} G(m_i)$ with polylogarithmic memory and a single pass over data stream; while
- For all functions G in our class that *do not* satisfy our algebraic characterization, we show a lower bound that requires greater then polylog memory for computing an approximation to $\sum_{i\in[n]} G(m_i)$ by *any* one-pass streaming algorithm.

Thus, we provide a zero-one law for all monotonically increasing functions G which are zero at the origin. Our results are quite general. As just one illustrative example, our main theorem implies a lower bound for $G(x) = (x(x-1))^{0.5\arctan(x+1)}$, while for a function $G(x) = (x(x+1))^{0.5\arctan(x+1)}$ our main theorem automatically yields a polylog memory one-pass $(1\pm\epsilon)$-approximation algorithm for computing $\sum_{i\in[n]} G(m_i)$. For both of these examples no lower or upper bounds were known. Of course, these are just illustrative examples, and there are many others. One might argue that these two functions may not be of interest in practical applications – we stress that our law works for **all** functions in this class, and the above examples illustrate the power of our method.

To the best of our knowledge, this is the first zero-one law in the streaming model for a wide class of functions, though we suspect that there are many more such laws to be discovered. Surprisingly, our upper bound requires only 4-wise independence and does not need the stronger machinery of Nisan's pseudorandom generators, even though our class captures multiple functions that previously required Nisan's generators. Furthermore, we believe that our methods can be extended to the more general models and complexity classes. For instance, the law also holds for a smaller class of non-decreasing and symmetric functions (i.e., $G(x) = G(-x)$ and $G(0) = 0$) which, due to negative values, allow deletions.

*Supported in part by NSF grants 0716835, 0716389, 0830803, 0916574.

†Supported in part by IBM Faculty Award, Xerox Innovation Group Award, the Okawa Foundation Award, Lockheed Martin, Intel, Teradata, NSF grants 0716835, 0716389, 0830803, 0916574, BSF grant and U.C. MICRO grant.

STOC'10, June 5–8, 2010, Cambridge, Massachusetts, USA.

Categories and Subject Descriptors

F.2 [**Theory of Computation**]: ANALYSIS OF ALGORITHMS AND PROBLEM COMPLEXITY

General Terms

Algorithms, Theory.

Keywords

Data Streams, Randomized Algorithms, Theory of Computation.

1. INTRODUCTION

Data streams emerged as a critical model for many applications with vast amounts of data. The importance of the streaming model is discussed, e.g., by Aggarwal (ed.) [1] and Muthukrishnan [41]. In the seminal AMS paper, Alon, Matias and Szegedy [2] studied the following basic model:

DEFINITION 1.1. *Let m, n be positive integers. A* stream *$D = D(n,m)$ is a sequence of size m of integers $p_1, \ldots, p_m$, where $p_i \in \{1, \ldots, n\}$. A* frequency vector *$M = M(D)$ is a vector of dimensionality n with* non-negative *entries $m_i, i \in [n]$ defined as:*

$$m_i = |\{j : 1 \le j \le m, p_j = i\}|.$$

AMS [2] studied the problem of approximating frequency moments with sublinear memory. They showed[1] that for $k = 0, 1, 2$ it is possible to approximate F_k with polylogarithmic space; for $k > 2$ they gave $O^*(n^{1-1/k})$ upper bound. Also, they gave $O^*(n^{1-5/k})$ lower bound for any $k > 5$. Indyk [30] presented a celebrated method of stable distributions for approximating L_p norms $p \in (0, 2]$ in a general model where deletions are allowed and updates can be larger then 1. Indyk and Woodruff [33] gave the first optimal algorithm for $F_k, k > 2$, proving $O^*(n^{1-2/k})$ upper bound. This result was later improved by polylog factors by Bhuvanagiri, Ganguly, Kesh and Saha [7]. Bar-Yossef, Jayram, Kumar and Sivakumar [3] used information theory to prove the first nearly matching lower bound of $\Omega(n^{1-(2+\epsilon)/k})$. Later Chakrabarti, Khot and Sun [17] improved the lower bound to $\Omega(n^{1-2/k})$ for one-pass algorithms. Indyk and Woodruff [32] and Woodruff [43] gave optimal lower bound in terms of error parameter. Many other results on frequency moments include, e.g., Flajolet and Martin [24], Bar-Yossef, Jayram, Kumar, and Sivakumar [4], Coppersmith and Kumar [19], Cormode, Datar, Indyk and Muthukrishnan [20], Feigenbaum, Kannan, Strauss and Viswanathan [23], Ganguly [25], Ganguly and Cormode [26], Li [39], and Kane, Nelson and Woodruff [35, 36], Braverman and Ostrovsky [9, 11]. Currently, many important frequency-based functions are well-understood in different models. Research on entropy, entropy norm and distributions included the works of Bhuvanagiri and Ganguly [6], Chakrabarti, Do Ba and Muthukrishnan [14], Chakrabarti, Cormode and McGregor [15], Guha, McGregor and Venkatasubramanian [28], Harvey, Nelson and Onak [29], Indyk and McGregor [31], Lall, Sekar, Ogihara, Xu and Zhang [38], Braverman, Chung, Liu, Mitzenmacher and Ostrovsky [8], Braverman and Ostrovsky [13]. The related question of frequent elements has been studied by Charikar, Chen and Farach-Colton [18], Cormode and Hadjieleftheriou [21], Cormode and Muthukrishnan [22]. The frequency-based functions were studied in extended models such as the read/write model (Beame, Jayram and Rudra [5]), and the randomized model (Chakrabarti, Cormode and McGregor [16], Jayram, McGregor, Muthukrishnan and Vee [34]).

The main question left open (and explicitly asked) by Alon, Matias and Szegedy [2] is:

AMS (informal): *What other frequency-based functions can be approximated on streams?*

[1]This is a very informal explanation. For precise statements see [2].

In 2006 Guha and Indyk [40] (Question 5) asked a related question:

Guha, Indyk (informal): *What distances can be computed between two distribution vectors V and U defined by two streams? Consider a function $\phi(x,y)$ such that $\phi(x,x) = 0$. What are the properties of ϕ such that $\sum_{i\in[n]} \phi(v_i, u_i)$ can be approximated with small memory and multiplicative error?*

To the best of our knowledge, the only work in this direction is the result of Guha, Indyk and McGregor [27]. They proved the Shift Invariant Theorem, a general result that gives a necessary condition for approximating a wide class of two-variable functions. The Shift Invariant Theorem says, very informally, that if $\frac{\phi(a,a+c)}{\phi(b,b+c)} > \alpha > 1$ for some a, b, c, then a linear lower bound can be shown. In fact, they showed a stronger result for *distributions*, i.e., vectors with entries m_i/m. As a corollary, they obtained a linear lower bound for all commonly used *divergences* and gave additive approximations instead. Guha, Indyk and McGregor suggested that any function $\phi(x,y)$ is not sketchable unless it is a function of $x - y$. Thus, it is important to understand what functions of a single variable can be approximated. Unfortunately, for such functions, the Shift Invariant Theorem is not applicable.

The questions of Alon, Matias and Szegedy [2] and Guha and Indyk [40] are still unresolved. Indeed, no sufficient and necessary conditions are known for a function to be computable; not even in the basic model of Alon, Matias and Szegedy [2]. Thus, to even approach the question posed by Guha and Indyk, we must first resolve the question of AMS [2]. This is exactly what we do in this paper. We limit ourselves to the basic streaming model (Definition 1.1) and consider a class of non-decreasing functions $G : R \mapsto R$ such that $G(0) = 0$. We discuss the following problem:

> G-sum(D, ϵ)
>
> Given: A stream $D = D(n,m)$ and $\epsilon = \Omega^*(1)^a$.
> Output: A real r such that r is a $(1 \pm \epsilon)$-approximation[b] of $\sum_{i\in[n]} G(m_i)$.
>
> [a]Given the parameters n, m, we use $O^*_{n,m}(g(n,m))$ to denote $O(log^{O(1)}(nm)g(n,m))$; $\Omega^*_{n,m}(g(n,m))$ is defined similarly. When the context is clear, we use O^* instead of $O^*_{n,m}$.
> [b]We say that x is a $(1 \pm \epsilon)$-approximation of y if $(1-\epsilon)y \le x \le (1+\epsilon)y$.

We ask whether or not it is possible to solve the G-Sum problem in polylog space, with a singe pass and a small probability of error. More precisely, we define the following class STREAM-POLYLOG class.

DEFINITION 1.2. *We say that a function G belongs to the* STREAM-POLYLOG *class if for any k there exist t and an algorithm $\mathfrak{A}$ such that for any n, m; any stream $D = D(n,m)$; and any[2] $\epsilon \ge \frac{1}{\log^k(nm)}$:*

[2]Here, polylog ϵ can also be replaced with a larger error which gives additional results as well; we defer these generalizations to the expanded version.

1. $\mathfrak{A}$ *makes a single pass over* D.

2. $\mathfrak{A}$ *solves* G*-Sum*(D,ϵ) *and errs with probability at most*[3] 0.3.

3. $\mathfrak{A}$ *uses* $O(\log^t(nm))$ *memory bits.*

Our main result is a sufficient and necessary condition (i.e., zero-one law) for any non-decreasing G such that $G(0) = 0$. An important strength of our result is that we consider functions which may not even be differentiable or continuous and can include "jumps":

DEFINITION 1.3. **Local jump.** *Define:*

$$\pi_\epsilon(x) = \min\{x, \min\{|z| \in \mathbb{N}^+ : |G(x) - G(x+z)| > \epsilon G(x)\}$$

Now, we are ready to introduce the following notion of "tractable" function:

DEFINITION 1.4. *Function* G *is* Tractable *if* $G(1) > 0$ *and:*

$$\forall k \exists N_0 \exists t \forall x, y \in \mathbb{N}^+, \forall R \in \mathbb{R}^+ \forall \epsilon :$$
$$\left(R > N_0,\ \frac{G(x)}{G(y)} = R,\ \epsilon > \frac{1}{\log^k(Rx)}\right) \implies \quad (1)$$
$$\left(\left(\frac{\pi_\epsilon(x)}{y}\right)^2 \geq \frac{R}{\log^t(xR)}\right).$$

Our main result is the following theorem:

THEOREM 1.5. **Main Theorem** *Let* G *be a non-decreasing function such that* $G(0) = 0$*:*

$G \in$ STREAM-POLYLOG **if and only if** $G \in$ Tractable

The precise formula of a tractable function is somewhat complicated; however, the notion of tractability is very intuitive, as we explain below.

HIGH-LEVEL INTERPRETATION OF OUR ZERO-ONE LAW: (We stress that here we only explain how our result should be interpreted, without getting into any technical details regarding the proof. We explain the intuition about our technical proof, that turned out to be highly nontrivial, in a different section below and explain why our result gives us the intuitively "right" characterization.) *The space complexity of* G*-Sum should depend on how fast* G *grows. Quadratic growth seems to be a "waterline" since any* $G(x) = x^{2+k}$ *can be approximated if and only if* $k \leq 0$. *Can we prove that* $G(x)$ *can be approximated if and only if* $G(x)$ *grows "slower" then* x^2*?* A careful elaboration of the above question gives us (1). We need to define precisely the notion of "growing slower then." It turns out that the right measure is the ratio between $G(x)/G(y)$ and $(x/y)^2$ for all pairs x, y. First, if $G(1) = 0$ then the maximal ratio is infinity. Indeed, we can generate vectors of arbitrary large dimensionality and still preserve a constant value of G-Sum. Intuitively it is clear that such a function cannot be approximated in a small space. This is indeed the case; similar observations were made, for example, for entropy norm $G(x) = x\log(x)$ in [14]. If $G(1) > 0$, then we can consider the ratio $G(x)/G(1)$. If it grows significantly faster (i.e., beyond polylog factors) than x^2 then we cannot approximate G-sum in polylog space (the lower bound follows from [17]). The above rule should be extended to any pair of positive integers $x > y$: $G(x)/G(y)$ cannot be significantly and asymptotically larger then x^2/y^2. Finally, can G grow very fast locally? Consider the following step function: $G(x) = 2^{\lfloor \log(x) \rfloor}$. It is not hard to see that we cannot obtain a small constant approximation of this function with sublinear space. Thus, in addition to the "global" growth of G, we also need to address its "local" jumps. We take one step further and define $\pi_\epsilon(x)$ as a minimal shift (to the left or the right of x) needed to "jump" beyond the $(1 \pm \epsilon)$ factor. It turns out that the ratio between $G(x)/G(y)$ and $\pi(x)^2/y^2$ is what we need to measure; this is exactly what (1) states.[4]

Our main contribution is the necessary and sufficient condition for a class of non-decreasing non-negative functions. To the best of our knowledge, this is the first zero-one law in the streaming model for a wide class of functions. In addition, our method has the following advantages.

RAMIFICATIONS OF OUR MAIN RESULT: Streaming algorithms typically employ a special treatment for every new function. For example, there are unique algorithms for F_2 [2, 30], F_0 [24, 20, 2] and for $L_p, 0 \leq p < 2$ [30, 39, 35]. Every new function so far required a new method or modification of existing methods and proofs. There is a natural question that one can ask:

Is there a general *algorithm for all tractable functions?*

We take the first step towards answering this fascinating general question. Our main technical contribution is a general algorithm and general proof for any function that satisfies (1).

Many of the existing methods first assume that totally random vectors are available, and later employ the celebrated pseudorandom generator of Nisan [42] to reduce the space for randomness. This brings another natural question:

Are pseudorandom generators necessary or can we directly work with k-wise independent distributions?

Surprisingly, we show that our general algorithm requires only 4-wise independence.

GENERALIZATIONS: Our methods can be extended to more general models and complexity classes. Our main theorem is immediately applicable to a more general model with deletions and larger updates. Here the law holds for a smaller class of non-decreasing and symmetric functions (i.e., $G(x) = G(-x)$).

Our methods may also shed some light on the fascinating open problem posed by Guha and Indyk in 2006. In fact, we believe that our methods are quite general and extend to other classes such as sublinear-space functions or distributions (i.e., to the functions $G(m_i/m)$.

RELATED WORK: Our paper is a generalization of many previous works and explicitly employs existing ideas as well as the development of several new general techniques, both for our algorithm and analysis. The major difference with

[3]We remark that 0.3 is for concreteness only and can be replaced by any 1/poly probability.

[4]In fact, the Shift Invariant Theorem gives a similar intuition for functions of two variables by measuring the ratio $G(x, x+a)/G(y, y+a)$.

previous works is that assumptions that may be true for specific functions are not true in general. This makes our task highly non-trivial. As a result, we needed to develop a general and novel framework with minimum assumptions. At the end, the only assumption we make is that G is non-decreasing.

In particular, our method was inspired by the seminal work of Indyk and Woodruff [33]; our work can be seen as a generalization and simplification of [33]. The most notable difference is that the Indyk and Woodruff's method was specifically developed to tackle F_k. They employ the strong relation between m_i and m_i^k; we cannot make this assumption. One example of Indyk and Woodruf method is a statement that if y is an $(1 \pm \epsilon)$-approximation of x then $G(y)$ is a $(1 \pm \epsilon')$-approximation of $G(x)$ for some $\epsilon' = \epsilon^{O(1)}$. The statement is correct for $G(x) = x^k$ for any constant k; but notice that it is not correct in general. In addition, and perhaps somewhat surprisingly, our method requires only 4-wise independence where as Indyk and Woodruff [33] employs pseudorandom generators of Nisan [42].

One of the key steps in our new method is an approximation of "heavy" elements $G(m_i)$. Heavy elements have been intensively studied, e.g., in the papers of Charikar, Chen and Farach-Colton [18] and Cormode and Muthukrishnan [22]. Unfortunately, these method are not directly applicable: we need G-heaviness, where [18, 22] address L_2 and L_1 heaviness respectfully. We thus developed a novel method for G-heaviness. Our method uses ideas developed in [18] and new techniques; both our method and [18] employ and build upon the AMS sketching for F_2 [2].

Main Technical Ideas: The lower bound follows from the reduction to set disjointness and index problems. Assume that $G(x)/G(y)$ is both arbitrarily large and significantly larger then $(x/y)^2$. Then set disjointness can be translated into a stream that contains only elements with frequency y or (in addition) one element with a frequency larger then x. Since G is non-decreasing, and with some additional work, by utilizing [17] we derive our lower bound. The detailed proof is technically more involved than the direct application of [17] and can be found in Section 3.

To prove the upper bound we apply two key steps: first, we reduce the problem of G-Sum to the question of estimating heavy elements; and second, we solve the heavy elements problem separately.

To address the first reduction, we generalize the machinery of Indyk and Woodruff. We split the domain of G into "intervals" and reduce G-Sum to the problem of counting the number of entries $G(m_i)$ that belong to a single interval. In fact, only a relaxed variant of interval counting should be solved. We always need to maintain a multiplicative upper bound; however, the lower bound is needed only for intervals that contribute nontrivially to the final answer. This task can be solved (if the number of entries in the interval is small) by reduction to finding heavy elements. Finally, we show how to reduce general counting to counting on intervals with a small number of elements.

To complete the proof, we need to approximate any $G(m_i)$ such that $G(m_i) = \Omega^*(\sum_{j \neq i} G(m_j))$. The definition of $\pi_\epsilon(m_i)$ implies that it is sufficient to approximate m_i with additive error smaller then $\pi_\epsilon(m_i)$. We need to verify that $G(m_i) = \Omega^*(\sum_{j \neq i} G(m_j))$, and that the additive error is less then $\pi_\epsilon(m_i)$. These generally hard problems can be solved for tractable functions. The key observation is that if G is tractable, then $G(m_i) = \Omega^*(\sum_{j \neq i} G(m_j))$ implies that $(\pi_\epsilon(m_i))^2 = \Omega^*(\sum_{j \neq i} m_j^2)$. This implies that to find heavy elements we only need to verify that $m_i^2 = \Omega^*(\sum_{j \neq i} m_j^2)$ and approximate m_i with additive error. With non-trivial technical effort we obtain an algorithm that reports only $(1 \pm \epsilon)$-approximations of $G(m_i)$, and with high probability finds all heavy $G(m_i)$. There is a possibility that the algorithm will report some extra $G(m_i)$. However, we show that the false positives do not affect the correctness of the final algorithm. Section 5 is devoted to this step.

2. PURIFEIR: AN ALTERNATIVE VIEW

In this paper and in our other STOC paper [13] we solve two very different problems. The models are incomparable: this paper addresses implicity defined tensors, and [13] describes how to approximate functions on explicit streaming frequencies. Moreover, our objectives are different. In [13] we improve the existing $\log(N)$-approximation to an $(1+\epsilon)$-approximation. In this paper we give new algorithms for previously unknown functions. As a result, our bottom-line techniques are different. Yet we use a single methodology for both problems, which seems quite general, and worth explaining.

Indyk and Woodruff proposed a seminal method of layering that has become folklore in the streaming applications. They show that the frequency moments problem can be reduced to a question of finding heavy hitters. Further, they show that it is possible to use F_2 (in particular the algorithm of [18]) to compute heavy hitters under F_k. Although the Indyk and Woodruff algorithm solves a particular problem, we believe that their methodology goes far beyond frequency moments. In fact our two papers can be seen as building upon methodology of Indyk and Woodruff and in fact generalization of their methodology. Thus, we would like to emphasize the importance of their methodology and explain our contribution.

In many cases the most non-trivial step of streaming computations can be seen as a summation (or counting) of entries of a very large vector that is implicitly defined by the stream. We claim that the Indyk and Woodruff methodology is applicable to many such functions. We were able to show that the layering method can be used for at least two general settings: frequency-based functions and tensors. In fact, we believe that it is possible to specify the set of problems and conditions for which the layering reduction is possible, something which we are currently exploring.

It seems that one such condition is separability, i.e. an ability to efficiently sample the target vector (not the stream). Generally speaking, the entries of this imaginary vector may have a very complex nature and be dependent on each other. Thus, sampling of the stream does not necessarily corresponds to the sampling of the implicit vector. Yet we show that for the Independence Problem from [13] it is possible to sample the vector without sampling the stream. Understanding which implicit vectors can be sampled efficiently is another important problem.

While the heavy hitters problem seems to be somewhat easier than to solve approximating the entire vector, it is generally not clear how to address this problem without computing the sum. Indeed, when the heavy hitter contributes almost entirely to the sum, those two problems coincide. Thus, it seems that in many cases finding the heavy hitter is the core obstacle. We are not aware of a general approach to tackling the heavy elements problem.[5] Thus, the key contribution of our methodology is such a method for tackling heavy elements. We present it very informally here; two specific examples of applying this methodology are in our two papers, and as these papers show, this methodology is quite flexible. Call an entry of a vector α-significant if it contributes at least α-fraction of the entire sum. Call a zero-one streaming function (α,β)-*certificate* for the vector $V = V(D)$ if $Certificate(D) = 1$ implies that there is a β-significant element in the vector $V = V(D)$; if there is a α-significant element in the implicit vector $V = V(D)$ then $Certificate(D) = 1$.

A function is a (β,τ)-mimic if an existence of a β-significant element v_i in $V = V(D)$ implies that $Mimic(D) \in [(1-\tau)|v_i|, (1+\tau)|v_i|]$.

Consider the case where we are given two such functions. Then there is a simple yet effective method for finding heavy hitters. We call this the **Purifier** method.

ALGORITHM 2.1. PURIFIER

1. $c = Certificate_{V,\alpha,\beta}(D)$.
2. $\mu = Mimic_{V,\beta}(D)$.
3. *If* $c = 1$ *output* μ; *else output* 0.

It is easy to see that **Purifier** solves the following promise problem. If a vector has an α-significant element then the output will be its approximation. If, on the other hand, there is no β-significant element, the output is 0. Generally speaking, we are able to find extremely heavy elements and to discard somewhat smaller ones.

It is a long way from this idea to a specific solution. To apply **Purifier**, we need to "guess" the right parameters, the certificate and the mimic function. In addition, we need to prove the correctness of the certificate and the mimic function, and prove memory bound for their computations. It is also important to note that mimic and certificate are problem specific. There might be other technical issues such as dealing with the probabilistic nature of the algorithms. The above tasks may be highly non-trivial. Still, the idea of **Purifier** provides a general framework for streaming algorithms; thus we believe it will be helpful for future applications.

We stress that Indyk and Woodruff were the first to implicitly use the **Purifier** method to tackle F_k heavy hitters. They observed that F_2 can be used as a certifier for F_k heavy hitters. In this paper we generalize this idea and show that F_2 is a litmus task of tractability; that is, any tractable frequency-based function can be both certified and mimicked by F_2. (From this, alternative perspective, in [13] we show that $\log(n)$-approximations can certify ϵ-heavy rows, and we give another, completely different function for mimicking.)

Purifier can be seen as a reduction from our target function to a mimic function under specific conditions. It gives a hierarchy of functions that can be reduced. We remark that it will also be very interesting to construct such complexity hierarchies for more general settings.

[5]It is important to note that heavy hitters were solved for many specific metrics [18, 22].

3. THE LOWER BOUND

To establish lower bounds, we will use SET DISJOINTNESS and INDEX problems from communication complexity [37]. Recall that SET DISJOINTNESS is the following promise problem: each of $t \geq 2$ players is given a set from the universe $[N]$; all sets have exactly one common element or disjoint. The lower bound on the communication complexity of this problem is $\Omega(\frac{N}{t})$ for the randomized one-way communication complexity [17]. INDEX is the following promise problem: there are two players: Alice and Bob. Alice is given a set S from the universe $[N]$; Bob is given a single element $x \in [N]$. The players must decide whether or not $x \in S$. The lower bound on the communication complexity of INDEX problem is $\Omega(N)$ for the randomized one-way communication complexity [37]. We stress that SET DISJOINTNESS and INDEX are common tools to prove lower bounds on streams. We start with the following observation.

FACT 3.1. *Let G be a non-decreasing function such that $G(1) = 0$. Then $G \notin$STREAM-POLYLOG.*

PROOF. Consider any algorithm that solves G-Sum$(D,2)$. Let $y = \min\{z \in \mathbb{N}^+ : G(z) > 0\}$. We have $y > x_0 \geq 1$. Consider the following reduction to the SET DISJOINTNESS problem with two players. Alice repeats each element of his set $y-1$ times. Then she evaluates the algorithm for G-Sum$(D,2)$ on the stream of repetitions D and sends the resulting memory to Bob. Bob continues its computations by feeding the same algorithm his input. The algorithm may have two outputs: 0 or 2-approximation of $G(y) > 0$. Clearly, it must distinguish between these two cases. Thus, any algorithm that solves G-Sum$(D,2)$ must use a linear memory. □

In the reminder of this paper we concentrate on the case where $G(x) > 0$ for all positive integers x. Further, we may assume that

$$G(1) = 1. \tag{2}$$

Indeed otherwise, we shall consider $G'(x) = \frac{G(x)}{G(1)}$, approximate $G'(M(D))$ and multiply by $G(1)$; the result is an approximation of $G(M)$.

THEOREM 3.2. *The Lower Bound for Non-Tractable Functions.*
Let G be a non-decreasing function such that $G(0) = 0$. If G is not tractable, then $G \notin$STREAM-POLYLOG.

PROOF. By Fact 3.1, it is sufficient to consider the case when $G(1) = 1$ and (1) does not hold. In particular:

$$\exists k \forall N_0 \forall t \exists x, y \in \mathbb{N}^+, \exists R \in \mathbb{R}^+ \exists \epsilon : \left(R > N_0,\ \frac{G(x)}{G(y)} = R,\ \epsilon > \frac{1}{\log^k(Rx)}\right) \cap \left(\left(\frac{\pi_\epsilon(x)}{y}\right)^2 < \frac{R}{\log^t(xR)}\right). \tag{3}$$

Consider the fixed k from (3) and let t, N_0 be any arbitrary large numbers. There exists $R \geq N_0$; a pair (x,y) and $\epsilon > \log^{-k}(Rx)$ such that (3) holds. Denote $N = \lfloor R \rfloor$; then $N \leq \frac{G(x)}{G(y)} < N+1$ and $\left(\frac{\pi_\epsilon(x)}{y}\right)^2 < \frac{N+1}{\log^t(xN)}$.

First, consider the case when $\pi_\epsilon(x) = x > y$; in this case we show that even a small constant approximation is not possible in polylogarithmic space. Consider a SET DISJOINTNESS on the domain of size $\Theta(N)$ with $s = \lceil \frac{x}{y} \rceil$ players. Consider the following reduction: the first player repeats y times every element of his subset, applies the streaming algorithm to the resulting stream, and sends the memory content to the second player. The second player and the rest of the players repeat their sets y times and continue the execution of the algorithm on the resulting stream. Consider the resulting stream $D(n,m)$, where $n = N$ and $m \leq n(x+1)$. If the sets are disjoint, then the resulting value of G-Sum should be $NG(y)$. If there is an intersection, then the resulting value should be at least $((N-1)G(y)+G(x)) \approx 2NG(y)$ for sufficiently large N. Thus, there exists a small constant c such that a c-approximation of G-Sum solves the SET DISJOINTNESS problem. Thus, any algorithm for G-Sum(D, c) must use $\Omega(\frac{N}{s^2})$ memory bits. However, (3) implies:

$$\frac{N}{s^2} \geq 0.5 \log^t(xN) \geq 0.5(0.5\log(nm))^t. \quad (4)$$

Next, consider the case that $\pi_\epsilon(x) < x$. W.l.o.g., assume that $G(x+\pi_\epsilon(x)) > (1+\epsilon)G(x)$. Assume that $\pi_\epsilon(x) \leq y$ and consider the following reduction to the INDEX problem of dimensionality N: Alice repeats elements of her set y times and Bob repeats his index x times. There are two possible outcomes for $G(M(D))$: either $G(M(D)) = NG(y) + G(x)$ or $G(M(D)) = (N-1)G(y)+G(x+\pi_\epsilon(x)) > (N-1)G(y)+(1+\epsilon)G(x)$. Since $G(x) \geq NG(y)$ it follows that there exists $\epsilon' = \Omega(\epsilon)$ such that any algorithm that solves G-Sum(D, ϵ') must solve INDEX. Thus, the lower bound is $N \geq \frac{N}{s^2}$; i.e., we obtain (4).

Finally, consider the case that $y < \pi_\epsilon(x) < x$. Consider a SET DISJOINTNESS problem with $s = \lceil \frac{\pi_\epsilon(x)}{y} \rceil$ players over a domain of size N. Consider the same reduction as in the case $x = \pi_\epsilon(x)$ with an additional modification. The last player does the following: for each element a of his set he simulates separately the insertion to the stream x copies of a. Thus, he simulates execution of the algorithm on streams $D_a = D', a, \dots, a$, where D' is the stream generated by the first $s-1$ players and a is an element from the s-th player set. Consider the outputs of G-Sum on all these streams. If the sets are disjoint then the output will be $N'G(y) + G(x)$ for all streams for some fixed $N' \leq N$. If there is an intersection, then exactly one answer will be $N'G(y)+G(x+\pi_\epsilon(x)) > N'G(y) + (1+\epsilon)G(x)$. Since $G(x) \geq NG(y)$, we conclude that there exists $\epsilon' = \Omega(\epsilon)$ such that any algorithm that solves G-Sum(D, ϵ') will distinguish between these two results. By repeating the above arguments, we also obtain (4). Finally, the case when $G(x - \pi_\epsilon(x)) < (1-\epsilon)G(x)$ can be handled similarly; instead of working with x we use $x - \pi_\epsilon(x)$.

To summarize, we have shown that there exists k such that for any t there exists $n, m, \epsilon \geq \log^k(nm)$ and a stream $D = D(n,m)$ such that any algorithm that solves G-Sum(D, ϵ) requires $\Omega(\log^t(nm))$ memory bits. Thus, and by Definition 1.2 we proved that $G \notin STREAM\text{-}POLYLOG$. $\square$

4. DEFINITIONS, NOTATIONS AND COMMENTS

In this section we summarize definitions and notations that we need to establish the upper bound. A probability p is *asymptotically equal* to a if $|p-a| = O^*(1/(nm))$; we denote this fact by $p \approx a$. A probability p is *negligible* if $p \approx 0$. We will extensively use the fact that a union of a polylogarithmic number of negligible events is a negligible event (i.e., occurs with negligible probability).

DEFINITION 4.1. *Major elements*
*Let V be a vector of dimensionality n with entries v_i. Let G be a function and d be a positive real number such that $d \geq 1$. An element v_i is a (G,d)-*major *with respect to V if:*

$$G(v_i) > d\sum_{j \neq i} G(v_j).$$

DEFINITION 4.2. *Sampled stream*
Let D be a stream and $H : [n] \mapsto \{0,1\}$ be a function. A sampled stream *D_H is a stream defined as $D \cap H^{-1}(1)$; i.e., D_H contains elements of D that are mapped to 1 by H.*

DEFINITION 4.3. *Residual second moment.*
For a vector V with $(F_2, 1)$-major entry v_i, define $F_2^{res}(V) = F_2(V) - v_i^2$. I.e., $F_2^{res}(V)$ is a second moment of V minus the square of the maximal element.

DEFINITION 4.4. *G-Vector*
Let G be a function and V be a vector of dimensionality n with entries $v_i, i \in [n]$. A G-vector *$G(V)$ is a vector of dimensionality n with i-th entry equal to $G(v_i)$.*

DEFINITION 4.5. *Hadamard product*
For two vectors of dimensionality n define $Had(V,U)$ to be their Hadamard product; i.e., $Had(V,U)$ is a vector of dimensionality n with entries $v_i u_i$.

Every vector H of dimensionality n with entries $h_i \in R$ defines a function $H : [n] \mapsto R$ as $H(i) = h_i$. We thus will freely interchange the notions of random vector and hash functions. In our auxiliary algorithms we use notations $D, M(D), \epsilon$, etc., to define an input of the auxiliary algorithm. It is important to distinguish between the parameters of auxiliary algorithms and the ones of the G-Sum problem.

5. COMPUTING G-CORE

In this section we solve the following problem:

G-Core(D, α)

Given: A stream D, and a real α.
Output: A set of positive numbers $S = \{s_1, \dots, s_l\}$ such that $l = O^*(1)$ and:

1. There exist a sequence $j_1 < \dots < j_l$ such that s_i is a $(1 \pm \alpha)$-approximation of a $G(m_{j_i})$.
2. If there is a $(G,1)$-major element m_i w.r.t. $M(D)$, then $i \in \{j_1, \dots, j_l\}$, i.e., S contains a $(1 \pm \alpha)$-approximation of a $G(m_i)$.

5.1 Preliminaries

FACT 5.1. *Let V be a vector with non-negative entries. Let H be a pairwise-independent random vector (of the same dimensionality as V) with zero-one entries h_i that are uniformly distributed. Let H' be a vector with entries $1 - h_i$.*

Denote $X = \langle V, H\rangle$ and $Y = \langle V, H'\rangle$, where $\langle,\rangle$ is an inner product. If for all i, $v_i < 0.01|V|$ then $P((X < \frac{1}{3}|V|) \cup (Y < \frac{1}{3}|V|)) < 0.1$.

PROOF. Clearly, $X = |V| - Y$ and $E(X) = E(Y) = 0.5|V|$. Further, since H is pairwise independent and by the condition of the lemma, we have that $Var(X) = 0.25F_2(V) \leq \frac{1}{400}|V|^2$. Thus, by Chebyshev inequality: $P((X < \frac{1}{3}|V|) \cup (Y < \frac{1}{3}|V|)) = P(|X - E(X)| \geq \frac{1}{6}|V| \leq \frac{36}{|V|^2}\frac{|V|^2}{400} < 0.1$. □

LEMMA 5.2. *Let V be a vector with non-negative entries. Let H be a pairwise independent random vector (of the same dimensionality as V) with zero-one entries h_i that are uniformly distributed. Let H' be a vector with entries $1 - h_i$. Denote $X = \langle V, H\rangle$ and $Y = \langle V, H'\rangle$. Let K be a parameter, $K > 10^4$. If there exists (L_1, K)-major element v_i then:*

$$P((X > KY) \vee (Y > KX)) = 1.$$

If there is no $(L_1, 10^{-4}K)$-major element then:

$$P((X > KY) \vee (Y > KX)) \leq 0.5.$$

PROOF. The first claim of the lemma follows directly. Indeed, w.l.o.g., assume that $v_1 > K\sum_{i>1} v_i$ and that $H(1) = 1$. Then $X \geq v_i > K\sum_{i>1} v_i \geq KY$.

To show the second claim, consider an entry v_i with maximal value. If $v_i < 0.01|V|$, we are done by Fact 5.1; thus we assume that $v_i \geq 0.01|V|$. Assume that there exists $v_j, j \neq i$ such that $v_j \geq \frac{100}{K}v_i$. We have:

$$Kv_j \geq 100v_i \geq |V|, \quad Kv_i \geq 0.01K|V| > |V|. \quad (5)$$

W.p. 0.5, $h_i \neq h_j$, in which case by (5) the event $(X > KY) \vee (Y > KX)$ cannot happen.

Finally, assume that for all $j \neq i$, we have:

$$v_j < \frac{100}{K}v_i < 0.01(|V| - v_i). \quad (6)$$

Consider vector V' that is equal to V for all entries and is equal to 0 on its i-th entry. Consider $X' = \langle V', H\rangle$ and $Y' = \langle V', H'\rangle$. By (6) and by Fact 5.1: $P((X' < \frac{1}{3}|V'|) \vee (Y' < \frac{1}{3}|V'|)) \leq 0.1$. But this implies that w.p. at least 0.9: $KX \geq KX' \geq \frac{K}{3}(|V| - v_i) \geq |V|$, $KY \geq KY' \geq \frac{K}{3}(|V| - v_i) \geq |V|$, in which case the event $(X > KY) \vee (Y > KX)$ cannot happen. □

LEMMA 5.3. *Let V be a vector with non-negative entries. Let H be a random vector (of the same dimensionality as V) with pairwise independent entries $h_i \sim U(\{-1, 1\})$. Denote $X = \langle V, H\rangle$. If there exists i such that v_i is $(F_2, 1)$-major with respect to V then:*

$$P(||X| - v_i| \geq 2(F_2^{res}(V))^{0.5}) \leq 0.25. \quad (7)$$

PROOF. Denote $Z = \sum_{j\neq i} h_i v_i$. By triangle inequality: $|X| \leq |Z| + |v_i|$. By inverse triangle inequality: $|X| = |v_i - (-Z)| \geq |v_i| - |Z|$. Since v_i is non-negative, we have: $v_i - |Z| \leq |X| \leq v_i + |Z|$.

By the linearity of expectation, $E(Z) = 0$. By pairwise independence of H, it follows that $Var(Z) = F_2(V) - v_i^2 = F_2^{res}$. Thus, by Chebyshev inequality: $P(|Z| \geq 2\sqrt{F_2^{res}(V)}) \leq 0.25$.

□

The following fact is folklore; a similar statement can found, e.g., in [7].

FACT 5.4. *Let D be a stream such that $M(D)$ contains a $(F_2, 2)$-major element m_i. There exists an algorithm that makes a single pass over D, uses a polylogarithmic memory and outputs r such that: $2(F_2^{res}(M))^{0.5} < r < 3(F_2^{res}(M))^{0.5}$. The algorithm errs with a negligible probability.*

PROOF. W.l.o.g, assume that m_1 is $(F_2, 2)$-major element. Let H be a zero-one hash function with pairwise independent entries. Consider two streams D_H and D_{1-H} and apply the AMS algorithm for F_2 on both streams. We require that the outputs be 1.1-approximations of the second moments with a negligible probability of error. Let a and b be two outputs. Thus $Z = 10min\{a, b\}$ is a 1.1 approximation of the following random variable:

$$X = 10\sum_{i>1} \mathbf{1}_{H(i)\neq H(1)} v_i^2.$$

Since H is pairwise independent we have that $E(X) = 5F^{res}(M)$. Since $0 \leq X \leq 10F_2^{res}(V)$, it follows that $Var(X) \leq E(X^2) \leq (10F_2^{res}(V))^2$. Let Y be an average of $C = O(1)$ independent X; it follows that $Var(Y) \leq C^{-1}(10F_2^{res}(V))^2$. Thus for sufficiently large C by Chebyshev inequality:

$$P(|Y - 5F_2^{res}| \geq 0.1F_2^{res}) \leq 0.1. \quad (8)$$

Taking a median of $O(\log(nm))$ independent averages drops the probability to negligible. Let Q be a median of $O(\log(nm))$ averages of C independent Zs. By the union bound all Z will be 1.1 approximations of corresponding Xs except with negligible probability. Thus and by (8), $r = Q^{0.5}$ satisfies the conditions of the fact except with negligible probability. □

FACT 5.5. *Let $\epsilon \leq 0.5$ and let $x, a, b \geq 0$ be such that $|x - a| \leq 0.1\pi_\epsilon(x)$ and $b < 0.1\pi_\epsilon(x)$. Then $(1-4\epsilon)G(a+b) \leq G(a) \leq (1+4\epsilon)G(a-b)$.*

PROOF. We have $a - b \geq x - 0.2\pi_\epsilon(x) > 0$ and $a + b \leq x + 0.2\pi_\epsilon(x)$. Thus[6] $(1-\epsilon)G(x) \leq G(a-b) \leq G(a) \leq G(a+b) \leq (1+\epsilon)G(x)$. Thus $(1+4\epsilon)G(a-b) \geq \frac{(1-\epsilon)(1+4\epsilon)}{(1+\epsilon)}G(a) \geq G(a)$. The second part can be proven similarly. □

FACT 5.6. *Let x, a, b be such that $|x - a| \leq b$. Then $(1 - \epsilon)G(a + b) \leq G(a) \leq (1 + \epsilon)G(a - b) \implies (1 - \epsilon)G(x) \leq G(a) \leq (1 + \epsilon)G(x)$.*

PROOF. Assume, on the contrary, that $G(a) > (1+\epsilon)G(x)$. Then since $x \geq a - b$ we have a contradiction: $G(a) > (1+\epsilon)G(x) \geq (1+\epsilon)G(a-b) \geq G(a)$. The second condition is proven similarly. □

5.2 Algorithms for G-Core

We define and solve the following problem:

> Hybrid-Major(D, ϵ)
>
> Given: A stream D, and a positive real ϵ.
> Output: A real $r \geq 0$ such that:
>
> 1. If $r \neq 0$ then r is an $(1 \pm 4\epsilon)$-approximation of a $G(m_j)$ for some m_j.
> 2. If there exists a $(F_2, 1)$-major element m_i (w.r.t. $M(D)$) such that $\pi_\epsilon(m_i) \geq 20^5(F_2^{res}(M(D)))^{0.5}$ then r is a $(1 \pm 4\epsilon)$-approximation of $G(m_i)$.

[6]In general, the inequality may not hold if $\pi_\epsilon(x) = 1$ since Definition 1.3 limits π to integers. However, in this case either G is not tractable or $x = O^*(1)$ and can be approximated precisely. We thus assume that $\pi_\epsilon(x) \neq 1$.

ALGORITHM 5.7. *Compute-Hybrid-Major*(D, ϵ)

1. *Repeat* $O(\log(nm))$ *times, independently and in parallel:*
   (a) *Generate uniform pairwise independent vector* $H' \in \{0,1\}^n$ *and compute* $a_t = |\langle M, H' \rangle|$.
2. *Compute* $a = median\{a_t\}$.
3. *Repeat* $O(\log(nm))$ *times, independently and in parallel:*
   (a) *Generate uniform pairwise independent vector* $H \in \{0,1\}^n$.
   (b) *Using the AMS algorithm*[a], *compute* 5/4-*approximations of second moments:* $X' = F_2(D_H)$ *and* $Y' = F_2(D_{(1-H)})$ *with negligible probability of error.*
   (c) *If* $X' < (20)^4 Y'$ *and* $Y' < (20)^4 X'$ *then output* 0 *and terminate the algorithm.*
4. *In parallel, apply the algorithm for the residual moment from Fact 5.4. Let* b *be the output of the algorithm.*
5. *If* $(1-4\epsilon)G(a+b) > G(a)$ *or* $G(a) > (1+4\epsilon)G(a-b)$ *then output* 0.
6. *Otherwise output* $G(a)$.

[a]The sketching algorithm for F_2 approximation from [2].

LEMMA 5.8. *Algorithm Compute-Hybrid-Major solves Hybrid-Major*(D, ϵ) *with negligible probability of error.*

PROOF. First, we show that if there is no $(F_2, 2)$-major entry, then the output is 0 except with negligible probability. Consider a single iteration of the main loop of the algorithm. Consider a vector M' with entries m_i^2 and denote $X = \langle M', H \rangle, Y = |M'| - \langle M', H \rangle$. By the properties of the AMS algorithm, with negligible probability of error, X' is 5/4-approximation of X and Y' is 5/4-approximation of Y. By Lemma 5.2, this implies that w.p. at most to $0.5 + o(1)$:

$$X' \le \frac{5}{4} X \le \frac{5}{2} (10)^4 Y < (20)^4 Y', \quad Y' < (20)^4 X'.$$

Thus, except with negligible probability, the algorithm will output 0.
Assume that there is a $(F_2, 2)$-major entry m_i. Then by Lemma 5.3 and by Chernoff bound, $|m_i - a| \le 2(F_2(M(D)))^{0.5}$ except with negligible probability. From Fact 5.4 it follows that $2(F_2^{res}(M(D)))^{0.5} < b < 3(F_2^{res}(M(D)))^{0.5}$ except with negligible probability. Thus, by Fact 5.6 it follows that if the algorithm outputs $G(a)$ then $G(a)$ is $(1 \pm 4\epsilon)$-approximation of $G(m_i)$. Thus, the first condition of Hybrid-Major follows.
Finally, assume that $\pi_\epsilon(m_i) \ge (20)^5 (F_2^{res}(M(D)))^{0.5}$. Definition 1.3 implies that $m_i \ge \pi_\epsilon(m_i)$ and thus m_i is $(F_2, 10^5)$-major w.r.t. M. Thus, by Lemma 5.2, we have (except with negligible probability): $X' > 20^4 Y'$ or $Y' > 20^4 X'$. Thus, except with negligible probability, the algorithm will not terminate before the last line. Also, $|m_i - a| \le 2F_2^{res}(M) < 0.01\pi_\epsilon(m_i)$, and $b \le 3F_2^{res}(M) < 0.01\pi_\epsilon(m_i)$. Thus, by Fact 5.5 the algorithm will output $G(a)$ which is a $(1 \pm 4\epsilon)$-approximation of $G(m_i)$. Thus, the second condition of Hybrid-Major follows. □

Lemma 5.10 states that for any $(G, 1)$-major entry of the vector $M(D)$, the square of its local jump π_ϵ is "heavy" with respect to $F_2^{res}(M)$ (at least after deleting a small number of entries). First, we need to establish the following simple corollary of tractability.

FACT 5.9. *If* G *is tractable then*

$$\exists N_1 \forall N > N_1 \in \mathbb{N}^+ : G(N) \le N^3. \tag{9}$$

PROOF. Indeed, if (9) does not hold then G cannot be tractable. In particular, there is an arbitrary large N such that $G(N) > N^3$ and thus $N^2 < \log^{-t}(NG(N))G(N)$ for any $t = O(1)$. By Definition 1.4, G is not tractable (for $k = 0$, arbitrary large t and $x = N, y = 1$). □

LEMMA 5.10. *Let* G *be a non-decreasing tractable function. Then for any* $k = O(1)$ *there exists* $t = O(1)$ *such that for any* n, m *and for any* $\epsilon > \log^{-k}(nm)$ *the following is true. Let* $D = D(n, m)$ *be a stream that defines frequency vector* $M = M(D)$. *If there exists a* $(G, 1)$-*major element* m_i *w.r.t.* M, *then there exists set* $S \subseteq [n]$ *such that* $|S| = O(\log(m))$ *and:*

$$(\pi_\epsilon(m_i))^2 = \Omega(\log^{-t}(nm) \sum_{j \notin S \cup \{i\}} m_j^2).$$

PROOF. W.l.o.g., assume that m_1 is the $(G, 1)$-major entry. Consider layers $S_s = \{j \in [n] : 2^s \le m_j < 2^{s+1}\}$ for $s = 0, 1, \ldots$. Let N_0 be the constant from Definition 1.4; and N_1 be the constant from Fact 9 (i.e., $G(x) \le x^3$ for $x > N_1$). Let $W = \{s : |S_s| \le N_0 + N_1\}$ and let $S = \cup_{s \in W} S_k$. Note that $m_i \le m$ for all $i \in [n]$; thus there are at most $\lceil \log(m) \rceil$ non-empty layers. Thus $|S| = O(\log(m))$, i.e., S satisfies the condition of the lemma.
Consider $X = \sum_{j \ne i, j \notin S} m_j^2$. If $X = 0$ then the lemma follows. Otherwise there exists at least one layer $S_l, l \notin W$ such that $\sum_{j \in S_l} m_j^2 \ge \frac{1}{\lceil \log(m) \rceil} X$. Since m_1 is $(G, 1)$-major w.r.t. M and by monotonicity of G, it follows that $G(m_1) \ge \sum_{j>1} G(m_j) \ge |S_l| G(2^l)$. Since $l \notin W$ we have that $|S_l| > N_0$; thus $\frac{G(m_1)}{G(2^l)} \ge |S_l| > N_0$. Since G is tractable, by Definition 1.4 of tractable functions there exists $t = t(k) = O(1)$ such that: $\left(\frac{\pi_\epsilon(m_1)}{2^l}\right)^2 \ge \frac{1}{\log^t(\left(\frac{G(m_1)}{G(2^l)}\right))} \left(\frac{G(m_1)}{G(2^l)}\right)$. Also, since $G(m_1) \ge |S_l| > N_1$ we conclude that $G(m_1) \le m_1^3 \le m^3$; thus $\log^t(\frac{G(m_1)}{G(2^l)}) \le (3\log(m))^t$. Thus, we summarize: $\left(\frac{\pi_\epsilon(m_1)}{2^l}\right)^2 \ge \frac{1}{(3\log(m))^t} |S^l|$; and finally:

$$(\pi_\epsilon(m_i))^2 \ge \frac{1}{(3\log(m))^t} 2^{2l} |S_l| \ge \frac{1}{(12\log(nm))^{t+1}} X.$$

□

Consider the following algorithm that solves G-Core.

> ALGORITHM 5.11. Compute-G-Core(D, ϵ, p)
>
> 1. *Generate a pairwise independent hash function* $H : [n] \mapsto \tau$, *where* $\tau = O^*(\frac{1}{p\epsilon})$.
> 2. *For each* $k \in [\tau]$ *compute in parallel* c_i = *Compute-Hybrid-Major*($D_{H_k}, 0.25\epsilon$), *where* $H_k(i) = \mathbf{1}_{H(i)=k}$.
> 3. *Output* $S = \{G(c_i) : c_i > 0\}$.

Finally, let us state the following claims which are a generalization of the arguments from [33] and can be seen as a variant of Lemmas 5.3 and 5.5 from our other paper [13]. (It is important to note, however, that while these results have similarities with the lemmas from [13], they are different. In this paper we consider frequency vectors, where in [13] we work with implicit tensors). We refer the reader to the full version [10] for details.

THEOREM 5.12. *Algorithm Compute-G-Core solves G-Core*(D, ϵ) *and errs w.p. asymptotically equal to p. Compute-G-Core uses* $O^*(1)$ *memory bits if* $p = \Omega^*(1)$ *and* $\epsilon = \Omega^*(1)$.

PROOF. First, except with negligible probability, every positive c_i is $(1 \pm \epsilon)$-approximation of some distinct entry $G(m_j)$. Second, assume that there exists a $(G, 1)$-dominant entry m_i. Denote $X = \sum_{j \neq i} v_i^2 \mathbf{1}_{H(j)=H(i)}$. By pairwise independence of H, we have $E(X) = \frac{1}{\tau}(F_2(M) - m_i^2)$. By Lemma 5.10 there exists a set S such that $|S| = O^*(1)$ and:

$$\pi_\epsilon(m_i)^2 = \Omega^*(\sum_{j \notin S} m_j^2). \quad (10)$$

Let $\mathcal{A}$ be an event that $\pi_\epsilon(m_i)^2 > (20)^5 X$ and $H(j) \neq H(i)$ for any $j \in S$. By Markov inequality, by pairwise independence of H and by (10), there exists $\tau = \Omega^*(\frac{1}{p})$ such that: $P(\mathcal{A}) \geq (1 - p)$. If $\mathcal{A}$ occurs, then by Lemma 5.8 $c_{H(i)}$ is $(1 \pm \epsilon)$-approximation of $G(m_i)$ except with negligible probability. Thus, the final probability of error is approximately equal to p.

Algorithm Compute-G-Core can be seen as a computational tree of a constant depth (after substituting the auxiliary algorithms). Each internal node in the tree has a polylogarithmic number of children. Each leaf is either a direct computation on a stream that requires polylog space or AMS algorithm for F_2 that also requires polylog space. Thus, the total space is polylogarithmic. In fact, for any $k = O(1)$ there exists $t = t(k) = O(1)$ such that we can solve G-Core($D(n, m), \epsilon$), where $\epsilon \geq \log^{-k}(nm)$ with $O(\log^{-t}(nm))$ space. □

THEOREM 5.13. *If there exists an algorithm that solves G-Core using memory* $O^*(1)$ *and a single pass over D with probability of error* $\Omega^*(1)$, *then there exists an algorithm that solves G-sum using memory* $O^*(1)$ *and a single pass over D with probability of error bounded at most* $1/3$.

5.3 Proof of the Main Theorem 1.5

PROOF. Theorem 3.2 proves that tractability is necessary. The sufficient condition, i.e., the existence of an algorithm that solves G-Sum for tractable G, follows from Theorem 5.13 and Theorem 5.12. □

6. ACKNOWLEDGEMENT

We thank Piotr Indyk for a helpful discussion and for pointing out Question 5 in [40].

7. REFERENCES

[1] C. C. Aggarwal. *Data Streams: Models and Algorithms (Advances in Database Systems)*. Springer-Verlag New York, Inc., Secaucus, NJ, USA, 2006.

[2] N. Alon, Y. Matias, and M. Szegedy. The space complexity of approximating the frequency moments. *J. Comput. Syst. Sci.*, 58(1):137–147, 1999.

[3] Z. Bar-Yossef, T. S. Jayram, R. Kumar, and D. Sivakumar. An information statistics approach to data stream and communication complexity. *J. Comput. Syst. Sci.*, 68(4):702–732, 2004.

[4] Z. Bar-Yossef, T. S. Jayram, R. Kumar, D. Sivakumar, and L. Trevisan. Counting distinct elements in a data stream. In *RANDOM '02: Proceedings of the 6th International Workshop on Randomization and Approximation Techniques*, pages 1–10, London, UK, 2002. Springer-Verlag.

[5] P. Beame, T. S. Jayram, and A. Rudra. Lower bounds for randomized read/write stream algorithms. In *STOC '07: Proceedings of the thirty-ninth annual ACM symposium on Theory of computing*, pages 689–698, New York, NY, USA, 2007. ACM.

[6] L. Bhuvanagiri and S. Ganguly. Estimating entropy over data streams. In *ESA'06: Proceedings of the 14th conference on Annual European Symposium*, pages 148–159, London, UK, 2006. Springer-Verlag.

[7] L. Bhuvanagiri, S. Ganguly, D. Kesh, and C. Saha. Simpler algorithm for estimating frequency moments of data streams. In *SODA*, pages 708–713, 2006.

[8] V. Braverman, K.-M. Chung, Z. Liu, M. Mitzenmacher, R. Ostrovsky, "AMS Without **4**-Wise Independence on Product Domains," STACS 2010.

[9] V. Braverman, R. Ostrovsky, "Effective Computations on Sliding Windows," SIAM J. Comput. Volume 39, Issue 6, pp. 2113-2131 (2010).

[10] V. Braverman, R. Ostrovsky, "Zero-One Frequency Laws," ArXiv, 2010.

[11] V. Braverman, R. Ostrovsky, "Smooth Histograms for Sliding Windows," In Proceedings of the 48th Annual IEEE Symposium on Foundations of Computer Science (October 21 - 23, 2007).

[12] V. Braverman, R. Ostrovsky, C. Zaniolo, "Optimal sampling from sliding windows," In Proceedings of the Twenty-Eighth ACM SIGMOD-SIGACT-SIGART Symposium on Principles of Database Systems (Providence, Rhode Island, USA, June 29 - July 01, 2009).

[13] V. Braverman, R. Ostrovsky, "Measuring Independence of Datasets," STOC 2010.

[14] A. Chakrabarti, K. D. Ba, and S. Muthukrishnan. Estimating entropy and entropy norm on data streams. In *In Proceedings of the 23rd International Symposium on Theoretical Aspects of Computer Science STACS 2006*. Springer, 2006.

[15] A. Chakrabarti, G. Cormode, and A. McGregor. A near-optimal algorithm for computing the entropy of a stream. In *SODA '07: Proceedings of the eighteenth*

annual ACM-SIAM symposium on Discrete algorithms, pages 328–335, Philadelphia, PA, USA, 2007. Society for Industrial and Applied Mathematics.

[16] A. Chakrabarti, G. Cormode, and A. McGregor. Robust lower bounds for communication and stream computation. In *STOC '08: Proceedings of the 40th annual ACM symposium on Theory of computing*, pages 641–650, New York, NY, USA, 2008. ACM.

[17] A. Chakrabarti, S. Khot, and X. Sun. Near-optimal lower bounds on the multi-party communication complexity of set disjointness. In *IEEE Conference on Computational Complexity*, pages 107–117, 2003.

[18] M. Charikar, K. Chen, and M. Farach-Colton. Finding frequent items in data streams. In *ICALP '02: Proceedings of the 29th International Colloquium on Automata, Languages and Programming*, pages 693–703, London, UK, 2002. Springer-Verlag.

[19] D. Coppersmith and R. Kumar. An improved data stream algorithm for frequency moments. In *SODA*, pages 151–156, 2004.

[20] G. Cormode, M. Datar, P. Indyk, and S. Muthukrishnan. Comparing data streams using hamming norms (how to zero in). *IEEE Trans. on Knowl. and Data Eng.*, 15(3):529–540, 2003.

[21] G. Cormode and M. Hadjieleftheriou. Finding frequent items in data streams. *Proc. VLDB Endow.*, 1(2):1530–1541, 2008.

[22] G. Cormode and S. Muthukrishnan. An improved data stream summary: the count-min sketch and its applications. *J. Algorithms*, 55(1):58–75, 2005.

[23] J. Feigenbaum, S. Kannan, M. Strauss, and M. Viswanathan. An approximate l1-difference algorithm for massive data streams. In *FOCS '99: Proceedings of the 40th Annual Symposium on Foundations of Computer Science*, page 501, Washington, DC, USA, 1999. IEEE Computer Society.

[24] P. Flajolet and G. N. Martin. Probabilistic counting algorithms for data base applications. *J. Comput. Syst. Sci.*, 31(2):182–209, 1985.

[25] S. Ganguly. Estimating frequency moments of data streams using random linear combinations. In *APPROX-RANDOM*, pages 369–380, 2004.

[26] S. Ganguly and G. Cormode. On estimating frequency moments of data streams. In *APPROX '07/RANDOM '07: Proceedings of the 10th International Workshop on Approximation and the 11th International Workshop on Randomization, and Combinatorial Optimization. Algorithms and Techniques*, pages 479–493, Berlin, Heidelberg, 2007. Springer-Verlag.

[27] S. Guha, P. Indyk, and A. McGregor. Sketching information divergences. *Mach. Learn.*, 72(1-2):5–19, 2008.

[28] S. Guha, A. McGregor, and S. Venkatasubramanian. Streaming and sublinear approximation of entropy and information distances. In *SODA '06: Proceedings of the seventeenth annual ACM-SIAM symposium on Discrete algorithm*, pages 733–742, New York, NY, USA, 2006. ACM.

[29] N. J. A. Harvey, J. Nelson, and K. Onak. Sketching and streaming entropy via approximation theory. In *FOCS '08: Proceedings of the 2008 49th Annual IEEE Symposium on Foundations of Computer Science*, pages 489–498, Washington, DC, USA, 2008. IEEE Computer Society.

[30] P. Indyk. Stable distributions, pseudorandom generators, embeddings, and data stream computation. *J. ACM*, 53(3):307–323, 2006.

[31] P. Indyk and A. McGregor. Declaring independence via the sketching of sketches. In *SODA '08: Proceedings of the nineteenth annual ACM-SIAM symposium on Discrete algorithms*, pages 737–745, Philadelphia, PA, USA, 2008. Society for Industrial and Applied Mathematics.

[32] P. Indyk and D. Woodruff. Tight lower bounds for the distinct elements problem. In *FOCS '03: Proceedings of the 44th Annual IEEE Symposium on Foundations of Computer Science*, page 283, Washington, DC, USA, 2003. IEEE Computer Society.

[33] P. Indyk and D. Woodruff. Optimal approximations of the frequency moments of data streams. In *STOC '05: Proceedings of the thirty-seventh annual ACM symposium on Theory of computing*, pages 202–208, New York, NY, USA, 2005. ACM.

[34] T. S. Jayram, A. McGregor, S. Muthukrishnan, and E. Vee. Estimating statistical aggregates on probabilistic data streams. In *PODS '07: Proceedings of the twenty-sixth ACM SIGMOD-SIGACT-SIGART symposium on Principles of database systems*, pages 243–252, New York, NY, USA, 2007. ACM.

[35] D. M. Kane, J. Nelson, and D. P. Woodruff. On the exact space complexity of sketching and streaming small norms. In *Proceedings of the 21st Annual ACM-SIAM Symposium on Discrete Algorithms (SODA 2010)*, 2010.

[36] D. M. Kane, J. Nelson, and D. P. Woodruff. An Optimal Algorithm for the Distinct Elements Problem. *PODS 2010*, 2010.

[37] E. Kushilevitz and N. Nisan. *Communication complexity*. Cambridge University Press, New York, NY, USA, 1997.

[38] A. Lall, V. Sekar, M. Ogihara, J. Xu, and H. Zhang. Data streaming algorithms for estimating entropy of network traffic. *SIGMETRICS Perform. Eval. Rev.*, 34(1):145–156, 2006.

[39] P. Li. Compressed counting. In *SODA '09: Proceedings of the Nineteenth Annual ACM -SIAM Symposium on Discrete Algorithms*, pages 412–421, Philadelphia, PA, USA, 2009. Society for Industrial and Applied Mathematics.

[40] A. McGregor. Open problems in data streams and related topics. In *IITK workshop on algorithms for data streams. http://www.cse.iitk.ac.in/users/sganguly/data-stream-probs.pdf, 2007.*, 2006.

[41] S. Muthukrishnan. Data streams: algorithms and applications. *Found. Trends Theor. Comput. Sci.*, 1(2):117–236, 2005.

[42] N. Nisan. Pseudorandom generators for space-bounded computations. In *STOC '90: Proceedings of the twenty-second annual ACM symposium on Theory of computing*, pages 204–212, 1990.

[43] D. Woodruff. Optimal space lower bounds for all frequency moments. In *SODA '04: Proceedings of the fifteenth annual ACM-SIAM symposium on Discrete algorithms*, pages 167–175, 2004.

Improved Algorithms for Computing Fisher's Market Clearing Prices

James B. Orlin*
MIT Sloan School of Management
Cambridge, MA 02139
jorlin@mit.edu

ABSTRACT

We give the first strongly polynomial time algorithm for computing an equilibrium for the linear utilities case of Fisher's market model. We consider a problem with a set B of buyers and a set G of divisible goods. Each buyer i starts with an initial integral allocation e_i of money. The integral utility for buyer i of good j is U_{ij}. We first develop a weakly polynomial time algorithm that runs in $O(n^4 \log U_{max} + n^3 e_{max})$ time, where $n = |B| + |G|$. We further modify the algorithm so that it runs in $O(n^4 \log n)$ time. These algorithms improve upon the previous best running time of $O(n^8 \log U_{max} + n^7 \log e_{max})$, due to Devanur et al. [5].

Categories and Subject Descriptors

F.2 [**Theory of Computation**]: Analysis of Algorithms and Problem Complexity

General Terms

Algorithms, Economics

Keywords

Market Equilibrium, Strongly Polynomial

1. INTRODUCTION

In 1891, Irving Fisher (see [3]) proposed a simple model of an economic market in which a set B of buyers with specified amounts of money were to purchase a collection G of diverse goods. In this model, each buyer i starts with an initial allocation e_i of money, and has a utility U_{ij} for purchasing all of good j. The utility received is assumed to be proportional to the fraction of the good purchased.

In 1954, Arrow and Debreu [2] provided a proof that a wide range of economic markets (including Fisher's model) have unique market clearing prices, that is, prices at which the total supply is equal to the total demand. However, their proof relied on Kakutani's fixed point theorem, and did not efficiently construct the market clearing prices. Eisenberg and Gale [8] transformed the problem of computing the Fisher market equilibrium into a concave cost maximization problem. They deserve credit for the first polynomial time algorithm because their concave maximization problem is solvable in polynomial time using the ellipsoid algorithm.

Devanur et al [5] gave the first combinatorial polynomial time algorithm for computing the exact market clearing prices under the assumption that utilities for goods are linear. For a problem with a total of n buyers and goods, their algorithm runs in $O(n^8 \log U_{max} + n^7 \log e_{max})$ time, where U_{max} is the largest utility and e_{max} is the largest initial amount of money of a buyer, and where all data are assumed to be integral. More precisely, it determines the market clearing prices as a sequence of $O(n^5 \log U_{max} + n^4 \log e_{max})$ maximum flow problems. (For details on solution techniques for maximum flows, see Ahuja et al. [1]).

Here we provide an algorithm that computes a market equilibrium in $O(n^4 \log U_{max} + n^3 \log e_{max})$ time. We also show how to modify the algorithm so that the running time is $O(n^4 \log n)$, resulting in the first strongly polynomial time algorithm for computing market clearing prices for the Fisher linear case.

The running time can be further improved to $O((n^2 \log n)(m+n \log n))$, where m is the number of pairs (i, j) for which $U_{ij} > 0$. Moreover, the algorithm can be used to provide an ϵ-approximate solution in $O((n \log 1/\epsilon)(m + n \log n))$ time, which is comparable to the running time of the algorithm by Garg and Kapoor [10] while using a stricter definition of ϵ-approximation.

1.1 A Formal Description of the Model

Suppose that p is a vector of prices, where p_j is the price of good j. Suppose that x is an allocation of money to goods; that is, x_{ij} is the amount of money that buyer i spends on good j. The *surplus cash* of buyer i is $c_i(x) = e_i - \sum_{j \in G} x_{ij}$. The *backorder amount* of good j is $b_j(p, x) = -p_j + \sum_{i \in B} x_{ij}$.

We assume that for each buyer i, there is a good j such that $U_{ij} > 0$. Otherwise, we would eliminate the buyer from the problem. Similarly, for each good j, we assume that there is a buyer i with $U_{ij} > 0$. Otherwise, we would eliminate the good from the problem.

For a given price vector p, the ratio U_{ij}/p_j is called the *bang-per-buck* of (i, j) with respect to p. For all $i \in B$, we let $\alpha_i(p) = \max\{U_{ij}/p_j : j \in G\}$, and refer to this ratio as

*Research supported in part by ONR grant N00014-05-1-0165.

STOC'10, June 5–8, 2010, Cambridge, Massachusetts, USA.

the *maximum bang-per-buck* for buyer i. A pair (i, j) is said to be an *equality edge* with respect to p if $U_{ij}/p_j = \alpha_i(p)$. We let $E(p)$ denote the set of equality edges.

A solution refers to any pair (p, x) of prices and allocations. We say that the solution is *optimal* if the following constraints are all satisfied:

i. *Cash constraints*: For each $i \in B$, $c_i(x) = 0$.

ii. *Allocation of goods constraints*: For each good $j \in G$, $b_j(p, x) = 0$.

iii. *Bang-per-buck constraints*: For all $i \in B$ and $j \in G$, if $x_{ij} > 0$, then $(i, j) \in E(p)$.

iv. *Non-negativity constraints*: $x_{ij} \geq 0, p_j \geq 0$ for all $i \in B$ and $j \in G$.

The above optimality conditions are the market equilibrium conditions specified by Fisher, as well as the optimality conditions for the Eisenberg-Gale program [8].

1.2 Other Algorithmic Results

The computation of market clearing prices is an important aspect of general equilibrium theory. Nevertheless, as pointed out in [5], there have been few results concerning the computation of market equilibrium. We refer the reader to [5] for these references. Papers that are particular relevant to this paper include papers by Garg and Karpur [10], Ghiyasvand and Orlin [11], and Vazirani [14]. Garg and Kapoor present a fully polynomial time approximation scheme (FPTAS) for computing approximate market clearing prices for the Fisher linear case as well as other cases. Ghiyasvand and Orlin develop a faster FPTAS while using a stronger (less relaxed) definition of approximate market equilibrium. Vazirani develops a weakly polynomial time algorithm for a generalization of the Fisher linear case in which utilities are piecewise linear functions of the amounts spent, and in which there is a utility of saving money. This more general utility function permits the modeling of several types of constraints, including upper bounds on the amount spent by buyer i in the purchase of good j.

1.3 Contributions of this Paper

The primary contributions of this paper are a strongly polynomial time algorithm for computing the market clearing prices, as well as a simple and efficient weakly polynomial time algorithm. Additional contributions of this paper include the following:

i. An algorithm for obtaining an ϵ-approximate solution that is comparable to the running time of the algorithm of Garg and Kapoor [10], while simultaneously having a stricter definition of ϵ-approximation.

ii. Our weakly polynomial and strongly polynomial time algorithms terminate after an optimal set of edges is identified, which may be much sooner than the termination criterion given by Devanur et al. [5].

1.4 Overview of the Weakly Polynomial Time Algorithm

The algorithm first determines an initial vector p^0 of prices (as described in Section 3.1). During the algorithm, prices are modified in a piecewise linear manner (as per Devanur et al. [5]) so that prices are always non-decreasing. The algorithm relies on a parameter Δ, called the *scaling parameter*. We say that a solution (p, x) is Δ*-feasible* if it satisfies the following conditions:

i. $\forall i \in B, c_i(x) \geq 0$;

ii. $\forall j \in G$, if $p_j > p_j^0$, then $0 \leq b_j(p, x) \leq \Delta$;

iii. $\forall i \in B$ and $\forall j \in G$, if $x_{ij} > 0$, then $(i, j) \in E(p)$, and x_{ij} is a multiple of Δ;

iv. $\forall i \in B$ and $\forall j \in G, x_{ij} \geq 0$ and $p_j \geq 0$.

We say that a solution (p, x) is Δ*-optimal* if it is Δ-feasible and if in addition

v. $\forall i \in B$, $c_i(x) < \Delta$.

The Δ-feasibility conditions modify the optimality conditions as follows: buyers may spend less than their initial allocation of money; it is possible for none of good j to be allocated if $p_j = p_j^0$; more than 100% of a good may be sold; and allocations are required to be multiples of Δ.

Our algorithm is a "scaling algorithm" as per Edmonds and Karp [7]. It initially creates a Δ-feasible solution for $\Delta = e_{max}$. It then runs a sequence of scaling phases. The input for the Δ-scaling phase is a Δ-feasible solution (p, x). The Δ-scaling phase transforms (p, x) into a Δ-optimal solution (p', x') via a procedure PriceAndAugment, which is called iteratively. The algorithm then transforms (p', x') into a $\Delta/2$-feasible solution. Then Δ is replaced by $\Delta/2$, and the algorithm goes to the next scaling phase. One can show that within $O(n \log U_{max} + e_{max})$ scaling phases, when the scaling parameter is less than $8n^{-2}(U_{max})^{-n}$, the algorithm determines an optimal solution.

1.5 Overview of the Strongly Polynomial Time Algorithm

If $x_{ij} \geq 3n\Delta$ at the beginning of the Δ-scaling phase, then $x'_{ij} \geq 3n(\Delta/2)$ for the solution x' at the beginning of the $\Delta/2$-scaling phase. We refer to edges (i, j) with $x_{ij} \geq 3n\Delta$ as "abundant." Once an edge becomes abundant, it remains abundant, and it is guaranteed to be positive in the optimal solution to which the scaling algorithm converges.

If a solution is "Δ-fertile" (as described in Section 4) at the end of the Δ-scaling phase, then there will be a new abundant edge within the next $O(\log n)$ scaling phases. If the solution (p, x) is not Δ-fertile, then the algorithm calls a special procedure that transforms (p, x) into a new solution (p', x') that is Δ'-fertile and Δ'-feasible for some $\Delta' \leq \Delta/n^2$. Since there are at most n abundant edges, the number of scaling phases is $O(n \log n)$ over all iterations.

2. PRELIMINARIES

We next state how to perturb the data so as to guarantee a unique optimal allocation. We then establish some results concerning feasible and optimal solutions.

For a feasible price vector p, it is possible that the set $E(p)$ of equality edges has cycles. If p is the optimal vector of prices, this leads to the possibility of multiple optimal solutions.

Here we perturb the utilities as follows: for all pairs i, j such that $U_{ij} > 0$, we replace U_{ij} by $U_{ij} + \epsilon^{in} + \epsilon^j$, where

ϵ is chosen arbitrarily close to 0. One can use lexicography to simulate perturbations without any increase in worst case running time. The advantage of perturbations is that it ensures that the set of equality edges is always cycle-free. Henceforth, we assume that the utilities have been perturbed, and the algorithm uses lexicography.

If E is the equality graph prior to perturbations, and if E' is the equality graph after perturbations, then E' is the maximum weight forest of E obtained by assigning edge (i, j) a weight of $in + j$. (This can be seen if one observes that (i, j) is an equality edge if $\log U_{ij} - \log p_j = \log \alpha_i$).

In the case that prices are changed and more than one edge is eligible to become an equality edge (prior to the perturbation), then the algorithm will select the edge with maximum weight for the perturbed problem. Henceforth, we assume that the utilities are perturbed, and we implement the algorithms using weights as a tie-breaking rule.

Suppose that $H \subseteq B \times G$. If H is cycle free, then the vector *BasicSolution*(H) is the unique vector p satisfying the following:

i. If $(i, j) \in H$ and if $(i, k) \in H$, then $U_{ij}/p_j = U_{ik}/p_k$.

ii. For each connected component C of H, $\sum_{i \in C} e_i = \sum_{j \in C} p_j$.

iii. If $(i, j) \notin H$, then $x_{ij} = 0$.

iv. For all $i \in B$, $\sum_{j \in G} x_{ij} = e_i$.

v. For all $j \in G$, $\sum_{i \in B} x_{ij} = p_j$.

The first two sets of constraints uniquely determine the vector p. The latter three sets of constraints uniquely determine the allocation vector x. The following lemma implies that an optimal solution can be obtained from its optimal set of edges.

LEMMA 1. *Suppose that (p^*, x^*) is the optimal solution for the Fisher Model. Let $H^* = \{(i, j) : x^*_{ij} > 0\}$. Then BasicSolution$(H^*) = (p^*, x^*)$. Moreover, if $x^*_{ij} > 0$, then $x^*_{ij} > e_{min}/D$, where $D = n(U_{max})^n$.*

PROOF. We first observe that H^* is cycle free because the perturbation ensures that there is a unique optimal solution. Suppose that $(\hat{p}, \hat{x}) = \text{BasicSolution}(H^*)$. The optimal price vector satisfies the $|B|$ constraints given in the first two sets of constraints for BasicSolution(H^*). Since these constraints are linearly independent, $p^* = \hat{p}$.

We next consider the remaining three sets of constraints that determines $\hat{x}$. For each component C of H^*, there are $|C|$ variables and $|C| + 1$ constraints, one of which is redundant because the sum of the moneys equals the sum of the prices. These constraints are all satisfied by x^*. Since there are $|H^*|$ variables that are not required to be 0, and there are $|H^*|$ linearly independent constraints, it follows that $x^* = \hat{x}$.

Any solution satisfying the above systems of equations is a rational number with denominator less than D by Cramer's rule. Moreover, if $j \in G$ is in component C, then the numerator of the rational number representing p_j is a multiple of $\sum_{i \in B} e_i$, which is at least e_{min}. □

In the following, the use of a set as a subscript indicates summation. For example, $e_S = \sum_{i \in S} e_i$. The following lemma is elementary and is stated without proof.

LEMMA 2. *Suppose that (p, x) is any solution and that $B' \subseteq B$, and $G' \subseteq G$. Then*
$e_{B'} - p_{G'} = c_{B'}(x) + b_{G'}(p, x)$.

3. THE SCALING ALGORITHM

3.1 The Initial Solution

We initialize as follows. Let $\Delta^0 = e_{max}/n$; $\forall i \in B$, let $U_{iG} = \sum_{j \in G} U_{ij}$; $\forall i \in B$ and $\forall j \in G$, let $\rho_{ij} = U_{ij} e_i / n U_{iG}$; $\forall j \in G$, let $p^0_j = \max\ \{\rho_{ij} : i \in B\}$; $\forall i \in B$ and $\forall j \in G$, $x^0_{ij} = 0$.

We note that the initial solution (p^0, x^0) is Δ^0-feasible. Moreover, it is easily transformed into a feasible solution by setting $x_{ij} = p_j$ for some i with $(i, j) \in E(p^0)$.

3.2 The Residual Network and Price Changes

Suppose that (p, x) is a Δ-feasible solution at some iteration during the Δ-scaling phase. We define the residual network $N(p, x)$ as follows: the node set is $B \cup G$. For each equality edge (i, j), there is an arc $(i, j) \in N(p, x)$. We refer to these arcs as the *forward arcs* of $N(p, x)$. For every (i, j) with $x_{ij} > 0$, there is an arc $(j, i) \in N(p, x)$. We refer to these arcs as the *backward arcs* of $N(p, x)$.

Let r be a *root node* of the residual network $N(p, x)$. The algorithm will select $r \in B$ with $c_r(x) \geq \Delta$. We let ActiveSet(p, x, r) be the set of nodes $k \in B \cup G$ such that there is a directed path in $N(p, x)$ from r to k; if $k \in$ ActiveSet(p, x, r), we say that k is *active* with respect to p, x and r.

As per price changes in [5], we will replace the price p_j of each active good j by $q \times p_j$ for some $q > 1$. This is accomplished by the following formula: $f(q) = \text{Price}(p, x, r, q)$, where

$$f_j(q) = \begin{cases} qp_j & \text{if } j \in \text{ActiveSet}(p, x, r) \\ p_j & \text{otherwise,} \end{cases}$$

and where q is below a certain threshold.

UpdatePrice(p, x, r) is the vector p' of prices obtained by setting $p' = \text{Price}(p, x, r, q')$, where q' is the maximum value of q such that (p', x) is Δ-feasible. At least one of two conditions will be satisfied by p': (i) there is an edge $(i, j) \in E(p') \backslash E(p)$, at which point node j becomes active; or (ii) there is an active node j with $b_j(p', x) \leq 0$. In the former case, PriceAndAugment will continue to update prices. In the latter case, it will carry out an "augmentation" from node r to node j. The following lemma is straightforward and is stated without proof.

LEMMA 3. *Suppose that (p, x) is Δ-feasible and p' is the vector of prices obtained by* Update-Price(p, x, r). *Then (p', x) is Δ-feasible.*

3.3 Augmenting Paths and Changes of Allocation

Suppose that (p, x) is a Δ-feasible solution. Any path $P \subseteq N(p, x)$ from a node in B to a node in G is called an *augmenting path*. A *Δ-augmentation* along the path P consists of replacing x by a vector x' where

$$x'_{ij} = \begin{cases} x_{ij} + \Delta & \text{if } (i, j) \in P \text{ is a forward arc of } N(p, x); \\ x_{ij} - \Delta & \text{if } (i, j) \in P \text{ is a backward arc of } N(p, x); \\ x_{ij} & \text{otherwise.} \end{cases}$$

LEMMA 4. *Suppose that (p, x) is Δ-feasible and that $c_r \geq \Delta$. Suppose further that P is an augmenting path from node r to a node $k \in G$ for which $b_j(p,x) \leq 0$. If x' is obtained by a Δ-augmentation along path P, then (p, x') is Δ-feasible. Moreover, $c_r(x') = c_r(x) - \Delta$, and $c_j(x') = c_j(x)$ for $j \neq r$.*

We present the procedures PriceAndAugment and ScalingAlgorithm next. We will establish their proof of correctness and running time in Subsection 3.4.

```
Algorithm 1. PriceAndAugment(p, x)
begin
    select a buyer r ∈ B with c_r(x) ≥ Δ;
    compute ActiveSet(p, x, r);
    until there is an active node j with b_j(p, x) ≤ 0 do
        replace p by UpdatePrice(p, x, r);
        recompute N(p, x), b(p, x), and ActiveSet(p, x, r);
    enduntil
    let P be a path in N(p, x) from r
        to an active node j with b_j(p, x) ≤ 0;
    replace x by carrying out a Δ-augmentation along P;
    recompute c(x) and b(p, x);
end
```

```
Algorithm 2. ScalingAlgorithm(e, U)
begin
    Δ := Δ^0; p := p^0; x := 0 (as per Section 3.1);
    ScalingPhase:
        while (p, x) is not Δ-optimal,
            replace (p, x) by PriceAndAugment(p, x);
        E' := {(i, j) : x_ij ≥ 4nΔ};
        if BasicSolution(E') is optimal, then quit;
        else continue;
        Δ := Δ/2;
        for each j ∈ G such that b_j(p, x) > Δ,
            decrease x_ij by Δ for some i ∈ B;
        return to ScalingPhase;
end
```

3.4 Running Time Analysis for each Scaling Phase and Proof of Correctness

Our bound on the number of calls of PriceAndAugment during a scaling phase will rely on a potential function argument. Let $\Phi(x, \Delta) = \sum_{i \in B} \lfloor c_i(x)/\Delta \rfloor$. We will show that $\Phi \leq n$ at the beginning of a scaling phase, $\Phi = 0$ at the end of a scaling phase, and each call of PriceAndAugment decreases Φ by exactly 1.

At the Δ-scaling phase, ScalingAlgorithm selects a buyer r with $c_r(x) \geq \Delta$. Ultimately it performs a Δ-augmentation. It continues the Δ-scaling phase until it obtains a Δ-optimal solution. Each Δ-augmentation reduces c_B by Δ. At the end of the scaling phase, ScalingAlgorithm does a check for optimality. If an optimal solution is not found, it divides Δ by 2, obtains a $\Delta/2$-optimal solution and goes to the next scaling phase.

THEOREM 1. *During the Δ-scaling phase,* ScalingAlgorithm *transforms a Δ-feasible solution into a Δ-optimal solution with at most n calls of* PriceAndAugment. *Each call of* PriceAndAugment *can be implemented to run in $O(m + n \log n)$ time. The number of scaling phases is $O(e_{max} + n \log U_{max})$; the algorithm runs in $O(n(m + n \log n)(e_{max} + n \log U_{max}))$ time.*

We will divide the proof of Theorem 1 into several parts. But first we deal with an important subtlety. We permit a good j in G to have no allocation if $p_j = p_j^0$. We need to establish that node j will receive some allocation eventually, and that $b_j(p, x) \geq 0$ at that time.

LEMMA 5. *Suppose that $\Delta < p_j^0/n$, and that that (p, x) is a Δ-feasible solution at the end of the Δ-scaling phase. Then $b_j(p, x) \geq 0$.*

PROOF. We prove the contrapositive of the lemma. Suppose that $b_j(p, x) < 0$. By Property (ii) of the definition of Δ-feasibility, $p_j = p_j^0$. Select node $i \in B$ such that $(i, j) \in E(p^0)$. We will show that $c_i(x) \geq \Delta$, which is a contradiction.

By construction, $p_j^0 \leq e_i/n$, and so $e_i/n \geq n\Delta$. Note that for each $k \in G$,

$$\frac{U_{ik}}{p_k} \leq \frac{U_{ik}}{p_k^0} \leq \frac{U_{ij}}{p_j^0} = \frac{U_{ij}}{p_j}.$$

Therefore, $(i, j) \in E(p)$. Let $K = \{k \in G : x_{ik} > 0\}$. Because $(i, k) \in E(p)$, the above inequalities hold with equality. Therefore, for each $k \in K$, $p_k = p_k^0$. Moreover, $p_k^0 \leq e_i/n$ for each $k \in K$, and $c_i(x) = e_i - \sum_{k \in K} x_{ik} \geq e_i - \sum_{k \in K}(p_k + \Delta) \geq e_i - |G|e_i/n - |G|\Delta = |B|e_i/n - |G|\Delta > \Delta$. □

We now return to the proof of Theorem 1.

Proof of correctness and number of calls of PriceAndAugment. By Lemma 3 and Lemma 4, if a solution is Δ-feasible at the beginning of a PriceAnd-Augment, then the sequence of solutions obtained during the procedure are all Δ-feasible.

We next bound the number of calls of PriceAndAugment during a scaling phase. Lemma 4 implies that each call of PriceAndAugment reduces Φ by exactly 1.

In the first scaling phase $c_i(x^0) \leq \Delta^0$ for all $i \in B$. Thus, $\Phi(x^0, \Delta^0) \leq |B| < n$.

Suppose next that Δ is a scaling parameter at any other scaling phase. Let (p, x) be the 2Δ-optimal solution at the end of the 2Δ-scaling phase. Thus $c_i(x) < 2\Delta$ for all $i \in B$. Therefore, $\Phi(x, \Delta) \leq |B|$. However, immediately after replacing 2Δ by Δ, the algorithm reduces by Δ the allocation to any good j with $b_j(p, x) > \Delta$. This transformation can increase Φ by as much as $|G|\Delta$. By Lemma 4, the number of calls of PriceAndAugment is at most $|B| + |G| = n$. □

Proof of time bound per phase. We next show how to implement PriceAndAugment in $O(m + |B| \log |B|)$ time. The time for identifying an augmenting path, and modifying the allocation x is $O(n)$. So, we need only consider the total time for UpdatePrice.

We cannot achieve the time bound if we store prices explicitly since the number of prices changes during PriceAndAugment is $O(|B|^2)$. So, we store prices implicitly. Suppose that p is the vector of prices that is the input for PriceAndAugment, and let p' be the vector of prices at some point during the execution of the procedure and prior to obtaining an augmenting path. Let r be the root node of PriceAndAugment, and choose v so that $(r, v) \in E(p)$. Rather than store the vector p' explicitly, we store the vector p, the price p'_v, and the vector $\alpha(p)$. In addition, for each active node k, we store γ_k, which is the price of node v at the iteration at which node k became active. If node $j \in G$ is not active with respect to p', then $p'_j = p_j$. If j is active then Then $p'_j = p_j \times p'_v/\gamma_j$.

An edge (i,j) has the possibility of becoming an equality edge at the next price update only if i is active and j is not active. Suppose that $(i,k) \in E(p)$. In such a case, (i,j) will become active when the updated price vector $\hat{p}$ satisfies $U_{ij}/\hat{p}_j = \alpha_i(\hat{p}) = \alpha_i(p)\gamma_i/\hat{p}_v$. Accordingly, if node $i \in B$ is active, and if node $j \in G$ is not active, then the price β_{ij} of node v at the iteration at which (i,j) becomes an equality edge is $\beta_{ij} = \gamma_i\alpha_i(p)p_j/U_{ij}$.

For all inactive nodes $j \in G$, we let $\beta_j = \min\ \{\beta_{ij} : i \text{ is active}\}$, and we store the β's in a Fibonacci heap, a data structure developed by Fredman and Tarjan [9]. The Fibonacci heap is a priority queue that supports "FindMin", "Insert", "Delete", and "Decrease Key". The FindMin and Decrease Key operations can each be implemented to run in $O(1)$ time in an amortized sense. The Delete and Insert operations each take $O(\log|B|)$ time when operating on $|B|$ elements.

We delete a node from the Fibonacci heap whenever the node becomes active. We carry out a Decrease Key whenever β_j is decreased for some j. This event may occur when node i becomes active and edge (i,j) is scanned, and β_{ij} is determined. Thus the number of steps needed to compute when edges become equality edges is $O(m+|B|\log|B|)$ during PriceAndAugment.

In addition, one needs to keep track of the price of v at the iteration at which b_j will equal 0. Suppose that node $i \in B$ is active. Let q' be the minimum value ≥ 1 such that $b_j(q'p,x) = 0 \bmod \Delta$. Thus $b_j = 0$ when the price of node v is $q'\gamma_j$. Accordingly, $\beta_j = q'\gamma_j$, and we store β_j in the same Fibonacci Heap as the inactive nodes of G. Thus the total time to determine all price updates is $O(m+|B|\log|B|)$. $\square$

3.5 Abundant Edges and Bounds on the Number of Scaling Phases

Before proving the bound on the number of phases given in Theorem 1, we introduce another concept and prove a lemma.

An edge (i,j) is called Δ-*abundant* if $x_{ij} \geq 3n\Delta$, where x is the allocation at the beginning of the Δ-scaling phase. (We could use $2n$ rather than $3n$ here, but $2n$ will not be sufficient for the strongly polynomial time algorithm.)

The concept of abundance was introduced by Orlin [12] for a strongly polynomial time algorithm for the minimum cost flow problem. (See also, [13] and Chapter 10 of Ahuja et al., [1].) The following lemma shows that once an edge (i,j) becomes abundant, it stays abundant at every successive iteration. (The reader may note that the following lemma suggests that it would be better to define "abundance" with a right hand side of 2Δ rather than 3Δ. However, a larger value is needed for the proof of Property (iv) of Lemma 13.)

LEMMA 6. *If edge (i,j) is abundant at the Δ-scaling phase, it is abundant at the $\Delta/2$-scaling phase, and at all subsequent scaling phases.*

PROOF. Let x' and x'' be the initial and final allocations during the Δ-scaling phase. If (i,j) is Δ-abundant, then $x''_{ij} \geq 3n\Delta - n\Delta = 2n\Delta = 4n(\Delta/2)$. If it is abundant at the $\Delta/2$-scaling phase, by induction it will be abundant at all subsequent scaling phases. $\square$

Proof of Theorem 1: the number of scaling phases. Suppose that (p^k, x^k) and Δ^k is the solution and scaling parameter at the beginning of the k-th scaling phase of the scaling algorithm. Because the change in any allocation and in any price is at most $n\Delta$ during the Δ-scaling phase, the sequences $\{p_k : k = 1,2,\ldots\}$ and $\{x_k : k = 1,2,\ldots\}$ both converge in the limit to the optimal solution (p^*, x^*).

Now suppose that $\Delta^k < D/8n$, where $D = (U_{max})^{-n}/n$. Let $E^k = \{(i,j) : x^k_{ij} > 4n\Delta^k\}$. We next claim that BasicSolution(E^k) is optimal. Consider edge (i,j). If $(i,j) \in E^k$, then (i,j) is Δ-abundant, and by Lemma 6, $x^*_{ij} > 0$. If $(i,j) \notin E^k$, then $x^*_{ij} < x^k_{ij} + 4n\Delta^k < 1/D$. By Lemma 1, $x^*_{ij} = 0$. We have thus shown that BasicSolution(E^k) is optimal. The number of scaling phases needed to ensure that $\Delta^k < 1/8nD$ is $O(\log e_{max} + n\log U_{max})$. $\square$

3.6 Finding Approximate Solutions

Suppose that $\epsilon > 0$. A solution (p,x) is said to be ϵ-*approximate* if it is Δ-optimal for $\Delta < \epsilon\sum_{j\in G} p_j$.

THEOREM 2. . ScalingAlgorithm *finds an ϵ-approximate solution after $O(\log(n/\epsilon))$ scaling phases. The running time is $O(n(m + n\log n)\log(n/\epsilon))$.*

PROOF. Recall that $\Delta^0 = e_{max}$. Within $O(\log(n/\epsilon))$ scaling phases, $\Delta < \epsilon\cdot e_{max}/2n$. Suppose (p,x) is the solution at the end of that phase, and let $k = \text{argmax}\{e_i : i \in B\}$. Then $c_i(x) < \Delta$ and so $\sum_{j\in G} p_j > e_i - c_i(x) > e_{max}/2 > n\Delta/\epsilon$. Therefore, $\Delta < \epsilon\sum_{j\in G} p_j$. $\square$

The above approach is the fastest method to determine an ϵ-approximate solution. Also, finding an approximate solution is quite practical. For example, if all initial endowments are in dollars and are bounded by $O(f(n))$ for some polynomial $f(\cdot)$, then ScalingAlgorithm determines a solution that is within 1 penny of optimal in $O(\log n)$ scaling phases.

3.7 A Simple Strongly Polynomial Time Algorithm if Utilities are Small

Devanur et al. [5] showed how to find an optimal solution in the case that $U_{ij} = 0$ or 1 for each (i,j). Here we provide a simple algorithm for finding an optimal solution if U_{ij} is polynomially bounded in n.

In the following, we assume that buyers have been reordered so that $e_i \geq e_{i+1}$ for all $i = 1$ to $|B| - 1$. We let Problem(j) be the market equilibrium problem as restricted to buyers 1 to j, and including all goods of G. In the following theorem, $M = 4n^2(U_{max})^n$. We also relax (iii) of the definition of Δ-feasibility. We do not require allocations in abundant edges (see Subsection 3.5) to be multiples of Δ.

THEOREM 3. *Suppose that $e_j > Me_{j+1}$, and that k is the next index after j for which $e_k > Me_{k+1}$. If one starts with an optimal solution for Problem(j), ScalingAlgorithm solves Problem(k) in $O(n(k-j)\log U_{max})$ scaling phases. By solving Problem(i) for each i such that $e_i > Me_{i+1}$, The total number of scaling phases to find an equilibrium is $O(n^2\log U_{max})$.*

PROOF. Suppose that (p', x') is the optimal solution for Problem(j). The algorithm solves Problem(k) starting with solution (p', x') and with scaling parameter $\Delta' = e_{j+1}$. We first show that this starting point is Δ'-feasible.

It is possible that allocations will not be a multiple of Δ'. However, if $x'_{il} > 0$ for some $i \leq j$, then by Lemma 1, $x'_{il} \geq e_j/D > 4ne_{j+1} = 4n\Delta'$. Thus (i,l) is abundant, and by Lemma 6, it remains abundant at all subsequent scaling phases.

We next bound the number of scaling phases for Problem(k). By Lemma 1, the optimum solution (p^*, x^*) for Problem(k) has the following property. If $x^*_{il} > 0$ for some $i \leq k$, then $x^*_{il} \geq e_k/D$. So, the algorithm will stop when the scaling parameter is less than $e_k/4nD$. Thus, the number of scaling phases is $O(\log 4nD(e_j/e_k)) = O(\log M^{k-j}) = O((k-j)(n) \log U_{max})$.

If we solve Problem(i) for each i such that $e_i > Me_{i+1}$, then the total number of scaling phases to find an equilibrium is $O(n^2 \log U_{max})$. □

4. A STRONGLY POLYNOMIAL TIME ALGORITHM

In this section, we develop a strongly polynomial time scaling algorithm, which we call StrongScaling. This algorithm is a variant of the scaling algorithm of Section 3. The number of scaling phases in StrongScaling is $O(n \log n)$, and the number of calls of PriceAndAugment is $O(n)$ at each phase. The total running time of the algorithm is $O((n^2 \log n)(m + n \log n))$.

4.1 Preliminaries

The algorithm StrongScaling relies on two new concepts: "surplus" of a subset of nodes and "fertile" price vectors. We also provide more details about abundant edges.

For the Δ-scaling phase, we let $A(\Delta)$ denote the set of Δ-abundant edges. We refer to each component in the graph defined by $A(\Delta)$ as a *Δ-component*. We let $\mathbf{C}(\Delta)$ denote the set of Δ-components.

Suppose that p is any price vector during the Δ-scaling phase. We let $N(p, \Delta)$ be the network in which the forward arcs are $E(p)$ and the backward arcs are the reversals of Δ-abundant edges. We refer to $N(p, \Delta)$ as the *Δ-residual network* with respect to p. We let $ActiveSet(p, \Delta, r)$ be the set of nodes reachable from r in the network $N(p, \Delta)$.

Suppose that $H \subseteq B \cup G$. We define the *surplus* of H with respect to a price vector p to be $s(p, H) = \sum_{i \in B \cap H} e_i - \sum_{j \in G \cap H} p_i$. Equivalently, $s(p, H) = e_H - p_H$.

Suppose that (p, x) is the solution at the beginning of the Δ-scaling phase. We say that a component H of $A(\Delta)$ is *Δ-fertile* if (i) H consists of a single node $i \in B$ and $e_i > \Delta/3n^2$, or if (ii) $s(p, H) \leq -\Delta/3n^2$. We say that the solution (p, x) is *Δ-fertile* if any of the components of $\mathbf{C}(\Delta)$ are Δ-fertile.

LEMMA 7. *Suppose that (p, x) is the solution obtained at the end of the Δ-scaling phase. For each fertile Δ-component, there will be a new abundant edge incident to H within $5 \log n + 5$ scaling phases.*

PROOF. Let Δ' be the scaling factor after at least $5 \log n + 4$ scaling phases. Then $\Delta' < \Delta/(16n^5)$. Let (p', x') be the solution at the beginning of the Δ'-scaling phase. If $H = \{i\}$, then $e_i > 3n^2\Delta'$, and so node i is incident to an edge (i, j) with $x'_{ij} > 3n\Delta'$. If H contains a node of G, then $s(p', H) \leq s(p, H) < -3n^2\Delta'$. Because $b_j(p', x') \geq 0$, it follows that there must be some edge (i, j) with $i \in B \backslash H$ and $j \in H \cap G$, such that $x'_{ij} \geq 3n\Delta'$, and so (i, j) is abundant at the Δ'-scaling phase. □

Because the set of optimal edges is cycle free, there are at most $n - 1$ optimal edges, and so there are at most $n - 1$ abundant edges. If the solution at the beginning of each scaling phase were fertile, then ScalingAlgorithm would identify all abundant edges in $O(n \log n)$ scaling phases, after which the algorithm would identify the optimal solution. However, it is possible that a solution is infertile at a scaling phase, as illustrated in the following example, which shows that ScalingAlgorithm is not strongly polynomial.

Example. $B = \{1\}$; $G = \{2, 3\}$; $e_1 = 1$; $U_{12} = 2^K$; $U_{13} = 1$, and K is a large integer. The unique optimal solution is: $p_2 = x_{12} = 2^K/(2^K + 1)$, and $p_3 = x_{13} = 1/(2^K + 1)$. At the k-th scaling phase for $k < K$, the Δ-optimal solution has $x_{12} = 1 - 2^k$ and $x_{13} = 2^k$. It takes more than K scaling phases before $(1, 3)$ is larger than $2n\Delta$ and the optimal solution is determined.

4.2 The Algorithm StrongScaling

In this section, we present the algorithm StrongScaling. Its primary difference from ScalingAlgorithm occurs when a solution is Δ-infertile at the beginning of a scaling phase. In this case, StrongScaling calls procedure MakeFertile, which produces a smaller parameter Δ' (perhaps exponentially smaller) and a feasible vector of prices p' that is Δ-fertile. It then returns to the Δ'-scaling phase.

In addition, there are two more subtle differences in the algorithm StrongScaling. The procedure MakeFertile permits allocations on abundant edges to be amounts other than a multiple of Δ. In addition, the procedure produces a solution (p', x') such that $b_j(p', x')$ is permitted to be negative, so long as $b_j(p', x') \geq \Delta'/n^2$.

```
Algorithm 3. StrongScaling(e, U)
begin
   Δ := Δ^0; p := p^0; x := 0; Threshold := Δ;
   ScalingPhase:
      if BasicSolution(A(Δ)) is optimal, then quit;
      while (p, x) is not Δ-optimal,
         replace (p, x) by PriceAndAugment(p, x);
      if no Δ-component is Δ-fertile, and if Δ ≤ Threshold,
         then MakeFertile(p, x)
      else do
         Δ := Δ/2;
         for each j ∈ G such that b_j(p, x) > Δ,
            decrease x_ij by Δ for some i ∈ B;
         return to ScalingPhase;
end
```

```
Algorithm 4. MakeFertile(p, x, Δ)
begin
   Δ' = GetParameter(p, Δ);
   if Δ' > Δ/n^2 then Threshold := Δ/n^5 and quit;
   else continue
   p' := GetPrices(p, Δ');
   x' := GetAllocations(p, Δ');
end
```

In the remainder of this section, we let (p, x) be the solution at the end of the Δ-scaling phase, and we assume that (p, x) is infertile. We use $\mathbf{C}$ instead of $\mathbf{C}(\Delta)$.

The procedure MakeFertile(p, Δ) has three subroutines. The first subroutine is called Get-Parameter(p, Δ). It determines the next value Δ' of the scaling parameter. If $\Delta' > \Delta/n^2$, the procedure sets Threshold to Δ/n^5 and returns to the Δ-scaling phase. (The purpose of the parameter Threshold is to prevent MakeFertile from being called for at least $5 \log n$ scaling phases.) In this case, even though p is not Δ-fertile, there will be a new abundant edge within $O(\log n)$ scaling phases. If $\Delta' \leq \Delta/n^2$, MakeFertile continues. The second subroutine is called GetPrice(p, Δ'), which determines a Δ'-feasible set of prices p'. The price vector p' is Δ'-fertile. In addition, $-\Delta'/2n \leq s(p', H) \leq \Delta'$ for all $H \in \mathbf{C}$. The third subroutine is called GetAllocations(p', Δ'). It obtains an allocation x' so that (p', x') is nearly Δ'-feasible, and where allocations are only made on abundant edges. Subsequently, StrongScaling runs the Δ'-scaling phase.

In the remainder of this section, we present the subroutines of MakeFertile. In addition, we will state lemmas concerning the properties of their outputs Δ', p', and x'. The algorithms GetParameter and GetPrices each rely on a procedure called SpecialPrice(p, H, t), where H is a Δ-component, and $t \geq 0$. The procedure produces a feasible price vector $\hat{p}$, which depends on H and t. The price vector p is increased until one of the following two events occurs: $s(\hat{p}, H) = t$, or there is a component $J \in \mathbf{C}$ with $s(\hat{p}, J) = -s(\hat{p}, H)/2n^2$.

The procedure GetParameter computes the next value of the scaling parameter. For each $H \in \mathbf{C}$ with at least one node in G, the procedure runs SpecialPrice$(p, H, 0)$ and computes the vector of prices as well as the scaling parameter, which we denote as Δ_H. If $H = \{i\}$ (and thus H has no node of G), then $\Delta_H := e_i$. The algorithm then sets $\Delta' = \max\{\Delta_H : H \in \mathbf{C}\}$.

The procedure GetPrices computes the next price vector. It computes SpecialPrice(p, H, Δ') for all $H \in \mathbf{C}$, and then lets p' be the component-wise maximum of the different price vectors.

These three procedures are presented next. (We will discuss the procedure GetAllocations later in this section.)

```
Procedure SpecialPrice(p, H, t)
begin
   p' := p;
   select a node v ∈ H ∩ G;
   while s(p', H) > t and s(p', J) > −s(p', H)/2n²,
   for all J ∈ C do
      compute the nodes ActiveSet(p', Δ, v);
      ∀ inactive nodes j ∈ G, p̂_j := p'_j;
      ∀ active nodes j ∈ G, p̂_j := q p'_j,
      where q > 1 is the least value so that
         (i) a new edge becomes an equality edge or
         (ii) s(p̂, H) = t or
         (iii) s(p̂, J) = −s(p̂, H)/2n² for some J ∈ C;
      p' := p̂;
   endwhile
end
```

```
Procedure GetParameter(p, Δ)
begin
   ∀ components H ∈ C do
      if H = {i} and i ∈ B, then Δ_H := e_i;
      else p̂ := SpecialPrice(p, H, 0), and Δ_H := s(p̂, H);
   Δ' := max {Δ_H : H ∈ C};
end
```

```
Procedure GetPrices(p, Δ')
begin
   ∀ components H ∈ C that contain a node of G do
      if s(p, H) ≤ Δ', then p^H := p;
      else p^H := SpecialPrice(p, H, Δ');
   ∀j ∈ G, p'_j := max {p_j^H : H ∈ C};
end
```

The following lemma concerns properties of Δ' and p' that are needed for the procedure GetAllocation. We let Δ_H and p^H denote parameters and prices calculated within GetParameter and GetPrices.

LEMMA 8. *Suppose that Δ' and p' are the output from* GetParameter *and* GetPrices. *Then the following are true:*

i. For all $H \in \mathbf{C}$, $s(p', H) \geq -\Delta'/n^2$.

ii. If $H \in \mathbf{C}$ and if $H = \{i\}$ and $i \in B$, then $e_i \leq \Delta'$.

iii. For all $H \in \mathbf{C}$, $s(p^H, H) = min\{s(p, H), \Delta'\}$.

iv. There is a component $H \in \mathbf{C}$, such that $p_H^H = p'_H$ and $s(p', H) = \Delta'$.

v. Either there is a node $i \in B$ with $e_i = \Delta'$, or there exists $J \in \mathbf{C}$ with $s(p', J) = -\Delta'/n^2$.

vi. If $s(p', J) < 0$, then there is $H \in \mathbf{C}$ with $s(p', H) = \Delta'$ and $J \subseteq ActiveSet(p', H)$.

PROOF. This lemma is highly technical, and the proof of Statements (iv), (v), and (vi) are involved. We first establish the correctness of Statements (i) to (iii). Prior to Proving Statements (iv), (v), and (vi), we will establish additional lemmas.

Proof of parts (i) to (iii). Consider Statement (i). There exists component K such that $s(p', H) = s(p^K, H) \geq -s(p^K, K)/n^2 \geq -\Delta'/n^2$, and so the statement is true. Now consider statement (ii). If $H = \{i\}$, then $\Delta_H = e_i \leq \Delta'$.

Consider statement (iii). If $s(p, H) < \Delta'$, then SpecialPrice(p, H, Δ') lets $p^H = p$. Otherwise, SpecialPrice increases the prices, and thus decreases the value $s(p^H, H)$, until $s(p^H, H) = \Delta'$. The other termination criteria do not play a role until $s(p^H, H) = \Delta_H \leq \Delta'$. □

4.3 The Auxiliary Network and Maximum Utility Paths

Before proving Statements (iv) to (vi) of Lemma 8, we develop some additional properties of prices and paths. We again assume that (p, x) is the input for MakeFertile. Let $A(\Delta)$ be the set of abundant edges. The *auxiliary network* is the directed graph N^* with node set $B \cup G$, and whose edge set is as follows. For every $i \in B$ and $j \in G$, there is an arc (i, j) with utility U_{ij}. For every $(i, j) \in A(\Delta)$, there is an arc (j, i) with utility $U_{ji} = 1/U_{ij}$. (There will also be an arc (i, j).) For every directed path $P \in N^*$, we let the utility of path P be $U(P) = \prod_{(i,j) \in P} U_{ij}$. For every pair of nodes j and k, we let $\mu(j, k) = \max\{U(P) : P$ is a directed path from j to k in $N^*\}$. That is, $\mu(j, k)$ is the maximum utility of a path from j to k.

LEMMA 9. *The utility of each cycle in the auxiliary network N^* is at most 1.*

PROOF. Let C be any cycle in the auxiliary network. For each edge (i,j) of the auxiliary network, let $U'_{ij} = U_{ij}/(\alpha_i(p)\cdot p_j)$. Since $U_{ij}/p_j \le \alpha_i(p)$, it follows that $U'_{ij} \le 1$ for all (i,j).

Let $U'(P) = \prod_{(i,j)\in P} U'_{ij}$. It follows that $U(P) = U'(P) \le 1$, and the lemma is true. □

We assume next that all components of $A(\Delta)$ have a single root node, and that the root node is in G whenever the component has a node of G. We extend μ to being defined on components as follows: $\mu(H,K) = \mu(v,w)$, where v is the root node of H, and w is the root node of K.

LEMMA 10. *Suppose that $K \in \mathbf{C}$ and that p^K = Special-Price(p, K, t). If component $H \subseteq$ ActiveSet(p^K, Δ, K), then $\mu(K,H) = p^K_H/p^K_K$.*

PROOF. For each (i,j) in the auxiliary network, let $U'_{ij} = U_{ij}/(\alpha_i(p^K)\cdot p^K_j)$. Then $U'_{ij} \le 1$ for all (i,j). Suppose next that P is any maximum utility path from a node v to a node w with respect to U. Then P is also a maximum utility path from v to w with respect to U'. Moreover, if $v \in G$ and $w \in G$, then $U'(P) = U(P)\cdot p^K_v/p^K_w$.

We now consider the path P' from the root of K to the root of H in the residual network $N(p^k, \Delta)$. Such a path exists because H is active. Then each arc of P' is an equality arc, and $U'(P') = 1$. It follows that P' is a maximum utility path. Moreover, $U(P) = U'(P)\cdot p^K_H/p^K_K = p^K_H/p^K_K$. □

LEMMA 11. *Suppose that K and H are components of $\mathbf{C}$, and that p^K and p^H are price vectors determined in* Get-Prices. *If $p^H_H < p^K_H$, then $p^H_H/p^K_K < \mu(H,K)$.*

PROOF. $p^H_H/p^K_K = p^H_H/p^K_H \times p^K_H/p^K_K$. By assumption, $p^H_H/p^K_H < 1$. This implies that $p_H < p^K_H$, and so component $H \subseteq ActiveSet(p^K, \Delta, K)$. By Lemma 10, $p^K_H/p^K_K = \mu(H,K)$. Therefore $p^H_H/p^K_K < \mu(H,K)$. □

4.4 The Rest of the Proof of Lemma 8

We are now ready to prove Statement (iv), (v), and (vi) of Lemma 8.

Proof of Statement (iv) of Lemma 8. We assume that there is no component H such that $s(p', H) = \Delta'$, and we will derive a contradiction. By statement (iii), if $s(p,H) \ge \Delta'$, then $s(p^H, H) = \Delta'$. By construction, if $s(p^H, H) = \Delta'$ and if $s(p', H) < \Delta'$, then there is some component K such that $s(p^K, K) = \Delta'$, and $p^H_H < p^K_H$. In such a case, we say that K dominates H.

Let H_1 be a component for which $s(p^H, H) = \Delta'$. By our assumption, there is a sequence of components $H_1, H_2, \ldots, H_k$ such that H_{i+1} dominates H_i for $i = 1$ to $k-1$, and H_k dominates H_1. For each component $J \in \mathbf{C}$, let $g(J) = p^J_J$. Let $H_{k+1} = H_1$. By Lemma 11,

$$\prod_{i=1}^{k} \mu(H_{i+1}, H_i) > \prod_{i=1}^{k} g(H_i)/g(H_{i+1}) = 1.$$

For $i = 1$ to k, let P_i be the max multiplier path from H_{i+1} to H_i, and let $P = P_1, P_2, \ldots, P_k$ be the closed walk obtained by concatenating the k paths. Then $U(P) = \prod_{i=1}^{k} \mu(H_{i+1}, H_i)$. But by Lemma 9, $U(P) \le 1$, which is a contradiction. We conclude that there is a component H such that $s(p', H) = \Delta'$. □

Proof of Statement (v) of Lemma 8. Choose H such that $s(p', H) = \Delta'$. If $H = \{i\}, \Delta' = e_i$. The remaining case in when H contains a node of G. Then the termination criteria for SpecialPrice$(p, H, 0)$ specifies that that there is a component J such that $s(p^H, J) = -\Delta'/n^2$. We claim that $s(p', J) = s(p^H, J) = -\Delta'/n^2$. Otherwise, there is a component K such that $p^K_J > p^H_J$. But then $s(p^K, J) < s(p^H, J) = -s(p^H, H)/n^2 = -\Delta'/n^2 \le -s(p^K, K)/n^2$, contradicting the termination rule for SpecialPrice(p, K, Δ'). □

Proof of Statement (vi) of Lemma 8. We first prove the statement in the case that $s(p', J) < s(p, J)$, and thus $p'_J > p_J$. In this case, there exists a component H such that $p'_J = p^H_J > p_J$. Let Q be the max utility path from H to J in N^*. We claim that $p'_H = p^H_H$. Otherwise, there is a component K that dominates H; that is, $p^K_H > p^H_H$. By Lemma 10, $p^K_J > p^H_J$. Therefore, $s(p^K, J) < s(p^H, J) = -s(p^H, H)/n^2 = -\Delta'/n^2 \le -s(p^K, K)/n^2$, a contradiction. Thus Statement (vi) is true in this case.

We will show that there is a component H with $s(p, H) \ge n\Delta'$ and $J \subseteq$ Activeset(p, Δ, H). In this case, $p'_J \ge p^H_J > p_J$, and thus Statement (vi) is true because it reduces to the case given above. We next determine an allocation $\hat{x}$ as restricted to the abundant edges and that is nearly Δ-feasible. We then use flow decomposition (see Ahuja et al. [1] pages 79-81) to determine the component H.

Consider the allocation $\hat{x}$ obtained from p that satisfies the following:

i. if $(i,j) \notin A(\Delta)$, then $\hat{x}_{ij} = 0$;

ii. $c(\hat{x}) \ge 0$; if $s(p, H) \ge 0$, then $c_H(\hat{x}) = s(p, H)$;

iii. $b(p, \hat{x}) \le 0$; if $s(p, H) < 0$, then $b_H(p, \hat{x}) = s(p, H)$.

Consider the flow decomposition of $y = x - \hat{x}$. The flow decomposition is the sum of nonnegative flows in paths in $N(p, \Delta)$, where each path is from a deficit node (a node v with $\sum_{k\in G} \hat{y}_{vk} > 0$) to an excess node (a node w with $\sum_{k\in B} \hat{y}_{kw} < 0$).

Consider the flow in the decomposition out of component J. We claim that J is a deficit component, and the deficit is at least $(n-1)\Delta/n$. To see that this claim is true, note that $b_J(p,x) \ge 0$, and $b_J(p, \hat{x}) = s(p, J) < 0$. Moreover, since x_{ij} is a multiple of Δ on non-abundant edges, it follows that $b_J(p,x) \equiv s(p,J) \mod \Delta$, and thus $b_J(p,x) \ge s(p,J) + \Delta > -\Delta/n^2 + \Delta > (n-1)\Delta/n$. Since $b_J(p, \hat{x}) \le 0$, it follows that there must be at least $(n-1)\Delta/n$ units of flow into component J in the flow decomposition. Accordingly, there must be at least one excess component H such that the flow from H to J in the flow decomposition is at least Δ/n. Since all flows in the decomposition are on equality edges, it follows that $J \subseteq$ ActiveSet(p, Δ, H). Moreover, $s(p, H) \ge \Delta/n \ge n\Delta'$, which is what we needed to prove. Therefore (vi) is true. □

4.5 Determining the Allocations

In procedure GetAllocations, for each Δ-component H with at least two nodes, we designate one node in $H \cap B$ as the *B-root* of H, and we designate one node in $H \cap G$ as the *G-root* of H. If H has a single node k, then k is the root.

The procedure will determine the allocation x' by first obtaining a basic feasible solution for a minimum cost flow problem. (See, e.g., [1].) In the procedure, we will let d_k

denote the supply/demand of node k. If $i \in B$, then $d_i \geq 0$. If $j \in G$, then $d_j \leq 0$.

```
Procedure GetAllocations(p', Δ')
begin
  ∀ components H ∈ C
    if i is the B-root of H, then d_i = max {0, e_H − p'_H};
    if j is the G-root of H, then d_j = min {0, e_H − p'_H};
    if k is not a B-root or G-root, then d_k = 0;
  select x' as the unique solution satisfying
    the supply/demand constraints and such that
    x'_ij = 0 for all non-abundant edges (i, j);
end
```

4.6 On the Correctness of StrongScaling and its Running Time

In this section, we provide lemmas that lead up to the theorem stating the correctness and time bounds for StrongScaling.

LEMMA 12. *Suppose that Δ' is the parameter obtained by running* GetParameter, *and suppose that $\Delta' > \Delta/n^2$. If the* Scaling-Algorithm *is run starting with solution (p, x) and with the Δ-scaling phase, then there will be a new abundant edge within $O(\log n)$ scaling phases.*

PROOF. By Lemma 8, we can select a component H such that $s(p^H, H) = \Delta'$. Then there must also be a component J with $s(p^H, J) = -\Delta_H/n^2$. (The termination criterion would not end with $e_i = \Delta'$ because (p, x) was not fertile.)

Because $\Delta' > \Delta/n^2$, StrongScaling went to the $\Delta/2$-scaling phase, starting with the solution (p, x). Suppose that $\hat{\Delta} < \Delta'/n^2$, and let $(\hat{p}, \hat{x})$ be a feasible solution at the end of the $\hat{\Delta}$-scaling phase. We will show that $(\hat{p}, \hat{x})$ or else $(\hat{p}, \hat{x})$ is $\hat{\Delta}$-fertile, and there will be a new abundant edge within $O(\log n)$ scaling phases. We consider two cases. Assume first that $\hat{p}_H \leq p^H_H$. In this case, $s(\hat{p}, H) \geq \Delta' \geq n^2\hat{\Delta}$, and there must be an abundant edge directed out of H.

In the second case, $\hat{p}_H > p^H_H$. In this case, $s(\hat{p}, J) \leq s(p^H, J) = -\Delta'/n^2 < -\hat{\Delta}/n^4$. In this case, J is $\hat{\Delta}$-fertile, and there will be a new abundant edge in O(log n) scaling phases. □

LEMMA 13. *Suppose that Δ' and (p', x') are the parameter and solution obtained by running* MakeFertile, *and suppose that $\Delta' \leq \Delta/n^2$. Then the following are true:*

i. (p', x') is Δ'-fertile.

ii. $c_i(x') \leq \Delta'$ for all $i \in B$.

iii. $-\Delta'/n^2 \leq b_j(p', x') \leq 0$ for all $j \in G$.

iv. If $(i, j) \in A(\Delta)$, then $x'_{ij} > 2n\Delta'$.

v. If $\Delta'' < \Delta/3n^2$, then the solution at the Δ''-scaling phase is Δ''-feasible. Within an additional $2\log n + 4$ scaling phases, there will be a new abundant edge.

PROOF. Statement (i) follows from Statements (iv) and (v) of Lemma 8. Statements (ii) and (iii) follow from Statements (i) and (iii) of Lemma 8, as well as the way that x' is constructed.

We next prove Statement (iv). Consider $\hat{x}$ described in the proof of Statement (vi) of Lemma 8. We first claim that $c_B(\hat{x}) < (n+1)\Delta$. The claim is true because $c_B(\hat{x}) + b_G(p, \hat{x}) = e_B - p_G = c_B(x) + b_G(p, x) \leq n\Delta$. Also, $b_j(p, \hat{x}) \geq -\Delta/n^2$. Thus $c_B(\hat{x}) \leq n\Delta - b_G(p, \hat{x}) < n\Delta + (|G|/n^2)\Delta < (n+1)\Delta$.

Now consider the flow decomposition of $y = x - \hat{x}$ in the proof of Statement (vi) of Lemma 8. The sum of the excesses is at most $c_B(\hat{x}) < (n+1)\Delta$. It follows that the total flow in the decomposition emanating from excess nodes is less than $(n+1)\Delta$. Therefore, $|\hat{x}_{ij} - x_{ij}| < (n+1)\Delta$ for all $(i, j) \in A(\Delta)$.

Now consider x' as determined by Procedure GetAllocations. Note that $\sum_{j \in G} p_j \leq \sum_{j \in G} p'_j \leq \sum_{j \in G} p_j + n\Delta$. Therefore, $|\hat{x}_{ij} - x'_{ij}| < n\Delta$ for all $(i, j) \in A(\Delta)$. Thus $|x_{ij} - x'_{ij}| < (2n+1)\Delta$. Because $x_{ij} \geq 3n\Delta$, $x'_{ij} > 3n\Delta - (2n+1)\Delta = (n-1)\Delta > (n^3 - n)\Delta'$, and thus (i, j) is abundant at the Δ'-scaling phase.

We next prove Statement (v). Let (p'', x'') be the solution at the Δ''-scaling phase, where $\Delta'' < \Delta'/4n^2$. Let J be a component with $s(p', J) < 0$. Statement (v) says that $b_J(p'', x'') \geq 0$.

So, suppose instead that $b_J(p'', x'') < 0$. We will derive a contradiction. We note that $p''_J = p'_J$. (Recall that a node j only increases its price when j is active and when there is no augmenting path. This cannot occur for a node j with $b_j < 0$.) We next claim that $p''_k = p'_k$ if $J \subset \text{ActiveSet}(p', \Delta, H)$. To see why, let Q' be a maximum multiplier path from k to J. Then by Lemma 10, $p'_J = p'_k \cdot \mu(k, J)$, and $p''_J \geq p''_k \cdot \mu(k, J)$. Since $p'_J = p''_J$, and $p''_k > p'_k$, it follows that $p''_k = p'_k$.

By Statement (vi) of Lemma 8, there is a component H with $s(p', H) = \Delta'$. In addition, $J \subseteq \text{ActiveSet}(p', \Delta, H)$. We are now ready to show to derive the contradiction, and thus show that $b_J(p'', x'') \geq 0$. Note that $s(p'', H) = \Delta'$, and $b(p'', H) \leq \Delta'' \leq \Delta/4n^2$. Now consider the flow decomposition $y' of x'' - x'$. The flow out of component H in y' is at least $(n-1)\Delta'/n$, and so there must be a flow of at least Δ'/n to some component K. Each arc in the flow decomposition is in $N(p', x')$. Then $p''_K = p''_H \cdot \mu(H, K)$, which implies that $p''_K = p'_K$. But then $b_K(p'', x'') = b_K(p', x'') > b_K(p', x') + \Delta'/n > (4n-1)\Delta''$, which is a contradiction. □

THEOREM 4. **Optimality of Strong Scaling**. *The algorithm* StrongScaling *finds an optimal solution (p^*, x^*) in $O(n \log n)$ scaling phases. It calls* MakeFertile *at most n times, and each call takes $O(n(m + n\log n))$ time. It calls* PriceAndAugment *$O(n)$ times per scaling phase. It runs in $O((n^2 \log n)(m + n\log n)$ time.*

PROOF. Once all of the abundant edges have been identified, the algorithm finds the optimal solution. And a new abundant edge is discovered at least once every $O(\log n)$ scaling phases. Thus the algorithm terminates with an optimal solution.

We now consider the running time. The algorithm calls MakeFertile at most n times because each call leads to a new abundant edge. Each call of MakeFertile takes $O(n(m + n\log n)$ time. There are $O(\log n)$ scaling phases between each call of MakeFertile, and each scaling phase takes $O(n(m + n\log n)$ time. Thus the running time of the algorithm is $O((n^2 \log n)(m + n\log n))$ time. □

5. SUMMARY

We presented a new scaling algorithm for computing the market clearing prices for Fisher's linear market model. We anticipate that this technique can be modified to solve extensions of the linear model.

We have also presented a strongly polynomial time algorithm. The strongly polynomial time algorithmic development may possibly be modified to solve extensions of the linear model; however, such modifications are challenging because of the technical aspects of the proof of validity.

6. ACKNOWLEDGEMENTS

The author gratefully acknowledges all of the help and advice from Dr. Mehdi Ghiyasvand.

7. REFERENCES

[1] R.K. Ahuja, T.L. Maganti, and J.B. Orlin. *Network Flows: Theory, Algorithms, and Applications.* Prentice Hall, N.J. 1993.

[2] K. Arrow and G. Debreu. Existance of an equilibrium for a competitive economy. *Econometrica* 22:265–290, 1954.

[3] W.C. Brainard, H.E. Scarf, D. Brown, F. Kubler, and K.R. Sreenivasan. How to compute equilibrium prices in 1891. Commentary. *The American Journal of Economics and Sociology* 64: 57-92, 2005.

[4] D. Chakrabarty, N. Devanur, and V. Vazirani. New results on rationality and strongly polynomial solvability in Eisenberg-Gale markets. In Proceedings of 2nd Workshop on Internet and Network Economics, 239-250, 2006.

[5] N.R. Devanur, C.H. Papadimitriou, A. Saberi, and V.V. Vazirani. Market equilibrium via a primal–dual algorithm for a convex program. *Journal of the ACM* 55: 1-18, 2008.

[6] N.R. Devanur and V.V. Vazirani. The spending constraint model for market equilibrium: algorithmic, existence and uniqueness results. Proceedings of 36th Symposium on the Theory of Computing, 519-528, 2004.

[7] J. Edmonds., and R.M. Karp. Theoretical improvements in algorithmic efficiency for network flow problems. *Journal of ACM* 19: 248-264, 1972.

[8] E. Eisenberg and D. Gale. Consensus of subjective probabilities: the Pari-Mutuel method. *Annals of Mathematical Statistics* 30: 165-168, 1959.

[9] M.L. Fredman, and R.E. Tarjan. Fibonacci heaps and their uses in improved network optimization algorithms. *Journal of ACM* 34: 596-615, 1987.

[10] R. Garg and S. Karpur. Price Roll-Backs and Path Auctions: An Approximation Scheme for Computing the Market Equilibrium Lecture Notes in Computer Science, Volume 4286/2006 Springer Berlin / Heidelberg 225-238, 2006.

[11] M. Ghiyasvand and J.B. Orlin An improved approximation algorithm for computing Arrow-Debreu market prices MIT Technical Paper. Submitted for publication. 2009.

[12] J.B. Orlin. Genuinely polynomial simplex and non-simplex algorithms for the minimum cost flow problem. Technical Report 1615-84, Sloan School of Management, MIT, Cambridge, MA. 1984.

[13] J.B. Orlin. A faster strongly polynomial minimum cost flow algorithm. *Operations Research* 41: 338-350, 1993.

[14] V.V. Vazirani. Spending constraint utilities, with applications to the Adwords market. Submitted to *Math of OR*, 2006.

[15] V.V. Vazirani. Combinatorial Algorithms for Market Equilibrium. in N. Nisan, T. Roughgarden, E'. Tardos, and V. Vazirani, editors, *Algorithmic Game Theory*, pages 103-134, Cambridge University Press, Cambridge, UK., 2007.

Bayesian Algorithmic Mechanism Design

[Extended Abstract]

Jason D. Hartline*
Northwestern University
Evanston, IL, USA
hartline@eecs.northwestern.edu

Brendan Lucier
University of Toronto
Toronto, ON, Canada
blucier@cs.toronto.edu

ABSTRACT

The principal problem in algorithmic mechanism design is in merging the incentive constraints imposed by selfish behavior with the algorithmic constraints imposed by computational intractability. This field is motivated by the observation that the preeminent approach for designing incentive compatible mechanisms, namely that of Vickrey, Clarke, and Groves; and the central approach for circumventing computational obstacles, that of approximation algorithms, are fundamentally incompatible: natural applications of the VCG approach to an approximation algorithm fails to yield an incentive compatible mechanism. We consider relaxing the desideratum of (ex post) incentive compatibility (IC) to Bayesian incentive compatibility (BIC), where truthtelling is a Bayes-Nash equilibrium (the standard notion of incentive compatibility in economics). For welfare maximization in single-parameter agent settings, we give a general black-box reduction that turns any approximation algorithm into a Bayesian incentive compatible mechanism with essentially the same[1] approximation factor.

Categories and Subject Descriptors

J.4 [**Social And Behavioral Sciences**]: Economics

General Terms

Algorithms, Economics, Theory

Keywords

Mechanism design, Bayesian incentive compatibility, algorithms, social welfare.

*Supported in part by NSF Grant CCF-0830773 and NSF Career Award CCF-0846113.

[1]More specifically, we obtain a polynomial time approximation scheme with an ϵ loss that is either additive or multiplicative, depending on the problem setting. This error term arises from statistical methods that seem necessary for a black-box reduction.

STOC'10, June 5–8, 2010, Cambridge, Massachusetts, USA.

1. INTRODUCTION

Can any approximation algorithm be converted into an approximation mechanism for selfish agents? This question is framed by a fundamental incompatibility between the standard economic approach for the design of mechanisms for selfish agents (the *Vickrey-Clarke-Groves* (VCG) mechanism) and the standard algorithmic approach for circumventing computational intractability (approximation algorithms). The conclusion from this incompatibility, driving much of the field of algorithmic mechanism design, is that incentive and algorithmic constraints must be dealt with simultaneously (See e.g., [15]). For a large, important class of problems, we arrive at the opposite conclusion: *there is a general approximation-preserving reduction from mechanism design to algorithm design!*

The goal of mechanism design is to construct the rules for a system of agents so that in the equilibrium of selfish agent behavior a desired objective is obtained. For settings of incomplete information the standard game theoretic equilibrium concept is *Bayes-Nash equilibrium* (BNE), which is defined by mutual best response when the *prior distribution* of agent payoffs is *common knowledge*. The *revelation principle* [18] suggests that when looking for mechanisms with desirable Bayes-Nash equilibria, one must look no further than those with truthtelling as a Bayes-Nash equilibrium, also known as *Bayesian incentive compatible* (BIC) mechanisms. Almost all of the computer science literature has focused on the BIC subclass of *ex post incentive compatible* (IC) mechanisms where truthtelling is a *dominant strategy*. While IC is aesthetically appealing because it is congruous with worst-case-style results, it is not generally without loss!

This loss is evident in the computer science theory of IC mechanism design, which is described most characteristically by impossibility. For instance, for single-minded combinatorial auctions of m items, the optimal worst-case approximation factor (under standard complexity theoretic assumptions) is $\sqrt{m}$ [17]. With such impossibility, a relevant theory must make relaxations. For many problems within the realm of computer systems; e.g., online auctions (eBay), advertising auctions (Google, Yahoo!, MSN), file sharing (BitTorrent), routing (TCP/IP), scheduling (SETI@home), and video streaming (YouTube); high volume should enable demand distributions to be estimated. With demand distributions, the natural algorithmic and mechanism design problems are Bayesian.

Agent incentives in Bayesian mechanism design are very well understood in single-parameter settings, where each agent has a single independent private value for receiving a service (see, e.g, [18]). For the single parameter setting it is known that a mechanism is BIC if and only if (a) the probability an agent is served (a.k.a. the *allocation rule*) is monotone non-decreasing in the agent's value for service, and (b) the agent's expected payment (a.k.a. the *payment rule*) is identified precisely from the allocation rule.[2]

The main challenge in reducing BIC (or IC) mechanism design to algorithm design is that approximation algorithms do not generally have monotone allocation rules. Our reduction shows that in a Bayesian setting we can convert any non-monotone allocation rule into a monotone one without compromising its social welfare. The main technical observation that enables this reduction is that, in a Bayesian setting, we can focus on a single agent for whom the allocation rule is not monotone, apply a transformation that fixes this non-monotonicity (and weakly improves our objective), and *no other agents are affected* (in a Bayesian sense). Therefore, we can apply the transformation independently to each agent. Our reduction is as follows:

1. For each agent, identify intervals in which the agent's allocation rule is non-monotone. (This is a property of the distribution and algorithm and can be done prior to considering any agent bids.)

2. For each agent, if their bid falls in an (above identified) interval, redraw the agent's bid from the prior distribution conditioned on being within the interval.

3. Run the approximation algorithm on the resulting bids and output its solution.

Notice that under the assumption that the original values are drawn according to the common prior, the redrawing of values does not alter this prior.

Three items must be clarified. First, there are many ways one might try to choose intervals in Step 1 of the reduction and most of them are incompatible with mechanism design. To address this issue, we develop a monotonizing technique for allocation rules (adapted from the standard *ironing procedure* from the field of Bayesian optimal mechanism design [18]). Second, we are unlikely to have access the functional form of the allocation rule. To address this issue, we estimate the allocation rule by sampling the distribution and making black-box calls to the algorithm. These estimates can be made precise enough to enable arbitrary small loss in welfare (i.e., a fully polynomial time approximation scheme). Finally, we must also determine payments for our monotonized allocation rule. For this, a general approach of Archer et al. [3] suffices.

Our results apply generally to single-parameter agent settings where the designer's objective is to maximize the social welfare (e.g., single-minded combinatorial auctions). Agents each have a private value for service. The designer either has a feasibility constraint on the set of agents that can be simultaneously served or a cost function over the set of served agents. The social welfare is the sum of the values of the agents served less the designer's cost.

For any ϵ, we give a black box reduction that, in polynomial time in the number of agents and $1/\epsilon$, converts any approximation algorithm into a BIC mechanism with an additive loss of ϵ to the social welfare. We also give a pseudo-polynomial time reduction to a BIC mechanism with a multiplicative loss of ϵ, and a fully polynomial time approximation scheme for the special case of downward-closed feasibility problems. Thus, the approximation complexity of social welfare in single-parameter settings is the same for algorithms and BIC mechanisms.

For the most studied single-parameter mechanism design problems, the performance of the best ex post IC approximation mechanism matches the best approximation algorithm (e.g., single-minded combinatorial auctions [17] and related machine scheduling [12]). None-the-less, our approach gives the best known BIC approximation mechanism for many problems, such as auctions under various graph constraints [2] and auctions of convex bundles [5].

Related Work. The design of ex post IC mechanisms for social welfare problems is well studied, notably for the specific settings of combinatorial auctions [3, 5, 16, 17]. Lehmann et al. [17] introduced the problem of polynomial time approximation of social welfare for single-minded combinatorial auctions and give a mechanism that matches the best algorithmic approximation factor. Archer et al. [3] considered the setting where there are many (at least logarithmic) copies of each item and gave a $(1 + \epsilon)$-approximation mechanism. Archer and Tardos [4] gave a (single-parameter) related machine scheduling mechanism that approximates the makespan. Dhangwatnotai et al. [12] gave a mechanism for related machine scheduling that approximates makespan and matches the algorithmic lower bound. All of the above results are for ex post incentive compatible mechanisms.

There has been a large literature on multi-parameter combinatorial auctions and approximation, but this is only tangentially related to our work so we do not cite it exhaustively.

There have been a few reductions of varying degrees of generality. Lavi and Swamy [16] consider IC mechanisms for multi-parameter packing problems and give a technique for constructing a (randomized) β-approximation mechanism from any β-approximation algorithm that verifies an integrality gap. Babaioff et al. [6] look at the equilibrium notion of *algorithmic implementation in undominated strategies* and gives a technique for turning a β-algorithm into a $\beta(\log v_{max})$-approximation mechanism. This solution concept requires that no agent plays a strategy that is dominated by an easy to find strategy. Their approach applies to single-valued combinatorial auctions and does not require the mechanism to know which bundles each agent desires.

There have been a few related studies of Bayes-Nash equilibrium. Christodoulou et al. [11] consider Bayes-Nash equilibria of simultaneous Vickrey auctions in a combinatorial setting and show that these give a 2-approximation when agents' valuations are submodular. Gairing et al. [14] consider Bayes-Nash equilibria of a routing game and study worst-case performance. Borodin and Lucier [8] study worst-case performance of Bayes-Nash equilibria in combinatorial mechanisms based on greedy algorithms.

There are many papers on profit maximization that consider Bayesian design settings. These papers do not tend to consider computational constraints and for many of these (non-computational) settings the restriction to ex post in-

[2]Probabilities and expectations above are taken with respect to both the distribution of agent values and possible randomization in the mechanism.

centive compatibility is without loss.[3] One exception exception is Bhattacharya et al. [7]. They focus on the problem of selling heterogeneous goods to agents with linear valuations, for which they construct a polynomial time 4-approximation mechanism. Their approximation result requires that the type distributions satisfy the monotone hazard rate assumption. In a spirit similar to this paper, they make heavy use of the Bayesian setting to obtain a polynomial runtime.

Organization. We describe in detail the model for single-parameter agents, Bayesian approximation, Bayesian incentive compatibility, and foundational economic theory in Section 2. In Section 3 we give the reduction in an ideal setting where the allocation rule of the algorithm for the given distribution on agent values is precisely known. This reduction is lossless. In Section 4 we develop the reduction in the black-box model where we must sample the distribution and run the algorithm to determine its allocation. Conclusions and open problems are discussed in Section 5.

2. MODEL AND DEFINITIONS

Algorithms. We consider algorithms for binary single-parameter agent settings. An algorithm in such a setting must select a set of agents to serve. This *allocation* is denoted by $\mathbf{x} = (x_1, \ldots, x_n)$ where x_i is an indicator for whether or not agent i is served. Agent i has *valuation* v_i for being served. Without loss for non-negative bounded-support distributions, we will assume $v_i \in [0, 1]$.[4] The vector $\mathbf{v} = (v_1, \ldots, v_n)$ of valuations is the *valuation profile*.

In the *general costs setting*, the seller may have some cost function $c(\cdot)$ over allocations representing the cost of serving the allocated set (e.g., Steiner tree problems [13]). The *general feasibility setting* is the special case where costs are zero (feasible) or infinity (infeasible). These include scheduling and public good problems. An important subclass are *downward-closed settings* where any subset of a feasible set is feasible. Downward closed settings include single-minded combinatorial auctions [17] and knapsack auctions [1].

An algorithm $\mathcal{A}$ is simply an *allocation rule* that maps valuation profiles to allocations. The allocation rule for $\mathcal{A}$ we will denote by $\mathbf{x}(\mathbf{v})$. Our objective is the *social welfare* which is $\mathcal{A}(\mathbf{v}) = \sum_i v_i x_i(\mathbf{v}) - c(\mathbf{x}(\mathbf{v}))$. We allow $\mathcal{A}$ to be randomized in which case $x_i(\mathbf{v})$ is a random variable; $\mathcal{A}(\mathbf{v})$ denotes the expected welfare of the algorithm for valuation profile $\mathbf{v}$. $\mathrm{OPT}(\mathbf{v})$ will denote the maximum social welfare.

We will consider these algorithmic problems in a Bayesian (a.k.a. stochastic) setting where the valuations of the agents are drawn from a product distribution $\mathbf{F} = F_1 \times \cdots \times F_n$. Agent i's *cumulative distribution* and *density* functions are denoted F_i and f_i, respectively. The distribution is assumed to be *common knowledge* to the agents and designer.

The pair $(c(\cdot), \mathbf{F})$ defines a setting for single-parameter algorithm design which we will take as implicit. For this setting, the optimal expected welfare is $\mathrm{OPT} = \mathbf{E}_{\mathbf{v}\sim\mathbf{F}}[\mathrm{OPT}(\mathbf{v})]$ and the algorithm's expected welfare is $\mathcal{A} = \mathbf{E}_{\mathbf{v}\sim\mathbf{F}}[\mathcal{A}(\mathbf{v})]$. An algorithm is a *worst-case β-approximation* if for all $\mathbf{v}$, $\mathcal{A}(\mathbf{v}) \geq \mathrm{OPT}(\mathbf{v})/\beta$. An algorithm is a *Bayesian β-approximation* if $\mathcal{A} \geq \mathrm{OPT}/\beta$.

Mechanisms. A mechanism $\mathcal{M}$ consists of an *allocation rule* and a *payment rule*. We denote by $\mathbf{x}(\mathbf{v})$ and $\mathbf{p}(\mathbf{v})$ the allocation and payment rule of an implicit mechanism $\mathcal{M}$. We assume agents are *risk neutral* and individually desire to maximize their expected *utilities*. Agent i's utility for allocation $\mathbf{x}$ and payments $\mathbf{p}$ is $v_i x_i - p_i$. We consider single-round, sealed-bid mechanisms where agents simultaneously bid and the mechanism then computes the allocation and payments.

Our goal is a mechanism that has good social welfare in equilibrium. The standard economic notion of equilibrium for games of incomplete information is *Bayes-Nash equilibrium* (BNE). The revelation principle says that any equilibrium that is implementable in BNE is implementable with truthtelling as the BNE strategies of the agents.[5] Meaning: an agent that believes the other agents are reporting their values truthfully as given by the distribution has a best response of also reporting truthfully. A mechanism with truthtelling as a BNE is *Bayesian incentive compatible* (BIC).[6]

It will be useful to consider agent i's expected payment and probability of allocation conditioned on their value. To this end, denote $p_i(v_i) = \mathbf{E}_{\mathbf{v},\mathcal{A}}[p_i(\mathbf{v}) \mid v_i]$ and $x_i(v_i) = \mathbf{E}_{\mathbf{v},\mathcal{A}}[x_i(\mathbf{v}) \mid v_i]$. The following theorem characterizes BIC mechanisms.

THEOREM 2.1. *[18] A mechanism is BIC if and only if for all agents i:*

- *$x_i(v_i)$ is monotone non-decreasing, and*
- *$p_i(v_i) = v_i x_i(v_i) - \int_0^{v_i} x_i(z)dz + p_i(0)$.*

Usually, $p_i(0)$ is assumed to be zero.

This motivates the following definition:

DEFINITION 2.1. *An allocation rule $\mathbf{x}(\cdot)$ is* monotone *for distribution $\mathbf{F}$ if $x_i(v_i)$ is monotone non-decreasing for all i. An algorithm is* monotone *if its allocation rule is monotone.*

From Theorem 2.1, BIC and monotone are equivalent and we will use them interchangeably for both algorithms and mechanisms, though we will prefer "BIC" when the focus is incentive properties and "monotone" when the focus is algorithmic properties.

Computation. Our main task in demonstrating that the approximation complexity of algorithms and BIC mechanisms is the same by giving an approximation-preserving reduction from the BIC mechanism design problem to the algorithm design problem. In other words, we use the algorithm's allocation rule to compute the mechanism's allocation and payment rules. As we are in a Bayesian setting this computation will also need access to the distribution.

[3]One non-computational setting where ex post incentive compatibility is with loss is when the profit maximizing seller has a strict no-deficit constraint [10].

[4]The bounded support assumption is unnecessary except for our results using sampling, where we believe it is realistic.

[5]The revelation principle holds even in computational settings; any BNE for which the agent strategies and the mechanism can be computed in polynomial time can be converted into a polynomial time BIC mechanism.

[6]Much of the computer science literature on mechanism design focuses on dominant strategy equilibrium (DSE) and *ex post incentive compatibility* (IC). This is not without loss in many settings and therefore should be considered with care when addressing computational questions in mechanism design.

We consider two models of computation: an *ideal model* and a *black-box model*. In the ideal model, we will assume we have explicit access to the functional form of the distribution and allocation rule and we will assume we can perform calculus on these functions. While this model is not realistic, we present it for the sake of clarity in explaining the economic theory that drives our results. In the black-box model we will assume we can query the algorithm on any input and that we can sample from the distribution on any subinterval of its support. Our philosophy is that the ideal model is predictive of what is implementable in polynomial time and we verify this philosophy by instantiating approximately the same reduction under the black-box model.

3. REDUCTION: IDEAL MODEL

In this section we prove that, in the ideal model, any Bayesian algorithm can be made BIC without loss of performance.

THEOREM 3.1. *In the ideal model and general cost settings, a BIC algorithm $\bar{\mathcal{A}}$ can be computed from any algorithm $\mathcal{A}$. Its Bayesian social welfare satisfies $\bar{\mathcal{A}} \geq \mathcal{A}$.*

Theorem 3.1 implies an immediate corollary for Bayesian approximation.

COROLLARY 3.2. *In the ideal model and general cost settings, a BIC Bayesian β-approximation $\bar{\mathcal{A}}$ can be computed from any Bayesian β-approximation algorithm, $\mathcal{A}$.*

Let us build some intuition for the requirements of Theorem 3.1. Suppose that we are given an algorithm $\mathcal{A}$ that is monotone for the distribution $\mathbf{F}$. Then $\mathcal{A}$ is already BIC and specifies the allocation rule $\mathbf{x}(\cdot)$, so we must only compute the payment rule. In our ideal model this is trivial given the formula from Theorem 2.1.

Now suppose we have a non-monotone Bayesian β-approximation algorithm $\mathcal{A}$ with allocation rule $\mathbf{x}(\cdot)$. We would like to use $\mathcal{A}$ to construct a monotone algorithm $\bar{\mathcal{A}}$ from which we can obtain a BIC mechanism by simply computing the payment rule as above. We must make sure that in doing so we do not reduce the algorithm's expected welfare. The key property of our approach which makes it tractable is that we monotonize each agent's allocation rule independently without changing (in a Bayesian sense) the allocation rule any other agent faces. This property is also important for the approximation factor as $\mathcal{A}$ is guaranteed to be a Bayesian β-approximation only for the given distribution $\mathbf{F}$, and may not be a good approximation for some other distribution.

In summary, the desiderata for monotonizing agent i are:

D1. monotone $\bar{x}_i(v_i)$,

D2. (weakly) improved social welfare $\mathbf{E}_{v_i}[v_i\bar{x}_i(v_i)] \geq \mathbf{E}_{v_i}[v_i x_i(v_i)]$, and

D3. other agents unaffected.

Notice that if we satisfy the last condition we can apply the process simultaneously to all agents.

3.1 Ironing via Resampling

There is a history of fixing non-monotonicities in Bayesian mechanism design. Myerson invented the technique of *ironing* which relies on the fact that if an allocation rule is constant over some interval then any agent within that interval

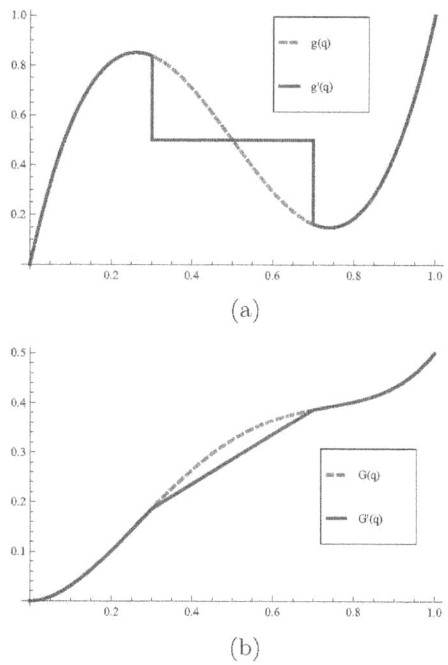

Figure 1: (a) A non-monotone ironing g' (solid) of curve g (dashed). (b) The corresponding integral curves G' (solid) and G (dashed) in probability space.

is effectively equivalent to a canonical "average" agent from that interval. Myerson applied this theory to iron *virtual valuation functions* which are used in Bayesian profit maximization [18]. We will apply this theory directly to allocation rules.

Before we describe our ironing procedure in full, let us develop some more intuition. Suppose allocation rule $x_i(\cdot)$ of $\mathcal{A}$ is non-monotone for agent i. A simple approach to flattening non-monotonicities is to choose some interval $[a, b]$ on which $x(\cdot)$ is non-monotone, and to treat the agent identically whenever on this interval. For example, whenever $v_i \in [a, b]$ we could choose to pretend that v_i is actually some other fixed value v' (e.g. $v' = a$) and pass this "pretend" value v' to the algorithm. Unfortunately, if we take this naïve approach, we would have changed the distribution of agent i's input to the algorithm (in particular, the probability of value v' would be increased) and violated D3. In order to maintain D3 we make a minor modification: instead of picking a fixed v', we will draw v' from F_i restricted to the interval $[a, b]$. Thus, we are replacing $v_i \in [a, b]$ with v' drawn from the same distribution. Other agents cannot tell the difference – this operation does not change the distribution of agent i's input! Moreover, agent i will indeed be treated identically whenever $v_i \in [a, b]$: the new probability of allocation will be precisely the distribution weighted average of $x_i(\cdot)$ over the interval $[a, b]$.

Let $x_i'(\cdot)$ represent the allocation rule we obtain from the following procedure (where $\mathbf{v}_{-i} \sim \mathbf{F}_{-i}$):

- if $v_i \in [a, b]$, redraw $v' \sim F_i$ restricted to $[a, b]$; else, set $v' = v_i$.

- run $\mathcal{A}(v', \mathbf{v}_{-i})$.

We say that $x_i'(\cdot)$ is the curve $x_i(\cdot)$ *ironed on interval* $[a,b]$. We note that $x_i'(v_i) = x_i(v_i)$ for $v_i \notin [a,b]$ and $x_i'(v_i) = \mathbf{E}_{v' \sim F_i}[x_i(v') \mid v' \in [a,b]]$ otherwise. Note that we can easily iron along multiple disjoint intervals, redrawing v' from whichever interval contains v_i' (if any).

We now explore a method for choosing intervals on which to iron in order to obtain monotonicity. It will be instructive to consider the *allocation rule in probability space* instead of valuation space, and the *cumulative allocation rule* (also in probability space).

- Let $g(q) = x_i(F_i^{-1}(q))$ be the allocation rule in probability space.
- Let $G(q) = \int_0^q g(z)dz$ be the cumulative allocation rule.

Notice that monotonicity of $x_i(\cdot)$ is equivalent to monotonicity of $g(\cdot)$ which is equivalent to convexity of $G(\cdot)$.

Let $x_i'(\cdot)$ be $x_i(\cdot)$ ironed along some interval $[a,b]$, and consider the corresponding curves $g'(\cdot)$ and $G'(\cdot)$. This ironing procedure corresponds to replacing $g(\cdot)$ with its average on $[a,b]$, or equivalently $G(\cdot)$ with the line segment connecting $G(F(a))$ to $G(F(b))$ (See Figure 1).[7] This latter line segment interpretation suggests that we can view our interval selection problem as the problem of replacing portions of curve G with straight line segments so that the resulting curve $\bar{G}$ will be convex. This is precisely the problem of finding the convex hull of G! Thus the choice of intervals that monotonizes $x_i(\ )$ (satisfying D1) is precisely the set of intervals defined by the convex hull of $G(\cdot)$. See Figure 2.

Finally, since the convex hull of $G(\cdot)$ lies below $G(\cdot)$, this transformation weakly improves welfare (satisfying D2). Informally speaking, in moving from cumulative allocation rule $G(\cdot)$ to $\bar{G}(\cdot)$, we lower the probability of low-value allocations in exchange for a corresponding increase in the probability that higher-valued allocations occur. This intuition is made more precise in Lemma 3.4, below.

3.2 The Ironed Algorithm

We are now ready to define our ironed algorithm $\bar{\mathcal{A}}$. Given distribution F and interval I, we will write $F[I]$ to mean F restricted to I.

DEFINITION 3.1 (RESAMPLE $(\mathcal{A}, \mathbf{\mathcal{I}})$). *Given algorithm* $\mathcal{A}$ *and a* profile of disjoint interval sets, $\mathbf{\mathcal{I}} = \{\mathcal{I}_1, \ldots, \mathcal{I}_n\}$, *the* resampled algorithm *for* $\mathcal{A}$ *with intervals* $\mathbf{\mathcal{I}}$ *is algorithm* RESAMPLE $(\mathcal{A}, \mathbf{\mathcal{I}})$:

1. *For each agent* i, *if* $v_i \in I \in \mathcal{I}_i$, *draw* $\bar{v}_i \sim F_i[I]$; *else, set* $\bar{v}_i = v_i$.
2. *Run* $\mathcal{A}(\bar{\mathbf{v}})$.

DEFINITION 3.2 (MONOINTS $(\mathbf{x})$). *The* set of monotonizing intervals for $\mathbf{x}(\cdot)$ *is* MONOINTS $(\mathbf{x}) = (\mathcal{I}_1, \ldots, \mathcal{I}_n)$ *defined by:*

1. *Let* $g_i(q) = x_i(F_i^{-1}(q))$ *be the allocation rule in probability space.*
2. *Let* $G_i(q) = \int_0^q g_i(z)dz$ *be the cumulative allocation rule.*
3. *Let* $\bar{G}_i(\cdot)$ *be the convex hull of* $G_i(\cdot)$.
4. *Let* $\mathcal{I}_i$ *be the set of intervals in valuation space on which* $G_i(F_i(\cdot)) > \bar{G}_i(F_i(\cdot))$.

[7]Note that the transformation to probability space (from valuation space) is necessary for obtaining this line-segment interpretation.

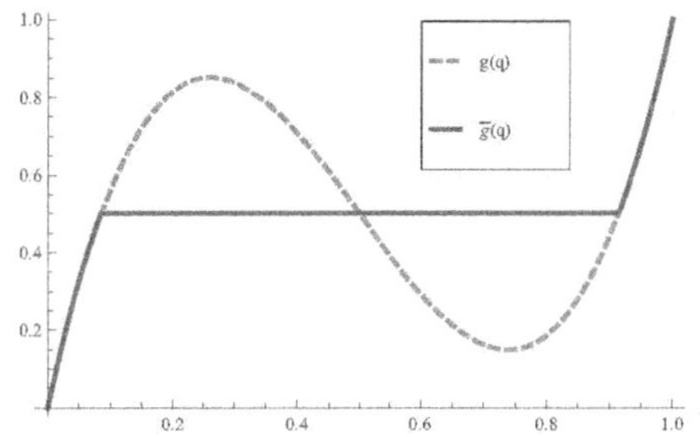

(a)

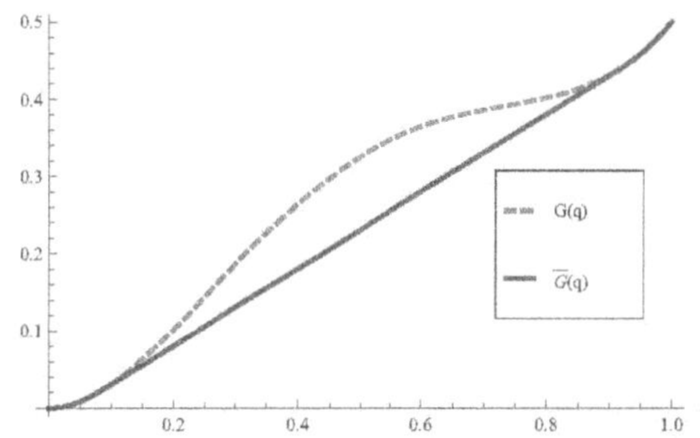

(b)

Figure 2: (a) A monotone ironing $\bar{g}$ (solid) of curve g (dashed). (b) The corresponding integral curves $\bar{G}$ (solid) and G (dashed) in probability space. Note $\bar{G}$ is the convex hull of G.

DEFINITION 3.3 ($\bar{\mathcal{A}}$). *The* ironed algorithm *corresponding to algorithm* $\mathcal{A}$ *is* $\bar{\mathcal{A}} =$ RESAMPLE $(\mathcal{A},$ MONOINTS $(\mathbf{x}))$.

LEMMA 3.3. $\bar{\mathcal{A}}$ *is monotone.*

PROOF. We must show that each agent has a monotone allocation rule. The allocation rule for agent i is precisely $\bar{x}_i(v_i) = \bar{g}(F_i(v_i))$, which is the derivative of a convex function and therefore monotone. □

LEMMA 3.4. *If* $\mathcal{A}$ *is a Bayesian* β*-approximation then* $\bar{\mathcal{A}}$ *is a Bayesian* β*-approximation.*

PROOF. First notice that the two allocation rules produce the same distribution over allocations and therefore expected costs are identical. We will show, for a single agent i, that $\mathbf{E}[v_i\bar{x}_i(v_i)] \geq \mathbf{E}[v_i x_i(v_i)]$, from which linearity of expectation implies the result. We have

$$\mathbf{E}[v_i x_i(v_i)] = \int_0^1 v x_i(v) f_i(v)\, dv = \int_0^1 F_i^{-1}(q) g_i(q)\, dq$$
$$= \int_0^1 \int_0^{F_i^{-1}(q)} g_i(q)\, dz\, dq = \int_0^1 \int_{F_i(z)}^1 g_i(q)\, dq\, dz$$
$$= \int_0^1 (G_i(1) - G_i(F_i(z)))\, dz$$

and similarly $\mathbf{E}[v_i\bar{x}_i(v_i)] = \int_0^1(\bar{G}_i(1) - \bar{G}_i(F_i(z)))dz$. We conclude $\mathbf{E}[v_i\bar{x}_i(v_i)] \geq \mathbf{E}[v_i x_i(v_i)]$ since $\bar{G}_i(1) = G_i(1)$ and $\bar{G}_i(F_i(z)) \leq G_i(F_i(z))$ for all $z \in [0,1]$. □

Theorem 3.1 follows from Lemmas 3.3 and 3.4.

4. REDUCTION: BLACK-BOX MODEL

We will use the ironing procedure from the previous section to monotonize an algorithm in the black-box model. However, instead of using direct knowledge of the allocation rule, we must use sampling to estimate it. This sampling introduces errors in the selection of interval sets for resampling, which must then be dealt with. Our analysis will proceed in the following steps.

1. We describe a method for computing payments in the black-box model.
2. We describe a method for combining sampling with ironing to obtain a nearly monotone algorithm. In fact, this algorithm will be ϵ-Bayesian incentive compatible.
3. We show that a convex combination of this nearly monotone algorithm with a blatantly monotone one will give a monotone algorithm, resulting in a BIC mechanism.

All of these steps approximately preserve social welfare. We obtain the following theorem.

THEOREM 4.1. *In the black-box model and general cost settings, for any $\epsilon > 0$, a BIC algorithm $\mathcal{A}'$ can be computed from any algorithm $\mathcal{A}$. Its Bayesian social welfare satisfies $\mathcal{A}' \geq \mathcal{A} - \epsilon$, and its runtime is polynomial in n and $1/\epsilon$.*

The additive error in Theorem 4.1 can be converted into a multiplicative error whenever the expected welfare of $\mathcal{A}$ is not too small. We obtain the following corollary.

COROLLARY 4.2. *In the black-box model and general cost settings, for any $\epsilon > 0$, a BIC algorithm $\mathcal{A}'$ can be computed from any algorithm $\mathcal{A}$. Its Bayesian social welfare satisfies $\mathcal{A}' \geq \mathcal{A}/(1+\epsilon)$, and its runtime is polynomial in n, $1/\epsilon$, and $1/\mathcal{A}'$.*

We note that it is possible to improve Theorem 4.1 by considering the expected values of the agents. This improvement is discussed in in Appendix C and enables, for example, a fully polynomial reduction for downward-closed settings.

In the remainder of this section we prove of Theorem 4.1.

4.1 Computing Payments

Suppose that $\mathcal{A}$ has monotone allocation rules. The problem of designing a mechanism to implement $\mathcal{A}$ then reduces to calculating appropriate payments. These payments are completely determined by the allocation rule of $\mathcal{A}$, but in the black-box model we do not have direct access to the functional form of the allocation rule. Archer et al. [3] solve this problem by computing an unbiased estimator of the desired payment rule using only black-box calls to the algorithm. For completeness we now summarize their approach.

DEFINITION 4.1 (BLACK-BOX PAYMENTS). *If algorithm $\mathcal{A}$ does not allocate to agent i, then agent i pays 0. Otherwise, we compute the payment of agent i as follows:*

1. *Choose v_i' uniformly from $[0, v_i]$*
2. *Draw $\mathbf{v}'_{-i} \sim \mathbf{F}_{-i}$ and run $\mathcal{A}(v_i', \mathbf{v}'_{-i})$*
3. *If $\mathcal{A}$ allocated to agent i in the previous step set $X = v_i$, otherwise set $X = 0$.*
4. *If $X \neq 0$, repeatedly draw values $\mathbf{v}'_{-i} \sim \mathbf{F}_{-i}$ and run $\mathcal{A}(v_i, \mathbf{v}'_{-i})$ until the algorithm allocates to player i, and let T be the number of iterations required.*
5. *Agent i's payment is $p_i = v_i - TX$.*

As was shown by Archer et al., this computation attains the appropriate expected payment.

CLAIM 4.3 (ARCHER ET AL. [3]). *In the black-box payment procedure, the expected payments are $p_i(v_i) = v_i x_i(v_i) - \int_0^{v_i} x_i(z)dz$.*

We note that since we execute this procedure for agent i only if he receives an allocation, which occurs with probability $x_i(v_i)$, the expected number of calls to $\mathcal{A}$ for each player is at most

$$x_i(v_i)\left(1 + \tfrac{1}{x_i(v_i)}\right) \leq 2.$$

Thus, in expectation, all payments can be computed with $2n$ calls to $\mathcal{A}$.

Note that any mechanism paired with the above payment scheme will be *individually rational* (IR), meaning that a truthtelling agent will never obtain negative utility. This is true even if the allocation rule is not monotone. This follows immediately from the fact that the payment for an agent that declares value v_i is never greater than v_i (indeed, it is defined as v_i minus a non-negative value).

4.2 Sampling and ϵ-Bayesian Incentive Compatibility

We will be estimating the allocation rule of a non-monotone algorithm and attempting to iron it. This will fail to result in an absolutely monotone rule. In this section we show that a nearly monotone rule results in truthtelling as an *ϵ-Bayes-Nash equilibrium* (ϵ-BNE): the most an agent can gain from a non-truthtelling strategy is an additive ϵ. We call such a mechanism *ϵ-Bayesian incentive compatible* (ϵ-BIC).

DEFINITION 4.2 (ϵ-BIC). *A mechanism is ϵ-Bayesian incentive compatible if truthtelling obtains at least as much utility as any other strategy, up to an additive ϵ, assuming all other agents truthtell. That is, for all i, v_i, and v', $v_i x_i(v_i) - p_i(v_i) \geq v_i x(v') - p_i(v') - \epsilon$.*

The main theorem of this section is the following.

THEOREM 4.4. *In the black-box model and general cost settings, for any $\epsilon > 0$, an ϵ-BIC algorithm $\mathcal{A}'$ can be computed from any algorithm $\mathcal{A}$. Its Bayesian social welfare satisfies $\mathcal{A}' \geq \mathcal{A} - \epsilon$, and its runtime is polynomial in n and $1/\epsilon$.*

The resampling procedure from the previous section is the main workhorse for Theorem 4.4. The construction of algorithm $\mathcal{A}'$ consists primarily to choosing interval sets on which to resample.

4.2.1 ϵ-closeness

We now formalize a closeness property under which an allocation rule that is close to monotone is ϵ-BIC (for some related ϵ).

DEFINITION 4.3 (ϵ-CLOSE). *Given allocation rules $x(\cdot)$ and $x'(\cdot)$ are ϵ-close if $|x(v) - x'(v)| < \epsilon$ for all v. Two algorithms or mechanisms are ϵ-close if each agent's allocation rules are ϵ-close.*

LEMMA 4.5. *If non-monotone $\mathcal{A}'$ is ϵ-close to a monotone $\mathcal{A}$, then $\mathcal{A}'$ is (2ϵ)-BIC.*

LEMMA 4.6. *If $\mathcal{A}$ and $\mathcal{A}'$ have the same expected costs*[8] *and are ϵ-close then $\mathcal{A}' \geq \mathcal{A} - n\epsilon$.*

LEMMA 4.7. *If algorithms $\mathcal{A}$ and $\mathcal{A}'$ are ϵ-close, then for any collection $\mathcal{I} = \{\mathcal{I}_1, \ldots, \mathcal{I}_n\}$ of interval sets, resampled algorithms* RESAMPLE $(\mathcal{A}, \mathcal{I})$ *and* RESAMPLE $(\mathcal{A}', \mathcal{I})$ *are ϵ-close.*

Appropriate payments to turn an algorithm that is ϵ-close to monotone into a mechanism that is 2ϵ-BIC can be computed by the same process we would use for monotone algorithms.

4.2.2 Discretization

A key step in our reduction will be in discretizing the allocation rules of the algorithm. This reduces the problem of estimating an allocation rule to estimating its value at a polynomial number of points. Moreover, our resulting allocation will not necessarily be monotone, but there will be only a polynomial number of points at which it can be non-monotone; we will use this to our advantage when fixing non-monotonicities in Section 4.3.

An algorithm is *k-piece piecewise constant* if for each i there is a partition of valuation space into at most k intervals such that the allocation rule for agent i is constant on each interval.

DEFINITION 4.4 ($\text{DISC}_\epsilon(\mathcal{A})$). *For a given $\epsilon > 0$ and algorithm $\mathcal{A}$, the* discretization of algorithm $\mathcal{A}$, $\text{DISC}_\epsilon(\mathcal{A})$, *is* RESAMPLE $(\mathcal{A}, \mathcal{I})$*, where $\mathcal{I} = \{\mathcal{I}_1, \ldots, \mathcal{I}_n\}$ is the collection of intervals defined by*

$$\mathcal{I}_i = \{[0, \epsilon)\} \cup \{[\epsilon(1+\epsilon)^t, \epsilon(1+\epsilon)^{t+1})\}_{0 \leq t \leq \log_{1+\epsilon}(1/\epsilon)}.$$

LEMMA 4.8. *$\text{DISC}_\epsilon(\mathcal{A})$ is $\log_{1+\epsilon}(1/\epsilon)$-piece piecewise constant and $\text{DISC}_\epsilon(\mathcal{A}) \geq \mathcal{A} - 2n\epsilon$.*

4.2.3 Statistical Estimation

We next describe a sampling procedure for estimating an allocation rule. This procedure will not form an algorithm, but rather generates an estimated allocation curve, which we will denote by $\mathbf{y}(\cdot)$. This estimate behaves like an allocation rule, but is not associated with an actual algorithm (and, in particular, need not be feasibly implementable).

DEFINITION 4.5 (ESTIMATE ALLOCATION RULE). *Given algorithm $\mathcal{A}$ which is k-piece piecewise constant and $\epsilon > 0$, an* estimated allocation rule *for $\mathcal{A}$ is a curve $\mathbf{y}(\cdot)$ found as follows:*

1. *for each agent i and valuation-space piece I_j, draw $\frac{4}{\epsilon^2}\log(2kn/\epsilon)$ samples from $\mathbf{F}$ conditional on $v_i \in I_j$, and run $\mathcal{A}$ on each of these samples.*
2. *let y_{ij} be the average allocation over the invocations to $\mathcal{A}$ above, for each i and j.*
3. *Define $\mathbf{y}$ by $y_i(v) = y_{ij}$ for all $v \in I_j$*

LEMMA 4.9. *If algorithm $\mathcal{A}$ is k-piece piecewise constant then, for any $\epsilon > 0$, an estimated allocation rule $\mathbf{y}(\cdot)$ for $\mathcal{A}$ is k-piece piecewise constant, and is $\frac{\epsilon}{2}$-close to $\mathbf{x}(\cdot)$ with probability at least $1 - \frac{\epsilon}{2}$. The number of black-box calls to $\mathcal{A}$ used in the construction of $\mathbf{y}(\cdot)$ is polynomial in n, k, and $1/\epsilon$.*

We now complete the proof of Theorem 4.4 by combining our sampling procedure with the ironing procedure from the ideal model.

DEFINITION 4.6 ($\text{IRON}_\epsilon(\mathcal{A})$). *Given piecewise constant algorithm $\mathcal{A}$, the* statistically ironed algorithm *for $\mathcal{A}$ with error $\epsilon > 0$ is $\text{IRON}_\epsilon(\mathcal{A})$ =* RESAMPLE $(\mathcal{A}, \text{MONOINTS}(\mathbf{y}))$ *where $\mathbf{y}(\cdot)$ is the estimated allocation rule for $\mathcal{A}$.*

Note that $\text{IRON}_\epsilon(\mathcal{A})$ is not simply a resampling of $\mathcal{A}$, but rather a convex combination of resamplings; construction of the interval set MONOINTS $(\mathbf{y})$ is randomized.

LEMMA 4.10. *$\text{IRON}_\epsilon(\mathcal{A})$ is 2ϵ-BIC and $\text{IRON}_\epsilon(\mathcal{A}) \geq \mathcal{A} - n\epsilon$.*

Proof of Theorem 4.4: Define $\mathcal{A}'$ to be the algorithm $\text{IRON}_{\epsilon'}(\text{DISC}_{\epsilon'}(\mathcal{A}))$, where $\epsilon' = \epsilon/3n$. Then, by Lemmas 4.8 and 4.10, $\mathcal{A}'$ is $2\epsilon'$-BIC, and hence ϵ-BIC, and $\mathcal{A}' \geq \text{DISC}_{\epsilon'}(\mathcal{A}) - n\epsilon' \geq \mathcal{A} - 3n\epsilon' = \mathcal{A} - \epsilon$. The runtime of $\mathcal{A}'$ (which is dominated by sampling in the construction of $\mathbf{y}$) is $O(nk\epsilon'^{-2}\log(2kn/\epsilon'))) = \tilde{O}(n^3\epsilon^{-3}\log(\epsilon^{-1}))$, where recall $k = \frac{1}{\epsilon}\log(1/\epsilon)$ is the number of discrete intervals in $\text{DISC}_{\epsilon'}(\mathcal{A})$. □

4.3 Bayesian Incentive Compatibility

In the previous section we showed how to construct an ϵ-BIC mechanism from any algorithm with almost no loss to the social welfare. Our goal now is to take such an ϵ-BIC algorithm $\mathcal{A}$ and make it BIC. In other words, we would like to "fix" the (small) non-monotonicities in $\mathcal{A}$. Fortunately, since each allocation curve of $\mathcal{A}$ is discretized, any non-monotonicities must occur only at a small number of predetermined points. Our approach for removing these points of non-monotonicity is simple: we will construct an alternative algorithm $\mathcal{A}'$ whose allocation curves are stair functions, with jumps in allocation probability occurring at each of those points. A convex combination of $\mathcal{A}$ and $\mathcal{A}'$ will then be monotone. This convex combination will be our final BIC algorithm.

It is important that this convex combination process not reduce social welfare by too much. This requires two things. First, we need the convex combination to be mostly $\mathcal{A}$ as only it has provably good welfare. This is possible by taking ϵ so small that the explicit monotonicities in $\mathcal{A}'$ heavily outweigh the non-monotonicities in $\mathcal{A}$ (which are at most ϵ). Second, we need to ensure that the expected social welfare of $\mathcal{A}'$ is not extremely negative.

How should we construct $\mathcal{A}'$? Suppose first that we are in a downward-closed feasibility setting. In this case, the singleton allocation $\{i\}$ is feasible for each agent i. The construction of $\mathcal{A}'$ with stair-function allocation curves is then straightforward: an agent i is chosen uniformly at random;

[8]Recall that the *expected cost* of an algorithm A with allocation rule $\mathbf{x}(\cdot)$ is $\mathbf{E}_{\mathbf{v}\sim\mathbf{F}}[c(\mathbf{x}(\mathbf{v}))]$.

the algorithm then either allocates to agent i or not, with the probability of allocation following a stair function. Since $\mathcal{A}'$ only returns feasible outcomes, its expected social welfare must be non-negative.

We would like to follow this same approach in general cost settings. However, it may be that, for some i, the particular allocation $\{i\}$ has an extremely high (or infinite) cost, in which case the above algorithm may have an extremely negative social welfare. Note, though, that in our construction we can replace $\{i\}$ with *any* allocation that includes agent i. It is therefore sufficient to find, for each i, some allocation that includes agent i and whose cost is not too high. Once these allocations are found, we can use them to construct the stair algorithm $\mathcal{A}'$.

In some cases finding low-cost allocations may be highly non-trivial. To get around this problem, we observe that as long as algorithm $\mathcal{A}$ has a reasonable probability of allocating to agent i, there must exist low-cost allocations that include i that are returned by $\mathcal{A}$. We can therefore find such allocations by repeatedly sampling outcomes of $\mathcal{A}$. If, on the other hand, we were to take many samples and not find any allocations that include agent i, then we can safely assume that agent i does not contribute much to the expected social welfare of $\mathcal{A}$. In this case, we can trivially monotonize agent i's allocation curve by ironing his entire allocation curve into a single interval, removing the need to find allocations that include him.

4.3.1 The Stair Algorithm

DEFINITION 4.7 (STAIR$(\mathcal{A})$). *Let $\mathcal{A}$ be a k-piece piecewise constant algorithm, and suppose $S_1, \dots, S_n$ and $T_1, \dots, T_n$ are allocations such that $i \in S_i$ and $i \notin T_i$ for all i. The* stair algorithm *for $\mathcal{A}$, STAIR$(\mathcal{A})$, does the following:*

1. *Pick an agent i uniformly from the n agents.*
2. *If v_i is in the jth highest piece of k pieces, allocate to S_i with probability $(j-1)/(k-1)$ and T_i otherwise.*

DEFINITION 4.8 (COMB$_\epsilon(\mathcal{A})$). *Suppose algorithm $\mathcal{A}$ is k-piece piecewise constant. Then COMB$_\epsilon(\mathcal{A})$ is the convex combination of $\mathcal{A}$ with probability $1-\delta$ and STAIR$(\mathcal{A})$ with probability δ, where $\delta = 2(k-1)n\epsilon$.*

LEMMA 4.11. *If $\mathcal{A}$ is ϵ-close to a monotone $\mathcal{A}'$, then algorithm COMB$_\epsilon(\mathcal{A})$ is BIC.*

4.3.2 Finding Low-Cost Sets

We now describe the choice of sets $S_1, \dots, S_n$ and $T_1, \dots, T_n$ for algorithm STAIR$(\mathcal{A})$. In many settings this is trivial (e.g., for downward-closed feasibility problems we can take $S_i = \{i\}$ and $T_i = \emptyset$), but for some problems it might be difficult to find feasible (or low-cost) allocations. Our approach is as follows. Since $\mathcal{A}$ never makes an allocation that generates negative social welfare, we can bound the cost of any allocation made by $\mathcal{A}$. This motivates us to look for a set $S_i \ni i$ returned by $\mathcal{A}$ on some input, for each i. This can be accomplished by sampling. In the event that we do not find a set S_i, it is likely that the probability of allocating to agent i is very low; we can therefore *iron together all intervals* for agent i, effectively removing the need for S_i, without causing much loss to the expected welfare. This operation can be viewed as trimming away agents that are very rarely allocated. The same holds for finding T_i.

DEFINITION 4.9 (TRIM$_\epsilon(\mathcal{A})$). *The trimmed algorithm for piece-wise constant $\mathcal{A}$ is TRIM$_\epsilon(\mathcal{A})$:*

1. *For each agent i and valuation-space piece $I_j \in \mathcal{I}_i$, draw $\frac{4}{\epsilon^2}\log(2n/\epsilon)$ samples from $\mathbf{F}$ conditional on $v_i \in I_j$, and run $\mathcal{A}$ on each of these samples.*
2. *If $\mathcal{A}$ is the same (always or never allocating) for i on every sample, define $\mathcal{I}'_i = \{[0,1]\}$; otherwise, $\mathcal{I}'_i = \mathcal{I}_i$ and we define S_i to be any observed allocation that includes agent i and T_i to be any observed allocation that does not include agent i.*
3. *Run RESAMPLE$(\mathcal{A}, \boldsymbol{\mathcal{I}}')$.*

Note that, for each i, either sets $S_i \ni i$ and $T_i \not\ni i$ will be found during the execution of TRIM$_\epsilon(\mathcal{A})$, or else the allocation rule of agent i will be made constant.

LEMMA 4.12. TRIM$_\epsilon(\mathcal{A}) \geq \mathcal{A} - n\epsilon$.

We are now ready to combine our tools into a BIC mechanism, proving Theorem 4.1.

DEFINITION 4.10 (MONO$_\epsilon(\mathcal{A})$). *Given an algorithm $\mathcal{A}$ and $\epsilon > 0$, the* monotonization *of $\mathcal{A}$, MONO$_\epsilon(\mathcal{A})$, is the algorithm COMB$_\epsilon$(IRON$_\epsilon$(TRIM$_\epsilon$(DISC$_\epsilon(\mathcal{A})$))).*

LEMMA 4.13. *MONO$_\epsilon(\mathcal{A})$ is BIC, and MONO$_\epsilon(\mathcal{A}) \geq \mathcal{A} - 6kn^2\epsilon$.*

Proof of Theorem 4.1: Let $\mathcal{A}'$ be the monotonized algorithm MONO$_{\epsilon'}(\mathcal{A})$, where $\epsilon' = \epsilon/6kn^2$. The result then follows immediately from Lemma 4.13. The runtime, which is dominated by sampling, is $O(kn(\epsilon')^{-2}) = \tilde{O}(\frac{n^5}{\epsilon^5}\log^3(1/\epsilon))$. $\square$

5. CONCLUSIONS

Our main result is for single-parameter agents and the objective of social welfare where we give a black-box reduction that converts any Bayesian approximation algorithm into a Bayesian incentive compatible mechanism. For these settings there is no gap separating the approximation complexity of algorithms and BIC mechanisms.

It is notable that our transformation from an approximation algorithm to a BIC mechanism cannot be duplicated by the agents acting on their own: there are non-monotone algorithms that, when coupled with an appropriate payment rule, do not have any BNE with near the expected welfare as the original algorithm on the true values. A concrete example is given in Appendix B.

While our main theorem is extremely general, the situations not covered by it are of notable interest.

1. Multi-parameter Bayesian mechanism design is not yet well understood, but there is every reason to believe that approximation (which has not been pursued much by the economics literature) has a very interesting and relevant role to play in providing positive results (See, e.g., [9]). For social welfare maximization, a recent lower bound by Papadimitriou et al. [19] for the combinatorial public project problem that shows that there is a gap separating the approximation complexity of algorithms and ex post IC mechanisms. This result, however, does not immediately extend to show a separation for BIC mechanisms. *Is there a black-box reduction from BIC mechanism design to algorithm design in multi-parameter settings?*

2. In the special case where our reduction is applied to a worst-case β-approximation (recall: our reduction applies more generally to Bayesian β-approximations), the resulting BIC mechanism is still only a β-approximation in the weaker Bayesian sense. *Is there a polynomial-time black-box reduction that turns any worst-case β-approximation algorithm into a BIC mechanism that is also a worst-case β-approximation?*

3. While Bayes-Nash equilibrium (i.e., BIC) is the standard equilibrium concept for implementation in economics, the stronger dominant strategy equilibrium (i.e., ex post IC) is the standard concept in computer science. The main challenge in obtaining a similar reduction for IC mechanisms is that the valuation space is exponentially big and monotonizing all points seems to require an exhaustive procedure. One potential approach would be to apply our ironing technique repeatedly, re-ironing an agent's curve whenever it is affected by an ironing of another agent's curve. Such a procedure will not generally give a monotone allocation rule; A concrete example is given in the full version of the paper. *Is there a polynomial-time reduction for turning any $f(n)$-approximation (worst-case or Bayesian) algorithm for a single-parameter domain into an ex post IC mechanism that is a (worst-case or Bayesian) $\Theta(f(n))$-approximation?*

The final question above is a refinement of what we consider to be the main open question of this work. *Is there a gap separating the approximation complexity of implementation by Bayesian incentive compatible and ex post incentive compatible mechanisms for single-parameter social welfare maximization?*

6. REFERENCES

[1] G. Aggarwal and J. Hartline. Knapsack auctions. In *Proceedings of the 17th Annual ACM-SIAM Symposium on Discrete Algorithms*, 2006.

[2] K. Akcoglu, J. Aspens, B. Dasgupta, and M. Kao. An opportunity-cost algorithm for combinatorial auctions. In *Applied Optimization: Computational Methods in Decision-Making, Economics, and Finance*, 2002.

[3] A. Archer, C. Papadimitriou, K. Talwar, and E. Tardos. An approximate truthful mechanism for combinatorial auctions with single parameter agents. In *Proc. 14th ACM Symp. on Discrete Algorithms*. ACM/SIAM, 2003.

[4] A. Archer and E. Tardos. Truthful mechanisms for one-parameter agents. In *Proc. 42nd IEEE Symp. on Foundations of Computer Science*, 2001.

[5] M. Babaioff and L. Blumrosen. Computationally-feasible truthful auctions for convex bundles. In *Proc. 7th Intl. Workshop on Approximation Algorithms for Combinatorial Optimization Problems*, 2004.

[6] M. Babaioff, R. Lavi, and E. Pavlov. Single-value combinatorial auctions and algorithmic implementation in undominated strategies. *Journal of the ACM*, 2009.

[7] S. Bhattacharya, G. Goel, S. Gollapudi, and K. Munagala. Budget constrained auctions with heterogeneous items. In *Proc. 41st ACM Symp. on Theory of Computing*, 2010.

[8] A. Borodin and B. Lucier. Price of anarchy for greedy auctions. In *Proc. 21st ACM Symp. on Discrete Algorithms*, 2010.

[9] S. Chawla, J. Hartline, D. Malec, and B. Sivan. Sequential posted pricing and multi-parameter mechanism design. In *Proc. 41st ACM Symp. on Theory of Computing*, 2010.

[10] S. Chawla, J. Hartline, U. Rajan, and R. Ravi. Bayesian optimal no-deficit mechanism design. In *Workshop on Internet and Network Economics (WINE)*, 2006.

[11] G. Christodoulou, A. Kovács, and Michael Schapira. Bayesian combinatorial auctions. In *Proc. 35st Intl. Colloq. on Automata, Languages and Programming*, pages 820–832, 2008.

[12] P. Dhangwatnotai, S. Dobzinski, S. Dughmi, and T. Roughgarden. Truthful approximation schemes for single-parameter agents. In *Proc. 49th IEEE Symp. on Foundations of Computer Science*, 2008.

[13] J. Feigenbaum, C. Papadimitriou, and S. Shenker. Sharing the cost of multicast transmissions. *Journal of Computer and System Sciences*, 63(1):21–41, 2001.

[14] M. Gairing, B. Monien, and K. Tiemann. Selfish routing with incomplete information. In *Proc. 17th ACM Symp. on Parallel Algorithms and Architectures*, 2005.

[15] R. Lavi. Computationally efficient approximation mechanisms. In N. Nisan, T. Roughgarden, É. Tardos, and V. Vazirani, editors, *Algorithmic Game Theory*, chapter 12, pages 301–329. Cambridge University Press, 2007.

[16] R. Lavi and C. Swamy. Truthful and near-optimal mechanism design via linear programming. In *Proc. 46th IEEE Symp. on Foundations of Computer Science*, 2005.

[17] D. Lehmann, L. I. O'Callaghan, and Y. Shoham. Truth revelation in approximately efficient combinatorial auctions. In *Proc. 1st ACM Conf. on Electronic Commerce*, pages 96–102. ACM Press, 1999.

[18] R. Myerson. Optimal auction design. *Mathematics of Operations Research*, 6:58–73, 1981.

[19] C. Papadimitriou, M. Schapira, and Y. Singer. On the hardness of being truthful. In *Proc. 49th IEEE Symp. on Foundations of Computer Science*, 2008.

APPENDIX

A. IRONING ALLOCATION RULES VS. IRONING VIRTUAL VALUATIONS

The ironing procedure described in this paper is reminiscent of the ironing procedure used by Myerson for maximizing revenue [18]. Myerson's optimal mechanism allocates to maximize virtual value (defined by $\phi_i(v_i) = v_i - \frac{1-F_i(v_i)}{f_i(v_i)}$ for agent i). When the virtual valuation functions are non-monotone, this mechanism first irons the virtual valuation functions, then allocates to maximize ironed virtual value. A natural question is whether this is identical to ironing the non-monotone allocation rule that would result from maximizing non-ironed virtual values. We now give an example demonstrating that these two mechanisms are distinct.

Consider an auction of a single indivisible item to multiple bidders with values drawn i.i.d. from distribution F. Suppose $\mathcal{A}$ assigns the item to the agent with highest virtual value. Let $\bar{\mathcal{A}}$ be the ironed algorithm corresponding to $\mathcal{A}$. Let $\mathcal{A}'$ be Myerson's algorithm, which assigns the item to the agent with the highest *ironed* virtual value. Let $x(\cdot)$, $x'(\cdot)$, and $\bar{x}(\cdot)$ denote the allocation curves of $\mathcal{A}$, $\mathcal{A}'$, and $\bar{\mathcal{A}}$, respectively (by symmetry, allocation curves are the same for each player). Our goal is to show that $\bar{x}(\cdot) \neq x'(\cdot)$.

Consider the following distribution F: with probability 1/2, the value is drawn uniformly from $[10, 11]$; otherwise, it is drawn uniformly from $[11, 15]$. The virtual valuation function corresponding to this distribution is

$$\phi(v) = \begin{cases} 2v - 12 & v \in [10, 11] \\ 2v - 15 & v \in (11, 15]. \end{cases}$$

Let $\phi'(\cdot)$ be the ironed function corresponding to $\phi(\cdot)$. It can be verified that $\phi'(10) < \phi'(v)$ for all $v \in [10, 15]$. This implies that $x'(10) = 0$.

On the other hand, $x(10) > 0$ (since $\phi(v) < \phi(10)$ for $v \in (11, 11.5)$), and furthermore $x(v) \geq 0$ for all $v \in [10, 15]$. Thus, from the definition of the ironing procedure, there is some $z \in [10, 15]$ such that $\bar{x}(10) = \mathbf{E}_v[x(v) \mid v \leq z] > 0$. We therefore conclude $x(\cdot) \neq \bar{x}(\cdot)$, and hence these two different ironing procedures result in different mechanisms.

B. EQUILIBRIA OF NON-MONOTONE ALGORITHMS

We have shown how to transform a non-monotone algorithm into a monotone one to obtain a mechanism that is BIC. It is notable that the agents could not do this on their own: there are non-monotone algorithms that, when coupled with any individually-rational and no-positive-transfer[9] payment rule, do not have any BNE with near the expected welfare as the original algorithm on the true values.

Choose parameter $X \gg n$. Consider an auction of a single indivisible item to n bidders with values drawn i.i.d. from the following distribution: with probability $1/n$ the value is X; with the remaining probability it is drawn uniformly from $[0, 1]$. Let $\mathcal{A}$ allocate to the bidder with the largest value in $\left[0, \frac{1}{n^2}\right]$, if any and breaking ties randomly; otherwise it allocates to the bidder with the largest value.

Consider the expected welfare of $\mathcal{A}$. Since with high probability an agent has value X and no agent has value $1/n^2$ or below, $\mathcal{A} = \Omega(X)$.

Next we show that in any BNE most agents will bid $1/n^2$ and the expected welfare will be the average value of the agents which is $O(X/n)$. Thus, the equiligrium is far from the algorithms Bayesian performance, i.e., the *price of stability* is linear.

Consider any mechanism that pairs $\mathcal{A}$ with an ex-post IR and no-positive-transfer payment scheme. We claim that in any BNE of such a mechanism, an agent with value greater than $\frac{1}{n^2}$ would instead report value $\frac{1}{n^2}$. To see this, consider a BNE and let p denote the probability that some agent declares value $\frac{1}{n^2}$. Suppose that $p < 1 - \frac{1}{n}$. If agent i has value $v_i \in \left[\frac{1}{8}, \frac{3}{8}\right]$ and he does not bid $\frac{1}{n^2}$, then his probability of allocation is at most $p(3/4 + o(1))$ (since otherwise, with high probability, there will be an agent with value at least $2v_i$ who could improve his utility by copying agent i's strategy). The expected utility of agent i is therefore at most $p(3v_i/4 + o(1))$. On the other hand, agent i could bid $\frac{1}{n^2}$ for an expected utility of at least $p\left(v_i - \frac{1}{n^2}\right) > p(v_i/2 + o(1))$ (since $v_i \geq 1/8$). Thus any agent with a value in $\left[\frac{1}{8}, \frac{3}{8}\right]$ will bid $\frac{1}{n^2}$, so $p \geq 1 - \frac{1}{n}$. We conclude by noting that if $p \geq 1 - \frac{1}{n}$, every player with value above $\frac{1}{n^2}$ maximizes his utility by declaring $\frac{1}{n^2}$.

[9]No positive transfers implies that losers have zero payment.

C. EXTENSION: GENERAL VALUATIONS

Theorem 4.1 states that an algorithm can be made BIC with an additive loss of ϵ to its social welfare, in time polynomial in ϵ^{-1}. As noted in Corollary 4.2, this error can be made multiplicative, but at a cost: our reduction is pseudo-polynomial, running in time polynomial in $1/\mathcal{A}$. This might be problematic if (for example) the expected value of each agent is exponentially small. In cases where expected values are very small, we require a stronger theorem to obtain meaningful results for fully polynomial time mechanisms.

In this section we discuss the following extension to Theorem 4.1, which is tailored to cases where the expected welfare of the given algorithm is very small. Let $\mu_{\max} = \max_i \mathbf{E}[v_i]$ be the maximum expected value of any agent.

THEOREM C.1. *In the black-box model and general cost settings, for any $\epsilon > 0$, a BIC algorithm $\mathcal{A}'$ can be computed from any Bayesian algorithm $\mathcal{A}$. Its social welfare satisfies $\mathcal{A}' \geq \mathcal{A} - \epsilon\mu_{\max}$, and its runtime is polynomial in n, $1/\epsilon$, and* $\log(1/\mu_{\max})$.

For the special case of downward-closed set systems for feasibility problems, we can assume that $\mathcal{A} \geq \mu_{\max}$, since the trivial algorithm that simply allocates to the single player with the highest input value attains this value. This implies the following corollary.

COROLLARY C.2. *In the black-box model and downward-closed feasibility settings, For any $\epsilon > 0$, a BIC Bayesian $\beta(1+\epsilon)$-approximation algorithm $\mathcal{A}'$ can be computed from any Bayesian β-approximation algorithm $\mathcal{A}$. Its runtime is polynomial in n, $1/\epsilon$, and* $\log(1/\mu_{\max})$.

The proof of Theorem C.1 closely follows the proof of Theorem 4.1 from Section 4. The main difference is in the conversion of an ϵ-BIC algorithm to a purely BIC algorithm (i.e. corresponding to the proof of Theorem 4.1 from Theorem 4.4 in Section 4.3). Our high-level approach is the same: we consider a convex combination of the almost-monotone algorithm from Theorem 4.4 with the blatantly monotone stair algorithm. Recall that in Section 4.3 some care was necessary when finding sets $S_1, \ldots, S_n$ such that $S_i \ni i$. This task becomes even more difficult in our extended setting, since we wish to bound our error with respect to $\mu_{\max}$. Thus, in addition to requiring that $S_i \ni i$ for each i, we also require that the cost of each set S_i is not too large relative to $\mu_{\max}$. We must therefore modify the sampling procedure in algorithm $\text{TRIM}_\epsilon(\mathcal{A})$ to search specifically for low-cost allocations. The details of this modification are deferred to the full version of the paper.

Multi-parameter Mechanism Design and Sequential Posted Pricing

Shuchi Chawla[*]
Computer Sciences Dept.
Univ. of Wisconsin - Madison
shuchi@cs.wisc.edu

Jason D. Hartline[†]
EECS
Northwestern University
hartline@eecs.northwestern.edu

David L. Malec[*]
Computer Sciences Dept.
Univ. of Wisconsin - Madison
dmalec@cs.wisc.edu

Balasubramanian Sivan[*]
Computer Sciences Dept.
Univ. of Wisconsin - Madison
balu2901@cs.wisc.edu

ABSTRACT

We study the classic mathematical economics problem of *Bayesian optimal mechanism design* where a principal aims to optimize expected revenue when allocating resources to self-interested agents with preferences drawn from a known distribution. In single parameter settings (i.e., where each agent's preference is given by a single private value for being served and zero for not being served) this problem is solved [20]. Unfortunately, these single parameter optimal mechanisms are impractical and rarely employed [1], and furthermore the underlying economic theory fails to generalize to the important, relevant, and unsolved multi-dimensional setting (i.e., where each agent's preference is given by multiple values for each of the multiple services available) [25].

In contrast to the theory of optimal mechanisms we develop a theory of sequential posted price mechanisms, where agents in sequence are offered take-it-or-leave-it prices. We prove that these mechanisms are approximately optimal in single-dimensional settings. These posted-price mechanisms avoid many of the properties of optimal mechanisms that make the latter impractical. Furthermore, these mechanisms generalize naturally to multi-dimensional settings where they give the first known approximations to the elusive optimal multi-dimensional mechanism design problem. In particular, we solve multi-dimensional multi-unit auction problems and generalizations to matroid feasibility constraints. The constant approximations we obtain range from 1.5 to 8. For all but one case, our posted price sequences can be computed in polynomial time.

This work can be viewed as an extension and improvement of the single-agent algorithmic pricing work of [9] to the setting of multiple agents where the designer has combinatorial feasibility constraints on which agents can simultaneously obtain each service.

[*]This author was supported in part by NSF award number CCF-0830494 and in part by a Sloan Foundation fellowship.

[†]This author was supported in part by NSF award number CCF-0830773.

STOC'10, June 5–8, 2010, Cambridge, Massachusetts, USA.

Categories and Subject Descriptors

J.4 [**Social and Behavioral Sciences**]: Economics; F.2.0 [**Analysis of Algorithms and Problem Complexity**]: General

General Terms

Algorithms, Economics, Theory

Keywords

Bayesian mechanism design

1. INTRODUCTION

Suppose that the local organizers for a prominent symposium on computer science need to arrange for suitable hotel accommodations in the Boston area for the attendees of the conference. There are a number of hotel rooms available with different features and attendees have preferences over the rooms. The organizers need a mechanism for soliciting preferences, assigning rooms, and calculating payments. Fortunately, they have distributional knowledge over the participants' preferences (e.g., from similar conferences). This is a stereotypical multi-dimensional setting for mechanism design that, for instance, also arises in most resource allocation problems in the Internet. What mechanism should the organizers employ to maximize their objective (e.g., revenue)?

The economic theory of optimal mechanism design is elegant and predictive in single-dimensional settings. Here Myerson's theory of virtual valuations and characterizations of incentive constraints via monotonicity guide the design of optimal incentive-compatible mechanisms [20] with practical (often non-incentive-compatible) implementations [1]. The challenge posed by multi-dimensional settings (e.g., in the likely case that conference attendees, i.e., agents, have different values for different hotel rooms) is two-fold. First, multi-dimensional settings are unlikely to permit succinct descriptions of optimal mechanisms [19, 22, 25]. Second, in multi-dimensional settings optimal mechanisms are unlikely to have practical implementations – even asking agents to report their true types across the many possible outcomes of the mechanism may be impractical. In summary, theory and practical considerations from optimal mechanism design in single-dimensional settings fail to generalize to multi-dimensional settings.

This paper approaches these issues through the lens of approximation. Our main results are simple, practical, approximately optimal mechanisms for a large class of multi-dimensional settings.

We consider the multi-dimensional setting through a single dimensional analogy wherein each multi-dimensional agent is represented by many independent single-dimensional agents (e.g., one for each hotel room). The optimal revenue for this single-dimensional setting is well understood and, due to increased competition among agents, upper-bounds that of the original multi-dimensional setting. We describe a "sequential posted price" mechanism for the single-dimensional setting that is practical and approximately optimal and, in contrast to the optimal single-dimensional mechanism, achieves its approximation without inter-agent competition. This gives a robustness to deviations in modeling assumptions and, for instance, the same mechanism continues to be approximately optimal in the original multi-dimensional setting. Therefore, our theory for approximately optimal single-dimensional mechanisms generalizes to multi-dimensional settings.

In the context of computer science literature this work is an extension of *algorithmic pricing* (e.g., [13]) to settings with multiple agents; it is unrelated to the standard computational questions of *algorithmic mechanism design* (e.g., [18, 21]). The central problem in algorithmic pricing can be viewed (for the most part) as Bayesian revenue maximization in a single agent setting (e.g., [13]). Algorithmic pricing is hard to approximate when the agent's values for different outcomes are generally correlated [7]; however, when the values are independent there is a 3-approximation [9]. In this context, our results improve and extend the independent case to settings with multiple agents and combinatorial feasibility constraints. Notice that the challenge in these problems is one imposed by the multi-dimensional incentive constraints and not one from an inherent complexity of an underlying non-game-theoretic optimization problem. (E.g., in the hotel example the underlying optimization problem is simply maximum weighted matching.) In contrast, most work in algorithmic mechanism design addresses settings where economic incentives are well understood but the underlying optimization problem is computationally intractable (e.g., combinatorial auctions [18]).

While our exposition focuses on revenue maximization, all of our techniques and results apply equally well to *social welfare*. Social welfare is unique among objectives in that designing optimal mechanisms in multi-dimensional settings is solved (by the VCG mechanism). Therefore, the interesting implication of our work on social welfare maximization is that sequential posted pricing approximates the welfare of the VCG mechanism and may be more practical.

Sequential Posted Pricing. Consider a single-parameter setting where each agent has a private value for service and there is a combinatorial feasibility constraint on the set of agents that can be simultaneously served. For this setting a *sequential posted pricing* (SPM) is a mechanism defined by a price for each agent, a sequence on agents, and the semantics that each agent is offered their corresponding price in sequence as a take-it-or-leave-it while-supplies-last offer. Meaning: if it is possible to serve the agent given the set of agents already being served then the agent is offered the price. A rational agent will accept if and only if the price is no more than their private value for service. That prices are associated with the agents and not the sequence reflects the possibility that agents may play asymmetric roles for a given feasibility constraint or value distribution.

Consider the following hotel rooms example with one room, two attendees, and attendee values independently and identically distributed uniformly between \$100 and \$200. The optimal mechanism is the Vickrey auction and its expected revenue is \$133. The optimal sequential posted pricing is for the organizers to offer the room to attendee 1 at a price of \$150. If the attendee accepts, then the room is sold, otherwise it is offered to attendee 2 for \$100. The expected revenue of this SPM is \$125.

We are interested in comparing the optimal mechanism to the optimal posted pricing in general settings. A special class of SPMs is one where mechanisms have provable performance guarantees for any sequence of the agents. These *order-oblivious posted pricings* (OPM) are mechanisms defined by a price for each agent and the semantics that each agent is offered their corresponding price in some arbitrary sequence as a take-it-or-leave-it while-supplies-last offer.

In single-dimensional settings, the advantages of sequential posted pricings speak to the many reasons optimal auctions are rarely seen in practice [1], and explain why posted pricings are ubiquitous [15]. First, take-it-or-leave-it offers result in trivial game dynamics: truthful responding is a dominant strategy. Second, SPMs satisfy strong notions of collusion resistance, e.g., *group strategyproofness* (see [12]): the only way in which an agent can "help" another agent is to decline an offer that he could have accepted, thereby hurting his own utility. Third, agents do not need to precisely know or report their value, they must only be able to evaluate their offer; therefore, they risk minimal exposure of their private information. Fourth, agents learn immediately whether they will be served or not. In conclusion, the robustness of SPMs in single-dimensional settings makes their approximation of optimal mechanisms independently worthy of study.

The final robustness property of SPMs, which is of paramount importance to our study of the multi-dimensional setting, is that they minimize the role of agent competition, implying that single-dimensional SPMs can be used "as-is" in multi-dimensional settings with only a constant factor loss in performance. In our translation from the multi-dimensional setting to the single-dimensional setting, each multi-dimensional agent has many single-dimensional representatives. A good OPM for the single-dimensional setting can be viewed as an OPM for the multi-dimensional setting by grouping all representatives of an agent together and making their offers simultaneously to the agent. The agent will of course accept the offer that maximizes their utility. The resulting mechanism is incentive compatible and achieves the same performance guarantee as the single-parameter OPM. For SPMs where we are not free to group each multi-dimensional agent's single-dimensional representatives together, an agent possibly faces a strategic dilemma of whether to accept an offer (e.g., for one hotel room) early on or wait for a later offer (e.g., another hotel room) which may or may not still be available. Our guarantee is robust to the actions of any agent with such a strategic option; if all agents with dominant strategies follow said strategies then our performance is a constant fraction of the original SPM's performance. (This is a non-standard notion of *dominant strategy implementation.*) Given the advantages of SPMs over standard dominant strategy mechanisms, these partially dominant strategy mechanisms may be more practically relevant.

Finally, we note that most of our results for posted pricings are constructive and there are efficient algorithms for them. A posted price mechanism has two components where computation is necessary: an offline computation of the prices to post (and for SPMs, the sequence of agents) and an online while-supplies-last offering of said prices.[1] The agents are only present for the online part where the mechanism is trivial. All of the computational burden for an SPM is in the offline part. The offline computation of our

[1]This is similar, for example, to nearest neighbor algorithms, where one distinguishes the time taken to construct a database, and the time taken to compute nearest neighbors over that database given a query.

posted price mechanisms is based on a subroutine that repeatedly samples the distribution of agent values and simulates Myerson's mechanism on the sample. This clearly requires more computation than just running Myerson's mechanism on the real agents in the first place; however, we benefit from the robustness that comes from the trivial online implementation of posted pricings.

Related work.

See [25] and references therein for work in economics on optimal multi-dimensional mechanism design. See [9] and references therein for work in computer science on multi-dimensional pricing for a single agent. We extend the setting from [9] to multiple agents and improve their approximation for a single agent from 3 to 2.

Sequential posted price mechanisms have been considered previously in single-dimensional settings. Sandholm and Gilpin [24] show experimentally that these mechanisms compare favorably to Myerson's optimal mechanisms. Blumrosen and Holenstein [6] show how to compute the optimal posted prices in the special case where agents' values are distributed identically, and also show that in this case the revenue of these mechanisms approaches the optimal revenue asymptotically. Several papers study revenue maximization through online posted pricings in the context of adversarial values, albeit in the simpler context of multi-unit auctions [5, 16, 4].

The question of whether simple mechanisms can achieve near-optimal revenue was considered recently by Hartline and Roughgarden [14]. Except for their result on single-item auctions with anonymous reserve prices, their VCG based mechanisms are likely to suffer the same impracticality criticisms as the optimal mechanism. The essay "The Lovely but Lonely Vickrey Auction" by Ausubel and Milgrom [1] discusses why this is the case. As a consequence of the near-optimality of sequential posted prices, we answer one of their open questions in the positive, namely, that the gap between the revenue optimal mechanism and a VCG mechanism with appropriate reserve prices is a constant (i.e., 2) in matroid settings but with arbitrary valuation distributions. This bound matches their result for regular distributions.

Our setting of sequential posted pricing with a matroid constraint is very closely related to the so-called matroid secretary problem [2, 3, 17], but there are two important differences: (a) they assume that agents' values are adversarial, whereas in our setting they are drawn from known distributions, and (b) in their setting agents arrive in random order, whereas we consider optimized and adversarial orderings. Some of our results are reminiscent of that work, but our techniques are necessarily different.

Finally, our results for OPMs in the multi-unit auction setting are based on work on prophet inequalities from optimal stopping theory. While that work applies directly to the analysis of OPMs in the single-item auction setting, we show that it extends to k-unit auctions with no loss in approximation factor.

2. PRELIMINARIES

2.1 Bayesian settings for mechanism design

The Bayesian multi-parameter unit-demand mechanism design problem (BMUMD for short) is an abstraction of the setting where a seller can provide a number of services to agents where each agent desires at most one service. An agent's value for each service may be different, but is drawn independently from known distributions. Formally we denote an instance of this problem as $(J, \mathcal{S}, \Pi, \mathbf{F})$ given as follows:

- $J = [m]$ is a set of m services.
- $\Pi = (J_1, \ldots, J_n)$ is a partitioning of the services among the n agents.[2] The services in J_i are the ones being targeted at agent i. These agents are *unit demand* in that they each desire at most one service from their partition.
- $\mathcal{S} \subset 2^J$ is a feasibility constraint. It specifies the sets of services the seller can simultaneously provide. We assume $\mathcal{S}$ is downward closed, i.e., for $S \in \mathcal{S}$ all subsets $S' \subset S$ are in $\mathcal{S}$. We assume $\mathcal{S}$ respects the partitioning Π and the unit-demand constraint, i.e., $S \in \mathcal{S}$ and $i \in [n]$ satisfies $|S \cap J_i| \leq 1$.
- $\mathbf{F} = F_1 \times \cdots \times F_m$ is the joint product distribution on agent values over the m services. I.e., v_j is drawn from distribution F_j with density function f_j.

The Bayesian single-parameter setting (BSMD for short) is an abstraction of the setting where each agent has a single private value for any "good outcome" of the mechanism. In this setting the mechanism can produce a good outcome for agent i in which case their valuation is v_i or a bad outcome in which case their valuation is zero. This can be represented as the special case of the multi-dimensional setting where there is exactly one service available to each agent, i.e., $n = m$ and $J_i = \{i\}$. We denote an instance of BSMD by the tuple $(J, \mathcal{S}, \mathbf{F})$.

Examples. In the multi-parameter hotel rooms example the set J of services is the set of edges in a bipartite graph between attendees and hotel rooms, J_i are the edges incident on attendee i, and $\mathcal{S}$ is the set of all matchings in the graph. In the single-parameter hotel rooms example, where each attendee has a set of desired rooms and the same valuation for each, the set J corresponds to attendees and the feasible sets $\mathcal{S}$ are sets of attendees that can be simultaneously matched, i.e., $\mathcal{S}$ is the set of all independent sets of the transversal matroid corresponding to matchings in the bipartite graph between attendees and their desired hotel rooms.

2.2 Posted-price mechanisms

We will consider sequential posted-price mechanisms based on the following high-level protocol that is parameterized by $\mathbf{p}$, a vector of prices, one for each service, and σ, an ordering over the services.

The generic sequential posted pricing protocol for $(\mathbf{p}, \sigma)$ is as follows:

1. Initialize $A \leftarrow \emptyset$.
2. For $j = 1$ through m, do:
   (a) If $A \cup \{\sigma(j)\} \in \mathcal{S}$, offer service $\sigma(j)$ at price p_j.
   (b) If the agent accepts, $A \leftarrow A \cup \{\sigma(j)\}$.
3. Provide the services in A to the corresponding agents.

We denote the revenue of this mechanism on valuation profile $\mathbf{v}$ by $\mathcal{R}^{(\mathbf{p},\sigma)}_{(J,\mathcal{S},\Pi,\mathbf{F})}(\mathbf{v})$. In the strategically-simple single-parameter setting this revenue can be calculated with the assumption that service j is accepted by the agent when offered if $v_j \geq p_j$. We defer the discussion of incentives in the more complicated multi-parameter setting to Section 2.3.

It is clear that it is always better from the designer's point of view to be able to choose the ordering σ. Unfortunately, this may not always be possible. We therefore distinguish between the following two kinds of posted-price mechanisms.

[2]This partitioning is for notational convenience only. Since we allow for an arbitrary feasibility constraint over the set J, the assumption that the sets J_i are disjoint is without loss of generality.

Sequenced Posted-Price Mechanisms. An SPM is given by $(\mathbf{p}, \sigma)$. Its expected revenue is:

$$\mathcal{R}^{(\mathbf{p},\sigma)}_{(J,\mathcal{S},\mathbf{F})} = \mathrm{E}_{\mathbf{v}\sim\mathbf{F}}[\mathcal{R}^{(\mathbf{p},\sigma)}_{(J,\mathcal{S},\mathbf{F})}(\mathbf{v})]$$

Order-oblivious Posted-pricing Mechanisms. An OPM is given simply by the pricing $\mathbf{p}$ where we allow the order over the services to be picked adversarially after the valuations of the agents are drawn. This pessimistically bounds the worst possible revenue for a given pricing. Formally:

$$\mathcal{R}^{\mathbf{P}}_{(J,\mathcal{S},\mathbf{F})} = \mathrm{E}_{\mathbf{v}\sim\mathbf{F}}[\min_\sigma \mathcal{R}^{(\mathbf{p},\sigma)}_{(J,\mathcal{S},\mathbf{F})}(\mathbf{v})]$$

When it is clear from the context we will omit the subscript $(J, \mathcal{S}, \Pi, \mathbf{F})$ or $(J, \mathcal{S}, \mathbf{F})$.

In some settings we consider randomized versions of SPMs and OPMs where the pricing $\mathbf{p}$ is picked randomly. In this case, we assume that the prices are drawn first and then the order σ is determined based on the prices (adversarially or by the designer).

2.3 Incentives

Most of the literature on mechanism design (especially in computer science) focuses on sealed-bid single-round direct-revelation mechanisms. These are mechanism that consist of two steps: first agents report bids, to be interpreted as their preferences over possible outcomes of the mechanisms, and second the mechanism selects an outcome and agent payments. In this context a mechanism is *incentive compatible* if each agent has a (weakly) dominant strategy of truthful reporting. It is assumed that agents report their true preferences in an incentive compatible mechanism.

Our posted price mechanisms do not take this general single-round form. Instead our mechanism will offer each agent a sequence of prices (and these offers may be arbitrarily interleaved among agents). Strategically, a bidder i when offered price p_j for $j \in J_i$ has two options. They can accept or reject the offer. An agent with value v_j for service j is *sincere* if they accept offers $p_j \leq v_j$ and reject offers $p_j > v_j$.

Sincere bidding is a dominant strategy for an agent only when the ordering σ respects the agent's incentives. Formally, we say that an ordering σ is J_i-respecting if for all $j_1, j_2 \in J_i$, $v_{j_1} - p_{j_1} > v_{j_2} - p_{j_2} \geq 0$ implies $\sigma^{-1}(j_1) < \sigma^{-1}(j_2)$. That is, the offers made to agent i are ordered by decreasing utility for the agent (although they may be interleaved arbitrarily with offers for other agents). An ordering is Π-respecting if it is J_i-respecting for all i. The following lemma formalizes the connection between sincere bidding and Π-respecting orderings.

LEMMA 1. *For $\mathbf{v}_{J_i}$ (the values of agent i) sincere bidding is a (weakly) dominant strategy for i in sequential posted pricing $(\mathbf{p}, \sigma)$ if and only if σ is J_i-respecting.*

It is easy to see that if the condition on σ is met then an agent will have no reason not to respond sincerely. If the condition is not met, an agent may strategize in the following way. When offered item j' at a desirable price $p_{j'}$, the agent might reject the offer in hopes of later being offered item j for which the agent has even higher utility.

The condition of the lemma is met in three special cases of interest:

1. When the agent is single dimensional, i.e., $|J_i| = 1$.
2. When the agent has positive utility for at most one service, i.e., $|\{j \in J_i \,:\, v_j - p_j > 0\}| \leq 1$
3. When the agent can choose the relative order of σ on J_i.

Given the last point, for an OPM in the multi-parameter setting we assume that orderings of interest are Π-respecting and define the worst-case revenue of the mechanism accordingly:

$$\mathcal{R}^{\mathbf{P}}_{(J,\mathcal{S},\Pi,\mathbf{F})} = \mathrm{E}_{\mathbf{v}\sim\mathbf{F}}\left[\min_{\sigma:\sigma \text{ is } \Pi\text{-respecting}} \mathcal{R}^{(\mathbf{p},\sigma)}_{(J,\mathcal{S},\Pi,\mathbf{F})}(\mathbf{v})\right]$$

In SPMs in multi-parameter settings, the ordering is not necessarily Π-respecting. We assume that all bidders for whom sincere bidding is a (weakly) dominant strategy indeed bid sincerely. We derive robust bounds on our mechanism performance in the presence of arbitrary manipulations of agents that do not have dominant strategies. This is a weaker form of implementation in dominant strategies, that we call *partial dominant strategy implementation.*

DEFINITION 1. *A mechanism is a* partial dominant-strategy (PDS) implementation *of a desired objective if that objective is met whenever every agent with a (weakly) dominant strategy plays that strategy (with other agents behaving arbitrarily).*

A mechanism is an α-approximation in partial dominant-strategy equilibrium (PDSE) *of a desired objective if it obtains an α approximation to the objective in expectation whenever every agent with a (weakly) dominant strategy plays that strategy.*

As is standard in mechanism design, we assume that the agents understand the mechanism. As our mechanisms are parameterized by prices $\mathbf{p}$, it is assumed that agents know these prices in advance. This assumption is only necessary for SPMs in multi-parameter settings where an agent i must know whether there is a future offer p_j for $j \in J_i$ such that $v_j - p_j > 0$.

2.4 Myerson's optimal mechanism

Myerson [20] describes the revenue maximizing mechanism for the Bayesian single-parameter mechanism design problem. *Virtual valuations* are given by the formula $\phi(v) = v - \frac{1-F(v)}{f(v)}$. When the value distributions F_i are *regular*, i.e., virtual valuations are monotone in valuations, the optimal mechanism first computes virtual values for each agent, and then allocates to a feasible subset of agents that maximizes the "virtual surplus"—the sum of the virtual values of agents in the set minus the cost of serving that set of agents [20].

When the distributions F_i are irregular, that is, virtual valuations are not monotone in valuations, Myerson's mechanism as described above will no longer be truthful. Myerson addressed this case by "ironing" the virtual valuation function and converting it into a monotone non-decreasing function called the ironed virtual value function denoted by $\bar{\phi}(v)$. We skip the description of this procedure; the reader is referred to [8, 9] for details.

We use $\mathcal{R}^{\mathcal{M}}_{\mathcal{I}}$ to denote the expected revenue of Myerson's mechanism on a single-parameter instance $\mathcal{I}$. For our analyses, we primarily require the following three characterizations of the expected revenue of any incentive compatible mechanism. See the appendix for a proof of Lemma 4.

PROPOSITION 2. *[20] When the distributions F_i are regular, the expected revenue of any incentive compatible single-parameter mechanism M is equal to its expected virtual surplus.*

PROPOSITION 3. *[20] The expected revenue of any incentive compatible single-parameter mechanism M is no more than its expected ironed virtual surplus. If the probability with which the mechanism serves agent i, as a function of v_i, is constant over any valuation range in which the ironed virtual value of i is constant, the expected revenue is equal to expected ironed virtual surplus.*

LEMMA 4. *If F_i is regular for each i, the revenue of any incentive compatible mechanism M over the n agents is bounded from above by $\sum_i p_i^M q_i^M$ where q_i^M is the probability (over $v_1, \cdots, v_n$) with which M allocates to agent i and $p_i^M = F_i^{-1}(1 - q_i^M)$.*

Furthermore for every i (with a regular or non-regular value distribution), there exist two prices $\underline{p_i}$ and $\overline{p_i}$ with corresponding probabilities $\underline{q_i}$ and $\overline{q_i}$, and a number $x_i \leq 1$, such that $x_i\underline{q_i} + (1 - x_i)\overline{q_i} = q_i^M$, and the expected revenue of M is no more than $\sum_i x_i\underline{p_i}\underline{q_i} + (1 - x_i)\overline{p_i}\overline{q_i}$.

2.5 Matroids and related set systems

Many of our techniques work for feasibility constraints $\mathcal{S}$ that are matroids or close to matroids. We define these set systems here. The set system $(X, \mathcal{S})$ over a universe X is called a matroid if it satisfies the following conditions:

1. (**heredity**) For every $A \in \mathcal{S}$, $B \subset A$ implies $B \in \mathcal{S}$.
2. (**augmentation**) For every $A, B \in \mathcal{S}$ with $|A| > |B|$, there exists $e \in A \setminus B$ such that $B \cup \{e\} \in \mathcal{S}$.

Sets in $\mathcal{S}$ are called independent, and maximal independent sets are called *bases*. A simple consequence of the above properties is that all bases are equal in size. The rank of a set $S \subseteq X$ is defined to be the size of any maximal independent subset of S. The *span* of a set $S \subseteq X$, $\mathrm{sp}(S)$, is the maximal set $T \supseteq S$ with $\mathrm{rank}(T) = \mathrm{rank}(S)$.

A k-uniform matroid on the universe X is a matroid where every subset of X of size at most k is independent. A partition matroid $(X, \mathcal{S})$ is a union of two or more uniform matroids $\{(X_i, \mathcal{M}_i)\}_i$, where $\{X_i\}_i$ is a partition of X and $\mathcal{S} = \{\cup_i A_i : A_i \in \mathcal{M}_i \ \forall i\}$.

A set system $(X, \mathcal{S})$ is called a matroid intersection if there are two (or more) matroids $(X, \mathcal{M}_1)$ and $(X, \mathcal{M}_2)$, such that $\mathcal{S} = \mathcal{M}_1 \cap \mathcal{M}_2$. An example of a matroid intersection is a matching in a bipartite graph.

Throughout this paper, the universe X is the set J of all services.

2.6 Computing the posted prices

For all but one of the approximately-optimal posted-price mechanisms that we present, prices and orderings can be computed efficiently in a computational model where we have black box access to the distribution $\mathbf{F}$. Please see the full version of this paper [11] for details.

3. REDUCING BMUMD TO BSMD

We now present a general reduction from the multi-parameter unit-demand mechanism design problem to the single-parameter problem. Using this reduction we can argue that if there exists an approximately optimal sequential posted-price mechanism in the single-parameter setting, there also exists one in the original multi-parameter setting. Understanding the properties of optimal mechanisms in multi-parameter settings is tricky so our approach is based on upper and lower bounds for single-parameter settings.

There are four main steps to give and instantiate our reduction. They are:

1. (Analogy) Define a single-parameter analog for any multi-parameter setting.
2. (Lower bound) Show that the revenue of the optimal single-dimensional analog is at least the revenue of the optimal multi-dimensional mechanism.
3. (Reduction) Show that if we had a sequential posted pricing for the single-dimensional analog, we can convert it into a posted pricing for the multi-dimensional setting without much loss in performance.
4. (Instantiation) Show for a given multi-dimensional setting that there exist sequential pricings that approximate the optimal mechanism for the single-parameter analog.

We give the analogy and lower bound here, as well as a reduction for OPMs. Section 4 instantiates this reduction in various settings of interest. While we do not obtain a general purpose reduction from SPMs, as we do for OPMs, in Section 5 we describe SPMs that obtain approximate optimality in PDSE in many single as well as multi-parameter settings.

The analogy

The main concept behind our reduction is a single-parameter analogy. Consider an instance $\mathcal{I} = (J, \mathcal{S}, \Pi, \mathbf{F})$ of the BMUMD with $n = |\Pi|$ agents and $m = |J|$ services. The *single-parameter analog* is the setting we get when we assume that each service is demanded by a distinct agent, i.e., $\mathcal{I}^{\text{reps}} = (J, \mathcal{S}, \mathbf{F})$. Formulaically, this analogy is trivial; intuitively, it replaces each agent i with $|J_i|$ distinct agents (called representatives or "reps" hereafter). Each rep is interested in a single service $j \in J_i$ and behaves independently of (and potentially to the detriment of) other reps. Notice that $\mathcal{I}^{\text{reps}}$ has $m = |J|$ agents and services.

Lower bound

Notice that $\mathcal{I}^{\text{reps}}$ is similar to $\mathcal{I}$ except that it involves more competition (among different reps of the same multi-parameter agent). Therefore it is natural to expect that a seller can obtain more revenue in the instance $\mathcal{I}^{\text{reps}}$ than in $\mathcal{I}$. The following lemma formalizes this (see the appendix for a proof).

LEMMA 5. *Let $\mathcal{A}$ be any individually rational and incentive compatible deterministic mechanism for instance $\mathcal{I}$ of the BMUMD. Then the expected revenue of $\mathcal{A}$, $\mathcal{R}^{\mathcal{A}}$, is no more than the expected revenue of Myerson's mechanism for the single-parameter instance $\mathcal{I}^{reps}$.*

A reduction for OPMs

The main advantage of a seller in the single-parameter analog is increased competition. Intuitively, if we can design mechanisms for the single-parameter setting that do not exploit competition, then it is reasonable to expect them to obtain similar performance in the multi-dimensional setting. Here, sequential posted pricings are exactly what is needed (see the appendix for a proof of the following).

THEOREM 6. *If OPM $\mathbf{p}$ is an α-approximation to the optimal mechanism for the single-parameter setting $\mathcal{I}^{reps}$ then it is an α-approximation in PDSE to the optimal mechanism for the multi-parameter setting $\mathcal{I}$.*

4. APPROXIMATION THROUGH OPMS

In this section we instantiate the reduction described in Section 3 for several different settings. We begin by discussing the hotel rooms assignment setting described in Section 1 and giving a simple 6.75 approximation for this setting. We then describe a (tight) 2-approximation for a simpler "k item auction" setting. We conclude this section by listing approximation factors for other settings of interest.

4.1 Intersections of partition matroids

Consider the instance $(J, \mathcal{S}, \mathbf{F})$ of the BSMD, where $\mathcal{S}$ is an intersection of two partition matroids $(\{X_a\}, \mathcal{S}_1)$ and $(\{Y_b\}, \mathcal{S}_2)$, with $\{X_a\}$ and $\{Y_b\}$ being partitions of the ground set $[m]$. Note that such an instance arises as the single-parameter analog $\mathcal{I}^{\text{reps}}$ of the hotel rooms assignment example discussed in the introduction; here the matroid $\mathcal{S}_1$ corresponds to the unit-demand constraint over the agents (i.e. any feasible allocation must contain at most one element in J_i for all i) and the matroid $\mathcal{S}_2$ corresponds to the supply constraints over hotel rooms (i.e. any feasible allocation must allocate any hotel room at most once).

THEOREM 7. *Let $\mathcal{I} = (J, \mathcal{S}, \mathbf{F})$ be an instance of the BSMD with $\mathcal{S}$ being an intersection of two partition matroids. Then, there exists a set of prices $\mathbf{p}$ such that $\mathcal{R}^{\mathbf{p}}_{\mathcal{I}} \geq \frac{1}{6.75}\mathcal{R}^{\mathcal{M}}_{\mathcal{I}}$.*

PROOF. We first consider the setting where the distributions F_j are regular. Recall from Lemma 4 that in this case the revenue of the optimal truthful mechanism for $\mathcal{I}$ is bounded by $\sum_j p_j^M q_j^M$, where q_j^M is the probability with which the optimal mechanism allocates service j and $p_j^M = F_j^{-1}(1 - q_j^M)$. We now describe the prices that achieve the claimed approximation. Let $q_j = q_j^M/3$. Our approximately optimal pricing is given by $\mathbf{p}$, where $p_i = F_j^{-1}(1 - q_j)$. Note that $p_j \geq p_j^M$.

Consider any ordering σ over the services, and let c_j denote the probability that service j gets offered under this ordering. We claim that $c_j \geq 4/9$ for all $j \in [m]$. Then, the expected revenue of the OPM $\mathbf{p}$ is given by

$$\mathcal{R}^{\mathbf{p}}_{\mathcal{I}} = \sum_j c_j p_j q_j \geq \sum_j (4/9) p_j^M (q_j^M/3) \geq \sum_j (1/6.75) p_j^M q_j^M.$$

This along with Lemma 4 implies the theorem.

To prove the claim, let $\mathcal{S}_1$ and $\mathcal{S}_2$ be the two partition matroids with $\mathcal{S} = \mathcal{S}_1 \cap \mathcal{S}_2$. Let j belong to the partition $X_a \subset [m]$ in $\mathcal{S}_1$ and the partition $Y_b \subset [m]$ in $\mathcal{S}_2$. Let k_a (resp. k_b) denote the maximum number of elements of X_a (resp. Y_b) that can be present in an independent set in $\mathcal{S}_1$ (resp. $\mathcal{S}_2$). Then, service j is offered if and only if the number of services in X_a that are offered prior to j in σ and are accepted is at most $k_a - 1$ and the number of services in Y_b that are offered prior to j in σ and are accepted is at most $k_b - 1$.

Note that by the feasibility of the allocation made by the optimal mechanism $\mathcal{M}$, we have

$$\sum_{j \in X_a} q_j = 1/3 \cdot \sum_{j \in X_a} q_j^M \leq k_a/3$$

$$\sum_{j \in Y_b} q_j = 1/3 \cdot \sum_{j \in Y_b} q_j^M \leq k_b/3$$

Therefore, using Markov's inequality, with probability at least $2/3$, at most $k_a - 1$ services in X_a are accepted if offered, and the same for Y_b. Using Baye's rule and noting that the two events are positively correlated, the probability that both the events happen is at least $4/9$, and so the claim holds.

When the distributions F_j are non-regular, we pick the prices p_j randomly as suggested by Lemma 4, such that the probability that service j is accepted if offered a randomized price is exactly $q_j^M/3$, and $\mathcal{R}^{\mathcal{M}}_{\mathcal{I}}$ is bounded from above by $3\sum_j \mathrm{E}\, p_j q_j$. To bound the expected revenue that the OPM obtains from allocating service j, we note that in any instantiation of the prices (and corresponding "worst" ordering over services), we can pessimistically defer offering service j until all other services have been offered. Then, following the above analysis, the probability that j is offered is at least $c_j \geq 4/9$. Then, the expected revenue from j is at least $4/9\, \mathrm{E}\, p_j q_j$, which is 4/27-th of the revenue that this service contributes to $\mathcal{R}^{\mathcal{M}}$. Therefore, the claimed approximation holds. □

4.2 k-uniform matroids

Next we present an improved (and tight) 2-approximation in the case where $\mathcal{S}$ is a k-uniform matroid. Our analysis follows an approach developed in the context of prophet inequalities in [23].

Recall from Section 2.4 that the expected revenue of any mechanism is equal to the expected virtual surplus from its allocation. Therefore, the optimal mechanism in this case allocates the k services with the largest virtual values. Let $\mathcal{O}$ denote this (random) set of services.

For a random variable X, let $(X)^+$ denote the positive portion of X, i.e. $(X)^+ = \max(0, X)$.

Our approximately optimal OPM chooses a virtual value r and sets $p_i = \phi_i^{-1}(r)$. The value r is chosen as the unique solution to $kr = \mathrm{E}[\sum_{i \in \mathcal{O}} (\phi_i(v_i) - r)^+]$. When the distributions F_j are non-regular, we use the same approach, except with ironed virtual valuations instead of virtual valuations. For the rest of this section, we assume that the distributions are regular.

THEOREM 8. *For any instance $\mathcal{I} = (J, \mathcal{S}, \mathbf{F})$ with a k-uniform matroid feasibility constraint, the OPM $\mathbf{p}$ described above achieves a 2-approximation to the optimal revenue, i.e., $\mathcal{R}^{\mathbf{p}}_{\mathcal{I}} \geq 1/2\mathcal{R}^{\mathcal{M}}_{\mathcal{I}}$.*

PROOF. Let σ be the worst-case ordering for the pricing $\mathbf{p}$. In particular, this corresponds to the order of increasing prices. Without loss of generality, we assume that $\sigma(i) = i$. Let S denote the (random) set of services allocated.

We upper bound the optimal revenue as

$$\begin{aligned}
\mathrm{E}\left[\sum_{i \in \mathcal{O}} \phi_i\right] &\leq \mathrm{E}\left[\sum_{i \in \mathcal{O}} r + (\phi_i - r)^+\right] \\
&\leq kr + \mathrm{E}\left[\sum_{i \in \mathcal{O}} (\phi_i - r)^+\right] \\
&= 2kr,
\end{aligned}$$

and lower bound the revenue of the OPM as

$$\mathrm{E}\left[\sum_{i \in S} \phi_i\right] = kr \Pr[|S| = k] + \mathrm{E}\left[\sum_{i \in S} \phi_i - r\right].$$

Let χ_i be the indicator random variable associated with the event $|S \cap \{1, 2, \ldots, i\}| < k$. We may then lower bound the second term above as

$$\begin{aligned}
\mathrm{E}\left[\sum_{i \in S} \phi_i - r\right] &= \sum_{i=1}^{n} \mathrm{E}[(\phi_i - r)^+ \cdot \chi_{i-1}] \\
&\geq \sum_{i=1}^{n} \mathrm{E}[(\phi_i - r)^+] \cdot \Pr[|S| < k] \\
&\geq kr \cdot \Pr[|S| < k].
\end{aligned}$$

Thus, we get

$$\mathrm{E}\left[\sum_{i \in S} \phi_i\right] \geq kr \cdot \Pr[|S| = k] + kr \cdot \Pr[|S| < k] = kr,$$

which implies the desired result. □

A lower bound of 2.

We now show that OPMs cannot approximate the optimal revenue to within a factor better than 2 even in the single-item setting. Consider a seller with one item and two agents. The first agent has a fixed value of 1. The second has a value of $1/\epsilon$ with probability

ϵ and 0 otherwise, for some small constant $\epsilon > 0$. Then, the optimal mechanism can obtain a revenue of $2 - \epsilon$ by first offering a price of $1/\epsilon$ to the second agent, and then a price of 1 to the first if the second declines the item. On the other hand, if the mechanism is forced to offer the item to the first agent first, then it has two choices: (1) offer the item at price 1 to agent 1; the agent always accepts, and (2) skip agent 1 and offer the item at price $1/\epsilon$ to agent 2; the agent accepts with probability ϵ. In either case, the expected revenue of the mechanism is 1.

4.3 Graphical matroids

While we do not know how to obtain constant factor approximations through OPMs for general matroid feasibility constraints, we now demonstrate that OPMs are constant factor optimal for a large class of matroids, namely graphical matroids. The ground set for a graphical matroid is the set of all edges of an undirected graph; A subset of edges is independent if it forms a forest (that is, it contains no cycles).

In order to obtain an approximation, however, we need to extend our definition of OPMs to allow the mechanism to be more restrictive in enforcing feasibility. Specifically, a **constrained order-oblivious posted-price mechanism** (COPM, for short) is given by the tuple $(\mathbf{p}, \mathcal{S}')$ where $\mathcal{S}' \subseteq \mathcal{S}$, and (as for OPMs) we allow the order σ over the agents to be picked adversarially, after the valuations of the agents are drawn. The selling protocol for a COPM offers a service j if the service along with previously allocated services is feasible in the set system $\mathcal{S}'$, and not merely in $\mathcal{S}$.

For graphical matroids, Babaioff et al. [3] and Korula and Pál [17] develop approaches for reducing this case to a partition matroid that in our setting yield a 8-approximation to the optimal revenue; we use a similar approach but exploit the connection between prophet inequalities and partition matroids to obtain a 3-approximation.

THEOREM 9. *Let $\mathcal{I}$ be an instance of the BSMD with a graphical matroid feasibility constraint. Then there is a COPM $(\mathbf{p}, \mathcal{S}')$, where $\mathcal{S}'$ is a partition matroid, that 3-approximates $\mathcal{R}^{\mathcal{M}}$ for $\mathcal{I}$.*

PROOF. Our technique here is to partition the elements of the matroid such that we may treat each part as a 1-uniform matroid yet still respect the original feasibility constraint, and achieve good revenue while doing so.

Let $G = (V, J)$ be the graph defining our matroid constraint, where J is the set of services/edges. As before, let q_j^M denote the probability with which edge (service) j is allocated by the optimal mechanism. Let $\delta(v)$ denote the set of edges incident on a vertex v, and for each $v \in V$ define $q_v = \sum_{j\in\delta(v)} q_j^M$. Now, we can see that

$$\sum_{v\in V} q_v = \sum_{j\in E} 2q_j^M \le 2(|V| - 1),$$

This implies that there exists a v for which $q_v \le 2$; Let $\delta(v)$ be one of our partitions. Note that the edge set $\delta(v)$ forms a cut in G, and so given an independent set of edges from $J \setminus \delta(v)$ we may add any single edge from $\delta(v)$ while retaining independence. We apply this argument recursively to $(V \setminus \{v\}, J \setminus \delta(v))$ to form the rest of our partition. At the end, we have a partition of J such that each part has total mass no more than 2 and any collection of edges using no more than one edge from each part is independent.

We first note how to obtain a simple 8-approximation and then describe the changes needed to obtain a 3-approximation. We define $\mathcal{S}'$ to be the union of 1-uniform matroids, each over the different parts of J defined above. The prices $\mathbf{p}$ for the 8-approximation are defined as follows: $q_j = q_j^M/4$ and $p_j = F_j^{-1}(1 - q_j)$. Then, the optimal revenue is at most $4\sum_j p_j q_j$, whereas, our mechanism offers each service with probability at least $1/2$, and therefore, obtains a revenue of $1/2\sum_j p_j q_j$.

To obtain a 3-approximation, we use the same constraint $\mathcal{S}'$ as before, but modify the prices employing the approach developed in the proof of Theorem 8. Let us focus on a single part, say $X \subset J$, in the partition of J defined above. Recall that $\sum_{j\in X} q_j \le 2$. Let $p_j^M = F_j^{-1}(1 - q_j^M)$, and r be defined such that $r = \sum_{j\in X} q_j^M (p_j^M - r)^+$. Let $p_j = p_j^M$ if $p_j^M \ge r$ and ∞ otherwise. Our COPM is given by $(\mathbf{p}, \mathcal{S}')$.

Then the optimal revenue over X can be bounded as

$$\sum_{j\in X} p_j^M q_j^M \le \sum_{j\in X} q_j^M (r + \left(p_j^M - r\right)^+) = r(1 + \sum_{j\in X} q_j^M) \le 3r.$$

On the other hand, following the proof of Theorem 8, the revenue of the COPM can be bounded as

$$r\,\Pr[\text{at least one service in } X \text{ is allocated}] + \left(\sum_{j\in X} q_j^M (p_j^M - r)^+\right) \Pr[\text{no service in } X \text{ is allocated}] = r$$

□

4.4 Non-matroids constraints

We now show that the approximations described above cannot extend to general non-matroid set systems. In particular, the example below describes a family of instances with i. i. d. agents and a symmetric non-matroid constraint for which the ratio between the expected revenue of Myerson's mechanism and that of the optimal OPM is $\Omega(\log n/\log\log n)$ where n is the number of agents. In fact the same lower bounds holds even for SPMs, that is, when we are able to choose the best ordering over offers.

EXAMPLE 1. *For a given k, set $n = k^{k+1}$. Partition $[n]$ into k^k groups $G_1, \cdots, G_{k^k}$ of size k each, with $G_i \cap G_j = \emptyset$ for all $i \ne j$. The set system $\mathcal{S}$ contains all subsets of the groups G_i, that is, $\mathcal{S} = \cup_i 2^{G_i}$ Each agent has a value of 1 with probability $1 - 1/k$ and k with probability $1/k$.*

For any given valuation profile, let us call the agents with a value of k to be good agents and the rest to be bad agents. The probability that a group contains k good agents is k^{-k}. Therefore in expectation one group has k good agents and Myerson's mechanism can obtain revenue k^2 from such a group: $\mathcal{R}^{\mathcal{M}} = \Omega(k^2)$.

Next consider any SPM. Once the mechanism commits to serving an agent, it can only serve agents within the same group in the future. These have a total expected value less than $2k$. Therefore, the revenue of any SPM is at most k from the first agent it serves and $2k$ in expectation from subsequent agents, for a total of $3k$. We get a gap of $\Omega(k) = \Omega(\log n/\log\log n)$.

4.5 Other feasibility constraints

Table 1 outlines the approximation factors we can achieve with OPMs, as well as lower bounds on achievable factors. Please see the full version of this paper [11] for details.

5. APPROXIMATION THROUGH SPMS

In this section we consider settings for the BSMD where we don't know of good approximations through OPMs. We show that we can achieve good approximations by picking the right ordering σ over offers, that is, through sequenced posted-price mechanisms.

Feasibility constraint $\mathcal{S}$	Gap from optimal upper bound	lower bound
Uniform matroid, Partition matroid	2	2
Graphical matroid	3	2
Intersection of two part. matroids	6.75	2
Graphical matroid ∩ partition matroid	10.66	2
General matroid	$O(\log k)$	2
Non-matroid downward closed	-	$\Omega(\frac{\log n}{\log\log n})$

Table 1: A summary of approximation factors for the BSMD achievable through OPMs. Here k is the rank of $\mathcal{S}$.

While there is no direct reduction from SPMs in multi-parameter settings to SPMs in single-parameter settings analogous to Theorem 6, we show that for matroid and matroid intersection settings our results carry over in an approximation preserving way to multi-parameter instances as well.

We begin with a 2 approximation to single-parameter instances with a general matroid feasibility constraint, and then describe an 8 approximation in PDSE to multi-parameter instances with a general matroid intersection constraint. We conclude this section with a table of approximation factors achievable through SPMs.

5.1 A 2-approximation for matroids

Consider the instance $\mathcal{I} = (J, \mathcal{S}, \mathbf{F})$ where $\mathcal{S}$ is a matroid with rank k. Assume first that all the distributions F_j are regular. Let $q_j = q_j^M$ be the probability with which the optimal truthful mechanism (Myerson's mechanism) allocates service j. Let $p_j = p_j^M = F_j^{-1}(1 - q_j^M)$. Let σ be the order of decreasing prices p_j over the services. Our approximately optimal SPM is given by $(\mathbf{p}, \sigma)$. When the distributions F_j are non-regular, we define the prices randomly as suggested by Lemma 4, and for each instantiation of the prices, pick the greedy ordering over services in order of decreasing prices.

THEOREM 10. *Let $\mathcal{I}$ be an instance of the BSMD with a matroid feasibility constraint. Then, the mechanism $(\mathbf{p}, \sigma)$ described above 2-approximates the revenue of Myerson's mechanism for $\mathcal{I}$.*

PROOF. We show that the mechanism $(\mathbf{p}, \sigma)$ achieves an expected revenue of at least $\frac{1}{2}\sum_i p_i q_i$. Once again we start with the assumption that all the distributions F_j are regular. Note that if the mechanism ignored the feasibility constraint $\mathcal{S}$, and offered the prices $\mathbf{p}$ to all agents, serving any agent that accepted its offered price, then its expected revenue would be exactly $\sum_i p_i q_i$. So our proof accounts for the total revenue lost due to agents "blocked" from getting an offer by previously served agents.

Formally, let $S = \{i_1 < i_2 < \cdots < i_\ell\}$ be the set of agents served, and let S_j denote the first j elements of S. Define the sets $B_j = (\mathrm{sp}(S_j) \setminus \mathrm{sp}(S_{j-1})) \cap \{i : i > i_j\}$. Note that the sets B_j partition the set of agents blocked by those previously served. Moreover, $p_i \le p_{i_j}$ for all $i \in B_j$, since $B_j \subseteq \{i : i > i_j\}$.

Denote the price offered to agent i_j by p^j. Then, the expected revenue lost given that S is served is

$$\sum_{j=1}^{\ell}\sum_{i\in B_j} p_i q_i$$

$$\le p^1\left(\sum_{i\in\mathrm{sp}(S_1)} q_i\right) + \sum_{j=2}^{\ell} p^j\left(\sum_{i\in\mathrm{sp}(S_j)} q_i - \sum_{i\in\mathrm{sp}(S_{j-1})} q_i\right)$$

$$= \sum_{j=1}^{\ell-1}\left((p^j - p^{j+1})\sum_{i\in\mathrm{sp}(S_j)} q_i\right) + p^\ell\left(\sum_{i\in\mathrm{sp}(S_\ell)} q_i\right)$$

$$\le \sum_{j=1}^{\ell-1}(p^j - p^{j+1})\cdot j + p^\ell\cdot\ell = \sum_{j=1}^{\ell-1} p^j,$$

which is the revenue obtained by serving S. Here we used the fact that $\sum_{i\in\mathrm{sp}(S_j)} q_i \le \mathrm{rank}(S_j) = |S_j| = j$. Therefore,

$$\mathrm{E}[\text{revenue lost}] \le \sum_S\sum_{j\in S} p^j \cdot \Pr[S \text{ is served}] = \mathcal{R}^{(\mathbf{p},\sigma)},$$

and so it follows that $\sum_i p_i q_i \le 2\mathcal{R}^{(\mathbf{p},\sigma)}$.

Next consider the case of non-regular distributions. As mentioned earlier, we pick prices randomly as suggested by Lemma 4. Let p_j be the average price offered for service j if j is the first service offered. Consider a hypothetical posted-price mechanism that orders the services in decreasing order of p_j, and then defers the instantiation of the prices to be offered to just before the service is offered. Then, the acceptance probabilities for the services are exactly q_j, and the previous analysis continues to work in this case. Our SPM, that picks the greedy ordering for every instantiation of prices performs no worse than this hypothetical mechanism and we obtain the same approximation factor as before. □

We note that this approximation factor is not known to be tight. Blumrosen et al. [6] show that the gap between the optimal SPM and Myerson's mechanism can be as large as $\sqrt{\pi/2} \approx 1.253$ even in the single item auction case with i. i. d. agents.

5.2 BMUMD with a matroid intersection constraint

Recall that Theorems 6 and 7 together show that we can achieve a constant factor approximation through OPMs to instances of the BMUMD with a feasibility constraint that is an intersection of two partition matroids. We now extend this result to general matroid intersections albeit through SPMs in a slightly weaker solution concept — partial dominant-strategy implementation.

The prices and ordering in our approximately optimal SPM is picked in a manner similar to the one employed in Section 5.1 for matroids. Specifically, let $\mathcal{I} = (J, \mathcal{S}, \Pi, \mathbf{F})$ be the instance of BMUMD that we are interested in. Assume, to begin with, that all the distributions F_j are regular. Consider the instance $\mathcal{I}^{\text{reps}} = (J, \mathcal{S}, \mathbf{F})$, and let q_j^M be the probability with which the optimal truthful mechanism (Myerson's mechanism) allocates service j in that setting. Let $p_j^M = F_j^{-1}(1 - q_j^M)$. We define q_j to be $q_j^M/2$ and $p_j = F_j^{-1}(1 - q_j)$. Let σ be the order of decreasing prices p_j over the services. Our approximately optimal SPM for $\mathcal{I}$ is $(\mathbf{p}, \sigma)$.

THEOREM 11. *Given any instance $\mathcal{I} = (J, \mathcal{S}, \Pi, \mathbf{F})$ of the BMUMD, if $\mathcal{S}$ is a matroid intersection set system, then the SPM $(\mathbf{p}, \sigma)$ described above is an 8-approximation in PDSE to the revenue of the optimal incentive compatible mechanism for $\mathcal{I}$.*

PROOF. Let the pricing $\mathbf{p}$ and ordering σ be as defined above. Recall that Lemmas 4 and 5 together imply that the revenue of any incentive compatible mechanism for $\mathcal{I}$ is bounded above by $\sum_j p_j^M q_j^M \le 2\sum_j p_j q_j$.

Now consider the SPM $(\mathbf{p}, \sigma)$. We say that an agent i desires a service $j \in J_i$ if $v_j > p_j$, and i uniquely desires j if j is the only service in J_i with that property. As noted in Section 2.3, for an agent that uniquely desires a service, sincere bidding is a (weakly) dominant strategy. We first note that for every agent i, with probability $1/2$, i bids sincerely. This follows from Markov's

Feasibility constraint S	Gap from optimal	
	upper bound	lower bound
General matroid	2	$\sqrt{\pi/2} \approx 1.25$
Uniform matroid, Partition matroid	$e/(e-1) \approx 1.58$	1.25
Intersection of two matroids (BSMD)	3	1.25
Intersection of two matroids (BMUMD)	8	1.25
Non-matroid downward closed	-	$\Omega(\log n/\log\log n)$

Table 2: A summary of approximation factors for the BSMD and the BMUMD achievable through SPMs.

inequality by noting that $\sum_{j\in J_i} \Pr[i \text{ desires } j] = \sum_{j\in J_i} q_j = 1/2\sum_{j\in J_i} q_j^M \leq 1/2$.

Now divide the set of all services into three groups—S, the set of *sold* services, B the set of services that are desired by their corresponding agents but "blocked" by services in S, and U the set of services that are desired by their corresponding agents and not in sets S or B. Note that these sets S, B, and U are random variables depending on the instantiation of agents' values. Then our observation above implies that services in U are not uniquely desired. Now, the expected total price in the union of the sets S, B and U is exactly $\sum_j p_j q_j$. Moreover, every desired service is uniquely desired with probability at least $1/2$; therefore, the expected total price in U is at most half the total price of all desired services, that is, at most $1/2\sum_j p_j q_j$. Finally, following the proof of Theorem 10, the expected total price in B conditioned on S is at most the total price contained in S. Therefore, putting everything together we get that the expected total price obtained from S is at least $1/4\sum_j p_j q_j$. By our choice of $\mathbf{p}$ and $\mathbf{q}$, this is an 8-approximation. □

5.3 Other feasibility constraints

Table 2 outlines the approximation factors we can achieve with SPMs, as well as lower bounds on achievable factors.

6. DISCUSSION

We presented constant factor approximations to revenue for several classes of multi-parameter mechanism design problems by designing approximately-optimal posted price mechanisms for single-parameter settings. The approximation factors we obtain in both the single-parameter and multi-parameter settings depend on the kind of feasibility constraint that the seller faces. The exact constants are summarized in Tables 1 and 2.

While these approximation factors are with respect to the optimal deterministic incentive compatible mechanism, in [10] we show that (slightly worse) constant-factor approximation guarantees can be obtained against the optimal randomized incentive compatible mechanism as well.

Our approach does not extend beyond matroid and matroid-like settings. However, it is possible that there is some other class of simple near-optimal mechanisms for non-matroid single-parameter settings that do not exploit competition among agents. Such mechanisms may lead to approximately-optimal multi-parameter mechanisms for a broader class of feasibility constraints.

More generally, two important assumptions underlie our work: (1) agents are unit-demand, and (2) their values for different services are distributed independently. In the absence of either of these assumptions the upper bound on the optimal revenue based on the single-parameter setting with representatives does not remain valid. An important open question is to design a reasonably tight upper bound in those cases, and use it to approximate the optimal mechanism. A partial result along these lines was obtained by [10] — they show that for a class of positively-correlated distributions, called the common base value model, the optimal revenue of the single-parameter analog still bounds from above the optimal revenue of the multi-parameter problem within a small constant factor.

7. REFERENCES

[1] Lawrence M. Ausubel and Paul Milgrom. The lovely but lonely vickrey auction. In P. Cramton, Y. Shoham, and R. Steinberg, editors, *Combinatorial Auctions*, chapter 1, pages 17–40. MIT Press, Cambridge, MA, 2006.

[2] M. Babaioff, N. Immorlica, and R. Kleinberg. Matroids, secretary problems, and online mechanisms. In *Proc. 19th ACM Symp. on Discrete Algorithms*, 2007.

[3] Moshe Babaioff, Michael Dinitz, Anupam Gupta, Nicole Immorlica, and Kunal Talwar. Secretary problems: weights and discounts. In *SODA '09: Proceedings of the Nineteenth Annual ACM -SIAM Symposium on Discrete Algorithms*, pages 1245–1254, Philadelphia, PA, USA, 2009. Society for Industrial and Applied Mathematics.

[4] A. Blum and J. Hartline. Near-optimal online auctions. In *Proc. 16th ACM Symp. on Discrete Algorithms*. ACM/SIAM, 2005.

[5] A. Blum, V. Kumar, A. Rudra, and F. Wu. Online learning in online auctions. *Theoretical Computer Science*, 324:137–146, 2004.

[6] L. Blumrosen and T. Holenstein. Posted prices vs. negotiations: an asymptotic analysis. In *Proc. 10th ACM Conf. on Electronic Commerce*, 2008.

[7] P. Briest. Towards hardness of envy-free pricing. Technical Report TR06-150, ECCC, 2006.

[8] J. Bulow and J. Roberts. The simple economics of optimal auctions. *The Journal of Political Economy*, 97:1060–90, 1989.

[9] S. Chawla, J. Hartline, and R. Kleinberg. Algorithmic pricing via virtual valuations. In *Proc. 9th ACM Conf. on Electronic Commerce*, pages 243–251, 2007.

[10] S. Chawla, D. Malec, and B. Sivan. The power of randomness in Bayesian optimal mechanism design. In *Proc. 12th ACM Conf. on Electronic Commerce*, 2010.

[11] Shuchi Chawla, Jason D. Hartline, David Malec, and Balu Sivan. Multi-parameter mechanism design and sequential posted pricing. *CoRR*, abs/0907.2435, 2009.

[12] A. Goldberg and J. Hartline. Collusion-resistant mechanisms for single-parameter agents. In *Proc. 16th ACM Symp. on Discrete Algorithms*, 2005.

[13] V. Guruswami, J. Hartline, A. Karlin, D. Kempe, C. Kenyon, and F. McSherry. On profit-maximizing envy-free pricing. In *Proc. 16th ACM Symp. on Discrete Algorithms*, 2005.

[14] J. Hartline and T. Roughgarden. Simple versus optimal mechanisms. In *Proc. 11th ACM Conf. on Electronic Commerce*, 2009.

[15] Catherine Holahan. Auctions on eBay: A Dying Breed. http://www.businessweek.com/technology/content/jun2008/tc2008062_112762.htm, June 3 2008.

[16] R. Kleinberg and T. Leighton. The value of knowing a demand curve: Bounds on regret for on-line posted-price auctions. In *Proc. 44th IEEE Symp. on Foundations of Computer Science*, 2003.

[17] Nitish Korula and Martin Pál. Algorithms for secretary problems on graphs and hypergraphs. In *ICALP '09: Proceedings of the 36th Internatilonal Collogquium on Automata, Languages and Programming*, pages 508–520, Berlin, Heidelberg, 2009. Springer-Verlag.

[18] D. Lehmann, L. I. O'Callaghan, and Y. Shoham. Truth revelation in approximately efficient combinatorial auctions. In *Proc. 1st ACM Conf. on Electronic Commerce*, pages 96–102. ACM Press, 1999.

[19] R.P. McAfee and J. McMillan. Multidimensional incentive compatibility and mechanism design. *Journal of Economic Theory*, 46(2):335–354, 1988.

[20] R. Myerson. Optimal auction design. *Mathematics of Operations Research*, 6:58–73, 1981.

[21] N. Nisan and A. Ronen. Algorithmic mechanism design. In *Proc. 31st ACM Symp. on Theory of Computing*, pages 129–140. ACM Press, 1999.

[22] Jean-Charles Rochet and Philippe Chone. Ironing, Sweeping, and Multidimensional Screening. *Econometrica*, 66(4):783–826, 1998.

[23] Ester Samuel-Cahn. Comparison of threshold stop rules and maximum for independent nonnegative random variables. *The Annals of Probability*, 12(4):1213–1216, 1984.

[24] Tuomas Sandholm and Andrew Gilpin. Sequences of take-it-or-leave-it offers: near-optimal auctions without full valuation revelation. In *AAMAS '06: Proceedings of the fifth international joint conference on Autonomous agents and multiagent systems*, pages 1127–1134, New York, NY, USA, 2006. ACM.

[25] D. Vincent and A. Manelli. Multidimensional mechanism design: Revenue maximization and the multiple-good monopoly. *Journal of Economic Theory*, 137(1):153–185, 2007.

[26] Robert B. Wilson. *Nonlinear Pricing*. Oxford University Press, 1997.

APPENDIX

In this section we prove Lemmas 4 and 5, as well as Theorem 6.

Proof of Lemma 4. We prove the regular case first. Consider the revenue that M draws from serving agent i. This is clearly bounded above by the optimal mechanism that sells to only i, but with probability at most q_i^M. By Proposition 2, such a mechanism should sell to agent i with probability 1 whenever the value of the agent is above $F_i^{-1}(1-q_i^M)$ and with probability 0 otherwise. The revenue of the optimal such mechanism is therefore $p_i^M q_i^M$.

In the non-regular case, note that the value p_i^M may fall in a valuation range that has constant ironed virtual value. Let $\underline{p_i}$ denote the infimum $\inf\{v : \bar{\phi}_i(v) = \bar{\phi}_i(p_i^M)\}$ of this range and $\overline{p_i}$ denote the supremum $\sup\{v : \bar{\phi}_i(v) = \bar{\phi}_i(p_i^M)\}$. Let $\underline{q_i} = 1 - F_i(\underline{p_i})$ and $\overline{q_i} = 1 - F_i(\overline{p_i})$. Then, $\overline{q_i} \le q_i^M \le \underline{q_i}$, and there exists an x_i such that $x_i\underline{q_i} + (1 - x_i)\overline{q_i} = q_i^M$. Now an easy consequence of Proposition 3 is that the optimal mechanism with selling probability q_i^M sells to the agent with probability x_i if the agent's value is between $\underline{p_i}$ and $\overline{p_i}$, and with probability 1 if the value is above $\overline{p_i}$. The revenue of this mechanism is exactly $x_i\underline{q_i}\underline{p_i} + (1 - x_i)\overline{q_i}\overline{p_i}$.

Proof of Lemma 5. Truthful mechanisms in multi-parameter settings satisfy the weak monotonicity condition defined below. For a Mechanism M, and a value vector $\mathbf{v}$, let $M_j(\mathbf{v})$ denote the probability with which M provides service j at value vector $\mathbf{v}$.

DEFINITION 2. *A mechanism M satisfies weak monotonicity if for any agent i and any two types $\mathbf{v}^1$ and $\mathbf{v}^2$ with $v_j^1 = v_j^2$ for all $j \in J \setminus J_i$, the following holds:*

$$\sum_{j \in J_i} \left(M_j(\mathbf{v}^1)v_j^1 + M_j(\mathbf{v}^2)v_j^2\right) \ge \sum_{j \in J_i} \left(M_j(\mathbf{v}^2)v_j^1 + M_j(\mathbf{v}^1)v_j^2\right)$$

We show that we can construct a truthful mechanism $\mathcal{A}^{\text{reps}}$ for the instance $\mathcal{I}^{\text{reps}}$ with revenue no less than that of $\mathcal{A}$. The lemma then follows from the optimality of Myerson's mechanism. Given a vector of values $\mathbf{v}$, the mechanism $\mathcal{A}^{\text{reps}}$ allocates to the set that $\mathcal{A}$ allocates to in $\mathcal{I}$ for the same value vector $\mathbf{v}$. We first claim that the allocation rule of $\mathcal{A}^{\text{reps}}$ is monotone non-decreasing in any v_j, implying that there exists a payment rule that makes the mechanism truthful. To prove the claim, fix any agent i and $j \in J_i$, and consider two value vectors $\mathbf{v}^1$ and $\mathbf{v}^2$ with $v_j^1 = x$, $v_j^2 = y$, and $v_{j'}^1 = v_{j'}^2$ for $j' \ne j$. Let α_x and α_y denote the probabilities of serving agent i with service j under the two value vectors respectively, and let β_x and β_y denote the total value that agent i obtains from other services $j' \in J_i$, $j' \ne j$, in the two cases respectively. Then the weak-monotonicity (Definition 2) of $\mathcal{A}$ implies that

$$(x\alpha_x + \beta_x) + (y\alpha_y + \beta_y) \ge (x\alpha_y + \beta_y) + (y\alpha_x + \beta_x).$$

This is equivalent to $(x - y)(\alpha_x - \alpha_y) \ge 0$ and so the claim holds.

It remains to prove that the expected revenue of $\mathcal{A}^{\text{reps}}$ given $\mathcal{I}^{\text{reps}}$ is no less than the expected revenue of $\mathcal{A}$ given $\mathcal{I}$. Note that any deterministic multi-parameter mechanism can be interpreted as offering a price menu with one price for each item or service to each agent as a function of other agents' bids [26]. The agent then chooses the item or service that brings her the most utility. Given this characterization, suppose that for a fixed set $\mathbf{v}$ of values, mechanism $\mathcal{A}$ offers a price menu with prices $\mathbf{p}$ to agent i. Then, it draws a revenue of p_j from i whenever service j is offered. On the other hand, mechanism $\mathcal{A}^{\text{reps}}$ charges the agent j the minimum amount it needs to bid to be served, which is no less than p_j, as $\mathcal{A}$ is individually rational.

Proof of Theorem 6. Let $\mathbf{p}$ be an α-approximate OPM for $\mathcal{I}^{\text{reps}}$. Consider its performance on I. For a fixed instantiation $\mathbf{v}$ of values let σ be any Π-respecting ordering that minimizes the revenue of the mechanism. Note that whenever the mechanism $(\mathbf{p}, \sigma)$ offers a service to agent i it is a dominant strategy for the agent to accept the service if and only if the agent gets non-negative value from the service. This is because any future offers that the agent gets can only bring him lower utility. Therefore, the sequence of offers and outcome of $(\mathbf{p}, \sigma)$ is identical under $\mathcal{I}$ and $\mathcal{I}^{\text{reps}}$, and, $\mathcal{R}_{\mathcal{I}}^{(\mathbf{p},\sigma)}(\mathbf{v}) = \mathcal{R}_{\mathcal{I}^{\text{reps}}}^{(\mathbf{p},\sigma)}(\mathbf{v}) \ge \mathcal{R}_{\mathcal{I}^{\text{reps}}}^{(\mathbf{p})}(\mathbf{v})$. Therefore, the revenue of $\mathbf{p}$ in the multi-parameter setting is no less than its revenue in the single-parameter setting. Then the result follows from Lemma 5.

Saving Space by Algebraization*

Daniel Lokshtanov
University of Bergen
PB 7803, N-5020
Bergen, Norway
daniello@ii.uib.no

Jesper Nederlof
University of Bergen
PB 7803, N-5020
Bergen, Norway
jesper.nederlof@ii.uib.no

ABSTRACT

The SUBSET SUM and KNAPSACK problems are fundamental $\mathcal{NP}$-complete problems and the pseudo-polynomial time dynamic programming algorithms for them appear in every algorithms textbook. The algorithms require pseudo-polynomial time and space. Since we do not expect polynomial time algorithms for SUBSET SUM and KNAPSACK to exist, a very natural question is whether they can be solved in *pseudo-polynomial time* and *polynomial space*. In this paper we answer this question affirmatively, and give the first pseudo-polynomial time, polynomial space algorithms for these problems.

Our approach is based on algebraic methods and turns out to be useful for several other problems as well. Then we show how the framework yields polynomial space exact algorithms for the classical TRAVELING SALESMAN, WEIGHTED SET COVER and WEIGHTED STEINER TREE problems as well. Our algorithms match the time bound of the best known pseudo-polynomial space algorithms for these problems.

Categories and Subject Descriptors

F.2.1 [**Analysis of Algorithms and Problem Complexity**]: Numerical Algorithms and Problems; F.2.2 [**Analysis of Algorithms and Problem Complexity**]: Nonnumerical Algorithms and Problems; G.2.1 [**Discrete Mathematics**]: Combinatorics; G.2.2 [**Discrete Mathematics**]: Graph Theory

General Terms

Algorithms, Theory

Keywords

Dynamic Programming, Space Efficient, Fourier, Möbius

*Supported by the Norwegian Research Council

1. INTRODUCTION

In the 1950's, Richard Bellman published his book "Bottleneck Problems and Dynamic Programming" [1], initiating the systematic study of *Dynamic Programming* (DP). Nowadays, DP is considered to be one of the most prominent techniques for designing algorithms, and many algorithmic results obtained by DP are not known to be obtainable by any other technique. Conceptually, a DP algorithm can be seen as a combination of a table and an algorithm computing table entries, usually formalized as a recurrence. An inherent property of DP algorithms is that they require a relatively big amount of working memory. This is because often, many previously computed table entries are required for efficient computation of new entries. For an elementary introduction to DP, see for example [7].

In this paper we identify sufficient conditions for being able to turn DP algorithms into algorithms with roughly the same running time and significantly lower space usage. In particular, we show that if a DP algorithm can be formalized as an expression using specific operators, then one can use algebraic transforms to evaluate the expression in a space-efficient manner.

Two of the canonical applications of DP are the SUBSET SUM and KNAPSACK problems. In the SUBSET SUM problem one is given a set of integers $S = \{w_1, \dots, w_n\}$ and an integer w. The question is whether there exist of subset $S' \subseteq S$ such that $\sum_{w_i \in S'} w_i = w$. In the KNAPSACK problem one is given an additional set of values $v_1, \dots, v_n$ and an integer v. Here the objective is to find a subset S' of items whose total weight is at most w and total value is at least v. The SUBSET SUM problem is the special case of KNAPSACK where $w = v$ and all items have weight equal to value. The classical $O(nw)$ time[1] for Subset Sum of Bellman [2] uses $O(w)$ space. Hence, the algorithm uses *pseudo-polynomial* time and space. A natural and fundamental question is whether it is possible to have a pseudo-polynomial time algorithm for SUBSET SUM using only polynomial space. We answer this question affirmatively by showing that Bellman's DP algorithm can be encoded as an expression with a restricted set of operators. In particular, we obtain an algorithm with running time $\tilde{\mathcal{O}}(n^3 t \log t)$ time and $\tilde{\mathcal{O}}(n^2)$ space. For the more general KNAPSACK problem we give an algorithm running in $\tilde{\mathcal{O}}(n^4 \log^2(vw)vw)$ time and $\tilde{\mathcal{O}}(n^2 \log(vw))$ space.

Our methodolody enables us to make many exponential-time and space DP algorithms run in polynomial space in-

[1]We make use of the $\mathcal{O}$, $\tilde{\mathcal{O}}$ and $\mathcal{O}^*$ notation which suppress factors constant, polylogarithmic in instance size, and polynomial in instance size respectively.

stead. This is useful because algorithms using both exponential time and space tend to run out of space long before they run out of time. Notable results in the direction of polynomial space exponential-time algorithms for $\mathcal{NP}$-hard problems include Karp's $\mathcal{O}^*(2^n)$ time algorithm [16] for HAMILTONIAN PATH, Björklund, Husfeldt and Koivisto's SET COVER[2] algorithm [4] running in time $\mathcal{O}^*(2^n)$ and Nederlof's $\mathcal{O}^*(2^k)$ time algorithm for UNWEIGHTED STEINER TREE [19]. Our method unifies these resukls, and gives improved algorithms for the weighted variants of these problems. An important open problem is whether TRAVELING SALESMAN can be solved in $O^*(2^n)$ time and polynomial space [21]. We make progress towards resolving this problem by giving a polynomial space algorithm for TRAVELING SALESMAN running in $O^*(2^n w)$ time. For the two other problems, WEIGHTED SET COVER and WEIGHTED STEINER TREE we make similar improvements. In particular our algorithms match the time bound of the best known pseudo-polynomial space algorithms for these problems.

The paper is organized as follows: In Section 2 we introduce the necessary notation. Then we briefly explain our approach in Section 3. In 4 we give sufficient conditions to be able to save space for DP on tables indexed by integers. In 5 we give sufficient conditions to be able to save space for DP on tables indexed by subsets. Finally, in Section 6 we combine the results from the two previous sections. All the latter three sections will be concluded by a few applications.

2. PRELIMINARIES AND NOTATION

We denote the naturals, the integers and the complex numbers by $\mathbb{N}$, $\mathbb{Z}$ and $\mathbb{C}$ respectively. For an integer i denote $\mathbb{N}_i$ for the set of integers $\{0,\ldots,i-1\}$, and $\mathbb{Z}_i$ for the ring of integers modulo i. For sets A and B, the set $A[B]$ is the set of all functions $f : B \to A$. One can think of $A[B]$ as a table with elements of B as keys and elements of A as values. Thus vectors of d integers are elements of $\mathbb{Z}[\mathbb{N}_d]$. For $\mathbf{v} \in A[B]$ we will use boldface for $\mathbf{v}$ if we think of $\mathbf{v}$ as a vector or table, and for $i \in B$, $\mathbf{v}[i]$ is the element of A associated with i - the i'th entry of $\mathbf{v}$. If we think of $\mathbf{f} \in A[B]$ as a function we will not use boldface for f and use $f(x)$ for f evaluated at $x \in B$. For a vector $v \in \mathbb{N}^d$, the set $\mathbb{N}_\mathbf{v} = \mathbb{N}_{\mathbf{v}[0]} \times \mathbb{N}_{\mathbf{v}[1]} \ldots \times \mathbb{N}_{\mathbf{v}[d]}$ where $\times$ is the cartesian product. For a set S, 2^S is the set of all subsets of S and $|S|$ is the cardinality of S.

We will instantiate vectors using $\langle$ and $\rangle$, that is, $\langle 3, 2\rangle$ is a vector with two entries whose first entry is 3 and second is 2. The $=$, $\leq$ and $<$ relations for vectors are pointwise so $\mathbf{u} \leq \mathbf{v}$ means $\mathbf{u}[i] \leq \mathbf{v}[i]$ for all i. The *absolute value* of a (complex) number a and the length of a vector $\mathbf{v}$ will be denoted by $\|a\|$ and $\|\mathbf{v}\|$ respectively.

We will be working with rings, semi-rings and generally sets that come with some operations on the elements. We let $+$ denote addition and $\cdot$ denote multiplication. For vectors, $\cdot$ means the dot product. We will often use the shorthand ab for $a \cdot b$. When working with elements of $A[B]$ where A comes with addition $(+)$ and a multiplication $(\cdot)$ operator, we define the *pointwise addition* operator $\oplus$ and the *pointwise multiplication* operator $\odot$ as follows. For $\mathbf{x}, \mathbf{y} \in A[B]$ and every $b \in B$,

$$(\mathbf{x} \oplus \mathbf{y})[b] = \mathbf{x}[b] + \mathbf{y}[b] \qquad (\mathbf{x} \odot \mathbf{y})[b] = \mathbf{x}[b] \cdot \mathbf{y}[b].$$

[2]with a polynomial number of sets

We will employ *Iverson's bracket notation* which works as follows. For a predicate b, $[b] = 1$ if b is true and 0 otherwise. When Iverson bracket notation is used in the context of a (semi-) ring $\mathcal{R}$, 1 will be $\mathcal{R}$'s identity element under multiplication and 0 will be $\mathcal{R}$'s identity under addition. We will sometimes use Iverson bracket notation to define functions. In that case x, $\mathbf{x}$ or X is implicitely assumed to be the parameter of the function. That is, for a fixed subset Y of a ground set V, $[X = Y]10$ is a function from 2^V to $\mathbb{N}$ which is 0 whenever $X \neq Y$ and 10 if $X = Y$. For sets A and B such that A has a 0 element, a *singleton* is an element $\mathbf{f}$ of $A[B]$ such that there is a $b \in B$ with $\mathbf{f}[x] = 0$ unless $x = b$.

For a set S and binary operators O_1, O_2 on S, a *circuit* C over $(S; O_1, O_2)$ is a directed acyclic graph $D = (N, A)$ with parallel arcs, such that every node of D is either a *constant* gate, O_1 gate or O_2 gate. Every node of D has indegree 0 or 2, the indegree 0 nodes are constants, and are labelled with elements of S. The indegree 2 nodes are either O_1 or O_2 gates. For an indegree 2 node, its two in-neighbours are its children. The *output* of a constant gate is the element it is labeled with. The output of an O_i gate is the result of performing O_i on the output of its two children. One gate c of C is additionally marked as the *output* gate. The output of C is the output of c. The *depth* $\Delta(C)$ of C is the size of the longest path, and the *size* of C is the size of the underlying graph. In this paper we will abuse notation, and refer by the same symbol both to a gate of C and to the output of that gate.

3. METHODOLOGY

A typical dynamic programming algorithm computes some basic tables, and then combines them using some operations in order to get an output table. Often we are only interested in a single element of the output table. In this paper we will formalize a dynamic programming algorithm as circuit C over a ring $(\mathcal{R}[S]; \oplus, O_2)$, where O_2 is a "complicated" convolution operator. Since S is very big, we are not allowed to store a single table. Thus, we cannot explicitely store the constants - the inputs to our circuit. Instead we will require the constants of our circuits to be singletons, and represent them implicitely - as the only key whose value is non-zero, together with the value associated to that key.

The main idea is to apply a linear transform on the circuit, such that the "complicated" operator O_2 is transformed into the much simpler $\odot$. This allows us to use C over $(\mathcal{R}, +, \cdot)$ to compute an entry of the transformed output table fast. Now we can obtain an entry of the original output of C by applying the inverse transformation.

4. SAVING SPACE BY THE DFT

4.1 The Discrete Fourier Transform

We recap Discrete Fourier Transform (DFT) and a few basic results about it. For every $\mathbf{N} \in \mathbb{N}^d$, the Discrete Fourier Transform is a linear transform $\mathcal{F} : \mathbb{C}[\mathbb{N}_\mathbf{N}] \to \mathbb{C}[\mathbb{N}_\mathbf{N}]$. Given $\mathbf{N}$ we let $\mathbf{t} \in \mathbb{C}^d$ so that $\mathbf{t}[j] = 2\pi\iota/\mathbf{N}[j]$, and $N = \Pi_{i=0}^{d-1}\mathbf{N}$. For a matrix $\mathbf{a} \in \mathbb{C}[\mathbb{N}_\mathbf{N}]$ the DFT of $\mathbf{a}$, $\mathcal{F}(\mathbf{a})$ is defined as follows.

$$(\mathcal{F}(\mathbf{a}))[\mathbf{x}] = \sum_{\mathbf{j} \in \mathbb{N}_\mathbf{N}} e^{(\mathbf{x} \odot \mathbf{t}) \cdot \mathbf{j}} \mathbf{a}[\mathbf{j}]$$

The inverse fourier transform $\mathcal{F}^{-1}(\mathbf{a})$ of $\mathbf{a}$ is defined as follows.

$$(\mathcal{F}^{-1}(\mathbf{a}))[\mathbf{x}] = \frac{1}{N}\sum_{\mathbf{j}\in\mathbb{N}_\mathbf{N}} e^{-(\mathbf{x}\odot\mathbf{t})\cdot\mathbf{j}}\mathbf{a}[\mathbf{j}]$$

The definitions of $\mathcal{F}$ and $\mathcal{F}^{-1}$ show that they both are linear transforms. That $\mathcal{F}^{-1}$ indeed is the inverse of $\mathcal{F}$ is stated in the next theorem.

THEOREM 4.1 ([7]). *For* $\mathbf{a} \in \mathbb{C}[\mathbb{N}_\mathbf{N}]$, $\mathcal{F}^{-1}(\mathcal{F}(\mathbf{a})) = \mathbf{a}$.

We now define the *convolution* operator which is central to our results. The convolution operator $\otimes$ takes two matrices $\mathbf{a}$ and $\mathbf{b}$ in $\mathbb{Z}[\mathbb{N}_\mathbf{N}]$ and produces a matrix $\mathbf{a}\otimes\mathbf{b}$ in $\mathbb{Z}[\mathbb{N}_\mathbf{N}]$, such that for any $\mathbf{x}$

$$(\mathbf{a}\otimes\mathbf{b})[\mathbf{x}] = \sum_{0\le\mathbf{j}\le\mathbf{x}} \mathbf{a}[\mathbf{j}]\mathbf{b}[\mathbf{x}-\mathbf{j}].$$

For $\mathbf{a}$ and $\mathbf{b} \in \mathbb{Z}[\mathbb{N}_\mathbf{N}]$ we say that the convolution $(\mathbf{a}\otimes\mathbf{b}$ *overflows* if there are vectors $\mathbf{x}, \mathbf{y} \in \mathbb{N}_\mathbf{N}$ such that $\mathbf{a}[\mathbf{x}] \neq 0$, $\mathbf{b}[\mathbf{y}] \neq 0$ and $x + y \not< \mathbf{N}$. If the elements of $\mathbb{Z}[\mathbb{N}_\mathbf{N}]$ are interpreted as d-variate polynomials with integer coefficients, convolution is equivalent to polynomial multiplication in coefficient form. From that viewpoint an overflow happens when the multiplication of two polynomials creates monomials of too high degree. It should be noted that the $\otimes$ operator generalizes to infinite tables like $\mathbb{Z}[\mathbb{N}]$ and to tables containing complex numbers like $\mathbb{C}[\mathbb{N}_\mathbf{N}]$ in the natural way. The next theorem is the reason why the DFT is useful for our purposes. The theorem states that the DFT translates the "complicated" $\otimes$ operator into $\odot$ which is much easier to work with. This comes in handy, as the dynamic programming algorithms for SUBSET SUM and KNAPSACK can be encoded using the $\oplus$ and the $\otimes$ operators.

THEOREM 4.2 (CONVOLUTION THEOREM [7]). *For* $\mathbf{a}, \mathbf{b}$ *in* $\mathbb{C}[\mathbb{N}_\mathbf{N}]$ *such that* $\mathbf{a}\otimes\mathbf{b}$ *does not overflow,* $\mathcal{F}(\mathbf{a}\otimes\mathbf{b}) = \mathcal{F}(\mathbf{a})\odot\mathcal{F}(\mathbf{b})$.

4.2 Numeric DP Without Tables

In this section we set up a general framework for turning pseudo-polynomial time and space algorithms that do a certain kind of dynamic programming on large d-dimensional tables into pseudo-polynomial time and space algorithms. We then show how our framework applies to the well-known algorithms for SUBSET SUM and KNAPSACK.

THEOREM 4.3. *Let* $\mathbf{N} \in \mathbb{N}^d$, $N = |\mathbb{N}_\mathbf{N}|$ *and* C *be a circuit over* $(\mathbb{Z}[\mathbb{N}_\mathbf{N}]; \oplus, \otimes)$ *with only singleton constants. Suppose that for any gate* $\mathbf{c} \in C$ *and any* $\mathbf{x} \in \mathbb{N}_\mathbf{N}$ *that* $|\mathbf{c}[\mathbf{x}]| \le m$ *and that no convolution gate overflows. Let* $\mathbf{f}$ *be the output of* C. *Then, given* $\mathbf{N}$, m, *and* $\mathbf{g} \in \mathbb{N}_\mathbf{N}$ *we can compute* $\mathbf{f}[\mathbf{g}]$ *in time* $\tilde{\mathcal{O}}((|C|N\log(N))\log(Nm)\Delta(C))$ *and space* $\mathcal{O}((|C| + \log(N))\log(Nm)\Delta(C))$.

PROOF. Since integers are also complex numbers, we can reinterpret the circuit C as a circuit over $(\mathbb{C}[\mathbb{N}_\mathbf{N}]; \oplus, \otimes)$. From the circuit C we construct another circuit C^1 over $\mathbb{C}[\mathbb{N}_\mathbf{N}]$ with the same directed graph as C, but with different gates. In particular, every constant gate $\mathbf{a} \in C$ is replaced with the constant gate $\mathbf{a}^1 = \mathcal{F}(\mathbf{a})$. Every convolution gate $(\otimes)$ is replaced by a pointwise multiplication gate $(\odot)$.

We prove that for any gate $\mathbf{a} \in C$ and its corresponding gate $\mathbf{a}^1$, we have $\mathbf{a}^1 = \mathcal{F}(\mathbf{a})$. The proof is by induction along a topological ordering of C. For the base case, if $\mathbf{a}$ is a constant gate the equality holds by construction. For the inductive step, let $\mathbf{a}$ be a gate with children $\mathbf{b}$ and $\mathbf{c}$, and let $\mathbf{a}^1$, $\mathbf{b}^1$ and $\mathbf{c}^1$ be the corresponding gates of C^1. By the inductive hypothesis $\mathbf{b}^1 = \mathcal{F}(\mathbf{b})$ and $\mathbf{c}^1 = \mathcal{F}(\mathbf{c})$. If $\mathbf{a}$ is an addition gate then $\mathbf{a}^1 = \mathcal{F}(\mathbf{b})\oplus\mathcal{F}(\mathbf{c}) = \mathcal{F}(\mathbf{b}\oplus\mathbf{c}) = \mathcal{F}(\mathbf{a})$. Finally, if $\mathbf{a}$ is a convolution gate then Theorem 4.2 implies that $\mathbf{a}^1 = \mathcal{F}(\mathbf{b})\odot\mathcal{F}(\mathbf{c}) = \mathcal{F}(\mathbf{b}\otimes\mathbf{c}) = \mathcal{F}(\mathbf{a})$.

We will use C^1 together with the fact that $\mathbf{f} = \mathcal{F}^{-1}(\mathcal{F}(\mathbf{f}))$ in order to compute $\mathbf{f}[\mathbf{g}]$. Writing out the definition of $\mathcal{F}^{-1}$ in $\mathbf{f} = \mathcal{F}^{-1}(\mathcal{F}(\mathbf{f}))$ we obtain the following equation for $\mathbf{f}[\mathbf{g}]$.

$$\mathbf{f}[\mathbf{g}] = \frac{1}{N}\sum_{\mathbf{j}\in\mathbb{N}_\mathbf{N}} e^{-(\mathbf{g}\odot\mathbf{t})\cdot\mathbf{j}}\cdot(\mathcal{F}(\mathbf{f}))[\mathbf{j}] \quad (1)$$

The algorithm computes $\mathbf{f}[\mathbf{g}]$ using Equation 1, using the circuit C^1 to compute the value of $(\mathcal{F}(\mathbf{f}))[\mathbf{j}]$ for each $\mathbf{j}$. We will now explain in detail how Equation 1 is used to compute $\mathbf{f}[\mathbf{g}]$. Before evaluating the sum in Equation 1 we compute $e^{\mathbf{t}[i]}$ and obtain $e^{-\mathbf{t}[i]}$ for every $i < d$ by taking complex conjugates.

The sum in Equation 1 is computed in the natural way - with d nested loops over the coordinates of $\mathbf{j}$. In each iteration we compute $e^{-(\mathbf{g}\odot\mathbf{t})\cdot\mathbf{j}}$ using Claim 1 below by noting that $e^{-(\mathbf{g}\odot\mathbf{t})\cdot\mathbf{j}} = \prod_{i\in\mathbb{N}_d}(e^{-\mathbf{t}[i]})^{\mathbf{g}[i]\cdot\mathbf{j}[i]}$. Thus, for each $\mathbf{j}$ we can compute $e^{-(\mathbf{g}\odot\mathbf{t})\cdot\mathbf{j}}$ by a circuit of size $\mathcal{O}(\sum_{i\in\mathbb{N}_d}\log(\mathbf{N}[i])) = \mathcal{O}(\log(N))$.

CLAIM 1. *Given* $a \in \mathbb{C}$ *and* $b \in \mathbb{N}$ *as input, we can construct a circuit* C^* *over* $(\mathbb{C}; +, \cdot)$ *computing* a^b *of size* $\mathcal{O}(\log b)$ *in* $\mathcal{O}(\log b)$ *time.*

PROOF. If b is even then $a^b = a^{b/2}\cdot a^{b/2}$ while if b is odd then $a^b = a\cdot a^{(b-1)/2}\cdot a^{(b-1)/2}$. Turning these recurrences into a circuit of size $\mathcal{O}(\log b)$ with a as its only constant is routine. □

Now we turn our attention to computing $(\mathcal{F}(\mathbf{f}))[\mathbf{j}]$ using the circuit C^1. Given C^1 and $\mathbf{j}$, define $C^1_\mathbf{j}$ to be a circuit over $(\mathbb{C}, +, \cdot)$ with the same directed graph as C^1. For every constant gate $\mathcal{F}(\mathbf{a})$ of C^1 the corresponding gate of $C^1_\mathbf{j}$ is $(\mathcal{F}(\mathbf{a}))[\mathbf{j}]$. Pointwise addition $(\oplus)$ gates of C^1 are replaced with $+$ gates and pointwise multiplication $(\odot)$ gates of C^1 are replaced with $\cdot$ gates in $C^1_\mathbf{j}$. It follows directly from the construction of $C^1_\mathbf{j}$ that it outputs $(\mathcal{F}(\mathbf{f}))[\mathbf{j}]$ using $|C^1| = |C|$ arithmetic operations, given that the constants of $C^1_\mathbf{j}$ are provided. Observe that for any singleton $\mathbf{a} = [\mathbf{x} = \mathbf{p}]v$ we have that

$$\begin{aligned}(\mathcal{F}(\mathbf{a}))[\mathbf{x}] &= \sum_{\mathbf{j}\in\mathbb{N}_\mathbf{N}} e^{(\mathbf{x}\odot\mathbf{t})\cdot\mathbf{j}}\cdot[\mathbf{j}=\mathbf{p}]v \quad (2)\\ &= v\prod_{i\in\mathbb{N}_d}(e^{\mathbf{t}[i]})^{\mathbf{p}[i]\cdot\mathbf{x}[i]}\end{aligned}$$

For a constant $\mathbf{a} = [\mathbf{x} = \mathbf{p}]v$ of C we compute the corresponding constant $(\mathcal{F}(\mathbf{a}))[\mathbf{j}]$ of $C^1_\mathbf{j}$ using Equation 2. By Claim 1 this can be done with a circuit of size $\mathcal{O}(\log(N))$.

To summarize the algorithm - we compute $\mathbf{f}[\mathbf{g}]$ using Equation 1, using the circuit $C^1_\mathbf{j}$ to compute the value of $(\mathcal{F}(\mathbf{f}))[\mathbf{j}]$ for each $\mathbf{j}$. The constants of $C^1_\mathbf{j}$ are computed using Equation 2. If we were able to store and manipulate complex numbers exactly, correctness would follow immediately from Equations 1 and 2. Of course, the algorithm cannot store and work with complex numbers. Instead, it will work with a binary representation of the numbers, both the real and the imaginary part, truncated ℓ bits after the decimal point for a properly chosen ℓ. It can easily be verified that the absolute value of any number in an intermediate step is bounded from above by $N^2 \cdot m$. Thus an estimation of each used number in $\mathbb{C}$ will be stored using $\mathcal{O}(\log(N) + \log(m) + \ell)$ bits.

The way the algorithm handles ℓ-bit precision is that some base numbers, the integers given in the input and $e^{\mathbf{t}[i]}$ for every $i < d$ are stored with *estimation error* $2^{-\ell}$, where estimation error is the distance in the complex plane between the number represented by the bitstring, and the number the bitstring is supposed to represent. Computing $e^{\mathbf{t}[i]}$ with estimation error $2^{-\ell}$ can be done in $\mathcal{O}(\ell^3)$ time and $\mathcal{O}(\ell)$ space using the Taylor series for sin and cos and a reasonable series expansion for π, such as the one provided by Chudnovsky and Chudnovsky [6]. All other numbers are obtained by performing addition and multiplication on the base numbers, truncating intermediate results ℓ bits after the decimal point. As more and more operations are required to obtain a number, the estimation error for that number increases. Since we know that $\mathbf{f}[\mathbf{g}]$ is an integer, the algorithm simply rounds the estimation of $\mathbf{f}[\mathbf{g}]$ to the nearest integer and outputs that as the answer. This answer is correct if the estimation error of $\mathbf{f}[\mathbf{g}]$ is less than 1/2. What remains is to show that chosing $\ell = \mathcal{O}(|C| + \log(N) + \log(m)\Delta(C))$ will yield estimation error less than 1/2 for $\mathbf{f}[\mathbf{g}]$. Let a' and b' be estimations of a and b respectively, let $c_1' = a' + b'$ truncated ℓ bits after the decimal point and $c_1 = a + b$. Then, we have that

$$\|c_1' - c_1\| \leq \|a' - a\| + \|b' - b\| + 2^{-\ell}. \quad (3)$$

Here, the $2^{-\ell}$ term comes from truncating c' ℓ bits after the decimal point. Now, suppose $c_2' = a' \cdot b'$ truncated ℓ bits after the decimal point and $c_2 = a \cdot b$. This yields the following error bound:

$$\begin{aligned}\|c_2' - c_2\| \leq \quad & \|a' - a\| \cdot \|b\| + \|b' - b\| \cdot \|a\| \\ + \quad & \|a' - a\| \cdot \|b' - b\| + 2^{-\ell}\end{aligned} \quad (4)$$

Equipped with Equations 3 and 4 we are ready to bound the error of the output of a circuit over $(\mathbb{C}, +, \cdot)$. The proof lends ideas from Knuth's analysis of the Schönhage-Strassen algorithm for integer multiplication[17].

Claim 2. *Let $\hat{C}$ be a circuit over $(\mathbb{C}; +, \cdot)$, and m and ℓ be positive integers such that for any gate $v \in \hat{C}$, $\|v\| \leq m$. Suppose estimations of the constants of $\hat{C}$ are given with error at most ϵ for each constant, such that $2^{-\ell} \leq \epsilon \cdot (4m)^{\Delta(\hat{C})} \leq 1$. Let c be the output of $\hat{C}$ and let c' be the estimate of c obtained by evaluating $\hat{C}$ on the estimations of its constants, truncating intermediate results ℓ bits after the decimal point. Then $\|c' - c\| \leq \epsilon \cdot (4m)^{\Delta(\hat{C})}$.*

Proof. We prove the statement by induction on $\Delta(\hat{C})$. For the base case, if $\Delta(\hat{C}) = 0$ then v is a constant and the statement of the claim holds. Otherwise, suppose the statement holds for all circuits of depth at most $k - 1$ and let $\hat{C}$ have depth k. Let u and v be the children of the output gate c and let $\hat{C}_u$ and $\hat{C}_v$ be the subcircuits of $\hat{C}$ rooted at u and v respectively. Let u' and v' be estimations of u and v obtained by evaluating $\hat{C}_u$ and $\hat{C}_v$ respectively on the estimations of their constants, truncating intermediate results ℓ bits after the decimal point. As $\Delta(\hat{C}_u) \leq k - 1$ and $\Delta(\hat{C}_v) \leq k - 1$, by the induction hypothesis we have $\|u' - u\| \leq \epsilon \cdot (4m)^{\Delta(\hat{C})-1}$ and $\|v' - v\| \leq \epsilon \cdot (4m)^{\Delta(\hat{C})-1}$. If c is an addition gate, Equation 3 yields

$$\|c' - c\| \leq \epsilon \cdot 2(4m)^{\Delta(\hat{C})-1} + 2^{-\ell}$$

which is at most $\epsilon \cdot (4m)^{\Delta(\hat{C})}$. On the other hand, if c is a multiplication gate, Equation 4 yields

$$\|c' - c\| \leq \epsilon \cdot 2m(4m)^{\Delta(\hat{C})-1} + (\epsilon \cdot (4m)^{\Delta(\hat{C})-1})^2 + 2^{-\ell}$$

which is at most $\epsilon \cdot (2m + 2)(4m)^{\Delta(\hat{C})-1}$ since

$$(\epsilon \cdot (4m)^{\Delta(\hat{C})-1})^2 \leq \epsilon \cdot (4m)^{\Delta(\hat{C})-1}$$

and $2^{-\ell} \leq \epsilon$. Since $m \geq 1$ this concludes the proof of the claim. □

For a fixed ℓ the estimation error of $e^{\mathbf{t}[i]}$ and $e^{-\mathbf{t}[i]}$ is $2^{-\ell}$ for every $i < d$. For every $\mathbf{j}$, $e^{-(\mathbf{g} \odot \mathbf{t}) \cdot \mathbf{j}}$ is computed by a circuit of size $\mathcal{O}(\log(N))$ and absolute value 1 in every step. Hence, by Claim 2 the estimation error of $e^{-(\mathbf{g} \odot \mathbf{t}) \cdot \mathbf{j}}$ is $2^{-\ell} 4^{\mathcal{O}(\log(N))}$. Similarly, for every $\mathbf{j}$ the constants of $C_{\mathbf{j}}^1$ are computed by circuits of size $\mathcal{O}(\log(N))$ and absolute value 1 in every step, the multiplication by v can be performed at the very end of the computation of Equation 2. Thus by Claim 2 the estimation error of the constants of $C_{\mathbf{j}}^1$ is bounded from above by

$$2^{-\ell} 4^{\mathcal{O}(\log(N))} 4v \leq 2^{-\ell + \mathcal{O}(\log(N) + \log(m))}.$$

Since C^1 computes $\mathcal{F}(\mathbf{a})$ for every gate $\mathbf{a}$ of C, and each of the N entries of $\mathbf{a}$ have absolute value at most m, the absolute value of the number computed by any gate of $C_{\mathbf{j}}^1$ is bounded by $m \cdot N$. Hence by Claim 2 the estimation error of $(\mathcal{F}(\mathbf{f}))[\mathbf{j}]$ is

$$2^{-\ell + \mathcal{O}(\log(N) + \log(m))} (4Nm)^{\Delta(C)} \leq 2^{-\ell + \mathcal{O}(\log(Nm)\Delta(C))}.$$

By Equation 3 the estimation error of $e^{-(\mathbf{g} \odot \mathbf{t}) \cdot \mathbf{j}} \cdot (\mathcal{F}(\mathbf{f}))[\mathbf{j}]$ is $2^{-\ell + \mathcal{O}(\log(Nm)\Delta(C))}$. Since the sum in Equation 1 runs over N elements and at the end we divide by N, the total estimation error becomes $2^{-\ell + \mathcal{O}(\log(Nm)\Delta(C))}$. Choosing $\ell = \mathcal{O}(\log(Nm)\Delta(C))$ yields estimation error less than 1/2 for $\mathbf{f}[\mathbf{g}]$.

Finally, we analyze the running time of the algorithm and bound the space used. The outer loop has N iterations, in each we evaluate at most $|C|$ circuits of size $\mathcal{O}(\log(N))$ to compute the constants of $C_{\mathbf{j}}^1$. Evaluating $C_{\mathbf{j}}^1$ takes $|C|$ arithmetic operations. Thus, the total number of arithmetic operations is $\mathcal{O}(|C|N\log(N))$ while the total number of comlpex numbers stored at any time is $\mathcal{O}(|C| + \log(N))$. The number of bits used to store each number is $\mathcal{O}(\log(Nm)\Delta(C))$. Thus the space used by the algorithm is $\mathcal{O}((|C| + \log(N))\log(Nm)\Delta(C))$. The time required to add two numbers is $\tilde{\mathcal{O}}(\log(Nm)\Delta(C))$ using a fast integer multiplication algorithm (see [11, 20]). Thus, the total running time becomes $\tilde{\mathcal{O}}((|C|N\log(N)\log(Nm)\Delta(C))$, completing the proof of the theorem. □

It is worth mentioning that a result similar to Theorem 4.3 can be obtained using modular arithmetic instead of complex numbers. Due to space constraints, details are deferred to the full version of the paper.

4.3 Applications

Subset Sum

We now show how to use Theorem 4.3 to give a pseudo-polynomial time, polynomial space algorithm for the SUBSET SUM problem, defined below.

SUBSET SUM
Instance: Set S of positive integers $w_1, \ldots, w_n$, an integer w.
Question: Does there exist a subset $S' \subseteq S$ such that $\sum_{w_i \in S'} w_i = w$?

Notice that SUBSET SUM can trivially be solved in $\mathcal{O}(2^n)$ time and polynomial space. This has been improved to $\mathcal{O}^*(2^{n/2})$ time and space by [14] and recently to $\mathcal{O}^*(2^{0.311n})$ time and $\mathcal{O}^*(2^{0.256}n)$ space [15]. Since a $w_i > w$ cannot participate in any solution we will assume that $w_i \leq w$ for every i. Also, if $w > 2^n$ then the trivial $\mathcal{O}(2^n)$ time algorithm runs in $\mathcal{O}(w)$ time and polynomial space. For every $1 \leq i \leq n$ and $x \leq nw$ let $\mathbf{s}_i[x]$ be the number of subsets $S' \subseteq \{1, \ldots, i\}$ such that $\sum_{j \in S'} w_j = x$. The well-known $\mathcal{O}(nw)$ time, $\mathcal{O}(w)$ space dynamic programming algorithm by Bellman (see [8]) can be reformulated as the following recurrence.

$$\begin{aligned} \mathbf{s}_1 &= [x = 0] \oplus [x = w_0] & (5)\\ \mathbf{s}_i &= \mathbf{s}_{i-1} \oplus (\mathbf{s}_{i-1} \otimes [x = w_i]) \qquad \text{for } i > 1. \end{aligned}$$

We are interested to know whether $\mathbf{s}_n[w] \neq 0$. Equation 5 can easily be translated into a circuit C over $(\mathbb{Z}[\mathbb{N}_{nw+1}]; \oplus, \otimes)$ with size and depth $\mathcal{O}(n)$ and the entries of any table computed by C can be bounded by 2^n since each entry of $\mathbf{s}_i$ counts subsets of $\{1, \ldots, i\}$. Thus, applying Theorem 4.3 would already yield a pseudo-polynomial time, polynomial space algorithm for SUBSET SUM. However, rearranging the recurrence before applying Theorem 4.3 gives a slightly better running time for the algorithm. The recurrence in Equation 5 can be rearranged as follows.

$$\mathbf{s}_i = \mathbf{s}_{i-1} \otimes ([x = 0] \oplus [x = w_i]) \qquad \text{for } i > 1.$$

Expanding this equation for $\mathbf{s}_n$ yields

$$\begin{aligned} \mathbf{s}_n = ([x = 0] \oplus [x = w_1]) \otimes ([x = 0] \oplus [x = w_2]) \quad (6)\\ \ldots \otimes ([x = 0] \oplus [x = w_n]) \end{aligned}$$

Since the $\otimes$ operator is commutative Equation 6 can be turned into a circuit C over $(\mathbb{Z}[\mathbb{N}_{nw+1}]; \oplus, \otimes)$ of size $\mathcal{O}(n)$ and depth $\mathcal{O}(\log(n))$, with maximum table entry bounded by 2^n. Applying Theorem 4.3 on C yields the following theorem.

THEOREM 4.4. *The* SUBSET SUM *problem can be solved in $\tilde{\mathcal{O}}(n^3 t \log t)$ time and $\tilde{\mathcal{O}}(n^2)$ space.*

Knapsack

Now we show that essentially the same approach as in the previous section can be taken to solve the KNAPSACK problem in pseudo-polynomial time using polynomial space. In KNAPSACK we are given a set of n items, each with a weight and a value. We have to select a set of items with total weight at most w and total value at least v. A formal definition of the problem is given below.

KNAPSACK
Instance: Set S of n pairs of positive integers $(v_1, w_1), \ldots, (v_n, w_n)$, two positive integers, v and w.
Question: Is there a subset $S' \subseteq \mathbb{N}_n$ such that $\sum_{i \in S'} v_i \geq v$ and $\sum_{i \in S'} w_i \leq w$?

Similarly to the SUBSET SUM problem, there is a trivial brute force algorithm running in $\mathcal{O}(2^n)$ time and polynomial space. Also, any item with weight more than w can not participate in the solution, and any item with weight at most w and value at least v constitutes a solution by itself. Hence we will assume that $\log w \leq n$, $\log v \leq n$ and that $w_i \leq w$ and $v_i \leq v$ for every i. For every $1 \leq i \leq n$ define $\mathbf{s}_i \in \mathbb{Z}[\mathbb{N}_{\langle 2nv+1, 2nw+1 \rangle}]$, where $\mathbf{s}_i[\langle x, y \rangle]$ is the number of subsets $S' \subseteq \{1, \ldots, i\}$ such that $x + \sum_{j \in S'} v_j = v \cdot i$ and $\sum_{j \in S'} w_j = y$. That is, for every $i \geq 1$, $\mathbf{s}_i[\langle x, y \rangle]$ counts the number of subsets of the first i items with total value $(v \cdot i) - x$ and total weight y. Then, the following recurrence holds for $\mathbf{s}_i$, $1 \leq i \leq n$.

$$\begin{aligned} \mathbf{s}_1 &= [\mathbf{x} = \langle v, 0 \rangle] \oplus [\mathbf{x} = \langle v - v_1, w_1 \rangle]\\ \mathbf{s}_i &= \mathbf{s}_{i-1} \oplus (\mathbf{s}_{i-1} \otimes [\mathbf{x} = \langle v - v_i, w_i \rangle]) \qquad \text{for } i > 1. \end{aligned}$$

Just as for SUBSET SUM, this recurrence can be rearranged to yield the following formula for $\mathbf{s}_n$.

$$\begin{aligned} \mathbf{s}_n &= ([\mathbf{x} = \mathbf{0} \oplus [\mathbf{x} = \langle v - v_1, w_1 \rangle])\\ &\otimes ([\mathbf{x} = \mathbf{0} \oplus [\mathbf{x} = \langle v - v_2, w_2 \rangle]) \qquad (7)\\ &\ldots \otimes ([\mathbf{x} = \mathbf{0} \oplus [\mathbf{x} = \langle v - v_n, w_n \rangle]) \end{aligned}$$

>From Equation 7 we construct a circuit C of size $\mathcal{O}(n)$ and depth $\mathcal{O}(\log n)$ computing $\mathbf{s}_n$. We are interested in whether there exists an $\mathbf{x} \leq \langle nv - v, w \rangle$ such that $\mathbf{s}_n[\mathbf{x}] \neq 0$. We could have used Theorem 4.3 and to find $\mathbf{s}_n[\mathbf{x}] \neq 0$ for each $\mathbf{x} \leq \langle nv - v, w \rangle$, but that creates an unnecessary overhead of $\mathcal{O}(vw)$ in the running time. Instead we will compute

$$(\mathbf{s}_n \otimes [\mathbf{x} \leq \langle nv - v, w \rangle])[\langle nv - v, w \rangle] \qquad (8)$$

since $(\mathbf{s}_n \otimes [\mathbf{x} \leq \langle nv - v, w \rangle])[\langle nv - v, w \rangle]$ is non-zero if and only if there is a $\mathbf{x} \leq \langle nv - v, w \rangle$ such that $\mathbf{s}_n[\mathbf{x}] \neq 0$. We need a circuit $\hat{C}$ to compute $[\mathbf{x} \leq \langle nv - v, w \rangle]$. For that we will use the following observation.

OBSERVATION 4.1. *For every integer p and $p < q$ there is a circuit $\hat{C}$ of size $\mathcal{O}(\log(p))$ over $(\mathbb{Z}[\mathbb{N}_q]; \oplus, \otimes)$ computing $[x \leq p]$.*

PROOF. If p is even then $[x \leq p] = [x \leq p] \oplus [x \leq p/2] \otimes [x \leq p/2]$. If p is odd then

$$[x \leq p] = [x \leq p] \oplus ([x \leq \lfloor p/2 \rfloor] \otimes [x \leq \lfloor p/2 \rfloor]) \oplus [x = p].$$

Transforming this recurrence into a circuit of size $O(\log(p))$ is routine. □

Of course, Observation 4.1 can also be used for circuits over $(\mathbb{Z}[\mathbb{N}_{\langle 2nv+1, 2nw+1 \rangle}]; \oplus, \otimes)$ in order to to make a circuit of size $\mathcal{O}(\log(nv))$ that computes $[\mathbf{x} \leq \langle nv - v, 0 \rangle]$ and another of size $\mathcal{O}(\log(w))$ that computes $[\mathbf{x} \leq \langle 0, w \rangle]$. Now,

$$[\mathbf{x} \leq \langle nv - v, w \rangle] = [\mathbf{x} \leq \langle nv - v, 0 \rangle] \otimes [\mathbf{x} \leq \langle 0, w \rangle].$$

Hence we have a circuit $\hat{C}$ of size $\mathcal{O}(n + \log v + \log w)$ and depth $\mathcal{O}(\log(n) + \log v + \log w)$ computing $(\mathbf{s}_n \otimes [\mathbf{x} \leq \langle nv - v, w \rangle])[\langle nv - v, w \rangle]$. Also for this circuit, the table entries are bounded by 2^n since they count subsets of n-sized sets. Applying Theorem 4.3 on $\hat{C}$ yields the following result.

THEOREM 4.5. *The* KNAPSACK *problem can be solved in* $\tilde{\mathcal{O}}(n^4 \log^2(cw)vw)$ *time and* $\tilde{\mathcal{O}}(n^2 \log(vw))$ *space.*

5. SAVING SPACE BY MÖBIUS INVERSION

In this section we will prove a general theorem that identifies sufficient conditions for turning exponential space dynamic programming algorithms over the subset lattice into polynomial space algorithms based on *Möbius Inversion.* While our theorem does not yield any new polynomial space algorithms, it unifies and generalizes several well-known results, such as the HAMILTONIAN PATH algorithm by Karp [16], the UNWEIGHTED SET COVER algorithm by Björklund et al [4] and the UNWEIGHTED STEINER TREE algorithm by Nederlof [19].

5.1 Möbius Inversion

Let V be a set and let $\mathcal{R}$ be a ring. We will consider circuits over $(\mathcal{R}[2^V]; \oplus, \diamond_u)$, where $\diamond_u$ is the *union product* operator [3], defined below:

$$(a \diamond_u b)(Y) = \sum_{A \cup B = Y} a(A)b(B)$$

For $f \in \mathcal{R}[2^V]$, the *zeta-transform* ζf and the *Möbius-transform* μf are defined as:

$$\zeta f[Y] = \sum_{X \subseteq Y} f[Y] \qquad \mu f[Y] = \sum_{X \subseteq Y} (-1)^{|Y \setminus X|} f[X]$$

Now the principle of *Möbius Inversion* can be summarized as the following theorem:

LEMMA 5.1 ([5]). *For any function* $f \in \mathcal{R}[2^V]$ *and* $Y \subseteq V$, *it holds that* $\mu(\zeta f)[Y] = f[Y]$.

Recall that $\odot$ denotes pointwise multiplication. Similarly to the DFT, Möbius Inversion is particularly useful because it transforms the "hard" to compute operator $\diamond_u$ into $\odot$. The following lemma follows from the discussion in [3]. We give a proof here for completeness.

LEMMA 5.2 ([3]). *For any function* $f, g \in \mathcal{R}[2^V]$ *and* $Y \subseteq V$, $\zeta(f \diamond_u g)[Y] = (\zeta f) \odot (\zeta g)$.

PROOF. We have to prove that for each $Y \subseteq V$

$$\sum_{X \subseteq Y} \sum_{A \cup B = X} f[A]g[B] = \Big(\sum_{A \subseteq Y} f[A]\Big)\Big(\sum_{B \subseteq Y} f[B]\Big)$$

To see that this equation holds, notice that for each $A, B \subseteq Y$, there exists exactly one $X \subseteq Y$ such that $A \cup B = X$, hence we can sum over each combination of two subsets A and B of Y. □

5.2 DP Over Subsets Without Tables

LEMMA 5.3. *Let* C *be a circuit over* $(\mathcal{R}[2^V]; \oplus, \diamond_u)$ *and output* s. *Then, there is a polynomial time algorithm that, given* $Y \subseteq V$, *creates a circuit* C^Y *over* $(\mathcal{R}; +, \cdot)$ *with the same underlying graph as* C, *such that for every gate* $a \in C$ *the corresponding gate in* C^Y *outputs* $(\zeta s)[Y]$.

PROOF. >From C we construct a circuit C' over $(\mathcal{R}[2^V]; \oplus, \odot)$, by relabelling all $\diamond_u$ gates with $\odot$, and replacing every constant gate $a \in C$ with the constant gate $a' = \zeta a$. We prove that for every gate $a \in C$ and corresponding gate $a' \in C'$, $a' = \zeta a$ by induction along a topological ordering of C. If a is a constant gate, equality follows by construction. Otherwise let b and c be the children of a and b' and c' be the corresponding gates in C'. If a is a $\oplus$ gate then $a' = b' \oplus c' = \zeta b \oplus \zeta c = \zeta(b \oplus c) = \zeta a$ since ζ is a linear transform. On the other hand, if a is a $\diamond_u$ gate then $a' = b' \odot c' = \zeta b \odot \zeta c = b \diamond_u c = \zeta a$, since Lemma 5.2 yields $\zeta b \odot \zeta c = b \diamond_u c$.

Since C' only uses pointwise addition and pointwise multiplication, it can be viewed as $2^{|V|}$ disjoint circuits over $(\mathcal{R}, +, \cdot)$, one circuit C_Y with output $(\zeta s)(Y)$ for each subset Y of V. For a fixed Y and constant gate $a = [X = S_a]v_a$ of C, the corresponfing constant gate $a_Y \in C_Y$ should be $(\zeta a)(Y)$ which is v_a if $S_a \subseteq Y$ and 0 otherwise. Given C and Y it is easy to construct C_Y in polynomial time. □

The idea is that the value $s[V]$ in which one is typically interested can be obtained by $\sum_{X \subseteq V} (-1)^{|V \setminus X|} \zeta s[V]$, where $(\zeta s)[V]$ can computed fast using the circuit obtained by the above lemma. However, in the next subsection another operator is introduced that turns out to be more useful for our applications, and there Lemma 5.3 will be used as an intermediate result.

5.3 Subset Convolution

Let V be a ground set. In this section we will study circuits over $(\mathcal{R}[2^V], \oplus, *_{\mathcal{R}})$, where $*_{\mathcal{R}}$ is the *subset convolution* operator over $\mathcal{R}$. We proceed to formally define $*_{\mathcal{R}}$.

DEFINITION 5.1 ([3]). *Let* V *be a set,* $\mathcal{R}$ *be a ring and let* $f, g \in \mathcal{R}[2^V]$. *The operator* subset convolution $*_{\mathcal{R}}$ *over* $\mathcal{R}$ *is defined as follows: for each* $Y \subseteq V$

$$(f *_{\mathcal{R}} g)[Y] = \sum_{X \subseteq Y} f[X]g[Y \setminus X] \tag{9}$$

where addition and multiplication are in the ring $\mathcal{R}$.

We consider circuits over $(\mathcal{R}[2^V], \oplus, *_{\mathcal{R}})$. We first embed subset convolution into the union product using the notion of relaxations, defined below.

DEFINITION 5.2. *A* relaxation *of a function* $f : \mathcal{R}[2^V]$ *is a sequence of functions* $\{f_i : f_i \in \mathcal{R}[2^V]\}$, *for* $0 \le i \le |V|$, *such that for every* $0 \le i \le |V|$, $Y \subseteq V$:

$$f_i[Y] = \begin{cases} f[Y] & \text{if } i = |Y| \\ 0 & \text{if } i < |Y| \end{cases}$$

We will denote the most common special case of subset convolution, being $*_{\mathbb{Z}}$, by $*$. Recall that $f \in \mathbb{Z}[2^V]$ is a singleton if $f = [X = S_f]v_f$ for some set S_f and integer v_f. The following theorem applies to circuits over $\mathbb{Z}[2^V]$ with pointwise addition and subset convolution.

THEOREM 5.1. *Let* V *be a set, and let* C *be a circuit over* $(\mathbb{Z}[2^V], \oplus, *)$. *Suppose* C *outputs* s, *all its constants are singletons, and* m *is an integer such that* $s[V] \le m$. *Then, given* C *and* m, $s[V]$ *can be computed using* $\mathcal{O}^*(2^{|V|})$ *time and* $\mathcal{O}(|V||C| \log m)$ *space.*

Before we prove this theorem, we first prove the following Lemma, which is also used in Section 6.

LEMMA 5.4. *Let* V *be a set and let* C *be a circuit over* $(\mathcal{R}[2^V]; \oplus, *_{\mathcal{R}})$. *Suppose* C *outputs* s *and all its constants are singletons. Then there exists a relaxation* $\{s_i\}$ *of* s *and a circuit* C' *over* $(\mathcal{R}[2^V]; \oplus, \diamond_u)$ *outputting* $s_{|V|}[V]$ *with* $|C'| = |C||V|$, *that can be constructed in polynomial time.*

PROOF. Let $|V| = n$. We construct C' by replacing every gate of $a \in C$ by n gates $a_1, \ldots, a_n \in C'$. For every constant gate $a = [X = S_a]v_a$, we set $a_i = 0$ if $i < |S|$ and $a_i = a$ otherwise. Notice that this means that all constant gates of C' are singletons. If a is not a constant gate, let b and c be the children of a in C. If $a = b \oplus c$, then for every i we set $a_i = b_i \oplus c_i$. Finally, if $a = b *_{\mathcal{R}} c$ we set $a_i = \sum_{j=0}^{i}(b_i \diamond_u c_{i-j})$. Clearly, the above procedure can be executed in polynomial time.

We prove that for every gate a, $\{a_i\}$ is a relaxation of a by induction along a topological order of C. If a is a constant gate this follows by construction. Otherwise, let b and c be the children of a. Then $\{b_i\}$ and $\{c_i\}$ are relaxations of b and c respectively by the induction hypothesis. If a is an addition gate ($a = b \oplus c$), then $\{a_i\}$ is a relaxation of a since

- for $i = |X|$, $a_i[X] = b_i[X] + c_i[X] = b[X] + c[X]$ since $b_i[X] = b[X]$ and $c_i[X] = c[X]$ by the induction hypothesis.

- for $i < |X|$, $a_i[X] = b_i[X] + c_i[X] = b[X] + c[X] = 0$ since both $b_i[X]$ and $c_i[X]$ are 0 by the induction hypothesis.

On the other hand if a is a subset convolution gate ($a = b *_{\mathcal{R}} c$), we have that for each $0 \leq i \leq n$,

$$a_i[X] = \sum_{i=0}^{i} \sum_{Y \cup Z = X} b_j[Y]c_{i-j}[Z].$$

Consider a summand $b_j[Y]c_{i-j}[Z]$. There are two cases:

- ($|X| > i$) Since $Y \cup Z = X$ we have that $|Y| + |Z| \geq |X| > i$. Now either $|Y| > j$ and $b_j[Y] = 0$, or $|Z| > i - j$ and $c_{i-j}[Z] = 0$, because $\{b_i\}$ and $\{c_i\}$ both are relaxations of b and c respectively. Then we have that $a_i[X] = 0$.

- ($|X| = i$) If $|Y| + |Z| > i$, either $|Y| > j$ or $|Z| > i - j$ and $a_j[A]b_{i-j}[B] = 0$ analogously to the first case. If $|Y| + |Z| = i$ then Y and Z are disjoint. Since only these pairs Y, Z will contribute to the sum, we match the definition of subset convolution and hence $a_i[X] = a[X]$.

Thus $\{a_i\}$ is a relaxation of a for all gates a, concluding the proof.

□

PROOF OF THEOREM 5.1. Note that C can as well be considered as a circuit over the ring $\mathbb{Z}_{m+1}$ since $s[V] \leq m+1$. Combining Lemma 5.4 and 5.3 there is a relaxation $\{s_i\}$ of s such that for every $Y \subseteq V$ we can construct a circuit C_Y over $(\mathbb{Z}_{m+1}; +, \cdot)$ of size $|V||C|$ outputting $(\zeta s_n)[Y]$. Möbius Inversion states that

$$s_n[V] = \sum_{Y \subseteq V} (-1)^{|V \setminus Y|} (\zeta s_n)[Y]$$

and now the theorem follows, since for every $Y \subseteq V$, we can evaluate C^Y in order to compute $s_n[Y]$ in $|C|$ operations in $\mathbb{Z}_{m+1}$ and $\mathcal{O}(|V||C| \log m)$ space. Using a fast integer multiplication algorithm (for example [11]), multiplication in $\mathbb{Z}_{m+1}$ takes $\mathcal{O}(\log m \log\log m \log^* m)$ time, which is $\mathcal{O}^*(1)$. This completes the proof of the theorem. □

5.4 An Application of Theorem 5.1

Now we will give an application of Theorem 5.1. In particular we will show that with our framework, the polynomial space algorithm of Nederlof [19] for UNWEIGHTED STEINER TREE follows directly from the Dreyfus-Wagner [9] recurrence. UNWEIGHTED STEINER TREE is defined as follows.

UNWEIGHTED STEINER TREE
Instance: A graph $G = (V, E)$, $T \subseteq V$ with $|T| = k$ and an integer $t \leq |V|$.
Question: Does there exist a subtree (V', E') of G such that $V' \leq t$ and $T \subseteq V'$?

A dynamic programming algorithm for this problem was given already in 1972 by Dreyfus and Wagner [9]. This algorithm uses $\mathcal{O}^*(3^k)$ time and $\mathcal{O}^*(2^k)$ space. In 2007, Björklund et al. [3] gave an improved algorithm using $\mathcal{O}^*(2^k)$ time and space. Finally, in 2009, Nederlof [19] gave a $\mathcal{O}^*(2^k)$ time and polynomial space algorithm. We show how the last result can be obtained from the first result using Theorem 5.1. Slightly reformulated, the dynamic programming of [9] can be summarized as follows. For every $1 \leq i \leq n$ and $v \in V$ define $f_i^v \in \mathbb{Z}[2^T]$ as

$$\begin{aligned} f_v^1 &= [X = \emptyset] && \text{for } v \notin T \\ f_v^1 &= [X = \{v\}] + [X = \emptyset] && \text{for } v \in T \qquad (10) \\ f_v^i &= \sum_{j=1}^{i-1} \sum_{w \in N(v)} f_w^j * f_v^{i-j} && \text{for } i > 1 \end{aligned}$$

The crux is that for every i, $f_v^i[X] > 0$ if and only if there exists a subtree (V', E') of G such that $|V'| \leq i$ and $X \cup \{v\} \subseteq V'$. This can be proved by induction on i: For $i = 1$ there exists such a subtree if and only if $X \subseteq \{v\}$ and $v \in T$ or $X = \emptyset$. For $i > 1$, note that there is a subtree (V', E') of the graph G such that $|V'| \leq i$ and $X \cup \{v\} \subseteq V'$ if and only if there are two subtrees $(A \cup \{v\}, E_1)$, $(B \cup \{w\}, E_2)$ such that $A \cup B \cup \{v, w\} = V'$, $|V_1| + |V_2| \leq i$ and $(v, w) \in E'$.

The instance of Unweighted Steiner Tree problem is a yes-instance if and only if $f_v^t[T] > 0$, where $v \in T$. Now we can apply Theorem 5.1 to compute $f_v^t[T]$. It is easy to see that the above recurrence implies a circuit with singleton constants, pairwise addition and convolution operators. Moreover, it can be easily be proved with induction on i that $f_v^i[X] \leq |V|^{3i}2^{|V|i}$ for every $X \subseteq T$ and $v \in V$, hence $f_v^t[T] \leq |V|^{3t}2^{|V|t}$. Thus, using $m = |V|^{3t}2^{|V|r}$ we obtain:

THEOREM 5.2 ([19]). *The Unweighted Steiner Tree problem can be solved in $\mathcal{O}^*(2^k)$ time and polynomial space.*

6. COMBINING DFT AND MÖBIUS TO SAVE SPACE

In this section we will combine the tools introduced in the previous two sections to obtain new polynomial space algorithms for several minimization problems. We obtain an analogue of Theorem 5.1 in the case where $\mathcal{R}$ is the min sum semi-ring $\mathcal{M}$ consisting of the set $\mathbb{N} \cup \infty$ with operators min and $+$. Notice that the identity of min is ∞ and the identity of $+$ is 0.

Evidently, Möbius Inversion is not applicable in this case since the addition operator of $\mathcal{M}$, minimization, does not have the inverse which is required for Möbius inversion. A commonly used solution to this is to embed $\mathcal{M}$ in the ring

$\mathbb{Z}[\mathbb{N}]$ with $\oplus$ and $\otimes$ as operators. Recall that $\oplus$ is pairwise addition $\otimes$ is convolution. We represent $a \in \mathcal{M}$ by $\mathbf{a}' \in \mathbb{Z}[\mathbb{N}]$ such that $\mathbf{a}[i] > 0$ for $i = a$ and $\mathbf{a}[i] = 0$ for $i < a$. Let $\mathbf{b}'$ represent b in a similar manner. Then we have that if

$$\min\{a,b\} = c \quad a+b = d \quad \mathbf{a}' \oplus \mathbf{b}' = \mathbf{c}' \quad \mathbf{a}' \otimes \mathbf{b}' = \mathbf{d}'$$

then c and d are exactly the minimum i such that $\mathbf{c}'[i] > 0$ and the minimum j such that $\mathbf{d}'[j] > 0$, respectively.

6.1 Minimization DP Without Tables

For dynamic programming algorithms, the special case of subset convolution $*_{\mathcal{R}}$ where $\mathcal{R} = \mathcal{M}$ is particularly useful. We refer to this special case as *min sum subset convolution*. Recalling Definition 5.1, $*_{\mathcal{M}}$ is defined as

$$(\mathbf{f} *_{\mathcal{M}} \mathbf{g})[X] = \min_{W \subseteq X} \mathbf{f}[W] + \mathbf{g}[X \setminus W]$$

For $\mathbf{f}$, $\mathbf{g} \in \mathbb{N}[2^V]$, the *pointwise minimization* operator min is defined as $(\mathbf{f} \min \mathbf{g})[X] = \min(\mathbf{f}[X], \mathbf{g}[X])$. The *pointwise maximization* operator max is defined similarly, that is, $(\mathbf{f} \max \mathbf{g})[X] = \max(\mathbf{f}[X], \mathbf{g}[X])$.

THEOREM 6.1. *Let V be a set and w be an integer. Let C be a circuit over $(\mathbb{N}[2^V], \min, *_{\mathcal{M}})$. Let $\hat{C}$ be obtained from C by replacing* min *with* max *gates, $*_{\mathcal{M}}$ with $\oplus$ gates and all constants with a table containing $w+1$ in all entries. Suppose all constants of C are singletons, and C and $\hat{C}$ output* $\mathbf{s}$ *and $\hat{\mathbf{s}}$ respectively. Then it can be decided whether $\mathbf{s}[V] \leq w$ using $\mathcal{O}^*(2^{|V|}u)$ time and polynomial space, where $\hat{\mathbf{s}}[Y] \leq u$ for every $Y \subseteq V$.*

Before proving Theorem 6.1 let us remark that there is an algorithm deciding whether $\hat{\mathbf{s}}[V] \leq w$ in $\mathcal{O}^*(3^n)$ time and $\mathcal{O}^*(2^n)$ space, by storing the elements of $\mathcal{M}$ for each subset and each gate and using Dynamic Programming, similarly to for example, [2, 9].

PROOF OF THEOREM 6.1. If $u \leq w$ we can return yes immediately because $\mathbf{s}[V] \leq \hat{\mathbf{s}}[V] \leq u \leq w$. Thus we assume that $w < u$. Also, we can assume $|V| \geq 2$ since otherwise we can decide whether $u \geq \hat{\mathbf{s}}[Y]$ in polynomial time using straight-forward dynamic programming techniques as mentioned above.

Let $\mathcal{P}$ be the ring $(\mathbb{Z}[\mathbb{N}]$ with addition operator $\oplus$ and multiplication $\otimes$. Embed the min sum semi-ring $\mathcal{M}$ into $\mathcal{P}$. Specifically, we construct a circuit C^0 over $(\mathcal{P}[2^V]; \oplus, *_{\mathcal{P}})$ from C by replacing all min gates by $\oplus$ gates, $\otimes$ gates by $*_{\mathcal{P}}$, and replacing the constant gates of C with different constant gates in the following manner. For a constant gate $\mathbf{a} \in C$, labeled with $z[X = S]$ with $z \in \mathbb{N} \cup \infty$ and $S \subseteq V$, the corresponding gate $\mathbf{a}' \in C^0$ is labeled with $\mathbf{e}[X = S]$, where $\mathbf{e} \in \mathcal{P}$ is defined as the vector such that

1. $\mathbf{e}[w+1] = 1$ and $\mathbf{e}[f] = 0$ for $f \leq w$ if $z = \infty$.

2. $\mathbf{e}[z] = 1$ and $\mathbf{e}[f] = 0$ for $f \neq z$, otherwise.

Let $Y \subseteq V$, $\mathbf{a} \in C$, $\mathbf{a}' \in C'$ be the gate corresponding to $\mathbf{a}$, and i be the minimum integer such that $(\mathbf{a}'[Y])[i] > 0$. By induction on $n(c)$ combined with the discussion of the previous subsection, it follows directly that $\mathbf{a}[Y] \geq w$ if $i = w$ and $\mathbf{a}[Y] < w$ otherwise.

Let $\mathtt{leq}^w$ be a circuit over $(\mathcal{P}; \oplus, *_{\mathcal{P}})$ outputting $\mathbf{d}$, where $(\mathbf{d}[S])[i] = 1$ if $S = \emptyset$ and $i \leq t$ and 0 otherwise. Using the circuit with the same underlying graph as in Observation 4.1 (and relabeling constants of labeled with $[x = p]$ with $[x = p][X = \emptyset]$), we can make sure that $|\mathtt{leq}^w|$ is $\mathcal{O}(\log w)$. We construct the circuit C^1 from C^0 as follows: add the circuit $\mathtt{leq}^w$ to C^0, and let the output of C^1 be the gate $\mathbf{t} = \mathbf{d} *_{\mathcal{P}} \mathbf{s}$. Now observe that $(\mathbf{t}[V])[w]] > 0$ if and only if $\mathbf{s}[V] \leq w$.

By Lemma 5.4 there exists a relaxation $\{\mathbf{t}_i\}$ of $\mathbf{t}$, such that for every Y we can in polynomial time construct a circuit C^2 over $(\mathcal{P}[2^V], \oplus, *_u)$ with $|C^2| = |C^1||V|$, outputting $(\zeta \mathbf{e}_n)[Y]$. This particular circuit C^2 will be related to $\hat{C}$ in the following claim. For this claim we need to introduce some notation.

For $\mathbf{p} \in \mathcal{P}$, denote $\alpha(\mathbf{p})$ for the largest i such that $\mathbf{p}[i] > 0$. Also, let $\beta(\mathbf{p})$ be the maximum value $\mathbf{p}[i]$ among all integers i. Finally for $\mathbf{a} \in C$, denote $n(\mathbf{a})$ for the number of gates $\mathbf{b} \in C$ such that there is a path from $\mathbf{b}$ to $\mathbf{a}$ in C.

CLAIM 3. *Suppose $|V| \geq 2$. For every gate $\mathbf{a} \in C$ with corresponding gates $\mathbf{a}_i \in C^2$ and $\hat{\mathbf{a}} \in \hat{C}$, it holds that for every $Y \subseteq V$, (i) $\alpha(\mathbf{a}_i) \leq \tilde{a}$ and (ii) $\beta(\mathbf{a}_i) \leq (|V|\tilde{a})^{n(\mathbf{a})}$, where $\tilde{a} = \max_{X \subseteq V}(\hat{\mathbf{a}})[X]$.*

PROOF. We prove the claim by induction on $n(\mathbf{a})$. In particular, we let $\mathbf{b}, \mathbf{c} \in C$ be the in-neighbors of $\mathbf{a}$ and $\mathbf{b}_i, \mathbf{c}_i \in C^2$ and $\hat{\mathbf{b}}, \hat{\mathbf{c}} \in \hat{C}$ be corresponding gates of $\mathbf{b}$ and $\mathbf{c}$ in C^2 and $\hat{C}$ respectively. We also refer to the integers $\tilde{b} = \max_{X \subseteq V}(\hat{\mathbf{b}})[X]$ and $\tilde{c} = \max_{X \subseteq V}(\hat{\mathbf{c}})[X]$.

Suppose $\mathbf{a}$ is a constant gate ($n(\mathbf{a}) = 1$), that is $\mathbf{a} = [X = Y]e$ where $e \in \mathbb{N}$. Then $(\mathbf{a}_i[Y])[k] = [Y = S][|Y| \geq i][k = e]$. Both equations (i) and (ii) are trivially true since $\tilde{a} = e$.

Suppose $\mathbf{a}$ is a min gate, then $\mathbf{a}_i$ is a $\oplus$ gate and (i) follows from the fact that

$$\alpha(\mathbf{a}_i) = \max\{\alpha(\mathbf{b}_i), \alpha(\mathbf{c}_i)\} \leq \max\{\tilde{b}, \tilde{c}\} \leq \tilde{a}$$

where the inequality is due to the induction hypothesis and the latter equality is due to fact that $\hat{\mathbf{a}}$ is a max gate. For (ii), notice that

$$\beta(\mathbf{a}_i) \leq \beta(\mathbf{b}_i) + \beta(\mathbf{c}_i) \leq (|V|\tilde{b})^{n(\mathbf{b})} + (|V|\tilde{c})^{n(\mathbf{c})} \leq (|V|\tilde{a})^{n(\mathbf{a})}$$

where the second inequality follows from the induction hypothesis and the third inequality follows from the fact that $\tilde{b}$ and $\tilde{c}$ are smaller than $\tilde{a}$, $|V| \geq 2$ and $n(\mathbf{b}) + n(\mathbf{c}) = n(\mathbf{a})$.

If $\mathbf{a}$ is a $*_{\mathcal{M}}$ gate, we have for every $\alpha(\mathbf{a}_i) = \alpha(\mathbf{b}_i) + \alpha(\mathbf{c}_i) \leq \tilde{a}$ by the induction hypothesis and (i) follows. Also, (ii) holds since $\beta(\mathbf{a}_i)$ is at most

$$|V|\tilde{a}\beta(\mathbf{b}_i)\beta(\mathbf{c}_i) \leq |V|\tilde{a}(|V|\tilde{b})^{n(b)}(|V|\tilde{c})^{n(c)} \leq (|V|\tilde{a})^{n(a)}$$

for the first inequality, recall that each table entry is the result of a sum of at most $|V|\tilde{a}$ products of table entries of $\mathbf{b}_j$ and $\mathbf{c}_{i-j}$ for some $j \leq i$. The second inequality is then due to the induction hypothesis, and the third inequality follows from $\tilde{b}, \tilde{c} \leq \tilde{a}$ and $n(b) + n(c) + 1 = n(a)$. □

Now Claim 3 implies that for all gates $a \in C$ and $0 \leq i \leq n$, $\alpha(\mathbf{a}_i) \leq \tilde{a}$ and $\beta(\mathbf{a}_i) \leq (n\tilde{a})^n$. For the gates $\mathbf{a}$ in C^2 coming from the added circuit $\mathtt{leq}^w$, we have that $\alpha(\mathbf{a}) \leq w$ and $\beta(\mathbf{a}) = 1$. For every $0 \leq i \leq n$, $\mathbf{t}_i = \mathbf{d} \diamond \mathbf{s}_i$, and it it follows that $\alpha(\mathbf{t}_i) \leq \tilde{a} + w$ and $\beta(\mathbf{e}_i) \leq (n\tilde{a})^n\tilde{a}$.

Now use Lemma 5.3 to obtain the circuit C^Y over the ring $(\mathbb{Z}[N]; \oplus, \otimes)$ such that for each $\mathbf{a}_i \in C^2$, the corresponding gate $\mathbf{a}_i^Y \in \mathbb{Z}[\mathbb{N}]$ outputs $(\zeta \mathbf{a}_i)[Y]$.

Since $\mathbf{a}_i^Y = \sum_{X \subseteq Y} \mathbf{a}_i[Y]$, it follows that $\mathbf{a}_i^Y[j] = 0$ for $j > \alpha(\mathbf{a}_i)$ and $\mathbf{a}_i^Y \leq 2^n \beta(\mathbf{a}_i)$. Now Theorem 4.3 can be used on C^Y to compute $((\zeta \mathbf{t}_n)[Y])[T]$. It is easily seen that C^Y only has singleton constants, and that $\Delta(C^Y)$ is polynomial in $|C|$. Moreover, since for all gates $\mathbf{g} \in C^Y$, $\alpha(\mathbf{g}) \leq \tilde{a}+w \leq 2u$ and $\beta(g) \leq 2^n\beta(\mathbf{a}_i) \leq (n\tilde{a})^n\tilde{a} \leq (nu)^{n+1}$, we can apply the theorem with $\mathbf{N}$ being the singleton vector $\langle 2W \rangle$ and m being nu^{n+1}. Hence for any $Y \subseteq V$, $((\zeta \mathbf{t})_n[Y])[T]$ can be computed in $\mathcal{O}^*(W)$ time and polynomial space.

Finally we use Möbius inversion to obtain $(\mathbf{t}_n[V])[w]$ from all values $((\zeta \mathbf{t}_n)[Y])[w]$ for every $Y \subseteq V$. Recall $(\mathbf{t}_n[V])[w] > 0$ if and only if $s[V] \leq w$, hence we can decide whether $\mathbf{s}[V] \leq w$ in the claimed time and space bound. □

6.2 Applications

We will now give a few applications of Theorem 6.1. We consider circuits using pointwise addition and the min-sum subset convolution $*_{\mathcal{M}}$. In the context of the min sum semiring, Iverson's bracket notation works as follows; $[b] = 0$ if $b = true$ and $[b] = \infty$ otherwise. Thus, a constant $[X = S]v$ is v if $X = S$ and $[X = S]v$ is ∞ otherwise. For a constant e we will shorthand $f *_{\mathcal{M}} [X = \emptyset]e$ as $f + e$, since min-sum subset convolution by $[X = \emptyset]e$ just adds e to all entries of f. Finally, we will denote by $\langle\langle x \rangle\rangle$ a table where all elements are x. We will only consider decision variants, but it should be noted that using binary search and standard self-reduction it is possible to extend these algorithms to construct an optimal solution, at the cost of a polynomial factor in the running time.

Traveling Salesman Problem

A Hamiltonian path of a graph is a path visiting all vertices exactly once. We study the following generalization of Hamiltonian path:

TRAVELING SALESMAN PROBLEM (TSP)
Instance: A graph $G = (V, E)$, a vertex s and a function $\phi : V \times V \to \{1, \ldots, d\}$ and an integer $t \leq |V|d$.
Question: Is there a Hamiltonian path $E' \in E$ of weight at most t?

Denote $n = |V|$. Early $\mathcal{O}^*(2^n)$ time and space DP algorithms are given in [2, 13]. Later, an algorithm running in time $\mathcal{O}^*(2^n d)$ using $O^*(d)$ space was given by Karp [16]. TSP can also be solved in $\mathcal{O}^*(4^n)$ time and polynomial space [12]. Recently, [18] proposed a combination of these two approaches to obtain a space-time trade off. It is an interesting open problem ([22]) whether TSP can be solved in $\mathcal{O}(2^n)$ time and polynomial space.

For $v \in V$ and $X \subseteq V\backslash\{s, v\}$, define $\mathbf{f}_v[X]$ as the minimum weight of a Hamiltonian path in $G[X \cup \{s, v\}]$ starting in s and ending in v. The Bellman-Held-Karp recurrence [2, 13] is:

$$\mathbf{f}_v[\emptyset] = w(s, v)$$
$$\mathbf{f}_v[X] = \min_{u \in N(v) \cap X} \mathbf{f}_u[X \setminus \{v\}] + w(u, v) \tag{11}$$

To see that the above equation holds, note that there only is one Hamiltonian path to consider if $X = \emptyset$ and its weight is $w(s, v)$. If X is not empty, any Hamiltonian path of $G[X \cup \{s, v\}]$ starting in s and ending in v consists of a Hamiltonian path of $G[X \cup \{s, u\}]$ starting in s and ending in u, and the edge (u, v). Hence, we can minimize over all the last edges a Hamiltonian path can have, and find the minimum weight such a Hamiltonian path can have using previously computed values and the value $w(u, v)$.

In order to turn the recurrence 11 into a circuit, we formulate it using min sum subset convolution

$$\mathbf{f}_v[\emptyset] = w(s, v)$$
$$\mathbf{f}_v[X] = \min_{u \in N(v)} (\mathbf{f}_u *_{\mathcal{M}} [X = \{u\}])[X] + w(u, v)$$

but the second case of this recurrence is *cyclic*, hence it can not be translated into a circuit. However, it is easy to see we can instead use the following recurrence:

$$\mathbf{f}_v^0 = [X = \emptyset] *_{\mathcal{M}} w(s, v)$$
$$\mathbf{f}_v^i = \min_{u \in N(v)} (\mathbf{f}_u^{i-1} *_{\mathcal{M}} [X = \{v\}]) + w(u, v) \qquad \text{for } 0 < i$$

since $\mathbf{f}_v^n[V] = \mathbf{f}_v[V]$ for every $v \in V \setminus \{s\}$. Now we can apply Theorem 6.1. To this end, we have to construct the circuit C', which can be formulated as the following recurrence:

$$\mathbf{g}_v^0 = \langle\langle t+1 \rangle\rangle \oplus \langle\langle t+1 \rangle\rangle$$
$$\mathbf{g}_v^i = \max_{u \in N(v)} \mathbf{g}_u^{i-1} \oplus \langle\langle t+1 \rangle\rangle \oplus \langle\langle t+1 \rangle\rangle \qquad \text{for } 0 < i$$

and it is easy to see that for every $X \subseteq V$, $\mathbf{g}_v^i[X] \leq 3(i+1)(t+1)$. Then Theorem 6.1 implies

THEOREM 6.2. *The Traveling Salesman problem can be solved in $\mathcal{O}^*(2^n d)$ time and polynomial space.*

Weighted Steiner Tree

In this section, we will extend the example of Subsection 5.4 to a weighted version of the Steiner Tree problem, which is the following:

WEIGHTED STEINER TREE (WST)
Instance: A graph $G = (V, E)$ with weight function $w : E \to \{1, \ldots, d\}$, terminals $T \subseteq V$ and an integer t such that $d \leq t \leq |V|d$.
Question: Does there exist a subtree (V', E') of G such that $\sum_{e \in E'} w(e) \leq t$ and $T \subseteq V'$?

The current fastest algorithm for this problem is due to [10], and uses $\mathcal{O}((2+\epsilon)^k n^{h(\epsilon)})$ time and space. It is an interesting question, whether there is a $\mathcal{O}^*(c^k)$ time, polynomial space algorithm for this problem. We again consider the algorithm of Dreyfus and Wagner [9], but now for the weighted case:

$$\mathbf{f}_v^1 = [X = \emptyset] \qquad \text{for } v \notin T$$
$$\mathbf{f}_v^1 = [X = \{v\}] \min[X = \emptyset] \qquad \text{for } v \in T \tag{12}$$
$$\mathbf{f}_v^i = \min_{j=1}^{i-1} \min_{w \in N(v)} \mathbf{f}_w^j *_{\mathcal{M}} \mathbf{f}_v^{i-j} + w(vw) \qquad \text{for } i > 1$$

Now $\mathbf{f}_v^n[T] \leq t$ if and only if there exists a subtree (V', E') of G such that $\sum_{e \in E'} w(e) \leq t$ with $T \subseteq V'$, analogously to the recurrence of subsection 5.4. We apply Theorem 6.1. To this end, we construct the circuit C', which can be formulated as the following recurrence:

$$\mathbf{g}_v^1 = \langle\langle t+1 \rangle\rangle$$
$$\mathbf{g}_v^i = \max_{j=1}^{i-1} \max_{w \in N(v)} \mathbf{g}_w^j \oplus \mathbf{g}_v^{i-j} \oplus \langle\langle t+1 \rangle\rangle \qquad \text{for } i > 1$$

Hence $\mathbf{g}_v^i[X] \leq 3(t+1)(i+1)$, yielding the following theorem.

THEOREM 6.3. *The Weighted Steiner Tree problem can be solved in $\mathcal{O}^*(2^{|T|}d)$ time and polynomial space.*

Weighted Set Cover

Our last application is for the following problem:

WEIGHTED SET COVER
Instance: A set V, a family of subsets $S_1, \ldots, S_m$, a weight function $w : \{1, \ldots, l\} \to \{1, \ldots, d\}$ and an integer $t \geq d$.
Question: Does there exist a $C \subseteq \{1, \ldots, l\}$ such that $\bigcup_{i \in C} S_i = V$ and $\sum_{i \in C} w(i) \leq t$?

The current fastest algorithm for WEIGHTED SET COVER due to [4] uses $\mathcal{O}^*(2^{|V|}d)$ time and $\mathcal{O}^*(d)$ space. In this variant of the problem, the sets are given explicitely and hence the number m is polynomial in input size. The standard dynamic programming algorithm for our the problem uses the following recurrence. For ease of notation, let $S_0 = \emptyset$, $w(0) = 0$ an for each $0 \leq i \leq n$, define $\mathbf{f}_i[X]$ as the minimum over all subsets C of $\{0, \ldots, i\}$ such that $\cup_{j \in C} S_j \supseteq X$. Then

$$\mathbf{f}^0 = [X = \emptyset]$$
$$\mathbf{f}^i = f^{i-1} *_{\mathcal{M}} \mathbf{s}^{S_i}$$

where $\mathbf{s}$ is defined as

$$\mathbf{s}^{\{e_1,\ldots e_l\}} = ([X = \{e_1\}] + [X = \emptyset]) *_{\mathcal{M}} \ldots *_{\mathcal{M}} ([X = \{e_l\}] + [X = \emptyset])$$

Note that $\mathbf{s}^W$ is 1 if $W \subseteq X$ and ∞ otherwise. Again, in order to apply Theorem 6.1 we have to consider the circuit $\hat{C}$ obtained by replacing min by max and $*_{\mathcal{M}}$ by $\oplus$:

$$\mathbf{g}^0 = \langle\langle t+1 \rangle\rangle$$
$$\mathbf{g}^i = \mathbf{g}^{i-1} \oplus \mathbf{r}^{S_i}$$
$$(\mathbf{r}^{\{e_1,\ldots e_l\}}] = \sum_{i=1}^{l} \langle\langle t+1 \rangle\rangle \max \langle\langle t+1 \rangle\rangle$$

And hence for every X $\mathbf{g}^i[X] \leq t + 1 + m|V|(t+1)$. Hence Theorem 6.1 yields the following result.

THEOREM 6.4. *The Weighted Set Cover problem can be solved in $\mathcal{O}^*(2^{|V|}d)$ time and polynomial space.*

Acknowledgements

We thank Fedor Fomin, Pinar Heggernes, Neeldhara Misra and Saket Saurabh for some useful discussions and help to improve the presentation of the paper.

7. REFERENCES

[1] R. Bellman. Bottleneck problems and dynamic programming. *Proceedings of the National Academy of Sciences of the United States of America*, 39(9):947, 1953.

[2] R. Bellman. Dynamic programming treatment of the travelling salesman problem. *J. ACM*, 9(1):61–63, 1962.

[3] A. Björklund, T. Husfeldt, P. Kaski, and M. Koivisto. Fourier meets möbius: Fast subset convolution. In *STOC*, pages 67–74, 2007.

[4] A. Bjorklund, T. Husfeldt, and M. Koivisto. Set partitioning via inclusion-exclusion. *SIAM Journal on Computing*, 39(2):546–563, 2009.

[5] P. J. Cameron. *Combinatorics*. Cambridge University Press, 1998.

[6] D. V. Chudnovsky and G. V. Chudnovsky. Approximations and complex multiplication according to ramanujan. *Ramanujan Revisited*, pages 375–396 and 468–472, 1988.

[7] T. Cormen, C. Leiserson, R. Rivest, and C. Stein. Introduction to algorithms, 2001.

[8] S. Dasgupta, C. H. Papadimitriou, and U. Vazirani. *Algorithms*. McGraw-Hill, 2006.

[9] S. Dreyfus and R. Wagner. The Steiner problem in graphs. *Networks*, 1:195–207, 1972.

[10] B. Fuchs, W. Kern, D. Mölle, S. Richter, P. Rossmanith, and X. Wang. Dynamic programming for minimum steiner trees. *Theory Comput. Syst.*, 41(3):493–500, 2007.

[11] M. Fürer. Faster integer multiplication. In *STOC*, pages 57–66, 2007.

[12] Y. Gurevich and S. Shelah. Expected computation time for hamiltonian path problem. *SIAM J. Comput.*, 16(3):486–502, 1987.

[13] M. Held and R. M. Karp. A dynamic programming approach to sequencing problems. *Journal of the Society for Industrial and Applied Mathematics*, 10(1):196–210, 1962.

[14] E. Horowitz and S. Sahni. Computing partitions with applications to the knapsack problem. *J. ACM*, 21(2):277–292, 1974.

[15] N. Howgrave-Graham and A. Joux. A new generic algorithm for hard knapsacks (to appear in *eurocrypt* 2010).

[16] R. M. Karp. Dynamic programming meets the principle of inclusion and exclusion. *Oper. Res. Lett.*, 1:49–51, 1982.

[17] D. E. Knuth. *The Art of Computer Programming, Volume II: Seminumerical Algorithms.* Addison-Wesley, 1969.

[18] M. Koivisto and P. Parviainen. A Space–Time Tradeoff for Permutation Problems.

[19] J. Nederlof. Fast polynomial-space algorithms using möbius inversion: Improving on steiner tree and related problems. In *ICALP '09*, pages 713–725. Springer-Verlag, 2009.

[20] A. Schönhage and V. Strassen. Schnelle multiplikation grosser zahlen. *Computing*, 7:281–292, 1971.

[21] G. J. Woeginger. Space and time complexity of exact algorithms: Some open problems (invited talk). In *IWPEC*, pages 281–290, 2004.

[22] G. J. Woeginger. Space and time complexity of exact algorithms: Some open problems (invited talk). In R. G. Downey, M. R. Fellows, and F. K. H. A. Dehne, editors, *IWPEC*, volume 3162 of *Lecture Notes in Computer Science*, pages 281–290. Springer, 2004.

On the Structure of Cubic and Quartic Polynomials

Elad Haramaty
Faculty of Computer Science
The Technion
Haifa, Israel
eladh@cs.technion.ac.il

Amir Shpilka
Faculty of Computer Science
The Technion
Haifa, Israel
shpilka@cs.technion.ac.il

ABSTRACT

In this paper we study the structure of polynomials of degree three and four that have high bias or high Gowers norm, over arbitrary prime fields. In particular we obtain the following results.

1. We give a canonical representation for degree three or four polynomials that have a significant bias (i.e. they are not equidistributed). This result generalizes the corresponding results from the theory of quadratic forms. It also significantly improves the results of [GT07] and [KL08] for such polynomials.
2. For the case of degree four polynomials with high Gowers norm we show that (a subspace of co-dimension $O(1)$ of) $\mathbb{F}^n$ can be partitioned to subspaces of dimension $\Omega(n)$ such that on each of the subspaces the polynomial is equal to some degree three polynomial.

It was shown in [GT07] and [LMS08] that a quartic polynomial with a high Gowers norm is not necessarily correlated with any cubic polynomial. Our result shows that a slightly weaker statement does hold. The proof is based on finding a structure in the space of partial derivatives of the underlying polynomial.

Categories and Subject Descriptors

F.0 [Theory of Computation]: General

General Terms

Theory

Keywords

Gowers Norm, Cubic Polynomials, Quartic Polynomials

1. INTRODUCTION

Assume that we are given a degree d polynomial f that, in some sense, 'behaves' differently from a random degree d polynomial. Is there anything that we can deduce about the structure of f just by knowing this fact? Recently this question received a lot of attention, where the 'behavior' of f was examined with respect to its bias or the more general notion of the Gowers norm.

Definition 1.1. *Let $f : \mathbb{F}^n \to \mathbb{F}$ be a function. The bias of f is defined as* $\text{bias}(f) = \left|\mathbb{E}_{\bar{a}\in\mathbb{F}^n}[\omega^{f(\bar{a})}]\right|$, *where* $\omega = e^{\frac{2\pi i}{|\mathbb{F}|}}$ *is a complex primitive root of unity of order* $|\mathbb{F}|$.

Intuitively, the bias of f measures how far is the distribution induced by f from the uniform distribution. We expect a random polynomial to have a vanishing small bias (as a function of the number of variables), so it is interesting to know what can be said when the bias is not too small. Indeed, Green and Tao [GT07] showed that if f is a degree d polynomial over $\mathbb{F}$, such that $d < |\mathbb{F}|$, and $\text{bias}(f) = \delta$ then f can be written as a function of a small number of lower degree polynomial. Formally, $f(x) = F(g_1, \ldots, g_{c_d})$ for some function F and $c_d = c_d(\text{bias}(f), |\mathbb{F}|)$ polynomials $\{g_i\}$ satisfying $\deg(g_i) < d$. Note that $c_d = c_d(\text{bias}(f), |\mathbb{F}|)$ does not depend on the number of variables, i.e. it is some constant. This result was later extended by Kaufman and Lovett [KL08] to arbitrary finite fields (i.e. without the restriction $d < |\mathbb{F}|$). Thus, if f has a noticeable bias, unlike a random degree d polynomial, then f is in fact very far from being random; simple counting arguments show that most degree d polynomials cannot be represented as functions of a few lower degree polynomials. This result is also interesting as it gives an average case - worst case reduction. Namely, if f has correlation δ with a lower degree polynomial then it is a function of a small number of lower degree polynomials. One drawback of the results of [GT07, KL08] is the dependance of the number of lower degree polynomials on the bias of f. In particular when $\deg(f) = 3$, [GT07, KL08] get the bound $c_3 = \exp(\text{poly}(1/\text{bias}(f)))$ and for $\deg(f) = 4$ they bound[1] c_4 by a tower of height c_3. On the other hand if $\deg(f) = 2$ and $\text{bias}(f) = \delta$ then it is known that f can be written as a function of at most $2\log(1/\delta) + 1$ linear functions. This can be immediately deduced from the following well known theorem.

Theorem 1.1 (Structure of quadratic polynomials). *(Theorems 6.21 and 6.30 in [LN97]). For every quadratic polynomial $f : \mathbb{F}^n \to \mathbb{F}$ over a prime field $\mathbb{F}$ there exists an invertible linear transformation T, a linear polynomial ℓ, and field elements $\alpha_1, \ldots \alpha_n$ (some of which may be 0) such that:*

[1] These numbers are not explicitly computed there, but this is what the recursive arguments in the papers imply.

STOC'10, June 5–8, 2010, Cambridge, Massachusetts, USA.

1. *If* char($\mathbb{F}$) = 2 *then* $(q \circ T)(x) = \sum_{1=i}^{\lfloor n/2 \rfloor} \alpha_i \cdot x_{2i-1} \cdot x_{2i} + \ell(x)$,

2. *If* char($\mathbb{F}$) *is odd then* $(q \circ T)(x) = \sum_{1=i}^{n} \alpha_i \cdot x_i^2 + \ell(x)$.

Moreover, the number of non zero α_i-s is invariant and depends only on f.

We thus see that there is a sharp contrast between the result for quadratic polynomials and the results for polynomials of degrees as low as three or four. We also note that the results of Kaufman and Lovett only guarantee that f can be represented as $f(x) = F(g_1, \ldots, g_c)$ but no nice structure like the one in Theorem 1.1 is known. It is thus an intriguing question whether a nice structural theorem exists for biased polynomials and what is the correct dependance of the number of lower degree polynomials on deg(f) and bias(f).

As mentioned above, a more general measure of randomness that was considered is the so called Gowers norm of f. Intuitively, the U^d Gower norm tests whether f behaves like a degree $d-1$ polynomial on d dimensional subspaces. To define the Gowers norm we first define the notion of a discrete partial derivative.

Definition 1.2. *(Discrete partial derivative) For a function $f : \mathbb{F}^n \to \mathbb{F}$ and a direction $y \in \mathbb{F}^n$ we define $\Delta_y(f)(x) \triangleq f(x+y) - f(x)$ to be the discrete partial derivative of f in direction y at the point x.*

It is not difficult to see that if deg(f) $= d$ then for every y, $\deg(\Delta_y(f)) \leq d-1$. We now define the d-th Gower norm of a function f.

Definition 1.3 (Gowers norm [AKK+05, Gow98, Gow01]). *The d-th Gower norm, U^d, of f is defined as*

$$\|f\|_{U^d} \triangleq |\mathbb{E}_{x,y_1,\ldots,y_d}[\omega^{\Delta_{y_d}\cdots\Delta_{y_1}(f)(x)}]|^{1/2^d} ,$$

where again $\omega = e^{\frac{2\pi i}{|\mathbb{F}|}}$.

Note that $\|f\|_{U^0} = \|f\|_{U^1} = \text{bias}(f)$. It is also clear that if deg(f) $= d-1$ then $\|f\|_{U^d} = 1$. For more properties of the Gowers norm we refer the reader to [Gow98, Gow01, GT08, Sam07, VW07].

In [AKK+05] Alon et. al. showed that if $\|f\|_{U^d} > 1 - \delta$, for some small δ (depending on d), then f can be well approximated by a degree $d-1$ polynomial. This raises the question whether any function that has a noticeable U^d norm is somewhat correlated with a lower degree polynomial and indeed in [Sam07, GT08] this was conjectured to be the case. This conjecture has become known as the inverse conjecture for the Gowers norm. Samorodnitsky [Sam07] proved that if $\|f\|_{U^3} = \delta$ where $f : \mathbb{F}_2^n \to \mathbb{F}_2$ is an arbitrary function, then f has an exponentially high (in δ) correlation with a quadratic polynomial. Namely, there exists a quadratic polynomial q such that $\Pr_{x\in\mathbb{F}_2^n}[f(x) = q(X)] \geq 1/2 + \exp(-\text{poly}(1/\delta))$. Independently, Green and Tao [GT08] obtained similar results for fields of odd characteristic. These results gave an affirmative answer for the case of the U^3 norm. More generally, Green and Tao proved that if $d < |\mathbb{F}|$ and f is a degree d polynomial with a high U^d norm then f is indeed correlated with a lower degree polynomial [GT07]. Recently, the case of large characteristic was solved by Tao and Ziegler [TZ08].[2] Using ideas from ergodic theory they proved that if $f : \mathbb{F}^n \to \mathcal{D}$ (where $\mathcal{D}$ is the unit disk in $\mathbb{C}$) is a function with high U^d norm and $d \leq |\mathbb{F}|$ then f is correlated with a degree $d-1$ phase polynomial.[3] This completely settled the conjecture for the case $d \leq |\mathbb{F}|$. On the other hand, for the U^4 norm it was shown, independently, by Lovett, Meshulam and Samorodnitsky [LMS08] and by Green and Tao [GT07] that no such result is possible when $\mathbb{F} = \mathbb{F}_2$. Namely, [LMS08] proved that the symmetric polynomial $S_4(x_1, \ldots, x_n) \triangleq \sum_{T\subset[n],|T|=4} \prod_{i\in T} x_i$, which is of degree four, has a high U^4 norm but has an exponentially (in n) small correlation with any lower degree polynomial. Similar examples where given for other fields (when d is large enough compared to the size of the field). These examples show that for small fields the inverse conjecture for the Gowers norm is not true in its current form. In their work, Tao and Ziegler [TZ08] proved a variant of the conjecture for the case of low characteristic ($d > |\mathbb{F}|$). Namely, that if a function f has high U^d norm then f is correlated with a phase polynomial of a certain constant degree (but not necessarily smaller than d). We note however, that if deg(f) $= d$ then the results of [TZ08] do not give any information on f. In fact, even if deg(f) $= 4$ and f has a high U^4 norm then nothing is known on the structure of f. It is thus a very interesting question to understand the structure of low degree polynomials having high Gowers norm over small fields.

Besides being natural questions on the own, results on the Gowers norms had many applications in mathematics and computer science. In his seminal work on finding arithmetic progressions in dense sets, Gowers first defined the U^d norm (for functions from $\mathbb{Z}_n$ to $\mathbb{Z}_n$) and proved an inverse theorem for them that was instrumental in his proofs [Gow98, Gow01]. Bogdanov and Viola [BV07] attempt for constructing a pseudo random generator for constant degree polynomials relied on the (erroneous) inverse conjecture for the Gowers norm, yet it paved the way for other papers solving the problem [Lov08, Vio08]. In [ST06] applications of an inverse theorem for the Gowers norm to PCP constructions was given. Samorodnitsky's proof of the inverse theorem for the U^3 norm [Sam07] implies a low degree test distinguishing quadratic functions from those that do not have a non trivial correlation with a quadratic function. This result also gives a test for checking the distance of a given word from the 2nd order Reed-Muller code, beyond the list decoding radius. For a more elaborate discussion of the connection between additive combinatorics and computer science see [Tre09].

1.1 Our results

In this work we are able to show analogs of Theorem 1.1 for polynomials of degree three and four. We also prove a structural result for the case that such a polynomial has a high Gowers norm. Our first main result is the following.

Theorem 1. *(biased cubic polynomials)Let $\mathbb{F}$ be a finite field and $f \in \mathbb{F}[x_1, \ldots, x_n]$ a cubic polynomial (deg(f) $= 3$) such that bias(f) $= \delta$. Then there exist $c_1 = O(\log(1/\delta))$ quadratic polynomials $q_1, \ldots, q_{c_1} \in \mathbb{F}[x_1, \ldots, x_n]$ and linear functions $\ell_1, \ldots, \ell_{c_1} \in \mathbb{F}[x_1, \ldots, x_n]$ and another $c_2 = O(\log^4(\frac{1}{\delta}))$ linear functions $\ell'_1, \ldots, \ell'_{c_2} \in \mathbb{F}[x_1, \ldots, x_n]$ such that $f = \sum_{j=1}^{c_1} \ell_j \cdot q_j + g(\ell'_1, \ldots, \ell'_{c_2})$, where g is cubic.*

[2]In fact,[TZ08] only get a qualitative result. No explicit connection is known between the Gowers norm and the correlation with polynomials.

[3]A degree $d-1$ phase polynomial is a function of the form $e^{2\pi i\theta}\omega^g$, for some degree $d-1-(p-1)t$ polynomial g where $\theta \in [0,1]$ and $\omega = e^{2\pi i/|\mathbb{F}|^t}$.

We note that if it weren't for the $g(\ell'_1, \ldots, \ell'_{c_2})$ part then this result would be quantitatively the same as Theorem 1.1 (and tight of course). It is an interesting open question to decide whether we can do only with the $\sum_{j=1}^{O(\log_{|\mathbb{F}|} 1/\delta)} \ell_i \cdot q_i$ part. Using the same techniques we show a similar result for the case that $\|f\|_{U^3} > \delta$.

Theorem 2. *(cubic polynomials with high U^3 norm)Let $\mathbb{F}$ be a finite field and $f \in \mathbb{F}[x_1, \ldots, x_n]$ a cubic polynomial such that $\|f\|_{U^3} = \delta$. Then there exist $c+1 = O(\log^2(\frac{1}{\delta}))$ quadratic polynomials $q_0, \ldots, q_c \in \mathbb{F}[x_1, \ldots, x_n]$ and c linear functions $\ell_1, \ldots, \ell_c \in \mathbb{F}[x_1, \ldots, x_n]$ such that $f = \sum_{j=1}^{c} \ell_j \cdot q_j + q_0$.*

Note that the difference between the structure of f in Theorems 1 and 2 is the number of quadratic function required. Recall that in [Sam07] Samorodnitsky proved that if an $\mathbb{F}_2$ function f has a high U^3 norm then it has an exponentially (in $\|f\|_{U^3}$) high correlation with a quadratic polynomial. Thus, our theorem shows that when f is a cubic polynomial then a much stronger statement holds. Namely, f has correlation $\exp(\log^2(1/\delta))$ with a quadratic polynomial, and further, has a nice structure.

Our second main result is an analog of Theorem 1 for the case of quartic polynomials (i.e. $\deg(f) = 4$).

Theorem 3. *(biased quartic polynomials) Let $\mathbb{F}$ be a finite field and $f \in \mathbb{F}[x_1, \ldots, x_n]$ a quartic polynomial ($\deg(f) = 4$) such that $\text{bias}(f) = \delta$. Then there exist $4c = \text{poly}(|\mathbb{F}|/\delta)$ polynomials $\{\ell_i, q_i, q'_i, g_i\}_{i=1}^{c}$, where the ℓ_i-s are linear, the q_i-s and q'_i-s are quadratic and the g_i-s are cubic such that $f = \sum_{j=1}^{c} \ell_j \cdot g_j + \sum_{j=1}^{c} q_j \cdot q'_j$.*

As mentioned above, prior to this result it was known that there exist C cubic polynomials $g_1, \ldots, g_C$ and a function F such that $f = F(g_1, \ldots, g_C)$, where C is a tower of height $\exp(\text{poly}(1/\delta))$ [GT07, KL08]. Thus, our result greatly improves the dependance on δ and gives a nice structure for the polynomial. We note that in their work Green and Tao do show that such a nice structure exists when $d < |\mathbb{F}|$ [GT07], but no such result was known for smaller fields (in addition C needs to be even larger for such a nice representation to hold).

Our third main result is for the case where $\deg(f) = 4$ and $\|f\|_{U^4} = \delta$. In such a case it is known [LMS08, GT07] that we cannot hope to get a nice structure as in Theorem 2 as it may be the case that f has an exponentially small (in n) correlation with all lower degree polynomials. However, we do manage to show that there is some subspace $U \subset \mathbb{F}^n$ such that when restricted to V, $f|_U$ is equal to some degree three polynomial. Thus, f does not have a correlation with a cubic polynomial in the entire space but instead there is a large subspace on which it is of degree three. In fact we show a more general result. Namely, that there is a large subspace V, of dimension $n - O(\log(1/\delta))$, that can be partitioned to subspaces of dimension $n/\exp(\log^2(1/\delta))$ such that the restriction of f to any of the subspaces in the partition is of degree three.

Theorem 4. *(quartic polynomials with high U^4 norm) Let $\mathbb{F}$ be a finite field and $f \in \mathbb{F}[x_1, \ldots, x_n]$ a degree four polynomial such that $\|f\|_{U^4} = \delta$. Then there exists a partition of a subspace $V \subseteq \mathbb{F}^n$, of dimension $\dim(V) \geq n - O(\log(1|/\delta))$, to subspaces $\{V_\alpha\}_{\alpha \in I}$, satisfying $\dim(V_\alpha) = \Omega(n/|\mathbb{F}|^{\log^2(1/\delta)})$, such that for every $\alpha \in I$, $f|_{V_\alpha}$ is a cubic polynomial.*

Remark 1.4. *Note that the structure guaranteed in Theorem 4 is shared by very few polynomials. Specifically, a random polynomial of degree four is unlikely to be equal to any degree three polynomial on any subspace of dimension larger than, say, $n^{0.9}$. To see this note that if $|\mathbb{F}| = p$ and $\dim(V) = d$ then there are roughly p^{d^3} cubic polynomials and p^{d^4} quartic polynomials over V. Furthermore, the map taking a quartic polynomial over $\mathbb{F}^n$ to its restriction is a linear map and so the fraction of quartic polynomials that equal a degree three polynomial on V is (roughly) $p^{-d^4+d^3}$. As the total number of subspaces can be bounded by p^{n^2} we get that the fraction of quartic polynomial that are equal to a degree three polynomial on some subspace of dimension greater than $n^{0.9}$ is at most $p^{n^2-n^{3.6}+n^3} = \exp(-n^{3.6})$.*

This result has the same flavor as the inverse U^3 norm theorem of [GT08]. There it was shown that if $f : \mathbb{F}_5^n \to \mathbb{F}_5$ satisfies $\|f\|_{U^3} = \delta$ then there exists a subspace V of codimension $\text{poly}(1/\delta)$, such that on an 'average' coset of V, f is correlated with a quadratic polynomial. Recently, Wolf [Wol09] proved a similar result for the case of characteristic two, thus extending Samorodnitsky's argument [Sam07]. The main difference between these results and our result is that ours only holds for polynomials of degree four whereas the results of [GT08, Sam07, Wol09] hold for arbitrary functions. On the other hand our result holds for the U^4 norm compared to the U^3 norm studied there. Moreover, when $\text{char}(\mathbb{F}) > 4$, using the same techniques we can actually show that f must have a structure similar to the one guaranteed by Theorem 3.

Theorem 5. *Let $\mathbb{F}$ be a finite field with $\text{char}(\mathbb{F}) > 4$ and $f \in \mathbb{F}[x_1, \ldots, x_n]$ a degree four polynomial such that $\|f\|_{U^4} = \delta$. Then $f = \sum_{i=1}^{R} \ell_i \cdot g_i + \sum_{i=1}^{r} q_i \cdot q'_i$, for $r = O(\log^2(1/\delta))$ and $R = \exp(\log^2(1/\delta))$ where ℓ_i is linear, q_i, q'_i are quadratic and g_i cubic.*

1.2 Proof Technique

The main approach in all the proofs is to consider the space of discrete partial derivatives of f and look for some structure there. We will explain the idea for the case of degree three polynomials and then its extension to degree four polynomials.

Let f be a degree three polynomials. Assume that f has high bias (respectively high U^3 norm). It can be shown that a constant fraction of its derivatives, which are degree 2 polynomials, have high bias (high U^2 norm). By Theorem 1.1 it follows that for a constant fraction of the directions, the partial derivatives depends on a small number of linear functions (same for the U^3 norm). Hence, in the space of partial derivatives, a constant fraction of the elements depend on a few linear functions. We now show that there must be a small number of linear functions that 'explain' this. More accurately, we show that there exist a subspace $V \subset \mathbb{F}^n$, of dimension $\dim(V) = n - O(1)$, and $O(1)$ linear functions $\ell_1, \ldots, \ell_c$, such that for every $y \in V$ it holds that $\Delta_y(f) = \sum_{i=1}^{c} \ell_i \cdot \ell_i^{(y)} + \ell_0^{(y)}$, where the $\ell_i^{(y)}$-s are linear functions determined by y.

We are now basically done. Consider the subspace $U = \{x : \ell_1(x) = \ldots = \ell_c(x) = 0\}$. Then, for every $y \in V$ it holds that $\Delta_y(f)|_U = \ell_0^{(y)}|_U$. This implies that $f|_V = \sum_{i=1}^{c} \ell_i \cdot q_i + q_0$, where the q_i-s are quadratic polynomials.

As $\dim(V) = n - O(1)$ we obtain the same structure (with a different constant c) for f.

To prove the result for biased degree four polynomials we follow the footsteps of [KL08] with two notable differences. Let f be such a polynomial. First, we pass to a subspace on which all the partial derivatives of f have low rank as degree three polynomials. This steps relies on our results for biased degree three polynomials. Then, as in [KL08], we show that f can be approximated by a function of a few of its derivatives. Because of the properties of the derivatives, this means that f can be approximated well by a function of a few quadratics and linear functions. We then show, again following [KL08], that in such a case f is actually a function of a few quadratics and linear functions. Here we heavily rely on properties of quadratic functions to avoid the blow up in the number of polynomials approximating f that occurs in [KL08, GT07]. Finally, we show that if a degree four polynomial is a function of several quadratic and linear functions then it actually have a nice structure.

The proof for the case of degree four polynomials with high U^4 norm is more delicate. Assume that f is such a polynomial. As before, a constant fraction of the partial derivatives of f are degree three polynomials with high U^3 norm. By the result for degree three polynomials we get that each of those partial derivatives is of the form $\Delta_y(f) = \sum_{i=1}^{c} \ell_i^{(y)} \cdot q_i^{(y)} + q_0^{(y)}$. Again we find a subspace V, of constant co-dimension, such that for every $y \in V$, $\Delta_y(f)$ has a nice structure. We now show that there exist a small number of linear and quadratic functions $\{\ell_i, q_i\}_{i=1}^{c}$ such that for every $y \in V$ it holds that $\Delta_y(f) = \sum_{i=1}^{c} \ell_i \cdot q_i^{(y)} + \sum_{i=1}^{c} \ell_i^{(y)} \cdot q_i + q_0^{(y)}$, where the polynomials $\{\ell_i^{(y)}, q_i^{(y)}\}$ depend on y. This is the technical heart of the proof. It now follows quite easily that there is a subspace $U \subseteq V$ of dimension $n/\exp(c)$ such that when restricted to U all the functions $\{\ell_i, q_i\}$ are fixed to constants. Thus, for every $y \in U$ it holds that $\deg(\Delta_y(f)) = 2$. So we get that $\deg(f|_U) = 3$. In fact, by closely examining the argument above we show an even stronger result. Namely, that we can partition a large subspace of $\mathbb{F}^n$ to (affine) subspaces of dimension $n/\exp(c)$ such that on each of the subspaces f is equal to some cubic polynomial (that may depend on the subspace).

1.3 Organization

In Section 2 we give some basic definitions and discuss properties of subadditive functions. In Section 3 we prove the theorems concerning degree three polynomials. In Section 4 we prove Theorem 3 and in Section 5 we prove Theorems 4 and 5.

2. PRELIMINARIES

In this paper $\mathbb{F}$ will always be a prime field. We denote with $\mathbb{F}_p$ the field with p elements. As we will be considering functions over $\mathbb{F}_p$ we will work modulo the polynomials $x_i^p - x_i$. In particular, when we write $f = g$, for two polynomials, we mean that they are equal as functions and not just as formal expressions. This will be mainly relevant when we consider quadratic polynomials (or higher degree polynomials) over $\mathbb{F}_2$. More generally, we shall say that a function f has degree d if there is a degree d polynomial g such that $f = g$. Note that this does not have an affect on the bias and the Gowers norm. Namely, the bias and U^d norm of f do not change when adding multiplies of $x_i^p - x_i$. Finally we note that if all the partial derivative of f have degree at most $d-1$ then there is a polynomial g of degree at most d such that $f = g$ (this is easily proved by observing that a degree k polynomial, all of whose individual degrees are smaller than $|\mathbb{F}|$, always has a partial derivative whose degree is $k-1$). From this point on we shall use the notion of a function and a polynomial arbitrarily without any real distinction.

We say that a function h ϵ-approximates a function f if $\Pr_x[f(x) \neq h(x)] \leq \epsilon$.

Definition 2.1. *Following [KL08] we say that the distribution induced by a set of functions $\{h_i\}_{i=1}^m$ (all from $\mathbb{F}^n$ to $\mathbb{F}$) is γ close to the uniform distribution if for every $\alpha_1, \ldots, \alpha_m \in \mathbb{F}$ it holds that*

$$\left| \Pr_{x \in \mathbb{F}^n}[\forall 1 \leq i \leq m,\ h_i(x) = \alpha_i] - |\mathbb{F}|^{-m} \right| \leq \gamma |\mathbb{F}|^{-m}.$$

2.1 Subadditive functions

As described in Section 1.2 our proofs are based on finding a structure for the space of partial derivatives of the underlying polynomial f. For this end we need the notion of rank.

Definition 2.2. *Let q be a degree two function over a prime field $\mathbb{F}$. We define $\mathrm{rank}_2(q) = r$, where r is the number of α_i-s that are non zero when considering the canonical representation of q in Theorem 1.1.*

The following lemma is immediate.

Lemma 2.3. *For two quadratic polynomials q, q' and a constant $\alpha \in \mathbb{F}$ we have that $\mathrm{rank}_2(\alpha q + q') \leq \mathrm{rank}_2(q) + \mathrm{rank}_2(q')$.*

The notion of subadditivity will play an important role in our proofs. Let $V \subset \mathbb{F}^n$ be a linear space. $\mathcal{F} : V \to \mathbb{R}^+$ is a *subadditive function* if for every $u, v \in V$ and $\alpha \in \mathbb{F}$ it holds that $\mathcal{F}(\alpha \cdot u + v) \leq \mathcal{F}(u) + \mathcal{F}(v)$. The next easy to verify lemma gives an interesting example of a subadditive function.

Lemma 2.4. *Let f be a cubic polynomial over a prime field $\mathbb{F}$. For every $y \in \mathbb{F}^n$ define $\mathcal{F}(y) = \mathrm{rank}_2(\Delta_y(f))$. Then $\mathcal{F}$ is a subadditive function.*

For this end we need a special case of a lemma of Bogolyubov (see e.g. [Gre]).

For a set $A \subseteq \mathbb{F}^n$ denote with $kA - kA$ the set

$$kA - kA = \{a_1 + \ldots + a_k - a_{k+1} - \ldots - a_{2k} \mid \forall i\ a_i \in A\}.$$

Lemma 2.5 (Bogolyubov). *Let $A \subseteq U$ be a subset of a linear space U such that $|A| = \mu_0 \cdot |U|$. Then, for some $k \leq \max(1, \lceil \frac{1}{2}(\log_{\frac{|\mathbb{F}|}{|\mathbb{F}|-1/2}}(2/\mu_0) + 2) \rceil)$, $kA - kA$ contains a subspace W of co-dimension at most $\log_{\frac{|\mathbb{F}|-1/2}{|\mathbb{F}|-1}}(1/2\mu_0)$.*

We will mainly apply the lemma on sets $A \subseteq \mathbb{F}^n$ of vectors with low $\mathcal{F}(v)$, for some subadditive function $\mathcal{F}$.

Lemma 2.6. *Let $\mathcal{F} : U \to \mathbb{R}^+$ be a subadditive function. Define, $A_r \triangleq \{x \in U \mid \mathcal{F}(x) \leq r\}$. If $|A_r| \geq \mu |U|$, then there exists a vector space V of co-dimension at most*

$\log_{\frac{|\mathbb{F}|-1/2}{|\mathbb{F}|-1}}(1/2\mu) = O(\log(1/\mu))$ *such that for every* $y \in V$ *it holds that* $\mathcal{F}(y) \leq 2r \cdot \lceil \frac{1}{2}(\log_{\frac{|\mathbb{F}|}{|\mathbb{F}|-1/2}}(2/\mu) + 2) \rceil + 2r = O(r\log(1/\mu))$.

Proof. The proof is immediate from Lemma 2.5. Let V be the subspace guaranteed by the lemma when applied on A_r. As $V \subseteq kA_r - kA_r$, for $k \leq \max(1, \lceil \frac{1}{2}(\log_{\frac{|\mathbb{F}|}{|\mathbb{F}|-1/2}}(2/\mu)+2) \rceil)$, we get that $\mathcal{F}(y) \leq 2kr$ for every $y \in V$. □ □

3. THE STRUCTURE OF CUBIC POLYNOMIALS

In this section we prove Theorems 1 and 2. As described in Section 1.2 both proofs are based on finding a structure for the space of partial derivatives of f.

3.1 Restricting the polynomial to a 'good' subspace

In this section we show that if a cubic f is biased or have a large U^3 norm then there is a large subspace $V \subseteq \mathbb{F}^n$ such that for every $y \in V$ the rank of $\Delta_y(f)$ is relatively small. We start from the following well known and easy to verify lemma.

Lemma 3.1. *Let f be a function.*

1. *If* $\text{bias}(f) = \delta$, *then for (at least) a* $\frac{\delta^2}{2}$ *fraction of* $y \in \mathbb{F}^n$ *it holds that* $\text{bias}(\Delta_y(f)) \geq \frac{2}{\delta^2}$.

2. *If* $\|f\|_{U^3} = \delta$, *then for (at least) a* $\frac{\delta^4}{2}$ *fraction of* $y \in \mathbb{F}^n$ *it holds that* $\|\Delta_y(f)\|_{U^2} \geq \frac{2}{\delta^2}$.

From the following lemma we get that if a partial derivative (which is a quadratic function) has a high bias then it depends on a few linear functions.

Lemma 3.2. *Let q be a quadratic polynomial over a prime field $\mathbb{F}$. Then* $\text{rank}_2(q) \leq \log_{|\mathbb{F}|}(\text{bias}(q))$.

Proof. See e.g. Lemmas 15-17 of [BV07]. □

The next lemma of Bogdanov and Viola [BV07] proves a similar result when a partial derivative has a high U^2 norm.

Lemma 3.3. *(Lemma 15 of [BV07]) For every quadratic polynomial q, over a prime field $\mathbb{F}$, it holds that* $\text{rank}_2(q) \leq \log_{|\mathbb{F}|}(1/\|q\|_{U^2})$.

We now combine Lemma 2.4 with Lemmas 3.1, 3.2 , 3.3 and Lemma 2.6 and obtain the following corollary.

Corollary 3.4. *Let f be a cubic polynomial. If* $\text{bias}(f) = \delta$ *or* $\|f\|_{U^2} = \delta$, *then there exists a subspace* $V \subseteq \mathbb{F}^n$ *such that* $\dim(V) \geq n - O(\log(\frac{1}{\delta}))$ *and such that for every* $y \in V$ *it holds that* $\text{rank}_2(\Delta_y(f)) = O(\log^2(\frac{1}{\delta}))$.

3.2 The structure of low rank spaces

So far we have established the existence of a subspace $V \subseteq \mathbb{F}^n$ such that for every $y \in V$ it holds that $\text{rank}_2(\Delta_y(f)) = O(\log^2(\frac{1}{\delta}))$. We now show that such spaces of low rank polynomials have a very restricted structure. Namely, there exist $r = O(\log^2(\frac{1}{\delta}))$ linear functions $\ell_1, \ldots, \ell_r$ such that every $\Delta_y(f)$ can be written as $\Delta_y(f) = \sum_{i=1}^r \ell_i \cdot \ell_i^{(y)} + \ell_0^{(y)}$, where the $\ell_i^{(y)}$-s are linear functions determined by y. The intuition behind this result is that $\text{rank}_2(q+q')$ can be much smaller than $\text{rank}_2(q) + \text{rank}_2(q')$ only if there is some basis with respect to which q and q' share many linear functions when represented in the form of Theorem 1.1. From this observation we deduce that if we consider some function of maximal rank, $q = \sum_{i=1}^r \ell_i \cdot \ell_i'$, and set $\{\ell_i, \ell_i'\}_{i=1}^r$ to zero (namely, consider the subspace on which they all vanish), then on this subspace, the rank of all the remaining quadratic functions decrease. So by repetition all those functions become linear.

Lemma 3.5. *Let M be a linear space of quadratic functions satisfying* $\text{rank}_2(p) \leq r$ *for all* $p \in M$. *Then there exists a subspace* $V \subseteq \mathbb{F}^n$ *of co-dimension* $\leq 4r$ *such that* $p|_V$ *is a linear function for all* $p \in M$.

We shall give the proof for the case $\mathbb{F} = \mathbb{F}_2$. The proof for odd characteristics is very similar (except that in the odd characteristic case we have that the co-dimension of V is $2r$ whereas in the even characteristic case it is $4r$).

Proof. Let $g \in M$ be such that $\text{rank}_2(g) = r$. By Theorem 1.1, g can be expressed as $g = \sum_{i=1}^r \ell_{2i-1} \cdot \ell_{2i} + \ell_0$. Denote $V \triangleq \{x \mid \ell_1(x) = \ell_2(x) = \ldots = \ell_{2r}(x) = 0\}$. We now show that for every $h \in M$ it holds that $\text{rank}_2(h|_V) \leq \frac{r}{2}$. Repeating this argument we get the required result.

Pick some $h \in M$ and denote $\text{rank}_2(h|_V) = s$. As before, $h|_V$ can be expressed as $h|_V = \sum_{i=1}^s m_{2i-1} \cdot m_{2i} + m_0$ (where the m_i-s are linear functions). Clearly the functions $\{\ell_1, \ldots, \ell_{2r}, m_1, \ldots, m_{2s}\}$ are linearly independent. We can therefore write $h = \sum_{i=1}^s m_{2i-1} \cdot m_{2i} + m_0 + \sum_{i=1}^{2r} \ell_i \cdot L_i$, where the L_i-s are linear functions. Write $L_i = \tilde{m}_i + \tilde{\ell}_i + \tilde{L}_i$ where $\tilde{m}_i \in \text{span}\{m_0, \ldots, m_{2s}\}$, $\tilde{\ell}_i \in \text{span}\{\ell_0, \ldots, \ell_{2r}\}$ and $\tilde{L}_i$ is linearly independent of the m_j-s and ℓ_j-s. Rearranging terms we get that $h = \sum_{i=1}^s (m_{2i-1} + \ell'_{2i-1}) \cdot (m_{2i} + \ell'_{2i}) + (m_0 + \ell'_0) + \tilde{h}(\ell_0, \ldots, \ell_{2r}, \tilde{L}_1, \ldots, \tilde{L}_{2r})$, where each ℓ'_i is in the span of the ℓ_i-s and $\tilde{h}$ is a quadratic polynomial. Denote $m'_i = m_i + \ell'_i$. It is clear that $\ell_0, \ldots, \ell_{2r}, \tilde{L}_1, \ldots, \tilde{L}_{2r}$ are linearly independent of the m'_i-s (and vice versa). Consequently, $\text{rank}_2(\sum_{i=1}^s m'_{2i-1} \cdot m'_{2i} + m'_0) + \text{rank}_2(\tilde{h}) = \text{rank}_2(h) \leq r$. Hence, $\text{rank}_2(\tilde{h}) \leq r - s$. We now get that

$r \geq \text{rank}_2(g+h) = \text{rank}_2(\sum_{i=1}^s m'_{2i-1} \cdot m'_{2i} + m'_0 + \tilde{h}(\ell_0, \ldots, \ell_{2r}, \tilde{L}_1, \ldots, \tilde{L}_{2r}) + g) = \text{rank}_2(\sum_{i=1}^s m'_{2i-1} \cdot m'_{2i} + m'_0) + \text{rank}_2(g + \tilde{h}(\ell_0, \ldots, \ell_{2r}, \tilde{L}_1, \ldots, \tilde{L}_{2r})) \geq s + (r - (r - s)) = 2s$,

where we used the fact that $\text{rank}_2(g+\tilde{h}) \geq \text{rank}_2(g) - \text{rank}_2(\tilde{h})$. As we showed that $r \geq 2s$ the proof is completed. □

3.3 Completing the proofs

We are now ready to complete the proofs of Theorems 1 and 2.

proof of Theorem 2. By Corollary 3.4 we get that if $\|f\|_{U^2} = \delta$, then there exists a subspace $V \subseteq \mathbb{F}^n$ such that $\dim(V) \geq n - O(\log(1/\delta))$ and such that for every $y \in V$ it holds that $\text{rank}_2(\Delta_y(f)) = O(\log^2(\frac{1}{\delta}))$. Lemma 3.5 implies that there are at most $r = O(\log^2(\frac{1}{\delta}))$ linear functions $\ell_1, \ldots, \ell_r$ such that for every $y \in V$ we have that $\Delta_y(f) = \sum_{i=1}^r \ell_i \cdot \ell_i^{(y)} + \ell_0^{(y)}$. Let $U = \{x \in V \mid \ell_1(x) = \ldots \ell_r(x) = 0\}$. Then U is a linear space of dimension $\dim(U) \geq n - O(\log^2(\frac{1}{\delta}))$. For every $y \in U$ we have that $\Delta_y(f)|_U = \ell_0^{(y)}|_U$. Hence, for every $y \in U$, $\deg(\Delta_y(f)) \leq 1$. Therefore, $\deg(f|_U) \leq 2$. Let $\ell'_1, \ldots, \ell'_t$ be linearly independent linear functions such that $x \in U$ iff $\ell'_1(x) = \ldots = \ell'_t(x) = 0$. It follows that we can write $f = \sum_{i=1}^t \ell'_i \cdot q_i + q_0$ for some quadratic polynomials $\{q_i\}$. As $t = n - \dim(U) = O(\log^2(\frac{1}{\delta}))$ the result follows. □

The proof of Theorem 1 is essentially the same except that we make another small optimization that reduces the required number of quadratic functions. Due to space constraint we only sketch the argument.

Proof Sketch of Theorem 1. By the same argument as above we get, possibly after a change of basis, that $f = \sum_{i=1}^t x_i \cdot q_i + q_0$ where $t = O(\log^2(\frac{1}{\delta}))$ (we changed basis so that instead of linear functions we have variables). We would like to show that t can be made small. Indeed, if it is not the case then there is some nonzero substitution $\alpha = (\alpha_1, \ldots, \alpha_t)$ to $(x_1, \ldots, x_t)$ so that $\text{bias}(\sum_{i=1}^t \alpha_i \cdot q_i + q_0) \geq \delta$ (we substitute α to $(x_1, \ldots, x_t)$). It follows that there is some nonzero combination of the q_i-s that is of high bias and therefore of low rank. We can thus replace the q_i-s by $t' = t-1$ quadratic polynomials and additional $O(\log(1/\delta))$ linear functions. We can continue this process until $t' = O(\log(1/\delta))$ in which case we cannot guarantee the existence of such nonzero α. □

4. THE STRUCTURE OF BIASED 4 DEGREE POLYNOMIALS

In this section we prove Theorem 3 on the structure of biased degree 4 polynomials. As in the case of cubic polynomials, we shall focus our attention on a subspace on which all of derivatives have a small rank (Definition 4.1). By a lemma of Bogdanov and Viola [BV07] (Lemma 4.3) we get that f can be well approximated by a function of a small number of its derivatives (which in our case, are all of low rank). Thus, f is well approximated by a function of a few linear and quadratic polynomials. By passing to a subspace we can assume that f is well approximated by a function of a small number of quadratic polynomials such that that every nontrivial linear combination of them has a high rank. We then show that in this case those quadratic functions are in fact *strongly regular* (a notion that we later explain) and therefore by a theorem of Kaufman and Lovett [KL08], f in fact equals a function in those quadratic (on the subspace). We then finish the proof by showing that in this case f also have a nice structure.

4.1 Restricting the polynomial to a 'good' subspace

In this section we prove an analogous result to Corollary 3.4. We first define the rank of a cubic polynomial.

Definition 4.1. *Let g be a degree three polynomial. We define* $\text{rank}_3(g)$ *to be the minimal integer r for which there are r linear functions $\ell_1, \ldots, \ell_r$ and $r+1$ quadratic functions $q_0, \ldots, q_r$ such that $g = \sum_{i=1}^r \ell_i q_i + q_0$.*

In a similar way to the proof of Corollary 3.4 (using Theorem 1 instead of Theorem 1.1) we can deduce the following lemma.

Lemma 4.2. *Let f be a degree four polynomial satisfying* $\text{bias}(f) = \delta$. *Then there exist a linear subspace $V \subseteq \mathbb{F}^n$ of dimension* $\dim(V) \geq n - O(\log_{|\mathbb{F}|}(1/\delta))$, *such that for every $y \in V$* $\text{rank}_3(\Delta_y(f)) = \log^{O(1)}(1/\delta)$.

By applying an invertible linear transformation we can assume that $V = \{x : x_1 = \ldots = x_m = 0\}$ for some $m = O(\log_{|\mathbb{F}|}(1/\delta))$. We now have

$$f = \sum_{i=1}^{m} x_i g_i + f' , \quad (1)$$

where $f' = f'(x_{m+1}, \ldots, x_n)$. Moreover, by Lemma 4.2 it follows that for every $y = (0, \ldots, 0, y_{m+1}, \ldots, y_n)$, $\text{rank}_3(\Delta_y(f)) = O(\log^5(\frac{1}{\delta}))$. Notice that for every such y it holds that $\Delta_y(f) = \sum_{i=1}^m x_i \Delta_y(g_i) + \Delta_y(f')$. Hence, $\text{rank}_3(\Delta_y(f')) \leq \text{rank}_3(\Delta_y(f)) + m$. We now fix some value to $x_1, \ldots, x_m$, such that $\text{bias}(f(\alpha_1, \ldots, \alpha_m, x_{m+1}, \ldots, x_n)) \geq \delta$. Let

$$\tilde{f}(x_{m+1}, \ldots, x_n) \triangleq f(\alpha_1, \ldots, \alpha_m, x_{m+1}, \ldots, x_n) . \quad (2)$$

It follows that $\text{bias}(\tilde{f}) \geq \delta$ and that for every $y = (y_{m+1}, \ldots, y_n)$, $\text{rank}_3(\Delta_y(\tilde{f})) = \text{rank}_3(\Delta_y(f')) = O(\log^5(\frac{1}{\delta}))$ (note that $\deg\left(\Delta_y(\tilde{f}) - \Delta_y(f')\right) = 2$ so they have the same rank). From now on we will only consider $\tilde{f}$ and not f. Observe that if we prove Theorem 3 for $\tilde{f}$ then by considering Equations (1) and (2) we get the required result for f itself.

4.2 Computing $\tilde{f}$ using a few quadratics

We now show that there is a large subspace on which f can be approximated by a function of a few quadratic polynomials. The following lemma of Bogdanov and Viola shows that if f is biased then it can be well approximated by a small set of partial derivatives.

Lemma 4.3. *(Lemma 24 from [BV07]) Let $f : \mathbb{F}^n \to \mathbb{F}$ be a function over a finite field $\mathbb{F}$ with* $\text{bias}(f) = \delta$. *Then there are t directions $a_1, ..., a_t$ and a function H such that $H(\Delta_{a_1}(f), \ldots, \Delta_{a_t}(f))$ ϵ-approximates f, where $t \leq (1 + \log\frac{1}{\epsilon})\left(|\mathbb{F}|/\delta\right)^{O(1)}$.*

By the construction of $\tilde{f}$ we know that each of its partial derivatives is of rank $\log^{O(1)}(1/\delta)$ and that $\text{bias}(\tilde{f}) \geq \delta$. Thus, Lemma 4.3 guarantees that $\tilde{f}$ can be well approximated using a few quadratics.

Corollary 4.4. *For every $\epsilon > 0$ there are $c = (1 + \log\frac{1}{\epsilon})\left(|\mathbb{F}|/\delta\right)^{O(1)}$ quadratic polynomials $Q_1, \ldots, Q_c$ and a function H such that $\tilde{f}$ is ϵ-approximated by $H(Q_1, \ldots, Q_c)$.*

The next lemma, which is the main lemma of [KL08] shows that if the approximation is good enough (i.e. ϵ is small), and if the quadratics satisfy the *strong regularity* property then $\tilde{f}$ can in fact be computed by a small number of quadratics.

Definition 4.5. *(strongly regular quadratic functions) We say that a family of quadratic functions $\{Q_i\}_{i=1}^m$ is γ-*strongly regular *if the following holds for every $x_0 \in \mathbb{F}^n$: for independent uniform random variables $Y_1, ..., Y_5$ the joint distribution of*

$$\left\{ Q_j\left(x_0 + \sum_{i \in I} Y_i\right) \mid j \in [m], I \subseteq [5], 1 \leq |I| \leq 2 \right\}$$

is γ close to the uniform distribution (recall Definition 2.1).

This definition is a restricted version of Definition 8 of [KL08] for quadratic polynomials. The interested reader is referred to that paper for the general definition for higher degree polynomials.

Lemma 4.6. *(Lemma 13 from [KL08]) Let $f(x)$ be a degree d polynomials, $h_1, ..., h_m$ polynomials of degree less than d satisfy $H : \mathbb{F}^m \to \mathbb{F}$ a function such that $H(h_1, ..., h_m)$ ϵ-approximates f where $\epsilon \leq 2^{-2(d+1)}$ and in addition $\{h_i\}_{i=1}^m$ is a γ-strongly regular family where $\gamma \leq \min\{2^{-d}, 2^{-m}\}$. Then there exists a function $F : \mathbb{F}^m \to \mathbb{F}$ such that $f = F(h_1, ..., h_m)$.*

In other words, the lemma says that if f is well approximated by a family of strongly regular functions then it can actually be computed everywhere by the functions in the family. We shall now show that if $q_1, \ldots, q_c$ are quadratic polynomials such that the rank of every nontrivial linear combination of them is high, then they are strongly regular. This will imply (by Corollary 4.4) that $\tilde{f}$ is a function of a few quadratics and therefore so is f.

By using the analogy between quadratic functions and matrices and the known fact that (for quadratic polynomials) high rank implies low bias one can show the following lemma.

Lemma 4.7. *Let $\{Q_i\}_{i=1}^m$ be a family of quadratic functions such that for every nontrivial linear combination, $\text{rank}_2(\sum_{i=1}^m \alpha_i Q_i) \geq R$. Then $\{Q_i\}_{i=1}^m$ is a γ-strongly regular family for $\gamma = |\mathbb{F}|^{3m/2-R/4}$.*

We now show that $\tilde{f}$ can be computed by a few quadratics.

Lemma 4.8. *Let $g : \mathbb{F}^n \to \mathbb{F}$ be a quartic polynomial such that for every y, $\text{rank}_3(\Delta_y(f)) \leq \text{poly}(1/\delta)$. Then there exist a subspace W, $c = \text{poly}(|\mathbb{F}|/\delta)$ quadratics $q'_1, \ldots, q'_c$ and a function G such that, $\dim(W) = n - \text{poly}(|\mathbb{F}|/\delta)$ and $g|_W = G(q'_1, \ldots, q'_c)$.*

Proof. Applying Lemma 4.3, and using the fact that every partial derivative of g has a low rank, we conclude that for $\epsilon = 2^{-20}$ there exist $c = \text{poly}(|\mathbb{F}|/\delta)$ linear and quadratic functions, and a function H, such that $H(\ell_1, \ldots, \ell_c, q_1, \ldots, q_c)$ ϵ-approximates g. Let $r = \text{poly}(|\mathbb{F}|/\delta)$ and $U = \{x : \ell_1(x) = \alpha_1, \ldots, \ell_c(x) = \alpha_c\}$ be some subspace such that $H(\alpha_1, \ldots, \alpha_c, q_1|_U, \ldots, q_c|_U)$ ϵ-approximates $g|_U$. By using the same arguments as in the proof of Theorem 1 we can assume that there exists a (possible affine) subspace $W \subseteq U$ and $c' \leq c$ such that: $\dim(W) \geq \dim(U) - (r+1)c \geq n - (r+2)c = n - \text{poly}(|\mathbb{F}|/\delta)$; w.l.o.g. for every $i = 1 \ldots c$, $q_i|_W \in \text{span}\{q_1|_W, \ldots, q_{c'}|_W\}$; any nontrivial linear combination of $q_1|_W, \ldots, q_{c'}|_W$ has rank larger than r; $g|_W$ is ϵ-approximated by $H(\ell_1|_W, \ldots, \ell_c|_W, q_1|_W, \ldots, q_c|_W)$ (this follows by picking an adequate shift of the linear space in the lemma). Hence, $g|_W$ is ϵ-approximated by $H(\ell_1|_W, \ldots, \ell_c|_W, q_1|_W, \ldots, q_c|_W) = H'(q_1|_W, \ldots, q_{c'}|_W)$ for some H'. The reason for passing to W is that now any nontrivial linear combination of $q_1|_W, \ldots, q_{c'}|_W$ has rank larger than r. We thus get by Lemma 4.6 and Lemma 4.7 that there is some function G such that $g|_W = G(q_1|_W, \ldots, q_{c'}|_W)$. ☐

Recall that we assume w.l.o.g. that for every $y \in \mathbb{F}^{n-m}$, $\text{rank}_3(\Delta_y(\tilde{f})) \leq \text{poly}(1/\delta)$. Thus, the lemma above implies the following corollary.

Corollary 4.9. *In the notations of the proof, there exist a subspace $Z \subset \mathbb{F}^{n-m}$ of dimension $\dim(Z) \geq n - \text{poly}(|\mathbb{F}|/\delta)$ such that $\tilde{f}|_Z = F(q_1, \ldots, q_c)$, for $c = \text{poly}(|\mathbb{F}|/\delta)$ quadratic polynomials and some function F.*

4.3 The structure of f

We now show that we can represent $\tilde{f}$ as $\tilde{f} = \sum_{i=1}^k \ell_i \cdot g_i + \sum_{i=1}^k q'_i \cdot q''_i$ where $k = \text{poly}(|\mathbb{F}|/\delta)$, the ℓ_i-s are linear functions, the q'_i-s and q''_i-s are quadratic polynomials and the g_i-s are cubic polynomials. To achieve this we use the notion of *disjoint polynomials*.

Definition 4.10. *We say that the quadratic polynomials $\{Q_i\}_{i=1}^m$ are disjoint if there is a linear transformation T, $2m$ variables $\{x_i\}_{i=1}^m \cup \{y_i\}_{i=1}^m$, where possibly for several i-s $x_i = y_i$, and quadratic functions $\{Q'_i\}_{i=1}^m$ such that for every $k \in [m]$, $Q_k \circ T = x_k y_k + Q'_k$ where no degree two monomial in Q'_k contains a variable from $\{x_i\}_{i=1}^m \cup \{y_i\}_{i=1}^m$.*

Let $\{Q_i\}_{i=1}^m$ be a family of polynomials. Assume that the monomial $x_k y_k$ appears in Q_k. By subtracting an appropriate multiple of Q_k from the other Q_i-s, one can assume that the monomial $x_k y_k$ appears only in Q_k. So we can assume w.l.o.g. that $Q_i = x_k \ell_i^k + y_k \tilde{\ell}_i^k + Q'_i$, where Q'_i does not contain x_k and y_k. By setting all the linear functions ℓ_i^k and $\tilde{\ell}_i^k$ to zero (i.e. by restricting the inputs to the corresponding subspace), we get that x_k and y_k only appear in Q_k (which contains $x_k y_k$). Repeating this process for each Q_k, we deduce the following lemma.

Lemma 4.11. *Let $q_1, \ldots, q_c$ be quadratic polynomials from $\mathbb{F}^n$ to $\mathbb{F}$. Assume that the rank of every nontrivial linear combination of them is at least r. Then there exist a subspace $V \subseteq \mathbb{F}^n$ of dimension $\geq n - 2c^2$ and $c' \leq c$ quadratic polynomials $q'_1, \ldots, q'_{c'} : V \to \mathbb{F}$ satisfying: the q'_i-s are disjoint; every nontrivial linear combination of the q'_i-s has rank at least $r - 2c^2$; $\text{span}(q'_1, \ldots, q'_{c'}) = \text{span}(q_1|_V, \ldots, q_c|_V)$.*

The usefulness Definition 4.10 is demonstrated in the following lemma.

Lemma 4.12. *Let $q_1, \ldots, q_c$ be disjoint quadratic polynomials. Assume that $\deg(f) = 2d$ and $f = F(q_1, \ldots, q_c)$ for some function $F(z_1, \ldots, z_c)$. Then as a polynomial over $\mathbb{F}$, $\deg(F) \leq d$.*

Proof. We shall give the proof over $\mathbb{F}_2$ but it is again similar over odd characteristic fields. Let $z_1^{e_1} \cdots z_c^{e_c}$ be a monomial of maximal degree in F. When composing it with $q_1, \ldots, q_c$ we get that $q_1^{e_1} \cdots q_c^{e_c}$ contains the monomial $\prod_{i=1}^c (x_i \cdot y_i)^{e_i}$. As $z_1^{e_1} \cdots z_c^{e_c}$ is of maximal degree and each x_i and y_i appear only as linear terms in all the q_j-s (except the monomial $x_i \cdot y_i$ in q_i) we see that this monomial cannot be cancelled by any other monomial created in $F(q_1, \ldots, q_c)$. Therefore the monomial $\prod_{i=1}^c (x_i \cdot y_i)^{e_i}$ belongs to f as well. Since $\deg(f) = 2d$ it must be the case that $2e_1 + \ldots + 2e_c \leq 2d$. Hence, $\deg(F) = \sum_{i=1}^c e_i \leq d$. ☐

We are now ready to complete the proof of Theorem 3.

Proof of Theorem 3. Combining Corollary 4.9, Lemma 4.12 and Lemma 4.11 we get that for the subspace Z of Corollary 4.9, there exist a subspace $Z' \subseteq Z$, of dimension $\dim(Z') \geq \dim(Z) - \text{poly}(|\mathbb{F}|/\delta)$, $b = \text{poly}(|\mathbb{F}|/\delta)$ quadratic polynomials $Q_1, \ldots, Q_b$ and a quadratic polynomial H such that $\tilde{f}|_{Z'} = H(Q_1, \ldots, Q_b)$. In other words $\tilde{f}|_{Z'} = \sum_{i \le j} \alpha_{i,j} Q_i Q_j + Q_0$.

As $f|_{Z'} = \tilde{f}|_{Z'}$ it follows that $f|_{Z'} = \sum_{i \le j} \alpha_{i,j} Q_i Q_j + Q_0$. Assume w.l.o.g. that Z' is defined as $Z' = \{x \mid x_1 = \beta_1, \ldots, x_k = \beta_k\}$ for some $k = \text{poly}(|\mathbb{F}|/\delta)$. Then it is clear that we can write $f = \sum_{i=1}^{k} x_i \cdot g_i + \sum_{i \le j} \alpha_{i,j} Q_i Q_j + g_0$ for cubic polynomials $g_0, \ldots, g_k$. □

5. QUARTIC POLYNOMIALS WITH HIGH U^4 NORM

In this section we prove Theorems 4 and 5. Intuitively, the notion of $d+1$ Gowers norm indicates how close a given function is to a degree d polynomial. In fact, it was conjectured that if the U^{d+1} norm is bounded away from zero then the function has a noticeable correlation with a degree d polynomial. This conjecture turned to be false even when the function is a degree four polynomial and $d = 3$ [LMS08, GT07]. Here we will show that for this special case a weaker conclusion holds. Namely, that for any degree four polynomial f there exists a subspace of dimension $n/\exp(\text{poly}(1/\|f\|_{U^4}))$ on which $f|_V$ is equal to some cubic polynomial. In fact an even stronger conclusion holds - there exists a partition of (a subspace of small codimension of) $\mathbb{F}^n$ to such subspaces on which f equals a cubic.

As in the proof of Theorem 2 we start by passing to a subspace of a constant codimension on which every derivative has low rank, i.e $\Delta_y(f) = \sum_{i=1}^{r} \ell_i Q_i + Q_0$. Then we shall deduce that there is some common 'basis' $\{\ell_i\}_{i=1}^{t_2}, \{Q_i\}_{i=1}^{t_1}$ to all the derivatives. Namely, every derivative $\Delta_y(F)$ can be expressed as $\sum_{i=1}^{t_1} \ell_i^y Q_i + \sum_{i=1}^{t_2} \ell_i Q_i^y + Q_0^y$ (where y in the exponent means that the polynomial may depend on y). This is the main technical difficulty of the proof and it is based on an extension of Lemma 3.5 to the case of low rank cubic polynomials. Then, we conclude that for every fixing of $\{\ell_i\}_{i=1}^{t_2}, \{Q_i\}_{i=1}^{t_1}$, to some set of values α, we obtain a subspace V_α on which all the derivative are quadratic polynomials, i.e $f|_{V_\alpha}$ is cubic.

5.1 Finding a 'basis' for a space of low rank cubic polynomials

In this section we present the main technical result showing that a subspace of degree 3 polynomials with low rank has a small 'basis'.

Lemma 5.1 (main lemma). *Let M be a vector space of cubic polynomials satisfying $\text{rank}_3(f) \le r$ for all $f \in M$. Then there exists a set of linear and quadratic functions $A = \{Q_i\}_{i=1}^{t_1} \cup \{\ell_i\}_{i=1}^{t_2}$, for $t_1 \le r$ and $t_2 = 2^{O(r)}$, such that every $f \in M$ can be represented as $f = \sum_{i=1}^{t_1} \ell_i^f Q_i + \sum_{i=1}^{t_2} \ell_i Q_i^f + Q_0^f$ for some linear and quadratic functions $\{\ell_i^f\}_{i=1}^{t_1} \cup \{Q_i^f\}_{i=0}^{t_2}$.*

Due to space limitations we only give an overview of the proof and omit the full proof from this version of the paper.

Proof Overview of Lemma 5.1. We construct the set A iteratively. We start with the empty set. In every iteration, we add some functions to A and consider the space $[M]_A$ which is M modulo the subspace

$$\mathcal{A} = \left\{ \sum_{i=1}^{t_1} \ell_i' Q_i + \sum_{i=1}^{t_2} \ell_i Q_i' + Q_0' \;\middle|\; \begin{matrix} \{\ell_i'\}_{i=1}^{t_1} \text{ linear funcs.} \\ \{Q_i'\}_{i=0}^{t_2} \text{ quadratics} \end{matrix} \right\}$$

First, we choose a function $g = \sum_{i=1}^{r} \ell_i^g Q_i^g \in [M]_A$ of maximal rank. Then, we add $\{Q_1^g\} \cup \{\ell_i^g\}_{i=1}^{r}$ to A. The point is that while every $h \in [M]_A$ may still have rank r, the number of high rank quadratic functions in its representation is reduced by at least one. Thus, after r steps we get that every function in $[M]_A$ can be represented as $\sum_{i=1}^{c} \ell_i^{(1)} \ell_i^{(2)} \ell_i^{(3)}$ where $c = O(1)$.

The second step is similar to the first but with a different potential function. For a function $f = \sum_{i=1}^{c} \ell_i^{f,(1)} \ell_i^{f,(2)} \ell_i^{f,(3)}$ we define $\dim_3^c(f)$ to be $\dim\left(\text{span}\left\{\ell_i^{f,(1)}, \ell_i^{f,(2)}, \ell_i^{f,(3)}\right\}_{i=1}^{c}\right)$. We choose some function $g = \sum_{i=1}^{c} \ell_i^{g,(1)} \ell_i^{g,(2)} \ell_i^{g,(3)}$ from $[M]_A$ such that $\dim_3^c(g)$ is maximal. We show that by adding all the functions $\left\{\ell_i^{g,(1)}, \ell_i^{g,(2)}, \ell_i^{g,(3)}\right\}_{i=1}^{c}$ to A, $\dim_3^c(h)$ is reduced by (at least) one, for every $h \in [M]_A$. By repeating this step $3c$ times we complete the proof. □

5.2 Completing the proof

We can now complete the proof of Theorem 4. We first give a lemma summarizing what we have achieved so far.

Lemma 5.2. *Let f be a degree four polynomial with $\|f\|_{U^4} = \delta$. Then for $r = O(\log^2(1/\delta))$ there exist a subspace V, satisfying $\dim(V) \ge n - O(\log(1/\delta))$, r quadratic polynomials $Q_1, \ldots, Q_r$ and $R = \exp(r)$ linear functions $\ell_1, \ldots, \ell_R$ such that for every $y \in V$ we have that $\Delta_y(f|_V) = \sum_{i=1}^{r} Q_i \cdot \ell_i^y + \sum_{i=1}^{R} \ell_i \cdot Q_i^y + Q_0^y$.*

Proof. Let f be a quartic function such that $\|f\|_{U^4} > \delta$. By Lemma 3.1, Theorem 2 and Lemma 2.6 there is a subspace V, satisfying $\dim(V) \ge n - O(\log(1/\delta))$, such that every partial derivative $f|_y$, for $y \in V$, is a cubic polynomial of rank at most $r = O(\log^2(1/\delta))$. Let $f' = f|_V$. Lemma 5.1 gives a set $A = \{Q_i\}_{i=1}^{r} \cup \{\ell_i\}_{i=1}^{\exp(r)}$ such that every $\Delta_y(f')$ can be written as $\Delta_y(f') = \sum_{i=1}^{r} Q_i \cdot \ell_i^y + \sum_{i=1}^{\exp(r)} \ell_i \cdot Q_i^y + Q_0^y$. Notice that the lemma concerns a linear space of cubic polynomials. In our case the linear space will be the span of all the partial derivatives of f'. As for every $y, z \in V$ it holds that $\deg(\Delta_y(f') + \Delta_z(f') - \Delta_{y+z}(f')) = 2$, we see that in order to 'close' the space we only need to add quadratic polynomials and so the assumption about the rank of the cubic polynomials in the space does not change. □

We now show that Theorem 4 easily follows from Lemma 5.2. Here we prove it to the case $\mathbb{F} = \mathbb{F}_2$ (the other case is similar).

Proof of Theorem 4. By Lemma 5.2 for $r = O(\log^2(1/\delta))$ there exist r quadratics $Q_1, \ldots, Q_r$ and $R = \exp(r)$ linear functions $\ell_1, \ldots, \ell_R$ such that for every $y \in V$ we have that $\Delta_y(f|_V) = \sum_{i=1}^{r} Q_i \cdot \ell_i^y + \sum_{i=1}^{R} \ell_i \cdot Q_i^y + Q_0^y$. By fixing the values of $\ell_1, \ldots, \ell_R$ we restrict ourself to a subspace with dimension $d_0 = n - R - O(\log^2(1/\delta))$ such that every derivative of f can be express as $\sum_{i=1}^{r} Q_i \cdot \ell_i^y + Q_0^y$. By Theorem 1.1 for every $1 \le i \le r$ we have that $Q_i = \sum_{i=1}^{d/2} \ell_{i,j} \cdot \ell_{i,j}' + \ell_{i,0}$. So, by fixing $d/2$ linear functions we can ignore one of the Q_i's (as it can be added to the degree two part of f). As a result the dimension of the subspaces is reduced by a factor of two. By repeating this argument r times we get a subspace V_α of dimension $(n - R - O(\log^2(1/\delta)))/2^r$ satisfying that every derivative of $f|_y$, for $y \in V_\alpha$, is a quadratic function. From it we can deduce that $f|_{V_\alpha}$ is cubic polynomial. We finish the proof by observing that it holds for any setting of the linear functions (it only yields a different subspace). Therefore the subspaces $\{V_\alpha\}_\alpha$ partition V. □

Combining the idea of the above proof with the notion of disjoint polynomials we prove Theorem 5.

Proof Sketch of Theorem 5. As in the proof of Theorem 4 we obtain linear $\{\ell_i\}_{i=1\ldots R}$ and quadratic $\{q_i\}_{i=1\ldots r}$, where $r = O(\log^2(1/\delta))$ and $R = \exp(r)$, that form a 'basis' to the set of partial derivatives. By passing to a subspace of codimension R and using Lemma 4.11 we can assume w.l.o.g. that the q_i-s are disjoint and that every partial derivative has the form $\Delta_y(f) = \sum_{i=1}^{r} q_i \cdot \ell_i^{(y)} + q_0^{(y)}$. As $\mathrm{char}(\mathbb{F}) > 4$ we can assume w.l.o.g. that $q_i = x_i^2 + q_i'$ and that x_j can appear in q_i' only as a linear term. We now subtract from f terms of the form $\alpha q_i q_j$ such that in the resulting polynomial f' there will be no monomial of the form $x_i^2 x_j^2$ for $i \leq j$. Note that f' also has the property that for every y, $\Delta_y(f') = \sum_{i=1}^{r} q_i \cdot {\ell'}_i^{(y)} + {q'}_0^{(y)}$. We now show that degree four monomials in f' may only contain x_i or x_i^3 but not x_i^2, for $i \in [r]$. Indeed, assume for a contrary that x_i^2 appears in a degree four monomial. Then, x_i appears in $\Delta_{x_i}(f')$ in a degree three monomial. This monomial comes from some $\ell_j^{(x_i)} q_j$ for $j \neq i$. Therefore, we also have the term $x_i x_j^2$ in $\Delta_{x_i}(f')$ (it is not difficult to see that this term cannot be cancelled by any other $\ell_k^{(x_i)} q_k$). As $\mathrm{char}(\mathbb{F}) > 4$, integration w.r.t. x_i gives that the term $x_i^2 x_j^2$ appears in f' in contradiction. We can thus write $f' = \sum_{i=1}^{r} x_i^3 \tilde{\ell}_i + f''$, where in f'' each x_i has degree at most one. Consider any y 'orthogonal' to $\{x_1, \ldots, x_r, \tilde{\ell}_1, \ldots, \tilde{\ell}_r\}$ (namely, substituting y in any of those linear functions gives zero). Then for each i, $\Delta_y(x_i^3 \tilde{\ell}_i) = 0$. Hence, x_i is the highest power of x_i appearing in $\Delta_y(f')$. As the q_i-s are disjoint and $\Delta_y(f') = \sum_{i=1}^{r} q_i \cdot {\ell'}_i^{(y)} + {q'}_0^{(y)}$ we obtain that it must be the case that $\deg(\Delta_y(f')) \leq 2$. Thus, f' can be rewritten as a polynomial in at most $2r$ variables plus a degree three polynomial. Therefore, possibly after a change of basis we can write $f = \sum_{i \leq j} \alpha_{i,j} q_i \cdot q_j + \sum_{i=1}^{2r+R} y_i \cdot g_i + g_0$ as needed. □

6. CONCLUSIONS

In this paper we gave strong structural results for degree three and four polynomials that have a high bias. It is a very interesting question whether such a structure exists for higher degree biased polynomials. Green and Tao [GT07] proved such a result when $\deg(f) < |\mathbb{F}|$ (with much worse parameters for degrees three and four), so this question is mainly open for small fields. Another interesting question is improving the parameters in the results of [GT07, KL08]. There it was shown that when $\deg(f) = d$ and f is biased then $f = F(g_1, \ldots, g_{c_d})$, where $\deg(g_i) < \deg(f)$. However, the dependence of c_d on the degree d and the bias δ is terrible. Basically, $c_3 = \exp(\mathrm{poly}(1/\delta)$ and c_d is a tower of height c_{d-1}. In contrast, our results give that $c_3 = \log^2(1/\delta)$ and $c_4 = \mathrm{poly}(1/\delta)$. Thus, it is an intriguing question to find the true dependence of c_d on δ. In particular, as far as we know, it may be the case that c_d is polynomial in $1/\delta$ (where the exponent may depend on d), or even $\mathrm{poly}(\log(1/\delta))$.

For the case of degree four polynomials with high U^4 norm we proved an inverse theorem showing that on many subspaces, of dimension $\Omega(n)$, f equals to a degree three polynomial (a different polynomial for each subspace). Such a result seems unlikely to be true for higher degrees. However, it may be the case that if $\deg(f) = d$ and f has a high U^d norm then f is correlated with a lower degree polynomial on a high dimensional subspace.

Acknowledgements

The authors would like to thank Shachar Lovett, Partha Mukhopadhyay and Alex Samorodnitsky for helpful discussions at various stages of this work. We are especially grateful to Shachar and Partha for many helpful comments on an earlier version of this paper. E.H would like to thank Noga Zewi for many helpful conversations and for her support. Finally, we thank Swastik Kopparty, Shubhangi Saraf and Madhu Sudan for pointing out an error in an earlier proof of Lemma 3.5.

7. REFERENCES

[AKK+05] N. Alon, T. Kaufman, M. Krivelevich, S. Litsyn, and D. Ron. Testing reed-muller codes. *IEEE Transactions on Information Theory*, 51(11):4032–4039, 2005.

[BV07] A. Bogdanov and E. Viola. Pseudorandom bits for polynomials. In *Proceedings of the 48th Annual FOCS*, pages 41–51, 2007.

[Gow98] T. Gowers. A New Proof of Szemerédi's Theorem for Arithmetic Progressions of Length Four. *Journal Geometric And Functional Analysis*, 8(3):529–551, 1998.

[Gow01] T. Gowers. A new proof of Szemerédi's theorem. *Journal Geometric And Functional Analysis*, 11(3):465–588, 2001.

[Gre] B. Green. The polynomial Freiman-Ruzsa conjecture. http://www.dpmms.cam.ac.uk/~bjg23/papers/PFR.pdf.

[GT07] B. Green and T. Tao. The distribution of polynomials over finite fields, with applications to the gowers norms. arXiv:0711.3191, 2007.

[GT08] B. Green and T. Tao. An inverse theorem for the Gowers U^3-norm, with applications. *Proc. Edinburgh Math. Soc.*, 51(1):73–153, 2008.

[KL08] T. Kaufman and S. Lovett. Worst case to average case reductions for polynomials. In *49th Annual FOCS*, pages 166–175, 2008.

[LMS08] S. Lovett, R. Meshulam, and A. Samorodnitsky. Inverse conjecture for the gowers norm is false. In *40th Annual STOC*, pages 547–556, 2008.

[LN97] R. Lidl and H. Niederreiter. *Finite Fields*, volume 20 of *Encyclopedia of mathematics and its applications*. Cambridge University Press, 2nd edition, 1997.

[Lov08] S. Lovett. Unconditional pseudorandom generators for low degree polynomials. In *40th Annual STOC*, pages 557–562, 2008.

[Sam07] A. Samorodnitsky. Low-degree tests at large distances. In *39th Annual STOC*, pages 506–515, 2007.

[ST06] A. Samorodnitsky and L. Trevisan. Gowers uniformity, influence of variables, and pcps. In *38th Annual STOC*, pages 11–20, 2006.

[Ste03] D. Stefankovic. Fourier transforms in computer

science. Master's thesis, University of Chicago, Department of Computer Science, 2003.

[Tre09] L. Trevisan. Additive combinatorics and theoretical computer science. *SIGACT News Complexity Column*, 63, 2009.

[TZ08] T. Tao and T. Ziegler. The inverse conjecture for the gowers norm over finite fields via the correspondence principle. arXiv:0810.5527v1, 2008.

[Vio08] E. Viola. The sum of d small-bias generators fools polynomials of degree d. In *Proceedings of the 23rd Annual IEEE Conference on Computational Complexity (CCC)*, pages 124–127, 2008.

[VW07] E. Viola and A. Wigderson. Norms, xor lemmas, and lower bounds for gf(2) polynomials and multiparty protocols. In *22nd Annual CCC*, pages 141–154, 2007.

[Wol09] J. Wolf. An inverse theorem for F_2^n. In preparation, 2009.

A Sparse Johnson–Lindenstrauss Transform

Anirban Dasgupta Ravi Kumar Tamás Sarlós
Yahoo! Research
701 First Avenue
Sunnyvale, CA 94089.
{anirban, ravikumar, stamas}@yahoo-inc.com

ABSTRACT

Dimension reduction is a key algorithmic tool with many applications including nearest-neighbor search, compressed sensing and linear algebra in the streaming model. In this work we obtain a *sparse* version of the fundamental tool in dimension reduction — the Johnson–Lindenstrauss transform. Using hashing and local densification, we construct a sparse projection matrix with just $\tilde{O}(\frac{1}{\epsilon})$ non-zero entries per column. We also show a matching lower bound on the sparsity for a large class of projection matrices. Our bounds are somewhat surprising, given the known lower bounds of $\Omega(\frac{1}{\epsilon^2})$ both on the number of rows of any projection matrix and on the sparsity of projection matrices generated by natural constructions.

Using this, we achieve an $\tilde{O}(\frac{1}{\epsilon})$ update time per non zero element for a $(1 \pm \epsilon)$-approximate projection, thereby substantially outperforming the $\tilde{O}(\frac{1}{\epsilon^2})$ update time required by prior approaches. A variant of our method offers the same guarantees for sparse vectors, yet its $\tilde{O}(d)$ worst case running time matches the best approach of Ailon and Liberty.

Categories and Subject Descriptors. F.2.0 [**Theory of Computation**]: Analysis of Algorithms and Problem Complexity—*General*; G.3 [**Mathematics of Computing**]: Probability and Statistics—*Probabilistic algorithms*

General Terms. Algorithms, Theory

Keywords. Johnson–Lindenstrauss transform, Dimensionality reduction

1. INTRODUCTION

Dimension reduction is a fundamental primitive with many algorithmic applications including nearest-neighbor search [2, 19], compressed sensing [11], data stream computations [5], computational geometry [13], numerical linear algebra [14, 17, 26, 28], machine learning [8, 33], graph sparsification [30], and more; see the monograph [32] for further applications. The seminal random projection method of Johnson and Lindenstrauss [20] consists of just multiplying the input vector by a suitably sampled random projection matrix — n vectors in d-dimensional space can be mapped into an $O(\frac{1}{\epsilon^2} \log n)$-dimensional subspace such that the length of each vector is distorted by at most $(1 \pm \epsilon)$. This simple and elegant method has the following desirable properties: (i) it is linear, (ii) it is oblivious to the input, (iii) it works with high probability for a given set of input points, and (iv) the target dimension is *independent* of d.

Given its algorithmic importance, much effort has been devoted to speeding up the mapping. One line of work achieves this goal by making the projection matrix sparse, and hence its multiplication with the input vectors faster. Sparsity is typically achieved by independently setting each matrix entry to zero with a certain probability [1, 2, 23]. There is however a limit on the extent of sparsity achievable by this approach: a result of Matousek [23, Theorem 4.1] states that such matrices need to contain $\tilde{\Omega}(\frac{\alpha^2}{\epsilon^2})$ non-zeroes in expectation per column, if they were to preserve the length of a unit vector with infinity norm at most α.

Our results. We obtain a sparse random projection matrix of size $k \times d$ that has $O(\frac{1}{\epsilon} \log^2(\frac{k}{\delta}) \log(\frac{1}{\delta}))$ non-zero entries per column, where $k = O(\frac{1}{\epsilon^2} \log(\frac{1}{\delta}))$. This is the *first* construction with $o(\frac{1}{\epsilon^2})$ non-zero entries in the projection matrix. (For our results to be improvements, we need to assume that $\log^2(\frac{k}{\delta}) = o(\frac{1}{\epsilon})$. Our analysis, however, does not need this assumption.)

A highlight of our approach is to construct the projection matrix itself with care. Instead of using independent random variables, as is typically done, we construct it out of a hash function that entails some dependency among the entries. This construction is implicit in the work of Langford et al. [21] and Weinberger et al. [33], where it played a role mostly as a practical heuristic. The hash-based construction introduces new technical difficulties, but ensures that we have exactly a fixed number of non-zero entries in each column, thereby relaxing the requirements on the density of input vectors.

Specifically, whereas prior work requires that for a unit vector x, $\|x\|_\infty = O(\epsilon)$, for a constant number of expected entries per column of the projection matrix, we only need $\|x\|_\infty = O(\sqrt{\epsilon})$. In order to achieve this level of densification, we can use a simple replication technique on x [33].

To manage the technical difficulties that arise from the dependencies, we show that the contribution from each hash bucket is bounded, and that the total amount of noise arising from the collisions in each hash bucket is small. The reduction in overall variance comes from the fact that each dimension is mapped to *exactly one* hash bucket, and the lack of self-collisions (which would be present if the entries in the matrix were i.i.d.) leads to a reduction in the variance of the cross-product error. There are several subtleties in analyzing this, in particular, the errors from different hash buckets being correlated. We handle this by an application of the FKG inequality on the product of the moment generating function of the random variables capturing the errors. This helps us in obtaining a

STOC'10, June 5–8, 2010, Cambridge, Massachusetts, USA.

concentration on the sum of the errors. Our choice of ± 1 random variables (instead of Gaussian random variables[1]) plays a critical role in making our proofs work.

Implications for sparse vectors. The resulting running time for an input vector x having $n_{\rm nz}(x)$ non-zeros is $\tilde{O}\left(\frac{n_{\rm nz}(x)}{\epsilon}\right)$ — better than the running time obtained by [22, 23] for sparse vectors in terms of the sparsity ratio $\frac{n_{\rm nz}(x)}{d}$ as well as by the factor $\frac{1}{\epsilon}$. Furthermore, using a block-Hadamard based preconditioner, instead of a global Hadamard transform, we can actually ensure that our running time for all vectors is $\tilde{O}(\min(\frac{n_{\rm nz}}{\epsilon}, d))$, which is once again an improvement over existing results. The qualitative difference in the running times is starker in the turnstile model of streaming. Since the updates in the stream come as (i, v_i), updating any sketch that requires computing a global Hadamard transform is very expensive, taking $\tilde{O}(d)$ time per update. Our update time, on the other hand, is only $\tilde{O}(\frac{1}{\epsilon})$ per entry.

Our technique speeds up nearest-neighbor computation for sparse vectors as well. We can use our construction to preprocess the input vectors before applying the algorithm as described in [2, Theorem 3.2]. The effective running time is then $\tilde{O}(\frac{n_{nz}(x)}{\epsilon} + \frac{1}{\epsilon^2}\log n + \frac{1}{\epsilon^3}\log n)$ instead of $O(d\log d + \frac{1}{\epsilon^3}\log n)$. For sparse vectors, this could represent a significant improvement.

Related work. Since the original Johnson–Lindenstrauss result, several authors have shown that the projection matrix could be constructed element-wise using Gaussian or uniform ± 1 variables [1, 7, 16, 19]. Alon showed a lower bound of $\Omega\left(\frac{\log n}{\epsilon^2\log(\frac{1}{\epsilon})}\right)$ on the target dimensionality [4].

In order to circumvent the sparsity lower bound of Matousek [23], the ingenious Fast Johnson–Lindenstrauss transform (FJLT) of Ailon and Chazelle preconditions the input with a randomized Hadamard transform thereby making it dense, and then applies a sparse projection matrix [2]. The computation of the Hadamard transform (via a fast Hadamard transform), however, forces an $\tilde{O}(d)$ running time *irrespective* of the number of non-zeros in the input vector. This makes it less desirable for sparse input vectors.

Ailon and Liberty [3] showed that the sparse projection matrix in [2] could be replaced by a dense, deterministic, but well-structured code matrix, and improved the running time to $O(d\log k)$ over a wide range of parameters; however, like before, the running time of these methods are unable to take advantage of the sparsity of the input vector. Liberty, Ailon, and Singer [22] proved that there exists projection matrices that are applicable in $O(d)$ time if the input satisfies density conditions that are significantly stricter than those required for hashing. Since hashing works in linear time, our work improves upon these results. Finally we remark that although [3, 22] contain a spectral condition derived from Talagrand's inequality that could be applied to our hashing construct[2], but the resulting bound is too weak; it fails to show that hashing improves over even the most basic Johnson–Lindenstrauss transform.

Charikar, Chen, and Farach-Colton [12] introduced the COUNT SKETCH data structure that used hash tables combined with pairwise independent ± 1 random variables for finding the most frequent items in a data stream. Thorup and Zhang [31] observed that this hashing trick could be used to speed up the celebrated AMS sketch [5] for estimating F_2; this was also noted by Cormode and Garofalakis [15]. Hashing decreases the update time from $O(\frac{1}{\epsilon^2}\log(\frac{1}{\delta}))$ to $O(\log(\frac{1}{\delta}))$. These estimators, however, are non-linear: they return the median of estimates obtained from $O(\log(\frac{1}{\delta}))$ independent hash functions, which makes them less desirable for some applications. Our results essentially show that by increasing the update time to $\tilde{O}(\frac{1}{\epsilon}\log(\frac{1}{\delta}))$, the median could be replaced by an average.

Lastly, we note that random projection using hashing has found practical applications in machine learning [21, 29, 33]. In particular, the densification by replication was suggested by Weinberger et al. [33]. Although they claim a concentration bound for hashing-based dimensionality reduction, unfortunately, their claim is false due to an error in the application of Talagrand's inequality.

2. MAIN RESULTS

Let $k = \frac{12}{\epsilon^2}\log(\frac{1}{\delta})$ and $c = \frac{16}{\epsilon}\log\left(\frac{1}{\delta}\right)\log^2\left(\frac{k}{\delta}\right)$. Let $r = \{r_j\}_{j\in[cd]}$ be a set of i.i.d. random variables such that for each $j \in [cd]$, $\Pr[r_j = 1] = \Pr[r_j = -1] = 1/2$. Let $\delta_{\alpha\beta} = 1$ iff $\alpha = \beta$ and zero otherwise. Let $n_{\rm nz}(x)$ denote the number of non-zero entries in vector x.

Let $h' : [cd] \to [k]$ be a hash function chosen uniformly at random and let $H' \in \{0, \pm 1\}^{k\times cd}$ be defined as $H'_{ij} = \delta_{ih'(j)} r_j$. Let the *pre-conditioner* $P \in \{0, \pm 1\}^{cd\times d}$ be defined as

$$P_{ij} = \begin{cases} \frac{1}{\sqrt{c}} \text{ for } (j-1)c + 1 \le i \le jc, \\ 0 \text{ otherwise.} \end{cases}$$

Let $\Phi = H'P$.

Theorem 1 *For any given vector $x \in \mathbb{R}^d$, with probability $1 - 4\delta$, Φ satisfies the following property:*

$$(1-\epsilon)\|x\|_2^2 \le \|\Phi x\|_2^2 \le (1+\epsilon)\|x\|_2^2. \tag{1}$$

The time required to compute Φx is $O\left(\frac{1}{\epsilon}\log^2(\frac{k}{\delta})\log(\frac{1}{\delta})\right)\cdot n_{\rm nz}(x)$.

This is easily implied by the following. Let $h : [d] \to [k]$ be a hash function chosen uniformly at random. Let $H \in \{0, \pm 1\}^{k\times d}$ be defined as $H_{ij} = \delta_{ih(j)} r_j$; note that the matrix H has only d non-zero entries, exactly one per column.

Theorem 2 *For any given vector $x \in \mathbb{R}^d$ such that $\|x\|_\infty \le \frac{1}{\sqrt{c}}$, for $\epsilon < 1$ and $\delta < \frac{1}{10}$, with probability $1 - 3\delta$, H satisfies the following property:*

$$(1-\epsilon)\|x\|_2^2 \le \|Hx\|_2^2 \le (1+\epsilon)\|x\|_2^2.$$

For dense vectors, Theorem 1 gives a run-time of $O(\frac{d}{\epsilon}\log^3(\frac{1}{\epsilon\delta}))$; this, for a small enough ϵ, could be significantly worse than the running time obtained by Ailon and Liberty in [3] and Matousek in [23]. However, we can modify the construction of the preconditioner so that we guarantee a running time of $O(d\log c\log\log c)$ for *all* vectors. Our new preconditioner is based on the randomized Hadamard construction by Ailon et al. [2, 3].

Theorem 3 *Let $d > 6c\log(\frac{3c}{\delta})$. There exists a preconditioner $G \in \Re^{d\times d}$ such that for any input vector $x \in \mathbb{R}^d$, with probability $1 - 4\delta$,*

$$(1-\epsilon)\|x\|_2^2 \le \|(HG)x\|_2^2 \le (1+\epsilon)\|x\|_2^2.$$

The time required to compute $(HG)x$ is given by

$$O\left(\min\left(\frac{n_{\rm nz}(x)}{\epsilon}\log^4\left(\frac{1}{\epsilon\delta}\right), d\right)\log\left(\frac{1}{\epsilon\delta}\right)\right).$$

[1]In fact, we need an average of $\frac{1}{\epsilon^2}$ Gaussians to get a $(1 \pm \epsilon)$-approximation.

[2]It is not hard to see that σ of [22] equals to $\max\{\sigma_i\}$ studied in Lemma 6.

3. PROOF OF THEOREM 2

3.1 Preliminaries

Without loss of generality, we can assume $\|x\|_2 = 1$. Let $Y_i = \sum_j H_{ij}x_j = \sum_j \delta_{ih(j)}r_jx_j$. and let $\sigma_i^2 = \mathrm{E}_r[Y_i^2]$, where E_r is the expectation taken with respect to the random variables $r = \{r_j\}$. Thus,

$$\sigma_i^2 = \mathrm{E}_r[Y_i^2] = \mathrm{E}_r\left[\left(\sum_{j\in[d]} \delta_{ih(j)}r_jx_j\right)^2\right] = \sum_{j\in[d]} \delta_{ih(j)}x_j^2,$$

since the cross-product terms cancel out by the independence i.e., $\mathrm{E}_r[r_jr_{j'}] = 0$ for $j \neq j'$. Let $Z_i = Y_i^2 - \mathrm{E}_r[Y_i^2] = Y_i^2 - \sigma_i^2$.

The outline of the proof is as follows. We need to prove that $\sum_i Y_i^2$ is concentrated around $\|x\|_2^2 = 1$. Instead of showing concentration of $\sum_i Y_i^2$, we will show that $\sum_i Z_i$ is concentrated around zero. Indeed, since our hash function guarantees that each coordinate $j \in [d]$ is mapped to one and exactly one hash bucket, we have that $\sum_{i=1}^k \sigma_i^2 = \|x\|_2^2 = 1$. Therefore, $\sum_{i=1}^k Y_i^2 = \sum_i \sigma_i^2 + \sum_i Z_i = 1 + \sum_{i=1}^k Z_i$. Showing that $\sum_i Z_i$ is concentrated around zero is thus enough.

We will utilize the following form of the FKG inequality [6, Theorem 6.2.1].

Theorem 4 (FKG inequality) *Let L be a finite distributive lattice and let $\mu : L \to \Re^+$ be a log-supermodular function. Then, for an increasing function f and a decreasing function g, we have that*

$$\sum_{x\in L} \mu(x)f(x)g(x) \sum_{x\in L} \mu(x) \leq \sum_{x\in L} \mu(x)f(x) \sum_{x\in L} \mu(x)g(x).$$

3.2 Notation

Recall that $k = \frac{12}{\epsilon^2}\log(\frac{1}{\delta})$. Define

$$\alpha = \alpha(k) = \frac{1}{\epsilon\ln(\frac{k}{\delta})}, \quad \sigma_*^2 = \frac{1+\alpha}{k}, \quad \text{and} \quad \theta = \frac{4\sigma_*^2 k}{\delta};$$

we will assume $\alpha \geq 3$. We define the following function as a shorthand to denote the upper bound on conditional expectation of the MGF with respect to the $\{r_j\}$ variables.

$$G(u,t) = 1 + \frac{1}{\theta^2}(\exp(u\theta) - 1 - u\theta)t + \frac{4\delta}{k}.$$

Definition 5 (Goodness) *A set $A \subseteq [d]$ is* good *if $\sum_{j\in A} x_j^2 \leq \sigma_*^2$. The ith hash bucket is* good *if $h^{-1}(i)$ is good, i.e., if $\sigma_i^2 = \sum_{j,h(j)=i} x_j^2 \leq \sigma_*^2$ and the hash function h is* good *if $h^{-1}(i)$ is good for all i.*

For a given h, let $\mathcal{G}_i$ denote the event that the ith hash bucket is good. Let $\mathcal{G}$ be the event that the hash function h is good. By abusing notation we use $\mathcal{G}$ and $\mathcal{G}_i$ to represent the indicator variables of the corresponding events.

3.3 Proof details

Recall that $Z_i = Y_i^2 - \mathrm{E}_r[Y_i^2]$, where $Y_i = \sum_j \delta_{ih(j)}r_jx_j$, i.e.,

$$Z_i = \sum_{j\neq j', j,j'\in[d]} \delta_{ih(j)}\delta_{ih(j')}r_jr_{j'}x_jx_{j'}.$$

Observe that $\mathrm{E}[Z_i] = 0$ and our goal is to show that $\sum_i Z_i$ is concentrated around 0.

Here is an overview of the proof. We first show in Lemma 6 that most h are good. In Lemma 7, we bound the moment generating function (MGF) of the random variable Z_i, for a fixed h. A usual step at this point would be to remove the effect of the bad choice of the random variables from the MGF by perhaps considering a truncated random variable $\hat{Z}_i = \min(Z_i, M)$. In our case, however, such a construction would introduce a dependence among the $\{r_j\}$ and h variables, which appears to be insurmountable when trying to apply the FKG inequality. We have to instead utilize the notion of goodness of h only in defining the truncated random variable $\hat{Z}_i$. Using the result of Lemma 7, we first get Corollary 8 that gives the expected and the worst-case bounds on the MGF for a good hash function h. We utilize these bounds to define $\hat{Z}_i$ in (5). Next, in Lemma 9, we define two set functions f_s and g_s and show that they are monotone, in accordance with the requirements of the FKG inequality (Theorem 4). These functions are then used in Lemma 10 to show that the MGF of $\sum_i Z_i$ can be bound by the product of the individual MGF's Z_i. We then bound the probability of an ϵ-deviation for $\sum_i Z_i$ in Theorem 11. Subsequently, we use Theorem 11 to prove Theorems 1 and 2. Section 4 gives the proof of Theorem 3.

Lemma 6 *If $c = \frac{16}{\epsilon}\log(\frac{1}{\delta})\log^2(\frac{k}{\delta})$, then $\Pr[\mathcal{G}] \geq 1-\delta$.*

The proof (Appendix 9.1) is an application of the Bernstein's inequality [24, Theorem 2.7] and utilizes the fact that since $\|x\|_\infty \leq \frac{1}{\sqrt{c}}$, and the hash function is random, with high probability, no σ_i can be too large. In essence, this generalizes well-known facts about the maximum load in the balls into bins problem for the weighted case[3].

The following lemma gives a bound on the MGF of the variable Z_i for a fixed h. The proof can be found in Appendix 9.2.

Lemma 7 *If $u < \frac{1}{4\sigma_i^2}$, then for a fixed h,*

$$\mathrm{E}_r[\exp(uZ_i)] \leq G(u, \mathrm{E}_r[Z_i^2]). \tag{2}$$

Lemma 7 leads to the following.

Corollary 8 *If $0 < u < \frac{1}{4\sigma_*^2}$, then the expectation of the MGF can be bounded as*

$$\mathrm{E}_{h,r}[\exp(uZ_i) \mid \mathcal{G}] \leq G(u, \frac{1}{k^2}). \tag{3}$$

Similarly,

$$\max_{h\in\mathcal{G}} \mathrm{E}_r[\exp(uZ_i)] \leq G(u, \sigma_*^4). \tag{4}$$

PROOF. By taking expectation over h and using

$$\mathrm{E}_h[\mathrm{E}_r[Z_i^2 \mid \mathcal{G}]] \leq 2\mathrm{E}[Z_i^2] \leq \frac{2}{k^2},$$

we have that

$$\begin{aligned}\mathrm{E}_{r,h}[\exp(uZ_i) \mid \mathcal{G}] &\leq 1 + \frac{2}{k^2\theta^2}(\exp(u\theta) - 1 - u\theta) + \frac{4\delta}{k}\\ &\leq \exp\left(\frac{2}{k^2\theta^2}(\exp(u\theta) - 1 - u\theta) + \frac{4\delta}{k}\right).\end{aligned}$$

[3]Sanders [27] contains a proof of the expected load for the weighted ball-and-bins problem, but does not contain a proof of the high probability statement.

The upper bound on $\mathrm{E}_r[\exp(uZ_i) \mid \mathcal{G}]$ is given by

$$\begin{aligned}
&\max_{h\in\mathcal{G}} \mathrm{E}_r[\exp(uZ_i)] \\
&\leq 1 + \frac{1}{\theta^2}(\exp(u\theta) - 1 - u\theta)\max_h \mathrm{E}_r[Z_i^2 \mid \mathcal{G}] + \frac{4\delta}{k} \\
&\leq 1 + \frac{1}{\theta^2}(\exp(u\theta) - 1 - u\theta)\sigma_*^4 + \frac{4\delta}{k},
\end{aligned}$$

where we use $\mathrm{E}_r[Z_i^2] < \sigma_*^4$. □

Next, we have to handle the fact that the Z_i variables are not independent. Yet, intuitively, since Z_i is roughly related to the cross-product of the set of entries x_j that map into the ith hash bucket, conditioned on the fact that one of the Z_i variables has achieved a large value, the probability that another $Z_{i'}$ is also large decreases. In fact, we show that we can apply the FKG inequality (Theorem 4) on the MGF of the Z_i random variables. Note that this situation is more involved that the simple negative dependence obtained on a set of random variables by conditioning their sum to be a constant — we cannot make such claims on $\sum_i Z_i$. For all $i = 1, \ldots, k$ let us define

$$\hat{Z}_i = \begin{cases} Z_i & \text{if } \mathcal{G}_i, \\ \frac{1}{u}\log G(u, \sigma_*^4) & \text{else.} \end{cases} \tag{5}$$

We first need the following lemma in preparation for the application of the FKG inequality (Theorem 4).

Lemma 9 *For $1 \leq s \leq k$, $u < \frac{1}{4\sigma_*^2}$ and $A \subseteq [d]$, let us define*

$$f_s(A) = \mathrm{E}_r\left[\exp\left(u\hat{Z}_s\right) \mid h^{-1}(s) = A\right] \text{ and}$$
$$g_s(A) = \mathrm{E}_{h,r}\left[\exp\left(u\sum_{i=1}^{s-1}\hat{Z}_i\right) \mid h^{-1}(s) = A\right].$$

Then f_s is an increasing and g_s is a decreasing set function.

PROOF. First we prove that f_s is increasing by showing that for all $A \subseteq [d]$ and for all $a \in [d] \setminus A$, it holds that $f_s(A \cup \{a\}) \geq f_s(A)$.

Observe that if $h^{-1}(s)$ is good (i.e., if $\mathcal{G}_s$ holds), then by Corollary 8, we have $\mathrm{E}_r[\exp(uZ_s)] \leq G(u, \sigma_*^4)$. Thus for all h and s, it holds from (5) that

$$\mathrm{E}_r[\exp(u\hat{Z}_s)] \leq G(u, \sigma_*^4). \tag{6}$$

There are two cases to consider. Suppose $A \cup \{a\}$ is bad. Then, $\hat{Z}_s = \frac{1}{u}\log G(u, \sigma_*^4)$ and hence $f_s(A \cup \{a\}) = G(u, \sigma_*^4) \geq f_s(A)$ from (6).

Suppose $A \cup \{a\}$ is good. Now, let us define

$$V_A = \sum_{j,g\in A, j\neq g} r_j r_g x_j x_g \quad \text{and} \quad W_A = x_a \sum_{j\in A} x_j r_j.$$

Also note that if $h^{-1}(s) = A \cup \{a\}$ and the sth bucket is good, then $\hat{Z}_s = Z_s = V_A + r_a W_A$ holds. Therefore we have that

$$\begin{aligned}
&f_s(A \cup \{a\}) = \mathrm{E}_r\left[\exp\left(u\hat{Z}_s\right) \mid h^{-1}(s) = A \cup \{a\}\right] \\
&= \mathrm{E}_r\left[\exp(uV_A + u \cdot r_a W_A) \mid h^{-1}(s) = A \cup \{a\}\right] \\
&= \mathrm{E}_r[\mathrm{E}_r\left[\exp(uV_A + u \cdot r_a W_A) \mid h^{-1}(s) = A \cup \{a\}, \{r_j\}_{j\in A}\right] \\
&\quad \mid h^{-1}(s) = A \cup \{a\}\,] \\
&\geq \mathrm{E}_r[\exp\left(\mathrm{E}_r\left[uV_A + u \cdot r_a W_A \mid h^{-1}(s) = A \cup \{a\}, \{r_j\}_{j\in A}\right]\right) \\
&\quad \mid h^{-1}(s) = A \cup \{a\}]. \\
&\quad\quad \text{(By Jensen's inequality, } \mathrm{E}[\exp(x)] \geq \exp(\mathrm{E}[x])) \\
&\overset{(a)}{=} \mathrm{E}_r\left[\exp(uV_A) \mid h^{-1}(s) = A \cup \{a\}\right] \\
&\overset{(b)}{=} \mathrm{E}_r\left[\exp(uV_A) \mid h^{-1}(s) = A\right] \\
&\overset{(c)}{=} f_s(A).
\end{aligned}$$

Here, (a) follows since only r_a is random in the inner expectation and

$$\mathrm{E}_r\left[uV_A + u \cdot r_a W_A \mid h^{-1}(s) = A \cup \{a\}, \{r_j\}_{j\in A}\right] = uV_A.$$

And, (b) follows since $a \notin A$ and V_A does not depend on $h(a)$ by the independence of the values of r and h. Finally, (c) follows since if $A \cup \{a\}$ is good then so is A; therefore if $h^{-1}(s) = A$, then we have that $\hat{Z}_s = Z_s = V_A$. The proof that f_s is increasing is complete.

The proof of g_s being a decreasing function is similar, and can be found in Appendix 9.3. □

Given our construction of the two functions, f_s and g_s, we can now proceed to apply the FKG inequality (Theorem 4) to show that the MGF of the random variable $\sum_{i=1}^k \hat{Z}_i$ is bounded by the product of the MGF's of each $\hat{Z}_i$ variable.

Lemma 10 *It holds that*

$$\mathrm{E}\left[\exp\left(u\sum_{i=1}^k \hat{Z}_i\right)\right] \leq \prod_{i=1}^k \mathrm{E}\left[\exp\left(u\hat{Z}_i\right)\right],$$

where the expectation is taken over both h and $r = \{r_j\}$.

PROOF. For all $1 \leq s \leq k$, we prove

$$\mathrm{E}\left[\exp\left(u\sum_{i=1}^s \hat{Z}_i\right)\right] \leq \prod_{i=1}^s \mathrm{E}\left[\exp\left(u\hat{Z}_i\right)\right], \tag{7}$$

by induction on s. The base case of $s = 1$ is obvious.

Now assume that the inductive hypothesis (7) holds for $s - 1$. For all $A \subseteq [d]$ let us define

$$\mu_s(A) = \Pr\left[h^{-1}(s) = A\right] = \prod_{j\in A}\Pr[h(j) = s]\prod_{j\notin A}\Pr[h(j) \neq s].$$

It is easy to check that μ_s is a log-supermodular measure[4] over the subsets of $[d]$. Recalling the definition of the increasing function f_s and the decreasing function g_s from Lemma 9 it follows from the FKG inequality (Theorem 4) that

$$\mathrm{E}_{\mu_s}[f_s g_s] \leq \mathrm{E}_{\mu_s}[f_s]\,\mathrm{E}_{\mu_s}[g_s].$$

[4]See [6, Section 6.2, page 87] for a precise definition and proof of this fact.

Furthermore, observe that for any random variable X we have

$$\mathrm{E}_{\mu_s}\left[\mathrm{E}\left[X \mid h^{-1}(s)=A\right]\right] = \sum_{A\subseteq[d]} \Pr\left[h^{-1}(s)=A\right]\mathrm{E}\left[X \mid h^{-1}(s)=A\right] = \mathrm{E}\left[X\right],$$

and consequently,

$$\mathrm{E}[\exp(u\sum_{i=1}^{s-1}\hat{Z}_i)\exp(u\hat{Z}_s)] \leq \mathrm{E}[\exp(u\sum_{i=1}^{s-1}\hat{Z}_i)]\mathrm{E}[\exp(u\hat{Z}_s)].$$

Combining the latter with the induction hypothesis for $s-1$ concludes the proof. □

Theorem 11 *For the variables Z_i we have*

(i) $$\Pr\left[\sum_i Z_i \geq \epsilon\right] \leq \exp\left(\frac{-3k\epsilon^2}{4(3+(1+\alpha)\epsilon\ln(\frac{k}{\delta}))}+4\delta\right)+\delta,$$

(ii) $$\Pr\left[\sum_i Z_i < -\epsilon\right] < \exp\left(-\frac{\epsilon^2 k}{12}\right)+\delta.$$

The proof of Theorem 11 involves a standard but tedious calculation that is similar to one done by Matousek [23]. The proof can be found in Appendix 9.4. Finally, we are ready to prove the main result.

PROOF. (**of Theorem 2**). Recall that $Y_i = \sum_j H_{ij}x_j$, thus $\|Hx\|_2^2 = \sum_i Y_i^2$. Also recall that $\sigma_i^2 = \mathrm{E}_r[Y_i^2]$. Thus, $\sum_{i=1}^k \sigma_i^2 = \|x\|_2^2 = 1$. Therefore, $\sum_{i=1}^k Y_i^2 = \sum_i \sigma_i^2 + \sum_i Z_i = 1 + \sum_{i=1}^k Z_i$. Recall that $k = \frac{12}{\epsilon^2}\log(\frac{1}{\delta})$, and $\alpha = \frac{1}{\epsilon\log(\frac{k}{\delta})}$. Plugging these values in Theorem 11(i), we have $\sum_i Z_i > \epsilon$, with probability at most $\exp(-\frac{9}{5}\ln(\frac{1}{\delta})+4\delta)+\delta < 2\delta$, for $\delta < \frac{1}{10}$. Similarly, from Theorem 11(ii), we have $\sum_i Z_i < -\epsilon$ with probability at most 2δ. Putting them together, with probability at least $1-4\delta$, $|\sum_i Y_i^2 - 1| = |\sum_i Z_i| < \epsilon$, and hence $|\|Hx\|_2^2 - \|x\|_2^2| < \epsilon\|x\|_2^2$. □

PROOF. (**of Theorem 1**). Theorem 1 easily follows from Theorem 2 by noting that if $y = Px$, then $\|y\|_2 = 1$ and $\|y\|_\infty \leq \frac{1}{\sqrt{c}}$. The running time is obtained as computing both $y = Px$ and Hy requires $O(c\cdot n_{nz}(x))$ time. □

4. PROOF OF THEOREM 3

Definition 12 (Randomized Hadamard matrix [2].) *Construct the $m\times m$ Hadamard matrix F as $F_{ij} = m^{-1/2}(-1)^{\langle i-1,j-1\rangle}$ and the diagonal matrix D by choosing each D_{ii} independently from $\{-1,1\}$ with probability $1/2$ for each value. The matrix $A = FD$ is defined to be an $m\times m$* randomized Hadamard matrix.

Using multiple small copies the randomized Hadamard matrix, we create the following preconditioner. Without loss of generality, we assume that $\frac{d}{b}$ is an integer, for the given value of b. We note that [3] also contains a similar construct; here we present a more straightforward analysis using a different vector norm.

Lemma 13 *Let $x\in\Re^d$, $\|x\| = 1$, and $1 > \delta > 0$, and $c \geq 1$. Define $b = 6c\log(\frac{3c}{\delta})$ and assume $b \leq d$. Construct $G \in \Re^{d\times d}$ to be a random block-diagonal matrix, where each of the d/b diagonal blocks of G consist of an independent copy of a $b\times b$ randomized Hadamard matrix. Then we have that*

$$\Pr\left[\|Gx\|_\infty \geq \frac{1}{\sqrt{c}}\right] \leq \delta.$$

PROOF. If A is $b\times b$ randomized Hadamard matrix, then for any b-dimensional vector z with $\|z\|_2 = 1$ it holds that $\|Az\|_2 = 1$. Using a Chernoff-type argument Ailon and Chazelle [2] showed

$$\Pr\left[\|Az\|_\infty \geq s\right] \leq 2b\exp\left(-\frac{s^2 b}{2}\right). \tag{8}$$

holds as well. Observe that the previous inequality trivially holds for $\|z\|_2 \leq 1$ as well. Let $y = Gx$, and G_j denote the jth diagonal block of G, and partition x and y into $\frac{d}{b}$ blocks x_j and define $y_j = G_j x_j$. Now for a block j, if $\|x_j\|_2 \leq \frac{1}{\sqrt{c}}$, then $\|y_j\|_\infty \leq \|y_j\|_2 \leq \frac{1}{\sqrt{c}}$ holds as well, since G_j is an isometry. Since x is unit length, there could be at most c blocks j such that $\|x_j\|_2 \geq \frac{1}{\sqrt{c}}$. Thus setting s to $\frac{1}{\sqrt{c}}$ in (8) and taking the union bound over these at most c blocks, we have that

$$\Pr\left[\|Gx\|_\infty \geq \frac{1}{\sqrt{c}}\right] \leq 2bc\exp\left(-\frac{b}{2c}\right) = \frac{12c^2\log(\frac{c}{\delta})\delta^3}{27c^3} \leq \delta,$$

establishing the claim. □

Using the block-Hadamard preconditioner, we are ready to prove Theorem 3. The ϵ-approximation guarantee of the projection matrix Φ follows trivially from the statements of Theorem 2 and of Lemma 13.

In order to bound the running time, let $n_{\mathrm{nzb}}(x)$ denote the number of blocks that have non-zero coordinates in x. Then the running time of the block-Hadamard based hashing is $O(n_{\mathrm{nzb}}(x)\cdot b\log b + n_{\mathrm{nzb}}(x)\cdot b)$. Now,

$$n_{\mathrm{nzb}}(x)\cdot b\log b \leq \min(n_{\mathrm{nz}}(x)b, d)\log b = O(\min(n_{\mathrm{nz}}(x)c\log(\frac{c}{\delta}), d)\log(\frac{c}{\delta}))$$

Now, $c\log(\frac{c}{\delta}) = O(\frac{1}{\epsilon}\log(\frac{1}{\delta})\log^2\frac{k}{\delta}\log(\frac{1}{\epsilon\delta}))$. Hence the final running time is

$$O\left(\min\left(\frac{n_{\mathrm{nz}}(x)}{\epsilon}\log\left(\frac{1}{\delta}\right)\log^2\left(\frac{k}{\delta}\right)\log\left(\frac{1}{\epsilon\delta}\right), d\right)\log\left(\frac{1}{\epsilon\delta}\right)\right).$$

Note that if δ is not too small then the running time of Theorem 3 is comparable to the best existing methods for dense vectors [3] yet it is much faster for sparse vectors. We remark that the localized Hadamard preconditioner presented in this section could also be combined with suitably sparse random matrices from [23] by making b larger, approximately equal to k. This variant would reproduce the results of [3], but it fails to show any improvement for sparse vectors over the naive construction as the running time would be $\tilde{\Omega}(\frac{1}{\epsilon^2})$ per non-zero element.

5. A LOWER BOUND

A random matrix Φ is said to have the *JL property* if for every vector x, Φx satisfies (1) with probability $1-\delta$ over the choice of Φ.

We show a lower bound on the sparsity for a class of constructions of matrices with the JL property. The construction of the matrix is modeled as a two stage process: first, the set of indices that have non-zero entries is chosen, and then each column is chosen independently random. Note that we do not assume that the random variables are independent within a column.

The lower bound argument of Matousek [23] shows that if the set of non-zero indices in the first stage is chosen by independent coin tosses and if the random variables in the second stage are independent (scaled) ±1 with equal probability, in expectation, then

$\tilde{\Omega}(\frac{\|x\|_\infty^2}{\epsilon^2})$ non-zero entries per column are needed to guarantee that the resulting matrix has the JL property.

We show a lower bound on the sparsity for the case when the non-zero indices are chosen arbitrarily. As mentioned earlier, if the random variables in the second stage are $N(0,1)$, then it is easy to obtain a lower bound of $\tilde{\Omega}(\frac{1}{\epsilon^2})$ on the number of non-zero entries per column: indeed, the lower bound follows since $\tilde{\Omega}(\frac{1}{\epsilon^2})$ such random variables are needed so that their sum is $(1 \pm \epsilon)$, w.h.p.

Under mild technical conditions on the random variables, we can prove the following lower bound stated in Theorem 14. It is easy to see that the conditions of Theorem 14 are satisfied if the random entries are independent (scaled) ± 1 or when they are generated by the replicated hashing construct of Theorem 1. Thus the upper bound of Theorem 1 is tight with respect to ϵ. The bound on the number of non-zeros per column implies a bound on the worst case update time over all vectors as well.

Theorem 14 *Let $1 \le c \le k < d$ be integers and M be an arbitrary, fixed or random, $k \times d$ 0-1 matrix with at most c non-zeroes per column. Let P be a $k \times d$ random matrix of the following form $P_{ij} = \begin{cases} 0 & \text{if } M_{ij} = 0 \\ U_{ij} & \text{if } M_{ij} = 1. \end{cases}$ Here the vector valued U_{*j} random variables are independent and for each j it holds that $\mathrm{E}[\sum_i P_{ij}^2] = 1$ and that $\mathrm{E}[\sum_i P_{ij}^4] = O(\frac{1}{c})$.*

Let $0 < \epsilon \le 1/4$. If P has JL property with probability at least $1 - \frac{o(1)}{d^2}$, then

$$c = \Omega\left(\min\left\{\frac{1}{\epsilon^2}, \frac{\sqrt{\log_k(d)}}{\epsilon}\right\}\right).$$

PROOF. For all $i = 1, \ldots, d$ let $C_i = \{s \in [k] | M_{si} \neq 0\}$ denote the index set of non-zeros in the ith column of P. Furthermore, let $V = \{e_1, \ldots, e_d\}$, where e_i denotes the ith unit vector. For $i \neq j$ we also define $X_{ij} = C_i \cap C_j$ and $S = \sum_{t \in X_{ij}} U_{ti} U_{tj}$. Then we have that

$$\|P(e_i + e_j)\|_2^2 = \|Pe_i\|_2^2 + \|Pe_j\|_2^2 + 2S. \quad (9)$$

Using the fourth moment method [9], we show that S has a large deviation with constant probability unless c is large enough. Towards this goal for all $t \in X_{ij}$ set $Y_t = U_{ti} U_{tj}$ and let $x_{ij} = |X_{ij}|$.

W.l.o.g. we can assume that each column of M contains exactly c non-zeroes and if $M_{ti} = 1$ then $\mathrm{E}[U_{ti}^2] = \frac{1}{c}$ and $\mathrm{E}[U_{ti}^4] = O(\frac{1}{c^2})$ hold as well; otherwise we replace P with a copy of P whose rows are randomly permuted. Furthermore we can also assume that $\mathrm{E}[U_{si} U_{ti}] = 0$ holds as multiplying each row of P with independent uniformly distributed ± 1 random variables does not change (9) or the theorem's conditions. Finally, w.l.o.g. we can assume that for all s, t_1, t_2, t_3 where $s \notin \{t_1, t_2, t_3\}$ it holds that $\mathrm{E}[Y_s Y_{t_1} Y_{t_2} Y_{t_3}] = 0$ as multiplying the rows of P with random ± 1 ensures the latter condition as well.

Now observe that $\mathrm{E}[S^2] = \mathrm{E}[\sum_t Y_t^2] + \sum_{s \neq t} \mathrm{E}[Y_s Y_t] = \frac{x_{ij}}{c^2}$ holds, since $\mathrm{E}[Y_t^2] = \mathrm{E}[U_{ti}^2 U_{tj}^2] = \mathrm{E}[U_{ti}^2]\mathrm{E}[U_{tj}^2] = \frac{1}{c^2}$ by the independence of columns. Moreover if $s \neq t$ then we have that $\mathrm{E}[Y_s Y_t] = \mathrm{E}[U_{si} U_{ti} U_{sj} U_{tj}] = \mathrm{E}[U_{si} U_{ti}]\mathrm{E}[U_{sj} U_{tj}] = 0$ by independence again.

Similarly note that

$$\mathrm{E}[S^4] = \mathrm{E}[\sum_t Y_t^4] + \sum_{s \neq t} \mathrm{E}[Y_s^2 Y_t^2] + \sum_{s \notin \{t_1, t_2, t_3\}} \mathrm{E}[Y_s Y_{t_1} Y_{t_2} Y_{t_3}] = O\left(\frac{x_{ij}^2}{c^4}\right).$$

By our assumptions it holds that $\mathrm{E}[Y_t^4] = \mathrm{E}[U_{ti}^4]\mathrm{E}[U_{tj}^4] = O(\frac{1}{c^4})$. If $s \neq t$ then $\mathrm{E}[Y_s^2 Y_t^2] = \mathrm{E}[U_{si}^2 U_{ti}^2]\mathrm{E}[U_{sj}^2 U_{tj}^2]$ holds by independence and hence from Hölder's inequality we have that $\mathrm{E}[U_{si}^2 U_{ti}^2] \le \sqrt{\mathrm{E}[U_{si}^4]\mathrm{E}[U_{ti}^4]}$. Thus it holds that $\mathrm{E}[Y_s^2 Y_t^2] \le O(\frac{1}{c^4})$. Lastly, recall that that for all s, t_1, t_2, t_3 where $s \notin \{t_1, t_2, t_3\}$ we have that $\mathrm{E}[Y_s Y_{t_1} Y_{t_2} Y_{t_3}] = 0$.

Now [9, Theorem 3.5] states that

$$\Pr\left[|S| \ge \frac{1}{2}\sqrt{\mathrm{E}[S^2]}\right] \ge \frac{(3/4)^2}{\frac{\mathrm{E}[S^4]}{\mathrm{E}[S^2]^2} - \frac{7}{16}}.$$

Therefore we have that

$$\Pr\left[|S| \ge \frac{\sqrt{x_{ij}}}{2c}\right] \ge \frac{(3/4)^2}{O(1) - \frac{7}{16}} = \Omega(1). \quad (10)$$

On the other hand, it follows from the assumed JL property of P that with probability $1 - o(1)$, for all $1 \le i < j \le d$, we have that $\left| \|P(e_i + e_j)\|_2^2 - 2 \right| \le 2\epsilon$ and that

$$\left| \|P(e_i\|^2 + \|Pe_j)\|_2^2 - 2 \right| \le 2\epsilon.$$

Therefore from combining equality (9) with inequality (10) it follows that $\frac{\sqrt{x_{ij}}}{c} \le 4\epsilon$ must hold for all $i \neq j$, or equivalently $|C_i \cap C_j| \le z$ with $z = 16\epsilon^2 c^2$ for all $i \neq j$.

If $z < 1$, then the C_i are pairwise disjoint and therefore $k \ge dc \ge d$, a contradiction. Thus $z \ge 1$, and hence $c \ge \frac{1}{16\epsilon}$ immediately. In what follows we strengthen the latter lower bound for a large range of d and k as claimed.

If $c \ge \frac{1}{32\epsilon^2}$ then the lemma clearly holds as $\Omega\left(\frac{1}{\epsilon^2}\right)$ is the largest of the lower bounds claimed.

Now note that $c \ge 2$. Since if $c = 1$ were to hold, then from $\epsilon < 1/4$ it follows that $z < 1$, which is a contradiction as before. Therefore if $c \le \frac{1}{32\epsilon^2}$ then all C_i's are distinct as $z + 1 = (c/2)(32\epsilon^2 c) + 1 \le c/2 + c/2 = c$ holds.

Observe that any $z + 1$ element set is contained in at most one C_i. Therefore the number of distinct C_i is at most

$$f(k, c, z+1) = \binom{k}{z+1} / \binom{c}{z+1},$$

a well known fact from block designs and set packing [18]. From the Stirling formula, for all $n \ge 1$, $\sqrt{2\pi n}\left(\frac{n}{e}\right)^n \le n! \le 1.1\sqrt{2\pi n}\left(\frac{n}{e}\right)^n$, and it follows that for all $1 \le y < x$ it holds that $\left(\frac{ex}{y}\right)^y \frac{0.8}{\sqrt{2\pi}}\sqrt{\frac{x-y}{xy}} \le \binom{x}{y} \le \left(\frac{ex}{y}\right)^y \frac{1.1}{\sqrt{2\pi}}\sqrt{\frac{x}{y(x-y)}}$. Therefore we have that

$$f(k, c, z+1) \le \left(\frac{k}{c}\right)^{z+1} 2k \le k^{z+3}. \quad (11)$$

Now observe that $d \le f(k, c, z+1)$ as all C_i are distinct. Combining the latter with inequality (11), we have that $\log_k(d) - 3 \le z$. Recalling that $1 \le z = 16\epsilon^2 c^2$ concludes the proof. □

Using a replication argument it is easy to see that if a matrix P only has the JL property for vectors x with $\frac{\|x\|_\infty}{\|x\|_2} \le \alpha$ for some α, then under the conditions of Theorem 14 we have that at least one column of P contains $\Omega\left(\alpha^2 \min\left\{\frac{1}{\epsilon^2}, \frac{\sqrt{\log_k(d)}}{\epsilon}\right\}\right)$ non-zeroes.

If the fourth moment of the random entries per column scales with the number of non-zeros per column, the next theorem strengthens the previous claim by bounding the average number of non-zeroes per column. This condition is satisfied, say, if the non-zero entries are independent scaled ± 1 random variables.

Theorem 15 *Let $0 < \epsilon \leq 1/4$ and M be an arbitrary $k \times d$ 0-1 matrix with $2k^2 < d$. Let c_j denote the number of non-zeroes in the jth column of M. Let P be a $k \times d$ random matrix of the following form $P_{ij} = \begin{cases} 0 & \text{if } M_{ij} = 0 \\ U_{ij} & \text{if } M_{ij} = 1. \end{cases}$ Here the vector valued U_{*j} random variables are independent and for each j it holds that $\mathrm{E}[\sum_i P_{ij}^2] = 1$ and $\mathrm{E}[\sum_i P_{ij}^4] = O(1/c_j)$.*

If P has JL property with probability at least $1 - \frac{o(1)}{d^2}$, then

$$\sum_{i=1}^{d} \frac{c_i}{d} = \Omega\left(\min\left\{\frac{1}{\epsilon^2}, \frac{\sqrt{\log_k(d)}}{\epsilon}\right\}\right).$$

PROOF. Set

$$s = \Omega\left(\min\left\{\frac{1}{\epsilon^2}, \frac{\sqrt{\log_k(d)}}{\epsilon}\right\}\right).$$

For all $j = 1, \ldots, k$, assemble the columns of P with $c_i = j$ into the $k \times n_j$ matrix P_j. For all j if $n_j > k$ then from assumed JL property of P it follows that P_j satisfies the conditions of Theorem 14 with $c = j$ and thus $j \geq s$.

Therefore for all $j < s$ we have that $n_j \leq k$. The number of non-zeroes in P is $\sum_{i=1}^{d} c_i = \sum_{j=1}^{k} n_j j$, which we lower bound as follows

$$\sum_{j=1}^{k} n_j j \geq \sum_{j=s}^{k} n_j s = \left(\sum_{j=1}^{k} n_j - \sum_{j=1}^{s-1} n_j\right) s \geq (d - sk)\, s$$
$$\geq (d - k^2)\, s \geq \frac{d}{2} s. \quad \square$$

6. EMBEDDING INTO ℓ_1

We can show the following result for the case that the target metric is ℓ_1. The result and the corresponding proof is similar to that of Ailon and Chazelle [2]. We construct the matrix H as follows: $H_{ij} = \delta_{ih(j)} r_j$, where r_j are now drawn i.i.d. random variables $N(0, 1)$ instead of being ± 1. We then have the following. Let $\beta_0 = \mathrm{E}[|z|]$ where $z \sim N(0, 1)$. By the 2-stability of the normal distribution, $Y_i = \sum_j x_j r_j \delta_{ih(j)} \sim N(0, \sigma_i)$ where $\sigma_i^2 = \sum_{j \in h^{-1}(i)} x_j^2$. Thus, $\mathrm{E}_r[|Y_i|] = \sigma_i \beta_0$.

Theorem 16 *There exists a constant ϵ_0 such that for all $\epsilon < \epsilon_0$, if $c = k/\epsilon$, and $k = O\left(\frac{1}{\epsilon^2}\log(\frac{1}{\delta})\right)$, $Y = \frac{1}{\beta_0\sqrt{k}} \sum_i |Y_i|$, we have that $\Pr[|Y - 1| > \epsilon] < \delta$.*

The proof is omitted in this version.

7. DISCUSSIONS

The most important open question is resolving the gap between the upper and lower bounds with respect to the error probability. It would be interesting to see whether our claims could be proven more directly using stronger concentration inequalities.

Application of the current result to streaming settings would also require proving the claims for a k-wise independent hash-function and ± 1 variables. The chief hurdle in applying the techniques of Clarkson and Woodruff [14] seems to be proving the FKG inequality for the limited independence case. Note that Nisan's pseudo-random number generator construction [25] can be used to derandomize the hash function, but the naive way of doing this increases the update time to k. We leave efficient derandomization as an open question.

It is worthwhile to note that the hash-function represents a bipartite expander. In a similar vein, Berinde et al. [10] use an unbalanced expander graph based construction to create matrices with restricted isometry property for sparse signal recovery. Their argument crucially uses two facts — that the error-norm is ℓ_1, and that the input vector is sparse. It would interesting to investigate possible connections between these results.

Acknowledgments. The authors would like to thank Flavio Chierichetti, Edo Liberty, and Alex Smola for helpful discussions. We also thank the anonymous reviewers for feedback and for suggesting future directions.

8. REFERENCES

[1] D. Achlioptas. Database-friendly random projections: Johnson–Lindenstrauss with with binary coins. *Journal of Computer and System Sciences*, 66(4):671–687, 2003.

[2] N. Ailon and B. Chazelle. The fast Johnson–Lindenstrauss transform and approximate nearest neighbors. *SIAM Journal on Computing*, 39(1):302–322, 2009.

[3] N. Ailon and E. Liberty. Fast dimension reduction using Rademacher series on dual BCH codes. *Discrete and Computational Geometry*, 42(4):615–630, 2009.

[4] N. Alon. Problems and results in extremal combinatorics, Part I. *Discrete Math*, 273:31–53, 2003.

[5] N. Alon, Y. Matias, and M. Szegedy. The space complexity of approximating the frequency moments. *Journal of Computer and System Sciences*, 58(1):137–147, 1999.

[6] N. Alon and J. H. Spencer. *The Probabilistic Method.* Wiley-Interscience, 2nd edition, 2000.

[7] R. I. Arriaga and S. Vempala. An algorithmic theory of learning: Robust concepts and random and random projection. In *Proc. 40th IEEE Symposium on Foundations of Computer Science*, pages 616–623, 1999.

[8] M. F. Balcan, A. Blum, and S. Vempala. Kernels as features: On kernels, margins, and low-dimensional mappings. *Machine Learning*, 65(1):79–94, 2006.

[9] B. Berger. The fourth moment method. *SIAM Journal on Computing*, 26(4):1188–1207, 1997.

[10] R. Berinde, A. Gilbert, P. Indyk, H. Karloff, and M. Strauss. Combining geometry and combinatorics: A unified approach to sparse signal recovery. In *46th Annual Allerton Conference*, pages 798–805, 2008.

[11] E. J. Candes and T. Tao. Near-optimal signal recovery from random projections: Universal encoding strategies? *IEEE Transactions on Information Theory*, 52(12):5406–5425, 2006.

[12] M. Charikar, K. Chen, and M. Farach-Colton. Finding frequent items in data streams. *Theoretical Computer Science*, 312(1):3–15, 2004.

[13] K. L. Clarkson. Tighter bounds for random projections of manifolds. In *Proc. 24th Annual Symposium on Computational geometry*, pages 39–48, 2008.

[14] K. L. Clarkson and D. P. Woodruff. Numerical linear algebra in the streaming model. In *Proc. 41st Annual ACM Symposium on Theory of Computing*, pages 205–214, 2009.

[15] G. Cormode and M. Garofalakis. Sketching streams through the net: Distributed approximate query tracking. In *Proc. 31st International Conference on Very Large Data Bases*, pages 13–24, 2005.

[16] S. Dasgupta and A. Gupta. An elementary proof of a theorem of Johnson and Lindenstrauss. *Random Structures and Algorithms*, 22(1):60–65, 2003.

[17] P. Drineas, M. W. Mahoney, S. Muthukrishnan, and T. Sarlós. Faster least squares approximation. *Arxiv preprint arXiv:0710.1435*, 2007.

[18] Z. Füredi and Z. Katona. Multiply intersecting families of sets. *Journal of Combinatorial Theory, Series A*, 106(2):315–326, 2004.

[19] P. Indyk and R. Motwani. Approximate nearest neighbors: Towards removing the curse of dimensionality. In *Proc. 20th Annual ACM Symposium on Theory of Computing*, pages 604–613, 1998.

[20] W. B. Johnson and J. Lindenstrauss. Extensions of Lipschitz mappings into a Hilbert space. *Contemporary Mathematics*, 26:189–206, 1984.

[21] J. Langford, L. Li, and A. Strehl. Vowpal wabbit online learning project. Technical report, http://hunch.net/?p=309, 2007.

[22] E. Liberty, N. Ailon, and A. Singer. Dense fast random projections and lean Walsh transforms. In *Proc. 12th International Workshop on Randomization and Approximation Techniques in Computer Science*, pages 512–522, 2008.

[23] J. Matousek. On variants of the Johnson–Lindenstrauss lemma. *Random Structures and Algorithms*, 33(2):142–156, 2008.

[24] C. McDiarmid. Concentration. In M. Habib, C. McDiarmid, J. Ramirez-Alfonsin, and B. Reed, editors, *Probabilistic Methods for Algorithmic Discrete Mathematics*, volume 16, pages 195–248. Springer, 1998.

[25] N. Nisan. Pseudorandom generators for space-bounded computation. *Combinatorica*, 12(4):449–461, 1992.

[26] V. Rokhlin, A. Szlam, and M. Tygert. A randomized algorithm for principal component analysis. *SIAM Journal on Matrix Analysis and Application*, 31(3):1100–1124, 2009.

[27] P. Sanders. On the competitive analysis of randomized static load balancing. In *Proc. 1st Workshop on Randomized Parallel Algorithms*, 1996.

[28] T. Sarlós. Improved approximation algorithms for large matrices via random projections. In *Proc.47th IEEE Symposium on Foundations of Computer Science*, pages 143–152, 2006.

[29] Q. Shi, J. Petterson, G. Dror, J. Langford, A. J. Smola, A. Strehl, and V. Vishwanathan. Hash kernels. In D. van Dyk and M. Welling, editors, *AISTATS 12*, 2009.

[30] D. A. Spielman and N. Srivastava. Graph sparsification by effective resistances. In *Proc. 40th Annual ACM Symposium on Theory of Computing*, pages 563–568, 2008.

[31] M. Thorup and Y. Zhang. Tabulation based 4-universal hashing with applications to second moment estimation. In *Proc. 15th Annual ACM-SIAM Symposium on Discrete Algorithms*, pages 615–624, 2004.

[32] S. Vempala. The random projection method. DIMACS Series in Discrete Mathematics and Theoretical Computer Science, 65. *American Mathematical Society, Providence, RI*, 2004.

[33] K. Weinberger, A. Dasgupta, J. Attenberg, J. Langford, and A. Smola. Feature hashing for large scale multitask learning. In *Proc. 26th International Conference on Machine Learning*, page 140, 2009.

9. APPENDIX

9.1 Proof of Lemma 6

PROOF. We show that $\sigma_1^2 \le \sigma_*^2$, with probability $1 - \delta/k$; the proof will then follow from the union bound.

Define the random variable $X_j = \delta_{1h(j)} x_j^2 - \frac{x_j^2}{k}$. Then, $\mathrm{E}_h[X_j] = 0$ and since $\|x\|_\infty < \frac{1}{\sqrt{c}}$, we have $X_j < \frac{1}{c}$. We also have $\mathrm{E}_h[X_j^2] = \mathrm{E}_h\left[\left(\delta_{1h(j)} x_j^2 - \frac{x_j^2}{k}\right)^2\right] = x_j^4\left(\frac{1}{k} + \frac{1}{k^2} - \frac{2}{k^2}\right) \le \frac{x_j^2}{c}\left(\frac{1}{k} - \frac{1}{k^2}\right)$, and

$$\sum_j \mathrm{E}_h[X_j^2] \le \sum_j \frac{x_j^2}{c}\left(\frac{1}{k} - \frac{1}{k^2}\right) \le \frac{1}{c}\left(\frac{1}{k} - \frac{1}{k^2}\right).$$

Also, $\sum_j X_j = \sigma_1^2 - \frac{1}{k}$. Plugging this into the Bernstein's inequality [24, Theorem 2.7],

$$\Pr\left[\sigma_1^2 - \frac{1}{k} > \frac{\alpha}{k}\right] = \Pr\left[\sum_j X_j > \frac{\alpha}{k}\right]$$
$$\le \exp\left(-\frac{(\alpha/k)^2/2}{\frac{1}{c}(\frac{1}{k} - \frac{1}{k^2}) + \frac{\alpha}{3ck}}\right) \le \exp\left(-\frac{c\alpha^2/2}{(k-1) + \alpha k/3}\right)$$
$$\le \exp\left(-\frac{c\alpha^2/2}{k + \alpha k/3}\right).$$

Since $\alpha \ge 3$,

$$\Pr\left[\sigma_1^2 - \frac{1}{k} > \frac{\alpha}{k}\right] \le \exp\left(-\frac{c\alpha^2/2}{2k\alpha/3}\right) \le \exp\left(-\frac{3c\alpha}{4k}\right).$$

Choosing $c = \frac{4k}{3\alpha}\log(\frac{k}{\delta})$, we get the above probability to be smaller than δ/k. Since $\alpha = \frac{1}{\epsilon\log(k/\delta)}$, and $k = \frac{12}{\epsilon^2}\log(1/\delta)$, we have that choosing $c = \frac{16}{\epsilon}\log(\frac{1}{\delta})\log^2(\frac{k}{\delta})$ is sufficient. □

9.2 Bounding the MGF's

We first compute the expectation of the MGF for different conditions on the hashing function. We begin by proving Lemma 7.

9.2.1 *Proof of Lemma 7*

PROOF. We have that $Z_i = \sum_{j \ne g \in h^{-1}(i)} r_j r_g x_j x_g$. Hence

$$Z_i = \left(\sum_{j:h(j)=i} x_j r_j\right)^2 - \sum_{j:h(j)=i} x_j^2 = Y_i^2 - \sigma_i^2$$

where $Y_i = \sum_{j:h(j)=i} x_j r_j$. Then,

$$\mathrm{E}_r[\exp(uY_i)] = \prod_{j:h(j)=i} \mathrm{E}_r[\exp(ur_j x_j)]$$
$$= \prod_{j:h(j)=i}\left(\frac{1}{2}\exp(ux_j) + \frac{1}{2}\exp(-ux_j)\right)$$
$$\le \prod_{j:h(j)=i}\exp\left(\frac{u^2 x_j^2}{2}\right) \le \exp\left(\frac{u^2\sigma_i^2}{2}\right).$$

By the Markov inequality, we get the probability of Y_i being larger than t as

$$\Pr[Y_i > t] \le \frac{\mathrm{E}_r[\exp(uY_i)]}{\exp(ut)} \le \frac{\exp\left(\frac{u^2\sigma_i^2}{2}\right)}{\exp(ut)} \le \exp\left(-\frac{t^2}{2\sigma_i^2}\right),$$

by choosing $u = \frac{t}{\sigma_i^2}$. Note that we do not need to worry about σ_i being zero, as then $Y_i = 0$. Then, we bound $\mathrm{E}_r[\exp(uZ_i)]$ as follows. Denote $p(t) = \Pr[Z_i = t]$. We first compute the expectation with respect to r. For any value of $\theta > 0$, we have

$$\mathrm{E}_r[\exp(uZ_i)] = \sum_{t\in(-\infty,\infty)} \exp(ut)p(t)$$
$$\le \sum_{t\in(-\infty,\theta]} \exp(ut)p(t) + \sum_{t>\theta} \exp(ut)p(t).$$

The first term can be bounded as follows:

$$\sum_{t\in(-\infty,\theta)} \exp(ut)p(t) \leq \sum_{t\in[0,\theta]} \left(1+ut+\sum_{j=2}^{\infty}\frac{u^j t^j}{j!}\right)p(t)$$
$$\leq \sum_{t\in(-\infty,\theta]} p(t) + \sum_{t\in(-\infty,\theta]} utp(t) + \sum_{t\in(-\infty,\theta]}\sum_{j=2}^{\infty}\frac{u^j t^j}{j!}dF(t)$$
$$\leq \sum_{t\in(-\infty,\infty)} p(t) + \sum_{t\in(-\infty,\infty)} utp(t) + \sum_{t\in(-\infty,\theta]}\sum_{j=2}^{\infty}\frac{u^j t^j}{j!}p(t),$$

where the last inequality follows since in the range $[\theta,\infty]$, the integral is positive. Then, the calculation can be simplified as follows:

$$\sum_{t\in(-\infty,\theta)} \exp(ut)p(t) \leq \sum_{t\in(-\infty,\infty)} (p(t)+utp(t))$$
$$+ \sum_{t\in(-\infty,\theta)}\sum_{j=2}^{\infty}\frac{u^j t^j}{j!}p(t)$$
$$\leq 1+0+\sum_{t\in(-\infty,\theta)}\sum_{j=2}^{\infty}\frac{u^j t^j}{j!}p(t)$$
$$\leq 1+\sum_{t\in(-\infty,\theta)}\frac{t^2}{\theta^2}\sum_{j=2}^{\infty}\frac{u^j\theta^j}{j!}p(t) \qquad \text{since } t<\theta \text{ in this range}$$
$$\leq 1+\frac{1}{\theta^2}(\exp(u\theta)-1-u\theta)\mathrm{E}_r[Z_i^2].$$

For the second term, we have

$$\sum_{t>\theta}\exp(ut)p(t)$$
$$\leq \sum_{\ell=u\theta}^{\infty}\exp(\ell+1)\left(\Pr\left[Z_i>\frac{\ell}{u}+1\right]-\Pr\left[Z_i>\frac{\ell}{u}\right]\right)$$
$$\leq \sum_{\ell=u\theta}^{\infty}\exp(\ell+1)\Pr\left[Z_i>\frac{\ell}{u}+1\right]$$
$$\leq \sum_{\ell=u\theta}^{\infty}\exp(\ell+1)\Pr\left[Y_i^2>\sigma_i^2+\frac{\ell}{u}+1\right]$$
$$\leq \sum_{\ell=u\theta}^{\infty}\exp(\ell+1)\exp\left(-\frac{\ell/u+\sigma_i^2}{2\sigma_i^2}\right)$$
$$\leq \sum_{\ell=u\theta}^{\infty}\exp\left(\ell+1-\frac{\ell}{2u\sigma_i^2}-\frac{1}{2}\right)$$
$$\leq \sqrt{e}\sum_{\ell=u\theta}^{\infty}\exp\left(\ell-\frac{\ell}{2u\sigma_i^2}\right).$$

By assumption of the lemma, since $u<\frac{1}{4\sigma_i^2}$, we have that $\ell-\frac{\ell}{2u\sigma_i^2}<-\frac{\ell}{4u\sigma_i^2}$. With this restriction,

$$\sum_{t>\theta}\exp(ut)p(t)\leq\sqrt{e}\cdot\sum_{\ell=u\theta}^{\infty}\exp\left(-\frac{\ell}{4u\sigma_i^2}\right)$$
$$\leq 2\sqrt{e}\cdot\exp\left(-\frac{u\theta}{4u\sigma_i^2}\right)=2\sqrt{e}\cdot\exp\left(-\frac{\theta}{4\sigma_i^2}\right)\leq 4\exp\left(-\frac{\theta}{4\sigma_*^2}\right).$$

By putting together the two parts, we have that

$$\mathrm{E}_r\left[\exp(uZ_i)\right]\leq\left(1+\frac{1}{\theta^2}(\exp(u\theta)-1-u\theta)\mathrm{E}_r[Z_i^2]\right)$$
$$+4\exp\left(-\frac{\theta}{4\sigma_*^2}\right).$$

Choosing $\theta=4\sigma_*^2\ln(k/\delta)$, the proof is complete. □

9.3 Continued proof of Lemma 9

We finish the proof of Lemma 9 by showing that g_s is decreasing. To this end, we prove that for all $A\subseteq[d]$ and for all $a\in[d]\setminus A$, $g_s(A\cup\{a\})\leq g_s(A)$. Recalling the definition of $g_s(A)$, we have

$$g_s(A)=\mathrm{E}\left[\exp\left(u\sum_{i=1}^{s-1}\hat{Z}_i\right)\mid h^{-1}(s)=A\right]$$
$$=\mathrm{E}\left[\mathrm{E}\left[\exp\left(u\sum_{i=1}^{s-1}\hat{Z}_i\right)\mid\forall j:h(j)\right]\mid h^{-1}(s)=A\right], \tag{12}$$

where the inner expectation is over the random variables $\{r_j\}$ only. Since h is completely independent we have that

$$g_s(A)=\sum_{\substack{(h_1,\ldots,h_d)\in[k]^d,\\ \forall j:h_j=s\Leftrightarrow j\in A}}\frac{\mathrm{E}\left[\exp\left(u\sum_{i=1}^{s-1}\hat{Z}_i\right)\mid\forall j:h(j)=h_j\right]}{(k-1)^{d-|A|}},$$

and similarly

$$g_s(A\cup\{a\})$$
$$=\sum_{\substack{(h_1,\ldots,h_d)\in[k]^d,\\ \forall j:h_j=s\Leftrightarrow j\in A\cup\{a\}}}\frac{\mathrm{E}\left[\exp\left(u\sum_{i=1}^{s-1}\hat{Z}_i\right)\mid\forall j:h(j)=h_j\right]}{(k-1)^{d-|A|-1}}.$$

Therefore it is sufficient to show that for all

$$(h_1,\ldots,h_{a-1},h_{a+1},\ldots,h_d)\in[k]^{d-1}$$

with $\forall j\neq a:h_j=s\Leftrightarrow j\in A$ it holds that

$$\sum_{h_a\in[k]\setminus\{s\}}\frac{\mathrm{E}\left[\exp\left(u\sum_{i=1}^{s-1}\hat{Z}_i\right)\mid\forall j:h(j)=h_j\right]}{k-1}$$
$$\geq\mathrm{E}\left[\exp\left(u\sum_{i=1}^{s-1}\hat{Z}_i\right)\mid\forall j\neq a:h(j)=h_j,h(a)=s\right].$$

We shall prove the following stronger inequality: for all $(h_1,\ldots,h_{a-1},h_{a+1},\ldots,h_d)\in[k]^{d-1}$ with $\forall j\neq a:h_j=s\Leftrightarrow j\in A$ and for all $h_a\in[k]\setminus\{s\}$ it holds that

$$\mathrm{E}\left[\exp\left(u\sum_{i=1}^{s-1}\hat{Z}_i\right)\mid\forall j:h(j)=h_j\right]$$
$$\geq\mathrm{E}\left[\exp\left(u\sum_{i=1}^{s-1}\hat{Z}_i\right)\mid\forall j\neq a:h(j)=h_j,h(a)=s\right].$$

Now observe that only r are random in the above expectations and that $\hat{Z}_i$ are conditionally independent given h. Therefore,

$$\mathrm{E}\left[\exp\left(\sum_{i=1}^{s-1}u\hat{Z}_i\right)\mid h\right]=\prod_{i=1}^{s-1}\mathrm{E}\left[\exp\left(u\hat{Z}_i\right)\mid h\right].$$

From the non-negativity of the exponential function, it follows that it is sufficient to show that for all $i = 1, \ldots, s-1$ and for all $(h_1, \ldots, h_{a-1}, h_{a+1}, \ldots, h_d) \in [k]^{d-1}$ with $\forall j \neq a : h_j = s \Leftrightarrow j \in A$ and for all $h_a \in [k] \setminus \{s\}$ it holds that

$$\mathrm{E}_L \geq \mathrm{E}_R, \text{ where} \tag{13}$$
$$\mathrm{E}_L = \mathrm{E}\left[\exp\left(u\hat{Z}_i\right) \mid \forall j : h(j) = h_j\right]$$
$$\mathrm{E}_R = \mathrm{E}\left[\exp\left(u\hat{Z}_i\right) \mid \forall j \neq a : h(j) = h_j, h(a) = s\right].$$

We prove inequality (13) by a case analysis. If $h_a \neq i$, then $\mathrm{E}_L = \mathrm{E}_R$ by definition. If $h_a = i$ and the ith bucket of E_L's hash function is bad, then $\mathrm{E}_L = G(u, \sigma_*^4) \geq \mathrm{E}_R$, as shown earlier in Corollary 8.

If $h_a = i$ and the ith bucket of E_L's hash function is good then, the ith bucket of E_R's hash function is also good. As before, define

$$V_a = \sum_{j \neq a} \sum_{g \neq a, j \neq g} r_j r_g x_j x_g \delta_{h(j)i} \delta_{h(g)i},$$

and

$$W_a = \sum_{j \neq a} r_j x_j x_a \delta_{h(j)i} \delta_{h(a)i}.$$

Again, note that if the ith bucket is good as assumed then $\hat{Z}_i = Z_i = V_a + r_a W_a$. Therefore we have that

$$\mathrm{E}_L = \mathrm{E}[\mathrm{E}\left[\exp\left(uV_a + u \cdot r_a W_a\right) \mid \forall j : h(j) = h_j, \forall j \neq a : r_j\right] \mid \forall j : h(j) = h_j]. \tag{14}$$

Now observe that only r_a is random in the inner expectation and

$$\mathrm{E}\left[uV_a + u \cdot r_a W_a \mid \forall j : h(j) = h_j, \forall j \neq a : r_j\right] = uV_a.$$

Thus from $\mathrm{E}[\exp(x)] \geq \exp(\mathrm{E}[x])$, it follows that

$$\mathrm{E}\left[\exp\left(uV_a + u \cdot r_a W_a\right) \mid \forall j : h(j) = h_j, \forall j \neq a : r_j\right] \geq \exp\left(uV_a\right)$$

as before. Plugging the latter into (14) we arrive at

$$\mathrm{E}_L \geq \mathrm{E}\left[\exp\left(uV_a\right) \mid \forall j : h(j) = h_j\right] \tag{15}$$
$$= \mathrm{E}\left[\exp\left(uV_a\right) \mid \forall j \neq a : h(j) = h_j, h(a) = s\right].$$

Here the last equality follows from the fact that all r and h values are independent and since V_a does not depend on a. If $h^{-1}(s) = A \cup \{a\}$ and the i hash bucket is good as assumed then $\hat{Z}_i = Z_i = V_a$ and we observe that

$$\mathrm{E}\left[\exp\left(uV_a\right) \mid \forall j \neq a : h(j) = h_j, h(a) = s\right] = \mathrm{E}_R \tag{16}$$

Combining (15) and (16), we conclude that $\mathrm{E}_L \geq \mathrm{E}_R$ for all cases and hence g_s is decreasing as claimed.

9.4 Proof of Theorem 11 (i)

PROOF. Recall that the random variable $\hat{Z}_i$ is defined as

$$\hat{Z}_i = \begin{cases} Z_i & \text{if } \mathcal{G}_i, \\ \frac{1}{u} \log G(u, \sigma_*^4) & \text{else.} \end{cases}$$

Note that $G(u, \sigma_*^4) > 1$, and hence for $u > 0$, $\frac{1}{u} \log G(u, \sigma_*^4) > 0$. Also recall that $\mathcal{G}_i$ is the indicator vector for bucket i being good, and $\mathcal{G}$ is the indicator for the hash function being good. By definition of $\hat{Z}_i$, since $\frac{1}{u} \log G(u, \sigma_*^4) > 0$, $\sum_i Z_i \wedge \mathcal{G} < \sum_i \hat{Z}_i$ and hence we have that,

$$\Pr\left[\sum_i Z_i > \epsilon\right] \leq \Pr\left[\sum_i Z_i > \epsilon \wedge \mathcal{G}\right] + \Pr[\bar{\mathcal{G}}]$$
$$\leq \Pr\left[\sum_i \hat{Z}_i > \epsilon\right] + \delta. \tag{17}$$

Thus, we prove a bound on $\mathrm{E}[\exp(u \sum_i \hat{Z}_i)]$ and thus bound on $\Pr[\sum_i \hat{Z}_i > \epsilon]$. Taking expectations over both r and h, and using $\Pr[\bar{\mathcal{G}}] < \delta$,

$$\mathrm{E}[\exp(u\hat{Z}_i)] \leq \mathrm{E}[\exp(uZ_i) \mid \mathcal{G}] \Pr[\mathcal{G}] + G(u, \sigma_*^4) \Pr[\bar{\mathcal{G}}]$$
$$\leq 1 + \frac{1}{\theta^2}(\exp(u\theta) - 1 - u\theta)\left(\frac{1}{k^2}(1-\delta) + \sigma_*^4 \delta\right) + \frac{4\delta}{k},$$

where we combined the appropriate terms from the two parts of the sum. Recall that $\sigma_*^4 < 1$. By choosing $\delta < \frac{1}{k^2}$, we have that

$$\mathrm{E}[\exp(u\hat{Z}_i)] \leq 1 + \frac{1}{\theta^2}(\exp(u\theta) - 1 - u\theta)\frac{2}{k^2} + \frac{4\delta}{k}$$
$$\leq \exp\left(\frac{2}{k^2\theta^2}(\exp(u\theta) - 1 - u\theta) + \frac{4\delta}{k}\right).$$

Taking the product over the k terms, by using Lemma 10,

$$\mathrm{E}[\prod_i \exp(u\hat{Z}_i)] \leq \prod_i \mathrm{E}[\exp(u\hat{Z}_i)]$$
$$\leq \exp\left(\frac{2}{k\theta^2}(\exp(u\theta) - 1 - u\theta) + 4\delta\right).$$

For completeness, we show how to determine the optimal u.

$$\Pr\left[\sum_i \hat{Z}_i > \epsilon\right] \leq \frac{\mathrm{E}[\exp(u\sum_i \hat{Z}_i)]}{\exp(u\epsilon)} \leq \prod_i \mathrm{E}[\exp(u\hat{Z}_i)]\exp(-u\epsilon)$$
$$\leq \exp\left(\frac{2}{k\theta^2}(\exp(u\theta) - 1 - u\theta) + \delta - u\epsilon\right) \leq \exp\left(H(u) + \delta\right),$$

where we define $H(u) = \frac{2}{k\theta^2}(\exp(u\theta) - 1 - u\theta) - u\epsilon$. Setting the derivative $H'(u) = 0$, we get $\frac{2}{k\theta^2}(\theta\exp(u\theta) - \theta) - \epsilon = 0$, and hence

$$u = \frac{1}{\theta}\ln\left(1 + \frac{k\epsilon\theta}{2}\right) = \frac{1}{4\sigma_*^2 \ln(k/\delta)} \ln\left(1 + \frac{4k\epsilon\sigma_*^2 \ln(k/\delta)}{2}\right).$$

Note that we need to restrict $u < \frac{1}{4\sigma_*^2}$. We need $\frac{\ln(1 + \frac{4k\epsilon\sigma_*^2 \ln(k/\delta)}{2})}{\ln(k/\delta)} < 1$, which is true if setting $\frac{4k\epsilon\sigma_*^2 \ln(k/\delta)}{2} < \frac{k}{2\delta}$, or $\epsilon < \frac{k}{4\delta(1+\alpha)\ln(k/\delta)}$, which is permissive. Using this value of u, we have that (skipping the simplifications)

$$H = \frac{2}{k\theta^2}\left(\frac{k\epsilon\theta}{2} - \left(1 + \frac{k\epsilon\theta}{2}\right)\ln\left(1 + \frac{k\epsilon\theta}{2}\right)\right)$$
$$\leq \frac{2}{k\theta^2}\frac{\frac{k^2\epsilon^2\theta^2}{4}}{2 + \frac{2k\epsilon\theta}{6}} \leq \frac{-k\epsilon^2}{2(2 + \frac{k\epsilon\theta}{3})},$$

which is the trick that Bernstein uses: $(1+x)\ln(1+x) - x \leq \frac{-x^2}{2+2x/3}$. Plugging in this value of H, we get that

$$\Pr\left[\sum_i \hat{Z}_i > \epsilon\right] \leq \exp\left(\frac{-3k\epsilon^2}{4(3 + (1+\alpha)\epsilon\ln(k/\delta))} + 4\delta\right). \quad \square$$

The proof of Theorem 11(ii) is similar to the above and is omitted in this version.

A Deterministic Single Exponential Time Algorithm for Most Lattice Problems based on Voronoi Cell Computations*

[Extended Abstract]

Daniele Micciancio
University of California, San Diego
daniele@cs.ucsd.edu

Panagiotis Voulgaris
University of California, San Diego
pvoulgar@cs.ucsd.edu

ABSTRACT

We give deterministic $\tilde{O}(2^{2n+o(n)})$-time algorithms to solve all the most important computational problems on point lattices in NP, including the Shortest Vector Problem (SVP), Closest Vector Problem (CVP), and Shortest Independent Vectors Problem (SIVP). This improves the $n^{O(n)}$ running time of the best previously known algorithms for CVP (Kannan, Math. Operation Research 12(3):415-440, 1987) and SIVP (Micciancio, Proc. of SODA, 2008), and gives a deterministic and asymptotically faster alternative to the $2^{O(n)}$-time (and space) randomized algorithm for SVP of (Ajtai, Kumar and Sivakumar, STOC 2001). The core of our algorithm is a new method to solve the closest vector problem with preprocessing (CVPP) that uses the Voronoi cell of the lattice (described as intersection of half-spaces) as the result of the preprocessing function. In the process, we also give algorithms for several other lattice problems, including computing the kissing number of a lattice, and computing the set of all Voronoi relevant vectors. All our algorithms are deterministic, and have $2^{O(n)}$ time and space complexity.

Categories and Subject Descriptors

F.2.2 [**Nonnumerical Algorithms and Problems**]: Computations on discrete structures

General Terms

Algorithms, Performance, Theory

Keywords

Lattice algorithms, SVP, CVP, SIVP, Voronoi Cell

*Supported in part by NSF grants CCF-0634909 and CNS-0831536. Any opinions, findings, and conclusions or recommendations expressed in this material are those of the author and do not necessarily reflect the views of the National Science Foundation.

STOC'10, June 5–8, 2010, Cambridge, Massachusetts, USA

1. INTRODUCTION

A d-dimensional lattice Λ is a discrete subgroup of the Euclidean space $\mathbb{R}^d$, and is customarily represented as the set of all integer linear combinations of $n \leq d$ basis vectors $\mathbf{B} = [\mathbf{b}_1, \ldots, \mathbf{b}_n] \in \mathbb{R}^{d \times n}$. There are many famous algorithmic problems on point lattices, the most important of which are:

- The shortest vector problem (SVP): given a basis $\mathbf{B}$, find a shortest nonzero vector in the lattice generated by $\mathbf{B}$.
- The closest vector problem (CVP): given a basis $\mathbf{B}$ and a target vector $\mathbf{t} \in \mathbb{R}^d$, find the lattice vector generated by $\mathbf{B}$ that is closest to $\mathbf{t}$.
- The shortest independent vectors problem (SIVP): given a basis $\mathbf{B}$, find n linearly independent lattice vectors in the lattice generated by $\mathbf{B}$ that are as short as possible.

Beside being classic mathematical problems in the study of the *geometry of numbers* [14], these problems play an important role in many computer science and communication theory applications. SVP and CVP have been used to solve many landmark algorithmic problems in theoretical computer science, like integer programming [34, 30], factoring polynomials over the rationals [33], checking the solvability by radicals [32], solving low density subset-sum problems [18] and breaking the Merkle-Hellman cryptosystem [44] (among many other cryptanalysis problems [29, 42].) SIVP is the main problem underlying the construction of lattice based cryptographic hash functions with worst-case/average-case connection [4, 40]. SVP and CVP also have many applications in communication theory, e.g., lattice coding for the Gaussian channel and vector quantization [17].

The complexity of lattice problems has been investigated intensively. All three problems mentioned above have been shown to be NP-hard both to solve exactly [53, 3, 12], or even approximate within small (constant or sub-polynomial in n) approximation factors [12, 8, 19, 13, 36, 31, 27]. Much effort has gone into the development and analysis of algorithms both to solve these problems exactly [30, 28, 25, 10, 5, 6, 11] or to efficiently find approximate solutions [33, 48, 47, 50, 49, 21, 22].

In this paper we focus on the complexity of finding exact solutions to these problems. Of course, as the problems are NP-hard, no polynomial time solution is expected to exist.

Still, the complexity of solving lattice problems exactly is interesting both because many applications (e.g., in mathematics and communication theory [17]) involve lattices in relatively small dimension, and because approximation algorithms for high dimensional lattices [47, 50, 21, 22] (for which exact solution is not feasible) typically involve the exact solution of low dimensional subproblems. The best deterministic polynomial time algorithm to solve any of these lattice problems exactly is still essentially the one discovered by Kannan [30] in 1983, running in time $n^{O(n)}$, where n is the dimension of the lattice. Subsequent work [28, 25] lead to improvements in the constant in the exponent, mostly through a better analysis, reducing the upper bound on the running time down to $n^{0.184n}$ for SVP and $n^{0.5n}$ for CVP and SIVP. The only problem that has seen asymptotically significant improvements in the exponent is SVP, for which Ajtai, Kumar and Sivakumar [5] gave a *randomized* algorithm running in time (and space) $2^{O(n)}$, typically referred to as the AKS Sieve. Following [5] much work has been devoted to better understand and improve the Sieve algorithm. Still the main questions posed in [5] didn't see much progress. Is the use of randomization (and exponential space) necessary to lower the time complexity of SVP from $n^{O(n)}$ to $2^{O(n)}$? Can algorithms with similar running time be devised for other lattice problems, like SIVP and CVP?

In [43, 41, 45], improved analysis and variants of the AKS sieve are studied, but still using the same approach leading to randomized algorithms. Extensions of the AKS sieve algorithm to other lattice problems like CVP and SIVP have been investigated in [6, 11], but only led to approximation algorithms which are not guaranteed (even probabilistically) to find the best solution, except for certain very special classes of lattices [11]. A possible explanation for the difficulty of extending the result of [5] to the exact solution of SIVP and CVP was offered by Micciancio in [38], where it is shown (among other things) that CVP, SIVP and all other lattice problems considered in [11], with the exception of SVP, are equivalent in their exact version under deterministic polynomial time dimension preserving reductions. So, either all of them are solvable in single exponential time $2^{O(n)}$, or none of them admits such an algorithm.

In this paper we resolve this question in the affirmative, giving a deterministic single exponential time algorithm for CVP, and therefore by the reductions in [23, 38], also to SVP, SIVP and several other lattice problems in NP considered in the literature. This improves the time complexity of the best previously known algorithm for CVP, SIVP, etc. [30] from $n^{O(n)}$ to $2^{O(n)}$. In the case of SVP, we achieve single exponential time as in [5, 43, 41, 45], but without using randomization and achieving a better constant in the exponent. In the process, we also provide deterministic single exponential time algorithms for various other classic computational problems in lattices, like computing the kissing number, and computing the list of all Voronoi relevant vectors.

We remark that all our algorithms, just like [5], use exponential space. So, the question whether exponential space is required to solve lattice problems in single exponential time remains open.

1.1 Our techniques.

At the core of all our results is a new technique for the solution of the closest vector problem with preprocessing (CVPP). We recall that CVPP is a variant of CVP where some side information about the lattice is given as a hint together with the input. The hint may depend on the lattice, but not on the target vector. Typically, in the context of polynomial time algorithms, the hint is restricted to have polynomial size, but since here we study exponential time algorithms, one can reasonably consider hints that have size $2^{O(n)}$. The hint used by our algorithm is a description of the Voronoi cell of the lattice. We recall that the Voronoi cell of a lattice is the set $\mathcal{V}$ of all points (in Euclidean space) that are closer to the origin than to any other lattice point. The Voronoi cell $\mathcal{V}$ is a convex body, symmetric about the origin, and can be described as the intersection of half-spaces $H_{\mathbf{v}}$, where for any nonzero lattice point $\mathbf{v}$, $H_{\mathbf{v}}$ is the set of all points that are closer to the origin than to $\mathbf{v}$. It is not necessary to consider all $\mathbf{v} \in V \setminus \{\mathbf{0}\}$ when taking this intersection. One can restrict the intersection to the so called *Voronoi relevant* vectors, which are the lattice vectors $\mathbf{v}$ such that $\mathbf{v}/2$ is the center of a facet of $\mathcal{V}$. Since the Voronoi cell of a lattice can be shown to have at most $2(2^n - 1)$ facets, $\mathcal{V}$ can be expressed as a finite intersection of at most $2(2^n - 1)$ half-spaces. Throughout this paper, we assume that the Voronoi cell of a lattice is always described by such a list of half-spaces.

The relation between the Voronoi cell and CVPP is well known, and easy to explain. In CVPP, we want to find the lattice point $\mathbf{v}$ closest to a given target vector $\mathbf{t}$. It is easy to see that this is equivalent to finding a lattice vector $\mathbf{v}$ such that $\mathbf{t} - \mathbf{v}$ belongs to the (closed) Voronoi cell of the lattice. In other words, CVP can be equivalently formulated as the problem of finding a point in the set $(\Lambda + \mathbf{t}) \cap \bar{\mathcal{V}}$, where $\bar{\mathcal{V}}$ is the topological closure of $\mathcal{V}$. The idea of using the Voronoi cell to solve CVP is not new. For example, a simple greedy algorithm for CVPP based on the knowledge of the Voronoi cell of the lattice is given in [52]. The idea behind this algorithm (called the Iterative Slicer) is to make $\mathbf{t}$ shorter and shorter by subtracting Voronoi relevant vectors from it. Notice that if $\mathbf{t} \notin H_{\mathbf{v}}$, then the length of $\mathbf{t}$ can be reduced by subtracting $\mathbf{v}$ from $\mathbf{t}$. So, as long as $\mathbf{t}$ is outside $\bar{\mathcal{V}}$, we can make further progress and find a shorter vector. Unfortunately, this simple strategy to solve CVPP using the Voronoi cell is not known to perform any better than previous algorithms. [52] only proves that the algorithm terminates after a finite number of iterations, and a close inspection of the proof reveals that the best upper bound that can be derived using the methods of [52] is of the form $n^{O(n)}$: the running time of the Iterative Slicer is bound by a volume argument, counting the number of lattice points of norm at most $\|\mathbf{t}\|$, and this can be well above $2^{O(n)}$ or even $n^{O(n)}$.

In the next two paragraphs we first sketch our new algorithm to solve CVPP using the Voronoi cell $\mathcal{V}$ in time $2^{O(n)}$, and then we show how to use the CVPP algorithm to recursively implement the preprocessing function and compute the Voronoi cell $\mathcal{V}$. Since both the preprocessing and CVPP computation take time $2^{O(n)}$, combining the two pieces gives an algorithm to solve CVP (and a host of other lattice problems, like SVP, SIVP, etc.) without preprocessing.

The CVPP algorithm.

Our CVPP algorithm works as follows. First we reduce the general CVPP to a special case where the target vector is guaranteed to belong to twice the Voronoi cell $2\bar{\mathcal{V}}$. This can be done very easily by a polynomial time Turing reduction. Next we solve the restricted CVPP problem using a variant of the Iterative Slicer of [52]. The main idea remains the same, if $\mathbf{t}_i \notin \bar{\mathcal{V}}$ we can select a relevant vector $\mathbf{v}_i$, such that $\mathbf{t}_{i+1} = \mathbf{t}_i - \mathbf{v}_i$ is shorter than $\mathbf{t}_i$. Starting with the target vector $\mathbf{t}$ and repeating this procedure the algorithm generates shorter and shorter points from the coset $\Lambda + \mathbf{t}$, until a vector $\mathbf{t}' \in \bar{\mathcal{V}} \cap \Lambda + \mathbf{t}$ is found. Then $\mathbf{t} - \mathbf{t}'$ is a closest lattice vector to $\mathbf{t}$. The novelty of our CVPP algorithm is a new selection strategy for $\mathbf{v}_i$, so that if $\mathbf{t}_i \in 2\bar{\mathcal{V}}$ then $\mathbf{t}_{i+1} = \mathbf{t}_i - \mathbf{v}_i$ is both shorter than $\mathbf{t}_i$ and in $2\bar{\mathcal{V}}$. So, given a target vector $\mathbf{t}$ in $2\bar{\mathcal{V}}$ all the generated points $\mathbf{t}_i$ are in $2\bar{\mathcal{V}}$. We use this property to bound the number of generated points $\mathbf{t}_i$ by 2^n and the running time by $\tilde{O}(2^{2n})$. This is an improvement over the graph traversal technique used in earlier versions of this paper with running time (at least) $\tilde{O}(2^{3n})$.

Computing the Voronoi cell.

We have sketched how to solve CVPP, given the Voronoi cell of the lattice. This leaves us with the problem of computing the Voronoi cell, a task typically considered even harder than CVP. To this end, we use a method of [1] to compute the Voronoi cell of a lattice Λ, making 2^n calls to a CVPP oracle for the same lattice Λ. We combine this with a standard rank reduction procedure implicit in enumeration algorithms [30, 25]. This procedure allows to solve CVPP in a lattice Λ of rank n making only $2^{o(n)}$ calls to a CVPP oracle for a certain sub-lattice Λ' with rank $n-1$. Combining all the pieces together we obtain an algorithm that computes the Voronoi cell of a lattice Λ by building a sequence of lattices $\Lambda_1 \subset \Lambda_2 \subset \cdots \subset \Lambda_n = \Lambda$ with rank $\text{rank}(\Lambda_i) = i$, and iteratively computing the Voronoi cell of Λ_{i+1} using the previously computed Voronoi cell of Λ_i.

Organization.

The rest of the paper is organized as follows. In the next subsection we mention some additional related work. In Section 2 we give some background about lattices. Our algorithms are described and analyzed in Section 3. Section 4 concludes with a discussion of open problems and directions for future research.

1.2 Related work

Most relevant work has already been described in the introduction. Here we mention a few more related papers. The closest vector problem with preprocessing has been investigated in several papers [35, 20, 46, 16, 7], mostly with the goal of showing that CVP is NP-hard even for fixed families of lattices, or devising polynomial time approximation algorithms (with super-polynomial time preprocessing). In summary, CVPP is NP-hard to approximate for any constant (or certain sub-polynomial) factors [7], and it can be approximated in polynomial time within a factor $\sqrt{n}$ [2], at least in its distance estimation variant. Here we use CVPP mostly as a building block to give a modular description of our CVP algorithm. We use CVPP to recursively implement the preprocessing function, and then to solve the actual CVP instance. It is an interesting open problem if a similar bootstrapping can be performed using the polynomial time CVPP approximation algorithm of [2], to yield a polynomial time solution to $\sqrt{n}$-approximate CVP.

The problem of computing the Voronoi cell of a lattice is of fundamental importance in many mathematics and communication theory applications. There are several formulations of this problem. In this paper we consider the problem of generating the list of facets ($(n-1)$-dimensional faces) of the Voronoi cell, as done also in [1, 52]. Sometime one wants to generate the list of vertices (i.e., one dimensional faces), or even a complete description including all faces in dimension 1 to $n-1$. This is done in [54, 51], but it is a much more complex problem, as in general the Voronoi cell can have as many as $n! = n^{\Omega(n)}$ vertices, so they cannot be computed in single exponential time. In [51] it is also shown that computing the number of vertices of the Voronoi cell of a lattice is $\#P$-hard.

2. PRELIMINARIES

In this section we give some background about lattices, and the algorithmic problems studied in this paper. For a more in-depth discussion, see [39]. The d-dimensional Euclidean space is denoted $\mathbb{R}^d$. We use bold lower case letters (e.g., $\mathbf{x}$) to denote vectors, and bold upper case letters (e.g., $\mathbf{M}$) to denote matrices. The ith coordinate of $\mathbf{x}$ is denoted x_i. For a set $S \subseteq \mathbb{R}^d$, $\mathbf{x} \in \mathbb{R}^d$ and $a \in \mathbb{R}$, we let $S + \mathbf{x} = \{\mathbf{y} + \mathbf{x} \colon \mathbf{y} \in S\}$ denote the translate of S by $\mathbf{x}$, and $aS = \{a\mathbf{y} \colon \mathbf{y} \in S\}$ denote the scaling of S by a. The Euclidean norm (also known as the ℓ_2 norm) of a vector $\mathbf{x} \in \mathbb{R}^d$ is $\|\mathbf{x}\| = (\sum_i x_i^2)^{1/2}$, and the associated distance is $\text{dist}(\mathbf{x}, \mathbf{y}) = \|\mathbf{x} - \mathbf{y}\|$. The linear space spanned by a set of vectors S is denoted $\text{span}(S) = \{\sum_i x_i \mathbf{s}_i : x_i \in \mathbb{R}, \mathbf{s}_i \in S\}$. The affine span of a set of vectors S is defined as $\mathbf{x} + \text{span}(S - \mathbf{x})$ for any $\mathbf{x} \in S$, and does not depend on the choice of $\mathbf{x}$.

Lattices.

A d-dimensional *lattice* of rank n is the set of all integer combinations

$$\left\{ \sum_{i=1}^{n} x_i \mathbf{b}_i \colon x_i \in \mathbb{Z} \text{ for } 1 \leq i \leq n \right\}$$

of n linearly independent vectors $\mathbf{b}_1, \ldots, \mathbf{b}_n$ in $\mathbb{R}^d$. The set of vectors $\mathbf{b}_1, \ldots, \mathbf{b}_n$ is called a *basis* for the lattice. A basis can be represented by the matrix $\mathbf{B} = [\mathbf{b}_1, \ldots, \mathbf{b}_n] \in \mathbb{R}^{d \times n}$ having the basis vectors as columns. The lattice generated by $\mathbf{B}$ is denoted $\mathcal{L}(\mathbf{B})$. Notice that $\mathcal{L}(\mathbf{B}) = \{\mathbf{B}\mathbf{x} \colon \mathbf{x} \in \mathbb{Z}^n\}$, where $\mathbf{B}\mathbf{x}$ is the usual matrix-vector multiplication. A sub-lattice of $\mathcal{L}(\mathbf{B})$ is a lattice $\mathcal{L}(\mathbf{S})$ such that $\mathcal{L}(\mathbf{S}) \subseteq \mathcal{L}(\mathbf{B})$.

The Gram-Schmidt orthogonalization of a basis $\mathbf{B}$ is the sequence of vectors $\mathbf{b}_1^*, \ldots, \mathbf{b}_n^*$, where $\mathbf{b}_i^*$ is the component of $\mathbf{b}_i$ orthogonal to $\text{span}(\mathbf{b}_1, \ldots, \mathbf{b}_{i-1})$.

The following two classical algorithms are used in this paper. The LLL basis reduction algorithm [33] runs in polynomial time, and on input a lattice basis, outputs a basis for the same lattice such that $\|\mathbf{b}_{i+1}^*\|^2 \geq \|\mathbf{b}_i^*\|^2/2$. (LLL reduced bases have other properties, but this is all we need here.) The Nearest Plane algorithm [9], on input a basis $\mathbf{B}$ and a target vector $\mathbf{t}$, finds a lattice point $\mathbf{v} \in \mathcal{L}(\mathbf{B})$ such that $\|\mathbf{v} - \mathbf{t}\| \leq (1/2)\sqrt{\sum_i \|\mathbf{b}_i^*\|^2}$.

Lattice problems.

In this paper we are mostly concerned with the SVP, CVP and SIVP problems defined in the introduction. Our results give algorithms of several other lattice problems like the Subspace Avoiding Problem (SAP) the Generalized Closest Vector Problem (GCVP), and the Successive Minima Problem (SMP) considered in the lattice algorithms literature [11,

38]. The results for all problems other than CVP and SVP are obtained in a back-box way by reduction to CVP [38], and we refer the reader to [11, 38] for details.

For simplicity in this paper we consider only inputs to lattice problems where all the entries in the basis matrix $\mathbf{B}$ have bit size polynomial in n, i.e., $\log(\|\mathbf{B}\|) = \text{poly}(n)$. This allows to express the complexity of lattice problems simply as a function of a single parameter, the lattice rank n. All the results in this paper can be easily adapted to the general case by introducing an explicit bound $\log\|\mathbf{B}\| \leq M$ on the size of the entries, and letting the time and space complexity bound depend polynomially in M. We will use $f = \tilde{O}(g)$ when $f(n)$ is bounded by $g(n)$ up to polylogarithmic factors, i.e., $f(n) \leq \log^c g(n) \cdot g(n)$ for some constant c and all sufficiently large n.

Voronoi cells.

The (open) Voronoi cell of a lattice Λ is the set

$$\mathcal{V}(\Lambda) = \{\mathbf{x} \in \mathbb{R}^n : \forall \mathbf{v} \in \Lambda \setminus \{\mathbf{0}\}. \|\mathbf{x}\| < \|\mathbf{x} - \mathbf{v}\|\}$$

of all points that are closer to the origin than to any other lattice point. We also define the closed Voronoi cell $\bar{\mathcal{V}}$ as the topological closure of $\mathcal{V}$. We omit Λ, and simply write $\mathcal{V}$, when the lattice is clear from the context. The Voronoi cell of a lattice point $\mathbf{v} \in \Lambda$ is defined similarly, and equals $\mathbf{v} + \mathcal{V}$. For any (lattice) point $\mathbf{v}$, define the half-space

$$H_{\mathbf{v}} = \{\mathbf{x} \colon \|\mathbf{x}\| < \|\mathbf{x} - \mathbf{v}\|\}.$$

Clearly, $\mathcal{V}$ is the intersection of $H_{\mathbf{v}}$ for all $\mathbf{v} \in \Lambda \setminus \{\mathbf{0}\}$. However, it is not necessary to consider all $\mathbf{v}$. The minimal set of lattice vectors V such that $\mathcal{V} = \bigcap_{\mathbf{v} \in V} H_{\mathbf{v}}$ is called the set of *Voronoi relevant* vectors. The Voronoi cell $\mathcal{V}$ is a polytope, and the Voronoi relevant vectors are precisely the centers of the ($(n-1)$ dimensional) facets of $2\mathcal{V}$.

3. THE ALGORITHM

In this section we describe and analyze our algorithms to solve CVP, and related lattice problems. The CVP algorithm has three components:

1. An $\tilde{O}(2^{2n})$-time algorithm to solve the *closest vector problem with preprocessing* (CVPP), where the output of the preprocessing function is the Voronoi cell of the input lattice, described as the intersection of half-spaces.

2. A *rank reduction* procedure that on input a lattice Λ of rank n, produces a basis $\{\mathbf{b}_1, \dots, \mathbf{b}_n\}$ for Λ such that for any $k = 1, \dots, n$, the CVP in the k-rank sub-lattice $\Lambda_k = \mathcal{L}(\mathbf{b}_1, \dots, \mathbf{b}_k)$ can be reduced to the solution of at most $2^{k/2}$ (or even $2^{o(k)}$) CVP computations in $\Lambda_{k-1} = \mathcal{L}(\mathbf{b}_1, \dots, \mathbf{b}_{k-1})$.

3. A reduction from computing the *Voronoi cell* of a lattice Λ to performing 2^n CVP computations in Λ.

We will see in subsection 3.4 that the last two components can be merged to get an asymptotically faster algorithm.

Notice that the rank reduction procedure immediately gives a recursive algorithm to solve CVP in arbitrary lattices. However, the obvious way to turn the rank reduction procedure into a recursive program leads to an algorithm with $2^{O(n^2)}$ running time, because each time the rank of the input lattice is reduced by 1, the number of recursive invocations gets multiplied by $2^{O(n)}$. We use the CVPP and Voronoi cell computation algorithms to give a more efficient transformation. The idea is to compute the Voronoi cells of all sub-lattices $\Lambda_k = \mathcal{L}(\mathbf{b}_1, \dots, \mathbf{b}_k)$ sequentially, where $\mathbf{b}_1, \dots, \mathbf{b}_n$ is the lattice basis produced by the rank reduction procedure. Notice that the Voronoi cell of the sub-lattice $\Lambda_1 = \mathcal{L}(\mathbf{b}_1)$ can be trivially computed, as the list of Voronoi relevant vectors is precisely $\{\mathbf{b}_1, -\mathbf{b}_1\}$. Next, assuming the Voronoi cell of Λ_{k-1} has already been computed, the Voronoi cell of Λ_k can be computed as follows:

1. Use the Voronoi cell computation algorithm to reduce the computation of the Voronoi cell of Λ_k to 2^k CVP computations in Λ_k.

2. Use the rank reduction procedure to perform each CVP computation in Λ_k by means of $2^{k/2}$ (or $2^{o(k)}$) CVP computations in Λ_{k-1}.

3. Use the knowledge of the Voronoi cell of Λ_{k-1} to solve each CVP instance in Λ_{k-1} using the $\tilde{O}(2^{2k})$ CVPP algorithm.

By combining the three steps, we see that the Voronoi cell of Λ_k can be computed from the Voronoi cell of Λ_{k-1} by means of $2^{k+o(k)}$ CVPP computations, each using 2^{2k} polynomial time computations. The total running time to compute the Voronoi cell of Λ_n is $\sum_{k=1}^{n} 2^{k+o(k)} \cdot \tilde{O}(2^{2k}) = \tilde{O}(2^{3n+o(n)})$. It is possible to lower the time complexity to $\tilde{O}(2^{2n+o(n)})$ by merging the first two steps. A thorough analysis of the faster variant will be given in the full version of the paper, but the main idea is described in subsection 3.4.

The following theorem immediately follows from the previous discussion, and the detailed description of the three components given in the next subsections.

THEOREM 3.1. *There is a deterministic $\tilde{O}(2^{2n+o(n)})$-time algorithm that on input a lattice $\mathbf{B}$, outputs a description of the Voronoi cell of the lattice as the intersection of at most 2^{n+1} half-spaces.*

From the description of the Voronoi cell, we immediately get a solution to many other lattice problems, e.g., the shortest vector problem (SVP) can be solved simply by picking the shortest vector in the list of lattice points describing the Voronoi cell, and the kissing number of the lattice can be computed as the number of vectors in the list achieving the same length as the shortest vector in the lattice.

COROLLARY 3.2. *There is a deterministic $\tilde{O}(2^{2n+o(n)})$-time algorithm to solve SVP, and to compute the kissing number of a lattice.*

Once the Voronoi cell of Λ_n has been computed, then we can solve CVP using the CVPP algorithm. Both the preprocessing and CVPP computation times are $\tilde{O}(2^{2n+o(n)})$, so the total running time to solve an arbitrary CVP instance is $\tilde{O}(2^{2n+o(n)})$. Algorithms for other lattice problems, like SIVP, SAP, GCVP, SMP, can be obtained by a reduction to CVP[38]

COROLLARY 3.3. *There is a deterministic $\tilde{O}(2^{2n+o(n)})$-time algorithm to solve CVP, SIVP, SAP, GCVP and SMP.*

Algorithm 1 Single exponential time for CVPP

```
function CVPP(t, B, V)
    t ← LinearSpan(t, B)
    Choose smallest k ∈ ℤ that t ∈ 2^k 𝒱
    x_k ← t
    for i = k downto 1 do
        x_{i-1} ← x_i − CVPP_{2𝒱}(x_i, 2^{i-1} V)
    return t − x_0

function CVPP_{2𝒱}(t, V)
    i ← 0
    t_0 ← t
    while t_i ∉ 𝒱 do
        Choose v_i ∈ V that maximizes ⟨t, v⟩/‖v‖²
        t_{i+1} ← t_i − v_i
        i ← i + 1
    return t_0 − t_i
```

3.1 CVP with preprocessing

We start with the most technical part of the algorithm. We give a single exponential time algorithm that on input a lattice Λ, a list V (of size at most 2^{n+1}) containing all Voronoi relevant vectors of Λ, and a target point $\mathbf{t}$, computes a lattice point closest to $\mathbf{t}$. (We can assume without loss of generality that $\mathbf{t}$ belongs to the linear span of Λ, otherwise, we simply project $\mathbf{t}$ orthogonally to that subspace.) We remark that here "single exponential time" means single exponential in the lattice rank n, rather than the size of V. The dependency of the running time on the length of the list V is linear. The dependency on the bit size of the target vector is polynomial.

Without loss of generality we may assume that the target vector $\mathbf{t}$ belongs to $2\bar{\mathcal{V}}$ (as justified below), the Voronoi cell of the lattice scaled up by a factor 2. The goal of the algorithm is to find a vector $\mathbf{x} \in \bar{\mathcal{V}}$ such that $\mathbf{x} \in \Lambda+\mathbf{t}$. Then, $\mathbf{t}-\mathbf{x}$ is a lattice point closest to $\mathbf{t}$. An algorithm for arbitrary target $\mathbf{t}$ (not necessarily in $2\bar{\mathcal{V}}$) is obtained as follows. Notice that membership in $c\cdot\bar{\mathcal{V}}$ (for any given c) can be efficiently tested by checking membership in each of the (scaled) half-spaces $c \cdot H_{\mathbf{v}}$ defining the Voronoi cell. Let k be an integer such that $\mathbf{t} \in 2^k\bar{\mathcal{V}}$. Such integer can be found by iteratively trying all possible values of k. Notice that $\mathbf{x}_k = \mathbf{t}$ is in $2(2^{k-1}\cdot\bar{\mathcal{V}})$, where $2^{k-1}\cdot\bar{\mathcal{V}}$ is the Voronoi cell of $2^{k-1}\Lambda$. So, we can use the basic algorithm to find a vector $\mathbf{x}_{k-1} \in 2^{k-1}\bar{\mathcal{V}}$ such that $\mathbf{x}_{k-1} - \mathbf{x}_k \in 2^k\Lambda \subset \Lambda$. We repeat this process k times, bringing the target $\mathbf{t} = \mathbf{x}_k$ into smaller and smaller multiples $2^i\bar{\mathcal{V}}$ of the Voronoi cell of the original lattice, until we get $\mathbf{x}_0 \in \bar{\mathcal{V}}$. At this point, the lattice point closest to $\mathbf{t}$ is obtained as $\mathbf{t} - \mathbf{x}_0$.

The basic CVPP$_{2\mathcal{V}}$ algorithm, is a variant of the Iterative Slicer of [52]. Given a target $\mathbf{t}$, and a list of relevant points V of a lattice Λ, the algorithm generates a sequence $\mathbf{t}_1 = \mathbf{t}, \mathbf{t}_2, \dots, \mathbf{t}_D$ of shorter and shorter points of the coset $\Lambda+\mathbf{t}$ by subtracting appropriate relevant vectors $\mathbf{v}_i$, so that $\mathbf{t}_{i+1} = \mathbf{t}_i - \mathbf{v}_i$. The algorithm terminates when a point $\mathbf{t}_D \in \bar{\mathcal{V}}\cap\Lambda+\mathbf{t}$ is found, and outputs $\mathbf{t} - \mathbf{t}_D$ which is a closest vector to the target $\mathbf{t}$. The main difference of our variant is that if the target vector $\mathbf{t}$ is in $2\bar{\mathcal{V}}$ all the generated points are restricted in $2\bar{\mathcal{V}}$. We first show that given this additional property the sequence length is upper bounded by 2^n and then we show how to choose appropriate $\mathbf{v}_i$ to achieve this property.

LEMMA 3.4. *Let Λ a n-rank lattice and $\mathbf{t}_1, \mathbf{t}_2, \dots, \mathbf{t}_D$ a sequence of vectors with strictly decreasing norm in $2\bar{\mathcal{V}} \cap \Lambda + \mathbf{t}_1$. The length of any such sequence is upper bounded by 2^n.*

Proof. Let $\mathbf{B}$ a basis of the lattice Λ, consider the partition of $\Lambda + \mathbf{t}$ to 2^n sets of the form:

$$C_{\mathbf{c}} = 2\Lambda + \mathbf{Bc} + \mathbf{t}_1, \mathbf{c} \in \{0,1\}^n$$

Every point $\mathbf{t}_i$ of the sequence is in one of these sets. We will prove the statement by contradiction. Assume that the length of the sequence is more than 2^n, then at least two points $\mathbf{t}_i, \mathbf{t}_j$, $i < j$ belong to the same set $C_{\mathbf{c}'}$. Notice that $\mathbf{t}_i \in 2\bar{\mathcal{V}}$ and consequently $\mathbf{t}_i$ is a minimum norm element of the coset $2\Lambda + \mathbf{t}_i$ which is exactly the set $C_{\mathbf{c}'}$. However $\mathbf{t}_j$ is also in $C_{\mathbf{c}'}$ and should have shorter norm than $\mathbf{t}_i$, because the norms strictly decrease. This is a contradiction, therefore the length cannot be more than 2^n. □

Now we are ready to show how to choose appropriate relevant vectors $\mathbf{v}_i$ to acquire a sequence with the required properties. Given a vector $\mathbf{t}_i \in 2\bar{\mathcal{V}}$ (but not in $\bar{\mathcal{V}}$) we can scale the voronoi cell by an appropriate factor k ($1 < k \leq 2$), such that $\mathbf{t}_i$ is exactly on the boundary of $k\bar{\mathcal{V}}$ and particularly on a facet corresponding to a scaled relevant vector $k\mathbf{v}_i$. The factor k and the corresponding $\mathbf{v}_i$ can be efficiently computed. It is not very hard to verify that $k = \max_{\mathbf{v}\in V}(2\langle\mathbf{t},\mathbf{v}\rangle/\|\mathbf{v}\|^2)$ and $\mathbf{v}_i$ is a relevant vector that maximizes the quantity above. We will show that the vector $\mathbf{t}_{i+1} = \mathbf{t}_i - \mathbf{v}_i$ is in $2\bar{\mathcal{V}}$ and strictly shorter than $\mathbf{t}_i$.

First we prove that $\mathbf{t}_{i+1}$ is in $2\bar{\mathcal{V}}$. Notice that if $\mathbf{t}_i$ is on the facet of $k\bar{\mathcal{V}}$ corresponding to $k\mathbf{v}_i$, it is also on the boundary of the voronoi cell centered on $k\mathbf{v}_i$. Notice that $\mathbf{t}_i \in k\bar{\mathcal{V}} + k\mathbf{v}_i$, directly gives that $\mathbf{t}_i - k\mathbf{v}_i \in k\bar{\mathcal{V}}$. So both $\mathbf{t}_i, \mathbf{t}_i - k\mathbf{v}_i$ are in $k\bar{\mathcal{V}}$ and by convexity of the voronoi cell we have that $\mathbf{t}_{i+1} = \mathbf{t}_i - \mathbf{v}_i$ is also in $k\bar{\mathcal{V}} \subseteq 2\bar{\mathcal{V}}$. Finally we show that $\|\mathbf{t}_{i+1}\| < \|\mathbf{t}_i\|$. Notice that if $\mathbf{t}_i$ is on the facet of $k\mathbf{v}_i$, $\|\mathbf{t}_i\| = \|\mathbf{t}_i - k\mathbf{v}_i\|$ which gives $2\langle\mathbf{t}_i, \mathbf{v}_i\rangle = k\|\mathbf{v}_i\|^2$, and we have:

$$\|\mathbf{t}_{i+1}\|^2 = \|\mathbf{t}_i\|^2 + (1-k)\|\mathbf{v}_i\|^2 < \|\mathbf{t}_i\|^2$$

which completes the proof.

COROLLARY 3.5. *Given $\mathbf{t} \in 2\bar{\mathcal{V}}$ and the set V of voronoi relevant points of a lattice Λ, CVPP$_{2\mathcal{V}}(\mathbf{t}, V)$ gives the closest vector to $\mathbf{t}$ after 2^{2n} polynomial time computations.*

Proof. For each point of the sequence $\mathbf{t}_1, \mathbf{t}_2, \dots \mathbf{t}_D$, the algorithm finds the relevant $\mathbf{v}_i$ that maximizes $2\langle\mathbf{t},\mathbf{v}\rangle/\|\mathbf{v}\|^2$ by trying all vectors on V. Therefore for each point $\mathbf{t}_i$ the algorithm does at most 2^n polynomial in the size of the vectors computations. We have already proved that the sequence length is upper bounded by 2^n and as a result we get a total of at most 2^{2n} polynomial time computations. □

3.2 The rank reduction procedure

The rank reduction procedure simply applies the LLL basis reduction algorithm [33] to the input lattice. This results in a basis $\mathbf{b}_1, \dots, \mathbf{b}_n$ such that $\|\mathbf{b}^*_{i+1}\|^2 \geq \|\mathbf{b}^*_i\|^2/2$ for all i, where $\mathbf{b}^*_1, \dots, \mathbf{b}^*_n$ are the Gram-Schmidt orthogonalized vectors. We now show how such a basis allows to reduce CVP computations in Λ_{k+1} to $2^{O(k)}$ CVP computations in Λ_k.

Algorithm 2 Voronoi cell Computation

```
function RelevantVectors(B)
    B ← LLL(B)
    V_1 = {(b_1, −b_1)}
    for k = 2 to n do
        V_k ← {}
        B_k ← [b_1, ..., b_k]
        for c in {{0,1}^k \ 0} do
            t ← −B_k c/2
            v ← CVP_rankred(t, B_k, V_{k−1})
            V_k ← V_k ∪ {±2(v − t)}
        RemoveNonRelevant(V_k)
    return V_n

function CVP_rankred(t, B_k, V_{k−1})
    h_t ← ⟨t, b*_k⟩/⟨b*_k, b*_k⟩
    best ← NearestPlaneCVP(t, B_k)
    for h such that: ||h − h_t|| · ||b*_k|| < ||best|| do
        v ← CVPP(t − h b_k, V_{k−1}) + h b_k
        if ||best|| < ||v|| then
            best ← v
    return best

function RemoveNonRelevant(V_k)
    for v_i ∈ V_k do
        if ∃v_j(≠ v_i) ∈ V_k : ||v_i/2 − v_j|| = ||v_i/2|| then
            V_k ← V_k \ {v_i, −v_i}
```

Let $\mathbf{t}$ be a target vector. We want to find a lattice point in Λ_{k+1} closest to $\mathbf{t}$. We can assume without loss of generality that $\mathbf{t}$ belongs to the linear span of Λ_{k+1}, otherwise, we simply project $\mathbf{t}$ orthogonally to that subspace. Partition the lattice Λ_{k+1} into layers of the form $h\mathbf{b}_{k+1} + \Lambda_k$, where $h \in \mathbb{Z}$. Notice that

- a lattice point within distance $\rho = \frac{1}{2}\sqrt{\sum_{j=1}^{k+1} \|\mathbf{b}_j^*\|^2}$ from any $\mathbf{t}$ can be computed using the nearest plane algorithm [9], therefore the distance of $\mathbf{t}$ to Λ_{k+1} is bounded by ρ.
- the distance of all lattice points in the layer $h\mathbf{b}_{k+1} + \Lambda_k$ from $\mathbf{t}$ is at least $|h - h_t| \cdot \|\mathbf{b}_{k+1}^*\|$, where $h_t = \langle \mathbf{t}, \mathbf{b}_{k+1}^*\rangle / \langle \mathbf{b}_{k+1}^*, \mathbf{b}_{k+1}^*\rangle$, because this is the distance between $\mathbf{t}$ and the entire affine space generated by the layer.
- From the property $\|\mathbf{b}_{i+1}^*\|^2 \geq \|\mathbf{b}_i^*\|^2/2$ of LLL reduced basis we have

$$\begin{aligned}\rho &= \frac{1}{2}\sqrt{\sum_{j=1}^{k+1}\|\mathbf{b}_j^*\|^2} \leq \frac{1}{2}\sqrt{\sum_{j=1}^{k+1} 2^{k+1-j}\|\mathbf{b}_{k+1}^*\|^2} \\ &= \frac{1}{2}\sqrt{2^{k+1}-1}\|\mathbf{b}_{k+1}^*\|.\end{aligned}$$

It follows from the above observations that the lattice points in Λ_{k+1} closest to $\mathbf{t}$ belong to layers $h\mathbf{b}_{k+1} + \Lambda_k$ such that $|h - h_t| \leq \frac{1}{2}\sqrt{2^{k+1}-1}$. So, in order to find a lattice point closest to $\mathbf{t}$ we can enumerate all $\sqrt{2^{k+1}-1}+1$ integers h such that $|h - h_t| \leq \frac{1}{2}\sqrt{2^{k+1}-1}$, and for each of them find a point in $h\mathbf{b}_{k+1} + \Lambda_k$ closest to $\mathbf{t}$. Notice that this is equivalent to finding a point in Λ_k closest to $\mathbf{t} - h\mathbf{b}_{k+1}$, i.e., a CVP computation in Λ_k. A lattice point closest to $\mathbf{t}$ is found selecting the best solution across all layers.

In summary, the rank reduction algorithm performs a polynomial time computation to preprocess the input lattice and produce a basis $\mathbf{b}_1, \ldots, \mathbf{b}_n$ such that any CVP computation in Λ_k can be reduced to $\sqrt{2^k - 1} < 2^{n/2}$ CVP computations in Λ_{k-1}. We remark that the number of CVP subproblems in Λ_{k-1} required to solve a CVP instance in Λ_k can be reduced to $2^{o(n)}$ using better basis reduction algorithms [22, 47]. This is the bound we use in the rest of the paper.

3.3 Voronoi cell computation

For this we use a simple variant of the RelevantVectors algorithm of [1] which reduces the computation of the Voronoi cell of a lattice to 2^n CVP instances, all for the same input lattice. The RelevantVectors algorithm works by iterating over all $(c_1, \ldots, c_n) \in \{0,1\}^n \setminus \{\mathbf{0}\}$, and for each one of them, do the following:

1. Find all lattice points in Λ that are closest to $\mathbf{t} = -\sum_i c_i \mathbf{b}_i/2$.
2. If there are precisely two solutions $\mathbf{v}, -(\mathbf{v}+2\mathbf{t})$, then include $\pm 2(\mathbf{v}-\mathbf{t})$ in the list of Voronoi relevant vectors.

For details, and a proof of correctness, the reader is referred to [1]. Notice that the RelevantVectors algorithm as just described uses an oracle that finds *all* solutions to a given CVP instance. Here we remark that this is not required. It is enough to find any of them $\mathbf{v}$, and just include $\pm 2(\mathbf{v}-\mathbf{t})$ to the list. This may result in a list that contains some redundant vectors, but it is guaranteed that all Voronoi relevant vectors will be in the list, and the list size is still bounded by 2^{n+1}. After creating the list we can easily remove the redundant vectors. It is not hard to prove that a vector $\mathbf{v}_i$ should be removed if there exist $\mathbf{v}_j \neq \mathbf{v}_i \in V$ such that $\|\mathbf{v}_j - \mathbf{v}_i/2\| = \|\mathbf{v}_i/2\|$.

3.4 Improving time complexity

The algorithm we described computes the voronoi cell V_k recursively for $k = 2, \ldots, n$ using the already computed voronoi cell V_{k-1}. This is achieved by solving CVP in Λ_k for 2^k targets of the form $-[\mathbf{b}_1, \ldots, \mathbf{b}_k] \cdot \mathbf{c}/2$ with $\mathbf{c} \in \{0,1\}^k$. For each of these 2^k targets, for $2^{o(k)}$ different hyperplanes, we solve lower rank CVPP instances using V_{k-1}. Each CVPP instance costs $\tilde{O}(2^{2k})$, so the total time complexity is $\tilde{O}(2^{3n+o(n)})$. We can lower the complexity to $\tilde{O}(2^{2n+o(n)})$ as follows. We first iterate over $2^{o(k)}$ hyperplanes and for each hyperplane we solve CVPP instances for all targets. Notice that all the targets are points of $\Lambda/2$. This greatly simplifies the problem and it is possible to solve CVPP for all 2^k targets in time $\tilde{O}(2^{2k})$. The number of hyperplanes we need to consider is $2^{o(k)}$ and the total complexity $\tilde{O}(2^{2k+o(k)})$. We will give a thorough description of this algorithm in the full version of the paper.

4. OPEN PROBLEMS, DIRECTIONS FOR FURTHER RESEARCH

We have shown that CVP, SVP, SIVP and many other lattice problems can be solved in deterministic single exponential time. Many open problems remain. Here we list those that we think are most important or interesting.

Our algorithm uses exponential space. It would be nice to find an algorithm running in exponential time and polynomial space.

We described an algorithm for the ℓ_2 norm. Many parts of the algorithm easily adapt to other norms as well, but it is not clear how to extend our results to all ℓ_p norms. The main technical problem is that the Voronoi cells in ℓ_p norms for $p \neq 2$ are not necessarily convex. So, extending the algorithm to all ℓ_p norms may require some substantially new idea. An important application of extending our algorithm to other ℓ_p norms is that it would immediately lead to single exponential time algorithms for integer programming [30].

As we have already discussed we can bring the constant in $2^{O(n)}$ down to 2. It seems possible to go even lower than 2 with better analysis of the CVPP algorithm. However, it is clear that our approach cannot possibly lead to constants in the exponent smaller than 1 (as achieved for example by randomized heuristics for SVP [43, 41].) Still, it may be possible to extend our ideas to develop an algorithm with running time proportional to the number of Voronoi relevant vectors. This may give interesting algorithms for special lattices whose Voronoi cell has a small description. Another possible research direction is to develop practical variants of our algorithm that use only a sublist of Voronoi relevant vectors, at the cost of producing only approximate solutions to CVP.

It would be nice to extend our algorithm to yield a single exponential time solution to the covering radius problem, or equivalently, the problem of computing the diameter of the Voronoi cell of a lattice. In principle, this could be done by enumerating the vertices of the Voronoi cell, and selecting the longest, but this would not lead to a single exponential time algorithm because the number of such vertices can be as large as $n^{\Omega(n)}$. No NP-hardness proof for the covering radius problem in the ℓ_2 norm is known (but see [26] for NP-hardness results in ℓ_p norm for large p). Still, the problem seems quite hard: the covering radius problem is not even known to be in NP, and it is conjectured to be Π_2-hard [37, 24] for small approximation factors. Counting the number of vertices of the Voronoi cell [51] or the number of lattice points of a given length [15] is also known to be $\#P$-hard.

5. REFERENCES

[1] E. Agrell, T. Eriksson, A. Vardy, and K. Zeger. Closest point search in lattices. *IEEE Transactions on Information Theory*, 48(8):2201–2214, Aug. 2002.

[2] D. Aharonov and O. Regev. Lattice problems in NP intersect coNP. *Journal of the ACM*, 52(5):749–765, 2005. Preliminary version in FOCS 2004.

[3] M. Ajtai. The shortest vector problem in L2 is NP-hard for randomized reductions (extended abstract). In *Proceedings of STOC '98*, pages 10–19. ACM, May 1998.

[4] M. Ajtai. Generating hard instances of lattice problems. *Complexity of Computations and Proofs, Quaderni di Matematica*, 13:1–32, 2004. Preliminary version in STOC 1996.

[5] M. Ajtai, R. Kumar, and D. Sivakumar. A sieve algorithm for the shortest lattice vector problem. In *Proceedings of STOC '01*, pages 266–275. ACM, July 2001.

[6] M. Ajtai, R. Kumar, and D. Sivakumar. Sampling short lattice vectors and the closest lattice vector problem. In *Proceedings of CCC '02*, pages 53–57. IEEE, May 2002.

[7] M. Alekhnovich, S. Khot, G. Kindler, and N. Vishnoi. Hardness of approximating the closest vector problem with pre-processing. In *Proceedings of FOCS 2005*. IEEE, Oct. 2005.

[8] S. Arora, L. Babai, J. Stern, and E. Z. Sweedyk. The hardness of approximate optima in lattices, codes, and systems of linear equations. *Journal of Computer and System Sciences*, 54(2):317–331, Apr. 1997. Preliminary version in FOCS'93.

[9] L. Babai. On Lovasz' lattice reduction and the nearest lattice point problem. *Combinatorica*, 6(1):1–13, 1986.

[10] J. Blömer. Closest vectors, successive minima and dual HKZ-bases of lattices. In *Proceedings of ICALP '00*, volume 1853 of *LNCS*, pages 248–259. Springer, July 2000.

[11] J. Blömer and S. Naewe. Sampling methods for shortest vectors, closest vectors and successive minima. *Theoretical Computer Science*, 410(18):1648–1665, Apr. 2009. Preliminary version in ICALP 2007.

[12] J. Blömer and J.-P. Seifert. On the complexity of computing short linearly independent vectors and short bases in a lattice. In *Proceedings of STOC '99*, pages 711–720. ACM, May 1999.

[13] J.-Y. Cai and A. P. Nerurkar. Approximating the SVP to within a factor $(1 + 1/dim^{\epsilon})$ is NP-hard under randomized reductions. *Journal of Computer and System Sciences*, 59(2):221–239, Oct. 1999. Prelim. version in CCC 1998.

[14] J. W. S. Cassels. *An introduction to the geometry of numbers*. Springer-Verlag, New York, 1971.

[15] D. X. Charles. Counting lattice vectors. *Journal of Computer and System Sciences*, 73(6):962 – 972, 2007.

[16] W. Chen and J. Meng. The hardness of the closest vector problem with preprocessing over ℓ_∞ norm. *IEEE Transactions on Information Theory*, 52(10):4603–4606, 2006.

[17] J. H. Conway and N. J. A. Sloane. *Sphere packings, lattices and groups*. Springer Verlag, 3rd edition, 1998.

[18] M. J. Coster, A. Joux, B. A. LaMacchia, A. M. Odlyzko, C.-P. Schnorr, and J. Stern. Improved low-density subset sum algorithms. *Computational Complexity*, 2(2):111–128, 1992. Preliminary versions in Eurocrypt '91 and FCT '91.

[19] I. Dinur, G. Kindler, R. Raz, and S. Safra. Approximating CVP to within almost-polynomial factors is NP-hard. *Combinatorica*, 23(2):205–243, 2003. Preliminary version in FOCS 1998.

[20] U. Feige and D. Micciancio. The inapproximability of lattice and coding problems with preprocessing. *Journal of Computer and System Sciences*, 69(1):45–67, 2003. Preliminary version in CCC 2002.

[21] N. Gama, N. Howgrave-Graham, H. Koy, and P. Nguyen. Rankin's constant and blockwise lattice reduction. In *Advances in Cryptology – Proceedings of CRYPTO 2006*, volume 4117 of *Lecture Notes in Computer Science*, pages 112–130. Springer, Aug. 2006.

[22] N. Gama and P. Q. Nguyen. Finding short lattice vectors within mordell's inequality. In *Proceedings of STOC '08*, pages 207–216. ACM, May 2008.

[23] O. Goldreich, D. Micciancio, S. Safra, and J.-P. Seifert. Approximating shortest lattice vectors is not harder than approximating closest lattice vectors. *Information Processing Letters*, 71(2):55–61, 1999.

[24] V. Guruswami, D. Micciancio, and O. Regev. The complexity of the covering radius problem. *Computational Complexity*, 14(2):90–121, jun 2005. Preliminary version in CCC 2004.

[25] G. Hanrot and D. Stehlé. Improved analysis of kannan's shortest lattice vector algorithm. In *Proceedings of CRYPTO '07*, volume 4622 of *LNCS*, pages 170–186. Springer, Aug. 2007.

[26] I. Haviv and O. Regev. Hardness of the covering radius problem on lattices. In *Proceedings of CCC '06*, pages 145–158. IEEE, July 2006.

[27] I. Haviv and O. Regev. Tensor-based hardness of the shortest vector problem to within almost polynomial factors. In *Proceedings of STOC '07*, pages 469–477. ACM, June 2007.

[28] B. Helfrich. Algorithms to construct Minkowski reduced and Hermite reduced lattice bases. *Theoretical Computer Science*, 41(2–3):125–139, Dec. 1985.

[29] A. Joux and J. Stern. Lattice reduction: A toolbox for the cryptanalyst. *Journal of Cryptology*, 11(3):161–185, 1998.

[30] R. Kannan. Minkowski's convex body theorem and integer programming. *Mathematics of operation research*, 12(3):415–440, Aug. 1987. Prelim. version in STOC 1983.

[31] S. Khot. Hardness of approximating the shortest vector problem in lattices. *Journal of the ACM*, 52(5):789–808, Sept. 2005. Preliminary version in FOCS 2004.

[32] S. Landau and G. L. Miller. Solvability by radicals is in polynomial time. *Journal of Computer and System Sciences*, 30(2):179–208, Apr. 1985. Preliminary version in STOC 1983.

[33] A. K. Lenstra, H. W. Lenstra, Jr., and L. Lovász. Factoring polynomials with rational coefficients. *Mathematische Annalen*, 261:513–534, 1982.

[34] H. W. Lenstra. Integer programming with a fixed number of variables. *Mathematics of Operations Research*, 8(4):538–548, Nov. 1983.

[35] D. Micciancio. The hardness of the closest vector problem with preprocessing. *IEEE Transactions on Information Theory*, 47(3):1212–1215, Mar. 2001.

[36] D. Micciancio. The shortest vector problem is NP-hard to approximate to within some constant. *SIAM Journal on Computing*, 30(6):2008–2035, Mar. 2001. Prelim. version in FOCS 1998.

[37] D. Micciancio. Almost perfect lattices, the covering radius problem, and applications to Ajtai's connection factor. *SIAM Journal on Computing*, 34(1):118–169, 2004. Preliminary version in STOC 2002.

[38] D. Micciancio. Efficient reductions among lattice problems. In *Proceedings of SODA 2008*, pages 84–93. ACM/SIAM, Jan. 2008.

[39] D. Micciancio and S. Goldwasser. *Complexity of Lattice Problems: a cryptographic perspective*, volume 671 of *The Kluwer International Series in Engineering and Computer Science*. Kluwer Academic Publishers, Boston, Massachusetts, Mar. 2002.

[40] D. Micciancio and O. Regev. Worst-case to average-case reductions based on Gaussian measure. *SIAM Journal on Computing*, 37(1):267–302, 2007. Preliminary version in FOCS 2004.

[41] D. Micciancio and P. Voulgaris. Faster exponential time algorithms for the shortest vector problem. In *Proceedings of SODA 2010*. ACM/SIAM, Jan. 2010.

[42] P. Nguyen and J. Stern. The two faces of lattices in cryptology. In *Proceedings of CaLC '01*, volume 2146 of *LNCS*, pages 146–180. Springer, Mar. 2001.

[43] P. Nguyen and T. Vidick. Sieve algorithms for the shortest vector problem are practical. *J. of Mathematical Cryptology*, 2(2):181–207, jul 2008.

[44] A. M. Odlyzko. The rise and fall of knapsack cryptosystems. In C. Pomerance, editor, *Cryptology and computational number theory*, volume 42 of *Procedings of Symposia in Applied Mathematics*, pages 75–88, Boulder, Colorado, 1989. AMS.

[45] X. Pujol and D. Stehlé. Solving the shortest lattice vector problem in time $2^{2.465n}$. *Cryptology ePrint Archive, Report 2009/605*, 2009.

[46] O. Regev. Improved inapproximability of lattice and coding problems with preprocessing. *IEEE Transactions on Information Theory*, 50(9):2031–2037, 2004. Preliminary version in CCC 2003.

[47] C.-P. Schnorr. A hierarchy of polynomial time lattice basis reduction algorithms. *Theoretical Computer Science*, 53(2–3):201–224, Aug. 1987.

[48] C.-P. Schnorr. A more efficient algorithm for lattice basis reduction. *Journal of Algorithms*, 9(1):47–62, Mar. 1988.

[49] C. P. Schnorr. Fast LLL-type lattice reduction. *Information and Computation*, 204(1):1–25, Jan. 2006.

[50] C.-P. Schnorr and M. Euchner. Lattice basis reduction: Improved practical algorithms and solving subset sum problems. *Mathematical programming*, 66(1-3):181–199, Aug. 1994. Preliminary version in FCT 1991.

[51] M. D. Sikirić, A. Schürmann, and F. Vallentin. Complexity and algorithms for computing Voronoi cells of lattices. *Mathematics of Computation*, 78(267):1713–1731, July 2009.

[52] N. Sommer, M. Feder, and O. Shalvi. Finding the closest lattice point by iterative slicing. *SIAM J. Discrete Math.*, 23(2):715–731, Apr. 2009.

[53] P. van Emde Boas. Another NP-complete problem and the complexity of computing short vectors in a lattice. Technical Report 81-04, Mathematische Instituut, University of Amsterdam, 1981. Available on-line at URL `http://turing.wins.uva.nl/~peter/`.

[54] E. Viterbo and E. Biglieri. Computing the Voronoi cell of a lattice: the diamond-cutting algorithm. *IEEE Trans. on Information Theory*, 42(1):161–171, Jan. 1996.

Sorting under Partial Information (without the Ellipsoid Algorithm)

Jean Cardinal, Samuel Fiorini, Gwenaël Joret*
Université Libre de Bruxelles (ULB)
Brussels, Belgium
jcardin,sfiorini,gjoret@ulb.ac.be

Raphaël M. Jungers*
Massachusetts Institute of Technology (MIT)
Cambridge (MA), USA
raphael.jungers@uclouvain.be

J. Ian Munro
University of Waterloo
Waterloo, Ontario, Canada
imunro@uwaterloo.ca

ABSTRACT

We revisit the well-known problem of sorting under partial information: sort a finite set given the outcomes of comparisons between some pairs of elements. The input is a partially ordered set P, and solving the problem amounts to discovering an unknown linear extension of P, using pairwise comparisons. The information-theoretic lower bound on the number of comparisons needed in the worst case is $\log e(P)$, the binary logarithm of the number of linear extensions of P. In a breakthrough paper, Jeff Kahn and Jeong Han Kim (STOC 1992) showed that there exists a polynomial-time algorithm for the problem achieving this bound up to a constant factor. Their algorithm invokes the ellipsoid algorithm at each iteration for determining the next comparison, making it impractical.

We develop efficient algorithms for sorting under partial information. Like Kahn and Kim, our approach relies on graph entropy. However, our algorithms differ in essential ways from theirs. Rather than resorting to convex programming for computing the entropy, we approximate the entropy, or make sure it is computed only once in a restricted class of graphs, permitting the use of a simpler algorithm. Specifically, we present:

1. an $O(n^2)$ algorithm performing $O(\log n \cdot \log e(P))$ comparisons;
2. an $O(n^{2.5})$ algorithm performing at most $(1+\varepsilon)\log e(P) + O_\varepsilon(n)$ comparisons;
3. an $O(n^{2.5})$ algorithm performing $O(\log e(P))$ comparisons.

All our algorithms are simple to implement.

*Postdoctoral Researcher of the *Fonds National de la Recherche Scientifique (F.R.S.-FNRS)*.

STOC'10, June 5–8, 2010, Cambridge, Massachusetts, USA.

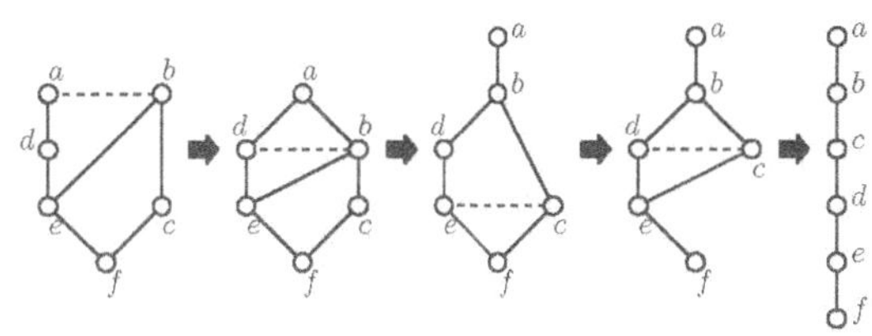

Figure 1. An instance of the problem of sorting under partial information. In this example, we use 4 comparisons (dashed edges). At every step, the Hasse diagram of the currently known partial order is shown.

Categories and Subject Descriptors: F.2.2 [Analysis of Algorithms and Problem Complexity]: Nonnumerical Algorithms and Problems; G.2.2 [Discrete Mathematics]: Graph Theory

General Terms: Algorithms, Theory

Keywords: Partial order, graph entropy

1. INTRODUCTION

Problem definition. We consider the following problem:

Let $V = \{v_1, \ldots, v_n\}$ be a set equipped with an unknown linear order $\leqslant$. Given a subset of the relations $v_i \leqslant v_j$, determine the complete linear order by queries of the form: "is $v_i \leqslant v_j$?".

This problem is called *Sorting under Partial Information.* We are given the outcomes of a number of comparisons between elements of a linearly ordered set, and we wish to "complete the sort" by performing more comparisons. The partially ordered set (poset) $P = (V, \leqslant_P)$ encoding these known outcomes is a partial information that should help reducing the number of comparisons performed. Denoting by $e(P)$ the number of linear extensions of P, it is obvious that the number of required comparisons is at least $\log e(P)$ in the worst case[1]. An example is given in Figure 1.

[1]Throughout the paper, $\log x$ denotes the binary logarithm of x.

Previous results. The problem was first posed by Fredman in 1976 [8]. He showed that there exists an algorithm that performs $\log e(P) + 2n$ additional comparisons between elements of V. However, the number of comparisons performed by Fredman's algorithm is not $O(\log e(P))$ in case $\log e(P)$ is sub-linear, and deciding what comparisons should be done takes super-polynomial time. At that time, it remained opened whether there existed, on the one hand, an algorithm performing $O(\log e(P))$ comparisons, and, on the other hand, an algorithm running in polynomial time.

The first question was answered by Kahn and Saks in 1984 [13]. They showed that there always exists a query of the form "is $v_i \leqslant v_j$?" such that the fraction of linear extensions in which v_i is smaller than v_j lies in the interval $(3/11, 8/11)$. This is a relaxation of the well-known 1/3–2/3 conjecture, a conjecture formulated independently by Fredman, Linial, and Stanley, see [17]. A simpler proof yielding weaker bounds was given by Kahn and Linial in 1991 [12]. Better bounds were later given by Brightwell, Felsner, and Trotter [2]. Iteratively choosing such a comparison yields an algorithm that performs $O(\log e(P))$ comparisons. However, finding the right comparisons remained intractable.

In 1995, Kahn and Kim published a breakthrough paper [11] in which they describe a polynomial-time algorithm performing $O(\log e(P))$ comparisons, thus answering both questions positively. Their key insight is to relate $\log e(P)$ to the entropy of the incomparability graph of P, a quantity that can be computed in polynomial time. Their algorithm, although polynomial, is still far from practical because it uses the ellipsoid algorithm $O(\log e(P)) = O(n \log n)$ times to determine the comparisons.

Contribution. Our results are described in the table below. We denote by $EA(n)$ the time needed for the ellipsoid algorithm to compute the entropy of a poset of order n. The original bound given by Kahn and Kim [11] on the number of comparisons performed by their algorithm is $54.45 \cdot \log e(P)$. The improved bound given in the table is a byproduct of our results.

Algorithm	Global complexity	Number of comparisons
K&K [11]	$O(n \log n \cdot EA(n))$	$\leq 9.82 \cdot \log e(P)$
ALGORITHM 1	$O(n^2)$	$O(\log n \cdot \log e(P))$
ALGORITHM 2	$O(n^{2.5})$	$\leq (1+\varepsilon) \log e(P) + O_\varepsilon(n)$
ALGORITHM 3	$O(n^{2.5})$	$\leq 15.09 \cdot \log e(P)$

We now compare these results to those of Kahn and Kim (shortly: K&K). In terms of global complexity, each of our algorithms greatly improves over that of K&K. Furthermore:

- If $\log e(P)$ is super-linear, the number of comparisons of our second algorithm is lower than that of K&K. By optimizing over ε, it can be shown that the number of comparisons is actually $\log e(P) + o(\log e(P)) + O(n)$ in this case (a number of comparisons comparable to that of Fredman's algorithm).
- If $\log e(P)$ is linear or sub-linear, the number of comparisons of our third algorithm is comparable to that of K&K (although the constant in front of $\log e(P)$ is still far from the best constant achieved by a super-polynomial algorithm [2]).
- Our first two algorithms have the following useful property: they compute a sorting strategy that can then be used to solve any given instance with the same partial information P, in time proportional to the number of comparisons, plus a term linear in n.

Outline and key ideas. K&K showed that graph entropy, as defined by Körner in 1973, plays a central role in the problem of sorting under partial information. Letting $H(\bar{P})$ be the entropy of the incomparability graph of P, they showed that $\log e(P) = \Theta(nH(\bar{P}))$. Every comparison performed by their algorithm decreases $nH(\bar{P})$ by at least some constant. Hence the total number of comparisons is $O(nH(\bar{P}))$ and thus $O(\log e(P))$. Furthermore, their algorithm is polynomial, since the entropy can be computed in polynomial time using convex programming algorithms.

Our goal is to obtain practical algorithms, without sacrificing the number of comparisons. Our first key idea is to compute a *greedy chain decomposition* of P, that is, a partition of P into chains (totally ordered subsets), obtained by iteratively extracting a longest chain. This allows us to get rid of the costly convex programming machinery and enables us to focus only on the relevant part of P. In [5], we have provided bounds on the amount of information (in terms of entropy) that is lost when we forget the relations of P between two distinct chains of a greedy chain decomposition.

We directly obtain a mergesort-like algorithm: find a greedy chain decomposition of P, and merge the chains using a simple linear-time merging algorithm. The number of comparisons performed by this algorithm can be shown to be close to $\log e(P)$, up to an arbitrarily small factor and a term linear in n. This is described in Section 4.

As noted above, our mergesort-like algorithm performs better than that of K&K provided the information theoretic lower bound $\log e(P)$ is super-linear. The algorithms are comparable (in terms of number of comparisons) if $\log e(P)$ is linear. If $\log e(P)$ is sub-linear, we have to use another strategy: instead of forgetting all the relations of P between the chains of a greedy chain decomposition, we keep some of them. Namely, we keep all the relations between the elements of the longest chain and the rest of P. When $\log e(P)$ is small compared to n, the longest chain contains a large fraction of the elements. Hence, this less radical strategy keeps most of the information contained in P.

Our second key idea is contained in the following algorithm: find a longest chain A, use the mergesort-like algorithm on $P - A$, yielding a chain B, and cautiously merge the chains A and B using the current partial information. Thus we reduce the general sorting problem to an easier subproblem known as *merging under partial information*. It is a special case of the problem of sorting under partial information in which P can be covered by exactly two chains, and has been studied in 1984 by Linial [17]. By using an algorithm for merging under partial information performing $O(\log e(P))$ comparisons, we obtain an algorithm for the general sorting problem performing $O(\log e(P))$ comparisons. This is shown in Section 5.

The problem of merging under partial information is tackled in Section 6. Although Linial [17] already provided an algorithm for the problem, we considerably improve on its complexity. We first show that in this special case, the entropy of the incomparability graph of P can be computed very easily. The computation relies on a structural lemma on the entropy of bipartite graphs by Körner and Marton [16], and on the additional structure exhibited by the incomparability graph of a poset covered by two chains.

Then, we show that given the vertex weights achieving the entropy, there exists a sequence of pairwise chain mergings, each of which decreases $nH(\bar{P})$ by an amount proportional to the number of comparisons performed. After each merging, the weights on the vertices can be updated efficiently. This yields the desired algorithm for merging under partial information, and thus an algorithm for sorting under partial information performing $O(\log e(P))$ comparisons. The global complexity of the algorithm is $O(n^{2.5})$.

Preliminaries on complexity measures, the entropy of a graph, and greedy chain decompositions, are given in Section 2. We also offer new results on the entropy, improving several aspects of K&K's analysis. Mainly, we prove the tight inequality $nH(\bar{P}) \leq 2\log e(P)$, whereas K&K show $nH(\bar{P}) \leq (1 + 7\log e)\log e(P) \simeq 11.1 \log e(P)$.

As a first simple example of a near-optimal algorithm for sorting under partial information, we give an analogue of insertion sort in Section 3. This algorithm has global complexity $O(n^2)$ and performs a number of comparisons within a $\log n$ factor only of the information-theoretic lower bound. We included an appendix at the end of the paper, in which we discuss the complexities of three important steps used in our algorithms, among which the construction of a greedy chain decomposition. Some proofs are omitted and can be found in the long version of the paper[2].

2. PRELIMINARIES

We give a number of definitions and summarize the contribution of K&K [11] to the problem. We also give an improved upper bound on the quantity $nH(\bar{P})$.

Complexity Measures. Consider an algorithm for sorting under partial information. The *query complexity* is the number of comparisons between elements of P that are done by the algorithm. The *preprocessing complexity* measures the computational work done before the first comparison is performed. The rest of the work is measured by the *sorting complexity*. The *preprocessing phase* and *sorting phases* are defined similarly. Thus, in the preprocessing phase, we are restricted to only process the input poset. The comparisons are performed during the sorting phase. The *global complexity* is simply the sum of the preprocessing and sorting complexities.

Our model of computation is a RAM machine with $\Theta(\log n)$-size words, and the global complexity is measured as the total number of arithmetic and logical operations on words.

Entropy and sorting. We recall that a subset S of vertices of a graph is a *stable set* (or *independent set*) if the vertices in S are pairwise nonadjacent. The *stable set polytope* of a graph G with vertex set V and order n is the n-dimensional polytope

$$\mathrm{STAB}(G) := \mathrm{conv}\{\chi^S \in \mathbb{R}^V : S \text{ stable set in } G\},$$

where χ^S is the characteristic vector of the subset S, assigning the value 1 to every vertex in S, and 0 to the others. The *entropy* of G is defined as (see [14, 7])

$$H(G) := \min_{x \in \mathrm{STAB}(G)} -\frac{1}{n}\sum_{v\in V} \log x_v. \tag{1}$$

Any point $x \in \mathrm{STAB}(G)$ describes a feasible solution of the convex program (1). The *entropy* of x is the value of the objective function of that program with respect to x.

For any given poset P, we consider two graphs: the *comparability graph* $G(P)$ and the *incomparability graph* $\bar{G}(P)$. The vertex set of $G(P)$ is the ground set of P and two distinct vertices v and w are adjacent in $G(P)$ whenever they are comparable in P. The incomparability graph $\bar{G}(P)$ is simply the complement of $G(P)$. We denote by $H(P)$ the entropy of $G(P)$ and by $H(\bar{P})$ the entropy of $\bar{G}(P)$.

Entropy plays an important role in the sorting under partial information problem. The first reason is explained by the following result due to K&K. In particular, it implies $\log e(P) = \Theta(nH(\bar{P}))$. Thus the information theoretic lower bound and the entropy of the incomparability graph of P are tightly related.

LEMMA 1 ([11]). *For any poset P of order n, $\log e(P) \leq nH(\bar{P}) \leq \min\{\log e(P) + \log e \cdot n, c_1 \log e(P)\}$, where $c_1 = (1 + 7\log e) \simeq 11.1$.*

The second reason is that, while computing $e(P)$ is #P-complete [3], computing $H(\bar{P})$ can be done in polynomial time by solving the convex minimization problem (1), as we now explain. When $G = \bar{G}(P)$, the stable set polytope $\mathrm{STAB}(G)$ has a known description in terms of linear inequalities. Although the number of inequalities is (in most cases) exponential, the corresponding separation problem can be solved efficiently. Hence (1) can be solved by the ellipsoid algorithm.

Much of this nice behaviour is due to the perfection of $\bar{G}(P)$. We recall that a graph G is *perfect* if $\omega(H) = \chi(H)$ holds for every induced subgraph H of G, where $\omega(H)$ and $\chi(H)$ denote the clique and chromatic numbers of H, respectively. If G is perfect, then its complement $\bar{G}$ is also perfect [18]. The comparability graph $G(P)$ of P is always perfect, hence the same holds for the incomparability graph $\bar{G}(P)$ of P. The following result is the easy part of a result by Csiszár, Körner, Lovász, Marton, and Simonyi.

LEMMA 2 ([7]). *Assume G is a perfect graph with vertex set V and order n, and let $x \in \mathbb{R}^V$ and $z \in \mathbb{R}^V$ be feasible solutions to (1) for G and $\bar{G}$, respectively. Then x and z are optimal iff $x_v z_v = 1/n$ for all $v \in V$. In particular, $H(G) + H(\bar{G}) = \log n$.*

The algorithm of K&K [11] is based on two main lemmas, Lemma 1 above and the next lemma. Whenever a and b are incomparable elements of P, we denote by $P(a < b)$ the poset obtained by adding the relation (a, b) to the partial order of P and closing transitively.

LEMMA 3 ([11]). *In any poset P of order n that is not a chain there are a, b incomparable such that*

$$\max\{nH(\overline{P(a < b)}), nH(\overline{P(b < a)})\} \leq nH(\bar{P}) - c_2,$$

where $c_2 = \log(1 + 17/112) \simeq 0.2$.

[2] http://arxiv.org/abs/0911.0086.

Let V denote the ground set of P. Given an optimal solution $x \in \mathbb{R}^V$ to (1) for $G(P)$, K&K show how to choose a pair a, b as in Lemma 3. Knowing the *primal* solution x, this choice can be done efficiently (in $O(n^2)$ time).

Comparing a and b gives a new partial information $P' \in \{P(a < b), P(b < a)\}$. The key is that for any outcome, $nH(\bar{P'}) \leq nH(\bar{P}) - c_2$. This is proved by modifying appropriately an optimal *dual* solution, that is, an optimal solution $z \in \mathbb{R}^V$ to (1) for $\bar{G}(P)$. By Lemma 2, $z_v = 1/(nx_v)$ for all $v \in V$. Knowing x, a new dual solution z' can be efficiently constructed (in $O(n^3)$ time).

To determine the next comparison, the K&K algorithm needs to compute an optimal solution x' to (1) for $G(P')$. Because the optimality of z' is not guaranteed, letting $x'_v = 1/(nz'_v)$ for $v \in V$ does not work. This explains why their algorithm uses the ellipsoid algorithm before each comparison.

We have shown in [5] that $H(P)$ can be expressed via a convex minimization problem with $2n$ variables and at most n^2 constraints, making possible the use of interior point algorithms for computing $H(P)$. Although this makes the K&K algorithm more practical, this does not make it competitive with our algorithms in terms of running time since it is unlikely that computing $H(P)$ using interior point algorithms can be done in less than $O(n^4)$ time (plugging in a straightforward way the number of variables and constraints in complexity bounds for interior point algorithms would yield a $O(n^6)$ complexity [1]).

A new result on the entropy of incomparability graphs. K&K conjectured that the value for the constant c_1 in Lemma 1 could be improved to $c_1 = 1 + \log e \simeq 2.44$. Using the same line of attack as above, we were able to show that one can actually take $c_1 = 2$, which is best possible.

LEMMA 4. *For any poset P of order n,*

$$nH(\bar{P}) \leq 2 \log e(P).$$

Note that this bound is tight, as shown by the poset consisting of two incomparable elements. The proof is omitted in this version of the paper.

Greedy chain decompositions. Suppose we want to approximate the entropy $H(G)$ of a given perfect graph G. We have shown [5] that the following greedy heuristic performs very well. First, iteratively remove a maximum stable set in G. Denote by $S_1, \ldots, S_k$ the stable sets extracted from G. Second, construct the *greedy point* $\tilde{x} := \sum_{i=1}^{k} \frac{|S_i|}{n} \chi^{S_i}$ in STAB(G). The entropy of this point is precisely the entropy of the distribution $\{\frac{|S_1|}{n}, \ldots, \frac{|S_k|}{n}\}$.

THEOREM 1 ([5]). *Let G be a perfect graph on n vertices and denote by $\tilde{g}$ the entropy of an arbitrary greedy point in* STAB(G). *Then, for every $\varepsilon > 0$,*

$$\tilde{g} \leq (1+\varepsilon)H(G) + (1+\varepsilon)\log\left(1 + \frac{1}{\varepsilon}\right).$$

In the context of the sorting under partial information problem, we apply the greedy heuristic to $\bar{G}(P)$. This gives a decomposition of P into chains $C_1, \ldots, C_k$ that we call a *greedy chain decomposition*. Although the fastest known algorithm for computing a maximum chain in a poset of order n has complexity $O(n^2)$ (see [9], Chapter 5), a greedy chain decomposition can be found in $O(n^{2.5})$ time, see Appendix A.

3. INSERTION SORT

We first propose an $O(n^2)$ sorting algorithm with query complexity $O(\log n \cdot \log e(P))$. It consists of first finding a maximum chain $C \subseteq P$, then iteratively inserting the remaining elements of $P \setminus C$ in the chain C, using binary search. We refer to this algorithm as ALGORITHM 1. In order to show that its query complexity is $O(\log n \cdot \log e(P))$, we need two lemmas.

LEMMA 5. *Let P be a poset of order n and let C be a maximum chain in P. Then $|C| \geq 2^{-H(\bar{P})}n$.*

PROOF. It is well known ([15, 4]) that the entropy of a graph on n vertices with stability number α is at least $-\log \frac{\alpha}{n}$. The result follows by applying this to $\bar{G}(P)$. □

LEMMA 6. *For all $x \in \mathbb{R}$, $1 - 2^{-x} \leq \ln 2 \cdot x$.*

Now the number of comparisons performed by the algorithm is at most

$$\begin{aligned} \log n \cdot (n - |C|) &\leq \log n \cdot (n - 2^{-H(\bar{P})}n) \quad \text{(Lemma 5)} \\ &\leq \log n \cdot \ln 2 \cdot nH(\bar{P}) \quad \text{(Lemma 6)} \\ &= O(\log n \cdot \log e(P)) \quad \text{(Lemma 1)}. \end{aligned}$$

This algorithm has the property that we can perform the preprocessing step only once, and sort all instances with the same partial information in time $O(\log n \cdot \log e(P)) + O(n)$. To achieve this, we store the maximum chain C in a balanced binary search tree in time $O(n)$ and insert each remaining element in time $O(\log n)$.

4. MERGE SORT

In order to improve on the previous algorithm, we can use an approach similar to mergesort.

ALGORITHM 2:

- **Phase 1 (Preprocessing):** find a greedy chain decomposition $C_1, \ldots, C_k$ of P; $\mathcal{C} \leftarrow \{C_1, \ldots, C_k\}$
- **Phase 2 (Sorting)**
  1. while $|\mathcal{C}| > 1$
     (a) pick the two smallest chains C and C' in $\mathcal{C}$
     (b) merge C and C' into a chain C'', in linear time
     (c) $\mathcal{C} \leftarrow \mathcal{C} \setminus \{C, C'\} \cup \{C''\}$
  2. return the chain in $\mathcal{C}$

Let $\tilde{g}$ denote the entropy of the distribution $\{\frac{|C_1|}{n}, \ldots, \frac{|C_k|}{n}\}$. Our next lemma bounds the query complexity of ALGORITHM 2 in terms on $\tilde{g}$. Its proof is omitted.

LEMMA 7. *The query complexity of* ALGORITHM 2 *is at most $(\tilde{g}+1)n$.*

The following theorem uses this bound and Theorem 1.

THEOREM 2. *For any $\varepsilon > 0$, the query complexity of* ALGORITHM 2 *is at most*

$$(1+\varepsilon)\log e(P) + (1+\varepsilon)\Big(\log e + \log\Big(1+\frac{1}{\varepsilon}\Big)\Big)\, n + n$$
$$= (1+\varepsilon)\log e(P) + O_\varepsilon(n).$$

PROOF. From Lemma 7, we infer that the query complexity is at most

$$\begin{aligned} & (\tilde{g}+1)\, n \\ \le\; & (1+\varepsilon) n H(\bar{P}) + (1+\varepsilon)\,\log\Big(1+\frac{1}{\varepsilon}\Big)\, n + n \text{ (Theorem 1)} \\ \le\; & (1+\varepsilon)\,(\log e(P) + \log e\cdot n) + (1+\varepsilon)\,\log\Big(1+\frac{1}{\varepsilon}\Big)\, n + n \\ & \text{(Lemma 1).} \end{aligned}$$

□

We conclude that ALGORITHM 2 is an $O(n^{2.5})$ algorithm with query complexity at most $(1+\varepsilon)\log e(P) + O_\varepsilon(n)$, for any $\varepsilon > 0$. Note that again, we can reuse the chain decomposition obtained in the preprocessing phase for sorting any instance with the same partial information in time proportional to the query complexity.

5. CAUTIOUS MERGE SORT

The query complexity of ALGORITHM 2 is not $O(\log e(P))$ because it completely ignores a large part of the partial information. Now, we show that using the partial information for the *last* merge suffices to obtain an algorithm with query complexity $O(\log e(P))$.

The subproblem at hand is that of *merging under partial information*. It is a special case of sorting under partial information, in which the given poset P is covered by two chains A and B, that is, P is of width at most 2. (The *width* of a poset P is the maximum size of an antichain of P.)

That problem was studied by Linial [17], who proposed an algorithm with query complexity $O(\log e(P))$. However, this algorithm requires computing polynomially many $\Theta(n)\times\Theta(n)$ determinants. In Section 6, we obtain an $O(n^2\log^2 n)$ algorithm for the problem with query complexity at most $6\log e(P)$.

THEOREM 3. *Suppose there exists an algorithm for the problem of merging under partial information with global complexity $T(n)$ and query complexity at most $c_3\log e(P')$, given as partial information a poset P' of order n and width at most 2. Then there exists an algorithm for the problem of sorting under partial information with global complexity $O(n^{2.5}) + T(n)$ and query complexity at most $(9.09 + c_3)\log e(P)$.*

PROOF. Let ALGORITHM 5 be the hypothesized algorithm for merging under partial information. (Such an algorithm will be given in Section 6.4.) Consider the following algorithm.

ALGORITHM 3:

1. find a maximum chain $A \subseteq P$
2. apply ALGORITHM 2 to the poset $P - A$, yielding a chain B
3. apply ALGORITHM 5 to the current partial information P'

From Lemma 5, we have $|A| \ge 2^{-H(\bar{P})}n$, and therefore (using Lemma 6):

$$|B| = |P - A| \le n(1 - 2^{-H(\bar{P})}) \le \ln 2\cdot nH(\bar{P}). \quad (2)$$

Now from Theorem 2 the number of comparisons in steps 2 and 3 is at most

$$\begin{aligned} & (1+\varepsilon)\log e(P-A) \\ & +\Big((1+\varepsilon)\big(\log e + \log(1+\tfrac{1}{\varepsilon})\big) + 1\Big)|P-A| + c_3\log e(P') \\ \le\; & (1+\varepsilon)\log e(P) + \Big((1+\varepsilon)(1+\ln(1+\tfrac{1}{\varepsilon})) + \ln 2\Big)\, nH(\bar{P}) \\ & + c_3\log e(P) \qquad \text{(from (2))} \\ \le\; & \Big(1+\varepsilon+2\Big((1+\varepsilon)(1+\ln(1+\tfrac{1}{\varepsilon})) + \ln 2\Big) + c_3\Big)\log e(P) \\ & \text{(from Lemma 4)} \\ \le\; & (9.09 + c_3)\log e(P) \qquad (\text{taking } \varepsilon = 0.35) \end{aligned}$$

The global complexity is $O(n^{2.5}) + T(n)$. □

6. MERGING UNDER PARTIAL INFORMATION

In this section, we assume that P is covered by two disjoint chains, denoted by A and B. First, we describe a structural result by Körner and Marton [16] concerning the entropy of a bipartite graph. Second, we show how to use this to obtain an $O(n^2\log^2 n)$ algorithm with query complexity at most $c_3\log e(P)$, with $c_3 = 6$.

6.1 The Entropy of Bipartite Graphs

Because the width of P is at most 2, the incomparability graph $\bar{G}(P)$ of P is a bipartite graph. Körner and Marton [16] describe a method for computing the entropy of any bipartite graph (see Theorem 3.8 in Simonyi's survey on graph entropy [19]). Below, $h(x) := -x\log x - (1-x)\log(1-x)$ is the binary entropy function (by convention, $h(0) = h(1) := 0$).

THEOREM 4 ([16]). *Let G be a bipartite graph of order n, with bipartition A, B. Then, one can find partitions $A = A_1\cup\cdots\cup A_k$ and $B = B_1\cup\cdots\cup B_k$ such that*

$$H(G) = \sum_{i=1}^{k}\frac{|A_i| + |B_i|}{n}\, h\left(\frac{|A_i|}{|A_i| + |B_i|}\right).$$

The partitions are constructed iteratively. Let $N_G(X)$ denote the neighborhood of a set X of vertices in the graph G. For $i \in \{1,\ldots,k\}$, Körner and Marton define A_i as any subset of $A' := A - A_1 - \cdots - A_{i-1}$ that maximizes

$$\frac{|A_i|}{|N_{G'}(A_i)|} \quad (3)$$

in the graph G' obtained from G by removing all vertices contained in some A_j or some B_j with $j < i$, and define B_i as $N_{G'}(A_i)$. By convention, if there is a vertex u in A' that is isolated, then we let $A_i = \{u\}$ and $B_i = \varnothing$. If A' is empty and $B' := B - B_1 - \cdots - B_{i-1}$ is not, we pick a vertex v in B', let $A_i = \varnothing$ and $B_i = \{v\}$.

Given partitions as in Theorem 4, the point $x \in \mathrm{STAB}(G)$ achieving the minimum in (1) is obtained by simply letting $x_u = |A_i|/(|A_i| + |B_i|)$ whenever $u \in A_i$ and $x_v = |B_i|/(|A_i| + |B_i|)$ whenever $v \in B_i$.

In Appendix B, we prove the following result.

LEMMA 8. *The entropy of a poset P of order n and width at most 2 can be computed in time $O(n^2 \log^2 n)$.*

6.2 Local Improvement of a Feasible Solution

Let $G = \bar{G}(P)$, and let E denote the edge set of G. Because G is bipartite, $\mathrm{STAB}(G) = \{x \in \mathbb{R}^V : x_u + x_v \leq 1\ \forall uv \in E,\ 0 \leq x_u \leq 1\ \forall u \in V\}$. Consider a point x in $\mathrm{STAB}(G)$. The point x is a feasible solution of the convex program (1). An edge $uv \in E$ is *tight* with respect to that solution if $x_u + x_v = 1$. Let $G(x)$ denote the graph whose vertices are those of G and whose edges are the edges of G that are tight. The point x is *locally optimal* if, letting $C_1, \ldots, C_k$ be the (connected) components of $G(x)$, and letting $A_i = C_i \cap A$ and $B_i = C_i \cap B$, for $i = 1, \ldots, k$, we have:

$$x_u = \frac{|A_i|}{|A_i| + |B_i|} \text{ if } u \in A_i, \text{ and } x_v = \frac{|B_i|}{|A_i| + |B_i|} \text{ if } v \in B_i. \tag{4}$$

In Appendix C, we prove that each A_i and each B_i is an interval of its respective chain, and that the components $C_i = A_i \cup B_i$ are linearly ordered by $\leqslant_P$, provided that x is locally optimal.

By convention, we always order the components $C_1, \ldots, C_k$ in such a way that the corresponding ratios $|A_i|/|B_i|$ are nonincreasing. (In particular, this is true if $A_1, \ldots, A_k$ and $B_1, \ldots, B_k$ are produced by the method of Körner and Marton described above.)

If $x \in \mathrm{STAB}(G)$ is not locally optimal, then one can efficiently find a locally optimal point $x' \in \mathrm{STAB}(G)$ with entropy at most that of x. We call this operation a *local improvement*. It will be used $O(n)$ times in ALGORITHM 4 and once in ALGORITHM 5. In both cases, we show that we can perform all necessary local improvements in $O(n^2)$ time, see Appendix C for a detailed discussion.

6.3 Iterated Hwang-Lin

Here, we explain how to solve "one half" of the problem of merging under partial information. Let again $G = \bar{G}(P)$. Consider a locally optimal point $x \in \mathrm{STAB}(G)$, the corresponding components $C_1, \ldots, C_k$ of $G(x)$ and partitions $A = A_1 \cup \cdots \cup A_k$ and $B = B_1 \cup \cdots \cup B_k$. Let $j \in \{1, \ldots, k\}$ be the last index for which A_j is nonempty. Thus, $j = k$ if G has no isolated point in B, and $j < k$ otherwise.

Now, assume $|A_j| \geq |B_j|$, that is, $|A_i| \geq |B_i|$ for all $i \in \{1, \ldots, j\}$. Provided this holds, we can use the following algorithm to merge A and B.

ALGORITHM 4: (*Iterated Hwang-Lin algorithm*)

1. while P is not a chain :
   (a) pick $j \in \{1, \ldots, k\}$ maximum such that $A_j \neq \varnothing$
   (b) merge A_j and B_j with the Hwang-Lin merging algorithm [10]
   (c) raise x_v to 1 for all $v \in B_j$
   (d) run local improvement on x, update partitions $A = A_1 \cup \cdots \cup A_k$ and $B = B_1 \cup \cdots \cup B_k$

We need the following lemma on the Hwang-Lin merging algorithm [10] (the proof is omitted).

LEMMA 9. *Provided $|A| \geq |B|$, the number of comparisons performed by the Hwang-Lin algorithm for merging two disjoint chains A and B is at most $|B| \log(4|A|/|B|)$.*

The analysis of the iterated Hwang-Lin algorithm is given in our next lemma.

LEMMA 10. *Let P be a poset of order n covered by two disjoint chains A, B, and let $G = \bar{G}(P)$. Assume that $x \in STAB(G)$ is a locally optimal point whose corresponding partitions $A = A_1 \cup \cdots \cup A_k$ and $B = B_1 \cup \cdots \cup B_k$ satisfy $|A_i| \geq |B_i|$ for all $i \in \{1, \ldots, k\}$ such that $A_i \neq \varnothing$. The iterated Hwang-Lin algorithm merges A and B in at most $2nh$ comparisons, where h denotes the entropy of x. Its global complexity is $O(n^2 \log^2 n)$.*

PROOF. Let P' denote the partial information after the merging operation 1b, and $G' = \bar{G}(P')$. Let also $x' \in \mathbb{R}^V$ be the point obtained from x by raising x_v to 1 for all $v \in B_j$.

Because x is locally optimal and belongs to $\mathrm{STAB}(G)$, in the graph G, none of the vertices in B_j is adjacent to a vertex in $A - A_j$. In other words, all elements of B_j are comparable to all elements in $A - A_j$ in P. Hence, all elements of B_j are comparable to all other elements in P'. It follows that $x' \in \mathrm{STAB}(G')$.

Consider the point x'' obtained by running the local improvement procedure described in Appendix C on x', and the corresponding bipartitions $A = A_1'' \cup \cdots \cup A_{k''}''$ and $B_1'' \cup \cdots \cup B_{k''}''$. Because $|A_i''| \geq |B_i''|$ still holds for all $i \in \{1, \ldots, k''\}$ such that $A_i'' \neq \varnothing$, we are allowed to iterate.

Letting h' denote the entropy of x', we have

$$nh - nh' \geq |B_j| \log \frac{|A_j| + |B_j|}{|B_j|} \geq \frac{1}{2} |B_j| \log \frac{4|A_j|}{|B_j|}.$$

By Lemma 9, we infer that the number of comparisons needed for merging A_j and B_j is at most twice the difference $nh' - nh$. The result follows. □

6.4 Two Iterated Hwang-Lin's Suffice

Finally, we can state our algorithm for merging under partial information. Again, we let $G = \bar{G}(P)$.

ALGORITHM 5:

1. compute the optimal solution x to (1), compute the components of $G(x)$ and the corresponding partitions $A = A_1 \cup \cdots \cup A_k$ and $B = B_1 \cup \cdots \cup B_k$
2. if $|A_i| \geq |B_i|$ for all i such that $A_i \neq \varnothing$, apply ALGORITHM 4
3. if $|B_i| \geq |A_i|$ for all i such that $B_i \neq \varnothing$, apply ALGORITHM 4, exchanging the roles of A and B
4. otherwise:

(a) pick j such that $|A_j| \geq |B_j| > 0$ and $0 < |A_{j+1}| \leq |B_{j+1}|$

(b) $H_1 \leftarrow \sum_{i=1}^{j} \frac{(|A_i|+|B_i|)}{n} h\left(\frac{|A_i|}{|A_i|+|B_i|}\right)$

(c) $H_2 \leftarrow \sum_{i=j+1}^{k} \frac{(|A_i|+|B_i|)}{n} h\left(\frac{|A_i|}{|A_i|+|B_i|}\right)$

(d) if $H_1 \leq H_2$: $A^\dagger \leftarrow A_1 \cup \cdots \cup A_j$; $B^\dagger \leftarrow B_1 \cup \cdots \cup B_j$

(e) if $H_2 < H_1$: $A^\dagger \leftarrow A_{j+1} \cup \cdots \cup A_k$; $B^\dagger \leftarrow B_{j+1} \cup \cdots \cup B_k$

(f) $P^\dagger \leftarrow$ subposet of P induced by $A^\dagger \cup B^\dagger$; $x^\dagger \leftarrow x$ restricted to $A^\dagger \cup B^\dagger$

(g) apply Algorithm 4 to $P^\dagger$ and $x^\dagger$, exchanging the roles of $A^\dagger$ and $B^\dagger$ if $H_2 < H_1$

(h) if $H_1 \leq H_2$: for all $v \in A^\dagger$: $x_v \leftarrow 1$; for all $v \in B^\dagger$: $x_v \leftarrow 1/2$

(i) if $H_2 < H_1$: for all $v \in B^\dagger$: $x_v \leftarrow 1$; for all $v \in A^\dagger$: $x_v \leftarrow 1/2$

(j) run local improvement on x, update partitions $A = A_1 \cup \cdots \cup A_k$ and $B = B_1 \cup \cdots \cup B_k$

(k) apply Algorithm 4 to P and x, exchanging the roles of A and B

Here is our final result:

Theorem 5. Algorithm 5 *is an* $O(n^2 \log^2 n)$ *algorithm solving the problem of merging under partial information with query complexity at most* $3nH(\bar{P})$ *hence, by Lemma 4, at most* $6 \log e(P)$.

Proof. Without loss of generality, by Lemma 10, we can assume that the algorithm enters step 4. Also, by symmetry, we can assume that $H_1 \leq H_2$. By Lemma 10, the query complexity of step 4f is at most $2nH_1$.

Let P' denote the partial information after step 4f and $G' = \bar{G}(P')$. By choice of j, steps 4g and 4h produce a point x' in $\mathrm{STAB}(G')$ whose entropy is at most that of x. Running the local improvement procedure on x' gives a new point $x'' \in \mathrm{STAB}(G')$, together with partitions $A_1'' \cup \cdots \cup A_{k''}''$ and $B_1'' \cup \cdots \cup B_{k''}''$, in time $O(n^2)$. Observe that $|B_i''| \geq |A_i''|$ for all $i = 1, \ldots, k''$ such that $B_i'' \neq \varnothing$. Thus we can apply the iterated Hwang-Lin algorithm to P' and x''.

By Lemma 10, the query complexity of step 4j is at most

$$2|B^\dagger| + 2nH_2 \leq 2(nH_1 + nH_2).$$

The total query complexity is thus at most

$$4nH_1 + 2nH_2 \leq 3(nH_1 + nH_2).$$

By Lemmas 8, 10 and 14, the global complexity of Algorithm 5 is $O(n^2 \log^2 n)$. □

References

[1] S. Boyd and L. Vandenberghe. *Convex optimization.* Cambridge University Press, Cambridge, 2004.

[2] G. R. Brightwell, S. Felsner, and W. T. Trotter. Balancing pairs and the cross product conjecture. *Order*, 2(4):327–349, 1995.

[3] G. R. Brightwell and P. Winkler. Counting linear extensions. *Order*, 8(3):225–242, 1991.

[4] J. Cardinal, S. Fiorini, and G. Joret. Minimum entropy coloring. *J. Comb. Opt.*, 16(4):361–377, 2008.

[5] J. Cardinal, S. Fiorini, G. Joret, R. Jungers, and J. I. Munro. An efficient algorithm for partial order production. In *STOC '09: 41st ACM Symposium on Theory of Computing*, 2009.

[6] T. Chan. All-pairs shortest paths with real weights in $O(n^3/\log n)$ time. *Algorithmica*, 50(2):236–243, 2008.

[7] I. Csiszár, J. Körner, L. Lovász, K. Marton, and G. Simonyi. Entropy splitting for antiblocking corners and perfect graphs. *Combinatorica*, 10(1):27–40, 1990.

[8] M. L. Fredman. How good is the information theory bound in sorting? *Theor. Comput. Sci.*, 1(4):355–361, 1976.

[9] M. C. Golumbic. *Algorithmic Graph Theory and Perfect Graphs, 2nd edition.* Annals of Discrete Mathematics. Elsevier, 2004.

[10] F. K. Hwang and S. Lin. A simple algorithm for merging two disjoint linearly-ordered sets. *SIAM J. Comput.*, 1(1):31–39, 1972.

[11] J. Kahn and J. H. Kim. Entropy and sorting. *J. Comput. Syst. Sci.*, 51(3):390–399, 1995.

[12] J. Kahn and N. Linial. Balancing extensions via Brunn-Minkowski. *Combinatorica*, 11:363–368, 1991.

[13] J. Kahn and M. E. Saks. Balancing poset extensions. *Order*, 1:113–126, 1984.

[14] J. Körner. Coding of an information source having ambiguous alphabet and the entropy of graphs. In *Transactions of the 6th Prague Conference on Information Theory*, pages 411–425, 1973.

[15] J. Körner. Fredman-Komlós bounds and information theory. *SIAM J. Algebraic and. Disc. Meth.*, 7(4):560–570, 1986.

[16] J. Körner and K. Marton. Graphs that split entropies. *SIAM J. Discrete Math.*, 1(1):71–79, 1988.

[17] N. Linial. The information-theoretic bound is good for merging. *SIAM J. Comput.*, 13(4):795–801, 1984.

[18] L. Lovász. Normal hypergraphs and the perfect graph conjecture. *Discrete Math.*, 2(3):253–267, 1972.

[19] Gábor Simonyi. Graph entropy: a survey. In *Combinatorial optimization (New Brunswick, NJ, 1992–1993)*, volume 20 of *DIMACS Ser. Discrete Math. Theoret. Comput. Sci.*, pages 399–441. Amer. Math. Soc., Providence, RI, 1995.

APPENDIX

We discuss the complexities of three crucial procedures used in our algorithms, namely, finding a greedy chain decomposition, computing the entropy of a poset covered by exactly two chains, and making a point locally optimal.

A. GREEDY CHAIN DECOMPOSITIONS

Any given poset P can be canonically decomposed into "levels". To construct this decomposition, we find the set L_1 of minimal elements of P (that is, the elements of P without predecessor), then set L_2 of minimal elements of $P - L_1$, and continue likewise until we find a set L_h such that $P - L_1 - \cdots - L_h$ is empty. The set L_i is the ith *level* of P, and h is the *height* of P. By construction, every element of L_i has a predecessor in L_{i-1}, for $i = 2, \ldots, h$. Thus P contains a chain of size h. Because each level is an antichain, the maximum size of a chain in P is precisely h.

The levels of a poset P of order n can be found in time $O(n^2)$. If, while constructing the levels, we record for each vertex in a level L_i with $i \geq 2$ one of its predecessors in the previous level L_{i-1}, a maximum chain of P can be then found in time $O(h)$.

PROPOSITION 1. *There is a $O(n^{2.5})$ algorithm finding a greedy chain decomposition of any poset of order n.*

PROOF. We assume we know all the relations of P. If needed, we compute a transitive closure in time $\tilde{O}(n^\omega)$, where ω is any real such that any two $n \times n$ matrices can be multiplied by performing $O(n^\omega)$ arithmetic operations, e.g., $\omega = 2.376$.

While the height of P exceeds $\sqrt{n}$, we repeat the following steps: build the decomposition of P into levels from scratch, find a maximum chain C in P, record C and remove C from P. This first phase takes $O(\sqrt{n}n^2) = O(n^{2.5})$ time.

Now the height of P is at most $\sqrt{n}$. We continue as before except that rebuilding the levels each time from scratch, we update them. To this end, we maintain for each element v of P a *table of predecessors*. Suppose v lies in level L_i. Then the jth entry of the table gives the list of predecessors of v lying j levels down, in level L_{i-j}.

Updating the levels is done as follows. First, for each element u of the chain C, we delete u from P and update the table of predecessors of every successor of u. We mark every element $v \in P - C$ such that the first component of the predecessor table for v becomes empty. Second, for $i = 1, \ldots, h$, we process the ith level L_i: For each element u that is marked, we determine the minimum index j such that the jth component of the predecessor table for u is non-empty, move u in level L_{i-j}, update the predecessor table for u and the predecessor table of every successor v of u. Again, we mark every element v such that the first component of the predecessor table for v becomes empty.

In order to analyze the algorithm, we assign to each relation of P a "score". The *score* of $u \leqslant_P v$ is $i+j$, where i and j are the indices of the levels containing u and v, respectively. Initially, the score of each relation is $O(\sqrt{n})$. Each time a relation is considered, its score is decreased by at least one. Hence, a given relation is considered $O(\sqrt{n})$ times through all the updates. Thus, the second phase of the algorithm also takes $O(n^2\sqrt{n}) = O(n^{2.5})$ time.

Therefore, a greedy chain decomposition can be found in $O(n^{2.5})$ time. □

B. COMPUTING THE ENTROPY OF WIDTH 2 POSETS

Consider a poset P of order n, covered by two disjoint chains A and B. If P is a chain, then $H(\bar{P}) = 0$. Now, assume that P is not a chain, so the width of P is exactly 2.

Let again G denote the incomparability graph of P, that is, $G = \bar{G}(P)$. The properties of G that we repeatedly use below are stated in the next lemma (the proof is omitted).

LEMMA 11. *Let P be a poset covered by two disjoint chains A and B, and let $G = \bar{G}(P)$. Then:*

(i) The graph G is bipartite, with bipartition A, B;

(ii) The neighborhood $N(u)$ of any vertex u in G is an interval in the opposite chain (thus, G is biconvex*);*

(iii) Consider two elements u and v of the same chain, say A, and such that $u \leqslant_P v$. Let $[c_u, d_u]$ and $[c_v, d_v]$ denote the intervals of A defined by $N(u)$ and $N(v)$, respectively. Then, we have $c_u \leqslant_P c_v$ and $d_u \leqslant_P d_v$. In particular, $N(w)$ is contained in the interval $[c_u, d_v]$ of A with endpoints c_u and d_v, whenever w belongs to A and $u \leqslant_P w \leqslant_P v$.

Suppose that, in the definition of the partitions $A = A_1 \cup \cdots \cup A_k$ and $B = B_1 \cup \cdots \cup B_k$ given after Theorem 4, each set A_i is chosen to be inclusion-wise minimal among the subsets of $A' = A - A_1 - \cdots - A_{i-1}$ maximizing the ratio (3). We claim that, with this choice of A_i, each A_i is an interval of the chain A and each B_i is an interval of the chain B. As precedingly, let $B' = B - B_1 - \cdots - B_{i-1}$ and let G' be the subgraph of G induced by $A' \cup B'$.

First, we show that the subgraph of G' induced by $A_i \cup B_i$ is connected, for every $i \in \{1, \ldots, k\}$. Suppose otherwise, that is, for some $i \in \{1, \ldots, k\}$, there are partitions $A_i = A_i^1 \cup A_i^2$ and $B_i = B_i^1 \cup B_i^2$ such that $N_{G'}(A_i^1) = B_i^1$ and $N_{G'}(A_i^2) = B_i^2$. Then, we have

$$\max\left\{\frac{|A_i^1|}{|B_i^1|}, \frac{|A_i^2|}{|B_i^2|}\right\} \geq \frac{|A_i^1| + |A_i^2|}{|B_i^1| + |B_i^2|} = \frac{|A_i|}{|B_i|},$$

contradicting the choice of A_i.

Second, we show that, for every $i \in \{1, \ldots, k\}$, the sets A_i and B_i are intervals in the chains A' and B', respectively. Let u and v be two elements of A_i such that $u <_P v$ and $w \notin A_i$ whenever $u <_P w <_P v$. By Lemma 11(iii), because $G'[A_i \cup B_i]$ is connected, the intervals $N_{G'}(u)$ and $N_{G'}(v)$ are non-disjoint. By the choice of A_i, the vertices u and v are consecutive in A' because adding to A_i any point $w \in A' - A_i$ with $u <_P w <_P v$ increases $|A_i|$ without changing $|N_{G'}(A_i)|$. It follows that A_i is an interval of the chain A', hence $B_i = N_{G'}(A_i)$ is an interval of the chain B'.

Third, this implies that, for every $i \in \{1, \ldots, k\}$, the sets A_i and B_i are intervals in the chains A and B, respectively. The claim follows.

Now, we are ready to prove that computing the entropy of a poset of width 2 can be done in $O(n^2 \log^2 n)$ time.

PROOF OF LEMMA 8. Let again $G = \bar{G}(P)$ and A, B be a bipartition of G. Initialize i to 1.

While A' contains a vertex u isolated in G', we let $A_i = \{u\}$ and $B_i = \varnothing$, and increase i.

While A' is not empty, we use the method of Körner and Marton to pick the next set A_i. Rather than allowing A_i be any subset of A' maximizing (3), we seek a set A_i maximizing (3) that is also an interval of A'. (By the above discussion, such a set exists.) We claim this can be done in $O(n \log^2 n)$ time.

Let $a_1, \ldots, a_\ell$ and $b_1, \ldots, b_m$ be enumerations of the elements of A' and B', respectively, such that $a_j \leqslant_P a_{j+1}$ for $j \in \{1, \ldots, \ell - 1\}$ and $b_j \leqslant_P b_{j+1}$ for $j \in \{1, \ldots, m-1\}$. We parametrize the intervals of A' by pairs (α, β) with $0 \leq \alpha < \beta \leq \ell$. The interval corresponding to the pair (α, β) is $[a_{\alpha+1}, a_\beta]$.

For a given $\alpha \in \{0, \ldots, \ell - 1\}$, we let γ be the smallest index such that b_γ is adjacent (that is, incomparable) to $a_{\alpha+1}$, and let $f(\alpha) = \gamma - 1$. For a given $\beta \in \{1, \ldots, \ell\}$, we let δ be the largest index such that b_δ is adjacent (that is, incomparable) to a_β, and let $g(\beta) = \delta$. Because no isolated vertex of G' belongs to A' (if such a vertex existed, it should have been included in A_{i-1}), $f(\alpha)$ and $g(\beta)$ are well-defined, and $f(\alpha) < g(\beta)$ whenever $0 \le \alpha < \beta \le \ell$.

By Lemma 11(iii), the neighborhood of the interval $[a_{\alpha+1}, a_\beta]$ corresponding to the pair (α, β) is the interval $[b_{f(\alpha)+1}, b_{g(\beta)}]$. It follows that the ratio (3) computed for $A_i = [a_{\alpha+1}, a_\beta]$ equals

$$\frac{\beta - \alpha}{g(\beta) - f(\alpha)}. \tag{5}$$

Let ρ be a guess on the maximum ratio (3) achieved by an interval A_i of A'. We wish to know if there exist indices α and β satisfying $0 \le \alpha < \beta \le \ell$ such that (5) is at least ρ. Equivalently, we wish to know if there exist $\alpha \in \{0, \dots, \ell-1\}$ and $\beta \in \{1, \dots, \ell\}$ such that

$$\alpha + 1 \le \beta \quad \text{and} \quad \alpha - \rho f(\alpha) \le \beta - \rho g(\beta).$$

If we can solve this subproblem in time $T(n)$, we can find the desired interval A_i in time $O(T(n) \log n)$ by a binary search over ρ.

Now, to each value α in $\{0, \dots, \ell - 1\}$ we associate a *blue* point $(\alpha+1, \alpha - \rho f(\alpha))$ in $\mathbb{R}^2$ and to each value β in $\{1, \dots, \ell\}$ we associate a *red* point $(\beta, \beta - \rho g(\beta))$ in $\mathbb{R}^2$. The subproblem amounts to finding a pair of points in $\mathbb{R}^2$, one blue and the other red, such that the blue point is coordinate-wise smaller or equal to the red point. Since this can easily be solved in $O(n \log n)$ time (see, e.g., [6]), the claim follows.

Then, we define B_i as $N_{G'}(A_i)$, increase i, and update G', A' and B'. We also update all values $f(\alpha)$ and $g(\beta)$.

Now A' is empty. While B' is not empty, we pick any element v in B', let $A_i = \varnothing$ and $B_i = \{v\}$, and increase i.

In time $O(n^2 \log^2 n)$, we obtain partitions $A = A_1 \cup \cdots \cup A_k$ and $B = B_1 \cup \cdots \cup B_k$. The optimal solution of (1) is obtained by letting $x_u = |A_i|/(|A_i| + |B_i|)$ and $x_v = |B_i|/(|A_i| + |B_i|)$ for $u \in A_i$ and $v \in B_i$. □

C. THE LOCAL IMPROVEMENT PROCEDURE

Now, we show that the weight updates (step 1d in ALGORITHM 4 and step 4i in ALGORITHM 5) can be implemented so that the total cost over all iterations is $O(n^2)$. The following lemma gives important structural information on locally optimal points. Below, when X and Y are two disjoint subsets of the poset P, we write $X \leqslant_P Y$ whenever $u \leqslant_P v$ holds for every $u \in X$ and every $v \in Y$.

LEMMA 12. *Let P be a poset covered by two disjoint chains A, B, and let $G = \bar{G}(P)$. Consider a point x in* STAB(G). *Let $C_1, \dots, C_k$ denote the components of $G(x)$ and, for $i = 1, \dots, k$, let $A_i = A \cap C_i$ and $B_i = B \cap C_i$. If x is locally optimal, then*

(i) each A_i and each B_i is an interval in its respective chain;

(ii) $A_i \leqslant_P A_j$ holds if and only if $B_i \leqslant_P B_j$ holds.

PROOF. (i) Suppose otherwise. Then there exists an index $i \in \{1, \dots, k\}$, distinct vertices u, u'' in A_i such that $u' \notin A_i$ whenever $u <_P u' <_P u''$, and a vertex w in $A - A_i$ such that $u <_P w <_P u''$. By Lemma 11(iii), because C_i is a component of $G(x)$ containing u and u'', there is a vertex v of B_i adjacent to both u and u'' in G.

By Lemma 11(ii), the neighborhood of v in G is an interval of A containing u and u''. Thus, it also contains w. Because w does not belong to C_i, the edge vw is not tight with respect to x. Thus, we have $x_v + x_w < 1$, that is, $x_w < x_u = x_{u''}$.

Let C_j denote the component of w in $G(x)$. Because x is locally optimal, w is not the only vertex of C_j because otherwise (4) would imply $x_w = 1$. Thus there exists a vertex v' in B adjacent to w. By Lemma 11(iii), this vertex is adjacent to u or u''. Without loss of generality, assume that v' is adjacent to u. Then we have $x_u + x_{v'} = x_u + (1 - x_w) > 1$, a contradiction.

(ii) By contradiction, suppose $A_i \leqslant_P A_j$ and at the same time $B_j \leqslant_P B_i$, for distinct indices i, j in $\{1, \dots, k\}$. Without loss of generality, assume that $|A_j|/|B_j| \ge |A_i|/|B_i|$. Now, let $u \in A_i$ and let $v \in B_j$. Because x is locally optimal and the components of $G(x)$ respectively containing u and v are distinct, u and v are comparable in P. If $u \leqslant_P v$ then also $\{u\} \leqslant_P B_i$, contradicting the fact that C_i is connected. If $v \leqslant_P u$ then also $\{v\} \leqslant_P A_j$, contradicting the fact that C_j is connected. □

LEMMA 13. *Step 1d of* ALGORITHM 4 *can be implemented in time $O(n)$.*

PROOF. As in the proof of Lemma 10, let P denote the partial information before the merging operation 1b, let $G = \bar{G}(P)$, let P' denote the partial information after the merging operation 1b, and let $G' = \bar{G}(P')$.

Computing the new incomparability graph. First, we compute the graph G' from G. For representing the incomparability graphs, it suffices to record the two endpoints of the interval of A or B defined by the neighborhood of each vertex (again, we use Lemma 11(ii)). Using that representation, we can efficiently compute G' from G, as follows.

Knowing the chain resulting from the merging of A_j and B_j, we partition A_j into three (possibly empty) sets A_j^1, A_j^2 and A_j^3. The first set A_j^1 consists of all elements u of A_j such that $\{u\} \leqslant_{P'} B_j$. The third set A_j^3 consists of all elements u of A_j such that $B_j \leqslant_{P'} \{u\}$. The second set A_j^2 contains the other elements of A_j. Notice that the elements in A_j^2, as the elements in B_j, are cutpoints of P' (that is, they are comparable to all other elements).

Because x is locally optimal, each element of $A - A_j$ is already comparable to all elements of B_j in P. The neighborhood of these elements is not affected by the merging operation. The neighborhood $N_{G'}(u)$ of an element u in A_j^1 (resp. A_j^3) can be obtained by removing from $N_G(u)$ all elements v such that $w \leqslant_P v$ (resp. $v \leqslant_P w$) for some w in B_j. For elements u in A_j^2, we have $N_{G'}(u) = \varnothing$.

This defines the edge set of G'. The neighborhood $N_{G'}(v)$ of each element v in B can obtained from its corresponding neighborhood $N_G(v)$ accordingly.

Updating the weights. Second, letting $x' \in \mathbb{R}^V$ denote the point obtained from x by raising x_v to 1 for all $v \in B_j$, we transform x' into a new point of STAB(G') that is locally optimal and whose entropy is at most that of x'. This is done by raising some weights in x' and decreasing some other weights in x'. During this process, we keep track of the way the initial partitions $A = A_1 \cup \cdots \cup A_k$ and $B = B_1 \cup \cdots \cup B_k$ evolve. By Lemma 12(i), each A_i is an interval in A

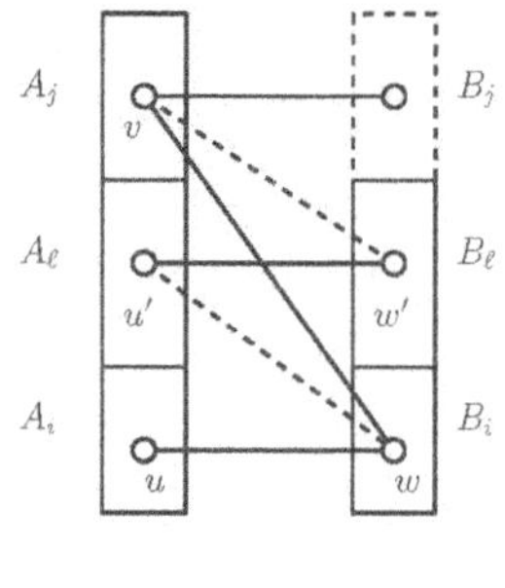

Figure 2. Illustration of the proof of Lemma 13.

and each B_i is an interval in B. Hence, we can represent these partitions by recording the endpoints of each interval involved.

Phase 1. First, we raise the weight x'_u to 1 for all vertices u of A_j that are isolated in G'. As the vertices of B_j, they become trivial components. Next, we raise the weights x'_v corresponding to vertices v of A_j that are not isolated in G', causing these vertices to move in components adjacent to A_j. The vertices of A_j that are not isolated in G' belong to either A_j^1 or A_j^3. They respectively form initial and final subintervals of A_j that we denote by I^1 and I^3.

For now, we focus on A_j^1 and I^1. Our handling of A_j^3 and I^3 is symmetric.

Assuming $I^1 \neq \varnothing$ (otherwise nothing has to be done), choose $\ell \in \{1, \ldots, k\}$ in such a way that the interval A_ℓ directly precedes A_j in $\leqslant_P$. By Lemma 12(ii), B_ℓ also directly precedes B_j in $\leqslant_P$. All elements of I^1 are adjacent to at least one element in B_ℓ and, in particular, to the maximum of B_ℓ. Now raise the weight x'_v for each $v \in I^1$ simultaneously, at the same speed, until some edge vw of G' becomes tight. (Proceed similarly for vertices in I^3.) Thus, we obtain a new point $x'' \in \mathrm{STAB}(G')$. We claim that w belongs to B_ℓ.

Suppose otherwise. Then w belongs to a component C_i distinct from C_ℓ. Necessarily, we have $A_i \leqslant_P A_\ell \leqslant_P A_j$ and $B_i \leqslant_P B_\ell \leqslant_P B_j$.

Let $u'w'$ be an edge of G' such that $u' \in A_\ell$ and $w' \in B_\ell$. Let also $u \in A_i$ be a neighbor of w in G'. Such an edge and such a neighbor exist because C_ℓ and C_i are non-trivial components of G'. Because the neighborhood of a vertex in G' is an interval in the opposite chain (Lemma 11(ii)), vw' and $u'w$ are edges of G', see Figure 2 for an illustration. Then, we have

$$\begin{aligned} x''_v &= 1 - x''_w \quad \text{(because } vw \text{ is tight)} \\ &> x''_{u'} \quad \text{(because } u'w \text{ is not tight)} \\ &= 1 - x''_{w'} \quad \text{(because } u'w' \text{ is tight)} \\ &\geq x''_v \quad \text{(because } vw' \text{ is an edge and } x'' \text{ is feasible)}, \end{aligned}$$

a contradiction. The claim follows.

Therefore, each component of $G'(x'')$ either is trivial, or is already a component of $G(x)$, or is obtained by moving the vertices of I^1 to the component C_ℓ of $G(x)$ directly preceding C_j in $\leqslant_P$, or the elements of I^3 to the component of $G(x)$ directly succeeding C_j in $\leqslant_P$.

Phase 2. Now, we adjust the weights in x'' for the updated component(s). Once again, we focus on the case of the component $C_\ell \cup I^1$ of $G'(x'')$.

The weights in $A_\ell \cup I^1$ and B_ℓ with respect to x'' are respectively $|A_\ell|/(|A_\ell| + |B_\ell|)$ and $|B_\ell|/(|A_\ell| + |B_\ell|)$. For turning x'' into a locally optimal point, the weights should become $(|A_\ell| + |I^1|)/(|A_\ell| + |B_\ell| + |I^1|)$ and $(|B_\ell|)/(|A_\ell| + |B_\ell| + |I^1|)$, respectively. Thus, the weights should be raised for elements in $A_\ell \cup I^1$ and decreased for elements in B_ℓ.

If no component of $G'(x'')$ precedes C_ℓ in $\leqslant_P$, then nothing can prevent this update. Otherwise, let C_m denote the component of $G'(x'')$ directly preceding C_ℓ. If there is no edge from $A_\ell \cup I^1$ to B_m in G', then we are fine again. Now assume that there is such an edge. Notice that this occurs if and only if the minimum element v of $A_\ell \cup I^1$ is adjacent to the maximum element w' of B_m.

We simultaneously raise the weights of the elements in $A_\ell \cup I^1$ and decrease the weights of the elements in B_ℓ. If some edge becomes tight, we stop. Let x''' denote the resulting point of $\mathrm{STAB}(G')$.

If some edge became tight, by the same argument used above (see Figure 2), the edges that became tight are precisely those that have one end in $A_\ell \cup I^1$ and the other end in B_m. (In particular, vw' became tight.) Then $A_\ell \cup I^1$, B_ℓ, A_m and B_m merge into a component of $G'(x''')$.

If no edge became tight, we can update the weights as initially planned.

Now, either x''' is locally optimal or we repeat the process, until we reach a locally optimal solution.

Finally, we note that the above local improvement procedure produces a point whose entropy is at most the entropy of x'. Indeed, in the first phase, we only increase weights, which always decreases the entropy. In the second phase, we re-balance some weights: letting $C_i = A_i \cup B_i$ denote a new component of $G'(x'')$ (e.g., $A_i = A_j \cup I^1$ and $B_i = B_j$), we increase x''_u towards $|A_i|/(|A_i|+|B_i|)$ for $u \in A_i$ and decrease x''_v towards $|B_i|/(|A_i| + |B_i|)$ for $v \in B_i$, while keeping that $x''_u + x''_v = 1$ for $u \in A_i$ and $v \in B_i$. This does not increase the entropy either, because the function

$$f(x) := \frac{|A_i|}{|A_i| + |B_i|} \log x + \frac{|B_i|}{|A_i| + |B_i|} \log(1 - x)$$

is strictly convex over the interval $(0, 1)$ with a minimum in $x = |A_i|/(|A_i| + |B_i|)$.

Computing the new incomparability graph and the first phase can both be done in $O(n)$ time. Each iteration of the second phase takes constant time. But there cannot be more than n iterations, as the number of components decreases by one every time. Thus the whole procedure has complexity $O(n)$. □

Note that an invariant of the main loop in ALGORITHM 4 is that for all components $C_i = A_i \cup B_i$ such that $A_i \neq \varnothing$, we have $|A_i| \geq |B_i|$. It is easy to check that this invariant is maintained throughout the above update operations.

By arguments similar to those used in the proof of Lemma 13, we easily get the following result.

LEMMA 14. *Step 4j of* ALGORITHM 5 *can be implemented in time* $O(n^2)$.

Matroid Matching: the Power of Local Search

[Extended Abstract]

Jon Lee
IBM Research
Yorktown Heights, NY
jonlee@us.ibm.com

Maxim Sviridenko
IBM Research
Yorktown Heights, NY
sviri@us.ibm.com

Jan Vondrák
IBM Research
San Jose, CA
jvondrak@us.ibm.com

ABSTRACT

We consider the classical *matroid matching* problem. Unweighted matroid matching for linear matroids was solved by Lovász, and the problem is known to be intractable for general matroids. We present a PTAS for unweighted matroid matching for general matroids. In contrast, we show that natural LP relaxations have an $\Omega(n)$ integrality gap and moreover, $\Omega(n)$ rounds of the Sherali-Adams hierarchy are necessary to bring the gap down to a constant.

More generally, for any fixed $k \geq 2$ and $\epsilon > 0$, we obtain a $(k/2+\epsilon)$-approximation for matroid matching in k-uniform hypergraphs, also known as the matroid k-parity problem. As a consequence, we obtain a $(k/2+\epsilon)$-approximation for the problem of finding the maximum-cardinality set in the intersection of k matroids. We have also designed a 3/2-approximation for the weighted version of a special case of matroid matching, the *matchoid problem.*

Categories and Subject Descriptors

F.2.2 [**Nonnumerical Algorithms and Problems**]: Computations on discrete structures

General Terms

Algorithms, Theory

Keywords

matroid, matching, local search, Sherali-Adams hierarchy

1. INTRODUCTION

The matroid matching problem was proposed by Lawler as a common generalization of two important polynomial-time solvable problems: the non-bipartite matching problem, and the matroid-intersection problem (see [32]). Unfortunately, it turns out that matroid matching for general matroids is intractable and requires an exponential number of queries if the matroid is given by an oracle (see [36, 26]). This result can be easily transformed into an NP-completeness proof for a concrete class of matroids (see [46]). An important result of Lovász is that (unweighted) matroid matching can be solved in polynomial time for *linear matroids* (see [35]). There have been several attempts to generalize Lovász' result to the weighted case. Polynomial-time algorithms are known for some special cases (see [49]), but for general linear matroids there is only a pseudopolynomial-time randomized exact algorithm (see [8, 40]).

In this paper, we revisit the matroid matching problem for general matroids. Our main result is that while LP-based approaches including the Sherali-Adams hierarchy fail to provide any meaningful approximation, a simple local-search algorithm gives a PTAS (in the unweighted case). This is the first PTAS for general matroid matching and to our knowledge also the first example of a problem where there is such a dramatic gap between the performance of the Sherali-Adams hierarchy and a simple combinatorial algorithm. We also provide approximation results for a generalization of the problem to hypergraphs; more details follow.

We assume familiarity with approximation algorithms (see [51], for example) and matroid algorithmics (see [46], for example). Throughout, we consider maximization problems. A *c-approximation algorithm* finds in polynomial time a solution of value at least OPT$/c$. Briefly, for a matroid $\mathcal{M}$, we denote the ground set of $\mathcal{M}$ by $V = V(\mathcal{M})$, its set of independent sets by $\mathcal{I} = \mathcal{I}(\mathcal{M})$, and its rank function by $r_{\mathcal{M}}$. For a given matroid $\mathcal{M}$, the associated *matroid constraint* is $S \in \mathcal{I}(\mathcal{M})$ or equivalently $|S| = r_{\mathcal{M}}(S)$.

In the *matroid hypergraph matching problem*, we are given a matroid $\mathcal{M} = (V, \mathcal{I})$ and a hypergraph $G = (V, \mathcal{E})$ where $\mathcal{E} \subseteq 2^V$. Note that the vertex set of the hypergraph G and the ground set of the matroid $\mathcal{M}$ are the same. The goal is to choose a maximum-cardinality collection of disjoint hyperedges $E^* \subseteq \mathcal{E}$ in hypergraph G, such that the set of vertices covered by hyperedges in E^* is an independent set in matroid $\mathcal{M}$. If G is a graph, we obtain the classical matroid matching problem.

The matroid hypergraph matching problem generalizes several classical optimization problems, namely:

1. If M is a *free matroid* (i.e., $\mathcal{I}(\mathcal{M}) = 2^V$), then the problem is the *maximum hypergraph matching problem* or the *maximum set-packing problem.* Set packing in general is NP-hard, but when G is a graph, it is the classical matching problem which led Edmonds to the notion of polynomial-time algorithms (see [15, 16]).

2. In the *k-matroid intersection problem* we are given k matroids $\mathcal{M}_1 = (V, \mathcal{I}_1), \ldots, \mathcal{M}_k = (V, \mathcal{I}_k)$ on the same

STOC'10, June 5–8, 2010, Cambridge, Massachusetts, USA.

ground set V, and the goal is to find a maximum cardinality set S of elements that is independent in each of the k matroids, i.e. $S \in \cap_{j=1}^{k} \mathcal{I}_j$. The k-matroid intersection problem is NP-hard for $k \geq 3$ but polynomially solvable for $k = 2$ (see [46]).

3. A problem of intermediate generality is the *k-uniform matchoid* problem, defined for $k = 2$ by Edmonds and studied by Jenkyns (see [27]). In this problem, we have a k-uniform hypergraph and a matroid $\mathcal{M}_v$ given for each vertex v, having ground set the set of hyperedges containing v. The goal is to choose a maximum collection of hyperedges S, such that for each v, the hyperedges in S containing v form an independent set in $\mathcal{M}_v$. This can be also seen as a packing problem with many matroid constraints, where each item participates in at most k of them.

   By taking each $\mathcal{M}_v$ to be the uniform matroid of rank 1, we get the set-packing problem. By taking k arbitrary matroids defined on k copies of the same ground set V and a hypergraph of n parallel hyperedges on the k copies of the same element from V, we get k-matroid intersection. On the other hand, the matchoid problem is a special case of matroid matching, as we show below. We remark that even for $k = 2$, the matchoid problem is NP-hard (see [36]).

4. The special case of the matroid hypergraph matching problem when each vertex belongs to a unique hyperedge, and all hyperedges have cardinality exactly k is known as the *matroid k-parity problem*, or simply the *matroid parity problem* when $k = 2$. As we show below, this problem is in fact equivalent to k-uniform matroid matching, even in terms of approximation.

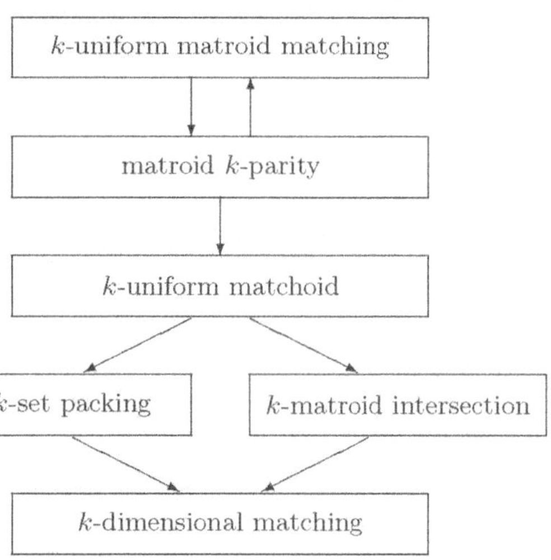

Next, we explain how the k-uniform matchoid problem is a special case of matroid k-parity. Given a hypergraph G, we can replace each vertex by n_v distinct copies, where n_v is the number of hyperedges containing v. We replace each hyperedge in G by a collection of distinct copies of its elements, so that we get a hypergraph G' where the hyperedges are disjoint. In the matchoid problem, we have a matroid $\mathcal{M}_v$ defined on the n_v copies of each vertex v, and we define a new matroid $\mathcal{M}'$ by taking the union of the matroids $\mathcal{M}_v$. Then matroid k-parity for $(G', \mathcal{M}')$ is equivalent to the original k-uniform matchoid for $(G, \mathcal{M}_v)$.

In fact, a similar construction implies that matroid k-parity includes (and therefore is equivalent to) matroid matching in k-uniform hypergraphs (or more generally in hypergraphs where each hyperedge has cardinality at most k, which can be shown by adding dummy elements). Given an instance of k-uniform matroid matching, we define n_v copies for each vertex v where n_v is the degree of v in the hypergraph $G = (V, \mathcal{E})$. We replace each hyperedge in G by a collection of distinct copies of its elements, so that the new hyperedges are disjoint. Let $G' = (V', \mathcal{E}')$ be the new hypergraph. We also define a new matroid $\mathcal{M}'$ on the ground set V', where the n_v copies of each vertex act as parallel copies. That is, a set of vertices $S' \subseteq V'$ is independent in $\mathcal{M}'$ if it contains at most one copy of each vertex from V and the respective set $S \subseteq V$ is independent in $\mathcal{M}$. It is not difficult to show that $\mathcal{M}'$ is a matroid.

Henceforth, we will discuss the matroid k-parity problem with the understanding that all our results can be easily extended to the k-uniform matroid matching problem. For the purposes of this paper, the terms *matroid matching* and *matroid parity* are essentially interchangeable.

Literature overview.

There are a few different lines of research relevant to our results. The matroid parity problem (for $k = 2$) was originally popularized by Lawler [31]. The maximum-cardinality matroid parity problem was shown to have exponential query complexity in general (see [36, 26]), and to be NP-hard for some concrete classes of matroids. If the matroid is linear over the reals, the problem is polynomially solvable (see [35, 20, 41, 42, 48]). For more on matroid parity, applications and closely related problems, see [6, 37, 43, 44]. The linear matroid k-parity problem also admits a polynomial time algorithm if k is a constant, and the rank of matroid $\mathcal{M}$ is $O(\log|V|)$ (see [4]). The special case of matroid intersection can be solved in polynomial time for arbitrary matroids (see for example [46]), even in the weighted case.

It is not difficult to show that a simple greedy algorithm that adds hyperedges one-by-one, as long as the current solution remains independent, gives a k-approximation for general weighted matroid k-parity and that this guarantee is tight. This follows from the work of Jenkyns on k-independence systems; see [28] (see also Section 2). Until our present work, this was the only algorithm known for the general matroid k-parity problem with a provable approximation guarantee. The only improvement to our knowledge has been achieved in the case of unweighted matroid matching ($k = 2$), where Fujito proved that a local-search algorithm gives a 3/2-approximation (see [19]).

Linear-programming relaxations for the matroid matching problem ($k = 2$) have been studied in [50, 11, 12, 21]. An LP proposed by Vande Vate (see [50]) has been shown to be half-integral, and moreover, there are polynomial-time algorithms to find a half-integral optimal solution in the unweighted case (see [11, 12]) and the general weighted case (see [21]). However, this approach has not yielded any approximation algorithms for matroid matching.

We now survey known results on the approximability of various special cases of the matroid k-parity problem. Local-search algorithms exploring a larger neighborhood for the k-set packing problem were analyzed in [25]. They showed that a local-search algorithm produces a solution with approximation guarantee $k/2 + \epsilon$ for any fixed $\epsilon > 0$ and constant k

in polynomial time. Hardness of approximation results are known for the maximum k-dimensional matching problem which is a special case of the maximum k-set packing problem and hence also matroid k-parity. The best known lower bound is the $\Omega(k/\log k)$ hardness of approximation of [24]. It is also known that a large-neighborhood local-search algorithm has a tight approximation guarantee of $k-1+\epsilon$ for the problem of (weighted) k-matroid intersection (see [33]). It should be noted though that unweighted versions of packing problems seem to be easier for algorithm design and analysis, and approximation guarantees for general linear objective functions can often be improved for an unweighted variants.

The Sherali-Adams hierarchy (see [47]) has been studied recently for a number of combinatorial optimization problems (see [29, 30] for surveys on the results in this area). Mathieu and Sinclair proved (see [38]) for the non-bipartite matching problem that r rounds of Sherali-Adams applied to the matching polytope have integrality gap $1+O(1/r)$ and hence provides a PTAS (while the problem can be solved exactly in polynomial time). Chan and Lau considered k-uniform hypergraph matching, i.e. k-set packing, and proved that that even after $O(n)$ rounds of Sherali-Adams, the standard LP has integrality gap at least $k-2$ (see [9]). In contrast, local search techniques yield a $(k/2+\epsilon)$-approximation (see [25]), and an alternative LP (using intuition from local search) has integrality gap at most $(k+1)/2$ (see [9]).

Our Results.

On the negative side, we show that the known linear relaxations of matroid parity do not yield any reasonable approximation guarantee (even for $k=2$ with unit weights). More precisely, all variants of the LPs that have been proposed have an $\Omega(n)$ integrality gap for instances with n pairs. Moreover, $\Omega(n)$ rounds of the Sherali-Adams hierarchy are required to generate an LP with a constant integrality gap.

In contrast, we prove that a very simple local-search algorithm gives a PTAS for unweighted matroid parity. Given the negative results for the matroid parity problem (see [36, 26]), this is the best type of worst-case result we could expect for this problem. It is also a strong manifestation of the fact that LP-based hierarchies do not always match the performance of combinatorial algorithms (which was, in a weaker sense, shown previously for the matching problem in graphs (see [38]) and hypergraphs (see [9])).

For the more general problem of unweighted matroid k-parity, we present a $(k/2+\epsilon)$-approximation, for any fixed $k\geq 2$ and $\epsilon>0$. As a special case, this subsumes the (unweighted) k-matroid intersection problem for which a k-approximation was known since 1976 (see [28]) and has been only recently improved to $k-1+\epsilon$ (see [33]).

The algorithm that we analyze is simple local search that in each iteration seeks to remove $s(\epsilon)$ hyperedges and add $s(\epsilon)+1$ hyperedges to the current solution in such a way that the new solution defines an independent set in matroid $\mathcal{M}$. We call this the *s-neighborhood local-search algorithm*. If there is no improvement the algorithm stops and outputs the current local optimum. Our analysis uses an idea from [25] to reduce inductively the instance, and given the performance of the local search on the smaller instance, to derive the guarantee on the original one. But the presence of the matroid independence constraint complicates matters significantly. In particular, to achieve the approximation guarantee of $1+\epsilon$ for the matroid parity problem we need to implement the local-search algorithm with $s(\epsilon)$ exponentially large in $1/\epsilon$, while it is well known that $s(\epsilon)=\lceil 1+1/\epsilon\rceil$ is enough for the maximum matching problem in graphs (the fixed-size augmenting-path algorithm could be viewed as a local-search algorithm). We do not know if having such a large neighborhood is necessary or if it is just an artifact of our analysis. Surprisingly, for $k\geq 3$, we show that to achieve $k/2+\epsilon$ approximation, it is enough to run the local-search algorithm with $s(\epsilon)$ polynomially bounded in $1/\epsilon$.

The rest of the paper is organized as follows. In §2, we show that matroid k-parity is a special case of a "k-independence system" which implies a greedy k-approximation. In §3, we present our PTAS for unweighted matroid parity. In §4, we consider various linear-programming relaxations for the matroid parity problem and present our lower bounds on their integrality gap. In §5, we present a $(k/2+\epsilon)$-approximation for matroid k-parity.

We have also developed a 3/2-approximation algorithm for the weighted matchoid problem, which is a special case of weighted matroid parity. This result uses an LP relaxation of the matchoid problem and its known half-integrality (see [11, 12, 21, 50] for closely related LPs). We provide an alternative proof that is very simple and intuitive which might be of independent interest. Unfortunately, the space here does not allow us to present these results, so we refer to [34].

2. RELATION TO INDEPENDENCE SYSTEMS

First, we show that the matroid k-parity falls in the framework of k-independence systems (see [28]). Such systems generalize intersections of k matroids, and in fact several definitions of various degrees of generality have been proposed (see also [39, 7]). Jenkyns' definition is as follows.

DEFINITION 1. *A family of sets $\mathcal{I}\subset 2^V$ is a* p-system, *if for all $W\subseteq V$,*

$$\max\{|B|\ :\ B\subseteq W, B\in\mathcal{I}\}\leq p\cdot\min\{|B|\ :\ B\subseteq W, B\in\mathcal{I}\}$$

LEMMA 1. *The independence system corresponding to matroid k-parity is a k-system.*

PROOF. Consider an independent collection of hyperedges $W=\{e_1,\dots,e_\ell\}$, and two bases (i.e., setwise maximal independent subsets) B_1,B_2 of W. Assume toward a contradiction that $|B_2|>k|B_1|$. Let $S_1=\bigcup\{e:e\in B_1\}$ and $S_2=\bigcup\{e:e\in B_2\}$; i.e. $|S_i|=k|B_i|$ and both S_1 and S_2 are independent in the matroid $\mathcal{M}$. By the matroid extension axiom, S_1 can be completed from S_2 to a set $S_1\cup S_2'$ independent in $\mathcal{M}$, where $S_2'\subseteq S_2\setminus S_1$ and $|S_2'|=|S_2|-|S_1|=k|B_2|-k|B_1|$. Note that S_2' is not necessarily a union of hyperedges. However, it must contain at least one hyperedge, otherwise $|S_2'|\leq(k-1)|B_2|<k|B_2|-k|B_1|$. Therefore, there is a hyperedge $e_i\in B_2\setminus B_1$ that we can add to B_1 which contradicts B_1 being a base of W. □

The work of [27, 18] for p-systems gives the following results (see also [7]).

THEOREM 1. *The greedy algorithm gives a p-approximation for maximizing a linear function over a p-system. Moreover, the greedy algorithm gives a $(p+1)$-approximation for maximizing a monotone submodular function over a p-system.*

COROLLARY 1. *The greedy algorithm gives a k-approximation for matroid k-parity even in the weighted version. Moreover, the greedy algorithm gives a $(k+1)$-approximation for maximizing a monotone submodular function over sets feasible for the matroid k-parity problem.*

We regard the greedy k-approximation for matroid k-parity as a "folklore" result and a starting point for further improvements. For unweighted matroid parity ($k=2$), this has been improved to a factor of 3/2 by Fujito [19]. For general k, no better approximation was known prior to our work.

3. PTAS FOR MATROID PARITY

Let us start with the case of $k=2$, i.e. matroid parity. In an instance of matroid parity, we have disjoint pairs, and we look for a maximum-cardinality collection of pairs whose union forms an independent set in a given matroid. We present a PTAS for this problem.

DEFINITION 2. *For feasible solutions A and B of matroid parity, a "local move of size s between A and B" is a choice of $s-1$ pairs $e_1,\dots,e_{s-1}$ inside A, and s pairs $e'_1,\dots,e'_s$ inside B, such that $(A\setminus\bigcup_{i=1}^{s-1}e_i)\cup\bigcup_{i=1}^{s}e'_i$ is again feasible.*

THEOREM 2. *For any $\epsilon>0$, a local-search algorithm which considers local moves of size up to $s(\epsilon)=5^{\lceil 1/(2\epsilon)\rceil}$ achieves a $(1+\epsilon)$-approximation for the matroid parity problem.*

The same result also holds for matroid matching, by a simple reduction that we outlined in the introduction. The theorem follows immediately from the following characterization of local optima.

LEMMA 2. *Let $t\ge 1$, and A,B feasible solutions to the matroid parity problem such that*

$$|A|<(1-1/2t)\,|B|.$$

Then there is a local move of size 5^{t-1} between A and B.

Assuming that B is an actual optimum and A is a local optimum with respect to local moves of size 5^{t-1}, this implies that A is a $2t/(2t-1)$-approximate solution. This means that for any fixed $\epsilon>0$, we can pick $t=\lceil 1/(2\epsilon)\rceil+1$ and $s=5^{t-1}$; the corresponding local-search algorithm achieves a $(1+\epsilon)$-approximation for matroid parity.

It remains to prove the lemma. Our proofs uses the standard notion of matroid contraction. For a set $S\subset V(\mathcal{M})$, $\mathcal{M}/S$ (read $\mathcal{M}$ *contract* S) is the matroid having ground set $V(\mathcal{M})\setminus S$ and set of independent sets $\{T\subseteq V(\mathcal{M})\setminus S : T\cup J\in\mathcal{I}(\mathcal{M})\}$, where J is an arbitrary maximal independent subset of S with respect to $\mathcal{M}$.

PROOF. Let A,B be feasible solutions as above. (We assume for simplicity that A and B are disjoint, otherwise we can contract the intersection, which only decreases the ratio $|A|/|B|$.) Because $|A|<|B|$, there exists $B_0\subset B, |B_0|=|B|-|A|$ such that $A\cup B_0$ is independent in $\mathcal{M}$. We proceed by induction on t.

Base case: $t=1$.

For $t=1$, we have $|A|<\frac{1}{2}|B|$. Then, $|B_0|=|B|-|A|>\frac{1}{2}|B|$. Because B decomposes into disjoint pairs, this means there must be a pair contained inside B_0. This pair can be added to A without violating independence, i.e. there is a local move of size one.

General case: $t\ge 2$.

We assume that $|A|=|B|-a$ where $a>\frac{1}{2t}|B|$. We also assume $a\le\frac{1}{2}|B|$, otherwise we are in the base case. We construct a set $B_0\subset B$ as above, with $A\cup B_0$ independent and $|B_0|=a$. Again, if there is a pair contained inside B_0, we can add it to A, and we are done. So let us assume that no pair is contained completely inside B_0.

Every pair intersecting B_0 also contains an element in $B\setminus B_0$; let us denote the elements matched with B_0 by B_1. We have $|B_1|=|B_0|=a$. Let $\mathcal{M}_0=\mathcal{M}/B_0$ denote the matroid where B_0 has been contracted. Because $A\cup B_0$ and $B_1\cup B_0$ are independent in $\mathcal{M}$ (by construction), we get that A and B_1 are independent in $\mathcal{M}_0$. Because $|A|=|B|-a\ge a=|B_1|$, we can extend B_1 by adding (possibly zero) elements from A, to form an $\mathcal{M}_0$-independent set $(A\setminus A_1)\cup B_1$ where $|A_1|=|B_1|=a$.

If A_1 contains a pair e then we can find a local move as follows: $A\setminus e$ is independent in $\mathcal{M}_0$, and so is the set $(A\setminus A_1)\cup B_1$. Therefore, $A\setminus e$ can be extended to a set $(A\setminus e)\cup\{x',x''\}$ independent in $\mathcal{M}_0$, such that $x',x''\in B_1$. The elements x',x'' are contained in pairs e',e'' whose remaining elements are in B_0. Because $(A\setminus e)\cup\{x',x''\}$ is independent in $\mathcal{M}_0=\mathcal{M}/B_0$, any elements of B_0 can be added for free, and $(A\setminus e)\cup e'\cup e''$ is independent in $\mathcal{M}$. This defines a local move of size two.

The rest of the proof deals with the case when there is no pair contained in A_1. Then, every pair intersecting A_1 also contains an element in $A\setminus A_1$; let us denote the elements matched with A_1 by A_2. We have $|A_2|=|A_1|=a$. Here is where we apply the inductive hypothesis.

The inductive step.

We define a new matroid $\mathcal{M}_1=\mathcal{M}_0/B_1=\mathcal{M}/(B_0\cup B_1)$. By construction, the sets $A^*=A\setminus(A_1\cup A_2)$ and $B^*=B\setminus(B_0\cup B_1)$ are both independent in $\mathcal{M}_1$. They both form a union of pairs and hence are feasible solutions to the matroid parity problem for $\mathcal{M}_1$. We have $|A^*|=|A|-2a$ and $|B^*|=|B|-2a$. Because $|A|=|B|-a$, we get

$$\frac{|A^*|}{|B^*|}=\frac{|A|-2a}{|B|-2a}=\frac{|B|-3a}{|B|-2a}=1-\frac{1}{|B|/a-2}.$$

Because we assumed $a>\frac{1}{2t}|B|$, we have $|B|/a<2t$ and $|A^*|<(1-\frac{1}{2t-2})|B^*|$, so we can apply the inductive hypothesis. There is a local move of size $s=5^{t-2}$ between A^* and B^*, i.e. a union of $s-1$ pairs $\tilde{A}\subseteq A^*$ and s pairs $\tilde{B}\subseteq B^*$ such that $(A^*\setminus\tilde{A})\cup\tilde{B}$ is independent in $\mathcal{M}_1$. Our goal is to find a local move of size $5s=5^{t-1}$ between A and B (in $\mathcal{M}$).

The set $(A^*\setminus\tilde{A})\cup\tilde{B}$ is independent in $\mathcal{M}_1$. Unfortunately, $(A\setminus\tilde{A})\cup\tilde{B}$ is not necessarily independent, even in $\mathcal{M}$. We have to proceed more carefully. The set $(A^*\setminus\tilde{A})\cup A_2=A\setminus(A_1\cup\tilde{A})$ is independent in $\mathcal{M}_1=\mathcal{M}_0/B_1$, because $(A\setminus A_1)\cup B_1$ was constructed to be independent in $\mathcal{M}_0$. Therefore, we can extend $(A^*\setminus\tilde{A})\cup\tilde{B}$ to a set $(A^*\setminus\tilde{A})\cup\tilde{B}\cup(A_2\setminus C_2)$ independent in $\mathcal{M}_1$, where $C_2\subseteq A_2$ and $|C_2|\le|\tilde{B}|$. (If $|A_2|\le|\tilde{B}|$, we can just set $C_2=A_2$.)

The new set $(A^*\setminus\tilde{A})\cup\tilde{B}\cup(A_2\setminus C_2)$ is also independent in $\mathcal{M}_0$ (a weaker condition). So is $(A^*\setminus\tilde{A})\cup(A_2\setminus C_2)\cup A_1$, as any subset of A is independent in $\mathcal{M}_0$. Therefore, we can extend $(A^*\setminus\tilde{A})\cup\tilde{B}\cup(A_2\setminus C_2)$ to a set $(A^*\setminus\tilde{A})\cup\tilde{B}\cup(A_2\setminus C_2)\cup(A_1\setminus C_1)$ in $\mathcal{M}_0$, where $C_1\subseteq A_1$ and $|C_1|\le|\tilde{B}|$.

The set we have obtained is not necessarily a union of pairs, so let us remove the whole pair for each element in C_1 and C_2. Let us denote by C' the union of all pairs intersecting $C_1 \cup C_2$. By our construction, we have $C_1 \cup C_2 \subseteq C' \subseteq A_1 \cup A_2$. Further, let us define $C'_1 = C' \cap A_1$ and $C'_2 = C' \cap A_2$. Each pair on $A_1 \cup A_2$ contains exactly one element in A_1 and one element in A_2, therefore $|C'_1| = |C'_2|$. Also, $|C'_1| = |C'_2| \leq |C_1 \cup C_2|$, because each each element of $C_1 \cup C_2$ contributes at most one pair to C'.

We obtain a feasible solution $A^+ = (A^* \setminus \tilde{A}) \cup \tilde{B} \cup (A_2 \setminus C'_2) \cup (A_1 \setminus C'_1)$ in $\mathcal{M}_0$. Now, consider the set $(A^+ \setminus A_1) \cup B_1 = (A^* \setminus \tilde{A}) \cup \tilde{B} \cup (A_2 \setminus C'_2) \cup B_1$. This is independent in $\mathcal{M}_0$, because $A^+ \setminus A_1$ was constructed to be independent in $\mathcal{M}_1 = \mathcal{M}_0/B_1$. Because A^+ misses some elements in A_1, namely C'_1, the cardinality of $(A^+ \setminus A_1) \cup B_1$ is actually larger than $|A^+|$, $|(A^+ \setminus A_1) \cup B_1| = |A^+| + |C'_1|$. Hence, we can extend A^+ by $|C'_1|$ elements of B_1, let us call them F_1, to obtain a set $A^+ \cup F_1$ independent in $\mathcal{M}_0$. The pairs touching F_1 have exactly 1 element in B_1 and the other element in B_0. Let F_0 be the elements of B_0 matched with F_1. We can add F_0 for free and obtain an independent set $A^+ \cup F_1 \cup F_0$ in $\mathcal{M}$. We have $|F_0| = |F_1| = |C'_1| = |C'_2|$. Now $A^+ \cup F_1 \cup F_0$ is a union of pairs and hence a feasible solution, of cardinality

$$|A^+ \cup F_1 \cup F_0| = |A^+ \cup C'_1 \cup C'_2| = |(A \setminus \tilde{A}) \cup \tilde{B}| > |A|.$$

Finally, let us estimate the size of this local move. We removed $\tilde{A} \cup C'_1 \cup C'_2$ from A, and added $\tilde{B} \cup F_1 \cup F_0$ instead. The size of C'_1 is bounded by $|C'_1| < |C_1 \cup C_2| < 2|\tilde{B}|$, hence $|F_1| = |C'_1| \leq 2|\tilde{B}|$. The size of F_0 is equal to the size of F_1, i.e. $|F_0 \cup F_1| = 2|F_1| \leq 4|\tilde{B}|$. In summary, we are adding at most $5|\tilde{B}|$ elements to A, i.e. the size of the local move is at most $5|\tilde{B}| = 5s = 5^{t-1}$. □

4. LP RELAXATIONS

In this section, we consider a linear-programming approach to matroid parity. Our results in this direction are mostly negative and indicate that linear programming in this case fails very badly compared to the local-search algorithm presented in the previous section. We formulate our linear programs for the general case of matroid k-parity but the case $k = 2$ is already sufficiently general to obtain our results.

We start with the following natural LP for the weighted matroid k-parity problem (equivalent to an LP studied in [21]). The variables y_e correspond to the hyperedges and the variables x_u correspond to the elements of the ground set. We assume here that each hyperedge alone is independent; otherwise we remove it from the instance.

$$\max \sum_{e \in \mathcal{E}} w_e y_e, \tag{1}$$

$$\sum_{u \in S} x_u \leq r_{\mathcal{M}}(S), \qquad \forall S \subseteq V, \tag{2}$$

$$x_u = y_e, \qquad \forall u \in e, e \in \mathcal{E}, \tag{3}$$

$$x_u, y_e \geq 0, \qquad \forall u \in V, e \in \mathcal{E}. \tag{4}$$

In the objective function (1) we are maximizing the total weight of chosen hyperedges. The constraints (3) correspond to the fact that we can choose a hyperedge only if we chose all its vertices. The constraints (2) are the standard rank constraints for the matroid $\mathcal{M}$ and any independent set of vertices must satisfy them.

For any set of elements $S \subseteq V$ let $\text{sp}(S) = \{u \in V \mid r_{\mathcal{M}}(S \cup \{u\}) = r_{\mathcal{M}}(S)\}$ be the *span* of S in matroid $\mathcal{M}$. $F \subseteq V$ is a *flat* if $\text{sp}(F) = F$ (for more information on these concepts, see [46], Chapter 39). Since $r_{\mathcal{M}}(\text{sp}(S)) = r_{\mathcal{M}}(S)$, it is easy to see that it is enough to write the constraints (2) for every flat $F \subseteq V$; the inequality for arbitrary $S \subset V$ is implied by the flat $F = \text{sp}(S)$.

Another set of valid inequalities (for $k = 2$) were suggested by Vande Vate [50] and studied in subsequent work [11, 12, 21, 50]. For a set $S \subseteq V$ and a hyperedge e, let $a(S, e) = r_{\mathcal{M}}(S \cap \text{sp}(e))$. In case of a flat F, the intuition is that $a(F, e)$ is the dimension of the subspace of F generated by e. The LP proposed by Vande Vate is as follows.

$$\max \sum_{e \in \mathcal{E}} w_e y_e, \tag{5}$$

$$\sum_{e \in \mathcal{E}} a(S, e) y_e \leq r_{\mathcal{M}}(S), \qquad \forall S \subseteq V, \tag{6}$$

$$y_e \geq 0, \qquad \forall e \in \mathcal{E}. \tag{7}$$

Again, it is equivalent to consider the inequalities (6) only for flats, which was the formulation given by Vande Vate. This LP is potentially stronger than LP (1-4), which can be equivalently obtained from (5-7) by replacing $a(S, e)$ with the smaller quantity $|S \cap e|$.

It is known that the linear program (5-7) is half-integral in the 2-uniform case. Moreover, there are polynomial time algorithms to find a half integral optimal solution in the unweighted 2-uniform case (see [11, 12]) and the weighted 2-uniform case (see [21]). The following lemma shows the validity of the LP (5–7) in the general k-uniform case. We could not find a published proof of validity (even for $k = 2$), so for completeness we provide a short proof.

LEMMA 3. *The inequalities (6) are valid for the matroid k-parity problem.*

PROOF. Consider any feasible solution, a collection of hyperedges $E^* = \{e_1, \ldots, e_k\}$ such that $e_1 \cup \ldots \cup e_k$ is an independent set in matroid $\mathcal{M}$. In the following, we denote the rank function of $\mathcal{M}$ simply by $r(S)$. Let $S_i = S \cap \text{sp}(e_i)$. Note that $r(S_i) = a(S, e_i)$. We claim that for any $i < k$, $r(S_1 \cup \ldots \cup S_i) = r(S_1 \cup \ldots \cup S_{i-1}) + r(S_i)$. By induction, we will get that $r(S_1 \cup \ldots \cup S_k) = \sum_{i=1}^k r(S_i) = \sum_{i=1}^k a(S, e_i)$ which implies the inequalities (6).

We let $r_A(S) = r(A \cup S) - r(A)$; due to submodularity, this is a non-increasing function of A. Let $A = S_1 \cup \ldots \cup S_{i-1}$ and $B = e_1 \cup \ldots \cup e_{i-1}$. Our goal is to prove that $r_A(S_i) = r(S_i)$. Because $A \subseteq \text{sp}(B)$, we get $r_A(S_i) \geq r_{\text{sp}(B)}(S_i) = r_B(S_i)$, using that $r(\text{sp}(B)) = r(B)$ and $r(S_i \cup \text{sp}(B)) = r(S_i \cup B)$. On the other hand, as e_i is independent of B, we have

$$\begin{aligned} r(\text{sp}(e_i)) = r_B(\text{sp}(e_i)) &= r_B(S_i) + r_{B \cup S_i}(\text{sp}(e_i))) \\ &\leq r_A(S_i) + r_{S_i}(\text{sp}(e_i)) \end{aligned}$$

using again the submodularity of r. This implies that $r_A(S_i) \geq r(\text{sp}(e_i)) - r_{S_i}(\text{sp}(e_i)) = r(S_i)$. The opposite inequality is obvious and hence $r_A(S_i) = r(S_i)$. □

In the following, we use examples where $e = \text{sp}(e)$ for all hyperedges $e \in \mathcal{E}$. Note that in this case, $a(S, e) = r_{\mathcal{M}}(S \cap \text{sp}(e)) = r_{\mathcal{M}}(S \cap e) = |S \cap e|$, and hence the two LPs are in fact equivalent.

4.1 Integrality gap example

It is known that the integrality gap of the LP relaxation (1–4) is $k-1+\frac{1}{k}$ for the maximum weighted hypergraph matching problem [9]. Therefore, it is tempting to conjecture that a similar result should hold for matroid hypergraph matching. Unfortunately, as we show below, the integrality gap of the linear-programming relaxation (1–4) is $\Omega(|\mathcal{E}|)$ even when $k=2$ and the matroid is linear over the rationals.

Example.

Consider a ground set $V=\{u_1,v_1,\dots,u_n,v_n\}$ of size $2n$, partitioned into pairs $e_i=\{u_i,v_i\}$. The weight of each pair is $w_{e_i}=1$. Given an integer parameter $t\geq 1$, we define a matroid $\mathcal{M}=(V,\mathcal{I})$ as follows. For a set $S\subseteq V$, let $p(S)$ be the number of pairs e_i such that $e_i\subseteq S$. Then let $S\in\mathcal{I}$ if $p(S)\leq t$.

It can be checked that $\mathcal{I}$ satisfies the matroid independence axioms: For any $S,T\in\mathcal{I}$, $|S|<|T|$, either T contains an element from a pair $\{u_i,v_i\}$ which is disjoint from S, or it contains more pairs than S. In either case, we can extend S by adding some element of T. Moreover, this matroid is is linear over the rationals (see [34]).

First, let us write down the LP for this particular example. We have variables y_i for $i=1,\dots,n$, which are constrained by $y_i\in[0,1]$. Since $\mathrm{sp}(e_i)=e_i$, the LPs (1-4) and (5-7) coincide. It is enough to write the constraints (6) for flats, and in particular only for collections of pairs $S=\bigcup_{i\in T}e_i$. This is because including only one element of a pair in S always increases $r_{\mathcal{M}}(S)$ by 1 and hence cannot strengthen the constraint. Also, for $S=\bigcup_{i\in T}e_i$ where $|T|\leq t$, the rank is $r_{\mathcal{M}}(S)=|S|$ and the respective constraint (6) is implied by $y_i\leq 1$. The only non-trivial constraints are for $S=\bigcup_{i\in T}e_i, |T|>t$, where we get $r_{\mathcal{M}}(S)=2t+(|T|-t)=t+|T|$. Also, $a(S,e_i)=2$ for all $i\in T$. Therefore, the LP is as follows.

$$\max\sum_{i=1}^{n} w_i y_i, \tag{8}$$

$$\sum_{i\in T} y_i \leq \frac{1}{2}(t+|T|), \qquad \forall T\subseteq[n], |T|>t \tag{9}$$

$$0\leq y_i\leq 1, \qquad \forall i. \tag{10}$$

LEMMA 4. *The integrality gap of LP (8–10) is $\Omega(n/t)$, even in the unweighted case.*

PROOF. It is easy to see that $y_i=1/2$ for all $i=1,\dots,n$ is a feasible fractional solution. Therefore, $LP\geq n/2$. However, only t pairs can be selected in an integral optimum, i.e. $OPT=t$. □

For $t=1$, we get an $\Omega(n)$ integrality gap. One way to improve the quality of linear-programming relaxations is to add valid inequalities that cut bad fractional solutions. One of the possible classes of valid inequalities are the so-called *clique inequalities* that were recently shown to reduce the integrality gap for unweighted hypergraph matching from $k-1$ to $(k+1)/2$ [9]. This motivates us to define the undirected graph $G'=(\mathcal{E},E')$ where the vertices are the hyperedges $e\in\mathcal{E}$ in our instance of matroid hypergraph matching and the edges are defined between "incompatible hyperedges" e and e', i.e. when $r(e\cup e')<|e\cup e'|$. A set of vertices C in graph G' is called a clique if it has an edge between every pair of vertices in C. Let $\mathcal{C}$ be the set of all cliques in graph G'. Then the following set of constraints is valid for the matroid hypergraph matching problem

$$\sum_{e\in C} y_e\leq 1, \quad \forall C\in\mathcal{C}. \tag{11}$$

However, as we can see in the example above (for $t\geq 2$), sometimes the clique inequalities do not add any non-trivial constraints and the LP effectively remains the same. More generally, we could add all the valid constraints for the stable-set polytope corresponding to G' (or perhaps consider the semidefinite program corresponding to the Lovász θ-function). The relaxation would still remain the same, since the graph G' is empty in our example.

In the next section, we consider the strongest known systematic way of generating valid constraints in linear programming, which is the *Sherali-Adams hierarchy.*

4.2 The Sherali-Adams hierarchy

The Sherali-Adams hierarchy produces progressively stronger refinements of a given LP by introducing new variables y_L indexed by subsets of the original variables, and then projecting back to the space of the original variables. We follow the formalism of [38]. To carry out r rounds of Sherali-Adams, we consider all pairs of disjoint subsets of variables I,J such that $|I\cup J|=r$. We multiply each constraint by $\prod_{i\in I}y_i\prod_{j\in J}(1-y_j)$, expand all the monomial terms and replace every square y_i^2 by y_i. Now all terms are multilinear, and we replace each occurrence of $\prod_{\ell\in L}y_\ell$ by a new variable y_L. We also do the same for the constraint $\prod_{i\in I}y_i\prod_{j\in J}(1-y_j)\geq 0$, for all disjoint I,J such that $|I\cup J|=r+1$. This defines the new LP; note that the variables y_L for $|L|>1$ play no role in the objective function and thus the polytope can be viewed as projected back to the original space.

LEMMA 5. *The integrality gap of LP (8–10) still remains $\Omega(n/r)$ after r rounds of the Sherali-Adams hierarchy.*

PROOF. Our starting point is LP (8–10), with the parameter t chosen equal to the desired number of rounds r. We have constraints $\sum_{\ell\in T}y_\ell\leq\frac{1}{2}(r+|T|)$ for all $|T|>r$. We multiply this constraint by $\prod_{i\in I}y_i\prod_{j\in J}(1-y_j)$ and obtain

$$\sum_{\ell\in T}y_\ell\prod_{i\in I}y_i\prod_{j\in J}(1-y_j)\leq\frac{1}{2}(r+|T|)\prod_{i\in I}y_i\prod_{j\in J}(1-y_j). \tag{12}$$

We expand the products, linearize the expressions, and replace monomials $\prod_{\ell\in L}y_\ell$ by new variables y_L as explained above. We also do the same thing for the constraints $\prod_{i\in I}y_i\prod_{j\in J}(1-y_j)\geq 0$ with $|I\cup J|=r+1$. We claim that $y_L=1/2^{|L|}$ for all $|L|\leq r+1$ is a feasible solution for the new LP.

To see this, first observe that whenever we have $\ell\in J$ on the left-hand side of (12), the corresponding term contains $y_\ell(1-y_\ell)=y_\ell-y_\ell^2$ which disappears after linearization. In terms where $\ell\in I$, we get y_ℓ^2 which gets linearized to y_ℓ. Equivalently, we can replace y_ℓ by 1 in its appearance before the product $\prod_{i\in I}y_i$, whenever $\ell\in I$. Variables outside of $I\cup J$ remain unchanged. Therefore, after linearization, the left-hand side is equal to $(|T\cap I|+\sum_{\ell\in T\setminus(I\cup J)}y_\ell)\prod_{i\in I}y_i\prod_{j\in J}(1-y_j)$.

Now we replace the monomials $\prod_{\ell\in L}y_\ell$ by y_L and substitute $y_L=1/2^{|L|}$. Note that this is equivalent to directly substituting $y_\ell = 1/2$ for all ℓ. Thus the left-hand side becomes

$$(|T \cap I| + \tfrac{1}{2}|T \setminus (I \cup J)|)\, 2^{-|I \cup J|}$$
$$= \tfrac{1}{2}(|T \cap I| + |T \setminus J|)\, 2^{-|I \cup J|} \leq \tfrac{1}{2}(r + |T|)\, 2^{-|I \cup J|}$$

using the fact that $|I| \leq r$. This verifies the linearized form of constraint (12).

The inequalities arising from $\prod_{i \in I} y_i \prod_{j \in J}(1 - y_j) \geq 0$ are easy to verify, since our assignment $y_L = 1/2^{|L|}$ is equivalent to substituting $y_i = 1/2$. Therefore, our fractional solution is feasible for r rounds of Sherali-Adams.

Finally, the value of our fractional solution is equal to $n/2$, because each singleton variable is $y_i = y_{\{i\}} = 1/2$. The integral optimum is $OPT = r$. □

To summarize, our LP (8–10) is an instance of the strongest "natural LP" for matroid matching we are aware of, namely the Vande Vate LP (5-7). The same LP (8–10) is obtained even with the added clique constraints (11) and other valid constraints for the stable-set polytope which are hard to optimize over in general. On top of this LP, we run the Sherali-Adams hierarchy and the gap still remains superconstant for $o(n)$ rounds.

4.3 Lower bound on Chvátal rank

Another popular way to derive progressively stronger linear-programming relaxations is to apply Chvátal-Gomory cuts (for example, see [45]). Let $P := \{x \in \mathbb{R}^n \ : \ \sum_{j=1}^n a_{i,j}x_j < b_i, \text{ for } i = 1, \ldots, m\}$ be a polyhedron defined by rational data. Let $\sum_j a_j x_j \leq b$ be a linear inequality satisfied by all points in P. Such an inequality is called a *valid (linear) inequality* for P.

Now, let $P_I := \operatorname{conv}(P \cap \mathbb{Z}^n)$. If $\sum_j a_j x_j \leq b$ is a valid linear inequality for P, and $a_j \in \mathbb{Z}$ for all j, then clearly $\sum_j a_j x_j \leq \lfloor b \rfloor$ is a valid linear inequality for P_I. Any such inequality is known as a *Chvátal-Gomory cut* with respect to P. Applying all Chvátal-Gomory cuts to P, we obtain the *first Chvátal closure* $P^{(1)}$ of P. It is a classical result that $P^{(1)}$ is again a polyhedron; that is, only a finite number of the Chvátal-Gomory cuts for P are needed to describe $P^{(1)}$. Now, we can repeatedly apply this closure operator, and we obtain after r repetitions the *r-th Chvátal closure* $P^{(r)}$ of P. If the linear inequality $\sum_j a_j x_j \leq b$ is valid for $P^{(r)}$ but not $P^{(r-1)}$, then we say that the inequality has *Chvátal rank* r. It is a classical result that when P is described by rational data, $P_I = P^{(r)}$ for some finite r.

Hartmann established lower bounds on the *Chvátal rank* for many classes of polytopes of interest in combinatorial optimization (see [22] and also [14]). Eisenbrand and Schulz established that for polytopes in $[0,1]^n$, the *Chvátal rank* is at most $3n^2 \log(n)$, and furthermore that there is a family of polytopes in the $[0,1]^n$ that has *Chvátal rank* at least $(1+\epsilon)n$ (see [17]).

The proof of the following lemma is a generalization of the geometric proof from [14] of the classical result by Chvátal [13] that a clique inequality involving n variables requires at least $\lfloor \log_2 n \rfloor$ rounds of the Chvátal-Gomory hierarchy. Let $\mathcal{P}_t$ be the polytope described by(8–10). So $\mathcal{P}_t^{(r)}$ is its r-th Chvátal closure.

LEMMA 6. *The point $y^r \in \mathbb{R}^n$ defined by $y_i^r = \frac{1}{2}(\frac{t}{t+1})^r$, for $i = 1, \ldots, n$, is in $\mathcal{P}_t^{(r)}$.*

PROOF. We prove the lemma by induction on the number r of rounds of the Chvátal closure. The base case $r = 0$ is trivial since the solution $(1/2, \ldots, 1/2)$ is obviously feasible for the linear program (8–10) for any parameter $t \geq 1$.

We assume that $y^{r-1} \in \mathcal{P}_t^{(r-1)}$. Let $\sum_{i=1}^n a_i y_i \leq b$ be a valid linear inequality for $\mathcal{P}_t^{(r-1)}$, with $a_i \in \mathbb{Z}$. Because $(0, \ldots, 0)$ is a feasible integral solution for the linear program (8–10), we obtain $(0, \ldots, 0) \in \mathcal{P}_t^{(r-1)}$, and therefore $b \geq 0$. If $a_i \leq 0$ for all $i = 1, \ldots, n$, then $\sum_{i=1}^n a_i y_i^r \leq 0 \leq \lfloor b \rfloor \leq b$.

Let $A^+ := \sum_{i | a_i > 0} a_i$. If the vector $(a_1, \ldots, a_n)$ has at most t strictly positive components, then $A^+ \leq b$ since any integral solution with at most t variables equal to one and the remaining variables equal to zero is a feasible integral solution for the linear program (8–10), which implies that such a solution must belong to $\mathcal{P}_t^{(r-1)}$. Moreover, because A^+ is an integer, we have $A^+ \leq \lfloor b \rfloor$. Therefore, we have $\sum_{i=1}^n a_i y_i^r < A^+ \leq \lfloor b \rfloor$.

Consider now an inequality in which the vector $(a_1, \ldots, a_n)$ has more than t strictly positive components. Recall that $a_i \in \mathbb{Z}$ and hence these coefficients are at least 1. An integral solution χ having any t of the respective coordinates equal to one and remaining coordinates equal to zero is feasible for (8–10); therefore $t \leq \sum_{i=1}^n a_i \chi_i \leq b$. We obtain

$$\sum_{i=1}^n a_i y_i^r = \frac{t}{t+1} \sum_{i=1}^n a_i y_i^{r-1} \leq \frac{t}{t+1} b \leq \lfloor b \rfloor,$$

which implies that $y^r \in \mathcal{P}^{(r)}$. □

COROLLARY 2. *The integrality gap of the linear-programming relaxation obtained from the linear-programming relaxation (8–10) after t rounds of Chvátal closure is $\Omega(n/t)$.*

PROOF. By the Lemma 6 there exists a feasible fractional solution of value $\frac{n}{2}(\frac{t}{t+1})^t = \Omega(n)$ in $\mathcal{P}_t^{(t)}$, while the value of the integral optimal solution is t. □

COROLLARY 3. *The Chvátal rank of the polytope defined by (8–10) with $t = n/4$ is at least $n/4$.*

PROOF. Consider the inequality $\sum_{i=1}^n y_i \leq t$. This inequality is valid for all integer feasible solutions of the linear programming relaxation (8–10). Let r be the smallest integer such that this inequality is valid for $\mathcal{P}_t^{(r)}$; i.e., r is the Chvátal rank of the inequality $\sum_{i=1}^n y_i \leq t$. By Lemma 6, we obtain $\frac{n}{2}(\frac{t}{t+1})^r \leq t$. Therefore,

$$r \geq \frac{\log_2 n - \log_2(2t)}{\log_2(1 + 1/t)} \geq t(\log_2 n - \log_2(2t)).$$

For $t = n/4$, the Chvátal rank is $r \geq n/4$. □

5. MATROID k-PARITY

Here we extend the analysis of local search to matroid k-parity; i.e. instead of pairs, we work with hyperedges of size k. We assume that $k \geq 3$. In an instance of matroid k-parity, all hyperedges are mutually disjoint. We remark that our analysis extends to k-uniform matroid matching where hyperedges need not be disjoint, by a standard reduction.

Interestingly, the analysis for $k \geq 3$ is slightly different and the complexity of our $(k/2+\epsilon)$-approximation for $k \geq 3$ has a much better dependence on ϵ than our PTAS for $k = 2$ (matroid matching). More precisely, while we need local moves of size exponential in $1/\epsilon$ in order to achieve a

$(1+\epsilon)$-approximation for matroid matching, local moves of size polynomial in $1/\epsilon$ are sufficient to achieve a $1/(2/k-\epsilon)$-approximation for matroid k-parity. We do not know whether our analysis is optimal in terms of this dependence.

DEFINITION 3. *For feasible solutions A, B of matroid k-parity,* a local move of size s between A and B *is a choice of $s-1$ hyperedges $e_1, \ldots, e_{s-1}$ from A, and s hyperedges $e'_1, \ldots, e'_s$ from B, such that $(A \setminus \bigcup_{i=1}^{s-1} e_i) \cup \bigcup_{i=1}^{s} e'_i$ is feasible.*

THEOREM 3. *For any $k \geq 3$ and $\epsilon > 0$, a local-search algorithm which considers local moves of size up to $s(\epsilon) = \lceil 1/\epsilon^3 \rceil$ achieves a $1/(2/k-\epsilon)$-approximation for the matroid k-parity problem.*

This follows easily from the following characterization of local optima.

LEMMA 7. *Let $k \geq 3$, $t \geq 1$, and A, B feasible solutions to the matroid k-parity problem such that*

$$|A| < \left(\frac{2}{k} - \frac{1}{(k-1)^t}\right)|B|.$$

Then there exists a local move of size $(2k+1)^{t-1}$ between A and B.

Note that in order to achieve a $1/(2/k-\epsilon)$-approximation, it suffices to pick $t = \lceil \log_{k-1}(1/\epsilon) \rceil$ and $s(\epsilon) = (2k+1)^{t-1} \leq 1/\epsilon^{\log_{k-1}(2k+1)}$. Then, if A is a local optimum and B is a global optimum, the lemma implies that $|A| \geq (2/k - 1/(k-1)^t)|B| \geq (2/k-\epsilon)|B|$. For simplicity, we replaced $1/\epsilon^{\log_{k-1}(2k+1)}$ by $1/\epsilon^3$ in the statement of the theorem, but for large k the dependency gets close to $1/\epsilon$.

It remains to prove the lemma.

PROOF. (Lemma 7). Let A, B be feasible solutions as above. (We assume for simplicity that A and B are disjoint, otherwise we can contract the intersection, which only decreases the ratio $|A|/|B|$.) Because $|A| < |B|$, there exists $B' \subset B, |B'| = |B| - |A|$ such that $A \cup B'$ is independent in $\mathcal{M}$. We proceed by induction on t.

Base case: $t = 1$.

Here, we have $|A| < (\frac{2}{k} - \frac{1}{k-1})|B| < \frac{1}{k}|B|$. Then, it is impossible that every hyperedge in B contains some element in $B \setminus B'$, because that would mean that $|A| = |B \setminus B'| \geq \frac{1}{k}|B|$. Hence, there must be a hyperedge contained completely inside B', which can be added to A without violating independence. This means there is a local move of size one.

General case: $t \geq 2$.

We assume that $|A| = (2/k-\epsilon)|B|$ and $\epsilon > \frac{1}{(k-1)^t}$. Again, if there is a hyperedge contained inside B', we can add it to A, and we are done. So let us assume that no hyperedge is contained completely inside B'.

We use a counting argument to show that there must be many hyperedges with exactly $k-1$ elements in B'. Let a denote the number of such hyperedges ($|e \cap B'| = k-1$), and b the number of hyperedges such that $|e \cap B'| \leq k-2$. All hyperedges in B fall into one of these two categories, hence $|B| = k(a+b)$. On the other hand, $|B'| \leq (k-1)a + (k-2)b$ which means that $|A| = |B| - |B'| \geq a + 2b$. We assumed that $|A| = (2/k-\epsilon)|B|$, which implies

$$a + 2b \leq |A| = (2/k-\epsilon)\,|B| = (2-k\epsilon)\,(a+b). \qquad (13)$$

We conclude that

$$a \geq k\epsilon(a+b). \qquad (14)$$

Let Q denote these a hyperedges in B and $V(Q)$ denote the elements of B that belongs to hyperedges in Q; each of them contains exactly one element in $B \setminus B'$ and $k-1$ elements in B'. Let $B_0 = V(Q) \cap B'$ and $B_1 = V(Q) \cap (B \setminus B')$. We have $|B_0| = (k-1)a$ and $|B_1| = a$.

Let $\mathcal{M}_0 = \mathcal{M}/B_0$ denote the matroid with B_0 contracted. Because $A \cup B_0 \subseteq A \cup B'$ and $B_1 \cup B_0 \subseteq B$, both of which are independent in $\mathcal{M}$, we get that A and B_1 are independent in $\mathcal{M}_0$. Because $|A| \geq a + 2b \geq |B_1|$, we can extend B_1 by adding (possibly zero) elements from A, to form a $\mathcal{M}_0$-independent set $(A \setminus A_1) \cup B_1$ where $|A_1| = |B_1| = a$.

If A contains any hyperedge e with $|e \cap A_1| \geq 2$, we find a local move of size two as follows: $((A \setminus e) \setminus A_1) \cup B_1$ is an independent set in $\mathcal{M}_0$, whose cardinality is at least $|A \setminus e| + 2$ (because A_1 contains ≥ 2 elements of e). Therefore, $A \setminus e$ can be extended to a set $(A \setminus e) \cup \{x', x''\}$ independent in $\mathcal{M}_0$, such that $x', x'' \in B_1$. The elements x', x'' are contained in hyperedges e', e'' whose remaining elements are in B_0. Because $(A \setminus e) \cup \{x', x''\}$ is independent in $\mathcal{M}_0 = \mathcal{M}/B_0$, any elements of B_0 can be added for free, and $(A \setminus e) \cup e' \cup e''$ is independent in $\mathcal{M}$. This defines a local move of size two.

The rest of the proof deals with the case in which there is no hyperedge in A with more than 1 element in A_1. Let P be the collection of hyperedges in A intersecting A_1; each such hyperedge satisfies $|e \cap A_1| = 1$, and so $|P| = |A_1| = a$. Let A_2 denote the remaining elements of P, i.e. $A_2 \subseteq A \setminus A_1$ and $|A_2| = (k-1)a$. Here we apply the inductive hypothesis.

The inductive step.

We define a new matroid $\mathcal{M}_1 = \mathcal{M}_0/B_1 = \mathcal{M}/(B_0 \cup B_1)$. By construction, the sets $A^* = A \setminus (A_1 \cup A_2)$ and $B^* = B \setminus (B_0 \cup B_1)$ are both independent in $\mathcal{M}_1$. They both form a union of hyperedges and hence feasible solutions to the matroid k-parity problem for $\mathcal{M}_1$. We have $|A^*| = |A| - ka$ and $|B^*| = |B| - ka = kb$. Using (13), we get

$$\frac{|A^*|}{|B^*|} = \frac{|A| - ka}{kb} = \frac{(2-k\epsilon)(a+b) - ka}{kb} = \frac{2}{k} - \epsilon - \frac{(k-2+k\epsilon)a}{kb}$$

and applying (14) to estimate $a \geq kb\epsilon$, we get

$$\frac{|A^*|}{|B^*|} \leq \frac{2}{k} - \epsilon - (k-2+k\epsilon)\epsilon \leq \frac{2}{k} - (k-1)\epsilon.$$

Because we assumed $\epsilon > \frac{1}{(k-1)^t}$, we have

$$|A^*| < \left(\frac{2}{k} - \frac{1}{(k-1)^{t-1}}\right)|B^*|,$$

and we can apply the inductive hypothesis. There is a local move of size $s = (2k+1)^{t-2}$ between A^* and B^*, i.e. a union of $s-1$ hyperedges $\tilde{A} \subseteq A^*$ and s hyperedges $\tilde{B} \subseteq B^*$ such that $(A^* \setminus \tilde{A}) \cup \tilde{B}$ is independent in $\mathcal{M}_1$. Our goal is to find a local move of size $(2k+1)s$ between A and B (in $\mathcal{M}$).

We accomplish this by a construction essentially identical to the case of matroid parity. The set $(A^* \setminus \tilde{A}) \cup \tilde{B}$ is independent in $\mathcal{M}_1$. Unfortunately, $(A \setminus \tilde{A}) \cup \tilde{B}$ is not necessarily independent, even in $\mathcal{M}$. However, the set $(A^* \setminus \tilde{A}) \cup A_2 = A \setminus (A_1 \cup \tilde{A})$ is independent in $\mathcal{M}_1 = \mathcal{M}_0/B_1$, because $(A \setminus A_1) \cup B_1$ was constructed to be independent in $\mathcal{M}_0$. Therefore, we can extend $(A^* \setminus \tilde{A}) \cup \tilde{B}$ to a set

$(A^* \setminus \tilde{A}) \cup \tilde{B} \cup (A_2 \setminus C_2)$ independent in $\mathcal{M}_1$, where $C_2 \subseteq A_2$ and $|C_2| \leq |\tilde{B}|$. (If $|A_2| \leq |\tilde{B}|$, we just take $C_2 = A_2$.)

The new set $(A^* \setminus \tilde{A}) \cup \tilde{B} \cup (A_2 \setminus C_2)$ is also independent in $\mathcal{M}_0$ (a weaker condition). So is $(A^* \setminus \tilde{A}) \cup (A_2 \setminus C_2) \cup A_1$, as any subset of A is independent in $\mathcal{M}_0$. So, we can extend $(A^* \setminus \tilde{A}) \cup \tilde{B} \cup (A_2 \setminus C_2)$ to a set $(A^* \setminus \tilde{A}) \cup \tilde{B} \cup (A_2 \setminus C_2) \cup (A_1 \setminus C_1)$ independent in $\mathcal{M}_0$, where $C_1 \subseteq A_1$ and $|C_1| \leq |\tilde{B}|$.

The set we have obtained is not necessarily a union of hyperedges, so let us remove the entire hyperedge for each element in C_1 and C_2. Let us denote by C' the union of all hyperedges intersecting $C_1 \cup C_2$. Note that due to our construction, $C_1 \cup C_2 \subseteq C' \subseteq A_1 \cup A_2$. We also define $C_1' = C' \cap A_1$ and $C_2' = C' \cap A_2$. We know that each hyperedge on $A_1 \cup A_2$ contains exactly one element in A_1 and $k-1$ elements in A_2. Therefore, $|C_2'| = (k-1)|C_1'|$, and also $|C_1'| = \frac{1}{k}|C'| \leq |C_1 \cup C_2|$, because each element of $C_1 \cup C_2$ contributes at most one hyperedge to C'.

We obtain a feasible solution $A^+ = (A^* \setminus \tilde{A}) \cup \tilde{B} \cup (A_2 \setminus C_2') \cup (A_1 \setminus C_1')$ in $\mathcal{M}_0$. Now, consider the set $(A^+ \setminus A_1) \cup B_1 = (A^* \setminus \tilde{A}) \cup \tilde{B} \cup (A_2 \setminus C_2') \cup B_1$. This is independent in $\mathcal{M}_0$, because $A^+ \setminus A_1$ was constructed to be independent in $\mathcal{M}_1 = \mathcal{M}_0 / B_1$. Because A^+ misses some elements in A_1, namely C_1', the cardinality of $(A^+ \setminus A_1) \cup B_1$ is actually larger than $|A^+|$, namely $|(A^+ \setminus A_1) \cup B_1| = |A^+| + |C_1'|$. Hence, we can extend A^+ by $F_1 \subseteq B_1$, $|F_1| = |C_1'|$, to obtain a set $A^+ \cup F_1$ independent in $\mathcal{M}_0$. The hyperedges touching F_1 have exactly 1 element in B_1 and the remaining $k-1$ elements in B_0 (denote these by F_0), hence we can add F_0 for free and obtain an independent set $A^+ \cup F_1 \cup F_0$ in $\mathcal{M}$. We have $|F_1| = |C_1'|$ and $|F_0| = (k-1)|F_1| = (k-1)|C_1'| = |C_2'|$. To conclude, we have found a feasible solution $A^+ \cup F_1 \cup F_0$ in $\mathcal{M}$, of cardinality

$$|A^+ \cup F_1 \cup F_0| = |A^+ \cup C_1' \cup C_2'| = |(A \setminus \tilde{A}) \cup \tilde{B}| > |A|.$$

Finally, let us estimate the size of this local move. We removed $\tilde{A} \cup C_1' \cup C_2'$ from A, and added $\tilde{B} \cup F_0 \cup F_1$ instead. The size of C_1' is bounded by $|C_1'| \leq |C_1 \cup C_2| \leq 2|\tilde{B}|$, hence $|F_0 \cup F_1| = k|C_1'| \leq 2k|\tilde{B}|$. In summary, we are adding at most $(2k+1)|\tilde{B}|$ elements to A, i.e. the size of the local move is at most $(2k+1)|\tilde{B}| = (2k+1)^{t-1}$. $\square$

6. CONCLUSION

We have seen that a simple combinatorial algorithm performs dramatically better than any known LP-based approach for matroid matching. Linear programming still holds some promise for the k-uniform matchoid problem. Our $\frac{3}{2}$-approximation for the weighted matchoid problem and the results from [9] on the integrality gap of the hypergraph matching problem motivate the following.

CONJECTURE 1. *The integrality gap of the LP relaxation (1-4) is $k - 1 + \frac{1}{k}$ for the maximum weighted k-matchoid problem and $k-1$ for the maximum weighted k-matroid intersection problem.*

In the case of weighted matroid k-parity, we have the following conjecture, which is true (and tight) for the weighted k-set packing problem due to [1, 3] and also for the weighted k-matroid intersection problem due to [33].

CONJECTURE 2. *The simple local-search algorithm for the weighted matroid k-parity problem that tries to add/remove a constant number of hyperedges in each iteration has approximation guarantee $k - 1 + \varepsilon$ for any $\varepsilon > 0$ (with running time depending on $1/\varepsilon$).*

A very intriguing open problem is to show that this simple local-search algorithm gives a PTAS for weighted matroid parity ($k = 2$). This problem is interesting even for the special case of linear matroids, because Lovász' polynomial-time algorithm applies only to the unweighted case (see [35]). For the weighted linear case, there is only a pseudopolynomial-time randomized exact algorithm [8] and pseudopolynomial-time randomized parallel exact algorithm [40].

Another interesting line of research is to analyze more sophisticated local-search algorithms (see [5, 10]) implemented for the weighted matroid k-parity problem. Such algorithms are known to provide improved approximation guarantees for the weighted set packing problem.

7. REFERENCES

[1] E. Arkin and R. Hassin, On local search for weighted k-set packing, *Math. of Op. Res.* 23(3) (1998) 640–648.

[2] M. Balinski, On maximum matching, minimum covering and their connections, in "Proceedings of Princeton Symp. on Math. Prog.," Eds. H. Kuhn, 303–312, Princeton Univ. Press, 1970.

[3] V. Bafna, B. Narayanan and R. Ravi, Nonoverlapping local alignments (weighted independent sets of axis-parallel rectangles), *Discrete Applied Mathematics* 71, (1996), no. 1-3, 41–53.

[4] A. Barvinok, New algorithms for linear k-matroid intersection and matroid k-parity problems, *Math. Program.* 69, 449–470 (1995).

[5] P. Berman, A $d/2$ approximation for maximum weight independent set in d-claw free graphs, *Nordic J. Comput.* 7(3) (2000), 178–184.

[6] P. Berman, M. Fűrer and A. Zelikovsky, Applications of the Linear Matroid Parity Algorithm to Approximating Steiner Trees, in "Proceedings of CSR 2006," *LNCS* v.3967, 70–79.

[7] G. Calinescu, C. Chekuri, M. Pál and J. Vondrák, Maximizing a submodular set function subject to a matroid constraint, to appear in *SIAM Journal on Computing*, special issue for STOC 2008.

[8] P. Camerini, G. Galbiati and F. Maffioli, Random pseudo-polynomial algorithms for exact matroid problems, *Journal of Algorithms,* 13:258-273, 1992.

[9] Y.H. Chan and L.C. Lau, On linear and semidefinite programming relaxations for hypergraph matching, to appear in SODA 2010.

[10] B. Chandra and M. Halldórsson, Greedy local improvement and weighted set packing approximation, *J. Algorithms* 39(2) (2001), 223–240.

[11] S. Chang, D. Llewellyn and J. Vande Vate, Matching 2-lattice polyhedra: finding a maximum vector, *Discrete Mathematics* 237 (2001), 29–61.

[12] S. Chang, D. Llewellyn and J. Vande Vate, Matching 2-lattice polyhedra: duality and extreme points, *Discrete Mathematics* 237 (2001), no. 1–3, 63–95.

[13] V. Chvátal, Edmonds polytopes and a hierarchy of combinatorial problems, *Disc. Math.* 4 (1973), 305–337.

[14] V. Chvátal, W. Cook and M. Hartmann, On cutting-plane proofs in combinatorial optimization, *Linear Algebra Appl.* 114/115 (1989), 455–499.

[15] J. Edmonds, Paths, trees, and flowers, *Canadian Journal of Mathematics* 17, 449–467, 1965.

[16] J. Edmonds, Maximum matching and a polyhedron with 0-1 vertices, *Journal of Research National Bureau of Standards, Section B* 69, 73–77, 1965.

[17] F. Eisenbrand and A.S. Schulz, Bounds on the Chvátal rank of polytopes in the 0/1-cube, *Combinatorica* 23, 245-261, 2003.

[18] M.L. Fisher, G.L. Nemhauser and L.A. Wolsey, An analysis of approximations for maximizing submodular set functions - II. *Math. Prog. Study*, 8:73–87, 1978.

[19] T. Fujito, A 2/3-approximation of the matroid matching problem, in "Proceedings of ISAAC 1993," *Lecture Notes in Computer Science* v.762, 185-190.

[20] H.N. Gabow and M. Stallmann, An augmenting path algorithm for linear matroid parity, *Combinatorica* 6, 123-150, 1986.

[21] D. Gijswijt and G. Pap, An algorithm for weighted fractional matroid matching, TR-2008-11, Technical Report of the Egervary Research Group, Budapest.

[22] M. Hartmann, "Cutting Plane Proofs and the Complexity of the Integer Hull," Ph.D. Thesis, Cornell University, Ithaca, 1988.

[23] D. Hausmann, B. Korte and T. Jenkyns. Worst case analysis of greedy type algorithms for independence systems, *Math. Prog. Study* 12 (1980), 120–131.

[24] E. Hazan, S. Safra and O. Schwartz. On the complexity of approximating k-set packing. *Computational Complexity,* 15(1), 20–39, 2006.

[25] C. Hurkens and A. Schrijver, On the size of systems of sets every t of which have an SDR, with an application to the worst-case ratio of heuristics for packing problems, *SIAM J. Disc. Math.* 2(1) (1989), 68–72.

[26] P.M. Jensen and B. Korte, Complexity of matroid property algorithms. *SIAM Journal on Computing* 11, 184-190, 1982.

[27] T.A. Jenkyns, "Matchoids: A generalization of matchings and matroids," Ph.D. thesis, University of Waterloo, Waterloo, Ontario, 1974.

[28] T.A. Jenkyns, The efficacy of the "greedy" algorithm, in: "Proc. of 7th SE Conf. on Comb., Graph Theory and Comp," 341–350, 1976.

[29] A. Karlin, C. Mathieu and C. Thach Nguyen, Integrality gaps of linear and semi-definite programming relaxations for knapsack, manuscript, 2009.

[30] M. Laurent, A comparison of the Sherali-Adams, Lovász-Schrijver and Lasserre relaxations for 0-1 programming. *Mathematics of Operations Research,* 28(3):470-496, 2003.

[31] E.L. Lawler, "Combinatorial Optimization: Networks and Matroids," Holt, Rinehart and Winston, 1976.

[32] E.L. Lawler, Matroids with parity conditions: a new class of combinatorial optimization problems, Memo. No. ERL-M334, Electronics Research Laboratory, College of Engineering, UC Berkeley, 1971.

[33] J. Lee, M. Sviridenko and J. Vondrák, Submodular maximization over multiple matroids via generalized exchange properties, "Proc. of APPROX," Springer *LNCS,* 244–257, 2009.

[34] J. Lee, M. Sviridenko and J. Vondrák, Matroid Matching: the Power of Local Search, IBM Research Report RC24898, 11/2009.

[35] L. Lovász, Matroid matching and some applications, *J. Comb. Th., Ser. B* 28, 208–236, 1980.

[36] L. Lovász, The matroid matching problem. In: L. Lovász, L., V.T. Sös (Eds.), "Algebraic Methods in Graph Theory, Vol. II," (Colloq. Szeged, 24–31 August 1978). *Colloq., Math. Soc. Janos Bolyai* 25, North-Holland, 495–517, 1981.

[37] L. Lovász and M.D. Plummer, "Matching Theory," *Annals of Disc. Math.* 29, North-Holland, 1986.

[38] C. Mathieu and A. Sinclair, Sherali-Adams relaxations of the matching polytope, in *Proc. STOC 2009.*

[39] J. Mestre, Greedy in approximation algorithms, in: "Proc. of ESA," 528–539, 2006.

[40] H. Narayanan, H. Saran and V. Vazirani, Randomized Parallel Algorithms for Matroid Union and Intersection, With Applications to Arboresences and Edge-Disjoint Spanning Trees, *SIAM Journal of Computing* 23(2), 387-397, (1994).

[41] J.B. Orlin, A fast, simpler algorithm for the matroid parity problem, In: A. Lodi, A. Panconesi and G. Rinaldi (Eds.), "Proceedings of the The 13th IPCO," (Bertinoro, Italy, 26–28 May 2008), *LNCS* 5035, 2008, 240–258.

[42] J.B. Orlin and J.H. Vande Vate, Solving the linear matroid parity problem as a sequence of matroid intersection problems," *Mathematical Programming,* 47, 81–106, 1990.

[43] A. Recski, "Matroid theory and its applications in electric network theory and in statics," *Algorithms and Combinatorics* 6, Springer Verlag, Berlin, 1989.

[44] A. Recski and J. Szabó, On the generalization of the matroid parity problem. In: A. Bondy, J. Fonlupt, J.-L. Fouquet, J.-C. Fournier, J.L. Ramïrez Alfonsïn (Eds.), "Graph Theory in Paris," Trends in Mathematics, Birkhauser, Basel, 2007, 347–354.

[45] A. Schrijver, "Theory of Linear and Integer Programming," Wiley, 1986.

[46] A. Schrijver, "Combinatorial Optimization: Polyhedra and Efficiency," Springer-Verlag, Berlin, 2003.

[47] H.D. Sherali and W.P. Adams, A hierarchy of relaxations between the continuous and convex hull representations for zero-one programming problems, *SIAM J. on Disc. Math.* 3, 411-430, 1990.

[48] M. Stallmann and H.N. Gabow, An augmenting path algorithm for the parity problem on linear matroids. In: "Proceedings of the 25th FOCS," (Singer Island, Florida, 24–26 October 1984). IEEE, Washington, DC, 1984, 217–228.

[49] P. Tong, E. Lawler and V. Vazirani, Solving the weighted parity problem for gammoids by reduction to graphic matching, In: "Progress in combinatorial optimization (Waterloo, Ont., 1982)," 363–374, Academic Press (Toronto, ON), 1984.

[50] J. Vande Vate, Fractional matroid matchings, *Journal of Combinatorial Theory, Series B* 55 (1992), 133–145.

[51] V.V. Vazirani, "Approximation Algorithms," Springer-Verlag, Berlin, 2001.

[52] D.J.A. Welsh, "Matroid Theory," Academic Press, London-New York, 1976.

[53] S.G. Williamson, "Combinatorics for computer science," Comput. Sci. Press, Rockville, MD, 1985.

Budget Constrained Auctions with Heterogeneous Items

Sayan Bhattacharya
Department of Computer Science
Duke University
Durham, NC 27708
bsayan@cs.duke.edu

Gagan Goel
College of Computing
Georgia Institute of Technology
Atlanta, GA 30332
gagang@cc.gatech.edu

Sreenivas Gollapudi
Microsoft Research
Silicon Valley
Mountain View, CA 94043
sreenig@research.microsoft.com

Kamesh Munagala*
Department of Computer Science
Duke University
Durham, NC 27708
kamesh@cs.duke.edu

ABSTRACT

In this paper, we present the first approximation algorithms for the problem of designing revenue optimal Bayesian incentive compatible auctions when there are multiple (heterogeneous) items and when bidders have arbitrary demand and budget constraints (and additive valuations). Our mechanisms are surprisingly simple: We show that a sequential all-pay mechanism is a 4 approximation to the revenue of the optimal ex-interim truthful mechanism with a discrete type space for each bidder, where her valuations for different items can be correlated. We also show that a sequential posted price mechanism is a $O(1)$ approximation to the revenue of the optimal ex-post truthful mechanism when the type space of each bidder is a product distribution that satisfies the standard hazard rate condition. We further show a logarithmic approximation when the hazard rate condition is removed, and complete the picture by showing that achieving a sub-logarithmic approximation, even for regular distributions and one bidder, requires pricing bundles of items. Our results are based on formulating novel LP relaxations for these problems, and developing generic rounding schemes from first principles.

Categories and Subject Descriptors

F.2 [**Theory of Computation**]: Analysis of Algorithms and Problem Complexity

*Supported by an Alfred P. Sloan Research Fellowship, and by NSF via CAREER award CCF-0745761 and grant CNS-0540347.

STOC'10, June 5–8, 2010, Cambridge, Massachusetts, USA.

General Terms

Algorithms, Economics, Theory

1. INTRODUCTION

In several scenarios, such as the Google TV ad auction [25] and the the FCC spectrum auctions [10], where auctions have been applied in the recent past, bidders are constrained by the amount of money they can spend. This leads to the study of auctions with budget-constrained bidders, which is the focus of this paper. The key difficulty with budgets is that the utility of a bidder is only quasi-linear as long as the price is below the budget constraint, but is $-\infty$ if the price exceeds the budget. As a consequence, well-known mechanisms such as the VCG mechanism are no longer directly applicable. Before proceeding further, we formally define our model.

1.1 Our Model

There are m bidders and n heterogeneous items. The *type* of a bidder is defined as the collection of her valuations for each item; we will assume throughout the paper that her valuations for different items are additive. Further, her type is private knowledge. We augment this basic model for bidder i with two publicly known constraints: A *demand constraint* n_i on the maximum number of items she is willing to buy, and a *budget constraint* B_i on the maximum total price she can afford to pay. Her utility is defined as follows: Suppose she gets a subset A of items where $|A| \leq n_i$, and pays a total price P_i. If v_{ij} denotes her valuation for item j, then her utility is given by $\sum_{j \in A} v_{ij} - P_i$ if $P_i \leq B_i$, and $-\infty$ otherwise. The goal of the auctioneer is to design a mechanism that maximizes its revenue, which is defined as $\sum_i P_i$. We require that the mechanism be *incentive compatible* in that no bidder gains in utility by misreporting her valuations, and *individually rational*, meaning that a bidder gets nonnegative utility by reporting the truth. Some of our results generalize to the case where the budget constraints are private knowledge.

There are two well-established ways of proceeding from here. In the adversarial setting, no assumptions are made on the valuations, while in the Bayesian setting, it is assumed the valuations are drawn from publicly known prior distributions. We take the latter Bayesian approach, which was pioneered by Myerson [24]. As mentioned above, in this setting, the bidders' private valuations are drawn from independent (but not necessarily identical) commonly known prior distributions. The auctioneer's goal is to maximize her expected revenue, where the expectation is over the prior distributions, and possible randomization introduced by the mechanism itself. In the Bayesian setting, the notions of truthfulness and individual rationality can be of two kinds:

Bayesian Incentive Compatible (BIC): Here, each bidder's expected utility is maximized by truth-telling, where the expectation is over the valuations of the other bidders (which are drawn according to their priors) and the randomness introduced by the mechanism. In other words, truth-telling is optimal only in expectation.

Dominant Strategy Incentive Compatible (DISC): In this setting, truth-telling is optimal for the bidder even if she knows the valuations of the other bidders and the random choices made by the mechanism.

We note that traditionally, the terms BIC and DSIC only refer to randomness introduced by other bidders' valuations via the prior distributions. Therefore, to be very precise, the space of mechanisms is two-dimensional, randomized versus universally truthful mechanisms on one dimension, and BIC versus DSIC mechanisms on the other. We collapse this space to randomized BIC versus universally truthful DSIC mechanisms, so as not to introduce additional terminology.

1.2 Our Results

Our results depend on the structure of the type space of each bidder. In particular, the results depend on whether the distributions of the valuations of a bidder for different items are correlated or independent. We note that the correlations if any are *only* for valuations of one bidder for different items; the distributions of the valuations of *different* bidders are always assumed to be independent. All our results can be viewed as presenting simple characterizations of approximately optimal mechanisms in these contexts.

We will first consider the situation when valuations of a bidder for different items are arbitrarily correlated, so that the type space of a bidder is simply specified as a poly-bounded discrete distribution. In Section 2, we present a simple *all-pay* mechanism: it charges each bidder a fixed price that depends only on its revealed type, while the allocation made to the bidder will be *random* depending on the types of other bidders. The resulting scheme is therefore only BIC; however, we show that it is a 4 approximation to the revenue of the optimal BIC scheme (Theorem 2.1).

An all-pay auction is unrealistic in several situations, since a bidder is forced to participate even if she obtains negative utility when the auction concludes. A natural question to ask is whether there exists a DSIC mechanism with good revenue properties. However, it is an easy exercise to show that the problem of designing an optimal DSIC mechanism for one unit-demand bidder ($n_i = 1$) whose type can take one of n arbitrarily correlated possibilities with equal probability, reduces to the problem of unlimited supply *envy-free pricing* with n bidders [19]. For the envy free pricing problem, the best known is a logarithmic approximation, and there is strong evidence that a better approximation is not possible [8]. Furthermore, in the correlated valuation setting, there are examples showing an unbounded gap between the revenues of the optimal randomized (BIC) and deterministic (DSIC) mechanisms [9]. This significantly dims the possibility of a constant factor approximate DSIC mechanism with discrete correlated types.

In view of the above negative result, we assume the valuations of a bidder for different items follow independent distributions. This *product distribution* assumption is also used by Chawla *et. al.* [11], who consider the special case of a single bidder with unit demand. In this special case, it is easy to see that any DSIC mechanism is a posted price mechanism, and they show a constant factor approximation to its revenue by an elegant connection to Myerson's mechanism [24]. Independently of our work, Chawla *et al.* [12] extend their result to show a $O(1)$ approximation for multiple unit-demand bidders. However, this result also crucially require the unit-demand assumption.

In Section 3.2, we show that for arbitrary demands and budgets, when the type of each bidder follows a product distribution where each dimension satisfies the standard monotone hazard rate (MHR), there is a constant factor approximation to the revenue of optimal BIC mechanism. Our mechanism is achieved by a DSIC mechanism with surprisingly simple structure: Consider the bidders sequentially in arbitrary order, and for each bidder, offer a subset of remaining items at a pre-computed price for each item; the bidder simply chooses the utility maximizing bundle of these items. This posted price mechanism shows a constant factor gap between the revenues of the optimal BIC and DSIC mechanisms (Theorem 3.6), which is in sharp contrast with the corresponding negative result [9] when the type space of a bidder is correlated. The surprising aspect of our result is that since the optimal DSIC mechanism for general demands and budgets will price bundles of items, there is *no a priori reason* to expect that the more simplistic scheme of posting prices for each item would be a constant approximation.

We show (Section 3.3) that the MHR condition is indeed necessary for our item pricing result: If this condition is slightly relaxed to regular product distributions and one bidder, the optimal DSIC mechanism will price *bundles of items*, and will have a logarithmic gap against the revenue of the optimal item pricing scheme. We show that this gap is tight by showing the existence of a posted price mechanism achieving this approximation ratio (Theorem 3.8). On a positive note, we conclude by proving that for regular distributions, if the space of feasible mechanisms is restricted to those that consider bidders in some adaptive order and post prices that may depend on the outcomes so far, there is a $O(1)$ approximation within this space, that considers bidders in an arbitrary but fixed order, and pre-computes the posted prices (Theorem 3.10).

1.3 Related Work

The Bayesian setting is widely studied in the economics literature [4, 10, 13, 14, 22, 23, 26, 27, 28]. In this setting, the optimal (either BIC or DSIC) mechanism can always be computed by encoding the incentive compatibility constraints in an integer program and maximizing expected revenue. However, the number of variables (and constraints) in this IP is exponential in the number of bidders, there being variables for the allocations and prices for each scenario of revealed types. Therefore, the key difficulty in the Bayesian mechanism design case is *computational: Can the optimal (or approximately optimal) auction be efficiently computed and implemented?*

Much of the literature in economics considers the case where the auctioneer has one item (or multiple copies of the item). In the absence of budget constraints, Myerson [24] presents the characterization of any BIC mechanism in terms of expected allocation made to a bidder: This allocation must be monotone in the revealed valuation of the bidder, and furthermore, the expected price is given by applying the VCG calculation to the expected allocation. This yields a linear-time computable optimal revenue-maximizing auction that is both BIC and DSIC. The key issue with budget constraints is that the allocations need to be thresholded in order for the prices to be below the budgets [13, 22, 26]. However, even in this case, the optimal BIC auction follows from a polymatroid characterization that can be solved by the Ellipsoid algorithm and an all-pay condition [6, 26]. By *all-pay*, we mean that the bidder pays a fixed amount given his revealed type, regardless of the allocation made. This also yields a DSIC mechanism that is $O(1)$ approximation to optimal BIC revenue [5], but the result holds only for homogeneous items.

An alternative line of work deals with the *adversarial setting*, where no distributional assumption is made on the bidders' private valuations. In this setting, the budget constrained auction problem is notorious mainly because standard auction concepts such as VCG, efficiency, and competitive equilibria do not directly carry over [25]. Most previous results deal with the case of multiple units of a homogeneous good. In this setting, based on the random partitioning framework of Goldberg *et al.* [18], Borgs *et al.* [7] presented a truthful auction whose revenue is asymptotically within a constant factor of the optimal revenue (see also [1]). If the focus is instead on optimizing social welfare, no non-trivial truthful mechanism can optimize social welfare [7]. Therefore, the focus has been on weaker notions than efficiency, such as Pareto-optimality, where no pair of agents (including the auctioneer) can simultaneously improve their utilities by trading with each other. Dobzinski *et al.* [16] present an ascending price auction based on the clinching auction of Ausubel [2], which they show to be the only Pareto-optimal auction in the public budget setting. This result was extended to the private budget setting by Bhattacharya *et al.* [5]; see [20] for a related result.

Finally, several researchers have considered the behavior specific types of auctions, for instance, auctions that are sequential by item and second price within each item [4, 17], and ascending price auctions [3, 10]. The goal here is to analyze the improvement in revenue (or social welfare) by optimal sequencing, or to study incentive compatibility of commonly used ascending price mechanisms. However, analyzing the performance of sequential or ascending price auctions is difficult in general, and there is little known in terms of optimal mechanisms (or even approximately optimal mechanisms) in these settings.

1.4 Our Techniques

If for every bidder, the valuations for different items are correlated (Section 2), then the optimal BIC revenue can be bounded from above by a linear program (LP1) that requires the incentive compatibility, voluntary participation, supply and demand constraints to hold *only in expectation*. We construct a BIC all pay auction (Figure 1) that basically implements a rounding scheme on the optimal solution to LP1, loosing a constant factor in revenue (Theorem 2.1). This approach is based on the techniques used in [5].

As mentioned before, Chawla *et. al.* [11] consider the Bayesian unit-demand pricing problem. There are n heterogeneous items, a single bidder with unit demand, and her valuations (v_j for item $j \in [1, \ldots, n]$) are drawn from independent distributions. They present an elegant pricing scheme that is a constant approximation to optimal revenue by upper bounding it using the revenue of Myerson's auction in the following setting: There is a single item, n bidders, and valuation of each bidder j follows the same distribution as that of v_j. However, this technique cannot be applied if the unit demand assumption is removed.

In contrast, our approach to the independent valuations setting (Section 3) does *not* require the unit-demand assumption, and is based on a novel LP relaxation (LPREV) for the problem (Lemma 3.1). Unlike the LP relaxation of Section 2 and perhaps surprisingly, LPREV does not encode any incentive compatibility constraints, and our DSIC mechanism (Figure 2), that competes against this LP, is in fact a constant approximation to optimal BIC revenue. One limitation of our approach is that we have to (necessarily) assume the bidders' valuations satisfy montone hazard rate (MHR). In the process of proving our main result (Theorem 3.6), we describe a crucial property of MHR distributions (Lemma 3.3) that can be used to extend the type of results shown in [21]. For example, in multi-item settings with only demand constraints, *posted price schemes generate revenue that is a constant factor of the optimal social welfare*, assuming MHR distributions (Corollary 3.7). The LP formulations also generalize the stochastic matching setting in Chen *et al.* [15].

2. CORRELATED VALUATIONS: BIC MECHANISMS

We first consider the problem of approximating the optimal Bayesian incentive compatible mechanism. There are m bidders and n indivisible items. The type t of a bidder is a n-vector $\langle v_{1t}, v_{2t}, \ldots, v_{nt} \rangle$, which specifies her valuations for the items. For bidder i, we assume the types follow a publicly known discrete distribution with polynomial support, where for $t = t_1, t_2, \ldots, t_K$, we have $f_i(t) = \Pr[\text{Type} = t]$. The distributions for different bidders are independent. Note that the above model allows the valuations of a bidder for different items to possibly be correlated. The bidder can afford to pay at most a publicly known budget B_i, and is interested in at most $n_i \geq 1$ items. (Our scheme extends to private budgets using the techniques in [5].) We will be interested in mechanisms that can be computed in time polynomial in the input size, *i.e.*, in n, m, and K.

For reported types $\vec{t}$, the auctioneer computes allocation of items $S_i(\vec{t})$ for each bidder i. It also computes prices $P_i(\vec{t})$. The subsets $S_i(\vec{t})$ of items need to be disjoint, and $P_i(\vec{t}) \leq B_i$. The utility of a bidder for obtaining subset S at price P when her type is t is $\sum_{j \in S} v_{jt} - P$. A mechanism should be incentive compatible in the following sense: For any bidder i, her expected utility, where the expectation is over the types of other bidders, is maximized if she reveals her true type. The auctioneer is interested in designing an incentive compatible mechanism that maximizes revenue: $\mathbf{E}_{\vec{t}}\left[\sum_i P_i(\vec{t})\right]$.

We now show an all-pay auction mechanism that is a 4-approximation to optimal revenue. Our LP relaxation and solution technique are inspired by the rounding scheme in [5] for multi-unit auctions.

Linear Programming Relaxation. Throughout, we will denote bidders by i, items by j, and types by t. For any feasible mechanism, let $x_{ij}(t)$ denote the probability that bidder i obtains item j if her reported type is t. Let $P_i(t)$ denote the expected price paid by bidder i when she bids type t. We have the following LP:

$$\text{Maximize} \quad \sum_{i,t} f_i(t)P_i(t) \qquad \text{(LP1)}$$

$$\begin{array}{rcll} \sum_{i,t} f_i(t)x_{ij}(t) & \leq & 1 & \forall j \\ \sum_j x_{ij}(t) & \leq & n_i & \forall i,t \\ \sum_j v_{jt}x_{ij}(t) - P_i(t) & \geq & \sum_j v_{jt}x_{ij}(s) - P_i(s) & \forall i,t,s \\ \sum_j v_{jt}x_{ij}(t) - P_i(t) & \geq & 0 & \forall i,t \\ x_{ij}(t) & \in & [0,1] & \forall i,j,t \\ P_i(t) & \in & [0,B_i] & \forall i,t \end{array}$$

The optimal Bayesian incentive compatible mechanism is feasible for the above constraints: The first constraint simply encodes that in expectation, each item is assigned to at most one bidder; the second constraint encodes the demand. The third and fourth constraints encodes Bayesian incentive compatibility and individual rationality. Therefore, the LP1 value is an upper bound on the expected revenue.

THEOREM 2.1. *The All Pay Auction (Figure 1) is Bayesian Incentive Compatible, and its revenue is a 4 approximation to the optimal BIC mechanism for heterogeneous items.*

PROOF. Note that $\sum_i X_{ij} \leq \frac{1}{2}$ for all items j, since we scaled down the LP variables. Furthermore, $Z_{ij} = \prod_{i'<i}(1 - X_{ij}) \geq 1 - \sum_{i'<i} X_{ij} \geq \frac{1}{2}$. This implies $\frac{1/2}{Z_{ij}} \leq 1$.

In Step 6, J denotes the set of available items. When bidder i is encountered in the predefined (but arbitrtary) ordering, the set W_i is initialized to $\emptyset$. In each group $\mathcal{G}_{it_ik}$, a single item j is selected with probability $\tilde{x}_{ij}(t_i)$. If $j \in J$, it is added to W_i with probability $\frac{1/2}{Z_{ij}}$ (which is at most 1), and regardless of the outcome of this random event, j is removed from J.

In the discussion below, all expectations are with respect the bids revealed by bidders $i' < i$ and the random choices made in constructing W_i. Since the values revealed by bidders $i' < i$ are independent, item j is available when bidder i is considered with probability exactly $\prod_{i'<i}(1 - X_{ij}) = Z_{ij}$. Therefore:

$$\Pr[j \in W_i] = Z_{ij} \cdot \tilde{x}_{ij}(t_i) \cdot 1/(2Z_{ij}) = \tilde{x}_{ij}(t_i)/2 = x^*_{ij}(t_i)/4$$

By linearity of expectation, the expected welfare of items allocated to bidder i is precisely $\frac{1}{4}\sum_j v_{jt_i}x^*_{ij}(t_i)$. Since bidder i pays a fixed price $P^*_i(t_i)/4$, both the expected welfare and expected price are scaled down by a factor exactly 4 relative to the LP values *regardless of her revealed type.* This preserves the incentive compatibility constraints in the LP, and makes the scheme be truthful and satisfy voluntary participation in expectation over the types of other bidders and the randomness introduced by the mechanism. The theorem follows. □

All Pay Auction

1. Choose an arbitrary but fixed ordering of all bidders and denote it by $1, \ldots, m$
2. Find the optimal solution to LP1, and denote the variable values by $\{x^*_{ij}(t), P^*_i(t)\}$
3. For all bidders i, items j, types t, let
   $\tilde{x}_{ij}(t) = x^*_{ij}(t)/2$,
   $X_{ij} = \sum_t f_i(t)\tilde{x}_{ij}(t)$,
   $Z_{ij} = \prod_{i'<i}(1 - X_{ij})$
4. FOR all bidders i, types t,
   Partition the items into n_i disjoint groups s.t. in each group $\mathcal{G}_{itk}$, $\sum_{j\in\mathcal{G}_{itk}} \tilde{x}_{ij}(t) \leq 1$
5. Collect the reported types of all bidders. Denote the reported type of bidder i by t_i
6. Initialize J to be the set of all items.
   FOR $i = 1, 2, \ldots m$,
   Initialize $W_i \leftarrow \emptyset$
   FOR $k = 1$ to n_i
   Pick a single item $j \in \mathcal{G}_{it_ik}$ w.p. $\tilde{x}_{ij}(t_i)$
   IF $j \in J$
   $W_i \leftarrow W_i \cup \{j\}$ w.p. $\frac{1/2}{Z_{ij}}$
   $J \leftarrow J \setminus \{j\}$
   Bidder i gets the (random) set W_i, and pays a (fixed) price $P^*_i(t_i)/4$

Figure 1: BIC Mechanism for correlated valuations

We note that by replacing the objective function with $\sum_{i,j,t} f_i(t)v_{jt}x_{ij}(t)$, the resulting scheme is a 4 approximation to the optimal expected social welfare (or any linear combination of revenue and welfare).

3. INDEPENDENT VALUATIONS: DSIC MECHANISMS

The All Pay Auction (Figure 1) satisfies the incentive compatibility constraints only in expectation over the valuations of the other bidders and randomness introduced by the mechanism. In practice, it is more desirable to consider mechanisms that satisfy these properties ex-post. As mentioned before (Section 1.2), in general, it is likely to be hard to approximate such mechanisms, and this hardness comes from the type space of a bidder being correlated. However, we show that for the important special case of product distributions with the hazard rate condition, a constant factor approximation follows from sequential posted price mechanisms. Such a mechanism considers the bidders sequentially in arbitrary order, and for each bidder, posts a subset of remaining items at certain price for each item, and lets the bidder choose the utility maximizing bundle of these items. Such a scheme is ex-post incentive compatible by definition.

Formally, there are n distinct indivisible goods each of unit quantity, and m bidders. Bidder i has publicly known budget B_i on the total price she is willing to pay. Her utility for paying more than this price is $-\infty$; as long as the budget constraint is satisfied, the utility for any item is quasi-linear, *i.e.*, the valuation obtained minus price, thresholded below at zero. The valuations for different items are additive, and she can buy more than one item, but at most some $n_i \geq 1$ items. Her valuation for item j is a positive integer-valued random variable $v_{ij} \in [1, L_{ij}]$ following publicly known distributions. Though we assume the distributions are defined at positive integer values, this is w.l.o.g., since we can discretize continuous distributions in powers of $(1+\epsilon)$ and apply the same arguments. This also holds when the values taken by the random variables are not polynomially bounded.

Key Assumption. We will present ex-post incentive compatible mechanisms under the following key *product distribution* assumption: The valuations v_{ij} for each (i, j) follow independent distributions.

Under the above assumption we consider two cases: (1) The random variables v_{ij} satisfy the monotone hazard rate condition (Section 3.2), and (2) The random variables v_{ij} are arbitrary integer valued variables over the domain $[1, L]$ (Section 3.3). In the former case, we show that sequential posted prices are a $O(1)$ approximation to the optimal BIC mechanism (Theorem 3.6), whereas in the latter case, they are a $O(\log L)$ approximation, and doing better necessarily requires pricing bundles of items rather than individual items (Theorem 3.8).

Proof Sketch of Theorem 3.6. First, observe that in order to enforce individual rationality, whenever item j is allocated to bidder i, the expected revenue generated across edge (i, j) is at most $\mathcal{V}_{ij} = \min(v_{ij}, B_i)$. Let $x_{ij}(r)$ denote the probability that bidder i gets item j when $\mathcal{V}_{ij} = r$. If we require the demand, budget and supply constraints to hold *only in expectation*, the revenue of any mechanism can be upper bounded by a linear program with variables $x_{ij}(r)$ (Lemma 3.1). Interestingly, this linear program (LPREV) does not encode incentive compatibility constraints. Thus, any DSIC scheme that is constant competitive against LPREV will also be a $O(1)$ approximation to optimal BIC revenue.

Note that if v_{ij} satisfies MHR, then $\mathcal{V}_{ij}$ also satisfies MHR (Claim 3.2). Next, we make the crucial observation that if the prior on a bidder's valuation is MHR, then with constant probability her virtual valuation is within a constant factor of her valuation (Lemma 3.3). Thus, replacing $\mathcal{V}_{ij}$ by the corresponding virtual valuation function φ_{ij}, we get a new linear program (LP2) that is still a good approximation to LPREV and hence to optimal revenue (Lemma 3.4). Using Myerson's characterization of virtual valuations [24], we show that the optimal solution to LP2 has a nice structure (Lemma 3.5). Roughly speaking, it treats each edge (i, j) as a separate bidder with valuation given by the random variable $\mathcal{V}_{ij}$. Finally, we employ an interesting rounding technique (Figure 2) on the optimal solution to LP2, and get a DSIC item pricing scheme that looses a constant factor in revenue. Since we need to apply Markov's inequality during the rounding phase, we revisit the definition of $\mathcal{V}_{ij}$ and scale down the reported budget by a suitable factor (Definition 1). This implies LPREV is an upper bound on optimal revenue up to a constant factor; rest of the proof remains the same.

One issue with auctions where bidders are budget and demand constrained is that given posted prices for the items, the bidder needs to solve a two-dimensional KNAPSACK problem to determine her optimal bundle, and this is NP-HARD in general. However, this aspect does not change our results: Our upper bound LP2 is the best possible revenue regardless of what optimization the bidders perform, and furthermore, our analysis of the algorithm in Figure 2 simply shows that with constant probability, the bidder solves a trivial knapsack instance where all items fit into the knapsack. Therefore, as long as the bidder uses any reasonable KNAPSACK heuristic, our results hold.

3.1 Linear Programming Relaxation

We first present a simple bound on the revenue of any BIC mechanism. In the ensuing discussion, we will denote bidders by i and items by j.

DEFINITION 1. *Define* $\mathcal{V}_{ij} = \min(v_{ij}, B_i/4)$ *and let its density function be* f_{ij}.

$$\text{Maximize} \quad \sum_{i,j}\sum_r r f_{ij}(r) x_{ij}(r) \qquad \text{(LPREV)}$$

$$\begin{array}{rcll} \sum_j \sum_r f_{ij}(r)x_{ij}(r) & \leq & n_i & \forall i \quad (1) \\ \sum_j \sum_r r f_{ij}(r)x_{ij}(r) & \leq & B_i & \forall i \quad (2) \\ \sum_i \sum_r f_{ij}(r)x_{ij}(r) & \leq & 1 & \forall j \quad (3) \\ x_{ij}(r) & \in & [0,1] & \forall i,j,r \quad (4) \end{array}$$

LEMMA 3.1. *The optimal value of the program (LPREV) is at least a factor 1/4 of the revenue of the optimal BIC mechanism. Furthermore, in the LP solution,* $x_{ij}(r)$ *is a monotonically non-decreasing function of* r.

PROOF. Without any loss of generality, we assume that whenever a bidder is allocated a bundle of items, the total price she has to pay is distributed amongst the individual items obtained. Since the mechanism satisfies the individual rationality condition in expectation, it is easy to ensure that the expected price on a single item is never greater than the valuation for the item or the overall budget. Let $x_{ij}(r)$ denote the expected amount of item j bidder i obtains when $\mathcal{V}_{ij} = r$, and let $p_{ij}(r)$ denote the expected price paid conditioned on obtaining the item. It is easy to see that $p_{ij}(r) \leq 4r$. The revenue of the optimal BIC mechanism can be relaxed as:

$$\text{Maximize} \quad \sum_{i,j}\sum_r p_{ij}(r) f_{ij}(r) x_{ij}(r)$$

$$\begin{array}{rcll} \sum_j \sum_r f_{ij}(r)x_{ij}(r) & \leq & n_i & \forall i \quad (1) \\ \sum_j \sum_r p_{ij}(r) f_{ij}(r)x_{ij}(r) & \leq & B_i & \forall i \quad (2) \\ \sum_i \sum_r f_{ij}(r)x_{ij}(r) & \leq & 1 & \forall j \quad (3) \\ x_{ij}(r) & \in & [0,1] & \forall i,j,r \quad (4) \\ p_{ij}(r) & \in & [0,4r] & \forall i,j,r \quad (5) \end{array}$$

The above program is nonlinear. Scale $p_{ij}(r)$ down by a factor of 4 so that $p_{ij}(r) \leq r$. This preserves the constraints and loses a factor of 4 in the objective. Now, for all i, j, if $p_{ij}(r) < r$, increase $p_{ij}(r)$ and decrease $x_{ij}(r)$ while preserving their product until $p_{ij}(r)$ becomes equal to r. This yields the constraints of (LPREV), and preserves the objective; but now, the objective becomes $\sum_{i,j}\sum_r r f_{ij}(r) x_{ij}(r)$.

This shows (LPREV) is a 4-approximation to the revenue of the optimal BIC mechanism.

To show that the objective is maximized when the $x_{ij}(r)$ are monotonically non-decreasing in r, for any (i, j), preserve $\sum_r r f_{ij}(r) x_{ij}(r)$ by increasing $x_{ij}(s_2)$ and decreasing $x_{ij}(s_1)$ for $s_1 < s_2$. In this process, $\sum_r f_{ij}(r) x_{ij}(r)$ must decrease, preserving all the constraints, which implies the monotonicity. □

We note that because of the presence of budget constraints, (LPREV) bounds only the expected revenue of the ex-post mechanism and *not* the expected social welfare, which can be larger by an unbounded amount. However, if the budget constraints are removed, the resulting LP also bounds the optimal social welfare.

3.2 Monotone Hazard Rates

We will now present a constant factor approximation to the optimal BIC mechanism via sequential posted price schemes, assuming the random variables v_{ij} satisfy the monotone hazard rate condition.

DEFINITION 2. *The distribution of* v_{ij} *satisfies the monotone hazard rate (MHR) condition if* $\Pr[v_{ij} > r]/Pr[v_{ij} = r]$ *is a non-increasing function of* r.

CLAIM 3.2. *If* v *is a random variable satisfying the monotone hazard rate condition, then* $\min(v, a)$ *satisfies the MHR condition for any integer* $a \geq 1$.

It follows that the $\mathcal{V}_{ij}$ also satisfy the MHR condition.

DEFINITION 3 (MYERSON [24]). *Let* $G_{ij}(r) = \Pr[\mathcal{V}_{ij} > r]$. *Define the* virtual valuation *as* $\varphi_{ij}(r) = r - G_{ij}(r)/f_{ij}(r)$. *This is said to be* regular *if it is a non-decreasing function of* r.

Clearly, MHR distributions are regular. We now present the crucial lemma for MHR distributions.

LEMMA 3.3. *Let* $\phi(v)$ *denote the virtual valuation function for a positive integer valued random variable* $v \in [1, L]$ *satisfying the MHR condition. Then,* $\Pr[\phi(v) \geq \frac{v}{2}] \geq \frac{1}{e^2}$.

PROOF. Let $f(t) = \Pr[v = t]$ and $G(t) = \Pr[v > t]$. Let $h(t) = f(t)/G(t)$ denote the hazard rate at t. Since f satisfies MHR, $\phi(t) < t/2$ iff $t \leq k$ for some integer $1 \leq k \leq L$. Furthermore, $\phi(k) = k - 1/h(k) \leq k/2$. This implies for all $t \leq k$, $h(t) \leq h(k) \leq 2/k$.

Therefore, $\Pr[\phi(t) \geq t/2] = \Pr[t > k]$. To bound the latter quantity, replace f with a continuous-valued distribution $\hat{f}$ whose density in $[t, t+1)$ for any integer $t \in [1, L]$ is precisely $f(t)$. It is easy to see that this new density also satisfies the hazard rate condition. Let $\hat{G}(t) = 1 - \int_{q=1}^{t+1} \hat{f}(q)dq$, and let $\hat{h}(t) = \frac{\hat{f}(t)}{\hat{G}(t)}$. Thus,

$$\Pr[\phi(t) \geq t/2] = \Pr[t > k] = G(k) = \hat{G}(k)$$
$$= e^{-\int_{t=1}^{k+1} \hat{h}(t)dt} \geq e^{-\int_{t=1}^{k+1} \frac{2}{k}dt} \geq e^{-2}$$

□

OBSERVATION 1. *Let* $v_{ij}^* = argmin_r\{\varphi_{ij}(r) \geq \frac{r}{2}\}$. *Then, Lemma 3.3 and Claim 3.2 imply* $\Pr[\mathcal{V}_{ij} \geq v_{ij}^*] \geq e^{-2}$.

3.2.1 *Incorporating Virtual Valuations*

Now consider the following linear program obtained from (LPREV).

$$\text{Maximize} \quad \sum_{i,j}\sum_r f_{ij}(r)\varphi_{ij}(r)x_{ij}(r) \qquad \text{(LP2)}$$

$$\begin{array}{rcll}
\sum_j \sum_r f_{ij}(r)x_{ij}(r) & \leq & n_i & \forall i \quad (1)\\
\sum_j \sum_r f_{ij}(r)\varphi_{ij}(r)x_{ij}(r) & \leq & B_i & \forall i \quad (2)\\
\sum_i \sum_r f_{ij}(r)x_{ij}(r) & \leq & 1 & \forall j \quad (3)\\
x_{ij}(r) & \in & [0,1] & \forall i,j,r \quad (4)
\end{array}$$

LEMMA 3.4. *The value of* (LP2) *is at least* $\frac{1}{2e^2}$ *times the value of* (LPREV).

PROOF. In the optimal solution to (LPREV), since $\Pr[\mathcal{V}_{ij} \geq v_{ij}^*] \geq e^{-2}$ by Lemma 3.3 and since $x_{ij}(r)$ is monotone in r, setting $x_{ij}(r) = 0$ for $r < v_{ij}^*$ loses a factor of at most e^2 in the objective value and preserves feasibility. Now replacing r by $\varphi_{ij}(r) \in [r/2, r]$ for $r \geq v_{ij}^*$ loses another factor of 2 by Lemma 3.3, and preserves feasibility. This shows a feasible solution to (LP2) of value at least $\frac{1}{2e^2}$ times that of (LPREV). □

LEMMA 3.5. *The optimal solution to* (LP2) *is as follows: For each* (i, j), *we have a convex combination of two solutions. The first (resp. second) solution has variables* $y_{ij}(r)$ *(resp.* $z_{ij}(r)$*), and value* $r_{ij}^* \leq B_i/4$ *(resp.* $s_{ij}^* = r_{ij}^* + 1 \leq B_i/4$*) so that if* $r < r_{ij}^*$, *then* $y_{ij} = 0$, *else* $y_{ij} = 1$. *Similarly, if* $r < s_{ij}^*$, *then* $z_{ij} = 0$, *else* $z_{ij} = 1$. *If the first solution has weight* p_{ij} *in the convex combination, and the second* $1 - p_{ij}$, *then:*

$$\sum_r f_{ij}(r)\varphi_{ij}(r)x_{ij}(r)$$
$$= p_{ij}r_{ij}^* \Pr[\mathcal{V}_{ij} \geq r_{ij}^*] + (1 - p_{ij})s_{ij}^* \Pr[\mathcal{V}_{ij} \geq s_{ij}^*] \qquad (1)$$

PROOF. For each (i, j) if $x_{ij}(r_1), x_{ij}(r_2) \in (0, 1)$ for $r_1 < r_2 \leq B_i/4$, then $x_{ij}(r_1)$ can be increased and $x_{ij}(r_2)$ can be decreased to preserve $\sum_r \varphi_{ij}(r)f_{ij}(r)x_{ij}(r)$. Since $\varphi_{ij}(r)$ is a monotonically non-decreasing function of r, this implies $\sum_r f_{ij}(r)x_{ij}(r)$ must decrease in this process, preserving all constraints. When this process terminates, we must have $x_{ij}(r) = 0$ for all $r < r^*$ and $x_{ij}(r) = 1$ for all $r > r^*$ for some r^*. This implies the optimal solution to (LP2) can be written in the fashion implied by the lemma, with $r_{ij}^* = r^*$ and $p_{ij} = x_{ij}(r^*)$. By Myerson's characterization of virtual valuations [24], we have:

$$\sum_r f_{ij}(r)\varphi_{ij}(r)x_{ij}(r) = \sum_r \left(f_{ij}(r)\left(rx_{ij}(r) - \sum_{s=1}^{r-1} x_{ij}(s)\right)\right)$$

Since $y_{ij}(r)$ is a 0/1 step function, it is easy to see that

$$\sum_r \left(f_{ij}(r)\left(ry_{ij}(r) - \sum_{s=1}^{r-1} y_{ij}(s)\right)\right) = r_{ij}^* \Pr[\mathcal{V}_{ij} \geq r_{ij}^*]$$

A similar equality holds for z_{ij}, and taking a convex combination completes the proof of the lemma. □

3.2.2 *Posted Price Mechanism and Analysis*

The posted price auction is described in Figure 2. Note that though the scheme is randomized, since it is posted price, it is universally and ex-post truthful and individually rational.

Posted Price Auction

1. Choose an arbitrary but fixed ordering of all bidders and denote it by $1, \ldots, m$
2. Solve LP2
3. FOR each (i, j)
   Independently pick one of the two solutions in the convex combination (see Lemma 3.5) w.p. equal to its weight in the combination.
4. Let $\tilde{r}_{ij}$ denote the threshold in the chosen solution where the allocation function $\tilde{y}_{ij}$ jumps from zero to one.
5. Initialize J to be the set of all items.
   FOR $i = 1, 2, \ldots, m$
   Initialize $W_i \leftarrow \emptyset$
   FOR each item $j \in J$
   $W_i \leftarrow W_i \cup \{j\}$ w.p. $\frac{1}{4}$
   Only the set of items W_i is offered to bidder i
   Each $j \in W_i$ is offered at a price $\tilde{r}_{ij}$
   Bidder i buys a subset of items $S_i \subseteq W_i$
   $J \leftarrow J \setminus S_i$

Figure 2: DSIC Mechanism for independent valuations

THEOREM 3.6. *The revenue of the posted price auction (Figure 2) is a $O(1)$ approximation to the optimal BIC mechanism, when the valuations of a bidder follow product distributions that satisfy the MHR condition.*

PROOF. We show that for every pair (i, j), the mechanism achieves revenue within $O(1)$ factor of $\sum_r f_{ij}(r)\varphi_{ij}(r)x_{ij}(r)$ in (LP2) for the pair. First note that if a price is posted according to the mechanism in Figure 2 just along edge (i, j), then by Equation (1), the expected revenue is simply:

$$p_{ij}r^*_{ij}\Pr[\mathcal{V}_{ij} \geq r^*_{ij}] + (1 - p_{ij})s^*_{ij}\Pr[\mathcal{V}_{ij} \geq s^*_{ij}] = \sum_r f_{ij}(r)\varphi_{ij}(r)x_{ij}(r)$$

We will now show that even in the presence of other items and bidders, a constant factor of this revenue is extracted. For pair (i, j), let X_{ij} be the 0/1 random variable denoting whether item j is taken by bidder i, and let P_{ij} denote the price at which it is taken (which is 0 if the item is not taken by the bidder). These are random variables that depend on the prior distributions as well as the random choices made in choosing the structured solution and the mechanism. Since the probability that any (i, j) is considered at all is $1/4$, the constraints of (LP2), when scaled down by factor 4, imply by linearity of expectation that for all i, j:

$$\mathbf{E}[\sum_{k\neq j} P_{ik}] \leq B_i/4, \qquad \mathbf{E}[\sum_{k\neq j} X_{ik}] \leq n_i/4,$$

$$\text{and} \qquad \mathbf{E}[\sum_{m\neq i} X_{mj}] \leq 1/4$$

Note that snce the valuation v_{ij} is independent of other valuations, this implies the above statements hold regardless of v_{ij}. Now applying Markov's inequality, we have for all i, j:

$$\Pr[\sum_{k\neq j} P_{ik} \geq 3B_i/4] \leq 1/3, \qquad \Pr[\sum_{k\neq j} X_{ik} \geq n_i] \leq 1/4,$$

$$\text{and} \qquad \Pr[\sum_{m\neq i} X_{mj} \geq 1] \leq 1/4$$

By union bounds, this implies that with probability at least $1/6$, we must have: $\sum_{k\neq j} P_{ik} < 3B_i/4$, $\sum_{k\neq j} X_{ik} < n_i$, and $\sum_{m\neq i} X_{mj} = 0$. In this event, item j is offered to bidder i w.p. $1/4$ (using one of two random choices of the posted price from Lemma 3.5). Furthermore, in this event, the bidder must take the item if $v_{ij} \geq \tilde{r}_{ij}$, since $\tilde{r}_{ij} \leq B_i/4$ (so that the bidder has sufficient budget to purchase this item), and the bidder has not exhausted his demand n_i. Since the valuation v_{ij} itself is independent of the event that the item j is offered to bidder i, this implies that with probability at least $1/6 \times 1/4$, the posted price mechanism obtains revenue $\sum_r f_{ij}(r)\varphi_{ij}(r)x_{ij}(r)$ along each (i, j) (using the definition of the latter quantity from Equation (1)). By linearity of expectation over all (i, j), we have a $O(1)$ approximation. □

COROLLARY 3.7. *Under the assumptions of Theorem 3.6, if there are no budget constraints, then the revenue of the sequential posted price mechanism is a constant factor approximation to the optimal social welfare.*

PROOF. If the Budget Constraint (2) is removed from (LPREV), it is an upper bound on the optimal social welfare that can be obtained by any mechanism. The rest of the analysis remains the same. □

3.3 General Distributions

The key point shown by Theorem 3.6 is that the optimal revenue of an ex-post truthful mechanism is approximated to a constant factor by a simple sequential posted price auction, where the prices are posted for each item and each bidder. This crucially used the monotone hazard rate condition. The natural question to ask is whether such a simple mechanism is a good approximation for more general classes of distributions. Note that even for one bidder, the optimal DSIC mechanism will in general price *bundles* of items. We show below that bundle pricing has a logarithmic advantage over item pricing even for regular distributions (see Definition 3), and that this gap is tight.

THEOREM 3.8. *Suppose $v_{ij} \in [1, L]$, are independent for different (i, j) but do not necessarily satisfy the monotone hazard rate condition. Then, there is a $\Theta(\log L)$ gap between the revenues of the optimal posted price scheme and the optimal DSIC mechanism. The lower bound holds for regular distributions and one bidder.*

PROOF. To show the lower bound, consider the following scenario: There is only one bidder, n items, and no budget or demand constraints. The valuations are *i.i.d.* for each item j, and follow the common distribution with $G(r) = \Pr[v \geq r] = \frac{1}{r}$, for $r = 1, 2, \ldots, n$, so that $n = L$. This distribution is regular, since $\varphi(r) = -1$ for $r < n$, and $\varphi(n) = n - 1$. We have $\mathbf{E}[v_{1j}] = H_n$ for all item j, and by Chernoff bounds,

$$\Pr[\sum_{j=1}^{n} v_{1j} \leq (1 - \epsilon)nH_n] \leq e^{\frac{-nH_n\epsilon^2}{2n}} = o(1)$$

Therefore, a scheme that sets a price of $nH_n(1 - \epsilon)$ for the bundle of n items sells the bundle with probability $1 - o(1)$, so that the expected revenue is $\Omega(n \log n)$. Any posted price scheme can extract a revenue of $\max_i i \cdot G(i) = 1$ from each item, so that the expected revenue from n items is at most n. This shows a gap of $\Omega(\log n) = \Omega(\log L)$.

The upper bound follows from a standard scaling argument. We start with (LPREV) which upper bounds the optimal achievable revenue. For each (i, j), group the r values in powers of 2 so that there are $O(\log L)$ groups. Let group $\mathcal{G}_k$ denote the interval $[2^k, 2^{k+1})$.

The first step is to solve (LPREV). Let its optimal value be OPT; note that this is a 4 approximation to the optimal ex-post incentive compatible scheme. Now, for each (i, j) perform the following rounding. Let

$$k_{ij} = \text{argmax}_k \sum_{r \in \mathcal{G}_k} r f_{ij}(r) x_{ij}(r)$$

$$r^*_{ij} = 2^{k_{ij}}$$

$$x^*_{ij} = \frac{\sum_{r \in \mathcal{G}_k} f_{ij}(r) x_{ij}(r)}{\sum_{r \in \mathcal{G}_k} f_{ij}(r)}$$

$$Q_{ij} = \Pr[\tilde{V}_{ij} \geq r^*_{ij}]$$

Since $x_{ij}(r)$ is monotone in r, it is easy to observe that:

1. $x^*_{ij} \leq x_{ij}(r)$ for $r \in \mathcal{G}_k$ for $k > k^*_{ij}$. This implies $x^*_{ij} Q_{ij} \leq \sum_r f_{ij}(r) x_{ij}(r)$.
2. $\sum_{r \in \mathcal{G}_{k_{ij}}} r f_{ij}(r) x_{ij}(r) \leq 2 r^*_{ij} x^*_{ij} \Pr[r \in \mathcal{G}_{k_{ij}}]$.
3. $\max_k \sum_{r \in \mathcal{G}_k} r f_{ij}(r) x_{ij}(r) = \Omega(1/\log L) \sum_r r f_{ij}(r) x_{ij}(r)$.
4. Therefore, $r^*_{ij} x^*_{ij} Q_{ij} = \Omega(1/\log L) \sum_r r f_{ij}(r) x_{ij}(r)$. Furthermore, $r^*_{ij} x^*_{ij} Q_{ij} \leq \sum_r r f_{ij}(r) x_{ij}(r)$.

The above directly implies $\sum_{i,j} r^*_{ij} x^*_{ij} Q_{ij} = \Omega(OPT/\log L)$, and the following constraints:

$$\begin{array}{rcll}
\sum_j x^*_{ij} Q_{ij} & \leq & n_i & \forall i \\
\sum_j r^*_{ij} x^*_{ij} Q_{ij} & \leq & B_i & \forall i \\
\sum_i x^*_{ij} Q_{ij} & \leq & 1 & \forall j \\
x^*_{ij} & \in & [0,1] & \forall i,j \\
r^*_{ij} & \in & [0, B_i/4] & \forall i,j
\end{array}$$

The final mechanism chooses an arbitrary ordering of bidders. When bidder i is encountered, let S_i denote the subset of items that have survived so far. For each item $j \in S_i$, with probability $x^*_{ij}/4$, post price r^*_{ij}, and with the remaining probability skip this item. This process is done simultaneously for all items, and the resulting items and prices are simultaneously offered to the bidder. Note that though the scheme is randomized, since it is posted price, it is universally and ex-post truthful and individually rational. Using the same proof as Theorem 3.6 now shows that this posted price scheme extracts revenue that is a constant factor of $\sum_{i,j} r^*_{ij} x^*_{ij} Q_{ij}$. This shows a $O(\log L)$ approximation. □

3.3.1 Adaptive Posted Price Schemes

The above implies we cannot generalize the result in Section 3.2 even to the class of regular distributions (see Definition 3). This is because an $\omega(1)$ gap is introduced in going from (LPREV) to (LP2). However, we can show that if the space of mechanisms is restricted, (LP2) itself is a good relaxation to the optimal revenue in this space.

In particular, suppose we restrict the space of mechanisms to be those that are posted price, and sequential by bidder: Depending on the subset of items and bidders left, the mechanism adaptively chooses the next bidder and posts prices for a subset of the remaining items. The bidder being a utility maximizer, solves a knapsack problem to choose the optimal subset of items. Once this bidder is dealt with, the mechanism again adaptively chooses the next bidder depending on the acceptance strategy of this bidder. Assuming the valuations of a bidder follow a product distribution, and v_{ij} follows a regular distribution, we will show a $O(1)$ approximation to the optimal mechanism.

Since the optimization problem the bidders need to solve is a two-dimensional KNAPSACK problem which is NP-HARD, we we assume bidders are *monotone optimizers* in the following sense: For any edge (i, j), if all valuations except v_{ij} are fixed, the quantity of item j taken by bidder i is monotonically non-decreasing in v_{ij}. This is true if the bidder solves KNAPSACK optimally. As with the posted price scheme in the previous section, our algorithm itself will allow arbitrary KNAPSACK heuristics as long as a bidder chooses all items if she is not constrained by either demand or budget.

LEMMA 3.9. *(LP2) is a 4-approximation to the revenue of the optimal adaptive posted price scheme assuming bidders are monotone optimizers.*

PROOF. In the discussion below, recall the definition $\mathcal{V}_{ij} = \min(v_{ij}, B_i/4)$ from Definition 1, and observe that its density function f_{ij} satisfies the regularity condition. For any adaptive mechanism, let $x_{ij}(r)$ denote the expected allocation of item j to bidder i conditioned on $\mathcal{V}_{ij} = r$, and let $p_{ij}(r)$ denote the corresponding expected price paid scaled down by a factor of 4. We will show that the LP relaxation that is a 4-approximation to maximizing expected revenue is the following:

$$\text{Maximize} \quad \sum_{i,j} \sum_r f_{ij}(r) p_{ij}(r) \qquad \text{(LPSEQ)}$$

$$\begin{array}{rcllr}
\sum_j \sum_r f_{ij}(r) x_{ij}(r) & \leq & n_i & \forall i & (1) \\
\sum_j \sum_r f_{ij}(r) p_{ij}(r) & \leq & B_i & \forall i & (2) \\
\sum_i \sum_r f_{ij}(r) x_{ij}(r) & \leq & 1 & \forall j & (3) \\
r x_{ij}(r) - \sum_{s=1}^{r-1} x_{ij}(s) & \geq & p_{ij}(r) & \forall i,j,r & (4) \\
x_{ij}(r) & \geq & x_{ij}(s) & \forall i,j,r \geq s \geq 0 & (5) \\
p_{ij}(r) & \geq & p_{ij}(s) & \forall i,j,r \geq s \geq 0 & (6) \\
x_{ij}(r) & \in & [0,1] & \forall i,j,r & (7)
\end{array}$$

To see this, fix all valuations except v_{ij}. If the mechanism considers item j for bidder i, then it posts a unique price $p^* \leq B_i$ for (i, j). Let $X_{ij}(r) \in [0, 1]$ denote the expected quantity taken when $\mathcal{V}_{ij} = r$, and let $P_{ij}(r) = p^* X_{ij}(r)$ denote the expected price paid. Note that as long as $r < B_i/4$, $v_{ij} = r$ and $X_{ij}(r)$ is either 0 or 1. However, at $r = B_i/4$, v_{ij} is not unique and $X_{ij}(r)$ can take a fractional value. Since the bidder is a utility maximizer, $X_{ij}(r)$ (and hence $P_{ij}(r)$) are monotone functions of r. Furthermore, it is easy to check that $r X_{ij}(r) - \sum_{s=1}^{r-1} X_{ij}(s) \geq p^* X_{ij}(r)/4 = P_{ij}(r)/4$. Defining $x_{ij}(r) = \mathbf{E}[X_{ij}(r)]$ and $p_{ij}(r) = \mathbf{E}[P_{ij}(r)]/4$, where the expectation is over the remaining valuations, we see that all constraints in the above LP hold.

Consider the optimal solution to (LPSEQ), and focus on edge (i, j). Let $g_{ij}(r) = r x_{ij}(r) - \sum_{s=1}^{r-1} x_{ij}(s)$. This is a monotone function of r, and so is $p_{ij}(r) \leq g_{ij}(r)$. Consider the *lexicographically maximal* solution where it cannot be the case that $p_{ij}(r)$ can be increased and some $p_{ij}(s)$ for $s > r$ can be decreased preserving all constraints and the objective. Let r_0 be the largest integer such that for all $r < r_0$, $g_{ij}(r) = p_{ij}(r)$. It is easy to see that for all $r \geq r_0$, we have $p_{ij}(r) = p_{ij}(r_0)$, else the lexicographic maximality property is violated. Now, reduce $x_{ij}(r_0)$ until $p_{ij}(r_0) = g_{ij}(r_0)$. Observe that if $x_{ij}(r)$ is set to $x_{ij}(r_0)$ for all $r > r_0$, all constraints are preserved and the objective is unchanged. This also ensures that $p_{ij}(r) = g_{ij}(r)$ for all $r \geq 0$. This makes Constraints (4) and (6) irrelevant since the former is tight and implies the latter via Constraint (5). Thus, (LPSEQ) reduces to:

$$\text{Maximize} \quad \sum_{i,j}\sum_{r} f_{ij}(r)\left(r x_{ij}(r) - \sum_{s=0}^{r-1} x_{ij}(s)\right)$$

$$\begin{array}{rcll} \sum_j \sum_r f_{ij}(r)x_{ij}(r) & \leq & n_i & \forall i \\ \sum_j \sum_r f_{ij}(r)\left(r x_{ij}(r) - \sum_{s=1}^{r-1} x_{ij}(s)\right) & \leq & B_i & \forall i \\ \sum_i \sum_r f_{ij}(r)x_{ij}(r) & \leq & 1 & \forall j \\ x_{ij}(r) & \in & [0,1] & \forall i,j,r \end{array}$$

Now, by Myerson's characterization [24], we have:

$$\sum_r \left(f_{ij}(r)\left(r x_{ij}(r) - \sum_{s=1}^{r-1} x_{ij}(s)\right)\right) = \sum_r f_{ij}(r)\varphi_{ij}(r)x_{ij}(r)$$

Plugging this formula into the objective and the second constraint completes the proof. □

The final mechanism and analysis are the same as in Section 3.2: Solve (LP2), decompose it into a convex combination of posted prices per edge, and sequentially post these prices for every bidder. To complete the analysis, note that Lemma 3.5 only requires that the distribution be regular. This shows the following theorem:

THEOREM 3.10. *There is a $O(1)$ approximation to the revenue of the optimal adaptive posted price scheme, when the types follow product distributions, and for each (i,j), the distribution of valuation is regular.*

Acknowledgments: We thank Shuchi Chawla, Vincent Conitzer, and Peng Shi for helpful discussions.

4. REFERENCES

[1] Z. Abrams. Revenue maximization when bidders have budgets. In *SODA*, pages 1074–1082, 2006.

[2] L. M. Ausubel. An efficient ascending-bid auction for multiple objects. *American Economic Review*, 94(5):1452 – 1475, 2004.

[3] L. M. Ausubel and P. Milgrom. Ascending auctions with package bidding. *Working Paper*, 2002.

[4] J. Benoit and V. Krishna. Multiple-object auctions with budget constrained bidders. *Review of Economic Studies*, 68:155 – 179, 2001.

[5] S. Bhattacharya, V. Conitzer, K. Munagala, and L. Xia. Incentive compatible budget elicitation in multi-unit auctions. In *SODA*, 2010.

[6] K. C. Border. Reduced form auctions revisited. *Economic Theory*, 31(1):167–181, 2007.

[7] C. Borgs, J. T. Chayes, N. Immorlica, M. Mahdian, and A. Saberi. Multi-unit auctions with budget-constrained bidders. In *ACM Conference on Electronic Commerce*, pages 44–51, 2005.

[8] P. Briest. Uniform budgets and the envy-free pricing problem. In *ICALP (1)*, pages 808–819, 2008.

[9] P. Briest, S. Chawla, R. D. Kleinberg, and S. M. Weinberg. Pricing randomized allocations. In *SODA*, 2010.

[10] S. Brusco and G. Lopomo. Simultaneous ascending bid auctions with privately known budget constraints. *Journal of Industrial Economics*, 56(1):113–142, 2008.

[11] S. Chawla, J. D. Hartline, and R. D. Kleinberg. Algorithmic pricing via virtual valuations. In *ACM Conference on Electronic Commerce*, pages 243–251, 2007.

[12] S. Chawla, J. D. Hartline, D. Malec, and B. Sivan. Sequential posted pricing and multi-parameter mechanism design. In *STOC*, 2010.

[13] Y. Che and J. Gale. Expected revenue of the all-pay auctions and first-price sealed bid auctions with budget constraints. *Economic Letters*, 50:373–380, 1996.

[14] Y. Che and J. Gale. The optimal mechanism for selling to a budget constrained buyer. *Journal of Economic Theory*, 92(2):198–233, 2000.

[15] N. Chen, N. Immorlica, A. R. Karlin, M. Mahdian, and A. Rudra. Approximating matches made in heaven. In *ICALP (1)*, pages 266–278, 2009.

[16] S. Dobzinski, R. Lavi, and N. Nisan. Multi-unit auctions with budget limits. In *FOCS*, pages 260–269, 2008.

[17] E. Elkind and S. S. Fatima. Maximizing revenue in sequential auctions. In *WINE*, pages 491–502, 2007.

[18] A. V. Goldberg, J. D. Hartline, and A. Wright. Competitive auctions and digital goods. In *SODA*, pages 735–744, 2001.

[19] V. Guruswami, J. D. Hartline, A. R. Karlin, D. Kempe, C. Kenyon, and F. McSherry. On profit-maximizing envy-free pricing. In *SODA*, pages 1164–1173, 2005.

[20] I. Hafalir, R. Ravi, and A. Sayedi. Sort-cut: A pareto optimal and semi-truthful mechanism for multi-unit auctions with budget-constrained bidders. *CoRR*, abs/0903.1450, 2009.

[21] J. D. Hartline and T. Roughgarden. Simple versus optimal mechanisms. In *ACM Conference on Electronic Commerce*, pages 225–234, 2009.

[22] J.-J. Laffont and J. Robert. Optimal auction with financially constrained buyers. *Economic Letters*, 52(2):181 – 186, 1996.

[23] A. M. Manellia and D. R. Vincent. Multidimensional mechanism design: Revenue maximization and the multiple-good monopoly. *Journal of Economic Theory*, 137(1):153–185, 2007.

[24] R. B. Myerson. Optimal auction design. *Mathematics of Operations Research*, 6(1):58–73, 1981.

[25] N. Nisan. Google's auction for tv ads. In *ESA*, page 553, 2009.

[26] M. Pai and R. Vohra. Optimal auctions with financially constrained bidders. *Working Paper*, 2008.

[27] J. Thanassoulis. Haggling over substitutes. *Journal of Economic Theory*, 117(2):217–245, 2004.

[28] R. B. Wilson. *Nonlinear Pricing*. Oxford University Press, 1997.

On the Searchability of Small-World Networks with Arbitrary Underlying Structure*

Pierre Fraigniaud
CNRS and Univ. Paris Diderot
Paris, France
pierre.fraigniaud@liafa.jussieu.fr

George Giakkoupis
CNRS and Univ. Paris Diderot
Paris, France
ggiak@liafa.jussieu.fr

ABSTRACT

Revisiting the "small-world" experiments of the '60s, Kleinberg observed that individuals are very effective at constructing short chains of acquaintances between any two people, and he proposed a mathematical model of this phenomenon. In this model, individuals are the nodes of a *base graph*, the square grid, capturing the *underlying structure* of the social network; and this base graph is augmented with additional edges from each node to a few *long-range contacts* of this node, chosen according to some natural distance-based distribution. In this augmented graph, a greedy search algorithm takes only a polylogarithmic number of steps in the graph size. Following this work, several papers investigated the correlations between underlying structure and long-range connections that yield efficient decentralized search, generalizing Kleinberg's results to broad classes of underlying structures, such as metrics of bounded doubling dimension, and minor-excluding graphs.

We focus on the case of *arbitrary* base graphs. We show that for a simple long-range contact distribution consistent with empirical observations on social networks, a slight variation of greedy search, where the next hop is to a distant node only if it yields sufficient progress towards the target, requires $n^{o(1)}$ steps, where n is the number of nodes. Precisely, the expected number of steps for any source–target pair is at most $2^{(\log n)^{1/2+o(1)}}$. This bound almost matches the best known lower bound of $\Omega(2^{\sqrt{\log n}})$ steps, which applies to a general class of search algorithms. In the context of social networks, our result could be interpreted as: individuals may well be able to construct short chains between people regardless of the underlying structure of the social network.

*Research supported in part by the ANR projects ALADDIN and PROSE, and by the INRIA project GANG.

STOC'10, June 5–8, 2010, Cambridge, Massachusetts, USA

Categories and Subject Descriptors

F.2.2 [**Nonnumerical Algorithms and Problems**]: Routing and layout; E.1 [**Data Structures**]: Graphs and networks; G.2.2 [**Graph Theory**]: Graph algorithms, Network problems; C.2.2 [**Network Protocols**]: Routing protocols

General Terms

Algorithms, Performance, Theory

Keywords

small worlds, decentralized search, social networks

1. INTRODUCTION

Small worlds have been an active research topic in many fields, including sociology, physics, and computer science. The scientific interest in small worlds began with the famous experiments conducted in the 1960s by sociologist S. Milgram [17]. These experiments quantified the *small-world phenomenon*, that is, the principle that all people are linked by short chains of acquaintances. Milgram's findings were subsequently confirmed by others (see, e.g., [3]). Revisiting Milgram's experiments, J. Kleinberg [9] observed another striking aspect of the small-world phenomenon: not only do short chains between people *exist*, but individuals are collectively very effective at *finding* them, using only local information. He then proposed a mathematical graph model for studying this aspect of small worlds (extending a model proposed in [19]). In the small-world model of [9], individuals are the nodes of a two-dimensional $n \times n$ grid graph, which is augmented with some additional *long-range* edges as follows. From each node u, one directed edge is added to some other node chosen at random, such that each node v is chosen with probability proportional to $d_{u,v}^{-\alpha}$, where $d_{u,v}$ is the grid distance between u and v, and $\alpha \geq 0$ is a parameter of the model. The edges of the augmented grid represent acquaintance relationships between people. Intuitively, the grid captures the *underlying structure* of the social network, defining a notion of distance between people (modeling, e.g., geographical distance). In this model, Kleinberg showed that if $\alpha \neq 2$ then *any* search algorithm that does not know the long-range edges of the nodes that have not been visited yet, requires an expected number of $\Omega(n^{\gamma})$ steps, for most source–target pairs, where $\gamma > 0$ depends on α but not on n. However, if $\alpha = 2$ then the simple *greedy search* algorithm (where greediness is with respect to the grid distance) performs in $n^{o(1)}$ steps. Precisely, for any source–target pair, greedy search takes an expected number of $O(\log^2 n)$ steps.[1]

Following [9], several papers explored further the correlations between underlying structure and long-range connections that yield efficiently-searchable small-world networks. Specifically, general models in which the results of [9] carry over have been proposed [1, 4, 5, 10, 15, 16, 18], and various non-greedy decentralized search algorithms have been studied [7, 12, 14, 15]. We consider a general framework for studying search in small worlds, which naturally extends the model in [9], and captures many of the models proposed in the follow-up work. In this framework, we show that for *any* underlying structure, we can construct a small-world network where search takes $n^{o(1)}$ steps. Specifically, this framework models a small world by a random graph, where nodes are individuals, and edges denote acquaintance relationships, as in [9]. It consists of three components:

- *Base graph:* It is a connected undirected graph G on the set of individuals. For any nodes u, v of G, their shortest-path distance in G, denoted by $d_{u,v}$, represents the distance between individuals u and v in the social network. This distance may capture various notions of proximity, such as geographic proximity, and/or similarity in occupation, culture, hobbies, etc. The neighbors of u in G, i.e., all v such that $d_{u,v} = 1$, are u's acquaintances with a profile most similar to that of u, and they are called the *local contacts* of u.[2] In this paper we will assume that G can be arbitrary; so, no extra assumptions about the underlying structure of the social network are imposed.

- *Augmentation scheme:* It is a collection $\{\varphi_u : u \in V(G)\}$ of probability distributions over the set of nodes $V(G)$ of G. The graph G is *augmented* with additional edges as follows: from each node u, one directed edge is added to a node chosen independently at random according to φ_u. This node is an acquaintance of u with, possibly, a very different profile than u's, and it is called the *long-range contact* of u.[3] We will use a simple and natural augmentation scheme, where φ_u depends on the "density" of G around u.

- *Search algorithm:* It is a decentralized algorithm that computes a path in the augmented graph from any source to any target, using *only* local information. More precisely, the decisions of the algorithm may depend on G and on the long-range contacts of the nodes visited so far, but not on the long-range contacts of nodes that have not been visited yet. We will consider a simple search algorithm, where the next hop is chosen based only on the current node's distance to its neighbors (in G), and on *their* distance to the target. A prominent example of such an algorithm is *greedy search*, where the next hop is to the neighbor of the current node that is closest to the target (in G).

[1]Note that paths of polylogarithmic length exist between nodes for a wide range of exponents α [16]; however, they can be efficiently discovered by a decentralized algorithm only when $\alpha = 2$.

[2]We could define the local contacts of u as all nodes with $d_{u,v} \leq k$, for some constant $k \geq 1$; however, this would not affect the asymptotic behavior of the model.

[3]Again, having a constant number $k \geq 1$ of long-range contacts per node would not essentially affect the model's behavior.

As mentioned earlier, a significant amount of work has focused on extending the results of [9] to underlying structures other than the grid. In fact, there has been an effort to identify the most general setting in which the results of [9] carry over. One motivation for that has been the observation that certain measures of social proximity, such as occupation, are not successfully captured by a grid-based model. Moreover, the underlying structure of a social network often results from the combination of several different measures of proximity. Therefore, it is highly unclear how this underlying structure should look.

The results of [9] were extended by [10] into hierarchical models, where the nodes are the leaves of a complete b-ary tree, and the distance between them is the length of the path between them in the tree. Also, [10] proposed a model generalizing both the grid-based and the hierarchical models, where the distance function is induced by certain families of node sets. Small-world networks with grid-like underlying structure were studied in [15, 16], where the diameter of these networks was computed. In [4], small-world networks where the base graph has a "bounded growth rate" property were considered. In [5], base graphs of bounded tree-width were studied. The case where the nodes are embedded in a metric space of bounded doubling dimension (instead of a base graph) was considered in [18]. Finally, weighted base graphs that exclude a fixed minor were studied in [1]. In all these cases, for suitable augmentation schemes, greedy search performs in a polylogarithmic expected number of steps, as a function of the number of nodes. (In [1] and [18], the expected number of steps is also a polylogarithmic function of the aspect ratio, i.e., the ratio of the largest to the smallest distance between nodes.)

For the case of *arbitrary* base graphs, the following results are known. An infinite family of graphs was described in [8], such that for any n-node base graph from this family, and any augmentation scheme, greedy search requires an expected number of $\Omega(2^{\sqrt{\log n}})$ steps, for some source–target pair. On the upper-bound side, a universal augmentation scheme was proposed in [6], such that for any n-node base graph augmented according to this scheme, the expected number of steps for greedy search is $\tilde{O}(n^{1/3})$.

Several non-greedy decentralized search algorithms have been suggested for grid-based small-world networks [7, 12, 14, 15]. Roughly speaking, all these algorithms construct shorter paths than greedy search, but they visit (or "consult") an additional, small number of nodes before the next hop is decided. Finally, there is work on lower-bounds on the performance of greedy search in grid-based small-world networks for arbitrary augmentation schemes (see, e.g., [2]).

For more background on search in small-world networks, see the survey [11].

1.1 Our contribution

In this paper, we show that for *any* base graph, there exists a simple, natural augmentation scheme, and a simple, natural search algorithm such that search in the augmented base graph takes $n^{o(1)}$ steps. Precisely, the expected number of steps for any source–target pair is at most $2^{(\log n)^{1/2+o(1)}}$. This bound almost matches the lower bound of $\Omega(2^{\sqrt{\log n}})$ steps of [8], which applies to any search algorithm that decreases the distance to the target in each step (see Theorem 2, in Section 2.3).

The augmentation scheme we consider is the one where

the probability $\varphi_u(v)$ that node $v \neq u$ is the long-range contact of node u is inversely proportional to the size of the smallest ball in the base graph that is centered at u and contains v. This scheme is inspired by the experimental observation of [13] that two-thirds of the friendships are geographically distributed as follows: the probability of befriending a particular person is inversely proportional to the number of closer people. This augmentation scheme is also a natural generalization to arbitrary graphs of the augmentation scheme with $\alpha = 2$ proposed in [9] for the grid.

Our search algorithm is a slight variation of greedy search, where the next hop may be to a distant neighbor of the current node only if this hop results in sufficient progress towards the target. Quantitatively, from the current node u, search moves to the node that is closest to the target t, among all the neighbors v of u for which the ratio of the "benefit" $\beta(u,v,t) = d_{u,t} - d_{v,t}$ of moving to v, over the distance $d_{u,v}$, is larger than some small threshold:

$$\beta(u,v,t)/d_{u,v} \geq 1/\operatorname{polylog} \beta(u,v,t).$$

(If this condition is replaced by $\beta(u,v,t)/d_{u,v} > 0$ then we obtain the standard greedy search.) This algorithm has a natural interpretation in the context of Milgram's experiments [17]: people make greedy choices, but are reluctant to forward the letter to an acquaintance located far away, unless they are sure this acquaintance is sufficiently closer to the target. This reluctance may result from the fact that people can only *approximate* the distances between their acquaintances and the target, and, typically, the further the acquaintance resides, the worse this approximation is.

In the context of social networks, our result could be interpreted as follows: individuals may well be able to construct short chains between people *regardless of the underlying structure of the social network.*

1.2 Comparison with previous work

All previous work except [6, 8] has focused on achieving polylogarithmic search performance, but for restricted underlying structures. In contrast, we assume that the underlying structure is a graph, but we impose no restrictions on the structure of this graph. In this general setting, the lower bound of [8] precludes achieving polylogarithmic search. Still, search in an n-node network in $n^{o(1)}$ steps could also be regarded as "efficient search." In [1], a *weighted* graph is used as a base graph. Our result can be extended to this case as well (see Section 3.3.5). In [18], a *metric space* of bounded doubling dimension is considered instead of a base graph. The concept of underlying metric is more general than that of base graph, and our result *cannot* be extend to *arbitrary* underlying metrics. Indeed, although a metric space can be seen as a weighted graph that induces a shortest-path metric, the edges of this graph are not necessarily present in the small-world network, unlike in the base graph approach. For our analysis to apply to an underlying metric, a condition that ensures that search can always make progress towards the target is necessary. In [18], this is achieved by combining the bounding doubling dimension condition, with a sufficiently large number of long-range contacts per node.

Our proof diverges significantly from the approach typically used in previous work. The standard approach has been to bound the number of steps until either the distance to the target is halved, or the size of the ball around the target containing the current node is halved. The target is then reached in a logarithmic number of such halvings. For the underlying structures that have been studied in previous work, this halving can be achieved in a polylogarithmic number of steps, because, intuitively, for any target, the long-range links that facilitate progress towards this target are frequent enough. This approach, however, does not work for arbitrary base graphs, essentially, because the "dimensionality" of the graph may be so large that for some destinations the useful long-range links are very rare (see [8]). In our approach, instead of evaluating progress in terms of big jumps, we focus on making progress "locally." Essentially, we recursively divide the search into smaller search subproblems, where in each subproblem either the distance between the source and the target is smaller, or the size of the part of the graph we focus on is smaller. To make this approach work we had to modify greedy search such that no long jumps with very small benefit are allowed, because such jumps could waste effort devoted to making progress locally, e.g., to overcoming a very dense part of the graph.

2. MODEL AND STATEMENT OF MAIN RESULT

In this section, we describe our augmentation scheme and search algorithm, and we state our main result.

2.1 Augmentation scheme

Recall that $d_{u,v}$ is the distance between the nodes u and v in the base graph G. We consider the augmentation scheme where the probability $\varphi_u(v)$ that v is the long-range contact of u is proportional to the *rank* of $d_{u,v}$ among the distances from u to all the other nodes; this scheme is called *rank-based augmentation*. Precisely, let $\mathbf{B}_u(r) = \{v \in V(G) : d_{u,v} \leq r\}$ be the ball of radius $\lfloor r \rfloor$ centered at u. ($\mathbf{B}_u(r) = \emptyset$, if $r < 0$.) In the *rank-based augmentation scheme*, for any nodes u, v with $v \neq u$,

$$\varphi_u(v) = \frac{1}{\nu_u \cdot |\mathbf{B}_u(d_{u,v})|}, \quad \text{where } \nu_u = \sum_{w \neq u} \frac{1}{|\mathbf{B}_u(d_{u,w})|}.$$

The normalizing factor ν_u is within the range:

$$1 - \frac{1}{n} \leq \nu_u \leq \sum_{i=2}^{n} \frac{1}{i} \leq \ln n. \tag{2.1}$$

The lower bound for ν_u follows from the fact that, for all $v \neq u$, $|\mathbf{B}_u(d_{u,v})| \leq n$. The upper bound follows from the fact that if $v_1, v_2, \ldots, v_{n-1}$ is an ordering of all the nodes excluding u, such that $d_{u,v_1} \leq d_{u,v_2} \leq \cdots \leq d_{u,v_{n-1}}$, then $|\mathbf{B}_u(d_{u,v_i})| \geq i + 1$.

2.2 Search algorithm

Let $\mathbf{N}_u$ denote the set of all neighbors of node u in the *augmented* graph, i.e., $\mathbf{N}_u$ consists of the neighbors of u in G, plus the long-range contact of u. In greedy search for target t, the next hop from node $u \neq t$ is to a node $v \in \mathbf{N}_u$ that *minimizes* the remaining distance $d_{v,t}$ to t, or, equivalently, that *maximizes* the *benefit*

$$\beta(u,v,t) = d_{u,t} - d_{v,t}$$

of moving to v. The search algorithm we consider in this paper, called *focused greedy*, is identical to greedy search, except that it ignores all nodes v for which the *relative benefit*

$\beta(u, v, t)/d_{u,v}$ is too small. Precisely, we define the *next-hop space* $\mathbf{D}_{u,t}$ of u for target t as

$$\mathbf{D}_{u,t} = \left\{ v \in V(G) : \frac{\beta(u, v, t)}{d_{u,v}} \geq \frac{1}{1 + \log \beta(u, v, t)} \right\}. \quad (2.2)$$

In *focused greedy search* for target t, if $u \neq t$ is the current node then the next hop is to a node $v \in \mathbf{N}_u \cap \mathbf{D}_{u,t}$ that minimizes the remaining distance $d_{v,t}$ to t. Note that $\mathbf{N}_u \cap \mathbf{D}_{u,t} \neq \emptyset$, because the first node after u in the shortest path in G from u to t is both in $\mathbf{N}_u$ and in $\mathbf{D}_{u,t}$. Thus, focused greedy search is well defined.

2.3 Main result

The main result of this paper is the following:

THEOREM 1 (UPPER BOUND). *For any base graph on n nodes augmented according to the rank-based augmentation scheme, the expected number of steps of focused greedy search from any source node to any target node is $o(2^{(\log n)^{1/2+\epsilon}})$, for any fixed $\epsilon > 0$.*

The upper bound of Theorem 1 almost matches the lower bound of [8] repeated below.[4]

THEOREM 2 (LOWER BOUND [8]). *There exists an infinite family of graphs such that, for any n-node base graph in this family, any augmentation scheme, and any search algorithm that reduces the distance to the target in each step, there exists a source–target pair for which search requires an expected number of $\Omega(2^{\sqrt{\log n}})$ steps.*

A family of graphs as described in Theorem 2 is the one consisting of the $\sqrt{\log n}$-dimensional grids where there are additional edges from each node to all its $2^{\sqrt{\log n}}$ diagonal neighbors. The source–target pairs for which search is hard consist of nodes that lie on the same diagonal.

3. ANALYSIS

We now present the proof of Theorem 1. We start with a sketch of this proof, in Section 3.1. In Section 3.2, we establish some properties of the next-hop space $\mathbf{D}_{u,t}$. The main proof is described in Section 3.3.

3.1 Proof sketch of Theorem 1

We begin with some properties of the next-hop space. $\mathbf{D}_{u,t}$ has a teardrop shape and is included in the ball $\mathbf{B}_t(d_{u,t} - 1)$, the analogue of $\mathbf{D}_{u,t}$ for greedy search (see Figure 1). Also, for any $v \in \mathbf{D}_{u,t}$, $\mathbf{D}_{v,t}$ is included in $\mathbf{D}_{u,t}$. Let $\varrho_u(v)$, for $v \in \mathbf{D}_{u,t}$, be the radius of the largest ball centered at v and included in $\mathbf{D}_{u,t}$; and let $r_u(v)$ be the radius of the smallest ball centered at t containing $\mathbf{D}_{v,t} \setminus \mathbf{B}_v(\varrho_u(v))$ (see Figure 3). We use ϱ_u to measure the progress of the search process. We have that for any $w \in \mathbf{D}_{v,t}$, $\varrho_u(w) - \varrho_u(v)$ is at least equal to some positive constant. In particular, if $w \in \mathbf{D}_{v,t} \cap \mathbf{B}_t(r_u(v))$ then $\varrho_u(w) - \varrho_u(v) \geq \varrho_u(v)/\operatorname{polylog} \varrho_u(v)$. This last property is at the core of our analysis, and it depends critically on the definition of the next-hop space.

The proof of the theorem proceeds by decomposing the search path into subpaths of certain types, and bounding the number and lengths of these subpaths. The decomposition is recursive, and it employs three types of subpaths: σ-paths, δ-paths, and π-paths. Subpaths of the last two types are also discomposed into smaller subpaths of the three types, while σ-paths are not decomposed further; so, the search path is eventually decomposed into a collection of σ-paths. Each σ-path P is associated with a *reference node* u such that if v is P's start node then $v \in \mathbf{D}_{u,t}$, and with a *target-ball radius* $r \geq r_u(v)$. P ends when a node $\hat{v}$ is reached such that (1) $\hat{v} \in \mathbf{B}_t(r)$, or (2) for some node $\hat{u}$ with $\hat{v} \in \mathbf{D}_{\hat{u},t}$, the set $\mathbf{D}_{\hat{u},t} \setminus \mathbf{B}_t(r)$ is at least $\kappa \approx n^{1/\sqrt{\log n}}$ times smaller than $\mathbf{D}_{u,t} \setminus \mathbf{B}_t(r)$—$\hat{u}$ will be the reference node of the next σ-path. Intuitively, if (1) occurs, search makes progress because ϱ_u increases, and if (2) occurs, because the size of the part of the base graph we focus on decreases. We show that for the rank-based augmentation scheme, the expected length of a σ-path is at most $\kappa \cdot \operatorname{polylog} n$. Also, the decomposition of the search path essentially yields a total number of $(\log n)^{O(\log_\kappa n)}$ σ-path—this result is based on the last property of the next-hop space mentioned above. The desired bound on the length of the search path then follows.

[4]This is what is actually proved in [8], although the authors only claim their result for greedy search.

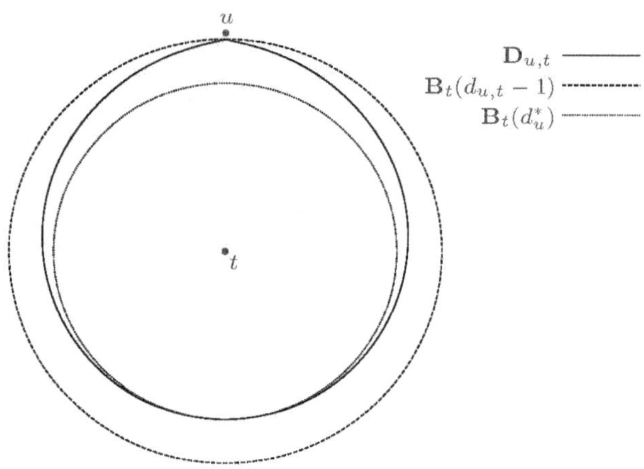

Figure 1: Illustration of Lemma 1(a). The next-hop space $\mathbf{D}_{u,t}$ is included in the ball $\mathbf{B}_t(d_{u,t} - 1)$, and includes the ball $\mathbf{B}_t(d_u^*)$, where $d_u^* = d_{u,t} - \Theta(d_{u,t}/\log d_{u,t})$.

3.2 Properties of next-hop space

Throughout this section, we assume that $u \neq t$. Also, the shorthand notations d_v and $\mathbf{D}_v$ are used for $d_{v,t}$ and $\mathbf{D}_{v,t}$, respectively. In the same spirit, in the notation we introduce we do not make explicit the dependence on t.

Let $f : [1, \infty) \to [1, \infty)$, with

$$f(x) = x(1 + \log x).$$

We can rewrite the definition in Equation (2.2) as

$$\mathbf{D}_u = \{v \in V(G) : d_{u,v} \leq f(d_u - d_v)\}.$$

Lemma 1 below describes the shape of $\mathbf{D}_u$ (see also Figures 1 and 2). As mentioned earlier, $\mathbf{D}_u$ has the shape of a teardrop. The distance from t to the "top" and to the "bottom" of this teardrop is $d_u - 1$ and d_u^*, respectively, where d_u^* is the solution of the following equation in x:

$$d_u + x = f(d_u - x).$$

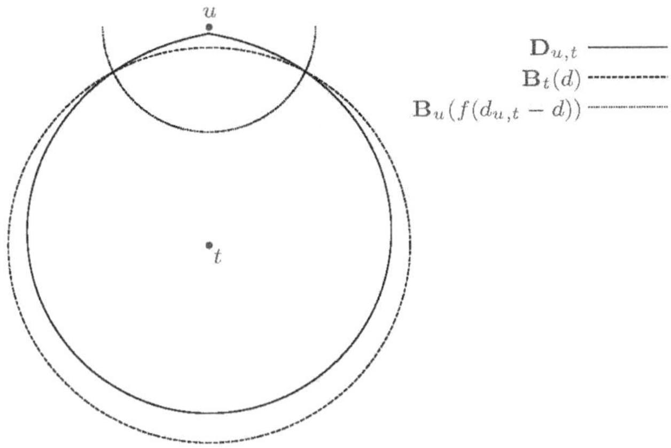

Figure 2: Illustration of Lemma 1(b). For any d with $d_u^* \le d \le d_{u,t}-1$, $\mathbf{D}_{u,t}$ is included in the union of $\mathbf{B}_t(d)$ and $\mathbf{B}_u(f(d_{u,t}-d))$, and includes their intersection.

Solving this equation, yields

$$d_u^* = d_u - \Theta(d_u/\log d_u).$$

LEMMA 1.

(a) $\mathbf{B}_t(d_u^*) \subseteq \mathbf{D}_u \subseteq \mathbf{B}_t(d_u-1)$.

(b) For all reals d with $d_u^* \le d \le d_u - 1$,

$$\mathbf{B}_t(d) \cap \mathbf{B}_u(f(d_u-d)) \subseteq \mathbf{D}_u \subseteq \mathbf{B}_t(d) \cup \mathbf{B}_u(f(d_u-d)).$$

(c) For all $v \in \mathbf{D}_u$, $\mathbf{D}_v \subseteq \mathbf{D}_u$.

PROOF. Part (a) is obtained as follows. If $v \in \mathbf{B}_t(d_u^*)$ then $d_v \le d_u^*$, so,

$$f(d_u-d_v) \ge f(d_u-d_u^*) = d_u + d_u^* \ge d_u + d_v \ge d_{u,v},$$

where the first relation holds because f is non decreasing, and the second follows from the definition of d_u^*. Thus, $v \in \mathbf{D}_u$. So, $\mathbf{B}_t(d_u^*) \subseteq \mathbf{D}_u$. If $v \in D_u$ then, by the definition of f, $d_u - d_v \ge 1$, so, $v \in \mathbf{B}_t(d_u-1)$. Hence, $\mathbf{D}_u \subseteq \mathbf{B}_t(d_u-1)$.

We now prove (b). If $v \in \mathbf{B}_t(d) \cap \mathbf{B}_u(f(d_u-d))$ then $d_v \le d$ and $d_{u,v} \le f(d_u-d)$. So, $f(d_u-d_v) \ge f(d_u-d) \ge d_{u,v}$, and, thus, $v \in \mathbf{D}_u$. Therefore, $\mathbf{B}_t(d) \cap \mathbf{B}_u(f(d_u-d)) \subseteq \mathbf{D}_u$. If $v \in \mathbf{D}_u \setminus \mathbf{B}_t(d)$ then $d_{u,v} \le f(d_u-d_v)$, and $d_v > d$. So, $d_{u,v} \le f(d_u-d)$, and, thus, $v \in \mathbf{B}_u(f(d_u-d))$. Therefore, $\mathbf{D}_u \subseteq \mathbf{B}_t(d) \cup \mathbf{B}_u(f(d_u-d))$.

Finally, for (c), we have that if $w \in \mathbf{D}_v$ then

$$d_{u,w} \le d_{u,v} + d_{v,w} \le f(d_u-d_v) + f(d_v-d_w) \le f(d_u-d_w),$$

where the last relation holds because $f(x)+f(y) \le f(x+y)$. So, $w \in \mathbf{D}_u$. Thus, $\mathbf{D}_v \subseteq \mathbf{D}_u$. □

We now introduce a quantity that plays a key role in our analysis. For any $v \in \mathbf{D}_u$, we define $\varrho_u(v)$ to be the solution of the following equation in x:

$$d_{u,v} + x = f(d_u - d_v - x),$$

Below, we will write ϱ_v instead of $\varrho_u(v)$. Intuitively, ϱ_v is a conservative estimate of the distance of v from the "border" of $\mathbf{D}_u$ (see Figure 3). The next lemma formalizes this intuition.

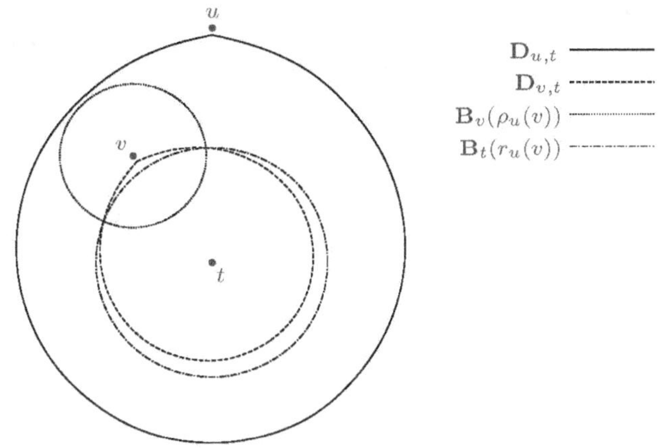

Figure 3: $\rho_u(v)$ is a lower bound on the radius of the largest ball centered at u and included in $\mathbf{D}_{u,t}$ (Lemma 2); $r_u(v)$ is such that $\mathbf{D}_{v,t}$ is included in the union of the balls $\mathbf{B}_v(\rho_u(v))$ and $\mathbf{B}_t(r_u(v))$, and includes their intersection (Lemma 3).

LEMMA 2. *For all $v \in \mathbf{D}_u$, (a) $0 \le \varrho_v \le d_u - d_v - 1$; and (b) $\mathbf{B}_v(\varrho_v) \subseteq \mathbf{D}_u$.*

PROOF. Part (a) is obtained as follows. The function $g(x) = f(d_u - d_v - x) - x$ is *strictly decreasing*. Also $g(0) = f(d_u - d_v) \ge d_{u,v}$, and $g(d_u - d_v - 1) = f(1) - (d_u - d_v - 1) = 2 - (d_u - d_v) \le 1 \le d_{u,v}$. Therefore, the equation $g(x) = d_{u,v}$ has a unique solution $x = \varrho_v$, and $0 \le \varrho_v \le d_u - d_v - 1$.

For (b), we have that if $w \in \mathbf{B}_v(\varrho_v)$ then

$$d_{u,w} \le d_{u,v} + \varrho_v = f(d_u - d_v - \varrho_v) \le f(d_u - d_w),$$

so, $w \in \mathbf{D}_u$. Thus, $\mathbf{B}_v(\varrho_v) \subseteq \mathbf{D}_u$. □

We also introduce another related quantity. For any $v \in \mathbf{D}_u$, we define

$$r_u(v) = \begin{cases} d_v - f^{-1}(\max\{1, \varrho_v\}), & \text{if } \varrho_v \le d_v + d_v^*; \\ -1, & \text{if } \varrho_v > d_v + d_v^*, \end{cases}$$

where f^{-1} is the inverse function of f. We will write r_v to denote $r_u(v)$. Informally, r_v is the radius of the smallest ball centered at t containing all the nodes in $\mathbf{D}_u$ that are not in $\mathbf{B}_v(\varrho_v)$ (see Figure 3). Precisely, we have the following lemma.

LEMMA 3. *For all $v \in \mathbf{D}_u$,*

$$\mathbf{B}_t(r_v) \cap \mathbf{B}_v(\varrho_v) \subseteq \mathbf{D}_v \subseteq \mathbf{B}_t(r_v) \cup \mathbf{B}_v(\varrho_v).$$

PROOF. If $\varrho_v < 1$ then $r_v = d_v - 1$. So,

$$\mathbf{B}_t(r_v) \cap \mathbf{B}_v(\varrho_v) = \mathbf{B}_t(d_v - 1) \cap \{v\} = \emptyset \subseteq \mathbf{D}_v.$$

Also, $\mathbf{B}_t(r_v) \cup \mathbf{B}_t(\varrho_v) \supseteq \mathbf{B}_v(d_v - 1) \supseteq \mathbf{D}_v$, by Lemma 1(a).

If $\varrho_v > d_v + d_v^*$ then $r_v = -1$ and $\mathbf{B}_t(r_v) = \emptyset$. So, $\mathbf{B}_t(r_v) \cap \mathbf{B}_v(\varrho_v) = \emptyset \subseteq \mathbf{D}_v$. Also, by Lemma 1(b),

$$\mathbf{D}_v \subseteq \mathbf{B}_t(d_v^*) \cup \mathbf{B}_v(f(d_v - d_v^*)) = \mathbf{B}_t(d_v^*) \cup \mathbf{B}_v(d_v + d_v^*)$$
$$= \mathbf{B}_v(d_v + d_v^*) \subseteq \mathbf{B}_v(\varrho_v) = \mathbf{B}_t(r_v) \cup \mathbf{B}_v(\varrho_v).$$

Finally, if $1 \le \varrho_v \le d_v + d_v^*$ then $d_v^* \le r_v \le d_v - 1$. So, by Lemma 1(b),

$$\mathbf{D}_v \supseteq \mathbf{B}_t(r_v) \cap \mathbf{B}_v(f(d_v - r_v)) = \mathbf{B}_t(r_v) \cap \mathbf{B}_v(\varrho_v),$$

and $\mathbf{D}_v \subseteq \mathbf{B}_t(r_v) \cup \mathbf{B}_v(f(d_v - r_v)) = \mathbf{B}_t(r_v) \cup \mathbf{B}_v(\varrho_v)$. □

The next lemma, Lemma 4, is the main result of this section. Lemma 4(a) says that if $v \in \mathbf{D}_u$ and $w \in \mathbf{D}_v$ then the difference between ϱ_w and ϱ_v is lower-bounded by a positive constant. This implies that when searching for t from a node in $\mathbf{D}_u$, the value of ϱ is increased by at least that constant in each step. Lemma 4(b) improves this bound to $\varrho_w - \varrho_v \geq \varrho_v/\operatorname{polylog}\varrho_v$, for the case where $w \in \mathbf{B}_t(r_v)$. Lemma 4(b) lies at the core of our analysis, and it depends critically on the fact that the threshold for $\beta(u,v,t)/d_{u,v}$ in Equation (2.2) is $1/\operatorname{polylog}\beta(u,v,t)$.[5]

LEMMA 4. *For all $v \in \mathbf{D}_u$ and $w \in \mathbf{D}_v$,*

(a) $\varrho_w \geq \varrho_v + 0.46$;

(b) if $w \in \mathbf{B}_t(r_v)$ then $\varrho_w \geq \varrho_v + h(\varrho_v)$, for some function h with $h(x) = \Omega(x/\log^2 x)$, and $h(x) \geq 0.46$ for all $x \geq 0$.

PROOF. Let $\Delta = \varrho_w - \varrho_v$. For (a) we must show that $\Delta \geq 0.46$. If $\varrho_w \geq d_u - d_v$ then $\Delta \geq d_u - d_v - \varrho_v \geq 1$, by Lemma 2(a). So, below we assume that $\varrho_w < d_u - d_v$.

By the definitions of ϱ_w and ϱ_v,

$$\Delta = f(d_u - d_w - \varrho_w) - f(d_u - d_v - \varrho_v) - d_{u,w} + d_{u,v}.$$

Also, $d_{u,w} \leq d_{u,v} + d_{v,w} \leq d_{u,v} + f(d_v - d_w)$, since $w \in \mathbf{D}_v$. So,

$$\Delta \geq f(d_u - d_w - \varrho_w) - f(d_u - d_v - \varrho_v) - f(d_v - d_w). \tag{3.1}$$

The difference $f(d_u - x - \varrho_w) - f(d_v - x)$ decreases when x increases, because $\varrho_w < d_u - d_v$ and f is convex. And, since $d_w \leq d_v - 1$, $f(d_u - d_w - \varrho_w) - f(d_v - d_w)$ is at least

$$f(d_u - d_v + 1 - \varrho_w) - f(1) = f(d_u - d_v - \varrho_v + 1 - \Delta) - 1.$$

Thus,

$$\Delta \geq f(d_u - d_v - \varrho_v + 1 - \Delta) - f(d_u - d_v - \varrho_v) - 1.$$

Suppose that $\Delta \leq 1$ (otherwise, $\Delta \geq 0.46$ holds). By a similar argument as above, we have that

$$f(d_u - d_v - \varrho_v + 1 - \Delta) - f(d_u - d_v - \varrho_v) \geq f(2 - \Delta) - 1,$$

since, by Lemma 2(a), $d_u - d_v - \varrho_v \geq 1$. Therefore, $\Delta \geq f(2 - \Delta) - 2$. Let $\alpha = 0.4696\ldots$ be the solution of the equation $\alpha = f(2-\alpha) - 2$. Then, we have $\Delta \geq \alpha$, because by assuming the opposite we have a contradiction:

$$\Delta < \alpha = f(2-\alpha) - 2 < f(2-\Delta) - 2 = \Delta.$$

We now proceed to prove (b). From (a), we have that $\Delta \geq 0.46$. So, we just have to show that $\Delta = \Omega(\varrho_v/\log^2\varrho_v)$. Since this result is asymptotic in ϱ_v, we can assume that ϱ_v is larger than some constant. We will assume that $\varrho_v \geq 8$.

Let $z = d_u - d_v - \varrho_v$. By the definition of ϱ_v,

$$z = f^{-1}(d_{u,v} + \varrho_v) \geq f^{-1}(\varrho_v) = \Omega(\varrho_v/\log\varrho_v) \tag{3.2}$$

Hence, if $\varrho_w \geq d_u - d_v$ then $\Delta \geq z = \Omega(\varrho_v/\log^2\varrho_v)$. So, below we assume that $\varrho_w < d_u - d_v$.

Inequality (3.1) still applies in the context of (b). Again we observe that $f(d_u - x - \varrho_w) - f(d_v - x)$ decreases as x increases. Also, since $w \in \mathbf{B}_t(r_v)$, $d_w \leq r_v = d_v - f^{-1}(\varrho_v)$ (since $\varrho_v \geq 8 > 1$). Thus, $f(d_u - d_w - \varrho_w) - f(d_v - d_w) \geq f(d_u - d_v + f^{-1}(\varrho_v) - \varrho_w) - \varrho_v$. Applying this to (3.1), we obtain

$$\Delta \geq f(z + f^{-1}(\varrho_v) - \Delta) - f(z) - \varrho_v. \tag{3.3}$$

Next we bound $f(z + f^{-1}(\varrho_v) - \Delta)$. We will use the following simple fact.

FACT 1.

(a) For all $x, y \geq 1$, $f(x+y) \geq f(x) + f(y) + \min\{x,y\}$.

(b) For all x, y with $x \geq 2y$ and $y \geq 1$, $f(x-y) \geq f(x) - f(y) - y\big(\log\frac{x}{y} + 2.2\big)$.

PROOF. For (a), suppose, w.l.o.g., that $x \geq y$. Then,

$$\begin{aligned} f(x+y) &= (x+y)(1+\log(x+y)) \\ &\geq x(1+\log x) + y(1+\log(2y)) = f(x) + f(y) + y. \end{aligned}$$

For (b), we have

$$f(x) - f(y) - f(x-y) = x\log\frac{x}{x-y} + y\log\frac{x-y}{y}.$$

Also, $\log\frac{x-y}{y} \leq \log\frac{x}{y}$, and

$$\begin{aligned} \log\frac{x}{x-y} &= \log\frac{1}{1-y/x} \leq \log\frac{1}{e^{-y/x-(y/x)^2}} \\ &= (y/x + (y/x)^2)\log e \leq \frac{3y}{2x}\log e \leq 2.2\frac{y}{x}, \end{aligned}$$

where for the second and the second-to-last relations we used the fact that $x \geq 2y$. Combining the above yields the desired inequality. □ {of Fact 1}

To apply the above result, we will need the condition

$$\Delta \leq \min\{f^{-1}(\varrho_v) - 1, f^{-1}(\varrho_v)/2\}. \tag{3.4}$$

Note, however, that if the above inequality does not hold then $\Delta = \Omega(f^{-1}(\varrho_v)) \subseteq \Omega(\varrho_v/\log^2\varrho_v)$. Also, we will have to make sure that $\Delta \geq 1$. This inequality, however, follows from our assumption that $\varrho_v \geq 8$, as we explain now. If $\Delta < 1$ then (3.3) yields

$$1 \geq f(z + f^{-1}(\varrho_v) - 1) - f(z) - \varrho_v.$$

Also, by (3.2), $z \geq f^{-1}(\varrho_v)$. Thus,

$$1 \geq f(2f^{-1}(\varrho_v) - 1) - 2f(f^{-1}(\varrho_v)).$$

Solving the above inequality numerically, yields $f^{-1}(\varrho_v) < 3$, which gives $\varrho_v < 8$, contradicting the assumption that $\varrho_v \geq 8$. Thus, $\Delta \geq 1$.

By Fact 1(a), we have

$$f(z + f^{-1}(\varrho_v) - \Delta) \geq f(z) + f(f^{-1}(\varrho_v) - \Delta) + f^{-1}(\varrho_v) - \Delta,$$

because, by (3.2), $z \geq f^{-1}(\varrho_v) - \Delta$, and, by (3.4), $f^{-1}(\varrho_v) - \Delta \geq 1$. Also, by Fact 1(b),

$$f(f^{-1}(\varrho_v) - \Delta) \geq \varrho_v - f(\Delta) - \Delta\Big(\log\frac{f^{-1}(\varrho_v)}{\Delta} + 2.2\Big),$$

because, by (3.4), $f^{-1}(\varrho_v) \geq 2\Delta$, and $\Delta \geq 1$. Combining the two results above with (3.3), yields

$$\Delta\Big(\log\frac{f^{-1}(\varrho_v)}{\Delta} + 4.2\Big) \geq f^{-1}(\varrho_v) - f(\Delta),$$

and solving for Δ we obtain that $\Delta \geq \frac{f^{-1}(\varrho_v)}{\log f^{-1}(\varrho_v) + 5.2} = \Theta(\frac{\varrho_v}{\log^2\varrho_v})$. □

[5] In particular, a threshold equal to $1/(\beta(u,v,t))^c$, for any constant $c > 0$, would yield $\varrho_w - \varrho_v \geq \varrho_v^{1-\Theta(1)}$; and a constant threshold would yield $\varrho_w - \varrho_v = \Omega(1)$.

3.3 Proof of Theorem 1

The proof describes a recursive decomposition of the search path into subpaths of certain types, and it establishes upper bounds on the number of those paths and on their lengths. In Section 3.3.1, we define the types of subpaths employed in the decomposition. The actual decomposition is described in Section 3.3.2. In Section 3.3.3, we bound the expected length of the base subpath type. In Section 3.3.4, we combine all the pieces to derive the theorem. We finish with some remarks, in Section 3.3.5.

3.3.1 Subpath types

We define three types of subpaths of a search path: σ-paths, δ-paths, and π-paths. A path P of any of the three types is identified by:

- a *starting node* v;
- a *reference node* u such that $\mathbf{D}_u$ contains all the nodes of P; $\mathbf{D}_u$ is called the *reference set* of P;[6] and
- an integer $r \geq 0$; the ball $\mathbf{B}_t(r)$ is the *target ball* of P.

The triple (v, u, r) satisfies some *pre-condition* that depends on the type of P. There is also a *post-condition*, depending on the type of P, that describes the last node of P. P is the *shortest* subpath of the search path from v to t such that the first node of P is v, and its last node satisfies the post-condition. Below, we described the pre- and post-condition for each path type.

The *σ-path* with parameters v, u, r is denoted $\sigma(v, u, r)$, and the pre-condition that v, u, r must satisfy is

$$\text{PRE}_\sigma(v, u, r): \ (v \in \mathbf{D}_u) \wedge (r_u(v) \leq r).$$

This condition implies that every node in $\mathbf{D}_v$ is in $\mathbf{B}_v(\varrho_u(v))$ or in the target ball $\mathbf{B}_t(r)$ (see Lemma 3). The following post-condition determines the last node $\hat{v}$ of $\sigma(v, u, r)$. For any node w, and any real d, define $N(w, d) = |\mathbf{D}_w \setminus \mathbf{B}_t(d)|$.

$$\text{POST}_\sigma(v, u, r, \hat{v}): \ \exists\, \hat{u}: (\hat{v} \in \mathbf{D}_{\hat{u}}) \wedge (N(\hat{u}, r) \leq N(u, r)/\kappa),$$

where $\kappa = 2^{\sqrt{\log n \log\log n}}$. Informally, $\text{POST}_\sigma(v, u, r, \hat{v})$ says that there is a smaller reference set $\mathbf{D}_{\hat{u}}$ containing $\hat{v}$, such that the size of its fraction that is outside the target ball is at least κ times smaller that the size of the corresponding fraction of the original reference set $\mathbf{D}_u$. Note that it is not required that $\hat{u}$ belong to the search path from v to t. We will denote by $\partial_\sigma(v, u, r)$ the node $\hat{u}$ described in $\text{POST}_\sigma(v, u, r, \hat{v})$.[7]

The *δ-path* with parameters v, u, r is denoted $\delta(v, u, r)$, and its pre-condition is

$$\text{PRE}_\delta(v, u, r): \ (v \in \mathbf{D}_u) \wedge (r_u(v) > r).$$

The post-condition specifying the last node $\hat{v}$ of $\delta(v, u, r)$ is

$$\text{POST}_\delta(v, u, r, \hat{v}): \ (\varrho_u(\hat{v}) \geq \varrho_u(v) + h(\varrho_u(v))) \vee (r_u(\hat{v}) \leq r),$$

where h is the function defined in the statement of Lemma 4. Informally, $\text{POST}_\delta(v, u, r, \hat{v})$ says that either the distance ϱ_u from the border of the reference set is increased sufficiently, or $\text{PRE}_\sigma(\hat{v}, u, r)$ is satisfied.

[6] As before, $\mathbf{D}_v$ and d_v are shorthand notations for $\mathbf{D}_{v,t}$ and $d_{v,t}$, respectively.

[7] If there are more such $\hat{u}$, one of them is selected deterministically.

The *π-path* with parameters v, u, r is denoted $\pi(v, u, r)$. Its pre-condition $\text{PRE}_\pi(v, u, r)$ is the same as $\text{PRE}_\sigma(v, u, r)$, and the post-condition specifying its last node $\hat{v}$ is

$$\text{POST}_\pi(v, u, r, \hat{v}): \ \exists\, \hat{u}: (\hat{v} \in \mathbf{D}_{\hat{u}}) \wedge (N(\hat{u}, r) \leq N(u, r)/\kappa) \wedge (r_{\hat{u}}(\hat{v}) \leq r),$$

that is, the conjunction of $\text{POST}_\sigma(v, u, r, \hat{v})$ and $\text{PRE}_\sigma(\hat{v}, \hat{u}, r)$. So, the triple $(\hat{v}, \hat{u}, r)$ satisfies the same conditions as (v, u, r), but $N(\hat{u}, r) \leq N(u, r)/\kappa$. We will denote by $\partial_\pi(v, u, r)$ the node $\hat{u}$ described in $\text{POST}_\pi(v, u, r, \hat{v})$.

The case of $u = \perp$. We extend the definitions of σ-paths and π-paths to the case where the reference set consists of all the nodes. Let $\mathbf{D}_\perp$ denote the set of all nodes, and let $\rho_\perp(v) = \infty$ and $r_\perp(v) = -1$, for any v. We define the paths $\sigma(v, \perp, r)$ and $\pi(v, \perp, r)$ using exactly the same definitions as for $\sigma(v, u, r)$ and $\pi(v, u, r)$, respectively, except that all occurrences of u in these definitions are replaced by $\perp$. E.g., the pre-condition for both $\sigma(v, \perp, r)$ and $\pi(v, \perp, r)$ is $(v \in \mathbf{D}_\perp) \wedge (r \geq r_\perp(v))$, which holds for any v and r.

3.3.2 Search-path decomposition

We now describe a decomposition of the search path into subpaths of the types above. The decomposition is defined recursively in Lemmata 5–7. Lemma 5 decomposes a π-path into a σ-path and a set of δ-paths; Lemma 6 decomposes a δ-path into a set of π-paths; and Lemma 7 decomposes a search path into a set of π-paths as well. In the first two lemmata, the union of the paths to which the initial path is decomposed may yield a larger path than the initial one. This is not a problem, however, since these results are used to obtain upper bounds on the length of the paths decomposed. Unlike δ-paths and π-paths, σ-paths are not decomposed into smaller paths; we bound the expected length of σ-paths in the next section.

Below, we denote the last node of path P by $\text{last}(P)$. Also, we assume that the starting node v is different than the target t of the search.

LEMMA 5. *$\pi(v, u, r)$ is a subpath of $\bigcup_{i=0}^{I} P_i$, where $P_0 = \sigma(v, u, r)$, for $i > 0$, $P_i = \delta(v_i, \hat{u}, r)$ with $v_i = \text{last}(P_{i-1})$ and $\hat{u} = \partial_\sigma(v, u, r)$, and $I = \min\{i : r_{\hat{u}}(v_{i+1}) \leq r\}$. Also, $I \leq c \log^3 d_v$, for some constant c.*

PROOF. First we show by induction that for all $i \leq I$, the pre-condition of P_i holds, thus, P_i is well defined. Clearly, the pre-condition $\text{PRE}_\sigma(v, u, r)$ of P_0 holds, since it is the same as $\text{PRE}_\pi(v, u, r)$. Let $0 < i \leq I$, and assume that the pre-condition of P_j holds, for all $j < i$. By the post-condition $\text{POST}_\sigma(v, u, r, v_1)$ of P_0, $v_1 \in \mathbf{D}_{\hat{u}}$, so, by Lemma 1(c), $v_i \in \mathbf{D}_{\hat{u}}$ as well. Also, $r_{\hat{u}}(v_i) > r$, since $I \geq i$. Therefore, the pre-condition $\text{PRE}_\delta(v_i, \hat{u}, r)$ of P_i holds.

Next, we prove the bound on I. If $0 < i < I$, by combining the post-condition $\text{POST}_\delta(v_i, \hat{u}, r, v_{i+1})$ of P_i and the fact that $r_{\hat{u}}(v_{i+1}) > r$ (since $I > i$), we obtain that $\varrho_{\hat{u}}(v_{i+1}) \geq \varrho_{\hat{u}}(v_i) + h(\varrho_{\hat{u}}(v_i))$. From this and the definition of h, it follows that for appropriate constants i_0 and $c' > 0$, if $i_0 \leq i < I$ then

$$\varrho_{\hat{u}}(v_{i+1}) \geq (1 + c'/\log^2 \varrho_{\hat{u}}(v_i))^{i - i_0}.$$

Also, since $r_{\hat{u}}(v_i) > r \geq 0$,

$$\varrho_{\hat{u}}(v_i) \leq d_{v_i} + d^*_{v_i} \leq 2d_{v_i} \leq 2d_v.$$

From the two inequalities above, it follows easily that $I \le c\log^3 d_v$, for some constant c.[8]

It remains to show that $\pi(v,u,r)$ is a subpath of $\bigcup_{i=0}^{I} P_i$. By the post-condition $\text{POST}_\sigma(v,u,r,v_1)$ of P_0, $v_1 \in \mathbf{D}_{\hat{u}}$, so, $v_{I+1} \in \mathbf{D}_{\hat{u}}$. From the same post-condition, we have that $N(\hat{u},r) \le N(u,r)/\kappa$. Also, $r_{\hat{u}}(v_{I+1}) \le r$, by the definition of I. Therefore, $\text{POST}_\pi(v,u,r,v_{I+1})$ holds, which implies that $\pi(v,u,r)$ is a subpath of $\bigcup_{i=0}^{I} P_i$.[9] □

LEMMA 6. *$\delta(v,u,r)$ is a subpath of $\bigcup_{i=0}^{I} \pi(v_i,u_i,\hat{r})$, where $v_0 = v$, $u_0 = u$, $\hat{r} = r_u(v)$, for $i > 0$, $v_i = \text{last}(\pi(v_{i-1},u_{i-1},\hat{r}))$ and $u_i = \partial_\pi(v_{i-1},u_{i-1},\hat{r})$, and $I = \min\{i : v_{i+1} \in \mathbf{B}_t(\hat{r})\}$. Also, $I \le \log_\kappa \max\{1, N(u,\hat{r})\}$.*

PROOF. It is similar to the proof of Lemma 5. First we show that for all $i \le I$, the pre-condition of $P_i = \pi(v_i,u_i,\hat{r})$ holds. The pre-condition $\text{PRE}_\pi(v,u,\hat{r})$ of P_0 holds because, by $\text{PRE}_\delta(v,u,r)$, $v \in \mathbf{D}_u$, and $\hat{r} = r_u(v)$. Also, if $0 < i \le I$, the pre-condition $\text{PRE}_\pi(v_i,u_i,\hat{r})$ of P_i follows from the post-condition $\text{POST}_\pi(v_{i-1},u_{i-1},\hat{r},v_i)$ of P_{i-1}.

Next, we derive the bound on I. Combining the post-conditions $\text{POST}_\pi(v_i,u_i,\hat{r},v_{i+1})$ of P_i, for all $i < I$, yields $N(u_I,\hat{r}) \le N(u,\hat{r})/\kappa^I$. Also, $N(u_I,\hat{r}) \ge 1$, since, otherwise, $v_I \in \mathbf{B}_t(\hat{r})$, which contradicts the definition of I. Therefore, $N(u,\hat{r})/\kappa^I \ge 1$, and, so, $I \le \log_\kappa \max\{1, N(u,\hat{r})\}$.

Finally, by the definition of I, $v_{I+1} \in \mathbf{B}_t(r_u(v))$, and, by applying Lemma 4(b), we obtain $\varrho_u(v_{I+1}) \ge \varrho_u(v) + h(\varrho_u(v))$. Hence, $\text{POST}_\delta(v,u,r,v_{I+1})$ holds, and, so, $\delta(v,u,r)$ is a subpath of $\bigcup_{i=0}^{I} P_i$. □

The proof of the next lemma is completely analogous to that of Lemma 6 and is omitted.

LEMMA 7. *The search path from node v to t is equal to $\bigcup_{i=0}^{I} \pi(v_i,u_i,0)$, where $v_0 = v$, $u_0 = \perp$, for $i > 0$, $v_i = \text{last}(\pi(v_{i-1},u_{i-1},0))$ and $u_i = \partial_\pi(v_{i-1},u_{i-1},0)$, and $I = \min\{i : v_{i+1} = t\}$. Also, $I \le \log_\kappa n$.*

3.3.3 Expected length of σ-path

In this section, we establish the following upper bound on the expected length of a σ-path. We denote the length of a path P by $\|P\|$.

LEMMA 8. $\mathbb{E}[\|\sigma(v,u,r)\|] = O(\kappa \log n)$.

PROOF. We show that if $\|\sigma(v,u,r)\|$ is larger than i then, with probability at least $1/\kappa \log n$, it is no larger than $i+2$. Formally, let $L = \|\sigma(v,u,r)\|$. We show that for all $i \ge 0$,

$$\mathbb{P}\text{r}[L \le i+2 \mid L > i] \ge 1/\kappa \log n.$$

From this it is immediate that $\mathbb{E}[L] = O(\kappa \log n)$. We now prove the above inequality.

Let the path $\sigma(v,u,r)$ be $v_0 v_1 \cdots v_L$. Suppose that $i < L$, and fix the value of v_i, say $v_i = w$. Let $\mathbf{A} = \mathbf{B}_w(x)$ for the *smallest* radius x such that $\mathbf{D}_w \subseteq \mathbf{B}_t(r) \cup \mathbf{B}_w(x)$. We describe two properties of the set $\mathbf{A}$ that we need for the proof. The first property is

$$\mathbf{A} \subseteq \mathbf{D}_u. \tag{3.5}$$

We can derive this inclusion as follows. Using the definitions of $r_u(w)$ and $r_u(v)$, and the inequalities $d_w \le d_v$, $d_w^* \le d_v^*$, and $\varrho_u(w) \ge \varrho_u(v)$, where the last one follows from Lemma 4(a), it is easy to show that $r_u(w) \le r_u(v)$. So, by $\text{PRE}_\sigma(v,u,r)$, $r_u(w) \le r$. And since, by Lemma 3, $\mathbf{D}_w \subseteq \mathbf{B}_t(r_u(w)) \cup \mathbf{B}_w(\varrho_u(w))$, $\mathbf{D}_w \subseteq \mathbf{B}_t(r) \cup \mathbf{B}_w(\varrho_u(w))$. Combining this and the definition of $\mathbf{A}$, yields $\mathbf{A} \subseteq \mathbf{B}_w(\varrho_u(w))$. And since, by Lemma 2(b), $\mathbf{B}_w(\varrho_u(w)) \subseteq \mathbf{D}_u$, (3.5) follows. The second property of $\mathbf{A}$ that we need is

$$\mathbf{B}_t(r) \cap \mathbf{A} \subseteq \mathbf{D}_w. \tag{3.6}$$

This can be shown by applying Lemmata 1(a) and (b) (for $\mathbf{D}_w$ and $d = r$), and using the definition of $\mathbf{A}$.

For the rest of the proof, we distinguish two cases. First we consider the case of $N(w,r) \le |\mathbf{A} \setminus \mathbf{B}_t(r)|/\kappa$. By (3.5),

$$N(w,r) \le |\mathbf{D}_u \setminus \mathbf{B}_t(r)|/\kappa = N(u,r)/\kappa,$$

and since $v_{i+1} \in \mathbf{D}_w$, $\text{POST}_\sigma(v,u,r,v_{i+1})$ holds. Therefore,

$$\mathbb{P}\text{r}[L = i+1 \mid (L > i) \wedge (v_i = w)] = 1.$$

We consider now the complementary case of $N(w,r) > |\mathbf{A} \setminus \mathbf{B}_t(r)|/\kappa$. Let r' be the *smallest* radius so that

$$|\mathbf{D}_w \cap \mathbf{B}_t(r') \setminus \mathbf{B}_t(r)| > |\mathbf{A} \setminus \mathbf{B}_t(r)|/\kappa.$$

Clearly, $r' > r$. Then,

$$\begin{aligned}
&\mathbb{P}\text{r}[v_{i+1} \in \mathbf{B}_t(r') \mid (L > i) \wedge (v_i = w)] \\
&\quad\ge \mathbb{P}\text{r}[v_{i+1} \in \mathbf{B}_t(r') \cap \mathbf{A} \mid (L > i) \wedge (v_i = w)] \\
&\quad\ge \sum_{v' \in \mathbf{B}_t(r') \cap \mathbf{A} \cap \mathbf{D}_w} \varphi_w(v') \\
&\quad\ge \frac{|\mathbf{B}_t(r') \cap \mathbf{A} \cap \mathbf{D}_w|}{\ln n \cdot |\mathbf{A}|} \\
&\quad\ge \frac{|\mathbf{B}_t(r') \cap \mathbf{A} \cap \mathbf{D}_w| - |\mathbf{B}_t(r) \cap \mathbf{A} \cap \mathbf{D}_w|}{\ln n \cdot (|\mathbf{A}| - |\mathbf{B}_t(r) \cap \mathbf{A} \cap \mathbf{D}_w|)},
\end{aligned}$$

where the second-to-last line is obtained by applying the definition of φ and (2.1), and the last by using the fact that $\frac{a}{b} \ge \frac{a-c}{b-c}$, for $0 \le c < a \le b$. It is

$$\begin{aligned}
&|\mathbf{B}_t(r') \cap \mathbf{A} \cap \mathbf{D}_w| - |\mathbf{B}_t(r) \cap \mathbf{A} \cap \mathbf{D}_w| \\
&\qquad = |\mathbf{B}_t(r') \cap \mathbf{A} \cap \mathbf{D}_w \setminus \mathbf{B}_t(r)| \\
&\qquad = |\mathbf{B}_t(r') \cap \mathbf{D}_w \setminus \mathbf{B}_t(r)|,
\end{aligned}$$

where the first relation holds because $r' \ge r$, and the second because, by the definition of $\mathbf{A}$, $\mathbf{A} \supseteq \mathbf{D}_w \setminus \mathbf{B}_t(r)$. Also,

$$|\mathbf{A}| - |\mathbf{B}_t(r) \cap \mathbf{A} \cap \mathbf{D}_w| = |\mathbf{A}| - |\mathbf{B}_t(r) \cap \mathbf{A}| = |\mathbf{A} \setminus \mathbf{B}_t(r)|,$$

where the first relation holds because of (3.6). Combining the above gives

$$\begin{aligned}
&\mathbb{P}\text{r}[v_{i+1} \in \mathbf{B}_t(r') \mid (L > i) \wedge (v_i = w)] \\
&\qquad \ge \frac{|\mathbf{D}_w \cap \mathbf{B}_t(r') \setminus \mathbf{B}_t(r)|}{\ln n \cdot |\mathbf{A} \setminus \mathbf{B}_t(r)|} \\
&\qquad \ge \frac{1}{\kappa \ln n},
\end{aligned} \tag{3.7}$$

by the definition of r'. If $v_{i+1} \in \mathbf{B}_t(r')$ then

$$\begin{aligned}
N(v_{i+1},r) &\le |\mathbf{D}_w \cap \mathbf{B}_t(r'-1) \setminus \mathbf{B}_t(r)| \\
&\le |\mathbf{A} \setminus \mathbf{B}_t(r)|/\kappa \\
&\le N(u,r)/\kappa,
\end{aligned}$$

[8]Note that this bound depends critically on function h, which is determined by the shape of the next-hop space; see also the footnote before the statement of Lemma 4.

[9]Note that, in general, $\pi(v,u,r) \ne \bigcup_{i=0}^{I} P_i$, since it is possible that $\partial_\pi(v,u,r) \ne \hat{u} = \partial_\sigma(v,u,r)$.

where the first inequality holds because $\mathbf{D}_{v_{i+1}} \subseteq \mathbf{D}_w \cap \mathbf{B}_t(r'-1)$, the second because of the minimality of r', and the last because of (3.5). So, if $v_{i+1} \in \mathbf{B}_t(r')$, $\textsc{Post}_\sigma(v, u, r, v_{i+2})$ holds, and, thus, $L \leq i+2$. Combining this and (3.7) yields

$$\mathbb{P}\mathrm{r}[L \leq i+2 \mid (L > i) \wedge (v_i = w)] \geq 1/\kappa \ln n. \quad \square$$

3.3.4 Expected length of search path

We are now ready to bound the expected length of the search path. Let $T_\sigma = \max_{v,u,r} \mathbb{E}[\|\sigma(v,u,r)\|]$, and, for $m \geq 1$, let

$$T_\delta(m) = \max\{\mathbb{E}[\|\delta(v,u,r)\|] : N(u,r) \leq m\};$$
$$T_\pi(m) = \max\{\mathbb{E}[\|\pi(v,u,r)\|] : N(u,r) \leq m\}.$$

Define also $T_\delta(0) = T_\pi(0) = 0$. By Lemma 5, we have

$$T_\pi(m) \leq T_\sigma + c\log^3 n \cdot T_\delta(\lfloor m/\kappa \rfloor).$$

Also, by Lemma 6 and the fact that $\hat{r} > r$,

$$T_\delta(m) \leq (1 + \log_\kappa m) \cdot T_\pi(m).$$

Combining yields

$$T_\pi(m) \leq T_\sigma + c\log^3 n \log_\kappa m \cdot T_\pi(\lfloor m/\kappa \rfloor),$$

and unfolding the recurrence we obtain

$$T_\pi(m) \leq T_\sigma \cdot \sum_{0 \leq i \leq \log_\kappa m} (c\log^3 n \log_\kappa m)^i$$
$$= \mathrm{O}(T_\sigma \cdot (c\log^3 n \log_\kappa m)^{\log_\kappa m}).$$

By Lemma 7, the expected length T of the search path from s to t is

$$T \leq (1 + \log_\kappa n) \cdot T_\pi(n),$$

and by Lemma 8, $T_\sigma = \mathrm{O}(\kappa \log n)$. Combining gives

$$T = \mathrm{O}(\log_\kappa n \cdot \kappa \log n \cdot (c\log^3 n \log_\kappa m)^{\log_\kappa n}).$$

Finally, substituting the value of $\kappa = 2^{\sqrt{\log n \log\log n}}$, we obtain $T = \mathrm{O}(2^{c'\sqrt{\log n \log\log n}})$, for some constant $c' > 0$. Therefore, $T = \mathrm{o}(2^{(\log n)^{1/2+\epsilon}})$, for any fixed $\epsilon > 0$. This completes the proof of Theorem 1.

3.3.5 Remarks

The bound we have shown above holds also with high probability (not only in expectation); i.e., with high probability, $2^{\mathrm{O}(\sqrt{\log n \log\log n})}$ steps are required, for all source–target pairs. This follows from the fact that, with high probability, $\|\sigma(v,u,r)\| = \mathrm{O}(\kappa \log n)$, which is immediate from the proof of Lemma 8. Our result can be extended to the case of arbitrary *weighted* base graphs. For this case, the bound is $2^{\mathrm{O}(\sqrt{\log n \log\log(n+\Delta)})}$ steps, where Δ is the aspect ratio, i.e., the ratio of the largest to the smallest distance between nodes.

4. OPEN PROBLEMS

We have established an $n^{\mathrm{o}(1)}$ bound on the expected number of steps of focused greedy search, a variant of greedy search, for any source–target pair, in any n-node base graph that has been augmented via some natural density-based distribution. This upper bound is essentially tight.

It would be interesting to determine if our bound holds for greedy search as well. In greedy search, the next-hop space of node u for target t consists of all nodes v with $\beta(u,v,t) = d_{u,t} - d_{v,t} > 0$, while in focused greedy, the next-hop space consists of those v with $\beta(u,v,t)/d_{u,v} \geq 1/\operatorname{polylog} \beta(u,v,t)$. Our proof works only for this specific threshold for $\beta(u,v,t)/d_{u,v}$. We do not know if this is intrinsically required for achieving search paths of length $n^{\mathrm{o}(1)}$, or if it is just an artifact of our proof.

The lower bound of Theorem 2 holds for the worst-case source-target pair, but not necessarily when the source–target pair is chosen at random. It may thus be the case that for a random pair, even greedy search takes a polylogarithmic expected number of steps, for any base graph (for a suitable augmentation). It is an open problem whether this is true.

Note also that Theorem 2 applies only to search algorithms that move closer to the target in each step. An interesting question is whether there is a combination of a decentralized search algorithm (which sometimes moves further away from the target) and a "natural" augmentation scheme, such as the rank-based augmentation, that achieves search paths of polylogarithmic expected length, for any base graph.

5. ACKNOWLEDGMENTS

We thank the anonymous referees of this paper for their helpful comments.

6. REFERENCES

[1] I. Abraham and C. Gavoille. Object location using path separators. In *Proc. 25th ACM Symp. on Principles of Distributed Computing (PODC)*, pages 188–197, 2006.

[2] M. Dietzfelbinger and P. Woelfel. Tight lower bounds for greedy routing in uniform small world rings. In *Proc. 41st ACM Symp. on Theory of Computing (STOC)*, pages 591–600, 2009.

[3] P. S. Dodds, R. Muhamad, and D. J. Watts. An experimental study of search in global social networks. *Science*, 301:827–829, 2003.

[4] P. Duchon, N. Hanusse, E. Lebhar, and N. Schabanel. Could any graph be turned into a small-world? In *Proc. 19th Int. Symp. on Distributed Computing (DISC)*, pages 511–513, 2005.

[5] P. Fraigniaud. Greedy routing in tree-decomposed graphs. In *Proc. 13th European Symp. on Algorithms (ESA)*, pages 791–802, 2005.

[6] P. Fraigniaud, C. Gavoille, A. Kosowski, E. Lebhar, and Z. Lotker. Universal augmentation schemes for network navigability: Overcoming the $\sqrt{n}$-barrier. In *Proc. 19th ACM Symp. on Parallelism in Algorithms and Architectures (SPAA)*, pages 1–7, 2007.

[7] P. Fraigniaud, C. Gavoille, and C. Paul. Eclecticism shrinks even small worlds. In *Proc. 23rd ACM Symp. on Principles of Distributed Computing (PODC)*, pages 169–178, 2004.

[8] P. Fraigniaud, E. Lebhar, and Z. Lotker. A lower bound for network navigability. *SIAM J. Discrete Math.*, to appear. (Preliminary version in *Proc. 13th ESA*, 2006.).

[9] J. Kleinberg. The small-world phenomenon: An algorithm perspective. In *Proc. 32nd ACM Symp. on Theory of Computing (STOC)*, pages 163–170, 2000.

[10] J. Kleinberg. Small-world phenomena and the dynamics of information. In *Proc. 15th Neural Information Processing Systems Conf. (NIPS)*, pages 431–438, 2001.

[11] J. Kleinberg. Complex networks and decentralized search algorithms. In *Proc. Int. Congress of Mathematicians (ICM)*, 2006.

[12] E. Lebhar and N. Schabanel. Almost optimal decentralized routing in long-range contact networks. In *Proc. 31st Int. Colloq. on Automata, Languages and Programming (ICALP)*, pages 894–905, 2004.

[13] D. Liben-Nowell, J. Novak, R. Kumar, P. Raghavan, and A. Tomkins. Geographic routing in social networks. *Proc. National Academy of Sciences of the USA*, 102(33):11623–11628, 2005.

[14] G. S. Manku, M. Naor, and U. Wieder. Know thy neighbor's neighbor: The power of lookahead in randomized P2P networks. In *Proc. 36th ACM Symp. on Theory of Computing (STOC)*, pages 54–63, 2004.

[15] C. Martel and V. Nguyen. Analyzing Kleinberg's (and other) small-world models. In *Proc. 23rd ACM Symp. on Principles of Distributed Computing (PODC)*, pages 179–188, 2004.

[16] C. Martel and V. Nguyen. Analyzing and characterizing small-world graphs. In *Proc. 16th ACM-SIAM Symp. on Discrete Algorithms (SODA)*, pages 311–320, 2005.

[17] S. Milgram. The small world problem. *Psychology Today*, 67(1):60–67, 1967.

[18] A. Slivkins. Distance estimation and object location via rings of neighbors. In *Proc. 24th ACM Symp. on Principles of Distributed Computing (PODC)*, pages 41–50, 2005.

[19] D. J. Watts and S. H. Strogatz. Collective dynamics of 'small-world' networks. *Nature*, 393:440–442, 1998.

Almost Tight Bounds for Rumour Spreading with Conductance*

Flavio Chierichetti, Silvio Lattanzi, Alessandro Panconesi
Dept. of Computer Science, Sapienza University of Rome
Rome, Italy
chierichetti@di.uniroma1.it, lattanzi@di.uniroma1.it, ale@di.uniroma1.it

ABSTRACT

We show that if a connected graph with n nodes has conductance ϕ then rumour spreading, also known as randomized broadcast, successfully broadcasts a message within $\tilde{O}(\phi^{-1} \cdot \log n)$, many rounds with high probability, regardless of the source, by using the PUSH-PULL strategy. The $\tilde{O}(\cdots)$ notation hides a polylog ϕ^{-1} factor. This result is almost tight since there exists graph of n nodes, and conductance ϕ, with diameter $\Omega(\phi^{-1} \cdot \log n)$.

If, in addition, the network satisfies some kind of uniformity condition on the degrees, our analysis implies that both both PUSH and PULL, by themselves, successfully broadcast the message to every node in the same number of rounds.

Categories and Subject Descriptors

G.3 [Mathematics of Computing]: Probability and Statistics.

General Terms

Algorithms, Theory.

Keywords

Conductance, rumor spreading, social networks.

1. INTRODUCTION

Rumour spreading, also known as randomized broadcast or randomized gossip (all terms that will be used as synonyms throughout the paper), refers to the following distributed algorithm. Starting with one source node with a message, the protocol proceeds in a sequence of synchronous rounds with the goal of *broadcasting* the message, i.e. to deliver it to every node in the network. In round $t \geq 0$, every node that knows the message selects a neighbour uniformly at random to which the message is forwarded. This is the so-called PUSH strategy. The PULL variant is symmetric. In round $t \geq 0$ every node that does not yet have the message selects a neighbour uniformly at random and asks for the information, which is transferred provided that the queried neighbour knows it. Finally, the PUSH-PULL strategy is a combination of both. In round $t \geq 0$, each node selects a random neighbour to perform a PUSH if it has the information or a PULL in the opposite case.

These three strategies have been introduced in [5] and since then have been intensely investigated (see the related work section). One of the most studied questions concerns their completion time: how many rounds will it take for one of the above strategies to disseminate the information to all nodes in the graph, assuming a worst-case source? In this paper we prove the following two results:

- If a network has conductance ϕ and n nodes, then, with high probability, PUSH-PULL reaches every node within $O\left(\frac{\log^2 \phi^{-1}}{\phi} \cdot \log n\right)$ many rounds, regardless of the source.
- If, in addition, the network satisfies the following condition for every edge uv and some constant $\alpha > 0$:
$$\max\left\{\frac{\deg(u)}{\deg(v)}, \frac{\deg(v)}{\deg(u)}\right\} \leq \alpha$$
then both PUSH and PULL, by themselves[1], reach every node within
$$O(c_\alpha \cdot \phi^{-1} \cdot \log n \cdot \log^2 \phi^{-1})$$
many rounds with high probability regardless of the source, where c_α is a constant depending only on α.

The first result is a significant improvement with respect to best current bound of $O(\log^4 n/\phi^6)$ [4]. (The proof of [4] is based on an interesting connection with spectral sparsification [19]. The approach followed here is entirely different.) The result is almost tight because $\Omega(\log n/\phi)$ is a lower bound[2] — in particular, the bound is tight in the case

*This research is partially supported by a grant of Yahoo! Research and by an IBM Faculty Award.

STOC'10, June 5–8, 2010, Cambridge, Massachusetts, USA.

[1]We observe that the star, a graph of conductance 1, is such that both the PUSH and the PULL strategy by themselves require $\Omega(n)$ many rounds to spread the information to each node, assuming a worst case, or even uniformly random, source. That is, conductance alone is not enough to ensure that PUSH, or PULL, spread the information fast.

[2]Indeed, choose any n, and any $\phi \geq n^{-1+\epsilon}$. Take any 3-regular graph of constant vertex expansion (a random 3-regular graph will suffice) on $O(n \cdot \phi)$ nodes. Then, substitute each edge of the regular graph with a path of $O(\phi^{-1})$ new nodes. The graph obtained is easily seen to have $O(n)$ nodes, diameter $O(\phi^{-1} \cdot \log n)$ and conductance $\Omega(\phi)$.

of constant conductance (for instance, this is the case for the almost-preferential-attachment graphs of [15].) The second result can be proved using the same approach we use for the main one. In this extended abstract we omit the details of its proof.

Our main motivation comes from the study of social networks. Loosely stated, we are looking for a theorem of the form *"Rumour spreading is fast in social networks"*. There is some empirical evidence showing that real social networks have high conductance. The authors of [14] report that in many different social networks there exist only cuts of small (logarithmic) size having small (inversely logarithmic) conductance – all other cuts appear to have larger conductance. That is, the conductance of the social networks they analyze is larger than a quantity seemingly proportional to an inverse logarithm.

Our work should also be viewed in the context of expansion properties of graphs, of which conductance is an important example, and their relationship with rumour spreading. In particular we observe how, interestingly, the convergence time of the PUSH-PULL process on graph of conductance ϕ is a factor of ϕ smaller than the worst-case mixing time of the uniform random walk on such graphs.

Conductance is one of the most studied measures of graph expansion. Edge expansion, and vertex expansion are two other notable measures. In the case of edge expansion there are classes of graphs for which the protocol is slow (see [3] for more details), while the problem remains open for vertex expansion.

In terms of message complexity, we observe first that it has been determined precisely only for very special classes of graphs (cliques [12] and Erdös-Rényi random graphs [8]). Apart from this, given the generality of our class, it is impossible to improve the trivial upper bound on the number of messages – that is, number of rounds times number of nodes. For instance consider the "lollipop graph." Fix $\omega(n^{-1}) < \phi < o(\log^{-1} n)$, and suppose to have a path of length ϕ^{-1} connected to a clique of size $n - \phi^{-1} = \Theta(n)$. This graph has conductance $\approx \phi$. Let the source be any node in the clique. After $\Theta(\log n)$ rounds each node in the clique will have the information. Furthermore, at least ϕ^{-1} steps will be needed for the information to be sent to the each node in the path. So, at least $n - \phi^{-1} = \Theta(n)$ messages are pushed (by the nodes in the clique) in each round, for at least $\phi^{-1} - \Theta(\log n) = \Theta(\phi^{-1})$ rounds. Thus, the total number of messages sent will be $\Omega(n \cdot \phi^{-1})$. Observing that the running time is $\Theta(\phi^{-1} + \log n) = \Theta(\phi^{-1})$, we have that the total number of rounds times n is (asymptotically) less than or equal to the number of transmitted messages.

2. RELATED WORK

The literature on the gossip protocol and social networks is huge and we confine ourselves to what appears to be more relevant to the present work.

Clearly, at least diameter-many rounds are needed for the gossip protocol to reach all nodes. It has been shown that $O(n \log n)$ rounds are always sufficient for each connected graph of n nodes [9]. The problem has been studied on a number of graph classes, such as hypercubes, bounded-degree graphs, cliques and Erdös-Rényi random graphs (see [9,11,17]). Recently, there has been a lot of work on "quasi-regular" expanders (i.e., expander graphs for which the ratio between the maximum and minimum degree is constant) — it has been shown in different settings [1, 6, 7, 10, 18] that $O(\log n)$ rounds are sufficient for the rumour to be spread throughout the graph. See also [13, 16]. Our work can be seen as an extension of these studies to graphs of arbitrary degree distribution. Observe that many real world graphs (e.g., facebook, Internet, etc.) have a very skewed degree distribution — that is, the ratio between the maximum and the minimum degree is very high. In most social networks' graph models the ratio between the maximum and the minimum degree can be shown to be polynomial in the graph order.

Mihail et al. [15] study the edge expansion and the conductance of graphs that are very similar to preferential attachment (PA) graphs. We shall refer to these as "almost" PA graphs. They show that edge expansion and conductance are constant in these graphs. Their result and ours together imply that rumor spreading requires $O(\log n)$ rounds on almost PA graphs.

For what concerns the original PA graphs, in [3] it is shown that rumour spreading is fast (requires time $O(\log^2 n)$) in those networks.

In [2] it is shown that high conductance implies that *non-uniform* (over neighbours) rumour spreading succeeds. By non-uniform we mean that, for every ordered pair of neighbours i and j, node i will select j with probability p_{ij} for the rumour spreading step (in general, $p_{ij} \neq p_{ji}$). This results does not extend to the case of uniform probabilities studied in this paper. In our setting (but not in theirs), the existence of a non uniform distribution that makes rumour spreading fast is a rather trivial matter. A graph of conductance ϕ has diameter bounded by $O(\phi^{-1} \log n)$. Thus, in a synchronous network, it is possible to elect a leader in $O(\phi^{-1} \log n)$ many rounds and set up a BFS tree originating from it. By assigning probability 1 to the edge between a node and its parent one has the desired non uniform probability distribution. Thus, from the point of view of this paper the existence of non uniform problem is rather uninteresting.

In [16] the authors consider a problem that at first sight might appear equivalent to ours. They consider the conductance ϕ_P of the *connection probability matrix* P, whose entry $P_{i,j}$, $1 \leq i, j \leq n$, gives the probability that i calls j in any given round. They show that if P is doubly stochastic then the running time of PUSH-PULL is $O(\phi_P^{-1} \cdot \log n)$. This might seem to subsume our result but this is not the case. The catch is that they consider the conductance of a doubly stochastic matrix instead of the actual conductance of the graph, as we do. Observe that the are graphs of high conductance that do not admit doubly stochastic matrices of high conductance. For instance, in the star, no matter how one sets the probabilities P_{ij}, there will always exist a leaf ℓ that will be contacted by the central node with probability $\leq \frac{1}{n-1}$. Since the matrix is doubly-stochastic this implies that ℓ will contact the central node with probability $O(n^{-1})$. Thus, at least $\Omega(n)$ rounds will be needed. Therefore their result gives too weak a bound for the uniform PUSH-PULL process that we analyze in this paper.

3. PRELIMINARIES

Observe that $\frac{1}{2}\operatorname{vol}(V) = |E|$. Given $S \subseteq V$, and $v \in S$, we define

$$N_S^+(v) = \{w \mid w \in V - S \wedge \{v, w\} \in E\}$$

and $d_S^+(v) = |N_S^+(v)|$. Analogously, we define $N_S^-(w) = N_{V-S}^+(w)$ and $d_S^-(w) = |N_S^-(w)|$. Recall that the conductance of a graph $G(V, E)$ is:

$$\Phi(G) = \min_{S \subset V : \operatorname{vol}(S) \le |E|} \frac{\operatorname{cut}(S, V-S)}{\operatorname{vol}(S)}$$

Where $\operatorname{cut}(S, V-S)$ is the number of edges in the cut between S and $V - S$ and $\operatorname{vol}(S)$ is the volume of S.

We now state and prove some technical lemmas that we will use in our analysis. The first one is an "inversion" of Markov's inequality.

LEMMA 1. *Suppose $X_1, X_2, \ldots, X_t$ are random variables, with X_i having co-domain $\{0, v_i\}$ and such that $X_i = v_i$ with probability p_i. Fix $p \le \min p_i$. Then, for each $0 < q < p$,*

$$\Pr\left[\sum_i X_i \ge \left(1 - \frac{1-p}{1-q}\right) \cdot \sum_i v_i\right] \ge q.$$

PROOF. Let $\overline{X}_i = v_i - X_i$. Observe that each X_i and each $\overline{X}_i$ is a non-negative random variable, of mean $p_i \cdot v_i$ and $(1 - p_i) \cdot v_i$, respectively. We use μ to denote the expected sum of the X_i, $\mu = \sum(p_i \cdot v_i)$, and $\overline{\mu}$ to denote the expected sum of the $\overline{X}_i$, $\overline{\mu} = \sum((1 - p_i) \cdot v_i)$. Observe that $\overline{\mu} \le (1-p) \cdot \sum v_i$.

By Markov's inequality, we have

$$\begin{aligned}
\Pr\left[\sum_i X_i \le \left(1 - \frac{1-p}{1-q}\right) \sum_i v_i\right] &\le \\
\Pr\left[\sum_i X_i \le \sum_i v_i - \frac{1}{1-q} \cdot \overline{\mu}\right] &= \\
\Pr\left[\sum_i \overline{X}_i \ge \frac{1}{1-q} \cdot \overline{\mu}\right] &\le 1 - q
\end{aligned}$$

Thus the claim. □

The next lemma gives some probabilistic bounds on the sum of binary random variables having "similar" expectation.

LEMMA 2. *Let $p \in (0, 1)$. Suppose $X_1, \ldots, X_t$ are independent 0/1 random variables, the i-th of which such that $\Pr[X_i = 1] = p_i$, with $\frac{1}{2} \cdot p \le p_i \le p$. Then,*

1. *if $\frac{pt}{2} > 1$, then $\Pr[\sum X_i \ge \frac{pt}{4}] \ge \frac{1}{32}$;*
2. *if $\frac{pt}{2} \le 1$, then $\Pr[\sum X_i \ge 1] \ge \frac{pt}{4}$;*
3. *in general, for $P = \min\left(\frac{1}{32}, \frac{pt}{4}\right)$, we have*

$$\Pr\left[\sum X_i \ge \frac{pt}{128 \cdot P}\right] \ge P.$$

PROOF. Let $X = \sum_{i=1}^t X_i$. In the first case, $E[X] \ge t \cdot \frac{p}{2}$; in particular, $E[X] \ge 1$. Therefore, by Chernoff's bound, we have

$$\begin{aligned}
\Pr\left[X < \frac{1}{2} \cdot E[X]\right] &\le e^{-\frac{1}{16}E[X]} \\
&\le e^{-\frac{1}{16}} \le 1 - \frac{1}{32},
\end{aligned}$$

where the last inequality follows from $e^{-x} \le 1 - \frac{x}{2}$ if $x \in [0, 1]$.

In the second case, we compute the probability that for no i, $X_i = 1$:

$$\begin{aligned}
\prod_{i=1}^t \Pr[X_i = 0] &\le \prod_{i=1}^t \left(1 - \frac{p}{2}\right) \\
&= \left(1 - \frac{p}{2}\right)^t = \left(\left(1 - \frac{p}{2}\right)^{\frac{2}{p}}\right)^{\frac{p}{2} \cdot t} \\
&\le e^{-\frac{p}{2} \cdot t} \le 1 - \frac{pt}{4}.
\end{aligned}$$

So, with probability $\ge \frac{pt}{4}$ at least one X_i will be equal to 1.

The third case, follows directly from the former two, by choosing — respectively — $P = \frac{1}{32}$, and $P = \frac{pt}{2}$. □

Finally we give a lemma that underlines symmetries in the PUSH-PULL strategy. Let $u \xrightarrow{t} v$ be the event that an information originated at u arrives to v in t rounds using the PUSH-PULL strategy. And let $u \xleftarrow{t} v$ the event that an information that is originally in v arrives to u in t rounds using the PUSH-PULL strategy. We have that:

LEMMA 3. *Let $u, v \in V$, then*

$$Pr[u \xrightarrow{t} v] = Pr[u \xleftarrow{t} v]$$

PROOF. Look at each possible sequence of PUSH-PULL requests done by the nodes of G in t rounds. We define the "inverse" of some sequence, as the sequence we would obtain by looking at the sequence starting from the last round to the first. Now the probability that the information spreads from u to v (resp., from v to u) in at most t steps is equal to the sum of the probabilities of sequences of length at most t that manage to pass the information from u to v (from v to u) — given that the probability of a sequence, and that of its inverse, are the same, the claim follows. □

4. A $O(\phi^{-2} \cdot \log N)$ BOUND

In this section we prove a completion time bound for the PUSH-PULL strategy of $O(\phi^{-2} \cdot \log n)$. Observe that this bound happens to be tight if $\phi \in \Omega(1)$. The general strategy is as follows:

- we will prove that, given any set S of informed nodes having volume $\le |E|$, after $O(\phi^{-1})$ rounds (that we call a *phase*) the new set S' of informed vertices, $S' \supseteq S$, will have volume $\operatorname{vol}(S') \ge (1 + \Omega(\phi)) \cdot \operatorname{vol}(S)$ with constant probability (over the random choices performed by nodes during those $O(\phi^{-1})$ rounds) — if this happens, we say that the phase was successful; this section is devoted to proving this lemma;

- given the lemma, it follows that PUSH-PULL informs a set of nodes of volume larger than $|E|$, starting from any single node, in time $O(\phi^{-2} \cdot \log n)$.

  Indeed, it suffices to observe that, if we flip $c \cdot \phi^{-1} \cdot \log n$ IID coins, each having $\Theta(1)$ head probability, we will end up with $f(c) \cdot \phi^{-1} \cdot \log n$ heads with high probability — with $f(c)$ increasing, and unbounded, in c. This implies that we can get enough (that is, $\Theta(\phi^{-1} \cdot \log n)$) successful phases for covering more than half of the graph's volume in at most $\Theta(\phi^{-1}) \cdot \Theta(\phi^{-1} \cdot \log n) = \Theta(\phi^{-2} \cdot \log n)$ rounds;

- applying lemma 3, we can then show that each uninformed node can get the information in the same amount of steps, if a set S of volume $> |E|$ is informed — completing the proof.

Our first lemma shows how one can always find a subset of nodes in the "smallest" part of a good conductance cut, that happen to hit many of the edges in the cut, and whose nodes have a large "fraction" of their degree that cross the cut.

LEMMA 4. *Let $G(V, E)$ be a simple graph.*
Let $A \subseteq B \subseteq V$, with $\mathrm{vol}(B) \leq |E|$ and $\mathrm{cut}(A, V - B) \geq \frac{3}{4} \cdot \mathrm{cut}(B, V - B)$. Suppose further that the conductance of the cut $(B, V - B)$ is at least ϕ, $\mathrm{cut}(B, V - B) \geq \phi \cdot \mathrm{vol}(B)$. If we let

$$U = U_B(A) = \left\{ v \in A \middle| \frac{d_B^+(v)}{d(v)} \geq \frac{\phi}{2} \right\},$$

then $\mathrm{cut}(U, V - B) \geq \frac{1}{4} \cdot \mathrm{cut}(B, V - B)$.

PROOF. We prove the lemma with the following derivation:

$$\sum_{v \in A} d_B^+(v) + \sum_{v \in B-A} d_B^+(v) = \mathrm{cut}(B, V - B)$$

$$\sum_{v \in A} d_B^+(v) = \mathrm{cut}(B, V - B) - \sum_{v \in B-A} d_B^+(v)$$

$$\sum_{v \in A \cap U} d_B^+(v) + \sum_{v \in A-U} d_B^+(v) = \mathrm{cut}(A, V - B)$$

$$\sum_{v \in U} d_B^+(v) + \sum_{v \in A-U} d_B^+(v) \geq \frac{3}{4} \cdot \mathrm{cut}(B, V - B),$$

then,

$$\sum_{v \in U} d_B^+(v) \geq \frac{3}{4} \cdot \mathrm{cut}(B, V - B) - \sum_{v \in A-U} d_B^+(v)$$

$$\sum_{v \in U} d_B^+(v) \geq \frac{3}{4} \cdot \mathrm{cut}(B, V - B) - \sum_{v \in A-U} \left(\frac{\phi}{2} \cdot d(v) \right)$$

$$\sum_{v \in U} d_B^+(v) \geq \frac{3}{4} \cdot \mathrm{cut}(B, V - B) - \frac{\phi}{2} \cdot \mathrm{vol}(B)$$

$$\sum_{v \in U} d_B^+(v) \geq \frac{3}{4} \cdot \mathrm{cut}(B, V - B) - \frac{1}{2} \cdot \mathrm{cut}(B, V - B)$$

$$\sum_{v \in U} d_B^+(v) \geq \frac{1}{4} \cdot \mathrm{cut}(B, V - B).$$

□

Given $v \in U = U_B(A)$, we define $N_U^{\ominus\rightarrow}(v)$ (to be read "N-push-U-v") and $N_U^{\oplus\leftarrow}(v)$(to be read "N-pull-U-v") as follows

$$N_U^{\ominus\rightarrow}(v) = \{u \in N_U^+(v) \mid d(u) \geq \frac{1}{3} d^+(v)\}$$

and

$$N_U^{\oplus\leftarrow}(v) = \{u \in N_U^+(v) \mid d(u) < \frac{1}{3} d^+(v)\}.$$

Then,

$$U^{\ominus\rightarrow} = \{v \in U \mid |N_B^{\ominus\rightarrow}(v)| \geq |N_B^{\oplus\leftarrow}(v)|\}$$

and

$$U^{\oplus\leftarrow} = \{v \in U \mid |N_B^{\oplus\leftarrow}(v)| > |N_B^{\ominus\rightarrow}(v)|\}.$$

Observe that $U^{\ominus\rightarrow} \cap U^{\oplus\leftarrow} = \varnothing$ and $U^{\ominus\rightarrow} \cup U^{\oplus\leftarrow} = U$. In particular, (at least) one of $\mathrm{vol}(U^{\ominus\rightarrow}) \geq \frac{1}{2} \cdot \mathrm{vol}(U)$ and $\mathrm{vol}(U^{\oplus\leftarrow}) \geq \frac{1}{2} \cdot \mathrm{vol}(U)$ holds. In the following, if $\mathrm{vol}(U^{\ominus\rightarrow}) \geq \frac{1}{2} \cdot \mathrm{vol}(U)$ we will "apply" the PUSH strategy on U; otherwise, we will "apply" the PULL strategy.

Given a vertex $v \in U$, we will simulate either the PUSH the PULL strategy, for $O\left(\frac{1}{\phi}\right)$ steps over it. The "gain" $g(v)$ of node v is then the volume of the node(s) that pull the information from v, or that v pushes the information to.

Our aim is to get a bound on the gain of the whole original vertex set S. This cannot be done by summing the gains of single vertices in S, because of the many dependencies in the process. For instance, different nodes $v, v' \in S$ might inform (or could be asked the information by) the same node in $V - S$.

To overcome this difficulty, we use an idea similar in spirit to the deferred decision principle. First of all, let us remark that, given a vertex set S having the information, we will run the PUSH-PULL process for $O\left(\frac{1}{\phi}\right)$ rounds. We will look at what happens to the neighbourhoods of different nodes in S sequentially, by simulating the $O\left(\frac{1}{\phi}\right)$ steps (which we call a phase) of each $v \in S$ and some of its peers in $N_S^+(v) \subseteq V - S$. Obviously, we will make sure that no node in $V - S$ performs more than $O\left(\frac{1}{\phi}\right)$ PULL steps in a single phase.

Specifically, we consider the following process:

1. at step i, we consider the sets A_i, B_i; at the first step, $i = 0$, we take $A_0 = B_0 = S$ and $H_0 = \varnothing$;
2. if $\mathrm{cut}(A_i, V - B_i) < \frac{3}{4} \cdot \mathrm{cut}(B_i, V - B_i)$, or $\mathrm{vol}(B_i) > |E|$, we stop; otherwise, apply lemma 4 to A_i, B_i, obtaining set $U_i = U_{B_i}(A_i)$;
3. we take a node v out of U_i, and we consider the effects of either the push or the pull strategy, repeated for $\left\lceil \frac{10}{\phi} \right\rceil$ steps, over v and $N_{B_i}^+(v)$;
4. $H_{i+1} \leftarrow H_i$;
5. each node $u \in N_{B_i}^+(v)$ that gets informed (either by a push of v, or by a pull from v) is added to the set of the "halted nodes" H_{i+1}; v is also added to the set H_{i+1};
6. let $A_{i+1} = A_i - \{v\}$, and $B_{i+1} = B_i \cup H_{i+1}$; observe that $B_{i+1} - A_{i+1} = H_{i+1}$;

7. iterate the process.

Observe that no vertex in $V - S$ will make more than $O\left(\frac{1}{\phi}\right)$ PULL steps in a single phase. Indeed, each time we run point 3 in the process, we *only* disclose whether some node $u \in V - S$ actually makes, or does not make, a PULL from v. If the PULL does not go through, and node u later tries to make a PULL to another node v', the probability of this second batch of PULL's (and in fact, of any subsequent batch) to succeed is actually larger than the probability of success of the first batch of PULL's of u (since at that point, we already know that the previous PULL batches made by u *never* reached any previous candidate node $v \in S$).

The next lemma summarize the gain, in a single step, of a node $v \in U_i$.

LEMMA 5. *If $v \in U_i^{\oplus}$, then*

$$\Pr\left[g(v) \geq \frac{1}{3} \cdot d^+_{B_i}(v)\right] \geq \frac{\phi}{4}.$$

On the other hand, if $v \in U_i^{\ominus}$ then

$$\Pr\left[g(v) \geq \frac{1}{20} \cdot d^+_{B_i}(v)\right] \geq \frac{1}{10}.$$

In general, if $v \in U_i$,

$$\Pr\left[g(v) \geq \frac{1}{20} \cdot d^+_{B_i}(v)\right] \geq \frac{\phi}{10}$$

PROOF. Suppose that $v \in U_i^{\oplus}$. Then, at least $\frac{1}{2}d^+_{B_i}(v)$ neighbours of $d(v)$ have degree $\geq \frac{1}{3}d^+_{B_i}(v)$. Since $v \in U_i$, we have that $\frac{d^+_{B_i}(v)}{d(v)} \geq \frac{\phi}{2}$. Thus, the probability that v pushes the information to one of its neighbours of degree $\geq \frac{1}{3}d^+_{B_i}(v)$ is $\geq \frac{\frac{1}{2}d^+_{B_i}(v)}{d(v)} \geq \frac{\phi}{4}$.

Now, suppose that $v \in U_i^{\ominus}$. Recall that $g(v)$ is the random variable denoting the gain of v; that is,

$$g(v) = \sum_{u \in N^{\ominus}_{B_i}(v)} g_u(v),$$

where $g_u(v)$ is a random variable equal to $d(u)$ if u pulls the information from v, and 0 otherwise.

Observe that $\mathrm{E}[g_u(v)] = 1$, so that $\mathrm{E}[g(v)] = \left|N^{\ominus}_{B_i}(v)\right|$, and that the variance of $g_u(v)$ is

$$\begin{aligned}\mathrm{Var}[g_u(v)] &= \mathrm{E}[g_u(v)^2] - \mathrm{E}[g_u(v)]^2 \\ &= \frac{1}{d(u)} \cdot d(u)^2 - 1 \\ &= d(u) - 1.\end{aligned}$$

Since the $g_{u_1}(v), g_{u_2}(v), \ldots$ are independent, we have

$$\begin{aligned}\mathrm{Var}[g(v)] &= \sum_{u \in N^{\ominus}_{B_i}(v)} \mathrm{Var}[g_u(v)] = \sum_{u \in N^{\ominus}_{B_i}(v)} (d(u) - 1) \\ &\leq \mathrm{vol}(N^{\ominus}_{B_i}(v)) \\ &\leq \frac{1}{3}\left(d^+_{B_i}(v)\right)\left|N^{\ominus}_{B_i}(v)\right|.\end{aligned}$$

In the following chain of inequalities we will apply Chebyshev's inequality to bound the deviation of $g(v)$, using the variance bound we have just obtained:

$$\begin{aligned}&\Pr\left[g(v) \leq \frac{1}{20} \cdot d^+_{B_i}(v)\right] \leq \\ &\Pr\left[g(v) \leq \mathrm{E}[g(v)] - \mathrm{E}[g(v)] + \frac{1}{20} \cdot d^+_{B_i}(v)\right] \leq \\ &\Pr\left[-g(v) + \mathrm{E}[g(v)] \geq \left|N^{\ominus}_{B_i}(v)\right| - \frac{1}{20} \cdot d^+_{B_i}(v)\right] \leq \\ &\Pr\left[\left|g(v) - \mathrm{E}[g(v)]\right| \geq \left|N^{\ominus}_{B_i}(v)\right| - \frac{1}{20} \cdot d^+_{B_i}(v)\right] \leq \\ &\Pr\left[\left|g(v) - \mathrm{E}[g(v)]\right| \geq \frac{\left|N^{\ominus}_{B_i}(v)\right| - \frac{1}{20}d^+_{B_i}(v)}{\sqrt{\frac{1}{3}d^+_{B_i}(v)\left|N^{\ominus}_{B_i}(v)\right|}} \cdot \sqrt{\mathrm{Var}[g(v)]}\right] \leq \\ &\frac{\frac{1}{3}d^+_{B_i}(v)\left|N^{\ominus}_{B_i}(v)\right|}{\left(\left|N^{\ominus}_{B_i}(v)\right| - \frac{1}{20}d^+_{B_i}(v)\right)^2} \leq \\ &\frac{\frac{1}{6}\left(d^+_{B_i}(v)\right)^2}{\left(\frac{1}{2}d^+_{B_i}(v) - \frac{1}{20}d^+_{B_i}(v)\right)^2} \leq \\ &\left(\frac{20}{9 \cdot \sqrt{6}}\right)^2 \leq \frac{9}{10}.\end{aligned}$$

This concludes the proof of the second claim. The third one is combination of the other two. □

Now we focus on v, and its neighbourhood $N^+_{B_i}(v)$, for $\left\lceil\frac{10}{\phi}\right\rceil$ many steps. What is the gain $G(v)$ of v in these many steps?

LEMMA 6. $\Pr[G(v) \geq \frac{1}{20} \cdot d^+_{B_i}(v)] \geq 1 - e^{-1}$.

PROOF. Observe that the probability that the event "$g(v) \geq \frac{1}{20} \cdot d^+_{B_i}(v)$" happens at least once in $\left\lceil\frac{10}{\phi}\right\rceil$ independent trials is lower bounded by

$$1 - \left(1 - \frac{\phi}{10}\right)^{\left\lceil\frac{10}{\phi}\right\rceil} \geq 1 - \left(1 - \frac{\phi}{10}\right)^{\frac{10}{\phi}} \geq 1 - e^{-1}.$$

The claim follows. □

For the process to finish, at some step t it must happen that either $\mathrm{vol}(B_t) > |E|$ (in which case, we are done — so we assume the contrary), or $\mathrm{cut}(A_t, V - B_t) < \frac{3}{4} \cdot \mathrm{cut}(B_t, V - B_t)$. Analogously,

$$\frac{1}{4} \cdot \mathrm{cut}(B_t, V - B_t) \leq \mathrm{cut}(B_t - A_t, V - B_t) = \mathrm{cut}(H_t, V - B_t).$$

But then,

$$\begin{aligned}\frac{1}{4} \cdot \phi \cdot \mathrm{vol}(S) &\leq \frac{1}{4} \cdot \phi \cdot \mathrm{vol}(B_t) \\ &\leq \frac{1}{4} \cdot \mathrm{cut}(B_t, V - B_t) \\ &\leq \mathrm{cut}(H_t, V - B_t) \\ &= \sum_{v \in H_t \cap S} d^+_{B_t}(v) + \sum_{v \in H_t \cap (V-S)} d^+_{B_t}(v) \\ &\leq \sum_{v \in H_t \cap S} d^+_{B_t}(v) + \sum_{v \in H_t \cap (V-S)} \mathrm{vol}(v)\end{aligned}$$

Consider the following two inequalities (that might, or might not, hold):

(a) $\sum_{v\in H_t\cap(V-S)} \mathrm{vol}(v) \geq \frac{1}{1000}\cdot\phi\cdot\mathrm{vol}(S)$, and

(b) $\sum_{v\in H_t\cap S} d^+_{B_t}(v) \geq \frac{249}{1000}\cdot\phi\cdot\mathrm{vol}(S)$.

At least one of (a) and (b) has to be true. We call *two-cases property* the disjunction of (a) and (b). If (a) is true, we are done, in the sense that we have captured enough volume to cover a constant fraction of the cut induced by S.

We lower bound the probability of (a) to be false given the truth of (b), since the negation of (b) implies the truth of (a).

Recall lemma 6. It states that — for each $v_i \in H_t \cap S$ — we had probability at least $1-e^{-1}$ of gaining at least $\frac{1}{20}\cdot d^+_{B_i}(v_i) \geq \frac{1}{20}\cdot d^+_{B_t}(v_i)$, since $i \leq t$ implies $B_i \subseteq B_t$.

For each v_i, let us define the random variable X_i as follows: with probability $1-e^{-1}$, X_i has value $\frac{1}{20}\cdot d^+_{B_t}(v_i)$, and with the remaining probability it has value 0. Then, the gain of v_i is a random variable that dominates X_i. Choosing $q = 1-2e^{-1}$, in lemma 1, we can conclude that

$$\Pr\left[\sum_{i:\,v_i\in H_t\cap S} X_i \geq \frac{1}{2}\cdot\sum_{v_i\in H_t\cap S}\left(\frac{1}{20}\cdot d^+_{B_t}(v_i)\right)\right] \geq 1-2e^{-1}.$$

Thus, with constant probability ($\geq 1-2e^{-1}$) we gain at least $\frac{1}{40}\cdot\sum_{v_i} d^+_{B_t}(v_i)$, which in turn, is at least

$$\frac{1}{40}\cdot\sum_{v_i\in H_t\cap S} d^+_{B_t}(v_i) \geq \frac{1}{40}\cdot\frac{249}{1000}\cdot\phi\cdot\mathrm{vol}(S) \geq \frac{6}{1000}\cdot\phi\cdot\mathrm{vol}(S).$$

Hence, (a) is true with probability at least $1-2e^{-1}$. So with constant probability there is a gain of $\frac{1}{1000}\cdot\phi\cdot\mathrm{vol}(S)$ in $\frac{1}{\phi}$ steps. Thus using the proof strategy presented at the beginning of the section we get a $O\left(\phi^{-2}\log n\right)$ bound on the completion time.

5. A TIGHTER BOUND

In this section we will present a tighter bound of

$$O\left(\frac{\log^2\frac{1}{\phi}}{\phi}\cdot\log n\right) = \tilde{O}\left(\frac{\log n}{\phi}\right).$$

Observe that, given the already noted diametral lower bound of $\Omega\left(\frac{\log n}{\phi}\right)$ on graphs of conductance $\phi \geq \frac{1}{n^{1-\epsilon}}$, the bound is almost tight (we only lose an exponentially small factor in ϕ^{-1}).

Our general strategy for showing the tighter bound will be close in spirit to the one we used for the $O\left(\frac{\log n}{\phi^2}\right)$ bound of the previous section.

The new strategy is as follows:

- we will prove in this section that, given any set S of informed nodes having volume at most $|E|$, for some $p = p(S) \geq \Omega(\phi)$, after $O(p^{-1})$ rounds (that we call a *p-phase*) the new set S' of informed vertices, $S' \supseteq S$, will have volume $\mathrm{vol}(S') \geq \left(1+\Omega\left(\frac{\phi}{p\cdot\log^2\phi^{-1}}\right)\right)\cdot\mathrm{vol}(S)$ with constant probability (over the random choices performed by nodes during those $O(p^{-1})$ rounds) — if this happens, we say that the phase was successful;
- given the previous statement, it follows that PUSH-PULL informs a set of nodes of volume larger than $|E|$, starting from any single node, in time $T \leq O(\phi^{-1}\cdot\log^2\phi^{-1}\cdot\log n)$ with high probability.

Indeed, at the end of a phase one has a multiplicative volume gain of

$$1+\Omega\left(\frac{\phi}{p\cdot\log^2\phi^{-1}}\right)$$

with constant probability $c > 0$. If one averages that gain over the $O(p^{-1})$ rounds of the phase, one can say that with constant probability c, each round in the phase resulted in a multiplicative volume gain of $1+\Omega\left(\frac{\phi}{\log^2\phi^{-1}}\right)$.

Of course, in this modified gain-accounting process, either one gets the $1+\Omega\left(\frac{\phi}{\log^2\phi^{-1}}\right)$ multiplicative volume gain at each round of the phase (this happens with probability c), or one does not gain anything during the phase. Furthermore, different phases will have different numbers of rounds. Still, one can use Chernoff bound to prove our desired upper bound on T, by partitioning phases in power-of-2 buckets according to their p's. The details of this argument are omitted in this version;

- by applying lemma 3, we can then show that each uninformed node can get the information in the same number of rounds, if a set S of volume $> |E|$ is informed — completing the proof.

Given $v \in U = U_B(A)$, we define $\widehat{N}^{\ominus}_U(v)$ (to be read "N-hat-push-U-v") and $\widehat{N}^{\oplus}_B(v)$(to be read "N-hat-pull-U-v") as follows

$$\widehat{N}^{\ominus}_B(v) = \{u \in N^+_B(v) \mid d(u) \geq \frac{1}{3}\cdot\phi^{-1}\cdot d^+_B(v)\}$$

and

$$\widehat{N}^{\oplus}_B(v) = \{u \in N^+_B(v) \mid d(u) < \frac{1}{3}\cdot\phi^{-1}\cdot d^+_B(v)\}.$$

Then, we define,

$$\widehat{U}^{\ominus} = \left\{v \in U \mid \left|\widehat{N}^{\ominus}_B(v)\right| \geq \left|\widehat{N}^{\oplus}_B(v)\right|\right\}$$

and

$$\widehat{U}^{\oplus} = \left\{v \in U \mid \left|\widehat{N}^{\oplus}_B(v)\right| > \left|\widehat{N}^{\ominus}_B(v)\right|\right\}.$$

As before, if $\mathrm{vol}(\widehat{U}^{\ominus}) \geq \frac{1}{2}\cdot\mathrm{vol}(U)$ we "apply" the PUSH strategy on U; otherwise, we "apply" the PULL strategy.

The following lemma is the crux of our analysis. It is a strengthening of lemma 5. A corollary of the lemma is that there exists a $p = p_v \geq \Omega(\phi)$, such that after p^{-1} rounds, with constant probability, node v lets us gain a new volume proportional to $\Theta\left(\frac{d^+_{B_i}(v)}{p\cdot\log\phi^{-1}}\right)$.

Lemma 5, that we used previously, only stated that with probability $\Omega(\phi)$ we gained a new volume of $\Theta(d^+_{B_i}(v))$ in a single step. Observe that if we do not allow v to go on for more than one step than the bounds of lemma 5 are sharp.

The insight of lemma 7 is that different nodes might require different number of rounds to give their "full" contribution in terms of new volume, but the more we have to wait for, the more we gain.

LEMMA 7. *Assume $v \in U_i$. Then, $\widehat{N}^{\oplus}_{B_i}(v)$ can be partitioned in at most $6 + \log \phi^{-1}$ parts, $S_1, S_2, \ldots$, in such a way that for each part i it holds that, for some $P_{S_i} \in (2^{-i+1}, 2^{-i}]$,*

$$\Pr\left[G_{S_i}(v) \geq \frac{|S_i|}{256 \cdot P_{S_i}}\right] \geq 1 - 2e^{-1},$$

where $G_{S_i}(v)$ is the total volume of nodes in S_i that perform a PULL *from v in $P^{-1}_{S_i}$ rounds.*

PROOF. If $v \in \widehat{U}^{\oplus}_i$, the same reasoning of lemma 5 applies. We assume that $v \in \widehat{U}^{\oplus}_i$.

We bucket the nodes in $\widehat{N}^{\oplus}_{B_i}(v)$ in $K = K_{B_i}(v) = \left\lceil \lg \frac{d^+_{B_i}(v)}{3 \cdot \phi} \right\rceil$ buckets in a power-of-two manner. That is, for $j = 1, \ldots, K$, R_j contains all the nodes u in $\widehat{N}^{\oplus}_{B_i}(v)$ having degree $2^{j-1} \leq d(u) < 2^j$. Observe that the R_j's are pairwise disjoint and that their union is equal to $\widehat{N}^{\oplus}_{B_i}(v)$.

Consider the buckets R_j, with $j > \lg \phi^{-1}$. We will empty some of them, in such a way that the total number of nodes removed from the union of the bucket is an ϵ fraction of the total (that is, of $d^+_{B_i}(v)$). This node removal step is necessary for the following reason: the buckets R_j, with $j > \lg \phi^{-1}$, contain nodes with a degree so high that any single one of them will perform a PULL operation on v itself with probability strictly smaller than ϕ. Roughly the motive behind this node removal is as follows: we want to guarantee that the probability of a "gain" is at least ϕ we are forced to remove nodes having too high degree, if their number is so small that — overall — the probability of any single one of them to actually perform a PULL on v is smaller than ϕ.

The node removal phase is as follows. If R'_j is the set of nodes in the j-th bucket after the node removal phase, then

$$R'_j = \begin{cases} R_j & |R_j| \geq \frac{1}{16} \cdot 2^j \cdot \phi \\ \varnothing & \text{otherwise} \end{cases}$$

Observe that the total number of nodes we remove is upper bounded by

$$\begin{aligned} \sum_{i=1}^{K} \left(\frac{1}{16} \cdot 2^i \cdot \phi\right) &\leq \frac{\phi}{16} \sum_{i=0}^{K} 2^i \leq \frac{\phi}{8} 2^{K+1} \\ &\leq \frac{\phi}{8} \cdot 4 \cdot \frac{d^+_{B_i}(v)}{3 \cdot \phi} = \frac{1}{6} \cdot d^+_{B_i}(v). \end{aligned}$$

Therefore, $\sum_j |R'_j| \geq \frac{1}{3} d^+_{B_i}(v)$, since $\sum_j |R_j| \geq \frac{1}{2} d^+_{B_i}(v)$.

Consider the random variable $g(v)$, which represent the total volume of the nodes in the different R'_j's that manage to pull the information from v. If we denote by $g_j(v)$ the contribution of the nodes in bucket R'_j to $g(v)$, we have $g(v) = \sum_{j=1}^{K} g_j(v)$.

Take any non-empty bucket R'_j. We want to show, via lemma 2, that

$$\Pr\left[g_j(v) \geq \frac{1}{128} \cdot \frac{|R'_j|}{p_j}\right] \geq p_j.$$

(If this event occurs, we say that bucket j succeeds.)

This claim follows directly from 2 by creating one X_i in the lemma for each $u \in R'_j$, and letting $X_i = 1$ iff node u pulls the information from v. The probability of this event is $p_i \in (2^{-j}, 2^{-j+1}]$, so we can safely choose the p of lemma 2 to be $p = 2^{-j+1}$.

Consider the different p_j's of the buckets. Fix some j. If p_j came out of case 2 then, since $|R'_j| \geq \frac{1}{16} \cdot 2^j \cdot \phi$, we have $p_j \geq \frac{1}{32} \cdot \phi$. If p_j came out of case 1, then $p_j = \frac{1}{32}$. In general, $p_j \geq \frac{\phi}{32}$, and $p_j \leq 1$.

Let us divide the unit into segments of exponentially decreasing length: that is, $[1, \frac{1}{2}), [\frac{1}{2}, \frac{1}{4}), \ldots, [2^{-j+1}, 2^{-j}), \ldots$. For each j, let us put each bucket R'_j into the segment containing its p_j. Observe that there are at most $\left\lceil \lg \frac{32}{\phi} \right\rceil \leq 6 + \lg \phi^{-1}$ segments.

Fix any non-empty segment ℓ. Let S_ℓ be the union of the buckets in segment ℓ. Observe that if we let the nodes in the buckets of S_ℓ run the process for 2^ℓ times, we have that, for each bucket R'_j,

$$\Pr\left[G_j(v) \geq \frac{1}{128} \cdot \frac{|R'_j|}{p_j}\right] \geq 1 - (1 - p_j)^{2^\ell} \geq 1 - e^{-1},$$

where $G_j(v)$ is the total volume of nodes in R'_j that perform a PULL from v in 2^ℓ rounds.

Now, we can apply lemma 1, choosing X_j to be equal $v_j = \frac{1}{128} \cdot \frac{|R'_j|}{p_j}$ if bucket R'_j in segment ℓ (buckets can be ordered arbitrarily) is such that $G_j(v) \geq v_j$, and 0 otherwise. Choosing $p = 1 - e^{-1}$ and $q = 1 - 2e^{-1}$, we obtain:

$$\Pr\left[G_{S_\ell}(v) \geq \frac{1}{256} \cdot \frac{|S_\ell|}{2^{-\ell}}\right] \geq 1 - 2e^{-1}.$$

□

The following corollary follows from lemma 7.

COROLLARY 8. *Assume $v_i \in U_i$. Then, there exists $p_i \in (\frac{\phi}{64}, 1]$ such that*

$$\Pr\left[G(v_i) \geq \frac{d^+_{B_i}(v_i)}{5000 \cdot p_i \cdot \lg \frac{2}{\phi}}\right] \geq 1 - 2e^{-1}.$$

where $G(v_i)$ is the total volume of nodes in $N^+_{B_i}(v_i)$ that perform a PULL *from v_i, or that v_i pushes the information to, in p_i^{-1} rounds.*

PROOF. If $v_i \in \widehat{U}^{\oplus}_i$, the same reasoning of lemma 5 applies. If $v_i \in \widehat{U}^{\oplus}_i$, then we apply lemma 7 choosing the part S with the largest cardinality. By the bound on the number of partitions, we will have

$$S \geq \frac{d^+_{B_i}(v_i)}{3} \cdot \frac{1}{6 + \lg \phi^{-1}} \geq \frac{d^+_{B_i}(v_i)}{18 \cdot \lg \frac{2}{\phi}},$$

which implies the corollary. □

The previous corollary is a generalization of lemma 5, which would lead to our result if we could prove an analogous of the *two-cases property* of the previous section. Unfortunately, the final gain we might need to aim for, could be larger than the cut — this inhibits the use of the *two-cases property*.

We say that an edge in the cut $(S, V-S)$ is *easy* if its endpoint w in $V-S$ is such that $\frac{d_S^-(w)}{d(w)} \geq \phi$. Then, to overcome the just noted issue, we consider two cases separately: (a) at least half of the edges in the cut are easy, or (b) less than half of the edges in the cut are easy.

In case (a) we bucket the easy nodes in $\Gamma(S)$ (the neighbourhood of S) in $\lceil \lg \frac{1}{\phi} \rceil$ buckets in the following way. Bucket D_i, $i = 1, \ldots, \lceil \lg \frac{1}{\phi} \rceil$, will contain all the nodes w in $\Gamma(S)$ such that $2^{-i} < \frac{d_S^-(w)}{d(w)} \leq 2^{-i+1}$. Now let D_j be the bucket of highest volume (breaking ties arbitrarily).

For any node $v \in D_j$ we have that its probability to pull the information in one step is at least 2^{-j}. So, the probability of v to pull the information in 2^j rounds is at least $1 - e^{-1}$. Hence, by applying lemma 1, we get that with probability greater than or equal to $1 - 2e^{-1}$ we gain a set of new nodes of volume at least $\frac{\text{vol}(D_j)}{2}$ in 2^j rounds. But,

$$\frac{\text{vol}(D_j)}{2} \geq 2^j \cdot \frac{\text{cut}(S, D_j)}{2} \geq 2^j \cdot \frac{\text{cut}(S, \Gamma(S))}{2\lceil \lg \frac{1}{\phi} \rceil} \geq 2^j \cdot \frac{\phi \cdot \text{vol}(S)}{2\lceil \lg \frac{1}{\phi} \rceil}.$$

Thus in this first case we gain with probability at least $1 - 2e^{-1}$ a set of new nodes of volume at least $2^j \cdot \frac{\phi \cdot \text{vol}(S)}{2\lceil \lg \frac{1}{\phi} \rceil}$ in 2^j rounds. By the reasoning presented at the beginning of section 5 the claim follows.

Now let us consider the second case, recall that in this case half of the edges in the cut point to nodes u in $\Gamma(S)$ having $\frac{d^-(u)}{d(u)} \geq \frac{1}{\phi}$.

We then replace the original *two-cases property* with the *strong two-cases property*:

(a') $\sum_{v \in H_t \cap (V-S)} d_{B_t}^-(v) \geq \frac{1}{1000} \cdot \text{cut}(S, V-S)$, and

(b') $\sum_{v \in H_t \cap S} d_{B_t}^+(v) \geq \frac{249}{1000} \cdot \text{cut}(S, V-S)$.

As before, at least one of (a') and (b') has to be true. If (a') happens to be true then we are done since the total volume of the new nodes obtains will be greater than or equal $\sum_{v \in H_t \cap (V-S)} d(v) \geq \phi^{-1} \sum_{v \in H_t \cap (V-S)} d_{B_t}^-(v) \geq \frac{1}{1000} \cdot \phi^{-1} \cdot \text{cut}(S, V-S)$. By Corollary 8, we will wait at most w rounds for the cut $(S, V-S)$, for some $w \leq O(\phi^{-1})$. Thus, if (a') holds, we are guaranteed to obtain a new set of nodes of total volume $\Omega\left(\frac{\text{cut}(S,V-S)}{w}\right)$ in w rounds. Which implies our main claim.

We now show that if (b') holds, then with $\Theta(1)$ probability our total gain will be at least $\Omega\left(\frac{\text{cut}(S,V-S)}{w \log^2 \phi^{-1}}\right)$ in w rounds, for some $w \leq (\phi^{-1})$.

Observe that each $v_i \in H_t \cap S$, when it was considered by the process, was given some probability $p_i \in \left(\frac{\phi}{64}, 1\right]$ by Corollary 8. We partition $H_t \cap S$ in buckets according to probabilities p_i. The j-th bucket will contain all the nodes v_i in $H_t \cap S$ such that $2^{-j} < p_i \leq 2^{-j+1}$. Recalling that B_i is the set of informed nodes when node v_i is considered, we let F be the bucket that maximizes $\sum_{v_i \in F} d_{B_t}^+(v_i)$.

Then,

$$\sum_{v_i \in F} d_{B_t}^+(v_i) \geq \frac{249}{1000\lceil \lg \frac{64}{\phi} \rceil} \cdot \text{cut}(S, V-S) \qquad (1)$$

By Corollary 8, we have that for each $v_i \in F$, there exists $p = p(F) \geq \frac{\phi}{64}$, such that with probability at least $1 - 2e^{-1}$, after $\lceil \frac{2}{p} \rceil$ round, we gain at least $\frac{1}{5000 \cdot p \cdot \lg \frac{2}{\phi}} \cdot d_{B_i}^+(v_i) \geq \frac{1}{5000 \cdot p \cdot \lg \frac{2}{\phi}} \cdot d_{B_t}^+(v_i)$ (since $i \leq t$ implies $B_i \subseteq B_t$). For each v_i, let us define the random variable X_i as follows: with probability $1 - 2e^{-1}$, X_i has value $\frac{1}{5000 \cdot p \cdot \lg \frac{2}{\phi}} \cdot d_{B_t}^+(v_i)$, and with the remaining probability it has value 0. Then, the gain of v_i is a random variable that dominates X_i. Choosing $q = 1 - \frac{5}{2}e^{-1}$, in lemma 1, we can conclude that

$$\Pr\left[\sum_{i: v_i \in F} X_i \geq \frac{4}{5} \cdot \sum_{v_i \in F}\left(\frac{1}{5000 \cdot p \cdot \lg \frac{2}{\phi}} \cdot d_{B_t}^+(v_i)\right)\right]$$
$$\geq 1 - \frac{5}{2}e^{-1} \geq 0.08.$$

Thus, in $\lceil \frac{2}{p} \rceil$ rounds, with constant probability we gain at least

$$\frac{1}{6250 \cdot \lg \frac{2}{\phi}} \cdot \sum_{v_i \in F} \frac{d_{B_t}^+(v_i)}{p},$$

which by equation 1, it is lower bounded by

$$\frac{1}{6250 \cdot p \cdot \lg \frac{2}{\phi}} \cdot \frac{249}{1000\lceil \lg \frac{64}{\phi} \rceil} \cdot \text{cut}(S, V-S) \geq$$
$$\geq \Omega\left(\frac{\text{cut}(S, V-S)}{p \cdot \log^2 \phi^{-1}}\right)$$

Thus applying the reasoning presented at the beginning of the section the claim follows.

6. PUSH AND PULL BY THEMSELVES

We now comment on how one can change our analysis to get a bound of $O\left(c_\alpha \cdot \phi^{-1} \cdot \log^2 \phi^{-1} \cdot \log n\right)$ on the completion time of PUSH or PULL by themselves. Observe that, if degrees of neighboring nodes have a constant ratio, then the probability that a single node $v_i \in S$ (in our analysis) to make a viable PUSH or to be hit by a PULL is $\Theta(\alpha\phi)$ (indeed, v will have at least $\phi \cdot d(v)$ neighboring nodes in $V-S$, each having at most its degree times α — an easy calculation shows that the probability bound for both PUSH and PULL is then $\Theta(\alpha\phi)$). Using this observation our analysis can be concluded as in the previous section.

7. REFERENCES

[1] P. Berenbrink, R. Elsässer and T. Friedetzky. Efficient randomized broadcasting in random regular networks with applications in peer-to-peer systems. *Proceedings of PODC*, 2006.

[2] S. P. Boyd, A. Ghosh, B. Prabhakar and D. Shah. Gossip algorithms: design, analysis and applications. *IEEE Transactions on Information Theory*, 2005.

[3] F. Chierichetti, S. Lattanzi and A. Panconesi. Rumor Spreading in Social Networks. *Proceedings of ICALP*, 2009.

[4] F. Chierichetti, S. Lattanzi and A. Panconesi. Rumour Spreading and Graph Conductance. *Proceedings of SODA*, 2010.

[5] A. J. Demers, D. H. Greene, C. Hauser, W. Irish, J. Larson, S. Shenker, H. E. Sturgis, D. C. Swinehart and D. B. Terry. Epidemic Algorithms for Replicated Database Maintenance. *Proceedings of PODC*, 1987.

[6] B. Doerr, T. Friedrich and T. Sauerwald. Quasirandom Rumor Spreading. *Proceedings of SODA*, 2008.

[7] B. Doerr, T. Friedrich and T. Sauerwald. Quasirandom Rumor Spreading: Expanders, Push vs. Pull, and Robustness. *Proceedings of ICALP*, 2009.

[8] R. Elsässer. On the Communication Complexity of Randomized Broadcasting in Random-like Graphs. *Proceedings of SPAA*, 2006.

[9] U. Feige, D. Peleg, P. Raghavan and E. Upfal. Randomized Broadcast in Networks. *Algorithms*, 1990.

[10] T. Friedrich and T. Sauerwald. Near-perfect load balancing by randomized rounding. *Proceedings of STOC*, 2009.

[11] A. Frieze and G. Grimmett. The shortest-path problem for graphs with random arc-lengths. *Algorithms*, 1985.

[12] R. Karp, C. Schindelhauer, S. Shenker and B. Vöcking. Randomized Rumor Spreading. *Proceedings of FOCS*, 2000.

[13] D. Kempe, A. Dobra and J. Gehrke. Gossip-based computation of aggregate information. *Proceedings of FOCS*, 2003.

[14] J. Leskovec, K. J. Lang, A. Dasgupta and M. W. Mahoney. Statistical properties of community structure in large social and information networks. *Proceedings of WWW*, 2008.

[15] M. Mihail, C. H. Papadimitriou and A. Saberi. On certain connectivity properties of the Internet topology. *J. Comput. Syst. Sci.*, 2006.

[16] D. Mosk-Aoyama and D. Shah. Fast Distributed Algorithms for Computing Separable Functions. *Transactions on Information Theory*, 2008.

[17] B. Pittel. On Spreading a Rumor. *SIAM Journal on Applied Mathematics*, 1987.

[18] T. Sauerwald. On Mixing and Edge Expansion Properties in Randomized Broadcasting. *Proceedings of ISAAC*, 2007.

[19] D. A. Spielman and S.-H. Teng. Nearly-linear time algorithms for graph partitioning, graph sparsification, and solving linear systems. *Proceedings of STOC*, 2004.

On the List-Decodability of Random Linear Codes

Venkatesan Guruswami*
Computer Science Dept.
Carnegie Mellon University
guruswami@cmu.edu

Johan Håstad†
School of Computer Science
and Communication
KTH
johanh@kth.se

Swastik Kopparty‡
CSAIL
MIT
swastik@mit.edu

ABSTRACT

We show that the list-decodability of random linear codes is as good as that of general random codes. Specifically, for every fixed finite field $\mathbb{F}_q$, $p \in (0, 1 - 1/q)$ and $\varepsilon > 0$, we prove that with high probability a random linear code C in $\mathbb{F}_q^n$ of rate $(1 - H_q(p) - \varepsilon)$ can be list decoded from a fraction p of errors with lists of size at most $O(1/\varepsilon)$.

This also answers a basic open question concerning the *existence* of highly list-decodable linear codes, showing that a list-size of $O(1/\varepsilon)$ suffices to have rate within ε of the "list decoding capacity" $1 - H_q(p)$. The best previously known list-size bound was $q^{O(1/\varepsilon)}$ (except in the $q = 2$ case where a list-size bound of $O(1/\varepsilon)$ was known).

The main technical ingredient in our proof is a strong upper bound on the probability that ℓ random vectors chosen from a Hamming ball centered at the origin have too many (more than $\Theta(\ell)$) vectors from their linear span also belong to the ball.

Categories and Subject Descriptors

E.4 [**Data**]: Coding and Information Theory

General Terms

Theory

Keywords

List error-correction, Linear Codes, Probabilistic method, List decoding capacity.

*Research supported by a Packard Fellowship, NSF CCF 0953155, and US-Israel BSF grant 2008293.

†Research supported by ERC grant 226203.

‡Work was partially done while the author was an intern at Microsoft Research, New England.

STOC'10, June 5–8, 2010, Cambridge, Massachusetts, USA.

1. INTRODUCTION

One of the central problems in coding theory is to understand the trade-off between the redundancy built into codewords (a.k.a. the rate of the code) and the fraction of errors the code enables correcting. Suppose we are interested in codes over the binary alphabet (for concreteness) that enable recovery of the correct codeword $c \in \{0,1\}^n$ from any noisy received word r that differs from c in at most pn locations. For each c, there are about $\binom{n}{pn} \approx 2^{H(p)n}$ such possible received words r, where $H(x) = -x \log_2 x - (1-x)\log_2(1-x)$ stands for the binary entropy function. Now for each such r, the error-recovery procedure must identify c as a possible choice for the true codeword. In fact, even if the errors are randomly distributed and not worst case, the algorithm must identify c as a candidate codeword for most of these $2^{H(p)n}$ received words, if we seek a low decoding error probability. This implies that there can be at most $\approx 2^{(1-H(p))n}$ codewords, or equivalently the largest rate R of the code one can hope for is $1 - H(p)$.

If we could pack about $2^{(1-H(p))n}$ pairwise disjoint Hamming balls of radius pn in $\{0,1\}^n$, then one can achieve a rate approaching $1 - H(p)$ while guaranteeing correct and unambiguous recovery of the codeword from an arbitrary fraction p of errors. Unfortunately, it is well known that such an asymptotic "perfect packing" of Hamming balls in $\{0,1\}^n$ does not exist, and the largest size of such a packing is at most $2^{(\alpha(p)+o(1))n}$ for $\alpha(p) < 1 - H(p)$ (in fact $\alpha(p) = 0$ for $p \geqslant 1/4$). Nevertheless, it turns out that it is possible to pack $2^{(1-H(p)-\varepsilon)n}$ such Hamming balls such that no $O(1/\varepsilon)$ of them intersect at a point, for any $\varepsilon > 0$. In fact a random packing has such a property with high probability.

1.1 List Decoding

This fact implies that it is possible to achieve rate approaching the optimal $1 - H(p)$ bound for correcting a fraction p of *worst-case* errors in a model called *list decoding*. List decoding, which was introduced independently by Elias and Wonzencraft in the 1950s [6, 17], is an error-recovery model where the decoder is allowed to output a small list of candidate codewords that must include all codewords within Hamming distance pn of the received word. Note that if at most pn errors occur, the list decoder's output will include the correct codeword. In addition to the rate R of the code and the error fraction p, list decoding has an important third parameter, the "list-size," which is the largest number L of codewords the decoder is allowed to output on any received word. The list-size thus bounds the maximum ambiguity in the output of the decoder.

For codes over an alphabet of size q, all the above statements hold with $H(p)$ replaced by $H_q(p)$, where $H_q(x) = x\log_q(q-1) - x\log_q x - (1-x)\log_q(1-x)$ is the q-ary entropy function.

DEFINITION 1 (COMBINATORIAL LIST DECODABILITY). *Let Σ be a finite alphabet of size q, $L \geqslant 1$ an integer, and $p \in (0, 1-1/q)$. A code $C \subseteq \Sigma^n$ is said to be (p, L)-list-decodable, if for every $x \in \Sigma^n$, there are at most L codewords of C that are at Hamming distance pn or less from x. Formally, $|B_n^q(x,p) \cap C| \leqslant L$ for every x, where $B_n^q(x,p) \subseteq \Sigma^n$ is the ball of radius pn centered at $x \in \{0,1\}^n$.*

We restrict $p < 1-1/q$ in the above definition since a random string differs from each codeword in at most a fraction $1-1/q$ of positions, and so over alphabet size q decoding from a fraction $1-1/q$ or more errors is impossible (except for trivial codes).

1.2 Combinatorics of list decoding

A fundamental question in list decoding is to understand the trade-off between rate, error-fraction, and list-size. For example, what list-size suffices if we want codes of rate within ε of the optimal $1 - H_q(p)$ bound? That is, if we define $L_{q,p}(\varepsilon)$ to be the minimum integer L for which there are q-ary (p, L)-list-decodable codes of rate at least $1 - H_q(p) - \varepsilon$ for infinitely many lengths n, how does $L_{q,p}(\varepsilon)$ behave for small ε (as we keep the alphabet size q and $p \in (0, 1-1/q)$ fixed)?

It is known that unbounded list-size is needed as one approaches the optimal rate of $1 - H_q(p)$. In other words, $L_{q,p}(\varepsilon) \to \infty$ as $\varepsilon \to 0$. This was shown for the binary case in [1], and his result implicitly implies $L_{2,p}(\varepsilon) \geqslant \Omega(\log(1/\varepsilon))$ (see [13] for an explicit derivation of this). For the q-ary case, $L_{q,p}(\varepsilon) = \omega_\varepsilon(1)$ was shown in [4, 5]. In the language of list-decoding, the above-mentioned result on "almost-disjoint" sphere packing states that for large enough block lengths, a random code of rate $1 - H_q(p) - \varepsilon$ is $(p, \frac{1}{\varepsilon})$-list-decodable with high probability. In other words, $L_{q,p}(\varepsilon) \leqslant 1/\varepsilon$. This result appears in [7] (and is based on a previous random coding argument for linear codes from [18]). The result is explicitly stated in [7] only for $q = 2$, but trivially extends for arbitrary alphabet size q. This result is also tight, in the sense that with high probability a *random* code of rate $1 - H_q(p) - \varepsilon$ is *not* $(p, c_{p,q}/\varepsilon)$-list-decodable w.h.p. for some constant $c_{p,q} > 0$ [13].

An interesting question is to close the exponential gap in the lower and upper bounds on $L_{2,p}(\varepsilon)$, and more generally pin down the asymptotic behavior of $L_{q,p}(\varepsilon)$ for every q. The upper bound of $O(1/\varepsilon)$ is perhaps closer to the truth, and it is probably the lower bound that needs strengthening.

1.3 Context of this work

In this work, we address another fundamental combinatorial question concerning list-decodable codes, namely the behavior of $L_{q,p}(\varepsilon)$ when restricted to *linear codes*. For q a prime power, a q-ary linear code is simply a subspace of $\mathbb{F}_q^n$ ($\mathbb{F}_q$ being the field of size q).

Most of the well-studied and practically used codes are linear codes. Linear codes admit a succinct representation in terms of its basis (called generator matrix). This aids in finding and representing such codes efficiently, and as a result linear codes are often useful as "inner" codes in concatenated code constructions.

In a linear code, by translation invariance, the neighborhood of every codeword looks the same, and this is often a very useful symmetry property. For instance, this property was recently used in [11] to give a black-box conversion of linear list-decodable codes to codes achieving capacity against a worst-case additive channel (the linearity of the list-decodable code is crucial for this connection). Lastly, list-decodability of linear codes brings to the fore some intriguing questions on the interplay between the geometry of linear spaces and Hamming balls, and is therefore interesting in its own right. For these and several other reasons, it is desirable to achieve good trade-offs for list decoding via linear codes.

Since linear codes are a highly structured subclass of all codes, proving the existence of linear codes which have list-decodability properties similar to general codes can be viewed as a strong "derandomization" of the random coding argument used to construct good list-decodable codes. A derandomized family of codes called "pseudolinear codes" were put forth in [10] since linear codes were not known to have strong enough list-decoding properties. Indeed, prior to this work, the results known for linear codes were substantially weaker than for general codes (we discuss the details next). *Closing this gap is the main motivation behind this work.*

1.4 Status of list-decodability of linear codes

Zyablov and Pinsker proved that a random binary linear code of rate $1 - H(p) - \varepsilon$ is $(p, 2^{O(1/\varepsilon)})$-list-decodable with high probability [18]. The proof extends in a straightforward way to linear codes over $\mathbb{F}_q$, giving list-size $q^{O(1/\varepsilon)}$ for rate $1 - H_q(p) - \varepsilon$. Let us define $L^{\mathrm{lin}}_{q,p}(\varepsilon)$ to be the minimum integer L for which there is an infinite family of (p, L)-list-decodable linear codes over $\mathbb{F}_q$ of rate at least $1 - H_q(p) - \varepsilon$. The results of [18] thus imply that $L^{\mathrm{lin}}_{q,p}(\varepsilon) \leqslant \exp(O_q(1/\varepsilon))$.

Note that this bound is *exponentially worse* than the $O(1/\varepsilon)$ bound known for general codes. In [7], Elias mentions the following as the most obvious problem left open left by the random coding results: *Is the requirement of the much larger list-size for linear codes inherent, or can one achieve list-size closer to the $O(1/\varepsilon)$ bound for general random codes?*

For the *binary* case, the *existence* of (p, L)-list-decodable linear codes of rate at least $1 - H(p) - 1/L$ is proven in [9]. This implies that $L^{\mathrm{lin}}_{2,p} \leqslant 1/\varepsilon$. There are some results which obtain lower bounds on the rate for the case of small fixed list-size (at most 3) [1, 2, 16]; these bounds are complicated and not easily stated, and as noted in [3], are weaker for the linear case for list-size as small as 5.

The proof in [9] is based on a carefully designed potential function that quantifies list-decodability, and uses the "semi-random" method to successively pick good basis vectors for the code. The proof only guarantees that such binary linear codes exist with positive probability, and does not yield a high probability guarantee for the claimed list-decodability property. Further, the proof relies crucially on the binary alphabet and extending it to work for larger alphabets (or even the ternary case) has resisted all attempts. Thus, for $q > 2$, $L_{q,p}(\varepsilon) \leqslant \exp(O_q(1/\varepsilon))$ remained the best known upper bound on list-size. A high probability result for the binary case, and an upper bound of $L_{q,p}(\varepsilon) \leqslant O(1/\varepsilon)$ for $\mathbb{F}_q$-linear codes, were conjectured in [8, Chap. 5].

1.5 Results

In this paper, we resolve the above open question concerning list-decodability of linear codes over *all* alphabets. In particular, we prove that $L^{\mathrm{lin}}_{q,p}(\varepsilon) \leqslant C_{q,p}/\varepsilon$ for a constant $C_{q,p} < \infty$. Up to constant factors, this matches the best known result for general, non-linear codes. Further, our result in fact shows that a random $\mathbb{F}_q$-linear code of rate $1 - H_q(p) - \varepsilon$ is $(p, C_{p,q}/\varepsilon))$-list-decodable *with high probability*. This was not known even for the case $q = 2$. The high probability claim implies an efficient randomized Monte Carlo construction of such list-decodable codes.

We now briefly explain the difficulty in obtaining good bounds for list-decoding linear codes and how we circumvent it. This is just a high level description; see the next section for a more technical description of our proof method.

Let us recall the straightforward random coding method that shows the list-decodability of random (binary) codes. We pick a code $C \subseteq \{0,1\}^n$ by uniformly and independently picking $M = 2^{Rn}$ codewords. To prove it is (p, L)-list-decodable, we fix a center y and a subset S of $(L+1)$ codewords of C. Since these codewords are independent, the probability that all of them land in the ball of radius pn around y is at most $(\frac{2^{H(p)n}}{2^n})^{L+1}$. A union bound over all 2^n choices of y and at most M^{L+1} choices of S shows that if $R \leqslant 1 - H(p) - 1/L$, the code fails to be (p, L)-list-decodable with probability at most $2^{-\Omega(n)}$.

Attempting a similar argument in the case of random linear codes, defined by a random linear map $A : \mathbb{F}_2^{Rn} \to \mathbb{F}_2^n$, faces several immediate obstacles. The 2^{Rn} codewords of a random linear code are not independent of one another; in fact the points of such a code are highly correlated and not even 3-wise independent (as $A(x+y) = Ax + Ay$). However, any $(L+1)$ distinct codewords $Ax_1, Ax_2, \ldots, Ax_{L+1}$ must contain a subset of $\ell \geqslant \log_2(L+1)$ independent codewords, corresponding to a subset $\{x_{i_1}, \ldots, x_{i_\ell}\}$ of *linearly independent* message vectors. This lets one mimic the argument for the random code case with $\log_2(L+1)$ playing the role of $L+1$. However, as a result, it leads to the exponentially worse list-size bounds.

To get a better result, we somehow need to control the "damage" caused by subsets of codewords of low rank. This is the crux of our new proof. Stated loosely and somewhat imprecisely, we prove a strong upper bound on the fraction of such low rank subsets, by proving that if we pick ℓ random vectors from the Hamming ball $B_n(0,p)$ (for some constant ℓ related to our target list-size L), it is rather unlikely that more than $\Theta(\ell)$ of the 2^ℓ vectors in their span will also belong to the ball $B_n(0,p)$. (See Theorem 3 for the precise statement.) This "limited correlation" between linear subspaces and Hamming balls is the main technical ingredient in our proof. It seems like a basic and powerful probabilistic fact that might find other applications. The argument also extends to linear codes over $\mathbb{F}_q$ after some adaptations.

2. RESULTS AND METHODS

Our main result is that random linear codes in $\mathbb{F}_2^n$ of rate $1 - H(p) - \varepsilon$ can be list-decoded from p-fraction errors with list-size only $O(\frac{1}{\varepsilon})$. We also show the analogous result for random q-ary linear codes.

THEOREM 2. *Let $p \in (0, 1/2)$. Then there exist constants $C_p, \delta > 0$, such that for all $\varepsilon > 0$ and all large enough integers n, letting $R = 1 - H(p) - \varepsilon$, if $\mathcal{C} \subseteq \mathbb{F}_2^n$ is a random linear code of rate R, then*

$$\Pr[\mathcal{C} \textit{ is } (p, \tfrac{C_p}{\varepsilon})\textit{-list-decodable}] > 1 - 2^{-\delta n}.$$

The proof begins by simplifying the problem to its combinatorial core. Specifically, we reduce the problem of studying the *list-decodability* of a random linear code of *linear* dimension to the problem of studying the *weight-distribution* of certain random linear codes of *constant* dimension. The next theorem analyzes the weight distribution of these constant dimensional random linear codes. The notation $B_n(x,p)$ refers to the Hamming ball of radius pn centered at $x \in \mathbb{F}_2^n$.

THEOREM 3 (SPAN OF RANDOM SUBSET OF $B_n(0,p)$). *For every $p \in (0, 1/2)$, there is a constant $C > 0$, such that for all n large enough and all $\ell = o(\sqrt{n})$, if $X_1, \ldots, X_\ell$ are picked independently and uniformly at random from $B_n(0,p)$, then*

$$\Pr[|\mathrm{span}(\{X_1, \ldots, X_\ell\}) \cap B_n(0,p)| > C \cdot \ell] \leqslant 2^{-5n}.$$

We now give a brief sketch of the proof of Theorem 3. Index the elements of $\mathrm{span}(\{X_1, \ldots, X_\ell\})$ as follows: for $v \in \mathbb{F}_2^\ell$, let X_v denote the random vector $\sum_{i=1}^\ell v_i X_i$. Fix an arbitrary $S \subseteq \mathbb{F}_2^\ell$ of cardinality $C \cdot \ell$, and let us study the event E_S: that all the vectors $(X_v)_{v \in S}$ lie in $B_n(0,p)$. If none of the events E_S occur, we know that $|\mathrm{span}(\{X_1, \ldots, X_\ell\}) \cap B_n(0,p)| \leqslant C \cdot \ell$.

The key technical step is a Ramsey-theoretic statememt (Lemma 5, stated below) which says that large sets S automatically have the property that some translate of S contains a certain structured subset (which we call an "increasing chain"). This structured subset allows us to give strong upper bounds on the probability that all the vectors $(X_v)_{v \in S}$ lie in $B_n(0,p)$. Applying this to each $S \subseteq \mathbb{F}_2^\ell$ of cardinality $C\ell$ and taking a union bound gives Theorem 3.

To state the Ramsey-theoretic lemma (Lemma 5), we first define increasing chains. For a vector $v \in \mathbb{F}_2^\ell$, the *support* of v, denoted $\mathrm{supp}(v)$, is defined to be the set of its nonzero coordinates.

DEFINITION 4. *A sequence of vectors $v_1, \ldots, v_d \in \mathbb{F}_2^\ell$ is called an c-increasing chain of length d, if for all $j \in [d]$,*

$$\left|\mathrm{supp}(v_j) \setminus \left(\bigcup_{i=1}^{j-1} \mathrm{supp}(v_i)\right)\right| \geqslant c.$$

We now state the Ramsey-theoretic lemma that plays the central role in Theorem 3. The proof appears in Section 5, where it is proved using the Sauer-Shelah lemma.

LEMMA 5. *For all positive integers c, ℓ and $L \leqslant 2^\ell$, the following holds. For every $S \subseteq \mathbb{F}_2^\ell$ with $|S| = L$, there is a $w \in \mathbb{F}_2^\ell$ such that $S + w$ has an c-increasing chain of length at least $\frac{1}{c}(\log \frac{L}{2}) - (1 - \frac{1}{c})(\log \ell)$.*

2.1 Larger alphabet

Due to their geometric nature, our arguments generalize to the case of q-ary alphabet (for arbitrary constant q) quite easily. Below we state our main theorem for the case of q-ary alphabet.

THEOREM 6. *Let q be a prime power and let $p \in (0, 1 - 1/q)$. Then there exist constants $C_{p,q}, \delta > 0$, such that for* *all $\varepsilon > 0$, letting $R = 1 - H_q(p) - \varepsilon$, if $\mathcal{C} \subseteq \mathbb{F}_q^n$ is a random linear code of rate R, then*

$$\Pr[\mathcal{C} \text{ is } (p, \tfrac{C_{p,q}}{\varepsilon})\text{-list-decodable}] > 1 - 2^{-\delta n}.$$

The proof of Theorem 6 has the same basic outline as the proof of Theorem 2. In particular, it proceeds via a q-ary analog of Theorem 3. The only notable deviation occurs in the proof of the q-ary analog of Lemma 5. The traditional generalization of the Sauer-Shelah lemma to larger alphabets turns out to be unsuitable for this purpose. Instead, we formulate and prove a non-standard generalization of the Sauer-Shelah lemma for the larger alphabet case which is more appropriate for this situation. Details appear in Section 6.

3. PROOF OF THEOREM 2

Let us start by restating our main theorem.

THEOREM 2 (RESTATED) *Let $p \in (0, 1/2)$. Then there exist constants $C_p, \delta > 0$, such that for all $\varepsilon > 0$ and all large enough integers n, letting $R = 1 - H(p) - \varepsilon$, if $\mathcal{C} \subseteq \mathbb{F}_2^n$ is a random linear code of rate R, then*

$$\Pr[\mathcal{C} \text{ is } (p, \tfrac{C_p}{\varepsilon})\text{-list-decodable}] > 1 - 2^{-\delta n}.$$

PROOF. Pick $C_p = 4C$, where C is the constant from Theorem 3. Pick $\delta = 1$. Take $L = \frac{C_p}{\varepsilon}$.

Let $\mathcal{C}$ be a random Rn dimensional linear subspace of $\mathbb{F}_2^n$. We want to show that

$$\Pr_{\mathcal{C}}[\exists x \in \mathbb{F}_2^n \text{ s.t. } |B_n(x,p) \cap \mathcal{C}| > L] < 2^{-\delta n}. \quad (1)$$

Let $x \in \mathbb{F}_2^n$ be picked uniformly at random. We will work towards Equation (1) by studying the following quantity.

$$\Delta \stackrel{\text{def}}{=} \Pr_{\mathcal{C},x}[|B_n(x,p) \cap \mathcal{C}| > L].$$

Note that to prove Equation (1), it suffices to show that[1]

$$\Delta < 2^{-\delta n} \cdot 2^{-n}.$$

Now for each $\ell \in [\log(L+1), L+1]$, let $\mathcal{F}_\ell$ be the set of all $(v_1, \ldots, v_\ell) \in B_n(0,p)^\ell$ such that $v_1, \ldots, v_\ell$ are linearly independent and $|\text{span}(v_1, \ldots, v_\ell) \cap B_n(0,p)| > L$. Let $\mathcal{F} = \bigcup_{\ell=\log(L+1)}^{L+1} \mathcal{F}_\ell$

For each $\mathbf{v} = (v_1, \ldots, v_\ell) \in \mathcal{F}$, let $\{\mathbf{v}\}$ denote the set $\{v_1, \ldots, v_\ell\}$.

We now bound Δ. Notice that if $|B_n(x,p) \cap \mathcal{C}| > L$, then there must be some $\mathbf{v} \in \mathcal{F}$ for which $B_n(x,p) \cap \mathcal{C} \supseteq x + \{\mathbf{v}\}$. Indeed, we can simply take $\mathbf{v}$ to be a maximal linearly independent subset of $(B_n(x,p) \cap \mathcal{C}) + x$ if this set has size at most $L+1$, and any linearly independent subset of $(B_n(x,p) \cap \mathcal{C}) + x$ of size $L+1$ otherwise.

Therefore, by the union bound,

$$\begin{aligned}\Delta &\leqslant \sum_{\mathbf{v} \in \mathcal{F}} \Pr_{\mathcal{C},x}[B_n(x,p) \cap \mathcal{C} \supseteq x + \{\mathbf{v}\}] \\ &= \sum_{\mathbf{v} \in \mathcal{F}} \Pr_{\mathcal{C},x}[B_n(0,p) \cap (\mathcal{C} + x) \supseteq \{\mathbf{v}\}] \\ &\leqslant \sum_{\mathbf{v} \in \mathcal{F}} \Pr_{\mathcal{C},x}[B_n(0,p) \cap (\mathcal{C} + \{0,x\}) \supseteq \{\mathbf{v}\}] \\ &\leqslant \sum_{\mathbf{v} \in \mathcal{F}} \Pr_{\mathcal{C}^*}[B_n(0,p) \cap \mathcal{C}^* \supseteq \{\mathbf{v}\}], \end{aligned} \quad (2)$$

where $\mathcal{C}^*$ is a random $Rn+1$ dimensional subspace containing $\mathcal{C} + \{0,x\}$ (explicitly, if $x \notin \mathcal{C}$, then $\mathcal{C}^* = \mathcal{C} + \{0,x\}$; otherwise $\mathcal{C}^* = \mathcal{C} + \{0,y\}$ where y is picked uniformly from $\mathbb{F}_2^n \setminus \mathcal{C}$). In particular, $\mathcal{C}^*$ is a uniformly random $Rn+1$ dimensional subspace.

The last probability can be bounded as follows. By the linear independence of $v_1, \ldots, v_\ell$, the probability that $v_j \in \mathcal{C}^*$ conditioned on $\{v_1, \ldots, v_{j-1}\} \subseteq \mathcal{C}^*$ is precisely the probability that a given point in a $n+1-j$ dimensional space lies in a $Rn+1-j$ dimensional subspace, and hence this conditional probability is exactly 2^{Rn+1-n}. We can hence conclude that

$$\Pr_{\mathcal{C}^*}[\mathcal{C}^* \supseteq \{\mathbf{v}\}] = \left(\frac{2^{Rn+1}}{2^n}\right)^\ell. \quad (3)$$

Putting together Equations (2) and (3), we have

$$\begin{aligned}\Delta &\leqslant \sum_{\mathbf{v} \in \mathcal{F}} \Pr_{\mathcal{C}^*}[B_n(0,p) \cap \mathcal{C}^* \supseteq \{\mathbf{v}\}] \\ &\leqslant \sum_{\ell=\log(L+1)}^{L+1} \sum_{\mathbf{v} \in \mathcal{F}_\ell} \Pr_{\mathcal{C}^*}[\mathcal{C}^* \supseteq \{\mathbf{v}\}] \\ &\leqslant \sum_{\ell=\log(L+1)}^{L+1} \sum_{\mathbf{v} \in \mathcal{F}_\ell} \left(\frac{2^{Rn+1}}{2^n}\right)^\ell \leqslant \sum_{\ell=\log(L+1)}^{L+1} |\mathcal{F}_\ell| \cdot \left(\frac{2^{Rn+1}}{2^n}\right)^\ell \end{aligned}$$

We now obtain an upper bound on $|\mathcal{F}_\ell|$. We have two cases depending on the size of ℓ.

- **Case 1:** $\ell < 4/\varepsilon$.

  In this case, note that $\frac{|\mathcal{F}_\ell|}{|B_n(0,p)|^\ell}$ is a lower bound on the probability that ℓ points $X_1, \ldots, X_\ell$ chosen uniformly at random from $B_n(0,p)$ are such that

  $$|\text{span}(\{X_1, \ldots, X_\ell\}) \cap B_n(0,p)| > L.$$

  Since $L > C \cdot \ell$, Theorem 3 tells us that this probability is bounded from above by 2^{-5n}. Thus, in this case

  $$|\mathcal{F}_\ell| \leqslant |B_n(0,p)|^\ell 2^{-5n} \leqslant 2^{n\ell H(p)} \cdot 2^{-5n}.$$

- **Case 2:** $\ell \geqslant 4/\varepsilon$. In this case, we have the trivial bound of $|\mathcal{F}_\ell| \leqslant |B_n(0,p)|^\ell \leqslant 2^{n\ell H(p)}$.

[1] We could even replace the 2^{-n} by $2^{-(1-R)n}$. Indeed, for every $\mathcal{C}$ for which there is a "bad" x, we know that there are 2^{Rn} "bad" x's (the translates of x by $\mathcal{C}$).

Thus, we may bound Δ by:

$$\begin{aligned}\Delta &\leqslant \sum_{\ell=\log L}^{\lfloor 4/\varepsilon\rfloor} |\mathcal{F}_\ell|\cdot\left(\frac{2^{Rn+1}}{2^n}\right)^\ell + \sum_{\ell=\lceil 4/\varepsilon\rceil}^{L} |\mathcal{F}_\ell|\cdot\left(\frac{2^{Rn+1}}{2^n}\right)^\ell\\ &\leqslant \sum_{\ell=\log L}^{\lfloor 4/\varepsilon\rfloor} 2^{n\ell H(p)}2^{-5n}\left(\frac{2^{Rn+1}}{2^n}\right)^\ell + \sum_{\ell=\lceil 4/\varepsilon\rceil}^{L} 2^{n\ell H(p)}\left(\frac{2^{Rn+1}}{2^n}\right)^\ell\\ &\leqslant 2^{-5n}\cdot 4/\varepsilon + L\cdot 2^{-(\varepsilon n)\cdot(4/\varepsilon)}\\ &\leqslant 2^{-\delta n}\cdot 2^{-n}\end{aligned}$$

as desired. □

4. PROOF OF THEOREM 3

In this section, we prove Theorem 3 which bounds the probability that the span of ℓ random points in $B_n(0,p)$ intersects $B_n(0,p)$ in more than $C\cdot\ell$ points, for some large constant C. We use the following simple fact.

LEMMA 7. *For every $p\in(0,1/2)$, there is a $\delta_p>0$ such that for all large enough integers n and every $x\in\mathbb{F}_2^n$, the probability that two uniform independent samples w_1,w_2 from $B_n(0,p)$ are such that $w_1+w_2\in B_n(x,p)$ is at most $2^{-\delta_p n}$.*

SKETCH OF PROOF. The point w_1+w_2 is essentially a random point in $B_n(0,2p-2p^2)$. The probability that it lies in the smaller ball $B_n(x,p)$ is easily seen to be maximal when $x=0$ and is then exponentially small. □

THEOREM 3 (RESTATED) *For every $p\in(0,1/2)$, there is a constant $C>0$, such that for all n large enough and all $\ell=o(\sqrt{n})$, if $X_1,\ldots,X_\ell$ are picked independently and uniformly at random from $B_n(0,p)$, then*

$$\Pr[|\mathrm{span}(\{X_1,\ldots,X_\ell\})\cap B_n(0,p)|>C\cdot\ell]\leqslant 2^{-5n}.$$

PROOF. Set $L=C\cdot\ell$ and let $c=2$. Let $\delta_p>0$ be the constant given by Lemma 7. Let

$$d=\left\lfloor\frac{1}{c}\log\frac{L}{2}-\left(1-\frac{1}{c}\right)\log\ell\right\rfloor\geqslant\frac{1}{2}\log\frac{L}{2\ell}-1=\frac{1}{2}\log\frac{C}{8}.$$

For a vector $u\in\mathbb{F}_2^\ell$, let X_u denote the random variable $\sum_i u_iX_i$.

We begin with a claim which bounds the probability of a particular collection of linear combinations of the X_i all lying within $B_n(0,p)$. At the heart of this claim lies the Ramsey-theoretic Lemma 5.

CLAIM 8. *For each $S\subseteq\mathbb{F}_2^\ell$ with $|S|=L+1$,*

$$\Pr[\forall v\in S, X_v\in B_n(0,p)]<2^n\cdot 2^{-\delta_p dn}. \tag{4}$$

PROOF. Let w and $v_1,\ldots,v_d\in S$ be as given by Lemma 5. That is, $v_1+w,v_2+w,\cdots,v_d+w$ is an c-increasing sequence. Then,

$$\begin{aligned}&\Pr[\forall v\in S,\ X_v\in B_n(0,p)]\\ &\qquad\leqslant\Pr[\forall j\in[d],X_{v_j}\in B_n(0,p)]\\ &\qquad=\Pr[\forall j\in[d],X_{v_j}+X_w\in B_n(X_w,p)]\\ &\qquad=\Pr[\forall j\in[d],X_{v_j+w}\in B_n(X_w,p)] \qquad (5)\end{aligned}$$

We now bound the probability that there exists $y\in\mathbb{F}_2^n$ such that for all $j\in[d]$, $X_{v_j+w}\in B_n(y,p)$. Fix $y\in\mathbb{F}_2^n$. We have:

$$\begin{aligned}&\Pr[\forall j\in[d],X_{v_j+w}\in B_n(y,p)]\\ &\qquad\leqslant\prod_{j=1}^{d}\Pr\left[X_{v_j+w}\in B_n(y,p)\middle|\left(X_t:t\in\bigcup_{i=1}^{j-1}\mathrm{supp}(v_i+w)\right)\right]\\ &\qquad\leqslant\left(2^{-\delta_p n}\right)^d. \qquad (6)\end{aligned}$$

The last inequality follows from applying Lemma 7 as follows: Let i_1 and i_2 be two distinct elements of $\mathrm{supp}(v_j+w)\setminus\left(\bigcup_{i=1}^{j-1}\mathrm{supp}(v_i+w)\right)$, guaranteed to exist because of the c-increasing property. We then apply Lemma 7 with w_1 and w_2 being vectors X_{i_1} and X_{i_2}, and with $x=y+\sum_{k\in[\ell],k\notin\{i_1,i_2\}}(v_j+w)_kX_k$.

Taking a union bound of Equation (6) over all $y\in\mathbb{F}_2^n$, we see that

$$\Pr[\exists y\in F_2^n\text{ s.t. }\forall j\in[d],X_{v_j+w}\in B_n(y,p)]\leqslant 2^n\cdot 2^{-\delta_p nd}.$$

Combining this with Equation (5) completes the proof of the claim. □

Given this claim, we now bound the probability that more than L elements of $\mathrm{span}(\{X_1,\ldots,X_\ell\})$ lie inside $B_n(0,p)$. This event occurs if and only if for some set $S\subseteq\mathbb{F}_2^\ell$ with $|S|=L+1$, it is the case that $\forall v\in S$, $X_v\in B_n(0,p)$. Taking a union bound of (4) over all such S, we see that the probability that there exists some $S\subseteq\mathbb{F}_2^\ell$ with $|S|=L+1$ such that $\forall v\in S,X_v\in B_n(0,p)$ is at most $2^{\ell(L+1)}\cdot 2^n\cdot 2^{-\delta_p dn}$. Taking C to be a large enough constant so that $d\geqslant\frac{1}{2}\log\frac{C}{8}>\frac{12}{\delta_p}$, the theorem follows.

5. PROOF OF THEOREM 5

In this section, we will prove Lemma 5, which finds a large c-increasing chain in some translate of any large enough set $S\subseteq\mathbb{F}_2^\ell$.

We will use the Sauer-Shelah Lemma.

LEMMA 9 (SAUER-SHELAH [14, 15]). *For all integers ℓ,c, and for any set $S\subseteq\{0,1\}^\ell$, if $|S|>2\ell^{c-1}$, then there exists some set of coordinates $U\subseteq[\ell]$ with $|U|=c$ such that $\{v|_U\mid v\in S\}=\{0,1\}^U$.*

LEMMA 5 (RESTATED) *For all positive integers c,ℓ and $L\leqslant 2^\ell$, the following holds. For every $S\subseteq\mathbb{F}_2^\ell$ with $|S|=L$, there is a $w\in\mathbb{F}_2^\ell$ such that $S+w$ has an c-increasing chain of length at least $\frac{1}{c}(\log\frac{L}{2})-(1-\frac{1}{c})(\log\ell)$.*

PROOF. We prove this by induction on ℓ. The claim holds trivially for $\ell\leqslant c$, so assume $\ell>c$.

If $L\leqslant 2\ell^{c-1}$, then again the lemma holds trivially. Otherwise, by the Sauer-Shelah lemma, we get a set U of c coordinates such that for each $u\in\mathbb{F}_2^U$, there is some $v\in S$ such that $v|_U=u$. We will represent elements of $\mathbb{F}_2^\ell$ in the form (u,v') where $u\in\mathbb{F}_2^U$ and $v'\in\mathbb{F}_2^{[\ell]\setminus U}$.

Let $u_0\in\mathbb{F}_2^U$ be a vector such that $|\{v\in S\mid v|_U=u_0\}|$ is at least $L/2^c$ (we know that such a u exists by averaging). Let $S'\subseteq\mathbb{F}_2^{[\ell]\setminus U}$ be given by $S'=\{v|_{[\ell]\setminus U}\mid v|_U=u\}$. By choice of u, we have $|S'|\geqslant L/2^c$.

By the induction hypothesis, there exist $w'\in\mathbb{F}_2^{\ell-c}$ and $v'_1,\ldots,v'_{d'}\in S'$ such that for each $j\in[d']$,

$$\left|\mathrm{supp}(v'_j+w')\setminus\left(\bigcup_{i=1}^{j-1}\mathrm{supp}(v'_i+w')\right)\right|\geqslant c.$$

for $d' \geqslant \frac{1}{c}\log(L/2^{c+1}) - (1-\frac{1}{c})\log(\ell - c)$.

Let $d = d'+1$. Note that $d \geqslant \frac{1}{c}\log(L/2) - (1-\frac{1}{c})\log(\ell - c) \geqslant \frac{1}{c}\log(L/2) - (1-\frac{1}{c})\log \ell$. For $i \in [d']$, let $v_i = (u_0, v_i') \in \mathbb{F}_2^\ell$. Let v_d be any vector in S with $(v_d)|_U = \neg u_0$, the bitwise complement of u_0. Let $w = (u_0, w')$. We claim that w and $v_1, \ldots, v_d$ satisfy the desired properties.

Indeed, for each $j \in [d']$, we have

$$\left|\text{supp}(v_j + w)\backslash\left(\bigcup_{i=1}^{j-1}\text{supp}(v_i+w)\right)\right| = \left|\text{supp}(v_j' + w') \setminus \left(\bigcup_{i=1}^{j-1}\text{supp}(v_i'+w')\right)\right| \geqslant c.$$

Also

$$\left|\text{supp}(v_d + w)\backslash\left(\bigcup_{i=1}^{d-1}\text{supp}(v_i+w)\right)\right| \geqslant \left|\text{supp}(v_d+w) \setminus ([\ell]\setminus U)\right| = |U| = c.$$

Thus for all $j \in [d]$, we have

$$\left|\text{supp}(v_j + w) \setminus (\bigcup_{i=1}^{j-1}\text{supp}(v_i+w))\right| \geqslant c\,,$$

as desired. □

6. LARGER ALPHABETS

As mentioned in the introduction the case of q-ary alphabet is nearly identical to the case of binary alphabet. We only highlight the differences. As before, the crux turns out to be the problem of studying the weight distribution of certain random constant-dimensional codes.

THEOREM 10 (SPAN OF RANDOM POINTS IN $B_n^q(0,p)$). *For every prime power q and every $p \in (0, 1-1/q)$, there is a constant $C_q > 0$, such that for all n large enough and all $\ell = o(\sqrt{n})$, if $X_1, \ldots, X_\ell$ are picked independently and uniformly at random from $B_n^q(0,p)$, then*

$$\Pr[|\text{span}(\{X_1,\ldots,X_\ell\}) \cap B_n^q(0,p)| > C_q \cdot \ell] \leqslant q^{-5n}.$$

The proof of Theorem 10 proceeds as before, by bounding the probability via a large c-increasing chain. The c-increasing chain itself is found in an analog of Lemma 5 for q-ary alphabet. We first need a definition.

DEFINITION 11. *A sequence of vectors $v_1, \ldots, v_d \in [q]^\ell$ is called an c-increasing chain of length d, if for all $j \in [d]$,*

$$\left|\text{supp}(v_j) \setminus \left(\bigcup_{i=1}^{j-1}\text{supp}(v_i)\right)\right| \geqslant c.$$

Now we have the following lemma.

LEMMA 12 (q-ARY INCREASING CHAINS). *For all positive integers c, ℓ, every prime power q, and $L \leqslant q^\ell$, the following holds. For every $S \subseteq \mathbb{F}_q^\ell$ with $|S| = L$, there is a $w \in \mathbb{F}_q^\ell$ such that $S + w$ has an c-increasing chain of length at least $\frac{1}{c}\log_q(\frac{L}{2}) - (1-\frac{1}{c})\log_q((q-1)\ell)$.*

The proof of Lemma 12 needs a non-standard generalization of the Sauer-Shelah lemma to larger alphabet described in the next section.

6.1 A q-ary Sauer-Shelah lemma

The traditional generalization of the Sauer-Shelah lemma to large alphabets is the Karpovsky-Milman lemma [12], which roughly states that given $S \subseteq [q]^\ell$ of cardinality at least $(q-1)^l l^{c-1}$, there is a set U of c coordinates such that for every $u \in [q]^U$, there is some $v \in S$ such that the restriction $v|_U$ equals u. Applying this lemma in our context, once $q > 2$, requires us to have a set $S > 2^\ell$, which turns out to lead to exponential list-size bounds. Fortunately, the actual property needed for us is slightly different. We want a bound B (ideally polynomial in ℓ) such that for any set $S \subseteq [q]^\ell$ of cardinality at least B, there is a set U of c coordinates such that for every $u \in [q]^U$, there is some $v \in S$ such that the restriction $v|_U$ *differs from u in every coordinate of U*. It turns out that this weakened requirement admits polynomial-sized B.

We state and prove this generalization of the Sauer-Shelah lemma below.

LEMMA 13 (q-ARY SAUER-SHELAH). *For all integers q, ℓ, c, for any set $S \subseteq [q]^\ell$, if $|S| > 2 \cdot ((q-1)\cdot \ell)^{c-1}$, then there exists some set of coordinates $U \subseteq [\ell]$ with $|U| = c$ such that for every $u \in [q]^U$, there exists some $v \in S$ such that u and $v|_U$ differ in every coordinate.*

PROOF. We prove this by induction on ℓ and c. If $c = 1$, then $|S| > 2$ and the result holds by letting U equal any coordinate on which not all elements of S agree.

Now assume $c > 1$. Represent an element x of $[q]^\ell$ as a pair (y, b), where $y \in [q]^{\ell-1}$ consists of the first $\ell - 1$ coordinates of x and $b \in [q]$ is the last coordinate of x.

Consider the following subsets of $[q]^{\ell-1}$.

$$S_1 = \{y \in [q]^{\ell-1} \mid \text{ for at least 1 value of } b \in [q],\ (y,b) \in S\}.$$

$$S_2 = \{y \in [q]^{\ell-1} \mid \text{ for at least 2 values of } b \in [q],\ (y,b) \in S\}.$$

Note that $|S| \leqslant (|S_1| - |S_2|) + q|S_2| = |S_1| + (q-1)|S_2|$. By assumption,

$$\begin{aligned}|S| &> 2\cdot((q-1)\cdot\ell)^{c-1}\\ &\geqslant 2\cdot((q-1)\cdot(\ell-1))^{c-1}\\ &\quad + (q-1)\left(2\cdot((q-1)\cdot(\ell-1))^{c-2}\right),\end{aligned}$$

(using the elementary inequality $\ell^{c-1} \geqslant (\ell-1)^{c-1} + (\ell-1)^{c-2}$). Thus, either $|S_1| > 2\cdot((q-1)\cdot(\ell-1))^{c-1}$, or else $|S_2| > 2\cdot((q-1)\cdot(\ell-1))^{c-2}$.

We now prove the desired claim in each of these cases.

Case 1: $|S_1| > 2\cdot((q-1)\cdot(\ell-1))^{c-1}$. In this case, we can apply the induction hypothesis to S_1 with parameters $\ell - 1$ and c, and get a subset of U of $[\ell-1]$ of cardinality c. Then the set U has the desired property.

Case 2: $|S_2| > 2\cdot((q-1)\cdot(\ell-1))^{c-2}$. In this case, we apply the induction hypothesis to S_2 with parameters $\ell - 1$ and $c-1$, and get a subset U of $[\ell-1]$ of cardinality $c-1$. Then the set $U \cup \{\ell\}$ has the desired property. Indeed, take any vector $u \in [q]^{U\cup\{\ell\}}$. Let $u' = u|_U$. By the induction hypothesis, we know that there is a $v \in S_2$ such that $v|_U$ differs from u' in every coordinate of U. Now we know that there are at least two $b \in [q]$ such that $(v, b) \in S$. At least one of these b will be such that (v, b) differs from u in every coordinate of $U \cup \{\ell\}$, as desired. $\square$

In the next section, we use the above lemma to prove the Ramsey-theoretic q-ary increasing chain claim (Lemma 12).

7. PROOF OF q-ARY INCREASING CHAIN LEMMA

In this section, we prove Lemma 12, which we restate below for convenience.

LEMMA 12 (RESTATED) *For every prime power q, and all positive integers c, ℓ and $L \leqslant q^\ell$, the following holds. For every $S \subseteq \mathbb{F}_q^\ell$ with $|S| = L$, there is a $w \in \mathbb{F}_q^\ell$ such that $S+w$ has an c-increasing chain of length at least $\frac{1}{c}\log_q(\frac{L}{2}) - (1-\frac{1}{c})\log_q((q-1)\ell)$.*

PROOF. We prove this by induction on ℓ. The claim holds trivially for $\ell \leqslant c$, so assume $\ell > c$.

If $L \leqslant 2((q-1)\cdot\ell)^{c-1}$, then again the lemma holds trivially. Otherwise, by Lemma 13 we get a set U of c coordinates such that for each $u \in \mathbb{F}_q^U$, there is some $v \in S$ such that $v|_U$ differs from u in every coordinate. We will represent elements of $\mathbb{F}_q^\ell$ in the form (u, v') where $u \in \mathbb{F}_q^U$ and $v' \in \mathbb{F}_q^{[\ell]\setminus U}$.

Let $u_0 \in \mathbb{F}_q^U$ be a vector such that $|\{v \in S \mid v|_U = u_0\}|$ is at least L/q^c (we know that such a u exists by averaging). Let $S' \subseteq \mathbb{F}_q^{[\ell]\setminus U}$ be given by $S' = \{v|_{[\ell]\setminus U} \mid v|_U = u\}$. By choice of u, we have $|S'| \geqslant L/q^c$.
By the induction hypothesis, for

$$d' \geqslant \frac{1}{c}\log\Big(\frac{L}{2q^c}\Big) - \Big(1-\frac{1}{c}\Big)\log((q-1)(\ell-c)) ,$$

there exist $w' \in \mathbb{F}_q^{\ell-c}$ and $v_1', \ldots, v_{d'}' \in S'$ such that for each $j \in [d']$,

$$\left|\mathrm{supp}(v_j' + w') \setminus \Big(\bigcup_{i=1}^{j-1} \mathrm{supp}(v_i' + w')\Big)\right| \geqslant c.$$

Let $d = d' + 1$. Note that

$$d \geqslant \frac{1}{c}\log_q\Big(\frac{L}{2}\Big) - \Big(1-\frac{1}{c}\Big)\log_q((q-1)\ell) .$$

For $i \in [d']$, let $v_i = (u_0, v_i') \in \mathbb{F}_q^\ell$. Let v_d be any vector in S where $(v_d)|_U$ differs from u_0 in every coordinate of U. Let $w = (-u_0, w')$. We claim that w and $v_1, \ldots, v_d$ satisfy the desired properties.
Indeed, for each $j \in [d']$, we have

$$\begin{aligned}\left|\mathrm{supp}(v_j + w)\setminus\Big(\bigcup_{i=1}^{j-1}\mathrm{supp}(v_i + w)\Big)\right| \\ &= \left|\mathrm{supp}(v_j' + w') \setminus \Big(\bigcup_{i=1}^{j-1}\mathrm{supp}(v_i' + w')\Big)\right| \\ &\geqslant c.\end{aligned}$$

Also,

$$\begin{aligned}\left|\mathrm{supp}(v_d + w)\setminus\Big(\bigcup_{i=1}^{d-1}\mathrm{supp}(v_i + w)\Big)\right| \\ &\geqslant \left|\mathrm{supp}(v_d + w) \setminus ([\ell] \setminus U)\right| \\ &= |U| = c.\end{aligned}$$

Thus for all $j \in [d]$, we have

$$\left|\mathrm{supp}(v_j + w) \setminus \Big(\bigcup_{i=1}^{j-1}\mathrm{supp}(v_i + w)\Big)\right| \geqslant c,$$

as desired. $\square$

Given Lemma 12, the proof of Theorem 10 is virtually identical to the proof of its binary analog Theorem 3. Theorem 6 can then be proved (using Theorem 10) in the same manner as Theorem 2 was proved.

Acknowledgements

Some of this work was done when we were all participating in the Dagstuhl seminar 09441 on constraint satisfaction. We thank the organizers of the seminar for inviting us, and Schloss Dagstuhl for the wonderful hospitality.

8. REFERENCES

[1] V. M. Blinovsky. Bounds for codes in the case of list decoding of finite volume. *Problems of Information Transmission*, 22(1):7–19, 1986.

[2] V. M. Blinovsky. *Asymptotic Combinatorial Coding Theory*. Kluwer Academic Publishers, Boston, 1997.

[3] V. M. Blinovsky. Lower bound for the linear multiple packing of the binary hamming space. *Journal of Combinatorial Theory, Series A*, 92(1):95–101, 2000.

[4] V. M. Blinovsky. Code bounds for multiple packings over a nonbinary finite alphabet. *Problems of Information Transmission*, 41(1):23–32, 2005.

[5] V. M. Blinovsky. On the convexity of one coding-theory function. *Problems of Information Transmission*, 44(1):34–39, 2008.

[6] P. Elias. List decoding for noisy channels. *Technical Report 335, Research Laboratory of Electronics, MIT*, 1957.

[7] P. Elias. Error-correcting codes for list decoding. *IEEE Transactions on Information Theory*, 37:5–12, 1991.

[8] V. Guruswami. *List decoding of error-correcting codes*. Number 3282 in Lecture Notes in Computer Science. Springer, 2004.

[9] V. Guruswami, J. Håstad, M. Sudan, and D. Zuckerman. Combinatorial bounds for list decoding. *IEEE Transactions on Information Theory*, 48(5):1021–1035, 2002.

[10] V. Guruswami and P. Indyk. Expander-based constructions of efficiently decodable codes. In *Proceedings of the 42nd Annual IEEE Symposium on Foundations of Computer Science*, pages 658–667, 2001.

[11] V. Guruswami and A. D. Smith. Explicit capacity-achieving codes for worst-case additive errors. Preprint, arxiv:0912.0965 [cs.IT], 2009.

[12] M. G. Karpovsky and V. D. Milman. Coordinate density of sets of vectors. *Discrete Math.*, 24(2):177–184, 1978.

[13] A. Rudra. Limits to list decoding random codes. In H. Q. Ngo, editor, *COCOON*, volume 5609 of *Lecture Notes in Computer Science*, pages 27–36. Springer, 2009.

[14] N. Sauer. On the density of families of sets. *J. Combinatorial Theory Ser. A*, 13:145–147, 1972.

[15] S. Shelah. A combinatorial problem; stability and order for models and theories in infinitary languages. *Pacific J. Math.*, 41:247–261, 1972.

[16] V. K. Wei and G.-L. Feng. Improved lower bounds on the sizes of error-correcting codes for list decoding. *IEEE Transactions on Information Theory*, 40(2):559–563, 1994.

[17] J. M. Wozencraft. List Decoding. *Quarterly Progress Report, Research Laboratory of Electronics, MIT*, 48:90–95, 1958.

[18] V. V. Zyablov and M. S. Pinsker. List cascade decoding. *Problems of Information Transmission*, 17(4):29–34, 1981 (in Russian); pp. 236-240 (in English), 1982.

Local List-Decoding and Testing of Random Linear Codes from High Error

Swastik Kopparty *
CSAIL
MIT
swastik@mit.edu

Shubhangi Saraf †
CSAIL
MIT
shibs@mit.edu

ABSTRACT

In this paper, we give surprisingly efficient algorithms for list-decoding and testing *random* linear codes. Our main result is that random sparse linear codes are locally list-decodable and locally testable in the *high-error* regime with only a *constant* number of queries. More precisely, we show that for all constants $c > 0$ and $\gamma > 0$, and for every linear code $\mathcal{C} \subseteq \{0,1\}^N$ which is:

- *sparse*: $|\mathcal{C}| \leq N^c$, and
- *unbiased*: each nonzero codeword in $\mathcal{C}$ has weight $\in (\frac{1}{2} - N^{-\gamma}, \frac{1}{2} + N^{-\gamma})$,

$\mathcal{C}$ is locally testable and locally list decodable from $(\frac{1}{2} - \epsilon)$ fraction worst-case errors using only $\text{poly}(\frac{1}{\epsilon})$ queries to a received word. We also give *subexponential time* algorithms for list-decoding arbitrary unbiased (but not necessarily sparse) linear codes in the high-error regime. In particular, this yields the first subexponential time algorithm even for the problem of (unique) decoding random linear codes of inverse-polynomial rate from a fixed positive fraction of errors.

Earlier, Kaufman and Sudan had shown that sparse, unbiased codes can be locally (unique) decoded and locally tested from a constant fraction of errors, where this constant fraction tends to 0 as the number of codewords grows. Our results significantly strengthen their results, while also having significantly simpler proofs.

At the heart of our algorithms is a natural "self-correcting" operation defined on codes and received words. This self-correcting operation transforms a code $\mathcal{C}$ with a received word w into a simpler code $\mathcal{C}'$ and a related received word w', such that w is close to $\mathcal{C}$ if and only if w' is close to $\mathcal{C}'$. Starting with a sparse, unbiased code $\mathcal{C}$ and an arbitrary received word w, a constant number of applications of the self-correcting operation reduces us to the case of local list-decoding and testing for the *Hadamard code*, for which the well known algorithms of Goldreich-Levin and Blum-Luby-Rubinfeld are available. This yields the constant-query local algorithms for the original code $\mathcal{C}$.

Our algorithm for decoding unbiased linear codes in subexponential time proceeds similarly. Applying the self-correcting operation to an unbiased code $\mathcal{C}$ and an arbitrary received word a super-constant number of times, we get reduced to the problem of *learning noisy parities*, for which non-trivial subexponential time algorithms were recently given by Blum-Kalai-Wasserman and Feldman-Gopalan-Khot-Ponnuswami. Our result generalizes a result of Lyubashevsky, which gave a subexponential time algorithm for decoding random linear codes of inverse-polynomial rate from *random errors*.

*This work was done while the author was an intern at Microsoft Research, New England.

†This work was done while the author was an intern at Microsoft Research, New England.

STOC'10, June 5–8, 2010, Cambridge, Massachusetts, USA.

Categories and Subject Descriptors

E.4 [**Data**]: Coding and Information Theory

General Terms

Theory

Keywords

List-decoding, Property testing, Random codes, dual-BCH codes, Noisy parity, Sublinear-time algorithms

1. INTRODUCTION

In this paper, we study the basic tasks of *error-correction* and *error-detection* for random linear codes in the presence of high error-rates. Our main result is that with high probability for a sparse random linear code $\mathcal{C}$, by inspecting just a *constant* number of coordinates of an arbitrary received word w, one can (i) decide whether the distance of w from $\mathcal{C}$ is at most 49% or not, and (ii) recover implicit descriptions of all the codewords of $\mathcal{C}$ which are 49%-close to w. We also give *subexponential time* algorithms for decoding random linear codes of inverse-polynomial rate from 49% errors.

We begin by setting up some notation. A linear code $\mathcal{C}$ in $\mathbb{F}_2^N$ is simply a linear subspace of $\mathbb{F}_2^N$. The elements of $\mathcal{C}$ are often referred to as "codewords". We say that $\mathcal{C}$ is sparse if $|\mathcal{C}| \leq N^c$ for some constant c. For a string $x \in \mathbb{F}_2^N$, we define its (normalized Hamming) weight $\text{wt}(x)$ to equal $\frac{1}{n} \times$ (the number of nonzero coordinates of x). We define the *bias* of the code $\mathcal{C}$ as $\max_{y \in \mathcal{C} \setminus \{0\}} \left| \frac{1 - \text{wt}(y)}{2} \right|$. Thus each nonzero codeword y of a code of bias β has $\text{wt}(y) \in$

$[(1-\beta)/2,(1+\beta)/2]$. For two strings $x, y \in \mathbb{F}_2^N$, we define the (normalized Hamming) distance between x and y, $\Delta(x,y)$, to be $\frac{1}{n}\times$ (the number of coordinates $i \in [N]$ where x_i and y_i differ). We then define the distance of a string x from the code $\mathcal{C}$, $\Delta(x,\mathcal{C})$ to be the minimum distance of x to some codeword of $\mathcal{C}$:

$$\Delta(x,\mathcal{C}) = \min_{y\in\mathcal{C}} \Delta(x,y).$$

The basic algorithmic tasks associated with codes are error-detection and error-correction. Here we are given an arbitrary received word $w \in \mathbb{F}_2^N$, and we want to (1) determine if $\Delta(w,\mathcal{C}) > \delta$, and (2) find all codewords $y \in \mathcal{C}$ such that $\Delta(w,\mathcal{C}) \leq \delta$. In recent years, there has been much interest in developing sublinear time algorithms (and in particular, highly query-efficient algorithms) for these tasks. In what follows, we will describe our results on various aspects of these questions.

1.1 Local list-decoding

Informally, a local list-decoder for $\mathcal{C}$ from δ-fraction errors is a randomized algorithm A that, when given oracle access to a received word $w \in \mathbb{F}_2^N$, recovers the list of all codewords c such that $\Delta(c,w) < \delta$, while querying w in very few coordinates. The codewords thus recovered are "implicitly represented" by randomized algorithms $A_1,\ldots,A_l$ with oracle access to w. Given a coordinate $j \in [N]$, A_i makes very few queries to w and is supposed to output the jth coordinate of the codeword that it implicitly represents.

A particular case of local list-decoding which is of significant interest is local list-decoding in the "high-error" regime. Specifically, for every constant $\epsilon > 0$, one wants to query-efficiently locally list-decode a code from $(\frac{1}{2}-\epsilon)$-fraction errors (the significance of $\frac{1}{2}-\epsilon$ is that it is just barely enough to to distinguish the received word from a random string in $\mathbb{F}_2^N$; for codes over large alphabets, one considers the problem of decoding from $(1-\epsilon)$-fraction errors). Local list-decoding in the high-error regime plays a particularly important role in the complexity-theoretic applications of coding theory (see [27], for example).

The first known local list-decoder (for any code) came from the seminal work of Goldreich and Levin [10], which gave time-efficient, low-query, local list-decoders for the Hadamard code in the high-error regime. In the following years, many highly non-trivial local list-decoders were developed for various codes, including multivariate polynomial based codes (in the works of Goldreich-Rubinfeld-Sudan [11], Arora-Sudan [4], Sudan-Trevisan-Vadhan [27], and Gopalan-Klivans-Zuckerman [12]) and combinatorial codes such as direct-product codes and XOR codes (in the works of Impagliazzo-Wigderson and Impagliazzo-Jaiswal-Kabanets-Wigderson [15, 13]). Many of these local list-decoders, especially the ones in the high-error regime, play a prominent role in celebrated results in complexity theory on hardness amplification and pseudorandomness [15, 27, 13].

To summarize, all known local list-decoding algorithms were for highly structured algebraic or combinatorial codes. Recently, Kaufman and Sudan [17] showed that *random* sparse linear codes can be locally (unique-)decoded from a small constant fraction of errors. This was the first result to show that query-efficient decoding algorithms could also be associated with random, unstructured codes. This result was proved by studying the weight distribution of these codes and their duals, and in particular was based on the MacWilliams identities and non-trivial information about the roots of Krawtchouk polynomials. In an earlier paper [19], we gave an alternate (and arguably simpler) proof of this result, as part of a more general attempt to characterize sparse codes that are locally decodable and testable in the low-error regime. Popular belief [26] suggested that these low-error local decoders for random codes could *not* be ex! tended to the high-error regime.

Our first main result is that even random codes *can* have query-efficient local list-decoders in the high-error regime. Specifically, we show that linear codes which are *sparse* and *unbiased* (both properties are possessed by sparse random linear codes with high probability) admit high-error local list-decoders with constant query complexity.

Informal Theorem A For every constant $c, \gamma > 0$, every linear code $\mathcal{C} \subseteq \mathbb{F}_2^N$ with N^c codewords and bias $N^{-\gamma}$ can be locally list-decoded from $(1/2-\epsilon)$-fraction errors using only poly$(\frac{1}{\epsilon})$ queries to a received word.

The formal statement appears in Theorem 4.

1.2 Local testing

Informally, a local tester for $\mathcal{C}$ is a randomized algorithm A, which when given oracle access to a received word $w \in \mathbb{F}_2^N$, makes very few queries to the received word w, and distinguishes between the case where $w \in \mathcal{C}$ and the case where w is "far" from all codewords of $\mathcal{C}$.

The first local tester (for any code) came from the seminal work of Blum, Luby and Rubinfeld [7], which gave an efficient, 3-query local tester for the Hadamard code. This result was subsequently generalized to the problem of local testing of low-degree multivariate polynomials [24, 3, 2, 1]. This body of work played a significant role in the proof of the PCP theorem and were the harbingers of the field of property testing.

A particular variant of local testability which is of significant interest is local testing in the "high-error" regime. Here, for every constant $\epsilon > 0$, one wants to query-efficiently distinguish between the cases $\Delta(w,\mathcal{C}) < 1/2-\epsilon$, i.e., w is "close" to $\mathcal{C}$, and $\Delta(w,\mathcal{C}) \approx 1/2$, i.e., w is as far from $\mathcal{C}$ as a random point is (for codes over large alphabets, 1/2 gets replaced by 1). For the Hadamard code, the existence of such testers follows from the Fourier-analytic proof of the BLR linearity test [5]. For the code of degree 2 multivariate polynomials over $\mathbb{F}_2$, local testers in the high-error regime were given by Samorodnitsky [25]. For the code of multivariate polynomials over large fields, local-testers in the high-error regime were given by Raz-Safra [23], Arora-Sudan [4] and Moshkovitz-Raz [22]. More recently, Dinur-Goldenberg [8] and Impagliazzo-Kabanets-Wigderson [14] gave query-efficient local testing algorithms in the high-error regime for the combinatorial families: the direct-product and XOR codes. These algebraic and combinatorial high-error local-testers led to some remarkable constructions of PCPs with high soundness.

As in the case of list-decodability, we have the situation that all known locally-testable codes in the high-error regime are for highly structured algebraic or combinatorial codes. Again, Kaufman and Sudan [17] showed that a random sparse linear code is locally testable in the low-error regime by studying its weight distribution and the weight distribution of its dual. We [19] had an alternate proof of this result too. Popular belief [26] again suggested that local-testability in the *high-error* regime could not be found in random linear codes.

Our second main result is that random codes *can* have query-efficient local testers in the high-error regime. Specifically, sparse and unbiased codes admit high-error local testers with constant query complexity.

Informal Theorem B For every constant $c, \gamma > 0$, every linear code $\mathcal{C} \subseteq \mathbb{F}_2^N$ with N^c codewords and bias $N^{-\gamma}$ can be locally tested from $(1/2-\epsilon)$-fraction errors using only $\text{poly}(\frac{1}{\epsilon})$ queries to a received word.

The formal theorem appears as Theorem 4, where we in fact show something stronger (called *distance estimation in the high-error regime*): for such codes, using constantly many queries, one can distinguish between $\Delta(w, \mathcal{C}) > 1/2 - \epsilon_1$ and $\Delta(w, \mathcal{C}) < 1/2 - \epsilon_2$ for every constants $0 < \epsilon_1 < \epsilon_2 < 1/2$.

1.3 Subexponential time list-decoding

The techniques we develop to address the previous questions turn out to be useful for making progress on another fundamental algorithmic question in coding theory: that of *time-efficient* worst-case decoding of random linear codes. Given a random linear code $\mathcal{C} \subseteq \mathbb{F}_2^N$ and an arbitrary received word $w \in \mathbb{F}_2^N$, we are interested in quickly finding all the codewords $c \in \mathcal{C}$ such that $\Delta(w, c) < \frac{1}{2} - \epsilon$, for constant $\epsilon > 0$. We show that this problem can be solved in *subexponential time*, using just the unbiasedness of $\mathcal{C}$. Our algorithm uses some recent breakthroughs on the problem of learning noisy-parities due to Blum-Kalai-Wasserman [6] and Feldman-Gopalan-Khot-Ponnuswami [9].

Informal Theorem C For all constants $\alpha, \gamma > 0$, for every linear code $\mathcal{C} \subseteq \mathbb{F}_2^N$ with dimension n, where $N = n^{1+\alpha}$, and bias $N^{-\gamma}$, and for every constant $\epsilon > 0$, $\mathcal{C}$ can be list-decoded from $(\frac{1}{2} - \epsilon)$-fraction errors in time $2^{O(n/\log\log n)}$.

The formal statement appears in Theorem 6.

In particular, the above theorem implies that if $\mathcal{C} \subseteq \mathbb{F}_2^N$ is a *random linear code* with dimension $n = N^{\frac{1}{1+\alpha}}$, then for every constant $\epsilon > 0$, $\mathcal{C}$ can be list-decoded from $(\frac{1}{2} - \epsilon)$-fraction errors in time $2^{O(n/\log\log n)}$.

Earlier, it was not even known how to *unique-decode* random linear codes from 0.1-*fraction* worst-case errors in time $2^{o(n)}$. For decoding random linear codes of inverse-polynomial rate from *random errors*, Lyubashevsky [21] gave a subexponential time algorithm, also based on algorithms for the Noisy Parity problem. Our result generalizes his in two ways: we decode from worst-case errors, and we give a natural, explicit criterion (namely low-bias) on the code $\mathcal{C}$ which guarantees the success of the algorithm.

1.4 Time-efficient local algorithms for dual-BCH codes

For the family of *dual-BCH* codes, perhaps the most important family of sparse, unbiased codes, we show that the constant-query local list-decoding and local testing algorithms can be made to run in a *time-efficient* manner too. The dual-BCH codes form a natural family of polynomial-based codes generalizing the Hadamard code. They have a number of extremal properties which give them an important role in coding theory. For example, the dual-BCH code $\mathcal{C} \subseteq \mathbb{F}_2^N$ with N^t codewords has bias as small as $O(t \cdot N^{-1/2})$, which is *optimal* for codes with N^t codewords!

The key to making our earlier query-efficient local list-decoding and local testing algorithms run in a time-efficient manner for dual-BCH codes, is a time-efficient efficient algorithm for a certain sampling problem that arises in the local list-decoder and tester. This sampling problem turns out to be closely related to an algorithmic problem that was considered in the context of low-error testing of dual-BCH codes [16], that of sampling constant-weight BCH codewords. A variant of the sampling algorithm of [16] turns out to suffice for our problem too, and this leads to the following result.

Informal Theorem D For every constant c, the dual-BCH code $\mathcal{C} \subseteq \mathbb{F}_2^N$ with N^c codewords, can be locally list-decoded and locally tested from $(1/2 - \epsilon)$-fraction errors in time $\text{poly}(\log N, \frac{1}{\epsilon})$ using only $\text{poly}(\frac{1}{\epsilon})$ queries to a received word.

The formal statement appears as Theorem 5. The original algorithm for sampling constant-weight BCH codewords given in [16], and was based on results on the weight distribution of BCH codes [20]. We give an alternate (and possibly simpler) analysis in in the full version of this paper [18].

Organization of this paper.

In Section 2, we give a brief overview of the techniques we use. In Section 3 we formally define local list-decoders and testers and state our main results. The proofs appear in Sections 4 and 5.

2. METHODS

In this section, we give an overview of the main ideas underlying our algorithms. Our goal in this section is to stress the simplicity and naturalness of our techniques.

The main component of our algorithms is a certain "self-correcting" operation which transforms a code $\mathcal{C}$ with a received word w into a simpler code $\mathcal{C}'$ and a related received word w', such that w is close to $\mathcal{C}$ if and only if w' is close to $\mathcal{C}'$. Repeated application of this self-correcting operation will allow us to reduce our list-decoding and testing problems for $\mathcal{C}$ to certain kinds of list-decoding and testing problems for a significantly simpler code $\mathcal{C}^*$ (in our case, $\mathcal{C}^*$ will be the Hadamard code). Query-efficient/time-efficient algorithms for the simpler code $\mathcal{C}^*$ then lead to query-efficient/time-efficient algorithms for the original code $\mathcal{C}$.

In order to simplify the description of the self-correcting operation, we first translate our problems into the language of list-decoding and testing under *distributions*. Let $\mathcal{C} \subseteq \{0,1\}^N$ be a linear code of dimension n, and let G be an $n \times N$ generator matrix for $\mathcal{C}$. Let $S = \{v_1, v_2, \ldots, v_N\} \subset \mathbb{F}_2^n$ denote the set of columns of G. We associate to $\mathcal{C}$ the distribution μ over $\mathbb{F}_2^n$ which is uniform over S. Note that if the code $\mathcal{C}$ has low bias, then the resulting distribution μ has small Fourier bias. Every word w in $\mathbb{F}_2^N$ can be viewed as a function $f_w : S \to \mathbb{F}_2$, where $f_w(v_i) = w_i$. Under this mapping, every *codeword* of $\mathcal{C}$ gets associated with a *linear* function.

Note that via this translation, the problem of testing if w is close to some codeword exactly translates into the problem of testing if f_w is close to some linear function *under the distribution* μ (where the distance of two functions g, h under

μ is measured by the probability that g and h differ on a random sample from μ). Similarly, the problem of local list-decoding, i.e. the problem of finding all codewords close to w, translates into the problem of finding all linear functions that are close to f_w under the distribution μ.

We now come to the self-correcting operation on f and μ. The operation has the property that it maintains the property "f correlates with a linear function under μ", and at the same time it results in a distribution that is "simpler" in a certain precise sense.

Define $\mu^{(2)}$ to be the convolution of μ with itself; i.e., it is the distribution of the sum of two independent samples from μ. We define $f^{(2)} : \mathbb{F}_2^n \to \mathbb{F}_2$ to be the (probabilistic) function, where for a given x, $f^{(2)}(x)$ is sampled as follows: first sample y_1 and y_2 independently and uniformly from μ conditioned on $y_1+y_2 = x$, and return $f(y_1)+f(y_2)$ (if there are no such y_1, y_2, then define $f^{(2)}(x)$ arbitrarily).

The following two simple facts are key to what follows:

- $\mu^{(2)}$ is "simpler" than μ: the statistical distance of $\mu^{(2)}$ to the uniform distribution on $\mathbb{F}_2^n$ is significantly smaller than the statistical distance of μ to the uniform distribution on $\mathbb{F}_2^n$ (this follows from the low Fourier bias of μ, which in turn came from the unbiasedness of $\mathcal{C}$).
- If f is $(\frac{1}{2}-\epsilon)$-close to a linear function g under μ, then $f^{(2)}$ is $(\frac{1}{2}-2\epsilon^2)$-close to g under $\mu^{(2)}$: this is a formal consequence of our definition of $f^{(2)}$. In particular, if f is noticeably-close to g under μ, then so is $f^{(2)}$ under $\mu^{(2)}$.

This leads to a general approach for list-decoding/testing for linear functions under μ. First pick k large, and consider the distribution $\mu^{(k)}$ and the function $f^{(k)}$ (defined analogously to $\mu^{(2)}$ and $f^{(2)}$). If k is chosen large enough, then $\mu^{(k)}$ will in fact be 2^{-10n}-close to the uniform distribution in statistical distance. Furthermore, if k is not too large, then $f^{(k)}$ will be noticeably-close under $\mu^{(k)}$ to the same linear functions that f is close to under μ. Thus, if k is suitable (as a function of the initial bias/sparsity of the code) $f^{(k)}$ is noticeably-close *under the uniform distribution* to the same linear functions that f is close to under μ. Now all we need to do is run a local list-decoding/testing algorithm on $f^{(k)}$ under the uniform distribution.

An important issue that was swept under the rug in this discussion, is the query/time-efficiency of working with $f^{(k)}$ and $\mu^{(k)}$. If we ignore running-time, one can simulate oracle access to $f^{(k)}$ using just a factor k larger number of queries to f. This leads to our query-efficient (but time-inefficient) algorithms for sparse, unbiased linear codes in the high-error regime (in this setting k only needs to be a constant). We stress that our proof of this result is significantly simpler and stronger than earlier analyses of local algorithms (in the low-error regime) of sparse, unbiased codes [16, 17].

The bottleneck for implementing these local, query-efficient algorithms in a time-efficient manner is the following algorithmic "back-sampling" problem: given a point $x \in \mathbb{F}_2^n$, produce a sample from the distribution of $y_1, \ldots, y_k$ picked independently from μ conditioned on $\sum y_i = x$. A time-efficient back-sampling algorithm would allow us to time-efficiently simulate oracle access to $f^{(k)}$ given oracle access to f. For random sparse linear codes, solving this problem in time sublinear in N is impossible; however for specific, interesting sparse unbiased codes, this remains an important problem to address. For the special case of dual-BCH codes, perhaps the most important family of sparse, unbiased codes, we observe that the back-sampling problem can be solved using a small variant of an algorithm of Kaufman-Litsyn [16]. Thus for dual-BCH codes, we get $\mathrm{poly}\log(N)$-time, constant-query local testing and local list-decoding algorithms in the high-error regime.

For subexponential time list-decoding, we follow the same plan. Here too we will self-correct f to obtain a function $f^{(k)}$, such that every linear function that correlates with f under the μ distribution, also correlates with $f^{(k)}$ under the uniform distribution over $\mathbb{F}_2^n$. However, since we are now paying attention to running time (and we do not know how to solve the back-sampling problem for μ efficiently in general), we cannot afford to allow the list-decoder over the uniform distribution over $\mathbb{F}_2^n$ to query the value of $f^{(k)}$ at any point that it desires (since this will force us to back-sample in order to compute $f^{(k)}$ at that point). Instead, we will use some recent remarkable list-decoders ([9, 6]), developed in the context of learning noisy parities, which can find all linear functions close (under the uniform distribution) to an arbitrary function h in subexponential time by simply querying the function h at independent uniformly random points of $\mathbb{F}_2^n$! Using the unbiasedness of μ, it turns out to be easy to evaluate $f^{(k)}$ at independent uniformly random points of $\mathbb{F}_2^n$. This leads to our subexponential time list-decoding algorithm.

Relationship to the k-wise XOR on codes.

Back in the language of codes, what happened here has a curious interpretation. Given a code $\mathcal{C} \subseteq \mathbb{F}_2^N$, the k-wise XOR of $\mathcal{C}$, $\mathcal{C}^{(\oplus k)}$, is the code contained in $\mathbb{F}_2^{N^k}$ defined as follows: for every codeword $c \in \mathcal{C}$, there is a codeword $c^{(\oplus k)} \in F_2^{[N]^k}$ whose value in coordinate $(i_1, \ldots, i_k)$ equals $c_{i_1} \oplus c_{i_2} \oplus \ldots \oplus c_{i_k}$. In terms of this operation, our algorithms simply do the following: given a code $\mathcal{C}$ and received word w, consider the code $\mathcal{C}^{(\oplus k)}$ with received word $w^{(\oplus k)}$. The crucial observation is, that for k chosen suitably as a function of the bias/sparsity of $\mathcal{C}$, the code $\mathcal{C}^{(\oplus k)}$ is essentially, up to repeating each coordinate a roughly-equal number of times, the Hadamard code! Additionally, $w^{(\oplus k)}$ is close to $c^{(\oplus k)}$ for a codeword c if and only if w is close c. Thus decoding/testing $w^{(\oplus k)}$ for the Hadamard code now suffices to complete the algorithm.

The k-wise XOR on codes is an operation that shows up often as a device for hardness amplification, to convert functions that are hard to compute into functions that are even harder to compute. Our algorithms use the XOR operation for "good": here the XOR operation is a vehicle to *transfer* query-efficient/time-efficient algorithms for the Hadamard code to query-efficient/time-efficient algorithms for arbitrary unbiased codes.

3. DEFINITIONS AND MAIN RESULTS

3.1 Codes

We begin by formalizing the notions of local list-decoding and local-testing of codes.

DEFINITION 1. *Let $r \in \mathbb{F}_2^N$. A randomized algorithm A is said to* implicitly compute r with error δ *if for all $j \in [N]$*

it holds that

$$\Pr[A(j) = r_j] \geq 1 - \delta,$$

where the probability is over the internal randomness of A.

Below we formally define local list-decoders. In what follows, we denote by A^w the randomized algorithm A with oracle access to w.

DEFINITION 2. *Let $\mathcal{C} \subseteq \mathbb{F}_2^N$ be a code. A (δ, q, l)-local list-decoder for $\mathcal{C}$ is a randomized algorithm A, such that for every $w \in \mathbb{F}_2^N$, A outputs a list of randomized algorithms $\{A_1, \ldots, A_l\}$, such that:*

- *For each $i \in [l]$, and for each input $j \in [N]$, the algorithm $A_i^w(j)$ makes at most q queries into w during its execution.*
- *With probability at least 2/3, for every codeword $c \in \mathcal{C}$ with $\Delta(w, c) < \delta$, there exists an index i such that the algorithm A_i^w implicitly computes c with error 1/3 (in the sense of Definition 1).*

We now define local-testers.

DEFINITION 3. *Let $\mathcal{C} \subseteq \mathbb{F}_2^N$ be a code. Let $0 < \delta_1 < \delta_2$. A (δ_1, δ_2, q)-local tester for $\mathcal{C}$ is a randomized algorithm A, such that for every $w \in \mathbb{F}_2^N$,*

- *A^w makes at most q oracle calls to w during its execution.*
- *If there is a codeword $c \in \mathcal{C}$ such that $\Delta(w, c) < \delta_1$, A^w accepts with probability at least 2/3.*
- *If for all $c \in \mathcal{C}$, $\Delta(w, c) > \delta_2$, then A^w rejects with probability at least 2/3.*

We can now formally state our main theorems regarding the local testability and local list-decodability of sparse unbiased codes.

THEOREM 4. *Let $C \subseteq \mathbb{F}_2^N$ be a linear code with N^c codewords and with bias $\beta = N^{-\gamma}$. Then,*

- **Local list-decoding:** *for all $0 < \epsilon < 1/2$, there exists a $\left(1/2 - \epsilon, \left(\frac{1}{\epsilon}\right)^{O(c/\gamma)}, \left(\frac{1}{\epsilon}\right)^{O(c/\gamma)}\right)$-local list-decoder for C.*
- **Local testing:** *for all constants ϵ_1, ϵ_2 such that $0 < \epsilon_1 < \epsilon_2 < 1/2$, there exists a $\left(1/2 - \epsilon_2, 1/2 - \epsilon_1, \left(\frac{1}{\epsilon_2 - \epsilon_1}\right)^{O(c/\gamma)}\right)$-local tester for C.*

The next theorem states that the above algorithms can be implemented in a time-efficient manner for the dual-BCH codes. The proof appears in the full version of this paper [18].

THEOREM 5. *Let t be a constant, and let N be an integer of the form $2^s - 1$. Let C be the dual-BCH code of length N and dimension st. Then,*

- **Local list-decoding:** *for all $0 < \epsilon < 1/2$, there exists a $\left(1/2 - \epsilon, \mathrm{poly}\left(\frac{1}{\epsilon}\right), \mathrm{poly}\left(\frac{1}{\epsilon}\right)\right)$-local list-decoder for C which runs in time $\mathrm{poly}(\log N, \frac{1}{\epsilon})$.*
- **Local testing:** *for all constants ϵ_1, ϵ_2 such that $0 < \epsilon_1 < \epsilon_2 < 1/2$, there exists a $\left(1/2 - \epsilon_2, 1/2 - \epsilon_1, \mathrm{poly}\left(\frac{1}{\epsilon_2 - \epsilon_1}\right)\right)$-local tester for C which runs in time $\mathrm{poly}(\log N, \frac{1}{\epsilon})$.*

Finally, we formally state our theorem on the subexponential time list-decoding of unbiased linear codes from worst-case errors. The proof appears in Section 5.

THEOREM 6. *For all constants $\alpha, \gamma, \epsilon > 0$, there is an algorithm* SubExpListDecode*, which when given:*

- *the generator matrix G of a n-dimensional binary linear code $\mathcal{C} \subseteq \mathbb{F}_2^N$, where $\mathcal{C}$ has bias $N^{-\gamma}$ and $N = n^{1+\alpha}$, and*
- *a vector $r \in \mathbb{F}_2^N$,*

runs in time $\exp(\frac{n}{\log \log n})$ and with high probability, finds all codewords $c \in \mathcal{C}$ such that $\Delta(c, r) < \frac{1}{2} - \epsilon$.

3.2 Distributions

As suggested earlier, it is greatly simplifying to work in the language of distributions over $\mathbb{F}_2^n$. We now formalize some notions in this context.

For sets $\mathcal{D}$ and $\mathcal{R}$, we will use the concept of a *probabilistic function* from $\mathcal{D}$ to $\mathcal{R}$. Formally, a probabilistic function h from $\mathcal{D}$ to $\mathcal{R}$ is given by a collection of distributions $(\nu_d)_{d \in \mathcal{D}}$, where each ν_d is a distribution over $\mathcal{R}$. Functionally, we view probabilistic functions as a black box, such that whenever an element $d \in \mathcal{D}$ is fed into this box, a sample from ν_d is returned by the box. The samples returned from different invocations of this box are mutually independent (in particular, two different calls to the box on the same input may return different values). Abusing notation, we write $h : \mathcal{D} \to \mathcal{R}$. Note that ordinary (deterministic) functions can be viewed as a special case of probabilistic functions.

For two probabilistic functions $h_1, h_2 : \mathbb{F}_2^n \to \mathbb{F}_2$ and a distribution μ over $\mathbb{F}_2^n$, we define the μ-distance between h_1 and h_2 by:

$$\Delta_\mu(h_1, h_2) = \Pr_{x \in \mu}[h_1(x) \neq h_2(x)],$$

where the probability is over x chosen according to μ, and $h_1(x)$ and $h_2(x)$ being sampled independently from the probabilistic functions h_1 and h_2.

We now introduce some terminology regarding linear functions and characters. Every linear function $g : \mathbb{F}_2^n \to \mathbb{F}_2$ is of the form $g(x) = a \cdot x \stackrel{\text{def}}{=} \sum_{i=1}^n a_i x_i$ for some $a \in \mathbb{F}_2^n$. A *character* of $\mathbb{F}_2^n$ is a function $\chi : \mathbb{F}_2^n \to \mathbb{R}$ such that for some linear function $g : \mathbb{F}_2^n \to \mathbb{F}_2$, we have $\chi(x) = (-1)^{g(x)}$ for all x. The character χ_0 with $\chi_0(x) = 1$ for all x is called the *trivial character.*

We can now define the analogous versions of local list-decoding and local testing for distributions.

DEFINITION 7. *Let μ be a distribution over $\mathbb{F}_2^n$. A (δ, q, l)-local list-decoder for linear functions under μ is a randomized algorithm A, such that for every probabilistic function $f : \mathbb{F}_2^n \to \mathbb{F}_2$, A outputs a list of randomized algorithms $\{A_1, \ldots, A_l\}$, such that:*

- *For each $i \in [l]$, and for each input $x \in \mathbb{F}_2^n$, the algorithm $A_i^f(x)$ makes at most q queries into f during its execution.*

- *With probability at least 2/3, for every linear function $g : \mathbb{F}_2^n \to \mathbb{F}_2$ such that $\Delta_\mu(f, g) < \delta$, there exists an index i such that the algorithm A_i^f implicitly computes g with error 1/3 (in the sense of Definition 1).*

DEFINITION 8. *Let μ be a distribution over $\mathbb{F}_2^n$. Let $0 < \delta_1 < \delta_2$. A (δ_1, δ_2, q)-local tester for linear functions, or linearity tester, under μ is a randomized algorithm A, such that for every probabilistic function $f : \mathbb{F}_2^n \to \mathbb{F}_2$,*

- *A makes at most q oracle calls to f.*
- *If there is a linear function $g : \mathbb{F}_2^n \to \mathbb{F}_2$ such that $\Delta_\mu(g, f) < \delta_1$, A^f accepts with probability at least 2/3*
- *If for all linear functions $g : \mathbb{F}_2^n \to \mathbb{F}_2$, $\Delta_\mu(g, f) > \delta_2$, then A^w rejects with probability at least 2/3*

We now state our main theorem on the local list-decoding and testing of linear functions under unbiased distributions. The proof appears in Section 4. In the next subsection, we will derive Theorem 4 from it.

THEOREM 9. *Let μ be a distribution over $\mathbb{F}_2^n$ such that for all nontrivial characters $\chi : \mathbb{F}_2^n \to \{-1, +1\}$,*

$$|\mathop{\mathbf{E}}_{x \in \mu}[\chi(x)]| < 2^{-\eta n}.$$

Then,

1. **Local list-decoding:** *for every $0 < \epsilon < 1/2$, there exists a $\left((1/2 - \epsilon), \left(\frac{1}{\epsilon}\right)^{O(1/\eta)}, \left(\frac{1}{\epsilon}\right)^{O(1/\eta)}\right)$-local list-decoder for linear functions under μ.*
2. **Local testing:** *for every $0 < \epsilon_1 < \epsilon_2 < 1/2$, there exists a $\left(1/2 - \epsilon_2, 1/2 - \epsilon_1, \left(\frac{1}{\epsilon_2 - \epsilon_1}\right)^{O(1/\eta)}\right)$-local tester for linear function under μ.*

3.3 From Distributions to Codes

In this subsection, we will use Theorem 9 on local algorithms for unbiased distributions to prove Theorem 4 on local algorithms for sparse, unbiased codes.

DEFINITION 10. *Let $\mathcal{C} \subseteq \{0, 1\}^N$ be a linear code of dimension n. Let G be any generator matrix for $\mathcal{C}$ (i.e., G is an $n \times N$ matrix whose rows are linearly independent and span $\mathcal{C}$). Then the* distribution associated to $\mathcal{C}$ via G *is distribution μ over $\mathbb{F}_2^n$ which is uniform over the columns of G.*

The connection between local algorithms for codes and local algorithms for distributions comes from the following simple theorem.

THEOREM 11. *Let $\mathcal{C}$ be a code and let μ be a distribution associated to $\mathcal{C}$ via G. Then,*

- **Local list-decoding:** *If there exists a (δ, q, l)-local list-decoder for linear function under μ, then there exists a (δ, q, l)-local list-decoder for $\mathcal{C}$.*
- **Local testing:** *If there exists a (δ_1, δ_2, q)-local tester for linear functions under μ, then there exists a (δ_1, δ_2, q)-local tester for $\mathcal{C}$.*

PROOF. Let $v_1, \ldots, v_N \in \mathbb{F}_2^n$ be the columns of G. Let $w \in \mathbb{F}_2^N$ be a received word.

Let $f : \mathbb{F}_2^n \to \mathbb{F}_2$ be the probabilistic function such that on input x, $f(x)$ is sampled as follows: If there exists $i \in [N]$ such that $x = v_i$, then pick an i uniformly at random from $\{i \in N \mid x = v_i\}$, and output w_i. If there is no $i \in [N]$ such that $x = v_i$, then output a uniformly random element of $\mathbb{F}_2$ (or define $f(x)$ arbitrarily).

Let $c = a \cdot G$ be a codeword of $\mathcal{C}$, and let $g : \mathbb{F}_2^n \to \mathbb{F}_2$ be the corresponding linear function given by $g(x) = a \cdot x$. Observe that our definition of f implies that

$$\Delta(c, w) = \Delta_\mu(g, f). \tag{1}$$

Also note that one can simulate oracle access to f given oracle access to w.

The local list-decoding and testing algorithms for $\mathcal{C}$ can now be easily described. Given a received word $w \in \mathbb{F}_2^N$, consider the corresponding probabilistic function $f : \mathbb{F}_2^n \to \mathbb{F}_2$, and run the algorithms for local list-decoding/testing for linear functions under μ on f. The local tester for $\mathcal{C}$ accepts if and only if the corresponding local tester for linear functions under μ accepts. The local list-decoding algorithm for $\mathcal{C}$ outputs, for each linear function $g(x) = a \cdot x$ in the list output by the list-decoding algorithm for linear functions under μ, the codeword $c = a \cdot G$. Correctness follows immediately from Equation (1). ☐

We now give a proof of the main theorem on local list-decodability and testability of sparse, unbiased codes, Theorem 4, assuming Theorem 9.

PROOF OF THEOREM 4. Let $\mathcal{C}$ be a linear code with $|\mathcal{C}| \leq N^c$ and bias $\leq N^{-\gamma}$. Let G be a generator matrix for $\mathcal{C}$. Let $n = \log |\mathcal{C}|$. Let μ be the distribution associated to $\mathcal{C}$ via G.

We first notice that our assumptions on the sparsity and the bias of the code $\mathcal{C}$ imply that for all nontrivial characters $\chi : \mathbb{F}_2^n \to \{-1, +1\}$,

$$|\mathop{\mathbf{E}}_{x \in \mu}[\chi(x)]| < 2^{-\eta n}, \tag{2}$$

where $\eta = \gamma / c$. Indeed, if $\chi(x) = (-1)^{a \cdot x}$, then the codeword $a \cdot G$ of the code $\mathcal{C}$ has weight $\frac{1 + \mathbf{E}_{x \in \mu}[\chi(x)]}{2}$. By assumption on the bias of $\mathcal{C}$, the weight of any nonzero codeword of $\mathcal{C}$ lies in the interval $(\frac{1 - N^{-\gamma}}{2}, \frac{1 + N^{-\gamma}}{2})$. By the sparsity of $\mathcal{C}$, this interval is contained in the interval $(\frac{1 - 2^{-\gamma n / c}}{2}, \frac{1 + 2^{-\gamma n / c}}{2})$, and Equation (2) follows.

Theorem 9 now implies the existence of suitable list-decoding and testing algorithms for linear functions under μ. By Theorem 11, this implies the existence of the desired local list-decoding and local testing algorithms for $\mathcal{C}$. ☐

4. LOCAL ALGORITHMS FOR DISTRIBUTIONS

In this section, we prove Theorem 9.

4.1 Some notation

We now introduce some notation.

Let U_n denote the uniform distribution over $\mathbb{F}_2^n$.

Let μ be a distribution over $\mathbb{F}_2^n$. For an integer $k > 0$, we let $\mu^{(k)}$ denote the distribution of $x_1 + \ldots + x_k$, where the x_i are picked independently from μ. The crucial fact that we need about this operation is given by the following lemma.

LEMMA 12. *Suppose that for every nontrivial character χ of $\mathbb{F}_2^n$, we have*

$$|\mathbb{E}_{x\in\mu}[\chi(x)]| < \beta.$$

Then the distribution $\mu^{(k)}$ is $\beta^k \cdot 2^n$-close to U_n in statistical distance.

For an integer $k > 0$ and $y \in \mathbb{F}_2^n$, we let $\mu^{(k,y)}$ denote the distribution of $(x_1, \ldots, x_k) \in (\mathbb{F}_2^n)^k$, where the x_i are picked independently from μ *conditioned* on $\sum_{i=1}^k x_i = y$.

For a probabilistic function $f : \mathbb{F}_2^n \to \mathbb{F}_2$, we define the *real function associated with* f to be the function $F : \mathbb{F}_2^n \to [-1, 1]$, where for each $x \in \mathbb{F}_2^n$, $F(x) = 2p_x - 1$, where p_x is the probability that $f(x)$ equals 0. Thus, if f was a deterministic function, then $F(x) = (-1)^{f(x)}$.

For functions $F, G : \mathbb{F}_2^n \to \mathbb{R}$ and a distribution μ over $\mathbb{F}_2^n$, we define the μ-correlation between F and G, denoted $\langle F, G\rangle_\mu$ be the quantity

$$\mathbb{E}_{x\in\mu}F(x)G(x).$$

Note that if f and g are probabilistic functions from $\mathbb{F}_2^n$ to $\mathbb{F}_2$, and F and G are the real functions associated with them, then

$$\langle F, G\rangle_\mu = 1 - 2\Delta_\mu(f, g). \quad (3)$$

4.2 Local algorithms for distributions

In this subsection, we will prove Theorem 9 on the local list-decoding and testing of linear functions under unbiased distributions μ.

Recall the setup: we have a distribution μ over $\mathbb{F}_2^n$ and a function $f : \mathbb{F}_2^n \to \mathbb{F}_2$. Our algorithms will work by reducing to the uniform distribution over $\mathbb{F}_2^n$. Specifically, we will produce a (probabilistic) function $h : \mathbb{F}_2^n \to \mathbb{F}_2$ (from which we can sample, given oracle access to f) such that the μ-distance of f from a linear function g "corresponds" to the U_n-distance of h from g. Then list-decoding and linearity-testing of h under the uniform distribution will enable us to list-decode and test the linearity of f under the μ-distribution.

We begin by introducing the local list-decoder for linear functions under the uniform distribution, given by the famous Goldreich-Levin algorithm[1].

THEOREM 13 ([10]). *For every $0 < \epsilon < 1/2$, there exists a $(\frac{1}{2} - \epsilon, \text{poly}(\frac{1}{\epsilon}), \text{poly}(\frac{1}{\epsilon}))$-local list-decoder for linear functions under U_n.*

This version of the Goldreich-Levin theorem, in conjunction with the BLR linearity test [7][2], easily implies a constant query local tester for linear functions under the uniform distribution in the *high error* regime.

THEOREM 14 ([10, 7]). *Then for every $0 < \epsilon_1 < \epsilon_2 < 1/2$, there exists a $\left(\frac{1}{2} - \epsilon_2, \frac{1}{2} - \epsilon_1, \text{poly}\left(\frac{1}{\epsilon_2 - \epsilon_1}\right)\right)$-local tester for linear functions under U_n.*

We now give a proof of the main result of this section, Theorem 9.

[1]To be precise, we state a generalization of the usual Goldreich-Levin theorem to handle probabilistic functions; inspecting the original proof of the theorem immediately reveals that it applies verbatim to probabilistic functions too.

[2]suitably generalized to handle probabilistic functions

THEOREM 9. *Let μ be a distribution over $\mathbb{F}_2^n$ such that for all nontrivial characters $\chi : \mathbb{F}_2^n \to \{-1, +1\}$,*

$$|\mathop{\mathbf{E}}_{x\in\mu}[\chi(x)]| < 2^{-\eta n}.$$

Then,

1. **Local list-decoding:** *For every ϵ such that $0 < \epsilon < 1/2$, there exists a $\left(\frac{1}{2} - \epsilon, (\frac{1}{\epsilon})^{O(1/\eta)}, (\frac{1}{\epsilon})^{O(1/\eta)}\right)$-local list-decoder for linear functions under μ.*
2. **Local testing:** *For every ϵ_1, ϵ_2 such that $0 < \epsilon_1 < \epsilon_2 < 1/2$, there exists a $\left(\frac{1}{2} - \epsilon_2, \frac{1}{2} - \epsilon_1, \left(\frac{1}{\epsilon_2 - \epsilon_1}\right)^{O(1/\eta)}\right)$-local tester for linear functions under μ.*

PROOF. Let $f : \mathbb{F}_2^n \to \mathbb{F}_2$ be the probabilistic function which we want to locally list-decode or locally test. Let k be an odd integer $\approx \frac{100}{\eta}$, and note that Lemma 12 implies that the distribution $\mu^{(k)}$ is 2^{-50n} close to U_n in statistical distance.

Let $h : \mathbb{F}_2^n \to \mathbb{F}_2$ be the probabilistic function defined as follows. For $y \in \mathbb{F}_2^n$, to sample $h(y)$, first sample $(x_1, \ldots, x_k)$ from $\mu^{(k,y)}$, and then output $\sum_{i=1}^k f(x_i)$. Clearly, any algorithm that is given oracle access to f can simulate oracle access to h with a $O(\frac{1}{\eta})$-blowup in the number of queries (although the *time complexity* of this simulation need not be bounded). See also the Remark following the proof.

We will assume without loss of generality in the rest of the proof that $(\frac{1}{\epsilon})^k$ and $(\frac{1}{\epsilon_2 - \epsilon_1})^k$ are all $2^{o(n)}$, since otherwise the trivial local testers and list-decoders that query the function at every point of the domain will satisfy the bounds in the theorem.

The crux of our algorithms is the following claim (the proof appears in the analysis of the algorithms).

CLAIM 15. *For every linear function $g : \mathbb{F}_2^n \to \mathbb{F}_2$, letting $\Delta_\mu(f, g) = \frac{1-\beta}{2}$ and $\Delta_{U_n}(h, g) = \frac{1-\alpha}{2}$, we have*

$$\alpha = \beta^k \pm 2^{-50n}.$$

We now present our local list-decoding and testing algorithms for linear functions. Both these algorithms will assume they have oracle access to the probabilistic function h, which by the earlier discussion, can be simulated by using oracle access to f.

Algorithm for Local List-Decoding.

Fix any ϵ such that $0 < \epsilon < 1/2$. We now describe a $\left(\frac{1}{2} - \epsilon, (\frac{1}{\epsilon})^{O(1/\eta)}, (\frac{1}{\epsilon})^{O(1/\eta)}\right)$-local list-decoder, D_μ, for linear functions under μ. Let $\alpha = \frac{(2\epsilon)^k - 2^{-50n}}{2}$.

By Theorem 13, there is a $(\frac{1}{2} - \alpha, \text{poly}(\frac{1}{\alpha}), \text{poly}(\frac{1}{\alpha}))$-local list-decoder, D_{U_n}, for linear functions under U_n. The list-decoder for linear functions under μ, D_μ^f, works as follows given oracle access to the probabilistic function f:

- Run D_{U_n} and get as output a list of randomized algorithms $\{D_1, \ldots, D_l\}$
- Return a list of randomized algorithms $\{D_{\mu,1}, \ldots, D_{\mu,l}\}$, where $D_{\mu,i}$ works as follows: The algorithm $D_{\mu,i}^f(x)$ simulates $D_i^h(x)$ (recall that given oracle access to f, one can simulate oracle access to h) and returns the value returned by $D_i^h(x)$.

Algorithm for Testing.
Fix any ϵ_1, ϵ_2 such that $0 < \epsilon_1 < \epsilon_2 < 1/2$. We now describe a $\left(\frac{1}{2}-\epsilon_2, \frac{1}{2}-\epsilon_1, \left(\frac{1}{\epsilon_2-\epsilon_1}\right)^{O(1/\eta)}\right)$-local tester, T_μ, for linear functions under μ.

Let $\alpha_1 = \frac{(2\epsilon_1)^k+2^{-50n}}{2}$ and let $\alpha_2 = \frac{(2\epsilon_2)^k-2^{-50n}}{2}$. By Theorem 14, there is a $\left(\frac{1}{2}-\alpha_2, \frac{1}{2}-\alpha_1, \text{poly}\left(\frac{1}{\alpha_2-\alpha_1}\right)\right)$-local tester, T_{U_n}, for linear functions under U_n.

The linearity-tester under μ, T_μ, works as follows given oracle access to the probabilistic function f:

- Simulate $T^h_{U_n}$ (again recall that given oracle access to f, one can simulate oracle access to h), and accept if and only if $T^h_{U_n}$ accepts.

Analysis.
The correctness of the algorithms will follow easily from Claim 15. We first prove this claim.

Let $F : \mathbb{F}_2^n \to [-1, +1]$ be the real function associated with f. Let $H : \mathbb{F}_2^n \to [-1, +1]$ be the real function associated with h.

Let χ_g be the real function associate with g. Note that since g is a deterministic function, $\chi_g(x)$ simply equals $(-1)^{g(x)}$.

Note that by definition,

$$H(x) = \mathbb{E}_{(x_1,\ldots,x_k)\in\mu^{(k,y)}}\left[\prod_{i=1}^k F(x_i)\right].$$

We want to estimate $\Delta_{U_n}(h, g)$ in terms of $\Delta_\mu(f, g)$. Equivalently, by Equation (3), we want to bound $\langle H, \chi_g\rangle_{U_n}$ in terms of $\langle F, \chi_g\rangle_\mu$. We begin by expanding out the definition of $\langle H, \chi_g\rangle_{U_n}$:

$$\begin{aligned}
&\langle H, \chi_g\rangle_{U_n}\\
&= \mathbb{E}_{y\in U_n}[H(y)\chi_g(y)]\\
&= \mathbb{E}_{y\in\mu^{(k)}}[H(y)\chi_g(y)] \pm 2^{-50n}\\
&\text{by Lemma 12 and choice of } k\\
&= \mathbb{E}_{y\in\mu^{(k)}}\left[\left(\mathbb{E}_{(x_1,\ldots,x_k)\in\mu^{(k,y)}}\left[\prod_{i=1}^k F(x_i)\right]\right)\chi_g(y)\right] \pm 2^{-50n}\\
&= \mathbb{E}_{y\in\mu^{(k)}}\left[\mathbb{E}_{(x_1,\ldots,x_k)\in\mu^{(k,y)}}\left[\prod_{i=1}^k (F(x_i)\chi_g(x_i))\right]\right] \pm 2^{-50n}\\
&= \mathbb{E}_{x_1,\ldots,x_k\in\mu}\left[\prod_{i=1}^k (F(x_i)\chi_g(x_i))\right] \pm 2^{-50n}\\
&= (\mathbb{E}_{x\in\mu}[F(x)\chi_g(x)])^k \pm 2^{-50n}.\\
&= \langle F, \chi_g\rangle_\mu^k \pm 2^{-50n}.
\end{aligned}$$

By Equation (3), we get that $\alpha = \beta^k \pm 2^{-50n}$. This proves the claim.

Analysis of decoder.
Claim 15 together with Equation (3) implies that if g is a linear function such that $\Delta_\mu(g, f) < 1/2 - \epsilon$, then $\Delta_{U_n}(g, h) < 1/2 - \alpha$, where $\alpha = \frac{(2\epsilon)^k-2^{-50n}}{2}$. Now, the decoder D^f_μ simulates $D^h_{U_n}$, and hence returns an algorithm computing every linear function g such that $\Delta_{U_n}(g, h) < 1/2 - \alpha$. Hence, it also returns an algorithm computing every linear function g such that $\Delta_\mu(g, f) < 1/2 - \epsilon$.

Observe that the query complexity of D^f_μ is given by the query complexity of $D^h_{U_n}$, but blown up by a factor of $k = O(1/\eta)$, since each each query to h is made by making k queries to f. Plugging in the parameters of D_{U_n}, we obtain the desired query complexity for D^f_μ.

Analysis of tester.
Just as we stated in the analysis of the decoder, Claim 15 together with Equation (3) implies that

- If g is a linear function such that $\Delta_\mu(g, f) < 1/2 - \epsilon_2$, then $\Delta_{U_n}(g, h) < 1/2 - \alpha_2$, where $\alpha_2 = \frac{(2\epsilon_2)^k-2^{-50n}}{2}$.
- If g is a linear function such that $\Delta_\mu(g, f) > 1/2 - \epsilon_1$, then $\Delta_{U_n}(g, h) > 1/2 - \alpha_1$, where $\alpha_1 = \frac{(2\epsilon_1)^k+2^{-50n}}{2}$. (For this implication we use that k is odd.)

Now, the tester T^f_μ simulates $T^h_{U_n}$, and outputs the output of $T^h_{U_n}$. If f is $1/2 - \epsilon_2$ close to a linear function under μ, then by the above implications, h is $1/2 - \alpha_2$ close to a linear function under U_n, and hence $T^h_{U_n}$ accepts. If f is $1/2 - \epsilon_1$ far from all linear function under μ, then by the above implications, h is $1/2 - \alpha_1$ far from all linear function under U_n, and hence $T^h_{U_n}$ rejects.

Just as in the case of the local list-decoder, observe that the query complexity of T^f_μ is given by the query complexity of $T^h_{U_n}$, but blown up by a factor of $k = O(1/\eta)$, since each each query to h is made by making k queries to f. Plugging in the parameters of T_{U_n}, we obtain the desired query complexity for T^f_μ □

Remark (Time Complexity). Suppose there is an algorithm μSample that runs in time T, which when given $y \in \mathbb{F}_2^n$, produces a vector $x \in (\mathbb{F}_2^n)^k$ whose distribution is λ-close to to $\mu^{(k,y)}$. Then in time poly(T), one can sample (upto λ-statistical distance) the value of $h(y)$ for any given y, using oracle access to f. This will allow the algorithms of the previous section to run in time which is a poly(T) factor larger than the corresponding running times of the invoked algorithms for the uniform distribution. In particular, if $\lambda < 2^{-\Omega(n)}$, the list-decoder will run in time $\text{poly}\left(T, \left(\frac{1}{\epsilon}\right)^{1/\eta}\right)$, and the linearity-tester will run in time $\text{poly}\left(T, \left(\frac{1}{\epsilon_2-\epsilon_1}\right)^{1/\eta}\right)$.

In the full version of this paper [18], we show how to implement the μSample algorithm in time poly(n) when μ is the distribution associated with the dual-BCH code via a particular generator matrix.

5. SUBEXPONENTIAL TIME LIST-DECODING

In this section, we prove Theorem 6 on the subexponential time list-decoding of unbiased linear codes.

As in the local algorithms given in Section 4, we first change our language to that of distributions on $\mathbb{F}_2^n$. Given a linear code $\mathcal{C}$ and a received word r from which we want to list-decode, we get a distribution μ and a function $f : \mathbb{F}_2^n \to \mathbb{F}_2$, and we want to find all linear functions $g : \mathbb{F}_2^n \to \mathbb{F}_2$ that are close to f in μ-distance.

Following the local algorithms, here too we will "self-correct" f to obtain a function h, such that every linear function that correlates with f under the μ distribution, also correlates with h under the uniform distribution over $\mathbb{F}_2^n$. However, since we are now paying attention to running time (and we do not know how to solve the μSample problem efficiently in general), we cannot afford to allow the list-decoder over the uniform distribution over $\mathbb{F}_2^n$ to query the value of h at any point that it desires. Instead, we will use some recent remarkable list-decoders, developed in the context of learning noisy parities, which can list-decode in subexponential time by simply querying the function h at independent uniformly random points of $\mathbb{F}_2^n$! Using the unbiasedness of μ, it turns out to be easy to evaluate h at independent uniformly random points of $\mathbb{F}_2^n$. This completes the informal description of the algorithm.

Below we state the result on agnostically learning parities ([9]) that gives a list-decoding algorithm for any function h over the uniform distribution over $\mathbb{F}_2^n$ in subexponential time, in the model where the algorithm receives independent and uniform samples from h. The parameters in Theorem 16 below are obtained by combining the parameters for the running time and query complexity of the Blum-Kalai-Wasserman [6] algorithm for learning *noisy parities* with random errors in subexponential time with the Feldman-Gopalan-Khot-Ponnuswami [9] algorithm for reducing the problem of learning noisy parities with agnostic errors to the problem of learning noisy parities with random errors.

THEOREM 16 ([9]). *There is an algorithm* AgnosticParity, *such that for every probabilistic function h : $\mathbb{F}_2^n \to \mathbb{F}_2$, every $\beta > 0$ and every choice of parameter $t > 0$,:*

- *If* AgnosticParity *is given as input the parameter β and $s \geq \exp(\log(1/\beta)n^{1/t} + \frac{tn}{\log n})$ independent samples $(x, h(x))$, where x is chosen uniformly $\mathbb{F}_2^n$, then with high probability* AgnosticParity *returns the set of all linear functions $g : \mathbb{F}_2^n \to \mathbb{F}_2$ such that $\Delta_{U_n}(h, g) < \frac{1-\beta}{2}$.*
- AgnosticParity *runs in time* $\exp(\log(1/\beta)n^{1/t} + \frac{tn}{\log n})$

We are now ready to prove our main theorem, Theorem 6, on the subexponential time list-decoding of unbiased codes.

THEOREM 6. *For all constants $\alpha, \gamma, \epsilon > 0$, there is an algorithm* SubExpListDecode, *which when given:*

- *the generator matrix G of a n-dimensional binary linear code $\mathcal{C} \subseteq \mathbb{F}_2^N$, where $\mathcal{C}$ has bias $N^{-\gamma}$ and $N = n^{1+\alpha}$, and*
- *a vector $r \in \mathbb{F}_2^N$,*

runs in time $\exp(\frac{n}{\log \log n})$ and with high probability, finds all codewords $c \in \mathcal{C}$ such that $\Delta(c, r) < \frac{1-\epsilon}{2}$.

PROOF. Let $\mathbf{v}_i$ the ith column of G.

Below we present the list-decoding algorithm. For concreteness will present the algorithm in the language of codes. The proof of correctness will employ the language of distributions over $\mathbb{F}_2^n$.

- Initialize the set $Z = \emptyset$.
- Set $k = \frac{100n}{\gamma \log N}$, $t = 2\frac{\log n}{\log \log n}$, and $s = \exp(\log(1/\epsilon)kn^{1/t} + \frac{tn}{\log n})$.
- Repeat s times:
  - Sample $i_1, \ldots, i_k$ uniformly at random from $[N]$.
  - Include $(\sum_{j=1}^k \mathbf{v}_{i_j}, \sum_{j=1}^k r_{i_j})$ in Z.
- Choose the parameter $t = 2\frac{\log n}{\log \log n}$, and feed $\epsilon^k/2$ and Z as input to AgnosticParity, and let its output be $\{g_1, \ldots, g_l\}$.
- For each $i \in [l]$, write the linear function g_i in the form $g_i(x) = a_i \cdot x$, and output the codeword $a_i \cdot G$.

Clearly, (by Theorem 16), this algorithm runs in time $\exp(\log(1/\epsilon)kn^{1/t} + \frac{tn}{\log n})$. By choice of k and t, and since ϵ is constant and $N = n^{1+\alpha}$ for constant α, this equals $\exp(\frac{n}{\log \log n})$.

We now show that this algorithm is indeed a list-decoder as claimed. Let $c = a \cdot G$ be a codeword of $\mathcal{C}$ such that $\Delta(c, r) < \frac{1-\epsilon}{2}$. Let $g : \mathbb{F}_2^n \to \mathbb{F}_2$ be the linear function given by $g(x) = a \cdot x$.

Let μ be the uniform distribution over the columns of G (i.e., μ is the distribution associated to $\mathcal{C}$ via G). Let $f : \mathbb{F}_2^n \to \mathbb{F}_2$ be a probabilistic function, where to sample $f(x)$, we pick an $i \in [N]$ uniformly at random from the set of all i such that $x = \mathbf{v}_i$, and output r_i (if there are no such i, then we can define $f(x)$ arbitrarily).

Let $h : \mathbb{F}_2^n \to \mathbb{F}_2$ be the probabilistic function defined as follows. For $y \in \mathbb{F}_2^n$, to sample $h(y)$, first sample $(x_1, \ldots, x_k)$ from $\mu^{(k,y)}$ (recall that $\mu^{(k,y)}$ denotes the distribution of $(x_1, \ldots, x_k) \in (\mathbb{F}_2^n)^k$, where the x_i are picked independently from μ *conditioned* on $\sum_{i=1}^k x_i = y$), and output $\sum_{i=1}^k f(x_i)$.

As in the local setting, we have the following claim. We omit the proof (which is identical to the proof Claim 15).

CLAIM 17. *Let $\Delta_{U_n}(h, g) = \frac{1-\alpha'}{2}$. Then,*

$$\alpha' > \epsilon^k \pm 2^{-50n}.$$

Now, if $\epsilon^k \leq 2^{-n}$, then the trivial brute force algorithm that searches over all possible linear function also satisfies the parameters of the theorem. Hence, from now on we assume without loss of generality that $\epsilon^k > 2^{-n}$. In particular, the claim above implies that $\alpha' > \epsilon^k/2$.

Let us analyze a single iteration of the loop in the algorithm. We will show that the distribution of the point $(\sum_j v_{i_j}, \sum_j r_{i_j})$ (which gets included in the set Z) is 2^{-50n}-close to the distribution of $(y, h(y))$, where y is sampled uniformly at random from $\mathbb{F}_2^n$, and $h(y)$ is sampled independently from the probabilistic function h.

Assuming this for the moment, it is easy to see that the algorithm will include c in its output. Indeed, the set of samples Z fed into the algorithm AgnosticParity is 2^{-50n}-close to the distribution of

$$((x_1, h(x_1)), (x_2, h(x_2)), \ldots, (x_s, h(x_s))),$$

where the x_i are independent. Thus by Theorem 16, since $\Delta_{U_n}(h, g) < \frac{1-\epsilon^k/2}{2}$, we see that the algorithm AgnosticParity will return g in its output. Thus c will be included in the output of the algorithm SubExpListDecode, as desired.

We now analyze the distribution of $(\sum_j v_{i_j}, \sum_j r_{i_j})$. By definition, the distribution of this is identical to the distribution of $(\sum_{j=1}^k x_j, \sum_{j=1}^k f(x_j))$, where $x_1, \ldots, x_k$ are sampled independently and uniformly from μ. By Lemma 12, the distribution of $\sum_{j=1}^k x_j$ is 2^{-50n}-close to uniformly distributed over $\mathbb{F}_2^n$. For any given $y \in \mathbb{F}_2^n$, conditioned on $\sum_{j=1}^k x_j = y$, the distribution of $\sum_{j=1}^{k} f(x_j)$ has a distribution identical to that of $h(y)$. Thus the distribution of $(\sum_j v_{i_j}, \sum_j r_{i_j})$ is 2^{-50n}-close to the distribution of $(y, h(y))$, for uniformly sampled y.

This completes the proof of correctness of the algorithm. □

Since the bias of random linear codes is small, we immediately get the following corollary.

COROLLARY 18. *For all constants $\alpha, \epsilon > 0$, there is an algorithm which when given the $n \times N$ generator matrix G of a random binary linear code $\mathcal{C}$, where $N = n^{1+\alpha}$, and when given a vector $r \in \mathbb{F}_2^N$, runs in time $\exp(\frac{n}{\log \log n})$ and finds all codewords $c \in \mathcal{C}$ such that $\Delta(c, r) < \frac{1}{2} - \epsilon$.*

Acknowledgements

We are very grateful to Madhu Sudan for suggesting these problems to us, for constant encouragement, valuable discussions and for conjecturing the impossibility of our results. We are also very grateful to Adam Kalai for his enthusiastic support and many helpful discussions. Many thanks also to Henry Cohn and Tali Kaufman for all their encouragement.

Finally, we would like to thank Microsoft Research, New England, for its hospitality.

6. REFERENCES

[1] N. Alon, T. Kaufman, M. Krivelevich, S. Litsyn, and D. Ron. Testing low-degree polynomials over GF(2). In *Proceedings of RANDOM 2003, LNCS, vol. 2764*, pages 188–199, New York, 2003. Springer.

[2] S. Arora, C. Lund, R. Motwani, M. Sudan, and M. Szegedy. Proof verification and the hardness of approximation problems. *Journal of the ACM*, 45(3):501–555, May 1998.

[3] S. Arora and S. Safra. Probabilistic checking of proofs: A new characterization of NP. *Journal of the ACM*, 45(1):70–122, January 1998.

[4] S. Arora and M. Sudan. Improved low degree testing and its applications. *Combinatorica*, 23(3):365–426, 2003. Preliminary version in Proceedings of ACM STOC 1997.

[5] M. Bellare, D. Coppersmith, J. Håstad, M. Kiwi, and M. Sudan. Linearity testing over characteristic two. *IEEE Transactions on Information Theory*, 42(6):1781–1795, November 1996.

[6] A. Blum, A. Kalai, and H. Wasserman. Noise-tolerant learning, the parity problem, and the statistical query model. *J. ACM*, 50(4):506–519, 2003.

[7] M. Blum, M. Luby, and R. Rubinfeld. Self-testing/correcting with applications to numerical problems. *Journal of Computer and System Sciences*, 47(3):549–595, 1993.

[8] I. Dinur and E. Goldenberg. Locally testing direct product in the low error range. In *FOCS*, pages 613–622. IEEE Computer Society, 2008.

[9] V. Feldman, P. Gopalan, S. Khot, and A. K. Ponnuswami. New results for learning noisy parities and halfspaces. In *FOCS*, pages 563–574, 2006.

[10] O. Goldreich and L. Levin. A hard-core predicate for all one-way functions. *Proceedings of the 21st Annual ACM Symposium on Theory of Computing*, pages 25–32, May 1989.

[11] O. Goldreich, R. Rubinfeld, and M. Sudan. Learning polynomials with queries: The highly noisy case. *SIAM Journal on Discrete Mathematics*, 13(4):535–570, November 2000.

[12] P. Gopalan, A. R. Klivans, and D. Zuckerman. List-decoding reed-muller codes over small fields. In *STOC*, pages 265–274, 2008.

[13] R. Impagliazzo, R. Jaiswal, V. Kabanets, and A. Wigderson. Uniform direct product theorems: simplified, optimized, and derandomized. In *STOC*, pages 579–588, 2008.

[14] R. Impagliazzo, V. Kabanets, and A. Wigderson. New direct-product testers and 2-query pcps. In *STOC*, pages 131–140, 2009.

[15] R. Impagliazzo and A. Wigderson. P = BPP if E requires exponential circuits: Derandomizing the XOR Lemma. *Proceedings of the 29th Annual ACM Symposium on Theory of Computing*, pages 220–229, May 1997.

[16] T. Kaufman and S. Litsyn. Almost orthogonal linear codes are locally testable. In *Proceedings of the Forty-sixth Annual Symposium on Foundations of Computer Science*, pages 317–326, 2005.

[17] T. Kaufman and M. Sudan. Sparse random linear codes are locally decodable and testable. In *FOCS*, pages 590–600. IEEE Computer Society, 2007.

[18] S. Kopparty and S. Saraf. Local list-decoding and testing of sparse random linear codes from high error. *Electronic Colloquium on Computational Complexity (ECCC)*, 9(115), 2009.

[19] S. Kopparty and S. Saraf. Tolerant linearity testing and locally testable codes. In *APPROX-RANDOM*, pages 601–614, 2009.

[20] I. Krasikov and S. Litsyn. On spectra of BCH codes. *IEEE Transactions on Information Theory*, 41(3):786–788, 1995.

[21] V. Lyubashevsky. The parity problem in the presence of noise, decoding random linear codes, and the subset sum problem. In *APPROX-RANDOM*, pages 378–389, 2005.

[22] D. Moshkovitz and R. Raz. Sub-constant error low degree test of almost-linear size. In J. M. Kleinberg, editor, *STOC*, pages 21–30. ACM, 2006.

[23] R. Raz and S. Safra. A sub-constant error-probability low-degree test, and a sub-constant error-probability PCP characterization of NP. In *Proceedings of the Twenty-Ninth Annual ACM Symposium on Theory of Computing*, pages 475–484, New York, NY, 1997. ACM Press.

[24] R. Rubinfeld and M. Sudan. Robust characterizations of polynomials with applications to program testing. *SIAM Journal on Computing*, 25(2):252–271, April 1996.

[25] A. Samorodnitsky. Low-degree tests at large distances. In D. S. Johnson and U. Feige, editors, *STOC*, pages 506–515. ACM, 2007.

[26] M. Sudan, 2009. Personal Communication.

[27] M. Sudan, L. Trevisan, and S. Vadhan. Pseudorandom generators without the XOR lemma. *Proceedings of the 31st Annual ACM Symposium on Theory of Computing*, pages 537–546, 1999.

Pseudorandom Generators for Polynomial Threshold Functions*

Raghu Meka†
UT Austin
raghu@cs.utexas.edu

David Zuckerman†
UT Austin
diz@cs.utexas.edu

ABSTRACT

We study the natural question of constructing pseudorandom generators (PRGs) for low-degree polynomial threshold functions (PTFs). We give a PRG with seed-length $\log n/\epsilon^{O(d)}$ fooling degree d PTFs with error at most ϵ. Previously, no nontrivial constructions were known even for quadratic threshold functions and constant error ϵ. For the class of degree 1 threshold functions or halfspaces, we construct PRGs with much better dependence on the error parameter ϵ and obtain the following results.

- A PRG with seed length $O(\log n \log(1/\epsilon))$ for error $\epsilon \geq 1/\text{poly}(n)$.
- A PRG with seed length $O(\log n)$ for $\epsilon \geq 1/\text{poly}(\log n)$.

Previously, only PRGs with seed length $O(\log n \log^2(1/\epsilon)/\epsilon^2)$ were known for halfspaces. We also obtain PRGs with similar seed lengths for fooling halfspaces over the n dimensional unit sphere.

The main theme of our constructions and analysis is the use of *invariance principles* to construct pseudorandom generators. We also introduce the notion of monotone read-once branching programs, which is key to improving the dependence on the error rate ϵ for halfspaces. These techniques may be of independent interest.

Categories and Subject Descriptors

G.3 [**Probability and Statistics**]: Random number generation

General Terms

Algorithms, Theory

*A full version of this paper is available at `http://arxiv.org/abs/0910.4122`

†Partially supported by NSF Grants CCF-0634811 and CCF-0916160 and THECB ARP Grant 003658-0113-2007.

Keywords

branching programs, halfspaces, invariance principles, polynomials, pseudorandom generators, threshold function

1. INTRODUCTION

Polynomial threshold functions are a fundamental class of functions with many important applications in complexity theory [Bei93], learning theory [KS04], quantum complexity theory [BBC+01], voting theory [ABFR94] and more. A polynomial threshold function (PTF) of degree d is a function $f : \{1,-1\}^n \to \{1,-1\}$ of the form $f(x) = \mathsf{sign}(P(x) - \theta)$, where $P : \{1,-1\}^n \to \mathbb{R}$ is a multi-linear polynomial of degree d. Of particular importance are the class of degree 1 threshold functions, also known as halfspaces which have been instrumental in the development of many fundamental tools in learning theory such as perceptrons, support vector machines and boosting.

Here we address the natural problem of explicitly constructing pseudorandom generators (PRGs) for PTFs. Derandomizing natural complexity classes is a fundamental problem in complexity theory, with several applications outside complexity theory. For instance, PRGs for PTFs facilitate estimating the accuracy of PTF classifiers in machine learning with a small number of deterministic samples; PRGs for spherical caps and PRGs for intersections of halfspaces can help derandomize randomized algorithms such as the Goemans-Williamson Max-Cut algorithm.

In this work, we give the first nontrivial pseudorandom generators for low-degree PTFs.

Definition 1.1. *A function $G : \{0,1\}^r \to \{1,-1\}^n$ is a PRG with error ϵ for (or ϵ-fools) PTFs of degree d, if*

$$\left| \mathop{\mathbb{E}}_{x \in_u \{1,-1\}^n}[f(x)] - \mathop{\mathbb{E}}_{y \in_u \{0,1\}^r}[f(G(y))] \right| \leq \epsilon,$$

for all PTFs f of degree at most d. (Here $x \in_u S$ denotes a uniformly random element of S.)

It can be shown by the probabilistic method that there exist PRGs that ϵ-fool degree d PTFs with *seed length* $r = O(d \log n + \log(1/\epsilon))$. However, despite their long history, until recently very little was known about explicitly constructing such PRGs, even for the special class of halfspaces.

In this work, we present a PRG that ϵ-fools degree d PTFs with seed length $O(\log n/\epsilon^{O(d)})$. Previously, PRGs with seed length $o(n)$ were not known even for degree 2 PTFs and constant ϵ.

THEOREM 1.2. *For $0 < \epsilon < 1$, there exists an explicit PRG fooling PTFs of degree d with error at most ϵ and seed length $2^{O(d)} \log n/\epsilon^{8d+3}$.*

For the $d = 1$ case of halfspaces, Diakonikolas et al. [DGJ+09] constructed PRGs with seed length $O(\log n)$ for constant error rates. PRGs with seed length $O(\log^2 n)$ for halfspaces with polynomially bounded weights follow easily from known results. However, nothing nontrivial was known for general halfspaces, for instance, when $\epsilon = 1/\sqrt{n}$. In this work we construct PRGs with exponentially better dependence on the error parameter ϵ.

THEOREM 1.3. *For all constants c, $\epsilon \geq 1/n^c$, there exists an explicit PRG fooling halfspaces with error at most ϵ and seed length $O(\log n \log(1/\epsilon))$.*

THEOREM 1.4. *For all constants c, $\epsilon \geq 1/\log^c n$, there exists an explicit PRG fooling halfspaces with error at most ϵ and seed length $O(\log n)$.*

We also obtain results similar to the above for spherical caps. The problem of constructing PRGs spherical caps was brought to our attention by Amir Shpilka; Karnin et al. [KRS09] were the first to obtain a PRG with parameters similar to those in Theorem 1.6 using different methods.

THEOREM 1.5. *There exists a constant $c > 0$ such that for all $\epsilon > c\log n/n^{1/4}$, there exists an explicit PRG fooling spherical caps with error at most ϵ and seed length $O(\log n \log(1/\epsilon))$.*

THEOREM 1.6. *For $\epsilon \geq 1/\text{poly}(\log n)$, there exists an explicit PRG fooling spherical caps with error at most ϵ and seed length $O(\log n)$.*

We briefly summarize the previous constructions for halfspaces.

1. Halfspaces with polynomially bounded integer weights can be computed by polynomial width read-once branching programs (ROBPs). Thus, the PRGs for ROBPs such as those of Nisan [Nis92] and Impagliazzo et al. [INW94] fool halfspaces with polynomially bounded integer weights with seed length $O(\log^2 n)$. However, a simple counting argument ([MT94], [Has94]) shows that most halfspaces have exponentially large weights.

2. Diakonikolas et al. [DGJ+09] showed that k-wise independent spaces fool halfspaces for $k = O(\log^2(1/\epsilon)/\epsilon^2)$. By using the known efficient constructions of k-wise independent spaces they obtain PRGs for halfspaces with seed length $O(\log n \log^2(1/\epsilon)/\epsilon^2)$.

3. Rabani and Shpilka [RS09] gave explicit constructions of polynomial size *hitting sets* for halfspaces.

The overarching theme behind all our constructions is the use of *invariance principles* to get pseudorandom generators. Broadly speaking, invariance principles for a class of functions say that under mild conditions (typically on the first few moments) the distribution of the functions is essentially invariant for all product distributions. Intuitively, invariance principles could be helpful in constructing pseudorandom generators as we can hope to exploit the invariance with respect to product distributions by replacing a product distribution with a "smaller product distribution" that still satisfies the conditions for applying the invariance principle. We believe that the above technique could be helpful for other derandomization problems.

Another aspect of our constructions is what we call the "monotone trick". The PRGs for small-width read-once branching programs (ROBP) from the works of Nisan [Nis92], Impagliazzo et al. [INW94], Nisan and Zuckerman [NZ96], have been a fundamental tool in derandomization with several applications [Siv02], [GR09]. An important ingredient in our PRG for halfspaces is our observation that any PRG for small-width ROBPs fools arbitrary width " monotone" ROBPs. Roughly speaking, we say a ROBP is monotone if there exists an ordering on the nodes in each layer of the program so that the corresponding sets of accepting strings *respect the ordering* (see Definition 2.3). We believe that this notion of monotone ROBP is quite natural and combined with the "monotone trick" could be useful elsewhere.

The above techniques have found recently other applications that we briefly describe in Section 1.2. We now give a high level view of our constructions and their analysis.

1.1 Outline of Constructions

Our constructions build mainly on the hitting set construction for halfspaces of Rabani and Shpilka. Although the constructions and analysis are similar in spirit for halfspaces and higher degree PTFs, for clarity, we deal with the two classes separately, at the cost of some repetition. The analysis is simpler for halfspaces and provides intuition for the more complicated analysis for higher degree PTFs.

1.1.1 PRGs for Halfspaces

Our first step in constructing PRGs for halfspaces is to use our "monotone trick" to show that PRGs for polynomial width read-once branching programs (ROBPs) also fool halfspaces. Previously, PRGs for polynomial width ROBPs were only known to fool halfspaces with polynomially bounded weights. Although the natural simulation of halfspaces by ROBP may require polynomially large width, we note that the resulting ROBP is what we call *monotone* (see Definition 2.3). We show that PRGs for polynomial width ROBP fool monotone ROBPs of arbitrary width.

THEOREM 1.7. *A PRG that δ-fools monotone ROBP of width $\log(4T/\epsilon)$ and length T fools monotone ROBP of arbitrary width and length T with error at most $\epsilon + \delta$.*

See Theorem 2.4 for a more formal statement. As a corollary we get the following.

COROLLARY 1.8. *For all $\epsilon > 0$, a PRG that δ-fools width $\log(4n/\epsilon)$ ROBPs fools halfspaces with error at most $\epsilon + \delta$.*

The above result already improves on the previous constructions for small ϵ, giving a PRG with seed length $O(\log^2 n)$ for $\epsilon = 1/\text{poly}(n)$. However, the randomness used is $O(\log^2 n)$ even for constant ϵ.

We next improve the dependence of the seed length on the error parameter ϵ to obtain our main results for fooling halfspaces. Following the approach of Diakonikolas et al. we first construct PRGs fooling *regular* halfspaces. A halfspace with coefficients $(w_1, \ldots, w_n)$ is regular if no coefficient is significantly larger than the others. Such halfspaces are easier to analyze because for regular w, the distribution of $\langle w, x\rangle$ with x uniformly distributed in $\{1,-1\}^n$ is close to a normal distribution by the Central Limit Theorem. Using a quantitative form of the above statement, the Berry-Esséen theorem, we show that a simplified version of the hitting set construction of Rabani and Shpilka gives a PRG fooling *regular* halfspaces.

Having fooled regular halfspaces, we use the structural results on halfspaces of Servedio [Ser06] and Diakonikolas et al. [DGJ+09] to fool arbitrary halfspaces. The structural results of Servedio and Diakonikolas et al. roughly show that either a halfspace is regular or is close to a function depending only on a small number of coordinates. Given this, we proceed by a case analysis as in Diakonikolas et al.: if a halfspace is regular, we use the analysis for regular halfspaces; else, we argue that bounded independence suffices.

The above analysis gives a PRG fooling halfspaces with seed length $O(\log n \log^2(1/\epsilon)/\epsilon^2)$, matching the PRG of Diakonikolas et al. [DGJ+09]. However, not only is our construction simpler to analyze (for the regular case), but we can also apply our "monotone trick" to derandomize the construction. Derandomizing using the PRGs for ROBPs of Nisan [Nis92], Impagliazzo et al. [INW94] gives Theorem 1.3 and derandomizing using the PRG of Nisan and Zuckerman [NZ96] gives Theorem 1.4.

For spherical caps, we give a simpler more direct construction based on our generator for regular halfspaces. We use an idea of Ailon and Chazelle [AC06] and the invariance of spherical caps with respect to unitary rotations to convert the case of arbitrary spherical caps to *regular spherical caps*. For lack of space, we defer the proofs of Theorems 1.5, 1.6 to the full version.

1.1.2 PRGs for PTFs

We next extend our PRG for halfspaces to fool higher degree polynomial threshold functions. The construction we use to fool PTFs is a natural extension of our *underandomized* PRG for halfspaces. The analysis, though similar in outline, is significantly more complicated and at a high level proceeds as follows.

As was done for halfspaces we first study the case of regular PTFs. The mainstay of our analysis for regular halfspaces is the Berry-Esséen theorem for sums of independent random variables. By using the generalized Berry-Esséen type theorem, or *invariance principle*, for low-degree multilinear polynomials, proved by Mossel et al. [MOO05], we extend our analysis for regular halfspaces to regular PTFs. We remark that unlike the case for halfspaces, we cannot use the invariance principle of Mossel et al. directly, but instead adapt their proof technique for our generator. In particular, we crucially use the fact that most of the arguments of Mossel et al. work even for distributions with bounded independence.

We then use structural results for PTFs of Diakonikolas et al. [DSTW10] and Harsha et al. [HKM09] that generalize the results of Servedio [Ser06] and Diakonikolas et al. [DGJ+09] for halfspaces. Roughly speaking, these results show the following: with at least a constant probability, upon randomly restricting a small number of variables, the resulting restricted PTF is either regular or has high bias. However, we cannot yet use the above observation to do a case analysis as was done for halfspaces; instead, we give a more delicate argument with recursive application of the results on random restrictions.

1.2 Other Applications

Gopalan et al. [GOWZ10] showed that our generator, when suitably modified, fools arbitrary functions of d halfspaces under product distributions where each coordinate has bounded fourth moment. To ϵ-fool any size-s, depth-d decision tree of halfspaces, their generator uses seed length $O((d\log(ds/\epsilon)+\log n)\cdot\log(ds/\epsilon))$. For monotone functions of k halfspaces, their seed length becomes $O((k\log(k/\epsilon)+\log n)\cdot\log(k/\epsilon))$. They get better bounds for larger ϵ; for example, to $1/\mathrm{poly}(\log n)$ fool all monotone functions of $(\log n)/\log\log n$ halfspaces, their generator requires a seed of length just $O(\log n)$.

In other subsequent work, building on techniques from this work and a new invariance principle for polytopes, Harsha et al. [HKM10] obtained pseudorandom generators that ϵ-fool certain classes of intersections of k halfspaces with seed length $(\log n)\cdot\mathrm{poly}(\log k, 1/\epsilon)$. As an application of their results, Harsha et al. obtained the first deterministic quasi-polynomial time approximate-counting algorithms for a large class of integer programs.

We first present our result on fooling arbitrary width *monotone* ROBPs with PRGs for small-width ROBPs.

2. PRGS FOR MONOTONE ROBPS

We start with some definitions.

DEFINITION 2.1 (ROBP). *An (S,D,T)-branching program M is a layered multi-graph with a layer for each $0\le i\le T$ and at most 2^S vertices (states) in each layer. The first layer has a single vertex v_0 and each vertex in the last layer is labeled with 0 (rejecting) or 1 (accepting). For $0\le i\le T$, a vertex v in layer i has at most 2^D outgoing edges each labeled with an element of $\{0,1\}^D$ and ending at a vertex in layer $i+1$.*

Note that by definition, an (S,D,T)-branching program is read-once. We also use the following notation. Let M be an (S,D,T)-branching program and v a vertex in layer i of M.

1. For $z=(z^i,z^{i+1},\ldots,z^T)\in(\{0,1\}^D)^{T+1-i}$ call (v,z) an *accepting* pair if starting from v and traversing the path with edges labeled z in M leads to an accepting state.

2. For $z\in(\{0,1\}^D)^T$, let $M(z)=1$ if (v_0,z) is an accepting pair, and $M(z)=0$ otherwise.

3. $A_M(v)=\{z:(v,z)$ is accepting in $M\}$ and $P_M(v)$ is the probability that (v,z) is an accepting pair for z chosen uniformly at random.

4. For brevity, let $\mathcal{U}$ denote the uniform distribution over $(\{0,1\}^D)^T$.

DEFINITION 2.2. *A function $G:\{0,1\}^r\to(\{0,1\}^D)^T$ is said to ϵ-fool (S,D,T)-branching programs if, for all (S,D,T)-branching programs M,*

$$|\Pr_{z\leftarrow\mathcal{U}}[M(z)=1]-\Pr_{y\in_u\{0,1\}^r}[M(G(y))=1]|\le\epsilon.$$

Nisan [Nis92] and Impagliazzo et al. [INW94] gave PRGs that fool (S, D, T)-branching programs with error δ and seed length $r = O((S + D)\log T + \log(T/\delta)\log T)$. For $T = \text{poly}(S, D)$, the PRG of Nisan and Zuckerman [NZ96] fools (S, D, T)-branching programs with seed length $r = O(S + D)$. Here we show that the above PRGs in fact fool arbitrary width monotone branching programs as defined below.

DEFINITION 2.3. *An (S, D, T)-branching program M is said to be monotone if for all $0 \leq i \leq T$, there exists an ordering $\{v_1 \prec v_2 \prec \ldots \prec v_{L_i}\}$ of the vertices in layer i such that for $1 \leq j < k \leq L_i$, $A_M(v_j) \subseteq A_M(v_k)$.*

THEOREM 2.4. *Let $0 < \epsilon < 1$ and $G : \{0,1\}^R \to (\{0,1\}^D)^T$ be a PRG that δ-fools monotone $(\log(4T/\epsilon), D, T)$-branching programs. Then G fools monotone (S, D, T)-branching programs for arbitrary S with error at most $\epsilon + \delta$.*

In particular, for $\delta = 1/\text{poly}(T)$ the above theorem gives a PRG fooling monotone (S, D, T)-branching programs with error at most $\delta+\epsilon$ and seed length $O(\log(1/\epsilon)\log T + D\log T + \log^2 T)$. Note that the seed length does not depend on the space S. Given the above result, Theorem 1.8 follows easily.

PROOF OF THEOREM 1.8. A halfspace with weight vector $w \in \mathbb{R}^n$ and threshold $\theta \in \mathbb{R}$ can be naturally computed by an $(S, 1, n)$-branching program $M_{w,\theta}$, for S large enough, by letting the states in layer i correspond to the partial sums $\sum_{j=1}^{i} w_j x_j$. It is easy to check that $M_{w,\theta}$ is monotone. The theorem now follows from Theorem 2.4. □

We now prove Theorem 2.4. The proof is based on the simple idea of "sandwiching" monotone branching programs between small-width branching programs. To this end, let M be a monotone (S, D, T)-branching program and call a pair of (s, D, T)-branching programs (M_{down}, M_{up}), ϵ-sandwiching for M if the following hold.

1. For all $z \in (\{0,1\}^D)^T$, $M_{down}(z) \leq M(z) \leq M_{up}(z)$.
2. $\Pr_{z \leftarrow \mathcal{U}}[M_{up}(z) = 1] - \Pr_{z \leftarrow \mathcal{U}}[M_{down}(z) = 1] \leq \epsilon$.

We first show that existence of small-width sandwiching branching programs suffices and then show the existence of small-width sandwiching branching programs for monotone branching programs. Theorem 2.4 follows directly from the following two lemmas.

LEMMA 2.5 (SEE FULL VERSION). *If a PRG G δ-fools (s, D, T)-branching programs, and there exist (s, D, T)-branching programs (M_{down}, M_{up}) that are ϵ-sandwiching for M, then G $(\epsilon + \delta)$-fools M.*

LEMMA 2.6. *For any monotone (S, D, T)-branching program M, there exist $(\log(2T/\epsilon), D, T)$-branching programs (M_{down}, M_{up}) that are (2ϵ)-sandwiching for M.*

PROOF. We first set up some notation. For $0 \leq i \leq T$, let the vertices in layer i in M be $V^i = \{v_1^i \prec v_2^i \prec \ldots \prec v_{l_i}^i\}$. Let $B^0 = \{v_0\}$ and for each $1 \leq i \leq T$, partition the vertices of layer i into at most $t_i \leq 2T/\epsilon$ intervals $J_1^i = \{v_1^i = v_{i_1}^i, v_{i_1+1}^i, \cdots, v_{i_2-1}^i\}$, $J_2^i = \{v_{i_2}^i, v_{i_2+1}^i, \ldots, v_{i_3-1}^i\}, \cdots, J_{t_i-1}^i = \{v_{i_{t_i-1}}^i, v_{i_{t_i-1}+1}^i, \ldots, v_{i_{t_i}}^i = v_{l_i}^i\}$ so that for $1 \leq k < t_i$

$$P_M(v_{i_{k+1}}^i) - P_M(v_{i_k}^i) \leq \epsilon/(2T) \quad \text{or} \quad i_{k+1} = i_k + 1. \tag{2.1}$$

Let $B^i = \{1 = i_1, i_2, \ldots, i_{t_i} = l_i\}$ be the set of separating indices for the intervals $J_1^i, J_2^i, \ldots, J_{t_i-1}^i$. Observe that, by definition, for any two nodes $v, v' \in J_k^i$ in the same interval,

$$|P_M(v) - P_M(v')| \leq \frac{\epsilon}{2T}. \tag{2.2}$$

Let $s = \log(2T/\epsilon)$ and define (s, D, T)-branching programs M_{up}, M_{down} as follows. The vertices in layer i of M_{up}, M_{down} are v_j^i for $j \in B^i$ and the edges are placed by *rounding* the edges of M *upwards and downwards* respectively as follows. For $j \in B^i$ suppose there is an edge labeled z between v_j^i and a vertex $v_l^{i+1} \in J_k^{i+1}$. If $|J_k^{i+1}| = 1$, we place an edge with label z between v_j^i and v_l^{i+1} in both M_{up} and M_{down}. Otherwise, we place an edge with label z from v_j^i to v_{k+1}^{i+1} in M_{up} and an edge with label z from v_j^i to v_k^{i+1} in M_{down}. We will show that M_{up}, M_{down} are ϵ-sandwiching for M.

CLAIM 2.7. *For $0 \leq i \leq T$ and $j \in B^i$, $A_{M_{down}}(v_j^i) \subseteq A_M(v_j^i) \subseteq A_{M_{up}}(v_j^i)$. In particular, for any z, $M_{down}(z) \leq M(z) \leq M_{up}(z)$.*

PROOF. Follows from the monotonicity of M. □

CLAIM 2.8. *For $0 \leq i \leq T$, and $j \in B^i$, $P_{M_{up}}(v_j^i) - P_{M_{down}}(v_j^i) \leq (T - i)\frac{\epsilon}{T}$. In particular, for z chosen uniformly at random, $\Pr[M_{up}(z) = 1] - \Pr[M_{down}(z) = 1] \leq 2\epsilon$.*

PROOF. The second part of the claim follows from the first. We will show the first part by showing the following: for $0 \leq i \leq T$ and $j \in B^i$,

$$|P_{M_{down}}(v_j^i) - P_M(v_j^i)| \leq \frac{(T-i)\epsilon}{2T} \tag{2.3}$$
$$|P_{M_{up}}(v_j^i) - P_M(v_j^i)| \leq \frac{(T-i)\epsilon}{2T}.$$

We prove the first equation above; the second equation can be proved similarly. The proof is by downward induction on i. For $i = T$, the statement is true trivially. Now, suppose the claim is true for all $j \geq i+1$. Let $v = v_j^i \in V^i$ for $j \in B^i$ and let $z = (z^i, \bar{z})$ be uniformly chosen from $(\{0,1\}^s)^{T+1-i}$ with $z^i \in_u \{0,1\}^s$. Let $w = \Gamma(v, z^i)$ be the vertex reached by taking the edge labeled z^i from v in M and let $w \in J_k^{i+1}$. Then, the edge labeled z^i from v goes to v_k^{i+1} in M_{down}. Now, by Equation (2.2), $|P_M(w) - P_M(v_k^{i+1})| \leq \epsilon/2T$. Therefore, for $j \in B^i$,

$$\begin{aligned}
P_M(v_j^i) &= \sum_{u \in \{0,1\}^s} \Pr[z^i = u]\, P_M(\Gamma(v_j^i, u)) \\
&\leq \sum_{u \in \{0,1\}^s} \Pr[z^i = u]\, (P_M(v_k^{i+1}) + \frac{\epsilon}{2T}) \\
&\leq \sum_{u \in \{0,1\}^s} \Pr[z^i = u] \left(P_{M_{down}}(v_k^{i+1}) + \frac{(T-i-1)\epsilon + \epsilon}{2T}\right) \\
&\qquad \text{(Induction hypothesis)} \\
&= \sum_{u \in \{0,1\}^s} \Pr[z^i = u]\, P_{M_{down}}(v_k^{i+1}) + \frac{(T-i)\epsilon}{2T} \\
&= P_{M_{down}}(v_j^i) + \frac{(T-i)\epsilon}{2T}. \\
&\qquad \text{(Definition of } M_{down})
\end{aligned}$$

Since by Claim 2.7, $P_{M_{down}}(v_j^i) \leq P_M(v_j^i)$, Equation (2.3) now follows from the above equation and induction. □

Lemma 2.6 now follows from Claims 2.7, 2.8.

3. MAIN GENERATOR CONSTRUCTION

We now describe our main construction G that serves as a blueprint for all of our constructions. The generator G is essentially a simplification of the hitting set construction of halfspaces for Rabani and Shpilka [RS09]. We use the following building blocks.

1. A family $\mathcal{H} = \{h : [n] \to [t]\}$ of hash functions that is α-pairwise independent. That is, for a fixed $k \in [t]$ and $i \neq j \in [n]$,

$$\Pr_{h \in_u \mathcal{H}}[h(i) = k \wedge h(j) = k] \leq \frac{1+\alpha}{t^2}. \quad (3.1)$$

Efficient constructions of size $|\mathcal{H}| = O(nt)$ are known for any constant α, even $\alpha = 0$.

2. A generator $G_0 : \{0,1\}^{r_0} \to \{1,-1\}^m$ of a δ-almost k-wise independent space over $\{1,-1\}^m$. We say a distribution $\mathcal{D}$ over $\{1,-1\}^m$ is δ-almost k-wise independent if, for all $\{i_1, \ldots, i_k\} \subseteq [m]$

$$\sum_{b_1,\ldots,b_k \in \{1,-1\}^k} \left| \Pr_{x \leftarrow D}[x_{i_1} = b_1, \ldots, x_{i_k} = b_k] - \frac{1}{2^k} \right| \leq \delta.$$

Efficient generators G_0 as above with seed length $r_0 = O(k + \log m + \log(1/\delta))$ are known [NN93].

Although efficient constructions of hash families $\mathcal{H}$ and generators G_0 as above are known even for $\alpha = 0$, $\delta = 0$ and constant k, we work with small but non-zero α, δ, as we will need the more general objects for our analysis.

The basic idea behind the generator is as follows. We first use the hash functions to distribute the *coordinates* ($[n]$) into buckets. The purpose of this step is to spread out the "influences" of the coordinates across buckets. Then, for each bucket we use an independently chosen sample from a δ-almost k-wise independent distribution to generate the bits for the coordinate positions mapped to the bucket. The purpose of this step is, roughly, to "match the first few moments" of functions restricted to the coordinates in each bucket. The hope then is to subsequently use invariance principles to show closeness in distribution.

Fix the error parameter $\epsilon > 0$ and let $t = \text{poly}(\log(1/\epsilon))/\epsilon^2$ to be chosen later. Let $m = n/t$ (assuming without loss of generality that t divides n) and let $\mathcal{H}$ be an α-pairwise independent hash family. To avoid some technicalities that can be overcome easily, we assume that every hash function $h \in \mathcal{H}$ is evenly distributed, meaning $\forall h, i \in [t]$, $|\{j : h(j) = i, j \in [n]\}| = n/t$. Let $G_0 : \{0,1\}^{r_0} \to \{1,-1\}^m$ generate a δ-almost k-wise independent space for $\delta \geq \text{poly}(\epsilon, 1/n)$ to be chosen later.

Define $G : \mathcal{H} \times (\{0,1\}^{r_0})^t \to \{0,1\}^n$ by

$$G(h, z^1, \ldots, z^t) = x, \text{ where } x_{|h^{-1}(i)} = G_0(z^i) \text{ for } i \in [t]. \quad (3.2)$$

We will show that for the parameters t, α, δ, k and $\mathcal{H}, G_0$ chosen appropriately, the above generator fools halfspaces as well as degree d PTFs. In particular, we fool progressively stronger classes, from halfspaces to degree d PTFs by choosing $\mathcal{H}$ and G_0 progressively stronger.

4. PRGS FOR HALFSPACES

In this section we show that for appropriately chosen parameters, G fools halfspaces. We first show that G fools "regular" halfspaces to obtain a PRG with seed length $O(\log n/\epsilon^2)$ for regular halfspaces. We then extend the analysis to arbitrary halfspaces to get a PRG with seed length $O(\log n \log^2(1/\epsilon)/\epsilon^2)$ and apply the monotone trick to prove Theorems 1.3 and 1.4.

In the following let $H_{w,\theta} : \{1,-1\}^n \to \{1,-1\}$ denote a halfspace $H_{w,\theta}(x) = \text{sign}(\langle w, x\rangle - \theta)$. Unless stated otherwise, we assume throughout that a halfspace $H_{w,\theta}$ is normalized, meaning $\|w\| = 1$ (here $\|\cdot\|$ is the l_2-norm). We measure distance between real-valued distributions P, Q by

$$d(P,Q) = \sup_{t\in\mathbb{R}} |\Pr_{x\leftarrow P}[x < t] - \Pr_{x\leftarrow Q}[x < t]|,$$

also known as Kolmogorov-Smirnov distance. In particular, we say two real-valued distributions P, Q are ε-close if $d(P,Q) \leq \varepsilon$. We use the fact that Kolmogorov-Smirnov distance is convex.

LEMMA 4.1. *For fixed Q, the distance function $d(P,Q)$ defined for probability distributions over $\mathbb{R}$ is a convex function.*

For $\sigma > 0$, let $\mathcal{N}(0,\sigma)$ denote the normal distribution with mean 0 and variance σ^2. We also assume that $\epsilon > 1/n^{.49}$ as otherwise, Theorem 1.3 follows from Corollary 1.8.

4.1 PRGs for Regular Halfspaces

As was done in Diakonikolas et al. we first deal with regular halfspaces.

DEFINITION 4.2. *A vector $w \in \mathbb{R}^n$ with $\|w\| = 1$ is ϵ-regular if $|w_i| \leq \epsilon$ for all i. A halfspace $H_{w,\theta}$ is ϵ-regular if w is ϵ-regular.*

Let $t = 1/\epsilon^2$. We claim that for $\mathcal{H}$ pairwise independent and G_0 generating an almost 4-wise independent distribution, G fools regular halfspaces. Note that the randomness used by G in this setting is $O(\log n/\epsilon^2)$.

THEOREM 4.3. *Let $\mathcal{H}$ be an α-almost pairwise independent family for $\alpha = O(1)$ and let G_0 generate a δ-almost 4-wise independent distribution for $\delta = \epsilon^2/4n^5$. Then, G defined by Equation 3.2 fools ϵ-regular halfspaces with error at most $O(\epsilon)$ and seed length $O(\log n/\epsilon^2)$. In particular, for $x \in \{1,-1\}^n$ generated from G and ϵ-regular w with $\|w\| = 1$, the distribution of $\langle w, x\rangle$ is $O(\epsilon)$-close to $\mathcal{N}(0,1)$.*

To prove the theorem we will need the Berry-Esséen theorem, which gives a quantitative form of the central limit theorem and can be seen as an *invariance principle* for halfspaces. We use the following corollaries of the standard Berry-Esséen theorem. We refer to the full version for their proofs.

COROLLARY 4.4. *Let $Y_1, \ldots, Y_t$ be independent random variables with $E[Y_i] = 0$, $\sum_i E[Y_i^2] = \sigma^2$, $\sum_i E[|Y_i|^4] \leq \rho_4$. Let $F(.)$ denote the cdf of the random variable $S_n = (Y_1 + \cdots + Y_n)/\sigma$, and $\Phi(.)$ denote the cdf of the normal distribution $\mathcal{N}(0,1)$. Then, for an absolute constant C*

$$\|F - \Phi\|_\infty = \sup_z |F(z) - \Phi(z)| \leq \frac{3\sqrt{\rho_4}}{\sigma^2}.$$

LEMMA 4.5. *For ϵ-regular w with $\|w\| = 1$ and $x \in_u \{1,-1\}^n$, the distribution of $\langle w, x\rangle$ is 3ϵ-close to $\mathcal{N}(0,1)$.*

The following lemma says that for a pairwise-independent family of hash functions $\mathcal{H}$ and $w \in \mathbb{R}^n$, the weight of the coefficients is *almost equidistributed* among the buckets.

LEMMA 4.6 (SEE FULL VERSION). *Let $\mathcal{H}$ be an α-almost pairwise independent family of hash functions from $[n]$ to $[t]$. For ϵ-regular w with $\|w\| = 1$, $\sum_{i=1}^t \mathbb{E}[\|w_{h^{-1}(i)}\|^4] \leq (1+\alpha)\epsilon^2 + \frac{1+\alpha}{t}$.*

PROOF OF THEOREM (4.3). Fix a hash function $h \in \mathcal{H}$. Let $w^i = w_{|h^{-1}(i)}$ for $i \in [t]$. Then,

$$\langle w, G(h,z)\rangle = \sum_{i=1}^{t} \langle w^i, G_0(z^i)\rangle.$$

Let random variables $Y_i^h \equiv Y_i \equiv \langle w^i, G_0(z^i)\rangle$ and $Y^h = Y_1 + \ldots + Y_t$. Then, $\mathbb{E}[Y_i] = 0$ and since $G_0(z^i)$ is δ-almost 4-wise independent, $|\,\mathbb{E}[Y_i^2] - \|w^i\|^2| \leq \delta n^2$. Further, for $1 \leq i \leq t$, $x \in_u \{1,-1\}^m$,

$$\mathop{\mathbb{E}}_x[\,\langle w^i, x\rangle^4\,] = \sum_{j=1}^{m} (w_j^i)^4 + 3 \sum_{p \neq q \in [m]} (w_p^i)^2 (w_q^i)^2 \leq 3\|w^i\|^4.$$

Since, the above equation depends only on the first four moments of random variable x and $G_0(Z^i)$ is δ-almost 4-wise independent, it follows that $\mathbb{E}[Y_i^4] \leq 3\|w^i\|^4 + \delta n^4$. Thus, $\sum_i \mathbb{E}[Y_i^2] \geq 1 - \delta n^2 t \geq 1/2$ and $\sum_{i=1}^t \mathbb{E}[Y_i^4] \leq 3\sum_{i=1}^t \|w^i\|^4 + \delta n^5$. Let $\rho_h = \sum_i \|w^i\|^4$. Then, by Corollary 4.4, since $\delta \leq \epsilon^2/4n^5$, for a fixed h the distribution of Y^h is $3(\sqrt{3\rho_h} + \epsilon)$-close to $\mathcal{N}(0,1)$.

Observe that for random h, z the distribution of $Y = \langle w, G(h,z)\rangle$ is a convex-combination of the distributions of Y^h for $h \in \mathcal{H}$. Thus, from Lemma 4.1, the distribution of Y is $O(\mathbb{E}[\sqrt{\rho_h}] + \epsilon)$-close to $\mathcal{N}(0,1)$. Now, by Cauchy-Schwarz $\mathbb{E}[\sqrt{\rho_h}] \leq \sqrt{\mathbb{E}[\rho_h]}$. Further, since w is ϵ-regular and $t = 1/\epsilon^2$, it follows from Lemma 4.6 that $\mathbb{E}[\rho_h] = \sum_i \mathbb{E}[\|w^i\|^4] = \sum_i \mathbb{E}[\|w_{h^{-1}(i)}\|^4] \leq 2(1+\alpha)\epsilon^2$. Thus, the distribution of Y is $O(\epsilon)$-close to $\mathcal{N}(0,1)$. The theorem now follows from combining this with Lemma 4.5. □

4.2 PRGs for Arbitrary Halfspaces

We now study arbitrary halfspaces and show that the generator G fools arbitrary halfspaces if the family of hash functions $\mathcal{H}$ and generator G_0 satisfy certain stronger properties. We use the following structural result on halfspaces that follows from the results of Servedio [Ser06] and Diakonikolas et al. [DGJ+09].

THEOREM 4.7. *Let $H_{w,\theta}$ be a halfspace with $w_1 \geq \ldots \geq w_n$, $\sum w_i^2 = 1$. There exists $K = K(\epsilon) = O(\log^2(1/\epsilon)/\epsilon^2)$ such that one of the following two conditions holds.*

1. *$w^K = (w_{K(\epsilon)+1}, \ldots, w_n)$ is ϵ-regular.*

2. *Let $w' = (w_1, \ldots, w_{K(\epsilon)})$ and $H_{w',\theta}(x) = \mathsf{sgn}(\sum_1^K w_i x_i - \theta)$. Then,*

$$|\mathop{\mathbb{E}}_{x \leftarrow \mathcal{D}}[H_{w,\theta}(x)] - \mathop{\mathbb{E}}_{x \leftarrow \mathcal{D}}[\mathsf{H}_{w',\theta}(x)]\,| \leq 2\epsilon. \qquad (4.1)$$

where $\mathcal{D}$ is any distribution satisfying the following conditions for $x \leftarrow \mathcal{D}$: (a) The distribution of $(x_1, \ldots, x_K)$ is ϵ-close to uniform. (b) With probability at least $1-\epsilon$ over the choice of $(x_1, \ldots, x_K)$, the distribution of $(x_{K+1}, \ldots, x_n)$ conditioned on $(x_1, \ldots, x_K)$ is $(1/n^2)$-almost pairwise independent.

Servedio and Diakonikolas et al. show the above result when $\mathcal{D}$ is the uniform distribution. However, their arguments extend straightforwardly to any distribution $\mathcal{D}$ as above.

Given the above theorem, we use a case analysis to analyze G. If the first condition of the theorem above holds, we use the results of the previous section, Theorem 4.3, showing that G fools regular halfspaces. If the second condition holds, we argue that for x distributed as the output of the generator, the distribution of $(x_1, \ldots, x_{K(\epsilon)})$ is $O(\epsilon)$-close to uniform.

Let $t = K(\epsilon)$. We need the family of hash functions $\mathcal{H} : [n] \to [t]$ in the construction of G to be *balanced* along with being α-pairwise independent as in Equation (3.1). Intuitively, a hash family is balanced if with high probability the maximum size of a bucket is small.

DEFINITION 4.8 (BALANCED HASH FUNCTIONS). *A family of hash functions $\mathcal{H} = \{h : [n] \to [t]$ is (L, β)-balanced if for any $S \subseteq [n]$, $|S| \leq t$,*

$$\mathop{\mathsf{Pr}}_{h \in_u \mathcal{H}}[\,\max_{j \in [t]} (|h^{-1}(j) \cap S|) \geq L\,] \leq \beta. \qquad (4.2)$$

It is known that a family of l-wise independent hash functions is balanced with appropriate parameters. For completeness, we include a proof of the following result in the full version. The distinction based on ϵ below will be useful later when derandomizing G for halfspaces.

THEOREM 4.9. *For $t = 1/\epsilon^2$, there exist $(L, 1/t^2)$-balanced hash families $\mathcal{H} : [n] \to [t]$ that are also pairwise independent with the following parameters.*

1. *For any constant $c \geq 0$, $\epsilon \geq 1/n^c$, $L = O(\log t) = O(\log(1/\epsilon))$ and $|\mathcal{H}| = n^{O(\log t)}$.*

2. *For any constant $c \geq 0$, $\epsilon \geq 1/(\log n)^c$, $L = O(\log n)$ and $|\mathcal{H}| = \mathrm{poly}(n)$.*

Let $m = n/t$ and fix L to be one of $O(\log t), O(\log n)$. We also need the generator $G_0 : \{0,1\}^{r_0} \to \{1,-1\}^m$ to be exactly 4-wise independent and δ-almost $(L+4)$-wise independent for $\delta = \epsilon^3/tn^5$. Generators G_0 as above with $r_0 = O(\log n + \log(1/\delta) + L) = O(\log(n/\epsilon))$ are known [NN93].

We now show that with $\mathcal{H}, G_0$ as above, G fools halfspaces with error $O(\epsilon)$. The randomness used by the generator is $\log|\mathcal{H}| + r_0 t = O(\log n \log^2(1/\epsilon)/\epsilon^2)$ and matches the randomness used in the results of Diakonikolas et al. [DGJ+09].

THEOREM 4.10. *With $\mathcal{H}, G_0$ chosen as above, G defined by Equation (3.2) fools halfspaces with error at most $O(\epsilon)$ and seed length $O(\log n \log^2(1/\epsilon)/\epsilon^2)$.*

PROOF. Let $H_{w,\theta}$ be a halfspace and without loss of generality suppose that $w_1 \geq \ldots \geq w_n$ and $\sum_i w_i^2 = 1$. Let $S = \{1, \ldots, K(\epsilon)\}$. Call a hash function S-*good* if for all $j \in [t]$, $|S_j| = |S \cap h^{-1}(j)| \leq L$. From Definition 4.8, a random hash function $h \in_u \mathcal{H}$ is S-good with probability at least $1 - 1/t^2$. Recall that $G(h, z^1, \ldots, z^t) = x$, where $x_{|h^{-1}(j)} = G_0(z^j)$ for $j \in [t]$. Let $\mathcal{D}$ denote the distribution of the output of G and let $x \leftarrow \mathcal{D}$.

CLAIM 4.11. *Given an S-good hash function h, the distribution of $x_{|S}$ is ϵ-close to uniform. Moreover, with probability at least $1-\epsilon$ over the random choices of $x_{|S}$, the distribution of x in the coordinates not in S conditioned on $x_{|S}$ is $(\epsilon^2/4n^5)$-almost 4-wise independent.*

PROOF. Fix an S-good hash function h. Since $z^1, \ldots, z^t$ are chosen independently, given the hash function h, $x|_{S_1}, \ldots, x|_{S_t}$ are independent of each other. Moreover, since the output of G_0 is δ-almost $(L+4)$-wise independent and $|S_j| \leq L$ for all $j \in [t]$, $x|_{S_j}$ is δ-close to uniform for all $j \in [t]$. It follows that given an S-good hash function h, $x|_S$ is $(t\delta)$-close to uniform. Further, by a similar argument, for any set $I \subseteq [n] \setminus S$ with $|I| = 4$, the distribution of $x_{|(S \cup I)}$ is $(t\delta)$-close to uniform. It follows that, with probability at least $1-\epsilon$, the distribution of $x_{|I}$ conditioned on $x_{|S}$ is $(t\delta/\epsilon)$-close to uniform. The claim now follows from the above observations and noting that $t\delta = \epsilon^3/4n^5$. □

We can now prove the theorem by a case analysis. Suppose that the weight vector w satisfies condition (2) of Theorem 4.7. Observe that from the above claim, $\mathcal{D}$ satisfies the conditions of Theorem 4.7 (2). Let $\mathsf{H}_{w_{|S},\theta}(x) = \mathsf{sgn}(\langle w_{|S}, x_{|S}\rangle - \theta)$. Then, from Equation (4.1),

$$| \mathop{\mathbb{E}}_{x \leftarrow U_n}[H_{w,\theta}(x)] - \mathop{\mathbb{E}}_{x \leftarrow U_n}[\mathsf{H}_{w_{|S},\theta}(x)] | \leq 2\epsilon,$$

$$| \mathop{\mathbb{E}}_{x \leftarrow \mathcal{D}}[H_{w,\theta}(x)] - \mathop{\mathbb{E}}_{x \leftarrow \mathcal{D}}[\mathsf{H}_{w_{|S},\theta}(x)] | \leq 2\epsilon.$$

Moreover, since the distribution of $x_{|S}$ is ϵ-close to uniform under $\mathcal{D}$ and $\mathsf{H}_{w_{|S},\theta}(x)$ only depends on $x_{|S}$,

$$| \mathop{\mathbb{E}}_{x \leftarrow U_n}[\mathsf{H}_{w_{|S},\theta}(x)] - \mathop{\mathbb{E}}_{x \leftarrow \mathcal{D}}[\mathsf{H}_{w_{|S},\theta}(x)]| \leq \epsilon.$$

Combining the above three equations, we get that

$$| \mathop{\mathbb{E}}_{x \leftarrow U_n}[H_{w,\theta}(x)] - \mathop{\mathbb{E}}_{x \leftarrow \mathcal{D}}[H_{w,\theta}(x)]| \leq 5\epsilon,$$

and thus G fools halfspace $H_{w,\theta}$ with error at most 5ϵ.

Now suppose that condition (1) of Theorem 4.7 holds and $w_{\bar{S}} = (w_{K(\epsilon)+1}, \ldots, w_n)$ is ϵ-regular. Fix an assignment to the variables $x_{|S} = u_{|S}$ and let $x_{\bar{S}} = (x_{k+1}, \ldots, x_n)$ and $H_u(x_{k+1}, \ldots, x_n) = \mathsf{sgn}(\langle w_{\bar{S}}, x_{\bar{S}}\rangle - \theta_u)$, where $\theta_u = \theta - \langle w_{|S}, x_{|S}\rangle$. We will argue that with probability at least $1-\epsilon$, conditioned on the values of $x_{|S}$, the output of G fools the ϵ-regular halfspace H_u with error $O(\epsilon)$. Given the last statement it follows that $\mathcal{D}$ fools the halfspace $H_{w,\theta}$ with error $O(\epsilon)$ since the distribution of $x_{|S}$ under $\mathcal{D}$ is ϵ-close to uniform.

Since $\mathcal{H}$ is a family of pairwise independent hash functions and a random hash function $h \in_u \mathcal{H}$ is S-good with probability at least $1-1/t^2$, even when conditioned on being S-good, a random hash function $h \in_u \mathcal{H}$ is α-pairwise independent for $\alpha = 1$. Further, from Claim 4.11, conditioned on the hash function h being S-good, with probability at least $1-\epsilon$, even conditioned on $x_{|S}$, the distribution of $x_{|[n]\setminus S}$ is $(\epsilon^2/4n^5)$-almost 4-wise independent. Thus, we can apply Theorem 4.3 showing that with probability at least $1-\epsilon$, conditioned on the values of $x_{|S}$, the output of G fools H_u with error $O(\epsilon)$.

4.3 Derandomizing G

We derandomize the generator G from above using the monotone trick to prove Theorems 1.3 and 1.4. The derandomization is motivated by the fact that for a fixed hash function h and $w \in \mathbb{R}^n, \theta \in \mathbb{R}$, $\mathsf{sgn}(\langle w, G(h, z^1, \ldots, z^t)\rangle - \theta)$ can be computed by a monotone ROBP with t layers. Given this observation, by Theorem 2.4, we can use PRGs for small-width ROBP to generate $z^1, \ldots, z^t$ instead of generating them independently as before. We leave the details to the full version.

5. PRGS FOR POLYNOMIAL THRESHOLD FUNCTIONS

We now extend our results from previous section to construct PRGs for degree d PTFs. We set the parameters of G as for halfspaces, with the main difference being that we take G_0 to generate a k-wise independent space for $k = O(\log^2(1/\epsilon)/\epsilon^{O(d)} + 4d)$ instead of $O(\log^2(1/\epsilon)/\epsilon^2)$ as was done for fooling halfspaces. The analysis of the construction is, however, more complicated and proceeds as follows.

1. We first use the invariance principle of Mossel et al. [MOO05] to deal with *regular* PTFs.

2. We then use the structural results on random restrictions of PTFs of Diakonikolas et al. [DSTW10] and Harsha et al. [HKM09] to reduce the case of fooling arbitrary PTFs to that of fooling *regular* PTFs and functions depending only on a few variables.

We carry out the first step above by an extension of the hybrid argument of Mossel et al. where we replace blocks of variables instead of single variables as done by Mossel et al. For this part of the analysis, we also need the *anti-concentration* results of Carbery and Wright [CW01] for low-degree polynomials over Gaussian distributions.

The second step relies on properties of random restrictions of PTFs similar in spirit to those for halfspaces. Roughly speaking, we use the following results. There exists a set $S \subseteq [n]$ of at most $L = 1/\epsilon^{\Omega(d)}$ variables such that for a random restriction of these variables, with probability at least $\Omega(1)$ one of the following happens.

1. The resulting PTF on the variables in $[n]/S$ is ϵ-regular.

2. The resulting PTF on the variables in $[n]/S$ has high bias.

We then finish the analysis by recursively applying the above claim to show that a generator fooling regular PTFs and having bounded independence also fools arbitrary PTFs.

5.1 PRGs for Regular PTFs

Here we extend our result for fooling regular halfspaces, Theorem 4.3, to *regular* PTFs.

DEFINITION 5.1. *Let $P(u_1, \ldots, u_n) = \sum_I \alpha_I \prod_{i \in I} u_i$ be a multi-linear polynomial of degree d. We will assume throughout that P is normalized with $\|P\|_2^2 = \sum_I \alpha_I^2 = 1$. Let the influence of i'th coordinate $\tau_i(P) = \sum_{I \ni i} \alpha_I^2$. We say P is ϵ-regular if $\sum_i \tau_i(P)^2 \leq \epsilon^2$. We say a polynomial threshold function $f(x) = \mathsf{sgn}(P(x) - \theta)$ is ϵ-regular if P is ϵ-regular.*

Fix $d > 0$. Let $t = 1/\epsilon^2, m = n/t$ and let $\mathcal{H}$ be an α-pairwise independent family as in Theorem 4.3. We assume $G_0 : \{0,1\}^{r_0} \to \{1,-1\}^m$ generates a $4d$-wise independent space, generalizing the assumption of 4-wise independence used for fooling regular halfspaces.

THEOREM 5.2. *Let $\mathcal{H}$ be an α-pairwise independent family for $\alpha = O(1)$ and let G_0 generate a $4d$-wise independent distribution. Then, G defined by Equation (3.2) fools ϵ-regular PTFs of degree at most d with error at most $O(d^3\, 9^d\, \epsilon^{2/(4d+1)})$.*

The following lemma generalizes Lemma 4.6 and says that for pairwise independent hash functions and regular polynomials, the total influence is *almost equidistributed* among the buckets. We also use (2, 4)-hypercontractivity for degree d polynomials.

LEMMA 5.3 (SEE FULL VERSION). *Let $\mathcal{H} = \{h : [n] \to [t]\}$ be a α-pairwise independent family of hash functions. Let P be a multilinear polynomial of degree d with coefficients $(\alpha_J)_{J\subseteq[n]}$ and $\|P\| \leq 1$. For $h \in \mathcal{H}$ let $\tau(h,i) = \sum_{J\cap h^{-1}(i)\neq\emptyset} \alpha_J^2$. Then, for $h \in_u \mathcal{H}$, $\mathbb{E}_h\left[\sum_{i=1}^t \tau(h,i)^2\right] \leq (1+\alpha)\sum_{i=1}^n \tau_i(P)^2 + (1+\alpha)d^2/t$.*

LEMMA 5.4 ((2, 4)-HYPERCONTRACTIVITY, [O'D08]). *For any degree d multilinear polynomial Q, and $X \in_u \{1,-1\}^n$, $\mathbb{E}_X[Q^4] \leq 9^d \cdot \mathbb{E}_X[Q^2]^2$.*

Following the approach of Mossel et al., we first show that our generator fools certain *nice* functions of regular polynomials, which are easier to analyze.

DEFINITION 5.5. *A function $\psi : \mathbb{R} \to \mathbb{R}$ is B-nice, if ψ is smooth and $|\psi''''(t)| \leq B$ for all $t \in \mathbb{R}$.*

LEMMA 5.6. *Let P be an ϵ-regular multilinear polynomial of degree at most d with $\|P\| = 1$. Let $\overline{Y} \in_u \{1,-1\}^n$ and $\overline{Z}$ be distributed as the output of G. Then, for any 1-nice function ψ, $|\, E[\psi(P(\overline{Y}))] - E[\psi(P(\overline{Z}))]\,| \leq \frac{1+\alpha}{6}\, d^2\, 9^d\, \epsilon^2$.*

Theorem 5.2 follows easily from the above lemma and using an *anti-concentration* result of Carbery and Wright [CW01] for polynomials over log-concave distributions. We defer the proof of Theorem 5.2 from Lemma 5.6 to the full version.

PROOF OF LEMMA 5.6. Fix a hash function $h \in \mathcal{H}$. Let $Z_1, \ldots, Z_t$ be t independent samples generated from the $4d$-wise independent space. Let $Y_1, \ldots, Y_t$ be t independent samples chosen uniformly from $\{1,-1\}^m$. We will prove the claim via a hybrid argument where we replace the blocks $Y_1, \ldots, Y_t$ with $Z_1, \ldots, Z_t$ progressively.

For $0 \leq i \leq t$, let X^i be the distribution with $X^i_{|h^{-1}(j)} = Z_j$ for $1 \leq j \leq i$ and $X^i_{|h^{-1}(j)} = Y_j$ for $i < j \leq t$. Then, for a fixed hash function h, X^0 is uniformly distributed over $\{1,-1\}^n$ and X^t is distributed as the output of the generator. For $i \in [t]$, let $\tau(h,i)$ be the influence of the i'th bucket under h, $\tau(h,i) = \sum_{J\cap h^{-1}(i)\neq\emptyset} \alpha_J^2$.

CLAIM 5.7. *For $1 \leq i \leq t$,*

$$|\,\mathbb{E}[\psi(P(X^i))] - \mathbb{E}[\psi(P(X^{i-1}))]| \leq \frac{9^d}{12}\tau(h,i)^2.$$

PROOF. Let $I = h^{-1}(i)$ be the variables that have been changed from X^{i-1} to X^i. Without loss of generality suppose that $I = \{1, \ldots, m\}$. Let

$$P(u_1, \ldots, u_n) = R(u_{m+1}, \ldots, u_n) + \sum_{J: J\cap[m]\neq\emptyset} \alpha_J \left(\prod_{j\in J} u_j\right),$$

where $R(\,)$ is a multi-linear polynomial of degree at most d. Let $S(u_1, \ldots, u_m, u_{m+1}, \ldots, u_n)$ denote the degree d multilinear polynomial given by the second term in the above expression.

Observe that X^{i-1}, X^i agree on coordinates not in $[m]$. Let $X^i = (Z_1, \ldots, Z_m, X_{m+1}, \ldots, X_n) = (Z, X)$ and $X^{i-1} = (Y_1, \ldots, Y_m, X_{m+1}, \ldots, X_n) = (Y, X)$. Then, $P(X^i) = R(X) + S(Z,X)$, $P(X^{i-1}) = R(X) + S(Y,X)$. Now, by using the Taylor series expansion for ψ at $R(X)$,

$$\mathbb{E}[\psi(P(X^i))] - \mathbb{E}[\psi(P(X^{i-1}))] = \mathbb{E}[\psi(R + S(Z,X))] -$$

$$E[\psi(R+S(Y,X))] = \mathbb{E}[\,\psi(R) + \psi'(R)S(Z,X) + \frac{\psi''(R)}{2}S(Z,X)^2$$

$$+\frac{\psi'''(R)}{6}S(Z,X)^3 + \{\leq \frac{1}{24}S(Z,X)^4\}\,] - \mathbb{E}[\,\psi(R) + \psi'(R)S(Y,X)$$

$$+\frac{\psi''(R)}{2}S(Y,X)^2 + \frac{\psi'''(R)}{6}S(Y,X)^3 + \{\leq \frac{1}{24}S(Y,X)^4\}\,].$$

Observe that X, Y, Z are independent of one another and are $4d$-wise independent individually. Since $S(\,)$ has degree at most d, it follows that for a fixed assignment of the variables $X_{m+1}, \ldots, X_n$ in X,

$$\mathbb{E}[S(Z,X)] = \mathbb{E}[S(Y,X)],\ \ \mathbb{E}[S(Z,X)^2] = \mathbb{E}[S(Y,X)^2],$$

$$\mathbb{E}[S(Z,X)^3] = \mathbb{E}[S(Y,X)^3],\ \ \mathbb{E}[S(Z,X)^4] = \mathbb{E}[S(Y,X)^4].$$

Combining the above equations we get

$$|\,\mathbb{E}[\psi(P(X^i))] - \mathbb{E}[\psi(P(X^{i-1}))]| \leq \frac{1}{12}\mathbb{E}[\,S(Y,X)^4\,]. \quad (5.1)$$

Now, using the fact that $S(\,)$ is a multi-linear polynomial of degree at most d and since (Y, X) is $4d$-wise independent, $\mathbb{E}[\,S(Y,X)^4\,] = \mathbb{E}[\,S(W)^4\,]$, where W is uniformly distributed over $\{1,-1\}^n$. Also note that

$$\mathbb{E}[S(W)^2] = \mathbb{E}\left[\left(\sum_{J:J\cap[m]\neq\emptyset} \alpha_J \left(\prod_{j\in J} W_j\right)\right)^2\right] = \sum_{J:J\cap I\neq\emptyset} \alpha_J^2 = \tau(h,i).$$

Therefore, using the (2, 4)-hypercontractivity inequality, Lemma 5.4, $\mathbb{E}[S(W)^4] \leq 9^d\, \mathbb{E}[S(W)^2]^2$ and Equation (5.1),

$$|\,\mathbb{E}[\psi(P(X^i))] - \mathbb{E}[\psi(P(X^{i-1}))]| \leq \frac{1}{12}\mathbb{E}[\,S(Y,X)^4\,] = \frac{1}{12}\mathbb{E}[\,S(W)^4\,] \leq \frac{9^d}{12}\,\mathbb{E}[S(W)^2]^2 = \frac{9^d}{12}\tau(h,i)^2.$$

□

PROOF LEMMA 5.6 CONTINUED. From Claim 5.7, for a fixed hash function h we have

$$|\,\mathbb{E}[\psi(P(\overline{Y}))] - \mathbb{E}[\psi(P(\overline{Z}))]| \leq \sum_{i=1}^{t} |\,\mathbb{E}[\psi(P(X^i))] - \mathbb{E}[\psi(P(X^{i-1}))]| \leq \frac{9^d}{12}\sum_{i=1}^{t}\tau(h,i)^2.$$

Therefore, for $h \in_u \mathcal{H}$, using Lemma 5.3 and $t = 1/\epsilon^2$,

$$|\,\mathbb{E}[\psi(P(\overline{Y}))] - \mathbb{E}[\psi(P(\overline{Z}))]| \leq \frac{9^d}{12}\,\mathbb{E}_h\left[\sum_i \tau(h,i)^2\right] = \frac{9^d}{12}(1+\alpha)(1+d^2)\epsilon^2 \leq \frac{(1+\alpha)\,d^2\,9^d\,\epsilon^2}{6}.$$

□

5.2 Random Restrictions of PTFs

To extend our PRG for regular PTFs to arbitrary PTFs we use the following structural results on random restrictions of Diakonikolas et al. [DSTW10] and Harsha et al. [HKM09]. We mainly refer to the exact statements from the work of Harsha et al., as the notion of regular polynomials from Diakonikolas et al. is slightly different from ours. Specifically, Diakonikolas et al. define regularity of a polynomial P by bounding $\max_i(\tau_i(P))$, but in our analysis we use the bound of $\sum_i \tau_i(P)^2$. Diakonikolas et al. have a statement similar to Lemma 5.10 below; however, we give a simple argument starting from the main lemmas of Harsha et al. in the full version.

We first introduce some notation.

DEFINITION 5.8. *A block decision tree T with block-size L is a decision tree with the following properties. Each internal node of the decision tree reads at most L variables. For each leaf node $\rho \in T$, the output upon reaching the leaf node ρ is a function $f_\rho : \{1,-1\}^{V_\rho} \to \{1,-1\}$, where V_ρ is the set of variables not occurring on the path to the node ρ. The depth of T is the length of the longest path from the root of T to a leaf in T.*

DEFINITION 5.9. *Given a block decision tree T computing a function f, we say that a leaf node $\rho \in T$ is (ϵ, d)-good if the function f_ρ satisfies one of the following two properties.*

1. *There exists $b \in \{1,-1\}$, such that for any $2d$-wise independent distribution D over $\{1,-1\}^{V_\rho}$, $Y \leftarrow D$, $\Pr[f_\rho(Y) \neq b] \leq \epsilon$.*
2. *f_ρ is a ϵ-regular degree d PTF.*

The following lemma states that arbitrary low-degree PTFs can be approximated by small depth decision trees in which the leaf nodes either compute a regular PTF or a function with high bias.

LEMMA 5.10 (SEE FULL VERSION). *There exist universal constants c'_d, c''_d such that the following holds for any degree d polynomial P and PTF $f = \mathsf{sign}(P() - \theta)$. There exists a block decision tree T computing f of block-size $L = c'_d \log(1/\epsilon)/\epsilon^2$ and depth at most $c''_d \log(1/\epsilon)$, such that with probability at least $1-\epsilon$ a uniformly random walk on the tree leads to an (ϵ, d)-good leaf node.*

5.3 PRGs for Arbitrary PTFs

We now study the case of arbitrary degree d PTFs. As was done for halfspaces, we will show that the generator G of Equation (3.2) fools arbitrary PTFs if the family of hash functions $\mathcal{H}$ and generator G_0 satisfy stronger properties.

Let $t = c_d c'_d \log^2(1/\epsilon)/\epsilon^2$, $m = n/t$, where c_d, c'_d are the constants from Lemma 5.10. We use a family of hash functions $\mathcal{H} : [n] \to [t]$ that are α-pairwise independent for $\alpha = O(1)$. We choose the generator $G_0 : \{0,1\}^{r_0} \to \{1,-1\}^m$ to generate a $(t+4d)$-wise independent space. Generators G_0 with $r_0 = O(t \log n)$ are known. We claim that with the above setting of parameter the generator G fools all degree d PTFs.

THEOREM 5.11. *With $\mathcal{H}, G_0$ chosen as above, G defined by Equation (3.2) fools degree d PTFs with error at most $O(\epsilon^{2/(4d+1)})$ and seed length $O_d(\log n \log^4(1/\epsilon)/\epsilon^4)$.*

The bound on the seed length of the generator follows directly from the parameter settings. By carefully tracing the constants involved in our calculations and those in the results of Harsha et al. we need, the exact seed length can be shown to be $a^d \log n \log^4(1/\epsilon)/\epsilon^4$ for a universal constant a.

Fix a polynomial P of degree d and a PTF $f(x) = \mathsf{sign}(P(x) - \theta)$ and let T denote the block-decision tree computing f as given by Lemma 5.10. Let $\mathcal{D}_{PTF}$ denote the output distribution of the generator G with parameters set as above. The intuition behind the proof of the theorem is as follows.

1. As $\mathcal{D}_{PTF}$ has sufficient bounded independence, the distribution on the leaf nodes of T obtained by taking a walk on T according to inputs chosen from $\mathcal{D}_{PTF}$ is the same as the case when inputs are chosen uniformly. In particular, a random walk on T according to $\mathcal{D}_{PTF}$ leads to a (ϵ, d)-good leaf node with high probability.
2. As G fools regular PTFs by Theorem 5.2, $\mathcal{D}_{PTF}$ will fool the function f_ρ computed at a (ϵ, d)-good leaf node. We also need to address the subtle issue that we really need $\mathcal{D}_{PTF}$ to fool a regular PTF f_ρ even when conditioned on reaching a particular leaf node ρ.

We first set up some notation. For a leaf node $\rho \in T$, let $U_\rho = [n] \setminus V_\rho$ be the set of variables seen on the path to ρ and let a_ρ be the corresponding assignment of variables in U_ρ that lead to ρ. Further, given an assignment x, let $\mathrm{Leaf}(x)$ denote the leaf node reached by taking a walk according to x on T.

LEMMA 5.12. *For any leaf node ρ of T,*

$$\Pr_{x \leftarrow \mathcal{D}_{PTF}}[\mathrm{Leaf}(x) = \rho] = \Pr_{x \in_u \{1,-1\}^n}[\mathrm{Leaf}(x) = \rho].$$

PROOF. Note that $\mathcal{D}_{PTF}$ is a t-wise independent distribution and for any ρ, $|U_\rho| \leq c_d c'_d \log^2(1/\epsilon)/\epsilon^2 = t$. Thus,

$$\Pr_{x \leftarrow \mathcal{D}_{PTF}}[\mathrm{Leaf}(x) = \rho] = \Pr_{x \leftarrow \mathcal{D}_{PTF}}[x_{|U_\rho} = a_\rho] = \frac{1}{2^{|U_\rho|}}$$
$$= \Pr_{x \in_u \{1,-1\}^n}[x_{|U_\rho} = a_\rho] = \Pr_{x \in_u \{1,-1\}^n}[\mathrm{Leaf}(x) = \rho].$$

□

LEMMA 5.13. *Fix an (ϵ, d)-good leaf node ρ of T. Then,*

$$\left| \Pr_{x \leftarrow \mathcal{D}_{PTF}}[f_\rho(x_{|V_\rho}) = 1 \mid x_{|U_\rho} = a_\rho] - \Pr_{y \leftarrow \{1,-1\}^{V_\rho}}[f_\rho(y) = 1] \right| = O(\epsilon^{2/(4d+1)}).$$

PROOF. We consider two cases depending on which of the two conditions of Definition 5.9 f_ρ satisfies.

Case (1) - f_ρ has high bias. Note that $\mathcal{D}_{PTF}$ is a $(t+4d)$-wise independent distribution. Since $|U_\rho| \leq t$, it follows that for $x \leftarrow \mathcal{D}_{PTF}$, even conditioned on $x_{|U_\rho} = a_\rho$, the distribution is $2d$-wise independent. The lemma then follows from the fact that for some $b \in \{1,-1\}$, f_ρ evaluates to b with high probability.

Case (2) - f_ρ is an ϵ-regular degree d PTF. We deal with this case by using Theorem 5.2. Let $x = G(h, z^1, \ldots, z^t)$ for $h \in_u \mathcal{H}$, $z^1, \ldots, z^t \in_u \{0,1\}^{r_0}$, so $x \leftarrow \mathcal{D}_{PTF}$ as in the definition of G. Let $h_\rho : V_\rho \to [t]$ be the restriction of a hash function h to indices in V_ρ. For brevity, let $x(\rho) = x_{|V_\rho}$ and let E_ρ be the event $x_{|U_\rho} = a_\rho$. We show that the distribution of $x(\rho)$, conditioned on E_ρ, satisfies the conditions of Theorem 5.2.

Observe that conditioning on E_ρ does not change the distribution of the hash function $h \in_u \mathcal{H}$ because $|U_\rho| \leq t$ and $\mathcal{D}_{PTF}$ is t-wise independent. Thus, even when conditioned on E_ρ, the hash functions h_ρ are almost pairwise independent. For a hash function h, $i \in [t]$, let $B_\rho(h,i) = h^{-1}(i) \setminus V_\rho = h_\rho^{-1}(i)$. Now, since G_0 generates a $(t+4d)$-wise independent distribution, even conditioned on E_ρ, for a fixed hash function h, the random variables $x(\rho)_{|B_\rho(h,1)}, x(\rho)_{|B_\rho(h,2)}, \ldots, x(\rho)_{|B_\rho(h,t)}$ are independent of one another. Moreover, each $x(\rho)_{|B_\rho(h,i)}$ is $4d$-wise independent for $i \in [t]$.

Thus, even conditioned on E_ρ, the distribution of $x(\rho)$ satisfies the conditions of Theorem 5.2 and hence fools the regular degree d PTF f_ρ with error at most $O(\epsilon^{2/(4d+1)})$. The lemma now follows. □

PROOF OF THEOREM 5.11. Observe that

$$\Pr_{x \leftarrow \{1,-1\}^n}[f(x)=1] = \sum_{\rho \in Leaves(T)} \Pr_{x \in_u \{1,-1\}^n}[x_{|U_\rho} = a_\rho] \cdot \Pr_{y \leftarrow \{1,-1\}^{V_\rho}}[f_\rho(y)=1].$$

Similarly, for $x \leftarrow \mathcal{D}_{PTF}$, and $\rho \in Leaves(T)$,

$$\Pr[f(x)=1] = \sum_\rho \Pr[x_{|U_\rho} = a_\rho] \cdot \Pr[f_\rho(x_{|V_\rho}) = 1 \mid x_{|U_\rho} = a_\rho].$$

From the above equations and Lemma 5.12 it follows that

$$\left|\Pr_{z \leftarrow \{1,-1\}^n}[f(z)=1] - \Pr[f(x)=1]\right| \leq \sum_\rho \left|\Pr[f_\rho(x_{|V_\rho}) = 1 \mid x_{|U_\rho} = a_\rho] - \Pr_{y \leftarrow \{1,-1\}^{V_\rho}}[f_\rho(y)=1]\right| \cdot \Pr[x_{|U_\rho} = a_\rho].$$

Now, by Lemma 5.13 for any (ϵ, d)-good leaf ρ the corresponding term on the right hand side of the above equation is $O(\epsilon^{2/(4d+1)})$. Further, from Lemma 5.10 we know that a random walk ends at a good leaf with probability at least $1-\epsilon$. It follows that

$$\left|\Pr_{x \leftarrow \{1,-1\}^n}[f(x)=1] - \Pr_{x \leftarrow \mathcal{D}_{PTF}}[f(x)=1]\right| \leq \epsilon t = O(\epsilon^{2/(4d+1)}).$$

□

Our main theorem on fooling degree d PTFs, Theorem 1.2, follows immediately from the above theorem.

Acknowledgements

We thank Amir Shpilka for drawing to our attention the problem of fooling spherical caps and pointing us to the work of Ailon and Chazelle. We thank Parikshit Gopalan, Prahladh Harsha, Adam Klivans and Ryan O'Donnell for useful discussions and comments.

6. REFERENCES

[ABFR94] J. Aspnes, R. Beigel, M. L. Furst, and S. Rudich. *The expressive power of voting polynomials.* Combinatorica, 14(2):135–148, 1994. (Preliminary version in *23rd STOC*, 1991).

[AC06] N. Ailon and B. Chazelle. *Approximate nearest neighbors and the fast johnson-lindenstrauss transform.* In *STOC*, pages 557–563. ACM, New York, NY, USA, 2006.

[BBC+01] Robert Beals, Harry Buhrman, Richard Cleve, Michele Mosca, and Ronald de Wolf. *Quantum lower bounds by polynomials.* Journal of the ACM, 48(4):778–797, 2001. (Preliminary version in *39th FOCS*, 1998). arXiv:quant-ph/9802049.

[Bei93] Richard Beigel. *The polynomial method in circuit complexity.* In *Proc. of 8th Annual Structure in Complexity Theory Conference*, pages 82–95. 1993.

[CW01] Anthony Carbery and James Wright. *Distributional and l^q norm inequalities for polynomials over convex bodies in $\mathbb{R}^n$.* Mathematical Research Letters, 8(3):233–248, 2001.

[DGJ+09] Ilias Diakonikolas, Parikshit Gopalan, Ragesh Jaiswal, Rocco A. Servedio, and Emanuele Viola. *Bounded independence fools halfspaces.* In *FOCS*. 2009.

[DSTW10] Ilias Diakonikolas, Rocco A. Servedio, Li-Yang Tan, and Andrew Wan. *A regularity lemma, and low-weight approximators, for low-degree polynomial threshold functions.* In *CCC, to appear*. 2010.

[GOWZ10] Parikshit Gopalan, Ryan O'Donnell, Yi Wu, and David Zuckerman. *Fooling functions of halfspaces under product distributions.* In *CCC, to appear*. 2010.

[GR09] Parikshit Gopalan and Jaikumar Radhakrishnan. *Finding duplicates in a data stream.* In *SODA*, pages 402–411. 2009.

[Has94] Johan Hastad. *On the size of weights for threshold gates.* SIAM J. Discret. Math., 7(3):484–492, 1994.

[HKM09] Prahladh Harsha, Adam Klivans, and Raghu Meka. *Bounding the sensitivity of polynomial threshold functions*, 2009. arXiv:0909.5175.

[HKM10] ———. *An invariance principle for polytopes.* In *STOC, to appear*. 2010.

[INW94] Russell Impagliazzo, Noam Nisan, and Avi Wigderson. *Pseudorandomness for network algorithms.* In *STOC*, pages 356–364. 1994.

[KRS09] Zohar Shay Karnin, Yuval Rabani, and Amir Shpilka. *Explicit dimension reduction and its applications.* ECCC, 16(121), 2009.

[KS04] Adam R. Klivans and Rocco A. Servedio. *Learning DNF in time $2^{O(n^{1/3})}$.* Journal of Computer and System Sciences, 68(2):303–318, 2004. (Preliminary version in *33rd STOC*, 2001).

[MOO05] Elchanan Mossel, Ryan O'Donnell, and Krzysztof Oleszkiewicz. *Noise stability of functions with low influences: invariance and optimality.* In *FOCS*, pages 21–30. 2005.

[MT94] Wolfgang Maass and György Turán. *How fast can a threshold gate learn?* In *Proceedings of a workshop on Computational learning theory and natural learning systems (vol. 1) : constraints and prospects*, pages 381–414. MIT Press, Cambridge, MA, USA, 1994.

[Nis92] Noam Nisan. *Pseudorandom generators for space-bounded computation.* Combinatorica, 12(4):449–461, 1992.

[NN93] Joseph Naor and Moni Naor. *Small-bias probability spaces: Efficient constructions and applications.* SIAM Journal on Computing, 22(4):838–856, 1993.

[NZ96] Noam Nisan and David Zuckerman. *Randomness is linear in space.* J. Comput. Syst. Sci., 52(1):43–52, 1996.

[O'D08] Ryan O'Donnell. *Some topics in analysis of boolean functions.* In *STOC*, pages 569–578. ACM, New York, NY, USA, 2008.

[RS09] Yuval Rabani and Amir Shpilka. *Explicit construction of a small epsilon-net for linear threshold functions.* In *STOC*, pages 649–658. 2009.

[Ser06] Rocco A. Servedio. *Every linear threshold function has a low-weight approximator.* In *CCC*, pages 18–32. 2006.

[Siv02] D. Sivakumar. *Algorithmic derandomization via complexity theory.* In *STOC*, pages 619–626. ACM, New York, NY, USA, 2002.

Efficiency Improvements in Constructing Pseudorandom Generators from One-way Functions

Iftach Haitner
Microsoft Research
New England Campus
iftach@microsoft.com

Omer Reingold*
Microsoft Research — Silicon Valley Campus & Weizmann Institute of Science
omreing@microsoft.com

Salil Vadhan†
School of Engineering & Applied Sciences
Harvard University
salil@seas.harvard.edu

ABSTRACT

We give a new construction of pseudorandom generators from any one-way function. The construction achieves better parameters and is simpler than that given in the seminal work of Håstad, Impagliazzo, Levin, and Luby [SICOMP '99]. The key to our construction is a new notion of *next-block pseudoentropy*, which is inspired by the notion of "inaccessible entropy" recently introduced in [Haitner, Reingold, Vadhan, and Wee, STOC '09]. An additional advantage over previous constructions is that our pseudorandom generators are parallelizable and invoke the one-way function in a non-adaptive manner. Using [Applebaum, Ishai, and Kushilevitz, SICOMP '06], this implies the existence of pseudorandom generators in NC^0 based on the existence of one-way functions in NC^1.

Categories and Subject Descriptors

F.0 [**Theory of Computation**]: General

General Terms

Theory

Keywords

One-way function, Pseudorandom generator, Pseudoentropy

1. INTRODUCTION

The result of Håstad, Impagliazzo, Levin, and Luby [13] that one-way functions imply pseudorandom generators is one of the centerpieces of the foundations of cryptography and the theory of pseudorandomness.

*Supported by US-Israel BSF grant 2006060.

†Supported by NSF grant CNS-0831289 and US-Israel BSF grant 2006060.

STOC'10, June 5–8, 2010, Cambridge, Massachusetts, USA.

From the perspective of cryptography, it shows that a very powerful and useful cryptographic primitive (namely, pseudorandom generators) can be constructed from the minimal assumption for complexity-based cryptography (namely, one-way functions). With this starting point, numerous other cryptographic primitives can also be constructed from one-way functions, such as private-key cryptography [5, 20], bit-commitment schemes [21], zero-knowledge proofs for NP [6], and identification schemes [3].

From the perspective of pseudorandomness, it provides strong evidence that pseudorandom bits can be generated very efficiently, with smaller computational resources than the "distinguishers" to whom the bits should look random. Such kinds of pseudorandom generators are needed, for example, for hardness results in learning [26] and the natural proofs barrier for circuit lower bounds [22]. Moreover, the paper of Håstad et al. introduced concepts and techniques that now permeate the theory of pseudorandomness, such as pseudoentropy and the Leftover Hash Lemma.

A drawback of the construction of Håstad et al., however, is that it is quite complicated. While it utilizes many elegant ideas and notions, the final construction combines these in a rather ad hoc and indirect fashion due to various technical issues. In addition to being less satisfactory from an aesthetic and pedagogical perspective, the complexity of the construction also has a significant impact on its efficiency. Indeed, it is too inefficient to be implemented even for very modest settings of parameters.

In the last few years, progress has been made on simplifying the construction of Håstad et al. [15] and improving its efficiency [9]. These constructions, however, still retain the overall structure of the Håstad et al. construction, and thus retain some of the complex and ad hoc elements.

In this paper, we present a significantly more direct and efficient construction of pseudorandom generators from one-way functions. The key to our construction is a new notion of *next-block pseudoentropy*, which is inspired by the recently introduced notion of "inaccessible entropy" [12].

1.1 The HILL Construction

Informally, a function $f : \{0,1\}^n \to \{0,1\}^n$ is a *one-way function* (OWF) if it is easy to compute (in polynomial time) and hard to invert even on random inputs. A polynomial-time computable function $G : \{0,1\}^n \to \{0,1\}^{m(n)}$ is a *pseudorandom generator* (PRG) if it is stretching (i.e., $m(n) > n$) and its output distribution is pseudorandom (i.e., $G(U_n)$ is computationally indistinguishable from $U_{m(n)}$). The theorem of Håstad et al. relates these notions:

THEOREM 1.1. *If there exists a one-way function, then there exists a pseudorandom generator.*

The key notion underlying their construction is the following generalization of pseudorandomness.

DEFINITION 1.2 (PSEUDOENTROPY, INFORMAL). *A random variable X has* pseudoentropy k *if there exists a random variable Y such that:*

1. *X is computationally indistinguishable from Y.*
2. *$\mathrm{H}(Y) \geq k$, where $\mathrm{H}(\cdot)$ denotes Shannon entropy.*[1]

A pseudoentropy generator (PEG)[2] *is a polynomial-time computable function $G : \{0,1\}^n \to \{0,1\}^{m(n)}$ such that $X = G(U_n)$ has pseudoentropy $\mathrm{H}(G(U_n)) + \Delta(n)$ for some $\Delta(n) \geq 1/\mathrm{poly}(n)$. We refer to $\Delta(n)$ as the* entropy gap *of G.*

That every pseudorandom generator $G : \{0,1\}^n \to \{0,1\}^{m(n)}$ is a pseudoentropy generator can be seen by taking $Y = U_{m(n)}$ and noting that $\mathrm{H}(Y) = m(n)$, but $\mathrm{H}(G(U_n)) \leq \mathrm{H}(U_n) = n$. Pseudoentropy generators are weaker in that Y may be very far from uniform, and may even have $\mathrm{H}(Y) < n$ (as long as $\mathrm{H}(G(U_n))$ is even smaller).

The construction of pseudorandom generators from one-way functions proceeds roughly in the following steps:

OWF to PEG: Given a one-way function $f : \{0,1\}^n \to \{0,1\}^n$, Håstad et al. define $\mathrm{PEG}(x, h, i) = (f(x), h, h(x)_{1\ldots i})$, where h is an appropriate hash function and $h(x)_{1\ldots i}$ denotes the first i bits of $h(x)$. PEG can be shown to be a pseudoentropy generator with an entropy gap of roughly $\Delta = \log n/n$ — Whenever $i = \log|f^{-1}(x)| + \Theta(\log n)$ (which happens with probability $\Theta(\log n/n)$) the first $\approx \log|f^{-1}(x)|$ bits of $h(x)$ extract all the entropy of x, and then we get $\Theta(\log n)$ bits of pseudoentropy by the Goldreich–Levin Hardcore-Bit Theorem [4].

Converting Shannon Entropy to Min-Entropy and Amplifying the Gap: Next, Håstad et al. use a direct product construction $\mathrm{PEG}'(x_1, \ldots, x_t) = (\mathrm{PEG}(x_1), \ldots, \mathrm{PEG}(x_t))$ to convert pseudoentropy into pseudo-*min*-entropy, and increase the entropy gap to be $\omega(\log n)$. This turns out to require taking roughly $t = (n/\Delta)^2$ copies.

Randomness Extraction: By hashing, Håstad et al. extract pseudorandom bits from the pseudo-min-entropy achieved so far. By also hashing the seed x to extract any remaining entropy, they obtain a pseudorandom generator. Specifically, they show that $G(x, h_1, h_2) = (h_1, h_2, h_1(\mathrm{PEG}'(x)), h_2(x))$ is a pseudorandom generator, if the output lengths of h_1 and h_2 are chosen appropriately. The choice of output lengths depends on the amount of min-entropy in the output of PEG′, which in turn depends on the amount of entropy in the output of PEG. Unfortunately, these quantities may be infeasible to compute; this is handled by the next step.

Enumeration: Håstad et al. enumerate over all $u = O(n/\Delta)$ possible values k for the output entropy of PEG (up to an accuracy of $\Delta/2$), construct a pseudorandom generator G_k for each, use composition to make each G_k stretch its seed by a factor of greater than u, and then take $G(x_1, \ldots, x_u) = G_1(x_1) \oplus \cdots \oplus G_u(x_u)$ as their final pseudorandom generator.

The total seed length in this informal description is roughly $n \cdot t \cdot u = O(n^4/\Delta^3) = O(n^7)$. In fact, we have been cheating a bit in order to present the construction in a more modular way than in [13]. (The issues we ignored have to do with the samplability of source Y in Definition 1.2.) The actual seed length in the main construction presented in [13] is of $O(n^{10})$ (and the construction involves additional complications). A construction of seed length $O(n^8)$ is outlined in [13], and has been formalized and proven in [15].

Above we see three main sources of inefficiency in the construction: (1) the entropy gap Δ being fairly small, (2) the conversion of Shannon entropy to min-entropy, and (3) enumerating guesses for the output entropy of the initial pseudoentropy generator. Haitner, Harnik, and Reingold [9] show how to save a factor of n in the enumeration step (by constructing a pseudoentropy generator in which more is known about how the entropy is distributed) to obtain a seed length of $O(n^7)$, but still all of the steps remain.

A further complication in the construction of Håstad et al. is that the reductions demonstrating the correctness of the construction are much more complex for uniform adversaries. This aspect of the proof has recently been simplified and made much more modular via Holenstein's uniform hardcore lemma [14, 15].

In case the one-way function is secure against exponential running time ($2^{\Omega(n)}$) adversaries, Holenstein [15] showed how to reduce the seed length to $O(n^4 \cdot \omega(\log n))$ (or $O(n^5)$ to obtain a PRG with exponential security), which was then improved by Haitner et al. [10] to $O(n \cdot \omega(\log n))$ (or $O(n^2)$ to obtain a PRG with exponential security).[3]

1.2 Our Approach

Our construction is based on a generalization of the notion of a pseudoentropy generator. It is motivated by the well-known fact that the pseudorandomness of a random variable X is equivalent to each bit of X being indistinguishable from uniform given the previous ones [27]. That is, $X = (X_1, \ldots, X_n)$ is computationally indistinguishable from $U_n = (Y_1, \ldots, Y_n)$ if and only if for every i, $(X_1, X_2, \ldots, X_{i-1}, X_i)$ is computationally indistinguishable from $(X_1, X_2, \ldots, X_{i-1}, Y_i)$. It is thus natural to consider what happens if we require not that X_i be pseudorandom given the previous bits, but only that X_i has *pseudoentropy* given the previous bits. More generally, we can allow the X_i's to be blocks instead of bits.

[1]The *Shannon entropy* of a random variable X is defined to be $\mathrm{E}_{x \stackrel{R}{\leftarrow} X}[\log(1/\Pr[X = x])]$.

[2]Håstad et al. [13] refer to such a generator as a *false entropy generator*, and require that a pseudoentropy generator to have output pseudoentropy $n + \Delta(n)$, rather than just $\mathrm{H}(G(U_n)) + \Delta(n)$. However, for the informal discussion here, we prefer not to introduce the additional term "false entropy".

[3]In more detail, Holenstein's construction generalizes [13] for OWFs of "any hardness", while Haitner et al. [10] take a totally different route (based on the"randomized iterate" of a function introduced by Goldreich et al. [7]) and obtain constructions based on exponentially hard OWFs, as well as on (unknown-)regular OWFs.

Definition 1.3 (NBP, informal). *A random variable $X = (X_1, \ldots, X_m)$ has* next-block pseudoentropy k *if there exists a set of random variables $Y = \{Y_1, \ldots, Y_m\}$, each jointly distributed with X, such that:*

1. *For every i, $(X_1, X_2, \ldots, X_{i-1}, X_i)$ is computationally indistinguishable from $(X_1, X_2, \ldots, X_{i-1}, Y_i)$.*
2. $\sum_i \mathrm{H}(Y_i|X_1, \ldots X_{i-1}) \geq k$.

A next-block pseudoentropy generator *(NBPEG) is a polynomial-time computable function $G : \{0,1\}^n \rightarrow (\{0,1\}^\ell)^m$ such that $(X_1, \ldots, X_m) = G(U_n)$ has next-block pseudoentropy $\mathrm{H}(G(U_n)) + \Delta(n)$, where again $\Delta(n)$ is called the* entropy gap.

That is, in total, the bits of X "look like" they have k bits of entropy given the previous ones. Note that the case of 1 block ($m = 1$) amounts to the definition of a pseudoentropy generator. Also note that, when $m > 1$, allowing Y to be correlated with X in this definition is essential: for example if all the blocks of X are always equal to each other (and have noticeable entropy), then there is no way to define Y that is independent of X and satisfies the first condition.

With this notion, our construction proceeds as follows.

OWF to NBPEG: Given a one-way function f, we define $G(x,h) = (f(x), h, h(x)_1, h(x)_2, \ldots, h(x)_n)$, where $h : \{0,1\}^n \rightarrow \{0,1\}^n$ is an appropriate hash function, and $h(x)_i$ is the i'th bit of $h(x)$. Notice that this is the same as the construction of Håstad et al., except that we do not randomly truncate the output. At first, this seems problematic; by revealing all of $h(x)$, it becomes easy for an adversary to compute x, and thus the pseudoentropy of output equals its real entropy (i.e., we have *zero* entropy gap). We show, however, that it does indeed have *next-block pseudoentropy* $n + \log n$, which is even larger than the seed length of G. We have gained in two ways here. First, the entropy gap is now $\Delta = \log n$ instead of $\Delta = \log n/n$. Second, we know the total amount of entropy in the output (though not the amount contributed by the individual blocks). These two advantages improve the the complexity and security of the rest of the construction. Furthermore, the fact that the next-block pseudoentropy is larger than the seed length simplifies the construction, as we do not need to extract any additional entropy from the seed.

Entropy Equalization: Here we use a technique from [12] to convert our knowledge about the total entropy (summed over all blocks) into knowledge about the entropy in the individual blocks. We evaluate G on $u = O(n/\Delta)$ independent seeds and concatenate the outputs, but randomly shifted by $i \xleftarrow{\mathrm{R}} [n]$ coordinates. This increases our seed length and our entropy by a multiplicatives factor of approximately u, but now almost all the blocks have pseudoentropy at least the average pseudoentropy of the blocks of G.

Converting Shannon Entropy to Min-Entropy and Amplifying the Gap: This works the same as in [13]. Again we take roughly $t = O(n/\Delta)^2$ copies, but concatenate them within each block to obtain an m-block generator G'. Now each of the m blocks is indistinguishable from having high *min-entropy* conditioned on the previous ones. Thus what we have is computational analogue of a *block source* [2], which are random sources in which each block has high min-entropy conditioned on the previous ones.

Randomness Extraction: For this step, we use a known method for block-source extraction [2, 28] and define $G(x,h) = (h, h(G'(x)_1), \ldots, h(G'(x)_m))$, where h is a universal hash function. Since we know how much pseudo-min-entropy is in each block, there is no difficulty in choosing the output length of h.

In total, our seed length is roughly $O(n \cdot u \cdot t) = O(n^4)$. For the case of exponentially hard one-way functions, we can obtain $\Delta = \Omega(n)$, and thus achieve seed $O(n \cdot \omega(\log n))$ matching [10] (but, unlike [10], our construction uses non-adaptive calls to the one-way function).

Note that our construction involves no "guessing" of entropies, neither in the construction of the initial NBPEG G, nor in an enumeration step at the end. While the entropy equalization "costs" the same (namely $u = O(n/\Delta)$) as enumeration did, it is actually doing more for us. Enumeration handled our lack of knowledge of a single entropy value (for which there were only $O(n/\Delta)$ choices), but here equalization is handling lack of knowledge for approximately n entropy values (one for each block), for which there are exponentially many choices. Moreover, enumeration required composing the pseudorandom generators to increase their stretch, resulting in a construction that is highly sequential and makes adaptive use of the one-way function. Our pseudorandom generators make nonadaptive use of the one-way function and are parallelizable (e.g., in NC^1), for getting pseudorandom generators with small stretch. Using Applebaum et al. [1], this implies the existence of pseudorandom generators in NC^0 based on the existence of one-way functions in NC^1.

1.3 Relation to Inaccessible Entropy

The notion of next-block pseudoentropy generators was inspired by the notion of *inaccessible entropy generators* in [12]. These are generators G that also produce m blocks $(x_1, \ldots, x_m)$ with the property that it is infeasible for an adversary to *generate* a sequence of blocks $(x_1, \ldots, x_m)$ that are consistent with the output of G in such a way that entropy of the individual blocks x_i is high (conditioned on the state of the adversary after generating the previous blocks). Thus, in a computational sense, the output of G has *low entropy*. For this reason, the notions of next-block pseudoentropy generators and inaccessible entropy generators seem to be dual to each other.

The initial construction of an inaccessible entropy generator in [12] is $G(x) = (f(x)_1, \ldots, f(x)_n, x)$, which is very similar to our construction of a next-block pseudoentropy generator except that there is no hashing and the bits of $f(x)$ instead of $h(x)$ are treated as separate blocks. This initial step is followed by entropy equalization and gap amplification steps that are exactly the same as the one we use (but analyzed with respect to dual notions). The final hashing step there (to construct statistically hiding commitment schemes) is more complex than ours and is necessarily interactive.

Interestingly, the notion of inaccessible entropy generator was introduced in an attempt to make the construction of statistically hiding commitment schemes from one-way functions "as simple" as the construction of pseudorandom generators from one-way functions, via manipulating notions of computational entropy. (The previous construction, from [11], was extremely complex.) In return, that effort has now inspired our simplifications and improvements to the construction of pseudorandom generators.

1.4 Paper Organization

Notations and definitions used through this paper are given in Section 2, where the new notion of a next-block pseudoentropy generator is formally defined in Section 3. In Section 4 we present our construction of next-block pseudoentropy generator from one-way functions, where in Section 5 we show how to use next-block pseudoentropy generators to get a pseudorandom generator. Finally, in Section 6 we use the above reductions to prove the main result of this paper.

2. PRELIMINARIES

2.1 Random Variables

Let X and Y be random variables taking values in a discrete universe $\mathcal{U}$. We adopt the convention that when the same random variable appears multiple times in an expression, all occurrences refer to the same instantiation. For example, $\Pr[X = X]$ is 1. The *support* of a random variable X is $\mathrm{Supp}(X) := \{x : \Pr[X = x] > 0\}$. We write $\Delta(X, Y)$ to denote the *statistical difference* (a.k.a. variation distance) between X and Y, i.e.

$$\Delta(X,Y) = \max_{T \subseteq \mathcal{U}} |\Pr[X \in T] - \Pr[Y \in T]| .$$

If $\Delta(X, Y) \leq \varepsilon$ (respectively, $\Delta(X, Y) > \varepsilon$), we say that X and Y are *ε-close* (resp., ε-far).

2.2 Entropy Measures

We will refer to several measures of entropy in this work. The relation and motivation of these measures is best understood by considering a notion that we will refer to as the *sample-entropy*. For a random variable X and $x \in \mathrm{Supp}(X)$, we define the sample-entropy of x with respect to X to be the quantity

$$\mathrm{H}_X(x) := \log(1/\Pr[X = x]).$$

The sample-entropy measures the amount of "randomness" or "surprise" in the specific sample x, assuming that x has been generated according to X. Using this notion, we can define the *Shannon entropy* $\mathrm{H}(X)$ and *min-entropy* $\mathrm{H}_\infty(X)$ as follows:

$$\mathrm{H}(X) := \mathop{\mathrm{E}}_{x \xleftarrow{R} X} [\mathrm{H}_X(x)]$$

$$\mathrm{H}_\infty(X) := \min_{x \in \mathrm{Supp}(X)} \mathrm{H}_X(x)$$

Flattening Shannon Entropy..

It is well-known that the Shannon entropy of a random variable can be converted to min-entropy (up to small statistical distance) by taking independent copies of this variable.

LEMMA 2.1. *1. Let X be a random variable taking values in a universe $\mathcal{U}$, let $t \in \mathbb{N}$, and let $\varepsilon > 0$. Then with probability at least $1 - \varepsilon - 2^{-\Omega(t)}$ over $x \xleftarrow{R} X^t$,*

$$|\mathrm{H}_{X^t}(x) - t \cdot \mathrm{H}(X)| \leq O(\sqrt{t \cdot \log(1/\varepsilon)} \cdot \log(|\mathcal{U}| \cdot t)).$$

2. Let X, Y be jointly distributed random variables where X takes values in a universe $\mathcal{U}$, let $t \in \mathbb{N}$, and let $\varepsilon > 0$. Then with probability at least $1 - \varepsilon - 2^{-\Omega(t)}$ over $(x, y) \xleftarrow{R} (X^t, Y^t) := (X, Y)^t$, we have that $|\mathrm{H}_{X^t|Y^t}(x|y) - t \cdot \mathrm{H}(X|Y)| \leq O(\sqrt{t \cdot \log(1/\varepsilon)} \cdot \log(|\mathcal{U}| \cdot t))$.

We omit the proof from this version.

2.3 One-way Functions

DEFINITION 2.2. *Let $f\colon \{0,1\}^n \mapsto \{0,1\}^m$ be a polynomial-time computable function, where n is a security parameter and $m = m(n)$. For $T = T(n)$ and $\varepsilon = \varepsilon(n)$, we say that f is a (T, ε)-*one-way function *if for every probabilistic algorithm A running in time T and all sufficiently large n, we have:*

$$\Pr[A(Y) \in f^{-1}(Y)] \leq \varepsilon,$$

where the probability is taken over $Y = f(U_n)$ and the coin tosses of A. We say that f is a one-way function *if it is a $(p(n), 1/p(n))$-one-way function for every polynomial p.*

2.4 Pseudorandom Generators

DEFINITION 2.3. *Let X be a random variable, depending on a security parameter n, and taking values in $\{0,1\}^m$, for $m = m(n)$. For $T = T(n)$ and $\varepsilon = \varepsilon(n)$, we say that X is (T, ε)-*pseudorandom *if for every probabilistic distinguisher D running in time T and all sufficiently large n, we have:*

$$|\Pr[D(X) = 1] - \Pr[D(U_m) = 1]| \leq \varepsilon.$$

*A polynomial-time computable function $G\colon \{0,1\}^n \mapsto \{0,1\}^m$ with $m = m(n) > n$ is a (T, ε)-*pseudorandom generator *if $G(U_n)$ is (T, ε)-pseudorandom.*

We say that X is pseudorandom *if it is $(p(n), 1/p(n))$-pseudorandom for every polynomial p. Similarly, G is a* pseudorandom generator *G if $G(U_n)$ is pseudorandom.*

3. NEXT-BLOCK PSEUDOENTROPY

In this section we formally define the new notion of next-block pseudoentropy, for the cases of both Shannon entropy and min-entropy. The definitions will differ from the informal definition given in the introduction (Definition 1.3) in the following two ways, both of which are important for the treatment of uniform adversaries:

- We will require indistinguishability even against algorithms that have an oracle for sampling from the joint distribution (X, Y_i). (This enables us to show, using a hybrid argument, that pseudoentropy increases when we taking many independent copies of X. In the case of nonuniform adversaries, no oracle for sampling from (X, Y_i) is needed, as the samples can be nonuniformly hardwired into the adversary.)
- In order to achieve the first item, we will allow the random variables Y_i to depend on the distinguisher.

Similar issues arise for treating uniform adversaries with standard pseudoentropy.

Definition 3.1. *(next-block (Shannon) pseudoentropy)* *Let X be a random variable taking values in $\mathcal{U}^m$, where X, $\mathcal{U}$, and m may all depend on a security parameter n. For $T = T(n)$, $k = k(n)$ and $\varepsilon = \varepsilon(n)$, we say that X has (T, ε)* next-block pseudoentropy *k if for every oracle-aided distinguisher $D^{(\cdot)}$ of running time at most T, there exists a set of random variables $\{Y_1, \ldots, Y_m\}$ over $\mathcal{U}$ such that:*

1. $\sum_{i=1}^{m} \mathrm{H}(Y_i \mid X_1, \ldots, X_{i-1}) \geq k$, *and*

2. $$\mathop{\mathrm{E}}_{i \stackrel{R}{\leftarrow} [m]} [\Pr[D^{O_{X,Y}}(X_1, \ldots, X_i) = 1] - \Pr[D^{O_{X,Y}}(X_1, \ldots, X_{i-1}, Y_i) = 1]] \leq L \cdot \varepsilon,$$

where $O_{X,Y}(i)$, for $i \in [m]$, samples according to the joint distribution (X, Y_i), and $L = L(n)$ is a bound on number of calls made by D to $O_{X,Y}$ (including the challenge itself).

We say that X has next-block pseudoentropy *k, if it has $(p(n), 1/p(n))$-next-block pseudoentropy k for every polynomial p. We say that* every block *of X has (T, ε)-next-block pseudoentropy $\alpha = \alpha(n)$, if condition (1) above is replaced with $\mathrm{H}(Y_i \mid X_{1,\ldots,i-1}) \geq \alpha$ for every $i \in [m]$.*

Note that we have omitted absolute values in the indistinguishability condition above (and below). This is purely for technical convenience, as D can use $O((m/\varepsilon)^2)$ random samples from its oracle to test whether the (signed) advantages inside the expectation are positive or negative to within an accuracy of $\pm\varepsilon/2m$ and negate itself for some values of i in order to ensure a positive advantage of at least $L\varepsilon/2$.

Definition 3.2. *(next-block pseudo-min-entropy) Let X be a random variable taking values in $\mathcal{U}^m$, where X, $\mathcal{U}$, and m may all depend on a security parameter n. For $T = T(n)$, $\alpha = \alpha(n)$, and $\varepsilon = \varepsilon(n)$, we say that* every block *of X has (T, ε)*-next-block pseudo-*min*-entropy *α, if for every oracle-aided distinguisher $D^{(\cdot)}$ running in time at most $T(n)$, there exists a set of random variables $\{Y_1, \ldots, Y_m\}$ over $\mathcal{U}$ such that:*

1. $\mathrm{H}_\infty(Y_i \mid X_{1,\ldots,i-1}) \geq \alpha$, *and*

2. $$\mathop{\mathrm{E}}_{i \stackrel{R}{\leftarrow} [m]} [\Pr[D^{O_{X,Y}}(X_1, \ldots, X_i) = 1] - \Pr[D^{O_{X,Y}}(X_1, \ldots, X_{i-1}, Y_i) = 1] \leq L \cdot \varepsilon,$$

where $O_{X,Y}$ and L is as in Definition 3.1.

We say that every block *of X has* next-block pseudo-min-entropy *α, if every block of X has $(p(n), 1/p(n))$-next-block pseudo-min-entropy α, for every polynomial p.*

Unless explicitly stated otherwise, in the following sections we view a distribution over $\{0,1\}^t$ as a t-block distribution. When we refer to the next-block pseudoentropy properties of a function $G : \{0,1\}^n \to \{0,1\}^m$, these refer to the random variable $G(U_n)$.

4. ONE-WAY FUNCTIONS TO NEXT-BLOCK PSEUDOENTROPY GENERATOR

This section will show how to construct a next-block pseudoentropy generator ${G_{nb}}^f$ out of a one-way function $f\colon \{0,1\}^n \mapsto \{0,1\}^n$.

Theorem 4.1. *(Next-block pseudoentropy generator from one-way functions) Let n be a security parameter and $f : \{0,1\}^n \mapsto \{0,1\}^n$ be a polynomial-time computable function. Then there exists a polynomial-time computable generator $G_{nb}\colon \{0,1\}^d \mapsto \{0,1\}^m$, with $d = d(n) \in O(n)$ and $m = m(n) \in O(n)$, such that the following holds:*

Security: *Assume that f is a (T, ε) one-way function for some $T = T(n)$ and $\varepsilon = \varepsilon(n)$. Then for any $\mathrm{poly}(n)$-time computable value of $\varepsilon' = \varepsilon'(n) > 2^{-n/4}$, G_{nb} has $(T \cdot (\varepsilon'/n)^{O(1)}, \varepsilon')$-next-block-pseudoentropy $k = d + \log(1/\varepsilon) - c \log n$, where c is a universal constant.*

Complexity: *G_{nb} is computable in NC^1 with one oracle call to f.*

When f is a standard one-way function, we can take $T = 1/\varepsilon = n^{c'}$ for an arbitrarily large constant c' and set $\varepsilon' = 1/n^{\gamma c'}$ for a small universal constant γ, to deduce that G_{nb} has $(n^{\Omega(c')}, 1/n^{\Omega(c')})$-next-block pseudoentropy $k = d + (c' - c) \log n$. In particular, G_{nb} has next-block pseudoentropy $k = d + \log n$.

Our construction employs a family of hash functions $\mathcal{Q} = \{\mathcal{Q}_n = \{q\colon \{0,1\}^n \mapsto \{0,1\}^n\}\}$. We will shortly discuss the properties needed from $\mathcal{Q}$. Given an appropriate family $\mathcal{Q}$, we can define ${G_{nb}}^f$ quite easily:

Construction 4.2. *On security parameter n, define the algorithm G_{nb} on domain $\{0,1\}^n \times \mathcal{Q}_n$, for $\mathcal{Q}_n = \{q\colon \{0,1\}^n \mapsto \{0,1\}^n\}$, and oracle $f : \{0,1\}^n \to \{0,1\}^n$ as follows:*

$$ {G_{nb}}^f(s, q) := (f(s), q, q(s)_1, \ldots, q(s)_n), $$

where s is n bits long and $q(s)_i$ denotes the ith bit of $q(s)$. (Note that we abuse notation and write q for both the function and its description.)

The following properties regarding the efficiency of ${G_{nb}}^f$ are immediate:

Lemma 4.3. *If $\mathcal{Q}$ is in NC^1 then ${G_{nb}}^f$ is in NC^1 with one oracle call to f. If the description length of $\mathcal{Q}_n$ is $O(n)$ then the input length of ${G_{nb}}^{(\cdot)}$ is linear in its first argument (as $|q| = O(|s|)$. Finally, ${G_{nb}}^f$ invokes f exactly once (and thus is non-adaptive with respect to f).*

Indeed, we will define $\mathcal{Q}$ that is both efficient and has a short description. The main requirement from $\mathcal{Q}$, however, has to do with ensuring that ${G_{nb}}^f$ is a next-block pseudoentropy generator. Let us start by presenting the following strategy showing that the entropy gap (i.e., $k - d$) for $\varepsilon = 1/n^{\Omega(\log n)}$ is at least $\log n$. Let $D_f(y) := \log |\{x \in \{0,1\}^n \colon f(x) = y\}|$ and let S be uniformly distributed over $\{0,1\}^n$. Then the distribution of S conditioned on $y = f(S)$ still has $D_f(y)$ bits of entropy. We would like $\mathcal{Q}$ to extract these bits and in addition to extract $\log n$ bits of pseudoentropy. More concretely, we ask that the first $D_f(y) + \log n$ bits of $q(S)$ are pseudorandom even given $y = f(S)$ and q (to simplify notation, we will ignore round-off errors and treat $D_f(y)$ as an integer). Given such a $\mathcal{Q}$, we are essentially done (at least when considering non-uniform security[4]). Consider the distributions $X = G_{nb}{}^f(S, Q)$ and the distribution $(Y_1, \ldots, Y_n) := (f(S), Q, R_1, \ldots R_k, Q(S)_{K+1}, \ldots, Q(S)_n)$, where S and Q are uniformly distributed, $K := D_f(f(S)) + \log n$ and the R_i's are uniformly random bits. By the above discussion, X and Y (more formally, X and $\{Y_i\}$) are next-block indistinguishable. In addition, we have:

$$\begin{aligned} & \sum_{i=1}^{m} \mathrm{H}(Y_i \mid X_{1,\ldots,i-1}) \\ \geq\ & \mathrm{H}(f(S)) + \mathrm{H}(Q) + \mathrm{H}(R_1, \ldots, R_K | f(S)) \\ =\ & \mathrm{H}(f(S)) + \mathrm{H}(Q) + \mathrm{E}[D_f(f(S)) + \log n] \\ =\ & n + \log|\mathcal{Q}_n| + \log n. \end{aligned}$$

and therefore $G_{nb}{}^f$ is indeed a next-block pseudoentropy generator.

The first remaining challenge is to construct such a family $\mathcal{Q}$. As we will discuss shortly, it is easy to obtain all the above properties with hash functions that have description length n^2. For better efficiency, we will settle on $\mathcal{Q}$ with slightly weaker properties (where the pseudorandom bits extracted by $q \in \mathcal{Q}$ will be pseudorandom up to advantage $1/n$ rather than an arbitrary inverse polynomial advantage). An additional challenge is achieving next-block pseudoentropy in the (more standard) uniform setting. The difficulty is that we need X and Y to be next-block indistinguishable even given oracles that sample these distributions. While X is efficiently samplable (and thus an oracle that samples X is easy to implement), Y may not be (as $D_f(y)$ may be hard to compute). To overcome this difficulty we employ Holenstein's Uniform Hardcore Lemma [14]. Employing the Hardcore Lemma also closes the gap between the properties of $\mathcal{Q}$ we obtain and the stronger properties in the discussion above (actually, we even achieve a stronger guarantee, where the entropy gap is roughly $\log(1/\varepsilon)$).

4.1 The family $\mathcal{Q}$ and unpredictability

A family $\mathcal{Q}$ with the above properties, but with description length n^2, is easy to come by. Simply define $q(s)$ to be As, where A is a uniformly chosen $n \times n$ matrix over GF(2). For a random $y = f(S)$, the Leftover Hash Lemma [19] yields that the first $D_f(y) - c \log n$ bits of $Q(S)$ are statistically close to uniform up to statistical distance $1/n^{\Omega(c)}$. An additional $(c+1) \cdot \log n$ bits are pseudorandom by reduction to the Goldreich-Levin hardcore predicate [4]. An interesting open problem is to come up with a family $\mathcal{Q}$ that has similar properties and in addition has description length n. Instead, in this paper we relax the requirements from $\mathcal{Q}$.

Defining $q(s) = As$ is equivalent to selecting each one of the output bits of $q(s)$ to be a uniformly selected location of the Hadamard encoding of s. If instead we let each bit be a location in a polynomially-long encoding of s, we get description length $n \log n$. As long as this encoding possesses good list-decoding properties, such a construction still suffices for our purposes. To save the final $\log n$ factor, we will look at an encoding of x into logarithmically long symbols (and thus will only need $n/\log n$ symbols as the output of $q(s)$). The following lemma formalizes the properties of the encoding we will use. As with the Hadamard Code, the code we will use will satisfy both the role of extracting $D_f(y) - O(\log n)$ truly random bits via the Leftover Hash Lemma and the role of extracting $O(\log n)$ pseudorandom bits similarly to a hardcore function.

LEMMA 4.4. *There exists an* NC^1 *algorithm* Enc *such that on input* $s \in \{0,1\}^n$, *the algorithm* Enc *produces* $t = \mathrm{poly}(n)$ *symbols* $\mathrm{Enc}(s)_1, \mathrm{Enc}(s)_2, \ldots, \mathrm{Enc}(s)_t$ *with each* $\mathrm{Enc}(s)_i \in \{0,1\}^\ell$ *for* $\ell = \lceil \log n \rceil$ *and such that the following properties hold:*

Almost 2-Universal: *For every two distinct* n*-bit strings* $s \neq s'$ *it holds that*

$$\Pr_{i \in [t]}[\mathrm{Enc}(s)_i = \mathrm{Enc}(s')_i] \leq 2^{-\ell} \cdot (1 + 1/(2n^5)).$$

List Decoding: *There exists a polynomial-time algorithm* Dec *that on input* 1^n *and given oracle access to a function* $\tilde{A} : [t] \times \{0,1\}^\ell \to \{0,1\}$, *outputs a list of* $\mathrm{poly}(n)$ *strings that includes every* $s \in \{0,1\}^n$ *satisfying the following:* $\Pr_{i \xleftarrow{R} [t]}[\tilde{A}(i, \mathrm{Enc}(s)_i) = 1] - \Pr_{i \xleftarrow{R} [t], z \xleftarrow{R} \{0,1\}^\ell}[\tilde{A}(i, z) = 1]] > 1/5n^2$.

Note that the oracle $\tilde{A}$ has a domain of size $t \cdot 2^\ell = \mathrm{poly}(n)$, so Dec has enough time to query it on all inputs (i.e. "local decoding" is not needed).

PROOF. Enc can be taken to be the concatenation of a Reed-Solomon Code (over a field of size a sufficiently large polynomial in n) and the Hadamard Code over $\mathrm{GF}(2^\ell)$. The almost-universality property follows from a standard argument: the probability that $\mathrm{Enc}(s) = \mathrm{Enc}(s')$ is bounded by the probability that a random symbol of two distinct Reed-Solomon codewords agree plus the probability that a random symbol in two distinct Hadamard codewords agree. By making the field of the Reed-Solomon encoding sufficiently larger than 2^ℓ (but still $\mathrm{poly}(n)$) we get the desired property. The list-decoding property follows from the list-decoding algorithm of Sudan [23] for the Reed–Solomon code, combined with brute-force decoding of the Hadamard code. □

CONSTRUCTION 4.5. *Let* n, Enc, t *and* ℓ *be as in Lemma 4.4. The description of a random hash function* $q \in \mathcal{Q}_n$ *is composed of* $\lceil n/\ell \rceil$ *random indices* $i_1, \ldots, i_{\lceil n/\ell \rceil} \in [t]$. *On input* s *define* $q(s)$ *to be the first* n *bits of* $\mathrm{Enc}(s)_{i_1} \ldots \mathrm{Enc}(s)_{i_{\lceil n/\ell \rceil}}$.

LEMMA 4.6. *Let* n *be a security parameter,* $\mathcal{Q}$ *be as in Construction 4.5, let* G_{nb} *be the oracle-aided algorithm for Construction 4.2 (with respect to* $\mathcal{Q}$*), and let* $f : \{0,1\}^n \to \{0,1\}^n$ *be a* (T, ε) *one-way function, for* $T = T(n) \geq n, \varepsilon = \varepsilon(n)$. *Then there exists a constant* $c > 0$ *such that*

$$\begin{aligned} & \sum_{i=0}^{n-1} \Pr[P(f(S), Q, Q(S)_1, \ldots, Q(S)_i) \neq Q(S)_{i+1}] \\ \geq\ & \frac{n - \mathrm{H}(f(S)) + \log(1/\varepsilon) - c \log n}{2}, \end{aligned}$$

even when P *is allowed to run in time* T/n^c, *where* S *and* Q *are uniformly distributed over* $\{0,1\}^n$ *and* $\mathcal{Q}_n$ *respectively.*

Note that above (and below) $Q(S)_1, \ldots, Q(S)_{i+1}$ refer to individual *bits* of $Q(S)$, not ℓ-bit blocks.

We omit the proof from this version.

[4]I.e., the distinguisher is non-uniform and does not get oracle access to $O_{X,Y}$.

4.2 Proving Next-block Pseudoentropy via Hardcore Lemma

Lemma 4.6 shows that the output of G_{nb} (after $f(S)$ and Q) satisfies a weak next-bit unpredictability. In this section we use Holenstein's "Uniform Hardcore Lemma" of Holenstein [14, 15, 16] (the uniform variant of the Impagliazzo [17] Hardcore Lemma), to translate this weak next-bit unpredictability into next-bit pseudoentropy, thereby proving Theorem 4.1. We begin with a statement of the the Hardcore Lemma. This translates weak unpredictability (of a single bit) into strong unpredictability on a noticeable fraction of inputs.

PROPOSITION 4.7. *Let n be a security parameter, and let $\ell = \ell(n)$, $h\colon \{0,1\}^n \mapsto \{0,1\}^\ell$, $V\colon \{0,1\}^n \mapsto \{0,1\}$, $\delta = \delta(n) \in (0,1) > 1/\operatorname{poly}(n)$, and $\gamma = \gamma(n) \in (0,1) > 2^{-n/3}$ all be $\operatorname{poly}(n)$-time computable functions. Assume that*

$$\Pr[M(h(U_n)) = V(U_n)] \leq 1 - \delta/2$$

for every probabilistic algorithm M running in time $T = T(n)$ and large enough n. Then there is a polynomial p such that for every oracle-aided predictor P running in time $T' = T/p(n, 1/\gamma)$ and all sufficiently large n, there exists a set $L \subseteq \{0,1\}^n$ of density at least δ such that

$$\Pr_{W \overset{R}{\leftarrow} L}[P^{\chi_L}(h(W)) = V(W)] < (1+\gamma)/2,$$

where χ_L is the characteristic function of L, provided that all the queries of P to χ_L are computed independently of the input $h(W)$.

We now reinterpret Holenstein's Hardcore Lemma in terms of conditional pseudoentropy, similarly to the reinterpretation of Impagliazzo's Hardcore Lemma in [24].

PROPOSITION 4.8. *Let n be a security parameter, and let $\ell = \ell(n)$, $\delta = \delta(n) \in (0,1) > 1/\operatorname{poly}(n)$, and $\gamma = \gamma(n) \in (0,1) > 2^{-n/3}$ all be $\operatorname{poly}(n)$-time computable functions, and let (A, B) be a poly-time samplable distribution on $\{0,1\}^\ell \times \{0,1\}$ such that*

$$\Pr[M(A) = B] \leq 1 - \delta/2$$

for every probabilistic algorithm M running in time $T = T(n)$ and large enough n. Then there is a polynomial p such that for every oracle-aided distinguisher D running in time $T' = T/p(n, 1/\gamma)$ and all sufficiently large n, there is a random variable C, jointly distributed with A, such that:

1. $\mathrm{H}(C|A) \geq \delta$.
2. $\Pr[D^{O_{A,B,C}}(A, B) = 1] - \Pr[D^{O_{A,B,C}}(A, C) = 1] \leq \gamma$.

PROOF. Let $(h, V) : \{0,1\}^n \to \{0,1\}^\ell \times \{0,1\}$ be the poly-time sampling algorithms for (A, B), i.e. $(h(U_n), V(U_n)) = (A, B)$. (By renaming the security parameter n, we may assume that the sampling algorithms use n coin tosses.) Thus we may apply Proposition 4.7 to the pair (h, V). For any given subset $L \subseteq \{0,1\}^n$ of density δ, we define a probabilistic function $V_L : \{0,1\}^n \to \{0,1\}$, where

$$V_L(r) = \begin{cases} V(r) & \text{if } r \notin L \\ \text{a random bit} & \text{if } r \in L. \end{cases}$$

From this we get a random variable C_L jointly distributed with A, defined by $(A, C_L) = (h(U_n), V_L(U_n))$. Notice that $\mathrm{H}(C_L|A)$ is at least the density of L, namely δ. We will show that taking $C = C_L$ for some L suffices. Suppose for contradiction that we have an oracle-aided distinguisher D running in time T' such that for every L of density δ, $\Pr[D^{O_{A,B,C_L}}(A, B) = 1] - \Pr[D^{O_{A,B,C_L}}(A, C_L) = 1] > \gamma$. Since B and C_L are identical when $U_n \notin L$, we have $\Pr[D^{O_{A,B,C_L}}(A, B) = 1 | U_n \in L] - \Pr[D^{O_{A,B,C_L}}(A, C_L) = 1 | U_n \in L] > \gamma$. Since C_L is a uniformly random bit when $U_n \in L$, we can apply the standard reduction from distinguishing to predicting to obtain an oracle-aided predictor P, running in time $T' + O(1)$ such that

$$\Pr[P^{\chi_L}(A) = B | U_n \in L] > (1 + \gamma)/2. \tag{1}$$

Specifically, on input x, P generates a random bit $b \overset{R}{\leftarrow} \{0,1\}$, runs $D^{O_{A,B,C_L}}(x, b)$, outputs b if D outputs 1, and outputs $\neg b$ if D outputs 0. P can simulate random samples from the oracle O_{A,B,C_L} by choosing $r \overset{R}{\leftarrow} \{0,1\}^n$ and outputting $(h(r), V(r), V_L(r))$, which can be efficiently computed using P's oracle access to χ_L. Equation (1) can be rewritten as:

$$\Pr_{W \overset{R}{\leftarrow} L}[P^{\chi_L}(h(W)) = V(W)] > (1 + \gamma)/2.$$

This contradicts Proposition 4.7. □

We can now use this form of the Hardcore Lemma to deduce Theorem 4.1 from Lemma 4.6. The proof is omitted from this version.

5. FROM NEXT-BLOCK PSEUDOENTROPY TO PSEUDORANDOM GENERATORS

In this section we show how to transform a next-block pseudoentropy generator into a pseudorandom generator.

THEOREM 5.1. *(Next-block pseudoentropy generator to pseudorandom generator) Let n be a security parameter, and let $m = m(n)$, $\Delta = \Delta(n) \in [1/\operatorname{poly}(n), n]$, and $\kappa = \kappa(n) \in \{1, \ldots, n\}$ be $\operatorname{poly}(n)$-time computable. For every polynomial-time computable, m-block generator $G_{nb}\colon \{0,1\}^n \mapsto \{0,1\}^m$, there exists a polynomial-time computable generator $G : \{0,1\}^d \to \{0,1\}^{d \cdot (1+\Omega(\Delta))}$ with $d = d(n) = O(m^2 \cdot (n/\Delta)^3 \cdot \kappa \cdot \log^2 n)$ such that the following holds:*

Security: *Assume that G_{nb} has (T, ε)-next-block pseudoentropy at least $n + \Delta$, for $T = T(n), \varepsilon = \varepsilon(n)$, then G is a $(T/\operatorname{poly}(n), \operatorname{poly}(n) \cdot (\varepsilon + 2^{-\kappa}))$-pseudorandom generator.*

Complexity: *G is computable in NC^1 with $O(d/n)$ oracle calls to G_{nb}.*

In Theorem 5.1, it may be convenient to view $\kappa(n)$ as the security parameter of the construction. In particular, when $\kappa(n)$ logarithmic in $1/\varepsilon(n)$ we get that $(T(n), \varepsilon(n))$-next-block pseudoentropy turns into an $(T(n)/\operatorname{poly}(n), \operatorname{poly}(n) \cdot \varepsilon(n))$-pseudorandom generator.

We prove Theorem 5.1 via the following sequence of reductions:

1. In Section 5.1 we show how to get a better handle on the output distribution of the G_{nb} — specifically, we apply a generic transformation on G_{nb}, to get a generator for which the (conditional) pseudoentropy of each of its output blocks is the same (i.e., $(n + \Delta)/m$).

2. In Section 5.2 we consider a direct product of the latter next-block pseudoentropy generator, and show that this action both increases the absolute gap between the next-block pseudoentropy of the generator and its real entropy (i.e., its input length), and transforms its next-block pseudoentropy into next-block pseudo-min-entropy.

3. In Section 5.3 we show to extract pseudorandomness from the output of the latter type of generators.

4. In Section 5.4 we put the above parts together to prove Theorem 5.1.

To simplify notations, we prove the first three steps with respect to arbitrary next-block pseudoentropy distributions. Given a distribution X over $\mathcal{U}^m$, a set of distributions $Y = \{Y_i\}_{i\in[m]}$ over $\mathcal{U}$, and an oracle-aided algorithm $D^{(\cdot)}$, we let $\delta^D_{X,Y} := \mathrm{E}_{i\overset{R}{\leftarrow}[m(n)]}[\delta^D_{X,Y,i} := \Pr[D^{O_{X,Y}}(X_1,\ldots,X_i) = 1] - \Pr[D^{O_{X,Y}}(X_1,\ldots,X_{i-1},Y_i) = 1]]$, where $O_{X,Y}(i)$ samples according to the joint distribution (X, Y_i) (see Definition 3.1). Finally, in all of the following claims we assume the description of the "universe" $\mathcal{U}$ is polynomial in n.

5.1 Entropy Equalization

In this section we show to manipulate a given distribution to gain a better characterization of its next-block pseudoentropy, without losing "too much" pseudoentropy. The following transformation is closely related to a similar reduction from [8]. The idea is the following: consider an m-block random variable X over $\mathcal{U}^m$ with next-block pseudoentropy k. Now generate $m \cdot \ell$ blocks by concatenating ℓ independent copies one after the other. Finally, for a random $j \in [m]$, erase the first j blocks and the last $m - j$ blocks. We now have a new variable $\widetilde{X}$ with $m \cdot (\ell - 1)$ blocks and for every location i the block in the ith location of $\widetilde{X}$ is a block of X in a random location. It is not hard to prove (as we do below) that the next-block pseudoentropy of each block is at least k/m. On the other hand, the real entropy of $\widetilde{X}$ is at most ℓ times that of X. Taking large enough ℓ we get that the (relative) difference between next-block pseudoentropy and real entropy has not significantly decreased.

For $j \in [m]$ and $z^{(1)},\ldots,z^{(\ell)} \in \mathcal{U}^m$, we let $\mathrm{Eq}(j, z^{(1)},\ldots,z^{(\ell)}) := (z^{(1)}_j,\ldots,z^{(1)}_m,\ldots,z^{(\ell)}_1,\ldots,z^{(\ell)}_{j-1})$.

CLAIM 5.2. *Let n be a security parameter, and let $m = m(n) = \mathrm{poly}(n)$ and $\ell = \ell(n) = \mathrm{poly}(n)$ be $\mathrm{poly}(n)$-time computable integer functions, where $\ell(n) > 1$. Let X be random variable over $\mathcal{U}^m$ with (T,ε)-next-block pseudoentropy at least k, for $T = T(n)$, $\varepsilon = \varepsilon(n)$ and $k = k(n)$. Let J be uniformly distributed over $[m]$ and let $\widetilde{X} = \mathrm{Eq}(J, X^{(1)},\ldots,X^{(\ell)})$, where the $X^{(i)}$'s are iid copies of X. Then $\widetilde{X}$ has $(T - O(\ell\cdot m\cdot\log|\mathcal{U}|), 2\ell\varepsilon)$ next-block pseudoentropy at least k/m.*

PROOF. Let $m' = (\ell - 1)\cdot m$ and let $Y = \{Y_1,\ldots,Y_m\}$ be a set of random variable jointly distributed with X. In the following we think of Y as a single random variable $Y = (Y_1,\ldots,Y_m)$ jointly distributed with X, though we only sample a single entry Y_i per instance of Y. Let $Y^{(1)},\ldots,Y^{(\ell)}$ be iid copies of Y and let $\widetilde{Y} = \mathrm{Eq}(J, Y^{(1)},\ldots,Y^{(\ell)})$ be jointly distributed with $\widetilde{X}$ in the natural way — J takes the same value as in $\widetilde{X}$, and for every $j \in [\ell]$, $Y^{(j)}$ is jointly distributed with $X^{(j)}$ according to the joint distribution (X, Y). Notice that $\widetilde{Y}_i = Y_{J+i-1 \bmod m}$ (where we define $m \bmod m$ to equal m rather than 0), and that $J + i - 1$ is uniformly distributed in $[m]$.

Thus, for every $i \in [m']$ we have that

$$\begin{aligned} &\mathrm{H}(\widetilde{Y}_i \mid \widetilde{X}_{1,\ldots,i-1}) \\ &\geq \mathrm{H}(Y_{J+i-1 \bmod m} | X_1,\ldots,X_{(J+i-1 \bmod m)-1}) \\ &= \mathop{\mathrm{E}}_{i'\overset{R}{\leftarrow}[m]}[\mathrm{H}(Y_{i'} \mid X_1,\ldots,X_{i'-1})]. \end{aligned} \tag{2}$$

Let $\widetilde{D}$ be an adversary the violates the next-block pseudoentropy of $\widetilde{X}$. We define D for breaking the next-block pseudoentropy of X as follows: on input $(x_1,\ldots,x_{i-1},z)$, D generates a random sample $x' = (x'_1,\ldots,x'_{m'})$ from $\widetilde{X}$ (using $O_{X,Y}$). It then selects $i' \in [m']$ uniformly at random such that $i' = j + i - 1 \bmod m$, where j is the value of J in the generation of x', and returns $\widetilde{D}^{O_{\widetilde{X},\widetilde{Y}}}(x'_1,\ldots,x'_{i'-i},x_1,\ldots,x_{i-1},z)$, while answering $\widetilde{D}$'s queries to $O_{\widetilde{X},\widetilde{Y}}$ using $O_{X,Y}$.

We note that D makes at most 2ℓ times more oracle queries than $\widetilde{D}$, and that D can be implemented in the running time of $\widetilde{D}$ plus $O(\ell\cdot m\cdot\log|\mathcal{U}|)$.

For every Y as above with $\sum_{i\in[m]}\mathrm{H}(Y_i \mid X_{1,\ldots,i-1}) \geq k$, Equation (2) yields that $\widetilde{Y}$ is a random variable that $\widetilde{D}$ should be able to next-block distinguish from $\widetilde{X}$. Since the query to $\widetilde{D}$ done by D is distributed identically to a random challenge to $\widetilde{D}$ with respect to the joint distribution $(\widetilde{X},\widetilde{Y})$, it follows that

$$\delta^{\widetilde{D}}_{\widetilde{X},\widetilde{Y}} = \delta^D_{X,Y} \leq L\cdot\varepsilon = \widetilde{L}\cdot(2\ell\varepsilon),$$

where L and $\widetilde{L}$ are the number of oracle calls made by D and $\widetilde{D}$, respectively. This is contradiction to the assumption about the next-block pseudoentropy of X. □

5.2 Next-block Pseudoentropy Converts to Pseudo-Min-Entropy

In this section we show how to transform next-block (Shannon) pseudoentropy to next-block pseudo-min-entropy, while increasing the overall entropy gap. The transformation of X is simply a t-fold parallel repetition of X (i.e., every block of the new random variable X^t is composed of t corresponding blocks of t independent copies of X). This generalizes an analogous transformation that was used by Håstad et al. [13] in the context of standard (i.e. single-block) pseudoentropy.

Given an m-block random variable V taking values in $\mathcal{U}^m$ and an integer $t > 0$, we let $V^t = ((V^{(1)}_1,\ldots,V^{(t)}_1),\ldots,(V^{(1)}_m,\ldots,V^{(t)}_m)) \in (\mathcal{U}^t)^m$, where $V^{(i)}$ for every $i \in [t]$ is an independent copy of V.

CLAIM 5.3. *Let n be a security parameter, and $m = m(n) = \mathrm{poly}(n)$, $t = t(n) = \mathrm{poly}(n)$, be $\mathrm{poly}(n)$-time computable functions, and let X be a random variable over $\mathcal{U}^m$ where every block of X has (T,ε) next-block pseudoentropy α, for $T = T(n)$, $\varepsilon = \varepsilon(n)$, $\alpha = \alpha(n)$. Then for every $\kappa = \kappa(n) > 0$ it holds that every block of X^t has (T',ε') next-block pseudo-min-entropy α', where*

- *$T' = T'(n) = T - O(m\cdot t\cdot\log|\mathcal{U}|)$.*
- *$\varepsilon' = \varepsilon'(n) = 2\cdot t^2\cdot(\varepsilon + 2^{-\kappa} + 2^{-c\cdot t})$ for a universal constant $c > 0$, and*

- $\alpha' = \alpha'(n) = t \cdot \alpha - \Gamma(t, \kappa, |\mathcal{U}|)$, *for* $\Gamma(t, \kappa, |\mathcal{U}|) \in O(\sqrt{t \cdot \kappa} \cdot \log(|\mathcal{U}| \cdot t))$.

Notice that the $t \cdot \alpha$ term is the largest we could hope for the pseudoentropy — getting α bits of pseudoentropy per copy. However, since we wish to move from a pseudo-form of Shannon entropy (measuring randomness on average) to a pseudo-form of min-entropy (measuring randomness with high probability), we may have a deviation that grows like $\sqrt{t}$. By taking t large enough, this deviation becomes insignificant.

In more detail, consider the case that X has next-block pseudoentropy α with polynomial security, i.e. T and $1/\varepsilon$ can be taken to be arbitrarily large polynomials in n, and we would like to deduce that X^t has next-block min-pseudoentropy α' with polynomial security. Moreover, assume $\mathcal{U} = \{0,1\}$. Then we should take κ and t to be an arbitrarily large multiples of $\log n$, and we have $\alpha' = t \cdot (\alpha - O(\sqrt{(\log n)/t}) \cdot \log t)$. So if we would like to have pseudo-min-entropy at least $t \cdot (\alpha - \delta)$, we should take t to be $\mathrm{polylog}(n)/\delta^2$. In our application, we have $\delta = \Theta(\Delta/n) = \Theta(\log n/n)$, so we take $t = \tilde{O}(n^2)$ copies.

We omit the proof from this version.

5.3 Next-block Pseudo-Min-Entropy to Pseudorandomness

For our final step, we assume that X is such that each of the m blocks of X has large next-block pseudo-min-entropy α. Using a two universal indopendont hash function S, we extract almost all its pseudo-min-entropy of each block individually. The result is a sufficiently long pseudorandom bit sequence. This is a computational analogue of block-source extraction in the literature on randomness extractors [2, 28].

CLAIM 5.4. *(from next-block pseudo-min-entropy to pseudorandomness) Let n be a security parameter, $m = m(n) = \mathrm{poly}(n)$, $t = t(n) = \mathrm{poly}(n)$, $\alpha = \alpha(n) \in [t(n)]$ and $\kappa = \kappa(n) \in [\alpha(n)]$ be $\mathrm{poly}(n)$-time computable integer functions. There exists an efficient procedure $\mathrm{Ext} \in \mathrm{NC}^1$ that on input $x \in (\{0,1\}^t)^m$ and $s \in \{0,1\}^t$, outputs a string $y \in (\{0,1\}^{\alpha-\kappa})^m$ such that the following holds.*

Let X be a random variable over $(\{0,1\}^t)^m$ such that every block of X has (T, ε) next-block pseudo-min-entropy α, for $T = T(n)$ and $\varepsilon = \varepsilon(n)$, then $\mathrm{Ext}(X, U_t)$ is $(T - m \cdot \mathrm{poly}(t), m \cdot \varepsilon + 2^{-\kappa/2})$ pseudorandom.

PROOF. Let $\mathrm{Ext}(x, s) := (s(x_1), \ldots, s(x_m))$, where s is interpreted as a member of a family of two-universal hash functions from t bits to $\alpha - \kappa$ bits in NC^1 (such as $s(x) := s \cdot x$ over $GF(2^t)$ truncated to $\alpha - \kappa$ bits). Let D_{PRG} be an adversary that violates the pseudorandomness of $\mathrm{Ext}(X, U_t)$, and let δ_{PRG} be its distinguishing advantage. We define D for breaking the next-block pseudoentropy of X as follows: on input $(x_1, \ldots, x_{i-1}, z)$, D returns $D_{\mathrm{PRG}}(s(x_1), \ldots, s(x_{i-1}), s(z), U_{(\alpha-\kappa)\cdot(m-i)})$, where s is uniformly chosen from $\{0,1\}^t$.

We note that D makes no oracle calls (and thus we count its query complexity as one), and that its running-time is at most that of D_{PRG} plus $m \cdot \mathrm{poly}(t)$.

Let $Z^{[i]}(W) := (S(X_1), \ldots, S(X_{i-1}), S(W), U_{(\alpha-\kappa)\cdot(m-i)})$, for a uniformly distributed hash function S and let $Y = \{Y_1, \ldots, Y_m\}$ be a set of random variable over $\mathcal{U}$ jointly distributed with X, with $\mathrm{H}_\infty(Y_i \mid x_{1,\ldots,i-1}) \geq \alpha$ for every $x \in \mathrm{Supp}(X)$ and $i \in [m]$. The Leftover Hash Lemma [19, 18] can be shown to yield that $\delta^D_{X,Y} \geq \varepsilon$ (further details are omitted from this version). This contradicts the assumption about the next-block pseudoentropy of X. □

5.4 Putting It Together

The proof of Theorem 5.1 follows the three steps given by the three previous subsection (entropy equalization, obtaining pseudo-min-entropy and finally obtaining pseudorandomness). We omit the proof from this version.

6. PUTTING IT TOGETHER

We are now ready to prove the main result of the paper.

THEOREM 6.1. *(Pseudorandom generator from one-way functions) Let n be a security parameter and $f : \{0,1\}^n \mapsto \{0,1\}^n$ a polynomial-time computable function. For all $\mathrm{poly}(n)$-time computable functions $\varepsilon = \varepsilon(n) \leq 1/n^c$ (where c is a universal constant) and $\kappa = \kappa(n) \in [n/4]$, there exists an efficient generator G from strings of length $d = d(n) = O(n^4 \cdot \kappa \cdot \log^2 n / \log^3(1/\varepsilon)$ to strings of length $d \cdot (1 + \Omega(\log(1/\varepsilon)/n)$, such that the following holds:*

Security: *Assume that f is a (T, ε) one-way function for $T = T(n)$, $\varepsilon = \varepsilon(n)$, and let $\varepsilon' = \varepsilon'(n) \geq 2^{-\kappa}$ be an $\mathrm{poly}(n)$-time computable function, then G is a $(T \cdot (\varepsilon'/n)^{O(1)}, \varepsilon' \cdot \mathrm{poly}(n))$-pseudorandom generator.*

Complexity: *G is computable in NC^1 with $O(d/n)$ oracle calls to f.*

We omit the proof from this version. The above theorem yields the following important corollaries.

COROLLARY 6.2. *(Pseudorandom generator from one-way functions — polynomial security case) Let n be a security parameter $f\colon \{0,1\}^n \mapsto \{0,1\}^n$ be a one-way function, then there exists a pseudorandom generator G from strings of length $d = d(n) \in \tilde{O}(n^4)$ to strings of length $d \cdot (1 + \Omega((\log n)/n))$.*

G is computable in NC^1 with $O(d/n)$ oracle calls to f.

PROOF. Applying Theorem 6.1 on f, $\varepsilon = 1/n^c$ and $\kappa = \log^2 n$, we get an efficient generator G of the stated input and output lengths. Assume now that G is not a pseudorandom generater. Namely, there exists $p \in \mathrm{poly}$ such that G is *not* $(p(n), 1/p(n))$ pseudorandom. Therefore, G is not $(T \cdot (\varepsilon'/n)^{O(1)}, \varepsilon' \cdot \mathrm{poly}(n))$-pseudorandom, for $\varepsilon' := 1/p(n) \cdot \mathrm{poly}(n) > 2^{-\kappa}$ and $T = \mathrm{poly}(n) \cdot p(n)$. It follows that f is not (T, ε)-one-way, in contradiction. □

COROLLARY 6.3. *(Pseudorandom generator from one-way functions —exponential hardness case) Let $f\colon \{0,1\}^n \mapsto \{0,1\}^n$ be a $(2^{\Omega(n)}, 2^{-\Omega(n)})$-one-way function, then*

1. *There exists a $(2^{\Omega(n)}, 2^{-\Omega(\log^2 n)})$-pseudorandom generator G from strings of length $d = d(n) \in \tilde{O}(n)$ to strings of length $d \cdot (1 + \Omega(1))$, and*

2. *There exists a $(2^{\Omega(n)}, 2^{-\Omega(n)})$-pseudorandom generator G from strings of length $d(n) \in \tilde{O}(n^2)$ to strings of length $d \cdot (1 + \Omega(1))$,*

G is computable in NC^1 with $O(d(n)/n)$ oracle calls to f.

PROOF. Immediate from Theorem 6.1, taking $\kappa = \log^2(n)$ and $\kappa \in \Omega(n)$ in the first and second cases respectively, and $\varepsilon' = 2^{-\kappa}$. □

Acknowledgments

We thank Benny Applebaum, Oded Goldreich, Thomas Holenstein, and Emanuele Viola for very helpful conversations.

References

[1] B. Applebaum, Y. Ishai, and E. Kushilevitz. Cryptography in NC^0. *SIAM Journal on Computing*, 36, 2006.

[2] B. Chor and O. Goldreich. Unbiased bits from sources of weak randomness and probabilistic communication complexity. *SIAM J. Comput.*, 17(2):230–261, Apr. 1988.

[3] U. Feige, A. Fiat, and A. Shamir. Zero-knowledge proofs of identity. *Journal of Cryptology*, 1(2):77–94, 1988.

[4] O. Goldreich and L. A. Levin. A hard-core predicate for all one-way functions. In *Proceedings of the 21st Annual ACM Symposium on Theory of Computing (STOC)*, pages 25–32, 1989.

[5] O. Goldreich, S. Goldwasser, and S. Micali. How to construct random functions. *Journal of the ACM*, 33 (4):792–807, 1986.

[6] O. Goldreich, S. Micali, and A. Wigderson. Proofs that yield nothing but their validity or all languages in NP have zero-knowledge proof systems. *Journal of the ACM*, 38(1):691–729, 1991. Preliminary version in *FOCS'86*.

[7] O. Goldreich, H. Krawczyk, and M. Luby. On the existence of pseudorandom generators. *SIAM Journal on Computing*, 22(6):1163–1175, 1993.

[8] I. Haitner, O. Reingold, S. Vadhan, and H. Wee. Inaccessible entropy. In *Proceedings of the 41st Annual ACM Symposium on Theory of Computing (STOC)*.

[9] I. Haitner, D. Harnik, and O. Reingold. On the power of the randomized iterate. In *Advances in Cryptology – CRYPTO 2006*, 2006.

[10] I. Haitner, D. Harnik, and O. Reingold. Efficient pseudorandom generators from exponentially hard one-way functions. In *Automata, Languages and Programming, 24th International Colloquium, ICALP*, 2006.

[11] I. Haitner, M. Nguyen, S. J. Ong, O. Reingold, and S. Vadhan. Statistically hiding commitments and statistical zero-knowledge arguments from any one-way function. *SIAM Journal on Computing*, 39(3):1153–1218, 2009.

[12] I. Haitner, O. Reingold, S. Vadhan, and H. Wee. Inaccessible entropy. In *Proceedings of the 41st Annual ACM Symposium on Theory of Computing (STOC '09)*, pages 611–620, 31 May–2 June 2009.

[13] J. Håstad, R. Impagliazzo, L. A. Levin, and M. Luby. A pseudorandom generator from any one-way function. *SIAM Journal on Computing*, 28(4):1364–1396, 1999. Preliminary versions in *STOC'89* and *STOC'90*.

[14] T. Holenstein. Key agreement from weak bit agreement. In *Proceedings of the 37th Annual ACM Symposium on Theory of Computing (STOC)*, pages 664–673, 2005.

[15] T. Holenstein. Pseudorandom generators from one-way functions: A simple construction for any hardness. In *Theory of Cryptography, Third Theory of Cryptography Conference, TCC 2006*, 2006.

[16] T. Holenstein. Strengthening key agreement using hard-core sets - PhD thesis, 2006.

[17] R. Impagliazzo. A personal view of average-case complexity. In *Proceedings of the Tenth Annual Structure in Complexity Theory Conference*, pages 134–147. IEEE Computer Society, 1995.

[18] R. Impagliazzo and D. Zuckerman. How to recycle random bits. In *Proceedings of the 30th Annual Symposium on Foundations of Computer Science (FOCS)*, pages 248–253, 1989.

[19] R. Impagliazzo, L. A. Levin, and M. Luby. Pseudo-random generation from one-way functions. In *Proceedings of the 21st Annual ACM Symposium on Theory of Computing (STOC)*, pages 12–24. ACM Press, 1989.

[20] M. Luby and C. Rackoff. How to construct pseudorandom permutations from pseudorandom functions. *SIAM Journal on Computing*, 17(2):373–386, 1988.

[21] M. Naor. Bit commitment using pseudorandomness. *Journal of Cryptology*, 4(2):151–158, 1991. Preliminary version in *CRYPTO'89*.

[22] A. A. Razborov and S. Rudich. Natural proofs. *Journal of Computer and System Sciences*, 55(1):24–35, Aug. 1997.

[23] M. Sudan. Decoding of Reed-Solomon codes beyond the error correction bound. *J. of Complexity*, 13:180–193, 1997.

[24] M. Sudan, L. Trevisan, and S. Vadhan. Pseudorandom generators without the XOR lemma. *Journal of Computer and System Sciences*, 62:236–266, 2001.

[25] S. P. Vadhan. Constructing locally computable extractors and cryptosystems in the bounded-storage model. *Journal of Cryptology*, 17(1):43–77, January 2004.

[26] L. G. Valiant. A theory of the learnable. *Communications of the ACM*, 27(11):1134–1142, 1984.

[27] A. C. Yao. Protocols for secure computations. pages 160–164, 1982.

[28] D. Zuckerman. Simulating BPP using a general weak random source. *Algorithmica*, 16(4/5):367–391, Oct./Nov. 1996.

The Limits of Buffering: A Tight Lower Bound for Dynamic Membership in the External Memory Model

Elad Verbin*
ITCS, Tsinghua University
Beijing, China
elad.verbin@gmail.com

Qin Zhang†
HKUST
Hong Kong, China
qinzhang@cse.ust.hk

ABSTRACT

We study the dynamic membership (or dynamic dictionary) problem, which is one of the most fundamental problems in data structures. We study the problem in the external memory model with cell size b bits and cache size m bits. We prove that if the amortized cost of updates is at most 0.999 (or any other constant < 1), then the query cost must be $\Omega(\log_{b \log n}(n/m))$, where n is the number of elements in the dictionary. In contrast, when the update time is allowed to be $1 + o(1)$, then a bit vector or hash table give query time $O(1)$. Thus, this is a *threshold phenomenon for data structures*.

This lower bound answers a folklore conjecture of the external memory community. Since almost any data structure task can solve membership, our lower bound implies a dichotomy between two alternatives: (i) make the amortized update time at least 1 (so the data structure does not buffer, and we lose one of the main potential advantages of the cache), or (ii) make the query time at least roughly logarithmic in n. Our result holds even when the updates and queries are chosen uniformly at random and there are no deletions; it holds for randomized data structures, holds when the universe size is $O(n)$, and does not make any restrictive assumptions such as *indivisibility*. All of the lower bounds we prove hold regardless of the space consumption of the data structure, while the upper bounds only need linear space.

The lower bound has some striking implications for external memory data structures. It shows that the query complexities of many problems such as 1D-range counting, predecessor, rank-select, and many others, are all the same in the regime where the amortized update time is less than 1, as long as the cell size is large enough ($b = polylog(n)$ suffices).

The proof of our lower bound is based on a new combinatorial lemma called the Lemma of Surprising Intersections (LOSI) which allows us to use a proof methodology where we first analyze the intersection structure of the positive queries by using encoding arguments, and then use statistical arguments to deduce properties of the intersection structure of *all* queries, even the negative ones. In most other data structure arguments that we know, it is difficult to argue anything about the negative queries. Therefore we believe that the LOSI and this proof methodology might find future uses for other problems.

Categories and Subject Descriptors

F.2.3 [**Theory of Computation**]: ANALYSIS OF ALGORITHMS AND PROBLEM COMPLEXITY—*Tradeoffs among Complexity Measures*; E.1 [**Data**]: DATA STRUCTURES

General Terms

Theory

Keywords

Data Structures, External Memory, Membership

*Elad Verbin was supported in part by the National Natural Science Foundation of China Grant 60553001, and the National Basic Research Program of China Grants 2007CB807900 and 2007CB807901.

†Qin Zhang was supported by Hong Kong Direct Allocation Grant (DAG 07/08) and Hong Kong CERG Grant 613507. Some of this work was done when he was visiting ITCS.

1. INTRODUCTION

Dynamic membership is one of the most fundamental problems in data structures. In this problem, we must design a data structure for maintaining a dynamic set $S \subset U$ ($|U| = u$) with $|S| = n \le u$.

- *Insert:* Insert an item $x \in U$ into S.
- *Delete:* Delete an item $x \in S$ from S.
- *Query:* Given any particular $x \in U$, decide whether $x \in S$.

A closely related problem is the dynamic dictionary problem, in which the insert operation gets two arguments: an item $x \in U$ and a data element y, which is to be associated with x; when querying x, if the answer is "yes", the data structure should also return x's associated data.

We study the problem in the *external memory* model (EM model) of Aggarwal and Vitter [1]. In this model, the data structure consists of a collection of b-bit cells (the disk) and a cache of m bits. The cost of an operation is measured by the number of cells that are *probed* (= read or written). Accesses to the cache and changes to it are free. Thus, the EM model is similar to Yao's cell probe model [31] with an additional free-to-access cache. The cache often drastically changes the behavior of the model, since it enables update operations to potentially take $o(1)$ amortized time, by writing the inserted elements to the cache (for free) and then, every few operations, writing them to the disk all at once using only one probe; this effect is called *buffering* or *batching* and it is one of the most interesting features of the EM model. Another difference between the EM model and the cell probe model is that in the cell probe model we are typically interested in cells of size $b \approx \log u$ bits, while in the EM model we typically care about $b = \text{polylog}(u)$ or even larger values of b. For more information on the EM model, see e.g. the book of Vitter [29]. About data structures in the EM model, also see e.g. [19, 2]. Recall that, in both the cell probe model and the EM model, computation is *free*; the only charge is for probing cells. Lower bounds in these models often have matching upper bounds in more realistic models (e.g. RAM) even though they are significantly stronger than real-world machines in their computational ability. This elucidates the point that in data structures, the bottleneck is often in collecting information for the computation, rather than in performing the computation itself.

It is interesting to note that buffering is the feature that captures the benefit of real-world caching (such as when using RAM as a cache for the hard drive, or using L2 cache as a cache for RAM, etc). In such real-world cases, the cost of accessing the cache is so small compared to accesses to the higher level memory, that it is essentially free. In some types of real-world caching, once a page becomes "full" we write it all back to higher-level memory, which is exactly what happens in the theoretical concept of *buffering*. Often, the goal of real-world caching is to enable faster data access and data modification. In this sense, the membership problem in the external memory model is a fundamental problem in the context of data access in real-world computing. It is well known that much of the machine time of databases, routers, search engines, and many other applications is taken by hashing and other types of membership searching, and that most of this time is spent on copying data from higher levels in the memory hierarchy. Thus, any improvement on membership in the external memory model would mean immediate and significant speedups in many applications. (And it is therefore somewhat tragic that in this paper we show that dramatic improvements on the current state of the art are impossible, at least under the EM theoretical model).

So, how fast can we solve membership in the EM model? When looking at the EM literature, it quickly becomes clear that there are two radically different approaches to solving the membership problem, which are disconnected from one another: hashing and buffering. In the hashing-type approaches (e.g. [29, chap. 10], [19, sec. 4]), a hash table is used, and the goal is to make the operations as efficient as possible, but it is always implicit that they cannot take less than 1 probe each (hence, no buffering is achieved). The query times are typically $O(1)$ with a very small constant in the big-Oh, or even $1 + o(1)$. The goal is to make the constants as good as possible, under various measures (worst case, average case, etc). On the other hand, in the buffering-type approaches (e.g. [29, chap. 11], [19, sec. 3.5]), various ways to achieve buffering are explored, and typical solutions such as the ubiquitous *buffer tree* (see Section 1.2) achieve an amortized update time of $o(1)$; in fact, the update time can be as small as $\frac{\log^2 u}{b}$, which is much smaller than 1 if b is large enough (see e.g. [3, 4, 9]; also, recall that b and m are measured in *bits*). However, all of these buffering-type approaches take query time roughly $\log n$ or $\frac{\log n}{\log \log n}$.

Few texts discuss why these two types of approaches are so different. Is there a way to get the best of both worlds: a data structure with amortized update time $o(1)$ and query time $O(1)$? This fundamental question has often been asked informally, and was also asked explicitly by Jensen and Pagh [12]. In this paper we give a very strong negative answer to this question: we prove a threshold result – that if the amortized update time is any constant bounded below 1 (for example, 0.999), then the query time must be roughly at least logarithmic in n, namely $\geq \Omega(\log_{b \log n}(n/m))$. See Theorem 1. This is an unusually delicate threshold behavior for data structures problems, and seems to say something deep about the EM model.

Since membership is one of the easiest data structures problems (in the sense that it is reducible to most other data structure problems) it follows that this lower bound applies for most other data structure problems as well (such as dictionary, predecessor, prefix sum, range counting, union find, rank-select, and many others; reductions will be formally proved in the full version of the paper).

Our lower bound means that for large enough b, for most of these data structures problems, one can either choose to use the optimal RAM solution (without doing any buffering), or one can achieve buffering using the buffer tree, but the query time is logarithmic, and there's nothing in between!

In the remainder of Section 1 we present our results, describe the buffer tree, and discuss previous work. In Section 2 we give a fake proof of our lower bound, which is quite simple (but not formally true) and captures many of the ideas behind our result. In Section 3 we present the real, formal, proof of our lower bound.

1.1 Our results

The statement of our lower bound is:

THEOREM 1. *Suppose we insert a sequence of n elements chosen uniformly at random, into any initially empty randomized data structure in the EM model with cell size b and cache size m. If the expected total cost of these insertions is $n \cdot t_u$, and the data structure is able to answer a membership query with expected average t_q probes,*[1] *then we have the following tradeoff: If $t_u \leq 0.9$, then $t_q \geq \Omega(\log_{b \log n}(n/m))$. This holds provided that $u \geq 10^{10000} n$. It holds even when we measure t_u only by the number of cells written.*

This theorem settles a folklore conjecture (explicitly proposed by Jensen and Pagh [12]), thereby completing the line of research of [30] and [33].

[1] That is, at any time during the updated sequence, if we query uniformly at random an element from the universe, then the expected cost of the query should be no more than t_q. All expectations are taken over all possible update sequences.

It is important to note that our bound does not assume indivisibility.[2] The ideas behind it might be useful for further bounds in the EM model that do not assume indivisibility.

As discussed before, the constant 0.9 is arbitrary, and can be replaced by any constant < 1. The constant 10^{10000} and the constants hidden in the big-Ω notation are quite wild, as is common with lower bounds. We did not make any effort to optimize them. We are reasonably sure that the "real" constants are quite tame, and since this makes a big difference in practice, it might be interesting to perform more careful analysis in order to pinpoint the right constants.

Theorem 1 is proved in Section 3, but only for deterministic data structures. The theorem can be generalized to hold for randomized data structures using a Minimax principle for data structures similar to that of [33]. The details are deferred to the full version due to space considerations.

Another contribution of this paper is the *Lemma of Surprising Intersections* (LOSI) which might be of independent interest. It is first discussed in Section 2, then discussed and proved in Section 3.4. The data-structural threshold phenomenon that we prove in fact arises from and corresponds to a threshold phenomenon in the LOSI.

1.2 The Buffer Tree

We describe here the ubiquitous buffer tree which supports very strong buffering in the EM model. It is relevant here for two reasons: first of all, since we are claiming to prove tight lower bounds, it makes sense to show how the corresponding upper bounds were obtained; secondly, our intuition for the lower bound can be seen to *match* the upper bound in some sense (this is quite common with tight lower bounds), so the upper bound actually helps to get intuition for the lower bound.

Here we sketch a construction of a buffer tree, which is a variant of the one in [3]. We assume $m \geq b$ and $b \geq \log^{1+\epsilon} u$ for some constant $\epsilon > 0$. $\lambda \geq 2$ is an adjustable parameter used to adjust the tradeoff between t_u and t_q. A buffer tree is a tree where the degrees of all nodes except the root are between $\lambda/4$ and λ. The height of the tree is $\Theta(\log_\lambda \frac{n}{m})$ The root consists of a buffer containing $m/\log u$ universe elements. Each internal node consists of a buffer containing $2b/\log u$ universe elements. The buffer of the root always resides in the cache, and the rest resides in the disk; each internal node is stored in $O(1)$ memory cells.

Intuitively, the buffer tree processes updates in a "lazy" fashion. For example, when we try to insert an item, we do not trace all the way down the tree and find the right place to perform the insertion. Instead, we just put it in the root. We do this until the root is half-full, and then we insert all of its items into the buffers of its children; the elements are distributed among the children according to their natural order, just like in a regular B-Tree. Similarly, whenever an internal node is half-full, we push all element in its buffer to its children. Deletions are done similarly (pushing them down until they encounter the element they are meant to delete). Queries can be done similarly, by lazily pushing them down the tree, if we are content with the data structure returning the answer to queries at a later time. Rebalance operations need to be done like in a B-Tree, but also lazily. In this way all the operations can be performed in a batched fashion, thus the amortized cost of each operation is $O(\frac{\lambda \log u}{b} \log_\lambda \frac{n}{m})$. However, if we want a query to be answered immediately, as is required in our problem, then we have to walk down a root-to-leaf path for each query in order to find the answer, which takes $\Theta(\log_\lambda \frac{n}{m})$ time.

It is thus interesting to note that the lower bound in this paper crucially relies on the need to answer queries immediately. If answers to queries can be delayed, a buffer tree can support both updates and queries in time $o(1)$ (when b is large enough).

By storing some additional data, the buffer tree can also be made to solve many other data structure problems with the same update times, see e.g. [3].

1.3 Previous Work

Dynamic membership has a long history of research. Here we review just the works that are most relevant to ours. On the upper bound side, Knuth [13] already showed that using hashing with standard collision resolution strategies (e.g. linear probing or chaining) gives a data structure for dynamic membership with both average query time (both successful and unsuccessful) and amortized update time only slightly larger than 1, namely $t_q = t_u = 1 + 1/2^{\Omega(b/\log u)}$. In a follow up work, Jensen and Pagh [12] showed how to design a hash table that uses close to $n \log u$ bits (which is roughly the optimal space) and has update time and query time both $1+O(1/\sqrt{b/\log u})$. If t_q is required to be worst case, Pagh and Rodler [21] proposed an interesting hashing method called *cuckoo hashing*; in this method $t_q = 2$ and t_u is still a constant in expectation. All these upper bounds work for both dynamic dictionary and dynamic membership. Intuitively, membership may have better upper bounds than dictionary, but we are not aware of any data structure that solves membership strictly better than dictionary. The *Bloom filter* [6] achieves better space utilization than all data structures that solve dictionary, but it has query and update cost larger than some constant> 1, and also contains false positives. All these are hashing-type data structures, and more related works on external hashing can be found in [10, 15, 14].

Another class of data structures that solve the dynamic membership problem is the buffering-type data structure, for example, the buffer tree and several of its variants developed by Brodal and Fagerberg [7]. All of these buffering-type data structures can achieve $t_u = o(1)$ (when b is large enough), but $t_q = \Omega(\log_b(n/m))$.

As for lower bounds, one of the previous works that is conceptually closest to ours is Brodal and Fagerberg [7]. They prove a lower bound of roughly

$$t_q \geq \log_{b/\log u}(n/m) ,$$

regardless of what t_u is, in the *comparison model*, which assumes that elements are indivisible and the only operation allowed on them is comparison. This model obviously does not support hashing, and is in general too weak to indicate what is possible on a real machine. One of the other lower bounds that they prove is very interesting – they prove roughly that $t_q \gtrsim \frac{n}{m}/(m/b)^{O(t_u b/\log u)}$ also in the comparison model. For $t_u = O(\log u/b)$ this gives $t_q \gtrsim \frac{n}{m}$. We believe that this is essentially true in the general EM model as well, but proving it might be outside the reach of current technology (in the common settings, the best type of bounds that the cell probe lower bound community can prove are $t_q \geq n^\epsilon$ where $\epsilon > 0$ is a problem-dependent constant which

[2]The indivisibility assumption assumes that each element should be stored atomically in the data structure.

is typically very small). See Section 4 for further discussion of this question.

What is known outside of the comparison model? If we consider the worst case operation cost, Pagh [20] proved that t_q must be at least 2, even for static membership, meaning that cuckoo hashing is optimal in terms of worst-case query time. In [8, 16, 28] some super-constant lower bounds on $\max\{t_q, t_u\}$ are shown but they are proved in models more restrictive than (or incomparable to) the EM model. There are very few lower bounds for dynamic membership in the RAM model. The reason might be that if there is no cache, then each update has to be committed immediately to the disk, thus t_u must be at least 1. Therefore Knuth's upper bound is already tight up to an $o(1)$ additive term. In the EM model, t_u does not necessary have to be at least 1 if the size of a cell is large, so there was some hope (dispelled by our lower bound) to get update time less than 1 while maintaining good query time. To prove this is impossible, [30, 33] gave a set of tradeoff curves between t_q and t_u. Concretely, they showed that the amortized update cost is at least $\Omega(1)$ if the average query cost is required to be no more than $1+\delta$ for any constant $\delta < 1/2$. This result already ruled out the possibility of achieving $t_q = 1 + o(1)$ and $t_u = o(1)$ simultaneously. [30] also studied the radically different case where we only measure the average query time for positive queries.[3] In this case, [30] show a data structure achieving both $t_q = 1 + o(1)$ and $t_u = o(1)$. Therefore, there is a gap between the case of supporting only successful queries and the case of also supporting unsuccessful ones.

Figure 1 depicts some of the known upper bounds and lower bounds.

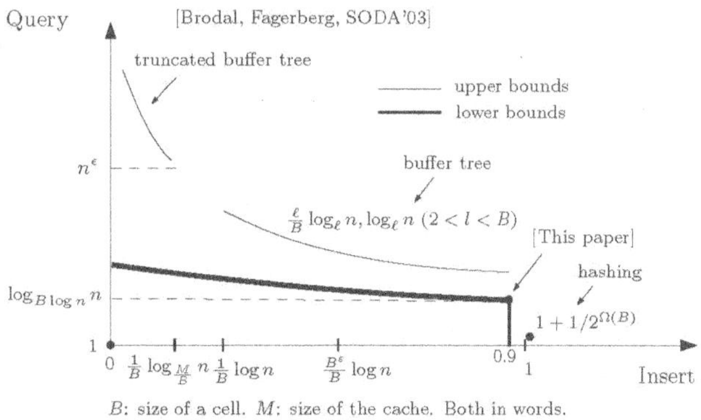

Figure 1: Some of the known upper and lower bounds on membership data structures in the external memory model. The thick line which represents our lower bound curls up as t_u decreases, in order to symbolize that our lower bound should improve as t_u decreases, although we did not deal with this issue in the current paper.

The techniques used in this paper are somewhat related to the recent lower bounds on succinct data structures in the cell probe model, of Golynski [11] and of Pătraşcu and Viola [26]. Their bounds can also be thought of as performing a "cache elimination" step (like we do in Section 2) interleaved with a "probe elimination" step. For the "probe elimination" step we use the LOSI, and their bounds use other ideas.

[3]That is, t_q is defined as the expected query cost of a random $x \in S$, instead of $x \in U$.

2. FAKE PROOF OF THE LOWER BOUND

In this section we provide an exposition of our results that is not strictly true, but captures many of our ideas in an easy-to-understand setting, and in fact represents the way that we came up with the solution in the first place. We believe that this section not only helps to explain our bound, but actually might be useful for novices to the field, by showing how very simple (but technically false) arguments give the "right" lower bounds, as well as the right intuition, for data structure lower bounds. These arguments can then be formalized into correct (but more complicated) proofs, which will be our task in the rest of the paper. Thus, this paper can also be read as a case study in getting a simple fake proof based on cache elimination, and then turning it into a correct proof based on encoding arguments.

In the presentation in this section we cheat constantly, with the goal of getting across most of our ideas, without the required hard work. Thus, we warn in advance that nothing in this section should be assumed to be strictly correct, and the whole section should be treated as just intuition.

We begin by discussing the cache elimination principle.

The Cache Elimination Principle. For most "reasonable" problems P, if there is a data structure for problem P with parameters (n, u, m, t_q, t_u) then there exists a data structure for problem P with parameters $(n/10m, u/10m, 0, t_q, t_u)$.

Here n, u, m, t_q, t_u denote the same quantities as defined in the introduction: the number of items, universe size, cache size (in bits), query time and update time, respectively.

Fix $t_u = 0.9$ (any other constant would work as well). The framework of the fake proof is to use the cache elimination principle alternately with the following reduction step:

LOSI-Based Cache Augmentation. For the membership problem, in the case where there is no cache, if there is a data structure with parameters $(n, u, 0, t_q, t_u)$ then there is a data structure with parameters $(n, u, t_q b, t_q - 0.2, t_u)$.

By using these two steps alternately, one can start with a structure with parameters (n, u, m, t_q, t_u) and end up with a structure with parameters

$$(n/m(10t_q b)^{5t_q}, u/m(10t_q b)^{5t_q}, 0, 0, t_u) ,$$

which implies that $n/m(10t_q b)^{5t_q} \leq 1$, and this gives

$$t_q = \Omega(\log_{bt_q}(n/m)) = \Omega(\log_{b \log n}(n/m)) ,$$

which is the lower bound that we desire.

It is interesting to observe that this string of "reductions" of parameters matches more or less the structure of the buffer tree. The LOSI-Based Cache Augmentation step corresponds, in some sense, to putting the root of the tree in the cache, thus saving one probe in each query.

We now give more details on the fake proof, in particular on the cache elimination principle and on the LOSI-Based Cache Augmentation step.

The cache elimination principle is analogous to the round elimination lemma of Miltersen et al. [17] or Sen [27] or the probe elimination lemma of Patrascu and Thorup [25]. It is also related (and arguably equivalent) to the notion of "published bits" found in various works of Patrascu and others (see for example [23]).

We omit here a more comprehensive discussion of the cache elimination principle, and defer it to Section 2.2. The principle will be easier to understand after we show how we use it.

The fake proof works only for non-adaptive queries, i.e. for the case where the set of cells $q(x)$ which are probed by query(x) depends only on x and not on the state of the cache or of the disk. Also, it works only when t_u is defined as the expected cost of a random update, rather than as the amortized cost. Both of these restrictions can be lifted, but we do not show here how to do so.

We now describe the LOSI-Based Cache Augmentation step. Let us start with a data structure for dynamic membership with parameters $(n, u, 0, t_q, t_u)$. We are going to heavily exploit the fact that there is no cache. Consider two uniformly random insertion operations, ins(x) and ins(y), which we assume are processed together, at a total expected cost of $2t_u$ probes. Since there is no cache, these operations must make at least one probe (in total). Denote by p the probability that they make exactly one probe in total. We know that their expected total cost is $\geq p + (1-p)\cdot 2$. Thus $2t_u \geq p + 2(1-p)$, which gives $p \geq 2(1-t_u)$. Therefore, with probability at least $2(1-t_u)$, these two updates make only one probe. From now on consider the case that they make only one probe in total. Denote by c the common cell that they probe. Consider the query operations query(x) and query(y). Since there is no cache, both of these operations must probe cell c, because it contains the only indication in the data structure that x and/or y were inserted.

We thus see that for two random elements x and y, with probability $\geq 2(1-t_u)$, the queries query(x) and query(y) probe a common cell.[4] We claim that this is a "surprising intersection" (or "surprising collision"). To see that this statistical behavior is surprising, consider hashing. In hashing, the queries are roughly equally split among the cells, and the collision probability of two random queries is roughly $1/n$. In our case, when $t_u = 0.9$, the collision probability is 0.2 – a constant!

Our main technical contribution in this paper is the Lemma Of Surprising Intersections (LOSI) which shows that if such surprising statistical behavior occurs, that must be because the queries have some rigid structure; namely, it shows there must be a set C that consists of only a few cells, such that C intersects a constant fraction of all query-paths $\{q(x) | x \in U\}$. Here is a trivial version of the LOSI, which suffices for our purposes in this fake proof. The full (and considerably more involved) LOSI can be found in Lemma 6.

LEMMA 1 (LOSI – VERY SIMPLE VERSION). *Let $\mathcal{F} = \{S_1, \ldots, S_u\}$ be a family of sets with the following property: When choosing two random elements $x, y \in U$, $\mathbf{Pr}_{x,y}[S_x \cap S_y \neq \emptyset] \geq 0.2$. Then if we pick $x \in U$ at random, we get that $\mathbf{E}_x[|\{y \in U \mid S_x \cap S_y \neq \emptyset\}|] \geq 0.2u$.*

PROOF. Choose x uniformly from U. Then by the condition, with probability 0.2 over the choice of y, it holds that $S_x \cap S_y \neq \emptyset$. The conclusion follows by using linearity of expectation. □

By substituting $S_x = q(x)$ (recall that the queries are non-adaptive), we see that when we choose x randomly, $q(x)$ intersects $0.2u$ $q(y)$'s. Also, since the average query time is t_q, the set $q(x)$ consists of roughly t_q elements.

Now, to get the LOSI-Based Cache Augmentation step, we take the elements of $q(x)$ and place them into the cache. This saved one probe for roughly 0.2-fraction of the universe, because any probe that used to read one of the elements of $q(x)$ can now read the cache instead. Thus, from our data structure that had parameters $(n, u, 0, t_q, t_u)$ we get a data structure with parameters $(n, u, t_q b, t_q - 0.2, t_u)$. (The $t_q b$ appears because we put t_q cells in the cache, and each cell consists of b bits).

After applying both types of reductions $5t_q$ times, we would get a data structure with parameters

$$(n/m(10t_q b)^{5t_q}, u/m(10t_q b)^{5t_q}, 0, 0, t_u) .$$

This is an absurdity – we get correct answers to queries, without having any cache and without any probes. Therefore, this must mean that the data data structure maintains less than one element, so that $n/m(10t_q b)^{5t_q} \leq 1$. This gives $t_q = \Omega(\log_{bt_q}(n/m)) = \Omega(\log_{b \log n}(n/m))$, which is the lower bound that we desired.

In Section 3 we turn this fake proof into a correct one. In particular, we develop a much stronger version of the LOSI, and we replace the cache elimination arguments (which are intuitive but incorrect) by encoding-based arguments (which are both intuitive *and* correct, but make the other arguments more complicated).

2.1 Discussion of the LOSI

One interesting thing to note about the LOSI is that it allows us to argue about the structure of negative queries (ones whose answer is "false") from statistical information that we know about (much fewer) positive queries. In a sense, the LOSI allows us to argue about the structure of queries *that we know nothing about*, from statistical properties of probe-sequences of queries that we do know something about.[5]

The LOSI might be of special importance in the dynamic membership problem, as explained by the fact that there is a data structure for dynamic membership in the EM model that uses update time $o(1)$ and average query time $1 + o(1)$ when the average is taken only over positive queries [30], so to get our lower bound we really need to argue about negative queries as well. This is a difficult task when using only traditional encoding-based techniques, since negative queries do not correspond to any inserts that were done, and thus do not correspond to any change to the data structure.

We thus suspect that the LOSI and the idea behind it (first proving statistical properties of certain queries using encoding arguments, and then using statistical reasoning to get implications about the set of all queries) might be of future use, particularly for problems where positive queries are easier to answer than negative queries. It seems like an interesting question to find data structure problems that exhibit this property, and in general to find further applications of our lower bound scheme.

[4]Note that if $t_u < 1/2$ then this probability is > 1 and this argument explodes. This is one way to see that we are cheating here. The strange behavior here comes from the fact that we ignored the error term created by cache elimination. However, we will just persist, and refer the suspicious reader to the full proof in Section 3.

[5]Of course, it seems odd to discuss at such length a lemma with a two-line proof; however, the strong LOSI (Lemma 6) is more involved, and it seems necessary when one wishes to get a non-fake proof of our results.

2.2 Justifying the Cache Elimination Principle

The intuition behind the cache elimination principle is that if we divide the domain into $10m$ parts then the cache contains, on average, 0.1 bits of information about each part. We then restrict our operations only to one part, chosen randomly among all $10m$ parts. Then, since we are working only in one part, the cache provides only roughly 0.1 bits of information, so it can be completely eliminated with a small increase in error (for example by using the average encoding lemma, see Sen [27]).

To make the cache elimination principle formally true, one has to introduce error, and to make some (not too restrictive) explicit demands on the problem P. Then one can prove the cache elimination principle for *static* data structure problems quite easily; one way to do so is to use an analogous proof to Sen's proof of the round elimination lemma [27]. However, for dynamic problems no formally-correct proof of anything like cache elimination is known, due to various technical difficulties that we do not detail here. It would be very interesting if a proof was found for something like the cache elimination principle, since this has the potential to simplify many lower bound proofs. In the present state of affairs, we use the cache elimination principle in the fake proof, and in the real proof we do not use anything like it, instead translating it to an encoding-based proof. It should be noted that this approach of obtaining lower bounds is well-known among data structure researchers [22], although we have not found a source where it is explicitly described.

Zeyuan Allen Zhu [34] observed that the cache elimination principle can also be used to obtain fake proofs for lower bounds for dynamic rank, for union-find, for dynamic prefix sum, and other problems.

3. THE LOWER BOUND

In this section we prove Theorem 1. First we describe the general framework of the proof. Following that we highlight two lemmas that express two key ideas, and they together give the lower bound. Finally we prove the two lemmas.

3.1 The framework of the proof

Let $\gamma = 1/800000$. Let l be chosen large enough such that $l \geq 64 \cdot 10^6 \cdot t_q b/\gamma$. We also assume that $t_q = O(\log n)$, since otherwise we are already done.

For any $x \in U$, let $q(x)$ be the query path of x, that is, the set of cells that are probed when querying x. $q(x)$ is actually determined by the cache state M and disk state D at the time of the query, and we write $q_{M,D}(x)$ explicitly whenever M and D are not clear from context. When we talk about $q(x)$ *at some time snapshot*, we mean $q(x)$ under the cache state and disk state at that time snapshot, and sometimes we denote this by $q_{\texttt{snapshot}}(x)$ for convenience.

We consider an update sequence of n insertions, each of which is chosen uniformly at random from U with replacement. We think of these n insertions as being performed on n subsequent "time steps", from time 1 to time n. In the sequel, we assume for simplicity that all insertions are different. It is quite easy to adapt the argument to the case where the inserted elements can have repetitions, but we do not show this here. The suspicious reader can choose the universe size to be at least n^3, in which case the birthday paradox guarantees that with probability $1 - O(1/n)$ there are indeed no repetitions and the rest of the argument goes through easily.

We pick a time snapshot, denoted by END uniformly at random between time $n/1000$ and n.[6] Most of our analysis will focus on the time END. We partition the insertions before END into exponentially growing epochs: The first epoch contains the set of insertions Y_1 ($|Y_1| = m/\gamma$) immediately before END and epoch i consists of the set of insertions Y_i ($|Y_i| = ml^{i-1}/\gamma$) immediately before epoch $i-1$. Note that we number the epochs in the reverse order: the first epoch consists of the insertions that are done last. The total number of epochs created is $d = \Theta(\log_l(n/m)) = \Omega(\log_{b \log n}(n/m))$.

For epoch i, let C_i^u be the set of cells that are probed during the insertion of Y_i. Let $\texttt{BEGIN}_i$ be the snapshot just before the i-th epoch.

Let Y_i' be a set of elements of size $|Y_i| + |Y_{i-1}| + \ldots + |Y_1|$ chosen uniformly at random from U. Let $\texttt{END}_i$' (sometimes just denoted END') be the snapshot at the same time as END created by inserting Y_i' instead of epochs 1 through i. Let $C_i'^u$ be the set of cells probed during the insertion of Y_i', and let $C_i'^q$ be the set of cells probed when querying all elements $y \in Y_i'$ in the state $(M_{\texttt{END}_i'}, D_{\texttt{BEGIN}_i})$. Let $C_i^* = C_i^u \cup C_i'^q$ and $C_{<i}^* = \bigcup_{j<i} C_j^*$. The lower bound follows from the following lemma:

LEMMA 2. *Suppose that $t_u \leq 0.9$ and pick $x \in U$ uniformly at random. Let $\mathcal{E}_i$ be the indicator random variable which is 1 if $q_{\texttt{END}}(x)$ intersects $C_i^* \backslash C_{<i}^*$. Then $\mathbf{E}[\mathcal{E}_i] \geq \Omega(1)$ for all $i = 1, 2, \ldots, d$.*

Lemma 2 directly implies by linearity of expectation that for a random x, $\mathbf{E}[|q_{\texttt{END}}(x)|] \geq \Omega(d)$ and this immediately gives Theorem 1. Thus, we just need to prove Lemma 2. From now on we concentrate on one epoch i and prove that $\mathbf{E}[\mathcal{E}_i] \geq \Omega(1)$.

3.2 Proof of Lemma 2

In this section we prove Lemma 2. We start by giving two lemmas that together imply the correctness of Lemma 2. Their proofs will be given in the next two subsections.

LEMMA 3. **(the encoding lemma)** *Let m be the cache size and suppose Y is the set of the last $|Y|$ insertions. Let C^u be the set of cells probed by the insertions in Y. Also assume that $m \leq \gamma |Y|$. Let END be the time after inserting Y and BEGIN be the time before inserting Y. Then with probability at least 0.999 over the choice of Y, both the following hold:*

1. $|\{y \in Y \mid q_{\texttt{END}}(y) \cap C^u \neq \emptyset\}| \geq 0.99\,|Y|$
2. $|\{y \in Y \mid q_{(M_{\texttt{END}}, D_{\texttt{BEGIN}})}(y) \cap C^u \neq \emptyset\}| \geq 0.99\,|Y|$.

LEMMA 4. **(application of LOSI)** *Under the same conditions as Lemma 3, let Y' be another randomly-drawn set of $|Y|$ insertions. Let END be the snapshot after inserting Y' instead of Y. Let $C'^q = \bigcup_{y \in Y'} q_{(M_{\texttt{END}'}, D_{\texttt{BEGIN}})}(y)$ and $C^* = C^u \cup C'^q$. If $|C^u| \leq 0.91 \cdot |Y|$ and $m \leq \gamma |Y|$, then with probability at least 0.999 over the choices of Y and Y', it holds that $|\{x \in U \mid q_{\texttt{END}}(x) \cap C^* \neq \emptyset\}| \geq \Omega(u)$.*

[6]This is done for technical reasons, in order to get the lower bound to apply for amortized update time. If one just wants t_u to denote the average time for a randomly-selected insert, then END can be selected to simply be time n.

Lemma 4 above implies the correctness of Lemma 2 for the first epoch by substituting $Y = Y_1$, $C = C_1$, etc. . To prove Lemma 2 for epoch $i > 1$, we make the following changes to the data structure:[7] We put all cells $C^*_{<i}$ into the cache. Then, every time that a probe wishes to read or change a cell that we put in the cache, we redirect it to the corresponding location in the cache. This new data structure can simulate the old one, and notice that for this new data structure, C^*_i is $C^*_i \backslash C^*_{<i}$. Furthermore, the following two properties are immediate consequences of our conceptual operation.

- The state of the disk at the end of epoch i is identical to that in END.
- The size of the cache in this modified data structure is $m_i = m + |C^*_{<i}|$.

We say epoch i is *good* if: (1) $|C^u_i| \leq 0.91 \cdot |Y_i|$, and (2) $m_i \leq \gamma |Y_i|$ after the conceptual operation. Note that Lemma 4 actually implies Lemma 2 provided that every epoch i ($1 \leq i \leq d$) is good with probability > 0.001, which indeed holds by the following lemma.

LEMMA 5. *Every epoch i ($1 \leq i \leq d$) is good with probability at least* 0.005. *over the random choices of* END, *and the choice of the insertion sequences.*

PROOF. Consider requirement (1). The expected update cost between time $n/1000$ and n is at most $0.9n$. Averaging over our choice of END, the total update cost of an epoch of length $|Y_i|$ is $\frac{1}{0.999} \cdot 0.9 |Y_i|$ in expectation. By Markov's inequality, the probability that this update cost is more than $0.91 |Y_i|$ is at most 0.006. As for requirement (2), we union bound over the events that any of the sets C^*_j ($j < i$) is too large. The expected size of this sets is tiny compared to Y_i, so this again follows easily from Markov's inequality. □

We give the proofs of Lemma 3 and 4 in Section 3.3 and 3.4, respectively. The proof of Lemma 3 uses an information theoretic argument and the proof of Lemma 4 explores the underlying combinatorial structures of the set of query paths $\{q(x) \mid x \in U\}$.

3.3 Proof of Lemma 3

PROOF. It is easy to see that if the first item of the lemma holds, then the second item holds, since the only changes to the disk between $D_{\texttt{BEGIN}}$ and $D_{\texttt{END}}$ are in the cells who are in C^u, so the set in item 1 and the set in item 2 are actually the same set. From now on we shall just prove the first item holds.

We consider all query paths $\{q(y) \mid y \in Y\}$. The idea behind the proof is to show how to "compress" (= to encode) the set Y by just specifying the elements $y \in Y$ that *do* touch C^u, and specifying the state of the cache at the end of the insertions. Then, since Y cannot be "compressed" beyond the standard information-theoretic limit, we get that the size of the encoding must be large, which means that many elements $y \in Y$ indeed *do* touch C^u, which is what we needed to prove.

The trick is to get convinced that this "compression algorithm" indeed compresses Y in a way that Y can be decoded from the compressed representation. Following is the full proof.

Let Z be the set of queries y in Y such that the query path $q(y)$ as it is performed at END *does* intersect C^u. We try to prove that with probability at least 0.999 over the choice of Y, it holds that $|Z| \geq 0.99 |Y|$.

In the encoding, we condition on the elements that were previously inserted. By "conditioning" we mean that both the compressor and the decompressor know which elements were inserted and in what order they were inserted. We call this the "shared information" (since it is shared between the compressor and the decompressor). It is easy to see that given the shared information, the decompressor can compute the state of the cache and of the disk at the beginning of the insertion of Y. (This uses the fact that the data structure is deterministic). The encoding of Y consists of the following.

1. The state of the cache at the end of the insertion of Y. This takes m bits.
2. The elements of Z. This takes at most $\log \binom{u}{|Z|}$ bits, which is at most $|Z| \log(eu/|Z|)$.[8]

We now observe that given the encoding of Y and the shared information, the decompressor can answer any query(x) ($x \in U$) correctly, as follows: (i) if x is already inserted before Y, answer "yes". (ii) If $x \in Z$, answer "yes". (iii) If both (i) and (ii) did not return "yes", then run the query algorithm with the state of the cache at END and with the state of the disk as it is *before* the insertion of Y. By the definition of Z, and since $x \notin Z$, this returns the right answer. Therefore, we managed to encode Y into $m + |Z| \log(eu/|Z|)$ bits.

Now, suppose in contradiction that with probability more than 0.001, $|Z| \leq 0.99 |Y|$. With the rest of the probability, $|Z|$ can be as large as $|Y|$. Then the expected size of the encoding is at most

$$\begin{aligned} & m + 0.999 |Y| \cdot \log \frac{eu}{|Y|} + 0.001 \cdot 0.99 |Y| \log \frac{eu}{0.99 |Y|} \\ \leq \quad & m + 0.99999 |Y| \log \frac{eu}{0.99 |Y|}. \end{aligned}$$

On the other hand, there are at least $\binom{u-n}{|Y|} \geq \binom{u/2}{|Y|} \geq 2^{|Y| \log \frac{u/2}{|Y|}}$ possibilities to choose Y. Since we can never encode x bits into $x - 1$ bits, we get that:

$$\begin{aligned} & m + 0.99999 |Y| \log \frac{eu}{0.99 |Y|} \geq |Y| \log \frac{u/2}{|Y|} \\ \Rightarrow \quad & m \geq |Y| \log \left(\left(\frac{u}{|Y|} \right)^{0.00001} \cdot \frac{1}{4e} \right) > 0.000005 \cdot |Y| \ . \end{aligned}$$

The last inequality holds since $u > c \cdot n \geq c|Y|$ for some sufficiently large constant c. This contradicts the fact that $m \leq \gamma |Y| < 0.000005 |Y|$. □

3.4 Proof of Lemma 4

In this section we first state and prove the LOSI. It is essentially an involved combinatorial argument that deduces a global behavior from an observed local behavior. We then prove Lemma 4, which is an application of the LOSI to our setting.

[7]We can change the data structure since we just need to prove Lemma 2 for epoch i. This is why it was important to use linearity of expectation.

[8]Technically speaking, we also have to encode the cardinality $|Z|$ itself, which takes another $\log u$ bits. This does not change the computation significantly, so we ignore it.

LEMMA 6. *[Lemma Of Surprising Intersections (LOSI)] Let k be an integer, and let $p \geq 2^{-k/40000}$. Let $\mathcal{F} = \{S_1, \ldots, S_u\}$ be a family of sets. Suppose that when we choose $Y \subseteq [u]$, $|Y| = k$, out of all size-k sets uniformly at random, with probability p the following holds:*

$$\begin{aligned} &\text{there exists a set } S \text{ such that:} \\ &(i)\ |S| \leq 0.91k, \text{ and} \\ &(ii)\ |\{y \in Y \mid S_y \cap S \neq \emptyset\}| \geq 0.99k\ . \end{aligned} \quad (1)$$

Then it follows that when we pick a family Z of k random sets from the collection, their union intersects $\Omega(1)$-fraction of the sets in expectation,[9] that is,

$$\mathbf{E}_{Z \subseteq U, |Z|=k}[|\{x \in U \mid \exists z \in Z, S_x \cap S_z \neq \emptyset\}|] \geq \Omega(u)\ .$$

The LOSI is tight, up to constants, in most of its parameters. In particular, it is not true that one can always choose Z to be of cardinality much smaller than k. To get one example for this, construct a family $\mathcal{F}$ such that $S_1 = S_2 = \ldots = S_{10^6 u/k} = \{1\}$, $S_{10^6 u/k+1} = S_{10^6 u/k+2} = \ldots = S_{2 \cdot 10^6 u/k} = \{2\}$, and so on. Then the condition of the LOSI holds, but to get the conclusion of the LOSI, Z really needs to be of size $\Omega(k)$.

What makes the LOSI non-trivial to prove is the fact that p can be exponentially small in k. If p was constant then the LOSI would be easy to prove using a simple averaging argument, similar to the proof of the simple LOSI in Section 2; but since p can be exponentially small we need to carefully use a concentration bound, which makes the LOSI somewhat more complicated to prove.

PROOF. (of Lemma 6). We first define an intersection graph that captures the combinatorial intersection structure of the family. The graph is $G = G_{\mathcal{F}} = (U, E)$, where two vertices $x, y \in U$ are connected by an edge if $S_x \cap S_y \neq \emptyset$. We now see that to prove the LOSI we just need to prove that a random set Z of k vertices will have $\mathbf{E}_Z[|N_G(Z)|] \geq \Omega(u)$, where $N_G(Z)$ is the set of vertices in G that have at least one neighbor in Z. In the sequel, whenever we say *k-set* we mean "a set of cardinality k".

For a subset $Z \subseteq U$, let $G[Z]$ denote the induced subgraph of G on Z, let MAX-IS$(G[Z])$ denote the size of a maximum independent set in $G[Z]$, and let $\deg_G(x)$ denote the degree of vertex x in G. We first show that if for a specific Y condition (1) holds, then MAX-IS$(G[Y]) \leq 0.96k$. To see this, observe that from (1) and from the pigeonhole principle, it follows that there exist y, y' such that S_y and $S_{y'}$ contain a common element from S. Thus y and y' are connected by an edge in the graph. Eliminate these two vertices, and repeat this argument. We can repeat the argument at least $(0.99k - 0.91k)/2 = 0.04k$ times, therefore there is a matching in $G[Y]$ of cardinality $0.04k$, and therefore MAX-IS$(G[Y]) \leq 0.96k$.

The condition (1) holds for a random k-set Y with probability p, so for a randomly selected k-set Y, it holds that $\mathbf{Pr}_Y[\text{MAX-IS}(G[Y]) \leq 0.96k] \geq p$. We thus see that many induced subgraphs do not have large independent sets. By applying Lemma 7 (whose statement and proof will be given shortly), we get that $|\{x \in U \mid deg(x) \leq u/100k\}| \leq 0.99$. And then by applying Lemma 8 (whose statement and proof we also give shortly), we get exactly the conclusion of the LOSI. □

[9]Notice that both the condition of the LOSI and the conclusion of the LOSI are deterministic statements, that use probability only to replace counting. We could formulate it as an entirely deterministic statement that uses no probabilistic notions. It is important to note that the LOSI is a combinatorial statement, not a probabilistic one.

Here are the two structural lemmas we used in the proof:

LEMMA 7. *Let $G = (U, E)$ be a simple graph such that*

$$\mathbf{Pr}_{Z \subseteq U, |Z|=k}[\text{MAX-IS}(G[Z]) \geq 0.97k] \leq 1 - e^{-k/40000}\ .$$

Then $|\{x \in U \mid deg(x) \leq u/100k\}| \leq 0.99$.

PROOF. Let W be the set of vertices in G that have degree at most $u/100k$, and let $S = U \backslash W$.

We prove the contrapositive of the lemma: that if $|W| > 0.99u$, then

$$\mathbf{Pr}_{Z \subseteq U, |Z|=k}[\text{MAX-IS}(G[Z]) \geq 0.97k] > 1 - e^{-k/40000}\ .$$

Consider a random variable which represents one of the vertices of Z, say the one chosen first. Call this random variable v. What is the probability that v has at least one neighbor in Z? It is at most

$$\mathbf{Pr}[v \in W] \cdot (k-1) \cdot 1/100k + \mathbf{Pr}[x \in S]\ . \quad (2)$$

This arises from the fact that if $v \in W$, then it has degree at most $u/100k$, and therefore each other vertex in Z has a probability of at most $1/100k$ to be v's neighbor. And we union bound on this over all $k-1$ neighbors.

An easy computation shows that (2) simplifies to $\leq 0.99 \cdot (k-1) \cdot 1/100k + (1 - 0.99) < 0.02$. Now write, for each vertex v in Z, an indicator random variable that is 1 if v has no neighbors in Z. By linearity of expectation, the expectation of the sum of these variables is $\geq 0.98k$, therefore $\mathbf{E}[|\text{MAX-IS}(G[Z])|] \geq 0.98k$.

To finish the proof of the lemma, we show that MAX-IS$(G[Z])$ is a highly concentrated random variable. To see this, define a martingale $X_0, X_1, \ldots, X_k$. X_0 is equal to $\mathbf{E}[\text{MAX-IS}(G[Z])]$ before any vertex of Z was chosen, thus X_0 is a deterministic value at least 0.98. X_1 is equal to $\mathbf{E}[\text{MAX-IS}(G[Z])]$ conditioning on the first vertex that is chosen. X_2 is the same value, conditioning on the first two vertices chosen, and so on. This martingale is thus the vertex-exposure martingale, where we expose vertices of Z one by one. It is easy to see that $|X_{i+1} - X_i| \leq 1$ for all $0 \leq i < k$. Then by Azuma's inequality, we have that with probability larger than $1 - e^{-k/40000}$ over the choices of Z, $X_k > (0.98 - 0.01)k = 0.97k$. □

We also have the following lemma.

LEMMA 8. *Let $G = (U, E)$ be a simple graph with the property that at least a 0.01 fraction of vertices have degrees at least $u/100k$. If we pick a subset $Z \subseteq U$ of size k uniformly at random, then the expected size of $N_G(Z)$ is at least $\Omega(u)$.*

PROOF. For any $v \in U$ whose degree is at least $u/100k$, the probability that it has a neighbor in Z is at least $1 - (1 - 1/100k)^k \geq 1 - e^{-1/100}$. Therefore we have

$$\mathbf{E}[N_G(Z)] \geq 0.01 \cdot \left(1 - e^{-1/100}\right) u \geq \Omega(u).$$

□

Now we are ready to prove Lemma 4.

PROOF. (of Lemma 4). Recall that Y is a set of the last $|Y| = k$ insertions done, and Y' is a set of random elements, also of cardinality k, chosen from U. Let BEGIN be the time before inserting Y, and recall that END is the snapshot after inserting Y and that END' is the snapshot after inserting Y' instead of Y. Let $M_{\texttt{BEGIN}}, M_{\texttt{END}}, M_{\texttt{END}'}$ be the states of the cache at BEGIN, END and END' respectively. Likewise, let $D_{\texttt{BEGIN}}, D_{\texttt{END}}, D_{\texttt{END}'}$ be the states of the disk at BEGIN, END and END'.

Now, the second item of Lemma 3 gives us the following:

CLAIM 1. *With probability at least* 0.999 *over the choices of* Y', *at least a* 0.99 *fraction of* Y' *will have query paths that intersect* C'^u *under* $(M_{\texttt{END}'}, D_{\texttt{BEGIN}})$.

To prove Lemma 4 it is enough to prove that

$$\left|\left\{x \in U \mid q_{\texttt{END}}(x) \bigcap \left(\bigcup_{y\in Y'} q_{(M_{\texttt{END}'},D_{\texttt{BEGIN}})}(y) \bigcup C^u\right) \neq \emptyset\right\}\right| \geq \Omega(u) . \quad (3)$$

Call x *good* if it is in the left-hand side of (3).

Consider some $x \in U$. If $q_{\texttt{END}}(x)$ intersects C^u then x is counted in the left-hand side of equation (3). Otherwise, $q_{\texttt{END}}(x) = q_{(M_{\texttt{END}},D_{\texttt{BEGIN}})}(x)$. We will now show how to use the LOSI to prove that for the family of queries $\{q_{(M_{\texttt{END}},D_{\texttt{BEGIN}})}(x)\}_x$, a constant fraction of them touches a small set of cells. That will prove (3). From now we concentrate on $\{q_{(M_{\texttt{END}},D_{\texttt{BEGIN}})}(x)\}_x$.

Now, recall that the set Y' is chosen uniformly at random. Therefore, we just need to show that $\{q_{(M_{\texttt{END}},D_{\texttt{BEGIN}})}(x)\}_{y\in Y'}$ satisfies the condition of the LOSI with probability $\geq p$. Claim 1 tells us that $\{q_{(M_{\texttt{END}'},D_{\texttt{BEGIN}})}(x)\}_{y\in Y'}$ satisfies the condition of the LOSI with probability ≥ 0.999. Thus, we just need to estimate the probability that $M_{\texttt{END}'} = M_{\texttt{END}}$. The probability of this is at least $1/2^m$, since $M_{\texttt{END}'}$ and $M_{\texttt{END}}$ are both drawn from the same distribution over a universe of cardinality 2^m. Therefore, the probability that $\{q_{(M_{\texttt{END}'},D_{\texttt{BEGIN}})}(x)\}_{y\in Y'}$ satisfies the condition of the LOSI is $0.999/2^m > p$, and we are done. □

4. CONCLUSIONS

In this paper we have resolved the complexity of dynamic membership in the external memory model, for the regime where t_u is just below 1. Consider the case $b \geq \log^{1+\epsilon} u$ for some large enough constant $\epsilon > 0$. For this case, our bounds are roughly tight all the way down to $t_u = O\left(\frac{\log(n/m)}{b^{1-\epsilon'}}\right)$ for some constant $\epsilon' > 1/(1+\epsilon)$. Namely, the lower bound shows that for such values of b, $t_q \geq \Omega(\log_b(n/m))$ whenever $t_u \leq 0.9$, and the upper bound shows that for such b, we can achieve $t_q = O(\log_b(n/m))$ and $t_u = O\left(\frac{\log(n/m)}{b^{1-\epsilon'}}\right)$ for some constant $\epsilon' > 1/(1+\epsilon)$. (For the upper bound part, see Section 1.3). For t_u smaller than this, the lower bound does not match the known upper bounds, and better lower bounds might be possible.

There are still a few regimes where our results are not tight:

1. For $t_u = 1 - o(1)$, it is interesting to see what our lower bound technique gives and whether that it tight.
2. For b which is smaller than $\log^{1+\epsilon} u$ for every $\epsilon > 0$, our lower bound is loose (in fact, for $b = 1$ it seems extremely loose) partly due to inherent limitations of the LOSI, and partly because we did not concentrate on such b. It is interesting whether the bound can be made tighter, and whether a variant of the LOSI suffices or another technique is needed.
3. For $t_u = O\left(\frac{\log u}{b}\right)$, we believe that the right behavior of the query time is something like $t_q \geq \Omega(n/m)$ or maybe $t_q \geq \Omega(n/bm)$. It seems interesting to try to prove this, but it is does not seem that the cell probe lower bound community has sufficiently advanced technology to achieve this. (Also see discussion in Section 1.3).

The first item in this list seems like it only requires playing around with the current result. The last two items, however, seem to not only require new ideas, but to be close to the boundaries of current lower bound technology. We are especially interested in the last one.

5. ACKNOWLEDGMENTS

The authors would like to thank Mihai Patrascu, Ke Yi and Zeyuan Allen Zhu for helpful discussions. We would like to thank the STOC reviewers for their insightful reviews.

6. REFERENCES

[1] A. Aggarwal and J. S. Vitter. The input/output complexity of sorting and related problems. *Communications of the ACM*, 31(9):1116–1127, 1988.

[2] L. Arge. *External Memory Data Structures*. Kluwer Academic Publishers, 2002.

[3] L. Arge. The buffer tree: A technique for designing batched external data structures. *Algorithmica*, 37(1):1–24, 2003.

[4] L. Arge, M. Bender, E. Demaine, B. Holland-Minkley, and J. I. Munro. Cache-oblivious priority-queue and graph algorithms. In *Proc. ACM Symposium on Theory of Computing*, pages 268–276, 2002.

[5] P. Beame and F. E. Fich. Optimal bounds for the predecessor problem and related problems. *Journal of Computer and System Sciences*, 65(1):38–72, 2002.

[6] B. H. Bloom. Space/time trade-offs in hash coding with allowable errors. *Communications of the ACM*, 13(7):422–426, 1970.

[7] G. S. Brodal and R. Fagerberg. Lower bounds for external memory dictionaries. In *Proc. ACM-SIAM Symposium on Discrete Algorithms*, pages 546–554, 2003.

[8] M. Dietzfelbinger, A. Karlin, K. Mehlhorn, F. Meyer auf der Heide, H. Rohnert, and R. E. Tarjan. Dynamic perfect hashing: upper and lower bounds. *SIAM Journal on Computing*, 23:738–761, 1994.

[9] R. Fadel, K. V. Jakobsen, J. Katajainen, and J. Teuhola. Heaps and heapsort on secondary storage. *Theoretical Computer Science*, 220(2):345–362, 1999.

[10] R. Fagin, J. Nievergelt, N. Pippenger, and H. Strong. Extendible hashing—a fast access method for dynamic files. *ACM Transactions on Database Systems*, 4(3):315–344, 1979.

[11] A. Golynski. Cell probe lower bounds for succinct data structures. In *Proc. ACM-SIAM Symposium on Discrete Algorithms*, pages 625–634, 2009.

[12] M. S. Jensen and R. Pagh. Optimality in external memory hashing. *Algorithmica*, 52(3):403–411, 2008.

[13] D. E. Knuth. *Sorting and Searching*, volume 3 of *The Art of Computer Programming*. Addison-Wesley, Reading MA, second edition, 1998.

[14] P. A. Larson. Performance analysis of linear hashing with partial expansions. In *ACM Transactions on Database Systems*, 1982.

[15] W. Litwin. Linear hashing: a new tool for file and table addressing. In *Proc. International Conference on Very Large Databases*, pages 212–223, 1980.

[16] K. Mehlhorn, S. Naher, and M. Rauch. On the complexity of a game related to the dictionary problem. In *Proc. IEEE Symposium on Foundations of Computer Science*, pages 546–548, 1989.

[17] P. B. Miltersen, N. Nisan, S. Safra, and A. Wigderson. On data structures and asymmetric communication complexity. In *Journal of Computer and System Sciences*, 1998.

[18] C. W. Mortensen, R. Pagh, and M. Pătraşcu. On dynamic range reporting in one dimension. In *Proc. ACM Symposium on Theory of Computing*, pages 104–111, 2005.

[19] R. Pagh. *Basic External Memory Data Structures*.

[20] R. Pagh. On the cell probe complexity of membership and perfect hashing. In *Proc. ACM Symposium on Theory of Computing*, pages 425–432, 2001.

[21] R. Pagh and F. F. Rodler. Cuckoo hashing. *Journal of Algorithms*, 51:122–144, 2004.

[22] M. Pătraşcu. Personal communication.

[23] M. Pătraşcu. Lower bound techniques for data structures. In *PhD Thesis*, 2008.

[24] M. Pătraşcu and E. D. Demaine. Tight bounds for the partial-sums problem. In *Proc. 15th ACM-SIAM Symposium on Discrete Algorithms*, pages 20–29, 2004.

[25] M. Pătraşcu and M. Thorup. Time-space trade-offs for predecessor search. In *Proc. ACM Symposium on Theory of Computing*, 2006.

[26] M. Pătraşcu and E. Viola. Cell-probe lower bounds for succinct partial sums. In *Proc. ACM-SIAM Symposium on Discrete Algorithms*, pages 117–122, 2010.

[27] P. Sen. Lower bounds for predecessor searching in the cell probe model. In *IEEE Conference on Computational Complexity*, 2003.

[28] R. Sundar. A lower bound for the dictionary problem under a hashing model. In *Proc. IEEE Symposium on Foundations of Computer Science*, pages 612–621, 1991.

[29] J. S. Vitter. *Algorithms and Data Structures for External Memory*. Now Publishers, 2008.

[30] Z. Wei, K. Yi, and Q. Zhang. Dynamic external hashing: The limit of buffering. In *Proc. ACM Symposium on Parallelism in Algorithms and Architectures*, 2009.

[31] A. C. Yao. Should tables be sorted? *Journal of the ACM*, 28(3):615–628, 1981.

[32] K. Yi. Personal communication.

[33] K. Yi and Q. Zhang. On the cell probe complexity of dynamic membership. In *Proc. ACM-SIAM Symposium on Discrete Algorithms*, 2010.

[34] Z. A. Zhu. Personal communication.

Maintaining a Large Matching and a Small Vertex Cover

Krzysztof Onak*
MIT
konak@mit.edu

Ronitt Rubinfeld†
MIT and Tel Aviv University
ronitt@csail.mit.edu

ABSTRACT

We consider the problem of maintaining a large matching and a small vertex cover in a dynamically changing graph. Each update to the graph is either an edge deletion or an edge insertion. We give the first randomized data structure that simultaneously achieves a constant approximation factor and handles a sequence of K updates in $K \cdot \text{polylog}(n)$ time, where n is the number of vertices in the graph. Previous data structures require a polynomial amount of computation per update.

Categories and Subject Descriptors

E.1 [**Data Structures**]: Graphs and Networks; F.2.2 [**Analysis of Algorithms and Problem Complexity**]: Nonnumerical Algorithms and Problems; G.2.2 [**Graph Theory**]: Graph Algorithms

General Terms

Algorithms

Keywords

dynamic algorithms, data structures, maximum matching, vertex cover

1. INTRODUCTION

Suppose one is given the task of solving a combinatorial problem, such as vertex cover or maximum matching, for a very large and constantly changing graph. In this setting, it is natural to ask, does one need to recompute the solution from scratch after every update?

*Supported by NSF grants 0732334 and 0728645.

†Supported by NSF grants 0732334 and 0728645, Marie Curie Reintegration grant PIRG03-GA-2008-231077, and the Israel Science Foundation grant nos. 1147/09 and 1675/09.

STOC'10, June 5–8, 2010, Cambridge, Massachusetts, USA.

Such questions have been asked before for various combinatorial quantities—examples include minimum spanning tree, shortest path length, min-cut, and many others (some examples include [3, 2, 6, 15, 8, 14]). Classic works for these problems have shown update times that are sublinear in the input size. For the problem of maximum matching, Sankowski [13] shows that it can be maintained with $O(n^{1.495})$ computation per update (n is the number of vertices in the graph), which for dense graphs is sublinear in the number of edges.

For very large graphs, it may be crucial to maintain the maximum matching with much faster, even polylogarithmic, update time. Note that this may be hard for maximum matching, since obtaining $o(\sqrt{n})$ update time, even in the case when only insertions are allowed, would improve on the 30-year-old algorithm of running time $O(m\sqrt{n})$ due to Micali and Vazirani [11], where m is the number of edges in the graph. Therefore, some kind of approximation may be unavoidable. Following similar considerations, Ivković and Lloyd [7] give a factor-2 approximation to both vertex cover and maximum matching, by maintaining a *maximal* matching (which is well known to give the desired approximation for maximum matching and minimum vertex cover). Their update time is nevertheless still polynomial in n. More precisely, it is $O((n+m)^{0.7072})$, which is $o(n)$ for sparse graphs.

In this paper, we concentrate on the setting in which slightly weaker, but still $O(1)$, approximation factors are acceptable, and in which it is crucial that update times be extremely fast, in particular, polylogarithmic in the graph size.

1.1 Problem Statement and Our Results

Recall that in the *maximum matching* problem, one wants to find the largest subset of vertex disjoint edges. In the *vertex cover* problem, one wants to find the smallest set of vertices such that each edge of the graph is incident to at least one vertex in the set.

Our goal here is to design a data structure that handles edge removals and edge insertions. The data structure provides access to a list of edges that constitute a large matching or a list of vertices that constitute a small vertex cover. We assume that we always start with an empty graph, and n is known in advance.

The main result of the paper is the following:

> *There is a randomized data structure for maximum matching and vertex cover that*
>
> *(a) achieves a constant approximation factor,*

(b) *runs in*

$$O\left(\min\{K,n^2\}\cdot\log n\cdot\log\frac{1}{\delta}+K\cdot\log^2 n\right)$$

time for a fixed sequence of K updates with probability $1-\delta$.

Furthermore, the first step in our presentation is a *deterministic* data structure for vertex cover. The data structure keeps a vertex cover that gives an $O(\log n)$ approximation to the minimum vertex cover. The amortized update time of the data structure is $O(\log^2 n)$. Though the approximation factor achieved by this algorithm is relatively weak, the algorithm may be of independent interest because of its relative simplicity and efficient update time.

1.2 Overview of Our Techniques

We present our main result in two stages.

A Deterministic $O(\log n)$-Approximation Data Structure: We construct a data structure that makes use of a carefully designed partition of vertices into a logarithmic number of subsets. The partition is inspired by a simple distributed algorithm of Parnas and Ron [12]. In [12], the first subset in the partition corresponds to removing vertices of degree approximately n. The second subset corresponds to removing vertices of degree close to $n/4$ from the modified graph. In general, the i-th subset is a set of vertices that are approximately $n/4^{i-1}$ in the graph with all previous subsets of vertices removed. Finally, after a logarithmic number of steps, the remaining graph has no edges. This implies that the union of all subsets removed so far constitutes a vertex cover. For each of the removed subsets, it is easy to show that the subset size is bounded by $O(\mathrm{VC}(G))$, where $\mathrm{VC}(G)$ is the size of the minimum vertex cover. Hence the total vertex cover is bounded by $O(\mathrm{VC}(G)\cdot\log n)$.

The main idea behind our data structure is to modify the partition of Parnas and Ron in order to allow efficient maintenance of this partition, under edge insertions and deletions. While this is not possible in the partition of Parnas and Ron, it is possible in our relaxed version of it. As edges are inserted and removed, we want to move vertices between subsets. In order to determine whether to move a vertex, we associate a potential function with every vertex, and we allow a vertex to jump from one set to another only if it has collected enough potential. To do this, we set two thresholds $\tau_1<\tau_2$ for each subset. A vertex can move into the subset from a subset corresponding to a lower degree if its number of neighbors in a specific graph is at least τ_2. Then the vertex can move back to a subset corresponding to a lower degree only if the number of edges decreases to τ_1 in the same graph. A slight technical difficulty is presented by the fact that moving vertices may increase the potential of other vertices. We overcome this obstacle by carefully selecting constants in the potential function so that the potential of the vertex that moves is spent on increasing the potential of its neighbors.

A Randomized $O(1)$-Approximation Data Structure: In this case, we redesign the partition, building upon the previous one. In the process of defining the partition, whenever we remove a large subset W of vertices of degree approximately $n/4^i$, we also show the existence of a matching M which is smaller than W by at most a constant factor. To build the next set of the partition, we not only remove W but also all vertices matched in M. In this way we achieve a matching and a vertex cover of sizes that are within a constant factor of each other. Therefore, both give a constant factor approximation to their respective optimal solutions.

Efficient maintenance of the new partition is more involved, as we are sometimes forced to recompute a matching. This can happen, for instance, when many edges in the matching are deleted from the graph. Unfortunately, the creation of a new matching is expensive, since we have modified the set of the vertices matched in M that are deleted together with W. If the edges in the matching are deleted too quickly, we have to create a new matching often, in which case we do not know how to maintain small update time. Fortunately, by picking a large *random* matching, we can ensure that it is unlikely that many edges from the matching get deleted in a short span of time. Thus, by the time the matching gets deleted, we are likely to have collected enough potential to pay for the creation of a new matching.

1.3 Other Related Work

A sequence of papers [5, 10, 16, 4] considers computing a large matching or a large weight matching (in the weighted case) in the semi-streaming model. The stream is a sequence of edges, and the goal of an algorithm is to compute a large matching in a small number of passes over the stream, using $O(n\cdot\log^{O(1)} n)$ space, and preferably at most polylog(n) update time. Results in this model correspond to results for dynamically changing graphs in which only edge insertions occur, except that the matching is only output once, at the end of the processing. To the best of our knowledge, it is not known how to achieve a better approximation factor than 2 in one pass for the maximum matching problem.

Lotker, Patt-Shamir, and Rosén [9] show how to maintain a large matching in a distributed network.

2. PRELIMINARIES

We assume that all the necessary simple set operations (insert, remove, find, ...) on ordered sets of size t can be implemented in $O(\log t)$ time. A number of tree based dictionaries (AVL trees, red-black trees, etc.) have this property (see for instance the textbook of Cormen *et al.* [1]). We also assume that the first s items in a set can be accessed in $O(s)$ time, which can usually easily be achieved by augmenting a given data structure with additional links.

Throughout the paper, α is a fixed integer greater than 1. We write k_α to denote $\lfloor\log_\alpha n\rfloor+2$. Moreover, $\mathrm{VC}(G)$ is the minimum vertex cover size in G, and $\mathrm{MM}(G)$ is the maximum matching size in G.

2.1 Basic Facts

FACT 1. *Let G be a graph, and let M be a matching in G. Then, $\mathrm{VC}(G)\geq|M|$.*

LEMMA 2. *Let G be a graph of maximum degree d. Let V' be a subset of vertices such that every vertex in V' has degree between d/γ and d. The following holds:*

- *There is a matching M of size at least $|V'|/(4\gamma)$ with each edge incident to a vertex in V'.*
- $|V'|\leq 4\gamma\cdot\mathrm{VC}(G)$.

PROOF. There are at least $X \stackrel{\text{def}}{=} \frac{d|V'|}{2\gamma}$ edges incident to vertices in V'. Each such edge is adjacent to at most $Y \stackrel{\text{def}}{=} 2(d-1)$ other such edges. This implies that G has a matching of size at least $X/(Y+1) \geq |V'|/(4\gamma)$. By Fact 1, $|V'| \leq 4\gamma \cdot \mathrm{VC}(G)$. □

2.2 Simple $O(d)$-Update-Time Data Structure

We now describe a straightforward data structure for maintaining a maximal matching in a graph of maximum degree bounded by d. To the best of our knowledge, the data structure was first described by Ivković and Lloyd [7].

For every vertex, the data structure maintains information indicating whether it is matched. Whenever an edge is inserted, the data structure checks if its endpoints are matched or not. If none of them are, the edge is added to the matching. Whenever an edge e in the maximal matching is removed, the data structure checks whether the remaining matching may be extended by adding edges incident to the endpoints of e. To do this, the data structure goes over $O(d)$ edges that were adjacent to e, and greedily tries to extend the matching with each of them.

It is easy to show that the matching held by the data structure is maximal. It can be used for obtaining a 2-approximation of both the minimum vertex cover (use the endpoints of edges in the matching) and the maximum matching (use the maximal matching itself). The `Insert` operation takes $O(1)$ time, and the `Delete` operation requires $O(d)$ time.

3. WARMUP: DETERMINISTIC $O(\log n)$-APPROXIMATION FOR VERTEX COVER

3.1 A Sequential Algorithm

Consider first the sequential Algorithm 1. The algorithm is a modification of a simple distributed algorithm for vertex cover that was used by Parnas and Ron [12].

Algorithm 1: A sequential $O(\log n)$-approximation algorithm for vertex cover

Input: graph G, integer $\alpha > 1$
$k_\alpha := \lfloor \log_\alpha n \rfloor + 2$
$G_{k_\alpha} := G$
for $i := k_\alpha$ **downto** 1 **do**
  $V_i := \{$vertices of degree $\geq \alpha^{i-1}$ in $G_i\}$
    $\cup\,\{$arbitrary subset of vertices of degree in $[\alpha^{i-2}, \alpha^{i-1})$ in $G_i\}$
  $G_{i-1} := G_i$ with vertices in V_i removed
return $\bigcup_{i=1}^{k_\alpha} V_i$

LEMMA 3. *Let α be an integer greater than 1. The size of each set V_i in Algorithm 1 is bounded by $4\alpha^2\,\mathrm{VC}(G)$. Algorithm 1 computes a vertex cover of size $\leq 4\alpha^2 \cdot k_\alpha \cdot \mathrm{VC}(G)$.*

PROOF. The algorithm repeatedly removes vertices and their adjacent edges from the original graph, and adds the removed vertices to the cover. To see that the algorithm computes a vertex cover, note that the final graph G_0 has no edges, which means that all edges of G have been covered by the output of the algorithm.

Let i be any integer between 1 and k_α. The maximum degree of G_i is bounded by α^i. By Lemma 2, $|V_i| \leq 4\alpha^2 \cdot \mathrm{VC}(G_i) \leq 4\alpha^2 \cdot \mathrm{VC}(G)$. This implies that the size of the cover returned by the algorithm is at most $k_\alpha \cdot 4\alpha^2\,\mathrm{VC}(G)$. □

3.2 The Data Structure

We design a data structure that keeps a partition of vertices into a logarithmic number of sets V_i, $0 \leq i \leq k_\alpha$. The partition is one that could potentially be created in an execution of Algorithm 1. We refer to sets V_i as *buckets*. The sets V_i with $i > 0$ are sets of vertices removed in consecutive executions of the loop of Algorithm 1, and V_0 is the set of vertices that are not removed from the graph by the algorithm. For $i > 0$, each V_i consists of vertices that at the time of removal, have degree between α^{i-2} and α^i. The union of V_i over $i > 0$ is the current vertex cover.

For every vertex v, we maintain the following variables:

`index`$[v]$: the index of the set V_i that contains v.

`neighbors`$[v, j]$ **for** $j \geq$ `index`$[v]$: the set of neighbors of v that that belong to V_j.

`below`$[v, j]$ **for** $j \geq$ `index`$[v]$: the total number of all neighbors of v in sets V_0 through V_j.

`lower-neighbors`$[v]$: the set of neighbors of v that belong to V_i for $i <$ `index`$[v]$.

We call the collection of vertices involving v the *structures of v*.

Initially, the graph is empty, so all sets of neighbors are empty, and `index`$[v] = 0$ and `below`$[v, j] = 0$ for all v and j.

We maintain the following invariants for each vertex v after each update to the graph:

- To ensure that v's bucket number `index`$[v]$ is not too high, i.e., that it has enough edges to nodes in lower buckets, we ask that if `index`$[v] > 0$, then `below`$[v,$ `index`$[v]] > \alpha^{\mathtt{index}[v]-2}$.
- On the other hand, to ensure that v's bucket number is not too low, i.e., that it should not have been placed in a higher bucket, we ask that for each $i \in \{$`index`$[v]+1, \ldots, k_\alpha\}$, `below`$[v, i] < \alpha^{i-1}$.

Note that if this is the case, then the sets V_i, $1 \leq i \leq k_\alpha$ defined as $V_i = \{v \in V :$ `index`$[v] = i\}$ could potentially be created by the non-deterministic Algorithm 1.

As a result of edge removals and insertions, the invariants may no longer hold. We first design a procedure `Restabilize` that given a set of vertices for which the invariant may not hold (we call such vertices *dirty*), attempts to fix the partition given by `index`$[\cdot]$. As long as there is a dirty vertex v, the procedure does the following.

- If there is an $i >$ `index`$[v]$, such that `below`$[v, i] \geq \alpha^{i-1}$, the procedure sets `index`$[v]$ to the highest such i. (This could happen if many edges adjacent to v have been added to the graph, or if many edges have been deleted from v's neighbors that were previously in higher buckets than the i-th, causing them to be demoted to lower buckets.)

  Let t and $t_\star$ be the new and old value of `index`$[v]$, respectively. The move of v from $V_{t_\star}$ to V_t may invalidate the invariant for neighbors of v in buckets V_t to

$V_{t_\star-1}$. Therefore, the procedure marks all of them as dirty.

Next, the procedure updates neighbors$[u]$, below$[u,\cdot]$, and lower-neighbors$[u]$ for all neighbors u of v in buckets V_0 through V_t. Then the procedure updates the structures for v as well. Note that updating all the structures takes at most $O(\texttt{below}[v,t]\cdot\log n)$ time, because this requires at most a constant number of set operations per each of the neighbors in consideration, and for each vertex u, the array below$[u,\cdot]$ can be updated in $O(k_\alpha) = O(\log n)$ time.

Finally, the procedure marks v as no longer dirty.

- Otherwise, if index$[v] > 0$, and $\texttt{below}[v, \texttt{index}[v]] \le \alpha^{\texttt{index}[v]-2}$, the procedure decreases index$[v]$ by one. (This could happen if many edges adjacent to v have been deleted, or if many edges are added to v's neighbors that were previously in lower buckets than v, causing them to jump to higher buckets.)

  Let t be the new value of index$[v]$. The move of v can affect the invariant for neighbors of v in sets V_0 through V_{t-1}, so the procedure marks all of them as dirty.

  The procedure also updates neighbors$[u]$, below$[u,\cdot]$, and lower-neighbors$[u]$ for all neighbors u of v in buckets V_0 to V_{t+1}. Next it does the same for the structures of v. In total, this takes $O(\texttt{below}[v,t+1]\cdot\log n)$ time, since at most a constant number of set operations per each of the neighbors in consideration is necessary, and for each of them below$[\cdot,\cdot]$ can be updated in $O(k_\alpha) = O(\log n)$ time.

  In this case, the procedure does not change the status of v. It still remains dirty, since the procedure may have to decrease index$[v]$ further[1].

- If none of the previous cases occurred, v is already in the right bucket, and there is no need to move it. The procedure marks the vertex as no longer dirty.

It is not immediately clear that the above procedure Restabilize always stops. We show that this is the case in Section 3.3.

It is easy to implement operations Insert and Delete that are responsible for inserting and removing an edge by using Restabilize. It suffices to modify first the corresponding below$[u,\cdot]$, neighbors$[u,\cdot]$, and lower-neighbors$[u]$ for each of the edge's endpoints u (this can be done in $O(\log n)$ time), mark the endpoints as dirty, and run Restabilize to fix the partition of vertices if necessary.

3.3 Complexity Analysis

THEOREM 4. *The amortized complexity of the operations* Insert *and* Delete *in the deterministic data structure is* $O(\log^2 n)$ *for* $\alpha = 4$.

PROOF. The use the following potential function. The potential of a vertex v equals

$$\Phi(v) \stackrel{\text{def}}{=} \Phi_1(v) + \Phi_2(v),$$

where

$$\Phi_1(v) \stackrel{\text{def}}{=} 0,$$

if index$[v] = 0$,

$$\Phi_1(v) \stackrel{\text{def}}{=} 8\cdot\min\Big\{ \max\left\{\alpha^{\texttt{index}[v]-1} - \texttt{below}[v,\texttt{index}[v]], 0\right\},\ \alpha^{\texttt{index}[v]-1} - \alpha^{\texttt{index}[v]-2}\Big\}$$

for index$[v] > 0$, and

$$\Phi_2(v) \stackrel{\text{def}}{=} 12\cdot \sum_{i=\texttt{index}[v]+1}^{k_\alpha} \max\left\{\texttt{below}[v,i] - \alpha^{i-2}, 0\right\}.$$

$\Phi_1(v)$ corresponds to losing neighbors. When v loses sufficiently many of them, there is enough potential to pay for decreasing index$[v]$. $\Phi_2(v)$ is related to the number of neighbors u with index$[u] >$ index$[v]$. We only increase index$[v]$ if there are sufficiently many of them, and then $\Phi_2(v)$ provides enough potential to conduct the operation. For the initial empty graph, all $\Phi(v) = 0$.

Each unit of the potential corresponds to $O(\log n)$ computation. Inserting or removing an edge can only change the potential of the endpoints of the edge, and the change is bounded by $O(k_\alpha)$, because each of $O(k_\alpha)$ terms can only change by a constant. We show that fixing the invariant of the data structure, i.e., executing the procedure Restabilize, is almost entirely paid for by potentials of vertices. More precisely, we show that the amortized complexity of Restabilize is the number of vertices that are initially marked as dirty times $O(\log n)$. Assuming this, the amortized cost of both Insert and Delete is $O(k_\alpha\cdot\log n) = O(\log^2 n)$.

Consider the case when Restabilize increases index$[v]$ for a vertex v. If this happens, index$[v]$ becomes t such that $\texttt{below}[v,t] \ge \alpha^{t-1}$. We can use up to $12\cdot(\texttt{below}[v,t] - \alpha^{t-2})$ units of the potential of v. This comes from the decrease in $\Phi(v)$, and more precisely in $\Phi_2(v)$. Once index$[v]$ is set to t, $\Phi_1(v)$ becomes 0, and $\Phi_2(v)$ only equals

$$\sum_{i=t+1}^{k_\alpha} \max\left\{\texttt{below}[v,i] - \alpha^{i-2}, 0\right\}.$$

Restabilize updates structures for all neighbors u of v such that index$[u] \le t$. It also marks some of them as dirty, and the potential has to pay also for checking later whether the invariant holds for them. This costs at most $O(\log n)\cdot\texttt{below}[v,t]$, that is, below$[v,t]$ units of potential. Additionally, modifying index$[v]$ can result in decreasing below$[u, \texttt{index}[u]]$ for some of the same neighbors u of v. The potential, therefore, has to pay another $8\cdot\texttt{below}[v,t]$ units to compensate for the change in $\Phi_1(u)$ for those neigh-

[1]One could immediately decrease index$[v]$ to the right value, but it is easier to analyze the complexity of this version of the procedure.

bors. The total expense can be bounded by

$$\begin{aligned}
&\texttt{below}[v,t] + 8\cdot\texttt{below}[v,t] \\
&= 9\cdot\frac{\texttt{below}[v,t]}{\texttt{below}[v,t]-\alpha^{t-2}}\cdot\left(\texttt{below}[v,t]-\alpha^{t-2}\right) \\
&\le 9\cdot\frac{\alpha^{t-1}}{\alpha^{t-1}-\alpha^{t-2}}\cdot\left(\texttt{below}[v,t]-\alpha^{t-2}\right) \\
&= \frac{9\alpha}{\alpha-1}\cdot\left(\texttt{below}[v,t]-\alpha^{t-2}\right) \\
&= 12\cdot\left(\texttt{below}[v,t]-\alpha^{t-2}\right),
\end{aligned}$$

which is not more than the available budget.

Consider now the other case when `Restabilize` decreases $\texttt{index}[v]$ by one for a vertex v. Let t be the new $\texttt{index}[v]$, i.e., the old $\texttt{index}[v]$ minus one. Note that the old $\Phi_1(v)$ equals $8\cdot(\alpha^t-\alpha^{t-1})$. `Restabilize` updates structures for at most α^{t-1} neighbors u of v, and it also marks some of them as dirty. This costs at most α^{t-1} units of potential together with checking later whether the invariant holds for them. Moving v may also increase $\texttt{below}[u,t]$ by one for all of them, and this may increase their potential Φ_2. The total increase is at most $12\cdot\alpha^{t-1}$ units of potential. Furthermore, the new potential $\Phi_1(v)$ can still be positive, but it can be bounded by $8\cdot(\alpha^{t-1}-\alpha^{t-2})$. Finally, we pay 1 for reverifying if the invariant holds for v after the modification of $\texttt{index}[v]$. The total expense is bounded by

$$\begin{aligned}
&\alpha^{t-1}+12\cdot\alpha^{t-1}+8\cdot(\alpha^{t-1}-\alpha^{t-2})+1 \\
&\le \left(\frac{13}{\alpha-1}+\frac{8}{\alpha}+\frac{1}{\alpha^t-\alpha^{t-1}}\right)\cdot(\alpha^t-\alpha^{t-1}) \\
&\le \left(\frac{13}{3}+2+\frac{4}{3}\right)\cdot(\alpha^t-\alpha^{t-1})\le 8\cdot(\alpha^t-\alpha^{t-1}),
\end{aligned}$$

which is the old $\Phi_1(v)$. □

4. RANDOMIZED $O(1)$-APPROXIMATION

We now describe a new data structure that maintains an $O(1)$ approximation for maximum matching and vertex cover. The data structure handles a sequence of ℓ updates in $\ell\cdot\mathrm{polylog}(n)$ time. In Section 4.1, we describe a new method of creating a partition of the vertices along with the properties that the partition satisifies. In Section 4.2, we describe how to generate a matching and vertex cover from the partition and bound the approximation factor. In Section 4.4, we give the implementation details which allow one to maintain the partition along with the required properties through the successive updates. In Section 4.5, we describe the amortized analysis of the update time.

In the following description, we use sufficiently large positive constants C_1, C_2, and C_T. We require that $C_2 \ll C_1$ and $C_2 \ll C_T$. As before, we assume that the α we use equals 4. Recall also that $k_\alpha = \lfloor\log_\alpha n+2\rfloor$, that is, $k_\alpha = O(\log n)$.

4.1 The new partition and its properties

As in the partition of Algorithm 1, we partition the vertices into a logarithmic number of sets. We remove a set of vertices at each of logarithmically many phases based on the degrees of the vertices being considered. However, whereas in Algorithm 1, only high degree vertices were removed at each phase, here we may remove additional vertices. In the following, we mainly focus on describing differences from the partition constructed by Algorithm 1.

Let $\Delta \stackrel{\text{def}}{=} 2+\lceil\log_\alpha 2k_\alpha\rceil$. For all $i\in\{1,\dots,k_\alpha\}$, recall that G_i is the graph remaining in the i-th loop of Algorithm 1, and V_i is the set of vertices of G_i. We define E_i as the edges incident to vertices in V_i in graph G_i. The new partition differs as follows:

1. We stop partitioning the graph when $i\le\Delta$ (i.e., step 3 of Algorithm 1 is changed to "for $i := k_\alpha$ to $\Delta+1$"). The graph G_Δ has degree bounded by $\alpha^\Delta \le 2\alpha^3 k_\alpha = O(\log n)$, and we use the simple data structure of Section 2.2 to maintain a maximal matching $M_\star$ in that graph. Each update costs $O(\log n)$.

2. For each $i>\Delta$, we select a set V_i in the same way as in Algorithm 1. Each $i>\Delta$ is either *heavy* or *light*. In general, when $|V_i|$ is sufficiently large, then i is heavy, and when $|V_i|$ is sufficiently small, then i is light, but there is a range of $|V_i|$ for which either alternative may be the case. In Section 4.4, we describe how the choice is made so that we can bound the amortized complexity of the data structure.

   For each $i>\Delta$, one of the following two is the case in the partition:

   heavy i: Apart from V_i, the partition also identifies a set of vertices V_i', and a matching $M_i\subseteq E_i$ such that $|M_i|\ge|V_i\cup V_i'|/C_1$, and each edge in M_i connects vertices in $V_i\cup V_i'$. G_{i-1} is created by removing not only vertices in V_i, but also those in V_i'. $V_i\cup V_i'$ is a part of the current approximate vertex cover.

   light i: A given i can only be light if $|E_i|\le C_T\cdot\alpha^i$. In this case, we create G_{i-1} by removing only vertices in V_i. V_i is a part of the current approximate vertex cover.

4.2 Approximating the Maximum Matching and the Minimum Vertex Cover

We now describe how the above partition is used to maintain a constant-factor approximation to both the maximum matching and the minimum vertex cover.

The current matching and the current vertex cover kept by the data structure are the following:

- At the end of every `Insert` and `Delete` operation, we compute a matching M_{light} that matches at least one vertex in V_i for each light i with non-empty V_i. We pick one vertex from each such V_i. There are at most k_α such vertices, and each of them has degree greater than $\alpha^\Delta/\alpha^2\ge 2k_\alpha$. This means that considering them in any order and going over the list of their neighbors, we eventually find a neighbor that has not yet been matched. This way, we get a matching of size at least half the number of light i. The whole procedure takes at most $O(\log^2 n)$ time, because we consider at most $O(\log^2 n)$ vertices, and for each of them we check whether it is already matched in M_{light}.

  We write M_{heavy} to denote the union of all M_i for i heavy. Note that $M_{\text{heavy}}\cup M_\star$ is a matching as well. Combining $M_{\text{heavy}}\cup M_\star$ with M_{light} gives a graph of degree at most 2, and we use the simple data structure of Section 2.2 to maintain a matching $\widetilde{M}$ of size at least $\frac{1}{2}\max\{|M_{\text{light}}|,|M_{\text{heavy}}|+|M_\star|\}$. $\widetilde{M}$ is the current matching.

- The current vertex cover $\widetilde{V}$ is the union of all V_i for $i > \Delta$, V_i' for heavy $i > \Delta$, and the vertices matched in $M_\star$.

Since $|\widetilde{M}| \leq \mathrm{MM}(G) \leq \mathrm{VC}(G) \leq |\widetilde{V}|$ (see Fact 1), it suffices to show that $|\widetilde{M}| \geq |\widetilde{V}|/C$, for some constant C to prove that $\widetilde{M}$ and $\widetilde{V}$ are constant factor approximations to maximum matching and vertex cover, respectively. Note that

$$\begin{aligned}\left|\bigcup_{\text{light } i} V_i\right| &\leq 2\cdot\alpha^2\cdot C_{\mathrm{T}}\cdot|M_{\text{light}}|,\\ \left|\bigcup_{\text{heavy } i}(V_i\cup V_i')\right| &\leq C_1\cdot|M_{\text{heavy}}|,\\ |\{\text{endpoints of edges in } M_\star\}| &\leq 2\cdot|M_\star|.\end{aligned}$$

Therefore,

$$\begin{aligned}\left|\widetilde{V}\right| &\leq 2\alpha^2 C_{\mathrm{T}}\cdot|M_{\text{light}}| + C_1\cdot|M_{\text{heavy}}| + 2\cdot|M_\star|\\ &\leq 2\alpha^2 C_{\mathrm{T}}\cdot|M_{\text{light}}| + 2C_1\cdot(|M_{\text{heavy}}|+|M_\star|)\\ &\leq 2\alpha^2 C_1 C_{\mathrm{T}}\cdot|M_{\text{light}}| + 2\alpha^2 C_1 C_{\mathrm{T}}\cdot(|M_{\text{heavy}}|+|M_\star|)\\ &\leq 4\alpha^2 C_1 C_{\mathrm{T}}\cdot\max\{|M_{\text{light}}|, |M_{\text{heavy}}|+|M_\star|\}\\ &= 8\alpha^2 C_1 C_{\mathrm{T}}\cdot\frac{1}{2}\max\{|M_{\text{light}}|, |M_{\text{heavy}}|+|M_\star|\}\\ &\leq 8\alpha^2 C_1 C_{\mathrm{T}}\cdot|\widetilde{M}|.\end{aligned}$$

4.3 Selecting a Large Matching M_i of V_i

We now describe how to select a large matching M_i for i heavy. The lemma states properties of our procedure, which we will use in the next section.

LEMMA 5. *Let G_i be a graph of maximum degree α^i. Let n be the number of vertices in G_i. Let V_i be a set of vertices in G_i, each with degree in $[\alpha^{i-2}, \alpha^i]$. Let E_i be the set of edges in G_i incident to at least one vertex in V_i, and let $|E_i| \geq C_{\mathrm{T}}\cdot\alpha^i$.*

Let $\mathcal{S}$ be the distribution on subsets of E_i created by independently selecting every edge in E_i with probability $p \stackrel{def}{=} 1/(C_2\alpha^i)$.

There is an algorithm $\mathcal{A}$ that with the following properties:

- *$\mathcal{A}$ selects a subset E' of edges from a distribution $\mathcal{S}'$ on subsets of E_i such that the statistical distance between $\mathcal{S}'$ and $\mathcal{S}$ is at most $1/1000$.*
- *The size of E' is at most $\frac{21}{20}\cdot p|E_i|$.*
- *With probability $998/1000$, $\mathcal{A}$ outputs a matching M that is a subset of E' and $|M| \geq \frac{9}{10}\cdot p|E_i|$.*

The running time of $\mathcal{A}$ is $O(|E_i|\log n)$.

PROOF. The set E' is selected as follows. The algorithm goes over all edges in E_i, and selects each edge independently with probability p. If at some point the number of selected edges reaches $\frac{21}{20}\cdot p|E_i|$, the procedure stops selecting new edges. If C_{T} and C_2 are large enough, then this does not happen with probability greater than $1/1000$ (via the Chernoff bound), so the statistical distance between $\mathcal{S}$ and $\mathcal{S}'$ is at most $1/1000$.

Suppose for now that E' is selected according to $\mathcal{S}$, not $\mathcal{S}'$. If C_2 is large enough, then the probability that a given edge in E' intersects with another edge in E' is small. Let M be the set of all those edges in E' that do not intersect with other edges in E'. For sufficiently large C_2 and C_{T} such that $C_2 \ll C_{\mathrm{T}}$, the size of M is close to its expectation via the Chernoff bound, and in particular $|M| \geq \frac{9}{10}p|E_i|$ with probability 999/1000. Since the statistical distance between $\mathcal{S}$ and $\mathcal{S}'$ is at most $1/1000$, $|M| \geq \frac{9}{10}p|E_i|$ with probability at least 998/1000, even if E' is selected from $\mathcal{S}'$. □

4.4 Maintaining the Partition

We now describe how the partition is maintained. As before the data structure keep a value $\mathtt{index}[v]$ for each vertex v. This time $\mathtt{index}[v]$ can only belong to the set $\{\Delta, \Delta+1, \Delta+2, \ldots, k_\alpha-1, k_\alpha\}$. The value Δ corresponds to v remaining in the graph G_Δ, for which a separate copy of the simple data structure is kept. Additionally, for each vertex v with $\mathtt{index}[v] > \Delta$, there is an additional Boolean variable $\mathtt{promoted}[v]$. If v belongs to $V_{\mathtt{index}[v]}$ in the partition, then $\mathtt{promoted}[v] = \mathbf{false}$. Otherwise, if v belongs to $V'_{\mathtt{index}[v]}$, then $\mathtt{promoted}[v] = \mathbf{true}$. Initially, each $j \in \{\Delta+1, \Delta+2, \ldots, k_\alpha-1, k_\alpha\}$ is set to *light*.

We wish that all vertices v obey the invariant that there be no $j > \mathtt{index}[v]$ such that the number of neighbors u of v with $\mathtt{index}[u] \leq j$ is at least α^{j-1}. Furthermore, we require that for v with $\mathtt{promoted}[v] = \mathbf{false}$ and $\mathtt{index}[v] > \Delta$, the number of neighbors u with $\mathtt{index}[u] \leq \mathtt{index}[v]$ be greater than $\alpha^{\mathtt{index}[v]-2}$. Note that the difference from the previous data structures is that some vertices, namely those with $\mathtt{promoted}[v] = \mathbf{true}$, do not obey the second invariant.

As before, some vertices will be marked as dirty in the course of the execution of the algorithm. When an edge is removed or added, we mark its endpoints as dirty and update its structures. Then our algorithm considers consecutive j starting with k_α and goes down to $\Delta+1$. For a given $i > \Delta$:

1. The algorithm checks if there are dirty vertices v with $\mathtt{index}[v] < i$ such that the number of neighbors u with $\mathtt{index}[u] \leq i$ is at least α^{i-1}. Those vertices have $\mathtt{index}[v]$ set to i, and the algorithms updates structures $\mathtt{below}[v,\cdot]$, $\mathtt{lower\text{-}neighbors}[v]$, and $\mathtt{neighbors}[v,\cdot]$ for them and for their neighbors u with $\mathtt{index}[u] \leq i$ accordingly, as we did for the deterministic data structures. Furthermore, if there are vertices v with $\mathtt{index}[v] = i$ and $\mathtt{promoted}[v] = \mathbf{true}$ with the same property of the number of neighbors, the algorithm sets $\mathtt{promoted}[v] = \mathbf{false}$ for them. Finally, if there are vertices v with $\mathtt{index}[v] = i$, $\mathtt{promoted}[v] = \mathbf{false}$, and the number of neighbors u with $\mathtt{index}[u] \leq i$ is at most α^{i-2}, the algorithm sets $\mathtt{index}[v] = i-1$ and updates all the structures accordingly, also marking specific neighbors as dirty whenever necessary.

2. **If i is heavy:**

   The algorithm checks if the old matching is large enough, and if not, the algorithm deletes it, and computes a new matching. More specifically, if it is no longer the case that $|M_i| \geq |V_i \cup V_i'|/C_1$, the algorithm goes over all v with $\mathtt{index}[v] = i$ and $\mathtt{promoted}[v] = \mathbf{true}$. For each such v, we set $\mathtt{promoted}[v]$ to $\mathbf{false}$. Moreover, for those v with the number of neighbors u with $\mathtt{index}[u] \leq i$ at most α^{i-2}, we set $\mathtt{index}[v] = i-1$ and mark them as dirty.

If now $|E_i|$ is at most $C_T \cdot \alpha^i$, we make i light. Otherwise, we use the procedure of Lemma 5 to select a new matching M_i. We set V_i' to the set of vertices matched by M_i that do not belong to V_i. As long as $|M_i| < \frac{9}{10}|E_i|/(C_2\alpha^i)$, we keep repeating the procedure of Lemma 5 until we succeed. For well chosen constants, $\frac{9}{10}|E_i|/(C_2\alpha^i) \geq |V_i \cup V_i'|/C_1$, since $C_1 \gg C_2$. Finally, for endpoints v of edges in the new M_i that have `index`$[v] < i$, we set `index`$[v] = i$ and `promoted`$[v] =$ **true**, and update all the structures for them and their neighbors accordingly, marking some of them as dirty.

3. **If i is light:**

   If $|E_i| > C_T \cdot \alpha^i$, we make i heavy and construct M_i in the same way as for heavy i.

   Otherwise, if $|E_i| \leq C_T \cdot \alpha^i$, and we do nothing.

4.5 Complexity Analysis

We use almost the same potential functions for vertices as before. The only difference is that we multiply all potentials by a constant factor so that when an edge is inserted into some set E_i or removed from it, we can pass one unit of potential to a special fund. We will use this fund to pay for the cost of recomputing matchings M_i. We will show that with large probability the fund deficit is small.

Whenever the data structure artificially moves a vertex v, creating or destroying some V_i', one has to cover the cost associated with changing `index`$[v]$. In the deterministic data structure the cost of moving vertices around was covered by the collected potential. Here, we have to find another source of funding.

Suppose that we want to create a matching M_i for a heavy i. We run the algorithm of Lemma 5, charging its running time to the fund. If M_i is sufficiently large, we spend $O(|V_i|\alpha^i)$ units of potential from the fund on moving vertices in V' from other buckets (where the constant hidden in the big O notation is very small). Later, moving vertices in V' back to their buckets will cost approximately the same, so we can assume that we charge this cost to the fund in advance. If M_i that has been generated is too small and the data structure has to rerun the process generating M_i, we say that we *lose*.

The matching M_i is relatively large compared to $|V_i \cup V_i'|$ right after we create it. The matching requires recomputation if it becomes relatively small compared to $|V_i \cup V_i'|$. For this to happen, at least one of the following two must be the case:

- A constant fraction of edges in M_i have been removed from E_i.
- The number of vertices in V_i must have grown by a constant factor.

Consider first the latter case. Since each new vertex in V_i contributes to the special fund at least α^{i-1} units of potential, it is easy to set constants so that we can afford to pay for moving vertices in V_i' (if their number is sufficiently small, which is the case if C_2 is large) and for the initial execution of the algorithm of Lemma 5, which requires only $\Theta(|V_i|\alpha^i)$ units of potential. We can also set the constants in the data structure such that in fact, we are left with a surplus of potential. We make sure that we collect a lot of potential. We say that we *win* in this case.

The former case requires probabilistic analysis, which we now describe. Recall that a well chosen M_i is at least a 4/5-fraction of a subset E' of edges E_i. Therefore, to delete at least half the edges of the initial M_i, one has to delete at least a 2/5-fraction of E'. We claim that with probability at least 3/4, one has to delete at least a 1/100-fraction of E_i in order to delete a 2/5-fraction of E'. We now sketch a proof of this claim.

> Suppose to the contrary that one can delete at least a 2/5-fraction of E' by deleting at most a 1/100-fraction of E_i with some probability greater than 1/4. Then, given how E' is selected in Lemma 5, one can delete at least $|E_i|/(5C_2\alpha^i)$ edges of E'' with probability at least $1/4 - 1/100$ (for well chosen constants) by selecting a subset of E_i of size $|E_i|/100$, where E'' is created by independently selecting each edge of E_i with probability $1/(C_2\alpha^i)$. Expressing the last sentence in a slightly different way, the sum of $|E_i|/100$ independent variables X_j is at least $|E_i|/(5C_2\alpha^i)$ with probability at least 24/100, where each X_j is 1 with probability $1/(C_2\alpha^i)$, and 0, otherwise. Using the Chernoff bound, one can show that this is not the case for well chosen constants.

The claim implies that with probability at least 3/4, we collect a lot of potential before a large fraction of M_i gets deleted, and also in this case, we say that we *win*. Otherwise, when the edges are deleted very quickly, we say that we *lose*.

Summarizing, we win with probability at least 2/3, in which case we collect a lot of potential (a large constant times the invested potential), which goes to the fund. We lose with probability at most 1/3, and in this case, the operation is paid by the fund. Consider a logarithmic number of ranges $[2^j, 2^{j+1})$ corresponding to different sizes of $|E_i|$ that may appear in the data structure. For a given range, we can assume that whenever we play, we lose at most $C \cdot 2^j$, for some constant C, and we win at least $10 \cdot C \cdot 2^j$. We initially provide the fund with enough potential to pay for the first $t_\star \stackrel{\text{def}}{=} C' \cdot \log \frac{\log n}{\delta}$ times we play the game, for every j of interest, where C' is a sufficiently large constant. Then, the probability that we ever spend more than we gain for a given j is bounded by $\frac{\delta}{2\log n}$. To prove this, it suffices to give an upper bound p_t on the probability that we spend more than win in t games. Using the Chernoff bound, one can show p_t's such that $p_{t+1} \leq p_t \cdot c$, for $t \geq t_\star$, where c is a constant in $(0,1)$. Using the Chernoff bound again, one can show that if C' is sufficiently large, $p_{t_\star} \leq (1-C)\frac{\delta}{2\log n}$, and $\sum_{t=t_\star}^{\infty} p_t \leq \frac{\delta}{2\log n}$. So by the union bound, the probability that we ever spend more than we gain for any j is bounded by δ.

Recall that K is the total number of graph operations, which gives a bound on the maximum size of E_i that can appear. The above analysis implies that for every j such that $2^j \leq n^2$ and $K \geq 2^j$, we can subsidize the fund with $O(2^j \cdot \log \frac{\log n}{\delta})$ units of potential to make sure that with probability $1 - \delta$, the fund's balance is always non-negative. In total, the aid for the fund is bounded by $O(\min\{K, n^2\} \cdot \log \frac{\log n}{\delta})$. Therefore, the total potential $\mathcal{P}$ spent by the algorithm can be bounded by

$$\begin{aligned}\mathcal{P} &= O\left(\min\{K, n^2\} \cdot \log \frac{\log n}{\delta} + K \cdot \log n\right) \\ &= O\left(\min\{K, n^2\} \cdot \log \frac{1}{\delta} + K \cdot \log n\right)\end{aligned}$$

with probability $1-\delta$. Recall that each unit of potential corresponds to $O(\log n)$ computation. Other operations, which include computing M_{light} and combining the three matchings, do not take more than $O(\log^2 n)$ time per update to the graph. Summarizing, we prove the following claim.

COROLLARY 6. *For any sequence of K updates, the randomized data structure runs in*

$$O\left(\min\{K, n^2\} \cdot \log n \cdot \log \frac{1}{\delta} + K \cdot \log^2 n\right)$$

time with probability $1 - \delta$, where $\delta \in (0, 1)$.

5. OPEN PROBLEMS

The two main questions left open by our paper are:

- Our approximation factors are large constants. How small can they be made with polylogarithmic update time? Can they be made 2? Can the approximation constant be made smaller than 2 for maximum matching?
- Is there a *deterministic* data structure that achieves a constant approximation factor with polylogarithmic update time?

6. REFERENCES

[1] T. H. Cormen, C. E. Leiserson, R. L. Rivest, and C. Stein. *Introduction to Algorithms, Second Edition.* The MIT Press and McGraw-Hill Book Company, 2001.

[2] D. Eppstein, Z. Galil, and G. F. Italiano. *Dynamic graph algorithms.* CRC Press, 1997.

[3] D. Eppstein, Z. Galil, G. F. Italiano, and A. Nissenzweig. Sparsification—a technique for speeding up dynamic graph algorithms. *J. ACM*, 44(5):669–696, 1997.

[4] L. Epstein, A. Levin, J. Mestre, and D. Segev. Improved approximation guarantees for weighted matching in the semi-streaming model. In *STACS*, 2010.

[5] J. Feigenbaum, S. Kannan, A. McGregor, S. Suri, and J. Zhang. On graph problems in a semi-streaming model. *Theor. Comput. Sci.*, 348(2-3):207–216, 2005.

[6] M. R. Henzinger and V. King. Randomized fully dynamic graph algorithms with polylogarithmic time per operation. *J. ACM*, 46(4):502–516, 1999.

[7] Z. Ivković and E. L. Lloyd. Fully dynamic maintenance of vertex cover. In *WG*, pages 99–111, 1993.

[8] P. N. Klein and S. Subramanian. A fully dynamic approximation scheme for shortest paths in planar graphs. *Algorithmica*, 22(3):235–249, 1998.

[9] Z. Lotker, B. Patt-Shamir, and A. Rosén. Distributed approximate matching. In *PODC*, pages 167–174, 2007.

[10] A. McGregor. Finding graph matchings in data streams. In *APPROX-RANDOM*, pages 170–181, 2005.

[11] S. Micali and V. V. Vazirani. An $O(\sqrt{|V|} \cdot |E|)$ algorithm for finding maximum matching in general graphs. In *FOCS*, pages 17–27, 1980.

[12] M. Parnas and D. Ron. Approximating the minimum vertex cover in sublinear time and a connection to distributed algorithms. *Theor. Comput. Sci.*, 381(1-3):183–196, 2007.

[13] P. Sankowski. Faster dynamic matchings and vertex connectivity. In *SODA*, pages 118–126, 2007.

[14] M. Thorup. Fully-dynamic min-cut. In *STOC*, pages 224–230, 2001.

[15] M. Thorup. Worst-case update times for fully-dynamic all-pairs shortest paths. In *STOC*, pages 112–119, 2005.

[16] M. Zelke. Weighted matching in the semi-streaming model. In *STACS*, pages 669–680, 2008.

Connectivity Oracles for Failure Prone Graphs*

Ran Duan
University of Michigan
duanran@umich.edu

Seth Pettie
University of Michigan
pettie@umich.edu

ABSTRACT

Dynamic graph connectivity algorithms have been studied for many years, but typically in the most general possible setting, where the graph can evolve in completely arbitrary ways. In this paper we consider a *dynamic subgraph* model. We assume there is some fixed, underlying graph that can be preprocessed ahead of time. The graph is subject only to vertices and edges flipping "off" (failing) and "on" (recovering), where queries naturally apply to the subgraph on edges/vertices currently flipped on. This model fits most real world scenarios, where the topology of the graph in question (say a router network or road network) is constantly evolving due to temporary failures but never deviates too far from the ideal failure-free state.

We present the first efficient *connectivity oracle* for graphs susceptible to vertex failures. Given vertices u and v and a set D of d failed vertices, we can determine if there is a path from u to v avoiding D in time polynomial in $d \log n$. There is a tradeoff in our oracle between the space, which is roughly mn^{ϵ}, for $0 < \epsilon \leq 1$, and the polynomial query time, which depends on ϵ. If one wanted to achieve the same functionality with existing data structures (based on edge failures or twin vertex failures) the resulting connectivity oracle would either need exorbitant space ($\Omega(n^d)$) or update time $\Omega(dn)$, that is, linear in the number of vertices. Our connectivity oracle is therefore the first of its kind.

As a byproduct of our oracle for vertex failures we reduce the problem of constructing an *edge*-failure oracle to 2D range searching over the integers. We show there is an $\tilde{O}(m)$-space oracle that processes any set of d failed edges in $O(d^2 \log\log n)$ time and, thereafter, answers connectivity queries in $O(\log\log n)$ time. Our update time is exponentially faster than a recent connectivity oracle of Pătraşcu and Thorup for bounded d, but slower as a function of d.

*This work is supported by NSF CAREER grant no. CCF-0746673 and a grant from the US-Israel Binational Science Foundation.

STOC'10, June 5–8, 2010, Cambridge, Massachusetts, USA

Categories and Subject Descriptors

G.2.2 [**Graph Theory**]: Graph algorithms

General Terms

Algorithms, Theory

Keywords

Connectivity

1. INTRODUCTION

Real world graphs and networks are vulnerable objects subject to unexpected node and link failures, fluctuations in congestion, and occasional augmentations of nodes and links. In the midst of such dynamism we would like to maintain as much information about the *current* network as possible and be able to perform basic tasks, for example, finding the (approximate) distance between two vertices, determining whether two vertices are simply connected (or k-vertex/edge connected) and to produce a shortest or nearly shortest path between two vertices if they are connected. Dynamic connectivity and shortest path problems have been studied since the late 1960s. However, decades of research on the subject focused on what is arguably an *un*naturally general model of a dynamic graph, namely, one subject to *completely arbitrary* insertions and deletions of nodes and links. In this paper we start from the assumption that there is some fixed underlying graph and that updates consist solely of flipping vertices and edges *on* or *off*, possibly with a restriction on the number of vertices flipped off at any time. In contrast to the general model of dynamic graphs, we will refer to this as the *dynamic subgraph* model. This model gives one the freedom to preprocess the underlying graph in order to facilitate more efficient updates and queries.

Our main result is a new, space efficient data structure that can quickly answer connectivity queries after recovering from d *vertex failures.* The recovery time is polynomial in d and $\log n$ but otherwise independent of the size of the graph. After processing the failed vertices, connectivity queries are answered in $O(d)$ time. The space used by the data structure is roughly mn^{ϵ}, for any fixed $\epsilon > 0$, where ϵ only affects the polynomial in the recovery time. The exact tradeoffs are given in Theorem 1.1. Our data structure is the first of its type. To achieve comparable query times using existing data structures we would need either $\Omega(n^d)$ space [11] or $\Omega(dn)$ recovery time [17].

Technical Challenges.

The obvious distinction between vertex failures and edge failures is proportionality: just a handful of d vertex failures can have huge impact on the graph connectivity that is completely divorced from d, whereas d edge failures have an effect proportional to d. In the happiest scenario the graph has constant degree and we can simply simulate vertex failures (with $O(1)$ slowdown) using Pătraşcu and Thorup's data structure [17] that processes a batch of edge deletions in $\tilde{O}(1)$ time per edge and answers connectivity queries in $\tilde{O}(1)$ time. Given this trivial observation, a natural (but doomed) way to attack the vertex-failure problem is to find a *sparse surrogate* of the graph that behaves like the input graph (in terms of connectivity) when there are at most d vertex failures, and that has low degree, say polynomial in d. It is easy to see that such sparse surrogates do not exist in general. However, in designing our data structure we *do* achieve something comparable, the details of which we will attempt to sketch.

The first component of our overall data structure is one that, given a spanning tree T, will recover from d vertex failures in time polynomial in the degrees of the failed vertices *in* T, but independent of their degrees in the overall graph. In other words, the *relevant degree* of a vertex can be much smaller than its actual degree and all but the relevant edges incident to a vertex can be deleted implicitly. (Our structure is essentially a reduction from a special subgraph connectivity problem to a 2D range reporting problem.)

The second component of our data structure is a redundant representation of the graph, parameterized by d, the maximum number of failures, and a degree threshold s, with the following properties: (1) there are roughly $n^{\log_{s/d} d}$ different representations of the graph such that (2) for any set of at most d vertex failures, in at least *one* of the graph representations, the *relevant* degree of each failed vertex is at most s, and (3) given the failed vertices, the correct graph representation can be selected in time polynomial in d. In other words, the redundant graph representation effectively sparsifies the graph, assuming that we only want to model the effect of d vertex failures. The space for each graph representation in (1) is roughly linear. If we select $s = d^{1+c}$, for $c \geq 1$, then the overall space for the data structure is roughly $mn^{1/c}$ and the time to recover from vertex failures is polynomial in d and s, i.e., polynomial in d. Notice that increasing c drives the space arbitrarily close to linear and increases the recovery time. Theorem 1.1 gives a precise statement of the capabilities and time-space tradeoffs of our structure:

THEOREM 1.1. *Let $G = (V, E)$ be a graph with m edges and n vertices and let $c \geq 1$ be an integer. A data structure with size $S = O(d^{1-2/c} mn^{1/c-1/(c\log(2d))} \log^2 n)$ can be constructed in $\tilde{O}(S)$ time that supports the following operations. Given a set D of at most d failed vertices, D can be processed in $O(d^{2c+4} \log^2 n \log\log n)$ time so that connectivity queries w.r.t. the graph induced by $V \backslash D$ can be answered in $O(d)$ time.*

To guarantee that the processing time is polynomial in $|D|$ rather than the upper bound d we simply build a version of the structure for $d = 2, 4, 8, \ldots$. Note that for $c \in \{1, 2\}$ the size of the structures is stable or geometrically decreasing with d and the overall space[1] is $\tilde{O}(mn^{1/c})$.

Prior Work on Subgraph Connectivity.

It is rather astonishing that dynamic *subgraph* connectivity problems—in which vertices and edges are flipped on and off—have been largely ignored until very recently [6, 7, 9, 11, 10, 5, 17, 13]. The premises of this graph model were laid out by Frigioni and Italiano [13] in 2000, who showed that in undirected planar graphs, flipping vertices and answering connectivity queries could all be performed in $O(\log^3 n)$ amortized time. Chan, Pătraşcu, and Roditty [6, 7] considered the same problem on general undirected graphs and showed that vertex flips can be supported in $\tilde{O}(m^{2/3})$ amortized time while answering connectivity queries in $\tilde{O}(m^{1/3})$ time. Pătraşcu and Thorup [17] gave a data structure that could process any d edge deletions in $O(d \log^2 n \log\log n)$ time and thereafter answer connectivity queries in $O(\log\log n)$ time. One downside of this data structure is its *exponential* construction time, due to the need to compute sparsest cuts. If one uses $O(\sqrt{\log n})$-approximate sparsest cuts [3, 2, 20], their construction time becomes polynomial and the deletion time becomes $O(d \log^{2.5} n \log\log n)$.

Demetrescu et al. [9] (see also [5]) considered the problem of answering *distance* queries in directed graphs in the absence of precisely one vertex or edge failure. They gave an $\tilde{O}(n^2)$-space structure that answered such queries in $O(1)$ time. This was later improved by Duan and Pettie [11], who showed that distance queries avoiding two edge/vertex failures could be answered in $O(\log n)$ time with a $\tilde{O}(n^2)$-space structure. No non-trivial results are known for three or more failures. For a survey of recent *fully* dynamic graph algorithms (i.e., not dynamic subgraph algorithms), refer to [15, 18, 22, 19, 8, 21].

Overview.

In Section 2 we present the *Euler tour structure*, which plays a key role in our vertex-failure oracle and can be used independently as an edge-failure oracle. In Sections 3 and 4 we define and analyze the redundant graph representation (called the *high degree hierarchy*) mentioned earlier. In Section 5 we provide algorithms to recover from vertex failures and answer connectivity queries.

2. THE EULER TOUR STRUCTURE

In this section we describe the *ET-structure* for handling connectivity queries avoiding multiple vertex and edge failures. When handling only d edge failures, the performance of the ET-structure is incomparable to that of Pătraşcu and Thorup [17] in nearly every respect.[2] The strength of the

[1] Also note that for moderate values of d the total space is $o(mn^{1/c})$, for any c. Specifically, for $d \ll 2^{\sqrt{(\log n)/c}}$ the factor $d^{1-2/c} n^{-1/(c\log(2d))} \log^2 n$ is $o(1)$. It is never worthwhile making $d > m^{1/(2c+4)}$ since we can trivially answer connectivity queries in $O(1)$ time after $O(m)$ preprocessing, so the maximum space is $\tilde{O}(m^{1+\frac{c-2}{c(2c+4)}} n^{1/c})$, which is always $o(mn^{2/c})$ since $m < n^2$.

[2] The ET-structure is significantly faster in terms of construction time (near-linear vs. a large polynomial or exponential time) though it uses slightly more space: $O(m \log^{\epsilon} n)$ vs. $O(m)$. It handles d edge deletions exponentially

ET-structure is that if the graph can be covered by a low-degree tree T, the time to delete a *vertex* is a function of its degree in T; incident edges not in T are deleted implicitly. We prove Theorem 2.1 in the remainder of this section.

THEOREM 2.1. *Let $G = (V, E)$ be a graph, with $m = |E|$ and $n = |V|$, and let $\mathcal{F} = \{T_1, \ldots, T_t\}$ be a set of vertex disjoint trees in G. (Each T_i does not necessarily span a connected component of G.) There is a data structure* $\mathbf{ET}(G, \mathcal{F})$ *occupying space $O(m \log^\epsilon n)$ (for any fixed $\epsilon > 0$) that supports the following operations. Suppose D is a set of failed edges, of which d are tree edges in $\mathcal{F}$ and d' are non-tree edges. Deleting D splits some subset of the trees in $\mathcal{F}$ into at most $2d$ trees $\mathcal{F}' = \{T'_1, \ldots, T'_{2d}\}$. In $O(d^2 \log\log n + d')$ time we can report which pairs of trees in $\mathcal{F}'$ are connected by an edge in $E \backslash D$. In $O(\min\{\log\log n, \log d\})$ time we can determine which tree in $\mathcal{F}'$ contains a given vertex.*

Our data structure uses as a subroutine Alstrup et al.'s data structure [1] for range reporting on the integer grid $[U] \times [U]$. They showed that given a set of N points, there is a data structure with size $O(N \log^\epsilon N)$, where $\epsilon > 0$ is fixed, such that given $x, y, w, z \in [U]$, the set of k points in $[x, y] \times [w, z]$ can be reported in $O(\log\log U + k)$ time. Moreover, the structure can be built in $O(N \log N)$ time.

For a tree T, let $L(T)$ be a list of its vertices encountered during an Euler tour of T (an undirected edge is treated as two directed edges), where we only keep the *first* occurrence of each vertex. One may easily verify that removing f edges from T partitions it into $f + 1$ connected subtrees and splits $L(T)$ into at most $2f + 1$ intervals, where the vertices of a connected subtree are the union of some subset of the intervals. To build $\mathbf{ET}(G = (V, E), \mathcal{F})$ we build the following structure for each pair of trees $(T_1, T_2) \in \mathcal{F} \times \mathcal{F}$; note that T_1 and T_2 may be the same. Let m' be the number of edges connecting T_1 and T_2. Let $L(T_1) = (u_1, \ldots, u_{|T_1|})$, $L(T_2) = (v_1, \ldots, v_{|T_2|})$, and let $U = \max\{|T_1|, |T_2|\}$. We define the point set $P \subseteq [U] \times [U]$ to be $P = \{(i, j) \mid (u_i, v_j) \in E\}$.[3] Suppose D is a set of edge failures including d_1 edges in T_1, d_2 in T_2, and d' non-tree edges. Removing D splits T_1 and T_2 into $d_1 + d_2 + 2$ connected subtrees and partitions $L(T_1)$ into a set $I_1 = \{[x_i, y_i]\}_i$ of $2d_1 + 1$ intervals and $L(T_2)$ into a set $I_2 = \{[w_i, z_i]\}_i$ of $2d_2 + 1$ intervals. For each pair i, j we query the 2D range reporting data structure for points in $[x_i, y_i] \times [w_j, z_j] \cap P$. However, we stop the query the moment it reports some point corresponding to a non-failed edge, i.e., one in $E \backslash D$. Since there are $(2d_1 + 1) \times (2d_2 + 1)$ queries and each failed edge in D can only be reported in *one* such query, the total query time is $O(d_1 d_2 \log\log U + |D|) = O(d_1 d_2 \log\log n + d')$. See Figure 1 for an illustration.

The space for the data structure (restricted to T_1 and T_2) is $O(|T_1| + |T_2| + m' \log^\epsilon n)$. We can assume without loss of generality that $|T_1| + |T_2| < 4m'$,[4] so the space for the ET-structure on T_1 and T_2 is $O(m' \log^\epsilon n)$. Since each non-tree edge only appears in one such structure the overall space for $\mathbf{ET}(G, \mathcal{F})$ is $O(m \log^\epsilon n)$. For the last claim of the Theorem, observe that if a vertex u lies in an original tree $T_1 \in \mathcal{F}$, we can determine which tree in $\mathcal{F}'$ contains it by performing a predecessor search over the left endpoints of intervals in I_1. This can be accomplished in $O(\min\{\log\log n, \log d_1\})$ query time using a van Emde Boas tree [23] or sorted list, whichever is faster.

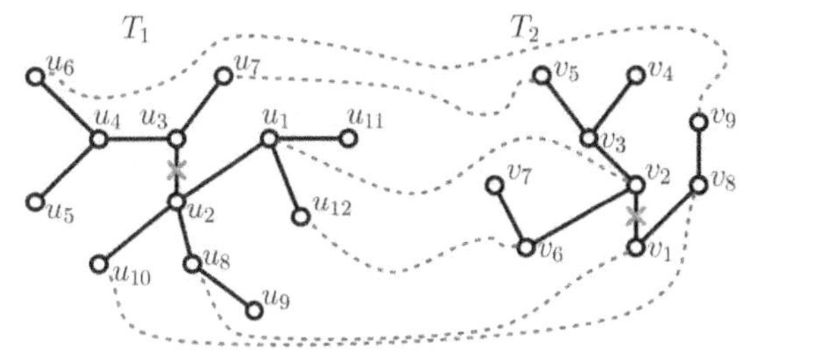

(a)

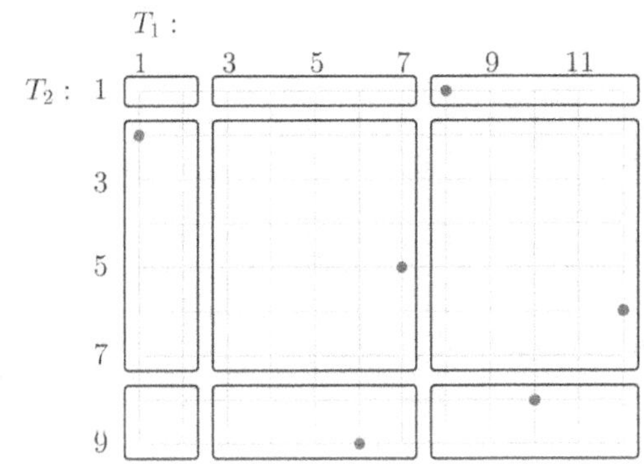

(b)

Figure 1: (a) Dashed edges connect trees T_1 and T_2. The edges (u_2, u_3) and (v_1, v_2) have failed. (b) The point (i, j) is in our point set if (v_i, u_j) is a non-tree edge. The set of 2D range queries are indicated by solid boxes.

Corollary 2.2 demonstrates how $\mathbf{ET}(G, \cdot)$ can be used to answer connectivity queries avoiding edge and vertex failures.

COROLLARY 2.2. *The data structure* $\mathbf{ET}(G, \{T\})$, *where T is a spanning tree of $G = (V, E)$, supports the following operations. Given a set $D \subset E$ of edge failures, D can be processed in $O(|D|^2 \log\log n)$ time so that connectivity queries in the graph $(V, E \backslash D)$ can be answered in $O(\min\{\log\log n, \log |D|\})$ time. If $D \subset V$ is a set of vertex failures, the update time is $O((\sum_{v \in D} \deg_T(v))^2 \log\log n)$ and the query time $O(\min\{\log\log n, \log(\sum_{v \in D} \deg_T(v))\})$. (Note that the update time is independent of $\sum_{v \in D} \deg(v)$.)*

PROOF. Let d be the number of failed edges in T (or edges in T incident to failed vertices). Using $\mathbf{ET}(G, \{T\})$ we split

faster for bounded d ($O(\log\log n)$ vs. $\Omega(\log^2 n \log\log n)$) but is slower as a function of d: $O(d^2 \log\log n)$ vs. $O(d \log^2 n \log\log n)$ time. The query time is the same for both structures, namely $O(\log\log n)$. Whereas the ET-structure naturally maintains a certificate of connectivity (a spanning tree), the Pătraşcu-Thorup structure requires modification and an additional logarithmic factor in the update time to maintain a spanning tree.

[3]The idea of representing the cross-product of trees as 2D point sets has been used in other contexts. See Grossi and Italiano [14].

[4]The idea is simply to remove irrelevant vertices and contract long paths of degree-2 vertices. We leave this as an exercise.

T into $d+1$ subtrees and $L(T)$ into a set I of $2d+1$ connected intervals, in which each connected subtree is made up of some subset of the intervals. Using $O(d^2)$ 2D range queries, in $O(d^2 \log\log n + |D|)$ time we find at most one edge connecting each pair in $I \times I$. In $O(d^2)$ time we find the connected components[5] of $V \backslash D$ and store with each interval a representative vertex from its component. To answer a query (u, v) we only need to determine which subtree u and v are in, which involves two predecessor queries over the left endpoints of intervals in I. This takes $O(\min\{\log\log n, \log d\})$ time. □

It is possible to reduce the query time using more complicated predecessor data structures [4, 12, 16]. However, in our vertex-failure connectivity oracle this cost is not the bottleneck.

3. CONSTRUCTING THE HIGH-DEGREE HIERARCHY

Theorem 2.1 and Corollary 2.2 demonstrate that given a spanning tree T with maximum degree t, we can processes d vertex failures in time roughly $(dt)^2$. However, there is no way to bound t as a function of d. Our solution is to build a *high-degree hierarchy* that represents the graph in a redundant fashion so that given d vertex failures, in some representation of the graph all failed vertices have low (relevant) degree.

3.1 Definitions

Let $\deg_H(v)$ be the degree of v in the graph H and let $\mathrm{Hi}(H) = \{v \in V(H) \mid \deg_H(v) > s\}$ be the set of *high degree* vertices in H, where $s = \Omega(d^2)$ is a fixed parameter of the construction and d is an *upper bound* on the number of vertex failures. Increasing s will increase the update time and decrease the space.

We assign arbitrary distinct weights to the edges of the input graph $G = (V, E)$, which guarantees that every subgraph has a unique minimum spanning forest. Let X and Y be arbitrary subsets of vertices. We define F_X to be the minimum spanning forest of the graph $G \backslash X$. (The notation $G \backslash X$ is short for "the graph induced by $V \backslash X$.") Let $F_X(Y)$ be the subforest of F_X that preserves the connectivity of $Y \backslash X$, i.e., an edge appears in $F_X(Y)$ if it is on the path in F_X between two vertices in $Y \backslash X$. If X is omitted it is $\emptyset$. Note that $F_X(Y)$ may contain branching vertices that are not in $Y \backslash X$.

LEMMA 3.1. *For sets* X, Y, $|\mathrm{Hi}(F_X(Y))| \le \lfloor \frac{|Y \backslash X| - 2}{s-1} \rfloor$.

PROOF. Note that all leaves of $F_X(Y)$ belong to $Y \backslash X$. We prove by induction that the maximum number of vertices with degree at least $s+1$ (the threshold for being high degree) in a tree with l leaves is precisely $\lfloor (l-2)/(s-1) \rfloor$. This upper bound holds whenever there is one internal vertex, and is clearly tight when $l \le s+1$. Given a tree with $l > s+1$ leaves and at least two internal vertices, select an internal vertex v adjacent to exactly one internal vertex and a maximum number of leaves. If v is incident to fewer than s leaves it can be spliced out without decreasing the number of high-degree vertices, so assume the number of incident leaves is at least s. Trimming the adjacent leaves of v leaves a tree with a net loss of $s-1$ leaves and 1 high degree vertex. The claim then follows from the inductive hypothesis. □

[5]This involves performing a depth first search of the graph whose vertices correspond to intervals in I.

3.2 The Hierarchy Tree and Its Properties

Definition 3.2 describes the hierarchy tree, and in fact shows that it is constructible in roughly linear time per hierarchy node. See Figure 2 for a diagram.

DEFINITION 3.2. *The* hierarchy tree *is a rooted tree that is uniquely determined by the graph* $G = (V, E)$, *its artificial edge weights, and the parameters* d *and* s. *Nodes in the tree are identified with subsets of* V. *The root is* V *and every internal node has precisely* d *children. A (not necessarily spanning) forest of* G *is associated with each node and each edge in the hierarchy tree. The tree is constructed as follows:*

1. *Let* W *be a node with parent* $p(W) = U$. *We associate the forest* $F(U)$ *with* U *and* $F_W(U)$ *with the edge* (U, W).
2. *Let* U *be a node. If* $F(U)$ *has no high degree vertices then* U *is a leaf; otherwise it has children* $W_1, \ldots, W_d$ *defined as follows. (Here* subtree(X) *is the set of descendants of* X *in the hierarchy, including* X.*)*

$$W_1 = \mathrm{Hi}(F(U))$$

$$W_i = W_{i-1} \cup \left[U \cap \left(\bigcup_{\substack{W' \in \mathrm{subtree}(W_{i-1}) \\ U' = p(W')}} \mathrm{Hi}(F_{W'}(U')) \right) \right]$$

In other words, W_i *inherits all the vertices from* W_{i-1} *and adds all vertices that are both in* U *and high-degree in some forest associated with an edge* (W', U'), *where* W' *is a descendant of* W_{i-1}. *Note that this includes the forest* $F_{W_{i-1}}(U)$.

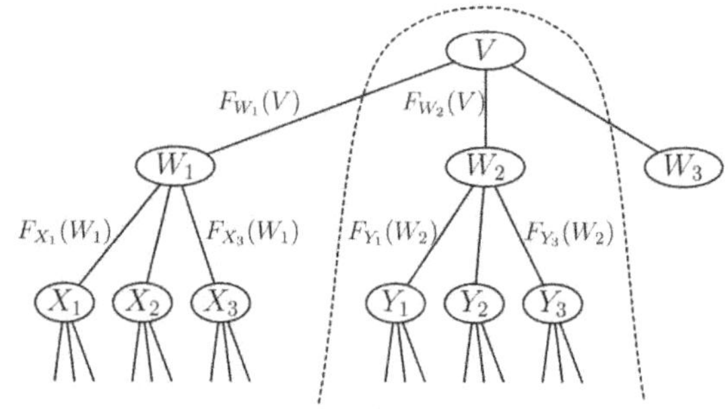

Figure 2: After W_1, W_2 and all their descendants have been constructed we construct W_3 as follows. Include all members of W_2 in W_3. Second, look at *all* hierarchy edges (X', U') where X' is in W_2's subtree and U' is the parent of X' (i.e., all edges under the dashed curve), and include all the high degree vertices in $F_{X'}(U')$ in W_3. In this example W_3 includes $\mathrm{Hi}(F_{W_2}(V)), \mathrm{Hi}(F_{Y_1}(W_2)), \mathrm{Hi}(F_{Y_2}(W_2))$, and so on.

It is regretful that Definition 3.2(2) is so stubbornly unintuitive. We do not have a clean justification for it, except that it guarantees all the properties we require of the hierarchy: that it is small, shallow, and effectively represents the

```
1. U_0 ← V
2. For i from 1 to ∞ : {
3.     If U_{i-1} is a leaf set p ← i − 1 and HALT. (I.e., U_{i-1} = U_p is the last node on the path.)
4.     Let W_1, ..., W_d be the children of U_{i-1} and artificially define W_0 = ∅ and W_{d+1} = W_d.
5.     Let j ∈ [0, d] be minimal such that D ∩ (W_{j+1}\W_j) = ∅.
6.     If j = 0 set p ← i − 1 and HALT. (I.e., U_{i-1} = U_p is the last node on the path.)
7.     Otherwise U_i ← W_j
8. }
```

Figure 3: A procedure for finding a path through the hierarchy, given a set D of failed vertices.

graph in many ways so that given d vertex failures, failed vertices have low degree in some graph representation. After establishing Lemmas 3.3–3.5, Definition 3.2(2) does not play any further role in the data structure whatsoever. Proofs of Lemmas 3.3 and 3.4 appear in the appendix.

LEMMA 3.3. **(Containment of Hierarchy Nodes)** *Let U be a node in the hierarchy tree with children $W_1, \ldots, W_d$. Then $\mathrm{Hi}(F(U)) \subseteq U$ and $W_1 \subseteq \cdots \subseteq W_d \subseteq U$.*

LEMMA 3.4. **(Hierarchy Size and Depth)** *Consider the hierarchy tree constructed with high-degree threshold $s = (2d)^{c+1} + 1$, for some integer $c \geq 1$. Then:*

1. *The depth of the hierarchy is at most*

$$k = \lceil \log_{(s-1)/2d} n \rceil \leq \lceil (\log n)/(c \log(2d)) \rceil.$$

2. *The number of nodes in the hierarchy is on the order of $d^{-2/c} n^{1/c - 1/(c \log 2d)}$.*

For the remainder of the paper the variable k is fixed, as defined above. Aside from bounds on its size and depth, the only other property we require from the hierarchy tree is that, for any set of d vertex failures, all failures have low degree in forests along *some* path in the hierarchy. More formally:

LEMMA 3.5. *For any set D of at most d failed vertices, there exists a path $V = U_0, U_1, \ldots, U_p$ in the hierarchy tree such that all vertices in D have low degree in the forests $F_{U_1}(U_0), \ldots, F_{U_p}(U_{p-1}), F(U_p)$. Furthermore, this path can be found in $O(d(p+1)) = O(dk)$ time.*

PROOF. We construct the path $V = U_0, U_1, \ldots$ one node at a time using the procedure in Figure 3. First let us note that in Line 5 there always exists such a j, since we defined the artificial set $W_{d+1} = W_d$, and that this procedure eventually halts since the hierarchy tree is finite. If, during the construction of the hierarchy, we record for each $v \in U_{i-1}$ the *first* child of U_{i-1} in which v appears, Line 5 can easily be implemented in $O(d)$ time, for a total of $O((p+1)d) = O(dk)$ time.

Define $D_i = D \cap U_i$. It follows from Lemma 3.3 that $U_0 \supseteq \cdots \supseteq U_p$ and therefore that $D = D_0 \supseteq \cdots \supseteq D_p$. In the remainder of the proof we will show that:

(A) When the procedure halts, in Line 3 or 6, D is disjoint from $\mathrm{Hi}(F(U_p))$.

(B) For each $i \in [1, p]$ and $i' \in [i, p]$, $D_{i-1} \backslash D_i$ is disjoint from $\mathrm{Hi}(F_{U_{i'}}(U_{i'-1}))$.

Regarding (B), notice that for $i' \in [1, i)$, $D_{i-1} \backslash D_i$ is trivially disjoint from $\mathrm{Hi}(F_{U_{i'}}(U_{i'-1}))$ because vertices in $D_{i-1} \backslash D_i \subseteq U_{i-1} \subseteq U_{i'}$ are specifically excluded from $F_{U_{i'}}(U_{i'-1})$. Thus, the lemma will follow directly from (A) and (B).

Proof of (A) Suppose the procedure halts at Line 3, i.e., $U_{i-1} = U_p$ is a leaf. By Definition 3.2(2), $\mathrm{Hi}(F(U_p)) = \emptyset$ and is trivially disjoint from D. The procedure would halt at Line 6 if $j = 0$, meaning $W_1 \backslash W_0 = W_1$ is disjoint from D, where W_1 is the first child of $U_{i-1} = U_p$. This implies $\mathrm{Hi}(F(U_p))$ is also disjoint from D since $W_1 = \mathrm{Hi}(F(U_p))$ *by definition*.

Proof of (B) Fix an $i \in [1, p]$ and let $W_j = U_i$ be the child of U_{i-1} selected in Line 5. We first argue that if $j = d$ there is nothing to prove, then deal with the case $j \in [1, d-1]$. If $j = d$ that means the d disjoint sets $W_1, W_2 \backslash W_1, \ldots, W_d \backslash W_{d-1}$ each intersect D, implying that $U_i = W_d \supseteq D$ and therefore $D_i = D$. Thus $D_{i-1} \backslash D_i = \emptyset$ is disjoint from any set. Consider now the case when $j < d$, i.e., the node W_{j+1} exists and $W_{j+1} \backslash W_j$ is disjoint from D. By Definition 3.2(2) and the fact that $U_i, \ldots, U_p$ are descendants of $W_j = U_i$, we know that W_{j+1} includes all the high-degree vertices in $F_{U_i}(U_{i-1}), \ldots, F_{U_p}(U_{p-1})$ that are also in U_{i-1}. By definition, $D_{i-1} \backslash D_i$ is contained in U_{i-1} and disjoint from $U_i, \ldots, U_p$, implying that no vertex in $D_{i-1} \backslash D_i$ has high-degree in $F_{U_i}(U_{i-1}), \ldots, F_{U_p}(U_{p-1})$. If one did, it would have been put in W_{j+1} (as dictated by Definition 3.2(2)) and $W_{j+1} \backslash W_j$ would not have been disjoint from D, contradicting the choice of j. □

4. INSIDE THE HIERARCHY TREE

Lemma 3.5 guarantees that for any set D of d vertex failures, there exists a path of hierarchy nodes $V = U_0, \ldots, U_p$ such that all failures have low degree in the forests $F_{U_1}(U_0), \ldots, F_{U_p}(U_{p-1}), F(U_p)$. Using the ET-structure from Section 2 we can delete the failed vertices and reconnect the disconnected trees in $O(d^2 s^2 \log \log n)$ time for each of the $p+1$ levels of forests. This will allow us to quickly answer connectivity queries *within one level*, i.e., whether two vertices are connected in the subgraph induced by $V(F_{U_{i+1}}(U_i)) \backslash D$. However, to correctly answer connectivity queries we must consider paths that traverse many levels.

Our solution, following an idea of Chan et al. [7], is to augment the graph with *artificial* edges that capture the fact that vertices at one level (say in $U_i \backslash U_{i+1}$) are connected by a path whose intermediate vertices come from lower levels, in $V \backslash U_i$. We do not want to add too many artificial edges, for two reasons. First, they take up space, which we want to conserve, and second, after deleting vertices from the graph some artificial edges may become invalid and must be removed, which increases the recovery time. (In other words, an artificial edge (u, v) between $u, v \in U_i \backslash U_{i+1}$ indicates a u-to-v path via $V \backslash U_i$. If $V \backslash U_i$ suffers vertex failures then this path may no longer exist and the edge (u, v) is presumed invalid.) We add artificial edges so that after d vertex failures, we only need to remove a number of artificial edges that is polynomial in d, s, and $\log n$.

4.1 Stocking the Hierarchy Tree

The data structure described in this section (as well as all notation) are for a *fixed* path $V = U_0, \ldots, U_p$ in the hierarchy tree. In other words, for *each* path from the root to a descendant in the hierarchy we build a completely distinct data structure. In order to have a uniform notation for the forests at each level we artificially define $U_{p+1} = \emptyset$, so $F(U_p) = F_{U_{p+1}}(U_p)$. Furthermore, we let $\mathcal{F}$ represent the collection of forests $F_{U_1}(U_0), \ldots, F_{U_{p+1}}(U_p)$, which we construe as having *disjoint* vertex sets. For $i > j$ we say vertices in $U_i \backslash U_{i+1}$ are at a *higher level* than those in $U_j \backslash U_{j+1}$ and say the trees in the forest $F_{U_{i+1}}(U_i)$ are at a higher level than those in $F_{U_{j+1}}(U_j)$. Recall that $F_{U_{i+1}}(U_i)$ is the minimum spanning forest connecting $U_i \setminus U_{i+1}$ in the graph $G \backslash U_{i+1}$ and may contain vertices at lower levels. See Figure 4 in the appendix. We distinguish these two types of vertices:

DEFINITION 4.1. **(Major Vertices)** *Vertices in $F_{U_{i+1}}(U_i)$ that are also in $U_i \setminus U_{i+1}$ are* major. *Let $T(u)$ be the* unique *tree in $\mathcal{F}$ in which u is a major vertex.*

It is not clear that the trees in $\mathcal{F}$ have any coherent organization. Lemma 4.3 shows that they naturally form a hierarchy, with trees in $F_{U_{p+1}}(U_p)$ on top. Below we give the definition of *ancestry* between trees and show each tree has exactly one ancestor at each higher level. See Figure 4 in the appendix for an illustration of Definitions 4.1 and 4.2.

DEFINITION 4.2. **(Ancestry Between Trees)** *Let $0 \leq j \leq i \leq p$ and let T and T' be trees in $F_{U_{j+1}}(U_j)$ and $F_{U_{i+1}}(U_i)$, respectively. Call T' an* ancestor *of T (and T a descendant of T') if T and T' are in the same connected component in the graph $G \backslash U_{i+1}$. Notice that T is both an ancestor and descendant of itself.*

LEMMA 4.3. **(Unique Ancestors)** *For $j \leq i \leq p$, each tree T in $F_{U_{j+1}}(U_j)$ has at most one ancestor in $F_{U_{i+1}}(U_i)$.*

PROOF. Let T_1, T_2 be ancestors of T in $F_{U_{i+1}}(U_i)$, i.e., T_1 and T_2 span connected components in $G \backslash U_{i+1}$. Since they are *both* connected to T in $G \backslash U_{i+1}$ (which contains T since $U_{i+1} \subseteq U_{j+1}$), T_1 and T_2 are connected in $G \backslash U_{i+1}$ and cannot be distinct trees in $F_{U_{i+1}}(U_i)$. □

Observe that the ancestry relation between trees T in $F_{U_{j+1}}(U_j)$ and T' in $F_{U_{i+1}}(U_i)$ is the *reverse* of the ancestry relation between the nodes U_j and U_i in the hierarchy tree. That is, if $j < i$, T' is an ancestor of T but U_j is an ancestor of U_i in the hierarchy tree.

DEFINITION 4.4. **(Descendant Sets)** *The* descendant set *of T is $\Delta(T) = \{v \mid T(v)$ is a descendant of $T\}$. Equivalently, if T is in $F_{U_{i+1}}(U_i)$ then $\Delta(T)$ is the set of vertices in the connected component of $G \backslash U_{i+1}$ containing T.*

Lemma 4.5 is a simple consequence of the definitions of ancestry and descendant set, and one that will justify the way we augment the graph with artificial edges.

LEMMA 4.5. **(Paths and Unique Descendant Sets)** *Consider a path between two vertices u and v and let w be an intermediate vertex (i.e., not u or v) with highest level. Then all intermediate vertices are in $\Delta(T(w))$ and each of $T(u)$ and $T(v)$ is either an ancestor or descendant of $T(w)$.*

PROOF. This follows from the definition of $\Delta(\cdot)$. □

Now that we have notions of ancestry and descendent sets, we are almost ready to describe exactly how we generate artificial edges. Recall that we are dealing with a fixed path $V = U_0, \ldots, U_p$ in the hierarchy tree. We construct a graph H that, among many other edges, includes all forest edges in $\mathcal{F}$. Since we interpret these forests as being on distinct vertex sets, H has at most $(p+1)n$ vertices, n of which are distinguished as major. In addition H includes all original edges of G, that is, for $(u, v) \in E(G)$ there is an edge in $E(H)$ connecting the major copies of u and v. Finally, H includes a collection of artificial edges; for each tree T in $\mathcal{F}$ there are edges that represent connectivity from ancestors of T via paths whose intermediate vertices are in $\Delta(T)$. To define the artificial edges with precision we must introduce some additional concepts. A d-adjacency list is essentially a path that is augmented to be resilient (in terms of connectivity) to up to d vertex failures.

DEFINITION 4.6. **(d-Adjacency List)** *Let $L = (v_1, \ldots, v_r)$ be a list of vertices and $d \geq 1$ be an integer. The* d-adjacency edges *$\Lambda_d(L)$ connect all vertices at distance at most $d+1$ in the list L:*

$$\Lambda_d(L) = \{(v_i, v_j) \mid 1 \leq i < j \leq r \text{ and } j - i \leq d + 1\}$$

Before proceeding we make some simple observations about d-adjacency lists.

LEMMA 4.7. **(Properties of d-Adjacency Lists)** *The following properties hold for any vertex list L:*

1. *$\Lambda_d(L)$ contains fewer than $(d+1)|L|$ edges.*
2. *If a set D of d vertices are removed from L, the subgraph of $\Lambda_d(L)$ induced by $L \backslash D$ remains connected.*
3. *If L is split into lists L_1 and L_2, then we must remove $O(d^2)$ edges from $\Lambda_d(L)$ to obtain $\Lambda_d(L_1)$ and $\Lambda_d(L_2)$.*

PROOF. Part (1) is trivial, as is (2), since each pair of consecutive undeleted vertices is at distance at most $d+1$, and therefore adjacent. Part (3) is also trivial: the number edges connecting any prefix and suffix of L is $O(d^2)$. □

We now have all the terminology necessary to define the graph H.

DEFINITION 4.8. **(The Graph H)** *The edge set of H includes the forests in $\mathcal{F}$, the original edges in G (connecting their major counterparts), and $\bigcup_T C(T)$, where the union is over all trees T in $\mathcal{F}$ and $C(T)$ is constructed as follows:*

- *Let the strict ancestors of T be $T_1, T_2, \ldots, T_q$.*
- *For $1 \leq i \leq q$, let $A(T, T_i)$ be a list of the major vertices in T_i that are incident to some vertex in $\Delta(T)$, ordered according to an Euler tour of T_i. (This is done exactly as in Section 2.) Let $A(T)$ be the concatenation of $A(T, T_1), \ldots, A(T, T_q)$.*
- *Define $C(T)$ to be the edge set $\Lambda_d(A(T))$.*

See Figure 5 in the appendix for an illustration of how $C(T)$ is constructed. Lemma 4.9 exhibits the two salient properties of H: that it encodes useful connectivity information and that it is economical to effectively destroy $C(T)$ when it is no longer valid, often in time sublinear in $|C(T)|$.

LEMMA 4.9. **(Disconnecting $C(T)$)** *Consider a $C(T) \subseteq E(H)$, where T is a tree in $\mathcal{F}$.*

1. *Suppose d vertices fail, none of which are in $\Delta(T)$, and let u and v be major vertices in ancestors of T that are adjacent to at least one vertex in $\Delta(T)$. Then u and v remain connected in the original graph and remain connected in H.*

2. *Suppose the proper ancestors of T are $T_1, \ldots, T_q$ and a total of f edges are removed from these trees, breaking them into subtrees $T'_1, \ldots, T'_{q+f}$. Then at most $O(d^2(q+f))$ edges must be removed from $C(T)$ such that no remaining edge in $C(T)$ connects distinct trees T'_i and T'_j.*

PROOF. For Part (1), the vertices u and v are connected in the original graph because they are each adjacent to vertices in $\Delta(T)$ and, absent any failures, all vertices in $\Delta(T)$ are connected, by definition. By Definition 4.8, u and v appear in $C(T)$ and, by Lemma 4.7, $C(T)$ remains connected after the removal of any d vertices. Turning to Part (2), recall from Definition 4.8 that $A(T)$ was the concatenation of $A(T, T_1), \ldots, A(T, T_q)$ and each $A(T, T_i)$ was ordered according to an Euler tour of T_i. Removing f edges from $T_1, \ldots, T_q$ separates their Euler tours (and, hence, the lists $\{A(T, T_i)\}_i$) into at most $2f + q$ intervals. (This is exactly the same reasoning used in Section 2.) By Lemma 4.7 we need to remove at most $(2f + q - 1) \cdot O(d^2)$ edges from $C(T)$ to guarantee that all remaining edges are internal to one such interval, and therefore internal to one of the trees $T'_1, \ldots, T'_{q+f}$. Note that $C(T)$ is now "logically" deleted since remaining edges internal to some T'_i do not add any connectivity. □

Finally, we associate the ET-structure $\mathbf{ET}(H, \mathcal{F})$ with the path $V = U_0, \ldots, U_p$. Lemma 4.10 bounds the space for the overall data structure.

LEMMA 4.10. **(Space Bounds)** *Given a graph G with m edges, n vertices, and parameters d and $s = (2d)^{c+1} + 1$, where $c \geq 1$, the space for a d-failure connectivity oracle is $O(d^{1-2/c} mn^{1/c - 1/(c \log(2d))} \log^2 n)$.*

PROOF. Recall that $k = \log_{(s-1)/2d} n < \log n$ is the height of the hierarchy. The graph H has at most $(p+1)n \leq kn$ vertices, and, we claim, less than $kn + [(d+1)k + 1]m$ edges. There are less than kn edges in the forests $\mathcal{F}$. Each original edge (u, v) appears in H and causes v to make an appearance in the list $A(T, T(v))$, whenever $u \in \Delta(T)$. There are at most k such lists. Moreover, v's appearance in $A(T, T(v))$ (and hence $A(T)$) contributes at most $d + 1$ edges to $C(T) = \Lambda_d(A(T))$. By Theorem 2.1, each edge in H contributes $O(\log n)$ space in $\mathbf{ET}(H, \mathcal{F})$ for a total of $O((dkm + kn) \log n) = O(dm \log^2 n)$ space for *one* hierarchy node. By Lemma 3.4 there are $d^{-2/c} n^{1/c - 1/(c \log(2d))}$ hierarchy tree nodes, which gives the claimed bound. □

5. RECOVERY FROM FAILURES

In this section we describe how, given up to d failed vertices, the structure can be updated in $O((dsk)^2 \log \log n)$ time such that connectivity queries can be answered in $O(d)$ time. Section 5.1 gives the algorithm to delete failed vertices and Section 5.2 gives the query algorithm.

5.1 Deleting Failed Vertices

Step 1. Given the set D of at most d failed vertices, we begin by identifying a path $V = U_0, \ldots, U_p$ in the hierarchy in which D have low degree in the $p + 1$ levels of forests $F_{U_1}(U_0), \ldots, F_{U_{p+1}}(U_p)$. By Lemma 3.5 this takes $O(d \log n)$ time.

In subsequent steps we delete all failed vertices in each of their appearances in the forests, i.e., up to $p + 1 \leq k$ copies for each failed vertex. Edges remaining in H (between vertices not in D) represent original edges, which are obviously still valid, or edges in $\bigcup_T C(T)$, which might no longer be valid. Recall that $C(T)$ represents connectivity via a path whose intermediate vertices are in the descendant set $\Delta(T)$. If $\Delta(T)$ contains failed vertices then that path may no longer exist, so *all edges* in $C(T)$ become suspect, and are presumed invalid. Although $C(T)$ may contain many edges, Lemma 4.9(2) implies that $C(T)$ can be *logically* destroyed in time polynomial in d and s. Before describing the next steps in detail we need to distinguish affected from unaffected trees.

DEFINITION 5.1. **(Affected Trees)** *If a tree T in $\mathcal{F}$ intersects the set of failed vertices D, T and all ancestors of T are* affected. *Equivalently, T is affected if $\Delta(T)$ contains a failed vertex. If T is affected, the connected subtrees of T induced by $V(T) \backslash D$ (i.e., the subtrees remaining after vertices in D fail) are called* affected subtrees.

LEMMA 5.2. **(The Number of Affected Trees)** *The number of affected trees is at most kd. The number of affected subtrees is at most $kd(s+1)$.*

PROOF. If u is a major vertex in T, u can only appear in ancestors of T. Thus, when u fails it can cause at most k trees to become affected. Since, by choice of U_p, all failed vertices have low degree in the trees in which they appear, at most kds tree edges are deleted, yielding $kd(s+1)$ affected subtrees. □

Step 2. We identify the affected trees in $O(kd)$ time and mark as deleted the tree edges incident to failed vertices in $O(kds)$ time. Deleting $O(kds)$ tree edges effectively splits the Euler tours of the affected trees into $O(kds)$ intervals, where each affected subtree is the union of some subset of the intervals.

Step 3. Recall from the discussion above that if T is an affected tree then $\Delta(T)$ contains failed vertices and the connectivity provided by $C(T)$ is presumed invalid. By Lemma 4.9 we can logically delete $C(T)$ by removing $O(d^2)$ edges for *each* edge removed from an ancestor tree of T i.e., $O(d^2 \cdot kds)$ edges need to be removed to destroy $C(T)$. (All remaining edges from $C(T)$ are internal to some affected subtree and can therefore be ignored; they do not provide additional connectivity.) There are at most dk affected trees T, so at most $O(k^2 d^4 s)$ edges need to be removed from H. Let H' be H with these edges removed.

Step 4. We now attempt to reconnect all affected subtrees using valid edges, i.e., those not deleted in Step 3. Let R be a graph whose vertices $V(R)$ represent the $O(kds)$ affected subtrees such that $(t_1, t_2) \in E(R)$ if t_1 and t_2 are connected by an edge from H'. Using the structure $\mathbf{ET}(H, \mathcal{F})$ (see Section 2, Theorem 2.1), we populate the edge set in time $O(|V(R)|^2 \log \log n + k^2 d^4 s)$, which is $O((dsk)^2 \log \log n)$ since $s > d^2$. In $O(|E(R)|) = O((dsk)^2)$ time we determine the connected components of R and store with each affected subtree a representative vertex of its component.

This concludes the deletion algorithm. The running time is dominated by Step 4.

5.2 Answering a Connectivity Query

The deletion algorithm has already identified the path $U_0, \ldots, U_p$. To answer a connectivity query between u and v we first check to see if there is a path between them that avoids affected trees, then consider paths that intersect one or more affected trees.

Step 1. We find $T(u)$ and $T(v)$ in $O(1)$ time; recall that these are trees in which u and v are major vertices. If $T(u)$ is unaffected, let T_1 be the most ancestral unaffected ancestor of $T(u)$, and let T_2 be defined in the same way for $T(v)$. If $T_1 = T_2$ then $\Delta(T_1)$ contains u and v but no failed vertices; if this is the case we declare u and v *connected* and stop. We can find T_1 and T_2 in $O(\log k) = O(\log \log n)$ time using a binary search over the ancestors of $T(u)$ and $T(v)$, or in $O(\log d)$ time using predecessor search and a level ancestor data structure.

Step 2. We now try to find vertices u' and v' in affected subtrees that are connected to u and v respectively. If $T(u)$ is affected then $u' = u$ clearly suffices, so we only need to consider the case when $T(u)$ is unaffected and T_1 exists. Recall from Definition 4.8 that $A(T_1)$ is the list of major vertices in proper ancestors of T_1 that are adjacent to some vertex in $\Delta(T_1)$. We scan $A(T_1)$ looking for *any* non-failed vertex u' adjacent to $\Delta(T_1)$. Since $\Delta(T_1)$ is unaffected, u is connected to u', and since T_1's parent is affected u' must be in an affected subtree. Since there are at most d failed vertices we must inspect at most $d + 1$ elements of $A(T_1)$. This takes $O(d)$ time to find u' and v', if they exist. If one or both of u' and v' does not exist we declare u and v *disconnected* and stop.

Step 3. Given u' and v', in $O(\min\{\log\log n, \log d\})$ time we find the affected subtrees t_1 and t_2 containing u' and v', respectively. Note that t_1 and t_2 are vertices in R, from Step 4 of the deletion algorithm. We declare u and v to be connected if and only if t_1 and t_2 are in the same connected component of R. This takes $O(1)$ time.

We now turn to the correctness of the query algorithm. If the algorithm replies *connected* in Step 1 or *disconnected* in Step 2 it is clearly correct. (This follows directly from the definitions of $\Delta(T_i)$ and $A(T_i)$, for $i \in \{1, 2\}$.) If u' and v' are discovered then u and v are clearly connected to u' and v', again, by definition of $\Delta(T_i)$ and $A(T_i)$. Thus, we may assume without loss of generality that the query vertices $u = u'$ and $v = v'$ lie in affected subtrees. The correctness of the procedure therefore hinges on whether the graph R correctly represents connectivity between affected subtrees.

LEMMA 5.3. **(Query Algorithm Correctness)** *Let u and v be vertices in affected subtrees t_u and t_v. Then there is a path from u to v avoiding failed vertices if and only if t_u and t_v are connected in R.*

PROOF. Edges in R represent either original graph edges (not incident to failed vertices) or paths whose intermediate vertices lie in some $\Delta(T)$, for an unaffected T. Thus, if there is a path in R from t_u to t_v then there is also a path from u to v avoiding failed vertices. For the reverse direction, let P be a path from u to v in the original graph avoiding failed vertices. If all intermediate vertices in P are from affected subtrees then P clearly corresponds to a path in R, since all inter-affected-tree edges in P are included in H' and eligible to appear in R. For the last case, let $P = (u, \ldots, x, x', \ldots, y', y, \ldots, v)$, where x' is the *first* vertex not in an affected tree and y is the first vertex following x' in an affected tree. That is, the subpath $(x', \ldots, y')$ lies entirely in $\Delta(T)$ for some unaffected tree T, which implies that x and y appear in $A(T)$. By Lemma 4.9, x and y remain connected in $C(T)$ even if d vertices are removed, implying that x and y remain connected in H'. Since all edges from H' are eligible to appear in R, t_x and t_y must be connected in R. Thus, u lies in t_u, which is connected to t_x in R, which is connected to t_y in R. The claim then follows by induction on the (shorter) path from y to v. □

6. CONCLUSION

We presented the first space-efficient data structure for one of the most natural dynamic graph problems: given that a set of vertices has *failed*, is there still a path from point A to point B avoiding all failures? Our connectivity oracle recovers from d vertex failures in time polynomial in d and answers connectivity queries in time linear in d. Are these types of time bounds intrinsic to the problem? Excluding polylogarithmic factors the best we could hope for is $\tilde{O}(m)$ space, $\tilde{O}(d)$ time to process vertex failues and $\tilde{O}(1)$ time for queries.

In addition to our vertex-failure oracle we presented a new edge-failure connectivity oracle that is incomparable to a previous structure of Pătraşcu and Thorup [17] in many ways. We note that it excels when the number of failures is small; for $d = O(1)$ the oracle recovers from failures in $O(\log \log n)$ time and answers connectivity queries in $O(1)$ time.

7. REFERENCES

[1] S. Alstrup, G. S. Brodal, and T. Rauhe. New data structures for orthogonal range searching. In *Proceedings 41st FOCS*, pages 198–207, 2000.

[2] S. Arora, E. Hazan, and S. Kale. $O(\sqrt{\log n})$ approximation to sparsest cut in $\tilde{O}(n^2)$ time. In *Proceedings 45th FOCS*, pages 238–247, 2004.

[3] S. Arora, S. Rao, and U. V. Vazirani. Expander flows, geometric embeddings and graph partitioning. *J. ACM*, 56(2), 2009.

[4] P. Beame and F. E. Fich. Optimal bounds for the predecessor problem and related problems. *J. Comput. Syst. Sci.*, 65(1):38–72, 2002.

[5] A. Bernstein and D. Karger. A nearly optimal oracle for avoiding failed vertices and edges. In *Proceedings 41st STOC*, pages 101–110, 2009.

[6] T. Chan. Dynamic subgraph connectivity with geometric applications. *SIAM J. Comput.*, 36(3):681–694, 2006.

[7] T. M. Chan, M. Pătraşcu, and L. Roditty. Dynamic connectivity: Connecting to networks and geometry. In *Proceedings 49th FOCS*, pages 95–104, 2008.

[8] C. Demetrescu and G. F. Italiano. Mantaining dynamic matrices for fully dynamic transitive closure. *Algorithmica*, 51(4):387–427, 2008.

[9] C. Demetrescu, M. Thorup, R. A. Chowdhury, and V. Ramachandran. Oracles for distances avoiding a failed node or link. *SIAM J. Comput.*, 37(5):1299–1318, 2008.

[10] R. Duan and S. Pettie. Bounded-leg distance and reachability oracles. In *Proceedings 19th ACM-SIAM Symposium on Discrete Algorithms (SODA)*, pages 436–445, 2008.

[11] R. Duan and S. Pettie. Dual-failure distance and connectivity oracles. In *Proceedings 20th ACM-SIAM Symposium on Discrete Algorithms (SODA)*, pages 506–515, 2009.

[12] M. L. Fredman and D. E. Willard. Surpassing the information-theoretic bound with fusion trees. *J. Comput. Syst. Sci.*, 47(3):424–436, 1993.

[13] D Frigioni and G. F. Italiano. Dynamically switching vertices in planar graphs. *Algorithmica*, 28(1):76–103, 2000.

[14] R. Grossi and G. F. Italiano. Efficient splitting and merging algorithms for order decomposable problems. *Information and Computation*, 154(1):1–33, 1999.

[15] J. Holm, K. de Lichtenberg, and M. Thorup. Poly-logarithmic deterministic fully-dynamic algorithms for connectivity, minimum spanning tree, 2-edge, and biconnectivity. *J. ACM*, 48(4):723–760, 2001.

[16] M. Pătraşcu and M. Thorup. Time-space trade-offs for predecessor search. In *Proceedings 38th ACM Symposium on Theory of Computing (STOC)*, pages 232–240, 2006.

[17] M. Pătraşcu and M. Thorup. Planning for fast connectivity updates. In *Proceedings 48th IEEE Symposium on Foundations of Computer Science (FOCS)*, pages 263–271, 2007.

[18] L. Roditty and U. Zwick. A fully dynamic reachability algorithm for directed graphs with an almost linear update time. In *Proceedings 36th ACM Symposium on Theory of Computing (STOC)*, pages 184–191, 2004.

[19] P. Sankowski. Faster dynamic matchings and vertex connectivity. In *Proceedings 8th ACM-SIAM Symposium on Discrete Algorithms (SODA)*, pages 118–126, 2007.

[20] J. Sherman. Breaking the multicommodity flow barrier for $O(\sqrt{\log n})$-approximations to sparsest cut. *CoRR*, abs/0908.1379, 2009.

[21] M. Thorup. Worst-case update times for fully-dynamic all-pairs shortest paths. In *Proceedings 37th ACM Symposium on Theory of Computing (STOC)*, pages 112–119, 2005.

[22] M. Thorup. Fully-dynamic min-cut. *Combinatorica*, 27(1):91–127, 2007.

[23] P. van Emde Boas. Preserving order in a forest in less than logarithmic time. In *Proceedings 39th FOCS*, pages 75–84, 1975.

APPENDIX

A. PROOFS AND FIGURES

Lemma 3.3 Let U be a node in the hierarchy tree with children $W_1, \ldots, W_d$. Then $\mathrm{Hi}(F(U)) \subseteq U$ and $W_1 \subseteq \cdots \subseteq W_d \subseteq U$.

PROOF. The second claim will be established in the course of proving the first claim. We prove the first claim by induction on the preorder (depth first search traversal) of the hierarchy tree. For the root node V, $\mathrm{Hi}(V)$ is trivially a subset of V. Let W_i be a node, U be its parent, and W_1 be U's first child, which may be the same as W_i. Suppose the claim is true for all nodes preceding W_i. If it is the case that $W_i = W_1$, we have that $W_1 = \mathrm{Hi}(F(U))$ (by Definition 3.2(2)) and $\mathrm{Hi}(F(U)) \subseteq U$ (by the inductive hypothesis). Since $F(W_1)$ is a subforest of $F(U)$ (this follows from the fact that for a vertex set Y we select $F(Y)$ to be the *minimum* forest spanning Y), every high degree vertex in $F(W_1)$ also has high degree in $F(U)$, i.e., $\mathrm{Hi}(F(W_1)) \subseteq \mathrm{Hi}(F(U)) = W_1$, which establishes the claim when $W_i = W_1$. Once we know that $W_1 \subseteq U$ it follows from Definition 3.2(2) that $W_1 \subseteq \cdots \subseteq W_d \subseteq U$. By the same reasoning as above, when $W_i \neq W_1$, we have that $W_i \subseteq U$, implying that $F(W_i)$ is a subforest of $F(U)$, which implies that $\mathrm{Hi}(F(W_i)) \subseteq \mathrm{Hi}(F(U)) = W_1 \subseteq W_i$. □

The claims of Lemma 3.4 will follow directly from Parts (1) and (3) of Lemma A.1

LEMMA A.1. *Consider the hierarchy tree constructed with high-degree threshold $s = (2d)^{c+1}+1$, for some integer $c \geq 1$. Let U be a non-root node in the hierarchy tree and $W_1, \ldots, W_d$ be its children, if U is not a leaf. Let $p(X)$ be the parent of X and* subtree(X) *be the set of descendants, including X, in the hierarchy tree. Then:*

1. *For $i \in [1, d]$, $|W_i| \leq 2i|U|/(s-1)$.*
2. *$\sum_{X \in \mathrm{subtree}(U)} |\,\mathrm{Hi}(F_X(p(X)))| \leq 2|p(U)|/(s-1)$.*
3. *The number of nodes in the hierarchy is on the order of $d^{-2/c} n^{1/c - 1/(c\log(2d))}$.*

PROOF. We prove Parts (1) and (2) by induction over the postorder of the hierarchy tree. In the base case U is a leaf, (1) is vacuous and (2) is trivial, since there is one summand, namely $|\,\mathrm{Hi}(F_U(p(U)))|$, which is at most $(|p(U)|-2)/(s-1)$ by Lemma 3.1. For Part (1), in the base case $|W_1| < |U|/(s-1)$. For $i \in [2, d]$ we have:

$$
\begin{aligned}
|W_i| &\leq |W_{i-1}| + \sum_{X \in \mathrm{subtree}(W_{i-1})} |\,\mathrm{Hi}(F_X(p(X)))| \\
&\leq \frac{2(i-1)|U|}{s-1} + \frac{2|U|}{s-1} \qquad \{\text{Ind. hyp. (1) and (2)}\} \\
&= \frac{2i|U|}{s-1}
\end{aligned}
$$

For Part (2) we have:

$$
\begin{aligned}
&\sum_{X \in \mathrm{subtree}(U)} |\,\mathrm{Hi}(F_X(p(X)))| \\
&= |\,\mathrm{Hi}(F_U(p(U)))| + \sum_{i=1}^{d} \sum_{X \in \mathrm{subtree}(W_i)} |\,\mathrm{Hi}(F_X(p(X)))| \\
&\qquad \{\text{Follows from defn. of subtree}\} \\
&< \frac{|p(U)|}{s-1} + \frac{2d|U|}{s-1} \qquad \{\text{Lemma 3.1, Ind. hyp. (2)}\} \\
&\leq \frac{|p(U)|}{s-1} + \frac{2d[2d|p(U)|/(s-1)]}{s-1} \qquad \{\text{Ind. hyp. (1)}\} \\
&\leq \frac{2|p(U)|}{s-1} \qquad \{s \geq 4d^2+1\}
\end{aligned}
$$

We prove Part (3) for a slight modification of the hierarchy tree in which U is forced to be a leaf if $|U| \leq 2ds$. This change has no effect on the running time of the algorithm.[6] Consider the set of intervals $\{B_j\}$ where $B_j = [(2d)^j, (2d)^{j+1})$, and let l_j be the maximum number of leaf descendants of a node U for which $|U| \in B_j$. If $|U| \leq (2d)s$ then U is a leaf, i.e., $l_j = 1$ for $j \leq c+1$. Part (1) implies that if $|U|$ lies in B_j then each child lies in either B_{j-c-1} or B_{j-c}. Hence, $l_j \leq d \cdot l_{j-c}$, and, by induction, $l_j \leq d^{\lfloor (j-2)/c \rfloor}$. Now suppose that n lies in the interval $[(2d)^{cx+2}, (2d)^{(c+1)x+2}) = B_{cx+2} \cup \cdots \cup B_{(c+1)x+1}$. Then the number of leaf descendants of V, the hierarchy tree root, is at most $d^c < n^{1/c} 2^{-x} d^{-2/c} \leq n^{1/c - 1/(c\log(2d))} d^{-2/c}$. □

[6] We only require that in a leaf node U, any set of d failed vertices are incident to a total of $O(ds)$ tree edges from $F(U)$, i.e., that the average degree in $F(U)$ is $O(s)$. We do not require that *every* failed vertex be low degree in $F(U)$.

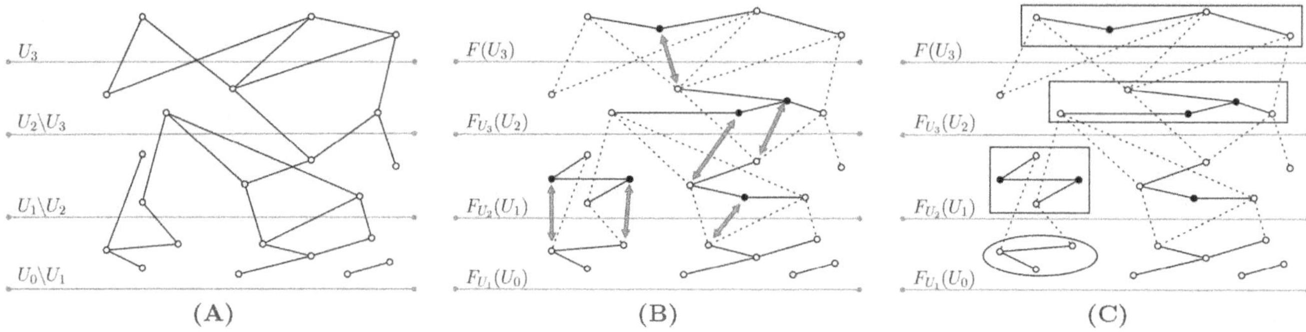

Figure 4: (A) A path $U_0, \ldots, U_3$ in the hierarchy tree (where $V = U_0$ is the root) naturally partitions the vertices into four levels $U_0\backslash U_1, U_1\backslash U_2, U_2\backslash U_3$, and U_3. (B) The forest $F_{U_{i+1}}(U_i)$ may contain "copies" of vertices from lower levels. (Hollow vertices are *major* vertices at their level; solid ones are copies from a lower level. Thick arrows associate a copy with its original major vertex.) (C) A tree T in $F_{U_{j+1}}(U_j)$ is a descendant of T' in $F_{U_{i+1}}(U_i)$ (where $j \leq i$) if T and T' are connected in $G\backslash U_{i+1}$. The tree inscribed in the oval is a descendant of those trees inscribed in rectangles.

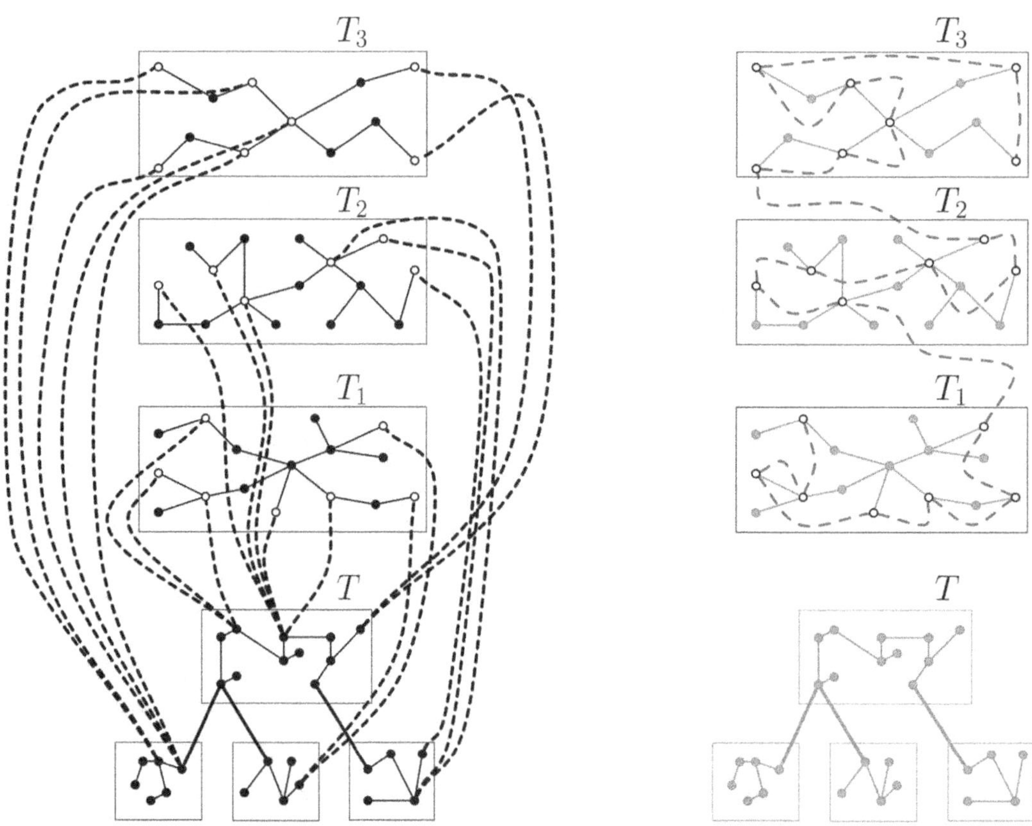

Figure 5: Left: T is a tree in some forest among $F_{U_1}(U_0), \ldots, F_{U_{p+1}}(U_p)$ having three strict descendants and three ancestors T_1, T_2, T_3. Dashed curves indicate edges connecting vertices from $\Delta(T)$ (all vertices in descendants of T) to major vertices in strict ancestors of T, which are drawn as hollow. Right: The set $C(T)$ consists of, first, linking up all hollow vertices in a list that is consistent with Euler tours of T_1, T_2, T_3 (indicated by dashed curves), and second, adding edges between all hollow vertices at distance at most $d+1$ in the list.

Approximate Sparse Recovery: Optimizing Time and Measurements

Anna C. Gilbert*
Department of Mathematics
University of Michigan
annacg@umich.edu

Yi Li†
Department of Electrical Engineering and Computer Science
University of Michigan
leeyi@umich.edu

Ely Porat
Department of Computer Science
Bar-Ilan University
porately@cs.biu.ac.il

Martin J. Strauss‡
Department of Mathematics and the Department of Electrical Engineering and Computer Science
University of Michigan
martinjs@umich.edu

ABSTRACT

A Euclidean *approximate sparse recovery* system consists of parameters k, N, an m-by-N *measurement matrix*, $\mathbf{\Phi}$, and a decoding algorithm, $\mathcal{D}$. Given a vector, $\mathbf{x}$, the system approximates $\mathbf{x}$ by $\widehat{\mathbf{x}} = \mathcal{D}(\mathbf{\Phi x})$, which must satisfy $\|\widehat{\mathbf{x}} - \mathbf{x}\|_2 \le C \|\mathbf{x} - \mathbf{x}_k\|_2$, where $\mathbf{x}_k$ denotes the optimal k-term approximation to $\mathbf{x}$. (The output $\widehat{\mathbf{x}}$ may have more than k terms). For each vector $\mathbf{x}$, the system must succeed with probability at least 3/4. Among the goals in designing such systems are minimizing the number m of measurements and the runtime of the decoding algorithm, $\mathcal{D}$.

In this paper, we give a system with $m = O(k \log(N/k))$ measurements—matching a lower bound, up to a constant factor—and decoding time $k \log^{O(1)} N$, matching a lower bound up to $\log(N)$ factors. We also consider the encode time (*i.e.*, the time to multiply $\mathbf{\Phi}$ by x), the time to update measurements (*i.e.*, the time to multiply $\mathbf{\Phi}$ by a 1-sparse x), and the robustness and stability of the algorithm (adding noise before and after the measurements). Our encode and update times are optimal up to $\log(k)$ factors. The columns of $\mathbf{\Phi}$ have at most $O(\log^2(k)\log(N/k))$ non-zeros, each of which can be found in constant time. Our full result, an FPRAS, is as follows. If $\mathbf{x} = \mathbf{x}_k + \nu_1$, where ν_1 and ν_2 (below) are arbitrary vectors (regarded as noise), then, setting $\widehat{\mathbf{x}} = \mathcal{D}(\Phi\mathbf{x} + \nu_2)$, and for properly normalized $\mathbf{\Phi}$, we get

$$\|\widehat{\mathbf{x}} - \mathbf{x}\|_2^2 \le (1+\epsilon)\|\nu_1\|_2^2 + \epsilon\|\nu_2\|_2^2,$$

using $O((k/\epsilon)\log(N/k))$ measurements and $(k/\epsilon)\log^{O(1)}(N)$ time for decoding.

Categories and Subject Descriptors

G.4 [**Mathematical Software**]: Algorithm design and analysis

General Terms

Algorithms, Theory

Keywords

Approximation, embedding, sketching, sparse approximation, sublinear algorithms

1. INTRODUCTION

Tracking heavy hitters in high-volume, high-speed data streams [4], monitoring changes in data streams [6], designing pooling schemes for biological tests [11] (e.g., high throughput sequencing, testing for genetic markers), localizing sources in sensor networks [17, 16], and combinatorial pattern matching [5] are all quite different technological challenges, yet they can all be expressed in the same mathematical formulation. We have a signal $\mathbf{x}$ of length N that is sparse or highly compressible; i.e., it consists of k significant entries ("heavy hitters") which we denote by $\mathbf{x}_k$ while the rest of the entries are essentially negligible. We wish to acquire a small amount of information (commensurate with the sparsity) about this signal in a linear, non-adaptive fashion and then use that information to quickly recover the significant entries. In a data stream setting, our signal is the distribution of items seen, while in biological group testing, the signal is proportional to the binding affinity of each drug compound (or the expression level of a gene in a particular organism). We want to recover the identities and values only

*Supported in part by DARPA/ONR N66001-08-1-2065.
†Supported in part by NSF CCF 0743372.
‡Supported in part by NSF CCF 0743372 and DARPA/ONR N66001-08-1-2065.

STOC'10, June 5–8, 2010, Cambridge, Massachusetts, USA

of the heavy hitters which we denote by $\mathbf{x}_k$, as the rest of the signal is not of interest. Mathematically, we have a signal $\mathbf{x}$ and an m-by-N measurement matrix $\mathbf{\Phi}$ with which we acquire measurements $\boldsymbol{y} = \mathbf{\Phi x}$, and, from these measurements $\boldsymbol{y}$, we wish to recover $\widehat{\mathbf{x}}$, with $O(k)$ entries, such that

$$\|\mathbf{x} - \widehat{\mathbf{x}}\|_2 \le C \|\mathbf{x} - \mathbf{x}_k\|_2 .$$

Our goal, which we achieve up to constant or log factors in the various criteria, is to design the measurement matrix $\mathbf{\Phi}$ and the decoding algorithm in an optimal fashion: (i) we minimize the number $m = O\big(k \log \frac{N}{k}\big)$ of measurements, (ii) the decoding algorithm runs in *sublinear* time $O\big(k \log \frac{N}{k}\big)$, and (iii) the encoding and update times are optimal $O\big(N \log \frac{N}{k}\big)$ and $O\big(k \log \frac{N}{k}\big)$, respectively. In order to achieve this, our algorithm is randomized; i.e., we specify a distribution on the measurement matrix $\mathbf{\Phi}$ and we guarantee that, for each signal, the algorithm recovers a good approximation with high probability over the choice of matrix.

In the above applications, it is important both to take as few measurements as possible and to recover the heavy hitters extremely efficiently. Measurements correspond to physical resources (e.g., memory in data stream monitoring devices, number of screens in biological applications) and reducing the number of necessary measurements is critical these problems. In addition, these applications require efficient recovery of the heavy hitters—we test many biological compounds at once, we want to quickly identify the positions of entities in a sensor network, and we cannot afford to spend computation time proportional to the size of the distribution in a data stream application.

Our result is robust to corruption of the measurements by an arbitrary noise vector ν_2, which is an important feature for such applications as high throughput screening and other physical measurement systems. (It is less critical for digital measurement systems that monitor data streams in which measurement corruption is less likely.) Our result is an FPRAS in both pre- and post- measurement noise.

1.1 Related Work

Do Ba et al. [2] give a lower bound of $\Omega(k \log(N/k))$ for the number of measurements for sparse recovery, in a model that is related to ours but different in some important respects. There are polynomial time algorithms [14, 3, 13] meeting this lower bound, both with high probability for each signal and the stronger setting, with high probability for all signals.[1] Previous sublinear time algorithms, whether in the "for each" model [4, 8] or in the "for all" model [12], however, used several additional factors of $\log(N)$ measurements. We summarize some previous algorithms in the "for each" signal model in Figure 1. The column sparsity denotes how many 1s there are per column of the measurement matrix and determines both the decoding and measurement update time and, for readability, we suppress $O(\cdot)$. The approximation error signifies the metric we use to evaluate the output; $\ell_j \le C\ell_k(+\ell_m)$ is shorthand for $\|\widehat{\mathbf{x}} - \mathbf{x}\|_j \le C\|\mathbf{x}_k - \mathbf{x}\|_k (+C\|\nu_2\|_m)$. (Some previous results that did not directly claim stability with respect to ν_2 can be modified easily to accomodate non-zero ν_2.)

[1] albeit with different error guarantees and different column sparsity depending on the error metric.

1.2 Our Result

We give a sublinear time recovery algorithm and a distribution over normalized measurement matrices that meet this lower bound (up to constant factors) in terms of the number of measurements and are within $\log(k)$ factors of optimal in the running time and the sparsity of the measurement matrix.

THEOREM 1. *There is an algorithm and distribution on matrices $\mathbf{\Phi}$ satisfying $\max_{\mathbf{x}} \mathbb{E}[\|\mathbf{\Phi x}\|_2 / \|\mathbf{x}\|_2] = 1$ such that, given $\mathbf{\Phi x}$, the parameters, and a concise description of $\mathbf{\Phi}$, the algorithm returns $\widehat{x}$ with approximation error $\|\mathbf{x} - \widehat{\mathbf{x}}\|_2^2 \le (1+\epsilon)\|\nu_1\|_2^2 + \epsilon\|\nu_2\|_2^2$ with probability $\frac{3}{4}$. The algorithm runs in time $\frac{k}{\epsilon}\log^{O(1)} N$ and $\mathbf{\Phi}$ has $O\big(\frac{k}{\epsilon}\log\frac{N}{k}\big)$ rows. In expectation, there are $O(\log^2(k)\log(N/k))$ non-zeros in each column of $\mathbf{\Phi}$.*

The approximation $\widehat{\mathbf{x}}$ may have more than k terms. From previous work, it is known that, if

$$\|\widehat{\boldsymbol{z}} - \mathbf{x}\|_2^2 \le (1+\epsilon^2)\|\mathbf{x}_k - \mathbf{x}\|_2^2 + \epsilon^2\|\nu_2\|_2^2,$$

then the truncation $\widehat{\boldsymbol{z}}_k$ of $\widehat{\boldsymbol{z}}$ to k terms satisfies

$$\|\widehat{\boldsymbol{z}}_k - \mathbf{x}\|_2^2 \le (1+\Theta(\epsilon))\|\mathbf{x}_k - \mathbf{x}\|_2^2 + \epsilon\|\nu_2\|_2^2.$$

So an approximation with exactly k terms is possible, but with cost $1/\epsilon^2$ versus $1/\epsilon$ for the general case.

1.3 Our Technical Contributions

Previous sublinear algorithms begin with the observation that if a signal consists of a single heavy hitter, then the trivial encoding of the positions 1 through N with $\log(N)$ bits, referred to as a bit tester, can identify the position of the heavy hitter, as in the following.

$$\begin{pmatrix} 1 & 1 & 1 & 1 & 1 & 1 & 1 & 1 \\ 0 & 0 & 0 & 0 & 1 & 1 & 1 & 1 \\ 0 & 0 & 1 & 1 & 0 & 0 & 1 & 1 \\ 0 & 1 & 0 & 1 & 0 & 1 & 0 & 1 \end{pmatrix} \begin{pmatrix} 0 \\ 0 \\ 7 \\ 0 \\ 0 \\ 0 \\ 0 \\ 0 \end{pmatrix} = \begin{pmatrix} 7 \\ 0 \\ 7 \\ 0 \end{pmatrix}.$$

The second observation in previous work is that a number of hash or Bernoulli functions drawn at random from a hash family are sufficient to isolate enough of the heavy hitters, which can then be identified by the bit tester. Depending on the type of error metric desired, the hashing matrix is pre-multiplied by random ± 1 vectors (for the ℓ_2 metric) in order to estimate the signal values. In this case, the measurements are referred to as the COUNT SKETCH in the data stream literature [4] and, without the premultiplication, the measurements are referred to as COUNT MEDIAN [7, 8] and give $\ell_1 \le C\ell_1$ error guarantees. In addition, the sublinear algorithms are typically greedy, iterative algorithms that recover portions of the heavy hitters with each iteration or that recover portions of the ℓ_2 (or ℓ_1) energy of the residual signal.

We build upon the COUNT SKETCH design but incorporate the following algorithmic innovations to ensure an optimal number of measurements:

- With a random assignment of N signal positions to $O(k)$ subsignals, we need to encode only $O(N/k)$ po-

Paper	No. Measurements	Column sparsity/ Update time	Decode time	Approx. error
[9, 3]	$k\log(N/k)$	$k\log(N/k)$	$\geq N$	$\ell_2 \leq (1/\sqrt{k})\ell_1 + \ell_2$
[4, 8]	$k\log^c N$	$\log^c N$	$k\log^c N$	$\ell_2 \leq C\ell_2$
[7]	$k\log^c N$	$\log^c N$	$k\log^c N$	$\ell_1 \leq C\ell_1$
This paper	$k\log(N/k)$	$\log^c N$	$k\log^c N$	$\ell_2 \leq C\ell_2 + \ell_2$

Table 1: Summary of the best previous results and the result obtained in this paper.

sitions, rather than N as in the previous approaches. Thus we can reduce the domain size which we encode.

- We use a good error-correcting code (rather than the trivial identity code of the bit tester).
- Our algorithm is an iterative algorithm but maintains a *compound* invariant: in our algorithm, the number of un-discovered heavy hitters decreases at each iteration while, simultaneously, the required error tolerance and failure probability become more stringent. Because there are fewer heavy hitters to find at each stage, we can use more measurements to meet more stringent guarantees.

We believe we are the first to consider a "for each" algorithm with post-measurement noise, ν_2. As we discuss below, we need to give a new definition of the appropriate metric under which to normalize $\mathbf{\Phi}$.

In Section 2 we detail the matrix algebra we use to describe the measurement matrix distribution which we cover in Section 3, along with the decoding algorithm. In Section 4, we analyze the foregoing recovery system.

2. PRELIMINARIES

2.1 Vectors

Let $\mathbf{x}$ denote a vector of length N. For each $k \leq N$, let $\mathbf{x}_k$ denote either the usual k'th component of $\mathbf{x}$ or the signal of length N consisting of the k largest-magnitude terms in $\mathbf{x}$; it will be clear from context. The signal $\mathbf{x}_k$ is the best k-term representation of $\mathbf{x}$. The energy of a signal $\mathbf{x}$ is $\|\mathbf{x}\|_2^2 = \sum_{i=1}^N |\mathbf{x}_i|^2$.

2.2 Matrices

In order to construct the overall measurement matrix, we form a number of different types of combinations of constituent matrices and to facilitate our description, we summarize our matrix operations in Table 2. The matrices that result from all of our matrix operations have N columns and, with the exception of the semi-direct product of two matrices $\ltimes_r$, all operations are performed on matrices $\boldsymbol{A}$ and $\boldsymbol{B}$ with N columns.

Next we give a full description of the matrix algebra defined in Table 2.

- **Row direct sum.** The row direct sum $\boldsymbol{A}\oplus_r\boldsymbol{B}$ is a matrix with N columns that is the vertical concatenation of $\boldsymbol{A}$ and $\boldsymbol{B}$.
- **Element-wise product.** If $\boldsymbol{A}$ and $\boldsymbol{B}$ are both $r \times N$ matrices, then $\boldsymbol{A}\odot\boldsymbol{B}$ is also an $r \times N$ matrix whose (i, j) entry is given by the product of the (i, j) entries in $\boldsymbol{A}$ and $\boldsymbol{B}$.
- **Semi-direct product.** Suppose $\boldsymbol{A}$ is a matrix of r_1 rows (and N columns) in which each row has exactly h non-zeros and $\boldsymbol{B}$ is a matrix of r_2 rows and h columns. Then $\boldsymbol{B}\ltimes_r\boldsymbol{A}$ is the matrix with r_1r_2 rows, in which each non-zero entry a of $\boldsymbol{A}$ is replaced by a times the j'th column of $\boldsymbol{B}$, where a is the j'th non-zero in its row.

  This matrix construction has the following interpretation. Consider $(\boldsymbol{B}\ltimes_r\boldsymbol{A})\mathbf{x}$ where $\boldsymbol{A}$ consists of a single row, $\boldsymbol{\rho}$, with h non-zeros and $\mathbf{x}$ is a vector of length N. Let $\boldsymbol{y} = \boldsymbol{\rho}\odot\mathbf{x}$ be the element-wise product of $\boldsymbol{\rho}$ and $\mathbf{x}$. If $\boldsymbol{\rho}$ is 0/1-valued, $\boldsymbol{y}$ picks out a subset of $\mathbf{x}$. We then remove all the positions in $\boldsymbol{y}$ corresponding to zeros in $\boldsymbol{\rho}$, leaving a vector $\boldsymbol{y}'$ of length h. Finally, $(\boldsymbol{B}\ltimes_r\boldsymbol{A})\mathbf{x}$ is simply the matrix-vector product $\boldsymbol{B}\boldsymbol{y}'$, which, in turn, can be interpreted as selecting subsets of $\boldsymbol{y}$, and summing them up. Note that we can modify this definition when $\boldsymbol{A}$ has fewer than h non-zeros per row in a straightforward fashion.

3. SPARSE RECOVERY SYSTEM

In this section, we specify the measurement matrix and detail the decoding algorithm.

3.1 Measurement matrix

The overall measurement matrix, $\mathbf{\Phi}$, is multi-layered. At the highest level, $\mathbf{\Phi}$ consists of a random permutation matrix $\boldsymbol{P}$ left-multiplying the row direct sum of $O(\log(k))$ summands, $\mathbf{\Phi}^{(j)}$, each of which is used in a separate iteration of the decoding algorithm. Each summand $\mathbf{\Phi}^{(j)}$ is the row direct sum of two separate matrices, an *identification* matrix, $\boldsymbol{D}^{(j)}$, and an *estimation* matrix, $\boldsymbol{E}^{(j)}$.

$$\mathbf{\Phi} = \boldsymbol{P}\begin{bmatrix} \mathbf{\Phi}^{(1)} \\ \hline \mathbf{\Phi}^{(2)} \\ \hline \vdots \\ \hline \mathbf{\Phi}^{(\log(k))} \end{bmatrix} \qquad \text{where } \mathbf{\Phi}^{(j)} = \boldsymbol{E}^{(j)}\oplus_r\boldsymbol{D}^{(j)}.$$

In iteration j, the identification matrix $\boldsymbol{D}^{(j)}$ consists of the row direct sum of $O(j)$ matrices, all chosen independently from the same distribution. We construct that distribution, $\frac{2^{-\Theta(j)}}{\sqrt{\log N/k}}(\boldsymbol{C}^{(j)}\ltimes_r\boldsymbol{H}^{(j)})\odot\boldsymbol{S}^{(j)}$, as follows. (The values of some parameters will be given later.)

- For $j = 1, 2, \ldots, \log(k)$, the matrix $\boldsymbol{H}^{(j)}$ is a hashing matrix with dimensions kc^j-by-N, where c in the range $1/2 < c < 1$ will be specified later. Each entry is 1 with probability $\Theta\left(1/(kc^j)\right)$ and zero otherwise. Each row is a pairwise independent family and the set of row seeds is pairwise dependent.
- The matrix $\boldsymbol{C}^{(j)}$ is an encoding of positions by an error-correcting code with constant rate and relative

operator	name	input	output dimensions and construction
$\oplus_r$	row direct sum	$A: r_1 \times N$ $B: r_2 \times N$	$M: (r_1 + r_2) \times N$ $M_{i,j} = \begin{cases} A_{i,j}, & 1 \le i \le r_1 \\ B_{i-r_1,j}, & 1 + r_1 \le i \le r_2 \end{cases}$
$\odot$	element-wise product	$A: r \times N$ $B: r \times N$	$M: r \times N$ $M_{i,j} = A_{i,j} B_{i,j}$
$\ltimes_r$	semi-direct product	$A: r_1 \times N$ $B: r_2 \times h$	$M: (r_1 r_2) \times N$ $M_{i+(k-1)r_2,\ell} = \begin{cases} 0, & A_{k,\ell} = 0 \\ A_{k,\ell} B_{i,j}, & A_{k,\ell} = j\text{th nonzero in row } \ell \end{cases}$

Table 2: Matrix algebra used in constructing an overall measurement matrix. The last column contains both the output dimensions of the matrix operation and its construction formula.

distance, together with several 1's. That is, fix an error-correcting code and encoding and decoding algorithms that encode messages of $\Theta(\log\log N)$ bits into longer codewords, also of length $\Theta(\log\log N)$, and can correct a constant fraction of errors. The i'th column of $C^{(j)}$ is the direct sum of $\Theta(\log\log N)$ copies of 1 with the direct sum of $E(i_1)$, $E(i_2)$, ..., where $i_1, i_2, \ldots$ are blocks of $O(\log\log N)$ bits each, whose concatenation is the binary expansion of i; $E(\cdot)$ is the encoding function for the error-correcting code. The number of columns in $C^{(j)}$ is the same as the maximum number of non-zeros in $H^{(j)}$, which is approximately the expected number, $\Theta\left(c^j N/k\right)$, where $c < 1$. The number of rows in $C^{(j)}$ is the logarithm of the number of columns, since the process of breaking the binary expansion of index i into blocks has rate 1 and encoding by $E(\cdot)$ has constant rate.

Note that error correcting encoding often is accomplished by a matrix-vector product, but we are *not* encoding a linear error-correcting code by the usual generator matrix process. Rather, our matrix explicitly lists all the codewords. The code may be non-linear.

- The matrix $S^{(j)}$ is a pseudorandom sign-flip matrix. Each row is a pairwise independent family of uniform ± 1-valued random variables. The sequence of seeds for the rows is a fully independent family. The size of $S^{(j)}$ matches the size of $C^{(j)} \ltimes_r H^{(j)}$.

Below, to achieve our claimed runtime, we will construct $C^{(j)}$ and $H^{(j)}$ together. See Figure 1.

The identification matrix at iteration j is of the form

$$D^{(j)} = \frac{2^{-\Theta(j)}}{\sqrt{\log N/k}} \begin{bmatrix} \left[2^{-\Theta(j)}(C^{(j)} \ltimes_r H^{(j)}) \odot S^{(j)}\right]_1 \\ \hline \vdots \\ \hline \left[(C^{(j)} \ltimes_r H^{(j)}) \odot S^{(j)}\right]_{O(j)} \end{bmatrix}.$$

In iteration j, the estimation matrix $E^{(j)}$ consists of the direct sum of $O(j + \log(1/\epsilon))$ matrices, all chosen independently from the same distribution, $\frac{2^{-\Theta(j)}}{\sqrt{\log N/k}} H'^{(j)} \odot S'^{(j)}$, so that the estimation matrix at iteration j is of the form

$$E^{(j)} = \frac{2^{-\Theta(j)}}{\sqrt{\log N/k}} \begin{bmatrix} \left[H'^{(j)} \odot S'^{(j)}\right]_1 \\ \hline \vdots \\ \hline \left[H'^{(j)} \odot S'^{(j)}\right]_{O(j)} \end{bmatrix}.$$

The construction of the distribution is similar to that of the identification matrix, but omits the error-correcting code and uses different constant factors for the number of rows, etc., compared with the analogs in the identification matrix.

- The matrix $H'^{(j)}$ is a hashing with dimensions $O(kc^j)$-by-N, for appropriate c, $1/2 < c < 1$. Each entry is 1 with probability $\Theta\left(1/(kc^j)\right)$ and zero otherwise. Each row is a pairwise independent family and the set of seeds is fully independent.

- The matrix $S'^{(j)}$ is a pseudorandom sign-flip matrix of the same dimension as $H'^{(j)}$. Each row of $S'^{(j)}$ is a pairwise independent family of uniform ± 1-valued random variables. The sequence of seeds for the rows is fully independent.

3.2 Measurements

The overall form of the measurements mirrors the structure of the measurement matrices. We do not, however, use all of the measurements in the same fashion. Upon receiving $\mathbf{\Phi x} + \nu_2$, the algorithm first applies the permutation P^{-1}. In iteration j of the algorithm, we use the measurements $y^{(j)} = \Phi^{(j)}\mathbf{x}$. As the matrix $\Phi^{(j)} = E^{(j)} \oplus_r D^{(j)}$, we have a portion of the measurements $w^{(j)} = D^{(j)}\mathbf{x}$ that we use for identification and a portion $z^{(j)} = E^{(j)}\mathbf{x}$ that we use for estimation. The $w^{(j)}$ portion is further decomposed into measurements $[v^{(j)}, u^{(j)}]$ corresponding to the run of $O(\log\log N)$ 1's in $C^{(j)}$ and measurements corresponding to each of the blocks in the error-correcting code. There are $O(j)$ i.i.d. repetitions in the identification part and $O(j + \log 1/\epsilon)$ repetitions in the estimation part.

3.3 Decoding

The decoding algorithm is shown in Figure 3.

4. ANALYSIS

In this section we analyze the decoding algorithm for correctness and efficiency.

4.1 Overview

The overall structure of our algorithm is greedy, similar to other algorithms in the literature. At each iteration, the algorithm recovers some of the signal, but introduce errors both through many coefficient estimates that are approximately but not perfectly correct, and also through a small number of terms that can be arbitrarily bad. The result is called a *residual signal*.

$\textsc{Recover}(\boldsymbol{\Phi}, \boldsymbol{y})$

Output: $\widehat{x} =$ approximate representation of x
 	
 $\boldsymbol{y} = \boldsymbol{P}^{-1}\boldsymbol{y}$
 $\boldsymbol{a}^{(0)} = 0$
 For $j = 0$ to $O(\log k)$ {
   $\boldsymbol{y} = \boldsymbol{y} - \boldsymbol{P}^{-1}\boldsymbol{\Phi}\boldsymbol{a}^{(j)}$
   split $\boldsymbol{y}^{(j)} = \boldsymbol{w}^{(j)} \oplus_{\mathrm{r}} \boldsymbol{z}^{(j)}$
   $\Lambda = \textsc{Identify}(\boldsymbol{D}^{(j)}, \boldsymbol{w}^{(j)})$
   $\boldsymbol{b}^{(j)} = \textsc{Estimate}(\boldsymbol{E}^{(j)}, \boldsymbol{z}^{(j)}, \Lambda)$
   $\boldsymbol{a}^{(j+1)} = \boldsymbol{a}^{(j)} + \boldsymbol{b}^{(j)}$
 }
 $\widehat{x} = \boldsymbol{a}^{(j)}$

$\textsc{Identify}(\boldsymbol{D}^{(j)}, \boldsymbol{w}^{(j)})$

Output: $\Lambda =$ list of positions
 	
 $\Lambda - \emptyset$
 Divide $\boldsymbol{w}^{(j)}$ into sections $[\boldsymbol{v}, \boldsymbol{u}]$ of size $O(\log(c^j(N/k)))$
 For each section {
   $u = \mathrm{median}(\lvert \boldsymbol{v}_\ell \rvert)$
   For each ℓ // threshold measurements
    $\boldsymbol{u}_\ell = \Theta(\boldsymbol{u}_\ell - u/2)$ // $\Theta(u) = 1$ if $u > 0$, $\Theta(u) = 0$ otherwise
   Divide $\boldsymbol{u}$ into blocks b_i of size $O(\log\log N)$
   For each b_i
    $\beta_i = \textsc{Decode}(b_i)$ // using error-correcting code
   $\lambda = \textsc{Integer}(\beta_1, \beta_2, \ldots)$ // integer represented by bits $\beta_1, \beta_2, \ldots$
   $\lambda = \textsc{Convert}(\lambda)$ // convert bucket index to signal index
   $\Lambda = \Lambda \cup \{\lambda\}$
 }

$\textsc{Estimate}(\boldsymbol{E}^{(j)}, \boldsymbol{z}^{(j)}, \Lambda)$

Output: $\boldsymbol{b} =$ vector of positions and values
 	
 $\boldsymbol{b} = \emptyset$
 For each $\lambda \in \Lambda$
   $\boldsymbol{b}_\lambda = \mathrm{median}_{\ell \text{ s.t.} \boldsymbol{H}^{(j)}_{\ell,\lambda} = 1}(\boldsymbol{z}^{(j)}_\ell \boldsymbol{S}^{(j)}_{\ell,\lambda})$
 For each $\lambda \in \Lambda$
   If $\lvert \boldsymbol{b}_\lambda \rvert$ is not among top $\Theta(k/2^j)$
    $\boldsymbol{b}_\lambda = 0$

Table 3: Pseudocode for the overall decoding algorithm.

The measurement and runtime costs of first iteration dominates the combined cost of all the others. In it, we reduce a bound on the number of heavy hitters to recover from k to $k/2$, while increasing the noise energy from 1 to $1+\epsilon/4$, using $O((k/\epsilon)\log(N/k))$ measurements. In subsequent iterations, the number of heavy hitters is reduced to $k/2^j$, which reduces the leading cost factor from k/ϵ to $2^{-j}k/\epsilon$. This gives the algorithm 2^j times more resources. In particular, the algorithm can tighten the approximation constant from $1+\epsilon/4$ to $1+(\epsilon/4)c^j$, for appropriate c in the range $1/2 < c < 1$, at cost factor $(1/c)^j < 2^j$, which is more than paid for by the $2^{-j} < 1$ savings in the leading factor. Similarly, the algorithm can simultaneously afford to have a smaller failure probability at iteration j. With the tightened approximation constant, the algorithm can tolerate additional ν_2 noise in later iterations, which, as we show below, saves resources.

To prove our result formally, we proceed as follows.

- We state a Loop Invariant maintained by our algorithm.
- We give a lemma (the Loop-Invariant Maintenance Lemma, or LIM lemma) that can be used to characterize a single iteration of the algorithm: how many measurements are used, how many non-zeros there are in each coluimn of the measurement matrix, the runtime, and the properties of the residual.

  To prove the LIM lemma, we proceed as follows.
- In Claim 1, we explain, structurally, how the conclusions of the lemma are met—what are the sources of errors, etc. We then examine the three subroutines in the algorithm—isolating heavy hitters, identifying them, and estimating coefficients.
- We discuss normalization of $\mathbf{\Phi}$ and show that it is, indeed, normalized.
- We conclude by analyzing the correctness and efficiency of the overall algorithm, using our results about each iteration.

4.2 Correctness

Formally, we maintain the following invariant.

INVARIANT 2 (LOOP INVARIANT). *At the beginning of iteration j, the residual signal has the form $\boldsymbol{r}^{(j)} = \sigma^{(j)} + \nu_1^{(j)}$ with*

$$\left\|\sigma^{(j)}\right\|_0 \le \frac{k}{2^j} \text{ and } \left\|\nu_1^{(j)}\right\|_2^2 \le \left(1+\epsilon\left(1-\left(\frac{3}{4}\right)^j\right)\right)\left\|\nu_1^{(j)}\right\|_2^2$$

except with probability $\frac{1}{4}(1-(\frac{1}{2})^j)$, where $\|\cdot\|_0$ is the number of non-zero entries. Furthermore, the algorithm has computed (the sparse partial representation) $\widehat{\mathbf{x}}^{(j)} = \mathbf{x} - \boldsymbol{r}^{(j)}$.

Clearly, the invariant holds at the start and maintaining the invariant is sufficient to prove the overall result. In order to show that the algorithm maintains the loop invariant, we demonstrate the following lemma, which, after proper instantiation of the lemma's variables, can be used to show the invariant is maintained.

4.2.1 Loop Invariant Maintenance

LEMMA 3 (LOOP INVARIANT MAINTENANCE). *Fix numerical parameters N, ℓ, δ, and η, with $\delta > 0$, and $\eta > 1/N$. Let $\boldsymbol{a}$ be a vector of length N that can be written as $\boldsymbol{a} = \sigma + \nu_1$, with $\|\sigma\|_0 \le \ell$. Let $\mathbf{\Phi}$ be of the form of $O(\log 1/\delta)$ repetitions of $(\boldsymbol{C}\ltimes_r\boldsymbol{H})\odot\boldsymbol{S}$ in row direct sum with $O(\log 1/(\delta\eta))$ repetitions of $\boldsymbol{H}'\odot\boldsymbol{S}'$ described in Section 3.1, where $\boldsymbol{H}$ and $\boldsymbol{H}'$ have $O(\ell/\eta)$ rows. Let ν_2 be a random noise vector, where each item has the same expected square magnitude.*

Then, except with probability δ, given $\mathbf{\Phi}, \boldsymbol{y} = \mathbf{\Phi}\boldsymbol{a} + \nu_2$, and appropriate parameters, the inner loop of the RECOVER algorithm in Figure 3 recovers $\boldsymbol{b}$ that can be written as $\boldsymbol{b} = \sigma' + \nu_1'$, with $\|\sigma'\|_0 \le \ell/2$ and $\|\nu_1'\|_2^2 \le (1+\eta)\|\nu_1\|_2^2 + \frac{\eta}{\gamma}\|\nu_2\|_2^2$, where γ is the common expected number of non-zeros in each column of $\mathbf{\Phi}$. Furthermore,

- *The number of rows in $\mathbf{\Phi}$ is $O(\ell/\eta)\log(N/\ell)\log(1/\delta)$.*
- *The computation time is*
$$(\ell/\eta)\log^{O(1)}(N/(\ell\delta\eta)).$$
- *The expected number γ of non-zeros in each column of $\mathbf{\Phi}$ is $O((\log N/\ell)\log(1/\delta))$.*

PROOF. Much of the algorithm and analysis is similar to previous work [4], so we sketch the proof, focusing on changes versus previous work. We first address the case $\nu_2 = 0$.

Recall that $\mathbf{\Phi}$ works by giving each element of the signal a random sign flip, hashing each item pairwise independently at random to each measurement, and encoding each index by an error-correcting code. We have:

CLAIM 1. *Except with probability $\delta/3$,*

- *The vector $\boldsymbol{b}$ contains all but at most $\ell/4$ terms of σ, with "good" estimates.*
- *The vector $\boldsymbol{b}$ contains at most $\ell/4$ terms with "bad" estimates, i.e., with square error greater than proportional to η/ℓ.*
- *The total sum square error over all "good" estimates is at most $\eta/4$.*

PROOF. To simplify notation, let T be the set of terms of $\boldsymbol{a}$ that are both among the top ℓ and have energy at least $\frac{\eta}{8\ell}\|\nu_1\|_2^2$. We know that $|T| \le O(\ell)$. The proof proceeds in three steps.

Step 1. Isolate heavy hitters with little noise. Consider the action of a hashing and sign-flip matrix $\boldsymbol{H}\odot\boldsymbol{S}$ with $O(\ell/\eta)$ rows. From previous work [4, 1], it follows that, if constant factors parametrizing the matrices are chosen properly,

LEMMA 4. *For each $t \in T$, the following holds with probability $1 - O(\delta\eta)$:*

- *The term t is hashed by at least one row ρ in $\boldsymbol{H}$.*
- *There are $O(\eta N/\ell)$ total positions (out of N) hashed by ρ.*
- *The dot product $(\rho\odot\boldsymbol{S})\boldsymbol{a}$ is $\boldsymbol{S}_t\boldsymbol{a}_t \pm O\left(\sqrt{\frac{\eta}{\ell}}\|\nu_1\|_2\right)$.*

PROOF. (Sketch) For intuition, note that the estimator $\boldsymbol{S}_t(\rho \odot \boldsymbol{S})\boldsymbol{a}$ is a random variable with mean $\boldsymbol{a}_t$ and variance $\|\nu_1\|_2^2$. Then the claims in the Lemma assert that the expected behavior happens, up to constant factors, with probability $\Omega(1)$.

In the favorable case, each row of $\boldsymbol{H}$ is hashed one term of T that dominates the other $\eta N/\ell$ terms hashed to that bucket. □

Step 2. Identify heavy hitters with little noise. Next, we show how to identify t. Since there are $\eta N/\ell$ positions hashed by $\boldsymbol{H}$, we need to learn the $O(\log(\eta N/k))$ bits describing t in this context. Previous sublinear algorithms [8, 12] used a trivial error correcting code, in which the t'th column was simply the binary expansion of t in direct sum with a single 1, for the matrix $\boldsymbol{C}$ in semi-direct product with $\boldsymbol{H}$. Thus, if the signal $\mathbf{x}$ consists of $\mathbf{x}_t$ in the t'th position and zeros elsewhere, the vector $(\boldsymbol{C} \ltimes_r \boldsymbol{H})\mathbf{x}$ would include $\mathbf{x}_t$ and $\mathbf{x}_t$ times the binary expansion of t (the latter interpreted as a string of 0's and 1's as real numbers). These algorithms require strict control on the failure probability of each measurement in order to use such a trivial encoding. In our case, each measurement succeeds only with probability $\Omega(1)$ and, generally, fails with probability $\Omega(1)$. So we need to use a more powerful error correcting code and a more reliable estimate of $|\mathbf{x}_t|$.

To get an estimate of $|\mathbf{x}_t|$ that is reliable, we use the $b = \Theta(\log\log N)$-parallel repetition code of all 1s. That is, we get b independent measurements of $|\mathbf{x}_t|$ and we decode by taking the median. Let p denote the success probability of each individual measurement. Then we expect the fraction p to be approximately correct estimates of $|\mathbf{x}_t|$, we achieve close to the expectation, and we can arrange that $p > 1/2$. It follows that the median is approximately correct. We use this value to threshold the subsequent measurements (i.e., the bits in the encoding) to 0/1 values.

Now, let us consider these bit estimates. In a single error-correcting code block of $b = \Theta(\log\log N)$ measurements, we will get close to the expected number, bp, of successful measurements, except with probability $1/\log(N)$, using the Chernoff bound. In the favorable case, we get a number of failures less than the (properly chosen) distance of the error-correcting code and we can recover the block using standard nearest-neighbor decoding. The number of error-correcting code blocks associated with t is $O(\log(\eta N/k)/\log\log N) \leq O(\log N)$, so we can take a union bound over all blocks and conclude that we recover t with probability $\Omega(1)$. Because the algorithm takes $O(\log 1/\delta)$ parallel independent repetitions, we guarantee that the failure probability is δ for each $t \in T$ and we expect $\delta|T| = O(\delta\ell)$ failures, overall. The probability of getting more than $\ell/4$ failures is at most $O(\delta)$.

Step 3. Estimate heavy hitters.

Many of the details in this step are similar to those in Lemma 4 (as well as to previous work as the function ESTIMATE is essentially the same as COUNT SKETCH), so we give only a brief summary.

The error-correcting code is not necessary. As above, random sign flips and hashing into $O(\ell/\eta)$ buckets suffices to isolate a term t so that the remaining terms hashed to t's bucket have expected energy $O(\eta/\ell)$ and realize energy $O(\eta/\ell)$ with constant probability. Another factor $\log 1/(\delta\eta)$ repetitions suffices to make the failure probability $\delta\eta$, so that, except with probability δ, we have $O(\eta|\Lambda|) = O(\ell)$ failures overall among the $|\Lambda| = \Theta(\ell/\eta)$ candidates whose coefficients we estimate.

This concludes the proof of the Claim.

Number of measurements.

We now consider the number of measurements in the matrix. The hashing matrix $\boldsymbol{H}$ contributes $O(\ell/\eta)$ rows. The constant-rate error-correcting code matrix $\boldsymbol{C}$ contributes an additional factor of $O(\log \eta N/\ell)$, to identify one index out of $\eta N/\ell$. The $O(\log 1/\delta)$ repetitions contribute that additional factor, to drive down the overall failure probability of identification from $1 - \Omega(1)$ to δ. The $\boldsymbol{S}$ matrix does not contribute to the number of rows. This gives a product of

$$O((\ell/\eta)(\log(\eta N/\ell)\log 1/\delta))$$

for identification. Similarly, for estimation, we have $O(\ell/\eta)$ rows for hashing. Since we are estimating coefficients for $O(\ell/\eta)$ candidates and can only afford $O(\ell)$ errors except with probability δ, the Markov inequality requires that each estimate fail with probability at most $\eta\delta$, which contributes the factor $O(\log 1/(\eta\delta))$. Thus we get $O((\ell/\eta)\log 1/(\eta\delta))$ for estimation, and

$$O((\ell/\eta)(\log(\eta N/\ell)\log 1/\delta + \log 1/(\eta\delta)),$$

overall. Note that we may assume $\eta > \ell/N$, since, otherwise, we may use $\ell/\eta > N$ measurements to recover trivially. Thus the overall number of measurements is

$$O((\ell/\eta)(\log(N/\ell)\log 1/\delta))$$

Number of non-zeros.

The expected number of non-zeros in each column of the identification part of $\boldsymbol{\Phi}$ is $O(1)$ from hashing, times the factor $O(\log \eta N/\ell)$ from the (generally, dense) error-correcting code, times $O(\log 1/\delta)$ for repetition. Analysis of the estimation part is similar. We get $O(\log(N/\ell)\log 1/\delta)$ non-zeros altogether.

Post-measurement noise.

Finally, consider the effect of ν_2. Suppose there are m rows in $\boldsymbol{\Phi}$. As in previous work, the sign-flip matrix $\boldsymbol{S}$ applied to $\boldsymbol{a}$ but not to ν_2 insures that, effectively, $\mathbb{E}[\nu_2] = 0$; our assumption about ν_2 then implies that the energy of ν_2 in each component has expectation $(1/m)\|\nu_2\|_2^2$. A careful inspection of the above proof indicates that ν_1 enters only through the expected energy in each bucket, which is $\Theta((\eta/\ell)\|\nu_1\|_2^2)$; the error-correcting code and parallel repetitions result in energy $\Theta((\eta/\ell)\|\nu_1\|_2^2) = \Theta((\gamma/m)\|\nu_1\|_2^2)$ in each component of $\boldsymbol{\Phi a}$. The error $(1+\eta)\|\nu_1\|_2^2$ represents the "inevitable" error $\|\nu_1\|_2^2$ due to terms outside the top $O(\ell)$ that are not recovered by the algorithm, plus "excess" error $\eta\|\nu_1\|_2^2$, due to missing large terms and introducing additional error through many small coefficient approximation errors and a few arbitrarily bad approximation errors, where the threshold for "good" depends on ν_1. Since ν_2 does not affect the inevitible error, we can replace $(\gamma/m)\|\nu_1\|_2^2$ with $(\gamma/m)\|\nu_1\|_2^2 + (1/m)\|\nu_2\|_2^2$ when figuring the excess error, giving the claimed result. (Below we will see that γ can be viewed as a normalization factor for $\boldsymbol{\Phi}$, that makes $\boldsymbol{\Phi}\nu_1$ and ν_2 comparable.) Full details will be given in the journal version of this paper.

This concludes the proof of the LIM lemma, Lemma 3.

4.2.2 Normalization of the Measurement Matrix

Next we consider the normalization of the overall matrix $\mathbf{\Phi}$ from Section 3.1.

As has been observed [2], $\mathbf{\Phi}$ should be normalized in the setting of $\nu_2 \neq 0$. Otherwise, the matrix $\mathbf{\Phi}$ can be scaled up by an arbitrary constant factor $c > 1$ which can be undone by the decoding algorithm: Let $\mathcal{D}'$ be a new decoding algorithm that calls the old decoding algorithm $\mathcal{D}$ as $\mathcal{D}'(\boldsymbol{y}) = \mathcal{D}(\frac{1}{c}\boldsymbol{y})$, so that $\mathcal{D}'(c\mathbf{\Phi x} + \nu_2) = \mathcal{D}(\mathbf{\Phi x} + \frac{1}{c}\nu_2)$. Thus we would be able to *reduce* the effect of ν_2 by an arbitrary factor $c > 1$. In our "for each, $\ell_2 \leq C\ell_2$" model, an appropriate way to normalize $\mathbf{\Phi}$ is as follows.

DEFINITION 5. *The $\|\mathbf{\Phi}\|_{2\rightsquigarrow 2}$ norm of a randomly constructed matrix $\mathbf{\Phi}$ is*

$$\max_{\boldsymbol{x}\neq 0} \mathbb{E}\left[\frac{\|\mathbf{\Phi}\boldsymbol{x}\|_2}{\|\boldsymbol{x}\|_2}\right].$$

Note that the usual 2-operator norm,

$$\|\mathbf{\Phi}\|_2 = \max_{\boldsymbol{x}\neq 0}\left[\frac{\|\mathbf{\Phi}\boldsymbol{x}\|_2}{\|\boldsymbol{x}\|_2}\right]$$

is typically much larger than $\|\mathbf{\Phi}\|_{2\rightsquigarrow 2}$, which would lead to a much weaker result. But it corresponds to an adversary choosing $\mathbf{x}$ and ν_2 knowing the outcome $\mathbf{\Phi}$, which is counter to the spirit of the "for each" model in previous work. Here we assume the adversary knows the distribution on $\mathbf{\Phi}$, but not the outcome, when choosing $\mathbf{x}$ and ν_2.

Now we bound $\|\mathbf{\Phi}\|_{2\rightsquigarrow 2}$ for our $\mathbf{\Phi}$. It is straightforward to see that this is the maximum column ℓ_2 norm. In the j'th iteration, there are at most $j \log N/k$ non-zero entries, each of magnitude $\sqrt{\frac{c^j}{\log N/k}}$ for some c in the range $1/2 < c < 1$. It follows that

$$\|\mathbf{\Phi}\|^2_{2\rightsquigarrow 2} \leq \left(\sum_j jc^j\right) \leq O(1),$$

if constants are chosen properly.

4.2.3 Invariant

Now we show that the invariant is satisfied, using the LIM lemma. That is all that remains to prove our main theorem:

Theorem 1 *There is an algorithm and distribution on matrices $\mathbf{\Phi}$ satisfying $\max_{\mathbf{x}} \mathbb{E}[\|\mathbf{\Phi x}\|_2 / \|\mathbf{x}\|_2] = 1$ such that, given $\mathbf{\Phi x}$, the parameters, and a concise description of $\mathbf{\Phi}$, the algorithm returns $\widehat{x}$ with approximation error $\|\mathbf{x} - \widehat{\mathbf{x}}\|_2^2 \leq (1+\epsilon)\|\nu_1\|_2^2 + \epsilon\|\nu_2\|_2^2$ with probability $\frac{3}{4}$. The algorithm runs in time $\frac{k}{\epsilon}\log^{O(1)} N$ and $\mathbf{\Phi}$ has $O(\frac{k}{\epsilon}\log\frac{N}{k})$ rows. In expectation, there are $O(\log^2(k)\log(N/k))$ non-zeros in each column of $\mathbf{\Phi}$.*

PROOF. First, note that the matrices described in Section 3.1 have two additional features, compared with the matrices in the LIM lemma. First, there is a single random permutation matrix $\boldsymbol{P}$ that multiplies all the error-correcting code, hashing, and sign-flip matrices, and, second, the matrices in iteration j are multiplied by $c^{j/2}$, where c is an appropriate constant in the range $1/2 < c < 1$. Also note that ν_2 is not *a priori* guaranteed to be symmetric in expectation, as stipulated by the LIM lemma.

Consider the effect of ν_2. We would like to argue that the noise vector ν_2 is "distributed" at random and each measurement is corrupted by $\frac{\|\nu_2\|_2^2}{m}$, where m is the number of measurements, approximately its fair share of $\|\nu_2\|_2^2$. Unfortunately, the contributions of ν_2 to the various measurements are not independent as ν_2 is permuted, so we cannot use such a simple analysis. Nevertheless, they are negatively correlated and we can achieve the result we want using [10]. Henceforth, we assume ν_2 does corrupt each measurement in $\mathbf{\Phi x}$ with the same expectation, just as in the LIM lemma.[2]

In iteration j, we make ℓ of the LIM lemma equal to $k/2^j$, η of the LIM lemma is $\Theta(\epsilon\beta^j)$, and $\delta = 2^{-j}$, for $\beta < 1$ to be specified below. Without loss of generality, assume $\|\nu_1\|_2 = \|\nu_2\|_2 = 1$, since our analysis can scale the signal (the algorithm does not need to know the scaling) and, if ν_1 and ν_2 have different energies, we can increase the weaker of the two. Then $\left\|\nu_1^{(0)}\right\|_2 = 1$.

It is straightforward to confirm that $\left\|\sigma^{(j+1)}\right\|_0 \leq k/2^{j+1}$, provided the invariant held at the previous iteration. We now turn to $\left\|\nu_1^{(j+1)}\right\|_2$.

At the beginning of the j'th iteration, $\left\|\nu_1^{(j)}\right\|_2^2 \leq 1 + \epsilon\left(1 - \left(\frac{3}{4}\right)^j\right)$. This means that $1 \leq \left\|\nu_1^{(j)}\right\|_2^2 \leq 2$ remains unchanged up to the factor 2. By the LIM lemma and the discussion at the beginning of 4.2.2, each repetition gives, with high probability, an estimate with $\left\|\nu_1^{(j+1)}\right\|_2^2 - \left\|\nu_1^{(j)}\right\|_2^2$ at most $\epsilon\beta^j\left(\left\|\nu_1^{(j)}\right\|_2^2 + c^{-j}\|\nu_2\|_2^2\right)$, where $\sqrt{c^j/\log N/k}$ is the magnitude of the $O(\log N/k)$ non-zeros in each repetition at iteration j. It follows that the median over repetitions of this estimate satisfies the same bound with high probability. Since $1 \ll c^{-j}$, it follows that $1 + c^{-j} \approx c^{-j}$. If we put $\beta \approx 5/8$ and $c \approx 5/6$, the invariant is satisfied. $\square$

4.3 Efficiency

4.3.1 Number of Measurements

The number of measurements in iteration j is computed as follows. There are $\log(\delta) = O(j)$ parallel repetitions in iteration j. They each consist of $O(k/(\epsilon\beta^j 2^j)\log(N/k))$ measurements, where $\beta = 5/8$. That is, the number of measurements is

$$\Theta\left(jk\left(\frac{4}{5}\right)^j \log\frac{N}{k}\right) = (k/\epsilon)\log\frac{N}{k}\left(\frac{4}{5} + o(1)\right)^j.$$

Thus we have a sequence bounded by a geometric sequence with ratio less than 1. The sum, over j, is bounded by $O((k/\epsilon)\log(N/k))$.

4.3.2 Encoding, Decoding, and Update Time

The encoding time is bounded by N times the number of non-zeros in each column of the measurement matrix. This was analyzed above in Section 4.2; there are $\log(j)\log(N/k)$ non-zeros per column in iteration j, for $j \leq O(\log(k))$, so the total is $\log^2(k)\log(N/k)$ non-zeros per column. This is

[2] Alternatively, note that one could plausibly model ν_2 as acting independently and identically on all measurements, leading to a weaker, but simpler and self-contained result.

suboptimal by the factor $\log^2(k)$. By comparison, however, some proposed methods use dense matrices, which are suboptimal by the exponentially-larger factor k.

When constructing the matrix for measuring the original signal or some intermediate representation, our algorithm will need to find, quickly, the bucket to which an index i is hashed and a codeword for i, where i is in the range $1 \leq i \leq N$. Note that it is crucial that we use $O(\log(N/B))$ bits for the codeword, where B is the number of buckets, and not $\log(N)$ bits. This means we need to find codewords for just the i's hashed to a particular bucket. Upon decoding, we need to be able to find i from its codeword, quickly.

We can use a pseudorandom number generator that hashes i to a bucket j if $jN/B \leq ai + b \bmod N < (j+1)N/B$ for random a and b. Then encode i by $E(ai+b)$, assuming quick encoding for numbers in the contiguous range 1 to N/B. To decode, we first recover $ai + b$, whence we easily recover i. An example is given in Figure 1.

Another issue is the time to find and to encode and to decode the error-correcting code. Observe that the length of the code is $O(\log\log N)$. We can afford time exponential in the length, *i.e.*, time $\log^{O(1)} N$, for finding, encoding, and decoding the code. These tasks are straightforward in that much time.

5. CONCLUSION AND OPEN PROBLEMS

In this paper, we construct an approximate sparse recovery system that is essentially optimal: the recovery algorithm is a sublinear algorithm (with near optimal running time), the number of measurements meets a lower bound, and the update time, encode time, and column sparsity are each within log factors of the lower bounds. We leave the following problems open, and make conjectures.

- We conjecture that with a few modifications to the distribution on measurement matrices, we can extend this result to the $\ell_1 \leq C\ell_1$ and $\ell_2 \leq (C/\sqrt{k})\ell_1$ error metric guarantees, still under the "for each" model. We do not, however, think that this approach can be extended to the "for all" signal model (all current sublinear algorithms use at least one factor $O(\log N)$ additional measurements) and leave open the problem of designing a sublinear time recovery algorithm and a measurement matrix with an optimal number of rows for this setting, under any suitable error metric.
- It remains to improve the number of nonzeros in the columns of our measurement matrix from

$$O(\log^2(k)\log(N/k))$$

to $O(\log(N/k))$.
- A straightforward way to encode a signal takes time proportional to the signal support size times the number of non-zeros per column of the measurement matrix. This is the case with our algorithm and the relevant related work. If the measurement matrix is properly structured, however—for example, if it consists of rows of a Fourier matrix in arithmetic progression—it is possible to multiply the measurement matrix by a vector faster than the trivial algorithm. Thus it would be interesting to improve the encode time of our algorithm (assuming a dense signal), even if one cannot improve the number of non-zeros per column.
- As discussed earlier, Do Ba et al. [2] give a lower bound of $\Omega(k\log(N/k))$ for the number of measurements, for constant ϵ, and Wainwright [15] gives a lower bound of $\Omega((k/\epsilon)\log(N/k))$, under certain restrictions, for problems and in models that are not exactly the same as ours. These lower bounds can be regarded as characterizing obstacles in our setting. It remains to give a lower bound for the dependence on ϵ, and to meet it.

  Note that the number of measurements used by our algorithm is

$$O((k/\epsilon)(\log(\epsilon N/k) + \log(1/\epsilon))).$$

  Above we quoted the larger expression

$$O((k/\epsilon)\log(N/k)).$$

  Note that we may assume that $\epsilon > k/N$ since, otherwise, we may use $k/\epsilon > N$ measurements and recover trivially. Also, if $\epsilon^{1.1} > k/N$ then

$$\log(1/\epsilon) \leq O(\log(\epsilon N/k)).$$

  Thus the number of measurements used by our algorithm is $O((k/\epsilon)\log(\epsilon N/k))$ except for the (rare?) cases of $k/N < \epsilon < (k/N)^{.9}$. Nevertheless, we conjecture that the lower bound is $\Omega((k/\epsilon)\log(N/k))$, which quantitatively matches the result in [15], and that this holds even if one of ν_1 and ν_2 is zero.

  The dependence on ϵ seems to increase from $1/\epsilon$ to $1/\epsilon^2$ for the recovery of an exactly-k-sparse representation. Characterizing precisely the lower bound here would be nice, too.

6. REFERENCES

[1] N. Alon, Y. Matias, and M. Szegedy. The Space Complexity of Approximating the Frequency Moments. *J. Comput. System Sci.*, 58(1):137–147, 1999.

[2] K. Do Ba, P. Indyk, E. Price, and D. Woodruff. Lower bounds for sparse recovery. In *ACM SODA*, page to appear, 2010.

[3] E. J. Candès, J. Romberg, and T. Tao. Stable signal recovery from incomplete and inaccurate measurements. *Comm. Pure Appl. Math.*, 59(8):1208–1223, 2006.

[4] M. Charikar, K. Chen, and M. Farach-Colton. Finding frequent items in data streams. *ICALP*, 2002.

[5] Raphaël Clifford, Klim Efremenko, Ely Porat, and Amir Rothschild. *k*-mismatch with don't cares. In *ESA*, pages 151–162, 2007.

[6] G. Cormode and S. Muthukrishnan. What's hot and what's not: Tracking most frequent items dynamically. In *Proc. ACM Principles of Database Systems*, pages 296–306, 2003.

[7] G. Cormode and S. Muthukrishnan. Improved data stream summaries: The count-min sketch and its applications. *FSTTCS*, 2004.

[8] G. Cormode and S. Muthukrishnan. Combinatorial algorithms for Compressed Sensing. In *Proc. 40th Ann. Conf. Information Sciences and Systems*, Princeton, Mar. 2006.

[9] D. L. Donoho. Compressed Sensing. *IEEE Trans. Info. Theory*, 52(4):1289–1306, Apr. 2006.

Figure 1: Example measurement matrix for identification. Here $N = 11$, $k = 3$, and, in the hashing $i \mapsto a + bi$, we have $a = 1$ and $b = 4$, so that the sequence $i = \langle 0, 1, 2, 3, 4, 5, 6, 7, 8, 9, 10 \rangle$ is mapped to $\langle 1, 5, 9, 2, 6, 10, 3, 7, 0, 4, 8 \rangle$. The three buckets are $\{i : 0 \leq a + bi < 4\}, \{i : 4 \leq a + bi < 8\}$, and $\{i : 8 \leq a + bi < 11\}$. We number starting from 0, so $0 \leq i < 11$. In this example, we use two rows of ones and the double repetition code instead of a good code.

$$\boldsymbol{H} = \begin{pmatrix} 1 & 0 & 0 & 1 & 0 & 0 & 1 & 0 & 1 & 0 & 0 \\ 0 & 1 & 0 & 0 & 1 & 0 & 0 & 1 & 0 & 1 & 0 \\ 0 & 0 & 1 & 0 & 0 & 1 & 0 & 0 & 0 & 0 & 1 \end{pmatrix}, \quad \boldsymbol{C} = \begin{pmatrix} 1 & 1 & 1 & 1 \\ 1 & 1 & 1 & 1 \\ 0 & 0 & 1 & 1 \\ 0 & 0 & 1 & 1 \\ 0 & 1 & 0 & 1 \\ 0 & 1 & 0 & 1 \end{pmatrix}$$

If ρ is the top row of $\boldsymbol{H}$, which maps $\langle 8, 0, 3, 6 \rangle$ to $\langle 0, 1, 2, 3 \rangle$, and with $\boldsymbol{S}$ arbitrary, then

$$(\rho \ltimes_{\mathrm{r}} \boldsymbol{C}) \odot \boldsymbol{S} = \begin{pmatrix} -1 & 0 & 0 & 1 & 0 & 0 & -1 & 0 & -1 & 0 & 0 \\ 1 & 0 & 0 & -1 & 0 & 0 & 1 & 0 & 1 & 0 & 0 \\ 0 & 0 & 0 & -1 & 0 & 0 & -1 & 0 & 0 & 0 & 0 \\ 0 & 0 & 0 & 1 & 0 & 0 & -1 & 0 & 0 & 0 & 0 \\ 1 & 0 & 0 & 0 & 0 & 0 & -1 & 0 & 0 & 0 & 0 \\ 1 & 0 & 0 & 0 & 0 & 0 & 1 & 0 & 0 & 0 & 0 \end{pmatrix}$$

[10] Devdatt Dubhashi, Volker Priebe, and Desh Ranjan. Negative dependence through the FKG inequality. In *Research Report MPI-I-96-1-020, Max-Planck-Institut für Informatik, Saarbrucken*, 1996.

[11] Yaniv Erlich, Kenneth Chang, Assaf Gordon, Roy Ronen, Oron Navon, Michelle Rooks, and Gregory J. Hannon. Dna sudoku—harnessing high-throughput sequencing for multiplexed specimen analysis. *Genome Research*, 19:1243—1253, 2009.

[12] A. C. Gilbert, M. J. Strauss, J. A. Tropp, and R. Vershynin. One sketch for all: fast algorithms for compressed sensing. In *ACM STOC 2007*, pages 237–246, 2007.

[13] P. Indyk and M. Ruzic. Near-optimal sparse recovery in the l_1 norm. *FOCS*, 2008.

[14] D. Needell and J. A. Tropp. CoSaMP: Iterative signal recovery from incomplete and inaccurate samples. *Appl. Comp. Harmonic Anal.*, 2008. To appear.

[15] M. Wainwright. Information-theoretic bounds on sparsity recovery in the high-dimensional and noisy setting. *IEEE Transactions on Information Theory*, 55(12):5728–5741, 2009.

[16] Y. H. Zheng, N. P. Pitsianis, and D. J. Brady. Nonadaptive group testing based fiber sensor deployment for multiperson tracking. *IEEE Sensors Journal*, 6(2):490–494, 2006.

[17] Y.H. Zheng, D. J. Brady, M. E. Sullivan, and B. D. Guenther. Fiber-optic localization by geometric space coding with a two-dimensional gray code. *Applied Optics*, 44(20):4306–4314, 2005.

The HOM Problem is Decidable

Guillem Godoy*
ggodoy@lsi.upc.edu

Omer Giménez
omer.gimenez@gmail.com

Lander Ramos
landertxu@gmail.com

Carme Àlvarez
alvarez@lsi.upc.edu

Universitat Politècnica de Catalunya
Departament de Llenguatges i Sistemes Informàtics
Jordi Girona 1, 08034, Barcelona, Spain

ABSTRACT

We provide an algorithm that, given a tree homomorphism H and a regular tree language L represented by a tree automaton, determines whether $H(L)$ is regular. This settles a question that has been open for a long time.

Along the way, we develop new constructions and techniques which are interesting by themselves, and provide several significant intermediate results. For example, we prove that the universality problem is decidable for languages represented by tree automata with equality constraints, and that the equivalence and inclusion problems are decidable for images of regular tree languages through tree homomorphisms.

Our algorithms are based on the following constructions. We describe a simple transformation for converting a tree automaton with equality constraints into a tree automaton with inequality constraints recognizing the complementary language. We also define a new class of automata with arbitrary inequality constraints and a particular kind of equality constraints. An automaton of this new class essentially recognizes the intersection of a tree automaton with inequality constraints and the image of a regular tree language through a tree homomorphism. We prove decidability of emptiness and finiteness for this class by a pumping mechanism.

Categories and Subject Descriptors

F.1.1 [**Computation by Abstract Devices**]: Automata, Computability Theory; F.4.2 [**Mathematical Logic and Formal Languages**]: Grammars and Other Rewriting Systems; F.4.3 [**Mathematical Logic and Formal Languages**]: Formal Languages

*All authors were supported by Spanish Ministry of Education and Science by the FORMALISM project (TIN2007-66523) and ALBCOM (SGR-2009-2013). The first and third authors were supported by the LOGICTOOLS-2 project (TIN2007-68093-C02-01).

General Terms

Algorithms, Languages, Theory, Verification

Keywords

Tree automata, Homomorphisms, Regular languages, Transducers

1. INTRODUCTION

We provide an algorithm that, given a tree homomorphism H and a regular tree language L represented by a tree automaton, determines whether $H(L)$ is regular. This settles a question that has been open for a long time.

A simple form of describing a finite automaton A is by giving a finite set of rules of the form $qa \to q'$, where q, q' are state symbols and a is an input symbol. Additionally, we must specify the initial state q_0 and the set of accepting states. A word w is accepted by A if $q_0 w$ can reach an accepting state by successive application of the rules. For example, the automaton $q_0a \to q_1$, $q_0b \to q_0$, $q_1a \to q_0$, $q_1b \to q_1$, where q_0 is the initial and the unique accepting state, recognizes the language W of words over the alphabet $\{a, b\}$ with an even number of occurrences of a. Word sets/languages recognized by automata are called regular.

Working with regular languages has several benefits. They are expressive enough in different settings, are closed under many natural operations, and there are efficient procedures for deciding most of their properties. In this paper, we focus on homomorphisms. A word homomorphism is any function H relating words which commutes with word concatenation, i.e. $H(xy) = H(x)H(y)$. Alternatively, any homomorphism H can be recursively defined by equations of the form $H(ax) = wH(x)$, where a is an alphabet symbol, x is a word variable and w is a word. In addition, $H(\lambda) = \lambda$ must hold for the empty word λ. For example, the image of the above language W by the homomorphism H defined by $H(ax) = aH(x)$, $H(bx) = H(x)$, $H(\lambda) = \lambda$ is the set of words over $\{a\}$ of even length. The advantage of homomorphic transformations on word languages is that they are regularity preserving, i.e. the image of a regular language by a word homomorphism is also regular.

In some contexts, terms, i.e. labeled trees, are more suited to express structured concepts than words. In a similar way to the definition of automata for words, one can define tree automata for trees. A (bottom-up) tree automaton (TA) is a set of rules of the form $f(q_1, \ldots, q_m) \to q$, where $q_1, \ldots, q_m, q$

are state symbols and f is an alphabet symbol which can be used for labeling some nodes of an input tree. Additionally, we must specify the set of accepting states. For example, consider the tree automaton A defined by the rules $a \rightarrow q_1$, $b \rightarrow q_0$, $f(q_0, q_0) \rightarrow q_0$, $f(q_0, q_1) \rightarrow q_1$, $f(q_1, q_0) \rightarrow q_1$, $f(q_1, q_1) \rightarrow q_0$, where q_0 is the only accepting state. It runs bottom-up on an input tree like $f(f(a, b), a)$ (see Figure 1) by successively applying the above rules. It accepts a tree if there is an execution reaching an accepting state. Our example accepts the tree language T of terms over binary f and nullaries a, b having an even number of a's.

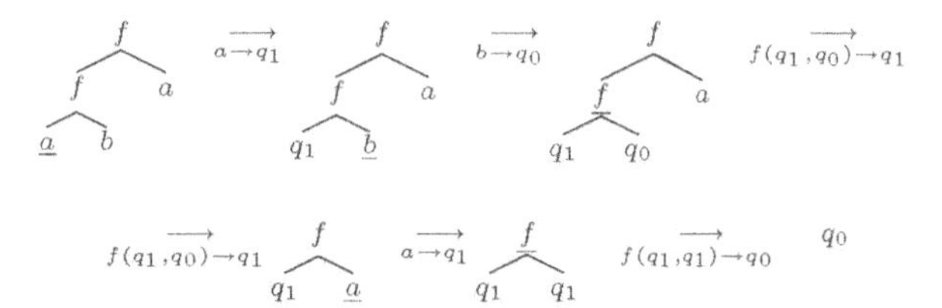

Figure 1: Execution of the tree automaton A on the input tree $f(f(a, b), a)$.

Regular tree languages, i.e. sets of terms recognized by tree automata, have almost all advantages of regular (word) languages. Nevertheless, they are not closed by homomorphisms. In the case of trees, homomorphisms can also be defined as functions commuting with a natural tree operator: application of substitution. Since this definition is not very intuitive, we prefer to just use the recursive alternative. A tree homomorphism can be defined by equations of the form $H(f(x_1, \ldots, x_n)) = t$, where t is a tree labeled by either alphabet symbols, or by $H(x_1), \ldots, H(x_n)$, which may only appear at the leaves. For example, the image of the above language T by the tree homomorphism H defined by $H(a) = a$, $H(b) = a$, $H(f(x_1, x_2)) = g(H(x_1), H(x_1))$ is the set of complete trees over binary g and nullary a (see Figure 2). It is not difficult to prove that this language is not regular. In general, non-linear tree homomorphisms like H (due to the duplication of the variable x_1) may produce non-regular images. The HOM problem questions for a given a regular tree language L described by a tree automaton and a tree homomorphism H, whether $H(L)$ regular.

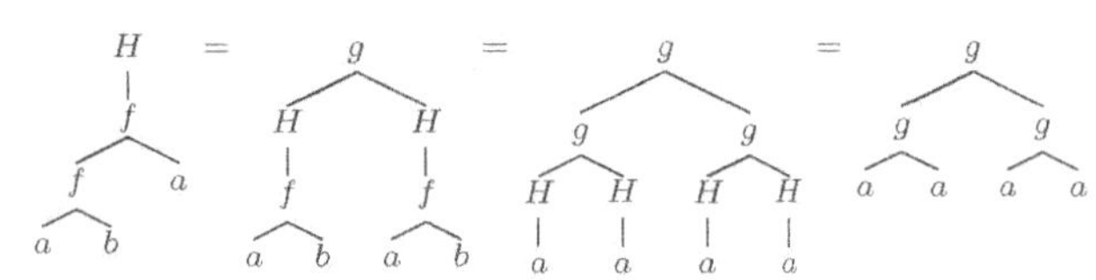

Figure 2: Recursive application of the tree homomorphism H to compute $H(f(f(a, b), a))$.

In order to increase expressiveness of the represented languages, several extensions of tree automata have been considered in literature. A well-studied case consists in allowing rules of the form $f(q_1, \ldots, q_m) \xrightarrow{c} q$, where c imposes an additional constraint for the rule application. Typically, c imposes equalities or inequalities between some subterms pending at certain positions relative to the rule application place. As an example of tree automaton with equality constraints consider the following: $a \rightarrow q$, $g(q, q) \xrightarrow{1=2} q$. The constraint $1 = 2$ imposes that the first and second subtrees must coincide for the application of the rule. Thus, the above automaton recognizes the set of complete trees over binary g and nullary a. We denote by $\mathrm{TA}_{\neq,=}$ the class of tree automata with equality and inequality constraints, and by $\mathrm{TA}_{=}$ and $\mathrm{TA}_{\neq}$ the respective subclasses allowing only equalities or only inequalities.

The gain of expressiveness of tree automata with constraints comes with the loss of good computational properties. For example, emptiness and finiteness of the language recognized by a $\mathrm{TA}_{=}$ are undecidable. In this paper we define two new classes of tree automata with constraints, called TA_{hom} and $\mathrm{TA}_{\neq,hom}$. TA_{hom} is a subclass of $\mathrm{TA}_{=}$ whose recognized languages are just the images of tree homomorphisms. $\mathrm{TA}_{\neq,hom}$ is the extension of TA_{hom} by allowing inequality constraints. Part of our contribution is to show that these classes are in the sweet spot for dealing with images of tree homomorphisms: they are expressive enough, but at the same time, they have several decidable interesting properties.

Finding an algorithm solving the HOM problem has been the focus of our research. But in the path of finding such an algorithm we have developed several ideas and techniques which are interesting by themselves and produce very significant intermediate results:

1. Given a $\mathrm{TA}_{=}$ A, a $\mathrm{TA}_{\neq}$ $\bar{A}$ can be constructed recognizing the complementary language of the first one. The size of $\bar{A}$ is exponential with respect to the size of A, and is constructed in exponential time.

2. The converse construction of a $\mathrm{TA}_{=}$ from a $\mathrm{TA}_{\neq}$ can also be done analogously.

3. As a consequence of item 1, the inclusion problem $\mathcal{L}(B) \subseteq \mathcal{L}(A)$ for a TA B and a $\mathrm{TA}_{=}$ A is shown decidable. The obtained time complexity is doubly exponential.

4. As a consequence of item 3 the universality problem for $\mathrm{TA}_{=}$, i.e. whether a given $\mathrm{TA}_{=}$ A accepts all terms, is decidable. The obtained time complexity is doubly exponential.

5. As a consequence of item 3, the inclusion problem $L_1 \subseteq H(L_2)$, for a given tree homomorphism H and regular tree languages L_1, L_2, is decidable. The obtained time complexity is doubly exponential.

6. As a consequence of item 1, regularity and universality of the language represented by a given $\mathrm{TA}_{\neq}$ are undecidable.

7. The emptiness of the language recognized by a given $\mathrm{TA}_{\neq,hom}$ is shown decidable. The obtained time complexity is a tower of five exponentials.

8. As a consequence of items 1 and 7, the inclusion problem $H_1(L_1) \subseteq H_2(L_2)$, for given tree homomorphisms H_1, H_2 and regular tree languages L_1, L_2 is decidable. The obtained time complexity is a tower of six exponentials.

9. As a consequence of item 8, the equivalence problem $H_1(L_1) = H_2(L_2)$, for given tree homomorphisms H_1, H_2 and regular tree languages L_1, L_2, is decidable. The obtained time complexity is a tower of six exponentials.

10. The finiteness of the language recognized by a given $TA_{\neq,hom}$is decidable. The obtained time complexity is a tower of five exponentials.

11. As a consequence of items 1 and 10, finiteness of the set $H_1(L_1) - H_2(L_2)$, for given tree homomorphisms H_1, H_2 and regular tree languages L_1, L_2, is decidable. The obtained time complexity is a tower of six exponentials.

12. The HOM problem is decidable. The obtained time complexity is a tower of four exponentials.

Our decision algorithm for the HOM problem has a very simple description. First, it generates a TA_{hom} A recognizing the language $H(L)$, for the given TA A and the given tree homomorphism H. Second, it linearizes A into a TA B by removing all equality constraints and replacing the involved positions in the constraints by all possible valid terms up to a certain height. Third, it checks $\mathcal{L}(A) = \mathcal{L}(B)$, concludes "regularity" in the affirmative case, and concludes "non-regularity" in the negative case.

Nevertheless, proving that this algorithm decides HOM is more complicated, and requires one to argue by intensively using the complementary construction of item 1, and the construction proving item 10.

Among all the above results, two of them (items 8 and 12) have direct implications in the context of XML. Extended DTD (document type descriptions) is a formalism expressively equivalent to tree automata. Thus, in this setting, a tree automaton is a type, i.e. it defines a set of valid descriptions, and HOM is equivalent to the following problem: given a type τ and an homomorphic transformation T, is $T(\tau)$ a type? We conclude that this question is decidable, and moreover, we are able to generate this type since our decision procedure of HOM is constructive. On the other hand, the decidability result of item 8 is at least as important as HOM in this setting. The most relevant static analysis problem for XML transformations is the TYPECHECKING problem [21], i.e., does a transformation T converts every input document of a type τ_1 into a document of a type τ_2? The TYPECHECKING problem has been shown undecidable for top-down tree transducers, which are machine-guided tree transformations. Our result on decidability of inclusion implies decidability of TYPECHECKING for the particular case where the tree transducer is, in fact, a tree homomorphism. It suffices to define L_1 as τ_1, L_2 as τ_2, H_1 as T and H_2 as the identity transformation, which is homomorphic.

To finish this introduction we provide some examples in order to see some contexts where tree automata and tree homomorphisms come up.

EXAMPLE 1.1. *Tree automata and regular tree languages are formalisms in which several XML document schema languages are based on. For instance, consider the following XML schema in DTD notation*

```
<!ELEMENT person(name,telephone*,email?)>
```

meaning the set of all XML trees consisting of a `person` *with a single* `name` *tag, any number of* `telephone` *tags and an optional* `email` *tag, like the following one:*

```
<person>
  <name>John</name>
  <telephone>666 1234</telephone>
  <telephone>666 5555</telephone>
  <email>johnfoo.com</email>
</person>
```

Note that XML trees can be represented as binary trees by using the well known left-child right-sibling bijection between arbitrary and binary trees,

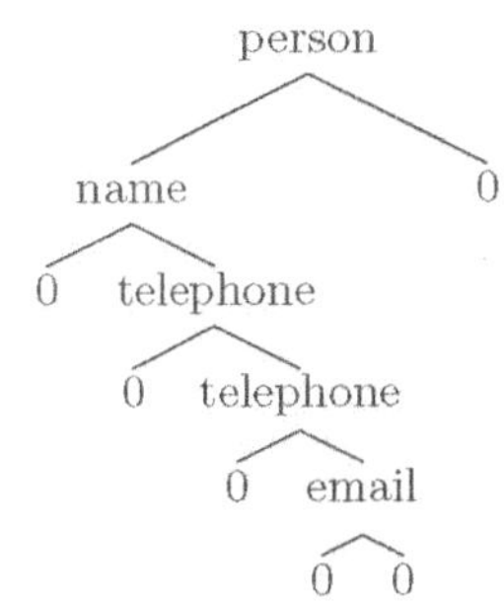

and that the set of binary trees satisfying the previous XML schema is the regular set recognized by the tree automata $0 \to q_0$, $0 \to q_t$, $\texttt{email}(q_0, q_0) \to q_t$, $\texttt{telephone}(q_0, q_t) \to q_t$, $\texttt{name}(q_0, q_t) \to q_n$, $\texttt{person}(q_n, q_0) \to q_p$, *where* q_p *is the only accepting state.*

EXAMPLE 1.2. *In computational linguistics tree automata are used to succinctly represent all possible readings of a sentence. In several practical cases, this representation allows for an exponential space reduction in contrast to keeping all such sentences explicitly. This is not the case of our example here, but it serves to figure out how this representation is made. The following tree automaton recognizes the finite tree language of all possible readings of the sentence "Every man likes a woman". The signature is* $\{\forall_x, \exists_y, \texttt{man}_x, \texttt{woman}_y, \texttt{loves}_{xy}\}$, *where* $\forall_x$ *and* $\exists_y$ *are binary, and the rest of symbols are nullary. The set of rules is* $\texttt{loves}_{xy} \to q_1$, $\texttt{man}_x \to q_{\texttt{m}}$, $\texttt{woman}_y \to q_{\texttt{w}}$, $\exists_y(q_{\texttt{w}}, q_1) \to q_{\texttt{wl}}$, $\forall_x(q_{\texttt{m}}, q_1) \to q_{\texttt{ml}}$, $\exists_y(q_{\texttt{w}}, q_{\texttt{ml}}) \to q_{\texttt{wml}}$, $\forall_x(q_{\texttt{m}}, q_{\texttt{wl}}) \to q_{\texttt{wml}}$, *and* $q_{\texttt{wml}}$ *is the only accepting state.*

Tree automata are useful in this context in order to compute the weakest readings, as the subset of normal forms with respect to a certain term rewrite system. Weakest readings are usually considered as the most appropriate interpretations of the sentence. In the example above $\forall_x(\texttt{man}_x, \exists_y(\texttt{woman}_y, \texttt{loves}_{xy}))$ *is the weakest reading by being the only normal form of the recognized regular tree language with respect to the term rewrite system* $\exists_y(z, \forall_x(u, v)) \to \forall_x(u, \exists_y(z, v))$. *Note that the right-hand side of this rule is entailed by the left-hand side, unless there is some clash with the involved names.*

EXAMPLE 1.3. *The set of reducible terms by a term rewrite system can always be represented as the image of a tree homomorphism. For example, consider the signature* $\Sigma = \{*, +, 0, 1\}$ *where* $*, +$ *are binary function symbols represented in infix notation and* $0, 1$ *are nullary symbols. The reducible terms by the rule* $(x * y) + (x * z) \to x * (y + z)$, *can be represented as the image of the tree homomorphism defined by* $H(x * y) = H(x) * H(y)$, $H(x + y) = H(x) + H(y)$, $H(\hat{*}(x, y, z)) = (H(x) * H(y)) + (H(x) * H(z))$, $H(0) = 0$, $H(1) = 1$ *applied to the set of all trees over* $\Sigma \cup \{\hat{*}\}$ *having at least one occurrence of the ternary symbol* $\hat{*}$, *which is a regular tree language.*

1.1 Related work

Finite-state tree automata (TA) [4] were introduced by Thatcher and Wright [23] in the context of circuit verification. Many famous researchers contributed to this school in the late 60's and the early 70's, establishing connections between automata and logic. In the 70's many new results were established concerning TA, which lose a bit their connections with the applications and were studied for their own. Applications of TA to program verification revived in the 80's, after the relative failure of automated deduction in this field. Automata, and in particular TA, also appeared as an approximation of programs on which fully automated tools can be used. New results were obtained connecting properties of programs or type systems or rewrite systems with automata. These applications are widely used nowadays and an extended matter of research.

Tree homomorphisms were defined in 1970 by Thatcher in [22], and by Engelfriet in [9], as a special case of tree transducers. As it can easily be derived from the fundamental results in [9], the HOM problem is equivalent to the following problem: given a bottom-up tree transducer T, is the range of T regular? Many variants, results and applications of tree transducers are studied along the 70's and 80's (see the book [12] and the handbook [13]). The oldest reference we know where the decidability of HOM is explicitly stated as a difficult open question is [14]. In the same paper, the particular case of the regularity of the reducible terms by a term rewrite system is also left as an open problem. This particular case is posted as the 7th problem in the RTA list of open problems in 1991 by Comon and Dauchet. It is solved independently in [18, 24, 20]. The HOM problem appears also in [10], where the more general case of regularity of the range of a top-down tree transducer is shown undecidable. In the more recent years, some other particularizations of the HOM problem have been taken into consideration. Tree automata with constraints are used to prove decidability of the HOM problem restricted to shallow homomorphisms in [2]. The HOM problem restricted to monadic signatures or to top-copying homomorphisms is proved decidable in [17]. The latter result is based on the decidability of first-order equational formulae with regular membership constraints proved in [5].

Emptiness of tree automata with inequality constraints is proved decidable in [6]. Exptime-completeness of this problem is proved in [7]. This result is developed in order to prove exptime-completeness of the ground reducibility problem. The decidability result in [6] is extended in [8] to the so-called class of reduction automata, which allow for arbitrary inequalities and a limited amount of equalities. Roughly speaking, a fixed number of equalities are permitted at each path of a run. This result is used to prove decidability of the first order theory of reduction. Emptiness and finiteness of tree automata with inequality and equality constraints between brothers (direct subtrees) is proved decidable in [3]. Regularity for this class was proved decidable in [2]. As a consequence, the HOM problem is proved decidable for the particular case of shallow homomorphisms, as we have mentioned above. But also, these results are key for proving decidability of preservation of regularity for shallow term rewrite systems and innermost rewriting in [16, 11]. Several other variants of tree automata with constraints have been developed, providing decidability results in logic and term rewriting, with application in protocol verification. We do not mention them since there are lots, and the provided techniques have not been used in this paper.

1.2 Organization of the paper

Due to the lack of space, some proofs, examples and explanations of this paper have been removed, but they can be found in the extended version [15]. For the sake of exposition, the organization of this contribution is the same as the one in such extended version. In Section 2 we introduce basic concepts on terms and tree automata. In Section 3 we present the construction transforming a $\mathrm{TA}_{=}$ into a $\mathrm{TA}_{\neq}$. In Section 4 we define $\mathrm{TA}_{\neq,hom}$ and TA_{hom} and their runs, state that the image of a regular tree language through a tree homomorphism can be recognized by a TA_{hom} and define the intersection of a TA_{hom} and a $\mathrm{TA}_{\neq}$. In Section 5 we state decidability of the emptiness and finiteness problems of $\mathrm{TA}_{\neq,hom}$. The proofs of these results (see [15]) are based on the concept of pumping of a run of a $\mathrm{TA}_{\neq,hom}$. In Section 6 we show all the significant intermediate consequences of our constructions. In Section 7 we use all the developed techniques to decide the HOM problem.

2. PRELIMINARIES

Due to the lack of space, we just recall the most basic definitions related to terms, regular tree languages and tree homomorphisms. For more detailed explanations see [1, 4, 15, 12, 13].

The set of symbols of arity m of a signature Σ is denoted as $\Sigma^{(m)}$. The set of terms over a signature Σ with variables in $\mathcal{X} = \{x_1, x_2, \dots\}$, denoted $\mathcal{T}(\Sigma \cup \mathcal{X})$ or $\mathcal{T}(\Sigma, \mathcal{X})$, is the set of terms over $\Sigma \cup \mathcal{X}$ where every symbol in $\mathcal{X}$ has arity zero, while $\mathcal{T}(\Sigma)$ denotes the set of ground (without variables) terms. By $|t|$ we denote the size of a term t. By $\mathtt{height}(t)$ we denote the height of t. Positions in terms are sequences of natural numbers. Given a term $f(t_1, \dots, t_m) \in \mathcal{T}(\Sigma)$, its set of positions $\mathtt{Pos}(t)$ is defined recursively as $\{\lambda\} \cup_{1 \le i \le m} \{i.p \mid p \in \mathtt{Pos}(t_i)\}$. λ denotes the empty sequence (position of the root node), and $p_1.p_2$, or simply p_1p_2, denotes concatenation of positions. The subterm of t at position p is denoted by $t|_p$, and we say that t at position p is labeled by $\mathtt{root}(t|_p)$. For a set Γ, we use $\mathtt{Pos}_\Gamma(t)$ to denote the set of positions of t that are labeled by symbols in Γ. For terms s, t and position $p \in \mathtt{Pos}(s)$, we denote by $s[t]_p$ the result of replacing the subterm at position p in s by the term t. A *substitution* σ is a mapping from variables to terms. It can be homomorphically extended to a function from terms to terms: $\sigma(t)$ denotes the result of simultaneously replacing in t every $x \in \mathtt{Dom}(\sigma)$ by $\sigma(x)$.

Along this paper, by $t|_{p_1} = t|_{p_2}$ we mean that p_1 and p_2 are positions in $\mathtt{Pos}(t)$ and the subterms of t at positions p_1 and p_2 coincide. On the other side, by $t|_{p_1} \neq t|_{p_2}$ we mean that either p_1 or p_2 is not in $\mathtt{Pos}(t)$, or that the subterms $t|_{p_1}$ and $t|_{p_2}$ are different. Note that, with this semantics, $t|_{p_1} \neq t|_{p_2}$ is the negation of $t|_{p_1} = t|_{p_2}$.

A *tree automaton*, TA for short, is a tuple $A = \langle Q, \Sigma, F, \Delta \rangle$, where Q is a set of states, Σ is a signature, $F \subseteq Q$ is the subset of final states, and Δ is a set of rules of the form $f(q_1, \dots, q_m) \to q$, where $q_1, \dots, q_m, q$ are in Q, and f is in $\Sigma^{(m)}$. The language recognized by A, denoted $\mathcal{L}(A)$, is the set of terms in $\mathcal{T}(\Sigma)$ reaching an accepting state by applying the rules of Δ. A term language L is *regular* if there exists a TA A satisfying $\mathcal{L}(A) = L$. We denote the extensions to TA with equality constraints, TA with inequality constraints and TA with equality and inequality constraints as $TA_=$, $TA_{\neq}$ and $TA_{\neq,=}$, respectively. For a definition of tree automata with constraints see [4, 15].

Let Σ_1, Σ_2 be two signatures. A *tree homomorphism* is a function $H : \mathcal{T}(\Sigma_1) \to \mathcal{T}(\Sigma_2)$ which can be defined as follows. Let X_m represent the set of variables $\{x_1, \ldots, x_m\}$ for each natural number m. The definition of a tree homomorphism $H : \mathcal{T}(\Sigma_1) \to \mathcal{T}(\Sigma_2)$ requires to define $H(f(x_1, \ldots, x_m))$ for each function symbol $f \in \Sigma_1$ of arity m as a term t_f in $\mathcal{T}(\Sigma_2 \cup X_m)$. After that, $H(f(t_1, \ldots, t_m))$ is defined, for each term $f(t_1, \ldots, t_m) \in \mathcal{T}(\Sigma_1)$, as $\{x_1 \mapsto H(t_1), \ldots, x_m \mapsto H(t_m)\}(t_f)$.

DEFINITION 2.1. *The HOM problem is defined as follows:*
Input: *A TA A and a tree homomorphism H.*
Question: *Is $H(\mathcal{L}(A))$ regular?*

3. THE COMPLEMENT OF A $TA_=$

For a given $TA_=$ $A = \langle Q, \Sigma, F, \Delta \rangle$ we want to construct a $TA_{\neq}$ B recognizing the complement of $\mathcal{L}(A)$. This construction is rather easy. We just need to consider 2^Q as the set of states of B. The intuitive meaning of each state $S \subseteq Q$ is that there exists a run with B of a term t with resulting state S if and only if, for each q in S, there is no run with A of t with resulting state q. In other words, using B we are computing sets of states which cannot be reached using A. The rules $f(S_1, \ldots, S_m) \xrightarrow{D} S$ of B are constructed to ensure that, for those states q in S, no rule of A with right-hand side q can be applied.

DEFINITION 3.1 (COMPLEMENT OF A $TA_=$). *Let $A = \langle Q, \Sigma, F, \Delta \rangle$ be a $TA_=$. Then, the complement $TA_{\neq}$ B of A is defined as the tuple $\langle 2^Q, \Sigma, \{F' \mid F \subseteq F' \subseteq Q\}, \Delta' \rangle$ where Δ' is the set of rules $f(S_1, \ldots, S_m) \xrightarrow{D} S$ satisfying the following:*

- *$S_1, \ldots, S_m, S \subseteq Q$.*
- *D is a conjunction of inequalities $p \neq q$ such that $p = q$ occurs in the constraint of some rule in Δ.*
- *For each q in S and each rule of the form $f(q_1, \ldots, q_m) \xrightarrow{c} q$ in Δ either there exists some i in $\{1, \ldots, m\}$ satisfying $q_i \in S_i$, or there exist positions p_1, p_2 such that $p_1 = p_2$ occurs in c and $p_1 \neq p_2$ occurs in D.*

EXAMPLE 3.2. *Let $A = \langle Q, \Sigma, F, \Delta \rangle$ be the $TA_=$ with $Q = \{q\}$, $\Sigma = \{f^{(2)}, a^{(0)}\}$, $F = \{q\}$, and where Δ contains the two rules $a \to q$ and $f(q, q) \xrightarrow{1=2} q$. This $TA_=$ recognizes the language of the complete trees. We can construct the complement $TA_{\neq}$ as follows. The set of states is $2^Q = \{\emptyset, \{q\}\}$, the signature is the same Σ, the set of accepting states is $F' = \{\{q\}\}$ and some of the rules in Δ' are:*

- $a \to \emptyset$
- $f(\emptyset, \emptyset) \to \emptyset$
- $f(\emptyset, \emptyset) \xrightarrow{1\neq 2} \{q\}$
- $f(\{q\}, \emptyset) \to \{q\}$
- $f(\emptyset, \{q\}) \to \{q\}$
- $f(\{q\}, \{q\}) \to \{q\}$

This automaton clearly recognizes the language of the non-complete trees (because at each position we can non-deterministically check that either at least one child is non-complete, or both children are not equal). According to the definition of the complement of a $TA_=$, there exist more rules in Δ' (like $f(\{q\}, \{q\}) \xrightarrow{1\neq 2} \{q\}$), but they are unnecessary or useless.

THEOREM 3.3. *Let $A = \langle Q, \Sigma, F, \Delta \rangle$ be a $TA_=$, and $B = \langle 2^Q, \Sigma, \{F' \mid F \subseteq F' \subseteq Q\}, \Delta' \rangle$ be its complement $TA_{\neq}$. Then, $\overline{\mathcal{L}(A)} = \mathcal{L}(B)$.*

Proceeding analogously we could transform a $TA_{\neq}$ into a $TA_=$ recognizing the complement of the first. We do not develop this transformation since it is very similar and we do not use it for the proof of the HOM problem, but state the analogous consequence as follows.

THEOREM 3.4. *Let $A = \langle Q, \Sigma, F, \Delta \rangle$ be a $TA_{\neq}$. Then, it can be computed a $TA_=$ $B = \langle 2^Q, \Sigma, \{F' \mid F \subseteq F' \subseteq Q\}, \Delta' \rangle$, called the complement $TA_=$ of A, such that $\overline{\mathcal{L}(A)} = \mathcal{L}(B)$.*

4. TREE AUTOMATA WITH INEQUALITY AND HOM EQUALITY CONSTRAINTS

Our aim is to define a new class of automata, with a certain kind of equality constraints, recognizing images of tree homomorphisms applied to regular tree languages. These will be the tree automata with HOM constraints, denoted TA_{hom}, and they essentially recognize the range of a bottom up tree transducer. But we will define a more general class including also arbitrary inequality constraints, denoted $TA_{\neq,hom}$. The reason is that we will need to argue about the intersection language of the languages represented by a TA_{hom} and a $TA_{\neq}$.

The definition of $TA_{\neq,hom}$ has differences from the definition of $TA_{\neq,=}$. The left-hand side of rules are not necessarily flat. Thus, they directly use information of states computed at relative positions deeper than 1. The inequality constraints are arbitrary, but the equality constraints are restricted. They always refer to positions with identical computed states. The rules are also labeled. The labels are not relevant at all for further definitions of run, pumping, etc. They are used when intersecting two automata, for keeping the necessary information to recover the runs of the two original automata from a run of their intersection automaton.

DEFINITION 4.1 (NEW AUTOMATA). *A tree automaton with inequality and HOM equality constraints, $TA_{\neq,hom}$ for short, is a tuple $A = \langle Q, \Sigma, F, \Delta \rangle$, where Q is a set of states, Σ is a signature, $F \subseteq Q$ is the subset of final states, and Δ is a set of labeled rules of the form $(I : s \xrightarrow{c} q)$, where I is the label, s is a term over $\mathcal{T}(\Sigma \cup Q) - Q$, interpreting the states of Q as 0-ary symbols, and c is a conjunction/set of atoms of the form $p_1 \neq p_2$ for arbitrary positions p_1, p_2, and atoms of the form $\hat{p}_1 = \hat{p}_2$, where $\hat{p}_1$ and $\hat{p}_2$ are different positions satisfying $s|_{\hat{p}_1} = s|_{\hat{p}_2} \in Q$. Moreover, for all positions $\hat{p}_1, \hat{p}_2, \hat{p}_3$, if $(\hat{p}_1 = \hat{p}_2)$ and $(\hat{p}_2 = \hat{p}_3)$ occur in c, then $(\hat{p}_1 = \hat{p}_3)$ also occurs in c. When no constraint in Δ contains a inequality, we say that A is a TA_{hom}.*

EXAMPLE 4.2. *As an example of TA_{hom} consider $A_{ex} = \langle Q, \Sigma, F, \Delta\rangle$, where $Q = F = \{q\}$, $\Sigma = \{f^{(3)}, h^{(1)}, a^{(0)}\}$, and Δ is the set of rules*

- $\rho_1 = I_1 : a \to q$
- $\rho_2 = I_2 : h(a) \to q$
- $\rho_3 = I_3 : h(f(q,q,q)) \xrightarrow{1.1=1.2} q.$

Note that the equality constraint refers to positions with the same state, which is mandatory for this kind of automata.

In order to define the concept of run of a $TA_{\neq,hom}$ we define the alphabet for describing runs on terms, which are just terms with additional labels indicating which rule has been applied at each node. The difference with respect to the case of plain tree automata with constraints is that now we may also use function symbols in Σ for defining runs, but not only rules. Roughly speaking, this is because the rules are not applied at all the positions of a term, since the left-hand sides of rules are not necessarily flat.

DEFINITION 4.3 (ALPHABET OF A RUN). *Let $A = \langle Q, \Sigma, F, \Delta\rangle$ be a $TA_{\neq,hom}$. The* alphabet of a run *of A is $\Sigma \cup \Delta$, where each rule $(I : s \xrightarrow{c} q)$ has the same arity as the one of the symbol* $\texttt{root}(s)$.

The resulting state *of a term r in $\mathcal{T}(\Sigma \cup \Delta)$ is q if r is of the form $(I : s \xrightarrow{c} q)(t_1, \dots, t_m)$.*

The projection *$\pi_\Sigma : \mathcal{T}(\Sigma \cup \Delta) \to \mathcal{T}(\Sigma)$ is recursively defined as $\pi_\Sigma(f(t_1, \dots, t_m)) = f(\pi_\Sigma(t_1), \dots, \pi_\Sigma(t_m))$ and as $\pi_\Sigma((I : s \xrightarrow{c} q)(t_1, \dots, t_m)) = (\texttt{root}(s))(\pi_\Sigma(t_1), \dots, \pi_\Sigma(t_m))$ for each rule $(I : s \xrightarrow{c} q)$ in Δ.*

Runs of $TA_{\neq,hom}$ are defined similarly to runs of $TA_{\neq,=}$. One of the differences is that, for a given equality ($p_1 = p_2$), while a $TA_{\neq,=}$ checks for equality of the projected terms at the relative positions p_1 and p_2, a $TA_{\neq,hom}$ checks for equality of the subruns at the relative positions p_1 and p_2, before projecting. This difference is not relevant, since by interpreting equalities in the usual way we would have the same expressiveness. We have chosen it making the proofs easier.

DEFINITION 4.4 (RUN). *Let $A = \langle Q, \Sigma, F, \Delta\rangle$ be a $TA_{\neq,hom}$. We define the concept of a* run *of A as a term in $\mathcal{T}(\Sigma \cup \Delta)$ satisfying certain conditions recursively as follows. Let $(I : s \xrightarrow{c} q)$ be a rule of Δ, where s is of the form $f(s_1, \dots, s_m)$. Let $P = \{\hat{p}_1, \dots, \hat{p}_n\}$ be the set of positions of s such that $(\hat{p} \in P \Leftrightarrow s|_{\hat{p}} \in Q)$ holds. Let $q_1, \dots, q_n$ be $s|_{\hat{p}_1}, \dots, s|_{\hat{p}_n}$, respectively. Let $r_1, \dots, r_n$ be runs of A with resulting states $q_1, \dots, q_n$, respectively. Let s' be $\pi_\Sigma(s[r_1]_{\hat{p}_1} \dots [r_n]_{\hat{p}_n})$. Suppose $r_i = r_j$ for each $(\hat{p}_i = \hat{p}_j) \in c$, and $s'|_{p_1} \neq s'|_{p_2}$ for each $(p_1 \neq p_2) \in c$. Then, $(I : s \xrightarrow{c} q)(s_1, \dots, s_m)[r_1]_{\hat{p}_1} \dots [r_n]_{\hat{p}_n}$ is a* run *of A.*

By $\mathcal{L}(A, q)$ we denote the set of terms t for which there exists a run r of A with resulting state q such that $\pi_\Sigma(r) = t$. The language accepted by A, denoted $\mathcal{L}(A)$, is $\bigcup_{q \in F} \mathcal{L}(A, q)$.

EXAMPLE 4.5. *(Following example 4.2) The term $r_{ex} = \rho_3(f(\rho_1, \rho_1, \rho_2(a)))$ is a run of A_{ex} with projection $\pi_\Sigma(r_{ex}) = h(f(a, a, h(a)))$.*

The following lemma establishes that TA_{hom} can be used to represent images of regular tree languages through tree homomorphisms.

PROPOSITION 4.6. *Let $B = \langle Q, \Sigma_1, F, \Delta\rangle$ be a TA. Let $H : \mathcal{T}(\Sigma_1) \to \mathcal{T}(\Sigma_2)$ be a tree homomorphism. Then, it can be computed a TA_{hom} A satisfying $H(\mathcal{L}(B)) = \mathcal{L}(A)$.*

EXAMPLE 4.7. *Let $A_r = \langle Q, \Sigma, F, \Delta\rangle$ be the TA satisfying $Q = F = \{q\}$, $\Sigma = \{a^{(0)}, b^{(0)}, g^{(2)}\}$ and $\Delta = \{a \to q, b \to q, g(q,q) \to q\}$. That is, a TA recognizing the set of all trees with a binary symbol g and leaves a and b. Let Σ_{ex} be the signature of the TA_{hom} A_{ex} of example 4.2. Let $H : \mathcal{T}(\Sigma) \to \mathcal{T}(\Sigma_{ex})$ be the tree homomorphism defined as follows:*

- $H(a) = a$
- $H(b) = h(a)$
- $H(g(x_1, x_2)) = h(f(x_2, x_2, x_1))$

The construction of Proposition 4.6 produces A_{ex}, and it is easy to prove that $H(\mathcal{L}(A_r)) = \mathcal{L}(A_{ex})$ holds.

The following lemma establishes that a TA_{hom} is essentially a particular case of a $TA_=$, that is, for each TA_{hom} we can construct a $TA_=$ recognizing the same language. It will be useful to obtain a $TA_{\neq}$ recognizing the complement of a TA_{hom}. The difficult point to prove this inclusion (see [15]) is the fact that equalities of a TA_{hom} ask for identical runs, while equalities of a $TA_=$ ask just for identically projected runs. But this is easy to solve by transforming a run of the constructed $TA_=$ in order to make those identically projected runs also identical as runs.

LEMMA 4.8. *Given a TA_{hom} $A_{hom} = \langle Q, \Sigma, F, \Delta\rangle$, a $TA_=$ $A_=$ can be computed satisfying $\mathcal{L}(A_{hom}) = \mathcal{L}(A_=)$.*

From Theorem 3.3 and Lemma 4.8 the following corollary follows.

COROLLARY 4.9. *Given a TA_{hom} $A_{hom} = \langle Q, \Sigma, F, \Delta\rangle$, a $TA_{\neq}$ $A_{\neq}$ can be computed satisfying $\overline{\mathcal{L}(A)} = \mathcal{L}(A_{\neq})$.*

DEFINITION 4.10. *Given a TA_{hom} A_{hom}, by $\overline{A_{hom}}$ we define the $TA_{\neq}$ provided by Corollary 4.9.*

Now, we show how to intersect a $TA_{\neq}$ and a TA_{hom} producing a $TA_{\neq,hom}$. Here is when the labels play an important role, keeping the necessary information of the original runs in order to be able to recover them by projection from a run of the produced $TA_{\neq,hom}$. These operations are necessary for the proof of decidability of the HOM problem (see [15]). We do not mind about the labels of the initial TA_{hom}, and obviate them.

DEFINITION 4.11 (INTERSECT. OF TA_{hom} AND $TA_{\neq}$). *Let $A = \langle Q_A, \Sigma, F_A, \Delta_A\rangle$ be a TA_{hom}. Let $B = \langle Q_B, \Sigma, F_B, \Delta_B\rangle$ be a $TA_{\neq}$. We define the $TA_{\neq,hom}$ $A \cap B$ as $\langle Q_A \times Q_B, \Sigma, F_A \times F_B, \Delta\rangle$, where Δ is the set of rules $(I : s \xrightarrow{c} \langle q_A, q_B\rangle)$ satisfying the following conditions.*

- *s is a term in $\mathcal{T}(\Sigma \cup (Q_A \times Q_B))$.*
- *there exists a rule $(s' \xrightarrow{c'} q_A)$ in Δ_A satisfying* $\texttt{Pos}_\Sigma(s') = \texttt{Pos}_\Sigma(s)$ *and for each $p \in$* $\texttt{Pos}_\Sigma(s')$, $\texttt{root}(s'|_p) = \texttt{root}(s|_p)$ *holds.*
- *For each $\hat{p} \in$* $\texttt{Pos}(s)$ *such that $s|_{\hat{p}}$ is of the form $\langle q'_A, q'_B\rangle$, $s'|_{\hat{p}}$ is q'_A.*

- $I : \texttt{Pos}_\Sigma(s) \rightarrow \Delta_B$ *is a mapping satisfying the following conditions for each p in* $\texttt{Pos}_\Sigma(s)$*: If* $I(p)$ *is of the form* $(f(q_{1B},\ldots,q_{mB}) \xrightarrow{c''} q'_B)$*, then* $\texttt{root}(s|_p)$ *is* f*, and for each* i *in* $\{1,\ldots,m\}$*, either* $s|_{p.i}$ *is a state of the form* $\langle \_, q_{iB}\rangle$*, or* $I(p.i)$ *is defined as a rule with right-hand side* q_{iB}*.*

- c *is the set* $c' \cup \{p.p_1 \neq p.p_2 | p \in \texttt{Pos}_\Sigma(s) \wedge \exists t, c'', q'_B : (I(p) = (t \xrightarrow{c''} q'_B) \wedge (p_1 \neq p_2) \in c'')\}$*. Moreover, for each* $\hat{p}_1 = \hat{p}_2$ *in* c'*,* $s|_{\hat{p}_1} = s|_{\hat{p}_2}$ *holds.*

EXAMPLE 4.12. *Let* $A_d = \langle Q', \Sigma, F', \Delta'\rangle$ *be a* $TA_{\neq}$ *with* $Q' = F' = \{q'\}$*,* $\Sigma = \Sigma_{ex}$ *(the signature of the* TA_{hom} A_{ex} *of example 4.2), and where* Δ' *contains the rules:*

- $\bar{\rho}_1 = a \rightarrow q'$
- $\bar{\rho}_2 = f(q', q', q') \xrightarrow{2 \neq 3} q'$
- $\bar{\rho}_3 = h(q') \xrightarrow{1.1 \neq 1.3} q'$
- $\bar{\rho}_4 = h(q') \xrightarrow{1.1 \neq 1.2} q'$

We can compute the $TA_{\neq,hom}$ $\hat{A} = A_{ex} \cap A_d$ *obtaining* $\langle Q \times Q', \Sigma, F \times F', \Delta\rangle$*, where* Δ *contains the following rules:*

- $\hat{\rho}_1 = I_1 : a \rightarrow \langle q, q'\rangle$*, with label* $I_1(\lambda) = \bar{\rho}_1$*.*

- $\hat{\rho}_2 = I_2 : h(a) \xrightarrow{1.1 \neq 1.3} \langle q, q'\rangle$*, with label* $I_2(\lambda) = \bar{\rho}_3$*,* $I_2(1) = \bar{\rho}_1$*. (Note that the constraint is always satisfied.)*

- $\hat{\rho}_3 = I_3 : h(a) \xrightarrow{1.1 \neq 1.2} \langle q, q'\rangle$*, with label* $I_3(\lambda) = \bar{\rho}_4$*,* $I_3(1) = \bar{\rho}_1$*. (Note that the constraint is always satisfied.)*

- $\hat{\rho}_4 = I_4 : h(f(\langle q, q'\rangle, \langle q, q'\rangle, \langle q, q'\rangle)) \xrightarrow{\substack{1.1 = 1.2 \\ 1.2 \neq 1.3 \\ 1.1 \neq 1.3}} \langle q, q'\rangle$*, with label* $I_4(\lambda) = \bar{\rho}_3$*,* $I_4(1) = \bar{\rho}_2$*.*

- $\hat{\rho}_5 = I_5 : h(f(\langle q, q'\rangle, \langle q, q'\rangle, \langle q, q'\rangle)) \xrightarrow{\substack{1.1 = 1.2 \\ 1.2 \neq 1.3 \\ 1.1 \neq 1.2}} \langle q, q'\rangle$*, with label* $I_5(\lambda) = \bar{\rho}_4$*,* $I_5(1) = \bar{\rho}_2$*, which is useless because the constraint is unsatisfiable.*

PROPOSITION 4.13. *Let* A *be a* TA_{hom}*. Let* B *be a* $TA_{\neq}$*. Then,* $\mathcal{L}(A \cap B) = \mathcal{L}(A) \cap \mathcal{L}(B)$*.*

5. PUMPINGS

Pumping is a traditional concept in automata theory, and in particular, they are very useful to reason about tree automata. The basic idea is to convert a given run r into another run by replacing a subterm at a certain position p in r by a run r', thus obtaining a run $r[r']_p$. In [15], for $TA_{\neq,hom}$ and when a term is big enough, the existence of a pumping decreasing the size and producing a correct run is proved. This allows to prove decidability of emptiness. The argumentation of this fact follows the ideas presented in [8].

THEOREM 5.1. *The emptiness problem is decidable for* $TA_{\neq,hom}$*.*

When a term is big enough, it can also be argued the existence of infinitely many pumpings increasing the size and producing correct runs. This allows to prove decidability of finiteness.

THEOREM 5.2. *The finiteness problem is decidable for* $TA_{\neq,hom}$*.*

Increasing pumpings are also used in the proof of decidability of the HOM problem. For future reference, we call $\check{h}(A)$ to the height, depending on A, which ensures the existence of infinitely many increasing pumpings in a given term. It is exponential on the size of A. See [15] for the precise definition of the bound $\check{h}(A)$.

6. CONSEQUENCES

We first mention the consequences from the construction for the complement.

THEOREM 6.1. *The inclusion problem* $\mathcal{L}(A) \supseteq \mathcal{L}(B)$ *is decidable for a* $TA_=$ A *and a TA* B *given as input.*

PROOF. By Theorem 3.3, the complement $TA_{\neq}$ $\bar{A}$ of A recognizes $\overline{\mathcal{L}(A)}$. It is well-known how to compute a new $TA_{\neq}$ recognizing the intersection of the languages represented by a $TA_{\neq}$ and a TA (in fact, our Definition 4.11 subsumes this construction). Thus, a $TA_{\neq}$ $\bar{A} \cap B$ recognizing $\overline{\mathcal{L}(A)} \cap \mathcal{L}(B)$ can be computed. It is well-known (see [6, 7]) that emptiness of a $TA_{\neq}$ is decidable (in fact, our Theorem 5.1 subsumes this result). Thus, we conclude by noting that deciding emptiness of $\overline{\mathcal{L}(A)} \cap \mathcal{L}(B)$ is equivalent to deciding $\mathcal{L}(A) \supseteq \mathcal{L}(B)$. $\square$

COROLLARY 6.2. *The universality problem is decidable for* $TA_=$*.*

PROOF. Deciding $\mathcal{L}(A) = \mathcal{T}(\Sigma)$ is equivalent to deciding $\mathcal{L}(A) \supseteq \mathcal{T}(\Sigma)$, and since $\mathcal{T}(\Sigma)$ is regular, from Theorem 6.1 it follows that universality is decidable. $\square$

COROLLARY 6.3. *The finiteness problem of* $\mathcal{L}(B) - \mathcal{L}(A)$ *is decidable for a* $TA_=$ A *and a TA* B *given as input.*

PROOF. As in the proof of Theorem 6.1, we can construct a $TA_{\neq}$ recognizing $\overline{\mathcal{L}(A)} \cap \mathcal{L}(B)$. In order to conclude, we mention that it is well-known that finiteness of a $TA_{\neq}$ is decidable (in fact, our Theorem 5.2 subsumes this result). $\square$

COROLLARY 6.4. *The regularity test is undecidable for* $TA_{\neq}$*, and thus, for reduction tree automata.*

PROOF. Since regularity is undecidable for $TA_=$, our transformation of a $TA_=$ into a $TA_{\neq}$ recognizing the complement is a reduction from this problem into regularity of a $TA_{\neq}$. Since $TA_{\neq}$ are a particular case of reduction automata, the second part of the statement follows, too. $\square$

Now, we mention the consequences of combining the construction for the complement and the decidability of emptiness and finiteness of $TA_{\neq,hom}$. Some of them generalize previous ones.

THEOREM 6.5. *The inclusion problem is decidable for images of tree homomorphisms, that is,* $\mathcal{L}(H_A(A)) \supseteq \mathcal{L}(H_B(B))$ *is decidable for a TA* A*, a TA* B*, and tree homomorphisms* H_A *and* H_B *given as input.*

PROOF. By Proposition 4.6, two TA$_=$ A' and B' recognizing $\mathcal{L}(H_A(A))$ and $\mathcal{L}(H_B(B))$, respectively, can be computed. By Lemma 4.8 and Theorem 3.3, the complement TA$_{\neq}$ $\bar{A}'$ of A' recognizes $\overline{\mathcal{L}(A')}$. By Proposition 4.13, $\bar{A}' \cap B'$ recognizes $\overline{\mathcal{L}(A')} \cap \mathcal{L}(B')$. By Theorem 5.1, emptiness of $\overline{\mathcal{L}(A')} \cap \mathcal{L}(B')$ is decidable. Thus, we conclude by noting that deciding emptiness of $\overline{\mathcal{L}(A')} \cap \mathcal{L}(B')$ is equivalent to deciding $\mathcal{L}(H_A(A)) \supseteq \mathcal{L}(H_B(B))$. □

COROLLARY 6.6. *The equivalence problem is decidable for images of tree homomorphisms, that is,* $\mathcal{L}(H_A(A)) = \mathcal{L}(H_B(B))$ *is decidable for a TA A, a TA B, and tree homomorphisms* H_A *and* H_B *given as input.*

COROLLARY 6.7. *The inclusion and equivalence problems are decidable for ranges of bottom-up tree transducers.*

COROLLARY 6.8. *The finiteness problem of* $\mathcal{L}(H_B(B)) - \mathcal{L}(H_A(A))$ *is decidable for a TA A, a TA B, and tree homomorphisms* H_A *and* H_B *given as input.*

PROOF. As in the proof of Theorem 6.5, we can construct a TA$_{\neq}$ recognizing $\overline{\mathcal{L}(H_A(A))} \cap \mathcal{L}(H_B(B))$. In order to conclude, we note that, by Theorem 5.2, finiteness of the previous set is decidable. □

7. DECISION OF THE HOM PROBLEM

In this section we state that the HOM problem is decidable. Due to the lack of space we just present the algorithm, which is simple. The proof that it works is considerably complicated (see [15] for the proof, examples and more intuition), and makes use of almost all results obtained for TA$_{\neq,hom}$ in the previous sections.

7.1 The algorithm deciding the HOM problem

DEFINITION 7.1 (LINEARIZATION OF A TA$_{hom}$). *Let* $A_{hom} = \langle Q, \Sigma, F, \Delta \rangle$ *be a* TA$_{hom}$. *Let* h *be a natural number. The* linearization *of* A_{hom} *by* h *is the* TA$_{hom}$ $\langle Q, \Sigma, F, \Delta' \rangle$, *denoted* $\texttt{linearize}(A_{hom}, \texttt{h})$, *where* Δ' *is the set of all rules of the form* $s[s_1]_{p_1} \ldots [s_n]_{p_n} \rightarrow q$ *such that:*

- *A rule of the form* $s \xrightarrow{c} q$ *occurs in* Δ.
- $p_1, \ldots, p_n$ *are the positions occurring in c.*
- *For each i in* $\{1, \ldots, n\}$, s_i *is a term in* $\mathcal{L}(A_{hom}, s|_{p_i})$ *such that* $\texttt{height}(s_i) \leq \texttt{h}$.
- *For each i, j in* $\{1, \ldots, n\}$ *such that* $(p_i = p_j)$ *occurs in c,* $s_i = s_j$ *holds.*

It is straightforward that a linearization of any TA$_{hom}$ is computable and recognizes a regular tree language, since no equality constraints appear. It is also clear that $\mathcal{L}(A_{hom})$ includes the language of any of its linearizations. Moreover, in the case where $\mathcal{L}(A_{hom})$ is included in some of its linearizations, we can conclude that $\mathcal{L}(A_{hom})$ is regular.

The key point for deciding the HOM problem using linearization is stated by the following lemma.

LEMMA 7.2. *Let* A_{hom} *be a* TA$_{hom}$. *Let* $\check{h}$ *be* $\check{h}(A_{hom} \cap \overline{A_{hom}})$. *Suppose that* $\mathcal{L}(A_{hom})$ *is not included in* $\mathcal{L}(\texttt{linearize}(A_{hom}, \check{h}))$. *Then,* $\mathcal{L}(A_{hom})$ *is not regular.*

The natural number $\check{h}$ is the one described at the end of Section 5. The proof of this lemma is partially done in the next subsections and completely in [15]. It provides a simple decision algorithm for the HOM problem, described as follows.

- Input: A tree automaton A and a tree homomorphism H.
- Construct a TA_{hom} A_{hom} recognizing $H(A)$.
- Construct the linearization B of A_{hom} by $\check{h} = \check{h}(A_{hom} \cap \overline{A_{hom}})$.
- If $\mathcal{L}(\texttt{linearize}(A_{hom}, \check{h}))$ includes $\mathcal{L}(A_{hom})$ then halt with output "REGULAR".
- Otherwise, halt with output "NON-REGULAR".

The construction of the second item can be done according to Proposition 4.6. The TA$_{\neq}$ $\overline{A_{hom}}$ is constructed according to Definitions 3.1 and 4.10. The TA$_{\neq,hom}$ $A_{hom} \cap \overline{A_{hom}}$ is constructed according to Definition 4.11. There is a straightforward algorithm based on a fixpoint computation for deciding the inclusion of the fourth item. Nevertheless, Theorem 6.5 provides a more general decision procedure.

THEOREM 7.3. *The HOM problem is decidable.*

To conclude, it remains to prove Lemma 7.2.

7.2 A non-terminating process detecting non-regularity

In order to prove Lemma 7.2, we describe a non-terminating process. We emphasize that this process is not executed in order to decide regularity (the algorithm has already been presented in the previous section). It will just help us to argue about the certainness of Lemma 7.2.

The process deals with sets of terms with equality constraints. They represent an infinite set of ground terms: the ones obtained by applying substitutions holding the constraints.

DEFINITION 7.4 (CONSTRAINED TERMS). *Let* $A_{hom} = \langle Q, \Sigma, F, \Delta \rangle$ *be a* TA$_{hom}$. *A* constrained term *with respect to* A_{hom} *is a pair* $t|c$, *where t is a term in* $\mathcal{T}(\Sigma \cup Q)$, *and c is a conjunction/set of equalities of positions* $(p_1 = p_2)$ *satisfying that* $t|_{p_1} = t|_{p_2} \in Q$ *holds and* p_1 *and* p_2 *are different. Moreover, if* $(p_1 = p_2), (p_2 = p_3)$ *occur in c, then* $(p_1 = p_3)$ *also occurs in c, for arbitrary positions* p_1, p_2, p_3. *We identify a term t with a constrained term* $t|\emptyset$, *that is, with an empty conjunction of equalities. We also define the replacement of a subterm* $t|_p$ *in a term t at position p by a constrained term* $s|c$, *denoted* $t[s|c]_p$, *as* $t[s]_p | \bigwedge_{(p_1=p_2) \in c} (p.p_1 = p.p_2)$.

An instance *of* $t|c$ *is a ground term of the form* $t[s_1]_{p_1} \ldots [s_n]_{p_n}$, *where* $\{p_1, \ldots, p_n\}$ *are the positions* p_i *satisfying* $t|_{p_i} \in Q$, $\{s_1, \ldots, s_n\}$ *are ground terms satisfying* $s_i \in \mathcal{L}(A_{hom}, t|_{p_i})$ *such that, for each* $(p_i = p_j)$ *occurring in c,* $s_i = s_j$ *holds. The set of instances of a constrained term* $t|c$ *with respect to* A_{hom} *is denoted by* $\texttt{instances}(t|c, A_{hom})$, *or by* $\texttt{instances}(t|c)$ *when* A_{hom} *is clear from the context. The set of instances of a set S of constrained terms with respect to a* TA$_{hom}$ A_{hom}, *denoted* $\texttt{instances}(S, A_{hom})$ *or* $\texttt{instances}(S)$ *when* A_{hom} *is clear from the context, is* $\bigcup_{(t|c) \in S}(\texttt{instances}(t|c))$.

DEFINITION 7.5 (LINEARIZATION OF TERMS). *Let $A_{hom} = \langle Q, \Sigma, F, \Delta \rangle$ be a TA_{hom}. Let* h *be a natural number. Let $t|c$ be a constrained term with respect to A_{hom}. The* linearization *of $t|c$ by* h*, denoted* $\texttt{linearize}(t|c, \texttt{h})$*, is the set of terms $t[s_1]_{p_1} \dots [s_n]_{p_n}$, where $\{p_1, \dots, p_n\}$ are the positions occurring in c, $\{s_1, \dots, s_n\}$ are ground terms satisfying $s_i \in \mathcal{L}(A_{hom}, t|_{p_i})$, each* $\texttt{height}(s_i)$ *is smaller than or equal to* h*, and for each $(p_i = p_j)$ occurring in c, $s_i = s_j$ holds.*

The process has a TA_{hom} $A_{hom} = \langle Q, \Sigma, F, \Delta \rangle$ as input, constructs a set S of constrained terms with respect to A_{hom}, and proceeds by modifying S until it (eventually) detects a condition implying non-regularity. The following invariants are satisfied at the beginning of each step of the process:

- I1. Each $t|c$ in S satisfies that c is $\emptyset$, i.e. S contains just terms.
- I2. $\texttt{instances}(S)$ is equal to $\mathcal{L}(A_{hom})$.
- I3. For each two terms t_1, t_2 in S and each two positions p_1, p_2 satisfying that $t_1|_{p_1}$ and $t_2|_{p_2}$ are in Q, $||p_2| - |p_1|| \leq h(A_{hom})$.

The description of the process is as follows

1. Input: A TA_{hom} $A_{hom} = \langle Q, \Sigma, F, \Delta \rangle$.
2. Assign $S := F$.
3. If all terms in S are in $\mathcal{T}(\Sigma)$, i.e. no state in Q occurs in S, then halt with output "REGULAR".
4. Otherwise, let p be a position minimal in size among $\{p' \mid \exists t \in S : t|_{p'} \in Q\}$. Let t be a term of S satisfying $t|_p \in Q$. Let q be $t|_p$. Assign $S := (S - \{t\}) \cup \{t[s|c]_p \mid (s \xrightarrow{c} q) \in \Delta\}$. (Note that, at this point, S satisfies all the invariants except I1).
5. While S does not satisfy I1 do:
   a. Let $t'|c'$ be a constrained term in S where c' is not empty.
   b. If there exists a position p' in c' and a term t'' in $\texttt{instances}(t'|c') - \texttt{instances}(S - \{t'|c'\})$ such that $\texttt{height}(t''|_{p'}) > \check{h}(A_{hom} \cap \overline{A_{hom}})$, then halt with output "NON-REGULAR".
   c. Otherwise, assign $S := (S - \{t'|c'\}) \cup \texttt{linearize}(t'|c', \check{h}(A_{hom} \cap \overline{A_{hom}}))$.
6. Go to 3.

It is clear that the above process satisfies all the invariants when it passes through item 3. We insist again that this process is not executed. Thus, it does not matter if the used instructions are computable (nevertheless they are).

LEMMA 7.6. *If the process does not halt with output "NON-REGULAR", then $\mathcal{L}(A_{hom}) \subseteq \mathcal{L}(\texttt{linearize}(A_{hom}, \check{h}(A_{hom} \cap \overline{A_{hom}})))$ holds.*

The contraposition of the statement in Lemma 7.6 says that, if $\mathcal{L}(A_{hom})$ is not included into $\mathcal{L}(\texttt{linearize}(A_{hom}, \check{h}(A_{hom} \cap \overline{A_{hom}})))$, then the process halts with output "NON-REGULAR". Hence, in order to prove Lemma 7.2, it rests to see that, when the process halts with output "NON-REGULAR", $\mathcal{L}(A_{hom})$ is not regular. This reduces to check that, when the condition in step 5b of the process is satisfied, it follows that $\mathcal{L}(A_{hom})$ is not regular. The proof is rather large and technical, and can be found in [15]. The next subsection tries to give intuition about why it holds.

7.3 Intuition behind the non-regularity condition

The proofs of the following subsection are very technical. Here, we briefly try to provide some intuition, in order to show one of the fundamental tricks of the proofs, and how the constructions of previous sections play an important role.

For simplifying, first we call A to A_{hom} and suppose that A is just a deterministic TA instead of an arbitrary TA_{hom}, and that S is the set of constrained terms $\{f(q_1, q_1)|(1 = 2),\ f(q_2, q_1)\}$ for different states q_1, q_2 of A. Also suppose that we have a "big enough" term $f(t, t)$ in $\texttt{instances}(f(q_1, q_1)|(1 = 2)) - \texttt{instances}(f(q_2, q_1))$. Our goal is to prove that $\texttt{instances}(S)$ is not regular. (Although these assumptions are not compatible with our context, since $\texttt{instances}(S) = \mathcal{L}(A)$ is not possible, they will be useful to our clarifying purposes).

Note that, by the definition of instance, t belongs to $\mathcal{L}(A, q_1)$, and since A is deterministic and q_1 and q_2 are different, t does not belong to $\mathcal{L}(A, q_2)$. Since $f(t, t)$ is "big", by means of pumpings on t we can construct infinite terms $t_1, t_2, \dots$ such that each t_i reaches q_1 with A. Thus, $f(t_i, t_i)$ is in $\texttt{instances}(f(q_1, q_1)|(1 = 2)) - \texttt{instances}(f(q_2, q_1))$ by the same reason, i.e. each t_i is in $\mathcal{L}(A, q_1)$, and hence, it is not in $\mathcal{L}(A, q_2)$.

Now, in order to prove that $\texttt{instances}(S)$ is not regular, we proceed by contradiction by assuming the existence of a TA C satisfying $\mathcal{L}(C) = \texttt{instances}(S)$. From the above infinite terms we can choose a t_i which is "big enough" with respect to the size of A and C. By means of a pumping on t_i, we can construct a new t'_i different from t_i but reaching the same state with A and the same state with C. Thus, $f(t'_i, t_i)$ reaches an accepting state with C, and t'_i reaches q_1 with A. Note that $f(t'_i, t_i)$ is not an instance of $f(q_1, q_1)|(1 = 2)$ because t'_i and t_i are different, neither an instance of $f(q_2, q_1)$ because t'_i reaches q_1 with A. Hence, we have reached a contradiction since $f(t'_i, t_i)$ is in $\mathcal{L}(C) - \texttt{instances}(S)$.

The previous ideas have a big obstacle when A is an arbitrary TA_{hom} instead of just a TA. The reason is that the starting tree homomorphism could be non-injective, and, in fact, TA_{hom} are inherently non-deterministic: thus, even when t reaches q_1 and not q_2 with A, it may happen that the generated $t_1, t_2, \dots$ by pumping reach both q_1 and q_2 with A. Hence, the new infinitely many terms $f(t_i, t_i)$ are not necessarily in $\texttt{instances}(f(q_1, q_1)|(1 = 2)) - \texttt{instances}(f(q_2, q_1))$, and we cannot repeat the argument above. Here is when $\overline{A}$ plays an important role. Note that there exists an execution of t with $\overline{A}$ reaching a set S containing q_2. If t is "big enough" with respect to the size of A and $\overline{A}$, then, we can perform infinite pumpings producing terms $t_1, t_2, \dots$ such that each t_i reaches q_1 with A, and S with $\overline{A}$, thus ensuring that each t_i cannot reach q_2 with A. This allows to reproduce the same argument as before.

8. CONCLUSION

We have closed affirmatively the open question of the decidability of the HOM problem. In [7] a propagation technique is presented for proving exptime-completeness of the emptiness problem for $TA_{\neq}$. It could be interesting to study the applicability of this technique to the case of $TA_{\neq,hom}$ in order to improve the time complexity. Also, it would be interesting to know whether $TA_{\neq,hom}$ could still be further extended in a meaningful way while still keeping at the same time its tractability.

Our result implies decidability of other related questions. For example, in [10] is questioned the decidability of the regularity of the range of a given tree homomorphism. This is a particular case of the HOM problem, and hence, we also close this question affirmatively.

THEOREM 8.1. *Given a tree homomorphism H, it is decidable whether the rank of H is regular.*

On the other side, tree homomorphisms are a particular case of bottom-up tree transducers. In [9] it is shown that for any given regular tree language L and any given bottom-up tree transducer T, a regular tree language L' and a tree homomorphism H can be computed such that $T(L) = H(L')$ holds. Thus, as a consequence of our result we have the following:

THEOREM 8.2. *Given a regular tree language L and a bottom-up tree transducer T, it is decidable whether $T(L)$ is regular.*

This is in contrast with top-down tree transducers: tree homomorphisms are also a particular case of top-down tree transducer, but it is well known [9, 10] that the regularity of the image of a given regular tree language through a top-down tree transducer is undecidable.

Acknowledgments: We greatly appreciate the comments of Z. Fülöp, F. Jacquemard and S. Maneth.

9. REFERENCES

[1] F. Baader and T. Nipkow. *Term Rewriting and All That.* Cambridge University Press, New York, 1998.

[2] B. Bogaert, F. Seynhaeve, and S. Tison. The recognizability problem for tree automata with comparison between brothers. In *Foundations of Software Science and Computation Structures (FOSSACS)*, pages 150–164, 1999.

[3] B. Bogaert and S. Tison. Equality and disequality constraints on direct subterms in tree automata. In *International Symposium on Theoretical Aspects of Computer Science (STACS)*, pages 161–171, 1992.

[4] H. Comon, M. Dauchet, R. Gilleron, C. Löding, F. Jacquemard, D. Lugiez, S. Tison, and M. Tommasi. Tree automata techniques and applications. Available at http://www.grappa.univ-lille3.fr/tata, 2007.

[5] H. Comon and C. Delor. Equational formulae with membership constraints. *Information and Computation*, 112:167–216, 1994.

[6] H. Comon and F. Jacquemard. Ground reducibility and automata with disequality constraints. In *International Symposium on Theoretical Aspects of Computer Science (STACS)*, pages 151–162, 1994.

[7] H. Comon and F. Jacquemard. Ground reducibility is EXPTIME-complete. In *Logic in Computer Science (LICS)*, pages 26–34, 1997.

[8] M. Dauchet, A.-C. Caron, and J.-L. Coquidé. Automata for reduction properties solving. *Journal of Symbolic Computation*, 20(2):215–233, 1995.

[9] J. Engelfriet. Bottom-up and top-down tree transformations - a comparison. *Mathematical Systems Theory*, 9(3):198–231, 1975.

[10] Z. Fülöp. Undecidable properties of deterministic top-down tree transducers. *Theoretical Computer Science*, 134:311–328, 1994.

[11] A. Gascón, G. Godoy, and F. Jacquemard. Closure of tree automata languages under innermost rewriting. *Electronic Notes Theoretical Computer Science*, 237:23–38, 2009.

[12] F. Gécseg and M. Steinby. *Tree Automata.* Akadémiai Kiadó, 1984.

[13] F. Gécseg and M. Steinby. Tree languages. In G. Rozenberg and A. Salomaa, editors, *Handbook of Formal Languages*, volume 3, pages 1–68. Springer-Verlag, 1997.

[14] R. Gilleron. Decision problems for term rewriting systems and recognizable tree languages. In *International Symposium on Theoretical Aspects of Computer Science (STACS)*, pages 148–159, 1991.

[15] G. Godoy, O. Giménez, L. Ramos, and C. Àlvarez. The hom problem is decidable. Available at `www.lsi.upc.edu/~ggodoy/publications.html`.

[16] G. Godoy and E. Huntingford. Innermost-reachability and innermost-joinability are decidable for shallow term rewrite systems. In *Term Rewriting and Applications (RTA)*, pages 184–199, 2007.

[17] G. Godoy, S. Maneth, and S. Tison. Classes of tree homomorphisms with decidable preservation of regularity. In *Foundations of Software Science and Computation Structures (FOSSACS)*, pages 127–141, 2008.

[18] D. Hofbauer and M. Huber. Computing linearizations using test sets. In *Third International Workshop on Conditional Term Rewriting Systems (CTRS)*, pages 287–301, 1992.

[19] Florent Jacquemard, Francis Klay, and Camille Vacher. Rigid tree automata. In *Language and Automata Theory and Applications (LATA)*, pages 446–457, 2009.

[20] G. Kucherov and M. Tajine. Decidability of regularity and related properties of ground normal form languages. *Information and Compuation*, 118:91–100, 1995.

[21] Thomas Schwentick. Automata for xml - a survey. *Journal of Computer and Systems Sciences*, 73(3):289–315, 2007.

[22] J. W. Thatcher. Generalized^2 sequential machine maps. *Computer and System Sciences*, 4:339–367, 1970.

[23] J. W. Thatcher and J. B. Wright. Generalized finite automata theory with an application to a decision problem of second-order logic. *Mathematical Systems Theory*, 2(1):57–81, 1968.

[24] S. Vágvölgyi and R. Gilleron. For a rewrite system it is decidable whether the set of irreducible, ground terms is regognizable. *Bulletin of the EATCS*, 48:197–209, 1992.

Complexity Theory for Operators in Analysis

Akitoshi Kawamura
University of Toronto
kawamura@cs.toronto.edu

Stephen Cook
University of Toronto
sacook@cs.toronto.edu

ABSTRACT

We propose a new framework for discussing computational complexity of problems involving uncountably many objects, such as real numbers, sets and functions, that can be represented only by approximation. The key idea is to use a certain class of string functions, which we call *regular functions*, as names representing these objects. These are more expressive than infinite sequences, which served as names in prior work that formulated complexity in more restricted settings. An important advantage of using regular functions is that we can define their *size* in the way inspired by higher-type complexity theory. This enables us to talk about computation on regular functions whose time or space is bounded polynomially in the input size, giving rise to more general analogues of the classes P, NP, and PSPACE. We also define NP- and PSPACE-completeness under suitable many-one reductions.

Because our framework separates machine computation and semantics, it can be applied to problems on sets of interest in analysis once we specify a suitable representation (encoding). As prototype applications, we consider the complexity of functions (operators) on real numbers, real sets, and real functions. The latter two cannot be represented succinctly using existing approaches based on infinite sequences, so ours is the first treatment of them. As an interesting example, the task of numerical algorithms for solving the initial value problem of differential equations is naturally viewed as an operator taking real functions to real functions. As there was no complexity theory for operators, previous results could only state how complex the solution can be. We now reformulate them to show that the operator itself is polynomial-space complete.

Categories and Subject Descriptors

F.1.3 [**Computation by Abstract Devices**]: Complexity Measures and Classes

General Terms

Theory

Keywords

computable analysis, computational complexity, higher-type complexity, second-order polynomials

1. INTRODUCTION

Computable analysis [19] studies problems involving real numbers, sets and functions from the viewpoint of computability. Uncountably many objects (such as real numbers) are represented by infinite sequences of approximations and processed by Turing machines. This framework is applicable not only to the real numbers but also with great generality to other spaces arising naturally in mathematical analysis. There is a unified way to discuss computability of real functions, sets of real numbers, operators taking real functions as inputs, and so on.

In contrast, the application of this approach to computational complexity has been limited in generality. For example, although there is a widely accepted notion of polynomial-time computable real functions $f : [0,1] \to \mathbb{R}$ on the compact interval that has been studied extensively [14], the same approach does not give a nice class of real functions on $\mathbb{R}$. Most of the complexity results in computable analysis to date (with a few exceptions [6, 18, 20]) are essentially limited to the complexity of either real functions with compact domain or of bounded subsets of $\mathbb{R}$. They do not address the complexity of, say, an operator F that takes real functions $f : [0,1] \to \mathbb{R}$ to another real function $F(f)$. There are many results [12] about such operators, but typically the positive and negative results are stated in the form

> if f is in the (small) complexity class X, then $F(f)$ is in complexity class Y, and
> there is f in complexity class X such that $F(f)$ is hard for Z.

More direct (and preferable) statements would be the "constructive" or "effectivized" form

> the operator F is in class $\mathcal{Y}$, and
> the operator F is $\mathcal{Z}$-hard,

where $\mathcal{Y}$ and $\mathcal{Z}$ are the "higher-order versions" of Y and Z. At the level of computability, it is common to ask, as soon as we see an ineffective result, whether it can be effectivized. For complexity, we cannot even ask this question because we do not know how to formulate $\mathcal{Y}$ and $\mathcal{Z}$. This limitation has been widely recognized; see, for example, [12, pp. 57–58], [20], and [3, p. 484].

The present paper addresses this problem. We start with the observation (Section 2) that the aforementioned limitation has to do with the fact that traditional formulations of computable analysis do not take into account the "size" of the infinite sequences given to the machine as input. We then propose (Section 3) an extension on the machine model by replacing infinite sequences by what we call *regular functions* from strings to strings. An important advantage of regular functions is that we can define their *size* in the way suggested by type-two complexity theory [16, 7]. This enables us to measure the growth of running time (or space) in terms of the input size—exactly what we do in the usual (type-one) Complexity Theory. We thus obtain the complexity classes analogous to P, NP, PSPACE (and function classes FP and FPSPACE) by bounding the time or space by *second-order polynomials* in the input size. Analogues of many-one reductions and NP- and PSPACE-hardness will also be introduced.

We apply this framework to a few specific problems in analysis by using suitable representations of real numbers, real sets, and real functions (Section 4). For real numbers, the induced complexity notions turn out to be equivalent to what has been studied by Ko–Friedman [10] and Hoover [6]. For sets and functions, our approach seems to be the first to provide complexity notions in a unified manner. This is of particular interest, because many numerical problems in the real world are naturally formulated as operators taking sets or functions. For example, consider the operator F that finds the solution $F(f)$ of the differential equation (of a certain class) given by a function f. As mentioned above, the existing ineffective results [11, 8] only tell us *how complex the solution $F(f)$ can be when f is easy*; precisely, they say that if f is polynomial-time computable, $F(f)$ is polynomial-space computable and can be polynomial-space hard. But the practical concern for numerical analysis would be *how hard it is to compute* F (i.e., to compute $F(f)$ given f). We formulate and prove the first result of this kind: F itself is a polynomial-space complete operator. Our contribution is in introducing the framework making such formulations possible, solving an important open problem as explained above. The technically hard parts of the proofs of the specific results are already done in the proofs of the ineffective versions, and all we need to do is to check that they effectivize in our sense. The original ineffective versions are now corollaries of the effectivized statements.

2. TYPE-TWO THEORY OF EFFECTIVITY

Computable Analysis dates back at least to Grzegorczyk [5], and there have been several equivalent formulations. Weihrauch's Type-Two Theory of Effectivity (TTE) is a powerful framework. In this section, we briefly introduce computable analysis through TTE and clarify its limitations in dealing with complexity.

2.0 Multi-functions

Before discussing TTE, we begin with a few words about *multi-valued functions*, or *multi-functions*. A multi-function F from a set X to a set Y is formally a subset of $X \times Y$. For $x \in X$, we write $F[x]$ for the set of $y \in Y$ such that (x, y) belongs to this subset. These y are the "allowable outputs" on input x. We denote by dom F the set of $x \in X$ for which $F[x]$ is nonempty. When $F[x]$ is a singleton, its unique element is denoted by $F(x)$, as usual. If $F[x]$ is a singleton for all $x \in \operatorname{dom} F$, we say that F is a *partial function*. When in addition dom $F = X$, we say that F is a *total function*, or simply a *function*.

Like some authors, we regard the so-called "function problems" (also called *search problems*) as multi-functions. The classes FP and FPSPACE are the sets of multi-functions from strings to strings that are computed by a machine whose time/space is polynomially bounded. Here, the word "compute" is interpreted according to the "allowable outputs" semantics of multi-functions: A machine is said to compute F if, on any input $x \in \operatorname{dom} F$, it outputs *some* element of $F[x]$. The classes FP^2 and $\mathsf{FPSPACE}^2$ that we will define later will also consist of multi-functions.

Note that we do not care what happens on inputs outside dom F, unlike some authors who require that such inputs be rejected explicitly. Thus, a multi-function can be easy to compute while having a nasty domain. We also note, however, that allowing dom F to be smaller than X is not so important in the context of time- or space-bounded computation, because a machine that runs past the time bound for some inputs can be modified so that it keeps track of the time and outputs an error message when it has run out of time.

2.1 Computability

In the usual Computability Theory, we introduce computability for functions from Σ^* to Σ^* under some machine model, where Σ^* is the set of strings. To discuss computation on other sets X, we specify an *encoding* of X—that is, a rule for interpreting an element of Σ^* as an element of X.

TTE roughly follows the same path. But since the countable set Σ^* cannot encode uncountable sets, such as the set $\mathbb{R}$ of real numbers, TTE uses the set $\Sigma^{\mathbb{N}}$ of *infinite sequences*.

Computability of functions from $\Sigma^{\mathbb{N}}$ to $\Sigma^{\mathbb{N}}$ is defined using Turing machines. The machine has an input tape, an output tape and a work tape, each of which is infinite to the right. We also assume that the output tape is one-way, that is, the only instruction for the output tape is "write $a \in \Sigma$ in the current cell and move the head to the right". The difference from the usual setting is in the convention by which the machine reads the input and delivers the output. The input is now an infinite string $a_0a_1 \ldots \in \Sigma^{\mathbb{N}}$, and is written on the input tape before the computation starts (with the tape heads at the leftmost cell). We say the machine outputs an infinite string $b_0b_1 \ldots \in \Sigma^{\mathbb{N}}$ if it never halts and writes the string indefinitely (that is, for each $n \in \mathbb{N}$, it eventually writes $b_0 \ldots b_{n-1}$ into the first n cells) on the output tape. This defines a class of (possibly partial) computable functions (without any time or space bound) from $\Sigma^{\mathbb{N}}$ to $\Sigma^{\mathbb{N}}$. The definition can be extended to multi-functions A: We say that a machine M computes A if M, on any input $\varphi \in \operatorname{dom} A$, always outputs some element of $A[\varphi]$.

A *representation* γ of a set X is formally a partial function from $\Sigma^{\mathbb{N}}$ to X which is surjective—that is, for each $x \in X$, there is at least one $\varphi \in \Sigma^{\mathbb{N}}$ with $\gamma(\varphi) = x$. We say that φ is a *γ-name* of x. Using representations, computability of multi-functions on represented sets is defined as follows.

Definition 2.1. Let γ and δ be representations of sets X and Y, respectively. We say that a machine *(γ, δ)-computes* a multi-function A from X to Y if it computes the multi-function $\delta^{-1} \circ A \circ \gamma$ given by

$$(\delta^{-1} \circ A \circ \gamma)[\varphi] = \begin{cases} \{\, \psi \in \operatorname{dom} \delta : \delta(\psi) \in A[\gamma(\varphi)] \,\} & \text{if } \varphi \in \operatorname{dom} \gamma, \\ \emptyset & \text{otherwise.} \end{cases} \tag{1}$$

In other words, whenever the machine is given a γ-name of an element $x \in \operatorname{dom} A$, it must output some δ-name of some element of $A[x]$ (Figure 1).

As an example, we define a representation $\rho_{\mathbb{R}}$ of $\mathbb{R}$, the set of real numbers. First, for each $n \in \mathbb{N}$, let $\mathbf{D}_n$ denote the set of strings of form

$$sx/1\underbrace{00\ldots0}_{n}, \tag{2}$$

where $s \in \{+, -\}$ and $x \in \{0, 1\}^*$. Let $\mathbf{D} = \bigcup_{n \in \mathbb{N}} \mathbf{D}_n$. A string in $\mathbf{D}$ *encodes* a rational number in the obvious sense (read (2) as a

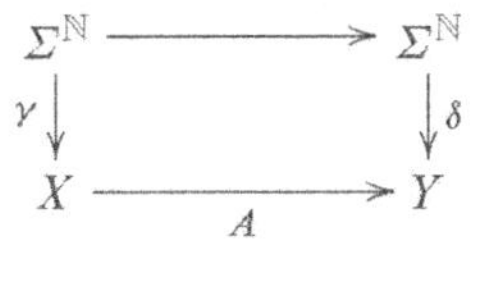

Figure 1: (γ, δ)-computing a multi-function A.

fraction whose numerator and denominator are integers written in binary with leading zeros allowed). We write $[\![u]\!]$ for the rational number encoded by $u \in \mathbf{D}$. We define a representation $\rho_{\mathbb{R}}$ of $\mathbb{R}$ by saying that an infinite string $\varphi \in \Sigma^{\mathbb{N}}$ is a $\rho_{\mathbb{R}}$-name of $x \in \mathbb{R}$ if φ is of the form $u_0\#u_1\#u_2\#\ldots$ (where # is a delimiter symbol not appearing in the u_i) such that $u_i \in \mathbf{D}$ and $|[\![u_i]\!] - x| < 2^{-i}$ for each $i \in \mathbb{N}$. Thus, this representation specifies a real number as a list of rational numbers converging to it.

It turns out that $\rho_{\mathbb{R}}$ is a natural representation with which to discuss computability of real functions. In particular, $\rho_{\mathbb{R}}$ is *admissible*, that is, it matches well with the usual topology of $\mathbb{R}$ [19, Lemma 4.1.6].

To deal with functions of two arguments, we define, for representations γ and δ of sets X and Y, a new representation $[\gamma, \delta]$ of $X \times Y$ by $[\gamma, \delta](a_0 b_0 a_1 b_1 a_2 b_2 \ldots) = (\gamma(a_0 a_1 a_2 \ldots), \delta(b_0 b_1 b_2 \ldots))$.

Example 2.2. Binary addition $+ : \mathbb{R} \times \mathbb{R} \to \mathbb{R}$ is $([\rho_{\mathbb{R}}, \rho_{\mathbb{R}}], \rho_{\mathbb{R}})$-computable. For suppose that we are given names $\varphi = u_0\#u_1\#\ldots$ and $\psi = v_0\#v_1\#\ldots$ of real numbers s and t. An approximation of $s + t$ with precision 2^{-m}, for each m, is given by $[\![u_{m+1}]\!] + [\![v_{m+1}]\!]$.

Example 2.3. Multiplication $\times : \mathbb{R} \times \mathbb{R} \to \mathbb{R}$ is $([\rho_{\mathbb{R}}, \rho_{\mathbb{R}}], \rho_{\mathbb{R}})$-computable. For suppose that we are given names $\varphi = u_0\#u_1\#\ldots$ and $\psi = v_0\#v_1\#\ldots$ of real numbers s and t. First, let $k = \max\{|u_0|, |v_0|\}$. Since $[\![u_0]\!]$ and $[\![v_0]\!]$ are near s and t, and it takes more than k digits to encode a number with absolute value $\geq 2^k$, we have $|s|, |t| < 2^k$. Hence, $s \times t$ is approximated with precision 2^{-m} by $[\![u_{m+k+1}]\!] \cdot [\![v_{m+k+1}]\!]$.

The strength of TTE is that, by using suitable representations, we can discuss computation over sets other than $\mathbb{R}$. Moreover, there are often standard ways to introduce representations of higher-type objects, such as sets or of functions. For example, since we have agreed on the representations $\rho_{\mathbb{R}}$ of $\mathbb{R}$, we can introduce a canonical representation of the set C[$\mathbb{R}$] of continuous real functions, and there are reasons to believe that this is the "right" representation [19, Chapter 3].

2.2 Complexity

Now we ask whether the computation runs in polynomial time. We ask whether the time it takes to output the nth prefix of the output is bounded by a polynomial in n (independently of φ):

Definition 2.4. A machine M runs in *polynomial time* if there is a polynomial p such that for all $\varphi \in \Sigma^{\mathbb{N}}$ and $n \in \mathbb{N}$, the machine M on input φ finishes writing the first n symbols of the output within $p(n)$ steps. Define *polynomial space* analogously by counting the number of visited cells on all (input, work and output) tapes.

Can we use this notion to define polynomial-time computability of, say, a real function?

2.2.1 Representations must be chosen carefully

A little thought shows that the simple combination of Definition 2.4 and the representation $\rho_{\mathbb{R}}$ is useless [19, Examples 7.2.1, 7.2.3]. On the one hand, the machine M could "cheat" by writing redundant $\rho_{\mathbb{R}}$-names: By writing $+10000/100000$ instead of $+1/10$, it gets more time to compute the next approximation. On the other hand, the machine may suffer by receiving redundant names as input, such as the one in which the first approximation is too long to even read in time.

Thus, to develop a meaningful complexity theory, we need to disallow redundancy carefully. This leads to the use of *signed digit representation* ρ_{sd} of $\mathbb{R}$ [19, Definition 7.2.4], defined as follows: dom ρ_{sd} consists of sequences $\varphi \in \Sigma^{\mathbb{N}}$ of form $a_k \ldots a_1 a_0 \bullet a_{-1} a_{-2} \ldots$ for some k, where each a_i is either 0, 1 or -1, such that either $k = 0$ or $(a_k, a_{k-1}) \in \{(1,0), (1,1), (-1,0), (-1,-1)\}$; if this is the case, set

$$\rho_{\text{sd}}(\varphi) = \sum_{i=-\infty}^{k} a_i \cdot 2^i \tag{3}$$

Thus, we read the digit sequence as a binary expansion of a real number (with decimal point $\bullet$) with digits 0, 1 and -1; we forbid certain patterns in the first two digits of the integer part in order to exclude redundancy. (See [19, Example 2.1.4.7] for the reason why the usual binary expansion without the "-1" digit does not work.)

Let $\rho_{\text{sd}}|^{[0,1]}$ denote the restriction of ρ_{sd} to (infinite sequences representing) real numbers in $[0, 1]$. By Definition 2.4, we know what it means for a real function $f : [0, 1] \to \mathbb{R}$ to be *polynomial-time* $(\rho_{\text{sd}}|^{[0,1]}, \rho_{\text{sd}})$*-computable*. This notion turns out to be robust and natural, and equivalent to the widely accepted polynomial-time computability of Ko and Friedman [10], so we will drop the prefix "$(\rho_{\text{sd}}|^{[0,1]}, \rho_{\text{sd}})$" from now on. The same goes for *polynomial-space computability*, and for functions on compact intervals or rectangles instead of $[0, 1]$ (use the pairing function as in Examples 2.2 and 2.3). It is routine to verify that, for example, addition and multiplication $+, \times : [0,1] \times [0,1] \to \mathbb{R}$ are polynomial-time computable. For more interesting results, see Ko's book [12], survey [14] or Weihrauch's book [19, Section 7.3].

2.2.2 Difficulties in generalizing to other spaces

Unfortunately, this approach does not extend much further. For example, a naive extension to real functions on $\mathbb{R}$ (instead of $[0, 1]$) does not work: polynomial-time $(\rho_{\text{sd}}, \rho_{\text{sd}})$-computability tends to fail for trivial reasons, as in the following example.

Example 2.5. Addition on $\mathbb{R}$ (Example 2.2) is not polynomial-time $([\rho_{\text{sd}}, \rho_{\text{sd}}], \rho_{\text{sd}})$-computable. For suppose that a machine $([\rho_{\text{sd}}, \rho_{\text{sd}}], \rho_{\text{sd}})$-computed it within polynomial time bound p. In particular, the machine has to write the first symbol of the output in $t := p(1)$ steps or fewer. Note that this first symbol must be 1 if the sum is greater than 1, and -1 if the sum is less than -1. In particular, it must be 1 if the two summands are 2^{t+100} and -2^{t+50}, and -1 if they are 2^{t+50} and -2^{t+100}. However, the machine cannot tell between these two cases, because it can read at most t symbols of the input in time.

The trouble seems to be that the time bound is independent of the input. Compare this with the addition of integers (written in binary) by the usual Turing machine. It is in polynomial time, because a large summand would make the "input size" big and thereby give the machine more time. For the same thing to happen for addition of the real numbers, we would need to talk about the "size" of the input and a time bound "polynomial in" it, but we do not have the notion of size for infinite sequences.

This problem is not just about real numbers. There are many other objects that we want to give representations to. The objects

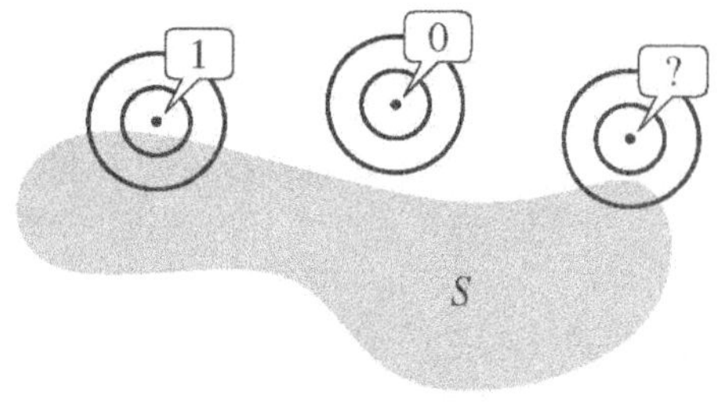

Figure 2: Computing a set S.

for which TTE gives reasonable notions of complexity are limited[1], compared to what we can do at the level of computability. This has long been recognized as a challenge; see, for example, [12, pp. 57–58], [20, Section 1], or [3, p. 484]. As a result of this limitation, the complexity of operators working on objects other than real numbers has been mostly formulated in non-constructive (ineffective) forms. We quote examples of such theorems below. We will reformulate them in effectivized forms later (Theorems 4.6 and 4.9).

2.2.3 *Ineffective results*

The first pair of results are the positive and negative statements about the operator of taking the convex hull $CH(S)$ of a closed set $S \subseteq [0,1]^2$.

Polynomial-time computability (deterministic or nondeterministic) of a set $S \subseteq [0,1]^2$ is defined using usual Turing machines as follows (see e.g. Braverman [4] for a discussion on this definition). We say that S is *(nondeterministic) polynomial-time computable* if there is a (nondeterministic) polynomial-time Turing machine that computes a function $\varphi : \Sigma^* \to \{0,1\}$ such that, for any $n \in \mathbb{N}$ and $u, v \in \mathbf{D}$,

- $\varphi(u, v, 0^n) = 1$ if $dist((\llbracket u \rrbracket, \llbracket v \rrbracket), S) < 2^{-n}$, and
- $\varphi(u, v, 0^n) = 0$ if $dist((\llbracket u \rrbracket, \llbracket v \rrbracket), S) > 2 \cdot 2^{-n}$,

where $dist(p, S) := \inf_{q \in S} \|p - q\|$ denotes the Euclidean distance of point $p \in \mathbb{R}^2$ from S (Figure 2).

Theorem 2.6 (Essentially[2] in [15, Corollary 4.3]). *If a set $S \subseteq [0,1]^2$ is polynomial-time computable, then $CH(S)$ is nondeterministic polynomial-time computable.*

Theorem 2.7 (Essentially[2] in [15, Corollary 4.6]). *Unless* $\mathsf{P} = \mathsf{NP}$, *there exists a set $S \subseteq [0,1]^2$ which is polynomial-time computable, but whose convex hull $CH(S)$ is not.*

For $A \subseteq \mathbb{R}^d$, let $\mathrm{C}[A]$ be the set of continuous functions from A to $\mathbb{R}$. The second pair of results concerns the differential equation

$$h(0) = 0, \qquad h'(t) = g(t, h(t)) \tag{4}$$

called the initial value problem (IVP), where $g \in \mathrm{C}[[0,1] \times \mathbb{R}]$ is given and $h \in \mathrm{C}[0,1]$ is the unknown. The *Picard–Lindelöf* (or *Cauchy–Lipschitz*) *Theorem* states that the solution h exists and is unique if g is *Lipschitz continuous* (in the second argument), i.e.,

$$|g(t, y_0) - g(t, y_1)| \le L \cdot |y_0 - y_1| \tag{5}$$

for some nonnegative constant L independent of t, y_0, y_1. The following results state how complex h can be, assuming that g is polynomial-time computable. Since polynomial-time computability is defined only for functions with compact domain, we restrict g to the rectangle $[0,1] \times [-1,1]$. If there is a solution $h \in \mathrm{C}[0,1]$ whose values stay in $[-1,1]$ (in which case h is unique, as mentioned above), we write *LipIVP*(g) for this h. Thus, *LipIVP* is a partial function from $\mathrm{CL}[[0,1] \times [-1,1]]$ to $\mathrm{C}[0,1]$, where the former set is the subset of $\mathrm{C}[[0,1] \times [-1,1]]$ consisting of functions Lipschitz continuous in the second argument.

Theorem 2.8 ([11, Section 4][3]). *If $g \in \operatorname{dom} LipIVP$ is polynomial-time computable, then LipIVP(g) is polynomial-space computable.*

Theorem 2.9 ([8, Theorem 3.2]). *There is a polynomial-time computable function $g \in \operatorname{dom} LipIVP$ such that LipIVP(g) is polynomial-space complete (in the sense defined in [13] or [8]).*

We can derive from Theorem 2.9 a statement of a similar form to Theorem 2.7: unless $\mathsf{P} = \mathsf{PSPACE}$, there is a real function $g \in \operatorname{dom} LipIVP$ which is polynomial-time computable but *LipIVP*(g) is not.

3. FUNCTIONS AS NAMES

We present the main definitions for our framework here.

As we have noted, the limitations of the TTE approach have to do with the fact that the information carried by infinite sequences in $\Sigma^{\mathbb{N}}$ is not rich enough, and in particular we do not have the notion of their size. We replace $\Sigma^{\mathbb{N}}$ with **Reg**, a class of string functions which we will use as names of real numbers, sets and functions[4]. This section develops a complexity theory for computation over **Reg**, introducing the analogues of classes P, NP, PSPACE and the notions of completeness under many-one reductions.

3.1 Computation over regular functions

We say that a (total) function $\varphi : \Sigma^* \to \Sigma^*$ is *regular* if it preserves relative lengths of strings in the sense that $|\varphi(u)| \le |\varphi(v)|$ whenever $|u| \le |v|$. We write **Reg** for the set of all regular functions (the motivation for considering these functions will become clear in Section 3.2 where we define their lengths).

Now we begin replacing the role of $\Sigma^{\mathbb{N}}$ in TTE (see Section 2.1) by **Reg**. This is a generalization, since an infinite string $a_0 a_1 \ldots \in \Sigma^{\mathbb{N}}$ can be identified with a regular function $\varphi \in$ **Reg** which

(a) takes values of length 1, and

(b) depends only on the length of the argument,

by setting $\varphi(0^n) = a_n$. In the following, observe that Definitions 3.1 and 3.2 extend their counterparts in TTE in this sense.

Since we will deal with an analogue of NP, and nondeterminism is better understood for predicates ($\{0,1\}$-valued functions), it sometimes makes sense to stop the generalization halfway, removing (b) only and keeping (a). Let **Pred** $\subseteq$ **Reg** be the set of $\{0,1\}$-valued regular functions.

Instead of the machine in TTE that converted infinite strings to infinite strings, we use an oracle Turing machine (henceforth just "machine") to convert regular functions to regular functions:

[1] We note, however, that Weihrauch [20] and Schröder [17] study how far we can get with the infinite string model.

[2] Ko and Yu state these results for *strong recognizability* instead of computability, but their proof almost works for computability as well. See Braverman [4] for a comparison of the two notions ([4] says *weak computability* for Ko's strong recognizability). In the present paper, Theorems 2.6 and 2.7 will be derived as corollaries of the effective version, Theorem 4.6.

[3] The original theorem is stated with a condition slightly weaker than Lipschitz continuity.

[4] Ko's formulation [12] already uses string functions instead of infinite strings of TTE, but it does not make full use of this extension.

Definition 3.1. 1. A deterministic machine *computes* a function $F : \mathbf{Reg} \to \mathbf{Reg}$ if, given φ as oracle and u as string input, it outputs $F(\varphi)(u)$ and halts.

2. A nondeterministic machine *computes* a function $F : \mathbf{Reg} \to \mathbf{Pred}$ if, given φ as oracle and u as input, it has at least one accepting branch exactly when $F(\varphi)(u) = 1$.

For the precise conventions for issuing and answering queries, follow any of [16, 7, 12].

As before, we can extend these definitions to multi-functions F by saying that a machine computes F if on any input $\varphi \in \operatorname{dom} F$ it outputs *some* element of $F[\varphi]$.

3.2 Polynomial time and space

Recall that regular functions are those that respect lengths in the sense explained at the beginning of Section 3.1. In particular, they map strings of equal lengths to strings of equal lengths. Therefore, it makes sense to define the *size* $|\varphi| : \mathbb{N} \to \mathbb{N}$ of a regular function φ by $|\varphi|(|u|) = |\varphi(u)|$. It is a non-decreasing function from $\mathbb{N}$ to $\mathbb{N}$.

Now we want to define what it means for a machine to run in polynomial time. Since $|\varphi|$ is a function, we begin by defining polynomials "in" a function, following the idea of Kapron and Cook [7]. *Second-order polynomials* (in type-1 variable $\mathtt{L}$ and type-0 variable $\mathtt{n}$) are defined inductively as follows: a positive integer is a second-order polynomial; the variable $\mathtt{n}$ is also a second-order polynomial; if P and Q are second-order polynomials, then so are $P + Q$, $P \cdot Q$ and $\mathtt{L}(P)$. An example is

$$\mathtt{L}\big(\mathtt{L}(\mathtt{n} \cdot \mathtt{n})\big) + \mathtt{L}\big(\mathtt{L}(\mathtt{n}) \cdot \mathtt{L}(\mathtt{n})\big) + \mathtt{L}(\mathtt{n}) + 4. \tag{6}$$

A second-order polynomial P specifies a function, which we also denote by P, that takes a function $p : \mathbb{N} \to \mathbb{N}$ to another function $P(p) : \mathbb{N} \to \mathbb{N}$ in the obvious way. For example, if P is the above second-order polynomial (6) and $p(x) = x^2$, then $P(p)$ is given by

$$\begin{aligned} P(p)(x) &= \big((x \cdot x)^2\big)^2 + (x^2 \cdot x^2)^2 + x^2 + 4 \\ &= x^8 + x^4 + x^2 + 4. \end{aligned} \tag{7}$$

As in this example, $P(p)$ is a (usual first-order) polynomial if p is.

Definition 3.2. A (deterministic or nondeterministic) machine M runs in *(second-order) polynomial time* if there is a second-order polynomial P such that, given any $\varphi \in \mathbf{Reg}$ as oracle and any $u \in \Sigma^*$ as input, M halts within $P(|\varphi|)(|u|)$ steps (regardless of the nondeterministic choices). Define *polynomial space* analogously by counting the number of visited cells on all (input, work, output and query) tapes.

When φ satisfies (a), the size $|\varphi|$ is a constant function, so the bound $P(|\varphi|)(|u|)$ reduces to a (usual first-order) polynomial in $|u|$. Therefore, Definition 3.2 can be viewed as an extension of Definition 2.4.

Definition 3.3. 1. We write FP^2 (resp. $\mathsf{FPSPACE}^2$) to denote the class of multi-functions from **Reg** to **Reg** computed by a deterministic machine that runs in second-order polynomial time (resp. space).

2. We write P^2 (resp. NP^2) for the class of multi-functions from **Reg** to **Pred** computed by a deterministic (resp. nondeterministic) machine M that runs in polynomial time.

Note that unlike FP and FPSPACE, it is easy to separate, e.g., FP^2 and $\mathsf{FPSPACE}^2$, because an $\mathsf{FPSPACE}^2$ machine can make exponentially many queries to the given oracle.

It is easy to see that the classes defined here respect the corresponding usual complexity classes:

Lemma 3.4. *1. Functions in FP^2 (resp. $\mathsf{FPSPACE}^2$) map regular functions in FP to FP (resp. FPSPACE to FPSPACE).*

2. Functions in P^2 (resp. NP^2) map regular functions in FP to P (resp. NP).

Why we restrict ourselves to regular functions

The idea of using second-order polynomial as a bound on time and space comes from Kapron and Cook's characterization [7] of Mehlhorn's class [16] of *polynomial-time computable operators*[5]. This is a class of (total) functionals $F : (\Sigma^* \to \Sigma^*) \times \Sigma^* \to \Sigma^*$, but they can be regarded as $F : (\Sigma^* \to \Sigma^*) \to (\Sigma^* \to \Sigma^*)$ by writing $F(\varphi)(x)$ instead of $F(\varphi, x)$. Kapron and Cook define the size of $\varphi : \Sigma^* \to \Sigma^*$ by

$$|\varphi|(n) = \max_{|u| \le n} |\varphi(u)|, \qquad n \in \mathbb{N}. \tag{8}$$

Note that our definition of size for regular φ is a special case of this. Then they defined the class of polynomial-time functionals in the same way as Definition 3.3.1. (We added $\mathsf{FPSPACE}^2$ by analogy.)

We have restricted attention to regular functions. This is because, in order to obtain reasonable complexity notions, it seems necessary to be able to simulate a given machine with known time bounds. Note that for usual (type-one) computation, it was easy to find $|x|$ given x, and thus to clock the machine with the time bound $p(|x|)$ for a fixed polynomial p. In contrast, finding the value (8) for a given φ in general requires exponentially many queries to φ and thus exponential time. For regular φ, we can easily find $|\varphi|(n)$ for each n, and thus the second-order polynomial $P(|\varphi|)(|u|)$ is a bound "time-constructible" from φ and u.

Regular functions φ suffice for our purpose, because our intention is to use φ as names of real numbers, sets and functions, and there seems to be little incentive to use irregular names. All representations in this paper (Section 4) will use regular functions only.

3.3 Reduction and completeness

Recall that the definition of the usual many-one reduction between multi-functions A, B from Σ^* to Σ^* is as follows: we say that A many-one reduces to B (written $A \le^1_{\mathrm{mF}} B$) if there are (total) functions r, $t \in \mathsf{FP}$ such that for any $u \in \operatorname{dom} A$, we have $r(v) \in A[u]$ whenever $v \in B[t(u)]$—that is, we have a function t that converts an input for A to an input for B, and another function r that converts an output of B to an output of A (we omit r in the many-one reduction $\le^1_{\mathrm{m}}$ between predicates). Since multi-functions over **Reg** also get a function as input, the analogous definition of reduction involves one more converter s:

Definition 3.5. 1. Let A and B be multi-functions from **Reg** to **Reg**. We say that *A many-one reduces* to B (written $A \le^2_{\mathrm{mF}} B$) if there are (total) functions r, s, $t \in \mathsf{FP}^2$ such that for any $\varphi \in \operatorname{dom} A$, we have $s(\varphi) \in \operatorname{dom} B$ and $r(\varphi) \circ \theta \circ t(\varphi) \in A[\varphi]$ whenever $\theta \in B[s(\varphi)]$ (Figure 3).

2. Let A and B be multi-functions from **Reg** to **Pred**. We write $A \le^2_{\mathrm{m}} B$ if there are functions s, $t \in \mathsf{FP}^2$ such that for any $\varphi \in \operatorname{dom} A$, we have $s(\varphi) \in \operatorname{dom} B$ and $\theta \circ t(\varphi) \in A[\varphi]$ whenever $\theta \in B[s(\varphi)]$.

[5] Kapron and Cook [7] call them *Basic Feasible Functionals* or *Basic Polynomial-Time Functionals*.

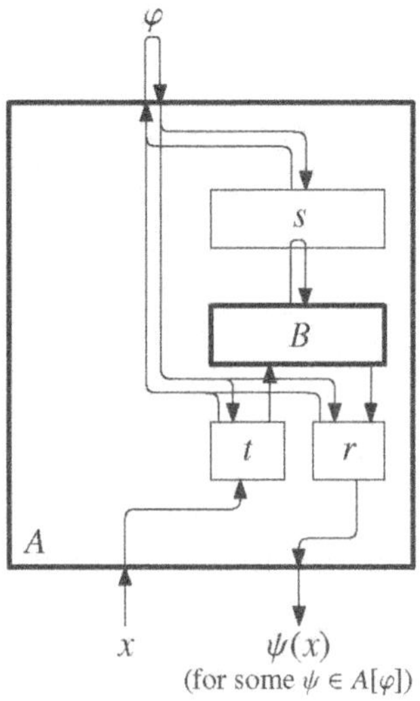

Figure 3: Reduction $A \leq^2_{\mathrm{mF}} B$.

Now that we have the classes (Definition 3.3) and reductions (Definition 3.5)[6], we can talk about completeness for these classes: we define $\mathsf{FPSPACE}^2$-completeness using the reduction $\leq^2_{\mathrm{mF}}$, and NP^2-completeness using $\leq^2_{\mathrm{m}}$.

The following lemma states that an $\mathsf{FPSPACE}^2$-complete multi-function maps some function in FP to an FPSPACE-complete function with respect to the usual many-one reduction $\leq^1_{\mathrm{mF}}$. But since a multi-function has several values, we need the following definition: For a set F of (single-valued) functions from X to Y, we write $\bigcup F$ to mean the multi-function from X to Y defined by $(\bigcup F)[x] = \{ f(x) : f \in F \}$.

Lemma 3.6. *1. Let B be an $\mathsf{FPSPACE}^2$-complete multi-function from* **Reg** *to* **Reg**. *Then there is $\psi \in \operatorname{dom} B \cap \mathsf{FP}$ such that $\bigcup(B[\psi])$ is* FPSPACE*-complete (with respect to $\leq^1_{\mathrm{mF}}$).*

2. Let B be an NP^2-complete multi-function from **Reg** *to* **Pred**. *Then there is $\psi \in \operatorname{dom} B \cap \mathsf{FP}$ such that $\bigcup(B[\psi])$ is* NP*-complete (with respect to $\leq^1_{\mathrm{m}}$).*

Proof. We only prove the first claim. There are a function $A \in \mathsf{FPSPACE}^2$ and a polynomial-time computable function $\varphi \in$ **Reg** such that $A(\varphi)$ is FPSPACE-complete. Since B is $\mathsf{FPSPACE}^2$-complete, there are total functions r, s, t as in Definition 3.5. Let $\psi = s(\varphi)$. Then $\psi \in \mathsf{FP}$. On the other hand, $\bigcup(B[\psi])$ is FPSPACE-complete. To see why, note that $r(\varphi)$ and $t(\varphi)$ are in FP and, by Definition 3.5, give a many-one reduction from $A(\varphi)$ to $\bigcup(B[\psi])$ in the usual sense. Since $A(\varphi)$ is FPSPACE-complete, so is $\bigcup(B[\psi])$. □

We define the pairing function for regular functions as follows: for $\varphi, \psi \in$ **Reg**, define $\langle \varphi, \psi \rangle \in$ **Reg** by setting $\langle \varphi, \psi \rangle(0u) = \varphi(u)10^{|\psi(u)|}$ and $\langle \varphi, \psi \rangle(1u) = \psi(u)01^{|\varphi(u)|}$ (we are padding the string to make $\langle \varphi, \psi \rangle$ regular). Let $\langle \varphi, \psi, \theta \rangle = \langle \langle \varphi, \psi \rangle, \theta \rangle$, etc.

[6]The design of these reductions is somewhat arbitrary. We chose this definition simply because it is strong enough to make our examples (Theorems 4.6 and 4.9) complete. What Beame et al. [2] call the *many-one reduction* between type-2 problems is slightly stronger in that it passes the string input x not only to t (Figure 3) but also to r and s.

3.4 Representations

As we have moved from $\Sigma^{\mathbb{N}}$ to **Reg**, we extend the notions of representations accordingly. A *representation* γ of a set X is a surjective partial function from **Reg** to X. Computation relative to representations is again formulated by Definition 2.1, now with the updated notion of representation. This defines what it means for a function F from X to Y, where X and Y are sets equipped with representations γ and δ, respectively, to be (γ, δ)-$\mathcal{C}$-computable, where $\mathcal{C}$ is one of the classes we have defined, such as FP^2 and $\mathsf{FPSPACE}^2$. This $\mathcal{C}$ can be P^2 or NP^2 if $\operatorname{dom} \delta \subseteq$ **Pred**. Also, we say that F is (γ, δ)-$\mathcal{C}$-complete (for $\mathcal{C} = \mathsf{FPSPACE}^2, \mathsf{NP}^2$) if $\delta^{-1} \circ F \circ \gamma$ (see Definition 2.1) is $\mathcal{C}$-complete.

We say that an element $x \in X$ is *γ-C-computable* (where C is a usual complexity class of string functions, such as FP and FPSPACE) if it has a γ-name in C. It is said to be *γ-C-complete* if $\bigcup(\gamma^{-1}[x])$ (where $\cdot^{-1}$ is the inverse image, and $\bigcup$ is defined before Lemma 3.6) is C-complete. Lemmas 3.4 and 3.6 yield:

Lemma 3.7. *Let γ and δ be representations of sets X and Y, respectively.*

1. *A (γ, δ)-FP^2-computable function from X to Y maps γ-FP-computable elements of X to δ-FP-computable elements of Y. Similarly for $\mathsf{FPSPACE}^2$ and FPSPACE replacing FP^2 and FP.*

2. *Suppose that $\operatorname{dom} \delta \subseteq$ **Pred**. Then a (γ, δ)-P^2-computable function from X to Y maps γ-FP-computable elements of X to δ-P-computable elements of Y. Similarly for NP^2 and NP replacing P^2 and P.*

Lemma 3.8. *Let γ and δ be representations of sets X and Y, respectively.*

1. *A (γ, δ)-$\mathsf{FPSPACE}^2$-complete function from X to Y maps some γ-FP-computable element of X to a δ-FPSPACE-complete element of Y.*

2. *Suppose that $\operatorname{dom} \delta \subseteq$ **Pred**. Then a (γ, δ)-NP^2-complete function from X to Y maps some γ-FP-computable element of X to a δ-NP-complete element of Y.*

For representations γ_0 and γ_1 of X_0 and X_1, respectively, we can define the representation $[\gamma_0, \gamma_1]$ of the Cartesian product $X_0 \times X_1$ by $[\gamma_0, \gamma_1](\langle \varphi_0, \varphi_1 \rangle) = (\gamma_0(\varphi_0), \gamma_1(\varphi_1))$.

4. APPLICATIONS

As we noted in Section 3.1, our formulation can be viewed as a generalization of TTE obtained by removing the conditions (a) and (b) on the oracle that we use as names. In the following three subsections, we will apply our theory to real numbers, real sets and real functions through representations $\rho_{\mathbb{R}}$, ψ, and $\delta_{\square}$. These three representations exploit the removal of (a), (b), and both, respectively.

4.1 Computation over real numbers

Recall the representation $\rho_{\mathbb{R}}$ of $\mathbb{R}$ in TTE (Section 2.1) where a $\rho_{\mathbb{R}}$-name of a real number x was an infinite list $u_0\#u_1\#\ldots$ of (encodings of) rational numbers $[\![u_i]\!]$ satisfying $|[\![u_i]\!] - x| < 2^{-i}$. We modify this in a straightforward way to define a representation $\rho_{\mathbb{R}}$ that encodes real numbers into regular functions (we keep writing $\rho_{\mathbb{R}}$ by abuse of notation): We say that $\varphi \in$ **Reg** is a $\rho_{\mathbb{R}}$-name of $x \in \mathbb{R}$ if $\varphi(0^i) \in \mathbf{D}$ and $|[\![\varphi(0^i)]\!] - x| < 2^{-i}$ for each $i \in \mathbb{N}$. Thus, we encode the same list into the values $\varphi(0^i)$. We write $\rho_{\mathbb{R}}|^{[0,1]}$ for the restriction of $\rho_{\mathbb{R}}$ to (names of) real numbers in the interval $[0, 1]$.

It turns out that $(\rho_{\mathbb{R}}|^{[0,1]}, \rho_{\mathbb{R}})$-$\mathsf{FP}^2$-computability coincides with the polynomial-time computability that was defined in Section 2.2.1 using the signed digit representation ρ_{sd}. Recall that in the definition of ρ_{sd}, we needed to forbid redundancy carefully so that the machine would not cheat by writing long names as output or suffer by reading long names as input. Observe how our formulation avoids these problems naturally: now we do not have to fret too much about defining concise representations.

Moreover, we obtain a reasonable notion of polynomial-time computability of real functions on $\mathbb{R}$ as well without additional work: $(\rho_{\mathbb{R}}, \rho_{\mathbb{R}})$-$\mathsf{FP}^2$-computability seems to be a reasonable notion and coincides with the one discussed by Hoover [6]. He extends the polynomial-time computability on [0, 1] to that on $\mathbb{R}$ by requiring that the 2^{-m}-approximation of the value $f(t)$ of function $f : \mathbb{R} \to \mathbb{R}$ should be delivered within time polynomial in m and $\log|t|$. An equivalent definition appears also in Takeuti [18], independently inspired by Pour-El's approach to computable analysis.

Example 4.1. It is easy to verify that binary addition and multiplication on $\mathbb{R}$ can be $([\rho_{\mathbb{R}}, \rho_{\mathbb{R}}], \rho_{\mathbb{R}})$-$\mathsf{FP}^2$-computed by the algorithms suggested by Examples 2.2 and 2.3.

Example 4.2. The exponential function $\exp : \mathbb{R} \to \mathbb{R}$ restricted to [0, 1] is $(\rho_{\mathbb{R}}|^{[0,1]}, \rho_{\mathbb{R}})$-$\mathsf{FP}^2$-computable, because $\exp t$ can be written as the sum of a series which is known to converge fast on [0, 1] (that is, given a desired precision, the machine can tell how many initial terms it needs to compute). However, exp on the whole real line $\mathbb{R}$ is not $(\rho_{\mathbb{R}}, \rho_{\mathbb{R}})$-$\mathsf{FP}^2$-computable, because it grows too fast.

Example 4.3. The sine function $\sin : \mathbb{R} \to \mathbb{R}$ is $(\rho_{\mathbb{R}}, \rho_{\mathbb{R}})$-$\mathsf{FP}^2$-computable. To see this, note that just like exp in the previous example, sin is polynomial-time computable if restricted to, say, [−4, 4]. It is also possible, given $t \in \mathbb{R}$ as oracle and a desired precision, to find efficiently a number in [−4, 4] which is close enough to t modulo 2π. We can compute $\sin t$ by combining these algorithms.

Example 4.4. A function can be $(\rho_{\mathbb{R}}, \rho_{\mathbb{R}})$-$\mathsf{FP}^2$-computable without even an explicit description known. The *trisector curves* between the points (0, 1) and (0, −1) in the plane are the pair of sets C_1, $C_2 \subseteq \mathbb{R}^2$ such that C_1 is the set of points equidistant from (0, 1) and C_2, and C_2 is the set of points equidistant from (0, −1) and C_1. Asano, Matoušek and Tokuyama [1] showed that such a pair (C_1, C_2) exists and is unique (see [9] for a simpler and more general proof), and that C_1 (as well as C_2, which is the mirror reflection) is a graph of a function $f : \mathbb{R} \to \mathbb{R}$ which is, in our terminology, $(\rho_{\mathbb{R}}, \rho_{\mathbb{R}})$-$\mathsf{FP}^2$-computable. Interestingly, they conjecture that the trisector curves are different from any curves that were previously known.

4.2 Computation over real sets

Let $\mathcal{A}$ be the set of closed subsets of $[0, 1]^2$. The operator *CH* of taking convex hulls (Section 2.2.3) is a function from $\mathcal{A}$ to $\mathcal{A}$. Define the representation ψ of $\mathcal{A}$ as follows[7]: let $\varphi \in$ **Pred** be a ψ-name of $S \in \mathcal{A}$ if φ and S satisfy the two itemized conditions in Section 2.2.3. Since $\operatorname{dom}\psi \subseteq$ **Pred**, it makes sense to talk about ψ-NP-computability, (ψ, ψ)-NP^2-computability, etc. The following is immediate from the definition of polynomial-time computability in Section 2.2.3.

Lemma 4.5. *A set in $\mathcal{A}$ is (nondeterministic) polynomial-time computable if and only if it is ψ-P-computable (ψ-NP-computable).*

[7]Note that this representation is more succinct than the one that we would be able to define in TTE using infinite sequences [20, Example 6.9].

Now we can state and prove the following effectivized version of Theorems 2.6 and 2.7.

Theorem 4.6. *CH is (ψ, ψ)-NP^2-complete.*

The proof is a straightforward effectivization of those of Theorems 2.6 and 2.7, but we need to modify the hardness proof slightly, because, as we noted in footnote 2, Ko and Yu's original results were about a different notion of computability; this will be explained in the full version of this paper.

As corollaries of Theorem 4.6, we get Theorem 2.6 by Lemmas 3.7.2 and 4.5, and Theorem 2.7 by Lemmas 3.8.2 and 4.5.

4.3 Computation over real functions

For $\mu : \mathbb{N} \to \mathbb{N}$, define $\overline{\mu} \in$ **Reg** by $\overline{\mu}(u) = 0^{\mu(|u|)}$. We say that μ is a *modulus of continuity* of a function $f \in$ C[0, 1] if $|t - t'| \le 2^{-\mu(n)}$ implies $|f(t) - f(t')| \le 2^{-n}$ (for all $n \in \mathbb{N}$ and t, $t' \in [0, 1]$).

Define the representation $\delta_\square$ of C[0, 1] as follows: for $\mu : \mathbb{N} \to \mathbb{N}$ and $\varphi \in$ **Reg**, we set $\delta_\square(\langle \overline{\mu}, \varphi \rangle) = f$ if and only if μ is a modulus of continuity of f and for every $n \in \mathbb{N}$ and $u \in \mathbf{D}_{\mu(n)}$, we have $v := \varphi(u) \in \mathbf{D}_n$ and $|f([\![u]\!]) - [\![v]\!]| < 2^{-n}$. This gives names to all functions in C[0, 1], because a continuous function on a compact interval is uniformly continuous.

Recall that the only reason that a real number can require long $\rho_{\mathbb{R}}$-names was having a large absolute value. In contrast, functions in C[0, 1] may have long $\delta_\square$-names for two possible reasons: having big values, and having a big modulus of continuity.

It is routine to prove the following.

Lemma 4.7. *A function in* C[0, 1] *is polynomial-time computable (resp. polynomial-space computable) if and only if it is $\delta_\square$-FP-computable (resp. $\delta_\square$-FPSPACE-computable).*

Lemma 4.8. *A function in* C[0, 1] *is* PSPACE*-complete in the sense of [8, Section 1.2] if it is $\delta_\square$-FPSPACE-complete.*

The above definitions and lemmas extend to compact domains other than [0, 1] (we keep writing $\delta_\square$ by abuse of notation). To discuss the complexity of the operator *LipIVP* (Section 2.2.3), we define a representation $\delta_{\square L}$ of the space CL[[0, 1]×[−1, 1]] of Lipschitz continuous functions: Let $\delta_{\square L}(\langle \varphi, \psi \rangle) = g$ if and only if φ is a $\delta_\square$-name of g and ψ is a constant function with value 0^L, where $L \in \mathbb{N}$ satisfies (5). Note that the Lipschitz constant is written in unary.

Now we can formulate the effectivized version of Theorems 2.8 and 2.9 as follows. The computability part can be verified by checking that the proof of Theorem 2.8 in [11] can be effectivized. For the hardness part, we need to modify slightly the construction in [8]; this will be worked out in the full version of this paper.

Theorem 4.9. *LipIVP is $(\delta_{\square L}, \delta_\square)$-$\mathsf{FPSPACE}^2$-complete.*

As corollaries, we have Theorem 2.8 by Lemmas 3.7.1 and 4.7, and Theorem 2.9 by Lemmas 3.8.1 and 4.8.

5. SUMMARY AND FUTURE WORK

- A TTE machine works on $\Sigma^{\mathbb{N}}$, the infinite strings. We replace $\Sigma^{\mathbb{N}}$ with **Reg**, the regular functions. This is a generalization in two ways: regular functions (a) can have values of length greater than 1, and (b) take arguments written in binary.
- For time and space bounds we use second-order polynomials in the input size, which are defined in the way suggested by

type-two complexity theory. We define complexity classes P^2, NP^2 and FP^2, $\mathsf{FPSPACE}^2$. With a suitable notion of polynomial-time reductions, we can also define NP^2- and $\mathsf{FPSPACE}^2$-completeness. Formulating other classes is left for future work.

- To apply this to real problems, we introduced representations $\rho_{\mathbb{R}}$, ψ and $\delta_{\square}$ of real numbers, sets and functions. Both aspects (a) and (b) of our generalization turn out to be useful. With respect to these representations, we showed that taking the convex hull of a set is NP^2-complete, and that solving the Lipschitz continuous initial value problem is $\mathsf{FPSPACE}^2$-complete. These are effectivized versions of what have been known in ineffective forms, and tell us more about the hardness of numerical problems in practice. It is interesting to investigate which other known ineffective results about operators do (or do not) effectivize and how.

6. ACKNOWLEDGEMENTS

We thank Kaveh Ghasemloo for comments on the manuscript that helped improve the presentation.

The first author is supported by the Nakajima Foundation, and both authors are supported by the Natural Sciences and Engineering Research Council of Canada.

7. REFERENCES

[1] T. Asano, J. Matoušek, and T. Tokuyama. The distance trisector curve. *Adv. Math.*, 212(1):338–360, 2007.

[2] P. Beame, S. Cook, J. Edmonds, R. Impagliazzo, and T. Pitassi. The relative complexity of NP search problems. *J. Comput. Syst. Sci.*, 57(1):3–19, 1998.

[3] V. Brattka, P. Hertling, and K. Weihrauch. A tutorial on computable analysis. In S. Barry Cooper, Benedikt Löwe, and Andrea Sorbi, editors, *New Computational Paradigms: Changing Conceptions of What is Computable*, pages 425–491. Springer, 2008.

[4] M. Braverman. On the complexity of real functions. In *Proc. 46th Annual IEEE Symposium on Foundations of Computer Science*, pages 155–164, 2005.

[5] A. Grzegorczyk. Computable functionals. *Fund. Math.*, 42:168–202, 1955.

[6] H. J. Hoover. Feasible real functions and arithmetic circuits. *SIAM J. Comput.*, 19(1):182–204, 1990.

[7] B. M. Kapron and S. A. Cook. A new characterization of type-2 feasibility. *SIAM J. Comput.*, 25(1):117–132, 1996.

[8] A. Kawamura. Lipschitz continuous ordinary differential equations are polynomial-space complete. *Comput. Complexity*, 2010, to appear.

[9] A. Kawamura, J. Matoušek, and T. Tokuyama. Zone diagrams in Euclidean spaces and in other normed spaces. In *Proc. 26th Annual ACM Symposium on Computational Geometry*, 2010, to appear.

[10] K. Ko and H. Friedman. Computational complexity of real functions. *Theoret. Comput. Sci.*, 20(3):323–352, 1982.

[11] K. Ko. On the computational complexity of ordinary differential equations. *Inform. Control*, 58:157–194, 1983.

[12] K. Ko. *Complexity Theory of Real Functions*. Birkhäuser Boston, 1991.

[13] K. Ko. On the computational complexity of integral equations. *Ann. Pure Appl. Log.*, 58(3):201–228, 1992.

[14] K. Ko. Polynomial-time computability in analysis. In Iurii Leonidovich Ershov et al., editors, *Handbook of Recursive Mathematics: Volume 2: Recursive Algebra, Analysis and Combinatorics*, vol. 139 of *Studies in Logic and the Foundations of Mathematics*, pages 1271–1317. North-Holland, 1998.

[15] K. Ko and F. Yu. On the complexity of convex hulls of subsets of the two-dimensional plane. In *Proc. 4th International Conference on Computability and Complexity in Analysis*, vol. 202 of *Electronic Notes in Theoretical Computer Science*, pages 121–135, 2008.

[16] K. Mehlhorn. Polynomial and abstract subrecursive classes. *J. Comput. Syst. Sci.*, 12(2):147–178, 1976.

[17] M. Schröder. Spaces allowing type-2 complexity theory revisited. *Math. Log. Q.*, 50(4-5):443–459, 2004.

[18] I. Takeuti. Effective fixed point theorem over a non-computably separable metric space. In Jens Blanck, Vasco Brattka, and Peter Hertling, editors, *Computability and Complexity in Analysis*, vol. 2064 of *Lecture Notes in Computer Science*, pages 310–322. Springer, 2001.

[19] K. Weihrauch. *Computable Analysis: An Introduction*. Texts in Theoretical Computer Science. Springer, 2000.

[20] K. Weihrauch. Computational complexity on computable metric spaces. *Math. Log. Q.*, 49(1):3–21, 2003.

Solving Polynomial Equations in Smoothed Polynomial Time and a Near Solution to Smale's 17th Problem

[Extended Abstract] *

Peter Bürgisser†
Institute of Mathematics
University of Paderborn
D-33098 Paderborn, Germany
pbuerg@upb.de

Felipe Cucker‡
Dept. of Mathematics
City University of Hong Kong
Kowloon Tong, Hong Kong
macucker@cityu.edu.hk

ABSTRACT

The 17th of the problems proposed by Steve Smale for the 21st century asks for the existence of a deterministic algorithm computing an approximate solution of a system of n complex polynomials in n unknowns in time polynomial, on the average, in the size N of the input system. A partial solution to this problem was given by Carlos Beltrán and Luis Miguel Pardo who exhibited a randomized algorithm, call it LV, doing so. In this paper we further extend this result in several directions. Firstly, we perform a smoothed analysis (in the sense of Spielman and Teng) of algorithm LV and prove that its smoothed complexity is polynomial in the input size and σ^{-1}, where σ controls the size of the random perturbation of the input systems. Secondly, we perform a condition-based analysis of LV. That is, we give a bound, for each system f, of the expected running time of LV with input f. In addition to its dependence on N this bound also depends on the condition of f. Thirdly, and to conclude, we return to Smale's 17th problem as originally formulated for deterministic algorithms. We exhibit such an algorithm and show that its average complexity is $N^{\mathcal{O}(\log \log N)}$. This is nearly a solution to Smale's 17th problem.

Categories and Subject Descriptors

F.2.1 [**Analysis of Algorithms and Problem Complexity**]: Numerical Algorithms and Problems—*computations on polynomials*; G.1.5 [**Numerical Analysis**]: Roots of Nonlinear Equations—*Continuation (homotopy) methods*

*A full version of this paper is available at `arxiv.org/abs/0909.2114`

†Partially supported by DFG grant BU 1371/2-1 and Paderborn Institute for Scientific Computation (PaSCo).

‡Partially supported by GRF grant CityU 100808.

General Terms

Algorithms

Keywords

polynomial equation solving, homotopy methods, approximate zero, complexity, polynomial time, smoothed analysis

1. INTRODUCTION

In 2000, Steve Smale published a list of mathematical problems for the 21st century [20]. The 17th problem in the list reads as follows:

> *Can a zero of n complex polynomial equations in n unknowns be found approximately, on the average, in polynomial time with a uniform algorithm?*

Smale pointed out that "it is reasonable" to homogenize the polynomial equations by adding a new variable and to work in projective space after which he made precise the different notions intervening in the question above. We provide these definitions in full detail in Section 2. Before doing so, in the remaining of this section, we briefly describe the recent history of Smale's 17th problem and the particular contribution of the present paper. The following summary of notations should suffice for this purpose.

We denote by $\mathcal{H}_{\mathbf{d}}$ the linear space of complex homogeneous polynomial systems in $n+1$ variables, with a fixed degree pattern $\mathbf{d} = (d_1, \ldots, d_n)$. We let $D = \max_i d_i$ and $N = \dim_{\mathbb{C}} \mathcal{H}_{\mathbf{d}}$. We endow this space with the unitarily invariant Bombieri-Weyl Hermitian product and consider the unit sphere $S(\mathcal{H}_{\mathbf{d}})$ with respect to the norm induced by this product. We then make this sphere a probability space by considering the uniform measure on it. The expression "on the average" refers to expectation on this probability space. Also, the expression "approximate zero" refers to a point for which Newton's method, starting at it, converges immediately, quadratically fast. Finally, the notion of "uniform polynomial time algorithm" refers to the so-called BSS-model [5], which is essentially a model of a random access machine operating with real numbers with infinite precision and at unit cost.

This is the setting underlying the series of papers [14, 15, 16, 17, 18] —commonly referred to as "the Bézout series"— written by Shub and Smale during the first half of the 1990s, a collection of ideas, methods, and results that pervade all the research done in Smale's 17th problem since this was proposed. The overall idea in the Bézout series is to use a linear homotopy. That is, one starts with a system g and a zero ζ of g and considers the segment $E_{f,g}$ with extremities f and g. Here f is the system whose zero we want to compute. Almost surely, when one moves from g to f, the zero ζ of g follows a curve in projective space to end in a zero of f. The homotopy method consists of dividing the segment $E_{f,g}$ in a number, say k, of subsegments E_i small enough to ensure that an approximate zero x_i of the system at the origin of E_i can be made into an approximate zero x_{i+1} of the system at its end (via one step of Newton's method). The difficulty of this overall idea lies in the following issues:

1. How does one choose the initial pair (g, ζ)?
2. How does one choose the subsegments E_i? In particular, how large k should be?

The state of the art at the end of the Bézout series, i.e., in [18], showed an incomplete picture. For (2), an adaptive algorithm is described which determines the interval E_{i+1} from data computed from the interval E_i. The analysis of the size of k, however, reveals a dependence on the initial pair (g, ζ) through a quantity involving the whole path $E_{f,g}$. Which brings us to issue (1). Concerning this issue, Shub and Smale proved that good initial pairs (g, ζ) (in the sense that the average number of iterations for the algorithm above was polynomial in the size of f) existed for each degree pattern $\mathbf{d}$, but they could not exhibit a procedure to generate one such pair.

The next breakthrough took a decade to come. Beltrán and Pardo proposed in [1, 2, 3] that the initial pair (g, ζ) should be randomly chosen. The consideration of randomized algorithms departs from the formulation of Smale's 17th problem but it is widely accepted that, in practical terms, such algorithms are as good as their deterministic siblings. And in the case at hand this departure turned out to pay off. The average (over f) of the expected (over (g, ζ)) number of iterations of the algorithm proposed in [3] is $\mathcal{O}(nND^{3/2})$. One of the most notable features of the ideas introduced by Beltrán and Pardo is the use of a measure on the space of pairs (g, ζ) which is friendly enough to perform a probabilistic analysis while, at the same time, does allow for an efficient sampling.

A first goal of this paper is to perform a smoothed analysis of a randomized algorithm (essentially Beltrán and Pardo's), which we call LV, that computes an approximate zero of f. The precise details of this smoothed analysis are in §3.3.

Average (or smoothed) complexity results do not provide information on the running time of an algorithm for the instance at hand. The second goal of this paper shows a bound of this kind for the expected running time of LV. This bound depends on the condition number of the input system f. The precise statement, Theorem 3.5, is in §3.5 below.

Last but not least, to close this introduction, we return to its opening theme: Smale's 17th problem. Even though randomized algorithms are efficient in theory and reliable in practice they do not offer an answer to the question of the existence of a *deterministic* algorithm computing approximate zeros of complex polynomial systems in average polynomial time. The third main result in this paper exhibits a deterministic algorithm computing approximate zeros in average time $N^{\mathcal{O}(\log\log N)}$. To do so we design and analyze a deterministic homotopy algorithm, call it MD, whose average complexity is polynomial in n and N and exponential in D. This already yields a polynomial-time algorithm when one restricts the degree D to be at most $n^{1-\varepsilon}$ for any fixed $\varepsilon > 0$ (and, in particular, when D is fixed as in a system of quadratic or cubic equations). Algorithm MD is fast when D is small. We complement it with an algorithm that uses a procedure proposed by Jim Renegar [10] and which computes approximate zeros similarly fast when D is large.

In order to prove the results described above we have relied on a number of ideas and techniques. Some of them — e.g., the use of the coarea formula or of the Bombieri-Weyl Hermitian inner product— are taken from the Bézout series and are pervasive in the literature on the subject. Some others —notably the use of the Gaussian distribution and its truncations in Euclidean space instead of the uniform distribution on a sphere or a projective space— are less common. The blending of these ideas has allowed us a development, which unifies the treatment of the several situations we consider for zero finding in this paper.

Acknowledgments. We thank Carlos Beltrán, Jean-Pierre Dedieu and Mike Shub for helpful criticism and comments. Part of the manuscript was written while the authors stayed at the Fields Institute in Toronto during the thematic program on the Foundations of Computational Mathematics. The stimulating working conditions there and the financial support are gratefully acknowledged.

2. PRELIMINARIES

2.1 Setting and Notation

Fix a degree pattern $\mathbf{d} = (d_1, \dots, d_n)$. The input space is the vector space $\mathcal{H}_\mathbf{d}$ of polynomial systems $f = (f_1, \dots, f_n)$ with $f_i = \sum_\alpha a^i_\alpha X^\alpha \in \mathbb{C}[X_0, \dots, X_n]$ homogeneous of degree d_i. We endow $\mathcal{H}_\mathbf{d}$ with the *Bombieri-Weyl Hermitian inner product* that is associated with the norm

$$\|f\|^2 := \sum_{|\alpha|=d_i} |a^i_\alpha|^2 \binom{d_i}{\alpha}^{-1}.$$

The reason to do so is that this inner product is invariant under the natural action of the unitary group $U(n+1)$, cf. [5, Chap. 12]. The quantity $N := \dim_\mathbb{C} \mathcal{H}_\mathbf{d}$ measures the size of the input system f and we further put $D := \max_i d_i$ and let $\mathcal{D} = \prod_i d_i$ be the *Bézout number.*

We look for solutions ζ of the equation $f(\zeta) = 0$ in the complex projective space $\mathbb{P}^n := \mathbb{P}(\mathbb{C}^{n+1})$. For $f, g \in \mathcal{H}_\mathbf{d} \setminus \{0\}$, we denote by $d_\mathbb{S}(f,g)$ the angle between f and g. Similarly we define $d_\mathbb{P}(x,y)$ for $x, y \in \mathbb{P}^n$. We define the *solution variety* to be

$$V_\mathbb{P} := \{(f,\zeta) \in \mathcal{H}_\mathbf{d} \times \mathbb{P}^n \mid f(\zeta) = 0\}.$$

This is a smooth submanifold of $\mathcal{H}_\mathbf{d} \times \mathbb{P}^n$. We denote by $V_\mathbb{P}(f)$ the zero set of $f \in \mathcal{H}_\mathbf{d}$ in $\mathbb{P}^n$. By Bézout's Theorem, it contains $\mathcal{D}$ points for almost all f. Let $Df(\zeta)_{|T_\zeta}$ denote the restriction of the derivative of $f\colon \mathbb{C}^{n+1} \to \mathbb{C}^n$ at ζ to the tangent space $T_\zeta := \{v \in \mathbb{C}^{n+1} \mid \langle v, \zeta\rangle = 0\}$ of $\mathbb{P}^n$ at ζ. The *discriminant variety* Σ is the set of systems f for which there exists a zero $\zeta \in \mathbb{P}^n$ such that $\mathsf{rank}\, Df(\zeta)_{|T_\zeta} < n$. Note that $f \notin \Sigma$ means all the zeros of f are simple.

The distribution of inputs will be modelled with isotropic Gaussians. We recall that the *Gaussian distribution* $N(\overline{f}, \sigma^2\mathrm{I})$ on $\mathcal{H}_\mathbf{d}$ with mean $\overline{f} \in \mathcal{H}_\mathbf{d}$ and covariance matrix $\sigma^2\mathrm{I}$, $\sigma > 0$, is given by the density

$$\rho_{\overline{f},\sigma}(f) = \Big(\frac{1}{\sigma\sqrt{2\pi}}\Big)^{2N} \exp\big(-\frac{\|f-\overline{f}\|^2}{2\sigma^2}\big).$$

2.2 Approximate zeros

In [12], Mike Shub introduced the following *projective version of Newton's method.* We associate to $f \in \mathcal{H}_{\mathbf{d}}$ a map $N_f : \mathbb{C}^{n+1} \setminus \{0\} \to \mathbb{C}^{n+1} \setminus \{0\}$ defined (almost everywhere) by

$$N_f(z) = z - Df(z)_{|T_z}^{-1} f(z).$$

Note that $N_f(z)$ is homogeneous of degree 0 in f so that N_f induces a rational map from $\mathbb{P}^n$ to $\mathbb{P}^n$.

It is well-known that when z is sufficiently close to a simple zero ζ of f, the sequence of Newton iterates beginning at z will converge quadratically fast to ζ. This property lead Steve Smale to define the following intrinsic notion of approximate zero.

DEFINITION 2.1. *By an* approximate zero *of $f \in \mathcal{H}_{\mathbf{d}}$ associated with a zero $\zeta \in \mathbb{P}^n$ of f we understand a point $z \in \mathbb{P}^n$ such that the sequence of Newton iterates $z_{i+1} := N_f(z_i)$ with initial point $z_0 := z$ converges immediately quadratically to ζ, i.e., $d_{\mathbb{P}}(z_i, \zeta) \leq 2^{-(2^i-1)}\, d_{\mathbb{P}}(z_0, \zeta)$ for all $i \in \mathbb{N}$.*

2.3 Condition Numbers

The so called α-theory of Smale [19] shows that the size of the basin of attraction of approximate zeros for a zero ζ of f is controlled by the following quantity:

$$\mu(f,\zeta) = \|f\| \cdot \|M^\dagger\|, \tag{1}$$

where (choosing a representative of ζ with $\|\zeta\| = 1$)

$$M := \Delta^{-1} Df(\zeta) \in \mathbb{C}^{n\times(n+1)},$$

with the diagonal matrix $\Delta := \mathsf{diag}(\sqrt{d_1}, \dots, \sqrt{d_n})$. Here $M^\dagger = M^*(MM^*)^{-1}$ denotes the Moore-Penrose inverse of M, and $\|M^\dagger\|$ its spectral norm. We note that the *condition number* $\mu(f,\zeta)$ is well defined for $(f,\zeta) \in \mathcal{H}_{\mathbf{d}} \times \mathbb{P}^n$.

Smale's α-theory [19] shows that, for z being an approximate zero of f associated with ζ, it is sufficient to have (cf. [13, 6])

$$d_{\mathbb{P}}(z,\zeta) \leq \frac{0.3}{D^{3/2}\mu(f,\zeta)}.$$

2.4 Coarea Formula

Suppose that X, Y are Riemannian manifolds of dimensions m, n, respectively such that $m \geq n$. Let $\varphi\colon X \to Y$ be differentiable. By definition, the derivative $D\varphi(x)\colon T_xX \to T_{\varphi(x)}Y$ at a regular point $x \in X$ is surjective. Hence the restriction of $D\varphi(x)$ to the orthogonal complement of its kernel yields a linear isomorphism. The absolute value of its determinant is called the *normal Jacobian* of φ at x and denoted $\mathrm{NJ}\varphi(x)$. We set $\mathrm{NJ}\varphi(x) := 0$ if x is not a regular point. We note that the fiber $F_y := \varphi^{-1}(y)$ is a Riemannian submanifold of X of dimension $m - n$ if y is a regular value of φ. Sard's lemma states that almost all $y \in Y$ are regular values.

The following result is the *coarea formula*, sometimes also called Fubini's Theorem for Riemannian manifolds. It tells us how probability distributions on Riemannian manifolds transform. A proof can be found e.g., in [9, Appendix].

PROPOSITION 2.2. *Suppose that X, Y are Riemannian manifolds of dimensions m, n, respectively, and let $\varphi\colon X \to Y$ be a surjective differentiable map. Put $F_y = \varphi^{-1}(y)$. Then we have for any function $\chi\colon X \to \mathbb{R}$ that is integrable with respect to the volume measure of X that*

$$\int_X \chi\, dX = \int_{y\in Y} \left(\int_{F_y} \frac{\chi}{\mathrm{NJ}\varphi}\, dF_y\right) dY.$$

3. STATEMENT OF MAIN RESULTS

3.1 The Homotopy Continuation Routine ALH

Suppose that we are given an input system $f \in \mathcal{H}_{\mathbf{d}}$ and an initial pair (g,ζ) in the solution variety $V_{\mathbb{P}}$ such that f and g are $\mathbb{R}$-linearly independent. Let $\alpha = d_{\mathbb{S}}(f,g)$ and consider the line segment $E_{f,g}$ in $\mathcal{H}_{\mathbf{d}}$ with endpoints f and g. We parameterize this segment by writing $E_{f,g} = \{q_\tau \in \mathcal{H}_{\mathbf{d}} \mid \tau \in [0,1]\}$ with q_τ being the only point in $E_{f,g}$ such that $d_{\mathbb{S}}(g, q_\tau) = \tau\alpha$. If $E_{f,g}$ does not intersect the discriminant variety Σ, there is a unique continuous map $\gamma\colon [0,1] \to V_{\mathbb{P}}, \tau \mapsto (q_\tau, \zeta_\tau)$ such that $(q_0,\zeta_0) = (g,\zeta)$, called the *lifting* of $E_{f,g}$ with origin (g,ζ).

The idea is to follow the path γ numerically: we adaptively choose a partition $\tau_0 = 0, \tau_1, \dots, \tau_k = 1$ and, writing $q_i := q_{\tau_i}$ and $\zeta_i := \zeta_{t_i}$, we successively compute approximations z_i of ζ_i by Newton's method starting with $z_0 := \zeta$. More specifically, we compute

$$z_{i+1} := N_{q_{i+1}}(z_i).$$

More precisely, we consider the following algorithm ALH (Adaptive Linear Homotopy) following an idea in Shub [13]. The stepsize parameter is set to $\lambda = 7.53 \cdot 10^{-3}$.

Algorithm ALH
input $f, g \in \mathcal{H}_{\mathbf{d}}$ and $\zeta \in \mathbb{P}^n$ such that $g(\zeta) = 0$
  $\alpha := d_{\mathbb{S}}(f,g)$, $r := \|f\|$, $s := \|g\|$
  $\tau := 0$, $q := g$, $z := \zeta$
  `repeat`
    $\Delta\tau := \frac{\lambda}{\alpha D^{3/2}\mu(q,z)^2}$
    $\tau := \min\{1, \tau + \Delta\tau\}$
    $t := \frac{s}{r\sin\alpha\cot(\tau\alpha) - r\cos\alpha + s}$
    $q := tf + (1-t)g$
    $z := N_q(z)$
  `until` $\tau = 1$
  `RETURN` z

In [13, 6] the following analysis of ALH was provided.

THEOREM 3.1. *The number of iterations $K(f,g,\zeta)$ of algorithm ALH in input f,g,ζ is bounded as*

$$K(f,g,\zeta) \;\leq\; 217\, D^{3/2}\, d_{\mathbb{S}}(f,g) \int_0^1 \mu(q_\tau,\zeta_\tau)^2\, d\tau.$$

The returned point z is an approximate zero of f with associated zero ζ_1.

3.2 Randomization and Complexity: the Algorithm LV

ALH will serve as the basic routine for a number of algorithms computing zeros of polynomial systems in different contexts. In these contexts both the input system f and the origin (g, ζ) of the homotopy may be randomly chosen: in the case of (g, ζ) as a computational technique and in the case of f in order to perform a probabilistic analysis of the algorithm's running time.

In both cases, a probability measure is needed: one for f and one for the pair (g, ζ). The measure for f will depend on the kind of probabilistic analysis (standard average-case or smoothed analysis) we perform. In contrast, we will consider only one measure on $V_{\mathbb{P}}$—which we denote by ρ_{st}— for the initial pair (g, ζ). It consists of drawing g from $\mathcal{H}_{\mathbf{d}}$ from the standard Gaussian distribution (defined via the isomorphism $\mathcal{H}_{\mathbf{d}} \simeq \mathbb{R}^{2N}$ given by the Bombieri-Weyl basis) and then choosing one of the (almost surely) $\mathcal{D}$ zeros of g from the uniform distribution on $\{1, \ldots, \mathcal{D}\}$. The above procedure is clearly non-constructive as computing a zero of a system is the problem we wanted to solve in the first place. One of the major contributions in [1] was to show that this drawback can be repaired.

PROPOSITION 3.2. *We can compute a random pair $(g, \zeta) \in V_{\mathbb{P}}$ according to the density ρ_{st} with $\mathcal{O}(N)$ choices of random real numbers from the standard Gaussian distribution and $\mathcal{O}(DnN + n^3)$ arithmetic operations (including square roots of positive numbers).*

Consider the following *Las Vegas algorithm* LV:

```
input f ∈ H_d
  draw (g,ζ) ∈ V_P from ρ_st
  run ALH on input (f,g,ζ)
```

For an input $f \in \mathcal{H}_{\mathbf{d}}$ algorithm LV either outputs an approximate zero z of f or loops forever. We write $t(f) := \mathbb{E}_{(g,\zeta)\sim\rho_{\mathrm{st}}}(t(f, g, \zeta))$ for the *expected running time* of LV on input f.

For all f, g, ζ_0, the running time $t(f, g, \zeta)$ is given by the *number of iterations* $K(f, g, \zeta)$ of ALH with input this triple, times the cost of an iteration, the latter being dominated by that of computing one Newton iterate (which is $\mathcal{O}(N + n^3)$ independently of the triple (f, g, ζ)). It therefore follows that analyzing the expected running time of LV amounts to do so for the expected value of $K(f, g, \zeta)$, over $(g, \zeta) \in V_{\mathbb{P}}$ drawn from ρ_{st}. We denote this expectation by

$$K(f) := \mathop{\mathbb{E}}_{(g,\zeta)\sim\rho_{\mathrm{st}}} (K(f, g, \zeta)).$$

Beltrán and Pardo [3] performed an average-case analysis of LV showing that

$$E_{f\in S(\mathcal{H}_{\mathbf{d}})} K(f) = \mathcal{O}(D^{3/2} Nn).$$

3.3 Smoothed Analysis of LV

A smoothed analysis of an algorithm consists of bounding, for all possible input data $\overline{f}$, the average of its running time (its expected running time if it is a Las Vegas algorithm) over small perturbations of $\overline{f}$. For the latter, for technical simplicity, we assume a truncated Gaussian defined as follows. For $\overline{f} \in \mathcal{H}_{\mathbf{d}}$ and $\sigma > 0$ we shall denote by $N(\overline{f}, \sigma^2\mathrm{I})$ the Gaussian distribution on $\mathcal{H}_{\mathbf{d}}$ with mean $\overline{f}$ and covariance matrix $\sigma^2\mathrm{I}$ (defined with respect to the Bombieri-Weyl basis). Further, let $A = \sqrt{2N}$ and $P_{A,\sigma} := \mathrm{Prob}\{\|f\| \le A \mid f \sim N(0, \sigma^2\mathrm{I})\}$ (it is known that $P_{A,\sigma} \ge \frac{1}{2}$ for all $\sigma \le 1$, cf. [8]). The *truncated Gaussian* $N_A(\overline{f}, \sigma^2\mathrm{I})$ with center $\overline{f} \in \mathcal{H}_{\mathbf{d}}$ is the probability measure on $\mathcal{H}_{\mathbf{d}}$ with density

$$\rho(f) = \begin{cases} \frac{\rho_{\overline{f},\sigma}(f)}{P_{A,\sigma}} & \text{if } \|f - \overline{f}\| \le A \\ 0 & \text{otherwise,} \end{cases} \tag{2}$$

where $\rho_{\overline{f},\sigma}$ denotes the density of $N(\overline{f}, \sigma^2\mathrm{I})$. We now state our smoothed analysis result for LV.

THEOREM 3.3. *For any $0 < \sigma \le 1$, Algorithm LV satisfies*

$$\sup_{\overline{f}\in S(\mathcal{H}_{\mathbf{d}})} \mathop{\mathbb{E}}_{f\sim N_A(\overline{f},\sigma^2\mathrm{I})} K(f) \le 3707\, D^{3/2} \Big(N + \sqrt{\frac{N}{2}}\Big)(n+1)\,\frac{1}{\sigma}.$$

3.4 The Main Technical Result

The technical heart of the proof of Theorem 3.3 is the following smoothed analysis of the *mean square condition number* $\mu_2(q)$ of $q \in \mathcal{H}_{\mathbf{d}}$, defined as

$$\mu_2(q) := \Big(\frac{1}{\mathcal{D}} \sum_{\zeta \mid q(\zeta)=0} \mu(q, \zeta)^2\Big)^{1/2}.$$

THEOREM 3.4. *Let $\overline{q} \in \mathcal{H}_{\mathbf{d}}$ and $\sigma > 0$. For $q \in \mathcal{H}_{\mathbf{d}}$ drawn from $N(\overline{q}, \sigma^2\mathrm{I})$ we have*

$$\mathop{\mathbb{E}}_{\mathcal{H}_{\mathbf{d}}} \Big(\frac{\mu_2(q)^2}{\|q\|^2}\Big) \le \frac{e(n+1)}{2\sigma^2}.$$

3.5 Condition-based Analysis of LV

We are here interested in estimating $K(f)$ for a fixed input system $f \in S(\mathcal{H}_{\mathbf{d}})$. Such an estimate will have to depend on, besides N, n, and D, the condition of f. We measure the latter using Shub and Smale's [14] condition number $\mu_{\max}(f)$ defined by $\mu_{\max}(f) := \max_{\zeta \mid f(\zeta)=0} \mu(f, \zeta)$. Our condition-based analysis of LV is summarized as follows.

THEOREM 3.5. *The expected number of iterations of Algorithm LV with input $f \in S(\mathcal{H}_{\mathbf{d}}) \setminus \Sigma$ is bounded as*

$$K(f) \le 157109\, D^3 N(n+1) \mu_{\max}(f)^2.$$

3.6 A Near Solution of Smale's 17th Problem

We finally want to consider *deterministic* algorithms finding approximate zeros of polynomial systems. Our goal is to exhibit one such algorithm working in nearly-polynomial average time, more precisely in average time $N^{\mathcal{O}(\log\log N)}$. A first ingredient to do so is a deterministic homotopy algorithm which is fast when D is small. This consists of algorithm ALH plus the initial pair $(\overline{U}, \boldsymbol{z}_1)$, where $\overline{U} = (\overline{U}_1, \ldots, \overline{U}_n) \in S(\mathcal{H}_{\mathbf{d}})$ with $\overline{U}_i = \frac{1}{\sqrt{2n}}(X_0^{d_i} - X_i^{d_i})$ and $\boldsymbol{z}_1 = (1 : 1 : \ldots : 1)$.

We consider the following algorithm MD (Moderate Degree):

```
input f ∈ H_d
  run ALH on input (f,Ū,z_1)
```

We write $K_{\overline{U}}(f) := K(f, \overline{U}, \boldsymbol{z}_1)$ for the number of iterations of algorithm MD with input f. We are interested in computing the average over f of $K_{\overline{U}}(f)$ for f randomly chosen in $S(\mathcal{H}_{\mathbf{d}})$ from the uniform distribution.

THEOREM 3.6. *The average number of iterations of Algorithm* MD *is bounded as*

$$\mathop{\mathbb{E}}_{f\in S(\mathcal{H}_{\mathbf{d}})} K_{\overline{U}}(f) \le 314217\, D^3\, N(n+1)^{D+1}.$$

Algorithm MD is efficient when D is small, say, when $D \le n$. For $D > n$ we use another approach, namely, a real number algorithm designed by Jim Renegar [10] which in this case has a performance similar to that of MD when $D \le n$. Putting both pieces together we reach our last main result.

THEOREM 3.7. *There is a* deterministic *real number algorithm that on input $f \in \mathcal{H}_{\mathbf{d}}$ computes an approximate zero of f in average time $N^{O(\log\log N)}$, where $N = \dim \mathcal{H}_{\mathbf{d}}$ measures the size of the input f. Moreover, if we restrict data to polynomials satisfying*

$$D \le n^{\frac{1}{1+\varepsilon}} \quad \text{or} \quad D \ge n^{1+\varepsilon},$$

for some fixed $\varepsilon > 0$, then the average time of the algorithm is polynomial in the input size N.

4. SMOOTHED ANALYSIS OF LV (PROOF)

We first state a consequence of Theorem 3.1.

PROPOSITION 4.1. *The expected number of iterations of* ALH *on input $f \in \mathcal{H}_{\mathbf{d}} \setminus \Sigma$ is bounded as*

$$K(f) \le 217\, D^{3/2} \mathop{\mathbb{E}}_{g\sim N(0,\mathrm{I})} \left(d_{\mathbb{S}}(f,g) \int_0^1 \mu_2(q_\tau)^2\, d\tau \right).$$

PROOF. Fix $g \in \mathcal{H}_{\mathbf{d}}$ such that the segment $E_{f,g}$ does not intersect the discriminant variety Σ (which is the case for almost all g, as $f \notin \Sigma$). To each of the zeros $\zeta^{(i)}$ of g there corresponds a lifting $[0,1] \to V, \tau \mapsto (q_\tau, \zeta_\tau^{(i)})$ of $E_{f,g}$ such that $\zeta_0^{(i)} = \zeta^{(i)}$. Theorem 3.1 states that

$$K(f,g,\zeta^{(i)}) \le 217\, D^{3/2}\, d_{\mathbb{S}}(f,g) \int_0^1 \mu(q_\tau, \zeta_\tau^{(i)})^2\, d\tau.$$

Since $\zeta_\tau^{(1)}, \ldots, \zeta_\tau^{(\mathcal{D})}$ are the zeros of q_τ, we have by the definition of $\mu_2(q_\tau)$,

$$\frac{1}{\mathcal{D}} \sum_{i=1}^{\mathcal{D}} K(f,g,\zeta^{(i)}) \le 217\, D^{3/2}\, d_{\mathbb{S}}(f,g) \int_0^1 \mu_2(q_\tau)^2\, d\tau. \quad (3)$$

Taking into account that

$$K(f) = \mathop{\mathbb{E}}_{(g,\zeta)\sim\rho_{\mathrm{st}}} (K(f,g,\zeta)) = \mathop{\mathbb{E}}_{g\sim N(0,\mathrm{I})} \Big(\frac{1}{\mathcal{D}} \sum_{i\le\mathcal{D}} K(f,g,\zeta^{(i)}) \Big).$$

the assertion follows. □

All our main results involve expectations —over random f and/or g— of the integral $\int_0^1 \mu_2(q_\tau)^2\, d\tau$. In all cases, we will eventually deal with such an expectation with f and g Gaussian. Since a linear combination (with fixed coefficients) of two such Gaussian systems is Gaussian as well, it is convenient to parameterize the interval $E_{f,g}$ by a parameter $t \in [0,1]$ representing a ratio of Euclidean distances (instead of a ratio of angles as τ does). Thus we write, abusing notation, $q_t = tf + (1-t)g$. For fixed t, as noted before, q_t follows a Gaussian law.

For this new parametrization we have the following result, whose elementary proof is omitted.

PROPOSITION 4.2. *Let $f, g \in \mathcal{H}_{\mathbf{d}}$ be $\mathbb{R}$-linearly independent and $\tau_0 \in [0,1]$. Then*

$$d_{\mathbb{S}}(f,g) \int_{\tau_0}^1 \mu_2(q_\tau)^2\, d\tau \le \int_{t_0}^1 \|f\|\,\|g\| \frac{\mu_2(q_t)^2}{\|q_t\|^2}\, dt,$$

where $\alpha = d_{\mathbb{S}}(f,g)$ and

$$t_0 = \frac{\|g\|}{\|g\| + \|f\|(\sin\alpha\cot(\tau_0\alpha) - \cos\alpha)}$$

is the fraction of the Euclidean distance $\|f-g\|$ corresponding to the fraction τ_0 of α.

As we will see, the factor $\|f\|\,\|g\|$ can be easily bounded and factored out the expectation. We will ultimately face the problem of estimating expectations of $\mu_2(q_t)^2/\|q_t\|^2$, where q_t follows a Gaussian law. This is provided by the crucial Theorem 3.4, whose sketch of proof is postponed to §5.

PROOF OF THEOREM 3.3. Fix $\overline{f} \in S(\mathcal{H}_{\mathbf{d}})$. We use Proposition 4.1 to obtain

$$\mathop{\mathbb{E}}_{f\sim N_A(\overline{f},\sigma^2\mathrm{I})} K(f) \le$$

$$217\, D^{3/2} \mathop{\mathbb{E}}_{f\sim N_A(\overline{f},\sigma^2\mathrm{I})}\ \mathop{\mathbb{E}}_{g\sim N_A(0,\mathrm{I})} \left(d_{\mathbb{S}}(f,g) \int_0^1 \mu_2(q_\tau)^2\, d\tau \right).$$

This follows from the fact that, since both $d_{\mathbb{S}}(f,g)$ and $\mu_2(q_\tau)^2$ are homogeneous of degree 0 in both f and g, we may replace the Gaussian $N(0,\mathrm{I})$ by any rotationally invariant distribution on $\mathcal{H}_{\mathbf{d}}$, in particular by the centered truncated Gaussian $N_A(0,\mathrm{I})$ defined in (2). Now we use Proposition 4.2 (with $\tau_0 = 0$) and $\|f\| \le \|\overline{f}\| + \|f - \overline{f}\| \le 1 + A$ to get

$$\mathop{\mathbb{E}}_{f\sim N_A(\overline{f},\sigma^2\mathrm{I})} K(f) \le \quad (4)$$

$$217 D^{3/2}(A+1)A \mathop{\mathbb{E}}_{f\sim N_A(\overline{f},\sigma^2\mathrm{I})}\ \mathop{\mathbb{E}}_{g\sim N_A(0,\mathrm{I})} \left(\int_0^1 \frac{\mu_2(q_t)^2}{\|q_t\|^2}\, dt \right).$$

Denoting by $\rho_{\overline{f},\sigma}$ and $\rho_{0,1}$ the densities of $N(\overline{f},\sigma^2\mathrm{I})$ and $N(0,\mathrm{I})$, respectively, the right-hand side of (4) equals

$$217\, D^{3/2} \frac{(A+1)A}{P_{A,\sigma}P_{A,1}} \cdot$$

$$\int_{\|f-\overline{f}\|\le A} \int_{\|g\|\le A} \int_0^1 \frac{\mu_2(q_t)^2}{\|q_t\|^2}\, \rho_{0,1}(g)\, \rho_{\overline{f},\sigma}(f)\, dt\, dg\, df$$

$$\le\ 217 D^{3/2} \frac{(A+1)A}{P_{A,\sigma}P_{A,1}} \mathop{\mathbb{E}}_{f\sim N(\overline{f},\sigma^2\mathrm{I})}\ \mathop{\mathbb{E}}_{g\sim N(0,\mathrm{I})} \left(\int_0^1 \frac{\mu_2(q_t)^2}{\|q_t\|}\, dt \right)$$

$$=\ 217 D^{3/2} \frac{(A+1)A}{P_{A,\sigma}P_{A,1}} \int_0^1 \mathop{\mathbb{E}}_{q_t\sim N(\overline{q}_t,\sigma_t^2\mathrm{I})} \left(\frac{\mu_2(q_t)^2}{\|q_t\|} \right) dt,$$

where the last equality follows from the fact that, for fixed t, the random polynomial system $q_t = tf + (1-t)g$ has a Gaussian distribution with law $N(\overline{q}_t, \sigma_t^2\mathrm{I})$ (with $\overline{q}_t = t\overline{f}$ and $\sigma_t^2 = (1-t)^2 + \sigma^2 t^2$). We now apply Theorem 3.4 to deduce

$$\int_0^1 \mathop{\mathbb{E}}_{q_t\sim N(\overline{q}_t,\sigma_t^2\mathrm{I})} \left(\frac{\mu_2(q_t)^2}{\|q_t\|^2} \right) dt$$

$$\le\ \frac{e(n+1)}{2} \int_0^1 \frac{dt}{(1-t)^2 + \sigma^2 t^2} = \frac{e\pi(n+1)}{4\sigma}.$$

Consequently, using that $\frac{(A+1)A}{P_{A,\sigma}P_{A,1}} \le 4(2N + \sqrt{2N})$, we get

$$\mathop{\mathbb{E}}_{f\sim N_A(\overline{f},\sigma^2\mathrm{I})} K(f) \le 217\, D^{3/2}\, 4(2N + \sqrt{2N})\, \frac{e\pi(n+1)}{4\sigma}. \quad \square$$

5. PROOF OF THEOREM 3.4

5.1 Reduction to Matrix Condition Number

We distinguish points $[\zeta] \in \mathbb{P}^n$ from their representatives ζ in the sphere $\mathbb{S}^n := \{\zeta \in \mathbb{C}^{n+1} \mid \|\zeta\| = 1\}$. Note that $[\zeta] \cap \mathbb{S}^n$ is a circle with radius one. We work with the "lifting"

$$V := \{(q, \zeta) \in \mathcal{H}_{\mathbf{d}} \times \mathbb{S}^n \mid q(\zeta) = 0\}$$

of the solution variety $V_{\mathbb{P}}$, which is a vector bundle over $\mathbb{S}^n$ with respect to the projection $\pi_2 \colon V \to \mathbb{S}^n, (q, \zeta) \mapsto \zeta$.

For $\zeta \in \mathbb{S}^n$ we consider the following subspace R_ζ of $\mathcal{H}_{\mathbf{d}}$ consisting of systems h that vanish at ζ of higher order:

$$R_\zeta := \{h \in \mathcal{H}_{\mathbf{d}} \mid h(\zeta) = 0, Dh(\zeta) = 0\}.$$

We further decompose the orthogonal complement $R_\zeta^\perp$ of R_ζ in $\mathcal{H}_{\mathbf{d}}$ (defined with respect to the Bombieri-Weyl Hermitian inner product). Let L_ζ denote the subspace of $R_\zeta^\perp$ consisting of the systems vanishing at ζ and let C_ζ denote its orthogonal complement in $R_\zeta^\perp$. Then we have an orthogonal decomposition

$$\mathcal{H}_{\mathbf{d}} = C_\zeta \oplus L_\zeta \oplus R_\zeta \tag{5}$$

parameterized by $\zeta \in \mathbb{S}^n$. In fact, this can be interpreted as an orthogonal decomposition of the trivial Hermitian vector bundle $\mathcal{H}_{\mathbf{d}} \times \mathbb{S}^n \to \mathbb{S}^n$ into subbundles C, L, and R over $\mathbb{S}^n$. Moreover, the vector bundle V is the orthogonal sum of L and R: we have $V_\zeta = L_\zeta \oplus R_\zeta$ for all ζ.

The following lemma is easily verified at $\zeta = (1, 0, \ldots, 0)$. (By unitary invariance this is sufficient.)

Lemma 5.1. *The space C_ζ consists of $(c_i \langle X, \zeta\rangle^{d_i})$ with $c_i \in \mathbb{C}$. The space L_ζ consists of the systems*

$$g = (\sqrt{d_i}\, \langle X, \zeta\rangle^{d_i - 1} \ell_i)$$

where ℓ_i is a linear form vanishing at ζ. Moreover, if $\ell_i = \sum_{j=0}^n m_{ij} X_j$ with $M = (m_{ij})$, then $\|g\| = \|M\|_F$.

Let $\mathscr{M}$ denote the space $\mathbb{C}^{n \times (n+1)}$ of matrices. In the special case, where all the degrees d_i are one, the solution manifold V specializes to the manifold

$$W := \{(M, \zeta) \in \mathscr{M} \times \mathbb{S}^n \mid M\zeta = 0\}$$

and π_2 specializes to the vector bundle $p_2 \colon W \to \mathbb{S}^n, (M, \zeta) \mapsto \zeta$ with the fibers

$$W_\zeta := \{M \in \mathscr{M} \mid M\zeta = 0\}.$$

Lemma 5.1 implies that we have *isometrical* linear maps

$$W_\zeta \to L_\zeta,\ M \mapsto g_{M,\zeta} := \big(\sqrt{d_i}\, \langle X, \zeta\rangle^{d_i - 1} \textstyle\sum_j m_{ij} X_j\big), \tag{6}$$

where $M = (m_{ij})$. In other words, the Hermitean vector bundles W and L over $\mathbb{S}^n$ are isometric.

We compose the orthogonal bundle projection $V_\zeta = L_\zeta \oplus R_\zeta \to L_\zeta$ with the bundle isometry $L_\zeta \simeq W_\zeta$ obtaining the map of vector bundles

$$\Psi \colon V \to W,\ (g_{M,\zeta} + h, \zeta) \mapsto (M, \zeta) \tag{7}$$

whose fibers $\Psi^{-1}(M, \zeta)$ are isometric to R_ζ. Another characterization of Ψ is $\Psi(q, \zeta) = (M, \zeta)$, where $M = \Delta^{-1} Dg_{M,\zeta}(\zeta)$. This shows that Ψ provides the link to the condition number: by the definition (1) we have

$$\frac{\mu(q, \zeta)}{\|q\|} = \|M^\dagger\|, \quad \text{where } (M, \zeta) = \Psi(q, \zeta). \tag{8}$$

Let $\rho_{\mathcal{H}_{\mathbf{d}}}$ denote the density of the Gaussian $N(\overline{q}, \sigma^2 \mathrm{I})$ on $\mathcal{H}_{\mathbf{d}}$, where $\overline{q} \in \mathcal{H}_{\mathbf{d}}$ and $\sigma > 0$. For fixed $\zeta \in \mathbb{S}^n$ we decompose the mean $\overline{q}$ as

$$\overline{q} = \overline{k}_\zeta + \overline{g}_\zeta + \overline{h}_\zeta \in C_\zeta \oplus L_\zeta \oplus R_\zeta$$

according to (5). If we denote by ρ_{C_ζ}, ρ_{L_ζ}, and ρ_{R_ζ} the densities of the Gaussian distributions in the spaces C_ζ, L_ζ, and R_ζ with covariance matrices $\sigma^2 \mathrm{I}$ and means $\overline{k}_\zeta, \overline{M}_\zeta$, and $\overline{h}_\zeta$, respectively, then the density $\rho_{\mathcal{H}_{\mathbf{d}}}$ factors as

$$\rho_{\mathcal{H}_{\mathbf{d}}}(k + g + h) = \rho_{C_\zeta}(k) \cdot \rho_{L_\zeta}(g) \cdot \rho_{R_\zeta}(h). \tag{9}$$

The Gaussian density ρ_{L_ζ} on L_ζ induces a Gaussian density ρ_{W_ζ} on the fiber W_ζ with the covariance matrix $\sigma^2 \mathrm{I}$ via the isometrical linear map (6), so that we have $\rho_{W_\zeta}(M) = \rho_{L_\zeta}(g_{M,\zeta})$.

By Bézout's theorem, the fiber $V(q)$ of the projection $\pi_1 \colon V \to \mathcal{H}_{\mathbf{d}}$ at $q \in \mathcal{H}_{\mathbf{d}}$ is a disjoint union of $\mathcal{D} = d_1 \cdots d_n$ unit circles and therefore has the volume $2\pi\mathcal{D}$, provided q does not lie in the discriminant variety.

Think now of choosing (q, ζ) at random from V by first choosing $q \in \mathcal{H}_{\mathbf{d}}$ from $N(\overline{q}, \sigma^2 \mathrm{I})$, then choosing one of its $\mathcal{D}$ zeros $[\zeta] \in \mathbb{P}^n$ at random from the uniform distribution on $\{1, \ldots, \mathcal{D}\}$, and finally choosing a representative ζ in the unit circle $[\zeta] \cap \mathbb{S}^n$ uniformly at random. The resulting probability density ρ_V on V is a natural extension of $\rho_{\mathbf{st}}$. With the coarea formula (Proposition 2.2) one can show that ρ_V has the following form

$$\rho_V(q, \zeta) := \frac{1}{2\pi\mathcal{D}}\, \rho_{\mathcal{H}_{\mathbf{d}}}(q)\, \mathrm{NJ}\pi_1(q, \zeta). \tag{10}$$

The plan to show Theorem 3.4 is now as follows. We have

$$\mathop{\mathbb{E}}_{\mathcal{H}_{\mathbf{d}}}\left(\frac{\mu_2(q)^2}{\|q\|^2}\right) = \mathop{\mathbb{E}}_{V}\left(\frac{\mu(q, \zeta)^2}{\|q\|^2}\right), \tag{11}$$

where $\mathbb{E}_{\mathcal{H}_{\mathbf{d}}}$ and $\mathbb{E}_V$ refer to the expectations with respect to the distribution $N(\overline{q}, \sigma^2 \mathrm{I})$ on $\mathcal{H}_{\mathbf{d}}$ and the probability density ρ_V on V, respectively. Moreover, by Equation (8),

$$\mathop{\mathbb{E}}_{V}\left(\frac{\mu(q, \zeta)^2}{\|q\|^2}\right) = \mathop{\mathbb{E}}_{\mathscr{M}}\left(\|M^\dagger\|^2\right),$$

where $\mathbb{E}_{\mathscr{M}}$ denotes the expectation with respect to the *push-forward density* $\rho_{\mathscr{M}}$ of ρ_V with respect to the map

$$\psi := p_1 \circ \Psi \colon V \to \mathscr{M},\ (q, \zeta) \mapsto M = \Delta^{-1} Dq(\zeta).$$

Proposition 5.2.

1. *For $M \in \mathscr{M}$ of rank n and $\zeta \in \mathbb{S}^n$ with $M\zeta = 0$ we have*

$$\rho_{\mathscr{M}}(M) = \rho_{C_\zeta}(0) \cdot \frac{1}{2\pi} \int_{\lambda \in S^1} \rho_{W_{\lambda\zeta}}(M)\, dS^1. \tag{12}$$

2. *If we put $c_\zeta := \mathbb{E}_{M \sim \rho_{W_\zeta}}(\det(MM^*))$, then $\rho_{\mathbb{S}^n}(\zeta) = \frac{c_\zeta}{2\pi} \rho_{C_\zeta}(0)$ is a probability density on $\mathbb{S}^n$ and*

$$\tilde{\rho}_{W_\zeta}(M) := c_\zeta^{-1}\, \rho_{W_\zeta}(M) \det(MM^*)$$

defines a probability density on W_ζ.

3. *The expectation of $\|M^\dagger\|^2$ with respect to the density $\rho_{\mathscr{M}}$ satisfies*

$$\mathop{\mathbb{E}}_{M \sim \rho_{\mathscr{M}}}\left(\|M^\dagger\|^2\right) = \mathop{\mathbb{E}}_{\zeta \sim \rho_{\mathbb{S}^n}}\left(\mathop{\mathbb{E}}_{M \sim \tilde{\rho}_{W_\zeta}}\left(\|M^\dagger\|^2\right)\right).$$

The formal proof of Proposition 5.2 is quite involved, and will be given in §5.2. However, Equation (12) has an easy heuristic explanation. We decompose a random $q \in \mathcal{H}_d$ according to the decomposition $\mathcal{H}_d = C_\zeta \oplus L_\zeta \oplus R_\zeta$ as $q = k + g + h$. Choose $\lambda \in \mathbb{C}$ with $|\lambda| = 1$ uniformly at random in the unit circle. Then we have $\Psi(q, \lambda\zeta) = (M, \lambda\zeta)$ iff $k = 0$ and g is mapped to M under the isometry in (6). The probability density for the event $k = 0$ equals $\rho_{C_\zeta}(0)$. The second event, conditioned on λ, has the probability density $\rho_{W_{\lambda\zeta}}(M)$.

For the proof of Theorem 3.4, according to Prop. 5.2(3), it is sufficient to show that for all ζ

$$\mathop{\mathbb{E}}_{M \sim \tilde{\rho}_{W_\zeta}} \left(\|M^\dagger\|^2\right) \leq \frac{e(n+1)}{2\sigma^2}. \tag{13}$$

This is achieved in §5.3. We note that the density $\tilde{\rho}_{W_\zeta}$ on the fiber W_ζ is closely related to a Gaussian. By unitary invariance we may assume that $\zeta = (1, 0, \ldots, 0)$. The matrices $M \in W_\zeta$ can then be identified with square matrices $A \in \mathbb{C}^{n \times n}$ and $M^\dagger$ corresponds to A^{-1}.

5.2 Proof of Proposition 5.2

We have already seen that the condition number $\mu(q, \zeta)$ can be described in terms of the map Ψ introduced in (7). Beltrán and Pardo in [3] proved that the normal Jacobian of the related bundle map

$$\Phi\colon V \to W,\ (q, \zeta) \mapsto (N, \zeta) = (Dq(\zeta), \zeta),$$

is constant. This is a crucial observation.

Proposition 5.3. *$\mathrm{NJ}\Phi(q, \zeta) = \mathcal{D}^n$ for all $(q, \zeta) \in V$.*

We also need the fact that $\mathrm{NJ}\pi_1(q, \zeta) = \mathrm{NJ}p_1(N, \zeta)$ where $N = Dq(\zeta)$ and $p_1\colon W \to \mathscr{M}, (N', \zeta) \mapsto N'$, cf. [15].

Using this fact, the factorization (9) of Gaussians, and (10), the density ρ_V can be written as

$$\rho_V(g_{M,\zeta} + h, \zeta) = \frac{1}{2\pi\mathcal{D}}\, \rho_{C_\zeta}(0)\, \rho_{L_\zeta}(g_{M,\zeta})\, \rho_{R_\zeta}(h)\, \mathrm{NJ}p_1(N, \zeta),$$

where $N = \Delta M$.

Applying the coarea formula (Proposition 2.2) to Φ and using $\mathrm{NJ}\Phi = \mathcal{D}^n$ (Proposition 5.3), we obtain for any measurable function $\chi\colon \mathscr{M} \to [0, \infty)$ that

$$\int_V (\chi \circ \psi)\, \rho_V\, dV =$$
$$\frac{1}{\mathcal{D}^n} \int_{(N,\zeta)\in W} \chi(M)\, \frac{\rho_{C_\zeta}(0)}{2\pi\mathcal{D}}\, \rho_{L_\zeta}(g_{M,\zeta})\, \mathrm{NJ}p_1(N, \zeta)\, dW,$$

where we have used that $\int_{R_\zeta} \rho_{R_\zeta}\, dR_\zeta = 1$.

We next apply the coarea formula to the projection p_1. For $N \in \mathscr{M}$ of rank n let $\zeta_N \in \mathbb{P}^n$ be given by $N\zeta_N = 0$. The fiber $V(N) = p_1^{-1}(N)$ is a circle consisting of all representations ζ of ζ_N with norm 1. Recall that ρ_{C_ζ} and ρ_{L_ζ} are independent of the choice of the representation of ζ. Moreover, $\rho_{L_{\zeta_N}}(g_{M,\zeta}) = \rho_{W_\zeta}(M)$. We can thus express the above integral as

$$\frac{1}{\mathcal{D}^n} \int_{N\in\mathscr{M}} \chi(M)\, \frac{\rho_{C_{\zeta_N}}(0)}{\mathcal{D}}\, I(M)\, d\mathscr{M},$$

where

$$I(M) := \frac{1}{2\pi} \int_{\zeta\in V(N)} \rho_{W_\zeta}(M)\, dV(N).$$

We finally perform the linear change of variables $\mathscr{M} \to \mathscr{M}, N \mapsto M$, that has the Jacobian determinant $\mathcal{D}^{n+1}$, and conclude that (note $\zeta_N = \zeta_M$)

$$\int_V (\chi \circ \psi)\, \rho_V\, dV = \int_{M\in\mathscr{M}} \chi(M)\, \rho_{C_{\zeta_M}}(0)\, I(M)\, d\mathscr{M}.$$

This proves that $\rho_{\mathscr{M}}(M) = \rho_{C_{\zeta_M}}(0)\, I(M)$ is the pushforward density of ρ_V with respect to ψ and shows the first assertion of Proposition 5.2.

For the second assertion, we apply the coarea formula first to $p_1\colon W \to \mathscr{M}$ and then to the projection $p_2\colon W \to \mathbb{S}^n, (M, \zeta) \mapsto \zeta$ with the fibers W_ζ and obtain for any measurable function $\chi\colon \mathscr{M} \to [0, \infty)$

$$\begin{aligned} 2\pi \int_{\mathscr{M}} \chi\, d\mathscr{M} &= \int_W (\chi \circ p_1)\, \mathrm{NJ}p_1\, dW \\ &= \int_{\zeta\in\mathbb{S}^n} \Big(\int_{W_\zeta} \chi\, \frac{\mathrm{NJ}p_1}{\mathrm{NJ}p_2}\, dW_\zeta \Big)\, d\mathbb{S}^n. \end{aligned}$$

In [15] (see also [5, Section 13.2, Lemmas 2-3]) it was shown that

$$\frac{\mathrm{NJ}p_1}{\mathrm{NJ}p_2}(M, \zeta) = \det(MM^*).$$

Using this, we obtain

$$\int_{\mathscr{M}} \chi\, d\mathscr{M} = \int_{\zeta\in\mathbb{S}^n} \Big(\int_{M\in W_\zeta} \frac{\chi(M)}{2\pi}\, \det(MM^*)\, d\mathscr{M}_\zeta \Big)\, d\mathbb{S}^n. \tag{14}$$

Applying this to $\chi = \rho_{\mathscr{M}}$, exchanging the order of the integrals and using S^1-invariance, we get

$$1 = \int_{\mathscr{M}} \rho_{\mathscr{M}}\, d\mathscr{M}_\zeta = \int_{\zeta\in\mathbb{S}^n} \frac{c_\zeta}{2\pi}\, \rho_{C_\zeta}(0)\, d\mathbb{S}^n,$$

where $c_\zeta := \mathbb{E}_{M\sim\rho_{W_\zeta}}(\det(MM^*))$. Hence $\frac{1}{2\pi} c_\zeta \rho_{C_\zeta}(0)$ defines a density on $\mathbb{S}^n$, showing the second assertion of Proposition 5.2. Finally, the third assertion follows by applying (14) to $\chi(M) = \|M^\dagger\|^2\, \rho_{\mathscr{M}}(M)$. □

5.3 Smoothed Analysis of a Matrix Condition Number

In the following we fix $\overline{A} \in \mathbb{C}^{n\times n}$, $\sigma > 0$ and denote by ρ the Gaussian density of $N(\overline{A}, \sigma^2 \mathrm{I})$ on $\mathbb{C}^{n\times n}$. Moreover, we consider the related density

$$\tilde{\rho}(A) = c^{-1}\, |\det A|^2\, \rho(A) \quad \text{where } c := \mathop{\mathbb{E}}_{A\sim\rho}(|\det A|^2).$$

The following result is akin to a smoothed analysis of the matrix condition number $\kappa(A) = \|A\| \cdot \|A^{-1}\|$ (compare Sankar et al. [11, §3]) with respect to the probability densities $\tilde{\rho}$ that are not Gaussian, but closely related to Gaussians.

Proposition 5.4. *For any $t > 0$ we have*

$$\mathop{\mathrm{Prob}}_{A\sim\tilde{\rho}} \left\{ \|A^{-1}\| \geq t \right\} \leq \frac{e^2(n+1)^2}{16\sigma^4}\, \frac{1}{t^4}.$$

This tail bound easily implies $\mathbb{E}_{A\sim\tilde{\rho}}(\|A^{-1}\|^2) \leq \frac{e(n+1)}{2\sigma^2}$, which proves inequality (13) and thus completes the proof of Theorem 3.4.

Recall that $\mathbb{S}^{n-1}$ denotes the unit sphere in $\mathbb{C}^n$.

LEMMA 5.5. *For any $v \in \mathbb{S}^{n-1}$ and any $t > 0$ we have*

$$\operatorname*{Prob}_{A\sim\widetilde{\rho}}\left\{\|A^{-1}v\| \geq t\right\} \leq \frac{1}{4\sigma^4 t^4}.$$

PROOF. We first claim that, because of unitary invariance, we may assume that $v = e_n := (0,\ldots,0,1)$. To see this, take $S \in U(n)$ such that $v = Se_n$. Consider the isometric map $A \mapsto B = S^{-1}A$ which transforms the density $\widetilde{\rho}(A)$ to a density of the same form, namely

$$\widetilde{\rho}'(B) = \widetilde{\rho}(A) = c^{-1}|\det A|^2\rho(A) = c^{-1}|\det B|^2\rho'(B),$$

where $\rho'(B)$ denotes the density of $N(S^{-1}\overline{A},\sigma^2\mathrm{I})$ and $c = \mathbb{E}_\rho(|\det A|^2) = \mathbb{E}_{\rho'}(|\det B|^2)$. Thus the assertion for e_n and random B (chosen from any isotropic Gaussian distribution) implies the assertion for v and A, noting that $A^{-1}v = B^{-1}e_n$. This proves the claim.

Let a_i denote the ith row of A. Almost surely, the rows $a_1,\ldots,a_{n-1}$ are linearly independent. We are going to characterize $\|A^{-1}e_n\|$ in a geometric way. Let S_n denote the span of $a_1,\ldots,a_{n-1}$ and denote by $a_n^\perp$ the orthogonal projection of a_n onto $S_n^\perp$. Consider $w := A^{-1}e_n$, which is the nth column of A^{-1}. Since $AA^{-1} = \mathrm{I}$ we have $\langle w, a_i\rangle = 0$ for $i = 1,\ldots,n-1$ and hence $w \in S_n^\perp$. Moreover, $\langle w, a_n\rangle = 1$, so $\|w\|\,\|a_n^\perp\| = 1$ and we arrive at

$$\|A^{-1}e_n\| = \frac{1}{\|a_n^\perp\|}. \tag{15}$$

Let $A_n \in \mathbb{C}^{(n-1)\times n}$ denote the matrix obtained from A by omitting a_n. We shall write $\mathsf{vol}(A_n) = \det(AA^*)^{1/2}$ for the $(n-1)$-dimensional volume of the parallelepiped spanned by the rows of A_n. Similarly, $|\det A|$ can be interpreted as the n-dimensional volume of the parallelepiped spanned by the rows of A.

Now we write $\rho(A) = \rho_1(A_n)\rho_2(a_n)$ where ρ_1 and ρ_2 are the density functions of $N(\overline{A}_n,\sigma^2\mathrm{I})$ and $N(\overline{a}_n,\sigma^2\mathrm{I})$, respectively (the meaning of $\overline{A}_n$ and $\overline{a}_n$ being clear). Moreover, note that

$$\mathsf{vol}(A)^2 = \mathsf{vol}(A_n)^2\,\|a_n^\perp\|^2.$$

Fubini's Theorem combined with (15) yields for $t > 0$

$$\int_{\|A^{-1}e_n\|\geq t} \mathsf{vol}(A)^2\rho(A)\,dA = \int_{A_n\in\mathbb{C}^{(n-1)\times n}} \mathsf{vol}(A_n)^2\,\rho_1(A_n) \cdot\left(\int_{\|a_n^\perp\|\leq 1/t} \|a_n^\perp\|^2\rho_2(a_n)\,da_n\right)dA_n. \tag{16}$$

We next show that for fixed, linearly independent $a_1,\ldots,a_{n-1}$ and $\lambda > 0$

$$\int_{\|a_n^\perp\|\leq\lambda} \|a_n^\perp\|^2\rho_2(a_n)\,da_n \leq \frac{\lambda^4}{2\sigma^2}. \tag{17}$$

For this, note that $a_n^\perp \sim N(\overline{a}_n^\perp,\sigma^2\mathrm{I})$ in $S_n^\perp \simeq \mathbb{C}$ where $\overline{a}_n^\perp$ is the orthogonal projection of $\overline{a}_n$ onto $S_n^\perp$. Thus, proving (17) amounts to showing

$$\int_{|z|\leq\lambda} |z|^2\rho_{\overline{z}}(z)dz \leq \frac{\lambda^4}{2\sigma^2}$$

for the Gaussian density $\rho_{\overline{z}}(z) = \frac{1}{2\pi\sigma^2}e^{-\frac{1}{2\sigma^2}|z-\overline{z}|^2}$ of $z \in \mathbb{C}$, where $\overline{z} \in \mathbb{C}$. Clearly, it is enough to show that

$$\int_{|z|\leq\lambda} \rho_{\overline{z}}(z)dz \leq \frac{\lambda^2}{2\sigma^2}.$$

Without loss of generality we may assume that $\overline{z} = 0$, since the integral in the left-hand side is maximized at this value of $\overline{z}$. Then, writing $z = \sigma w$, we have

$$\begin{aligned}\int_{|z|\leq\lambda} \rho_0(z)dz &= \int_{|w|\leq\frac{\lambda}{\sigma}} \frac{1}{2\pi}e^{-\frac{1}{2}|w|^2}\,dw \\ &= \int_0^{\frac{\lambda}{\sigma}} \frac{1}{2\pi}e^{-\frac{1}{2}r^2}2\pi r\,dr \\ &= -e^{-\frac{1}{2}r^2}\Big|_0^{\frac{\lambda}{\sigma}} = 1 - e^{-\frac{\lambda^2}{2\sigma^2}} \leq \frac{\lambda^2}{2\sigma^2},\end{aligned}$$

which proves inequality (17).

A similar argument shows that

$$2\sigma^2 \leq \int |z|^2\rho_{\overline{z}}(z)dz = \int \|a_n^\perp\|^2\rho_2(a_n)\,da_n. \tag{18}$$

Plugging in this inequality into (16) (with $t = \infty$) we conclude that

$$2\sigma^2 \mathop{\mathbb{E}}_{\rho_1}\left(\mathsf{vol}(A_n)^2\right) \leq \mathop{\mathbb{E}}_{\rho}\left(\mathsf{vol}(A)^2\right). \tag{19}$$

On the other hand, plugging in (17) with $\lambda = \frac{1}{t}$ into (16), we obtain

$$\int_{\|A^{-1}e_n\|\geq t} \mathsf{vol}(A)^2\rho(A)\,dA \leq \frac{1}{2\sigma^2 t^4}\mathop{\mathbb{E}}_{\rho_1}\left(\mathsf{vol}(A_n)^2\right).$$

Combined with (19) this yields

$$\int_{\|A^{-1}e_n\|\geq t} \mathsf{vol}(A)^2\rho(A)\,dA \leq \frac{1}{4\sigma^4 t^4}\mathop{\mathbb{E}}_{\rho}\left(\mathsf{vol}(A)^2\right).$$

By the definition of the density $\widetilde{\rho}$, this means that

$$\operatorname*{Prob}_{A\sim\widetilde{\rho}}\{\|A^{-1}e_n\| \geq t\} \leq \frac{1}{4\sigma^4 t^4},$$

which was to be shown. □

The following is a consequence of [7, Lemma 2.1].

LEMMA 5.6. *For fixed $u \in \mathbb{S}^{n-1}$, $0 \leq s \leq 1$, and v uniformly chosen at random in $\mathbb{S}^{n-1}$, we have*

$$\operatorname*{Prob}_{v}\left\{|u^{\mathrm{T}}v| \geq s\right\} = (1-s^2)^{n-1}.$$

PROOF OF PROPOSITION 5.4. We use an idea in Sankar et al. [11, §3]. For any invertible $A \in \mathbb{C}^{n\times n}$ there exists $u \in \mathbb{S}^{n-1}$ such that $\|A^{-1}u\| = \|A^{-1}\|$. For almost all A, the vector u is uniquely determined up to a scaling factor θ of modulus 1. We shall denote by u_A a representative of such u.

The following is an easy consequence of the singular value decomposition of $\|A^{-1}\|$: for any $v \in \mathbb{S}^{n-1}$ we have

$$\|A^{-1}v\| \geq \|A^{-1}\|\cdot|u_A^{\mathrm{T}}v|. \tag{20}$$

We choose now a random pair (A,v) with A following the law $\widetilde{\rho}$ and, independently, $v \in \mathbb{S}^{n-1}$ from the uniform distribution. Lemma 5.5 implies that

$$\operatorname*{Prob}_{A,v}\left\{\|A^{-1}v\| \geq t\sqrt{\frac{2}{n+1}}\right\} \leq \frac{(n+1)^2}{16\sigma^4 t^4}.$$

On the other hand, we have by (20)

$$\begin{aligned}\operatorname*{Prob}_{A,v}&\left\{\|A^{-1}v\| \geq t\sqrt{2/(n+1)}\right\}\\ &\geq \operatorname*{Prob}_{A,v}\left\{\|A^{-1}\| \geq t \text{ and } |u_A^{\mathrm{T}} v| \geq \sqrt{2/(n+1)}\right\}\\ &\geq \operatorname*{Prob}_{A}\left\{\|A^{-1}\| \geq t\right\}\\ &\quad\cdot \operatorname*{Prob}_{A,v}\left\{|u_A^{\mathrm{T}} v| \geq \sqrt{2/(n+1)} \;\Big|\; \|A^{-1}\| \geq t\right\}.\end{aligned}$$

Lemma 5.6 tells us that for any fixed $u \in \mathbb{S}^{n-1}$ we have

$$\operatorname*{Prob}_{v}\left\{|u^{\mathrm{T}} v| \geq \sqrt{2/(n+1)}\right\} = (1-2/(n+1))^{n-1} \geq e^{-2},$$

the last inequality as $(\frac{n+1}{n-1})^{n-1} = (1+\frac{2}{n-1})^{n-1} \leq e^2$. We thus obtain

$$\begin{aligned}\operatorname*{Prob}_{A}\left\{\|A^{-1}\| \geq t\right\} &\leq e^2 \operatorname*{Prob}_{A,v}\left\{\|A^{-1}v\| \geq t\sqrt{\frac{2}{n+1}}\right\}\\ &\leq \frac{e^2(n+1)^2}{16\sigma^4 t^4},\end{aligned}$$

as claimed. □

6. SKETCH OF REMAINING PROOFS

6.1 Homotopies with a Fixed Extremity

The next two cases we wish to analyze (the condition-based analysis of LV and a solution for Smale's 17th problem with moderate degrees) share the feature that one endpoint of the homotopy segment is fixed, not randomized. This sharing actually allows one to derive both corresponding results (Theorems 3.5 and 3.6, respectively) as a consequence of the following statement.

THEOREM 6.1. *For $g \in S(\mathcal{H}_{\mathbf{d}}) \setminus \Sigma$ we have*

$$\begin{aligned}\mathop{\mathbb{E}}_{f\in S(\mathcal{H}_{\mathbf{d}})}&\left(d_{\mathbb{S}}(f,g)\int_0^1 \mu_2(q_\tau)^2\,d\tau\right)\\ &\leq 724\,D^{3/2}N(n+1)\mu_{\max}(g)^2 + 0.01.\end{aligned}$$

The idea to prove Theorem 6.1 is simple. For small values of τ the system q_τ is close to g and therefore, the value of $\mu_2(q_\tau)^2$ can be bounded by a small multiple of $\mu_{\max}(g)^2$. For the remaining values of τ, the corresponding $t = t(\tau)$ is bounded away from 0 and therefore so is the variance σ_t^2 in the distribution $N(\overline{q}_t, \sigma_t^2 \mathrm{I})$ for q_t. This allows one to control the denominator in the right-hand side of Theorem 3.4 when using this result.

6.2 Condition-based Analysis of LV (proof of Theorem 3.5)

It follows immediately by combining Proposition 4.1 with Theorem 6.1, with the roles of f and g swapped. □

6.3 The Complexity of a Deterministic Homotopy Continuation

We next prove Theorem 3.6. The unitary group $\mathcal{U}(n+1)$ naturally acts on $\mathbb{P}^n$ as well as on $\mathcal{H}_{\mathbf{d}}$ via $(\nu, f) \mapsto f \circ \nu^{-1}$. The following lemma results from the unitary invariance of our setting. The proof is immediate.

LEMMA 6.2. *Let $g \in \mathcal{H}_{\mathbf{d}}$, $\zeta \in \mathbb{P}^n$ be a zero of g, and $\nu \in \mathcal{U}(n+1)$. Then $\mu(g,\zeta) = \mu(g\circ\nu^{-1}, \nu\zeta)$. Moreover, for $f \in \mathcal{H}_{\mathbf{d}}$, we have $K(f,g,\zeta) = K(f\circ\nu^{-1}, g\circ\nu^{-1}, \nu\zeta)$.*

Denote by $z_{(i)}$ a d_ith primitive root of unity. The $\mathcal{D}$ zeros of $\overline{U} = (\overline{U}_1, \ldots, \overline{U}_n)$ are the points $\boldsymbol{z}_j = \left(1 : z_{(1)}^{j_1} : \ldots : z_{(n)}^{j_n}\right) \in \mathbb{P}^n$ for all the possible tuples $j = (j_1, \ldots, j_n)$ with $j_i \in \{0, \ldots, d_i - 1\}$. Clearly, each $\boldsymbol{z}_j$ can be obtained from $\boldsymbol{z}_1 := (1 : 1 : \ldots : 1)$ by a unitary transformation ν_j, which leaves $\overline{U}$ invariant, that is, $\nu_j \boldsymbol{z}_1 = \boldsymbol{z}_j$, $\overline{U}\circ\nu_j^{-1} = \overline{U}$. Hence Lemma 6.2 implies $\mu(\overline{U}, \boldsymbol{z}_j) = \mu(\overline{U}, \boldsymbol{z}_1)$ for all j. In particular, $\mu_{\max}(\overline{U}) = \mu(\overline{U}, \boldsymbol{z}_1)$. It also implies the following result.

PROPOSITION 6.3. *$K_{\overline{U}}(f) = K(f, \overline{U}, \boldsymbol{z}_1)$ satisfies*

$$\mathop{\mathbb{E}}_{f\in S(\mathcal{H}_{\mathbf{d}})} K_{\overline{U}}(f) = \mathop{\mathbb{E}}_{f\in S(\mathcal{H}_{\mathbf{d}})}\Big(\frac{1}{\mathcal{D}}\sum_{j=1}^{\mathcal{D}} K(f, \overline{U}, \boldsymbol{z}_j)\Big).$$

The following lemma follows in a straightforward way from the definition of μ.

LEMMA 6.4. *We have*

$$\mu_{\max}(\overline{U})^2 < 2n\max_i \frac{1}{d_i}(n+1)^{d_i-1} \leq 2\,(n+1)^D.$$

PROOF OF THEOREM 3.6. Equation (3) in the proof of Proposition 4.1 implies for $g = \overline{U}$ that

$$\frac{1}{\mathcal{D}}\sum_{i=1}^{\mathcal{D}} K(f, \overline{U}, z_i) \leq 217\,D^{3/2}\,d_{\mathbb{S}}(f, \overline{U})\int_0^1 \mu_2(q_\tau)^2\,d\tau.$$

Using Proposition 6.3 we get

$$\mathop{\mathbb{E}}_{f\in S(\mathcal{H}_{\mathbf{d}})} K_{\overline{U}}(f) \leq 217\,D^{3/2} \mathop{\mathbb{E}}_{f\in S(\mathcal{H}_{\mathbf{d}})}\Big(d_{\mathbb{S}}(f,\overline{U})\int_0^1 \mu_2(q_\tau)^2\,d\tau\Big).$$

Applying Theorem 6.1 with $g = \overline{U}$ we obtain

$$\mathop{\mathbb{E}}_{f\in S(\mathcal{H}_{\mathbf{d}})} K_{\overline{U}}(f) \leq 217\,D^{3/2}\left(724\,D^{3/2}N(n+1)\,\mu_{\max}(\overline{U})^2 + 0.01\right).$$

We now plug in the bound $\mu_{\max}(\overline{U})^2 \leq 2(n+1)^D$ of Lemma 6.4 to obtain

$$\mathop{\mathbb{E}}_{f\in S(\mathcal{H}_{\mathbf{d}})} K_{\overline{U}}(f) \leq 314216\,D^3\,N(n+1)^{D+1} + 2.17\,D^{3/2}.$$

This is bounded from above by $314217\,D^3\,N(n+1)^{D+1}$, which completes the proof. □

6.4 A Near Solution to Smale's 17th Problem

We finally proceed with the proof of Theorem 3.7. The algorithm we will exhibit uses different routines for $D \leq n$ and $D > n$.

6.4.1 The case $D \leq n$

Theorem 3.6 bounds the number of iterations of Algorithm MD as

$$\mathop{\mathbb{E}}_{f\in S(\mathcal{H}_{\mathbf{d}})} K_{\overline{U}}(f) = \mathcal{O}(D^3 N n^{D+1}).$$

For comparing the order of magnitude of this upper bound to the input size $N = \sum_{i=1}^n \binom{n+d_i}{n}$ we need the following technical lemma (which will be useful for the case $D > n$ as well).

LEMMA 6.5. *For $D \le n$ we have $n^D \le N^{2\ln\ln N + \mathcal{O}(1)}$.*

Theorem 3.6 combined with Lemma 6.5 implies that

$$\mathop{\mathbb{E}}_{f} K_{\overline{U}}(f) = N^{2\ln\ln N+\mathcal{O}(1)} \quad \text{if } D \le n. \tag{21}$$

Note that this bound is nearly polynomial in N.

6.4.2 The case $D > n$

The homotopy continuation algorithm MD is not efficient for large degrees—the main problem being that we do not know how to deterministically compute a starting system g with small $\mu_{\max}(g)$. However, it turns out that an iterative procedure ItRen using an algorithm due to Jim Renegar [10] is fast for large degrees. We prove the following result.

PROPOSITION 6.6. *Let $T(f)$ denote the running time of algorithm* ItRen *on input f. Then, for standard Gaussian $f \in \mathcal{H}_{\mathbf{d}}$, $\mathbb{E}_f T(f) = (nN\mathcal{D})^{\mathcal{O}(1)}$.*

PROOF OF THEOREM 3.7. We use Algorithm MD if $D \le n$ and Algorithm ItRen if $D > n$. We have already shown (see (21)) that the assertion holds if $D \le n$. For the case $D > n$ we use Proposition 6.6 together with the inequality $\mathcal{D}^{\mathcal{O}(1)} \le D^{\mathcal{O}(n)} \le N^{\mathcal{O}(\log\log N)}$ which follows from Lemma 6.5 with the roles of D and n swapped. □

7. REFERENCES

[1] C. Beltrán and L. M. Pardo. On Smale's 17th problem: a probabilistic positive solution. *Found. Comput. Math.*, 8(1):1–43, 2008.

[2] C. Beltrán and L.M. Pardo. Smale's 17th problem: average polynomial time to compute affine and projective solutions. *J. Amer. Math. Soc.*, 22(2):363–385, 2009.

[3] C. Beltrán and L. M. Pardo. Fast linear homotopy to find approximate zeros of polynomial systems. Manuscript 2008.

[4] C. Beltrán and M. Shub. Complexity of Bézout's theorem VII: Distance estimates in the condition metric. *Found. Comput. Math.*, 9(2):179–195, 2009.

[5] L. Blum, F. Cucker, M. Shub, and S. Smale. *Complexity and Real Computation*. Springer, 1998.

[6] P. Bürgisser, and F. Cucker. On a problem posed by Steve Smale. `arxiv.org/abs/0909.2114`

[7] P. Bürgisser, F. Cucker, and M. Lotz. Smoothed analysis of complex conic condition numbers. *J. Math. Pures et Appl.*, 86:293–309, 2006.

[8] K. P. Choi. On the medians of gamma distributions and an equation of Ramanujan. *Proc. Amer. Math. Soc.*, 121(1):245–251, 1994.

[9] R. Howard. The kinematic formula in Riemannian homogeneous spaces. *Mem. Amer. Math. Soc.*, 106(509):vi+69, 1993.

[10] J. Renegar. On the worst-case arithmetic complexity of approximating zeros of systems of polynomials. *SIAM J. Comput.*, 18:350–370, 1989.

[11] A. Sankar, D. A. Spielman, and S.-H. Teng. Smoothed analysis of the condition numbers and growth factors of matrices. *SIAM J. Matrix Anal. Appl.*, 28(2):446–476 (electronic), 2006.

[12] M. Shub. Some remarks on Bezout's theorem and complexity theory. In *From Topology to Computation: Proceedings of the Smalefest (Berkeley, CA, 1990)*, pages 443–455. Springer, New York, 1993.

[13] M. Shub. Complexity of Bézout's theorem VI: Geodesics in the condition (number) metric. *Found. Comput. Math.*, 9(2):171–178, 2009.

[14] M. Shub and S. Smale. Complexity of Bézout's theorem. I. Geometric aspects. *J. Amer. Math. Soc.*, 6(2):459–501, 1993.

[15] M. Shub and S. Smale. Complexity of Bézout's theorem II: volumes and probabilities. In F. Eyssette and A. Galligo, editors, *Computational Algebraic Geometry*, volume 109 of *Progress in Mathematics*, pages 267–285. Birkhäuser, 1993.

[16] M. Shub and S. Smale. Complexity of Bézout's theorem III: condition number and packing. *Journal of Complexity*, 9:4–14, 1993.

[17] M. Shub and S. Smale. Complexity of Bézout's theorem IV: probability of success; extensions. *SIAM J. of Numer. Anal.*, 33:128–148, 1996.

[18] M. Shub and S. Smale. Complexity of Bézout's theorem V: polynomial time. *Theoretical Computer Science*, 133:141–164, 1994.

[19] S. Smale. Newton's method estimates from data at one point. In *The merging of disciplines: new directions in pure, applied, and computational mathematics (Laramie, Wyo., 1985)*, pages 185–196. Springer, New York, 1986.

[20] S. Smale. Mathematical problems for the next century. In *Mathematics: frontiers and perspectives*, pages 271–294. Amer. Math. Soc., Providence, RI, 2000.

[21] D. A. Spielman and S.-H. Teng. Smoothed analysis of algorithms. In *Proceedings of the International Congress of Mathematicians*, volume I, pages 597–606, 2002.

Distributed Computation in Dynamic Networks

Fabian Kuhn
Faculty of Informatics,
University of Lugano
Lugano, Switzerland 6904
fabian.kuhn@usi.ch

Nancy Lynch
Computer Science and AI
Laboratory, MIT
Cambridge, MA 02139
lynch@csail.mit.edu

Rotem Oshman
Computer Science and AI
Laboratory, MIT
Cambridge, MA 02139
rotem@csail.mit.edu

ABSTRACT

In this paper we investigate distributed computation in dynamic networks in which the network topology changes from round to round. We consider a worst-case model in which the communication links for each round are chosen by an adversary, and nodes do not know who their neighbors for the current round are before they broadcast their messages. The model captures mobile networks and wireless networks, in which mobility and interference render communication unpredictable. In contrast to much of the existing work on dynamic networks, we do not assume that the network eventually stops changing; we require correctness and termination even in networks that change continually. We introduce a stability property called *T-interval connectivity* (for $T \geq 1$), which stipulates that for every T consecutive rounds there exists a stable connected spanning subgraph. For $T = 1$ this means that the graph is connected in every round, but changes arbitrarily between rounds.

We show that in 1-interval connected graphs it is possible for nodes to determine the size of the network and compute any computable function of their initial inputs in $O(n^2)$ rounds using messages of size $O(\log n + d)$, where d is the size of the input to a single node. Further, if the graph is T-interval connected for $T > 1$, the computation can be sped up by a factor of T, and any function can be computed in $O(n + n^2/T)$ rounds using messages of size $O(\log n + d)$. We also give two lower bounds on the token dissemination problem, which requires the nodes to disseminate k pieces of information to all the nodes in the network.

The T-interval connected dynamic graph model is a novel model, which we believe opens new avenues for research in the theory of distributed computing in wireless, mobile and dynamic networks.

Categories and Subject Descriptors:
F.2.2 [Analysis of Algorithms and Problem Complexity]: Non-numerical Algorithms and Problems—*computations on discrete structures*
G.2.2 [Discrete Mathematics]: Graph Theory—*graph algorithms*
G.2.2 [Discrete Mathematics]: Graph Theory—*network problems*

General Terms: Algorithms, Theory

Keywords: distributed algorithms, dynamic networks

1. INTRODUCTION

The study of dynamic networks has gained importance and popularity over the last few years. Driven by the growing ubiquity of the Internet and a plethora of mobile devices with communication capabilities, novel distributed systems and applications are now within reach. The networks in which these applications must operate are inherently dynamic; typically we think of them as being large and completely decentralized, so that each node can have an accurate view of only its local vicinity. Such networks change over time, as nodes join, leave, and move around, and as communication links appear and disappear.

In some networks, e.g., peer-to-peer, nodes participate only for a short period of time, and the topology can change at a high rate. In wireless ad-hoc networks, nodes are mobile and move around unpredictably. Much work has gone into developing algorithms that are guaranteed to work in networks that eventually stabilize and stop changing; this abstraction is unsuitable for reasoning about truly dynamic networks.

The objective of this paper is to make a step towards understanding the fundamental possibilities and limitations for distributed algorithms in dynamic networks in which eventual stabilization of the network is not assumed. We introduce a general dynamic network model, and study computability and complexity of essential, basic distributed tasks. Under what conditions is it possible to elect a leader or to compute an accurate estimate of the size of the system? How efficiently can information be disseminated reliably in the network? To what extent does stability in the communication graph help solve these problems? These and similar questions are the focus of our current work.

1.1 The Dynamic Graph Model

In the interest of broad applicability our dynamic network model makes few assumptions about the behavior of the network, and we study it from the worst-case perspective. In the current paper we consider a fixed set of nodes that operate in synchronized rounds and communicate by broadcast. In each round the communication graph is chosen adversarially, under an assumption of *T-interval connectivity*: throughout every block of T consecutive rounds there must exist a connected spanning subgraph that remains stable.

We consider the range from 1-interval connectivity, in which the communication graph can change completely from one round to the next, to ∞-interval connectivity, in which there exists some stable connected spanning subgraph that is not known to the nodes in advance. We note that edges that do not belong to the stable subgraph can still change arbitrarily from one round to the next, and nodes do not know which edges are stable and which are not. We do not assume that a neighbor-discovery mechanism is available to the nodes; they have no means of knowing ahead of time which nodes will receive their message.

In this paper we are mostly concerned with deterministic algorithms, but we also include a randomized algorithm and a randomized lower bound. The computation model is as follows. In every round, the adversary first chooses the edges for the round; for this choice it can see the nodes' internal states at the beginning of the round. At the same time and independent of the adversary's choice of edges, each node tosses private coins and uses them to generate its message for the current round. Deterministic algorithms generate the message based on the interal state alone. In both cases the nodes do not know which edges were chosen by the advesary. Each message is then delivered to the sender's neighbors, as chosen by the adversary; the nodes transition to new states, and the next round begins. Communication is assumed to be bidirectional, but this is not essential. We typically assume that nodes initially know nothing about the network, and communication is limited to $O(\log n)$ bits per message.

To demonstrate the power of the adversary in the dynamic graph model, consider the problem of *local token circulation*: each node u has a local Boolean variable $token_u$, and if $token_u = 1$, node u is said to "have the token". In every round exactly one node in the network has the token, and it can either keep the token or pass it to one of its neighbors. The goal is for all nodes to eventually have the token in some round. This problem is impossible to solve in 1-interval connected graphs: in every round, the adversary can see which node u has the token, and provide that node with only one edge $\{u, v\}$. Node u then has no choice except to eventually pass the token to v. After v receives it, the adversary can turn around and remove all of v's edges except $\{u, v\}$, so that v has no choice except to pass the token back to u. In this way the adversary can prevent the token from ever visiting any node except u, v.

Perhaps surprisingly given our powerful adversary, even in 1-interval connected graphs it is possible to reliably compute any computable function of the initial states of the nodes, and even have all nodes output the result at the same time (simultaneity).

The dynamic graph model we suggest can be used to model various dynamic networks. Perhaps the most natural scenario is mobile networks, in which communication is unpredictable due to the mobility of the agents. There is work on achieving continual connectivity of the communication graph in this setting (e.g., [14]), but currently little is known about how to take advantage of such a service. The dynamic graph model can also serve as an abstraction for static or dynamic wireless networks, in which collisions and interference make it difficult to predict which messages will be delivered, and when. Finally, dynamic graphs can be used to model traditional communication networks, replacing the traditional assumption of a bounded number of failures with our connectivity assumption.

Although we assume that the node set is static, this is not a fundamental limitation. We defer in-depth discussion to future work; however, our techniques are amenable to standard methods such as logical time, which could be used to define the permissible outputs for a computation with a dynamic set of participants.

1.2 Contribution

In this paper we focus on two problems in the context of dynamic graphs. The first problem is *counting*, in which nodes must determine the size of the network. The second is *k-token dissemination*, in which k pieces of information, called *tokens*, are handed out to some nodes in the network, and all nodes must collect all k tokens.

We are especially interested in the variant of k-token dissemination where the number of tokens is equal to the number of nodes in the network, and each node starts with exactly one token. This variant of token dissemination allows any function of the initial states of the nodes to be computed. However, it requires counting, since nodes do not know in advance how many tokens they need to collect. We show that both problems can be solved in $O(n^2)$ rounds in 1-interval connected graphs. Then we extend the algorithm for T-interval connected graphs with known $T > 1$, obtaining an $O(n+n^2/T)$-round protocol for counting or all-to-all token dissemination. When T is not known, we show that both problems can be solved in $O(\min\{n^2, n + n^2\log(n)/T\})$ rounds. Finally, we give a randomized algorithm for approximate counting that assumes an *oblivious* adversary, and terminates with high probability in almost-linear time.

We also give two lower bounds, both concerning token-forwarding algorithms for token dissemination. A *token-forwarding algorithm* is one that does not combine or alter tokens, only stores and forwards them. First, we give an $\Omega(n \log k)$ lower bound on k-token dissemination in 1-interval connected graphs. This lower bound holds even against centralized algorithms, in which each node is told which token to broadcast by some central authority that can see the entire state of the network. We also give an $\Omega(n + nk/T)$ lower bound on k-token dissemination in T-interval connected graphs for a restricted class of randomized algorithms, in which the nodes' behavior depends only on the set of tokens they knew in each round up to the current one. This includes the algorithms in the paper, and other natural strategies such as round robin, choosing a token to broadcast uniformly at random, or assigning a probability to each token that depends on the order in which the tokens were learned.

For simplicity, the results we present here assume that all nodes start the computation in the same round. It is generally not possible to solve any non-trivial problem if some nodes are initially asleep and do not participate. However, if 2-interval connectivity is assumed, it becomes possible to solve k-token dissemination and counting even when computation is initiated by one node and the rest of the nodes are asleep.

1.3 Related Work

For static networks, information dissemination and basic network aggregation tasks have been extensively studied (see e.g. [5, 20, 34]). In particular, the token dissemination problem is analyzed in [40], where it is shown that k tokens can always be broadcast in time $O(n + k)$ in a static graph. The various problems have also been studied in the context of alternative communication models. A number of papers look at the problem of broadcasting a single message (e.g. [9, 27]) or multiple messages [13, 30] in wireless networks. Gossiping protocols are another style of algorithm in which it is assumed that in each round each node communicates with a small number of randomly-chosen neighbors. Various information dissemination problems for the gossiping model have been considered [21, 23, 25]; gossiping aggregation protocols that can be used to approximate the size of the system are described in [24, 36]. The gossiping model differs from our dynamic graph model in that the neighbors for each node are chosen at random and not adversarially, and in addition, pairwise interaction is usually assumed where we assume broadcast.

A dynamic network topology can arise from node and link failures; fault tolerance, i.e., resilience to a bounded number of faults, has been at the core of distributed computing research from its very beginning [5, 34]. There is also a large body of previous work on general dynamic networks. However, in much of the existing work, topology changes are restricted and assumed to be "well-behaved" in some sense. One popular assumption is eventual stabilization (e.g., [1, 7, 8, 41, 22]), which asserts that changes eventually stop occuring; algorithms for this setting typically guarantee safety throughout the execution, but progress is only guaranteed to occur after the network stabilizes. Self-stabilization is a useful property in this context: it requires that the system converge to a valid configuration from any arbitrary starting state. We refer to [15] for a comprehensive treatment of this topic. Another assumption, studied for example in [26, 28, 35], requires topology changes to be infrequent and spread out over time, so that the system has enough time to recover from a change before the next one occurs. Some of these algorithms use link-reversal [18], an algorithm for maintaining routes in a dynamic topology, as a building block.

Protocols that work in the presence of continual dynamic changes have not been as widely studied. Early work (e.g., [6]) considered the problem of end-to-end message delivery in continually changing networks under an assumption of *eventual connectivity*, which asserts that the source and the destination are connected by a path whose links appear infinitely often during the execution. There is some work on handling nodes that join and leave continually in peer-to-peer overlay networks [19, 31, 33]. Most closely related to the problems studied here is [37], where a few basic results in a similar setting are proved; mainly it is shown that in 1-interval connected dynamic graphs (the definition in [37] is slightly different), if nodes have unique identifiers, it is possible to globally broadcast a single message and have all nodes eventually stop sending messages. The time complexity is at least linear in the value of the largest node identifier. In [2], Afek and Hendler give lower bounds on the message complexity of global computation in asynchronous networks with arbitrary link failures.

The time required for global broadcast has been studied in a probabilistic version of the edge-dynamic graph model, where edges are independently formed and removed according to simple Markov processes [10, 11, 12]. Similar edge-dynamic graphs have also been considered in control theory literature, e.g. [38, 39]. In [12] the authors also consider a worst-case dynamic graph model which is similar to ours, except that the graph is not always connected and collisions are modelled explicitly. This lower-level model does not admit a deterministic algorithm for global broadcast; however, [12] gives a randomized algorithm that succeeds with high probability.

A variant of T-interval connectivity was used in [29], where two of the authors studied clock synchronization in *asynchronous* dynamic networks. In [29] it is assumed that the network satisfies T-interval connectivity for a small value of T, which ensures that a connected subgraph exists long enough for each node to send one message. This is analogous to 1-interval connectivity in synchronous dynamic networks.

Finally, a somewhat related computational model results from population protocols, introduced in [3], where the system is modeled as a collection of finite-state agents with pairwise interactions. Population protocols typically (but not always) rely on a strong fairness assumption which requires every pair of agents to interact infinitely often in an infinite execution. We refer to [4] for a survey. Unlike our work, population protocols compute some function in the limit, and nodes do not know when they are done. This can make sequential composition of protocols challenging, since it is not possible to execute a protocol until it terminates, then take the final result and use it as input for some other computation. (Instead, one may use *self-stabilizing* population protocols, which are resilient to inputs that fluctuate and eventually stabilize to some value; but this is not always possible [16]). In our model nodes must eventually output the result of the computation, and sequential composition is straightforward.

2. PRELIMINARIES

We assume that nodes have unique identifiers (UIDs) drawn from a namespace $\mathcal{U}$. We use $x_u(r)$ to denote the value of node u's local variable x at the beginning of round r.

A synchronous dynamic network is modeled as a dynamic graph $G = (V, E)$, where V is a static set of nodes, and $E : \mathbb{N} \to \{\{u, v\} \mid u, v \in V\}$ is a function mapping a round number $r \in \mathbb{N}$ to a set of undirected edges $E(r)$. We make the following assumption about connectivity in the network graph.

DEFINITION 2.1 (T-INTERVAL CONNECTIVITY). *We say a dynamic graph $G = (V, E)$ is* T-interval connected *for $T \geq 1$ if for all $r \in \mathbb{N}$, the static graph $G_{r,T} := (V, \bigcap_{i=r}^{r+T-1} E(r))$ is connected. The graph is said to be* ∞-interval connected *if there is a connected static graph $G' = (V, E')$ such that for all $r \in \mathbb{N}$, $E' \subseteq E(r)$.*

For the current paper we are mainly interested in the following problems.

Counting. An algorithm is said to solve the counting problem if whenever it is executed in a dynamic graph comprising n nodes, all nodes eventually terminate and output n.

k-verification. Closely related to counting, the k-verification problem requires nodes to determine whether or not $n \leq k$. All nodes begin with k as their input, and must eventually terminate and output "yes" or "no". Nodes must output "yes" if and only if there are at most k nodes in the network.

k-token dissemination. An instance of k-token dissemination is a pair (V, I), where $I : V \to \mathcal{P}(\mathcal{T})$ assigns a set of tokens from some domain $\mathcal{T}$ to each node, and $|\bigcup_{u \in V} I(v)| = k$. An algorithm solves k-token dissemination if for all instances (V, I), when the algorithm is executed in any dynamic graph $G = (V, E)$, all nodes eventually terminate and output $\bigcup_{u \in V} I(u)$. We assume that each token in the nodes' input is represented using $O(\log n)$ bits. Nodes may or may not know k, depending on the context.

All-to-all token dissemination. A restricted class of k-token dissemination in which $k = n$ and for all $u \in V$ we have $|I(u)| = 1$. The nodes know that each node starts with a unique token, but they do not know n.

k-committee election. As a useful step towards solving counting and token dissemination we introduce a new problem called k-committee election. In this problem, nodes must partition themselves into sets, called *committees*, such that

(a) The size of each committee is at most k, and

(b) If $k \geq n$, then there is just one committee containing all nodes.

Each committee has a unique committee ID, and the goal is for all nodes to eventually output a committee ID such that the two conditions are satisfied.

3. BASIC FACTS

In this section we state several basic properties of the dynamic graph model, which we later use in our algorithms. The first key fact pertains to the way information spreads in connected dynamic networks.

PROPOSITION 3.1. *It is possible to solve 1-token dissemination in 1-interval connected graphs in $n - 1$ rounds, if nodes are not required to halt after they output the token.*[1]

[1]Prop. 3.1 is intended only as an illustration; in the rest of our algorithms nodes can halt after they perform the output action.

PROOF SKETCH. We simply have all nodes that know the token broadcast it in every round; when a node receives the token, it outputs it immediately, but continues broadcasting it. In any given round, consider a cut between the nodes that already received the token and those that have not. From 1-interval connectivity, there is an edge in the cut; the token is broadcast on that edge and some new node receives it. Since one node initially knows the message and there are n nodes, after $n-1$ rounds all nodes have the token. □

To make this intuition more formal we use Lamport's causal order [32], which formalizes the notion of one node "influencing" another through a chain of messages originating at the first node and ending at the latter (possibly going through other nodes in between). We use $(u,r) \rightsquigarrow (v,r')$ to denote the fact that node u's state in round r influences node v's state in round r', and the formal definition is as follows.

DEFINITION 3.1 (LAMPORT CAUSALITY). *Given a dynamic graph $G = (V,E)$ we define an order $\rightarrow \subseteq (V \times \mathbb{N})^2$, where $(u,r) \rightarrow (v,r')$ iff $r' = r+1$ and $\{u,v\} \in E(r)$. The* causal order *$\rightsquigarrow \subseteq (V \times \mathbb{N})^2$ is defined to be the reflexive and transitive closure of $\rightarrow$.*

The following lemma shows that 1-interval connectivity is sufficient to guarantee that the number of nodes that have influenced a node u grows by at least one in every round, and so does the number of nodes that u itself has influenced.

LEMMA 3.2. *For any node $u \in V$ and round $r \geq 0$ we have*
(a) $|\{v \in V : (u,0) \rightsquigarrow (v,r)\}| \geq \min\{r+1, n\}$, *and*
(b) $|\{v \in V : (v,0) \rightsquigarrow (u,r)\}| \geq \min\{r+1, n\}$.

The proof of the lemma is similar to that of Proposition 3.1, and it is omitted here. We can now re-state the principle behind Proposition 3.1 as a corollary of Lemma 3.2.

COROLLARY 3.3. *For all $u,v \in V$ it holds that $(v,0) \rightsquigarrow (u,n-1)$.*

PROOF. Lemma 3.2 shows that in round $r = n-1$ we have $|\{v \in V : (v,0) \rightsquigarrow (u,n-1)\}| \geq n$, and the claim follows. □

If we have an upper bound on the size of the network, we can use Corollary 3.3 to compute simple functions which serve as building blocks for algorithms.

PROPOSITION 3.4. *Given an upper bound N on the size of the network, functions such as the minimum or maximum of inputs to the nodes can be computed in $N-1$ rounds.*

Corollary 3.3 guarantees that if nodes always broadcast the smallest (resp. largest) value they have heard, all nodes will have the true min or max value after $n-1$ rounds; the upper bound N is needed for nodes to *know* when they have the true min or max. One application is leader election, which can be implemented by choosing the node with the smallest UID as the unique leader. We also note that having an upper bound on the size allows the use of randomized algorithms for data aggregation which rely on computing the max or the min of random variables chosen by the nodes [17, 36]; see Section 7.

The remainder of the paper focuses on counting and solving the token dissemination problem. The two problems are intertwined, and both are useful as a starting point for distributed computing in dynamic networks. We remark that when message sizes are not limited, both problems can be solved in linear time by having nodes constantly broadcast all the information they have collected so far.

PROPOSITION 3.5. *Counting and all-to-all token dissemination can be solved in $O(n)$ rounds in 1-interval connected graphs, using messages of size $O(n \log n)$.*

PROOF. Consider a simple protocol for counting. Each node maintains a set A containing all the UIDs it has heard about so far, where initially $A_u(0) = \{u\}$ for all $u \in V$. In each round r, node u broadcasts A_u and adds to A_u any UIDs it receives from other nodes. If $r > |A_u|$, node u halts and outputs $|A_u|$; otherwise node u continues on to the next round.

It is not hard to see that for all $u, v \in V$ and rounds r, if $(v,0) \rightsquigarrow (u,r)$ then $v \in A_u(r)$. Thus, $\{v \in V : (v,0) \rightsquigarrow (u,r)\} \subseteq A_u(r)$. Correctness of the protocol follows from Lemma 3.2: if node u halts in round r, then $r > |A_u(r)| \geq |\{v \in V : (v,0) \rightsquigarrow (u,r)\}|$, and Lemma 3.2 shows that $r > n$. Next, using Corollary 3.3 we have that in this case $V \subseteq A_u(r)$. And finally, since obviously $A_u(r) \subseteq V$, it follows that $A_u(r) = V$ and node u's output is correct. Termination also follows from Lemma 3.2 and the fact that $A_u(r) \subseteq V$ in every round r.

To solve all-to-all token dissemination, we have nodes attach every token they have heard so far to every message they send. □

In the sequel we describe solutions which use only $O(\log n)$ bits per message.

4. COUNTING THROUGH k-COMMITTEE

In this section we show how k-committee election can be used to solve counting and token dissemination.

Our counting algorithm works by successive doubling: at each point the nodes have a guess k for the size of the network, and attempt to verify whether or not $k \geq n$. If it is discovered that $k < n$, the nodes double k and repeat; if $k \geq n$, the nodes halt and output the count. We defer the problem of determining the exact count until the end of the section, and focus for now on the k-verification problem, that is, checking whether or not $k \geq n$.

Suppose that nodes start out in a state that represents a solution to k-committee election: each node has a committee ID, such that no more than k nodes have the same ID, and if $k \geq n$ then all nodes have the same committee ID. The problem of checking whether $k \geq n$ is then equivalent to checking whether there is more than one committee: if $k \geq n$ there must be one committee only, and if $k < n$ there must be more than one. Nodes can therefore check if $k \geq n$ by executing a simple k-round protocol that checks if there is more than one committee in the graph.

The k-verification protocol. Each node has a local variable x, which is initially set to 1. While $x_u = 1$, node u broadcasts its committee ID. If it hears from some neighbor a different committee ID from its own, or the special value $\perp$, it sets $x_u \leftarrow 0$ and broadcasts $\perp$ in all subsequent rounds. After k rounds, all nodes output the value of their x variable.

LEMMA 4.1. *If the initial state of the execution represents a solution to k-committee election, at the end of the k-verification protocol each node outputs 1 iff $k \geq n$.*

PROOF SKETCH. First suppose that $k \geq n$. In this case there is only one committee in the graph; no node ever hears a different committee ID from its own. After k rounds all nodes still have $x = 1$, and all output 1.

Next, suppose $k < n$. We can show that after the ith round of the protocol, at least i nodes in each committee have $x = 0$. In any round of the protocol, consider a cut between the nodes that belong to a particular committee and still have $x = 1$, and the rest of the nodes, which either belong to a different committee or have $x = 0$. From 1-interval connectivity, there is an edge in the cut, and some node u in the committee that still has $x_u = 1$ hears either a different committee ID or $\bot$. Node u then sets $x_u \leftarrow 0$, and the number of nodes in the committee that still have $x = 1$ decreases by at least one. Since each committee initially contains at most k nodes, after k rounds all nodes in all committees have $x = 0$, and all output 0. □

Our strategy for solving the counting problem is as follows: for $k = 1, 2, 4, 8, \ldots$, solve the k-committee election problem, then execute the k-verification protocol. If $k \geq n$, terminate and output the count; else, continue to the next value of k. Here we use the fact that our model is amenable to sequential composition.

The strategy outlined above requires all nodes to begin the k-verification protocol in the same round. Our protocol for solving k-committee election ensures that this occurs. The protocol also has the useful property that if $k \geq n$, every node knows the UIDs of all other nodes in the graph at the end of the protocol. Thus, when $k \geq n$, nodes can determine the exact count.

5. A k-COMMITTEE PROTOCOL FOR 1-INTERVAL CONNECTED GRAPHS

To solve k-committee election in 1-interval connected graphs, we imagine that there is a unique leader in the network, and this leader invites k nodes to join its committee. Of course we do not truly have a pre-elected leader in the network; we will soon show how to get around this problem. The protocol proceeds in k cycles, each consisting of two phases.

- **Polling phase:** For $k - 1$ rounds, all nodes in the network propagate the UID of the smallest node they have heard about that has not yet joined a committee. Initially each node broadcasts its own UID if it has not joined a committee, or $\bot$ if it has; in each round nodes remember the smallest value they have sent or received so far in the execution, and broadcast that value in the next round.
- **Invitation phase:** The leader selects the smallest UID it heard during the polling phase, and issues a message inviting that node to join its committee. The message carries the UID of the leader and of the invited node. The invitation is propagated by all nodes for $k - 1$ rounds. At the end of the invitation phase, a node that received an invitation joins the leader's committee.

At the end of the k cycles, nodes that have joined the leader's committee output the leader's UID as their committee ID. Any node that has not been invited to join a committee joins its own committee, using its UID as the committee ID.

Because we do not initially have a unique leader in the network, *all* nodes start out thinking they are the leader, and continue to play the role of a leader until they hear a UID smaller than their own. At that point they switch to playing the role of a non-leader. However, once nodes join a committee they do not change their minds.

THEOREM 5.1. *The protocol sketched above solves k-committee election in $O(k^2)$ rounds.*

PROOF SKETCH. The first condition of k-committee election requires each committee to be of size at most k. This condition is satisfied because no node ever invites more than k nodes to join its committee (each node issues at most one invitation per cycle). For the second condition we must show that if $k \geq n$ then all nodes join the same committee. Thus, suppose that $k \geq n$. The polling phase of the first cycles lasts for $k - 1 \geq n - 1$ rounds, and from Corollary 3.3, this is sufficient for all nodes to hear the UID of the smallest node in the network. Thus, after the first polling phase there is only one leader, and no other node ever issues an invitation.

Using Corollary 3.3 we see that the $k - 1$ rounds of each polling phase are sufficient for the leader to successfully identify the smallest node that has not yet joined its committee. Similarly, the invitation phase is long enough for that node to receive the leader's invitation, so in every cycle one node joins the leader's committee. Since there are $k \geq n$ cycles, all nodes join the leader's committee, and all output the leader's UID as their committee ID. □

We remark that when $k \geq n$, the k-committee election protocol can also be used to solve all-to-all token dissemination. To do so we simply have nodes attach their token to their UID in every message they send. Each node is "singled out" for $k - 1 \geq n - 1$ rounds during which it is invited to join the leader's committee, and the invitation reaches all nodes in the graph. Thus, nodes can collect all the tokens by recording the tokens attached to all invitations they hear. In particular, if node UIDs are used as tokens, nodes can collect all the UIDs in the network.

COROLLARY 5.2. *When used together with the k-verification protocol from Section 4, the k-committee election protocol yields an $O(n^2)$-round protocol for counting or all-to-all token dissemination.*

6. COUNTING AND TOKEN DISSEMINATION IN MORE STABLE GRAPHS

In this section we show that in T-interval connected graphs the computation can be sped up by a factor of T. To do this we employ a neat pipelining effect, using the temporarily stable subgraphs that T-interval connectivity guarantees; this allows us to disseminate information more quickly. For convenience we assume that the graph is $2T$-interval connected for some $T \geq 1$.

6.1 Fast T-Token Dissemination in $2T$-Interval Connected Graphs

Procedure `disseminate` gives an algorithm for exchanging at least T pieces of information in n rounds when the dynamic graph is $2T$-interval connected. The procedure takes three arguments: a set of tokens A, the parameter T, and a guess k for the size of the graph. If $k \geq n$, each node is guaranteed to learn the T smallest tokens that appeared in the input to all the nodes.

The execution of procedure `disseminate` is divided into $\lceil k/T \rceil$ phases, each consisting of $2T$ rounds. During each phase, each node maintains the set A of tokens it has already learned and a set S of tokens it has already broadcast in the current phase (initially empty). In each round of the phase, the node broadcasts the smallest token it has not yet broadcast in the current phase, then adds that token to S.

```
S ← ∅
for i = 0, ..., ⌈k/T⌉ − 1 do
    for r = 0, ..., 2T − 1 do
        if S ≠ A then
            t ← min (A \ S)
            broadcast t
            S ← S ∪ {t}
        receive t_1, ..., t_s from neighbors
        A ← A ∪ {t_1, ..., t_s}
    S ← ∅
return A
```

Procedure `disseminate` (A, T, k)

Because the graph is $2T$-interval connected, in each phase i there is a stable connected subgraph G_i that persists throughout the phase. We use $A_u^i(r), S_u^i(r)$ for the values of node u's local variables A, S at the beginning of round r of phase i. We say that u *knows* token t whenever $t \in A_u$.

Let $K_i(t)$ denote the set of nodes that know t at the beginning of phase i, and let $\mathrm{tdist}_i(u,t)$ denote the minimal distance in G_i between node u and any node in $K_i(t)$. Correctness hinges on the following property.

LEMMA 6.1. *For any node $u \in V$, token $t \in \bigcup_{v \in V} A_v(0)$ and round r such that $\mathrm{tdist}_i(u,t) \le r \le 2T$, either $t \in S_u^i(r+1)$ or $S_u(r+1)$ includes at least $(r - \mathrm{tdist}_i(u,t))$ tokens that are smaller than t.*

The intuition behind Lemma 6.1 is that if $r \ge \mathrm{tdist}_i(u,t)$, then r rounds are "enough time" for u to receive t. If u has not received t and sent it on, the path between u and the nearest node that knows t must have been blocked by smaller tokens, which node u received and sent on.

Using Lemma 6.1 we can show:

LEMMA 6.2. *If $k \ge n$, at the end of procedure `disseminate` the set A_u of each node u contains the T smallest tokens.*

PROOF SKETCH. Let $N_i^d(t) := \{u \in V \mid \mathrm{tdist}_i(u,t) \le d\}$ denote the set of nodes at distance at most d from some node that knows t at the beginning of phase i, and let t be one of the T smallest tokens.

From Lemma 6.1, for each node $u \in N_i^T(t)$, either $t \in S_u^i(2T+1)$ or $S_u^i(2T+1)$ contains at least $2T - T = T$ tokens that are smaller than t. But t is one of the T smallest tokens, so the second case is impossible. Therefore all nodes in $N_i^T(t)$ know token t at the end of phase i. Because G_i is connected we have $|N_i^T(t)| \ge \min\{n - |K_i(t)|, T\}$; that is, in each phase T new nodes learn t, until all the nodes know t. Since there are no more than k nodes and we have $\lceil k/T \rceil$ phases, at the end of the last phase all nodes know t. □

Remark 1. If each stable subgraph G_i enjoys good expansion then `disseminate` requires fewer than n phases. For example, if G_i is always f-connected for some parameter f, then each token is learned by $f \cdot T$ new nodes in each phase until all nodes know it, and we only require $\lceil n/f \rceil$ phases. Similarly, if G_i is always a vertex expander we only require $O(\log n)$ phases.

6.2 Counting and Token Dissemination

To solve counting and token dissemination with up to n tokens, we use Procedure `disseminate` to speed up the k-committee election protocol from Section 5. Instead of inviting one node in each cycle, we can use `disseminate` to have the leader learn the UIDs of the T smallest nodes in the polling phase, and use procedure `disseminate` again to extend invitations to all T smallest nodes in the selection phase. Thus, in $O(k+T)$ rounds we can increase the size of the committee by T.

THEOREM 6.3. *It is possible to solve k-committee election in $O(k + k^2/T)$ rounds in T-interval connected graphs. When used in conjunction with the k-verification protocol, this approach yields an $O(n+n^2/T)$-round counting all-to-all token dissemination protocol.*

6.3 Unknown Interval Connectivity

The protocol sketched above assumes that all nodes know the degree of interval connectivity present in the communication graph; if the graph is not $2T$-interval connected, invitations may not reach their destination, and the committees formed may contain less than k nodes even when $k \ge n$. However, even when the graph is not $2T$-interval connected, no committee ever contains *more* than k nodes, simply because no node ever issues more than k invitations. Thus, if nodes guess a value for T and use the protocol to check if $k \ge n$, their error is one-sided: if their guess for T is too large they may falsely conclude that $k < n$ when in fact $k \ge n$, but they will never conclude that $k \ge n$ when $k < n$.

This one-sided error allows us to try different values for k and T without fear of mistakes. We can count in $O(n \log n + n^2 \log n/T)$ time in graphs where T is *unknown* by iterating over various combinations of k and T until we reach a pair (k,T) such that $k \ge n$ and the graph is T-interval connected.

In the worst case, the graph is 1-interval connected, and we need to try all the values $T = 1, 2, 4, \ldots, k$ for each k; we pay a $\log n$ factor in the round complexity. This only improves upon the original $O(n^2)$ algorithm when the graph is $\omega(\log n)$-interval connected. However, we can execute the original algorithm in parallel with the adaptive one, and terminate when the first of the two terminates. In this way we can solve counting or token dissemination in $O(\min\{n^2, n \log n + n^2 \log n/T\})$ rounds when T is unknown.

Using similar ideas we can also adapt to unknown expansion of the graph, e.g., we might guess that it is always f-connected for some initial value of f, and decrease f until we find the right value.

7. APPROXIMATE COUNTING

In this section we show that under certain restrictions on the dynamic-graph adversary, it is possible to use randomization to compute an approximate count in almost-linear time, even when the dynamic graph is only 1-interval connected. The techniques we use are based on a gossiping protocol from [36]. We assume that nodes know some (potentially loose) upper bound N on the size n of the network; this upper bound determines the message size.

For any $\varepsilon > 0$, the algorithm computes a $(1+\varepsilon)$-approximation of the number of nodes n. There are two variants of the algorithm: the first terminates in $O(n)$ time with high probability (in N) and uses messages of size $O(\log N \cdot (\log\log N + \log(1/\varepsilon)/\varepsilon^2))$; the second requires $O(n \cdot (\log\log N + \log(1/\varepsilon)/\varepsilon^2))$ rounds with high probability, but uses messages of size only $O(\log N)$.

Both versions of the algorithm assume that the dynamic graph is generated by an *oblivious* adversary, which determines the complete sequence of graphs before the execution begins. In particular, the adversary is not privy to the results of the nodes' coin tosses in previous rounds, and it also cannot see their states and their messages, which reveal the results of those coin tosses.

For simplicity, we describe here only the algorithm that runs in $O(n)$ rounds w.h.p. but uses slightly larger messages.

The algorithm relies on the following lemma from [36], which shows how the size of the network can be estimated by computing the minimum of exponential random variables (and repeating this procedure to decrease the error probability).

LEMMA 7.1 ([36]). *Let S be a set of ℓ-tuples of independent exponential variables with rate 1: $S = \left\{\left(Y_1^{(1)}, \ldots, Y_\ell^{(1)}\right), \ldots, \left(Y_1^{(m)}, \ldots, Y_\ell^{(m)}\right)\right\}$. Define*

$$\hat{n}(S) := \frac{\ell}{\sum_{i=1}^{\ell} \min_{1 \le j \le |S|} Y_i^{(j)}}.$$

Then

$$\Pr\left(|\hat{n}(S) - |S|| > \frac{2}{3}\epsilon \cdot |S|\right) \leq 2e^{-\varepsilon^2 \ell/27}.$$

For parameters $\varepsilon \in (0, 1/2)$ and $c > 0$, we define $\ell := \lceil (2 + 2c) \cdot 27 \ln(N)/\varepsilon^2 \rceil$.

The scheme for approximate counting is given in Alg 2. The main idea is as follows. Initially, each node $v \in V$ computes ℓ independent exponential random variables $Y_1^{(v)}, \ldots, Y_\ell^{(v)}$ with rate 1. The objective of all nodes is to compute $\hat{n}(V)$, which is a good estimate for n with high probability. To do this they must compute $\min_{v \in V} Y_i^{(v)}$ for each $i \in [\ell]$.

From Proposition 3.4 we know that nodes can find $\min_{v \in V} Y_i^{(v)}$ by propagating the smallest value they have heard so far for $n - 1$ rounds. However, n is not known to the nodes (we could wait $N - 1$ rounds, but N may be a very loose upper bound). We use a combination of Lemma 3.2 and Lemma 7.1 to decide when to stop.

Let $C_u(r) := \{v \in V : (v, 0) \rightsquigarrow (u, r)\}$ be the set of nodes whose value $Y_i^{(v)}$ has reached u by round r. In round r node u is able to compute $\min_{v \in C_u(r)} Y_i^{(v)}$, but it cannot "see" values $Y_i^{(v)}$ for $v \notin C_u(r)$. Therefore we want node u to halt only when $C_u(r) = V$.

From Lemma 3.2 we know that $|C_u(r)| \geq r + 1$ for all $r \leq n - 1$. Because we assume an oblivious adversary, the set $C_u(r)$ is chosen before the nodes choose their random variables. We can use Lemma 7.1 to show that with high probability, if $(1 - \varepsilon)r > \hat{n}_u(C_u(r))$, then $C_u(r) = V$. We use this criterion to know when to terminate. (Recall that in Proposition 3.5 we used a deterministic version of this test: we halted exactly when $r > |C_u(r)|$.)

Sending exact values for $Y_i^{(v)}$ would require nodes to send real numbers, which cannot be represented using a bounded number of bits. Instead nodes send rounded and range-restricted approximations $\tilde{Y}_i^{(v)}$ for $Y_i^{(v)}$; we omit the technical details here. Each value $\tilde{Y}_i^{(v)}$ can be represented using $O(\log \log N + \log(1/\varepsilon))$ bits.

$\underline{Z}^{(u)} \leftarrow (\tilde{Y}_1^{(u)}, \ldots, \tilde{Y}_\ell^{(u)})$
for $r = 1, 2, \ldots$ **do**
  broadcast $\underline{Z}^{(u)}$
  receive $\underline{Z}^{(v_1)}, \ldots, \underline{Z}^{(v_s)}$ from neighbors
  for $i = 1, \ldots, \ell$ **do**
    $Z_i^{(u)} \leftarrow \min\left\{Z_i^{(u)}, Z_i^{(v_1)}, \ldots, Z_i^{(v_s)}\right\}$
  $\tilde{n}_u(r) \leftarrow \ell / \sum_{i=1}^{\ell} Z_i^{(u)}$
  if $(1 - \varepsilon)r > \tilde{n}_u(r)$ **then** terminate and output $\tilde{n}_u(r)$

Algorithm 2: Randomized approximate counting in linear time (code for node u)

For lack of space, the following theorem is given without proof.

THEOREM 7.2. *For $\varepsilon \in (0, 1/2)$ and $c > 0$, with probability at least $1 - 1/N^c$,*

(a) every node in the graph computes the same value $\tilde{n}_v(r) =: \tilde{n}$, and furthermore,

(b) $|\tilde{n} - n| \leq \varepsilon n$.

8. LOWER BOUNDS ON TOKEN DISSEMINATION

Our algorithms for token dissemination do not combine tokens or alter them in anyway, only store and forward them. We call this style of algorithm a *token-forwarding algorithm*. Formally, let $A_u(r)$ denote the set of messages node u has received by the beginning of round r, plus node u's input $I(u)$. A token-forwarding algorithm satisfies: (a) for all $u \in V$ and $r \geq 0$, the message sent by u in round r is a member of $A_u(r) \cup \{\bot\}$, where $\bot$ denotes the empty message; and (b) node u cannot halt in round r unless $A_u(r) = \bigcup_{v \in V} I(v)$, that is, node u has received all the tokens either in messages from other nodes or in its input.

In this section we give two lower bounds on token dissemination with token-forwarding algorithms.

8.1 Lower Bound on Centralized Token Dissemination

For this lower bound we assume that in each round r, some central authority provides each node u with a value $t_u(r) \in A_u(r)$ to broadcast in that round. The centralized algorithm can see the state and history of the entire network, but it does not know which edges will be scheduled in the current round. Centralized algorithms are more powerful than distributed ones, since they have access to more information. To simplify, we begin with each of the k tokens known to exactly one node (this restriction is not essential).

We observe that while the nodes only know a small number of tokens, it is easy for the algorithm to make progress; for example, in the first round of the algorithm at least k nodes learn a new token, because connectivity guarantees that k nodes receive a token that was not in their input. However, as nodes learn more tokens, it becomes harder for the algorithm to provide them with tokens they do not already know.

Accordingly, our strategy is to charge a cost of $1/(k - i)$ for the i-th token learned by each node: the first token each node learns comes at a cheap $1/k$, and the last token learned costs dearly (a charge of 1). Formally, the potential of the system in round r is given by

$$\Phi(r) := \sum_{u \in V} \sum_{i=0}^{|A_u(r)|-1} \frac{1}{k - i}.$$

In the first round we have $\Phi(0) = 1$, because k nodes know one token each. If the algorithm terminates in round r then we must have $\Phi(r) = n \cdot H_k = \Theta(n \log k)$, because all n nodes must know all k tokens. We construct an execution in which the potential increase is bounded by a constant in every round; this gives us an $\Omega(n \log k)$ bound on the number of rounds required.

THEOREM 8.1. *Any deterministic centralized algorithm for k-token dissemination in 1-interval connected graphs requires at least $\Omega(n \log k)$ rounds to complete in the worst case.*

PROOF. We construct the communication graph for each round r in three stages (independently of previous or future rounds).

Stage I: adding the free edges. An edge $\{u, v\}$ is said to be *free* if $t_u(r) \in A_v(r)$ and $t_v(r) \in A_u(r)$; that is, if when we connect u and v, neither node learns anything new. Let $F(r)$ denote the set of free edges in round r; we add all of them to the graph. Let $C_1, \ldots, C_\ell$ denote the connected components of the graph $(V, F(r))$. Observe that any two nodes in different components must send different values, otherwise they would be in the same component.

We choose representatives $v_1 \in C_1, \ldots, v_\ell \in C_\ell$ from each component arbitrarily. Our task now is to construct a connected subgraph over $v_1, \ldots, v_\ell$ and pay only a constant cost. We assume that $\ell \geq 12$, otherwise we can connect the nodes arbitrarily for a constant cost. Let $missing(u) := k - |A_u(r)|$ denote the number of tokens node u does not know at the beginning of round r.

Stage II. We split the nodes into two sets, *Top* and *Bottom*, according to the number of tokens they know, with nodes that know many tokens "on top": $Top := \{v_i \mid missing(v_i) \le \ell/6\}$ and $Bottom := \{v_i \mid missing(v_i) > \ell/6\}$.

Since top nodes know many tokens, connecting to them could be expensive. We will choose our edges in such a way that no top node will learn a new token. Bottom nodes are cheaper, but still not free; we will ensure that each bottom node will learn at most three new tokens (see Fig. 1).

We begin by bounding the size of *Top*. To that end, notice that $\sum_{u \in Top} missing(u) \ge \binom{|Top|}{2}$: for all i, j such that $u, v \in Top$, either $t_u(r) \notin A_v(r)$ or $t_v(r) \notin A_u(r)$, otherwise $\{u, v\}$ would be a free edge and u, v would be in the same component. Therefore each pair $u, v \in Top$ contributes at least one missing token to the sum, and $\sum_{u \in Top} missing(u) \ge \binom{|Top|}{2}$. On the other hand, since each node in *Top* is missing at most $\ell/6$ tokens, it follows that $\sum_{u \in Top} missing(u) \le |Top| \cdot (\ell/6)$. Putting the two facts together we obtain $|Top| \le \ell/3 + 1$, and consequently also

$$|Bottom| - |Top| \ge \ell - 2|Top| \ge \ell - \frac{2\ell}{3} - 2 \overset{(\ell \ge 12)}{\ge} \frac{\ell}{6}.$$

Next we show that because there are many more bottom nodes than top nodes, we have enough flexibility to use only "cheap" edges to connect to top nodes.

Stage III: Connecting the nodes. The bottom nodes are relatively cheap to connect to, so we connect them in an arbitrary line (see Fig. 1). In addition we want to connect each top node to a bottom node, such that no top node learns something new, and no bottom node is connected to more than one top node. That is, we are looking for a matching between *Top* and *Bottom*, using only edges in $P = \{\{u, v\} : u \in Top, v \in Bottom \text{ and } t_v \in A_u(r)\}$.

Since each top node is missing at most $\ell/6$ tokens, and each bottom node broadcasts a different value from all other bottom nodes, for each top node there are at least $|Bottom| - \ell/6$ edges in P to choose from. To construct the matching, we go through the top nodes in arbitrary order $v_0, \ldots, v_p \in Top$, and choose for each v_i some unmatched bottom node u_i such that $\{v_i, u_i\} \in P$ and $u_i \ne u_j$ for all $j < i$. Before each step i the number of unmatched bottom nodes is at least $|Bottom| - i > |Bottom| - |Top| \ge \ell/6$. We already saw that each top node is connected to all but $\ell/6$ bottom nodes in P, so there is always some unmatched P-neighbor of v_i to choose in step i.

What is the total cost of the graph? Top nodes learn no tokens, and bottom nodes learn at most two tokens from other bottom nodes and at most one token from a top node. Thus, the total cost is bounded by

$$\sum_{u \in Bottom} \sum_{i=1}^{\min\{3, missing(u)\}} \frac{1}{missing(u) - (i-1)}$$
$$\le |Bottom| \cdot \frac{6}{\frac{\ell}{6}} \le \ell \cdot \frac{36}{\ell} = 36.$$

□

8.2 Lower Bound on Token Dissemination with Knowledge-Based Algorithms

A token-forwarding randomized algorithm for k-token dissemination is said to be *knowledge-based* if the distribution that determines which token is broadcast by node u in round r is a function of the UID of u, the sequence $A_u(0), \ldots, A_u(r-1)$, where A_i is the set of tokens received by u by the beginning of round i (including its input), and the sequence of u's coin tosses up to round r (inclusive).

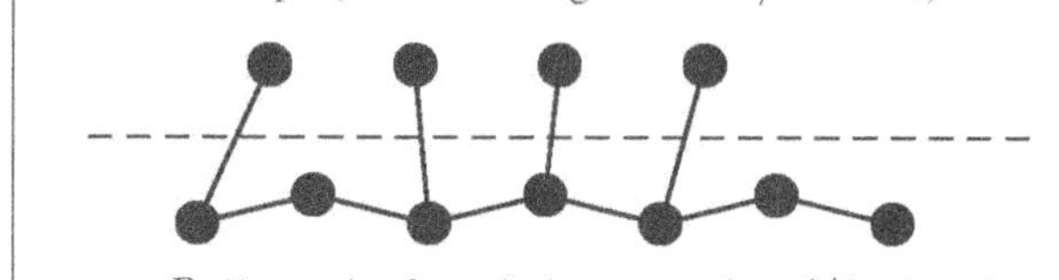

Figure 1: Illustration for the proof of Theorem 8.1

Knowledge-based algorithms can base their decisions on the set of tokens currently known, the order in which tokens were acquired, and even the round in which each token was acquired; however, they cannot rely on other factors, such as the number of times a particular token was heard, or which tokens were received in the previous round. Nevertheless, the class of knowledge-based algorithms includes many natural strategies for solving the token dissemination problem, and it includes the algorithms in this paper. (Other knowledge-based strategies include round-robin over the known tokens, choosing a token to broadcast uniformly at random, and choosing each token with a probability that depends on how long ago that token was acquired.)

Knowledge-based algorithms have the property that once a node learns all the tokens, the distribution of tokens broadcast in future rounds is fixed and does not depend on the dynamic graph. We use this property to show the following lower bound.

THEOREM 8.2. *Any knowledge-based algorithm for k-token dissemination in T-interval connected graphs requires $\Omega(n + nk/T)$ rounds to succeed with probability $1/2$. Further, if the size of the namespace for UIDs $|\mathcal{U}| = \Omega(n^2 k/T)$, then deterministic algorithms require $\Omega(n + nk/T)$ rounds even when each node starts with exactly one token.*

PROOF SKETCH. An $\Omega(n)$ lower bound is trivially demonstrated in a static line graph where some token starts at one end of the line. Thus we assume that $k > 1$. For simplicity, we choose an input assignment in which some node u knows all the tokens, and the other nodes have no tokens.

Let $r_0 = (n-1)(k-1)/(4T) - 2 = \Theta(nk/T)$. We say that a token t is *infrequent* in a given execution if node u broadcasts t less than $(n-1)/(2T)$ times in rounds $0, \ldots, r_0$ of the execution.

Since node u knows all the tokens, its behavior is determined: regardless of the dynamic graph we choose in rounds $0, \ldots, r_0$, the distribution of tokens broadcast by node u in these rounds is fixed. In particular, since $r_0 < (n-1)(k-1)/(4T) - 1$, the linearity of expectation and Markov's inequality show that there is some token t such that in any dynamic graph, token t will be infrequent with probability at least $1/2$. We will construct a specific dynamic graph G in which whenever t is infrequent, the algorithm does not terminate by round r_0. Thus, in the graph we construct, the algorithm requires $\Omega(nk/T)$ rounds w.p. at least $1/2$.

Initially there are $n-1$ nodes that do not know t (all nodes but u). Our goal in constructing G is to ensure that every time node u broadcasts t, at most $2T$ new nodes learn t. Recall that t is said to be infrequent when it is broadcast less than $(n-1)/(2T)$ times by round r_0. Hence, whenever t is infrequent, some node in G has still not learned t by round r_0 and algorithm cannot terminate.

We construct the dynamic graph in phases of two types. When

u has not broadcast t for a while (T rounds to be precise), the network is in a *quiet phase*. A quiet phase extends until the first time u broadcasts t (including that round). During quiet phases the communication graph remains static and comprises two components (see Fig. 2(a)): component U (for "unaware", shown as white nodes in Fig. 2(a)) contains nodes that are guaranteed not to know t, arranged in a line $v_{i_1}, \ldots, v_{i_\ell}$. The first node in the line, v_{i_1}, is connected to node u. (Note that $u \notin U$, because u knows t from the start). The other component, K (for "knowledgeable"), contains the remaining nodes. These nodes may or may not know t, and we connect them to each other arbitrarily. Initially, $K = \{u\}$ and $U = V \setminus \{u\}$, with the nodes in U ordered arbitrarily.

A quiet phase ends immediately after u broadcasts token t. At this point $v_{i_1} \in U$ knows t; if we leave the network static, the nodes in U may forward t to each other, until in $|U| - 1$ rounds all nodes in U know t. Recall that we want to ensure that at most $2T$ nodes learn t after every time u broadcasts it. To contain the propagation of t, we begin an *active phase*.

If we wanted to satisfy only 1-interval connectivity, we would simply move v_{i_1} from U to K and connect u to v_{i_2} instead. This would prevent v_{i_1} from spreading t to other nodes in U, but it violates T-interval connectivity for $T > 1$. In order to move nodes from U to K we need more edges, so that we can remove some without breaking connectivity.

Thus, at the beginning of an active phase we connect u to v_{i_ℓ}, closing the line to form a ring (see Fig. 2(b)). Then we wait for T rounds. Finally, we remove edge $\{v_{i_{2T}}, v_{i_{2T+1}}\}$ (see Fig. 2(c)). This ends the active phase. Note that T-interval connectivity is preserved along the line $v_{i_{2T+1}}, v_{i_{2T+2}}, \ldots, v_{i_\ell}, u, v_{i_1}, \ldots, v_{i_{2T}}$ (shown in bold lines in the figures). This is why we use a ring instead of a line.

At the beginning of an active phase, token t may be known only by nodes $v_{i_1}, \ldots, v_{i_T}$ in the ring. (If the preceding phase was quiet, only node v_{i_1} knows t; if the preceding phase was active more nodes may know t, see below.) An active phase lasts T rounds. During this time, token t propagates in one of two ways:

(1) Nodes $v_{i_1}, \ldots, v_{i_T}$ may forward t to nodes $v_{i_{T+1}}, \ldots, v_{i_{2T}}$.

(2) Node u may broadcast t again during the phase, in which case nodes $v_{i_\ell}, \ldots, v_{i_{\ell-T}}$ (indicated in cross-hatching in Fig. 2(c)) may also learn it.

At the end of the phase we remove the link $\{v_{i_{2T}}, v_{i_{2T+1}}\}$, cutting off the propagation of t along that side of the ring, and set $U \leftarrow U \setminus \{v_{i_1}, \ldots, v_{i_{2T}}\}$. Notice that now the only node in U to which u is connected is v_{i_ℓ}. To retain consistency in notation we reverse the line, renaming as follows: $\ell' \leftarrow \ell - 2T, i_1' \leftarrow i_\ell, i_2' \leftarrow i_{\ell-1}, \ldots, i_{\ell}' \leftarrow i_{2T+1}$.

If u did not broadcast t during the phase (that is, case (2) above did not occur), then no remaining node in U knows t, and we begin another quiet phase. If u did broadcast t, at most $v_{i_1'}, \ldots, v_{i_T'}$ (which were labelled $v_\ell, \ldots, v_{\ell-T}$ before the renaming) know it, and we begin another active phase.

The construction above allows us to charge at most $2T$ nodes to each time u broadcasts t: an active phase is only triggered when u broadcasts t, and each active phase ends with the removal of $2T$ nodes from U. If t is infrequent in an execution, then there are less than $(n-1)/(2T)$ active phases by round r_0 of the execution; since initially $|U| = n - 1$, by round $r_0 = \Omega(nk/T)$ there is still some node in U which does not know t, and the algorithm is not done. Since t is infrequent w.p. at least $1/2$, this shows that any knowledge-based algorithm for k-token dissemination requires $\Omega(nk/T)$ rounds w.p. at least $1/2$. □

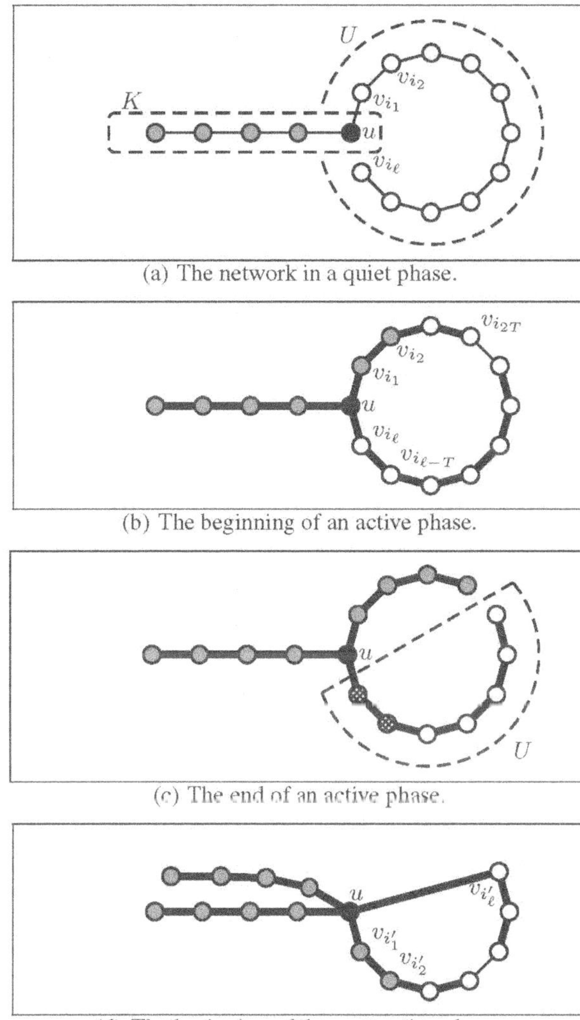

(a) The network in a quiet phase.

(b) The beginning of an active phase.

(c) The end of an active phase.

(d) The beginning of the next active phase.

Figure 2: The construction for Theorem 8.2, with $T = 2$. Nodes that do not know t are shown in white, nodes that may know t are shown in grey. Edges along which T-interval connectivity is preserved are shown in bold.

9. CONCLUSION

In this work we consider a model for dynamic networks which makes very few assumptions about the network. The model can serve as an abstraction for wireless or mobile networks, to reason about the fundamental unpredictability of communication in this type of system. We do not restrict the mobility of the nodes except for retaining connectivity, and we do not assume that geographical information or neighbor discovery are available. Nevertheless, we show that one can efficiently compute any computable function in our model, taking advantage of stability if it exists in the network.

We believe that the T-interval connectivity property provides a natural and general way to reason about dynamic networks. It is easy to see that without any connectivity assumption no non-trivial function can be computed, except possibly in the sense of computation in the limit (as in [3]). However, our connectivity assumption is easily weakened to only require connectivity once every constant number of rounds, or to only require eventual connectivity in the style of Prop. 3.1, with a known bound on the number of rounds.

There are many open problems related to the model. We hope to strengthen our lower bounds for token dissemination and obtain an $\Omega(nk/T)$ general lower bound, and to determine whether counting is in fact as hard as token dissemination. Other natural problems, such as consensus and leader election, can be solved in linear time once a (possibly approximate) count is known, but can they be solved more quickly without first counting? Is it possible to compute an approximate upper bound for the size of the network in less than the time required for counting exactly? These and other questions remain intriguing open problems.

10. REFERENCES

[1] Y. Afek, B. Awerbuch, and E. Gafni. Applying static network protocols to dynamic networks. In *Proc. of 28th Symp. on Foundations of Computer Science (FOCS)*, pages 358–370, 1987.

[2] Y. Afek and D. Hendler. On the complexity of gloabl computation in the presence of link failures: The general case. *Distributed Computing*, 8(3):115–120, 1995.

[3] D. Angluin, J. Aspnes, Z. Diamadi, M. Fischer, and R. Peralta. Computation in networks of passively mobile finite-state sensors. *Distributed Computing*, 18(4):235–253, 2006.

[4] J. Aspnes and E. Ruppert. An introduction to population protocols. In B. Garbinato, H. Miranda, and L. Rodrigues, editors, *Middleware for Network Eccentric and Mobile Applications*, pages 97–120. Springer-Verlag, 2009.

[5] H. Attiya and J. Welch. *Distributed Computing: Fundamentals, Simulations, and Advanced Topics*. John Wiley and Sons, Inc., 2nd edition, 2004.

[6] B. Awerbuch, Y. Mansour, and N. Shavit. Polynomial end-to-end communication. In *Proc. of 30th Symp. on Foundations of Computer Science (FOCS)*, pages 358–363, 1989.

[7] B. Awerbuch, B. Patt-Shamir, D. Peleg, and M. E. Saks. Adapting to asynchronous dynamic networks. In *Proc. of the 24th Annual ACM Symposium on Theory of Computing (STOC)*, pages 557–570, 1992.

[8] B. Awerbuch and M. Sipser. Dynamic networks are as fast as static networks. In *Proc. of 29th Symp. on Foundations of Computer Science (FOCS)*, pages 206–220, 1988.

[9] R. Bar-Yehuda, O. Goldreich, and A. Itai. On the time complexity of broadcast in radio networks: An exponential gap between determinism and randomization. *Journal of Computer and System Sciences (JCSS)*, 45(1):104–126, 1992.

[10] H. Baumann, P. Crescenzi, and P. Fraigniaud. Parsimonious flooding in dynamic graphs. In *Proc. of 28th Symp. on Principles of Distributed Computing (PODC)*, pages 260–269, 2009.

[11] A. Clementi, C. Macci, A. Monti, F. Pasquale, and R. Silvestri. Flooding time in edge-markovian dynamic graphs. In *Proc. of 27th Symp. on Principles of Distributed Computing (PODC)*, pages 213–222, 2008.

[12] A. E. F. Clementi, A. Monti, F. Pasquale, and R. Silvestri. Broadcasting in dynamic radio networks. *J. Comput. Syst. Sci.*, 75(4):213–230, 2009.

[13] A. E. G. Clementi, A. Monti, and R. Silvestri. Distributed multi-broadcast in unknown radio networks. In *Proc. of 20th Symp. on Principles of Distributed Computing (PODC)*, pages 255–263, 2001.

[14] A. Cornejo, F. Kuhn, R. Ley-Wild, and N. A. Lynch. Keeping mobile robot swarms connected. In *Proc. of 23rd Conference on Distributed Computing (DISC)*, pages 496–511, 2009.

[15] S. Dolev. *Self-Stabilization*. MIT Press, 2000.

[16] M. Fischer and H. Jiang. Self-stabilizing leader election in networks of finite-state anonymous agents. In *Proc. of 10th Int. Conf. on Principles of Distributed Systems (OPODIS)*, pages 395–409, 2006.

[17] P. Flajolet and G. N. Martin. Probabilistic counting algorithms for data base applications. *Journal of Computer and System Sciences*, 31(2):182 – 209, 1985.

[18] E. Gafni and D. Bertsekas. Distributed algorithms for generating loop-free routes in networks with frequently changing topology. *IEEE Transactions on Communication*, 29(1):11–18, 1981.

[19] T. P. Hayes, J. Saia, and A. Trehan. The forgiving graph: A distributed data structure for low stretch under adversarial attack. In *Proc. of 28th Symp. on Principles of Distributed Computing (PODC)*, pages 121–130, 2009.

[20] S. M. Hedetniemi, S. T. Hedetniemi, and A. L. Liestman. A survey of gossiping and broadcasting in communication networks. *Networks*, 18:319–349, 1988.

[21] J. Hromkovič, R. Klasing, B. Monien, and R. Peine. Dissemination of information in interconnection networks (broadcasting & gossiping). *Combinatorial Network Theory*, pages 125–212, 1996.

[22] R. Ingram, P. Shields, J. E. Walter, and J. L. Welch. An asynchronous leader election algorithm for dynamic networks. In *Proc. of 23rd IEEE Int. Symp. on Parallel and Distributed Processing (IPDPS)*, pages 1–12, 2009.

[23] R. Karp, C. Schindelhauer, S. Shenker, and B. Vöcking. Randomized rumor spreading. In *Proc. of 41st Symp. on Foundations of Computer Science (FOCS)*, pages 565–574, 2000.

[24] D. Kempe, A. Dobra, and J. Gehrke. Gossip-based computation of aggregate information. In *Proc. of 44th Symp. on Foundations of Computer Science (FOCS)*, pages 482–491, 2003.

[25] D. Kempe and J. Kleinberg. Protocols and impossibility results for gossip-based communication mechanisms. In *Proc. of 43rd Symp. on Foundations of Computer Science (FOCS)*, pages 471–480, 2002.

[26] A. Korman. Improved compact routing schemes for dynamic trees. In *Proc. of 27th Symp. on Principles of Distributed Computing (PODC)*, pages 185–194, 2008.

[27] D. Kowalski and A. Pelc. Broadcasting in undirected ad hoc radio networks. In *Proc. of 22nd Symp. on Principles of Distributed Computing (PODC)*, pages 73–82, 2003.

[28] D. Krizanc, F. Luccio, and R. Raman. Compact routing schemes for dynamic ring networks. *Theory of Computing Systems*, 37:585–607, 2004.

[29] F. Kuhn, T. Locher, and R. Oshman. Gradient clock synchronization in dynamic networks. In *Proc. of 21st ACM Symp. on Parallelism in Algorithms and Architectures (SPAA)*, pages 270–279, 2009.

[30] F. Kuhn, N. A. Lynch, and C. C. Newport. The abstract MAC layer. In *Proc. of 23rd Conference on Distributed Computing (DISC)*, pages 48–62, 2009.

[31] F. Kuhn, S. Schmid, and R. Wattenhofer. A self-repairing peer-to-peer system resilient to dynamic adversarial churn. In *Proc. of 4th Int. Workshop on Peer-To-Peer Systems (IPTPS)*, 2005.

[32] L. Lamport. Time, clocks, and the ordering of events in a distributed system. *Commun. ACM*, 21(7):558–565, 1978.

[33] X. Li, M. J, and C. Plaxton. Active and Concurrent Topology Maintenance. In *Proc. of 18th Conference on Distributed Computing (DISC)*, 2004.

[34] N. A. Lynch. *Distributed Algorithms*. Morgan Kaufmann Publishers, 1996.

[35] N. Malpani, J. L. Welch, and N. Vaidya. Leader election algorithms for mobile ad hoc networks. In *DIALM '00: Proceedings of the 4th international workshop on Discrete algorithms and methods for mobile computing and communications*, pages 96–103, New York, NY, USA, 2000. ACM.

[36] D. Mosk-Aoyama and D. Shah. Computing separable functions via gossip. In *Proc. of 25th Symp. on Principles of Distributed Computing (PODC)*, pages 113–122, 2006.

[37] R. O'Dell and R. Wattenhofer. Information dissemination in highly dynamic graphs. In *Proc. of 9th Joint Workshop on Foundations of Mobile Computing (DIALM-POMC)*, pages 104–110, 2005.

[38] R. Olfati-Saber and R. M. Murray. Consensus problems in networks of agents with switching topology and time-delays. *IEEE Transactions on Automatic Control*, 49(9):1520–1533, 2004.

[39] W. Ren and R. W. Beard. Consensus of information under dynamically changing interaction topologies. In *Proc. of American Control Conference*, pages 4939–4944, 2004.

[40] D. M. Topkis. Concurrent broadcast for information dissemination. *IEEE Transactions on Software Engineering*, SE-11(10), 1985.

[41] J. E. Walter, J. L. Welch, and N. H. Vaidya. A mutual exclusion algorithm for ad hoc mobile networks. *Wireless Networks*, 7(6):585–600, 2001.

Optimal Bounds for Sign-Representing the Intersection of Two Halfspaces by Polynomials

Alexander A. Sherstov
Microsoft Research
1 Memorial Drive
Cambridge, MA 02142 USA
sherstov@cs.utexas.edu

ABSTRACT

The *threshold degree* of a function $f:\{0,1\}^n \to \{-1,+1\}$ is the least degree of a real polynomial p with $f(x) \equiv \operatorname{sgn} p(x)$. We prove that the intersection of two halfspaces on $\{0,1\}^n$ has threshold degree $\Omega(n)$, which matches the trivial upper bound and completely answers a question due to Klivans (2002). The best previous lower bound was $\Omega(\sqrt{n})$. Our result shows that the intersection of two halfspaces on $\{0,1\}^n$ only admits a trivial $2^{\Theta(n)}$-time learning algorithm based on sign-representation by polynomials, unlike the advances achieved in PAC learning DNF formulas and read-once Boolean formulas. The proof introduces a new technique of independent interest, based on Fourier analysis and matrix theory.

Categories and Subject Descriptors

F.0 [**Theory of Computation**]: General; F.1.3 [**Computation by Abstract Devices**]: Complexity Measures and Classes

General Terms

Theory

Keywords

Polynomial representations of Boolean functions, PAC learning, halfspaces, intersections of halfspaces

1. INTRODUCTION

A well-studied notion in computational learning theory is that of a *perceptron*. This term stands for the representation of a given Boolean function $f:\{0,1\}^n \to \{-1,+1\}$ in the form $f(x) \equiv \operatorname{sgn} p(x)$ for a real polynomial p of some degree d. The least degree d for which f admits such a representation is called the *threshold degree* of f, denoted $\deg_\pm(f)$. In other words, $\deg_\pm(f)$ is the least degree of a real polynomial that agrees with f in sign. Perceptrons are appealing from a learning standpoint because they immediately lead to efficient learning algorithms. In more detail, let $f:\{0,1\}^n \to \{-1,+1\}$ be an unknown function of threshold degree d. Then by definition, f has a representation of the form

$$f(x) \equiv \operatorname{sgn}\left(\sum_{|S|\leqslant d} \lambda_S \prod_{i\in S} x_i\right)$$

for some reals λ_S and is therefore a halfspace in $N = \binom{n}{0} + \binom{n}{1} + \cdots + \binom{n}{d}$ dimensions. As a result, f can be PAC learned in time polynomial in N, using any of a variety of halfspace learning algorithms. (Throughout this paper, the term "PAC learning" refers to Valiant's standard model [40] of learning under arbitrary distributions.)

The study of perceptrons dates back forty years to the seminal monograph of Minsky and Papert [25], who examined the threshold degree of several common functions. Today, the perceptron-based approach yields the fastest known PAC learning algorithms for several concept classes. One such is the class of DNF formulas of polynomial size, posed a challenge in Valiant's original paper [40] and extensively studied over the past two decades. The fastest known algorithm for PAC learning DNF formulas runs in time $\exp\{\tilde{O}(n^{1/3})\}$ and is due to Klivans and Servedio [18]. Specifically, the authors of [18] prove an upper bound of $O(n^{1/3}\log n)$ on the threshold degree of polynomial-size DNF formulas, which essentially matches a classical lower bound of $\Omega(n^{1/3})$ due to Minsky and Papert [25].

Another success story of the perceptron-based approach is the concept class of Boolean formulas, i.e., Boolean circuits with fan-out 1 at every gate. O'Donnell and Servedio [29] proved an upper bound of $\sqrt{s}\log^{O(d)} s$ on the threshold degree of Boolean formulas of size s and depth d, giving the first subexponential algorithm for a family of formulas of superconstant depth. This upper bound on the threshold degree was improved to $s^{0.5+o(1)}$ for any depth d by Ambainis et al. [2], building on a quantum query algorithm of Farhi et al. [10]. More recently, Lee [24] sharpened the upper bound to $O(\sqrt{s})$, which is tight. This line of research gives the fastest known algorithm for PAC learning Boolean formulas.

Another extensively studied problem in computational learning theory, and the subject of this paper, is the problem of learning *intersections of halfspaces*, i.e., conjunctions of functions of the form $f(x) = \operatorname{sgn}(\sum \alpha_i x_i - \theta)$ for some reals $\alpha_1, \ldots, \alpha_n, \theta$. While solutions are known [7, 23, 41, 3, 17, 19, 16] to several restrictions of this problem, no algorithm has been discovered for PAC learning the intersection of even two halfspaces in time faster than $2^{\Theta(n)}$. Progress on proving hardness results has also been scarce. Indeed, all known hardness results [8, 1, 20, 14] either require polynomially many halfspaces or assume *proper* learning. In particular, we are not aware of any representation-independent hardness results for PAC learning the intersection of $O(1)$ halfspaces.

STOC'10, June 5–8, 2010, Cambridge, Massachusetts, USA.

Our Results

Since the perceptron-based approach yields the fastest known algorithms for PAC learning DNF formulas and read-once Boolean formulas, it is natural to wonder whether it can yield any nontrivial results for the intersection of two halfspaces. Letting $D(n)$ stand for the maximum threshold degree over all intersections of two halfspaces on $\{0,1\}^n$, the question becomes whether $D(n)$ is a nontrivial (sublinear) function of the dimension n. This question has been studied by several authors, as summarized in Table 1. Forty years ago, Minsky and Papert [25] used a compactness argument to show that $D(n) = \omega(1)$, the function in question being the intersection of two majorities on disjoint sets variables. O'Donnell and Servedio [29] studied the same function using a rather different approach and thereby proved that $D(n) = \Omega(\log n/\log\log n)$. No nontrivial upper bounds on $D(n)$ being known, Klivans [15, §7] formally posed the problem of proving a lower bound substantially better than $\Omega(\log n)$ or an upper bound of $o(n)$.

It was recently shown in [34] that $D(n) = \Omega(\sqrt{n})$, solving Klivans' problem and ruling out an $n^{o(\sqrt{n})}$-time PAC learning algorithm based on perceptrons. It is clear, however, that a PAC learning algorithm for the intersection of two halfspaces in time $n^{\Theta(\sqrt{n})}$ would still be a breakthrough in computational learning theory, comparable to the advances in the study of DNF formulas and read-once Boolean formulas. The main contribution of this paper is to prove that $D(n) = \Omega(n)$, which matches the trivial upper bound and definitively rules out the perceptron-based approach for learning the intersection of two halfspaces in nontrivial time.

THEOREM 1 (Main result). *For $n = 1,2,3,\ldots$, let $D(n)$ denote the maximum threshold degree of a function of the form $f(x)\wedge g(x)$, where $f,g\colon\{0,1\}^n \to \{-1,+1\}$ are halfspaces. Then*

$$D(n) = \Theta(n).$$

To be more precise, we give a randomized algorithm which with probability at least $1 - e^{-n/12}$ constructs two halfspaces on $\{0,1\}^n$ whose intersection has threshold degree $\Theta(n)$. In Section 6, we develop several refinements of Theorem 1. For example, we show that the intersection of two halfspaces on $\{0,1\}^n$ requires a perceptron with $\exp\{\Theta(n)\}$ monomials, i.e., does not have a sparse sign-representation. We also give an essentially tight lower bound on the threshold degree of the intersection of a halfspace and a majority function, improving quadratically on the previous bound in [34].

In summary, unlike DNF formulas and read-once Boolean formulas, the intersection of two halfspaces does not admit a nontrivial sign-representation. Apart from computational learning theory, lower bounds on the threshold degree have played a key role in several works on circuit complexity [30, 39, 21, 22, 36], Turing complexity classes [4, 6, 5], and communication complexity [36, 35, 37, 31]. For this reason, we consider Theorem 1 and the techniques used to obtain it to be of interest outside of computational learning.

Theorem 1 and much previous work suggest that the nature of a PAC learning problem changes significantly when, instead of Valiant's original arbitrary-distribution setting, one considers learning with respect to restricted distributions. For example, the uniform distribution on the sphere $\mathbb{S}^{n-1}$ or hypercube $\{0,1\}^n$ allows the use of tools other than sign-representing polynomials, such as Fourier analysis. In particular, polynomial-time algorithms are known for the uniform-distribution learning of intersections of a constant number of halfspaces on the sphere [7, 41] and hypercube [17]. Furthermore, if membership queries are allowed, DNF formulas are known to be learnable in polynomial time with respect to the uniform distribution on the hypercube [12].

Result	*Reference*
$D(n) = \omega(1)$	[25]
$D(n) = \Omega(\log n/\log\log n)$	[29]
$D(n) = \Omega(\sqrt{n})$	[34]
$D(n) = \Theta(n)$	this paper

Table 1: Lower bounds for the intersection of two halfspaces.

Our Techniques

Let $f\wedge f$ denote the conjunction of two copies of a given Boolean function f, each on an independent set of variables. It was shown in [34] that the threshold degree of $f\wedge f$ equals, up to a small multiplicative constant, the least degree of a rational function R with $\|f - R\|_\infty \leqslant 1/3$. With this characterization in hand, the equality $\deg_\pm(f\wedge f) = \Theta(\sqrt{n})$ was derived in [34] by solving the rational approximation problem for the halfspace

$$f(x) = \operatorname{sgn}\left(1 + \sum_{i=1}^{\sqrt{n}}\sum_{j=1}^{\sqrt{n}} 2^i x_{ij}\right).$$

Unfortunately, the $\Theta(\sqrt{n})$ barrier is fundamental to the analysis in [34]. To prove that in fact $D(n) = \Theta(n)$, we pursue a rather different approach.

The intuition behind our work is as follows. Let $\alpha_1, \alpha_2, \ldots, \alpha_n$ be given nonzero integers, and let $f\colon\{0,1\}^n \to \{-1,+1\}$ be a given Boolean function such that $f(x)$ is completely determined by the sum $\sum \alpha_i x_i$. When approximating f pointwise by polynomials and rational functions of a given degree, can one restrict attention to those approximants that are, like f, functions of the sum $\sum \alpha_i x_i$ alone rather than the individual bits $x_1, x_2, \ldots, x_n$? If true, this claim would dramatically simplify the analysis of the threshold degree of f by reducing it to a univariate question. Minsky and Papert [25] showed that the claim is indeed true in the highly special case $\alpha_1 = \alpha_2 = \cdots = \alpha_n$. For the purposes of this paper, however, the nonzero coefficients $\alpha_1, \alpha_2, \ldots, \alpha_n$ must be of increasing orders of magnitude and in particular must satisfy

$$\max_{i,j}\left|\frac{\alpha_i}{\alpha_j}\right| > \exp\{\Omega(n)\}.$$

Minsky and Papert's argument breaks down completely in this setting, and with good reason: coefficients $\alpha_1, \ldots, \alpha_n$ are easily constructed [5] for which the passage to univariate approximation increases the degree requirement from 1 to n.

To overcome this difficulty, we use techniques from Fourier analysis and matrix perturbation theory. Specifically, we define an appropriate distribution on n-tuples $(\alpha_1, \ldots, \alpha_n)$ and study the behavior of the sum $\sum \alpha_i x_i$ as the vector x ranges over $\{0,1\}^n$. We prove that for a typical n-tuple $(\alpha_1, \ldots, \alpha_n)$ and any collection of sums $S \subset \mathbb{Z}$ of interest, the subset $X_S \subset \{0,1\}^n$ that induces the sums in S is highly random in that membership in X_S is uncorrelated with any polynomial of degree up to $\Theta(n)$. With some additional work, this allows the sought passage to a univariate question. In particular, we are able to prove the existence of a halfspace $f\colon\{0,1\}^n \to \{-1,+1\}$ such that any multivariate rational approximant for f gives a univariate rational approximant for the sign function on $\{\pm1, \pm2, \pm3, \ldots, \pm2^{\Theta(n)}\}$ with the same degree and error. The univariate question being well-understood, we infer that f requires a rational function of degree $\Omega(n)$ for pointwise approximation within $1/3$ and hence $\deg_\pm(f\wedge f) \geqslant \Omega(n)$ by the characterization from [34].

2. PRELIMINARIES

We will view Boolean functions as mappings $X \to \{0,1\}$ or $X \to \{-1,+1\}$ for some finite set X, where the output value 1 corresponds to "true" in the former case and "false" in the latter. We adopt the following standard definition of the sign function:

$$\operatorname{sgn} x = \begin{cases} -1, & x < 0, \\ 0, & x = 0, \\ 1, & x > 0. \end{cases}$$

The complement of a set S is denoted $\overline{S}$. We denote the symmetric difference of sets S and T by $S \oplus T = (S \cap \overline{T}) \cup (\overline{S} \cap T)$. For a finite set X, the symbol $\mathscr{P}(X)$ denotes the family of all $2^{|X|}$ subsets of X. For functions $f, g\colon X \to \mathbb{R}$ on a finite set X, we use the notation

$$\langle f, g\rangle = \frac{1}{|X|} \sum_{x \in X} f(x)g(x).$$

We let $\log x$ stand for the logarithm of x to the base 2. The binary entropy function $H\colon[0,1] \to [0,1]$ is given by $H(p) = -p\log p - (1-p)\log(1-p)$ and is strictly increasing on $[0,1/2]$. The following bound is well known [13, p. 283]:

$$\sum_{i=0}^{k} \binom{n}{i} \leqslant 2^{H(k/n)n}, \qquad k = 0,1,2,\dots,\lfloor n/2\rfloor. \tag{2.1}$$

For elements x, y of a given set, we use the Kronecker delta

$$\delta_{x,y} = \begin{cases} 1, & x = y, \\ 0, & x \neq y. \end{cases}$$

The symbol P_k stands for the family of all univariate real polynomials of degree up to k. The majority function $\mathrm{MAJ}_n\colon\{0,1\}^n \to \{-1,+1\}$ has the usual definition:

$$\mathrm{MAJ}_n(x) = \begin{cases} -1, & x_1 + x_2 + \cdots + x_n > n/2, \\ 1, & \text{otherwise.} \end{cases}$$

Fourier Transform

Consider the vector space of functions $\{0,1\}^n \to \mathbb{R}$, equipped with the inner product

$$\langle f, g\rangle = 2^{-n} \sum_{x \in \{0,1\}^n} f(x)g(x).$$

For $S \subseteq \{1,2,\dots,n\}$, define $\chi_S\colon\{0,1\}^n \to \{-1,+1\}$ by $\chi_S(x) = (-1)^{\sum_{i\in S} x_i}$. Then $\{\chi_S\}_{S\subseteq\{1,2,\dots,n\}}$ is an orthonormal basis for the inner product space in question. As a result, every function $f\colon\{0,1\}^n \to \mathbb{R}$ has a unique representation of the form

$$f = \sum_{S\subseteq\{1,2,\dots,n\}} \hat{f}(S)\chi_S,$$

where $\hat{f}(S) = \langle f, \chi_S\rangle$. The reals $\hat{f}(S)$ are called the *Fourier coefficients of f*. The orthonormality of $\{\chi_S\}$ immediately yields *Parseval's identity*:

$$\sum_{S\subseteq\{1,2,\dots,n\}} \hat{f}(S)^2 = \langle f, f\rangle = \mathop{\mathbf{E}}_{x\in\{0,1\}^n}[f(x)^2]. \tag{2.2}$$

Matrices

The symbol $\mathbb{R}^{m\times n}$ refers to the family of all $m \times n$ matrices with real entries. A matrix $A \in \mathbb{R}^{n\times n}$ is called *strictly diagonally dominant* if

$$|A_{ii}| > \sum_{\substack{j=1 \\ j\neq i}}^{n} |A_{ij}|, \qquad i = 1,2,\dots,n.$$

A well-known result in matrix perturbation theory, due to Gershgorin [11], states that the eigenvalues of a matrix lie in the union of certain disks in the complex plane centered around the diagonal entries of the matrix. We will need the following very special case, which corresponds to showing that the eigenvalues are all nonzero.

THEOREM 2.1 (Gershgorin). *Let $A \in \mathbb{R}^{n\times n}$ be strictly diagonally dominant. Then A is nonsingular.*

PROOF (Gershgorin). Fix a nonzero vector $x \in \mathbb{R}^n$ and choose i such that $|x_i| = \|x\|_\infty$. Then by strict diagonal dominance,

$$|(Ax)_i| = \left|\sum_{j=1}^{n} A_{ij}x_j\right| \geqslant |A_{ii}|\|x\|_\infty - \sum_{\substack{j=1 \\ j\neq i}}^{n} |A_{ij}|\|x\|_\infty > 0,$$

so that $Ax \neq 0$. □

Rational Approximation

The degree of a rational function $p(x)/q(x)$, where p and q are polynomials on $\mathbb{R}^n$, is the maximum of the degrees of p and q. Consider a function $f\colon X \to \{-1,+1\}$, where $X \subseteq \mathbb{R}^n$. For $d \geqslant 0$, define

$$R(f,d) = \inf_{p,q} \sup_{x\in X} \left| f(x) - \frac{p(x)}{q(x)} \right|,$$

where the infimum is over multivariate polynomials p and q of degree up to d such that q does not vanish on X. In words, $R(f,d)$ is the least error in an approximation of f by a multivariate rational function of degree up to d. A closely related quantity is

$$R^+(f,d) = \inf_{p,q} \sup_{x\in X} \left| f(x) - \frac{p(x)}{q(x)} \right|,$$

where the infimum is over multivariate polynomials p and q of degree up to d such that q is positive on X. These two quantities are related in a straightforward way:

$$R^+(f,2d) \leqslant R(f,d) \leqslant R^+(f,d).$$

The second inequality here is trivial. The first follows from the fact that every rational approximant $p(x)/q(x)$ of degree d gives rise to a degree-$2d$ rational approximant with the same error and a positive denominator, namely, $\{p(x)q(x)\}/q(x)^2$.

The infimum in the definitions of $R(f,d)$ and $R^+(f,d)$ cannot in general be replaced by a minimum [32], even when X is finite subset of $\mathbb{R}$. This contrasts with the more familiar setting of a finite-dimensional normed linear space, where least-error approximants are guaranteed to exist.

For $S \subseteq \mathbb{R}$, we let

$$R^+(S,d) = \inf_{p,q} \sup_{x\in S} \left| \operatorname{sgn} x - \frac{p(x)}{q(x)} \right|,$$

where the infimum ranges over $p, q \in P_d$ such that q is positive on S. The study of the rational approximation of the sign function dates back to seminal work by Zolotarev [42] in the late

19th century. A much later result due to Newman [28] gives highly accurate estimates of $R^+([-n,-1]\cup[1,n],d)$ for all n and d. Newman's work in particular provides upper bounds on $R^+(\{\pm1,\pm2,\ldots,\pm n\},d)$, which in [34] were sharpened and complemented with matching lower bounds to the following effect:

THEOREM 2.2 (Sherstov). *Let n,d be positive integers, $R = R^+(\{\pm1,\pm2,\ldots,\pm n\},d)$. For $1\leqslant d\leqslant \log n$,*

$$\exp\left\{-\Theta\left(\frac{1}{n^{1/(2d)}}\right)\right\} \leqslant R < \exp\left\{-\frac{1}{n^{1/d}}\right\}.$$

For $\log n < d < n$,

$$R = \exp\left\{-\Theta\left(\frac{d}{\log(2n/d)}\right)\right\}.$$

For $d\geqslant n$,

$$R = 0.$$

Theorem 2.2 has the following corollary [34, Thm. 1.7], in which we adopt the notation $\mathrm{rdeg}_\varepsilon(f) = \min\{d : R^+(f,d)\leqslant \varepsilon\}$.

THEOREM 2.3 (Sherstov). *Let $\mathrm{MAJ}_n\colon\{0,1\}^n\to\{-1,+1\}$ denote the majority function. Then*

$$\mathrm{rdeg}_\varepsilon(\mathrm{MAJ}_n) = \begin{cases}\Theta\left(\log\left\{\frac{2n}{\log(1/\varepsilon)}\right\}\cdot\log\frac{1}{\varepsilon}\right), & 2^{-n}<\varepsilon<1/3,\\[2mm] \Theta\left(1+\frac{\log n}{\log\{1/(1-\varepsilon)\}}\right), & 1/3\leqslant\varepsilon<1.\end{cases}$$

Threshold Degree

Let $f\colon X\to\{-1,+1\}$ be a given Boolean function, where $X\subset\mathbb{R}^n$ is finite. The *threshold degree* of f, denoted $\deg_\pm(f)$, is the least degree of a polynomial $p(x)$ such that $f(x)\equiv \operatorname{sgn} p(x)$. The term "threshold degree" appears to be due to Saks [33]. Equivalent terms in the literature include "strong degree" [4], "voting polynomial degree" [21], "polynomial threshold function degree" [29], and "sign degree" [9].

Given functions $f\colon X\to\{-1,+1\}$ and $g\colon Y\to\{-1,+1\}$, we let the symbol $f\wedge g$ stand for the function $X\times Y\to\{-1,+1\}$ given by $(f\wedge g)(x,y) = f(x)\wedge g(y)$. Note that in this notation, f and $f\wedge f$ are completely different functions, the former having domain X and the latter $X\times X$. An elegant observation, due to Beigel et al. [6], relates the notions of sign-representation and rational approximation for conjunctions of Boolean functions.

THEOREM 2.4 (Beigel, Reingold, and Spielman). *Consider functions $f\colon X\to\{-1,+1\}$ and $g\colon Y\to\{-1,+1\}$, where $X,Y\subseteq\mathbb{R}^n$. Let d be an integer with $R^+(f,d)+R^+(g,d)<1$. Then*

$$\deg_\pm(f\wedge g)\leqslant 2d.$$

PROOF (Beigel, Reingold, and Spielman). Consider rational functions $p_1(x)/q_1(x)$ and $p_2(y)/q_2(y)$ of degree at most d such that q_1 and q_2 are positive on X and Y, respectively, and

$$\sup_X\left|f(x)-\frac{p_1(x)}{q_1(x)}\right| + \sup_Y\left|g(y)-\frac{p_2(y)}{q_2(y)}\right| < 1.$$

Then

$$\begin{aligned} f(x)\wedge g(y) &\equiv \operatorname{sgn}\{1+f(x)+g(y)\}\\ &\equiv \operatorname{sgn}\left\{1+\frac{p_1(x)}{q_1(x)}+\frac{p_2(y)}{q_2(y)}\right\}.\end{aligned}$$

Multiplying the last expression by the positive quantity $q_1(x)q_2(y)$ leads to $f(x)\wedge g(y) \equiv \operatorname{sgn}\{q_1(x)q_2(y)+p_1(x)q_2(y)+p_2(y)q_1(x)\}$. □

We will also need a converse to Theorem 2.4, proved recently in [34, Thm. 3.9].

THEOREM 2.5 (Sherstov). *Let $f\colon X\to\{-1,+1\}$ and $g\colon Y\to\{-1,+1\}$ be given functions, where $X,Y\subset\mathbb{R}^n$ are arbitrary finite sets. Assume that f and g are not identically false. Let $d=\deg_\pm(f\wedge g)$. Then*

$$R^+(f,4d)+R^+(g,2d)<1.$$

Symmetric Functions

Let S_n denote the symmetric group on n elements. For $\sigma\in S_n$ and $x\in\{0,1\}^n$, we denote $\sigma x = (x_{\sigma(1)},\ldots,x_{\sigma(n)})\in\{0,1\}^n$. For $x\in\{0,1\}^n$, we define $|x| = x_1+x_2+\cdots+x_n$. A function $\phi\colon\{0,1\}^n\to\mathbb{R}$ is called *symmetric* if $\phi(x)=\phi(\sigma x)$ for every $x\in\{0,1\}^n$ and every $\sigma\in S_n$. Equivalently, ϕ is symmetric if $\phi(x)$ is uniquely determined by $|x|$. Symmetric functions on $\{0,1\}^n$ are intimately related to univariate polynomials, as borne out by Minsky and Papert's *symmetrization argument* [25]:

PROPOSITION 2.6 (Minsky and Papert). *Let $\phi\colon\{0,1\}^n\to\mathbb{R}$ be a polynomial of degree d. Then there is a polynomial $p\in P_d$ such that*

$$\mathop{\mathbf{E}}_{\sigma\in S_n}[\phi(\sigma x)] = p(|x|), \qquad x\in\{0,1\}^n.$$

We will need the following consequence of Minsky and Papert's technique for rational functions, pointed out in [34, Prop. 2.7].

PROPOSITION 2.7. *Let $n_1,\ldots,n_k$ be positive integers. Consider a function $F\colon\{0,1\}^{n_1}\times\cdots\times\{0,1\}^{n_k}\to\{-1,+1\}$ such that $F(x_1,\ldots,x_k)\equiv f(|x_1|,\ldots,|x_k|)$ for some $f\colon\{0,1,\ldots,n_1\}\times\cdots\times\{0,1,\ldots,n_k\}\to\{-1,+1\}$. Then for all d,*

$$R^+(F,d) = R^+(f,d).$$

3. ANALYSIS OF RANDOM HALFSPACES

In this section, we prove a certain structural property of random halfspaces. Specifically, we will fix integers $w_1,w_2,\ldots,w_n$ at random from a suitable range and analyze the sum

$$\sum_{i=1}^n w_ix_i$$

as x ranges over $\{0,1\}^n$. Our objective will be to show that, for a typical choice of the weights $w_1,w_2,\ldots,w_n$, the distribution of this sum modulo $2^{\Theta(n)}$ is highly random. More precisely, we will show that the subset $X_s\subset\{0,1\}^n$ that induces any particular sum s modulo $2^{\Theta(n)}$ is relatively large and that membership in X_s is almost uncorrelated with any polynomial of low degree. We start with a technical lemma.

LEMMA 3.1. *Let $f, g: \{0,1\}^n \to \{0,1\}$ be given functions. Fix an integer k with $0 \leqslant k \leqslant n/2$. For a set $S \subseteq \{1,2,\ldots,n\}$, define $F_S: \{0,1\}^n \to \{0,1\}$ by*

$$F_S(x) = f(x) \wedge \left(g(x) \oplus \bigoplus_{i \in S} x_i \right).$$

Fix a positive real ζ. Then with probability no smaller than $1 - 2^{-n+H(k/n)n+2\zeta n}$ over a uniformly random choice of $S \in \mathscr{P}(\{1,2,\ldots,n\})$, one has

$$\left| \hat{F}_S(T) - \frac{1}{2}\hat{f}(T) \right| \leqslant 2^{-\zeta n - 1}, \qquad |T| \leqslant k. \tag{3.1}$$

PROOF. Define $\phi: \{0,1\}^n \to [-1/2, 1/2]$ by $\phi(x) = f(x)g(x) - \frac{1}{2}f(x)$. Define $\mathscr{S} \subseteq \mathscr{P}(\{1,2,\ldots,n\})$ by $\mathscr{S} = \{S : |\hat{\phi}(S)| \geqslant 2^{-\zeta n - 1}\}$. By Parseval's identity (2.2),

$$|\mathscr{S}| \leqslant 4^{\zeta n}. \tag{3.2}$$

Since $F_S(x) = \frac{1}{2}f(x) + (-1)^{\sum_{i \in S} x_i}\phi(x)$, we have

$$\left| \hat{F}_S(T) - \frac{1}{2}\hat{f}(T) \right| = |\hat{\phi}(S \oplus T)|, \qquad S, T \subseteq \{1,2,\ldots,n\}. \tag{3.3}$$

For a uniformly random set $S \in \mathscr{P}(\{1,2,\ldots,n\})$, the family $\{S \oplus T : |T| \leqslant k\}$ contains any fixed element of $\mathscr{P}(\{1,2,\ldots,n\})$ with probability $2^{-n}\sum_{i=0}^{k}\binom{n}{i}$. By the union bound, we infer that

$$\mathop{\mathbf{P}}_S[\{S \oplus T : |T| \leqslant k\} \cap \mathscr{S} \neq \varnothing] \leqslant |\mathscr{S}| 2^{-n} \sum_{i=0}^{k} \binom{n}{i},$$

which in view of (2.1) and (3.2) is at most $2^{-n+H(k/n)n+2\zeta n}$. This observation, along with (3.3), completes the proof. $\square$

Using Lemma 3.1 and induction, we now obtain a key intermediate result.

LEMMA 3.2. *Fix an integer $k \geqslant 0$ and reals $\varepsilon, \zeta \in (0, 1/2)$. Choose sets $S_0, S_1, \ldots, S_k \in \mathscr{P}(\{1,2,\ldots,n\})$ uniformly at random. Fix any integer s and define $f: \{0,1\}^n \to \{0,1\}$ by*

$$f(x) = 1 \quad \Leftrightarrow \quad \sum_{i=0}^{k} 2^i \sum_{j \in S_i} x_j \equiv s \pmod{2^{k+1}}. \tag{3.4}$$

Then with probability at least $1 - (k+1)2^{-n+H(\varepsilon)n+2\zeta n}$ over the choice of $S_0, S_1, \ldots, S_k$, one has

$$\left| \hat{f}(T) - \frac{\delta_{T,\emptyset}}{2^{k+1}} \right| \leqslant 2^{-\zeta n}, \qquad |T| \leqslant \varepsilon n. \tag{3.5}$$

PROOF. In view of the modular counting in (3.4), one may assume that $0 \leqslant s < 2^{k+1}$ and therefore $s = \sum_{i=0}^{k} 2^i b_i$ for some $b_0, b_1, \ldots, b_k \in \{0,1\}$. The proof of the lemma is by induction on k for a fixed s.

The base case $k = 0$ corresponds to letting $f(x) = \frac{1}{2} + \frac{1}{2}(-1)^{b_0}\chi_{S_0}(x)$. One obtains (3.5) by conditioning on the event $|S_0| > \varepsilon n$, which in view of (2.1) occurs with probability no smaller than $1 - 2^{-n+H(\varepsilon)n}$.

We now consider the inductive step. Define $f': \{0,1\}^n \to \{0,1\}$ by

$$f'(x) = 1 \quad \Leftrightarrow \quad \sum_{i=0}^{k-1} 2^i \sum_{j \in S_i} x_j \equiv \sum_{i=0}^{k-1} 2^i b_i \pmod{2^k}.$$

Let E_1 be the event, over the choice of sets $S_0, \ldots, S_{k-1}$, that $|\widehat{f'}(T) - 2^{-k}\delta_{T,\emptyset}| \leqslant 2^{-\zeta n}$ for $|T| \leqslant \varepsilon n$. By the inductive hypothesis,

$$\mathbf{P}[E_1] \geqslant 1 - k2^{-n+H(\varepsilon)n+2\zeta n}. \tag{3.6}$$

Let E_2 be the event, over the choice of sets $S_0, \ldots, S_k$, that $|\hat{f}(T) - \frac{1}{2}\widehat{f'}(T)| \leqslant 2^{-\zeta n - 1}$ for $|T| \leqslant \varepsilon n$. In this terminology, it suffices to show that

$$\mathbf{P}[E_1 \wedge E_2] \geqslant 1 - (k+1)2^{-n+H(\varepsilon)n+2\zeta n}. \tag{3.7}$$

Observe that

$$f(x) = f'(x) \wedge \left(g(x) \oplus \bigoplus_{i \in S_k} x_i \right),$$

where $g: \{0,1\}^n \to \{0,1\}$ is the function such that $g(x) = 1$ if and only if b_k is the $(k+1)$st least significant bit of the integer

$$\sum_{i=0}^{k-1} 2^i \sum_{j \in S_i} x_j.$$

As a result, Lemma 3.1 shows that $\mathbf{P}[E_2] \geqslant 1 - 2^{-n+H(\varepsilon)n+2\zeta n}$. This bound, along with (3.6), settles (3.7) and thereby completes the induction. $\square$

We have reached the main result of this section.

THEOREM 3.3 (Key property of random halfspaces). *Fix an integer $k \geqslant 0$ and reals $\varepsilon, \zeta \in (0, 1/2)$. Choose integers $w_1, w_2, \ldots, w_n$ uniformly at random from $\{0, 1, \ldots, 2^{k+1} - 1\}$. For $s \in \mathbb{Z}$, define $f_s: \{0,1\}^n \to \{0,1\}$ by*

$$f_s(x) = 1 \quad \Leftrightarrow \quad \sum_{i=1}^{n} w_i x_i \equiv s \pmod{2^{k+1}}. \tag{3.8}$$

Then with probability at least $1 - (k+1)2^{-n+H(\varepsilon)n+2\zeta n+k+1}$ over the choice of $w_1, w_2, \ldots, w_n$, one has

$$\left| \hat{f}_s(T) - \frac{\delta_{T,\emptyset}}{2^{k+1}} \right| \leqslant 2^{-\zeta n}, \qquad |T| \leqslant \varepsilon n, \quad s \in \mathbb{Z}.$$

PROOF. In view of the modular counting in (3.8), it suffices to prove the theorem for $s \in \{0, 1, \ldots, 2^{k+1} - 1\}$. The functions f_s have the following equivalent definition: pick sets $S_0, S_1, \ldots, S_k \in \mathscr{P}(\{1,2,\ldots,n\})$ uniformly at random and define

$$f_s(x) = 1 \quad \Leftrightarrow \quad \sum_{i=0}^{k} 2^i \sum_{j \in S_i} x_j \equiv s \pmod{2^{k+1}}.$$

The proof is now complete by Lemma 3.2 and the union bound over all possible values of s. $\square$

4. ZEROING OUT CORRELATIONS BY A CHANGE OF DISTRIBUTION

Recall the setting of the previous section, where we fixed integers $w_1, w_2, \ldots, w_n$ at random from a suitable range and analyzed the sum $\sum_{i=1}^{n} w_i x_i$ as x ranged over $\{0,1\}^n$. We showed that the subset $X_s \subset \{0,1\}^n$ that induces any particular sum s modulo $2^{\Theta(n)}$ is relatively large and that membership in X_s has *almost* zero correlation with any given polynomial of low degree. For the purposes of this paper, the correlations with low-degree polynomials need to be *exactly* zero. In this section we show that, with respect to a suitable distribution μ_s on each X_s, membership in X_s will indeed have zero correlation with any low-degree polynomial.

A starting point in our discussion is a general statement on zeroing out the correlations of given Boolean functions $\chi_1, \chi_2, \dots, \chi_k$ with another Boolean function f. Recall that for functions $f, g\colon X \to \mathbb{R}$ on a finite set X, we use the notation

$$\langle f, g\rangle = \frac{1}{|X|}\sum_{x\in X} f(x)g(x).$$

THEOREM 4.1. *Let $f, \chi_1, \dots, \chi_k\colon X \to \{-1,+1\}$ be given functions on a finite set X. Suppose that*

$$\sum_{i=1}^{k} |\langle f, \chi_i\rangle| < \frac{1}{2}, \tag{4.1}$$

$$\sum_{\substack{j=1\\ j\neq i}}^{k} |\langle \chi_i, \chi_j\rangle| \leqslant \frac{1}{2}, \qquad i = 1, 2, \dots, k. \tag{4.2}$$

Then there exists a probability distribution μ on X such that

$$\mathop{\mathbf{E}}_{\mu}[f(x)\chi_i(x)] = 0, \qquad i = 1, 2, \dots, k.$$

REMARK 4.2. A comment is in order on the hypothesis of Theorem 4.1. The theorem states that if $\chi_1, \chi_2, \dots, \chi_k$ each have a small correlation with f and, in addition, have small pairwise correlations, then a distribution exists with respect to which f is completely uncorrelated with $\chi_1, \chi_2, \dots, \chi_k$. The latter part of the hypothesis, namely the requirement (4.2) of small pairwise correlations for $\chi_1, \chi_2, \dots, \chi_k$, may seem unnecessary at first. In actuality, it is vital. Exponential lower bounds on the weights of linear perceptrons [27, 38] imply, by linear programming duality, the existence of functions $f, \chi_1, \chi_2, \dots, \chi_k\colon X \to \{-1,+1\}$ such that $|\langle f, \chi_i\rangle| = \exp\{-\Theta(k)\}$, $i = 1, 2, \dots, k$, and yet

$$f(x) \equiv \operatorname{sgn}\left(\sum_{i=1}^{k} \alpha_i\chi_i(x)\right) \tag{4.3}$$

for some fixed reals $\alpha_1, \dots, \alpha_k$. In this construction, the correlation of f with each χ_i is small, in fact exponentially smaller than what is assumed in Theorem 4.1; nevertheless, the representation (4.3) rules out a distribution μ with respect to which f could have zero correlation with each χ_i, for such a distribution μ would have to obey

$$0 < \mathop{\mathbf{E}}_{\mu}\left[\left|\sum_{i=1}^{k}\alpha_i\chi_i(x)\right|\right] = \mathop{\mathbf{E}}_{\mu}\left[f(x)\sum_{i=1}^{k}\alpha_i\chi_i(x)\right] = \sum_{i=1}^{k}\alpha_i \mathop{\mathbf{E}}_{\mu}[f(x)\chi_i(x)] = 0.$$

PROOF OF THEOREM 4.1. Consider the linear system

$$M\alpha = \gamma \tag{4.4}$$

in the unknown $\alpha \in \mathbb{R}^k$, where $M = [\langle \chi_i, \chi_j\rangle]_{i,j}$ is a matrix of order k and $\gamma = (\langle f, \chi_1\rangle, \dots, \langle f, \chi_k\rangle) \in \mathbb{R}^k$. Then (4.2) shows that M is strictly diagonally dominant and hence nonsingular by Theorem 2.1. Fix the unique solution α to the system (4.4). Then $2|\alpha_i| - \sum_{j=1}^{k}|\alpha_j\langle \chi_i, \chi_j\rangle| \leqslant |\langle f, \chi_i\rangle|$ for $i = 1, 2, \dots, k$. Summing these k inequalities, we obtain

$$2\sum_{i=1}^{k}|\alpha_i| - \sum_{j=1}^{k}|\alpha_j|\sum_{i=1}^{k}|\langle \chi_i, \chi_j\rangle| \leqslant \sum_{i=1}^{k}|\langle f, \chi_i\rangle|,$$

which in view of (4.1) and (4.2) shows that $\sum_{i=1}^{k}|\alpha_i| < 1$. Therefore, the function $\mu\colon X \to \mathbb{R}$ given by

$$\mu(x) = \varepsilon\left(1 - f(x)\sum_{i=1}^{k}\alpha_i\chi_i(x)\right)$$

is a probability distribution on X for a suitable normalizing factor $\varepsilon > 0$. At last,

$$\mathop{\mathbf{E}}_{\mu}[f(x)\chi_i(x)] = \varepsilon|X|\left(\langle f, \chi_i\rangle - \sum_{j=1}^{k}\alpha_j\langle \chi_i, \chi_j\rangle\right) = 0,$$

where the final equality holds by (4.4). $\square$

We are now in a position to prove the main result of this section.

THEOREM 4.3. *Let $\alpha > 0$ be a sufficiently small absolute constant. Choose integers $w_1, w_2, \dots, w_n$ uniformly at random from $\{0, 1, \dots, 2^{\lfloor \alpha n\rfloor+1} - 1\}$. For $s \in \mathbb{Z}$, define*

$$X_s = \left\{x \in \{0,1\}^n : \sum_{i=1}^{n} w_ix_i \equiv s \pmod{2^{\lfloor \alpha n\rfloor+1}}\right\}. \tag{4.5}$$

Then with probability at least $1 - \mathrm{e}^{-n/3}$ over the choice of $w_1, w_2, \dots, w_n$, there is a distribution μ_s on X_s (for each s) such that

$$\mathop{\mathbf{E}}_{\mu_s}[p(x)] = \mathop{\mathbf{E}}_{\mu_t}[p(x)] \tag{4.6}$$

for any $s, t \in \mathbb{Z}$ and any polynomial p of degree at most $\lfloor \alpha n\rfloor$.

PROOF. Let $\alpha > 0$ be sufficiently small. We will assume throughout the proof that $n \geqslant 1/\alpha$, the theorem being trivial otherwise. Set $\varepsilon = 2\alpha$, $\zeta = 1/5$, and $k = \lfloor \alpha n\rfloor$ in Theorem 3.3. Then with probability at least $1 - \mathrm{e}^{-n/3}$ over the choice of $w_1, w_2, \dots, w_n$, one has

$$\left|\hat{f}_s(T) - \frac{\delta_{T,\emptyset}}{2^{\lfloor \alpha n\rfloor+1}}\right| \leqslant 2^{-n/5}, \qquad |T| \leqslant 2\alpha n, \quad s \in \mathbb{Z}, \tag{4.7}$$

where $f_s\colon \{0,1\}^n \to \{0,1\}$ is given by $f_s(x) = 1 \Leftrightarrow x \in X_s$. It follows that for each s,

$$|X_s| = 2^n\hat{f}_s(\emptyset) \geqslant 2^n(2^{-\lfloor \alpha n\rfloor-1} - 2^{-n/5}). \tag{4.8}$$

For $f, g\colon \{0,1\}^n \to \mathbb{R}$, we will write

$$\langle f, g\rangle_{X_s} = |X_s|^{-1}\sum_{x\in X_s} f(x)g(x).$$

Let $\mathscr{S} \subset \mathscr{P}(\{1, 2, \dots, n\})$ be the system of nonempty subsets of at most αn elements. Fix any $T \in \mathscr{S}$. Then for each s,

$$\sum_{\substack{S\in\mathscr{S}\\ S\neq T}} |\langle \chi_S, \chi_T\rangle_{X_s}| = \frac{2^n}{|X_s|}\sum_{\substack{S\in\mathscr{S}\\ S\neq T}} |\hat{f}_s(S\oplus T)| \leqslant \frac{2^n}{|X_s|}\cdot|\mathscr{S}|2^{-n/5} < \frac{1}{2}, \tag{4.9}$$

where the final two inequalities follow from (2.1), (4.7), and (4.8). Similarly, for each s,

$$\sum_{S\in\mathscr{S}} |\langle f_s, \chi_S\rangle_{X_s}| = \frac{2^n}{|X_s|}\sum_{S\in\mathscr{S}} |\hat{f}_s(S)| \leqslant \frac{2^n}{|X_s|}\cdot|\mathscr{S}|2^{-n/5} < \frac{1}{2}. \tag{4.10}$$

In view of (4.9) and (4.10), Theorem 4.1 provides a distribution μ_s on $\{0,1\}^n$ that is supported on X_s and obeys $\hat{\mu}_s(S) = 0$ for $S \in \mathscr{S}$. Since μ_s is a probability distribution, we additionally have $\hat{\mu}_s(\emptyset) = 2^{-n}$ for all s. In particular, the distributions μ_s have identical Fourier spectra up to coefficients of order αn, which is another way of stating (4.6). □

5. REDUCTION TO A UNIVARIATE PROBLEM

Recall from the Introduction that the crux of our proof is to establish the existence of a halfspace $f\colon\{0,1\}^n \to \{-1,+1\}$ that requires a rational function of degree $\Theta(n)$ for pointwise approximation within $1/3$. The purpose of this section is to reduce this task, for a suitably chosen random halfspace, to a univariate problem. The univariate problem pertains to the uniform approximation of the sign function on the set $\{\pm1,\pm2,\pm3,\dots,\pm2^{\Theta(n)}\}$ and has been solved in previous work. Key to this univariate reduction will be the construction of probability distributions in the previous two sections.

THEOREM 5.1 (Reduction to a univariate problem). *Put $k = \lfloor\alpha n\rfloor$, where $\alpha > 0$ is the absolute constant from Theorem 4.3. Choose $w_1, w_2, \dots, w_n$ uniformly at random from $\{0,1,\dots,2^{k+1}-1\}$. Define $f\colon\{0,1\}^n \times \{0,1,2,\dots,n\} \to \{-1,+1\}$ by*

$$f(x,t) = \operatorname{sgn}\left(\frac{1}{2} + \sum_{i=1}^n w_i x_i - 2^{k+1}t\right).$$

Then with probability at least $1 - e^{-n/3}$ over the choice of $w_1, w_2, \dots, w_n$, one has

$$R^+(f,d) \geqslant R^+(\{\pm1,\pm2,\pm3,\dots,\pm2^k\},d), \qquad d = 0,1,\dots,k. \tag{5.1}$$

PROOF. For $s = \pm1,\pm2,\pm3,\dots,\pm2^k$, define $X_s \subseteq \{0,1\}^n$ by (4.5). Then by Theorem 4.3, with probability at least $1 - e^{-n/3}$ there is a distribution μ_s on X_s for each s such that

$$\mathop{\mathbf{E}}_{\mu_s}[p(x)] = \mathop{\mathbf{E}}_{\mu_r}[p(x)] \tag{5.2}$$

for any $s, r \in \{\pm1,\pm2,\pm3,\dots,\pm2^k\}$ and any polynomial p of degree no greater than k. In the remainder of the proof, we will work with a fixed choice of weights $w_1, w_2, \dots, w_n$ for which the described distributions μ_s exist.

Suppose that $R^+(f,d) < \varepsilon$ where $0 < \varepsilon < 1$ and $0 \leqslant d \leqslant k$. Then there are degree-$d$ polynomials p, q on $\mathbb{R}^n \times \mathbb{R}$ such that on the domain of f,

$$0 < (1-\varepsilon)q(x,t) \leqslant p(x,t)f(x,t) \leqslant (1+\varepsilon)q(x,t). \tag{5.3}$$

On the support of μ_s (for $s = \pm1,\pm2,\pm3,\dots,\pm2^k$), the linear form

$$\ell(x,s) = 2^{-k-1}\left(\sum_{i=1}^n w_i x_i - s\right)$$

obeys $\ell(x,s) \in \{0,1,2,\dots,n\}$ and $f(x,\ell(x,s)) = \operatorname{sgn} s$. Letting $t = \ell(x,s)$ in (5.3) and passing to expectations,

$$\begin{aligned} 0 < \mathop{\mathbf{E}}_{x\sim\mu_s}[q(x,\ell(x,s))](1-\varepsilon) &\leqslant \mathop{\mathbf{E}}_{x\sim\mu_s}[p(x,\ell(x,s))]\operatorname{sgn} s \\ &\leqslant \mathop{\mathbf{E}}_{x\sim\mu_s}[q(x,\ell(x,s))](1+\varepsilon). \end{aligned}$$

It follows from (5.2) that $\mathbf{E}_{\mu_s}[p(x,\ell(x,s))] = P(s)$ and $\mathbf{E}_{\mu_s}[q(x,\ell(x,s))] = Q(s)$ for some $P, Q \in P_d$ and all s. As a result, $R^+(\{\pm1,\pm2,\pm3,\dots,\pm2^k\},d) \leqslant \varepsilon$, the approximant in question being P/Q. □

It remains to rewrite the previous theorem in terms of functions on the hypercube $\{0,1\}^{2n}$ rather than the set $\{0,1\}^n \times \{0,1,2,\dots,n\}$.

THEOREM 5.2. *Put $k = \lfloor\alpha n\rfloor$, where $\alpha > 0$ is the absolute constant from Theorem 4.3. Choose $w_1, w_2, \dots, w_n$ uniformly at random from $\{0,1,\dots,2^{k+1}-1\}$. Define $f\colon\{0,1\}^{2n} \to \{-1,+1\}$ by*

$$f(x) = \operatorname{sgn}\left(\frac{1}{2} + \sum_{i=1}^n w_i x_i - 2^{k+1}\sum_{i=n+1}^{2n} x_i\right).$$

Then with probability at least $1 - e^{-n/3}$ over the choice of $w_1, w_2, \dots, w_n$, one has

$$R^+(f,d) \geqslant R^+(\{\pm1,\pm2,\pm3,\dots,\pm2^k\},d), \qquad d = 0,1,\dots,k.$$

PROOF. Immediate from Proposition 2.7 and Theorem 5.1. □

6. MAIN RESULT AND GENERALIZATIONS

We now combine the newly obtained result on rational approximation with known results from Section 2 to prove the main theorem of this work.

THEOREM 6.1 (Main result). *Fix sufficiently small absolute constants $\alpha > 0$ and $\beta = \beta(\alpha) > 0$. Choose integers $w_1, w_2, \dots, w_n \in \{0,1,\dots,2^{\lfloor\alpha n\rfloor+1}-1\}$ uniformly at random. Then with probability at least $1-e^{-n/3}$, the function $f\colon\{0,1\}^{2n} \to \{-1,+1\}$ given by*

$$f(x) = \operatorname{sgn}\left(\frac{1}{2} + \sum_{i=1}^n w_i x_i - 2^{\lfloor\alpha n\rfloor+1}\sum_{i=n+1}^{2n} x_i\right)$$

obeys

$$\deg_\pm(f \wedge f) \geqslant \lfloor\beta n\rfloor. \tag{6.1}$$

PROOF. Theorem 5.2 shows that with probability no smaller than $1 - e^{-n/3}$ over the choice of $w_1, w_2, \dots, w_n$, one has

$$R^+(f,d) \geqslant R^+(S,d), \qquad d = 0,1,\dots,\lfloor\alpha n\rfloor, \tag{6.2}$$

where $S = \{\pm1,\pm2,\pm3,\dots,\pm2^{\lfloor\alpha n\rfloor}\}$ and $\alpha > 0$ is the absolute constant from Theorem 4.3. In the remainder of the proof, we will condition on this event.

Suppose now that $\deg_\pm(f \wedge f) < \lfloor\beta n\rfloor$, where β is a constant to be chosen later subject to $0 < \beta < \alpha/4$. Then Theorem 2.5 implies that $R^+(f,\lfloor4\beta n\rfloor) < 1/2$, which in view of (6.2) leads to $R^+(S,\lfloor4\beta n\rfloor) < 1/2$. The last inequality violates Theorem 2.2 for small enough $\beta > 0$. Thus, (6.1) holds for β small enough. □

Recall that the technical crux of this paper is an optimal lower bound for the rational approximation of a halfspace. We will have occasion to appeal to this result again, and for this reason we formulate it as a theorem in its own right.

THEOREM 6.2. *A family of halfspaces* $h_n: \{0,1\}^n \to \{-1,+1\}$, $n = 1,2,3,\ldots,$ *exists such that*

$$R^+(h_n, d) = 1 - \exp\left\{-\Theta\left(\frac{n}{d}\right)\right\}, \qquad d = 1,2,\ldots,\Theta(n). \tag{6.3}$$

PROOF. The lower bound in (6.3) is immediate from Theorem 5.2 and the univariate lower bounds in Theorem 2.2.

Next, every halfspace $h_n: \{0,1\}^n \to \{-1,+1\}$ constructed in Theorem 5.2 trivially obeys $R^+(h_n, 1) < 1 - \exp\{-\Theta(n)\}$. For $0 < \xi < 1$, Newman's classical work [28] shows that $R^+([-1,-\xi] \cup [\xi, 1], d) \leqslant 1 - \xi^{\Theta(1/d)}$, whence by composition of the approximants one obtains the upper bound in (6.3). □

Mixed Intersection

Theorem 6.1 shows that the intersection of two halfspaces has the asymptotically highest threshold degree. At the same time, Beigel et al. [6] showed that the intersection of a constant number of majority functions on $\{0,1\}^n$, which are particularly simple halfspaces, has threshold degree $O(\log n)$. We now derive a lower bound of $\Omega(\sqrt{n \log n})$ on the threshold degree of the intersection of a halfspace and a majority function, which improves quadratically on the previous bound in [34] and essentially matches the upper bound, $O(\sqrt{n}\log n)$, given below in Remark 6.4.

THEOREM 6.3. *A family of halfspaces* $h_n: \{0,1\}^n \to \{-1,+1\}$, $n = 1,2,3,\ldots,$ *exists such that*

$$\deg_\pm(h_n \wedge \mathrm{MAJ}_n) = \Theta(\sqrt{n \log n}). \tag{6.4}$$

PROOF. The lower bound in (6.4) is immediate from Theorems 2.3, 2.5, and 6.2. The upper bound in (6.4) is immediate from Theorems 2.3, 2.4, and 6.2. □

REMARK 6.4. The construction of Theorem 6.3 is essentially best possible in that every sequence of halfspaces $h_n: \{0,1\}^n \to \{-1,+1\}$, $n = 1,2,3,\ldots,$ obeys

$$\deg_\pm(h_n \wedge \mathrm{MAJ}_n) = O(\sqrt{n}\log n). \tag{6.5}$$

To derive this upper bound, recall that $R^+(h_n, 1) < 1 - \exp\{-\Theta(n \log n)\}$ for every halfspace $h_n: \{0,1\}^n \to \{-1,+1\}$, by a classical result due to Muroga [26]. Since $R^+([-1,-\xi] \cup [\xi,1], d) < 1 - \xi^{\Theta(1/d)}$ for $0 < \xi < 1$ by Newman [28], we obtain by composition of approximants that $R^+(h_n, d) < 1 - \exp\{-\Theta(\{n \log n\}/d)\}$. This settles (6.5) in view of Theorems 2.3 and 2.4.

Threshold Density

In addition to threshold degree, several other complexity measures are of interest when sign-representing Boolean functions by real polynomials. One such complexity measure is *density*, i.e., the least k for which a given function can be sign-represented by a linear combination of k parity functions. Formally, for a given function $f: \{0,1\}^n \to \{-1,+1\}$, the *threshold density* $\mathrm{dns}(f)$ is the minimum size $|\mathscr{S}|$ of a family $\mathscr{S} \subseteq \mathscr{P}(\{1,2,\ldots,n\})$ such that

$$f(x) \equiv \mathrm{sgn}\left(\sum_{S \in \mathscr{S}} \lambda_S \chi_S(x)\right)$$

for some reals λ_S, $S \in \mathscr{S}$. It is clear from the definition that $\mathrm{dns}(f) \leqslant 2^n$ for all functions $f: \{0,1\}^n \to \{-1,+1\}$, and we will show that the intersection of two halfspaces on $\{0,1\}^n$ has threshold density $2^{\Theta(n)}$.

To this end, we recall an elegant technique for converting Boolean functions with high threshold degree into Boolean functions with high threshold density, discovered by Krause and Pudlák [21, Prop. 2.1]. Their construction sends a function $f: \{0,1\}^n \to \{-1,+1\}$ to the function $f^{\mathrm{KP}}: (\{0,1\}^n)^3 \to \{-1,+1\}$ given by

$$f^{\mathrm{KP}}(x,y,z) = f(\ldots, (\overline{z_i} \wedge x_i) \vee (z_i \wedge y_i), \ldots).$$

THEOREM 6.5 (Krause and Pudlák). *Every Boolean function* $f: \{0,1\}^n \to \{-1,+1\}$ *obeys*

$$\mathrm{dns}(f^{KP}) \geqslant 2^{\deg_\pm(f)}.$$

We are now in a position to obtain the desired density results.

THEOREM 6.6. *A family of halfspaces* $h_n: \{0,1\}^n \to \{-1,+1\}$, $n = 1,2,3,\ldots,$ *exists such that*

$$\mathrm{dns}(h_n \wedge h_n) \geqslant \exp\{\Theta(n)\} \tag{6.6}$$

and

$$\mathrm{dns}(h_n \wedge \mathrm{MAJ}_n) \geqslant \exp\{\Theta(\sqrt{n \log n})\}. \tag{6.7}$$

PROOF. The parity of several parity functions is another parity function. As a result,

$$\max_{h_n}\{\mathrm{dns}(h_n \wedge h_n)\} \geqslant \max_F\{\mathrm{dns}(F \wedge F)\}, \tag{6.8}$$

where the maximum on the left is over all halfspaces $h_n: \{0,1\}^n \to \{-1,+1\}$ and the maximum on the right is over arbitrary functions $F: \{0,1\}^m \to \{-1,+1\}$ (for arbitrary m) such that $\mathrm{dns}(F) \leqslant n$. For each $n = 1,2,3,\ldots,$ Theorem 6.1 ensures the existence of a halfspace $f_n: \{0,1\}^n \to \{-1,+1\}$ with $\deg_\pm(f_n \wedge f_n) \geqslant \Omega(n)$. By Theorem 6.5, the function $(f_n \wedge f_n)^{\mathrm{KP}} = {f_n}^{\mathrm{KP}} \wedge {f_n}^{\mathrm{KP}}$ has threshold density $\exp\{\Omega(n)\}$. Since $\mathrm{dns}({f_n}^{\mathrm{KP}}) \leqslant 4n+1$, the right member of (6.8) is at least $\exp\{\Omega(n)\}$.

This completes the proof of (6.6). The proof of (6.7) is closely analogous, with Theorem 6.3 used instead of Theorem 6.1. □

The lower bounds in Theorem 6.6 are essentially optimal. Specifically, (6.6) is tight for trivial reasons, whereas the lower bound (6.7) nearly matches the upper bound of $\exp\{\Theta(\sqrt{n}\log^2 n)\}$ that follows from (6.5).

We also note that Theorem 6.5 readily generalizes to linear combinations of conjunctions rather than parity functions. In other words, if a function $f: \{0,1\}^n \to \{-1,+1\}$ has threshold degree d and $f^{\mathrm{KP}}(x,y,z) \equiv \mathrm{sgn}(\sum_{i=1}^N \lambda_i T_i(x,y,z))$ for some conjunctions $T_1,\ldots,T_N$ of the literals $x_1, y_1, z_1, \ldots, x_n, y_n, z_n$, $\neg x_1, \neg y_1, \neg z_1, \ldots, \neg x_n, \neg y_n, \neg z_n$, then $N \geqslant 2^{\Omega(d)}$. With this remark in mind, Theorem 6.6 and its proof readily carry over to this alternate definition of density.

7. ACKNOWLEDGMENTS

The author is thankful to Adam Klivans, Ryan O'Donnell, Rocco Servedio, and the anonymous reviewers for their feedback on this manuscript.

8. REFERENCES

[1] M. Alekhnovich, M. Braverman, V. Feldman, A. R. Klivans, and T. Pitassi. The complexity of properly learning simple concept classes. *J. Comput. Syst. Sci.*, 74(1):16–34, 2008.

[2] A. Ambainis, A. M. Childs, B. Reichardt, R. Špalek, and S. Zhang. Any AND-OR formula of size N can be evaluated in time $N^{1/2+o(1)}$ on a quantum computer. In *Proc. of the 48th Symposium on Foundations of Computer Science (FOCS)*, pages 363–372, 2007.

[3] R. I. Arriaga and S. Vempala. An algorithmic theory of learning: Robust concepts and random projection. *Mach. Learn.*, 63(2):161–182, 2006.

[4] J. Aspnes, R. Beigel, M. L. Furst, and S. Rudich. The expressive power of voting polynomials. *Combinatorica*, 14(2):135–148, 1994.

[5] R. Beigel. Perceptrons, PP, and the polynomial hierarchy. *Computational Complexity*, 4:339–349, 1994.

[6] R. Beigel, N. Reingold, and D. A. Spielman. PP is closed under intersection. *J. Comput. Syst. Sci.*, 50(2):191–202, 1995.

[7] A. Blum and R. Kannan. Learning an intersection of a constant number of halfspaces over a uniform distribution. *J. Comput. Syst. Sci.*, 54(2):371–380, 1997.

[8] A. L. Blum and R. L. Rivest. Training a 3-node neural network is NP-complete. *Neural Networks*, 5:117–127, 1992.

[9] H. Buhrman, N. K. Vereshchagin, and R. de Wolf. On computation and communication with small bias. In *Proc. of the 22nd Conf. on Computational Complexity (CCC)*, pages 24–32, 2007.

[10] E. Farhi, J. Goldstone, and S. Gutmann. A quantum algorithm for the Hamiltonian NAND tree. *Theory of Computing*, 4(1):169–190, 2008.

[11] S. A. Gershgorin. Über die Abgrenzung der Eigenwerte einer Matrix. *Izv. Akad. Nauk. U.S.S.R. Otd. Fiz.-Mat. Nauk*, 7:749–754, 1931.

[12] J. C. Jackson. An efficient membership-query algorithm for learning DNF with respect to the uniform distribution. *J. Comput. Syst. Sci.*, 55(3):414–440, 1997.

[13] S. Jukna. *Extremal Combinatorics with Applications in Computer Science*. Springer-Verlag, Berlin, 2001.

[14] S. Khot and R. Saket. On hardness of learning intersection of two halfspaces. In *Proc. of the 40th Symposium on Theory of Computing (STOC)*, pages 345–354, 2008.

[15] A. R. Klivans. *A Complexity-Theoretic Approach to Learning*. PhD thesis, MIT, 2002.

[16] A. R. Klivans, P. M. Long, and A. K. Tang. Baum's algorithm learns intersections of halfspaces with respect to log-concave distributions. In *Proc. of the 13th Intl. Workshop on Randomization and Computation*, pages 588–600, 2009.

[17] A. R. Klivans, R. O'Donnell, and R. A. Servedio. Learning intersections and thresholds of halfspaces. *J. Comput. Syst. Sci.*, 68(4):808–840, 2004.

[18] A. R. Klivans and R. A. Servedio. Learning DNF in time $2^{\tilde{O}(n^{1/3})}$. *J. Comput. Syst. Sci.*, 68(2):303–318, 2004.

[19] A. R. Klivans and R. A. Servedio. Learning intersections of halfspaces with a margin. *J. Comput. Syst. Sci.*, 74(1):35–48, 2008.

[20] A. R. Klivans and A. A. Sherstov. Cryptographic hardness for learning intersections of halfspaces. *J. Comput. Syst. Sci.*, 75(1):2–12, 2009.

[21] M. Krause and P. Pudlák. On the computational power of depth-2 circuits with threshold and modulo gates. *Theor. Comput. Sci.*, 174(1–2):137–156, 1997.

[22] M. Krause and P. Pudlák. Computing Boolean functions by polynomials and threshold circuits. *Comput. Complex.*, 7(4):346–370, 1998.

[23] S. Kwek and L. Pitt. PAC learning intersections of halfspaces with membership queries. *Algorithmica*, 22(1/2):53–75, 1998.

[24] T. Lee. A note on the sign degree of formulas, 2009. Available at `http://arxiv.org/abs/0909.4607`.

[25] M. L. Minsky and S. A. Papert. *Perceptrons: An Introduction to Computational Geometry*. MIT Press, Cambridge, 1969.

[26] S. Muroga. *Threshold Logic and Its Applications*. John Wiley & Sons, New York, 1971.

[27] J. Myhill and W. H. Kautz. On the size of weights required for linear-input switching functions. *IRE Trans. on Electronic Computers*, 10(2):288–290, 1961.

[28] D. J. Newman. Rational approximation to $|x|$. *Michigan Math. J.*, 11(1):11–14, 1964.

[29] R. O'Donnell and R. A. Servedio. New degree bounds for polynomial threshold functions. In *Proc. of the 35th Symposium on Theory of Computing (STOC)*, pages 325–334, 2003.

[30] R. Paturi and M. E. Saks. Approximating threshold circuits by rational functions. *Inf. Comput.*, 112(2):257–272, 1994.

[31] A. A. Razborov and A. A. Sherstov. The sign-rank of AC^0. *SIAM J. Comput.*, 39(5):1833–1855, 2010. Preliminary version in 49th FOCS, 2008.

[32] T. J. Rivlin. *An Introduction to the Approximation of Functions*. Dover Publications, New York, 1981.

[33] M. E. Saks. Slicing the hypercube. *Surveys in Combinatorics*, pages 211–255, 1993.

[34] A. A. Sherstov. The intersection of two halfspaces has high threshold degree. In *Proc. of the 50th Symposium on Foundations of Computer Science (FOCS)*, 2009.

[35] A. A. Sherstov. The pattern matrix method. *SIAM J. Comput.*, 2010. To appear. Preliminary version in 40th STOC, 2008.

[36] A. A. Sherstov. Separating AC^0 from depth-2 majority circuits. *SIAM J. Comput.*, 38(6):2113–2129, 2009. Preliminary version in 39th STOC, 2007.

[37] A. A. Sherstov. The unbounded-error communication complexity of symmetric functions. In *Proc. of the 49th Symposium on Foundations of Computer Science (FOCS)*, pages 384–393, 2008.

[38] K.-Y. Siu and J. Bruck. On the power of threshold circuits with small weights. *SIAM J. Discrete Math.*, 4(3):423–435, 1991.

[39] K.-Y. Siu, V. P. Roychowdhury, and T. Kailath. Rational approximation techniques for analysis of neural networks. *IEEE Transactions on Information Theory*, 40(2):455–466, 1994.

[40] L. G. Valiant. A theory of the learnable. *Commun. ACM*, 27(11):1134–1142, 1984.

[41] S. Vempala. A random sampling based algorithm for learning the intersection of halfspaces. In *Proc. of the 38th Symposium on Foundations of Computer Science (FOCS)*, pages 508–513, 1997.

[42] E. I. Zolotarev. Application of elliptic functions to questions of functions deviating least and most from zero. *Izvestiya Imp. Akad. Nauk*, 30(5), 1877.

Bounding the Average Sensitivity and Noise Sensitivity of Polynomial Threshold Functions

Ilias Diakonikolas
Columbia University
ilias@cs.columbia.edu

Prahladh Harsha
Tata Institute of Fundamental Research
prahladh@tifr.res.in

Adam Klivans
University of Texas at Austin
klivans@cs.utexas.edu

Raghu Meka
University of Texas at Austin
raghu@cs.utexas.edu

Prasad Raghavendra
Microsoft Research, New England
prasad@cs.washington.edu

Rocco A. Servedio
Columbia University
rocco@cs.columbia.edu

Li-Yang Tan
Columbia University
liyang@cs.columbia.edu

ABSTRACT

We give the first non-trivial upper bounds on the average sensitivity and noise sensitivity of degree d polynomial threshold functions (PTFs). These bounds hold both for PTFs over the Boolean hypercube $\{-1,1\}^n$ and for PTFs over $\mathbb{R}^n$ under the standard n-dimensional Gaussian distribution $\mathcal{N}(0, I_n)$. Our bound on the Boolean average sensitivity of PTFs represents progress towards the resolution of a conjecture of Gotsman and Linial [17], which states that the symmetric function slicing the middle d layers of the Boolean hypercube has the highest average sensitivity of all degree-d PTFs. Via the L_1 polynomial regression algorithm of Kalai et al. [22], our bounds on Gaussian and Boolean noise sensitivity yield polynomial-time agnostic learning algorithms for the broad class of constant-degree PTFs under these input distributions.

The main ingredients used to obtain our bounds on both average and noise sensitivity of PTFs in the Gaussian setting are tail bounds and anti-concentration bounds on low-degree polynomials in Gaussian random variables [20, 7]. To obtain our bound on the Boolean average sensitivity of PTFs, we generalize the "critical-index" machinery of [37] (which in that work applies to halfspaces, i.e. degree-1 PTFs) to general PTFs. Together with the "invariance principle" of [30], this lets us extend our techniques from the Gaussian setting to the Boolean setting. Our bound on Boolean noise sensitivity is achieved via a simple reduction from upper bounds on average sensitivity of Boolean PTFs to corresponding bounds on noise sensitivity.

STOC'10, June 5–8, 2010, Cambridge, Massachusetts, USA.

Categories and Subject Descriptors

F.2.2 [**Nonnumerical Algorithms and Problems**]: Computations on Discrete Structures, I.2.6 [**Learning**]: [Concept Learning]

General Terms

Theory

Keywords

Boolean function; Fourier analysis; Average Sensitivity; Noise Sensitivity; Polynomial Threshold Function

1. INTRODUCTION

A degree-d polynomial threshold function (PTF) over a domain $X \subseteq \mathbb{R}^n$ is a Boolean-valued function $f : X \to \{-1, +1\}$,

$$f(x) = \text{sign}(p(x_1, \ldots, x_n))$$

where $p : X \to \mathbb{R}$ is a degree-d polynomial with real coefficients. When $d = 1$ polynomial threshold functions are simply linear threshold functions (also known as halfspaces or LTFs), which play an important role in complexity theory, learning theory, and other fields such as voting theory. Low-degree PTFs (where d is greater than 1 but is not too large) are a natural generalization of LTFs which are also of significant interest in these fields.

Over more than twenty years much research effort in the study of Boolean functions has been devoted to different notions of the "sensitivity" of a Boolean function to small perturbations of its input, see e.g. [21, 6, 5, 14, 2, 38, 29, 30, 32, 33] and many other works. In this work we focus on two natural and well-studied measures of this sensitivity, the "average sensitivity" and the "noise sensitivity." As our main results, we give the first non-trivial upper bounds on average sensitivity and noise sensitivity of low-degree PTFs. These bounds have several applications in learning theory and complexity theory as we describe later in this introduction.

We now define the notions of average and noise sensitivity in the setting of Boolean functions $f : \{-1,1\}^n \to \{-1,1\}$. (Our paper also deals with average sensitivity and noise sensitivity of functions $f : \mathbb{R}^n \to \{-1,1\}$ under the Gaussian distribution, but the precise definitions are more involved than in the Boolean case so we defer them until later.)

1.1 Average Sensitivity and Noise Sensitivity

The *sensitivity* of a Boolean function $f : \{-1,1\}^n \to \{-1,1\}$ on an input $x \in \{-1,1\}^n$, denoted $s_f(x)$, is the number of Hamming neighbors $y \in \{-1,1\}^n$ of x (i.e. strings which differ from x in precisely one coordinate) for which $f(x) \neq f(y)$. The *average sensitivity* of f, denoted $\mathrm{AS}(f)$, is simply $\mathbf{E}[s_f(x)]$ (where the expectation is with respect to the uniform distribution over $\{-1,1\}^n$). An alternate definition of average sensitivity can be given in terms of the influence of individual coordinates on f. For a Boolean function $f : \{-1,1\}^n \to \{-1,1\}$ and a coordinate index $i \in [n]$, the *influence of coordinate i on f* is the probability that flipping the i-th bit of a uniform random input $x \in \{-1,1\}^n$ causes the value of f to change, i.e. $\mathrm{Inf}_i(f) = \mathbf{Pr}[f(x) \neq f(x^{\oplus i})]$ (where the probability is with respect to the uniform distribution over $\{-1,1\}^n$). The sum of all n coordinate influences, $\sum_{i=1}^n \mathrm{Inf}_i(f)$, is called the *total influence* of f; it is easily seen to equal $\mathrm{AS}(f)$. Bounds on average sensitivity have been of use in the structural analysis of Boolean functions (see e.g. [21, 14, 38]) and in developing computationally efficient learning algorithms (see e.g. [6, 33]).

The average sensitivity is a measure of how f changes when a single coordinate is perturbed. In contrast, the noise sensitivity of f measures how f changes when a random collection of coordinates are all perturbed simultaneously. More precisely, given a noise parameter $0 \leq \epsilon \leq 1$ and a Boolean function $f : \{-1,1\}^n \to \{-1,1\}$, the *noise sensitivity of f at noise rate ϵ* is defined to be

$$\mathrm{NS}_\epsilon(f) = \mathbf{Pr}_{x,y}[f(x) \neq f(y)]$$

where x is uniform from $\{-1,1\}^n$ and y is obtained from x by flipping each bit independently with probability ϵ. Noise sensitivity has been studied in a range of contexts including Boolean function analysis, percolation theory, and computational learning theory [2, 25, 29, 36, 26].

1.2 Main Results: Upper Bounds on Average Sensitivity and Noise Sensitivity

1.2.1 Boolean PTFs

In 1994 Gotsman and Linial [17] conjectured that the symmetric function slicing the middle d layers of the Boolean hypercube has the highest average sensitivity among all degree-d PTFs. Since this function has average sensitivity $\Theta(d\sqrt{n})$ for every $1 \leq d \leq \sqrt{n}$, this conjecture implies (and is nearly equivalent to) the conjecture that every degree-d PTF f over $\{-1,1\}^n$ has $\mathrm{AS}(f) \leq d\sqrt{n}$.

Our first main result is an upper bound on average sensitivity which makes progress toward this conjecture:

THEOREM 1.1. *For any degree-d PTF f over $\{-1,1\}^n$, we have $\mathrm{AS}(f) \leq 2^{O(d)} \cdot \log n \cdot n^{1-1/(4d+2)}$.*

Using a completely different set of techniques, we also prove a different bound which improves on Theorem 1.1 for $d \leq 4$:

THEOREM 1.2. *For any degree-d PTF f over $\{-1,1\}^n$, we have $\mathrm{AS}(f) \leq 2n^{1-1/2^d}$.*

We give a simple reduction which translates any upper bound on average sensitivity for degree-d PTFs over Boolean variables into a corresponding upper bound on their noise sensitivity. Combining this reduction with Theorems 1.1 and 1.2, we establish:

THEOREM 1.3. *For any degree-d PTF f over $\{-1,1\}^n$ and any $0 \leq \epsilon \leq 1$, we have*

$$\mathrm{NS}_\epsilon(f) \leq 2^{O(d)} \cdot \epsilon^{1/(4d+2)} \log(1/\epsilon)$$
$$\mathrm{NS}_\epsilon(f) \leq O(\epsilon^{1/2^d}).$$

1.2.2 Gaussian PTFs

Looking beyond the Boolean hypercube, there are well-studied notions of average sensitivity and noise sensitivity for Boolean-valued functions over $\mathbb{R}^n$, where we view $\mathbb{R}^n$ as endowed with the standard multivariate Gaussian distribution $\mathcal{N}(0, I_n)$ [4, 30]. Given $f : \mathbb{R}^n \to \mathbb{R}$ that is square-integrable under the Gaussian measure $\mathcal{N}(0,1)$ and $i \in [n]$, the *Gaussian influence of co-ordinate i on f* is defined to be $\mathrm{GI}_i(f) = \mathbf{E}_{x_{-i} \sim \mathcal{N}^{n-1}}[\mathrm{Var}_{x_i \sim \mathcal{N}}[f]]$where x_{-i} denotes all but the ith coordinate of x. The *Gaussian average sensitivity of f* is defined as $\mathrm{GAS}(f) = \sum_{i \in [n]} \mathrm{GI}_i(f)$. The *Gaussian noise sensitivity of f at noise rate $\epsilon \in [0,1]$* is defined to be $\mathrm{GNS}_\epsilon(f) = \mathbf{Pr}_{x,z}[f(x) \neq f(y)]$ where $x \sim \mathcal{N}^n$ and $y \stackrel{\text{def}}{=} (1-\epsilon)x + \sqrt{2\epsilon - \epsilon^2}\, z$ for an independent Gaussian *noise vector* $z \sim \mathcal{N}^n$. These are natural analogues of their uniform-distribution Boolean hypercube counterparts defined above.) We prove upper bounds on Gaussian average sensitivity and Gaussian noise sensitivity of low-degree PTFs:

THEOREM 1.4. *For any degree-d PTF f over $\mathbb{R}^n$, we have* $\mathrm{GAS}(f) \leq O(d^2 \cdot \log n \cdot n^{1-1/2d})$.

THEOREM 1.5. *For any degree-d PTF f over $\mathbb{R}^n$ and any $0 \leq \epsilon \leq 1$, we have* $\mathrm{GNS}_\epsilon(f) \leq O(d \cdot \log^{1/2}(1/\epsilon) \cdot \epsilon^{1/2d})$.

We note that in subsequent work D. Kane [24] has given an optimal upper bound $\mathrm{GNS}_\epsilon(f) \leq O(d\sqrt{\epsilon})$ on the Gaussian noise sensitivity of any degree-d PTF.

1.3 Application: agnostically learning constant-degree PTFs in polynomial time

Our bounds on noise sensitivity, together with machinery developed in [25, 22, 26], yield the first efficient agnostic learning algorithms for low-degree polynomial threshold functions. In this section we state our new learning results; details are given in the full version.

We begin by briefly reviewing the fixed-distribution agnostic learning framework that has been studied in several recent works, see e.g. [22, 26, 3, 15, 23, 39]. Let $\mathcal{D}_X$ be a (fixed, known) distribution over an example space X such as the uniform distribution over $\{-1,1\}^n$ or the standard multivariate Gaussian distribution $\mathcal{N}(0, I_n)$ over $\mathbb{R}^n$. Let $\mathcal{C}$ denote a class of Boolean functions, such as the class of all degree-d PTFs. An algorithm A is said to be an *agnostic learning algorithm for $\mathcal{C}$ under distribution $\mathcal{D}_X$* if it has the following property: Let $\mathcal{D}$ be any distribution over $X \times \{-1,1\}$ such that the marginal of $\mathcal{D}$ over X is $\mathcal{D}_X$. Then if A is run on a sample of labeled examples drawn independently from $\mathcal{D}$, with high probability A outputs a hypothesis $h : X \to \{-1,1\}$ such that $\mathbf{Pr}_{(x,y)\sim\mathcal{D}}[h(x) \neq y] \leq \mathsf{opt} + \epsilon$, where $\mathsf{opt} = \min_{f \in \mathcal{C}} \mathbf{Pr}_{(x,y)\sim\mathcal{D}}[f(x) \neq y]$. In words, A's hypothesis is nearly as accurate as the best hypothesis in the class $\mathcal{C}$.

Kalai et al. [22] gave an agnostic learning algorithm based on L_1 polynomial regression. More precisely, they showed that for a class $\mathcal{C}$ of functions and a distribution $\mathcal{D}$, if every function in $\mathcal{C}$ has a low-degree polynomial approximator (in the L_2 norm) under the marginal distribution $\mathcal{D}_X$, then the L_1 polynomial regression algorithm is an efficient agnostic learning algorithm for $\mathcal{C}$ under $\mathcal{D}_X$. Together with the existence of low-degree polynomial approximators for halfspaces (under the uniform distribution on $\{-1,1\}^n$ and the standard Gaussian distribution $\mathcal{N}(0, I_n)$ on $\mathbb{R}^n$), the L_1 polynomial regression algorithm yields a $n^{O(1/\epsilon^4)}$-time agnostic learning algorithm for halfspaces under these distributions.

Using ingredients from [25], upper bounds on Boolean noise sensitivity (such as Theorem 1.3) imply the existence of low-degree L_2-norm polynomial approximators under the uniform distribution on $\{-1,1\}^n$. Hence we obtain the following agnostic learning result:

THEOREM 1.6. *The class of degree-d PTFs is agnostically learnable under the uniform distribution on $\{-1,1\}^n$ in time $n^{2^{O(d^2)}(\log 1/\epsilon)^{4d+2}/\epsilon^{8d+4}}$. For $d \leq 4$, this bound can be improved to $n^{O(1/\epsilon^{2^{d+1}})}$.*

Similarly, using ingredients from [26], upper bounds on Gaussian noise sensitivity (such as Theorem 1.5) imply the existence of low-degree L_2-norm polynomial approximators under $\mathcal{N}(0, I_n)$. This lets us obtain

THEOREM 1.7. *The class of degree-d PTFs is agnostically learnable under any n-dimensional Gaussian distribution in time $n^{(d/\epsilon)^{O(d)}}$.*

For ϵ constant, these results are the first polynomial-time agnostic learning algorithms for constant-degree PTFs.

1.4 Other applications

The results and approaches of this paper have found other recent applications beyond the agnostic learning results presented above; we describe two of these below.

Gopalan and Servedio [16] have combined the average sensitivity bound given by Theorem 1.1 with techniques from [27] to give the first sub-exponential time algorithms for learning AC^0 circuits augmented with a small (but super-constant) number of arbitrary threshold gates, i.e. gates that compute arbitrary LTFs which may have weights of any magnitude. (Previous work using different techniques [19] could only handle AC^0 circuits augmented with majority gates.)

In other recent work Diakonikolas et al. [10] and Harsha et al. [18] have refined the approach used to prove Theorem 1.1 to establish a "regularity lemma" for low-degree polynomial threshold functions. Roughly speaking, this lemma says that any degree-d PTF can be decomposed into a constant number of subfunctions, almost all of which are "regular" degree-d PTFs. [10] apply this regularity lemma to extend the positive results on the existence of low-weight approximators for LTFs, proved in [37], to low-degree PTFs.

1.5 Techniques

In this section we give a high-level overview of how Theorems 1.1, 1.4 and 1.5 are proved. (As mentioned earlier, Theorem 1.2 is proved using completely different techniques; see Section 5.) The arguments are simpler for the Gaussian setting so we begin with these.

1.5.1 The Gaussian case

We sketch the argument for the Gaussian average sensitivity bound Theorem 1.4; the Gaussian noise sensitivity bound Theorem 1.5 follows along similar lines.

Let $f = \mathrm{sign}(p)$ where $p : \mathbb{R}^n \to \mathbb{R}$ is a degree-d polynomial. The Gaussian average sensitivity $\mathrm{GAS}(f)$ of f is equal to the sum of individual Gaussian influences $\mathrm{GI}_i(f) = 2\,\mathbf{Pr}_{x,x^i}[f(x) \neq f(x^i)]$, where $x \sim \mathcal{N}^n$ and x^i is obtained by replacing the ith coordinate of x by an independent random sample from $\mathcal{N}$. Central to the proof of Theorem 1.4 is a bound on $\mathrm{GI}_i(f)$ by $\mathrm{GI}_i(p)$, the influence of variable i in the polynomial p. Let $i = 1$, and express $p(x)$ as a univariate polynomial in x_1 as follows: $p(x) = p(x_1, \ldots, x_n) = \sum_{i=0}^{d} p_i(x_2, \ldots, x_n) \cdot h_i(x_1)$, where $h_i(x_1)$ is the univariate degree-i Hermite polynomial. Intuitively, the event $f(x) \neq f(x^1)$ can only take place if either:

- $|p_0(g_2, \ldots, g_n)|$ is "small", or
- $|p_i(g_2, \ldots, g_n)|$ is "large" for some $i \in [d]$.

We use an anti-concentration result for polynomials in Gaussian random variables, due to Carbery and Wright [7], to show that $|p_0(g_2, \ldots, g_n)|$ is "small" only with low probability. For the second bullet, we apply tail bounds for low-degree polynomials in independent Gaussian random variables [20] to show, for each $i \in [d]$, that $|p_i(g_2, \ldots, g_n)|$ is "large" only with low probability. We can thus argue that $\mathbf{Pr}_{x,x^1}[f(x) \neq f(x^1)]$ is low, bounding the Gaussian influence of variable 1 on f in terms of $\mathrm{GI}_1(p)$. By normalizing $\mathrm{Var}[p] = 1$ and applying a convexity argument, we see that $\mathrm{GI}(f)$ is maximized when $\mathrm{GI}_i(p) = d/n$ for each $i \in [n]$, establishing Theorem 1.4.

1.5.2 The Boolean case

One advantage of working over the Boolean domain $\{-1,1\}^n$ is that without loss of generality we may consider only *multilinear* PTFs, where $f = \mathrm{sign}(p(x))$ for p a multilinear polynomial. However, this advantage is offset by the fact that the uniform distribution on $\{-1,1\}^n$ is less symmetric than the Gaussian distribution; for example, every degree-1 PTF under the Gaussian distribution $\mathcal{N}^n$ is equivalent simply to $\mathrm{sign}(x_1 - \theta)$, but this is of course not true for degree-1 PTFs over $\{-1,1\}^n$. Our upper bound on Boolean average sensitivity uses ideas from the Gaussian setting but also requires significant additional ingredients.

An important notion in the Boolean case is that of a "regular" PTF; this is a PTF $f = \mathrm{sign}(p)$ where every variable *in the polynomial* p has low influence. (See Section 2 for a definition of the influence of a variable on a real-valued function; note that the definition from Section 1.1 applies only for Boolean-valued functions.) If f is a regular PTF, then the "invariance principle" of [30] tells us that $p(x)$ (where x is uniform from $\{-1,1\}^n$) behaves much like $p(\mathcal{G})$ (where $\mathcal{G}$ is drawn from $\mathcal{N}(0, I_n)$), and essentially the arguments from the Gaussian case can be used.

It remains to handle the case where f is not a regular PTF, i.e. some variable has high influence in p. To accomplish this, we generalize the notion of the "critical-index" of a halfspace (see [37, 11]) to apply to PTFs. We show that a carefully chosen random restriction (one which fixes only the variables up to the critical index – very roughly speaking, only the highest-influence variables – and leaves the other ones free) has non-negligible probability of causing f to collapse down to a regular PTF. This lets us give a recursive bound on average sensitivity which ends up being not much worse than the bound that can be obtained for the regular case; see Section 4.2 for a detailed explanation of the recursive argument.

1.6 Organization

Due to space constraints, this proceedings version contains only a selection of our results with high-level arguments. Full proofs are provided in [8, 18].

Formal definitions of average sensitivity and noise sensitivity (especially in the Gaussian case), along with mathematical tools we use such as tail bounds and anticoncentration results for low degree polynomials, are presented in Section 2.

In Section 3, we outline the proof of an upper bound on the Gaussian average sensitivity of PTFs (Theorem 1.4); the missing details can be found in the full version. The main result of the paper – a bound on the Boolean average sensitivity (Theorem 1.1) – is outlined in Section 4 (again details are in the full version). In Section 5, an alternate bound is established for Boolean average sensitivity that is better than Theorem 1.1 for degrees $d \leq 4$ (Theorem 1.2). This is followed by a reduction from Boolean average sensitivity bounds to corresponding noise sensitivity bounds (Theorem 6.1) in Section 6.

2. DEFINITIONS AND BACKGROUND

2.1 Basic Definitions

In this subsection we record the basic notation and definitions used throughout the paper. For $n \in \mathbb{N}$, we denote by $[n]$ the set $\{1, 2, \ldots, n\}$. We write $\mathcal{N}$ to denote the standard univariate Gaussian distribution $\mathcal{N}(0, 1)$.

For a degree-d polynomial $p : X \to \mathbb{R}$ we denote by $\|p\|_2$ its l_2 norm, $\|p\|_2 = \mathbf{E}_x[p(x)^2]^{1/2}$, where the intended distribution over $x \in \mathbb{R}^n$ (which will always be either uniform over $\{-1,1\}^n$, or the $\mathcal{N}^n$ distribution) will always be clear from context. We note that for multilinear p the two notions are always equal (see e.g. Proposition 3.5 of [30]).

We now proceed to define the notion of influence for real-valued functions in a product probability space. Throughout this paper we consider either the uniform distribution on the hypercube $\{\pm 1\}^n$ or the standard n-dimensional Gaussian distribution in $\mathbb{R}^n$. However, for the sake of generality, we adopt this more general setting.

Let $(\Omega_1, \mu_1), \ldots, (\Omega_n, \mu_n)$ be probability spaces and let $(\Omega = \otimes_{i=1}^n \Omega_i, \mu = \otimes_{i=1}^n \mu_i)$ denote the corresponding product space. Let $f : \Omega \to \mathbb{R}$ be any square integrable function on (Ω, μ), i.e. $f \in L^2(\Omega, \mu)$. The influence of the ith coordinate on f [30] is

$$\mathrm{Inf}_i^{\mu}(f) \stackrel{\mathrm{def}}{=} \mathbf{E}_{\mu}[\mathrm{Var}_{\mu_i}[f]]$$

and the total influence of f is $\mathrm{Inf}^{\mu}(f) \stackrel{\mathrm{def}}{=} \sum_{i=1}^n \mathrm{Inf}_i^{\mu}(f)$.

For a function $f : \{-1,1\}^n \to \mathbb{R}$ over the Boolean hypercube endowed with the uniform distribution, the influence of variable i on f can be expressed in terms of the Fourier coefficients of f as $\mathrm{Inf}_i(f) = \sum_{S \ni i} \widehat{f}(S)^2$, and as mentioned in the introduction it is easily seen that $\mathrm{AS}(f) = \mathrm{Inf}(f)$ for Boolean-valued functions $f : \{-1,1\}^n \to \{-1,1\}$.

In this paper we are concerned with variable influences for functions defined over $\{-1,1\}^n$ under the uniform distribution, and over $\mathbb{R}^n$ under $\mathcal{N}(0, I_n)$; we shall adopt the convention that $\mathrm{Inf}_i(f)$ denotes the former and $\mathrm{GI}_i(f)$ the latter. We also denote by $\mathrm{GAS}(f) = \sum_{i \in [n]} \mathrm{GI}_i(f)$ the Gaussian average sensitivity.

Note that for a function $f : \mathbb{R}^n \to \{-1,1\}$, the Gaussian influence $\mathrm{GI}_i(f)$ can be equivalently written as: $\mathrm{GI}_i(f) = 2\,\mathbf{Pr}_{x,x^i}[f(x) \neq f(x^i)]$, where $x \sim \mathcal{N}^n$ and x^i is obtained by replacing the ith coordinate of x by an independent random sample from $\mathcal{N}$.

Fourier and Hermite Analysis. We assume familiarity with the basics of Fourier analysis over the Boolean hypercube $\{-1,1\}^n$. We will also require similar basics of Hermite analysis over the space $\mathbb{R}^n$ equipped with the standard n-dimensional Gaussian distribution $\mathcal{N}^n$; a brief review is provided in the full version.

2.2 Probabilistic Facts

In this subsection, we record the basic probabilistic tools we use in our proofs.

We first recall the following well-known consequence of hypercontractivity (see e.g. Lecture 16 of [31] for the boolean setting and [4] for the Gaussian setting):

THEOREM 2.1. *Let $p : X \to \mathbb{R}$ be a degree-d polynomial, where X is either $\{-1,1\}^n$ under the uniform distribution or $\mathbb{R}^n$ under $\mathcal{N}^n$, and fix $q > 2$. Then*

$$\|p\|_q^2 \leq (q-1)^d \|p\|_2^2.$$

We will need a concentration bound for low-degree polynomials over independent random signs or standard Gaussians. It can be proved (in both cases) using Markov's inequality and hypercontractivity, see e.g. [20, 31, 1].

THEOREM 2.2 ("DEGREE-d CHERNOFF BOUND"). *Let $p(x)$ be a degree-d polynomial. Let x be drawn either from the uniform distribution in $\{-1,1\}^n$ or from $\mathcal{N}^n$. For any $t > e^d$, we have*

$$\mathbf{Pr}_x[|p(x)| \geq t\|p\|_2] \leq \exp(-\Omega(t^{2/d})).$$

The second fact is a powerful anti-concentration bound for low-degree polynomials over Gaussian random variables. (We note that this result does not hold in the Boolean setting.)

THEOREM 2.3 ([7]). *Let $0 \neq p : \mathbb{R}^n \to \mathbb{R}$ be a degree-d polynomial. Then for all $\epsilon > 0$, we have*

$$\mathbf{Pr}_{x \sim \mathcal{N}^n}[|p(x)| \leq \epsilon\|p\|_2] \leq O(d\epsilon^{1/d}).$$

We also make essential use of a (weak) anti-concentration property of low-degree polynomials over the hypercube $\{-1,1\}^n$:

THEOREM 2.4 ([12, 1]). *Let $p : \{-1,1\}^n \to \mathbb{R}$ be a degree-d polynomial with $\mathrm{Var}[p] \equiv \sum_{0<|S|\leq d} \widehat{p}(S)^2 = 1$ and $\mathbf{E}[p] = \widehat{p}(\emptyset) = 0$. Then we have*

$$\mathbf{Pr}[p(x) > 1/2^{O(d)}] > 1/2^{O(d)}$$

and hence,

$$\mathbf{Pr}[|p(x)| \geq 1/2^{O(d)}] > 1/2^{O(d)}.$$

The following is a restatement of the invariance principle, specifically Theorem 3.19 under hypothesis **H4** in [30].

THEOREM 2.5 ([30]). *Let* $p(x) = \sum_{|S|\le d} \widehat{p}(S) x_S$ *be a degree-d multilinear polynomial with* $\sum_{0<|S|\le d} \widehat{p}(S)^2 = 1$. *Suppose each variable* $i \in [n]$ *has low influence* $\mathrm{Inf}_i(p) \le \tau$, *i.e.* $\sum_{S \ni i} \widehat{p}(S)^2 \le \tau$. *Let* x *be drawn uniformly from* $\{-1,1\}^n$ *and* $\mathcal{G} \sim \mathcal{N}^n$. *Then,*

$$\sup_{t\in\mathbb{R}} |\mathbf{Pr}[p(x) \le t] - \mathbf{Pr}[p(\mathcal{G}) \le t]| \le O(d\tau^{1/(4d+1)}).$$

3. GAUSSIAN AVERAGE SENSITIVITY

The following lemma, which relates the influence of a variable on $f = \mathrm{sign}(p)$ to its influence on the polynomial p, is central to the proof of Theorem 1.4.

LEMMA 3.1. *Let* $p : \mathbb{R}^n \to \mathbb{R}$ *be a degree-d polynomial over Gaussian inputs with* $\|p\|_2 = 1$ *and let* $f = \mathrm{sign}(p)$. *Then for each* $i \in [n]$, *we have* $\mathrm{GI}_i(f) \le O(d^2 \cdot \mathrm{GI}_i(p)^{1/(2d)} \cdot \log(1/\mathrm{GI}_i(p)))$.

PROOF OF LEMMA 3.1. Let $p(x)$ be a degree-d polynomial with $\|p\|_2 = 1$. For notational convenience let us fix $i = 1$ and let $\tau = \mathrm{GI}_1(p)$. We may assume that $\tau < 1/4$ since otherwise the claimed bound holds trivially. We express $p(x)$ as a univariate polynomial in x_1 as follows,

$$p(x) = p(x_1, \ldots, x_n) = \sum_{i=0}^{d} p_i(x_2, \ldots, x_n) \cdot h_i(x_1)$$

where $h_i(x_1)$ is the univariate degree-i Hermite polynomial. Note that for any multi-index $S = (S_2, \ldots, S_n) \in \mathbb{N}^{n-1}$ and $0 \le i \le d$, we have $\widehat{p_i}(S) = \widehat{p}(S')$ where $S' = (i, S_2, \ldots, S_n) \in \mathbb{N}^n$. As a result, using Parseval's identity for the Hermite basis, we have that $\|p\|^2 = \sum_{i=0}^{d} \|p_i\|^2$.

We further have

$$\|p_i\|^2 = \sum_{S\in\mathbb{N}^{n-1}} \widehat{p_i}(S)^2 \quad \text{and} \quad \mathrm{GI}_i(p) = \sum_{S:S_i>0} \widehat{p}(S)^2.$$

Consequently the 2-norms of $p_1, \ldots, p_d$ are "small" and the 2-norm of p_0 is "large":

$$\sum_{i=1}^{d} \|p_i\|^2 = \sum_{S:S_1>0} \widehat{p}(S)^2 = \tau, \text{ and } \|p_0\|^2 = 1 - \tau > 1/2.$$

Let $t = C^{d/2}\tau^{1/2}\log^{d/2}(1/\tau)$ and $\gamma = d^2 \cdot \tau^{1/2d}\log(1/\tau)$ where C is an absolute constant. We can assume that $\gamma < 1/10$ since otherwise the bound of Lemma 3.1 holds trivially. For these values of t and γ, the proof strategy is as follows:

- We use the anti-concentration bound Theorem 2.3 to argue that with high probability $p_0(g_2, \ldots, g_n)$ is not too small: more precisely, $\mathbf{Pr}_{\mathcal{N}^{n-1}}[|p_0(g_2, \ldots, g_n)| \le td(2ed\log(1/\gamma))^{d/2}] \le O(\gamma)$.
- We use the "degree-d Chernoff bound" (Theorem 2.2) to argue that with high probability each $p_i(g_2, \ldots, g_n)$, $i \in [d]$, is not too large: more precisely, $\mathbf{Pr}_{\mathcal{N}^{n-1}}[|p_i(g_2, \ldots, g_n)| \ge t] \le O(\gamma)$.
- We use elementary properties of the $\mathcal{N}(0,1)$ distribution to argue that if $|a| \ge td(2ed\log(1/\gamma))^{d/2}$ and $|b_i| \le t$, then the function $\mathrm{sign}(a + \sum_{i=1}^{d} b_i h_i(g_1))$ (a function of one $\mathcal{N}(0,1)$ random variable g_1) is $O(\gamma)$-close to the constant function $\mathrm{sign}(a)$.
- Thus with probability at least $1 - O(\gamma)$ over the choice of $g_2, \ldots, g_n$, we have $\mathrm{Var}_{g_1}[\mathrm{sign}(p(g_1, \ldots, g_n))] \le O(\gamma(1-\gamma)) \le O(\gamma)$. For the remaining (at most) $O(\gamma)$ fraction of outcomes for $g_2, \ldots, g_n$ we always have $\mathrm{Var}_{g_1}[\mathrm{sign}(p(g_1, \ldots, g_n))] \le 1$, so overall we get $\mathrm{GI}_1(\mathrm{sign}(p)) \le O(\gamma)$.

Proofs of the three aforementioned claims are presented in the full version. □

We now sketch the proof of Theorem 1.4 using Lemma 3.1. The idea is simple: by normalizing we may assume that $\mathrm{Var}[p] = 1$, and consequently the total influence $\mathrm{GI}(p) = \sum_{i=1}^{n} \mathrm{GI}_i(p)$ of p is at most d since p is a degree-d polynomial. Intuitively, Lemma 3.1 tells us that the largest possible total value of $\mathrm{GI}(f)$ is obtained if each $\mathrm{GI}_i(p)$ equals d/n; a convexity argument, presented in the full version, makes this precise and establishes Theorem 1.4.

We remark that in the case of degree-d *multilinear* PTFs it is possible to obtain a slightly stronger bound of $\mathrm{GAS}(f) \le O(d \cdot \log n \cdot n^{1-1/2d})$ using our approach; we omit the details.

4. BOOLEAN AVERAGE SENSITIVITY

Let $\mathrm{AS}(n,d)$ denote the maximum possible average sensitivity of any degree-d PTF over n Boolean variables. In this section we outline the proof of the claimed bound in Theorem 1.1:

$$\mathrm{AS}(n,d) \le 2^{O(d)} \cdot \log n \cdot n^{1-1/(4d+2)}. \quad (1)$$

For $d = 1$ (linear threshold functions) it is well known that $\mathrm{AS}(n,1) = 2^{-n}\binom{n}{n/2} = \Theta(\sqrt{n})$. Also, notice that the RHS of (1) is larger than n for $d = \omega(\sqrt{\log n})$, yielding a trivial bound of $\mathrm{AS}(n,d) \le n$. Therefore throughout this section we shall assume d satisfies $2 \le d \le O(\sqrt{\log n})$.

4.1 Regularity and the critical index of polynomials

The proof of Theorem 1.1 is a combination of a case analysis and a recursive bound. The case analysis is based on the notion of critical index for polynomials that we define below.

In [37] a notion of the "critical index" of a linear form was defined and subsequently used in [34, 9, 11]. This notion is generalized below to the case of polynomials.

DEFINITION 1. *Let* $0 \ne p : \{-1,1\}^n \to \mathbb{R}$ *and* $\tau > 0$. *Assume the variables are ordered such that* $\mathrm{Inf}_i(f) \ge \mathrm{Inf}_{i+1}(f)$ *for all* $i \in [n-1]$. *The* τ-critical index *of* f *is the least* i *such that:*

$$\mathrm{Inf}_{i+1}(p) \le \tau \cdot \sum_{j=i+1}^{n} \mathrm{Inf}_j(p). \quad (2)$$

If (2) does not hold for any i *we say that the* τ*-critical index of* p *is* $+\infty$. *If* p *is has* τ*-critical index 0, we say that* p *is* τ-regular.

The following simple lemma will be useful for us. It says that the total influence $\sum_{i=j+1}^{n} \mathrm{Inf}_i(p)$ goes down exponentially as a function of j prior to the critical index:

LEMMA 4.1. *Let* $p : \{-1,1\}^n \to \mathbb{R}$ *and* $\tau > 0$. *Let* k *be the* τ*-critical index of* p. *For* $0 \le j \le k$ *we have* $\sum_{i=j+1}^{n} \mathrm{Inf}_i(p) \le (1-\tau)^j \cdot \mathrm{Inf}(p)$.

PROOF. The lemma trivially holds for $j = 0$. In general, since j is at most k, we have that $\mathrm{Inf}_j(p) \geq \tau \cdot \sum_{i=j}^{n} \mathrm{Inf}_i(p)$, or equivalently $\sum_{i=j+1}^{n} \mathrm{Inf}_i(p) \leq (1-\tau) \cdot \sum_{i=j}^{n} \mathrm{Inf}_i(p)$ which yields the claimed bound. □

4.2 Overview of proof

The high-level approach to proving Theorem 1.1 is a combination of a case analysis and a recursive bound.

By the invariance principle (see Section 2.2), the behaviour of τ-regular PTFs in the boolean and Gaussian settings is nearly the same. Therefore, we can argue directly that the average sensitivity is small using arguments similar to the Gaussian case (in fact simpler since now the polynomial is multilinear). In particular, we show the following lemma:

LEMMA 4.2. *Fix $\tau = n^{-\Theta(1)}$. Let f be a τ-regular degree-d PTF. Then,* $\mathrm{AS}(f) \leq O(d \cdot n \cdot \tau^{1/(4d+1)})$.

The following claim is a direct consequence of the above lemma.

CLAIM 4.3. *Suppose $f = \mathrm{sign}(p)$ is a τ-regular degree-d PTF where $\tau \stackrel{def}{=} n^{-(4d+1)/(4d+2)}$. Then,*

$$\mathrm{AS}(f) \leq O(d \cdot n^{1-1/(4d+2)}).$$

For PTFs that are not τ-regular, we show that there is a not-too-large value of k (at most $K \stackrel{\mathrm{def}}{=} 2d \log n/\tau$), and a collection of k variables (the variables whose influence in p are largest), such that the following holds: if we consider all 2^k subfunctions of f obtained by fixing the variables in all possible ways, a "large" (at least $1/2^{O(d)}$) fraction of the restricted functions have low average sensitivity. More precisely, we show:

CLAIM 4.4. *Let $K \stackrel{def}{=} 2d \log n/\tau$ where $\tau \stackrel{def}{=} n^{-(4d+1)/(4d+2)}$. Suppose $f = \mathrm{sign}(p)$ is a degree-d PTF that is not τ-regular. Then for some $1 \leq k \leq K$, there is a set of k variables with the following property: for at least a $1/2^{O(d)}$ fraction of all 2^k assignments ρ to those k variables, we have*

$$\mathrm{AS}(f_\rho) \leq O(d \cdot (\log n)^{1/4} \cdot n^{1-1/(4d+2)}).$$

The proof of Claim 4.4 is given in Section 4.3.3. We do this by generalizing the "critical index" case analysis from [37]. We define a notion of the τ-critical index of a degree-d polynomial; a τ-regular polynomial p is one for which the τ-critical index is 0. If the τ-critical index of p is some value $k \leq 2d \log n/\tau$, we restrict the k largest-influence variables (see Section 4.3.1). If the τ-critical index is larger than $2d \log n/\tau$, we restrict the $k = 2d \log n/\tau$ largest-influence variables in p (see Section 4.3.2).

4.2.1 *Proof of main result (Theorem 1.1) assuming Claim 4.3 and Claim 4.4*

Given these two claims it is not difficult to obtain the final result. In Claim 4.4, we note that the k restricted variables may each contribute at most 1 to the average sensitivity of f (recall that average sensitivity is equal to the sum of influences of each variable), and that the total influence of the remaining variables on f is equal to the expected average sensitivity of f_ρ, where the expectation is taken over all 2^k restrictions ρ. Since each function f_ρ is itself a degree-d PTF over at most n variables, we have the following recursive constraint on $\mathrm{AS}(n, d)$:

$$\mathrm{AS}(n,d) \leq \max\{O(d \cdot n^{1-1/(4d+2)}),$$

$$\max_{\substack{1 \leq k \leq K \\ 1/2^{O(d)} \leq \alpha \leq 1}} \{k + \alpha \cdot O(d \cdot (\log n)^{1/4} \cdot n^{1-1/(4d+2)}) + (1-\alpha)\mathrm{AS}(n,d)\}\}.$$

It is easy to see that the maximum possible value of $\mathrm{AS}(n, d)$ subject to the above constraint is at most the maximum possible value of $\mathrm{AS}'(n, d)$ that satisfies the following weaker constraint:

$$\mathrm{AS}'(n,d) \leq K + \left(1 - \frac{1}{2^{O(d)}}\right) \mathrm{AS}'(n,d)$$

which is satisfied by $\mathrm{AS}'(n,d) \leq 2^{O(d)} \cdot \log n \cdot n^{1-1/(4d+2)}$.

4.3 Non τ-regular PTFs

The proof of Claim 4.4 is divided into two cases based on the value of the critical index.

4.3.1 *The small critical index case*

Let $f = \mathrm{sign}(p)$ be such that the τ-critical index of p is some value k between 1 and $K = 2d \log n/\tau$. By definition, the sequence of influences $\mathrm{Inf}_{k+1}(p), \ldots, \mathrm{Inf}_n(p)$ is τ-regular. We essentially reduce this case to the regular case for a regularity parameter τ' somewhat larger than τ.

Consider a random restriction ρ of all the variables up to the critical index. We will show the following:

LEMMA 4.5. *For a $1/2^{O(d)}$ fraction of restrictions ρ, the sequence of influences $\mathrm{Inf}_{k+1}(p_\rho), \ldots, \mathrm{Inf}_n(p_\rho)$ is τ'-regular, where $\tau' \stackrel{def}{=} (3 \log n)^d \cdot \tau$.*

By our choice of $\tau = n^{-(4d+1)/(4d+2)}$, we have that $\tau' = n^{-\Theta(1)}$, and so we may apply Lemma 4.2 to these restrictions to conclude that the associated PTFs have average sensitivity at most $O(d \cdot n \cdot (\tau')^{1/(4d+1)})$.

PROOF. Since the sequence of influences $\mathrm{Inf}_{k+1}(p), \ldots, \mathrm{Inf}_n(p)$ is τ-regular, we have

$$\mathrm{Inf}_i(p) \leq \tau \cdot \sum_{j=k+1}^{n} \mathrm{Inf}_j(p)$$

for all $i \in [k+1, n]$.

We want to prove that for a $1/2^{O(d)}$ fraction of all 2^k restrictions ρ to $x_1, \ldots, x_k$ we have

$$\mathrm{Inf}_i(p_\rho) \leq \tau' \cdot \sum_{j=k+1}^{n} \mathrm{Inf}_j(p_\rho) \qquad (3)$$

for all $i \in [k+1, n]$.

To do this we proceed as follows: First we show that for a low-degree polynomial, a random restriction with very high probability does not cause any variable's influence to increase by more than a $\mathrm{polylog}(n)$ factor. Formally, we prove the following lemma in the full version:

LEMMA 4.6. *Let $p(x_1, \ldots, x_n)$ be a degree-d polynomial. Let ρ be a randomly chosen assignment to the variables $x_1, \ldots, x_k$. Fix any $t > e^{2d}$ and any $\ell \in [k+1, n]$. With probability at least $1 - \exp(-\Omega(t^{1/d}))$ over the choice of ρ, we have*

$$\mathrm{Inf}_\ell(p_\rho) \leq t \cdot 3^d \mathrm{Inf}_\ell(p).$$

In particular, for $t = \log^d n$, we have that with probability at least $1 - n^{-\omega(1)}$, every variable $\ell \in [k+1, n]$ has $\mathrm{Inf}_\ell(p_\rho) \leq (3 \log n)^d \cdot \mathrm{Inf}_\ell(p)$.

Lemma 4.6 implies that, with very high probability over the random restrictions, we have $\text{Inf}_i(p_\rho) \le (3\log n)^d \cdot \text{Inf}_i(p)$, for all $i \in [k+1, n]$. We need to show that for a $1/2^{O(d)}$ fraction of all restrictions the sum on the RHS of (3) is at least $\sum_{j=k+1}^{n} \text{Inf}_j(p)$ (its expected value). The lemma then follows by a union bound.

We consider the degree-$2d$ polynomial $A(\rho_1, \dots, \rho_k) \stackrel{\text{def}}{=} \sum_{j=k+1}^{n} \text{Inf}_j(p_\rho)$ in variables $\rho_1, \dots, \rho_k$. The expected value of A is $\mathbf{E}_\rho[A] = \sum_{j=k+1}^{n} \text{Inf}_j(p) = \widehat{A}(\emptyset)$. We apply Theorem 2.4 to the polynomial $B = (A - \widehat{A}(\emptyset))/\text{Var}[A]$. We get $\mathbf{Pr}_\rho[B > 0] > 1/2^{O(d)}$, which implies $\mathbf{Pr}_\rho[A > \mathbf{E}_\rho[A]] > 1/2^{O(d)}$ and we are done. □

4.3.2 The large critical index case

Finally we consider PTFs $f = \text{sign}(p)$ with τ-critical index greater than $K = 2d\log n/\tau$. Let ρ be a restriction of the first K variables $\mathcal{H} = \{1, \dots, K\}$; we call these the "head" variables. We will show the following:

LEMMA 4.7. *For a $1/2^{O(d)}$ fraction of restrictions ρ, the function $\text{sign}(p_\rho(x))$ is a constant function.*

PROOF. By Lemma 4.1, the surviving variables $x_{K+1}, \dots, x_n$ have very small total influence in p:

$$\sum_{i=K+1}^{n} \text{Inf}_i(p) = \sum_{i=K+1}^{n} \sum_{S \ni i} \widehat{p}(S)^2 \le (1-\tau)^K \cdot \text{Inf}(p) \le d/n^{2d}. \tag{4}$$

Therefore, if we let p' be the truncation of p comprising only the monomials with all variables in $\mathcal{H}$,

$$p'(x_1, \dots, x_k) = \sum_{S \subset \mathcal{H}} \widehat{p}(S) x_S,$$

we know that almost all of the original Fourier weight of p is on the coefficients of p':

$$1 \ge \sum_{\substack{S \subset \mathcal{H} \\ |S|>0}} \widehat{p}(S)^2 \ge 1 - \sum_{i=K+1}^{n} \text{Inf}_i(p) \ge 1 - d/n^{2d}.$$

Applying Theorem 2.4 to p' [1] we get $\mathbf{Pr}_{x \in \{-1,1\}^K}[|p'(x)| \ge 1/2^{O(d)}] \ge 1/2^{O(d)}$. In words, for a $1/2^{O(d)}$ fraction of all restrictions ρ to $x_1, \dots, x_K$, the value $p'(\rho)$ has magnitude at least $1/2^{O(d)}$.

For any such restriction, if the function $f_\rho(x)$ is not a constant function it must necessarily be the case that:

$$\sum_{\emptyset \ne S \subseteq \{K+1, \dots, n\}} |\widehat{p_\rho}(S)| \ge 1/2^{O(d)}.$$

As noted in (4), each tail variable $\ell > K$ has very small influence in p: $\text{Inf}_\ell(p) \le \sum_{i=K+1}^{n} \text{Inf}_i(p) = d/n^{2d}$.

Applying Lemma 4.6, we get that for the overwhelming majority of the $1/2^{O(d)}$ fraction of restrictions mentioned above, the influence of ℓ in p_ρ is not much larger than the influence of ℓ in p:

$$\text{Inf}_\ell(p_\rho) \le (3\log n)^d \cdot \text{Inf}_\ell(p) \le d \cdot (3\log n)^d / n^{2d} \tag{5}$$

[1]after a very slight rescaling so the non-constant Fourier coefficients of p' have sum of squares equal to 1; this does not affect the bound we get because of the big-O.

Using Cauchy-Schwarz, we have

$$\begin{aligned} & \sum_{S \ni \ell, S \subseteq \{x_{K+1}, \dots, x_n\}} |\widehat{p_\rho}(S)| \\ \le\ & n^{d/2} \cdot \sqrt{\sum_{S \ni \ell, S \subseteq \{x_{K+1}, \dots, x_n\}} \widehat{p_\rho}(S)^2} \\ =\ & n^{d/2} \sqrt{\text{Inf}_\ell(p_\rho)} \le n^{-\Omega(1)} \end{aligned}$$

where we have used (5) (and our upper bound on d). From this we easily get that

$$\sum_{0 < |S| \subseteq \{x_{K+1}, \dots, x_n\}} |\widehat{p_\rho}(S)| \le n^{-\Omega(1)} \ll 1/2^{O(d)}.$$

We have established that for a $1/2^{O(d)}$ fraction of all restrictions to $x_1, \dots, x_K$, the function $f_\rho = \text{sign}(p_\rho)$ is a constant function, and the lemma is proved. □

4.3.3 Proof of Claim 4.4

If f is a degree-d PTF that is not τ-regular, then its τ-critical index is either in the range $\{1, \dots, K\}$ or it is greater than K.

In the first case (small critical index case), as shown in Section 4.3.1, we have that for a $1/2^{O(d)}$ fraction of restrictions ρ to variables $x_1, \dots, x_k$, the total influence of $f_\rho = \text{sign}(p_\rho)$ is at most

$$O(d \cdot n \cdot (\tau')^{1/(4d+1)}) = O(d \cdot (\log n)^{1/4} \cdot n^{1-1/(4d+2)}),$$

so the conclusion of Claim 4.4 holds in this case.

In the second case (large critical index case), as shown in Section 4.3.2, for a $1/2^{O(d)}$ fraction of restrictions ρ to $x_1, \dots, x_K$ the function f_ρ is constant and hence has zero influence, so the conclusion of Claim 4.4 certainly holds in this case as well. □

5. BOOLEAN AVERAGE SENSITIVITY: A FOURIER-ANALYTIC BOUND

In this section, we present a simple proof of the following upper bound on the average sensitivity of a degree-d PTF (Theorem 1.2): $\text{AS}(n,d) \le 2n^{1-1/2^d}$.

We recall here the definition of the formal derivative of a function $f : \{-1,1\}^n \to \mathbb{R}$.

$$D_i f(x) = \sum_{S \ni i} \hat{f}_S x_{S-\{i\}}.$$

It is easy to see that,

$$D_i f(x) = \frac{1}{2} x_i [f(x) - f(x^{\oplus i})] = \frac{1}{2}\left(\frac{f(x) - f(x^{\oplus i})}{x_i}\right) \tag{6}$$

where "$x^{\oplus i}$" means "x with the i-th bit flipped."

For a Boolean function f, we have $D_i f(x) = \pm 1$ iff flipping the ith bit flips f; otherwise $D_i f(x) = 0$. So we have

$$\text{Inf}_i(f) = \mathbf{E}[|D_i f(x)|].$$

LEMMA 5.1. *Fix $i \ne j \in [n]$. Let $f, g : \{-1,1\}^n \to \mathbb{R}$ be functions such that f is independent of the ith bit x_i and g is independent of the jth bit x_j. Then*

$$\mathbf{E}_x[x_i x_j f(x) g(x)] \le \frac{\text{Inf}_i(g) + \text{Inf}_j(f)}{2}.$$

PROOF. First, note that the influence of ith coordinate on a function f can be written as $\text{Inf}_i(f) =$

$$\begin{aligned} \mathbf{E}_{x_{-i}}[\text{Var}_{x_i}[f(x)]] &= \mathbf{E}_x\left[\left(\frac{|f(x^{\oplus i}) - f(x)|}{2}\right)^2\right] \\ &= \mathbf{E}_{x_{-i}}\left[|\mathbf{E}_{x_i}[x_i f(x)]|^2\right] \quad (7) \end{aligned}$$

As f is independent of x_i and g is independent of x_j, we can write,

$$\begin{aligned} \mathbf{E}_x[x_i x_j f(x) g(x)] &= \mathbf{E}_{x_{-\{i,j\}}} \mathbf{E}_{x_i, x_j}[x_i x_j f(x) g(x)] \\ &= \mathbf{E}_{x_{-\{i,j\}}}\left[\mathbf{E}_{x_i}[x_i g(x)]\, \mathbf{E}_{x_j}[x_j f(x)]\right] \\ &\leq \mathbf{E}_{x_{-\{i,j\}}}\left[\frac{1}{2}|\mathbf{E}_{x_i}[x_i g(x)]|^2 + \frac{1}{2}|\mathbf{E}_{x_j}[x_j f(x)]|^2\right] \\ &\leq \frac{\text{Inf}_j(f) + \text{Inf}_i(g)}{2}. \end{aligned}$$

where the first inequality uses $ab \leq \frac{1}{2}(a^2+b^2)$ and the second uses Equation 7. □

Theorem 1.2 is shown using an inductive argument over the degree d. Central to this inductive argument is the following lemma relating the influences of a degree-d PTF $\text{sign}(p(x))$ to the degree-$(d-1)$ PTFs obtained by taking formal derivatives of p.

LEMMA 5.2. *For a PTF $f = \text{sign}(p(x))$ on n variables and $i \in [n]$, $\text{Inf}_i(f) = \mathbf{E}[f(x) x_i \text{sign}(D_i p(x))]$.*

The following simple claim will be useful in the proof of the above lemma.

CLAIM 5.3. *For two real numbers a, b, if $\text{sign}(a) \neq \text{sign}(b)$ then $\text{sign}(\text{sign}(a) - \text{sign}(b)) = \text{sign}(a - b)$.*

PROOF OF LEMMA 5.2. The influence of the ith coordinate is given by,

$$\begin{aligned} \text{Inf}_i(f) &= \mathbf{E}\left[\frac{1}{2}|f(x) - f(x^{\oplus i})|\right] \\ &= \mathbf{E}\left[\frac{1}{2}\left(f(x) - f(x^{\oplus i})\right)\text{sign}\left(f(x) - f(x^{\oplus i})\right)\right] \quad (8) \end{aligned}$$

Consider an x for which $f(x) \neq f(x^{\oplus i})$. In this case, we can use Claim 5.3 to conclude:

$$\begin{aligned} \text{sign}\left(f(x) - f(x^{\oplus i})\right) &= \text{sign}\left(p(x) - p(x^{\oplus i})\right) \\ &= \text{sign}(2x_i D_i p(x)) = x_i \text{sign}(D_i p(x)), \end{aligned}$$

using (6). Hence for an x with $f(x) \neq f(x^{\oplus i})$,

$$\begin{aligned} &\left(f(x) - f(x^{\oplus i})\right)\text{sign}\left(f(x) - f(x^{\oplus i})\right) \\ = &\left(f(x) - f(x^{\oplus i})\right) x_i \text{sign}(D_i p(x)). \end{aligned}$$

On the other hand, if $f(x) = f(x^{\oplus i})$ then the above equation continues holds since both the sides evaluate to 0. Substituting this equality into Equation 8 yields,

$$\begin{aligned} \text{Inf}_i(f) &= \frac{1}{2}\mathbf{E}[f(x) x_i \text{sign}(D_i p(x))] \\ &- \frac{1}{2}\mathbf{E}\left[f(x^{\oplus i}) x_i \text{sign}(D_i p(x))\right]. \end{aligned}$$

Notice that the ith coordinate $(x^{\oplus i})_i$ of $x^{\oplus i}$ is given by $-x_i$. Since $D_i p$ is independent of the ith coordinate x_i, we have $D_i p(x) = D_i p(x^{\oplus i})$. Rewriting the above equation, we get

$$\begin{aligned} \text{Inf}_i(f) &= \frac{1}{2}\mathbf{E}[f(x) x_i \text{sign}(D_i p(x))] \\ &+ \frac{1}{2}\mathbf{E}\left[f(x^{\oplus i})(x^{\oplus i})_i \text{sign}(D_i p(x^{\oplus i}))\right] \\ &= \mathbf{E}[f(x) x_i \text{sign}(D_i p(x))] \end{aligned}$$

□

THEOREM 5.4. *Let $\text{AS}(n, d)$ denote the max possible average sensitivity of any degree-d PTF on n variables. Then we have*

$$\text{AS}(n, d) \leq \sqrt{n + n \cdot \text{AS}(n, d-1)}.$$

PROOF.

$$\begin{aligned} \text{Inf}(f) &= \sum_i \text{Inf}_i(f) \\ &= \sum_i \mathbf{E}[f(x) x_i \text{sign}(D_i p(x))] \qquad \text{(by Lemma 5.2)} \\ &= \mathbf{E}[f(x) \sum_i x_i \text{sign}(D_i p(x))] \\ &\leq \sqrt{\mathbf{E}[f(x)^2]} \cdot \sqrt{\mathbf{E}[(\sum_i x_i \text{sign}(D_i p(x)))^2]} \qquad (9) \\ &= 1 \cdot \sqrt{\mathbf{E}[\sum_{i,j} x_i x_j \text{sign}(D_i p(x)) \text{sign}(D_j p(x))]} \qquad (10) \\ &\leq \sqrt{\mathbf{E}[\sum_i x_i^2 \text{sign}(D_i p(x))^2] + \sum_{i \neq j} \text{Inf}_i(\text{sign}(D_j p(x)))} \\ &= \sqrt{n + \sum_{i \neq j} \text{Inf}_i(\text{sign}(D_j p(x)))}. \end{aligned}$$

Here (9) is the Cauchy-Schwarz inequality, (10) is expanding the square. The last inequality uses Lemma 5.1 which we may apply since $D_i p(x)$ does not depend on x_i.

Observe that for any fixed j', we have $D_{j'} p(x)$ is a degree-$(d-1)$ polynomial and $\text{sign}(D_{j'} p(x))$ is a degree-$(d-1)$ PTF. Hence, by definition we have,

$$\sum_{i \neq j'} \text{Inf}(\text{sign}(D_{j'} p(x))) \leq \text{AS}(n, d-1),$$

for all $j' \in [n]$. Therefore the quantity $\sum_{i \neq j} \text{Inf}(\text{sign}(D_j p(x))) \leq n \cdot \text{AS}(n, d-1)$, finishing the proof. □

The bound on average sensitivity (Theorem 1.2) follows immediately from the above recursive relation.

PROOF OF THEOREM 1.2. Clearly, we have $\text{AS}(n, 0) = 0$. For $d = 1$, Theorem 5.4 yields $\text{AS}(n, 1) \leq \sqrt{n}$. Now suppose $\text{AS}(n, d) = 2n^{1-1/2^d}$ for $d \geq 1$, then by Theorem 5.4,

$$\text{AS}(n, d+1) \leq \sqrt{n + n \cdot \text{AS}(n, d)} \leq \sqrt{4n^{2-1/2^d}} = 2n^{1-1/2^{d+1}},$$

finishing the proof. □

6. BOOLEAN AVERAGE SENSITIVITY VS NOISE SENSITIVITY

Our results on Boolean noise sensitivity are obtained via the following simple reduction which translates any upper bound on average sensitivity for degree-d PTFs over Boolean variables into a corresponding upper bound on noise sensitivity. This theorem is inspired by the proof of noise sensitivity of halfspaces by Peres [35].

THEOREM 6.1. *Let* $\mathrm{NS}(\epsilon, d)$ *denote the maximum noise sensitivity of a degree d-PTF at a noise rate of* ϵ. *For all* $0 \leq \epsilon \leq 1$ *if* $m = \lfloor \frac{1}{\epsilon} \rfloor$ *then* $\mathrm{NS}(\epsilon, d) \leq \frac{1}{m}\mathrm{AS}(m, d)$.

Theorem 1.3 follows immediately from this reduction along with our bounds on Boolean average sensitivity (Theorems 1.1 and 1.2), so it remains for us to prove Theorem 6.1.

6.1 Proof of Theorem 6.1

Let $f(x) = \mathrm{sign}(p(x))$ be a degee d-PTF. Let us denote $\delta = \frac{1}{m}$. As $\delta \geq \epsilon$, by the monotonicity of noise sensitivity we have $\mathrm{NS}_\epsilon(f) \leq \mathrm{NS}_\delta(f)$. In the following, we will show that $\mathrm{NS}_\delta(f) \leq \frac{1}{m}\mathrm{AS}(m, d)$ which implies the intended result. Recall that $\mathrm{NS}_\delta(f)$ is defined as

$$\mathrm{NS}_\delta(f) = \mathbf{Pr}_{x \sim_\delta y}[f(x) \neq f(y)],$$

where $x \sim_\delta y$ denotes that y is generated by flipping each bit of x independently with probability δ. An alternate way to generate y from x is as follows:

- Sample $r \in \{1, \ldots, m\}$ uniformly at random.
- Partition the bits of x into $m = \frac{1}{\delta}$ sets $S_1, S_2, \ldots, S_m$ by independently assigning each bit to a uniformly random set. Formally, a partition α is specified by a function $\alpha : \{1, \ldots, n\} \to \{1, \ldots, m\}$ mapping bit locations to their partition numbers, i.e., $i \in S_{\alpha(i)}$. A uniformly random partition is picked by sampling $\alpha(i)$ for each $i \in \{1, \ldots, n\}$ uniformly at random from $\{1, \ldots, m\}$.
- Flip the bits of x contained in the set S_r to obtain y.

Each bit of x belongs to the set S_r independently with probability $\frac{1}{m} = \delta$. Therefore, the vector y generated by the above procedure can equivalently be generated by flipping each bit of x with probability δ.

Inspired by the above procedure, we now define an alternate equivalent procedure to generate the pair $x \sim_\delta y$.

- Sample $a \in \{-1, 1\}^n$ uniformly at random.
- Sample a uniformly random partition $\alpha : \{1, \ldots, n\} \to \{1, \ldots, m\}$ of the bits of a.
- Sample $z \in \{-1, 1\}^m$ uniformly at random.
- Sample $r \in \{1, \ldots, m\}$ uniformly at random. Let $\tilde{z} = z^{\oplus r}$ and let $x_i = a_i z_{\alpha(i)}$, $y_i = a_i \tilde{z}_{\alpha(i)}$

Notice that x is uniformly distributed in $\{-1, 1\}^n$, since both a and z are uniformly distributed in $\{-1, 1\}^n$ and $\{-1, 1\}^m$ respectively. Furthermore, $\tilde{z}_i = z_i$ for all $i \neq r$ and $\tilde{z}_r = -z_r$. Therefore, y is obtained by flipping the bits of x in the coordinates belonging to the rth partition. As the partition α is generated uniformly at random, this amounts to flipping each bit of x with probability exactly $\frac{1}{m} = \delta$.

The noise sensitivity of f can be rewritten as,

$$\mathrm{NS}_\delta(f) = \mathbf{Pr}_{a,\alpha,z,r}[f(x) \neq f(y)]$$

For a fixed choice of a and α, $f(x)$ is a function of z. In this light, let us define the function $f_{a,\alpha} : \{-1, 1\}^m \to \{-1, 1\}$ for each a, α as $f_{a,\alpha}(z) = f(x)$. Returning to the expression for noise sensitivity we get:

$$\begin{aligned}
\mathrm{NS}_\delta(f) &= \mathbf{Pr}_{a,\alpha,z,r}[f_{a,\alpha}(z) \neq f_{a,\alpha}(\tilde{z})] \\
&= \mathbf{E}_{a,\alpha,z,r}\left[\mathbf{1}[f_{a,\alpha}(z) \neq f_{a,\alpha}(z^{\oplus r})]\right] \\
&= \mathbf{E}_{a,\alpha,z}\left[\frac{1}{m}\sum_{r=1}^{m} \mathbf{1}\left[f_{a,\alpha}(z) \neq f_{a,\alpha}(z^{\oplus r})\right]\right] \\
&= \mathbf{E}_{a,\alpha}\left[\frac{1}{m}\sum_{r=1}^{m} \mathbf{E}_z\left[\mathbf{1}\left[f_{a,\alpha}(z) \neq f_{a,\alpha}(z^{\oplus r})\right]\right]\right].
\end{aligned}$$

In the above calculation, the notation $\mathbf{1}[E]$ refers to the indicator function of the event E. Recall that, by definition of influences,

$$\mathrm{Inf}_r(f_{a,\alpha}) = \mathbf{E}_z\left[\mathbf{1}\left[f_{a,\alpha}(z) \neq f_{a,\alpha}(z^{\oplus r})\right]\right],$$

for all r. Thus, we can rewrite the noise sensitivity of f as

$$\mathrm{NS}_\delta(f) = \mathbf{E}_{a,\alpha}\left[\frac{1}{m}\sum_{r=1}^{m} \mathrm{Inf}_r(f_{a,\alpha})\right] = \frac{1}{m}\mathbf{E}_{a,\alpha}[\mathrm{Inf}(f_{a,\alpha})]. \tag{11}$$

We claim that $f_{a,\alpha}$ is a degree d-PTF in m variables. To see this observe that

$$f_{a,\alpha}(z) = \mathrm{sign}(p(x_1, \ldots, x_n)) = \mathrm{sign}\left(p(a_1 z_{\alpha(1)}, \ldots, a_n z_{\alpha(n)})\right),$$

which for a fixed choice of a, α is a degree d-PTF in z. Consequently, by definition of $\mathrm{AS}(m, d)$ we have $\mathrm{Inf}(f_{a,\alpha}) \leq \mathrm{AS}(m, d)$ for all a and α. Using this in (11), the result follows.

7. ACKNOWLEDGMENT

Ilias Diakonikolas is supported by NSF grant CCF-0728736, and by an Alexander S. Onassis Foundation Fellowship. Part of this work was done while visiting IBM Almaden. Prahladh Harsha is supported by THECB ARP grant 003658-0161-2007. Research done while the author was at the University of Texas at Austin. Adam Klivans is supported by NSF grants CCF-0643829, CCF-0728536 and THECB ARP grant 003658-0161-2007. Raghu Meka is partially supported by NSF grants CCF-0634811 and CCF-0916160 and THECB ARP grant 003658-0113-2007. Prasad Raghavendra is supported by NSF CCF-0343672. Part of this research was done while at the University of Washington and visiting Carnegie Mellon University. Rocco A. Servedio is supported by NSF grants CCF-0347282, CCF-0523664 and CNS-0716245, and by DARPA award HR0011-08-1-0069. Li-Yang Tan is supported by DARPA award no. HR0011-08-1-0069 and NSF Cybertrust grant no. CNS-0716245.

8. REFERENCES

[1] P. Austrin and J. Håstad. Randomly supported independence and resistance. In *Proc. 41st Annual ACM Symposium on Theory of Computing (STOC)*, pages 483–492. ACM, 2009.

[2] I. Benjamini, G. Kalai, and O. Schramm. Noise sensitivity of Boolean functions and applications to percolation. *Inst. Hautes Études Sci. Publ. Math.*, 90:5–43, 1999.

[3] E. Blais, R. O'Donnell, and K. Wimmer. Polynomial regression under arbitrary product distributions. In *Proc. 21st Annual Conference on Learning Theory (COLT)*, pages 193–204, 2008.

[4] V. Bogachev. *Gaussian measures.* Mathematical surveys and monographs, vol. 62, 1998.

[5] J. Bourgain and G. Kalai. Influences of variables and threshold intervals under group symmetries. *GAFA*, 7:438–461, 1997.

[6] N. Bshouty and C. Tamon. On the Fourier spectrum of monotone functions. *Journal of the ACM*, 43(4):747–770, 1996.

[7] A. Carbery and J. Wright. Distributional and L^q norm inequalities for polynomials over convex bodies in R^n. *Mathematical Research Letters*, 8(3):233–248, 2001.

[8] I. Diakonikolas, P. Raghavendra, R. Servedio, and L.-Y. Tan. Average sensitivity and noise sensitivity of polynomial threshold functions, 2009. Available at http://arxiv.org/abs/0909.5011.

[9] I. Diakonikolas and R. Servedio. Improved approximation of linear threshold functions. In *Proc. 24th Annual IEEE Conference on Computational Complexity (CCC)*, pages 161–172, 2009.

[10] I. Diakonikolas, R. Servedio, L.-Y. Tan, and A. Wan. A regularity lemma, and low-weight approximators, for low-degree polynomial threshold functions. manuscript, 2009.

[11] I. Diakoniokolas, P. Gopalan, R. Jaiswal, R. Servedio, and E. Viola. Bounded independence fools halfspaces. In *Proc. 50th IEEE Symposium on Foundations of Computer Science (FOCS)*, pages 171–180, 2009.

[12] I. Dinur, E. Friedgut, G. Kindler, and R. O'Donnell. On the Fourier tails of bounded functions over the discrete cube. In *Proc. 38th ACM Symp. on Theory of Computing*, pages 437–446, 2006.

[13] W. Feller. *An introduction to probability theory and its applications.* John Wiley & Sons, 1968.

[14] E. Friedgut. Boolean functions with low average sensitivity depend on few coordinates. *Combinatorica*, 18(1):474–483, 1998.

[15] P. Gopalan, A. Kalai, and A. Klivans. Agnostically learning decision trees. In *Proc. 40th Annual ACM Symposium on Theory of Computing (STOC)*, pages 527–536, 2008.

[16] P. Gopalan and R. Servedio. Learning threshold-of-AC^0 circuits. Manuscript, 2009.

[17] C. Gotsman and N. Linial. Spectral properties of threshold functions. *Combinatorica*, 14(1):35–50, 1994.

[18] P. Harsha, A. Klivans, and R. Meka. Bounding the sensitivity of polynomial threshold functions. Available at http://arxiv.org/abs/0909.5175, 2009.

[19] J. Jackson, A. Klivans, and R. Servedio. Learnability beyond AC^0. In *Proc. 34th Annual ACM Symposium on Theory of Computing (STOC)*, pages 776–784, 2002.

[20] S. Janson. *Gaussian Hilbert Spaces.* Cambridge University Press, Cambridge, UK, 1997.

[21] J. Kahn, G. Kalai, and N. Linial. The influence of variables on boolean functions. In *Proc. 29th Annual Symposium on Foundations of Computer Science (FOCS)*, pages 68–80, 1988.

[22] A. Kalai, A. Klivans, Y. Mansour, and R. Servedio. Agnostically learning halfspaces. *SIAM Journal on Computing*, 37(6):1777–1805, 2008.

[23] A. Kalai, Y. Mansour, and E. Verbin. On agnostic boosting and parity learning. In *Proc. 40th Annual ACM Symposium on Theory of Computing (STOC)*, pages 629–638, 2008.

[24] D. Kane. The Gaussian surface area and noise sensitivity of degree-d polynomial threshold functions. CCC 2010, to appear, 2010.

[25] A. Klivans, R. O'Donnell, and R. Servedio. Learning intersections and thresholds of halfspaces. *Journal of Computer & System Sciences*, 68(4):808–840, 2004.

[26] A. Klivans, R. O'Donnell, and R. Servedio. Learning geometric concepts via Gaussian surface area. In *Proc. 49th IEEE Symposium on Foundations of Computer Science (FOCS)*, pages 541–550, 2008.

[27] N. Linial, Y. Mansour, and N. Nisan. Constant depth circuits, Fourier transform and learnability. *Journal of the ACM*, 40(3):607–620, 1993.

[28] E. Mossel. Lecture 4. Available at http://www.stat.berkeley.edu/˜mossel/teach/206af05/scribes/sep8.pdf, 2005.

[29] E. Mossel and R. O'Donnell. On the noise sensitivity of monotone functions. *Random Structures and Algorithms*, 23(3):333–350, 2003.

[30] E. Mossel, R. O'Donnell, and K. Oleszkiewicz. Noise stability of functions with low influences: invariance and optimality. In *Proc. 46th Symposium on Foundations of Computer Science (FOCS)*, pages 21–30, 2005.

[31] R. O'Donnell. Lecture 16: The hypercontractivity theorem. Available at http://www.cs.cmu.edu/˜odonnell/boolean-analysis/lecture16.pdf, 2007.

[32] R. O'Donnell, M. Saks, O. Schramm, and R. Servedio. Every decision tree has an influential variable. In *Proc. 46th Symposium on Foundations of Computer Science (FOCS)*, pages 31–39, 2005.

[33] R. O'Donnell and R. Servedio. Learning monotone decision trees in polynomial time. *SIAM J. Comput.*, 37(3):827–844, 2007.

[34] R. O'Donnell and R. Servedio. The Chow Parameters Problem. In *Proc. 40th Annual ACM Symposium on Theory of Computing (STOC)*, pages 517–526, 2008.

[35] Y. Peres. Noise stability of weighted majority, 2004.

[36] O. Schramm and J. Steif. Quantitative noise sensitivity and exceptional times for percolation. Ann. Math., to appear.

[37] R. Servedio. Every linear threshold function has a low-weight approximator. *Computational Complexity*, 16(2):180–209, 2007.

[38] Y. Shi. Lower bounds of quantum black-box complexity and degree of approximating polynomials by influence of boolean variables. *Inform. Process. Lett.*, 75(1-2):79–83, 2000.

[39] S. S. Shwartz, O. Shamir, and K. Sridharan. Agnostically learning halfspaces with margin errors. TTI Technical Report, 2009.

An Invariance Principle For Polytopes

[Extended Abstract] *

Prahladh Harsha†
TIFR, Mumbai
prahladh@tifr.res.in

Adam Klivans‡
UT Austin
klivans@cs.utexas.edu

Raghu Meka§
UT Austin
raghu@cs.utexas.edu

ABSTRACT

Let X be randomly chosen from $\{-1,1\}^n$, and let Y be randomly chosen from the standard spherical Gaussian on $\mathbb{R}^n$. For any (possibly unbounded) polytope P formed by the intersection of k halfspaces, we prove that

$$|\Pr[X \in P] - \Pr[Y \in P]| \leq \log^{8/5} k \cdot \Delta,$$

where Δ is a parameter that is small for polytopes formed by the intersection of "regular" halfspaces (i.e., halfspaces with low influence). The novelty of our invariance principle is the polylogarithmic dependence on k. Previously, only bounds that were at least linear in k were known.

We give two important applications of our main result:

- A bound of $\log^{O(1)} k \cdot \varepsilon^{1/6}$ on the Boolean noise sensitivity of intersections of k "regular" halfspaces (previous work gave bounds linear in k). This gives a corresponding agnostic learning algorithm for intersections of regular halfspaces.
- A pseudorandom generator (PRG) with seed length $O(\log n \operatorname{poly}(\log k, 1/\delta))$ that δ-fools *all* polytopes with k faces with respect to the Gaussian distribution.

We also obtain PRGs with similar parameters that fool polytopes formed by intersection of regular halfspaces over the hypercube. Using our PRG constructions, we obtain the first deterministic quasi-polynomial time algorithms for approximately counting the number of solutions to a broad class of integer programs, including dense covering problems and contingency tables.

*A full version of this paper is available at (`http://eccc.uni-trier.de/report/2009/144/`).

†Research done while the author was at UT Austin and was supported by THECB ARP Grant 003658-0161-2007

‡Supported by NSF grants CCF-0643829 and CCF-0728536 and THECB ARP Grant 003658-0161-2007.

§Partially supported by NSF Grants CCF-0634811 and CCF-0916160 and THECB ARP Grant 003658-0113-2007

STOC'10, June 5–8, 2010, Cambridge, Massachusetts, USA.

Categories and Subject Descriptors

G.3 [**Probability and Statistics**]: Random number generation

General Terms

Algorithms, Theory

Keywords

agnostic learning, average sensitivity, contingency tables, halfspaces, intersections, invariance principles, limit theorems, noise sensitivity, polytopes, pseudorandom generators

1. INTRODUCTION

An important theme in theoretical computer science over the last two decades has been the usefulness of translating a combinatorial problem over a discrete domain (e.g., $\{-1,1\}^n$) to a problem in continuous space. The notion of convex relaxation, for example, is now a standard technique in the design of algorithms for optimization problems. More recently, the study of analytic properties of Boolean functions (e.g., Fourier spectra and sensitivity) has been a fundamental tool for proving results in hardness of approximation [O'D08] and learning theory [Man94].

The work of Mossel, O'Donnell, and Oleszkiewicz [MOO05] proving the "Majority Is Stablest" conjecture has led to a rich collection of hardness results for constraint satisfaction problems, most notably for the Max-Cut problem. The crux of their work is an invariance principle relating the behavior of low-degree polynomials over the uniform distribution on $\{-1,1\}^n$ to their behavior with respect to Gaussians:

THEOREM 1.1 (INVARIANCE PRINCIPLE [MOO05]). *Let P be a multilinear polynomial such that $\|P\| = 1$. Then, for any $t \in \mathbb{R}$,*

$$\left| \Pr_{x \in_u \{-1,1\}^n}[P(x) > t] - \Pr_{x \leftarrow \mathcal{N}^n}[P(x) > t] \right| \leq \tau.$$

Here $\mathcal{N}^n$ is the standard multivariate spherical Gaussian distribution on $\mathbb{R}^n$; the parameter τ depends on the coefficients of P and is small if P is "regular" in the sense that the "influence" of each variable in P is small.

Roughly speaking, the above invariance principle says that the cumulative distribution function (cdf) of a polynomial over $\{-1,1\}^n$ is close to the cdf of a polynomial over $\mathcal{N}^n$ if the coefficients of the polynomial are sufficiently regular.

Although developed in the context of hardness of approximation, their invariance principle has also found applications in the theory of social choice [O'D08] and more recently to the construction of pseudorandom generators for polynomial threshold functions [MZ10].

The main result of this paper is an invariance principle for characteristic functions of polytopes. Recall that a polytope $\mathcal{K}$ is a (possibly unbounded) convex set in $\mathbb{R}^n$ formed by the intersection of some finite number of supporting halfspaces. We refer to $\mathcal{K}$ as a k-polytope if it is equal to the intersection of k halfspaces. Our main theorem is as follows (see Theorem 3.1 for exact statement):

THEOREM 1.2 (INVARIANCE PRINCIPLE FOR POLYTOPES). *Let $\mathcal{K}$ be a k-polytope. Then,*

$$\left| \Pr_{x \in_u \{-1,1\}^n} [x \in \mathcal{K}] - \Pr_{x \leftarrow \mathcal{N}^n} [x \in \mathcal{K}] \right| \leq \log^{8/5} k \cdot \Delta.$$

The parameter Δ depends on the coefficients of the bounding hyperplanes of $\mathcal{K}$ and is small if these coefficients are sufficiently regular. In particular, if $\mathcal{K}$ equals $\{x \mid W^T x \leq \theta\}$ for $W \in R^{n \times k}$ and $\theta \in R^k$, and each column u of W is ε-regular, i.e., satisfies $\sum_{i=1}^n u_i^4 \leq \varepsilon^2 \|u\|_2^2$, then Δ is less than $\varepsilon^{1/6}$. Note that there is no restriction on the vector θ and that some assumption on the "regularity" of hyperplanes bounding $\mathcal{K}$ is necessary even for the case $k = 1$ (eg., $\mathcal{K} = \{x : x_1 \leq 1\}$). Our invariance principle also holds more generally for any product distribution that is hypercontractive and whose first four moments are appropriately bounded.

The novelty of our theorem is the dependence of the error on k. Applying a recent result due to Mossel [Mos08], it is possible to obtain a statement similar to Theorem 1.2 with an error term that has a polynomial dependence on k. Achieving polylogarithmic dependence on k, however, is much harder, and we need to use some nontrivial results from the analysis of convex sets in Gaussian space.

The case $k = 1$, a single halfspace, is equivalent to the classical Berry-Esséen theorem [Fel71], a fundamental theorem from probability and statistics giving a quantitative version of the Central Limit Theorem. We can therefore view our principle as a generalization of the Berry-Esséen theorem for polytopes. Further, understanding the structure of integer points in polytopes (that is, solutions to integer programs) is an important topic in computer science [BV08], optimization [Zie95], and combinatorics [BR07], and we believe our invariance principle will find many applications.

In this paper, we use our invariance principle to derive new results in learning theory and derandomization.

1.1 Results on Noise Sensitivity of Intersections of Halfspaces

Noise sensitivity of Boolean functions introduced in the seminal works of [KKL88], [BKS99] is an important notion in the *analysis* of Boolean functions. Roughly speaking, the noise sensitivity of a Boolean function f measures the probability over a randomly chosen input x that f changes sign if each bit of x is flipped independently with probability δ.

Bounds on the noise sensitivity of Boolean functions have direct applications in hardness of approximation [Hås01], [KKMO07], hardness amplification [O'D04], circuit complexity [LMN93], the theory of social choice [Kal05], and quantum complexity [Shi00]. Here, we focus on applications in learning theory, where it is known that bounds on the noise sensitivity of a class of Boolean functions yield learning algorithms that succeed in harsh noise models such as the agnostic model of learning [KKMS08].

A direct application of our invariance principle Theorem 1.2 gives the following new bound on the noise sensitivity of intersections of regular halfspaces:

THEOREM 1.3 (NOISE SENSITIVITY APPLICATION). *Let f be the Boolean function defined by the intersection of k, ε-regular halfspaces. Then the noise sensitivity of f for noise rate ε is at most $(\log k)^{O(1)} \cdot \varepsilon^{1/6}$.*

Applying a result of Kalai et al. [KKMS08] and Klivans et al. [KOS04], the above theorem implies that intersections of k, ε-regular halfspaces are agnostically learnable with respect to the uniform distribution on $\{-1,1\}^n$ in time $n^{(\log^{O(1)} k)}$ for any constant error parameter. In particular, intersections of $\{-1,1\}$ halfspaces (oriented majorities) are ε-regular and fall into this class. The previous best algorithm for learning this concept class, even in the easier PAC model, ran in time $n^{O(k^2)}$ ([KOS04, KKMS08]).

The current best bound for the noise sensitivity of intersection of k arbitrary halfspaces is $O(k\sqrt{\varepsilon})$. This bound is obtained by starting with the $\sqrt{\varepsilon}$ noise sensitivity bound for a single halfspace due to Peres [Per04] and applying a union bound over k halfspaces. On the other hand, optimal bounds of $\Theta(\sqrt{\log k}\sqrt{\varepsilon})$ for the related Gaussian noise sensitivity were obtained recently by Klivans et al. [KOS08]. We believe that the right order for Boolean noise sensitivity of intersection of k halfspaces is $\Theta(\sqrt{\log k}\sqrt{\varepsilon})$ as well.

Improving the bounds for Boolean noise sensitivity would be of considerable interest, particularly for the learning theory applications, as learning the class of intersections of halfspaces even with respect to specific distributions such as the uniform distribution over $\{1,-1\}^n$ is an important open problem in learning theory. We feel that our result is an important step towards improving noise sensitivity bounds for intersections of arbitrary (not necessarily regular) halfspaces.

1.2 Results on Pseudorandom Generators for Polytopes

Our invariance principle also yields new results for several problems in derandomization. Recall the following definition of pseudorandom generators (PRGs):

DEFINITION 1.4. *Let μ be a distribution over $\mathbb{R}$. A function $G : \{0,1\}^r \to \{1,-1\}^n$ is said to δ-fool a polytope $\mathcal{K}$ with respect to μ if the following holds.*

$$\left| \Pr_{y \in_u \{0,1\}^r} [G(y) \in \mathcal{K}] - \Pr_{X \leftarrow \mu^n} [X \in \mathcal{K}] \right| \leq \delta.$$

Combining our invariance principle with a PRG similar to a recent construction of Meka and Zuckerman [MZ10], we obtain a black-box algorithm for approximately counting the number of $\{-1,1\}^n$ points in polytopes formed by the intersection of regular halfspaces:

THEOREM 1.5 (PRGS FOR REGULAR POLYTOPES). *For all $\delta \in (0,1)$, there exists an explicit PRG $G : \{0,1\}^r \to \{1,-1\}^n$ with $r = O((\log n \log k)/\varepsilon)$ that δ-fools all polytopes formed by the intersection of k ε-regular halfspaces with respect to all proper and hypercontractive distributions μ for $\varepsilon = \delta^5/(\log^{8.1} k)(\log(1/\delta))$.*

The constants above depend on the hypercontractivity constants of μ. We define proper and hypercontractive distributions in the next section and remark that the uniform distribution over $\{-1,1\}^n$ is an example of such a distribution.

Theorem 1.5 implies quasi-polynomial time, deterministic, approximate counting algorithms for a broad class of integer programs. For example, dense covering programs such as dense set-cover, and $\{0,1\}$-contingency tables correspond to polytopes formed by the intersection of ε-regular halfspaces. For these types of integer programs, we can deterministically approximate, to within an additive error ε, the number of integer solutions in quasi-polynomial time.

As stated, our invariance principle applies to polytopes whose bounding hyperplanes have coefficients that are sufficiently regular. In some cases, however, we can randomly rotate an arbitrary polytope so that all the bounding hyperplanes become regular. As such, after applying a suitable random transformation (which we derandomize), we can build PRGs for *arbitrary* polytopes if the underlying distribution is spherically symmetric (e.g., Gaussian):

THEOREM 1.6 (PRGS FOR GAUSSIAN SPACE). *For a universal constant $c > 0$ and all $\delta > c\log^2 k/n^{1/11}$, there exists an explicit PRG $G_{\mathcal{N}} : \{0,1\}^r \to \mathbb{R}^n$ with $r = O((\log n)(\log^{9.1} k)/\delta^{5.1})$ that δ-fools all k-polytopes with respect to $\mathcal{N}$.*

Additionally, we prove an invariance principle for polytopes with respect to the uniform distribution over the n-dimensional sphere S^{n-1}. This allows us to easily modify our PRG for polytopes in Gaussian space and build PRGs for intersections of spherical caps:

THEOREM 1.7 (PRGS FOR SPHERICAL CAPS). *For a universal constant $c > 0$ and all $\delta > c\log^2 k/n^{1/11}$, there exists an explicit PRG $G_{sp} : \{0,1\}^r \to S^{n-1}$ with $r = O((\log n)(\log^{9.1} k)/\delta^{5.1})$ that δ-fools all k-polytopes with respect to the uniform distribution over S^{n-1}.*

An immediate consequence of the above PRG construction is a polynomial time derandomization of the Goemans-Williamson approximation algorithm for Max-Cut [GW95] and other similar hyperplane based randomized rounding schemes. Observe that this derandomization is a *black-box* derandomization as opposed to some earlier derandomizations of the Goemans-Williamson algorithm, which are instance-specific (e.g., [MH99]).

1.3 Proof Outline

In this section, we give a high level outline of the proof of our invariance principle and contrast it with the works of Mossel et al. [MOO05] and Mossel [Mos08]. The proof proceeds in two steps.

Step One: As in Mossel et al. [MOO05] and Mossel [Mos08], we first use the Lindeberg method (see [PR89]) to prove an invariance principle for smooth functions. By this we mean proving that

$$\left|\mathop{\mathbb{E}}_X[\Psi(\ell_1(X),\ldots,\ell_k(X))] - \mathop{\mathbb{E}}_Y[\Psi(\ell_1(Y),\ldots,\ell_k(Y))]\right| \le \gamma, \tag{1.1}$$

where $X \in_u \{1,-1\}^n, Y \leftarrow \mathcal{N}^n$ and $\ell_1,\ldots,\ell_k$ are linear functions (corresponding to the normals of the faces of the k-polytope) and Ψ is a smoothing function. The value γ will depend on k, the coefficients of the ℓ_p's and the derivatives of Ψ. The function Ψ is often called a "test" function and is smooth if there is a uniform bound on its fourth derivative. Notice here that Ψ maps $\mathbb{R}^k$ to $\mathbb{R}$; in [MOO05], they were concerned with the value $\Psi(Q(X))$ for a low-degree polynomial Q and a univariate test function Ψ.

At this point, we could use the k-wise product of a test function constructed by Mossel et al. to approximate the logical AND function. Further, Mossel provides a very general framework for multivariate test functions and gives bounds for the overall error incurred by the hybrid argument. Here we run into our first difficulty: the standard hybrid argument as used by Mossel et al. and Mossel results in a bad dependence on the coefficients of the ℓ_p's. In particular, the resulting error term is not small even for polytopes formed by the intersection of regular halfspaces.

To solve this problem, we use a non-standard hybrid argument that groups the input variables into blocks. We observe that it is irrelevant in which order we replace X_i's with Y_i's – in fact a random order would suffice. Further, we can group the X_i's into blocks and proceed blockwise with the hybrid argument. To implement this intuition, we partition $[n]$ randomly into a set of blocks and replace all the X_i's within a block by the corresponding Y_i's one block at a time. Proceeding in this fashion with a random partitioning has a "smoothing effect" on the coefficients of the linear functions resulting in a much better bound on the error in terms of the coefficients.

Roughly speaking, if ℓ_{pi} denotes the i'th coefficient of ℓ_p, then the standard hybrid arguments of [PR89], [MOO05], [Mos08] incur an error proportional to $\sum_{i\in[n]}(\max_{p\in[k]}\ell_{pi}^4)$, which can be as large as $\Omega(k)$ even for regular functions ℓ_p. In contrast, our *randomized-blockwise-hybrid* argument only suffers an error of $(\log k)\cdot\max_{p\in[k]}\sum_i \ell_{pi}^4$, which is small for regular functions. It turns out that in the above analysis, we can choose the random partitioning into blocks in a $\Theta(\log k)$-wise independent manner, instead of uniformly at random, and this is crucial for our PRG constructions.

Step Two: Given the above invariance principle for smooth functions, we now aim to translate the closeness in expectation for smooth functions to closeness in cdf distance. Here the smoothness of the test function Ψ becomes important, and we run into our second problem: the natural choice of test function Ψ (the multivariate version of the test function from Mossel et al.) leads to an error bound on the order of k, rather than poly$(\log k)$. To get around this problem, we first observe that in Mossel's proof of the multivariate invariance principle as in our *randomized-blockwise-hybrid* argument, it suffices to bound the 'l_1-norm' of the fourth derivative $\sup_{x\in\mathbb{R}^k}(\sum_{p,q,r,s\in[k]}|\partial_p\partial_q\partial_r\partial_s\Psi(x)|)$, instead of uniformly bounding the fourth derivative $\sup_{x\in\mathbb{R}^k,p,q,r,s\in[k]}(|\partial_p\partial_q\partial_r\partial_s\Psi(x)|)$. Thus, it suffices to obtain a smooth approximation of the AND function for which the former quantity is small. Fortunately for us, we uncovered a beautiful result due to Bentkus [Ben90], who constructs a smooth approximation of the AND function with precisely this property.

The final difficulty for translating closeness in expectation as in Equation 1.1 to closeness in cdf distance is to prove that Ψ differs from the characteristic function only on a set of small Gaussian measure. To this end, we show that it suffices to bound the Gaussian measure of l_∞-neighborhoods around the boundary of k-polytopes. For an l_∞-neighborhood of width λ, a union bound would imply Gaussian measure on the order of $k\lambda$. At this point, however, we can apply a nontrivial result due to Nazarov [Naz03] on the Gaussian surface area of k-polytopes to get the much better bound of $\sqrt{\log k}\,\lambda$. This result of Nazarov was used before by Klivans et al. [KOS08] in the context of learning intersections of halfspaces with respect to Gaussian distributions.

We give an outline of the proofs of the applications of the invariance principle to noise sensitivity and PRGs in the corresponding sections.

1.4 Related Work

As mentioned earlier, the classical Berry-Esséen theorem [Fel71] from probability, a quantitative version of the Central Limit Theorem, gives an invariance principle for the case of a single halfspace (i.e., $k = 1$). More precisely, for any $w \in \mathbb{R}^n$, such that $\|w\| = 1$ and each coefficient of w is at most ε, the Berry-Esséen theorem states that

$$\left| \Pr_{x\in\{-1,1\}^n}[\langle w,x\rangle \geq t] - \Pr_{x\leftarrow\mathcal{N}^n}[\langle w,x\rangle \geq t] \right| \leq O(\varepsilon).$$

Bentkus [Ben03] proves a multidimensional Berry-Esséen theorem for sums of vector-valued random variables each with identity covariance matrix, whose error term depends on the Gaussian surface area of the test set. Although his paper deals with topics related to our work, his result seems to have no implications in our setting.

There is a long history of research on approximately counting the number of solutions to integer programs, especially with regard to contingency tables [JS97, CD03]. However, not much is known in terms of *deterministic* algorithms, and we believe that our deterministic quasi-polynomial time algorithms for dense covering problems and dense set cover instances is the first result of its kind.

Regarding contingency tables, Dyer [Dye03] gave a deterministic, relative-error approximation for counting solutions to contingency tables that runs in time exponential in the number of rows. In contrast, we obtain an algorithm that runs in quasi-polynomial time in the number of rows (however, we do not give a relative-error approximation). Although not stated explicitly before, it is easy to see that the pseudorandom generator for small space machines of Impagliazzo et al. [INW94] yields a deterministic algorithm for counting $n \times k$ contingency tables with additive error at most ε and run time $\exp(O(\log^2(nk/\varepsilon)))$. This is incomparable to our algorithm for contingency tables which has run time $\exp((\log n)\cdot \mathrm{poly}(\log k, 1/\varepsilon))$. In our case, we obtain a polynomial-time, black-box derandomization for contingency tables with a constant number of rows (for $\varepsilon = O(1)$).

For PRGs for intersections of halfspaces, recently Gopalan et al. [GOWZ10] and Diakonikolas et al. [DKN09] gave results incomparable to ours. Gopalan et al. give generators for arbitrary intersections of k halfspaces with seed length linear in k but logarithmic in $1/\delta$. Diakonikolas et al. show that bounded independence fools intersections of quadratic threshold functions and in particular, get generators with seed length $O((\log n)\cdot \mathrm{poly}\ (k, 1/\varepsilon))$ fooling intersections of k halfspaces. Due to the at least linear dependence on k, the results of the above works do not yield good algorithms for counting solutions to integer programs, as in this setting k is typically large (e.g., $\mathrm{poly}(n)$).

2. NOTATION AND PRELIMINARIES

We use the following notation.

1. For $W \in \mathbb{R}^{n\times k}$, $\theta \in \mathbb{R}^k$, $\mathcal{K}(W,\theta)$ denotes the polytope $\mathcal{K}(W,\theta) = \{x : W^T x \leq \theta\}$. We say a polytope $\mathcal{K}(W,\theta)$ as above has k faces.

2. Unless stated otherwise, we work with the same polytope $\mathcal{K}(W,\theta)$ and assume that the columns of the matrix W have norm one. We often shorten $\mathcal{K}(W,\theta)$ to $\mathcal{K}$ if W, θ are clear from context. We assume that $k \geq 2$.

3. For $A \in \mathbb{R}^{m_1\times m_2}$, A^T denotes the transpose of A and for $p \in [m_2]$, A^p denotes the p'th column of A.

4. The all ones vector in $\mathbb{R}^k$ is denoted by 1_k.

5. For $u \in \mathbb{R}^k$, define rectangle $\mathsf{Rect}(u) = (-\infty, u_1] \times (-\infty, u_2] \times \cdots \times (-\infty, u_k]$. Note that $x \in \mathcal{K}(W,\theta)$ if and only if $W^T x \in \mathsf{Rect}(\theta)$.

6. $\mathcal{N}^n$ (where $\mathcal{N} = \mathcal{N}(0,1)$) denotes the standard multivariate spherical Gaussian distribution over $\mathbb{R}^n$ with mean 0 and identity covariance matrix.

7. For a smooth function $\psi : \mathbb{R}^k \to \mathbb{R}$, let $\|\psi^{(4)}\|_1 = \sup\{\sum_{p,q,r,s\in[k]} |\partial_p\partial_q\partial_r\partial_s\,\psi(a_1,\ldots,a_k)| : (a_1,\ldots,a_k) \in \mathbb{R}^k\}$.

8. We denote all universal constants by c, C, even when we have in mind different constants in the same equation.

DEFINITION 2.1 (REGULARITY). *A vector $u \in \mathbb{R}^n$ is ε-regular if $\sum_i u_i^4 \leq \varepsilon^2\|u\|^4$. A matrix $W \in \mathbb{R}^{n\times k}$ is ε-regular if every column of W is ε-regular. A polytope $\mathcal{K} = \mathcal{K}(W,\theta)$ is ε-regular if W is ε-regular* [1].

The main results of this paper are applicable to a large class of product distributions that satisfy the following two properties.

DEFINITION 2.2 (PROPER DISTRIBUTIONS). *A distribution μ over $\mathbb{R}$ is proper if for $X \leftarrow \mu$, $\mathbb{E}[X] = 0$, $\mathbb{E}[X^2] = 1$ and $\mathbb{E}[X^3] = 0$.*

DEFINITION 2.3 (HYPERCONTRACTIVE DISTRIBUTIONS). *A distribution μ over $\mathbb{R}$ is hypercontractive, if there exists a constant c such that the following holds. For any m, vector $u \in \mathbb{R}^m$, and any $q \geq 2$,*

$$\left(\mathop{\mathbb{E}}_{X\leftarrow\mu^m}[\,|\langle u,X\rangle|^q\,]\right)^{1/q} \leq c\sqrt{q}\left(\mathop{\mathbb{E}}_{X\leftarrow\mu^m}[\,|\langle u,X\rangle|^2\,]\right)^{1/2}.$$

Two important examples of distributions that are proper and hypercontractive are the uniform distribution over the hypercube $\{1,-1\}^n$ and the multivariate spherical Gaussian $\mathcal{N}^n$.

We also use the following hypercontractivity inequality for degree d multilinear polynomials over the hypercube (see [O'D08]).

[1] "Regular polytopes" have a different meaning in combinatorics, but for the purpose of this paper, we will abuse notation and say a polytope is ε-regular if it is formed by the intersection of ε-regular halfspaces as in Definition 2.1.

LEMMA 2.4 ((2, q)-HYPERCONTRACTIVITY). *For any $q \geq 2$ and any degree d multilinear polynomial $P : \{1,-1\}^n \to \mathbb{R}$, $X \in_u \{1,-1\}^n$,*

$$\left(\mathbb{E}\left[\,|P(X)|^q\,\right]\right)^{1/q} \leq q^{d/2} \left(\mathbb{E}\left[\,|P(X)|^2\,\right]\right)^{1/2}.$$

3. INVARIANCE PRINCIPLE FOR POLYTOPES

Our main invariance principle for polytopes $\mathcal{K}(W,t)$ is as follows:

THEOREM 3.1 (INVARIANCE PRINCIPLE FOR POLYTOPES). *For any proper and hypercontractive distribution μ over $\mathbb{R}$ there exists a constant C such that the following holds. For any ε-regular k-polytope $\mathcal{K}$, $X \leftarrow \mu^n$, $Y \leftarrow \mathcal{N}^n$,*

$$|\Pr[X \in \mathcal{K}] - \Pr[Y \in \mathcal{K}]| \leq C\,(\log^{8/5} k)\,(\varepsilon\,\log(1/\varepsilon))^{1/5}. \tag{3.1}$$

The proof of the theorem can be divided into three parts.

1. We establish an invariance principle for smooth functions on polytopes (Theorem 3.2) using an extension of Lindeberg's method; Section 4 is devoted to proving this part.
2. We prove that for random variables A, B over $\mathbb{R}^k$, closeness with respect to smooth functions and anti-concentration bounds for one of the variables imply closeness with respect to rectangles (Lemma 3.3). To do so, we use a nontrivial result of Bentkus [Ben90] on smooth approximations for the l_∞ norm.
3. We use a result of Nazarov [Naz03] on Gaussian surface area of polytopes to bound the Gaussian measure of "l_∞-neighborhoods" of polytopes in $\mathbb{R}^n$ (Lemma 3.4).

We begin by stating an invariance principle (IP) for smooth functions $\psi : \mathbb{R}^k \to \mathbb{R}$. The proof is involved, making use of the randomized-blockwise-hybrid argument alluded to in the introduction. For clarity we present the proof in the next section (Section 4).

THEOREM 3.2 (IP FOR SMOOTH FUNCTIONS). *For any proper and hypercontractive distribution μ over $\mathbb{R}$ there exists a constant C such that the following holds. For any ε-regular W and smooth function $\psi : \mathbb{R}^k \to \mathbb{R}$,*

$$\left|\mathop{\mathbb{E}}_{X \leftarrow \mu^n}[\psi(W^T X)] - \mathop{\mathbb{E}}_{Y \leftarrow \mathcal{N}^n}[\psi(W^T Y)]\right| \leq C\|\psi^{(4)}\|_1\,(\log^3 k)\,(\varepsilon\,\log(1/\varepsilon)).$$

The following lemma shows that for two random variables A, B over $\mathbb{R}^k$, closeness with respect to smooth functions and *anti-concentration bounds* for the variable B imply closeness with respect to rectangles. Note that to use the lemma we do not need anti-concentration bounds for the random variable A.

LEMMA 3.3 (SMOOTH APPROXIMATION OF AND). *Let A, B be two random variables over $\mathbb{R}^k$ satisfying the following conditions:*

- *There exists $\Delta > 0$, such that for all smooth functions $\psi : \mathbb{R}^k \to \mathbb{R}$, $|\mathbb{E}[\psi(A)] - \mathbb{E}[\psi(B)]| \leq \Delta\,\|\psi^{(4)}\|_1$.*
- *For a function $g_k : [0,1] \to [0,1]$ the following holds: for all $\lambda \in [0,1]$, $\theta \in \mathbb{R}^k$, $\Pr[B \in \mathsf{Rect}(\theta + \lambda 1_k) \setminus \mathsf{Rect}(\theta)\,] \leq g_k(\lambda)$.*

Then, for all $\theta \in \mathbb{R}^k$, $0 < \lambda < 1$, $|\Pr[A \in \mathsf{Rect}(\theta)] - \Pr[B \in \mathsf{Rect}(\theta)]| \leq C\Delta \log^3 k/\lambda^4 + C g_k(\lambda)$.

Finally, we use the following anti-concentration bound that follows from Nazarov's estimate on the Gaussian surface area of polytopes [Naz03]:

LEMMA 3.4. *For $0 < \lambda < 1$,*

$$\mathop{\Pr}_{x \leftarrow \mathcal{N}^n}\left[W^T x \in \mathsf{Rect}(\theta) \setminus \mathsf{Rect}(\theta - \lambda 1_k)\right] = O(\lambda\sqrt{\log k}).$$

We first prove Theorem 3.1 using the above three results and then prove Lemmas 3.3 and 3.4 in Sections 3.1 and 3.2. Theorem 3.2 is then proved in Section 4.

PROOF OF THEOREM 3.1. Let $X \leftarrow \mu^n$, $Y \leftarrow \mathcal{N}^n$ and let random variables $A = W^T X$, $B = W^T Y$. Then, by Lemma 3.4 and Theorem 3.2,

$$\Pr[B \in \mathsf{Rect}(\theta + \lambda 1_k) \setminus \mathsf{Rect}(\theta)] \leq C\sqrt{\log k}\,\lambda,$$

$$|\mathbb{E}[\psi(A)] - \mathbb{E}[\psi(B)]| \leq C\,(\log^3 k)\,\varepsilon\,\log(1/\varepsilon)\,\|\psi^{(4)}\|_1,$$

where $\psi : \mathbb{R}^k \to \mathbb{R}$ is any smooth function, $\theta \in \mathbb{R}^k$ and $\lambda \in (0,1)$. Therefore, by Lemma 3.3, for $\theta \in \mathbb{R}^k$,

$$|\Pr[A \in \mathsf{Rect}(\theta)] - \Pr[B \in \mathsf{Rect}(\theta)]| \leq C\,(\log^6 k)\,\log(1/\varepsilon)\varepsilon/\lambda^4 + C\sqrt{\log k}\,\lambda.$$

Setting $\lambda = O((\log^{11/10} k)\,(\varepsilon\log(1/\varepsilon))^{1/5})$ gives us the theorem. □

3.1 Smooth approximation of AND

We now prove Lemma 3.3. For this, we use the following nontrivial result of Bentkus [Ben90] on smooth approximations for the l_∞ norm.

THEOREM 3.5 (BENTKUS [BEN90]). *For every $\alpha > 0$ and $0 < \lambda < 1$, there exists a function $\psi \equiv \psi_{\alpha,\lambda} : \mathbb{R}^k \to \mathbb{R}$ such that $\|\psi^{(4)}\|_1 \leq C\log^3 k/\lambda^4$ and*

$$\psi(a) = \begin{cases} 1 & \text{if } \|a\|_\infty \leq \alpha \\ 0 & \text{if } \|a\|_\infty > \alpha + \lambda \\ \in [0,1] & \text{otherwise.} \end{cases}$$

COROLLARY 3.6. *For all $u \in \mathbb{R}^k$, $0 < \lambda < 1$, $T > \|u\|_\infty$, there exists a function $\psi \equiv \psi_{u,\lambda,T} : \mathbb{R}^k \to \mathbb{R}$ such that $\|\psi^{(4)}\|_1 \leq C\log^3 k/\lambda^4$ and*

$$\psi(a) = \begin{cases} 1 & \text{if } \forall l \in [k], -T + u_l \leq a_l \leq u_l \\ 0 & \text{if } \exists l \in [k], a_l > u_l + \lambda \\ \in [0,1] & \text{otherwise.} \end{cases}$$

PROOF. Let $\psi_{T/2,\lambda}$ be the function from Theorem 3.5 with $\alpha = T/2$. It is easy to check that $\psi_{u,\lambda,T} : \mathbb{R}^k \to \mathbb{R}$ by $\psi_{u,\lambda,T}(a) = \psi_{T/2,\lambda}(a - u + (T/2)1_k)$ satisfies the conditions of the theorem. □

PROOF OF LEMMA 3.3. Fix $\theta \in \mathbb{R}^k$, $0 < \lambda < 1$. Choose $T \in \mathbb{R}$ large enough so that $T > \|\theta\|_\infty$, $\Pr[\|A\|_\infty \geq T] < \Delta$ and $\Pr[\|B\|_\infty \geq T] < \Delta$. Let $\psi : \mathbb{R}^k \to \mathbb{R}$ be the function obtained from applying Corollary 3.6 to θ, λ, T. Then,

$$|\Pr[A \in \mathsf{Rect}(\theta)] - \Pr[A \in \mathsf{Rect}_T(\theta)]| \leq \Delta,$$
$$|\Pr[B \in \mathsf{Rect}(\theta)] - \Pr[B \in \mathsf{Rect}_T(\theta)]| \leq \Delta, \tag{3.2}$$

where $\mathsf{Rect}_T(\theta) = [-T+\theta_1, \theta_1] \times [-T+\theta_2, \theta_2] \times \cdots \times [-T+\theta_k, \theta_k] \subseteq \mathbb{R}^k$. Observe that from the definition of ψ in Corollary 3.6 and Equation 3.2

$$\Pr[A \in \mathsf{Rect}(\theta)] \leq \mathbb{E}[\psi(A)] + \Delta \leq \mathbb{E}[\psi(B)] + \Delta\|\psi^{(4)}\|_1 + \Delta.$$

Similarly, from the definition of g_k,

$$\mathbb{E}[\psi(B)] \leq \Pr[B \in \mathsf{Rect}(\theta + \lambda 1_k)] = \Pr[B \in \mathsf{Rect}(\theta)] + \Pr[B \in \mathsf{Rect}(\theta+\lambda 1_k) \setminus \mathsf{Rect}(\theta)] \leq \Pr[B \in \mathsf{Rect}(\theta)] + g_k(\lambda).$$

Combining the above two equations we get

$$\Pr[A \in \mathsf{Rect}(\theta)] \leq \Pr[B \in \mathsf{Rect}(\theta)] + 2\Delta\|\psi^{(4)}\|_1 + g_k(\lambda) \leq \Pr[B \in \mathsf{Rect}(\theta)] + \frac{C\Delta \log^3 k}{\lambda^4} + g_k(\lambda).$$

Proceeding similarly for the function $\psi_L : \mathbb{R}^k \to \mathbb{R}$ obtained by applying Corollary 3.6 to $t - \lambda 1_k, \lambda, T$, we get

$$\Pr[A \in \mathsf{Rect}(\theta)] \geq \Pr[B \in \mathsf{Rect}(\theta)] - \frac{C\Delta \log^3 k}{\lambda^4} - g_k(\lambda).$$

Therefore,

$$|\Pr[A \in \mathsf{Rect}(\theta)] - \Pr[B \in \mathsf{Rect}(\theta)]| \leq \frac{C\Delta \log^3 k}{\lambda^4} + g_k(\lambda).$$

□

3.2 Anti-concentration bound for ℓ_∞ neighborhood of rectangles

Lemma 3.4 follows straightforwardly from the following result of Nazarov [Naz03]. For a convex body $K \subseteq \mathbb{R}^n$ with boundary ∂K, let $\Gamma(K)$ denote the Gaussian surface area of K defined by

$$\Gamma(K) = \int_{y \in \partial K} e^{\frac{-\|y\|^2}{2}} d\sigma(y),$$

where $d\sigma(y)$ denotes the surface element at $y \in \partial K$.

THEOREM 3.7 (NAZAROV; SEE [KOS08]). *For a polytope $\mathcal{K}$ with at most k faces, $\Gamma(\mathcal{K}) \leq C\sqrt{\log k}$.*

PROOF OF LEMMA 3.4. Consider an increasing (under set inclusion) family of polytopes $\mathcal{K}_\rho$ for $0 \leq \rho \leq \lambda$ such that $\mathcal{K}_0 = \{x : W^T x \in \mathsf{Rect}(\theta - \lambda 1_k)\}$ and $\mathcal{K}_\lambda = \{x : W^T x \in \mathsf{Rect}(\theta)\}$. Then,

$$\Pr_{x \leftarrow \mathcal{N}^n}\left[W^T x \in \mathsf{Rect}(\theta) \setminus \mathsf{Rect}(\theta - \lambda 1_k)\right] = \int_{\rho=0}^{\lambda} \Gamma(\mathcal{K}_\rho) d\rho \leq C\sqrt{\log k}\,\lambda,$$

where the last inequality follows from Theorem 3.7 □

4. INVARIANCE PRINCIPLE FOR SMOOTH FUNCTIONS OVER POLYTOPES

We now prove Theorem 3.2. The proof of the theorem is based on Lindeberg's method. Let $t = 1/\varepsilon$ and let $\mathcal{H} = \{h : [n] \to [t]\}$ be a family of $(2\log k)$-wise independent functions. That is, for all $I \subseteq [n], |I| \leq 2\log k$ and $b \in [t]^I$, $\Pr_{h \in_u \mathcal{H}}[\forall i \in I,\ h(i) = b_i] = \frac{1}{t^{|I|}}$.

We remark that to prove Theorem 3.2 we could take the hash family to be the set of all functions. However, we work with a $(2\log k)$-wise independent family as the analysis is no more complicated and we need to work with such hash families while constructing pseudorandom generators. For $S \subseteq [n]$, let W_S be the matrix formed by the rows of W with indices in S. Define

$$\mathcal{H}(W) \stackrel{\text{def}}{=} \sum_{i=1}^{t} \left(\mathop{\mathbb{E}}_{h}\left[\sum_{p=1}^{k} \|W^p_{h^{-1}(i)}\|^{4\log k} \right] \right)^{1/\log k}.$$

Theorem 3.2 follows from the following two lemmas.

LEMMA 4.1. *For ε-regular W, $\mathcal{H}(W) = O((\log k)\varepsilon \log(1/\varepsilon))$.*

LEMMA 4.2. *For any smooth function $\psi : \mathbb{R}^k \to \mathbb{R}$,*

$$\left| \mathop{\mathbb{E}}_{X \leftarrow \mu^n}\left[\psi(W^T X)\right] - \mathop{\mathbb{E}}_{Y \leftarrow \mathcal{N}^n}\left[\psi(W^T Y)\right] \right| \leq 4\,(\log^2 k)\,\mathcal{H}(W)\|\psi^{(4)}\|_1.$$

We defer the proof of Lemma 4.1 to the full version and prove Lemma 4.2 below. The proof uses a blockwise hybrid argument and careful applications of hypercontractivity as sketched in the proof outline in the introduction. To gain some intuition of the advantage of our randomized blockwise hybrid argument over the standard Lindeberg method, it might be helpful to compare both arguments for the following two cases (for lack of space, we do not go into the details of the examples):

Example 1: The bounding hyperplanes of $\mathcal{K}$ are oriented majorities: $W \in \{1/\sqrt{n}, -1/\sqrt{n}\}^{n \times k}$. In this case, the standard Lindeberg method in conjunction with Bentkus's smoothing function and Nazarov's surface area bound as used in Lemmas 3.3, 3.4 can be adapted (without having to do a blockwise hybrid argument) to get a bound as in Theorem 3.1.

Example 2: The bounding hyperplanes of $\mathcal{K}$ are oriented majorities on disjoint sets of variables: For $m = n/k$ and each $p \in [k]$, $m = n/k$, $W^p_i = 1/\sqrt{m}, (p-1)m + 1 \leq i \leq pm$ and $W^p_i = 0$ otherwise. In this case, when $m \geq 1/\varepsilon^2$ and each bounding hyperplane is regular, the Lindeberg method even when used with Lemmas 3.3, 3.4 leads to an error bound that is at least linear in k.

We use the following form of the standard Taylor series expansion. For a smooth function $\psi : \mathbb{R}^k \to \mathbb{R}$, $x \in \mathbb{R}^k$ and $p_1, \ldots, p_r \in [k]$, let $\partial_{p_1,\ldots,p_r}\psi(x) = \partial_{p_1}\partial_{p_2}\cdots\partial_{p_r}\psi(x)$. For indices $p_1, \ldots, p_r \in [k]$, let $(p_1, \ldots, p_r)! = s_1!s_2!\ldots s_k!$, where, for $l \in [k]$, s_l denotes the number of occurrences of l in $(p_1, \ldots, p_r)$.

FACT 4.3 (TAYLOR'S THEOREM). *For any smooth function $\psi : \mathbb{R}^k \to \mathbb{R}$, and $x, y \in \mathbb{R}^k$,*

$$\psi(x+y) = \psi(x) + \sum_{p \in [k]} \partial_p \psi(x)\, y_p + \sum_{p,q \in [k]} \frac{1}{(p,q)!} \partial_{p,q}\psi(x)\, y_p y_q + \sum_{p,q,r \in [k]} \frac{1}{(p,q,r)!} \partial_{p,q,r}\psi(x)\, y_p y_q y_r + \mathsf{err}(x,y),$$

where $|\mathsf{err}(x,y)| \leq \|\psi^{(4)}\|_1 \cdot \max_{p \in [k]} |y_p|^4$.

PROOF OF LEMMA 4.2. Let $\overline{X} \leftarrow \mu^n$ and $\overline{Y} \leftarrow \mathcal{N}^n$. We first partition $[n]$ into blocks using a random hash function $h \in_u \mathcal{H}$ and then use a blockwise-hybrid argument. Fix a hash function $h \in \mathcal{H}$. View $\overline{X}$ as $X^1, \ldots, X^t$, where each $X^l = \overline{X}_{h^{-1}(l)}$ is chosen independently and uniformly from $\mu^{|h^{-1}(l)|}$. Similarly, view $\overline{Y}$ as $Y^1,\dots,Y^t$ where each $Y^l = \overline{Y}_{h^{-1}(l)}$ is chosen independently and uniformly from $\mathcal{N}^{|h^{-1}(l)|}$. We prove the claim via a hybrid argument where we replace the blocks $X^1,\dots,X^t$ with $Y^1,\dots,Y^t$ one at a time.

For $0 \le i \le t$, let Z^i be the distribution with $Z^i_{|h^{-1}(j)} = X^j$ for $i < j \le t$ and $Z^i_{|h^{-1}(j)} = Y^j$ for $1 \le j \le i$. Then, Z^0 is distributed as μ^n and Z^t is distributed as $\mathcal{N}^n$. For $l \in [t]$, let

$$h(W,l) = \left(\sum_{p=1}^k \|W^p_{h^{-1}(l)}\|^{4\log k}\right)^{1/\log k}.$$

CLAIM 4.4. *For $1 \le l \le t$, and fixed $h \in \mathcal{H}$,*

$$\left|\mathop{\mathbb{E}}_{X,Y}\left[\psi(W^T Z^l)\right] - \mathop{\mathbb{E}}_{X,Y}\left[\psi(W^T Z^{l-1})\right]\right| \le C\log^2 k\,\|\psi^{(4)}\|_1\, h(W,l).$$

PROOF. Without loss of generality, suppose that $h^{-1}(l) = \{1,\dots,m\}$. Note that Z^l, Z^{l-1} have the same random variables in positions $m+1,\dots,n$. Let

$$Z^{l-1} = (X_1,\dots,X_m, Z_{m+1},\dots,Z_n),$$

$$Z^l = (Y_1,\dots,Y_m, Z_{m+1},\dots,Z_n),$$

where $(X_1,\dots,X_m)$ has distribution μ^m and $(Y_1,\dots,Y_m)$ is uniform over $\mathcal{N}^m$. Note that $(Z_{m+1},\dots,Z_n)$ is independent of $(X_1,\dots,X_m)$, $(Y_1,\dots,Y_m)$.

Let $W_1 \in \mathbb{R}^{m\times k}$ be the matrix formed by the first m rows of W and similarly let $W_2 \in \mathbb{R}^{(n-m)\times k}$ be the matrix formed by the last $n-m$ rows of W. Lastly, let $V = W_2^T(Z_{m+1},\dots,Z_n)$ and U be one of $X = (X_1,\dots,X_m)$ or $Y = (Y_1,\dots,Y_m)$. Now, by using a Taylor expansion of ψ at V as in Fact 4.3,

$$\begin{aligned}\psi(W^T(U_1,\dots,U_m,Z_{m+1},\dots,Z_n)) &= \psi(W_1^T U + V) \\ &= \psi(V) + \sum_{p\in[k]} \partial_p\psi(V)\,\langle W_1^p, U\rangle + \\ &\sum_{p,q\in[k]} \frac{1}{(p,q)!}\partial_{p,q}\psi(V)\,\langle W_1^p,U\rangle\,\langle W_1^q,U\rangle \\ &+ \sum_{p,q,r\in[k]} \frac{1}{(p,q,r)!}\partial_{p,q,r}\psi(V)\,\langle W_1^p,U\rangle\,\langle W_1^q,U\rangle\,\langle W_1^r,U\rangle + \\ &\mathsf{err}(V, W_1^T U). \quad (4.1)\end{aligned}$$

Now, using the fact that $\|z\|_\infty \le \|z\|_{\log k}$ for $z \in \mathbb{R}^k$,

$$\left|\mathsf{err}(V,W_1^TU)\right| \le \|\psi^{(4)}\|_1 \cdot \max_{p\in[k]} |\langle W_1^p, U\rangle|^4 \le \|\psi^{(4)}\|_1 \left(\sum_{p=1}^k |\langle W_1^p,U\rangle|^{4\log k}\right)^{1/\log k}. \quad (4.2)$$

Now, by hypercontractivity of μ,

$$\begin{aligned}\mathop{\mathbb{E}}_X\left[\left(\sum_{p=1}^k |\langle W_1^p, X\rangle|^{4\log k}\right)^{1/\log k}\right] &\le \left(\mathop{\mathbb{E}}_X\left[\sum_{p=1}^k |\langle W_1^p,X\rangle|^{4\log k}\right]\right)^{1/\log k} \\ &= \left(\sum_{p=1}^k \mathop{\mathbb{E}}_X\left[|\langle W_1^p,X\rangle|^{4\log k}\right]\right)^{1/\log k} \\ &\le \left(\sum_{p=1}^k (C\log k)^{2\log k}\,\|W_1^p\|^{4\log k}\right)^{1/\log k} \\ &\le C(\log^2 k)\,h(W,l), \quad (4.3)\end{aligned}$$

where the first inequality follows from power-mean inequality and the third from hypercontractivity of μ. Similarly, by hypercontractivity of $\mathcal{N}$,

$$\mathop{\mathbb{E}}_Y\left[\left(\sum_{p=1}^k |\langle W_1^p, Y\rangle|^{4\log k}\right)^{1/\log k}\right] \le C(\log^2 k)\,h(W,l). \quad (4.4)$$

Further, since μ is proper, for any $u^1, u^2, u^3 \in \mathbb{R}^m$,

$$\mathbb{E}[\langle u^1, X\rangle] = \mathbb{E}[\langle u^1, Y\rangle]$$

$$\mathbb{E}[\langle u^1, X\rangle\,\langle u^2,X\rangle] = \mathbb{E}[\langle u^1, Y\rangle\,\langle u^2,Y\rangle]$$

$$\mathbb{E}[\langle u^1, X\rangle\,\langle u^2,X\rangle\,\langle u^3,X\rangle] = \mathbb{E}[\langle u^1, Y\rangle\,\langle u^2,Y\rangle\,\langle u^3,Y\rangle].$$

From the above equations, Equations (4.1), (4.2), (4.3), (4.4) and the fact that X, Y, V are independent of one another, it follows that

$$|\,\mathbb{E}[\psi(W^TZ^l) - \psi(W^TZ^{l-1})]| \le C(\log^2 k)\,\|\psi^{(4)}\|_1 h(W,l).$$

□

Lemma 4.2 now follows from the above claim, summing from $l = 1,\dots,t$, and taking expectation with respect to $h \in_u \mathcal{H}$.

5. NOISE SENSITIVITY OF INTERSECTIONS OF REGULAR HALFSPACES

We now describe how our invariance principle yields a bound on the average and noise sensitivity of intersections of regular halfspaces. We begin by defining the (Boolean) noise sensitivity of a Boolean function:

DEFINITION 5.1. *Let $f : \{1,-1\}^n \to \{1,-1\}$ be a Boolean function. For any $\delta \in (0,1)$, let X be a random element of the hypercube $\{1,-1\}^n$ and Z a δ-perturbation of X defined as follows: for each i independently, Z_i is set to X_i with probability $1-\delta$ and $-X_i$ with probability δ. The noise sensitivity of f, denoted $\mathbb{NS}_\delta(f)$, for noise δ is then defined as follows: $\mathbb{NS}_\delta(f) = \Pr[f(X) \ne f(Z)]$.*

Let $f^1,\dots,f^k : \{1,-1\}^n \to \{1,-1\}$ be halfspaces with $f^p(x) = \mathsf{sign}(\langle W^p, x\rangle - \theta_p)$ and let $f^{\wedge k} : \{1,-1\}^n \to \{1,-1\}$ be their intersection, $f^{\wedge k} = f^1 \wedge f^2 \wedge \dots \wedge f^k$.

THEOREM 5.2. *For $f^{\wedge k}$ ε-regular,*

$$\mathbb{NS}_\delta(f^{\wedge k}) \le C(\log^{1.6}(k/\delta))\,(\varepsilon^{1/6} + \delta^{1/2}).$$

We prove the theorem by first reducing bounding noise sensitivity of $f^{\wedge k}$ to bounding the Boolean volume of ℓ_∞ neighborhoods of polytopes. We then use our invariance principle, Theorem 3.1, to prove the required bounds on the Boolean volume of boundaries of polytopes. As mentioned before, the above theorem implies a $n^{\log^{O(1)} k}$ algorithm for learning intersections of regular halfspaces in the agnostic model for any constant error rate. We defer the details to the full version.

6. PSEUDORANDOM GENERATORS FOR POLYTOPES

We now prove our main theorems for constructing pseudorandom generators for polytopes with respect to a variety of distributions (Theorems 1.5, 1.6, and 1.7).

The results in this section are based on a recent PRG construction due to Meka and Zuckerman [MZ10] for polynomial threshold functions using the invariance principle of Mossel et al. [MOO05]. A closer look at their construction reveals a general program for constructing PRGs from invariance principles. Given this observation, it is natural to ask if our invariance principle can be used to construct PRGs for regular polytopes. Indeed it can, and we use the Meka and Zuckerman generator but with a different setting of its parameters. The analysis, however, is a little more complicated in our setting (even given our invariance principle) and requires a careful application of hypercontractivity.

6.1 Main Generator Construction

We begin by describing the construction of the PRG we use; it is a slightly modified version of the PRG used by Meka and Zuckerman [MZ10] to fool regular *halfspaces* (i.e., the case $k=1$).

Give $\delta \in (0,1)$, let $\varepsilon = \Omega(\delta^6/\log^{9.6} k)$ be such that $(\log^{1.6} k)(\varepsilon \log(1/\varepsilon))^{1/5} = \delta$. Let $t = 1/\varepsilon$ and let $\mathcal{H} = \{h : h : [n] \to [t]\}$ be a $(2\log k)$-wise independent family of hash functions. That is, for all $I \subseteq [n], |I| \leq 2\log k$ and $b \in [t]^I$,

$$\Pr_{h \in_u \mathcal{H}}[\forall i \in I,\ h(i) = b_i] = \frac{1}{t^{|I|}}.$$

Efficient constructions of hash families $\mathcal{H}$ as above with $|\mathcal{H}| = O(n^{2\log k})$ are known. To avoid some technical issues that can be overcome easily, we assume that every hash function $h \in \mathcal{H}$ is equi-distributed in the following sense: for all $j \in [t]$, $|\{i : h(i) = j\}| = n/t$.

Let $m = n/t$ and let $G_0 : \{0,1\}^s \to \{1,-1\}^m$ generate a $(4\log k)$-wise independent distribution over $\{1,-1\}^m$. That is, for all $I \subseteq [n], |I| \leq 2\log k$ and $b \in \{1,-1\}^I$,

$$\Pr_{x = G_0(z), z \in_u \{0,1\}^s}[\forall i \in I,\ x_i = b_i] = \frac{1}{2^{|I|}}.$$

Efficient constructions of generators G_0 as above with $s = O(\log k \log n)$ are known [NN93].

Given a hash family and generator G_0 as above, we consider the following generator. Define $G : \mathcal{H} \times (\{0,1\}^s)^t \to \{1,-1\}^n$ by $G(h, z^1, \ldots, z^t) = x$, where $x_{|h^{-1}(i)} = G_0(z^i)$ for $i \in [t]$.

6.2 Pseudorandom Generators for Regular Polytopes

We now argue that the generator G defined in the last section fools regular polytopes and prove Theorem 1.5.

PROOF OF THEOREM 1.5. The bound on the seed length of the generator G follows from the construction. The following statement follows from an argument similar to that of the proof of Theorem 3.2: for any smooth function $\psi : \mathbb{R}^k \to \mathbb{R}$ and ε-regular W,

$$\left| \mathop{\mathbb{E}}_{y \in_u \{0,1\}^r}[\psi(W^T G(y))] - \mathop{\mathbb{E}}_{Y \leftarrow \mathcal{N}^n}[\psi(W^T Y)] \right| \leq C \log^3 k\,(\varepsilon \log(1/\varepsilon))\,\|\psi^{(4)}\|_1. \quad (6.1)$$

Indeed, to observe that Lemma 4.1 holds for any $(2\log k)$-wise independent family of hash functions and the proof of Lemma 4.2 relies only on two key properties of $X \leftarrow \mu^n$: (1) For a fixed hash function h, the blocks $X_{h^{-1}(1)}, X_{h^{-1}(2)}, \ldots, X_{h^{-1}(t)}$ are independent of one another. (2) For a fixed hash function h, and $j \in [t]$, the distribution of each block $X_{h^{-1}(j)}$ satisfies $(2, 2\log k)$ hypercontractivity for all $j \in [t]$. In other words, we used the property that for all $j \in [t]$, $u \in \mathbb{R}^{|h^{-1}(j)|}$,

$$\mathbb{E}[|\langle u, X_{h^{-1}(j)}\rangle|^{4\log k}] \leq (C\log k)^{2\log k}\,\|u\|^{4\log k}. \quad (6.2)$$

Note that X generated according to the generator G satisfies both the above conditions: 1) For a fixed function h, the blocks are independent by definition and 2) the hypercontractivity inequality 6.2 only involves the first $(4\log k)$-moments of the distribution of $X_{h^{-1}(j)}$. As a consequence, inequality 6.2 holds for any $(4\log k)$-wise independent distribution over $\{1,-1\}^{|h^{-1}(j)|}$.

We can now move from closeness in expectation to closeness in cdf distance by an argument similar to the proof of Theorem 3.1, where we use Equation 6.1 instead of Theorem 3.2, to get

$$\left| \Pr_{y \in_u \{0,1\}^r}[G(y) \in \mathcal{K}] - \Pr_{Y \leftarrow \mathcal{N}^n}[Y \in \mathcal{K}] \right| \leq \delta.$$

The theorem now follows from the above equation and Theorem 3.1. □

6.2.1 *Approximate Counting for Integer Programs*

The PRG from Theorem 1.5 coupled with enumeration over all possible seeds immediately implies a quasi-polynomial time, deterministic algorithm for approximately counting, within a small additive error, the number of solutions to "regular" $\{0,1\}$-integer programs. It turns out that "regular" integer programs correspond to a broad class of well-studied combinatorial problems. For example, we obtain deterministic, approximate counting algorithms for *dense* set cover problems and $\{0,1\}$-contingency tables. We obtain quasi-polynomial time algorithms even when there are a polynomial number of constraints (or polynomial number of rows in the contingency table setting). As far as we know, there is no prior work giving nontrivial *deterministic* algorithms for counting solutions to integer programs with many constraints.

Here we discuss the case of *dense* set cover instances and remark that we get similar results for the special case of counting contingency tables. Covering integer programs are a fundamental class of integer programs and can be formulated as follows.

$$\min \sum_i X_i$$
$$\text{s.t. } \sum_i a_{ij} X_i \geq c_j,\ j = 1, \ldots, k, \qquad (6.3)$$
$$X \in \{0,1\}^n,$$

where the coefficients of the constraints a_{ij} and c_j are all non-negative. An important special class of covering integer programs is set cover, which in turn is a generalization of many important problems in combinatorial optimization such as edge cover and multidimensional $\{0,1\}$-knapsack.

In the standard set cover problem, the input is a family of sets $S_1, \ldots, S_n$ over a universe U of size k and an integer t. The goal is to find a subfamily of sets $\mathcal{C}$ such that $|\mathcal{C}| \leq t$ and the union of all the sets in $\mathcal{C}$ equals U. This corresponds to a covering program as above with k constraints and n unknowns from $\{0,1\}$. Call an instance of set cover ε-dense if each element in U appears in at least $1/\varepsilon^2$ of the different sets S_i. It is easy to verify that with this restriction, after translating from $\{0,1\}$ to $\{1,-1\}$ and appropriate normalization, all the linear constraints in the corresponding integer program as in Equation 6.3 are ε-regular. Thus, using the generator from Theorem 1.5 and enumerating over all seeds to the generator, we have the following:

THEOREM 6.1. *There exists a deterministic algorithm that, given instance of an ε-dense set covering problem with k constraints over a universe of size n, approximates the number of solutions to within an additive factor of δ in time $n^{\mathrm{poly}(\log k, 1/\delta)}$ as long as $\varepsilon \leq \delta^5/(\log^{8.1} k)(\log(1/\delta))$.*

We now briefly elaborate on approximately counting the number of $\{0,1\}$ contingency tables. The problem of counting $\{0,1\}$-contingency tables is the following. Given, positive integers n, k $n > k$, $\mathbf{r} = (r_1, \ldots, r_n) \in \mathbb{Z}^n$, $\mathbf{c} = (c_1, \ldots, c_k) \in \mathbb{Z}^k$ we wish to count the number of solutions, $\mathsf{CT}(\mathbf{r}, \mathbf{c})$, to the following integer program whose solutions are matrices $X \in \{0,1\}^{n\times k}$ with row and column sums given by $\mathbf{r}, \mathbf{c}$.

$$\text{Find } X \in \{0,1\}^{n\times k}$$
$$\text{s.t. } \sum_j X_{ij} = r_i, 1 \leq i \leq n,$$
$$\sum_i X_{ij} = c_j, 1 \leq j \leq k.$$

Observe that, after translating from $\{0,1\}$ to $\{1,-1\}$ and appropriately normalizing, solutions to the above integer program correspond to points from $\{1,-1\}^{n\times k}$ that lie in an intersection of $2(n+k)$-halfspaces each of which is $(1/\sqrt{k})$-regular (recall that the notion of regularity does not depend on the value of the c_i's or r_j's). Thus, as with dense instances of set cover, we can use Theorem 1.5 to count the number of $\{0,1\}$-contingency tables:

THEOREM 6.2. *There exists a deterministic algorithm that on input $\mathbf{r} \in \mathbb{Z}^n$, $\mathbf{c} \in \mathbb{Z}^k$, approximates $\mathsf{CT}(\mathbf{r}, \mathbf{c})/2^{nk}$, the fraction of $\{0,1\}$-contingency tables with sums $\mathbf{r}, \mathbf{c}$, to within additive error δ, and runs in time $n^{\mathrm{poly}(\log k, 1/\delta)}$.*

We remark that using results of Wolff [Wol07], who shows hypercontractivity for various discrete distributions, we can approximately count number of solutions to dense set cover instances and contingency tables over most natural domains.

6.3 Pseudorandom Generators for Polytopes in Gaussian Space

We now briefly sketch the details of Theorem 1.6. The proof is based on an idea of Ailon and Chazelle [AC06] and the invariance of the Gaussian measure to unitary rotations to obtain PRGs with respect to $\mathcal{N}^n$ for *all* polytopes. Similar ideas were used by Meka and Zuckerman to obtain PRGs for spherical caps (i.e., the case of one hyperplane). In our setting, we must prove that, with respect to a random rotation, *all* of the bounding hyperplanes become regular with high probability. We refer the readers to the full version for details.

6.4 Pseudorandom Generators for Intersections of Spherical Caps

Theorem 1.7 follows from Theorem 1.6 and the following new invariance principle for polytopes over S^{n-1}:

LEMMA 6.3. *For any polytope $\mathcal{K}$ with k faces, $X \in_u S^{n-1}$, $Y \leftarrow \mathcal{N}^n$,*

$$\left|\Pr[X \in \mathcal{K}] - \Pr\left[Y/\sqrt{n} \in \mathcal{K}\right]\right| \leq C \log n \, \log k/\sqrt{n}.$$

The proof is based on Nazarov's bound on Gaussian surface area and large deviation bounds for the norm of random Gaussian vectors. We defer the details to the full version.

7. DISCUSSION AND FUTURE WORK

Here we discuss some possible extensions and applications of our work.

We believe that our main invariance principle, Theorem 3.1, has the right dependence on the number of halfspaces k and the regularity ε up to polynomial factors. Although we do not have any lower bounds to this effect, the lower bounds on Gaussian surface area (see [Naz03] and references therein) suggest that the right dependence of the error term on the number of halfspaces is $\Theta(\sqrt{\log k})$.

One obvious weakness of our applications to noise sensitivity bounds (Theorem 1.3) and PRGs over the hypercube (Theorem 1.5) is the regularity requirement. Recent results on sensitivity bounds and PRGs for halfspaces and PTFs ([DHK+10, MZ10]) use certain *regularity lemmas* which allow one to "reduce" the problem for arbitrary functions to the regular case and then use invariance to handle the regular case. Unfortunately, applying the reductions to the regular case as in the above works leads to bounds that are at least linear in k, even when using our stronger bounds for the regular case. We (optimistically) believe that the above difficulty could be overcome and a better reduction to the regular case can be achieved.

Acknowledgments

Thanks to Fedja Nazarov for helping us compute an integral. We had useful conversations with Carly Klivans, Ryan O'Donnell, Alistair Sinclair, Eric Vigoda, and David Zuckerman.

8. REFERENCES

[AC06] N. AILON and B. CHAZELLE. *Approximate nearest neighbors and the fast Johnson Lindenstrauss transform*. In *STOC*, pages 557–563. 2006.

[Ben90] Vidmantas K. Bentkus. *Smooth approximations of the norm and differentiable functions with bounded support in Banach space l^k_∞.* Lithuanian Mathematical Journal, 30(3):223–230, July 1990.

[Ben03] ———. *On the dependence of the BerryâĂŞ-Esseen bound on dimension.* Journal of Statistical Planning and Inference, 113(2):385–402, May 2003.

[BKS99] Itai Benjamini, Gil Kalai, and Oded Schramm. *Noise sensitivity of Boolean functions and applications to percolation.* Inst. Hautes Études Sci. Publ. Math., 90(1):5–43, 1999. arXiv:math/9811157.

[BR07] Matthias Beck and Sinai Robins. *Computing the Continuous Discretely: Integer-point Enumeration in Polyhedra.* Undergraduate Texts in Mathematics. Springer, 1st edition, 2007.

[BV08] Alexander Barvinok and Ellen Veomett. *The computational complexity of convex bodies.* In Jacob E. Goodman, János Pach, and Richard Pollack, eds., *Surveys on Discrete and Computational Geometry: Twenty Years Later,* volume 453 of *Contemporary Mathematics,* pages 117–137. AMS, 2008. arXiv:math/0610325.

[CD03] Mary Cryan and Martin E. Dyer. *A polynomial-time algorithm to approximately count contingency tables when the number of rows is constant.* J. Comp. Sys. Sci., 67(2):291–310, 2003.

[DHK+10] I. Diakonikolas, P. Harsha, A. Klivans, R. Meka, P. Raghavendra, R. Servedio, and L. Tan. *Bounding the average sensitivity and noise sensitivity of polynomial threshold functions.* In *STOC, to appear.* 2010.

[DKN09] Ilias Diakonikolas, Daniel M. Kane, and Jelani Nelson. *Bounded independence fools degree-2 threshold functions,* 2009. arXiv:0911.3389.

[Dye03] M. E. Dyer. *Approximate counting by dynamic programming.* In *STOC,* pages 693–699. 2003.

[Fel71] William Feller. *An Introduction to Probability Theory and Its Applications, Volume 2.* Wiley, 2nd edition, 1971.

[GOWZ10] P. Gopalan, R. O'Donnell, Y. Wu, and D. Zuckerman. *Fooling functions of halfspaces under product distributions.* In *CCC, to appear.* 2010.

[GW95] Michel X. Goemans and David P. Williamson. *Improved approximation algorithms for maximum cut and satisfiability problems using semidefinite programming.* J. ACM, 42(6):1115–1145, 1995. (Preliminary version in *26th STOC,* 1994).

[Hås01] Johan Håstad. *Some optimal inapproximability results.* J. ACM, 48(4):798–859, July 2001. (Preliminary Version in *29th STOC,* 1997).

[INW94] Russell Impagliazzo, Noam Nisan, and Avi Wigderson. *Pseudorandomness for network algorithms.* In *STOC,* pages 356–364. 1994.

[JS97] Mark Jerrum and Alistair Sinclair. *The Markov chain Monte Carlo method: An approach to approximate counting and integration.* In Dorit S. Hochbaum, ed., *Approximation Algorithms for NP-hard Problems.* PWS Publishing Company, 1997.

[Kal05] Gil Kalai. *Noise sensitivity and chaos in social choice theory.* Technical Report 399, Center for Rationality and Interactive Decision Theory, Hebrew University of Jerusalem, 2005.

[KKL88] Jeff Kahn, Gil Kalai, and Nathan Linial. *The influence of variables on Boolean functions (extended abstract).* In *FOCS,* pages 68–80. 1988.

[KKMO07] Subhash Khot, Guy Kindler, Elchanan Mossel, and Ryan O'Donnell. *Optimal inapproximability results for MAX-CUT and other 2-variable CSPs?* SIAM J. Computing, 37(1):319–357, 2007.

[KKMS08] Adam Tauman Kalai, Adam R. Klivans, Yishay Mansour, and Rocco A. Servedio. *Agnostically learning halfspaces.* SIAM J. Computing, 37(6):1777–1805, 2008. (Preliminary version in *46th FOCS,* 2005).

[KOS04] Adam R. Klivans, Ryan O'Donnell, and Rocco A. Servedio. *Learning intersections and thresholds of halfspaces.* J. Comp. Sys. Sci., 68(4):808–840, 2004. (Preliminary version in *43rd FOCS,* 2002).

[KOS08] ———. *Learning geometric concepts via Gaussian surface area.* In *FOCS,* pages 541–550. 2008.

[LMN93] Nathan Linial, Yishay Mansour, and Noam Nisan. *Constant depth circuits, Fourier transform, and learnability.* J. ACM, 40(3):607–620, 1993. (Preliminary version in *30th FOCS,* 1989).

[Man94] Yishay Mansour. *Learning Boolean functions via the Fourier transform.* In Vwani P. Roychowdhury, Kai-Yeung Siu, and Alon Orlitsky, eds., *Theoretical Advances in Neural Computation and Learning,* pages 391–424. Kluwer Academic Publishers, 1994.

[MH99] Sanjeev Mahajan and Ramesh Hariharan. *Derandomizing approximation algorithms based on semidefinite programming.* SIAM J. Computing, 28(5):1641–1663, 1999. (Preliminary version in *36th FOCS,* 1995).

[MOO05] Elchanan Mossel, Ryan O'Donnell, and Krzysztof Oleszkiewicz. *Noise stability of functions with low in.uences invariance and optimality.* In *FOCS,* pages 21–30. 2005. arXiv:math/0503503.

[Mos08] Elchanan Mossel. *Gaussian bounds for noise correlation of functions and tight analysis of long codes.* In *FOCS,* pages 156–165. 2008. arXiv:math/0703683.

[MZ10] R. Meka and D. Zuckerman. *Pseudorandom generators for polynomial threshold functions.* In *STOC,to appear.* 2010. arXiv:0910.4122.

[Naz03] Fedor Nazarov. *On the maximal perimeter of a convex set in $\mathbb{R}^n$ with respect to a Gaussian measure.* In *Geometric Aspects of Functional Analysis (Israel Seminar 2001–2002),* volume 1807/2003 of *Lecture Notes in Mathematics,* pages 169–187. Springer, 2003.

[NN93] Joseph Naor and Moni Naor. *Small-bias probability spaces: Efficient constructions and applications.* SIAM J. Computing, 22(4):838–856, August 1993. (Preliminary Version in *22nd STOC,* 1990).

[O'D04] Ryan O'Donnell. *Hardness amplification within NP.* J. Comp. Sys. Sci., 69(1):68–94, 2004. (Preliminary version in *34th STOC,* 2002).

[O'D08] ———. *Some topics in analysis of Boolean functions.* In *STOC,* pages 569–578. 2008. eccc:TR08-055.

[Per04] Yuval Peres. *Noise stability of weighted majority,* 2004. arXiv:math/0412377.

[PR89] Vygantas Paulauskas and Alfredas Račkauskas. *Approximation Theory in the Central Limit Theorem: Exact Results in Banach Spaces.* Kluwer Academic Publishers, 1989. (Translated from Russian).

[Shi00] Yaoyun Shi. *Lower bounds of quantum black-box complexity and degree of approximating polynomials by influence of Boolean variables.* Inf. Process. Lett., 75(1-2):79–83, 2000. arXiv:quant-ph/9904107.

[Wol07] Pawel Wolff. *Hypercontractivity of simple random variables.* Studia Math, 180(3):219–236, 2007.

[Zie95] Günter M. Ziegler. *Lectures on polytopes,* volume 152 of *Graduate texts in Mathematics.* Springer, 1995.

Efficiently Learning Mixtures of Two Gaussians

Adam Tauman Kalai[*]
Microsoft Research, New England
Cambridge, MA 02139
adum@microsoft.com

Ankur Moitra[†]
Massachusetts Institute of Technology
Cambridge, MA 02139
moitra@mit.edu

Gregory Valiant[‡]
University of California, Berkeley
Berkeley, CA 94720
gvaliant@eecs.berkeley.edu

ABSTRACT

Given data drawn from a mixture of multivariate Gaussians, a basic problem is to accurately estimate the mixture parameters. We provide a polynomial-time algorithm for this problem for the case of two Gaussians in n dimensions (even if they overlap), with provably minimal assumptions on the Gaussians, and polynomial data requirements. In statistical terms, our estimator converges at an inverse polynomial rate, and no such estimator (even exponential time) was known for this problem (even in one dimension). Our algorithm reduces the n-dimensional problem to the one-dimensional problem, where the *method of moments* is applied. One technical challenge is proving that noisy estimates of the first six moments of a univariate mixture suffice to recover accurate estimates of the mixture parameters, as conjectured by Pearson (1894), and in fact these estimates converge at an inverse polynomial rate.

As a corollary, we can efficiently perform near-optimal clustering: in the case where the overlap between the Gaussians is small, one can accurately cluster the data, and when the Gaussians have partial overlap, one can still accurately cluster those data points which are not in the overlap region. A second consequence is a polynomial-time density estimation algorithm for arbitrary mixtures of two Gaussians, generalizing previous work on axis-aligned Gaussians (Feldman *et al*, 2006).

*Microsoft Research New England. Part of this work was done while the author was at Georgia Institute of Technology, supported in part by NSF CAREER-0746550, SES-0734780, and a Sloan Fellowship.

†This research was supported in part by a Fannie and John Hertz Foundation Fellowship. Part of this work was done while the author was an intern at Microsoft Research New England.

‡This research was supported in part by an NSF Graduate Research Fellowship. Part of this work was done while the author was an intern at Microsoft Research New England.

STOC'10, June 5–8, 2010, Cambridge, Massachusetts, USA.

Categories and Subject Descriptors

G.3 [**Probability and Statistics**]: multivariate statistics

General Terms

Algorithms, Theory

Keywords

Gaussians, Finite Mixture Models, method of moments

1. INTRODUCTION

The problem of estimating the parameters of a mixture of Gaussians has a rich history of study in statistics and more recently, computer science. This natural problem has applications across a number of fields, including agriculture, economics, medicine, and genetics. Consider a mixture of two *different* multinormal distributions, each with *mean* $\mu_i \in \mathbf{R}^n$, *covariance matrix* $\Sigma_i \in \mathbf{R}^{n\times n}$, and *weight* $w_i > 0$. With probability w_1 a sample is chosen from $\mathcal{N}(\mu_1, \Sigma_1)$, and with probability $w_2 = 1 - w_1$, a sample is chosen from $\mathcal{N}(\mu_2, \Sigma_2)$. The mixture is referred to as a Gaussian Mixture Model (GMM), and if the two multinormal densities are F_1, F_2, then the GMM density is,

$$F = w_1 F_1 + w_2 F_2.$$

The problem of *identifying* the mixture is that of estimating $\hat{w}_i$, $\hat{\mu}_i$, and $\hat{\Sigma}_i$ from m independent random samples drawn from the GMM.

In this paper, we prove that the parameters can be estimated at an inverse polynomial rate. In particular, we give an algorithm and polynomial bounds on the number of samples and runtime required under provably minimal assumptions, namely that w_1, w_2 and the statistical distance between the Gaussians are all bounded away from 0 (Theorem 1). No such bounds were previously known, even in one dimension. Our algorithm for accurately identifying the mixture parameters can also be leveraged to yield the first provably efficient algorithms for near-optimal clustering and density estimation (Theorems 3 and 2) for mixtures of two Gaussians. We start with a brief history, and then give the formal definition of the learning problem we consider and our main results and approach.

1.1 Brief history

In one of the earliest GMM studies, Pearson [19] fit a mixture of two univariate Gaussians to data (see Figure 1) using the *method of moments.* In particular, he computed empirical estimates of the first six (raw) moments

$E[x^i] \approx \frac{1}{m}\sum_{j=1}^{m} x_j^i$, for $i = 1, 2, \ldots, 6$ from sample points $x_1, \ldots, x_m \in \mathbf{R}$. Using only the first five moments, he solved a cleverly constructed ninth-degree polynomial *by hand* from which he derived a set of candidate mixture parameters. Finally, he heuristically chose the candidate set of parameters among them whose sixth moment most closely agreed with the empirical estimate.

Later work showed that "identifiability" is theoretically possible – every two distinct mixtures of Gaussians (i.e. the mixtures are not equivalent after some permutation of the labels) have different probability distributions [22]. However, this work shed little light on convergence *rates*: this result is based on demonstrating that distinct mixtures of Gaussians exhibit different behavior in the density tails, and even obtaining a single sample from the density tails could require an enormous number of random samples. In fact, previous work left open the possibility that distinguishing between GMMs that are ϵ-different (see Theorem 1 for our definition of ϵ-close) might require an amount of data that grows exponentially in $1/\epsilon$.

The problem of *clustering* is that of partitioning the points into two sets, with the hope that the points in each set are drawn from different Gaussians. Given an accurate clustering of sufficiently many points, one can recover good estimates of the mixture parameters. Starting with Dasgupta [5], a line of computer scientists designed *polynomial time* algorithms for identifying and clustering in high dimensions [2, 7, 24, 13, 1, 4]. However, even if we were given the parameters of the mixture, we could not hope to cluster many points accurately unless the Gaussians have little *overlap* (statistical distance near 1). Thus this line of work must make such an assumption in order to cluster, and learn good estimates for the mixture from such a clustering. Here we are able to learn good estimates of the mixture parameters for a GMM of two Gaussians without clustering, and we do so using provably minimal assumptions on the GMM.

There is a vast literature that we have not touched upon (see, e.g., [8]), including the popular EM and K-means algorithms.

1.2 Main results

In identifying a GMM $F = w_1F_1 + w_2F_2$, three limitations are immediately apparent:

1. Since permuting the two Gaussians does not change the resulting density, one cannot distinguish permuted mixtures. Hence, at best one hopes to estimate the parameter set, $\{(w_1, \mu_1, \Sigma_1), (w_2, \mu_2, \Sigma_2)\}$.
2. If $w_i = 0$, then one cannot hope to estimate F_i because no samples will be drawn from it. And, in general, at least $\Omega(1/\min\{w_1, w_2\})$ samples will be required in order to obtain any reasonable estimate.
3. If $F_1 = F_2$ (i.e., $\mu_1 = \mu_2$ and $\Sigma_1 = \Sigma_2$) then it is impossible to estimate w_i. If the statistical distance between the two Gaussians is Δ, then at least $\Omega(1/\Delta)$ samples will be required.

Hence, the number of examples required will depend on the smallest of w_1, w_2, and the statistical distance between F_1 and F_2 denoted by $D(F_1, F_2)$ (see Section 2 for a precise definition).

Our goal is, given m independently drawn samples from a GMM F, to construct an estimate GMM $\hat{F} = \hat{w}_1\hat{F}_1 + \hat{w}_2\hat{F}_2$.

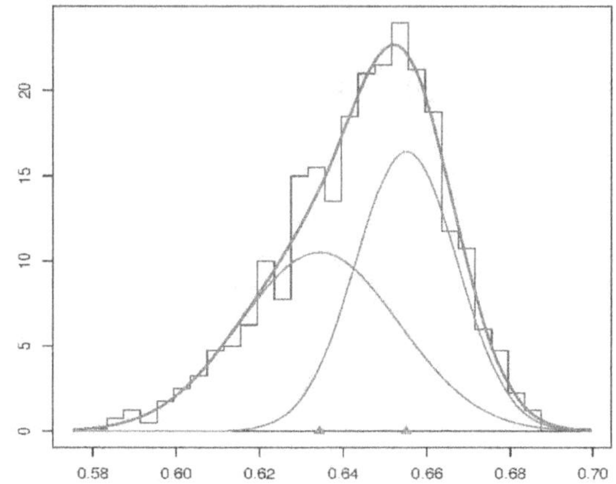

Figure 1: A fit of a mixture of two univariate Gaussians to the Pearson's data on Naples crabs [19]. The hypothesis was that the data was in fact a mixture of two different species of crabs. Although the empirical data histogram is single-peaked, the two constituent Gaussian parameters may be estimated. This density plot was created by Peter Macdonald using *R* [18] .

We will say that $\hat{F}$ is accurate to within ϵ if $|\hat{w}_i - w_i| \le \epsilon$ and $D(F_i, \hat{F}_i) \le \epsilon$ for each $i = 1, 2$. This latter condition is affine invariant and more appealing than bounds on the difference between the estimated and true parameters. In fact for arbitrary Gaussians, estimating parameters, such as the mean μ, to any given additive error ϵ is impossible without further assumptions since scaling the data by a factor of s will scale the error $\|\mu - \hat{\mu}\|$ by s. We would like the algorithm to succeed in this goal using polynomially many samples. And we would also like the algorithm itself to be computationally efficient, i.e., a polynomial-time algorithm.

Our main theorem is the following.

THEOREM 1. *For any $n \ge 1$, $\epsilon, \delta > 0$, and any GMM $F = w_1F_1 + w_2F_2$ in n dimensions, using m independent samples from F, there is an algorithm that outputs GMM $\hat{F} = \hat{w}_1\hat{F}_1 + \hat{w}_2\hat{F}_2$ such that, with probability $\ge 1 - \delta$ (over the samples and randomization of the algorithm), is ϵ-close - i.e. there is a permutation $\pi : \{1, 2\} \to \{1, 2\}$ such that,*

$$D(\hat{F}_i, F_{\pi(i)}) \le \epsilon \text{ and } |\hat{w}_i - w_{\pi(i)}| \le \epsilon, \text{for each } i = 1, 2.$$

And the runtime (in the Real RAM model) and number of samples drawn by the algorithm is at most $\text{poly}(n, \frac{1}{\epsilon}, \frac{1}{\delta}, \frac{1}{w_1}, \frac{1}{w_2}, \frac{1}{D(F_1, F_2)})$

The guarantee in the main theorem implies that the estimated parameters are off by an additive $O(\epsilon\sigma_{max}^2)$, where σ_{max}^2 is the largest (projected) variance of either Gaussian in any direction.

Due to space considerations, we do not give the algorithm here but we give a detailed algorithm for the case in which F is in isotropic position in Algorithm 4, and the algorithm in the above theorem begins with a step where samples are used to put the distribution (nearly) in isotropic position, which suffices for the analysis.

Our primary goal is to understand the statistical and computational complexities of this basic problem, and the distinction between polynomial and exponential is a natural step. While the order of the polynomial in our analysis is quite large, to the best of our knowledge these are the first bounds on the convergence rate for the problem in this general context. In some cases, we have favored clarity of presentation over optimality of bounds. The challenge of achieving optimal bounds (optimal rate) is very interesting, and will most likely require further insights and understanding.

As mentioned, our approximation bounds are in terms of the statistical distance between the estimated and true Gaussians. To demonstrate the utility of this type of bound, we note the following corollaries. For both problems, no assumptions are necessary on the underlying mixture. The first problem is simply that of approximating the density F itself.

COROLLARY 2. *For any $n \geq 1, \epsilon, \delta > 0$ and any GMM $F = w_1 F_1 + w_2 F_2$ in n dimensions, using m independent samples from F, there is an algorithm that outputs a GMM $\hat{F} = \hat{w}_1 \hat{F}_1 + \hat{w}_2 \hat{F}_2$ such that with probability $\geq 1-\delta$ (over the samples and randomization of the algorithm) $D(F, \hat{F}) \leq \epsilon$ And the runtime (in the Real RAM model) and number of samples drawn from the oracle is at most* $\text{poly}(n, \frac{1}{\epsilon}, \frac{1}{\delta})$.

The second problem is that of clustering the m data points. In particular, suppose that during the data generation process, for each point $x \in \mathbf{R}^n$, a secret label $y_i \in \{1, 2\}$ (called *ground truth*) is generated based upon which Gaussian was used for sampling. A *clustering algorithm* takes as input m points and outputs a *classifier* $C : \mathbf{R}^n \to \{1, 2\}$. The *error* of a classifier is minimum, over all label permutations, of the probability that the the label of the classifier agrees with ground truth. Of course, achieving a low error is impossible in general. For example, suppose the Gaussians have equal weight and statistical distance 1/2. Then, even armed with the correct mixture parameters, one could not identify with average accuracy greater than 3/4, the label of a randomly chosen point. However, it is not difficult to show that given the correct mixture parameters, the optimal clustering algorithm (minimizing expected errors) simply clusters points based on which Gaussian has a larger posterior probability. We are able to approach the error rate of this classifier and achieve near optimal clustering without *a priori* knowledge of the distribution parameters. See Section 6 for precise details.

COROLLARY 3. *For any $n \geq 1, \epsilon, \delta > 0$ and any GMM $F = w_1 F_1 + w_2 F_2$ in n dimensions, using m independent samples from F, there is an algorithm that outputs a classifier $C_{\hat{F}}$ such that with probability $\geq 1 - \delta$ (over the samples and randomization of the algorithm), the error of $C_{\hat{F}}$ is at most ϵ larger than the error of any classifier, $C' : \mathbf{R}^n \to \{1, 2\}$. And the runtime (in the Real RAM model) and number of samples drawn from the oracle is at most* $\text{poly}(n, \frac{1}{\epsilon}, \frac{1}{\delta})$

In a recent extension of Principal Component Analysis, Brubaker and Vempala [4] give a polynomial-time clustering algorithm that will succeed, with high probability, whenever the Gaussians are nearly separated by any hyperplane. (See 2c for an example.) This algorithm inspired the present work, and our algorithm follows theirs in that both are invariant to affine transformations of the data. Figure 2d illustrates a mixture where clustering is possible although the two Gaussians are not separable by a hyperplane.

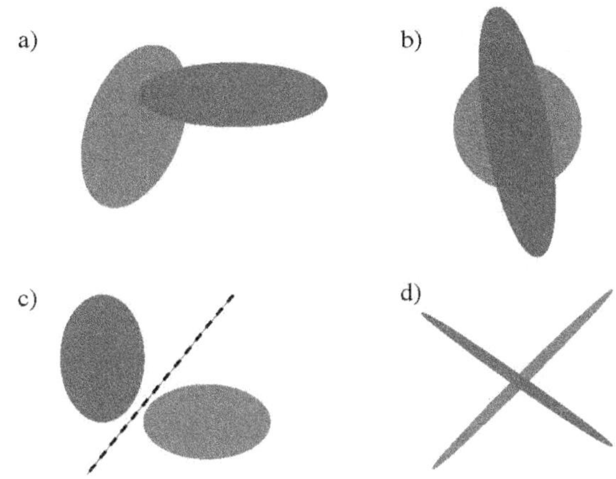

Figure 2: Mixtures of two multinormal distributions, with varying amounts of overlap. Our algorithm will learn the parameters in all cases.

1.3 Outline of Algorithm and Analysis

The problem of identifying Gaussians in high dimensions is surprising in that much of the difficulty seems to be present in the one-dimensional problem. We first briefly explain our reduction from n to 1 dimensions, based upon the fact that the projection of a multivariate GMM is a univariate GMM to which we can apply a one-dimensional algorithm.

When the data is projected down onto a line, each pair $(mean, variance)$ recovered in this direction gives some direct information about the corresponding $(mean, variance)$ pair in n dimensions. Lemma 12 states that for a suitably chosen *random* direction[1], two different Gaussians (statistical distance bounded away from 0) will project down to two reasonably distinct one-dimensional Gaussians, with high probability. For a single Gaussian, knowing the approximate value of the projected mean and variance in $O(n^2)$ linearly independent directions is enough to recover a good approximation for the Gaussian. The remaining challenge is identifying which univariate Gaussian in one projection corresponds to which univariate Gaussian in another projection; one must correctly *match up* the many pairs of univariate Gaussians in each one-dimensional problem. In practice, the mixing weights may be somewhat different, i.e., $|w_1 - w_2|$ is bounded from 0. In such cases, matching would be quite easy because each one-dimensional problem should have one Gaussian with weight close to the true w_1. In the general case, however, we must do something more sophisticated. The solution we employ is simple but certainly not the most efficient – we project to $O(n^2)$ directions which are all very close to each other, so that with high probability the means and variances change very little and are easy to match up. The idea of using random projection for this problem has been used in a variety of theoretical and practical contexts. Independently, Belkin and Sinha considered using random projections to one dimension for the problem of learning a mixture of multiple identical spherical Gaussians [3].

We now proceed to describe how to identify univariate GMMs. Like many one-dimensional problems, it is algorithmically *easy* because simple brute-force algorithms (like

[1]The random direction is not uniform but is chosen in accordance with shape (covariance matrix) of the data, making the algorithm affine invariant.

that of [10]) will work. The surprising difficulty is proving that such brute force algorithms cannot return wrong (or spurious) estimates. What if there were two mixtures where all four Gaussians were at least ϵ-different in statistical distance, yet the resulting mixtures were exponentially close in statistical distance? Ruling out this possibility is, in fact, a central hurdle in this work.

We appeal to the old method of moments. In particular, the key fact is that univariate mixtures of two Gaussians are *polynomially robustly identifiable*–that is, if two mixtures have parameter sets differing by ϵ then one of the low-order moments will differ: i.e. $|\mathrm{E}_{x\sim F}[x^i] - \mathrm{E}_{x\sim F'}[x^i]|$ will be at least $\mathrm{poly}(\epsilon)$ for some $i \leq 6$.

> **Polynomially Robust Identifiability (Informal version of Theorem 4):** Consider two one-dimensional mixtures of two Gaussians, F, F', where F's mean is 0 and variance is 1. If the parameter sets differ by ϵ, then at least one of the first six raw moments of F will differ from that of F' by $\mathrm{poly}(\epsilon)$.

Using this theorem, a brute force search will work correctly: First normalize the data so that it has mean 0 and variance 1 (called *isotropic position*). Then perform a brute-force search over mixture parameters, choosing the one whose moments best fit the empirical moments and this will necessarily be a good estimate for the parameters. We now describe the proof of Theorem 4. The two ideas are to relate the statistical distance of two mixtures to the discrepancy in the moments, and *deconvolution*.

1.3.1 Relating statistical distance and discrepancy in moments

If two (bounded or almost bounded) distributions are statistically close, then their low-order moments must be close. However, the converse is not true in general. For example, consider the uniform distribution over $[0, 1]$ and the distribution whose density is proportional to $|\sin(Nx)|$ over $x \in [0, 1]$, for very large N. Crucial to this example is that the difference in the two densities oscillate many times, which cannot happen for mixtures of two univariate Gaussians. Lemma 8 shows that if two univariate GMMs have nonnegligible statistical distance, then they must have a nonnegligible difference in one of the first six moments. Hence statistical distance and moment discrepancy are closely related.

We very briefly describe the proof of Lemma 8. Denote the difference in the two probability density functions by $f(x)$; by assumption, $\int |f(x)|dx$ is nonnegligible. We first argue that $f(x)$ has at most six zero-crossings (using a general fact about the effect of convolution by a Gaussian on the number of zeros of a function), from which it follows that there is a degree-six polynomial whose sign always matches that of $f(x)$. Call this polynomial p. Intuitively, $\mathrm{E}[p(x)]$ should be different under the two distributions; namely $\int_{\mathbf{R}} p(x)f(x)dx$ should be bounded from 0 (provided we make sure that the mass of $f(x)$ is not too concentrated near any zero). Then if the coefficients of $p(x)$ are bounded, this implies $\mathrm{E}[x^i]$ differs under the two distributions, for some $i \leq 6$.

1.3.2 Deconvolving Gaussians

The convolution of two Gaussians is a Gaussian, just as the sum of two normal random variables is normal. Hence, we can also consider the "deconvolution" of the mixture by a Gaussian of variance, say, α – this is a simple operation which subtracts α from the variance of each Gaussian in the mixture. In fact, it affects all the moments in a simple, predictable fashion, and we show that a discrepancy in the low-order moments of two mixtures is roughly preserved by convolution. (See Lemma 6).

If we choose α close to the smallest variance of the four Gaussians that comprise the two mixtures, then after deconvolving, one of the mixtures has a Gaussian component that is very skinny – nearly a Dirac Delta function. When one of the four Gaussians is very skinny, it is intuitively clear that unless this skinny Gaussian is closely matched by a similar skinny Gaussian in the other mixture, the two mixtures will have large statistical distance. And if instead there are two closely matched Gaussians, these can be removed from the respective mixtures and we can compare the remaining Gaussians directly and obtain a large statistical distance directly (see Lemma 5).

The proof of Theorem 4 then follows: (1) after deconvolution, at least one of the four Gaussians is very skinny; (2) combining this with the fact that the parameters of the two GMMs are slightly different, the deconvolved GMMs have nonnegligible statistical distance; (Lemma 5) (3) nonnegligible statistical distance implies nonnegligible moment discrepancy (Lemma 8); and (4) if there is a discrepancy in one the low-order moments of two GMMs, then after convolution by a Gaussian, there will still be a discrepancy in some low-order moment (Lemma 6).

2. NOTATION AND PRELIMINARIES

Let $\mathcal{N}(\mu, \Sigma)$ denote the multinormal distribution with mean $\mu \in \mathbf{R}^n$ and $n \times n$ covariance matrix Σ, with density

$$\mathcal{N}(\mu, \Sigma, x) = (2\pi)^{-n/2}|\Sigma|^{-1/2}e^{-\frac{1}{2}(x-\mu)^T\Sigma^{-1}(x-\mu)}.$$

For probability distribution F, define the *mean* $\mu(F) = \mathrm{E}_{x\sim F}[x]$ and *covariance matrix*

$$\mathrm{var}(F) = \mathrm{E}_{x\sim F}[xx^T] - \mu(F)(\mu(F))^T$$

A distribution is *isotropic* or in *isotropic position* if the mean is zero and the covariance matrix is the identity matrix.

For distributions F and G with densities f and g, define the ℓ_1 distance $\|F - G\|_1 = \int_{\mathbf{R}^n} |f(x) - g(x)|dx$. Define the *statistical distance* or *variation distance* by $D(F, G) = \frac{1}{2}\|F - G\|_1 = F(S) - G(S)$, where $S = \{x | f(x) \geq g(x)\}$.

For vector $v \in \mathbf{R}^n$, Let P_v be the projection onto v, i.e., $P_v(w) = v \cdot w$, for vector $w \in \mathbf{R}^n$. For probability distribution F over $\mathbf{R}^n$, $P_v(F)$ denotes the marginal probability distribution over $\mathbf{R}$, i.e., the distribution of $x \cdot v$, where x is drawn from F. For Gaussian G, we have that $\mu(P_v(G)) = v \cdot \mu(G)$ and $\mathrm{var}(P_v(G)) = v^T \mathrm{var}(G)v$.

Let $\mathbb{S}_{n-1} = \{x \in \mathbf{R}^n : \|x\| = 1\}$. We write $\Pr_{u\in\mathbb{S}_{n-1}}$ over u chosen uniformly at random from the unit sphere. For probability distribution F, we define an *sample oracle* $\mathrm{SA}(F)$ to be an oracle that, each time invoked, returns an independent sample drawn according to F. Note that given $\mathrm{SA}(F)$ and a vector $v \in \mathbf{R}^n$, we can efficiently simulate $\mathrm{SA}(P_v(F))$ by invoking $\mathrm{SA}(F)$ to get sample x, and then returning $v \cdot x$.

For probability distribution F over $\mathbf{R}$, define $M_i(F) = \mathrm{E}_{x\sim F}[x^i]$ to be the ith (raw) moment.

3. THE UNIVARIATE PROBLEM

In this section, we will show that one can efficiently learn one-dimensional mixtures of two Gaussians. To be most useful in the reduction from n to 1 dimensions, Theorem 9 will be stated in terms of achieving estimated parameters that are off by a small additive error (and will assume the true mixture is in isotropic position).

The main technical hurdle in this result is showing the *polynomially robust identifiability* of these mixtures: that is, given two such mixtures with parameter sets that differ by ϵ, we show that one of the first six raw moments will differ by at least poly(ϵ). Given this result, it will be relatively easy to show that by performing essentially a brute-force search over a sufficiently fine (but still polynomial-sized) mesh of the set of possible parameters, one will be able to efficiently learn the 1-d mixture.

3.1 Polynomially Robust Identifiability

Throughout this section, we will consider two mixtures of one-dimensional Gaussians:

$$F(x) = \sum_{i=1}^{2} w_i \mathcal{N}(\mu_i, \sigma_i^2, x), \text{ and } F'(x) = \sum_{i=1}^{2} w_i' \mathcal{N}(\mu_i', \sigma_i'^2, x).$$

DEFINITION 1. *We will call the pair F, F' ϵ-standard if $\sigma_i^2, \sigma_i'^2 \leq 1$ and if ϵ satisfies:*

1. $w_i, w_i' \in [\epsilon, 1]$
2. $|\mu_i|, |\mu_i'| \leq \frac{1}{\epsilon}$
3. $|\mu_1 - \mu_2| + |\sigma_1^2 - \sigma_2^2| \geq \epsilon$ *and* $|\mu_1' - \mu_2'| + |\sigma_1'^2 - \sigma_2'^2| \geq \epsilon$
4. $\epsilon \leq \min_\pi \sum_i \left(|w_i - w_{\pi(i)}'| + |\mu_i - \mu_{\pi(i)}'| + |\sigma_i^2 - \sigma_{\pi(i)}'^2|\right)$, *where the minimization is taken over all permutations π of $\{1, 2\}$.*

THEOREM 4. *There is a constant $c > 0$ such that, for any $\epsilon < c$ and any ϵ-standard F, F',*

$$\max_{i \leq 6} |M_i(F) - M_i(F')| \geq \epsilon^{67}$$

In order to prove this theorem, we rely on "deconvolving" by a Gaussian with an appropriately chosen variance (this corresponds to running the heat equation in reverse for a suitable amount of time). We define the operation of deconvolving by a Gaussian of variance α as $\mathcal{F}_\alpha$; applying this operator to a mixture of Gaussians has a particularly simple effect: subtract α from the variance of each Gaussian in the mixture (assuming that each constituent Gaussian has variance at least α).

DEFINITION 2. *Let $F(x) = \sum_{i=1}^{n} w_i \mathcal{N}(\mu_i, \sigma_i^2, x)$ be the probability density function of a mixture of Gaussian distributions, and for any $\alpha < \min_i \sigma_i^2$, define*

$$\mathcal{F}_\alpha(F)(x) = \sum_{i=1}^{n} w_i \mathcal{N}(\mu_i, \sigma_i^2 - \alpha, x).$$

Consider any two mixtures of Gaussians that are ϵ-standard. Ideally, we would like to prove that these two mixtures have statistical distance at least poly(ϵ). We settle instead for proving that there is some α for which the resulting mixtures (after applying the operation $\mathcal{F}_\alpha$) have large statistical distance. Intuitively, this deconvolution operation allows us to isolate Gaussians in each mixture and then we can reason about the statistical distance between the two mixtures locally, without worrying about the other Gaussian in the mixture. We now show that we can always choose an α so as to yield a large ℓ_1 distance between $\mathcal{F}_\alpha(F)$ and $\mathcal{F}_\alpha(F')$.

LEMMA 5. *Suppose F, F' are ϵ-standard. There is some α such that $D(\mathcal{F}_\alpha(F), \mathcal{F}_\alpha(F')) \geq \Omega(\epsilon^4)$, and such an α can be chosen so that the smallest variance of any constituent Gaussian in $\mathcal{F}_\alpha(F)$ and $\mathcal{F}_\alpha(F')$ is at least ϵ^{12}.*

The proof of the above lemma is through an analysis of several cases. Assume without loss of generality that the first constituent Gaussian of mixture F has the minimal variance among all Gaussians in F and F'. Consider the difference between the two density functions. We lower-bound the ℓ_1 norm of this function on $\mathbf{R}$. The first case to consider is when both Gaussians in F' either have variance significantly larger than σ_1^2, or means far from μ_1. In this case, we can pick α so as to show that there is $\Omega(\epsilon^4)$ statistical distance in a small interval around μ_1 in $\mathcal{F}_\alpha(F) - \mathcal{F}_\alpha(F')$. In the second case, if one Gaussians in F' has parameters that very closely match σ_1, μ_1, then if the weights do not match very closely, we can use a similar approach as to the previous case. If the weights do match, then we choose an α very, very close to σ_1^2, to essentially make one of the Gaussians in each mixture nearly vanish, except on some tiny interval. We conclude that the parameters σ_2, μ_2 must not be closely matched by parameters of F', and demonstrate an $\Omega(\epsilon^4)$ statistical distance coming from the mismatch in the second Gaussian components in $\mathcal{F}_\alpha(F)$ and $\mathcal{F}_\alpha(F')$. The details are laborious, and are deferred to the the full version of our paper.

Unfortunately, the transformation $\mathcal{F}_\alpha$ does not preserve the statistical distance between two distributions. However, we show that it, at least roughly, preserves the disparity in low-order moments of the distributions. Specifically, we show that if there is an $i \leq 6$ such that the ith raw moment of $\mathcal{F}_\alpha(F)$ is at least poly(ϵ) different than the ith raw moment of $\mathcal{F}_\alpha(F')$ then there is a $j \leq 6$ such that the jth raw moment of F is at least poly(ϵ) different than the jth raw moment of F'.

LEMMA 6. *Suppose that each constituent Gaussian in F or F' has variances in the interval $[\alpha, 1]$. Then*

$$\frac{\sum_{i=1}^{k} |M_i(\mathcal{F}_\alpha(F)) - M_i(\mathcal{F}_\alpha(F'))|}{\sum_{i=1}^{k} |M_i(F) - M_i(F')|} \leq \frac{(k+1)!}{\lfloor k/2 \rfloor !},$$

The key observation here is that the moments of F and $\mathcal{F}_\alpha(F)$ are related by a simple linear transformation; and this can also be viewed as a recurrence relation for Hermite polynomials. We defer a proof to the full version of our paper.

To complete the proof of the theorem, we must show that the poly(ϵ) statistical distance between $\mathcal{F}_\alpha(F)$ and $\mathcal{F}_\alpha(F')$ gives rise to a poly(ϵ) disparity in one of the first six raw moments of the distributions. To accomplish this, we show that there are at most 6 zero-crossings of the difference in densities, $f = \mathcal{F}_\alpha(F) - \mathcal{F}_\alpha(F')$, using properties of the evolution of the heat equation, and then we construct a degree six polynomial $p(x)$ that always has the same sign as $f(x)$, so that when $p(x)$ is integrated against $f(x)$ the result is at least poly(ϵ). We construct this polynomial so that the coefficients are bounded, and this implies that there is some raw moment i (at most the degree of the polynomial) for which the difference between the ith raw moment of $\mathcal{F}_\alpha(F)$ and of $\mathcal{F}_\alpha(F')$ is large.

Our first step is to show that $\mathcal{F}_\alpha(D)(x) - \mathcal{F}_\alpha(D')(x)$ has a constant number of zeros.

PROPOSITION 1. *Given $f(x) = \sum_{i=1}^k a_i \mathcal{N}(\mu_i, \sigma_i^2, x)$, the linear combination of k one-dimensional Gaussian probability density functions, such that $\sigma_i^2 \neq \sigma_j^2$ for $i \neq j$, assuming that not all the a_i's are zero, the number of solutions to $f(x) = 0$ is at most $2(k-1)$. Furthermore, this bound is tight.*

Using only the facts that quotients of Gaussians are Gaussian and that the number of zeros of a differentiable function is at most one more than the number of zeros of its derivative, one can prove that linear combinations of k Gaussians have at most 2^k zeros. However, since the number of zeros dictates the number of moments that we must match in our univariate estimation problem, we will use more powerful machinery to prove the tighter bound of $2(k-1)$ zeros. Our proof of Proposition 1 will hinge upon the following Theorem, due to Hummel and Gidas [12], and we defer the details to the full version of our paper.

THEOREM 7 (THM 2.1 IN [12]). *Given $f(x) : \mathbb{R} \to \mathbb{R}$, that is analytic and has n zeros, then for any $\sigma^2 > 0$, the function $g(x) = f(x) \circ \mathcal{N}(0, \sigma^2, x)$ has at most n zeros.*

Let $f(x) = \mathcal{F}_\alpha(F)(x) - \mathcal{F}_\alpha(F')(x)$, where α is chosen according to Lemma 5 so that $\int_x |f(x)|dx = \Omega(\epsilon^4)$.

LEMMA 8. *There is some $i \leq 6$ such that*

$$\left|\int_x x^i f(x) dx\right| = |M_i(\mathcal{F}_\alpha(F)) - M_i(\mathcal{F}_\alpha(F'))| = \Omega(\epsilon^{66})$$

A sketch of the proof of the above lemma is as follows: Let $x_1, x_2, \ldots, x_k$ be the zeros of $f(x)$ which have $|x_i| \leq \frac{2}{\epsilon}$. Using Proposition 1, the number of such zeros is at most the total number of zeros of $f(x)$ which is bounded by 6. We prove that there is some $i \leq 6$ for which $|M_i(\mathcal{F}_\alpha(F)) - M_i(\mathcal{F}_\alpha(F'))| = \Omega(poly(\epsilon))$ by constructing a degree 6 polynomial (with bounded coefficients) $p(x)$ such that the integral of $p(x)$ against $f(x)$ is at least $\Omega(poly(\epsilon))$. Then if the coefficients of $p(x)$ can be bounded by some polynomial in $\frac{1}{\epsilon}$ we can conclude that there is some $i \leq 6$ for which the ith moment of F is different from the ith moment of $\hat{F}$ by at least $\Omega(poly(\epsilon))$. So we choose $p(x) = \pm \prod_{i=1}^k (x - x_i)$ and we choose the sign of $p(x)$ so that $p(x)$ has the same sign as $f(x)$ on the interval $I = [\frac{-2}{\epsilon}, \frac{2}{\epsilon}]$. Lemma 5 together with tail bounds imply that $\int_I |f(x)|dx \geq \Omega(\epsilon^4)$. To finish the proof, we show that $\int_I p(x)f(x)dx$ is large, and that $\int_{\mathbb{R}\setminus I} p(x)f(x)dx$ is negligibly small. We defer a full proof to the full version of our paper.

These tools are enough to yield a proof of Theorem 4.

3.2 The Univariate Algorithm

We now leverage the robust identifiability shown in Theorem 4 to prove that we can efficiently learn the parameters of 1-d GMM via a brute-force search over a set of candidate parameter sets. Roughly, the algorithm will take a polynomial number of samples, compute the first 6 sample moments, and compare those with the first 6 (analytic) moments of each of the candidate parameter sets. The algorithm then returns the parameter set whose moments most closely match the sample moments. Theorem 4 guarantees that if the first 6 sample moments closely match those of the chosen parameter set, then the parameter set must be nearly accurate. To conclude the proof, we argue that a polynomial-sized set of candidate parameters suffices to guarantee that at least one set of parameters will yield moments sufficiently close to the sample moments. We state the theorem below, and defer the details of the algorithm, and the proof of its correctness to the full version of our paper.

THEOREM 9. *Suppose we are given access to independent samples from any* **isotropic** *mixture $F = w_1F_1 + w_2F_2$, where $w_1 + w_2 = 1$, $w_i \geq \epsilon$, and each F_i is a univariate Gaussian with mean μ_i and variance σ_i^2, satisfying $|\mu_1 - \mu_2| + |\sigma_1^2 - \sigma_2^2| \geq \epsilon$,. Then Algorithm 1 will use $\text{poly}(\frac{1}{\epsilon}, \frac{1}{\delta})$ samples and with probability at least $1-\delta$ will output mixture parameters $\hat{w}_1, \hat{w}_2, \hat{\mu}_1, \hat{\mu}_2, \hat{\sigma_1}^2, \hat{\sigma}_2^2$, so that there is a permutation $\pi : \{1,2\} \to \{1,2\}$ so that for each $i = 1, 2$*

$$|w_i - \hat{w}_{\pi(i)}| \leq \epsilon, \quad |\mu_i - \hat{\mu}_{\pi(i)}| \leq \epsilon, \quad |\sigma_i^2 - \hat{\sigma}_{\pi(i)}^2| \leq \epsilon$$

The brute-force search in the univariate algorithm is rather inefficient – we presented it for clarity of intuition, and ease of description and proof. Alternatively, we could have proceeded along the lines of Pearson's work [19]: using the first five sample moments, one generates a ninth degree polynomial whose solutions yield a small set of candidate parameter sets (which, one can argue, includes one set whose sixth moment closely matches the sixth sample moment). After picking the parameters whose sixth moment most closely matches the sample moment, we can use Theorem 4 to prove that the parameters have the desired accuracy.

4. THE N-DIMENSIONAL ALGORITHM

In this section, via a series of projections and applications of the univariate parameter learning algorithm of the previous section, we show how to efficiently learn the mixture parameters of an n-dimensional GMM. Let $\epsilon > 0$ be our target error accuracy. Let $\delta > 0$ be our target failure probability. For this section, we will suppose further that $w_1, w_2 \geq \epsilon$ and $D(F_1, F_2) \geq \epsilon$.

We first analyze our algorithm in the case where the GMM F is in *isotropic position*. This means that $\mathrm{E}_{x\sim F}[x] = 0$ and, $\mathrm{E}_{x\sim F}[xx^T] = I_n$. The above condition on the co-variance matrix is equivalent to $\forall u \in \mathbb{S}_{n-1}\ \ \mathrm{E}_{x\sim F}[(u \cdot x)^2] = 1$. In the full version of our paper we explain the general case which involves first using a number of samples to put the distribution in (approximately) isotropic position, and then running the isotropic algorithm.

Given a mixture in isotropic position, we first argue that we can get ϵ-close additive approximations to the weights, means and variances of the Gaussians. This does not suffice to upper-bound $D(F_i, \hat{F}_i)$ in the case where F_i has small variance along one dimension. For example, consider a univariate GMM $F = \frac{1}{2}\mathcal{N}(0, 2-\epsilon') + \frac{1}{2}\mathcal{N}(0, \epsilon')$, where $\epsilon' \ll \epsilon$ is arbitrarily small (even possibly 0 – the Gaussian is a point mass). Note that an additive error of ϵ, say $\hat{\sigma}_2 = \epsilon' + \epsilon$ leads to a variation distance near $\frac{1}{2}$. In this case, however, $D(\hat{F}_1, \hat{F}_2)$ must be very close to 1, i.e., the Gaussians nearly do not overlap.[2] The solution is to use the additive approx-

[2]We are indebted to Santosh Vempala for suggesting this idea, namely, that if one of the Gaussians is very thin, then they must be almost non-overlapping and therefore clustering may be applied.

ALGORITHM 1. UNIVARIATE ESTIMATION
Input: $\epsilon > 0, \delta > 0$, sample oracle SA(F).
Output: For $i = 1, 2$, $(\hat{w}_i, \hat{\mu}_i, \hat{\sigma}_i) \in \mathbf{R}^3$.
(* Note: this algorithm assumes that the mixture is isotropic position, i.e., $\mathrm{E}[x] = 0, \mathrm{E}[x^2] = 1$. *)

1. Let $\hat{M}_1 = 0$, $\hat{M}_2 = 1$.
2. Let $\alpha = \epsilon^{150}$, and choose $m, N \in \mathbb{N}$ such that $m \geq \frac{500^2}{\alpha^2 \delta}$, and $N \geq \frac{1}{\alpha \epsilon^3}$.
3. For $i = 3, 4, 5, 6$:
   - Let $\hat{M}_i = \frac{1}{m} \sum_{j=1}^{m} x_i^j$, where $x_1, x_2, \ldots, x_m$ are m samples drawn from SA(F).

   (* Brute-force search: *)
4. Let $\mathcal{A} = \{\frac{1}{N}, \frac{2}{N}, \ldots, \frac{N-1}{N}\}$, $\mathcal{B} = \{-N, -N + \frac{1}{N}, -N + \frac{2}{N}, \ldots, N\}$.
5. For each $(\hat{w}_1, \hat{\mu}_1, \hat{\sigma}_1, \hat{\mu}_2, \hat{\sigma}_2) \in \mathcal{A} \times \mathcal{B}^4$, let:

$$\hat{w}_2 = 1 - \hat{w}_1 \tag{1}$$

$$\text{for } i = 1, 2, \ldots, 6: \quad \tilde{M}_i = M_i\left(\hat{w}_1 \mathcal{N}(\hat{\mu}_1, \hat{\sigma}_1^2) + \hat{w}_2 \mathcal{N}(\hat{\mu}_2, \hat{\sigma}_2^2)\right) \tag{2}$$

$$\mathrm{disc}_{\hat{w}_1, \hat{\mu}_1, \hat{\sigma}_1^2, \hat{w}_2, \hat{\mu}_2, \hat{\sigma}_2^2} = \max_{i \in \{1,2,\ldots,6\}} \left|\hat{M}_i - \tilde{M}_i\right| \tag{3}$$

6. Output $(\hat{w}_1, \hat{\mu}_1, \hat{\sigma}_1^2, \hat{w}_2, \hat{\mu}_2, \hat{\sigma}_2^2)$ of minimal $\mathrm{disc}_{\hat{w}_1, \hat{\mu}_1, \hat{\sigma}_1^2, \hat{w}_2, \hat{\mu}_2, \hat{\sigma}_2^2}$ that satisfies $|\hat{\mu}_1 - \hat{\mu}_2| + |\hat{\sigma}_1^2 - \hat{\sigma}_2^2| > \epsilon$.

Figure 3: The one-dimensional estimation algorithm. For (2), evaluation of the moments of the distributions may be done exactly using explicit formulas for the first six moments of a Gaussian, given in Appendix ??.

imation to the Gaussians to then cluster the data. From clustered data, the problem is simply one of estimating a single Gaussian from random samples, which is easy to do in polynomial time.

4.1 Additive approximation

LEMMA 10. *For any $n \geq 1$, $\epsilon, \delta > 0$, for any any* isotropic *GMM mixture $F = w_1 F_1 + w_2 F_2$, where $w_1 + w_2 = 1$, $w_i \geq \epsilon$, and each F_i is a Gaussian in $\mathbf{R}^n$ with $D(F_1, F_2) \geq \epsilon$, with probability $\geq 1 - \delta$, (over the samples and randomization of the algorithm), Algorithm 2 will output GMM $\hat{F} = \hat{w}_1 \hat{F}_1 + \hat{w}_2 \hat{F}_2$ such that there exists a permutation $\pi : [2] \to [2]$ so that for each $i = 1, 2$*

$$\|\hat{\mu}_i - \mu_{\pi(i)}\| \leq \epsilon, \|\hat{\Sigma}_i - \Sigma_{\pi(i)}\|_F \leq \epsilon, \text{ and } |\hat{w}_i - w_{\pi(i)}| \leq \epsilon$$

And the runtime and number of samples drawn by Algorithm 2 is at most $\mathrm{poly}(n, \frac{1}{\epsilon}, \frac{1}{\delta})$.

Algorithm 2 is given in Figures 4 and 5. The rest of this section gives an outline of the proof of this lemma. We first state two geometric lemmas (Lemmas 11 and 12) that are independent of the algorithm.

LEMMA 11. *For any $\mu_1, \mu_2 \in \mathbf{R}^n, \delta > 0$, over uniformly random unit vectors u,*

$$\Pr_{u \in \mathbb{S}_{n-1}}\left[|u \cdot \mu_1 - u \cdot \mu_2| \leq \delta \|\mu_1 - \mu_2\| / \sqrt{n}\right] \leq \delta.$$

PROOF. If $\mu_1 = \mu_2$, the lemma is trivial. Otherwise, let $v = (\mu_1 - \mu_2)/\|\mu_1 - \mu_2\|$. The lemma is equivalent to claiming that

$$\Pr_{u \in \mathbb{S}_{n-1}}[|u \cdot v \leq t] \leq t\sqrt{n}.$$

This is a standard fact about random unit vectors (see, e.g., Lemma 1 of [6]). □

We next prove that, given a random unit vector r, with high probability either the projected means onto r or the projected variances onto r of F_1, F_2 must be different by at least $\mathrm{poly}(\epsilon, \frac{1}{n})$. A qualitative argument as to why this lemma is true is roughly: suppose that for most directions r, the projected means $r^T \mu_1$ and $r^T \mu_2$ are close, and the projected variances $r^T \Sigma_1 r$ and $r^T \Sigma_2 r$ are close, then the statistical distance $D(F_1, F_2)$ must be small too. So conversely, given $D(F_1, F_2) \geq \epsilon$ and $w_1, w_2 \geq \epsilon$ (and the distribution is in isotropic position), for most directions r either the projected means or the projected variances must be different.

LEMMA 12. *Let $\epsilon, \delta > 0$, $t \in (0, \epsilon^2)$. Suppose that $\|\mu_1 - \mu_2\| \leq t$. Then, for uniformly random r,*

$$\Pr_{r \in \mathbb{S}_{n-1}}\left[\min\{r^T \Sigma_1 r, r^T \Sigma_2 r\} > 1 - \frac{\epsilon \delta^2 (\epsilon^3 - t^2)}{12 n^2}\right] \leq \delta.$$

This lemma holds under the assumptions that we have already made about the mixture in this section (namely isotropy and lower bounds on the weights and statistical distance). While the above lemma is quite intuitive, the proof involves a probabilistic analysis based on the eigenvalues of the two covariance matrices, and is deferred to the full version.

Next, suppose that $r^T \mu_1 - r^T \mu_2 \geq poly(\epsilon, \frac{1}{n})$. Continuity arguments imply that if we choose a direction $r^{i,j}$ sufficiently

ALGORITHM 2. HIGH-DIMENSIONAL ISOTROPIC ADDITIVE APPROXIMATION
Input: Integers $n \geq 1$, reals $\epsilon, \delta > 0$, sample oracle $\text{SA}(F)$.
Output: For $i = 1, 2$, $(\hat{w}_i, \hat{\mu}_i, \hat{\Sigma}_i) \in \mathbf{R} \times \mathbf{R}^n \times \mathbf{R}^{n \times n}$.

1. Let $\epsilon_4 = \frac{\epsilon\delta}{100n}$, and $\epsilon_i = \epsilon_{i+1}^{10}$, for $i = 3, 2, 1$.
2. Choose uniformly random orthonormal basis $B = (b_1, \ldots, b_n) \in \mathbf{R}^{n \times n}$. Let $r = \sum_{i=1}^n b_i/\sqrt{n}$. Let $r^{ij} = r + \epsilon_2 b_i + \epsilon_2 b_j$ for each $i, j \in [n]$.
3. Run $\text{UNIVARIATE}(\epsilon_1, \frac{\delta}{3n^2}, \text{SA}(P_r(F)))$ to get a univariate mixture of Gaussians $\hat{w}_1 G_1^0 + \hat{w}_2 G_2^0$.
4. If $\min\{\hat{w}_1, \hat{w}_2\} < \epsilon_3$ or $\max\{|\mu(G_1^0) - \mu(G_2^0)|, |\text{var}(G_1^0) - \text{var}(G_2^0)|\} < \epsilon_3$, then halt and output $FAIL$ ELSE:
5. If $|\mu(G_1^0) - \mu(G_2^0)| > \epsilon_3$, then:
   - Permute G_1^0, G_2^0 (and $\hat{w}_1, \hat{w}_2$) as necessary so that $\mu(G_1^0) < \mu(G_2^0)$. ELSE
   - Permute G_1^0, G_2^0 (and $\hat{w}_1, \hat{w}_2$) as necessary so $\text{var}(G_1^0) < \text{var}(G_2^0)$.
6. For each $i, j \in [n]$:
   - Run $\text{UNIVARIATE}(\epsilon_1, \frac{\delta}{3n^2}, \text{SA}(P_{r^{ij}}(F)))$ to get estimates of a univariate mixture of two Gaussians, G_1^{ij}, G_2^{ij}. (* We ignore the weights returned by the algorithm. *)
   - If $\mu(G_2^0) - \mu(G_1^0) > \epsilon_3$, then:
     - Permute G_1^{ij}, G_2^{ij} as necessary so that $\mu(G_1^{ij}) < \mu(G_2^{ij})$. ELSE
     - Permute G_1^{ij}, G_2^{ij} as necessary so that $\text{var}(G_1^{ij}) < \text{var}(G_2^{ij})$.
7. Output $\hat{w}_1, \hat{w}_2$, and for $\ell \in \{1, 2\}$, and output

$$(\hat{\mu}_\ell, \hat{\Sigma}_\ell) = \text{SOLVE}\left(n, \epsilon_2, B, \mu(G_\ell^0), \text{var}(G_\ell^0), \left\langle \mu(G_\ell^{ij}), \text{var}(G_\ell^{ij}) \right\rangle_{i,j \in [n]}\right)$$

Figure 4: A dimension reduction algorithm. Although ϵ_4 is not used by the algorithm, it is helpful to define it for the analysis. We choose such ridiculously small parameters to make it clear that our efforts are placed on simplicity of presentation rather than tightness of parameters.

ALGORITHM 3. SOLVE
Input: $n \geq 1$, $\epsilon_2 > 0$, basis $B = (b_1, \ldots, b_n) \in \mathbf{R}^{n \times n}$, means and variances m^0, v^0, and $m^{ij}, v^{ij} \in \mathbf{R}$ for each $i, j \in [n]$.
Output: $\hat{\mu} \in \mathbf{R}^n$, $\hat{\Sigma} \in \mathbf{R}^{n \times n}$.

1. Let $v^i = \frac{1}{n} \sum_{j=1}^n v^{ij}$ and $v = \frac{1}{n^2} \sum_{i=1}^n v^{ij}$.
2. For each $i \leq j \in [n]$, let

$$V_{ij} = \frac{\sqrt{n}(v - v^i - v^j)}{(2\epsilon_2 + \sqrt{n})2\epsilon_2^2} - \frac{v^{ii} + v^{jj}}{(2\epsilon_2 + \sqrt{n})4\epsilon_2} - \frac{v^0}{2\epsilon_2\sqrt{n}} + \frac{v^{ij}}{2\epsilon_2^2}.$$

3. For each $i > j \in [n]$, let $V_{ij} = V_{ji}$. (* So $V \in \mathbf{R}^{n \times n}$ *)
4. Output

$$\hat{\mu} = \sum_{i=1}^n \frac{m^{ii} - m^0}{2\epsilon_2} b_i, \quad \hat{\Sigma} = B\left(\arg\min_{M \succeq 0} \|M - V\|_F\right) B^T.$$

Figure 5: Solving the equations. In the last step, we project onto the set of positive semidefinite matrices, which can be done in polynomial time using semidefinite programming.

close to r, then $(r^{i,j})^T\mu_1 - (r^{i,j})^T\mu_2$ will not change much from $r^T\mu_1 - r^T\mu_2$. So given a univariate algorithm that computes estimates for the mixture parameters in direction r and in direction $r^{i,j}$, we can determine a pairing of these parameters so that we now have estimates for the mean of F_1 projected on r and estimates for the mean of F_1 projected on $r^{i,j}$, and similarly we have estimates for the projected variances (on r and $r^{i,j}$) of F_1. From sufficiently many of these estimates in different directions $r^{i,j}$, we can hope to recover the mean and covariance matrix of F_1, and similarly for F_2. An analogous statement will also hold in the case that for direction r, the projected variances are different in which case choosing a direction $r^{i,j}$ sufficiently close to r will result in not much change in the projected variances, and we can similarly use these continuity arguments (and a univariate algorithm) to again recover many estimates in different directions.

LEMMA 13. *For r, r^{ij} of Algorithm 2, (a) With probability $\geq 1-\delta$ over the random unit vector r, $|r\cdot(\mu_1-\mu_2)| > 2\epsilon_3$ or $|r^T(\Sigma_1-\Sigma_2)r| > 2\epsilon_3$, (b) $|(r^{ij}-r)\cdot(\mu_1-\mu_2)| \leq \epsilon_3/3$, and (c) $|(r^{ij})^T(\Sigma_1-\Sigma_2)r^{ij} - r^T(\Sigma_1-\Sigma_2)r| \leq \epsilon_3/3$.*

The proof, based on Lemma 12, is given in the full version. We then argue that SOLVE outputs the desired parameters. Given estimates of the projected mean and projected variance of F_1 in n^2 directions $r^{i,j}$, each such estimate yields a linear constraint on the mean and covariance matrix. Provided that each estimate is close to the correct projected mean and projected variance, we can recover an accurate estimate of the parameters of F_1, and similarly for F_2. Thus, using the algorithm for estimating mixture parameters for univariate GMMs $F = w_1F_1 + w_2F_2$, we can get a polynomial time algorithm for estimating mixture parameters in n-dimensions for isotropic Gaussian mixtures. Further details are deferred to the full version.

LEMMA 14. *Let $\epsilon_2, \epsilon_1 > 0$. Suppose $|m^0 - \mu\cdot r|, |m^{ij} - \mu\cdot r^{ij}|$, $|v^0 - r^T\Sigma r|, |v^{ij} - (r^{ij})^T\Sigma r^{ij}|$ are all at most ϵ_1. Then* SOLVE *outputs $\hat{\mu}\in\mathbf{R}^n$ and $\hat{\Sigma}\in\mathbf{R}^{n\times n}$ such that $\|\hat{\mu}-\mu\| < \epsilon$, and $\|\hat{\Sigma}-\Sigma\|_F \leq \epsilon$. Furthermore, $\hat{\Sigma}\succeq 0$ and $\hat{\Sigma}$ is symmetric.*

4.2 Statistical approximation

It remains to achieve, with high probability, approximations to the Gaussians that are close in terms of variation distance. An additive bound on error yields bounded variation distance, only for Gaussians that are relatively "round," in the sense that their covariance matrix has a smallest eigenvalue that is bounded away from 0. However, if, for isotropic F, one of the Gaussians has a very small eigenvalue, then this means that they are practically nonoverlapping, i.e., $D(F_1, F_2)$ is close to 1. In this case, our estimates from Algorithm 2 are good enough, with high probability, to cluster a polynomial amount of data into two clusters based on whether it came from Gaussian F_1 or F_2. After that, we can easily estimate the parameters of the two Gaussians. The statistical approximation algorithm is given in Algorithm 4, and proof of the lemma is deferred to the full version.

LEMMA 15. *For any $n\geq 1$, $\epsilon,\delta > 0$, for any any* isotropic *GMM mixture $F = w_1F_1 + w_2F_2$, where $w_1+w_2 = 1$, $w_i \geq \epsilon$, and each F_i is a Gaussian in $\mathbf{R}^n$ with $D(F_1,F_2)\geq\epsilon$, with probability $\geq 1-\delta$, (over its own randomness and the samples), Algorithm 4 will output GMM $\hat{F} = \hat{w}_1\hat{F}_1 + \hat{w}_2\hat{F}_2$ such that there exists a permutation $\pi : [2]\rightarrow[2]$ with,*

$$D(\hat{F}_i, F_{\pi(i)}) \leq \epsilon, \text{ and } |\hat{w}_i - w_{\pi(i)}| \leq \epsilon, \text{for each } i = 1, 2.$$

The runtime and number of samples drawn by Algorithm 4 is at most $\mathrm{poly}(n, \frac{1}{\epsilon}, \frac{1}{\delta})$.

5. DENSITY ESTIMATION

The problem of PAC learning a distribution (or density estimation) was introduced in [14]: Given parameters $\epsilon, \delta > 0$, and given oracle access to a distribution F (in n dimensions), the goal is to learn a distribution $\hat{F}$ so that with probability at least $1-\delta$, $D(F,\hat{F})\leq\epsilon$ in time polynomial in $\frac{1}{\epsilon}$, n, and $\frac{1}{\delta}$. Here we apply our algorithm for learning mixtures of two arbitrary Gaussians to the problem of polynomial-time density estimation (aka PAC learning distributions) for arbitrary mixtures of two Gaussians without any assumptions. We show that given oracle access to a distribution $F = w_1F_1 + w_2F_2$ for $F_i = \mathcal{N}(\mu_i,\Sigma_i)$, we can efficiently construct a mixture of two Gaussians $\hat{F} = \hat{w}_1\hat{F}_1 + \hat{w}_2\hat{F}_2$ for which $D(F,\hat{F})\leq\epsilon$. Previous work on this problem [10] required that the Gaussians be axis aligned.

The algorithm for density estimation and a proof of correctness is deferred to the full version.

6. CLUSTERING

It makes sense that knowing the mixture parameters should imply that one can perform optimal clustering, and approximating the parameters should imply approximately optimal clustering. In this section, we formalize this intuition. For GMM F, it will be convenient to consider the *labeled distribution* $\ell(F)$ over $(x,y)\in\mathbf{R}^n\times\{1,2\}$ in which a *label* $y\in\{1,2\}$ is drawn with probability w_i of i, and then a sample x is chosen from F_i.

A clustering algorithm takes as input m examples and outputs a classifier $C : \mathbf{R}^n \rightarrow \{1,2\}$ for future data (a similar analysis could be done in terms of partitioning data $x_1,\ldots,x_m$). The *error* of a classifier C is defined to be,

$$\mathrm{err}(C) = \min_{\pi} \Pr_{(x,y)\sim\ell(F)}[C(x)\neq y],$$

where the minimum is over permutations $\pi : \{1,2\}\rightarrow\{1,2\}$. In other words, it is the fraction of points that must be relabeled so that they are partitioned correctly (actual label is irrelevant).

For any GMM F, define C_F to be the classifier that outputs whichever Gaussian has a greater posterior: $C_F(x) = 1$ if $w_1F_1(x)\geq w_2F_2(x)$, and $C(x) = 2$ otherwise. It is not difficult to see that this classifier has minimum error.

Corollary 3 implies that given a polynomial number of points, one can cluster *future samples* with near-optimal expected error. But using standard reductions, this also implies that we can learn and accurately cluster our training set as well. Namely, one could run the clustering algorithm on, say, $\sqrt{m}$ of the samples, and then use it to partition the data. The algorithm for near-optimal clustering is given in the full version, along with a proof for correctness.

7. ACKNOWLEDGMENTS

We are grateful to Santosh Vempala, Charlie Brubaker, Yuval Peres, Daniel Stefankovic, and Paul Valiant for helpful discussions.

ALGORITHM 4. HIGH-DIMENSIONAL ISOTROPIC VARIATION-DISTANCE APPROXIMATION
Input: Integers $n \geq 1$, reals $\epsilon, \delta > 0$, sample oracle $\mathrm{SA}(F)$.
Output: n-dimensional GMM

1. Let $\varepsilon_1, \varepsilon_2, \varepsilon_3 =$
2. Run Algorithm $2(n, \varepsilon_1, \delta/3, \mathrm{SA}(F))$ to get $\hat{F} = \hat{w}_1\hat{F}_1 + \hat{w}_2\hat{F}_2$.
3. Permute $\hat{w}_i, \hat{F}_i$ so that the *smallest* eigenvalue of $\mathrm{var}(\hat{F})_1$ is no larger than the smallest eigenvalue of $\mathrm{var}(\hat{F})_2$.
4. If the smallest eigenvalue of $\mathrm{var}(\hat{F}_1)$ is greater than ε_2, then halt and output the mixture $\hat{F}$. ELSE: (* Clustering step *)
   (a) Let λ, v be a smallest eigenvalue and corresponding unit eigenvector of $\hat{F}_1$.
   (b) Draw $m = \varepsilon_4^{-1}$ samples $x_1, \ldots, x_m$ from $\mathrm{SA}(F)$.
   (c) Partition the data into two sets, $D_1 \cup D_2 = \{x_1, \ldots, x_m\}$, where,
   $$D_1 = \left\{x_i : \left|P_v(x_i) - P_v(\mu(\hat{F}_1))\right| \leq \frac{\sqrt{\varepsilon_2}}{\varepsilon_3}\right\}.$$
   (d) Output GMM $\hat{G} = \hat{w}_1\hat{G}_1 + \hat{w}_2\hat{G}_2$, where $\hat{G}_i$ is the Gaussian with mean and covariance matrix that matches the empirical mean and covariance on set D_i, and $\hat{w}_i$ are those from Step 2.

Figure 6: The algorithm that guarantees low variation distance.

8. REFERENCES

[1] D. Achlioptas and F. McSherry. On spectral learning of mixtures of distributions. In *COLT*, pages 458–469, 2005.

[2] S. Arora and R. Kannan. Learning mixtures of arbitrary Gaussians. In *STOC*, pages 247–257, 2001.

[3] M. Belkin and K. Sinha. Learning Gaussian mixtures with arbitrary separation. *CoRR*, 2009.

[4] S. C. Brubaker and S. Vempala. Isotropic PCA and affine-invariant clustering. In *FOCS*, pages 551-560, 2008.

[5] S. Dasgupta. Learning mixtures of Gaussians. In *FOCS*, pages 634–644, 1999.

[6] S. Dasgupta, A. T. Kalai, and C. Monteleoni. Analysis of perceptron-based active learning. In *COLT*, pages 249–263, 2005.

[7] S. Dasgupta and L. J. Schulman. A two-round variant of EM for Gaussian mixtures. In *UAI*, pages 152–159, 2000.

[8] A. P. Dempster, N. M. Laird, and D. B. Rubin. Maximum likelihood from incomplete data via the EM Algorithm. *J. Roy. Statist. Soc. Ser. B*, 39:1–38, 1977.

[9] A. Dinghas. Über eine klasse superadditiver mengenfunktionale von brunn–minkowski–lusternik-schem typus. *Math. Zeitschr.*, 68:111–125, 1957.

[10] J. Feldman, R. A. Servedio, and R. O'Donnell. PAC learning axis-aligned mixtures of Gaussians with no separation assumption. In *COLT*, pages 20–34, 2006.

[11] A. A. Giannopoulos and V. D. Milman. Concentration property on probability spaces. *Adv. Math.*, 156:77–106, 2000.

[12] R. A. Hummel and B. C. Gidas. Zero crossings and the Heat Equation. *Technical Report Number 111, Courant Institute of Mathematical Sciences at NYU*, 1984.

[13] R. Kannan, H. Salmasian, and S. Vempala. The spectral method for general mixture models. *SIAM J. Comput.*, 38(3):1141–1156, 2008.

[14] M. J. Kearns, Y. Mansour, D. Ron, R. Rubinfeld, R. E. Schapire, and L. Sellie. On the learnability of discrete distributions. In *STOC*, pages 273–282, 1994.

[15] L. Leindler. On a certain converse of Hölder's Inequality ii. *Acta Sci. Math. Szeged*, 33:217–223, 1972.

[16] B. Lindsay. *Mixture models: theory, geometry and applications*. American Statistical Association, 1995.

[17] L. Lovász and S. Vempala. The geometry of logconcave functions and sampling algorithms. *Random Struct. Algorithms*, 30(3):307–358, 2007.

[18] P. Macdonald. Personal Communication, 2010

[19] K. Pearson. Contributions to the mathematical theory of evolution. *Phil. Trans. R. Soc. Lond. A*, 1894.

[20] A. Prékopa. Logarithmic concave measures and functions. *Acta. Sci. Math. Szeged*, 34:335–343, 1973.

[21] M. Rudelson. Random vectors in the isotropic position. *J. Funct. Anal*, 164:60–72, 1999.

[22] H. Teicher. Identifiability of mixtures. *Ann. Math. Statist.*, 32(1):244–248, 1961.

[23] L. Valiant. A theory of the learnable. *Comm. ACM*, 27(11):1134–1142, 1984.

[24] S. Vempala and G. Wang. A spectral algorithm for learning mixture models. *J. Comput. Syst. Sci.*, 68(4):841–860, 2004.

[25] C. F. J. Wu. On the convergence properties of the EM Algorithm. *Ann. Stat.*, 11(1):95–103, 1983.

Augmenting Undirected Node-Connectivity by One *

László A. Végh†
MTA-ELTE Egerváry Research Group and
Department of Operations Research, Eötvös University,
Pázmány P. stny. 1/c
H-1117 Budapest, Hungary
veghal@cs.elte.hu

ABSTRACT

We present a min-max formula for the problem of augmenting the node-connectivity of a graph by one and give a polynomial time algorithm for finding an optimal solution. We also solve the minimum cost version for node-induced cost functions.

Categories and Subject Descriptors

G.2.1 [**Combinatorics**]: Combinatorial algorithms

General Terms

Algorithms, Theory, Reliability

Keywords

node-connectivity, connectivity augmentation

1. INTRODUCTION

An undirected graph $G = (V, E)$ is **k-node-connected**, or shortly, **k-connected** if $|V| \geq k+1$ and after the deletion of any set of at most $k-1$ nodes, the remaining graph is still connected. By Menger's well-known theorem, a graph is k-connected if and only if it contains k internally disjoint paths between any two nodes. The node connectivity augmentation problem consists of finding a minimum number of edges whose addition to a given graph G results in a k-connected graph. The complexity of this problem is a long-standing open question. In this paper we give a min-max formula and a polynomial time algorithm for augmenting connectivity by one, the special case when the input graph G is already $(k-1)$-connected. This special case itself has attracted considerable attention see for example [13, 14, 10, 16, 15]. Kortsarz and Nutov [15] referred to its complexity status as a major open question in graph connectivity.

Besides node-connectivity, one may study edge-connectivity as well, and both augmentation problems can also be asked for directed graphs. The other three among these four basic connectivity augmentation problems were solved beforehand: undirected edge-connectivity by Watanabe and Nakamura [18], directed edge-connectivity by Frank [6], and directed node-connectivity by Frank and Jordán [8].

For the undirected node-connectivity version, the best previously known result is due to Jackson and Jordán [12]. They gave a polynomial time algorithm for finding an optimal augmentation for any fixed k. The running time is bounded by $O(|V|^5 + f(k)|V|^3)$, where $f(k)$ is an exponential function of k. For some special classes of graphs they prove even stronger results: for example, the running time of the algorithm is polynomial in $|V|$ if the minimum degree is at least $2k-2$. Liberman and Nutov [16] gave a polynomial time algorithm for augmenting connectivity by one for the graphs satisfying the following property: there exists a set $B \subseteq V$ with $|B| = k-1$ so that $G - B$ has at least k connected components. (It can be decided in polynomial time whether a graph contains such a set, see Cheriyan and Thurimella [3].)

Prior to these results, the cases $k = 2, 3, 4$ were solved by Eswaran and Tarjan [4], Watanabe and Nakamura [19] and Hsu [10], respectively. For $k = |V| - 2$ it is easy to verify that connectivity augmentation is equivalent to finding a maximum matching in the complement graph of G. Similarly, the case $k = |V| - 3$ is equivalent to finding a maximum square-free 2-matching in the complement. This is still open, however, augmentation by one (or equivalently, finding a maximum square-free 2-matching in a subcubic graph) was recently solved by Bérczi and Kobayashi [1], see also [2].

It is straightforward to give a 2-approximation for connectivity augmentation by replacing each edge by two oppositely directed egdes and using that directed node-connectivity can be augmented optimally (see [8]). For augmenting connectivity by one, Jordán [13, 14] gave an algorithm for finding an augmenting edge set larger than the optimum by at most $\lceil \frac{k-2}{2} \rceil$. Jackson and Jordán [11] extended this result for general connecitivity augmentation with an additive term of $\left\lceil \frac{k(k-1)}{2} \right\rceil$. (The running time of these algorithms can be bounded by polynomials of $|V|$.)

Let us now formulate our theorem, conjectured by Frank

*Dedicated to András Frank on the occasion of his 60th birthday. A full version of the paper is available at the EGRES homepage `http://www.cs.elte.hu/egres`, as Technical Report TR-2009-10.

†Supported by the Hungarian National Foundation for Scientific Research (OTKA), grants K60802 and NK67867.

STOC'10, June 5–8, 2010, Cambridge, Massachusetts, USA.

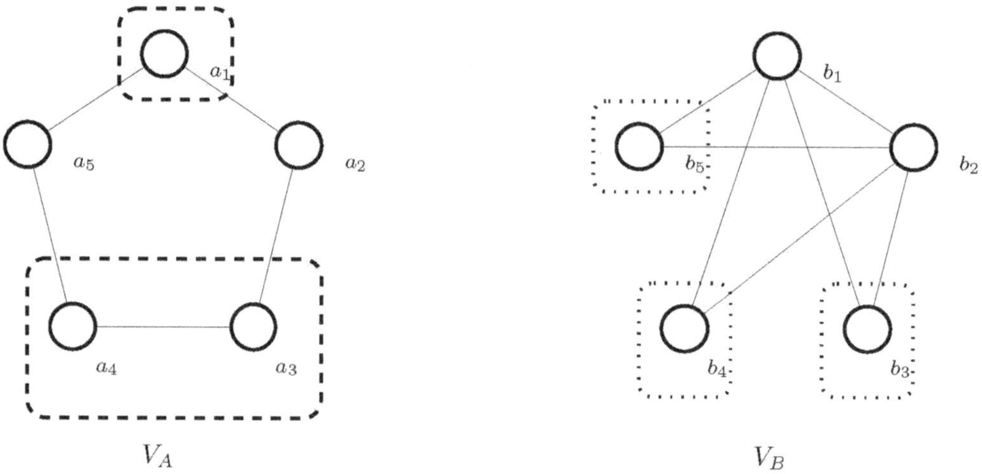

Figure 1: Let G be the graph on the figure with the addition of a complete bipartite graph between V_A and V_B and let $k = 8$. G is 7-connected, and it can be made 8-connected by adding the five edges $a_1a_3, a_2a_4, a_3a_5, b_3b_4$ and b_4b_5. Two clumps $(\{a_1\}, \{a_3, a_4\})$ and $(\{b_3\}, \{b_4\}, \{b_5\})$ are shown on the figure. A grove Π with $def(\Pi) = 5$ consists of the shrub $\mathcal{B}_0 = \{(\{b_3\}, \{b_4\}, \{b_5\})\}$ and the bush $\mathcal{B}_1 = \{(\{a_1\}, \{a_3, a_4\}), (\{a_2\}, \{a_4, a_5\}), (\{a_3\}, \{a_5, a_1\}), (\{a_4\}, \{a_1, a_2\}), (\{a_5\}, \{a_2, a_3\})\}$.

and Jordán [7] in 1994. In the $(k-1)$-connected graph $G = (V, E)$, a subpartition $X = (X_1, \ldots, X_t)$ of V with $t \geq 2$ is called a **clump** if $|V - \bigcup X_i| = k-1$ and $d(X_i, X_j) = 0$ for any $i \neq j$. The sets X_i are called the **pieces** of X while $|X|$ is used to denote t, the number of pieces. If $t = 2$ then X is a **small clump**, while for $t \geq 3$ it is a **large clump**. (The set $V - \bigcup X_i$ is often called **separator** in the literature, and **shredder** if $t \geq 3$.) An edge $uv \in \binom{V}{2}$ **connects** X if u and v lie in different pieces of X.[1] Two clumps are said to be **independent** if there is no edge in $\binom{V}{2}$ connecting both. As an example, consider the complete bipartite graph $G = K_{k-1,k-1}$ on two colour classes of size $k-1$. The subpartition consiting of singleton nodes in one colour class forms a clump of size $k-1$; the two clumps corresponding to the two colour classes are independent.

A **bush** $\mathcal{B}$ is a set of pairwise different small clumps, so that each edge in $\binom{V}{2}$ connects at most two of them. A **shrub** is a set consisting of pairwise independent (possibly large) clumps. For a bush $\mathcal{B}$, let $def(\mathcal{B}) = \left\lceil \frac{|\mathcal{B}|}{2} \right\rceil$, and for a shrub $\mathcal{S}$ let $def(\mathcal{S}) = \sum_{K \in \mathcal{S}} (|K| - 1)$. Observe that if $G + F$ is k-connected, then F must contain at least $|K| - 1$ edges connecting a clump K. An edge may connect at most two clumps in a bush and at most one in a shrub, therefore $def(\mathcal{B})$ and $def(\mathcal{S})$ are lower bounds on the number of edges in F connecting all clumps in $\mathcal{B}$ and $\mathcal{S}$, respectively.

A **grove** is a set consisting of some (possibly zero) bushes and one (possibly empty) shrub, so that the clumps belonging to different bushes are independent, and a clump belonging to a bush is independent from all clumps belonging to the shrub. For a grove Π consisting of the shrub $\mathcal{B}_0$ and bushes $\mathcal{B}_1, \ldots, \mathcal{B}_\ell$, let $def(\Pi) = \sum_{i=0}^{\ell} def(\mathcal{B}_i)$. For a $(k-1)$-connected graph $G = (V, E)$, let $\tau(G)$ denote the minimum number of edges whose addition makes G k-connected, and let $\nu(G)$ denote the maximum value of $def(\Pi)$ over all groves Π. Again, it is clear that $def(\Pi)$ is a lower bound on $\tau(G)$ for any grove Π. Consequently, $\nu(G) \leq \tau(G)$.

[1]By $\binom{V}{2}$ we denote the set of all undirected edges on V, while V^2 stands for the set of all arcs (directed edges) on V.

THEOREM 1.1. *Let $G = (V, E)$ be a $(k-1)$-connected graph with $|V| \geq k+1$. Then $\nu(G) = \tau(G)$.*

The theorem is illustrated on Figure 1. Both the proof and the algorithm are motivated by the algorithm given by Frank and the author [9] for augmenting directed node-connectivity by one. Let us now state the min-max formula for this problem. In a digraph $D = (V, A)$, an ordered pair (K^-, K^+) of disjoint non-empty subsets of V is called a **one-way pair** if $|V - (K^- \cup K^+)| = k-1$ and there is no arc in A from K^- to K^+. An arc $uv \in V^2$ **covers** (K^-, K^+) if $u \in K^-$, $v \in K^+$, and two one-way pairs are **independent** if they cannot be covered by the same arc.

THEOREM 1.2 (FRANK AND JORDÁN, 1995 [8]). *For a $(k-1)$-connected digraph $D = (V, A)$ with $|V| \geq k+1$, the minimum number of new arcs whose addition results in a k-connected digraph equals the maximum number of pairwise independent one-way pairs.*

Let us briefly outline the argument of [9]. A natural partial order $\preceq$ can be defined on the set of one-way pairs: $(K^-, K^+) \preceq (L^-, L^+)$ if $K^- \subseteq L^-$ and $K^+ \supseteq L^+$. A subset $\mathcal{K}$ of one-way pairs is called **cross-free** if any two non-independent pairs in $\mathcal{K}$ are comparable with respect to $\preceq$; such a $\mathcal{K}$ maximal for inclusion is called a **skeleton**. The two main ingredients of the proof are as follows: (i) for a cross-free $\mathcal{K}$, the maximum number of pairwise independent one-way pairs in $\mathcal{K}$ along with an arc set F of the same cardinality covering all one-way pairs in $\mathcal{K}$ can be determined using Dilworth's theorem on finding a maximum antichain and a minimum chain cover of a poset; (ii) an arc set F covering all one-way pairs in a skeleton $\mathcal{K}$ can be transformed to an arc set F' of the same cardinality covering every one-way pair in D.

Our proof for Theorem 1.1 will follow similar lines. Although no natural partial order can be defined on the set of clumps, nestedness may be introduced as a natural analogoue of comparability: a cross-free system will be a set of clumps so that any two non-independent clumps are nested and by skeleton we mean a maximal cross-free system. For a cross-free $\mathcal{K}$ we will be able to determine an edge set F covering all clumps in $\mathcal{K}$ along with a grove with deficiency $|F|$, consisting of a shrub and bushes formed by clumps in $\mathcal{K}$. Instead of Dilworth's theorem, we apply a reduction to Fleiner's theorem [5] on covering a symmetric poset by symmetric chains. For part (ii), the argument of [9] may be adapted with minor modifications.

While Dilworth's theorem can be derived from the Kőnig-Hall theorem on finding a maximum matching in bipartite graphs, Fleiner's theorem can be deduced from the Berge-Tutte theorem on the size of a maximum matching in general graphs. The relation between directed and undirected connectivity augmentation is somewhat analogous: for example, the formula in Theorem 1.1 involves parity. This is a reason why the strikingly simple original proof for Theorem 1.2 by Frank and Jordán [8] cannot be adapted for the undirected case.

Another difficulty is that in contrast to one-way pairs, clumps may have more than two pieces. Fortunately, it turns out that large clumps are nested with every other clump they are dependent with. Therefore, although large clumps will cause certain difficulties in the first part of the proof, they play only little role in the second part.

For the algorithm, we are going to construct a subroutine determining the dual optimum value $\nu(G)$ for a $(k-1)$-connected graph G. Based on Theorem 1.1, this gives rise to the following simple algorithm for finding an optimal augmenting edge set. First compute $\nu(G)$, and let $J = \binom{V}{2} - E$ be the complement of E. In each step choose an edge $e \in J$, compute $\nu(G+e)$, and remove e from J. If $\nu(G+e) = \nu(G) - 1$ then add e to E, otherwise keep the same G. Note that Theorem 1.1 ensures the existence of an edge e with $\nu(G+e) = \nu(G) - 1$.

The rest of the paper is organized as follows. We introduce the necessary concepts and prove some basic claims in Section 2. Section 3 contains the proof of Theorem 1.1, while the algorithm is given in Section 4. Finally, Section 5 describes the node-induced cost version and discusses possible further directions. Due to space limitations, some proofs are omitted; these are included in the full version.

2. PRELIMINARIES

For an undirected graph $G = (V, E)$ and a subset $B \subseteq V$, $d(B) = d_G(B) = d_E(B)$ denotes the degree of B, and $N(B) = N_G(B)$ the set of neighbours of B, that is, $\{v \in V - B, \exists u \in B, uv \in E\}$. B^* is used to denote the set $V - (B \cup N(B))$. For subsets $B, C \subseteq V$, $d(B, C)$ is the number of edges between $B - C$ and $C - B$. For $u \in V$, u sometimes refers to the set $\{u\}$, for example, $B + v$ and $B - v$ denote the sets $B \cup \{v\}$ and $B - \{v\}$, respectively. Similar notation is used concerning edges. Let $n = |V|$, the number of nodes.

First we give a brief motivation for the concepts related to clumps. In a $(k-1)$-connected graph G, we may have sets $B \subsetneq V$ with $|B| = k - 1$, so that $V - B$ has $t \geq 2$ connected components. The components of $V - B$ form a clump, and any partition of these components to at least two sets forms a clump as well, since in the definition, the pieces are not required to be connected. In order to make G k-connected, we have to add at least $t - 1$ edges between different components of $V - Z$. For $t = 2$, an arbitrary edge suffices between the two components, however the situation is more complicated if $t \geq 3$. As already mentioned, such a set B is often called a **shredder** in the literature.

Now we list some definitions. For a clump $X = (X_1, X_2, \ldots, X_t)$, let $N_X = V - \bigcup_i X_i$. X is called **basic** if all pieces X_i are connected. The clump Y is **derived** from the basic clump X if each piece of Y is the union of some pieces of X. By $D(X)$ we mean the set of all clumps derived from X, while $D_2(X)$ is used for the set of small clumps derived from X. Let $\mathcal{C}$ denote the set of all basic clumps. For a set $\mathcal{F} \subseteq \mathcal{C}$, $D(\mathcal{F})$ denotes the union of the sets $D(X)$ with $X \in \mathcal{F}$. The clumps being in the same set $D(X)$ can easily be characterized (see e.g. [13, 14, 16]):

CLAIM 2.1. *(i) Two clumps X and Y are derived from the same basic clump if and only if $N_X = N_Y$. (ii) If two basic clumps X and Y have a piece in common, then $X = Y$.* □

For a clump X and an edge set F, let F/X be the graph obtained from (V, F) by deleting N_X and shrinking the components X_i to single nodes. Let $c_F(X)$ denote the number of connected components of F/X. F **covers** X if F/X is connected, that is, $c_F(X) = 1$. To cover X, we need at least $|X| - 1$ edges of F connecting X. If X is a small clump, then F covers X if and only if F connects X. We say that F covers (resp. connects) $\mathcal{H} \subseteq D(\mathcal{C})$ if it covers (resp. connects) all clumps in $\mathcal{H}$. Clearly, F is an augmenting edge set if and only if it covers $D(\mathcal{C})$. The following simple claim shows that in order to cover a set $\mathcal{F}$ of clumps, it suffices to connect every small clump derived from the members of $\mathcal{F}$.

CLAIM 2.2. *For an edge set $F \subseteq \binom{V}{2}$ and $\mathcal{F} \subseteq \mathcal{C}$, the following three statements are equivalent: (i) F covers $\mathcal{F}$; (ii) F covers $D(\mathcal{F})$; and (iii) F connects $D_2(\mathcal{F})$.* □

We have already defined when two clumps are independent: if no edge in $\binom{V}{2}$ connects both. Two clumps are **dependent**, if they are not independent. In the rest of the section we introduce the concept of nestedness of clumps and uncrossing for dependent clumps, and furthermore we define crossing and cross-free subsets of clumps. The reader may find useful to compare these to the concepts related to one-way pairs in case of directed connectivity augmentation as in [8]. These will also be defined later in this section as we will also use them directly. A major difference between the undirected and directed setting is that in the directed case, a natural partial order can be defined for the one-way pairs, which cannot be done for clumps. Nestedness will be the natural analogue of comparability for clumps.

We say that two clumps $X = (X_1, \ldots, X_t)$ and $Y = (Y_1, \ldots, Y_h)$ are **nested** if $X = Y$ or for some $1 \leq a \leq t$ and $1 \leq b \leq h$, $Y_i \subsetneq X_a$ for all $i \neq b$ and $X_j \subsetneq Y_b$ for all $j \neq a$. We call X_a the **dominant piece** of X with respect to Y, and Y_b the dominant piece of Y w.r.t X. The following important lemma shows that a large basic clump is automatically nested with any other basic clump (see also in [16]).

LEMMA 2.3. *Assume X is a large basic clump, and Y is an arbitrary basic clump. If X and Y are dependent then X and Y are nested.*

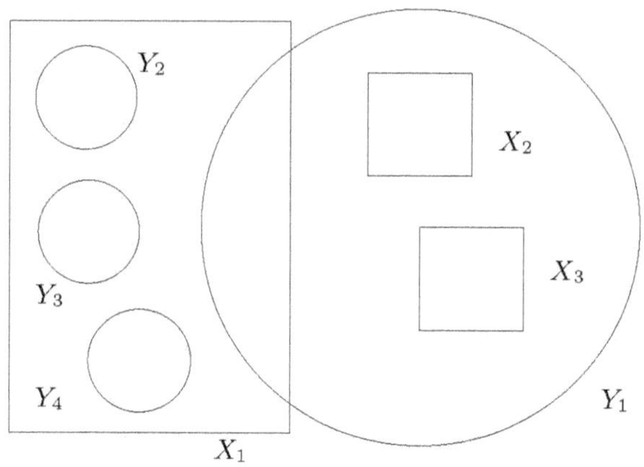

Figure 2: The nested clumps $X = (X_1, X_2, X_3)$ and $Y = (Y_1, Y_2, Y_3, Y_4)$ with dominant pieces X_1 and Y_1.

To prove this, first we need two simple claims.

CLAIM 2.4. *For the basic clumps $X = (X_1, \ldots, X_t)$ and $Y = (Y_1, \ldots, Y_h)$, $X_i \cap N_Y = \emptyset$ implies $X_i \subseteq Y_j$ for some $1 \le j \le h$.* □

CLAIM 2.5. *Let $X = (X_1, \ldots, X_t)$ and $Y = (Y_1, \ldots, Y_h)$ be two different clumps both basic or both small. If $X_s \subsetneq Y_b$ for some $1 \le s \le t$, $1 \le b \le h$, then X and Y are nested with Y_b being the dominant piece of Y w.r.t X.*

PROOF. Consider an $\ell \neq b$. $X_s \subseteq Y_b$ implies $d(X_s, Y_\ell) = 0$, thus $Y_\ell \cap N_X = \emptyset$. Hence $Y_\ell \subseteq X_a$ for some $a \neq s$ follows either by Claim 2.4 or by $t = 2$. We claim that this a is always the same independently from the choice of ℓ. Indeed, assume that for some $\ell' \notin \{b, \ell\}$, $Y_{\ell'} \subseteq X_{a'}$ with $a' \neq a$.

The same argument applied with changing the role of X and Y (by making use of $Y_\ell \subseteq X_a$) shows that $X_{a'} \subseteq Y_j$ for some j, giving $Y_{\ell'} \subseteq Y_j$, a contradiction. $X_i \subseteq Y_b$ for $i \neq a$ can be proved by changing the role of X and Y again. Thus X and Y are nested with dominant pieces X_a and Y_b. □

PROOF OF LEMMA 2.3. The dependence implies $X_1 \cap Y_1 \neq \emptyset$, $X_2 \cap Y_2 \neq \emptyset$ by possibly changing the indices. Let $x_i = |N_Y \cap X_i|$, $y_i = |N_X \cap Y_i|$, $n_0 = |N_X \cap N_Y|$. Then $k - 1 \le |N(X_1 \cap Y_1)| \le n_0 + x_1 + y_1$. Since $k - 1 = |N_Y| = n_0 + \sum_i y_i$ this implies $\sum_{i \neq 1} y_i \le x_1$ and similarly $\sum_{i \neq 1} x_i \le y_1$. The same argument for $X_2 \cap Y_2$ gives $\sum_{i \neq 2} y_i \le x_2$ and $\sum_{i \neq 2} x_i \le y_2$.

Thus we have $x_i = y_i = 0$ for $i \ge 3$. This gives $X_3 \cap N_Y = \emptyset$ and hence $X_3 \subseteq Y_i$ for some i by Claim 2.4. The nestedness of X and Y follows by the previous claim. □

The notion of one-way pairs from the directed connectivity augmentation setting will also be used. A **one-way pair** $K = (K^-, K^+)$ is an ordered pair of disjoint sets with $|V - (K^- \cup K^+)| = k - 1$ and $d(K^-, K^+) = 0$, or equivalently, the subpartition consisting of K^- and K^+ forms a (small) clump. K^- is called the **tail**, while K^+ the **head** of K. For each small clump X, there are two corresponding one-way pairs, called the orientations of X. For a large clump X, we mean by the orientations of X the **orientations** of the small clumps in $D_2(X)$.

For a one-way pair K, $\underline{K}$ denotes the corresponding small clump. An arc (directed edge) $uv \in V^2$ **covers** the one-way pair $K = (K^-, K^+)$, if $u \in K^-$, $v \in K^+$. Note that if uv covers K, then vu does not cover it. If an edge $uv \in \binom{V}{2}$ connects a small clump X, then the arc $uv \in V^2$ covers exactly one of its two orientations (in the directed sense). For the one-way pair $K = (K^-, K^+)$, its reverse is $\overleftarrow{K} = (K^+, K^-)$.

Two one-way pairs are **independent**, if no arc covers both or equivalently, if either their tails or their heads are disjoint. Two non independent set pairs are called **dependent**. Let us define a partial order $\preceq$ on the one-way pairs as follows. For the one-way pairs $K = (K^-, K^+)$ and $L = (L^-, L^+)$, $K \preceq L$ if $K^- \subseteq L^-$, $K^+ \supseteq L^+$. For dependent one-way pairs K and L, let $K \wedge L = (K^- \cap L^-, K^+ \cup L^+)$ and $K \vee L = (K^- \cup L^-, K^+ \cap L^+)$. A simple argument (e.g. in [8]) shows that these are also one-way pairs.

Take two dependent small clumps $X = (X_1, X_2)$ and $Y = (Y_1, Y_2)$. We say that their orientations L_X and L_Y are **compatible** if they are dependent one-way pairs. Clearly, any two dependent one-way pairs admit compatible orientations, and if L_X and L_Y are compatible, then so are $\overleftarrow{L_X}$ and $\overleftarrow{L_Y}$. X and Y are said to be **simply dependent** if for an orientation L_X of X, there is exactly one compatible orientation L_Y of Y and **strongly dependent** if both possible choices of L_Y are compatible with L_X. (Note that the definition does not depend on the choice of L_X). X and Y are strongly dependent if and only if $X_i \cap Y_j \neq \emptyset$ for every $i = 1, 2$, $j = 1, 2$. The following claim is easy to see.

CLAIM 2.6. *Two small clumps X and Y are nested if and only if for some orientations K_X and K_Y, $K_X \preceq K_Y$.* □

We are ready to define uncrossing of clumps. By uncrossing the dependent one-way pairs K and L we mean replacing them by $K \wedge L$ and $K \vee L$ (which coincide with K and L if K and L are comparable). For dependent basic clumps X and Y, we will define a set $\Upsilon(X, Y)$ consisting of two or four pairwise nested clumps in the analogous sense. If X and Y are nested, then let $\Upsilon(X, Y) = \{X, Y\}$. By Lemma 2.3, this is always the case if one of X and Y is large. For the small basic clumps X and Y, consider some compatible orientations L_X and L_Y. If X and Y are simply dependent then let $\Upsilon(X, Y) = \{\underline{L_X \wedge L_Y}, \underline{L_X \vee L_Y}\}$. (Altough there are two possible choices for L_X and L_Y, the set $\Upsilon(X, Y)$ will be the same.) If they are strongly dependent, then L_X is also compatible $\overleftarrow{L_Y}$. In this case let

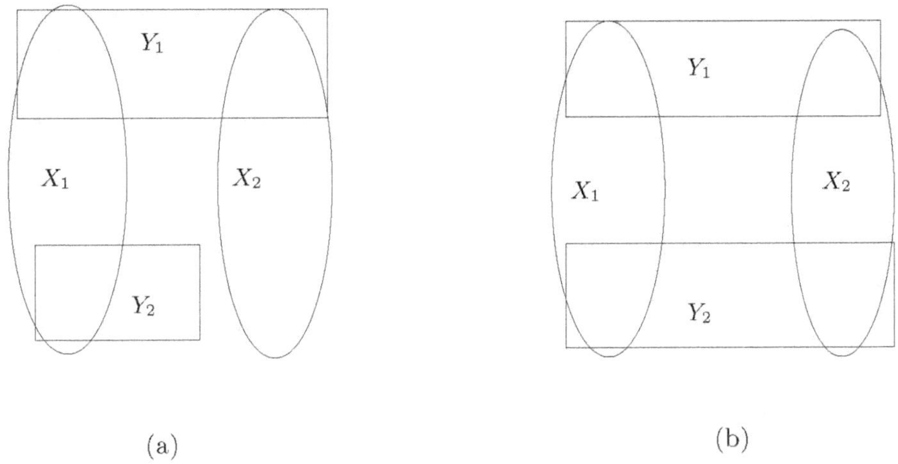

Figure 3: Simply dependent one-way pairs (a), and strongly dependent ones (b).

$\Upsilon(X,Y) = \{\underline{L_X \wedge L_Y}, \underline{L_X \vee L_Y}, \underline{L_X \wedge \overleftarrow{L_Y}}, \underline{L_X \vee \overleftarrow{L_Y}}\}$. It is easy to see that the clumps in $\Upsilon(X,Y)$ are nested with X and Y and with each other in both cases. The following claim is straightforward.

CLAIM 2.7. *For dependent basic clumps X, Y, if an edge uv connects a clump in $\Upsilon(X,Y)$ then it connects at least one of X and Y.* □

We say that two clumps are **crossing** if they are dependent but not nested. Again by Lemma 2.3, two basic clumps may be crossing only if both are small. A subset $\mathcal{F} \subseteq \mathcal{C}$ is called **crossing**, if for any two dependent clumps $X, Y \in \mathcal{F}$, $\Upsilon(X,Y) \subseteq D(\mathcal{F})$. The reason for assuming containment in $D(\mathcal{F})$ instead of $\mathcal{F}$ is that there might be non basic members of $\Upsilon(X,Y)$. Note that $\mathcal{C}$ itself is crossing. For a crossing system $\mathcal{F}$ and a clump $K \in \mathcal{F}$, let $\mathcal{F} \div K$ denote the set of clumps in $\mathcal{F}$ independent or nested with K. Similarly, for a subset $\mathcal{K} \subseteq \mathcal{F}$, $\mathcal{F} \div \mathcal{K}$ denotes the set of clumps in $\mathcal{F}$ not crossing any clump in $\mathcal{K}$. An $\mathcal{F} \subseteq \mathcal{C}$ is **cross-free** if it contains no crossing clumps, that is, any two dependent clumps in $\mathcal{F}$ are nested. (Note that a cross-free system is crossing as well.) A cross-free $\mathcal{K}$ is called a **skeleton** of $\mathcal{F}$ if it is maximal cross-free in $\mathcal{F}$, that is, $\mathcal{F} \div \mathcal{K} = \mathcal{K}$. By Lemma 2.3, a skeleton of $\mathcal{C}$ should contain every large clump.

LEMMA 2.8. *For a crossing system $\mathcal{F} \subseteq \mathcal{C}$ and $K \in \mathcal{F}$, $\mathcal{F} \div K$ is a crossing system as well.* □

Finally, the sequence $K_1, K_2, \ldots, K_\ell$ of clumps is called a **chain** if they admit orientations $L_1, L_2, \ldots, L_\ell$ with $L_1 \preceq L_2 \preceq \ldots \preceq L_\ell$. If $u \in L_1^-$, $v \in L_\ell^+$ then the edge uv connects all members of the chain.

3. PROOF OF THEOREM 1.1

For a crossing system $\mathcal{F} \subseteq \mathcal{C}$, let $\tau(\mathcal{F})$ denote the minimum cardinality edge set covering $\mathcal{F}$. Let $\nu(\mathcal{F})$ denote the maximum of $def(\Pi)$ over groves consisting of a shrub and bushes of clumps in $D(\mathcal{F})$. First, we give the proof of the following slight generalization of Theorem 1.1 based on two lemmas proved in the following subsections.

THEOREM 3.1. *For a crossing system $\mathcal{F} \subseteq \mathcal{C}$, $\nu(\mathcal{F}) = \tau(\mathcal{F})$.*

It is an easy consequence of the following two lemmas.

LEMMA 3.2. *For a cross-free system $\mathcal{F}$, $\nu(\mathcal{F}) = \tau(\mathcal{F})$.*

LEMMA 3.3. *For a cross-free system $\mathcal{F}$ and a $K \in \mathcal{F}$, if an edge set F covers $\mathcal{F} \div K$, then there exists an F' covering $\mathcal{F}$ with $|F'| = |F|$, and furthermore $d_{F'}(v) = d_F(v)$ for every $v \in V$.*

PROOF OF THEOREM 3.1. $\nu \leq \tau$ is straightforward. The proof of $\nu \geq \tau$ is by induction on $|\mathcal{F}|$. If $\mathcal{F}$ is cross-free, we are done by Lemma 3.2. Otherwise, consider two crossing clumps $K, K' \in \mathcal{F}$ and let $\mathcal{F}' = \mathcal{F} \div K$, a crossing system by Lemma 2.8. As $K' \notin \mathcal{F}'$, we may apply the inductive statement for $\mathcal{F}'$ giving a grove Π and an edge set F covering $\mathcal{F}'$ with $def(\Pi) = |F|$. The proof is finished using Lemma 3.3. □

The following theorem may be seen as a reformulation of this proof, however, it will be more convenient for the aim of the algorithm and to handle the minimum cost version for node induced cost functions.

THEOREM 3.4. *For a crossing system $\mathcal{F} \subseteq \mathcal{C}$ and a skeleton $\mathcal{K}$ of $\mathcal{F}$, $\nu(\mathcal{K}) = \nu(\mathcal{F})$. Furthermore, if an edge set F covers $\mathcal{K}$, then there exists an F' covering $\mathcal{F}$ with $|F'| = |F|$ and $d_{F'}(v) = d_F(v)$ for every $v \in V$.* □

3.1 Covering cross-free systems

This section is devoted to the proof of Lemma 3.2. The analogous statement in the case of directed connectivity augmentation simply follows by Dilworth' theorem, which is a well-known consequence of the Kőnig-Hall theorem on the size of a maximum matching in a bipartite graph. In contrast, Lemma 3.2 is deduced from Fleiner's theorem, which is proved via a reduction to the Berge-Tutte theorem on maximum matchings in general graphs.

We need the following notion to formulate Fleiner's theorem. A triple $P = (U, \preceq, M)$ is called a **symmetric poset** if $(U, \preceq)$ is a finite poset and M a perfect matching on U with the property that $u \preceq v$ and $uu', vv' \in M$ implies $u' \succeq v'$. The edges of M will be called **matches**. A subset $\{u_1v_1, \ldots, u_kv_k\} \subseteq M$ is called a **symmetric chain** if

$u_1 \preceq u_2 \preceq \ldots \preceq u_k$ (and thus $v_1 \succeq v_2 \succeq \ldots \succeq v_k$). The symmetric chains $S_1, S_2, \ldots, S_t$ **cover** P if $M = \bigcup S_i$.

A set $\mathcal{L} = \{L_1, L_2 \ldots, L_\ell\}$ of disjoint subsets of M forms a **legal subpartition** if $uv \in L_i$, $u'v' \in L_j$, $u \preceq u'$ yields $i = j$, and no symmetric chain of length three is contained in any L_i. The value of $\mathcal{L}$ is $val(\mathcal{L}) = \sum_i \left\lceil \frac{|L_i|}{2} \right\rceil$.

THEOREM 3.5 (FLEINER, 1997 [5]). *Let $P = (U, \preceq, M)$ be a symmetric poset. The minimum number of symmetric chains covering P is equal to the maximum value of a legal subpartition of P.*

Note that the max $\leq$ min direction follows easily since a symmetric chain may contain at most two matches belonging to one class of a legal subpartition. This theorem gives a common generalization of Dilworth's theorem and of the well-known min-max formula on the minimum size edge cover of a graph (a theorem equivalent to the Berge-Tutte theorem).

First we show that Lemma 3.2 is a straigthforward consequence if $\mathcal{F}$ contains only small clumps. Consider the cross-free family $\mathcal{F}$ of clumps, and let U be the set of all orientations of one-way pairs in $\mathcal{F}$. The matches in M consist of the two orientations of the same clump, while $\preceq$ is the usual partial order on one-way pairs. A symmetric chain corresponds to a chain of clumps. Since all clumps in a chain can be connected by a single edge, a symmetric chain cover gives a cover of $\mathcal{F}$ of the same size. On the other hand, a legal subpartition yields a grove with a shrub and bushes consisting of the clumps corresponding to the one-way pairs in L_i.

Let us now turn to the general case when $\mathcal{F}$ may contain large clumps as well. An edge set F **semi-covers** the clump $X = (X_1, \ldots, X_t)$ if F contains at least $|X| - 1$ edges connecting X, and furthermore each clump (X_i, X_i^*) is connected for $i = 1, \ldots, t$. (Note that $X_i^* = \bigcup_{j \neq i} X_j$.) F semi-covers $\mathcal{F}$ if it semi-covers every $X \in \mathcal{F}$. Although a semi-cover is not necessarly a cover, the following lemma shows that it can be transformed into a cover of the same size.

LEMMA 3.6. *If F is a semi-cover of $\mathcal{F}$, then there exists an edge set H covering $\mathcal{F}$ with $|F| = |H|$ and $d_H(v) = d_F(v)$ for every $v \in V$.*

PROOF. We are done if F covers all clumps in $\mathcal{F}$. Otherwise, consider a clump $X \in \mathcal{F}$ semi-covered but not covered. X is large, since semi-covered small clumps are automatically covered. Since X is connected by at least $|X| - 1$ edges of F, there is an edge $e = x_1y_1 \in F$ connecting X with $c_F(X) = c_{F-e}(X)$. Each (X_i, X_i^*) is connected, hence we may consider an edge $x_2y_2 \in F$ connecting X with x_2y_2 being in a component of F/X different from the one containing x_1y_1. Let $F' = F - \{x_1y_1, x_2y_2\} + \{x_1y_2, x_2y_1\}$. Clearly, $c_{F'}(X) = c_F(X) - 1$. We show that $c_{F'}(Y) \leq c_F(Y)$ for every $Y \in \mathcal{F} - X$, hence by a sequence of such steps we finally arrive at an H covering $\mathcal{F}$.

Indeed, assume $c_{F'}(Y) > c_F(Y)$ for some $Y \in \mathcal{F}$. X and Y are dependent since at least one of x_1y_1 and x_2y_2 connects both. By Lemma 2.3, X and Y are nested; let X_a and Y_b denote their dominant pieces. The nodes x_1, y_1, x_2, y_2 lie in four different pieces of X and thus at least three of them are contained in Y_b. Consequently, $c_{F'}(Y) = c_F(Y)$ yields a contradiction. □

In what follows, we show how a semi-cover F of $\mathcal{F}$ can be found based on a reduction to Fleiner's theorem. For a basic clump $X = (X_1, \ldots, X_t)$, let $u_i^X = (X_i, X_i^*)$, $v_i^X = (X_i^*, X_i)$ and $U^X = \{u_i^X, v_i^X : i = 1, \ldots, t\}$. Let $U = \bigcup_{X \in \mathcal{F}} U^X$. We say that the members of U^X are of type X. Let the matching M consist of the matches $u_i^X v_i^X$; such a match is called an **X-match**.

If X is small ($t = 2$), then $u_1^X = v_2^X$ and $v_1^X = u_2^X$, thus $|U^X| = 2$. If X is large, then $|U^X| = 2t$. In this case, let u_1^X and v_1^X be called the **special one-way pairs** w.r.t X. $u_1^X v_1^X$ is called a **special match**. Note that it matters here, which piece of X is denoted by X_1 (arbitrarily chosen though). Let the partial order $\preceq'$ on U be defined as follows. If x and y are one-way pairs of different type, then let $x \preceq' y$ if and only if $x \preceq y$ for the standard partial order $\preceq$ on one-way pairs. If x and y are both of type X for a large clump X, then let $x \preceq y$ if either $x = u_1^X$, $y = v_i^X$, or $x = u_i^X$, $y = v_1^X$ for some $i > 1$. In other words, $\preceq'$ is the same as $\preceq$ except that x and y are uncomparable whenever x and y are of the same type X, and neither of them is special.

CLAIM 3.7. *$P = (U, \preceq', M)$ is a symmetric poset.* □

The following simple claim establishes the connection between dependency of clumps and comparability in P.

CLAIM 3.8. *In a cross-free system $\mathcal{F}$, the clumps $X, Y \in \mathcal{F}$ are dependent if and only if for arbitrary i, j, u_i^X is comparable with either u_j^Y or v_j^Y.* □

Take a symmetric chain cover $S_1, \ldots, S_t$ and a legal subpartition $\mathcal{L} = \{L_1, L_2, \ldots, L_\ell\}$ with $val(\mathcal{L}) = t$. Let us choose $\mathcal{L}$ so that ℓ is maximal, and subject to this, $\bigcup_{i=1}^{\ell} L_i$ contains the maximum number special matches. A symmetric chain S_i naturally corresponds to a chain of the clumps (X_j, X_j^*) for $u_j^X v_j^X \in S_i$. These can be covered by a single edge; hence a symmetric chain cover corresponds to an edge set F of the same size. A symmetric chain may contain both $u_j^X v_j^X$ and $u_{j'}^X v_{j'}^X$ for $j \neq j'$ only if $j = 1$ or $j' = 1$. Consequently, F is a semi-cover as there are at least $|X| - 1$ different edges in F connecting X, and all (X_j, X_j^*)'s are connected.

It is left to show that $\mathcal{L}$ can be transformed to a grove Π with $def(\Pi) = val(\mathcal{L})$. For a clump X, let $B(X)$ denote the set of indices j with $u_j^X v_j^X \in \bigcup_{i=1}^{\ell} L_i$. Most efforts are needed to ensure that the bushes consit of small clumps; allowing large clumps would enable a simpler argument.

CLAIM 3.9. *For any clump X, the X-matches corresponding to $B(X)$ are either all contained in the same L_i or are all singleton L_i's. $1 \in B(X)$ always gives the first alternative.*

PROOF. There is nothing to prove for $|X| = 2$, so let us assume $|X| \geq 3$. As $\mathcal{L}$ is chosen with ℓ maximal, if $u_j^X v_j^X \in L_i$ with $|L_i| > 1$, then there is an $u_h^Y v_h^Y \in L_i$ with u_h^Y comparable with either u_j^X or v_j^X. If $Y \neq X$, then Claim 3.8 gives that u_h^Y is also comparable with $u_{j'}^X$ or $v_{j'}^X$ for any $j' \in B(X)$. If $Y = X$ then either $j = 1$ or $h = 1$ follows, implying $u_{j'}v_{j'} \in L_i$ for every $j' \in B(X)$. This argument also shows that $1 \in B(X)$ leads to the first alternative. □

Let $\beta(X) = i$ in the first alternative if L_i is not a singleton, and $\beta(X) = 0$ in the second alternative. Let $\mathcal{I}$ denote the set of indices for which L_i is a singleton. Take a clump X with $\beta(X) = i > 0$ (and thus $i \notin \mathcal{I}$). Let us say that a piece X_j is a **dominant piece** of X, if for some $Y \neq X$ with $\beta(Y) = i$, X_j is the dominant piece of X w.r.t. Y. Let $U(X)$ denote the set of the indices of the dominant pieces of X; note that the set $U(X) - B(X)$ is possibly nonempty.

CLAIM 3.10. *If $\beta(X) = i > 0$, then $|B(X)| \geq 2$ implies $|B(X) \cap U(X)| = \emptyset$.*

PROOF. First assume $B(X) \cap U(X) \neq \emptyset$ and $|U(X)| \geq 2$. Consider arbitrary $j \in B(X) \cap U(X)$ and $j' \in U(X) - \{j\}$, say, X_j is the dominant piece of X w.r.t. Y and $X_{j'}$ the one w.r.t. Y' with $\beta(Y) = \beta(Y') = i$. It is easy to see that L_i contains a symmetric chain of lenght three consisting of a Y-match, $u_j^X v_j^X$ and a Y'-match.

Thus $B(X) \cap U(X) \neq \emptyset$ implies $|U(X)| = 1$. Let $U(X) = \{j\}$. Assume again that X_j is the dominant piece of X w.r.t. Y with $\beta(Y) = i$. We claim that $1 \notin B(X)$. Indeed, if $1 \in B(X)$ and $j \neq 1$, then a Y-match, $u_j^X v_j^X$ and $v_1^X u_1^X$ would form a symmetric chain in L_i. If $j = 1$, then a Y-match, $u_1^X v_1^X$ and $v_h^X u_h^X$ form a symmetric chain for arbitrary $h \in B(X) - \{1\}$.

Let us replace L_i by $L_i' = L_i - \{u_j^X v_j^X\} + \{u_1^X v_1^X\}$. By Claim 3.8, any element of L_i' is incomparable to any element of L_h for $h \neq i$. It is easy to verify that L_i' does not contain any symmetric chain of length three given that L_i did not contain any. This is a contradiction as $\mathcal{L}$ was chosen to contain the maximal possible number of special matches. □

Let us construct the grove Π as follows. For any X with $\beta(X) = 0$, $B(X) \neq \emptyset$, let $\tilde{X} \in D(X)$ denote the clump consisting of pieces X_i with $i \in B(X)$ and the piece $\bigcup_{j \notin B(X)} X_j$. The latter set is nonempty since $1 \notin B(X)$ by Claim 3.9, thus $|\tilde{X}| - 1 = |B(X)|$. Define the shrub as $\mathcal{B}_0 = \{\tilde{X} : \beta(X) = 0\}$. For $i \notin \mathcal{I}$, let $\mathcal{B}_i = \{(X_j, X_j^*) : u_j^X v_j^X \in L_i\}$. The following easy claim completes the proof.

CLAIM 3.11. *Π is a grove with $def(\mathcal{B}_0) = |\mathcal{I}|$ and $def(\mathcal{B}_i) = \left\lceil \frac{|L_i|}{2} \right\rceil$ if $i \notin \mathcal{I}$.*

PROOF. Since the elements of different L_i's are pairwise incomparable, Claim 3.8 implies that clumps in different bushes are independent from each other and from those in $\mathcal{B}_0$. Assume an edge $uv \in \binom{V}{2}$ covers three clumps in some $\mathcal{B}_i$. If these three clumps were derived from different basic clumps, then L_i would contain a symmetric chain of length three. Thus we need to have two clumps derived from the same basic clump X: uv covers (X_j, X_j^*), $(X_{j'}, X_{j'}^*)$ and (Y_h, Y_h^*) for $\beta(X) = \beta(Y) = i$. This is also impossible since either X_j or $X_{j'}$ would need to be the dominant piece of X w.r.t Y, a contradiction to Claim 3.10. □

3.2 Proof of Lemma 3.3.

First we need the following lemmas.

LEMMA 3.12. *Assume that for three small clumps $X = (X_1, X_2)$, $Y = (Y_1, Y_2)$, $Z = (Z_1, Z_2)$, all four sets $X_1 \cap Y_1 \cap Z_1$, $X_1 \cap Y_2 \cap Z_2$, $X_2 \cap Y_1 \cap Z_2$, $X_2 \cap Y_2 \cap Z_1$ are nonempty. Then all of X, Y and Z are derived from the same basic clump (and thus none of them is basic itself).*

PROOF. Let $X_c = N_X$, $Y_c = N_Y$, $Z_c = N_Z$. By A_s for a sequence s of three literals each 1,2 or c, we mean the intersection of the corresponding sets. For example, $A_{12c} = X_1 \cap Y_2 \cap Z_c$.

The conditions mean that the sets A_{111}, A_{122}, A_{212}, A_{221} are nonempty. $V - (A_{111} \cup N(A_{111})) \neq \emptyset$ as there is no edge between A_{111} and X_2, thus $|N(A_{111})| \geq k - 1$ as G is $(k-1)$-connected. This implies

$$k - 1 \leq |A_{c11} \cup A_{1c1} \cup A_{11c} \cup A_{1cc} \cup A_{c1c} \cup A_{cc1} \cup A_{ccc}|$$

as $N(A_{111})$ is a subset of the set on the RHS. Let us take the sum of these types of inequalities for all A_{111}, A_{122}, A_{212}, A_{221}. This gives $4(k-1) \leq S_1 + 2S_2 + 4|A_{ccc}|$, where S_1 is the sum of the cardinalities of the sets having exactly one c in their indices, while S_2 is the same for two c's.

On the other hand, $|X_c| = |Y_c| = |Z_c| = k - 1$. This gives $3(k-1) = S_1 + 2S_2 + 3|A_{ccc}|$. These together imply $S_1 = S_2 = 0$, $|A_{ccc}| = k - 1$. We are done by Claim 2.1, since $N_X = N_Y = N_Z = A_{ccc}$. □

LEMMA 3.13. *[9] (i) Let L_1, L_2, L_3 be one-way pairs with L_1 and L_2 dependent, $L_1 \wedge L_2$ and L_3 also dependent, but L_2 and L_3 independent. Then $L_1^- - L_2^- \subseteq L_3^-$. (ii) Let L_1, L_2, L_3 be one-way pairs with L_1 and L_2 dependent, $L_1 \vee L_2$ and L_3 also dependent, but L_2 and L_3 independent. Then $L_1^+ - L_2^+ \subseteq L_3^+$.*

PROOF. (i) The dependence of $L_1 \wedge L_2$ and L_3 implies $L_2^- \cap L_3^- \neq \emptyset$, so L_2 and L_3 can only be independent if $L_2^+ \cap L_3^+ = \emptyset$. Consider now the pair $N = (L_1 \wedge L_2) \vee L_3$. $N^+ = (L_1^+ \cup L_2^+) \cap L_3^+ = L_1^+ \cap L_3^+$, hence $N^+ \subseteq L_1^+$. By Claim 2.5, $N^- \supseteq L_1^-$, implying the claim. (ii) follows from (i) by reverting the orientations of all pairs. □

PROOF OF LEMMA 3.3. Let $\mathcal{F}' = \mathcal{F} \div K$. If K is large then $\mathcal{F}' = \mathcal{F}$ by Lemma 2.3, therefore K will be assumed to be small with an orientation L_K.

If F covers $\mathcal{F}'$ but not $\mathcal{F}$, then by Claim 2.2 there exists a small clump $X \in D_2(\mathcal{F}) - D_2(\mathcal{F}')$ not connected by F, thus X and K are crossing. Choose X with the orientation L_X compatible with L_K so that L_X is minimal to these properties w.r.t. $\preceq$ (that is, there exists no other uncovered X' with orientation $L_{X'}$ compatible with L_K so that $L_{X'} \prec L_X$.) Choose Y not connected by F with $L_X \preceq L_Y$, and L_Y maximal in the analogous sense ($X = Y$ is allowed).

$L_X \wedge L_K$ and $L_Y \vee L_K$ are nested with L_K and thus connected by edges $x_1y_1, x_2y_2 \in F$ with $x_1 \in L_X^- \cap L_K^-$, $y_2 \in L_Y^+ \cap L_K^+$. As X and Y are not connected, $y_1 \in L_K^+ - L_X^+$, $x_2 \in L_K^- - L_Y^-$ follows. Let $F' = F - \{x_1y_1, x_2y_2\} + \{x_1y_2, x_2y_1\}$. F' connects X and Y, and we shall prove that F' connects all small clumps in $D_2(\mathcal{F})$ connected by F. Hence after a finite number of such operations all small clumps in $D_2(\mathcal{F})$ will be connected, so by Claim 2.2, $\mathcal{F}$ will be covered.

For a contradiction, assume there is a small clump S connected by F but not by F'. (S is not necessarly basic.) No edge in $F \cap F'$ may connect S, hence either exactly one of x_1y_1 and x_2y_2 connects it, or if both then x_1 and y_2 are in the same piece, and y_1 and x_2 in the other piece of S. In this latter case, K and S are strongly dependent.

(I) First, assume that only x_1y_1 connects S, and choose the orientation L_S with $x_1 \in L_S^-$, $y_1 \in L_S^+$. We claim that L_S and L_Y are also dependent. Indeed, if they are independent, then Lemma 3.13(i) is applicable for $L_1 = L_K$, $L_2 = L_Y$, $L_3 = L_S$, since $L_K \wedge L_Y$ and L_S are dependent because x_1y_1 covers both. This gives $x_2 \in L_K^- - L_Y^- \subseteq L_S^-$, that is, x_2y_1 connects S, a contradiction.

Hence we may consider the one-way pair $L_S \vee L_Y$. $L_S \vee L_Y$ is strictly larger than L_Y, as if $L_S \preceq L_Y$ held, then S would be connected by x_1y_2. By the maximal choice of L_Y, $L_S \vee L_Y$ is connected by some edge $f \in F$. By Claim 2.7, f

also connects S or Y, implying $f = x_1y_1$. This is a contradiction as $x_1 \in L_S^- \cup L_Y^-$ and $y_1 \notin L_S^+ \cap L_Y^+$.

(II) If x_2y_2 is the only edge connecting S, we may use the same argument by exchanging $\vee$ and $\wedge$, X and Y, "minimal" and "maximal" everywhere and applying Lemma 3.13(ii) instead of (i).

(III) Finally, if both x_1y_1 and x_2y_2 cover S, let L_S be chosen with $x_1, y_2 \in L_S^-$, $y_1, x_2 \in L_S^+$. The argument in (I) may be applied with the only difference that at the end $f = x_2y_2$ is also possible. This gives $x_2 \in L_Y^+ \cap L_S^+$, thus $x_2 \in L_X^+$. Analogously, the argument in (II) applies for $\overleftarrow{L_S}$, and we get $y_1 \in L_X^- \cap L_S^+$, thus $y_1 \in L_X^-$.

Now the clumps K, S and X satisfy the condition in Lemma 3.12, witnessed by nodes x_1, x_2, y_2, y_1. This contradicts the assumption that K was a basic clump. □

4. THE ALGORITHM

As outlined in the Introduction, our algorithm is a simple iterative application of a subroutine determining the dual optimum $\nu(G)$. Theorem 3.1(ii) shows that $\nu(G) = \nu(\mathcal{K})$ for an arbitrary skeleton $\mathcal{K}$. Given a skeleton $\mathcal{K}$, $\nu(\mathcal{K})$ can be determined based on Fleiner's theorem: [5] gives a proof of Theorem 3.5 based on a (linear time) reduction to maximum matching in general graphs. Hence the only nontrivial question is how a skeleton can be found. A naive approach would be choosing clumps greedily so that they do not cross the previously selected ones. The difficulty arises from the fact that the number of the clumps might be exponentially large, forbiding us to check all clumps one-by-one. In fact, it is not even clear how to decide whether a given cross-free system is a skeleton. To overcome these difficulties, we restrict ourselves to a special class of cross-free systems. The proofs and technical details are omitted here and can be found in the full version.

DEFINITION 4.1. *A cross-free set of $\mathcal{H} \subseteq \mathcal{C}$ is* **stable** *if U crosses some element of $\mathcal{H}$ whenever $U \in \mathcal{C} - \mathcal{H}$ and there exist clumps $K, K' \in \mathcal{H}$ so that K, U, K' forms a chain.*

Let us now introduce some new notation concerning pieces. If the set $B \subseteq V$ is a piece of the basic clump X, then let $B^\sharp$ denote X. Let $\mathcal{Q}$ be the set of all (connected) pieces of all basic clumps, whereas $\mathcal{Q}_1$ the set of all (not necessarily connected) pieces of all clumps. For a subset $\mathcal{A} \subseteq \mathcal{Q}$, $\mathcal{A}^\sharp$ is the set of corresponding basic clumps (e.g. $\mathcal{Q}^\sharp = \mathcal{C}$). For a set $\mathcal{H} \subseteq \mathcal{C}$, by $\bigcup \mathcal{H}$ we denote the set of all pieces of clumps in $\mathcal{H}$.

Clearly, $\mathcal{H} = \emptyset$ is stable, and every skeleton is stable as well. Let $\mathcal{M} \subseteq \mathcal{P}$ denote the set of the pieces minimal for inclusion. Based on the following claim, we will be able to determine when a stable cross-free system is a skeleton.

CLAIM 4.2. *The stable cross-free system $\mathcal{H} \subseteq \mathcal{C}$ is a skeleton if and only if $\mathcal{M}^\sharp \subseteq \mathcal{H}$.* □

Assume $\mathcal{H}$ is a stable cross-free system, but not a skeleton. In the following, we show how $\mathcal{H}$ may be extended to a stable cross-free system larger by one. By the above claim, there is an $M \in \mathcal{M}$ with $M^\sharp \in \mathcal{C} - \mathcal{H}$. Let

$$\begin{aligned} \mathcal{L}_1 &:= \{X \in \mathcal{H} : X \text{ and } M^\sharp \text{ are nested}\}, \\ \mathcal{L}_2 &:= \{X \in \mathcal{H} : X \text{ and } M^\sharp \text{ are independent}\}. \end{aligned} \tag{1}$$

CLAIM 4.3. *If $\mathcal{L}_1 = \emptyset$, then $\mathcal{H} + M^\sharp$ is a stable cross-free system.* □

In the sequel we assume therefore $\mathcal{L}_1 \neq \emptyset$. The key concept of the algorithm will be "fitting". We shall define when a piece $C \in \mathcal{Q}$ **fits** the pair $(\mathcal{H}, M)$. The definition being significantly more complicated, we formulate the main lemma in advance:

LEMMA 4.4. *Let C be a minimal member of $\mathcal{P} - \bigcup \mathcal{H}$ fitting $(\mathcal{H}, M)$. Then $\mathcal{H} + C^\sharp$ is a stable cross-free system.* □

There exists a C satisfying the conditions of this lemma, as according to the definition, the pieces of $M^\sharp$ different from M (that is, the connected components of M^*) fit $(\mathcal{H}, M)$. Such a C can be found using standard bipartite matching theory similarly as in [9].

The minimality of M implies that for any $X \in \mathcal{L}_1$, the dominant piece of $M^\sharp$ w.r.t. X is a connected component of M^*. One simple notion before giving the definition of fitting is the following. For pieces $B, C \in \mathcal{Q}$, we say that B **supports** C if $B \subseteq C \subseteq M^*$. $B \in \mathcal{Q}$ supports $Y \in \mathcal{C}$ if B supports some piece of Y; $X \in \mathcal{C}$ supports $B \in \mathcal{Q}$ if a piece of X supports B.

DEFINITION 4.5. *The piece $C \in \mathcal{Q}$* **fits** *the pair $(\mathcal{H}, M)$ if*

(a) $C^\sharp \in \mathcal{C} - \mathcal{H}, C \subseteq M^*$.

(b) There exists a $W \in \mathcal{L}_1$ supporting C.

(c) Take any clump $X \in \mathcal{L}_1$ with dominant piece X_a w. r. t. $M^\sharp$, and an arbitrary other piece X_i with $i \neq a$. Then either $X_i \subsetneq C$ or $X_i \cap C = \emptyset$, and if $X_a \cap C \neq \emptyset$ then $X_i \cap C^* = \emptyset$.

(d) $C^\sharp$ is independent from every $X \in \mathcal{L}_2$.

The proof of Lemma 4.4 is based on the following claim:

CLAIM 4.6. *Let $C \in \mathcal{Q} - \bigcup \mathcal{H}$, $C \subseteq M^*$ supported by some $W \in \mathcal{L}_1$. The following two properties are equivalent: (i) C fits $(\mathcal{H}, M)$; (ii) $\mathcal{H} + C^\sharp$ is cross-free.* □

4.1 Running times

To determine the value of $\nu(G)$, first we construct a skeleton $\mathcal{K}$ as described above, and apply the reduction to Theorem 3.5, which can be further reduced to the Berge-Tutte theorem. Bounds given by Jordán [13, 14] on the size of an optimal augmenting edge set can be used to get an upper bound n^2 on the size of $\mathcal{K}$. A bound $O(kn^5)$ can be given for a single call of the Dual Oracle. As indicated in the Introduction, at most n^2 calls of the Dual Oracle enable us to compute an optimal augmentation. This gives a total running time $O(kn^7)$.

5. FURTHER REMARKS

5.1 Node-induced cost function

The problem of finding a minimum cost edge set whose addition makes a $(k-1)$-connected graph k-connected is NP-complete as already making the graph $G = (V, \emptyset)$ connected by adding a minimum cost edge set generalizes the TSP problem, even for 0-1-valued cost functions. However, there is a special type of cost-functions for which directed connectivity augmentation and also directed and undirected edge-connectivity augmentation are solvable: the node-induced cost functions. We show that augmenting undirected connectivity by one is also tractable for such cost functions.

A cost function $c' : E \to \mathbb{R}$ is **node-induced** if there exists a $c : V \to \mathbb{R}$ so that $c'(uv) = c(u) + c(v)$ for every $uv \in E$. By the last part of Theorem 3.1(ii), for a skeleton $\mathcal{K}$ and a node-induced cost function c', the minimum cost of an edge set covering $\mathcal{C}$ is the same as the minimum cost cover of $\mathcal{K}$. Hence it is enough to construct an oracle for determining the minimum cost $\nu_c(\mathcal{K})$ of a cover of $\mathcal{K}$. A minimum cost edge set whose addition makes G k-connected can be found by iteratively calling this oracle. $\nu_c(\mathcal{K})$ can be determined by the following weighted version of Fleiner's theorem, which reduces to maximum cost matching in general graphs.

Given a symmetric poset $P = (U, \preceq, M)$ and a cost function $w : U \to \mathbb{R}$, let us define the cost of the symmetric chain $S = \{u_1v_1, \ldots, u_\ell v_\ell\} \subseteq M$ with $u_1 \preceq \ldots \preceq u_\ell$, $v_1 \succeq \ldots \succeq v_\ell$ by $w(S) = w(u_\ell) + w(v_1)$. Our aim is to find a chain cover of minimum total cost.

This problem can be solved easily based on the reduction of Fleiner's theorem to the Berge-Tutte theorem.

5.2 Degree sequences

What can we say about the degree sequences of the augmenting edge sets? It is well-known that in a graph G with some cost function on the edges, the sets of nodes covered by a minimum cost matching form the bases of a matroid. A natural generalization of matroid bases are base polyhedra. For undirected edge-connectivity augmentation, the degree sequences of the optimal augmenting edge sets form a base polyhedron, and the same holds for the in- and out-degree sequences for directed connectivity augmentation (see e.g. [6]). This is also true in case of directed connectivity augmentation [8]. Moreover, all these results can be generalized for node-induced cost functions: the degree (resp. in- and out-degree) sequences of the minimum cost augmenting edge sets form a base polyhedron. Hence a natural conjecture is the following:

CONJECTURE 5.1. *Given a $(k-1)$-connected graph G and a node-induced cost function, the degree sequences of the minimum cost augmenting edge sets form base polyhedron.*

This was essentially proved by Szabó in his master's thesis [17] for $k = n - 2$. His result holds even without the assumption that the graph is $(k-1)$-connected, indicating that the conjecture might hold for arbitrary graphs as well.

5.3 Future directions

Let us discuss some possible generalizations and extension of the above results. For directed connectivity augmentation, Theorem 1.2 is only a special case of covering crossing families of set pairs [8, Theorem 2.5], which is still only special case of the general theorem on covering positively crossing bisupermodular functions [8, Theorem 2.3]. Here, the size of a minimum covering equals the maximum sum of p-values over pairwise independent set pairs for a function p. For connectivity augmentation of the (not necessarly $(k-1)$-connected) digraph $D = (V, A)$, we define $p(K^-, K^+) = \max(0, k - |V - (K^- \cup K^+)| - \delta_A(K^-, K^+))$ for nonempty disjoint $K^-, K^+ \subseteq V$ pairs. The proof is astonishingly simple even for this most general version.

The first natural question is whether it is possible to give a generalization of Theorem 1.1 for abstract structures, as for crossing families of set pairs in the directed case. Indeed, it would be possible to formulate such an abstract theorem for describing coverings of a systems $\mathcal{C}$ of "basic clumps", where under basic clump we simply mean a subpartition of a set satisfying certain properties. However, it is not easy to extract the abstract properties $\mathcal{C}$ needs to fulfill for the argument to work. In particular, we need to ensure Claim 2.1, Lemma 2.3, Claims 2.4 and 2.5, Lemma 3.12. It may be verified that whenever $\mathcal{C}$ satisfies these, all other proofs carry over; for the algorithm we also need to know the representation how $\mathcal{C}$ is given.

Since the argument is already quite abstract and complicated, and we could not find an elegant list of properties that ensure all these claims, we did not formulate such an abstract theorem in order to avoid the addition of a new level of complexity. Furthermore, we believe that there should be a relatively simple abstract generalization of Theorem 1.1, which does not rely on all claims listed above. For comparison, the argument given in [9] for proving Theorem 1.2 strongly relies on properties of one-way pairs in a a $(k-1)$-connected digraph. Nevertheless, these are not needed (and in fact, not necessarly true) for the general theorem for crossing families, which admits a much simpler proof.

Another question is if we may hope a simple generalization of Theorem 1.1 for general connectivity augmentation. By "simple", we mean an analogous situation as in the directed case. Such an approach would be the following. Let a clump be a subpartition $X = (X_1, \ldots, X_\ell)$ of V with $d(X_i, X_j) = 0$ (we do not assume $|N_X| = k - 1$), and let $p(X)$ be a lower bound on the number of edges needed to cover X. There are multiple possible candidates for $p(X)$ and let us not commit to any of them, but assume only that $(\star)$ $p(X) = \max(0, k - |N_X|)$ whenever $|X| = 2$; and $p(X) = 0$ whenever $|N_X| \geq k$. Hence a natural conjecture is the following: the minimum size of an augmenting edge set equals the maximum deficiency of a grove, where in the definition of deficiency, each term $|X| - 1$ is replaced by $p(X)$. Unfortunately, it can be shown by an example (see the full version) that this conjecture fails even if $(\star)$ is the only assumption on $p(X)$.

Despite this example, we expect not only that general connectivity augmentation should be polynomially solvable, but that it should also admit a relatively simple abstract generalization such as the general Frank-Jordán theorem in the directed case. This generalization should be applicable, besides Theorem 1.1, to rooted connectivity augmentation and problems like maximum $K_{t,t}$-free t-matching (see [2]).

Acknowledgement

The author is grateful to Kristóf Bérczi and András Frank for several fruitful discussions on this topic and for their valuable ideas and suggestions.

6. REFERENCES

[1] K. Bérczi and Y. Kobayashi. An algorithm for $(n-3)$-connectivity augmentation problem: Jump system approach. Technical Report METR 2009-12, Department of Mathematical Engineering, University of Tokyo, April 2009.

[2] K. Bérczi and L. A. Végh. Restricted b-matchings in degree-bounded graphs. Technical Report TR-2009-12, Egerváry Research Group, Budapest, 2009. `www.cs.elte.hu/egres`.

[3] J. Cheriyan and R. Thurimella. Fast algorithms for k-shredders and k-node connectivity augmentation. *Journal of Algorithms*, 33(1):15–50, 1999.

[4] K. Eswaran and R. Tarjan. Augmentation problems. *SIAM J. Computing*, 5(4):653–665, 1976.

[5] T. Fleiner. Covering a symmetric poset by symmetric chains. *Combinatorica*, 17(3):339–344, 1997.

[6] A. Frank. Augmenting graphs to meet edge-connectivity requirements. *SIAM J. Discret. Math.*, 5(1):25–53, 1992.

[7] A. Frank and T. Jordán. Presented at the Workshop on Network Design, Budapest, October 1994.

[8] A. Frank and T. Jordán. Minimal edge-coverings of pairs of sets. *J. Comb. Theory Ser. B*, 65(1):73–110, 1995.

[9] A. Frank and L. A. Végh. An algorithm to increase the node-connectivity of a digraph by one. *Discrete Optimization*, 5:677–684, 2008.

[10] T.-S. Hsu. On four-connecting a triconnected graph. *J. Algorithms*, 35(2):202–234, 2000.

[11] B. Jackson and T. Jordán. A near optimal algorithm for vertex connectivity augmentation. In *ISAAC '00: Proceedings of the 11th International Conference on Algorithms and Computation*, pages 312–325, London, UK, 2000. Springer-Verlag.

[12] B. Jackson and T. Jordán. Independence free graphs and vertex connectivity augmentation. *J. Comb. Theory Ser. B*, 94(1):31–77, 2005.

[13] T. Jordán. On the optimal vertex-connectivity augmentation. *J. Comb. Theory Ser. B*, 63(1):8–20, 1995.

[14] T. Jordán. A note on the vertex-connectivity augmentation problem. *J. Comb. Theory, Ser. B*, 71(2):294–301, 1997.

[15] G. Kortsarz and Z. Nutov. Approximating minimum cost connectivity problems. In T. F. Gonzalez, editor, *Handbook on Approximation Algorithms and Metaheuristics*, chapter 58. Chapman & Hall/CRC, 2007.

[16] G. Liberman and Z. Nutov. On shredders and vertex connectivity augmentation. *J. of Discrete Algorithms*, 5(1):91–101, 2007.

[17] J. Szabó. Jump systems and matroid parity (in hungarian). Master's thesis, Eötvös University, Budapest, 2002. Available online at `http://www.cs.elte.hu`.

[18] T. Watanabe and A. Nakamura. Edge-connectivity augmentation problems. *J. Comput. Syst. Sci.*, 35(1):96–144, 1987.

[19] T. Watanabe and A. Nakamura. A minimum 3-connectivity augmentation of a graph. *J. Comput. Syst. Sci.*, 46(1):91–128, 1993.

QIP = PSPACE

Rahul Jain* Zhengfeng Ji† Sarvagya Upadhyay‡ John Watrous‡

*Department of Computer Science and Centre for Quantum Technologies
National University of Singapore
Republic of Singapore

†Perimeter Institute for Theoretical Physics
Waterloo, Ontario, Canada
and
State Key Laboratory of Computer Science
Institute of Software, Chinese Academy of Sciences
Beijing, China

‡Institute for Quantum Computing and School of Computer Science
University of Waterloo
Waterloo, Ontario, Canada

ABSTRACT

We prove that the complexity class QIP, which consists of all problems having quantum interactive proof systems, is contained in PSPACE. This containment is proved by applying a parallelized form of the matrix multiplicative weights update method to a class of semidefinite programs that captures the computational power of quantum interactive proofs. As the containment of PSPACE in QIP follows immediately from the well-known equality IP = PSPACE, the equality QIP = PSPACE follows.

Categories and Subject Descriptors

F.1.3 [**Theory of Computation**]: Computation by Abstract Devices—*Complexity Measures and Classes*

General Terms

Theory

Keywords

Quantum interactive proof systems, quantum computation, matrix multiplicative weights update method, semidefinite programming

1. INTRODUCTION

Efficient proof verification is a fundamental notion in computational complexity theory. The most direct complexity-theoretic abstraction of efficient proof verification is represented by the complexity class NP, wherein a deterministic polynomial-time verification procedure decides whether a polynomial-length proof string is valid for a given input. One cannot overstate the importance of this notion—it is essential to complexity theory and finds applications throughout the broad range of scientific fields that make use of the theory of NP-completeness.

In the mid-1980's, Babai [4] and Goldwasser, Micali, and Rackoff [21] introduced a computational model that extends the notion of efficient proof verification to an *interactive* setting. (Journal versions of these papers appeared later as [5] and [22].) In this model, which is known as the *interactive proof system* model, a computationally bounded *verifier* interacts with a *prover* of unlimited computation power. The interaction comprises one or more rounds of communication between the prover and verifier, and the verifier may make use of randomly generated bits during the interaction. After the rounds of communication are finished, the verifier makes a decision to *accept* or *reject* based on the interaction.

A decision problem A, which we may take to be a *promise problem* [15, 19] in the interest of generality, is said to have an interactive proof system if there exists a polynomial-time verifier that meets two conditions: the *completeness* condition and the *soundness* condition. The completeness condition formalizes the requirement that true statements can be proved, which in the present setting means that if an input string x is a yes-instance of A, then there exists a course of action for the prover that causes the verifier to accept with high probability. The soundness condition formalizes the requirement that false statements cannot be proved, meaning in this case that if an input string x is a no-instance of A, then the verifier will reject with high probability no matter what course of action the prover takes. One denotes by IP the collection of decision problems having interactive proof systems that meet these conditions.

The computational power of interactive proof systems was not known when they were first introduced, but it was soon determined to coincide with PSPACE, the class of problems solvable deterministically in polynomial space. The containment IP $\subseteq$ PSPACE is fairly straightforward—it was first proved in [17], and a proof may also be found in [43]. Known proofs of the reverse containment PSPACE $\subseteq$ IP, on the other hand, are not straightforward, and make essential use of the technique commonly known as *arithmetization* [33, 41, 42].

STOC'10, June 5–8, 2010, Cambridge, Massachusetts, USA.

Many variants of interactive proof systems have been studied, including public-coin interactive proofs [4, 5, 23], zero-knowledge interactive proofs [21, 22, 20], multi-prover interactive proofs [7], and interactive proofs with competing provers [16].

The present paper is concerned with *quantum interactive proof systems*, which were first studied roughly a decade after IP = PSPACE was proved [45, 30]. The fundamental notions of this model are the same as those of classical interactive proof systems, except that the prover and verifier may now process and exchange quantum information. Similar to the classical case, several variants of quantum interactive proof systems have been studied, including those considered in [24, 25, 29, 32, 31, 35, 46].

The complexity class QIP is defined as the class of decision problems having complete and sound quantum interactive proof systems. QIP trivially contains IP, as the ability of a verifier to process quantum information is never a hindrance: a quantum verifier can simulate a classical verifier, and a single computationally unbounded prover can never use quantum information to an advantage against a verifier behaving classically. The inclusion PSPACE $\subseteq$ QIP is therefore immediate. The best upper bound on QIP known prior to the present paper was QIP $\subseteq$ EXP, where EXP denotes the class of problems solvable in deterministic exponential-time. This containment was proved in [30] through the use of semidefinite programming: the optimal probability with which a given verifier can be made to accept in a quantum interactive proof system can be represented as an exponential-size semidefinite program, and known polynomial-time algorithms for semidefinite programming provide the required tool to prove the containment. It has been an open problem for the last decade to establish more precise bounds on the class QIP.

It is known that quantum information offers at least one significant advantage to the interactive proof system model under a reasonable complexity-theoretic assumption. Specifically, quantum interactive proof systems can be *parallelized* to three messages, meaning that quantum interactive proof systems in which just three messages are exchanged between the prover and verifier already have the full power of quantum interactive proofs having a polynomial number of messages [30]. Classical interactive proofs cannot have this property unless the polynomial-time hierarchy collapses to the second level [5, 23].

Three of us [26] recently showed that QIP(2), the class of problem having 2-message quantum interactive proof systems, is contained in PSPACE. Our proof made use of a parallel algorithm, based on a method known as the *matrix multiplicative weights update method*, to approximate optimal solutions for a class of semidefinite programs that represent the maximum acceptance probabilities for verifiers in two-message quantum interactive proofs. In the present paper we extend this result to all of QIP, establishing the relationship QIP = PSPACE. Similar to [26], we use the matrix multiplicative weights update method, together with parallel methods for matrix computations.

The multiplicative weights method is a framework for algorithm design having its origins in various fields, including learning theory, game theory, and optimization. Its matrix variant, as discussed in the survey paper [2] and the PhD thesis of Kale [28], gives an iterative way to approximate the optimal value of semidefinite programs [3, 44]. In addition to its application in [26], it was applied to quantum complexity in [27] to prove the containment of a different quantum complexity class QRG(1) in PSPACE. The key strength of this method for these applications is that it can be parallelized for some special classes of semidefinite programs.

A key result that allows the matrix multiplicative weights update method to be applied to the entire class QIP is a characterization of QIP in terms of *quantum Arthur–Merlin games* that was proved in [35]. This characterization is described in greater detail later in the paper.

2. PRELIMINARIES

We assume the reader has familiarity with complexity theory and the basics of quantum computing, and refer readers who do not to [1] and [39]. The purpose of this section is to clarify some of the notation, terminology, and background knowledge on quantum information and basic linear algebra that we use or assume later in the paper.

A *quantum register* refers simply to a collection of qubits that we wish to assign a name. The 2^n-dimensional complex vector space associated with an n-qubit quantum register X is denoted $\mathcal{X}$, and a similar convention is used for other register names. The space associated with a tuple of quantum registers is given by the tensor product of the spaces associated with the individual registers.

For any vector space $\mathcal{X}$ associated with one or more quantum registers and any two linear operators (or matrices) A and B mapping $\mathcal{X}$ to itself, we define the inner product

$$\langle A, B \rangle = \operatorname{Tr}(A^* B),$$

where A^* denotes the adjoint (or conjugate transpose) of A. (We will only refer to such inner products for Hermitian operators A and B, so one may safely view that $\langle A, B \rangle = \operatorname{Tr}(AB)$ throughout this paper.) We write $\operatorname{Pos}(\mathcal{X})$ to refer to the set of all positive semidefinite operators on $\mathcal{X}$, and $\operatorname{D}(\mathcal{X})$ to refer to the set of all density operators on $\mathcal{X}$. For Hermitian operators A and B, the notations $A \leq B$ and $B \geq A$ mean that $B - A$ is positive semidefinite. An operator $\Pi \in \operatorname{Pos}(\mathcal{X})$ is a *projection* if all of its eigenvalues are either 0 or 1. The identity operator on $\mathcal{X}$ is denoted $\mathbb{1}_{\mathcal{X}}$, or simply by $\mathbb{1}$ when $\mathcal{X}$ can safely be taken as implicit.

A *quantum state* of a quantum register X is a density operator $\rho \in \operatorname{D}(\mathcal{X})$, and a *measurement* on X is a collection

$$\{P_b : b \in \Gamma\} \subseteq \operatorname{Pos}(\mathcal{X})$$

satisfying

$$\sum_{b \in \Gamma} P_b = \mathbb{1}_{\mathcal{X}}.$$

The set Γ is the set of *measurement outcomes*, and when such a measurement is performed on X while it is in the state ρ, each outcome $b \in \Gamma$ occurs with probability $\langle P_b, \rho \rangle$. A *projective measurement* is one in which each P_b is a projection.

For spaces $\mathcal{X}$ and $\mathcal{Y}$, one defines the *partial trace* $\operatorname{Tr}_{\mathcal{Y}}$ to be the unique linear mapping that satisfies $\operatorname{Tr}_{\mathcal{Y}}(A \otimes B) = (\operatorname{Tr} B)A$ for all operators A on $\mathcal{X}$ and B on $\mathcal{Y}$. A similar notation is used for the partial trace over $\mathcal{X}$ rather than $\mathcal{Y}$, as well as for partial traces defined on three or more tensor factors. When a pair of registers (X, Y) is viewed as a single register and has the quantum state $\rho \in \operatorname{D}(\mathcal{X} \otimes \mathcal{Y})$, one defines the state of X to be $\operatorname{Tr}_{\mathcal{Y}}(\rho)$. In other words, the partial trace describes the action of destroying, or simply ignoring, a given quantum register.

The *spectral norm* of an operator A mapping $\mathcal{X}$ to itself is defined as

$$\|A\| = \max\{\|Ax\| : x \in \mathcal{X}, \|x\| = 1\},$$

where $\|Ax\|$ and $\|x\|$ refer to the Euclidean norm on $\mathcal{X}$. The spectral norm is sub-multiplicative: $\|AB\| \leq \|A\| \|B\|$ for all operators A and B. It holds that $\|P\|$ is equal to the largest eigenvalue of P for every positive semidefinite operator P.

For any operator A, the exponential of A is defined as

$$\exp(A) = \mathbb{1} + A + A^2/2 + A^3/6 + \cdots$$

The *Golden-Thompson Inequality* (see Section IX.3 of [8]) states that, for any two Hermitian operators A and B on $\mathcal{X}$, we have

$$\operatorname{Tr}[\exp(A+B)] \leq \operatorname{Tr}[\exp(A)\exp(B)].$$

3. SEMIDEFINITE PROGRAMS FOR QIP

The first step in our proof that QIP $\subseteq$ PSPACE is the identification of a family of semidefinite programs based on quantum interactive proof systems with the following form:

1. On any given input string x, the prover begins by sending a quantum register X to the verifier.
2. Upon receiving X from the prover, the verifier generates a bit $a \in \{0,1\}$ uniformly at random and sends this bit to the prover.
3. The prover responds with a second quantum register Y. (There is no loss of generality in assuming Y has the same number of qubits as X.)
4. The verifier performs one of two binary-valued measurements, determined by the value of the random bit a, on the pair (X, Y). A measurement outcome of 1 is interpreted as *acceptance*, while the outcome 0 is interpreted as *rejection*.

Such a proof system is an example of a *quantum Arthur-Merlin game* given that the verifier's messages to the prover consist entirely of uniformly generated random bits (which is analogous to the classical definition [4, 5]). It was proved in [35] that every problem $A \in$ QIP has a quantum interactive proof system of the above form, where the completeness is perfect and the soundness error is bounded by $1/2 - \varepsilon$ for any desired constant $\varepsilon > 0$. It may, in addition, be assumed that the measurements performed by the verifier in step 4 are projective measurements.

Now, for a given proof system of the above form, and for a fixed input string x, let us denote by $\mathcal{X}$ and $\mathcal{Y}$ the complex vector spaces corresponding to the registers X and Y, respectively. Let us suppose further that

$$\{\Pi_b^a : a, b \in \{0,1\}\} \subset \operatorname{Pos}(\mathcal{X} \otimes \mathcal{Y})$$

are the projection operators on $\mathcal{X} \otimes \mathcal{Y}$ that describe the measurements performed by the verifier in step 4 (meaning that $\{\Pi_0^a, \Pi_1^a\}$ describes the binary-valued measurement that is performed for each $a \in \{0,1\}$). We claim that the maximum probability with which the prover can cause the verifier to accept (or output 1) in this proof system is given by the optimal value of the following semidefinite optimization problem:

$$\begin{aligned}
\text{maximize:} \quad & \frac{1}{2}\left\langle \Pi_1^0, \rho_0 \right\rangle + \frac{1}{2}\left\langle \Pi_1^1, \rho_1 \right\rangle \\
\text{subject to:} \quad & \operatorname{Tr}_{\mathcal{Y}}(\rho_0) = \operatorname{Tr}_{\mathcal{Y}}(\rho_1), \\
& \rho_0, \rho_1 \in \mathrm{D}(\mathcal{X} \otimes \mathcal{Y}).
\end{aligned}$$

The density operators ρ_0 and ρ_1 represent the possible states of the register pair (X, Y) conditioned on the verifier choosing $a = 0$ and $a = 1$, respectively. As one ranges over all actions for the prover, the possible state-pairs (ρ_0, ρ_1) that may result are precisely those states that agree on X, i.e., those satisfying

$$\operatorname{Tr}_{\mathcal{Y}}(\rho_0) = \operatorname{Tr}_{\mathcal{Y}}(\rho_1).$$

It is clear that this condition is necessary, as the prover sends X before learning a, while its sufficiency follows from the well-known principle in quantum information theory sometimes called the *unitary equivalence of purifications*.

Now, for the sake of the algorithm to be discussed in the next section, it is necessary that we consider a relaxation of the above semidefinite program. First, for any choice of $\alpha > 0$, let us introduce a block matrix

$$P_\alpha = \begin{pmatrix} \Pi_1^0 + \alpha \Pi_0^0 & 0 \\ 0 & \Pi_1^1 + \alpha \Pi_0^1 \end{pmatrix}, \tag{1}$$

whose inverse is given by

$$P_\alpha^{-1} = \begin{pmatrix} \Pi_1^0 + \frac{1}{\alpha}\Pi_0^0 & 0 \\ 0 & \Pi_1^1 + \frac{1}{\alpha}\Pi_0^1 \end{pmatrix}.$$

By taking $\mathcal{A}$ to be a complex vector space of dimension 2, which intuitively corresponds to the verifier's random bit a, we may view that $P_\alpha \in \operatorname{Pos}(\mathcal{A} \otimes \mathcal{X} \otimes \mathcal{Y})$. Along similar lines, the density operators ρ_0 and ρ_1 may be combined into a single block density matrix

$$\rho = \begin{pmatrix} \frac{1}{2}\rho_0 & 0 \\ 0 & \frac{1}{2}\rho_1 \end{pmatrix} \in \mathrm{D}(\mathcal{A} \otimes \mathcal{X} \otimes \mathcal{Y}).$$

Finally, we introduce an auxiliary variable $\sigma \in \mathrm{D}(\mathcal{X})$ in order to express the equality $\operatorname{Tr}_{\mathcal{Y}}(\rho_0) = \operatorname{Tr}_{\mathcal{Y}}(\rho_1)$ in the form of two inequalities. With these operators in mind, we consider the following semidefinite program:

$$\begin{aligned}
\text{maximize:} \quad & \left\langle P_\alpha^{-2}, \rho \right\rangle \\
\text{subject to:} \quad & \operatorname{Tr}_{\mathcal{Y}}(\rho) \leq \frac{1}{2}\mathbb{1}_{\mathcal{A}} \otimes \sigma, \\
& \rho \in \operatorname{Pos}(\mathcal{A} \otimes \mathcal{X} \otimes \mathcal{Y}), \\
& \sigma \in \mathrm{D}(\mathcal{X}).
\end{aligned}$$

This semidefinite program has an optimal value that is at least as large as the optimal value of the original problem, and is at most $1/\alpha^2$ plus that value.

An equivalent formulation of this problem, which we take to be the formal statement of the semidefinite program that is to be considered in the next section, is as follows:

Primal problem

$$\begin{aligned}
\text{maximize:} \quad & \operatorname{Tr}(\rho) \\
\text{subject to:} \quad & \operatorname{Tr}_{\mathcal{Y}}(P_\alpha \rho P_\alpha) \leq \frac{1}{2}\mathbb{1}_{\mathcal{A}} \otimes \sigma, \\
& \operatorname{Tr}(\sigma) \leq 1, \\
& \rho \in \operatorname{Pos}(\mathcal{A} \otimes \mathcal{X} \otimes \mathcal{Y}), \\
& \sigma \in \operatorname{Pos}(\mathcal{X}).
\end{aligned}$$

The dual problem takes the following form:

Dual problem

$$\begin{aligned} \text{minimize:} \quad & \frac{1}{2}\left\|\operatorname{Tr}_{\mathcal{A}}(Q)\right\| \\ \text{subject to:} \quad & P_\alpha(Q\otimes \mathbb{1}_{\mathcal{Y}})P_\alpha \geq \mathbb{1}_{\mathcal{A}\otimes\mathcal{X}\otimes\mathcal{Y}}, \\ & Q \in \operatorname{Pos}(\mathcal{A}\otimes\mathcal{X}). \end{aligned}$$

4. A PARALLEL SDP ALGORITHM

We now present a parallel algorithm that operates as follows. It takes as input four projection operators

$$\Pi_0^0,\ \Pi_1^0,\ \Pi_0^1,\ \Pi_1^1 \in \operatorname{Pos}(\mathcal{X}\otimes\mathcal{Y})$$

satisfying $\Pi_0^0+\Pi_1^0 = \mathbb{1}_{\mathcal{X}\otimes\mathcal{Y}} = \Pi_0^1+\Pi_1^1$, where $\mathcal{X}$ and $\mathcal{Y}$ are complex vector spaces, both having dimension N. Under the promise that the semidefinite program described in the previous section has an optimal value that is either close to 1 or close to $1/2$, it determines which is the case (accepting if the optimal value is close to 1 and rejecting when it is close to $1/2$). The algorithm is as follows.

1. Let

$$\alpha = 4, \quad \gamma = \frac{4}{3}, \quad \varepsilon = \frac{1}{64} \quad \text{and} \quad \delta = \frac{\varepsilon}{\alpha^2},$$

and let P_α be as defined in (1). Set the number of iterations to be performed by the algorithm to

$$T = \left\lceil \frac{8\log(N)}{\varepsilon^2\delta} \right\rceil$$

and initialize

$$\begin{aligned} X_0 &= \mathbb{1}_{\mathcal{A}\otimes\mathcal{X}\otimes\mathcal{Y}}, & \rho_0 &= X_0/\operatorname{Tr}(X_0), \\ Y_0 &= \mathbb{1}_{\mathcal{X}}, & \sigma_0 &= Y_0/\operatorname{Tr}(Y_0). \end{aligned}$$

2. Repeat the following steps for each $t = 0,\dots,T-1$.

   (a) Let Δ_t be the projection operator onto the positive eigenspace of

$$\operatorname{Tr}_{\mathcal{Y}}\left(P_\alpha\rho_t P_\alpha\right) - \frac{\gamma}{2}\mathbb{1}_{\mathcal{A}}\otimes\sigma_t,$$

   and let

$$\beta_t = \langle P_\alpha(\Delta_t\otimes\mathbb{1}_{\mathcal{Y}})P_\alpha, \rho_t\rangle.$$

   If $\beta_t \leq \varepsilon$ then *halt and accept*.

   (b) Let

$$X_{t+1} = \exp\left(-\varepsilon\delta\sum_{j=0}^{t} P_\alpha\left(\Delta_j\otimes\mathbb{1}_{\mathcal{Y}}\right)P_\alpha/\beta_j\right),$$

$$Y_{t+1} = \exp\left(\varepsilon\delta\sum_{j=0}^{t}\operatorname{Tr}_{\mathcal{A}}\left(\Delta_j/\beta_j\right)\right),$$

   and let

$$\rho_{t+1} = \frac{X_{t+1}}{\operatorname{Tr}(X_{t+1})} \quad \text{and} \quad \sigma_{t+1} = \frac{Y_{t+1}}{\operatorname{Tr}(Y_{t+1})}.$$

3. If acceptance did not occur in step 2, then *halt and reject*.

4.1 Analysis (ignoring precision)

We now show that the algorithm answers correctly, meaning that (i) if the optimal value of the semidefinite program from the previous section is sufficiently close to 1, then the algorithm accepts, and (ii) if the optimal value is sufficiently close to $1/2$, then the algorithm rejects. We first do this in the idealized situation where all of the matrix operations are performed exactly, as this analysis better illustrates the basic principles of the algorithm. The finite-precision case is discussed in the subsection following this one.

Assume first that the algorithm accepts. This must happen during some iteration of step 2, and for whichever iteration t it is we will write ρ, σ, Δ, and β rather than ρ_t, σ_t, Δ_t, and β_t to simplify our notation. Define $\rho' \in \operatorname{Pos}(\mathcal{A}\otimes\mathcal{X}\otimes\mathcal{Y})$ and $\sigma' \in \operatorname{Pos}(\mathcal{X})$ as follows:

$$\begin{aligned} \rho' &= \frac{\rho}{\gamma+4\beta}, \\ \sigma' &= \frac{\gamma\sigma + 4\operatorname{Tr}_{\mathcal{A}}\left[\Delta\operatorname{Tr}_{\mathcal{Y}}\left(P_\alpha\rho P_\alpha\right)\Delta\right]}{\gamma+4\beta}. \end{aligned}$$

We will prove that (ρ',σ') is a primal feasible point of our semidefinite program that achieves an objective value significantly larger than $1/2$. By the definition of Δ it holds that

$$\operatorname{Tr}_{\mathcal{Y}}(P_\alpha\rho P_\alpha) - \frac{\gamma}{2}\mathbb{1}_{\mathcal{A}}\otimes\sigma \leq \Delta\left(\operatorname{Tr}_{\mathcal{Y}}(P_\alpha\rho P_\alpha) - \frac{\gamma}{2}\mathbb{1}_{\mathcal{A}}\otimes\sigma\right)\Delta,$$

and given that σ is positive semidefinite it is immediate that

$$\Delta\left(\operatorname{Tr}_{\mathcal{Y}}(P_\alpha\rho P_\alpha) - \frac{\gamma}{2}\mathbb{1}_{\mathcal{A}}\otimes\sigma\right)\Delta \leq \Delta\operatorname{Tr}_{\mathcal{Y}}\left(P_\alpha\rho P_\alpha\right)\Delta.$$

Finally, by Lemma 1 (which is stated below) it holds that

$$\Delta\operatorname{Tr}_{\mathcal{Y}}(P_\alpha\rho P_\alpha)\Delta \leq 2\mathbb{1}_{\mathcal{A}}\otimes\operatorname{Tr}_{\mathcal{A}}\left[\Delta\operatorname{Tr}_{\mathcal{Y}}\left(P_\alpha\rho P_\alpha\right)\Delta\right],$$

and so we conclude that

$$\operatorname{Tr}_{\mathcal{Y}}(P_\alpha\rho P_\alpha) \leq \frac{1}{2}\mathbb{1}_{\mathcal{A}}\otimes\left(\gamma\sigma + 4\operatorname{Tr}_{\mathcal{A}}\left[\Delta\operatorname{Tr}_{\mathcal{Y}}\left(P_\alpha\rho P_\alpha\right)\Delta\right]\right).$$

It therefore holds that

$$\operatorname{Tr}_{\mathcal{Y}}(P_\alpha\rho' P_\alpha) \leq \frac{1}{2}\mathbb{1}_{\mathcal{A}}\otimes\sigma',$$

and it is clear that $\operatorname{Tr}(\sigma') = 1$, so (ρ',σ') is primal feasible as claimed. The objective value achieved by the point (ρ',σ') is given by

$$\operatorname{Tr}(\rho') \geq \frac{1}{\gamma+4\beta} \geq \frac{1}{\gamma+4\varepsilon} > \frac{5}{8}.$$

Now assume that the algorithm rejects, and define

$$Q = \frac{1+4\varepsilon}{T}\sum_{t=0}^{T-1}\Delta_t/\beta_t.$$

We will prove that Q is dual feasible and achieves a dual objective value that is significantly smaller than 1.

To prove the dual feasibility of Q, let us first observe that for each choice of $t = 0,\dots,T-1$ we have

$$\operatorname{Tr}\left(X_{t+1}\right) \leq \operatorname{Tr}\left(X_t\exp\left(-\frac{\varepsilon\delta}{\beta_t}P_\alpha(\Delta_t\otimes\mathbb{1}_{\mathcal{Y}})P_\alpha\right)\right)$$

by the Golden-Thompson inequality. As we have assumed that the algorithm rejects, it holds that $\beta_t > \varepsilon$, and therefore

$$\left\|\frac{\delta}{\beta_t}P_\alpha(\Delta_t\otimes\mathbb{1}_{\mathcal{Y}})P_\alpha\right\| \leq \frac{\delta\alpha^2}{\varepsilon} \leq 1.$$

By Lemma 2 (which is also stated below) this implies that

$$\exp\left(-\frac{\varepsilon\delta}{\beta_t}P_\alpha(\Delta_t\otimes\mathbb{1}_\mathcal{Y})P_\alpha\right)\leq\mathbb{1}-\frac{\varepsilon\delta\exp(-\varepsilon)}{\beta_t}P_\alpha(\Delta_t\otimes\mathbb{1}_\mathcal{Y})P_\alpha,$$

and therefore

$$\begin{aligned}\operatorname{Tr}(X_{t+1})&\leq\operatorname{Tr}\left(X_t\left(\mathbb{1}-\frac{\varepsilon\delta\exp(-\varepsilon)}{\beta_t}P_\alpha(\Delta_t\otimes\mathbb{1}_\mathcal{Y})P_\alpha\right)\right)\\&\leq\operatorname{Tr}(X_t)\left(1-\frac{\varepsilon\delta\exp(-\varepsilon)}{\beta_t}\langle P_\alpha(\Delta_t\otimes\mathbb{1}_\mathcal{Y})P_\alpha,\rho_t\rangle\right)\\&=\operatorname{Tr}(X_t)(1-\varepsilon\delta\exp(-\varepsilon))\\&\leq\operatorname{Tr}(X_t)\exp(-\varepsilon\delta\exp(-\varepsilon)),\end{aligned}$$

where the last inequality follows from $1+z\leq\exp(z)$, which holds for all real numbers z. By applying the above inequality recursively we obtain the inequality

$$\begin{aligned}\operatorname{Tr}(X_T)&\leq\operatorname{Tr}(X_0)\exp(-T\varepsilon\delta\exp(-\varepsilon))\\&=2N^2\exp(-T\varepsilon\delta\exp(-\varepsilon)).\end{aligned}$$

On the other hand, we have that

$$\begin{aligned}\operatorname{Tr}(X_T)&=\operatorname{Tr}\left(\exp\left(-\varepsilon\delta\sum_{t=0}^{T-1}P_\alpha(\Delta_t\otimes\mathbb{1}_\mathcal{Y})P_\alpha/\beta_t\right)\right)\\&\geq\exp\left(-\varepsilon\delta\lambda_{\min}\left(\sum_{t=0}^{T-1}P_\alpha(\Delta_t\otimes\mathbb{1}_\mathcal{Y})P_\alpha/\beta_t\right)\right),\end{aligned}$$

where the function $\lambda_{\min}$ is defined as the smallest eigenvalue of its argument. Thus, we have

$$\begin{aligned}&2N^2\exp(-T\varepsilon\delta\exp(-\varepsilon))\\&\quad\geq\exp\left(-\varepsilon\delta\lambda_{\min}\left(\sum_{t=0}^{T-1}P_\alpha\left(\Delta_t\otimes\mathbb{1}_\mathcal{Y}\right)P_\alpha/\beta_t\right)\right),\end{aligned}$$

and therefore

$$\begin{aligned}&\lambda_{\min}\left(\sum_{t=0}^{T-1}P_\alpha\left(\Delta_t\otimes\mathbb{1}_\mathcal{Y}\right)P_\alpha/\beta_t\right)\\&\qquad\geq T\exp(-\varepsilon)-\frac{\log(2N^2)}{\varepsilon\delta}.\end{aligned}$$

Consequently

$$\begin{aligned}&\lambda_{\min}(P_\alpha(Q\otimes\mathbb{1}_\mathcal{Y})P_\alpha)\\&\qquad\geq(1+4\varepsilon)\left(\exp(-\varepsilon)-\frac{\log(2N^2)}{T\varepsilon\delta}\right)\geq 1,\end{aligned}$$

and therefore $P_\alpha(Q\otimes\mathbb{1}_\mathcal{Y})P_\alpha\geq\mathbb{1}_{\mathcal{A}\otimes\mathcal{X}\otimes\mathcal{Y}}$, which implies that Q is dual feasible as claimed.

It remains to prove an upper bound on the dual objective value achieved by Q. For each $t=0,\ldots,T-1$ we have

$$\operatorname{Tr}(Y_{t+1})\leq\operatorname{Tr}\left(Y_t\exp\left(\varepsilon\delta\operatorname{Tr}_\mathcal{A}(\Delta_t/\beta_t)\right)\right).$$

We again make use of the inequality $\beta_t>\varepsilon$, this time to conclude that $\|\delta\operatorname{Tr}_\mathcal{A}(\Delta_t/\beta_t)\|<1$. Using Lemma 2 again, we have

$$\exp\left(\varepsilon\delta\operatorname{Tr}_\mathcal{A}(\Delta_t/\beta_t)\right)\leq\mathbb{1}+\varepsilon\delta\exp(\varepsilon)\operatorname{Tr}_\mathcal{A}(\Delta_t/\beta_t).$$

Thus we have

$$\begin{aligned}\operatorname{Tr}(Y_{t+1})&\leq\operatorname{Tr}(Y_t)\left(1+\varepsilon\delta\exp(\varepsilon)\langle\operatorname{Tr}_\mathcal{A}(\Delta_t/\beta_t),\sigma_t\rangle\right)\\&=\operatorname{Tr}(Y_t)\left(1+\frac{\varepsilon\delta\exp(\varepsilon)}{\beta_t}\langle\Delta_t,\mathbb{1}_\mathcal{A}\otimes\sigma_t\rangle\right).\end{aligned}$$

We now make use of the fact that

$$\left\langle\Delta_t,\operatorname{Tr}_\mathcal{Y}(P_\alpha\rho_tP_\alpha)-\frac{\gamma}{2}\mathbb{1}_\mathcal{A}\otimes\sigma_t\right\rangle\geq 0,$$

which implies that

$$\langle\Delta_t,\mathbb{1}_\mathcal{A}\otimes\sigma_t\rangle\leq\frac{2}{\gamma}\langle\Delta_t,\operatorname{Tr}_\mathcal{Y}(P_\alpha\rho_tP_\alpha)\rangle=\frac{2\beta_t}{\gamma}.$$

We therefore have

$$\begin{aligned}\operatorname{Tr}(Y_{t+1})&\leq\operatorname{Tr}(Y_t)\left(1+\frac{2\varepsilon\delta\exp(\varepsilon)}{\gamma}\right)\\&\leq\operatorname{Tr}(Y_t)\exp\left(\frac{2\varepsilon\delta\exp(\varepsilon)}{\gamma}\right).\end{aligned}$$

By applying this inequality recursively we find that

$$\operatorname{Tr}(Y_T)\leq N\exp\left(\frac{2T\varepsilon\delta\exp(\varepsilon)}{\gamma}\right).$$

On the other hand we have

$$\begin{aligned}\operatorname{Tr}(Y_T)&=\operatorname{Tr}\left[\exp\left(\varepsilon\delta\sum_{t=0}^{T-1}\operatorname{Tr}_\mathcal{A}(\Delta_t/\beta_t)\right)\right]\\&\geq\exp\left(\varepsilon\delta\left\|\sum_{t=0}^{T-1}\operatorname{Tr}_\mathcal{A}(\Delta_t/\beta_t)\right\|\right),\end{aligned}$$

and therefore

$$\left\|\sum_{t=0}^{T-1}\operatorname{Tr}_\mathcal{A}(\Delta_t/\beta_t)\right\|\leq\frac{2T\exp(\varepsilon)}{\gamma}+\frac{\log(N)}{\varepsilon\delta}.$$

The dual objective value obtained by Q therefore satisfies

$$\begin{aligned}\frac{1}{2}\|\operatorname{Tr}_\mathcal{A}(Q)\|&\leq(1+4\varepsilon)\left(\frac{\exp(\varepsilon)}{\gamma}+\frac{\log(N)}{2T\varepsilon\delta}\right)\\&\leq\frac{1+8\varepsilon}{\gamma}<\frac{7}{8}.\end{aligned}$$

Now, to complete the analysis, suppose that the optimal value of the semidefinite program described in the previous section is greater than $7/8$. Then it cannot be that the algorithm rejects, so the algorithm must accept. Similarly, if the optimal value is smaller than $5/8$, then the algorithm cannot accept, so it must reject. These bounds are sufficient for the application of this algorithm to the containment of QIP in PSPACE to be presented in Section 5.

It remains to state and prove the two lemmas used in the analysis above.

LEMMA 1. *Let* $R\in\operatorname{Pos}(\mathcal{A}\otimes\mathcal{Z})$ *be a positive semidefinite operator, and assume* $\dim(\mathcal{A})=2$. *Then* $R\leq 2\mathbb{1}_\mathcal{A}\otimes\operatorname{Tr}_\mathcal{A}(R)$.

PROOF. Let σ_x, σ_y and σ_z denote the Pauli operators on $\mathcal{A}$. In matrix form they are

$$\sigma_x=\begin{pmatrix}0&1\\1&0\end{pmatrix},\quad\sigma_y=\begin{pmatrix}0&-i\\i&0\end{pmatrix}\quad\text{and}\quad\sigma_z=\begin{pmatrix}1&0\\0&-1\end{pmatrix}.$$

As each of these operators is Hermitian, we have that

$$\begin{aligned}&(\sigma_x\otimes\mathbb{1}_\mathcal{Z})R(\sigma_x\otimes\mathbb{1}_\mathcal{Z}),\\&(\sigma_y\otimes\mathbb{1}_\mathcal{Z})R(\sigma_y\otimes\mathbb{1}_\mathcal{Z}),\\&(\sigma_z\otimes\mathbb{1}_\mathcal{Z})R(\sigma_z\otimes\mathbb{1}_\mathcal{Z})\end{aligned}$$

are all positive semidefinite. It therefore holds that

$$\begin{aligned}2\mathbb{1}_{\mathcal{A}} \otimes \operatorname{Tr}_{\mathcal{X}}(R) &= R + (\sigma_x \otimes \mathbb{1}_{\mathcal{Z}})R(\sigma_x \otimes \mathbb{1}_{\mathcal{Z}}) \\ &\quad + (\sigma_y \otimes \mathbb{1}_{\mathcal{Z}})R(\sigma_y \otimes \mathbb{1}_{\mathcal{Z}}) \\ &\quad + (\sigma_z \otimes \mathbb{1}_{\mathcal{Z}})R(\sigma_z \otimes \mathbb{1}_{\mathcal{Z}}) \\ &\geq R\end{aligned}$$

as required. □

LEMMA 2. *Let R be an operator satisfying $0 \leq R \leq \mathbb{1}$. Then for every real number $\eta > 0$, the following two inequalities hold:*

$$\exp(\eta R) \leq \mathbb{1} + \eta \exp(\eta) R,$$
$$\exp(-\eta R) \leq \mathbb{1} - \eta \exp(-\eta) R.$$

PROOF. It is sufficient to prove the inequalities for R replaced by a scalar $\lambda \in [0,1]$, for then the operator inequalities follow by considering a spectral decomposition of R. If $\lambda = 0$ both inequalities are immediate, so let us assume $\lambda > 0$. By the Mean Value Theorem there exists a value $\lambda_0 \in (0, \lambda)$ such that

$$\frac{\exp(\eta\lambda) - 1}{\lambda} = \eta \exp(\eta\lambda_0) \leq \eta \exp(\eta),$$

from which the first inequality follows. Similarly, there exists a value $\lambda_0 \in (0, \lambda)$ such that

$$\frac{\exp(-\eta\lambda) - 1}{\lambda} = -\eta \exp(-\eta\lambda_0) \leq -\eta \exp(-\eta),$$

which yields the second inequality. □

4.2 Comments on precision

The analysis in the previous subsection has assumed that all computations performed by the algorithm are exact. It is, however, necessary for our implementation of the algorithm to take some of the computations to be approximate. In particular, the computation of the positive eigenspace projections in step 2(a) and the matrix exponentials in step 2(b) will need to be approximate computations. Fortunately this is not a significant obstacle; when the approximate computations are performed with sufficient accuracy, a similar analysis to the one presented in the previous subsection shows that the correct answer is obtained. Here we provide a brief sketch of this analysis.

Based on the specific implementation of the algorithm to be discussed in the next subsection, we may make the following assumptions about the algorithm's accuracy.

1. For each $t = 0, \ldots, T-1$, Δ_t is a positive semidefinite operator and satisfies
$$\left\| \sqrt{\Delta_t} - \Lambda_t \right\| < \frac{\varepsilon^2}{8\alpha^2 N} \tag{2}$$
for Λ_t being the true projection operator onto the positive eigenspace of $\operatorname{Tr}_{\mathcal{Y}}(P_\alpha \rho_t P_\alpha) - \frac{\gamma}{2}\mathbb{1}_{\mathcal{A}} \otimes \sigma_t$. Although it is not essential, we may also assume for the sake of convenience that each Δ_t satisfies $\Delta_t \leq \mathbb{1}$.
2. For each $t = 0, \ldots, T-1$ it holds that ρ_{t+1} and σ_{t+1} are density operators and satisfy
$$\|\rho_{t+1} - X_{t+1}/\operatorname{Tr}(X_{t+1})\| < \frac{\varepsilon^2}{2\alpha^2 N^2},$$
$$\|\sigma_{t+1} - Y_{t+1}/\operatorname{Tr}(Y_{t+1})\| < \frac{\varepsilon^2}{4N},$$
where X_{t+1} and Y_{t+1} are exactly as defined by the algorithm:
$$X_{t+1} = \exp\left(-\varepsilon\delta \sum_{j=0}^{t} P_\alpha(\Delta_j \otimes \mathbb{1}_{\mathcal{Y}})P_\alpha/\beta_j\right),$$
$$Y_{t+1} = \exp\left(\varepsilon\delta \sum_{j=0}^{t} \operatorname{Tr}_{\mathcal{A}}\left(\Delta_j/\beta_j\right)\right).$$
(In other words, we do not need to view X_{t+1} and Y_{t+1} as being variables stored by the algorithm, because their only purpose is to define ρ_{t+1} and σ_{t+1}.)
3. The values $\beta_0, \ldots, \beta_{T-1}$ are computed exactly, meaning that $\beta_t = \langle P_\alpha(\Delta_t \otimes \mathbb{1}_{\mathcal{Y}})P_\alpha, \rho_t\rangle$ for $t = 0, \ldots, T-1$. The remaining variables (α, γ, ε, δ, T, and P_α) can obviously be stored exactly as well.

Now, under the assumption (2) it can be shown that

$$\begin{aligned}&\sqrt{\Delta_t}\left(\operatorname{Tr}_{\mathcal{Y}}(P_\alpha\rho_t P_\alpha) - \frac{\gamma}{2}\mathbb{1}_{\mathcal{A}} \otimes \sigma_t\right)\sqrt{\Delta_t} \\ &\geq \Lambda_t\left(\operatorname{Tr}_{\mathcal{Y}}(P_\alpha\rho_t P_\alpha) - \frac{\gamma}{2}\mathbb{1}_{\mathcal{A}} \otimes \sigma_t\right)\Lambda_t - \frac{\varepsilon^2}{4N}\mathbb{1}_{\mathcal{A}\otimes\mathcal{X}}.\end{aligned} \tag{3}$$

For the case that the algorithm accepts, we use this inequality when performing a similar analysis to the exact case, this time taking

$$\rho' = \frac{\rho}{\gamma + 4\beta + \varepsilon},$$

$$\sigma' = \frac{\gamma\sigma + 4\operatorname{Tr}_{\mathcal{A}}\left[\sqrt{\Delta}\operatorname{Tr}_{\mathcal{Y}}(P_\alpha\rho P_\alpha)\sqrt{\Delta}\right] + (\varepsilon/N)\mathbb{1}_{\mathcal{X}}}{\gamma + 4\beta + \varepsilon},$$

to conclude that the primal objective value is at least

$$\frac{1}{\gamma + 5\varepsilon} > \frac{5}{8}.$$

(The inequality (3) is slightly stronger than what is needed to obtain this bound, but we will benefit from the stronger form for the case of rejection.)

For the case that the algorithm rejects we again proceed as in the error-free case, except that this time we may make use of the bounds on $\|\rho_{t+1} - X_{t+1}/\operatorname{Tr}(X_{t+1})\|$ to obtain the inequality

$$\operatorname{Tr}(X_{t+1}) \leq \operatorname{Tr}(X_t)\exp(-\varepsilon\delta(1-\varepsilon)\exp(-\varepsilon))$$

for each $t = 0, \ldots, T-1$, and therefore

$$\begin{aligned}&\lambda_{\min}(P_\alpha(Q \otimes \mathbb{1}_{\mathcal{Y}})P_\alpha) \\ &\geq (1 + 4\varepsilon)\left((1-\varepsilon)\exp(-\varepsilon) - \frac{\log(2N^2)}{T\varepsilon\delta}\right) \geq 1.\end{aligned}$$

Thus, dual feasibility still holds for Q in the approximate case. Along similar lines, we apply the assumed bound on $\|\sigma_{t+1} - Y_{t+1}/\operatorname{Tr}(Y_{t+1})\|$ as well as (3) to obtain

$$\operatorname{Tr}(Y_{t+1}) \leq \operatorname{Tr}(Y_t)\exp\left(\frac{2\varepsilon\delta(1+\varepsilon)\exp(\varepsilon)}{\gamma}\right),$$

so that the dual objective value obtained by Q satisfies

$$\begin{aligned}\frac{1}{2}\|\operatorname{Tr}_{\mathcal{A}}(Q)\| &\leq (1+4\varepsilon)\left(\frac{(1+\varepsilon)\exp(\varepsilon)}{\gamma} + \frac{\log(N)}{2T\varepsilon\delta}\right) \\ &\leq \frac{1+8\varepsilon}{\gamma} < \frac{7}{8}.\end{aligned}$$

4.3 An NC implementation of the algorithm

In this subsection we explain how the algorithm above can be implemented by an NC computation. Recall that the class NC may be defined as the class of all functions (including predicates that represent decision problems) computable by logarithmic-space uniform Boolean circuits of polylogarithmic depth.

The matrices stored and processed by our algorithm will have entries with rational real and imaginary parts, and naturally we assume that rational numbers are represented as pairs of integers in binary notation. All other rational numbers processed by the algorithm are represented in a similar way. With these assumptions in place, we first note that elementary matrix operations, including sums, products, tensor products, inverses, and iterated sums and products of matrices, are known to be in NC. There is an extensive literature on this topic, and we refer the reader to the survey of von zur Gathen [18] for more details.

As was mentioned in the previous subsection, the positive eigenspace computation in step 2(a) and the matrix exponential computation in step 2(b) of the algorithm will not be computed exactly in our implementation. Based on the discussion of precision above, however, it will suffice that the following computational problems can be performed by NC computations.

Matrix exponentials

Input: An $n \times n$ matrix M, a positive rational number η, and an integer k expressed in unary notation (i.e., 1^k).

Promise: $\|M\| \leq k$.

Output: An $n \times n$ matrix X such that $\|\exp(M) - X\| < \eta$.

Positive eigenspace projection

Input: An $n \times n$ Hermitian matrix H and a positive rational number η.

Output: An $n \times n$ positive semidefinite matrix $\Delta \leq \mathbb{1}$ such that

$$\|\Delta - \Lambda\| < \eta,$$

for Λ being the projection operator onto the positive eigenspace of H.

Indeed, the fact that these computations can be performed in NC provides significantly more precision than is needed for our algorithm.

The fact that matrix exponentials can be approximated in NC follows by truncating the series

$$\exp(M) = \mathbb{1} + M + M^2/2 + M^3/6 + \cdots$$

to a number of terms linear in $k + \log(1/\eta)$. (From a numerical point of view this is not necessarily a good way to compute matrix exponentials [37], but it is arguably the simplest way to prove that the stated problem is in NC.) In the case that M is Hermitian it holds that $\exp(M)$ is positive semidefinite, and one may ensure that the approximation X is positive semidefinite as well by taking an odd number of terms in the truncated series for $\exp(M)$.

That positive eigenspace projections can be approximated in NC relies on the fact that roots of integer polynomials can be approximated to very high precision in NC. This was proved first for polynomials having only real roots in [6], and an alternate proof appears in [9]. While the real-root case is sufficient for our needs, we note that the general case, which allows for complex roots, was solved in [38]. It is important to note that distinct roots of integer polynomials can neither be too close to one another nor to zero [34, 12], and that the accuracy with which the roots may be approximated in NC can be taken to be small even relative to this minimal separation. This allows one to determine without error which root approximations correspond to positive roots (in the real-root case).

Given that the characteristic polynomial of a matrix can be computed in NC [13], it follows that an NC algorithm exists for approximating the eigenvalues of a Hermitian matrix to high precision. Given a sufficiently accurate approximation κ to an eigenvalue λ of a Hermitian matrix H, one may obtain a close approximation of the projection Π onto the eigenspace of H corresponding to λ by dividing the matrix

$$(\kappa\mathbb{1} - H)^{-1}$$

by a close approximation to its eigenvalue of maximum absolute value. (One may perturb κ slightly in the event that $\kappa = \lambda$.) By summing the approximate projections onto the eigenspaces corresponding to distinct positive eigenvalues of H, we obtain a close approximation Δ to Λ as claimed.

Once each of the matrix computations required by the algorithm has been implemented as an NC computation, it is straightforward to implement the entire algorithm by an NC computation. We may agree from the start that the real and imaginary parts of each entry of the matrices $\Delta_0, \ldots, \Delta_{T-1}$, $\rho_0, \ldots, \rho_T$ and $\sigma_0, \ldots, \sigma_T$ is to be stored by the algorithm as an integer divided by 2^K, for $K = O(N)$ (or even $K = O(\log N)$ if one prefers), as rounding in this way can only introduce small errors that are within our accuracy requirements. This ensures that the size of the entire computation remains polynomially bounded. As the number of iterations of the algorithm is logarithmic in N, and therefore logarithmic in the size of the input to the algorithm, a composition of the computations described above yields an NC implementation of the algorithm.

5. CONTAINMENT OF QIP IN PSPACE

With the algorithm from the previous section in hand, the containment QIP $\subseteq$ PSPACE may be proved as described in this section.

First, we consider a scaled-up variant of NC, which is the complexity class NC(*poly*) that consists of all functions computable by polynomial-space uniform families of Boolean circuits having polynomial-depth. (The notation NC(2^{poly}) has also previously been used for this class [11].) For decision problems, it is known that NC(*poly*) = PSPACE [10]. Thus, it suffices for us to prove QIP $\subseteq$ NC(*poly*).

A basic property of NC and NC(*poly*) that we now require is that functions in NC and NC(*poly*) compose well. Specifically, if F is a function in NC(*poly*) and G is a function in NC, then the composition $G \circ F$ is also in NC(*poly*). This follows from the most straightforward way of composing the families of circuits that compute F and G.

Now, assume that A is a promise problem in QIP. Our goal is to prove that $A \in$ NC(*poly*). As $A \in$ QIP there must exist a quantum interactive proof of the sort described in Section 3 that has perfect completeness and soundness error at most $1/2 - \varepsilon$ for $\varepsilon = 1/64$. (Any other sufficiently small positive constant would do, and in fact one can replace ε with an exponentially small value—but this choice is sufficient for our needs.) We consider a two-step computation as follows:

1. Compute from a given input string x an explicit description of the projections Π_0^0, Π_1^0, Π_0^1, and Π_1^1 that determine the quantum interactive proof system for A that is under consideration.
2. Run an NC implementation of the algorithm described in Section 4 on Π_0^0, Π_1^0, Π_0^1, and Π_1^1.

If it is the case that x is a yes-instance of A, then the optimal value of the semidefinite program described in Section 3 is at least 1, and therefore the algorithm accepts. If x is a no-instance of A, then the optimal value of the semidefinite program is at most $1/2 + \varepsilon + 1/\alpha^2 < 5/8$, and therefore the algorithm rejects.

It remains to observe that the computation can be implemented in NC(*poly*). The first step of this computation can be implemented exactly in NC(*poly*) by computing explicit matrix representations of all of the gates in the quantum circuit specifying the verifier's measurements, followed by elementary matrix computations that yield Π_0^0, Π_1^0, Π_0^1, and Π_1^1. The second step has been described in the previous section. We have that the composition of the two steps is an NC(*poly*) computation, and therefore $A \in$ NC(*poly*) as required.

6. OPEN PROBLEMS

We will conclude this paper by discussing two directions for future research.

The question that is perhaps most clearly raised by this paper is: which semidefinite programs can be solved approximately in parallel (by NC algorithms)? We do not have an answer to this question, and believe it is certainly deserving of further investigation. The fact that the algorithm presented in this paper can be implemented in NC relies heavily on the specific form of the semidefinite program it approximates, and we do not know to what extent the method can be applied to more general classes of semidefinite programs. It is, of course, highly unlikely that all semidefinite programs can be approximated to high accuracy in NC—for even if this were true just for linear programs it would imply NC = P [14, 40, 36].

A second open problem relating to this paper is whether QRG(2) = PSPACE. The class QRG(2) contains all problems having two-turn (i.e., one-round) quantum refereed games, or, in other words, competing-prover quantum interactive proof systems in which the verifier asks each prover a question (in parallel), receives their answers, and makes a decision to accept or reject. The optimal accept/reject probabilities for quantum refereed games can be represented by semidefinite programs [24] and the classical analogue of this class is known to coincide with PSPACE [16].

7. ACKNOWLEDGEMENTS

We thank Xiaodi Wu for helpful discussions. Rahul Jain's research is supported by the internal grants of the Centre for Quantum Technologies, which is funded by the Singapore Ministry of Education and the Singapore National Research Foundation. Zhengfeng Ji acknowledges support from NSF of China (Grant Nos. 60736011 and 60721061); his research at the Perimeter Institute is supported by the Government of Canada through Industry Canada and by the Province of Ontario through the Ministry of Research and Innovation. Sarvagya Upadhyay's research is supported by NSERC, CIFAR, MITACS, QuantumWorks, Industry Canada, Ontario's Ministry of Research and Innovation, and the U.S. ARO. John Watrous's research is supported by NSERC, CIFAR, and QuantumWorks.

8. REFERENCES

[1] S. Arora and B. Barak. *Computational Complexity: A Modern Approach*. Cambridge University Press, 2009.

[2] S. Arora, E. Hazan, and S. Kale. Fast algorithms for approximate semidefinite programming using the multiplicative weights update method. In *Proceedings of the 46th Annual IEEE Symposium on Foundations of Computer Science*, pages 339–348, 2005.

[3] S. Arora and S. Kale. A combinatorial, primal-dual approach to semidefinite programs. In *Proceedings of the Thirty-Ninth Annual ACM Symposium on Theory of Computing*, pages 227–236, 2007.

[4] L. Babai. Trading group theory for randomness. In *Proceedings of the 17th Annual ACM Symposium on Theory of Computing*, pages 421–429, 1985.

[5] L. Babai and S. Moran. Arthur-Merlin games: a randomized proof system, and a hierarchy of complexity classes. *Journal of Computer and System Sciences*, 36(2):254–276, 1988.

[6] M. Ben-Or, E. Feig, D. Kozen, and P. Tiwari. A fast parallel algorithm for determining all roots of a polynomial with real roots. In *Proceedings of the 18th Annual ACM Symposium on Theory of Computing*, pages 340–349, 1986.

[7] M. Ben-Or, S. Goldwasser, J. Kilian, and A. Wigderson. Multi-prover interactive proofs: how to remove intractability assumptions. In *Proceedings of the 20th Annual ACM Symposium on Theory of Computing*, pages 113–131, 1988.

[8] R. Bhatia. *Matrix Analysis*. Springer, 1997.

[9] D. Bini and V. Pan. Computing matrix eigenvalues and polynomial zeros where the output is real. *SIAM Journal on Computing*, 27(4):1099–1115, 1998.

[10] A. Borodin. On relating time and space to size and depth. *SIAM Journal on Computing*, 6:733–744, 1977.

[11] A. Borodin, S. Cook, and N. Pippenger. Parallel computation for well-endowed rings and space-bounded probabilistic machines. *Information and Control*, 58:113–136, 1983.

[12] Y. Bugeaud. *Approximation by Algebraic Numbers*, volume 160 of *Cambridge Tracts in Mathematics*. Cambridge University Press, Cambridge, 2004.

[13] L. Csanky. Fast parallel matrix inversion algorithms. *SIAM Journal on Computing*, 5(4):618–623, 1976.

[14] D. Dobkin, R. Lipton, and S. Reiss. Linear programming is log-space hard for P. *Information Processing Letters*, 8(2):96–97, 1979.

[15] S. Even, A. Selman, and Y. Yacobi. The complexity of promise problems with applications to public-key cryptography. *Information and Control*, 61(2):159–173, 1984.

[16] U. Feige and J. Kilian. Making games short. In *Proceedings of the 29th Annual ACM Symposium on Theory of Computing*, pages 506–516, 1997.

[17] P. Feldman. The optimum prover lies in PSPACE. Manuscript, 1986.

[18] J. von zur Gathen. Parallel linear algebra. In J. Reif, editor, *Synthesis of Parallel Algorithms*, chapter 13. Morgan Kaufmann Publishers, Inc., 1993.

[19] O. Goldreich. On promise problems (a survey in memory of Shimon Even [1935–2004]). Electronic Colloquium on Computational Complexity, Report TR05-018, 2005.

[20] O. Goldreich, S. Micali, and A. Wigderson. Proofs that yield nothing but their validity or all languages in NP have zero-knowledge proof systems. *Journal of the ACM*, 38(1):691–729, 1991.

[21] S. Goldwasser, S. Micali, and C. Rackoff. The knowledge complexity of interactive proof systems. In *Proceedings of the 17th Annual ACM Symposium on Theory of Computing*, pages 291–304, 1985.

[22] S. Goldwasser, S. Micali, and C. Rackoff. The knowledge complexity of interactive proof systems. *SIAM Journal on Computing*, 18(1):186–208, 1989.

[23] S. Goldwasser and M. Sipser. Private coins versus public coins in interactive proof systems. In S. Micali, editor, *Randomness and Computation*, volume 5 of *Advances in Computing Research*, pages 73–90. JAI Press, 1989.

[24] G. Gutoski and J. Watrous. Toward a general theory of quantum games. In *Proceedings of the 39th Annual ACM Symposium on Theory of Computing*, pages 565–574, 2007.

[25] S. Hallgren, A. Kolla, P. Sen, and S. Zhang. Making classical honest verifier zero knowledge protocols secure against quantum attacks. In *Proceedings of the 35th International Colloquium on Automata, Languages and Programming*, volume 5126 of *Lecture Notes in Computer Science*, pages 592–603. Springer, 2008.

[26] R. Jain, S. Upadhyay, and J. Watrous. Two-message quantum interactive proofs are in PSPACE. In *Proceedings of the 50th Annual IEEE Symposium on Foundations of Computer Science*, pages 534–543, 2009.

[27] R. Jain and J. Watrous. Parallel approximation of non-interactive zero-sum quantum games. In *Proceedings of the 24th IEEE Conference on Computational Complexity*, pages 243–253, 2009.

[28] S. Kale. *Efficient algorithms using the multiplicative weights update method*. PhD thesis, Princeton University, 2007.

[29] J. Kempe, H. Kobayashi, K. Matsumoto, and T. Vidick. Using entanglement in quantum multi-prover interactive proofs. *Computational Complexity*, 18(2):273–307, 2009.

[30] A. Kitaev and J. Watrous. Parallelization, amplification, and exponential time simulation of quantum interactive proof system. In *Proceedings of the 32nd Annual ACM Symposium on Theory of Computing*, pages 608–617, 2000.

[31] H. Kobayashi. General properties of quantum zero-knowledge proofs. In *Proceedings of the Fifth IACR Theory of Cryptography Conference*, volume 4948 of *Lecture Notes in Computer Science*, pages 107–124. Springer, 2008.

[32] H. Kobayashi and K. Matsumoto. Quantum multi-prover interactive proof systems with limited prior entanglement. *Journal of Computer and System Sciences*, 66(3):429–450, 2003.

[33] C. Lund, L. Fortnow, H. Karloff, and N. Nisan. Algebraic methods for interactive proof systems. *Journal of the ACM*, 39(4):859–868, 1992.

[34] K. Mahler. *Lectures on Diophantine Approximations*, volume 1. Cushing Malloy, 1961.

[35] C. Marriott and J. Watrous. Quantum Arthur-Merlin games. *Computational Complexity*, 14(2):122–152, 2005.

[36] N. Megiddo. A note on approximate linear programming. *Information Processing Letters*, 42(1):53, 1992.

[37] C. Moler and C. V. Loan. Nineteen dubious ways to compute the exponential of a matrix, twenty-five years later. *SIAM Review*, 45(1):3–49, 2003.

[38] C. A. Neff. Specified precision polynomial root isolation is in NC. *Journal of Computer and System Sciences*, 48(3):429–463, 1994.

[39] M. A. Nielsen and I. L. Chuang. *Quantum Computation and Quantum Information*. Cambridge University Press, 2000.

[40] M. Serna. Approximating linear programming is log-space complete for P. *Information Processing Letters*, 37(4):233–236, 1991.

[41] A. Shamir. IP = PSPACE. *Journal of the ACM*, 39(4):869–877, 1992.

[42] A. Shen. IP = PSPACE: simplified proof. *Journal of the ACM*, 39(4):878–880, 1992.

[43] M. Sipser. *Introduction to the Theory of Computation*. Thomson Course Technology, second edition, 2005.

[44] M. Warmuth and D. Kuzmin. Online variance minimization. In *Proceedings of the 19th Annual Conference on Learning Theory*, volume 4005 of *Lecture Notes in Computer Science*, pages 514–528. Springer, 2006.

[45] J. Watrous. PSPACE has constant-round quantum interactive proof systems. In *Proceedings of the 40th Annual IEEE Symposium on Foundations of Computer Science*, pages 112–119, 1999.

[46] J. Watrous. Zero-knowledge against quantum attacks. *SIAM Journal on Computing*, 39(1):25–58, 2009.

An Improved LP-based Approximation for Steiner Tree[*]

Jarosław Byrka[†]
Institute of Mathematics, EPFL
Lausanne, Switzerland
jaroslaw.byrka@epfl.ch

Fabrizio Grandoni[‡]
University of Tor Vergata
Rome, Italy
grandoni@disp.uniroma2.it

Thomas Rothvoß
Institute of Mathematics, EPFL
Lausanne, Switzerland
thomas.rothvoss@epfl.ch

Laura Sanità[§]
Institute of Mathematics, EPFL
Lausanne, Switzerland
laura.sanita@epfl.ch

ABSTRACT

The *Steiner tree* problem is one of the most fundamental **NP**-hard problems: given a weighted undirected graph and a subset of terminal nodes, find a minimum-cost tree spanning the terminals. In a sequence of papers, the approximation ratio for this problem was improved from 2 to the current best 1.55 [Robins,Zelikovsky-SIDMA'05]. All these algorithms are purely combinatorial. A long-standing open problem is whether there is an LP-relaxation for Steiner tree with integrality gap smaller than 2 [Vazirani,Rajagopalan-SODA'99].

In this paper we improve the approximation factor for Steiner tree, developing an LP-based approximation algorithm. Our algorithm is based on a, seemingly novel, *iterative randomized rounding* technique. We consider a directed-component cut relaxation for the k-restricted Steiner tree problem. We sample one of these components with probability proportional to the value of the associated variable in the optimal fractional solution and contract it. We iterate this process for a proper number of times and finally output the sampled components together with a minimum-cost terminal spanning tree in the remaining graph. Our algorithm delivers a solution of cost at most $\ln(4)$ times the cost of an optimal k-restricted Steiner tree. This directly implies a $\ln(4) + \varepsilon < 1.39$ approximation for Steiner tree.

As a byproduct of our analysis, we show that the integrality gap of our LP is at most 1.55, hence answering to the mentioned open question. This might have consequences for a number of related problems.

Categories and Subject Descriptors

F.2.2 [**Computations on discrete structures**]: Non-numerical Algorithms and Problems

General Terms

Algorithms, Theory

Keywords

Network design, approximation algorithms, linear programming relaxations, randomized algorithms

1. INTRODUCTION

Given an undirected n-node graph $G = (V, E)$, with edge costs (or weights) $c : E \rightarrow \mathbb{Q}^+$, and a subset of nodes $R \subseteq V$ (*terminals*), the *Steiner tree* problem asks for a tree S spanning the terminals, of minimum cost $c(S) := \sum_{e \in S} c(e)$. Note that S might contain some other nodes, besides the terminals (*Steiner nodes*). Steiner tree is one of the classical and, probably, most fundamental problems in Computer Science and Operations Research, with great theoretical and practical relevance. This problem emerges in a number of contexts, such as the design of VLSI, optical and wireless communication systems, as well as transportation and distribution networks (see, e.g., [27]).

The Steiner tree problem appears already in the list of **NP**-hard problems in the book by Garey and Johnson [19]. In fact, it is **NP**-hard to find solutions of cost less than $\frac{96}{95}$ times the optimal cost [5, 10]. Hence, the best one can hope for is an approximation algorithm with a small but constant approximation guarantee. Without loss of generality, we can replace the weighted graph given as input by its metric closure[1]. It is well-known that a minimum-cost *terminal spanning tree* T is a 2-approximation for the Steiner tree problem [20, 41]. A terminal spanning tree is a Steiner tree without Steiner nodes: such a tree always exists in the metric closure of the graph. A sequence of improved approximation algorithms appeared in the literature [29, 35,

[1]The *metric closure* of a weighted graph is a complete weighted graph on the same node set, with weights given by shortest path distances with respect to original weights.

*Extended abstract.

†Partially supported by MNISW grant number N N206 1723 33, 2007 - 2010.

‡Developed while visiting EPFL.

§Supported by Swiss National Science Foundation within the project "Robust Network Design"

38, 42], culminating with the famous $1+\frac{\ln(3)}{2}+\varepsilon<1.55$ approximation algorithm by Robins and Zelikovsky [38] (here $\varepsilon>0$ is an arbitrary small constant).

All the mentioned improvements are based on the following idea. A *full component* (or, for short, *component*) of a Steiner tree is a maximal subtree whose terminals coincide with its leaves. Note that the edge set of the Steiner tree is partitioned by its components. A *k-restricted* Steiner tree is a Steiner tree whose components contain no more than k terminals (*k-component*). The following result by Borchers and Du [6] shows that, in order to obtain a good approximation factor, it is sufficient to restrict our attention to k-restricted Steiner trees. We let Opt and Opt_k denote an optimal Steiner tree and an optimal k-restricted Steiner tree, respectively. Moreover, $opt := c(Opt)$ and $opt_k := c(Opt_k)$.

THEOREM 1. *[6] Let ρ_k be the k-Steiner ratio, i.e. the supremum of the ratio opt_k/opt. Then $\rho_k = \frac{(r+1)2^r+s}{r2^r+s} \leq 1+\frac{1}{\lfloor \log_2 k\rfloor}$, where r and s are non-negative integers such that $k=2^r+s$ and $s<2^r$.*

We remark that, given an optimal k-restricted Steiner tree S^*, its components are optimal Steiner trees connecting the corresponding terminals. For any fixed k, a list $\{Z_1,\ldots,Z_q\}$, $q=O(n^k)$, of all potential k-components can be computed in polynomial time by considering all subsets R' of at most k terminals, and computing an optimal Steiner tree[2] on terminals R'. Unfortunately, selecting the cheapest subset of $\{Z_1,\ldots,Z_q\}$ spanning the terminals is an **NP**-hard problem already for $k\geq 4$ [18]. For this reason, [38] and previous papers rather select a subset of the Z_i's with a local-search approach. The idea is to start with a minimum-cost terminal spanning tree T^0 (which is formed by 2-components), and iteratively improve it. At each step, one considers each Z_i, and checks *how much* adding Z_i to the current solution (and removing redundant edges) *improves* the solution itself. The algorithm each time selects the Z_i leading to the largest improvement, and halts when no further improvement is possible. Different algorithms (essentially) differ in the way the improvement is evaluated.

Despite the efforts of many researchers in the last 10 years, the approach above did not provide any further improvement after [38]. This motivated our search for alternative methods. One standard approach is to exploit a proper LP-relaxation (see, e.g., [21] for a list of LP-relaxations for Steiner tree). A natural formulation for the problem is the *undirected cut formulation* (see [22, 41]), where we have a variable for each edge of the graph and a constraint for each cut separating the set of terminals. Each constraint forces to pick at least one edge crossing the corresponding cut. Considering its linear relaxation, 2-approximation algorithms can be obtained either using primal-dual schemes [22] or iterative rounding [28]. However, this relaxation has an integrality gap of 2 already in the spanning tree case, i.e., when $R=V$ (see example 22.10 in [41]).

Another well-studied but more promising LP is the so called *bidirected cut relaxation* [8, 12, 36]. Let us fix an arbitrary terminal r (*root*). Replace each edge $\{u,v\}$ by two

[2]We recall that, given k terminals, the dynamic-programming algorithm by Dreyfus and Wagner [11] computes an optimal Steiner tree among them in $O(3^k n+2^k n^2+n^3)$ worst-case time. A faster parameterized algorithm can be found in [33].

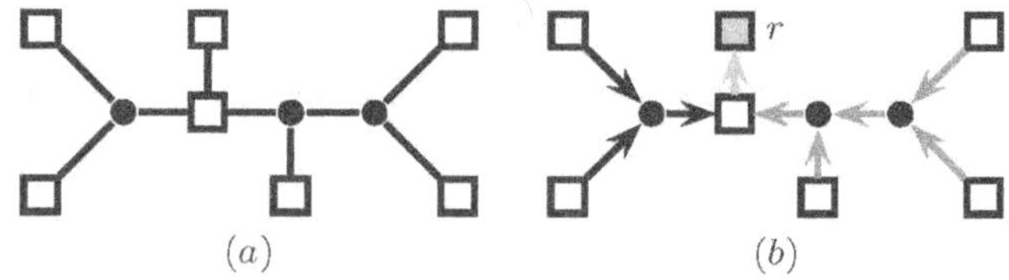

Figure 1: (a) A 4-restricted Steiner tree S, where rectangles denote terminals and circles represent Steiner nodes. (*b*) Edges of S are directed towards a root r. The resulting directed components are depicted with different colors.

directed edges (u,v) and (v,u) of cost $c(\{u,v\})$. For a given cut $U\subseteq V$, define $\delta^+(U)=\{(u,v)\in E \mid u\in U,\ v\notin U\}$ as the set of edges leaving U. The mentioned relaxation is

$$\min \sum_{e\in E} c(e)z_e \qquad \text{(BCR)}$$
$$\sum_{e\in\delta^+(U)} z_e \geq 1 \qquad \forall U\subseteq V\setminus\{r\}: U\cap R\neq\emptyset$$
$$z_e\geq 0 \qquad \forall e\in E.$$

We can consider the value z_e as the capacity which we are going to install on the directed edge e. The LP can then be interpreted as computing the minimum-cost capacities that support a flow of 1 from each terminal to the root. In a seminal work, Edmonds [12] showed that BCR is integral in the spanning tree case.

THEOREM 2. *[12] For $R=V$, the polyhedron of BCR is integral.*

The best-known lower bound on the integrality gap of BCR is 8/7 [31, 41]. The best-known upper bound is 2, though BCR is believed to have a smaller integrality gap than the undirected cut relaxation [36]. The authors in [8] report that the structure of the dual to BCR is highly asymmetric, which complicates a primal-dual approach. Moreover, iterative rounding based on picking a single edge cannot yield good approximations, as was pointed out in [36].

Finding a better-than-2 LP-relaxation for the (k-restricted) Steiner tree problem is a long-standing open problem [8, 36]. We remark that good LP-bounds, besides potentially leading to better approximation algorithms for Steiner tree, might have a much wider impact. This is because Steiner tree appears as a building block in several other problems, and the best approximation algorithms for some of those problems are LP-based. Strong LPs are also important in the design of (practically) efficient and accurate heuristics.

1.1 Our Results and Techniques

We next state the main result of this paper (see Section 4.1 for a derandomization of this result).

THEOREM 3. *For any constant $\varepsilon>0$, there is a polynomial-time randomized approximation algorithm for the Steiner tree problem with expected approximation ratio $\ln(4)+\varepsilon$.*

Our algorithm is based on the following *directed-component cut relaxation* for the k-restricted Steiner tree problem (see also [34]). Consider a k-restricted Steiner tree S with the edges directed towards the chosen root terminal r (see Figure 1). Consider the (undirected) k-components Z_i introduced before. Make a copy C of each Z_i for each choice of one (*sink*) terminal u_i in it, and direct all the edges of C towards u_i. Let $C_1, \ldots, C_h$ be the resulting *directed k-components*. Observe that $h = O(kn^k)$ is polynomially bounded for any fixed k. We denote by $c(C_j)$ the cost of C_j. Recall that $c(C_j)$ is the cost of an optimal Steiner tree over $R \cap V(C_j)$, and that this tree can be computed in polynomial time (for constant k). We also let $sink(C_j)$ be the sink terminal of C_j, and $sources(C_j) := V(C_j) \cap R \setminus \{sink(C_j)\}$ be the other terminals (*sources* of C_j). We say that a component C_j *crosses* $U \subseteq R$ if C_j has at least one source in U and the sink outside. By $\delta_k^+(U)$ we denote the set of k-components crossing U. Our LP-relaxation is then:

$$\min \sum_j c(C_j) x_j \qquad (k\text{-DCR})$$

$$\sum_{C_j \in \delta_k^+(U)} x_j \geq 1 \quad \forall U \subseteq R \setminus \{r\},\ R \neq \emptyset$$

$$x_j \geq 0 \quad \forall j = 1, \ldots, h.$$

The LP above can be solved in polynomial time (see Section 2).

We remark that k-DCR is a relaxation for the k-restricted Steiner tree problem. In fact, consider the optimal integral solution Opt_k. As already observed, we can direct all its edges towards an arbitrary root terminal r. At this point, Opt_k consists of a set of directed k-components C_j, where each C_j is an optimal Steiner tree over $R \cap V(C_j)$. Setting $x_j = 1$ for those components, and the remaining variables to zero, provides a feasible solution to k-DCR of cost exactly opt_k.

We combine our LP with a (to the best of our knowledge) novel *iterative randomized rounding* technique. We solve the LP, sample one component C_j with probability proportional to its value x_j in the optimal fractional solution x, contract C_j into its sink node $sink(C_j)$, and reoptimize the LP. We iterate this process for a suitable number of times. With a simple analysis we can show that a minimum-cost terminal spanning tree on the remaining terminals plus the sampled components cost (in expectation) at most 3/2 times the cost of the optimal k-restricted Steiner tree (see Section 3). With a refined analysis, we improve this bound to $\ln(4)$ (see Section 4). A $\ln(4)\rho_k \leq \ln(4)(1 + \frac{1}{\lfloor \log_2 k \rfloor}) < 1.39$ approximation for Steiner tree immediately follows from Theorem 1 by choosing k large enough[3]. This bound can be further improved for special graph classes, as for example for quasi-bipartite graphs, where non-terminal nodes are not adjacent (details will be given in the journal version of the paper).

We remark that our algorithm combines features of *randomized rounding* (where typically variables are rounded randomly, but simultaneously) and *iterative rounding* (where variables are rounded iteratively, but deterministically). We believe that our iterative randomized rounding technique will also find other applications, and is henceforth of independent interest.

The key insight in our analysis is to quantify the expected reduction of the cost of the optimal terminal spanning tree and optimal Steiner tree in each iteration. To show this, we exploit a *Bridge Lemma*, relating the cost of terminal spanning trees with the cost of fractional solutions to k-DCR. The proof of the lemma is based on Edmonds' Theorem 2

[3]Observe that our approach provides approximation factors strictly better than 2 for any $k \geq 6$, since $\rho_6 = 1.4$

[12]. In our opinion, our analysis is simpler (or at least more intuitive) than the one in [38].

As an easy consequence of our analysis, we obtain that the integrality gap of k-DCR is at most $1 + \ln(2) < 1.694$, hence answering to the mentioned open problem in [8, 36] (for the k-restricted case). A more technical analysis, based on an adaptation of the analysis of Robins and Zelikovsky which exploits our Bridge Lemma, leads to the following improved result (see Section 5).

THEOREM 4. *For any constant k, there is a polynomial-time algorithm which computes a solution for k-restricted Steiner tree of cost at most $1 + \frac{\ln(3)}{2} < 1.55$ times the cost of the optimal fractional solution to k-DCR.*

As mentioned before, integrality gap results of this type often provide new insights to variants and generalizations of the original problem. We expect that this will be the case with the above theorem as well, since Steiner tree appears as a building block in many other problems.

1.2 Related Work

One reason for the importance of Steiner tree is that it appears either as a subproblem or as a special case of many other problems in network design. A (certainly incomplete) list contains Steiner Forest [1, 22], Prize-Collecting Steiner tree [3, 22], Virtual Private Network [13, 14, 25], Single-Sink Rent-or-Buy [15, 16, 26], Connected Facility Location [15, 16, 39] and Single-Sink Buy-At-Bulk [23, 26, 40].

Both the previously cited primal-dual and iterative rounding approximation techniques apply to a more general class of problems. In particular, the iterative rounding technique introduced by Jain [28] provides a 2-approximation for the generalized Steiner network problem, and the primal-dual framework developed by Goemans and Williamson [22] gives the same approximation factor for a large class of constrained forest problems.

Regarding the integrality gap of LP relaxations for the Steiner tree problem, upper bounds better than 2 are known only for special graph classes. For example, BCR has an integrality gap smaller than 2 on quasi-bipartite graphs, where non-terminal nodes induce an independent set. For such graphs Rajagopalan and Vazirani [36] (see also Rizzi [37]) gave an upper bound of 3/2 on the gap. This was recently improved to 4/3 by Chakrabarty, Devanur and Vazirani [8]. Still, for this class of graphs the lower bound of 8/7 holds [31, 41]. Könemann, Pritchard and Tan [31] showed that for a different LP formulation, which is stronger than BCR, the integrality gap is upper-bounded by $\frac{2b+1}{b+1}$, where b is the maximum number of Steiner nodes in full components.

Finally, we remark that under additional constraints, Steiner tree admits better approximations. In particular, a PTAS can be obtained by the technique of Arora [4] if the nodes are points in a fixed-dimension Euclidean space, and using the algorithm of Borradaile, Kenyon-Mathieu and Klein [7] for planar graphs.

2. A DIRECTED-COMPONENT CUT RELAXATION

We now prove some crucial properties of our k-DCR. The optimal fractional solution to k-DCR is denoted by Opt_k^f, and opt_k^f is its cost. For a given (directed or undirected) component C', $R(C') := R \cap V(C')$ is the set of its terminals. Recall that k is a constant, hence k-DCR has a polynomial number of variables. Despite the fact that k-DCR has an exponential number of constraints, it can be solved to optimality using the Ellipsoid method [24, 30], since we can solve the separation problem in polynomial time.

LEMMA 5. *k-DCR can be solved in polynomial time, for any constant k.*

PROOF. We show how to solve the separation problem in polynomial time. Create a new directed graph G', on node set $V' = R \cup \{v_j \mid j = 1, \ldots, h\}$. For every component C_j, insert edges (u, v_j) for any $u \in \mathit{sources}(C_j)$, and one edge $e_j = (v_j, \mathit{sink}(C_j))$. Set the capacity of each e_j to $w(e_j) := x_j$, and let $w(e) := \infty$ for the remaining edges. It is not hard to see that, for a terminal $s \in R \setminus \{r\}$, there is an s-r cut $U' \subseteq V'$ of minimum capacity $\sum_{e \in \delta^+(U')} w(e)$, consisting of edges e_j only. Moreover, given a non-empty subset $R' \subseteq R \setminus \{r\}$, there is a cut U' such that

$$\sum_{e \in \delta^+(U')} w(e) = \sum_{e_j : C_j \in \delta_k^+(R')} w(e_j) = \sum_{C_j \in \delta_k^+(R')} x_j.$$

It then follows that a non-empty subset $R' \subseteq R \setminus \{r\}$ minimizing $\sum_{C_j \in \delta_k^+(R')} x_j$ can be computed via $|R|-1$ minimum-cut computations in G'. The claim follows. □

Note that one can solve k-DCR alternatively by a compact LP formulation which computes a minimum-cost multicommodity flow in G' (setting the cost of e_j to $c(C_j)$). This can be done even in strongly-polynomial time using the framework of Frank and Tardos [17] (see also Theorem 6.6.3 in [24]). Details will appear in the full version of the paper.

Let T^0 be a minimum-cost terminal spanning tree, i.e., T^0 spans R, but does not contain any Steiner node. It is a well-known fact that $c(T^0) \leq 2 \cdot \mathit{opt}$ (see e.g. Theorem 3.3 in [41]). Extending the standard proof, this bound also holds w.r.t. our LP relaxation:

LEMMA 6. *For any k, $c(T^0) \leq 2 \cdot \mathit{opt}_k^f$.*

PROOF. For each component C_j of Opt_k^f, obtain a TSP tour on $R(C_j)$ of cost at most $2c(C_j)$, remove one edge of the tour, and direct the remaining edges towards $\mathit{sink}(C_j)$. This induces a fractional solution to k-DCR of cost at most $2 \cdot \mathit{opt}_k^f$, with the property that only components with 2 terminals and without Steiner nodes are used. This provides a feasible fractional solution to BCR of the same cost. Since BCR without Steiner nodes is integral [12], the claim follows. □

We next prove our Bridge Lemma, which is the heart of our analysis. This lemma relates the cost of any terminal spanning tree to the cost of any fractional solution to k-DCR via the notion of bridges, and its proof is based on Edmonds' Theorem 2.

Before proving the lemma, we need a few intermediate results. Let R' be a subset of k' terminals. Consider a given tree S, with edge weights c, containing the terminals R'. The weight function c associated to S will be clear from the context. Let us collapse the terminals R' into one node, and consider the minimum-cost tree $S' \subseteq S$ in the resulting (possibly, multi-)graph, spanning all nodes of S. Observe that S' will contain all the edges of S but $k' - 1$ edges, since collapsing R' decreases the number of nodes in S by $k' - 1$.

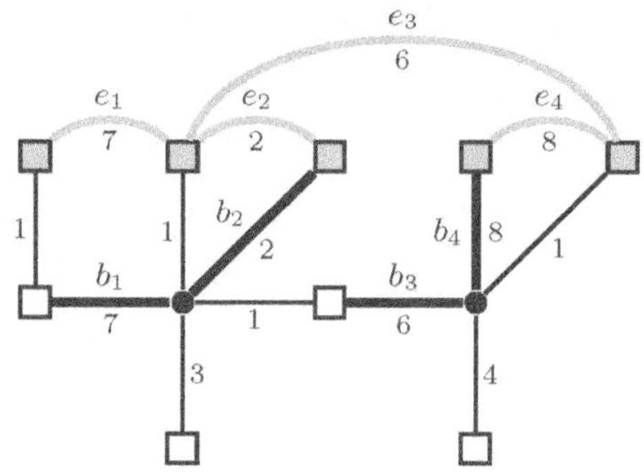

Figure 2: Steiner tree S is drawn in black. Terminals of R' are gray shaded. Bold black edges indicate $Br_S(R') = \{b_1, \ldots, b_4\}$. The corresponding edges $e_1, \ldots, e_4$ of Y' are drawn in gray and labeled with $w(e_i)$. Note that $w(e_i) = c(b_i)$. Observe also that b_3 is the unique bridge on the cycle contained in $S \cup \{e_3\}$.

We call the latter edges the *bridges* of S w.r.t. R', and denote them by $Br_S(R')$[4]. Intuitively, if we imagine to add zero cost dummy edges between the terminals R', $Br_S(R')$ is a maximum-cost subset of edges that we could remove from S and still have a connected spanning subgraph (see Figure 2). In other terms, $Br_S(R')$ is equal to

$$\operatorname{argmax}\left\{c(B) \mid B \subseteq S,\ S \backslash B \cup \tbinom{R'}{2} \text{ connects } V(S)\right\}.$$

Let us abbreviate $br_S(R') := c(Br_S(R'))$. For a (directed or undirected) component C', we use $Br_S(C')$ and $br_S(C')$ as shortcuts for $Br_S(R(C'))$ and $br_S(R(C'))$, respectively.

A key ingredient in the proof of our Bridge Lemma is the construction of a proper weighted terminal spanning tree as described in the following lemma. We define a *bridge weight function* $w : R \times R \to \mathbb{Q}_+$ as follows: For any terminal pair $u, v \in R$, the quantity $w(u, v)$ is the maximum cost of any edge in the unique u-v path in S.

LEMMA 7. *Let $R' \subseteq R$ and $Br_S(R') = \{b_1, \ldots, b_{k'-1}\}$ with $k' := |R'|$. Then one can construct a spanning tree $Y' = \{e_1, \ldots, e_{k'-1}\}$ on R' such that, for $i = 1, \ldots, k' - 1$,*

(a) *$w(e_i) = c(b_i)$ (hence $w(Y') = br_S(R')$).*

(b) *b_i is the only bridge edge on the cycle in $S \cup \{e_i\}$.*

PROOF. Observe that $S \setminus Br_S(R')$ is a forest of trees $F_1, \ldots, F_{k'}$, where each F_i contains exactly one terminal $r_i \in R'$. Each bridge b_i connects exactly two trees $F_{i'}$ and $F_{i''}$. For each b_i, we add edge $e_i = \{r_{i'}, r_{i''}\}$ to Y'. Clearly Y' is a spanning tree on R'. The path P_i between $r_{i'}$ and $r_{i''}$ contains b_i and no other bridge. Hence b_i is a maximum-cost edge on P_i and $w(e_i) = c(b_i)$ (see Figure 2). □

The following lemma is the heart of our analysis.

LEMMA 8. *[Bridge Lemma] Let T be a terminal spanning tree and x be a k-DCR solution. Then*

$$c(T) \leq \sum_j x_j \cdot br_T(C_j).$$

[4]As usual, we break ties according to edge indexes.

(1) For $t = 1, 2, \ldots, \mu$
  (1a) Compute an optimal fractional solution x^t to k-DCR (w.r.t. the current instance).
  (1b) Sample one component C^t, where $C^t = C_j$ with probability $x_j^t / \sum_i x_i^t$. Contract C^t.
(2) Compute a terminal spanning tree T^μ in the remaining instance.
(3) Output $T^\mu \cup \bigcup_{t=1}^{\mu} C^t$.

Figure 3: A 3/2-approximation algorithm for k-restricted Steiner tree.

PROOF. For every component C_j we construct a spanning tree Y_j on $R(C_j)$ with weight $w(Y_j) = br_T(C_j)$ according to Lemma 7. Then we direct the edges of Y_j towards $sink(C_j)$. We define a directed capacity reservation $y : R \times R \to \mathbb{Q}_+$ as follows: For every j, install capacity x_j in a cumulative manner on Y_j. In other terms, $y(u, v) := \sum_{Y_j \ni (u,v)} x_j$. The directed tree Y_j supports at least the same flow as component C_j with respect to $R(C_j)$. It then follows that y supports one unit of flow from each terminal to the root. In other terms, y is a feasible fractional solution to BCR. By Theorem 2, BCR is integral when no Steiner node is used. As a consequence there is an (integral) terminal spanning tree F that is not more costly than the fractional solution y, i.e. $w(F) \leq \sum_{e \in R \times R} w(e)y(e)$.

Recall that $w(u, v)$, for $u, v \in R$, is the maximum cost of any edge of the unique cycle in $T \cup \{u, v\}$. It follows from the classical cycle rule for minimum-cost spanning tree computation that $w(F) \geq c(T)$ (see, e.g., Theorem 6.2 in [32]). Altogether

$$\sum_j x_j br_T(C_j) = \sum_j x_j w(Y_j) = \sum_{e \in R \times R} w(e)y(e) \geq w(F) \geq c(T). \quad \square$$

3. ITERATIVE RANDOMIZED ROUNDING

In this section we present our approximation algorithm for k-restricted Steiner tree. To highlight the novel ideas of the approximation technique more than the approximation factor itself, we present a simplified analysis providing a weaker 3/2 approximation factor (which is already an improvement on the previous best 1.55 approximation). The more complex analysis leading to ln(4) is postponed to Section 4.

Our 3/2-approximation algorithm for k-restricted Steiner tree is described in Figure 3. Let x^t be the optimal fractional solution to k-DCR at a generic iteration t. By *sampling* a component C^t, we mean selecting one of the components C_j with probability $x_j^t / \sum_i x_i^t$. *Contracting* a component C^t means collapsing all its terminals into its sink $sink(C^t)$, which inherits all the edges incident to C^t (in case of parallel edges, we only keep the cheapest one).

Recall that $h = O(kn^k)$ is the number of potential k-components. Observe that the quantity $\Sigma^t := \sum_i x_i^t$ might vary over the iterations t. In order to simplify the analysis, we apply the above algorithm to a slightly different LP where we add a dummy component C_{h+1} formed by the root only (hence of cost zero), and add the constraint $x_{h+1} = \Sigma - \sum_{i=1}^h x_i$. Here $\Sigma = O(h)$ is an upper bound on the possible sum of the x_i's in the original LP. The number μ of iterations is fixed to $\delta\Sigma$, where δ is a proper constant to be chosen later. (W.l.o.g., $\delta\Sigma$ is integral). It is easy to see that the running time of the algorithm is polynomial.

We first outline the analysis of our algorithm. Let Opt_k^t be the optimal k-restricted Steiner tree at the beginning of iteration t, and let opt_k^t be its cost. By $opt_k^{f,t} := \sum_j x_j^t \cdot c(C_j)$ we denote the cost of the optimal fractional solution at the beginning of iteration t. Lemma 9 bounds the expected cost of the final terminal spanning T^μ. The basic idea is showing that the current terminal spanning tree is getting cheaper by a factor $(1 - \frac{1}{\Sigma})$ at each iteration (in expectation): This is an easy consequence of the Bridge Lemma. Lemma 13 bounds the expected cost of each sampled component C^t. For this component we pay in expectation a $\frac{1}{\Sigma}$ fraction of $opt_k^{f,t}$, which is in turn upper bounded by opt_k^t. Hence it is sufficient to bound the cost of opt_k^t (Corollary 12). In order to do that, we show that the cost of the optimal Steiner tree decreases by a factor $(1 - \frac{1}{2\Sigma})$ at each iteration (Lemma 12). Also in this case the proof relies crucially on the Bridge Lemma.

The next lemma bounds the cost of the final terminal spanning tree.

LEMMA 9. *One has* $E[c(T^\mu)] \leq (1 - \frac{1}{\Sigma})^\mu \cdot 2opt_k^f$.

PROOF. Let T^t (T^0, resp.) be the minimum cost terminal spanning tree at the end of iteration t (for the original instance, resp.). Consider an arbitrary iteration $t = 1, \ldots, \mu$. The reduction in the cost of T^t w.r.t. T^{t-1} is at least $br_{T^{t-1}}(C^t)$. Therefore:

$$\begin{aligned} E[c(T^t)] &\leq c(T^{t-1}) - E[br_{T^{t-1}}(C^t)] \\ &= c(T^{t-1}) - \frac{1}{\Sigma}\sum_j x_j^t \cdot br_{T^{t-1}}(C_j) \\ &\overset{\text{Bridge Lem 8}}{\leq} \left(1 - \frac{1}{\Sigma}\right) \cdot c(T^{t-1}). \end{aligned}$$

It follows that

$$E[c(T^\mu)] \leq \left(1 - \frac{1}{\Sigma}\right)^\mu \cdot c(T^0) \overset{\text{Lem 6}}{\leq} \left(1 - \frac{1}{\Sigma}\right)^\mu \cdot 2opt_k^f. \quad \square$$

It remains to bound the cost of the sampled components. The proof of the following technical lemma is based on standard techniques (see, e.g., [29]).

LEMMA 10. *For any Steiner tree* S, $br_S(R) \geq \frac{1}{2}c(S)$.

PROOF. Turn S into a binary tree with leaves R by adding dummy Steiner nodes and zero cost edges. For each Steiner node of S, mark the most expensive edge out of the edges going to its 2 children. Let $B \subseteq S$ be the set of marked edges. Observe that $c(B) \geq \frac{1}{2}c(S)$. Furthermore, after contracting R, one can remove B while keeping S connected. From the definition of bridges it follows that $br_S(R) \geq c(B) \geq \frac{1}{2}c(S)$. $\square$

The next lemma and corollary bound the expected decrease of the cost of the optimal Steiner tree after each contraction.

LEMMA 11. *Let S be any Steiner tree and x be a feasible solution to k-DCR. Sample a component C randomly w.r.t. x. Then there is a subgraph $S' \subseteq S$ such that $S' \cup C$ spans R and*

$$E[c(S')] \leq \left(1 - \frac{1}{2\Sigma}\right) \cdot c(S).$$

PROOF. Let $Br_S(R) = \{b_1, \ldots, b_q\}$. We apply Lemma 7 to S to obtain a terminal spanning tree Y consisting of edges $e_1, \ldots, e_q$ such that $w(e_i) = c(b_i)$ (hence $w(Y) = br_S(R)$) and b_i is the unique bridge on $S \cup \{e_i\}$. Choose

$$S' := S \backslash \{b_i \mid e_i \in Br_Y(C)\}.$$

(Here $Br_Y(C)$ is computed w.r.t. weights $w(e_i)$). Observe that $S' \cup C$ spans R. In fact, consider any edge $e_i = \{u_i, v_i\} \in Y \backslash Br_Y(C)$. The u_i-v_i path in S contains only one potential bridge edge, namely b_i. Hence, if two terminals are connected by $Y \backslash Br_Y(C)$, then they are so in S'. The claim follows since $(Y \backslash Br_Y(C)) \cup C$ is connected due to the definition of bridges. We conclude

$$\begin{aligned} E[c(S')] &= c(S) - E[br_Y(C)] \\ &= c(S) - \frac{1}{\Sigma}\sum_j x_j br_Y(C_j) \\ &\overset{\text{Bridge Lem 8}}{\leq} c(S) - \frac{1}{\Sigma} w(Y) \\ &= c(S) - \frac{1}{\Sigma} br_S(R) \\ &\overset{\text{Lem 10}}{\leq} \left(1 - \frac{1}{2\Sigma}\right) c(S). \quad \square \end{aligned}$$

COROLLARY 12. *For every* $t = 1, \ldots, \mu$,

$$E[opt_k^t] \leq \left(1 - \frac{1}{2\Sigma}\right)^{t-1} \cdot opt_k.$$

PROOF. Observe that, in Lemma 11, if the initial Steiner tree S is k-restricted, then $S' \cup C$ is k-restricted as well. Hence, this lemma implies that $E[opt_k^{t+1}] \leq (1 - \frac{1}{2\Sigma}) \cdot opt_k^t$ for any iteration $t = 1, \ldots, \mu - 1$. The claim follows. $\square$

Corollary 12 immediately provides an upper bound on $opt_k^{f,t}$. An upper bound on the expected cost of the sampled components easily follows.

LEMMA 13. *For every* $t = 1, \ldots, \mu$,

$$E[c(C^t)] \leq \frac{1}{\Sigma}\left(1 - \frac{1}{2\Sigma}\right)^{t-1} \cdot opt_k.$$

PROOF. One has

$$\begin{aligned} E[c(C^t)] &= \frac{1}{\Sigma} E[\textstyle\sum_j x_j^t \cdot c(C_j)] \\ &= \frac{1}{\Sigma} E[opt_k^{f,t}] \\ &\leq \frac{1}{\Sigma} E[opt_k^t] \\ &\overset{\text{Cor 12}}{\leq} \frac{1}{\Sigma}\left(1 - \frac{1}{2\Sigma}\right)^{t-1} \cdot opt_k. \quad \square \end{aligned}$$

We now have all the ingredients to show a 3/2-approximation factor for the problem.

THEOREM 14. *For any* $k = O(1)$, *there is a polynomial-time randomized approximation algorithm for k-restricted Steiner tree with expected approximation ratio* 3/2.

PROOF. Consider the algorithm of Figure 3 with $\mu = \delta\Sigma$ and $\delta = \ln(4)$. The cost of the computed solution is $c(T^\mu) + \sum_{t=1}^{\mu} c(C^t)$. The expected approximation ratio satisfies

$$\begin{aligned} E\left[\frac{c(T^\mu) + \sum_{t=1}^{\mu} c(C^t)}{opt_k}\right] &\overset{\text{Lem 9 + 13}}{\leq} 2 \cdot \left(1 - \frac{1}{\Sigma}\right)^{\mu} + \frac{1}{\Sigma}\sum_{t=1}^{\mu}\left(1 - \frac{1}{2\Sigma}\right)^{t-1} \\ &= 2 \cdot \left(1 - \frac{1}{\Sigma}\right)^{\delta \cdot \Sigma} + 2 - 2 \cdot \left(1 - \frac{1}{2\Sigma}\right)^{\delta \cdot \Sigma} \\ &\leq 2e^{-\delta} + 2 - 2 \cdot e^{-\delta/2} = \frac{3}{2}. \end{aligned}$$

In the last inequality we used the fact that $(1 - \frac{1}{y})^{\delta y} - (1 - \frac{1}{2y})^{\delta y}$ is an increasing function of $y > 1$, and that $\lim_{y \to \infty}(1 - \frac{1}{y})^y = \frac{1}{e}$. $\square$

Theorems 1 and 14 immediately imply an expected $(3/2+\varepsilon)$-approximation algorithm for the Steiner tree problem.

(1) For $t = 1, 2, \ldots$

- (1a) Compute an optimal fractional solution x^t to k-DCR (w.r.t. the current instance).
- (1b) Sample one component C^t, where $C^t = C_j$ with probability $x_j^t / \sum_i x_i^t$. Contract C^t.
- (1c) If the instance consists only of the root, return $\bigcup_{i=1}^{t} C^i$.

Figure 4: A ln(4)-approximation algorithm for k-restricted Steiner tree.

4. A REFINED APPROXIMATION

In this section, we present a $(\ln(4) + \varepsilon)$-approximation for Steiner tree. The algorithm is the same as in the previous section, with the difference that now we let it run until all the terminals collapse into the root. The set of sampled components provides the desired solution (see Figure 4).

We first give a high-level description of our analysis. Let $S^* := Opt_k$ be the optimal k-restricted Steiner tree for the original instance (in particular, $c(S^*) = opt_k$). Each time we sample a component C^t, we will delete a proper subset of edges from S^*. Consider the sequence $S^* = S^1 \supseteq S^2 \supseteq \ldots$ of subgraphs of S^* which are obtained this way. We will guarantee that at any iteration t, the edge set S^t plus the previously sampled components yields a subgraph that connects all terminals. Furthermore, we will prove that a fixed edge $e \in S^*$ is deleted after an expected number of at most $\ln(4) \cdot \Sigma$ iterations. This immediately implies the approximation factor of $\ln(4)$.

In order to track which edges can be safely deleted from S^*, we will construct an artificial terminal spanning tree Y (the *witness tree*) and assign a random subset $W(e)$ of edges of Y to each edge $e \in S^*$. The choice of $W(e)$ guarantees (deterministically) that, if a pair of terminals is connected by $Y' \subseteq Y$, then they are as well connected by $\{e \in S^* \mid W(e) \cap Y' \neq \emptyset\}$.

At each iteration, when component C^t is sampled, we mark a proper *random* subset $\overline{Br}_Y(C^t)$ of edges of Y. This set guarantees that $(Y \backslash \overline{Br}_Y(C^t)) \cup C^t$ is connected (deterministically). The intuitive reason for using $\overline{Br}_Y(C^t)$ rather than $Br_Y(C^t)$ is that we want to sample each edge of Y *more uniformly*. When all the edges in $W(e)$ are marked, we delete e from S^*. Summarizing, we consider the following random process:

> For $t = 1, 2, \ldots$, sample one component C^t from x^t and *mark* the edges in $\overline{Br}_Y(C^t)$. *Delete* an edge e from S^* as soon as all edges in $W(e)$ are marked.

The subgraph S^t is given by the edges of S^* which are not yet deleted at the beginning of iteration t.

We next give the details of our analysis. A combination of Farkas' Lemma together with our Bridge Lemma provides the existence of random sets $\overline{Br}_Y(C_j)$ such that every edge in Y is marked with probability at least $\frac{1}{\Sigma}$ per iteration.

LEMMA 15. *Let Y be any terminal spanning tree and x be any k-DCR solution with $\Sigma = \sum_j x_j$. Then there exist random sets $\overline{Br}_Y(C_j) \subseteq Y$ such that if we sample a component C randomly w.r.t. x one has*

(1) $\Pr[e \in \overline{Br}_Y(C)] \geq \frac{1}{\Sigma}$ *for all* $e \in Y$;

(2) $Y \backslash \overline{Br}_Y(C_j) \cup C_j$ *connects* $V(Y)$ *for all* C_j.

PROOF. For a component C_j, let the set of *candidate* bridges $\mathcal{B}_Y(C_j)$ be

$$\{B \subseteq Y \mid |B| = |R(C_j)| - 1, (Y \backslash B) \cup C_j \text{ connects } V(Y)\}.$$

By definition any $B \in \mathcal{B}_Y(C_j)$ satisfies Property (2). For a proper probability distribution w, we let $\Pr[\overline{Br}_Y(C_j) = B] := w_{jB}$. In particular, $\sum_{B \in \mathcal{B}_Y(C_j)} w_{jB} = 1$. We will show that there is a w with

$$\sum_{(B,j): B \in \mathcal{B}_Y(C_j), e \in B} x_j w_{jB} \geq 1$$

for all $e \in Y$. This implies Property (1) since

$$\Pr[e \in \overline{Br}_Y(C)] = \sum_{(B,j): B \in \mathcal{B}_Y(C_j), e \in B} \frac{x_j}{\Sigma} \cdot w_{jB} \geq \frac{1}{\Sigma}.$$

Suppose by contradiction that such a distribution w does not exist. Then the following system of linear inequalities has no solution[5]

$$\begin{aligned} \sum_{B \in \mathcal{B}_Y(C_j)} w_{jB} &\leq 1 \quad \forall j \\ \sum_{(B,j): B \in \mathcal{B}_Y(C_j), e \in B} x_j w_{jB} &\geq 1 \quad \forall e \in Y \\ w &\geq \mathbf{0}. \end{aligned}$$

Farkas' Lemma[6] yields that there is a vector $(y, c) \geq \mathbf{0}$ with

$$(a) \quad y_j \geq \sum_{e \in B} c_e x_j \quad \forall (B, j) : B \in \mathcal{B}_Y(C_j);$$

$$(b) \quad \sum_j y_j < \sum_{e \in Y} c_e = c(Y).$$

In particular,

$$y_j \overset{(a)}{\geq} x_j \cdot \max\{c(B) \mid B \in \mathcal{B}_Y(C_j)\} = x_j \cdot br_Y(C_j).$$

[5]We can replace the "=" constraint with "≤" without affecting feasibility since all coefficients of w_{jB} are non-negative.

[6]$\exists x \geq \mathbf{0} : Ax \leq b \dot\vee \exists z \geq \mathbf{0} : z^T A \geq 0, z^T b < 0$

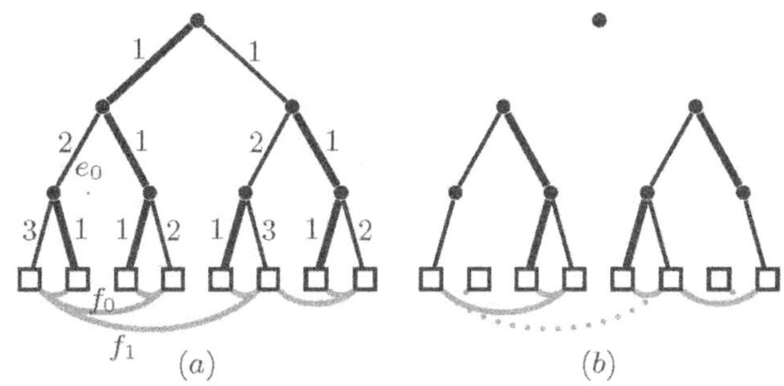

Figure 5: (a) Optimal Steiner tree S^* in black, where bold edges indicate B, and the associated terminal spanning tree Y in gray. Edges e in S^* are labeled with $|W(e)|$. For example $W(e_0) = \{f_0, f_1\}$. (b) Marked edges in Y at a given iteration t are drawn dotted; the non-deleted edges in S^* (i.e. edges of S^t) are drawn in black. Non-marked edges of Y and non-deleted edges of S^* support the same connectivity on R.

Then

$$\sum_j x_j \cdot br_Y(C_j) \leq \sum_j y_j \overset{(b)}{<} c(Y),$$

which contradicts the Bridge Lemma 8. □

Next, we define the witness tree Y and the sets $W(e)$ for each $e \in S^*$. Without loss of generality any Steiner node in S^* has degree 3 or more. By adding dummy Steiner nodes and zero cost edges, we can assume that S^* is a (not necessarily complete) binary tree, rooted at some Steiner node, of height at most $|R| - 1$. For each Steiner node, choose uniformly at random one of the two edges to its children. Let B denote the chosen edges. Clearly $\Pr[e \in B] = \frac{1}{2}$ for any $e \in S^*$. Let $P_{uv} \subseteq S^*$ be the unique u-v path in S^*. The witness tree is

$$Y := \{\{u, v\} \in \tbinom{R}{2} \mid |P_{uv} \cap B| = 1\}.$$

Similarly to arguments in Lemma 7, Y is a spanning tree on R. Furthermore, for each edge $e \in S^*$, we define

$$W(e) := \{\{u, v\} \in Y \mid e \in P_{uv}\}.$$

See Figure 5(a) for an illustration. Note that $1 \leq |W(e)| \leq |Y| = |R| - 1$. Observe also that $|W(e)| = 1$ if $e \in B$. Indeed, the expected cardinality of $W(e)$ is small also for the remaining edges.

LEMMA 16. *For any edge $e \in S^*$ at level $k_e \leq |R| - 1$ (edges incident to the root are at level one), one has*

$$\Pr[|W(e)| = q] = \begin{cases} 1/2^q & \text{if } 1 \leq q < k_e; \\ 2/2^q & \text{if } q = k_e; \\ 0 & \text{otherwise.} \end{cases}$$

PROOF. Consider the path $v_0, v_1, \ldots, v_{k_e}$ from e towards the root. In particular, $e = \{v_0, v_1\}$. If (v_{q-1}, v_q) is the first edge from B on this path, then $|W(e)| = q$. This is because, for each node v_j, $j \geq 1$, there is one distinct path P_{uv} with $\{u, v\} \in Y$ that contains e (see also Figure 5(a)). This event happens with probability $1/2^q$. Otherwise, $|W(e)| = k_e$ by a similar argument. The latter event happens with probability $1/2^{k_e}$. The claim follows. □

For $W \subseteq Y$, let $M(W)$ denote the first iteration when all the edge in W are marked. The choice for the sequence $S^* = S^1 \supseteq S^2 \supseteq \ldots$ is given by $S^t = \{e \in S^* \mid M(W(e)) \geq t\}$. In other words, S^t is the set of edges which are not yet deleted at the beginning of iteration t.

LEMMA 17. *The graph* $S^t \cup \bigcup_{t'=1}^{t-1} C^{t'}$ *spans* R.

PROOF. Let $Y' \subseteq Y$ be the set of edges which are not yet marked at the beginning of iteration t (see also Figure 5(b)). Then, by definition of bridges, $Y' \cup \bigcup_{t'=1}^{t-1} C^{t'}$ spans R. Consider any edge $\{u, v\} \in Y'$. Then $\{u, v\} \in W(e)$ for all $e \in P_{uv}$. Hence no edge on P_{uv} is deleted. Therefore u and v are also connected in S^t. The claim follows. □

Recall that $H_q := \sum_{i=1}^{q} \frac{1}{i}$ is the *qth harmonic number.*

LEMMA 18. *Let* $W \subseteq Y$. *Then the expected number of iterations until all edges in* W *are marked satisfies*

$$E[M(W)] \leq H_{|W|} \cdot \Sigma.$$

PROOF. Let m_q be the best possible upper bound on the expected number of iterations until all out of a given set W of q edges are marked (over all feasible probability distributions). We will prove that $m_q \leq H_q \cdot \Sigma$ by induction on q. For $q = 1$, the only edge in W is marked with probability at least $\frac{1}{\Sigma}$ in each iteration, hence $m_1 \leq \Sigma$. Next, let $q > 1$ and consider the first iteration. Consider the probability distribution $p = (p_0, \ldots, p_q)$ where p_i gives the probability that i edges are sampled in the first iteration. Of course, since the expected number of marked edges must be at least $q \cdot \frac{1}{\Sigma}$ in the first iteration, this distribution has to satisfy the constraint

$$\sum_{i=0}^{q} p_i = 1; \quad \sum_{i=0}^{q} i \cdot p_i \geq \frac{q}{\Sigma}; \quad p_i \geq 0, \forall i = 0, \ldots, q. \quad (1)$$

If we condition on the event that $i \in \{0, \ldots, q\}$ edges are marked in the first iteration, we need in expectation at most m_{q-i} more iterations until the remaining $q - i$ edges are marked. Hence we obtain the bound

$$m_q \leq 1 + \sum_{i=0}^{q} p_i \cdot m_{q-i}. \quad (2)$$

Assume pessimistically that p is the distribution which maximizes the right-hand side of (2) under Constraint (1). The value of p is an optimal fractional solution of a linear program. In particular, we can assume that p is a vertex of the polyhedron induced by (1). Hence all but (at most) two entries of p are zero. Suppose $p_0 = 0$. In this case we would mark deterministically at least one edge. The claim follows since, conditioning on the number $i \in \{1, \ldots, q\}$ of sampled edges, one obtains $m_q \leq 1 + m_{q-i} \leq 1 + H_{q-i} \cdot \Sigma \leq H_q \cdot \Sigma$. Here we use $q \leq |Y| = |R| - 1 \leq \Sigma$. Otherwise, there must be an $i > 0$ such that $p_i = \frac{q}{i\Sigma}$, $p_0 = 1 - \frac{q}{i\Sigma}$, and $p_j = 0$ for all $0 < j \neq i$. Hence

$$m_q \leq 1 + \frac{q}{i\Sigma} \cdot H_{q-i}\Sigma + \left(1 - \frac{q}{i\Sigma}\right) m_q.$$

Rearranging terms yields

$$m_q \leq \Sigma \cdot \left(\frac{i}{q} + H_{q-i}\right) \leq \Sigma \cdot H_q,$$

and the assertion follows. □

Eventually, we prove the expected approximation of $\ln(4)$, as claimed in Theorem 3.

PROOF OF THEOREM 3. For an edge $e \in S^*$, we define $D(e) = \max\{t \mid e \in S^t\}$ as the iteration in which e is deleted. One has

$$\begin{aligned}
E[D(e)] &= \sum_{q=1}^{k_e} \Pr[|W(e)| = q] \cdot E[D(e) \mid |W(e)| = q] \\
&\overset{\text{Lem 18}}{\leq} \sum_{q=1}^{k_e} \Pr[|W(e)| = q] \cdot H_q \cdot \Sigma \\
&\overset{\text{Lem 16}}{=} \sum_{q=1}^{k_e - 1} \left(\frac{1}{2}\right)^q \cdot H_q \cdot \Sigma + \frac{2}{2^{k_e}} \cdot H_{k_e} \cdot \Sigma \\
&\leq \sum_{q \geq 1} \left(\frac{1}{2}\right)^q \cdot H_q \cdot \Sigma \\
&= \Sigma \cdot \sum_{q \geq 1} \frac{1}{q} \sum_{i \geq 0} \left(\frac{1}{2}\right)^{q+i} \\
&= \Sigma \cdot \sum_{q \geq 1} \frac{1}{q} \left(\frac{1}{2}\right)^{q-1} = \ln(4) \cdot \Sigma.
\end{aligned}$$

The expected cost of the approximate solution satisfies

$$\begin{aligned}
E\Big[\sum_{t \geq 1} c(C^t)\Big] &= \sum_{t \geq 1} \frac{1}{\Sigma} E\left[opt_k^{f,t}\right] \\
&\leq \frac{1}{\Sigma} \sum_{t \geq 1} E\left[c(S^t)\right] \\
&= \frac{1}{\Sigma} \sum_{e \in S^*} E[D(e)] \cdot c(e) \leq \ln(4) \cdot opt_k.
\end{aligned}$$

The claim follows. □

4.1 Derandomization

After submitting the preliminary version of this paper, we found a way to derandomize our algorithm via the method of *limited independence* (see, e.g., Alon and Spencer [2]). The basic idea is to partition the sequence of iterations into a (large) constant number of *phases*. In each phase, we sample a proper number of random components (rather than just one component). The LP is updated only from phase to phase. This sampling is performed in such a way that only $O(\log n)$ random bits are needed. Hence, the algorithm can be derandomized by considering all the (polynomially-many) choices for the random bits. The approximation ratio grows by a factor $(1 + \varepsilon)$. The proof of the following theorem will appear in the journal version of this paper.

THEOREM 19. *For any* $k = O(1)$ *and any constant* $\varepsilon > 0$, *there is a polynomial time deterministic* $(\ln(4) + \varepsilon)$*-approximation algorithm for k-restricted Steiner tree.*

COROLLARY 20. *For any constant* $\varepsilon > 0$, *there is a polynomial-time deterministic* $(\ln(4) + \varepsilon)$*-approximation algorithm for Steiner tree.*

5. INTEGRALITY GAP

In this section we bound the integrality gap of k-DCR. Note that, despite the fact that our analysis is based on an LP relaxation of the problem, it does not imply a $\ln(4)$ (nor even a 1.5) bound on the integrality gap of the studied

LP. (This is because the LP changes during the iterations of the algorithm). However, an easy adaptation of the analysis from previous sections proves the following claim.

THEOREM 21. *There is a polynomial-time algorithm which computes a solution to the k-restricted Steiner tree problem of expected cost at most $1 + \ln(2) < 1.694$ times the cost of the optimal fractional solution to k-DCR.*

PROOF. Consider the algorithm from Figure 3 with $\mu = \delta\Sigma$ and $\delta = \ln(2)$. Observe that, for any $t \geq 1$, $opt_k^{f,t} \leq opt_k^f$ (contracting components does not increase the cost of the fractional solution). Hence

$$
\begin{aligned}
E\Big[c(T^\mu) + \sum_{t=1}^{\mu} c(C^t)\Big] & \\
&\overset{\text{Lem 9}}{\leq} 2 \cdot \left(1 - \frac{1}{\Sigma}\right)^{\mu} opt_k^f + \frac{1}{\Sigma}\sum_{t=1}^{\mu} opt_k^{f,t} \\
&\leq 2 \cdot \left(1 - \frac{1}{\Sigma}\right)^{\mu} opt_k^f + \frac{\mu}{\Sigma} opt_k^f \\
&\leq (2e^{-\delta} + \delta) opt_k^f = (1 + \ln(2)) opt_k^f. \quad \square
\end{aligned}
$$

In order to achieve the better 1.55 bound on the integrality gap claimed in Theorem 4, we prove that another algorithm, namely the algorithm of Robins and Zelikovsky [38], produces solutions of cost bounded with respect to the optimal fractional solutions to k-DCR. Our alternative analysis of this algorithm is, to some extent, inspired by an analogous argument of Charikar and Guha [9] in the context of the facility location problem. Our argument is essentially a combination of the analysis in [38] with our new Bridge Lemma 8. For this reason, the proof of Theorem 4 is postponed to the full version of the paper.

We leave it as an interesting open problem to prove a $\ln(4)$ (or even 1.5) bound on the integrality gap of k-DCR (if possible). This might involve the development of a fractional version of Lemma 11.

We conclude the paper with a comparison between BCR and k-DCR. It is easy to see that any feasible solution to k-DCR can be turned into a feasible solution to BCR of the same cost. In fact, it is sufficient to split each component into the corresponding set of edges.

Interestingly enough, the reverse is not true, as observed in [34]. In other words, for any k, k-DCR is a relaxation strictly stronger than BCR. In particular, the 1.55 upper bound on the integrality gap of k-DCR does not imply the same bound on the integrality gap of BCR. Nevertheless, Skutella's graph [31] implies an 8/7 lower bound also on the integrality gap of our relaxation. It remains as a challenging open problem to show whether the integrality gap of BCR is smaller than 2 or not.

Acknowledgements.

The authors wish to thank C. Chekuri, F. Eisenbrand, M. X. Goemans, J. Könemann, D. Pritchard, F. B. Shepherd, and R. Zenklusen for helpful discussions. The second author is grateful to F. Eisenbrand for supporting his visit at EPFL (during which part of this paper was developed). We thank the anonymous reviewers for many suggestions on how to improve the presentation.

6. REFERENCES

[1] A. Agrawal, P. Klein, and R. Ravi. When trees collide: an approximation algorithm for the generalized Steiner problem on networks. *SIAM Journal on Computing*, 24(3): 440–456, 1995.

[2] N. Alon and J. Spencer. *The probabilistic method.* Wiley-Interscience Series in Discrete Mathematics and Optimization. John Wiley & Sons Inc., Hoboken, NJ, third edition, 2008.

[3] A. Archer, M. Bateni, M. Hajiaghayi, and H. Karloff. Improved approximation algorithms for prize-collecting Steiner tree and TSP. In *FOCS*, pages 427–436, 2009.

[4] S. Arora. Polynomial time approximation schemes for Euclidean traveling salesman and other geometric problems. *Journal of the ACM*, 45(5):753–782, 1998.

[5] M. Bern and P. Plassmann. The Steiner problem with edge lengths 1 and 2. *Information Processing Letters*, 32(4):171–176, 1989.

[6] A. Borchers and D. Du. The k-Steiner ratio in graphs. *SIAM Journal on Computing*, 26(3):857–869, 1997.

[7] G. Borradaile, C. Kenyon-Mathieu, and P. Klein. A polynomial-time approximation scheme for Steiner tree in planar graphs. In *SODA*, pages 1285–1294, 2007.

[8] D. Chakrabarty, N. R. Devanur, and V. V. Vazirani. New geometry-inspired relaxations and algorithms for the metric Steiner tree problem. In *IPCO*, pages 344–358, 2008.

[9] M. Charikar and S. Guha. Improved combinatorial algorithms for facility location problems. *SIAM Journal on Computing*, 34:803–824, 2005.

[10] M. Chlebík and J. Chlebíková. The Steiner tree problem on graphs: Inapproximability results. *Theoretical Computer Science*, 406(3):207–214, 2008.

[11] S. E. Dreyfus and R. A. Wagner. The Steiner problem in graphs. *Networks*, 1:195–207, 1972.

[12] J. Edmonds. Optimum branchings. *J. Res. Nat. Bur. Standards*, B71:233–240, 1967.

[13] F. Eisenbrand and F. Grandoni. An improved approximation algorithm for virtual private network design. In *SODA*, pages 928–932, 2005.

[14] F. Eisenbrand, F. Grandoni, G. Oriolo, and M. Skutella. New approaches for virtual private network designs. *SIAM Journal on Computing* 37(3): 706-721, 2007.

[15] F. Eisenbrand, F. Grandoni, T. Rothvoß, and G. Schäfer. Approximating connected facility location problems via random facility sampling and core detouring. In *SODA*, pages 1174–1183, 2008.

[16] F. Eisenbrand, F. Grandoni, T. Rothvoß, and G. Schäfer. Connected Facility Location via Random Sampling and Core Detouring. *Journal of Computer and System Sciences*. To appear.

[17] A. Frank and É. Tardos. An application of simultaneous Diophantine approximation in combinatorial optimization. *Combinatorica*, 7:49–65, 1987.

[18] M. R. Garey and D. S. Johnson. The rectilinear Steiner tree problem is NP-complete. *SIAM Journal on Applied Mathematics*, 32:826–834, 1977.

[19] M. R. Garey and D. S. Johnson. *Computers and*

intractability. W. H. Freeman and Co., San Francisco, Calif., 1979. A guide to the theory of NP-completeness, A Series of Books in the Mathematical Sciences.

[20] E. N. Gilbert and H. O. Pollak. Steiner minimal trees. *SIAM Journal on Applied Mathematics*, 16(1):1–29, January 1968.

[21] M. X. Goemans and Y. S. Myung. A catalog of Steiner tree formulations. *Networks*, 23:19–28, 1993.

[22] M. X. Goemans and D.P. Williamson. A general approximation technique for constrained forest problems. *SIAM Journal on Computing*, 24:296–317, 1995.

[23] F. Grandoni and G. F. Italiano. Improved approximation for single-sink buy-at-bulk. In *ISAAC*, pages 111–120, 2006.

[24] M. Grötschel, L. Lovasz, and A. Schrijver. The ellipsoid method and its consequences in combinatorial optimization. *Combinatorica*, 1:169–197, 1981.

[25] A. Gupta, J. Kleinberg, A. Kumar, R. Rastogi, and B. Yener. Provisioning a virtual private network: a network design problem for multicommodity flow. In *STOC*, pages 389–398, 2001.

[26] A. Gupta, A. Kumar, M. Pál, and T. Roughgarden. Approximation via cost sharing: simpler and better approximation algorithms for network design. *Journal of the ACM*, 54(3):11, 2007.

[27] F.K. Hwang, D.S. Richards, and P. Winter. *The Steiner tree problem*. Monograph in Annals of Discrete Mathematics, 53. Elsevier, Amsterdam, 1992.

[28] K. Jain. A factor 2 approximation algorithm for the generalized Steiner network problem. In *FOCS*, pages 448–457, 1998.

[29] M. Karpinski and A. Zelikovsky. New approximation algorithms for the Steiner tree problems. *Journal of Combinatorial Optimization*, 1(1):47–65, 1997.

[30] L. G. Khachiyan. A polynomial algorithm for linear programming. *Soviet Math. Doklady*, 20:191–194, 1979. (Russian original in Doklady Akademiia Nauk SSSR, 244:1093–1096).

[31] J. Könemann, D. Pritchard, and K. Tan. A partition-based relaxation for Steiner trees. *CoRR*, abs/0712.3568, 2007.

[32] B. Korte and J. Vygen. *Combinatorial Optimization - Theory and Algorithms*. Springer-Verlag, Second Edition, 2002.

[33] D. Mölle, S. Richter, and P. Rossmanith. A faster algorithm for the Steiner tree problem. In *STACS 2006*, pages 561–570, 2006.

[34] T. Polzin and S. V. Daneshmand. On Steiner trees and minimum spanning trees in hypergraphs. *Operations Research Letters*, 31:12–20, 2003.

[35] H. J. Prömel and A. Steger. A new approximation algorithm for the Steiner tree problem with performance ratio 5/3. *Journal of Algorithms*, 36:89–101, 2000.

[36] S. Rajagopalan and V. V. Vazirani. On the bidirected cut relaxation for the metric Steiner tree problem. In *SODA*, pages 742–751, 1999.

[37] R. Rizzi. On Rajagopalan and Vazirani's 3/2-approximation bound for the Iterated 1-Steiner heuristic. *Information Processing Letters*, 86(6):335–338, 2003.

[38] G. Robins and A. Zelikovsky. Tighter bounds for graph Steiner tree approximation. *SIAM Journal on Discrete Mathematics*, 19(1):122–134, 2005. A preliminary version appeared in SODA 2000.

[39] C. Swamy and A. Kumar. Prima-dual algorithms for connected facility location problems. *Algorithmica*, 40(4):245–269, 2004.

[40] K. Talwar. The single-sink buy-at-bulk LP has constant integrality gap. In *IPCO*, pages 475–486, 2002.

[41] V. V. Vazirani. *Approximation Algorithms*. Springer-Verlag, 2001.

[42] A. Z. Zelikovsky. An 11/6-approximation algorithm for the network Steiner problem. *Algorithmica*, 9:463–470, 1993.

Changing Base without Losing Space

Yevgeniy Dodis[*]
New York University
dodis@cs.nyu.edu

Mihai Pătraşcu
AT&T Labs
mip@alum.mit.edu

Mikkel Thorup
AT&T Labs
mthorup@research.att.com

ABSTRACT

We describe a simple, but powerful local encoding technique, implying two surprising results:

1. We show how to represent a vector of n values from Σ using $\lceil n \log_2 \Sigma \rceil$ bits, such that reading or writing any entry takes $O(1)$ time. This demonstrates, for instance, an "equivalence" between decimal and binary computers, and has been a central toy problem in the field of succinct data structures. Previous solutions required space of $n \log_2 \Sigma + n/\log^{O(1)} n$ bits for constant access.

2. Given a stream of n bits arriving online (for any n, not known in advance), we can output a *prefix-free* encoding that uses $n + \log_2 n + O(\log \log n)$ bits. The encoding and decoding algorithms only require $O(\log n)$ bits of memory, and run in constant time per word. This result is interesting in cryptographic applications, as prefix-free codes are the simplest counter-measure to extensions attacks on hash functions, message authentication codes and pseudorandom functions. Our result refutes a conjecture of [Maurer, Sjödin 2005] on the hardness of online prefix-free encodings.

Categories and Subject Descriptors

E.1 [**Data**]: Data Structures; E.2 [**Data**]: Data Storage Representations; E.4 [**Data**]: Coding and Information Theory; H.3.2 [**Information Systems**]: Information Storage

General Terms

Algorithms, Theory, Security

Keywords

Succinct Data Structures, Prefix-Free Encoding, Streaming Algorithms, Domain Extension of Hash Functions, Arithmetic Coding.

[*]Supported by NSF Grants 0831299, 0716690, 0515121.

1. INTRODUCTION

Suppose we want to represent a vector $A[1\,..\,n]$, where each element comes from some finite alphabet Σ. The optimal space is $\lceil n \log_2 \Sigma \rceil$ bits,[1] and it can be achieved by treating the vector as a big number between 0 and $\Sigma^n - 1$, and converting this number to binary. Unfortunately, this encoding has very poor locality: (1) we cannot encode a stream of symbols with a low-memory algorithm; (2) we cannot read or write a single element $A[i]$ faster than decoding the entire vector.

In this paper, we give a surprisingly simple technique that solves both of these problems optimally. We can represent A using $\lceil n \log_2 \Sigma \rceil$ bits, while reading/writing $A[i]$ in constant time. Additionally, given a stream of symbols in Σ, we can encode (and later decode) it into a binary stream of optimal size, while using $O(\log(n\Sigma))$ bits of memory and constant processing time per symbol. As an unexpected application of this result, we show how to encode/decode a stream of a-priori unknown length in a prefix-free manner, using essentially optimal overhead and memory.

1.1 Representing a Vector

The field of succinct data structures is preoccupied with representing data in close to optimal space, while still supporting useful queries. Representing a vector to support reads and writes to individual entries is perhaps the most foundational problem in the field, and thus has been a toy problem of particular interest.

The naïve way of supporting local access is to encode each element separately using $\lceil \log_2 \Sigma \rceil$ bits (cf. Hamming codes versus arithmetic codes). This has a redundancy of $\Omega(n)$ bits when Σ is not a power of two; for instance, it wastes around $0.68n$ bits for decimal digits, $\Sigma = \{0, 1, \dots, 9\}$.

Standard techniques in succinct data structure, dating back to [17], could achieve constant access time using $n \log_2 \Sigma + O(n/\log n)$ bits of space. More recently, Golynski et al. [12] proposed an encoding with $O(n/\log^2 n)$ redundancy and constant access time. Pătraşcu [21] showed how to use recursion in succinct encodings, and achieved query time $O(t)$ with a redundancy of $O(n/(\frac{\log n}{t})^t)$. Setting $t = O(1)$, we get redundancy $n/\log^{O(1)} n$ with constant query time.

For a growing body of problems, we have strong redundancy lower bounds of $\Omega(n/t)$ [13], $\Omega(n/t^2)$ [15], or $n/\log^{O(t)} n$ [22]. Combining this with the non-locality of known optimal encodings (e.g., arithmetic coding described

[1]When clear from context, we will abuse the notation and use Σ to denote both the alphabet set and its cardinality.

in Section 1.3), one may conjecture that any representation of a vector will require some nontrivial trade-off between the redundancy and query time.

In this paper, we show that this is not the case, and a surprising optimal result is possible:

THEOREM 1. *On a Word RAM, one can represent a vector $A[1..n]$ of elements from a finite alphabet Σ using $\lceil n \log_2 \Sigma \rceil$ bits, such that any element of the vector can be read or written in constant time. The data structure requires $O(\log n)$ precomputed word constants.*

From a conceptual perspective, the statement that a binary computer can represent data in any radix with no penalty has an inherent appeal.

From a theoretical perspective, our result forms a nice contrast with the lower bounds of [22]. An overwhelming majority of succinct data structures rely crucially on the so-called rank/select problem. But it is proved in [22] that the redundancy needs to be at least $n/\log^{O(t)} n$, essentially matching the upper bound [21]. Two scenarios are plausible: either (1) the use of rank/select is inherent, and we need stronger lower bound techniques that apply to a broader class of problems; or (2) one can surpass the rank/select barrier by alternative techniques.

In this paper, we illustrate scenario (2) for a natural, central question. One can hope that this opens the door to further improvements. For example, an important target is the dictionary problem (a.k.a. set membership) — perhaps the most important remaining open problem in this field — where the state-of-the-art remains [21].

FURTHER DISCUSSION. The model of computation throughout this paper is the Word RAM, which is meant to formalize what is possible in imperative programming languages. The memory allows random access, and is organized into words of w bits, where $w = \Omega(\log n)$ in order to allow indices and pointers. A standard set of unit-cost operations is specified (in this paper, we only require addition, multiplication, and division).

In the (unrealistic but mathematically cleaner) bit-probe model, Viola [25] has recently shown that, if the query is allowed t bit probes, the redundancy must be at least $n/2^{O(t)}$. Our new result provides a matching upper bound: simply simulate the actions of a RAM with t-bit words.

It is unclear whether the abstract vector-representation problem has direct applications in practice. Applications to compressed Bloom filters are suggested by [18]. In addition, extreme compression is of interest in current database applications. In many databases, columns have few common possibilities (as few as 3-5), so they can be compressed to an alphabet with these possibilities plus a letter indicating "other." After pruning many rows using indexes, database queries degenerate into linear scans over ranges, and such scans are often memory-bound. Thus, it is worth using a (slightly) more CPU intensive algorithm for tighter compression of the records. In this context, not wasting one bit for small fields might be valuable. We mention that algorithms that exploit packing small fields into bits *are* currently deployed in a large commercial database [24, 16]; in fact, this was the initial motivation behind our theoretical investigation.

1.2 Online Prefix-Free Encoding

Suppose one is to represent some n bits of information using a prefix-free code, where n is not fixed (i.e. it should be implicitly included in the code). In information theory, this task is known as *universal coding*, whereas in Computer Science, the term "prefix-free" is more often used (ambiguously). The term "self-delimiting code" is also in use.

The textbook solution to this problem is given by Elias codes. For example, to encode a vector of n bits using the Elias delta-code, one can write: (1) as many zeros as there are bits in $\log_2 n$, followed by a one; (2) the number n written in binary, using as many bits as indicated in part 1; (3) the n bits of data. This achieves $n + O(\log n)$ bits, for any n. Applying this idea recursively, one obtains the Elias omega-code, which represents n input bits using $n + \log_2 n + \log_2 \log_2 n + \cdots + O(\log^* n)$ output bits. This bound is optimal.

Prefix-free encodings are essential for communicating or storing any type of data, except fixed-size records. Less obviously, prefix-free encodings are often essential to ensure security of iterative constructions in cryptography, such as CBC-MAC [6] and cascade constructions [14, 4, 10, 20]. In particular, prefix-freeness gives the simplest provably-secure counter-measure to various forms of *extension attacks* on hash functions, message authentication codes and pseudorandom functions, as discussed in Appendix A.

In many natural applications, including those in cryptography, the message comes online, as a stream of bits, and the length of the stream is not known in advance. Elias codes are unusable in this setting. Instead, one wishes to design a simple code that can be encoded and decoded in one pass by algorithms maintaining small state (ideally, $O(\log n)$ bits), and using lower overhead (ideally, $O(1)$ time per input word).

In practice, one typically assumes that the input comes in large blocks, say, $b = 128$ bits; the last block may be padded if it is incomplete. Then, one can append one bit after each block, indicating whether we have reached the end of file. With $b = 128$, this code has an overhead of almost 1%, which is acceptable, but a fairly steep price to pay just for encoding the length of the stream. More problematically, many cryptographic standards include workarounds that eliminate the need for prefix-freeness, creating theoretical and practical burdens.

In theory, the naïve block-based solution gives a linear trade-off between redundancy and the space of the algorithm, by buffering b bits (e.g., one block) of input, and including an end-of-file marker before each block.

Maurer and Sjödin [20] conjectured that a linear redundancy might be necessary for small-space online prefix-free encoding. This would explain why cryptographic standards tend to use ad hoc solutions instead, since a proportional increase in the stream size is unacceptable. Fortunately, we disprove this conjecture, by constructing a simple prefix-free code with ideal space and running time.

As the first step, we point out the fallacy in the linear trade-off between space and redundancy: thinking in terms of integral bits. Let us imagine that the stream consists of n blocks of b bits each, and we are guaranteed that $n \le 2^b$. We can augment the alphabet of $[2^b]$ with an end-of-file symbol, EOF, making the stream prefix-free. If we can *efficiently* move from this alphabet of $2^b + 1$ to a binary alphabet (not wasting one bit per block), then the stream will take $(n+1)\log_2(2^b+1)$ bits. This means an overhead of $(n+1)\log_2(2^b+1) - n\cdot b = n\log_2(1+\frac{1}{2^b}) + b + O(\frac{1}{2^b}) = O(\frac{n}{2^b}) + b$. Since we were guaranteed $n \le 2^b$, the overhead is $b + O(1)$. To remove this assumption, we can use slowly growing blocks ("guessing" n up to a factor of two). This gives an overhead of $O(\log n)$.

In this paper, we give an efficient online algorithm that converts base 2^b+1 to base 2^b (or, equivalently, to binary), thus refuting the conjecture of [20]. In fact, we describe two solutions in Sections 2 and 5.

The first algorithm assumes $b \ge 2\log_2 n + 2$ and wastes at most two blocks. It benefits from extreme simplicity and very fast running time, so we expect it to be the method of choice in practical implementations. A slightly more complicated version of the algorithm achieves optimal encoding size ($n+1$ blocks) as long as $b \ge 2\log_2 n + 3$.

Our algorithm has excellent locality properties. During normal operation, the algorithm outputs a pair of blocks for each pair of blocks it reads. This takes constant processing time, and the memory maintained is $O(1)$ blocks. At the end of the file, the algorithm outputs the last $O(1)$ blocks of the encoding, which is now guaranteed to be prefix-free. The decoding algorithm has the same behavior. We can also decode or modify any block by reading/writing only $O(1)$ code blocks. In addition, we can append to the stream or delete blocks from the end in $O(1)$ time.

In Section 5, we consider the case of binary streams, and show how to match the optimal Elias bound up to $O(\log\log n)$:

THEOREM 2. *There exists a universal code mapping n bits to $n + \log_2 n + O(\log\log n)$ bits, which can be encoded and decoded by algorithms that use $O(\log n)$ bits of space and take $O(1)$ time per operation.*

APPLICATIONS TO CRYPTOGRAPHY. As we already mentioned, prefix-free encodings (PFEs) are also essential for proving security of many natural cryptographic constructions which need to process variable-length messages. We will give many popular examples in Appendix A, but start with explaining the general reason why PFEs are useful in this context. In all such constructions, one first designs a "secure" *compression function* $f : \{0,1\}^s \times \{0,1\}^b \to \{0,1\}^s$, where b is called the block-length, and s is called the buffer-length. (Depending on the application, such f could be keyed or unkeyed, as we survey in Appendix A.) Intuitively, though, f allows one to securely process short, b-bit messages: given an initial buffer $IV \in \{0,1\}^s$ (which could be a key or a fixed constant), the hash of $m \in \{0,1\}^b$ is simply $y = f(IV, m)$. Then, to process an arbitrarily long message M, one first splits M into b-bits blocks $m_1 \dots m_n$ (so $n \approx |M|/b$),[2] and then iteratively process M via the *cascade mode-of-operation*, parameterized by the compression function f and the *initialization vector* $IV \in \{0,1\}^s$ (see Figure 1):

CASCADE(M, f, IV):
  Split M into b-bit blocks $m_1 \dots m_n$, where
    $m_i \in \{0,1\}^b$ and $n = \lceil |M|/b \rceil$;

[2]We will assume that $|M|$ is a multiple of b. If not, one can always pad M with 1 followed by several (at most $(b-1)$) zeros to make the last block m_n full. Hence, w.l.o.g. we assume $M \in (\{0,1\}^b)^*$.

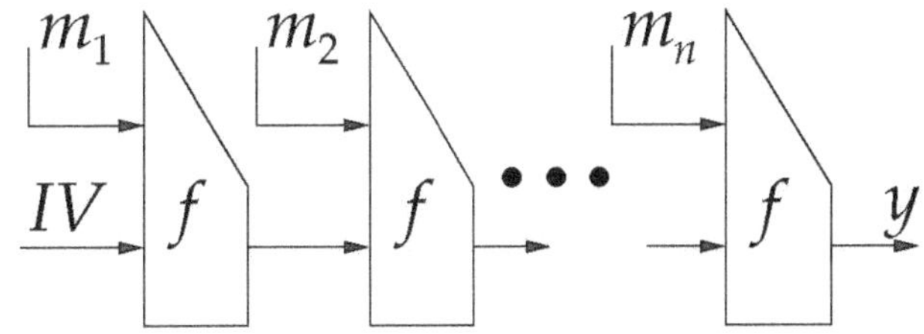

Figure 1: The Cascade Mode of Operation CASCADE(M, f, IV).

  Set $x_0 = IV$;
  For $i = 1$ to n
    Set $x_i = f(x_{i-1}, m_i)$;
  Output $y = x_n$;

Typically, one can prove the following result: if the compression function f is "secure" *and M is encoded in prefix-free form*, then CASCADE(M, f, IV) is "secure" (where IV is either a cryptographic key or a constant, depending on the application). Intuitively, one can imagine building 2^b-ary tree T, whose root is labeled by the IV, and each internal node $m_1 \dots m_n$ at "depth" n is labeled by CASCADE$(m_1 \dots m_n, f, IV)$. Typically, f is designed in a way that its ancestor-descendant node pairs might be related in a "meaningful way" (e.g., CASCADE$(MM', f, IV) =$ CASCADE$(M', f,$ CASCADE$(M, f, IV))$), while all other pairs of nodes are not related. Thus, if no two messages M_1 and M_2 are in the ancestor-descendant relationship, then the construction is secure. But this precisely corresponds to the fact that the messages are encoded in a prefix-free way.

Moreover, in all known examples (see Appendix A), one can actually break the security of the construction if the PFE constraint is not enforced. Such attacks are typically referred to as *extension attacks*. Of course, if efficient one-line PFEs were known, one can easily prevent extension attacks using an on-line PFE. Unfortunately, since prior to our work it was believed (and explicitly conjectured by [20]) that one-line PFE comes at a significant cost, extension attacks are typically handled using various ad-hoc methods, different for each specific application. Specific examples are discussed in Appendix A, and include CBC-MAC [6], cascade pseudorandom functions [4], Merkle-Damgård hash functions [10], domain extension of message authentication codes [20] and multi-property preservation [7, 8]. In each of these examples, applying the cascade transform to the *prefix-free encoding* of the message gives the simplest-to-understand domain extension for the given cryptographic application. Thus, one application of our results is that previously used ad hoc methods might not be necessary in these applications.

1.3 Comparison to Arithmetic Coding

From an information-theoretic view point, the standard approach to converting from one base to another is *arithmetic coding*. To encode n independently chosen symbols from some distribution $\mathcal{D}$, arithmetic codes use $n \cdot \mathrm{H}(\mathcal{D}) + O(1)$ bits in expectation, where $\mathrm{H}(\cdot)$ denotes binary entropy. In our case, $\mathcal{D}$ is the uniform distribution over an alphabet Σ, so $n\log_2\Sigma + O(1)$ bits are used. Unfortunately, a closer look at arithmetic coding reveals that it does not have the kind of worst-case locality properties that our applications require.

The basic idea in arithmetic coding is to map the space of possible inputs A to the interval $[0,1]$. To represent the first letter, $[0,1]$ is broken into $|\Sigma|$ intervals, and each letter $a \in \Sigma$ gets an interval of length $p_{\mathcal{D}}(a)$. The process continues recursively, subdividing the interval corresponding to $A[1]$ in order to represent $A[2]$, etc. After the (tiny) interval corresponding to A has been identified, one simply outputs the shortest binary number inside it.

The challenge is to implement this conceptual idea efficiently with bounded precision arithmetic. The ubiquitous implementation, due to Witten et al. [26, 19], can perform encoding and decoding of a stream in $O(1)$ time per bit, using $O(\log n)$ space.

It is instructive to briefly review this algorithm, as it highlights the inherently non-local nature of arithmetic codes. Imagine encoding a stream of symbols sequentially, and maintaining a subinterval of $[0,1]$ that represents the data so far. Whenever the interval is fully contained in $[0,\frac{1}{2}]$, a zero bit can be output, and we can re-normalize $[0,\frac{1}{2}] \mapsto [0,1]$ to gain precision. Similarly, once the interval is in $[\frac{1}{2},1]$, a one bit is output and we map $[\frac{1}{2},1] \mapsto [0,1]$. Alas, this is not enough to keep the required precision bounded, as the interval may become $[\frac{1}{2}-\varepsilon, \frac{1}{2}+\varepsilon]$ for exponentially small ε.

The trick of [26, 19] is to re-normalize $[\frac{1}{4},\frac{3}{4}] \mapsto [0,1]$ whenever the current interval is fully contained in $[\frac{1}{4},\frac{3}{4}]$. Since the next bit is not known, the algorithm simply increments a counter of "outstanding bits." When the interval finally gets below or above the middle point, a burst of zeros or ones is written.

This demonstrates that the encoding of one particular character may depend non-trivially on many surrounding characters. It is thus impossible, for worst-case data, to access a symbol in the middle of the vector without linear decoding time. For prefix-free encoding/decoding, arithmetic coding would lead to bursty behavior where many blocks may be written after one block is read.

1.4 Organization

In Section 2, we begin by describing a very simple algorithm for prefix-free encoding in the streaming model. This algorithm assumes that the input comes in blocks of $b \geq 2\log_2 n + 2$ bits, and outputs a code of at most $n+3$ blocks (or, $n+1$ blocks with a more complicated algorithm). While restrictive, this scenario is of interest in cryptography, where common message authentication schemes work with at least 128 bits at a time. The algorithm is very simple, and we expect it to be the practical choice for these application.

Using the intuition from this algorithm, we formulate a general concept (information carriers) in Section 3. Used appropriately, this construct implies an optimal data structure for representing a vector (Section 4), and an online prefix-free encoding of size $n + \log_2 n + O(\log\log n)$ (Section 5).

2. THE SOLE PREFIX-FREE ENCODING

For the simplest algorithm, assume that the input stream consists of blocks of $b \geq 2\log_2 n + 2$ bits, and that n is odd (we can pad with an additional EOF block otherwise). Under these conditions, our algorithm will output an encoding of $n+2$ blocks. For each block, the algorithm uses $O(1)$ arithmetic operations on b-bit integers.

Let $B = 2^b$ be the alphabet of a block, and we write $[B]$ to denote the range $\{0,\ldots,B-1\}$. Adding a special end-of-file symbol (EOF), we obtain an alphabet of size $B+1$. Our goal is to encode $n+1$ letters from this alphabet (including the final EOF) using $n+2$ blocks of b bits.

Block #	1	2	3	4	5	6	...
Input alp.	B	B	B	B	B	B	...
With EOF	$B+1$	$B+1$	$B+1$	$B+1$	$B+1$	$B+1$	...
Pass 1	B	$B+3$	$B-3$	$B+6$	$B-6$	$B+9$	...
Regroup	B	$B+3$	$B-3$	$B+6$	$B-6$	$B+9$	...
Pass 2	B	B	B	B	B	B	...

Figure 2: Short-Odd Long-Even (SOLE) Encoding.

The algorithm is best illustrated by Figure 2. Intuitively, it is simplest to view the algorithm as two separate passes through the stream.

In *Pass 1*, we consider pairs of elements on positions $(2i+1, 2i+2)$, for $i \geq 0$. Grouped together, the elements form a number in range $[(B+1)^2]$. We decompose this number into two values: one in range $[B-3i]$, and one in range $[B+3i+3]$. The smaller range is placed on odd positions, while the larger one on even positions, hence the name "Short-Odd Long-Even (SOLE)[3] Encoding."

The decomposition is simply a division by $B-3i$, using the remainder as the first block and the quotient as the next one. The transformation is valid as long as:

$$(B+1)^2 \leq (B-3i)(B+3i+3) \iff B \geq 1 + 9i(i+1)$$

which easily follows from the fact that $i \leq \frac{n+1}{2}$ and $B \geq 4n^2$.

In *Pass 2*, we regroup the elements, considering pairs on positions $(2i, 2i+1)$ for $i \geq 1$. These elements come from range $[B+3i]$ and $[B-3i]$, respectively. Since $(B+3i)(B-3i) < B^2$, we can group them together as a number in range $[B^2]$. This uses a multiplication by $B+3i$. Hence, we have obtained $2b$ bits (a "double-block"), which we output immediately.

It is clear that these two conceptual passes can be implemented as a single pass in an online streaming algorithm. We simply need to remember the state of each pass (at most two integers each). The decoding algorithm is the straightforward inversion of this process, implementing Figure 2 bottom-up. One can immediately observe the following locality property:

PROPERTY 3. *Output blocks $2i$ and $2i+1$ can be computed from input blocks $2i-1,\ldots,2i+2$. Input blocks $2i+1$ and $2i+2$ can be decoded from output blocks $2i,\ldots,2i+3$.*

TERMINATION. An important component of the algorithm that we have not described is the termination behavior, once EOF is received. We assumed that n was odd, i.e. EOF appears at some even position $n+1 = 2i$. The final element after Pass 1 is in range $[B+3i]$. We artificially insert a zero value in range $[B-3i]$ into the stream output by Pass 1. After regrouping and Pass 2, this completes a double-block at positions $2i$ and $2i+1$, which is output.

When the decoding algorithm has decoded the EOF symbol, it stops immediately. Thus, we need to argue that the decoding stops before reading past the end of the encoded file. This follows from Property 3, as the last block needed in the decoding of EOF is $2i+1$.

[3] Coincidentally, one meaning of the word "sole" is "exclusive, not shared with others".

ADDITIONAL PROPERTIES. Based on Property 3, one can support random access to the encoding in constant time. Decoding a block in the middle of the file requires reading 4 output blocks. Modifying an input block will read and change 4 consecutive output blocks. For instance, to modify block 3 in Figure 2, we first read output blocks 2, ..., 5. From these, we compute the input block 4, and blocks 2 and 5 output by Pass 1. From the new value of block 3 and the old block 4, we can rerun Pass 1 to update the intermediate blocks 3 and 4. We now know the intermediate blocks 2,..., 5, so the output blocks can be computed by running Pass 2. Appending to the file and truncating can be reduced to write operations.

A TIGHTER ENCODING. The previous algorithm wasted up to 3 blocks (when n is even). If $n \geq 2$ and $b \geq 2\log_2 n + 3$, we can instead obtain an optimal encoding that always uses $n+1$ output blocks. The first idea is to conceptually insert the EOF symbol two blocks before the actual termination of the input stream. This can be done by buffering the last two blocks, and ensures that EOF will be followed by two output blocks. Hence, by Property 3, the usual decoding algorithm will certainly observe the EOF without reading past the end of the encoding. At this point, we switch to a special termination procedure for the last two blocks.

Imagine that, after EOF appearing on position $n-1$, and the last two blocks on positions n and $n+1$, an infinite stream of zeros follows in the input stream. Then, it is not hard to see that block $n+2$ of the usual encoding will be 0 or 1 (henceforth "the final bit"), and the remaining blocks are guaranteed to be zero. In the new algorithm, we will output the usual output values of blocks up to $n+1$.

Instead of wasting block $n+2$ for the final bit, we will use the following hack: we will have two end-of-file symbols, EOF_0 and EOF_1, coding this bit. We note that there is no circular dependence, since block $n+2$ (the final bit) does not depend on block $n-1$ (the EOF) by Property 3. The price we pay is increasing the alphabet to $B+2$, instead of $B+1$. Now ranges of the form $[B \pm 3i]$ become $[B \pm 5i]$. The encoding is possible as long as:

$$(B+2)^2 \leq (B-5i)(B+5i+5) \iff B \geq 25i(i+1)+4$$

Since $i \leq \frac{n+1}{2}$, this requires $b \geq 2\log_2 n + 3$.

This scheme is further improved in Section 5, which also uses multiple EOF symbols, and moves EOF ahead of the file termination.

PRACTICAL CONSIDERATIONS. To ensure fast arithmetic operations, one would set $b = 32$ or $b = 64$. While the algorithm uses arithmetic on double precision ($2b$ bits), it is standard to implement division and multiplication by $2^b \pm x$ using fast, single-precision operations.

For a given b, our basic algorithm can process a stream of up to $n_0 = 2^{b/2-1}$ blocks. For $n > n_0$ blocks, we can trivially obtain an encoding with overhead $\frac{n}{n_0} + O(1)$ blocks, by applying SOLE on each chunk of n_0 blocks. Specifically, one block is wasted for each chunk except the last one, where 3 blocks may be wasted.

With a minimal setting of $b = 32$ bits, our encoding adds a block (4 bytes) per each $2^{15} = 32,768$ blocks (128Kb), making our overhead roughly $2^{-15} \approx 0.003\%$. For comparison, the naïve encoding will waste 1 bit per block, which is $\frac{1}{32} = 3.125\%$, a factor of 1024 worse than our encoding. E.g., a 32Gb file will have a negligible 1Mb overhead with our encoding, and 1Gb overhead with the naïve encoding.

Block #	1	2	3	4	5	6	...
Input alp.	B	B	B	B	B	B	...
With EOF	$B+1$	$B+1$	$B+1$	$B+1$	$B+1$	$B+1$	...
Pass 1	$B+1$	$B-1$	$B+4$	$B-4$	$B+7$	$B-7$	...
Regroup	$B+1$	$B-1$	$B+4$	$B-4$	$B+7$	$B-7$	...
Pass 2	B	B	B	B	B	B	...

Figure 3: Long-Odd Short-Even (LOSE) Encoding.

LOSE ENCODINGS. An alternative scheme with almost identical properties is the Long-Odd Short-Even (LOSE) encoding; see Figure 3.

3. INFORMATION CARRIERS

Let us re-examine the behavior of SOLE encodings for intuition. After seeing $2n$ blocks, the algorithm has written $2n-1$ blocks to the output, and is left with a number in range $[B+3n]$. In keeping with the terminology of [21], we shall call this number a *spill*.

The algorithm proceeds by grabbing two more blocks, i.e. a number in $[(B+1)^2]$. Its first worry is to *complete* the spill with some information, to obtain two full blocks of output. That means that the spill must be combined with a value in range $\lfloor \frac{B^2}{B+3n} \rfloor \approx B - 3n$.

To identify some useful information in range $[B-3n]$, the algorithm takes the new number in $[(B+1)^2]$ modulo $B-3n$. The result is combined with the spill and immediately output. Remaining now is the quotient of the division, a number in range $\frac{(B+1)^2}{B-3n} \approx B+3n+3$. This is the new spill.

More abstractly, imagine the current spill as a value y in some range $[Y]$. We would like to store y immediately, but, unfortunately, the range $[Y]$ is not a power of two, so we cannot simply write y to memory without losing entropy. Instead, we use some unrelated x in some appropriately bigger range $[X]$ as an "information carrier." The purpose of x is to help commit y to memory without much waste. The pair (x, y) is injectively mapped into the immediate output m and the next spill s, such that:

- m comes from some range $[2^M]$, meaning that it can be written to memory *in bits*, without losing entropy;
- m stores enough information to recover the old spill y we care about, meaning that y can be immediately recovered from memory.
- the entropy loss of going from (x, y) to (m, s) can be made arbitrarily small, by making the range $[X]$ of the information carrier appropriately large.

For instance, in the SOLE encoding, we had $Y = B+3n$. By making $X = (B+1)^2$, we could store the spill y in $M = 2b$ bits of memory, and the new spill s had only a marginally larger range $[S] = [B+3n+3]$. This means that the entropy loss of this operation was at most $\log_2(B+3n+3) - \log_2(B+3n) = O(1/B)$ bits.

The discussion above motivates us to formulate the following general lemma, where we optimized the parameters M and S to minimize the entropy loss:

LEMMA 4. *Let $X, Y \leq 2^w$. Then, for some values M and S, we can injectively map $(x, y) \in [X] \times [Y]$ to $(m, s) \in [2^M] \times [S]$, with the following properties:*

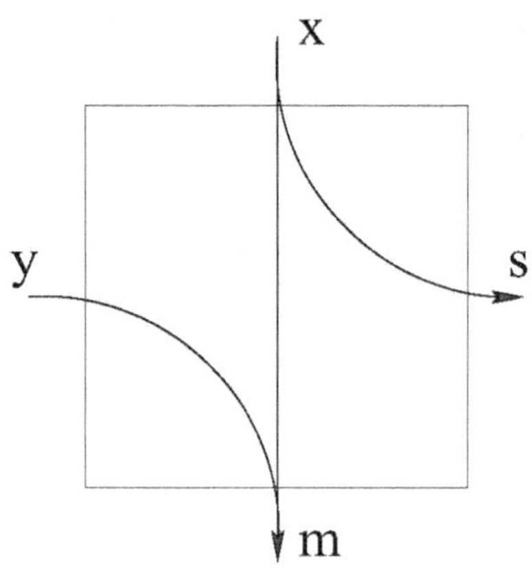

Figure 4: Lemma 4 implements the box depicted.

- *S and M are chosen as functions of X and Y, but satisfy $S = O(\sqrt{X})$ and $2^M = O(Y\sqrt{X})$;*
- *the map can be evaluated in $O(1)$ time;*
- *x can be decoded from m and s, in $O(1)$ time;*
- *y can be decoded from m alone, in $O(1)$ time;*
- *the redundancy of this encoding scheme is:*

$$(M + \log_2 S) - (\log_2 X + \log_2 Y) \;=\; O\left(\tfrac{1}{\sqrt{X}}\right).$$

The lemma could be graphically depicted by Figure 4. The current spill value y is combined with the information carrier x, producing the memory content m (from which one can recover y) and the new spill value s.

PROOF. Say we will use M memory bits. The entire information about y must be in these M bits. In addition to y, the bits can store a quantity from the universe $C = \lfloor 2^M/Y \rfloor$. The redundancy in doing this rounding is at most:

$$\begin{aligned} R_1 &= M - \log_2\left(Y \cdot \left\lfloor \frac{2^M}{Y} \right\rfloor\right) \;\le\; M - \log_2\left(2^M - Y\right) \\ &= \log_2\left(\frac{1}{1 - Y/2^M}\right) \;=\; O\left(\frac{Y}{2^M}\right) = O\left(\frac{1}{C}\right). \end{aligned}$$

Now x is broken into two components: a value in the universe $[C]$, to be combined with y, and a spill of size $S = \lceil X/C \rceil$. This decomposition introduces a redundancy of:

$$\begin{aligned} R_2 &= \left(\log_2 C + \log_2 \left\lceil \frac{X}{C} \right\rceil\right) - \log_2 X \\ &\le \log_2\left(\frac{X + C}{X}\right) \;\le\; O\left(\frac{C}{X}\right). \end{aligned}$$

Balancing the two redundancies, $R_1 = R_2$, we find that we should set $C = \Theta(\sqrt{X})$ and obtain $R_1 = R_2 = O(\frac{1}{\sqrt{X}})$. The overall redundancy is, by the chain rule:

$$\begin{aligned} &(M + \log_2 S) - (\log_2 X + \log_2 Y) \\ &\quad = (M - \log_2 Y - \log_2 C) + (\log_2 C + \log_2 S - \log_2 X) \\ &\quad = R_1 + R_2. \end{aligned}$$

Mapping (x, y) to (m, s) takes one division and one multiplication. (We assume here that X and Y are fixed, so constant like C are precomputed.) Extracting y from m takes one division, and extracting x from (m, s) takes one division and one multiplication. In practice, it is standard to replace any integer division by a constant with two multiplications (precomputing the multiplicative inverse to w bits of precision). ∎

4. REPRESENTING A VECTOR

4.1 A First Attempt

We now turn to the problem of representing a vector $A[1\,..\,n]$ of elements from Σ, supporting local access. A direct approach is to simply iterate Lemma 4. Formally, we group elements of A into blocks of size $O(\log_\Sigma n)$, so that each block can be interpreted as an element x in range $[X]$, where $X = \Theta(n^2)$. This gives us $N = O(n/\log_\Sigma n)$ larger elements $x_1, \ldots, x_N$ from a universe of size $\Theta(n^2)$. Initially, we start with a null spill, $Y_0 = 0$. Applying the lemma, we obtain some memory bits M_0 (which we write to memory), and some spill Y_1. Then, we store the spill from Y_1 by using x_2 as the information carrier, and obtain a spill Y_2, etc. Observe that, while the spill size Y_i may depend non-trivially on Y_{i-1}, our lemma guarantees that $Y_i = O(\sqrt{X})$, i.e. the spill universe doesn't grow without bounds.

The redundancy introduced in each step is $O(1/\sqrt{X}) = O(1/n)$. Thus, the overall redundancy is $O(\frac{N}{n}) = o(1)$, plus one bit at the end, when we simply write down the last spill. To prove this formally, note that our definition of redundancy admits a chain rule:

$$\begin{aligned} &\left(\lceil \log_2 Y_n \rceil + \sum_i M_i\right) - n \log_2 \Sigma \\ &\le 1 + \sum_i (M_i + \log_2 Y_i - \log_2 Y_{i-1}) - N \log_2 X \\ &= 1 + \sum_i (M_i + \log_2 Y_i - \log_2 Y_{i-1} - \log_2 X) \\ &\le 1 + N \cdot O\left(\tfrac{1}{\sqrt{X}}\right) \end{aligned}$$

To read an element $A[i]$, we first calculate to which x_j it belongs. Then, we recover the spill y_j from the memory written in step $j+1$. Finally, we recover x_j from the spill y_j and the memory written in step j. Updating an x_j can be done by recomputing the actions of steps j and $j+1$. Spill y_j may change in the process, but this only affect the memory written in step $j+1$, and does not propagate to y_{j+1}.

Unfortunately, this approach requires $N = O(n/\log n)$ precomputed constants. Indeed, each Y_j is distinct, and even the number of bits written to memory in each step varies. This was not a problem in the SOLE encoding, as $X = 2^b + 1$, so the Y_j values could be approximated by an arithmetic progression. Here, X can be far from a power of two, and the behavior of the Y_j's can be rather irregular inside a universe of $O(n)$.

4.2 A Tree Representation

To reduce the number of precomputed constants to $O(\log n)$, we will use a tree structure. As before, we group elements into N values from universe $X = \Theta(n^2)$. Group these values into a binary tree, as in the standard representation of a heap. This is an implicit representation, i.e. we simply *define* $2i$ and $2i+1$ as the children of node i, and $\lfloor i/2 \rfloor$ as the parent of node i.

Each node will receive two spills, one from each child. It will combine these into a single value y_i, and use its own value $x_i \in [X]$ as the information carrier to store y_i. The resulting new spill is propagated to the parent. Note that, even though spills are propagated up, there is no recursion happening at query time. To obtain a value stored in a node v, we go to v's parent and obtain v's spill from the parent's memory bits. Then, we compute v's value from the spill and its own memory bits. To update some x_i, we simply reconstruct the encoding of node i and its parent.

The advantage of the arboral representation is that all nodes on a level are handled using $O(1)$ precomputed constants. We have three types of nodes on level $\lceil \log_2 n \rceil - k$:

- A prefix of the nodes have subtrees that are complete binary trees of height k.
- Following this, at most one node has a subtree that is not complete.
- The remaining nodes have subtrees that are complete binary trees of height $k-1$.

The nodes in each of these three classes, from a given level, have identical constants generated by Lemma 4, since the spills from the children are identical by induction. Therefore, for each class of nodes on each level, we need to remember the following information:

- the number of nodes in this class;
- the location of the memory bits from the first node in the class;
- the spill sizes received from the two children;
- the constants of Lemma 4.

The level of node i is $\lfloor \log_2 i \rfloor$. We note that this can be computed by $O(1)$ Word RAM operations, as shown in [11]. Once the level is known, we can determine in constant time the class of the node, and retrieve the constants and memory locations necessary for decoding.

THE LAST BIT. By the construction from above, the total redundancy introduced by the applications of Lemma 4 is $o(1)$ bits. Up to one bit of redundancy is then lost by rounding when the final spill is stored. Thus, we use $\lceil n \log_2 \Sigma + o(1) \rceil$, which could be equal to $\lceil n \log_2 \Sigma \rceil + 1$.

As a theoretical amusement, we mention that the space can be reduced to the optimal $\lceil n \log_2 \Sigma \rceil + 1$. The idea is that the $o(1)$ term can be made $O(n^{-c})$, for any constant c, if one increases X and uses arithmetic on $O(c \log n)$-bit integers. But results on linear forms in logarithms show [2] that $n \log_2 \Sigma$ is bounded away from an integer by $1/n^{O(1)}$, for any constant Σ. Thus, setting c high enough will ensure that $n \log_2 \Sigma + O(1/n^c) \leq \lceil n \log_2 \Sigma \rceil$. (For instance, when $\Sigma = \{0, 1, 2\}$, it suffices to set $c = 1,179,648$.)

5. PREFIX-FREE CODES VIA INFORMATION CARRIERS

In this section, we show how to obtain online prefix-free codes of size $n + \log_2 n + O(\log \log n)$, getting exponentially closer to the Elias bound of $n + \log_2 n + \log_2 \log_2 n + \dots$

We view the input as partitioned into blocks of slowly growing size: after n bits have been seen, the next block (block i) consists of the subsequent $2k_i = 2\lceil \log_2 n \rceil$ bits. Let N be the number of blocks. As the N-th block may contain anywhere between 1 and $2\lceil \log_2 n \rceil$ bits, we treat it specially. We will encode the first $N-1$ blocks in a prefix-free way, and then append an Elias encoding for the last block. This Elias code brings an overhead of $O(\log k_N) = O(\log \log n)$ bits.

We view a block as coming from the alphabet $[2^{k_i}]^2$. The reason for blocks of around $2 \log_2 n$ bits is the information carrier lemma: when working with a domain of X, we obtain a redundancy of $O(1/\sqrt{X})$. Thus, a block universe of $O(n^2)$ is needed to control the redundancy introduced in each block.

Unfortunately, we cannot afford one block for the EOF symbol, since this would cost some $2 \log_2 n$ bits. Instead, in Pass 1 we convert each block of $[2^{k_i}]^2$ to a block of $[2^{k_i}] \times \left([2^{k_i}] \cup \{\text{EOF}\}\right)$. More precisely, we use a buffer of $O(\log n)$ bits to introduce a 3-block lag, effectively learning about the end of file 3 blocks in advance. If block $N-2$ has value $(a,b) \in [2^{k_{N-2}}]^2$, we replace it by (a, EOF), and append b at the very end of the stream (in plaintext). This transformation costs $k_{N-2} \leq \log_2 n$ bits for the EOF symbol. In addition, we pay $\log_2 \left(2^{k_i}(2^{k_i}+1)\right) - \log_2 \left(2^{2k_i}\right) = O(2^{-k_i})$ for enlarging the alphabet of block i. To understand $\sum_i 2^{-k_i}$, note that there are $O(2^K/K)$ blocks with a fixed value $k_i = K$, so the total cost from fixed K is $O(1/K)$. Summing for K from 1 to $\log_2 n$, we obtain $O(\log \log n)$ bits of redundancy.

In Pass 2, we convert each block from alphabet $[2^{k_i}] \times \left([2^{k_i}] \cup \{\text{EOF}\}\right)$ to binary. This proceeds like in Section 4.1, by applying Lemma 4 sequentially to all blocks, and feeding one spill into the next application. The redundancy introduced at step i is $O(2^{-k_i})$, since the domain is $X = O(2^{2k_i})$. As shown above, $\sum_i 2^{-k_i} = O(\log \log n)$. For the decoding, observe that EOF was encoded in block $N-2$, so it will be detected after output block $N-1$ is read (which allows one to decode the spill of input block $N-2$, and thus the entire $N-2$ block). The decoder can thus stop in time at block $N-1$, and run the special decoding for block N, and the second half of block $N-2$ displaced by EOF.

Overall, the overhead was $\log_2 n + O(\log \log n)$, and the running time per block was constant.

6. REFERENCES

[1] Jee Hea An, Mihir Bellare, *Constructing VIL-MACs from FIL-MACs: Message Authentication under Weakened Assumptions*, CRYPTO 1999, pages 252-269.

[2] Alan Baker and Gisbert Wüstholz. Logarithmic forms and group varieties. *Journal für die reine und angewandte Mathematik*, 442:19–62, 1992.

[3] Mihir Bellare, *New Proofs for NMAC and HMAC: Security without Collision-Resistance*, Advances in Cryptology - Crypto 2006 Proceedings, Springer-Verlag, 2006.

[4] Mihir Bellare, Ran Canetti, and Hugo Krawczyk, *Pseudorandom Functions Re-visited: The Cascade Construction and Its Concrete Security*, In Proc. 37th FOCS, pages 514-523. IEEE, 1996.

[5] Mihir Bellare, Ran Canetti, Hugo Krawczyk: *Keying Hash Functions for Message Authentication.* CRYPTO 1996: pp. 1–15.

[6] Mihir Bellare, Joe Kilian, and Phillip Rogaway. The Security of Cipher Block Chaining. In *Crypto '94*, pages 341–358, 1994. LNCS No. 839.

[7] Mihir Bellare and Thomas Ristenpart, *Multi-Property-Preserving Hash Domain Extension and the EMD Transform*, In Advances in Cryptology - Asiacrypt 2006, pp. 299-314.

[8] Mihir Bellare and Thomas Ristenpart, *Hash Functions in the Dedicated-Key Setting: Design Choices and MPP Transforms*, ICALP 2007, pp. 399-410.

[9] Mihir Bellare and Phillip Rogaway. Random Oracles are Practical: A Paradigm for Designing Efficient Protocols. In *Proceedings ACM Conference on Computer and Communications Security* (1993), 62-73.

[10] Jean-Sebastian Coron, Yevgeniy Dodis, Cecile Malinaud and Prashant Puniya, *Merkle-Damgård Revisited: How to Construct a Hash Function*, Advances in Cryptology, Crypto 2005 Proceedings: 430-448, Springer-Verlag, 2006.

[11] Michael L. Fredman and Dan E. Willard. Surpassing the information theoretic bound with fusion trees. *Journal of Computer and System Sciences*, 47(3):424–436, 1993. See also STOC'90.

[12] Alexander Golynski, Roberto Grossi, Ankur Gupta, Rajeev Raman, and S. Srinivasa Rao. On the size of succinct indices. In *Proc. 15th European Symposium on Algorithms (ESA)*, pages 371–382, 2007.

[13] Anna Gál and Peter Bro Miltersen. The cell probe complexity of succinct data structures. In *Proc. 30th International Colloquium on Automata, Languages and Programming (ICALP)*, pages 332–344, 2003.

[14] Oded Goldreich, Shafi Goldwasser, and Silvio Micali. How to construct random functions. *Journal of the ACM*, 33(4):792–807, October 1986.

[15] Alexander Golynski. Cell probe lower bounds for succinct data structures. In *Proc. 20th ACM/SIAM Symposium on Discrete Algorithms (SODA)*, pages 625–634, 2009.

[16] Allison L. Holloway, Vijayshankar Raman, Garret Swart, and David J. DeWitt. How to barter bits for chronons: compression and bandwidth trade offs for database scans. In *Proc. ACM SIGMOD International Conference on Management of Data*, pages 389–400, 2007.

[17] Guy Jacobson. Space-efficient static trees and graphs. In *Proc. 30th IEEE Symposium on Foundations of Computer Science (FOCS)*, pages 549–554, 1989.

[18] Michael Mitzenmacher. Compressed Bloom filters. *IEEE/ACM Transactions on Networking*, 10(5):604–612, 2002. See also PODC'01.

[19] Alistair Moffat, Radford M. Neal, and Ian H. Witten. Arithmetic coding revisited. *ACM Transactions on Information Systems (TOIS)*, 16(3):256–294, 1998. See also DCC'95.

[20] Ueli M. Maurer and Johan Sjödin. Single-key AIL-MACs from any FIL-MAC. In *Proc. 32nd International Colloquium on Automata, Languages and Programming (ICALP)*, pages 472–484, 2005.

[21] Mihai Pătraşcu. Succincter. In *Proc. 49th IEEE Symposium on Foundations of Computer Science (FOCS)*, pages 305–313, 2008.

[22] Mihai Pătraşcu and Emanuele Viola. Cell-probe lower bounds for succinct partial sums. In *Proc. 21st ACM/SIAM Symposium on Discrete Algorithms (SODA)*, 2010.

[23] Erez Petrank, Charles Rackoff, *CBC MAC for Real-Time Data Sources*, J. Cryptology 13(3): 315-338 (2000).

[24] Vijayshankar Raman and Garret Swart. How to wring a table dry: Entropy compression of relations and querying of compressed relations. In *Proc. 32nd International Conference on Very Large Data Bases (VLDB)*, pages 858–869, 2006.

[25] Emanuele Viola. Bit-probe lower bounds for succinct data structures. In *Proc. 41st ACM Symposium on Theory of Computing (STOC)*, pages 475–482, 2009.

[26] Ian H. Witten, Radford M. Neal, and John G. Cleary. Arithmetic coding for data compression. *Communications of the ACM*, 30(6):520–540, 1987.

APPENDIX

A. APPLICATIONS TO CRYPTOGRAPHY

We now discuss several applications of prefix-free encodings (PFEs) in cryptography. As discussed in the the Introduction, all these applications could be viewed as processing the given n-block message $M = (m_1, \ldots, m_n)$ by the *cascade mode of operation*, parameterized by the appropriate *compression function* $f : \{0,1\}^s \times \{0,1\}^b \to \{0,1\}^s$ and the *initialization vector* $IV \in \{0,1\}^s$. (Depending on the application, such f could be keyed or unkeyed, and the IV could be a key or a constant.) For completeness, we repeat this definition of the cascade mode below (see also Figure 1):

```
CASCADE(M, f, IV):
    Split M into b-bit blocks m_1 ... m_n, where
        m_i ∈ {0,1}^b and n = ⌈|M|/b⌉;
    Set x_0 = IV;
    For i = 1 to n
        Set x_i = f(x_{i-1}, m_i);
    Output y = x_n;
```

CBC-MAC. The CBC-MAC is a very popular way to build a message authentication code (MAC) from a block cipher. Such block-cipher g can be viewed as a keyed permutation $g_k(m)$, where $|m| = b$, k is the secret key and m is the message. The CBC-MAC of M is defined by $\textsc{Cascade}(M, f_k, 0^b)$, where the compression function $f_k(x,m) = g_k(x \oplus m)$ is keyed and the buffer-length $s = b$. Namely,

$$\text{CBC-MAC}(k, M) = g_k(m_n \oplus g_k(\ldots \oplus g_k(m_2 \oplus g_k(m_1))\ldots))$$

It is well known that CBC-MAC is secure if the encoding M is prefix-free [6]. In contrast, CBC-MAC is easy to break otherwise. For example, if $y = \text{CBC-MAC}(k, m_1) = g_k(m_1)$, then setting $m_2 = m_1 \oplus y$, we get $\text{CBC-MAC}(k, m_1 m_2) = g_k(m_2 \oplus y) = g_k(m_1) = y$, meaning that it is easy to forge the MAC of (m_1, m_2) after learning the MAC of m_1.

The practical fix for the above problem (see [23]) is to use "encrypted CBC-MAC": namely, have a fresh key k' in addition to k, and output $g_{k'}(\text{CBC-MAC}(k, M))$. Although this fix is quite simple, it doubles the size of the secret key, which could be undesirable for some applications. On the other hand, our method makes at most one more calls to the block cipher (due to adding two more blocks in our encoding), and also adds a little bit of complexity due to encoding and decoding procedure (which are simple, but nevertheless need to be done).

CASCADE PRF. Another natural application of the cascade mode is to extend the domain of a pseudorandom function (PRF). Specifically, assume g_k is a keyed PRF from b bits to s bits, where s is simultaneously the size of the key k and the output length of $g_k(m)$. Define the compression function $f(x, m) = g_x(m)$, and set the initial $IV = k$. Then the classical cascade construction is defined as $F_k(M) = \text{CASCADE}(M, f, k)$. Namely, the cascade state x_i keeps the current PRF key (initially equal to the actual key k), with each iteration using the next message block m_i to set the new key x_i to the the PRF of the message block m_i under the old key x_{i-1}. We also remark that the classical GGM [14] construction of a PRF F_k from a length-doubling pseudorandom generator (PRG) $G : \{0,1\}^s \to \{0,1\}^{2s}$ is also a special case of the cascade construction with $b = 1$. Indeed, the PRG $G(k) = (G_0(k), G_1(k))$ above, where $|G_m(k)| = s$ and $m \in \{0,1\}$, yields a 1-bit PRF $g_k(m) = G_m(k)$.

It is well known [14, 4] that the cascade construction is a secure PRF of variable-length messages if and only if the messages are encoded in a prefix-free form. Intuitively, as long as any two message "diverge" at some point, the resulting key values become random and unrelated. In contrast, the extension attack is particularly simple and devastating. If $M_2 = M_1 M'$, then $F_k(M_2) = F_{F_k(M_1)}(M')$, so one can easily compute the PRF of any "descendant" (M_1, M_2) from the PRF of the "ancestor" M_1, breaking the pseudorandomness of F_k.

The clean fix is to use the NMAC variant [5, 3], where a fresh key k' is stored in addition to k, and one defines $\text{NMAC}_{k,k'}(M) = g_{k'}(G_k(M))$. Once again, although simple, this doubles the key size of our PRF. Hence, in practice an hoc variant of NMAC is used, called HMAC [5, 3]. HMAC uses a single key $\tilde{k}$, and essentially calls NMAC with $k = g_c(\tilde{k} + ipad)$ and $k' = g_c(\tilde{k} + opad)$, where $c, ipad, opad$ are specific constants hardwired into the design of HMAC. This regains the short key size, but now the security analysis requires an ad hoc assumption about our initial PRF g, beyond the fact that it is a PRF. In contrast, using a PFE, one naturally regains a singe key k, has the same number of calls to g_k, but adds a little bit of complexity due to on-line encoding/decoding, which is not needed in HMAC.

MERKLE-DAMGÅRD HASH FUNCTIONS. The cascade mode of operation is the main technique for building cryptographic hash functions. Such a hash function H should take an arbitrary long message $M = (m_1, \ldots, m_n)$, and produce a short, s-bit hash value $H(M)$. The minimal requirement for such hash functions is collision-resistance: it should be hard to find $M_1 \neq M_2$ such that $H(M_1) = H(M_2)$. However, in many applications even stronger properties are needed from H: intuitively, a new value $H(M)$ should look random and independent from all previous values $H(M')$ for $M' \neq M$. This is formalized by modeling H as a *random oracle* [9]. Of course, in practice one uses concrete hash function H. In fact, practical hash functions, including the current standard SHA and the vast majority of other popular hash functions, precisely use the cascade mode of operations, applied to an appropriate compression function f.[4]

Specifically, $H(M)$ is precisely $\text{CASCADE}(M, f, IV)$, where f is a publicly known unkeyed hash function from $(s + b)$ to s bits, and IV is a fixed constant. As observed by many papers, and formally addressed by Coron et al. [10], such design of H makes it very different from a "monolithic" random oracle, even if the compression function f is modeled as a fixed-length random oracle. In particular, the extension attack here is as follows: given $y = H(M)$ for any *unknown* value M, one can easily compute the value $y' = H(M, M') = \text{CASCADE}(M', f, y)$, for any suffix M'. Clearly, this should not be possible if H was a true random oracle.[5]

Coron et al. [10] formally defined what it means to securely extend the domain of a random oracle, and gave four simple ways to *provably* circumvent extension (and all other generic) attacks. The cleanest solution is to simply encode the message in a PFE! However, prior to our work it was considered too wasteful. The second solution is to truncate a non-trivial fraction of the output bits. Unfortunately, this method suffers from relatively poor exact security (and, of course, gives shorter output). The third solution is similar in spirit to the NMAC PRF solution above, and requires an independent compression function f'. which is then applied to $\text{CASCADE}(M, f, IV)$. Unfortunately, it is not practically convenient to design two different compression functions f and f'.[6] Finally, the last method is similar to the HMAC PRF method above, and could be viewed as an ad hoc trick to avoid having two independent compression functions: it outputs $\text{CASCADE}(\text{CASCADE}(0^b M, f, IV), f, IV)$. Until our work, this was considered the method of choice, since only one compression function is used, the message can be processed on-line, and only two extra calls to f are made are made. With our on-line PFE, however, we end up making the same number of calls to f, but, arguably, obtain a result which is simpler to understand and explain (in terms of security).

DOMAIN EXTENSION OF MACS. Another natural usage of the cascade mode is to extend the domain of a message authentication code (MAC) $f_k : \{0,1\}^{b+s} \to \{0,1\}^s$. This is different from the CBC-MAC and the cascade-PRF applications above because the building block here is only assumed to be unpredictable, as opposed to pseudorandom (indeed, it is easy to see that the CBC-MAC and the cascade constructions are *not* always secure if the block cipher or the

[4]Actually, one uses the so called *strengthened Merkle-Damgård Transform*, where the length of the message is appended as the last message block. However, this detail does not affect our discussion below, so we stick with "plain Merkle-Damgård", which is precisely the cascade mode.

[5]While this attack might appear theoretical, consider a simple PRF construction $F_k(M) = H(k, M)$. It is clearly secure if H is a random oracle, but completely insecure (due to the extension attack above) when H is implemented by the cascade mode.

[6]Ironically, one way to design two independent compression functions f_0 and f_1 from a single compression function f is to prepend 0 when calling f_0, and 1 — when calling f_1. However, this is *equivalent* to the classical "wasteful" PFE, where each but last block is prepended with 0, and the last block is prepended with 1. Clearly, our PFE will result in a much less wasteful solution.

b-bit PRF are only assumed unpredictable [1]). Still, we can still define Cascade-MAC$(k, M) = $ CASCADE$(M, f_k, 0^s)$, where our compression function f_k is keyed by the same key k throughout (so called dedicated-key setting [8]).

It was observed by Maurer and Sjödin [20] that the Cascade-MAC is secure if M is encoded in a prefix-free form. (The extension attack here is a bit more complicated; we refer to [8].) On the other hand, without using on-line PFE (which was conjectured to be too wasteful by Maurer and Sjödin), several techniques to overcome this problem are known. The simplest one is to use, once again, an additional key k', and apply $f_{k'}$ to the output of the Cascade-MAC(k, M) (see [20], which slightly optimizes the earlier suggestion of [1]). Without having two keys, several ad hoc solutions were developed by [20, 8]. While offering comparable efficiency to using the basic cascade construction with our PFE, these solutions are arguably less intuitive than the basic cascade construction.

We also notice that the dedicated key setting can be used for the domain extension of PRFs as well, when f_k is a assumed a PRF rather than a MAC (but one gets a PRF back as well). The discussion here is similar to the MAC case.

MULTI-PROPERTY PRESERVATION. As we have seen, in all the applications that we mentioned, applying the PFE followed by the cascade construction works. Thus, the PFE followed by the cascade construction can be seen as a *multi-property preserving* transform (MPPT). As advocated by Bellare and Ristenpart [7, 8], devising MPPTs is advantageous in terms of reusing the existing implementations of hash functions, by designing compression functions which simultaneously satisfy several desired properties. However, since online PFEs were considered impractical, Bellare and Ristenpart [7, 8] had to work relatively hard to design their MPPTs. Arguably, the "PFE-then-Cascade" is a much simpler MPPT to understand and explain than the MPPTs developed by [7, 8]. Given that our work gives a very efficient PFE, our MPPT also offers roughly the same efficiency than the MPPTs of [7, 8], so it could be an attractive alternative to those MPPTs.

Towards Polynomial Lower Bounds for Dynamic Problems

Mihai Pătraşcu
AT&T Labs

ABSTRACT

We consider a number of dynamic problems with no known poly-logarithmic upper bounds, and show that they *require* $n^{\Omega(1)}$ time per operation, unless 3SUM has strongly subquadratic algorithms. Our result is modular:

1. We describe a carefully-chosen dynamic version of set disjointness (the *multiphase problem*), and conjecture that it requires $n^{\Omega(1)}$ time per operation. All our lower bounds follow by easy reduction.

2. We reduce 3SUM to the multiphase problem. Ours is the first *nonalgebraic* reduction from 3SUM, and allows 3SUM-hardness results for combinatorial problems. For instance, it implies hardness of reporting all triangles in a graph.

3. It is plausible that an unconditional lower bound for the multiphase problem can be established via a number-on-forehead communication game.

Categories and Subject Descriptors

F.1.3 [**Complexity Measures and Classes**]: Reducibility and completeness; E.1 [**Data**]: Data Structures

General Terms

Algorithms, Performance, Theory

Keywords

3SUM, dynamic data structures, lower bounds

1. INTRODUCTION

1.1 Dynamic Problems

Consider the following problems in the field of dynamic data structures:

dynamic reachability [7, 11, 12, 17, 18]
Maintain a directed graph G under:

- insertions and deletions of edges;
- reachability queries (is there a directed path from u to v?).

dynamic shortest paths [6, 21]
Maintain an undirected graph G, under:

- insertions and deletions of edges;
- queries for the length of the shortest path from u to v.

subgraph connectivity [4, 5]
Preprocess an undirected graph G, and support:

- node updates: turn a node on/off;
- connectivity queries (is there a path of *on* nodes from u to v?).

Langerman's problem. Maintain an array $A[1..n]$ of integers under:

- value updates, $A[i] = x$;
- searching for a zero partial sum (is there a k such that $\sum_{i=1}^{k} A[i] = 0$?).

Pagh's problem. Motivated by information retrieval applications that employ set intersection queries on inverted lists, this problem asks to preprocess a family of sets $X_1, X_2, \cdots \subseteq [n]$ and support:

- create a new set $X_{new} = X_i \cap X_j$, where X_i and X_j remain intact;
- a query whether some element z belongs to some set X_i.

Erickson's problem. Preprocess a matrix of integers, and support:

- increment all values in a specified row or column;
- queries for the maximum value in the matrix.

(The last problems were communicated to us by Stefan Langerman, Rasmus Pagh, and Jeff Erickson, respectively.)

For the sake of uniformity, let N denote the number of bits needed to describe the current state, in all problems. These problems do not currently have solutions running in time polylog(N) per operation, with $N \cdot$ polylog(N) preprocessing (where appropriate). In some cases, it is generally accepted that polylogarithmic solutions are impossible, and we would like lower bounds to formally prove it. In others, polylogarithmic solutions remain an intriguing open question.

Unfortunately, the current state of the art in dynamic lower bounds means that that any progress on these problems can only come from the upper bound side. Indeed, the

STOC'10, June 5–8, 2010, Cambridge, Massachusetts, USA.

highest known dynamic lower bound in the cell-probe model remains $\Omega(\lg N)$, for *any* explicit problem [16].

1.2 The Multiphase Problem

Our first contribution is an easy criterion for arguing that a problem may not admit solutions in polylogarithmic time. Let us define the following *multiphase problem*, which is essentially a dynamic version of set disjointness:

Phase I. We are given k sets, $S_1, \ldots, S_k \subset [n]$. We may preprocess the sets in time $O(nk \cdot \tau)$.

Phase II. We are given another set $T \subseteq [n]$, and have time $O(n \cdot \tau)$ to read and update memory locations from the data structure constructed in Phase I.

Phase III. Finally, we are given an index $i \in [k]$ and must, in time $O(\tau)$, answer whether S_i is disjoint from T.

Observe that the sizes of the sets are not prescribed (except that $|S_i|, |T| \leq n$). The input in Phase I consists of $O(n \cdot k)$ bits, the input of Phase II of $O(n)$ bits, and the input of Phase III of $O(\lg n)$ bits (one word in the Word RAM model). Thus, the running time allowed in each phase is proportional to the maximum input size in that phase, with τ as the proportionality factor. We set forth the following conjecture about the hardness of the multiphase problem, expressed in terms of our unifying parameter τ.

CONJECTURE 1. *There exist constants $\gamma > 1$ and $\delta > 0$ such that the following holds. If $k = \Theta(n^\gamma)$, any solution to the multiphase problem in the Word RAM model requires $\tau = \Omega(n^\delta)$.*

We briefly motivate the setting of parameters in the conjecture. Certainly, $\tau \leq n$, since Phase III can simply examine all the elements of S_i and T. Furthermore, it seems somewhat questionable to assume anything beyond $\tau = \Omega(\sqrt{n})$, since the conjecture would fail for random sets (as sets of density much higher than $\sqrt{n}$ intersect with high probability). We only assume $\tau = \Omega(n^\delta)$ for generality.

The conjecture is safer for $k \gg n \cdot \tau$. Indeed, Phase II can try to compute the intersection of T with all sets S_i (a boolean vector of k entries), making Phase III trivial. This is achieved naively in time $O(k \cdot n)$, but faster algorithms are possible via fast matrix multiplication. However, if Phase II only has time $n \cdot \tau \ll k$, it cannot hope to output a vector of size k with all answers.

On the other hand, we do not want k to be too high: we ask that $k \approx n^\gamma$, since we want a polynomial lower bound in terms of the total input size (that is, we need $n^\delta = (kn)^{\Omega(1)}$).

Implications. The value of this conjecture lies in the easy reductions from it to the problems listed in Section 1.1. In particular, we obtain:

THEOREM 2. *If the multiphase problem is hard (in the sense of Conjecture 1), then for every problem listed in §1.1, there exists a constant $\varepsilon > 0$ such that the problem cannot be solved with $o(N^\varepsilon)$ time per operation and $o(N^{1+\varepsilon})$ preprocessing time.*

PROOF SKETCH. The proof appears in Appendix A. Here, we briefly illustrate the ease of these reductions by proving the hardness of Erickson's problem.

Assume we have a fast data structure for this problem. To construct a solution for the multiphase problem, each phase runs as follows:

I. The data structure is asked to preprocess a matrix M of $k \times n$ boolean values, where $M[i][j] = 1$ iff $j \in S_i$.

II. For each element $j \in T$, increment column j in M.

III. Given the index i, increment row i in M, and then ask for the maximum value in the matrix. Report that S_i intersects T iff the maximum value is 3.

Observe that a maximum value of $M[i][j] = 3$ can only happen if: (1) the element was originally one, meaning $j \in S_i$; (2) the column was incremented in Phase II, meaning $j \in T$; (3) the row was incremented in Phase III, indicating S_i was the set of interest. Thus, $M[i][j] = 3$ iff $S_i \cap T \neq \emptyset$.

The input size for Erickson's problem is $O(nk)$ bits. If the preprocessing is done in $O((nk)^{1+\varepsilon})$ and each operation is supported in $O((nk)^\varepsilon)$ time, then the running time in the multiphase problem will be: $O((nk)^{1+\varepsilon})$ for Phase I; $O(n \cdot (nk)^\varepsilon)$ in Phase II; and $O((nk)^\varepsilon)$ in Phase III. Thus, we have a solution with $\tau = (nk)^\varepsilon$.

This contradicts Conjecture 1 for $(\gamma + 1)\varepsilon < \delta$. Thus, we have shown a lower bound of $\Omega\big((nk)^{\delta/(\gamma+1)}\big) = \Omega(N^{\delta/(\gamma+1)})$ for Erickson's problem. □

1.3 On 3SUM-Hardness

The 3SUM problem asks, given a set S of n numbers, to find distinct $x, y, z \in S$ such that $x + y = z$. The problem can be solved easily in $O(n^2)$ time, and it is a long-standing conjecture that this is essentially the best possible (see below).

Just like progress on dynamic cell-probe lower bounds has been too slow to impact many natural dynamic problems, progress on lower bounds for offline algorithms (or, in particular, circuit lower bounds) is unlikely to answer many of our pressing questions very soon. Instead, it would be of great interest to argue, based on some widely-believed hardness assumption, that natural algorithmic problems like finding maximum flow or computing the edit distance require superlinear time.

The 3SUM conjecture is perhaps the best proposal for this hardness assumption, since it is accepted quite broadly, and it gives a rather sharp lower bound for a very simple problem in the low regime of polynomial time. Unfortunately, the hope of using 3SUM appears too optimistic when contrasted with the current state of 3SUM reductions.

Gajentaan and Overmars [10] were the first to use 3SUM hardness to argue $\Omega(n^2)$ lower bounds in computational geometry, for problems such as finding 3 collinear points, minimum area triangle, separating n line segments by a line, determining whether n rectangles cover a given rectangle, etc. Subsequently, further problems such as polygon containment [3] or testing whether a dihedral rotation will cause a chain to self-intersect [20] were also shown to be 3SUM-hard.

All these reductions talk about transforming the condition $x + y = z$ into some geometric condition on, e.g., the collinearity of points. Formally, such reductions work even in an algebraic model, morphing the 3SUM instance into an instance of the other problem by common arithmetic. By contrast, we would like reductions to purely combinatorial questions, talking about graphs, strings, etc. Such problems may not even have *numbers* in them, so the reductions must be nonalgebraic. In this paper, we give the first examples of such nonalgebraic reductions, which use hashing (and thus, must assume finite precision numbers, i.e. the Word RAM model).

Most interestingly, we prove that the multiphase conjecture is implied by the hardness of 3SUM, which can be considered as very significant evidence in favor of our new conjecture. The following is shown in Section 2:

THEOREM 3. *Under the 3SUM conjecture, the multiphase problem with $k = \Theta(n^{2.5})$ requires $\tau \geq n^{0.5-o(1)}$ on the Word RAM.*

Combining this with Theorem 2, one can shortcut our multiphase conjecture entirely, and obtain conclusions of the form: "solving Erickson's problem in $O(N^{1/7-\varepsilon})$ time per operation is 3SUM-hard." Pending an unconditional proof of the multiphase conjecture, we believe 3SUM-hardness is a very satisfactory indication of hardness for our dynamic problems.

Our new reduction technique from 3SUM also leads to a few results outside the realm of data structures:

THEOREM 4. *In a weighted graph with m edges, finding a triangle of prescribed weight in $O(m^{1.5-\varepsilon})$ time is 3SUM-hard.*

THEOREM 5. *In a graph with m edges, reporting m triangles in $O(m^{4/3-\varepsilon})$ time is 3SUM-hard.*

Theorem 4 is a direct improvement over a recent result of Vassilevka and Williams [23], which showed that it is 3SUM-hard to find a triangle of a given weight in $O(n^{2.5-\varepsilon})$ time, when $m = \Theta(n^2)$. Our result implies $O(n^{3-\varepsilon})$ for dense graphs, thus ruling out the possibility of any improvement via matrix multiplication. This improved result hinges on the first innovation in our 3SUM reductions (a certain *convolution* version of 3SUM).

With regards to Theorem 5, we observe that *testing* whether a graph contains a triangle can be done in $\widetilde{O}(m^{4/3})$ time, assuming Fast Matrix Multiplication in $\widetilde{O}(n^2)$ time. (While such an algorithm for matrix multiplication is not known at present, it seems unlikely that 3SUM-hardness could be used to rule it out.) It would be very interesting to extend the lower bound of Theorem 5 to the computationally-easier case of testing.

Clarification of the 3SUM conjecture. To formalize this conjecture in the RAM model, which is of interest to us, we assume the set S consists of n integers from $\{-u, \dots, u\}$, where the word size is $O(\lg u)$. In this model, the problem can be solved in $O(n^2 \cdot \frac{\lg^2 \lg n}{\lg^2 n})$ expected time [2]. (Note that the model allows word-level parallelism on $\lg n$ bits, and the algorithm essentially saves a factor of $\lg^2 n$, confirming the quadratic nature of 3SUM.)

For maximal generality, we will assume that 3SUM requires $n^{2-o(1)}$ time. One may also choose to assume an $n^2/\lg^{O(1)} n$ lower bound, with corresponding improvements in the lower bounds that 3SUM-hardness implies. Since our reductions will be randomized, we must assume that 3SUM requires $n^{2-o(1)}$ expected running time for zero-error algorithms. It is also possible to build a theory based on bounded-error hardness, with minor technical complications in the proofs.

For a bounded universe u, 3SUM may also be solved in $O(u \lg u)$ time by the Fast Fourier Transform, so the conjecture can only hold for large enough u. Using the techniques of [2], one can show that for $u \gg n^3$, it is possible to hash down the universe to $O(n^3)$, while maintaining the expected running time. (This only applies to the version where a solution must be reported, but the search version is equivalent to the decision version up to a logarithm.) Thus, the Word RAM version of the 3SUM conjecture need only talk about a universe of $u = O(n^3)$.

We say obtaining a specified time bound for a problem is "3SUM-hard" if doing so would violate the following:

CONJECTURE 6 (3SUM-HARDNESS). *In the Word RAM model with words of $O(\lg n)$ bits, any algorithm requires $n^{2-o(1)}$ time in expectation to determine whether a set $S \subset \{-n^3, \dots, n^3\}$ of $|S| = n$ integers contains a triple of distinct $x, y, z \in S$ with $x + y = z$.*

While this conjecture appears to be widely accepted, formal evidence in its favor is circumstantial. Erickson [9] showed that 3SUM requires $\Omega(n^2)$ time in a restricted class of algebraic decision trees; see also [1] for improvements in this model. Recently, [15] showed that the d-SUM problem requires time $n^{\Omega(d)}$, unless k-SAT can be solved in $2^{o(n)}$ time for any constant k. While this result does not imply anything for 3SUM, it demonstrates that the complexity must eventually grow as d-SUM-hardness would predict.

1.4 An Attack on the Multiphase Conjecture

The statement of the multiphase problem meets three independent goals: (1) it is easy give reductions to most dynamic problems; (2) hardness can be proved conditionally, based on 3SUM-hardness; (3) there is a plausible attack on an unconditional proof of the conjecture. We now give details on the final goal: we describe a 3-party number-on-forehead communication game, the analysis of which would lead to a lower bound for the multiphase problem.

The three players have the following information on their foreheads (i.e. they can see the information on the foreheads of the other players, but not their own):

Alice: an index $i \in [k]$.

Bob: a family of sets $S_1, \dots, S_k \subseteq [n]$.

Carmen: a set $T \subseteq [n]$.

The goal of the communication is to decide whether $S_i \cap T = \emptyset$. The communication proceeds as follows. First, Alice sends a message of $n \cdot M$ bits privately to Bob; thereafter, Alice is silent. Bob and Carmen engage in bidirectional communication, taking a total of M bits, and announce the answer at the end.

CONJECTURE 7. *There exist constants $\gamma > 1$ and $\delta > 0$ such that the following holds. For $k = \Theta(n^\gamma)$, any solution to the 3-party communication problem requires $M = \Omega(n^\delta)$.*

Observe that it is essential that Alice's message is sent privately to Bob. As the message contains more than n bits, it could describe the entire set T. If Carmen saw it, she would know the entire input, and could announce the result with no further communication.

One must also ensure that $\gamma > 1 + \delta$. Otherwise, Alice's message would have $n \cdot M \geq k$ bits, and could include a k-bit vector specifying whether S_i intersects T, for all i. Then, Bob could immediately announce the answer.

Finally, it is essential that Alice only speak in the beginning. Otherwise, Bob or Carmen could announce the $O(\lg k)$ bits of input on Alice's forehead, and Alice would immediately announce the result.

It is easy to see that a strong lower bound of this communication game would imply a strong version of the multiphase conjecture:

OBSERVATION 8. *Conjecture 7 implies Conjecture 1. This holds even in the stronger cell-probe model, and even if Phase I is allowed unbounded time.*

PROOF. We assume a solution for the multiphase conjecture, and obtain a communication protocol. Alice sees $S_1, \ldots, S_k$ and T, and thus can simulate the actions of Phase I and Phase II. Her message describes all cells written during Phase II, including their addresses and contents. This takes $n \cdot M = O(n\tau w)$ bits, where w is the word size.

Subsequently, Bob will execute the actions of the algorithm in Phase III. For every cell read, he first tests whether it was included in the message from Alice. If not, he communicates the address (w bits) to Carmen.

Carmen sees $S_1, \ldots, S_k$ and can thus simulate Phase I. Therefore, she knows that contents of all cells written during Phase I, and can reply to Bob with the contents of all cells he wants to read.

In total, Bob and Carmen communicate $M = O(\tau w)$ bits. Assuming $w = O(\lg n)$, an $\Omega(n^{\delta})$ lower bound on M implies an $\Omega(n^{\delta'})$ lower bound on τ. □

Relation to other communication problems. The formulation of our communication game is inspired by the round elimination lemma [13, 19]. In this two-player setting, Alice receives $S_1, \ldots, S_k$ and Bob receives T and $i \in [k]$. Alice begins by sending a message of $o(k)$ bits. Then, it is possible to prove that the message can be eliminated, while fixing i in a way that increases the error of the protocol by $o(1)$. The idea is that the message can be fixed a priori. Alice will receive only the relevant S_i, and she will manufacture $S_1, \ldots S_{i-1}, S_{i+1}, \ldots, S_k$ in a way that makes the fixed message be correct. This is possible with probability $1 - o(1)$, as the message only contains $o(1)$ bits of information about S_i.

Unfortunately, in our 3-party setting, the initial message of $o(k)$ bits may depend on both the inputs of Bob and Carmen. Thus, Carmen cannot, by herself, manufacture a vector of S_j's ($j \neq i$) that is consistent with the message. However, the information theoretic intuition of the lemma holds, and it is conceivable that the message of Alice can be eliminated in a black-box fashion for any communication problem of the appropriate direct-sum structure:

CONJECTURE 9. *Consider a 3-party number-on-forehead game in which Alice holds $i \in [k]$, Bob holds $y_1, \ldots, y_k \in \mathcal{Y}$, and Carmen holds $x \in \mathcal{X}$. The goal is to compute $f(x, y_i)$, for some arbitrary $f : \mathcal{X} \times \mathcal{Y} \to \{0, 1\}$.*

If there is a protocol in which Alice begins with a private message to Bob of $o(k)$ bits, followed by M bits of bidirectional communication between Bob and Carmen, then the 2-party communication complexity of f is $O(M)$.

In general, number-on-forehead communication games are considered difficult to analyze. In particular, the asymmetric setup in our problem appears similar to a 3-party communication game proposed by Valiant [22, 14]. A strong enough lower bound on Valiant's game would rule out linear-size, logarithmic-depth circuits for some explicit problems. Fortunately, our game may be easier to analyze, since we are satisfied with much weaker bounds (in Valiant's setting, even an $\Omega(n^{1-\varepsilon})$ lower bound would not suffice).

2. USING 3SUM HARDNESS

2.1 Convolution 3SUM

The first issue that we must overcome for effective use of 3SUM hardness is the following "gap" in the problem's combinatorial structure: the test $x + y = z$ must be iterated over $\binom{n}{3}$ triples, yet the (tight) lower bound is only quadratic.

We define the *Convolution-3SUM* problem as follows: given an array $A[1\,..\,n]$, determine whether there exist $i \neq j$ with $A[i] + A[j] = A[i + j]$. Observe that this problem has a much more rigid structure, as the predicate is only evaluated $O(n^2)$ times. Another way to highlight the additional structure is to note that Convolution-3SUM *obviously* has an $O(n^2)$ algorithm, whereas this is less obvious for 3SUM.

THEOREM 10. *If 3SUM requires $\Omega(n^2/f(n))$ expected time, Convolution-3SUM requires $\Omega\big(n^2/f^2(n \cdot f(n))\big)$ expected time.*

In particular, if 3SUM requires $n^{2-o(1)}$ time, then so does Convolution-3SUM. Furthermore, if 3SUM requires $n/\lg^{O(1)} n$ time, so does Convolution-3SUM. As an immediate application of this result, we mention that plugging it into the reduction from [23] to finding a given-weight triangle, one immediately obtains our improved bound from Theorem 4.

PROOF. Our reduction from 3SUM to Convolution-3SUM is the first point of departure from algebraic reductions: we will use hashing. Conceptually, our idea is fairly simple. Assume that we had some injective hash map $h : S \to [n]$, which is *linear* in the sense $h(x) + h(y) = h(z)$. Then, we could simply place every 3SUM element $x \in S$ into the location $A[h(x)]$. If there exist $x, y, z \in S$ with $x + y = z$, then $h(x) + h(y) = h(z)$ and therefore $A[h(x)] + A[h(y)] = A[h(x) + h(y)]$. Thus, the triple will be discovered by the Convolution-3SUM algorithm (no false negatives). On the other hand, there are clearly no false positives, since the array A is filled with elements from S, so any $A[i] + A[j] = A[k]$ is a valid answer to 3SUM.

Unfortunately, we do not have linear perfect hashing. Instead, we use a family of hash functions introduced by Dietzfelbinger [8]. The hash function is defined by picking a random *odd* integer a on w bits, where w is the machine word size. To obtain values in range $\{0, \ldots, 2^s - 1\}$, the hash function multiplies x by the random odd value a (modulo 2^w) and keeps the high order s bits of the result as the hash code. In C notation, the word x is mapped to `(unsigned) (a*x) >> (w-s)`.

This function was also used in the upper bound for 3SUM [2], where the following crucial properties were shown:

almost linearity: For any x and y, either $h(x) + h(y) = h(x + y) \pmod{2^s}$, or $h(x) + h(y) + 1 = h(x + y)$

(mod 2^s). This property follows because $a \cdot x + a \cdot y = a \cdot (x+y) \pmod{2^w}$, and chopping off the low order $w - s$ bits can at most generate an off-by-one error, losing the carry.

few false positives: By the above, we declare that $x + y = z$ with good probability if they pass the test $h(z) \in h(x) + h(y) + \{0, 1\} \pmod{2^s}$. The probability of passing the test for any $x + y \neq z$ is $O(1/2^s)$.

good load balancing: Assume that we place n items into $R = 2^s$ buckets using a random function from the family. The average load of a bucket is n/R. In expectation, at most $O(R)$ elements will reside in buckets with load exceeding $\frac{3n}{R}$ (buckets with three times the expected load).

Let $R = 2^s = \frac{\varepsilon n}{f(n)}$ for a small enough constant $\varepsilon > 0$. We place each value x from the 3SUM problem into bucket $h(x)$. By the load-balancing properties, at most $O(R)$ elements are expected to be in buckets with load exceeding $3n/R = O(f(n))$. For each of these elements, we can, in $O(n)$ time, determine whether they participate in a solution to the 3SUM problem (see [2]). The expected running time in dealing with high-load elements is thus $O(\frac{\varepsilon n}{f(n)} \cdot n)$, which is less than half the time required by 3SUM, for small enough ε.

It remains to deal with the buckets of load at most $3n/R = O(f(n))$. The idea is to form $O(f^3(n))$ instances of Convolution-3SUM on arrays of size $O(R)$, which test all triplets of elements that may lead to a solution.

We iterate over all triples $i, j, k \in \{0, \ldots, 3n/R\}$. For some (i, j, k), we are looking for solutions $x + y = z$, where x is the i-th element in its bucket, y the j-th element, and z the k-th element. We map all elements to an array of size $8R$. From each bucket $t \in [R]$, we map the i-th element to $8t + 1$, the j-th element to $8t + 3$, and the k-th element to $8t + 4$. The locations of the array that remain unfilled get the value $2(\max S) + 1$, ensuring that they cannot participate in any sum.

It is easy to check that the set of $\{1, 3, 4\}$ has only one solution to $x + y = z$ modulo 8. Thus, we cannot find false positives involving a repeated element.

Unfortunately, we have some false-negative situations, stemming from two sources. The first is modular arithmetic: since Convolution-3SUM only checks for $A[i] + A[j] = A[i + j]$, it misses pairs where $h(x) + h(y) \geq R$ (a wrap-around happens modulo R). To fix this, we double the array size, including two identical copies. This simulates the wrap-around effect.

The second reason we may miss a solution is the nonlinearity of the hash function: we miss triples $x + y = z$ which nonetheless have $h(z) = h(x) + h(y) + 1 \pmod{R}$. This is easily fixed by, in addition to the above, trying instances where $h(x)$ is incremented by one. In other words, the i-th element from bucket t is mapped to $8(t + 1) + 1$.

Overall, we run $O(f^3(n))$ instances of Convolution-3SUM on arrays of size $O(n/f(n))$. Since the lower bound on the overall time is $\Omega(n^2/f(n))$, it follows that one cannot support such instances in $o\big((\frac{n}{f(n)})^2/f^2(n)\big)$ time. □

2.2 Hardness of Reporting Triangles

We now describe the following reduction from Convolution-3SUM to reporting triangles in a graph.

LEMMA 11. *Assume Convolution-3SUM requires $\Omega(n^2/f(n))$ expected time, and let R be:*

$$\omega\big(\sqrt{n \cdot f(n)}\big) < R < o\big(n/f(n)\big).$$

Then, $\Omega(n^2/f(n))$ expected time is needed to report $O(n^2/R)$ triangles in a tripartite graph where:

- *the three parts are A, B, C, of sizes $|A| = |B| = R\sqrt{n}$ and $|C| = n$;*
- *each vertex in $A \cup B$ has $O(n/R)$ neighbors in C;*
- *there are $O(nR)$ edges in $A \times B$.*

This reduction is parametrized by R for the sake of our later reduction to the multiphase problem. To derive hardness of triangle reporting (Theorem 5), we simply assume $f(n) = n^{o(1)}$ as per the 3SUM conjecture, and set $R = n^{0.5+o(1)}$. Our graph will have $O(R\sqrt{n}) = n^{1+o(1)}$ vertices, $m = O(nR + \frac{n}{R} \cdot R\sqrt{n}) = n^{1.5+o(1)}$ edges, and $O(\frac{n^2}{R}) = o(n^{1.5})$ triangles. We obtain a lower bound of $n^{2-o(1)} = m^{4/3-o(1)}$.

PROOF. We being by applying linear hashing to every value in the Convolution-3SUM problem. Unlike our previous reduction, however, we now use a hash range $[R]$ with $R \ll n$. Thus, the linear hashing only acts as a filter. By the filter property of the hash family, for any triple with $x + y \neq z$, $\Pr[h(x) + h(y) = h(z) \pmod{R}] = O(\frac{1}{R})$. Since Convolution-3SUM is concerned with $O(n^2)$ different triples (of the form $A[i], A[j], A[i + j]$), in expectation we will have $O(n^2/R)$ false positives.

For some $x \in \{0, \ldots, R - 1\}$, let the bucket of x be $\mathcal{B}(x) = \{i \in [n] \mid h(A[i]) = x\}$. By the load balancing property of the hash family, the buckets with more than $\frac{3n}{R}$ elements only contain a total of $O(R)$ elements in expectation. For each such element z, run the linear-time algorithm to test whether there exist x, y with $x + y = z$. The expected running time is $O(nR)$, a lower-order term.

From now on, we may assume that all buckets have $O(n/R)$ elements. To solve Convolution-3SUM, proceed as follows:

```
1  for i = 1 to n
2      x = h(A[i])
3      for y = 0 to R − 1
4          T = {j − i | j ∈ B((x + y) mod R)}
               // shift B(x + y) to left by i positions
5          T' = {j − i | j ∈ B((x + y + 1) mod R)}
6          if B(y) ∩ T ≠ ∅ or B(y) ∩ T' ≠ ∅
7              for j ∈ B(y)        // exhaustive search
8                  if A[i] + A[j] = A[i + j]
                       return Solution Found!
9  return No Solution!
```

Let us explain the condition in line 6. Say $j \in \mathcal{B}(y) \cap T$. On the one hand, this implies $h(A[j]) = y$. On the other hand $i + j \in \mathcal{B}((x + y) \bmod R)$, so $h(A[i + j]) = x + y \pmod{R}$. Thus, $h(A[i]) + h(A[j]) = h(A[i + j]) \pmod{R}$, i.e. any intersection found in line 5 indicates either a solution or a false position to the test $h(x) + h(y) = h(z) \pmod{R}$. Similarly, $j \in \mathcal{B}(y) \cap T'$ indicates $h(A[i]) + h(A[j]) + 1 = h(A[i + j]) \pmod{R}$. Since the hash function is almost linear, any solution with satisfy either $h(A[i]) + h(A[j]) = h(A[i + j])$ or $h(A[i]) + h(A[j]) + 1 = h(A[i + j])$, so it will be found (no false negative).

As noted above, the expected number of false positives is $O(n^2/R)$. Each one will have a cost of $O(n/R)$, given by the exhaustive search in lines 7-8. Thus, the running time of the algorithm, excluding the intersections in line 5, is $O(nR + \frac{n^3}{R^2})$ in expectation. Since $R = \omega(\sqrt{nf(n)})$ and $R = o(n/f(n))$, this time is $o(n^2/f(n))$.

However, we assumed the Convolution-3SUM requires time $\Omega(n^2/f(n))$, implying that the total cost of the intersection operations in line 6 must be $\Omega(n^2/f(n))$.

We now implement these intersections in terms of finding triangles in a tripartite graph, obtaining the desired reduction. The goal is to get rid of the set-shift operations in lines 4-5. We accomplish this by breaking a shift by some $i \in [n]$ into a shift by $i \bmod \sqrt{n}$, and a shift by $\lfloor \frac{i}{\sqrt{n}} \rfloor \cdot \sqrt{n}$.

Formally, let the parts in our graph be $A = B = [R] \times [\sqrt{n}]$, and $C = [n]$. We interpret an element $(x, i) \in A$ as the set $\mathcal{B}(x) - i$. The edges from A to C represent the elements of these sets: an edge exists from (x, i) to some $j \in B$ iff $j \in \mathcal{B}(x) - i$. An element $(x, i) \in B$ is interpreted as the set $\mathcal{B}(x) + i \cdot \sqrt{n}$. The edges from B to C represent the elements of these sets: an edge exists from (x, i) to $j \in B$ iff $j \in \mathcal{B}(x) + i \cdot \sqrt{n}$.

Finally, the edges from A to B represent the $2n \cdot R$ intersection questions that we ask in line 6. To ask whether $\mathcal{B}(y)$ intersects $\mathcal{B}(x+y) - i$, we ask whether $\mathcal{B}(y) + \lfloor \frac{i}{\sqrt{n}} \rfloor \sqrt{n}$ intersects $\mathcal{B}(x + y) - i \bmod \sqrt{n}$.

For each triangle reported, we run the exhaustive search in lines 7-8. We expect $O(n^2/R)$ triangles. If this expectation is exceeded by a constant (the triangle reporting algorithm reports too many elements), we rehash. □

2.3 Reduction to the Multiphase Problem

In this final step, we reduce triangle reporting to the multiphase problem. Combined with Theorem 10 and Lemma 11, this establishes the reduction from 3SUM to the multiphase problem claimed in Theorem 3.

In the beginning, we take edges from A to C, and construct $k = R\sqrt{n}$ sets indicating the neighbors of each vertex from A. These are the sets given in Phase I.

We then run $R\sqrt{n}$ copies of Phase II. Each copy corresponds to a vertex of B, and the set T represents the neighbors of the vertex in C. Each execution of Phase II starts with the memory state after Phase I. Any cells written during Phase II are saved in a separate hash table for each execution.

Finally, we run a query (Phase III) for each of the $O(nR)$ edges between A and B. For each such edge, we need to test the intersection of the neighborhood of a vertex from A with the neighborhood of a vertex from B. This is done by running a Phase III with the index of the A vertex, on top of the Phase II memory state corresponding to the B vertex.

By Lemma 11, we only need to deal with $O(n^2/R)$ triangles in the graph. Whenever some Phase III query returns an intersection, we enumerate the two sets of $O(n/R)$ size and find the intersection (and thus, a triangle). The total running time of this search is $O(n^3/R^2) = o(n^2/f(n))$.

Thus, the running time must be dominated by the multiphase problem, and we obtain an $\Omega(n^2/f(n))$ bound for running Phase I, $O(R\sqrt{n})$ copies of Phase II, and $O(nR)$ copies of Phase III.

The final obstacle is the universe of the sets in the multiphase problem. Since the running time is assumed to be $O(U \cdot \tau)$, where each set comes from the universe $[U]$, we need to decrease the universe from the current $U = n$ to get a superconstant lower bound. Notice that our sets are very sparse, each having $O(n/R)$ values. This suggests that we should hash each set by a universal function to a universe of $U = c \cdot (\frac{n}{R})^2$, for large enough constant c.

By universality of the hash function, if two sets are disjoint, a false intersection is introduced with small constant probability. We repeat the construction with $O(\lg n)$ hash functions chosen independently. We only perform the exhaustive search if a query returns true in all the $O(\lg n)$ instances. This means that the expected number of false positives only increases by $o(1)$, so the analysis of the running time is unchanged.

The total running time of each of the $O(\lg n)$ instances is given by:

- Phase I, taking time $O(k \cdot U\tau) = O(R\sqrt{n} \cdot \frac{n^2}{R^2}\tau) = O(n^{2.5}\tau/R)$.
- $O(R\sqrt{n})$ executions of Phase II, taking time $R\sqrt{n} \cdot O(U\tau) = O(n^{2.5}\tau/R)$.
- $O(nR)$ executions of Phase III, taking time $O(nR\tau)$.

To balance the costs of $O(n^{2.5}\tau/R)$ and $O(nR\tau)$, we set $R = n^{0.75}$, which is in the range permitted by Lemma 11. This gives a lower bound of $\tau \geq n^{0.25-o(1)}$. To rephrase the bound in the language of Theorem 3, observe that $k = R\sqrt{n} = n^{1.25}$ and $N = O(n^2/R^2) = O(\sqrt{n})$. Thus, $k = O(N^{2.5})$, and $\tau \geq N^{0.5-o(1)}$.

3. REFERENCES

[1] N. Ailon and B. Chazelle. Lower bounds for linear degeneracy testing. In *Proc. 36th ACM Symposium on Theory of Computing (STOC)*, pages 554–560, 2004.

[2] I. Baran, E. D. Demaine, and M. Pătraşcu. Subquadratic algorithms for 3SUM. *Algorithmica*, 50(4):584–596, 2008. See also WADS 2005.

[3] G. Barequet and S. Har-Peled. Polygon-containment and translational min-Hausdorff-distance between segment sets are 3SUM-hard. In *Proc. 10th ACM/SIAM Symposium on Discrete Algorithms (SODA)*, page 862âĂŞ863, 1999.

[4] T. M. Chan. Dynamic subgraph connectivity with geometric applications. In *Proc. 34th ACM Symposium on Theory of Computing (STOC)*, pages 7–13, 2002.

[5] T. M. Chan, M. Pătraşcu, and L. Roditty. Dynamic connectivity: Connecting to networks and geometry. In *Proc. 49th IEEE Symposium on Foundations of Computer Science (FOCS)*, pages 95–104, 2008.

[6] C. Demetrescu and G. F. Italiano. A new approach to dynamic all pairs shortest paths. *Journal of the ACM*, 51(6):968–992, 2004. See also STOC'03.

[7] C. Demetrescu and G. F. Italiano. Trade-offs for fully dynamic transitive closure on DAGs: breaking through the $O(n^2)$ barrier. *Journal of the ACM*, 52(2):147–156, 2005. See also FOCS'00.

[8] M. Dietzfelbinger. Universal hashing and k-wise independent random variables via integer arithmetic without primes. In *Proc. 13th Symposium on Theoretical Aspects of Computer Science (STACS)*, pages 569–580, 1996.

[9] J. Erickson. Bounds for linear satisfiability problems. *Chicago Journal of Theoretical Computer Science*, 1999.

[10] A. Gajentaan and M. H. Overmars. On a class of $O(n^2)$ problems in computational geometry. *Computational Geometry: Theory and Applications*, 5:165–185, 1995.

[11] V. King. Fully dynamic algorithms for maintaining all-pairs shortest paths and transitive closure in digraphs. In *Proc. 40th IEEE Symposium on Foundations of Computer Science (FOCS)*, pages 81–91, 1999.

[12] V. King and G. Sagert. A fully dynamic algorithm for maintaining the transitive closure. *Journal of Computer and System Sciences*, 65(1):150–167, 2002. See also STOC'99.

[13] P. B. Miltersen, N. Nisan, S. Safra, and A. Wigderson. On data structures and asymmetric communication complexity. *Journal of Computer and System Sciences*, 57(1):37–49, 1998. See also STOC'95.

[14] N. Nisan and A. Wigderson. Rounds in communication complexity revisited. *SIAM Journal on Computing*, 22(1):211–219, 1993. See also STOC'91.

[15] M. Pătraşcu and R. Williams. On the possibility of faster sat algorithms. In *Proc. 21st ACM/SIAM Symposium on Discrete Algorithms (SODA)*, 2010. To appear.

[16] M. Pătraşcu and E. D. Demaine. Logarithmic lower bounds in the cell-probe model. *SIAM Journal on Computing*, 35(4):932–963, 2006. See also SODA'04 and STOC'04.

[17] L. Roditty and U. Zwick. A fully dynamic reachability algorithm for directed graphs with an almost linear update time. In *Proc. 36th ACM Symposium on Theory of Computing (STOC)*, pages 184–191, 2004.

[18] P. Sankowski. Dynamic transitive closure via dynamic matrix inverse. In *Proc. 45th IEEE Symposium on Foundations of Computer Science (FOCS)*, pages 509–517, 2004.

[19] P. Sen and S. Venkatesh. Lower bounds for predecessor searching in the cell probe model. *Journal of Computer and System Sciences*, 74(3):364–385, 2008. See also ICALP'01, CCC'03.

[20] M. A. Soss, J. Erickson, and M. H. Overmars. Preprocessing chains for fast dihedral rotations is hard or even impossible. *Computational Geometry*, 26(3):235–246, 2003.

[21] M. Thorup. Worst-case update times for fully-dynamic all-pairs shortest paths. In *Proc. 37th ACM Symposium on Theory of Computing (STOC)*, pages 112–119, 2005.

[22] L. G. Valiant. Graph-theoretic arguments in low-level complexity. In *Proc. 6th Mathematical Foundations of Computer Science (MFCS)*, pages 162–176, 1977.

[23] V. Vassilevska and R. Williams. Finding, minimizing, and counting weighted subgraphs. In *Proc. 41st ACM Symposium on Theory of Computing (STOC)*, pages 455–464, 2009.

APPENDIX

A. REDUCTIONS TO DYNAMIC PROBLEMS

Dynamic reachability. The vertex set consists of a vertex for every set S_i, a vertex for every element of $[n]$, and a sink v. In Phase I, we insert edges from S_i to j whenever $j \in S_i$. This takes $O(nk)$ updates. In Phase II, we insert edges from j to the sink v whenever $j \in T$. This takes $O(n)$ updates. In Phase III, we query whether a directed path exists from S_i to v. This happens iff $S_i \cap T \neq \emptyset$.

We obtain that the update or query time must be $\Omega(n^\delta)$.

Dynamic shortest paths. The reduction is the same as above, except that the edges are undirected. A path of length 2 exists iff $S_i \cap T \neq \emptyset$.

Subgraph connectivity. As before, the vertex set contains vertex for every set S_i, a vertex for every element of $[n]$, and a sink v. The edge set is constructed during Phase I, and the preprocessing algorithm is called on the graph. There will be an edge from every S_i to every j such that $j \in S_i$, and from all j to the sink v. Initially, all nodes are off, except the sink.

In Phase II, we turn on all nodes from T. In Phase III, we turn on the node S_i, and query whether S_i and v are connected. Since only the T nodes are on, the only possible path is an intersection between T and S_i.

Langerman's problem. We consider an array of $1 + n \cdot (2k+2)$ elements. The first element is special; beyond this, every block of $k+2$ elements has the following structure:

- among the first and last element, one is 0 and one is $-2k$. If $i \in T$, the first element in block is $-2k$ and the last in 0; otherwise, the values are swapped.
- elements on position $2j$ and $2j+1$ in block i indicate whether $i \in S_j$. If $i \in S_j$, both elements are $+1$; otherwise, the first is $+2$ and the second is 0.

Assume the first element is $2x+1$. Every block has a total sum of 0, so blocks behave "independently." No block that begins with 0 can have a partial sum equal to zero, since one first increments the (already positive) partial sum, and only in the last element subtract $2k$. But if $i \in T$ (the i-th block begins with $-2k$) a zero partial sum is possible. The partial sum after the block head is $2j+1-2k$. Each pair of items increments this by 2. Then, the partial sum reaches zero only if the $(k-x)$-th pair of items is $+1, +1$. If it is $0, +2$, then the sum skips past zero, and then stay positive. In other words, a zero partial sum exists iff $i \in S_{k-x}$, for some $i \in T$. That is, a zero sum exists iff $S_{k-x} \cap T \neq \emptyset$.

In Phase I, we update the $O(nk)$ elements corresponding to the sets S_i. In Phase II, we update the $O(n)$ elements corresponding to the set T. In Phase III, we update the first element, and run the query.

Pagh's problem. In Phase I, we create n sets from a universe of $[k]$. Each set X_i contains all j such that $i \notin S_j$. In Phase II, create a new set X as the intersection of X_i for all $i \in T$ (this takes $|T|-1$ updates). In Phase III, query whether $i \in X$. If so, it means $i \in X_j$, for all $j \in T$. That is equivalent to $j \notin S_i$, for all $j \in T$, i.e. S_i and T are disjoint.

An Optimal Ancestry Scheme and Small Universal Posets*

Pierre Fraigniaud, and Amos Korman
CNRS and Univ. Paris Diderot
Paris, France
pierre.fraigniaud@liafa.jussieu.fr, amos.korman@liafa.jussieu.fr

ABSTRACT

In this paper, we solve the *ancestry problem*, which was introduced more than twenty years ago by Kannan et al. [STOC '88], and is among the most well-studied problems in the field of informative labeling schemes. Specifically, we construct an *ancestry labeling scheme* for n-node trees with label size $\log_2 n + O(\log\log n)$ bits, thus matching the $\log_2 n + \Omega(\log\log n)$ bits lower bound given by Alstrup et al. [SODA '03]. Besides its optimal label size, our scheme assigns the labels in linear time, and guarantees that any ancestry query can be answered in constant time.

In addition to its potential impact in terms of improving the performances of XML search engines, our ancestry scheme is also useful in the context of partially ordered sets. Specifically, for any fixed integer k, our scheme enables the construction of a *universal* poset of size $O(n^k \log^{4k} n)$ for the family of n-element posets with tree-dimension at most k. This bound is almost tight thanks to a lower bound of $n^{k-o(1)}$ due to Alon and Scheinerman [Order '88].

Categories and Subject Descriptors

G.2.2 [**Discrete Mathematics**]: Graph Theory—*Graph algorithms, Graph labeling, Network problems*; E.1 [**Data structures**]: [Distributed data structures, Trees]

General Terms

Algorithms, Theory

Keywords

XML, informative labeling schemes, partially ordered sets

*This research is supported in part by the ANR projects ALADDIN and PROSE, and by the INRIA project GANG.

STOC'10, June 5–8, 2010, Cambridge, Massachusetts, USA.

1. INTRODUCTION

1.1 Background

How to represent a graph in a compact manner is a fundamental data structure question. In most traditional graph representations, the names (or identifiers) given to the nodes serve merely as pointers to entries in a data structure, and thus reveal no information about the graph structure per se. Hence, in a sense, some memory space is wasted for the storage of content-less data. In contrast, Kannan, Naor, and Rudich [23] introduced the notion of *informative labeling schemes*, which involves a mechanism for assigning short, yet informative, labels to nodes. Specifically, the goal of such schemes is to assign labels to nodes in such a way that allows one to infer information regarding any two nodes *directly from their labels*. Hence in essence, this mechanism bases the entire graph representation on the set of labels alone. One important question in the framework of informative labeling schemes is how to efficiently encode the ancestry relation in trees. This was formalized in the seminal work of Kannan et al. [23] as follows.

1.1.1 The ancestry problem

Given any n-node rooted tree T, label the nodes of T using the shortest possible labels (bit strings) such that, given any pair of nodes u and v in T, one can determine whether u is an *ancestor* of v in T by merely inspecting the labels of u and v.

The following simple ancestry scheme was suggested in [23]. Given a rooted n-node tree T, perform a DFS traversal in T starting at the root, and provide each node u with a DFS number, $\text{DFS}(u)$, in the range $[0, n-1]$. (Recall, in a DFS traversal, a node is visited before any of its children, thus, the DFS number of a node is smaller than the DFS number of any of its descendants). The label of a node u is simply the interval $I(u) = [\text{DFS}(u), \text{DFS}(v)]$, where v is the descendant of u with the largest DFS number. An ancestry query then amounts to an interval containment query between the corresponding labels: a node u is an ancestor of a node v if and only if $I(v) \subset I(u)$. Clearly, the *label size*, namely, the maximal size of a label assigned by this ancestry scheme to any node in any n-node tree, is bounded by $2\log n$ bits[1].

The $2\log n$ bits scheme of [23] initiated an extensive research [1, 3, 7, 13, 21, 22, 26] whose goal was to reduce the label size of ancestry schemes as much as possible. The

[1]All logarithms in this paper are taken in base 2.

main motivation behind these works lies in the fact that a small improvement in the label size of ancestry schemes can contribute to a significant improvement in the performances of XML search engines. Indeed, to implement sophisticated queries, XML documents are viewed as labeled trees, and typical queries over the documents amount to testing relationships between document items, which correspond to ancestry queries among the corresponding tree nodes [2, 10, 31, 32]. XML search engines process such queries using an index structure that summarizes this ancestry information. To allow good performances, a large portion of the XML index structure resides in the main memory. A main factor which determines the index size is the length of the labels. Thus, due to the enormous size of the Web data, even a small reduction in the label size can contribute significantly to both memory cost reduction and performance improvement. A more detailed explanation regarding this application can be found in various papers on ancestry labeling schemes, e.g., [1, 22].

In [4], Alstrup et al. constructed a lower bound of $\log n + \Omega(\log\log n)$ bits for the label size of an ancestry scheme. On the other hand, the current state of the art upper bound is $\log n + O(\sqrt{\log n})$ bits [1]. Thus, a large gap is still left between the best known upper and lower bounds on the label size. This paper closes this gap, by constructing an ancestry labeling scheme whose label size matches the aforementioned lower bound.

In addition to its potential impact on the performances of XML search engines, our ancestry scheme finds applications also in the context of *partially ordered sets* (posets). To elaborate more on this application, let us first recall several notions from order theory. A poset $(X, \leq_X)$ contains a poset $(Y, \leq_Y)$ as an *induced suborder* if there exists an injective mapping $\phi : Y \rightarrow X$ such that for any two elements $a, b \in Y$: we have $a \leq_Y b \iff \phi(a) \leq_X \phi(b)$. A poset $(X, \leq)$ is called *universal* for a family of posets $\mathcal{P}$ if $(X, \leq)$ contains every poset in $\mathcal{P}$ as an induced suborder. Given a family of posets $\mathcal{P}$, a natural problem consists of determining what is the smallest size (in term of number of elements) of a universal poset for $\mathcal{P}$. When considering infinite posets, it is known that a countable universal poset for the family of all countable posets exists. This classical result was proved several times [11, 16, 17] and, in fact, as mentioned in [15], has motivated the whole research area of category theory.

If $(X, \leq)$ and $(X, \leq')$ are orders on the set X, we say that $(X, \leq')$ is an *extension* of $(X, \leq)$ if $x \leq y$ implies $x \leq' y$ for any two elements $x, y \in X$. A common way to characterize a poset $(X, \leq)$ is by its *dimension*, i.e., the smallest number of linear (i.e., total order) extensions of $(X, \leq)$ the intersection of which gives rise to $(X, \leq)$ [27]. It can be easily seen that the smallest size of a universal poset for the family of n-element posets with dimension at most k is at most n^k. Another way of characterizing a poset $(X, \leq)$ is by its *tree-dimension*. A poset $(X, \leq)$ is a *tree*[2] [9, 29] if, for every pair x and y of incomparable elements in X, there does not exist an element $z \in X$ such that $x \leq z$ and $y \leq z$. (Observe that the Hasse diagram [27] of a tree poset is a forest of rooted trees). The *tree-dimension* [9] of a poset $(X, \leq)$ is the smallest number of tree extensions of $(X, \leq)$ the intersection of which gives rise to $(X, \leq)$. It is well known that the dimension of a poset is at most twice its tree-dimension.

[2]Note that the term "tree" for ordered sets is used in various senses in the literature, see e.g., [28].

Thus, the smallest size of a universal poset for the family of all n-element posets with tree-dimension at most k is at most n^{2k}. On the other hand, Alon and Scheinerman [8] showed that for fixed k, the number of n-element posets of dimension at most k is $n^{n(k-o(1))}$. Since the dimension of a poset is at least its tree-dimension, it follows[3] that a universal poset for the family of all n-element posets with tree-dimension at most k has number of elements at least $n^{k-o(1)}$. As we show, it turns out that the real bound is much closer to this lower bound than to the n^{2k} upper bound.

1.2 Our results

This paper constructs an ancestry labeling scheme for n-node rooted trees, whose label size is $\log n + O(\log\log n)$ bits. By doing that, we solve the ancestry problem which is among the main open problems in the field of informative labeling schemes. Moreover, our scheme assigns the labels to the nodes of any tree in linear time, and guarantees that any ancestry query is answered in constant time.

In addition, we establish a simple relation between compact ancestry schemes and small universal posets. Specifically, we show that there exists a *consistent* ancestry labeling scheme for n-node forests with label size ℓ (see next section for the definition of consistent ancestry schemes for forests) if and only if, for any integer $k \geq 1$, there exists a universal poset with $2^{k\ell}$ elements for the family of n-element posets with tree-dimension at most k. Using this equivalence, and slightly modifying our ancestry scheme, we prove that for any integer k, there exists a universal poset of size $O(n^k \log^{4k} n)$ for the family of all n-element posets with tree-dimension at most k.

1.3 Related work

As mentioned before, following the $2\log n$-bit ancestry scheme in [23], a considerable amount of research has been devoted to improve the upper bound on the label size as much as possible. Specifically, [3] gave a first non-trivial upper bound of $\frac{3}{2}\log n + O(\log\log n)$ bits. In [21], a scheme with label size $\log n + O(d\sqrt{\log n})$ bits was constructed to detect ancestry only between nodes at distance at most d from each other. An ancestry labeling scheme with label size of $\log n + O(\log n/\log\log n)$ bits was given in [26]. The current state of the art upper bound of $\log n + O(\sqrt{\log n})$ bits was given in [7] (that scheme is described in detail in the journal publication [1] joint with [3]).

Following the aforementioned results on ancestry labeling schemes for general rooted trees, two other works were published, which focused on particular types of trees. Specifically, an experimental comparison of different ancestry labeling schemes on XML trees that appear in real life can be found in [22]. More recently, [13] gave an ancestry labeling scheme that is efficient for trees of small depth: for n-node trees with depth d, the scheme uses labels of size $\log n + 2\log d + O(1)$ bits. This study was motivated by the observation that in real-life data, the typical depth of an XML tree is very small, which may strengthen the assumption that most nodes in the collection of all XML trees

[3]To see this, observe that the proof of Theorem 1 in [8] implies that the number of non-isomorphic n-element posets with tree-dimension at most k is at least $n^{n(k-o(1))}/n!$. Let M be the size of a universal poset for the family of n-element posets with tree-dimension at most k. We must have $n^{n(k-o(1))}/n! \leq \binom{M}{n}$, and thus $M \geq n^{k-o(1)}$.

belong to trees of small depth. If this is indeed the case, the scheme of [13] would incur a very good *average* label size for XML trees. This would be efficient if one considers a variable-length representation of the labels, but not very useful if the representation is fixed-length (the same amount of space must be used for each label) — see [22] for a more detailed discussion on the label representation.

The following *parenthood* problem can be viewed as a variant of the ancestry problem: given a rooted tree T, label the nodes of T in the most compact way such that one can determine whether u is a *parent* of v in T by merely inspecting the corresponding labels. The parenthood problem was also introduced in [23], and a very simple parenthood scheme was constructed there, using labels of size at most $2\log n$ bits. (Actually, [23] considered *adjacency* schemes in trees rather than parenthood schemes, however, such schemes are equivalent up to a constant number of bits in the label size[4]). By now, the parenthood problem is almost completely closed thanks to Alstrup and Rauhe [6], who constructed a parenthood scheme for n-node trees with label size $\log n + O(\log^* n)$ bits. In particular, this bound indicates that encoding ancestry in trees is strictly more costly than encoding parenthood.

Informative labeling schemes were also proposed for other decision problems, including distance [4, 14, 25], routing [12, 26], flow [18, 20], vertex connectivity [18, 19], and nearest common ancestor [5, 24].

The $2\log n$-bit ancestry scheme of [23] is consistent, and thus provides yet another evidence for the existence of a universal poset with n^{2k} elements for the family of all n-element posets with tree-dimension at most k. It is not clear whether the ancestry schemes in [3, 7, 21, 26] can be somewhat modified to be consistent and still maintain the same label size. However, even if this is indeed the case, the universal poset for the family of all n-element posets with tree-dimension at most k that would be obtained from those schemes, would be of size $\Omega(n^k 2^{k\sqrt{\log n}})$.

The lower bound of [4] implies a lower bound of $\Omega(n \log n)$ for the number of elements in a universal poset for the family of n-element posets with tree-dimension 1. As mentioned earlier, for fixed $k > 1$, the result of Alon and Scheinerman [8] implies a lower bound of $n^{k-o(1)}$ for the number of elements in a universal poset for the family of n-element posets with tree-dimension at most k.

2. PRELIMINARIES

Let T be a *rooted* tree, i.e., a tree with a designated node r referred as the *root* of T. The *depth* of a node $u \in T$ is defined as the distance from u to the root of T, i.e., the number of edge traversals from u to the root. In particular, the depth of the root is 0. For two nodes u and v in T, we say that u is an *ancestor* of v if $u \neq v$ and u is one of the nodes on the shortest path connecting v and r in T. For every non-root node u, let parent(u) denote the parent of u, i.e., the ancestor of u at distance 1 from it. A node v is a *descendant* of u if and only if u is an ancestor of v. The *size* of T, denoted by $|T|$, is the number of nodes in T. The *weight* of a node $u \in T$, denoted by weight(u), is defined as 1 plus the number of descendants of u, i.e., weight(u) is the size of the subtree hanging down from u. In particular, the weight of the root is weight$(r) = |T|$. For every integer n, let $\mathcal{T}(n)$ denote the family of all rooted trees of size at most n. For two nodes u and v in some forest F of rooted trees, we say that u is an *ancestor* of v in F iff u and v belong to the same rooted tree in F and u is an ancestor of v in that tree. For every integer n, let $\mathcal{F}(n)$ denote the family of all forests of rooted trees, were each forest in $\mathcal{F}(n)$ has at most n nodes.

For two nodes u and v in a tree T, let $P[u,v]$ denote the shortest path connecting u and v in T (including u and v), and let $P[u,v) = P[u,v] \setminus \{v\}$. For two integers $a \leq b$, let $[a,b]$ denote the set of integers $\{a, a+1, \cdots, b\}$. We refer to this set as an *interval*. For two intervals $I = [a,b]$ and $I' = [a',b']$, we say that $I \prec I'$ if $b < a'$. The *size* of an interval $I = [a,b]$ is $|I| = b - a + 1$, namely, the number of integers in I.

An *ancestry labeling scheme* $(\mathcal{M}, \mathcal{D})$ for a family $\mathcal{F}$ of forests of rooted trees is composed of the following components:

1. A *marker* algorithm $\mathcal{M}$ that assigns labels (i.e., bit strings) to the nodes of all forests in $\mathcal{F}$.
2. A *decoder* algorithm $\mathcal{D}$ that given any two labels ℓ_1 and ℓ_2 in the output domain of $\mathcal{M}$, returns a boolean $\mathcal{D}(\ell_1, \ell_2)$.

These components must satisfy that if $L(u)$ and $L(v)$ denote the labels assigned by the marker algorithm to two nodes u and v in some rooted forest $F \in \mathcal{F}$, then

$$\mathcal{D}(L(u), L(v)) = 1 \iff u \text{ is an ancestor of } v \text{ in } F.$$

It is important to note that the decoder algorithm $\mathcal{D}$ is independent of the forest F. That is, given the labels of two nodes, the decoder algorithm decides the ancestry relationship between the corresponding nodes without knowing to which forest in $\mathcal{F}$ they belong.

The most common complexity measure used for evaluating an ancestry scheme is the *label size*, that is, the maximum number of bits in a label assigned by $\mathcal{M}$, taken over all nodes in all forests in $\mathcal{F}$. When considering the *query time* of the decoder algorithm, we use the RAM model of computation, and assume that the length of a computer word is $\Omega(\log n)$ bits. Similarly to previous works on ancestry schemes, our decoder algorithm uses only basic RAM operations (which are assumed to take constant time). Specifically, the basic operations used by our decoder algorithm are the following: addition, substraction, left/right shifts, less-than comparisons, and extraction of the least significant bit. Our scheme avoids the sometimes more costly operations such as multiplication or division.

Let $\mathcal{F}$ be a family of forests of rooted trees. We say that an ancestry labeling scheme $(\mathcal{M}, \mathcal{D})$ for $\mathcal{F}$ is *consistent* if (1) the marker algorithm $\mathcal{M}$ assigns pairwise distinct labels to the nodes of any forest $F \in \mathcal{F}$, and (2) the decoder algorithm $\mathcal{D}$ satisfies the following conditions, for any three labels ℓ_1, ℓ_2 and ℓ_3 in the output domain of $\mathcal{M}$:

- *Anti-symmetry*: if $\mathcal{D}(\ell_1, \ell_2) = 1$ then $\mathcal{D}(\ell_2, \ell_1) = 0$, and

[4]To see this equivalence, observe that one can construct a parenthood scheme from an adjacency scheme in trees, as follows. Given a rooted tree T, first label the nodes of T using the adjacency scheme (with ignores the fact that T is rooted). Then, for each node u, in addition to the label given to it by the adjacency scheme, add two more bits, for encoding $d(u)$, the distance from u to the root calculated modulo 3. Now the parenthood scheme follows by observing that for any two nodes u and v in a tree, u is a parent of v iff u and v are adjacent and $d(u) = d(v) - 1$ modulo 3.

- *Transitivity*: if $\mathcal{D}(\ell_1, \ell_2) = 1$ and $\mathcal{D}(\ell_2, \ell_3) = 1$ then $\mathcal{D}(\ell_1, \ell_3) = 1$.

Note that by the definition of an ancestry scheme $(\mathcal{M}, \mathcal{D})$, the decoder algorithm $\mathcal{D}$ trivially satisfies the two conditions above if $\ell_i = L(u_i)$ for $i = 1, 2, 3$, and u_1, u_2 and u_3 belong to the same forest in $\mathcal{F}$.

3. THE ANCESTRY LABELING SCHEME

This section is dedicated to the proof of the following theorem:

THEOREM 1. *There exists an ancestry labeling scheme for $\mathcal{T}(n)$ with label size $\log n + O(\log\log n)$ bits. Moreover, given a tree $T \in \mathcal{T}(n)$, the labels can be assigned to the nodes of T in $O(n)$ time, and any ancestry query can be answered in constant time.*

A natural approach for constructing an ancestry labeling scheme is to label each node u in the given tree T by a pointer to some interval $I(u)$, in a way such that for any two nodes u and v in T, u is an ancestor of v if and only if $I(v) \subset I(u)$. Thus, to check ancestry, the decoder algorithm can simply apply the interval containment test. This approach relates the partial order defined by ancestry to the natural partial order defined on intervals through containment. It was used, for example, by the original ancestry scheme of [23]. There, the set of intervals U that could potentially be used to label nodes is of size at most n^2, and the $2\log n$ bits label size follows.

The idea behind the ancestry scheme of [13] was to find a much smaller set of intervals U to which one can map the nodes of trees in such an order preserving manner. Indeed, this method works well when the depths of the given trees are small. Unfortunately, however, the approach is no longer efficient if the input trees can have long paths. Informally, enforcing the decoder algorithm to be merely an interval containment test imposes a strong constraint on the way the intervals must be organized in U. For arbitrary trees, we could not find a way to bypass this constraint while keeping U small. Instead, this paper introduces a decoder algorithm which performs according to a different principle. At a very high level, our new decoder algorithm exploits the fact that intervals can be partially ordered not only by the containment relation, but also by the relation " $\prec$ " introduced in the previous section. By combining these two partial orders on intervals, we define a new relation[5] between *pairs* of intervals. This relation is defined such that the nodes of any tree can be mapped to a limited set of pairs of intervals in an "order preserving manner", i.e., the ancestry relation in the tree is compatible with the new relation defined on pairs of intervals.

More formally, given any node u in some rooted tree T, we first associate u with a *supervisor* node, denoted by $\sup(u)$, which is either u itself or one of its ancestors. For this purpose, we first mark each node as either *heavy* or *light* as follows. For every non-leaf node u of T, let $H(u)$ be the set of children v of u that satisfy $\text{weight}(v) \geq \text{weight}(w)$ for every child w of u. Among the nodes in $H(u)$, select an arbitrary node, and call it *heavy*. A node which is not heavy is called *light*. (In particular, the root is light). For each node $u \in T$, define the *supervisor* of u, denoted by $\sup(u)$, as the light node of largest depth on the path $P[u, r]$ connecting u to the root r. Note that if u is light then $\sup(u)$ is u itself; in particular, $\sup(r) = r$, and $\sup(\sup(u)) = \sup(u)$. Observe also that if u is an ancestor of v, then either $\sup(u) = \sup(v)$, or $\sup(u)$ is an ancestor of $\sup(v)$. See Figure 1.

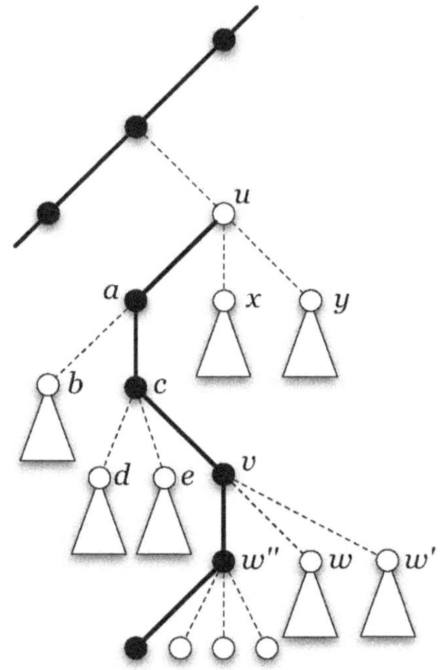

Figure 1: The heavy nodes are depicted in black, while the light nodes are depicted in white. In the figure, $\sup(v) = u$ and $\sup(w) = w$. We have $\text{parent}(w) = v$. Hence, the local quasi ancestors of w are the set of nodes $\text{lqa}(w) = \{x, y, a, b, c, d, e, v, w'\}$ if $\text{DFS}(w) > \text{DFS}(w')$, and $\text{lqa}(w) = \{x, y, a, b, c, d, e, v\}$, otherwise. Similarly, we have $\text{lqa}(x) = \emptyset$ if $\text{DFS}(y) > \text{DFS}(x)$, and $\text{lqa}(x) = \{y\}$, otherwise.

The marker algorithm $\mathcal{M}$ now assigns an interval $I(u)$ to each node $u \in T$, and associates u with the pair of intervals $I(u)$ and $I(\sup(u))$. More formally, the marker algorithm $\mathcal{M}$ assigns a label $L(u)$ to each node u, in a way such that the intervals $I(u)$ and $I(\sup(u))$ can be extracted from $L(u)$ in constant time. Given the labels $L(u)$ and $L(v)$ assigned by our marker algorithm $\mathcal{M}$ to two nodes u and v in some rooted tree, our boolean decoder algorithm $\mathcal{D}$ outputs 1 if and only if the "decoding conditions" defined below hold at u w.r.t. v.

DEFINITION 1. *Consider a set of pairwise distinct intervals $\{I(u),\ u \in T\}$ for a tree T (i.e., $I(u) \neq I(v)$ for any two different nodes u and v). We say that the* decoding conditions *hold at u w.r.t. v if and only if:*

- D1: *$I(v) \subset I(sup(u))$, and*
- D2: *$I(u) \prec I(v)$ or $I(u) = I(sup(u))$.*

[5]As explained in Section 4, this relation is "almost" a partial order on the set of labels (each label corresponds to a pair of intervals) which are assigned by the marker algorithm. Indeed, only a slight modification of the decoder algorithm (for making our ancestry scheme consistent) suffices to induce a partial order on that set.

Before dwelling into the details of our construction, we would like to point out that storing both intervals $I(u)$ and $I(\sup(u))$ explicitly in the label of u may consume too many bits. In fact, it will follow from our construction that the encoding of a single interval may already consume $\log n + O(\log\log n)$ bits, in worst case. To overcome this problem, we shall use the fact that for every node u, $I(u) \subseteq I(\sup(u))$. This fact, together with specific constraints which are imposed on the intervals, will allow the decoder algorithm to recover the interval $I(\sup(u))$ from the interval $I(u)$ using only additional $O(\log\log n)$ bits.

3.1 The marker algorithm $\mathcal{M}$

Assume without loss of generality that n is a power of 2, and fix a tree $T \in \mathcal{T}(n)$. For our scheme to be correct, the marker algorithm $\mathcal{M}$ must assign the interval $I(u)$ to each node u in T in a way such that for every two nodes u and v in T, u is an ancestor of v if and only if the decoding conditions hold at u w.r.t. v. For this purpose, we first show that it is sufficient to provide an assignment of intervals that satisfies more "local" conditions.

3.1.1 The local conditions

Let us first assign numbers from 0 to $n-1$ to the nodes according to a DFS traversal that starts at the root, and visits light children first. We denote by DFS(u) the DFS number of u. Let $P_u = P[\text{parent}(u), \sup(\text{parent}(u))]$. We define the *local quasi-ancestors* of a non-root node u, denoted by lqa(u), as all nodes in P_u, together with their light children, but removing u, $\sup(\text{parent}(u))$, and all nodes that have DFS numbers higher than u. See Figure 1 for an example. Note that the local quasi-ancestors of a node may not form a connected subtree of T.

DEFINITION 2. *Let us consider a set of pairwise distinct intervals $\{I(u),\ u \in T\}$ for a tree T. For every non-root node u, we say that u satisfies the* local conditions *if the two conditions below are satisfied:*

- L1: $I(u) \subseteq I(sup(u)) \cap I(sup(parent(u)))$;
- L2: $I(x) \prec I(u)$ *for every* $x \in lqa(u)$.

The following lemma relates the decoding conditions to the local conditions.

LEMMA 1. *If every non-root node u satisfies the local conditions* L1 *and* L2, *then for every two different nodes u and v, u is an ancestor of v if and only if the decoding conditions* D1 *and* D2 *hold at u w.r.t. v.*

PROOF. Let us assume that every non-root node u satisfies the local conditions L1 and L2. We first prove the following claim:

Claim 1. For any light node u, and any descendent v of u, we have $I(v) \subset I(u)$.

We establish the claim by induction on the distance between u and v. If $\text{dist}(u,v) = 1$ then the claim holds as v satisfies L1 and u is light. Fix $d \geq 1$ and assume that the claim holds for all pairs of nodes u and v such that $\text{dist}(u,v) \leq d$. Consider now a pair of nodes u and v such that $\text{dist}(u,v) = d+1$. If $u = \sup(\text{parent}(v))$ then the claim follows as v satisfies L1. On the other hand, if $u \neq \sup(\text{parent}(v))$ then there exists a light node $w \notin \{u,v\}$ on the shortest path connecting u to v, namely $w = \sup(\text{parent}(v))$. The claim then follows by induction.

To establish the lemma, consider first the case where u is an ancestor of v. Since v is a descendent of u, either $\sup(v) = \sup(u)$ or $\sup(v)$ is a descendent of $\sup(u)$. Thus, by Claim 1, $I(v) \subseteq I(\sup(v)) \subseteq I(\sup(u))$. Since $v \neq u$, $I(v) \subset I(\sup(u))$, i.e., D1 follows. If u is light then the fact that u and v satisfy D2 follows trivially from the fact that, in this case, $\sup(u) = u$. So assume now that u is heavy. If $u \in \text{lqa}(v)$, then D2 follows from L2. On the other hand, if $u \notin \text{lqa}(v)$, then there exists a light node w that is an ancestor of v, and such that $u \in \text{lqa}(w)$. D2 follows by combining L2 with Claim 1.

Consider now the case where u is not an ancestor of v. We need to show that either D1 or D2 does not hold. Let w be the light node of largest depth on the path $P[v,r]$, which is an ancestor of u. If w is v itself then $\sup(u)$ is either v or a descendant of v. Therefore, by Claim 1, we have $I(\sup(u)) \subseteq I(v)$, and thus D1 is not satisfied. In the remaining of the proof we thus assume that $w \neq v$. For a node x which is a descendant of w, and which satisfies $\sup(x) \neq w$, let $f(x)$ be the light node of smallest depth on the path $P[x,w)$.

Assume first that $\sup(u) = w$. If also $\sup(v) = w$ then $v \in \text{lqa}(u)$, and thus, by L2, $I(v) \prec I(u)$. Since $u \neq w$, we have $I(u) \neq I(\sup(u))$, and therefore D2 is not satisfied. If, on the other hand, $\sup(v) \neq w$ then we have $f(v) \in \text{lqa}(u)$ and, by Claim 1, $I(v) \subset I(f(v))$. In a way similar to the previous case where $\sup(v) = w$, we then get that D2 is not satisfied.

Assume now that $\sup(u) \neq w$. We have $I(\sup(u)) \subseteq I(f(u))$. If v is an ancestor of $f(u)$ then $v \in \text{lqa}(f(u))$. Consequently, $I(v) \prec I(f(u))$ and thus D1 does not hold. On the other hand, if v is not an ancestor of $f(u)$ then we are left with two cases: $\sup(v) = w$ and $\sup(v) \neq w$. If $\sup(v) = w$ then $I(f(u)) \prec I(v)$ since $f(u) \in \text{lqa}(v)$. Thus D1 does not hold. Finally, if $\sup(v) \neq w$ then either $f(u) \in \text{lqa}(f(v))$ or $f(v) \in \text{lqa}(f(u))$. Since $I(\sup(u)) \subseteq I(f(u))$ and $I(v) \subseteq I(f(v))$, it follows that D1 does not hold. □

3.1.2 The interval assignment

By Lemma 1, one of our goals is to let the marker algorithm assign intervals that satisfy the local conditions at each non-root node. For integers a, b and k, let

$$I_{k,a,b} = [2^k a,\ 2^k(a+b)].$$

For $k \in [1, \log n]$, define the set of intervals:

$$\mathcal{I}_k = \{I_{i,a,b} \mid i \in [1,k], a \in [1, n\log n/2^{i-2}], \text{ and } b \in [1, 4i]\}$$

Denote $\mathcal{I} = \mathcal{I}_{\log n}$.

DEFINITION 3. *Let $T \in \mathcal{T}(n)$. A mapping $I : V(T) \to \mathcal{I}$ is called a* legal interval-mapping *if I is one-to-one, and $\{I(u), u \in T\}$ satisfies the local conditions at each non-root node of T.*

In order to show that there exists a legal interval-mapping from every tree in $\mathcal{T}(n)$ into $\mathcal{I}$, we use the following notation. For any interval $J \subseteq [1, 4n\log n]$, and, for any k, $1 \leq k \leq \log n$, let

$$\mathcal{I}_k(J) = \{I_{i,a,b} \in \mathcal{I}_k \mid I_{i,a,b} \subseteq J\}.$$

LEMMA 2. *For every $k \in [1, \log n]$, every tree $T \in \mathcal{T}(2^k)$, and every interval $J \subseteq [1, 4n\log n]$, such that $|J| = 4k|T|$,*

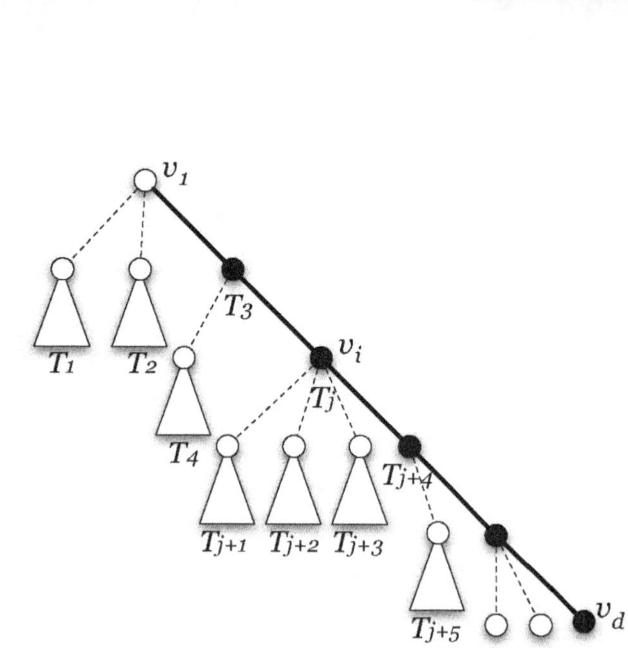

Figure 2: Tree decomposition as in the proof of Lemma 2. In the figure, the DFS traversal that visits light nodes first is supposed to proceed by visiting children from left to right.

there exists a legal interval-mapping of T into $\mathcal{I}_k(J)$. Moreover this mapping can be computed in $O(|T|)$ time.

PROOF. We prove the lemma by induction on k. For $k = 1$, the fact that the lemma holds can be easily verified. Assume now that the lemma holds for k with $1 \leq k < \log n$, and let us show that it also holds for $k+1$. Clearly, if $|T| \leq 2^k$ then we are done by induction. Consider now the case where T is of size $2^k < |T| \leq 2^{k+1}$, and let $J \subseteq [1, 4n \log n]$ be an interval, such that $|J| = 4(k+1)|T|$. Our goal is to construct a legal-interval mapping of T into $\mathcal{I}_{k+1}(J)$.

We make use of the following decomposition of T. Let H be the path from the root of T to a leaf of T such that every non-root node in H is heavy. Let $v_1, v_2, \cdots, v_d$ be the nodes of H, ordered top-down, i.e., v_1 is the root of T, v_d is a leaf of T, and for every $1 \leq i < d$, v_i is the parent of v_{i+1}.

For every $1 \leq i \leq d$, let $T_i^1, T_i^2, \cdots, T_i^{t_i}$ be the rooted trees hanging down from the light children of v_i. (If v_i does not have any light child, which is the case, for example, for $i = d$, then this set of trees is empty, or, in other words, $t_i = 0$). One important property of these trees is that, for every i and j, $1 \leq j \leq t_i$, we have $|T_i^j| < |T|/2 \leq 2^k$.

Let us now group the nodes in $T \setminus \{r\}$ in disjoint trees $T_1, T_2, \cdots, T_m$, where $m = d - 1 + \sum_{\ell=1}^{d} t_\ell$ as follows. A tree T_i is either a single heavy node v_j, for $j > 1$, or a subtree hanging down from a light child of some v_j, $j \geq 1$. Moreover, the trees are enumerated according to the DFS numbers of their roots as follows. Recall that $\text{DFS}(u)$ denotes the DFS number of node u in T. The trees are ordered such that if r_j denotes the root of T_j then $\text{DFS}(r_j) < \text{DFS}(r_{j+1})$ for all $j = 1, \ldots, m-1$. See Figure 2.

Consider now the given interval $J \subseteq [1, 4n \log n]$, and express it as $J = [\alpha, \alpha + 4(k+1)|T| - 1]$ for some integer α. Let a be the smallest integer such that $\alpha \leq a\, 2^{k+1}$, and let b be the smallest integer such that $4k|T| \leq b\, 2^{k+1}$. First, we assign the root r to the interval $J' = [a 2^{k+1}, (a+b)2^{k+1}]$. We now show that indeed $J' \in \mathcal{I}_{k+1}(J)$. By definition of a and b, we have

$$(a+b)2^{k+1} = 2^{k+2} + ((a-1)+(b-1))2^{k+1} \leq 2^{k+2} + \alpha + 4k|T| - 2.$$

Since $2^k < |T|$, we get that

$$(a+b)2^{k+1} < \alpha + (4k+4)|T| - 1.$$

Thus

$$J' = [a\, 2^{k+1}, (a+b)2^{k+1}] \subset [\alpha, \alpha + (4k+4)|T| - 1] = J.$$

Therefore, since $a - 1 < \alpha/2^{k+1} < 4n \log n/2^{k+1}$, and since n is a power of 2, we get $1 \leq a \leq 4n \log n/2^{k+1}$. Combining this with the fact that $1 \leq b \leq 4k$, we obtain that $J' \in \mathcal{I}_{k+1}(J)$.

The rest of the nodes in T are mapped as follows. First note that $|J'| > 4k|T|$, and recall that $\sum_{i=1}^{m} |T_i| = |T| - 1$. Let $J_1', J_2', \cdots, J_m'$ be m pairwise disjoint consecutive subintervals of J' such that, for each $1 \leq i \leq m$, we have $|J_i'| = 4k|T_i|$, and for $1 \leq i < m$, $J_i' \prec J_{i+1}'$. For each $1 \leq i \leq m$, we now use the induction hypothesis to map the nodes in T_i to $\mathcal{I}_k(J_i')$ via a legal interval-mapping (recall that $|T_i| \leq 2^k$).

The fact that the above recursive mapping can be performed in linear time is obvious. It remains to show that the above mapping of T into $\mathcal{I}_{k+1}(J)$ is indeed a legal interval-mapping. That is, we have to show that the set of intervals satisfies the local conditions L1 and L2 at each non-root node u. The fact that the local conditions hold at every node u in $T_i \setminus r_i$ follows from the induction hypothesis, since $\sup(u)$, $\sup(\text{parent}(u))$, and $\text{lqa}(u)$ are all contained in T_i. Finally, consider the root r_i of T_i. (Note that if r_i is heavy then $T_i = \{r_i\}$). L1 holds trivially for r_i because J' contains J_i', and, by induction, the interval assigned to r_i is contained in the interval J_i'. To establish that L2 holds, first observe that $\text{lqa}(r_i) = \{r_1, \ldots, r_{i-1}\}$. On the other hand, for every $j = 1, \ldots, i-1$, $\text{DFS}(r_j) < \text{DFS}(r_i)$, and thus $J_j' \prec J_i'$. Hence L2 holds for r_i as well. Our mapping is thus a legal interval-mapping of T into $\mathcal{I}_{k+1}(J)$. The lemma follows. □

COROLLARY 1. *Let $T \in \mathcal{T}(n)$. There exists a legal interval-mapping of T into $\mathcal{I}$, which takes $O(|T|)$ time.*

3.1.3 The label assignment

After mapping T into $\mathcal{I}$ using the legal-interval mapping given by Corollary 1, the marker algorithm $\mathcal{M}$ assigns the label $L(u)$ to each node u as follows. Given a node u, the marker algorithm uses the first $\log n + \log\log n + O(1)$ least significant bits of $L(u)$ to encode the interval $I(u)$. This can be done explicitly as $I(u) = I_{k,a,b}$ for some $k \in [1, \log n]$, $a \in [1, n \log n/2^{k-2}]$ and $b \in [1, 4k]$. Specifically, the first $\lceil \log k \rceil$ bits in $L(u)$ are set to 0 and the following bit is set to 1. The next $2\log k + O(1)$ bits are used for encoding k and b, and the following $\log n + \log\log n - k + O(1)$ bits to encode a.

Finally, the marker algorithm aims at encoding $I(\sup(u))$ in the label of u. However, using the method above to encode $I(\sup(u))$ would consume yet another $\log n + \log\log n + O(1)$ bits, which is obviously undesired. Instead, we use the following trick. Let k', a', and b' be such that $I(\sup(u)) = I_{k',a',b'}$. Clearly, $2\log\log n + O(1)$ bits suffice to encode both k' and b'. To encode a', the marker algorithm acts as follows. Let $I(u) = [\alpha, \beta]$, and let a'' be the largest integer such that $2^{k'} a'' \leq \alpha$. Recall that by definition $I(\sup(u)) =$

$[2^{k'}a', 2^{k'}(a'+b')]$. We have, $a'' - 4\log n \le a'' - b'$ because $b' \le 4\log n$. Since $I(u) \subseteq I(\sup(u))$, we also have $2^{k'}(a'+b') \ge \beta \ge \alpha \ge 2^{k'}a''$. Thus $a'' - b' \le a'$. Finally, again since $I(u) \subseteq I(\sup(u))$, we have $2^{k'}a' \le \alpha$, and thus $a'' \ge a'$. Combining the above inequalities, we get that $a' \in [a'' - 4\log n, a'']$. The marker algorithm now encodes the integer $t \in [0, 4\log n]$ such that $a' = a'' - t$. This is done in consuming another $\log\log n + O(1)$ bits. Hence, we obtain:

LEMMA 3. *Given a tree $T \in \mathcal{T}(n)$, the marker algorithm $\mathcal{M}$ assigns labels to the nodes of T in linear time, and each label is encoded using* $\log n + 4\log\log n + O(1)$ *bits.*

3.2 The decoder algorithm $\mathcal{D}$

Now, we describe our decoder algorithm $\mathcal{D}$. Given the labels $L(u)$ and $L(v)$ assigned by $\mathcal{M}$ to two different nodes in some tree T, the decoder algorithm $\mathcal{D}$ needs to find whether u is an ancestor of v in T. (Observe that since each node receives a distinct label, the decoder algorithm can easily find out if u and v are in fact the same node, and, in this trivial case, it simply outputs 0.)

The decoder algorithm first extracts $I(u)$ by inspecting the first $\log n + \log\log n + O(1)$ least significant bits of $L(u)$. This is done as follows. Recall that $I(u) = I_{k,a,b}$ for some integers k, a and b. The decoder algorithm first extracts $\lceil \log k \rceil$ by finding the least significant bit that equals to 1. It then inspects the next $2\log k + O(1)$ bits to obtain k and b, and the next $\log n + \log\log n - k + O(1)$ bits to extract a. Once $I(u) = [\alpha, \beta]$ has been reconstructed from $L(u)$, the decoder algorithm aims at extracting $I(\sup(u))$. For this purpose, it first reconstructs k' and b' that have been explicitly encoded in the next $2\log\log n + O(1)$ bits of $L(u)$. Then, it computes the largest integer a'' such that $2^{k'}a'' \le \alpha$. The decoder algorithm then proceeds by extracting t, and computes $a' = a'' - t$. At this point, $\mathcal{D}$ has reconstructed both $I(u)$ and $I(\sup(u))$. Similarly, $\mathcal{D}$ extracts $I(v)$ by inspecting $L(v)$.

Finally, the boolean decoder algorithm $\mathcal{D}$ outputs 1 if and only if the two decoding conditions D1 and D2 hold at u w.r.t. v (see Definition 1).

LEMMA 4. *Let $L(u)$ and $L(v)$ be two labels assigned by $\mathcal{M}$ to two nodes in T. The decoder algorithm $\mathcal{D}(L(u), L(v))$ performs in constant time, and satisfies $\mathcal{D}(L(u), L(v)) = 1$ if and only if u is an ancestor of v in T.*

PROOF. The fact that $\mathcal{D}(L(u), L(v)) = 1$ if and only if u is an ancestor of v in T follows by combining Lemma 1 with the fact that the intervals are assigned by the marker algorithm via a legal-interval mapping (cf. Corollary 1). Since $I(u) = I_{k,a,b} = [2^k a, 2^k(a+b)]$ with all three parameters k, a, and b stored explicitly, computing $I(u)$ from $L(u)$ can be achieved in constant time. (Note that $2^k a$, for example, can be obtained from a by a simple shift of k bits.) Similarly, $I(v)$ can be extracted from $L(v)$ in constant time. Computing $I(\sup(u))$ just needs a subtraction operation and a division by a power of 2, which again amounts to a simple shift operation. The lemma follows. □

Theorem 1 follows by combining Lemma 3 with Lemma 4. Observe now that a rooted forest $F \in \mathcal{F}(n)$ can be viewed as a subgraph of T, where T is the rooted tree with $n+1$ nodes obtained by adding another root node and connecting it to the roots of all trees in F. Thus, by slightly modifying our marker algorithm $\mathcal{M}$, we obtain an new ancestry scheme $(\mathcal{M}', \mathcal{D})$ that can handle forests as well. Specifically, we have:

COROLLARY 2. *$(\mathcal{M}', \mathcal{D})$ is an ancestry scheme for $\mathcal{F}(n)$ with label size* $\log n + 4\log\log n + O(1)$ *bits.*

4. SMALL UNIVERSAL POSETS

For any two positive integers n and k, let $\mathcal{P}(n,k)$ denote the family of all n-element posets with tree-dimension at most k. Recall that an ancestry labeling scheme $(\mathcal{M}, \mathcal{D})$ for $\mathcal{F}(n)$ is consistent if $\mathcal{M}$ assigns distinct labels to the nodes of any $F \in \mathcal{F}(n)$ and $\mathcal{D}$ satisfies the anti-symmetry and transitivity conditions. Our next theorem relates compact consistent ancestry labeling schemes with small universal posets.

THEOREM 2. *There exists a consistent ancestry labeling scheme for $\mathcal{F}(n)$ with label size ℓ if and only if for every integer k, there exists a universal poset of size $2^{k\ell}$ for $\mathcal{P}(n,k)$.*

PROOF. Assume first that for every integer k there exists a universal poset $(\mathcal{P}, \le)$ of size $2^{k\ell}$ for $\mathcal{P}(n,k)$. In particular, there exists a universal poset $(\mathcal{P}, \le)$ of size 2^ℓ for $\mathcal{P}(n,1)$, i.e., for the family of n-element posets with tree-dimension 1. We construct the following ancestry scheme $(\mathcal{M}, \mathcal{D})$ for $\mathcal{F}(n)$. The marker algorithm $\mathcal{M}$ first considers some bijective mapping $\phi : \mathcal{P} \to [1, |\mathcal{P}|]$. Given a rooted forest $F \in \mathcal{F}(n)$, view F as a poset whose Hasse diagram is F. Obviously, F is a poset with tree-dimension 1. Now, let $\rho : F \to \mathcal{P}$ be a mapping that preserves the partial order of F. The marker algorithm assigns the label $L(u) = \phi(\rho(u))$ to each node $u \in F$. Given the labels $L(u)$ and $L(v)$ of two nodes u and v in some $F \in \mathcal{F}(n)$, the decoder algorithm $\mathcal{D}$ outputs 1 if and only if $L(u) \ne L(v)$ and $\phi^{-1}(L(u)) \le \phi^{-1}(L(v))$. Obviously, $(\mathcal{M}, \mathcal{D})$ is a consistent ancestry labeling scheme for $\mathcal{F}(n)$ with label size $\log|\mathcal{P}| = \ell$.

For the other direction, assume that there exists a consistent ancestry labeling scheme for $\mathcal{F}(n)$ with label size ℓ. Let $\mathcal{P} = [1, 2^\ell]^k$. We define a relation $\le$ between pairs of elements in $\mathcal{P}$. For two elements $x, y \in \mathcal{P}$, where $x = (x_1, x_2, \cdots, x_k)$ and $y = (y_1, y_2, \cdots, y_k)$, we say that $x \le y$ if and only if, for every i, $1 \le i \le k$, either $x_i = y_i$ or $\mathcal{D}(x_i, y_i)$ is defined and equals 1. It can be easily verified that $(\mathcal{P}, \le)$ is a universal poset for $\mathcal{P}(n,k)$. The theorem follows. □

For the objective of constructing a small universal poset for $\mathcal{P}(n,k)$, let us consider the ancestry labeling scheme $(\mathcal{M}', \mathcal{D})$ for $\mathcal{F}(n)$ given by Corollary 2. We now define a new decoder algorithm $\mathcal{D}'$ as follows: $\mathcal{D}'(L(u), L(v)) = 1$ if and only if $\mathcal{D}(L(u), L(v)) = 1$ and $I(\sup(v)) \subseteq I(\sup(u))$.

LEMMA 5. *$(\mathcal{M}', \mathcal{D}')$ is a consistent ancestry labeling scheme for $\mathcal{F}(n)$ with label size* $\log n + 4\log\log n + O(1)$ *bits.*

PROOF. The fact that $(\mathcal{M}', \mathcal{D}')$ is an ancestry labeling scheme for $\mathcal{F}(n)$ is obvious, since the condition $I(\sup(v)) \subseteq I(\sup(u))$ always holds if u is an ancestor of v in some forest (see Claim 1 in the proof of Lemma 1). Moreover, the required label size of $(\mathcal{M}', \mathcal{D}')$ follows directly from Corollary 2.

We now turn to prove that $(\mathcal{M}', \mathcal{D}')$ is consistent. The fact that $\mathcal{M}'$ assigns disjoint labels to the nodes of any forest

$F \in \mathcal{F}(n)$ is obvious from its construction. Consider now any three labels ℓ_1, ℓ_2 and ℓ_3 in the domain of $\mathcal{M}'$, and let u, v and w be three nodes each belonging to some forest in $\mathcal{F}(n)$ (not necessarily the same forest) where $\ell_1 = L(u)$, $\ell_2 = L(v)$ and $\ell_3 = L(w)$. Assume now that $\mathcal{D}'(L(u), L(v)) = 1$ and let us show that $\mathcal{D}'(L(v), L(u)) = 0$. By definition of $\mathcal{D}'$, the decoding conditions between u and v must hold, i.e., we have (1) $I(v) \subset I(\sup(u))$, and (2) $I(u) \prec I(v)$ or $I(u) = I(\sup(u))$. (Note, by definition, these conditions must hold also if u and v belong to different forests). If $I(u) = I(\sup(u))$ then $I(v) \subset I(u)$. If also $\mathcal{D}'(L(v), L(u)) = 1$ then we must have $I(v) = I(\sup(v))$ which contradicts the condition $I(u) \subset I(\sup(v))$. If on the other hand $I(u) \neq I(\sup(u))$ then $I(u) \prec I(v)$. If also $\mathcal{D}'(L(v), L(u)) = 1$ then we must have $I(v) = I(\sup(v))$, and therefore since $I(u) \subset I(\sup(v))$, we get $I(u) \subset I(v)$, contradiction.

Let us now show that the transitivity condition holds, i.e., we assume that $\mathcal{D}'(L(u), L(v)) = 1$ and $\mathcal{D}'(L(v), L(w)) = 1$, and our goal is to show that $\mathcal{D}'(L(u), L(w)) = 1$. The fact that $I(\sup(w)) \subseteq I(\sup(u))$ is immediate. Since $I(w) \subset I(\sup(v))$ and $I(\sup(v)) \subseteq I(\sup(u))$, we obtain that $I(w) \subset I(\sup(u))$, i.e., the first decoding condition between u and w holds. We now show that the second decoding condition also holds. If $I(u) = I(\sup(u))$ then we are done, therefore, assume $I(u) \neq I(\sup(u))$. The fact that $\mathcal{D}'(L(u), L(v)) = 1$ now implies that $I(u) \prec I(v)$. Observe, if $I(v) \prec I(w)$ then $I(u) \prec I(w)$ and we are done. Otherwise, the fact that $\mathcal{D}'(L(u), L(w)) = 1$ implies that $I(v) = I(\sup(v))$. Therefore, $I(w) \subset I(\sup(v)) = I(v)$. Combining this with the fact that $I(u) \prec I(v)$, we obtain $I(u) \prec I(w)$. This completes the proof of the lemma. □

By combining Theorem 2 and Lemma 5, we obtain the following.

THEOREM 3. *For every integer k, there exists a universal poset of size $O(n^k \log^{4k} n)$ for $\mathcal{P}(n,k)$.*

Acknowledgments. The authors are very thankful to William T. Trotter, Sundar Vishwanathan and Jean-Sebastien Sereni for helpful discussions.

5. REFERENCES

[1] S. Abiteboul, S. Alstrup, H. Kaplan, T. Milo and T. Rauhe. Compact labeling schemes for ancestor queries. *SIAM Journal on Computing* **35**, (2006), 1295–1309.

[2] S. Abiteboul, P. Buneman and D. Suciu. Data on the Web: From Relations to Semistructured Data and XML. *Morgan Kaufmann*, (1999).

[3] Abiteboul, S., Kaplan, H., and Milo, T.: Compact labeling schemes for ancestor queries. In *Proc. 12th ACM-SIAM Symp. on Discrete Algorithms* (SODA), 2001.

[4] S. Alstrup, P. Bille and T. Rauhe. Labeling Schemes for Small Distances in Trees. In *Proc. 14th ACM-SIAM Symp. on Discrete Algorithms* (SODA), 2003.

[5] S. Alstrup, C. Gavoille, H. Kaplan and T. Rauhe. Nearest Common Ancestors: A Survey and a new Distributed Algorithm. *Theory of Computing Systems* **37**, (2004), 441–456.

[6] S. Alstrup and T. Rauhe. Small induced-universal graphs and compact implicit graph representations. In *Proc. 43rd IEEE Symp. on Foundations of Computer Science* (FOCS), 2002.

[7] S. Alstrup and T. Rauhe. Improved labeling scheme for ancestor queries. In *Proc. 13th ACM-SIAM Symposium on Discrete Algorithms* (SODA), pages 947-953, 2002.

[8] N. Alon and E. R. Scheinerman. Degrees of Freedom Versus Dimension for Containment Orders. In *Order* **5** (1988), 11–16.

[9] G. Behrendt. On trees and tree dimension of ordered sets. *Order* **10(2)**, (1993), 153–160.

[10] A. Deutsch, M. Fernández, D. Florescu, A. Levy and D. Suciu. A Query Language for XML. *Computer Networks* **31**, (1999), 1155-1169.

[11] R. Fraisse Theory of relations. *North-Holland*, Amsterdam, 1953.

[12] P. Fraigniaud and C. Gavoille. Routing in trees. In Proc. 28th Int. Colloq. on Automata, Languages, and Programing (ICALP), LNCS 2076, pages 757–772, Springer, 2001.

[13] P. Fraigniaud and A. Korman. Compact Ancestry Labeling Schemes for XML Trees. In Proc. 21st ACM-SIAM Symp. on Discrete Algorithms (SODA), 2010.

[14] C. Gavoille, D. Peleg, S. Pérennes and R. Raz. Distance labeling in graphs. In Proc. 12th ACM-SIAM Symp. on Discrete Algorithms (SODA), pages 210–219, 2001.

[15] J. Hubicka and J. NeŽetril. Universal partial order represented by means of oriented trees and other simple graphs. *Euro. J. of Combinatorics* **26(5)**, (2005), 765 – 778.

[16] B. Jonson. Universal relational systems. *Math Scan.* **4**, (1956), 193–208.

[17] J. B. Johnston. Universal infinite partially ordered sets. *Proc. Amer. Math. Soc.* **7**, (1957), 507–514.

[18] M. Katz, N.A. Katz, A. Korman, and D. Peleg. Labeling schemes for flow and connectivity. *SIAM Journal on Computing* **34** (2004),23–40.

[19] A. Korman. Labeling Schemes for Vertex Connectivity. *ACM Transactions on Algorithms*, to appear.

[20] A. Korman and S. Kutten. Distributed Verification of Minimum Spanning Trees. *Distributed Computing* **20**(4): 253-266 (2007).

[21] H. Kaplan and T. Milo. Short and simple labels for small distances and other functions. In *Workshop on Algorithms and Data Structures*, Aug. 2001.

[22] H. Kaplan, T. Milo and R. Shabo. A Comparison of Labeling Schemes for Ancestor Queries. In Proc. 19th ACM-SIAM Symp. on Discrete Algorithms (SODA), 2002.

[23] S. Kannan, M. Naor, and S. Rudich. Implicit representation of graphs. *SIAM J. on Discrete Math* **5**, (1992), 596–603.

[24] D. Peleg. Informative labeling schemes for graphs. *Theoretical Computer Science* **340(3)**, (2005), 577–593.

[25] M. Thorup. Compact oracles for reachability and

approximate distances in planar digraphs. *J. of the ACM* **51**, (2004), 993–1024.

[26] M. Thorup and U. Zwick. Compact routing schemes. In Proc. 13th ACM Symp. on Parallel Algorithms and Architecture (SPAA), pages 1–10, 2001.

[27] W. T. Trotter. Combinatorics and partially ordered sets: Dimension theory. *The Johns Hopkins University Press*, (1992).

[28] W.T. Trotter and J. I. Moore. The dimension of planar posets *J. Comb. Theory B* **22**, (1977), 54–67.

[29] E.S. Wolk. The comparability graph of a tree. *Proc. Amer. Math. Soc.* **3**, (1962), 789–795.

[30] W3C.Extensive markup language (XML) 1.0. http://www.w3.org/TR/REC-xml.

[31] W3C. Exensive stylesheet language (xsl) 1.0. http://www.w3.org/Style/XSL/.

[32] W3C. Xsl transformations (xslt) specification. http://www.w3.org/TR/WD-xslt

Bilipschitz Snowflakes and Metrics of Negative Type

[Extended Abstract]

James R. Lee*
University of Washington
jrl@cs.washington.edu

Mohammad Moharrami†
University of Washington
mohammad@cs.washington.edu

ABSTRACT

We show that there exists a metric space (X,d) such that $(X,\sqrt{d})$ admits a bilipschitz embedding into L_2, but (X,d) does not admit an equivalent metric of negative type. In fact, we exhibit a strong quantitative bound: There are n-point subsets $Y_n \subseteq X$ such that mapping (Y_n,d) to a metric of negative type requires distortion $\widetilde{\Omega}(\log n)^{1/4}$. In a formal sense, this is the first lower bound specifically against bilipschitz embeddings into negative-type metrics, and therefore unlike other lower bounds, ours cannot be derived from a 1-dimensional Poincaré inequality.

This answers an open question about the strength of strong vs. weak triangle inequalities in a number of semi-definite programs. Our construction sheds light on the power of various notions of "dual flows" that arise in algorithms for approximating the Sparsest Cut problem. It also has other interesting implications for bilipschitz embeddings of finite metric spaces.

Categories and Subject Descriptors

F.2 [**Analysis of Algorithms and Problem Complexity**]: Geometrical problems and computations

General Terms

Algorithms, Theory

Keywords

Metric embeddings, Semi-definite programming, Sparsest Cut

1. INTRODUCTION

Beginning with the works [LLR95, AR98], it became apparent that the embeddability of finite metric spaces into various normed spaces (predominantly L_1 and L_2) was intimately tied to the efficacy of certain mathematical programs for approximating the Sparsest Cut problem in graphs. Subsequently, such tools were used to achieve new approximation results for an array of well-known problems, many of which were unapproachable via other methods.

We now recall the Sparsest Cut problem. Given a finite set V on n points, and two symmetric non-negative functions $\mathsf{cap}, \mathsf{dem} : V \times V \to \mathbb{R}_{\geq 0}$, one defines the *sparsity* of the subset $S \subseteq V$ by

$$\Phi_{\mathsf{cap},\mathsf{dem}}(S) = \frac{\mathsf{cap}(S,\bar{S})}{\mathsf{dem}(S,\bar{S})},$$

where we use the notation $f(S,\bar{S}) = \sum_{x\in S, y\notin S} f(x,y)$ for $f \in \{\mathsf{cap},\mathsf{dem}\}$. The value of the instance $(V,\mathsf{cap},\mathsf{dem})$ is then given by $\Phi(\mathsf{cap},\mathsf{dem}) = \min\{\Phi_{\mathsf{cap},\mathsf{dem}}(S) : S \subseteq V\}$. We recall that the instance is said to be *uniform* if $\mathsf{dem}(u,v) = 1$ for all $u,v \in V$.

It was shown in [LLR95, AR98, GNRS99] that the integrality gap for a natural (and well-studied) linear-programming relaxation (see [LR99]) is precisely $\sup\{c_1(X,d) : (X,d)\}$, where (X,d) ranges over all metric spaces on n-points, and $c_1(X,d)$ denotes the minimal distortion required to embed (X,d) into an L_1 space (see Section 1.2 for formal definitions). Bourgain's embedding theorem [Bou85] shows that this bound is $O(\log n)$, and in [LLR95, AR98], it was shown that this is tight for the path metric on expander graphs.

The Goemans-Linial SDP. In order to achieve better approximations, one can consider the Goemans-Linial SDP:

$$\min\left\{ \frac{\sum_{u,v} \mathsf{cap}(u,v)\|x_u - x_v\|_2^2}{\sum_{u,v} \mathsf{dem}(u,v)\|x_u - x_v\|_2^2} : \{x_u\}_{u\in V} \subseteq \mathbb{R}^n \text{ and } \|\cdot\|_2^2 \text{ is a metric on } \{x_u\}_{u\in V} \right\}.$$

In other words, we optimize over sets of n vectors $W \subseteq \mathbb{R}^n$ which satisfy, for every $x,y,z \in W$, the condition

$$\|x-y\|_2^2 \leq \|x-z\|_2^2 + \|z-y\|_2^2.$$

In general, we say that a metric space (X,d) is of *negative type* if there exist a mapping $f : X \to L_2$ such that

$$\|f(x) - f(y)\|^2 = d(x,y)$$

for all $x,y \in X$.

As before (see [Mat02a, Ch. 15]), the integrality gap of this relaxation is exactly the solution to an embedding problem. The gap is precisely the supremum of $c_1(X,d)$ over all n-point metric spaces of negative type. In [ARV04], the

*Research supported by NSF grants CCF-0644037 and CCF-0915251, and a Sloan Research Fellowship.

†Research supported by NSF grant CCF-0644037.

STOC'10, June 5–8, 2010, Cambridge, Massachusetts, USA.

Goemans-Linial SDP was used to achieve an $O(\sqrt{\log n})$-approximation for the *uniform* case of Sparsest Cut, and building on these techniques as well as various tools from the theory of metric embeddings, one can obtain $c_1(X,d) \le O(\sqrt{\log n}\log\log n)$ for any n-point space of negative type ([ALN08], following an earlier bound of [CGR05]). This yields the same bound for approximating the general Sparsest Cut problem.

Given the effectiveness of this approach, and generally the power of the $\|\cdot\|_2^2$ triangle inequality constraints in relaxations for other fundamental problems (see e.g. [FHL05, ACMM05, Kar09, CMM06]), it becomes a matter of fundamental importance to understand the geometry of negative-type metrics, and the effect of the negative-type constraints on mathematical programming relaxations.

Integrality gaps and the ease of snowflaking. In order to crystalize this goal, Goemans and Linial conjectured (see [Mat02a, Ch. 15], [Lin02]) that $c_1(X,d) \le O(1)$ for every metric space (X,d) of negative type. Khot and Vishnoi subsequently disproved this in [KV05]. The most ingenious part of their work involves the construction of the lower bound space (X,d), and the most intricate technical analysis goes toward showing that (X,d) is of negative type. Subsequently, [KR06] and [DKSV06] proved a stronger quantitative bound of $\Omega(\log\log n)$, where notably the latter lower bound holds in the uniform case. The first paper uses exactly the Khot-Vishnoi construction, while the second paper relies heavily on the analysis techniques of [KV05].

In [LN06], a new integrality gap construction was proposed, based on the 3-dimensional Heisenberg group $\mathbb{H}^3$. Again, the bulk of the work in [LN06] goes into proving that $\mathbb{H}^3$ admits an interesting metric of negative type. The lower bound analysis uses work of Cheeger and Kleiner [CK06b, CK06a, CK09]. Building on this analysis, it was recently proved in [CKN09] that this construction achieves an integrality gap of $(\log n)^{\delta_0}$ for some small constant $\delta_0 > 0$.

We now express a property that all these lower bounds share. For a metric space (X,d) and a number $\alpha \in (0,1]$, we use (X,d^α) to denote the metric space where X is equipped with the distance $d^\alpha(x,y) = d(x,y)^\alpha$. For values $\alpha < 1$, such constructions are commonly referred to as "snowflakes." Let us call a metric space (X,d) a *D-half-snowflake* if $c_2(X,\sqrt{d}) \le D$, i.e. $(X,\sqrt{d})$ admits a Euclidean embedding with distortion D. It is immediate from the definition that *metrics of negative type are precisely* 1*-half-snowflakes.*

In all the above constructions of integrality gaps, it is relatively easy to show that that space in question is an $O(1)$-half-snowflake. In the case of [KV05]-based constructions, this can be done in a page of analysis (see, e.g. [KL08]). Since the Heisenberg group $\mathbb{H}^3$ (equipped with the Carnot-Caratheodory metric) is doubling, a classical result of Assouad [Ass83] shows that it is already an $O(1)$-half-snowflake. Indeed, in all these cases, the fact that one could construct an $O(1)$-half-snowflake was taken as evidence and motivation that eventually a negative-type metric could be constructed. This leads to the following natural question (see the "Isometric vs. isomorphic L_2 squared" problem [Mat02b] posed by the first author in 2003) whose affirmative answer would make the construction of integrality gaps a significantly easier process.

QUESTION 1. *Can every $O(1)$-half-snowflake be embedded into a metric of negative type with $O(1)$ distortion?*

The main theorem of this paper shows that the answer is negative, in a very strong sense.

THEOREM 1.1. *There exists an $O(1)$-half-snowflake for which any embedding into a metric of negative type incurs distortion $\widetilde{\Omega}(\log n)^{1/4}$.*

The power of snowflakes. To give more motivation for obtaining an answer to Question 1, we observe the ubiquity of snowflakes in embeddings and analysis of the Goemans-Linial SDP and related algorithms. It is a common observation that the algorithms and analysis of [ARV04, Lee05, CGR05, ALN08] do not require the vector solution $W \subseteq \mathbb{R}^n$ to actually satisfy the full triangle inequalities, but only the weaker form: For every sequence $w_1, w_2, \ldots, w_k \in W$,

$$\|w_1 - w_k\|_2^2 \le C \sum_{i=1}^{k-1} \|w_i - w_{i+1}\|_2^2,$$

for some constant $C \ge 1$ independent of the sequence. This is merely the half-snowflake condition in disguise: It simply says that W is the image of an $O(1)$-half-snowflake embedding of some metric space. In all known algorithmic applications, it is only the $O(1)$-half-snowflake condition that is needed. Furthermore, results like [LMN05] show e.g. that planar graphs always admit $O(1)$-half-snowflake embeddings, while the question of whether they admit negative-type embeddings was posed by Rabinovich, and is still open. (This is related to another well-known conjecture in the theory of multi-commodity flows: that the shortest-path metric of a planar graph embeds into L_1 with $O(1)$ distortion [GNRS99].)

Far more than being a curiousity of the analysis, the fact that a weaker condition suffices is actually the basis for algorithmis which find sparse cuts in graphs without solving a semi-definite program. In [AHK04], the authors give an $O(\sqrt{\log n})$-approximation to the uniform Sparsest Cut problem that runs in $\widetilde{O}(n^2)$ time. In [She09], such an approximation is obtained in $\widetilde{O}(m+n^{3/2+\varepsilon})$-time for every $\varepsilon > 0$. Both of these algorithms are primal-dual, with the algorithm and analysis being guided by the structure of the Goemans-Linial SDP and its dual. A key aspect lending to their efficiency is that they do not need the full power of the dual; indeed, they operate by finding an "expander flow" [ARV04], which is a solution that corresponds precisely to a weakening of the triangle inequalities in the primal. Our lower bound shows that, in the non-uniform setting, such approaches can be significantly less powerful than finding full-fledged dual solutions. In particular, we give an $\widetilde{\Omega}(\log n)^{1/4}$ lower bound on the approximation ratio of any algorithm for non-uniform Sparsest Cut that relies on finding the non-uniform analog of expander flows. We refer to the full version for a detailed explanation.

Additional implications in metric embeddings. We mention two additional consequences of our result for the theory of bilipschitz metric embeddings, which have played a fundamental role in approximation algorithms.

Scale gluing for L_1. The first application is to "scale-gluing" results for embeddings into L_1. Specifically, suppose that (X,d) is an n-point metric space, and furthermore that for every value $k \in \mathbb{Z}$, there exists a 1-Lipschitz map $\varphi_k : X \to L_1$ such that for $x, y \in X$ satisfying $d(x,y) \geq 2^k$, we have

$$\|\varphi_k(x) - \varphi_k(y)\|_1 \geq \frac{2^k}{\alpha}. \quad (1)$$

On the one hand, we have the following.

THEOREM 1.2. *[Lee05] There exists an embedding of (X, d) into L_1 with distortion $O(\sqrt{\alpha \log n})$.*

Such scale-gluing results have played a central role in the best-known approximation algorithms for Sparsest Cut [KLMN05, Lee05, CGR05, ALN08] and Graph Bandwidth [Rao99, KLMN05, Lee09], and have found applications in approximate multi-commodity max-flow/min-cut theorems in graphs [Rao99, KLMN05]. The work of Cheeger and Kleiner [CK06a] shows that even if $\alpha = O(1)$, the distortion can go to infinity, and [CKN09] gives a definite bound of $\Omega(\log n)^{\delta_0}$ for some small $\delta_0 > 0$. Our construction and analysis yield the following lower bound.

THEOREM 1.3. *There exist n-point metric spaces (X, d) which satisfy (1) with $\alpha = 2$, but such that $c_1(X,d) = \tilde{\Omega}(\log n)^{1/4}$. In fact, we even have $c_{\mathsf{NEG}}(X,d) = \tilde{\Omega}(\log n)^{1/4}$.*

The k-sum embedding conjecture. In [LS09], it is conjectured that if a family of finite graphs $\mathcal{F}$ is such that every shortest-path metric supported on a member of $\mathcal{F}$ embeds into L_1 with distortion $O(1)$, then the family $\oplus_k \mathcal{F}$ has the same property, for every $k \in \mathbb{N}$, where the $\oplus_k(\cdot)$ notation denotes the closure of $\mathcal{F}$ under the operation of taking k-sums along cliques (see [LS09] for a formal description). This authors refer to this as the "k-sum embedding conjecture." The conjecture is open even for $k = 2$. One of the main results of [LS09] is that the k-sum embedding conjecture, combined with the well-known planar embedding conjecture, implies the GNRS max-flow/min-cut conjecture in excluded-minor families [GNRS99].

Our results show that there exists an unweighted graph G whose shortest-path metric embed into L_1 with distortion 2, but that by taking repeated 2-sums of G with itself, one obtains a graph whose L_1 distortion becomes arbitrarily large. This does not disprove the k-sum conjecture, because we have only considered a single shortest-path metric on G, but it does show that the proof must use something about the entire set of embeddings for metrics on G, as opposed to merely an embedding of the given metric on G.

1.1 Efficiency, embeddings, and iterated graphs

We now describe our main construction, and the steps that go into a exhibiting a separation between half-snowflakes and metrics of negative type. Various aspects are simplified here for the sake of exposition, and some finer points of the construction are left unmentioned. The analysis is based on a "differentiation"-type argument. At a very broad level, we first argue that any low-distortion embedding must be well-controlled on a small piece of our lower bound space, and then show that any well-controlled embedding is quite rigid in structure, allowing us to prove a lower bound.

Generalizations of classical differentiation theory have played a prominent role in proving the non-existence of bi-Lipschitz embeddings between various spaces, when the target space Z is sufficiently nice (e.g. if Z is a Banach space with the Radon-Nikodym property); see, for instance [Pan89, Che99, LN06, BL00, CK06c]. But this approach does not apply to targets like L_1 which don't have the Radon-Nikodym property; in particular, even Lipschitz mappings $f : \mathbb{R} \to L_1$ are not guaranteed to be differentiable in the classical sense.

More recently, however, Cheeger and Kleiner [CK06a, CK06b] have successfully applied weaker notions of differentiability to the study of L_1 embeddings of the Heisenberg group. Subsequent papers [LR07, CK09, CKN09] continue this theme. Ours is the first work to apply these techniques to lower bounds against negative-type metrics.

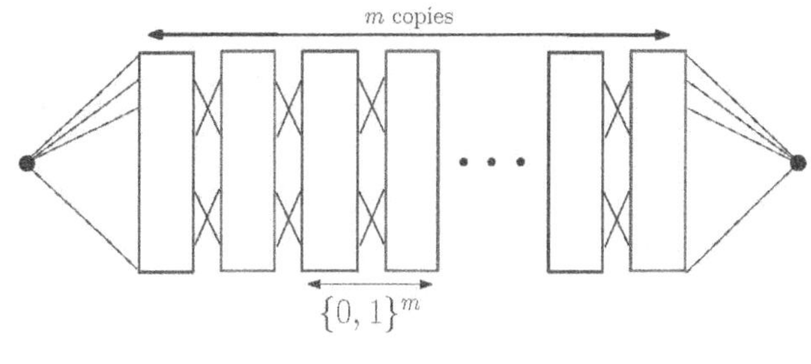

Figure 1: The "string of cubes" graph, which we recursively compose with itself.

The construction. Let G be an unweighted graph with two distinguished vertices $s, t \in V(G)$. As in [LR07], we use $G^{\oslash k}$ to denote the following iterated graph: $G^{\oslash 0}$ is a single edge, and $G^{\oslash k+1}$ arises by replacing every edge of $G^{\oslash k}$ with a copy of G, with s and t taking the place of the endpoints of the edge. See Section 2 for a formal definition.

For a parameter $m \in \mathbb{N}$, consider now the graph H_m constucted as follows. Let Q_m be the m-dimensional hypercube graph, and write $V(Q_m) = B_m \cup R_m$, where B_m and R_m denote the nodes of even and odd parity, respectively. Then Q_m is bipartite with respect to the partition (B_m, R_m). H_m is the graph which consists of $2m$ layers of the form

$$B_m^{(1)} R_m^{(1)} B_m^{(2)} R_m^{(2)} B_m^{(3)} R_m^{(3)} \cdots B_m^{(m)} R_m^{(m)}, \quad (2)$$

where $B_m^{(i)}$ and $R_m^{(i)}$ denote disjoint copies of B_m and R_m for $i = 1, 2, \ldots, m$, and hypercube edges are presently between every pair of adjacent layers.

We also add to H_m two distinguished nodes: s connected to all the nodes of $B_m^{(1)}$ by paths of length m and a t connected the nodes of $R_m^{(m)}$ by paths of length t. We call H_m the "string of cubes" graph. See Figure 1. Our final construction is of the form $G_{k,m} = H_m^{\oslash k}$ for appropriate values of $k, m \in \mathbb{N}$. We use $d_{k,m}$ to denote the shortest-path metric on $G_{k,m}$. Our goal is now to show that $G_{k,m}$ is an $O(1)$-half-snowflake for all $k, m \in \mathbb{N}$, while $\lim_{m\to\infty} \lim_{k\to\infty} c_{\mathsf{NEG}}(G_{k,m}) = \infty$.

Efficiency. A central role will be played by the *efficiency* of various "paths" in metric spaces, following [EFW06, LR07]. Consider a finite sequence of points equipped with a non-negative symmetric function dist (which may *not* satisfy the triangle inequality), $\mathcal{S} = \{x_1, x_2, \ldots, x_k\}$. We say that $\mathcal{S}$ is *ε-efficient (with respect to* dist*)* if

$$\sum_{i=1}^{k-1} \mathsf{dist}(x_i, x_{i+1}) \leq (1+\varepsilon)\,\mathsf{dist}(x_1, x_k).$$

Note that if dist is a metric, then the left-hand side is always at least $\mathsf{dist}(x_1, x_k)$, by the triangle inequality.

The first key aspect of our approach is that we reduce the embeddability of $G^{\oslash k}$ to the study of specific types of embeddings for the base graph G. For a graph G and two nodes $s, t \in V(G)$, let $\mathcal{P}_{s,t}(G)$ denote the set of all s-t shortest-paths in G. In Section 2, we prove a quantitative variant of the following theorem, based on the "coarse differentiation" methodology of [EFW06].

THEOREM 1.4. *Let (Y, d_Y) be any metric space, and suppose that $c_Y(G^{\oslash k}) \le D$ for all $k = 1, 2, \ldots$. Then for every $\varepsilon > 0$, there exists an embedding $f : G \to Y$ with distortion at most D, and such that for every sequence $\{x_1, x_2, \ldots, x_r\} \in \mathcal{P}_{s,t}(G)$, the sequence $\{f(x_1), f(x_2), \ldots, f(x_r)\}$ is ε-efficient in (Y, d_Y).*

A more general result was proved in [LR07]. The novel aspect of our approach in Section 2, is that in the special case of iterated graphs, we are able to gain an exponential improvement in a quantitative version of this theorem (which is necessary to obtain our strong lower bounds). In particular, the dependence of k on D is logarithmic (as opposed to linear as in [LR07]).

Snowflake embedding: On the other hand, in the setting of half-snowflakes, we have a partial converse to the preceding theorem. If there is an embedding

$$f : (G, \sqrt{d_G}) \to L_2$$

with distortion D, and such that for every sequence

$$\{x_1, x_2 \ldots, x_r\} \in \mathcal{P}_{s,t}(G),$$

the sequence $\{f(x_1), f(x_2), \ldots, f(x_r)\}$ is ε-efficient with respect to the distance $\|f(x_i) - f(x_j)\|_2^2$, then for every $k = O(1/\varepsilon)$, the graph $G^{\oslash k}$ is an $O(D)$-half-snowflake. (We are actually only able to prove this for a modification of the graph $G^{\oslash k}$.) Due to lack of space, the proof of this fact is deferred to the full version.

Because of these two results, we are able to focus on a separation between embeddings of our base graph H_m into negative-type metrics and half-snowflakes, respectively, with the additional property that the embeddings are ε-efficient on s-t shortest-paths. Analyzing efficient (and approximately efficient embeddings) is the technical core of our approach, which we now address.

A lower bound for efficient embeddings into NEG: Poincaré boosting. Recall that H_m consists of m hypercubes $C_1, C_2, \ldots, C_m$ strung together as in (2). First, we recall the classical Poincaré inequality of Enflo [Enf69] for the discrete m-cube. For any $f : Q_m \to \mathbb{R}$, we have

$$\mathbb{E}_{x \in Q_m} |f(x) - f(\bar{x})|^2 \le \sum_{i=1}^{m} \mathbb{E}_{x \in Q_m} |f(x) - f(x \oplus e_i)|^2, \quad (3)$$

where we use $\bar{x}$ to denote x with all coordinates flipped, and $x \oplus e_i$ to denote x with the ith coordinate flipped. By integrating, we easily conclude that for any $f : Q_m \to L_2$,

$$\mathbb{E}_{x \in Q_m} \|f(x) - f(\bar{x})\|^2 \le \sum_{i=1}^{m} \mathbb{E}_{x \in Q_m} \|f(x) - f(x \oplus e_i)\|^2. \quad (4)$$

Obviously, this inequality does not yield any lower bound on the distortion for embedding Q_m into NEG (since it embeds into L_1, and hence NEG isometrically).

But suppose we are given an embedding $g : H_m \to L_2$ which is an isometric negative-type embedding, in the sense that $\|g(x) - g(y)\|^2 = d_{H_m}(x, y)$ for all $x, y \in H_m$. Now, for each i, let $g_i = g|_{C_i} : Q_m \to L_2$ be the restriction of g to the ith copy of Q_m in H_m, where we think of all the maps $\{g_i\}_{i=1}^m$ as having the same domain. If we simply applied (4) to each $f = g_i$ and summed the resulting inequalities, we would again achieve no non-trivial lower bound.

Instead, we apply (4) to the mapping $f = g_1 + g_2 + \cdots + g_m$. By the strictness of the property that g is an isometry (when the range is considered with the squared norm $\|\cdot\|^2$), all the vectors $\{g_i(x) - g_i(\bar{x})\}_{i=1}^m$ are colinear, and one concludes that,

$$\|f(x) - f(\bar{x})\|^2 = \left(\sum_{j=1}^{m} \|g_j(x) - g_j(\bar{x})\| \right)^2. \quad (5)$$

On the other hand, if we (by abuse of notation) consider a shortest-path in H_m of the form

$$x - x \oplus e_i - x - x \oplus e_i - x - x \oplus e_i - \cdots$$

(where the elements of the path lie in the respective sets $B_m^{(1)}, R_m^{(1)}, B_m^{(2)}, R_m^{(2)}, \ldots$), then by the fact that g is an isometry, for any pairs of adjacent nodes x, x' and y, y' in such a path, we have $g(x) - g(x')$ and $g(y) - g(y')$ being orthogonal. This implies that for every $x \in Q_m$ and $i \in [m]$, we have for every $j, k \in [m]$, the property that $g_j(x) - g_j(x \oplus e_i)$ and $g_k(x) - g_k(x \oplus e_i)$ are orthogonal (actually, this only holds for j and k of the same parity, but ignore this small issue).

We conclude that if $f = g_1 + g_2 + \cdots g_m$, then

$$\|f(x) - f(x \oplus e_i)\|^2 = \sum_{j=1}^{m} \|g_j(x) - g_j(x \oplus e_i)\|^2. \quad (6)$$

From (5), (6), and (4), we get a "boosted" Poincaré inequality of the form

$$\mathbb{E}_{x \in Q_m} \left(\sum_{j=1}^{m} \|g_j(x) - g_j(\bar{x})\| \right)^2 \quad (7)$$

$$\le \sum_{j=1}^{m} \sum_{i=1}^{m} \mathbb{E}_{x \in Q_m} \|g_j(x) - g_j(x \oplus e_i)\|^2.$$

Notice that to obtain this inequality, we needed to use the fully high-dimensional version (4) instead of (3), because we used the high-dimensional relationship between the various maps $\{g_i\}_{i=1}^m$.

Now, if we were told in advance that (7) holds, and also that each g_j has distortion at most D (again, when the range is considered with the squared distance $\|\cdot\|^2$), it would immediately yield a lower bound of $D \ge m$. (Assuming each g_j is 1-Lipschitz, the right-hand side is at most m^2, while the left-hand side is at least m^3/D.)

Of course, we started with the assumption that g was isometric, so this simply proves that H_m does not admit an isometric negative-type embedding. But now the main point is that every aspect of the preceding argument is *robust.* In Section 3, we prove a stable version of (5) using a distortion bound for g, and a stable version of (6) using the assumption that g is ε-efficient on a large fraction of s-t shortest-paths in H_m.

Combining all this together in Section 3 shows that H_m does not admit a low-distortion negative-type metric which is ε-efficient on most s-t paths (for ε small enough). Combined with a differentiation theorem like Theorem 1.4, this shows that the iterated graph $G_{k,m}$ does not admit a low-distortion negative-type metric for k, m large enough.

An upper bound for efficient embeddings into half-snowflakes. The preceding discussion yields only part of the separation between half-snowflakes and negative-type metrics. For the other side, using the "snowflake embedding" method mentioned earlier for the iterated graph $G_{k,m}$, it suffices to construct an embedding $f : (H_m, \sqrt{d_{H_m}}) \to L_2$ which has small distortion, and such that every s-t shortest-path in H_m is mapped 0-efficiently, when the range is considered with the squared distance $\|\cdot\|^2$. To illustrate how this is done, we will argue for the path metric P on the points $\{1, 2, \ldots, n\}$. In the actual construction, the following argument is carried out for all the shortest s-t paths simulataneously.

Suppose that $f : P \to L_2$ satisfies, for all $x, y \in P$,

$$\frac{|x-y|}{D} \leq \|f(x) - f(y)\|^2 \leq |x-y|. \tag{8}$$

Let $v_0 = \frac{f(n)-f(1)}{\|f(n)-f(1)\|}$, and put $\alpha_i = \langle v_0, f(i)\rangle$. We will also need to make the assumption that

$$\alpha_1 \leq \alpha_2 \leq \cdots \leq \alpha_n, \tag{9}$$

which will be satisfied in our constructions.

Now, write every point $i \in P$ in the form

$$f(i) = \alpha_i v_0 + v_i,$$

where $\langle v_i, v_0\rangle = 0$. Consider the mapping $g(i) = \alpha_i v_0 + \delta v_i$, for some $\delta \in [0, 1]$.

In this case, we have

$$\begin{aligned}\sum_{i=1}^{n-1} \|g(i+1) - g(i)\|^2 &= \sum_{i=1}^{n-1} (\alpha_{i+1} - \alpha_i)^2 + \delta^2 \|v_{i+1} - v_i\|^2 \\ &\leq \sum_{i=1}^{n-1} (\alpha_{i+1} - \alpha_i)^2 + \delta^2 n,\end{aligned}$$

where in the last inequality we have used (8).

Note that $\|f(n) - f(1)\| = \sum_{i+1} |\alpha_{i+1} - \alpha_i|$ by (9), and we have $|\alpha_{i+1} - \alpha_i| \leq 1$ by (8), hence

$$\sum_{i=1}^{n-1} (\alpha_{i+1} - \alpha_i)^2 \leq \|f(n) - f(1)\|.$$

On the other hand, $\|g(n) - g(1)\|^2 = \|f(n) - f(1)\|^2 \geq n/D$. It follows that for some value $\delta \gtrsim 1/\sqrt{D}$, we will have

$$\|g(n) - g(1)\|^2 = \sum_{i=1}^{n-1} \|g(i+1) - g(i)\|^2,$$

i.e. the image will of P will be 0-efficient. This gives us a general way to obtain 0-efficient embeddings for half-snowflakes, which would not work for negative-type embeddings (because in the process of decreasing δ, triangle inequalities that may have been satisfied in the image could become violated).

1.2 Preliminaries

For a graph G, we will use $V(G), E(G)$ to denote the sets of vertices and edges of G, respectively. Sometimes we will equip G with a non-negative length function $\mathsf{len} : E(G) \to \mathbb{R}_+$, and we let d_{len} denote the shortest-path pseudo-metric on G. We refer to the pair (G, len) as a *metric graph*, and often len will be implicit, in which case we use d_G to denote the path metric.

Given two expressions E and E' (possibly depending on a number of parameters), we write $E = O(E')$ to mean that $E \leq CE'$ for some constant $C > 0$ which is independent of the parameters. Similarly, $E = \Omega(E')$ implies that $E \geq CE'$ for some $C > 0$. We also write $E \lesssim E'$ as a synonym for $E = O(E')$. Finally, we write $E \asymp E'$ to denote the conjunction of $E \lesssim E'$ and $E \gtrsim E'$.

Embeddings and distortion. If $(X, d_X), (Y, d_Y)$ are metric spaces, and $f : X \to Y$, then we write

$$\|f\|_{\mathrm{Lip}} = \sup_{x \neq y \in X} \frac{d_Y(f(x), f(y))}{d_X(x, y)}.$$

If f is injective, then the *distortion of* f is defined by $\mathsf{dist}(f) = \|f\|_{\mathrm{Lip}} \cdot \|f^{-1}\|_{\mathrm{Lip}}$. A map with distortion D will sometimes be referred to as D*-bi-lipschitz*. If $d_Y(f(x), f(y)) \leq d_X(x, y)$ for every $x, y \in X$, we say that f is *non-expansive*. If $d_Y(f(x), f(y)) \geq d_X(x, y)$ for every $x, y \in X$, we say that f is *non-contracting*. For a metric space X, we use $c_p(X)$ to denote the least distortion required to embed X into some L_p space.

A metric space (X, d) is said to be of *negative type* if $c_2(X, \sqrt{d}) = 1$. We use $c_{\mathsf{NEG}}(X, d)$ to denote the least distortion required to embed X into some metric space of negative type. We will abuse notation in the following way. We write $f : (X, d) \to \mathsf{NEG}$ to denote the fact that f takes values in L_2, and that its image is a metric when equipped with the distance induced from the square of the L_2 norm. In this case, the image is always thought to be equipped with the metric $\|f(x) - f(y)\|_2^2$, for $x, y \in X$ (e.g. for notions like the distortion of f).

2. ITERATED GRAPHS AND COARSE DIFFERENTIATION

In the present section, we define formally a key part of our graph construction process (marked $\oslash$ products), and give a differentiation theorem for iterated product graphs.

2.1 Marked $\oslash$-products

An s-t graph G is a graph which has two distinguished vertices $s, t \in V(G)$. For an s-t graph, we use $s(G)$ and $t(G)$ to denote the vertices labeled s and t, respectively. We define the length of an s-t graph G as $\mathsf{len}(G) = d_{\mathsf{len}}(s, t)$. Throughout the paper, we will only be concerned with *symmetric* s-t graphs, i.e. graphs for which there is an automorphism which maps s to t. We assume that all s-t graphs are symmetric in the following definitions. A *marked graph* $G = (V, E)$ is one which carries an additional subset $E_M(G) \subseteq E$ of *marked edges*. Every graph is assumed to be equipped with the trivial marking $E_M(G) = E(G)$ unless a marking is otherwise specified.

Definition 2.1 (Composition of s-t graphs). *Given two marked s-t graphs H and G, define $H \oslash G$ to be the s-t graph obtained by replacing each* marked *edge $(u, v) \in E_M(H)$ by a copy of G. Formally,*

- $V(H \oslash G) = V(H) \cup (E_M(H) \times (V(G) \setminus \{s(G), t(G)\}))$.

- *For every edges $(u,v) \in E(H) \setminus E_M(H)$, there is a corresponding edge in $H \oslash G$.*
- *For every edge $e = (u,v) \in E_M(H)$, there are $|E(G)|$ edges,*

$$\left\{\Big((e,v_1),(e,v_2)\Big) \mid (v_1,v_2) \in E(G), v_1, v_2 \notin \{s(G),t(G)\}\right\}$$
$$\cup \left\{\Big(u,(e,w)\Big) \mid (s(G),w) \in E(G)\right\}$$
$$\cup \left\{\Big((e,w),v\Big) \mid (w,t(G)) \in E(G)\right\}$$

- *The marked edges of $H \oslash G$ are precisely those introduced in the previous step which correspond to marked edges in G.*
- *$s(H \oslash G) = s(H)$ and $t(H \oslash G) = t(H)$.*

If H and G are equipped with length functions $\mathsf{len}_H, \mathsf{len}_G$, respectively, we define $\mathsf{len} = \mathsf{len}_{H \oslash G}$ as follows. Using the preceding notation, for every edge $e = (u,v) \in E_M(H)$,

$$\begin{aligned}
\mathsf{len}\left((e,v_1),(e,v_2)\right) &= \frac{\mathsf{len}_H(e)}{d_{\mathsf{len}_G}(s(G),t(G))}\mathsf{len}_G(v_1,v_2)\\
\mathsf{len}\left(u,(e,w)\right) &= \frac{\mathsf{len}_H(e)}{d_{\mathsf{len}_G}(s(G),t(G))}\mathsf{len}_G(s(G),w)\\
\mathsf{len}\left((e,w),v\right) &= \frac{\mathsf{len}_H(e)}{d_{\mathsf{len}_G}(s(G),t(G))}\mathsf{len}_G(w,t(G)).
\end{aligned}$$

This choice implies that $H \oslash G$ contains an isometric copy of $(V(H), d_{\mathsf{len}_H})$.

DEFINITION 2.2 (RECURSIVE COMPOSITION). *Given a marked s-t graph G and a number $k \in \mathbb{N}$, we define $G^{\oslash k}$ inductively by letting $G^{\oslash 0}$ be a single edge of unit length, and setting $G^{\oslash k} = G^{\oslash k-1} \oslash G$.*

The following result is straightforward.

LEMMA 2.3 (ASSOCIATIVITY OF $\oslash$). *For any three graphs A, B, C, we have $(A \oslash B) \oslash C = A \oslash (B \oslash C)$, both graph-theoretically and as metric spaces.*

DEFINITION 2.4. *For two graphs G, H, a subset of vertices $X \subseteq V(H)$ is said to be a copy of G if there exists a bijection $f : V(G) \to X$ with distortion 1.*

Now we make the following two simple observations about copies of H and G in $H \oslash G$.

OBSERVATION 2.5. *The graph $H \oslash G$ contains $|E_M(H)|$ distinguished copies of the graph G, one copy corresponding to each edge in H.*

OBSERVATION 2.6. *The subset of vertices $V(H) \subseteq V(H \oslash G)$ form an isometric copy of H.*

2.2 Coarse differentiation

Let G be an s-t graph, (X,d) a metric space, and consider a mapping $f : V(G) \to X$. Recalling that $\mathcal{P}_{s,t}(G)$ is the set of s-t shortest-paths in G, let μ be a measure on $\mathcal{P}_{s,t} = \mathcal{P}_{s,t}(G)$. We say that f is *ε-efficient with respect to μ* if it satisfies

$$\mathbb{E}_{\gamma\sim\mu} \sum_{uv\in\gamma} d(f(u),f(v)) \le (1+\varepsilon)\, d(f(s),f(t)).$$

For a marked s-t graph G, we define its *marked length* by

$$\mathsf{len}_M(G) = \min_{\gamma\in\mathcal{P}_{s,t}} \sum_{uv\in\gamma:(u,v)\in E_M(G)} \mathsf{len}_G(u,v).$$

THEOREM 2.7. *Let G be a marked s-t graph. Then for any $D \ge 1$ and $\varepsilon \ge 2D\left(1 - \frac{\mathsf{len}_M(G)}{\mathsf{len}(G)}\right)$, there exists a $k = O(\frac{1}{\varepsilon}\log D)$ such that the following holds. For every metric space (X,d) and mapping $f : V(G^{\oslash k}) \to X$ with distortion D, there exists a copy of G in $G^{\oslash k}$ such that $f|_G$ is ε-efficient with respect to μ.*

PROOF. Assume, without loss of generality, that f is 1-Lipschitz. We claim that if f is not ε-efficient with respect to μ on any copy of G in $G^{\oslash k}$, then

$$\mathbb{E}_{\gamma\sim\mu^{\oslash k}} \sum_{uv\in\gamma} d(f(u),f(v)) \ge \left(1+\frac{\varepsilon}{2}\right)^k d\left(f(s(G^{\oslash k})), f(t(G^{\oslash k}))\right), \tag{10}$$

where $\mu^{\oslash k}$ is the natural iterated measure on $s(G^{\oslash k})$-$t(G^{\oslash k})$ shortest-paths in $G^{\oslash k}$. We prove this by induction on k, where the case $k=0$ is trivial.

Now, write $G^{\oslash k+1} = G \oslash G^{\oslash k}$. We have one copy of $G^{\oslash k}$ in $G^{\oslash k+1}$ for every marked edge $e = (u,v) \in E_M(G)$. Denoting this copy by H_e, by the induction hypothesis, we have

$$\mathbb{E}_{\gamma\sim(\mu^{\oslash k})_e} \sum_{uv\in\gamma} d(f(u),f(v)) \ge \left(1+\frac{\varepsilon}{2}\right)^k d\left(f(s(H_e)), f(t(H_e))\right), \tag{11}$$

where we use $(\mu^{\oslash k})_e$ to denote the path measure on H_e. Denote now the outer copy of G by G_0, and observe that if it is not mapped ε-efficiently by f, then

$$\begin{aligned}
\mathbb{E}_{\gamma\sim\mu} \sum_{uv\in\gamma} d(f(u),f(v)) &\ge (1+\varepsilon)\, d(f(s(G_0)), f(t(G_0)))\\
&= (1+\varepsilon)\, d\left(f(s(G^{\oslash k+1})), f(t(G^{\oslash k+1}))\right),
\end{aligned}$$

where the distribution μ here is over $s(G_0)$-$t(G_0)$ paths in $G_0 \cong G$.

Consider now a term of the form $\sum_{uv\in\gamma} d(f(u),f(v))$ on the left-hand side. Since f is 1-Lipschitz, we have

$$\begin{aligned}
&\sum_{uv\in\gamma:(u,v)\in E_M(G_0)} d(f(u),f(v))\\
&\ge \sum_{uv\in\gamma} d(f(u),f(v)) - \left(1 - \frac{\mathsf{len}_M(G_0)}{\mathsf{len}(G_0)}\right) d_G(s(G_0),t(G_0))\\
&\ge \sum_{uv\in\gamma} d(f(u),f(v)) - \frac{\varepsilon}{2D} d(f(s(G_0)), f(t(G_0)))\\
&\ge \left(1+\frac{\varepsilon}{2}\right) d(f(s(G_0)), f(t(G_0))).
\end{aligned}$$

But now since each marked edge is replaced by a copy of $G^{\oslash k}$ in G, every term in the sum $\sum_{uv\in\gamma:(u,v)\in E_M} d(f(u),f(v))$ corresponds to the right-hand side of an instance of (11), yielding

$$\mathbb{E}_{\gamma\sim\mu^{\oslash k+1}} \sum_{uv\in\gamma} d(f(u),f(v)) \ge \left(1+\frac{\varepsilon}{2}\right)^{k+1} d\left(f(s(G^{\oslash k+1})), f(t(G^{\oslash k+1}))\right). \tag{12}$$

This preceding line completes our proof of (10) by induction. Now, combining the triangle inequality and the fact that f is 1-Lipschitz, the left-hand side of (10) is at most $\mathsf{len}(G^{\oslash k})$, while the right-hand side is at least

$$\frac{\mathsf{len}(G^{\oslash k})}{D}\left(1+\frac{\varepsilon}{2}\right)^k,$$

yielding a contradiction for $k \asymp \frac{\log D}{\varepsilon}$. □

3. LOWER BOUND FOR NEG

We now formally present our lower bound construction and prove a lower bound on the distortion required to embed these graphs into NEG.

3.1 Graph construction

We will refer to the graphs H_m described in Section 1.1. We use $[Q_m]_i$ to denote the ith copy of Q_m in H_m, and for a vertex $x \in V(Q_m)$, we use $[x]_i$ to denote the copy of x in $[Q_m]_i$. For a directed edge $\vec{e} = (u, v)$, we define $f(\vec{e}) = f(u) - f(v)$.

For $m, h \in \mathbb{N}$, we define the graph $I_{m,h}$ as follows. We begin with a copy of H_m where all the edges are marked. Then, we relabel the vertices s and t in H_m as s' and t'. Next, we add two distinguished vertices s and t and and connect s to s' and t to t' by a path of length $1000\lceil\sqrt{m}\rceil$. All the edges in this new path are unmarked. Finally, we replace each marked edge with a path of length $1000\lceil\sqrt{m}\rceil h$, all of whose edges are marked. Our final construction is of the form $I_{m,h}^{\oslash k}$ for appropriate choices of $m, h, k \in \mathbb{N}$. We equip these graphs with the unweighted shortest-path metric, which we denote $d_{m,h,k}$.

3.2 Distortion lower bound

The main result of this section is the following theorem.

THEOREM 3.1. *For $m \geq 1$ and $k = \lceil m\log^2 m\rceil$, any embedding of $I_{m,m^2}^{\oslash k}$ into NEG requires distortion $\tilde{\Omega}(\log^{1/4} N)$ where $N = |V(H_m^{\oslash k})| \asymp 2^{O(mk)}$.*

We will use Theorem 2.7 to reduce our task to proving lower bounds on efficient embeddings. Let μ_m be the uniform measure over s-t shortest paths in H_m of the form

$$(s, \ldots, [x]_1, [x \oplus e_k]_1, [x]_2, [x \oplus e_k]_2, \ldots, [x]_m, [x \oplus e_k]_m, \ldots, t),$$

where $k \in \{1, 2, \ldots, m\}$ and $x \in Q_m$ are chosen uniformly at random.

LEMMA 3.2. *For any mapping $f : H_m \to$ NEG, if f is $O(\frac{1}{m\log m})$-efficient with respect to μ_m, then $\mathsf{dist}(f) \gtrsim m^{1/2}$.*

Using the preceding lemma, the Theorem 3.1 follows quickly.

PROOF OF THEOREM 3.1. Suppose that $f : I_{m,m^2}^{\oslash k} \to$ NEG has distortion at most $\sqrt{m}$. By Theorem 2.7, there must exist an isometric copy of $(I_{m,m^2}, d_{m,m^2,1})$, in $I_{m,m^2}^{\oslash k}$ such that $f|_{I_{m,m^2}}$ is $\frac{1}{m\log m}$-efficient with respect to μ_m. Now, I_{m,m^2} possesses an isometric copy of (H_m, d_{H_m}) as a subgraph.

We restrict f further to H_m. The map $f|_{H_m} : H_m \to$ NEG is $\frac{1}{m\log m} + O(1/m^2)\mathsf{dist}(f)$-efficient, and is thus $O(\frac{1}{m\log m})$-efficient. By Lemma 3.2, any such embedding of H_m has distortion $\Omega(\sqrt{m})$. We have $\log N \lesssim m^2\log^2 m$, hence $\mathsf{dist}(f) \gtrsim m^{1/2} \gtrsim \frac{(\log N)^{1/4}}{\log\log N}$. □

Before we prove Lemma 3.2, we start with a couple of general lemmas. Let $\vec{E}(Q_m)$ be the set of all ordered pairs (u, v) where $\{u, v\}$ is an edge of Q_m (in other words, replace every undirected edge by two directed edges).

LEMMA 3.3. *Let $\mathcal{F}$ be a set of functions $f : Q_m \to L_2$ such that*

i) $\mathbb{E}_{f,g\in\mathcal{F},\vec{e}\in\vec{E}(Q_m)}[f(\vec{e})\cdot g(\vec{e})] \leq c_1$,

ii) $\mathbb{E}_{f,g\in\mathcal{F},x\in V(Q_m)}[(f(x) - f(\bar{x}))\cdot(g(x) - g(\bar{x}))] \geq c_2$.

Then,

$$m \geq \frac{c_2}{c_1}.$$

PROOF. Let $F(x) = \mathbb{E}_{f\in\mathcal{F}}f(x)$. Therefore,

$$\begin{aligned}
c_2 &\leq \mathbb{E}_{f,g\in\mathcal{F},x\in V(Q_m)}[(f(x) - f(\bar{x}))\cdot(g(x) - g(\bar{x}))]\\
&= \mathbb{E}_{x\in V(Q_m)}[\mathbb{E}_{f\in\mathcal{F}}(f(x) - f(\bar{x}))\cdot\mathbb{E}_{g\in\mathcal{F}}(g(x) - g(\bar{x}))]\\
&= \mathbb{E}_{x\in V(Q_m)}[(F(x) - F(\bar{x}))\cdot(F(x) - F(\bar{x}))]\\
&= \mathbb{E}_{x\in V(Q_m)}[\|F(x) - F(\bar{x})\|_2^2].
\end{aligned}$$

Therefore (4) implies,

$$\begin{aligned}
c_2 &\leq m\cdot\mathbb{E}_{\vec{e}\in\vec{E}(Q_m)}[\|F(\vec{e})\|_2^2]\\
&= m\cdot\mathbb{E}_{\vec{e}\in\vec{E}(Q_m)}[(F(\vec{e}))\cdot(F(\vec{e}))]\\
&= \mathbb{E}_{\vec{e}\in\vec{E}(Q_m)}[\mathbb{E}_{f\in\mathcal{F}}f(\vec{e})\cdot\mathbb{E}_{g\in\mathcal{F}}g(\vec{e})]\\
&= \mathbb{E}_{f,g\in\mathcal{F},\vec{e}\in\vec{E}(Q_m)}[f(\vec{e})\cdot g(\vec{e})]\\
&= m\cdot c_1
\end{aligned}$$

□

The main idea in the proof of Lemma 3.2 is to apply Lemma 3.3 to some family $\mathcal{F} \subseteq \{f|_{[Q_m]_i} : 1 \leq i \leq m\}$. In the rest of the section, we are mainly concerned with bounding the values c_1 and c_2 based on efficiency and distortion.

LEMMA 3.4. *For all $i, j \in [m]$, and for any non-expansive map $f : V(H_m) \to$ NEG with distortion at most D, the following inequality holds,*

$$(f([x]_i) - f([\bar{x}]_i))(f([x]_j) - f([\bar{x}]_j)) \geq \frac{m}{D} - 4(|j - i|). \quad (13)$$

PROOF. We prove this inequality using the following bounds.

i) Non-expanding property: $\|f([x]_j) - f([x]_i)\|_2^2 \leq 2|i - j|$ and $\|f([\bar{x}]_i) - f([\bar{x}]_j)\|_2^2 \leq 2|i - j|$.

ii) Distortion bound: $\|f([x]_i) - f([\bar{x}]_i)\|_2^2 \geq \frac{m}{D}$ and $\|f([x]_j) - f([\bar{x}]_j)\|_2^2 \geq \frac{m}{D}$.

To prove (13),

$$\begin{aligned}
&\frac{m}{D} - 4|i - j|\\
&\leq \frac{m}{D} - \|(f([x]_i) - f([x]_j))\|_2^2 - \|(f([\bar{x}]_j) - f([\bar{x}]_i))\|_2^2\\
&\leq \frac{m}{D} - \frac{\|(f([x]_i) - f([x]_j)) + (f([\bar{x}]_j) - f([\bar{x}]_i))\|_2^2}{2}\\
&= \frac{m}{D} - \frac{\|(f([x]_i) - f([\bar{x}]_i) - (f([(x]_j) - f([\bar{x}]_j))\|_2^2}{2}\\
&\leq \frac{m}{D} - \frac{\frac{m}{D} + \frac{m}{D} - 2(f([x]_i) - f([\bar{x}]_i))(f([x]_j) - f([\bar{x}]_j))}{2}\\
&= (f([x]_i) - f([\bar{x}]_i))(f([x]_j) - f([\bar{x}]_j)).
\end{aligned}$$

□

COROLLARY 3.5. *For all $i, j \in [m]$ such that $|i-j| \le \frac{m}{8D}$, and for any non-expansive map $f : V(H_m) \to \mathsf{NEG}$ with distortion at most D, the following inequality holds,*

$$(f([x]_i) - f([\bar{x}]_i))\,(f([x]_j) - f([\bar{x}]_j)) \ge \frac{m}{2D}.$$

LEMMA 3.6. *Let $f : H_m \to \mathsf{NEG}$ be a non-expansive mapping. Furthermore, suppose that $\mathsf{dist}(f) \le D$ and f is ε-efficient with respect to μ_m, then there exist an index $p \in [m]$ such that,*

$$\mathbb{E}_{\vec{e} \in \vec{E}(Q_m)} \mathbb{E}_{i,j \in \{p,\cdots,p+\ell\}} f([\vec{e}]_i) f([\vec{e}]_j) \lesssim \frac{D}{m} + \frac{\varepsilon m}{D}, \quad (14)$$

where $\ell = \lfloor \frac{m}{8D} \rfloor$.

PROOF. To prove this lemma first we bound the slack on sub-paths. Let s_p denote the expectation of the following quantum when $x \in Q_m$ and $k \in [m]$ are chosen uniformly at random

$$\sum_{r=p}^{p+\ell} \left(\|f([x]_r) - f([x \oplus e_k]_r)\|_2^2 + \|f([x]_{r+1}) - f([x \oplus e_k]_r)\|_2^2\right) - \|f([x]_p) - f([x \oplus e_k]_{p+\ell})\|_2^2 .$$

Since f is ε-efficient with respect to μ_m, we have

$$\mathbb{E}_{p \in [m-\ell]} s_p \lesssim \varepsilon \ell,$$

and therefore there must exist an index p such that $s_p \lesssim \varepsilon \ell$. We show that any such p satisfies (14).

We bound the sum,

$$\mathbb{E}_{\vec{e} \in \vec{E}(Q_m)} \left\| \sum_{i=p}^{p+\ell} f([\vec{e}]_i) \right\|_2^2 \quad (15)$$
$$\asymp \ell^2 \left(\mathbb{E}_{\vec{e} \in \vec{E}(Q_m)} \mathbb{E}_{i,j \in \{p,\cdots,p+\ell\}} f([\vec{e}]_i) f([\vec{e}]_j)\right)$$

by splitting it into two parts:

$$\left\| \sum_{i=p}^{p+\ell} f([\vec{e}]_i) \right\|_2^2 = \sum_{i=p}^{p+\ell} \|f([\vec{e}]_i)\|_2^2 + \sum_{i,j=p: i \ne j}^{p+\ell} f([\vec{e}]_i) f([\vec{e}]_j).$$

The map f is non-expansive, therefore $\|f([\vec{e}]_i)\|_2^2 \le 1$, and

$$\left\| \sum_{i=p}^{p+\ell} f([\vec{e}]_i) \right\|_2^2 \lesssim \ell + \sum_{i,j=p: i \ne j}^{p+\ell} f([\vec{e}]_i) f([\vec{e}]_j).$$

By bounding,

$$\sum_{i,j=p: i \ne j}^{p+\ell} f([\vec{e}]_i) f([\vec{e}]_j), \quad (16)$$

we can bound the overall sum and complete the proof.

For a given p and e, let

$$\nu_{p,\vec{e}} = \max_{i \ne j \in \{p,\ldots,p+\ell\}} f([\vec{e}]_i) f([\vec{e}]_j),$$

and let $i_0 < j_0$ be the indices were the maximum is achieved. We show that $s_p \lesssim \mathbb{E}_{e \in E(Q_m)} \nu_{p,\vec{e}}$ and then bound (15) by

$$\left\| \sum_{i=p}^{p+\ell} f([\vec{e}]_i) \right\|_2^2 \lesssim \ell + s_p \ell^2 \lesssim \ell^2 \left(\frac{1}{\ell} + \varepsilon \ell\right) \asymp \ell^2 \left(\frac{D}{m} + \frac{\varepsilon m}{D}\right),$$

to complete the proof.

For an edge $\vec{e} = (x, x \oplus e_k)$, we can write the triangle inequality for $\|\cdot\|_2^2$ among $[x]_{i_0}$, $[x]_{j_0}$ and $[x \oplus e_k]_{j_0}$ as

$$\begin{aligned} 0 &\ge (f([x]_{i_0}) - f([x]_{j_0})) \cdot (f([x]_{j_0}) - f([x \oplus e_k]_{j_0})) \\ &= (f([x]_{i_0}) - f([x \oplus e_k]_{i_0}) \cdot (f([x]_{j_0}) - f([x \oplus e_k]_{j_0}) \\ &\quad + f([x \oplus e_k]_{i_0}) - f([x]_{j_0})) \cdot (f([x]_{j_0}) - f([x \oplus e_k]_{j_0})) \\ &\ge \nu_{p,\vec{e}} + (f([x \oplus e_k]_{i_0}) - f([x]_{j_0})) \cdot (f([x]_{j_0}) - f([x \oplus e_k]_{j_0})), \end{aligned}$$

hence

$$\|f([x \oplus e_k]_{i_0}) - f([x]_{j_0})\|_2^2 + \|f([x]_{j_0}) - f([x \oplus e_k]_{j_0})\|_2^2 \ge \|f([x \oplus e_k]_{i_0}) - f([x \oplus e_k]_{j_0})\|_2^2 + 2\nu_{p,\vec{e}}.$$

Using the triangle inequality, we obtain

$$\begin{aligned} &\|f([x]_p) - f([x \oplus e_k]_{p+\ell})\|_2^2 \\ &\quad \le \|f([x]_p) - f([x \oplus e_k]_{i_0})\|_2^2 \\ &\quad\quad + \|f([x \oplus e_k]_{i_0}) - f([x \oplus e_k]_{j_0})\|_2^2 \\ &\quad\quad + \|f([x \oplus e_k]_{j_0}) - f([x \oplus e_k]_{p+\ell})\|_2^2 \\ &\quad \le -2\nu_{p,\vec{e}} + \sum_{r=p}^{p+\ell} \|f([x]_r) - f([x \oplus e_k]_r)\|_2^2 \\ &\quad\quad + \|f([x]_{r+1}) - f([x \oplus e_k]_r)\|_2^2 . \end{aligned}$$

Therefore, $s_p \gtrsim \mathbb{E}_{\vec{e} \in \vec{E}(Q_m)} \nu_{p,\vec{e}}$ and the proof is complete. □

Now we can present the proof of Lemma 3.2.

PROOF OF LEMMA 3.2. Let $f : H_m \to \mathsf{NEG}$ be a non-expansive map which is ε-efficient with respect to μ_m, where $\varepsilon = O(\frac{1}{m \log m})$. Let p satisfy the conclusion of Lemma 3.6. Let $f_i(x) = f([x]_i)$. Furthermore, let

$$\mathcal{F} = \left\{ f_i : p \le i \le p + \left\lfloor \frac{m}{8D} \right\rfloor \right\}.$$

An immediate application of Lemma 3.6 yields,

$$\mathbb{E}_{f,g \in \mathcal{F}, \vec{e} \in \vec{E}(Q_m)} [f(\vec{e}) \cdot g(\vec{e})] \lesssim \frac{D}{m} + \frac{\varepsilon m}{D}.$$

From Corollary 3.5 we have,

$$\mathbb{E}_{f,g \in \mathcal{F}, x \in V(Q_m)} [(f(x) - f(\bar{x})) \cdot (g(x) - g(\bar{x}))] \ge \frac{m}{2D}.$$

Applying Lemma 3.3 with the given bounds, we must have

$$m \gtrsim \frac{\frac{m}{D}}{\frac{D}{m} + \frac{\varepsilon m}{D}} \gtrsim \frac{1}{\varepsilon + \frac{D^2}{m^2}},$$

therefore

$$m\varepsilon + \frac{D^2}{m} \gtrsim 1,$$

and $D \gtrsim m^{1/2}$. □

Acknowledgements

We are grateful to Alex Jaffe for his participation in the early phases of this work. We also thank Sushant Sachdeva for pointing out a quantitative improvement in our lower bound argument.

4. REFERENCES

[ACMM05] A. Agarwal, M. Charikar, K. Makarychev, and Y. Makarychev. $O(\sqrt{\log n})$ approximation algorithms for Min UnCut, Min 2CNF Deletion, and directed cut problems. In *37th Annual ACM Symposium on Theory of Computing*. ACM, 2005.

[AHK04] S. Arora, E. Hazan, and S. Kale. $O(\sqrt{\log n})$ approximation to SPARSEST CUT in $\tilde{O}(n^2)$ time. In *45th Annual Syposium on Foundations of Computer Science*, pages 238–247. IEEE Computer Society, 2004.

[ALN08] Sanjeev Arora, James R. Lee, and Assaf Naor. Euclidean distortion and the Sparsest Cut. *J. Amer. Math. Soc.*, 21(1):1–21, 2008.

[AR98] Yonatan Aumann and Yuval Rabani. An $O(\log k)$ approximate min-cut max-flow theorem and approximation algorithm. *SIAM J. Comput.*, 27(1):291–301 (electronic), 1998.

[ARV04] Sanjeev Arora, Satish Rao, and Umesh Vazirani. Expander flows, geometric embeddings, and graph partitionings. In *36th Annual Symposium on the Theory of Computing*, pages 222–231, 2004.

[Ass83] Patrice Assouad. Plongements lipschitziens dans $\mathbf{R}^n$. *Bull. Soc. Math. France*, 111(4):429–448, 1983.

[BL00] Yoav Benyamini and Joram Lindenstrauss. *Geometric nonlinear functional analysis. Vol. 1*, volume 48 of *American Mathematical Society Colloquium Publications*. American Mathematical Society, Providence, RI, 2000.

[Bou85] J. Bourgain. On Lipschitz embedding of finite metric spaces in Hilbert space. *Israel J. Math.*, 52(1-2):46–52, 1985.

[CGR05] S. Chawla, A. Gupta, and H. Räcke. An improved approximation to sparsest cut. In *Proceedings of the 16th Annual ACM-SIAM Symposium on Discrete Algorithms*, Vancouver, 2005. ACM.

[Che99] J. Cheeger. Differentiability of Lipschitz functions on metric measure spaces. *Geom. Funct. Anal.*, 9(3):428–517, 1999.

[CK06a] J. Cheeger and B. Kleiner. Differentiating maps into L^1 and the geometry of BV functions. arXiv:math.MG/0611954, 2006.

[CK06b] Jeff Cheeger and Bruce Kleiner. Generalized differential and bi-Lipschitz nonembedding in L^1. *C. R. Math. Acad. Sci. Paris*, 343(5):297–301, 2006.

[CK06c] Jeff Cheeger and Bruce Kleiner. On the differentiability of Lipschitz maps from metric measure spaces to Banach spaces. In *Inspired by S. S. Chern*, volume 11 of *Nankai Tracts Math.*, pages 129–152. World Sci. Publ., Hackensack, NJ, 2006.

[CK09] J. Cheeger and B. Kleiner. Metric differentiation, monotonicity and maps to L^1. arXiv:0907.3295, 2009.

[CKN09] J. Cheeger, B. Kleiner, and A. Naor. A $(\log n)^{\Omega(1)}$ integrality gap for the Sparsest Cut SDP. In *50th Annual Symposium on Foundations of Computer Science*. IEEE Computer Soc., Los Alamitos, CA, 2009.

[CMM06] Eden Chlamtac, Konstantin Makayrchev, and Yury Makarychev. How to play unique game using embeddings. In *47th Annual Syposium on Foundations of Computer Science*, 2006.

[DKSV06] N. Devanur, S. Khot, R. Saket, and N. K. Vishnoi. Integrality gaps for sparsest cut and minimum linear arrangement problems. In *38th Annual Symposium on the Theory of Computing*, 2006.

[EFW06] A. Eskin, D. Fisher, and K. Whyte. Quasi-isometries and rigidity of solvable groups. Preprint, 2006.

[Enf69] P. Enflo. On the nonexistence of uniform homeomorphisms between L_p-spaces. *Ark. Mat.*, 8:103–105, 1969.

[FHL05] U. Feige, M. T. Hajiaghayi, and J. R. Lee. Improved approximation algorithms for minimum-weight vertex separators. In *37th Annual ACM Symposium on Theory of Computing*. ACM, 2005. To appear, *SIAM J. Comput.*

[GNRS99] A. Gupta, I. Newman, Y. Rabinovich, and A. Sinclair. Cuts, trees and l_1-embeddings of graphs. In *40th Annual Symposium on Foundations of Computer Science*, pages 399–408. IEEE Computer Soc., Los Alamitos, CA, 1999.

[Kar09] George Karakostas. A better approximation ratio for the vertex cover problem. *ACM Trans. Algorithms*, 5(4):Art. 41, 8, 2009.

[KL08] A. Kolla and J. R. Lee. Sparsest cut on quotients of the hypercube. Preprint, 2008.

[KLMN05] R. Krauthgamer, J. R. Lee, M. Mendel, and A. Naor. Measured descent: a new embedding method for finite metrics. *Geom. Funct. Anal.*, 15(4):839–858, 2005.

[KR06] Robert Krauthgamer and Yuval Rabani. Improved lower bounds for embeddings into l_1. In *Proceedings of the 17th annual ACM-SIAM symposium on Discrete algorithm*, pages 1010–1017. ACM Press, 2006.

[KV05] Subhash Khot and Nisheeth Vishnoi. The unique games conjecture, integrality gap for cut problems and embeddability of negative type metrics into ℓ_1. In *Proceedings of the 46th Annual IEEE Conference on Foundations of Computer Science*, pages 53–62, 2005.

[Lee05] James R. Lee. On distance scales, embeddings, and efficient relaxations of the cut cone. In *SODA '05: Proceedings of the sixteenth annual ACM-SIAM symposium on Discrete algorithms*, pages 92–101, Philadelphia, PA, USA, 2005. Society for Industrial and Applied Mathematics.

[Lee09] J. R. Lee. Volume distortion for subsets of Euclidean spaces. *Discrete Comput. Geom.*, 41(4):590–615, 2009.

[Lin02] Nathan Linial. Finite metric-spaces—combinatorics, geometry and algorithms. In *Proceedings of the International Congress of Mathematicians, Vol. III (Beijing, 2002)*, pages 573–586, Beijing, 2002. Higher Ed. Press.

[LLR95] N. Linial, E. London, and Y. Rabinovich. The geometry of graphs and some of its algorithmic applications. *Combinatorica*, 15(2):215–245, 1995.

[LMN05] James R. Lee, Manor Mendel, and Assaf Naor. Metric structures in L_1: dimension, snowflakes, and average distortion. *European J. Combin.*, 26(8):1180–1190, 2005.

[LN06] J. R. Lee and A. Naor. L_p metrics on the Heisenberg group and the Goemans-Linial conjecture. In *47th Annual Symposium on Foundations of Computer Science*. IEEE Computer Soc., Los Alamitos, CA, 2006.

[LR99] Tom Leighton and Satish Rao. Multicommodity max-flow min-cut theorems and their use in designing approximation algorithms. *J. ACM*, 46(6):787–832, 1999.

[LR07] J. R. Lee and P. Rhagevendra. Coarse differentiation and multi-flows in planar graphs. To appear, *Disc. Comp. Geom.*, 2007.

[LS09] J. R. Lee and A. Sidiropoulos. On the geometry of graphs with a forbidden minor. In *STOC'09: Proceedings of the 41st Annual ACM Symposium on Theory of Computing*. ACM, 2009.

[Mat02a] J. Matoušek. *Lectures on discrete geometry*, volume 212 of *Graduate Texts in Mathematics*. Springer-Verlag, New York, 2002.

[Mat02b] Jiri Matoušek. Open problems on embeddings of finite metric spaces. *Available at http://kam.mff.cuni.cz/~matousek/haifaop.ps*, 2002.

[Pan89] Pierre Pansu. Métriques de Carnot-Carathéodory et quasiisométries des espaces symétriques de rang un. *Ann. of Math. (2)*, 129(1):1–60, 1989.

[Rao99] Satish Rao. Small distortion and volume preserving embeddings for planar and Euclidean metrics. In *Proceedings of the 15th Annual Symposium on Computational Geometry*, pages 300–306, New York, 1999.

[She09] J. Sherman. Breaking the multicommodity flow barrier for $\sqrt{\log n}$-approximations to Sparsest Cut. In *50th Annual Symposium on Foundations of Computer Science*. IEEE Computer Soc., Los Alamitos, CA, 2009.

Approximations for the Isoperimetric and Spectral Profile of Graphs and Related Parameters

Prasad Raghavendra
MSR New England
Cambridge, MA

David Steurer*
Princeton University
Princeton, NJ

Prasad Tetali
Georgia Tech
Atlanta, GA

ABSTRACT

The spectral profile of a graph is a natural generalization of the classical notion of its Rayleigh quotient. Roughly speaking, given a graph G, for each $0 < \delta < 1$, the spectral profile $\Lambda_G(\delta)$ minimizes the Rayleigh quotient (from the variational characterization) of the spectral gap of the Laplacian matrix of G over vectors with support at most δ over a suitable probability measure. Formally, the spectral profile Λ_G of a graph G is a function $\Lambda_G : [0, 1/2] \to \mathbb{R}$ defined as:

$$\Lambda_G(\delta) \stackrel{\mathrm{def}}{=} \min_{\substack{x \in \mathbb{R}^V \\ d(\mathrm{supp}(x)) \leqslant \delta}} \frac{\sum g_{ij}(x_i - x_j)^2}{\sum_i d_i x_i^2}.$$

where g_{ij} is the weight of the edge (i, j) in the graph, d_i is the degree of vertex i, and $d(\mathrm{supp}(x))$ is the fraction of edges incident on vertices within the support of vector x.

While the notion of the spectral profile has numerous applications in Markov chain, it is also is closely tied to its isoperimetric profile of a graph. Specifically, the spectral profile is a relaxation for the problem of approximating edge expansion of small sets in graphs.

In this work, we obtain an efficient algorithm that yields a $\log(1/\delta)$-factor approximation for the value of $\Lambda_G(\delta)$. By virtue of its connection to edge-expansion, we also obtain an algorithm for the problem of approximating edge expansion of small linear sized sets in a graph. This problem was recently shown to be intimately connected to the Unique Games Conjecture in [18].

Finally, we extend the techniques to obtain approximation algorithms with similar guarantees for restricted eigenvalue problems on diagonally dominant matrices.

Categories and Subject Descriptors

F.2.2 [**Theory of Computation**]: Analysis of Algorithms and Problem Complexity—*Nonnumerical Algorithms and Problems*

*Supported by NSF grants 0830673, 0832797, 528414. Part of this work done while at Microsoft Research New England.

General Terms

Algorithms, Theory

Keywords

Spectral Profile, Graph Expansion, Semidefinite Programming, Approximation Algorithm, Small-Set Expansion, Sparse Principal Component Analysis

1. INTRODUCTION

Motivated by the need for improvements over the elementary bounds on total variation mixing times of a Markov chain using spectral gap and conductance, Lovász and Kannan [15] introduced the notion of an average conductance, which takes into account the gain from large expansion small sets (of states of a Markov chain). By deriving bounds on the stronger L^2-mixing time, Morris and Peres [17] further strengthened the above result, using the notion of *evolving sets*. A corresponding functional analog of the average conductance was then derived in the form of the spectral profile by Goel-Montegro-Tetali [14], building on and further simplifying earlier works in the continuous setting of heat kernels on manifolds [5, 10]. As explained in detail in [16], besides providing tighter estimates on mixing times for various walks (by avoiding the penalty of a slow start), the approach to mixing time in L^2 using the spectral profile facilitated easier derivation of estimates on mixing using other functional approaches – notably the logarithmic Sobolev and Nash inequalities.

Generalizing the standard Cheeger-type inequality relating the spectral gap and conductance (or sparsest cut in the context of a graph), [14] also showed a Cheeger-type inequality relating the spectral profile to the average conductance (or isoperimetric profile). Since one is often interested in knowing when *small sets* expand (as this is sufficient for many applications of expanders), the question of computing or approximating the spectral profile becomes relevant and interesting – with the hope of obtaining a certificate for such small-set expansion. In this work we consider a very natural semidefinite relaxation of the profile and obtain a logarithmic factor approximation. A precise statement of our results appears below.

Inspired by recent applications in optimization over sparse subspaces, we consider a natural extension of the notion of spectral profile to the class of diagonally dominant matrices. Recall that a matrix (over the reals) is diagonally dominant if in every row, the diagonal entry is larger or equal (in absolute value) to the sum of the absolute values of the off-diagonal entries. The Laplacian matrix of a graph (being the diagonal matrix of degrees minus the adjacency matrix), with a row and a corresponding column removed, is easily seen to be a special case of such matrices. Our second main contribution is in formulating the spectral profile problem for the diagonally dominant matrices and providing a similar logarithmic factor approximation. This turns out to be a rather nontrivial extension of our first result for graphs. Once again, the precise statement of our second main theorem is provided below.

In the following we briefly mention some recent related work. In the currently active topic of sparse principal component analysis [11, 12, 13], a general problem is to decompose a covariance matrix as a combination of projections on orthogonal "sparse subspaces". A related problem to this turns out to be to maximize a quadratic form over sparse vectors. For this problem, d'Aspremont et al. [13] consider a semidefinite relaxation very similar to the one considered in our work. We show the first approximation algorithm for this problem. If the covariance matrix is diagonally dominant, then we can find sparse vectors that are almost maximally correlated with this covariance matrix (see Theorem 1.6 for a more precise statement).

1.1 Results

Let $G = (g_{ij})$ be a weighted graph with vertex set $V = \{1, \dots, n\}$. Let $d = (d_1, \dots, d_n)$ be the *degree vector* of G, that is, $d_i := \sum_j g_{ij}$. We assume that the weights of G are scaled such that $\sum_i d_i = 1$. Hence, we can think of d as a probability measure on V and we denote $d(S) := \sum_{i \in S} d_i$ for a subset $S \subseteq V$. For a vector $x \in \mathbb{R}^V$, let $\operatorname{supp}(x) := \{i \in V \mid x_i \neq 0\}$ denote its *support*. We define the *spectral profile* of G as

$$\Lambda_G(\delta) \stackrel{\text{def}}{=} \min_{\substack{x \in \mathbb{R}^V \\ d(\operatorname{supp}(x)) \leqslant \delta}} \frac{\sum_{ij} g_{ij}(x_i - x_j)^2}{\sum_i d_i x_i^2}. \tag{1.1}$$

We consider a natural semidefinite programming relaxation $\tilde{\Lambda}_G$ for the spectral profile of G (see §2.1, (2.3)). Our main result is the following relation of the spectral profile and its SDP relaxation. (The theorem follows by combining Theorem 3.1 and Theorem 3.2 in Section 3.)

THEOREM 1.1. *For every graph G and all $\varepsilon, \delta > 0$,*

$$\tilde{\Lambda}_G(\delta) \leqslant \Lambda_G(\delta) \leqslant \tilde{\Lambda}_G(\delta/1+\varepsilon) \cdot O\left(\log(1/\delta)/\varepsilon^3\right).$$

In the theorem above, we can think of ε as an absolute constant, say $\varepsilon = 0.01$, and δ as tending to zero.

Standard arguments also show that the rounding can be implemented efficiently, yielding approximation algorithms for the spectral profile of graphs. In particular, given a graph G and a parameter $\delta > 0$, we can compute a vertex set of volume $O(\delta)$ such that the corresponding principal submatrix of $\mathcal{L}_G$ has smallest eigenvalue $\lambda \leqslant \Lambda_G(\delta) \cdot O(\log(1/\delta))$. Given such a submatrix, we can efficiently find a vertex set S of volume $O(\delta)$ with conductance $\Phi(S) \leqslant O(\sqrt{\lambda})$ [14, 8]. Recall that the conductance $\Phi(S)$ of a vertex set S is the weight of the edge leaving the set divided by the weight of all edges incident to the set.

The combination of these results leads to following approximation algorithm for SMALL-SET EXPANSION (as considered in [18]).

THEOREM 1.2. *There exists a polynomial time algorithm that given a graph G and a parameter $\delta > 0$, finds a set $S \subseteq [n]$ with volume $d(S) = O(\delta)$ and conductance*

$$\Phi(S) \leqslant O\big(\tilde{\Lambda}(\delta)\log(1/\delta)\big)^{1/2}.$$

To the best of our knowledge, there are no previous approximation results for SMALL-SET EXPANSION mentioned in the literature (at least for the regime where the optimal conductance is small but constant).

We observe that the approximation algorithm for SPARSEST CUT based on Cheeger's inequality [1, 2] implies quite easily a somewhat worse approximation for SMALL-SET EXPANSION. The rough idea is to apply this algorithm SPARSEST CUT recursively until the graph is partitioned into sets of volume not much more than δ. We can then argue that one of these sets has conductance $O(\log(1/\delta)\sqrt{\varepsilon})$ if the optimal conductance of a set of volume δ was ε. Theorem 1.2 improves this approximation guarantee by a factor $\sqrt{\log(1/\delta)}$.

We note that one can prove Theorem 1.2 also directly, without going through the approximation for the spectral profile. The idea is to combine the techniques of [6, 7] with the techniques in this paper.

We also note that the approximations of Theorem 1.1 and Theorem 1.2 are optimal (up to constant factors) with respect to the relaxation we are using. The Gaussian noise graph in $\mathbb{R}^n$ (Ornstein-Uhlenbeck operator) is an integrality gap instance with matching parameters.

Finally, we remark that the approximation algorithms for SMALL-SET EXPANSION and the spectral profile can be implemented with quasi-linear running time if $\tilde{\Lambda}(\delta)$ is lower-bounded by a constant. (We measure the instance size by the number of edges in the graph.) In this case, we can compute near-optimal solutions for the SDP relaxation $\tilde{\Lambda}(\delta)$ in quasi-linear time using the framework of Arora and Kale [3] (also [19]).

Diagonally Dominant Matrices.

Let $A = (a_{ij}) \in \mathbb{R}^{n \times n}$ be a symmetric diagonally dominant[1] matrix. Let μ be some probability measure on the coordinate set $[n]$. Let $R_A(x) = \sum_{ij} a_{ij} x_i x_j / \sum_i \mu_i x_i^2$ be the Rayleigh quotient of A at x. We define the spectral profile of A as $\Lambda_A(\delta) = \min_{x \in \mathbb{R}^n, \mu(\operatorname{supp}(x)) \leqslant \delta} R_A(x)$. We consider a natural semidefinite relaxation $\tilde{\Lambda}_A(\delta)$ of the spectral profile. We can generalize Theorem 1.1 in the following way. (The theorem follows by combining Theorem 4.1 and Theorem 4.3 in Section 4.)

THEOREM 1.3. *There exists an absolute constant $c > 0$ such that for every matrix A as above and all $\delta > 0$,*

$$\tilde{\Lambda}_A(\delta) \leqslant \Lambda_A(\delta) \leqslant \tilde{\Lambda}_A(c\delta) \cdot O\big(\log(1/\delta)\big).$$

The rounding that achieves the above bounds is quite different from our construction for Theorem 1.1.

A relatively straight-forward modification of the construction for Theorem 1.1 achieves almost the above bound, but with an additional additive error of $\tilde{\Lambda}_A(c\delta)\log(1/\tilde{\Lambda}_A(c\delta))$. We present the significantly simpler analysis of this slightly suboptimal construction in Section 4.2.

Again the rounding can be implemented efficiently.

[1] diagonally dominant means $a_{ii} \geqslant \sum_{j \neq i} |a_{ij}|$ for all $i \in [n]$

THEOREM 1.4. *There exists a polynomial time algorithm that given a matrix A as above and a parameter $\delta > 0$, finds an $O(\delta)$-sparse vector x such that*

$$R_A(x) \leqslant \tilde{\Lambda}_A(c\delta) \cdot O\big(\log(1/\delta)\big).$$

Trevisan [20] showed that Cheeger's inequality also applies in this setting.

THEOREM 1.5. *There exists a polynomial time algorithm that given a matrix A as above and a parameter $\delta > 0$, finds an $O(\delta)$-sparse vector $x \in \{-1,0,1\}^n$ such that*

$$R_A(x) \leqslant O\Big(\tilde{\Lambda}_A(c\delta) \cdot \log(1/\delta)\Big)^{1/2}.$$

As before, the framework of Arora and Kale [3] allows us to implement these approximation algorithms in quasi-linear if $\tilde{\Lambda}_A(c\delta)$ is bounded from below by a constant.

D'Aspremont et al. [13] consider the problem of maximizing $R_A(x)$ over sparse vectors x. If the measure μ is proportional to the diagonal of A (which is a natural assumption), this problem reduces to the problem of computing the spectral profile of the matrix $A' = 2\operatorname{diag}(A) - A$. (In words, A' has the same diagonal as A, but all off-diagonal entries are negated.) Notice that A' is diagonally dominant if and only if A is so. Hence, we can apply Theorem 1.4 to A'. In this way, we get the following approximation algorithm for the problem of maximizing $R_A(x)$ over sparse vectors x.

THEOREM 1.6. *Let A be a matrix as above and let $\delta > 0$. Suppose the measure μ is proportional to the diagonal of A. If there exists a δ-sparse vector x such that $R_A(x) \geqslant (2-\eta)\operatorname{Tr} A$, then we can find in polynomial time a $O(\delta)$-sparse vector y such that*

$$R_A(y) \geqslant \big(2 - O(\eta \cdot \log(1/\delta))\big)\operatorname{Tr} A.$$

(In our normalization, 2 is the maximum possible value that $R_A(x)$ can achieve.)

1.2 Proof Overview and Techniques

SDP Relaxation of sparsity constraints.

Let G be a graph on vertex set $\{1,\ldots,n\}$. For the sake of simplicity, let us assume that G is unweighted and regular. Our goal is to find a vector x with about δn non-zero coordinates that minimizes the following Rayleigh quotient (from the variational characterization of the spectral gap)

$$R_G(x) \stackrel{\text{def}}{=} \frac{\sum_{i\sim j}(x_i - x_j)^2}{\sum_i x_i^2}.$$

We note that without loss of generality, it is enough to consider non-negative vectors (the Rayleigh quotient can only decrease if we replace every coordinate by its absolute value). Ignoring the sparsity constraint, the minimization of $R_G(x)$ is equivalent to a semidefinite program, where we minimize the function $\sum_{i\sim j}\|v_i - v_j\|^2$ over all collections of vectors $\{v_i\}$ such that $\sum_i\|v_i\|^2 = 1$. The challenge is to deal with the sparsity constraint. Since every δ-sparse vector x satisfies $\|x\|_1^2 \leqslant \delta n\|x\|_2^2$, we can relax the sparsity constraint to $\|\sum_i v_i\|^2 \leqslant \delta n \sum_i\|v_i\|^2$ in the SDP. In addition to this constraint, we also include non-negativity constraints for the inner products, $\langle v_i, v_j\rangle \geqslant 0$ for all $i,j \in [n]$. We note that unlike for other SDP relaxations (e.g. for UNIQUE GAMES), these non-negativity constraints are crucial. (Without these constraints the SDP value for two disjoint cliques would be 0 for all $\delta > 0$, even though the spectral profile is close to 1 for small enough $\delta > 0$.)

Before describing the rounding, we mention a natural generalization: For a symmetric positive semidefinite matrix $A = (a_{ij})$, let $R_A(x) = \langle x, Ax\rangle / \langle x, x\rangle$ be its Rayleigh quotient. Our goal is to minimize this quotient over all δ-sparse vectors x. The objective of our SDP relaxation for this problem is $\sum_{ij} a_{ij}\langle v_i, v_j\rangle / \sum_i\|v_i\|^2$. In contrast to the previous case, we can no longer assume that the coordinates of the minimizer x are non-negative. Hence, we cannot include non-negativity constraints for the inner products. Instead, we add the constraint $\sum_{ij}|\langle v_i, v_j\rangle| \leqslant \delta n \sum_i\|v_i\|^2$. The resulting SDP relaxation has been suggested in [13] (for the related problem of maximizing $R_A(x)$ over sparse vectors x).

Two-phase rounding.

Our rounding proceeds in two phases: In the first phase, we start with an optimal solution to the SDP relaxation and produce a new SDP solution that satisfies a stronger relaxation of the sparsity constraint. In this phase, our objective value increases by at most a factor of order $\log(1/\delta)$. In the second phase, we extract a sparse vector from the SDP solution that satisfies the stronger sparsity constraint. In this phase, we only increase the objective value by a constant factor.

The advantage of this two-phase rounding is that it allows us to separate local and non-local arguments. In the first phase, the transformation of the SDP solution is quite drastic (we lose a $\log(1/\delta)$ factor in the objective). However, the transformation in this phase is completely local. In fact, every vector gets mapped to a new vector in a way that is oblivious to all other vectors in the SDP solution. On the other hand, the rounding in the second phase is inherently non-local, because it has to ensure that the resulting vector x is sparse. In particular, the rounding for the ith coordinate of x cannot be oblivious to all other coordinates. What allows us to analyze the non-local rounding in this phase, is the stronger sparsity constraint that we established in the first phase.

The stronger sparsity constraint that is established in the first phase has the form

$$\Big\|\textstyle\sum_i |v_i|\Big\|^2 \leqslant \delta n \displaystyle\sum_i \|v_i\|^2, \tag{1.2}$$

where $|v_i|$ is the vector v_i with each coordinate replaced by its absolute value. In Section 3.1, we show that vectors satisfying this constraints can be rounded to a sparse vector x such that $R_G(x)$ is not much larger than the SDP value of the vectors $v_1,\ldots,v_n$. The main ingredient is the following lemma (see Lemma 2.5 and its consequences Lemma 3.6 and Lemma 4.7): Suppose x satisfies $\|x\|_1^2 \leqslant \delta n\|x\|_2^2$. Then, we can choose a parameter $t > 0$ such that the vector y defined as $y_i = \mathsf{soft\text{-}chop}_t(x_i)$ is 3δ-sparse (say) and at the same time $\|y\|_2^2 \geqslant \frac{1}{3}\|x\|_2^2$ (a good fraction of the mass is preserved). Here, $\mathsf{soft\text{-}chop}_t$ is the soft-thresholding function, defined as $\mathsf{soft\text{-}chop}_t(x) = x - t$ if $x > t$, $\mathsf{soft\text{-}chop}_t(x) = 0$ if $|x| \leqslant t$, and $\mathsf{soft\text{-}chop}_t(x) = x + t$ if $x < -t$.

This lemma allows us to show that in order to approximate $\Lambda_G(\delta)$, it is enough to find a vector x such that $R_G(x)$ is small and $\|x\|_1^2 \leqslant \delta n\|x\|_2^2$. More concretely, it is easy to show that $R_G(y) \leqslant 3R_G(x)$ where y is the 3δ-sparse vector obtained from x by soft-thresholding as above. (This argument works not only for Laplacian matrices but also for symmetric diagonally dominant matrices, see Section 4.1.)

In the first phase of the rounding, our task is to transform an arbitrary SDP solution to a solution that satisfies the stronger sparsity constraint (1.2). For Laplacian matrices, we use the same transformation as Barak et al. [4]. This transformation has the property that it maps arbitrary vectors to vectors with only non-negative coordinates and it preserves distances in an approximate sense (see Section 3.2). For diagonally dominant matrices, we require that the transformation is symmetric (an antipodal pair of vectors gets mapped to an antipodal pair again). A straight forward adaptation of the transformation for Laplacian matrices already gives a relatively good approximation for diagonally dominant matrices (see Section 4.2). Unfortunately, this construction incurs an additional additive error term and therefore the final approximation guarantee is not multiplicative. In Section 4.3, we describe a transformation that is quite different from the construction of Barak et al. [4] and avoids the additional additive error even for diagonally dominant matrices. The disadvantage of this construction is that the analysis is technically more involved (it relies on Gaussian noise sensitivity bounds for soft threshold functions, see Section B).

2. PRELIMINARIES

2.1 Semidefinite Relaxation for the Spectral Profile of Graphs

Let $G = (g_{ij})$ be a weighted graph with vertex set $V = \{1, \ldots, n\}$. Let $d = (d_1, \ldots, d_n)$ be the *degree vector* of G, that is, $d_i := \sum_j g_{ij}$. We assume that the weights of G are scaled such that $\sum_i d_i = 1$. We denote $d(S) := \sum_{i \in S} d_i$ for a subset $S \subseteq V$. For a vector $x \in \mathbb{R}^V$, let $\mathrm{supp}(x) := \{i \in V \mid x_i \neq 0\}$ denote its *support*. The *spectral profile* of G is defined as

$$\Lambda_G(\delta) \stackrel{\text{def}}{=} \min_{\substack{x \in \mathbb{R}^V \\ d(\mathrm{supp}(x)) \leqslant \delta}} \frac{\sum_{ij} g_{ij}(x_i - x_j)^2}{\sum_i d_i x_i^2}. \tag{2.1}$$

Note that $\Lambda_G(\delta)$ is monotonically decreasing in δ. It is easy to show that $\Lambda_G(1/2)$ is up to constant factors equal to the usual spectral gap of G (e.g., see [14]). The spectral profile is characterized by the smallest eigenvalues of certain restrictions of the Laplacian of G (Dirichlet eigenvalues). Let $\mathcal{L}$ denote the normalized Laplacian of G (as defined e.g. in [9]). For a set $S \subseteq V$, let $\mathcal{L}_S$ be the $S \times S$ submatrix of $\mathcal{L}$. Then,

$$\Lambda_G(\delta) = \min_{\substack{S \subseteq V \\ d(S) \leqslant \delta}} \lambda_{\min}(\mathcal{L}_S). \tag{2.2}$$

We consider the following semidefinite programming relaxation for the spectral profile,

$$\tilde{\Lambda}_G(\delta) \stackrel{\text{def}}{=} \min_{v_1, \ldots, v_n \in \mathbb{R}^n} \frac{\sum_{ij} g_{ij} \|v_i - v_j\|^2}{\sum_i d_i \|v_i\|^2}, \tag{2.3}$$

where the minimum is over all vector configurations $v_1, \ldots, v_n \in \mathbb{R}^n$ that satisfy

$$\left\|\sum_i d_i v_i\right\|^2 \leqslant \delta \cdot \sum_i d_i \|v_i\|^2, \tag{2.4}$$

$$\langle v_i, v_j \rangle \geqslant 0. \qquad (i, j \in V) \tag{2.5}$$

Let us show that $\tilde{\Lambda}_G(\delta)$ is indeed a relaxation of the spectral profile. Let v_0 be any unit vector in $\mathbb{R}^n$. For a vector $x \in \mathbb{R}^V$ with $S = \mathrm{supp}(x)$ and $d(S) \leqslant \delta$, define vectors $v_1, \ldots, v_n \in \mathbb{R}^n$ as $v_i = |x_i| \cdot v_0$. Let $\mathbb{1}_S \in \{0,1\}^V$ denote the indicator function of the set S. By Cauchy–Schwarz,

$$\begin{aligned} \|\textstyle\sum d_i v_i\|^2 &= \Big(\sum_i d_i |x_i|\Big)^2 \\ &\leqslant \sum_i d_i \mathbb{1}_S(i) \cdot \sum_i d_i x_i^2 \leqslant \delta \cdot \sum_i d_i \|v_i\|^2 . \end{aligned}$$

Furthermore, it is easy to verify that $\langle v_i, v_j \rangle \geqslant 0$ for all $i, j \in V$ and that $\sum_{ij} g_{ij} \|v_i - v_j\|^2 \leqslant \sum_{ij} g_{ij}(x_i - x_j)^2$. It follows that $\tilde{\Lambda}_G(\delta)$ is indeed a relaxation for the spectral profile.

LEMMA 2.1. *For every graph G and all $\delta > 0$,*

$$\tilde{\Lambda}_G(\delta) \leqslant \Lambda_G(\delta).$$

2.2 Semidefinite Relaxation for the Spectral Profile of Matrices

Let $A = (a_{ij}) \in \mathbb{R}^{n \times n}$ be a symmetric positive semidefinite matrix and let μ be a probability measure on $\{1, \ldots, n\}$.

We define the *spectral profile* $\Lambda_A \colon [0,1] \to \mathbb{R}$ as

$$\Lambda_A(\delta) \stackrel{\text{def}}{=} \min_{\substack{x \in \mathbb{R}^n \\ \mu(\mathrm{supp}(x)) \leqslant \delta}} \frac{\sum_{ij} a_{ij} x_i x_j}{\sum_i \mu_i x_i^2}.$$

Let $D \in \mathbb{R}^{n \times n}$ be the diagonal matrix with entries $\mu_1, \ldots, \mu_n$. Note that

$$\Lambda_A(\delta) = \min_{\substack{S \subseteq [n] \\ \mu(S) \leqslant \delta}} \lambda_{\min}(D_S^{-1/2} A_S D_S^{-1/2}),$$

where D_S and A_S denote the principal submatrices of D and A corresponding to the coordinate set S.

We consider the following semidefinite programming relaxation for the spectral profile,

$$\tilde{\Lambda}_A(\delta) \stackrel{\text{def}}{=} \min_{v_1, \ldots, v_n \in \mathbb{R}^n} \frac{\sum_{ij} a_{ij} \langle v_i, v_j \rangle}{\sum_i \mu_i \|v_i\|^2}, \tag{2.6}$$

where the minimum is over all vector configurations $v_1, \ldots, v_n \in \mathbb{R}^n$ that satisfy

$$\sum_{ij} \mu_i \mu_j |\langle v_i, v_j \rangle| \leqslant \delta \cdot \sum_i \mu_i \|v_i\|^2 . \tag{2.7}$$

This semidefinite relaxation has been introduced in [13] (for the corresponding maximization problem).

Note that the constraint (2.7) is weaker than the previous constraints (2.4) and (2.5). We have to use the weaker constraint (2.7) for $\tilde{\Lambda}_A$ because we can no longer assume that the optimal vector $x \in \mathbb{R}^n$ has only nonnegative coordinates. As before, it is easy to verify that $\tilde{\Lambda}_A$ is a relaxation of Λ_A.

LEMMA 2.2. *For every symmetric matrix A and all $\delta > 0$,*

$$\tilde{\Lambda}_A(\delta) \leqslant \Lambda_A(\delta).$$

2.3 Gaussian Distributions

Let λ^n denote the usual Lebesgue measure on $\mathbb{R}^n$. Let $N(0, \sigma^2)^n$ be the Gaussian measure on $\mathbb{R}^n$ with mean 0 and covariance $\sigma^2 I$ (each coordinate is independent Gaussian with mean 0 and standard deviation σ). Let $\phi_\sigma \colon \mathbb{R}^n \to \mathbb{R}_+$

be the density of $N(0,\sigma^2)^n$ with respect to the Lebesgue measure,

$$\phi_\sigma(x) \stackrel{\text{def}}{=} \frac{1}{(\sigma\sqrt{2\pi})^n} e^{-\|x\|^2/2\sigma^2}.$$

Let T_u be the translation operator, i.e.,

$$T_u f(x) \stackrel{\text{def}}{=} f(x-u).$$

We will use the following bound on the (Hellinger) affinity of translated Gaussians (e.g. in Barak et al. [4]).

LEMMA 2.3 ([4]). *Let u and v be two unit vectors in $\mathbb{R}^n$. Then*

$$\int \sqrt{T_u\phi_\sigma \cdot T_v\phi_\sigma}\ \mathrm{d}\lambda^n = e^{-\|u-v\|^2/8\sigma^2}.$$

PROOF. Immediate from the identity

$$\sqrt{T_u\phi_\sigma \cdot T_v\phi_\sigma} = e^{-\|u-v\|^2/8\sigma^2} T_{\frac{1}{2}(u+v)}\phi_\sigma. \quad \square$$

We equip the space $\{f\colon \mathbb{R}^n \to \mathbb{R}\}$ with the inner product $\langle f,g\rangle := \int fg\,\mathrm{d}\lambda^n$ and define the corresponding norm $\|f\| := \langle f,f\rangle^{1/2}$. Consider the mapping

$$u \mapsto f_u := \|u\|\sqrt{T_{\bar{u}}\phi_\sigma}.$$

Here, $\bar{u}$ denotes the unit vector in the direction of u. In §3.2, we will use this mapping to transform arbitrary SDP solutions to non-negative SDP solutions. Notice that $\|f_u\| = \|u\|$ for every vector $u \in \mathbb{R}^n$. Furthermore, for unit vectors $u,v \in \mathbb{R}^n$ that are close, say $\|u-v\|^2 \leqslant \varepsilon$, we have $\|f_u - f_v\|^2 \leqslant O(\varepsilon/\sigma^2)$. On the other hand, for unit vectors $u,v \in \mathbb{R}^n$ that are far apart, say $\langle u,v\rangle \leqslant 1/2$, we have $\langle f_u, f_v\rangle \leqslant 2^{-\Omega(1/\sigma^2)}$. In this sense, $u \mapsto f_u$ is a distance preserving mapping from the sphere in $\mathbb{R}^n$ to the non-negative orthant of the space $\mathbb{R}^n \to \mathbb{R}$.

The following technical fact shows that in order for a mapping to preserve distances it is enough to preserve lengths and distances of unit vectors (angles).

FACT 2.4. *For any two vectors $u,v \in \mathbb{R}^n$, we have*

$$\|u-v\|^2 = (\|u\|-\|v\|)^2 + \|u\|\,\|v\|\cdot\|\bar{u}-\bar{v}\|^2.$$

2.4 Nonnegative Random Variables

The following technical lemma shows the following intuitive fact. If a non-negative random variable X satisfies $\mathbb{E}X^2 > (1+\varepsilon)k(\mathbb{E}X)^2$, then a significant fraction of the 2-norm of X has to be on values larger than $\tau = k\,\mathbb{E}X$, in the sense that the 2-norm of the variable $Y = \max\{X-\tau, 0\}$ is comparable to the 2-norm of X.

LEMMA 2.5. *Let X be a non-negative random variable with mean μ. For $k \geqslant 1$, let $Y = \max\{X-k\mu, 0\}$. Then, for every $\varepsilon > 0$,*

$$\mathbb{E}Y^2 \geqslant \varepsilon^2\cdot\left(\mathbb{E}X^2 - k\mu^2/(1-\varepsilon)\right).$$

PROOF. For $u = \varepsilon^2$, let A be the event $Y^2 \geqslant uX^2$ and let B denote the complementary event. In other words, B is the event $(1-\varepsilon)X \leqslant k\mu$. Let $\mathbb{1}_A$ and $\mathbb{1}_B$ be 0/1-indicator variables for these events. We can lower bound $\mathbb{E}Y^2$ as follows

$$\begin{aligned}\mathbb{E}Y^2 &\geqslant u\,\mathbb{E}\,\mathbb{1}_A X^2\\ &= u\left(\mathbb{E}X^2 - \mathbb{E}\,\mathbb{1}_B X^2\right)\\ &\geqslant u\left(\mathbb{E}X^2 - \mathbb{E}X\cdot k\mu/(1-\varepsilon)\right). \quad \square\end{aligned}$$

3. SPECTRAL PROFILE OF GRAPHS

We prove the following two theorems in this section (one for each phase of our rounding). Putting them together yields Theorem 1.1.

Let $G = (g_{ij})$ be a graph with vertex set $V = \{1,\ldots,n\}$ and degrees $d_1,\ldots,d_n$ such that $\sum_i d_i = 1$.

THEOREM 3.1. *For all $\delta > 0$ and $t \geqslant 1$, there exist non-negative functions $f_1,\ldots,f_n\colon \mathbb{R}^n \to \mathbb{R}_+$ such that*

$$\frac{\sum_{ij} g_{ij}\|f_i - f_j\|^2}{\sum_i d_i\|f_i\|^2} \leqslant t\cdot\tilde{\Lambda}_G(\delta)$$

and

$$\|\textstyle\sum_i d_i f_i\|^2 \leqslant (\delta + e^{-t})\sum_i d_i\|f_i\|^2.$$

THEOREM 3.2. *Let $f_1,\ldots,f_n\colon \mathbb{R}^n \to \mathbb{R}_+$ be non-negative functions that satisfy*

$$\left\|\textstyle\sum_i d_i f_i\right\|^2 \leqslant \delta\sum_i d_i\,\|f_i\|^2. \tag{3.1}$$

Then for every $\varepsilon > 0$,

$$\Lambda_G(\delta/1-2\varepsilon) \leqslant \frac{\sum_{ij} g_{ij}\|f_i-f_j\|^2}{\varepsilon^3\sum_i d_i\|f_i\|^2}.$$

3.1 From Non-negative SDP Solutions to Sparse Vectors (Theorem 3.2)

Let $f_1,\ldots,f_n\colon \mathbb{R}^n \to \mathbb{R}_+$ be non-negative functions that satisfy the constraint (3.1). For $\delta' := \delta/(1-2\varepsilon)$, let $t\colon \mathbb{R}^n \to \mathbb{R}_+$ be the function

$$t \stackrel{\text{def}}{=} \tfrac{1}{\delta'}\sum_i d_i f_i.$$

Define non-negative functions $f_1',\ldots,f_n'\colon \mathbb{R}^n \to \mathbb{R}_+$ as

$$f_i' \stackrel{\text{def}}{=} \max\{f_i - t, 0\}.$$

Let $F'\colon \mathbb{R}^n \to \mathbb{R}_+^n$ denote $F' := (f_1',\ldots,f_n')$.

For the next lemma we crucially rely on the fact that the functions $f_1,\ldots,f_n$ are non-negative (in fact it is the only part of the proof where the non-negativity is used).

LEMMA 3.3. *For every $x \in \mathbb{R}^n$,*

$$d(\operatorname{supp}(F'(x))) \leqslant \delta'.$$

PROOF. The lemma is a consequence of Markov's inequality. Imagine that we choose i at random with probability d_i. Then $d(\operatorname{supp}(F'(x)))$ is the probability that $f_i(x)$ is larger than $t(x)$. On the other hand, $\sum_i d_i f_i(x)$ is the expected value of $f_i(x)$ if i is chosen from this distribution. (Here it is important that $f_i(x)$ is non-negative.) Thus,

$$t(x)\cdot d(\operatorname{supp}(F'(x))) \leqslant \sum_i d_i f_i(x).$$

By the choice of t, it follows that $d(\operatorname{supp}(F'(x))) \leqslant \delta'$. $\square$

LEMMA 3.4.

$$\Lambda_G(\delta') \leqslant \frac{\sum_{ij} g_{ij}\|f_i' - f_j'\|^2}{\sum_i d_i\|f_i'\|^2}.$$

PROOF. For every $x \in \mathbb{R}^n$, the support of the vector $F'(x)$ has weight at most δ' (Lemma 3.3) and therefore,

$$\Lambda_G(\delta') \leqslant \frac{\sum_{ij} g_{ij}(f_i'(x) - f_j'(x))^2}{\sum_i d_i f_i'(x)^2}.$$

Furthermore, by an averaging argument, there exists an $x \in \mathbb{R}^n$ such that

$$\frac{\sum_{ij} g_{ij}(f_i'(x) - f_j'(x))^2}{\sum_i d_i f_i'(x)^2} \leqslant \frac{\sum_{ij} g_{ij}\|f_i' - f_j'\|^2}{\sum_i d_i\|f_i'\|^2}.$$

The combination of the previous two equations implies the lemma. □

LEMMA 3.5.

$$\sum_{ij} g_{ij}\|f_i' - f_j'\|^2 \leqslant \sum_{ij} g_{ij}\|f_i - f_j\|^2.$$

PROOF. The truncation operation is contractive, i.e., for any two functions f and g, we have $\|\max\{f,0\} - \max\{g,0\}\| \leqslant \|f - g\|$. This fact implies the lemma. □

LEMMA 3.6.

$$\sum_i d_i\|f_i'\|^2 \geqslant \varepsilon^3 \sum_i d_i\|f_i\|^2.$$

PROOF. By Lemma 2.5, for every $x \in \mathbb{R}^n$,

$$\sum_i d_i f_i'(x)^2 \geqslant \varepsilon^2\Big(\sum_i d_i f_i(x)^2 - \Big(\sum_i d_i f_i(x)\Big)^2 \tfrac{1}{\delta'(1-\varepsilon)}\Big).$$

Hence,

$$\begin{aligned}\sum_i d_i\|f_i'\|^2 &\geqslant \varepsilon^2 \cdot \Big(\sum_i d_i\|f_i\|^2 - \Big\|\sum_i d_i f_i\Big\|^2 \tfrac{1}{\delta'(1-\varepsilon)}\Big)\\ &\geqslant \varepsilon^2 \cdot \Big(1 - \tfrac{\delta}{\delta'(1-\varepsilon)}\Big)\sum_i d_i\|f_i\|^2 \qquad \text{(by (3.1))}\\ &= \varepsilon^2 \cdot \tfrac{\varepsilon}{1-\varepsilon}\sum_i d_i\|f_i\|^2 \qquad \text{(choice of } \delta'). \;\square\end{aligned}$$

Putting together the previous three lemmas (Lemma 3.4, Lemma 3.5 and Lemma 3.6) yields Theorem 3.2.

3.2 From Arbitrary SDP Solutions to Non-negative SDP Solutions (Theorem 3.1)

Let $v_1, \ldots, v_n \in \mathbb{R}^n$ be an optimal solution for the SDP relaxation $\tilde{\Lambda}_G(\delta)$ (see (2.3)–(2.5)). The vectors satisfy

$$\Big\|\sum_i d_i v_i\Big\|^2 \leqslant \delta \sum_i d_i\|v_i\|^2, \qquad (3.2)$$

$$\langle v_i, v_j\rangle \geqslant 0. \qquad (i,j \in V) \qquad (3.3)$$

We define non-negative functions $f_1, \ldots, f_n \colon \mathbb{R}^n \to \mathbb{R}_+$ as

$$f_i := \|v_i\| \cdot \sqrt{T_{\bar{v}_i}\phi_\sigma}.$$

Here, $T_{\bar{v}_i}\phi_\sigma$ is the density function of the Gaussian distribution with mean $\bar{v}_i$ and standard deviation $\sigma \leqslant 1/2$ in each coordinate (see §2.3 for the formal definitions).

The following lemma shows that up to factor $O(1/\sigma^2)$ the functions $f_1, \ldots, f_n$ have the same objective value as the SDP solution $v_1, \ldots, v_n$ (which we assumed to be optimal).

LEMMA 3.7.

$$\frac{\sum_{ij} g_{ij}\|f_i - f_j\|^2}{\sum_i d_i\|f_i\|^2} \leqslant \frac{\sum_{ij} g_{ij}\|v_i - v_j\|^2}{4\sigma^2\sum_i d_i\|v_i\|^2}.$$

PROOF. Since $\|v_i\| = \|f_i\|$, it is enough to show that we have $\|f_i - f_j\|^2 \leqslant \|v_i - v_j\|^2/4\sigma^2$ for all $i,j \in V$. From Lemma 2.3 and the fact $1 - x \leqslant e^{-x}$, it follows that

$$\|\bar{f}_i - \bar{f}_j\|^2 = 2 - 2e^{-\|\bar{v}_i - \bar{v}_j\|^2/8\sigma^2} \leqslant \|\bar{v}_i - \bar{v}_j\|^2/4\sigma^2$$

Together with Fact 2.4, we get as desired

$$\begin{aligned}\|f_i - f_j\|^2 &= (\|v_i\| - \|v_j\|)^2 + \|v_i\|\,\|v_j\| \cdot \|\bar{f}_i - \bar{f}_j\|^2\\ &\leqslant (\|v_i\| - \|v_j\|)^2 + \|v_i\|\,\|v_j\| \cdot \|\bar{v}_i - \bar{v}_j\|^2/4\sigma^2\\ &\leqslant \|v_i - v_j\|^2/4\sigma^2.\end{aligned}$$

The last inequality uses the assumption $\sigma \leqslant 1/2$ and again Fact 2.4. □

In the next lemma, we crucially use that the vectors $v_1, \ldots, v_n$ satisfy the constraints (3.2) and (3.3). In fact, it is the only part of the proof where these constraints are important.

LEMMA 3.8.

$$\Big\|\sum_i d_i f_i\Big\|^2 \leqslant (e^{-1/4\sigma^2} + \delta)\sum_i d_i\|v_i\|^2.$$

PROOF. Using Lemma 2.3 and the fact $e^{cx} \leqslant 1 - (1 - e^c)x$ for $x \in [0,1]$, we can bound the inner products of the normalized functions by

$$\begin{aligned}\langle \bar{f}_i, \bar{f}_j\rangle &= e^{-(1-\langle \bar{v}_i, \bar{v}_j\rangle)/4\sigma^2}\\ &\leqslant 1 - (1 - e^{-1/4\sigma^2})(1 - \langle \bar{v}_i, \bar{v}_j\rangle) \leqslant e^{-1/4\sigma^2} + \langle \bar{v}_i, \bar{v}_j\rangle.\end{aligned}$$

(Both inequalities above use the non-negativity of $\langle v_i, v_j\rangle$.) This bound allows us to estimate the length of $\sum_i d_i f_i$,

$$\begin{aligned}\Big\|\sum_i d_i f_i\Big\|^2 &\leqslant \sum_{ij} d_i d_j\|v_i\|\,\|v_j\|\big(e^{-1/4\sigma^2} + \langle \bar{v}_i, \bar{v}_j\rangle\big)\\ &= e^{-1/4\sigma^2}\Big(\sum_i d_i\|v_i\|\Big)^2 + \Big\|\sum_i d_i v_i\Big\|^2.\end{aligned}$$

By Jensen's inequality, the first term contributes not more than $e^{-1/4\sigma^2}\sum_i d_i\|v_i\|^2$. From (3.2) it follows that the second term is at most $\delta\sum_i d_i\|v_i\|^2$. The lemma follows. □

Putting together the previous two lemmas (Lemma 3.7 and Lemma 3.8) yields Theorem 3.1 (for $t = 1/4\sigma^2$).

4. SPECTRAL PROFILE OF DIAGONALLY DOMINANT MATRICES

We will prove Theorem 1.3 in this section. The proof has the same outline as the proof of Theorem 1.1 in the previous section (§3). The main difference is in the transformation that is used to map an optimal SDP solution to a collection of functions that satisfies a stronger relaxation of the sparsity constraint.

Let $A \in \mathbb{R}^{n\times n}$ be a symmetric diagonally dominant matrix and let $\mu = (\mu_1, \ldots, \mu_n)$ be a probability measure on $[n]$ (natural choices for μ are uniform, $\mu_i = 1/n$, or proportional to the diagonal of the matrix, $\mu_i = a_{ii}/\mathrm{Tr}\,A$).

In §4.1, we prove the following analog of Theorem 3.2.

THEOREM 4.1. *Let $f_1, \ldots, f_n \colon \mathbb{R}^n \to \mathbb{R}$ be functions that satisfy*

$$\sum_{ij} \mu_i\mu_j\langle |f_i|, |f_j|\rangle \leqslant \delta\sum_i \mu_i\|f_i\|^2. \qquad (4.1)$$

Here, $|f|$ is the function $x \mapsto |f(x)|$. Then for every $\varepsilon > 0$,

$$\Lambda_A(\delta/1-2\varepsilon) \leqslant \frac{\sum_{ij} a_{ij}\langle f_i, f_j\rangle}{\varepsilon^3\sum_i \mu_i\|f_i\|^2}.$$

In §4.2, we prove an analog of Theorem 3.1. However, in addition to a multiplicative error there is also an additive error. (Furthermore, we can control this additive error only when μ is proportional to the diagonal of A.) The construction is a relatively straight-forward modification of the construction we used for Laplacian matrices.

THEOREM 4.2. *Suppose that μ is proportional to the diagonal of A. For all $\delta > 0$ and $t \geqslant 1$, there exist functions $f_1, \ldots, f_n : \mathbb{R}^n \to \mathbb{R}$ such that*

$$\sum_{ij} \mu_i \mu_j \langle |f_i|, |f_j| \rangle \leqslant (\delta + O(2^{-t})) \sum_i \mu_i \|f_i\|^2$$

and

$$\frac{\sum_{ij} a_{ij} \langle f_i, f_j \rangle}{\sum_i \mu_i \|f_i\|^2} \leqslant O(t) \cdot \tilde{\Lambda}_A(\delta) + 2^{-t} \sum_i a_{ii} .$$

In §4.3, we prove an analog of Theorem 3.1 that avoids the additive error of the previous theorem. The construction here is quite different from the previous constructions. Our analysis of the construction is unfortunately somewhat more involved.

THEOREM 4.3. *For all $\delta > 0$ and $t \geqslant 1$, there exist functions $f_1, \ldots, f_n : \mathbb{R}^n \to \mathbb{R}$ such that*

$$\sum_{ij} \mu_i \mu_j \langle |f_i|, |f_j| \rangle \leqslant O(\delta + 2^{-t}) \sum_i \mu_i \|f_i\|^2$$

and

$$\frac{\sum_{ij} a_{ij} \langle f_i, f_j \rangle}{\sum_i \mu_i \|f_i\|^2} \leqslant O(t) \cdot \tilde{\Lambda}_A(\delta) .$$

Putting together Theorem 4.1 and Theorem 4.3 yields an approximation for the spectral profile of diagonally dominant matrices (Theorem 1.3).

4.1 From SDP Solutions with Small 1-Norms to Sparse Vectors (Theorem 4.1)

Let $f_1, \ldots, f_n : \mathbb{R}^n \to \mathbb{R}$ be functions that satisfy (4.1). For $\delta' := \delta/(1-2\varepsilon)$, let $t : \mathbb{R}^n \to \mathbb{R}_+$ be the function

$$t \stackrel{\text{def}}{=} \tfrac{1}{\delta'} \sum_i \mu_i |f_i| .$$

Define non-negative functions $f'_1, \ldots, f'_n : \mathbb{R}^n \to \mathbb{R}$ as

$$f'_i(x) \stackrel{\text{def}}{=} \begin{cases} f_i(x) - t(x) & \text{if } f_i(x) > t(x), \\ 0 & \text{if } -t(x) \leqslant f_i(x) \leqslant t(x), \\ f_i(x) + t(x) & \text{if } f_i(x) < -t(x). \end{cases}$$

This method of "sparsifying" the functions is known as *soft thresholding* [21]. Let $\mathsf{soft\text{-}chop}_\tau : \mathbb{R} \to \mathbb{R}$ denote the soft-thresholding function $\mathsf{soft\text{-}chop}_\tau(a) = \operatorname{sign}(a) \cdot \max\{|a| - \tau, 0\}$. Note that $f'_i(x) = \mathsf{soft\text{-}chop}_{t(x)} f_i(x)$. Let $F' : \mathbb{R}^n \to \mathbb{R}^n_+$ denote $F' := (f'_1, \ldots, f'_n)$.

The proof of the next lemma is the same as the proof of Lemma 3.3 (essentially Markov's inequality).

LEMMA 4.4. *For every $x \in \mathbb{R}^n$,*

$$\mu(\operatorname{supp}(F'(x))) \leqslant \delta' .$$

The proof of the next lemma is the same as the proof of Lemma 3.4. (An averaging argument shows that we can find $x \in \mathbb{R}^n$ such that the Rayleigh quotient of A at the vector $F'(x)$ is at most the right-hand side of the equation below. By the previous lemma, this vector $F'(x)$ is δ'-sparse.)

LEMMA 4.5.

$$\Lambda_A(\delta') \leqslant \frac{\sum_{ij} a_{ij} \langle f'_i, f'_j \rangle}{\sum_i \mu_i \|f'_i\|^2} .$$

The next lemma corresponds to Lemma 3.5. In the proof of Lemma 3.5 we used properties specific to Laplacians. In the next lemma, we show that the same bound holds also for diagonally dominant matrices.

LEMMA 4.6.

$$\sum_{ij} a_{ij} \langle f'_i, f'_j \rangle \leqslant \sum_{ij} a_{ij} \langle f_i, f_j \rangle .$$

PROOF. Since $\mathsf{soft\text{-}chop}_\tau$ is contractive (has Lipschitz constant at most 1) and symmetric (an odd function), i.e., $\sigma \cdot \mathsf{soft\text{-}chop}_\tau(b) = \mathsf{soft\text{-}chop}_\tau(\sigma \cdot b)$, we have for all $a, b \in \mathbb{R}$, $\sigma \in \{\pm 1\}$, and $\tau \geqslant 0$,

$$|\mathsf{soft\text{-}chop}_\tau(a) - \sigma \cdot \mathsf{soft\text{-}chop}_\tau(b)| \leqslant |a - \sigma \cdot b| .$$

In particular, $\|f'_i - \sigma f'_j\| \leqslant \|f_i - \sigma f_j\|$ for all $i, j \in [n]$ and $\sigma \in \{\pm 1\}$. By Lemma A.1, there exist matrices $B \in \mathbb{R}^{n \times n}_+$ and $C \in \{1, -1\}^{n \times n}$ such that $\sum_{ij} a_{ij} x_i x_j = \sum_{ij} b_{ij}(x_i - c_{ij} x_j)^2$ for all $x \in \mathbb{R}^n$. We conclude

$$\begin{aligned} \sum_{ij} a_{ij} \langle f_i, f_j \rangle &= \sum_{ij} b_{ij} \|f_i - c_{ij} f_j\|^2 \\ &\leqslant \sum_{ij} b_{ij} \|f'_i - c_{ij} f'_j\|^2 = \sum_{ij} a_{ij} \langle f'_i, f'_j \rangle . \quad \square \end{aligned}$$

The next lemma has the same proof as Lemma 3.6.

LEMMA 4.7.

$$\sum_i \mu_i \|f'_i\|^2 \geqslant \varepsilon^3 \sum_i \mu_i \|f_i\|^2 .$$

Putting together the previous three lemmas (Lemma 4.5, Lemma 4.6, and Lemma 4.7) yields Theorem 4.1.

4.2 From Arbitrary SDP Solutions to SDP Solutions with Small 1-Norms (Theorem 4.2)

Let $v_1, \ldots, v_n \in \mathbb{R}^n$ be an optimal solution to the semidefinite relaxation $\tilde{\Lambda}_A(\delta)$. The vectors satisfy

$$\sum_{ij} \mu_i \mu_j |\langle v_i, v_j \rangle| \leqslant \delta \sum_i \mu_i \|v_i\|^2 . \tag{4.2}$$

For a parameter $\sigma \geqslant 0$ (which will be determined later), we define functions $f_1, \ldots, f_n : \mathbb{R}^n \to \mathbb{R}$ as

$$f_i := \tfrac{1}{\sqrt{2}} \|v_i\| \cdot \sqrt{T_{\bar{v}_i} \phi_\sigma} - \tfrac{1}{\sqrt{2}} \|v_i\| \cdot \sqrt{T_{-\bar{v}_i} \phi_\sigma} . \tag{4.3}$$

(Recall the notation from §2.3.) Using Lemma 2.3, we compute the inner products of the functions $f_1, \ldots, f_n$ as

$$\langle f_i, f_j \rangle = \|v_i\| \, \|v_j\| \left(e^{-\|\bar{v}_i - \bar{v}_j\|^2 / 8\sigma^2} - e^{-\|\bar{v}_i + \bar{v}_j\|^2 / 8\sigma^2} \right) . \tag{4.4}$$

For the rest of the proof, we will use the following bounds on these inner products.

LEMMA 4.8. *For all $i, j \in \{1, \ldots, n\}$,*

1. $\|f_i\|^2 = \left(1 - e^{-1/2\sigma^2}\right)\|v_i\|^2$,

2. $\langle |\bar{f}_i|, |\bar{f}_i|\rangle \leqslant |\langle \bar{v}_i, \bar{v}_j\rangle| + 2e^{-1/4\sigma^2}$,

3. $\|\bar{f}_i - \bar{f}_j\|^2 \leqslant {}^1\!/\!{}_{4\sigma^2}\|\bar{v}_i - \bar{v}_j\|^2 + 2e^{-1/4\sigma^2}$,

4. $\|\bar{f}_i + \bar{f}_j\|^2 \leqslant {}^1\!/\!{}_{4\sigma^2}\|\bar{v}_i + \bar{v}_j\|^2 + 2e^{-1/4\sigma^2}$,

PROOF. Item 1 is immediate from (4.4). To demonstrate Item 2, we bound the inner product of $|\bar{f}_i|$ and $|\bar{f}_j|$ analog to (4.4) by

$$\langle |\bar{f}_i|, |\bar{f}_j|\rangle \leqslant e^{-(1-\langle \bar{v}_i,\bar{v}_j\rangle)/4\sigma^2} + e^{-(1+\langle \bar{v}_i,\bar{v}_j\rangle)/4\sigma^2}.$$

By symmetry, we may assume $\langle \bar{v}_i, \bar{v}_j\rangle \geqslant 0$. In this case, the second term on the right hand side is at most $e^{-1/4\sigma^2}$, and the first term on the right hand side is at most

$$1 - (1 - e^{-1/4\sigma^2})(1 - \langle \bar{v}_i, \bar{v}_j\rangle/4\sigma^2) \leqslant e^{-1/4\sigma^2} + \langle \bar{v}_i, \bar{v}_j\rangle/4\sigma^2.$$

Here, we used the bound $e^{cx} \leqslant 1 - (1 - e^c)x$ for $x \in [0, 1]$ as in the proof of Lemma 3.8. Item 2 follows by combining the bounds on the two terms. Towards proving Item 3, we bound the inner product of $\bar{f}_i$ and $\bar{f}_j$ from below. If $\langle \bar{v}_i, \bar{v}_j\rangle \geqslant 0$, then $\|\bar{v}_i + \bar{v}_j\|^2 \geqslant 2$ and thus we get from (4.4),

$$\langle \bar{f}_i, \bar{f}_j\rangle \geqslant 1 - \|\bar{v}_i - \bar{v}_j\|^2/8\sigma^2 - e^{-1/4\sigma^2},$$

using the approximation $e^{-x} \geqslant 1 - x$ for $x \in \mathbb{R}$. Otherwise, if $\langle \bar{v}_i, \bar{v}_j\rangle < 0$, we get from (4.4),

$$\langle \bar{f}_i, \bar{f}_j\rangle \geqslant (1 - e^{-1/4\sigma^2})(1 + \langle \bar{v}_i, \bar{v}_j\rangle) - 1 \geqslant \langle \bar{v}_i, \bar{v}_j\rangle - e^{-1/4\sigma^2},$$

using $-e^{cx} \geqslant (1 - e^c)x - 1$ for $x \in [0, 1]$. In both cases, our bound on the inner product $\langle \bar{f}_i, \bar{f}_j\rangle$ implies Item 3. To prove Item 4, we note that the transformation (4.3) is symmetric, i.e., if v is mapped to f, then $-v$ is mapped to $-f$. Hence, Item 3 implies Item 4. □

The next lemma corresponds to Lemma 3.7. However, in our current construction, an additive error term appears (in contrast to the purely multiplicative error in Lemma 3.7). We can control the error by decreasing the standard deviation σ of the Gaussians in our construction.

LEMMA 4.9.

$$\frac{\sum_{ij} a_{ij}\langle f_i, f_j\rangle}{\sum_i \mu_i\|f_i\|^2} \leqslant O(\tfrac{1}{\sigma^2})\frac{\sum_{ij} a_{ij}\langle v_i, v_j\rangle}{\sum_i \mu_i\|v_i\|^2} + 2^{-\Omega(\sigma^{-2})}\sum_j a_{jj}.$$

PROOF. Using Fact 2.4 (similar to the proof of Lemma 3.7), Item 3 and Item 4 of Lemma 4.8 imply for all $i, j \in [n]$ and $\sigma \in \{\pm 1\}$,

$$\|f_i - \sigma f_j\|^2 \leqslant O(\tfrac{1}{\sigma^2})\|v_i - v_j\|^2 + 2^{-\Omega(\sigma^{-2})}\|v_i\|\,\|v_j\|.$$

Let $B \in \mathbb{R}_+^{n\times n}$ and $C \in \{1, -1\}^{n\times n}$ as in Lemma A.1. Then,

$$\begin{aligned}\sum_{ij} a_{ij}\langle f_i, f_j\rangle &= \sum_{ij} b_{ij}\|f_i - c_{ij}f_j\|^2\\ &\leqslant O(\tfrac{1}{\sigma^2})\sum_{ij} b_{ij}\|v_i - c_{ij}v_j\|^2 + 2^{-\Omega(\sigma^{-2})}\sum_{ij} b_{ij}\|v_i\|\,\|v_j\|\\ &\leqslant O(\tfrac{1}{\sigma^2})\sum_{ij} a_{ij}\langle v_i, v_j\rangle + 2^{-\Omega(\sigma^{-2})}\sum_i a_{ii}\|v_i\|^2.\end{aligned}$$

In the last inequality, we used $2\|v_i\|\,\|v_j\| \leqslant \|v_i\|^2 + \|v_j\|^2$ and the observation that $\sum_j b_{ij} \leqslant a_{ii}$. The lemma follows because $\|f_i\|^2 = \Theta(\|v_i\|^2)$ and $\mu_i = a_{ii}/\sum_j a_{jj}$ (one of the assumptions of Theorem 4.2 was that μ is proportional to the diagonal of A). □

The next lemma corresponds to Lemma 3.8. In this section, it is a straight-forward consequence of Item 2 of Lemma 4.8 and the fact that the vectors satisfy (4.2).

LEMMA 4.10.

$$\sum_{ij} \mu_i\mu_j\langle |f_i|, |f_j|\rangle \leqslant (\delta + 2^{-\Omega(1/\sigma^2)})\sum_i \mu_i\|f_i\|^2.$$

PROOF. From Item 2 of Lemma 4.8, it follows that $\langle |f_i|, |f_j|\rangle \leqslant |\langle v_i, v_j\rangle| + \|v_i\|\,\|v_j\|e^{-1/4\sigma^2}$. Therefore,

$$\sum_{ij} \mu_i\mu_j\langle |f_i|, |f_j|\rangle \leqslant \sum_{ij} \mu_i\mu_j|\langle v_i, v_j\rangle| + e^{-1/4\sigma^2}\left(\textstyle\sum_i \mu_i\|v_i\|\right)^2.$$

Since the vectors satisfy (4.2), the first term of the right-hand side is at most $\delta\sum_i \mu_i\|v_i\|^2$. By convexity, the second term contributes at most $e^{-1/4\sigma^2}\sum_i \mu_i\|v_i\|^2$, as desired. □

Theorem 4.2 follows from Lemma 4.9 and Lemma 4.10.

4.3 Better Construction for Diagonally Dominant Matrices (Theorem 4.3)

Suppose $v_1, \ldots, v_n$ is an optimal solution for the SDP relaxation $\tilde{\Lambda}_A(\delta)$. Recall the soft-thresholding function $\mathsf{soft\text{-}chop}_t(x) = \operatorname{sign}(x)\max\{|x| - t, 0\}$. For a parameter $t > 0$, we define functions $f_1, \ldots, f_n$ as

$$f_i(x) = \|v_i\| \cdot \mathsf{soft\text{-}chop}_t(\langle \bar{v}_i, x\rangle)/\|\mathsf{soft\text{-}chop}_t\|_\gamma.$$

Here, $\|\cdot\|_\gamma$ denotes the 2-norm with respect to the Gaussian measure γ. We equip the space $\{f\colon \mathbb{R}^n \to \mathbb{R}\}$ with the corresponding inner product $\langle f, g\rangle_\gamma = \int f(x)g(x)\,\mathrm{d}\gamma^n(x)$, where γ^n denotes the n-dimensional Gaussian measure. With these definitions, we can check that $\|f_i\|_\gamma = \|v_i\|$ for all $i \in [n]$.

In the next section (§B), we show that the functions satisfy the following properties.

LEMMA 4.11. *For all $i, j \in \{1, \ldots, n\}$,*

1. $\langle |\bar{f}_i|, |\bar{f}_j|\rangle \leqslant O(1)|\langle \bar{v}_i, \bar{v}_j\rangle| + 2^{-\Omega(t^2)}$,

2. $\|\bar{f}_i - \bar{f}_j\|^2 \leqslant O(t^2)\|\bar{v}_i - \bar{v}_j\|^2$

3. $\|\bar{f}_i + \bar{f}_j\|^2 \leqslant O(t^2)\|\bar{v}_i + \bar{v}_j\|^2$

PROOF OF THEOREM 4.3. In the previous section (§4.2) we showed that the properties asserted by Lemma 4.11 are enough to conclude as desired

$$\frac{\sum_{ij} a_{ij}\langle f_i, f_j\rangle}{\sum_i \mu_i\|f_i\|^2} \leqslant O(t^2)\frac{\sum_{ij} a_{ij}\langle v_i, v_j\rangle}{\sum_i \mu_i\|v_i\|^2},$$

and

$$\sum_{ij} \mu_i\mu_j\langle |f_i|, |f_j|\rangle \leqslant O(\delta + 2^{-\Omega(1/\sigma^2)})\sum_i \mu_i\|f_i\|^2. \quad \square$$

5. REFERENCES

[1] N. Alon. Eigenvalues and expanders. *Combinatorica*, 6(2):83–96, 1986. Theory of computing (Singer Island, Fla., 1984).

[2] N. Alon and V. D. Milman. λ_1, isoperimetric inequalities for graphs, and superconcentrators. *J. Combin. Theory Ser. B*, 38(1):73–88, 1985.

[3] S. Arora and S. Kale. A combinatorial, primal-dual approach to semidefinite programs. In *STOC*, pages 227–236, 2007.

[4] B. Barak, M. Hardt, I. Haviv, A. Rao, O. Regev, and D. Steurer. Rounding parallel repetitions of unique games. In *FOCS*, pages 374–383, 2008.

[5] M. Barlow, T. Coulhon, and A. Grigor'yan. Manifolds and graphs with slow heat kernel decay. *Invent. Math.*, 144:609–649, 2001.

[6] M. Charikar, K. Makarychev, and Y. Makarychev. Near-optimal algorithms for unique games. In *STOC*, pages 205–214, 2006.

[7] E. Chlamtac, K. Makarychev, and Y. Makarychev. How to play unique games using embeddings. In *FOCS*, pages 687–696, 2006.

[8] F. Chung. Random walks and local cuts in graphs. *Linear Algebra Appl.*, 423(1):22–32, 2007.

[9] F. R. K. Chung. *Spectral graph theory*, volume 92 of *CBMS Regional Conference Series in Mathematics*. Published for the Conference Board of the Mathematical Sciences, Washington, DC, 1997.

[10] T. Coulhon, Grigor'yan, and C. Pittet. A geometric approach to on-diagonal heat kernel lower bound on groups. *Ann. Inst. Fourier*, 51:1763–1827, 2001.

[11] A. d'Aspremont, F. R. Bach, and L. E. Ghaoui. Full regularization path for sparse principal component analysis. In *ICML*, pages 177–184, 2007.

[12] A. d'Aspremont, F. R. Bach, and L. E. Ghaoui. Optimal solutions for sparse principal component analysis. *CoRR*, abs/0707.0705, 2007.

[13] A. d'Aspremont, L. E. Ghaoui, M. I. Jordan, and G. R. G. Lanckriet. A direct formulation for sparse pca using semidefinite programming. In *NIPS*, 2004.

[14] S. Goel, R. Montenegro, and P. Tetali. Mixing time bounds via the spectral profile. *Electron. J. Probab.*, 11:no. 1, 1–26 (electronic), 2006.

[15] L. Lovász and R. Kannan. Faster mixing via average conductance. In *Proc. of the Symp. on Theory of Computing*, volume 31 of *STOC*, pages 282–287. ACM, ACM, 1999.

[16] R. Montenegro and P. Tetali. *Mathematical Aspects of Mixing Times in Markov Chains*, volume 1 of *Foundations and Trends in Theoretical Computer Science*. NOW, Boston-Delft, 2006.

[17] B. Morris and Y. Peres. Evolving sets, mixing and heat kernel bounds. *Probab. Th. and Related Fields*, 133(2):245–266, 2005.

[18] P. Raghavendra and D. Steurer. Graph expansion and the unique games conjecture. In *STOC*, 2010.

[19] D. Steurer. Fast SDP algorithms for constraint satisfaction problems. In *SODA*, 2010. To appear.

[20] L. Trevisan. Max cut and the smallest eigenvalue. In *STOC*, pages 263–272, 2009.

[21] H. Zou, T. Hastie, and R. Tibshirani. Sparse principal component analysis. *J. Comput. Graph. Statist.*, 15(2):265–286, 2006.

APPENDIX

A. CHARACTERIZATION OF DIAGONALLY DOMINANT MATRICES

The following lemma is easy to show, e.g., by induction on the number of non-zero entries of the matrix A.

LEMMA A.1. *Let $A = (a_{ij}) \in \mathbb{R}^{n\times n}$ be a symmetric diagonally dominant matrix. Then, there exists a non-negative matrix $B = (b_{ij}) \in \mathbb{R}_+^{n\times n}$ and a sign matrix $C = (c_{ij}) \in \{1,-1\}^{n\times n}$ such that for every $x \in \mathbb{R}^n$,*

$$\langle x, Ax\rangle = \sum_{ij} b_{ij}(x_i - c_{ij}x_j)^2 .$$

B. PROPERTIES OF TRUNCATED GAUSSIANS

In this section, we will prove Lemma 4.11. For brevity, we write $\theta_t = \text{soft-chop}_t$ for the soft-thresholding function. We think of θ_t as a member of $L_2(\mathbb{R},\gamma)$, where γ is the standard Gaussian measure on $\mathbb{R}$. In §4.3, we implicitly considered the following mapping T from $\mathbb{R}^n$ to $L_2(\mathbb{R}^n,\gamma^n)$,

$$T(u)\colon g \mapsto \|u\| \cdot \theta_t(\langle g, \bar{u}\rangle)/\|\theta_t\| .$$

In the following, we will show that for any two unit vectors $u, v \in \mathbb{R}^n$,

$$\langle |T(u)|, |T(v)|\rangle \leqslant |\langle u,v\rangle| + 2^{-\Omega(t^2)}, \tag{B.1}$$

$$\|T(u) - T(v)\|^2 \leqslant O(t^2)\|u-v\|^2 . \tag{B.2}$$

Since $T(-u) = -T(u)$, the bounds (B.1) and (B.2) directly imply Lemma 4.11.

For $\rho \in [-1,1]$, let U_ρ denote the operator on $L_2(\mathbb{R})$

$$\langle f, U_\rho f\rangle = \int f(x) f(\rho x + \sqrt{1-\rho^2} y)\,\mathrm{d}\gamma(x)\,\mathrm{d}\gamma(y) .$$

For any two unit vectors $u, v \in \mathbb{R}^n$ with inner product $\langle u,v\rangle = \rho$, the distribution of $(\langle g,\bar{u}\rangle, \langle g,\bar{v}\rangle)$ for a random Gaussian vector $g \in \mathbb{R}^n$ is the same as the distribution of $(x, \rho x + \sqrt{1-\rho^2}y)$ for two independent Gaussians x and y. Hence, $\langle T(u), T(v)\rangle = \langle \theta_t, U_\rho\theta_t\rangle$ and $\langle |T(u)|, |T(v)|\rangle = \langle |\theta_t|, U_\rho|\theta_t|\rangle$. The quantity $\langle \theta_t, U_\rho\theta_t\rangle$ is the Gaussian noise sensitivity of the function θ_t. In the rest of this section, we derive bounds on this sensitivity that imply the bounds (B.1) and (B.2) and thereby Lemma 4.11.

B.1 Gaussian noise sensitivity bounds for soft threshold functions

For $x \in \mathbb{R}$, let $(x)_+ = \max\{x, 0\}$. Note that $\theta_t = \operatorname{sign}(x)(|x| - t)_+$. Recall that $\mathrm{d}\gamma(x) = (\sqrt{2\pi})^{-1}e^{-x^2/2}\,\mathrm{d}x$.

We need the following fact about moments of the exponential distribution.

FACT B.1. *For $k \in \mathbb{N}$ and $z \geqslant 1/t$,*

$$\int_{u=0}^{z} u^k t e^{-tu}\mathrm{d}u = \tfrac{k!}{t^{k+1}} \quad \pm e^{-tz}\cdot O_k(tz)^k .$$

LEMMA B.2. $\|\theta_t\|^2 = \Theta(e^{-t^2/2}/t^3)$.

PROOF. We have

$$\|\theta_t\|^2 = 2\int (x-t)_+^2\,\mathrm{d}\gamma(x) = 2e^{-t^2/2}\int_{u\geqslant 0} u^2 e^{-tu}\,\mathrm{d}\gamma(u) .$$

The lemma follows from Fact B.1 and the fact that $\mathrm{d}\gamma(u) \approx \mathrm{d}u/\sqrt{2\pi}$ for small enough u. □

LEMMA B.3. *If $|\rho| \leqslant 1/2$, then for $\alpha = \sqrt{4/3}$*

$$\langle |\theta_t|, U_\rho|\theta_t|\rangle \leqslant 6\|\theta_{\alpha t}\|^2 .$$

PROOF. Define $\vartheta_t(x) = (x-t)_+$. Let $\tau = \sqrt{1-\rho^2}$. First, we estimate $\langle \vartheta_t, U_\rho \vartheta_t\rangle$,

$$\begin{aligned}
&\int (x-t)_+(\rho x + \tau y - t)_+ \,\mathrm{d}\gamma(x,y) \\
&\leqslant \int (x + \rho x + \tau y - 2t)_+^2 \,\mathrm{d}\gamma(x,y) \qquad \text{(pointwise)} \\
&= \int (\sqrt{2(1+\rho)}\, z - 2t)_+^2 \,\mathrm{d}\gamma(z) \quad \text{(Gaussians are 2-stable)} \\
&= 2(1+\rho) \int \left(z - \sqrt{2/1+\rho}\; t\right)_+^2 \mathrm{d}\gamma(z) \\
&= (1+\rho)\|\theta_{t'}\|^2 \qquad (\text{for } t' = \sqrt{2/1+\rho}\; t) \\
&\leqslant 3/2 \cdot \|\theta_{\alpha t}\|^2 \qquad (\text{for } \alpha = \sqrt{4/3} \leqslant t'/t)
\end{aligned}$$

Let $z = \rho x + \sqrt{1-\rho^2} y$. Notice that

$$|\theta_t(x)\theta_t(z)| = \vartheta_t(|x|)\vartheta_t(|z|) = \sum_{\sigma,\sigma' \in \{\pm 1\}} \vartheta_t(\sigma x)\vartheta_t(\sigma' z)\,.$$

It follows that $\langle |\theta_t|, U_\rho |\theta_t|\rangle = 2\langle \vartheta_t, U_\rho \vartheta_t\rangle + 2\langle \vartheta_t, U_{-\rho}\vartheta_t\rangle$, which implies the lemma using the previous bound $\langle \vartheta_t, U_{\pm\rho}\vartheta_t\rangle \leqslant 3/2 \cdot \|\theta_{\alpha t}\|^2$. □

As a direct consequence of previous two lemmas, we get the following bound on $\langle |\theta_t|, U_\rho |\theta_t|\rangle$.

LEMMA B.4.

$$\langle |\theta_t|, U_\rho|\theta_t|\rangle \leqslant 2|\rho|\|\theta_t\|^2 + O(e^{-t^2/6})\|\theta_t\|^2\,.$$

PROOF. Since U_ρ is a Markov operator, $\langle |\theta_t|, U_\rho|\theta_t|\rangle \leqslant \|\theta_t\|^2$. Hence the lemma is trivially true if $|\rho| \geqslant 1/2$. Otherwise, if $|\rho| \leqslant 1/2$, Lemma B.3 asserts $\langle |\theta_t|, U_\rho|\theta_t|\rangle \leqslant \|\theta_{\alpha t}\|^2$ for $\alpha = \sqrt{4/3}$. By Lemma B.2, $\|\theta_{\alpha t}\|^2 = \|\theta_t\|^2 \cdot \Theta(e^{-t^2/6})$. □

LEMMA B.5. *If $\rho = 1 - \varepsilon$, then*

$$\langle \theta_t, (I - U_\rho)\theta_t\rangle \leqslant O(t^2\varepsilon)\|\theta_t\|^2$$

PROOF. Let $\tau = \sqrt{1-\rho^2} \approx \sqrt{2\varepsilon}$ and let $f(x,y) = \theta_t(x) - \theta_t(\rho x + \tau y)$. The inner product $\langle \theta_t, (I-U_\rho)\theta_t\rangle$ is equal to

$$\tfrac{1}{2}\int \left(\theta_t(x) - \theta_t(\rho x + \tau y)\right)^2 \mathrm{d}\gamma^2(x,y) = \tfrac{1}{2}\int f^2 \,\mathrm{d}\gamma^2\,.$$

The function f is invariant under the following isometries,

$$(x,y) \mapsto (-x,-y) \text{ and } (x,y) \mapsto (\rho x + \tau y, \tau x - \rho y).$$

Since the Gaussian measure is also invariant under these isometries, it follows that the integrals of f^2 over the sets $\{(x,y) \mid x \geqslant t\}$, $\{(x,y) \mid x \leqslant -t\}$, $\{(x,y) \mid \rho x + \tau y \geqslant t\}$, and $\{(x,y) \mid \rho x + \tau y \leqslant -t\}$ have the same value. Since these four sets cover the support of f, it follows that

$$\int f^2 \,\mathrm{d}\gamma^2 \leqslant 4 \int_{x \geqslant t} f^2 \,\mathrm{d}\gamma^2(x,y)\,.$$

Since θ_t is 1-Lipschitz, we can bound $|f(x,y)|$ by

$$\begin{aligned}
|\theta_t(x) - \theta_t(\rho x + \tau y)| &\leqslant |\theta_t(x) - \theta_t(\rho x)| + |\theta_t(\rho x) - \theta_t(\rho x + \tau y)| \\
&\leqslant \varepsilon|x| + \tau|y|\,.
\end{aligned}$$

If $x \geqslant t$, then $f(x,y) = x - t - \theta_t(\rho x + \tau y)$. Therefore,

$$\int_{x\geqslant t} f^2 \,\mathrm{d}\gamma^2(x,y) \leqslant 2\varepsilon^2 \int_{x \geqslant t} x^2 \,\mathrm{d}\gamma(x) + 2\tau^2 \int_{x \geqslant t} 1 \,\mathrm{d}\gamma(x)\,.$$

The standard Gaussian tail bound asserts

$$\int_{x \geqslant t} 1 \,\mathrm{d}\gamma(x) \leqslant \tfrac{1}{\sqrt{2\pi}} e^{-t^2/2}/t = t^2\|\theta_t\|^2\,.$$

Similarly, it is also straight forward to show

$$\int_{x \geqslant t} x^2 \,\mathrm{d}\gamma(x) \leqslant O(te^{-t^2/2}) = t^4\|\theta_t\|^2\,.$$

Putting the two bounds together, we can conclude

$$\langle \theta_t, (I - U_\rho)\theta_t\rangle \leqslant O(\varepsilon^2 t^4)\|\theta_t\|^2 + O(\varepsilon t^2)\|\theta_t\|^2.$$

This bound implies the lemma, since we can assume $\varepsilon t^2 \leqslant 1$ (otherwise, the lemma is trivially true). □

Weighted Geometric Set Cover via Quasi-Uniform Sampling

Kasturi Varadarajan*
Department of Computer Science
University of Iowa
Iowa City, IA 52242
kvaradar@cs.uiowa.edu

ABSTRACT

There has been much progress on geometric set cover problems, but most known techniques only apply to the unweighted setting. For the weighted setting, very few results are known with approximation guarantees better than that for the combinatorial set cover problem. In this article, we employ the idea of *quasi-uniform sampling* to obtain improved approximation guarantees in the weighted setting for a large class of problems for which such guarantees were known in the unweighted case. As a consequence of this sampling method, we obtain new results on the fractional set cover packing problem.

Categories and Subject Descriptors

F.2.2 [**Analysis of Algorithms and Problem Complexity**]: Nonnumerical Algorithms and Problems—*Geometrical problems and computations*

General Terms

Algorithms, Theory

Keywords

Set cover, epsilon nets, approximation

1. INTRODUCTION

The combinatorial set cover problem has a privileged place in computer science for the wealth of theoretical results known about it and its applications. Here one is given a ground set X together with a family $\mathcal{F} = \{S_1, S_2, \ldots, S_n\}$ where each S_i is a subset of X and has associated with it a non-negative weight $w(S_i)$. The family $\mathcal{F}$ covers X, that is, X is contained in the union of the elements of $\mathcal{F}$. The goal is to find a minimum weight subfamily $\mathcal{G} \subseteq \mathcal{F}$ that also covers X. Here, the weight of a subfamily $\mathcal{G}$ is simply the sum of the weights of the elements in it. This NP-hard problem admits several different polynomial time algorithms that guarantee an approximation factor of $O(\log |X|)$ – some of these are combinatorial greedy algorithms and some are based on (randomized) rounding of the natural linear programming relaxation [33]. These results hold for both the weighted and the unweighted case, which is obtained when $w(S_i) = 1$ for each i. This approximation factor has also been shown to be the best possible under standard complexity theoretic assumptions [30].

We are interested in the geometric set cover problem where X is a (usually finite) subset of some fixed dimensional Euclidean space – in this paper we will assume this to be the two dimensional plane unless stated otherwise. The family $\mathcal{F}$ of subsets of X is induced by some family of objects, for example, disks, triangles, or visibility polygons. In the set cover problem with disks, for instance, we are given a set $\{D_1, D_2, \ldots, D_n\}$ of disks along with their weights, and we wish to find the minimum weight subset of disks that cover (whose union contains) X. This is clearly an instance of the combinatorial set cover problem by computing $S_i = X \cap D_i$. Given the constraints imposed by geometry, it is reasonable to expect that we can obtain approximation factors better than $O(\log |X|)$ for the combinatorial version. Indeed, as we review below, we now have a few techniques that yield better approximation factors for certain types of objects. However, these techniques have hitherto worked only for the unweighted case. Our main aim in this paper is to extend some of these techniques to the weighted case.

We now review the techniques that have yielded improved approximation factors for the unweighted case. Combinatorial algorithms cleverly designed for the problem at hand have been successful for some problems, see for example [22, 6]. Very recently, the general technique of local search has been shown, quite surprisingly, to yield polynomial time approximation schemes (PTAS's) for some problems [9, 27]. For instance, this approach yields a PTAS for set cover with disks [27]. However, it has recently been shown that such a PTAS does not exist (unless P = NP) for fairly "nice" objects, for example, fat triangles of roughly the same size [19]. An interesting question that is open is whether local search or other combinatorial approaches can be shown to give weaker but sub-logarithmic approximation guarantees for other classes of objects.

Such guarantees can often be obtained by rounding the natural linear programming relaxation of the set cover problem. The approximation factor obtained by such rounding is related to the well known combinatorial problem of bound-

*Supported by NSF grant CCF 0915543.

ing the size of an ε-*net*. Suppose that we have a collection of n disks and an integer $1 \le L \le n$. An $\frac{L}{n}$-net is a subset of the disks that covers all points in the plane that are L-deep, that is, contained within at least L of the disks. The question is, what is a good upper bound on the size of an $\frac{L}{n}$-net over all families of n disks and all $1 \le L \le n$? Clearly this bound must be at least $\frac{n}{L}$ and we want to know how much larger it must be. We know [7, 16] that if for any type of object (disks, triangles, axes-parallel rectangles) there are $\frac{L}{n}$-nets of size at most $\frac{n}{L}g(\frac{n}{L})$ (and we can efficiently compute such nets), then the integrality gap and the approximation factor obtained via the natural linear programming relaxation of the problem is $O(g(\frac{n}{L}))$. Nets of size $O(\frac{n}{L}\log\frac{n}{L})$ are known to exist for fairly general geometric objects, those of "constant description complexity" – this includes disks, triangles, rectangles, and by far all the types we are concerned with in this paper [11, 20]. In fact, a random sample of this size is a net with constant probability. Thus for these objects we obtain an approximation guarantee of $O(\log \lambda^*)$ where λ^* is the size of the optimal solution.

There is hope that nets of size $O(\frac{n}{L})$ should exist for very general subclasses of these objects, but this is an outstanding open problem. One situation where nets of size better than $O(\frac{n}{L}\log\frac{n}{L})$ are known to exist is when the *combinatorial complexity of the boundary of the union* (for brevity, union complexity) is near-linear [13, 4, 32]. Given m disks, the boundary of their union is a set of one-dimensional components each of which can be obtained by gluing together pieces of the boundaries of the disks; the union complexity is roughly the number of such pieces. We refer the reader to [31] for more precise definitions. If for a certain type of object, the union complexity of m of the objects is at most $mh(m)$, then there are $\frac{L}{n}$-nets of size $O(\frac{n}{L}\log h(\frac{n}{L}))$, and we thus obtain an $O(\log h(\lambda^*))$ approximation for the corresponding set cover problem [4]. Objects for which improved approximation algorithms are obtained using this approach include disks and fat triangles.

1.1 Our Contribution

Compared to this wealth of results for the unweighted setting, very few instances are known in the weighted setting where we have an approximation guarantee that is better than $O(\log|X|)$, where X, we remind the reader, is the ground set in the input for set cover. Two such instances are *unit* disks in the plane, for which constant factor approximations are known based on dynamic programming [3] and the linear programming approach [29], and the problem of guarding a one-dimensional terrain for which a constant factor approximation is given based on the linear programming approach [15]. A third and somewhat easier instance is when the objects doing the covering are translates of a fixed polygon, and here a constant factor approximation is implied by results in [18]. In these three instances, very special structure of the problem at hand is exploited. Thus, even for arbitrary disks and fat triangles, we do not currently have an approximation guarantee that is better than $O(\log|X|)$. It is easy to set up examples in the weighted setting where the basic local search approach doesn't yield improved bounds even for object types on which it yields a PTAS in the unweighted setting. Turning to the linear programming approach, we are now interested in an upper bound on the *weight* of an $\frac{L}{n}$-net and not its size. Clearly, this bound on the weight is at least as large as $\frac{W}{L}$, where W is the total weight of all the objects, and can be shown to be $O(\frac{W}{L}\log n)$ for fairly general geometric objects [16]. A bound of $O(\frac{W}{L}g(n))$ on the maximum weight of a net implies an approximation guarantee of $O(g(n))$ for the corresponding weighted set cover problem. Unfortunately, a bound better than $O(\frac{W}{L}\log n)$ on the maximum weight of a net is not known even for objects with small union complexity such as fat triangles or disks.

Why do the approaches in [13, 4, 32], which yield improved nets for objects such as fat triangles and disks, fail to do so in the weighted case? The answer is that they resort to random sampling methods that are in effect non-uniform. That is, while they guarantee that the number of objects in the net is small in the aggregate, they do not bound the probability of any particular object being in the net. This shortcoming is explicitly identified in [32].

The main contribution of this article is a method for computing nets based on *quasi-uniform sampling*, where the probability of any object being in the $\frac{L}{n}$-net is close to $\frac{1}{L}$, the natural bound. The method yields low weight nets for objects with near-linear union complexity, but for concreteness we state it for fat triangles. A triangle is ρ-fat if the ratio of the radius of its smallest circumscribing circle to the radius of its largest inscribed circle is bounded by ρ. By a fat triangle, we mean one that is ρ-fat for some arbitrary constant ρ. The union complexity of m fat triangles is bounded by $O(m\log\log m)$ [25]. Our main result is the following theorem on computing nets by quasi-uniform sampling:[1]

THEOREM 1. *There is a probabilistic polynomial time algorithm that takes as input a set T of n fat triangles and a parameter $1 \le L \le n$, and outputs a subset $T' \subset T$ that covers all points that are L-deep with respect to T, and has the following property: for any triangle $t \in T$, the probability that t is in the output T' is at most*

$$\frac{O(\log\log\log n)}{L}.$$

Clearly, this algorithm outputs an $\frac{L}{n}$-net whose expected weight is $O(\log\log\log n)\frac{W}{L}$ and we obtain an $O(\log\log\log n)$ approximation to the weighted set cover problem with fat triangles. At a high level, the theorem proceeds by showing a variant of it where we allow the sampling probability to be $\frac{O(\log L)}{L}$, but we ensure that L-deep points are $\log L$-deep with respect to the sample. This variant exploits the sparsity of the *shallow level* and in this sense it is similar to [32] and an algorithm of [9] for the independent set problem. But there are crucial differences needed to obtain the quasi-uniformity. The variant is then applied again to the sample, but with L now set to be $\log L$. (This is similar to [32].) Three such iterations suffice to obtain the Theorem.

For disks in the plane, our version of the theorem has a sampling probability bounded by $\frac{2^{O(\log^* n)}}{L}$, and we obtain a $2^{O(\log^* n)}$ approximation for the corresponding set cover problem. For objects with union complexity $mh(m)$, we obtain an approximation factor of $2^{O(\log^* n)}\log h(n)$, but this bound can sometimes be tightened further.

[1]The reader may find the flavor of the statement similar to that in completely different contexts, such as probabilistic approximation of metrics by tree metrics [5, 17].

1.2 Consequences for Set Cover Packing

In the *set cover packing problem*, we are given a ground set X, a family $\mathcal{F} = \{S_1, S_2, \ldots, S_n\}$ where each S_i is a subset of X, and the goal is to partition $\mathcal{F}$ into as many blocks as possible so that each block is a cover for X. In the *fractional set cover packing problem*, we want to compute a set of blocks plus a fraction $0 \leq f(B) \leq 1$ corresponding to each block B, so that (a) each block covers X, and (b) for each i the sum of the fractions of the blocks to which S_i belongs is at most 1, and the objective is to maximize the sum of the fractions. One motivation for both problems comes from the world of sensors [8] – here X is a region that needs to be monitored, S_i is the sub-region monitored by the i-th sensor, each sensor has a battery life of one time unit, and the goal is find a schedule for the sensors so that X remains monitored for as long as possible. The set cover packing problem corresponds to the *non-preemptive* scenario where once a sensor is turned on, it runs for one continuous unit of time. The fractional version corresponds to the *preemptive* scenario where we may turn a sensor on and off as often as we like.

In the combinatorial setting the best approximations for these problems is logarithmic (see [1, 8, 14] and the references therein). Given the motivation from sensors, geometric versions of the problem have been extensively studied recently. Let L denote the *load* of the instance, that is, the largest integer value so that each point in X is contained in at least L of the sets in $\mathcal{F}$. Clearly, the load is an upper bound on the objective function value in both versions of the problem. Previous work has shown that we can obtain a solution whose objective function value is (a) $\Omega(\frac{1}{\log(n/L)})$ of the load for the integral problem when the sets S_i are induced by fairly general geometric objects [8]; (b) $\Omega(1)$ of the load for the integral problem when the sets S_i are induced by *translates* of a fixed convex polygon [2, 18]; (c) $\Omega(1)$ of the load for the fractional problem when the sets S_i are induced by unit disks [29].

Our results on quasi-uniform sampling extend the frontier for such results:

COROLLARY 2. *Given an instance of the fractional set cover packing problem with X being a set of points in the plane, and $\mathcal{F}$ consisting of subsets induced by a set T of n fat triangles, there is a solution whose value is at least $\Omega(\frac{1}{\log\log\log n})$ of the load L.*

PROOF. Consider the algorithm of Theorem 1 for computing an $\frac{L}{n}$-net for T, and the distribution over covers of all L-deep points that it induces. For any cover B that is output by this distribution, set $f(B) = \Pr(B) * \frac{L}{c \log\log\log n}$, where $c > 0$ is a sufficiently large constant, and $\Pr(B)$ is the probability that B is output. □

The algorithm that outputs this fractional set cover packing is of course not polynomial, because it needs to compute the distribution corresponding to the output of the algorithm of Theorem 1. However, as we describe in some detail in this paper, we can obtain a randomized polynomial algorithm that computes a packing that is nearly as good by sampling from this distribution.

Organization of the Paper. In Section 2 we review some rather standard notions that we need. In Section 3, we establish Theorem 1. In Sections 4 and 5, we derive its consequences for the weighted set cover problem and the fractional set cover packing, respectively. We conclude in 6 with some remarks on generalizing these results to object families with small union complexity and with some open problems.

2. PRELIMINARIES

In this section, we review the notion of an arrangement of triangles in the plane, and state the well known result bounding the number of shallow cells when the triangles are fat.

A triangle t can be partitioned into seven *features* – the three vertices, the three edges (we don't include the endpoints of an edge when we talk about it as a feature), and its interior. Now given a set T of triangles in the plane, we can define an equivalence relation on the plane – two points are related if they are contained in exactly the same set of features. The connected components of the resulting equivalence classes are the *cells* in the *arrangement* of T. A cell can be a point (thus zero-dimensional), a line segment (thus one-dimensional), or an open polygonal region (thus two-dimensional).

We define the *level* or *depth* of a point in a given set T of triangles to be the number of triangles it is contained in. Note that two points that belong to the same cell have the same level, because they are contained in the same set of triangles. Thus we can speak of the level or depth of a cell. The level of a point is an integer between 0 and $|T|$. We will say that a point is k-*deep* with respect to a set T of triangles if its level is at least k.

We will need the following well known result, which follows from the fact that the union complexity of m fat triangles is $O(m \log\log m)$ [25] and a certain application of the probabilistic method [12]. The lemma bounds the number of cells that are at level at most α, and it is through this that the union complexity comes into play in our results.

LEMMA 3. *Let F be a set of m ρ-fat triangles in general position, and $1 \leq \alpha \leq m$ be a parameter. The number of cells with level at most α in the arrangement of F is $O(\alpha m \log\log \frac{m}{\alpha})$.*

3. QUASI-UNIFORM SAMPLING

In this section, we establish the main result of this paper, which is Theorem 1. Throughout this section, let $\phi(x)$ denote the function $\log\log x$. We first need the following:

THEOREM 4. *Let F be a set of fat triangles in the plane, and let $1 \leq \alpha \leq |F|$ be a parameter. There is a probabilistic polynomial-time algorithm that outputs a subset F' of F that has at least $\log \alpha$ triangles covering each α-deep point in F, and has the following property: For any triangle $t \in F$, the probability that $t \in F'$ is at most $\frac{O(\max\{\log \alpha, \log \phi(|F|/\alpha)\})}{\alpha}$.*

PROOF. For notational convenience, let $m = |F|$. To prove the theorem we first describe a probabilistic process that outputs a cover that has at least $\log \alpha$ triangles covering each cell of the arrangement of F whose depth is between α and 2α. With this in mind, let $\beta = \max\{\log \alpha, \log \phi(m/\alpha)\}$. We need a certain ordering of the triangles in F.

Let $N = F$ initially. Let $\mathcal{C}$ denote the set of cells in the arrangement of N with level at most 2α. So the size of $\mathcal{C}$ is $O(|N|\alpha\phi(|N|/\alpha))$, due to Lemma 3. The number of pairs in $(t, \tau) \in N \times \mathcal{C}$ such that triangle t contains cell τ is bounded by $|\mathcal{C}| \cdot 2\alpha \leq d|N|\alpha^2\phi(\frac{|N|}{\alpha})$, where $d > 0$ is some constant. So there is a triangle in N that contains at most $d\alpha^2\phi(\frac{|N|}{\alpha}) \leq d\alpha^2\phi(\frac{m}{\alpha})$ cells in $\mathcal{C}$.

We remove such a triangle t from N, and recursively compute a sequence for the resulting N and append this sequence to t. By "recursively compute a sequence for N", we simply mean: find a triangle t' in the new N that contains at most $d\alpha^2\phi(\frac{m}{\alpha})$ cells in the arrangement of the new N with level at most 2α, recursively compute a sequence for $N \setminus \{t'\}$, and append to it t'. The recursion bottoms out when all triangles have been removed, that is, N becomes empty.

Now, let σ be the *reverse* of the sequence of triangles we just computed. Recall that our goal is a probabilistic algorithm that outputs a cover with at least $\log\alpha$ triangles covering any point at depth between α and 2α in F. We consider the triangles of σ in order and looking at each one we make an instant decision about adding it to our cover. When considering triangle t, we add it if t covers some point p at depth between α and 2α in F, and not adding t would result in having less than $\log\alpha$ triangles covering p in our cover. More precisely, suppose that n_1 triangles that contain p have been already added to the cover, and there are n_2 triangles that contain p and have not yet been considered; we add t if $n_1+1+n_2 \leq \log\alpha$. Let us call this a *forced addition* of t. If t is not forced, we add it with probability $\frac{c\beta}{\alpha}$, where c is a sufficiently large positive constant.

Clearly, at the end we have a cover that has at least $\log\alpha$ triangles covering each point whose depth in F is between α and 2α. Fix a triangle t. We argue that the probability that t is added to the cover is $\frac{O(\beta)}{\alpha}$. Clearly, it suffices to show that the probability of a forced addition of t is bounded by $1/\alpha$.

Consider the set N corresponding to which t makes an appearance in (the reverse of) sequence σ. So t is a triangle that contains at most $d\alpha^2\phi(\frac{m}{\alpha})$ cells in the set $\mathcal{C}$ of cells in the arrangement of N with depth at most 2α. For any cell τ in the set $\mathcal{C}$, let Z_τ denote the triangles in N containing τ, minus the triangle t itself.

If t is forced, there is a point p contained in some cell $\tau \in \mathcal{C}$ so that (a) t contains τ, (b) $|Z_\tau| \geq \alpha - \log\alpha$, and (c) less than $\log\alpha$ triangles in Z_τ have been added.

Consider a cell τ for which (a) and (b) hold. We can now bound the probability that (c) happens. Note that $|Z_\tau| \geq \alpha - \log\alpha \geq \frac{\alpha}{2}$. The probability that (c) happens is upper bounded by the probability that in a sequence of $\frac{\alpha}{2}$ independent and identical coin tosses with a probability of heads being $\frac{c\beta}{\alpha}$, less that $\log\alpha$ coins turn up heads. The expected number of heads in such a sequence is $\mu \equiv \frac{c\beta}{2}$. Since $\log\alpha \leq \beta = \max\{\log\alpha, \log\phi(m/\alpha)\}$, it suffices to bound the probability that there are fewer than β heads. For c sufficiently large, $\beta \leq \mu/2$. By applying the Chernoff bound (see for instance Theorem 4.5 (2) of [26]), we can thus bound the probability of (c) by $1/e^{c\beta/16}$, which is at most $\frac{1}{d(\alpha\phi(m/\alpha))^4}$ for c sufficiently large. Since there are at most $d\alpha^2\phi(m/\alpha)$ cells in $\mathcal{C}$ for which (a) and (b) hold, the probability of a forced addition of t is at most

$$\frac{d\alpha^2\phi(m/\alpha)}{(\alpha\phi(m/\alpha))^4} \leq \frac{1}{\alpha}.$$

Thus we have a probabilistic algorithm that outputs a set that covers points at depth between α and 2α in F at least $\log\alpha$ times, and has the property that the probability that a given triangle is added to our cover is bounded by $\frac{O(\max\{\log\alpha, \log\phi(m/\alpha)\})}{\alpha}$.

We repeat the same algorithm for points at depth between α_i and $2\alpha_i$ in F, for each $1 \leq i \leq \log_2 m$, where $\alpha_i = 2^i\alpha$. For a fixed value of i, we output a set that covers any point at such a depth at least $\log(\alpha_i)$ times; the probability that a certain triangle t is added to the set is bounded by $\frac{O(\max\{\log\alpha_i, \log\phi(m/\alpha_i)\})}{\alpha_i}$.

We output F', the union of the sets output for each i. A summation over i shows that the probability of a particular triangle being in F' is still bounded by

$$\frac{O(\max\{\log\alpha, \log\phi(m/\alpha)\})}{\alpha}.$$

□

3.1 Proof of Theorem 1

The following is the algorithm that corresponds to Theorem 1. Recall that the input to this algorithm is a set T of n fat triangles and a parameter $1 \leq L \leq n$.

1. Let $F \leftarrow T$ and $\alpha \leftarrow L$.
2. While $\alpha > \log\phi(n)$:
   (a) Run the algorithm of Theorem 4 with F and α to obtain output F',
   (b) Reset $F \leftarrow F'$, and reset $\alpha \leftarrow \log\alpha$.
3. Return $T' = F$.

From the guarantee of Theorem 4, it follows that the T' that is output is a cover for all points that are L-deep with respect to T. We now bound the probability that a particular triangle t is part of T'.

Let τ denote the number of times the body of the While loop is executed. If in an iteration of this loop we have $\alpha \leq \phi(|F|/\alpha)$ in Step 2a, then this is the final iteration of the loop. This is because the next time the condition in the While statement is checked, we will have $\alpha \leq \log\phi(n)$. Thus, in all iterations but the last, we can invoke Theorem 4 to bound the probability that t is output by the algorithm in Step 2a (conditioned on t being in F) by

$$\frac{O(\max\{\log\alpha, \log\phi(|F|/\alpha)\})}{\alpha} = \frac{O(\log\alpha)}{\alpha}.$$

In the last iteration, we bound this probability simply by

$$\frac{O(\max\{\log\alpha, \log\phi(|F|/\alpha)\})}{\alpha}.$$

A simple calculation shows that the probability that $t \in T'$ is bounded above by

$$2^{O(\tau)}\frac{\log\phi(n)}{L}.$$

(Illustration: if $\tau = 3$, the probability that $t \in T'$ is bounded by

$$\frac{O(\log L)}{L} \times \frac{O(\log\log L)}{\log L} \times \frac{O(\max\{\log\log\log L, \log\phi(|F|/\log\log L)\})}{\log\log L},$$

where F denotes its value the last time Step 2a is executed.)

Now, τ is at most 3, since $\alpha \leq n$ initially and the While loop terminates when $\alpha \leq \log\phi(n)$. Thus the probability that t is output is at most $\frac{O(\log\phi(n))}{L}$.

4. WEIGHTED SET COVER

Suppose we are given a set P of k points in the plane, and a set T_1 of fat triangles, each triangle t with a positive integer weight $\mathrm{w}(t)$. The union of the triangles covers P, and we seek the minimum weight subset of T_1 that also covers P. We now describe an efficient approximation algorithm for the problem that is based on solving the natural linear programming relaxation and then applying Theorem 1 to do the rounding. As we have remarked in Section 1, the fact that an algorithm for constructing nets can be used for rounding is well known [7, 23, 16].

Since two triangles that contain the same subset of P are equivalent, we may assume that $|T_1| \le k^6$. (This may be seen by an ad hoc argument; for a more principled derivation, we can use the methods in Chapter 10 of [24].) Let λ^* denote the weight of the optimal cover. Solving in polynomial time the linear programming relaxation of the set cover problem, we find numbers $0 \le x_t \le 1$ for each $t \in T_1$, so that

$$\sum_{t \in T_1 : p \in t} x_t \ge 1 \text{ for each } p \in P,$$

and $\lambda \equiv \sum_{t \in T_1} \mathrm{w}(t) x_t \le \lambda^*$. For each t such that $x_t \ge \frac{1}{2k^6}$, we make $\left\lfloor \frac{x_t}{1/(2k^6)} \right\rfloor$ copies of it, each with weight $\mathrm{w}(t)$. For each t with $x_t < \frac{1}{2k^6}$, we make no copy (we discard it). Let T denote the resulting set of triangles. Clearly, $\mathrm{w}(T) \le 2k^6\lambda$. For any $p \in P$, the number of triangles in T containing p is at least

$$\begin{aligned}\sum_{t \in T_1 : p \in t, x_t \ge \frac{1}{2k^6}} \left\lfloor \frac{x_t}{1/(2k^6)} \right\rfloor &\ge k^6 \sum_{t \in T_1 : p \in t, x_t \ge \frac{1}{2k^6}} x_t \\ &\ge k^6 \left(1 - \sum_{t \in T_1 : p \in t, x_t < \frac{1}{2k^6}} x_t\right) \\ &\ge k^6 \left(1 - \frac{|T_1|}{2k^6}\right) \\ &\ge \frac{k^6}{2}.\end{aligned}$$

We also have $|T| \le 2k^6 |T_1| \le 2k^{12}$. Applying the algorithm in Theorem 1 with $L = k^6/2$, we get a cover of P whose expected weight is at most

$$\begin{aligned}O(\log\log\log |T|) \frac{\mathrm{w}(T)}{L} &= O(\log\log\log k) \cdot \lambda \\ &= O(\log\log\log k) \cdot \lambda^*.\end{aligned}$$

We conclude:

THEOREM 5. *Given a set P of k points in the plane, and a set T_1 of fat triangles, each with a positive weight, whose union covers P, we can, in polynomial time, compute a subset of T_1 with expected weight $O(\log\log\log k) * \lambda^*$ that covers P, where λ^* is the weight of the min-weight subset of T_1 that covers P.*

5. FRACTIONAL SET COVER PACKING

In this section, we show how the fractional set cover packing problem with fat triangles can be approximated via Theorem 1. An instance of such a fractional set cover packing problem consists of a set X of points in the plane, and a family $\mathcal{F}$ consisting of subsets induced by a set T of n fat triangles. The goal is to compute $B_1, B_2, \ldots, B_r$, where each $B_i \subseteq T$ covers X, together with non-negative fractions $f(B_i)$ so that $\sum_i f(B_i)$ is maximized subject to the constraint that for each $t \in T$, $\sum_{i: t \in B_i} f(B_i) \le 1$.

Let L be the *load*, that is, the largest integer so that each $x \in X$ is in at least L of the triangles in T. The load L is clearly an upper bound on the objective function value. In Section 1, we saw that there is a solution with value $\Omega(\frac{L}{\log\log\log n})$, but this may take exponential time to construct.

We now describe a variant that runs in polynomial time and returns a solution that is nearly as good with high probability. Let N be a sufficiently large integer, to be chosen below. We run the algorithm of Theorem 1 N times independently; if B is a cover output by the algorithm, then we set

$$f(B) = \frac{\text{No. of times } B \text{ is output}}{N} * \frac{L}{c \log\log\log n},$$

where $c > 0$ is a sufficiently large constant.

We readily check that the objective function value of this solution to the fractional set cover problem is $\Omega(\frac{L}{\log\log\log n})$.

To show that the packing constraint is satisfied for each triangle, it suffices to argue that with high probability no triangle is chosen in more than $\frac{O(\log\log\log n)}{L} * N$ of the covers that are output. We choose $N = c_1 L \log n$ for sufficiently large $c_1 > 0$. Fix a triangle t. Since the probability that it is part of a single cover is $\frac{O(\log\log\log n)}{L}$, a Chernoff-bound argument implies that with probability at least $1 - \frac{1}{n^2}$, it is chosen in at most $\frac{O(\log\log\log n)}{L} * N$ of the covers. The union bound implies that with probability at least $1 - 1/n$, this event happens for every triangle in T.

THEOREM 6. *For the fractional set cover packing problem with points X and a set T of n fat triangles, there is a randomized polynomial time algorithm that with high probability outputs a solution that is within a factor of $O(\log\log\log n)$ of the load (and hence the best possible solution).*

6. CONCLUSIONS

We now state our result on quasi-uniform sampling for a family of disks in the plane.

THEOREM 7. *There is a probabilistic polynomial time algorithm that takes as input a set D of n disks and a parameter $1 \le L \le n$, and outputs a subset $D' \subset D$ that covers all points that are L-deep with respect to D, and has the following property: for any disk $d \in D$, the probability that it is output is at most*

$$\frac{2^{O(\log^* n)}}{L}.$$

The proof for this is almost exactly the same as that for fat triangles in Section 3: we just let the function $\phi(x) = 2$, since the version of Lemma 3 for disks has the number of cells at level at most α being $O(m\alpha)$. This in turn follows from the fact that union complexity for m disks is $O(m)$ [21].

We obtain corresponding a approximation guarantee of $2^{O(\log^* n)}$ for the weighted set cover problem and the fractional set cover packing problem with disks.

Similar remarks apply to other object families with near-linear union complexity, e.g., half-spaces in $\Re^3$. One question that remains is whether the approximation guarantee can be improved to match that of the unweighted case in [4]. Can we obtain an $O(1)$ guarantee for disks, for instance? A natural idea is to try to employ shallow cuttings as in [10], but at present, we do not know how to do this effectively.

Another interesting direction concerns the fractional set cover packing problem. Can we find interesting and natural geometric examples where the ratio of the load to the best fractional packing is not bounded by a constant? By an interesting example, we mean one for which we do not yet have super-linear lower bounds on the size of an epsilon net. Our hope is that perhaps this question is more tractable than super-linear lower bounds on epsilon nets. We note that there are already good lower bounds for *integral* set cover packing [28], but these do not work for the fractional case.

Acknowledgements. I thank Chandra Chekuri for his thought provoking remarks on the connections between the weighted set cover and fractional set cover packing problems via duality. Duality is not explicit here because the link has been made in a more elementary way. I also thank Esther Ezra and Sariel Har-Peled for very useful feedback, and the reviewers for their comments.

7. REFERENCES

[1] Z. Abrams, A. Goel, and S. Plotkin. Set k-cover algorithms for energy efficient monitoring in wireless sensor networks. In *Proceedings of the third international symposium on Information processing in sensor networks (ISPN)*, pages 424–432, 2004.

[2] G. Aloupis, J. Cardinal, S. Collette, S. Langerman, D. Orden, and P. Ramos. Decomposition of multiple coverings into more parts. In *Proceedings of the ACM -SIAM Symposium on Discrete Algorithms* (SODA), pages 302-310, 2009.

[3] C. Ambuhl, T. Erlebach, M. Mihalak, and M. Nunkesser. Constant-factor approximation for minimum-weight (connected) dominating sets in unit disk graphs. In *Proceedings of APPROX-RANDOM*, pages 3–14, 2006.

[4] B. Aronov, E. Ezra, and M. Sharir. Small-size ε-nets for axis-parallel rectangles and boxes. In *Proceedings of ACM Symposium on the Theory of Computing* (STOC), pages 639–648, 2009.

[5] Y. Bartal. Probabilistic approximations of metric spaces and its algorithmic applications. In *Proceedings of IEEE Symposium on Foundations of Computer Science* (FOCS), pages 184–193, 1996.

[6] B. Ben-Moshe, M. J. Katz, and J. S. B. Mitchell. A constant-factor approximation algorithm for optimal terrain guarding. *Proc. ACM-SIAM Symposium on Discrete Algorithms* (SODA), 515–524, 2005.

[7] H. Brönnimann and M. T. Goodrich. Almost optimal set covers in finite VC-dimension. *Discrete Comput. Geom.*, 14:263–279, 1995.

[8] A. L. Buchsbaum, A. Efrat, S. Jain, S. Venkatasubramanian, and K. Yi. Restricted strip covering and the sensor cover problem. In *Proceedings of the ACM-SIAM symposium on Discrete algorithms* (SODA), 1056–1063, 2007.

[9] T. M. Chan and S. Har-Peled. Approximation algorithms for maximum independent set of pseudo-disks. In *Proceedings of the Symposium on Computational Geometry*, pages 333–340, 2009.

[10] C. Chekuri, K. L. Clarkson, S. Har-Peled. On the set multi-cover problem in geometric settings In *Proceedings of the Symposium on Computational Geometry*, pages 341–350, 2009.

[11] K. L. Clarkson. New applications of random sampling in computational geometry. *Discrete Comput. Geom.*, 2:195–222, 1987.

[12] K. L. Clarkson and P. Shor. Applications of random sampling in computational geometry, II. *Discrete and Computational Geometry*, 4:387–421, 1989.

[13] K. Clarkson and K. Varadarajan. Improved approximation algorithms for geometric set cover. *Discrete and Computational Geometry*, 37:43–58, 2007,

[14] A. Deshpande, S. Khuller, A. Malekian, and M. Toossi. Energy efficient monitoring in sensor networks. In *Proceedings of LATIN*, LNCS volume 4957, pages 436–448, 2008.

[15] K. Elbassioni, E. Krohn, D. Matijevic, J. Mestre, and D. Severdija. Improved Approximation Algorithms for 1.5D Terrain Guarding. In *Proceedings of STACS*, 361–371, 2009.

[16] G. Even, D. Rawitz, and S. Shahar. Hitting sets when the VC-dimension is small. Information Processing Letters 95(2): 358–362, 2005.

[17] J. Fakcharoenphol, S. Rao, and K. Talwar. A tight bound on approximating arbitrary metrics by tree metrics. In *Proceedings of the ACM Symposium on Theory of Computing* (STOC), pages 448–455, 2003.

[18] M. R. Gibson and K. Varadarajan. Decomposing multiple coverings and the planar sensor cover problem. In *Proceedings of IEEE Symposium on Foundations of Computer Science* (FOCS), 159–168, 2009.

[19] S. Har-Peled. Being fat and friendly is not enough. *CoRR*, abs/0908.2369, 2009.

[20] D. Haussler and E. Welzl. Epsilon-nets and simplex range queries. *Discrete Comput. Geom.*, 2:127–151, 1987.

[21] K. Kedem, R. Livne, J. Pach, and M. Sharir. On the union of Jordan regions and collision free translational motion amidst polygonal obstacles. *Discrete Comput. Geom.*, 1:59–71, 1986.

[22] V. S. A. Kumar and H. Ramesh. Covering rectilinear polygons with axis-parallel rectangles. *SIAM J. Comput.*, 32(6):1509–1541, 2003.

[23] P. M. Long. Using the pseudo-dimension to analyze approximation algorithms for integer programming. In *Proceedings of the 7th Workshop on Algorithms and Data Structures*, LNCS vol. 2125, 26–37, 2001.

[24] J. Matoušek. *Lectures on Discrete Geometry*. Springer-Verlag, 2002.

[25] J. Matoušek, J. Pach, M. Sharir, S. Sifrony, and E. Welzl. Fat triangles determine linearly many holes. *SIAM J. Comput.*, 23:154–169, 1994.

[26] M. Mitzenmacher and E. Upfal. *Probability and Computing.* Cambridge University Press, 2005.

[27] N. H. Mustafa and S. Ray. PTAS for geometric hitting set problems via local search. In *Proceedings of the Symposium on Computational Geometry*, pages 17–22, 2009.

[28] J. Pach, G. Tardos, and G. Toth. Indecomposable coverings. In *Proceedings of the China-Japan joint Conference on Discrete Geometry, Combinatorics, and Graph Theory* (CJCDGCGT 05), LNCS vol. 4381, 135–148, 2007.

[29] S. Pandit, S. V. Pemmaraju, and K. Varadarajan. Approximation algorithms for domatic partitions of unit disk graphs. In *Proceedings of APPROX-RANDOM*, pages 312–325, 2009.

[30] R. Raz and S. Safra. A sub-constant error-probability low-degree test, and a sub-constant error-probability PCP characterization of NP. In *Proceedings of the ACM Symposium on Theory of Computing* (STOC), pages 475–484, 1997.

[31] M. Sharir and P. K. Agarwal. *Davenport-Schinzel Sequences and Their Geometric Applications.* Cambridge University Press, New York, 1995.

[32] K. Varadarajan. Epsilon nets and union complexity. In *Proceedings of the Symposium on Computational Geometry*, pages 11–16, 2009.

[33] V. V. Vazirani. *Approximation Algorithms.* Springer, 2001.

Deterministic Identity Testing of Depth-4 Multilinear Circuits with Bounded Top Fan-in

Zohar S. Karnin, Partha Mukhopadhyay, Amir Shpilka, Ilya Volkovich

Faculty of Computer Science, Technion - Israel Institute of Technology
Haifa 32000, Israel.
{zkarnin,partha,shpilka,ilyav}@cs.technion.ac.il

ABSTRACT

We give the first sub-exponential time deterministic polynomial identity testing algorithm for depth-4 multilinear circuits with a small top fan-in. More accurately, our algorithm works for depth-4 circuits with a plus gate at the top (also known as $\Sigma\Pi\Sigma\Pi$ circuits) and has a running time of $\exp(\text{poly}(\log(n), \log(s), k))$ where n is the number of variables, s is the size of the circuit and k is the fan-in of the top gate. In particular, when the circuit is of polynomial (or quasi-polynomial) size, our algorithm runs in quasi-polynomial time. In [AV08], it was shown that derandomizing polynomial identity testing for general $\Sigma\Pi\Sigma\Pi$ circuits implies a derandomization of polynomial identity testing in general arithmetic circuits. Prior to this work sub-exponential time deterministic algorithms were known for depth-3 circuits with small top fan-in and for very restricted versions of depth-4 circuits.

The main ingredient in our proof is a new structural theorem for multilinear $\Sigma\Pi\Sigma\Pi(k)$ circuits. Roughly, this theorem shows that any nonzero multilinear $\Sigma\Pi\Sigma\Pi(k)$ circuit contains an 'embedded' nonzero multilinear $\Sigma\Pi\Sigma(k)$ circuit. Using ideas from previous works on identity testing of sums of read-once formulas and of depth-3 multilinear circuits, we are able to exploit this structure and obtain an identity testing algorithm for multilinear $\Sigma\Pi\Sigma\Pi(k)$ circuits.

Categories and Subject Descriptors

F.2.0 [**Theory of Computation**]: Analysis of Algorithms and Problem Complexity

General Terms

Algorithms, Theory

Keywords

Identity Testing, Arithmetic Circuits, Bounded Depth Circuits, Multilinear circuits, Derandomization

STOC'10, June 5–8, 2010, Cambridge, Massachusetts, USA.

1. INTRODUCTION

Polynomial Identity Testing (PIT) is one of the central problems in algebraic complexity theory: Given an arithmetic circuit C over a field $\mathbb{F}$ with input variables $x_1, x_2, \cdots, x_n$, can we check efficiently whether C computes the identically zero polynomial in the polynomial ring $\mathbb{F}[x_1, x_2, \cdots, x_n]$? The same question can be asked in the black-box model too. In the black-box model, C is accessed by a black-box where we are allowed to substitute field elements $a_i \in \mathbb{F}$ for x_i and the black-box returns the value of $C(a_1, a_2, \cdots, a_n)$.

A randomized polynomial-time algorithm (more precisely a coRP algorithm) for this problem is known due to the Schwartz-Zippel Lemma [Sch80, Zip79]. Over the years PIT has played a significant role in our understanding of important complexity theoretic and algorithmic problems. Well-known examples are the randomized NC algorithms for the matching problem in graphs [Lov79, MVV87], and the AKS primality test [AKS04]. The PIT problem has also played an indirect role in important complexity results such as IP = PSPACE [LFKN92, Sha90] and the old proof of PCP theorem [ALM+98].

The main open problem is to come up with a deterministic polynomial-time (or at least subexponential-time) algorithm for PIT. In 2003, Kabanets and Impagliazzo [KI03] show that giving a deterministic polynomial-time (even subexponential-time) identity testing algorithm means either NEXP $\not\subset$ P/poly or that the integer Permanent has no polynomial size arithmetic circuit. Considering the black-box derandomization of PIT, Agrawal further strengthen the connection of PIT with proving circuit lower bounds [Agr05]. More precisely, he shows that the black-box derandomization of PIT implies that an explicit multilinear polynomial has no subexponential size arithmetic circuit.

The results of [KI03] and [Agr05] have triggered a large amount of research for PIT derandomization. So far, most of the derandomization results are known for depth-3 $\Sigma\Pi\Sigma(k,d)$ circuits when the top Σ gate is of bounded fan-in k (d is the fan-in of the Π gates which can be unbounded) [DS06, KS07, KS08, SS09, KS09]. In an important discovery, Agrawal and Vinay [AV08] justified the lack of progress beyond depth-3. What they show is that the *black-box* derandomization of PIT for only depth-4 $\Sigma\Pi\Sigma\Pi$ circuits is almost as hard as that for *general* arithmetic circuits. Their result is based on a depth reduction technique [VSBR83, AJMV98] that converts any arithmetic circuits C to a depth-4 circuit C' such that C and C' compute the same polynomial. Thus, their reduction is suitable for *black-box*

PIT derandomization. This connection makes the problem of black-box derandomization of PIT for depth-4 circuits an intriguing open problem.

So far all the black-box derandomization algorithms for depth-3 $\Sigma\Pi\Sigma(k,d)$ circuits [DS06, KS08, SS09, KS09] exploit one common theme: The subspace spanned by the linear forms of an *identically zero* $\Sigma\Pi\Sigma$ circuit (viewing each linear form as a vector in $\mathbb{F}^n$) is of low dimension. More precisely, over a finite field, the current best known bound for the dimension is $\mathcal{O}(k^3 \log d)$ [SS09] and over the field $\mathbb{Q}$ of rational numbers, the bound is $2^{\mathcal{O}(k \log k)}$ which is still a constant for a constant k [KS09]. For multilinear $\Sigma\Pi\Sigma(k,d)$ circuits, over any characteristic, the dimension is bounded by $\mathcal{O}(k^3 \log(k))$ [DS06, SS09]. Yet, the algorithm with the best running time [SV09] was obtained using a different approach. For depth-4 circuits, the situation is very different. It seems unlikely that the method of black-box derandomization for $\Sigma\Pi\Sigma$ circuits can be adopted/extended for depth-4 circuits. The main difficulty is that there seems to be no notion of a linear space, spanned by the circuit components, that can be used.

In this paper, we study the black-box PIT problem for multilinear depth-4 circuits with bounded fan-in at the top Σ gate. We give new techniques and come up with an efficient black-box algorithm which runs in time *quasi-polynomial* in the input size. We first formally define a depth-4 circuit. A depth-4 $\Sigma\Pi\Sigma\Pi$ circuit has four layers of alternating Σ and Π gates. The top gate is a Σ gate (at level one).[1] The circuit computes a polynomial $C(x_1, x_2, \cdots, x_n)$ of the form $C(x_1, x_2, \cdots, x_n) = \sum_{i=1}^{k} \prod_{j=1}^{d_i} P_{ij}$, where k is the fan-in of the top Σ gate and d_i are the fan-in's of the Π gates at the second level. P_{ij}-s are the polynomials computed at the third level of the circuit (which is a $\Sigma\Pi$ component). It is clear that the number of monomials in each P_{ij} is bounded by the fan-in of the Σ gates at the third level, and in particular, bounded by the circuit size s. In the rest of the paper, we refer to the polynomials P_{ij} as s-sparse polynomials where the sparsity should be understood as a parameter of the circuit size. Also for notational convenience, we denote depth-4 circuits whose top Σ fan-in is at most k by $\Sigma\Pi\Sigma\Pi(k)$ circuits.

We consider the identity testing problem of $\Sigma\Pi\Sigma\Pi(k)$ circuits when each multiplication gate $\prod_{j=1}^{d_i} P_{ij}$ computes a multilinear polynomial and the fan-in of the top Σ gate is a constant k. We call such circuits depth-4 multilinear $\Sigma\Pi\Sigma\Pi$ circuits. We give a deterministic *black-box* PIT algorithm for this model with a running time $\exp(\text{poly}(\log(n), \log(s), k))$ (s is the size of the circuit) which is *quasi-polynomial* in the input size. More formally, we prove the following theorem.

THEOREM 1. *Let k, n, s be integers. There is an explicit set $\mathcal{H}$ of size $n^{\mathcal{O}(k^6 \log(k) \log^2 s)}$, that can be constructed in time $n^{\mathcal{O}(k^6 \log(k) \log^2 s)}$ such that the following holds. Let $P \in \mathbb{F}[x_1, x_2, \ldots, x_n]$ be a non-zero polynomial computed by a multilinear $\Sigma\Pi\Sigma\Pi(k)$ circuit of size s on n variables. Then there is some $\bar{\alpha} \in \mathcal{H}$ such that $P(\bar{\alpha}) \neq 0$.*

To the best of our knowledge, prior to our work, efficient deterministic algorithm were known only in the non black-box setting for very restricted classes of depth-4 circuits [AM07, Sax08, SV09]. For higher depths, efficient black-box algorithms are known only for read-once formulas [SV08, SV09]. Designing efficient PIT algorithms for multilinear circuits is an important problem and our result makes the first step for the important class of depth-4 circuits.

1.1 Overview of Our Algorithm and Proof Technique

To start with, we briefly define the notion of generators and hitting sets for arithmetic circuits which are important for our algorithm. Intuitively, a generator $\mathcal{G}$ for a class of polynomials $\mathcal{M}$, is a function that stretches q independent variables into $n >> q$ dependent variables that can be *plugged* into any polynomial $P \in \mathcal{M}$ without vanishing it. A set $\mathcal{H} \subseteq \mathbb{F}^n$ is a hitting set for a class of polynomials $\mathcal{M}$, if for every nonzero polynomial $P \in \mathcal{M}$, there exists $\bar{a} \in \mathcal{H}$, such that $P(\bar{a}) \neq 0$. In identity testing, the role of generators and hitting sets are equivalent. The image of a generator for a class of circuits always contains a hitting set for the same class of circuits. Conversely, given a hitting set for a class of arithmetic circuits, it is fairly easy to construct a generator.

In our algorithm, we use a recursive technique (on the fan-in k of the top Σ gate) to find a generator for $\Sigma\Pi\Sigma\Pi(k)$ circuits and in every stage of the recursion we also construct a hitting set. Recall that the sparsity of the polynomials P_{ij} is bounded by the circuit size s. For $k = 1$, we need to build a generator for product of s-sparse polynomials. It is easy to see that a generator for a single s-sparse polynomial is also a generator for a product of s-sparse polynomials and the construction of a generator for a s-sparse polynomial is well known [KS01].

For $k > 1$, we construct the generator via the following procedure: Let P be a non-zero n-variate polynomial computed by a $\Sigma\Pi\Sigma\Pi(k)$ circuit C of size s and let $\mathcal{G}_{k-1}$ be a generator for $\Sigma\Pi\Sigma\Pi(k-1)$ circuits of size s. We prove that there exist a set $U \subseteq [n]$ of size $\text{poly}(\log s)$ such that a substitution of the generator $\mathcal{G}_{k-1}$ to the variables (indexed by) $[n] \setminus U$ leads to a non-zero polynomial. By going over all possible sets of choice for U, we can produce a small size hitting set for $\Sigma\Pi\Sigma\Pi(k)$ circuits, which in turn is transformed into a generator using the techniques of [SV09]. Notice that the number of choices for U is bounded by $n^{\text{poly}(\log s)}$, which is *quasi-polynomial* in s. Now we justify the existence of U which is enough to justify the correctness of our algorithm. We describe the construction of U in two different cases.

Case I: Assume that there exists some large constant r (that depends on k) such that for each i, j, the polynomial P_{ij} depends on at most n/r variables. We show that there exists a subset of the variables $V \subseteq [n]$ of size roughly r/k such that every P_{ij} has at most one variable x_ℓ such that $\ell \in V$. Now, let $\mathcal{G}_{k-1}$ be a generator for $\Sigma\Pi\Sigma\Pi(k-1)$ circuits. Then by suitably fixing the variables whose indices are in $[n] \setminus V$ from the image set of $\mathcal{G}_{k-1}$, we obtain a multilinear depth-3 $\Sigma\Pi\Sigma(k)$ circuit [2]. Using a structural theorem of identically zero depth-3 circuits from [DS06, SS09], our fixing ensures that the resulting depth-3 circuit computes a nonzero polynomial.

[1]One can consider $\Pi\Sigma\Pi\Sigma$ circuits, however, for identity testing purposes the interesting case is the $\Sigma\Pi\Sigma\Pi$ model.

[2]Notice that after the substitution, at most one variable remains alive in each P_{ij}.

Case II: We prove that for any polynomial P that can be computed by a $\Sigma\Pi\Sigma\Pi(k)$ circuit, there exists a set $W \subseteq [n]$ of size poly($\log s$) (recall that s is the size of the given circuit) such that the following property holds: For a set $S \subseteq [n]$, let $m(S)$ be the multilinear monomial $\prod_{i\in S} x_i$. Express the polynomial P as $P = \sum_{S\subseteq W} m(S)P_S$ where each polynomial P_S is over $x_{[n]\setminus W}$. We prove that there exists a subset S such that P_S can be computed by a $\Sigma\Pi\Sigma\Pi(k)$ circuit C' and each polynomial P'_{ij} computed in the third level of C' depends only on a small fraction of the total number of variables (which gives a reduction to the first stage). We now explain how to find the set W. Fix r suitably. Let C be the given $\Sigma\Pi\Sigma\Pi(k)$ circuit. Write C as $C = \sum_{i=1}^{k} N_i \cdot A_i$ where $N_i = \prod_j P_{ij}$ such that each P_{ij} depends on at most n/r variables. Similarly, let A_i be the product of the rest of the polynomials under the i-th Π gate. So by definition, each P_{ij} in A_i depends on at least n/r variables. Hence, by multilinearity, each A_i is a product of at most r many P_{ij}-s. We *eliminate* A_i-s by the following process: Consider a variable appearing in some A_i. By either setting the variable to zero or taking a partial derivative with respect to it, we can get rid of at least half of the monomials in A_i. Moreover, we show that such a variable exists with the additional property that both the choices (either setting to zero or taking partial derivative) will result in a non-zero polynomial. Repeating this process at most $\mathcal{O}(\log s)$ times, we can eliminate *all* such A_i.

The final set U that our algorithm considers is defined as $U \triangleq W \cup V$ (the union of the sets found at the first and second stages).

1.2 Organization

We start by giving the required definitions in Sections 2 and 3. We prove our main theorem (Theorem 4.11) in Section 4, showing a construction of a generator for $\Sigma\Pi\Sigma\Pi(k)$ circuits. In Section 4.5 we give as an easy corollary a hitting set for $\Sigma\Pi\Sigma\Pi(k)$ circuits.

2. PRELIMINARIES

For a positive integer n denote $[n] = \{1,\ldots,n\}$. Let $\mathbb{F}$ be a field and $\bar{\mathbb{F}}$ be its algebraic closure. For a polynomial $P(x_1,\ldots,x_n)$, a variable x_i, and $\alpha \in \mathbb{F}$, $P|_{x_i=\alpha}$ is the polynomial resulting after substituting α to the variable x_i. The following definitions are for polynomials $P, Q \in \mathbb{F}[x_1, x_2, \ldots, x_n]$. We say that P *depends* on x_i if there exist $\bar{a} \in \bar{\mathbb{F}}^n$ and $b \in \bar{\mathbb{F}}$ such that:

$$P(a_1,\ldots,a_i,\ldots,a_n) \neq P(a_1,\ldots,a_{i-1},b,a_{i+1},\ldots,a_n).$$

We denote $\text{var}(P) \triangleq \{x_i \mid P \text{ depends on } x_i\}$. Intuitively, P depends on x_i if x_i appears when P is listed as a sum of monomials. Given a subset $I \subseteq [n]$ and an assignment $\bar{a} \in \mathbb{F}^n$ we define $P|_{x_I=\bar{a}_I}$ to be the polynomial resulting from substituting a_i to the variable x_i for every $i \in I$. Let P, Q be two non-constant polynomials. We say that P and Q are *similar* and denote $P \sim Q$ if there exist $\alpha, \beta \in \mathbb{F}\setminus\{0\}$ such that $\alpha \cdot P = \beta \cdot Q$. Let $D_i(P,Q)$ be the polynomial defined as follows:

$$D_i(P,Q)(\bar{x}) \triangleq \left|\begin{pmatrix} P & P|_{x_i=0} \\ Q & Q|_{x_i=0}\end{pmatrix}\right|(\bar{x}) =$$

$$(P\cdot Q|_{x_i=0} - P|_{x_i=0}\cdot Q)(\bar{x})$$

over $\mathbb{F}$. The following is an easy observation.

Observation 2.1. *Let $P, Q \in \mathbb{F}[x_1, x_2, \ldots, x_n]$ be two multilinear polynomials such that $x_i \in \text{var}(P)\cap\text{var}(Q)$. If $P \sim Q$ then $D_i(P,Q) \equiv 0$.*

2.1 Mappings and Generators for arithmetic circuits

In this section, we formally define the notion of generators and hitting sets for polynomials and describe a few useful properties. A mapping $\mathcal{G} = (\mathcal{G}^1,\ldots,\mathcal{G}^n) : \mathbb{F}^q \to \mathbb{F}^n$, is a *generator* for the circuit class $\mathcal{M}$ if for every non-zero n-variate polynomial $P \in \mathcal{M}$, it holds that $P(\mathcal{G}) \not\equiv 0$. The image of the map $\mathcal{G}$ is denoted as $\text{Im}(\mathcal{G}) = \mathcal{G}(\bar{\mathbb{F}}^q)$. Ideally, q should be very small compared to n. A set $\mathcal{H} \subseteq \mathbb{F}^n$ is a hitting set for a circuit class $\mathcal{M}$, if for every nonzero polynomial $P \in \mathcal{M}$, there exists $\bar{a} \in \mathcal{H}$, such that $P(\bar{a}) \neq 0$. A generator can also be viewed as a mapping containing a hitting set for $\mathcal{M}$ in its image. That is, for every nonzero $P \in \mathcal{M}$ there exists $\bar{a} \in \text{Im}(\mathcal{G})$ such that $P(\bar{a}) \neq 0$. In [SV09] an efficient method of constructing a generator from a hitting set, for a (relatively) *small* q, is given.

Lemma 2.2 (Lemma 4.8 in [SV09]). *Let $|\mathbb{F}| > n$. Given a hitting set $\mathcal{H} \subseteq \mathbb{F}^n$ for a circuit class $\mathcal{M}$ there is an algorithm that in time* poly$(|\mathcal{H}|, n)$ *constructs a mapping $L(\bar{y}) : \mathbb{F}^q \to \mathbb{F}^n$, which is a generator for $\mathcal{M}$ with $q \triangleq \lceil \log_n |\mathcal{H}| \rceil$ and the individual degrees of L^i are bounded by $n-1$.*

The following is an immediate and important property of a generator:

Observation 2.3. *Let $P = P_1 \cdot P_2 \cdot \ldots \cdot P_k$ be a product of non-zero polynomials $P_i \in \mathcal{M}$ and let $\mathcal{G}$ be a generator for $\mathcal{M}$. Then $P(\mathcal{G}) \not\equiv 0$.*

At times we would like to use only a partial substitution generator to a polynomial. Given a subset $I \subseteq [n]$ we define the mapping: $\mathcal{G}^I$ as $(\mathcal{G}^I)_i = \mathcal{G}^i$ when $i \in I$ and $(\mathcal{G}^I)_i = x_i$ when $i \notin I$. In addition, we define $P|_{x_I=\mathcal{G}^I}$ to be the polynomial resulting from substituting the function $\mathcal{G}^i$ to the variable x_i for each $i \in I$. The following is an immediate observation:

Observation 2.4. *Let $\mathcal{M}$ be a class of polynomials and let $\mathcal{G}$ be a generator for n-variate polynomials in $\mathcal{M}$. Let $I \subseteq [n]$ and $P \in \mathcal{M}$ be a non-zero polynomial. Then $P|_{x_I=\mathcal{G}^I} \not\equiv 0$. Moreover, there exists $\bar{a} \in \text{Im}(\mathcal{G}^I)$ such that $P(\bar{a}) \neq 0$.*

2.2 Partial Derivatives

Discrete partial derivatives will play an important role in the analysis of our algorithms.

Definition 2.5. *Let P be an n-variate polynomial over a field $\mathbb{F}$. We define the* discrete partial derivative *of P with respect to x_i as $\frac{\partial P}{\partial x_i} = P|_{x_i=1} - P|_{x_i=0}$. For a non-empty subset $I \subseteq [n]$, $I = \{i_1,\ldots,i_{|I|}\}$, we define the* iterated partial derivative *with respect to I in the following way:*

$$\partial_I P \triangleq \frac{\partial^{|I|} P}{\partial x_{i_1}\partial x_{i_2}\partial x_{i_3}\cdots\partial x_{i_{|I|}}}.$$

Notice that if P is a multilinear polynomial then this definition coincides with the "analytical" one when $\mathbb{F} = \mathbb{R}$

or $\mathbb{F} = \mathbb{C}$. We now state some easy facts about discrete partial derivatives that can be easily verified. Let $P \in \mathbb{F}[x_1, x_2, \ldots, x_n]$ be a multilinear polynomial. Then, P depends on x_i if and only if $\frac{\partial P}{\partial x_i} \not\equiv 0$. For every i and j,

$$\frac{\partial^2 P}{\partial x_i \partial x_j} = \frac{\partial}{\partial x_i}\left(\frac{\partial P}{\partial x_j}\right) = \frac{\partial^2 P}{\partial x_j \partial x_i}$$

For two different variables x_i, x_j, derivative and substitution commutes: $\frac{\partial P}{\partial x_i}|_{x_j=a} = \frac{\partial}{\partial x_i}(P|_{x_j=a})$.

2.3 Known Results

In this section, we recall some known results about sparse polynomials and depth-3 $\Sigma\Pi\Sigma$ circuits which play an important role in the design of our algorithm. A *m-sparse polynomial* is a polynomial with at most m non-zero monomials. Equivalently, it is a polynomial computed by a depth-2 circuit with top fan-in m. Using a result of [KS01], we can construct an efficient generator for sparse polynomials.

LEMMA 2.6 (THEOREM 10 OF [KS01]). *In time polynomial in m, n, d and $\log|\mathbb{F}|$, one can output a hitting set $\mathcal{H}$ of cardinality $|\mathcal{H}| = \text{poly}(n, m, d)$ for n-variate m-sparse polynomials of degree d over a field $\mathbb{F}$. If $\mathbb{F} = \mathbb{R}$ then each element of each vector in the set has bit-length at most $\mathcal{O}(\log(nd))$. If $\mathbb{F}$ is a finite field with less than $(nd)^6$ elements, then the elements of the vectors lie in the smallest extension of $\mathbb{F}$ with at least $(nd)^6$ elements; otherwise, the vectors contain just elements of $\mathbb{F}$.*

Using Lemma 2.2, we can construct a generator from the hitting set output by the above result.

LEMMA 2.7. *There exists a generator $\mathcal{S}_m \triangleq (\mathcal{S}_m^1, \mathcal{S}_m^2, \ldots, \mathcal{S}_m^n) : \mathbb{F}^q \to \mathbb{F}^n$ for m-sparse multilinear polynomials with the individual degrees of each $\mathcal{S}_m^i$ are bounded by $n-1$ and $q(n, m) = \mathcal{O}(\log_n m)$.*

PROOF. Since the degree of a multilinear polynomial is bounded by n, we apply Lemma 2.2 on the hitting set $\mathcal{H}$ output by Lemma 2.6. Note that as $|\mathcal{H}| = \text{poly}(n, m)$, we obtain that $q(n, m) = \mathcal{O}(\log_n m)$. □

The proof technique of our main result involves a reduction from identity testing of a class of depth-4 circuits to depth-3 circuits. Here, we define depth-3 circuits formally and recall some of their relevant properties. A depth-3 $\Sigma\Pi\Sigma(k, d)$ circuit C computes a polynomial of the form

$$C(\bar{x}) = \sum_{i=1}^{k} F_i(\bar{x}) = \sum_{i=1}^{k} \prod_{j=1}^{d_i} L_{ij}(\bar{x})$$

where the $L_{ij}(\bar{x})$-s are linear functions $L_{ij}(\bar{x}) = \sum_{\ell} a_{ij\ell} x_\ell + a_{ij0}$ with $a_{ij\ell} \in \mathbb{F}$, and $d_i \leq d$. We refer to the F_m-s as the multiplication gates of the circuit. A *subcircuit* of C is defined as a sum of a subset of the multiplication gates in C. Let $\gcd(C) \triangleq \gcd(F_1, F_2, \ldots, F_k)$. We say that a circuit is *simple* if $\gcd(C) = 1$. We say that a circuit is *minimal* if no proper subcircuit of C computes the zero polynomial. Define the *rank* of C, denoted by $\text{rank}(C)$, as the rank of its linear functions, viewed as $(n+1)$-dimensional vectors over $\mathbb{F}^{n+1}$. That is, $\text{rank}(C) \triangleq \dim(\text{span}\{L_{ij}\})$.

A *multilinear* $\Sigma\Pi\Sigma(k, d)$ circuit has the additional requirement that each F_i is a multilinear polynomial. We require an important structural theorem regarding the rank of an identically zero $\Sigma\Pi\Sigma(k, d)$ multilinear circuit.

THEOREM 2.8. *[DS06, SS09] There exists an increasing integer function $R(k)$ upper bounded by $\mathcal{O}(k^3 \log(k))$ with the following property: Let C be an n-variate multilinear, simple and minimal $\Sigma\Pi\Sigma(k, d)$ circuit computing the zero polynomial. Then* $\text{rank}(C) < R(k)$.

We conclude this section with a well-known lemma concerning polynomials, giving a trivial (yet possibly large) hitting set. A proof can be found in [Alo99].

LEMMA 2.9. *Let $P \in \mathbb{F}[x_1, x_2, \ldots, x_n]$ be a polynomial. Suppose that for every $i \in [n]$ the individual degree of x_i is bounded by d_i, and let $S_i \subseteq \mathbb{F}$ be such that $|S_i| > d_i$. We denote $S = S_1 \times S_2 \times \cdots \times S_n$ then $P \equiv 0$ iff $P|_S \equiv 0$.*

3. DEPTH-4 MULTILINEAR CIRCUITS

In this section, we recall the model of depth-4 multilinear circuits and present a simple structural property of such circuits which is useful for our main result.

DEFINITION 3.1. *A multilinear depth-4 $\Sigma\Pi\Sigma\Pi(k)$ circuit C has four layers of alternating Σ and Π gates (the top Σ gate is at level one) and it computes a polynomial of the form*

$$C(\bar{x}) = \sum_{i=1}^{k} F_i(\bar{x}) = \sum_{i=1}^{k} \prod_{j=1}^{d_i} P_{ij}(\bar{x})$$

where the $P_{ij}(\bar{x})$-s are multilinear polynomials computed by the last two layers of $\Sigma\Pi$ gates of the circuit and are the inputs to the Π gates at the second level. Each multiplication gate F_i computes a multilinear polynomial.

Note that the requirement that the F_i-s compute multilinear polynomials implies that for each i the polynomials $\{P_{ij}\}_{j\in[d_i]}$ are variable-disjoint. It is clear that if the circuit size is s, then the number of monomials in P_{ij} (i.e. its sparsity) is bounded by s. In this paper, we often refer to the polynomials P_{ij} as s-sparse where the sparsity should be understood in terms of the circuit size s. Similar to the case of depth-3 circuits, a (proper) subcircuit of C is defined as the sum of a (proper) subset of multiplication gates of C. Also, a $\Sigma\Pi\Sigma\Pi(k)$ circuit is simple when no P_{ij} appears in all the multiplication gates at the second level. Namely, $\gcd(C) \triangleq \gcd(F_1, \ldots, F_k) = 1$. When C is not simple we define its simplification to be

$$\text{sim}(C) \triangleq C/\gcd(C)\ .$$

Note that $\text{sim}(C)$ is a simple $\Sigma\Pi\Sigma\Pi(k)$ circuit.

Our identity testing algorithm builds on a reduction from identity testing of multilinear $\Sigma\Pi\Sigma\Pi(k)$ circuits to identity testing of a special type of such circuits where for every i, j, $|\text{var}(P_{ij})| \leq n/r$. We call such circuits *r-compressed* circuits. Now we prove an easy structural property of r-compressed circuits which is useful for our algorithm design.

LEMMA 3.2. *Let $P \in \mathbb{F}[x_1, x_2, \ldots, x_n]$ be computed by a $\Sigma\Pi\Sigma\Pi(k)$ multilinear r-compressed circuit $C = \sum_{i=1}^{k}\prod_{j=1}^{d_i} P_{ij}(\bar{x})$. Then there exists a set $V \subseteq [n]$ of size $|V| \geq r/k$ such that for each i, j: $|V \cap \text{var}(P_{ij})| \leq 1$.*

PROOF. The first element of V can be arbitrarily set to x_1. Let $T_1 \subseteq [n]$ be the set of variables that appear in some P_{ij} along with x_1. As $|\text{var}(P_{ij})| \leq n/r$, we get that $|T_1| \leq k \cdot (\frac{n}{r} - 1)$. Hence, the set $W = [n] \setminus (T_1 \cup \{x_1\})$ is non empty. We pick one arbitrarily (say, the one with lowest index) from W and construct a set analogical to T_1 for it. Due to the size restriction of T_1 (and the other T's), we can continue this process at least r/k times. The set V is the set of these (at least) r/k chosen indices. □

4. BLACK-BOX PIT

In this section we give an efficient black-box PIT algorithm for multilinear $\Sigma\Pi\Sigma\Pi(k)$ circuits. We construct a generator for such circuits, which gives us a small hitting set. We start by describing the construction of a polynomial map which we eventually use as our generator.

4.1 The Construction and Some Easy Properties

In this section we construct a map from $\mathbb{F}^{2t}$ to $\mathbb{F}^n$ with the following property: Its image contains all vectors $\bar{a} \in \mathbb{F}^n$ with at most t non-zero entries. This map will later be put to use in the construction of the generator for depth-4 circuits. We assume that $|\mathbb{F}| > n$ as we are allowed to use elements from an appropriate extension field. Throughout the entire section we fix a set $A = \{\alpha_1, \alpha_2, \ldots, \alpha_n\} \subseteq \mathbb{F}$ of n distinct elements.

DEFINITION 4.1. *For every $i \in [n]$ let $u_i(w) : \mathbb{F} \to \mathbb{F}$ be the i-th Lagrange Interpolation polynomial for the set A. That is, each $u_i(w)$ is polynomial of degree $n-1$ satisfying $u_i(\alpha_j) = 1$ if $i = j$ and zero otherwise. For every $i \in [n]$ and $t \geq 1$ we define $G_t^i(y_1, \ldots, y_t, z_1, \ldots, z_t) : \mathbb{F}^{2t} \to \mathbb{F}$ as*

$$G_t^i(y_1, \ldots, y_t, z_1, \ldots, z_t) \triangleq \sum_{j=1}^{t} u_i(y_j) \cdot z_j .$$

Finally, let $G_t(y_1, \ldots, y_t, z_1, \ldots, z_t) : \mathbb{F}^{2t} \to \mathbb{F}^n$ be defined as

$$G_t(y_1, \ldots, y_t, z_1, \ldots, z_t) \triangleq (G_t^1, G_t^2, \ldots, G_t^n) =$$
$$\left(\sum_{j=1}^{t} u_1(y_j) \cdot z_j, \sum_{j=1}^{t} u_2(y_j) \cdot z_j, \ldots, \sum_{j=1}^{t} u_n(y_j) \cdot z_j \right).$$

We will use the following immediate observations:

OBSERVATION 4.2. *For every $t \geq 1$, it holds $G_t(\bar{y}, \bar{0}) \equiv 0$.*

OBSERVATION 4.3. *Denote with $\bar{e}_i \in \{0,1\}^n$ the vector that has 1 in the i-th coordinate and 0 elsewhere. Then*

$$G_{t+1} = G_t + \sum_{i=1}^{n} u_i(y_{t+1}) \cdot z_{t+1} \cdot \bar{e}_i .$$

Hence, for every $t \geq 1$ and $\alpha_m \in A$ we have that

$$G_{t+1}|_{y_{t+1} = \alpha_m} = G_t + z_{t+1} \cdot \bar{e}_m .$$

We now state a simple but crucial property of the generator G that follows from the above observations. (Recall the notation above Observation 2.4).

OBSERVATION 4.4. *Let $\ell, t \in \mathbb{N}$, $I \subseteq [n]$ and $|I| \leq t$. Then, it holds that*

$$\text{Im}\left(G_\ell^{[n]\setminus I}\right) \subseteq \text{Im}\left(G_{\ell+t}\right).$$

4.2 A Restricted Case: r-compressed $\Sigma\Pi\Sigma\Pi(k)$ Circuits

In this section we consider a restricted class of $\Sigma\Pi\Sigma\Pi(k)$ circuits: For a fixed r, we assume that the polynomial is computed by a simple r-compressed $\Sigma\Pi\Sigma\Pi(k)$ circuit of size s. Using a generator that works for sparse polynomials as well as for $\Sigma\Pi\Sigma\Pi(k-1)$ circuits of size s, we construct a generator for r-compressed $\Sigma\Pi\Sigma\Pi(k)$ circuits of size s. To do so, the key idea is to use the set $V \subseteq [n]$ that we obtain from Lemma 3.2. Recall that V has the following property: The size of V is at least r/k and for every P_{ij} in C, $|V \cap \text{var}(P_{ij})| \leq 1$. Let $\mathcal{G}_{k-1}$ be a generator for $\Sigma\Pi\Sigma\Pi(k-1)$ circuits and for sparse polynomials of suitable sparsity. In the following lemma we show that if $r = R(k) \cdot k$ then when we restrict the variables in $[n] \setminus V$ to $\mathcal{G}_{k-1}$, we obtain a non-zero polynomial.

LEMMA 4.5. *Let $k \geq 2$ and $P \in \mathbb{F}[x_1, x_2, \ldots, x_n]$ be a non-zero polynomial computed by a simple, multilinear, $k \cdot R(k)$-compressed $\Sigma\Pi\Sigma\Pi(k)$ circuit of size s. In addition, let $\mathcal{G}_{k-1}$ be a generator for $\Sigma\Pi\Sigma\Pi(k-1)$ circuits of size s and $(2s^2)$-sparse polynomials.[3] Then there exists a subset $V \subseteq \text{var}(P)$ of size $|V| \leq R(k)$ such that*

$$P|_{x_{\text{var}(P)\setminus V} = \mathcal{G}_{k-1}^{\text{var}(P)\setminus V}} = P \circ \mathcal{G}_{k-1}^{\text{var}(P)\setminus V} \not\equiv 0 .$$

PROOF. Let $C = \sum_{i=1}^{k} \prod_{j=1}^{d_i} P_{ij}(\bar{x})$ be a simple, multilinear, and $(k \cdot R(k))$-compressed $\Sigma\Pi\Sigma\Pi(k)$ circuit of size s, computing P. If C is not minimal, then P can be computed by a $\Sigma\Pi\Sigma\Pi(k-1)$ circuit of size s and we are done (set $V = \emptyset$). Assume w.l.o.g. that C is minimal. Let V be a set promised by Lemma 3.2. We can assume w.l.o.g that $|V| = k \cdot R(k)/k = R(k)$ by keeping $R(k)$ arbitrary indices. Define the set T as $T = [n] \setminus V$.

We now describe a way to find an assignment for x_T such that the resulting polynomial is non-zero. We do so via a reduction to depth-3 circuits. Let $C_1, \ldots, C_{2^k-2}$ be the proper subcircuits of C (excluding the empty circuit). Clearly they are all $\Sigma\Pi\Sigma\Pi(k-1)$ circuits of size s. For any $P_{i_1 j_1}$ and $P_{i_2 j_2}$ appearing in C, and a variable x_ℓ such that $\text{var}(P_{i_1 j_1}) \cap \text{var}(P_{i_2 j_2}) \cap V = \{x_\ell\}$, define the polynomial Q as $D_\ell(P_{i_1 j_1}, P_{i_2 j_2})$ (recall D_ℓ and its property from Observation 2.1). Let $\mathcal{Q}$ be the set of all non-zero such Q's. The following lemma gives a sufficient condition that a given partial assignment for x_T results in a simple, minimal and nonzero depth-3 circuit.

LEMMA 4.6. *Let*

$$\varphi = \prod_{i=1}^{2^k-1} C_i \cdot \prod_{Q \in \mathcal{Q}} Q.$$

Let $\bar{a} \in \bar{\mathbb{F}}^n$ be such that $\varphi|_{x_T = \bar{a}_T} \not\equiv 0$. Then $C|_{x_T = \bar{a}_T}$ is a simple, minimal multilinear $\Sigma\Pi\Sigma(k)$ circuit.

PROOF. The minimality of $C|_{x_T = \bar{a}_T}$ is clear since all of the subcircuits of C are factors of φ. If one of them is zero, then so is $\varphi|_{x_T = \bar{a}_T}$. Notice that due to the same reason, no P_{ij} is reduced to zero. In order to prove that $C|_{x_T = \bar{a}_T}$ is simple, notice two following simples facts. First, by the definition of V, for every i, j it holds that $|\text{var}(P_{ij}|_{x_T = \bar{a}_T})| \leq$

[3]Namely, $\mathcal{G}_{k-1}$ is a generator for both models.

1. Second, consider $i_1 \neq i_2$ and j_1, j_2 such that $P_{i_1 j_{i_1}} \nsim P_{i_2 j_{i_2}}$. If $\text{var}(P_{i_1 j_{i_1}}|_{x_T=\bar{a}_T}) \neq \text{var}(P_{i_2 j_{i_2}}|_{x_T=\bar{a}_T})$ then we still have $P_{i_1 j_{i_1}}|_{x_T=\bar{a}_T} \nsim P_{i_2 j_{i_2}}|_{x_T=\bar{a}_T}$. If, on the other hand, $\text{var}(P_{i_1 j_{i_1}}|_{x_T=\bar{a}_T}) = \text{var}(P_{i_2 j_{i_2}}|_{x_T=\bar{a}_T}) = \{x_\ell\}$, then $D_\ell(P_{i_1 j_{i_1}}, P_{i_2 j_{i_2}})$ is a factor of φ and so

$$D_\ell(P_{i_1 j_{i_1}}, P_{i_2 j_{i_2}})|_{x_T=\bar{a}_T} =$$

$$D_\ell(P_{i_1 j_{i_1}}|_{x_T=\bar{a}_T}, P_{i_2 j_{i_2}}|_{x_T=\bar{a}_T}) \not\equiv 0\,.$$

Hence, by Observation 2.1, $P_{i_1 j_{i_1}}|_{x_T=\bar{a}_T} \nsim P_{i_2 j_{i_2}}|_{x_T=\bar{a}_T}$. Since C is itself a simple circuit, the claim follows from those two facts. □

Now we return to the proof of Lemma 4.5. The polynomial φ is a product of $(2s^2)$-sparse polynomials and $\Sigma\Pi\Sigma\Pi(k-1)$ circuits of size s. By Observations 2.3 and 2.4 we get that $\varphi|_{x_T=\mathcal{G}^T_{k-1}} \not\equiv 0$. It follows that there exists some $\bar{a} \in \text{Im}(\mathcal{G}_{k-1})$ for which $C|_{x_T=\bar{a}_T}$ is a simple, minimal, and multilinear $\Sigma\Pi\Sigma(k)$ circuit. Notice now that $C|_{x_T=\bar{a}_T}$ contains $R(k)$ variables (the previous proof shows that all the variables in V 'survived') and any linear function appearing in it contains only one variable. Hence, the rank of $C|_{x_T=\bar{a}_T}$ is $R(k)$. By the definition of $R(k)$ (Theorem 2.8) it cannot be a zero circuit. We thus proved that $P|_{x_T=\mathcal{G}^T_{k-1}} \not\equiv 0$.

4.3 A Reduction to r-compressed Multilinear $\Sigma\Pi\Sigma\Pi(k)$ Circuits

In this section we prove a structural theorem for multilinear $\Sigma\Pi\Sigma\Pi(k)$ circuits. This theorem enables us to reduce the identity testing of multilinear $\Sigma\Pi\Sigma\Pi(k)$ circuits to the identity testing of r-compressed multilinear $\Sigma\Pi\Sigma\Pi(k)$ circuits for any $r > 0$. Roughly, the theorem says that there exists a small set of variables W with the following property. Let $P = \sum_{T \subseteq W} m(T) F_T$, where F_T are polynomials defined over the variables $[n] \setminus W$ and $m(T) = \prod_{i \in T} x_i$. Then there exists T such that F_T can be computed by an r-compress $\Sigma\Pi\Sigma\Pi(k)$ circuit of size s. Now we state the theorem formally.

THEOREM 4.7. *Let $P \in \mathbb{F}[x_1, x_2, \ldots, x_n]$ be a non-zero polynomial computed by a multilinear $\Sigma\Pi\Sigma\Pi(k)$ circuit of size s. Let $r > 0$ be a parameter. Then there exists a set W of size $|W| \leq 2\log n \cdot \log s \cdot kr$ for which the following holds: Write*

$$P = \sum_{T \subseteq W} m(T) F_T$$

where the F_T's are non-zero polynomials independent of the variables in W. Then there exists at least one set $T \subseteq W$ for which $F_T = Q \cdot H$ where Q is a product of s-sparse polynomials and H is computable by a simple, r-compressed $\Sigma\Pi\Sigma\Pi(k)$ circuit of size s.

An alternative view of the theorem states that there exist two sets I, J of the following properties: If we set the variables of J to zero and take a partial derivative w.r.t. I (i.e. compute $\partial_I P|_{x_J=\bar{0}_J}$) then we get an r-compressed $\Sigma\Pi\Sigma\Pi(k)$ circuit of size s, multiplied by s-sparse polynomials. The set I corresponds to the variables in the monomial (i.e. T) and J to the variables of W outside the monomial (i.e. $W \setminus T$). We find this alternative view more convenient for the purpose of proving the theorem.

LEMMA 4.8. *Let $n, s, r, k > 1$ be integers. Let $P \in \mathbb{F}[x_1, x_2, \ldots, x_n]$ be a non-zero polynomial computed by a multilinear $\Sigma\Pi\Sigma\Pi(k)$ circuit C of size s. Then there exist disjoint subsets $I, J \subseteq [n]$ such that $|I| + |J| \leq 2kr\log(s)$ and $\partial_I P|_{x_J=\bar{0}_J}$ is a non-zero polynomial computed by a $\Sigma\Pi\Sigma\Pi(k)$ circuit C_{IJ} with at least one of the following properties:*

- $\text{var}(\text{sim}(C_{IJ})) < \text{var}(\text{sim}(C))/2$ *(recall the definition of* $\text{sim}(C)$ *from Section 3).*
- $\text{sim}(C_{IJ})$ *is an r-compressed $\Sigma\Pi\Sigma\Pi(k)$ circuit of size s.*

PROOF. Assume that C itself does not meet any of the needed conditions. Let $\text{sim}(C) = \sum_{j=1}^{k} M_j$ where each M_j is a multiplication gate of a $\Sigma\Pi\Sigma\Pi(k)$ circuit of size s. Write $M_j = N_j \cdot A_j$ where N_j is a product of s-sparse polynomials which are defined on at most $|\text{var}(\text{sim}(C))|/2r$ variables and $A_j = M_j/N_j$. Clearly, A_j is a product of s-sparse polynomials, each defined on at least $|\text{var}(\text{sim}(C))|/2r$ variables. Hence, due to the multilinearity of M_j, A_j must be s^{2r}-sparse. Let $\text{mon}(A)$ denote the number of monomials in a polynomial A. Let $\Phi(C) \triangleq \sum_{j=1}^{k} \log(\text{mon}(A_j))$ be a potential function that will aid us during the proof. We assume w.l.o.g. that $\Phi(C)$ is minimal w.r.t. all possible $\Sigma\Pi\Sigma\Pi(k)$ circuits of size s computing P. Notice that $\Phi(C) \leq 2kr\log(s)$.

Let $I_0 = J_0 = \emptyset$, $P_0 = P$ and $A_{j,0} = A_j$ for each $j \in [k]$. We now describe an algorithm that produces the required sets I, J. The algorithm is composed of enumerated steps, starting from 1. At each step, we add a single element either to I or J. Denote by I_ℓ and J_ℓ the sets at the end of step ℓ. Correspondingly, define $P_\ell = \partial_{I_\ell} P|_{x_{J_\ell}=\bar{0}_{J_\ell}}$. Also, define

$$C_\ell = \text{gcd}(C_\ell) \cdot \text{sim}(C_\ell) = \text{gcd}(C_\ell) \cdot \sum_{j=1}^{k} N_{j,\ell} A_{j,\ell}$$

where the $N_{j,\ell}$'s are s-sparse polynomials that rely on at most $|\text{var}(\text{sim}(C))|/2r$ variables (notice that we used C and not C_ℓ) and $C_\ell \equiv P_\ell$. Let $\Phi_C(C_\ell) \triangleq \sum_{j=1}^{k} \log(\text{mon}(A_{j,\ell}))$.[4] Define C_ℓ as the circuit achieving the minimal Φ_C among all size s $\Sigma\Pi\Sigma\Pi(k)$ circuits computing P_ℓ.

We now describe the process of adding a single variable to I or J. The idea is to take a variable appearing in some $A_{j,\ell}$ and add it to a set that will result in a maximal reduction to the monomials of $A_{j,\ell}$. One of the choices must reduce the number of monomials by a factor of 2 and thus reduce the Φ_C function by at least 1. This is since adding the variable to I means keeping only monomials in which it appears and adding it to J means keeping only the monomials in which it does not appear. The problem is to ensure that the resulting circuit computes a non-zero polynomial. The following lemma guarantees the existence of a variable for which neither action would result in a non-zero polynomial.

[4]We use a different notation (Φ_C and not Φ) as $\text{var}(\text{sim}(C))$ affects the definition of the $A_{j,\ell}$-s.

LEMMA 4.9. *Let $\ell \geq 0$. Assume that $P_\ell \not\equiv 0$ and that C_ℓ does not meet the conditions of Lemma 4.8. Then there exist some $i \in [n]$ and $j \in [k]$ such that $A_{j,\ell}$ and P_ℓ depend on x_i and x_i is not a factor of P_ℓ.*

PROOF. Assume that the claim is false. We have one of the following cases:
case 1: For some i, j, $A_{j,\ell}$ depends on x_i and P_ℓ does not. We can replace $A_{j,\ell}$ with $A_{j,\ell}|_{x_i=0}$ and result in a circuit C' computing the same polynomial P with a $\Phi(C') < \Phi(C_\ell)$. This is a contradiction to the minimality of C_ℓ.
case 2: All the $A_{j,\ell}$'s are constant. That is: $C_\ell = \gcd(C_\ell) \cdot \sum_{j=1}^{k} N_{j,\ell}$. In this case, either $\mathrm{var}(\mathrm{sim}(C_\ell)) < \mathrm{var}(\mathrm{sim}(C))/2$ or $\mathrm{sim}(C_\ell)$ is an r-compressed $\Sigma\Pi\Sigma\Pi(k)$ circuit of size s. Either way this is a contradiction.
case 3: There exists a variable x_i in $A_{j,\ell}$ that divides P_ℓ. Let $C' \triangleq C|_{x_i=1} \cdot x_i$. Then $P_\ell \equiv C'$ and $\Phi_C(C') < \Phi_C(C_\ell)$. This is a contradiction to the minimality of C_ℓ w.r.t. Φ_C. □

We return to the proof of lemma 4.8. Due to the lemma, there exist some x_i that appears in some $A_{j,\ell}$ where both $\frac{\partial P_\ell}{\partial x_i}$ and $P_\ell|_{x_i=0}$ are non-zero polynomials. Clearly, one of these choices for $P_{\ell+1}$ results in a non-zero polynomial for which $\Phi_C(C_{\ell+1}) \leq \Phi_C(C_\ell) - 1$. Since Φ_C is always non-negative, after at most $2kr\log(s)$ (the initial value for Φ) steps, we get the required circuit.

By repeating Lemma 4.8 at most $\log n$ times, we get Theorem 4.7 (indeed, in each step if we do not have the conclusion of 4.7 then $|\mathrm{var}(\mathrm{sim}(C_\ell))|$ is reduced by a factor of 2).

4.4 Rounding the Components Together

In the previous sections we found that there exists a small set of variables W and an additional disjoint small set of variables V with the following properties: When picking the variables outside of W and V from a generator for $\Sigma\Pi\Sigma\Pi(k-1)$ circuits and for $(2s^2)$-sparse polynomials, we get a non-zero polynomial. The following is the formal claim:

LEMMA 4.10. *Let $k \geq 2$ and Let $P \in \mathbb{F}[x_1, x_2, \ldots, x_n]$ be a non-zero polynomial computed by a multilinear $\Sigma\Pi\Sigma\Pi(k)$ circuit of size s. In addition, let $\mathcal{G}_{k-1}$ be a generator for $\Sigma\Pi\Sigma\Pi(k-1)$ circuits of size s and $(2s^2)$-sparse polynomials. Then there exists a subset $U \subseteq [n]$, depending only on P (i.e. U does not depend on the generator), of size $|U| \leq 3k^2R(k)\log(s)\log(n)$ such that $P|_{x_{[n]\setminus U}=\mathcal{G}_{k-1}^{[n]\setminus U}} \not\equiv 0$ for any such generator.*

PROOF. Let T_0 and W be the sets guaranteed by Theorem 4.7. Namely, when writing $P = \sum_{T\subseteq W} m(T)F_T$, we have that $F_{T_0} = Q \cdot H$ where Q is a product of s-sparse polynomials and H can be computed by a simple, multilinear $(k \cdot R(k))$-compressed $\Sigma\Pi\Sigma\Pi(k)$ circuit. Note that Q, H are defined on $[n] \setminus W$ (that is $\mathrm{var}(Q) \cup \mathrm{var}(H) \subseteq [n] \setminus W$). By Lemma 4.5 there exists a subset $V \subseteq \mathrm{var}(H)$ of size $|V| \leq R(k)$ such that

$$H|_{x_{\mathrm{var}(H)\setminus V}=\mathcal{G}_{k-1}^{\mathrm{var}(H)\setminus V}} \not\equiv 0 .$$

Let $U \triangleq V \cup W$. It holds that

$$H|_{x_{[n]\setminus U}=\mathcal{G}_{k-1}^{[n]\setminus U}} \not\equiv 0 .$$

As Q is a product of s-sparse polynomials we get, by Observations 2.3 and 2.4, that

$$Q|_{x_{[n]\setminus U}=\mathcal{G}_{k-1}^{[n]\setminus U}} \not\equiv 0 .$$

It follows that under the restriction $x_{[n]\setminus U} = \mathcal{G}_{k-1}^{[n]\setminus U}$, F_{T_0} is a non-zero polynomial. As we did not substitute anything to the variables in W the claim clearly follows. □

We now establish the generator for $\Sigma\Pi\Sigma\Pi(k)$ circuits. This is our main theorem and it guarantees that we get the required black-box algorithm. In particular Theorem 1 is an immediate corollary.

THEOREM 4.11 (MAIN). *Let $P \in \mathbb{F}[x_1, x_2, \ldots, x_n]$ be a non-zero polynomial computed by a multilinear $\Sigma\Pi\Sigma\Pi(k)$ circuit of size s. Then for every $\ell \geq 3k^3R(k)\log(s)\log(n)$ it holds that $P(G_\ell(\bar{y}, \bar{z}) + \mathcal{S}_{2s^2}(\bar{w})) \not\equiv 0$, where $\bar{y}, \bar{z}$ and $\bar{w}$ are new sets of variables.*

PROOF. We prove the claim by induction on k. For $k = 1$ we note that P is a product of $(2s^2)$-sparse polynomials. By definition of $\mathcal{S}_{2s^2}$ (recall Lemma 2.7), and Observations 2.3 and 4.2, we get that $P(G_\ell + \mathcal{S}_{2s^2}) \not\equiv 0$ and the claim follows. Assume that $k \geq 2$. Let $U \subseteq [n]$ be the subset guaranteed by Lemma 4.10. By the induction hypothesis, we get that for $v = \lceil 3(k-1)^3R(k-1)\log(s)\log(n)\rceil$ the mapping $G_v(\bar{y}, \bar{z}) + \mathcal{S}_{2s^2}(\bar{w})$ is a generator for both $\Sigma\Pi\Sigma\Pi(k-1)$ circuits and for $(2s^2)$-sparse polynomials. From Lemma 4.10 and Observation 2.4 it follows that $\mathrm{Im}\left(G_v^{[n]\setminus U} + \mathcal{S}_{2s^2}^{[n]\setminus U}\right)$ contains a point $\bar{a}$ for which $P(\bar{a}) \neq 0$. Since $|U| \leq 3k^2R(k)\log(s)\log(n) \leq \ell - v$, Observation 4.4 gives

$$\mathrm{Im}\left(G_v^{[n]\setminus U} + \mathcal{S}_{2s^2}^{[n]\setminus U}\right) \subseteq \mathrm{Im}\left(G_v^{[n]\setminus U} + \mathcal{S}_{2s^2}\right) \subseteq \mathrm{Im}\left(G_\ell + \mathcal{S}_{2s^2}\right)$$

and thus $\bar{a} \in \mathrm{Im}(G_\ell(\bar{y}, \bar{z}) + \mathcal{S}_{2s^2}(\bar{w}))$ and the claim holds. □

4.5 An explicit hitting set

The hitting set for $\Sigma\Pi\Sigma\Pi(k)$ circuit is an immediate corollary of Theorem 4.11. Basically, as $G_\ell(\bar{y}, \bar{z}) + \mathcal{S}_{2s^2}(\bar{w})$ are (relatively) low degree polynomials defined on $m = O(k^3R(k)\log(s)\log(n))$ many variables, we can simply evaluate $P \circ (G_\ell(\bar{y}, \bar{z}) + \mathcal{S}_{2s^2}(\bar{w}))$ on all inputs from E^m where $E \subseteq \mathbb{F}$ is a set of size $\mathrm{poly}(n)$. Algorithm 1 follows exactly this intuition and produces the hitting set.

```
Input: n, k, s ∈ ℕ.
Output: A set H
Let W ⊆ F be of size |W| = n²;
Let ℓ ≜ ⌈3k³R(k) log(s) log(n)⌉ where R(k) is defined in Theorem 2.8;
Let q ≜ q(n, 2s²) as defined in Lemma 2.7;
Initialize H = ∅;
foreach ā, b̄ ∈ W^ℓ and c̄ ∈ W^q do
  | Evaluate G_ℓ(ā, b̄) + S_{2s²}(c̄) and add it to H.
end
```

Algorithm 1: Construction of a hitting set for $\Sigma\Pi\Sigma\Pi(k)$ circuits

THEOREM 4.12. *Let $n, s, k > 0$. Algorithm 1, given n, s, k as input runs in $n^{\mathcal{O}(k^3 R(k) \log^2 s)} = n^{\mathcal{O}(k^6 \log(k) \log^2 s)}$ time. The set $\mathcal{H}$ it produces is of size $n^{\mathcal{O}(k^3 R(k) \log^2 s)} = n^{\mathcal{O}(k^6 \log(k) \log^2 s)}$ and is a hitting set for n-variate polynomials that can be computed by a $\Sigma\Pi\Sigma\Pi(k)$ circuit of size s.*

PROOF. Let $P \in \mathbb{F}[x_1, x_2, \ldots, x_n]$ be a polynomial computed by a multilinear $\Sigma\Pi\Sigma\Pi(k)$ circuit of size s. Let $\mathcal{H}$ be the set given by Algorithm 1. We claim that $P \equiv 0$ if and only if $P|_{\mathcal{H}} \equiv 0$. If $P \equiv 0$ then the claim is trivial. If $P \not\equiv 0$, by Theorem 4.11 we get that $P(G_\ell + \mathcal{S}_{2s^2}) \not\equiv 0$. According to their definition, the degrees of all the output variables of G_ℓ and $\mathcal{S}_{2s^2}$ are at most $n-1$. Therefore, the degrees of the variables in $P(G_\ell + \mathcal{S}_{2s^2})$ are bounded by $(n-1)n < n^2$. Since $P(G_\ell + \mathcal{S}_{2s^2}) \not\equiv 0$, Lemma 2.9 implies that $P|_{\mathcal{H}} \not\equiv 0$.

We now bound the size of $\mathcal{H}$ and the time required to construct it. From their definition, G_ℓ depends on 2ℓ variables and $\mathcal{S}_{2s^2}$ depends on $\mathcal{O}(\log_n s)$ variables. Hence,

$$|\mathcal{H}| \leq n^{4\ell + 2q(n, 2s^2)} = n^{\mathcal{O}(k^3 R(k) \log s \log n \cdot \log_n s)} =$$

$$n^{\mathcal{O}(k^3 R(k) \log^2 s)}.$$

The time required to construct $\mathcal{S}_{2s^2}$ and G_ℓ is polynomial in n, s. The time to evaluate $(G_\ell + \mathcal{S}_{2s^2})$ on a point from $W^{2\ell + q(n, 2s^2)}$ is polynomial in n. Hence, the time to construct $\mathcal{H}$ is $|\mathcal{H}| \cdot (ns)^{\mathcal{O}(1)} = n^{\mathcal{O}(k^3 R(k) \log^2 s)}$. □

5. CONCLUSION

Derandomizing the Polynomial Identity Testing problem for depth-4 arithmetic circuits is an outstanding open problem in complexity theory [AV08]. Any efficient derandomized algorithm for depth-4 circuits will imply strong lower bounds [KI03, Agr05]. So far, the progress in depth-4 identity testing is very limited [AM07, Sax08, SV09]. In this paper, we improve the situation by giving a quasi-polynomial time *black-box* identity testing algorithm for depth-4 multilinear circuits with bounded fan in top gate. Our algorithm is based on new structural theorems about such circuits.

In identity testing and explicit lower bound proofs, multilinear circuits have already received significant attention from the community [DS06, KS08, SV08, SV09, Raz04a, Raz04b, RSY08, RY08]. In [Raz04a], Raz asked whether one could design efficient identity testing algorithms for multilinear formulas. The best algorithms today are for sums of read-once formulas [SV09] and for set-multilinear depth-3 formulas (non black-box) [RS05]. For depth-4 multilinear circuits with bounded fan in top gate, our result gives the first efficient identity testing algorithm.

It will be very interesting to generalize our result for non-multilinear circuits with bounded fan in top gate. Another problem is to give a deterministic *polynomial time* identity testing algorithm for such circuits in *non black-box* model.

6. ACKNOWLEDGMENTS

The research was supported in part by the Israel Science Foundation (grant number 439/06) and Aly Kaufman Fellowship.

7. REFERENCES

[Agr05] M. Agrawal. Proving lower bounds via pseudo-random generators. In *Proceedings of the 25th FSTTCS*, volume 3821 of *LNCS*, pages 92–105, 2005.

[AJMV98] E. Allender, J. Jiao, M. Mahajan, and V. Vinay. Non-commutative arithmetic circuits: Depth reduction and size lower bounds. *Theor. Comput. Sci.*, 209(1-2):47–86, 1998.

[AKS04] M. Agrawal, N. Kayal, and N. Saxena. Primes is in P. *Annals of Mathematics*, 160(2):781–793, 2004.

[ALM+98] S. Arora, C. Lund, R. Motwani, M. Sudan, and M. Szegedy. Proof verification and the hardness of approximation problems. *JACM*, 45(3):501–555, 1998.

[Alo99] N. Alon. Combinatorial nullstellensatz. *Combinatorics, Probability and Computing*, 8:7–29, 1999.

[AM07] V. Arvind and P. Mukhopadhyay. The monomial ideal membership problem and polynomial identity testing. In *Proceedings of the 18th ISAAC*, pages 800–811, 2007.

[AV08] M. Agrawal and V. Vinay. Arithmetic circuits: A chasm at depth four. In *Proceedings of the 49th Annual FOCS*, pages 67–75, 2008.

[DS06] Z. Dvir and A. Shpilka. Locally decodable codes with 2 queries and polynomial identity testing for depth 3 circuits. *SIAM J. on Computing*, 36(5):1404–1434, 2006.

[KI03] V. Kabanets and R. Impagliazzo. Derandomizing polynomial identity tests means proving circuit lower bounds. In *Proceedings of the 35th Annual STOC*, pages 355–364, 2003.

[KS01] A. Klivans and D. Spielman. Randomness efficient identity testing of multivariate polynomials. In *Proceedings of the 33rd Annual STOC*, pages 216–223, 2001.

[KS07] N. Kayal and N. Saxena. Polynomial identity testing for depth 3 circuits. *Computational Complexity*, 16(2):115–138, 2007.

[KS08] Z. S. Karnin and A. Shpilka. Deterministic black box polynomial identity testing of depth-3 arithmetic circuits with bounded top fan-in. In *Proceedings of the 23rd Annual CCC*, pages 280–291, 2008.

[KS09] N. Kayal and S. Saraf. Blackbox polynomial identity testing for depth 3 circuits. *Electronic Colloquium on Computational Complexity (ECCC)*, (32), 2009.

[LFKN92] C. Lund, L. Fortnow, H. Karloff, and N. Nisan. Algebraic methods for interactive proof systems. *JACM*, 39(4):859–868, 1992.

[Lov79] L. Lovasz. On determinants, matchings, and random algorithms. In L. Budach, editor, *Fundamentals of Computing Theory*. Akademia-Verlag, 1979.

[MVV87] K. Mulmuley, U. Vazirani, and V. Vazirani. Matching is as easy as matrix inversion. *Combinatorica*, 7(1):105–113, 1987.

[Raz04a] R. Raz. Multi-linear formulas for permanent and determinant are of super-polynomial size.

In *Proceedings of the 36th Annual STOC*, pages 633–641, 2004.

[Raz04b] R. Raz. Multilinear $NC_1 \neq$ Multilinear NC_2. In *Proceedings of the 45th Annual FOCS*, pages 344–351, 2004.

[RS05] R. Raz and A. Shpilka. Deterministic polynomial identity testing in non commutative models. *Computational Complexity*, 14(1):1–19, 2005.

[RSY08] R. Raz, A. Shpilka, and A. Yehudayoff. A lower bound for the size of syntactically multilinear arithmetic circuits. *SIAM J. on Computing*, 38(4):1624–1647, 2008.

[RY08] R. Raz and A. Yehudayoff. Lower bounds and separations for constant depth multilinear circuits. In *IEEE Conference on Computational Complexity*, pages 128–139, 2008.

[Sax08] N. Saxena. Diagonal circuit identity testing and lower bounds. In *ICALP (1)*, pages 60–71, 2008.

[Sch80] J. T. Schwartz. Fast probabilistic algorithms for verification of polynomial identities. *JACM*, 27(4):701–717, 1980.

[Sha90] Adi Shamir. IP=PSPACE. In *Proceedings of the Thirty First Annual Symposium on Foundations of Computer Science*, pages 11–15, 1990.

[SS09] N. Saxena and C. Seshadhri. An almost optimal rank bound for depth-3 identities. In *Proceedings of the 24th annual CCC*, 2009.

[SV08] A. Shpilka and I. Volkovich. Read-once polynomial identity testing. In *Proceedings of the 40th Annual STOC*, pages 507–516, 2008.

[SV09] A. Shpilka and I. Volkovich. Improved polynomial identity testing for read-once formulas. In *APPROX-RANDOM*, pages 700–713, 2009.

[VSBR83] L. G. Valiant, S. Skyum, S. Berkowitz, and C. Rackoff. Fast parallel computation of polynomials using few processors. *SIAM J. on Computing*, 12(4):641–644, November 1983.

[Zip79] R. Zippel. Probabilistic algorithms for sparse polynomials. In *Symbolic and algebraic computation*, pages 216–226. 1979.

Tensor-Rank and Lower Bounds for Arithmetic Formulas

Ran Raz*
Weizmann Institute
ran.raz@weizmann.ac.il

ABSTRACT

We show that any explicit example for a tensor $A : [n]^r \to \mathbb{F}$ with tensor-rank $\geq n^{r \cdot (1-o(1))}$, (where $r \leq \log n / \log\log n$), implies an explicit super-polynomial lower bound for the size of general arithmetic formulas over $\mathbb{F}$. This shows that strong enough lower bounds for the size of arithmetic formulas of depth 3 imply super-polynomial lower bounds for the size of general arithmetic formulas.

One component of our proof is a new approach for homogenization and multilinearization of arithmetic formulas, that gives the following results:

We show that for any n-variate homogenous polynomial f of degree r, if there exists a (fanin-2) formula of size s and depth d for f then there exists a homogenous formula of size $O\left(\binom{d+r+1}{r} \cdot s\right)$ for f. In particular, for any $r \leq \log n$, if there exists a polynomial size formula for f then there exists a polynomial size homogenous formula for f. This refutes a conjecture of Nisan and Wigderson [10] and shows that super-polynomial lower bounds for homogenous formulas for polynomials of small degree imply super-polynomial lower bounds for general formulas.

We show that for any n-variate set-multilinear polynomial f of degree r, if there exists a (fanin-2) formula of size s and depth d for f then there exists a set-multilinear formula of size $O((d+2)^r \cdot s)$ for f. In particular, for any $r \leq \log n / \log\log n$, if there exists a polynomial size formula for f then there exists a polynomial size set-multilinear formula for f. This shows that super-polynomial lower bounds for set-multilinear formulas for polynomials of small degree imply super-polynomial lower bounds for general formulas.

*Research supported by the Israel Science Foundation (ISF), the Binational Science Foundation (BSF) and the Minerva Foundation.

Categories and Subject Descriptors

F.2.0 [**Analysis of Algorithms and Problem Complexity**]: [General]

General Terms

Theory

Keywords

arithmetic circuits, lower bounds, tensor rank, homogenous circuits, multilinear circuits

1. INTRODUCTION

1.1 Arithmetic Formulas

Let $\mathbb{F}$ be a field and let $\{x_1, \ldots, x_n\}$ be a set of input variables. An *arithmetic formula* is a directed tree whose edges are directed from the leaves to the root. Every leaf of the tree is labeled with either an input variable or a field element. Every other node of the tree is labeled with either $+$ or $\times$; in the first case the node is a *sum gate* and in the second case a *product gate*. The *size* of a formula is the number of edges in it. The *depth* of a formula is the length of the longest directed path in it[1]. The *fanin* of a gate is its in-degree.

Every node of an arithmetic formula computes a polynomial in the ring $\mathbb{F}[x_1, \ldots, x_n]$ as follows. A leaf just computes the input variable or field element that labels it. A sum gate computes the sum of the polynomials computed by its children. A product gate computes the product of the polynomials computed by its children. The *output* of the formula is the polynomial computed by the root. The root of the formula is also called the *output node*.

An *arithmetic circuit* is defined in the same way as arithmetic formula, except that the underlying graph is a general directed acyclic graph (rather than a directed tree). For simplicity, we assume that every circuit has exactly one output node.

Proving super-polynomial lower bounds for the size of arithmetic circuits and formulas (for explicit polynomials) is one of the most interesting and most challenging open problems in computational complexity. Such lower bounds are only known for restricted cases. For example, super-polynomial lower bounds were proved for non-commutative

[1]When counting the depth of a formula, it is customary not to count *scalar-products*, that is, product gates of fanin 2 that at least one of their children is a leaf labeled by a field element.

formulas [9], for depth 3 formulas over finite fields [5, 6], and for multilinear formulas [11, 12].

1.2 Homogenous Formulas

A polynomial f in the ring $\mathbb{F}[x_1,\ldots,x_n]$ is *homogenous* if all the monomials that occur in f are of the same degree. An arithmetic formula (or circuit) is *homogenous* if the polynomial computed by each of its nodes is homogenous.

A standard (and straightforward) homogenization technique by Strassen [17] shows that for any homogenous polynomial $f \in \mathbb{F}[x_1,\ldots,x_n]$ of degree r, if there exists a formula of size s for f then there exists a homogenous formula of size $\text{poly}(s^{\log r})$ for f. It was conjectured (see for example [10]) that this technique is optimal for every degree r. We show that this is not the case. In particular, we show that for any homogenous polynomial $f \in \mathbb{F}[x_1,\ldots,x_n]$ of degree $r \leq O(\log n)$, if there exists a polynomial size formula for f then there exists a polynomial size homogenous formula for f. Thus, super-polynomial lower bounds for homogenous formulas of degree up to $O(\log n)$ imply super-polynomial lower bounds for general arithmetic formulas.

1.3 Set-Multilinear Formulas

Let $X_1,\ldots,X_r$ be sets of variables. A polynomial f over the set of variables $X_1 \cup \ldots \cup X_r$ is *set-multilinear* in the sets $X_1,\ldots,X_r$ if every monomial that occurs in f is multilinear and contains exactly one variable from each set X_i. An arithmetic formula (or circuit) is *set-multilinear* in the sets $X_1,\ldots,X_r$ if the polynomial computed by its output node is set-multilinear in the sets $X_1,\ldots,X_r$ and the polynomial computed by each of its other nodes is set-multilinear in a subset of $\{X_1,\ldots,X_r\}$.

A standard (and straightforward) multilinearization technique shows that for any set-multilinear polynomial f over the sets $X_1,\ldots,X_r$, if there exists a formula of size s for f then there exists a set-multilinear formula of size $\text{poly}(s^r)$ for f. We show that this technique is not optimal. In particular, we show that for any set-multilinear polynomial f of degree $r \leq O(\log n/\log\log n)$, if there exists a polynomial size formula for f then there exists a polynomial size set-multilinear formula for f. Thus, super-polynomial lower bounds for set-multilinear formulas of degree up to $O(\log n/\log\log n)$ imply super-polynomial lower bounds for general arithmetic formulas.

Set-multilinear formulas were first studied in [10]. Super-polynomial lower bounds for multilinear formulas (that are more general than set-multilinear formulas) were proved in [11, 12] (see also [1, 14, 15, 16]). These techniques however do not give super-polynomial lower bounds for polynomials of very small degree.

1.4 Tensor-Rank

A tensor $A : [n]^r \to \mathbb{F}$ is of rank 1 if there exist r vectors $a_1,\ldots,a_r : [n] \to \mathbb{F}$ such that $A = a_1 \otimes \ldots \otimes a_r$ (where $\otimes$ denotes tensor product). More generally, the *tensor-rank* of A is the minimal k such that there exist k tensors $A_1,\ldots,A_k : [n]^r \to \mathbb{F}$ of rank 1 such that $A = \sum_{i=1}^k A_i$. This is a natural generalization of matrix-rank.

Given a tensor $A : [n]^r \to \mathbb{F}$ and r sets of variables $X_1,\ldots,X_r$, where $X_i = \{x_{i,1},\ldots,x_{i,n}\}$, one can define the set-multilinear polynomial f_A as follows

$$f_A(x_{1,1},\ldots,x_{r,n}) = \sum_{i_1,\ldots,i_r \in [n]} A(i_1,\ldots,i_r) \cdot \prod_{j=1}^{r} x_{j,i_j}$$

A beautiful well known and straightforward insight, going back to [17] (see [4] for a survey), shows that the tensor-rank of tensors of order $r = 3$ is very related to *bilinear complexity* and hence also to general arithmetic circuit complexity. In particular (using also [3]), if the tensor-rank of $A : [n]^3 \to \mathbb{F}$ is k then the smallest circuit for f_A is of size $\Omega(k)$. Thus, one can prove lower bounds for arithmetic circuit size by proving lower bounds for tensor-rank. Note, however, that the tensor-rank of $A : [n]^3 \to \mathbb{F}$ is bounded by $O(n^2)$. Hence, this approach can only give lower bounds of up to $\Omega(n^2)$ for arithmetic circuit size. We note also that to date no lower bound better than $\Omega(n)$ is known for the tensor-rank of any explicit tensor $A : [n]^3 \to \mathbb{F}$.

Here we consider tensors $A : [n]^r \to \mathbb{F}$ where $r = r(n)$ is super-constant and satisfies $r \leq O(\log n/\log\log n)$. We show that for any such A, if there exists an arithmetic formula of size n^c for f_A then the tensor-rank of A is at most $n^{r\cdot(1-2^{-O(c)})}$. Thus, a lower bound of $n^{r\cdot(1-o(1))}$ for the tensor-rank of A implies a super-polynomial lower bound for the size of any arithmetic formula for[2] f_A.

Since the tensor-rank of A corresponds to computations of f_A by depth-3 (set-multilinear) formulas, our result shows that strong enough lower bounds for the size of arithmetic formulas of depth 3 imply super-polynomial lower bounds for the size of general arithmetic formulas. Previously, it was well known that strong enough lower bounds for the size of arithmetic circuits of depth 4 imply exponential lower bounds for the size of general arithmetic circuits (see for example [15, 13]). Moreover, a striking recent result of Agrawal and Vinay (based on [18]) shows that *any* exponential lower bound for the size of arithmetic circuits of depth 4 implies an exponential lower bound for the size of general arithmetic circuits [2].

We note that it is very easy to give lower bounds of $n^{\lfloor r/2 \rfloor}$ for the tensor-rank of tensors $A : [n]^r \to \mathbb{F}$ (by taking a full-rank matrix of size $n^{\lfloor r/2 \rfloor} \times n^{\lfloor r/2 \rfloor}$). We are not aware of any better lower bound. We note also that it was proved by Håstad that computing the tensor-rank is an NP-complete problem [7].

1.5 Preliminaries

We say that an arithmetic formula (or circuit) is of *fanin* 2 if the fanin of every gate in it is 2. We say that an arithmetic formula (or circuit) is of *product-fanin-*2 if the fanin of every product gate in it is 2. The *product-depth* of a product-fanin-2 formula (or circuit) is the maximal number of product gates along a directed path in it.

For a formula (or circuit) Φ and a node u in it, we denote by Φ_u the sub-formula of Φ rooted at u and by $\hat{\Phi}_u$ the polynomial computed by the formula Φ_u.

It is well known that for any fanin-2 formula Φ of size s, one can assume without loss of generality that the depth of Φ is $O(\log s)$. That is, there exists a formula of size poly(s)

[2]Moreover, it was noted to us by Amir Yehudayoff that by the completeness of the permanent, if the tensor A is "explicit" the super-polynomial lower bound holds for the permanent.

and depth $O(\log s)$ that computes the same polynomial computed by Φ.

1.6 Discussion

A well known approach, first suggested by Strassen [17], is to consider the tensor-product of tensors of high tensor-rank as a candidate for a larger tensor with high tensor-rank.

Let n, m, r be such that $m^r = n$, and for simplicity assume that $\mathbb{F}$ is a finite field. Let $A_1, \ldots, A_r : [m]^r \to \mathbb{F}$ be random tensors, and let $A = A_1 \otimes \ldots \otimes A_r : [n]^r \to \mathbb{F}$ be their tensor-product, defined by

$$A((i_{1,1}, \ldots, i_{1,r}), \ldots, (i_{r,1}, \ldots, i_{r,r})) =$$

$$A_1(i_{1,1}, \ldots, i_{r,1}) \cdots A_r(i_{1,r}, \ldots, i_{r,r}).$$

Since $A_1, \ldots, A_r$ are random, with high probability their tensor-rank is high. If one can prove that with probability larger than 0 the tensor-rank of A is at least $n^{r\cdot(1-o(1))}$, one obtains super-polynomial lower bounds for arithmetic formulas for the polynomial f_A, where the entries of the tensors $A_1, \ldots, A_r$ are viewed as additional input variables (note that there are only $r \cdot n$ such entries).

2. HOMOGENIZATION

For a polynomial $f \in \mathbb{F}[x_1, \ldots, x_n]$, denote by f_i the homogenous part of f of degree i. That is, $f = \sum_i f_i$ where each f_i is a homogenous polynomial of degree i. In the same way, for a formula (or circuit) Φ and a node u in it denote by $\hat{\Phi}_{u,i}$ the homogenous part of degree i of the polynomial $\hat{\Phi}_u$.

Obviously, if u is a fanin-2 sum gate with children v, w then for every i

$$\hat{\Phi}_{u,i} = \hat{\Phi}_{v,i} + \hat{\Phi}_{w,i} \tag{1}$$

and if u is a fanin-2 product gate with children v, w then for every i

$$\hat{\Phi}_{u,i} = \sum_{j=0}^{i} \hat{\Phi}_{v,j} \cdot \hat{\Phi}_{w,i-j} \tag{2}$$

Let Φ be a fanin-2 circuit of size s and depth d that computes a homogenous polynomial of degree r. There is a standard and straightforward technique to turn Φ into a fanin-2 homogenous circuit of size $s \cdot \text{poly}(r)$ and depth $O(d \cdot \log r)$ that computes the same polynomial [17]. The main idea of the homogenization technique is to split every node u in the circuit into $r+1$ nodes $u_0, \ldots, u_r$, where each node u_i in the new circuit computes the homogenous part of degree i of the polynomial computed by u; that is, u_i computes the polynomial $\hat{\Phi}_{u,i}$. The computation of each $\hat{\Phi}_{u,i}$ is done recursively using Equation 1 and Equation 2. If u is the output node of the original circuit, the output node of the new circuit is the node u_r that computes the polynomial $\hat{\Phi}_{u,r} = \hat{\Phi}_u$ (since we assumed that the original circuit computes a homogenous polynomial of degree r). The size of the new circuit is $s \cdot \text{poly}(r)$. When we turn the new circuit into a fanin-2 circuit its depth may increase to $O(d \cdot \log r)$ since the sum in Equation 2 is on up to $r+1$ elements.

Let Φ be a formula of size s that computes a homogenous polynomial of degree r. The standard homogenization technique turns Φ into a homogenous formula of size $\text{poly}(s^{\log r})$ that computes the same polynomial, as follows. First, assume for simplicity and without loss of generality that Φ is a fanin-2 formula, and assume without loss of generality that the depth of Φ is $O(\log s)$ (see Section 1.5) - this step may increase the size of Φ polynomially. Next, use the homogenization technique described above to turn Φ into a fanin-2 homogenous circuit of depth $O(\log s \cdot \log r)$ for the same polynomial. Finally, turn that circuit into a formula of size $2^{O(\log s \cdot \log r)} = \text{poly}(s^{\log r})$.

It was conjectured in [10] that the increase in the formula-size by a power of $O(\log r)$ in the exponent is necessary. We note also that for the special case of multilinear formulas, it was recently proved in [8] that for $r = \text{poly}(n)$ this is indeed the case.

2.1 A New Homogenization Theorem

Our approach can be viewed as a tighter analysis of the standard technique described above. For simplicity and without loss of generality we state and prove our theorem for fanin-2 formulas.

THEOREM 1. *Let Φ be a fanin-2 formula of size s and product-depth d that computes a homogenous polynomial of degree r. Then there exists a fanin-2 homogenous formula Ψ of size $O\left(\binom{d+r+1}{r} \cdot s\right)$ and product-depth d that computes the same polynomial*[3].

PROOF. For every node u in the formula Φ, denote by $\text{path}(u)$ the set of all nodes on the directed path from u to the root (including the node u). For every node u denote by N_u the set of all functions $D : \text{path}(u) \to \{0, \ldots, r\}$ such that:

1. For every $v, w \in \text{path}(u)$ such that v is a sum gate and w is a child of v, $D(v) = D(w)$.
2. For every $v, w \in \text{path}(u)$ such that v is a product gate and w is a child of v, $D(v) \geq D(w)$.

Intuitively, a function $D \in N_u$ describes a possible progress of the degree of a monomial along the path from u to the root.

Construction of Ψ:

The formula Ψ is constructed as follows. For every node u in Φ and $D \in N_u$ we will have a node (u, D). Every node (u, D) will compute in Ψ the polynomial

$$\hat{\Psi}_{(u,D)} = \hat{\Phi}_{u,D(u)}$$

that is, the homogenous part of degree $D(u)$ of the polynomial $\hat{\Phi}_u$ computed by u in Φ. To compute $\hat{\Phi}_{u,D(u)}$, the node (u, D) will only use the outputs of nodes (v, D') such that v is a child of u and D' extends D. This is done inductively in a straightforward manner (using Equation 1 and Equation 2) as follows:

1. u **is a leaf:** If u is a leaf in Φ then for every $D \in N_u$ the node (u, D) will be a leaf. If u is labeled by a field element, (u, D) is labeled by the same field element if $D(u) = 0$ and by 0 if $D(u) \neq 0$. If u is labeled by an input variable, (u, D) is labeled by the same input variable if $D(u) = 1$ and by 0 if $D(u) \neq 1$. By the definitions, for every $D \in N_u$,

$$\hat{\Psi}_{(u,D)} = \hat{\Phi}_{u,D(u)}$$

[3]In the same way, if the polynomial computed by Φ is not homogenous and is of an arbitrary degree, and r is an integer, there exists Ψ as above that computes the homogenous part of degree r of the polynomial computed by Φ.

2. u **is a sum gate:** Assume that u is a sum gate in Φ with children v, w. For every $D \in N_u$ denote by $D_v \in N_v$ the function that agrees with D on path(u) and satisfies $D_v(v) = D(u)$, and in the same way denote by $D_w \in N_w$ the function that agrees with D on path(u) and satisfies $D_w(w) = D(u)$. The node (u, D) will sum the outputs of the nodes (v, D_v) and (w, D_w). By the induction hypothesis and Equation 1 we have

$$\hat{\Psi}_{(u,D)} = \hat{\Psi}_{(v,D_v)} + \hat{\Psi}_{(w,D_w)} = \hat{\Phi}_{v,D_v(v)} + \hat{\Phi}_{w,D_w(w)}$$

$$= \hat{\Phi}_{v,D(u)} + \hat{\Phi}_{w,D(u)} = \hat{\Phi}_{u,D(u)}$$

3. u **is a product gate:** Assume that u is a product gate in Φ with children v, w. For every $D \in N_u$ and $i \in \{0, \ldots, D(u)\}$ denote by $D_{v,i} \in N_v$ the function that agrees with D on path(u) and satisfies $D_{v,i}(v) = i$, and in the same way denote by $D_{w,i} \in N_w$ the function that agrees with D on path(u) and satisfies $D_{w,i}(w) = i$. The node (u, D) will compute $\hat{\Psi}_{(u,D)}$ from the outputs of the nodes $\{(v, D_{v,i}) : i \in \{0, \ldots, D(u)\}\}$ and $\{(w, D_{w,i}) : i \in \{0, \ldots, D(u)\}\}$ by the formula

$$\hat{\Psi}_{(u,D)} = \sum_{i=0}^{D(u)} \hat{\Psi}_{(v,D_{v,i})} \cdot \hat{\Psi}_{(w,D_{w,D(u)-i})}$$

By the induction hypothesis and Equation 2 we have

$$\hat{\Psi}_{(u,D)} = \sum_{i=0}^{D(u)} \hat{\Psi}_{(v,D_{v,i})} \cdot \hat{\Psi}_{(w,D_{w,D(u)-i})}$$

$$= \sum_{i=0}^{D(u)} \hat{\Phi}_{v,D_{v,i}(v)} \cdot \hat{\Phi}_{w,D_{w,D(u)-i}(w)}$$

$$= \sum_{i=0}^{D(u)} \hat{\Phi}_{v,i} \cdot \hat{\Phi}_{w,D(u)-i} = \hat{\Phi}_{u,D(u)}$$

We fix the output node of Ψ to be the node (u, D) such that u is the output node of Φ and $D \in N_u$ is the function that satisfies $D(u) = r$.

Comment: Note that in the construction above there may be nodes (u, D) that are not connected by a path to the output node of Ψ. These nodes do not contribute to the functionality of Ψ and should be removed so that the final Ψ is a tree rather than a union of trees.

Functionality of Ψ*:*

We proved by induction that every node (u, D) in Ψ computes the polynomial $\hat{\Psi}_{(u,D)} = \hat{\Phi}_{u,D(u)}$. In particular, the output node (u, D) computes the polynomial $\hat{\Psi}_{(u,D)} = \hat{\Phi}_{u,D(u)} = \hat{\Phi}_{u,r} = \hat{\Phi}_u$, which is the polynomial computed by Φ.

Properties of Ψ*:*

To see that Ψ is a formula note that the output of a node (v, D') is only used by a node (u, D) such that u is a parent of v and D agrees with D' on path(u), and there is at most one such node (u, D). Thus, the out-degree of every node is at most 1.

Ψ is homogenous since each of its nodes computes a homogenous polynomial.

The product-depth of Ψ is the same as the product-depth of Φ since the "product-depth" of Equation 1 is 0 and the "product-depth" of Equation 2 is 1.

Finally, since the size of every N_u is bounded by $\binom{d+r+1}{r}$, the size of Ψ is at most $O\left(\binom{d+r+1}{r} \cdot s\right)$. □

COROLLARY 2. *Let $f \in \mathbb{F}[x_1, \ldots, x_n]$ be a homogenous polynomial of degree $\leq O(\log n)$. If there exists a polynomial size formula for f then there exists a polynomial size homogenous formula for f.*

PROOF. Let Φ be a polynomial size formula for f. Without loss of generality Φ is a fanin-2 formula of depth $O(\log n)$. The proof hence follows from Theorem 1. □

3. MULTILINEARIZATION

For vectors $a, b \in \{0,1\}^r$, we say that $b \leq a$ if for every $i \in \{1, \ldots, r\}$, $b(i) \leq a(i)$.

Let $X_1, \ldots, X_r$ be sets of variables. For a vector $a \in \{0,1\}^r$ and a monomial q in the set of variables $X_1 \cup \ldots \cup X_r$, we say that q is set-multilinear of type a if it is multilinear and contains exactly one variable from each set X_i such that $a(i) = 1$ and no variables from sets X_i such that $a(i) = 0$. For a polynomial f over the set of variables $X_1 \cup \ldots \cup X_r$, and a vector $a \in \{0,1\}^r$, denote by f_a the set-multilinear part of f of type a. That is, f_a is the sum of all the set-multilinear monomials of type a that occur in f with the same coefficient as their occurrence in f.

In the same way, for a formula (or circuit) Φ and a node u in it denote by $\hat{\Phi}_{u,a}$ the set-multilinear part of type a of the polynomial $\hat{\Phi}_u$.

Obviously, if u is a fanin-2 sum gate with children v, w then for every a

$$\hat{\Phi}_{u,a} = \hat{\Phi}_{v,a} + \hat{\Phi}_{w,a} \quad (3)$$

and if u is a fanin-2 product gate with children v, w then for every a

$$\hat{\Phi}_{u,a} = \sum_{b \in \{0,1\}^r \text{ s.t. } b \leq a} \hat{\Phi}_{v,b} \cdot \hat{\Phi}_{w,a-b} \quad (4)$$

Let Φ be a fanin-2 circuit of size s and depth d that computes a set-multilinear polynomial in the sets $X_1, \ldots, X_r$. There is a standard and straightforward technique to turn Φ into a fanin-2 set-multilinear circuit of size $s \cdot \text{poly}(2^r)$ and depth $O(d \cdot r)$ that computes the same polynomial. The main idea of the multilinearization technique is to split every node u in the circuit into 2^r nodes $\{u_a\}_{a \in \{0,1\}^r}$, where each node u_a in the new circuit computes the set-multilinear part of type a of the polynomial computed by u; that is, u_a computes the polynomial $\hat{\Phi}_{u,a}$. The computation of each $\hat{\Phi}_{u,a}$ is done recursively using Equation 3 and Equation 4. If u is the output node of the original circuit, the output node of the new circuit is the node $u_{\vec{1}}$ (where $\vec{1} \in \{0,1\}^r$ denotes the vector $(1, \ldots, 1)$) that computes the polynomial $\hat{\Phi}_{u,\vec{1}} = \hat{\Phi}_u$ (since we assumed that the original circuit computes a set-multilinear polynomial in the sets $X_1, \ldots, X_r$). The size of the new circuit is $s \cdot \text{poly}(2^r)$. When we turn the new circuit into a fanin-2 circuit its depth may increase to $O(d \cdot r)$ since the sum in Equation 4 is on up to 2^r elements.

Let Φ be a formula of size s that computes a set-multilinear polynomial in the sets $X_1, \ldots, X_r$. The standard multilinearization technique turns Φ into a set-multilinear formula of size poly(s^r) that computes the same polynomial, as follows. First, assume for simplicity and without loss of generality that Φ is a fanin-2 formula, and assume without loss of generality that the depth of Φ is $O(\log s)$ (see Section 1.5) - this step may increase the size of Φ polynomially. Next, use the multilinearization technique described above to turn Φ into a fanin-2 set-multilinear circuit of depth $O(\log s \cdot r)$ for the same polynomial. Finally, turn that circuit into a formula of size $2^{O(\log s \cdot r)} = \text{poly}(s^r)$.

3.1 A New Multilinearization Theorem

Our approach can be viewed as a tighter analysis of the standard technique described above. For simplicity and without loss of generality we state and prove our theorem for fanin-2 formulas. The technique that we use is very similar to the technique that we used in Section 2.1.

THEOREM 3. *Let Φ be a fanin-2 formula of size s and product-depth d that computes a set-multilinear polynomial over the sets $X_1, \ldots, X_r$. Then there exists a fanin-2 set-multilinear formula Ψ of size $O\left((d+2)^r \cdot s\right)$ and product-depth d that computes the same polynomial.*

PROOF. For every node u in the formula Φ, denote by path(u) the set of all nodes on the directed path from u to the root (including the node u). For every node u denote by N_u the set of all functions $D : \text{path}(u) \to \{0,1\}^r$ such that:

1. For every $v, w \in \text{path}(u)$ such that v is a sum gate and w is a child of v, $D(v) = D(w)$.
2. For every $v, w \in \text{path}(u)$ such that v is a product gate and w is a child of v, $D(v) \geq D(w)$.

Intuitively, a function $D \in N_u$ describes a possible progress of the type of a set-multilinear monomial along the path from u to the root.

Construction of Ψ:

The formula Ψ is constructed as follows. For every node u in Φ and $D \in N_u$ we will have a node (u, D). Every node (u, D) will compute in Ψ the polynomial

$$\hat{\Psi}_{(u,D)} = \hat{\Phi}_{u,D(u)}$$

that is, the set-multilinear part of type $D(u)$ of the polynomial $\hat{\Phi}_u$ computed by u in Φ. To compute $\hat{\Phi}_{u,D(u)}$, the node (u, D) will only use the outputs of nodes (v, D') such that v is a child of u and D' extends D. This is done inductively in a straightforward manner (using Equation 3 and Equation 4) as follows:

1. u **is a leaf:** If u is a leaf in Φ then for every $D \in N_u$ the node (u, D) will be a leaf. If u is labeled by a field element, (u, D) is labeled by the same field element if $D(u) = \vec{0}$ and by 0 if $D(u) \neq \vec{0}$ (where $\vec{0}$ denotes the 0 vector in $\{0,1\}^r$). If u is labeled by an input variable from the set X_i, (u, D) is labeled by the same input variable if $D(u) = \vec{e_i}$ and by 0 if $D(u) \neq \vec{e_i}$ (where $\vec{e_i} \in \{0,1\}^r$ is defined by $\vec{e_i}(j) = 1$ iff $j = i$). By the definitions, for every $D \in N_u$,
$$\hat{\Psi}_{(u,D)} = \hat{\Phi}_{u,D(u)}$$
2. u **is a sum gate:** Assume that u is a sum gate in Φ with children v, w. For every $D \in N_u$ denote by $D_v \in N_v$ the function that agrees with D on path(u) and satisfies $D_v(v) = D(u)$, and in the same way denote by $D_w \in N_w$ the function that agrees with D on path(u) and satisfies $D_w(w) = D(u)$. The node (u, D) will sum the outputs of the nodes (v, D_v) and (w, D_w). By the induction hypothesis and Equation 3 we have
$$\hat{\Psi}_{(u,D)} = \hat{\Psi}_{(v,D_v)} + \hat{\Psi}_{(w,D_w)} = \hat{\Phi}_{v,D_v(v)} + \hat{\Phi}_{w,D_w(w)}$$
$$= \hat{\Phi}_{v,D(u)} + \hat{\Phi}_{w,D(u)} = \hat{\Phi}_{u,D(u)}$$
3. u **is a product gate:** Assume that u is a product gate in Φ with children v, w. For every $D \in N_u$ and $a \in \{0,1\}^r$ such that $a \leq D(u)$ denote by $D_{v,a} \in N_v$ the function that agrees with D on path(u) and satisfies $D_{v,a}(v) = a$, and in the same way denote by $D_{w,a} \in N_w$ the function that agrees with D on path(u) and satisfies $D_{w,a}(w) = a$. The node (u, D) will compute $\hat{\Psi}_{(u,D)}$ from the outputs of the nodes $\{(v, D_{v,a}) : a \leq D(u)\}$ and $\{(w, D_{w,a}) : a \leq D(u)\}$ by the formula
$$\hat{\Psi}_{(u,D)} = \sum_{a \leq D(u)} \hat{\Psi}_{(v,D_{v,a})} \cdot \hat{\Psi}_{(w,D_{w,D(u)-a})}$$
By the induction hypothesis and Equation 4 we have
$$\hat{\Psi}_{(u,D)} = \sum_{a \leq D(u)} \hat{\Psi}_{(v,D_{v,a})} \cdot \hat{\Psi}_{(w,D_{w,D(u)-a})}$$
$$= \sum_{a \leq D(u)} \hat{\Phi}_{v,D_{v,a}(v)} \cdot \hat{\Phi}_{w,D_{w,D(u)-a}(w)}$$
$$= \sum_{a \leq D(u)} \hat{\Phi}_{v,a} \cdot \hat{\Phi}_{w,D(u)-a} = \hat{\Phi}_{u,D(u)}$$

We fix the output node of Ψ to be the node (u, D) such that u is the output node of Φ and $D \in N_u$ is the function that satisfies $D(u) = \vec{1}$.

Comment: Note that in the construction above there may be nodes (u, D) that are not connected by a path to the output node of Ψ. These nodes do not contribute to the functionality of Ψ and should be removed so that the final Ψ is a tree rather than a union of trees.

Functionality of Ψ:

We proved by induction that every node (u, D) in Ψ computes the polynomial $\hat{\Psi}_{(u,D)} = \hat{\Phi}_{u,D(u)}$. In particular, the output node (u, D) computes the polynomial $\hat{\Psi}_{(u,D)} = \hat{\Phi}_{u,D(u)} = \hat{\Phi}_{u,\vec{1}} = \hat{\Phi}_u$, which is the polynomial computed by Φ.

Properties of Ψ:

To see that Ψ is a formula note that the output of a node (v, D') is only used by a node (u, D) such that u is a parent of v and D agrees with D' on path(u), and there is at most one such node (u, D). Thus, the out-degree of every node is at most 1.

Ψ is set-multilinear since each of its nodes computes a set-multilinear polynomial.

The product-depth of Ψ is the same as the product-depth of Φ since the "product-depth" of Equation 3 is 0 and the "product-depth" of Equation 4 is 1.

Finally, since the size of every N_u is bounded by $(d+2)^r$, the size of Ψ is at most $O\left((d+2)^r \cdot s\right)$. $\square$

COROLLARY 4. *Let f be a set-multilinear polynomial over sets $X_1, \ldots, X_r$ of size n each, where $r \leq O(\log n / \log logn)$. If there exists a polynomial size formula for f then there exists a polynomial size set-multilinear formula for f.*

PROOF. Let Φ be a polynomial size formula for f. Without loss of generality Φ is a fanin-2 formula of depth $O(\log n)$. The proof hence follows from Theorem 3. □

4. TENSOR-RANK AND FORMULA SIZE

Recall that given a tensor $A : [n]^r \to \mathbb{F}$ and r sets of variables $X_1, \ldots, X_r$, where $X_i = \{x_{i,1}, \ldots, x_{i,n}\}$, we defined the set-multilinear polynomial f_A by

$$f_A(x_{1,1}, \ldots, x_{r,n}) = \sum_{i_1,\ldots,i_r \in [n]} A(i_1, \ldots, i_r) \cdot \prod_{j=1}^{r} x_{j,i_j}$$

In this section, we show that for any tensor $A : [n]^r \to \mathbb{F}$ with $r \leq O(\log n / \log\log n)$, if there exists a polynomial size formula for the polynomial f_A then the tensor-rank of A is not too high.

THEOREM 5. *Let $A : [n]^r \to \mathbb{F}$ be a tensor such that $r \leq O(\log n / \log\log n)$. If there exists a formula of size n^c for the polynomial f_A then the tensor-rank of A is at most $n^{r\cdot(1-2^{-O(c)})}$.*

PROOF. Let Φ be a formula of size n^c for f_A. Without loss of generality Φ is a fanin-2 formula of depth $O(\log(n^c))$. Hence, by Theorem 3 we can assume without loss of generality that Φ is a set-multilinear formula (in the sets $X_1, \ldots, X_r$) of size $n^{O(c)}$.

Formulas in Normal Form:

It will be convenient in this proof to allow a leaf of a formula to be labeled by a product of a field element and an input variable (rather than by only one of them). The polynomial computed by such a leaf is the product that labels it.

We will say that a set-multilinear formula is in a *normal form* if it satisfies the following properties (that can be assumed without loss of generality):

1. The fanin of every product gate in the formula is 2.
2. The sum gates in the formula are collapsed so that a child of a sum gate is never a sum gate.
3. No node of the formula computes the 0 polynomial.
4. Every leaf of the formula is labeled by a product of a field element (different than 0) and an input variable (and hence the polynomial computed by any node in the formula is of degree larger than 0).

Without loss of generality we assume that the formula Φ is in normal form.

Tensor-Rank:

We will use the following 3 (straightforward) properties of tensor-rank:

1. For any $A' : [n]^{r'} \to \mathbb{F}$, (where $r' > 0$),
$$\text{rank}(A') \leq n^{r'-1} \qquad (5)$$
2. For any $A_1, \ldots, A_k : [n]^{r'} \to \mathbb{F}$,
$$\text{rank}\left(\sum_{i=1}^{k} A_i\right) \leq \sum_{i=1}^{k} \text{rank}(A_i) \qquad (6)$$
3. For any $A_1 : [n]^{r_1} \to \mathbb{F}$ and $A_2 : [n]^{r_2} \to \mathbb{F}$
$$\text{rank}\,(A_1 \otimes A_2) \leq \text{rank}(A_1) \cdot \text{rank}(A_2) \qquad (7)$$
(where $A_1 \otimes A_2 : [n]^{r_1+r_2} \to \mathbb{F}$ is the tensor-product of A_1 and A_2, defined by $A_1 \otimes A_2(i_1, \ldots, i_{r_1+r_2}) = A_1(i_1, \ldots, i_{r_1}) \cdot A_2(i_{r_1+1}, \ldots, i_{r_1+r_2})$).

Syntactic-Rank:

For a set-multilinear formula Ψ in normal form in the sets of variables $X_1, \ldots, X_r$, we define the *syntactic-rank* of Ψ inductively as follows:

1. If u is a leaf,
$$\text{syn-rank}(\Psi_u) = 1$$
2. If u is a sum gate with children $u_1, \ldots, u_k$,
$$\text{syn-rank}(\Psi_u) = \min\left(n^{r'-1}\ ;\ \sum_{i=1}^{k} \text{syn-rank}(\Psi_{u_i})\right)$$
where r' is the degree of $\hat{\Psi}_u$ (and note that since Ψ is in normal form, $r' > 0$).
3. If u is a product gate with children u_1, u_2,
$$\text{syn-rank}(\Psi_u) = \text{syn-rank}(\Psi_{u_1}) \cdot \text{syn-rank}(\Psi_{u_2})$$

By Equation 5, Equation 6, and Equation 7, it is straightforward to verify by induction on the formula that the syntactic-rank bounds the tensor-rank in the following sense: if A_Ψ is the tensor such that the formula Ψ computes the polynomial f_{A_Ψ} then $\text{rank}(A_\Psi) \leq \text{syn-rank}(\Psi)$. Hence, in order to bound the tensor-rank of A it's sufficient to bound the syntactic-rank of Φ.

Extended-Formulas:

It will be convenient to extend the definition of a set-multilinear formula in normal form (in the sets of variables $X_1, \ldots, X_r$), so that each node in the formula can be labeled (in addition to its label in the formula) by an additional real number larger or equal to 1, referred to as the *weight* of the node (if the node is not labeled we think of the weight as 1). We refer to such formulas as *extended-formulas* (in the sets of variables $X_1, \ldots, X_r$). (Note that *extended-formula* already means that the formula is set-multilinear in normal form).

Intuitively, one should think of a weight w of a node as indicating that the sub-formula rooted at that node is duplicated w times and all the w copies are summed. Note however that w is a real number and not necessarily integer. An extended-formula is not viewed as a computational device and we will not care about its functionality; we define it in order to explore the relations between size and syntactic-rank of a formula.

Size of an Extended-Formula:

We define the *size* of an extended-formula to be the sum over all the leaves of the formula of the product of all weights along the path from that leaf to the root of the formula. Note that if all weights are 1, the size of an extended-formula is the number of leaves in the formula. This is different than our definition of the size as the number of edges in a formula, but the two notions differ by a factor of at most 2 and hence the difference will not be important.

Note that if in an extended-formula Ψ, u is a node with children $u_1, \ldots, u_k$, then

$$\text{size}(\Psi_u) = \text{weight}(u) \cdot \sum_{i=1}^{k} \text{size}(\Psi_{u_i}) \tag{8}$$

(where $\text{size}(\Psi_u)$ and $\text{size}(\Psi_{u_i})$ denote the sizes of the extended-formulas Ψ_u and Ψ_{u_i}).

Syntactic-Degree of an Extended Formula:

We define the *syntactic-degree* of an extended-formula Ψ inductively as follows:

1. If u is a leaf, $\text{syn-deg}(\Psi_u) = 1$.
2. If u is a sum gate with children $u_1, \ldots, u_k$, $\text{syn-deg}(\Psi_u) = \text{syn-deg}(\Psi_{u_1})$, (note that for every i, j, $\text{syn-deg}(\Psi_{u_i}) = \text{syn-deg}(\Psi_{u_j})$).
3. If u is a product gate with children u_1, u_2, $\text{syn-deg}(\Psi_u) = \text{syn-deg}(\Psi_{u_1}) + \text{syn-deg}(\Psi_{u_2})$.

Syntactic-Rank of an Extended Formula:

We extend the definition of syntactic-rank to extended-formulas. We define the *syntactic-rank* of an extended-formula Ψ (in the sets of variables $X_1, \ldots, X_r$) inductively as follows:

1. If u is a leaf,
$$\text{syn-rank}(\Psi_u) = 1 \tag{9}$$
2. If u is a sum gate with children $u_1, \ldots, u_k$,
$$\text{syn-rank}(\Psi_u) = \tag{10}$$
$$\min\left(n^{r'-1} \; ; \; \text{weight}(u) \cdot \sum_{i=1}^{k} \text{syn-rank}(\Psi_{u_i})\right)$$
where $r' = \text{syn-deg}(\Psi_u)$ (and note that $r' > 0$).
3. If u is a product gate with children u_1, u_2,
$$\text{syn-rank}(\Psi_u) = \tag{11}$$
$$\min\left(n^{r'-1}; \text{weight}(u) \cdot \text{syn-rank}(\Psi_{u_1}) \cdot \text{syn-rank}(\Psi_{u_2})\right)$$
where $r' = \text{syn-deg}(\Psi_u)$ (and note that $r' > 0$).

Note that if all weights are 1 the definition coincides with the original definition of syntactic-rank.

By the definition, for any node u in Ψ, $\text{syn-rank}(\Psi_u) \leq n^{r'-1}$, where $r' = \text{syn-deg}(\Psi_u)$. We say that a node u in Ψ is of *full-rank* if $\text{syn-rank}(\Psi_u) = n^{r'-1}$.

Size versus Syntactic-Rank of an Extended-Formula:

For a fixed $s = n^{c'}$, where $1 \leq c' \leq \log r - 3$, consider all the extended-formulas Ψ' (in the sets of variables $X_1, \ldots, X_r$) such that $\text{syn-deg}(\Psi') = r$ and $\text{size}(\Psi') \leq s$; and let Ψ be an extended-formula with the largest syntactic-rank among all these formulas (if there are many extended-formulas with the same syntactic-rank, take Ψ to be an extended-formula with the smallest size among all these formulas). We will show that without loss of generality the extended-formula Ψ is of a very specific form.

First we claim that without loss of generality we can assume that every sum gate in Ψ is of fanin 1. Let u be a sum gate in Ψ, with children $u_1, \ldots, u_k$ (where $k > 1$). Note that for every i, $\text{syn-deg}(\Psi_u) = \text{syn-deg}(\Psi_{u_i})$. Let $i \in \{1, \ldots, k\}$ be such that $\text{syn-rank}(\Psi_{u_i})/\text{size}(\Psi_{u_i})$ is maximal, and let $q = \sum_{j=1}^{k} \text{size}(\Psi_{u_j})$. We will multiply the weight of u_i by $q/\text{size}(\Psi_{u_i})$ and remove all children of u (together with the sub-trees below them) except u_i. By Equation 8, $\text{size}(\Psi_u)$ and hence also $\text{size}(\Psi)$ didn't change, while by Equation 10 (using also Equation 9 and Equation 11), $\text{syn-rank}(\Psi_u)$ and hence also $\text{syn-rank}(\Psi)$ may only increase. Thus, we have turned u into a fanin 1 gate without increasing the size of the extended-formula and without decreasing its syntactic-rank. By repeating this process we can assume that every sum gate in Ψ is of fanin 1.

Next we claim that without loss of generality we can assume that there are no sum gates in Ψ. This is obvious because any sum gate u of fanin 1 can be removed by connecting its child directly to its parent (or just removing u if it has no parent) and passing its weight to its child (that is, multiplying the weight of the child of u by $\text{weight}(u)$). We can hence assume that Ψ has no sum gates. Thus, Ψ is a Binary tree and every non-leaf node in it is a product gate. Since $\text{syn-deg}(\Psi) = r$, the number of leaves in Ψ is r.

We will now analyze the possible weights of the nodes of Ψ.

First we claim that for every leaf u, $\text{weight}(u) = 1$. This is because for every leaf u, $\text{syn-rank}(\Psi_u) = 1$ (regardless of its weight). Therefore, $\text{weight}(u) = 1$, since a higher weight increases the size of the extended-formula without increasing its syntactic-rank.

Let u be a non-leaf node with children u_1, u_2. Denote $r_1 = \text{syn-deg}(\Psi_{u_1})$ and $r_2 = \text{syn-deg}(\Psi_{u_2})$. Thus, $\text{syn-deg}(\Psi_u) = r_1 + r_2$. We know that $\text{syn-rank}(\Psi_{u_1}) \leq n^{r_1-1}$ and $\text{syn-rank}(\Psi_{u_2}) \leq n^{r_2-1}$. We claim the following:

1. If $\text{weight}(u) > 1$ then u_1, u_2 are of full-rank. *Proof:* Assume for a contradiction that $\text{weight}(u) > 1$, and u_1 is not of full-rank. (In particular, u_1 is not a leaf). Then by multiplying $\text{weight}(u_1)$ by $1 + \epsilon$ and dividing $\text{weight}(u)$ by $1 + \epsilon$ (for a small enough ϵ) we preserve the syntactic-rank of Ψ_u (by Equation 11) while decreasing its size (by Equation 8). Thus, we preserve the syntactic-rank of Ψ while decreasing its size, in contradiction to the definition of Ψ.

2. If u is of full-rank then $\text{weight}(u) = n$. *Proof:* Since u is of full-rank, $\text{syn-rank}(\Psi_u) = n^{r_1+r_2-1}$. Hence by Equation 11, $\text{weight}(u) \geq n$. Thus, by 1, u_1, u_2 are of full-rank. Thus, $\text{syn-rank}(\Psi_{u_1}) = n^{r_1-1}$ and $\text{syn-rank}(\Psi_{u_2}) = n^{r_2-1}$. Hence, by Equation 11, $\text{weight}(u) = n$ (otherwise, by reducing $\text{weight}(u)$ to n

we preserve the syntactic-rank of Ψ while decreasing its size, in contradiction to the definition of Ψ).

3. By 1, 2, if u is of full-rank then both u_1, u_2 are of full-rank.

Consider the nodes along a path from a leaf to the root in Ψ. The leaf is always of full-rank and, as we saw, the weight of the leaf is 1. By 1,2,3, following the leaf we have a certain number of full-rank nodes with weight n. After that we have at most one node that is not of full-rank and its weight is larger than 1, and after that we have nodes that are not of full-rank and are with weight 1. Since the size of Ψ is $s = n^{c'}$, the number of full-rank nodes with weight n along a path from a leaf to the root in Ψ is at most $\log_n(s) = c'$.

Denote by V the set of non-leaf nodes in Ψ that are not of full-rank and their weight is 1. Thus, from any leaf of Ψ we can reach a node in the set V by a path of length at most $c' + 2$. Hence, since the number of leaves in Ψ is r and since Ψ is a Binary tree, $|V| \geq \frac{r}{2^{c'+2}}$. Also, by 1,2,3, V is a Binary tree (of product gates) such that if $v \in V$ and v is a child of u then $u \in V$.

Denote by U the set of nodes that are not in V but are connected to V by an edge. Let $l = |U|$ and let $u_1, \ldots, u_l$ be the nodes in U and let $r_i = \text{syn-deg}(\Psi_{u_i})$. Note that $l > |V|$ and that for every i, $\text{syn-rank}(\Psi_{u_i}) \leq n^{r_i - 1}$. Since V is a Binary tree of product gates $\sum_{i=1}^{l} r_i = \text{syn-deg}(\Psi) = r$, and since the weight of every node in V is 1, by Equation 11 (applied $|V|$ times)

$$\text{syn-rank}(\Psi) \leq \prod_{i=1}^{l} \text{syn-rank}(\Psi_{u_i}) \leq n^{\sum_{i=1}^{l} r_i - l} \leq n^{r - r/2^{c'+2}}$$

Since Ψ was chosen to be the extended-formula with the highest syntactic-rank among all the extended-formulas of size $n^{c'}$, we have the same bound for every extended-formula (as a function of its size). In particular, since Φ is a formula of size $n^{O(c)}$,

$$\text{rank}(A) \leq \text{syn-rank}(\Phi) \leq n^{r - r/2^{O(c)}}$$

□

COROLLARY 6. *Let $A : [n]^r \to \mathbb{F}$ be a tensor such that $r \leq O(\log n / \log\log n)$. If the tensor-rank of A is $\geq n^{r \cdot (1-o(1))}$ then there is no polynomial size formula for the polynomial f_A.*

(Note that the corollary is interesting only when $r = r(n)$ is super-constant. For $r = O(1)$, the corollary holds trivially since the tensor-rank of any $A : [n]^r \to \mathbb{F}$ is at most n^{r-1}).

5. REFERENCES

[1] S. Aaronson. Multilinear Formulas and Skepticism of Quantum Computing. STOC 2004: 118-127

[2] M. Agrawal, V. Vinay. Arithmetic Circuits: A Chasm at Depth Four. FOCS 2008: 67-75

[3] W. Baur, V. Strassen. The Complexity of Partial Derivatives. *Theor. Comput. Sci.* 22: 317-330 (1983)

[4] J. von zur Gathen. Algebraic Complexity Theory. *Ann. Rev. Computer Science* 3: 317-347 (1988)

[5] D. Grigoriev, M. Karpinski. An Exponential Lower Bound for Depth 3 Arithmetic Circuits. STOC 1998: 577-582

[6] D. Grigoriev, A. A. Razborov. Exponential Lower Bounds for Depth 3 Arithmetic Circuits in Algebras of Functions over Finite Fields. *Applicable Algebra in Engineering, Communication and Computing* 10(6): 465-487 (2000) (preliminary version in FOCS 1998)

[7] J. Håstad. Tensor Rank is NP-Complete. *J. Algorithms* 11(4): 644-654 (1990) (preliminary version in ICALP 1989)

[8] P. Hrubeš, A. Yehudayoff. Homogeneous Formulas and Symmetric Polynomials, Manuscript 2009

[9] N. Nisan. Lower Bounds for Non-Commutative Computation. STOC 1991: 410-418

[10] N. Nisan, A. Wigderson. Lower Bounds on Arithmetic Circuits Via Partial Derivatives. *Computational Complexity* 6(3): 217-234 (1996) (preliminary version in FOCS 1995)

[11] R. Raz. Multi-Linear Formulas for Permanent and Determinant are of Super-Polynomial Size. *J. ACM 56(2)* (2009) (Preliminary version in STOC 2004)

[12] R. Raz. Separation of Multilinear Circuit and Formula Size. *Theory Of Computing* 2(6) (2006) (preliminary version in FOCS 2004, title: Multilinear-$NC_1 \neq$ Multilinear-NC_2)

[13] R. Raz. Elusive Functions and Lower Bounds for Arithmetic Circuits. STOC 2008: 711-720

[14] R. Raz, A. Shpilka, A. Yehudayoff. A Lower Bound for the Size of Syntactically Multilinear Arithmetic Circuits. *SIAM J. Comput.* 38(4): 1624-1647 (2008) (preliminary version in FOCS 2007)

[15] R. Raz, A. Yehudayoff. Multilinear Formulas, Maximal-Partition Discrepancy and Mixed-Sources Extractors. FOCS 2008: 273-282

[16] R. Raz, A. Yehudayoff. Lower Bounds and Separations for Constant Depth Multilinear Circuits. *IEEE Conference on Computational Complexity* 2008: 128-139

[17] V. Strassen. Vermeidung von Divisionen. *J. Reine Angew. Math.* 264: 182-202 (1973)

[18] L. G. Valiant, S. Skyum, S. Berkowitz, C. Rackoff. Fast Parallel Computation of Polynomials Using Few Processors. *SIAM J. Comput.* 12(4): 641-644 (1983)

Non-Commutative Circuits and the Sum-of-Squares Problem

[Extended Abstract]*

Pavel Hrubeš†
School of Mathematics
Institute for Advanced Study
Princeton, USA
pahrubes@gmail.com

Avi Wigderson†
School of Mathematics
Institute for Advanced Study
Princeton, USA
avi@ias.edu

Amir Yehudayoff†
School of Mathematics
Institute for Advanced Study
Princeton, USA
amir.yehudayoff@gmail.com

ABSTRACT

We initiate a direction for proving lower bounds on the size of non-commutative arithmetic circuits. This direction is based on a connection between lower bounds on the size of *non-commutative* arithmetic circuits and a problem about *commutative* degree four polynomials, the classical sum-of-squares problem: find the smallest n such that there exists an identity

$$(x_1^2+x_2^2+\cdots+x_k^2)\cdot(y_1^2+y_2^2+\cdots+y_k^2) = f_1^2+f_2^2+\cdots+f_n^2, \quad (1)$$

where each $f_i = f_i(X,Y)$ is bilinear in $X = \{x_1,\ldots,x_k\}$ and $Y = \{y_1,\ldots,y_k\}$. Over the complex numbers, we show that a sufficiently strong *super-linear* lower bound on n in (1), namely, $n \geq k^{1+\epsilon}$ with $\varepsilon > 0$, implies an *exponential* lower bound on the size of arithmetic circuits computing the non-commutative permanent.

More generally, we consider such sum-of-squares identities for any biquadratic polynomial $h(X,Y)$, namely

$$h(X,Y) = f_1^2 + f_2^2 + \cdots + f_n^2. \quad (2)$$

Again, proving $n \geq k^{1+\epsilon}$ in (2) for *any* explicit h over the complex numbers gives an *exponential* lower bound for the non-commutative permanent. Our proofs relies on several new structure theorems for non-commutative circuits, as well as a non-commutative analog of Valiant's completeness of the permanent.

We proceed to prove such super-linear bounds in some restricted cases. We prove that $n \geq \Omega(k^{6/5})$ in (1), if $f_1,\ldots,f_n$ are required to have *integer* coefficients. Over the *real* numbers, we construct an explicit biquadratic polynomial h such that n in (2) must be at least $\Omega(k^2)$. Unfortunately, these results do not imply circuit lower bounds.

We also present other structural results about non-commutative arithmetic circuits. We show that any non-commutative circuit computing an *ordered* non-commutative polynomial can be efficiently transformed to a syntactically multilinear circuit computing that polynomial. The permanent, for example, is ordered. Hence, lower bounds on the size of syntactically multilinear circuits computing the permanent imply unrestricted non-commutative lower bounds. We also prove an exponential lower bound on the size of non-commutative syntactically multilinear circuit computing an explicit polynomial. This polynomial is, however, not ordered and an unrestricted circuit lower bound does not follow.

†Research supported by NSF Grant DMS-0835373.

*Full version can be found at ECCC website http://eccc.hpi-web.de.

STOC'10, June 5–8, 2010, Cambridge, Massachusetts, USA.

Categories and Subject Descriptors

F.2.1 [**Theory of computation**]: Numerical Algorithms and Problems

General Terms

Theory

1. INTRODUCTION

1.1 Non-commutative computation

Arithmetic complexity theory studies computation of formal polynomials over some field or ring. Most of this theory is concerned with computation of commutative polynomials. The basic model of computation is that of *arithmetic circuit*. Despite decades of work, the best size lower bound for general circuits computing an explicit n-variate polynomial of degree d is $\Omega(n \log d)$, due to Baur and Strassen [29, 2]. Better lower bounds are known for a variety of more restricted computational models, such as monotone circuits, multilinear or bounded depth circuits (see, e.g., [6, 3]).

In this paper we deal with a different type of restriction. We investigate *non-commutative* polynomials and circuits; the case when the variables do not multiplicatively commute, i.e., $xy \neq yx$ if $x \neq y$, as in the case when the variables represent matrices over a field[1]. In a non-commutative circuit, a multiplication gate is given with an order in which its inputs are multiplied. Precise definitions appear in Section 2. A simple illustration of how absence of commutativity limits computation is the polynomial $x^2 - y^2$. If x, y commute,

[1]As in this case, addition remains commutative, as well as multiplication by constants.

the polynomial can be computed as $(x-y)(x+y)$ using one multiplication. In the non-commutative case, two multiplications are required to compute it.

Surprisingly, while interest in non-commutative computations goes back at least to 1970 [32], no better lower bounds are known for general non-commutative circuits than in the commutative case. The seminal work in this area is [21], where Nisan proved exponential lower bounds on non-commutative *formula* size of determinant and permanent. He also gives an explicit polynomial that has linear size non-commutative circuits but requires non-commutative formulas of exponential size, thus separating non-commutative formulas and circuits.

One remarkable aspect of non-commutative computation is its connection with the celebrated approximation scheme for the (commutative) permanent [14]. The series of papers [7, 16, 1, 5] reduce the problem of approximating permanent to the problem of computing determinant of a matrix whose entries are elements of (non-commutative) Clifford algebras. However, already in the case of quaternions (the third Clifford algebra), determinant cannot be efficiently computed by means of arithmetic formulas. This was shown by Chien and Sinclair [4] who extend Nisan's techniques to this and other non-commutative algebras.

In this paper, we propose new directions towards proving lower bounds on non-commutative circuits. We present structure theorems for non-commutative circuits, which enable us to reduce circuit size lower bounds to apparently simpler problems. The foremost such problem is the so called sum-of-squares problem, a classical question on a border between algebra and topology. We also outline a connection with multilinear circuits, in which exciting progress was made in recent years. We then make modest steps towards the lower-bound goal, and present results some of which are of independent interest. Before we describe the results, we take a detour to briefly describe the sum-of-squares problem and its long history.

1.2 The sum-of-squares problem

In this section all variables commute. Consider the polynomial

$$\mathsf{SOS}_k = (x_1^2 + x_2^2 + \cdots + x_k^2) \cdot (y_1^2 + y_2^2 + \cdots + y_k^2). \quad (3)$$

Given a field (or a ring) $\mathbb{F}$, define $\mathcal{S}_{\mathbb{F}}(k)$ as the smallest n such that there exists a polynomial identity

$$\mathsf{SOS}_k = z_1^2 + z_2^2 + \cdots + z_n^2\,, \quad (4)$$

where each $z_i = z_i(X, Y)$ is a bilinear form in variables $X = \{x_1, \ldots, x_k\}$ and $Y = \{y_1, \ldots, y_k\}$ over the field $\mathbb{F}$.

We refer to the problem of determining the value $\mathcal{S}_{\mathbb{F}}(k)$ as the *sum-of-squares* problem. Note that the problem is not interesting if $\mathbb{F}$ has characteristic two, for then $\mathcal{S}_{\mathbb{F}}(k) = 1$. Over other fields, the trivial bounds are

$$k \leq \mathcal{S}_{\mathbb{F}}(k) \leq k^2\,.$$

In Section 1.3, we describe the connection between the sum-of-squares problem and arithmetic complexity. At this point, let us discuss the mathematical significance of the sum-of-squares problem (much more can be found, e.g., in [28]). We focus on real sums of squares, for they are of the greatest historical importance[2]. Nontrivial identities exhibiting $\mathcal{S}_{\mathbb{R}}(k) = k$ initiated this story.

When $k = 1$, we have $x_1^2 y_1^2 = (x_1 y_1)^2$. When $k = 2$, we have

$$(x_1^2 + x_2^2) \cdot (y_1^2 + y_2^2) = (x_1 y_1 - x_2 y_2)^2 + (x_1 y_2 + x_2 y_1)^2.$$

Interpreting (x_1, x_2) and (y_1, y_2) as complex numbers α and β, this formula expresses the property

$$|\alpha|^2 |\beta|^2 = |\alpha\beta|^2 \quad (5)$$

of multiplication of complex numbers. The case $k = 1$ trivially expresses the same fact (5) for *real* α and β. In 1748, motivated by the number theoretic problem of expressing every integer as a sum of four squares, Euler proved an identity showing that $\mathcal{S}_{\mathbb{R}}(4) = 4$. When Hamilton discovered the *quaternion* algebra in 1843, this identity was quickly realized to express (5) for mutiplying quaternions. This was repeated in 1848 with the discovery of the *octonions* algebra, and the 8-square identity expressing (5) for octonions. Motivated by the study of division algebras, mathematicians tried to prove a 16-square identity in the following 50 years. Finally Hurwitz in 1898 proved that it is impossible, obtaining the first nontrivial lower bound:

THEOREM 1.1. ([11]) *$\mathcal{S}_{\mathbb{R}}(k) > k$, except if $k \in \{1, 2, 4, 8\}$.*

The following interpretation of the sum-of-squares problem got topologists interested in this problem: if $z_1, \ldots, z_n$ satisfy (4), the map $z = (z_1, \ldots, z_n) : \mathbb{R}^k \times \mathbb{R}^k \to \mathbb{R}^n$ is a bilinear *normed* map. Namely, it satisfies $|z(\bar{x}, \bar{y})| = |\bar{x}||\bar{y}|$ for every $\bar{x}, \bar{y} \in \mathbb{R}^k$, where $|\cdot|$ is the Euclidean norm. This rigid structure allows for topological and algebraic geometry tools to yield the following, best known lower bound, which unfortunately gains only a factor of two over the trivial bound:

THEOREM 1.2. ([13, 18]) *$\mathcal{S}_{\mathbb{R}}(k) \geq (2 - o(1))k$.*

As it happens, the trivial upper bound can be improved as well. There exists a normed bilinear map as above from $\mathbb{R}^k \times \mathbb{R}^{\rho(k)}$ to $\mathbb{R}^k$, with $\rho(k) = \Theta(\log k)$. This was shown by Radon and Hurwitz [24, 12], who computed the exact value of the optimal $\rho(k)$. Interestingly, such a map exists even if we require the polynomials z_i to have *integer*[3] coefficients, see [35, 19]. The existence of this integer bilinear normed map turns out to be related to Clifford algebras as well: it can be obtained using a matrix representation of a Clifford algebra with $\rho(k)$ generators. This can be seen to imply

FACT 1.3. $\mathcal{S}_{\mathbb{Z}}(k) \leq O(k^2/\log k)$.

This is the best known upper bound on $\mathcal{S}_{\mathbb{R}}$, or $\mathcal{S}_{\mathbb{F}}$ for any other field with char $\mathbb{F} \neq 2$. This motivated researchers to study integer sums of squares, and try to prove lower bounds on $\mathcal{S}_{\mathbb{Z}}$. Despite the effort [18, 33, 28], the asymptotic bounds on $\mathcal{S}_{\mathbb{Z}}$ remained as wide open as in the case of reals. One of the contributions of this paper is the first super-linear lower bound in the integer case. We show that $\mathcal{S}_{\mathbb{Z}}(k) \geq \Omega(k^{6/5})$.

To illustrate the subtlety of proving lower bounds on the sum-of-squares problem, let us mention that if we allow the z_i's to be *rational* functions rather than polynomials, the

[2]The assumption that the z_i's in (4) are bilinear is satisfied automatically if the z_i's are real polynomials.

[3]The coefficients of the z_i's can actually be taken to be in $\{-1, 0, 1\}$.

nature of the problem significantly changes. In 1965, Pfister [23] proved that if the z_i's are rational functions, SOS_k can be written as a sum of k squares whenever k is a power of two.

1.3 Non-commutative circuits and bilinear complexity

Conditional lower bounds on circuit complexity.
The connection between the sum-of-squares problem and non-commutative lower bounds is that a sufficiently strong lower bound on $\mathcal{S}(k)$ implies an exponential lower bound for permanent. Here we present our main results, for a more detailed discussion, see Section 2.1. In the non-commutative setting, there are several options to define the permanent, we define it row-by-row, that is,

$$\mathrm{PERM}_n(X) = \sum_{\pi} x_{1,\pi(1)} x_{2,\pi(2)} \cdots x_{n,\pi(n)},$$

where π is a permutation of $[n] = \{1, \ldots, n\}$. The advertised connection can be summarized as follows[4].

THEOREM 1.4. *Let $\mathbb{F}$ be an algebraically closed field. Assume that $\mathcal{S}_{\mathbb{F}}(k) \geq \Omega(k^{1+\varepsilon})$ for a constant $\varepsilon > 0$. Then* PERM_n *requires non-commutative circuits of size $2^{\Omega(n)}$.*

Theorem 1.4 is an instance of a general connection between non-commutative circuits and commutative degree four polynomials, which we now proceed to describe.

Let f be a *commutative* polynomial of degree four over a field $\mathbb{F}$. We say that f is *biquadratic* in variables $X = \{x_1, \ldots, x_k\}$ and $Y = \{y_1, \ldots, y_k\}$, if every monomial in f has the form $x_{i_1} x_{i_2} y_{j_1} y_{j_2}$. If f is biquadratic in variables X and Y, we define

sum-of-squares complexity: $\mathcal{S}_{\mathbb{F}}(f)$ is the smallest[5] n so that f can be written as

$$f = z_1^2 + \cdots + z_n^2,$$

bilinear complexity: $\mathcal{B}_{\mathbb{F}}(f)$ is the smallest n so that f can be written as

$$f = z_1 z_1' + \cdots + z_n z_n',$$

where each z_i and z_i' are bilinear forms in X, Y. We thus have $\mathcal{S}_{\mathbb{F}}(\mathsf{SOS}_k) = \mathcal{S}_{\mathbb{F}}(k)$, as defined in the previous section.

Let us first note that over certain fields, $\mathcal{S}_{\mathbb{F}}(f)$ and $\mathcal{B}_{\mathbb{F}}(f)$ are virtually the same:

REMARK 1.5. *Clearly, $\mathcal{B}_{\mathbb{F}}(f) \leq \mathcal{S}_{\mathbb{F}}(f)$. If $\mathbb{F}$ is algebraically closed with char $\mathbb{F} \neq 2$, then $\mathcal{S}_{\mathbb{F}}(f) \leq 3\mathcal{B}_{\mathbb{F}}(f)$. This holds since $2zz' = (z+z')^2 + (\sqrt{-1}z)^2 + (\sqrt{-1}z')^2$.*

We now define the non-commutative version of SOS_k: the non-commutative *identity polynomial* is

$$\mathsf{ID}_k = \sum_{i,j \in [k]} x_i y_j x_i y_j. \tag{6}$$

We show that a lower bound on $\mathcal{B}_{\mathbb{F}}(\mathsf{SOS}_k)$ implies a lower bound on the size of non-commutative circuit computing ID_k.

[4]If char $\mathbb{F} = 2$, the theorem holds trivially, since $\mathcal{S}_{\mathbb{F}}(k) = 1$.
[5]When no such n exists, $\mathcal{S}_{\mathbb{F}}(f)$ is infinite.

THEOREM 1.6. *Over a field $\mathbb{F}$, the size of a non-commutative circuit computing ID_k is at least $\Omega(\mathcal{B}_{\mathbb{F}}(\mathsf{SOS}_k))$.*

Theorem 1.6 is proved in Section 4. The lower bound given by the theorem is reminiscent of the tensor rank approach to lower bounds for commutative circuits, where a lower bound on tensor rank implies circuit lower bounds [30]. In the non-commutative case we can prove a much stronger implication. For every $\varepsilon > 0$, a $k^{1+\varepsilon}$ lower bound on $\mathcal{B}_{\mathbb{F}}(\mathsf{SOS}_k)$ gives an exponential lower bound for the permanent. Theorem 1.7, which is proved in Section 5, together with Remark 1.5 imply Theorem 1.4.

THEOREM 1.7. *Assume that $\mathcal{B}_{\mathbb{F}}(\mathsf{SOS}_k) \geq \Omega(k^{1+\varepsilon})$, for some $\varepsilon > 0$. Then* PERM_n *requires non-commutative circuits of size $2^{\Omega(n)}$ over $\mathbb{F}$.*

The theorem is reminiscent of a result in Boolean complexity, where a sufficient *linear* lower bound on complexity of a bipartite graph implies an *exponential* circuit lower bound for a related function (see [15] for discussion.)

An important property that the non-commutative permanent shares with its commutative counterpart is its completeness for the class of explicit polynomials. This enables us to generalize Theorem 1.7 to the following theorem, which is proved in Section 5.1. Let $\{f_k\}$ be a family of commutative biquadratic polynomials such that the number of variables in f_k is polynomial in k. We call $\{f_k\}$ *explicit*, if there exists a polynomial-time algorithm which, given k and a degree four monomial α as inputs[6], computes the coefficient of α in f_k. The polynomial SOS_k is clearly explicit.

THEOREM 1.8. *Let $\mathbb{F}$ be a field such that char $\mathbb{F} \neq 2$. Let $\{f_k\}$ be a family of explicit biquadratic polynomials. Assume that $\mathcal{B}_{\mathbb{F}}(f_k) \geq \Omega(k^{1+\epsilon})$ for some $\epsilon > 0$. Then* PERM_n *requires non-commutative circuits of size $2^{\Omega(n)}$ over $\mathbb{F}$.*

Lower bounds on sum-of-squares complexity in special cases.
Remark 1.5 tells us that for some fields, $\mathcal{B}_{\mathbb{F}} = \Theta(\mathcal{S}_{\mathbb{F}})$, and hence to prove a circuit lower bound, it is sufficient to prove a lower bound on $\mathcal{S}_{\mathbb{F}}$. We prove lower bounds on $\mathcal{S}_{\mathbb{F}}(k)$ in some restricted cases. For more details, see Section 2.2.

Over $\mathbb{R}$, we find an explicit 'hard' polynomial

THEOREM 1.9. *There exists an explicit family $\{f_k\}$ of real biquadratic polynomials with coefficients in $\{0,1,2,4\}$ such that $\mathcal{S}_{\mathbb{R}}(f_k) = \Theta(k^2)$.*

By Theorem 1.8, if the construction worked over the complex numbers $\mathbb{C}$ instead of $\mathbb{R}$, we would have an exponential lower bound on the size of non-commutative circuits for the permanent. Such a construction is not known.

We investigate sums of squares over integers. We prove the following:

THEOREM 1.10. $\mathcal{S}_{\mathbb{Z}}(k) \geq \Omega(k^{6/5})$.

This result, too, does not imply a circuit lower bound. However, if we knew how to prove the same for $\mathbb{Z}[\sqrt{-1}]$ instead of $\mathbb{Z}$, we would get lower bounds for circuits over $\mathbb{Z}$. Such lower bounds are not known.

[6]We think of the input as given in a binary representation; the algorithm thus runs in time polynomial in $\log k$.

1.4 Ordered and multilinear circuits

An important restriction on computational power of circuits is multilinearity. This restriction has been extensively investigated in the commutative setting. A polynomial is multilinear, if every variable has individual degree at most one in it. Syntactically multilinear circuits are those in which every product gate multiplies gates with disjoint sets of variables. This model was first considered in [22], where lower bounds on constant depth multilinear circuits were proved (and later improved in [26]). In a breakthrough paper, Raz [25] proved super-polynomial lower bounds on multilinear formula size for the permanent and determinant. These techniques were extended by [27] to give a lower bound of about $n^{4/3}$ for the size multilinear *circuits*.

An interesting observation about non-commutative circuits is that if they compute a polynomial of a specific form, they are without loss of generality multilinear. Let us call a non-commutative polynomial f *ordered*, if the variables of f are divided into disjoint sets $X_1, \dots, X_d$ and every monomial in f has the form $x_1 \cdots x_d$ with $x_i \in X_i$. The non-commutative permanent, as defined above, is thus ordered. An *ordered circuit* is a natural model for computing ordered polynomials. Roughly, we require every gate to take variables from the sets X_i in the same interval $I \subset [d]$. One property of ordered circuits is that they are automatically syntactically multilinear.

We show that any non-commutative circuit computing an ordered polynomial can be efficiently transformed to an ordered circuit, hence a multilinear one, computing the same polynomial. Such a reduction is not known in the commutative case, and gives hope that a progress on multilinear lower bounds for permanent or determinant will yield general non-commutative lower bounds.

THEOREM 1.11. *Let f be an ordered polynomial of degree d. If f is computed by a non-commutative circuit of size s, it can be computed by an ordered circuit of size $O(d^3 s)$.*

Again, we fall short of utilizing this connection for general lower bounds. By a simple argument, we manage to prove an exponential lower bound on non-commutative multilinear circuits, as we state in the next theorem. However, the polynomial AP_k in question is not ordered, and we cannot invoke the previous result to obtain an unconditional lower bound. (Theorem 1.12 is proved in Section 6).

THEOREM 1.12. *Let*

$$\mathsf{AP}_k = \sum_{\sigma} x_{\sigma(1)} x_{\sigma(2)} \cdots x_{\sigma(k)},$$

where σ is a permutation of $[k]$. Then every non-commutative multilinear circuit computing AP_k is of size at least $2^{\Omega(k)}$.

1.5 A different perspective: lower bounds using rank

An extremely appealing way to obtain lower bounds is by using sub-additive measures, and matrix rank is perhaps the favorite measure across many computational models. It is abundant in communication complexity, and in circuit complexity it has also found its applications. Often, one cannot hope to find a unique matrix whose rank would capture the complexity of the investigated function. Instead, we can associate the function with a family of matrices, and the complexity of the function is related to the *minimum* rank of matrices in that family. Typically, the family consists of matrices which are in some sense "close" to some fixed matrix.

For arithmetic circuits, many of the known structure theorems [8, 21, 25, 9] invite a natural rank interpretation. This interpretation, however, has lead to lower bounds only for restricted circuits. We sketch below the rank problem which arises in the case of commutative circuits, and explain why it is considerably simpler in the case of non-commutative ones.

Let f be a commutative polynomial of degree d. Consider $N \times N$ matrices whose entries are elements of some field, andÊ rows and columns are labelled by monomials of degree roughly $d/2$. Hence N is in general exponential in the degree of f. Associate with f a family $\mathcal{M}$ of all $N \times N$ matrices M with the following property: for every monomial α of degree d, the sum of all entries M_{β_1,β_2}, such that $\beta_1\beta_2 = \alpha$, is equal to the coefficient of α in f. In other words, we partition M into subsets T_α corresponding to the possible ways to write α as a product of two monomials, and we impose a condition on the sum of entries in every T_α. It can be shown that the circuit complexity of f can be lower bounded by the minimal rank of the matrices in $\mathcal{M}$.

Note that the sets T_α are of size exponential in d, the degree of f. The structure of the sets is not friendly either. Our first structure theorem for non-commutative circuits, which decomposes non-commutative polynomials to central polynomials, translates to a similar rank problem. However, the matrices $M \in \mathcal{M}$ will be partitioned into sets of size only d (instead of exponential in d). This is thanks to the fact that there are much fewer options to express a non-commutative monomial as a product of other monomials. Our second structure theorem, concerning block-central polynomials, gives a partition into sets of size at most two. The structure of these sets is quite simple too. However, not simple enough to allow us to prove a rank lower bound. In the rank formulation of circuit lower bounds, we can therefore see non-commutative circuits as a first step towards understanding commutative circuit lower bounds.

2. OVERVIEW OF PROOFS

We now outline proofs of the main theorems of the paper. Theorems 1.4 - 1.8 will be proved in Sections 3 - 5, and Theorem 1.12 in Section 6. Proofs of the rest of the theorems are omitted due to space restrictions.

2.1 Conditional lower bounds on non-commutative circuit size

In this section we describe the path that leads from non-commutative circuit complexity to bilinear complexity.

Preliminaries.

Let $\mathbb{F}$ be a field. A *non-commutative polynomial* is a formal sum of products of variables and field elements. We assume that the variables do not multiplicatively commute, that is, $xy \neq yx$ whenever $x \neq y$. However, the variables commute with elements of $\mathbb{F}$. The reader can imagine the variables as representing square matrices.

A *non-commutative arithmetic circuit* Φ is a directed acyclic graph as follows. Nodes (or gates) of in-degree zero are labelled by either a variable or a field element in $\mathbb{F}$. All the other nodes have in-degree two and they are labelled by either + or $\times$. The two edges going into a gate v labelled by $\times$ are labelled by *left* and *right*. We denote by $v = v_1 \times v_2$ the fact that (v_1, v) is the left edge going into v, and (v_2, v) is the right edge going into v. (This is to determine the order of multiplication.) The *size* of a circuit Φ is the number of edges in Φ. The integer $\mathcal{C}(f)$ is the size of a smallest circuit computing f.

Note. Unless stated otherwise, we refer to non-commutative polynomials as polynomials, and to non-commutative circuits as circuits.

The proof is presented in three parts, which are an exploration of the structure of non-commutative circuits.

Part I: structure of circuits.

The starting point is the structure of polynomials computed by non-commutative circuits, which we now explain. The methods we use are elementary, and are an adaptation of works like [8, 9] to the non-commutative world.

We start by defining the 'building blocks' of polynomials, which we call central polynomials. A homogeneous[7] polynomial f of degree d is called *central*, if there exist integers m and d_0, d_1, d_2 satisfying $d/3 \le d_0 < 2d/3$ and $d_0+d_1+d_2 = d$ so that

$$f = \sum_{i \in [m]} h_i g \bar{h}_i, \tag{7}$$

where

(*i*). the polynomial g, which we call the *body*, is homogeneous of degree $\deg g = d_0$,

(*ii*). for every $i \in [m]$, the polynomials $h_i, \bar{h}_i$ are homogeneous of degrees $\deg h_i = d_1$ and $\deg \bar{h}_i = d_2$.

The *width* of a homogeneous polynomial f of degree d, denoted $w(f)$, is the smallest integer n so that f can be written as

$$f = f_1 + f_2 + \cdots f_n, \tag{8}$$

with each f_i a central polynomial. In Section 3.1 we show that the width of f is at most $O(d^3 \mathcal{C}(f))$, and so lower bounds on width imply lower bounds on circuit complexity. We prove this by induction on the circuit complexity of f.

Part II: degree-four.

In the first part, we argued that a lower bound on width implies a lower bound on circuit complexity. In the case of degree-four, a central polynomial has a very simple structure: d_0 is always 2, and so the body must reside in one of three places: left (when $d_1 = 0$), center (when $d_1 = 1$), and right (when $d_1 = 2$). For a polynomial of degree four, we can thus write (8) with n at most order $\mathcal{C}(f)$, and each f_i of this special form.

This observation allows us to relate width and bilinear complexity, as the following proposition shows. For a more general statement, see Proposition 4.1, which also shows that the width and bilinear complexity are in fact equivalent.

[7]Recall that a polynomial f is *homogeneous*, if all monomials with a non-zero coefficient in f have the same degree, and that circuit Φ is homogeneous, if every gate in Φ computes a homogeneous polynomial.

PROPOSITION 2.1. $w(\mathsf{ID}_k) \ge \mathcal{B}(\mathsf{SOS}_k)$.

Part I and Proposition 2.1 already imply Theorem 1.6, which states that a lower bound on bilinear complexity implies a lower bound on circuit complexity of ID_k.

Part III: general degree to degree-four.

The argument presented in the second step can imply at most a quadratic lower bound on circuit size. To get exponential lower bounds, we need to consider polynomials of higher degrees. We think of the degree of a degree-$4r$ polynomial as divided into 4 groups, for which we try to mimic the special structure from part II: A *block-central* polynomial is a central polynomial so that $d_0 = 2r$ and $d_1 \in \{0, r, 2r\}$. The structure of block-central polynomials is similar to the structure of degree-four central polynomials in that the body is of fixed degree and it has three places it can reside in: left (when $d_1 = 0$), center (when $d_1 = r$), and right (when $d_1 = 2r$). In Section 5 we show that a degree-$4r$ polynomial f can be written as a sum of at most $O(r^3 2^r \mathcal{C}(f))$ block-central polynomials.

We thus reduced the analysis of degree-$4r$ polynomials to the analysis of degree-four polynomial. This reduction comes with a price, a loss of a factor of 2^r. We note that this loss is necessary. The proof is a rather technical case distinction. The idea behind it is a combinatorial property of intervals in the set $[4r]$, which allows us to transform a central polynomial to a sum of 2^r block-central polynomials.

Here is an example of this reduction in the case of the identity polynomial. The *lifted identity polynomial*, LID_r, is the polynomial in variables z_0, z_1 of degree $4r$ defined by

$$\mathsf{LID}_r = \sum_{e \in \{0,1\}^{2r}} z_e z_e \,,$$

where for $e = (e_1, \ldots, e_{2r}) \in \{0,1\}^{2r}$, define $z_e = \prod_{i=1}^{2r} z_{e_i}$. The lifted identity polynomial is the high-degree counterpart of the identity polynomial, which allows us to prove that a super-linear lower bound implies an exponential one (the corollary is proved in Section 5):

COROLLARY 2.2. *If $\mathcal{B}(\mathsf{SOS}_k) \ge \Omega(k^{1+\epsilon})$ for some $\epsilon > 0$, then $\mathcal{C}(\mathsf{LID}_r) \ge 2^{\Omega(r)}$.*

To complete the picture, we show that LID_r is reducible to the permanent of dimension $4r$.

LEMMA 2.3. *There exists a matrix M of dimension $4r \times 4r$ whose nonzero entries are variables z_0, z_1 so that the permanent of M is LID_r.*

To prove the lemma, the matrix M is constructed explicitly, see Section 5. The conditional lower bound on the permanent, Theorem 1.7, follows from Corollary 2.2 and Lemma 2.3.

An important property that non-commutative permanent shares with its commutative counterpart is completeness for the class of explicit polynomials. This enables us to argue that a super-linear lower bound on the bilinear complexity of an explicit degree-four polynomial implies an exponential lower bound on permanent. In the commutative setting, this a consequence of the VNP completeness of permanent, as given in [31]. In the non-commutative setting, one can prove a similar result [10].

2.2 Lower bounds on sum-of-squares complexity in restricted cases

We now discuss the lower bounds for restricted sum-of-squares problems we prove: an explicit lower bound over $\mathbb{R}$ and a lower bound for SOS_k over integers.

We phrase the problem of lower bounding $\mathcal{S}_{\mathbb{R}}(g)$ in terms of matrices of real vectors. Let $V = \{\mathbf{v}_{i,j} : i, j \in [k]\}$ be a $k \times k$ matrix whose entries are vectors in $\mathbb{R}^n$. We call V a *vector matrix*, and n is called the *height* of V. The matrix V defines a biquadratic polynomial $f(V)$ in $X = \{x_1, \ldots, x_k\}$ and $Y = \{y_1, \ldots, y_k\}$ by

$$f(V) = \sum_{i_1 \leq i_2, j_1 \leq j_2} a_{i_1,i_2,j_1,j_2} x_{i_1} x_{i_2} y_{j_1} y_{j_2},$$

where a_{i_1,i_2,j_1,j_2} is equal to $\mathbf{v}_{i_1,j_1} \cdot \mathbf{v}_{i_2,j_2} + \mathbf{v}_{i_1,j_2} \cdot \mathbf{v}_{i_2,j_1}$, up to a small correction factor which is not important at this point. We can think of the coefficients as given by the permanent of the 2×2 sub-matrix[8] of V defined by i_1, i_2 and j_1, j_2.

The following lemma gives the connection between sum-of-squares complexity and vector matrices.

LEMMA 2.4. *Let g be a biquadratic polynomial. Then $\mathcal{S}_{\mathbb{R}}(g) \leq n$ is equivalent to the existence a vector matrix V of height n so that $g = f(V)$.*

As long as it is finite, the height of a vector matrix for any polynomial does not exceed k^2, and a counting argument shows that this holds for "almost" all polynomials. The problem is to construct explicit polynomials that require large height. Even a super-linear lower bound seems nontrivial, since the permanent condition does not talk about inner products of pairs of vectors, but rather about the sum of inner products of two such pairs. We manage to construct an explicit polynomial which requires near-maximal height $\Omega(k^2)$. In our proof, the coefficients impose (through the 2×2 permanent conditions) either equality or orthognality constraints on the vectors in the matrix, and eventually the existence of many pairwise orthogonal ones. In a crucial way, we employ the fact that over $\mathbb{R}$, if two unit vectors have inner product one, they must be equal. This property[9] fails over $\mathbb{C}$, but it is still possible that even over $\mathbb{C}$ our construction has similar height (of course, if this turns out to be even $k^{1+\epsilon}$, we get an exponential lower bound for non-commutative circuits).

The construction, however, does not shed light on the classical sum-of-squares problem which is concerned specifically with the polynomial SOS_k. In the case of SOS_k, the conditions on the matrix V from Lemma 2.4 are especially nice and simple: (1) all vectors in V are unit vectors, (2) in each row and column the vectors are pairwise orthogonal, and (3) every 2×2 permanent (of inner products) must be zero.

As mentioned in the introduction, the best upper bounds for the sum-of-squares problem have *integer* coefficients, and so a lot of effort was invested into proving lower bounds in the integer case. Despite that, previously known lower bounds do not even reach $2k$. We prove the first super-linear lower bound, $\mathcal{S}_{\mathbb{Z}}(k) = \Omega(k^{6/5})$. Over integers, we take advantage of the fact that the unit vectors in V must have entries in $\{-1, 0, 1\}$ and there is exactly one nonzero entry in each vector. The nonzero coordinate can be thus thought of as a "color" in $[n]$, which is signed by plus or minus. This gives rise to the earlier studied notion of *intercalate matrices* (see, [33] and the book [28]). The integer sum-of-squares problem can thus be phrased in terms of minimizing the number of colors in a signed intercalate matrix, which can be approached as an elementary combinatorial problem.

Our strategy for proving the integer lower bound has three parts. The first step uses a simple counting argument to show that there must exist a sub-matrix in which one color appears in every row and every column. In the second step we show that the permanent conditions give rise to a "forbidden configuration" in such sub-matrices. In the last step we conclude that any matrix without this forbidden configuration must have many colors.

[8] In some cases, e.g., when $i_1 = i_2$, this matrix can become 1×2, 2×1 or even 1×1, but we still think of it as a 2×2 matrix. This is also where the correction factor comes from.

[9] Here, the inner product of two complex vectors a, b is $\sum_i a_i b_i$, rather than $\sum_i a_i \bar{b}_i$, with $\bar{b}$ the complex conjugate of b.

3. NON-COMMUTATIVE CIRCUITS

We use the following notation. For a node v in a circuit Φ, we denote by Φ_v the sub-circuit of Φ rooted at v. Every node v computes a polynomial $\widehat{\Phi}_v$ in the obvious way. A *monomial* α is a product of variables, and $\mathsf{COEF}_\alpha(f)$ is the coefficient of α in the polynomial f. Denote by $\deg f$ the degree of f, and if v is a node in a circuit Φ, denote by $\deg v$ the degree of $\widehat{\Phi}_v$.

3.1 Structure of non-commutative circuits

In this section we describe the structure of the polynomials computed by non-commutative circuits. The methods we use are elementary, and are an adaptation of works like [8, 9] to the non-commutative world.

We start by defining the 'building blocks' of polynomials, which we call central polynomials. Recall that a polynomial f is *homogeneous*, if all monomials with a non-zero coefficient in f have the same degree, and that circuit Φ is homogeneous, if every gate in Φ computes a homogeneous polynomial. A homogeneous polynomial f of degree d is called *central*, if there exist integers m and d_0, d_1, d_2 satisfying

$$d/3 \leq d_0 < 2d/3 \quad \text{and} \quad d_0 + d_1 + d_2 = d$$

so that

$$f = \sum_{i \in [m]} h_i g \bar{h}_i, \tag{9}$$

where

(i). the polynomial g is homogeneous of degree $\deg g = d_0$,

(ii). for every $i \in [m]$, the polynomials $h_i, \bar{h}_i$ are homogeneous of degrees $\deg h_i = d_1$ and $\deg \bar{h}_i = d_2$.

REMARK 3.1. *In the definition of central polynomial, no assumption on the size of m is made. Hence we can without loss of generality assume that $h_i = c_i \alpha_i$ and $\bar{h}_i = \beta_i$, where α_i is a monomial of degree d_1, β_i is a monomial of degree d_2, and c_i is a field element.*

The *width* of a homogeneous polynomial f of degree d, denoted $w(f)$, is the smallest integer n so that f can be written as

$$f = f_1 + f_2 + \cdots + f_n,$$

where $f_1, \dots, f_n$ are central polynomials of degree d. The following proposition shows that the width of a polynomial is a lower bound for its circuit complexity. We will later relate width and bilinear complexity.

PROPOSITION 3.2. *Let f be a homogeneous polynomial of degree $d \geq 2$. Then*

$$\mathcal{C}(f) \geq \Omega(d^{-3} w(f)).$$

PROOF. We start by observing that the standard homogenization of commutative circuits [30, 3] works also for non-commutative circuits.

LEMMA 3.3. *Let g be a homogeneous polynomial of degree d. Then there exists a homogeneous circuit of size $O(d^2\mathcal{C}(f))$ computing g.*

Assume that we have a homogeneous circuit Φ of size s computing f. We will show that $w(f) \leq ds$. By Lemma 3.3, this implies that $w(f) \leq O(d^3\mathcal{C}(f))$, which completes the proof. Without loss of generality, we can also assume that no gate v in Φ computes the zero polynomial (gates that compute the zero polynomial can be removed, decreasing the circuit size).

For a multiset of pairs of polynomials $\mathcal{H} = \{\langle h_i, \overline{h}_i\rangle : i \in [m]\}$, define

$$g \times \mathcal{H} = \sum_{i \in [m]} h_i g \overline{h}_i .$$

Let $\mathcal{G} = \{g_1, \dots, g_t\}$ be the set of homogeneous polynomials g of degree $d/3 \leq \deg g < 2d/3$ so that there exists a gate in Φ computing g. We show that for every gate v in Φ so that $\deg v \geq d/3$ there exist multisets of pairs of homogeneous polynomials $\mathcal{H}_1(v), \dots, \mathcal{H}_t(v)$ satisfying

$$\widehat{\Phi}_v = \sum_{i \in [t]} g_i \times \mathcal{H}_i(v). \tag{10}$$

We prove (10) by induction on the depth of Φ_v. If $\deg(v) < 2d/3$ then $\widehat{\Phi}_v = g_i \in \mathcal{G}$ for some $i \in [t]$. Thus (10) is true, setting $\mathcal{H}_i(v) = \{\langle 1, 1\rangle\}$ and $\mathcal{H}_j(v) = \{\langle 0, 0\rangle\}$ for $j \neq i$ in $[t]$. Otherwise, we have $\deg v \geq 2d/3$. When $v = v_1 + v_2$, we do the following. Since Φ is homogeneous, v_1, v_2 and v have the same degree which is at least $2d/3$. Induction thus implies: for every $e \in \{1, 2\}$,

$$\widehat{\Phi}_{v_e} = \sum_{i \in [t]} g_i \times \mathcal{H}_i(v_e).$$

This gives

$$\widehat{\Phi}_v = \widehat{\Phi}_{v_1} + \widehat{\Phi}_{v_2} = \sum_{i \in [t]} g_i \times \big(\mathcal{H}_i(v_1) \cup \mathcal{H}_i(v_2)\big).$$

When $v = v_1 \times v_2$, we have $\deg v = \deg v_1 + \deg v_2$. Since $\deg v \geq 2d/3$, either (a) $\deg v_1 \geq d/3$ or (b) $\deg v_2 \geq d/3$. In the case (a), by induction,

$$\widehat{\Phi}_{v_1} = \sum_{i \in [t]} g_i \times \mathcal{H}_i(v_1) .$$

Defining $\mathcal{H}_i(v) = \{\langle h, \overline{h}\widehat{\Phi}_{v_2}\rangle \ : \ \langle h, \overline{h}\rangle \in \mathcal{H}_i(v_1)\}$, we obtain

$$\widehat{\Phi}_v = \widehat{\Phi}_{v_1}\widehat{\Phi}_{v_2} = \Big(\sum_{i \in [t]} g_i \times \mathcal{H}_i(v_1)\Big)\widehat{\Phi}_{v_2} = \sum_{i \in [t]} g_i \times \mathcal{H}_i(v).$$

Since $\widehat{\Phi}_{v_2}$ is a homogeneous polynomial, $\mathcal{H}_i(v)$ consists of pairs of homogeneous polynomials. In case (b), let $\mathcal{H}_i(v) = \{\langle \widehat{\Phi}_{v_1} h, \overline{h}\rangle \ : \ \langle h, \overline{h}\rangle \in \mathcal{H}_i(v_2)\}$.

Applying (10) to the output gate of Φ, we obtain

$$f = \sum_{i \in [t]} g_i \times \mathcal{H}_i ,$$

where $\mathcal{H}_i$ are multisets of pairs of homogeneous polynomials. For every $i \in [t]$ and every $r \leq d - \deg g_i$, define $\mathcal{H}_i^r = \{\langle h, \overline{h}\rangle \in \mathcal{H}_i \ : \ \deg(h) = r, \ \deg \overline{h} = d - \deg g_i - r\}$. Then $g_i \times \mathcal{H}_i^r$ is a central polynomial. Moreover, since f is homogeneous of degree d, we obtain

$$f = \sum_{i \in [t]} \sum_{r=0}^{d - \deg g_i} g_i \times \mathcal{H}_i^r .$$

Since $t \leq s$, the proof is complete. □

3.2 Degree four polynomials

Before we describe the specific structure of degree four polynomials, let us give a general definition. Let $X_1, \dots, X_r$ be (not necessarily disjoint) sets of variables. For a polynomial f, let $f[X_1, \dots, X_r]$ be the homogeneous polynomial of degree r so that for every monomial α, we have: i) $\mathsf{COEF}_\alpha(f[X_1, \dots, X_r]) = \mathsf{COEF}_\alpha(f)$, if $\alpha = x_1 x_2 \cdots x_r$ with $x_i \in X_i$ for every $i \in [r]$, and ii) $\mathsf{COEF}_\alpha(f[X_1, \dots, X_r]) = 0$, otherwise.

We easily obtain the following refinement of structure of degree-four polynomials:

LEMMA 3.4. *If $f = f[X_1, X_2, X_3, X_4]$, then $w(f)$ is the smallest n so that f can be written as $f = f_1 + \cdots + f_n$, where for every $t \in [n]$, either*

(a) $f_t = g_t[X_1, X_2] h_t[X_3, X_4]$, or

(b) $f_t = \sum_{i \in [m]} h_{t,i}[X_1] g_t[X_2, X_3] \overline{h}_{t,i}[X_4]$,

where $g_t, h_t, h_{t,i}, \overline{h}_{t,i}$ are some polynomials.

4. DEGREE FOUR AND BILINEAR COMPLEXITY

We consider polynomials of a certain structure. Let f be a polynomial in variables $X, Y = \{x_1, \dots, x_k\}, \{y_1, \dots, y_k\}$ so that $f = f[X, Y, X, Y]$, i.e.,

$$f = \sum_{i_1, j_1, i_2, j_2 \in [k]} a_{i_1, j_1, i_2, j_2} x_{i_1} y_{j_1} x_{i_2} y_{j_2} . \tag{11}$$

For a non-commutative polynomial g, we define $g^{(c)}$ to be the polynomial g understood as a commutative polynomial. For example, if $g = xy + yx$, then $g^{(c)} = 2xy$.

In particular, if f is of the form (11), the polynomial $f^{(c)}$ is biquadratic. In the following proposition, we relate the width of a polynomial f and $\mathcal{B}(f^{(c)})$.

PROPOSITION 4.1. *Let f be a homogeneous polynomial of degree four of the form (11). Then $\mathcal{B}(f^{(c)}) \leq w(f)$.*

PROOF. Using Lemma 3.4, we can write $f = f_1 + \cdots + f_n$, where for every $t \in [n]$, either

(a) $f_t = g_t[X, Y] h_t[X, Y]$, or

(b) $f_t = \sum_{i \in [m]} h_{t,i}[X] g_t[Y, X] \overline{h}_{t,i}[Y]$.

The commutative polynomial $f_t^{(c)}$ is a product of two bilinear forms in X and Y: in case (a), of $g_t[X,Y]^{(c)}$ and $h_t[X,Y]^{(c)}$, in case (b), of $g_t[Y,X]^{(c)}$ and $\sum_i h_{t,i}[X]\overline{h}_{t,i}[Y]$. Altogether $f^{(c)} = f_1^{(c)} + \cdots + f_n^{(c)}$, where each $f_t^{(c)}$ is a product of two bilinear forms, and hence $\mathcal{B}(f^{(c)}) \leq n$. $\square$

PROOF OF THEOREM 1.6.. Recall the definition of the identity polynomial,

$$\mathsf{ID}_k = \sum_{i,j\in[k]} x_i y_j x_i y_j .$$

The commutative polynomial $\mathsf{ID}_k^{(c)}$ is the polynomial SOS_k

$$\mathsf{SOS}_k = \sum_{i\in[k]} x_i^2 \sum_{j\in[k]} y_j^2 .$$

The theorem follows from Proposition 3.2 and 4.1. $\square$

Let us note that it is not necessary to separate variables in ID_k into two disjoint sets X and Y. In the non-commutative setting, this is just a cosmetic detail:

REMARK 4.2. $w(\mathsf{ID}_k) = w(\sum_{i,j\in[k]} x_i x_j x_i x_j)$.

5. HIGHER DEGREES

In this section, we show that a sufficiently strong lower bound on the width of a degree four polynomial implies an exponential lower bound on the width, and hence circuit size, of a related high degree polynomial.

Let f be a homogeneous polynomial of degree $4r$. We assume that f contains only two variables z_0 and z_1. We define $f^{(\lambda)}$ to be the polynomial obtained by replacing degree r monomials in f by new variables. Formally, for every monomial α of degree r in variables z_0, z_1, introduce a new variable x_α. The polynomial $f^{(\lambda)}$ is defined as the homogeneous degree four polynomial in the 2^r variables $X = \{x_\alpha : \deg \alpha = r\}$ satisfying

$$\mathsf{COEF}_{x_{\alpha_1} x_{\alpha_2} x_{\alpha_3} x_{\alpha_4}}(f^{(\lambda)}) = \mathsf{COEF}_{\alpha_1\alpha_2\alpha_3\alpha_4}(f). \quad (12)$$

REMARK 5.1. *Let g be a homogeneous degree four polynomial in k variables. If $k \leq 2^r$, then there exists a polynomial f of degree $4r$ in variables z_0, z_1 such that $g = f^{(\lambda)}$ (up to a renaming of variables).*

We now relate $w(f)$ and $w(f^{(\lambda)})$. To do so, we need a modified version of Proposition 3.2. Let f be a homogeneous polynomial of degree $4r$. We say that f is *block-central*, if either

I. $f = gh$, where g, h are homogeneous polynomials with $\deg g = \deg h = 2r$, or

II. $f = \sum_{i\in[m]} h_i g \overline{h}_i$, where $g, h_i, \overline{h}_i$ are homogeneous polynomials of degrees $\deg g = 2r$ and $\deg h_i, \deg \overline{h}_i = r$ for every $i \in [m]$.

Every block-central polynomial is also central. The following lemma shows that every central polynomial can be written as a sum of 2^r block-central polynomials. The lemma thus enables us to consider a simpler problem, i.e., lower bounding the width with respect to block-central polynomials. However, this simplification comes with a price, namely, a loss of a factor of 2^r.

LEMMA 5.2. *Let f be a central polynomial of degree $4r$ in two variables z_0, z_1. Then there exist $n \leq 2^r$ and block-central polynomials $f_1, \ldots, f_n$ so that $f = f_1 + \cdots + f_n$.*

PROOF. The proof is by a rather long case distinction, and we omit it. $\square$

We can now relate the width of f and $f^{(\lambda)}$.

PROPOSITION 5.3. *Let f be a homogeneous polynomial of degree $4r$ in the variables z_0, z_1. Then $w(f) \geq 2^{-r} w(f^{(\lambda)})$.*

PROOF. Assume $w(f) = n$. Lemma 5.2 implies $f = f_1 + \cdots + f_{n'}$, where $n' \leq 2^r n$ and f_j are block-central polynomials. Equation (12) implies

$$f^{(\lambda)} = f_1^{(\lambda)} + \cdots + f_{n'}^{(\lambda)} .$$

It is thus sufficient to show that every $f_t^{(\lambda)}$ is a central polynomial, for then $w(f^{(\lambda)}) \leq n' \leq 2^r n$.

In order to do so, let us extend the definition of $(.)^{(\lambda)}$ as follows. If g is a polynomial of degree ℓr in the variables z_0, z_1, let $g^{(\lambda)}$ be the homogeneous polynomial of degree ℓ in X so that

$$\mathsf{COEF}_{x_{\alpha_1}\cdots x_{\alpha_k}}(g^{(\lambda)}) = \mathsf{COEF}_{\alpha_1\cdots\alpha_k}(g).$$

If g, h are homogeneous polynomials whose degree is divisible by r, we obtain $(gh)^{(\lambda)} = g^{(\lambda)} h^{(\lambda)}$. Hence if $f_t = g_t h_t$ a block-centralpolynomial of type I, then $f_t^{(\lambda)} = g_t^{(\lambda)} h_t^{(\lambda)}$ is a central polynomial of type (a) according to Lemma 3.4 with $X = X_1 = X_2 = X_3 = X_4$. If $f_t = \sum_i h_{t,i} g_t \overline{h}_{t,i}$ is a block-centralpolynomial of type II, $f_t^{(\lambda)} = \sum_i h_{t,i}^{(\lambda)} g_t^{(\lambda)} \overline{h}_{t,i}{}^{(\lambda)}$, and hence $f_t^{(\lambda)}$ is a centralpolynomial of type (b) according to Lemma 3.4. $\square$

By Remark 5.1, we can start with a degree four polynomial in $k \leq 2^r$ variables and "lift" it to a polynomial f of degree $4r$ such that $f^{(\lambda)} = g$. We can then deduce that a sufficiently strong lower bound on the bilinear complexity of g implies an exponential lower bound for the circuit complexity of f. We apply this to the specific case of the identity polynomial. The *lifted identity polynomial*, LID_r, is the polynomial in variables z_0, z_1 of degree $4r$ defined by

$$\mathsf{LID}_r = \sum_{e\in\{0,1\}^{2r}} z_e z_e ,$$

where for $e = (e_1, \ldots, e_s) \in \{0,1\}^s$, we define $z_e = \prod_{i=1}^s z_{e_i}$.

COROLLARY 5.4 (COROLLARY 2.2 RESTATED). *If $\mathcal{B}(\mathsf{SOS}_k) \geq \Omega(k^{1+\epsilon})$ for some $\epsilon > 0$, then $\mathcal{C}(\mathsf{LID}_r) \geq 2^{\Omega(r)}$.*

PROOF. The definition of LID_r can be equivalently written as

$$\mathsf{LID}_r = \sum_{e_1,e_2\in\{0,1\}^r} z_{e_1} z_{e_2} z_{e_1} z_{e_2} .$$

By definition, $\mathsf{LID}_r^{(\lambda)} = \sum_{i,j\in[k]} x_i x_j x_i x_j$ with $k = 2^r$. Thus, by Remark 4.2, $w(\mathsf{LID}_r^{(\lambda)}) = w(\mathsf{ID}_k)$. By Proposition 5.3, $w(\mathsf{LID}_r) \geq 2^{-r} w(\mathsf{LID}_r^{(\lambda)})$. Hence $w(\mathsf{LID}_r) \geq 2^{-r} w(\mathsf{ID}_k)$. By Proposition 4.1, $w(\mathsf{ID}_k) \geq \mathcal{B}(\mathsf{ID}_k)$. If $\mathcal{B}(\mathsf{ID}_k) \geq ck^{1+\epsilon}$ for some constants $c, \epsilon > 0$, we have $w(\mathsf{LID}_r) \geq c2^{-r}2^{r(1+\epsilon)} = c2^{\epsilon r}$. By Proposition 3.2, $\mathcal{C}(\mathsf{LID}_r) \geq \Omega(r^{-3}2^{\epsilon r}) = 2^{\Omega(r)}$. $\square$

One motivation for studying the lifted identity polynomial is that we believe it is hard for non-commutative circuits. However, note that an apparently similar polynomial has small circuit size. For $e = (e_1, \ldots, e_s) \in \{0,1\}^s$, let $e^\star = (e_s, \ldots, e_1)$. The polynomial

$$\sum_{e \in \{0,1\}^{2r}} z_e z_{e^\star} ,$$

has a non-commutative circuit of linear size. This result can be found in [21], where it is also shown that the non-commutative formula complexity of this polynomial is exponential in r.

We now show that LID_r is reducible to the permanent of dimension $4r$.

LEMMA 5.5 (LEMMA 2.3 RESTATED). *There is a matrix M of dimension $4r \times 4r$ whose nonzero entries are variables z_0, z_1 so that the permanent of M is LID_r.*

PROOF. For $j \in \{0,1\}$, let D_j be the $2r \times 2r$ matrix with z_j on the diagonal and zero everywhere else. The matrix M is defined as

$$M = \begin{bmatrix} D_0 & D_1 \\ D_1 & D_0 \end{bmatrix}.$$

The permanent of M taken row by row is

$$\mathsf{PERM}(M) = \sum_\sigma M_{1,\sigma(1)} M_{2,\sigma(2)} \cdots M_{4r,\sigma(4r)},$$

where σ is a permutation of $[4r]$. The permutations that give nonzero value in $\mathsf{PERM}(M)$ satisfy: for every $i \in [2r]$, if $\sigma(i) = i$ then $\sigma(2r+i) = 2r+i$, and if $\sigma(i) = 2r+i$ then $\sigma(2r+i) = i$. By definition of M, this means that for every such σ and $i \in [2r]$, $M_{i,\sigma(i)} = M_{i+2r,\sigma(i+2r)}$. Moreover, given the values of such a σ on $[2r]$, it can be uniquely extended to all of $[4r]$. □

Theorem 1.7 follows from Corollary 2.2 and Lemma 2.3.

5.1 Explicit polynomials and completeness of non-commutative permanent

We now turn to Theorem 1.8. Let $\{f_k\}$ be an infinite family of non-commutative polynomials over $\mathbb{F}$ so that every f_k has at most $p(k)$ variables and degree at most $p(k)$, where $p : \mathbb{N} \to \mathbb{N}$ is a polynomial. We call $\{f_k\}$ *explicit*, if there exists a polynomial time algorithm which, given k and a monomial α is input, computes $\mathsf{COEF}_\alpha(f_k)$. Hence PERM_k and other families of polynomials are explicit in this sense. In the commutative setting, the following theorem is a consequence of the VNP completeness of permanent, as given in [31]. In the non-commutative setting, one can prove a similar result:

THEOREM 5.6. ([10]) *Assume that $\{f_k\}$ is an explicit family of non-commutative polynomials such that $C(f_k) \geq 2^{\Omega(k)}$. Then $C(\mathrm{PERM}_k) \geq 2^{\Omega(k)}$.*

PROOF OF THEOREM 1.8. For a commutative biquadratic polynomial in k variables

$$f = \sum_{i_1,j_1,i_2,j_2 \in [k]} a_{i_1,j_1,i_2,j_2} x_{i_1} y_{j_1} x_{i_2} y_{j_2} ,$$

define f' as the non-commutative polynomial

$$f' = \sum_{i_1,j_1,i_2,j_2 \in [k]} a_{i_1,j_1,i_2,j_2} x_{i_1} y_{j_1} x_{i_2} y_{j_2} .$$

This is to guarantee that $f' = f'[X,Y,X,Y]$ and $(f')^{(c)} = f$ is as required in Proposition 4.1. Let r be the smallest integer so that $2^r \geq 2k$. Let $f^\star$ be the polynomial given by Remark 5.1 so that $(f^\star)^{(\lambda)} = f'$. If f is explicit, $f^\star$ is explicit.

Let $\{f_k\}$ be as in the assumption. As in the proof of Corollary 5.4, we conclude that $f_k^\star$ require exponential size non-commutative circuits. By Theorem 5.6, this implies an exponential lower bound for permanent. □

6. MULTILINEAR CIRCUITS

In this section we prove an exponential lower bound on the size of non-commutative syntactically multilinear circuits (a circuit Φ is *syntactically multilinear*, if for every product gate $v = v_1 \times v_2$ in Φ, the two circuits Φ_{v_1} and Φ_{v_2} do not share variables). Note that an ordered circuit is automatically syntactically multilinear. By means of Theorem 1.11, a lower bound on syntactically multilinear circuits computing an ordered polynomial would imply an unconditional lower bound. However, our lower bound involves a polynomial which is *not* ordered.

We now define the multilinear version of central polynomials. Let f be a multilinear polynomial of degree d. We say that f is *ml-central*, if f is central as in (9), and for every $i \in [m]$, the polynomial $h_i g \overline{h}_i$ is multilinear; in particular, the polynomials $h_i, g, \overline{h}_i$ have distinct variables.

The following lemma describes the structure of multilinear circuits.

LEMMA 6.1. *Let f be a homogeneous multilinear polynomial of degree $d \geq 2$. Assume that there is a syntactically multilinear circuit Φ of size s computing f. Then there exist $n \leq O(d^3 s)$ and ml-central polynomials $f_1, \ldots, f_n$ such that $f = f_1 + \cdots + f_n$.*

PROOF. Almost identical to Proposition 3.2. □

Our lower bound is based on counting monomials. The following lemma is the basic observation for the lower bound.

LEMMA 6.2. *Let f be a ml-central polynomial of degree k in k variables. Then f has at most $2^{-\Omega(k)} k!$ monomials with nonzero coefficients.*

PROOF. Write f as $f = \sum_{i \in [m]} h_i g \overline{h}_i$ with every $h_i g \overline{h}_i$ multilinear. Let X be the set of variables in f and X_0 the set of variables in g. Every monomial with a nonzero coefficient in f has the form $\alpha_1 \gamma \alpha_2$, where (1) γ is a multilinear monomial of degree d_0 in variables X_0, and (2) α_1, α_2 are multilinear monomials in the variables $X \setminus X_0$ of degrees d_1, d_2, and α_1, α_2 have distinct variables. Since $d_0 + d_1 + d_2 = k$, we have $|X_0| = d_0$. There are thus $d_0!$ βs in (1), and at most $(d_1 + d_2)!$ pairs α_1, α_2 in (2). Hence f contains at most

$$d_0!(d_1+d_2)! = d_0!(k-d_0)! = \frac{k!}{\binom{k}{d_0}}$$

monomials with non-zero coefficients. Since $k/3 \leq d_0 < 2k/3$, this is at most $2^{-\Omega(k)} k!$. □

Define the all-permutations polynomial, AP_k, as a polynomial in variables $x_1, \ldots, x_k$

$$\mathsf{AP}_k = \sum_\sigma x_{\sigma(1)} x_{\sigma(2)} \cdots x_{\sigma(k)} ,$$

where σ is a permutation of $[k]$. Note that $\mathsf{AP}_k^{(ord)}$ is a polynomial in k^2 variables,

$$\mathsf{AP}_k^{(ord)} = \sum_{\sigma} x_{1,\sigma(1)} x_{2,\sigma(2)} \cdots x_{k,\sigma(k)}.$$

In other words, $\mathsf{AP}_k^{(ord)} = \mathrm{PERM}_k$.

PROOF OF THEOREM 1.12.. Assume that AP_k has been computed by such a circuit of size s. By Lemma 6.1, AP_k can be written as a sum of $O(k^3 s)$ ml-central polynomials. By Lemma 6.2, AP_k can thus have at most $O(2^{-\Omega(k)} k! k^3 s)$ monomials with nonzero coefficients. However, AP_k has $k!$ monomials. □

7. REFERENCES

[1] A. Barvinok. A simple polynomial time algorithm to approximate the permanent within a simply exponential factor. Random Structures and Algorithms 14(1), pages 29–61, 1999.

[2] W. Baur and V. Strassen. The complexity of partial derivatives. Theoretical computer science (22), pages 317–330, 1983.

[3] P. Burgisser. Completeness and reduction in algebraic complexity theory. Springer-Verlag Berlin Heidelberg 2000.

[4] S. Chien and A. Sinclair. Algebras with polynomial identities and computing the determinant. SIAM Journal on Computing 37, pages 252–266, 2007.

[5] S. Chien, L. Rasmussen and A. Sinclair. Clifford algebras an approximating the permanent. STOC 02', pages 222-231, 2002.

[6] J. von zur Gathen. Algebraic complexity theory. Ann. Rev. Comp. Sci. (3), pages 317–347, 1988.

[7] C. Godsil and I. Gutman. On the matching polynomial of a graph. Algebraic Methods in Graph Theory, pages 241–249, 1981.

[8] L. Hyafil. On the parallel evaluation of multivariate polynomials. SIAM J. Comput. 8(2), pages 120–123, 1979.

[9] P. Hrubeš and A. Yehudayoff. Homogeneous formulas and symmetric polynomials. arXiv:0907.2621

[10] P. Hrubeš, A. Wigderson and A. Yehudayoff. Relationless completeness and separations. To appear in CCC.

[11] A. Hurwitz. Über die Komposition der quadratischen Formen von beliebigvielen Variabeln. *Nach. Ges. der Wiss. Göttingen*, pages 309–316, 1898.

[12] A. Hurwitz. Über die Komposition der quadratischen Formen. *Math. Ann.*, 88, pages 1–25, 1923.

[13] I. M. James. On the immersion problem for real projective spaces. *Bull. Am. Math. Soc.*, 69, pages 231–238, 1967.

[14] M. Jerrum, A. Sinclair and E. Vigoda. A polynomial-time approximation algorithm for the permanent of a matrix with nonnegative entries. J. ACM 51(4), pages 671–697, 2004.

[15] S. Jukna Boolean function complexity: advances and frontiers. Book in preparation.

[16] N. Karmarkar, R. Karp, R. Lipton, L. Lovasz and M. Luby. A Monte-Carlo algorithm for estimating the permanent. SIAM Journal on Computing 22(2), pages 284–293, 1993.

[17] T. Kirkman. On pluquatemions, and horaoid products of sums of n squares. *Philos. Mag. (ser. 3)*, 33, pages 447–459; 494-509, 1848.

[18] K. Y. Lam. Some new results on composition of quadratic forms. *Inventiones Mathematicae.*, 1985.

[19] T. Y. Lam and T. Smith. On Yuzvinsky's monomial pairings. *Quart. J. Math. Oxford. (2)*, 44, pages 215–237, 1993.

[20] K. Mulmuley. On P vs. NP, Geometric Complexity Theory, and the Riemann Hypothesis. Technical Report, Computer Science department, The University of Chicago, 2009.

[21] N. Nisan. Lower bounds for non-commutative computation. STOC 91', pages 410–418, 1991.

[22] N. Nisan and A. Wigderson. Lower bounds on arithmetic circuits via partial derivatives. Computational Complexity, vol. 6, pages 217–234, 1996.

[23] A. Pfister. Zur Darstellung definiter Funktionen als Summe von Quadraten. *Inventiones Mathematicae.*, 1967.

[24] J. Radon. Lineare scharen orthogonalen matrizen. *Abh. Math. Sem. Univ. Hamburg 1*, pages 2–14, 1922.

[25] R. Raz. Multi-linear formulas for permanent and determinant are of super-polynomial size. Journal of the Association for Computing Machinery 56 (2), 2009.

[26] R. Raz and A. Yehudayoff. Lower bounds and separation for constant depth multilinear circuits. Proceedings of Computational Complexity, pages 128-139, 2008.

[27] R. Raz, A. Shpilka and A. Yehudayoff. A lower bound for the size of syntactically multilinear arithmetic circuits. SIAM Journal on Computing 38 (4), pages 1624-1647, 2008.

[28] D. B. Shapiro. Composition of quadratic forms. W. de Gruyter Verlag, 2000.

[29] V. Strassen. Die berechnungskomplexitat von elementarsymmetrischen funktionen und von interpolationskoeffizienten. Numerische Mathematik (20), pages 238–251, 1973.

[30] V. Strassen. Vermeidung von Divisionen. J. Reine Angew. Math. 264, pages 182–202, 1973.

[31] L. G. Valiant. Completeness classes in algebra. STOC '79, pages 249–261.

[32] S. Winograd. On the number of multiplications needed to compute certain functions. Comm. on Pure and Appl. Math. (23), pages 165–179, 1970.

[33] P. Yiu. Sums of squares formulae with integer coefficients. *Canad. Math. Bull.* , 30, pages 318-324, 1987.

[34] P. Yiu. On the product of two sums of 16 squares as a sum of squares of integral bilinear forms. *Quart. J. Math. Oxford. (2)* , 41, pages 463–500, 1990.

[35] S. Yuzvinsky. A series of monomial pairings. *Linear and multilinear algebra*, 15, pages 19–119, 1984.

On the Hardness of the Noncommutative Determinant

Vikraman Arvind
Institute of Mathematical Sciences
CIT Campus, Taramani
Chennai, India
arvind@imsc.res.in

Srikanth Srinivasan
Institute of Mathematical Sciences
CIT Campus, Taramani
Chennai, India
srikanth@imsc.res.in

ABSTRACT

In this paper we study the computational complexity of computing the *noncommutative* determinant. We first consider the arithmetic circuit complexity of computing the noncommutative determinant polynomial. Then, more generally, we also examine the complexity of algorithms computing the determinant over noncommutative domains. Our hardness results are summarized below:

- We show that if the noncommutative determinant polynomial has small noncommutative arithmetic circuits then so does the noncommutative permanent. Consequently, the commutative permanent polynomial has small commutative arithmetic circuits.
- For any field $\mathbb{F}$ we show that computing the $n \times n$ permanent over $\mathbb{F}$ is polynomial-time reducible to computing the $2n \times 2n$ (noncommutative) determinant whose entries are $O(n^2) \times O(n^2)$ matrices over the field $\mathbb{F}$.
- We also derive as a consequence that computing the $n \times n$ permanent over the nonnegative rationals is polynomial-time reducible to computing the noncommutative determinant over Clifford algebras of dimension $n^{O(1)}$.

Our techniques are elementary and use primarily the notion of the *Hadamard Product* of noncommutative polynomials introduced in an earlier paper [AJS09].

Categories and Subject Descriptors: F.2 [Analysis of Algorithms and Problem Complexity]: Miscellaneous.

General Terms: Algorithms, Theory.

Keywords: Determinant, Permanent, Arithmetic Circuits, Noncommutative Rings.

STOC'10, June 5–8, 2010, Cambridge, Massachusetts, USA.

1. INTRODUCTION

Arithmetic circuits, computing polynomials in the commutative ring $\mathbb{F}[x_1, x_2, \ldots, x_n]$, are a natural model of computation to study the complexity of many important algorithmic problems such as Matrix Multiplication, the Fast Fourier Transform, computing the determinant and permanent, etc. Therefore, it is a fundamental goal of Complexity Theory to prove explicit lower bounds in this model. However, despite much effort over the last four decades or so, not much progress has been made on this front. Even in the case of depth-3 circuits computing polynomials over the rationals, no superpolynomial lower bounds are known (which is less than what we know even for Boolean circuits).

Motivated by our inability to prove lower bounds in the *commutative* setting, in a seminal paper [N91], Nisan studied the apparently simpler problem of proving lower bounds for *noncommutative* arithmetic circuits: arithmetic circuits that compute polynomials in the free algebra $\mathbb{F}\langle x_1, x_2, \ldots, x_n\rangle$. (Note that, analogous to commutative arithmetic circuits, this computation model captures natural algorithms for computing polynomials over noncommutative algebras over $\mathbb{F}$.) In his central result based on a rank argument, Nisan shows that the noncommutative permanent or determinant polynomials in the ring $\mathbb{F}\langle x_{1,1}, \ldots, x_{n,n}\rangle$ require exponential size noncommutative algebraic branching programs (defined in Section 2). Nisan's results are over the *free* noncommutative ring $\mathbb{F}\langle x_1, x_2, \ldots, x_n\rangle$. Chien and Sinclair, in [CS04], explore the same question over other noncommutative algebras. They refine Nisan's rank argument to show exponential size lower bounds for formulas computing the permanent or determinant over specific noncommutative algebras, like the algebra of 2×2 matrices over $\mathbb{F}$, the quaternion algebra, and a host of other examples.

However, the question of whether there is a small noncommutative *circuit* for the determinant or permanent (or indeed any explicit polynomial) remains unanswered. Since the existence of small noncommutative arithmetic circuits for the permanent would imply the existence of small *commutative* arithmetic circuits for the permanent, we have a good reason to believe that the permanent does not have small noncommutative arithmetic circuits. However, as far as we know, no such argument has been given for the case of the noncommutative *determinant.* Indeed, since Nisan [N91] has also shown an exponential separation between the power of noncommutative formulas and circuits, it may very well be that the noncommutative determinant has polynomial-sized arithmetic circuits. One of our motivations is to show that the noncommutative determinant polynomial, unlike its commutative counterpart, is indeed hard to compute.

Another important motivation for an algorithmic study of the noncommutative determinant is for its role in a long-standing approach [GG81, KKL+93] to the design of randomized approximation algorithms for the 0-1 permanent through good unbiased estimators based on the determinant. Of specific interest are the works of Barvinok [B]; Chien, Rasmussen, and Sinclair [CRS03]; and more recently that of Moore and Russell [MR09]. Barvinok [B] defines a variant of the noncommutative determinant called the *symmetrized determinant* and shows that given inputs from a *constant dimensional* matrix algebra, the symmetrized determinant over these inputs can be evaluated in polynomial time. He uses these to define a series of algorithms that he conjectures might yield progressively better randomized approximation algorithms for the (commutative) permanent. Chien, Rasmussen, and Sinclair [CRS03] show that efficient algorithms to compute the determinant over Clifford algebras of polynomial dimension would yield efficient approximation algorithms for the permanent. Moore and Russell [MR09] provide evidence that Barvinok's approach might not work, but their results also imply that computing either the symmetrized or standard noncommutative determinant over polynomial dimensional matrix algebras would give a good estimator for the permanent.

Our results

1. We provide evidence that the noncommutative determinant is hard. We show that if the noncommutative determinant can be computed by a small noncommutative arithmetic circuit, then so can the noncommutative permanent and therefore, the commutative permanent has small commutative arithmetic circuits. This is in marked contrast to the commutative case, where the determinant is known to be computable by polynomial sized circuits, but the permanent is not known (or expected) to have subexponential sized arithmetic circuits. Note that we haven't yet formally defined the noncommutative determinant polynomial. There are, in fact, several ways of doing it as we will see in Section 2.

2. We show that computing the noncommutative determinant over matrix algebras of polynomial dimension is as hard as computing the commutative permanent. We also derive as a consequence that computing the $n \times n$ permanent over the nonnegative rationals is polynomial-time reducible to computing the noncommutative determinant over Clifford algebras of poly(n) dimension. This points to the intractability of carrying over Barvinok's approach for large dimension, and also to the possibility that the approach of Chien, Rasmussen, and Sinclair might be computationally infeasible.

   We stress that our result here is more relevant from an algorithmic point of view than showing a noncommutative *circuit* lower bound for the determinant. For, an arithmetic circuit lower bound result would not rule out the possibility of a polynomial-time algorithm for the noncommutative determinant over even polynomial dimension matrix algebras. For example, Barvinok's algorithm [B] computes the symmetrized determinant over constant dimensional matrix algebras, whereas any algebraic branching program that computes the symmetrized determinant over constant dimensional matrix algebras must be of exponential size [CS04].

2. PRELIMINARIES

For any set of variables X, let $\mathbb{F}\langle X\rangle$ denote the ring of *noncommuting* polynomials over X. Let $\mathcal{M}(X)$ denote the set of noncommutative monomials over X; given $d \in \mathbb{N}$, let $\mathcal{M}_d(X)$ denote the monomials over X of degree exactly d. For $f \in \mathbb{F}\langle X\rangle$ and $m \in \mathcal{M}(X)$, we will denote by $f(m)$ the coefficient of the monomial m in f.

For any ring R, we use $M_n(R)$ to denote the ring of $n \times n$ matrices with entries from R.

Fix $X = \{x_1, x_2, \ldots, x_m\}$ and $Y = \{y_1, y_2, \ldots, y_n\}$, two sets of variables. Given $f \in \mathbb{F}\langle X\rangle$, matrices $A_i \in M_k(\mathbb{F}\langle Y\rangle)$ for $1 \leq i \leq m$, and $i_0, j_0 \in [k]$, we use $f(A_1, A_2, \ldots, A_m)(i_0, j_0)$ to denote the $(i_0, j_0)^{th}$ entry of the matrix $f(A_1, A_2, \ldots, A_m) \in M_k(\mathbb{F}\langle Y\rangle)$.

2.1 Noncommutative determinant and permanent

Given $X = \{x_{i,j} \mid 1 \leq i, j \leq n\}$ for $n \in \mathbb{N}$, we define the $n \times n$ noncommutative determinant and permanent polynomials over the set of variables X. By fixing the order of multiplication in each monomial of the *commutative* determinant/permanent polynomials in different ways, one can obtain many different reasonable ways of defining the $n \times n$ noncommutative determinant and permanent, and indeed many of these definitions have been studied (see [A96], which surveys various flavours of the noncommutative determinant). The most straightforward definitions are those of the *Cayley determinant* and *Cayley permanent* – we will denote these by $\mathrm{Cdet}_n(X)$ and $\mathrm{Cperm}_n(X)$ respectively – which use the row order of multiplication. That is,

$$\mathrm{Cdet}_n(X) = \sum_{\sigma \in S_n} \mathrm{sgn}(\sigma)\; x_{1,\sigma(1)} \cdot x_{2,\sigma(2)} \cdots x_{n,\sigma(n)},$$

$$\mathrm{Cperm}_n(X) = \sum_{\sigma \in S_n} x_{1,\sigma(1)} \cdot x_{2,\sigma(2)} \cdots x_{n,\sigma(n)}.$$

We also define the *Moore determinant* and *Moore permanent* – denoted $\mathrm{Mdet}_n(X)$ and $\mathrm{Mperm}_n(X)$ respectively – by ordering the variables in each monomial using the cyclic order of the corresponding permutation. Given $\sigma \in S_n$, we write it as a product of disjoint cycles $(n^\sigma_{11} \cdots n^\sigma_{1l_1})(n^\sigma_{21} \cdots n^\sigma_{2l_2}) \cdots (n^\sigma_{r1} \cdots n^\sigma_{rl_r})$ such that $\forall i \in [r]$ and $j \in [l_r] \setminus \{1\}$, we have $n^\sigma_{i1} < n^\sigma_{ij}$ and $n^\sigma_{11} > n^\sigma_{21} > \cdots > n^\sigma_{r1}$. For each permutation $\sigma \in S_n$ define the (noncommuting) monomial

$$\mathrm{term}_\sigma(X) = x_{n^\sigma_{11}, n^\sigma_{12}} \cdots x_{n^\sigma_{1l_1}, n^\sigma_{11}} \cdots x_{n^\sigma_{r1}, n^\sigma_{r2}} \cdots x_{n^\sigma_{rl_r}, n^\sigma_{r1}}.$$

Then the Moore determinant and permanent are defined as

$$\mathrm{Mdet}_n(X) = \sum_{\sigma \in S_n} \mathrm{sgn}(\sigma)\mathrm{term}_\sigma(X),$$

$$\mathrm{Mperm}_n(X) = \sum_{\sigma \in S_n} \mathrm{term}_\sigma(X).$$

Over a characteristic zero field $\mathbb{F}$, Barvinok has studied another variant of the noncommutative determinant in [B].

This variant is called the *symmetrized determinant* and is denoted by $\mathrm{sdet}_n(X)$. It is defined as follows:

$$\mathrm{sdet}_n(X) = \frac{1}{n!}\sum_{\sigma,\tau\in S_n} \mathrm{sgn}(\sigma)\mathrm{sgn}(\tau)\prod_{i=1}^{n} x_{\tau(i),\sigma(i)},$$

where $\prod_{i=1}^{n} x_{\tau(i),\sigma(i)}$ denotes the noncommuting monomial $x_{\tau(1),\sigma(1)}x_{\tau(2),\sigma(2)}\cdots x_{\tau(n),\sigma(n)}$.
Let $\mathcal{B}$ be any *constant* dimensional associative algebra $\mathcal{B}$ over a characteristic zero field $\mathbb{F}$. Barvinok shows that there is a polynomial-time algorithm that computes $\mathrm{sdet}_n(A)$ for an $n\times n$ matrix A with entries from $\mathcal{B}$. It is not known whether such algorithms exist for the Cayley or Moore determinants.

2.2 Models for noncommutative arithmetic computation

A *noncommutative arithmetic circuit* C over a field $\mathbb{F}$ is defined as follows: C is a directed acyclic graph. Every node of indegree 0 in C is an *input* node and it is labelled with either an input variable from the set of variables X or an element from $\mathbb{F}$. Every internal node of C is labelled by either $(+)$ or $(\times)$ – meaning that it is either an addition or multiplication gate respectively – and has fanin two. Since we are working over noncommutative domains, we will assume that each multiplication gate has a designated left child and a designated right child. Each gate of the circuit computes a polynomial in $\mathbb{F}\langle X\rangle$ in the natural way. Each input node computes the variable or scalar element that labels it. The polynomial computed at an internal node labelled by $+$ (respectively, $\times$) is the sum (respectively, the product in left-to-right order) of the polynomials computed at its children. The polynomial computed by the circuit C is the polynomial computed at a designated *output* node of the circuit.
We also recall the definition of an Algebraic Branching Program (ABP) computing a noncommutative polynomial in $\mathbb{F}\langle X\rangle$ ([N91], [RS05]). An ABP is a directed acyclic graph with one vertex of in-degree zero, which is called the *source*, and one vertex of out-degree zero, which is called the *sink*. The vertices of the graph are partitioned into levels numbered $0, 1, \ldots, d$. Edges may only go from level i to level $i+1$ for $0 \le i \le d-1$. The source is the only vertex at level 0 and the sink is the only vertex at level d. Each edge is labeled with a homogeneous linear form in the variables X. The size of the ABP is the number of vertices in it.
A d layered ABP, as defined above, computes a degree d homogeneous polynomial $f \in \mathbb{F}\langle X\rangle$ in the following sense. Consider a path γ from source to sink in the ABP with edges $e_1, e_2, \ldots, e_d$, where e_i is the edge from level $i-1$ to level i. Let ℓ_i denote the linear form labelling edge e_i. We denote by f_γ the homogeneous degree d polynomial $\ell_1\cdot\ell_2\cdots\ell_d$ (note that the order of multiplication is important). The polynomial f computed by the ABP is simply

$$f = \sum_{\gamma\in\mathcal{P}} f_\gamma$$

where $\mathcal{P}$ is the set of all paths from the source to the sink.

3. THE HADAMARD PRODUCT

A key notion we require for all our reductions is the Hadamard product of polynomials that was introduced in [AJS09].

DEFINITION 1. *Given polynomials $f, g \in \mathbb{F}\langle X\rangle$, their* Hadamard product *$h = f\circ g$ is defined as follows: h is the unique polynomial in $\mathbb{F}\langle X\rangle$ such that for any monomial $m\in\mathcal{M}(X)$, the coefficient $h(m) = f(m)\cdot g(m)$.*

In [AJS09, Theorem 5] we show that given a noncommutative circuit for polynomial f and an ABP for polynomial g we can efficiently compute a noncommutative circuit for their Hadamard product $f\circ g$. However, the construction we present in [AJS09] modifies the noncommutative circuit for the polynomial f. Hence, it will not work if we are allowed only black-box access to f, which we require for certain applications in this paper.
Suppose we have an efficient *black-box* algorithm for evaluating the polynomial $f\in\mathbb{F}\langle X\rangle$, where the variables in X take values in some matrix algebra (say, $n\times n$ matrices over the field $\mathbb{F}$). Furthermore, suppose we have an *explicit* ABP for the polynomial g. *Ideally,* we would like to obtain an efficient algorithm for computing their Hadamard product $f\circ g$ over the same matrix algebra.
However, what we can show is that we can put together the ABP and the black-box algorithm for f to obtain an efficient algorithm that computes $f\circ g$ over $\mathbb{F}$. This turns out to be sufficient to prove all our hardness results for the different noncommutative determinants.

THEOREM 1. *Fix $d\in\mathbb{N}$. Let $Z = \{z_1, z_2, \ldots, z_m\}$ be a set of noncommuting variables and $g\in\mathbb{F}\langle Z\rangle$ be a homogeneous polynomial of degree d such that g is computed by an ABP P of size S. Then, there exist matrices $A_1, A_2, \ldots, A_n \in M_S(\mathbb{F})$ such that for any homogeneous polynomial $f\in\mathbb{F}\langle Z\rangle$ of degree d, $f\circ g = f(A_1z_1, A_2z_2, \ldots, A_nz_n)(1, S)$. Moreover, given the ABP P, the matrices $A_1, A_2, \ldots, A_n$ can be computed in time polynomial in the size of the description of P.*

PROOF. Let the vertices of P be named $1, 2, \ldots, S$ where 1 is the source of the ABP and S is the sink. Define the matrices $A_1, A_2, \ldots, A_n \in M_S(\mathbb{F})$ as follows: $A_i(k,l)$ is the coefficient of the variable z_i in the linear form labelling the edge that goes from vertex k to vertex l; if there is no such edge, the entry $A_i(k,l) = 0$. For any monomial $m = z_{i_1}z_{i_2}\cdots z_{i_d}\in\mathcal{M}_d(Z)$, let A_m denote the matrix $A_{i_1}A_{i_2}\cdots A_{i_d}$. Furthermore, let $\prod_{j=1}^{d} z_{i_j}$ denote the monomial $z_{i_1}z_{i_2}\cdots z_{i_d}$ and let $\prod_{j=1}^{d} A_{i_j}z_{i_j}$ denote the product $(A_{i_1}z_{i_1})(A_{i_2}z_{i_2})\cdots(A_{i_d}z_{i_d})$. Now, we first observe that

$$f(A_1z_1, \ldots, A_nz_n) = \sum_{i_1,i_2,\ldots,i_d\in[n]} f(z_{i_1}z_{i_2}\cdots z_{i_d})\prod_{j=1}^{d} A_{i_j}z_{i_j}.$$

Since $\prod_{j=1}^{d} A_{i_j}z_{i_j} = (\prod_{j=1}^{d} A_{i_j})(\prod_{j=1}^{d} z_{i_j}) = A_m m$, where m denotes the degree d monomial $\prod_{j=1}^{d} z_{i_j}$, we can write

$$f(A_1z_1, A_2z_2, \ldots, A_nz_n) = \sum_{m\in\mathcal{M}_d(Z)} f(m)A_m m.$$

Now, consider the homogeneous degree-d polynomial g computed by by the ABP P. Note that the coefficient $g(m)$ of any monomial $m = z_{i_1}z_{i_2}\cdots z_{i_d}$ in g is just

$$A_m(1, S) = \sum_{k_1,k_2,\ldots,k_{d-1}\in[S]}\prod_{j=1}^{d} A_{i_j}(k_{j-1}, k_j),$$

where $k_0 = 1$ and $k_d = S$. Putting the above observations together, we see that $f(A_1z_1, A_2z_2, \ldots, A_nz_n)(1, S) =$

$\sum_{m \in \mathcal{M}_d(Z)} f(m) A_m(1,S) m = \sum_{m \in \mathcal{M}_d(Z)} f(m) g(m) m = f \circ g$. Since the entries of the matrices $A_1, A_2, \ldots, A_n$ can be read off the labels of P, it can be seen that $A_1, A_2, \ldots, A_n$ can be computed in polynomial time given the ABP P. This completes the proof. □

REMARK 1. *We note that the matrices A_i in the statement of Theorem 1 can actually be computed from the ABP even more efficiently, say, in uniform AC^0.*

The following corollary is immediate.

COROLLARY 1. *[AJS09] Given a noncommutative circuit of size S' for $f \in \mathbb{F}\langle Z \rangle$ and an ABP of size S for $g \in \mathbb{F}\langle Z \rangle$, in deterministic polynomial time (indeed, even in deterministic logspace) we can compute a noncommutative circuit of size $O(S'S^3)$ for $f \circ g$.*

The next corollary is the more useful version for this paper.

COROLLARY 2. *Let $Z = \{z_1, z_2, \ldots, z_n\}$. Suppose $\mathcal{P}$ is a polynomial-time algorithm for computing a homogeneous degree d polynomial $f \in \mathbb{F}\langle Z \rangle$ for matrix inputs from $M_S(\mathbb{F})$ (the statement can be generalized to any unital algebra in place of the field $\mathbb{F}$.) Given as input an ABP P, with S nodes, computing a homogeneous degree d polynomial $g \in \mathbb{F}\langle Z \rangle$, and scalars $a_1, a_2, \ldots, a_n \in \mathbb{F}$, we can compute $f \circ g(a_1, a_2, \ldots, a_n)$ in polynomial time.*

PROOF. We first compute matrices $A_1, A_2, \ldots, A_n$, described in the Theorem 1, in time polynomial in the description of the ABP P. Then we invoke the given algorithm $\mathcal{P}$ on input $(A_1a_1, A_2a_2, \ldots, A_na_n)$ to obtain as output an $S \times S$ matrix whose $(1,S)^{th}$ entry contains $f \circ g(a_1, a_2, \ldots, a_n)$. Clearly, the simulation runs in polynomial time. □

4. THE HARDNESS OF THE CAYLEY DETERMINANT

We consider polynomials over an arbitrary field $\mathbb{F}$ (for the algorithmic results $\mathbb{F}$ is either rational numbers or a finite field). The main result of this section is that if there is a polynomial-time algorithm that computes the $2n \times 2n$ Cayley determinant over inputs from $M_S(\mathbb{F})$ for $S = c \cdot n^2$ (for a suitable constant c) then there is a polynomial-time algorithm that computes the $n \times n$ permanent over $\mathbb{F}$.

Throughout this section let X denote $\{x_{i,j} \mid 1 \le i,j \le 2n\}$, and Y denote $\{y_{ij} \mid 1 \le i,j \le n\}$. Our aim is to show that if there is a polynomial-time algorithm for computing $\mathrm{Cdet}_{2n}(X)$ where $x_{i,j}$ takes values in $M_S(\mathbb{F})$ then there is a polynomial-time algorithm that computes $\mathrm{Cperm}_n(Y)$ where y_{ij} takes values in $\mathbb{F}$.

The $2n \times 2n$ determinant has $(2n)!$ many signed monomials of degree $2n$ of the form $x_{1,\sigma(1)} x_{2,\sigma(2)} \cdots x_{2n,\sigma(2n)}$ for $\sigma \in S_{2n}$. We will identify $n!$ of these monomials, all of which have the same sign. More precisely, we will design a small ABP with which we will be able to pick out these $n!$ monomials of the same sign.

We now define these $n!$ many permutations from S_{2n} which have the same sign and the corresponding monomials of Cdet_{2n} that can be picked out by a small ABP.

DEFINITION 2. *Let $n \in \mathbb{N}$. For each permutation $\pi \in S_n$, we define a permutation $\rho(\pi)$ in S_{2n}, called the* interleaving *of π, as follows:*

$$\rho(\pi)(i) = \begin{cases} \pi(\frac{i+1}{2}), & \text{if } i \text{ is odd,} \\ n + \pi(\frac{i}{2}), & \text{if } i \text{ is even.} \end{cases}$$

That is, the elements $\rho(\pi)(1), \rho(\pi)(2), \cdots, \rho(\pi)(2n)$ are simply $\pi(1), (n+\pi(1)), \pi(2), (n+\pi(2)), \cdots, \pi(n), (n+\pi(n))$.

We will use 1_n to denote the *identity permutation* in the permutation group S_n, for each n.

The following lemma states a crucial property of the permutation $\rho(\pi)$.

LEMMA 1. *The sign of the permutation $\rho(\pi)$ is independent of π. More precisely, for every $\pi \in S_n$, we have $\mathrm{sgn}(\rho(\pi)) = \mathrm{sgn}(\rho(1_n))$.*

PROOF. For each $\pi \in S_n$ we can define the permutation $\pi_2 \in S_{2n}$ as $\pi_2(i) = \pi(i)$ for $1 \le i \le n$ and $\pi_2(n+j) = n + \pi(j)$ for $1 \le j \le n$. It is easy to verify that $\mathrm{sgn}(\pi_2) = \mathrm{sgn}(\pi)^2 = 1$ for every $\pi \in S_n$. To see this we write π_2 as a product of disjoint cycles and notice that every cycle occurs an even number of times. Furthermore, we can check that $\rho(\pi) = \rho(1_n)\pi_2$, where we evaluate products of permutations from left to right. Hence it follows that $\mathrm{sgn}(\rho(\pi)) = \mathrm{sgn}(\rho(1_n))\mathrm{sgn}(\pi_2) = \mathrm{sgn}(\rho(1_n))$. □

We will denote by ρ_0 the permutation $\rho(1_n)$.

For a permutation $\sigma \in S_{2n}$, we will denote by m_σ the monomial $x_{1,\sigma(1)} x_{2,\sigma(2)} \cdots x_{2n,\sigma(2n)} \in \mathcal{M}(X)$. For $\sigma, \tau \in S_{2n}$, we will denote the monomial $x_{\sigma(1),\tau(1)} x_{\sigma(2),\tau(2)} \cdots x_{\sigma(2n),\tau(2n)}$ by $m_{\sigma,\tau}$.

In the next lemma we show that there is an ABP that will filter out monomials that are not of the form $m_{\rho(\pi)}$ from among the m_σ.

LEMMA 2. *There is an ABP P of size $O(n^2)$ that computes a homogeneous polynomial $F \in \mathbb{F}\langle X \rangle$ of degree $2n$ such that for any $\sigma, \tau \in S_{2n}$,*

- *$F(m_\sigma) = 1$ if $\sigma = \rho(\pi)$ for some $\pi \in S_n$, and 0 otherwise.*
- *$F(m_{\sigma,\tau}) = 0$ unless $\sigma = 1_{2n}$.*

Moreover, the above ABP P can be computed in time polynomial in n.

PROOF. The ABP is essentially just a finite automaton over the alphabet X with the following properties: for input monomials of the form m_σ it accepts only those monomials that are of the form $m_{\rho(\pi)}$. Further, for input monomials of the form $m_{\sigma,\tau}$ it accepts only those monomials of the form $m_{1_{2n},\tau}$. We give the formal description of this ABP P below.

The ABP P contains $2n+1$ layers, labelled $\{0, 1, \ldots, 2n\}$. For each even $i \in \{0, 1, \ldots, 2n\}$ the ith layer has exactly one node q_i. For each odd $i \in \{0, 1, \ldots, 2n\}$, there are n nodes $p_{i,1}, p_{i,2}, \ldots, p_{i,n}$ in the ith*layer*. We now describe the edges of the ABP P. For each even integer $i \in \{0, 1, \ldots, 2n-2\}$ and $j \in [n]$ there is an edge from q_i to $p_{i+1,j}$ labelled $x_{i+1,j}$. For each odd integer $i \in \{0, 1, \ldots, 2n\}$ and $j \in [n]$, there is an edge from $p_{i,j}$ to q_{i+1} labelled $x_{i+1,n+j}$.

It is easy to see that P as defined above satisfies the requirements of the statement of the lemma. It is also clear that this ABP P can be computed in polynomial time. □

Note that the ABP P of Lemma 2 can in fact be constructed in uniform AC^0.

REMARK 2. *For this section we require only the first part of Lemma 2. The second part of Lemma 2 is used in Section 6.*

We are now ready to prove that if there is a small noncommutative arithmetic circuit that computes the Cayley determinant polynomial, then there is a small noncommutative arithmetic circuit that computes the Cayley permanent polynomial.

THEOREM 2. *For any $n \in \mathbb{N}$, if there is a circuit C of size s computing $\mathrm{Cdet}_{2n}(X)$, then there is a circuit C' of size polynomial in s and n that computes $\mathrm{Cperm}_n(Y)$.*

PROOF. Assuming the existence of the circuit C as stated above, by Corollary 1, there is a noncommutative arithmetic circuit C'' of size $\mathrm{poly}(s,n)$ that computes the polynomial $F'' = \mathrm{Cdet}_{2n} \circ F$, where F is the polynomial referred to in Lemma 2. For any monomial m, if $m \neq m_\sigma$ for any $\sigma \in S_{2n}$, then $\mathrm{Cdet}_{2n}(m) = 0$ and hence, in this case, $F''(m) = 0$; moreover, for $m = m_\sigma$, we have $F(m) = 1$ if $\sigma = \rho(\pi)$ for some $\pi \in S_n$, and 0 otherwise. Hence, we see that

$$F''(X) = \sum_{\pi \in S_n} \mathrm{sgn}(\rho(\pi)) m_{\rho(\pi)} = \mathrm{sgn}(\rho_0) \left(\sum_{\pi \in S_n} m_{\rho(\pi)} \right)$$

where the last equality follows from Lemma 1.
Let C' be the circuit obtained from C'' by substituting $x_{i,j}$ with $y_{\frac{1+i}{2},j}$ if i is odd and $j \in [n]$, and by 1 if i is even or $j \notin [n]$, and by multiplying the output of the resulting circuit by $\mathrm{sgn}(\rho_0)$. Let F' denote the polynomial computed by C'. Then, we have

$$F'(Y) = \sum_{\pi \in S_n} m'_{\rho(\pi)}$$

where $m'_{\rho(\pi)}$ denotes the monomial obtained from $m_{\rho(\pi)}$ after the substitution. It can be checked that for any $\pi \in S_n$, the monomial $m'_{\rho(\pi)} = y_{1,\pi(1)} y_{2,\pi(2)} \cdots y_{n,\pi(n)}$. Hence, the polynomial F' computed by C' in indeed $\mathrm{Cperm}_n(Y)$. It is easily seen that the size of C' is $\mathrm{poly}(s,n)$. □

We now show that evaluating the polynomial Cdet_{2n} over $M_S(\mathbb{F})$, for $S = c \cdot n^2$ for suitable $c > 0$, is at least as hard as evaluating the permanent over $\mathbb{F}$.

THEOREM 3. *If there is a polynomial-time algorithm $\mathcal{P}$ that computes the $2n \times 2n$ Cayley determinant of matrices with entries in $M_S(\mathbb{F})$, for $S = c \cdot n^2$ for suitable $c > 0$, then there is a polynomial-time algorithm that computes the $n \times n$ permanent over $\mathbb{F}$.*

PROOF. This is an easy consequence of Corollary 2. Consider the algorithm given by Corollary 2 for computing $\mathrm{Cdet}_{2n} \circ F$ over the field $\mathbb{F}$, where the ABP in Corollary 2 is the ABP of Lemma 2 computing F.
In order to evaluate the permanent over inputs $a_{ij}, 1 \leq i,j \leq n$ we will substitute $x_{2i-1,j} = a_{ij}$ for $1 \leq i,j \leq n$ and we put $x_{i,j} = 1$ when i is even or $j > n$. As in the proof of Theorem 2 it follows that for this substitution the algorithm computing $\mathrm{Cdet}_{2n} \circ F$ will output $\mathrm{sgn}(\rho_0)\mathrm{Cperm}_n(a_{11}, \ldots, a_{nn})$. Since $\mathrm{sgn}(\rho_0)$ can be easily computed, we have a polynomial-time algorithm for computing the $n \times n$ permanent over $\mathbb{F}$. □

REMARK 3. *The above result has a stronger consequence: for any fixed $\varepsilon > 0$, if there is a polynomial-time algorithm that computes the $m \times m$ Cayley determinant over $M_{m^\varepsilon}(\mathbb{F})$, then there is a polynomial-time algorithm that computes $\Omega(m^{\varepsilon/2}) \times \Omega(m^{\varepsilon/2})$ permanents over $\mathbb{F}$, hence implying that permanent over $\mathbb{F}$ is polynomial-time computable.*

5. THE CAYLEY DETERMINANT OVER CLIFFORD ALGEBRAS

We now consider the complexity of computing the determinant over real Clifford algebras of polynomially large dimension. We show via a polynomial-time reduction that computing the permanent over the rationals is reducible to this problem. Indeed, by inspecting our result we can observe that even *approximating* the determinant over such Clifford algebras would yield similar approximation algorithms for the permanent over the reals.
We first define the basic notions in the theory of Clifford algebras. A thorough treatment can be found in [LS09]. Fix $m \in \mathbb{N}$. The (real) *Clifford algebra* CL'_m is a 2^m-dimensional vector space over $\mathbb{R}$ with basis elements of the form $e_{i_1} e_{i_2} e_{i_3} \cdots e_{i_k}$ where $i_1 < i_2 < i_3 \cdots < i_k$ are elements from $[m]$. Multiplication between elements of the basis is defined by the following rules: $e_i^2 = 1$ and $e_i e_j = -e_j e_i$ for distinct $i,j \in [m]$; this is extended linearly to all pairs of elements from the Clifford algebra. Given $i_1 < i_2 < \cdots < i_k$ from $[m]$, we denote by e_S the basis element $e_{i_1} e_{i_2} \cdots e_{i_k}$, where $S = \{i_1, i_2, \ldots, i_k\}$. Each element of the Clifford algebra is uniquely expressible as $\sum_{S \subseteq [m]} c_S e_S$, where $c_S \in \mathbb{R}$ for each S. (Note that $e_\emptyset$ and 1 both refer to the multiplicative identity of the algebra.) An *idempotent* of the Clifford algebra is an element e such that $e^2 = e$. Given $h = \sum_{S \subseteq [m]} c_S e_S$ in CL'_m, we define its *norm* $|h|$ to be $\sqrt{\sum_{S \subseteq [m]} c_S^2}$.
The subset of basis elements $\{e_S \mid S \text{ has even cardinality}\}$ generates a strict subalgebra of CL'_m. We will denote this subalgebra by CL_m. This is the algebra of interest to us. The term 'Clifford algebra' will henceforth refer to CL_m for some $m \in \mathbb{N}$.
Chien, Rasmussen, and Sinclair [CRS03] have shown that a polynomial-time algorithm that, when given as input an $n \times n$ matrix B with entries from CL_m for

$$m = 2 \log n + 2,$$

computes $|\mathrm{Cdet}_n(B)|^2$ can be used to design a randomized polynomial time algorithm to approximate the 0-1 permanent (over $\mathbb{Q}$).
In this section, we prove that if there is a polynomial-time algorithm to compute either $|\mathrm{Cdet}_n(B)|^2$ or $\mathrm{Cdet}_n(B)$, then the permanent (over inputs from $\mathbb{Q}$) can actually be computed in polynomial time. For an $n \times n$ real matrix A, let $\mathrm{perm}_n(A)$ denote the permanent of A.

REMARK 4. *In a sense, our result in this section should not be surprising. We have already proved (in Theorem 3) that computing the determinant over matrix algebras is at least as hard as computing the permanent. Also, it is known that Clifford algebras of polynomial dimension are isomorphic to matrix algebras of polynomial dimension (see, for example, [LS09, Chapter 5]). However, in this section we actually give an explicit polynomial-time reduction showing that computing the permanent over the reals is reducible to computing either $|\mathrm{Cdet}_n(B)|^2$ or $\mathrm{Cdet}_n(B)$ where the entries of B are from the Clifford algebra CL_m.*

Suppose we wish to compute the permanent of an $n \times n$ matrix with entries from $\mathbb{Q}$. W.l.o.g., we assume that $n = 2^\ell$ for some $\ell \in \mathbb{N}$. Let m denote 5ℓ. The next lemma is about the existence of certain elements in the algebra CL_m useful for the reduction.

LEMMA 3. *Let n, ℓ, m be as above. Then, there exist $h_1, h_2, \ldots, h_n, h'_1 h'_2, \ldots, h'_n \in CL_m$ and an idempotent $e \in CL_m$ such that:*

- *For all j, $h_j h'_j = e$.*
- *For all $j \neq k$, $h_j h'_k = 0$.*
- $|e|^2 = \frac{1}{2^\ell}$.

Moreover, the elements $h_1, h_2, \ldots, h_n, h'_1, h'_2, \ldots, h'_n$ and e can be constructed in time polyomial in n.

We defer the proof of the above lemma and first prove the main result of this section.

THEOREM 4. *Let the parameters n, ℓ, m be defined as above. Then there is a polynomial-time algorithm which takes as input any matrix $A \in M_n(\mathbb{R})$ and computes a matrix $B \in M_{2n}(CL_m)$ such that $|\mathrm{Cdet}_{2n}(B)|^2 = \frac{\mathrm{perm}_n(A)^2}{2^\ell}$.*

PROOF. The matrix B will be the following: for any odd $i \in [2n]$ and any $j \in [2n]$, set $B(i,j)$ – the $(i,j)^{th}$ entry of B – to be $A(\frac{i+1}{2}, j)h_j$ if $j \leq n$ and 0 if $j > n$; for any even $i \in [2n]$ and $j \in [2n]$, set $B(i,j)$ to be h'_{j-n} if $j > n$ and 0 otherwise. Clearly, B can be computed in polynomial time given A. Note the following property of B: for any odd $i \in [2n]$ and $j, k \in [2n]$

$$B(i,j)B(i+1,k) = \begin{cases} A(\frac{i+1}{2}, j)e & \text{if } j \leq n \text{ and } k = n+j, \\ 0 & \text{otherwise.} \end{cases}$$

Here e denotes the idempotent from Lemma 3. Using the above fact, the following claim is easy to see.

CLAIM 1. *For any permutation $\sigma \in S_{2n}$, the product $\prod_{i=1}^{2n} B(i, \sigma(i)) = (\prod_{i=1}^{n} A(i, \pi(i)))e$ if $\sigma = \rho(\pi)$ for some $\pi \in S_n$ and it is 0 otherwise.*

Let us consider $\mathrm{Cdet}_{2n}(B)$.

$$\begin{aligned}\mathrm{Cdet}_{2n}(B) &= \sum_{\sigma \in S_{2n}} \mathrm{sgn}(\sigma) \prod_{i=1}^{2n} B(i, \sigma(i)) \\ &= \sum_{\pi \in S_n} \mathrm{sgn}(\rho(\pi))(\prod_{i=1}^{n} A(i, \pi(i)))e \\ &= \mathrm{sgn}(\rho_0)\mathrm{perm}_n(A)e.\end{aligned}$$

It follows from the above equations that $|\mathrm{Cdet}_{2n}(B)|^2 = \mathrm{perm}_n(A)^2 |e|^2 = \frac{\mathrm{perm}_n(A)^2}{2^\ell}$. □

We have the following easy consequence of the above theorem.

COROLLARY 3. *Fix any $\varepsilon > 0$, and suppose there is a polynomial-time algorithm that computes $|\mathrm{Cdet}_n(B)|^2$ on input an $n \times n$ matrix B with entries from CL_m for $m = \varepsilon \log n$. Then there is a polynomial-time algorithm that computes the $n \times n$ permanent of matrices with nonnegative rational entries.*

PROOF. The corollary is a direct consequence of Theorem 4 for $m = \lceil 5 \log n \rceil$. To prove hardness for $m = \varepsilon \log n$, we note that a polynomial-time algorithm to compute $|\mathrm{Cdet}_n(B)|^2$ over $CL_{\varepsilon \log n}$ can be used to compute $|\mathrm{Cdet}_{n^{\varepsilon/5}}(B)|^2$ over $CL_{5 \log n^{\varepsilon/5}}$ in polynomial time. □

A δ-approximation algorithm $\mathcal{P}$ for a function $f : \Sigma^* \longrightarrow \mathbb{Q}$ is an algorithm such that for each $x \in \Sigma^*$

$$(1-\delta)f(x) \leq \mathcal{P}(x) \leq (1+\delta)f(x).$$

Our reduction from computing the permanent for nonnegative entries to computing $|\mathrm{Cdet}_n(B)|^2$ actually yields an approximation preserving reduction. We formalize this in the next corollary.

COROLLARY 4. *Fix any $\delta > 0$ and $\varepsilon > 0$. Suppose there is a polynomial-time δ-approximation algorithm for the function that on input an $n \times n$ matrix B with entries from CL_m for $m = \varepsilon \log n$ takes the value $|\mathrm{Cdet}_n(B)|^2$. Then there is a polynomial-time δ-approximation algorithm for the $n \times n$ permanent with nonnegative rational entries.*

We now prove Lemma 3.

PROOF PROOF OF LEMMA 3. Let $e_1, e_2, \ldots, e_m$ be the generators of CL'_m. Partition the set $[m]$ into ℓ subsets of size 5 as follows: set $S_i = \{5(i-1)+j \mid j \in [5]\}$ for each $i \in [\ell]$. For each $i \in [\ell]$, let $S_{i,0} = \{5(i-1)+1, 5(i-1)+2, 5(i-1)+3, 5(i-1)+5\}$ and $S_{i,1} = \{5(i-1)+2, 5(i-1)+3, 5(i-1)+4, 5(i-1)+5\}$.
Using the fact that $e_i^2 = 1$ and $e_i e_j = -e_j e_i$ for $i \neq j$ it easily follows that for any two *disjoint* sets $S, T \subseteq [m]$ such that $|S|, |T|$ are even, we have $e_S e_T = e_T e_S$. Hence, the elements $e_{S_{i,b_1}}$ and $e_{S_{j,b_2}}$ commute for $i \neq j$ and any $b_1, b_2 \in \{0,1\}$. Furthermore, for all $i \in [\ell]$ and $b \in \{0,1\}$ we have $e^2_{S_{i,b}} = 1$. Also, we have $e_{S_{i,0}} e_{S_{i,1}} = -e_{S_{i,1}} e_{S_{i,0}}$. Finally, notice that $e_{S_{i,b}}$ for $1 \leq i \leq \ell$ and $b \in \{0,1\}$ are all elements of CL_m.
For $i \in [\ell]$ and $b \in \{0,1\}$, set $g_{i,0} = \frac{1+e_{S_{i,1}}}{2}$ and $g_{i,1} = \frac{e_{S_{i,0}}(1-e_{S_{i,1}})}{2}$. Also, set $g'_{i,0} = g_{i,0}$ and $g'_{i,1} = \frac{e_{S_{i,0}}(1+e_{S_{i,1}})}{2}$.
Notice that $g^2_{i,0} = g_{i,0}$ and $e_{S_{i,0}}(1-e_{S_{i,1}}) = (1+e_{S_{i,1}})e_{S_{i,0}}$. Using these we can easily derive the following crucial properties of these elements of CL_m.

- For each $i \in [\ell]$ and $b \in \{0,1\}$, $g_{i,b} g'_{i,b} = g_{i,0}$.
- For each $i \in [\ell]$ and $b \in \{0,1\}$, $g_{i,b} g'_{i,1-b} = 0$.
- For $i_1 \neq i_2$ and any $b_1, b_2 \in \{0,1\}$, the elements g_{i_1,b_1} and g'_{i_2,b_2} commute.

Finally, we define h_j, h'_j for a fixed $j \in [n]$. Let $b_1 b_2 \ldots b_\ell$ be the binary representation of the integer $j-1$ (recall that $n = 2^\ell$). We define $h_j = g_{1,b_1} g_{2,b_2} \cdots g_{\ell,b_\ell}$ and $h'_j = g'_{1,b_1} g'_{2,b_2} \cdots g'_{\ell,b_\ell}$. Also, we define e to be $g_{1,0} g_{2,0} \cdots g_{\ell,0}$, which is the same as h_1 and h'_1.
We now prove that the h_j, h'_j ($j \in [n]$) and e satisfy the properties claimed in the statement of the lemma. Fix any $j \in [n]$ and let $b_1 b_2 \ldots b_\ell$ be the binary representation of $j-1$. We have

$$\begin{aligned} h_j h'_j &= g_{1,b_1} g_{2,b_2} \cdots g_{\ell,b_\ell} g'_{1,b_1} g'_{2,b_2} \cdots g'_{\ell,b_\ell} \\ &= (g_{1,b_1} g'_{1,b_1}) \cdot (g_{2,b_2} g'_{2,b_2}) \cdots (g_{\ell,b_\ell} g'_{\ell,b_\ell}) \\ &= g_{1,0} g_{2,0} \cdots g_{\ell,0} = e \end{aligned}$$

The second equality follows from the fact that $g_{i_1,b}$ and $g'_{i_2,b}$ commute for any distinct i_1 and i_2. The third equality follows from the fact that for any i and b, $g_{i,b} g'_{i,b} = g_{i,0}$. This proves the first property claimed in the statement of the lemma. Similarly, we can see that e is an idempotent: $e^2 = h_1^2 = e$.

Fix any distinct $j, k \in [n]$. Let $b_1 b_2 \ldots b_\ell$ and $b'_1 b'_2 \ldots b'_\ell$ be the binary representations of j and k. Since $j \neq k$, we can fix some i such that $b_i \neq b'_i$. We have

$$\begin{aligned} h_j h'_k &= g_{1,b_1} g_{2,b_2} \cdots g_{\ell,b_\ell} g'_{1,b'_1} g'_{2,b'_2} \cdots g'_{\ell,b'_\ell} \\ &= (g_{1,b_1} g'_{1,b_1}) \cdot (g_{2,b_1} g'_{2,b_2}) \cdots (g_{i,b_i} g'_{i,b'_i}) \cdots (g_{\ell,b_\ell} g'_{\ell,b_\ell}) \\ &= (g_{1,b_1} g'_{1,b_1}) \cdot (g_{2,b_1} g'_{2,b_2}) \cdots 0 \cdots (g_{\ell,b_\ell} g'_{\ell,b_\ell}) = 0 \end{aligned}$$

where the third equality follows from the fact that we have $g_{i,b} g'_{i,1-b} = 0$. This proves the second claim made in the lemma.

Finally, we note that

$$\begin{aligned} |e|^2 = |g_{1,0} g_{2,0} \cdots g_{\ell,0}|^2 &= \left| \frac{1}{2^\ell} \sum_{T \subseteq \ell} \prod_{i \in T} e_{S_{i,1}} \right|^2 \\ &= \frac{1}{4^\ell} \left| \sum_{T \subseteq \ell} \prod_{i \in T} e_{S_{i,1}} \right|^2 = \frac{2^\ell}{4^\ell} = \frac{1}{2^\ell} \end{aligned}$$

It is easily seen from their definitions that the h_j, h'_j and e can be computed in time polynomial in n. This completes the proof of the lemma. □

6. THE SYMMETRIZED AND MOORE DETERMINANTS

In this section, we will prove that the symmetrized and Moore determinants are also hard to compute. As in the case of the Cayley determinant, we will show that the symmetrized determinant over matrix algebras of polynomial dimension cannot be computed in polynomial time unless the permanent over the underlying field $\mathbb{F}$ can be computed in polynomial time. For the Moore determinant, we will be able to prove something stronger: when $\mathbb{F}$ is of characteristic k, the Moore determinant cannot be computed over matrix algebras of polynomial dimension unless there is a polynomial-time algorithm to count the number of directed Hamilton cycles in a directed graph modulo k.

We first consider the symmetrized determinant. We observe that the $2n \times 2n$ symmetrized determinant over $O(n^2)$-dimensional matrix algebras is at least as hard to compute as the permanent. This stands in marked contrast to the result of Barvinok [B], who shows that over *constant-dimensional* matrix algebras, the symmetrized determinant is polynomial-time computable.

Let $\mathbb{F}$ be a characteristic zero field. We define sets of indeterminates

$$X = \{x_{i,j} \mid 1 \leq i, j \leq 2n\},$$
$$Y = \{y_{i,j} \mid 1 \leq i, j \leq n\}.$$

For permutations $\sigma, \tau \in S_{2n}$, we recall the monomial definitions from Section 4:

$$m_{\sigma,\tau} = x_{\sigma(1),\tau(1)} x_{\sigma(2),\tau(2)} \cdots x_{\sigma(2n),\tau(2n)},$$
$$m_\sigma = x_{1,\sigma(1)} x_{2,\sigma(2)} \cdots x_{2n,\sigma(2n)}.$$

THEOREM 5. *If the* $\mathrm{sdet}_{2n}(X)$ *polynomial over* $\mathbb{F}$ *can be computed by a polynomial-sized noncommutative arithmetic circuit, then the polynomial* $\mathrm{Cperm}_n(Y)$ *can also be computed by a polynomial-sized noncommutative arithmetic circuit.*

PROOF. Assume that $\mathrm{sdet}_{2n}(X)$ is computed by a circuit C of size s. As in Theorem 2, we will proceed by taking Hadamard product. Let P be the ABP defined in Lemma 2 and $F(X)$ the polynomial it computes. Let F'' denote the polynomial $\mathrm{sdet}_{2n}(X) \circ F$. Note that by Corollary 1, F'' can be computed by a circuit C'' of size $\mathrm{poly}(s, n)$. From Lemma 2, we have $F(m_{\sigma,\tau}) = 0$ unless $\sigma = 1_{2n}$, the identity permutation in S_{2n}; moreover, we also have $F(m_{1_{2n},\tau}) = F(m_\tau)$ which is 1 if $\tau = \rho(\pi)$ for some $\pi \in S_n$ and 0 otherwise. By the above reasoning,

$$F''(X) = \frac{1}{(2n)!} \sum_{\pi \in S_n} \mathrm{sgn}(\rho(\pi)) m_{\rho(\pi)} = \frac{\mathrm{sgn}(\rho_0)}{(2n)!} \sum_{\pi \in S_n} m_{\rho(\pi)}$$

Now, we substitute each $x_{i,j}$ by $y_{\frac{1+i}{2},j}$ if i is odd and $j \in [n]$ and by 1 if i is even or $j \notin [n]$ in the circuit C''. The effect of this substitution is to transform $m_{\rho(\pi)}$ into $y_{1,\pi(1)} y_{2,\pi(2)} \cdots y_{n,\pi(n)}$ for each $\pi \in S_n$. Hence, the resulting polynomial is simply $\frac{\mathrm{sgn}(\rho_0)\mathrm{Cperm}_n(Y)}{(2n)!}$. Thus, by multiplying by $\mathrm{sgn}(\rho_0)(2n)!$, we obtain a circuit C' of size $\mathrm{poly}(s, n)$ that computes $\mathrm{Cperm}_n(Y)$. □

THEOREM 6. *If there is a polynomial-time algorithm* $\mathcal{P}$ *that computes the* $2n \times 2n$ *symmetrized determinant of matrices with entries in* $M_S(\mathbb{F})$*, for* $S = c \cdot n^2$ *for suitable* $c > 0$*, then there is a polynomial-time algorithm that computes the* $n \times n$ *permanent over* $\mathbb{F}$.

PROOF. The proof is almost exactly identical to that of Theorem 3. Consider the algorithm given by Corollary 2 for computing $\mathrm{sdet}_{2n} \circ F$ over the field $\mathbb{F}$, where the ABP in Corollary 2 is the ABP of Lemma 2 computing F.

In order to evaluate the permanent over inputs $a_{ij}, 1 \leq i, j \leq n$ we will substitute $x_{2i-1,j} = a_{ij}$ for $1 \leq i, j \leq n$ and we put $x_{i,j} = 1$ when i is even or $j > n$. As in the proof of Theorem 5, it follows that for this substitution the algorithm computing $\mathrm{sdet}_{2n} \circ F$ will output $\frac{\mathrm{sgn}(\rho_0)}{(2n)!} \mathrm{Cperm}_n(a_{11}, \ldots, a_{nn})$. Since $\mathrm{sgn}(\rho_0)$ and $(2n)!$ are easily computable, we have a polynomial-time algorithm for computing the $n \times n$ permanent over $\mathbb{F}$. □

We now consider the Moore determinant. We first demonstrate by a simple reduction that the Moore determinant and permanent are interreducible. We then show that the computing the Moore determinant over a field of characteristic zero is at least as hard as counting the number of directed Hamilton Cycles of a directed graph, which is a well-known #P-complete problem. If the field is of characteristic k, then computing the Moore determinant over the field is at least as hard as counting the number of Hamilton cycles of a directed graph modulo the prime k, which is hard for the complexity class $\mathrm{Mod}_k\mathrm{P}$.

Assume $X = \{x_{i,j} \mid 1 \leq i, j \leq n\}$. Given a permutation $\sigma \in S_n$, we write σ as a product of disjoint cycles as follows: $(n^\sigma_{11} \cdots n^\sigma_{1l_1})(n^\sigma_{21} \cdots n^\sigma_{2l_2}) \cdots (n^\sigma_{r1} \cdots n^\sigma_{rl_r})$ with $n^\sigma_{i1} < n^\sigma_{ij}$ for all $i \in [r]$ and $j \in [l_r] \setminus \{1\}$ and satisfying $n^\sigma_{11} > n^\sigma_{21} > \cdots > n^\sigma_{r1}$. Recall that term_σ denotes the monomial $x_{n^\sigma_{11},n^\sigma_{12}} \cdots x_{n^\sigma_{1l_r},n^\sigma_{11}} \cdots x_{n^\sigma_{r1},n^\sigma_{r2}} \cdots x_{n^\sigma_{rl_r},n^\sigma_{r1}}$. Finally, let $\mathbb{F}$ be an arbitrary field.

Let C_n denote the set of all n-cycles in S_n, i.e permutations whose cycle decomposition consists of a single cycle of length n. Define the polynomial $\mathrm{HC}_n(x_{1,1}, \ldots, x_{n,n}) \in \mathbb{F}\langle X \rangle$ to be

$$\mathrm{HC}_n(x_{1,1}, \ldots, x_{n,n}) = \sum_{\sigma \in C_n} \mathrm{term}_\sigma.$$

Fix any directed graph G on n vertices with adjacency matrix A. Let $H(G)$ denote $\mathrm{HC}_n(A(1,1),\ldots,A(n,n))$. The quantity $H(G)$ has a simple description: if $\mathbb{F}$ is of characteristic zero, then $H(G)$ is the number of directed Hamiltonian cycles in G; and if $\mathbb{F}$ is of characteristic k, then $H(G)$ is the number of directed Hamiltonian cycles of G modulo k.
We have the following easy lemma:

LEMMA 4. *There are ABPs P_1' and P_2' of size $O(n^2)$ that compute homogeneous polynomials $F_1', F_2' \in \mathbb{F}\langle X\rangle$ of degree n such that for any $\sigma \in S_n$, we have*

- $F_1'(\mathrm{term}_\sigma) = \mathrm{sgn}(\sigma)$.
- $F_2'(\mathrm{term}_\sigma) = \mathrm{sgn}(\sigma)$ *if $\sigma \in C_n$ and 0 otherwise.*

Moreover, the above ABPs can be computed in time polynomial in n.

PROOF. Recall that given a permutation $\sigma \in S_n$, the quantity $\mathrm{sgn}(\sigma)$ is $(-1)^{n+c_\sigma}$, where c_σ is the number of disjoint cycles in σ. Moreover, note that if σ as a product of disjoint cycles is $(n_{11}^\sigma\cdots n_{1l_1}^\sigma)(n_{21}^\sigma\cdots n_{2l_2}^\sigma)\cdots(n_{r1}^\sigma\cdots n_{rl_r}^\sigma)$ as above, the value c_σ is simply the number of *left-to-right minima* in this representation, i.e the number of n_{ij}^σ such that $n_{ij}^\sigma < n_{kl}^\sigma$ for all n_{kl}^σ to the *left* of n_{ij}^σ. Using this observation, it is easy to design an ABP P_1' that keeps track of the sign of the permutation and computes a polynomial F_1' as above. The ABP P_2' can be constructed similarly. The main difference from the case of P_1' is that the ABP P_2' must produce the coefficient 0 unless $n_{11}^\sigma = 1$. We omit the easy details in a formal description of P_1' and P_2'. □

The analogue of Theorem 2 for the Moore determinant follows below. The statement here is stronger: we show that the arithmetic circuit complexity of $\mathrm{Mdet}_n(X)$ is polynomial *if and only if* the arithmetic circuit complexity of $\mathrm{Mperm}_n(X)$ is polynomial.

THEOREM 7. *The Moore determinant $\mathrm{Mdet}_n(X)$ can be computed by a polynomial-sized noncommutative arithmetic circuit if and only if the Moore permanent polynomial $\mathrm{Mperm}_n(X)$ can be computed by a polynomial-sized noncommutative arithmetic circuit.*

PROOF. As in the proof of Theorem 2, we will use the Hadamard product; this time, it can be used to erase or introduce the signs of the permutations corresponding to each monomial term_σ. Formally, we have $\mathrm{Mperm}_n(X) = \mathrm{Mdet}_n(X) \circ F_1'(X)$ and $\mathrm{Mdet}_n(X) = \mathrm{Mperm}_n(X) \circ F_1'(X)$, where $F_1'(X)$ is the polynomial defined in the statement of Lemma 4. Hence, if $\mathrm{Mdet}_n(X)$ (respectively, $\mathrm{Mperm}_n(X)$) is computed by a noncommutative arithmetic circuit of size s, then by applying Corollary 1, we see that $\mathrm{Mperm}_n(X)$ (respectively, $\mathrm{Mdet}_n(X)$) is computed by a noncommutative arithmetic circuit of size $\mathrm{poly}(s,n)$. □

REMARK 5. *Note that Theorem 7 proves an equivalence (up to polynomial factors) between the arithmetic circuit complexities of the Moore determinant and permanent. This is a stronger statement than we obtained in the case of the Cayley determinant and permanent, where we only showed (roughly) that the Cayley determinant is at least as hard to compute as the Cayley permanent. The reason for this is that we are unable to obtain a small ABP that performs the function of P_1' for the monomials m_σ (defined in Section 4): that is, a small ABP computing a polynomial F_1 such that $F_1(m_\sigma) = \mathrm{sgn}(m_\sigma)$ for every $\sigma \in S_n$. However, we are unable to rule out the possibility that such an ABP exists. If it does, then as above, we can obtain a simple equivalence between the complexities of the Cayley determinant and permanent.*

We now consider the complexity of computing the Moore determinant over matrix algebras of polynomial dimension. We can, as in the previous sections, show that this is at least as hard as computing the permanent over matrices with entries from $\mathbb{F}$, but we take a different route this time. We show that if the Moore determinant over a field of characteristic k can be computed in polynomial time, then there is a polynomial-time algorithm to compute the number of directed Hamilton cycles $H(G)$ modulo k for an input directed graph G. This allows us to draw stronger consequences, namely that the Moore determinant is hard to compute even when the field $\mathbb{F}$ is of characteristic 2, something that would not follow if we reduced the permanent to this problem (since the permanent is polynomial-time computable over fields of characteristic 2).

THEOREM 8. *If there is a polynomial-time algorithm $\mathcal{P}$ that computes the $n\times n$ Moore determinant of matrices with entries in $M_S(\mathbb{F})$, for $S = c\cdot n^2$ for suitable $c > 0$, then there is a polynomial-time algorithm that, on input a directed graph G, computes $H(G)$.*

PROOF. Note that we can write the polynomial $\mathrm{HC}_n(X)$ as $\mathrm{HC}_n(X) = \mathrm{Mdet}_n(X) \circ F_2'$, where F_2' is the polynomial computed by ABP P_2' constructed in Lemma 4. Moreover, $H(G) = \mathrm{HC}_n(A(1,1),\ldots,A(n,n))$, where A is the adjacency matrix of the graph G. Hence, to compute $H(G)$, we need to compute $\mathrm{HC}_n(A(1,1),\ldots,A(n,n))$, which can be done in polynomial time by Corollary 2. □

7. COMPLETENESS RESULTS

In this section we observe that the noncommutative Cayley determinant over integer matrices is complete for GapP w.r.t. polynomial-time Turing reductions. Likewise, the noncommutative Cayley determinant over a finite field of characteristic $k \neq 2$ is hard for the modular counting complexity class $\mathrm{Mod}_k\mathrm{P}$ w.r.t. polynomial-time Turing reductions. These observations also hold for the symmetrized determinant. For the Moore determinant, we prove the above results without any restriction on the characteristic of the underlying field. We formally describe these observations.

DEFINITION 3. *[FFK94],[BG92] A function $f : \Sigma^* \longrightarrow \mathbb{Z}$ is in GapP if there is a polynomial time NDTM M such that for each $x \in \Sigma^*$ the value $f(x)$ is $\mathrm{acc}_M(x) - \mathrm{rej}_M(x)$.*
For a prime k, the class $\mathrm{Mod}_k P$ consist of languages $L \subseteq \Sigma^*$ such that for some function $f \in$ GapP we have $x \in L$ if and only if $f(x) \equiv 0 (mod\ k)$.

By Valiant's result [V79] it is known that the integer permanent is GapP-complete with respect to polynomial-time Turing reductions. Furthermore, the permanent over $\mathbb{F}_k$ is $\mathrm{Mod}_k\mathrm{P}$-hard for prime $k \neq 2$.
Now, for $n \in \mathbb{N}$, consider the Cayley determinant for $2n \times 2n$ matrices with entries from $M_S(\mathbb{Z})$, where $S = cn^2$ for some constant c. By Theorem 3, there is a fixed $c > 0$ such that computing the integer permanent for $n \times n$ matrices

is polynomial-time reducible to computing the $(1, S)^{th}$ entry of such a Cayley determinant. The same observation holds modulo k for a prime k.
Furthermore, the problem of computing the $(1, S)^{th}$ entry of such a Cayley determinant over $\mathbb{Z}$ is easily seen to be in GapP: we can design a polynomial-time NDTM which takes as input a $2n \times 2n$ matrix with entries from $M_S(\mathbb{Z})$ and the difference in the number of accepting and rejecting paths is the $(1, S)^{th}$ entry of its Cayley determinant. Hence we have the following.

COROLLARY 5. *There exists a constant c such that the following holds. For $S = cn^2$, computing the $(1, S)^{th}$ entry of the Cayley determinant for $2n \times 2n$ matrices with entries from $M_S(\mathbb{Z})$ is GapP-complete w.r.t. polynomial-time Turing reductions. Given a finite field $\mathbb{F}$ of characteristic $k \neq 2$, computing the $(1, S)^{th}$ entry of the Cayley determinant for $2n \times 2n$ matrices over $M_S(\mathbb{F})$ is hard w.r.t. polynomial-time Turing reductions for Mod$_k$P.*

We have similar GapP-completeness and Mod$_k$P-hardness consequences for the symmetrized determinant from the results in Sections 6. For the Moore determinant, by Theorem 8, we additionally obtain hardness for $\oplus$P over fields of characteristic 2.

COROLLARY 6. *There exists a constant c such that the following holds. For $S = cn^2$, computing the $(1, S)^{th}$ entry of the Moore determinant for $2n \times 2n$ matrices with entries from $M_S(\mathbb{Z})$ is GapP-complete w.r.t. polynomial-time Turing reductions. Given a finite field $\mathbb{F}$ of any characteristic $k > 1$, computing the $(1, S)^{th}$ entry of the Moore determinant for $2n \times 2n$ matrices over $M_S(\mathbb{F})$ is hard w.r.t. polynomial-time Turing reductions for Mod$_k$P.*

PROOF. The result follows from Theorem 8 and the following observations: computing $H(G)$ over the rationals on an input graph G is GapP-complete w.r.t. polynomial-time Turing reductions; similarly, computing $H(G)$ over a field $\mathbb{F}$ of characteristic k (including $k = 2$) is hard for Mod$_k$P w.r.t. polynomial-time Turing reductions. □

8. DISCUSSION

Our work raises further interesting questions regarding the complexity of the noncommutative determinant.
An important open question is the complexity of computing the noncommutative determinant over constant dimensional matrix algebras. Theorem 3 can be easily used to show that assuming that the permanent of an $n \times n$ matrix over $\mathbb{F}$ cannot be computed in subexponential time, the $n \times n$ noncommutative Cayley, symmetrized, and Moore determinants with entries from $M_{(\log n)^{\omega(1)}}(\mathbb{F})$ cannot be computed in polynomial time. Can one strengthen this result to one that says something about computing the Cayley or Moore determinant over matrices with entries from $M_c(\mathbb{F})$ for some absolute constant c? (Recall that the symmetrized determinant, on the other hand, *is* efficiently computable over constant dimensional matrix algebras.) It is interesting to note that [CS04] have shown an exponential lower bound for the ABP complexity of the Cayley determinant over even 2×2 matrices.
As mentioned in Remark 5, an interesting technical question is whether or not there is a polynomial size ABP that computes a polynomial F of degree n such that $F(x_{1,\sigma(1)} \ldots x_{n,\sigma(n)}) = \mathrm{sgn}(\sigma)$ for every $\sigma \in S_n$. Such an ABP would make the proofs of Theorems 2 and 3 much more transparent. It would also easily imply, analogous to Theorem 7, that the Cayley permanent is at least as hard to compute as the Cayley determinant.
Finally, note that our results do not imply that the Cayley determinant is hard to compute over $M_k(\mathbb{F})$ when $\mathbb{F}$ is a field of characteristic 2, since the permanent is known to be polynomial-time computable over such fields. On the other hand, we have proved that the Moore determinant over such domains (where k is polynomial) is hard for $\oplus$P. Can we prove an analogous result for the Cayley determinant?

Acknowledgements. We are grateful to the referees for their comments and suggestions. Special thanks are due to Avi Wigderson and Amir Yehudayoff for their valuable comments on the paper.

9. REFERENCES

[AJS09] V. ARVIND, P. S. JOGLEKAR, S. SRINIVASAN. Arithmetic Circuits and the Hadamard Product of Polynomials *CoRR abs/0907.4006: (2009).* http://arxiv.org/abs/0907.4006. Proceedings of *IARCS Annual Conference on Foundations of Software Technology and Theoretical Computer Science, FSTTCS 2009, December 15 17, 2009, IIT Kanpur, India,* pp.25-36.

[AS09] V. ARVIND, S. SRINIVASAN. On the Hardness of the Noncommutative Determinant. *Electronic Colloquium of Computational Complexity, TR09-103.* http://eccc.hpi-web.de/report/2009/103/

[A96] H. ASLAKSEN. Quaternionic determinants. *Math. Intelligencer 18 (1996), no. 3,* 57-65.

[B] A. BARVINOK. New Permanent Estimators via Non-Commutative Determinants. Preprint available at http://www.math.lsa.umich.edu/~barvinok/det.ps.

[BG92] R. BEIGEL, J. GILL. Counting Classes: Thresholds, Parity, Mods, and Fewness. *Theor. Comput. Sci.* 103(1): 3-23 (1992).

[CS04] S. CHIEN, A. SINCLAIR. Algebras with polynomial identities and computing the determinant *In Proc. Annual IEEE Sym. on Foundations of Computer Science,*352-361, 2004.

[CRS03] S. CHIEN, L. E. RASMUSSEN, A. SINCLAIR. Clifford algebras and approximating the permanent. *J. Comput. Syst. Sci. 67(2)*: 263-290 (2003).

[FFK94] S. A. FENNER, L. FORTNOW, S. A. KURTZ. Gap-Definable Counting Classes. *J. Comput. Syst. Sci.* 48(1): 116-148 (1994).

[GG81] C. GODSIL, I. GUTMAN. On the matching polynomial of a graph, *Algebraic Methods in Graph Theory, 1981*, pp. 241-249.

[KKL+93] N. KARMARKAR, R. M. KARP, R. J. LIPTON, L. LOVÀSZ, MICHAEL LUBY. A Monte-Carlo Algorithm for Estimating the Permanent. *SIAM J. Comput.* 22(2): 284-293 (1993).

[LS09] D. LUNDHOLM, L. SVENSSON. Clifford algebra, geometric algebra, and applications. Available at http://arxiv.org/abs/0907.5356

[MR09] C. Moore, A. Russell. Approximating the Permanent via Nonabelian Determinants, *CoRR abs/0906.1702: (2009).* http://arxiv.org/abs/0906.1702

[N91] N. Nisan. Lower bounds for noncommutative computation *In Proc. of 23rd ACM Sym. on Theory of Computing*, 410-418, 1991.

[RS05] R. Raz, A. Shpilka. Deterministic polynomial identity testing in non commutative models *Computational Complexity*,14(1):1-19, 2005.

[V79] L. G. Valiant. The Complexity of Computing the Permanent. *Theor. Comput. Sci.* 8: 189-201 (1979).

A Shorter Proof of the Graph Minor Algorithm – The Unique Linkage Theorem –*

[Extended Abstract] †

Ken-ichi Kawarabayashi‡
National Institute of Informatics
2-1-2 Hitotsubashi, Chiyoda-ku
Tokyo, Japan
k_keniti@nii.ac.jp

Paul Wollan
Department of Computer Science
University of Rome, *La Sapienza*
Rome, Italy
wollan@di.uniroma1.it

ABSTRACT

At the core of the seminal Graph Minor Theory of Robertson and Seymour is a powerful theorem which describes the structure of graphs excluding a fixed minor. This result is used to prove Wagner's conjecture and provide a polynomial time algorithm for the disjoint paths problem when the number of the terminals is fixed (i.e, the Graph Minor Algorithm). However, both results require the full power of the Graph Minor Theory, i.e, the structure theorem.

In this paper, we show that this is not true in the latter case. Namely, we provide a new and much simpler proof of the correctness of the Graph Minor Algorithm. Specifically, we prove the "Unique Linkage Theorem" without using Graph Minors structure theorem. The new argument, in addition to being simpler, is much shorter, cutting the proof by at least 200 pages. We also give a new full proof of correctness of an algorithm for the well-known edge-disjoint paths problem when the number of the terminals is fixed, which is at most 25 pages long.

Categories and Subject Descriptors

G.2.2 [**Discrete Mathematics**]: Graph Theory—*Graph algorithms, Path and circuit problems*

General Terms

Algorithms, Theory

*This work was partially supported by MOU grant at National Institute of Informatics.

†A full version of this paper is available at `http://reseach.nii.ac.jp/~k_keniti/uniquelink.pdf`

‡Research partly supported by Japan Society for the Promotion of Science, Grant-in-Aid for Scientific Research, by C and C Foundation, by Kayamori Foundation and by Inoue Research Award for Young Scientists.

Keywords

Disjoint paths problem, Graph Minors, linkages

1. INTRODUCTION

1.1 Graph Minors Algorithm

One of the deepest and most important bodies of work in graph theory is the Graph Minor Theory developed by Robertson and Seymour. At the heart of this theory is a theorem [33, Theorem 1.3] describing the structure of all graphs excluding a fixed graph as a minor. At a high level, the theorem says that every such graph can be decomposed into a collection of graphs each of which can "almost" be embedded into a bounded-genus surface, combined in a tree structure. Much of the Graph Minors series of articles is devoted to the proof of this structure theorem.

The main algorithmic result of the Graph Minor Theory is a polynomial-time algorithm for testing the existence of a fixed minor [31] which, combined with the proof of Wagner's Conjecture, implies the existence of a polynomial-time algorithm for deciding any minor-closed graph property. The existence of such a polynomial time algorithm has in turn been used to show the existence of polynomial-time algorithms for several graph problems, some of which were not previously known to be decidable [10]. It also leads to the framework of parameterized complexity developed by Downey and Fellows [8], which is perhaps one of the most active areas in the study of algorithms.

This algorithm is one of the most important polynomial time algorithms in theoretical computer science. The algorithm is relatively easy to describe. However, the proof of correctness of the algorithm (that is, the proof that the algorithm does in fact correctly determine the presence of a fixed graph as a minor) uses the full power of the Graph Minor Theory. More precisely, we can immediately reduce the problem to the case when the input graph has no large clique minor. However, the analysis of this case requires the development of the structure theorem. Our goal is to provide a new proof for the correctness of this algorithm that avoids many of the difficulties and technicalities in the original proof of Robertson and Seymour, and, specifically, avoids the use of the structure theorem.

The main purpose of this paper is to show the correctness of the Graph Minor Algorithm without using the structure theorem. This leads to a dramatically shorter and more simple proof of the correctness for the algorithm.

Much of the proof of the correctness of Graph Minor Algorithm in fact focuses on developing an algorithm for the disjoint paths problem. It will be more convenient for us, as well, to focus on the disjoint paths problem. We discuss this further in the next subsection.

1.2 The Graph Minors Algorithm vs. the k-disjoint paths problem

In the edge- (vertex-) disjoint paths problem, we are given a graph G and a set of k pairs of vertices, called *terminals*, in G, and we have to decide whether or not G has k edge- (vertex-) disjoint paths connecting given pairs of terminals. The problem of testing whether a given graph contains a fixed graph H as a minor can be trivially reduced to a bounded number of vertex disjoint path problems. Thus, a polynomial time algorithm for the k disjoint paths problem yields a polynomial time algorithm for minor testing, albeit with a worse runtime than that of the Graph Minors Algorithm. Moreover, the arguments for minor testing and the disjoint paths problem are analogous, although somewhat simpler to explain in the case of the disjoint paths problem. Finally, the k disjoint paths problem is also a classic problem the theory of algorithms, widely studied in its own right. For all these reasons, for the remainder of the article we will restrict our attention to the k disjoint paths problem. We will return only briefly to Graph Minors Algorithm to show how our results yield a short argument for the correctness of the Graph Minors Algorithm.

1.3 Background on the disjoint paths problem

The k disjoint paths problem, both in it's vertex and edge disjoint versions, is a central problem in algorithmic graph theory and combinatorial optimization. See the surveys [11, 36]. It has attracted attention in the contexts of transportation networks, VLSI layout and virtual circuit routing in high-speed networks or on the internet. A basic technical problem here is to interconnect certain prescribed "channels" on a chip such that wires belonging to different pins do not touch each other. In this simplest form, the problem mathematically amounts to finding disjoint trees in a graph or disjoint paths in a graph, each connecting a given set of vertices.

We now quickly look at previous results on the k disjoint paths problem. If k is as a part of the input of the problem, then this is one of Karp's original NP-complete problems [13], and it remains NP-complete even if G is restricted to be planar (Lynch [22]). The seminal work of Robertson and Seymour says that there exists a polynomial time algorithm (the actual runtime of the algorithm is $O(n^3)$. The time complexity is improved to $O(n^2)$ in [18]) for the disjoint paths problem when the number of terminals, k, is fixed. In the next subsection, we give an outline of this algorithm.

1.4 Robertson-Seymour Algorithm

In this subsection, we sketch Robertson and Seymour's algorithm for the k disjoint paths problem (see also [27]). At a high level, Robertson-Seymour's algorithm is based on the following two cases: either a given graph G has bounded tree-width (bounded by some function of k) or else it has large tree-width.

Case 1. Tree-width of G is bounded.

In this case, one can apply a dynamic programming argument to a tree-decomposition of bounded tree-width, see [1, 2, 31].

Case 2. Tree-width of G is large.

This second case again breaks into two cases depending on whether G has a large clique minor or not.

Case 2.1. G has a large clique minor.

If there exist disjoint paths from the terminals to this clique minor, then we can use this clique minor to link up the terminals in any desired way. Otherwise, there is a small cut set such that the large clique minor is cut off from the terminals by this cut set. In this case, we can prove that there is a vertex v in the clique minor which is *irrelevant*, i.e., the k disjoint paths problem is feasible in G if and only if it is also feasible in $G - v$. We then recursively apply the algorithm to $G - v$.

Case 2.2. G does not have a huge clique minor.

In this case, one can prove that, after deleting a bounded number of vertices, there is a huge subgraph which is essentially planar. Moreover, this huge planar subgraph itself has very large tree width. This makes it possible to prove that the middle vertex v of this wall is irrelevant. Again, we recursively apply the algorithm to $G - v$.

The analysis of Cases 1 and 2.1 is relatively easy. It is the analysis of Case 2.2 that gives rise to the majority of the work. The analysis of this case requires the whole series of graph minor papers and the structure theorem of [33].

1.5 Our main contributions – Unique linkage theorem

The analysis of Case 2 in the previous subsection can be reduced to the Unique Linkage Theorem without excessive difficulty. It is then the proof of the Unique Linkage Theorem that requires much of the graph minors machinery. In fact, in the corresponding argument for the Graph Minors Algorithm, this is the only place in the proof of correctness which requires the full structure theorem. Before stating the theorem, we give some notation.

A *linkage* is a graph where every component is a path (possibly trivial). The *order* of the linkage is the number of components. In slightly sloppy notation, we will use $P \in \mathcal{P}$ to refer to a component P of the linkage $\mathcal{P}$. Two linkages $\mathcal{P}$ and $\mathcal{P}'$ are *equivalent* if they have the same order and for every component P of $\mathcal{P}$, there exists a component P' of $\mathcal{P}'$ such that P and P' have the same endpoints. We say a linkage $\mathcal{P}$ in a graph G is *unique* if for all linkages $\mathcal{P}'$ in G equivalent to $\mathcal{P}$, we have that $V(\mathcal{P}') = V(\mathcal{P})$.

We are now ready to state the theorem, which is the main result of Graph Minors XXI [34].

Theorem 1 (The Unique Linkage Theorem [34]). *For all $k \geq 1$, there exists a value $w(k)$ such that the following holds. Let $\mathcal{P}$ be a linkage of order k in a graph G with $V(G) = V(\mathcal{P})$. If $\mathcal{P}$ is unique, then the tree-width of G is at most $w(k)$.*

The current proof given by Robertson and Seymour [34] needs the full power of the graph minor structure theorem, but they predicted that there exists a simpler proof avoiding the use of the Graph Minor structure theorem. Our main contribution is to confirm that they are right– we provide such a short proof. Our proof less is than 25 pages, and gives rise to an explicit bound for the tree-width $w(k)$, while the original algorithm does not.

We now mention several consequences of our new shorter proof. First, we clarify how the unique linkage theorem implies that the vertex v in Case 2 is irrelevant. This was easy to prove for Case 2.1. The formal argument is given in Sections 5 and 6 in [31]. We are left with Case 2.2. The main result in [35] says that the existence of the irrelevant vertex in Case 2.2 can be reduced to the unique linkage problem. Let us observe that the arguments in [35] does NOT use the graph minor structure theorem. It is totally self-contained. Our proof of the Unique Linkage Theorem currently uses several tools from [29] for graphs embedded on surfaces of bounded genus (again, these tools do not depend on the structure theorem). Thus together with [35] and [29], our proof of the Unique Linkage Theorem provides a proof of the correctness of the k-disjoint paths algorithm which avoids the use of the graph minor structure theorem. At the moment, we believe that we also have a much shorter proof of the main result in [35] and the aspects of [29] which we use. This would lead to a correspondingly short, self-contained proof of the k-vertex disjoint paths algorithm.

Second, when we consider instead the k-edge disjoint paths problem, we are able to avoid the need for the work of [35]. This allows us to give a self-contained argument for the proof of correctness of the k-edge disjoint paths problem. We present the argument in the next subsection.

Finally, one of the original applications of the Unique Linkage Theorem is to verify the "intertwining conjecture" of Lovász [21] and Milgram and Unger [24]. The conjecture states that for every two graphs G_1 and G_2, there is a finite list $H_1, \dots, H_n$ of graphs, such that G topologically contains both G_1 and G_2 if and only if it topologically contains one of $H_1, \dots, H_n$ (G *topologically* contains H if some subgraph of G is isomorphic to a subdivision of H). A proof of this conjecture follows from the unique linkage theorem, as proved in [34]. But our proof, together with the proof in Section 11 of [34] gives rise to a short self-contained proof of this conjecture, which is, we believe, of independent interest. As pointed out in [34], our proof yields an algorithm that given two graphs G_1 and G_2, computes $H_1, \dots, H_n$ above.

We conclude with a few words on possible applications of our new proof. Kernelization is a technique for creating algorithms for fixed-parameter tractable problems. This concept has attracted recent interest within the framework of parameterized complexity. See, for example, [3]. The approach is based on the observation that a problem is fixed-parameter tractable if and only if it is kernelizable and decidable. The idea of kernelization is to reduce the size of the input X to a function of k in polynomial time. When the input is bounded by k, we can use any exponential time algorithm, for example brute-force search, to find a solution of the problem. A basic technique in kernelization arguments is to find an "irrelevant" vertex for the problem, and reduce the size of the input. This is exactly what we do for the disjoint paths problem, hence we hope that our new short proof might yield new technical methods in this line of inquiry.

Algorithms for H-minor-free graphs for a fixed graph H have been studied extensively; see e.g. [4, 5, 6, 12]. In particular, it is generally believed that algorithms for planar graphs can often be generalized to H-minor-free graphs for any fixed H. Results from graph minors, and the unique linkage theorem in particular, are essential for these arguments. For example, the topological embedding algorithms given in [14, 15, 16, 17, 23] partially depend on the unique linkage theorem. Also, linear time algorithms for the disjoint paths problem when an input graph is planar [26] or an input graph is bounded genus [9, 20] heavily depend on the unique linkage theorem. Thus we anticipate that our new proof will have further applications along these lines.

1.6 The edge-disjoint paths problem

Using our new proof of Unique Linkage Theorem, we give a short proof of correctness for the *k-edge disjoint paths problem*.

Input: A graph G with n vertices and m edges, k pairs of vertices (s_i, t_i), called *terminals*, $i = 1, \dots, k$, in G.

Output : Edge-disjoint paths $P_1, P_2, \dots, P_k$ in G such that P_i joins s_i and t_i for $i = 1, 2, \dots, k$.

We assume that k is fixed. We will need the following definitions. For a vertex set X in a graph $G = (V, E)$, let $\delta(X)$ be the set of edges between X and $V \setminus X$. For a graph $G = (V, E)$, its *line graph* $L(G)$ is the graph whose vertex set is E such that two vertices of $L(G)$ are adjacent if and only if their corresponding edges share a common endpoint in G. To simplify the description, when we consider the line graph of a graph with terminals, we assume that exactly one edge is incident to each terminal by adding a new terminal and a single edge to G. Let $\tilde{s}_1, \dots, \tilde{s}_k, \tilde{t}_1, \dots, \tilde{t}_k$ be the edges incident with the terminals $s_1, \dots, s_k, t_1, \dots, t_k$ in G, respectively. Then, one can see that the edge-disjoint paths problem in G with respect to the terminals $s_1, \dots, s_k, t_1, \dots, t_k$ is equivalent to the vertex-disjoint paths problem in $L(G)$ with respect to the terminals $\tilde{s}_1, \dots, \tilde{s}_k, \tilde{t}_1, \dots, \tilde{t}_k$.

As proved in [19], an instance of the k edge-disjoint paths problem can be reduced to an instance satisfying the following conditions:

(R1) All vertices have degree at most $2k - 1$.

(R2) G has no vertex set X such that $|X| \geq 2$, X contains no terminals, and $|\delta(X)| \leq 3$.

(R3) G and $L(G)$ has no clique minor of size $3k$.

We call these operations *simple reductions*. Although it is easy to find a vertex of high degree (as in (R1)) and a ≤ 3-edge-cut in a given graph (as in (R2)), it is not easy to find a large clique minor.

The following theorem, which is the main result in [19], characterizes the instances of the edge-disjoint paths problem, and shows a way to find a large clique minor.

Theorem 2. *For any instance of the k-edge-disjoint paths problem and for any integer $h \geq 2$, there exists an integer $f(k, h)$ such that one of the following holds:*

(A) The instance violates at least one of (R1), (R2), and (R3). That is, one of the simple reductions can be applied to the instance.

(B) The input graph has tree-width at most $f(k, h)$.

(C) The input graph contains a wall W of size h with the outer face boundary C with the following properties:

(a) $G - C$ consists of two parts X and Y such that $X \cup C$ contains the whole wall W.

(b) Every vertex of $X \cup C$ has degree at most three.

(c) $X \cup C$ does not contain any terminal.

(d) $X \cup C$ can be embedded in a plane with the outer face boundary C.

We can find one of (A), (B) and (C) in $O(m)$ time. Furthermore, if the instance satisfies (R1) and (R2), but does not satisfy (B) and (C), then we can find a clique minor of size $3k$ in G or $L(G)$ in $O(m)$ time (For definitions of the tree-width and the wall, we refer the reader to the appendix).

Having Theorem 2, we are ready to describe our $O(mn)$ time algorithm for the edge disjoint path problem more precisely. The algorithm below has appeared in [19], but for the completeness, we include the whole algorithm. We set $h = 4w(k) + 4$, where $w(k)$ is the value given by Theorem 1.

Algorithm for the edge-disjoint paths problem

Step 1. We first apply Theorem 2. If (A) in Theorem 2 occurs, we apply a simple reduction as in (A) and recurse on a smaller graph. If (B) occurs, we apply the standard dynamic programming argument [1, 2]. Thus we may assume outcome (C).

Step 2. If (C) happens, it is possible to throw away a vertex v (*irrelevant vertex*) in the deep inside the wall W if h is large enough (i.e, the vertex in the middle brick of W).

We then recursively apply our algorithm to $G - v$. Since Theorem 2 can be done in $O(m)$ time, the whole algorithm runs in $O(mn)$ time (this improves the time complexity of [31] that gives an $O(m^3)$ algorithm for the edge-disjoint paths problem).

Correctness of the Algorithm

For the correctness of the algorithm, it suffices to prove that v is an irrelevant vertex in Step 2. We now give a proof, which is very similar to that given in [35], Theorem (3.1). We shall essentially reduce the correctness of the algorithm to the unique linkage theorem.

It is easy to see that if G does not have the desired k edge-disjoint paths, then $G - v$ does not have them either. Thus it remains to show that if the desired k edge-disjoint paths exist in G, then $G - v$ has them as well. Let G' be the line graph $L(G)$. We begin with the following:

(1) The line graph of $X \cup C$ described in (C) of Theorem 2 is still a plane graph.

This is because each vertex in $X \cup C$ has degree at most three in $X \cup C$. Hereafter, let H be the plane subgraph of G' induced by $X \cup C$.

Let $C_1, \dots, C_s$ be disjoint cycles in the plane graph H. Let D_i be the disc in the plane with boundary C_i. We say that they are *concentric* if we have the property that $D_s \subsetneq \cdots \subsetneq D_1$. Let $C_1, \dots, C_{h/2}$ be concentric cycles in H and $\mathcal{P} = \{P_1, \dots, P_k\}$ be a linkage in G'. Note that since $X \cup C$ contains a wall of height h, it follows that H also contains these $h/2$ concentric cycles.

We assume that the vertices of G' that correspond to the edges incident with v in Step 2 are contained in $D_{h/2} - C_{h/2}$ (again such a choice is possible by the above remark). Let $M = C_1 \cup \cdots \cup C_h$. We only need to prove is the following:

(2) Suppose M exists in G'. Then the desired k vertex-disjoint paths in G' exist such that the vertices of G' that correspond to the edges incident with v in G are not in any of the paths.

This will clearly suffice to complete the proof of the theorem. We prove (2) by induction on the number of vertices of G'. Note that we do not preserve line graph in the inductive step, i.e, when we make a smaller graph and apply induction, it may not be the line graph of some graph. We only require that our graph is contained in H as a subgraph, i.e, $h/2$ concentric cycles in a subgraph of the plane graph H.

Proceeding, if there is a vertex u that is not in $M \cup \mathcal{P}$, then we can delete u from G', and apply induction to $G' - u$. Similarly, consider the case when there exists an edge e that is in C_i, $i \leq t/2$, but one of the endpoints is not used in $\mathcal{P}$. We can contract e and still preserves the existence of concentric cycles $C_1, \dots, C_i/e, \dots, C_{h/2}$ (and a plane subgraph H/e), unless $|C_i| = 3$. But if $|C_i| = 3$, then we can clearly reroute the paths in $\mathcal{P}$ so that they do not touch any vertex inside the disk D_i, except for the vertices in C_i, and so find a linkage avoiding the edges incident v. Thus, after contracting e, we can apply induction to the resulting graph. We conclude that $V(M \cup \mathcal{P}) = V(G')$.

Let $w(k)$ be the value given by Theorem 3. By a *dive* we mean a subpath of a path in $\mathcal{P}$ contained in the disc D_1 with both ends in C_1 and at least one vertex in C_l for some $l \geq w(k) + 1$ We now claim the following:

(3) There are at most $w(k)$ dives.

If there is another linkage $\mathcal{P}'$ equivalent to $\mathcal{P}$ such that $|V(\mathcal{P}')| < |V(\mathcal{P})|$, then there is a vertex u of G' that is not in $\mathcal{P}'$. If u is not in M, then we delete u from G', and apply induction to $G' - u$. Similarly, if u is in M, then there is an edge e with one endpoint u in M. In this case, we contract e as above. After contracting e, we can apply the inductive hypothesis to the resulting graph. Thus we may assume that $\mathcal{P}$ is a unique linkage.

We now use the unique linkage theorem to prove (3). Suppose for a contradiction that the linkage $\mathcal{P}$ contains at least $w(k) + 1$ dives. Then since H is a plane subgraph of G' and M is contained in H, there are dives $P_1, P_2, \dots, P_{w(k)+1}$ that are pairwise disjoint and all intersect C_i for $i = 1, \dots, w(k)+1$. This implies that $P_1, P_2, \dots, P_{w(k)+1}$ all intersect each of $C_1, C_2, \dots, C_{w(k+1)}$, and hence $C_1 \cup P_1, C_2 \cup P_2, \dots, C_{w(k)+1} \cup P_{w(k)+1}$ is a "bramble" in G' of "order" at least $w(k) + 1$ (for the definition of the bramble, we refer the reader to [25]). By [25] the graph G' has tree-width at least $w(k) + 1$, a contradiction to the unique linkage theorem. This proves (3).

We are now ready to finish the proof. We claim that no dive intersects $C_{2w(k)+1}$. The *depth* of a dive P is the maximum index i such that $P \cap C_i \neq \emptyset$. To see this, observe that if P is a dive of depth i, then if C_{i-1} does not intersect any path of $\mathcal{P}$, we can reroute the component of $\mathcal{P}$ containing $\mathcal{P}$ to avoid the vertex $P \cap C_i$. Thus, some component (other than the one containing P) of $\mathcal{P}$ intersects C_{i-1}. By planarity, it follows that there exists a dive of depth $i - 1$. Thus, if there exists a dive of depth $2w(k) + 2$, we see that there exist $w(k) + 1$ dives, a contradiction to (3).

If we assume that $h \geq 4w(k)+4$, we see that no component of $\mathcal{P}$ can intersect $C_{t/2}$. This completes the proof of (2), and the theorem. □

In the next section, we give an outline of our proof of the unique linkage theorem. To help the reader see how the proof goes, we shall give a short proof of the case $k = 2$.

2. OUTLINE OF THE PROOF OF THE UNIQUE LINKAGE THEOREM

In this section, we give an overview for our proof of the unique linkage theorem[1]. The proof proceeds by analyzing what we will call *traversing linkages*. Before we give the exact definition, we first give some intuition of what a traversing linkage is. Let $\mathcal{P}$ be a k-linkage. A linkage $\mathcal{Q}$ traverses $\mathcal{P}$ if when we follow the linkage $\mathcal{Q}$ from beginning to end, we intersect the linkage $\mathcal{P}$ repeatedly in a regular, uniform way. Moreover, these intersections are independent of each other in a sense. That is, the first intersections of $\mathcal{P}$ and $\mathcal{Q}$ are contained in a small subpath of $\mathcal{P}$, and $\mathcal{Q}$ never returns to that subpath. We reduce the proof of the Unique Linkage Theorem to showing the following theorem.

Theorem 3. *There exists functions $l(k)$ and $w(k)$ such that the following holds. Let $\mathcal{P}$ be a linkage of order k, and let $\mathcal{Q}$ be a linkage traversing $\mathcal{P}$ of order $w(k)$ and length $l(k)$. Then $\mathcal{P}$ is not unique in $\mathcal{P} \cup \mathcal{Q}$.*

Traversing linkages have two nice properties we use repeatedly in the proof of Theorem 3. First, the graph consists of the union of just two linkages, and so is dramatically simpler than the general graphs typically analyzed in the theory of graph minors. Second, there is an element of symmetry allowing us to move back and forth between analyzing first the linkage $\mathcal{P}$, and then the linkage $\mathcal{Q}$, and back again.

We now give the exact definition of a traversing linkage. We recall that a *ladder of length t* is a graph consisting of two paths of length P_1, P_2 with the vertices of P_i equal to $v_1^i, \dots, v_t^i$ for $i = 1, 2$ as well as edges of the form $v_j 1 v_j 2$ for $1 \leq j \leq t$.

Definition 4. Let $\mathcal{P}$ be a linkage. The linkage $\mathcal{Q}$ *traverses* $\mathcal{P}$ (or, equivalently, is a traversing linkage) if there exist disjoint subpaths $B_1, \dots, B_l$ in $\mathcal{P}$ such that the following hold:

a. The linkage $\mathcal{Q}$ intersects $\mathcal{P}$ only in the subpaths $B_1, \dots, B_l$, i.e. $V(\mathcal{Q}) \cap V(\mathcal{P}) \subseteq \bigcup_1^l V(B_i)$.

b. For all $Q \in \mathcal{Q}$ and $1 \leq i \leq l$, $Q \cap B_i$ is a (possibly trivial) subpath of B_i.

c. For every element $Q \in \mathcal{Q}$, we may traverse the path Q from one end to the other, we encounter the paths $B_1, B_2, \dots, B_l$ in that order.

d. If we look at the Z the set of subpaths of $\mathcal{Q}$ with one end in B_i and another end in B_{i+1} for $1 \leq i \leq l-1$, then $Z \cup B_i \cup B_{i+1}$ forms a subdivided ladder after possibly deleting vertices of degree one.

The paths $B_1, B_2, \dots, B_l$ are called the *basis subpaths* of the traversing linkage $\mathcal{Q}$. The value l is the *length* of the traversing linkage $\mathcal{Q}$. Again, the order of the traversing linkage is the number of components. Fix labels s_P, t_P to the endpoints of every component $P \in \mathcal{P}$. If we consider the ladder in d, there are two distinct possibilities. Let P and P' be the components of $\mathcal{P}$ containing B_i and B_{i+1}, respectively. We say that $\mathcal{Q}$ *twists between B_i and B_{i+1}* if for all j, the jth component of Z we intersect traveling P from s_P to t_P is the $(w-j+1)^{th}$ when traversing P' from $s_{P'}$ to $t_{P'}$ (where w is the order of $\mathcal{Q}$).

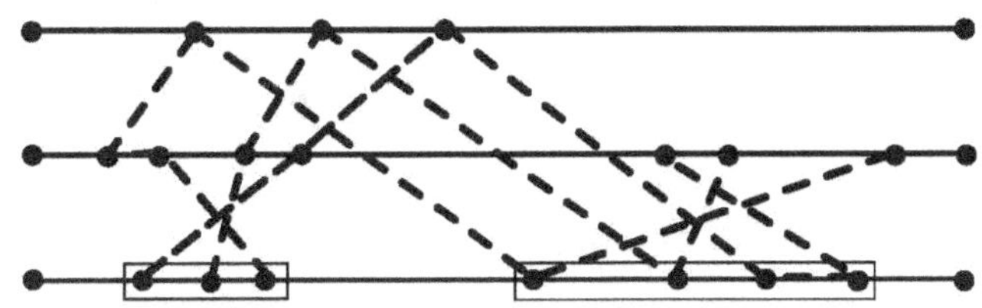

Figure 1: The dashed linkage is a traversing linkage of order three and length five traversing the solid linkage. The first and fourth basis subpaths are indicated with boxes. The dashed linkage twists between the first and second basis subpaths.

Observe, that if we swap the labels s_P and t_P on a component $P \in \mathcal{P}$, then if we consider some basis subpath B_i contained in P, if $\mathcal{Q}$ twists between B_i and B_{i+1} before the swap, then $\mathcal{Q}$ will not twist between the two basis subpaths after the swap (and vice versa: if $\mathcal{Q}$ does not twist before the swap, then it will twist after the swap).

We briefly describe now how we reduce the Unique Linkage Theorem to the proof of Theorem 3. The analysis is somewhat similar to the proof of the edge disjoint version of the disjoint paths problem. We proceed in two basic steps. First, we pick a prospective counter-example to the Unique Linkage Theorem: a linkage $\mathcal{P}$ contained in a graph G with $V(G) = V(\mathcal{P})$ such that G does not contain an equivalent linkage on fewer vertices. Moreover, we make the assumption that the tree width of the graph is huge. We first show that such a counterexample G cannot contain a large clique minor, and then using what we call the Weak Structure Theorem, we show that there exists a large planar subgraph H containing a huge wall such that the linkage $\mathcal{P}$ interacts with H planarly. In other words, even if there exist vertices with neighbors in the center of H, the components of $\mathcal{P}$ intersect H in a way that always respects the planar embedding of H. We then, as in the proof of the edge disjoint version, take a large number of concentric cycles such that they intersect the linkage $\mathcal{P}$ in a clean way. The concentric cycles as they travel through the linkage $\mathcal{P}$ will then provide the traversing linkage $\mathcal{Q}$.

The proof of Theorem 3 will be the main work in our proof of the Unique Linkage Theorem. The remainder of this section will be devoted to a brief outline of the proof of Theorem 3.

The proof of Theorem 3 proceeds by finding many sublinkages in $\mathcal{Q}$ forming what we will call $\mathcal{Q}$-bumps. Let $\mathcal{P}$ be a linkage and $\mathcal{Q}$ be a traversing linkage of order w. Let $B_1, \dots, B_l$ be the basis subpaths. A *$\mathcal{Q}$-bump* is a sublinkage $\overline{\mathcal{Q}}$ of $\mathcal{Q}$ of order w such that there exist indices i and i' and a path $P \in \mathcal{P}$ such that

a. every component of $\overline{\mathcal{Q}}$ has one endpoint in B_i and one endpoint in $B_{i'}$ and no internal vertex in P, and

b. B_i and $B_{i'}$ are both contained in P.

$\mathcal{Q}$-bumps can be thought of as a cylindrical set of subpaths wrapping around a sublinkage of the linkage $\mathcal{P}$. A $\mathcal{Q}$ bump allows one to reroute the linkage $\mathcal{P}$ - not to find an equivalent

[1]A full version of this paper is available at `http://reseach.nii.ac.jp/~k_keniti/uniquelink.pdf`

linkage - but rather to cyclically shift by one some subset of the paths. We make this more explicit in the following observation.

Observation 5. *Let $\mathcal{P}$ be a linkage of order k with components P_i for $1 \le i \le k$. Let s_i and t_i be the endpoints of P_i for $1 \le i \le k$. Let $\mathcal{Q}$ be a traversing linkage of order $k+1$ with basis subpaths $B_1, \dots, B_l$. Let $\overline{\mathcal{Q}}$ be a $\mathcal{Q}$-bump of length $l'+1$ with basis subpaths $\overline{B}_1, \dots, \overline{B}_{l'+1}$ satisfying the following properties.*

i. Assume $\overline{B}_i$ is contained in P_i for $1 \le i \le l'$. Specifically, note $\overline{B}_i$ and $\overline{B}_{i'}$ are contained in distinct components of $\mathcal{P}$ for $1 \le i < i' \le l'$.

ii. For all i, $1 \le i < l'+1$, $\mathcal{Q}$ does not twist between B_i and B_{i+1}.

Then $\mathcal{P} \cup \overline{\mathcal{Q}}$ contains disjoint paths $P'_1, \dots, P'_k$ such that the endpoints of P'_i are s_i and t_{i+1} for $1 \le i \le l'$ (taken modulo l') and the ends of P_i are s_i and t_i for $i > l'$. Moreover, the paths $P'_1, \dots, P'_k$ can be chosen to avoid some vertex of $\mathcal{P}$.

We illustrate the observation in Figure 2.

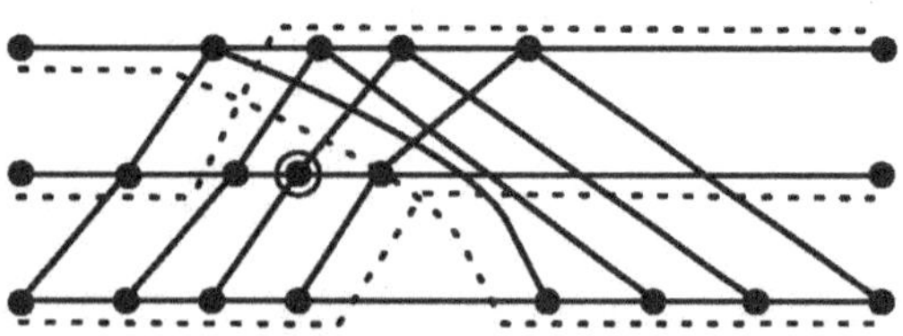

Figure 2: A bump of order 4 traversing a linkage of order 3. The rerouted paths guaranteed by Observation 5 are indicated as dotted paths. Note that the circled vertex is avoided by the new linkage.

Let $\mathcal{R}_1$ and $\mathcal{R}_2$ be two vertex disjoint $\mathcal{Q}$-bumps, and assume that there exists a component P of $\mathcal{P}$ containing all the endpoints of $\mathcal{R}_1$ and $\mathcal{R}_2$. Let $\pi(i)$ and $\sigma(i)$ be values, for $i = 1, 2$ such that $\mathcal{R}_i$ has endpoints in $B_{\pi(i)}$ and $B_{\sigma(i)}$. Consider the subpath of P_i of P connecting the ends of R_i, i.e. let P_i be the minimal subpath of P containing $B_{\pi(i)}$ and $B_{\sigma(i)}$ for $i = 1, 2$. Then $\mathcal{R}_1$ and $\mathcal{R}_2$ are *independent* if P_1 and P_2 are disjoint.

We now have everything in place to outline the argument for the proof of Theorem 3. Let $\mathcal{P}$ be our linkage of order k which we would like to reroute, and let $\mathcal{Q}$ be a *very* long traversing linkage of *huge* order. Fix a path P_1 in the linkage $\mathcal{P}$.

First, we observe that for some component P_1 of $\mathcal{P}$, the linkage $\mathcal{Q}$ must return frequently to the path P_1.

If there existed many disjoint independent $\mathcal{Q}$-bumps with ends in P_1, it would be relatively easy to ensure that some subset large satisfies the necessary properties to apply Observation 5. Then using at most k bumps satisfying the conditions of Observation 5, we repeatedly rotate and find an equivalent linkage avoiding some vertex.

The difficulty is how to find many disjoint independent $\mathcal{Q}$-bumps. We switch perspectives at this point and consider how the components of $\mathcal{P}$ intersect with $\mathcal{Q}$. The path P_1 repeatedly crosses the linkage $\mathcal{Q}$, always hitting the paths of $\mathcal{Q}$ in order. Then there are two possible cases. First, it is possible that some subpath P'_1 of P_1 intersects $\mathcal{Q}$ in a somewhat regular manner, yielding many disjoint, independent $\mathcal{Q}$-bumps on P'_1. In this case, we apply Observation 5 to find a linkage equivalent to $\mathcal{P}$ avoiding some vertex. Alternatively, no such path P'_1 exists and the path P_1 intersects $\mathcal{Q}$ in a more complex fashion. In this case we are able to find a large complete minor in $\mathcal{P} \cup \mathcal{Q}$. As we have already discussed, a large clique minor allows us to find an equivalent linkage avoiding some vertex of $\mathcal{P}$. In each case, we find an equivalent linkage avoiding some vertex of $\mathcal{P}$, completing the proof.

We expand, for a moment, on these ideas for interested readers with some familiarity with the graph minors techniques. We return to a more general discussion below. Let $\mathcal{P}$ be a linkage of order k and $\mathcal{Q}$ be a traversing linkage of order w and length l. Let the basis subpaths of $\mathcal{Q}$ be $B_1, B_2, \dots, B_l$.

We contract all the edges incident a vertex of degree at most two, as well as edges of $E(\mathcal{Q}) \cap E(\mathcal{P})$. Thus we may assume that:

1. there are no edges contained in $\mathcal{Q} \cap \mathcal{P}$, and

2. there are no vertices in $V(\mathcal{Q}) \setminus V(\mathcal{P})$.

We can fix a labeling $Q_1, Q_2, \dots, Q_w$ of the components of $\mathcal{Q}$ of order w, so that every component $P \in \mathcal{P}$ satisfies the following. The path P can be decomposed into subpaths $R_1, \dots, R_t$ and edges $e_1, \dots, e_{t-1}$ that are pairwise disjoint so that e_i connects the ends of R_i and R_{i+1} and each R_i has one end in Q_1, the other end in Q_w, and intersects the paths of $\mathcal{Q}$ in order, i.e. $Q_1, Q_2, \dots, Q_w$. (In fact, the paths R_i are the basis subpaths of $\mathcal{Q}$ on P, ordered by traversing P).

If we look at the graph formed by $P \cup \mathcal{Q}$, we see that $\mathcal{Q} \cup \bigcup_1^t R_i$ forms a subdivision W of the $(w \times t)$-grid. The horizontal paths of the grid are the Q_i for $1 \le i \le w$, and the vertical paths are the R_i, $1 \le i \le t$. The edges e_i form a matching with the ends contained in $Q_1 \cup Q_w$. We keep the grid W aside, and for the rest of the proof focus on the edges e_i. As we described above, there are essentially two cases. If these edges are relatively well behaved, all but a small number of them can be embedded in a low genus surface. In this case, this will allow us to reroute the linkage $\mathcal{P}$ avoiding some vertex using techniques of Robertson and Seymour for the disjoint paths problem in the bounded genus case [29]. Alternatively, the edges e_i are not tame. In this case, we will find a large clique minor. Then, again we see that $\mathcal{P}$ can again be rerouted to avoid some vertex v.

The edges e_i, together with the outer face boundary of W, comprise a *society*, one of the key topics in Graph Minors Theory [30]. Our proof builds on results in [30], and extending them in such a way that the outcomes include "genus addition", i.e, a handle addition and a crosscap addition. We further adapt some ideas in [32, 33] to grow a graph on the surface with large representativity. This process stops when we have a huge clique minor, because, as mentioned above, if there is a huge clique minor, we can reroute the linkage $\mathcal{P}$ to avoid some vertex. We reiterate that our proof does not need most of the heavy machinery in Graph Minor theory. This is for several reasons. First, because our society consists of only a matching, the analysis is simplified. Second, we do not have to worry about global connectivity issues as the society vertices are the vertices of the outer ring of a grid. And, finally, certain degenerate cases will allow us to easily find many disjoint $\mathcal{Q}$-bumps, an outcome not available in the general graph minors arguments. This final point will allow us to evade the topic of "vortices", a major savings in time and effort. Further ingredients of the graph minors series which we are able to avoid include, "embedding up to 3-separations", "tangle, respectful tangle" etc.

We return now to a more general overview of the proof. A technicality we ignored in this outline is the following. Given that we find many disjoint independent $\mathcal{Q}$-bumps on the subpath P_1' of P_1, how do use the bumps to reroute the linkage? We do so by *splitting* on edges. Given an edge e in a linkage $\mathcal{P}$, we say that the linkage $\mathcal{P} - e$ is obtained from $\mathcal{P}$ by splitting $\mathcal{P}$ on e. We note that the property of being a unique linkage is preserved upon splitting a linkage on a given edge:

Observation 6. *Let $\mathcal{P}$ be a unique linkage in a graph G, and let $\overline{\mathcal{P}}$ be obtained from splitting $\mathcal{P}$ on some edge e. Then $\overline{\mathcal{P}}$ is a unique linkage in G. Moreover, if $\mathcal{Q}$ is a traversing linkage of $\mathcal{P}$ of length l, with basis subpaths $B_1, B_2, \ldots, B_l$, then if $e \notin E(B_i)$ for all $1 \leq i \leq l$, then $\mathcal{Q}$ is a traversing sublinkage of $\overline{\mathcal{P}}$.*

Thus we perform possibly two edge splits on $\mathcal{P}$ to obtain a new linkage with a component equal to P_1'. Given that we have many disjoint, independent $\mathcal{Q}$ bumps attaching to P_1', we contradict that the new linkage is unique, and by the observation, that the original linkage $\mathcal{P}$ is unique.

In conclusion, we give a complete proof of the $k = 2$ case of Theorem 3. Robertson and Seymour [34] observe that this can be easily shown directly; however, we give a proof using traversing linkages in the hopes that it further illustrates the tools and techniques of the main result.

Theorem 7. *Let $\mathcal{P}$ be a linkage of order 2. Let $\mathcal{Q}$ be a traversing linkage of order five and length 33. Then there exists a vertex $v \in V(\mathcal{P})$ such that $(\mathcal{P} \cup \mathcal{Q}) - v$ contains a linkage $\mathcal{P}'$ equivalent to $\mathcal{P}$.*

PROOF. Let the components of $\mathcal{P}$ be P_1 and P_2, and label the ends of P_i s_i and t_i for $i = 1, 2$. Let the basis subpaths of $\mathcal{Q}$ be $B_1, B_2, \ldots, B_{33}$. We assume, to reach a contradiction, that there do not exist paths P_1', P_2' that avoid some vertex of $\mathcal{P}$ such that the endpoints of P_i' are s_i and t_i.

The linkage $\mathcal{Q}$ repeatedly passes back and forth between P_1 and P_2. To simplify the picture somewhat, we consider the following auxiliary graph H with vertices equal to the set of basis subpaths B_i for $1 \leq i \leq 33$ and two vertices B_i and B_j connected by an edge if either there is a subpath of P_i connecting them avoiding all other basis subpaths, or if $|j - i| = 1$. It follows that $E(H)$ is comprised of three edge disjoint paths: one for each of the paths P_i and one for the linkage $\mathcal{Q}$. The edges of H of the form B_iB_{i+1} have two distinct types - the linkage $\mathcal{Q}$ can either twist between B_i and B_{i+1} or not. We will refer to the edges B_iB_{i+1} where $\mathcal{Q}$ twists as the *odd* edges of H; every other edge of H will be called *even*. If Σ is the set of odd edges, then by swapping the labels s_i and t_i, the resulting set of odd edges is $\Sigma \triangle X$ where $\triangle$ denotes the symmetric difference and X is the set of all edges of the form B_iB_{i+1}.

First, observe that there does not exist an index i such both the edge $B_{i-1}B_i$ and B_iB_{i+1} are even in H. Otherwise, we can find paths P_1' and P_2' equivalent to $\mathcal{P}$ avoiding an internal vertex of B_i. Similarly, there does not exist an index i such that $\mathcal{Q}$ does twist between both B_{i-1} and B_i and between B_i and B_{i+1}. This is because we could swap the labels on the ends P_1 so that $\mathcal{Q}$ does not twist between B_{i-1} and B_i and between B_i and B_{i+1}. If we let R be the path in H of consisting of the edges of the form B_iB_{i+1} for $1 \leq i \leq 32$, it follows that the edges of R alternate between edges in Σ and edges not in Σ.

Also, observe that for indices i and j such that both the edges B_iB_{i+1} and B_jB_{j+1} are not in Σ, we have that the edges do not "cross" in H. That is, if B_i and B_j are both contained P_1, say, and occur on P_1 in that order when traversing from s_1 to t_1, then B_{i+1} occurs before B_{j+1} on P_2 when traversing from s_2 to t_2. Otherwise, we would be able to find an equivalent linkage avoiding some vertex of $\mathcal{P}$. Similarly, if i and j are two indices such that both the edges B_iB_{i+1} and B_jB_{j+1} are in Σ, and if both B_i and B_j are contained in P_1 in that order, then it follows that B_{j+1} and B_{i+1} occur on that order when traversing P_2 from s_2 to t_2.

After possibly swapping the labels s_i and t_i for one or possibly both values of i, we see by examining the graph H that the following must hold for $\mathcal{Q} \cup \mathcal{P}$. Traversing P_1 from s_1 to t_1, we see $B_2, B_6, \ldots, B_{26}, B_{30}, B_{32}, B_{28}, \ldots, B_8, B_4$ in that order, and traversing P_2 from s_2 to t_2, we see $B_1, B_5, \ldots, B_{29}, B_{33}, B_{31}, B_{27}, \ldots, B_7, B_3$ in that order. Moreover, $\mathcal{Q}$ twists between B_i and B_{i+1} if and only if i is even. Let e_1 be an edge of P_1 separating B_{30} from B_{32}, and let e_2 be an edge of P_2 separating B_{33} from B_{31}. If we split the linkage $\mathcal{P}$ on e_1 and e_2, we have a linkage $\mathcal{P}'$ of order four. Moreover, by appropriately choosing the labels for the endpoints of components of $\mathcal{P}'$, we may assume that $\mathcal{Q}$ does not twist between any two basis subpaths in $\mathcal{P}'$. We label the components of $\mathcal{P}'$ as P_i' for $1 \leq i \leq 4$ such that the endpoints of $\mathcal{Q}$ are contained in P_1'.

By examination, we see that there exist four disjoint independent $\mathcal{Q}$-bumps with endpoints in P_1' satisfying *i.* and *ii.* in Observation 5. Moreover, if we let the endpoints of P_i' be s_i' and t_i', then for each such bump, the rerouting guaranteed by Observation 5 results in paths with endpoints s_i' and t_{i+1}'. By using all four re-routings, we see that we wrap around and find a linkage $\overline{\mathcal{P}}$ equivalent to $\mathcal{P}'$ avoiding some vertex of $\mathcal{P}'$. Then Observation 6 implies a contradiction to our choice of $\mathcal{P}$ to be a unique linkage, proving the claim.

3. REFERENCES

[1] S. Arnborg and A. Proskurowski, Linear time algorithms for NP-hard problems restricted to partial k-trees, *Discrete Appl. Math.* **23** (1989), 11–24.

[2] H. L. Bodlaender, A linear-time algorithm for finding tree-decomposition of small treewidth, *SIAM J. Comput.* **25** (1996), 1305–1317.

[3] H. L. Bodlaender, F. Fomin, D. Lokshtanov, E. Penninkx, S. Saurabh and D. Thilikos, (Meta) kernelization, to appear in *50th Annual Symposium on Foundations of Computer Science (FOCS 2009).*

[4] E. D. Demaine, F. Fomin, M. Hajiaghayi, and D. Thilikos, Subexponential parameterized algorithms on bounded-genus graphs and H-minor-free graphs, *J. ACM* **52** (2005), 1–29.

[5] E. D. Demaine, M. Hajiaghayi, and K. Kawarabayashi, Algorithmic graph minor theory: Decomposition, approximation and coloring, *Proc. 46th Annual Symposium on Foundations of Computer Science (FOCS'05)*, 637–646, (2005).

[6] E. D. Demaine, M. Hajiaghayi, and B. Mohar, Approximation algorithms via contraction decomposition, *Proc. 18th Annual ACM-SIAM Symposium on Discrete Algorithms (SODA'07)*, 278–287, (2007).

[7] R. Diestel, Graph Theory, 3rd Edition, Springer, 2005.

[8] R.G. Downey and M.R. Fellows, Parameterized complexity, Springer-Verlag, 1999.

[9] Z. Dvorak, D. Kral and R. Thomas, Coloring triangle-free graphs on surfaces, *ACM-SIAM Symposium on Discrete Algorithms (SODA)*, 2009, 120–129.

[10] M.R. Fellows and M. A. Langston, Nonconstructive tools for proving polynomial-time decidability, *J. ACM* **35**, (1988), 727–739.

[11] A. Frank, Packing paths, cuts and circuits – a survey, in *Paths, Flows and VLSI-Layout*, B. Korte, L. Lovász, H. J. Promel and A. Schrijver (Eds.), Springer-Verlag, Berlin, 1990, 49–100.

[12] M. Grohe, Local tree-width, excluded minors, and approximation algorithms. *Combinatorica* **23**, (2003), 613–632.

[13] R. M. Karp, On the computational complexity of combinatorial problems, *Networks* **5** (1975), 45–68.

[14] K. Kawarabayashi, Planarity allowing few error vertices in linear time, *50th Annual Symposium on Foundations of Computer Science (FOCS 2009)*, 639–648, (2009).

[15] K. Kawarabayashi and B. Reed, Computing crossing number in linear time, *Proc. 39th ACM Symposium on Theory of Computing (STOC'07)*, 382–390, (2007).

[16] K. Kawarabayashi and B. Mohar, Graph and Map Isomorphism and all polyhedral embeddings in linear time, *Proc. 40th ACM Symposium on Theory of Computing (STOC'08)*, 471–480, (2008).

[17] K. Kawarabayashi, B. Mohar and B. Reed, A simpler linear time algorithm for embedding graphs into an arbitrary surface and the genus of bounded tree-width graphs, *Proc. 49th Annual Symposium on Foundations of Computer Science (FOCS'08)*, 771–780, (2008).

[18] K. Kawarabayashi, Y. Kobayashi and B. Reed, The disjoint paths problem in quaratic time, *submitted.*

[19] K. Kawarabayashi and Y. Kobayashi, The edge-disjoint paths problem for 4-edge-connected graphs and Eulerian graphs, *ACM-SIAM Symposium on Discrete Algorithms (SODA)*, 345–353, (2010).

[20] Y. Kobayashi and K. Kawarabayashi, Algorithms for finding an induced cycle in planar graphs and bounded genus graphs, *ACM-SIAM Symposium on Discrete Algorithms (SODA)*, 1146–1155, (2009).

[21] L. Lovász, in *Combinatorics, Proc. Fifith Hungarian Combin. Colloq.*, Keszthely, 1976, Vol. II, p.1208, North-Holland, Amsterdam, 1978.

[22] J. F. Lynch, The equivalence of theorem proving and the interconnection problem, *ACM SIGDA Newsletter* **5** (1975), 31–65.

[23] D. Marx and I. Schlotter, Obtaining a planar graph by vertex deletion, *Proc. the 33rd Workshop on Graph-Theoretic Concepts in Computer Scienece*, 292–303, (2007).

[24] M. Milgram and P. Ungar, *Amer. Math. Monthly*, **85**, (1978), 664–668.

[25] B. Reed, Tree width and tangles: a new connectivity measure and some applications, in *"Surveys in Combinatorics, 1997 (London)"*, London Math. Soc. Lecture Note Ser. **241**, Cambridge Univ. Press, Cambridge, 87–162, (1997).

[26] B. Reed, N. Robertson, A. Schrijver and P. D. Seymour, Finding disjoint trees in planar graphs in linear time, Contemp. Math., 147, Amer. Math. Soc., Providenc, RI, 1993, 295–301.

[27] N. Robertson and P. D. Seymour, An outline of a disjoint paths algorithm, in *Paths, Flows, and VLSI-Layout*, B. Korte, L. Lovász, H. J. Prömel, and A. Schrijver (Eds.), Springer-Verlag, Berlin, 1990, 267–292.

[28] N. Robertson and P. D. Seymour, Graph minors. VI. Disjoint paths across a disk, *J. Combin. Theory Ser. B*, **41** (1986), 115–138.

[29] N. Robertson and P. D. Seymour, Graph minors. VII. Disjoint paths on a surface, *J. Combin. Theory Ser. B*, **45** (1988), 212–254.

[30] N. Robertson and P. D. Seymour, Graph minors IX. Disjoint crossed paths, *J. Combin. Theory Ser. B*, **49** (1990), 40–77.

[31] N. Robertson and P. D. Seymour, Graph minors. XIII. The disjoint paths problem, *J. Combin. Theory Ser. B* **63** (1995), 65–110.

[32] N. Robertson and P. D. Seymour, Graph minors. XV. Giant Steps, *J. Combin. Theory Ser. B* **68** (1996), 112–148.

[33] N. Robertson and P. D. Seymour, Graph minors. XVI. Excluding a non-planar graph, *J. Combin. Theory Ser. B* **89** (2003), 43–76.

[34] N. Robertson and P. D. Seymour, Graph minors. XXI. Graphs with unique linkages, *J. Combin. Theory Ser. B* **99** (2009), 583–616.

[35] N. Robertson and P. D. Seymour, Graph minors. XXII. Irrelevant vertices in linkage problems, to appear in *J. Combin. Theory Ser. B.*

[36] A. Schrijver, Combinatorial Optimization: Polyhedra and Efficiency, number 24 in Algorithm and Combinatorics, Springer Verlag, 2003.

Odd Cycle Packing*

[Extended Abstract] †

Ken-ichi Kawarabayashi‡
National Institute of Informatics
2-1-2 Hitotsubashi, Chiyoda-ku
Tokyo, Japan
k_keniti@nii.ac.jp

Bruce Reed§
Canada Research Chair in Graph Theory
McGill University
Montreal, Canada
breed@cs.mcgill.ca

ABSTRACT

We consider the following problem, which is called the *odd cycle packing problem*.

Input: A graph G with n vertices and m edges, and an integer k.

Output : k vertex disjoint odd cycles.

We also consider the edge disjoint case, and the node-and arc-disjoint directed case. This problem is known to be NP-hard, even for planar graphs, if k is part of input.

In this paper, we first present the integrality gap and hardness results for these problems. We prove that the integrality gap of the standard LP-relaxation of the odd cycle packing problem is $\Theta(\sqrt{n})$. This result is obtained by giving an algorithm to compute an odd cycle packing, which gives rise to an $O(\sqrt{n})$ approximating algorithm for the fractional odd cycle packing problem (this gives rise to an upper bound), and by showing that there is a graph G such that there is an $O(\sqrt{n})$ half-integral odd cycle packing in G, but there are no two disjoint odd cycle in G (this gives rise to a lower bound).

For the hardness result, we prove that for any ε, the node-disjoint directed odd cycle packing problem is NP-hard to approximate within $m^{1/2-\varepsilon}$, where m is the number of arcs of a given digraph G. This is true not only for the node-disjoint directed odd cycle packing problem but also for the arc-disjoint directed odd cycle packing problem. In addition, we prove that there is an $O(m^{1/2})$-approximation algorithm for the node- and arc- directed odd cycle packing problems. Thus this approximation algorithm almost matches the hardness result.

For the positive side, we consider the case when the number of odd cycles, k, is fixed. This is a natural direction, for example, the seminal result of Robertson and Seymour for the disjoint paths problem in the graph minors project.

We present an $O(m\alpha(m,n)n)$ algorithm for any fixed k, where the function $\alpha(m,n)$ is the inverse of the Ackermann function (see by Tarjan [72]). This is the first polynomial time algorithm for this problem (and in fact, it is the first fixed parameter tractable algorithm). This proves a conjecture by Lovász and Schrijver in early 1980's, who gave a polynomial time algorithm for the case $k = 2$.

Our algorithm can be applied to decide whether or not G has k edge disjoint odd cycle with the same time complexity for any fixed k. We also show that our algorithm gives rise to the Graph Minor Algorithm for the k vertex-disjoint paths problem by Robertson and Seymour for any fixed k. Thus our algorithm is beyond the framework of the Graph Minor Theory.

Our algorithm has several appealing features: We use the odd S-path theorem, which is a generalization of the well-known S-paths theorem by Mader. We also introduce an odd clique minor, which can be viewed as a clique minor with some parity condition.

As with the Robertson-Seymour algorithm to solve the k disjoint paths problem for any fixed k, in each iteration, we would like to either use a huge clique minor as a "crossbar", or exploit the structure of graphs in which we cannot find such a minor. Here, however, we must maintain the parity of the cycles and can only use an "odd clique minor". We must also describe the structure of those graphs in which we cannot find such a minor and discuss how to exploit it. This part needs the seminal result of Robertson and Seymour for the graph minor decomposition theorem for H-minor-free graphs. We also use some deep results of Robertson and Seymour that are needed to prove the correctness of their algorithm for the disjoint paths problem.

Categories and Subject Descriptors

G.2 [**Discrete Math**]: Combinatorics; G.2.2 [**Graph Theory**]: Combinatorics—*Graph algorithms*

*This work was done as a part of an INRIA-NII collaboration under MOU grant, and partially supported by MEXT Grant-in-Aid for Scientific Research on Priority Areas "New Horizons in Computing"

†A full version of this paper is available at `http://reseach.nii.ac.jp/~k_keniti/oddpack.pdf`

‡Research partly supported by Japan Society for the Promotion of Science, Grant-in-Aid for Scientific Research, by C and C Foundation, by Kayamori Foundation and by Inoue Research Award for Young Scientists.

§Project Mascotte, INRIA, Laboratoire I3S, CNRS, Sophia-Antipolis, France

STOC'10, June 5–8, 2010, Cambridge, Massachusetts, USA.

General Terms

Algorithm, Theory

Keywords

Odd cycles packing, the integrality gap

1. INTRODUCTION

1.1 Background and Overview

Finding a minimum vertex cover (or vertex transversal) for the set of odd cycles in a given graph G (which we call the *Odd Cycle Cover Problem*) is a fundamental problem in both combinatorial optimization and theoretical computer science. Determining a minimum edge cover for the set of odd cycles is equivalent to one of the most important NP-complete problem called the *maximum cut problem*. In the positive side, the maximum cut problem is solvable for planar graphs (by Hadlock [18]), and Reed et al. [50] presented an $O(mn)$ algorithm to determine whether or not a given graph with m edges and n vertices has an odd cycle cover of order at most k for any fixed k (recently, the time complexity is improved to almost linear time by the authors [37]).

In this paper, we are interested in a similar problem, which is called the *odd cycle packing problem*. This problem may be viewed as the "dual" problem of the odd cycle cover problem (and hence it is also connected to the maximum cut problem).

The Odd Cycle Packing Problem

Input: A graph G with m edges and n vertices, and an integer k.

Output: Does G have k vertex-(or edge-)disjoint odd cycles?

We also consider the directed version of the problem. Both the odd cycle packing problem and the odd cycle covering problem are well-studied in combinatorial optimization. The odd cycle packing problem is known to be NP-hard, even for planar graphs, if k is part of input, see [13]. For more details in this context, we refer the reader to the book by Schrijver [67]. It also has direct applications in combinatorial biology (see for example, [52]). We remark that packing *disjoint cycles*, i.e, no parity requirement, has been also studied extensively. It is one of the most fundamental problems in graph theory with applications to several areas (see [2, 40]).

In order to consider the odd cycle packing problem, it is natural to consider the "fractional" version of the problem. Given a graph G, the *fractional odd cycle packing* is a function f from $\mathcal{C}$ of odd cycles in G to $[0,1]$ satisfying $\sum_{C:v\in C} f(C) \leq 1$ for each vertex v in G. Letting $|f| = \sum_{C\in\mathcal{C}} f(C)$, the *fractional odd cycle packing number* is defined to be the maximum of $|f|$ taken over the fractional odd cycle packing f in G. If each vertex is used in at most two of these odd cycles, then we call it *the half-integral* odd cycle packing.

We now formulate the odd cycle packing problem and the odd cycl covering problem as integer programs whose linear program relaxations are duals. Letting V denote the vertex set of G and $\mathcal{O}$ denote the set of odd cycles in G, these duals LPs are;

The Odd Cycle Covering LP

Minimize $\sum_{v\in V} y_v$, subject to

1. $\sum_{v:v\in C} y_v \geq 1$, for each odd cycle C in $\mathcal{O}$;
2. $y_v \geq 0$, for each vertex v in G.

The Odd Cycle Packing LP

Maximize $\sum_{C\in\mathcal{O}} x_C$, subject to

1. $\sum_{C:v\in C} x_C \leq 1$, for each vertex v in G;
2. $x_C \geq 0$, for each odd cycle C in $\mathcal{O}$.

Let us observe that both the odd cycle covering problem and the odd cycle packing problem are NP-hard, even for planar graphs [13]. Goemans and Williamson [16] proved that the integrality gap of the odd cycle covering LP is at most 9/4 for planar graphs. Fiorini et al. [13] proved that the integrality gap of the odd cycle packing LP is bounded by a constant for planar graphs. But for general graphs, these are not true. In this paper, we prove that the integrality gap of the odd cycle packing LP is $\Theta(\sqrt{n})$. We also prove that for any ε, the directed odd cycles packing problem is NP-hard to approximate within $m^{1/2-\varepsilon}$. This is true not only for the node-disjoint directed odd cycle packing problem but also for the arc-disjoint directed odd cycle packing problem. We also obtain an $O(\sqrt{m})$-approximation algorithm for the directed odd cycle packing problem. Thus, this approximation algorithm almost matches the hardness result.

The integrality gap result is obtained by giving an algorithm to compute an odd cycle packing, which gives rise to an $O(\sqrt{n})$ approximating algorithm for the fractional odd cycle packing problem (this gives rise to an upper bound), and by showing that there is a graph G such that there is an $O(\sqrt{n})$ half-integral odd cycle packing in G, but there are no two disjoint odd cycle in G (this gives rise to a lower bound). In the second case, the example we shall provide has been known for over 25 years. It is provided by Lovász and Schrijver (see [70]) who characterized graphs without two vertex-disjoint odd cycles. The example appears in their characterization. Their proof heavily depends on the seminal result by Seymour [68] for decomposing regular matroids.

The characterization by Lovász and Schrijver results in polynomial time algorithm for testing whether or not a given graph contains two disjoint odd cycles. No such characterization or algorithm has been known for k disjoint odd cycles for any fixed k, even $k = 3$, until the present paper. In fact, Lovász and Schrijver considered this problem in early 1980's, and conjectured that the problem of deciding if a given graph G contains k disjoint odd cycles for any fixed k can be done in polynomial time (Actually, it seems that Gerards, Seymour and Thomassen also considered this problem in early 1980's). One may argue that the difficulty lies in the fact that the collection of odd cycles does not possess the Erdős-Pósa property (see the next subsection).

Motivated by this fact, our positive main result is to give an $O(mn)$ algorithm to test whether or not a given graph G with m edges and n vertices has k disjoint odd cycles for any fixed k. This is the first polynomial time algorithm (and in fact, it is the first fixed parameter tractable algorithm) for the odd cycles packing problem for any fixed k. This settles the above mentioned conjecture by Lovász and Schrijver. By *disjoint*, we mean vertex-disjoint. But our proof certainly works for the edge-disjoint case. In addition, we give an approximate structure for graphs without k disjoint odd cycles for any fixed k.

Let us observe that our algorithm gives rise to the graph minor algorithm for the k vertex-disjoint paths problem by Robertson and Seymour [60] for fixed k. We shall clarify this point later.

To appreciate why the odd cyclespacking problem for any fixed k is difficult, as pointed out above, it is useful to consider the Erdős-Pósa property and odd disjoint cycles. Let us observe that Reed [47] proved that the Erdős-Pósa property holds for the half-integral odd cycle packing. It follows from this property that there is a polynomial time algorithm to test whether or not a given graph has a half-integral k odd cycle packing for any fixed k.

1.2 Erdős-Pósa property and odd disjoint cycles

A family $\mathcal{F}$ of graphs is said to have the *Erdős-Pósa property*, if for every integer k there is an integer $f(k, \mathcal{F})$ such that every graph G contains k vertex-disjoint subgraphs each isomorphic to a graph in $\mathcal{F}$ or a set C of at most $f(k, \mathcal{F})$ vertices such that $G-C$ has no subgraph isomorphic to a graph in $\mathcal{F}$. The term *Erdős-Pósa property* arose because in [11], Erdős and Pósa proved that the family of cycles (without any parity condition) has this property.

On the other hand, for cycles with odd length, the situation is different. The Erdős-Pósa property does not hold for odd cycles in general. Let us give an example. We need some definitions. For a graph G an *odd cycle cover* is a set of vertices $C \subseteq V(G)$ such that $G - C$ is bipartite.

An *Escher wall of height h* consists of a wall of height h: W, and h vertex disjoint paths $P_1,\dots,P_h$ such that:

(i) Each P_i has both endpoints on W but is otherwise disjoint from W.

(ii) One endpoint of P_i is in the ith brick of the top row of bricks of W, the other is in the $(h+1-i)$th brick of the bottom row of W. Furthermore, both of these vertices are in only one brick of W.

(iii) W is bipartite but for each i, $W \cup P_i$ contains an odd cycle.

See Figure 1 for an example. Note that if the height is odd, then the length of each P_i is odd.

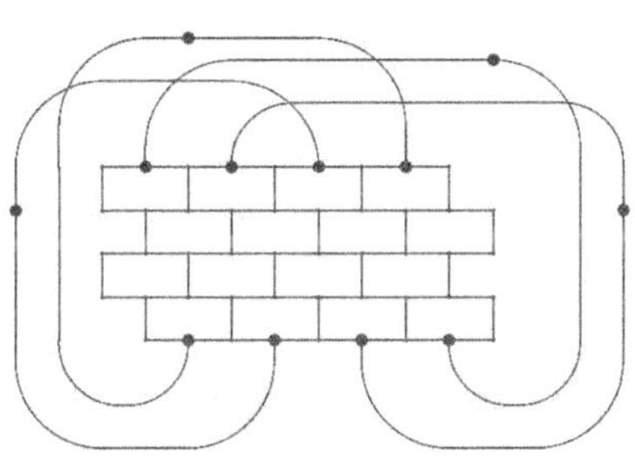

Figure 1: An Escher Wall of height 4

Let us recall that an *r-grid* is a graph which is isomorphic to the graph W_r obtained from the Cartesian product of paths $P_r \square P_r$, with vertex set $V(W_r) = \{v_{i,j} \mid 1 \leq i \leq r,\ 1 \leq j \leq r\}$ in which two vertices $v_{i,j}$ and $v_{i',j'}$ are adjacent if and only if one of the following possibilities holds:

(1) $i' = i$ and $j' \in \{j-1, j+1\}$.

(2) $j' = j$ and $i' = i + (-1)^{i+j}$.

We can define an *Escher grid of height r* in a natural way.

We remark that, as pointed out by Lovász and Schrijver (see [70]), an Escher wall W of height h contains neither 2 vertex disjoint odd cycles nor an odd cycle cover with fewer than h vertices (the first follows from the fact that for any Escher wall $W, P_1, \dots, P_h$, the planar embedding of W can be extended to an embedding of the Escher wall in the projective plane so that every odd cycle is non-null homotopic by routing the P_i through a cross-cap; the fact that there is no odd cycle cover of size $h-1$ follows from the fact that if X is a set of $h-1$ vertices then X fails to intersect some path along the top of a level of bricks of W and then, as is easily verified, there is some i such that P_i is disjoint from X and both endpoints of P_i are connected to this row in $W - X$. Hence the two endpoints of this P_i are connected by a path Q in $W - X$ and then $P_i + Q$ is an odd cycle in $G - X$. The latter fact was also given in the book by Mohar and Thomassen [42]). This shows that the Erdős-Pósa property does not hold for odd cycles (in fact, it holds for the cycles of length p *mod* m if and only if p is congruent to 0 *mod* m see [7] and [76]).

However, Reed [47] proved that the Erdős-Pósa property holds for odd cycles in planar graphs. This result was extended to an orientable fixed surface in [29]. Note that the Erdős-Pósa property does not hold for odd cycles in nonorientable surfaces, even for projective planar graphs, because of the Escher wall of large height.

The difficulty for testing k disjoint odd cycles is that, since the Erdős-Pósa property does not hold for odd cycles (even $k = 2$), so, we cannot reduce the problem to the disjoint paths problem in bipartite graphs. If the Erdős-Pósa property would hold for odd cycles, then we could just guess a vertex set X that has bounded number of vertices such that $G - X$ is bipartite. Because every odd cycle would pass through at least one vertex of X, and there are at most $|X|^k$ ways for k disjoint odd cycles to pass through the vertex set X, so we could use the algorithm of Robertson and Seymour with respect to the terminals in X to test whether or not there are k disjoint odd cycles (note that we do not have to worry about parity of disjoint paths in the bipartite graph $G - X$). But this argument does not work simply because the Erdős-Pósa property does not hold for odd cycles (even $k = 2$). This also suggests that the parity version of the disjoint paths problem is much harder than the nonparity version.

But on the other hand, for the half-integral odd cycles packing problem, Reed [47] proved that the Erdős-Pósa property does hold. Consequently, Reed's result [47] implies the following.

Theorem 1.1. *For any fixed k, there is a polynomial time algorithm for testing whether or not there is a half-integral k disjoint odd cycles packing.*

Later, Reed, Smith and Vetta [50] gave an $O(mn)$ algorithm by using Reed's theorem in [47]. Finally authors gives an almost linear time algorithm [37].

Reed [47] actually proved the following.

Theorem 1.2. *For any fixed k and a given graph G, either there are k disjoint odd cycles in G, or there is a vertex set X of order at most $f(k)$ (for some function f of k) such that $G - X$ is bipartite, or there is an Escher wall of large height in G.*

Reed [47] then proved that an Escher wall W of large height contains many odd cycles such that each vertex in W is on at most two of these odd cycles. Together with Theorem 1.2, this implies Theorem 1.1.

1.3 Main Results

Let G be a graph with m edges and n vertices.

In this paper, we first give the integrality gap in the odd cycles packing problem. Specifically:

Theorem 1.3. *The standard LP-relaxation of the odd cycle packing problem has the integrality gap $\Theta(\sqrt{n})$.*

Theorem 1.3 follows from the following two results.

Theorem 1.4. *There is an algorithm to compute an odd cycle packing, which gives rise to an $O(\sqrt{n})$-approximation algorithm for the fractional odd cycles packing problem.*

Theorem 1.5. *There is a graph G such that an $O(\sqrt{n})$ half-integral odd cycle packing exists in G, but no two disjoint odd cycles exist in G.*

Note that the first gives an upper bound, while the second gives a lower bound for the integrality gap.

For the directed case, we give the following hardness result.

Theorem 1.6. *For any $\varepsilon > 0$, the directed odd cycle packing problem (for both the arc-disjoint and the node-disjoint cases) is NP-hard to approximate within $m^{1/2-\varepsilon}$.*

Our proof of Theorem 1.6 is very simple and it does not depend on the PCP theorem.

Actually, Theorem 1.6 almost matches the following approximation algorithm.

Theorem 1.7. *There is an $O(m^{1/2})$-approximation algorithm for the directed odd cycle packing problem (for both the arc-disjoint and the node-disjoint cases).*

The proof of Theorem 1.7 is also simple. So for the directed odd cycle packing problem, we already have both hardness and almost best possible approximation results. But for the undirected case, we are not sure yet. The proof of Theorem 1.7 certainly does not work for the undirected case.

Let us remark that the similar situation happens for the well-known edge-disjoint paths problem (EDP). One can easily get an $O(\sqrt{m})$-approximation algorithm for the EDP (and the directed EDP), but the EDP for the directed case is NP-hard to approximate within $m^{1/2-\varepsilon}$ for any $\varepsilon > 0$. On the other hand, if we fix the number of terminals, k, for the EDP, then there is a seminal result by Robertson-Seymour which gives an $O(m^3)$-algorithm to decide the undirected EDP. This is also a fixed parameter tractable algorithm too.

In view of the above results, one might expect that the same happens here, and this is our main motivation in this paper. In fact, we shall prove that our result below (Theorem 1.8) gives rise to the above mentioned result by Robertson-Seymour which gives an $O(m^3)$-algorithm to decide the undirected EDP (and VDP) for any fixed k.

In the main part of this paper, we shall focus on the case when k is any fixed constant. Then we can give the following.

Theorem 1.8. *For any fixed k, there is an $O(m\alpha(m,n)n)$ algorithm to decide whether or not G has k disjoint odd cycles. If the answer is yes, the algorithm finds k disjoint odd cycles.*

This settles the above mentioned conjecture by Lovász and Schrijver. In fact, this is the first polynomial time algorithm (and in fact, this is the first fixed parameter tractable algorithm) for the odd cycle packing problem for any fixed k. Let us observe that if k is part of input, then the odd cycles packing problem is NP-hard, even for planar graphs [13].

We now show why Theorem 1.8 implies the graph minor algorithm by Robertson and Seymour [60] for the k vertex-disjoint paths problem when k is fixed. Suppose we are given a graph $G = (V, E)$ with n vertices, m edges, and k pairs of vertices $(s_1, t_1), (s_2, t_2), \ldots, (s_k, t_k)$ in G. For each edge e in G, we subdivide once, i.e, we insert a vertex to e such that the new vertex has degree two. Let G' be the resulting graph, and let V' be all the new vertices we added. It follows that G' is bipartite with bipartition (V, V'). Thus for each pair (s_i, t_i), any path with endpoints s_i, t_i must have even length. We now add edges s_it_i for $i = 1, \ldots, k$, and let G'' be the resulting graph. Since each odd cycle must pass through at least one edge s_it_i, and at most k edges s_it_i are added to G', it is easy to see that the followings are equivalent:

1. G has vertex-disjoint paths $P_1, \ldots, P_k$ such that P_i joins s_i and t_i for $i = 1, 2, \ldots, k$.

2. G'' has k disjoint odd cycles.

So, our algorithm, Theorem 1.8, gives rise to an $O(m^2)$ algorithm for the graph minor algorithm by Robertson and Seymour [60] for the k vertex-disjoint paths problem when k is fixed (note that G'' has $m + n$ vertices and $2m$ edges).

Our algorithm has several appealing features: We use the odd S-path theorem, which is a generalization of the well-known S-paths theorem by Mader. We also introduce an "odd clique minor", which can be viewed as a clique minor with some parity condition.

As with the Robertson-Seymour algorithm to solve the k disjoint paths problem for any fixed k, in each iteration, we would like to either use a huge clique minor as a "crossbar", or exploit the structure of graphs in which we cannot find such a minor. Here, however, we must maintain the parity of the cycles and can only use an "odd clique minor". We must also describe the structure of those graphs in which we cannot find such a minor and discuss how to exploit it. This part needs the seminal result of Robertson and Seymour for the graph minor decomposition theorem for H-minor-free graphs. We also use some deep results of Robertson and Seymour that are needed to prove the correctness of their algorithm for the disjoint paths problem.

2. HARDNESS RESULTS

We now modify the Escher grid to give a proof of Theorem 1.6. In this section, we only consider the directed case of the odd cycles packing problem. In addition, we only consider the arc-disjoint directed odd cycles packing, as the node-disjoint case can be dealt with in a similar way.

The proofs below are inspired by Guruswami et al. [17] and Krivelvech et al. [40]. In fact, the examples are quite similar to those in [17, 40], but let us emphasize that Lovász and Schrijver had already come with this example in early 1980's (to characterize graphs without two disjoint odd cycles).

Proof of Theorem 1.6.

We just need to prove the following:

> For any $\varepsilon > 0$, it is NP-hard to distinguish given a directed instance G with m arcs, whether there are two arc-disjoint directed odd cycles or there are $m^{1/2-\varepsilon}$ arc-disjoint directed odd cycles.

The proof is by a reduction from the following well-known NP-hard problem [12]:

The two arc-disjoint directed paths problem
Instance: A directed graph H' (with N vertices and M arcs) with four distinct vertices x_1, x_2, y_1, y_2.
Question: Are there two arc-disjoint directed paths P_1, P_2 such that P_i starts at x_i and ends at y_i in H for $i = 1, 2$?

We now subdivide each arc in H', i.e, for each arc $e = xy$ with tail x and head y, we add a vertex z to e so that there are two arcs e_1, e_2 with tail x and head z, and tail z and head y, respectively. Then clearly each path between x_i and y_i is even for $i = 1, 2$. The resulting graph H has $N + M$ vertices and $2M$ arcs. This graph H is the key for our argument.

We start with the Escher grid T (a grid W, and paths $P_1, \dots, P_{\sqrt{n}}$) of height $\sqrt{n}$, where $n = |M|^{1/(2\varepsilon)}$ (thus T has n vertices and $2n + \sqrt{n}$ edges. We assume that $\sqrt{n}$ is odd). We follow the notation for the Escher wall given in the previous subsection, whet it explains the Erdős-Pósa-property. For each row, we direct each edge from left to right, i.e, the head is $v_{i,j+1}$ and the tail is $v_{i,j}$. For each column, we direct each edge from top to bottom, i.e, the head is $v_{i,j}$, and the tail is $v_{i+1,j}$. For each path P_i, the tail is in the bottom row and the head is in the top row. Note that $v_{i,j}$ means that it is at ith row and jth column, where the first row is the bottom row, the $\sqrt{n}$th row is the top row, and the column appears from the left to the right.

For each vertex $v_{i,j}$ (with $2 \leq i, j \leq \sqrt{n}-1$) in T, we split it into four vertices $v_{i,j,1}, v_{i,j,2}, v_{i,j,3}, v_{i,j,4}$ such that

1. there is an arc with the head $v_{i,j,1}$ and the tail $v_{i,j-1,3}$,
2. there is an arc with the head $v_{i,j,2}$ and the tail $v_{i+1,j,4}$,
3. there is an arc with the tail $v_{i,j,3}$ and the head $v_{i,j+1,1}$, and
4. there is an arc with the tail $v_{i,j,4}$ and the head $v_{i-1,j,2}$.

We then take $(\sqrt{n}-2)^2$ copies of H with x_1, x_2, y_1, y_2 such that, for $2 \leq i, j \leq \sqrt{n} - 1$,

1. x_1 is identified to $v_{i,j,1}$,
2. x_2 is identified to $v_{i,j,2}$,
3. y_1 is identified to $v_{i,j,3}$, and
4. y_2 is identified to $v_{i,j,4}$.

Let G be the resulting digraph. Note that if we contract each graph H into a single point, then we get the Escher grid T with each arc having the above direction. At the moment, G has $4\sqrt{n} - 4 + (N + M) \times (\sqrt{n} - 2)^2$ nodes and $2M \times (\sqrt{n} - 2)^2 + 2n + \sqrt{n}$ arcs.

We now prove the following claim.

Claim 2.1. *If there are two arc-disjoint directed paths P_1, P_2 in H, then there are $\sqrt{n}/2-2$ arc-disjoint odd directed cycles in G.*

Proof. We just need to find $\sqrt{n}/2 - 2$ directed arc-disjoint paths $P'_2, \dots, P'_{\sqrt{n}/2-1}$ such that each P'_i connects from the ending point of P_i to the starting point of P_i. This is rather straightforward, thus we omit the details, and leave them to the reader. Informally, we can select one row S in order (except for the top and bottom rows), for each of the paths $P'_2, P'_3, \dots, P'_{\sqrt{n}/2-1}$ in order, such that each path P'_i goes through only the vertices in S for the rows of W. In addition, each column is used in exactly one path of P'_i. In this way, for each ending point of P_i (for $i = 2, \dots, \sqrt{n}/2 - 1$), we can go through one column from it to reach S, and for each starting point of P_i (for $i = 2, \dots, \sqrt{n}/2 - 1$), we can go through one column from S to reach it. □

On the other hand, by the remarks in the previous section, where it explains the Erdős-Pósa-property, it is easy to see that:

Claim 2.2. *If there are two arc-disjoint odd directed cycles in G, then there must be two arc-disjoint directed paths P_1, P_2 in H.*

Claims 2.1 and 2.2 imply that YES instances of the two arc-disjoint directed paths problem are mapped to instances of the directed odd cycles packing problem with $(\sqrt{n}/2 - 2)$-arc-disjoint odd directed cycles, while NO instances are mapped to instances of the directed odd cycles packing problem with only one directed odd cycle. Thus we cannot distinguish between $(\sqrt{n}/2-2)$-arc-disjoint directed odd cycles and two arc-disjoint directed odd cycles. Since the number of arcs in G is $2M \times (\sqrt{n} - 2)^2 + 2n + \sqrt{n} = O(n^{1+2\varepsilon})$, so it is NP-hard to distinguish two arc-disjoint directed odd cycles and $m^{1/2+\varepsilon}$ arc-disjoint directed odd cycles. (Recall that $n = M^{1/(2\varepsilon)}$, since $\varepsilon > 0$ is arbitrary.) This completes the proof. □

As pointed out at the beginning of this section, the node-disjoint case can be also done in a similar way. It is still NP-hard to decide whether or not there are two node-disjoint directed paths with specified endpoints in a given directed graph [12]. So we just need to replace the graph H' in the above proof by the graph H'' with the instance for the two node-disjoint directed paths problem. The rest of the proof is exactly same. So we omit the details.

3. INTEGRALITY GAP

In this section, we give a proof of Theorem 1.3. In addition, we also give a proof of Theorem 1.7. Actually, it is almost identical to that of Theorem 1.4, so we first give a proof of Theorem 1.4, and then give a sketch of proof of Theorem 1.7.

Proof of Theorem 1.4.

The following algorithm uses the ideas similar to those in Chekuri and Khanna [5] (for the edge-disjoint paths problem). It will be convenient to describe the algorithm with a certain parameter l, which will be eventually set to $l = \sqrt{n}$. The algorithm starts with $\mathbf{C_1}, \mathbf{C_2} = \emptyset$ and in the end, outputs $\mathbf{C_1} \cup \mathbf{C_2}$, which is an odd cycle packing.

Phase 1: As long as there is an odd cycle of length at most l, find such a cycle, and then add it to $\mathbf{C_1}$. Then delete its vertices from the graph.

This can be done as follows: Take a vertex v. For $k = 1, \dots, l/2$, let the k-th level I_k be defined as the set of vertices at distance exactly k from v, and let $N_k = \bigcup_{0 \le i \le k} I_i$ be the set of vertices at distance at most k from v. If there is an odd cycle C of length l, then there must exist a vertex u such that C is contained in the graph induced by $N_{l/2}$ (for u), and in addition, C contains exactly two vertices from I_i for $i = 1, \dots, l/2$. So, we just need to find an odd cycle through u in the graph H induced by N_i (for $i = 1, \dots, l/2$) but we are allowed to delete all the edges with both endpoints in N_i (for $i = 1, \dots, l/2 - 1$). This can be done in polynomial time, because we just need to find a cycle through u in H, such that it contains only one edge with both endpoints in $I_{l/2}$, and does not contain any edge with both endpoints in I_j for $1 \le j \le l/2 - 1$. Then go to Phase 2 below.

Phase 2: If G is not bipartite, take an odd cycle C, and add it to $\mathbf{C_2}$.

It remains to prove that this is, actually, an $O(\sqrt{n})$ approximation algorithm for the fractional odd cycles packing.

Let us now fix an optimal fractional odd cycles packing f', and let f'_1 be the restriction of f' to odd cycles that intersect some odd cycles from $\mathbf{C_1}$, and $f'_2 = f' - f'_1$. Since every odd cycle from $\mathbf{C_1}$ has length at most l, it follows that $|f'_1| \le l|\mathbf{C_1}|$.

Let G_2 be the graph at the beginning of Phase 2. For each vertex v in G_2, let $f'_2(v)$ be the restriction of f'_2 to the odd cycles in G_2 containing v. By our choice, for every vertex v of G_2, clearly $|\mathbf{C_2}| \ge |f'_2(v)|$. Note that if G_2 is bipartite, then $|\mathbf{C_2}| = |f'_2(v)| = 0$ for each vertex v. Since every odd cycle in $\mathbf{C_2}$ has length at least l, so $n|\mathbf{C_2}| \ge \sum_{v \in V(G)} |f'_2(v)| \ge l|f'_2|$. Thus $|\mathbf{C_2}| \ge l|f'_2|/n = |f'_2|/l$.

Therefore, $|\mathbf{C_1}| + |\mathbf{C_2}| \ge (|f'_1| + |f'_2|)/l = |f'|/l$. Thus this is an $O(\sqrt{n})$ algorithm for the fractional odd cycles packing. □

Let us observe that the above proof works for the edge-disjoint case as well. The proof is essentially same (in Phase 1, in place of deleting vertices on the odd cycles, we shall delete edges on the odd cycles).

We remark that the above proof also works for the directed odd cycles packing problem. We first set $l = \sqrt{m}$. Finding a directed odd cycle is easy, see the book by Schrijver [67]. Thus in Phase 2, we can find a directed odd cycle, if one exists in G. In Phase 1, we need to find a directed odd cycle of length at most l. This can be done by mimicking the proof of Phase 1, together with a method to find a directed path between two vertices, see [67]. Thus the above algorithm and the above proof of the correctness of the algorithm can be applied to the directed odd cycles case (for both the arc-disjoint case and the node-disjoint case). Thus we can obtain Theorem 1.7.

As we mentioned in the introduction, Theorem 1.3 would follow if we could prove Theorem 1.5.

Proof of Theorem 1.5.

We need to provide a graph such that there are no two disjoint odd cycles in it, but there are $\sqrt{n} - 2$ odd cycles in it such that each vertex is on at most two of them (which is a half-integral odd cycles packing). We just consider an Escher grid T (a grid W and paths $P_1, \dots, P_{\sqrt{n}}$) of height $\sqrt{n}$. Note that this graph has no vertex of degree 2, if $\sqrt{n}$ is odd. We follow the notation for the Escher wall given in the previous subsection, explaining the Erdős-Pósa-property.

As pointed out there, there are no two disjoint odd cycles in T. To see why there are $\sqrt{n} - 2$ odd cycles such that each vertex is on at most two of them, we just need to find $\sqrt{n} - 2$ paths $P'_2, \dots, P'_{\sqrt{n}-1}$ in the grid W such that P'_i connects the endpoints of P_i for $i = 2, \dots, \sqrt{n} - 1$, and each vertex in W is on at most two of these paths. This is rather straightforward, thus we omit the details, and leave them to the reader. Informally, we can select one row S in order (except for the top and bottom rows), for each of the paths $P'_2, P'_3, \dots, P_{\sqrt{n}-1}$ in order, such that each path P'_i goes through only the vertices in S for the rows of W. In addition, each column is used in exactly two paths of P'_i. In this way, for each endpoint of P_i, we can go through one column to reach S. □

Let us observe that since we can construct an Escher wall of height $O(\sqrt{n})$ such that each vertex has degree exactly three, so Theorem 1.3 holds for the edge-disjoint odd cycle case as well, because if a given graph is 3-regular, vertex-disjoint cycles and edge-disjoint cycles are same.

4. OVERVIEW OF PROOF OF MAIN THEOREM

How do we prove Theorem 1.8? Recall that, given a graph G with m edges and n vertices, and for any fixed k, we have to decide whether or not G has k disjoint odd cycles.

Before giving an overview, let us give our intuition. We feel that the situation for the odd cycle packing problem is close to the well-known edge-disjoint paths problem (EDP). One can easily get an $O(\sqrt{m})$-approximation algorithm for the EDP (and the directed EDP), but the EDP for the directed case is NP-hard to approximate within $m^{1/2-\varepsilon}$ for any $\varepsilon > 0$. On the other hand, if we fix the number of terminals k for the EDP, then there is a seminal result by Robertson-Seymour which gives an $O(m^3)$-algorithm to decide the undirected EDP for any fixed k. In fact, as mentioned before, our result gives rise to the above mentioned result by Robertson-Seymour. So, we thought that we could adapt some of the techniques developed in graph minor theory. Here is overview of our proof for Theorem 1.8.

Although the Erdős-Pósa property does not hold for odd cycles, and thus we cannot directly reduce the odd cycles packing problem (for any fixed k) to the disjoint paths problem with fixed number of terminals, our approach makes use of the ideas in Robertson-Seymour's algorithm [60], together with some apparently new algorithmic techniques. So, let us first sketch the Robertson-Seymour's algorithm on the disjoint paths problem first. At a high level, it is based on the following two cases: either a given graph G has bounded tree-width or else it has a large tree-width. In the first case, one can apply dynamic programming to a tree-decomposition of bounded tree-width, see [1, 3, 60]. The second case again breaks into two cases. If G has a large clique minor, then one can use this clique minor to link up a subset of the terminals in any desired way. So, suppose G does not have a huge clique minor. Then one can prove that, after deleting bounded number of vertices, there is a huge wall which is essentially planar. This makes it possible to prove that the middle vertex v of this wall is irrelevant, i.e, the disjoint paths problem for any fixed k is feasible in G if and only if it is in $G - v$. This requires the whole graph minor papers, and the structure theorem of graph minors [61]. Therefore, this part is the most difficult and complicated.

Our algorithm is based on following the same line of Robertson and Seymour's. The first step is to examine whether or not the tree-width is bounded. Again, if the tree-width is bounded, we are done. In fact, in this case, the Erdős-Pósa-property holds, see [76]. Thus we can decide whether or not there are k disjoint odd cycles in an input graph G.

But when tree-width of a given graph is large, the Robertson-Seymour's algorithmic framework is not enough to solve our problem, since we need to control the parity of the cycles. More precisely, as with the Robertson-Seymour algorithm to solve the disjoint paths problem for any fixed k, in each iteration, we would like to either use a huge clique minor as a "crossbar", or exploit the structure of graphs in which we cannot find such a minor. Here, however, we must maintain the parity of the cycles and can only use an "odd clique minor" (we shall define it in a moment). We must also describe the structure of those graphs in which we cannot find such a minor and discuss how to exploit it. This motivates us to introduce an odd clique minor to attack this problem. In fact, the odd clique minor appears in many ares of combinatorial optimization. So, it seems us that this approach is quite natural. For more details and literatures concerning odd clique minors, we refer the reader to the book by Schrijver [67]. But let us address what the odd clique minor is.

Recall that a graph H is a *minor* of G if H can be obtained by contracting and deleting edges in G. Equivalently, H is a minor of G precisely if there are $|V(H)|$ vertex-disjoint trees in G, one tree T_v for each vertex v of H, such that for every edge $e = \{v, w\}$ in H there is an edge $\hat{e}$ in G connecting the two corresponding trees T_v and T_w. Now H is an *odd minor* of G if, in addition, all the vertices of the trees can be two-colored in such a way that (1) the edges of each tree T_v are bichromatic, while (2) the edge $\hat{e}$ connecting trees T_v and T_w corresponding to each edge $e = \{v, w\}$ of H is monochromatic. Let us observe that any three trees give rise to an odd cycle. Thus an odd clique minor of order $3k$ contains k disjoint odd cycles.

The class of odd-H-minor-free graphs (excluding a fixed graph H as an odd minor) is more general than the class of H-minor-free graphs (excluding a fixed graph H as a minor). Indeed, the class of odd-H-minor-free graphs is strictly more general: the complete bipartite graph $K_{n/2,n/2}$ certainly contains a K_k-minor for $k \leq n/2$, but on the other hand, it does not contain K_k as an odd minor for $k \geq 3$. Also, any K_k-minor-free graph G is $O(k\sqrt{\log k})$-degenerate, i.e, every induced subgraph has a vertex of degree at most $O(k\sqrt{\log k})$; see [74, 39]. Thus, any K_k-minor-free graph G has $O(k\sqrt{\log k}n)$ edges. On the other hand, some odd-K_k-minor-free graphs such as $K_{n/2,n/2}$ may have $\Theta(n^2)$ edges.

Let us come back to overview of our main result.

We shall find an irrelevant vertex v, i.e, the odd cycles packing problem for any fixed k is feasible in G if and only if it is in $G - v$. . To do so, we need to consider the following three cases.

1. A big odd clique minor with a huge clique minor.
2. A huge clique minor, but no big odd clique minor.
3. A wall W of huge height, but no huge clique minor.

More precisely, the third case needs the following two subcases.

(a) A flat wall W of huge height with some odd faces.

(b) A bipartite flat wall W of huge height.

We now remark that we can take all the above configurations so that they are "attached" to a specific highly connected part of the graph. When speeding up the time complexity of Theorem 1.8 to $O(m\alpha(m, n) + n \log n)$, we need this fact, because this allows us to throw away almost half of the vertices when we perform a reduction. For now, let us just try to find an irrelevant vertex.

Suppose there is a huge clique minor. Robertson and Seymour also excluded a huge clique minor for the k disjoint paths problem for any fixed k, and that step is not hard. But our problem setting is much harder since we need to figure out the parity of each cycle. To do so, we first need to exclude a big odd clique minor. So this corresponds to the case 1 above. If there is an odd clique minor of order $3k$, then clearly there are k disjoint odd cycles, and hence we are done.

One question is: how do we find a big clique odd minor? It turns out that we have a nice structure theorem which tells us that if we have a huge clique minor, then either we can get a big odd minor or else we can get a vertex set X of bounded size (depending on k) such that the component of $G - X$ containing most of the nodes of the huge clique minor is "essentially" bipartite. This can be shown with help of the recent result by Geelen et al. [15]. Let us observe that, in order to obtain a big odd clique minor from a huge clique minor, we need some recent deep results concerning odd S-paths from [15] (which generalize the well-known S-paths theorem by Mader).

Then we need to discuss the case when there is a huge clique minor, but no big odd clique minors. So this corresponds to the case 2 above. In this case, by the above result, we can conclude that a given graph has an induced subgraph which is "essentially" bipartite. More precisely, the following holds:

> There is a separation (A, B) of order at most $25k$ in G (that is, $|A \cap B| \leq 25k$), such that $A - B$ is bipartite, and contains a clique minor Q of order at least $52k$.

Note that each odd cycle must contain a vertex in B since $A - B$ is bipartite. Since the separation (A, B) has order $25k$, so, if there are desired k disjoint odd cycles, then they passes across the vertices in $A \cap B$ at most $25k/2$ times, and hence there are at most $25k^k$ ways for k disjoint odd cycles to pass through the vertex set $A \cap B$ toward A. In addition, we do not have to worry about the parity of the paths in $A - B$ since it is bipartite. So, as demonstrated in the subsection 1.2 for the Erdős-Pósa property, we could use the algorithm of Robertson and Seymour for the disjoint paths problem in

A, with respect to the terminals in $A \cap B$ (thus the number of terminals is at most $25k$, and there are at most $25k^k$ ways for the k disjoint odd cycles to pass through the vertex set $A \cap B$ toward A). This allows us to find an irrelevant vertex in the clique minor Q by using a result in Graph Minors, see [60]. In summary, if there is a huge clique minor, we can always find an irrelevant vertex in the clique.

Thus we come to the point where there is no huge clique minor. So this corresponds to the case 3 above, but we need to look at the cases (a) and (b). In the case (a), it is not so hard to prove the following;

> Either W has k disjoint odd faces, or there is a vertex set X of order at most $100k$ such that $W - X$ has no odd faces.

This allows us to reduce to the final case (b). This case is the hardest case, and in fact, this corresponds to the hardest case of Robertson and Seymour's algorithm.

(Recall that Robertson and Seymour proved that the middle vertex v of a flat wall of huge height is irrelevant, i.e., the disjoint paths problem for any fixed k is feasible in G if and only if it is in $G - v$. This requires the whole graph minor papers, and the structure theorem of graph minors [61].

Actually, we prove the following theorem, which corresponds to the parity version of the main correctness theorem in [60].

Theorem 4.1. *There are computable constants $g(k), f'(k)$ satisfying the following:*

If there is a subset $X \subset V(G)$ of order at most $\binom{96k\sqrt{\log k}}{2}$ such that there is a flat wall W of height $f'(k)$ in $G - X$ with the following properties:

1. *all the components $A_1, \ldots, A_l$ (Roughly, each component of $A_1, \ldots, A_l$ is attached to a face in the planar graph induced by the wall W, with at most three vertices.) have tree-width at most $g(k)$, and*
2. *the compass of the wall W in $G - X$ is bipartite, i.e, the graph induced by the wall W is bipartite,*

then there is a vertex v in W such that v is irrelevant, i.e, the odd cycles packing problem for any fixed k is feasible in G if and only if it is in $G - v$. Furthermore, given such a wall W, we can find in linear time the irrelevant vertex v.

The proof needs the whole graph minor structure theorem, techniques and methods in [61]. Fortunately, by carefully analyzing the structure in [61], together with some results in Algebraic Topology and the results in [63, 64], we are able to manage to reduce Theorem 4.1 to the main correctness theorem of the disjoint paths problem for any fixed k in graph minors in [60].

Theorem 4.2. *There are computable constants $g(k), f(k)$ satisfying the following:*

If there is a subset $X \subset V(G)$ of order at most $\binom{3k}{2}$ such that there is a flat wall W of height $f(k)$ in $G - X$ with the property that all the components $A_1, \ldots, A_l$ (Roughly, each component of $A_1, \ldots, A_l$ is attached to a face in the planar graph induced by the wall W, with at most three vertices.) have tree-width at most $g(k)$, then there is a vertex v in W such that v is irrelevant, i.e, the disjoint paths problem for any fixed k is feasible in G if and only if it is in $G - v$. Furthermore, given such a wall W, we can find in linear time the irrelevant vertex v.

We now sketch how we can reduce Theorem 4.1 to Theorem 4.2. Assume that the structure as in Theorem 4.2 is given. In fact, as in the result in [64], the structure in Theorem 4.2 is a part of an "almost-embeddable" graph. After deleting a bounded number of vertices, and putting them in the apex vertex set of a given graph G, it can be show that G is an almost embeddable graph such that

1. each component that is attached to the bounded genus part (of the almost embeddable graph, up to 3-separations) is bipartite,
2. each face in the surface (of the almost embeddable graph) is even,
3. each vortex is bipartite,
4. each odd cycle in the surface (of the almost embeddable graph) is one-sided, i.e, each odd cycle must pass through one specified crosscap, and
5. each odd cycle in the almost embeddable graph must go through either a vertex in the apex vertex set, or the crosscap or both.

Note that 4 needs some results in Algebraic Topology Let us observe that the structure in 4 contains an Escher wall of large height. This is an obstruction for odd cycles to have Erdős-Pósa property, as observed by Lóvasz and Schrijver.

By 5, if we delete the apex vertex set and the edges in the special cross cap from G, then the resulting graph G' is bipartite. The number of apex vertices is bounded (in terms of k). It remains to prove that

> [F] if there are k disjoint odd cycles in G, then we can modify k disjoint odd cycles in G, so that the total number of times that these k disjoint odd cycles pass through the special crosscap, can be bounded in terms of k.

Since G' is bipartite, so we do not have to worry about the parity of paths in G'. Thus if we could prove the statement [F], this could reduce Theorem 4.1 to Theorem 4.2 because we only have to consider the disjoint paths problem with specified terminals in G'. In addition, the number of these terminals is bounded in terms of k.

The proof of the statement [F] follows from the result in [55], together with some additional analysis on the parity of paths. Roughly, the result in [55] says that if there are desired k disjoint paths in a graph which is embedded on a fixed surface S of Euler genus g, then one can modify these k disjoint paths so that each of the paths can go across one specific homotopic type (of the surface S) at most $f(k, g)$ times for some function f of k, g. This helps proving the statement [F], because we just need to prove that each odd cycle can go across the crosscap only bounded number of times.

We learned from Jim Geelen that his student, Tony Huynh, also worked on a similar problem in his Ph. D thesis [20].

5. REFERENCES

[1] S. Arnborg and A. Proskurowski, Linear time algorithms for NP-hard problems restricted to partial k-trees, *Discrete Appl. Math.*, **23** (1989), 11–24.

[2] P. Balister, packing digraphs with directed closed trails, *Combin. Probab. Comput.*, **12** (2003), 1–15.

[3] H. L. Bodlaender, A linear-time algorithm for finding tree-decomposition of small treewidth, *SIAM J. Comput.*, **25** (1996), 1305–1317.

[4] T. Böhme, K. Kawarabayashi, J. Maharry and B. Mohar, Linear connectivity forces large complete bipartite minors, *J. Combin. Theory Ser. B.*, **99** (2009), 557–582.

[5] C. Chekuri and S. Khanna, Edge disjoint paths revisited, *ACM-SIAM Symposium on Discrete Algorithms (SODA'03)*, 628–637, (2003).

[6] M. Chudnovsky, J. Geelen, B. Gerards, L. Goddyn, M. Lohman and P. Seymour, Packing non-zero A-paths in group labelled graphs, *Combinaorica*, **26** (2006), 521–532.

[7] I. Dejter and V. Neumann-lara, Unboundedness for generalized odd cycle traversability and a Gallai conjecture, paper presented at the Fourth Caribbean Conference on Computing, Puerto Rico, 1985.

[8] E. D. Demaine, M. Hajiaghayi, and K. Kawarabayashi, Algorithmic graph minor theory: Decomposition, approximation and coloring, *Proc. 46th Annual Symposium on Foundations of Computer Science (FOCS'06)*, 637–646, (2005).

[9] R. Diestel, K. Yu. Gorbunov, T. R. Jensen, and C. Thomassen, Highly connected sets and the excluded grid theorem, *J. Combin. Theory Ser. B*, **75** (1999), 61–73.

[10] R. Diestel, K. Kawarabayashi, T. Müller and P. Wollan, On the structure theorem of the excluded minor theorem of large tree-width, *submitted.*

[11] P. Erdös and L. Pósa, On the maximal number of disjoint circuits of a graph, *Publ. Math. Debrecen*, **9** (1962), 3–12.

[12] S. Fortune, J.E. Hopcroft and J. Wyllie, The directed subgraph homeomorphism problem, *Theor. Comput. Sci.*, **10** (1980), 111–121.

[13] S. Fiorini, N. Hardy, B. Reed and A. Vetta, Approximate min-max relations for odd cycles in planar graphs, *Mathematical Programming*, **110** (2007), 71–91.

[14] A. Frank, Packing paths, cuts and circuits – a survey, in *Paths, Flows and VLSI-Layout* B. Korte, L. Lovász, H.J. Promel and A. Schrijver. Eds. Berlin: Springer-Verlag 1990, 49-100.

[15] J. Geelen, B. Gerards, B. Reed, P. Seymour and A. Vetta, On the odd variant of Hadwiger's conjecture, *J. Combin. Theory Ser. B.*, **99** (2009), 20–29.

[16] M. X. Goemans and D.P. Williamson, Primal-dual approximation algorithms for feedback problems in planar graphs, *Combinatorica*, **18** (1998), 37–59.

[17] V. Guruswami, S. Khanna, R. Rajaraman, B. Sherphard, and M. Yannakakis, Near-optimal hardness results and apprixmaiton algorithms for edge-disjoint paths and related problems, *J. Comp. Styst. Science*, **67** (2003), 473–496. Also, *Proc. 31st ACM Symposium on Theory of Computing, (STOC'99)*, 19–28, (1999).

[18] F. Hadlock, Finding a maximum cut of a planar graph in polynomial time, *Siam J. Comput.*, **4** (1975), 221–225.

[19] R. Halin, S-function for graphs, *J. Geometry*, **8** (1976), 171–186.

[20] T. Hunyh, The linkage problem for group-labelled graphs, Ph. D Thesis, University of Waterloo, 2009.

[21] T. Ibaraki and H. Nagamochi, A linear time algorithm for finding a sparse k-connected spanning subgraph of a k-connected graph, *Algorithmica*, **7** (1992), 583–596.

[22] R. Kapadia, Z. Li and B. Reed, A linear time algorithm to test the 2-paths problem, *submitted.*

[23] K. Kawarabayashi, On the connectivity of minimal counterexamples to Hadwiger's conjecture, *J. Combin. Theory Ser. B*, **97** (2007), 144–150.

[24] K. Kawarabayashi, Rooted minors problem in highly connected graphs, *Discrete Math.*, **287** (2004), 121–123.

[25] K. Kawarabayashi, Improved alogirthm for find a cycle through elements, *IPCO'08*, 374–384.

[26] K. Kawarabayashi, Note on coloring graphs with no odd-K_k-minors, *J. Combin. Theory Ser. B.*, **99** (2009), 738–741.

[27] K. Kawarabayashi and P. Wollan, Non-zero disjoint cycles in highly connected group-labelled graphs, *J. Combin. Theory Ser. B*, **96** (2006), 296–301.

[28] K. Kawarabayashi and Z. Song, Some remarks on the odd Hadwiger's conjecture, *Combinatorica*, **27** (2007), 429–438.

[29] K. Kawarabayashi and A. Nakamoto, The Erdős-Pósa property for odd cycles on an orientable fixed surface, *Discrete Math.*, **307** (2007), 764–768.

[30] K. Kawarabayashi and B. Reed, Computing crossing number in linear time, *Proc. 39th ACM Symposium on Theory of Computing (STOC'07)*, 382–390, (2007).

[31] K. Kawarabayashi and B. Mohar, Graph and Map Isomorphism and all polyhedral embeddings in linear time, *Proc. 40th ACM Symposium on Theory of Computing (STOC'08)*, 471–480, (2008).

[32] K. Kawarabayashi and B. Reed, A nearly linear time algorithm for the half disjoint paths packing, *ACM-SIAM Symposium on Discrete Algorithms (SODA'08)*, 446–454, (2008).

[33] K. Kawarabayashi and B. Reed, A nearly linear time algorithm for the half integral parity disjoint paths packing problem (with B. Reed), *ACM-SIAM Symposium on Discrete Algorithms (SODA'09)*, 1183–1192, (2009).

[34] K. Kawarabayashi and B. Reed, Highly parity linked graphs, *Combinatorica*, **29** (2009), 215–225.

[35] K. Kawarabayashi, B. Mohar and B. Reed, A simpler linear time algorithm for embedding graphs into an arbitrary surface and the genus of bounded tree-width graphs, *Proc. 49th Annual Symposium on Foundations of Computer Science (FOCS'08)*, 771–780, (2008).

[36] K. Kawarabayashi, Y. Kobayashi and B. Reed, The disjoint paths problem in quaratic time, *submitted.*

[37] K. Kawarabayashi and B. Reed, An (almost) linear time algorithm for odd cycles transversal, *ACM-SIAM Symposium on Discrete Algorithms, (SODA'10)*, 365–378, (2010).

[38] R. M. Karp, On the computational complexity of combinatorial problems, *Network*, **5** (1975), 45–68.

[39] A. Kostochka, Lower bound of the Hadwiger number of graphs by their average degree, *Combinatorica*, **4** (1984), 307–316.

[40] M. Krivelevich, Z. Nutov, M. R. Salavatipour, J. Verstaete, and R. Yuster, Approximating algorithms and hardness results for cycle packing problems, *ACM transaction on Algorithms*, **3** (2007), article 48. Also, SODA 2005 and IPCO 2005.

[41] B. Mohar, Combinatorial local planarity and the width of graph embeddings, *Canad. J. Math.*, **44** (1992), 1272–1288.

[42] B. Mohar and C. Thomassen, Graphs on Surfaces, Johns Hopkins University Press, Baltimore, MD, 2001.

[43] L. Perkovic and B. Reed, An improved algorithm for finding tree decompositions of small width, *International Journal on the Foundations of Computing Science*, **11** (2000), 81–85.

[44] B. Reed, Finding approximate separators and computing tree width quickly; STOC 1992, Victoria B.C., 1992.

[45] B. Reed, Rooted Routing in the Plane, *Discrete Applied Mathematics*, **57** (1995), 213–227.

[46] B. Reed, Tree width and tangles: a new connectivity measure and some applications, in *"Surveys in Combinatorics, 1997 (London)"*, London Math. Soc. Lecture Note Ser. **241**, Cambridge Univ. Press, Cambridge, 1997, pp. 87–162.

[47] B. Reed, Mangoes and blueberries, *Combinatorica*, **19** (1999), 267–296.

[48] B. Reed, Rooted Routing via Graph Minors, to appear.

[49] B. Reed, N. Robertson, A. Schrijver and P. D. Seymour, Finding disjoint trees in planar graphs in linear time. Graph structure theory (Seattle, WA, 1991), 295–301, Contemp. Math., 147, Amer. Math. Soc., Providenc, RI, 1993.

[50] B. Reed, K. Smith and A. Vetta, Finding odd cycle transversals, *Operation Research Letter*, **32** (2004), 299–301.

[51] B. Reed and D. Wood, A linear time algorithm to find a separator in a graph with an excluded minor, *submitted.*

[52] R. Rizzi, V. Bafna, S. Istrail, G. Lancia, Practical algorithms and fixed parameter tractability for the single individual SNP haplotyping problem, Algorithms in Bioinformatics: Second international workshop, Lecture notes in computer scienece, **2452**, Springer, Berlin, 2002, 29–43.

[53] N. Robertson and P. D. Seymour, Graph minors. III. Planar tree-width, *J. Combin. Theory Ser. B*, **36** (1984), 49–63.

[54] N. Robertson and P. D. Seymour, Graph minors. V. Excluding a planar graph, *J. Combin. Theory Ser. B*, **41** (1986), 92–114.

[55] N. Robertson and P. D. Seymour, Graph minors. VII. Disjoint paths on a surface, *J. Combin. Theory Ser. B*, **45** (1988), 212–254.

[56] N. Robertson and P. D. Seymour, Graph minors. IX. Disjoint crossed paths, *J. Combin. Theory Ser. B*, **49** (1990), 40–77.

[57] N. Robertson and P. D. Seymour, Graph minors. X. Obstructions to tree-decomposition, *J. Combin. Theory Ser. B*, **52** (1991), 153–190.

[58] N. Robertson and P. D. Seymour, Graph minors. XI. Circuits on a surface, *J. Combin. Theory Ser. B*, **60** (1994), 72–106.

[59] N. Robertson and P. D. Seymour, Graph minors. XII. Distance on a surface, *J. Combin. Theory, Ser. B*, **64** (1995), 240–272.

[60] N. Robertson and P. D. Seymour, Graph minors. XIII. The disjoint paths problem, *J. Combin. Theory Ser. B*, **63** (1995), 65–110.

[61] N. Robertson and P. D. Seymour, Graph minors. XVI. Excluding a non-planar graph, *J. Combin. Theory Ser. B*, **89** (2003), 43–76.

[62] N. Robertson and P. D. Seymour, Graph minors. XVII. Taming a vortex, *J. Combin. Theory Ser. B*, **77** (1999), 162–210.

[63] N. Robertson and P. D. Seymour, Graph Minors XXI. Graphs with uniquely linkages, to appear in *J. Combin. Theory Ser. B.*

[64] N. Robertson and P. D. Seymour, Graph Minors XXII. Irrelevant vertices in linkage problems, to appear in *J. Combin. Theory Ser. B.*

[65] N. Robertson and P. D. Seymour, An outline of a disjoint paths algorithm, in: *"Paths, Flows, and VLSI-Layout,"* B. Korte, L. Lovász, H. J. Prömel, and A. Schrijver (Eds.), Springer-Verlag, Berlin, 1990, pp. 267–292.

[66] N. Robertson, P. D. Seymour and R. Thomas, Quickly excluding a planar graph, *J. Combin. Theory Ser. B*, **62** (1994), 323–348.

[67] A. Schrijver, Combinatorial Optimization: Polyhedra and Efficiency, number 24 in Algorithm and Combinatorics, Springer Verlag, 2003.

[68] P.D. Seymour, Decomposition of regular matroids. *J. Combin. Theory, Ser. B*, **28** (1980), 305–359.

[69] P. Seymour, *Disjoint paths in graphs, Discrete Mathematics*, **29** (1980), 293 - 309.

[70] P. Seymour, Matroid minors, *Handbook of Combinatorics*, (Eds.: R. L. Graham, M. Grötschel and L. Lóvasz). North-Holland, Amsterdam, 1985, 419–431.

[71] P. Seymour and R. Thomas, Graph searching and a min-max theorem for tree-width, *J. Combin. Theory Ser. B*, **58** (1993), 22–33.

[72] R.E. Tarjan, Data Structures and network algorithms, SIAM, Philadelphia, PA, 1983.

[73] T. Tholey, Solving the 2-disjoint paths problem in nearly linear time, *Theory of computing systems*, **39** (2004), 51–78.

[74] A. Thomason, An extremal function for contractions of graphs, *Math. Proc. Cambridge Philos. Soc.*, **95** (1984), 261–265.

[75] C. Thomassen, 2-linked graph, *European J. Combinatorics*, **1** (1980), 371 - 378.

[76] C. Thomassen, On the presence of disjoint subgraphs of a specified type, *J. Graph Theory*, **12** (1988), 101 - 111.

[77] K. Wagner, *Über eine Eigenschaft der ebenen Komplexe, Math. Ann.*, **114** (1937), 570–590.

On the Geometry of Differential Privacy

Moritz Hardt*
Center for Computational Intractability
Department of Computer Science
Princeton University
mhardt@cs.princeton.edu

Kunal Talwar
Microsoft Research
Silicon Valley
kunal@microsoft.com

ABSTRACT

We consider the noise complexity of differentially private mechanisms in the setting where the user asks d linear queries $f\colon \mathbb{R}^n \to \mathbb{R}$ non-adaptively. Here, the database is represented by a vector in $\mathbb{R}^n$ and proximity between databases is measured in the ℓ_1-metric. We show that the noise complexity is determined by two geometric parameters associated with the set of queries. We use this connection to give tight upper and lower bounds on the noise complexity for any $d \le n$. We show that for d random linear queries of sensitivity 1, it is necessary and sufficient to add ℓ_2-error $\Theta(\min\{d\sqrt{d}/\epsilon, d\sqrt{\log(n/d)}/\epsilon\})$ to achieve ϵ-differential privacy. Assuming the truth of a deep conjecture from convex geometry, known as the Hyperplane conjecture, we can extend our results to arbitrary linear queries giving nearly matching upper and lower bounds. Our bound translates to error $O(\min\{d/\epsilon, \sqrt{d\log(n/d)}/\epsilon\})$ per answer. The best previous upper bound (Laplacian mechanism) gives a bound of $O(\min\{d/\epsilon, \sqrt{n}/\epsilon\})$ per answer, while the best known lower bound was $\Omega(\sqrt{d}/\epsilon)$. In contrast, our lower bound is strong enough to separate the concept of differential privacy from the notion of approximate differential privacy where an upper bound of $O(\sqrt{d}/\epsilon)$ can be achieved.

Categories and Subject Descriptors

F.2 [**ANALYSIS OF ALGORITHMS AND PROBLEM COMPLEXITY**]: General

General Terms

Algorithms, Theory

1. INTRODUCTION

The problem of Privacy-preserving data analysis has attracted a lot of attention in recent years. Several databases, e.g. those held by the Census Bureau, contain private data provided by individuals, and protecting the privacy of those individuals is an important concern. *Differential Privacy* is a rigorous notion of privacy that allows statistical analysis of sensitive data while providing strong privacy guarantees even in the presence of an adversary armed with arbitrary auxiliary information. We refer the reader to the survey of Dwork [7] and the references therein for further motivation and background information.

We consider the following setup: A *database* is represented by a vector $x \in \mathbb{R}^n$. The *queries* that the analyst may ask are *linear* combinations of the entries of x. In general, a multidimensional query is a map $F\colon \mathbb{R}^n \to \mathbb{R}^d$, and we will restrict ourselves to linear maps F with coefficients in the interval $[-1, 1]$. Thus F is a $d\times n$ matrix with entries in $[-1, 1]$. In this work, we assume throughout that $d \le n$. A mechanism is a randomized algorithm which holds a database $x \in \mathbb{R}^n$, receives a query $F\colon \mathbb{R}^n \to \mathbb{R}^d$ and answers with some $a \in \mathbb{R}^d$. Informally, we say a mechanism satisfies differential privacy in this setting if the densities of the output distributions on inputs $x, x' \in \mathbb{R}^n$ with $\|x - x'\|_1 \le 1$ are point wise within an $\exp(\epsilon)$ multiplicative factor of each other. Here and in the following, $\epsilon > 0$ is a parameter that measures the strength of the privacy guarantee (smaller ϵ being a stronger guarantee). The *error* of a mechanism is the expected Euclidean distance between the correct answer Fx and the actual answer a. Here the expectation is taken over the coin tosses of the mechanism; we consider the worst case error over all databases.

In this work, we use methods from convex geometry to determine a nearly optimal trade-off between privacy and error. We give a lower bound on how much error any differentially private mechanism must add. And we present a mechanism whose error nearly matches this lower bound.

The above setup is fairly general. To illustrate it and facilitate comparison with previous work, we will describe some specific instantiations below.

Histograms.

Suppose we have a database $D \in [n]^m$, containing private information about m individuals. We can think of each individual as belonging to one of n types. The database D can then naturally be translated to a histogram $x \in \mathbb{R}^n$, i.e., x_i counts the number of individuals of type i. In this case, the parameter m corresponds to the sparsity of x. Note that in the definition of differential privacy, we require the mechanism to be defined for all $x \in \mathbb{R}^n$ and demand that the output distributions be close whenever $\|x - x'\|_1 \le 1$.

*Supported by NSF grants CCF-0426582 and CCF-0832797. Part of this work has been done while the author visited Microsoft Research Silicon Valley.

STOC'10, June 5–8, 2010, Cambridge, Massachusetts, USA.

This is a stronger requirement than asserting this property only for integer vectors x and x'. It only makes our upper bounds stronger. For the lower bounds, this strengthening allows us to ignore the discretization issues that would arise in the usual definition. Our lower bounds can be extended for the usual definition for very small ϵ and large enough m. We note that better mechanisms do exist for small m. Now, our upper bound holds for any linear query on the histogram. This includes some well-studied and natural classes of queries. For instance, *contingency tables* (see, e.g., [1]) and counting queries are both linear queries on the histogram.

Private bits.

In the setting looked at by Dinur and Nissim [6], the database $D \in \{0,1\}^m$ consists of one private bit for each individual and each query ask for the number of 1's amongst a (random) subset on $[m]$. Given d such queries, one can define $n \le 2^d$ types of individuals, depending on the subset of the queries that ask about an individual. The database D then maps to a histogram x in the natural way with x_i denoting the number of individuals of type i with their private bit set to 1. Our results then imply a lower bound of $\Omega(d/\epsilon)$ per answer for any ϵ-differentially private mechanism. This improves on the $\Omega(\sqrt{d})$ bound for $d = m$ from [6] for a weaker privacy definition (blatant non-privacy). A closely related rephrasing is to imagine each individual having d private $\{0,1\}$ attributes so that $n = 2^d$. The d queries that ask for the 1-way marginals of the input naturally map to a matrix F and Theorem 1.1 implies a lower bound of $\Omega(d/\epsilon)$ noise per marginal for such queries. In contrast $O(\sqrt{d \log \frac{1}{\delta}}/\epsilon)$ error is attainable under the relaxed notion of (ϵ,δ)-differential privacy.

Other settings.

One can also look at x itself as a database where each individuals private data is in $[0,1]$; in this setting the dimension of the data n equals the number of individuals m. Our results lead to better upper bounds for this setting. Finally, there are settings such as the recent work of [23] on private recommendation systems, where the private data is transformed with a stability guarantee so that nearby databases get mapped to vectors at ℓ_1 distance at most 1.

1.1 Our results

We first relate the noise complexity of differentially private mechanisms to geometric properties of the image of the unit ℓ_1-ball B_1^n when applying the linear mapping F. We will denote the resulting convex polytope by $K = FB_1^n$. Our first result lower bounds the noise any ϵ-differentially private mechanism must add in terms of the volume of K.

THEOREM 1.1. *Let $\epsilon > 0$ and suppose $F\colon \mathbb{R}^n \to \mathbb{R}^d$ is a linear map. Then, every ϵ-private mechanism M has error at least $\Omega(\epsilon^{-1} d\sqrt{d} \cdot \mathrm{Vol}(K)^{1/d})$ where $K = FB_1^n$.*

Recall, the term *error* refers to the expected Euclidean distance between the output of the mechanism and the correct answer to the query F. As mentioned before, our lower bounds make use of the fact that the mechanism M is defined on all points $x \in \mathbb{R}^n$ rather than only on $x \in \mathbb{Z}_+^n$. While all mechanism we are aware of satisfy this stronger requirement, we remark that it would be interesting to achieve the same lower bound under the weaker assumption.

We then describe a differentially private mechanism whose error depends on the expected ℓ_2 norm of a randomly chosen point in K. Our mechanism is an instantiation of the exponential mechanism [24] with the score function defined by the (negative of the) norm $\|\cdot\|_K$. Hence, we will refer to this mechanism as the K-norm mechanism.

THEOREM 1.2. *Let $\epsilon > 0$ and suppose $F\colon \mathbb{R}^n \to \mathbb{R}^d$ is a linear map with $K = FB_1^n$. Then, the K-norm mechanism is ϵ-differentially private and has error at most $O(\epsilon^{-1} d\, \mathbb{E}_{z\in K} \|z\|_2)$.*

As it turns out, when F is a random Bernoulli ± 1 matrix our upper bound matches the lower bound up to constant factors. In this case, K is a random polytope and its volume and average Euclidean norm have been determined rather recently. Specifically, we apply a volume lower bound of Litvak et al. [22], and an upper bound on the average Euclidean norm due to Klartag and Kozma [21]. Quantitatively, we obtain the following theorem.

THEOREM 1.3. *Let $\epsilon > 0$ and $d \le n/2$. Then, for almost all matrices $F \in \{-1,1\}^{d\times n}$, any ϵ-differentially private mechanism M has error $\Omega(d/\epsilon)\cdot \min\{\sqrt{d}, \sqrt{\log(n/d)}\}$. On the other hand, the K-norm mechanism is ϵ-differentially private with error $O(d/\epsilon)\cdot \min\{\sqrt{d}, \sqrt{\log(n/d)}\}$.*

We remark that Litvak et al. also give an explicit construction of a mapping F realizing the lower bound.

More generally, we can relate our upper and lower bounds whenever the body K is in *approximately isotropic position.* Informally, this condition implies that $\mathbb{E}_{z\in K}\|z\| \sim \sqrt{d}\cdot \mathrm{Vol}(K)^{1/d} L_K$. Here, L_K denotes the so-called *isotropic constant* which is defined in Section 5.2.

THEOREM 1.4. *Let $\epsilon > 0$ and suppose $F\colon \mathbb{R}^n \to \mathbb{R}^d$ is a linear map such that $K = FB_1^n$ is in approximately isotropic position. Then, the K-norm mechanism is ϵ-differentially private with error at most $O(\epsilon^{-1} d\sqrt{d}\cdot \mathrm{Vol}(K)^{1/d} L_K)$, where L_K denotes the isotropic constant of K.*

Notice that the bound in the previous theorem differs from the lower bound by a factor of L_K. A central conjecture in convex geometry, sometimes referred to as the "Hyperplane Conjecture" or "Slicing Conjecture" (see [21] for further information) states that $L_K = O(1)$. Unfortunately, in general the polytope K could be very far from isotropic. In this case, both our volume-based lower bound and the K-norm mechanism can be quite far from optimal. We give a recursive variant of our mechanism and a natural generalization of our volume-based lower bound which are nearly optimal even if K is non-isotropic.

THEOREM 1.5. *Let $\epsilon > 0$. Suppose $F\colon \mathbb{R}^n \to \mathbb{R}^d$ is a linear map. Further, assume the Hyperplane Conjecture. Then, the mechanism introduced in Section 6 is ϵ-differentially private and has error at most $O(\log^{3/2} d)\cdot \mathrm{GLB}(F,\epsilon)$, where $\mathrm{GLB}(F,\epsilon)$ is a lower bound on the error of the optimal ϵ-differentially private mechanism.*

While we restricted our theorems to $F \in [-1,1]^{d\times n}$, they apply more generally to any linear mapping F. We remark that unlike the Laplace mechanism which can deal with

Mechanism	ℓ_2-error
Laplacian noise [9]	$\epsilon^{-1}d\sqrt{d}$
K-norm (here)	$\epsilon^{-1}d\sqrt{\log(n/d)}$
lower bound [6]	$\Omega(\epsilon^{-1}d)$
lower bound (here)	$\Omega(\epsilon^{-1}d)\min\{\sqrt{\log(n/d}, \sqrt{d}\}$

Figure 1: Summary of results in comparison to best previous work for d *random* linear queries each of sensitivity 1 where $1 \le d \le n$. Note that informally the average per coordinate error is smaller than the stated bounds by a factor of $\sqrt{d}$.

queries being presented one at a time, and chosen adaptively, we require knowledge of the full matrix F of queries in advance. We leave open the question of relaxing this constraint.

Efficient Mechanisms.

Our mechanism is an instantiation of the exponential mechanism and involves sampling random points from rather general high-dimensional convex bodies. This is why our mechanism is not efficient as it is. However, we can use rapidly mixing geometric random walks for the sampling step. These random walks turn out to approach the uniform distribution in a metric that is strong enough for our purposes. It will follow that both of our mechanisms can be implemented in polynomial time.

THEOREM 1.6. *The mechanisms given in Theorem 1.2 and Theorem 1.5 can be implemented in time polynomial in $n, 1/\epsilon$ such that the stated error bound remains the same up to constant factors, and the mechanism achieves ϵ-differential privacy.*

We point our that our lower bound GLB can also be approximated up to a constant factor.Together these results give polynomial time computable upper and lower bounds on the error of any differentially private mechanism, that are always within an $O(\log^{3/2} d)$ of each other assuming the Hyperplane conjecture.

Figure 1.1 summarizes our results. Note that we state our bounds in terms of the total ℓ_2 error, which is a $\sqrt{d}$ factor larger than the average per coordinate error.

1.2 Previous Work

Queries of the kind described above have *sensitivity* d, and hence the work of Dwork et al. [9] shows that adding Laplace noise with parameter d/ϵ to each entry of Fx ensures ϵ-differential privacy. Moreover, adding Laplace noise to the histogram x itself leads to another private mechanism. Thus such questions can be answered with noise $\min(d/\epsilon, \sqrt{n}/\epsilon, m)$ per entry of Fx. Some specific classes of queries can be answered with smaller error. Nissim, Raskhodnikova and Smith [26] show that one can add noise proportional to a smoothed version of the *local sensitivity* of the query, which can be much smaller than the global sensitivity for some *non-linear* queries. Building on [24], Blum, Ligett and Roth [4] show that it is possible to answer d counting queries (a special case of linear queries) with error $O(m^{2/3}\text{poly}\log(n,d))$. This bound is better than ours when $d \gg m$. Feldman et al. [13] construct private core sets for the k-median problem, enabling approximate computation of the k-median cost of any set of k facilities in $\mathbb{R}^d$. Private mechanisms with small error, for other classes of queries have also been studied in several other works, see e.g. [3, 1, 24, 5, 19, 16].

Dinur and Nissim [6] initiated the study of lower bounds on the amount of noise private mechanisms must add. They showed that any private mechanism that answers $\tilde{O}(m)$ random subset sum queries about a set of m people each having a private bit must add noise $\Omega(\sqrt{m})$ to avoid nearly full disclosure of the database (*blatant non-privacy*). This implies that as one answers more and more questions, the amount of error needed per answer must grow to provide any kind of privacy guarantee. These results were strengthened by Dwork, McSherry and Talwar [10], and by Dwork and Yekhanin [11]. However all these lower bounds protect against blatant non-privacy and cannot go beyond noise larger than $\min(\sqrt{d}, \sqrt{m})$ per answer, for d queries. Kasiviswanathan, Rudelson and Smith [18] show lower bounds of the same nature ($\min(\sqrt{d}, \sqrt{m})$ for d questions) for a more natural and useful class of questions. Their lower bounds also apply to (ϵ, δ)-differential privacy and are tight when ϵ and δ are constant. For the case of $d = 1$, Ghosh, Roughgarden and Sundararajan [14] show that adding Laplace noise is in fact optimal in a very general decision-theoretic framework, for any symmetric decreasing loss function. For the case that all sum queries need to be answered (i.e. all queries of the form $f_P(D) = \sum_{i=1}^{m} P(D_i)$ where P is a 0-1 predicate), Dwork et al. [9] show that any differentially private mechanism must add noise $\Omega(m)$. Rastogi et al [27] show that half of such queries must have error $\Omega(\sqrt{m})$. Blum, Ligett and Roth [4] show that any differentially private mechanism answering all (real-valued) halfspace queries must add noise $\Omega(m)$.

1.3 Overview and organization of the paper

In this section we will give a broad overview of our proof and outline the remainder of the paper.

We prove our lower bound in Section 3. Given a query $F\colon \mathbb{R}^n \to \mathbb{R}^d$, our lower bound depends on the d-dimensional volume of $K = FB_1^n$. If the volume of K is large, then a packing argument shows that we can pack exponentially many points inside K so that each pair of points is far from each other. We then scale up K by a suitable factor λ. By linearity, all points within λK have preimages under F that are still λ-close in ℓ_1-distance. Hence, the definition of ϵ-differential privacy (by transitivity) enforces some constraint between these preimages. We can combine these observations so as to show that any differentially private mechanism M will have to put significant probability mass in exponentially many disjoint balls. This forces the mechanism to have large expected error.

We then introduce the K-norm mechanism in Section 4. Our mechanism computes Fx and then adds a noise vector to Fx. The key point here is that the noise vector is not independent of F as in previous works. Instead, informally speaking, the noise is tailored to the exact shape of $K = FB_1^n$. This is accomplished by picking a particular noise vector z with probability proportional to $\exp(-\epsilon\|z\|_K)$. Here, $\|\cdot\|_K$ denotes the (Minkowski) norm defined by K. While our mechanism depends upon the query F, it does not depend on the particular database x. We can analyze our mechanism in terms of the expected Euclidean distance from the origin of a random point in K, i.e., $\mathbb{E}_{z\in K}\|z\|_2$. Arguing optimality of our mechanism hence boils down to relating

$\mathbb{E}_{z\in K}\|z\|_2$ to the volume of K. Indeed, using several results from convex geometry, we observe that our lower and upper bounds match up to constant factors when F is drawn at random from $\{-1,1\}^{d\times n}$. The polytope K can be interpreted as the symmetric convex hull of the row vectors of F. When F is a random matrix, K is a well-studied random polytope. Some recent results on random polytopes give us suitable lower bounds on the volume and upper bounds on the average Euclidean norm. More generally, our bounds are tight whenever K is in isotropic position (as pointed out in Section 5.2). This condition intuitively gives a relation between volume and average distance from the origin. Our bounds are actually only tight up to a factor of L_K, the isotropic constant of K. A well-known conjecture from convex geometry, known as the Hyperplane Conjecture or Slicing Conjecture, implies that $L_K = O(1)$.

The problem is that when F is not drawn at random, K could be very far from isotropic. In this case, the K-norm mechanism by itself might actually perform poorly. We thus give a recursive variant of the K-norm mechanism in Section 6 which can handle non-isotropic bodies. Our approach is based on analyzing the covariance matrix of K in order to partition K into parts on which our earlier mechanism performs well. Assuming the Hyperplane conjecture, we derive bounds on the error of our mechanism that are optimal to within polylogarithmic factors.

While our mechanisms are not efficient as they are, we finally show how they can actually be implemented in polynomial time. Our result follow from efficient sampling techniques for convex bodies using geometric random walks.

Acknowledgments.

We would like to thank Frank McSherry, Aaron Roth, Katrina Ligett, Indraneel Mukherjee, Nikhil Srivastava for several useful discussions, and Adam Smith for discussions and comments on a previous version of the paper.

2. PRELIMINARIES

Notation.

We will write B_p^d to denote the unit ball of the p-norm in $\mathbb{R}^d$. When $K \subseteq \mathbb{R}^d$ is a centrally symmetric convex set, we write $\|\cdot\|_K$ for the (Minkowski) norm defined by K (i.e. $\|x\|_K = \inf\{r : x \in rK\}$). The ℓ_p-norms are denoted by $\|\cdot\|_p$, but we use $\|\cdot\|$ as a shorthand for the Euclidean norm $\|\cdot\|_2$. Given a function $F : \mathbb{R}^{d_1} \to \mathbb{R}^{d_2}$ and a set $K \in \mathbb{R}^{d_1}$, FK denotes the set $\{F(x) : x \in K\}$.

2.1 Differential Privacy

DEFINITION 2.1. *A* mechanism M *is a family of probability measures* $M = \{\mu_x : x \in \mathbb{R}^n\}$ *where each measure* μ_x *is defined on* $\mathbb{R}^d$. *A mechanism is called* ϵ-differentially private, *if for all* $x, y \in \mathbb{R}^n$ *such that* $\|x-y\|_1 \le 1$, *we have* $\sup_{S\subseteq\mathbb{R}^d} \frac{\mu_x(S)}{\mu_y(S)} \le \exp(\epsilon)$, *where the supremum runs over all measurable subsets* $S \subseteq \mathbb{R}^d$.

A common weakening of ϵ-differential privacy is the following notion of *approximate* privacy.

DEFINITION 2.2. *A mechanism is called δ-approximate ϵ-*differentially private, *if for all* $x, y \in \mathbb{R}^n$ *such that* $\mu_x(S) \le \exp(\epsilon)\mu_y(S) + \delta$ *for all measurable subsets* $S \subseteq \mathbb{R}^n$ *whenever* $\|x-y\|_1 \le 1$,

The definition of privacy is transitive in the following sense.

FACT 2.3. *If M is an ϵ-differentially private mechanism and $x, y \in \mathbb{R}^n$ satisfy $\|x-y\|_1 \le k$, then for measurable $S \subseteq \mathbb{R}^d$ we have* $\frac{\mu_x(S)}{\mu_y(S)} \le \exp(\epsilon k)$.

Let $F : \mathbb{R}^n \to \mathbb{R}^d$ and $\ell : \mathbb{R}^d \times \mathbb{R}^d \to \mathbb{R}^+$. We define the *$\ell$-error* of a mechanism M as

$$\mathrm{err}_\ell(M, F) = \sup_{x\in\mathbb{R}^n} \mathop{\mathbb{E}}_{a\sim\mu_x} \ell(a, Fx).$$

Unless otherwise specified, we take ℓ to be the Euclidean norm ℓ_2. We will consider mappings F which possess the Lipschitz property, $\sup_{x\in B_1^n} \|Fx\|_1 \le d$. In this case, we will say that F has *sensitivity* d.

Our goal is to show trade-offs between privacy and error. The following standard upper bound, usually called the Laplacian mechanism, is known.

THEOREM 2.4 ([9]). *For any mapping $F : \mathbb{R}^n \to \mathbb{R}^d$ of sensitivity d and any $\epsilon > 0$, there exists an ϵ-differentially private mechanism M with* $\mathrm{err}(M, F) = O(d\sqrt{d}/\epsilon)$.

When it comes to approximate privacy, the Gaussian mechanism [8] shows that for any mapping $F : \mathbb{R}^n \to \mathbb{R}^d$ of sensitivity d there exists a δ-approximate ϵ-differentially private mechanism M with $\mathrm{err}(M, F) = O(d\sqrt{\log(1/\delta)}/\epsilon)$.

2.2 Isotropic Position

DEFINITION 2.5 (ISOTROPIC POSITION). *We say a convex body $K \subseteq \mathbb{R}^d$ is in* isotropic position *with isotropic constant L_K if for every unit vector $v \in \mathbb{R}^d$,*

$$\frac{1}{\mathrm{Vol}(K)} \int_K |\langle z, v\rangle|^2 dz = L_K^2 \mathrm{Vol}(K)^{2/d}. \tag{1}$$

A standard fact is that for every convex body $K \subseteq \mathbb{R}^d$, there is a volume-preserving linear transformation T such that TK is in isotropic position. For an arbitrary convex body K, its isotropic constant L_K can then be defined to be L_{TK} where T brings L to isotropic position. It is known (e.g. [25]) that T is unique up to an orthogonal transformation and thus this is well-defined. We refer the reader to the paper of Milman and Pajor [25], as well as the extensive survey of Giannopoulos [15] for a proof of this fact and other facts regarding the isotropic constant.

2.3 Gamma Distribution

The *Gamma distribution* with shape parameter $k > 0$ and scale $\theta > 0$, denoted $\mathrm{Gamma}(k, \theta)$, is given by the probability density function $f(r; k, \theta) = r^{k-1}\frac{e^{-r/\theta}}{\Gamma(k)\theta^k}$. Here, $\Gamma(k) = \int e^{-r} r^{k-1} dr$ denotes the Gamma function. The m-th moment of $r \sim \mathrm{Gamma}(k, \theta)$ is given by

$$\mathbb{E}[r^m] = \frac{\theta^m \Gamma(k+m)}{\Gamma(k)}. \tag{2}$$

3. LOWER BOUNDS FROM VOLUME ESTIMATES

In this section we show that lower bounds on the volume of the convex body $FB_1^n \subseteq \mathbb{R}^d$ give rise to lower bounds on the error that any private mechanism must have with respect to F. For that we will need a formal definition of private mechanism and its error.

DEFINITION 3.1. *A mechanism M is a family of probability measures $M = \{\mu_x : x \in \mathbb{R}^n\}$ where each measure μ_x is defined on $\mathbb{R}^d$. A mechanism is called* ϵ-differentially private, *if for all $x, y \in \mathbb{R}^n$ such that $\|x - y\|_1 \leq 1$, we have $\sup_{S \subseteq \mathbb{R}^d} \frac{\mu_x(S)}{\mu_y(S)} \leq \exp(\epsilon)$, where the supremum runs over all measurable subsets $S \subseteq \mathbb{R}^d$.*

For a mapping $F : \mathbb{R}^n \to \mathbb{R}^d$, we define the ℓ_2-error *of a mechanism M as* $\mathrm{err}(M, F) = \sup_{x \in \mathbb{R}^n} \mathbb{E}_{a \sim \mu_x} \|a - Fx\|_2$.

DEFINITION 3.2. *A set of points $Y \subseteq \mathbb{R}^d$ is called a* r-packing *if $\|y - y'\|_2 \geq r$ for any $y, y' \in Y, y \neq y'$.*

FACT 3.3. *Let $K \subseteq \mathbb{R}^d$ such that $R = \mathrm{Vol}(K)^{1/d}$. Then, K contains an $\Omega(R\sqrt{d})$-packing of size at least* $\exp(d)$.

PROOF. Since $\mathrm{Vol}(B_2^d)^{1/d} \sim \frac{1}{\sqrt{d}}$, the body K has the volume of a ball of radius $r \in \Omega(R\sqrt{d})$. Any maximal $\frac{r}{4}$-packing then has the desired property. □

THEOREM 3.4. *Let $\epsilon > 0$ and suppose $F : \mathbb{R}^n \to \mathbb{R}^d$ is a linear map and let $K = FB_1^n$. Then, every ϵ-differentially private mechanism M must have* $\mathrm{err}(M, F) \geq \Omega(\epsilon^{-1} d\sqrt{d} \cdot \mathrm{Vol}(K)^{1/d})$.

PROOF. Let $\lambda \geq 1$ be some scalar and put $R = \mathrm{Vol}(K)^{1/d}$. By Fact 3.3 and our assumption, $\lambda K = \lambda FB_1^n$ contains an $\Omega(\lambda R\sqrt{d})$-packing Y of size at least $\exp(d)$. Let $X \subseteq \mathbb{R}^n$ be a set of arbitrarily chosen preimages of $y \in Y$ so that $|X| = |Y|$ and $FX = Y$. By linearity, $\lambda FB_1^n = F(\lambda B_1^n)$ and hence we may assume that every $x \in X$ satisfies $\|x\|_1 \leq \lambda$.

We will now assume that $M = \{\mu_x : x \in \mathbb{R}^n\}$ is an ϵ-differentially private mechanism with error $cd\sqrt{d}R/\epsilon$ and lead this to a contradiction for small enough $c > 0$. For this we set $\lambda = d/2\epsilon$. By the assumption on the error, Markov's inequality implies that for all $x \in X$, we have $\mu_x(B_x) \geq \frac{1}{2}$, where B_x is a ball of radius $2cd\sqrt{d}R/\epsilon = 4c\lambda R\sqrt{d}$ centered at Fx. Since $Y = FX$ is an $\Omega(\lambda R\sqrt{d})$-packing, the balls $\{B_x : x \in X\}$ are disjoint for small enough constant $c > 0$.

Since $\|x\|_1 \leq \lambda$, it follows from the transitivity of ϵ-differential privacy (shown in Fact 2.3) that $\mu_0(B_x) \geq \exp(-\epsilon\lambda)\mu_x(B_x) \geq \frac{1}{2}\exp(-d/2)$. Since the balls B_x are pairwise disjoint,

$$1 \geq \mu_0(\cup_{x \in X} B_x) = \sum_{x \in X} \mu_0(B_x) \geq \exp(d)\tfrac{1}{2}\exp(-d/2) > 1 \tag{3}$$

for $d \geq 2$. We have thus obtained a contradiction. □

We denote by $\mathrm{LB}(F, \epsilon))$ the lower bound resulting from the above theorem. In other words

$$\mathrm{LB}(F, \epsilon) = \epsilon^{-1} d\sqrt{d} \cdot \mathrm{Vol}(FB_1^n)^{1/d}.$$

Thus any ϵ-differentially private mechanism must add noise $\Omega(\mathrm{LB}(F, \epsilon))$.

We will later need the following modification of the previous argument which gives a lower bound in the case where K is close to a lower dimensional subspace and hence the volume inside this subspace may give a stronger lower bound. Suppose P is the orthogonal projection operator of a k-dimensional subspace of $\mathbb{R}^d$ for some $1 \leq k \leq d$. Then, we claim that every ϵ-differentially private mechanism M for $F : \mathbb{R}^n \to \mathbb{R}^d$ must have

$$\mathrm{err}(M, F) \geq \Omega(\epsilon^{-1} k\sqrt{k} \cdot \mathrm{Vol}_k(PK)^{1/k}). \tag{4}$$

To see this note that a differentially private answer a to F can be projected down to a (differentially private) answer Pa to PF and P is norm 1 operator. We will therefore denote by $\mathrm{GLB}(F, \epsilon)$ the best lower bound obtainable in this manner, i.e.,

$$\mathrm{GLB}(F, \epsilon) = \sup_{k,P} \epsilon^{-1} k\sqrt{k} \cdot \mathrm{Vol}_k(PFB_1^n)^{1/k} \tag{5}$$

where the supremum is taken over all k and all k-dimensional orthogonal projections P.

A separation result.

We use this paragraph to point out that our lower bound immediately implies a separation between approximate differential privacy (see Definition 2.2) and exact differential privacy (as used throughout the paper). The Gaussian mechanism gives a mechanism providing δ-approximate ϵ-differential privacy with error $o(\epsilon^{-1}\sqrt{\log(n/d)})$ as long as $\delta \geq 1/n^{o(1)}$. Our lower bound in Theorem 5.2 on the other hand states that the error of any ϵ-differentially private mechanism must be $\Omega(\epsilon^{-1}\sqrt{\log(n/d)})$ (assuming $d \gg \log(n)$). We get the strongest separation when $d \leq \log(n)$ and δ is constant. In this case, our lower bound is a factor $\sqrt{d}$ larger than the upper bound for approximate differential privacy.

4. THE *K*-NORM MECHANISM

In this section we describe a new differentially private mechanism, which we call the K-norm mechanism.

DEFINITION 4.1 (K-NORM MECHANISM). *Given a linear map $F : \mathbb{R}^n \to \mathbb{R}^d$ and $\epsilon > 0$, we let $K = FB_1^n$ and define the mechanism $\mathbf{KM}(F, d, \epsilon) = \{\mu_x : x \in \mathbb{R}^n\}$ so that each measure μ_x is given by the probability density function*

$$f(a) = Z^{-1} \exp(-\epsilon\|Fx - a\|_K) \tag{6}$$

defined over $\mathbb{R}^d$. Here Z denotes the normalization constant

$$Z = \int_{\mathbb{R}^d} \exp(-\epsilon\|Fx - a\|_K) da = \Gamma(d+1)\mathrm{Vol}(\epsilon^{-1}K),$$

which is independent of x.

A more concrete view of the mechanism is provided by Figure 2 and justified in the next remark.

REMARK 4.2. *We can sample from the distribution μ_x as follows: First, sample r from the Gamma distribution with parameter $d+1$ and scale ϵ^{-1}, denoted* $\mathrm{Gamma}(d+1, \epsilon^{-1})$. *That is, r is distributed as*

$$\Pr(r > R) = \frac{1}{\epsilon^{-d}\Gamma(d+1)} \int_R^\infty e^{-\epsilon t} t^d dt.$$

KM(F, d, ϵ):
1. Sample z uniformly at random from $K = FB_1^n$ and sample $r \sim \mathrm{Gamma}(d+1, \epsilon^{-1})$.
2. Output $Fx + rz$.

Figure 2: Description of the d-dimensional K-norm mechanism. Here, $\mathrm{Gamma}(d+1,\epsilon^{-1})$ denotes the $(d+1)$-dimensional Gamma distribution with scaling ϵ^{-1}.

Second, sample a uniformly from $Fx + rK$. Indeed, if $\|a - Fx\|_K = R$, then the distribution of a as above follows the probability density function

$$g(a) = \frac{1}{\epsilon^{-(d+1)}\Gamma(d+1)} \int_R^\infty \frac{e^{-\epsilon t}t^d}{\mathrm{Vol}(tK)}\mathrm{d}t = \frac{\int_R^\infty e^{-\epsilon t}\mathrm{d}t}{\epsilon^{-1}\Gamma(d+1)\mathrm{Vol}(\epsilon^{-1}K)} = \frac{e^{-\epsilon R}}{\Gamma(d+1)\mathrm{Vol}(\epsilon^{-1}K)},$$

using the fact that $\int_R^\infty e^{-\epsilon t}\mathrm{d}t = \epsilon^{-1}e^{-\epsilon R}$. We conclude that $g(a) = f(a)$.

The next theorem shows that the K-norm mechanism is indeed differentially private. Moreover, we can express its error in terms of the *expected distance from the origin* of a random point in K.

THEOREM 4.3. *Let $\epsilon > 0$. Suppose $F\colon \mathbb{R}^n \to \mathbb{R}^d$ is a linear map and put $K = FB_1^n$. Then, the mechanism* **KM**(F,d,ϵ) *is ϵ-differentially private, and for every $p > 0$ achieves the error bound $\mathbb{E}_{a\sim\mu_x} \|Fx - a\|^p \le \frac{\Gamma(d+1+p)}{\epsilon^p\Gamma(d)} \mathbb{E}_{z\in K}\|z\|_2^p$. In particular, the ℓ_2-error is at most $\frac{d+1}{\epsilon}\mathbb{E}_{z\in K}\|z\|_2$.*

PROOF. To argue the error bound, we will follow Remark 4.2. Let $D = \mathrm{Gamma}(d+1, 1/\epsilon)$. For all $x \in \mathbb{R}^n$,

$$\mathop{\mathbb{E}}_{a\sim\mu_x}\|Fx - a\|^p = \mathop{\mathbb{E}}_{a\sim\mu_0}\|a\|^p = \mathop{\mathbb{E}}_{r\sim D}\mathop{\mathbb{E}}_{a\in rK}\|a\|^p$$
$$= \left[\mathop{\mathbb{E}}_{r\sim D} r^p\right]\mathop{\mathbb{E}}_{z\in K}\|z\|^p = \frac{\Gamma(d+1+p)}{\epsilon^p\Gamma(d+1)}\mathop{\mathbb{E}}_{z\in K}\|z\|^p$$

where we used Equation 2 in the last step. When $p = 1$, $\frac{\Gamma(d+1+p)}{\Gamma(d+1)} = d+1$.

Privacy follows from the fact that the mechanism is a special case of the exponential mechanism [24]. For completeness, we repeat the argument. Suppose that $\|x\|_1 \le 1$. It suffices to show that for all $a \in \mathbb{R}^d$, the densities of μ_0 and μ_x are within multiplicative $\exp(\epsilon)$, i.e.,

$$\frac{Z^{-1}e^{-\epsilon\|a\|_K}}{Z^{-1}e^{-\epsilon\|Fx-a\|_K}} = e^{\epsilon(\|Fx-a\|_K - \|a\|_K)} \le e^{\epsilon\|Fx\|_K} \le e^\epsilon.$$

where in the first inequality we used the triangle inequality for $\|\cdot\|_K$. In the second step we used that $x \in B_1^n$ and hence $Fx \in FB_1^n = K$ which means $\|Fx\|_K \le 1$. Hence, the mechanism satisfies ϵ-differential privacy. □

5. OPTIMALITY FOR RANDOM QUERIES AND ISOTROPIC BODIES

In this section, we will show that our upper bound matches our lower bound when F is a random query. A key observation is that FB_1^n is the *symmetric* convex hull of n (random) points $\{v_1, \ldots, v_n\} \subseteq \mathbb{R}^d$, i.e., the convex hull of $\{\pm v_1, \ldots, \pm v_n\}$, where $v_i \in \mathbb{R}^d$ is the ith column of F. The symmetric convex hull of random points has been studied extensively in the theory of random polytopes. A recent result of Litvak, Pajor, Rudelson and Tomczak-Jaegermann [22] gives the following lower bound on the volume of the convex hull.

THEOREM 5.1 ([22]). *Let $2d \le n \le 2^d$ and let F denote a random $d \times n$ Bernoulli matrix. Then,*

$$\mathrm{Vol}(FB_1^n)^{1/d} \ge \Omega(1)\sqrt{\log(n/d)/d}\,, \tag{7}$$

with probability $1 - \exp(-\Omega(d^\beta n^{1-\beta}))$ for any $\beta \in (0, \frac{1}{2})$. Furthermore, there is an explicit construction of n points in $\{-1,1\}^d$ whose convex hull achieves the same volume.

The bound in (7) is tight up to constant factors. A well known result [2] shows that the volume of the convex hull of any n points on the sphere in $\mathbb{R}^d$ of radius $\sqrt{d}$ is bounded by

$$\mathrm{Vol}(K)^{1/d} \le O(1)\sqrt{\log(n/d)/d}\,. \tag{8}$$

Notice, that in our case $K = FB_1^n \subseteq B_\infty^d \subseteq \sqrt{d}B_2^d$ and in fact the vertices of K are points on the $(d-1)$-dimensional sphere of radius $\sqrt{d}$. However, equation (7) states that the normalized volume of the random polytope K will be proportional to the volume of the Euclidean ball of radius $\sqrt{\log(n/d)}$ rather than $\sqrt{d}$. When $d \gg \log n$, this means that the volume of K will be tiny compared to the volume of the infinity ball B_∞^d. Note that (7) does not apply when $d \le \log n$. But in that case it is easy to get a lower bound as follows: Simply consider F corresponding to all n points of the boolean hypercube $\{-1,1\}^d$. Now, $FB_1^n \supseteq [-1,1]^d$ and hence $\mathrm{Vol}(FB_1^n)^{1/d} \ge 2$. This explains why we get qualitatively different answers below and above $d = \log(n)$. By combining the volume lower bound with Theorem 3.4, we get the following lower bound on the error of private mechanisms.

THEOREM 5.2. *Let $\epsilon > 0$ and $0 < d \le n/2$. Then, for almost all matrices $F \in \{-1,1\}^{d\times n}$, every ϵ-differentially private mechanism M must have*

$$\mathrm{err}(M, F) \ge \Omega(d/\epsilon)\cdot\min\left\{\sqrt{d}, \sqrt{\log(n/d)}\right\}.$$

5.1 Upper bound on average Euclidean norm

Klartag and Kozma [21] recently gave a bound on the quantity $\mathbb{E}_{z\sim K}\|z\|$ when $K = FB_1^n$ for random F.

THEOREM 5.3 ([21]). *Let F be a random $d \times n$ Bernoulli matrix and put $K = FB_1^n$. Then, there is a constant $C > 0$ so that with probability greater than $1 - Ce^{-O(n)}$, $\mathbb{E}_{z\in K}\|z\|^2 \le C\log(n/d)$.*

An application of Jensen's inequality thus gives us the following corollary.

COROLLARY 5.4. *Let $\epsilon > 0$ and $0 < d \le n/2$. Then, for almost all matrices $F \in \{-1,1\}^{d\times n}$, the mechanism* **KM**$(F,d,\epsilon)$ *is ϵ-differentially private with error at most $O(d/\epsilon)\cdot\min\left\{\sqrt{d}, \sqrt{\log(n/d)}\right\}$.*

5.2 Approximately isotropic bodies

The following definition is a relaxation of nearly isotropic position used in literature (e.g., [17])

DEFINITION 5.5 (APPROXIMATELY ISOTROPIC POSITION). *We say a convex body* $K \subseteq \mathbb{R}^d$ *is in* c-approximately isotropic position *if for every unit vector* $v \in \mathbb{R}^d$, $\mathbb{E}_{z\in K}|\langle z, v\rangle|^2 \le c^2 L_K^2 \mathrm{Vol}(K)^{\frac{2}{d}}$.

The results of Klartag and Kozma [21] referred to in the previous section show that the symmetric convex hull n random points from the d-dimensional hypercube are in $O(1)$-approximately isotropic position and have $L_K = O(1)$. More generally, the K-norm mechanism can be shown to be approximately optimal whenever K is nearly isotropic.

THEOREM 5.6 (THEOREM 1.2 RESTATED). *Let* $\epsilon > 0$. *Suppose* $F\colon \mathbb{R}^n \to \mathbb{R}^d$ *is a linear map such that* $K = FB_1^n$ *is in c-approximately isotropic position. Then, the* K*-norm mechanism is* ϵ*-differentially private and has error at most* $O(cL_K)\cdot \mathrm{LB}(F,\epsilon)$.

We can see that the previous upper bound is tight up to a factor of cL_K. Estimating L_K for general convex bodies is a well-known open problem in convex geometry. The best known upper bound for a general convex body $K \subseteq \mathbb{R}^d$ is $L_K \le O(d^{1/4})$ due to Klartag [20], improving over the estimate $L_K \le O(d^{1/4}\log d)$ of Bourgain from '91. The conjecture is that $L_K = O(1)$.

CONJECTURE 5.7 (HYPERPLANE CONJECTURE). *There exists* $C > 0$ *such that for every* d *and every convex set* $K \subseteq \mathbb{R}^d$, $L_K < C$.

Assuming this conjecture we get matching bounds for approximately isotropic convex bodies.

THEOREM 5.8. *Let* $\epsilon > 0$. *Assuming the hyperplane conjecture, for every* $F \in [-1,1]^{d\times n}$ *such that* $K = FB_1^n$ *is c-approximately isotropic, the* K*-norm mechanism* $\mathbf{KM}(F,d,\epsilon)$ *is* ϵ*-differentially private with error at most* $O(c)\cdot \mathrm{LB}(F,\epsilon) \le O(cd/\epsilon)\cdot \min\left\{\sqrt{d}, \sqrt{\log(n/d)}\right\}$.

6. NON-ISOTROPIC BODIES

While the mechanism of the previous sections is near-optimal for near-isotropic queries, it can be far from optimal if K is far from isotropic. For example, suppose the matrix F has random entries from $\{+1,-1\}$ in the first row, and (say) from $\{\frac{1}{d^2}, -\frac{1}{d^2}\}$ in the remaining rows. While the Laplacian mechanism will add $O(\frac{1}{\epsilon})$ noise to the first co-ordinate of Fx, the K-norm mechanism will add noise $O(d/\epsilon)$ to the first co-ordinate. Moreover, the volume lower bound LB is at most $O(\epsilon^{-1}\sqrt{d})$. Rotating F by a random rotation gives, w.h.p., a query for which the Laplacian mechanism adds ℓ_2 error $O(d/\epsilon)$. For such a body, the Laplacian and the K-norm mechanisms, as well as the LB are far from optimal.

In this section, we will design a recursive mechanism that can handle such non-isotropic convex bodies. To this end, we will need to introduce a few more notions from convex geometry.

Suppose $K \subseteq \mathbb{R}^d$ is a centered convex body, i.e. $\int_K x\,dx = 0$. The *covariance matrix of* K, denoted M_K is the $d\times d$ matrix with entry ij equal to $M_{ij} = \frac{1}{\mathrm{Vol}(K)}\int_K x_i x_j dx$. That is, M_K is the covariance matrix of the uniform distribution over K.

> $\mathbf{NIM}(F,d,\epsilon)$:
> 1. Let $K = FB_1^n$. Let $\sigma_1 \ge \sigma_2 \ge \cdots \ge \sigma_d$ denote the eigenvalues of the covariance matrix M_K. Pick a corresponding orthonormal eigenbasis $u_1,\dots,u_d$.
> 2. Let $d' = \lfloor d/2 \rfloor$ and let $U = \mathrm{span}\{u_1,\dots,u_{d'}\}$ and $V = \mathrm{span}\{u_{d'+1},\dots,v_d\}$.
> 3. Sample $a \sim \mathbf{KM}(F,d,\epsilon)$.
> 4. If $d = 1$, output $P_V a$. Otherwise, output $\mathbf{NIM}(P_U F, d', \epsilon) + P_V a$.

Figure 3: Mechanism for non-isotropic bodies

6.1 A recursive mechanism

Having defined the covariance matrix, we can describe a recursive mechanism for the case when K is not in isotropic position. The idea of the mechanism is to act differently on different eigenspaces of the covariance matrix. Specifically, the mechanism will use a lower-dimensional version of $\mathbf{KM}(F,d',\epsilon)$ on subspaces corresponding to few large eigenvalues.

Our mechanism, called $\mathbf{NIM}(F,d,\epsilon)$, is given a linear mapping $F\colon \mathbb{R}^n \to \mathbb{R}^d$, and parameters $d \in \mathbb{N}, \epsilon > 0$. The mechanism proceeds recursively by partitioning the convex body K into two parts defined by the middle eigenvalue of M_K. On one part it will act according to the K-norm mechanism. On the other part, it will descend recursively. The mechanism is described in Figure 6.1. We remark that the image of $P_U F$ is a d'-dimensional subspace of $\mathbb{R}^d$. We assume that in the recursive call $\mathbf{NIM}(P_U F, d', \epsilon)$, the K-norm mechanism is applied to a basis of this subspace. However, formally the output is a d-dimensional vector.

To analyze our mechanism, first observe that the recursive calls terminate after at most $\log d$ steps. For each recursive step $m \in \{0,\dots,\log d\}$, let a_m denote the distribution over the output of the K_m-norm mechanism in step 3. Here, K_m denotes the d_m-dimensional body given in step m.

LEMMA 6.1. *The mechanism* $\mathbf{NIM}(F,d,\epsilon)$ *satisfies* $(\epsilon\log d)$*-differential privacy.*

PROOF. We claim that for every step $m \in \{0,\dots,\log d\}$, the distribution over a_m is ϵ-differentially private. Notice that this claim implies the lemma, since the joint distribution of $a_0, a_1, \dots, a_m$ is $\epsilon\log(d)$-differentially private. In particular, this is true for the final output of the mechanism as it is a function of $a_0,\dots,a_m$. To see why the claim is true, observe that each K_m is the d_m-dimensional image of the ℓ_1-ball under a linear mapping. Hence, the K_m-norm mechanism guarantees ϵ-differential privacy by Theorem 4.3. □

The error analysis of our mechanism requires more work. In particular, we need to understand how the volume of $P_U K$ compares to the norm of $P_V a$. As a first step we will analyze the volume of $P_U K$.

6.2 Volume in eigenspaces of the covariance matrix

Our goal in this section is to express the volume of K in eigenspaces of the covariance matrix in terms of the eigenvalues of the covariance matrix. This will be needed in the analysis of our mechanism for non-isotropic bodies.

We start with a formula for the volume of central sections of isotropic bodies. This result can be found in [25].

PROPOSITION 6.2. *Let $K \subseteq \mathbb{R}^d$ be an isotropic body of unit volume. Let E denote a k-dimensional subspace for $1 \le k \le d$. Then,*

$$\mathrm{Vol}_k(E \cap K)^{1/(d-k)} = \Theta\left(\frac{L_{B_K}}{L_K}\right).$$

Here, B_K is an explicitly defined isotropic convex body.

From here on, for an isotropic body K, let $\alpha_K = \Omega(L_{B_K}/L_K)$ be a lower bound on $\mathrm{Vol}_k(E \cap K)^{1/(d-k)}$ implied by the above proposition. For a non-isotropic K, let α_K be α_{TK} when T is the map the brings K into isotropic position. Notice that if the Hyperplane Conjecture is true, then $\alpha_K = \Omega(1)$. Moreover, α_K is $\Omega(d^{\frac{1}{4}})$ due to the results of [20].

COROLLARY 6.3. *Let $K \subseteq \mathbb{R}^d$ be an isotropic body with $\mathrm{Vol}(K) = 1$. Let E denote a k-dimensional subspace for $1 \le k \le d$ and let P denote an orthogonal projection operator onto the subspace E. Then, $\mathrm{Vol}_k(PK)^{1/(d-k)} \ge \alpha_K$.*

PROOF. Observe that the PK contains $E \cap K$ since P is the identity on E. □

We cannot immediately use these results since they only apply to isotropic bodies and we are specifically dealing with non-isotropic bodies. The trick is to apply the previous results after transforming K into an isotropic body while keeping track how much this transformation changed the volume.

As a first step, the following lemma relates the volume of projections of an arbitrary convex body K to the volume of projections of TK for some linear mapping T.

LEMMA 6.4. *Let $K \subseteq \mathbb{R}^d$ be a symmetric convex body. Let T be a linear map which has eigenvectors $u_1, \dots, u_d$ with eigenvalues $\lambda_1, \dots, \lambda_d$. Let $1 \le k \le d$ and suppose $E = \mathrm{span}\{u_1, u_2, \dots, u_k\}$, Denote by P be the projection operator onto the subspace E. Then,*

$$\mathrm{Vol}_k(PK) \ge \mathrm{Vol}_k(PTK) \prod_{i=1}^{k} \lambda_i^{-1}.$$

PROOF. For simplicity, we assume that the eigenvectors of T are the standard basis vectors $e_1, \dots, e_d$; this is easily achieved by applying a rotation to K. Now, it is easy to verify that $P = PT^{-1}T = SPT$ where

$$S = \mathrm{diag}(\lambda_1^{-1}, \lambda_2^{-1}, \dots, \lambda_k^{-1}, 0, \dots, 0).$$

Thus we can write

$$\mathrm{Vol}_k(PK) = \det(S_{|E})\mathrm{Vol}_k(PTK) = \frac{1}{\prod_{i=1}^{k} \lambda_i} \mathrm{Vol}_k(PTK).$$

□

Before we can finish our discussion, we will need the fact that the isotropic constant of K can be expressed in terms of the determinant of M_K.

FACT 6.5 ([15, 25]). *Let $K \subseteq \mathbb{R}^d$ be a convex body of unit volume. Then, $L_K^2 \mathrm{Vol}(K)^{\frac{2}{d}} = \det(M_K)^{1/d}$. Moreover, K is in isotropic position iff $M_K = L_K^2 \mathrm{Vol}(K)^{2/d} I$.*

We conclude with the following Proposition 6.6.

PROPOSITION 6.6. *Let $K \subseteq \mathbb{R}^d$ be a symmetric convex body. Let M_k have eigenvectors $u_1, \dots, u_d$ with eigenvalues $\sigma_1, \dots, \sigma_d$. Let $1 \le k \le \lceil \frac{d}{2} \rceil$ with and suppose $E = \mathrm{span}\{u_1, u_2, \dots, u_k\}$, Denote by P be the projection operator onto the subspace E. Then,*

$$\mathrm{Vol}_k(PK)^{1/(d-k)} \ge \Omega(1) \cdot \alpha_K \left(\prod_{i=1}^{k} \sigma_i^{1/2}\right)^{1/(d-k)}, \tag{9}$$

where α_K is $\Omega(1/d^{\frac{1}{4}})$. Moreover, assuming the Hyperplane conjecture, $\alpha_K \ge \Omega(1)$.

PROOF. Consider the linear mapping $T = M_K^{-1/2}$. this is well defined since M_K is a positive symmetric matrix. It is easy to see that after applying T, we have $M_{TK} = I$. Hence, by Fact 6.5, TK is in isotropic position and has volume $\mathrm{Vol}(TK)^{1/d} = 1/L_{TK} = 1/L_K$, since $\det(M_{TK}) = 1$. Scaling TK by $\lambda = L_K^{1/d}$ hence results in $\mathrm{Vol}(\lambda TK) = 1$. Noting that λT has eigenvalues $\lambda\sigma_1^{-\frac{1}{2}}, \lambda\sigma_2^{-\frac{1}{2}}, \dots, \lambda\sigma_d^{-\frac{1}{2}}$, we can apply Lemma 6.4 and get

$$\mathrm{Vol}_k(PK) \ge \mathrm{Vol}_k(P\lambda TK) \prod_{i=1}^{k} \frac{\sqrt{\sigma_i}}{\lambda}$$

Since λTK is in isotropic position and has unit volume, Corollary 6.3 implies that

$$\mathrm{Vol}_k(P\lambda TK)^{1/(d-k)} \ge \alpha_K. \tag{10}$$

Thus the required inequality holds with an additional $\lambda^{-\frac{k}{d-k}}$ term. By assumption on k, $\frac{k}{d-k}$ is at most 2. Moreover, $\lambda = L_K^{1/d} \le d^{1/d} \le 2$, so that this additional term is a constant. As discussed above, α_K is $\Omega(d^{-\frac{1}{4}})$ by [20], and $\Omega(1)$ assuming the Hyperplane Conjecture 5.7. Hence the claim. □

6.3 Arguing near optimality of our mechanism

Our next lemma shows that the expected squared Euclidean error added by our algorithm in each step is bounded by the square of the optimum. We will first need the following fact.

FACT 6.7. *Let $K \subseteq \mathbb{R}^d$ be a centered convex body. Let $\sigma_1 \ge \sigma_2 \ge \dots \ge \sigma_d$ denote the eigenvalues of M_K with a corresponding orthonormal eigenbasis $u_1, \dots, u_d$. Then, for all $1 \le i \le d$, $\sigma_i = \max_\theta \mathbb{E}_{x \in K}\langle \theta, x\rangle^2$ where the maximum runs over all $\theta \in \mathbb{S}^{d-1}$ such that θ is orthogonal to $u_1, u_2, \dots, u_{i-1}$.*

LEMMA 6.8. *Let a denote the random variable returned by the K-norm mechanism in step (3) in the above description of* **NIM**(F, d, ϵ). *Then,*

$$\mathrm{GLB}(F, \epsilon)^2 \ge \Omega(\alpha_K^2)\,\mathbb{E}\,\|P_V a\|_2^2.$$

PROOF. For simplicity, we will assume that d is even and hence $d - d' = d'$. The analysis of the K-norm mechanism (Theorem 4.3 with $p = 2$) shows that the random variable a

returned by the K-norm mechanism in step (3) satisfies

$$\begin{aligned}\mathbb{E}\,\|P_V a\|_2^2 &= \frac{\Gamma(d+3)}{\epsilon^2\Gamma(d+1)} = \frac{(d+2)(d+1)}{\epsilon^2}\mathop{\mathbb{E}}_{z\in K}\|P_V z\|_2^2 \\ &= O\left(\frac{d^2}{\epsilon^2}\right)\sum_{i=d'+1}^{d}\mathop{\mathbb{E}}_{z\in K}\langle z,u_i\rangle^2 \\ &= O\left(\frac{d^2}{\epsilon^2}\right)\sum_{i=d'+1}^{d}\sigma_i \quad \text{(by Fact 6.7)} \\ &\le O\left(\frac{d^3}{\epsilon^2}\right)\cdot\sigma_{d'+1}. \qquad (11)\end{aligned}$$

On the other hand, by the definition of GLB,

$$\begin{aligned}\mathrm{GLB}(F,\epsilon)^2 &\ge \Omega\left(\frac{d^3}{\epsilon^2}\right)\cdot \mathrm{Vol}_{d'}(P_U K)^{2/d'} \\ &\ge \Omega\left(\frac{d^3}{\epsilon^2}\right)\alpha_K^2\left(\prod_{i=1}^{d'}\sigma_i\right)^{1/d'} \\ &\qquad\text{(by Proposition 6.6)} \\ &\ge \Omega\left(\frac{d^3}{\epsilon^2}\right)\alpha_K^2\sigma_{d'}.\end{aligned}$$

Since $\sigma_{d'} \ge \sigma_{d'+1}$, it follows that

$$\mathrm{GLB}(F,\epsilon)^2 \ge \Omega(\alpha_K^2)\,\mathbb{E}\,\|P_V a\|^2. \qquad (12)$$

The case of odd d is similar except that we define K' to be the projection onto the first $d'+1$ eigenvectors. □

LEMMA 6.9. *Assume the hyperplane conjecture. Then, the ℓ_2-error of the mechanism* $\mathbf{NIM}(F,d,\epsilon)$ *is at most* $O(\sqrt{\log(d)}\cdot\mathrm{GLB}(F,\epsilon))$.

PROOF. We have to sum up the error over all recursive calls of the mechanism. To this end, let $P_{V_m}a_m$ denote the output of the K-norm mechanism a_m in step m projected to the corresponding subspace V_m. Also, let $a\in\mathbb{R}^d$ denote the final output of our mechanism. We then have,

$$\begin{aligned}\mathbb{E}\,\|a\|_2 &\le \sqrt{\mathbb{E}\,\|a\|_2^2} \qquad \text{(Jensen's inequality)} \\ &= \sqrt{\sum_{m=1}^{\log d}\mathbb{E}\,\|P_{V_m}a_m\|_2^2} \\ &\le \sqrt{\sum_{m=1}^{\log d}O(\alpha_{K_m}^{-2})\cdot\mathrm{GLB}(F,\epsilon)^2} \qquad \text{(by Lemma 6.9)} \\ &\le O(\sqrt{\log d})\left(\max_m \alpha_{K_m}^{-1}\right)\mathrm{GLB}(F,\epsilon).\end{aligned}$$

Here we have used the fact that $\mathrm{GLB}(F,\epsilon)\ge\mathrm{GLB}(P_UF,\epsilon)$. Finally, the hyperplane conjecture implies $\max_m \alpha_{K_m}^{-1} = O(1)$. □

COROLLARY 6.10. *Let $\epsilon > 0$. Suppose $F\colon\mathbb{R}^n\to\mathbb{R}^d$ is a linear map. Further, assume the hyperplane conjecture. Then, there is an ϵ-differentially private mechanism M with error* $\mathrm{err}(M,F)\le O(\log(d)^{3/2}\cdot\mathrm{GLB}(F,\epsilon))$.

PROOF. The mechanism $\mathbf{NIM}(F,d,\epsilon/\log(d))$ satisfies ϵ-differential privacy, by Lemma 6.1. The error is at most $\log(d)\sqrt{\log d}\cdot\mathrm{GLB}(F,\epsilon)$ as a direct consequence of Lemma 6.9. □

7. EFFICIENT IMPLEMENTATION

The costly step in our mechanism is sampling uniformly from high-dimensional convex bodies such as $K = FB_1^n$. To implement the sampling step efficiently, we will use geometric random walks [12, 28]. It can be shown that these random walks approach the uniform distribution over K in time polynomial in n. We will actually need convergence bounds in the relative ℓ_∞-metric, a metric strong enough to entail guarantees about exact differential privacy. We also need to implement a separation oracle for K which can be done using standard convex programming arguments.

Some complications arise, since we need to repeat the privacy and optimality analysis of our mechanisms in the presence of approximation errors (such as an approximate covariance matrix and an approximate separation oracle for K). For details we refer the reader to the full version of this paper.

8. REFERENCES

[1] B. Barak, K. Chaudhuri, C. Dwork, S. Kale, F. McSherry, and K. Talwar. Privacy, accuracy, and consistency too: a holistic solution to contingency table release. In *Proc. 26th PODS*, pages 273–282. ACM, 2007.

[2] I. Barany and Z. Furedi. Approximation of the sphere by polytopes having few vertices. *Proceedings of the American Mathematical Society*, 102(3):651–659, 1988.

[3] A. Blum, C. Dwork, F. McSherry, and K. Nissim. Practical privacy: the sulq framework. In *PODS '05: Proceedings of the twenty-fourth ACM SIGMOD-SIGACT-SIGART symposium on Principles of database systems*, pages 128–138, New York, NY, USA, 2005. ACM.

[4] A. Blum, K. Ligett, and A. Roth. A learning theory approach to non-interactive database privacy. In *STOC '08: Proceedings of the 40th annual ACM symposium on Theory of computing*, pages 609–618, New York, NY, USA, 2008. ACM.

[5] K. Chaudhuri and C. Monteleoni. Privacy-preserving logistic regression. In *Proceedings of the Twenty-Second Annual Conference on Neural Information Processing Systems (NIPS)*, pages 289–296, 2008.

[6] I. Dinur and K. Nissim. Revealing information while preserving privacy. In *Proc. 22nd PODS*, pages 202–210. ACM, 2003.

[7] C. Dwork. Differential privacy: A survey of results. In *Proc. 5th TAMC*, pages 1–19. Springer, 2008.

[8] C. Dwork, K. Kenthapadi, F. McSherry, I. Mironov, and M. Naor. Our data, ourselves: Privacy via distributed noise generation. In *Proc. 25th EUROCRYPT*, pages 486–503. Springer, 2006.

[9] C. Dwork, F. McSherry, K. Nissim, and A. Smith. Calibrating noise to sensitivity in private data analysis. In *Proc. 3rd TCC*, pages 265–284. Springer, 2006.

[10] C. Dwork, F. McSherry, and K. Talwar. The price of privacy and the limits of LP decoding. In *Proc. 39th STOC*, pages 85–94. ACM, 2007.

[11] C. Dwork and S. Yekhanin. New efficient attacks on statistical disclosure control mechanisms. In *Proc. 28th CRYPTO*, pages 469–480. Springer, 2008.

[12] M. E. Dyer, A. M. Frieze, and R. Kannan. A random polynomial time algorithm for approximating the volume of convex bodies. *J. ACM*, 38(1):1–17, 1991.

[13] D. Feldman, A. Fiat, H. Kaplan, and K. Nissim. Private coresets. In *Proceedings of the 41st annual ACM symposium on Symposium on theory of computing*, pages 361–370. ACM New York, NY, USA, 2009.

[14] A. Ghosh, T. Roughgarden, and M. Sundararajan. Universally utility-maximizing privacy mechanisms. In *STOC*, pages 351–360, 2009.

[15] A. Giannopoulos. Notes on isotropic convex bodies. Preprint, 2003.

[16] A. Gupta, K. Ligett, F. McSherry, A. Roth, and K. Talwar. Differentially private approximation algorithms. In *Proceedings of the Twenty First Annual ACM-SIAM Symposium on Discrete Algorithms*, 2010. To appear.

[17] R. Kannan, L. Lovász, and M. Simonovits. Random walks and an $o^*(n^5)$ volume algorithm for convex bodies. *Random Struct. Algorithms*, 11(1):1–50, 1997.

[18] S. Kasiviswanathan, M. Rudelson, and A. Smith. The price of privately releasing contingency tables and the spectra of random matrices with correlated rows. Manuscript, 2009.

[19] S. P. Kasiviswanathan, H. K. Lee, K. Nissim, S. Raskhodnikova, and A. Smith. What can we learn privately? In *FOCS '08: Proceedings of the 2008 49th Annual IEEE Symposium on Foundations of Computer Science*, pages 531–540, Washington, DC, USA, 2008. IEEE Computer Society.

[20] B. Klartag. On convex perturbations with a bounded isotropic constant. *Geometric and Functional Analysis (GAFA)*, 16(6):1274–1290, December 2006.

[21] B. Klartag and G. Kozma. On the hyperplane conjecture for random convex sets. *Israel Journal of Mathematics*, 170(1):253–268, 2009.

[22] A. E. Litvak, A. Pajor, M. Rudelson, and T.-J. N. Smallest singular value of random matrices and geometry of random polytopes. *Adv. Math.*, 195(2):491–523, 2005.

[23] F. McSherry and I. Mironov. Differentially private recommender systems: building privacy into the net. In *Proc. 15th KDD*, pages 627–636. ACM, 2009.

[24] F. McSherry and K. Talwar. Mechanism design via differential privacy. In *Proc. 48th FOCS*, pages 94–103. IEEE, 2007.

[25] V. Milman and A. Pajor. Isotropic position and inertia ellipsoids and zonoids of the unit ball of a normed n-dimensional space. *Geometric Aspects of Functional Analysis*, 1376:64–104, 1989.

[26] K. Nissim, S. Raskhodnikova, and A. Smith. Smooth sensitivity and sampling in private data analysis. In *STOC '07: Proceedings of the thirty-ninth annual ACM symposium on Theory of computing*, pages 75–84, New York, NY, USA, 2007. ACM.

[27] V. Rastogi, D. Suciu, and S. Hong. The boundary between privacy and utility in data publishing. In *VLDB '07: Proceedings of the 33rd international conference on Very large data bases*, pages 531–542. VLDB Endowment, 2007.

[28] S. Vempala. Geometric random walks: a survey. *MSRI Volume on Combinatorial and Computational Geometry*, 52:577–616, 2005.

Differential Privacy Under Continual Observation

Cynthia Dwork
Microsoft Research
Mountain View, CA, USA
dwork@microsoft.com

Moni Naor*
Weizmann Institute of Science
Rehovot, Israel
moni.naor@weizmann.ac.il

Toniann Pitassi†
University of Toronto
Toronto, Canada
toni@cs.toronto.edu

Guy N. Rothblum‡
Princeton University
Princeton, NJ, USA
rothblum@alum.mit.edu

ABSTRACT

Differential privacy is a recent notion of privacy tailored to privacy-preserving data analysis [11]. Up to this point, research on differentially private data analysis has focused on the setting of a trusted curator holding a large, static, data set; thus every computation is a "one-shot" object: there is no point in computing something twice, since the result will be unchanged, up to any randomness introduced for privacy.

However, many applications of data analysis involve repeated computations, either because the entire goal is one of monitoring, *e.g.*, of traffic conditions, search trends, or incidence of influenza, or because the goal is some kind of adaptive optimization, *e.g.*, placement of data to minimize access costs. In these cases, the algorithm must permit continual observation of the system's state. We therefore initiate a study of *differential privacy under continual observation*. We identify the problem of maintaining a counter in a privacy preserving manner and show its wide applicability to many different problems.

Categories and Subject Descriptors

F.2.0 [**Theory of Computation**]: Analysis of Algorithms and problem complexity—*General*

*Research supported by a grant from the Israel Science Foundation. Part of this work was done while visiting MSR and the Center for Computational Intractability at Princeton University.

†Research supported by Nserc. Part of this work was done while visiting MSR.

‡Research supported by NSF Grants CCF-0635297, CCF-0832797 and by a Computing Innovation Fellowship. Parts of this work were done while visiting and interning at MSR.

STOC'10, June 5–8, 2010, Cambridge, Massachusetts, USA.

General Terms

Algorithms, Security, Theory, Privacy, Private Data Analysis

1. INTRODUCTION

Differential privacy is a recent privacy guarantee tailored to the problem of statistical disclosure control: how to publicly release statistical information about a set of people without compromising the privacy of any individual [11] (see [8, 9, 6] for motivation of the definition, history, basic techniques, and pointers to recent results). In a nutshell, differential privacy requires that the probability distribution on the published results of an analysis is "essentially the same," independent of whether any individual opts in to, or opts out of, the data set. (The probabilities are over the coin flips of the privacy mechanism.) Statistical databases are frequently created to achieve a social goal, and increased participation in the databases permits more accurate analyses. The differential privacy guarantee supports the social goal by assuring each individual that she incurs little risk by joining the database: anything that can happen is essentially equally likely to do so whether she joins or abstains.

Up to this point, research on differentially private data analysis has focused on the setting of a trusted curator holding a large, static, data set, in a permanently infrangible storage system. The curator either responds to queries (the *interactive* case) or prepares some sort of summary or synthetic database intended to answer all queries of a particular type (the *non-interactive* case)[1]. A line of work investigates the way in which the accuracy of the responses to the queries may need to deteriorate with the number, sensitivity (a metric describing how much the addition or deletion of a member of the database can change affect the outputs), and geometry of the query sequence [5, 12, 16, 17], and general techniques have been developed that in some cases match these bounds [15, 2, 11, 19, 17, 3, 14].

In all previous work every computation is a "one-shot" object: there is no point in computing something twice, since the result will be unchanged, up to any perturbations introduced for privacy. However, many applications of data analysis involve repeated computations, either because the

[1]The one exception considers a distributed setting, in which each data holder controls her own data and decides in which analyses to participate [10]. However, this is done by emulating the curator via secure multiparty computation.

entire goal is one of monitoring, *e.g.*, of traffic conditions, search trends, or incidence of influenza, typically with a goal of preparing some appropriate response, or the goal is to optimize the placement of data to minimize access costs. In such an application the system is required to continually produce outputs. We therefore initiate a study of *differential privacy under continual observation.* We illustrate the design goals of our continual observation algorithms by appeal to a real-life example.

Continual Observation. Consider a website for H1N1 self-assessment[2]. Individuals can interact with the site to learn whether symptoms they are experiencing may be indicative of the H1N1 flu. The user fills in some demographic data (age, zipcode, sex), and responds to queries about his symptoms (fever over 100.4°F?, sore throat?, duration of symptoms?). We would like to *continually* analyze aggregate information of consenting users in order to monitor regional health conditions, with the goal, for example, of organizing improved flu response. Can we do this in a differentially private fashion with reasonable accuracy (despite the fact that the system is continually producing outputs)?

We would expect a given individual to interact very few times with the H1N1 self-assessment site. For simplicity, let us say this is just once (the general case is an easy extension). In such a setting, it is sufficient to ensure *event-level* privacy, in which the privacy goal is to hide the presence or absence of a single event (interaction of one user with the self-assessment site). That is, the probability of any output sequence should be essentially the same, independent of the presence or absence of any single interaction with the site.

The privacy statement at the H1N1 self-assessment site encourages users to allow their data to be shared:

> "This information can be very helpful in monitoring regional health conditions, plan flu response, and conduct health research. By allowing the responses to the survey questions to be used for public health, education and research purposes, you can help your community."

But the site also describes conditions under which the data may be disclosed:

> "...if required to do so by law or in the good faith belief that such action is necessary to (a) conform to the edicts of the law or comply with legal process served on Microsoft or the Site; (b) protect and defend the rights or property of Microsoft and our family of Web sites; or (c) act in urgent circumstances to protect the personal safety of users of Microsoft products or members of the public."

Pan-Privacy. This raises the following question, orthogonal to that of continual observation: Is it possible to maintain a differentially private *internal state*, so that a consenting user has privacy even against a subpoena or other intrusion into the local state? Algorithms with this property are called *pan-private*, as they are private inside (internal state) and out (output sequence). This notion was recently introduced in [13]. The goal of pan-privacy is to provide a mathematically rigorous way of (essentially) eliminating the risk – of anything – incurred by sharing one's information, *even in the presence of an intrusion*, further encouraging participation. Another motivation is the prevention of "mission creep" for data, protecting the data curator from the (very real!) pressure to allow data to be used for purposes other than that for which they were collected. This fits well with streaming algorithms with small state, which can at most store a few data items, and [13] does focus on the streaming model. However, nothing prevents a streaming algorithm from storing in its state an event of a person of interest. Event-level pan-privacy rules this out, since the internal state must have essentially the same distribution, independent of whether an event of the person of interest has, or has not, appeared in the stream.

We remark that, since an intrusion can occur at an unpredictable time, designing pan-private algorithms is interesting even when the system will generate only a single output. This was studied in [13]. The current paper addresses pan-privacy under continual observation. We emphasize that continual output and pan-privacy are each interesting and non-trivial properties and, generally speaking, they are independent of each other[3]. Their combination is, of course, more powerful than each individually.

Adjacency notions: User-Level vs. Event-Level Privacy. We have made the reasonable assumption that a single individual interacts with the H1N1 self-assessment site at most a small number of times (one). Such an assumption is not reasonable for other kinds of websites, such as a search engine. We ask: what kinds of statistics can we gather while preserving the privacy of an individual's entire history of accesses to the website? That is, what can we compute if we require that, no matter how many times an individual accesses the website, and no matter how these accesses are interleaved with those of others, the distribution on outputs, or, in the case of *user-level pan-privacy*, the distribution on pairs (internal state, output sequence), should be essentially the same, independent of presence or absence of any individual's data in the stream? All the algorithms of [13] enjoy user-level pan-privacy. In this paper we construct several algorithms that exhibit user-level pan-privacy under continual observation.

2. OVERVIEW OF OUR RESULTS

Counter. We identify the problem of maintaining a counter in a privacy preserving manner and show its wide applicability to many different problems. We construct a continual observation low-error pan-private *counter* estimating, at all times, the answer to the question "How many times has an event of interest happened so far?"

One-shot → Continual Observation. We describe a general transformation that, roughly speaking, converts a large class of (possibly user-level possibly pan-private) one-shot algorithm and produces an algorithm with the same types of privacy guarantees under continual observation. This class contains algorithms for monotonically increasing or decreasing functions with a bounded range, as well as functions that are "close to" monotonic, provided the algorithm satisfies a condition we call (k, d)-unvarying. Roughly speaking, this condition says that the output can change by an additive d

[2]https://h1n1.cloudapp.net is such a website. User-supplied data are stored for analysis only if the user consents.

[3]The extreme case of continual intrusion also implies continual output

amount at most k times. The loss of accuracy deteriorates as k and d increase.

Applications of the Counter. Counting is a fundamental computational primitive. We illustrate the utility of the counter by obtaining event-level pan-private algorithms for sophisticated tasks, such as following expert advice. We obtain an event-level pan-private under continual observation version of *Follow the Perturbed Leader* [18].

Negative Results. Pan-privacy comes at a price that increases with the number of intrusions: we prove that any counter providing pan-privacy against a number k of intrusions on the internal state must have error at least $\sqrt{k}$. In [13] Dwork *et al.* obtained an accurate, one-shot, pan-private algorithm for modular incidence counting. Unlike all the other problems addressed in that work, for this problem there is no reasonably accurate algorithm providing user-level privacy under continual observation, even without pan-privacy. This result generalizes to any function whose value "many times" increases by "a lot" (the accuracy deteriorates with the product of "many" and "a lot;" see Section 4.2).

3. DEFINITIONS AND TOOLS

3.1 Differential Privacy Basics

In the literature, a differentially private mechanism operates on a *database*, or *data set*. This is a collection of *rows*, where the data of an individual are held in a single row. Differential privacy ensures that the ability of an adversary to inflict harm (or good, for that matter) – of any sort, to any set of people – is essentially the same, independent of whether any individual opts in to, or opts out of, the dataset. This is done indirectly, simultaneously addressing all possible forms of harm and good, by focusing on the probability of any given output of a privacy mechanism and how this probability can change with the addition or deletion of any row. We will concentrate on pairs of databases (D, D') differing only in one row, meaning one is a subset of the other and the larger database contains just one additional row.

DEFINITION 3.1. *[11] A randomized function $\mathcal{K}$ gives ε-*differential privacy *if for all data sets D and D' differing in at most one row, and all $S \subseteq Range(\mathcal{K})$,*

$$\Pr[\mathcal{K}(D) \in S] \quad \leq \quad \exp(\varepsilon) \times \Pr[\mathcal{K}(D') \in S], \qquad (1)$$

where the probability is over the coin flips of $\mathcal{K}$.

The multiplicative nature of the guarantee implies that an output whose probability is zero on a given database must also have probability zero on any neighboring database, and hence, by repeated application of the definition, on any other database. The parameter ε is public, and its selection is a social question. We tend to think of ε as, say, 0.01, 0.1, or in some cases, $\ln 2$ or $\ln 3$.

DEFINITION 3.2. *[11] For $f : \mathcal{D} \rightarrow \mathbf{R}^d$, the* L_1 sensitivity *of f is $\Delta f = \max_{D,D'} \|f(D) - f(D')\|_1$ for all D, D' differing in at most one row.*

The Laplace distribution with parameter b, denoted *Lap*(b), has density function $\Pr(z|b) = \frac{1}{2b}\exp(-|z|/b)$ and variance $2b^2$. Taking $b = 1/\varepsilon$ we have that the density at z is proportional to $e^{-\varepsilon|z|}$. This distribution has highest density at 0 (good for accuracy), and for any z, z' such that $|z - z'| \leq 1$ the density at z is at most e^{ε} times the density at z'. Finally, the distribution gets flatter as ε decreases: smaller ε means better privacy, so the noise density should be less "peaked" at 0 and change more gradually as the magnitude of the noise increases.

THEOREM 3.1. *[11] For $f : \mathcal{D} \rightarrow \mathbf{R}^d$, the mechanism $\mathcal{K}$ that adds independently generated noise with distribution Lap$(\Delta f/\varepsilon)$ to each of the d output terms enjoys ε-differential privacy.*

THEOREM 3.2. *[11] The composition of an ε_1-differentially private mechanism and an ε_2-differentially private mechanism is at worst $(\varepsilon_1 + \varepsilon_2)$-differentially private.*

3.2 Event-Level and User-Level (Pan-)Privacy

Speaking intuitively, we think of continual observation algorithms as taking steps at discrete time intervals; at each step the algorithm receives an input, computes, and produces output. We model this formally with a streaming algorithm. Computation proceeds in a sequence of atomic steps. At each step the algorithm receives an input from the stream, computes (changes state), and produces outputs. Thus the intuitive notion of "t time periods" corresponds to processing a sequence of t elements in the stream. Intrusions may only occur *between* atomic steps.

Because we are modeling real systems, where time is a factor (computers have clocks, as do the adversaries), we will occasionally need to model the fact that "nothing has happened" in a given time unit. We may do this by means of a "nothing happened" element. For example, the motivation behind the counter primitive below is to count the number of times that something has occurred since the algorithm was started (the counter is very general; we don't specify *a priori* what it is counting). This is modeled by an input stream over $\{0, 1\}$. Here, "0" means "nothing happened," "1" means the event of interest occurred, and for $t = 1, 2, \ldots$ the algorithm outputs an approximation to the number of 1's seen in the length t prefix of the stream.

To define privacy, we need a notion of adjacent stream prefixes. The definition of adjacency in [13] permitted strings of radically different lengths to be adjacent. To be able to capture time, we modify the definition as follows. Let X be the universe of possible input symbols. Let S and S' be stream prefixes (ie, finite streams) of symbols drawn from X. Then $\mathrm{Adj}(S, S')$ ("S is adjacent to S'") if and only if there exist $x, x' \in X$ so that if we change some of the instances of x in S to instances of x', then we get S'. More formally, $\mathrm{Adj}(S, S')$ iff $\exists x, x' \in X$ and $\exists T \subseteq [|S|]$, such that $S|_{T:x\rightarrow x'} = S'$. Here, T is a set of indices in the stream prefix S, and $S|_{T:x\rightarrow x'}$ is the result of replacing all the occurrences of x at these indices with x' (note that w.l.o.g we can assume $S|_T$ contains only occurrences of x).

The definition of adjacency anticipates user-level privacy, where the behavior of the algorithm should remain the same independent of the number or pattern of instances of any single symbol x in the stream. A special case of adjacency is *event-level adjacency*, in which the number of instances of one symbol replaced by another is at most 1. Naturally, this will be used for defining event-level privacy. With these definitions, adjacent prefixes are always of the same length.

DEFINITION 3.3. *Let* **Alg** *be an algorithm. Let* I *denote the set of internal states of the algorithm, and σ the set of possible output sequences. Then algorithm* **Alg** *mapping data* *stream prefixes to the range* $\mathrm{I} \times \sigma$, *is* user-level pan-private (against a single intrusion) *if for all sets* $\mathrm{I}' \subseteq \mathrm{I}$ *and* $\sigma' \subseteq \sigma$, *and for all pairs of* X*-adjacent data stream prefixes* S, S'

$$\Pr[\mathbf{Alg}(S) \in (\mathrm{I}', \sigma')] \leq e^{\varepsilon} \Pr[\mathbf{Alg}(S') \in (\mathrm{I}', \sigma')]$$

where the probability is over the coin flips of **Alg**.

We typically omit the term ε-differential when discussing pan-privacy. However, every claim of pan-privacy must describe the privacy loss.

Event-level pan-privacy is defined analogously, with the requirement restricted to event-level adjacent streams. In the case of one-shot algorithms the output sequence has length 1. In the case of continual observation the output sequence is as long as the stream prefix processed by the algorithm. Ordinary user-level, respectively, event-level, privacy (as opposed to pan-privacy) is just differential privacy for user-level, respectively, event-level, adjacent streams.

Note that popular techniques from the streaming literature, such as Count-Min Sketch and subsampling, cannot be pan-private.

4. EVENT-LEVEL PRIVATE COUNTING

In this section we introduce the web-counter problem, and present algorithms and lower bounds.

Monitoring events, such as the spread of an epidemic or the traffic at a website, frequently can be cast in terms of counting the number of "interesting" events that have occurred over time. Formally, we view time as a series of time periods, named by the natural numbers. In each time period there are two possibilities: an event occurs or no event occurs. We model this as a binary stream, with 1's corresponding to periods in which an event occurs and 0's corresponding to periods in which no event occurs. Informally, the *web counter problem* is to continually produce an accurate, but not necessarily exact, estimate of the number of events that have occurred "so far," while obscuring, for each time period t, whether or not an event actually occurs at t.

DEFINITION 4.1. *A randomized streaming algorithm yields a* (T, α, β) counter *if, in every execution, with probability at least* $1 - \beta$ *over the coin flips of the algorithm, simultaneously, for all* $1 \leq t \leq T$*, after processing a prefix of length* t*, the current output contains an estimate of the number of 1's in the prefix that differs from the true weight of the prefix by at most an additive* α *amount.*

with T and $1/\beta$. In the remainder of this section we present an event-level counter[4] for which α grows as roughly $\log(1/\beta)\log^{2.5} T$. There is a narrow gap between this and the lower bound (see Section 4.1). The algorithm is pan-private against a single intrusion; it appears in Figure 1.

It will be convenient to number the time periods $0, 1, \ldots, T-1$, so that in time period t the algorithm is processing the $(t+1)$st element in the input stream. Similarly, we will number the elements of the stream beginning with 0, so on stream x at time t the algorithm is processing x_t. The algorithm requires the following set of (time) *segments*. For $i \in \{1, \ldots, \log T\}$, associate with each string $s \in \{0,1\}^i$ the time segment S of $2^{\log T - i}$ time periods $\{s \circ 0^{\log T - i}, \ldots s \circ 1^{\log T - i}\}$. We say the segment *begins in time* $s \circ 0^{\log T - i}$ and *ends in time* $s \circ 1^{\log T - i}$.

[4]Our original algorithm (see full version of this paper or [7]) had worse performance guarantees. Several people, including Ilya Mironov, Kobbi Nissim, and Adam Smith (thanks guys!), immediately suggested an approach closely resembling the one presented here, based on the Bentley-Saxe method of converting static data structures to dynamic ones [1]. Our algorithm is slightly different, in order to ensure pan-privacy.

THEOREM 4.1. *The counter algorithm of Figure 1 run with parameters* $T, \varepsilon, \beta > 0$*, yields a* $(T, 4\log(1/\beta) \cdot \log^{2.5} T/\varepsilon, \beta)$ *counter enjoying* ε*-differential pan-privacy against a single intrusion.*

PROOF. We first argue about the accuracy of the algorithm, and then prove event-level differential pan-privacy.

Accuracy. Let S be a segment. The noise value η_S is stored in the algorithm's internal state during the first time period contained in S, and is deleted during the atomic step occurring in the last time period contained in S. Thus, all the noise values for segments containing t are in memory in Step 3 when we generate time period t's output.

We add $1 + \log T$ independently chosen Laplace noise variables to the true answer: the $\log T$ segment noises, and the noise with which we initialize *count*. Each of these variables has variance $2(\log T/\varepsilon)^2$, Thus, in each round, with probability at least $1 - \beta/T$ probability, the sum of noises is within magnitude $2\log(1/\beta) + \log T$ standard deviations, so by a union bound, with probability at least $1 - \beta$, in all rounds simultaneously, this sum of noises has magnitude smaller than $4\log(1/\beta) \cdot \log^{2.5} T/\varepsilon$.

Pan-Privacy. During an intrusion between atomic steps t^* and $t^* + 1$, that is, immediately following the processing of element t^* in the input stream (recall that we begin numbering the elements with 0), the view of the adversary consists of (1) the noisy count, (2) the segment noise values η_S in memory when the intrusion occurs, and (3) the complete sequence of all of the algorithm's outputs. Consider adjacent databases x and x', which differ in time t, say, without loss of generality, $x_t = 1$ and $x'_t = 0$, and an intrusion immediately following time period $t^* \geq t$ (we will discuss the case $t^* < t$ below). We will describe a bijection between the vector of noise values used in executions on x and executions on x', such that corresponding noise values induce identical adversary views on x and x', and the probabilities of adjacent noise values differ only by an e^{ε} multiplicative factor. This implies ε-differential pan-privacy.

By assumption, the true count just after the time period $t^* \geq t$ is larger when the input is x than it is when the input is x'. Fix an arbitrary execution E_x when the input stream is x. This amounts to fixing the randomness of the algorithm, which in turn fixes the noise values generated. We will describe the corresponding execution $E_{x'}$ by describing how its noise values differ from those in E_x.

The program variable *count* was initialized with Laplace noise. By increasing this noise by 1 in $E_{x'}$ the value of *count* just after step t^* is identical in $E_{x'}$ and E_x. The noise variables in memory immediately following period t^* are independent of the input; these will be unchanged in $E_{x'}$. We will make the sequence of outputs in $E_{x'}$ *identical* to those in E_x by changing a collection of $\log T$ segment noise values η_S that are *not* in memory when the adversary intrudes, so that the sum of *all* noise values in all rounds up through $t-1$ is unchanged, but the sum from round t on is larger by 1 for database x' than for x. Since we *increased* the initialization noise for *count*, we now need to *decrease*

Counter (T, ε)

Initialization. Initialize $\xi = (1 + \log T)/\varepsilon$, and sample $count \sim Lap(\xi)$.

Segments. For $i \in \{1, \ldots, \log T\}$, associate with each string $s \in \{0,1\}^i$ the time segment S of $2^{\log T - i}$ time periods $\{s \circ 0^{\log T - i}, \ldots s \circ 1^{\log T - i}\}$. The segment *begins in time* $s \circ 0^{\log T - i}$ and *ends in time* $s \circ 1^{\log T - i}$.

Processing. In time period $t \in \{0, 1, \ldots, T-1\}$, let $x_t \in \{0,1\}$ be the t-th input bit:

1. $count \leftarrow count + x_t$;
2. For every segment S which begins in time t, sample noise $\eta_S \sim Lap(\xi)$;
3. Let $S_1, \ldots, S_{\log T}$ be the $\log T$ segments that contain t. Output $count + \sum_{i=1}^{\log T} \eta_{S_i}$.
4. For every segment S that ends in time t, erase η_S.

Figure 1: Event-Level Counter Algorithm

the sum of segment noise values for periods $0, \ldots, t-1$ by 1, and leave unchanged the sum of segment noise values from period t.

To do this, we find a collection of disjoint segments whose union is $\{0, \ldots, t-1\}$. There is always such a collection, and it is always of size at most $\log T$. We can construct it iteratively by, for i decreasing from $\lfloor \log(t-1) \rfloor$ to 0, choosing the segment of size 2^i that is contained in $\{0, \ldots, t-1\}$ and is not contained in a previously chosen segment (if such a segment exists). Given this set of disjoint segments, we notice also that they all end at time $t - 1 < t \leq t^*$, and so their noises are not in memory when the adversary intrudes (just following period t^*). In total (taking into account also changing the initial noise value for *count*), the complete view seen by the adversary is identical and the probabilities of the (collection of) noise values used for x and x' differ by at most an e^{ε} multiplicative factor.

Note that we assumed $t^* \geq t$. If $t^* < t$ then the initial noise added to *count* in $E_{x'}$ will be the same as in E_x, and we need to add 1 to the sum of segment noises in every time period from t through T (the sum of segment noises before time t remains unchanged). This is done as above, by finding a disjoint collection of at most $\log T$ segments that exactly covers $\{t, \ldots, T-1\}$. The noise values for these segments are not yet in memory when the intrusion occurs in time $t^* < t$, and the proof follows similarly. □

We note also that in every round *individually* (rather than in all rounds simultaneously), with all but β probability, the error has magnitude at most $O(\log(1/\beta) \cdot \log^{1.5} T/\varepsilon)$.

4.1 A Logarithmic (in T) Lower Bound

Given the upper bound of Theorem 4.1, where the error depends only poly-logarithmically on T, it is natural to ask whether *any* dependence is inherent. In this section we show that a logarithmic dependence on T is indeed inherent. The proof is omitted from this extended abstract.

THEOREM 4.2. *Any differentially private event-level algorithm for counting over T rounds must have error $\Omega(\log T)$ (even with $\varepsilon = 1$).*

4.2 Lower Bound for Counting with Intrusions

THEOREM 4.3. *Any counter that is ε-pan-private under continual observation while tolerating n intrusions must have additive error $\Omega(\sqrt{n})$ with probability at least $1/2 - 2\delta$, for any $\delta > 0$.*

PROOF. Let A be an ε-pan-private algorithm for counting the number of 1's in x, $|x| = n$, with continual intrusions. At each step, A reads the next bit, x_i, of x, updates its state from s_{i-1} to s_i, and must reveal the entire state s_i (including the updated count.)

Fix a constant k that depends on δ. We define two distributions on inputs of length n: I_0 and I_1. I_0 puts all of its weight on the all 0 string. A string is drawn from I_1 as follows. For each bit position i, set $i = 0$ with probability $1 - 1/k\sqrt{n}$ and set $i = 1$ with probability $1/k\sqrt{n}$. We will show that for any continual-intrusion pan-private algorithm, A, the statistical distance between D_0 and D_1 is at most δ, where D_0 is the distribution on states when running A on I_0, and D_1 is the distribution on states when running A on I_1. Thus there exists two input sequences, s_0, the all 0 input, and s^*, an input with $O(\sqrt{n})$ 1's and the rest zeroes, such that the statistical distance between the distribution of states when run on s_0 versus s^* is at most δ. This in turn implies that for one of these two inputs, the algorithm must make an additive $\Omega(\sqrt{n})$ error with probability at least $1/2 - 2\delta$. (If on input s^* A outputs a count that is smaller than $k'\sqrt{n}$ with probability at least $1/2$, then we are done. Otherwise A outputs a count that is at least $k'\sqrt{n}$ with probability at least $1/2$ on s^*. In this case, since the statistical distance between the states on s_0 and s^* is at most δ, this implies that with probability at least $(1/2 - 2\delta)$, A outputs a count that is at least $k'\sqrt{n}$ on s_0, completing the argument.)

It is left to show that for any ε-pan-private algorithm A with continuous intrusion, the statistical distance between D_0 and D_1 is at most δ. Let $p_0^s(x)$ be the probability, over the random coin tosses of algorithm A, of going to state x from state s, upon seeing a 0. Similarly let $p_1^s(x)$ be the probability of going to state x from state s, upon seeing a 1. We want to compare two distributions: the distribution D_0 induced on the possible states of A, when running A starting in s_0 on the distribution I_0 for n steps, and the distribution D_1 induced on the states of A when running A on I_1 for n steps, still starting from s_0. Let $q_0^s = p_0^s$ and let $q_1^s = (1 - \frac{1}{k\sqrt{n}})p_0^s + \frac{1}{k\sqrt{n}}p_1^s$. D_0 is the distribution induced on the states if you start in the start state, s_0, and run for n steps using probabilities q_0^s and similarly D_1 is the distribution induced on the states running for n steps, using the probabilities q_1^s.

The details of the proof are omitted for lack of space. We provide some intuition and the statements of the key lemma. *Randomized response* is a popular technique in the social sciences for obtaining answers to questions about embarrassing or even illegal behaviors [20]. We can abstract randomized response as follows. Consider a question for which there are two possible answers, say, $\{0,1\}$. We define two trivial distributions: *Zero* and *One*, which place all their weight, respectively, on 0 and 1. We now define two *answer* distributions A_0 and A_1. A respondent whose answer is $b \in \{0,1\}$ chooses from A_b. Both A_0 and A_1 are convex combinations of *Zero* and *one*. The intuition for randomized response is that the probability of producing any specific value $v \in \{0,1\}$ when drawing from A_0 is sufficiently close to the probability of producing v when drawing from A_1 to provide "plausible deniability" to the respondent, while the statistician, knowing the descriptions of A_0 and A_1 can "reverse engineer" the responses to obtain statistical information about the distribution of true answers. This completes the abstract description of randomized response. The intuition for our proof is that any counter that provides privacy is carrying out some form of randomized response.

Formally, we show (Lemma 4.4) the existence of two specific distributions $C'(x)$ and $C''(x)$ such that the distributions $q_0^s(x)$ and $q_1^s(x)$ are specific convex combinations of these distributions, say, $q_0^s(x) = z_0C'(x) + z_1C''(x)$ and $q_1^s(x) = w_0C'(x) + w_1C''(x)$. To upper bound the distance between $q_0^s(x)$ and $q_1^s(x)$ we replace $C'(x)$ and $C''(x)$ with distributions that are, intuitively, as far apart as possible, specifically, we replace $C'(x)$ with the trivial *Zero* distribution and $C''(x)$ with the trivial *One* distribution, and bound the distance between $z_0Zero+z_1One$ and $w_0Zero+w_1One$.

LEMMA 4.4. *If the algorithm is ε-differentially pan private, then for every state s, distributions q_0^s and q_1^s can be written in the following form:*

$$\begin{aligned} q_0^s(x) &= \frac{1}{2}C'(x) + \frac{1}{2}C''(x) \\ q_1^s(x) &= (\frac{1}{2} - \frac{1}{k\sqrt{n}})C'(x) + (\frac{1}{2} + \frac{1}{k\sqrt{n}})C''(x), \text{ where} \\ C'(x) &= \frac{k\sqrt{n}}{2}q_0^s(x) + q_0^s(x) - \frac{k\sqrt{n}}{2}q_1^s(x) \\ C''(x) &= q_0^s(x) - \frac{k\sqrt{n}}{2}q_0^s(x) + \frac{k\sqrt{n}}{2}q_1^s(x) \end{aligned}$$

That is, q_0^s is obtained by choosing either C' or C'' with equal probability, and then sampling uniformly from the chosen distribution; q_1^s is obtained via biased sampling from the distributions C' and C'': choose C'' with probability $(1/2 + 1/k\sqrt{n})$ and C' with probability $(1/2 - 1/k\sqrt{n})$, and then sample uniformly from the chosen distribution.

□

5. A GENERAL TRANSFORMATION

Our main result in this section will be a general transformation that converts a single-output streaming algorithm into a streaming algorithm that continually produces outputs. As an example, consider a single-output algorithm **Alg** for a monotone function, such as counting. Given a stream σ, the true count is the number of 1's in σ, and $\mathbf{Alg}(\sigma)$ produces an approximation to this true count. The transformed algorithm will be a counting algorithm as defined in the previous section of this paper: after processing any prefix of σ the output will be an approximation to the number of 1's in the prefix.

Our transformation works for single algorithms for any monotonic or "nearly monotonic" (see below) functions. User-level privacy and pan-privacy are preserved by the transformation, so if the original algorithm enjoys either or both of these properties then so will the transformed algorithm.

REMARK 5.1. *Throughout this section, we focus on the properties of the* algorithm *being transformed, such as the probability with which it produces output of specific accuracy, and we obtain results describing how these properties change (typically, deteriorate) in the transformed algorithm.*

Fix a single-output streaming algorithm **Alg**. We begin with the notion of a k-snapshot. Intuitively, this is a snapshot of the algorithm's outputs from k different time periods. Of course, our algorithm to be transformed is a single-output algorithm, so there is only one output, and not k outputs. However, for a fixed length T input stream σ and a fixed sequence τ of coin tosses, given a k-tuple $t_1, \ldots, t_k$ of times in $[T]$, we can fix the algorithm's coin tosses and run it on the k prefixes of length, respectively, $t_1, t_2, \ldots, t_k$. Each time we start from the beginning of σ and τ, and obtain a single output. This gives a well defined notion of the outputs at k different times.

DEFINITION 5.1 (k-SNAPSHOT). *For a fixed T-round execution of an algorithm* **Alg** *(i.e. fixing the algorithm's random coins τ and its input stream σ), a k-snapshot is a set of k pairs $(t_1, a_1), \ldots, (t_k, a_k)$, where, for $1 \le i \le t$, a_i is the output produced by* **Alg** *when run on the length t_i prefix of σ, using coin sequence τ (not all coins in τ need be read). We say that a snapshot is d-varying if for all $1 \le i \le k$ it holds that $|a_{i+1} - a_i| \ge d$.*

The deterioration in accuracy of the transformed algorithm is affected by the number of times the output can change by at least an additive factor of d. When k and d are both small the accuracy hit will be low.

DEFINITION 5.2 ((k,d,γ)-UNVARYING ALGORITHM). *An algorithm* **Alg** *is (k,d,γ)-unvarying if in every execution, with all but γ probability over the algorithm's coins, there does not exist a d-varying k-snapshot for the execution. I.e., the number of times the algorithm's output varies by at least d is at most k.*

Intuitively, any accurate algorithm computing a monotone function cannot vary too often or too wildly. In particular, when the range of the function to be computed is bounded, for example, when the range is contained in the interval $[0,1]$, then the output can change by an additive d amount at most $1/d$ times. We now make this precise.

CLAIM 5.1. *Let* **Alg** *be an algorithm for computing a* monotonically increasing *function whose output is in $[0,1]$.*[5] *If in every execution, with all but γ probability, the outputs of* **Alg** *are all within an α additive error, then for any $0 < d < 1$,* **Alg** *is $(1/d, d + 2\alpha, \gamma)$-unvarying. The claim also holds for monotonically decreasing functions.*

[5] A monotonically increasing function is one whose value can only increase as more data items are processed. For example, density estimation is a monotone increasing function.

PROOF. With probability at least $1-\beta$, the algorithm's outputs are all α-accurate. Assuming we are in this high probability case, for any $k > 0$ consider any k-snapshot $(t_1, a_1), \ldots, (t_k, a_k)$. For any $0 < d < 1$ and any $j \in \{1, \ldots, k\}$, a $d + 2\alpha$-change in the algorithm's output between t_j and t_{j+1} corresponds to a change of at least $1/k$ in the *value of the function* between t_j and t_{j+1} (because of α-accuracy in time periods t_j and in t_{j+1}). Since the function is monotone, this change in its value can only be an increase, and since the output is bounded to be between 0 and 1, there can only be $1/d$ such increases. We conclude that $k \le 1/d$. □

Before presenting our general transformation, we provide some intuition. Assume **Alg** is a (user-level pan-private) algorithm for a monotonic function f with range in $[0,1]$. Fix an input stream σ and sequence τ of random coins. Let $\mathbf{Alg}_t$ denote the output that the algorithm would produce after a prefix of length t. Recall that the transformed algorithm will have output at every step; let out_t denote this output after processing the t-length prefix of σ. The first idea is to change out infrequently, that is, only when it becomes very inconsistent with $\mathbf{Alg}_t$. In other words, for "suitably chosen" d, at each time t:

> If $\mathbf{Alg}_t - out_{t-1} > d$ then $out_t \leftarrow \mathbf{Alg}_t$,
> else $out_t \leftarrow out_{t-1}$.

As noted above, we will expect at most about $1/d$ changes to out. For privacy, we now have two problems. First, if there is no change at time t but there is a change at time $t+1$, this leaks information about σ_{t+1}, the $(t+1)$st symbol in σ, so, still speaking intuitively, we will need to add some noise to the comparison. For a similar reason, we need to add noise to the output.

Since we expect a change to occur only about $1/d$ times, we can scale the noise to this amount and abort the execution if the number of updates exceeds this.

> At time t: if $\mathbf{Alg}_t$ + fresh noise $- out_{t-1} \le d$
> then $out_t \leftarrow out_{t-1}$ (no change in output); else
> $out_t \leftarrow \mathbf{Alg}_t$ + fresh noise (update output).

This approach leads to an algorithm ensuring a weaker form of privacy known as (ε, δ)-differential privacy. Intuitively, the obstacle to pure differential privacy is that information is also leaked by the fact that an update to out does *not* occur. A long sequence of non-updates may be much more likely on an input σ', than on an adjacent input σ. For example, still speaking intuitively, this might happen if the true value of the function on a given prefix is close to triggering an update in σ and slightly farther in σ', and then for a large number of steps there is no input, so the value of the function does not change. Although in each of these steps the ratio of the probability of no update in σ' to the probability of no update in σ may be relatively small, say, e^{ε}, the ratio of probabilities of no update during this entire input-free stretch in σ' to the probability of no update during this stretch in σ may be very large ($e^{m\varepsilon}$ for a stretch of length m). To address this, we introduce a "soft" threshold: instead of comparing to d we compare to $d+$fresh noise, where fresh noise is chosen anew at each step. This fresh noise will be generated using the same segment-based techniques as were used in the counter construction. These involve relatively few variables at any one time ($\log T$), while simultaneously providing a dynamic set of thresholds for comparison, changing at every step.

The general transformation is presented in Figure 2. As we will see, the transformation preserves user-level pan-privacy.

THEOREM 5.2. *For any (k, d, γ)-unvarying algorithm* **Alg** *with (α_0, β_0)-accuracy, ε_0 (pan-)privacy, and user-level sensitivity ρ, the transformation of Figure 2, run with parameters as above and with any $T, \varepsilon, \beta > 0$, yields a T-round continual output algorithm with $(\varepsilon_0 + 3\varepsilon)$ (pan-)privacy. With all but $(\beta + \beta_0 + \gamma)$ probability, the error in all time periods is at most:*

$$d + \alpha_0 + (4\rho \cdot (\log(1/\beta) + \log T) \cdot (k + \log^2 T)/\varepsilon)$$

PROOF. We first argue about the accuracy of the algorithm, and then prove differential pan-privacy (for *pan*-privacy we assume that **Alg** itself is pan-private, otherwise we get only standard differential privacy for continual observation).

Accuracy. Assume that (1) the answers produced by **Alg** are all α-accurate ("**Alg** is accurate"); (2) the sequence of answers returned is (k, d)-unvarying, and (3) all the Laplace noise values have magnitude at most $(\log(1/\beta) + \log T + O(1))$ times their scale ("the noise is never large"). Taking a union bound, all of these conditions above are satisfied (in all rounds simultaneously) with all but $(\beta+\beta_0+\gamma)$ probability.

If $\widehat{compare}_t \le \widehat{thresh}_t$, so the conditional in Step 3 of round t evaluates to "true", then we say round t is *light*. Otherwise, that is, if $\widehat{compare}_t > \widehat{thresh}_t$, then we say round t is *heavy*. Fix a round t, and let $h < t$ be the last heavy round preceding round t, if one exists; otherwise let $h = -1$. Conditioned on assumption (3) that the noise is never large, the "noisy" difference $\widehat{compare}_t - \widehat{thresh}_t$ and the "true" difference $(|answer_h - answer_t|) - thresh$ differ by at most 2α (see the definition of α in Figure 2). This means that in every heavy round t, the difference between $answer_h$ and $answer_t$ is at least d. Since, by Assumption (2), **Alg** is (k, d)-unvarying, we conclude that the with all but $(\beta + \beta_0 + \gamma)$ probability, the algorithm does not terminate by the HALT instruction Step 3b.

Given that the algorithm never terminates in Step 3b, what is its error? Still under our assumptions (1) and (3) that **Alg** is accurate and the noise is never large, if the comparison of Step 3 evaluates to "true," so the round in light, we have that $out_t = out_{t-1} = \cdots = out_h$ is within a $d + 4\alpha$ error of $\mathbf{Alg}_t$. If t is heavy, then out_t is within an α error of $\mathbf{Alg}_t$. We conclude that with all but $(\beta + \beta_0 + \gamma)$ probability, the error in all rounds (simultaneously) is indeed at most $(d + 4\alpha)$ plus the error of **Alg**, i.e. the total error is at most:

$$d + \alpha_0 + (4\rho \cdot (\log(1/\beta) + \log T) \cdot (k + \log^2 T)/\varepsilon).$$

Privacy. To argue pan-privacy, we first use the ε_0 pan-privacy of **Alg** (and the composition of differential privacy) to argue that **Alg**'s internal state during an intrusion is privacy preserving. The proof of privacy for the combination of the internal state and the *times* of updates, *i.e.*, the set of the heavy rounds, is similar in spirit to the proof of pan-privacy for the counter. Given this, and using composition of differential privacy, the actual updated outputs in the at most k heavy rounds will only incur an additional ε-cost in privacy.

Fix two adjacent databases x and x'. Fix an arbitrary execution E_x when the input stream is x. This amounts to fixing the randomness of the algorithm, which in turn fixes the noise values generated. We will describe a corresponding

Transformation for Alg with parameters $(T, \varepsilon, \beta, \rho, k, d, \gamma)$

Initialization. Initialize $\xi_{thresh} = \rho \cdot \log T/\varepsilon$, $\xi_{compare}, \xi_{answer} = 2\rho \cdot (k+1)/\varepsilon$, $m = 0$, $answer_{-1} = 0$, accuracy $\alpha = \rho \cdot (\log(1/\beta) + \log T) \cdot (k + \log^2 T)/\varepsilon$ and $thresh = d + 2\alpha$.

Noise. At time period $0 \leq t < T$, choose noise values $\eta_{compare,t} \sim Lap(\xi_{compare})$ and $\eta_{answer,t} \sim Lap(\xi_{answer})$. We also associate $\log T$ threshold noise values with every time period t. To do this, view $t \in [T]$ as a string in $\{0,1\}^{\log T}$. For the i-bit prefix $t_{|i}$ of t (where $i \geq 1$), sample the noise value $\eta_{thresh,t_{|i}} \sim Lap(\xi_{thresh})$.

Persistent State. The value $\eta_{thresh,t_{|i}}$ is sampled and stored in round $(t_{|i} \circ 0^{\log T - i})$, and is erased by the end of round $(t_{|i} \circ 1^{\log T-i})$. There are $2T-2$ of these noise values in total. The values $\eta_{compare,t}$ and $\eta_{answer,t}$ are sampled in round t and erased by the end of round t; that is, they do *not* persist.

Processing. For $t \in \{0, 1, \ldots, T-1\}$, let $answer_t$ denote the answer computed by **Alg** at time t (recall that we enumerate time and input symbols starting with 0). inputs

1. $\widehat{compare}_t \leftarrow |out_{last} - answer_t + \eta_{compare,t}|$
2. $\widehat{thresh}_t \leftarrow thresh + \sum_{i=1}^{\log T} \eta_{thresh,t_{|i}}$
3. If $\widehat{compare}_t \leq \widehat{thresh}_t$ then $out_t \leftarrow out_{t-1}$ else DO:
   (a) $out_t \leftarrow answer_t + \eta_{answer,t}$
   (b) If $m < k$ then $m \leftarrow m+1$ else HALT.

Figure 2: Continual Output Transformation for Algorithm Alg

execution $E_{x'}$ by describing how its noise values differ from those in E_x. The adversary's view in $E_{x'}$ will be identical to its view in E_x; moreover the probabilities of corresponding noise values differ only by an $e^{3\varepsilon}$ ratio. This implies 3ε differential pan-privacy.

Let η be the noise vector in execution E_x. The adversary's view consists of the incidence vector v for the set of heavy rounds (these are the rounds in which the output changes), the values of the heavy rounds' outputs, and the internal noise values seen in the intrusion. Let the intrusion occur immediately following round t^* of E_x. Then the observed noise values are a subset of $\{\eta_{thresh,t^*_{|i}}\}_{i=1}^{\log T}$. In constructing the noise vector for $E_{x'}$ we will only change noise values *other than* the threshold noises in round t^*; thus we only change noise values that the are *not* observed during the intrusion.

First, to ensure that all light rounds in E_x are also light for in $E_{x'}$, we want to increase the sum of threshold noises in every round except t^* by ρ. This can be done by increasing the values of $\log T$ threshold noises as described below. For $t \in \{0, 1, \ldots, T-1\}$, and $i \in \{1, \ldots, \log T\}$, we view the noise value $\eta_{thresh,t_{|i}}$ as "covering" or "corresponding to" the segment of $2^{\log T - i}$ time periods $\{t_{|i} \circ 0^{\log T-i}, \ldots, t_{|i} \circ 1^{\log T - i}\}$.

For every round t^*, there exists a set S^* of exactly $\log T$ segments, such that every time period *except* t^* is covered by exactly one of these segments. To see this, we start with S^* being empty, and then for each i going from 1 to $\log T$, we choose the one segment of size $2^{\log T - i}$ that isn't covered by previously chosen segments and does not cover t^*. In each of these iterations we cover half of the remaining segments, and all of the segments we choose are disjoint. This means that after $\log T$ iterations, every time period except t^* is covered by exactly one segment. Now in η' we increase the noise values of each of these segments in S^* by ρ. This guarantees that when running with noise η' the sum of threshold noises in each round except t^* is larger by ρ than in the run on x (with noise η). In particular, since the sensitivity of **Alg** is at most ρ, with the possible exception of round t^*, light rounds in E_x with noise η will also be light in $E_{x'}$ with noise η'. Because the threshold noises were chosen from the Laplace distribution with magnitude $\rho \cdot \log T/\varepsilon$, the probabilities of these new values differ by at most an e^{ε} factor from the original noise values.

Now to ensure that heavy rounds in E_x are also heavy in $E_{x'}$, we need to change the noise $\eta_{compare,t}$ by at most 2ρ between η and η' for every heavy round t: we may need a change of ρ to handle the sensitivity of **Alg**, and another change of ρ to handle the increased sum of noisy thresholds. Note that the decision as to whether the noise is increased or decreased depends on $\mathbf{Alg}_t$ and the noise in previous rounds, but this dependence is fixed and so indeed we have a bijection between the vector of noise values. There are at most k heavy rounds in any execution, and so E_x has at most k heavy rounds. We choose the comparison noises from a Laplace distribution with magnitude $2\rho \cdot (k+1) \cdot \varepsilon$. This change in the noise values changes the noise probabilities by at most an $e^{\varepsilon k/(k+1)}$.

Finally, to ensure that if round t^* is light in E_x then it is also light in $E_{x'}$, we may change the comparison noise $\eta_{compare,t^*}$. This poses no risk to privacy as this value does not persist after round t^*, and so will not be seen during the intrusion.

Thus, we have obtained an identical incidence vector by changing the noise probabilities by at most an $e^{2\varepsilon}$ factor. To argue privacy for the actual answers generated in the heavy rounds, we simply note that there are at most k such answers and this incurs another ε cost in privacy. In total, the transformed algorithm is $(\varepsilon_0 + 3\varepsilon)$-differentially pan private with continual outputs. If the original algorithm **Alg** was not pan-private, then the transformed one is not pan-private either, but its collection of outputs is still 3ε-differentially private. □

5.1 Lower Bounds for User-Level Continual Output Privacy

In the previous section, we saw that it is possible to accurately approximate a wide class of functions with user-level privacy even under continual observation (and moreover some of these algorithms are even pan-private). In particular, this was the case for unvarying functions. In contrast, consider a highly varying function such as modular incidence counting, where we want to estimate the number (between 0 and n) of users that appear an odd number of times (or more generally i times $\pmod k$). Each occurrence of each user is a significant event. Over many time periods, the value of this function can vary wildly many times. Thus, the general transformation of Section 5 does not yield a privacy-preserving algorithm. This is no accident. Indeed, the following theorem shows that there is no user-level differentially private continual-output algorithm for any highly varying function. (See Definition 5.2 for the definition of unvarying algorithms.) As this includes modular incidence counting, we obtain a natural statistic that can be computed pan-privately (see [13]), but that cannot be computed privately in the continual output setting (even without pan-privacy).

DEFINITION 5.3. *Let f be a function defined over a database with n users, with the property that f on a blank symbol does not change value. f is (k, d)-varying if there exists an input y and k indices, $t_1 < t_2 < \ldots < t_k$, such that for all i, $1 \le i \le k$, $|f(y_{t_i}) - f(y_{t_{i+1}})| \ge d$. That is, the function f on y jumps by at least d units k times.*

THEOREM 5.3. *Let f be a (k, d)-varying function defined over a database with n users. Then every differentially private, continual output algorithm must have additive error $\Omega(dk/n)$ (even with $\varepsilon = 1$).*

PROOF SKETCH.. We assume throughout that the global sensitivity is $\rho = O(dk/n)$. Otherwise, if $\rho = \Omega(dk/n)$, then by a standard argument for ε-privacy the error must be $\Omega(dk/n)$.

First we claim that if f is (k, d)-varying, then there exists a set S of 2^k inputs such that for every pair x, y of inputs from S, there exists an index i such that $|f(x_1, \ldots, x_i) - f(y_1, \ldots, y_i)| \ge d$. Let y be the input such that f jumps by d at least k times. That is, there exist indices $t_1, \ldots, t_k$ such that $|f(y_{t_i}) - f(y_{t_{i+1}})| \ge d$. We partition y into k intervals, $I_1, \ldots, I_k$, as follows. The interval I_l begins at $t_{l-1} + 1$ and ends at t_l. Each input $v \in S$ will consist of k intervals, and the total length of each v will be $2|y|$. Letting $v(\alpha_1, \ldots, \alpha_k)$ denote a particular string in S, where $\alpha_i \in \{0, 1\}$, the ith interval of $z(\alpha_1, \ldots, \alpha_k)$ is defined as follows: (i) if $\alpha_i = 0$, then the ith interval will contain a copy of I_i followed by $|I_i|$ blank symbols; (ii) otherwise if $\alpha_i = 1$, then the ith interval will contain $|I_i|$ blank symbols followed by a copy of I_i. This defines a set of 2^k inputs.

Now consider two distinct inputs $v(\alpha), v(\beta)$ from S. We want to show that at some location l, the output of f after reading the lth bits of $v(\alpha)$, $v(\beta)$ differs by at least d. By construction, $v(\alpha)$ and $v(\beta)$ must differ in at least one interval. Suppose it is interval j, so that the jth interval of $v(\alpha)$ consists of I_j followed by an equal number of blanks, and $v(\beta)$ consists of $|I_j|$ blanks followed by I_j. At the location immediately preceding the jth interval of $v(\alpha)$, the value of f on $v(\alpha)$ and $v(\beta)$, is the same, and is equal to the value of f on the first $j - 1$ intervals of y. At the first location in the j-th interval of $v(\alpha)$, the value of f jumps by d, whereas the value of f on $v(\beta)$ on the same length substring has not changed from its previous value. Thus the claim is proven.

Secondly we note that if f is (k, d)-varying, then f is also $(t, dk/t)$-varying, as long as $\rho \le dk/2t$. If the sensitivity is ρ, then for any $a < d/2\rho$, we can split up an interval with a "jump" (change in the function value from the interval's beginning to its end) of d, into a subintervals where each subinterval has a jump of at least d/a (this uses the upper bound on the function's sensitivity). Setting $a = t/k$, which is less than $d/(2\rho)$ as long as $\rho \le dk/2t$, we end up with t intervals in total, each with a jump of at least dk/t.

Now let S be the set of 2^t inputs, with the property that for every pair of inputs in S, there exists a time period where the output of f differs by at least $d' = dk/t$. If A is accurate, then w.h.p. its output is within $d'/2$ of the correct answer in every time period. If we associate with each input in S an event, corresponding to the algorithm being with $d'/2$ of the correct answer on that input in every round, then this set of events is disjoint. By privacy, however, each of these events has some (exponentially small in n) probability on every input. This implies a contradiction, since there are $|S| = 2^t$ disjoint events, and for $t > n$ the sum of these probabilities is larger than 1. See the full version for details (there we also rule out even algorithms that are accurate in a large fraction of the rounds). □

Note that the lower bound here is not tight with the upper bound of Theorem 5.2. Finding a tight characterization is an intriguing direction for future work.

6. HOW TO USE EXPERT ADVICE

The goal of this section is demonstrating that continual observation counters can be applied to obtain privacy preserving solutions to fairly complex problems, especially in online environments. There are several algorithms in various settings that rely on counting a number of "successes" or "accesses", determining their action based on this count. An underlying principle behind many such algorithms is aggregating the advice of several experts, and choosing a response that is not much worse than any of the experts (regret minimization). In this section out goal is showing that such algorithms can be utilized *without revealing the advice given by the experts*. I.e., we protect the experts' privacy. The main issue is whether the accuracy of the approximate counter is good enough for the application considered. In this extended abstract we focus on the problem of combining expert advice (in the full version we also consider problems such as list access or list update, and how to run many different counters simultaneously).

We present a method for combining expert advice that is competitive with the best expert in hindsight. The setting is that there is a sequence of actions by n experts. At each round each expert decides on an action, and following the round the cost associated with the action is revealed (it is a value in $[0, 1]$). The combiner has to choose one of the experts at each round, and act by following that expert, where all the information the combiner has is the cost of the previous actions by the experts. The goal is to minimize *regret*, that is to compare the combiner's performance to the best expert in hindsight. Known performance guarantees for this problem (without privacy concerns) are of the form $(1 + \gamma)(\text{best expert}) + O(\log n/\gamma)$, for any γ. That is, there are combiner strategies that only incur an $(1 + o(1))$ multiplicative overhead over the best expert in hindsight.

The problem has a long history, see the survey by Blum and Mansour [4]. Our goal is performing the same sort of aggregation, but while protecting the privacy of each expert's action with respect to an observer that sees which expert is being followed. That is, for any time period t and expert i we guarantee ε-differential privacy for expert i's decision in step t. Here we aim for *event level* privacy.[6]

Most of the combining algorithms in the literature rely, when making a decision at the tth round, on the costs incurred by the experts so far, and not, say, on when exactly these costs occurred. This suggests applying privacy-preserving counters to this problem. The issue, however, is showing that the *approximate* estimation of the cost given by the privacy-preserving counter still serves the combiner of the experts problem (almost) as well as an exact computation of the cost. Some of the well known combining algorithms, like Randomized Weighted Majority, use multiplicative weights or more involved functions of the cost, making this a non-trivial obstacle.

Kalai and Vempala [18] suggested a very simple additive algorithm called *Follow the Perturbed Leader*: For each round $t = 1, 2, \ldots, T$: (1) for each expert $i \in [n]$ pick weight $p_t[i]$ independently chosen according to the exponential distribution with parameter γ, and (2) for each expert i let $C_t(i)$ be the total cost so far. Pick the expert minimizing $C_t(i) - p_t(i)$ and act accordingly.

For this algorithm, as well as Randomized Weighted Majority, the regret (w.r.t the best expert in hindsight) is bounded by γ(best expert) $+ \log n/\gamma$. The natural way to adapt this algorithm is to have, for each expert, a private counter counting the cost incurred so far (it is easy to adapt the counter to work with continuous, rather than discrete, increments).

The problem is that we do not have access to the real cost, rather we have access to an approximation C'_t where we are guaranteed to have $C_t(i) \in C'(t) \pm \log^{1.5} t$ (w.h.p in each round). A possible approach to the problem is to show that this is true for *any* adversarial approximation, that is at each point in time the estimate C' of the cost so far is guaranteed to be with Δ of the real cost C, but an adversary may set the approximation as it wishes within these bounds, and the question is what combining algorithm is appropriate. It is not clear whether such a general approach will work.

Suppose, instead, that the approximation works by adding noise, where at any point in time the distribution of the noise is identical. This, in fact, is the case for the counter algorithm of Section 4: in each round, the noise is the sum of (the same number of) identically distributed Laplace variables. Consider the cost of the expert combining algorithm. It is equal to $\sum_{t=1}^{T} Y_t$ where Y_t is a random variable representing the cost of the combining algorithm at step t. The r.v's $\{Y_t\}$ depend on the noise added at each step and the randomness of the combining algorithm (the perturbations in the Kalai-Vempala algorithm). From linearity of expectation $E[\sum_{t=1}^{T} Y_t] = \sum_{t=1}^{T} E[Y_t]$. The expectation of the random variables Y_t remains the same when the algorithm is run on counters where exactly the same noise is added at all the steps: that is, the noise is generated only for one round and then *exactly the same noise* is added at all rounds. If this is the case (i.e. the same noise added at all rounds), then we can think of the algorithm as running with a prefix of steps where the cost of each expert in that prefix equals the noise added to it. Now take the guarantee on the regret w.r.t to the best expert. The difference between the real leading expert and the leading expert with the approximation noise is at most the maximal noise. So we get that the new combining algorithm is within the bound the original algorithm was plus the maximum of n random variables, each a sum of $(1+\log T)$ Laplacians with magnitude $\epsilon/\log T$, that is an additional $O(\log n \cdot log^{1.5} T/\epsilon)$ term to the regret. Note that here we use the fact that in each round individually, w.h.p. the noise added by the counter has magnitude $O(\log^{1.5} T/\varepsilon)$ (see the discussion following Theorem 4.1).

[6]In fact, it can be shown that it is impossible to obtain any non trivial result with respect to user level privacy.

7. REFERENCES

[1] J. L. Bentley and J. B. Saxe. Decomposable searching problems i: Static-to-dynamic transformation. *J. Algorithms*, 1(4):301–358, 1980.

[2] A. Blum, C. Dwork, F. McSherry, and K. Nissim. Practical privacy: The SuLQ framework. 24th PODS, 2005.

[3] A. Blum, K. Ligett, and A. Roth. A learning theory approach to non-interactive database privacy. In *Proceedings of STOC*, 2008.

[4] A. Blum and Y. Mansour. Learning, regret minimization, and equilibria. In *Algorithmic Game Theory*. Cambridge University Press, 2007.

[5] I. Dinur and K. Nissim. Revealing information while preserving privacy. In *Proceedings of 22nd PODS*, pages 202–210, 2003.

[6] C. Dwork. A firm foundation for private data analysis. *Communications of the ACM (to appear)*.

[7] C. Dwork, Differential privacy in new settings. *Proc. ACM-SIAM SODA*, 2010.

[8] C. Dwork. An ad omnia approach to defining and achieving private data analysis. In *Privacy, Security, and Trust in KDD, First ACM SIGKDD International (PinKDD), Revised Selected Papers*, volume 4890 of *Lecture Notes in Computer Science*, pages 1–13. Springer, 2007.

[9] C. Dwork. The differential privacy frontier. In *Proceedings of TCC*, 2009.

[10] C. Dwork, K. Kenthapadi, F. McSherry, I. Mironov, and M. Naor. Our data, ourselves: privacy via distributed noise generation. In *Advances in Cryptology: Proceedings of EUROCRYPT*, pages 486–503, 2006.

[11] C. Dwork, F. McSherry, K. Nissim, and A. Smith. Calibrating noise to sensitivity in private data analysis. In *Proceedings of TCC*, pages 265–284, 2006.

[12] C. Dwork, F. McSherry, and K. Talwar. The price of privacy and the limits of lp decoding. In *Proceedings of STOC*, pages pp. 85–94, 2007.

[13] C. Dwork, M. Naor, T. Pitassi, G. N. Rothblum, and S. Yekhanin. Pan-private streaming algorithms. In *Proceedings of ICS*, 2010.

[14] C. Dwork, M. Naor, O. Reingold, G. Rothblum, and S. Vadhan. When and how can privacy-preserving data release be done efficiently? In *Proceedings of STOC*, 2009.

[15] C. Dwork and K. Nissim. Privacy-preserving datamining on vertically partitioned databases. In *Proceedings of CRYPTO 2004*, volume 3152, pages 528–544, 2004.

[16] C. Dwork and S. Yekhanin. New efficient attacks on statistical disclosure control mechanisms. In *Proceedings of CRYPTO 2008*, pages 468–480, 2008.

[17] M. Hardt and K. Talwar. On the geometry of differential privacy. arXiv:0907.3754v2, 2009.

[18] A. T. Kalai and S. Vempala. Efficient algorithms for online decision problems. *J. Comput. Syst. Sci.*, 71(3):291–307, 2005.

[19] F. McSherry and K. Talwar. Mechanism design via differential privacy. In *Proceedings of FOCS 2007*.

[20] S. Warner. Randomized response: a survey technique for eliminating evasive answer bias. *JASA*, pages 63–69, 1965.

On the Complexity of #CSP

Martin Dyer and David Richerby*
School of Computing
University of Leeds
Leeds LS2 9JT
United Kingdom
{M.E.Dyer,D.M.Richerby}@leeds.ac.uk

ABSTRACT

Bulatov (2008) has given a dichotomy for the *counting constraint satisfaction problem*, #CSP. A problem from #CSP is characterized by a constraint language Γ, which is a fixed, finite set of relations over a finite domain. An instance of the problem uses these relations to constrain the values taken by a finite set of variables. Bulatov showed that, for any fixed Γ, the problem of counting the satisfying assignments of instances of any problem from #CSP is either in polynomial time (FP) or #P-complete, according on the structure of the constraint language Γ. His proof draws heavily on techniques from universal algebra and cannot be understood without a secure grasp of that field.

We give an elementary proof of Bulatov's dichotomy, based on succinct representations, which we call *frames*, of a class of highly structured relations, which we call *strongly rectangular*. We show that these are precisely the relations that are invariant under a *Mal'tsev polymorphism*. En route, we give a simplification of a decision algorithm for strongly rectangular constraint languages due to Bulatov and Dalmau (2006). Out proof uses no universal algebra, except for the straightforward concept of the Mal'tsev polymorphism and is accessible to readers with little background in #CSP.

Categories and Subject Descriptors

F.2.2 [**Theory of Computation**]: Analysis of algorithms and problem complexity

General Terms

Theory, Algorithms

Keywords

Constraint satisfaction problem, counting problems, complexity dichotomy

*Supported by EPSRC grant EP/E062172/1 "The Complexity of Counting in Constraint Satisfaction Problems".

STOC'10, June 5–8, 2010, Cambridge, Massachusetts, USA.

1. INTRODUCTION

The constraint satisfaction problem (CSP) is ubiquitous in computer science. Problems in such diverse areas as Boolean logic, graph theory, database query evaluation, type inference, scheduling and artificial intelligence can be expressed naturally in the setting of assigning values from some domain to a collection of variables, subject to constraints on the combination of values that can be taken by given subsets of the variables [17]. CSP is directly equivalent to the problem of evaluating conjunctive queries on databases [22] and to the homomorphism problem for relational structures [17]. Weighted versions of the problem appear in statistical physics, where the total weight of all solutions corresponds to the so-called partition function of a spin system [14].

For example, suppose we wish to know if a graph is 3-colourable. The question we are trying to answer is whether we can assign a colour (domain value) to each vertex (variable) such that, whenever two vertices are adjacent in the graph, they receive a different colour (constraints). Similarly, by asking if a 3-CNF formula is satisfiable, we are asking if we can assign a truth value to each variable such that every clause contains at least one true literal.

Since it includes both 3-COLOURABILITY and 3-SAT, this general form of the CSP, known as *uniform* CSP, is NP-complete. Therefore, attention has focused on *non-uniform* CSP. Here, we fix a domain and a finite *constraint language* Γ, a set of relations over that domain. Having fixed Γ, we only allow constraints of the form, "the values assigned to the variables $v_1, \dots, v_r$ must be a tuple in the r-ary relation $R \in \Gamma$" (we give formal definitions in Section 2). We write CSP(Γ) to denote non-uniform CSP with the constraint language Γ. To express 3-COLOURABILITY in this setting, we just take Γ to be the disequality relation on a set of three colours. 3-SAT is also expressible: for example, the clause $\neg x \vee y \vee \neg z$ corresponds to the relation $\{\mathtt{t},\mathtt{f}\}^3 \setminus \{\mathtt{t},\mathtt{f},\mathtt{t}\}$, where t indicates "true" and f "false"; the other seven possible patterns of negations within a clause can be expressed as similar ternary relations.

Thus, there are languages Γ for which CSP(Γ) is NP-complete. Of course, the methods above can be adapted to express polynomial-time problems such as 2-COLOURABILITY and 2-SAT. Feder and Vardi [17] conjectured that these are the only possibilities: that is, for all Γ, CSP(Γ) is either in P or is NP-complete. To date, this conjecture remains open but it is known to hold in several special cases [1, 20, 24]. Recent efforts to resolve the conjecture have focused on techniques from universal algebra [10].

There can be no dichotomy for the whole of NP, since Ladner [23] has shown that either P = NP or there is an infinite hierarchy of complexity classes between them. In the latter case there are, therefore, problems in NP that are neither complete for the class nor in P. However, it is not unreasonable to conjecture a dichotomy for CSP, since there are problems in NP, such as graph Hamiltonicity and even connectivity, that cannot be expressed as CSP(Γ) for any finite Γ. (This fact follows from results of Fagin, later improved with Stockmeyer and Vardi, on the expressive power of monadic existential second-order logic [15, 16]). Further, Ladner's proof is by a diagonalization that does not seem to be expressible in CSP [17].

In this paper, we consider the *counting* version of CSP(Γ), which we denote #CSP(Γ). Rather than ask whether an instance of CSP(Γ) has a satisfying assignment, we ask how many satisfying assignments there are. The corresponding conjecture is that, for every Γ, #CSP(Γ) is either computable in polynomial time or complete for #P. We give formal definitions in the next section but, informally, #P is the analogue of NP for counting problems. Again, a modification of Ladner's proof shows that there can be no dichotomy for the whole of #P. The decision version of any problem in NP is trivially reducible to the corresponding counting problem in #P: if we can count the solutions, we can certainly determine whether one exists. However, the converse appears not to be the case: there are well-known polynomial-time algorithms that determine whether a graph admits a perfect matching but it is #P-complete to count perfect matchings even in bipartite graphs [26].

Dichotomies for #CSP(Γ) are known in several special cases [8, 9, 11, 13, 14], each consistent with the conjecture that #CSP(Γ) is always either polynomial-time computable or #P-complete. However, Bulatov recently made a major breakthrough by proving a dichotomy for all Γ [2, 3].

Bulatov's proof makes heavy use of the techniques of universal algebra. Geiger [19] showed that an algebra can be associated with the set of pp-definable relations over a constraint language Γ and Bulatov examines detailed properties of this algebra's *congruence lattice*. The structure of quotients in the lattice must have certain algebraic properties, which can be derived from *tame congruence theory* [21] and *commutator theory* [18]. Bulatov constructs an algorithm for the easy cases, where counting is in FP, by decomposing this congruence lattice and using the structure of its quotients. He is only able to do this, in general, by transforming the relation corresponding to the input instance to one which is a *subdirect power*. It is even nontrivial to prove that this transformation inherits the required property of the original. His paper runs to some 43 pages, and is very difficult to follow for anyone who is not expert in these areas. The criterion of Bulatov's dichotomy, which is based on an infinite class of algebras constructed from Γ, is not known to be decidable. It also seems difficult to apply his criterion to recover the special cases mentioned above.

Our main result is a new and elementary proof of Bulatov's theorem. It follows Bulatov's approach in working with the relation over Γ determined by the input, but requires almost no machinery from universal algebra. The little that is used is defined and explained below. We use a different criterion for the dichotomy, based on properties of ternary relations definable in Γ. We construct a simple iterative algorithm for the tractable cases, which uses no algebraic properties but operates by constructing a succinct representation of the set of satisfying assignments.

Our criterion can be shown to be equivalent to Bulatov's, but we have been unable so far to show that it is decidable. It appears more suited to proving special cases of the dichotomy for restricted constraint languages, but we do not explore this, here.

1.1 Our proof

Our proof is largely self-contained, and is accessible to readers with no knowledge of universal algebra and little background in CSP. We use reductions from three previous papers on counting complexity, by Dyer and Greenhill [14], Bulatov and Dalmau [5] and Bulatov and Grohe [6]. The last two of these papers deal partly with ideas from universal algebra, but we make no use of that. We use only one concept from universal algebra, that of a *Mal'tsev polymorphism* and the condition that one exists [10], which we define and explain in Section 2 below. The proof of the condition we use is quite simple, but we do not repeat it here.

Our proof is based around a succinct representation for relations that are preserved by a Mal'tsev polymorphism. We call such relations *strongly rectangular*, for reasons which will become clear. Our representations, which we call *frames*, are similar to the *compact representations* of Bulatov and Dalmau [4] but are smaller because they avoid some redundancy in the representation.

We define a *frame* for a relation $R \subseteq D^n$ to be a relation $F \subseteq R$ such that, whenever R contains a tuple with ith component a, F also contains such a tuple and, whenever R contains tuples $a_1 \ldots a_n$ and $a_1 \ldots a_{i-1} b_i \ldots b_n$, F also contains tuples whose ith elements are a_i and b_i and which agree on the first $i-1$ elements. We show that every n-ary strongly rectangular relation over D has a *small* frame of size linear in n and $|D|$, whereas R may have $|D|^n$ tuples. Further, we show how to construct such a small frame efficiently and how to recover a strongly rectangular relation R from any of its frames.

Now, suppose we have an instance Φ of #CSP(Γ) for some strongly rectangular constraint language Γ, with m constraints in n variables. Using methods similar to Bulatov and Dalmau [4], we construct a frame for the solution set of Φ in polynomial time, by starting with a frame for D^n (i.e., the solution set of the n-variable instance with no constraints) and introducing the constraints one at a time. A frame is empty if, and only if, it represents the empty relation so, at this point, we have re-proven Bulatov and Dalmau's result that there is a polynomial-time algorithm for the decision problem CSP(Γ), for any strongly rectangular constraint language Γ. We give an explicit time complexity for this algorithm, which is $O(n^4)$ for fixed Γ. Bulatov and Dalmau [4] gave no time estimate, showing only that their procedure is polynomial time.

Any ternary relation $R \subseteq A_1 \times A_2 \times A_3$ (where the A_i need not be disjoint) induces a matrix $M = (m_{xy})$ with rows and columns indexed by A_1 and A_2 and with

$$m_{xy} = |\{z : (x, y, z) \in R\}|.$$

We say that R is *balanced* if every block of M has rank one, and that a relation $R \subseteq D^n$ for any $n > 3$ is balanced if every expression of it as a ternary relation in $D^k \times D^\ell \times D^m$ $(k, \ell, m \geq 1,\ k + \ell + m = n)$ is balanced. A constraint language Γ is *strongly balanced* if every relation of arity at least three that is pp-definable over Γ is balanced. Via a brief detour through weighted #CSP, we show that #CSP(Γ) is #P-complete if Γ is not strongly balanced.

If Γ is strongly balanced, we compute the number of satisfying assignments to a CSP(Γ) instance as follows. Let $R \subseteq D^n$ be the set of satisfying assignments. First, we construct a small frame F for R, as above. If R is unary, we have $F = R$ so we return $|F|$ and we are done.

Otherwise, for $2 \le i < j \le n$, let $N_{i,j}(a)$ be the number of prefixes $u_1 \dots u_{i-1}$ such that there is a tuple $u_1 \dots u_n \in R$ with $u_j = a$. In particular, then, summing the values of $N_{n,n}(\cdot)$ gives $|R|$. Since the function $N_{2,j}$ can be calculated easily, we just need to show how to compute $N_{i+1,j}$ for each $j > i$, given $N_{i,j}$ for each $j \ge i$. Writing $[k]$ for the set $\{1, \dots, k\}$, we can consider the projection

$$\mathsf{pr}_{[i]\cup\{j\}} R = \{u_1 \dots u_i u_j : u_1 \dots u_n \in R\}$$

to be a ternary relation on $\mathsf{pr}_{[i-1]} R \times \mathsf{pr}_i R \times \mathsf{pr}_j R$. R is strongly balanced, so the matrix given by

$$M_{xy} = |\{\mathbf{u} : (\mathbf{u}, x, y) \in \mathsf{pr}_{[i]\cup\{j\}}\}|$$

is a rank-one block matrix. The sum of the a-indexed row of this matrix is $N_{i+1,j}(a)$.

By taking certain quotients, we obtain another rank-one block matrix $\widehat{M}$, whose block structure and row and column sums we can determine. A key fact about rank-one block matrices is that this information is sufficient to recover the entries of the matrix. This allows us to recover M and, hence, compute the values $N_{i+1,j}(a)$ for each j and a. Iterating, we can determine the function $N_{n,n}$, from which we can easily compute $|R|$.

The above discussion assumes that the constraint language Γ is fixed: that is, we are considering uniform CSP. In particular, this means that $q = O(1)$. We have extended our results to non-uniform CSP, the case where Γ is included as part of the input, but we do not consider this case in the present paper.

1.2 Organization of the paper

Preliminary definitions and notation are given in Section 2. In Section 3, we define the notion of strong rectangularity that we use throughout the paper and, in Section 4, we further study the properties of strongly rectangular relations and introduce frames, our succinct representations of these relations. We give an efficient procedure for constructing frame for the solution set of a CSP instance in Section 5.

In Section 6, we introduce counting problems and, in Section 7, we define the key notion of a strongly balanced constraint language and prove the dichotomy that #CSP(Γ) is solvable in polynomial time if Γ is strongly balanced and is #P-complete, otherwise. Concluding remarks appear in Section 8.

2. DEFINITIONS AND NOTATION

We write $[n]$ for the set $\{1, 2, \dots, n\}$ for any natural number n. Boldface letters indicate tuples of some appropriate arity, such as $\mathbf{t} = (t_1, \dots, t_r)$. Sometimes, we just write $t_1 \dots t_r$ for this tuple.

Suppose $\varphi\colon D^k \to D$ and let $\mathbf{u}_1, \dots, \mathbf{u}_k \in D^r$, with $\mathbf{u}_i = (u_{i,1}, u_{i,2}, \dots, u_{i,r})$. We implicitly extend the function φ to r-tuples and write $\varphi(\mathbf{u}_1, \dots, \mathbf{u}_r)$ for the r-tuple $\mathbf{v} = v_1 \dots v_r$, where $v_i = \varphi(u_{1,i}, u_{2,i}, \dots, u_{k,i})$ for each $i \in [r]$.

2.1 Constraint satisfaction problems

Let $D = \{d_1, d_2, \dots, d_q\}$ be a finite *domain* with $q = |D|$. We will always consider q to be a constant. A *constraint language* Γ is a finite set of (finitary) relations on D, including the binary equality relation $=$. We will call (D, Γ) a *relational structure*. We may view an r-ary relation H on D with $\ell = |H|$ as an $\ell \times r$ matrix with elements in D. Then a tuple $\mathbf{t} \in H$ is any row of this matrix. We define the size of H as $\|H\| = \ell r$, the number of elements in its matrix, and the size of Γ as $\|\Gamma\| = \sum_{H \in \Gamma} \|H\|$.

Let $V = \{\nu_1, \nu_2, \dots, \nu_n\}$ be a finite *codomain*. An *assignment* is a function $\mathbf{x}\colon V \to D$. We will abbreviate $\mathbf{x}(\nu_i)$ to x_i. If $\{i_1, i_2, \dots, i_r\} \subseteq [n]$, we write $H(x_{i_1}, x_{i_2}, \dots, x_{i_r})$ for the relation $\Theta = \{\mathbf{x} : (x_{i_1}, x_{i_2}, \dots, x_{i_r}) \in H\}$, and we refer to this as a *constraint*. Then $(\nu_{i_1}, \nu_{i_2}, \dots, \nu_{i_r})$ is the *scope* of the constraint, and we say that $\mathbf{x}$ is a *satisfying* assignment for the constraint if $\mathbf{x} \in \Theta$.

A Γ-*formula* Φ in a set of variables $\{x_1, x_2, \dots, x_n\}$ is a conjunction of constraints $\Theta_1 \wedge \dots \wedge \Theta_m$. We will identify the variables with the x_i above, although strictly they are only a *model* of the formula. A Γ-formula Φ describes an instance of the *constraint satisfaction problem* (CSP) with *constraint language* Γ. A satisfying assignment for Φ is an assignment that satisfies all Θ_i $(i \in [m])$. The set of all satisfying assignments for Φ is the Γ-*definable* relation R_Φ over D. We will make no distinction between Φ and R_Φ, unless this could cause confusion.

An equivalent view is to regard Φ as a finite structure with domain V and relations determined by the scopes of the constraints. Thus we have relations $\tilde{H}$, where $(i_1, i_2, \dots, i_r) \in \tilde{H}$ if $H(x_{i_1}, x_{i_2}, \dots, x_{i_r})$ is a constraint. In this view, a satisfying assignment $\mathbf{x}$ is a *homomorphism* from Φ to Γ.

2.2 Projections

If R is an n-ary relation and $I \subseteq [n]$, then $\mathsf{pr}_I R$ is the *projection* of R on I, the relation corresponding to existentially quantifying $R(x_1, \dots, x_n)$ on the variables x_i where $i \notin I$. If $I = \{i\}$, we just write $\mathsf{pr}_i R$, and if $I = \{i, j\}$, we write $\mathsf{pr}_{i,j} R$. For the relation $\{\mathbf{t}\}$, where $\mathbf{t}$ is a single n-tuple, we write $\mathsf{pr}_I \mathbf{t}$ rather than $\mathsf{pr}_I \{\mathbf{t}\}$.

2.3 Definability and clones

A *primitive positive* (pp) formula Ψ is a Γ-formula Φ with existential quantification over some subset of the variables. A satisfying assignment for Ψ is any satisfying assignment for Φ. The unquantified (free) variables then determine the *pp-definable* relation R_Ψ, a projection of R_Φ. Again, we make no distinction between Ψ and R_Ψ.

The set of all Γ-definable relations is denoted by CSP(Γ), and the set of all pp-definable relations is the *relational clone* $\langle\Gamma\rangle$. If $\Gamma = \{H, =\}$, we will just write #CSP(H) and $\langle H\rangle$. An *equivalence relation* in $\langle\Gamma\rangle$ is called a *congruence*.

2.4 Polymorphisms

A *Mal'tsev polymorphism* of Γ is any function $\varphi\colon D^3 \to D$ that preserves all relations in Γ and has the property that $\varphi(a, b, b) = \varphi(b, b, a) = a$ for all $a, b \in D$. (So, in particular, $\varphi(a, a, a) = a$.) φ preserves the r-ary relation $H \in \Gamma$ if, whenever $\mathbf{u}, \mathbf{v}, \mathbf{w} \in H$, then

$$\varphi(\mathbf{u}, \mathbf{v}, \mathbf{w}) = \big(\varphi(u_1, v_1, w_1), \dots, \varphi(u_r, v_r, w_r)\big) \in H\,.$$

It is well known, and easy to prove, that any polymorphism of Γ preserves every relation in $\langle\Gamma\rangle$. See, for example, [7]. In general, polymorphisms may be of any arity but we do not require this.

For clarity, we usually present calculations involving a Mal'tsev polymorphism φ as a four-row table. The first three rows give the triple of "input" tuples $\mathbf{t}_1, \mathbf{t}_2, \mathbf{t}_3$ and the fourth row gives the "output" $\varphi(\mathbf{t}_1, \mathbf{t}_2, \mathbf{t}_3)$. For example, the following table indicates $\varphi(a\mathbf{u}, a\mathbf{v}, b\mathbf{w}) = (b, \varphi(\mathbf{u}, \mathbf{v}, \mathbf{w}))$.

$$\begin{array}{cc} a & \mathbf{u} \\ a & \mathbf{v} \\ b & \mathbf{w} \\ \hline b & \varphi(\mathbf{u}, \mathbf{v}, \mathbf{w}). \end{array}$$

2.5 Complexity

For any alphabet Σ, we denote by FP the class of functions $f\colon \Sigma^* \to \mathbb{N}$ for which there is a deterministic, polynomial-time Turing machine that, given input $x \in \Sigma^*$, writes $f(x)$ (in binary) to its output tape. The class #P is the class of functions $f\colon \Sigma^* \to \mathbb{N}$ for which there is a nondeterministic, polynomial-time Turing machine that has exactly $f(x)$ accepting computations for every input $x \in \Sigma^*$.

Completeness for #P is defined in terms of Turing reductions [27]. Let $f, g\colon \Sigma^* \to \mathbb{N}$. A *Turing reduction* from f to g is a polynomial-time oracle Turing machine that computes f using an oracle for g. A function f is *#P-hard* if there is a Turing reduction to f from every problem in #P and a *#P-complete* function is a #P-hard function in #P.

The class #P plays a role in the complexity of counting problems that is analogous to NP's role in decision problems. Note, however, that, subject to standard complexity-theoretic assumptions, #P-complete problems are computationally much harder than NP-complete problems. Toda has shown that $\mathsf{P}^{\#\mathsf{P}}$ includes the whole of the polynomial time hierarchy [25], of which P^{NP} just one level.

3. RECTANGULAR RELATIONS

A binary relation $B \subseteq A_1 \times A_2$ is called *rectangular* if $(a,c), (a,d), (b,d) \in B$ implies $(b,c) \in B$ for all $a, b \in A_1$, $c, d \in A_2$. We may view B as an undirected bipartite graph $\mathcal{G}_B$, with vertex bipartition A_1, A_2 and edge set $E_B = \{\{a_1, a_2\} : (a_1, a_2) \in B\}$. Note that we do not insist that $A_1 \cap A_2 = \emptyset$ but, if $a \in A_1 \cap A_2$, a is regarded as labelling two distinct vertices, one in A_1 and one in A_2. Formally, A_1 and A_2 should be replaced by the disjoint vertex sets $\{1\} \times A_1$ and $\{2\} \times A_2$ but this would unduly complicate the notation. We will assume that $\mathsf{pr}_i B = A_i$ $(i = 1, 2)$, so that $\mathcal{G}_B$ has no isolated vertices. Where appropriate, we do not distinguish between B and $\mathcal{G}_B$. We will often refer to a bipartite clique in $\mathcal{G}_B$ as a *block*.

Rectangular relations have very simple structure, as shown by the following lemma and its corollaries. The proofs are straightforward.

LEMMA 1. *If B is rectangular, $\mathcal{G}_B$ comprises k bipartite cliques, for some $k \le \min\{|A_1|, |A_2|\}$.*

COROLLARY 2. *The relations*

$$\theta_1(x_1, x_2) \equiv \exists y\, (B(x_1, y) \wedge B(x_2, y))$$
$$\theta_2(y_1, y_2) \equiv \exists x\, (B(x, y_1) \wedge B(x, y_2))$$

are equivalence relations on $\mathsf{pr}_1 B$, $\mathsf{pr}_2 B$ respectively and their equivalence classes are in one-to-one correspondence.

COROLLARY 3. *If Γ is a constraint language, and $B \in \langle\Gamma\rangle$ is rectangular, then the relations θ_1 and θ_2 of Corollary 2 are congruences in $\langle\Gamma\rangle$.*

We call a constraint language Γ *strongly rectangular* if every binary relation $B \in \langle\Gamma\rangle$ is rectangular. If $R \in \langle\Gamma\rangle$ for a strongly rectangular Γ, then R is also strongly rectangular, since $\langle R\rangle \subseteq \langle\Gamma\rangle$. From the definition, it is not clear whether the strong rectangularity of Γ is even decidable, since $\langle\Gamma\rangle$ is an infinite set. However, the key fact is given by the following lemma and decidability follows.

LEMMA 4. *Γ is strongly rectangular if, and only if, it has a Mal'tsev polymorphism.*

PROOF. It is known that $\langle\Gamma\rangle$ has a Mal'tsev polymorphism if, and only if, it is *congruence permutable*. See, for example, [10]. For our purposes, this has the following meaning. Let ρ_1 and ρ_2 be congruences on $A \subseteq D^r$ and define

$$\psi(\mathbf{x}, \mathbf{y}) \equiv \exists \mathbf{z}\, (\rho_1(\mathbf{x}, \mathbf{z}) \wedge \rho_2(\mathbf{z}, \mathbf{y}))\,.$$

Clearly ψ is a pp-definable binary relation on D^r. We say ρ_1 and ρ_2 are permutable if $\psi(\mathbf{u}, \mathbf{v})$ implies $\psi(\mathbf{v}, \mathbf{u})$ for all $\mathbf{u}, \mathbf{v} \in A$. $\langle\Gamma\rangle$ is congruence permutable if all pairs of congruences it contains are permutable.

Suppose that Γ is strongly rectangular and contains congruences ρ_1 and ρ_2, and that $(\mathbf{u}, \mathbf{v}) \in \psi$. Then, we have $(\mathbf{u}, \mathbf{u})$, $(\mathbf{u}, \mathbf{v})$, $(\mathbf{v}, \mathbf{v}) \in \psi$, since ρ_1 and ρ_2 are congruences. But this implies $(\mathbf{v}, \mathbf{u}) \in \psi$ since ψ is rectangular. Thus, strong rectangularity implies permutability of congruences, and hence the existence of a Mal'tsev polymorphism.

Conversely, if Γ has a Mal'tsev polymorphism φ, consider any pp-definable binary relation $B \subseteq D^r \times D^s$. If $(\mathbf{t}, \mathbf{v}), (\mathbf{t}, \mathbf{w}), (\mathbf{u}, \mathbf{w}) \in B$ then we have

$$(\varphi(\mathbf{t}, \mathbf{t}, \mathbf{u}), \varphi(\mathbf{v}, \mathbf{w}, \mathbf{w})) = (\mathbf{u}, \mathbf{v}) \in B\,,$$

from the definition of a Mal'tsev polymorphism. Hence B is rectangular and Γ is strongly rectangular. □

As a result, we can determine whether Γ is strongly rectangular in time $O(\|\Gamma\|^4)$ by testing whether any of the $q^{q(q-1)}$ Mal'tsev operations over D is a polymorphism. In fact, we can do this in time polynomial in $q = |D|$ but we do not pursue the details here, as our focus in the present paper is on the case $q = O(1)$.

Note that the decomposition of a relation R as a binary relation on $A_1 \times A_2$ is not necessarily unique. A consequence Lemma 4 is that, if a relation is strongly rectangular for some such decomposition, it is strongly rectangular for all decompositions. We will use this fact repeatedly, and consider a relation $R \subseteq D^n$ for some $n > 2$ to be a binary relation on $D^k \times D^{n-k}$ or a ternary relation on $D^k \times D^\ell \times D^{n-k-\ell}$ where appropriate. In particular, then, a constraint language is strongly rectangular if every binary relation is rectangular and every n-ary relation with $n > 2$ is rectangular for every decomposition as a binary relation on $D^k \times D^{n-k}$ for all $1 \le k < n$.

Strongly rectangular constraint languages have another useful property. For each $a \in D$, define the *constant relation* $\chi_a = \{(a)\}$. Then the constraint $\chi_a(x_i)$ fixes the value of x_i to be a. Any Mal'tsev operation φ has $\varphi(a, a, a) = a$ so preserves χ_a. This gives the following.

LEMMA 5. *If Γ is strongly rectangular, then $\Gamma' = \Gamma \cup \{\chi_a\}$ also is strongly rectangular.*

In the light of the above results, we may assume that $\{\chi_a : a \in D\} \subseteq \Gamma$, for any strongly rectangular Γ and that we have determined a Mal'tsev polymorphism φ for Γ.

4. THE STRUCTURE OF STRONGLY RECTANGULAR RELATIONS

Let R be a strongly rectangular relation. For any $i \in [n]$, we say that an n-tuple $\mathbf{t} \in R$ is a *witness* for (a, i) if $t_i = a$. If $\mathbf{t} = (\mathbf{u}, a, \mathbf{v}) \in R$ for some $\mathbf{v}$, we call $\mathbf{u}$ a *prefix* for a. Now, for each $i \in [n]$, define a relation $\sim_i$ on $\mathsf{pr}_i R$ by $a \sim_i b$ if, and only if, a and b have a common prefix $\mathbf{u} \in D^{i-1}$.

LEMMA 6. *$\sim_i$ is an equivalence relation on $\mathsf{pr}_i R$, and a congruence in $\langle R \rangle$.*

For $i \in [n]$, let $\sim_i$ have $\kappa_i \leq q$ equivalence classes, and denote these by $\mathcal{E}_{i,k}$ $(1 \leq k \leq \kappa_i)$. Observe that $\kappa_1 = 1$, since all $a \in \mathsf{pr}_1 R$ have witnesses with the common empty prefix. More generally, we have the following.

COROLLARY 7. *For each $k \in [\kappa_i]$ and $i \in [n]$, there is a common prefix $\mathbf{u}_{i,k} \in D^{i-1}$ for all $a \in \mathcal{E}_{i,k}$, and we can choose $\mathbf{u}_{i,k}$ to be any prefix of any $a \in \mathcal{E}_{i,k}$.*

Following Bulatov and Dalmau [4], if H is any relation and φ a Mal'tsev operation, then we write $\mathsf{cl}_\varphi H$ for the smallest relation closed under φ that contains H. That is, $\mathsf{cl}_\varphi H$ is the $\subseteq$-least relation H' that contains H and has the property that $\varphi(\mathbf{u}, \mathbf{v}, \mathbf{w}) \in H'$ for all $\mathbf{u}, \mathbf{v}, \mathbf{w} \in H'$. (So we have $H' \subseteq H''$ for any other H'' that contains H and is closed under φ.) $\mathsf{cl}_\varphi H$ is strongly rectangular and, by definition, has polymorphism φ. We say that the H *generates* $\mathsf{cl}_\varphi H$. The following observation is from [4].

LEMMA 8. *Let H be an n-ary relation. For any $I \subseteq [n]$, we have $\mathsf{cl}_\varphi \mathsf{pr}_I H = \mathsf{pr}_I \mathsf{cl}_\varphi H$.*

Let $S = \{\mathbf{t}_1, \mathbf{t}_2, \ldots, \mathbf{t}_s\}$ be a set of n-tuples, presented as an $s \times n$ matrix. For $I \subseteq [n]$, we will need to compute efficiently a relation $T \subseteq \mathsf{cl}_\varphi S$ such that $\mathsf{pr}_I T = \mathsf{cl}_\varphi \mathsf{pr}_I S = \mathsf{pr}_I \mathsf{cl}_\varphi S$.

LEMMA 9. *If $\ell = |\mathsf{pr}_I \mathsf{cl}_\varphi S|$ and $s = |S|$, then a relation $T \subseteq \mathsf{cl}_\varphi S$ such that $\mathsf{pr}_I T = \mathsf{pr}_I \mathsf{cl}_\varphi S$ can be computed in time $O(n\ell^3 + s\ell^4)$.*

PROOF. By the following algorithm CLOSURE(I).

```
1: ℓ ← s, j1 ← 2
2: while j1 ≤ ℓ do
3:   for j2 ∈ [j1] do
4:     for j3 ∈ [j2] do
5:       for all permutations (k1, k2, k3) of {j1, j2, j3}
         such that k2 ≠ k1, k3 do
6:         u ← φ(t_k1, t_k2, t_k3)
7:         if there is no j ∈ [ℓ] such that pr_I t_j = pr_I u
           then
8:           ℓ ← ℓ + 1, t_ℓ ← u
9:   j1 ← j1 + 1
```

The correctness of CLOSURE is trivial. At termination, all ℓ^3 triples (k_1, k_2, k_3) with $k_1, k_2, k_3 \in [\ell]$ have been considered for generating new n-tuples (in line 6), so we have computed $\mathsf{cl}_\varphi \mathsf{pr}_I S$. The analysis is equally easy. There are ℓ^3 triples (k_1, k_2, k_3). For each triple, the generation in line 6 takes $O(n)$ time and the search in line 7 requires $O(s\ell)$ time, with the obvious implementations. Thus, the total time is $O(n\ell^3 + s\ell^4)$. $\square$

The procedure outlined in [4] has complexity $O(n\ell^4 + s\ell^5)$, since the same triple (k_1, k_2, k_3) can appear $\Omega(\ell)$ times. The procedure CLOSURE simply avoids this.

Now we define a *frame* for an n-ary relation R to be a set $F \subseteq R$ such that:

(a) $\mathsf{pr}_i F = \mathsf{pr}_i R$ for each $i \in [n]$; and

(b) for each equivalence class $\mathcal{E}_{i,k}$ of $\sim_i$, there is a $\mathbf{v}_{i,k} \in D^{i-1}$ such that, for each $a \in \mathcal{E}_{i,k}$, there exists a $\mathbf{w}_a \in F$ with $\mathsf{pr}_{[i]} \mathbf{w}_a = \mathbf{v}_{i,k} a$.

Clearly, R itself satisfies the definition of a frame, so every relation has at least one frame. However, we will show that strongly rectangular relations have frames that can be much smaller than R and we call a frame for a strongly rectangular relation $R \subseteq D^n$ *small* if $|F| \leq 1 + n(q-1)$.

A *witness function* for a frame F of the relation R is a function $\boldsymbol{\omega}$ with codomain F such that $\boldsymbol{\omega}(a, i)$ witnesses (a, i) for all $a \in \mathsf{pr}_i R$ and $i \in [n]$ and $\mathsf{pr}_{[i-1]} \boldsymbol{\omega}(a, i) = \mathsf{pr}_{[i-1]} \boldsymbol{\omega}(b, i)$ when $a \sim_i b$.

LEMMA 10. *Let F be a frame for a strongly rectangular relation $R \subseteq D^n$. We can determine a small frame F' for R and a surjective witness function $\boldsymbol{\omega}' : D \times [n] \to F'$ in time $O(\|F\| + n^2)$.*

PROOF. For each $i \in [n]$ and $a \in \mathsf{pr}_i F$, determine a witness $\mathbf{w} \in F$ for (a, i) and set $\boldsymbol{\omega}(a, i) \leftarrow \mathbf{w}$. Then, for any $\mathbf{t} \in F$ such that $\boldsymbol{\omega}^{-1}(\mathbf{t}) = \emptyset$, set $F \leftarrow F \setminus \{\mathbf{t}\}$. Now we have a surjective witness function $\boldsymbol{\omega}$, and the computation clearly requires $O(\|F\|)$ time. Since $\boldsymbol{\omega}$ is surjective, we now have $|F| \leq |D \times [n]| = nq$. However, F is not necessarily a frame any more.

Now we construct F' and $\boldsymbol{\omega}'$ as follows. Choose any $\mathbf{f} \in F$, and set $F' = \{\mathbf{f}\}$. Then, for each $i = 1, 2, \ldots, n$, do the following. First check whether $\boldsymbol{\omega}(f_i, i) = \mathbf{g} \neq \mathbf{f}$. If so, set $\boldsymbol{\omega}'(f_i, i) \leftarrow \mathbf{f}$. Now, for each $a \neq f_i$ with $a \sim_i f_i$, suppose $\mathbf{h} = \boldsymbol{\omega}(a, i)$. Note that $\mathbf{g}$ and $\mathbf{h}$ have the same prefix $\mathbf{u}' \in D^{i-1}$, since F is a frame, and suppose $\mathbf{f}$ has prefix $\mathbf{u} \in D^{i-1}$. Then set $\mathbf{h}' \leftarrow \varphi(\mathbf{f}, \mathbf{g}, \mathbf{h})$, $F' \leftarrow F' \cup \{\mathbf{h}'\}$ and $\boldsymbol{\omega}'(a, i) \leftarrow \mathbf{h}'$. Since

$$\begin{array}{ccccc} \mathbf{f} & : & \mathbf{u} & f_i & \mathbf{v} \\ \mathbf{g} & : & \mathbf{u}' & f_i & \mathbf{v}' \\ \mathbf{h} & : & \mathbf{u}' & a & \mathbf{v}_a \\ \hline \mathbf{h}' & : & \mathbf{u} & a & \varphi(\mathbf{v}, \mathbf{v}', \mathbf{v}_a), \end{array}$$

this ensures that F' retains property (b) of a frame. Now, for all $a \in \mathsf{pr}_i F$ with $a \not\sim_i f_i$, set $F' \leftarrow F' \cup \{\boldsymbol{\omega}(a, i)\}$ and $\boldsymbol{\omega}'(a, i) \leftarrow \boldsymbol{\omega}(a, i)$.

The final size of F' can be bounded as follows. The tuple $\mathbf{f}$ witnesses (f_i, i) for all $i \in [n]$. Then, for each $i \in [n]$, there is at most one tuple in F' witnessing (a, i) for each $a \in \mathsf{pr}_i R \setminus \{f_i\}$. Since there are, in total,

$$\sum_{i=1}^{n} (|\mathsf{pr}_i R| - 1) \leq n(q-1)$$

such pairs (a, i), it follows that F' is a small frame.

The time bound is easy. Given the function $\boldsymbol{\omega}$, we can determine the $\mathbf{h}'$ in $O(n)$ time for each $i \in [n]$. All other operations require $O(1)$ time for each $i \in [n]$. Thus we need only $O(n^2)$ time once we have determined $\boldsymbol{\omega}$. The total time is, therefore, $O(\|F\| + n^2)$. $\square$

The bound $\|F\| \leq n(q-1)+1$ is tight: the complete relation D^n has no smaller frame. However, other relations have smaller frames. In particular, any n-ary relation R with fewer than $n(q-1)+1$ tuples has the small frame $F = R$. Bulatov and Dalmau's *compact representations* [4] are not necessarily frames, and can have size $nq^2/2$. However, it appears that a frame could be constructed efficiently from such a representation using methods similar to those of Lemma 10.

We assume from this point that all frames are small, implicitly applying Lemma 10 as needed. We have not defined frames for R as being able to generate R, since this is entailed by the following.

LEMMA 11. *If R is strongly rectangular, and F is a frame for R, then $\mathsf{cl}_\varphi F = R$.*

PROOF. $F \subseteq R$ so $\mathsf{cl}_\varphi F \subseteq \mathsf{cl}_\varphi R = R$.

For the converse inclusion, we inductively construct any $\mathbf{t} = (t_1, t_2, \ldots, t_n) \in R$. Suppose we have constructed $\mathbf{t}' \in R$ so that $\mathsf{pr}_{[i-1]}\mathbf{t}' = \mathsf{pr}_{[i-1]}\mathbf{t} = \mathbf{u}$, say. The base case $i = 1$ is trivial. For $i > 1$, write $\mathbf{t} = (\mathbf{u}, t_i, \mathbf{v})$ and take any $\mathbf{t}' = (\mathbf{u}, t'_i, \mathbf{v}') \in R$, with $t_i \sim_i t'_i$. F contains witnesses $(\mathbf{u}', t_i, \mathbf{w})$ and $(\mathbf{u}', t'_i, \mathbf{w}')$ for (t_i, i) and (t'_i, i) with a common prefix $\mathbf{u}'$. Thus we have

$$\begin{array}{ccc} \mathbf{u} & t'_i & \mathbf{v}' \\ \mathbf{u}' & t'_i & \mathbf{w}' \\ \mathbf{u}' & t_i & \mathbf{w} \\ \hline \mathbf{u} & t_i & \varphi(\mathbf{v}', \mathbf{w}', \mathbf{w}). \end{array}$$

Writing $\mathbf{t}''$ for this last tuple, we have $\mathbf{t}'' \in \mathsf{cl}_\varphi F$ and $\mathsf{pr}_{[i]}\mathbf{t}'' = \mathsf{pr}_{[i]}\mathbf{t}$, continuing the induction. □

Given φ and the matrix for F, the procedure of Lemma 11 can be used to decide $\mathbf{t} \in R$ in time $O(n^2)$. If the procedure fails at any step, then we have $t'_i \not\sim_i t_i$. Suppose there is any $\mathbf{t}'' \in R$ which agrees with t in its first $i-1$ places. Then $t'_i \sim_i t_i$ and (t_i, i) and (t'_i, i) will have witnesses in F with a common prefix, so the procedure will not fail. Thus $\mathbf{t}''$ cannot exist and so either $\mathbf{t} \notin R$ or we have shown that R is not strongly rectangular.

The following lemma will be used repeatedly to manipulate frames.

LEMMA 12. *Given a frame F for a relation $R(x_1, \ldots, x_n)$, a frame for*

$$R(a_1, \ldots, a_i, x_{i+1}, \ldots, x_n) = \{\mathbf{t} \in R : (t_1, \ldots, t_i) = (a_1, \ldots, a_i)\}$$

can be constructed in $O(n^3)$ time.

PROOF. We write $R(a, \cdot)$ for $R(a, x_2, \ldots, x_n)$ and show that we can construct a frame for this relation in $O(n^2)$ time. The result follows by a simple induction on $i \leq n$.

For each $j = 2, \ldots, n$, determine $\mathsf{cl}_\varphi \mathsf{pr}_{1,j} F = \mathsf{pr}_{1,j} \mathsf{cl}_\varphi F = \mathsf{pr}_{1,j} R$. We perform the calculation on all n columns of R. Note that $|\mathsf{pr}_{1,j} R| \leq q^2 = O(1)$, so this requires $O(n)$ time for each i, and $O(n^2)$ time in total.

We have $(a, b) \in \mathsf{pr}_{1,j} R$ if, and only if, $b \in \mathsf{pr}_j R(a, \cdot)$. Also, we have calculated a witness for each $b \in \mathsf{pr}_j R(a, \cdot)$. Let $\sim_j$ be the usual congruence for R and $\sim'_j$ the corresponding congruence for $R(a, \cdot)$. Clearly $b \sim'_j c$ implies $b \sim_j c$, since there are witnesses $(a, \mathbf{u}, b, \mathbf{v}), (a, \mathbf{u}, c, \mathbf{v}') \in R$. On the other hand, if $b \sim_j c$ and $b \in \mathsf{pr}_j R(a, \cdot)$, then $b \sim'_j c$, since we have

$$\begin{array}{cccc} a & \mathbf{u} & b & \mathbf{v} \\ a' & \mathbf{u}' & b & \mathbf{v}' \\ a' & \mathbf{u}' & c & \mathbf{v}'' \\ \hline a & \mathbf{u} & c & \varphi(\mathbf{v}, \mathbf{v}', \mathbf{v}''). \end{array}$$

Thus, the equivalence classes of $\sim'_j$ are a subset of those of $\sim_j$. Therefore, we can easily construct $\sim'_j$, and a witness for each $b \in \mathsf{pr}_j R(a, \cdot)$, using F and the n-tuples from the calculation of $\mathsf{pr}_{1,j} R$. □

5. CONSTRUCTING A FRAME

If R is Γ-definable, then $\mathbf{t} \in R$ can be decided in polynomial time by checking that $\mathbf{t}$ satisfies each of the defining constraints. However we cannot use this method to decide efficiently whether $R = \emptyset$. But we can decide whether $R = \emptyset$ trivially using any frame F for R, since $R = \emptyset$ if, and only if, $F = \emptyset$. If $F \neq \emptyset$, then any $\mathbf{f} \in F$ is a certificate that $R \neq \emptyset$. Similarly, given a frame for R and any tuple $(a_1, \ldots, a_i)$, we can determine whether there is any $\mathbf{t} \in R$ such that $(t_1, \ldots, t_i) = (a_1, \ldots, a_i)$, using Lemma 12.

We must be able to construct some frame F for R efficiently. If Γ is strongly rectangular, we show how to determine a frame for a Γ-formula Φ having m constraints in n variables, in time polynomial in m, n and $\|\Gamma\|$. This is achieved, as in [4], by adding constraints sequentially. If the m constraints are $\Theta_1, \Theta_2, \ldots, \Theta_m$, let $\Phi_s = \Theta_1 \wedge \Theta_2 \wedge \cdots \wedge \Theta_s$. Thus $\Phi_0 = D^n$ and $\Phi_m = \Phi$.

LEMMA 13. *A small frame F_0 for Φ_0 can be constructed in $O(n^2)$ time.*

PROOF. Let d be any element of D, and let $F_0 = \{\mathbf{t}^d\} \cup \{\mathbf{t}^{a,i} : i \in [n], a \in D \setminus d\}$, where

$$t^d_j = d \quad \text{and} \quad t^{a,i}_j = \begin{cases} a & \text{if } j = i \\ d & \text{otherwise} \end{cases} \qquad (j \in [n]). \qquad \square$$

Note that the frame constructed has size $1 + n(q-1)$. It is not hard to see that no smaller frame exists for the complete relation, which establishes that the bound on the size of small frames is strict.

Now, we show how to determine a frame for Φ_s given a frame for Φ_{s-1}. We show that this can be done in polynomial time when $\|\Gamma\| = O(1)$, which is non-uniform CSP, the most important case. We can also construct a frame in time polynomial in $\|\Gamma\|$ and Φ but our focus here is on the non-uniform case.

LEMMA 14. *Given a frame F for Φ and a constraint Θ, a frame F' for $\Phi' = \Phi \wedge \Theta$ can be constructed in $O(n^4)$ time.*

PROOF. Suppose that $\Theta = H(x_{i_1}, x_{i_2}, \ldots, x_{i_r})$, where $H \in \Gamma$ has arity r. We will assume that $x_{i_1}, x_{i_2}, \ldots, x_{i_r}$ are distinct since, otherwise, we can consider a smaller relation H' over the distinct variables. Let $I = \{i_1, i_2, \ldots, i_r\}$. For each $i \in [n]$, let $J = I \cup \{i\}$, and determine $T_i \subseteq \Phi$ such that $\mathsf{pr}_J T_i = \mathsf{cl}_\varphi \mathsf{pr}_J \Phi$ using CLOSURE. If $\ell = |\mathsf{pr}_I \Phi|$, then $|T_i| \leq q\ell$, so this takes time $O(n\ell^3 + r\ell^4)$ by Lemma 9. But, since $\|\Gamma\| = O(1)$, we have $r = O(1)$, $\ell \leq q^r = O(1)$ and $O(n\ell^3 + r\ell^4) = O(n)$. The entire computation for all i therefore takes time $O(n^2)$, and we have $\sum_i |T_i| = O(n)$.

Determine U_i, the set of tuples in T_i that are consistent with Θ, so $U_i \subseteq \Phi'$. Now U_i contains a witness for each $a \in \mathsf{pr}_i\Phi'$, since

$$\begin{aligned}\mathsf{pr}_J U_i &= \mathsf{cl}_\varphi \mathsf{pr}_J F \cap \Theta \\ &= \mathsf{pr}_J \Phi \cap \Theta \\ &= \mathsf{pr}_J(\Phi \wedge \Theta) \\ &= \mathsf{pr}_J \Phi'.\end{aligned}$$

Thus, in particular, $\mathsf{pr}_i U_i = \mathsf{pr}_i \Phi'$. We now do the following for each $i \in [n]$.

Let $\mathcal{A} \leftarrow \mathsf{pr}_i U_i$, and repeat the following until $\mathcal{A} = \emptyset$. Choose $\mathbf{t} \in U_i$ with $t_i \in \mathcal{A}$. Determine a frame $F^\star$ for $\Phi(t_1, \ldots, t_{i-1}, x_i, \ldots, x_n)$ by Lemma 12. We have $\mathbf{t} \in \mathsf{cl}_\varphi F^\star$, so $F^\star \neq \emptyset$. Now determine the intersection of the relation $R^\star$ generated by $F^\star$ with Θ, using CLOSURE, as above. This takes $O(n)$ time; let the resulting relation be R°. Now, by Corollary 7, $\mathsf{pr}_i R^\circ$ is the equivalence class $\mathcal{E} = \{a : a \sim'_i t_i\}$ of t_i in Φ'. For each $a \in \mathcal{E}$, we can find a witness $\omega'(a, i) \in R^\circ$ for $a \in \mathsf{pr}_i \Phi'$, all with common prefix $(t_1, \ldots, t_{i-1})$. We set $\mathcal{A} \leftarrow \mathcal{A} \setminus \mathcal{E}$, and repeat.

At the end of this process, ω' is a witness function for a frame F' for Φ'. The total time required is $O(n^3|F'|) = O(n^4)$. □

COROLLARY 15. *A frame F for Φ can be constructed in time $O(mn^4)$.*

PROOF. Construct Φ_0 in $O(n^2)$ time. Then, for each $i \in [m]$, apply Lemma 14 to construct a frame F_i for Φ_i from a frame F_{i-1} for Φ_{i-1}. At termination, we have $\Phi \leftarrow \Phi_m$ and $F \leftarrow F_m$. □

Since a relation has $\emptyset$ for a frame if, and only if, it is empty (and $\emptyset$ has no other frame), we can determine in time $O(mn^4)$ whether there is a satisfying assignment to a CSP instance in a fixed strongly rectangular vocabulary. By Lemma 4, we have re-proven the main result of [4], which states that there is a polynomial-time algorithm for CSP(Γ) for any constraint language Γ that has a Mal'tsev polymorphism. We improve on that result by giving an explicit time bound for our algorithm.

6. COUNTING PROBLEMS

We consider the problem #CSP(Γ) of determining $|R_\Phi|$, which we abbreviate to $|\Phi|$, where Φ is a Γ-formula with m constraints and n variables. For fixed Γ, we require the computations to be done in time polynomial in the size of the input Φ. This is bounded by a polynomial in n, since there are only $O(n^r)$ distinct constraints in an r-ary relation in Γ and repeated constraints may be discarded without changing R_Φ. We use the following result, due to Bulatov and Dalmau [5], which we restate in our terminology; the corollary is immediate.

THEOREM 16. *Let (D, Γ_1) and (D, Γ_2) be relational structures with $\Gamma_2 \subseteq \langle\Gamma_1\rangle$. Then #CSP($\Gamma_2$) is polynomial time reducible to #CSP(Γ_1).*

COROLLARY 17. *If $H \in \langle\Gamma\rangle$ and #CSP(H) is #P-complete, then #CSP(Γ) is #P-complete.*

First, we apply Corollary 17 to give a short proof of the main result of [5].

LEMMA 18. *#CSP(Γ) is #P-complete for any Γ that is not strongly rectangular.*

PROOF. Clearly #CSP(Γ) ∈ #P for any Γ. If Γ is not strongly rectangular, there is a non-rectangular binary $B \in \langle\Gamma\rangle$. Let $G = (V, E)$ be an undirected bipartite graph with bipartition V_1, V_2. Let Φ_1 be the Γ-formula with a constraint $B(x_i, x_j)$ for each $\{\nu_i, \nu_j\} \in E$ with $\nu_i \in V_1$, $\nu_j \in V_2$. Define Φ_2 analogously, but with constraints $B(x_j, x_i)$.

$|\Phi_1| + |\Phi_2|$ is the number of graph homomorphisms from G to $\mathcal{G}_B$ and computing this is #P-complete by [14], since $\mathcal{G}_B$ has a component which is not a complete bipartite graph. Thus #CSP(B) is #P-complete, and hence #CSP(Γ) is #P-complete by Corollary 17. □

There is an important generalisation of the counting problem to *weighted* problems which we now describe briefly; see [6, 12] for details. The relations $H \subseteq D^r$ in Γ are replaced by functions $f\colon D^r \to \mathbb{Q}^+$, where $\mathbb{Q}^+$ denotes the non-negative rationals.[1] Thus Γ is replaced by a set of functions $\mathcal{F}$. We will call $(D, \mathcal{F})$ a *weighted structure*. The *underlying relation* of $f \in \mathcal{F}$ is $\{\mathbf{u} \in D^r : f(\mathbf{u}) > 0\}$. Note that a relation H can be identified with a function $f_H\colon D^r \to \{0, 1\}$, where $f_H(\mathbf{u}) = 1$ if, and only if, $\mathbf{u} \in H$. Then H is the underlying relation of f_H and we may write H to denote the function f_H without any ambiguity.

Now, using notation similar to the relational case, an instance $\mathcal{I}$ of #CSP($\mathcal{F}$) is defined as follows. A constraint Θ has the form $f(\nu_{i_1}, \nu_{i_2}, \ldots, \nu_{i_r})$ for some r-ary function $f \in \mathcal{F}$. Thus $(\nu_{i_1}, \nu_{i_2}, \ldots, \nu_{i_r})$ is the scope of Θ. Suppose we have constraints $\Theta_1, \ldots, \Theta_m$, where Θ_s applies the function $f_s \in \mathcal{F}$. Write $\mathbf{x}_s$ for $(x_{i_1}, x_{i_2}, \ldots, x_{i_r})$, where $(\nu_{i_1}, \nu_{i_2}, \ldots, \nu_{i_r})$ is the scope of the Θ_s. Then, the *weight* of an assignment $\mathbf{x}\colon V \to D$ is the product of the weights generated by the constraints:

$$\mathsf{W}(\mathbf{x}) = \prod_{s=1}^{m} f_s(\mathbf{x}_s).$$

The computational problem #CSP($\mathcal{F}$) is then to compute the *partition function*

$$Z(\mathcal{I}) = \sum_{\mathbf{x}\colon V \to D} \mathsf{W}(\mathbf{x}).$$

If $\mathcal{F} = \{f\}$ for a single function f, we write #CSP(f).

We use the following generalization of a result of Dyer and Greenhill [14] to the weighted case, due to Bulatov and Grohe [6]. The result applies to more general classes of weights but natural numbers suffice for our requirements.

THEOREM 19. *Let $f\colon A_1 \times A_2 \to \mathbb{N}$ be a binary function. Then #CSP(f) is in FP if there is a rectangular relation B and functions $\alpha_1\colon A_1 \to \mathbb{N}$ and $\alpha_2\colon A_2 \to \mathbb{N}$ such that $f(x, y) = \alpha_1(x)\alpha_2(y)B(x, y)$, for all $x \in A_1$, $y \in A_2$. Otherwise #CSP(f) is #P-hard.*

We may view a binary function $f\colon A_1 \times A_2 \to \mathbb{N}$ as a matrix with elements in $\mathbb{N}$ and rows and columns indexed by A_1 and A_2. A binary function f satisfying the condition of Theorem 19 will be called a *rank-one block matrix*, as the condition is equivalent to the matrix f decomposing into blocks of rank one (which implies that the underlying relation is rectangular).

[1]More generally, we can take the function values to be non-negative algebraic numbers.

LEMMA 20. *A rank-one block matrix $f\colon A_1 \times A_2 \to \mathbb{Q}^+$ is uniquely determined by its underlying relation and row and column totals.*

PROOF. Let B be the underlying (rectangular) relation. Consider any block C of B, with $\mathsf{pr}_1 C = S_1$, $\mathsf{pr}_2 C = S_2$. Then there exist $\alpha_1 : S_1 \to \mathbb{Q}^+$ and $\alpha_2 : S_2 \to \mathbb{Q}^+$ such that $f(x_1, x_2) = \alpha_1(x_1)\alpha_2(x_2)$ for every $x_1 \in S_1$ and $x_2 \in S_2$. Now, let

$$f(x_1,\cdot) = \sum_{x_2\in S_2} f(x_1,x_2) = \alpha_1(x_1)\sum_{x_2\in S_2}\alpha_2(x_2)$$
$$f(\cdot,x_2) = \sum_{x_1\in S_1} f(x_1,x_2) = \alpha_2(x_2)\sum_{x_1\in S_1}\alpha_1(x_1)$$
$$f(\cdot,\cdot) = \sum_{x_1\in S_1} f(x_1,\cdot) = \sum_{x_1\in S_1}\alpha_1(x_1)\sum_{x_2\in S_2}\alpha_2(x_2)$$

be the row, column and grand totals of $f(x_1, x_2)$, for $x_1 \in S_1$ and $x_2 \in S_2$. A simple calculation gives

$$f(x_1,x_2) = \frac{f(x_1,\cdot)f(\cdot,x_2)}{f(\cdot,\cdot)}. \qquad \square$$

7. THE DICHOTOMY THEOREM

We are now ready to introduce the dichotomy. We saw in the previous section that (assuming that $\mathsf{FP} \neq \#\mathsf{P}$) strong rectangularity is a necessary condition for tractability. In this section, we introduce a stronger condition, based on certain rank-one block matrices and show that it characterizes the FP/#P-complete dichotomy for #CSP.

We say that a ternary relation $H(x, y, z)$ on $A_1 \times A_2 \times A_3$ is *balanced* if the *balance matrix*

$$M(x,y) = |\{z \in A_3 : (x,y,z) \in H\}| \qquad (x \in A_1,\ y \in A_2)$$

is a rank-one block matrix. A relation $R \subseteq D^n$ of arity $n > 4$ is balanced if every expression of it as a ternary relation in $D^k \times D^\ell \times D^m$ ($k, \ell, m \geq 1$, $k+\ell+m = n$) is balanced. We say that Γ is *strongly balanced* if every pp-definable relation of arity three or more is balanced. It is straightforward to show that every strongly-balanced relation is strongly rectangular. Below, we refer to ternary relations, which may be relations over powers of D, as well as relations in D^3.

We will prove the following. Although we phrase the criterion rather differently, Theorem 21 can be shown to be equivalent to Bulatov's dichotomy [3] that $\#\mathsf{CSP}(\Gamma)$ is in FP if Γ is "congruence-singular" and #P-complete, otherwise.

THEOREM 21. *If Γ is strongly balanced, $\#\mathsf{CSP}(\Gamma)$ is in FP. Otherwise $\#\mathsf{CSP}(\Gamma)$ is #P-complete.*

PROOF. If Γ is strongly balanced, $\#\mathsf{CSP}(\Gamma) \in \mathsf{FP}$ by Lemma 22 below.

Otherwise, there is an unbalanced ternary relation $H \in \langle\Gamma\rangle$. Let E be a binary relation with $V = V_1 \cup V_2$, $V_1 \cap V_2 = \emptyset$ and $\mathsf{pr}_i E = V_i$ ($i = 1, 2$). Let Φ be the Γ-formula with a constraint $H(x_i, x_j, z_{ij})$ for each $(\nu_i, \nu_j) \in E$. Thus Φ has $|V| + |E|$ variables and $|E|$ constraints. Let $M\colon A_1 \times A_2 \to \mathbb{Q}^+$ be Φ's balance matrix.

We have $|\Phi| = Z(\mathcal{I})$, where $Z(\mathcal{I})$ is the partition function for an instance $\mathcal{I}$ of $\#\mathsf{CSP}(M)$ with input E. But this problem is #P-hard by Theorem 19, which means that $\#\mathsf{CSP}(H)$ is #P-complete. Therefore, $\#\mathsf{CSP}(\Gamma)$ is #P-complete by Corollary 17. $\square$

It remains to prove the polynomial-time case.

LEMMA 22. *Let Γ be strongly balanced and let $R \in \langle\Gamma\rangle$ be an n-ary relation. Given a frame F for R, $|R|$ can be computed in $O(n^5)$ time.*

PROOF. If $n = 1$ then $R = \mathsf{pr}_1 R = \mathsf{pr}_1 F = F$ so $|R| = |F|$ and we are done. We may, therefore, assume that $n \geq 2$. For $2 \leq i \leq\leq j \leq n$, define the function $N_{i,j}\colon \mathsf{pr}_j R \to \mathbb{N}$ by

$$N_{i,j}(a) = |\{(\mathbf{u}, a) \in \mathsf{pr}_{[i-1]\cup\{j\}} R\}|.$$

Thus

$$N_{2,j}(a) = |\{b \in \mathsf{pr}_1 R : (b,a) \in \mathsf{pr}_{1,j} R\}|$$

for each $j \in [2, n]$. By Lemma 9, we can use F to determine each $\mathsf{pr}_{1,j} R$, in total time $O(n\ell^3 + |F|\ell^4)$, where $\ell = |\mathsf{pr}_{1,j} R|$. We have $\ell \leq q^2 = O(1)$ and F may be assumed to be small so $|F| = O(n)$. Therefore, we can determine the functions $N_{2,j}$ in total time $O(n^2)$.

Since we have

$$|R| = \sum_{a\in \mathsf{pr}_n R} N_{n,n}(a),$$

we need to compute the function $N_{n,n}$. We do this using $N_{i,i}$ and $N_{i,j}$ to compute $N_{i+1,j}$ for $j = i+1, \ldots, n$. We repeat these computations for each $i = 2, \ldots, n$.

Fix i and j. Let $J = [i] \cup \{j\}$, and let $H = \mathsf{pr}_J R$, which we express as a ternary relation

$$H = \{(\mathbf{u}, x, y) \in \mathsf{pr}_J R : \mathbf{u} \in \mathsf{pr}_{[i-1]} R,\ x \in \mathsf{pr}_i R,\ y \in \mathsf{pr}_j R\}.$$

Since R is strongly balanced, the balance matrix

$$M(x,y) = |\{\mathbf{u} \in \mathsf{pr}_{[i-1]} R : (\mathbf{u}, x, y) \in H\}|$$

is a rank-one block matrix. The block structure of M is given by the relation $\mathsf{pr}_{i,j} R$, since if $(x, y) \in \mathsf{pr}_{i,j} R$, there is a $\mathbf{t} \in R$ such that $\mathsf{pr}_i \mathbf{t} = x$ and $\mathsf{pr}_j \mathbf{t} = y$. By Lemma 9, we can compute $\mathsf{pr}_{i,j} R$ in $O(n)$ time, using F.

For notational simplicity, let us write $\mathcal{D}_i = \mathsf{pr}_i R$. Consider the y column of M, $M(\cdot, y)$.

$$\begin{aligned}\sum_{x\in\mathcal{D}_i} M(x,y) &= \sum_{x\in\mathcal{D}_i} |\{\mathbf{u} : (\mathbf{u},x,y) \in H\}| \\ &= |\{(\mathbf{u},x) : (\mathbf{u},x,y) \in H\}| \\ &= N_{i+1,j}(y). \end{aligned} \tag{1}$$

By Lemma 5, the relation

$$B_y(\mathbf{u}, x) = \{(\mathbf{u}, x) : (\mathbf{u}, x, y) \in H\}$$

is rectangular. Let $S_y(x) = \{\mathbf{u} : (\mathbf{u}, x, y) \in H\}$. By Corollary 2, there is an equivalence relation on $\mathcal{D}_j$, given by

$$\theta_y(x_1, x_2) \equiv \exists \mathbf{u}\,(H(\mathbf{u}, x_1, y) \wedge H(\mathbf{u}, x_2, y)),$$

such that $S_y(x_1)$ and $S_y(x_2)$ are equal, if $\theta_y(x_1, x_2)$, and disjoint, otherwise. Thus, if $\mathcal{S}(y) \subseteq \mathcal{D}_i$ contains one representative of each equivalence class of θ_y, then

$$\sum_{x\in\mathcal{S}(y)} M(x,y) = |\{\mathbf{u} : \exists x\,(\mathbf{u},x,y) \in H\}| = N_{i,j}(y). \tag{2}$$

Now suppose that $\theta_y(x_1, x_2)$ and $y' \neq y$. Thus, $H(\mathbf{u}, x_1, y)$, $H(\mathbf{u}, x_2, y)$ for some $\mathbf{u}$, so $(x_1, y), (x_2, y) \in C$ for some block C of $\mathsf{pr}_{i,j} R$. There is $\mathbf{u}'$ such that $H(\mathbf{u}', x_1, y')$ if, and only if, $(x_1, y') \in C$. But then we have

$$\begin{array}{ccc} \mathbf{u}' & x_1 & y' \\ \mathbf{u} & x_1 & y \\ \mathbf{u} & x_2 & y \\ \hline \mathbf{u}' & x_2 & y', \end{array}$$

and, hence, $\theta_{y'}(x_1, x_2)$. Thus the equivalence relations θ_y depend only on the block C containing y.

We now define the relations

$$\begin{aligned} x_1 \sim_{i,j} x_2 &\iff \exists \mathbf{u}, y\,(H(\mathbf{u}, x_1, y) \wedge H(\mathbf{u}, x_2, y)) \\ y_1 \sim_{j,i} y_2 &\iff \exists \mathbf{u}, x\,(H(\mathbf{u}, x, y_1) \wedge H(\mathbf{u}, x, y_2)). \end{aligned}$$

The notation is unambiguous, since $i < j$. These relations can be shown to be congruences in $\langle R \rangle$ and computable in time $O(n^5)$. We may deduce the equivalence classes of θ_y from $\mathsf{pr}_{i,j}R$ and the classes of $\sim_{i,j}$. It follows that M has identical columns corresponding to the equivalence classes of $\sim_{i,j}$ and, similarly, identical rows according to $\sim_{j,i}$. If the $S'(x)$ contain one representative of each class of the corresponding congruence θ'_x, we have

$$\sum_{y \in S'(x)} M(x,y) = |\{\mathbf{u} : \exists y\,(\mathbf{u}, x, y) \in H\}| = N_{i,i}(x). \quad (3)$$

Now the matrix $\widehat{M}$, obtained by choosing one representative from each of the equivalence classes of $\sim_{i,j}$ and $\sim_{j,i}$, is also a rank-one block matrix. Moreover, we know the block structure, row and column sums of $\widehat{M}$, from $\mathsf{pr}_{i,j}R$, $\sim_{i,j}$, $\sim_{j,i}$, (2) and (3). Hence, by Lemma 20, we can reconstruct all the entries of $\widehat{M}$. Then, using $\mathsf{pr}_{i,j}R$, $\sim_{i,j}$ and $\sim_{j,i}$, we can reconstruct the matrix M. Finally we compute the row sums, as in equation (1), to give the values of $N_{i+1,j}(a)$ for each $a \in \mathsf{pr}_j R$.

Note that the time complexity of the algorithm is $O(n)$ for a given i and j, even in the bit-complexity model. Since there are $O(n^2)$ pairs i, j, the overall complexity is $O(n^3)$. However, our algorithm for computing the congruences $\sim_{i,j}$ and $\sim_{j,i}$ takes total time $O(n^5)$. □

The time complexity of this algorithm is $O(n^5)$ but constructing F already takes time $O(mn^4)$. We may assume that $m = \Omega(n)$ as, otherwise, there is a variable which appears in no constraint and can be removed to give an instance on the remaining variables. Thus the cost of the counting algorithm is no worse than the $O(mn^4) = O(n^5)$ complexity of computing F.

8. CONCLUSIONS

The principal question that remains open is the decidability of strong balance and, hence, of the dichotomy. We believe it to be decidable but, so far, we have not succeeded in proving this. We have not yet dealt with the extension to the weighted counting problem but, again, we believe this can be done. A third issue is to see how known counting dichotomies can be recovered from this general theorem and we have some preliminary results in this direction.

Finally, a deeper question that arises from our proof is to what extent the detailed properties of the algebras associated with CSP instances are of real significance. In recent years, the algebraic approach has proven very successful in the study of CSP, but it is possible that these algebras are, in fact, more complicated objects than the relations they are intended to capture.

9. ACKNOWLEDGMENTS

The authors are grateful to Jin-Yi Cai, Xi Chen and Andrei Krokhin for their comments on drafts of this paper. We also thank Andrei Bulatov for explaining parts of his proof, and Leslie Ann Goldberg, for useful discussions.

10. REFERENCES

[1] A. A. Bulatov. A dichotomy theorem for constraint satisfaction problems on a 3-element domain. *Journal of the ACM*, 53(1):66–120, 2006.

[2] A. A. Bulatov. The complexity of the counting constraint satisfaction problem. *Electronic Colloquium on Computational Complexity*, **14**(093), 2007. (Revised Feb. 2009).

[3] A. A. Bulatov. The complexity of the counting constraint satisfaction problem. In *Proc. 35th International Colloquium on Automata, Languages and Programming (Part 1)*, LNCS **5125**, pages 646–661. Springer, 2008.

[4] A. A. Bulatov and V. Dalmau. A simple algorithm for Mal'tsev constraints. *SIAM Journal on Computing*, 36(1):16–27, 2006.

[5] A. A. Bulatov and V. Dalmau. Towards a dichotomy theorem for the counting constraint satisfaction problem. *Information and Computation*, 205(5):651–678, 2007.

[6] A. A. Bulatov and M. Grohe. The complexity of partition functions. *Theoretical Computer Science*, 348(2–3):148–186, 2005.

[7] A. A. Bulatov, P. Jeavons and A. A. Krokhin. Classifying the complexity of constraints using finite algebras. *SIAM Journal on Computing*, 34(3):720–742, 2005.

[8] J.-Y. Cai, P. Lu and M. Xia. Holant problems and counting CSP. In *Proc. 41st Annual ACM Symposium on Theory of Computing*, pages 715–724, 2009.

[9] N. Creignou and M. Hermann. Complexity of generalized satisfiability counting problems. *Information and Computation*, 125(1):1–12, 1996.

[10] K. Denecke and S. L. Wismath. *Universal Algebra and Applications in Theoretical Computer Science.* Chapman and Hall/CRC, 2002.

[11] M. E. Dyer, L. A. Goldberg and M. Jerrum. A complexity dichotomy for hypergraph partition functions. arXiv:0811.0037, 2008.

[12] M. E. Dyer, L. A. Goldberg and M. R. Jerrum. The complexity of weighted Boolean #CSP. *SIAM Journal on Computing*, 38(5):1970–1986, 2009.

[13] M. E. Dyer, L. A. Goldberg and M. S. Paterson. On counting homomorphisms to directed acyclic graphs. *Journal of the ACM*, 54(6), 2007.

[14] M. E. Dyer and C. S. Greenhill. The complexity of counting graph homomorphisms. *Random Structures and Algorithms*, 17(3–4):260–289, 2000. (Corrigendum in *Random Structures and Algorithms*, 25(3):346–352, 2004.)

[15] R. Fagin. Monadic generalized spectra. *Zeitschrift für Mathematische Logik und Grundlagen der Mathematik*, 21:89–96, 1975.

[16] R. Fagin, L. J. Stockmeyer and M. Y. Vardi. On

monadic NP vs monadic co-NP. *Information and Computation*, 120(1):78–92, 1995.

[17] T. Feder and M. Y. Vardi. The computational structure of monotone monadic SNP and constraint satisfaction: A study through Datalog and group theory. *SIAM Journal on Computing*, 28(1):57–104, 1998.

[18] R. Freese and R. McKenzie. *Commutator Theory for Congruence Modular Varieties*. Cambridge University Press, 1987.

[19] D. Geiger. Closed systems of functions and predicates. *Pacific Journal of Mathematics*, 27:95–100, 1968.

[20] P. Hell and J. Nešetřil. On the complexity of H-coloring. *Journal of Combinatorial Theory (Series B)*, 48(1):92–110, 1990.

[21] D. Hobby and R. McKenzie. *The Structure of Finite Algebras*, volume 76 of *Contemporary Mathematics*. AMS, 1988.

[22] P. G. Kolaitis and M. Y. Vardi. Conjunctive-query containment and constraint satisfaction. In *Proc. 17th ACM Symposium on Principles of Database Systems*, pages 205–213, 1998.

[23] R. E. Ladner. On the structure of polynomial time reducibility. *Journal of the ACM*, 22(1):155–171, 1975.

[24] T. Schaefer. The complexity of satisfiability problems. In *Proc. 10th Annual ACM Symposium on Theory of Computing*, pages 216–226, 1978.

[25] S. Toda. On the computational power of PP and $\bigoplus$P. In *Proc. 30th Annual Symposim on Foundations of Computer Science*, pages 514–519. IEEE Computer Society, 1989.

[26] L. G. Valiant. The complexity of computing the permanent. *Theoretical Computer Science*, 8:189–201, 1979.

[27] L. G. Valiant. The complexity of enumeration and reliability problems. *SIAM Journal on Computing*, 8(3):410–421, 1979.

Tractable Hypergraph Properties for Constraint Satisfaction and Conjunctive Queries*

Dániel Marx†
School of Computer Science
Tel Aviv University
Tel Aviv, Israel
dmarx@cs.bme.hu

ABSTRACT

An important question in the study of constraint satisfaction problems (CSP) is understanding how the graph or hypergraph describing the incidence structure of the constraints influences the complexity of the problem. For binary CSP instances (i.e., where each constraint involves only two variables), the situation is well understood: the complexity of the problem essentially depends on the treewidth of the graph of the constraints [19, 24]. However, this is not the correct answer if constraints with unbounded number of variables are allowed, and in particular, for CSP instances arising from query evaluation problems in database theory. Formally, if $\mathcal{H}$ is a class of hypergraphs, then let CSP($\mathcal{H}$) be CSP restricted to instances whose hypergraph is in $\mathcal{H}$. Our goal is to characterize those classes of hypergraphs for which CSP($\mathcal{H}$) is polynomial-time solvable or fixed-parameter tractable, parameterized by the number of variables. In the applications related to database query evaluation, we usually assume that the number of variables is much smaller than the size of the instance, thus parameterization by the number of variables is a meaningful question.

The most general known property of $\mathcal{H}$ that makes CSP($\mathcal{H}$) polynomial-time solvable is bounded fractional hypertree width. Here we introduce a new hypergraph measure called *submodular width,* and show that bounded submodular width of $\mathcal{H}$ (which is a strictly more general property than bounded fractional hypertree width) implies that CSP($\mathcal{H}$) is fixed-parameter tractable. In a matching hardness result, we show that if $\mathcal{H}$ has unbounded submodular width, then CSP($\mathcal{H}$) is not fixed-parameter tractable (and hence not polynomial-time solvable), unless the Exponential Time Hypothesis (ETH) fails. The algorithmic result uses tree decompositions in a novel way: instead of using a single decomposition depending on the hypergraph, the instance is split into a set of instances (all on the same set of variables as the original instance), and then the new instances are solved by choosing a different tree decomposition for each of them. The reason why this strategy works is that the splitting can be done in such a way that the new instances are "uniform" with respect to the number extensions of partial solutions, and therefore the number of partial solutions can be described by a submodular function. For the hardness result, we prove via a series of combinatorial results that if a hypergraph H has large submodular width, then a 3SAT instance can be efficiently simulated by a CSP instance whose hypergraph is H. To prove these combinatorial results, we need to develop a theory of (multicommodity) flows on hypergraphs and vertex separators in the case when the function $b(S)$ defining the cost of separator S is submodular.

Categories and Subject Descriptors

F.2 [**Theory of Computing**]: Analysis of Algorithms and Problem Complexity

General Terms

Algorithms, Design, Performance, Theory

Keywords

constraint satisfaction, conjunctive queries, submodular width, fixed-parameter tractability

1. INTRODUCTION

There is a long line of research devoted to identifying hypergraph properties that make the evaluation of conjunctive queries tractable (see e.g. [15, 31, 18, 19]). In the early 80s, it has been noted that acyclicity is one such property [5, 11, 32, 4]. Later, more general such properties were identified in the literature: for example, bounded query width [7], bounded hypertree width [15], and bounded fractional hypertree width [25, 20]. Our main contribution is giving a complete theoretical answer to this question: in a very precise technical sense, we characterize those hypergraph properties that imply tractability for the evaluation of a query. Efficient evaluation of queries is originally a question of database theory; however, the problem can be treated as a constraint satisfaction problem [23, 17, 31].

Constraint satisfaction. Constraint Satisfaction Problems (CSP) form a general framework that includes many standard algorithmic problems such as satisfiability, graph

†Research supported by ERC Advanced Grant DMMCA.

*The full version of the paper is available at `http://arxiv.org/abs/0911.0801`

STOC'10, June 5–8, 2010, Cambridge, Massachusetts, USA.

coloring, database queries, etc. [18, 12]. A CSP instance consists of a set V of variables, a domain D, and a set C of constraints, where each constraint is a relation on a subset of the variables. The task is to assign a value from D to each variable in such a way that every constraint is satisfied. It is easy to see that Boolean Conjunctive Query can be formulated as the problem of deciding if a CSP instance has a solution: the variables of the CSP instance correspond to the variables appearing in the query and the constraints correspond to the database relations. A distinctive feature of CSP instances obtained this way is that the number of variables is small (as queries are typically small), while the domain of the variables are large (as the database relations usually contain a large number of entries). This has to be contrasted with typical CSP problems from AI, such as 3-colorability and satisfiability, where the domain is small, but the number of variables is large. As our motivation is database-theoretic, in the rest of the paper the reader should keep in mind that we are envisioning scenarios where the number of variables is small and the domain is large.

A natural question is to investigate the effect of *structural restrictions* on the complexity of CSP; that is, what kind of restrictions on the structure induced by the constraints on the variables make the problem tractable. The *hypergraph* of a CSP instance is defined to be a hypergraph on the variables of the instance such that for each constraint $c \in C$ there is a hyperedge e_c containing exactly the variables appearing c. If the hypergraph of the CSP instance has simple structure, then the instance is easy to solve. It is well-known that a CSP instance I with hypergraph H can be solved in time $\|I\|^{O(\mathrm{tw}(H))}$ [14], where $\mathrm{tw}(H)$ denotes the treewidth of H and $\|I\|$ is the size of the representation of I.

Our goal is to characterize the "easy" and "hard" hypergraphs from the viewpoint of constraint satisfaction. However, formally speaking, CSP is polynomial-time solvable for every fixed hypergraph H: since H has a constant number k of vertices, every CSP instance with hypergraph H can be solved by trying all $\|I\|^k$ possible combinations on the k variables. It makes more sense to characterize those *classes* of hypergraphs where CSP is easy. For a class $\mathcal{H}$ of hypergraphs, let CSP($\mathcal{H}$) be the restriction of CSP to instances whose hypergraphs are in $\mathcal{H}$. For the characterization of the complexity of CSP($\mathcal{H}$), we can investigate two notions of tractability. CSP($\mathcal{H}$) is *polynomial-time solvable* if there is an algorithm solving every instance of CSP($\mathcal{H}$) in time $(\|I\|)^{O(1)}$, where $\|I\|$ is the length of the representation of I in the input. For example, if $\mathcal{H}$ is class of hypergraphs with bounded treewidth, then CSP($\mathcal{H}$) is polynomial-time solvable. The following notion interprets tractability in a less restrictive way: CSP($\mathcal{H}$) is *fixed-parameter tractable (FPT)* if there is an algorithm solving every instance I of CSP($\mathcal{H}$) in time $f(H)(\|I\|)^{O(1)}$, where f is an arbitrary function.

The case of bounded arities. If the constraints have bounded arity (i.e., the edge size in $\mathcal{H}$ is bounded by a constant r), then CSP($\mathcal{H}$) is well understood: bounded treewidth is the only polynomial-time solvable case.

THEOREM 1.1 ([19]). *If $\mathcal{H}$ is a recursively enumerable class of hypergraphs with bounded edge size, then (assuming* FPT $\neq$ W[1]*) the following are equivalent:*

1. *CSP($\mathcal{H}$) is polynomial-time solvable.*
2. *CSP($\mathcal{H}$) is fixed-parameter tractable.*
3. *$\mathcal{H}$ has bounded treewidth.*

Theorem 1.1 proves the surprising result that whenever CSP($\mathcal{H}$) is fixed-parameter tractable, it is polynomial-time solvable as well. The following sharpening of Theorem 1.1 shows that there is no algorithm whose running time is significantly better than the $\|I\|^{O(\mathrm{tw}(H))}$ bound of the treewidth based algorithm. The result is proved under the Exponential Time Hypothesis (ETH) [22], a somewhat stronger assumption than FPT $\neq$ W[1]: it is assumed that there is no $2^{o(n)}$ time algorithm for n-variable 3SAT.

THEOREM 1.2 ([24]). *If there is a function f and a recursively enumerable class $\mathcal{H}$ of hypergraphs with bounded edge size and unbounded treewidth such that CSP($\mathcal{H}$) can be solved in time $f(H)\|I\|^{o(\mathrm{tw}(H)/\log \mathrm{tw}(H))}$ for instances I with hypergraph $H \in \mathcal{H}$, then ETH fails.*

Unbounded arities. The situation is less understood in the unbounded arity case, i.e., when there is no bound on the maximum edge size in $\mathcal{H}$. First, the complexity in the unbounded-arity case depends on how the constraints are represented. In the bounded-arity case, if each constraint contains at most r variables (r being a fixed constant), then every reasonable representation of a constraint has size $|D|^{O(r)}$. Therefore, the size of the different representations can differ only by a polynomial factor. On the other hand, if there is no bound on the arity, then there can be exponential difference between the size of succinct representations (e.g., formulas [8]) and verbose representations (e.g., truth tables [26]). The running time of an algorithm is expressed as a function of the input size, hence the complexity of the problem can depend on how the input is represented: longer representation means that it is potentially easier to obtain a polynomial-time algorithm.

The most well-studied representation of constraints is listing all the tuples that satisfy the constraint. This representation is perfectly compatible with our database-theoretic motivation: the constraints are relations of the database, and a relation is physically stored as a table containing all the tuples in the relation. For this representation, there are classes $\mathcal{H}$ with unbounded treewidth such that CSP restricted to this class is polynomial-time solvable. A trivial example is the class $\mathcal{H}$ of all hypergraphs having only a single hyperedge of arbitrary size. There are other classes of hypergraphs with unbounded treewidth such that CSP($\mathcal{H}$) is solvable in polynomial time: for example, classes with bounded *(generalized) hypertree width* [16], bounded *fractional edge cover number* [20], and bounded *fractional hypertree width* [20, 25]. Thus treewidth is not the right measure for characterizing the complexity of the problem.

Our results. We introduce a new hypergraph width measure that we call *submodular width.* Small submodular width means that for every monotone submodular function b on the vertices of the hypergraph H, there is a tree decomposition where $b(B)$ is small for every bag B of the decomposition. (This definition makes sense only if we normalize the considered functions: for this reason, we require that $b(e) \leq 1$ for every edge e of H.) The main result of the paper is showing that bounded submodular width is the property that precisely characterizes the complexity of CSP($\mathcal{H}$):

THEOREM 1.3 (MAIN). *Let $\mathcal{H}$ be a recursively enumerable class of hypergraphs. Assuming ETH, CSP($\mathcal{H}$) parameterized by the hypergraph H is fixed-parameter tractable if and only if $\mathcal{H}$ has bounded submodular width.*

Theorem 1.3 has an algorithmic side (algorithm for bounded submodular width) and a complexity side (hardness result for unbounded submodular width). Unlike previous width measures in the literature, where small value of the measure suggests a way of solving CSP($\mathcal{H}$) it is not at all clear how bounded submodular width is of any help. In particular, it is not obvious what submodular functions have to do with CSP instances. The main idea of our algorithm is that a CSP instance can be "split" into a small number of "uniform" CSP instances; for this purpose, we use a partitioning procedure inspired by a result of Alon et al. [3]. Conceptually, our algorithm goes beyond previous decomposition techniques in two ways. First, the tree decomposition that we use depends not only on the hypergraph, but on the actual constraint relations in the instance (we remark that this idea first appeared in [26] in a different context that does not directly apply to our problem). Second, we are not only decomposing the set of variables, but we also split the constraint relations. This way, we can apply different decompositions to different parts of the solution space.

The proof of the complexity side of Theorem 1.3 follows the same high-level strategy as the proof of Theorem 1.2 in [24]. In a nutshell, the argument of [24] is the following: if treewidth is large, then there is subset of vertices which is highly connected in the sense that the set does not have a small balanced separator; such a highly connected set implies that there is uniform concurrent flow (i.e., a compatible set of flows connecting every pair of vertices in the set); the paths in the flows can be used to embed the graph of a 3SAT formula; and finally this embedding can be used to reduce 3SAT to CSP. These arguments build heavily on well-known characterizations of treewidth and results from combinatorial optimization (such as the $O(\log k)$ integrality gap of sparsest cut). The proof of Theorem 1.3 follows this outline, but now no such well-known tools are available: we are dealing with hypergraphs and submodular functions in a way that was not explored before in the literature. One of the main difficulties of obtaining Theorem 1.3 is that we have to work in three different domains:

- **CSP instances.** As our goal is to investigate the existence of algorithms solving CSP, the most obvious domain is CSP instances. In light of previous results, we are especially interested in algorithms based on tree decompositions. For such algorithms, what matters is the existence of subsets of vertices such that restricting the instance to any of these subsets gives an instance with "small" number of solutions. In order to solve the instance, we would like to find a tree decomposition where every bag is such a small set.

- **Submodular functions.** Submodular width is defined in terms of submodular functions, thus submodular functions defined on hypergraphs is our second natural domain. We need to understand what large submodular width means, that is, what property of the submodular function and the hypergraph makes it impossible to obtain a tree decomposition where every bag has small value.

- **Flows and embeddings in hypergraphs.** In the hardness proof, our goal is to embed the graph of a 3SAT formula into a hypergraph. Thus we need to define an appropriate notion of embedding and study what guarantees the existence of embeddings with suitable properties. As in [24], we use the paths appearing in flows to construct embeddings. For our purposes, the right notion of flow is a collection of weighted paths where the total weight of the paths intersecting each hyperedge is at most 1. This notion of flows has not been studied in the literature before, thus we need to obtain basic tools and results on such flows.

A key question is how to find connections between these domains. As mentioned above and detailed in Section 3, we have a procedure that reduces a CSP instance into a set of uniform CSP instances, and the number of solutions on the different subsets of variables in a uniform CSP instance can be described by a submodular function. This method allows us to move from the domain of CSP instances to the domain of submodular functions. Section 4 is devoted to showing that if submodular width of a hypergraph is large, then there is a certain "highly connected" set in the hypergraph. Highly connected set is defined as a property of the hypergraph and has no longer anything to do with submodular functions. Thus this connection allows us to move from the domain of submodular functions to the study of hypergraphs. In Section 5, we show that a highly connected set in a hypergraph means that graphs can be efficiently embedded into the hypergraph. In particular, the graph of a 3SAT formula can be embedded into the hypergraph, which gives us (as shown in Section 6) a reduction from 3SAT to CSP($\mathcal{H}$). This connection allows us to move from the domain of embeddings back to the domain of CSP instances.

We can show that bounded submodular width is a strictly more general property than bounded fractional hypertree width, which was previously the most general property known to make CSP($\mathcal{H}$) FPT (see the full version of the paper). Thus Theorem 1.3 not only gives a complete characterization of the parameterized complexity of CSP($\mathcal{H}$), but its algorithmic side proves fixed-parameter tractability in a strictly more general case than what was known before.

2. PRELIMINARIES

Constraint satisfaction problems. We briefly recall the most important notions related to CSP. For more background, see e.g., [18, 12]. An instance of a *constraint satisfaction problem* is a triple (V, D, C), where: V is a set of variables, D is a domain of values, C is a set of constraints, $\{c_1, c_2, \dots, c_q\}$. Each constraint $c_i \in C$ is a pair $\langle s_i, R_i \rangle$, where s_i is a tuple of variables of length m_i, called the *constraint scope,* and R_i is an m_i-ary relation over D, called the *constraint relation.*

For each constraint $\langle s_i, R_i \rangle$ the tuples of R_i indicate the allowed combinations of simultaneous values for the variables in s_i. The length m_i of the tuple s_i is called the *arity* of the constraint. A *solution* to a constraint satisfaction problem instance is a function f from the set of variables V to the domain of values D such that for each constraint $\langle s_i, R_i \rangle$ with $s_i = \langle v_{i_1}, v_{i_2}, \dots, v_{i_m} \rangle$, the tuple $\langle f(v_{i_1}), f(v_{i_2}), \dots, f(v_{i_m}) \rangle$ is a member of R_i. We say that an instance is *binary* if each constraint relation is binary, i.e., $m_i = 2$ for each constraint. It can be assumed that the instance does not contain two constraints $\langle s_i, R_i \rangle$, $\langle s_j, R_j \rangle$ with $s_i = s_j$, since in this case the two constraints can be replaced by the constraint $\langle s_i, R_i \cap R_j \rangle$. In the input, the relation in a constraint is represented by listing all the tuples of the constraint. We denote by $\|I\|$ the size of the representation of the instance $I = (V, D, C)$.

Let $I = (V, D, C)$ be a CSP instance and let $V' \subseteq V$ be a nonempty subset of variables. The *projection* $\mathrm{pr}_{V'} I$ of I to V' is a CSP $I' = (V', D, C')$, where C' is defined the following way: For each constraint $c = \langle (v_1, \ldots, v_k), R \rangle$ having at least one variable in V', there is a corresponding constraint c' in C'. Suppose that $v_{i_1}, \ldots, v_{i_\ell}$ are the variables among $v_1, \ldots, v_k$ that are in V'. Then the constraint c' is defined as $\langle (v_{i_1}, \ldots, v_{i_\ell}), R' \rangle$, where the relation R' is the projection of R to the components $i_1, \ldots, i_\ell$, that is, R' contains an ℓ-tuple $(d'_1, \ldots, d'_\ell) \in D^\ell$ if and only if there is a k-tuple $(d_1, \ldots, d_k) \in R$ such that $d'_j = d_{i_j}$ for $1 \le j \le \ell$. Clearly, if f is a solution of I, then $f_{|V'}$ (*f restricted to V'*) is a solution of $\mathrm{pr}_{V'} I$. For a subset $V' \subseteq V$, we denote by $\mathrm{sol}_I(V')$ the set of all solutions of $\mathrm{pr}_{V'} I$. If the instance I is clear from the context, we drop the subscript.

The *primal graph* (or *Gaifman graph*) of a CSP instance $I = (V, D, C)$ is a graph with vertex set V such that $u, v \in V$ are adjacent if and only if they appear together in the scope of some constraint. The *hypergraph* of a CSP instance $I = (V, D, C)$ is a hypergraph H with vertex set V, where $e \subseteq V$ is an edge if and only if there is a constraint whose scope is e. Let $\mathrm{CSP}(\mathcal{H})$ be the problem restricted to instances whose hypergraph is in $\mathcal{H}$.

Paths, separators, and flows in hypergraphs. A *path* P in hypergraph H is an ordered sequence $v_0, v_1, \ldots, v_r$ of vertices such that v_i and v_{i-1} are adjacent for every $1 \le i < r$. We distinguish the endpoints of a path: vertex v_0 is the *first endpoint* of P and v_r is the *second endpoint* of P. A path is an $X - Y$ *path* if its first endpoint is in X and its second endpoint is in Y.

Let H be a hypergraph and $X, Y \subseteq V(H)$ be two (not necessarily disjoint) sets of vertices. An *(X, Y)-separator* is a set $S \subseteq V(H)$ of vertices such that every $X - Y$ path of H contains at least one vertex of S. In particular, this means that $X \cap Y \subseteq S$. An assignment $s : E(H) \to \mathbb{R}^+$ is a *fractional (X, Y)-separator* if every $X - Y$ path P is *covered* by s, that is, $\sum_{e \in E(H), e \cap P \neq \emptyset} s(e) \ge 1$. The *weight* of the fractional separator s is $\sum_{e \in E(H)} s(e)$.

Let H be a hypergraph and let $\mathcal{P}$ be the set of all paths in H. A *flow* of H is an assignment $f : \mathcal{P} \to \mathbb{R}^+$ such that $\sum_{P \in \mathcal{P}, P \cap e \neq \emptyset} f(P) \le 1$ for every $e \in E(H)$. The *value* of the flow f is $\sum_{P \in \mathcal{P}} f(P)$. We say that a path P *appears* in flow f, or simply P is a *path of f* if $f(P) > 0$. For some $X, Y \subseteq V(H)$, an *(X, Y)-flow* is a flow f such that only $X - Y$ paths appear in f. A standard LP duality argument shows that the minimum weight of a fractional (X, Y)-separator is equal to the maximum value of an (X, Y)-flow. If f, f' are flows such that $f'(P) \le f(P)$ for every path P, then f' is a *subflow* of f. The *sum* of the flows $f_1, \ldots, f_r$ is a mapping that assigns weight $\sum_{i=1}^{r} f_i(P)$ to each path P. If the sum of $f_1, \ldots, f_r$ is a flow, then we say that $f_1, \ldots, f_r$ are *compatible*.

Highly connected sets. An important step in understanding various width measures is showing that if the measure is large, then the (hyper)graph contains a highly connected set (in a certain sense). We define here the notion of highly connected that will be used in the paper. First, recall that a *fractional independent set* of a hypergraph H is a mapping $\mu : V(H) \to [0, 1]$ such that $\sum_{v \in e} \mu(v) \le 1$ for every $e \in E(H)$. We extend functions on the vertices of H to subsets of vertices of H the natural way by setting $\mu(X) := \sum_{v \in X} \mu(v)$.

Let μ be a fractional independent set of hypergraph H and let $\lambda > 0$ be a constant. We say that a set $W \subseteq V(H)$ is *(μ, λ)-connected* if for any two disjoint sets $A, B \subseteq W$, the minimum weight of a fractional (A, B)-separator is at least $\lambda \cdot \min\{\mu(A), \mu(B)\}$. Note that if W is (μ, λ)-connected, then W is (μ, λ')-connected for every $\lambda' < \lambda$ and every $W' \subseteq W$ is also (μ, λ)-connected. Informally, if W is (μ, λ)-lambda connected for some fractional independent set μ such that $\mu(W)$ is "large", then we call W a highly connected set. For $\lambda > 0$, we denote by $\mathrm{con}_\lambda(H)$ the maximum of $\mu(W)$, taken over all (μ, λ)-connected set W of H. Throughout the paper, λ can be thought of as a sufficiently small universal constant, say, 0.001.

Embeddings. The hardness result presented in the paper and earlier hardness results for $\mathrm{CSP}(\mathcal{H})$ [19, 26, 24] are based on embedding some other problem (with a certain graph structure) in a CSP instance whose hypergraph is a member of $\mathcal{H}$. Thus we need appropriate notions of embedding a graph in a (hyper)graph. A crucial difference between the proof of Theorem 1.1 in [19] and the proof of Theorem 1.2 in [24] is that the former result is a based on finding a minor embedding of a grid, while the latter result uses an embedding where the images of distinct vertices are not necessarily disjoint, but can overlap in a controlled way. We define such embeddings the following way. We say that two sets of vertices $X, Y \subseteq V(H)$ *touch* if either $X \cap Y \neq \emptyset$, or there is an edge $e \in E(H)$ intersecting both X and Y. An *embedding* of graph G into hypergraph H is a mapping ψ that maps each vertex of H to a connected subset of $V(G)$ such that if u and v are adjacent in G, then $\psi(u)$ and $\psi(v)$ touch. The *depth* of a vertex $v \in V(H)$ in embedding ψ is $d_\psi(v) := |\{u \in V(G) \mid v \in \psi(u)\}|$, the number of vertices of G whose images contain v. The *vertex depth* of the embedding is $\max_{v \in V(H)} d_\psi(v)$. Because in our case we want to control the size of the constraint relations, we need a notion of depth that is sensitive to "what the edges see." We define *edge depth* of ψ to be $\max_{e \in E(H)} \sum_{v \in e} d_\psi(v)$. Equivalently, we can define edge depth as the maximum of $\sum_{v \in V(G)} |\psi(v) \cap e|$, taken over all edges of e of H.

Trivially, for any graph G and hypergraph H, there is an embedding of G into H having vertex depth and edge depth at most $|V(G)|$. If G has m edges and no isolated vertices, then $|V(G)|$ is at most $2m$. We are interested in how much we can gain compared to this trivial solution of depth $O(m)$. We define the *embedding power* $\mathrm{emb}(H)$ to be the maximum (supremum) value of α for which there is an integer m_α such that every graph G with $m \ge m_\alpha$ edges has an embedding into H with edge depth m/α.

Width parameters We follow the framework of width functions introduced by Adler [1]. A *tree decomposition* of a hypergraph H is a tuple $(T, (B_t)_{t \in V(T)})$, where T is a tree and $(B_t)_{t \in V(T)}$ is a family of subsets of $V(H)$ satisfying the following two conditions: (1) for each $e \in E(H)$ there is a node $t \in V(T)$ such that $e \subseteq B_t$, and (2) for each $v \in V(H)$ the set $\{t \in V(T) \mid v \in B_t\}$ is connected in T. The sets B_t are called the *bags* of the decomposition. Let $f : 2^{V(H)} \to \mathbb{R}^+$ be a function that assigns a nonnegative real number to each nonempty subset of vertices. The *f-width* of a tree-decomposition $(T, (B_t)_{t \in V(T)})$ is $\max\{f(B_t) \mid t \in V(T)\}$. The *$f$-width* of a hypergraph H is the minimum of the f-widths of all its tree decompositions. In other words,

f-width$(H) \leq w$ if and only if there is a tree decomposition of H where $f(B) \leq w$ for every bag B.

The main idea of tree decomposition based algorithms is that if we have a tree decomposition for instance I such that at most C assignments on B_t have to be considered for each bag B_t, then the problem can be solved by dynamic programming in time polynomial in C and $\|I\|$. The various width notions try to guarantee the existence of such decompositions. For example, the simplest such notion, treewidth, can be defined as $\text{tw}(H) := s\text{-width}(H)$, where $s(B) = |B| - 1$. Further width notions defined in the literature, such as generalized hypertree width and fractional hypertree width can also be conveniently defined using this setup, see [1].

We generalize the notion of f-width from a single function f to a class of functions $\mathcal{F}$. Let $\mathcal{F}$ be an arbitrary (possibly infinite) class of functions that assign nonnegative real numbers to nonempty subsets of vertices. The *$\mathcal{F}$-width* of a hypergraph H is $\mathcal{F}\text{-width}(H) := \sup\{f\text{-width}(H) \mid f \in \mathcal{F}\}$. Thus if $\mathcal{F}\text{-width}(H) \leq k$, then for every $f \in \mathcal{F}$, hypergraph H has a tree decomposition with f-width at most k. Note that this tree decomposition can be different for the different functions f. For normalization purposes, we consider only functions f on $V(H)$ that are *edge-dominated:* $f(e) \leq 1$ holds for every $e \in E(H)$. The main new definition of the paper is submodular width:

DEFINITION 2.1. *A function $b : 2^{V(H)} \to \mathbb{R}^+$ is* submodular *if $b(X) + b(Y) \geq b(X \cap Y) + b(X \cup Y)$ holds for every $X, Y \subseteq V(H)$. Given a hypergraph H, let $\mathcal{F}$ contain the edge-dominated monotone submodular functions on $V(H)$. The* submodular width $\text{subw}(H)$ *of hypergraph H is $\mathcal{F}$-width(H).*

3. FROM CSP INSTANCES TO SUBMODULAR FUNCTIONS

We prove the main algorithmic result in this section: CSP($\mathcal{H}$) is FPT if $\mathcal{H}$ has bounded submodular width.

THEOREM 3.1. *Let $\mathcal{H}$ be a class of hypergraphs such that $\text{subw}(H) \leq c_0$ for every $H \in \mathcal{H}$. Then CSP($\mathcal{H}$) can be solved in time $2^{2^{O(|V(H)|)}} \cdot \|I\|^{O(c_0)}$.*

The proof of Theorem 3.1 is based on two main ideas:

1. A CSP instance I can be decomposed into a bounded number of "uniform" CSP instances $I_1, \ldots, I_t$ (Lemma 3.9). Here uniform means that if $B \subseteq A$ are two sets of variables, then every solution of $\text{pr}_B I_j$ has roughly the same number of extensions to $\text{pr}_A I_j$.
2. If I is a uniform CSP instance, then (the logarithm of) the number of solutions on the different projections of I can be described by an edge-dominated submodular function (Lemma 3.10). Therefore, if the hypergraph H of I has bounded submodular width, then it follows that there is a tree decomposition where every bag has a small number of solutions.

In the implementation of the first idea (Lemma 3.9), we guarantee uniformity only to subsets of variables that are "small" in the following hereditary sense:

DEFINITION 3.2. *For a CSP instance I and $M \geq 1$, a set $S \subseteq V$ is* M-small *if $|\text{sol}_I(S')| \leq M$ for every $S' \subseteq S$.*

It is not difficult to find all the M-small sets, and every solution of the instances projected onto these sets:

LEMMA 3.3. *Let $I = (V, D, C)$ be a CSP instance and $M \geq 1$ an integer. There is an algorithm with running time $2^{O(|V|)} \cdot \text{poly}(\|I\|, M)$ that finds the set $\mathcal{S}$ of all M-small sets $S \subseteq V$ and constructs $\text{sol}_I(S)$ for each such $S \in \mathcal{S}$.*

The following definition gives the precise notion of uniformity that we use:

DEFINITION 3.4. *Let $I = (V, D, C)$ be a CSP instance. For $B \subseteq A \subseteq V$ and an assignment $b : B \to D$, let $\text{sol}_I(A|B = b) := \{a \in \text{sol}_I(A) \mid a(x) = b(x) \text{ for every } x \in B\}$, the set of all extensions of b to a solution of $\text{pr}_A I$. Let $\max_I(A|B) = \max_{b \in \text{sol}_I(B)} |\text{sol}_I(A|B = b)|$. We say that $A \subseteq V$ is* c-uniform *(for some integer c) if, for every $B \subseteq A$, $\max_I(A|B) \leq c|\text{sol}_I(A)|/|\text{sol}_I(B)|$. We define $\max_I(A|\emptyset) = |\text{sol}_I(A)|$ and $\max_I(\emptyset|\emptyset) = 1$. An instance is* (N, c, ϵ)-uniform *if every N^c-small set is N^ϵ-uniform.*

PROPOSITION 3.5. *For every $B \subseteq A \subseteq V$ and $C \subseteq V$, we have*

1. $\max(A|B) \geq |\text{sol}(A)|/|\text{sol}(B)|$,
2. $\max(A|B) \geq \max(A \cup C|B \cup C)$.

We want to avoid dealing with assignments $b \in \text{sol}(B)$ that cannot be extended to a member of $\text{sol}(A)$ for some $A \supseteq B$ (that is, $\text{sol}(A|B = b) = \emptyset$). We require that there is no such unextendable b if A and B are M-small:

DEFINITION 3.6. *A CSP instance is* M-consistent *if $\text{sol}(B) = \text{pr}_A \text{sol}(A)$ for all M-small sets $B \subseteq A$. A CSP instance is* nontrivial *if $\text{sol}(\{v\}) \neq \emptyset$ for any $v \in V$.*

PROPOSITION 3.7. *If I is an M-consistent nontrivial CSP instance, then $\text{sol}(S) \neq \emptyset$ for every M-small set S.*

We can achieve M-consistency by throwing away partial solutions that violate the requirements. Instance $I' = (V, D, C')$ is a *refinement* of $I = (V, D, C)$ if for every $\langle s, R\rangle \in C$, there is a $\langle s, R'\rangle \in C'$ such that $R' \subseteq R$.

LEMMA 3.8. *Let $I = (V, D, C)$ be a CSP instance and $M \geq 1$ an integer. There is an algorithm with running time $2^{O(|V|)} \cdot \text{poly}(\|I\|, M)$ that produces an M-consistent CSP instance I' that is a refinement of I with $\text{sol}(I) = \text{sol}(I')$.*

Our algorithm for decomposing a CSP instance into uniform CSP instances is inspired by a combinatorial result of Alon et al. [3], which shows that, for every fixed n, an n-dimensional point set S can be partitioned into polylog$(|S|)$ $O(1)$-uniform classes. We follow the same proof idea: the instance is split into two instances if uniformity is violated somewhere, and we analyze the change of a weight function to bound the number of splits performed. However, the parameter setting is different in our proof: we want to partition into $f(|V|)$ classes, but we are satisfied with weaker uniformity. A minor difference is that we require uniformity only on N^c-small sets.

LEMMA 3.9. *Let $I = (V, D, C)$ be a CSP instance and let N, c be integers and $\epsilon > 0$. There is an algorithm with running time $2^{2^{O(|V|)} \cdot c/\epsilon} \cdot \text{poly}(\|I\|, N^c)$ that produces a set of (N, c, ϵ)-uniform N^c-consistent nontrivial instances $I_1, \ldots, I_t$ with $0 \leq t \leq 2^{2^{O(|V|)} \cdot c/\epsilon}$, all on the set V of variables, such that*

1. every solution of I is a solution of exactly one I_i,

2. for every $1 \le i \le t$, instance I_i is a refinement of I.

PROOF. The main step of the algorithm takes a CSP instance I and either makes it (N,c,ϵ)-uniform and N^c-consistent, or splits it into two instances I_{small}, I_{large}. By applying the main step recursively on I_{small} and I_{large}, we eventually arrive to a set of (N,c,ϵ)-uniform N^c-consistent instances. We will argue that the number of constructed instances is $2^{2^{O(|V|)} \cdot c/\epsilon}$.

In the main step, we first check if the instance is trivial; in this case we can stop with $t = 0$. Otherwise, we invoke the algorithm of Lemma 3.8 to obtain an N^c-consistent refinement of the instance, without losing any solution. Next we check if this N^c-consistent instance I is (N,c,ϵ)-uniform. This can be tested in time $2^{O(|V|)} \cdot \text{poly}(\|I\|, N^c)$ if we use Lemma 3.3 to find all the N^c-small sets and the corresponding sets of solutions. Suppose that N^c-small sets $B \subseteq A$ violate uniformity, that is, $\max(A|B) > M^\epsilon |\text{sol}(A)|/|\text{sol}(B)|$. Let $\text{sol}_{\text{small}}(B)$ contain those tuples b for which $|\text{sol}(A|B = b)| \le \sqrt{M^\epsilon}|\text{sol}(A)|/|\text{sol}(B)|$ and let $\text{sol}_{\text{large}}(B) = \text{sol}(B) \setminus \text{sol}_{\text{small}}(B)$. Note that

$$|\text{sol}(A)| \ge |\text{sol}_{\text{large}}(B)| \cdot (\sqrt{M^\epsilon}|\text{sol}(A)|/|\text{sol}(B)|)$$

(as every tuple $b \in \text{sol}_{\text{large}}(B)$ has at least $\sqrt{M^\epsilon}|\text{sol}(A)|/|\text{sol}(B)|$ extensions to A), hence $|\text{sol}_{\text{large}}(B)| \le |\text{sol}(B)|/\sqrt{M^\epsilon}$. Let instance I_{small} (resp., I_{large}) be obtained from I by adding the constraint $\langle B, \text{sol}_{\text{small}}(B)\rangle$ (resp., $\langle B, \text{sol}_{\text{large}}(B)\rangle$). Clearly, the set of solutions of I is the disjoint union of the sets of solutions of I_{small} and I_{large}. This completes the description of the main step.

It is clear that if the recursive procedure stops, then the instances at the leaves of the recursion satisfy the two requirements. We show that the height of the recursion tree can be bounded from above by a function $h(|V|, c, \epsilon)$ depending only on $|V|$, c, and ϵ; in particular, this shows that the recursive algorithm eventually stops and produces at most $2^{h(|V|,c,\epsilon)}$ instances.

Let us consider a path in the recursion tree starting at the root, and let $I^1, I^2, \ldots, I^p$ be the corresponding N^c consistent instances. If a set S is N^c-small in I^j, then it is N^c-small in $I^{j'}$ for every $j' > j$: the main step cannot increase $|\text{sol}(S)|$ for any S. Thus, with the exception of at most $2^{|V|}$ values of j, instances I^j and I^{j+1} have the same N^c-small sets. Let us consider a subpath $I^x, \ldots, I^y$ such that all these instances have the same N^c-small sets. We show that the length of this subpath is at most $O(3^{|V|} \cdot c/\epsilon)$, hence $p = O(2^{|V|} \cdot 3^{|V|} \cdot c/\epsilon)$.

For the instance I^j, let us define the following weight:

$$W^j = \sum_{\substack{\emptyset \subseteq B \subseteq A \subseteq V \\ A,\, B \text{ are } N^c\text{-small}}} \log \max_{I^j}(A|B).$$

We bound the length of the subpath $I^x, \ldots, I^y$ by analyzing how this weight changes in I_{large} and I_{small} compared to I. Note that $0 \le W^j \le 3^{|V|} \log N^c = 3^{|V|} \cdot c \log N$: the sum consists of at most $3^{|V|}$ terms and (as A is N^c-small and the instance I^j is N^c consistent and nontrivial) $\max_{I^j}(A|B)$ is between 1 and N^c. We show that $W^{j+1} \le W^j - (\epsilon/2)\log N$, which immediately implies that the length of the subpath is $O(3^{|V|} \cdot c/\epsilon)$. Let us inspect how W^{j+1} changes compared to W^j. Since I^j and I^{j+1} have the same N^c-small sets, no new term can appear in W^{j+1}. It is clear that $\max_{I^{i+1}}(A|B)$ cannot be greater than $\max_{I^i}(A|B)$ for any A, B. However, there is at least one term that strictly decreases. Suppose first that I^{j+1} was obtained from I^j by adding the constraint $\langle B, \text{sol}_{\text{small}}(B)\rangle$. Then

$$\log \max_{I^{j+1}}(A|B) \le \log \sqrt{N^\epsilon}\frac{|\text{sol}_{I^j}(A)|}{|\text{sol}_{I^j}(B)|}$$
$$\le \log(\max_{I^j}(A|B)/\sqrt{N^\epsilon}) = \log \max_{I^j}(A|B) - (\epsilon/2)\log N.$$

On the other hand, if I^{j+1} was obtained by adding the constraint $\langle B, \text{sol}_{\text{large}}(B)\rangle$, then

$$\log \max_{I^{j+1}}(B|\emptyset) = \log|\text{sol}_{I^{j+1}}(B)|$$
$$\le \log(|\text{sol}_{I^j}(B)|/\sqrt{N^\epsilon}) = \log \max_{I^j}(B|\emptyset) - (\epsilon/2)\log N.$$

In both cases, we get that at least one term decreases by at least $(\epsilon/2)\log N$. □

Assume for a moment that we have a 1-uniform instance I with hypergraph H. Note that by Prop 3.5(1), this means that $\max(A|B) = |\text{sol}(A)|/|\text{sol}(B)|$. Suppose that every constraint contains at most N tuples and let us define the function $b(S) = \log_N|\text{sol}(S)|$. For every edge $e \in E(H)$, there is a corresponding constraint, which has at most N tuples by the definition of N. Thus $|\text{sol}(e)| \le N$ and hence $b(e) \le 1$ for every $e \in E(H)$, that is, b is edge dominated. The crucial observation of this section is that this function b is submodular:

$$\begin{aligned}
&b(X) + b(Y)\\
&= \log_N|\text{sol}(X)| + \log_N\left(|\text{sol}(X\cap Y)|\frac{|\text{sol}(Y)|}{|\text{sol}(X\cap Y)|}\right)\\
&= \log_N|\text{sol}(X)| + \log_N(|\text{sol}(X\cap Y)|\max(Y|X\cap Y))\\
&\ge \log_N|\text{sol}(X)| + \log_N(|\text{sol}(X\cap Y)|\max(X\cup Y|X))\\
&= \log_N\left(|\text{sol}(X)|\frac{|\text{sol}(X\cup Y)|}{|\text{sol}(X)|}\right) + \log_N|\text{sol}(X\cap Y)|\\
&= b(X\cap Y) + b(X\cup Y)
\end{aligned}$$

(the equalities follow from 1-uniformity; the inequality uses Prop. 3.5(2) with $A = Y$, $B = X\cap Y$, $C = X$). Therefore, if $\text{subw}(H) \le c$, then H has a tree decomposition where $b(B) \le c$ and hence $|\text{sol}(B)| \le N^c$ for every bag B. This allows us to solve the problem by dynamic programming in time polynomial in N^c.

Lemma 3.9 guarantees some uniformity for the created instances, but not perfect 1-uniformity and only for the N^c-small sets. In Lemma 3.10, we define b in a slightly different way: we add small terms to correct errors arising from weaker uniformity and we truncate the function at large values (i.e., for sets that are not N^c-small).

LEMMA 3.10. *Let $I = (V, D, C)$ be a CSP instance with hypergraph H such that $|\text{sol}(e)| \le N$ for every $e \in E(H)$. If I is N^c-consistent and (N, c, ϵ^3)-uniform for some $c \ge 1$ and $\epsilon := 1/|V|$, then the following function b is an edge-dominated, monotone, submodular function on $V(H)$:*

$$b(S) := \begin{cases} (1-\epsilon)\log_N|\text{sol}(S)| + 2\epsilon^2|S| - \epsilon^3|S|^2 & \textit{if } S \textit{ is } N^c\textit{-small,}\\ (1-\epsilon)c + 2\epsilon^2|S| - \epsilon^3|S|^2 & \textit{otherwise.}\end{cases}$$

If $\mathrm{subw}(H) \le (1-\epsilon)c$, then there is a tree decomposition where every bag is N^c-small, and we can use this tree decomposition to find a solution. In fact, in this case N^c-consistency implies that every nontrivial instance has a solution. Putting together this observation with Lemmas 3.9 and 3.10, the proof of Theorem 3.1 follows.

4. FROM SUBMODULAR FUNCTIONS TO HIGHLY CONNECTED SETS

The aim of this section is to show that if a hypergraph H has large submodular width, then there is a large highly connected set in H. The main result is the following:

THEOREM 4.1. *For every sufficiently small constant $\lambda > 0$, the following holds. Let b be an edge-dominated monotone submodular function of H. If the b-width of H is greater than $\frac{3}{2}(w+1)$, then $\mathrm{con}_\lambda(W) \ge w$.*

For the proof of Theorem 4.1, we need to show that if there is no tree decomposition where $b(B)$ is small for every bag B, then a highly connected set exists. There is a standard recursive procedure that either builds a tree decomposition or finds a highly connected set (see e.g., [13, Section 11.2]). Simplifying somewhat, the main idea is that if a the graph can be decomposed into smaller graphs by splitting a certain set of vertices into two parts, then a tree decomposition for each part is constructed using the algorithm recursively, and the tree decompositions for the parts are joined in an appropriate way to obtain a tree decomposition for the original problem. On the other hand, if the set of vertices cannot be split, then we can conclude that it is highly connected. This high-level idea has been applied for various notions of tree decompositions [30, 28, 2, 29], and it turns out to be useful in our context as well. However, we need to overcome two major difficulties:

1. Highly connected set in our context is defined as not having certain *fractional separators* (i.e., weight assignments). However, if we want to build a tree decomposition in a recursive manner, we need *integer separators* (i.e., subsets of vertices) that decompose the hypergraph into smaller parts.
2. Measuring the sizes of sets with a submodular function b can lead to problems, since the size of the union of two sets can be much smaller the sum of the sizes of the two sets. We need the property that, roughly speaking, removing a "large" part from a set makes it "much smaller." For example, if A and B are components of $H \setminus S$, and both $b(A)$ and $b(B)$ are large, then we need the property that both of them are much smaller than $b(A \cup B)$. Adler [1, Section 4.2] investigates the relation between some notion of highly connected set and f-width, but assumes that f is additive: if A and B do not touch, then $f(A \cup B) = f(A) + f(B)$. However, for a submodular function b, it very well may be that $b(A) = b(B) = b(A \cup B)$.

To overcome the first difficulty, we have to understand what fractional separation really means. We show that if there is a fractional (A, B)-separator of weight w, then for *every* edge-dominated monotone submodular function b, there is an (A, B)-separator S with $b(S) = O(w)$. Note that this separator S can be different for different functions b, so we are not claiming that there is a single (A, B)-separator S that is small in every b. The converse is also true (we omit the proof), thus this gives a novel characterization of fractional separation, tight up to a constant factor. This result is the key idea that allows us to move from the domain of submodular functions to the domain of pure hypergraph properties: if there is no (A, B)-separator such that $b(S)$ is small, then we know that there is no small fractional (A, B)-separator, which is a property of the hypergraph H only and has no longer anything to do with the submodular function b.

To overcome the second difficulty, we introduce a transformation that turns a monotone submodular function b on $V(H)$ into a function b^* that encodes somehow the neighborhood structure of H as well. The new function b^* is no longer monotone and submodular, but is has a number of remarkable properties, for example, b^* remains edge dominated and $b^*(S) \ge b(S)$ for every set $S \subseteq V(H)$, implying that b^*-width is not smaller than b-width. The main idea is to prove Theorem 4.1 for b^*-width instead of b-width. Because of the way b^* encodes the neighborhoods, the second difficulty will disappear: for example, it will be true that $b^*(A \cup B) = b^*(A) + b^*(B)$ if there are no edges between A and B, that is, b^* is additive on disjoint components. Lemma 4.3 formulates (in a somewhat technical way) the exact property of b^* that we will need. It turns out that the result mentioned in the previous paragraph remains true with b replaced by b^*: if there is a fractional (A, B)-separator of weight w, then there is an (A, B)-separator S such that not only $b(S)$, but even $b^*(S)$ is $O(w)$.

The function b^*. We define the function b^* the following way. Let H be a hypergraph and let b be a monotone submodular function defined on $V(H)$. Let $S_{V(H)}$ be the set of all permutations of $V(H)$. For a permutation $\pi \in S_{V(H)}$, let $N^-_\pi(v)$ be the neighbors of v preceding v in the ordering π. For $\pi \in S_{V(H)}$ and $Z \subseteq V(H)$, we define

$$\partial b_{\pi,Z}(v) := b(v \cup (N^-_\pi(v) \cap Z)) - b(N^-_\pi(v) \cap Z).$$

In other words, $\partial b_{\pi,Z}(v)$ is the marginal value of v with respect to the set of its neighbors in Z preceding it. We abbreviate $\partial b_{\pi,V(H)}$ by ∂b_π. We extend the definition to subsets by $\partial b_{\pi,Z}(S) := \sum_{v \in S} \partial b_{\pi,Z}(v)$. Next, we define

$$b_\pi(Z) := \partial b_{\pi,Z}(Z) = \sum_{v \in Z} \partial b_{\pi,Z}(v) \qquad b^*(Z) := \min_{\pi \in S_{V(H)}} b_\pi(Z).$$

Thus $b_\pi(Z)$ is the sum of the marginal values with respect to a given ordering, while $b^*(Z)$ is the smallest possible sum taken over all possible orderings.

PROPOSITION 4.2. *Let H be a hypergraph and let b be a monotone submodular function defined on $V(H)$. For every $\pi \in S_{V(H)}$ and $Z \subseteq V(H)$ we have*

1. $b_\pi(Z) \ge b(Z)$,
2. $b^*(Z) \ge b(Z)$,
3. $b_\pi(Z) = b(Z)$ *if Z is a clique,*
4. $\partial b_{\pi,Z_1}(v) \le \partial b_{\pi,Z_2}(v)$ *if $Z_2 \subseteq Z_1$,*
5. $\partial b_\pi(v) \le \partial b_{\pi,Z}(v)$,
6. $b^*(X \cup Y) \le b^*(X) + b^*(Y)$.

The following property of b^* allows us to avoid the second difficulty described at the beginning of Section 4.

LEMMA 4.3. *Let H be a hypergraph, let b be a monotone submodular function defined on $V(H)$ and let W be a set of* *vertices. Let π_W be an ordering of $V(H)$, and let $\mu(v) := \partial b_{\pi_W,W}(v)$ for $v \in W$ and $\mu(v) = 0$ otherwise. Let $A, B \subseteq W$ be two disjoint sets, and let S be an (A, B)-separator. If $b^*(S) < \mu(A), \mu(B)$, then $b^*((C \cap W) \cup S) < \mu(W)$ for every component C of $H \setminus S$.*

Next we show that having a small fractional (A, B)-separator means that for every monotone edge-dominated submodular function b, there is an (A, B)-separator S such that $b^*(S)$ (and hence $b(S)$) is small. The proof is based on a standard trick that is often used for rounding fractional solutions for separation problems: we define a distance function and show by an averaging argument that cutting at some distance t gives a small separator. However, in our setting, we need significant new ideas to make this trick work: the main difficulty is that the cost function b is defined on *subsets* of vertices and is not a function defined by the cost of vertices. To overcome this problem, we use the function $\partial b_\pi(v)$ to assign a cost to every single vertex.

THEOREM 4.4. *Let H be a hypergraph, $X, Y \subseteq V(H)$ two sets of vertices, and $b : V(H) \to \mathbb{R}^+$ an edge-dominated monotone submodular function. Suppose that s is a fractional (X, Y)-separator of weight at most w. Then there is an (X, Y)-separator $S \subseteq V(H)$ with $b^*(S) = O(w)$.*

PROOF. Let us define $x(v) := \max\{1, \sum_{e \in E(H), v \in e} s(e)\}$. It is clear that if P is a path from X to Y, then $\sum_{v \in P} x(v) \geq 1$. We define the distance $d(v)$ to be the minimum of $\sum_{v' \in P} x(v')$, taken over all paths from X to v (this means that $d(v) > 0$ is possible for some $v \in X$). It is clear that $d(v) \geq 1$ for every $v \in Y$. Let us associate the closed interval $\iota(v) = [d(v) - x(v), d(v)]$ to each vertex v. If v is in X, then the left endpoint of $\iota(v)$ is 0, while if v is in Y, then the right endpoint of $\iota(v)$ is at least 1. The following claim is easy to see:

Claim 1: If u and v are adjacent, then $\iota(u) \cap \iota(v) \neq \emptyset$.

The *class* of a vertex $v \in V(H)$ is the largest integer $\kappa(v)$ such that $x(v) \leq 2^{-\kappa(v)}$, and we define $\kappa(v) := \infty$ if $x(v) = 0$. Recall that $x(v) \leq 1$, thus $\kappa(v)$ is nonnegative. The *offset* of a vertex v is the unique value $0 \leq \alpha < 2 \cdot 2^{-\kappa(v)}$ such that $d(v) = i(2 \cdot 2^{-\kappa(v)}) + \alpha$ for some integer i. Let us define an ordering $\pi = (v_1, \dots, v_n)$ of $V(H)$ such that $\kappa(v)$ is nondecreasing, and among vertices having the same class, the offset is nondecreasing.

Let directed graph D be the orientation of the primal graph of H such that if v_i and v_j are adjacent and $i < j$, then there is a directed edge $\overrightarrow{v_iv_j}$ in D. If P is a directed path in D, then the *width* of P is the length of the interval $\bigcup_{v \in P} \iota(v)$ (note that by Claim 1, this union is indeed an interval). The following claim bounds the maximum possible width of a directed path:

Claim 2: If P is a directed path D starting at v, then the width of P is at most $16x(v)$.

To prove Claim 2, we first show that if every vertex of P has the same class $\kappa(v)$, then the width of P is at most $4 \cdot 2^{-\kappa(v)}$. Since the class is nondecreasing along the path, we can partition the path into subpaths such that every vertex in a subpath has the same class and the classes are distinct on the different subpaths. The width of P is at most the sum of the widths of the subpaths, which is at most $\sum_{i \geq \kappa(v)} 4 \cdot 2^{-i} = 8 \cdot 2^{-\kappa(v)} \leq 16x(v)$.

Suppose now that every vertex of P has the same class $\kappa(v)$ as the first vertex v and let $h := 2^{-\kappa(v)}$. As the offset is nondecreasing, path P can be partitioned into two parts: a subpath P_1 containing vertices with offset at least h, followed by a subpath P_2 containing vertices with offset less than h (one of P_1 and P_2 can be empty). We show that each of P_1 and P_2 has width at most $2h$, which implies that the width of P is at most $4h$. Observe that if $v \in P_1$ and $\iota(v)$ contains a point $i \cdot 2h$ for some integer i, then, considering $x(v) \leq h$ and the bounds on the offset of v, this is only possible if $\iota(v) = [i \cdot 2h, i \cdot 2h + h]$, i.e., $i \cdot 2h$ is the left endpoint of $\iota(v)$. Thus if $I_1 = \bigcup_{v \in P_1} \iota(v)$ contains $i \cdot 2h$, then it is the left endpoint of I_1. Therefore, I_1 can contain $i \cdot 2h$ for at most one value of i, which immediately implies that the length of I_1 is at most $2h$. We can argue similarly for P_2.

Claim 3: $\sum_{v \in V(H)} x(v)c(v) \leq w$ for $c(v) := \partial b_\pi(v)$.

Let us examine the contribution of an edge $e \in E(H)$ with value $s(e)$ to the sum. For every $v \in e$, edge e increases the value $x(v)$ by at most $s(e)$. Thus the total contribution of e is at most

$$s(e) \cdot \sum_{v \in e} c(v) = s(e) \cdot \sum_{v \in e} \partial b_\pi(v) \leq s(e) \cdot \sum_{v \in e} \partial b_{\pi,e}(v) = s(e) b_\pi(e) \leq s(e) b(e) \leq s(e),$$

where the first inequality follows Prop. 4.2(5); the second inequality follows form Prop. 4.2(3); the last inequality follows from the fact that b is edge dominated. Therefore, $\sum_{v \in V(H)} x(v)c(v) \leq \sum_{e \in E(H)} s(e) \leq w$, proving Claim 3.

We define $\mathcal{C}(S)$ to be the set of all vertices from which a vertex of S is reachable on a directed path in D.

Claim 4: For every $S \subseteq V(H)$, $\sum_{v \in \mathcal{C}(S)} c(v) = b_\pi(\mathcal{C}(S))$.

Observe that for any $v \in \mathcal{C}(S)$, every inneighbor of v is also in $\mathcal{C}(S)$, hence $N_\pi^-(v) \subseteq \mathcal{C}(S)$. Therefore, $\partial b_{\pi,\mathcal{C}(S)}(v) = \partial b_\pi(v) = c(v)$ and Claim 4 follows.

Now we are ready to prove the lemma. Let $S(t)$ be the set of all vertices $v \in V(H)$ for which $t \in \iota(v)$ and let $S_C(t) = \mathcal{C}(S(t))$. Observe that for every $0 \leq t \leq 1$, the set $S(t)$ (and hence $S_C(t)$) separates X from Y. We use an averaging argument to show that there is a $0 \leq t \leq 1$ for which $b_\pi(S_C(t))$ is $O(w)$. As $b^*(S_C(t)) \leq b_\pi(S_C(t))$, the set $S_C(t)$ satisfies the requirement of the lemma.

If we can show that $\int_0^1 b_\pi(S_C(t))dt = O(w)$, then the existence of the required t follows. Let $I_v(t) = 1$ if $v \in S_C(t)$ and let $I_v(t) = 0$ otherwise. If $I_v(t) = 1$, then there is a path P in D from v to $S(t)$. By Claim 2, the width of this path is at most $16x(v)$, thus $t \in [d(v) - 16x(v), d(v) + 15x(v)]$. Therefore, $\int_0^1 I_v(t)dt \leq 31x(v)$. Now we have

$$\int_0^1 b_\pi(S_C(t))dt = \int_0^1 \sum_{v \in S_C(t)} c(v)dt = \int_0^1 \sum_{v \in V(H)} c(v)I_v(t)dt = \sum_{v \in V(H)} c(v) \int_0^1 I_v(t)dt \leq 31 \sum_{v \in V(H)} x(v)c(v) \leq 31w$$

(we used Claim 4 in the first equality and Claim 3 in the last inequality). □

By Prop 4.2(2), the following lemma implies Theorem 4.1. The proof is a recursive procedure finding a tree decomposition, using Lemmas 4.3 and 4.4 to overcome the difficulties described at the beginning of the section.

LEMMA 4.5. *Let b be an edge-dominated monotone submodular function of H. If b^*-width$(H) > \frac{3}{2}(w+1)$, then $\mathrm{con}_\lambda(W) \geq w$ (for some universal constant λ).*

5. FROM HIGHLY CONNECTED SETS TO EMBEDDINGS

We show that the existence of highly connected sets implies that the hypergraph has large embedding power:

THEOREM 5.1. *For every sufficiently small $\lambda > 0$ and hypergraph H, there is a constant $m_{H,\lambda}$ such that every graph G with $m \geq m_{H,\lambda}$ edges has an embedding into H with edge depth $O(m/(\lambda^{\frac{3}{2}} \mathrm{con}_\lambda(H)^{\frac{1}{4}}))$.*

Our strategy is similar to [24]: we show that a highly connected set implies that a uniform concurrent flow exists; the paths appearing in the uniform concurrent flow can be used to embed the line graph of a complete graph; and every graph has an appropriate embedding in the line graph of a complete graph. To make this strategy work, we need generalizations of concurrent flows, multicuts, and multicommodity flows in our hypergraph setting and we need to obtain results that connect these concepts to highly connected sets. Let W be a set of vertices and let $(X_1, \ldots, X_k)$ be a partition of W. A *uniform concurrent flow of value ϵ on $(X_1, \ldots, X_k)$* is a compatible set of $\binom{k}{2}$ flows $F_{i,j}$ $(1 \leq i < j \leq k)$ where $F_{i,j}$ is an (X_i, X_j)-flow of value ϵ. We will need a uniform concurrent flow connecting a set of cliques, thus our first goal is to find a highly connected set that can be partitioned into k cliques in an appropriate way. (Proofs of this section appear in the full version of the paper.)

LEMMA 5.2. *Let H be a hypergraph and let $0 < \lambda < 1/16$ be a constant. Then there is fractional independent set μ, a $(\mu, \lambda/6)$-connected set W, and a partition $(K_1, \ldots, K_k)$ of W such that $k = \Omega(\lambda\sqrt{\mathrm{con}_\lambda(H)})$, and for every $1 \leq i \leq k$, K_i is a clique with $\mu(K_i) \geq 1/2$.*

If H is connected, then the maximum value of a uniform concurrent flow on $(X_1, \ldots, X_k)$ is at least $1/\binom{k}{2} = \Omega(k^{-2})$: if each of the $\binom{k}{2}$ flows has value $1/\binom{k}{2}$, then they are clearly compatible. The following lemma shows that if $X_1, \ldots, X_r$ are appropriate cliques of a (μ, λ)-connected set, then we can guarantee a better bound $\Omega(k^{-\frac{3}{2}})$.

LEMMA 5.3. *Let H be a hypergraph, μ a fractional independent set of H, and $W \subseteq V(H)$ a (μ, λ)-connected set of W for some $0 < \lambda < 1$. Let $(K_1, \ldots, K_k)$ be a partition of W such that K_i is a clique and $\mu(K_i) \geq 1/2$ for every $1 \leq i \leq k$. Then there is a uniform concurrent flow of value $\Omega(\lambda/k^{\frac{3}{2}})$ on $(K_1, \ldots, K_k)$.*

Intuitively, the intersection structure of the paths appearing in a uniform concurrent flow on cliques $K_1, \ldots, K_r$ is reminiscent of the edges of the complete graph on r vertices: if $\{i_1, j_1\} \cap \{i_2, j_2\} \neq \emptyset$, then every path of F_{i_1,j_1} touches every path of F_{i_2,j_2}. We use the following result from [24] (restated using the terminology of this paper), which shows that line graphs of cliques have good embedding properties. Let L_k be the line graph of the k-clique.

LEMMA 5.4. *For every $k > 1$ there is a constant $n_k > 0$ such that for every $G(V, E)$ with $|E| > n_k$ and no isolated vertices, the graph G has an embedding into L_k with vertex depth $O(|E|/k^2)$.*

The proof of Theorem 5.1 uses Lemmas 5.2 and 5.3 to find highly connected set and a uniform concurrent flow on it, and then uses Lemma 5.4 to embed the vertices of G into the paths appearing in the flows.

6. FROM EMBEDDINGS TO HARDNESS OF CSP

We prove the main hardness result in this section:

THEOREM 6.1. *Let $\mathcal{H}$ be a recursively enumerable class of hypergraphs with unbounded submodular width. If there is an algorithm $\mathbb{A}$ and a function f such that $\mathbb{A}$ solves every instance I of CSP($\mathcal{H}$) with hypergraph $H \in \mathcal{H}$ in time $f(H) \cdot \|I\|^{o(\mathrm{subw}(H)^{\frac{1}{4}})}$, then the Exponential Time Hypothesis fails.*

In particular, Theorem 6.1 implies that CSP($\mathcal{H}$) for such a $\mathcal{H}$ is not fixed-parameter tractable:

COROLLARY 6.2. *If $\mathcal{H}$ is a recursively enumerable class of hypergraphs with unbounded submodular width, then CSP($\mathcal{H}$) is not fixed-parameter tractable, unless ETH fails.*

The Exponential Time Hypothesis (ETH) states that there is no $2^{o(n)}$ time algorithm for n-variable 3SAT. The Sparsification Lemma of Impagliazzo, Paturi, and Zane [22] shows that ETH is equivalent to the assumption that there is no algorithm for 3SAT whose running time is subexponential *in the number of clauses*. This result will be crucial for our hardness proof, as our reduction from 3SAT is sensitive to the number of clauses.

To prove Theorem 6.1, we show that a "too fast" algorithm $\mathbb{A}$ implies that a subexponential-time algorithm for 3SAT exists. We use the characterization of submodular width from Section 4 and the embedding results of Section 5 to reduce 3SAT to CSP($\mathcal{H}$) by embedding the incidence graph of a 3SAT formula into a hypergraph $H \in \mathcal{H}$. The basic idea of the proof is that if the 3SAT formula has m clauses and the edge depth of the embedding is m/r, then we can gain a factor r in the exponent of the running time. If submodular width is unbounded in $\mathcal{H}$, then we can make this gap r between the number of clauses and the edge depth arbitrary large, and hence the exponent can be arbitrarily smaller than the number of clauses, i.e., the algorithm is subexponential in the number of clauses.

The following simple lemma gives a transformation that turns a 3SAT instance into a binary CSP instance.

LEMMA 6.3 ([24]). *Given an instance of 3SAT with n variables and m clauses, it is possible to construct in polynomial time an equivalent CSP instance with $n + m$ variables, $3m$ binary constraints, and domain size 3.*

Next we show that an embedding from graph G to hypergraph H can be used to simulate a binary CSP instance I_1 having primal graph G by a CSP instance I_2 whose hypergraph is H. The size of the constraint relations of I_2 can grow very large: the edge depth of the embedding determines how large is this increase.

LEMMA 6.4. *Let $I_1 = (V_1, D_1, C_1)$ be a binary CSP instance with primal graph G and let ϕ be an embedding of G into a hypergraph H with edge depth q. Given I_1, H, and the embedding ϕ, it is possible to construct (in time polynomial in the size of the output) an equivalent CSP instance $I_2 = (V_2, D_2, C_2)$ with hypergraph H where the size of every constraint relation is at most $|D_1|^q$.*

With these tools at hand, we can prove Theorem 6.1 the following way. We show that if there is a class $\mathcal{H}$ of hypergraphs with unbounded submodular width and an algorithm $\mathbb{A}$ as in Theorem 6.1, then this algorithm can be used to solve 3SAT in subexponential time. The main ingredients are the embedding result of Theorem 5.1, and Lemmas 6.3 and 6.4 above on reduction to CSP. Furthermore, we need a way of choosing an appropriate hypergraph from the set $\mathcal{H}$. As discussed earlier, the larger the submodular width of the hypergraph is, the more we gain in the running time. However, we should not spend too much time on constructing the hypergraph and on finding an embedding. Therefore, we use the same technique as in [24]: we enumerate a certain number of hypergraphs and we try all of them simultaneously. The number of hypergraphs enumerated depends on the size of the 3SAT instance. This will be done in such a way that guarantees that we do not spend too much time on the enumeration, but eventually every hypergraph in $\mathcal{H}$ is considered for sufficiently large input sizes.

7. REFERENCES

[1] I. Adler. *Width functions for hypertree decompositions.* PhD thesis, Albert-Ludwigs-Universität Freiburg, 2006.

[2] I. Adler, G. Gottlob, and M. Grohe. Hypertree width and related hypergraph invariants. *European J. Combin.*, 28(8):2167–2181, 2007.

[3] N. Alon, I. Newman, A. Shen, G. Tardos, and N. Vereshchagin. Partitioning multi-dimensional sets in a small number of "uniform" parts. *European J. Combin.*, 28(1):134–144, 2007.

[4] C. Beeri, R. Fagin, D. Maier, A. O. Mendelzon, J. D. Ullman, and M. Yannakakis. Properties of acyclic database schemes. In *STOC*, pages 355–362, 1981.

[5] C. Beeri, R. Fagin, D. Maier, and M. Yannakakis. On the desirability of acyclic database schemes. *J. Assoc. Comput. Mach.*, 30(3):479–513, 1983.

[6] A. K. Chandra and P. M. Merlin. Optimal implementation of conjunctive queries in relational data bases. In *STOC*, pages 77–90, 1977.

[7] C. Chekuri and A. Rajaraman. Conjunctive query containment revisited. *Theoret. Comput. Sci.*, 239(2):211–229, 2000.

[8] H. Chen and M. Grohe. Constraint satisfaction problems with succinctly specified relations, 2006. Manuscript. Preliminary version in *Dagstuhl Seminar Proceedings 06401: Complexity of Constraints.*

[9] F. R. K. Chung, R. L. Graham, P. Frankl, and J. B. Shearer. Some intersection theorems for ordered sets and graphs. *J. Combin. Theory Ser. A*, 43(1):23–37, 1986.

[10] R. G. Downey and M. R. Fellows. *Parameterized Complexity.* Monographs in Computer Science. Springer, New York, 1999.

[11] R. Fagin. Degrees of acyclicity for hypergraphs and relational database schemes. *J. Assoc. Comput. Mach.*, 30(3):514–550, 1983.

[12] T. Feder and M. Y. Vardi. The computational structure of monotone monadic SNP and constraint satisfaction: a study through Datalog and group theory. *SIAM J. Comput.*, 28(1):57–104, 1999.

[13] J. Flum and M. Grohe. *Parameterized Complexity Theory.* Springer, Berlin, 2006.

[14] E. C. Freuder. Complexity of k-tree structured constraint satisfaction problems. In *Proc. of AAAI-90*, pages 4–9, Boston, MA, 1990.

[15] G. Gottlob, N. Leone, and F. Scarcello. Hypertree decompositions and tractable queries. *Journal of Computer and System Sciences*, 64:579–627, 2002.

[16] G. Gottlob, F. Scarcello, and M. Sideri. Fixed-parameter complexity in AI and nonmonotonic reasoning. *Artificial Intelligence*, 138(1-2):55–86, 2002.

[17] G. Gottlob and S. Szeider. Fixed-parameter algorithms for artificial intelligence, constraint satisfaction and database problems. *The Computer Journal*, 51(3):303–325, 2008.

[18] M. Grohe. The structure of tractable constraint satisfaction problems. In *MFCS'06*, pages 58–72, 2006.

[19] M. Grohe. The complexity of homomorphism and constraint satisfaction problems seen from the other side. *J. ACM*, 54(1):1, 2007.

[20] M. Grohe and D. Marx. Constraint solving via fractional edge covers. In *SODA'06*, pages 289–298, 2006.

[21] M. Grohe and D. Marx. On tree width, bramble size, and expansion. *J. Combin. Theory Ser. B*, 99(1):218–228, 2009.

[22] R. Impagliazzo, R. Paturi, and F. Zane. Which problems have strongly exponential complexity? *J. Comput. System Sci.*, 63(4):512–530, 2001.

[23] P. G. Kolaitis and M. Y. Vardi. Conjunctive-query containment and constraint satisfaction. *J. Comput. Syst. Sci.*, 61(2):302–332, 2000.

[24] D. Marx. Can you beat treewidth? To appear in *Theory of Computing.*

[25] D. Marx. Approximating fractional hypetree width. In *SODA'09*, pages 902–911, 2009.

[26] D. Marx. Tractable structures for constraint satisfaction with truth tables. In *STACS'09*, pages 649–660, 2009.

[27] R. Niedermeier. *Invitation to fixed-parameter algorithms*, volume 31 of *Oxford Lecture Series in Mathematics and its Applications.* Oxford University Press, Oxford, 2006.

[28] S. Oum. Approximating rank-width and clique-width quickly. In *WG'05*, pages 49–58, 2005.

[29] S. Oum and P. Seymour. Testing branch-width. *J. Combin. Theory Ser. B*, 97(3):385–393, 2007.

[30] S.-i. Oum and P. Seymour. Approximating clique-width and branch-width. *J. Combin. Theory Ser. B*, 96(4):514–528, 2006.

[31] F. Scarcello, G. Gottlob, and G. Greco. Uniform constraint satisfaction problems and database theory. In *Complexity of Constraints*, pages 156–195, 2008.

[32] M. Yannakakis. Algorithms for acyclic database schemes. In *VLDB*, pages 82–94, 1981.

Conditional Hardness of Precedence Constrained Scheduling on Identical Machines

Ola Svensson
KTH – Royal Institute of Technology
Stockholm, Sweden
osven@kth.se

ABSTRACT

Already in 1966, Graham showed that a simple procedure called list scheduling yields a 2-approximation algorithm for the central problem of scheduling precedence constrained jobs on identical machines to minimize makespan. Till this date it has remained the best algorithm and whether it can or cannot be improved has become a major open problem in scheduling theory.

We address this problem by establishing a quite surprising relation between the approximability of the considered problem and that of scheduling precedence constrained jobs on a single machine to minimize weighted completion time. More specifically, we prove that if the single machine problem is hard to approximate within a factor of $2-\epsilon$ then the considered parallel machine problem, even in the case of unit processing times, is hard to approximate within a factor of $2-\zeta$, where ζ tends to 0 as ϵ tends to 0. Combining this with Bansal & Khot's recent hardness result for the single machine problem gives that it is NP-hard to improve upon the approximation ratio obtained by Graham, assuming a new variant of the unique games conjecture.

Categories and Subject Descriptors

F.2 [**Analysis of Algorithms and Problem Complexity**]: Nonnumerical Algorithms and Problems—*Sequencing and scheduling*

General Terms

Theory

1. INTRODUCTION

One of the first approximation algorithms with a worst-case analysis can be traced back to 1966, when Graham [20] studied the following central scheduling problem (known as $P|prec|C_{max}$ in standard scheduling notation [19]): There is a set N of n jobs to be scheduled on m identical parallel machines. Each machine can process at most one job at a time and each job $j \in N$ requires p_j uninterrupted units of processing on one of the machines. Jobs also have precedence constraints between them that are specified by a partial order P on N, where $(i,j) \in P$ implies that job i must be completed before job j can be started. The goal is to find a schedule that minimizes the makespan $C_{max} = \max_j C_j$, where C_j is the time at which job j completes in the given schedule.

Arguably the simplest algorithm for many scheduling problems is the so called *list scheduling* procedure, where we order the jobs in a preference list and schedule the first available job(s) from the list whenever a machine falls idle. In his seminal paper [20], Graham showed that for $P|prec|C_{max}$, the list scheduling procedure has a worst-case performance guarantee of $2-1/m$.

Considering the special case with no precedence constraints, denoted by $P||C_{max}$, Graham [21] later refined his analysis and showed that the list scheduling procedure has a worst-case performance guarantee of $4/3-1/(3m)$, assuming the priority list is obtained by arranging jobs according to non-increasing processing times. Using more complex techniques, Hochbaum & Shmoys [22] improved upon the $4/3-1/(3m)$ approximation guarantee by giving a polynomial time approximation scheme for $P||C_{max}$. This gives a tight result since $P||C_{max}$ is known to be strongly NP-hard and hence does not admit a fully polynomial time approximation scheme [15]. We remark that the problem where the number of machines is fixed, i.e., not part of the input, is also resolved in terms of approximability: Sahni [33] gave a fully polynomial approximation scheme and it is easily seen to be weakly NP-hard by a reduction from partition. In summary, the considered problem is well understood in the absence of precedence constraints.

Unfortunately, understanding the complexity in the presence of precedence constraints has turned out to be much more challenging and remains limited. The mentioned $(2-1/m)$-approximation algorithm obtained by Graham in 1966, remains the algorithm of choice for this problem. The last progress in understanding whether it can or cannot be improved, was made over 30 years ago by Lenstra & Rinnooy Kan [29] who showed that it is NP-hard to approximate $P|prec|C_{max}$ within a factor less than 4/3. Closing this gap is mentioned as "Open Problem 1" in Woeginger and Schuurman's list of ten open problems in scheduling theory [35]. Furthermore, the computational complexity of finding an exact solution to $Pm|prec, p_j = 1|C_{max}$ (the problem with a fixed number m of machines and unit processing times),

STOC'10, June 5–8, 2010, Cambridge, Massachusetts, USA.

open problem "OPEN8" from the original list of Garey and Johnson [16], is still open.

We remark that Du, Leung & Young [11] showed that $P2|prec|C_{max}$ is strongly NP-hard. Whereas, $P2|prec, p_j = 1|C_{max}$ is known to be polynomially solvable by techniques from matching theory (Fujii, Kasami & Ninomiya [13]). The best algorithm for problem $P3|prec, p_j = 1|C_{max}$ is a 4/3-approximation algorithm by Lam & Sethi [27][1] who analyzed an algorithm by Coffman & Graham [9]. In a recent paper [14], Gangal & Ranade showed that Graham's $(2 - 1/m)$-approximation algorithm can be improved to a $(2 - \frac{7}{3m+1})$-approximation algorithm in case of unit processing times and $m > 3$. Older results by Hu [23] and Garey, Johnson, Tarjan, & Yannakakis [17] give polynomial time algorithms in the case of unit processing times and special cases of precedence constraints. We refer the interested reader to the surveys [7] and [19] for further information on these and other algorithms for special cases of $P|prec|C_{max}$.

1.1 Our Results

We make the first progress in settling the approximability of $P|prec|C_{max}$ in the last 30 years: assuming a new possibly stronger version of the unique games conjecture (introduced by Bansal & Khot [4]), we show that it is NP-hard to approximate the scheduling problem $P|prec|C_{max}$ within any factor strictly less than 2, even in the case of unit processing times. The result is obtained by establishing a quite surprising connection between $P|prec|C_{max}$ and the scheduling problem of minimizing weighted completion time with precedence constraints ($1|prec|\sum w_j C_j$), studied in [4].

The problem $1|prec|\sum w_j C_j$ is another classical scheduling problem that has been studied since the 70's [36, 28, 30, 32]. Despite much interest, there was, until recently, a relatively large gap in our understanding of the approximability of $1|prec|\sum w_j C_j$. On the algorithmic side, several different techniques and linear programming formulations have been used to obtain 2-approximation algorithms for it (see e.g. [34, 6, 8, 31]). On the hardness side, before 2007, only NP-hardness for the exact problem was known [28, 30].

However, in contrast to $P|prec|C_{max}$, several recent results have lead to increased understanding of $1|prec|\sum w_j C_j$. In a series of papers [8, 10, 1] it was in fact established that $1|prec|\sum w_j C_j$ is a special case of weighted vertex cover; a result exploited to obtain improved approximation algorithms for special cases of precedence constraints [2]. Furthermore, new techniques have been used to obtain inapproximability results. Ambühl, Mastrolilli & the author [3] used the Quasi-random PCP due to Khot [25] to rule out the possibility of a polynomial time approximation scheme. More importantly, Bansal & Khot [4] settled the approximability of $1|prec|\sum w_j C_j$ assuming a certain conjecture. More specifically, they proved, assuming a new variant of the unique games conjecture (see Hypothesis 1 described in Appendix B), that it is NP-hard to approximate the value of an optimal schedule to $1|prec|\sum w_j C_j$ within a factor of $2 - \epsilon$ for any $\epsilon > 0$.

Our main result lets us profit from the hardness of $1|prec|\sum w_j C_j$ to obtain hardness of $P|prec|C_{max}$:

[1]Also see [5] for a correction of an error in [27].

THEOREM 1. *For any $\epsilon > 0$ and $\zeta \geq \zeta(\epsilon)$ where $\zeta(\epsilon)$ tends to 0 as ϵ tends to 0: if $1|prec|\sum w_j C_j$ has no $(2-\epsilon)$-approximation algorithm[2] then $P|prec|C_{max}$ has no $(2-\zeta)$-approximation algorithm, even in the case of unit processing times.*

The relation between the approximability of $1|prec|\sum w_j C_j$ and that of $P|prec|C_{max}$ is interesting on its own. In particular, even if the new variant of the unique games conjecture is false it might very well be that $1|prec|\sum w_j C_j$ (and thus $P|prec|C_{max}$ by the above theorem) is NP-hard to approximate within a factor $2 - \epsilon$, for any $\epsilon > 0$.

Proof overview 1. The proof is made in two steps. First in Section 2, we show that if $1|prec|\sum w_j C_j$ has no $(2-\epsilon)$-approximation algorithm then the following bipartite ordering problem is also hard: given an n by n bipartite graph $G(V, W, E)$ determine for a small $\zeta > 0$ whether

- (YES Case): G has a permutation $\pi : V \mapsto \{1, \ldots n\}$ such that for $i = 1, 2, \ldots, n$, the set
$$\{w \in W : \max_{\{v,w\} \in E} \pi(v) \leq i\}$$
has size at least $i - \zeta n$.
- (NO Case): For each permutation $\pi : V \mapsto \{1, \ldots n\}$, the set
$$\{w \in W : \max_{\{v,w\} \in E} \pi(v) \leq (1-\zeta)n\}$$
has size at most ζn.

The proof of the hardness of this problem is based on some new observations together with several older results regarding the structure of problem $1|prec|\sum w_j C_j$.

Second in Section 3, we provide a reduction from the bipartite graph problem to $P|prec|C_{max}$. The intuition of the reduction is the following. Let $\delta > \zeta$ be a small constant and Let $G(V, W, E)$ be an instance of the bipartite ordering problem. Consider the instance $\mathcal{I}$ of $P|prec|C_{max}$ with $(1-\delta)n$ machines, a job with processing time 1 for each vertex in G, and a precedence constraint from $v \in V$ to $w \in W$ if $\{v, w\} \in E$. Now suppose G is a YES instance, then there is a permutation π so that the set $\{w \in W : \max_{\{v,w\} \in E} \pi(v) \leq (1-\delta)n\}$ has size at least $(1-\delta)n - \zeta n \geq (1-2\delta)n$. This means that there is a schedule of $\mathcal{I}$ that completes the jobs corresponding to the first (according to π) $(1-\delta)n$ vertices in V at time 1; schedules the remaining jobs in V (at most δn many) and $(1-2\delta)n$ jobs in $\{w \in W : \max_{\{v,w\} \in E} \pi(v) \leq (1-\delta)n\}$ during time interval [1, 2]; and finally completes the remaining jobs in W at time 3. On the other hand if G is a NO instance, then it is easy to see that any schedule will have completed only a fraction ζ of the jobs in W at time 2. It follows that any schedule will need to schedule at least a fraction $1 - \zeta > 1 - \delta = m$ of the W-jobs from time 2 and will thus have makespan at least 4.

To amplify this "gap", we form a new instance $\mathcal{I}'$ that consists of several copies of $\mathcal{I}$ that are related by precedence constraints. For a hardness factor close to 2, a careful balance between the number of copies and the number of

[2]Recall that an α-approximation algorithm is a polynomial time algorithm that approximates the value of an optimal solution within a factor of α.

machines is needed. With our current techniques ϵ must be significant smaller than ζ and as a result a strong hardness result (close to 2) is needed for $1|prec|\sum w_jC_j$ to obtain a good hardness result for $P|prec|C_{max}$. □

The above theorem together with the result of Bansal & Khot [4], gives us the following corollary.

COROLLARY 1. *Assuming a new variant of the unique games conjecture (Hypothesis 1), it is NP-hard to approximate $P|prec|C_{max}$ within a factor $(2-\zeta)$, for any $\zeta > 0$.*

2. BIPARTITE ORDERING AND SCHEDULING PROBLEM $1|PREC|\sum W_J C_J$

Problem $1|prec|\sum w_jC_j$ is the problem of scheduling a set N of n jobs on a single machine, which can process at most one job at a time. Each job $j \in N$ has a processing time p_j and a weight w_j. Jobs also have precedence constraints between them that are specified in the form of a partial order P on N. The goal is to find a schedule that minimizes $\sum_{j\in N} w_jC_j$, where C_j is the time at which job j completes in the given schedule. In this section we shall see that if $1|prec|\sum w_jC_j$ has no $(2-\epsilon)$-approximation algorithm for some $\epsilon > 0$, then there is no polynomial algorithm that distinguishes between certain bipartite graphs (see Theorem 2). This will then be used to prove our main result in Section 3.

Before presenting the result of this section we need the following definition.

Definition 1. For an n by n bipartite graph $G = (V, W, E)$ and a permutation $\pi : V \mapsto \{1, \ldots, n\}$, define

$$V_i^\pi = \{v \in V : \pi(v) \le i\} \quad \text{for } i = 1, \ldots, n$$

$$W_i^\pi = \{w \in W : \max_{\{v,w\}\in E} \pi(v) \le i\} \quad \text{for } i = 0, 1, \ldots, n.$$

THEOREM 2. *For any $\epsilon > 0$ and ζ such that $\zeta^2 > 2\epsilon$: if no polynomial algorithm approximates $1|prec|\sum w_jC_j$ within a factor of $(2-\epsilon)$, then there is no polynomial algorithm that distinguishes between n by n bipartite graphs*

- *that have a permutation π of V that satisfies*

$$|W_i^\pi| \ge i - \zeta n \qquad \text{for } i = 1, 2, \ldots, n$$

- *and those for which each permutation π of V satisfies*

$$|W_{(1-\zeta)n}^\pi| \le \zeta n.$$

PROOF. Woeginger [37] proved that the general case of $1|prec|\sum w_jC_j$ is no harder to approximate than the following bipartite case:

1. The set N of jobs are partitioned into two sets A and B so that the set P of precedence constraints is a subset of $A \times B$.
2. The jobs in A have processing time 1 and weight 0 and the jobs in B have processing time 0 and weight 1.

We can thus restrict our attention to such bipartite instances. Structural results by Sidney [36] and algorithmic results by Lawler [28] imply that an α-approximation algorithm for bipartite instances that are so called non-Sidney-decomposable gives an α-approximation algorithm for all bipartite instances.[3]

[3]We remark that we have restricted ourselves to bipartite instances of $1|prec|\sum w_jC_j$, but the results by Sidney and Lawler hold for general instances (see [18] for a nice exposition of these results).

A bipartite instance is non-Sidney-decomposable if for each $A' \subseteq A$ the number of jobs in B with no predecessors in $A\backslash A'$ is at most $\frac{|A'|}{|A|}|B|$. We can thus further restrict ourselves to bipartite instances that are non-Sidney-decomposable.

When analyzing non-Sidney-decomposable bipartite instances it will be convenient to work with the so-called 2D Gantt chart, first introduced by Eastman et al. [12] and later revived by Goemans and Williamson [18] to give elegant proofs for various results related to $1|prec|\sum w_jC_j$. In a 2D Gantt chart, we have a horizontal axis of processing time and a vertical axis of weight. For a scheduling instance of the above form, the chart starts at point $(0, |B|)$ and ends at point $(|A|, 0)$. A job j is represented by a rectangle of length p_j and height w_j. Hence, a job of A is represented by a horizontal line of length 1 and a job of B is represented by a vertical line of length 1. Any schedule is represented in the 2D Gantt chart by placing the corresponding rectangles of the jobs in the order of the schedule such that the startpoint of a job is the endpoint of the previous job (or $(0, |B|)$ for the first job). The value $\sum_j w_jC_j$ of a schedule is then the area under the "work line" (see the shaded area in Figure 1-a).

Recall that a bipartite instance is non-Sidney-decomposable if for each $A' \subseteq A$ the number of jobs in B with no predecessors in $A \setminus A'$ is at most $\frac{|A'|}{|A|}|B|$. It follows that any schedule for such an instance will have its work line always above the diagonal in the 2D Gantt chart. Hence, any schedule of a non-Sidney-decomposable bipartite instance has value at least $|A||B|/2$. This was discovered independently in the general case by Chekuri and Motwani [6] and Margot et al. [31]; and later shown by Goemans and Williamson [18] using 2D Gantt charts.

As non-Sidney-decomposable bipartite instances are the hardest instances to approximate and any schedule of such an instance with job sets A and B has value at least $|A||B|/2$, we have the following. If there is no $(2-\epsilon)$-approximation algorithm for $1|prec|\sum w_jC_j$ then there is no polynomial algorithm that distinguishes between non-Sidney-decomposable bipartite instances with value $\frac{1+2\epsilon}{2}|A||B|$ and those with value $(1-\epsilon)|A||B|$, for any $\epsilon > 0$. Indeed, suppose there exists a polynomial time algorithm $\mathcal{A}$ that outputs "YES" if the scheduling instance has value at most $\frac{1+2\epsilon}{2}|A||B|$ and outputs "NO" if the scheduling instance has value at least $(1-\epsilon)|A||B|$. Then the following is a $(2-\epsilon)$-approximation algorithm: given a non-Sidney-decomposable bipartite instance with job sets A and B, run $\mathcal{A}$ on the instance and

- if $\mathcal{A}$ outputs "YES" then approximate the value of the instance to be $(1-\epsilon)|A||B|$ (since any schedule has value at least $|A||B|/2$ this is a $(2-2\epsilon)$-approximation);
- else approximate the value of the instance to be $|A||B|$ (since any schedule then has value at least $\frac{1+2\epsilon}{2}|A||B|$ this is a $\frac{2}{1+2\epsilon} \le (2-\epsilon)$-approximation).

Now let $\mathcal{I}$ be a non-Sidney-decomposable bipartite instance with the jobs partitioned into sets A and B and precedence constraints P. Let $n_A = |A|, n_B = |B|$, and $n = n_An_B$. With $\mathcal{I}$ we associate an n by n bipartite graph $G(V, W, E)$ where there are n_B vertices in V for each $a \in A$ referred to as V_a, n_A vertices in W for each $b \in B$ referred to as W_b, and an edge between all vertices in V_a and all vertices in W_b if $(a, b) \in P$. In other words, G is the undirected graph of the precedence constraints where each job in A has

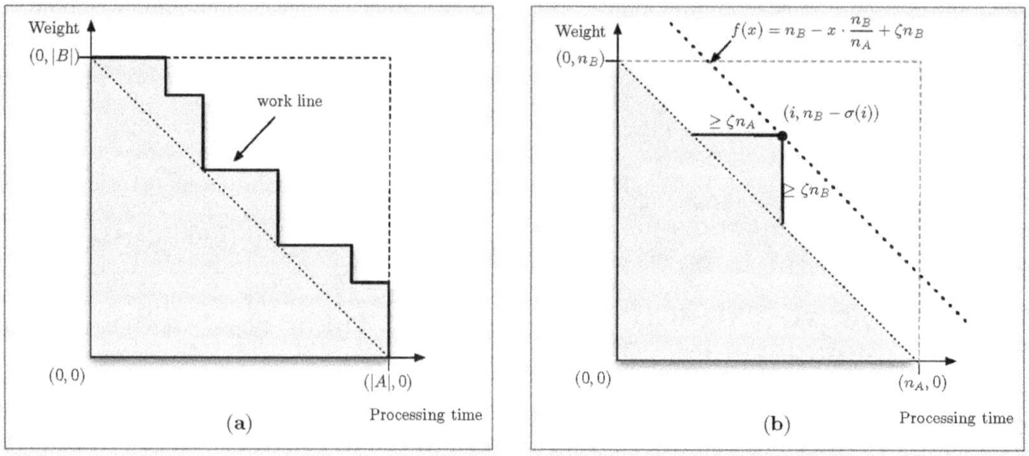

Figure 1: (a): An example of a 2D Gantt diagram. (b): An illustration of the argument used to prove Claim 1-a.

been copied n_B times and each job in B has been copied n_A times. The following claim completes the proof of the theorem.

CLAIM 1. *For any $\zeta > 0$ such that $\zeta^2 > 2\epsilon$:*

(a) If $\mathcal{I}$ has a schedule of value at most $\frac{1+2\epsilon}{2}n$ then G has a permutation π of V that satisfies

$$|W_i^\pi| \geq i - \zeta n \qquad \text{for } i = 1, 2, \ldots, n$$

(b) If all schedules of $\mathcal{I}$ have value at least $(1-\epsilon)n$ then each permutation π of V satisfies

$$|W_{(1-\zeta)n}^\pi| \leq \zeta n.$$

Proof of claim 1. (a): Let σ be a schedule of $\mathcal{I}$ with value at most $\frac{1+2\epsilon}{2}n$. For $i = 0, 1, 2, \ldots, n_A$, we let $\sigma(i)$ denote the number of jobs in B that have been scheduled when at most i jobs in A have completed. Now suppose toward contradiction that there exists an integer $i = 1, 2, \ldots, n_A$ such that $\sigma(i) \leq i\frac{n_B}{n_A} - \zeta n_B$ and consider the the 2D Gantt chart of σ. As σ will have its work line above both the diagonal and the point $(i, n_B - \sigma(i))$ on the dotted line(see Figure 1-b), the value of σ will be at least

$$n_B \cdot n_A/2 + \zeta n_A \cdot \zeta n_B/2 \quad = \quad \frac{1+\zeta^2}{2}n,$$

which is, by the choice of ζ, strictly greater than $\frac{1+2\epsilon}{2}n$. A contradiction since we assumed the value of σ to be at most $\frac{1+2\epsilon}{2}n$. Hence, for all $i = 1, 2, \ldots, n_A$ we have $\sigma(i) > i\frac{n_B}{n_A} - \zeta n_B$. Now let π be a permutation that orders all vertices in V_a before the vertices in $V_{a'}$ if σ schedules a before a'. Note that by the definition of G and π

$$|W_{i \cdot n_B}^\pi| \geq n_A \cdot \sigma(i) \qquad \text{for } i = 1, \ldots, n_A.$$

It follows that for $i = 1, 2, \ldots, n$

$$|W_i^\pi| \geq n_A \cdot \sigma(i/n_B) = i - \zeta n_A n_B = i - \zeta n.$$

We remarked that we assumed for simplicity that i/n_b evaluates to an integer. However, it is easy to see that a more careful analysis with $\lfloor i/n_b \rfloor$ will not have any impact on the final result.

(b): Assume all schedules of $\mathcal{I}$ have value at least $(1-\epsilon)n$ and suppose toward contradiction that there is a permutation π of V that satisfies $|W_{(1-\zeta)n}^\pi| > \zeta n$. Let σ be a schedule of $\mathcal{I}$ such that

1. for each $a, a' \in A$, σ schedules a before a' if $\max_{v \in V_a} \pi(v) \leq \max_{v' \in V_{a'}} \pi(v')$
2. and a job in B is scheduled as soon as its predecessors are finished.

Since $|W_{(1-\zeta)n}^\pi| > \zeta n$ at least ζn_B jobs in B are scheduled when at most $(1-\zeta)n_A$ jobs are completed in σ. It follows that the value of σ is at most

$$(1-\zeta)n_A \cdot \zeta n_B + n_A \cdot (1-\zeta)n_B = (1-\zeta^2)n.$$

A contradiction since $\zeta^2 > 2\epsilon$ and hence $(1-\zeta^2) < (1-\epsilon)$.

The proof of the above claim completed the proof of Theorem 2. □

3. PROOF OF MAIN RESULT

Here, we shall use Theorem 2 to establish the connection between $1|prec|\sum w_j C_j$ and $P|prec|C_{max}$. Given an n by n bipartite graph $G(V, W, E)$ and an integer d, we will construct an instance $\mathcal{I}(d)$ of $P|prec, p_j = 1|C_{max}$ such that for a small $\zeta > 0$ that only depends on d:

- *(Completeness)* If G has a permutation π of V that satisfies

$$|W_i^\pi| \geq i - \zeta n \qquad \text{for } i = 1, 2, \ldots, n$$

  then $\mathcal{I}(d)$ has a schedule of makespan $d+1$.

- *(Soundness)* If each permutation π of V satisfies

$$|W_{(1-\zeta)n}^\pi| \leq \zeta n.$$

  then any schedule of $\mathcal{I}(d)$ has makespan $2d$.

Theorem 1 then follows by combining Theorem 2 with the above reduction. We first present the reduction in Section 3.1 followed by the completeness and soundness analyses in Sections 3.2 and 3.3, respectively.

3.1 Construction

The final instance $\mathcal{I}(d)$ will consist of several copies of a set of precedence constrained jobs. This set will be referred to as the "building block" and is actually the only part of the construction that depends on G. The number of copies of the building block is carefully selected and precedence constraints between the copies are added to obtain the final instance $\mathcal{I}(d)$. We first present the building block, then we set the parameters that control the number of copies of the building block and the precedence constraints that are added between those copies. Finally, we present the instance $\mathcal{I}(d)$.

Building Block.

Let $\mathcal{B}$ denote the building block. The set of jobs is $V \cup W$ and there is a precedence constraint from $v \in V$ to $w \in W$ if $\{v, w\} \in E$. In addition the jobs in V, referred to as V-jobs, have processing time 1 and the jobs in W, referred to as W-jobs, have processing time 0. We remark that the jobs with processing time 0 — the W-jobs — are superfluous in the sense that removing them will not change the length of any schedule. Instead, they are included because they make the exposition much cleaner.

Parameters.

Before describing instance $\mathcal{I}(d)$ we need to define some parameters. Select $\gamma_d = \frac{1}{10}$ and let $\gamma_{\ell-1} = \gamma_\ell^{10}$ for $\ell = d, d-1 \ldots, 1$. Furthermore, let $\delta_{\ell+1} = 1/\gamma_\ell^5$ for $\ell = 1, 2, \ldots, d$. Note that $\delta_2, \ldots, \delta_{d+1}, 1/\gamma_1, \ldots, 1/\gamma_d$ are all integers. The parameters are also selected such that the following bounds hold (they will be used in the completeness and soundness analyses).

LEMMA 1. *For each* $\ell = 1, \ldots, d$

$$(1 - 4\gamma_{\ell-1})^{\delta_{\ell+1}} \geq 1 - 2\gamma_\ell \tag{1}$$

$$\left(1 - \frac{\gamma_\ell}{4}\right)^{\delta_{\ell+1}} \leq \gamma_\ell/2 \tag{2}$$

The proof of the above bounds is straightforward and can be found in Appendix A. Finally, we select

$$\zeta = \gamma_0^{10}. \tag{3}$$

Instance.

Instance $\mathcal{I}(d)$ has m machines (selected below (4)) and consists of several copies of $\mathcal{B}$ related to each other by precedence constraints. Conceptually, it will be useful to partition these copies into d *layers*. The copies in layer $\ell = 1, 2, \ldots, d$ will then in turn be subdivided into several *groups*. We will denote the set of groups in layer ℓ by $\mathcal{L}_\ell$. We continue by a formal definition of the layers and will then define the precedence constraints between the layers (see also Figure 2 for an example of the construction):

- Layer 1 consists of a set

$$\mathcal{L}_1 = \{B^{(1,i)} : i \in \{1, \ldots, n\}\}$$

of $|\mathcal{L}_1| = n$ groups and each group $B^{(1,i)} \in \mathcal{L}_1$ contains $(1 + \gamma_1)\frac{m}{n \cdot |\mathcal{L}_1|}$ copies of $\mathcal{B}$.

- Layer $\ell = 2, 3, \ldots, d$ consists of a set

$$\mathcal{L}_\ell = \left\{ B^{(\ell,i,X)} : \begin{array}{c} i \in \{1, \ldots, n\}, \\ \text{X is a multi-set consisting of} \\ \delta_\ell \text{ groups from } \mathcal{L}_{\ell-1} \end{array} \right\}$$

of $|\mathcal{L}_\ell| = n \cdot |\mathcal{L}_{\ell-1}|^{\delta_\ell}$ groups and each group $B^{(\ell,i,X)} \in \mathcal{L}_\ell$ contains $(1 + \gamma_\ell)\frac{m}{n \cdot |\mathcal{L}_\ell|}$ copies of $\mathcal{B}$.

Note that the number of V-jobs and the number of W-jobs in layer $\ell = 1, \ldots, d$ are both $(1 + \gamma_\ell)m$.

We are now ready to define the precedence constraints between the different layers. For a group $B^{(\ell,i,X)} \in \mathcal{L}_\ell$ with $\ell \geq 2$, there are precedence constraints from all the jobs that correspond to w_i in the groups $\mathcal{L}_{\ell-1} \cap X$ to all the jobs in $B^{(\ell,i,X)}$.

Finally, we select the number of machines so as to guarantee that $(1 + \gamma_\ell)\frac{m}{n|\mathcal{L}_\ell|}$ is an integer for $\ell = 1, \ldots, d$. As $|\mathcal{L}_\ell|$ divides $|\mathcal{L}_d|$ for $\ell = 1, \ldots, d$, we let

$$m = \left(\prod_{i=0}^{d} \frac{1}{\gamma_i}\right) \cdot n \cdot |\mathcal{L}_d| = \left(\prod_{i=0}^{d} \frac{1}{\gamma_i}\right) \cdot n \cdot n^{1+\sum_{i=2}^{d}\prod_{j=i}^{d}\delta_j} \tag{4}$$

Note that m is a polynomial in n whose degree only depends on d and since layer $\ell = 1, 2, \ldots, d$ contains $(1+\gamma_\ell)m$ V-jobs and $(1 + \gamma_\ell)m$ W-jobs the construction is polynomial in n for any fixed d.

3.2 Completeness

Let π be a permutation of V that satisfies

$$|W_i^\pi| \geq i - \zeta n \qquad \text{for } i = 1, 2, \ldots, n \tag{5}$$

and let

$$t_i = \lfloor (1 - \gamma_i)n \rfloor \text{ for } i = 1, 2, \ldots, d.$$

The key lemma for the completeness is the following:

LEMMA 2. *For each* $\ell = 1, \ldots, d$ *there exists a schedule* σ_ℓ *of all the jobs in layers* $1, \ldots, \ell$ *satisfying:*
for each $k = 1, \ldots, \ell$

(i) in at least a fraction $1 - 4\gamma_{k-1}$ *of layer* k*'s groups, all jobs corresponding to the vertices in* $V_{t_k}^\pi \cup W_{t_k}^\pi$ *are scheduled during time interval* $[k-1, k]$*;*

(ii) the set of remaining jobs of layer k *that were not scheduled during* $[k-1, k]$ *contains at most* $4\gamma_k m$ V*-jobs and are scheduled during time interval* $[k, k+1]$*.*

As σ_d will schedule all the jobs and have makespan $d + 1$, this will imply the completeness analysis.

PROOF. We proceed by induction on ℓ.

Base Case.

For $\ell = 1$, consider schedule σ_1 defined as follows. During time interval

$[0, 1]$: σ_1 first schedules the jobs in layer 1 that correspond to the vertices in $V_{t_1}^\pi$ followed (at time 1) by the jobs that correspond to the vertices in $W_{t_1}^\pi$.

$[1, 2]$: σ_1 first schedules the remaining V-jobs of layer 1 followed (at time 2) by the remaining W-jobs of layer 1.

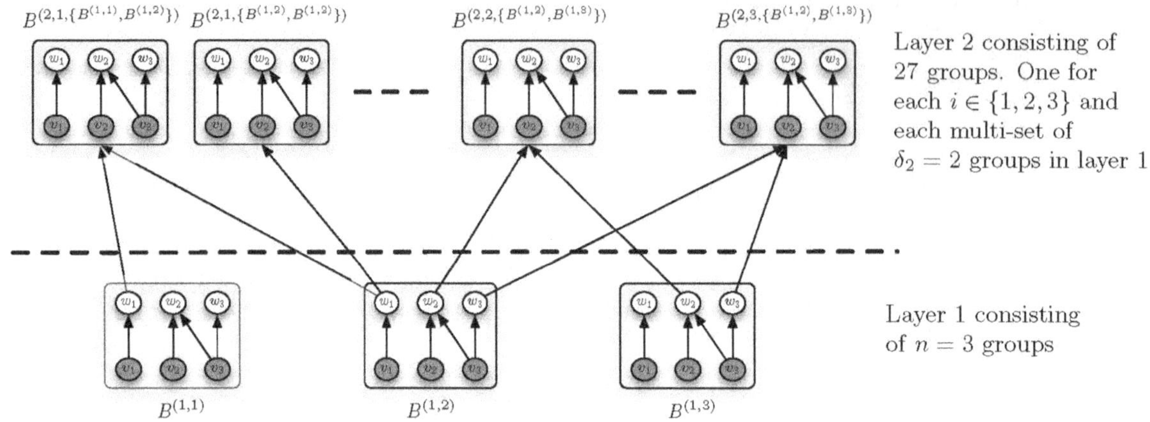

Figure 2: An example of the groups in $\mathcal{I}(2)$ with $\delta_2 = 2$ arising from the bipartite graph with $V = \{v_1, v_2, v_3\}$, $W = \{w_1, w_2, w_3\}$, and $E = \{\{v_1, w_1\}, \{v_2, w_2\}, \{v_3, w_3\}, \{v_3, w_2\}\}$. Each rectangle represents a group that contains a layer dependent number of copies of the building block. The V-jobs and W-jobs are depicted in gray and white, respectively.

Before showing that σ_1 satisfies conditions (i) and (ii), we prove that σ_1 is a feasible schedule, i.e., no precedence constraints are violated and σ_1 does not schedule more than m jobs at any time. Note that there might only be a precedence constraint between two jobs in layer 1 if they correspond to two vertices $v \in V$ and $w \in W$ with $\{v, w\} \in E$. By Definition 1 there are no edges between the vertices in $V \setminus V^{\pi}_{t_1}$ and the vertices in $W^{\pi}_{t_1}$. It follows that no precedence constraints are violated by σ_1. To show σ_1 feasible, it remains to verify that σ_1 does not schedule more jobs than machines at any time. As the W-jobs have 0 processing time, they can be scheduled sequentially without increasing the makespan. It is thus sufficient to verify that no more than m V-jobs are scheduled at any time. During time interval $[0, 1]$, σ_1 schedules a fraction $t_1/n \leq (1 - \gamma_1)$ of the V-jobs. The total number of V-jobs scheduled during $[0, 1]$ is thus at most $(1 - \gamma_1)(1 + \gamma_1)m = (1 - \gamma_1^2)m \leq m$. Similarly, during time interval $[1, 2]$, σ_1 schedules the remaining $1 - t_1/n \leq 2\gamma_1$ fraction of the V-jobs. The total number of V-jobs scheduled during $[1, 2]$ is thus at most $2\gamma_1 m$.

We shall now see that σ_1 satisfies conditions (i) and (ii). Since we have proved that the remaining jobs scheduled by σ_1 during time interval $[1, 2]$ contains at most $2\gamma_1 m$ V-jobs, we know that σ_1 satisfies condition (ii) in the induction hypothesis. To see that σ_1 satisfies condition (i), it is sufficient to observe that in all layer 1's groups, all jobs corresponding to the vertices in $V^{\pi}_{t_1} \cup W^{\pi}_{t_1}$ are scheduled during time interval $[0, 1]$. This completes the proof of the base case.

Inductive Step.

Suppose we already defined schedules $\sigma_1, \sigma_2, \ldots, \sigma_\ell$ that satisfy conditions (i) and (ii), for $\ell < d$. We shall now define a schedule $\sigma_{\ell+1}$ that schedules all jobs in layers $1, 2, \ldots, \ell+1$ and satisfies conditions (i) and (ii).

Before defining schedule $\sigma_{\ell+1}$ we need to introduce some new notation. A group $B \in \mathcal{L}_\ell$ is called *early* if σ_ℓ has completed all the jobs in B that correspond to the vertices in $V^{\pi}_{t_\ell} \cup W^{\pi}_{t_\ell}$ at time ℓ. Let

$$\mathcal{L}^{no\text{-}pre}_{\ell+1} = \left\{ B^{(\ell+1,i,X)} \in \mathcal{L}_{\ell+1} : \begin{array}{c} w_i \in W^{\pi}_{t_\ell} \text{ and} \\ \text{each } B \in X \text{ is early} \end{array} \right\}.$$

Note that $\mathcal{L}^{no\text{-}pre}_{\ell+1}$ is defined so that σ_ℓ has scheduled all the predecessors of the V-jobs in $\mathcal{L}^{no\text{-}pre}_{\ell+1}$ at time ℓ.

We are now ready to define $\sigma_{\ell+1}$. Schedule $\sigma_{\ell+1}$ is an extension of σ_ℓ in the sense that $\sigma_{\ell+1}$ schedules all the jobs in layers $1, 2, \ldots, \ell$ in the same way as σ_ℓ. The jobs in layer $\ell+1$ are scheduled by $\sigma_{\ell+1}$ as follows. During time interval

- $[\ell, \ell+1]$: $\sigma_{\ell+1}$ first schedules the jobs in $\mathcal{L}^{no\text{-}pre}_{\ell+1}$ that correspond to the vertices in $V^{\pi}_{t_{\ell+1}}$ followed (at time $\ell+1$) by the jobs in $\mathcal{L}^{no\text{-}pre}_{\ell+1}$ that correspond to the vertices in $W^{\pi}_{t_{\ell+1}}$.
- $[\ell+1, \ell+2]$: $\sigma_{\ell+1}$ first schedules the remaining V-jobs of layer $\ell+1$ followed (at time $\ell+2$) by the remaining W-jobs of layer 1.

As in the base case we start by showing that $\sigma_{\ell+1}$ is feasible. The proof that $\sigma_{\ell+1}$ satisfies conditions (i) and (ii) will then follow in a straightforward manner.

To show that $\sigma_{\ell+1}$ is feasible we need to prove that no precedence constraints are violated and the number of scheduled jobs does not exceed the number of machines m at any time.

We start by showing that no precedence constraints are violated. Since σ_ℓ does not violate any precedence constraints between jobs of layers $1, 2, \ldots, \ell$ neither does $\sigma_{\ell+1}$. Now consider the precedence constraints where at least one job is in layer $\ell+1$. As already noted, σ_ℓ and thus $\sigma_{\ell+1}$ has finished all the predecessors of the V-jobs in $\mathcal{L}^{no\text{-}pre}_{\ell+1}$ at time ℓ. Similarly, by condition (ii) in the induction hypothesis σ_ℓ and thus $\sigma_{\ell+1}$ has finished all the predecessor of all V-jobs in layer $\ell+1$ at time $\ell+1$. It follows that no precedence constraint from a job in a different layer than $\ell+1$ to a job in layer $\ell+1$ is violated. Now consider the precedence constraints between jobs in layer $\ell+1$. As in the base case, there might only be a precedence constraint between two jobs in the same layer if they correspond to two vertices $v \in V$ and

$w \in W$ with $\{v, w\} \in E$. By Definition 1 there are no edges between the vertices in $V \setminus V^{\pi}_{t_{\ell+1}}$ and the vertices in $W^{\pi}_{t_{\ell+1}}$. Hence, no precedence constraints are violated.

We continue by verifying that $\sigma_{\ell+1}$ does not schedule more than m jobs at any time. As noted in the base case, it is sufficient to verify that no more than m V-jobs are scheduled at any time. Since $\sigma_{\ell+1}$ and σ_ℓ do not differ during time interval $[0, \ell]$, we only need to verify $\sigma_{\ell+1}$ during time intervals $[\ell, \ell+1]$ and $[\ell+1, \ell+2]$. By condition (ii) in the induction hypothesis, σ_ℓ and thus $\sigma_{\ell+1}$ schedules at most $4\gamma_\ell m$ V-jobs from layer ℓ during time interval $[\ell, \ell+1]$. In addition $\sigma_{\ell+1}$ schedules a fraction $\frac{t_{\ell+1}}{n} \cdot \frac{|\mathcal{L}^{no\text{-}pre}_{\ell+1}|}{|\mathcal{L}_{\ell+1}|}$ of the V-jobs from layer $\ell+1$ during $[\ell, \ell+1]$. The total number of V-jobs scheduled by $\sigma_{\ell+1}$ during $[\ell, \ell+1]$ is thus at most

$$4\gamma_\ell m + \frac{t_{\ell+1}}{n} \cdot \frac{|\mathcal{L}^{no\text{-}pre}_{\ell+1}|}{|\mathcal{L}_{\ell+1}|} \cdot (1+\gamma_{\ell+1})m. \qquad (6)$$

During interval $[\ell+1, \ell+2]$, $\sigma_{\ell+1}$ schedules the remaining V-jobs from layer $\ell+1$. The number of such jobs is thus

$$\left(1 - \frac{t_{\ell+1}}{n} \cdot \frac{|\mathcal{L}^{no\text{-}pre}_{\ell+1}|}{|\mathcal{L}_{\ell+1}|}\right)(1+\gamma_{\ell+1})m. \qquad (7)$$

The following claim completes the proof that $\sigma_{\ell+1}$ is feasible.

CLAIM 2. *We have that (6) $\le m$ and (7) $\le 4\gamma_{\ell+1}m$.*

Proof of claim 2. We start with proving (6) $\le m$. As $\frac{|\mathcal{L}^{no\text{-}pre}_{\ell+1}|}{|\mathcal{L}_{\ell+1}|} \le 1$ and $\frac{t_{\ell+1}}{n} \le 1 - \gamma_{\ell+1}$, we have that

$$(6) \le 4\gamma_\ell + (1-\gamma_{\ell+1})(1+\gamma_{\ell+1})m \le m,$$

where we used that $4\gamma_\ell = 4\gamma_{\ell+1}^{10} \le \gamma_{\ell+1}^2$ for the last inequality.

To prove (7) $\le 4\gamma_{\ell+1}m$ we need to bound the size of $\frac{|\mathcal{L}^{no\text{-}pre}_{\ell+1}|}{|\mathcal{L}_{\ell+1}|}$. Recall that

$$\mathcal{L}^{no\text{-}pre}_{\ell+1} = \left\{ B^{(\ell+1,i,X)} \in \mathcal{L}_{\ell+1} : \begin{array}{c} w_i \in W^{\pi}_{t_\ell} \text{ and} \\ \text{each } B \in X \text{ is early} \end{array} \right\}.$$

We can thus write $\frac{|\mathcal{L}^{no\text{-}pre}_{\ell+1}|}{|\mathcal{L}_{\ell+1}|}$ as

$$\Pr_{B^{(\ell+1,i,X)} \in \mathcal{L}_{\ell+1}} [w_i \in W^{\pi}_{t_\ell} \text{ and each } B \in X \text{ is early}],$$

which in turn equals

$$\frac{|W^{\pi}_{t_\ell}|}{|W|} \cdot \left(\Pr_{B \in \mathcal{L}_\ell} [B \text{ is early}] \right)^{\delta_{\ell+1}}.$$

By condition (i) in the induction hypothesis,

$$\Pr_{B \in \mathcal{L}_\ell} [B \text{ is early}] \ge 1 - 4\gamma_{\ell-1}$$

and by assumption (5) and the fact that $\zeta = \gamma_0^{10} << \gamma_\ell$ we have

$$\frac{|W^{\pi}_{t_\ell}|}{|W|} \ge \frac{\lfloor (1-\gamma_\ell)n \rfloor - \zeta n}{n} \ge 1 - 2\gamma_\ell.$$

Substituting in these bounds gives us that

$$\begin{aligned} \frac{|\mathcal{L}^{no\text{-}pre}_{\ell+1}|}{|\mathcal{L}_{\ell+1}|} &\ge (1-2\gamma_\ell) \cdot (1-4\gamma_{\ell-1})^{\delta_{\ell+1}} \\ &\ge (1-2\gamma_\ell)^2 \qquad \text{(by (1) in Lemma 1)} \\ &\ge 1 - 4\gamma_\ell \end{aligned}$$

We are now ready to prove (7) $\le 4\gamma_{\ell+1}m$:

$$\begin{aligned} (7) &= \left(1 - \frac{t_{\ell+1}}{n} \cdot \frac{|\mathcal{L}^{no\text{-}pre}_{\ell+1}|}{|\mathcal{L}_{\ell+1}|}\right)(1+\gamma_{\ell+1})m \\ &\le (1 - (1-2\gamma_{\ell+1}) \cdot (1-4\gamma_\ell))(1+\gamma_{\ell+1})m \\ &= (4\gamma_\ell + 2\gamma_{\ell+1} - 8\gamma_\ell\gamma_{\ell+1})(1+\gamma_{\ell+1})m \\ &\le (4\gamma_\ell + 2\gamma_{\ell+1})(1+\gamma_{\ell+1})m \\ &= (4\gamma_{\ell+1}^{10} + 2\gamma_{\ell+1})(1+\gamma_{\ell+1})m \\ &\le 4\gamma_{\ell+1}m \qquad (\text{since } \gamma_{\ell+1} \le 1/10) \end{aligned}$$

We have thus proved that (6) $\le m$ and (7) $\le 4\gamma_{\ell+1}m$ as required. □

We continue by proving that $\sigma_{\ell+1}$ satisfies conditions (i) and (ii) of the induction hypothesis. Since $\sigma_{\ell+1}$ is an extension of σ_ℓ, conditions (i) and (ii) are satisfied for $k = 1, 2, \ldots, \ell$. We continue by verifying the induction hypothesis for $k = \ell+1$. To see that $\sigma_{\ell+1}$ satisfies condition (i), note that $\sigma_{\ell+1}$ schedules all jobs in $\mathcal{L}^{no\text{-}pre}_{\ell+1}$ that correspond to the vertices in $V^{\pi}_{t_{\ell+1}} \cup W^{\pi}_{t_{\ell+1}}$ during time interval $[\ell, \ell+1]$. As $\Pr_{B \in \mathcal{L}_{\ell+1}}[B \in \mathcal{L}^{no\text{-}pre}_{\ell+1}] \ge 1 - 4\gamma_\ell$ (see proof of the claim above), $\sigma_{\ell+1}$ satisfies condition (i). Now consider condition (ii). Obviously $\sigma_{\ell+1}$ schedules all the remaining jobs of layer $\ell+1$ during time interval $[\ell+1, \ell+2]$. Furthermore, as proved above, the set of remaining jobs contains (7) V-jobs with (7) $\le 4\gamma_{\ell+1}m$.

By the above arguments the schedule $\sigma_{\ell+1}$ is feasible and satisfies conditions (i) and (ii). This concludes the inductive step and the completeness analysis. □

3.3 Soundness

By assumption we have that each permutation π of V satisfies

$$|W^{\pi}_{(1-\zeta)n}| \le \zeta n. \qquad (8)$$

Fix any feasible schedule σ. The key lemma for soundness is the following:

LEMMA 3. *For each $\ell = 1, \ldots, d$, schedule σ has at time $2 \cdot (\ell - 1)$ completed at most a fraction $\gamma_{\ell-1}$ of the V-jobs in layer ℓ.*

As there are $(1+\gamma_d)m$ V-jobs in layer d and $\gamma_d > \gamma_{d-1}$, this implies that the schedule must have makespan at least $2(d-1) + 2 = 2d$.

PROOF. We proceed by induction on ℓ.

Base case.

For $\ell = 1$ the induction hypothesis is obviously true, because σ has completed no jobs at time 0.

Inductive Step.

Suppose we already proved the induction hypothesis for $1, 2, \ldots, \ell$ for $\ell < d$. We shall now prove that at time 2ℓ, σ

has completed at most a fraction γ_ℓ of the V-jobs in layer $\ell+1$.

Let $t = 2(\ell-1)$. For each $i = 1, \ldots, n$ and each $B \in \mathcal{L}_\ell$, let $X_i^{(B)}$ be the indicator variable defined

$$X_i^{(B)} = \begin{cases} 1, & \text{If at time } t+1,\ \sigma \text{ has completed all the jobs in group } B \text{ that correspond to } w_i \in W. \\ 0, & \text{Otherwise.} \end{cases}$$

Moreover, for $i \in \{1, \ldots, n\}$, let X_i denote the indicator variable that takes value 1 if $\mathbb{E}_{B\in\mathcal{L}_\ell}[X_i^{(B)}] \geq 1 - \frac{\gamma_\ell}{4}$ and 0 otherwise.

CLAIM 3. *We have* $\mathbb{E}_i[X_i] \leq 4\zeta$.

Proof of claim 3. Suppose toward contradiction that $\mathbb{E}_i[X_i] > 4\zeta$ and hence there are more than a fraction 4ζ of the indicator variables that equals 1. Let $a = \lceil 4\zeta n \rceil$ and assume without loss of generality that $X_1 = X_2 = \cdots = X_a = 1$. By the definition of X_i's,

$$\mathbb{E}_{i\in[a],B\in\mathcal{L}_\ell}[X_i^{(B)}] \geq 1 - \frac{\gamma_\ell}{4}.$$

It follows that

$$\Pr_{B\in\mathcal{L}_\ell}[E_{i\in[a]}[X_i^{(B)}] \geq 1/2] \geq 1 - \frac{\gamma_\ell}{2}.$$

By letting the expectation be over $[n]$ instead of $[a]$,

$$\Pr_{B\in\mathcal{L}_\ell}[E_{i\in[n]}[X_i^{(B)}] \geq 2\zeta] \geq 1 - \frac{\gamma_\ell}{2}.$$

Call a group $B \in \mathcal{L}_\ell$ *good* if $\mathbb{E}_{i\in[n]}[X_i^{(B)}] \geq 2\zeta$. By the inequality above, at least a fraction $1 - \frac{\gamma_\ell}{2}$ of the groups in $\mathcal{L}_\ell$ are good.

Now consider a good group $B \in \mathcal{L}_\ell$. As $\mathbb{E}_{i\in[n]}[X_i^{(B)}] \geq 2\zeta$, σ schedules all jobs in B that correspond to a subset $W' \subseteq W$ of vertices with $|W'| \geq 2\zeta n$. By assumption (8), σ must have completed more than a fraction $1-\zeta$ of the V-jobs in B before all jobs corresponding to W' are scheduled. Hence, we can conclude that for each good block σ has completed at least a fraction $1-\zeta$ of the V-jobs. As layer ℓ consists of $(1+\gamma_\ell)m$ V-jobs and at least a fraction $1-\gamma_\ell/2$ of them belong to good groups, the total number of the V-jobs completed by σ at time $t+1$ is at least $(1+\gamma_\ell)(1-\gamma_\ell/2)(1-\zeta)m$. However this leads to the following contradiction. By the induction hypothesis, σ has completed at most a fraction $\gamma_{\ell-1}$ of the V-jobs in layer ℓ at time t. Thus during time interval $[t, t+1]$, the number of V-jobs σ must schedule is at least

$$(1+\gamma_\ell)(1-\gamma_\ell/2)(1-\zeta)m - \gamma_{\ell-1}(1+\gamma_\ell)m,$$

which is strictly greater than m since $(1+\gamma_\ell)(1-\gamma_\ell/2) \geq 1+\gamma_\ell/4$, $\zeta = \gamma_0^{10} << \gamma_\ell$, and $\gamma_{\ell-1} = \gamma_\ell^{10} << \gamma_\ell$. A contradiction. $\square$

Without loss of generality, let $X_1, X_2, \ldots, X_k$ be the indicator variables with value 1. By the claim above we have that $k \leq 4\zeta$. A group $B^{(\ell+1,i,X)} \in \mathcal{L}_{\ell+1}$ can be scheduled at time $t+1$ if all of its predecessors have been completed at that time. All predecessors of $B^{(\ell+1,i,X)}$ have been completed at time $t+1$ if $X_i^{(B)} = 1$ for each $B \in X$. We can thus write the fraction of groups in $\mathcal{L}_{\ell+1}$ for which all predecessors have been completed at time $t+1$ as

$$\Pr_{B^{(\ell+1,i,X)}\in\mathcal{L}_{\ell+1}}[\forall B \in X, X_i^{(B)} = 1], \tag{9}$$

which is at most the sum of $\Pr_{B^{(\ell+1,i,X)}\in\mathcal{L}_{\ell+1}}[i \leq k]$ and $\Pr_{B^{(\ell+1,i,X)}\in\mathcal{L}_{\ell+1}}[i > k \text{ and } \forall B \in X, X_i^{(B)} = 1]$. As $k \leq 4\zeta$ and $\mathbb{E}_B[X_i^{(B)}] < 1 - \frac{\gamma_\ell}{4}$ for $i > k$, we have that (9) is bounded from above by

$$\begin{aligned} 4\zeta + \left(1 - \frac{\gamma_\ell}{4}\right)^{|X|} &= 4\zeta + \left(1 - \frac{\gamma_\ell}{4}\right)^{\delta_{\ell+1}} \\ &\leq 4\zeta + \gamma_\ell/2 \text{ (by (2) in Lemma 1)} \\ &\leq \gamma_\ell \quad \text{(since } \zeta = \gamma_0^{10} < \gamma_\ell/8) \end{aligned}$$

Hence, σ has at time $t+2 = 2\ell$ completed at most a fraction γ_ℓ of the V-jobs in layer $\ell+1$. This concludes the inductive step and the soundness analysis.

4. ACKNOWLEDGEMENTS

I would like to thank Johan Håstad for many useful comments on an early version of this paper. I would also like to thank Monaldo Mastrolilli for suggesting to do the reduction to $P|prec|C_{max}$ from $1|prec|\sum w_jC_j$ instead of from the new variant of the unique games conjecture.

This research is supported by ERC Advanced investigator grant 226203 and the Swiss National Science Foundation project "Approximation Algorithms for Machine Scheduling Through Theory and Experiments III" Project N. 200020-122110/1.

5. REFERENCES

[1] C. Ambühl and M. Mastrolilli. Single machine precedence constrained scheduling is a vertex cover problem. *Algorithmica*, 53(4):488–503, 2009.

[2] C. Ambühl, M. Mastrolilli, N. Mutsanas, and O. Svensson. Scheduling with precedence constraints of low fractional dimension. In *Proceedings of the 12th Conference on Integer Programming and Combinatorial Optimization (IPCO)*, pages 130–144, 2007.

[3] C. Ambühl, M. Mastrolilli, and O. Svensson. Inapproximability results for sparsest cut, optimal linear arrangement, and precedence constrained scheduling. In *Proceedings of the 48th Annual IEEE Symposium on Foundations of Computer Science (FOCS)*, pages 329–337, 2007.

[4] N. Bansal and S. Khot. Optimal long code test with one free bit. In *Proceedings of the 50th Annual IEEE Symposium on Foundations of Computer Science (FOCS)*, pages 453–462, 2009.

[5] B. Braschi and D. Trystram. A new insight into the coffman-graham algorithm. *SIAM Journal on Computing*, 23(3):662–669, 1994.

[6] C. Chekuri and R. Motwani. Precedence constrained scheduling to minimize sum of weighted completion times on a single machine. *Discrete Applied Mathematics*, 98(1-2):29–38, 1999.

[7] B. Chen, C. N. Potts, and G. J. Woeginger. A review of machine scheduling: Complexity, algorithms and approximability. *Handbook of Combinatorial Optimization*, 3:21–169, 1998.

[8] F. A. Chudak and D. S. Hochbaum. A half-integral linear programming relaxation for scheduling precedence-constrained jobs on a single machine. *Operations Research Letters*, 25:199–204, 1999.

[9] E. Coffman and R. Graham. Optimal scheduling for two-processor systems. *Acta Informatica*, 1:200–213, 1972.

[10] J. R. Correa and A. S. Schulz. Single machine scheduling with precedence constraints. *Mathematics of Operations Research*, 30(4):1005–1021, 2005.

[11] J. Du, J. Y.-T. Leung, and G. H. Young. Scheduling chain-structured tasks to minimize makespan and mean flow time. *Information and Computation*, 92(2):219–236, 1991.

[12] W. L. Eastman, S. Even, and I. M. Isaacs. Bounds for the optimal scheduling of n jobs on m processors. *Management Science*, 11(2):268–279, 1964.

[13] M. Fujii, T. Kasami, and K. Ninomiya. Optimal sequencing of two equivalent processors. *SIAM Journal on Applied Mathematics*, 17(4):784–789, 1969.

[14] D. Gangal and A. Ranade. Precedence constrained scheduling in $(2 - 73p + 1)$·optimal. *Journal of Computer and System Sciences*, 74(7):1139–1146, 2008.

[15] M. R. Garey and D. S. Johnson. " strong " np-completeness results: Motivation, examples, and implications. *Journal of the ACM*, 25(3):499–508, 1978.

[16] M. R. Garey and D. S. Johnson. *Computers and intractability; a guide to the theory of NP-completeness*. W.H. Freeman, 1979.

[17] M. R. Garey, D. S. Johnson, R. E. Tarjan, and M. Yannakakis. Scheduling opposing forests. *SIAM Journal on Algebraic and Discrete Methods*, 1(4):72–93, 1983.

[18] M. X. Goemans and D. P. Williamson. Two-dimensional Gantt charts and a scheduling algorithm of Lawler. *SIAM Journal on Discrete Mathematics*, 13(3):281–294, 2000.

[19] R. Graham, E. Lawler, J. Lenstra, and A. R. Kan. Optimization and approximation in deterministic sequencing and scheduling: A survey. *Annals of Discrete Mathematics*, 5:287–326, 1979.

[20] R. L. Graham. Bounds for certain multiprocessing anomalies. *Bell System Technical Journal (BSTJ)*, 45:1563–1581, 1966.

[21] R. L. Graham. Bounds on multiprocessing timing anomalies. *SIAM Journal on Applied Mathematics*, 17(2):416–429, 1969.

[22] D. S. Hochbaum, , and D. B. Shmoys. Using dual approximation algorithms for scheduling problems theoretical and practical results. *Journal of the ACM*, 34(1):144–162, 1987.

[23] T. C. Hu. Parallel Sequencing and Assembly Line Problems. *Operations Research*, 9(6):841–848, 1961.

[24] S. Khot. On the power of unique 2-prover 1-round games. In *Proceedings of the 34th annual ACM symposium on Theory of computing (STOC)*, pages 767–775, 2002.

[25] S. Khot. Ruling out PTAS for graph min-bisection, dense k-subgraph, and bipartite clique. *SIAM Journal on Computing*, 36(4):1025–1071, 2006.

[26] S. Khot and O. Regev. Vertex cover might be hard to approximate to within $2 - \varepsilon$. *Journal of Computer and System Sciences*, 74(3):335–349, 2008.

[27] S. Lam and R. Sethi. Worst case analysis of two scheduling algorithms. *SIAM Journal on Computing*, 6(3):518–536, 1977.

[28] E. L. Lawler. Sequencing jobs to minimize total weighted completion time subject to precedence constraints. *Annals of Discrete Mathematics*, 2:75–90, 1978.

[29] J. K. Lenstra and A. H. G. R. Kan". Complexity of scheduling under precedence constraints. *Operations Research*, 26(1):22–35, 1978.

[30] J. K. Lenstra and A. H. G. R. Kan. The complexity of scheduling under precedence constraints. *Operations Research*, 26:22–35, 1978.

[31] F. Margot, M. Queyranne, and Y. Wang. Decompositions, network flows and a precedence constrained single machine scheduling problem. *Operations Research*, 51(6):981–992, 2003.

[32] C. N. Potts. An algorithm for the single machine sequencing problem with precedence constraints. *Mathematical Programming Study*, 13:78–87, 1980.

[33] S. K. Sahni. Algorithms for scheduling independent tasks. *Journal of the ACM*, 23(1):116–127, 1976.

[34] A. S. Schulz. Scheduling to minimize total weighted completion time: Performance guarantees of LP-based heuristics and lower bounds. In *Proceedings of the 5th Conference on Integer Programming and Combinatorial Optimization (IPCO)*, pages 301–315, 1996.

[35] P. Schuurman and G. J. Woeginger. Polynomial time approximation algorithms for machine scheduling: ten open problems. *Journal of Scheduling*, 2(5):203–213, 1999.

[36] J. B. Sidney. Decomposition algorithms for single-machine sequencing with precedence relations and deferral costs. *Operations Research*, 23:283–298, 1975.

[37] G. J. Woeginger. On the approximability of average completion time scheduling under precedence constraints. *Discrete Applied Mathematics*, 131(1):237–252, 2003.

APPENDIX

A. PROOF OF LEMMA 1

Recall that the parameters were selected to be $\gamma_d = \frac{1}{10}$, $\gamma_{\ell-1} = \gamma_\ell^{10}$ and $\delta_{\ell+1} = 1/\gamma_\ell^5$ for $\ell = 1, \ldots, d$. To prove the bounds we shall use Bernoulli's inequality:

$$1+nx \leq (1+x)^n \qquad \text{for all } x \in [-1, \infty] \text{ and for all } n = 1, 2, \ldots$$

Bound (1),i.e., $(1-4\gamma_{\ell-1})^{\delta_{\ell+1}} \geq 1 - 2\gamma_\ell$ now follows trivially. Indeed by Bernoulli's inequality and the selection of parameters we have

$$\begin{aligned}(1-4\gamma_{\ell-1})^{\delta_{\ell+1}} &\geq 1 - 4\gamma_{\ell-1}\cdot\delta_{\ell+1}\\ &= 1 - 4\gamma_\ell^{10}\cdot 1/\gamma_\ell^5\\ &= 1 - 4\gamma_\ell^5\\ &\geq 1 - 2\gamma_\ell\end{aligned}$$

We continue by showing Bound (2), i.e., $(1-\frac{\gamma_\ell}{4})^{\delta_{\ell+1}} \leq \gamma_\ell/2$:

$$\begin{aligned}\left(1-\frac{\gamma_\ell}{4}\right)^{\delta_{\ell+1}} &= \left(\frac{4/\gamma_\ell - 1}{4/\gamma_\ell}\right)^{\delta_{\ell+1}}\\ &= \frac{1}{\left(\frac{4/\gamma_\ell}{4/\gamma_\ell - 1}\right)^{\delta_{\ell+1}}}\\ &= \frac{1}{\left(1+\frac{1}{4/\gamma_\ell - 1}\right)^{\delta_{\ell+1}}}\\ &\leq \frac{1}{1+\frac{\delta_{\ell+1}}{(4/\gamma_\ell - 1)}} \qquad \text{(by Bernoulli's inequality)}\\ &\leq \frac{4}{\gamma_\ell\cdot\delta_{\ell+1}}\\ &= \frac{4}{\gamma_\ell\cdot 1/\gamma_\ell^5}\\ &\leq \gamma_\ell/2\end{aligned}$$

□

B. THE NEW STRONGER UNIQUE GAMES CONJECTURE

Although we do not directly use the new stronger version of the unique games conjecture, we define it here for the sake of completeness. An instance of unique games $\mathcal{L} = (G(V,W,E),[n],\{\pi_{v,w}\}_{(v,w)})$ consists of a regular bipartite graph $G(V,W,E)$ and a set $[n]$ of labels. For each edge $(v,w) \in E$ there is a constraint specified by a permutation $\pi_{v,w} : [n] \mapsto [n]$. The goal is to find a labeling $\ell : (V \cup W) \mapsto [n]$ so as to maximize $val(\ell) := \Pr_{e\in E}[\ell \text{ satisfies } e]$, where a labeling ℓ is said to satisfy an edge $e = (v,w)$ if $\ell(v) = \pi_{v,w}(\ell(w))$. For a unique game instance $\mathcal{L}$, we let $OPT(\mathcal{L}) = \max_{\ell:V\cup W\mapsto[n]} val(\ell)$. The now famous unique games conjecture that has been extensively used to prove strong hardness of approximation results can be stated as follows.

Conjecture 1 ([24]). *For any constants $\zeta,\gamma > 0$, there is a sufficiently large constant $n = n(\zeta,\gamma)$ such that, for unique game instances $\mathcal{L}$ with label set $[n]$, it is NP-hard to distinguish between $OPT(\mathcal{L}) \geq 1-\zeta$ and $OPT(\mathcal{L}) \leq \gamma$.*

To address the scheduling problem $1|prec|\sum w_jC_j$, Bansal & Khot introduced the following variant of the unique games conjecture:

Hypothesis 1 ([4]). *For arbitrarily small constants $\zeta,\gamma,\delta > 0$, there exists an integer $n = n(\zeta,\gamma,\delta)$ such that for a unique games instance $\mathcal{L} = (G(V,W,E),[n],\{\pi_{v,w}\}_{(v,w)\in E})$, it is NP-hard to distinguish between:*

- *(YES Case:) There are sets $V' \subseteq V, W' \subseteq W$ such that $|V'| \geq (1-\zeta)|V|$ and $|W'| \geq (1-\zeta)|W|$ and an assignment to $\mathcal{L}$ such that all the edges between the sets (V',W') are satisfied.*
- *(NO Case:) No assignment to $\mathcal{L}$ satisfies even a γ fraction of the edges. Moreover, the instance satisfies the following expansion property. For every set $S \subseteq V, |S| = \delta|V|$, we have $\Gamma(S) \geq (1-\delta)|W|$, where $\Gamma(S) = \{w \in W | \exists v \in S, (v,w) \in E\}$.*

One can see that Hypothesis 1 differs from Conjecture 1 in two ways. In the YES case, Hypothesis 1 requires that there exists a labeling that satisfies all constraints between to large sets $V' \subseteq V, W' \subseteq W$. Whereas Conjecture 1 only requires that almost all constraints are satisfied by a labeling. Furthermore, in the NO case Hypothesis 1 has the additional assumption that the instance satisfy the (arguably weak) expansion property that any two sets of relative size δ has an edge between them.

As remarked in [4], no algorithmic results rule out Hypothesis 1. Furthermore, each of the two extra properties (one in the YES case and the other in the NO case) can be achieved by suitable transformations from the standard unique games conjecture. (The property in the NO case can be achieved by imposing a dummy expander and Khot & Regev [26] showed how to transform a unique game instance into one with the property in the YES case preserving low soundness.) However, it remains an open problem whether assuming both properties simultaneously is equivalent to the standard unique games conjecture.

Graph Expansion and the Unique Games Conjecture

Prasad Raghavendra
MSR New England
Cambridge, MA

David Steurer*
Princeton University
Princeton, NJ

ABSTRACT

The edge expansion of a subset of vertices $S \subseteq V$ in a graph G measures the fraction of edges that leave S. In a d-regular graph, the edge expansion/conductance $\Phi(S)$ of a subset $S \subseteq V$ is defined as $\Phi(S) = \frac{|E(S,V\setminus S)|}{d|S|}$. Approximating the conductance of small linear sized sets (size δn) is a natural optimization question that is a variant of the well-studied SPARSEST CUT problem. However, there are no known algorithms to even distinguish between almost complete edge expansion ($\Phi(S) = 1 - \varepsilon$), and close to 0 expansion.

In this work, we investigate the connection between Graph Expansion and the Unique Games Conjecture. Specifically, we show the following:

–We show that a simple decision version of the problem of approximating small set expansion reduces to UNIQUE GAMES. Thus if approximating edge expansion of small sets is hard, then UNIQUE GAMES is hard. Alternatively, a refutation of the UGC will yield better algorithms to approximate edge expansion in graphs.

This is the first non-trivial "reverse" reduction from a natural optimization problem to UNIQUE GAMES.

–Under a slightly stronger UGC that assumes mild expansion of small sets, we show that it is UG-hard to approximate small set expansion.

–On instances with sufficiently good expansion of small sets, we show that UNIQUE GAMES is easy by extending the techniques of [4].

Categories and Subject Descriptors

F.2.2 [**Theory of Computation**]: Analysis of Algorithms and Problem Complexity—*Nonnumerical Algorithms and Problems*

*Supported by NSF grants 0830673, 0832797, 528414. Part of this work done while at Microsoft Research New England.

STOC'10, June 5–8, 2010, Cambridge, Massachusetts, USA.

General Terms

Algorithms, Theory.

Keywords

Graph Expansion, Unique Games Conjecture, Hardness of Approximation, Spectral profile.

1. INTRODUCTION

The phenomenon of vertex and edge expansion in graphs has been a subject of intense study with applications pervading almost all branches of theoretical computer science. From an algorithmic standpoint, approximating expansion or lack thereof (finding good cuts or separators) is a fundamental optimization problem with numerous applications. Yet, the computational complexity of detecting and approximating expansion in graphs is not very well understood.

Among the two notions of expansion, this work will concern mostly with edge expansion. For simplicity, let us first consider the case of a d-regular graph $G = (V, E)$. The edge expansion of a subset of vertices $S \subseteq V$ measures the fraction of edges that leave S. Formally, the edge expansion $\Phi(S)$ of a subset $S \subseteq V$ can be defined as,

$$\Phi_G(S) = \frac{|E(S, V \setminus S)|}{d|S|},$$

where $E(S, V \setminus S)$ denotes the set of edges with one endpoint in S and the other endpoint in $V \setminus S$. The conductance or the Cheeger's constant associated with the graph G is the minimum of $\Phi(S)$ over all sets S with at most half the vertices, i.e.,

$$\Phi_G = \min_{|S| \leqslant n/2} \Phi_G(S).$$

The definitions of conductance of sets $\Phi_G(S)$ and the graph Φ_G can be extended naturally to non-regular graphs, and finally to arbitrary weighted graphs. For the sake of simplicity, we restrict our attention to regular graphs here, and defer the discussion of general weighted graphs to the full version. Henceforth, we will use the notation $\mu(S)$ to denote the normalized set size $\mu(S) = |S|/n$.

The problem of approximating Φ_G also referred to as the the uniform SPARSEST CUT (equivalent within a factor of 2), is among the fundamental problems in approximation algorithms. Efforts towards approximating Φ_G have led to a rich body of work with strong connections to spectral techniques and metric embeddings.

The first approximation for conductance was obtained by discrete analogues of the Cheeger inequality [9] shown by

Alon-Milman [2] and Alon [1]. Specifically, they show the following:

THEOREM 1.1 (CHEEGER'S INEQUALITY). *If λ_2 denotes the second largest eigenvalue of the suitably normalized adjacency matrix of a graph G then,*

$$\frac{1-\lambda_2}{2} \leqslant \Phi_G \leqslant \sqrt{2(1-\lambda_2)}\,.$$

Since the second eigenvalue λ_2 can be efficiently computed, Cheeger's inequality yields an approximation algorithm for Φ_G, indeed one that is used heavily in practice for graph partitioning. However, the approximation for Φ_G obtained via Cheeger's inequality is poor in terms of a approximation ratio, especially when the value of Φ_G is small (λ_2 is close to 1).

An $O(\log n)$ approximation algorithm for Φ_G was obtained by Leighton and Rao [17]. Later work by Linial et al. [18] and Aumann and Rabani [6] established a strong connection between the SPARSEST CUT problem and the theory of metric spaces, in turn spurring a large and rich body of literature. More recently, in a breakthrough result Arora et al. [5] obtained an $O(\sqrt{\log n})$ approximation for the problem using semidefinite programming techniques.

Small Set Expansion.

Note that the Φ_G is a fairly coarse measure of edge expansion, in that it is the worst case edge expansion over sets S of all sizes. In a typical graph (say a random d-regular graph), smaller sets of vertices expand to a larger extent than sets with half the vertices. For instance, all sets S of δn vertices in a random d-regular graph have $\Phi(S) \approx 1 - \frac{2}{d}$ with very high probability, while the conductance Φ_G of the entire graph is roughly $\frac{1}{2}$. Moreover, the stronger expansion exhibited by small sets has numerous applications in graph theory.

A natural finer measure of the edge expansion of a graph is its expansion profile. Specifically, for a regular graph G the expansion profile is given by the curve [1]

$$\Phi_G(\delta) = \min_{\mu(S)=\delta} \Phi(S) \qquad \forall \delta \in [0, 1/2]\,.$$

The problem of approximating the expansion profile is seemingly far-less tractable than approximating Φ_G itself. For instance, there is no known algorithm for the following easily stated decision problem concerning the expansion profile:

Problem 1. GAP-SMALL-SET EXPANSION (η, δ) Given a graph G and constants $\eta, \delta > 0$, distinguish whether

$$\Phi_G(\delta) \geqslant 1 - \eta \qquad \text{or} \qquad \Phi_G(\delta) \leqslant \eta\,.$$

Spectral techniques fail in approximating the expansion of small sets in graphs. On one hand, even with the largest possible spectral gap, the Cheeger's inequality cannot yield a lower bound greater than $1/2$ for the conductance $\Phi_G(\delta)$. More importantly, there exists graphs such as hypercube where there are sets S of half the vertices with small conductance ($\Phi(S) < \eta$), yet every sufficiently small set S satisfies $\Phi(S) \geqslant 1 - \eta$. This implies that Φ_G (and the second eigen value λ_2) do not yield any information about $\Phi_G(\delta)$ for small δ.

Unique Games Conjecture.

The Unique Games Conjecture (UGC) of Khot [13] is among the central open problems in hardness of approximation, and has fueled many developments in the area in recent years. The UGC is shown to imply optimal inapproximability results for classic problems like MAX CUT [14], VERTEX COVER [15] and SPARSEST CUT [16] and constraint satisfaction problems [19].

For the sake of concreteness, we formally state the unique games conjecture here. The UNIQUE GAMES problem is defined as follows:

Definition 1. An instance of UNIQUE GAMES represented as $\Upsilon = (\mathcal{V}, \mathcal{E}, \Pi, [R])$ consists of a graph over vertex set $\mathcal{V}$ with the edges $\mathcal{E}$ between them. Also part of the instance is a set of labels $[R] = \{1, \ldots, R\}$, and a set of permutations $\pi_{v\leftarrow w} : [R] \to [R]$ for each edge $e = (w, v) \in \mathcal{E}$. An assignment $\mathcal{A}$ of labels to vertices is said to satisfy an edge $e = (w, v)$, if $\pi_{v\leftarrow w}(\mathcal{A}(w)) = \mathcal{A}(v)$. The objective is to find an assignment $\mathcal{A}$ of labels that satisfies the maximum number of edges.

As is customary in hardness of approximation, one defines a gap-version of the UNIQUE GAMES problem as follows:

Problem 2. (UNIQUE GAMES $(R, 1-\varepsilon, \eta)$) Given a UNIQUE GAMES instance $\Upsilon = (\mathcal{V}, \mathcal{E}, \Pi = \{\pi_{v\leftarrow w} : [R] \to [R] \mid e = (w, v) \in \mathcal{E}\}, [R])$ with number of labels R, distinguish between the following two cases:

- $(1-\varepsilon)$- satisfiable instances: There exists an assignment $\mathcal{A}$ of labels that satisfies a $1-\varepsilon$ fraction of edges.
- Instances that are not η-satisfiable: No assignment satisfies more than a η-fraction of the edges $\mathcal{E}$.

The Unique Games Conjecture asserts that the above decision problem is NP-hard when the number of labels is large enough. Formally,

CONJECTURE 1.2 (UNIQUE GAMES CONJECTURE [13]). *For all constants $\varepsilon, \eta > 0$, there exists large enough constant R such that* UNIQUE GAMES $(R, 1-\varepsilon, \eta)$ *is NP-hard.*

While the implications of the conjecture are well-understood, there has been much slower progress towards its resolution. Results supporting the truth of UGC have been especially difficult to show. In particular, it is unknown whether many of the implications of UGC are equivalent to the conjecture. In other words, it is entirely consistent with existing literature that all the implications of UGC on problems like MAX CUT and VERTEX COVER hold, but the conjecture itself is false. More precisely, although the UNIQUE GAMES problem is known to efficiently reduce to classic problems like MAX CUT and VERTEX COVER, there are no known "reverse" reductions from these problems back to UNIQUE GAMES.

The only *reverse* reduction towards which there is any literature is the reduction from MAX CUT to UNIQUE GAMES. Note that the MAX CUT problem is a special case of UNIQUE GAMES over the binary alphabet $\{0, 1\}$. Hence a MAX CUT instance is readily reduced to a UNIQUE GAMES instance by using parallel repetition. With a sufficiently strong parallel repetition theorem (conjectured by Feige et al. [11]), this would yield a *reverse* reduction from MAX CUT to UNIQUE GAMES. Unfortunately, a strong parallel repetition theorem of this nature was shown not to hold by Raz [24]. Subsequent work by Barak et al. [7] almost entirely ruled out this approach to reduce MAX CUT to UNIQUE GAMES.

[1] In irregular graphs, it is more convenient to permit sets S within a range of sizes say $[\delta, 10\delta]$, since in an arbitrary (non-regular) graph there could be no sets satisfying $\mu(S) = \delta$.

Expansion and Unique Games.

Vertex and edge expansion in graphs appear to be closely tied to the hard instances for linear and semidefinite programming relaxations. Many integrality gap instances have been constructed for problems like VERTEX COVER or MAX CUT against the linear programming hierarchies such as Lovász–Schriver and Sherali–Adams hierarchies (see [8, 25] and the references therein). Not only do most of these instances consist of expanding graphs but the arguments rely crucially on either vertex or edge expansion.

The situation is little bit more subtle in case of semidefinite programming. Semidefinite programs can approximate MAX CUT well on instances that have very good conductance (spectral gap). Hence, the SDP integrality gap instances known are graphs where small sets expand well, while the larger sets do not. Indeed, SDP integrality gap constructions for MAX CUT [10, 16, 21], VERTEX COVER [12], UNIQUE GAMES [16, 20] and SPARSEST CUT [16] all have near-perfect edge expansion for small sets.

In case of UNIQUE GAMES, not only do all known integrality gap instances have near-perfect edge expansion of small sets, even the analysis relies directly on this property. Furthermore, it is known that the best possible soundness for UNIQUE GAMES with label size R and completeness $1-\varepsilon$ is a constant $\eta(R,\varepsilon)$ which is roughly $\frac{1}{R^{\varepsilon/2}}$. The constant $1-\eta$ arises directly from the expansion of sets of size $\frac{1}{R}$ in a certain graph defined over the Gaussian space.

While this suggests that UNIQUE GAMES is closely tied to expansion of small sets in graphs, somewhat contrastingly, Arora et al. [4] show that UNIQUE GAMES is easy when the constraint graph involved is a good spectral expander, i.e., has a non-trivial spectral gap for the Laplacian.

Motivated by the above reasons, we investigate the connection between graph expansion and UNIQUE GAMES in this work.

1.1 Results

The main result of this work is a reduction from the problem of approximating expansion of small sets to the UNIQUE GAMES problem. The main implication of the result can be succinctly stated as follows.

Let us consider the following hardness assumption about the complexity of the GAP-SMALL-SET EXPANSION problem.

CONJECTURE 1.3. *(Gap-Small-Set Expansion Conjecture) For every $\eta > 0$, there exists δ such that the problem* GAP-SMALL-SET EXPANSION (η,δ) *is NP-hard.*

Then, an immediate consequence of the reduction presented in this work is,

THEOREM 1.4. *The* GAP-SMALL-SET EXPANSION *conjecture implies the Unique Games Conjecture.*

To the best of our knowledge, this is the first non-trivial "reverse" reduction from a natural combinatorial optimization problem to UNIQUE GAMES. On one hand, it connects the somewhat non-standard problem of UNIQUE GAMES to the much well-studied problem of approximating graph expansion. Furthermore, the result makes concrete the conspicious presence of small set expansion in SDP integrality gaps for UNIQUE GAMES and related problems.

While a confirmation of UGC was known to imply optimal inapproximability results for fundamental problems, a refutation of UGC was not known to formally imply any new algorithmic technique. An important implication of the above result is that a refutation of the UGC would yield an algorithm for approximating edge expansion (only in a certain regime) in graphs – a basic optimization problem. Now we state the main result of the paper from this algorithmic standpoint. To this end, we formally state a hypothesis that would be emerge from a refutation of UGC.

HYPOTHESIS 1.5 (UNIQUE GAMES IS EASY). *There exists a constant $\varepsilon > 0$ and a function $f\colon \mathbb{N} \to \mathbb{N}$ such that given a* UNIQUE GAMES *instance Υ with n vertices and k labels, it is possible distinguish between the cases* $\mathrm{opt}(\Upsilon) \geqslant 1-\varepsilon$ *and* $\mathrm{opt}(\Upsilon) \leqslant \varepsilon$ *in time $n^{f(k)}$.*

THEOREM 1.6. *Suppose the above hypothesis (*UNIQUE GAMES *is easy) holds for a constant ε_0 and a function f, then there exists a function $g\colon [0,1] \to \mathbb{N}$ such that given any graph G with n vertices, and it is possible to distinguish whether $\Phi_G(\delta) \leqslant \varepsilon_1$ or $\Phi_G(\delta) > 1-\varepsilon_1$ for some absolute constant ε_1 in time $n^{g(\delta)}$.*

A somewhat stronger consequence of the UNIQUE GAMES *is easy* hypothesis follows using the parallel repetition theorem. The following corollary is an immediate consequence of the parallel repetition theorem of Rao [23] and our reduction from GAP-SMALL-SET EXPANSION to UNIQUE GAMES.

COROLLARY 1.7. *Suppose the hypothesis –* UNIQUE GAMES *instance is easy) holds for a constant ε_0 and a function f. Then, given a graph G with n vertices and parameters ε,δ such that $\varepsilon < \varepsilon_1$ for some absolute constant ε_1, we can distinguish the following cases in time $n^{g(\varepsilon,\delta)}$ for some $g : [0,1]^2 \to \mathbb{N}$.*

1. *There exists $S \subseteq V$ with $\mu(S) = \delta$ and $\Phi(S) \leqslant \varepsilon$*
2. *Every set $S \subseteq V$ with $\mu(S) \leqslant 1500\delta/\varepsilon$ satisfies $\Phi(S) \geqslant 1500\sqrt{\varepsilon}$.*

1.1.1 Towards an Equivalence

A natural question that arises from Theorem 1.4 is whether the Unique Games Conjecture is equivalent to the GAP-SMALL-SET EXPANSION conjecture. More specifically, could it be true that Unique Games Conjecture implies the GAP-SMALL-SET EXPANSION conjecture.

Showing a result of this nature amounts to obtaining a reduction from UNIQUE GAMES to GAP-SMALL-SET EXPANSION. Despite the large number of UG reductions and a fairly thorough understanding of how to construct reductions from UNIQUE GAMES, obtaining reductions to graph expansion problems is often problematic.

The main issue is that hardness reductions via local gadgets do not alter the global structure of the graph. For example, if the UNIQUE GAMES instance is disconnected, the resulting graph produced by a gadget reduction is also disconnected. Hence, to show a UG-hardness result for a global property such as expansion, it often seems necessary to assume the corresponding global property on the constraint graph of the UNIQUE GAMES. More specifically, in our case we require that the UNIQUE GAMES instance has good local expansion, in that sufficiently small sets have conductance close to 1. The formal statement of the modified Unique Games Conjecture with mild expansion on small sets is given below:

CONJECTURE 1.8. *(UNIQUE GAMES WITH SMALL SET EXPANSION Conjecture) For every $\varepsilon > 0$, there exists δ such that for all $\eta > 0$ the following problem is NP-hard with a sufficiently large $R = R(\varepsilon, \eta)$:*

Given an instance $\Upsilon = (\mathcal{V}, \mathcal{E}, \Pi = \{\pi_{v\leftarrow w} : [R] \to [R]\}, [R])$ of UNIQUE GAMES with alphabet size $R \geqslant R_0$ distinguish between the following cases:

- *Completeness There exists an assignment $\mathcal{A} : \mathcal{V} \to [R]$ that satisfies at least $1 - \varepsilon$ fraction of edges.*
- *Soundness Every assignment $\mathcal{A} : \mathcal{V} \to [R]$ satisfies at most η fraction of edges and the constraint graph $(\mathcal{V}, \mathcal{E})$ satisfies the following expansion property:*
  - *(Local Expansion Property) For every set S with $\mu(S) \leqslant \delta$, $\Phi(S) \geqslant 1 - \varepsilon$.*

The above conjecture assumes fairly mild expansion in that *sufficiently small* sets have conductance close to 1. In fact, existing SDP integrality gap instances for UNIQUE GAMES (see [16, 20]) satisfy the above local expansion property. Under this stronger Unique Games Conjecture stated above, we show the following hardness result for GAP-SMALL-SET EXPANSION.

THEOREM 1.9. *The Unique Games with Small Set Expansion conjecture implies the* GAP-SMALL-SET EXPANSION *conjecture.*

As an immediate consequence of the UG hardness reduction we also obtain super-constant hardness of approximation for the k-DENSEST SUBGRAPH PROBLEM.

THEOREM 1.10. *Assuming the Unique Games with Small Set Expansion conjecture, it is NP-hard to approximate the k-*DENSEST SUBGRAPH PROBLEM *to any constant factor.*

Using standard techniques, the UG-hardness reductions can be used to construct SDP integrality gaps for the GAP-SMALL-SET EXPANSION and the k-DENSEST SUBGRAPH PROBLEM. Due to space constraints, we defer the proofs of Theorem 1.9 and Theorem 1.10 to the full version.

1.2 Unique Games with Small Set Expansion are Easy

Further exploring the connection between UNIQUE GAMES and small set expansion, we show that the UNIQUE GAMES problem is easy when there is sufficiently high expansion of small sets. This result generalizes the work of [4] which showed that UNIQUE GAMES is easy when the associated constraint graph is a good spectral expander.

We will use an analytic notion of a graph being a small set expander for this purpose. This is akin to spectral expansion of a graph instead of combinatorial expansion.

Definition 2. For a graph G and $\delta > 0$, define $\tilde{\Lambda}_G(\delta)$ as the minimum of

$$\mathop{\mathbb{E}}_{(u,v)\sim G} \|\boldsymbol{X}_u - \boldsymbol{X}_v\|^2$$

over all collection of vectors $\{\boldsymbol{X}_v\}_{v\in V}$ that satisfy the constraints

$$\mathop{\mathbb{E}}_{u,v\sim V} \langle \boldsymbol{X}_u, \boldsymbol{X}_v \rangle \leqslant \delta\,, \qquad (1.1)$$

$$\mathop{\mathbb{E}}_{u\sim V} \|\boldsymbol{X}_u\|^2 = 1\,. \qquad (1.2)$$

Unlike the combinatorial small set expansion $\Phi_G(\delta)$, the quantity $\tilde{\Lambda}_G(\delta)$ is efficiently computable, thus making it easy to recognize graphs that satisfy the required expansion property. Raghavendra et al. [22] show that this parameter approximates the combinatorial expansion profile $\Phi_G(\delta)$ as follows:

$$\tilde{\Lambda}_G(\delta) \leqslant \Phi_G(\delta) \leqslant O\left(\tilde{\Lambda}_G(\delta/2)\log(1/\delta)\right)^{1/2}.$$

In this work, we show that UNIQUE GAMES is easy if the constraint graph G has sufficiently large $\tilde{\Lambda}_G(\delta)$. The formal statement of the result is as follows:

THEOREM 1.11. *Let Υ be unique game with SDP value $1 - \varepsilon$ and constraint graph G. Suppose there exists $\delta > 0$ such that*

$$\tilde{\Lambda}_G(\delta) > 10^6 \varepsilon \log(1/\varepsilon\delta)\,,$$

then the integral value of Υ is at least $\delta/10$.

COROLLARY 1.12. *If the constraint graph G associated with a unique games instance Υ satisfies $\tilde{\Lambda}_G(\delta) > 10^6\varepsilon\log(1/\varepsilon\delta)$, then it is easy to distinguish whether instance has value $1 - \varepsilon$ or less than δ.*

Independent of this work, Arora et al. [3] also show that UNIQUE GAMES is easy if the underlying constraint graph has sufficient local expansion using different techniques. Due to space constraints, we defer the proof of Theorem 1.11 to the full version.

Relation with Conjecture 1.8: For $\delta < 2^{-1/\varepsilon}$ the quantity $10^6\varepsilon\log(1/\varepsilon\delta) > 1$, while $\tilde{\Lambda}_G(\delta) \leqslant 1$ for all graphs G and all $\delta > 0$. Hence, Theorem 1.11 is not applicable on graphs with expansion of sets of size $\delta < 2^{-1/\varepsilon}$. In Conjecture 1.8, there is no lower bound on the size δ of sets with local expansion. Consequently, Theorem 1.11 only yields an upper bound on the choice of the set size δ in Conjecture 1.8.

2. PRELIMINARIES

Notation: Unless otherwise stated, all graphs considered henceforth can be assumed to be regular unweighted graphs. The proofs and results generalize to arbitrary weighted graphs, but we defer its discussion to the full version.

Given a graph $G = (V, E)$, we will use $v \sim V$ to denote a vertex sampled from the probability distribution given by degrees $\deg(v)$ (in this case, the uniform distribution). Furthermore, for a set $S \subseteq V$, $\mu(S) = \mathbb{P}_{v\sim V}\{v \in S\}$. Similarly, the notation $e \sim E$ will denote an edge sampled from a distribution proportional to the weights (the uniform distribution in unweighted graphs). We denote by $E(A, B)$ the set of edges with one endpoint in A and the other endpoint in B. For a subset of edges $E' \subseteq E$, $|E'|$ will denote the sum of the edge weights within E'. Therefore for a subset of edges E', $\mathbb{P}_{e\sim E}[e \in E'] = |E'|/|E| = 2|E'|$.

Definition 3. For a vertex subset $S \subseteq V$, we define

$$\partial(S) \stackrel{\text{def}}{=} |E(S, V \setminus S)| \qquad \text{and} \qquad \mu(S) \stackrel{\text{def}}{=} \sum_{s\in S} \deg(s)\,.$$

Definition 4. (Conductance) The conductance/Cheeger's constant associated with a subset $S \subseteq V$ is given by $\Phi(S) = \frac{\partial(S)}{\mu(S)}$. The conductance/Cheeger's constant for the graph G is $\Phi_G = \min_{\mu(S)\leqslant\frac{1}{2}} \Phi(S)$.

Due to space constraints we omit the proofs of the following simple facts.

FACT 2.1. *For all* $a, b \in [0,1]$, $|a^2 - b^2| \leqslant 2a + 2b - 4ab$.

LEMMA 2.2 (GLORIFIED MARKOV INEQUALITY). *Let* Ω *be a probability space and let* $X, Y : \Omega \to \mathbb{R}_+$ *be two jointly distributed non-negative random variables over* Ω. *Suppose* $\mathbb{E}X \leqslant \gamma \mathbb{E}Y$. *Then, there exists* $\omega \in \Omega$ *such that* $X(\omega) \leqslant 2\gamma Y(\omega)$ *and* $Y(\omega) \geqslant \mathbb{E}Y/2$.

Partial 2-prover games: A general 2-prover game Γ is specified by a vertex set V, an edge set E, an alphabet Σ, and a collection of predicates $\{\Pi_{u,v}\}$ indexed by vertex pairs $u, v \in V$. The value of the game Γ is defined as the maximum success probability

$$\underset{uv \in E}{\mathbb{P}} \left\{ (F(u), F(v)) \in \Pi_{u,v} \right\},$$

over all strategies $F : V \to \Sigma$.

Given a 2-prover game Γ, a *partial game* is one in which the provers are permitted to *refuse* to answer the question. The provers win only if both of them refuse to answer the question or else they both answer correctly as per the game Γ. To preclude the trivial strategy that always refuses to answer questions, we require that the provers answer at least an α-fraction of the questions for some constant $\alpha > 0$. Formally, we define the *α-partial value* of a 2-prover game Γ as the maximum success probability

$$\underset{uv \in E}{\mathbb{P}} \left\{ (F(u), F(v)) \in \Pi_{u,v} \right\} / \underset{u \sim V}{\mathbb{P}} \left\{ F(u) \neq \perp \right\},$$

over all α-partial strategies $F : V \to \Sigma \cup \{\perp\}$. Here, $\perp$ is a designated symbol (not a member of Σ) and an *α-partial strategy* is an assignment $F : V \to \Sigma \cup \{\perp\}$ such that $\mathbb{P}_{u \sim V} \{F(u) \neq \perp\} \geqslant \alpha$. As usual, the notation $v \sim V$ means that v is sampled with probability proportional to its degree.

Organization: In the remainder of the paper, we present the reduction from GAP-SMALL-SET EXPANSION to UNIQUE GAMES and its analysis. For conceptual clarity, we subdivide the reduction in to two parts: In the first part (Section 3), we reduce GAP-SMALL-SET EXPANSION to a *partial* Unique games, and then in Section 4 exhibit a generic reduction from *partial* 2-prover games to a corresponding traditional 2-prover game. Finally, in Section 5 we wrap up the proof of the main result of this work - Theorem 1.4.

3. FROM GAP-SMALL-SET-EXPANSION TO PARTIAL UNIQUE GAMES

In this section, we outline the key ideas of the reduction from GAP-SMALL-SET EXPANSION to Partial UNIQUE GAMES.

First Attempt.

Let $G = (V, E)$ be an instance of the GAP-SMALL-SET EXPANSION (η, δ) problem. For the sake of simplicity, let G be a d-regular unweighted graph. We define the following unique game:

- Fix $R = \lceil \frac{1}{\delta} \rceil$. The referee/verifier picks R edges $M = \{(u_1, v_1), \ldots, (u_R, v_R)\}$ uniformly at random from G.
- The referee sends a random permutation of the tuple $U = (u_1, \ldots, u_R)$ to the first prover, and a random permutation of the tuple $V = (v_1, \ldots, v_R)$ to second prover.
- The provers are expected to pick one of the vertices of the tuple they receive. Specifically, the answer set of the first prover is $\{u_1, \ldots, u_R\}$, while the second prover's answer set is $\{v_1, \ldots, v_R\}$.
- The provers win if they pick two vertices (u_i, v_i) corresponding to some edge in the set M.

Completeness: Let us suppose there exists a set S of δn vertices such that $\Phi(S) \leqslant \varepsilon$. In this case, the provers can use the following simple strategy: If exactly one vertex from S appears in the tuple, return that vertex, else refuse to answer the question.

The set S is of size δn and a question $U \in V^R$ has $\lceil \frac{1}{\delta} \rceil$ vertices. Therefore, with constant probability (at least 0.01) exactly one of the vertices from S appears in the question U, and the provers answer the question. Consequently, the above strategy is a valid partial strategy. Observe that if the set S has small conductance $\Phi(S) \leqslant \varepsilon$, a random edge incident on S is with high probability completely contained within S. In other words, if $u_i \in S$ then with very high probability its neighbour v_i also belongs to S. This implies that whenever the first prover decides to answer the vertex u_i, the second prover also answers v_i with very high probability. Hence a small non-expanding set S translates directly in to a *good* partial strategy for the unique game.

Soundness: Let $F : V^R \to [R]$ be a strategy for the two provers that succeeds with probability at least $\frac{1}{2}$. For a vertex sequence $U \in V^{R-1}$, let $U +_i x \in V^R$ denote the vertex sequence obtained by inserting x at index i.

For every vertex sequence $U \in V^{R-1}$ and an index $i \in [R]$, let us define a $\{0,1\}$-valued function $F_U^{(i)}$ as follows:

$$F_U^{(i)}(x) = 1 \text{ if } F(U +_i x) = i \text{ else it is } 0$$

Specifically, $F_U^{(i)}$ is the indicator function of the set of vertices x such that the strategy decides to pick up the vertex x, when it is inserted at the ith location in U.

Notice that, for the strategy proposed in the completeness case, for every setting of U, the set $F_U^{(i)}$ is either the non-expanding set S or the empty set. Extrapolating from here, it is natural to look for non-expanding sets by considering the set $F_U^{(i)}$ for a a random choice of $U \in V^{R-1}$ and i. This is the basic intuition behind the soundness analysis presented in Section 3.1.

Over a random choice of $U \in V^{R-1}$ and i, the expected size of $F_U^{(i)}$ is indeed roughly $\Theta(\frac{1}{R}) = \Theta(\delta)$. However, it could be possible that with very high probability over the choice of U and i, $F_U^{(i)}$ is either too large or too small a set. To rule out this possibility, we modify the above unique game by including random noise in to the questions. More specifically, the referee changes each vertex of the questions U, V independently with probability ε, before sending it to the provers. In the modified game, we bound the second moment of the random variable – the size of $F_U^{(i)}$ over a random choice of U and i.

Formal Reduction.

Here we present the details of the reduction from GAP-SMALL-SET EXPANSION problem to Partial UNIQUE GAMES.

For a vertex $v \in V$ and $\varepsilon > 0$, we define a distribution $\mathcal{N}_\varepsilon(v)$ on V as follows: with probability $1 - \varepsilon$, we output $u := v$ and with probability ε, we output $u \sim V$. For a vertex sequence $v_1, \dots, v_R$, the notation $\mathcal{N}_\varepsilon(v_1, \dots, v_R)$ refers to the product distribution $\mathcal{N}_\varepsilon(v_1) \otimes \cdots \otimes \mathcal{N}_\varepsilon(v_R)$ on V^R.

For an edge $e \in E$, we define $\mathcal{D}(e)$ to be the distribution that picks a random endpoint of e (uniformly). For a edge sequence $e_1, \dots, e_R$, the distribution $\mathcal{D}(e_1, \dots, e_R)$ on V^R is the product of the distributions $\mathcal{D}(e_1), \dots, \mathcal{D}(e_R)$. For a permutation $\pi\colon [R] \to [R]$ and a sequence $A \in V^R$, we write $A' = \pi.A$ to denote the permutation of A according to π, i.e., $A'_{\pi(i)} = A_i$ for all $i \in [R]$.

Let $R \in \mathbb{N}$. We define a Unique Games instance $\Upsilon = \Upsilon_{R,\varepsilon}(G)$ with vertex set V^R and alphabet $\Sigma = [R]$. The edge constraints in Υ are given by the tests performed by the following verifier.

> SSE-to-UG Reduction
>
> Let $F : V^R \to \Sigma$ be an assignment to the instance Υ. The value of the assignment is the success probability of the following test:
>
> 1. Sample R random edges $e_1, \dots, e_R$ from E and let $M := (e_1, \dots, e_R)$.
> 2. Sample $A \sim \mathcal{D}(M)$ and $B \sim \mathcal{D}(M)$.
> 3. Sample $\tilde{A} \sim \mathcal{N}_\varepsilon(A)$ and $\tilde{B} \sim \mathcal{N}_\varepsilon(B)$.
> 4. Sample two permutations $\pi_1, \pi_2\colon [R] \to [R]$.
> 5. Output **Success** if
>
> $$\pi_1^{-1}\left(F(\pi_1.\tilde{A})\right) = \pi_2^{-1}\left(F(\pi_2.\tilde{B})\right). \qquad (3.1)$$

In the remainder of the section, we will show the following theorem.

Theorem 3.1. *For $\eta < \frac{1}{24}$, given a graph $G = (V, E)$, the 3 reduction produces an instance Υ of* Unique Games *such that:*

–Completeness: *If $\Phi(S) \leqslant \eta$ for some S with $\mu(S) \in \left[\frac{1}{20R}, \frac{1}{R}\right]$ then there exists a $1/10e$-partial strategy of value at least $1 - 40e\eta - 4\varepsilon$.*

–Soundness: *If there exists a α-partial strategy with value $1-\eta$ for the* Unique Games *instance Υ, then there exists a set $S \subseteq V$ with $\Phi(S) \leqslant 96\eta$ and $\mu(S) \in \left[\frac{\alpha}{4R}, \frac{6}{\varepsilon\eta R}\right]$.*

Due to space limitations, we defer the somewhat straightforward proof of the completeness case to the full version. The soundness claim of the above theorem is proven in the next section (Lemma 3.3).

3.1 Soundness

Let $F\colon V^R \to [R] \cup \{\perp\}$ be a partial assignment for the unique game Υ. For $U \in V^{R-1}$ and $x \in V$, we let $f(U, x) \in [0, 1]$ denote the probability that F selects the coordinate of x after we place it at a random position of U and permute the sequence randomly, i.e.,

$$f(U, x) \stackrel{\text{def}}{=} \mathop{\mathbb{P}}_{\substack{i \in [R] \\ \pi}} \left\{F(\pi.(U +_i x)) = \pi(i)\right\}. \qquad (3.2)$$

Here, $U +_i x$ denotes the vertex sequence in V^R obtained from U by inserting x as the i-th coordinate (the original coordinates $i, \dots, R-1$ of U are moved by one to the right).

For $M \in E^{R-1}$, we define a function $f_M\colon V \to [0, 1]$ as follows

$$f_M(x) \stackrel{\text{def}}{=} \mathop{\mathbb{E}}_{U \sim \mathcal{D}(M)} \; \mathop{\mathbb{E}}_{(\tilde{U}, \tilde{x}) \sim \mathcal{N}_\varepsilon(U, x)} f(\tilde{U}, \tilde{x}). \qquad (3.3)$$

We establish the following three relatively straight-forward properties of the functions f_M.

Proposition 3.2. *Suppose that F has value $1 - \eta$ for the game Υ and that F differs from $\perp$ on exactly an α fraction of the inputs, i.e., $\alpha := \mathbb{P}_{X \sim V^R}\{F(X) \neq \perp\}$. Then the following hold,*

$$\mathop{\mathbb{E}}_{M \in E^{R-1}} \mathop{\mathbb{E}}_{x \sim V} f_M(x) = \tfrac{\alpha}{R}, \qquad (3.4)$$

$$\mathop{\mathbb{E}}_{x \sim V} f_M(x) \leqslant \tfrac{2}{\varepsilon R} \quad \forall M \in E^{R-1} \qquad (3.5)$$

$$\mathop{\mathbb{E}}_{M \in E^{R-1}} \mathop{\mathbb{E}}_{e \in E} \left(\mathop{\mathbb{E}}_{x \sim \mathcal{D}(e)} f_M(x)\right)^2 = (1 - \eta)\tfrac{\alpha}{R}. \qquad (3.6)$$

Before proving the proposition, we will first show that the existence of such functions $\{f_M\}$ as outlined in the proposition, suffices to finish the soundness analysis.

Lemma 3.3. *Suppose there exists a collection of functions $\{f_M\}$ satisfying the three conditions of 3.2 for some $\eta \leqslant \frac{1}{24}$. Then there exists a set $S \subseteq V$ with $\mu(S) \in \left[\frac{\alpha}{4R}, \frac{6}{\varepsilon R}\right]$ and $\Phi(S) \leqslant 96\eta$*

Proof. Let X and Y be the following non-negative random variables over the probability space E^{R-1},

$$X(M) := \mathop{\mathbb{E}}_{xy \in E} f_M(x) f_M(y) \qquad Y(M) := \mathop{\mathbb{E}}_{x \sim V} f_M(x).$$

Since $X \leqslant Y$ (pointwise), $X' = Y - X$ is also a non-negative random variable over E^{R-1}. The conditions (3.6) and (3.4) imply that $\mathbb{E}\, X' \leqslant 2\eta\, \mathbb{E}\, Y$ and $\mathbb{E}\, Y = \alpha/R$. Hence, Lemma 2.2 (Glorified Markov Inequality) asserts that there exists an edge sequence $M^* \in E^{R-1}$ such that $X'(M^*) \leqslant 4\eta Y(M^*)$ and $Y(M^*) \geqslant \mathbb{E}\, Y/2$. In other words,

$$\mathop{\mathbb{E}}_{xy \in E} f_{M^*}(x) f_{M^*}(y) \geqslant (1 - 4\eta) \mathop{\mathbb{E}}_{x \sim V} f_{M^*}(x), \qquad (3.7)$$

$$\mathop{\mathbb{E}}_{x \sim V} f_{M^*}(x) \geqslant \tfrac{\alpha}{2R}. \qquad (3.8)$$

By condition (3.5), we can also upper bound the expectation of f_{M^*},

$$\mathop{\mathbb{E}}_{x \sim V} f_{M^*}(x) \leqslant \tfrac{2}{\varepsilon R}. \qquad (3.9)$$

Lemma 3.4 shows that we can round the function f_{M^*} to a cut S^* that satisfies

$$\Phi(S^*) \leqslant 96\eta, \qquad \text{and} \qquad \mu(S^*) \in \left[\tfrac{\alpha}{4R}, \tfrac{6}{\varepsilon R}\right].$$

□

Lemma 3.4. *Let G be a graph with vertex set V and edge set E. Suppose $f\colon V \to [0, 1]$ is a bounded function on V such that*

$$\mathop{\mathbb{E}}_{xy \sim E} f(x) f(y) \geqslant (1 - \eta) \mathop{\mathbb{E}}_{x \sim V} f(x), \qquad (3.10)$$

for $\eta < \frac{1}{6}$. Let $\beta := \mathbb{E}_{x \sim V} f(x)$. Then, there exists a vertex set $S^* \subseteq V$ such that $\mu(S^*) \in \left[\frac{\beta}{2}, 3\beta\right]$ and $\Phi(S^*) \leqslant 24\eta$.

Proof. Define a distribution over sets S given by the following sampling procedure:

1. sample a threshold $t \in [1/9, 4/9]$ uniformly at random,
2. output the set $S := \{x \mid f^2(x) > t\}$.

Since $\mathbb{E} f = \beta$ the set S always satisfies

$$\mu(S) \leqslant \frac{\mathbb{E}[f]}{1/3} = 3\beta. \tag{3.11}$$

Note that condition (3.10) implies

$$(1-\eta)\beta \leqslant \mathop{\mathbb{E}}_{xy\sim E} f(x)f(y) \leqslant \mathop{\mathbb{E}}_{xy\sim E} \tfrac{1}{2}(f^2(x)+f^2(y)) = \mathop{\mathbb{E}}_{x\sim V} f^2.$$

Therefore we have $\mathbb{E}_{x\sim V} f(1-f) \leqslant \eta\beta$. Rewriting the previous inequality,

$$\begin{aligned}\eta\beta &\geqslant \mathbb{P}[f < 2/3] \mathop{\mathbb{E}}_{x\sim V} [f(1-f) | f < 2/3] \\ &\geqslant \frac{1}{3}\mathbb{P}[f < 2/3] \mathop{\mathbb{E}}_{x\sim V} [f | f < 2/3]\,.\end{aligned}$$

This implies a lower bound on the size of the set S as follows,

$$\begin{aligned}\mu(S) &\geqslant \mathbb{P}[f \geqslant 2/3] \geqslant \mathbb{P}[f \geqslant 2/3] \mathop{\mathbb{E}}_{x\sim V} [f | f \geqslant 2/3] \\ &= \mathbb{E}[f] - \mathbb{P}[f < 2/3] \mathop{\mathbb{E}}_{x\sim V} [f | f < 2/3] \geqslant \beta(1-3\eta)\,.\end{aligned} \tag{3.12}$$

Finally, we estimate the boundary of the set S.

$$\begin{aligned}\partial(S) &= \mathop{\mathbb{E}}_{xy\sim E} [|\mathbb{1}_S(x) - \mathbb{1}_S(y)|] \leqslant \mathop{\mathbb{E}}_{xy\sim E} [3\,|f^2(x) - f^2(y)|] \\ &\leqslant 12 \mathop{\mathbb{E}}_{x} f - 12 \mathop{\mathbb{E}}_{xy\sim E} f(x)f(y) \quad (\because 0 \leqslant f \leqslant 1 \text{ and Fact 2.1}) \\ &\leqslant 12\eta\beta\end{aligned} \tag{3.13}$$

The claim follows from (3.11),(3.12) and (3.13). □

3.2 Proof of Proposition 3.2

Let $F\colon V^R \to [R] \cup \{\perp\}$ be a partial strategy of value $1-\eta$ for the game Υ. Suppose F differs from $\perp$ on exactly an α fraction of inputs, i.e., $\mathbb{P}_{X\sim V}\{F(X) \in [R]\} = \alpha$. We prove the three conditions of 3.2 in the following lemmas.

LEMMA 3.5. $\mathbb{E}_{M\in E^{R-1}} \mathbb{E}_{x\sim V} f_M(x) = \frac{\alpha}{R}$.

PROOF. We unroll the definition of $f_M(x)$,

$$\begin{aligned}&\mathop{\mathbb{E}}_{M\in E^{R-1}} \mathop{\mathbb{E}}_{x\sim V} f_M(x) \\ &= \mathop{\mathbb{E}}_{\substack{M\in E^{R-1}, U\sim\mathcal{D}(M) \\ x\sim V, (\tilde{U},\tilde{x})\sim\mathcal{N}_\varepsilon(U,x)}} \mathop{\mathbb{P}}_{\substack{i\in[R] \\ \pi}} \left\{F(\pi.(\tilde{U} +_i \tilde{x})) = \pi(i)\right\} \\ &= \mathop{\mathbb{P}}_{X\sim V^R,\ r\in[R]} \{F(X) = r\} = \tfrac{\alpha}{R}\,.\end{aligned}$$

In the last equality, we use that the joint distribution of $\pi.(\tilde{U} +_i \tilde{x})$ and $\pi(i)$ is the same as the joint distribution of X and r. □

LEMMA 3.6. $\mathbb{E}_{M\in E^{R-1}}\ \mathbb{E}_{e\in E}\left(\mathbb{E}_{x\sim\mathcal{D}(e)} f_M(x)\right)^2 = (1-\eta)\frac{\alpha}{R}$.

PROOF. For an edge sequence $M \in E^R$ and $r \in [R]$, the notation M^{-r} refers to the edge sequence in E^{R-1} obtained from M by removing the r-th coordinate. Similarly, M_r denotes the r-th coordinate of M. Recall that F is a partial strategy with value $(1-\eta)\cdot\alpha$ on the game Υ. Expressing this fact we get,

$$\begin{aligned}&(1-\eta)\tfrac{\alpha}{R} = \\ &\mathop{\mathbb{E}}_{\substack{M\in E^R, A,B\sim\mathcal{D}(M) \\ \tilde{A}\sim\mathcal{N}_\varepsilon(A),\ \tilde{B}\sim\mathcal{N}_\varepsilon(B) \\ r\in[R]}} \mathop{\mathbb{P}}_{\pi_1,\pi_2} \left\{F(\pi_1.\tilde{A}) = \pi_1(r) \ \wedge\ F(\pi_2.\tilde{B}) = \pi_2(r)\right\} \\ &= \mathop{\mathbb{E}}_{\substack{M\in E^R, \\ r\in[R]}} \Big(\mathop{\mathbb{E}}_{A\sim\mathcal{D}(M)} \mathop{\mathbb{E}}_{\tilde{A}\sim\mathcal{N}_\varepsilon(A)} \mathop{\mathbb{P}}_{\pi} \left\{F(\pi.\tilde{A}) = \pi(r)\right\} \Big)^2 \\ &= \mathop{\mathbb{E}}_{\substack{M\in E^R, \\ r\in[R]}} \Big(\mathop{\mathbb{E}}_{\substack{x\sim\mathcal{D}(M_r) \\ U\sim\mathcal{D}(M^{-r}) \\ (\tilde{U},\tilde{x})\sim\mathcal{N}_\varepsilon(U,x)}} \mathop{\mathbb{P}}_{\pi} \left\{F(\pi.(\tilde{U} +_r \tilde{x})) = \pi(r)\right\} \Big)^2 \\ &= \mathop{\mathbb{E}}_{\substack{M\in E^R, \\ r\in[R]}} \Big(\mathop{\mathbb{E}}_{x\sim\mathcal{D}(M_r)} \mathop{\mathbb{E}}_{U\sim\mathcal{D}(M^{-r})} \mathop{\mathbb{E}}_{(\tilde{U},\tilde{x})\sim\mathcal{N}_\varepsilon(U,x)} f(\tilde{U},\tilde{x}) \Big)^2 \\ &= \mathop{\mathbb{E}}_{\substack{M\in E^R, \\ r\in[R]}} \Big(\mathop{\mathbb{E}}_{x\sim\mathcal{D}(M_r)} f_{M^{-r}}(x) \Big)^2 \\ &= \mathop{\mathbb{E}}_{M'\in E^{R-1}} \mathop{\mathbb{E}}_{e\in E} \Big(\mathop{\mathbb{E}}_{x\sim\mathcal{D}(e)} f_{M'}(x) \Big)^2\,.\end{aligned}$$

In the second equality, we use the fact that the events $F(\pi_1.\tilde{A}) = \pi_1(r)$ and $F(\pi_2.\tilde{B}) = \pi_2(r)$ are independent given $M \in E^R$ and $r \in [R]$. In the third equality, e_r denotes the edge in the r-th coordinate of M. □

LEMMA 3.7. *Suppose εR is sufficiently large. Then for every $M \in E^{R-1}$,*

$$\mathop{\mathbb{E}}_{x\sim V} f_M(x) \leqslant \tfrac{2}{\varepsilon R}\,.$$

PROOF. As before, we first unroll the definition of $f_M(x)$

$$\begin{aligned}\mathop{\mathbb{E}}_{x\sim V} f_M(x) &= \mathop{\mathbb{E}}_{U\sim\mathcal{D}(M)} \mathop{\mathbb{E}}_{x\sim V} \mathop{\mathbb{E}}_{(\tilde{U},\tilde{x})\sim\mathcal{N}_\varepsilon(U,x)} f(\tilde{U}+\tilde{x},\tilde{x}) \\ &= \mathop{\mathbb{E}}_{U\sim\mathcal{D}(M)} \mathop{\mathbb{E}}_{x\sim V} \mathop{\mathbb{E}}_{(\tilde{U},\tilde{x})\sim\mathcal{N}_\varepsilon(U,x)} \mathop{\mathbb{P}}_{\substack{i\in[R] \\ \pi}} \left\{F(\pi.(\tilde{U} +_i \tilde{x}))) = \pi(i)\right\}\end{aligned} \tag{3.14}$$

To estimate this expectation, we generate random variables $\pi.(\tilde{U} +_i \tilde{x})$ and $\pi(i)$ in an different fashion. Let $\circledast$ denote a placeholder symbol (not a member of V). Consider the following randomized procedure generating $A \in V^R$, $r \in [R]$:

1. Sample $U \sim \mathcal{D}(M)$, a permutation $\pi\colon [R] \to [R]$ and an index $i \in [R]$. Set $B := \pi.(U +_i \circledast)$.
2. Generate $B' \in (V \cup \{\circledast\})^R$ by changing each coordinate of B randomly to $\circledast$ with probability ε. Let $\mathcal{I} \subseteq [R]$ denote the set of coordinates of B' that contain $\circledast$.
3. Generate $A \in V^R$ by replacing all the placeholders in B' by vertices sampled from V.
4. Sample $r \in \mathcal{I}$ uniformly at random.

We claim that the joint distribution of A and r is the same as the joint distribution of $\pi.(\tilde{U} +_i \tilde{x})$ and $\pi(i)$ in (3.14). By construction, the joint distribution of A and $\pi(i)$ is the same as the joint distribution of $\pi.(\tilde{U} +_i \tilde{x})$ and $\pi(i)$ in (3.14) (with an obvious coupling). From the description of the construction, it is also clear that the r-th coordinate of A has the same distribution as the $\pi(i)$-th coordinate of A (both are sampled from V).

Since the pair (A, r) is identical in distribution to the pair $(\pi.(\tilde{U} +_i x), \pi(i))$, we can finish the proof of the lemma as follows

$$\mathop{\mathbb{E}}_{x\sim V} f_M(x) = \mathop{\mathbb{E}}_{\substack{U\sim\mathcal{D}(M), x\sim V\\ (\tilde{U},\tilde{x})\sim\mathcal{N}_\varepsilon(U,x)}} \mathop{\mathbb{P}}_{\substack{i\in[R]\\ \pi}} \left\{F(\pi.(\tilde{U} +_i \tilde{x}))) = \pi(i)\right\}$$

(by (3.14))

$$= \mathop{\mathbb{P}}_{A,r}\left\{F(A) = r\right\} \quad (A \text{ and } r \text{ generated as above})$$

$$= \mathop{\mathbb{E}}_{A,\ \mathcal{I}} \mathop{\mathbb{P}}_{r\in\mathcal{I}}\left\{F(A) = r\right\} \quad (A \text{ and } \mathcal{I} \text{ generated as above})$$

$$= \mathop{\mathbb{E}}_{A,\ \mathcal{I}} \tfrac{1}{|\mathcal{I}|}\mathbb{1}_{\{F(A)\in\mathcal{I}\}}$$

$$\leqslant \mathop{\mathbb{E}}_{t\sim\text{Binom}(R-1,\varepsilon)} \tfrac{1}{t+1} \quad (\because |\mathcal{I}| \sim 1 + \text{Binom}(R-1,\varepsilon))$$

$$\leqslant \tfrac{1.5}{\varepsilon R} + \mathop{\mathbb{P}}_{t\sim\text{Binom}(R-1,\varepsilon)} \{t + 1 \leqslant \varepsilon R/1.5\}$$

$$\leqslant \tfrac{1.5}{\varepsilon R} + 2^{-\Omega(\varepsilon R)} \quad \text{(using Chernoff bound)}$$

$$\leqslant \tfrac{2}{\varepsilon R} \quad (\text{for sufficiently large } \varepsilon R)$$

□

4. FROM PARTIAL 2-PROVER GAMES TO TOTAL 2-PROVER GAMES

We show a general reduction from a partial 2-prover game Γ to a corresponding 2-prover game Γ'.

Recall that in the partial game Γ, the provers are allowed to refuse to answer questions. However, in the game Γ' no such choice should be available. To achieve this, the referee gives multiple questions from Γ simultaneously and the provers have to answer any question of their choice.

Specifically, the questions in Γ' consists of a sequence of c questions from the game Γ. The provers are required to choose one of the c questions to answer, and return the answer. The provers win only if they pick the corresponding pair of questions (say the ith question), and also answer the question correctly as per the game Γ. Formally, we will show the following theorem in the remainder of the section.

THEOREM 4.1. *For all positive integers c, given a 2-prover game Γ with n vertices, there is a reduction to another 2-prover game Γ' running in time $n^{O(c)}$ such that:*

- Completeness *If the α-partial value of Γ is at least $1-\varepsilon$, then the value of Γ' is at least $1 - \varepsilon - e^{-\alpha\cdot c}$.*
- Soundness *If the value of Γ' is at least $1-\eta$, then the $1/3c$-partial value of Γ is at least $1 - 12\eta$.*

Furthermore, the reduction preserves the uniqueness property of the games.

We will assume that the edge set E of the game Γ does not contain any self-loops. We denote by $E_{\circlearrowleft}$ the following distribution over vertex pairs $(u, v) \in V^2$: sample a random edge $e \in E$ and let u and v be (independent) random endpoints of e (in particular, $u = v$ with probability 1/2). We add predicates $\Pi_{u,u} = \{(a, a) \mid a \in \Sigma\}$ for all self-loops $(u, u) \in V^2$ to the collection $\{\Pi_{u,v}\}$. For a parameter $c \in \mathbb{N}$, let Γ' be the following 2-prover game:

Reduction from a partial 2-prover game Γ to a total 2-prover game Γ'

1. Sample c vertex pairs $(u_1, v_1), \ldots, (u_c, v_c) \sim E_{\circlearrowleft}$.
2. Send the vertex sequence $u_1, \ldots, u_c$ to the first prover and the sequence $v_1, \ldots, v_c$ to the second prover.
3. Let (i, a) and (j, b) be their answers.
4. The provers win if $i = j$ and $(a, b) \in \Pi_{u_i,v_j}$.

We observe that the reduction preserves the uniqueness property.

OBSERVATION 4.2. *If Γ is a unique game, then Γ' is a unique game as well.*

We will show Theorem 4.1 in two parts: Lemma 4.3 and Lemma 4.4.

LEMMA 4.3 (COMPLETENESS). *If the α-partial value of Γ is at least $1-\varepsilon$, then the value of Γ' is at least $1-\varepsilon-e^{-\alpha\cdot c}$.*

PROOF. Let $F\colon V \to \Sigma \cup \{\perp\}$ be an α-partial strategy of value $1-\varepsilon$. We consider the following strategy F' for Γ'.

$$F'(u_1,\ldots,u_c) := \begin{cases} (i,a) & \text{if } (F(u_i)\in\Sigma) \wedge (\forall j<i, F(u_j)=\perp), \\ (1,1) & \text{if } F(u_1)=\ldots=F(u_c)=\perp. \end{cases}$$

(In words, the prover answers with the first answer in the list $F(u_1), \ldots, F(u_c)$ (ignoring $\perp$). If the partial strategy refuses to answer on all inputs $u_1, \ldots, u_c$, then the prover returns an arbitrary answer.)

Let $u_1v_1, \ldots, u_cv_c$ be a sequence of c vertex pairs, independently drawn from $E_{\circlearrowleft}$. The probability of the event $F(u_1) = \ldots = F(u_c)$ is at most $(1-\alpha)^c \leqslant e^{-\alpha c}$. Let us condition on the complementary event, i.e., the event that $F(u_i) \neq \perp$ for at least one coordinate $i \in [c]$. Let i_0 be the first coordinate such that $F(u_{i_0}) \neq \perp$ or $F(u_{i_0}) \neq \perp$. The winning probability of the provers (conditioned on the event that $F(u_i) \neq \perp$ for at least one coordinate $i \in [c]$) is equal to

$$\mathbb{P}\left\{(F(u_{i_0}), F(v_{i_0})) \in \Pi_{u_{i_0},v_{i_0}}\right\}$$

$$= \mathop{\mathbb{P}}_{uv\sim E_{\circlearrowleft}}\left\{(F(u),F(v))\in\Pi_{u,v} \;\middle|\; F(u)\in\Sigma \vee F(v)\in\Sigma\right\}$$

$$= \frac{\mathbb{P}_{uv\sim E_{\circlearrowleft}}\{(F(u),F(v))\in\Pi_{u,v}\}}{\mathbb{P}_{uv\sim E_{\circlearrowleft}}\{F(u)\in\Sigma\vee F(v)\in\Sigma\}}$$

$$= \frac{\mathbb{P}_{uv\sim E_{\circlearrowleft}}\{(F(u),F(v))\in\Pi_{u,v}\}}{2\,\mathbb{P}_{u\sim V}\{F(u)\in\Sigma\} - \mathbb{P}_{uv\sim E_{\circlearrowleft}}\{F(u),F(v)\in\Sigma\}}.$$

Without loss of generality, we may assume $\mathbb{P}_{u\sim V}\{F(u)\in\Sigma\} = \alpha$. Since the partial strategy F' has value $1-\varepsilon$, we have $\mathbb{P}_{uv\in E_{\circlearrowleft}}\{(F(u),F(v))\in\Pi_{u,v}\} \geqslant 1/2\cdot(1-\varepsilon)\alpha + 1/2\cdot\alpha$. Therefore, also $\mathbb{P}_{uv\in E_{\circlearrowleft}}\{F(u),F(v)\in\Sigma\} \geqslant (1-\varepsilon/2)\alpha$. We can conclude

$$\mathop{\mathbb{P}}_{uv\sim E_{\circlearrowleft}}\left\{(F(u),F(v))\in\Pi_{u,v} \;\middle|\; F(u)\in\Sigma\vee F(v)\in\Sigma\right\}$$

$$\geqslant \tfrac{(1-\varepsilon/2)\alpha}{(1+\varepsilon/2)\alpha} \geqslant 1-\varepsilon.$$

It follows that the value of the strategy F' for the game Γ' is at least $1-\varepsilon-e^{-\alpha c}$. □

LEMMA 4.4 (SOUNDNESS). *If the value of Γ' is at least $1-\eta$, then the $1/3c$-partial value of Γ is at least $1-12\eta$.*

PROOF. Let $F'\colon V^c \to [c]\times\Sigma$ be a strategy for Γ' of value $1-\eta$. We first construct a partial strategy for Γ that uses shared randomness. For $i\in[c]$ and $\underline{u}\in V^{c-1}$, we define a partial strategy $F_{i,\underline{u}}\colon V\to\Sigma\cup\{\bot\}$ as

$$F_{i,\underline{u}}(u) := \begin{cases} a & \text{if } F'(\underline{u} +_i u) = (i,a)\,, \\ \bot & \text{otherwise.}\end{cases}$$

Here, $\underline{u} +_i u$ denotes the vertex sequence $\underline{u}'\in V^c$ obtained from $\underline{u}$ by inserting u as the i-th coordinate (the original coordinates $i,\ldots,c-1$ of $\underline{u}$ are moved by one to the right).

It is clear that

$$\mathop{\mathbb{P}}_{i\in[c],\ \underline{u}\in V^{c-1},\ u\sim V}\Big\{F_{i,\underline{u}}(u)\in\Sigma\Big\} = 1/c\,. \tag{4.1}$$

Since the value of F' is $1-\eta$, we have

$$\begin{aligned}(1-\eta)/c &= \mathop{\mathbb{P}}_{i\in[c],\ \underline{uv}\sim E_{\circlearrowleft}^{c-1},\ uv\sim E_{\circlearrowleft}}\Big\{(F_{i,\underline{u}}(u),F_{i,\underline{v}}(v))\in\Pi_{u,v}\Big\}\\ &= \tfrac{1}{2}\mathop{\mathbb{P}}_{i\in[c],\ \underline{uv}\in E_{\circlearrowleft}^{c-1},\ uv\in E}\Big\{(F_{i,\underline{u}}(u),F_{i,\underline{v}}(v))\in\Pi_{u,v}\Big\}\\ &+ \tfrac{1}{2}\mathop{\mathbb{P}}_{i\in[c],\ \underline{uv}\in E_{\circlearrowleft}^{c-1},\ u\sim V}\Big\{F_{i,\underline{u}}(u)=F_{i,\underline{v}}(u)\in\Sigma\Big\}\end{aligned}$$

From (4.1), it follows that both probabilities in the previous equation are at most $1/c$. Hence, for their average to be $(1-\eta)/c$, both of them have to be at least $(1-2\eta)/c$,

$$\mathop{\mathbb{P}}_{i\in[c],\ \underline{uv}\in E_{\circlearrowleft}^{c-1},\ uv\in E}\Big\{(F_{i,\underline{u}}(u),F_{i,\underline{v}}(v))\in\Pi_{u,v}\Big\}\geqslant(1-2\eta)/c\,, \tag{4.2}$$

$$\mathop{\mathbb{P}}_{i\in[c],\ \underline{uv}\in E_{\circlearrowleft}^{c-1},\ u\sim V}\Big\{F_{i,\underline{u}}(u)=F_{i,\underline{v}}(u)\in\Sigma\Big\}\geqslant(1-2\eta)/c\,. \tag{4.3}$$

To further analyze the partial strategies, we define two random variables

$$\begin{aligned}\mathsf{Vol}(i,\underline{u},\underline{v}) &:= \mathop{\mathbb{P}}_{u\sim V}\Big\{F_{i,\underline{u}}(u)\in\Sigma\vee F_{i,\underline{v}}(u)\in\Sigma\Big\}\,,\\ \mathsf{Val}(i,\underline{u},\underline{v}) &:= \mathop{\mathbb{P}}_{uv\sim E_{\circlearrowleft}}\Big\{(F_{i,\underline{u}}(u),F_{i,\underline{v}}(v))\in\Pi_{u,v}\Big\}\,.\end{aligned}$$

The measure on $(i,\underline{u},\underline{v})$ is as follows: We choose $i\in[c]$ uniformly at random, and sample $\underline{uv}$ from $E_{\circlearrowleft}^{c-1}$. It is clear that $\mathsf{Val}\leqslant\mathsf{Vol}$ (pointwise) and

$$\begin{aligned}\mathbb{E}\,\mathsf{Vol} &= \mathop{\mathbb{E}}_{i\in[c],\ \underline{uv}\sim E_{\circlearrowleft}^{c-1}}\Big[\mathop{\mathbb{P}}_{u\sim V}\{F_{i,\underline{u}}(u)\in\Sigma\} \qquad (4.4)\\ &+\mathop{\mathbb{P}}_{u\sim V}\{F_{i,\underline{v}}(u)\in\Sigma\}-\mathop{\mathbb{P}}_{u\sim V}\Big\{F_{i,\underline{u}}(u),F_{i,\underline{v}}(u)\in\Sigma\Big\}\Big]\\ &= 2/c-\mathop{\mathbb{P}}_{i\in[c],\ \underline{uv}\sim E_{\circlearrowleft}^{c-1},\ u\sim V}\Big\{F_{i,\underline{u}}(u),F_{i,\underline{v}}(u)\in\Sigma\Big\}\\ &\leqslant(1+2\eta)/c\qquad(\text{using (4.3)})\,. \qquad (4.5)\end{aligned}$$

On the other hand, since the value of F' is $1-\eta$, $\mathbb{E}\,\mathsf{Val}$ is given by,

$$\mathop{\mathbb{P}}_{i\in[c],\ \underline{uv}\sim E_{\circlearrowleft}^{c-1},\ uv\sim E_{\circlearrowleft}}\Big\{(F_{i,\underline{u}}(u),F_{i,\underline{v}}(v))\in\Pi_{u,v}\Big\}=(1-\eta)/c\,. \tag{4.6}$$

At this point, we could use Lemma 2.2 (Glorified Markov Inequality) to argue that there exists a triple $(i,\underline{u},\underline{v})$ such that $\mathsf{Val}(i,\underline{u},\underline{v})\geqslant(1-O(\eta))\mathsf{Vol}(i,\underline{u},\underline{v})$ and $\mathsf{Vol}(i,\underline{u},\underline{v})\geqslant\mathbb{E}\,\mathsf{Vol}/2\geqslant1/2c$.

For the reader's convenience, we repeat the (short) argument: Let $\eta'\leqslant3\eta$ be such that $1-\eta'=(1-\eta)/(1+2\eta)$. Let Good be the event $\mathsf{Val}\geqslant(1-2\eta')\mathsf{Vol}$ and let Bad be the complementary event. We denote by $\mathbb{1}_{\mathsf{Good}}$ and $\mathbb{1}_{\mathsf{Bad}}$ the indicator variables of these events. We can relate $\mathbb{E}\,\mathbb{1}_{\mathsf{Good}}\mathsf{Vol}$ and $\mathbb{E}\,\mathsf{Vol}$ as follows

$$\begin{aligned}0 &\leqslant \mathbb{E}\,\mathsf{Val}-(1-\eta')\,\mathbb{E}\,\mathsf{Vol}\qquad(\text{using (4.5) and (4.6)})\\ &\leqslant\mathbb{E}\,\mathbb{1}_{\mathsf{Good}}\mathsf{Vol}+(1-2\eta')\,\mathbb{E}\,\mathbb{1}_{\mathsf{Bad}}\mathsf{Vol}-(1-\eta')\,\mathbb{E}\,\mathsf{Vol}\\ &=2\eta'\,\mathbb{E}\,\mathbb{1}_{\mathsf{Good}}\mathsf{Vol}-\eta'\,\mathbb{E}\,\mathsf{Vol}\,.\end{aligned}$$

Hence, we can find i, $\underline{u}$, and $\underline{v}$ such that $\mathbb{1}_{\mathsf{Good}}(i,\underline{u},\underline{v})=1$ and $\mathsf{Vol}(i,\underline{u},\underline{v})\geqslant\mathbb{E}\,\mathsf{Vol}/2$, i.e.,

$$\begin{aligned}&\mathop{\mathbb{P}}_{uv\sim E_{\circlearrowleft}}\Big\{(F_{i,\underline{u}}(u),F_{i,\underline{v}}(v))\in\Pi_{u,v}\Big\}\\ &\quad\geqslant(1-2\eta')\cdot\mathop{\mathbb{P}}_{u\sim V}\Big\{F_{i,\underline{u}}(u)\in\Sigma\vee F_{i,\underline{v}}(u)\in\Sigma\Big\}\,, \qquad (4.7)\\ &\mathop{\mathbb{P}}_{u\sim V}\Big\{F_{i,\underline{u}}(u)\in\Sigma\vee F_{i,\underline{v}}(u)\in\Sigma\Big\}\geqslant(1-2\eta)/2c\,. \qquad (4.8)\end{aligned}$$

We claim that the two conditions (4.7) and (4.8) allows us to construct an $O(1/c)$-partial strategy of value $1-O(\eta)$. More concretely, we can modify $F_{i,\underline{u}}$ and $F_{i,\underline{v}}$ in such a way that $F_{i,\underline{u}}(u)=F_{i,\underline{v}}(u)$ for all $u\in V$ while maintaining the conditions (4.7) and (4.8). (Here, we use the fact that with probability $1/2$, we test $F_{i,\underline{u}}(u)=F_{i,\underline{v}}(u)\in\Sigma$.) In this way, we get an assignment $F^*\colon V\to\Sigma\cup\{\bot\}$ such that $F^*(u)=\bot$ if $F_{i,\underline{u}}(u)=F_{i,\underline{v}}=\bot$ and $F^*(u)\in\{F_{i,\underline{u}}(u),F_{i,\underline{v}}(u)\}\cap\Sigma$ otherwise. Furthermore, the assignment F^* satisfies

$$\begin{aligned}&\mathop{\mathbb{P}}_{u\sim V}\Big\{F^*(u)\in\Sigma\Big\}=\mathop{\mathbb{P}}_{u\sim V}\Big\{F_{i,\underline{u}}(u)\in\Sigma\vee F_{i,\underline{v}}(u)\in\Sigma\Big\}\,,\\ &\mathop{\mathbb{P}}_{uv\sim E_{\circlearrowleft}}\Big\{(F^*(u),F^*(v))\in\Pi_{u,v}\Big\}\\ &\qquad\geqslant\mathop{\mathbb{P}}_{uv\sim E_{\circlearrowleft}}\Big\{(F_{i,\underline{u}}(u),F_{i,\underline{v}}(v))\in\Pi_{u,v}\Big\}\,.\end{aligned}$$

Let $\alpha=\mathbb{P}_{u\sim V}\{F^*(u)\in\Sigma\}$. We have

$$\begin{aligned}(1-2\eta')\cdot\alpha &\leqslant\mathop{\mathbb{P}}_{uv\sim E_{\circlearrowleft}}\Big\{(F^*(u),F^*(v))\in\Pi_{u,v}\Big\}\\ &=\tfrac{1}{2}\mathop{\mathbb{P}}_{uv\in E}\Big\{(F^*(u),F^*(v))\in\Pi_{u,v}\Big\}+\tfrac{1}{2}\alpha\end{aligned}$$

It follows that $\mathbb{P}_{uv\in E}\{(F^*(u),F^*(v))\in\Pi_{u,v}\}\geqslant(1-4\eta')\cdot\alpha$. We can conclude that F^* is an $(1-2\eta)/2c$-partial strategy of value at least $1-4\eta'\geqslant1-12\eta$ for Γ. □

5. WRAPPING UP

The main result of this work namely Theorem 1.4 is an immediate consequence of the following theorem.

THEOREM 5.1. *Given a regular graph G of size n and parameters $\varepsilon,\delta>0$ such that $\delta=m/n$ for some integer m, we can compute in polynomial time a* UNIQUE GAMES *instance Υ with $(n/\varepsilon)^{O(1/\delta)}$ variables and with $\mathrm{poly}(1/\varepsilon\delta)$ labels such that the following holds with $C=1500$:*

–Completeness: *For all $\eta>0$ if*

$$\Phi_G(\delta)\leqslant\eta\implies\mathrm{opt}(\Upsilon)\geqslant1-C(\eta+\varepsilon)$$

–Soundness:

$$\Phi_G(\delta)\geqslant1-\varepsilon^2/2C^2\log^2(1/\varepsilon)\implies\mathrm{opt}(\Upsilon)\leqslant1-\frac{1}{2C}$$

PROOF. Execute the SSE-TO-UG reduction with parameters $R = \lfloor \frac{1}{\delta} \rfloor$ and ε on the input graph $G = (V, E)$. This yields a UNIQUE GAMES instance Υ^* on alphabet size R. Apply the reduction from partial UNIQUE GAMES to UNIQUE GAMES presented in Section 4 with parameter $c = 40e\log(1/\varepsilon)$, to get the UNIQUE GAMES instance Υ.

Completeness If $\Phi_G(\delta) \leqslant \eta$ then there exists a subset S such that $\mu(S) \in [\delta/10, \delta]$ and $\Phi(S) \leqslant \varepsilon$. By choice of R, we have $\mu(S) \in [\frac{1}{20R}, \frac{1}{R}]$. Hence by Theorem 3.1, there exists a $1/20e$-partial strategy with value $(1 - 40e\eta - 4\varepsilon)$ for Υ^*. Finally, by Theorem 4.1 there exists a strategy for the game Υ succeeding with probability at least $1 - 40e\eta - 4\varepsilon - \varepsilon^2$.

Soundness Let $\beta = \frac{1}{2C}$. Suppose not, let us say $\mathrm{opt}(\Upsilon) \geqslant 1 - \beta$. By Theorem 4.1, if $\mathrm{opt}(\Upsilon) \geqslant 1 - \beta$ then there exists a $\frac{1}{3c}$-partial strategy for Υ^* with value at least $1 - 12\beta$. Applying Theorem 3.1, we get that there exists a set S with $\Phi(S) \leqslant 1152\beta$ and

$$\mu(S) \in \left[\frac{\delta}{480e\log(1/\varepsilon)}, \frac{6\delta}{\varepsilon}\right].$$

If $\mu(S) < \delta$ then pad it with arbitrary vertices to construct a set S' such that $\mu(S') = \delta$. On the other hand, if $\mu(S) > \delta$, randomly subsample a subset $S' \subseteq S$ of volume δ. In either case, it is easy to check that $\Phi(S') \leqslant 1 - (1 - 1152\beta)\varepsilon^2/C^2\log^2(1/\varepsilon) \leqslant 1 - \varepsilon^2/2C^2\log^2(1/\varepsilon)$. □

Acknowledgments: We thank Boaz Barak for suggesting the notion of partial games, which helped to improve the presentation of the results. We also thank Sanjeev Arora, Venkatesan Guruswami, Oded Regev and Prasad Tetali for insightful discussions.

6. REFERENCES

[1] N. Alon. Eigenvalues and expanders. *Combinatorica*, 6(2):83–96, 1986.

[2] N. Alon and V. D. Milman. λ_1, isoperimetric inequalities for graphs, and superconcentrators. *Journal of Combinatorial Theory. Series B*, 38:73–88, 1985.

[3] S. Arora, R. Impagliazzo, W. Matthews, and D. Stuerer. Improved algorithms for unique games via divide and conquer. In *Electronic Colloquium on Computational Complexity ECCCTR: TR10-041*, 2010.

[4] S. Arora, S. Khot, A. Kolla, D. Steurer, M. Tulsiani, and N. K. Vishnoi. Unique games on expanding constraint graphs are easy: extended abstract. In *STOC*, pages 21–28. ACM, 2008.

[5] S. Arora, S. Rao, and U. Vazirani. Expander flows, geometric embeddings and graph partitioning. In *Proceedings of the thirty-sixth annual ACM Symposium on Theory of Computing (STOC-04)*, pages 222–231, June 13–15 2004.

[6] Y. Aumann and Y. Rabani. An $O(\log k)$ approximate min-cut max-flow theorem and approximation algorithm. *SIAM Journal on Computing*, 27(1):291–301, Feb. 1998.

[7] B. Barak, M. Hardt, I. Haviv, A. Rao, O. Regev, and D. Steurer. Rounding parallel repetitions of unique games. In *FOCS*, pages 374–383. IEEE Computer Society, 2008.

[8] M. Charikar, K. Makarychev, and Y. Makarychev. Integrality gaps for sherali-adams relaxations. In *STOC*, pages 283–292. ACM, 2009.

[9] J. Cheeger. A lower bound on smallest eigenvalue of a laplacian. *Problems in Analysis (Papers dedicated to Salomon Bochner)*, pages 195–199, 1970.

[10] Feige and Schechtman. On the optimality of the random hyperplane rounding technique for MAX CUT. *RSA: Random Structures Algorithms*, 20, 2002.

[11] U. Feige, G. Kindler, and R. O'Donnell. Understanding parallel repetition requires understanding foams. In *IEEE Conference on Computational Complexity*, pages 179–192, 2007.

[12] K. Georgiou, A. Magen, T. Pitassi, and I. Tourlakis. Integrality gaps of 2 - o(1) for vertex cover SDPs in the lovész-schrijver hierarchy. In *FOCS*, pages 702–712. IEEE Computer Society, 2007.

[13] S. Khot. On the power of unique 2-prover 1-round games. In *STOC*, pages 767–775. ACM, 2002.

[14] S. Khot, G. Kindler, E. Mossel, and R. O'Donnell. Optimal inapproximability results for max-cut and other 2-variable csps? *SIAM J. Comput.*, 37(1):319–357, 2007.

[15] S. Khot and O. Regev. Vertex cover might be hard to approximate to within 2-ε. *J. Comput. Syst. Sci.*, 74(3):335–349, 2008.

[16] S. Khot and N. K. Vishnoi. The unique games conjecture, integrality gap for cut problems and embeddability of negative type metrics into l_1. In *FOCS*, pages 53–62. IEEE Computer Society, 2005.

[17] F. T. Leighton and S. Rao. Multicommodity max-flow min-cut theorems and their use in designing approximation algorithms. *J. ACM*, 46(6):787–832, 1999.

[18] N. Linial, E. London, and Y. Rabinovich. The geometry of graphs and some of its algorithmic applications. *Combinatorica*, 15(2):215–245, 1995.

[19] P. Raghavendra. Optimal algorithms and inapproximability results for every CSP? In *STOC*, pages 245–254. ACM, 2008.

[20] P. Raghavendra and D. Steurer. How to round any CSP. In *FOCS*, pages 586–594. IEEE Computer Society, 2009.

[21] P. Raghavendra and D. Steurer. Integrality gaps for strong SDP relaxations of UNIQUE GAMES. In *FOCS*, pages 575–585. IEEE Computer Society, 2009.

[22] P. Raghavendra, D. Steurer, and P. Tetali. Approximations for the isoperimetric and spectral profile of graphs and for restricted eigenvalues of diagonally-dominant matrices. In *STOC*. ACM, 2010. To Appear.

[23] A. Rao. Parallel repetition in projection games and a concentration bound. In *STOC*, pages 1–10. ACM, 2008.

[24] R. Raz. A counterexample to strong parallel repetition. In *FOCS*, pages 369–373. IEEE Computer Society, 2008.

[25] G. Schoenebeck, L. Trevisan, and M. Tulsiani. A linear round lower bound for Lovász-Schrijver SDP relaxations of vertex cover. In *IEEE Conference on Computational Complexity*, pages 205–216, 2007.

Interactive Privacy via the Median Mechanism

Aaron Roth*
Carnegie Mellon University
5000 Forbes Avenue
Pittsburgh, PA 15217
alroth@cs.cmu.edu

Tim Roughgarden†
Stanford University
353 Serra Mall
Stanford, CA 94305
tim@cs.stanford.edu

ABSTRACT

We define a new interactive differentially private mechanism — the *median mechanism* — for answering arbitrary predicate queries that arrive online. Given fixed accuracy and privacy constraints, this mechanism can answer exponentially more queries than the previously best known interactive privacy mechanism (the Laplace mechanism, which independently perturbs each query result). With respect to the number of queries, our guarantee is close to the best possible, even for non-interactive privacy mechanisms. Conceptually, the median mechanism is the first privacy mechanism capable of identifying and exploiting correlations among queries in an interactive setting.

We also give an efficient implementation of the median mechanism, with running time polynomial in the number of queries, the database size, and the domain size. This efficient implementation guarantees privacy for all input databases, and accurate query results for almost all input distributions. The dependence of the privacy on the number of queries in this mechanism improves over that of the best previously known efficient mechanism by a super-polynomial factor, even in the non-interactive setting.

Categories and Subject Descriptors

F.2 [**ANALYSIS OF ALGORITHMS AND PROBLEM COMPLEXITY**]: Miscellaneous

General Terms

Theory, Algorithms

*Supported in part by an NSF Graduate Research Fellowship. Portions of this work were done while visiting Stanford University.

†Supported in part by NSF CAREER Award CCF-0448664, an ONR Young Investigator Award, an ONR PECASE Award, an AFOSR MURI grant, and an Alfred P. Sloan Fellowship.

STOC'10, June 5–8, 2010, Cambridge, Massachusetts, USA.

1. INTRODUCTION

Managing a data set with sensitive but useful information, such as medical records, requires reconciling two objectives: providing utility to others, perhaps in the form of aggregate statistics; and respecting the privacy of individuals who contribute to the data set. The field of *private data analysis*, and in particular work on *differential privacy*, provides a mathematical foundation for reasoning about this utility-privacy trade-off and offers methods for non-trivial data analysis that are provably privacy-preserving in a precise sense. For a recent survey of the field, see Dwork [Dwo08].

More precisely, consider a domain X and database size n. A *mechanism* is a randomized function from the set X^n of databases to some range. For a parameter $\alpha > 0$, a mechanism M is *α-differentially private* if, for every database D and fixed subset S of the range of M, changing a single component of D changes the probability that M outputs something in S by at most an e^α factor. The output of a differentially private mechanism (and any analysis or privacy attack that follows) is thus essentially independent of whether or not a given individual "opts in" or "opts out" of the database.

Achieving differential privacy requires "sufficiently noisy" answers [DN03]. For example, suppose we're interested in the result of a query f — a function from databases to some range — that simply counts the fraction of database elements that satisfy some predicate φ on X. A special case of a result in Dwork et al. [DMNS06] asserts that the following mechanism is α-differentially private: if the underlying database is D, output $f(D)+\Delta$, where the output perturbation Δ is drawn from the Laplace distribution $\mathrm{Lap}(\frac{1}{n\alpha})$ with density $p(y) = \frac{n\alpha}{2}\exp(-n\alpha|y|)$. Among all α-differentially private mechanisms, this one (or rather, a discretized analog of it) maximizes user utility in a strong sense [GRS09].

What if we care about more than a single one-dimensional statistic? Suppose we're interested in k predicate queries $f_1, \ldots, f_k$, where k could be large, even super-polynomial in n. A natural solution is to use an independent Laplace perturbation for each query answer [DMNS06]. To maintain α-differential privacy, the magnitude of noise has to scale linearly with k, with each perturbation drawn from $\mathrm{Lap}(\frac{k}{n\alpha})$. Put another way, suppose one fixes "usefulness parameters" ϵ, δ, and insists that the mechanism is *(ϵ, δ)-useful*, meaning that the outputs are within ϵ of the correct query answers with probability at least $1-\delta$. This constrains the magnitude of the Laplace noise, and the privacy parameter α now suffers linearly with the number k of answered queries. This dependence limits the use of this mechanism to a sublinear $k = o(n)$ number of queries.

Can we do better than independent output perturbations? For special classes of queries like predicate queries, Blum, Ligett, and Roth [BLR08] give an affirmative answer (building on techniques of Kasiviswanathan et al. [KLN+08]). Specifically, in [BLR08] the exponential mechanism of McSherry and Talwar [MT07] is used to show that, for fixed usefulness parameters ϵ, δ, the privacy parameter α only has to scale *logarithmically* with the number of queries.[1] This permits simultaneous non-trivial utility and privacy guarantees even for an exponential number of queries. Moreover, this dependence on $\log k$ is necessary in every differentially private mechanism (see the full version of [BLR08]).

The mechanism in [BLR08] suffers from two drawbacks, however. First, it is *non-interactive*: it requires all queries $f_1, \ldots, f_k$ to be given up front, and computes (noisy) outputs of all of them at once.[2] By contrast, independent Laplace output perturbations can obviously be implemented interactively, with the queries arriving online and each answered immediately. There is good intuition for why the non-interactive setting helps: outperforming independent output perturbations requires correlating perturbations across multiple queries, and this is clearly easier when the queries are known in advance. Indeed, prior to the present work, no interactive mechanism better than independent Laplace perturbations was known.

Second, the mechanism in [BLR08] is *inefficient*. Here by "efficient" we mean has running time polynomial in n, k, and $|X|$; Dwork et al. [DNR+09] prove that this is essentially the best one could hope for (under certain cryptographic assumptions). The mechanism in [BLR08] is not efficient because it requires sampling from a non-trivial probability distribution over an unstructured space of exponential size. Dwork et al. [DNR+09] recently gave an efficient (non-interactive) mechanism that is better than independent Laplace perturbations, in that the privacy parameter α of the mechanism scales as $2^{\sqrt{\log k}}$ with the number of queries k (for fixed usefulness parameters ϵ, δ).

Very recently, Hardt and Talwar [HT10] gave upper and lower bounds for answering noninteractive linear queries which are tight in a related setting. These bounds are not tight in our setting, however, unless the number of queries is small with respect to the size of the database. When the number of queries is large, our mechanism actually yields error significantly less than required in general by their lower bound [3]. This is not a contradiction, because when translated into the setting of [HT10], our database size n becomes a sparsity parameter that is not considered in their bounds.

[1] More generally, linearly with the VC dimension of the set of queries, which is always at most $\log_2 k$.

[2] Or rather, it computes a compact representation of these outputs in the form of a synthetic database.

[3] We give a mechanism for answering k "counting queries" with coordinate-wise error $O(n^{2/3} \log k (\log |X|/\alpha)^{1/3})$. This is less error than required by their *lower* bound of roughly $\Omega(\sqrt{k \log(|X|/k)}/\alpha)$ unless $k \leq \tilde{O}((n\alpha/\log|X|)^{4/3})$. We can take k to be as large as $k = \tilde{\Omega}(2^{(n\alpha/\log|X|)^{1/3}})$, in which case our upper bound is a significant improvement – as are the upper bounds of [BLR08] and [DNR+09].

1.1 Our Results

We define a new interactive differentially private mechanism for answering k arbitrary predicate queries, called the *median mechanism.*[4] The basic implementation of the median mechanism interactively answers queries $f_1, \ldots, f_k$ that arrive online, is (ϵ, δ)-useful, and has privacy α that scales with $\log k \log |X|$; see Theorem 4.1 for the exact statement. These privacy and utility guarantees hold even if an adversary can adaptively choose each f_i after seeing the mechanism's first $i-1$ answers. *This is the first interactive mechanism better than the Laplace mechanism, and its performance is close to the best possible even in the non-interactive setting.*

The basic implementation of the median mechanism is not efficient, and we give an efficient implementation with a somewhat weaker utility guarantee. (The privacy guarantee is as strong as in the basic implementation.) This alternative implementation runs in time polynomial in n, k, and $|X|$, and satisfies the following (Theorem 5.1): for every sequence $f_1, \ldots, f_k$ of predicate queries, for all but a negligible fraction of input distributions, the efficient median mechanism is (ϵ, δ)-useful.

This is the first efficient mechanism with a non-trivial utility guarantee and polylogarithmic privacy cost, even in the non-interactive setting.

1.2 The Main Ideas

The key challenge to designing an interactive mechanism that outperforms the Laplace mechanism lies in determining the appropriate correlations between different output perturbations on the fly, without knowledge of future queries. It is not obvious that anything significantly better than independent perturbations is possible in the interactive setting.

Our median mechanism and our analysis of it can be summarized, at a high level, by three facts. First, among any set of k queries, we prove that there are $O(\log k \log |X|)$ "hard" queries, the answers to which completely determine the answers to all of the other queries (up to $\pm\epsilon$). Roughly, this holds because: (i) by a VC dimension argument, we can focus on databases over X of size only $O(\log k)$; and (ii) every time we answer a "hard" query, the number of databases consistent with the mechanism's answers shrinks by a constant factor, and this number cannot drop below 1 (because of the true input database). Second, we design a method to privately release an indicator vector which distinguishes between hard and easy queries online. We note that a similar private 'indicator vector' technique was used by Dwork et al. [DNR+09]. Essentially, the median mechanism deems a query "easy" if a majority of the databases that are consistent (up to $\pm\epsilon$) with the previous answers of the mechanism would answer the current query accurately. The median mechanism answers the small number of hard queries using independent Laplace perturbations. It answers an easy query (accurately) using the median query result given by databases that are consistent with previous answers. A key intuition is that if a user knows that query i is easy, *then it can generate the mechanism's answer on its own.* Thus answering an easy query communicates only a single new bit of information: that the query is easy. Finally, we show how to release the classification of queries as "easy" and "hard" with

[4] The privacy guarantee is (α, τ)-differential privacy for a negligible function τ; see Section 2 for definitions.

low privacy cost; intuitively, this is possible because (independent of the database) there can be only $O(\log k \log |X|)$ hard queries.

Our basic implementation of the median mechanism is not efficient for the same reasons as for the mechanism in [BLR08]: it requires non-trivial sampling from a set of super-polynomial size. For our efficient implementation, we pass to *fractional* databases, represented as fractional histograms with components indexed by X. Here, we use the random walk technology of Dyer, Frieze, and Kannan [DFK91] for convex bodies to perform efficient random sampling. To explain why our utility guarantee no longer holds for every input database, recall the first fact used in the basic implementation: every answer to a hard query shrinks the number of consistent databases by a constant factor, and this number starts at $|X|^{O(\log k)}$ and cannot drop below 1. With fractional databases (where polytope volumes play the role of set sizes), the lower bound of 1 on the set of consistent (fractional) databases no longer holds. Nonetheless, we prove a lower bound on the volume of this set for almost all fractional histograms (equivalently probability distributions), which salvages the $O(\log k \log |X|)$ bound on hard queries for databases drawn from such distributions.

2. PRELIMINARIES

We briefly formalize the setting of the previous section and record some important definitions. We consider some finite domain X, and define a database D to be an unordered set of elements from X (with multiplicities allowed). We write $n = |D|$ to denote the size of the database. We consider the set of Boolean functions (predicates) $f : X \rightarrow \{0, 1\}$. We abuse notation and define a predicate query $f(D) : X^* \rightarrow [0, 1]$ as $|\{x \in D : f(X) = 1\}|/|D|$, the function that computes the fraction of elements of D that satisfy predicate f. We say that an answer a_i to a query f_i is ϵ*-accurate* with respect to database D if $|f_i(D) - a_i| \leq \epsilon$. A mechanism $M(D, (f_1, \ldots, f_k))$ is a function from databases and queries to distributions over outputs. In this paper, we consider mechanisms that answer predicate queries numerically, and so the range of our mechanisms is $\mathbb{R}^k$.[5]

Definition 1. A mechanism M is (ϵ, δ)*-useful* if for every sequence of queries $(f_1, \ldots, f_k)$ and every database D, with probability at least $1 - \delta$ it provides answers $a_1, \ldots, a_k$ that are ϵ-accurate for $f_1, \ldots, f_k$ and D.

Recall that differential privacy means that changing the identity of a single element of the input database does not affect the probability of any outcome by more than a small factor. Formally, given a database D, we say that a database D' of the same size is a *neighbor* of D if it differs in only a single element: $|D \cap D'| = |D| - 1$.

Definition 2. A mechanism M satisfies (α, τ)*-differential privacy* if for every subset $S \subseteq \mathbb{R}^k$, every set of queries $(f_1, \ldots, f_k)$, and every pair of neighboring databases D, D':

$$\Pr[M(D) \in S] \leq e^{\alpha} \cdot \Pr[M(D') \in S] + \tau.$$

We are generally interested in the case where τ is a *negligible function* of some of the problem parameters, meaning one that goes to zero faster than x^{-c} for every constant c.

[5]From ϵ-accurate answers, one can efficiently reconstruct a synthetic database that is consistent (up to $\pm\epsilon$) with those answers, if desired [DNR+09].

Finally, the *sensitivity* of a real-valued query is the largest difference between its values on neighboring databases. For example, the sensitivity of every non-trivial predicate query is precisely $1/n$.

3. THE MEDIAN MECHANISM: BASIC IMPLEMENTATION

We now describe the median mechanism and our basic implementation of it. As described in the Introduction, the mechanism is conceptually simple. It classifies queries as "easy" or "hard", essentially according to whether or not a majority of the databases consistent with previous answers to hard queries would give an accurate answer to it (in which case the user already "knows the answer"). Easy queries are answered using the corresponding median value; hard queries are answered as in the Laplace mechanism.

To explain the mechanism precisely, we need to discuss a number of parameters. We take the privacy parameter α, the accuracy parameter ϵ, and the number k of queries as input; these are hard constraints on the performance of our mechanism.[6] Our mechanism obeys these constraints with a value of δ that is inverse polynomial in k and n, and a value of τ that is negligible in k and n, provided n is sufficiently large (at least polylogarithmic in k and $|X|$, see Theorem 4.1). Of course, such a result can be rephrased as a nearly exponential lower bound on the number of queries k that can be successfully answered as a function of the database size n.[7]

The median mechanism is shown in Figure 1, and it makes use of several additional parameters. For our analysis, we set their values to:

$$m = \frac{160000 \ln k \ln \frac{1}{\epsilon}}{\epsilon^2}; \tag{1}$$

$$\alpha' = \frac{\alpha}{720 m \ln |X|} = \Theta\left(\frac{\alpha\epsilon^2}{\log |X| \log k \log \frac{1}{\epsilon}}\right); \tag{2}$$

$$\gamma = \frac{4}{\alpha' \epsilon n} \ln \frac{2k}{\alpha} = \Theta\left(\frac{\log |X| \log^2 k \log \frac{1}{\epsilon}}{\alpha\epsilon^3 n}\right). \tag{3}$$

The denominator in (2) can be thought of as our "privacy cost" as a function of the number of queries k. Needless to say, we made no effort to optimize the constants.

The value r_i in Step 2(a) of the median mechanism is defined as

$$r_i = \frac{\sum_{S \in C_{i-1}} \exp(-\epsilon^{-1}|f_i(D) - f_i(S)|)}{|C_{i-1}|}. \tag{4}$$

For the Laplace perturbations in Steps 2(a) and 2(d), recall that the distribution Lap(σ) has the cumulative distribution function

$$F(x) = 1 - F(-x) = 1 - \frac{1}{2}e^{-x/\sigma}. \tag{5}$$

[6]We typically think of α, ϵ as small constants, though our results remain meaningful for some sub-constant values of α and ϵ as well. We always assume that α is at least inverse polynomial in k. Note that when α or ϵ is sufficiently small (at most c/n for a small constant c, say), simultaneously meaningful privacy and utility is clearly impossible.

[7]In contrast, the number of queries that the Laplace mechanism can privately and usefully answer is at most linear.

1. Initialize $C_0 = \{$ databases of size m over X $\}$.

2. For each query $f_1, f_2, \ldots, f_k$ in turn:

   (a) Define r_i as in (4) and let $\hat{r}_i = r_i + \mathrm{Lap}(\frac{2}{\epsilon n \alpha'})$.

   (b) Let $t_i = \frac{3}{4} + j \cdot \gamma$, where $j \in \{0, 1, \ldots, \frac{1}{\gamma}\frac{3}{20}\}$ is chosen with probability proportional to 2^{-j}.

   (c) If $\hat{r}_i \geq t_i$, set a_i to be the median value of f_i on C_{i-1}.

   (d) If $\hat{r}_i < t_i$, set a_i to be $f_i(D) + \mathrm{Lap}(\frac{1}{n\alpha'})$.

   (e) If $\hat{r}_i < t_i$, set C_i to the databases S of C_{i-1} with $|f_i(S) - a_i| \leq \epsilon/50$; otherwise $C_i = C_{i-1}$.

   (f) If $\hat{r}_j < t_j$ for more than $20m \log|X|$ values of $j \leq i$, then halt and report failure.

Figure 1: The Median Mechanism.

The motivation behind the mechanism's steps is as follows. The set C_i is the set of size-m databases consistent (up to $\pm\epsilon/50$) with previous answers of the mechanism to hard queries. The focus on databases with the small size m is justified by a VC dimension argument, see Proposition 4.6. Steps 2(a) and 2(b) choose a random value $\hat{r}_i$ and a random threshold t_i. The value r_i in Step 2(a) is a measure of how easy the query is, with higher numbers being easier. A more obvious measure would be the fraction of databases S in C_{i-1} for which $|f_i(S) - f_i(D)| \leq \epsilon$, but this is a highly sensitive statistic (unlike r_i, see Lemma 4.9). The mechanism uses the perturbed value $\hat{r}_i$ rather than r_i to privately communicate which queries are easy and which are hard. In Step 2(b), we choose the threshold t_i at random between 3/4 and 9/10. This randomly shifted threshold ensures that, for every database D, there is likely to be a significant gap between r_i and t_i; such gaps are useful when optimizing the privacy guarantee. Steps 2(c) and 2(d) answer easy and hard queries, respectively. Step 2(e) updates the set of databases consistent with previous answers to hard queries. We prove in Lemma 4.7 that Step 2(f) occurs with at most inverse polynomial probability.

Finally, we note that the median mechanism is defined as if the total number of queries k is (approximately) known in advance. This assumption can be removed by using successively doubling "guesses" of k; this increases the privacy cost by an $O(\log k)$ factor.

4. ANALYSIS OF MEDIAN MECHANISM

This section proves the following privacy and utility guarantees for the basic implementation of the median mechanism.

THEOREM 4.1. *For every sequence of adaptively chosen predicate queries $f_1, \ldots, f_k$ arriving online, the median mechanism is (ϵ, δ)-useful and (α, τ)-differentially private, where τ is a negligible function of k and $|X|$, and δ is an inverse polynomial function of k and n, provided the database size n satisfies*

$$n \geq \frac{30 \ln \frac{2k}{\alpha} \log_2 k}{\alpha' \epsilon} = \Theta\left(\frac{\log|X| \log^3 k \log \frac{1}{\epsilon}}{\alpha \epsilon^3}\right). \qquad (6)$$

We prove the utility and privacy guarantees in Sections 4.1 and 4.2, respectively.[8]

4.1 Utility of the Median Mechanism

Here we prove a utility guarantee for the median mechanism.

THEOREM 4.2. *The median mechanism is (ϵ, δ)-useful, where $\delta = k \exp(-\Omega(\epsilon n \alpha'))$.*

Note that under assumption (6), δ is inverse polynomial in k and n.

We give the proof of Theorem 4.2 in three pieces: with high probability, every hard query is answered accurately (Lemma 4.4); every easy query is answered accurately (Lemmas 4.3 and 4.5); and the algorithm does not fail (Lemma 4.7). The next two lemmas follow from the definition of the Laplace distribution (5), our choice of δ, and trivial union bounds.

LEMMA 4.3. *With probability at least $1 - \frac{\delta}{2}$, $|r_i - \hat{r}_i| \leq 1/100$ for every query i.*

LEMMA 4.4. *With probability at least $1 - \frac{\delta}{2}$, every answer to a hard query is $(\epsilon/100)$-accurate for D.*

The next lemma shows that median answers are accurate for easy queries.

LEMMA 4.5. *If $|r_i - \hat{r}_i| \leq 1/100$ for every query i, then every answer to an easy query is ϵ-accurate for D.*

PROOF. For a query i, let $G_{i-1} = \{S \in C_{i-1} : |f_i(D) - f_i(S)| \leq \epsilon\}$ denote the databases of C_{i-1} on which the result of query f_i is ϵ-accurate for D. Observe that if $|G_{i-1}| \geq .51 \cdot |C_{i-1}|$, then the median value of f_i on C_{i-1} is an ϵ-accurate answer for D. Thus proving the lemma reduces to showing that $\hat{r}_i \geq 3/4$ only if $|G_{i-1}| \geq .51 \cdot |C_{i-1}|$.

Consider a query i with $|G_{i-1}| < .51 \cdot |C_{i-1}|$. Using (4), we have

$$\begin{aligned} r_i &= \frac{\sum_{S \in C_{i-1}} \exp(-\epsilon^{-1}|f_i(D) - f_i(S)|)}{|C_{i-1}|} \\ &\leq \frac{|G_{i-1}| + e^{-1}|C_{i-1} \setminus G_{i-1}|}{|C_{i-1}|} \\ &\leq \frac{(\frac{51}{100} + \frac{49}{100e})|C_{i-1}|}{|C_{i-1}|} \\ &< \frac{74}{100}. \end{aligned}$$

Since $|r_i - \hat{r}_i| \leq 1/100$ for every query i by assumption, the proof is complete. □

Our final lemma shows that the median mechanism does not fail and hence answers every query, with high probability; this will conclude our proof of Theorem 4.2. We need the following preliminary proposition, which instantiates the standard uniform convergence bound with the fact that the VC dimension of every set of k predicate queries is at most $\log_2 k$ [Vap96]. Recall the definition of the parameter m from (1).

[8]If desired, in Theorem 4.1 we can treat n as a parameter and solve for the error ϵ. The maximum error on any query (normalized by the database size) is $O(\log k \log^{1/3}|X|/n^{1/3}\alpha^{1/3})$; the unnormalized error is a factor of n larger.

PROPOSITION 4.6 (UNIFORM CONVERGENCE BOUND). *For every collection of k predicate queries $f_1, \ldots, f_k$ and every database D, a database S obtained by sampling points from D uniformly at random will satisfy $|f_i(D) - f_i(S)| \leq \epsilon$ for all i except with probability δ, provided*

$$|S| \geq \frac{1}{2\epsilon^2}\left(\log k + \log \frac{2}{\delta}\right).$$

In particular, there exists a database S of size m such that for all $i \in \{1, \ldots, k\}$, $|f_i(D) - f_i(S)| \leq \epsilon/400$.

In other words, the results of k predicate queries on an arbitrarily large database can be well approximated by those on a database with size only $O(\log k)$.

LEMMA 4.7. *If $|r_i - \hat{r}_i| \leq 1/100$ for every query i and every answer to a hard query is $(\epsilon/100)$-accurate for D, then the median mechanism answers fewer than $20m \log |X|$ hard queries (and hence answers all queries before terminating).*

PROOF. The plan is to track the contraction of C_i as hard queries are answered by the median mechanism. Initially we have $|C_0| \leq |X|^m$. If the median mechanism answers a hard query i, then the definition of the mechanism and our hypotheses yield

$$r_i \leq \hat{r}_i + \frac{1}{100} < t_i + \frac{1}{100} \leq \frac{91}{100}.$$

We then claim that the size of the set $C_i = \{S \subset C_{i-1} : |f_i(S) - a_i| \leq \epsilon/50\}$ is at most $\frac{94}{100}|C_{i-1}|$. For if not,

$$\begin{aligned} r_i &= \frac{\sum_{S \in C_{i-1}} \exp(-\epsilon^{-1}|f_i(S) - f_i(D)|)}{|C_{i-1}|} \\ &\geq \frac{94}{100} \cdot \exp\left(-\frac{1}{50}\right) > \frac{92}{100}, \end{aligned}$$

which is a contradiction.

Iterating now shows that the number of consistent databases decreases exponentially with the number of hard queries:

$$|C_k| \leq \left(\frac{94}{100}\right)^h |X|^m \qquad (7)$$

if h of the k queries are hard.

On the other hand, Proposition 4.6 guarantees the existence of a database $S^* \in C_0$ for which $|f_i(S^*) - f_i(D)| \leq \epsilon/100$ for every query f_i. Since all answers a_i produced by the median mechanism for hard queries i are $(\epsilon/100)$-accurate for D by assumption, $|f_i(S^*) - a_i| \leq |f_i(S^*) - f_i(D)| + |f_i(D) - a_i| \leq \epsilon/50$. This shows that $S^* \in C_k$ and hence $|C_k| \geq 1$. Combining this with (7) gives

$$h \leq \frac{m \ln |X|}{\ln(50/47)} < 20m \ln |X|,$$

as desired. □

4.2 Privacy of the Median Mechanism

This section establishes the following privacy guarantee for the median mechanism.

THEOREM 4.8. *The median mechanism is (α, τ)- differentially private, where τ is a negligible function of $|X|$ and k when n is sufficiently large (as in (6)).*

We can treat the median mechanism as if it has two outputs: a vector of answers $a \in \mathbb{R}^k$, and a vector $d \in \{0,1\}^k$ such that $d_i = 0$ if i is an easy query and $d_i = 1$ if i is a hard query. A key observation in the privacy analysis is that answers to easy queries are a function only of the previous output of the mechanism, and incur no additional privacy cost beyond the release of the bit d_i. Moreover, the median mechanism is guaranteed to produce no more than $O(m \log |X|)$ answers to hard queries. Intuitively, what we need to show is that the vector d can be released after an unusually small perturbation.

Our first lemma states that the small sensitivity of predicate queries carries over, with a $2/\epsilon$ factor loss, to the r-function defined in (4).

LEMMA 4.9. *The function $r_i(D) = (\sum_{S \in C} \exp(-\epsilon^{-1}|f(D) - f(S)|)/|C|$ has sensitivity $\frac{2}{\epsilon n}$ for every fixed set C of databases and predicate query f.*

PROOF. Let D and D' be neighboring databases. Then

$$\begin{aligned} r_i(D) &= \frac{\sum_{S \in C} \exp(-\epsilon^{-1}|f(D) - f(S)|)}{|C_i|} \\ &\leq \frac{\sum_{S \in C_i} \exp(-\epsilon^{-1}(|f(D') - f(S)| - n^{-1}))}{|C_i|} \\ &= \exp\left(\frac{1}{\epsilon n}\right) \cdot r_i(D') \\ &\leq \left(1 + \frac{2}{\epsilon n}\right) \cdot r_i(D') \\ &\leq r_i(D') + \frac{2}{\epsilon n} \end{aligned}$$

where the first inequality follows from the fact that the (predicate) query f has sensitivity $1/n$, the second from the fact that $e^x \leq 1 + 2x$ when $x \in [0, 1]$, and the third from the fact that $r_i(D') \leq 1$. □

The next lemma identifies nice properties of "typical executions" of the median mechanism. Consider an output (d, a) of the median mechanism with a database D. From D and (d, a), we can uniquely recover the values $r_1, \ldots, r_k$ computed (via (4)) in Step 2(a) of the median mechanism, with r_i depending only on the first $i - 1$ components of d and a. We sometimes write such a value as $r_i(D, (d, a))$, or as $r_i(D)$ if an output (d, a) has been fixed. Call a possible threshold t_i *good* for D and (d, a) if $d_i = 0$ and $r_i(D, (d, a)) \geq t_i + \gamma$, where γ is defined as in (3). Call a vector t of possible thresholds *good* for D and (d, a) if all but $180m \ln |X|$ of the thresholds are good for D and (d, a).

LEMMA 4.10. *For every database D, with all but negligible $(\exp(-\Omega(\log k \log |X|/\epsilon^2)))$ probability, the thresholds t generated by the median mechanism are good for its output (d, a).*

PROOF. The idea is to "charge" the probability of bad thresholds to that of answering hard queries, which are strictly limited by the median mechanism. Since the median mechanism only allows $20m \ln |X|$ of the d_i's to be 1, we only need to bound the number of queries i with output $d_i = 0$ and threshold t_i satisfying $r_i < t_i + \gamma$, where r_i is the value computed by the median mechanism in Step 2(a) when it answers the query i.

Let Y_i be the indicator random variable corresponding to the (larger) event that $r_i < t_i + \gamma$. Define Z_i to be 1 if and only if, when answering the ith query, the median mechanism chooses a threshold t_i and a Laplace perturbation Δ_i such that $r_i + \Delta_i < t_i$ (i.e., the query is classified as hard). If the median mechanism fails before reaching query i, then we define $Y_i = Z_i = 0$. Set $Y = \sum_{i=1}^k Y_i$ and $Z = \sum_{i=1}^k Z_i$. We can finish the proof by showing that Y is at most $160m \ln |X|$ except with negligible probability.

Consider a query i and condition on the event that $r_i \geq \frac{9}{10}$; this event depends only on the results of previous queries. In this case, $Y_i = 1$ only if $t_i = 9/10$. But this occurs with probability $2^{-3/20\gamma}$, which using (3) and (6) is at most $1/k$.[9] Therefore, the expected contribution to Y coming from queries i with $r_i \geq \frac{9}{10}$ is at most 1. Since t_i is selected independently at random for each i, the Chernoff bound implies that the probability that such queries contribute more than $m \ln |X|$ to Y is

$$\exp(-\Omega((m \log |X|)^2)) = \exp(-\Omega((\log k)^2 (\log |X|)^2/\epsilon^4)).$$

Now condition on the event that $r_i < \frac{9}{10}$. Let T_i denote the threshold choices that would cause Y_i to be 1, and let s_i be the smallest such; since $r_i < \frac{9}{10}$, $|T_i| \geq 2$. For every $t_i \in T_i$, $t_i > r_i - \gamma$; hence, for every $t_i \in T_i \setminus \{s_i\}$, $t_i > r_i$. Also, our distribution on the j's in Step 2(b) ensures that $\Pr[t_i \in T_i \setminus \{s_i\}] \geq \frac{1}{2} \Pr[t_i \in T_i]$. Since the Laplace distribution is symmetric around zero and the random choices Δ_i, t_i are independent, we have

$$\begin{aligned} \mathrm{E}[Z_i] &= \Pr[t_i > r_i + \Delta_i] \\ &\geq \Pr[t_i > r_i] \cdot \Pr[\Delta_i \leq 0] \\ &\geq \tfrac{1}{4} \Pr[t_i > r_i - \gamma] \\ &= \tfrac{1}{4} \mathrm{E}[Y_i]. \end{aligned} \tag{8}$$

The definition of the median mechanism ensures that $Z \leq 20m \ln |X|$ with probability 1. Linearity of expectation, inequality (8), and the Chernoff bound imply that queries with $r_i < \frac{9}{10}$ contribute at most $159m \ln |X|$ to Y with probability at least $1 - \exp(-\Omega(\log k \log |X|/\epsilon^2))$. The proof is complete. □

We can now prove Theorem 4.8.

Proof of Theorem 4.8: Recall Definition 2 and fix a database D, queries $f_1, \ldots, f_k$, and a subset S of possible mechanism outputs. For simplicity, we assume that all perturbations are drawn from a discretized Laplace distribution, so that the median mechanism has a countable range; the continuous case can be treated using similar arguments. Then, we can think of S as a countable set of output vector pairs (d, a) with $d \in \{0,1\}^k$ and $a \in \mathbb{R}^k$. We write $MM(D, f) = (d, a)$ for the event that the median mechanism classifies the queries $f = (f_1, \ldots, f_k)$ according to d and outputs the numerical answers a. If the mechanism computes thresholds t while doing so, we write $MM(D, f) = (t, d, a)$. Let $G((d, a), D)$ denote the vectors that would be good thresholds for (d, a) and D. (Recall that D and (d, a) uniquely define the corresponding $r_i(D, (d, a))$'s.)

We have

$$\Pr[MM(D,f) \in S] = \sum_{(d,a) \in S} \Pr[MM(D,f) = (d,a)]$$

$$\leq \tau + \sum_{(d,a) \in S} \Pr[MM(D,f) = (t,d,a)]$$

$$= \tau + \sum_{(d,a) \in S} \sum_{t \in G((d,a),D)} \Pr[MM(D,f) = (t,d,a)]$$

with some t good for (d, a), D, and where τ is the negligible function of Lemma 4.10. We complete the proof by showing that, for every neighboring database D', possible output (d, a), and thresholds t good for (d, a) and D,

$$\Pr[MM(D,f) = (t,d,a)] \leq e^{\alpha} \cdot \Pr[MM(D',f) = (t,d,a)]. \tag{9}$$

Fix a neighboring database D', a target output (d, a), and thresholds t good for (d, a) and D. The probability that the median mechanism chooses the target thresholds t is independent of the underlying database, and so is the same on both sides of (9). For the rest of the proof, we condition on the event that the median mechanism uses the thresholds t (both with database D and database D').

Let $\mathcal{E}_i$ denote the event that $MM(D, f)$ classifies the first i queries in agreement with the target output (i.e., query $j \leq i$ is deemed easy if and only if $d_j = 0$) and that its first i answers are $a_1, \ldots, a_i$. Let $\mathcal{E}'_i$ denote the analogous event for $MM(D', f)$. Observe that $\mathcal{E}_k, \mathcal{E}'_k$ are the relevant events on the left- and right-hand sides of (9), respectively (after conditioning on t). If (d, a) is such that the median mechanism would fail after the ℓth query, then the following proof should be applied to $\mathcal{E}_\ell, \mathcal{E}'_\ell$ instead of $\mathcal{E}_k, \mathcal{E}'_k$. We next give a crude upper bound on the ratio $\Pr[\mathcal{E}_i | \mathcal{E}_{i-1}] / \Pr[\mathcal{E}'_i | \mathcal{E}'_{i-1}]$ that holds for every query (see (10), below), followed by a much better upper bound for queries with good thresholds.

Imagine running the median mechanism in parallel on D, D' and condition on the events $\mathcal{E}_{i-1}, \mathcal{E}'_{i-1}$. The set C_{i-1} is then the same in both runs of the mechanism, and $r_i(D), r_i(D')$ are now fixed. Let b_i (b'_i) be 0 if $MM(D, f)$ ($MM(D', f)$) classifies query i as easy and 1 otherwise. Since $r_i(D') \in [r_i(D) \pm \frac{2}{\epsilon n}]$ (Lemma 4.9) and a perturbation with distribution $\mathrm{Lap}(\frac{2}{\alpha' \epsilon n})$ is added to these values before comparing to the threshold t_i (Step 2(a)),

$$\Pr[b_i = 0 \,|\, \mathcal{E}_{i-1}] \leq e^{\alpha'} \Pr[b'_i = 0 \,|\, \mathcal{E}'_{i-1}]$$

and similarly for the events where $b_i, b'_i = 1$. Suppose that the target classification is $d_i = 1$ (a hard query), and let s_i and s'_i denote the random variables $f_i(D) + \mathrm{Lap}(\frac{1}{\alpha' n})$ and $f_i(D') + \mathrm{Lap}(\frac{1}{\alpha' n})$, respectively. Independence of the Laplace perturbations in Steps 2(a) and 2(d) implies that

$$\Pr[\mathcal{E}_i | \mathcal{E}_{i-1}] = \Pr[b_i = 1 \,|\, \mathcal{E}_{i-1}] \cdot \Pr[s_i = a_i \,|\, \mathcal{E}_{i-1}]$$

and

$$\Pr[\mathcal{E}'_i | \mathcal{E}'_{i-1}] = \Pr[b'_i = 1 \,|\, \mathcal{E}'_{i-1}] \cdot \Pr[s'_i = a_i \,|\, \mathcal{E}'_{i-1}].$$

Since the predicate query f_i has sensitivity $1/n$, we have

$$\Pr[\mathcal{E}_i \,|\, \mathcal{E}_{i-1}] \leq e^{2\alpha'} \cdot \Pr[\mathcal{E}'_i \,|\, \mathcal{E}'_{i-1}] \tag{10}$$

when $d_i = 1$.

Now suppose that $d_i = 0$, and let m_i denote the median value of f_i on C_{i-1}. Then $\Pr[\mathcal{E}_i | \mathcal{E}_{i-1}]$ is either 0 (if $m_i \neq a_i$) or $\Pr[b_i = 0 \,|\, \mathcal{E}_{i-1}]$ (if $m_i = a_i$); similarly, $\Pr[\mathcal{E}'_i | \mathcal{E}'_{i-1}]$ is either 0 or $\Pr[b'_i = 0 \,|\, \mathcal{E}'_{i-1}]$. Thus the bound in (10) continues to hold (even with $e^{2\alpha'}$ replaced by $e^{\alpha'}$) when $d_i = 0$.

[9]For simplicity, we ignore the normalizing constant in the distribution over j's in Step 2(b), which is $\Theta(1)$.

Since α' is not much smaller than the privacy target α (recall (2)), we cannot afford to suffer the upper bound in (10) for many queries. Fortunately, for queries i with good thresholds we can do much better. Consider a query i such that t_i is good for (d, a) and D and condition again on $\mathcal{E}_{i-1}, \mathcal{E}'_{i-1}$, which fixes C_{i-1} and hence $r_i(D)$. Goodness implies that $d_i = 0$, so the arguments from the previous paragraph also apply here. We can therefore assume that the median value m_i of f_i on C_{i-1} equals a_i and focus on bounding $\Pr[b_i = 0 \mid \mathcal{E}_{i-1}]$ in terms of $\Pr[b'_i = 0 \mid \mathcal{E}'_{i-1}]$. Goodness also implies that $r_i(D) \geq t_i + \gamma$ and hence $r_i(D') \geq t_i + \gamma - \frac{2}{\epsilon n} \geq t_i + \frac{\gamma}{2}$ (by Lemma 4.9). Recalling from (3) the definition of γ, we have

$$\begin{aligned}\Pr[b'_i = 0 \mid \mathcal{E}'_{i-1}] &\geq \Pr[r_i - \hat{r}_i < \tfrac{\gamma}{2}] \\ &= 1 - \tfrac{1}{2}e^{-\gamma\alpha'\epsilon n/4} \\ &= 1 - \frac{\alpha}{4k} \qquad (11)\end{aligned}$$

and of course, $\Pr[b_i = 0 \mid \mathcal{E}_{i-1}] \leq 1$.

Applying (10) to the bad queries — at most $180m \ln |X|$ of them, since t is good for (d, a) and D — and (11) to the rest, we can derive

$$\begin{aligned}\Pr[\mathcal{E}_k] &= \prod_{i=1}^{k} \Pr[\mathcal{E}_i : \mathcal{E}_{i-1}] \\ &\leq \underbrace{e^{360\alpha' m \ln |X|}}_{\leq e^{\alpha/2} \text{ by } (2)} \cdot \underbrace{(1 - \frac{\alpha}{4k})^{-k}}_{\leq (1+\frac{\alpha}{2k})^k \leq e^{\alpha/2}} \cdot \prod_{i=1}^{k} \Pr[\mathcal{E}'_i : \mathcal{E}'_{i-1}] \\ &\leq e^{\alpha} \cdot \Pr[\mathcal{E}'_k],\end{aligned}$$

which completes the proof of both the inequality (9) and the theorem. ■

5. THE MEDIAN MECHANISM: EFFICIENT IMPLEMENTATION

The basic implementation of the median mechanism runs in time $|X|^{\Theta(\log k \log(1/\epsilon)/\epsilon^2)}$. This section provides an efficient implementation, running in time polynomial in n, k, and $|X|$, although with a weaker usefulness guarantee.

THEOREM 5.1. *Assume that the database size n satisfies (6). For every sequence of adaptively chosen predicate queries $f_1, \ldots, f_k$ arriving online, the efficient implementation of the median Mechanism is (α, τ)-differentially private for a negligible function τ. Moreover, for every fixed set $f_1, \ldots, f_k$ of queries, it is (ϵ, δ)-useful for all but a negligible fraction of* fractional *databases (equivalently, probability distributions).*

Specifically, our mechanism answers exponentially many queries for all but an $O(|X|^{-m})$ fraction of probability distributions over X drawn from the unit ℓ_1 ball, and from databases drawn from such distributions. Thus our efficient implementation always guarantees privacy, but for a given set of queries $f_1, \ldots, f_k$, there might be a negligibly small fraction of fractional histograms for which our mechanism is not useful for all k queries.

We note however that even for the small fraction of fractional histograms for which the efficient median mechanism may not satisfy our usefulness guarantee, it does not output incorrect answers: it merely halts after having answered a sufficiently large number of queries using the Laplace mechanism. Therefore, even for this small fraction of databases, the efficient median mechanism is an improvement over the Laplace mechanism: in the worst case, it simply answers every query using the Laplace mechanism before halting, and in the best case, it is able to answer many more queries.

We give a high-level overview of the proof of Theorem 5.1 which we then make formal. First, why isn't the median mechanism a computationally efficient mechanism? Because C_0 has super-polynomial size $|X|^m$, and computing r_i in Step 2(a), the median value in Step 2(c), and the set C_i in Step 2(e) could require time proportional to $|C_0|$. An obvious idea is to randomly sample elements of C_{i-1} to approximately compute r_i and the median value of f_i on C_{i-1}; while it is easy to control the resulting sampling error and preserve the utility and privacy guarantees of Section 4, it is not clear how to sample from C_{i-1} efficiently.

We show how to implement the median mechanism in polynomial time by redefining the sets C_i to be sets of probability distributions over points in X that are consistent (up to $\pm\frac{\epsilon}{50}$) with the hard queries answered up to the ith query. Each set C_i will be a convex polytope in $\mathbb{R}^{|X|}$ defined by the intersection of at most $O(m \log |X|)$ halfspaces, and hence it will be possible to sample points from C_i approximately uniformly at random in time poly$(|X|, m)$ via the grid walk of Dyer, Frieze, and Kannan [DFK91]. Lemmas 4.3, 4.4, and 4.5 still hold (trivially modified to accommodate sampling error). We have to reprove Lemma 4.7, in a somewhat weaker form: that for all but a diminishing fraction of input databases D, the median mechanism does not abort except with probability $k \exp(-\Omega(\epsilon n \alpha'))$. As for our privacy analysis of the median mechanism, it is independent of the representation of the sets C_i and the mechanisms' failure probability, and so it need not be repeated — the efficient implementation is provably private for *all* input databases and query sequences.

We now give a formal analysis of the efficient implementation.

5.1 Redefining the sets C_i

We redefine the sets C_i to represent databases that can contain points fractionally, as opposed to the finite set of small discrete databases. Equivalently, we can view the sets C_i as containing probability distributions over the set of points X.

We initialize C_0 to be the ℓ_1 ball of radius m in $\mathbb{R}^{|X|}$, $mB_1^{|X|}$, intersected with the non-negative orthant:

$$C_0 = \{F \in \mathbb{R}^{|X|} : F \geq 0, ||F||_1 \leq m\}.$$

Each dimension i in $\mathbb{R}^{|X|}$ corresponds to an element $x_i \in X$. Elements $F \in C_0$ can be viewed as fractional histograms. Note that integral points in C_0 correspond exactly to databases of size at most m.

We generalize our query functions f_i to fractional histograms in the natural way:

$$f_i(F) = \frac{1}{m} \sum_{j: f_i(x_j)=1} F_j.$$

The update operation after a hard query i is answered is the same as in the basic implementation:

$$C_i \leftarrow \left\{F \in C_{i-1} : |f_i(F) - a_i| \leq \frac{\epsilon}{50}\right\}.$$

Note that each updating operation after a hard query merely intersects C_{i-1} with the pair of halfspaces:

$$\sum_{j:f_i(x_j)=1} F_j \le ma_i + \frac{\epsilon m}{50} \quad \text{and} \quad \sum_{j:f_i(x_j)=1} F_j \ge ma_i - \frac{\epsilon m}{50};$$

and so C_i is a convex polytope for each i.

Dyer, Kannan, and Frieze [DFK91] show how to δ-approximate a random sample from a convex body $K \in \mathbb{R}^{|X|}$ in time polynomial in $|X|$ and the running time of a membership oracle for K, where δ can be taken to be exponentially small (which is more than sufficient for our purposes). Their algorithm has two requirements:

1. There must be an efficient membership oracle which can in polynomial time determine whether a point $F \in \mathbb{R}^{|X|}$ lies in K.
2. K must be 'well rounded': $B_2^{|X|} \subseteq K \subseteq |X|B_2^{|X|}$, where $B_2^{|X|}$ is the unit ℓ_2 ball in $\mathbb{R}^{|X|}$.

Since C_i is given as the intersection of a set of explicit halfspaces, we have a simple membership oracle to determine whether a given point $F \in C_i$: we simply check that F lies on the appropriate side of each of the halfspaces. This takes time poly$(|X|, m)$, since the number of halfspaces defining C_i is linear in the number of answers to hard queries given before time i, which is never more than $20m \ln |X|$. Moreover, for each i we have $C_i \subseteq C_0 \subset mB_1^{|X|} \subset mB_2^{|X|} \subset |X|B_2^{|X|}$. Finally, we can safely assume that $B_2^X \subseteq C_i$ by simply considering the convex set $C_i' = C_i + B_2^X$ instead. This will not affect our results.

Therefore, we can implement the median mechanism in time poly$(|X|, k)$ by using sets C_i as defined in this section, and sampling from them using the grid walk of [DFK91]. Estimation error in computing r_i and the median value of f_i on C_{i-1} by random sampling rather than brute force is easily controlled via the Chernoff bound and can be incorporated into the proofs of Lemmas 4.3 and 4.5 in the obvious way. It remains to prove a continuous version of Lemma 4.7 to show that the efficient implementation of the median mechanism is (ϵ, δ)-useful on all but a negligibly small fraction of fractional histograms F.

5.2 Usefulness for Almost All Distributions

We now prove an analogue of Lemma 4.7 to establish a usefulness guarantee for the efficient version of the median mechanism.

Definition 3. With respect to any set of k queries $f_1, \dots, f_k$ and for any $F^* \in C_0$, define

$$\text{Good}_\epsilon(F^*) = \{F \in C_0 : \max_{i \in \{1,2,\dots,k\}} |f_i(F) - f_i(F^*)| \le \epsilon\}$$

as the set of points that agree up to an additive ϵ factor with F^* on every query f_i.

Since databases $D \subset X$ can be identified with their corresponding histogram vectors $F \in \mathbb{R}^{|X|}$, we can also write $\text{Good}_\epsilon(D)$ when the meaning is clear from context.

For any F^*, $\text{Good}_\epsilon(F^*)$ is a convex polytope contained inside C_0. We will prove that the efficient version of the median mechanism is (ϵ, δ)-useful for a database D if

$$\frac{\text{Vol}(\text{Good}_{\epsilon/100}(D))}{\text{Vol}(C_0)} \ge \frac{1}{|X|^{2m}}. \qquad (12)$$

We first prove that (12) holds for almost every fractional histogram. For this, we need a preliminary lemma.

LEMMA 5.2. *Let $\mathcal{L}$ denote the set of integer points inside C_0. Then with respect to an arbitrary set of k queries,*

$$C_0 \subseteq \bigcup_{F \in \mathcal{L}} \text{Good}_{\epsilon/400}(F).$$

PROOF. Every rational valued point $F \in C_0$ corresponds to some (large) database $D \subset X$ by scaling F to an integer-valued histogram. Irrational points can be arbitrarily approximated by such a finite database. By Proposition 4.6, for every set of k predicates $f_1, \dots, f_k$, there is a database $F^* \subset X$ with $|F^*| = m$ such that for each i, $|f_i(F^*) - f_i(F)| \le \epsilon/400$. Recalling that the histograms corresponding to databases of size at most m are exactly the integer points in C_0, the proof is complete. □

LEMMA 5.3. *All but an $|X|^{-m}$ fraction of* fractional *histograms F satisfy*

$$\frac{\text{Vol}(\text{Good}_{\epsilon/200}(F))}{\text{Vol}(C_0)} \ge \frac{1}{|X|^{2m}}.$$

PROOF. Let

$$\mathcal{B} = \left\{ F \in \mathcal{L} : \frac{\text{Vol}(\text{Good}_{\epsilon/400}(F))}{\text{Vol}(C_0)} \le \frac{1}{|X|^{2m}} \right\}.$$

Consider a randomly selected fractional histogram $F^* \in C_0$. For any $F \in \mathcal{B}$ we have:

$$\Pr[F^* \in \text{Good}_{\epsilon/400}(F)] = \frac{\text{Vol}(\text{Good}_{\epsilon/400}(F))}{\text{Vol}(C_0)} < \frac{1}{|X|^{2m}}$$

Since $|\mathcal{B}| \le |\mathcal{L}| \le |X|^m$, by a union bound we can conclude that except with probability $\frac{1}{|X|^m}$, $F^* \notin \text{Good}_{\epsilon/400}(F)$ for any $F \in \mathcal{B}$. However, by Lemma 5.2, $F^* \in \text{Good}_{\epsilon/400}(F')$ for some $F' \in \mathcal{L}$. Therefore, except with probability $1/|X|^m$, $F' \in \mathcal{L} \setminus \mathcal{B}$. Thus, since $\text{Good}_{\epsilon/400}(F') \subseteq \text{Good}_{\epsilon/200}(F^*)$, except with negligible probability, we have:

$$\frac{\text{Vol}(\text{Good}_{\epsilon/200}(F^*))}{\text{Vol}(C_0)} \ge \frac{\text{Vol}(\text{Good}_{\epsilon/400}(F'))}{\text{Vol}(C_0)} \ge \frac{1}{|X|^{2m}}.$$

□

We are now ready to prove the analogue of Lemma 4.7 for the efficient implementation of the median mechanism.

LEMMA 5.4. *For every set of k queries $f_1, \dots, f_k$, for all but an $O(|X|^{-m})$ fraction of fractional histograms F, the efficient implementation of the median mechanism guarantees that: The mechanism answers fewer than $40m \log |X|$ hard queries, except with probability $k \exp(-\Omega(\epsilon n \alpha'))$,*

PROOF. We assume that all answers to hard queries are $\epsilon/100$ accurate, and that $|r_i - \hat{r}_i| \le \frac{1}{100}$ for every i. By Lemmas 4.3 and 4.4 — the former adapted to accommodate approximating r_i via random sampling — we are in this case except with probability $k \exp(-\Omega(\epsilon n \alpha'))$.

We analyze how the volume of C_i contracts with the number of hard queries answered. Suppose the mechanism answers a hard query at time i. Then:

$$r_i \le \hat{r}_i + \frac{1}{100} < t_i + \frac{1}{100} \le \frac{91}{100}.$$

Recall $C_i = \{F \in C_{i-1} : |f_i(F) - a_i| \le \epsilon/50\}$. Suppose that $\text{Vol}(C_i) \ge \frac{94}{100}\text{Vol}(C_{i-1})$. Then

$$r_i = \frac{\int_{C_{i-1}} \exp(-\epsilon^{-1}|f_i(F) - f_i(D)|)dF}{\text{Vol}(C_{i-1})}$$

$$\ge \frac{94}{100}\exp\left(-\frac{1}{50}\right) > \frac{92}{100},$$

a contradiction. Therefore, we have

$$|C_k| \le \left(\frac{94}{100}\right)^h \text{Vol}(C_0), \tag{13}$$

if h of the k queries are hard.

Since all answers to hard queries are $\epsilon/100$ accurate, it must be that $\text{Good}_{\epsilon/100}(D) \in C_k$. Therefore, for an input database D that satisfies (12) — and this is all but an $O(|X|^{-m})$ fraction of them, by Lemma 5.3 — we have

$$\text{Vol}(C_k) \ge \text{Vol}(\text{Good}_{\epsilon/100}(D)) \ge \frac{\text{Vol}(C_0)}{|X|^{2m}}. \tag{14}$$

Combining inequalities (13) and (14) yields

$$h \le \frac{2m \ln |X|}{\ln \frac{50}{47}} < 40m \ln |X|,$$

as claimed. □

Lemmas 4.4, 4.5, and 5.4 give the following utility guarantee.

THEOREM 5.5. *For every set $f_1, \dots, f_k$ of queries, for all but a negligible fraction of fractional histograms F, the efficient implementation of the median mechanism is (ϵ, δ)-useful with $\delta = k\exp(-\Omega(\epsilon n\alpha'))$.*

5.3 Usefulness for Finite Databases

Fractional histograms correspond to probability distributions over X. Lemma 5.3 shows that most probability distributions are 'good' for the efficient implementation of the Median Mechanism; in fact, more is true. We next show that finite databases *sampled* from randomly selected probability distributions also have good volume properties. Together, these lemmas show that the efficient implementation of the median mechanism will be able to answer nearly exponentially many queries with high probability, in the setting in which the private database D is drawn from some 'typical' population distribution.

DatabaseSample($|D|$):

1. Select a fractional point $F \in C_0$ uniformly at random.
2. Sample and return a database D of size $|D|$ by drawing each $x \in D$ independently at random from the probability distribution over X induced by F (i.e. sample $x_i \in X$ with probability proportional to F_i).

LEMMA 5.6. *For $|D|$ as in (6) (as required for the Median Mechanism), a database sampled by* ***DatabaseSample***$(|D|)$ *satisfies (12) except with probability at most $O(|X|^{-m})$.*

PROOF. By lemma 5.3, except with probability $|X|^{-m}$, the fractional histogram F selected in step 1 satisfies

$$\frac{\text{Vol}(\text{Good}_{\epsilon/200}(F))}{\text{Vol}(C_0)} \ge \frac{1}{|X|^{2m}}.$$

By lemma 4.6, when we sample a database D of size $|D| \ge O((\log |X| \log^3 k \log 1/\epsilon)/\epsilon^3)$ from the probability distribution induced by F, except with probability $\delta = O(k|X|^{-\log^3 k/\epsilon})$, $\text{Good}_{\epsilon/200}(F) \subset \text{Good}_{\epsilon/100}(D)$, which gives us condition (12). □

We would like an analogue of lemma 5.3 that holds for all but a diminishing fraction of *finite* databases (which correspond to lattice points within C_0) rather than fractional points in C_0, but it is not clear how uniformly randomly sampled lattice points distribute themselves with respect to the volume of C_0. If $n >> |X|$, then the lattice will be fine enough to approximate the volume of C_0, and lemma 5.3 will continue to hold. We now show that *small* uniformly sampled databases will also be good for the efficient version of the median mechanism. Here, small means $n = o(\sqrt{|X|})$, which allows for databases which are still polynomial in the size of X. A tighter analysis is possible, but we opt instead to give a simple argument.

LEMMA 5.7. *For every n such that n satisfies (6) and $n = o(\sqrt{|X|})$, all but an $O(n^2/|X|)$ fraction of databases D of size $|D| = n$ satisfy condition (12).*

PROOF. We proceed by showing that our **DatabaseSample** procedure, which we know via lemma 5.6 generates databases that satisfy (12) with high probability, is close to uniform. Note that **DatabaseSample** first selects a *probability distribution* F uniformly at random from the positive quadrant of the ℓ_1 ball, and then samples D from F.

For any particular database D^* with $|D^*| = n$ we write $\Pr_U[D = D^*]$ to denote the probability of generating D^* when we sample a database uniformly at random, and we write $\Pr_N[D = D^*]$ to denote the probability of generating D^* when we sample a database according to **DatabaseSample**. Let R denote the event that D^* contains no duplicate elements. We begin by noting by symmetry that: $\Pr_U[D = D^*|R] = \Pr_N[D = D^*|R]$ We first argue that $\Pr_U[R]$ and $\Pr_N[R]$ are both large. We immediately have that the expected number of repetitions in database D when drawn from the uniform distribution is $\binom{n}{2}/|X|$, and so $\Pr_U[\neg R] \le \frac{n^2}{|X|}$. We now consider $\Pr_N[R]$. Since F is a uniformly random point in the positive quadrant of the ℓ_1 ball, each coordinate F_i has the marginal of a Beta distribution: $F_i \sim \beta(1, |X| - 1)$. (See, for example, [Dev86] Chapter 5). Therefore, $E[F_i^2] = \frac{2}{|X|(|X|+1)}$ and so the expected number of repetitions in database D when drawn from **DatabaseSample** is $\binom{n}{2}\sum_{i=1}^{|X|} E[F_i^2] = \frac{2\binom{n}{2}}{|X|+1} \le \frac{2n^2}{|X|}$. Therefore, $\Pr_N[\neg R] \le \frac{2n^2}{|X|}$.

Finally, let B be the event that database D fails to satisfy (12). We have:

$$\begin{aligned}
\Pr_U[B] &= \Pr_U[B|R] \cdot \Pr_U[R] + \Pr_U[B|\neg R] \cdot \Pr_U[\neg R] \\
&= \Pr_N[B|R] \cdot \Pr_U[R] + \Pr_U[B|\neg R] \cdot \Pr_U[\neg R] \\
&\le \Pr_N[B|R] \cdot \Pr_U[R] + \Pr_U[\neg R] \\
&\le \Pr_N[B] \cdot \frac{\Pr_U[R]}{\Pr_N[R]} + \Pr_U[\neg R] \\
&\le \frac{\Pr_N[B]}{1 - \frac{2n^2}{|X|}} + \frac{n^2}{|X|} \\
&= O(\frac{n^2}{|X|})
\end{aligned}$$

where the last equality follows from lemma 5.6, which states that $\Pr_N[B]$ is negligibly small. □

We observe that we can substitute either of the above lemmas for lemma 5.3 in the proof of lemma 5.4 to obtain versions of Thoerem 5.5:

COROLLARY 5.8. *For every set $f_1, \ldots, f_k$ of queries, for all but a negligible fraction of databases sampled by* ***DatabaseSample****, the efficient implementation of the median mechanism is (ϵ, δ)-useful with $\delta = k\exp(-\Omega(\epsilon n\alpha'))$.*

COROLLARY 5.9. *For every set $f_1, \ldots, f_k$ of queries, for all but an $n^2/|X|$ fraction of uniformly randomly sampled databases of size n, the efficient implementation of the median mechanism is (ϵ, δ)-useful with $\delta = k\exp(-\Omega(\epsilon n\alpha'))$.*

6. CONCLUSION

We have shown that in the setting of predicate queries, interactivity does not pose an information theoretic barrier to differentially private data release. In particular, our dependence on the number of queries k nearly matches the optimal dependence of $\log k$ achieved in the *offline* setting by [BLR08]. We remark that our dependence on other parameters is not necessarily optimal: in particular, [DNR+09] achieves a better (and optimal) dependence on ϵ. We have also shown how to implement our mechanism in time $\text{poly}(|X|, k)$, although at the cost of sacrificing worst-case utility guarantees. The question of an interactive mechanism with $\text{poly}(|X|, k)$ runtime and worst-case utility guarantees remains an interesting open question. More generally, although the lower bounds of [DNR+09] seem to preclude mechanisms with run-time $\text{poly}(\log |X|)$ from answering a superlinear number of generic predicate queries, the question of achieving this runtime for specific query classes of interest (offline or online) remains largely open. Recently a representation-dependent impossibility result for the class of conjunctions was obtained by Ullman and Vadhan [UV10]: either extending this to a representation-independent impossibility result, or circumventing it by giving an efficient mechanism with a novel output representation would be very interesting.

Acknowledgments

The first author wishes to thank a number of people for useful discussions, including Avrim Blum, Moritz Hardt, Katrina Ligett, Frank McSherry, and Adam Smith. He would particularly like to thank Moritz Hardt for suggesting trying to prove usefulness guarantees for a continuous version of the BLR mechanism, and Avrim Blum for suggesting the distribution from which we select the threshold in the median mechanism.

7. REFERENCES

[BLR08] A. Blum, K. Ligett, and A. Roth. A learning theory approach to non-interactive database privacy. In *Proceedings of the 40th annual ACM symposium on Theory of computing*, pages 609–618. ACM New York, NY, USA, 2008.

[Dev86] L. Devroye. *Non-uniform random variate generation.* 1986.

[DFK91] M. Dyer, A. Frieze, and R. Kannan. A random polynomial-time algorithm for approximating the volume of convex bodies. *Journal of the ACM (JACM)*, 38(1):1–17, 1991.

[DMNS06] C. Dwork, F. McSherry, K. Nissim, and A. Smith. Calibrating noise to sensitivity in private data analysis. In *Proceedings of the Third Theory of Cryptography Conference TCC*, volume 3876 of *Lecture Notes in Computer Science*, page 265. Springer, 2006.

[DN03] I. Dinur and K. Nissim. Revealing information while preserving privacy. In *22nd ACM SIGACT-SIGMOD-SIGART Symposium on Principles of Database Systems (PODS)*, pages 202–210, 2003.

[DNR+09] C. Dwork, M. Naor, O. Reingold, G.N. Rothblum, and S. Vadhan. On the complexity of differentially private data release: efficient algorithms and hardness results. In *Proceedings of the 41st annual ACM symposium on Symposium on theory of computing*, pages 381–390. ACM New York, NY, USA, 2009.

[Dwo08] C. Dwork. Differential privacy: A survey of results. In *Proceedings of Theory and Applications of Models of Computation, 5th International Conference, TAMC 2008*, volume 4978 of *Lecture Notes in Computer Science*, page 1. Springer, 2008.

[GRS09] A. Ghosh, T. Roughgarden, and M. Sundararajan. Universally utility-maximizing privacy mechanisms. In *Proceedings of the 41st annual ACM symposium on Symposium on theory of computing*, pages 351–360. ACM New York, NY, USA, 2009.

[HT10] M. Hardt and K. Talwar. On the Geometry of Differential Privacy. In *The 42nd ACM Symposium on the Theory of Computing, 2010. STOC'10*, 2010.

[KLN+08] S.P. Kasiviswanathan, H.K. Lee, K. Nissim, S. Raskhodnikova, and A. Smith. What Can We Learn Privately? In *IEEE 49th Annual IEEE Symposium on Foundations of Computer Science, 2008. FOCS'08*, pages 531–540, 2008.

[MT07] F. McSherry and K. Talwar. Mechanism design via differential privacy. In *Proceedings of the 48th Annual Symposium on Foundations of Computer Science*, 2007.

[UV10] J. Ullman and S. Vadhan. PCPs and the Hardness of Generating Synthetic Data . *Manuscript*, 2010.

[Vap96] V. Vapnik. Structure of statistical learning theory. *Computational Learning and Probabilistic Reasoning*, page 3, 1996.

The Price of Privately Releasing Contingency Tables and the Spectra of Random Matrices with Correlated Rows*

Shiva Prasad Kasiviswanathan
CCS-3, Los Alamos National Laboratory
kasivisw@gmail.com

Mark Rudelson
Department of Mathematics
University of Missouri
rudelsonm@missouri.edu

Adam Smith
Department of Computer Science and Engineering
Pennsylvania State University
asmith@cse.psu.edu

Jonathan Ullman
SEAS, Harvard University
jullman@seas.harvard.edu

ABSTRACT

Marginal (contingency) tables are the method of choice for government agencies releasing statistical summaries of categorical data. In this paper, we derive lower bounds on how much distortion (noise) is necessary in these tables to ensure the privacy of sensitive data. We extend a line of recent work on impossibility results for private data analysis [9, 12, 13, 15] to a natural and important class of functionalities.

Consider a database consisting of n rows (one per individual), each row comprising d binary attributes. For any subset of T attributes of size $|T| = k$, the marginal table for T has 2^k entries; each entry counts how many times in the database a particular setting of these attributes occurs. We provide lower bounds for releasing all $\binom{d}{k}$ k-attribute marginal tables under several different notions of privacy.

(1) We give efficient polynomial time attacks which allow an adversary to reconstruct sensitive information given insufficiently perturbed marginal table releases. In particular, for a constant k, we obtain a tight bound of $\tilde{\Omega}(\min\{\sqrt{n}, \sqrt{d^{k-1}}\})$[1] on the average distortion per entry for any mechanism that releases all k-attribute marginals while providing "attribute" privacy (a weak notion implied by most privacy definitions).

(2) Our reconstruction attacks require a new lower bound on the least singular value of a random matrix with correlated rows. Let $M^{(k)}$ be a matrix with $\binom{d}{k}$ rows formed by taking all possible k-way entry-wise products of an underlying set of d random vectors from $\{0,1\}^n$. For constant k, we show that the least singular value of $M^{(k)}$ is $\tilde{\Omega}(\sqrt{d^k})$ with high probability (the same asymptotic bound as for independent rows).

(3) We obtain stronger lower bounds for marginal tables satisfying *differential privacy.* We give a lower bound of $\tilde{\Omega}(\min\{\sqrt{n}, \sqrt{d^k}\})$, which is tight for $n = \tilde{\Omega}(d^k)$. We extend our analysis to obtain stronger results for mechanisms that add *instance-independent* noise and weaker results when k is super-constant.

*The full version [20] contains proofs omitted here.

[1]The $\tilde{\Omega}(\cdot)$ notation hides inverse polylogarithmic factors in d, n, k.

STOC'10, June 5–8, 2010, Cambridge, Massachusetts, USA.
Copyright 2010 ACM 978-1-4503-0050-6/10/06 ...$10.00.

Categories and Subject Descriptors

F.2.0 [**Analysis of Algorithms and Problem Complexity**]: General

General Terms

Algorithms, Security, Theory

1. INTRODUCTION

The goal of *private data analysis* is to provide global, statistical properties of a data set of sensitive information while protecting the privacy of the individuals whose records the data set contains. There is a vast body of work on this problem in statistics and computer science. However, until recently, most schemes proposed in the literature lacked rigor: typically, the schemes had either no formal privacy guarantees or ensured security only against a specific suite of attacks.

The seminal results of Dinur and Nissim [9] initiated a rigorous study of the tradeoff between privacy and utility. The notion of *differential privacy* [12] that emerged from this line of work provides rigorous guarantees even in the presence of a malicious adversary with access to arbitrary side information. Differential privacy requires, roughly, that any single individual's data have little effect on the outcome of the analysis. Recently, many techniques have been developed for designing differentially private algorithms (see [10, 11] for two recent surveys). A typical objective is to release as accurate an approximation as possible to some function f evaluated on the database D.

A complementary line of work seeks to establish lower bounds on how much distortion (noise) is necessary for particular functions f. Some of these bounds apply only to differential privacy (e.g., [12, 18, 19]); other bounds rule out *any* reasonable notion of privacy by showing how to reconstruct almost all of the data D given sufficiently accurate approximations to $f(D)$ [9, 13, 15]. We refer to the latter works as lower bounds for *minimal* privacy.

In this paper, we investigate lower bounds on the distortion necessary for releasing a set of *marginal contingency tables* (marginal tables, in short), under both minimal and differential privacy. A database D in our setting consists of n rows, each row comprising values for d binary attributes $x_1, \ldots, x_d$. For any subset of T attributes of size $|T| = k$, the marginal table for T has 2^k entries; each entry counts how many times in the database a particular setting of these attributes occurs. Alternatively, we may think of the table as counting the number of rows in the database that satisfy each of the 2^k possible *conjunctions* on the k attributes in T. We call a marginal table for a set of k attributes a k-way marginal table. The d-attribute marginal table is the "full" contingency table for the data set.

Marginal tables are the workhorses of categorical data analysis and, in particular, of data analysis in the medical, social and behavioral sciences (e.g., clinical trials, public health studies, and education statistics). In addition to being easy to interpret, they are sufficient statistics for popular classes of probabilistic models [4]. (As a simple example: for binary data, the mean vector and covariance matrix, which capture linear dependencies among attributes, are equivalent to the set of all 2-attribute marginal tables.) Because of this, they are the format of choice for data release by government statistical bureaus [3]. However, many of the fields in which categorical data are used generate highly sensitive data. Researchers and government agencies have ethical and legal responsibilities to protect the confidentiality of the individuals whose data they collect. Consequently, the confidentiality of contingency table releases has been an active topic of research in statistics for over thirty years (see, for example, [17, 30]). Understanding the extent to which marginal tables can be released while guaranteeing a rigorous, meaningful notion of privacy is an important problem.

1.1 Our Contributions

Let $\mathcal{C}_k(D)$ be the set of all k-way marginal tables (equivalently, the frequencies of all possible k-way conjunctions) for a database $D \in (\{0,1\}^d)^n$. There are $\binom{d}{k}$ such tables; however, it is convenient to think of $\mathcal{C}_k(D)$ as a single real vector of length $2^k\binom{d}{k}$. We give lower bounds for simultaneously estimating all the entries of $\mathcal{C}_k(D)$ privately. As a point of reference, for constant k, the best-known differentially private algorithms [5, 6, 14] add an $\widetilde{O}(\min\{n, (n^2d)^{1/3}, 2^{\sqrt{\log d}}\sqrt{nd}, \sqrt{d^k}\})$ average distortion per entry. Here, the $\widetilde{O}(\cdot)$ notation hides polylogarithmic factors in d, n, k. Our lower bounds match this upper bound in different respects.

(1) Lower Bounds for Minimal Privacy: We show that algorithms that do not sufficiently distort the marginal tables fail to satisfy a large class of "privacy" definitions. We define two violations of privacy[2]: *attribute non-privacy* and *row non-privacy*.

Each of these rules out a large class of popular definitions of privacy. Row non-privacy rules out definitions that protect an entire row of the database even given leakage of other rows; such definitions include differential privacy as well as several definitions popular in the *randomized response* literature [33, 1, 16]. Attribute non-privacy rules out any definition that guarantees the secrecy of a particular "sensitive" attribute even when all other attributes are known to an attacker; such definitions include K-anonymity [32] and its variants [23, 22, 7, 24, 34], as well as the notions ruled out by row non-privacy.

Using a "reconstruction" attack outlined below **(2)**, we show that for any constant k, releasing $\mathcal{C}_k(D)$ with distortion $o(\min\{\sqrt{n}, \sqrt{d^{k-1}}\})$ per entry allows an adversary to efficiently reconstruct large fraction of the sensitive attribute entries given the nonsensitive values, thus *violating* attribute privacy (the bound holds even for releasing only all those k-way tables that involve the sensitive attribute and $k-1$ other attributes). Moreover, releasing $\mathcal{C}_k(D)$ with distortion $o(\min\{\sqrt{n}, \sqrt{d^k}\})$ per entry allows an adversary to efficiently reconstruct large fraction of the rows of D, even though this would not be possible without the release, thus *violating* row privacy. Both these bounds are (almost) tight, as there is an algorithm which is neither attribute non-private nor row non-private and which for every database D adds $\widetilde{O}(\min\{\sqrt{n}, \sqrt{d^k}\})$ distortion per entry of $\mathcal{C}_k(D)$. The formal bounds for these privacy notions are stated in Table 1 and discussed in Section 2.

(2) Reconstruction Attack & the Least Singular Value of Random Matrices with Correlated Rows: The bounds on minimal privacy **(1)** above require significantly different techniques from previous work. Previous lower bounds [9, 13, 15] were based on variants of the following reconstruction problem: given a real-valued matrix M, and a corrupted "codeword" $Ms + e$, the goal is to compute an approximation $\hat{s}$ to s such that the "reconstruction error" $\hat{s} - s$ is somehow bounded in terms of the noise vector e. Typically, assuming some norm $\|e\|_p$ is small, one can bound a related norm of $\hat{s} - s$.

Returning to data privacy: if $s \in \mathbb{R}^n$ is a database with one number assigned per person, we can think of $y = Ms + e$ as a vector of (distorted) estimates of the quantities $\langle M_i, s\rangle$, where M_i is the ith row of M. Any private data release that allows a user to estimate $\langle M_i, s\rangle$, allows an attacker to obtain y. Therefore, an algorithm for approximating s from y can be used to infer sensitive data from the release.

Previous lower bounds rely heavily on the freedom to design M by selecting the rows of M independently (either at random [9, 13, 15] or from an algebraic code [15]). When $k = 1$ a similar flexibility is available in our lower bounds; the matrix $M^{(1)}$ that arises in our lower bounds is a $\{0,1\}^{d\times n}$ matrix with independent random entries. However, for $k > 1$ the rows of the matrix $M^{(k)}$ that arises in our lower bounds are highly correlated: the matrix $M^{(k)}$ has d^k rows which are formed by taking all possible k-way *entry-wise products*[3] of the rows of the random matrix $M^{(1)}$. The techniques of previous work, from the literature on both privacy and random matrices, break down. We show that reconstruction procedures using these matrices can in fact be analyzed, by showing for any constant k that a random $(0,1)$-matrix with *correlated* rows has approximately the same least singular value as a random $(0,1)$-matrix with *independent* rows.

Tight bounds are known on the least singular values of various types of matrices (e.g., square, rectangular) with independent random entries (see, e.g., [28, 29, 27]

[2]Alternatively, we might call these "attribute leakage" and "row leakage". We use "non-privacy" for consistency with the previous works [9, 13, 15].

[3]The entry-wise product of k vectors $p_1, \ldots, p_k \in \mathbb{R}^n$ is the vector in $q \in \mathbb{R}^n$ with entries $q_i = \prod_{j=1}^k p_{j_i}$.

and references therein). The least singular value of an $N \times n$ matrix with $(0,1)$ independent random entries and $N \geq n$ is $\Theta(\sqrt{N})$ with exponentially high probability (in fact, even non-asymptotic bounds are known, see [29]). To deal with the dependencies, we develop several new tools, which may be of independent interest. We show that for any constant k if the random matrix $M^{(1)}$ has less than $d^k/\log^{k-2} n$ columns, then the least singular value of $M^{(k)}$ is $\tilde{\Omega}(\sqrt{d^k})$ with exponentially high probability. Therefore, the least singular value of $M^{(k)}$ is asymptotically comparable to that of a $d^k \times n$ random matrix with independent entries, but $M^{(k)}$ (constructed out of $M^{(1)}$) uses far lower randomness.

The proof is challenging because correlations make powerful measure concentration tools hard to apply. We first reduce the problem to bounding the least singular value of a (related) random centered matrix $\tilde{\Pi}$. The smallest singular value of $\tilde{\Pi}$ is the minimum of $\|\tilde{\Pi}x\|$, over x from the unit sphere. An important tool in the proof is bounding the *small ball probability*, which is the probability that $\|\tilde{\Pi}x\|$ is small for a *fixed* vector x. To obtain a uniform lower bound for $\|\tilde{\Pi}x\|$, we decompose the unit sphere into many pieces, and for each piece use epsilon-net arguments tailored according to the small ball probability. Then, we obtain a uniform lower estimate on the net, which is then extended to the whole unit sphere by approximation.

In the privacy context, our spectral lower bound allows for a reconstruction algorithm of the form

$$\hat{s} = \text{round}(M_{inv}^{(k)} \cdot (M^{(k)}s + e)),$$

where s is a $(0,1)$-vector, $M_{inv}^{(k)}$ is an appropriate pseudoinverse of $M^{(k)}$ and round(z) rounds the entries of a vector z to the nearer of 0 and 1. We show that releasing $M^{(k)}s$ with distortion $o(\sqrt{n})$ per entry allows the adversary to reconstruct $n - o(n)$ bits of s (that is, to find $\hat{s}$ that agrees in almost all entries of s), as long as $n = o(d^k)$. One can extend the result to get a lower bound of $\tilde{\Omega}(\min\{\sqrt{n}, \sqrt{d^k}\})$ for all n.

(3) Lower Bounds for Differential Privacy: Using a disjoint set of techniques, we show a stronger lower bound for releasing k-way marginal tables under the notion of (ϵ, δ)-differential privacy. The precise bounds are stated in Table 1 and discussed in Section 4. Here, we treat ϵ and δ as constants.

For constant k, the best-known (ϵ, δ)-differentially private algorithms [5, 6, 14] yield an average distortion per entry of $\tilde{O}(\min\{n, (n^2d)^{1/3}, 2^{\sqrt{\log d}}\sqrt{nd}, \sqrt{d^k}\})$, while our lower bound is $\tilde{\Omega}(\min\{\sqrt{n}, \sqrt{d^k}\})$. Our bounds imply that the technique of Blum *et al.* [5], which adds Gaussian noise to each entry in $\mathcal{C}_k$ is tight for large databases (when $n = \tilde{\Omega}(d^k)$). Moreover, for a natural and popular class of algorithms based on adding *instance-independent* noise [5, 12, 3], we strengthen this bound to $\Omega(\sqrt{d^k})$, which is tight for all n.

Our lower bounds for differential privacy extend even to a non-constant k, and here we show a lower bound of $\tilde{\Omega}(\min\{\sqrt{n}, \sqrt{\binom{d}{k}}\}/2^k)$ on the average distortion per entry. For $n = \tilde{\Omega}(\binom{d}{k})$, this is loose by a factor of $\sqrt{2^k}$ when compared to the best-known upper bound. This lower bound can again be strengthened for the instance-independent case (see Table 1).

Let $\mathcal{A}$ be a differentially private algorithm for $\mathcal{C}_k$. The rough idea behind these differential privacy lower bounds is to start with a particular database D and then bound the projection of the *mean squared error*(MSE) matrix of $\mathcal{A}(D)$ along a large set of directions. If the algorithm adds instance-independent noise then we show that this set of directions contains an (almost) orthonormal basis, allowing us to lower bound the trace of the MSE matrix, and hence the average distortion per entry. In the general case (when the distortion is instance-dependent), we use concentration inequalities for matrix-valued random variables to show that for appropriately chosen *random* databases, the trace of the MSE matrix is large with high probability.

We expect the linear algebraic techniques developed for this bound to be useful for bounding the required distortion of a wide range of differentially private releases.

1.2 Significance of the Privacy Lower Bounds

Dinur and Nissim [9] showed that if a mechanism answers (or allows the user to compute) $O(n \log n)$ arbitrary inner product queries on a database (vector) $s \in \{0,1\}^n$ with noise $o(\sqrt{n})$ per response, then an adversary can reconstruct $n - o(n)$ entries of s. Their attack was subsequently extended to use a linear number of queries [13], allow a small fraction of answers to be arbitrarily distorted [13], and run significantly more quickly [15]. These reconstruction attacks provide lower bounds for various minimal notions of privacy; our results extend the scope of these bounds significantly.

There were also several known lower bounds specific to differential privacy, though they are not directly relevant to marginal tables [12, 26, 18]. Subsequently to our work, Hardt and Talwar [19] gave upper and lower bounds for releasing a variety of linear functions (including marginal tables) for the special case of "pure" ϵ-differential privacy (with $\delta = 0$). For the case of 1-attribute marginal tables, their bound of $\Omega(d/\epsilon)$ improves on ours; we conjecture that their techniques lead to a bound of $\tilde{\Omega}(d^k/\epsilon)$ for releasing constant k-way marginal tables under ϵ-differential privacy. However, their techniques break down for even slightly relaxed privacy notions such as (ϵ, δ)-differential privacy.

We see our new lower bounds as interesting for several reasons.

Natural symmetric functions. In their simplest form, the inner product queries considered by [9, 13, 15] require the adversary to be able to "name rows", that is, specify a coefficient for each entry of the vector s.

Thus, the lower bound does not apply directly to any functionality that is symmetric in the rows of the data set such as marginal tables. It was pointed out in [8] that in databases with more than one entry per row, random inner product queries (on, say, attribute x_d) can be simulated via hashing: for example, the adversary could ask for the sum of the function $H(x_1, \ldots, x_{d-1}) \cdot x_d$ over the whole database, where $H : \{0,1\}^{d-1} \rightarrow \{0,1\}$ is an appropriate hash function. This is a symmetric query, but it might seem odd to a statistician (with, e.g., a 2-wise independent hash function). The lower bounds we give for marginal table releases are the first for symmetric functions regularly released by official statistical agencies; one can think of our reconstruction attacks as using *conjunctions* as weak hash functions to implement the idea of [8].

Privacy Guarantee	Upper Bound on Noise	Lower Bound on Noise
Attribute privacy	$\widetilde{O}(\min\{\sqrt{n}, \sqrt{d^k}\})$	$\widetilde{\Omega}\left(\min\left\{\sqrt{n}, \sqrt{d^{k-1}}\right\}\right)$
Row privacy	$\widetilde{O}(\min\{\sqrt{n}, \sqrt{d^k}\})$	$\widetilde{\Omega}\left(\min\left\{\sqrt{n}, \sqrt{d^{k}}\right\}\right)$
(ϵ, δ)-differential privacy (instance indep. noise)	$O\left(\frac{\sqrt{\binom{d}{k}\log(1/\delta)}}{\sqrt{2^k}\epsilon}\right)$ [5, 3]	$\Omega\left(\frac{\sqrt{\binom{d}{k}(1-\delta/\epsilon)}}{2^k\epsilon}\right)$
(ϵ, δ)-differential privacy (with $\delta = 1/\text{poly}(n)$)	$\widetilde{O}\left(\min\left\{n, \left(\frac{n^2 dk}{\epsilon}\right)^{\frac{1}{3}}, \frac{\sqrt{nd}}{\epsilon} \cdot 2^{\sqrt{k \log d}}, \frac{\sqrt{\binom{d}{k}}}{\epsilon\sqrt{2^k}}\right\}\right)$ [3, 6, 14]	$\widetilde{\Omega}\left(\min\left\{\frac{\sqrt{n}}{2^k\sqrt{\epsilon}}, \frac{\sqrt{\binom{d}{k}}}{2^k\epsilon}\right\}\right)$

Table 1: *Upper and lower bounds on the average noise per cell entry for releasing all k-way marginal tables (or equivalently all k-way conjunction predicates) under various privacy guarantees. The results on attribute non-privacy and row non-privacy are for constant k. The n term in the upper bound for (ϵ, δ)-differential privacy (last row) comes from an algorithm that releases a vector of $n/2$'s for all D's. All the uncited results appear in this paper.*

When is distortion acceptably low? It is natural to ask at what point the distortion required for privacy interferes with statistical analysis. There is no simple answer, but for the "predicate queries" considered here, where each entry counts the number of occurrences of a predicate in the underlying data set, there is a large class of statistical models which inherently have "sampling error", that is standard deviation of the observed statistics, of $\Omega(\sqrt{n})$. A crude rule of thumb, then, is that the distortion interferes seriously when it is not $o(\sqrt{n})$ [12, 3, 31]. Our lower bounds of $\widetilde{\Omega}(\min(\sqrt{n}, \sqrt{d^k}))$ show that for even modest values of d and k, the data set n must be very large to get distortion $o(\sqrt{n})$.

The "dimension" of marginal tables. The reconstruction attacks [9, 13, 15] above show a lower bound of roughly $\min\{\sqrt{n}, \sqrt{m}\}$ on the distortion required to answer a set of m random, independent queries about a data set of size n. However, the bounds heavily rely on independence of the queries. This raises the question of whether certain interesting classes of queries could be answered with much less noise. For example, if a set of queries is linearly dependent, then one can compute noisy answers to only a few queries (a spanning set), and deduce the rest using the linear relationships. Both of our bounds can be interpreted as showing that the marginal statistics of a data set are, in a sense that depends on the notion of privacy, *far* from any low dimensional subspace. In particular, we show that the $\binom{d}{k}2^k$ different entries of the k-way marginal tables hide a set of $\Omega(d^k)$ "nearly independent" underlying features – as far as privacy is concerned, they have dimension close to $\binom{d}{k}$. It is natural to ask: what properties of a set of queries lead to this type of behavior, in general? Our techniques suggest that the right notion is related to inapproximability by low-dimensional linear spaces, however, it is unclear how to formulate this notion precisely.

1.3 Known Upper Bounds for Diff. Privacy

In [5, 12] it was shown that addition of carefully calibrated noise to functions satisfying a Lipschitz condition is enough to ensure differential privacy. Applied to conjunctions, they show that random noise drawn from a normal distribution with mean 0 and standard deviation $\sqrt{2\binom{d}{k}\log(1/\delta)}/\epsilon$ to each entry in $\mathcal{C}_k(D)$ guarantees (ϵ, δ)-differential privacy [5], while adding random noise drawn from a Laplacian distribution with mean 0 and standard deviation $2\binom{d}{k}/\epsilon$ to each entry in $\mathcal{C}_k(D)$ guarantees ϵ-differential privacy (with $\delta = 0$) [12]. Barak *et al.* [3] improve the dependency on k in these results, saving a factor of approximately $\sqrt{2^k}$ in the required distortion.

In a different vein, Blum *et al.* [6] adapt the exponential sampling technique of [25] to release a synthetic data set. One can use their techniques to release $\mathcal{C}_k(D)$ with distortion $\widetilde{O}((n^2dk/\epsilon)^{2/3})$ in each entry . The dependency on d and k in [6] is much better than in the additive noise mechanisms, but the dependency on n is significantly worse; in particular, our results show that one cannot significantly reduce the dependency on n without incurring a dependency on d^k. Finally, Dwork *et al.* [14] provide a similar, but incomparable, synthetic data mechanism, which allows one to release all k-way conjunctions with distortion $\widetilde{O}(\frac{\sqrt{nd}}{\epsilon}2^{\sqrt{k\log d}})$.

1.4 Preliminaries

We use $[n]$ to denote the set $\{1, 2, \ldots, n\}$. We use $negl(n)$ denotes a function that is asymptotically smaller than $1/n^c$ for all $c > 0$. Vectors used in the paper are by default column vectors. For a vector v, $v^\top$ denotes its transpose (row vector), $\|v\|$ denotes its Euclidean norm, and v_i denotes its ith entry. We use u_v to denote the unit vector corresponding to v (i.e., $u_v = v/\|v\|$). For two vectors v_1 and v_2, $\langle v_1, v_2\rangle$ denotes the inner product of v_1 and v_2. The length of projection of v_1 onto v_2 is then $\langle v_1, v_2\rangle/\|v_2\|$. For a matrix M, $tr(M)$ denotes the trace and $\|M\|_\infty$ denotes the operator norm. We use $diag(a_1, \ldots, a_n)$ to denote an $n \times n$ diagonal matrix with entries $a_1, \ldots, a_n$ along the main diagonal. Let $\mathbb{I}_d$ denote the identity matrix of dimension d. We use m_k to denote $\binom{d}{k}$.

Let M be an $N \times n$ real matrix with $N \geq n$. The singular values $\sigma_j(M)$ are the eigenvalues of $\sqrt{M^\top M}$ arranged in non-increasing order. Of particular importance in this paper is the smallest singular value $\sigma_n(M) = \inf_{z:\|z\|=1}\|Mz\|$.

Boolean Conjunctions. It is convenient to describe the results in terms of releasing conjunction predicates over the domain $\{0,1\}^d$. Each $x \in \{0,1\}^d$ is interpreted as an assignment to d Boolean variables $x_1, \ldots, x_d$. A conjunction predicate $c_v : \{0,1\}^d \to \{0,1\}$ for $v \in \{-1,0,1\}^d$ is defined as $c_v(x) = 1$ iff for all $i \in [d], x_i = 1$ if $v_i = 1$ and $x_i = 0$ if $v_i = -1$. The value of v_i indicates whether the variable x_i appears as not negated (if $v_i = 1$), negated (if $v_i = -1$), or absent (if $v_i = 0$). The length of a conjunction predicate is the number of coordinates of v that are non-zero. We will refer to a conjunction predicate of length k as a k-way conjunction. Let $\mathcal{C}_k$ be the function class of all k-way conjunction predicates on variables $x_1, \ldots, x_d$. The size of $\mathcal{C}_k$, $|\mathcal{C}_k| = 2^k\binom{d}{k}$. Let $D \in (\{0,1\}^d)^n$ be a database. Each row of D represents information contributed by one individual. The ith column of D contains the assignments to variable x_i. For a predicate $c_v \in \mathcal{C}_k$, define $c_v(D) = \sum_{x \in D} c_v(x)$. We use $\mathcal{C}_k(D)$ to represent the vector of all predicates in $\mathcal{C}_k$ evaluated on D.

2. LOWER BOUNDS – MINIMAL PRIVACY

In this section, we introduce a reconstruction attack based on analyzing the least singular value of a random matrix with correlated entries. We then use the reconstruction attack to establish lower bounds on the noise needed for releasing k-way marginal tables under the notions of attribute non-privacy and row non-privacy. We treat k as a constant in this section.

The lower bounds for our minimal privacy definitions proceed by "reducing" an instance of the reconstruction problem for a matrix with correlated rows into a marginal table release problem. To define the reduction from the reconstruction problem, we need the following definition of entry-wise product of vectors and matrices.

DEFINITION 2.1. *The entry-wise product of vectors $p, q \in \mathbb{R}^n$ is the vector in $p \odot q \in \mathbb{R}^n$ with entries $(p \odot q)_i = p_i \cdot q_i$. If A is an $N_1 \times n$ matrix, and B is an $N_2 \times n$ matrix, denote by $A \odot B$ an $N_1 \cdot N_2 \times n$ matrix, whose rows are entry-wise products of the rows of A and B: $(A \odot B)_{i,k} = A_i \odot B_k$, where $(A \odot B)_{j,k}, A_j, B_k$ denote rows of the corresponding matrices.*

We now formally define attribute non-privacy and row non-privacy, and explain the reductions from the reconstruction problem.

DEFINITION 2.2 (ATTRIBUTE NON-PRIVACY). *An algorithm $\mathcal{A}$ for releasing all k-way conjunction predicates is* attribute non-private *if there exists a polynomial time adversary such that for every $s \in \{0,1\}^n$ there exists a database $D_{at}(s) \in (\{0,1\}^d)^n$ whose last column is s, such that the adversary with input $\mathcal{A}(D_{at}(s))$ and the first $d-1$ columns of $D_{at}(s)$, can reconstruct at least $\widetilde{\Omega}(\min\{n, d^{k-1}\})$ entries of s with probability $1 - negl(d)$.*

This definition captures a common model in the data privacy literature (e.g., [32, 23, 22, 7, 24, 34]) where one assumes that a database (with d attributes) consists of $d-1$ *nonsensitive* attributes (e.g., demographic information), which can be learned from other sources, and one *sensitive* attribute (e.g., disease). The attribute non-privacy lower bound applies to any notion of privacy that purports to protect individual values of the sensitive attribute (the lower bound applies in particular, to differential privacy but also, e.g., to the notion of privacy implicit in the popular "K-anonymization" scheme [32] and its recent variants [23, 22, 7, 24, 34]).

Reduction from the Reconstruction Problem to Attribute Non-Privacy: Consider a matrix $M \in \{0,1\}^{d \times n}$. Let $M^{(k)} = M \odot M \odot \ldots \odot M$ be the dimension $d^k \times n$ matrix obtained by applying $\odot$ operator $k-1$ times. Let $s \in \{0,1\}^n$. Consider the database $D = (M^\top | s) \in (\{0,1\}^{d+1})^n$. That is, the first d columns of D are given by the rows of M, and the last column is s. Then $\mathcal{C}_k(D)$ contains the vector $M^{(k-1)}s$, i.e., $M^{(k-1)}s \subset \mathcal{C}_k(D)$. Now, any algorithm that allows an adversary to reconstruct a large fraction of s given $M^{(k-1)}s$ is attribute non-private. This reduction holds for every $M \in \{0,1\}^{d \times n}$, but in the analysis, we use a random matrix M.

DEFINITION 2.3 (ROW NON-PRIVACY). *An algorithm $\mathcal{A}$ for releasing all k-way conjunction predicates is* row non-private *if there exists a distribution of databases $\mathbb{D}$ over the domain $(\{0,1\}^d)^n$ under which the rows of the databases are statistically independent and there exists a set $S \subseteq [n]$ whose size is at least $\widetilde{\Omega}(\min\{n, d^k\})$ satisfying the following:*

1. *For any (not-necessarily polynomial time) adversary if $D \sim \mathbb{D}$, the adversary can output any row of D indexed by the elements of S with probability at most a constant (say $2/3$);*
2. *There exists a polynomial time adversary such that if $D \sim \mathbb{D}$, the adversary on input $\mathcal{A}(D)$ can output $1 - o(1)$ fraction of the rows of D indexed by the elements of S with probability $1 - negl(d)$.*

The row non-privacy lower bound applies, roughly, to any notion of privacy that seeks to protect any complete row of the database (as opposed to only individual entries). This includes differential privacy as well as its relaxations to metrics on probability distributions such as total variation distance or KL divergence [12, 33, 1, 16].

Reduction from the Reconstruction Problem to Row Non-Privacy: Consider a matrix $M \in \{0,1\}^{d \times n}$. Consider the database $D = diag(s) \cdot M^\top \in (\{0,1\}^d)^n$, where $diag(s)$ is an $n \times n$ diagonal matrix with diagonal s. Because s is a $(0,1)$-vector, this corresponds to a world where person i's data is either $M_i^\top$ or 0^d, according to the ith bit of s (where M_i is the ith row of M). Then $\mathcal{C}_k(D)$ contains the vector $M^{(k)}s$. Again, this reduction holds for every $M \in \{0,1\}^{d \times n}$, but in the analysis, we use a random matrix M.

2.1 Lower Bounds – Reconstruction Problem

Let $s = (s_1, \ldots, s_n) \in \{0,1\}^n$ be some (secret) vector. Let c_k be a constant (we will define it later in Theorem 2.5). Let the integer $a = \min\{n, c_k d^k / \log^{2k-2} n\}$ (to simplify the exposition, we shall ignore rounding issues). Let $s|_a = (s_1, \ldots, s_a)$ be the first a entries of s. Let $\Phi \in \{0,1\}^a$ be a vector with independent entries taking values 0 and 1 with probability 1/2. Let $\Phi_1, \ldots, \Phi_d \in \{0,1\}^a$ be d independent copies of Φ. Let M be a $d \times a$ matrix whose rows are $\Phi_1, \ldots, \Phi_d$. Again, we consider the matrix $M^{(k)}$ constructed from M.

The attack works as follows: for every row R in $M^{(k)}$, the adversary asks inner product of R with $s|_a$, and receives noisy responses. Consider a privacy mechanism $\mathcal{A}$. Let $p = \mathcal{A}(M^{(k)}s|_a)$ be the vector of noisy answers generated by $\mathcal{A}$. Define the error (noise) vector as $e = p - M^{(k)}s|_a$. Let $M^{(k)} = P\Gamma Q$ be the singular value decomposition of $M^{(k)}$. Here, P is a $d^k \times d^k$ orthogonal matrix, Γ is a $d^k \times a$ diagonal matrix, and Q is an $a \times a$ orthogonal matrix. Let $\mathbf{0}$ be a $(d^k - a) \times a$ matrix with all entries zero. Define $\Gamma^{-1} = (diag(\sigma_1(M^{(k)})^{-1}, \ldots, \sigma_a(M^{(k)})^{-1}) | \mathbf{0}^\top)$. The dimension of Γ^{-1} is $a \times d^k$. Define $M_{inv}^{(k)} = Q^\top \Gamma^{-1} P^\top$.

Now, given p, the adversary uses $M_{inv}^{(k)}$ to construct $\hat{s} = (\hat{s}_1, \ldots, \hat{s}_a)$ as follows: $\hat{s}_i = 1$ if the ith entry in $M_{inv}^{(k)} p \geq$

1/2, and 0 otherwise. Now, the claim is that $\hat{s}$ is a good reconstruction of $s|_a$. The idea behind the analysis is that $M^{(k)}_{inv}p = s|_a + M^{(k)}_{inv}e$, and therefore (as P and Q are orthogonal matrices),

$$\|M^{(k)}_{inv}e\| = \|Q^\top \Gamma^{-1} P^\top e\| = \|\Gamma^{-1} P^\top e\| \\ \leq \|\Gamma^{-1}\|_\infty \|P^\top e\| = \|e\|/\sigma_a(M^{(k)}).$$

Corollary 2.6 shows that with high probability $\sigma_a(M^{(k)}) = \tilde{\Omega}(\sqrt{d^k})$. If an algorithm only adds $o(\sqrt{n})$ noise to each query (i.e., all the entries in e are $o(\sqrt{n})$) then $\|e\| = o(\sqrt{d^k n})$, and therefore, $\|M^{(k)}_{inv}e\| \approx o(\sqrt{n})$ with high probability. In particular, if $a = n$, then this implies that with high probability $M^{(k)}_{inv}e$ cannot have $\Omega(n)$ entries with absolute value above 1/2, and therefore, the Hamming distance between $\hat{s}$ and $s|_a$ is $o(a) = o(n)$ (as the adversary only fails to recover those entries of $s|_a$ whose corresponding $M^{(k)}_{inv}e$ entries are greater than 1/2). The following proposition formalizes this observation. The proof uses some ideas from a recent reconstruction attack proposed by Dwork and Yekhanin [15].

PROPOSITION 2.4. *Let k be a constant. If an algorithm adds*

$$o(\min\{\sqrt{n}/\log^{(k^2+k+1)} n, \sqrt{d^k}/\log^{(k^2+3k-1)} n\})$$

noise to each entry in $M^{(k)}s|_a$, then there exists an adversary that can reconstruct $1 - o(1)$ fraction of $s|_a$ with probability at least $1 - negl(d)$.

The proof of the above proposition relies heavily on the following theorem that lower bounds the least singular value of a random matrix with correlated rows. A proof outline of the theorem is given in the Section 3.

THEOREM 2.5. *Let k, m, d be natural numbers such that $m \leq c_k d^k/\log^{2k-2} m$ where c_k depends only on k, and let A be a $d \times m$ matrix with independent entries taking values 0 and 1 with probability 1/2. Then there exists numbers C_k, c'_k which depend only on k such that the k-times entry-wise product $\tilde{A} = A \odot A \odot \ldots \odot A$ is a $d^k \times m$ matrix satisfying*

$$\Pr\left[\sigma_m(\tilde{A}) \leq \frac{c'_k \sqrt{d^k}}{\log^{(k^2+k+1)} m}\right] \leq 2\exp\left(-C_k d/\log^{2k-2} m\right).$$

Now, as M is a $d \times a$ matrix with independent entries taking values 0 and 1 with probability 1/2, and $a \leq c_k d^k/\log^{2k-2} n$, we can apply the above theorem to conclude the following.

COROLLARY 2.6. $\Pr\left[\sigma_a(M^{(k)}) \leq \frac{\sqrt{d^k}}{\log^{(k^2+k+1)} n}\right] \leq negl(d)$.

2.2 Attribute Non-Privacy

We use the reduction from the reconstruction attack described earlier. Define, a vector $\hat{\Phi}_j \in \{0,1\}^n$ as follows: the ith entry in $\hat{\Phi}_j$ is the ith entry of Φ_i if $i \leq a$, and is 0 otherwise. For a vector $s \in \{0,1\}^n$, define a database $D_{at}(s) \in (\{0,1\}^d)^n$ as follows: the first d columns are $\hat{\Phi}_1, \ldots, \hat{\Phi}_{d-1}$, the last column is s. The following theorem uses Proposition 2.4 to show that there exists an adversary that can reconstruct $1 - o(1)$ fraction of the first $\tilde{\Omega}(\min\{n, d^{k-1}\})$ entries of s if given too accurate vector $\mathcal{C}_k(D_{at}(s))$.

THEOREM 2.7. *Let k be a constant. Any algorithm $\mathcal{A}$ for releasing all k-way marginal tables (or equivalently all k-way conjunction predicates) that for every database $D \in (\{0,1\}^d)^n$ adds*

$$o\left(\min\left\{\sqrt{n}/\log^{(k^2-k+1)} n, \sqrt{d^{k-1}}/\log^{(k^2+k-3)} n\right\}\right)$$

noise to each entry in $\mathcal{A}(D)$ is attribute non-private.

2.3 Row Non-Privacy

Again, we use the reduction from the reconstruction attack described earlier. For a vector $s \in \{0,1\}^n$, define a database $D_{st}(s) \in (\{0,1\}^d)^n$ as follows: (i,j)th entry of $D_{st}(s)$ is s_i if the ith entry in $\hat{\Phi}_j = 1$, and 0 otherwise. We assume that the adversary has access to $\Phi_1, \ldots, \Phi_d$.

Define a distribution $\mathbb{D}$ over the set of databases as follows: draw a vector s_r uniformly at random from $\{0,1\}^n$ and output $D_{st}(s_r)$. Let consider some ith row where $i \in [a]$. Let E be the event that there exists a Φ_j such that ith entry in Φ_j is 1. Conditioned on event E, an adversary can only predict the ith row of $D_{st}(s_r)$ by guessing the ith entry in s_r. Since s_r is picked uniformly at random, this implies that conditioned on E no adversary can guess the ith row of $D_{st}(s_r)$ with probability more than 1/2. Finally, since $\Pr[\bar{E}] = 1/2^d$, therefore, no adversary (even with access to $\Phi_1, \ldots, \Phi_d$) can guess the ith row of $D_{st}(s_r)$ with probability more than $1/2 + 1/2^d \leq 2/3$. Thus, $\mathbb{D}$ satisfies the first condition of Definition 2.3 for every set S. The following theorem uses this distribution $\mathbb{D}$ to obtain a lower bound on the noise needed for row privacy.

THEOREM 2.8. *Let k be a constant. Any algorithm for releasing all k-way marginal tables (or equivalently all k-way conjunction predicates) that for every database $D \in (\{0,1\}^d)^n$ adds*

$$o\left(\min\left\{\sqrt{n}/\log^{(k^2+k+1)} n, \sqrt{d^k}/\log^{(k^2+3k-1)} n\right\}\right)$$

noise to each entry in $\mathcal{A}(D)$ is row non-private.

3. PROOF OUTLINE OF THEOREM 2.5

Estimating the smallest singular value of the matrix $\tilde{A}$ presents two challenges. The entries of this matrix are interdependent, which makes powerful measure concentration tools hard to apply. Also, the entries are non-centered, and hence its operator norm is of order $\sqrt{d^k n}$ with high probability. The norm of the matrix enters many probabilistic bounds involved in the proof, and such a large norm would render most of these bounds meaningless. To remove these obstacles, we apply a simple decoupling and symmetrization argument to reduce the problem to bounding the smallest singular value of a matrix $\tilde{\Pi}$, which is an entry-wise product of $\Pi_1, \ldots, \Pi_k$, where each Π_i is a $d \times n$ matrix with independent random entries taking values -1 with probability 1/4, 1 with probability 1/4, and 0 with probability 1/2. Note that the entries in Π_i are centered. Analysis of the behavior of the least singular value of $\tilde{\Pi}$ is the core of the argument.

The first step in this analysis is obtaining a probabilistic bound for the operator norm of $\tilde{\Pi}$. This bound is proved by induction on k, with Talagrand's measure concentration inequality for convex functions (see [21], Corollary 4.10) applied at each step. We show that with high probability,

$$\|\tilde{\Pi}|_J\|_\infty \leq c''_k (d^{k/2} + \sqrt{|J|} \cdot \log^{k/2} n) \cdot \log^{(k-1)/2} n \quad (1)$$

for all non-empty subsets $J \subset \{1, \ldots, n\}$. Here $\tilde{\Pi}|_J$ denotes the submatrix of $\tilde{\Pi}$ with columns belonging to J, and c''_k is a constant depending on k only.

The smallest singular value of $\tilde{\Pi}$ is the minimum of $\|\tilde{\Pi}x\|$, over x from the unit sphere. Before we analyze this quantity in full generality, we consider a simpler question of estimating *the small ball probability*. This is the probability that $\|\tilde{\Pi}x\|$ is small for a fixed vector x. Measure concentration plays a prominent role in this estimate as well. To apply measure concentration tools, we have to represent $\|\tilde{\Pi}x\|$ as a function of independent random variables. This is done by conditioning on the matrices $\Pi_1, \ldots, \Pi_{l-1}$ and $\Pi_{l+1}, \ldots, \Pi_k$, for some $l \in \{1, \ldots, k\}$. In this case the random variable $\|\tilde{\Pi}x\|$ depends only on the matrix Π_l with independent entries.

The number $l \in \{1, \ldots, k\}$ is chosen to match the level of *compressibility* of the vector x. A vector is compressible if its norm is concentrated on a small number of coordinates. Note that the coordinates of the vector $\tilde{\Pi}x$ consist of d^{k-l} blocks $(\Pi_1 \odot \ldots \odot \Pi_l)y_i^\top$, where y_i denotes the ith row of the matrix $\Pi_{l+1} \odot \ldots \Pi_k \odot x^\top$. We show that with high probability most of the vectors y_i have norm and degree of compressibility comparable to those of x. This reduces the small ball probability bound for the vector $\tilde{\Pi}x$ to a similar bound for each vector $(\Pi_1 \odot \ldots \odot \Pi_l)y_i^\top$. To obtain such a bound, we decompose the coordinates of this vector in a similar fashion in d blocks $(\Pi_1 \odot \ldots \odot \Pi_{l-1} \odot \Pi_l(j))y_i^\top$, where $\Pi_l(j)$ is the j-th row of the matrix Π_l.

For any matrix A with n columns, and any vectors $u, v \in \mathbb{R}^n$, $(A \odot u^\top)v = (A \odot v^\top)u$. Using this elementary identity, we rewrite $(\Pi_1 \odot \ldots \odot \Pi_{l-1} \odot \Pi_l(j))y_i^\top$ as $(\Pi_1 \odot \ldots \odot \Pi_{l-1} \odot y_i)\Pi_l(j)^\top$. After conditioning on $B := \Pi_1 \odot \ldots \odot \Pi_{l-1}$ this becomes the product of a fixed matrix $B \odot y_i$ and a random vector $\Pi_l(j)^\top$ with independent coordinates. The small ball probability bound for such vector can be obtained by applying Talagrand's concentration theorem for convex functions to the function $F(w) = \|(B \odot y_i)w\|$. The level of concentration is determined by the Lipschitz constant of the function F, i.e., by the norm of the matrix $B \odot y_i$. This norm, in turn, is controlled using the inequality (1) applied to the matrix B.

We can obtain a uniform bound for the entire sphere via a net argument. Unfortunately, since the small ball probability for $\|\tilde{\Pi}x\|$ depends significantly on the vector x, it is impossible to construct one net that would work for the whole sphere. Therefore, we decompose the sphere in numerous regions, and estimate the probability that $\|\tilde{\Pi}x\|$ is small for each part separately. The regions are defined by the small ball probability, which depends on the compressibility of the vectors. For each part we apply a net argument especially tailored for a certain degree of compressibility. Namely, the region is discretized, by using a γ-net for appropriate γ. Then we obtain a uniform lower estimate on the net, using the small ball probability and the union bound. This estimate is extended to the whole region by approximation. This method requires a careful balance between the small ball probability and the size of the net. The better the small ball probability is, the bigger a net we can consider, and so the bigger region we can cover. This balance dictates the aforementioned decomposition of the sphere.

We start with obtaining a uniform estimate of $\|\tilde{\Pi}x\|$ over a set of all vectors x having a given level of sparsity. We then extend the bound from the set of sparse vectors to the set of compressible vectors with a certain level of compressibility. Finally, we show that the whole sphere can be assembled from these sets. This allows to finish the proof by using the union bound. See the full version [20] for a complete proof.

4. LOWER BOUNDS – DIFF. PRIVACY

In this section, we establish lower bounds on the noise needed for releasing all k-way marginal tables under the popular notion of differential privacy. A database D' is said to be a neighbor of a database D if it differs from D in exactly one row. A randomized algorithm is *differentially private* if neighbor databases induce nearby distributions on the outputs.

DEFINITION 4.1 ((ϵ, δ)-DIFFERENTIAL PRIVACY [12]). *A randomized algorithm $\mathcal{A}$ is (ϵ, δ)-differentially private if for all neighboring databases D, D', and for all sets $\mathcal{S}$ of possible outputs*

$$\Pr[\mathcal{A}(D) \in \mathcal{S}] \leq \exp(\epsilon) \cdot \Pr[\mathcal{A}(D') \in \mathcal{S}] + \delta.$$

The probability is taken over the random coins of the algorithm $\mathcal{A}$. If $\mathcal{A}$ is $(\epsilon, 0)$-differentially private (i.e., $\delta = 0$), then we say it is ϵ-differentially private.

Let X and Y be random variables taking values in a set $\mathcal{O}$. We use $X \approx_{\epsilon,\delta} Y$ to indicate that random variables X and Y are (ϵ, δ)-indistinguishable, i.e.,

$$\forall \mathcal{S} \subseteq \mathcal{O}, \Pr[X \in \mathcal{S}] \leq \exp(\epsilon) \cdot \Pr[Y \in \mathcal{S}] + \delta \quad \text{and}$$
$$\Pr[Y \in \mathcal{S}] \leq \exp(\epsilon) \cdot \Pr[X \in \mathcal{S}] + \delta.$$

We also use $X \approx_\epsilon Y$ to indicate that random variables X and Y are $(\epsilon, 0)$-indistinguishable.

Our bounds are tight under a natural and popular class of differentially private algorithms based on adding instance-independent noise. This class contains algorithms that for all inputs add noise from a fixed distribution (i.e., the noise distribution is independent of the input). Formally, if an algorithm $\mathcal{A}$ for a function class $\mathcal{F}$ adds instance-independent noise from a distribution Z then for all D, $\mathcal{A}(D) = \mathcal{F}(D) + Z$. Therefore, for D' a neighbor of D, $\mathcal{A}(D') = \mathcal{A}(D) + \mathcal{F}(D') - \mathcal{F}(D)$. The SuLQ algorithm of Blum *et al.* [5] is an example of an algorithm that adds instance-independent noise.

In Section 4.1, we consider (ϵ, δ)-differentially private algorithms for $\mathcal{C}_k$ that add instance-independent noise. For an instance-independent differentially private algorithm $\mathcal{A}$, we can measure the perturbation introduced by $\mathcal{A}$ either by using the mean squared error matrix

$$\Sigma_{\mathcal{A}}(D) = \mathbb{E}[(\mathcal{A}(D) - \mathcal{C}_k(D))(\mathcal{A}(D) - \mathcal{C}_k(D))^\top]$$

or the covariance matrix of $\mathcal{A}(D)$, and the results are the same with either choice. Define the average mean squared error of $\mathcal{A}(D)$ as the trace of $\Sigma_{\mathcal{A}}(D)$ divided by the size of $\mathcal{A}(D)$. Let $m_k = \binom{d}{k}$. We show that if for every database D, $\mathcal{A}(D)$ has an average mean squared error (or variance) of $o(m_k(1-\delta/\epsilon)^2/(2^{2k}\epsilon^2))$, then $\mathcal{A}$ is *not* (ϵ, δ)-differentially private. To do so, we analyze projections onto various directions. The idea is to show that for any neighboring databases D and D' with $\mathcal{C}_k(D') - \mathcal{C}_k(D) = \Delta$, the indistinguishability requirement of differential privacy forces both the expected squared length of the projection of $\mathcal{A}(D) - \mathcal{C}_k(D)$ on Δ and the expected squared length of the projection of $\mathcal{A}(D') - \mathcal{C}_k(D')$ on Δ to be at least square of the length of Δ.

Of particular interest to us are the direction vectors Δ's with large lengths (close to the largest possible length of $\sqrt{m_k}$). Then, using a careful argument involving geometries of these Δ vectors we show that there exists a database D^* such that the trace of $\Sigma_{\mathcal{A}}(D^*)$ is at least $m_k^2(1-\delta/\epsilon)^2/(2^k\epsilon^2)$. The result follows by dividing the trace by the size of $\mathcal{A}(D^*)$.

In Section 4.2, we consider general (ϵ,δ)-differentially private algorithms for $\mathcal{C}_k$. For a "general" differentially private algorithm $\mathcal{A}$, we *need*[4] to use the mean squared error matrix to measure the perturbation. We show that if for every database D, $\mathcal{A}(D)$ has an average mean squared error of $o(\min\{m_k(1-\delta/\epsilon)^2/(2^{2k}\epsilon^2), n(1-\delta/\epsilon)^2/(2^{2k}\epsilon\log m_k)\})$, then $\mathcal{A}$ is *not* (ϵ,δ)-differentially private. Again for neighboring databases D and D' with $\mathcal{C}_k(D')-\mathcal{C}_k(D)=\Delta$, we investigate the expected squared length of the projections of $\mathcal{A}(D)-\mathcal{C}_k(D)$ and $\mathcal{A}(D')-\mathcal{C}_k(D')$ on Δ. The analysis of the general case is harder, because now the indistinguishability requirement forces only one among these two projection lengths to be greater than the squared length of Δ. Our proof looks at random databases and shows that for a random database D_r with high probability the trace of $\Sigma_{\mathcal{A}}(D_r)$ is at least $\min\{m_k^2(1-\delta/\epsilon)^2/(2^k\epsilon^2), nm_k(1-\delta/\epsilon)^2/(2^k\epsilon\log m_k)\}$.

Inner Products. In our analysis, (for simplicity) instead of conjunctions, we consider inner products over the domain $\{-1,1\}^d$. An inner product predicate $i_v:\{-1,1\}^d\to\{-1,1\}$ is defined as $i_v(x)=\prod_i x_i\cdot v_i$, where the value of v_i indicates whether x_i is present (if $v_i=1$) or not (if $v_i=0$). Similar to $\mathcal{C}_k$, let $\mathcal{I}_k$ be the class of all k-way inner product predicates. Let D be a database from $(\{-1,1\}^d)^n$. For a predicate $i_v\in\mathcal{I}_k$, define $i_v(D)=\sum_{x\in D} i_v(x)$. Let $\mathcal{I}_k(D)$ be the vector of all predicates in $\mathcal{I}_k$ evaluated on D. In the full version [20], we provide the relationship between releasing conjunctions and inner products. Informally, what we show is that if there exists a database $D_o\in(\{-1,1\}^d)^n$ such that no (ϵ,δ)-differentially private algorithm $\mathcal{B}$ for $\mathcal{I}_k$ has $tr(\Sigma_{\mathcal{B}}(D_o))\le T$, then there exists a database $D_z\in(\{0,1\}^d)^n$ such that no (ϵ,δ)-differentially private algorithm $\mathcal{A}$ for $\mathcal{C}_k$ has $tr(\Sigma_{\mathcal{A}}(D_z))\le T/2^k$.

4.1 Instance-independent Additive Case

For simplicity, we set $\delta=0$ in the following discussion (we will introduce δ in Theorem 4.6). We start by proving a very useful property about differential privacy. We state the lemma in terms of a general function class $\mathcal{F}$ and later use if for our specific function class $\mathcal{I}_k$. Let $\mathcal{A}$ be an ϵ-differentially private algorithm for $\mathcal{F}$ that adds instance-independent noise. The lemma shows that both $\mathbb{E}[\langle\mathcal{A}(D)-\mathcal{F}(D),\Delta\rangle^2]$ and $\mathbb{E}[\langle\mathcal{A}(D')-\mathcal{F}(D'),\Delta\rangle^2]$ are $\Omega(\langle\Delta,\Delta\rangle^2/\epsilon^2)$ where $\Delta=\mathcal{F}(D')-\mathcal{F}(D)$. The proof uses the fact that projections onto direction Δ need to be ϵ-indistinguishable for $\mathcal{A}(D)$ and $\mathcal{A}(D')$.

LEMMA 4.2. *Let $\mathcal{F}$ be a function class of Boolean predicates, and let $\mathcal{A}$ be an ϵ-differentially private algorithm for $\mathcal{F}$ that adds instance-independent noise. Let $\mathcal{A}(D)=\mathcal{F}(D)+Z$. Let $\Delta=\mathcal{F}(D')-\mathcal{F}(D)$, and let $\mathcal{A}(D)\approx_\epsilon\mathcal{A}(D')=\mathcal{A}(D)+\Delta$. Then, $\mathbb{E}[\langle\mathcal{A}(D)-\mathcal{F}(D),\Delta\rangle^2]=\Omega(\langle\Delta,\Delta\rangle^2/\epsilon^2)$.*

[4]This is because an algorithm could always add noise such that the output released is always a 0 vector for every database. This is clearly *not* a good algorithm as the deviation from the true answer could be quite big. But this algorithm clearly satisfies all the privacy requirements and also the variance in each coordinate of $\mathcal{A}(D)$ is 0.

One-way Inner products. If $k=1$ (i.e., 1-way inner products), then the remaining analysis is quite simple. Let D_e be any database which has at least a row of both $(-1)^d$ and $(1)^d$. Consider a vector $\Delta\in\{-2,2\}^d$, construct D_Δ from D_e by replacing the row $(-1)^d$ is replaced by $\Delta/2$ and the row $(1)^d$ by $\Delta/2$. The Hamming distance between D_e and D_Δ is 2 and $\mathcal{I}_1(D_\Delta)-\mathcal{I}_1(D_e)=\Delta$. Also, $\langle\Delta,\Delta\rangle^2=16d^2$. We use the above construction to create for every $\Delta=\{-2,2\}^d$ a corresponding database D_Δ. The idea now is to use the fact that this set of Δ's (which contains every vector from $\{-2,2\}^d$) contains an orthogonal (Hadamard) basis $\Delta_1,\ldots,\Delta_d$, and therefore, by invoking Lemma 4.2 for $\mathcal{I}_1$, and noting that $\sum_{i=1}^d\Delta_i\Delta_i^\top=4d\cdot\mathbb{I}_d$, we have

$$\begin{aligned}\Omega\left(\frac{d^3}{\epsilon^2}\right)&=\sum_{\Delta_i} tr(\mathbb{E}[\langle\mathcal{A}(D_e)-\mathcal{I}_1(D_e),\Delta_i\rangle^2])\\&=\sum_{\Delta_i} tr(\Delta_i^\top\Sigma_{\mathcal{A}}(D_e)\Delta_i)=\sum_{\Delta_i} tr(\Sigma_{\mathcal{A}}(D_e)\Delta_i\Delta_i^\top)\\&=tr(\Sigma_{\mathcal{A}}(D_e)\cdot 4d\cdot\mathbb{I}_d)=4d\cdot tr(\Sigma_{\mathcal{A}}(D_e)).\end{aligned}$$

PROPOSITION 4.3. *Let $\mathcal{A}$ be an ϵ-differentially private algorithm for $\mathcal{I}_1$ that adds instance-independent noise. Let D_e be any database which has at least a row of both $(-1)^d$ and $(1)^d$. Then, $tr(\Sigma_{\mathcal{A}}(D_e))=\Omega(d^2/\epsilon^2)$.*

Extension to k-way inner products. The analysis for $k>1$ (k not necessarily a constant) is trickier, as we don't get a set of orthogonal Δ vectors. Here, we start with a special database $D_c=((1)^d)^n$ (a database of all 1's), and look at the neighbors of D_c obtained by replacing a row of D_c by a vector from $\{-1,1\}^d$. Let D'_c be a neighbor of D_c, and let $\tilde{z}=\mathcal{I}_k(D'_c)-\mathcal{I}_k(D_c)$. Assume that D'_c is obtained from D_c by replacing the jth row of D_c by a vector $d'_c\in\{-1,1\}^d$. Therefore, $\tilde{z}=(n)^{m_k}-((n-1)^{m_k}+\mathcal{I}_k(d'_c))=(1)^{m_k}-\mathcal{I}_k(d'_c)$ has lots of 0 entries making $\|\tilde{z}\|$ "small". This is true for many different choices of D'_c. To overcome this problem we analyze projections of $\mathcal{A}(D)-\mathcal{I}_k(D)$ onto direction $\pi\tilde{z}$ where $\pi=\mathbb{I}_{m_k}-oo^\top/\langle o,o\rangle$ ($\pi\tilde{z}$ is the orthogonal projection of $\tilde{z}$ onto the orthogonal complement of $o=(1)^{m_k}$). These projections have the advantage that $\|\pi\tilde{z}\|=\|\pi\cdot\mathcal{I}_k(d'_c)\|$ is "big" with probability at least 1/2 over random choices of $\tilde{z}$. The idea now is to use Lemma 4.2 to show that $\mathbb{E}[\langle\mathcal{A}(D_c)-\mathcal{I}_k(D_c),\pi\tilde{z}\rangle^2]=\Omega(\langle\pi\tilde{z},\pi\tilde{z}\rangle^2/\epsilon^2)$.

LEMMA 4.4. *Let $\mathcal{A}$ be an ϵ-differentially private algorithm for $\mathcal{I}_k$ that adds instance-independent noise. Let $D_c=((1)^d)^n$. Let $D'_c\in(\{-1,1\}^d)^n$ be a neighbor of D_c. Let $\tilde{z}=\mathcal{I}_k(D'_c)-\mathcal{I}_k(D_c)$, $z=\mathcal{I}_k(D'_c)-(n-1)^{m_k}$, and $\pi=\mathbb{I}_{m_k}-oo^\top/\langle o,o\rangle$ where $o=(1)^{m_k}$. Then,*

$$\mathbb{E}[\langle\mathcal{A}(D_c)-\mathcal{I}_k(D_c),\pi\tilde{z}\rangle^2]=\Omega\left(\frac{\langle\pi\tilde{z},\pi\tilde{z}\rangle^2}{\epsilon^2}\right)=\Omega\left(\frac{\langle\pi z,\pi z\rangle^2}{\epsilon^2}\right).$$

In the proof, we use random directions z. The following lemma analyzes the structure of $\mathbb{E}_z[zz^\top]$ (where the randomness is over the choice of z).

LEMMA 4.5. *Let $r\in\{-1,1\}^d$ be a random vector with independent entries taking values -1 and 1 with probability 1/2. Let $m_k=\binom{d}{k}$. Define a random vector z_r of length m_k as $z_r=\mathcal{I}_k(r)$. Define a matrix $B=\mathbb{E}_{z_r}[z_rz_r^\top]$ where* *the randomness is over z_r. Then, $B = \mathbb{I}_{m_k}$ where $\mathbb{I}_{m_k}$ is an identity matrix of dimension m_k.*

The following theorem uses Lemmata 4.4 and 4.5 to show that every instance-independent differentially private algorithm needs to add a lot of noise to release $\mathcal{I}_k(D_c)$. The idea is to analyze $\mathbb{E}_{z_r}[(\pi z_r)^\top \Sigma_\mathcal{A}(D_c)(\pi z_r)]$. Since, $\mathbb{E}_{z_r}[z_r z_r^\top] = \mathbb{I}_{m_k}$ (from Lemma 4.5), we have

$$\begin{aligned}\mathbb{E}_{z_r}[(\pi z_r)^\top \Sigma_\mathcal{A}(D_c)(\pi z_r)] &= \mathbb{E}_{z_r}[tr((\pi z_r)^\top \Sigma_\mathcal{A}(D_c)(\pi z_r))]\\ &= \mathbb{E}_{z_r}[tr(\pi^\top \Sigma_\mathcal{A}(D_c)\pi z_r z_r^\top)] = tr(\pi^\top \Sigma_\mathcal{A}(D_c)\pi \mathbb{I}_{m_k})\\ &\le tr(\Sigma_\mathcal{A}(D_c))\|\pi\|_\infty \|\mathbb{I}_{m_k}\|_\infty = tr(\Sigma_\mathcal{A}(D_c)).\end{aligned}$$

The third equality follows as trace and expectation commute. The last equality follows as π is a projection matrix. Now, using Lemma 4.4, we show that

$$\mathbb{E}_{z_r}[(\pi z_r)^\top \Sigma_\mathcal{A}(D_c)(\pi z_r)] = \Omega(m_k^2/\epsilon^2),$$

and therefore, $tr(\Sigma_\mathcal{A}(D_c)) = \Omega(m_k^2/\epsilon^2)$. As explained earlier, a lower bound for releasing k-way inner products can be converted to a lower bound for releasing k-way conjunctions.

THEOREM 4.6. *Let $m_k = \binom{d}{k}$. Any algorithm $\mathcal{A}$ for releasing all k-way marginal tables (or equivalently all k-way conjunction predicates) that adds instance-independent noise and that for every database $D \in (\{0,1\}^d)^n$ has a root mean squared error (or standard deviation) of*

$$o(\sqrt{m_k}(1-\delta/\epsilon)/(2^k\epsilon))$$

for each entry of $\mathcal{A}(D)$ is not *(ϵ,δ)-differentially private.*

4.2 Lower Bounds – General Case

Again our analysis looks at the related problem of releasing inner products. We initially prove the lower bound by fixing ϵ to 1/2. We start by proving an extension of Lemma 4.2 to general differentially private algorithms. Let $\mathcal{F}$ be a function class, and let $\mathcal{A}$ be an (ϵ,δ)-differentially private algorithm for $\mathcal{F}$. Let $\mathcal{A}(D) \approx_{1/2,\delta} \mathcal{A}(D')$, and let $\Delta = \mathcal{F}(D') - \mathcal{F}(D)$. Unlike in the instance-independent case (Lemma 4.2) both $\mathbb{E}[\langle \mathcal{A}(D) - \mathcal{F}(D), \Delta\rangle^2]$ and $\mathbb{E}[\langle \mathcal{A}(D') - \mathcal{F}(D'), \Delta\rangle^2]$ needn't be $\|\Delta\|^4$, but the following lemma shows that at least one of them is $\|\Delta\|^4$ (this one-sided behavior is in fact unavoidable and is explained in the full version [20]).

LEMMA 4.7. *Let $\mathcal{F}$ be a function class of Boolean predicates, and let $\mathcal{A}$ be a $(1/2,\delta)$-differentially private algorithm for $\mathcal{F}$. Let $\mathcal{A}(D) \approx_{1/2,\delta} \mathcal{A}(D')$. Let $\Delta = \mathcal{F}(D') - \mathcal{F}(D)$. Then, at least one of $\mathbb{E}[\langle \mathcal{A}(D) - \mathcal{F}(D), \Delta\rangle^2]$ or $\mathbb{E}[\langle \mathcal{A}(D') - \mathcal{F}(D'), \Delta\rangle^2]$ is $\Omega(\langle \Delta, \Delta\rangle^2(1-\delta)^2)$.*

For a database $D \in (\{-1,1\}^d)^n$, consider the n neighboring databases[5] $\widetilde{D}_1, \dots, \widetilde{D}_n$ where $\widetilde{D}_i$ is obtained by replacing ith row of D by $(1)^d$. Let $T_k(D) = \{z_1, \dots, z_n\}$ denote the (multi) set such that $\mathcal{I}_k(\widetilde{D}_i) - \mathcal{I}_k(D) = \tilde{z}_i$ and $z_i = o - \tilde{z}_i$. Let $\pi = \mathbb{I}_{m_k} - oo^\top/\langle o, o\rangle$ be an orthogonal projection matrix. Notice that, $\pi\tilde{z}_i = -\pi z_i$. For the reasons same as in the instance-independent case, we analyze projections onto $\pi\tilde{z}_i$ (or equivalently $-\pi z_i$). Let u_{z_i} be the unit vector corresponding to z_i. Define

$$S_k(D) = \{z \in T_k(D) | \mathbb{E}[(\pi z)^\top \Sigma_\mathcal{A}(D)(\pi z)] = \Omega(m_k^2(1-\delta)^2)\},$$

$$U_k(D) = \sum_{z\in S_k(D)} u_z u_z^\top \quad \text{and} \quad V_k(D) = \sum_{z \in T_k(D)} u_z u_z^\top.$$

For a database D it is possible that the expected squared length of the projection of $\mathcal{A}(D) - \mathcal{I}_k(D)$ onto $\Delta = \mathcal{I}_k(D') - \mathcal{I}_k(D)$ is $o(\|\Delta\|^2(1-\delta)^2)$ for many neighbors D' of D. For example, it could happen that the expected squared length of the projection $\mathcal{A}(D') - \mathcal{I}_k(D')$ onto Δ is $\Omega(\|\Delta\|^2(1-\delta)^2)$, whereas the expected squared length of the projection of $\mathcal{A}(D) - \mathcal{I}_k(D)$ onto Δ is only $o(\|\Delta\|^2(1-\delta)^2)$. To overcome this problem we use random databases. Let D_r be a database drawn uniformly at random from $(\{-1,1\}^d)^n$. The idea is as follows,

$$\begin{aligned}\Omega(m_k^2(1-\delta)^2|S_k(D_r)|) &= \sum_{z\in S_k(D_r)} \mathbb{E}[\langle \mathcal{A}(D_r) - \mathcal{I}_k(D_r), \pi z\rangle^2]\\ &= \sum_{z\in S_k(D_r)} (\pi z)^\top \Sigma_\mathcal{A}(D_r)(\pi z) = \sum_{z\in S_k(D_r)} tr(\pi^\top \Sigma_\mathcal{A}(D_r)\pi z z^\top)\\ &= tr(\pi^\top \Sigma_\mathcal{A}(D_r)\pi \sum_{z\in S_k(D_r)} zz^\top) = tr(\pi^\top \Sigma_\mathcal{A}(D_r)\pi m_k U_k(D_r)).\end{aligned}$$

The last step follows from the definition of $U_k(D_r)$. Now, since π, $\Sigma_\mathcal{A}(D_r)$, and $U_k(D_r)$ are all positive semidefinite, therefore,

$$\begin{aligned}tr(\pi^\top \Sigma_\mathcal{A}(D_r)\pi U_k(D_r)) &\le tr(\Sigma_\mathcal{A}(D_r))\|\pi\|_\infty \|U_k(D_r)\|_\infty\\ &= tr(\Sigma_\mathcal{A}(D_r))\|U_k(D_r)\|_\infty.\end{aligned}$$

Putting together,

$$\Omega(m_k^2(1-\delta)^2|S_k(D_r)|) = m_k tr(\Sigma_\mathcal{A}(D_r))\|U_k(D_r)\|_\infty.$$

Therefore, to lower bound $tr(\Sigma_\mathcal{A}(D_r))$, we need good upper bound on the largest eigenvalue of $U_k(D_r)$. Lemma 4.8 does that by using the matrix-valued Chernoff bound from Ahlswede and Winter [2].

LEMMA 4.8. *For all $D \in (\{-1,1\}^d)^n$, we have $\|U_k(D)\|_\infty \le \|V_k(D)\|_\infty$, and with probability at least $1 - 1/n$ over the choice of D_r, $\|V_k(D_r)\|_\infty = O(\max\{n/m_k, \log m_k\})$.*

Let $\widetilde{\mathcal{D}}$ be the set of all databases from $(\{-1,1\}^d)^n$ which have at least one row of $(1)^d$. If with high probability, $|S_k(D_r)|$ is $\Omega(n)$, then the upper bound on $\|U_k(D_r)\|_\infty$ from Lemma 4.8 will give us the lower bound on $tr(\Sigma_\mathcal{A}(D_r))$. But it is not necessary that $|S_k(D_r)| = \Omega(n)$ (as in constructing $S_k(D_r)$ we only consider the neighbors of D_r belonging to $\widetilde{\mathcal{D}}$). In that case, we show that one could pick a database $\widetilde{D}_r$ uniformly at random from $\widetilde{\mathcal{D}}$, and use a similar analysis to lower bound $tr(\Sigma_\mathcal{A}(\widetilde{D}_r))$. We show that if the expected size of $S_k(D_r)$ is small (less than $n/4$), then the expected size of $\widetilde{S}_k(\widetilde{D}_r)$ is greater than $n/4$ (i.e., at least one of the two expected sizes is greater than $n/4$). The following proposition uses these ideas to show that every differentially private algorithm with probability $\Omega(1-1/n)$ needs to add a lot of noise to either $\mathcal{I}_k(D_r)$ or $\mathcal{I}_k(\widetilde{D}_r)$.

PROPOSITION 4.9. *Let $\mathcal{A}$ be a $(1/2,\delta)$-differentially private algorithm for $\mathcal{I}_k$. Let D_r be a database chosen uniformly at random from $(\{-1,1\}^d)^n$ and $\widetilde{D}_r$ be a database*

[5]If D has a row of $(1)^d$ (say the ith), then $D = \widetilde{D}_i$. For uniformity, we will still treat D and $\widetilde{D}_i$ as neighbors.

chosen uniformly at random from $\widetilde{\mathcal{D}}$. Then, with probability $\Omega(1-1/n)$, at least one of $tr(\Sigma_{\mathcal{A}}(D_r))$ or $tr(\Sigma_{\mathcal{A}}(\widetilde{D}_r))$ is $\Omega(\min\{m_k^2(1-\delta)^2, nm_k(1-\delta)^2/(\log m_k)\})$.

This previous lower bound for $(1/2,\delta)$-differentially private algorithms can be converted into a lower bound for (ϵ,δ)-differentially private algorithms. Details are deferred to the full version [20]. We now summarize the result.

THEOREM 4.10. *Let $m_k = \binom{d}{k}$. Any algorithm $\mathcal{A}$ for releasing all k-way marginal tables (or equivalently all k-way conjunction predicates) that for every database $D \in (\{0,1\}^d)^n$ has a root mean squared error of*

$$o(\min\{\sqrt{m_k}(1-\delta/\epsilon)/(2^k\epsilon), \sqrt{n}(1-\delta/\epsilon)/(2^k\sqrt{\epsilon\log m_k})\})$$

for each entry of $\mathcal{A}(D)$ is not *(ϵ,δ)-differentially private.*

5. REFERENCES

[1] R. Agrawal and R. Srikant. Privacy-preserving data mining. In *SIGMOD*, pages 439–450. ACM, 2000.

[2] R. Ahlswede and A. Winter. Strong converse for identification via quantum channels. *IEEE Transactions on Information Theory*, 48(3), 2002.

[3] B. Barak, K. Chaudhuri, C. Dwork, S. Kale, F. McSherry, and K. Talwar. Privacy, accuracy, and consistency too: a holistic solution to contingency table release. In *PODS*, pages 273–282. ACM, 2007.

[4] Y. Bishop, S. Fienberg, and P. Holland. *Discrete Multivariate Analysis: Theory and Practice.* MIT Press, Cambridge MA, 1975.

[5] A. Blum, C. Dwork, F. McSherry, and K. Nissim. Practical privacy: The SuLQ framework. In *PODS*, pages 128–138. ACM, 2005.

[6] A. Blum, K. Ligett, and A. Roth. A learning theory approach to non-interactive database privacy. In *STOC*, pages 609–618. ACM, 2008.

[7] B.-C. Chen, R. Ramakrishnan, and K. LeFevre. Privacy skyline: Privacy with multidimensional adversarial knowledge. In *VLDB*, pages 770–781, 2007.

[8] I. Dinur, C. Dwork, and K. Nissim. Revealing information while preserving privacy, full version of [9], in preparation, 2010.

[9] I. Dinur and K. Nissim. Revealing information while preserving privacy. In *PODS*, pages 202–210. ACM, 2003.

[10] C. Dwork. Differential privacy: A survey of results. In *TAMC*, pages 1–19. Springer, 2008.

[11] C. Dwork. The differential privacy frontier. In *TCC*, pages 496–502. Springer, 2009.

[12] C. Dwork, F. McSherry, K. Nissim, and A. Smith. Calibrating noise to sensitivity in private data analysis. In *TCC*, pages 265–284. Springer, 2006.

[13] C. Dwork, F. McSherry, and K. Talwar. The price of privacy and the limits of LP decoding. In *STOC*, pages 85–94. ACM, 2007.

[14] C. Dwork, M. Naor, O. Reingold, G. Rothblum, and S. Vadhan. On the complexity of differentially private data release: efficient algorithms and hardness results. In *STOC*, pages 381–390, 2009.

[15] C. Dwork and S. Yekhanin. New efficient attacks on statistical disclosure control mechanisms. In *CRYPTO*, pages 469–480. Springer, 2008.

[16] A. Evfimievski, R. Srikant, R. Agrawal, and J. Gehrke. Privacy preserving mining of association rules. In *KDD*, pages 217–228. ACM, 2002.

[17] S. Fienberg and L. C. R. J. Willenborg. Special issue on disclosure control. *Journal of Official Statistics*, 14(4), 1998.

[18] A. Ghosh, T. Roughgarden, and M. Sundararajan. Universally utility-maximizing privacy mechanisms. In *STOC*, pages 351–360. ACM, 2009.

[19] M. Hardt and K. Talwar. On the geometry of differential privacy. In *these proceedings*. ACM, 2010.

[20] Full version of this abstract. Available from the authors, 2010.

[21] M. Ledoux. The concentration of measure phenomenon, volume 89 of Mathematical Surveys and Monographs. *American Mathematical Society*, 208:2005–2006, 2001.

[22] N. Li, T. Li, and S. Venkatasubramanian. t-closeness: Privacy beyond k-anonymity and l-diversity. In *ICDE*, pages 106–115. IEEE, 2007.

[23] A. Machanavajjhala, J. Gehrke, D. Kifer, and M. Venkitasubramaniam. l-diversity: Privacy beyond k-anonymity. *ACM TKDD*, 1(1):3, 2007.

[24] D. J. Martin, D. Kifer, A. Machanavajjhala, J. Gehrke, and J. Y. Halpern. Worst-case background knowledge for privacy-preserving data publishing. In *ICDE*, pages 126–135. IEEE, 2007.

[25] F. McSherry and K. Talwar. Mechanism design via differential privacy. In *FOCS*, pages 94–103. IEEE, 2007.

[26] V. Rastogi, S. Hong, and D. Suciu. The boundary between privacy and utility in data publishing. In *VLDB*, pages 531–542, 2007.

[27] M. Rudelson and R. Vershynin. The least singular value of a random square matrix is $O(n^{-1/2})$. *Comptes rendus-Mathématique*, 2008.

[28] M. Rudelson and R. Vershynin. The Littlewood–Offord problem and invertibility of random matrices. *Advances in Mathematics*, 218(2):600–633, 2008.

[29] M. Rudelson and R. Vershynin. The smallest singular value of a random rectangular matrix. *Communications on Pure and Applied Mathematics*, pages 1707 – 1739, 2009.

[30] C. Skinner and N. Shlomo. Assessing identification risk in survey microdata using log-linear models. *Journal of the American Statistical Association*, 103(483):989–1001, 2008.

[31] A. Smith. Efficient, differentially private point estimators. *CoRR*, abs/0809.4794, 2008.

[32] L. Sweeney. k-anonymity: A model for protecting privacy. *International Journal on Uncertainty, Fuzziness and Knowledge-based Systems*, 10(5):557–570, 2002.

[33] S. L. Warner. Randomized response: A survey technique for eliminating evasive answer bias. *Journal of the American Statistical Association*, 60(309):63–69, 1965.

[34] X. Xiao and Y. Tao. M-invariance: towards privacy preserving re-publication of dynamic datasets. In *SIGMOD*, pages 689–700. ACM, 2007.

Privacy Amplification with Asymptotically Optimal Entropy Loss

Nishanth Chandran[*]
Department of Computer Science
UCLA
nishanth@cs.ucla.edu

Bhavana Kanukurthi[†]
Department of Computer Science
Boston University
bhavanak@cs.bu.edu

Rafail Ostrovsky[‡]
Department of Computer Science and Mathematics
UCLA
rafail@cs.ucla.edu

Leonid Reyzin[†]
Department of Computer Science
Boston University
reyzin@cs.bu.edu

ABSTRACT

We study the problem of "privacy amplification": key agreement between two parties who both know a weak secret w, such as a password. (Such a setting is ubiquitous on the internet, where passwords are the most commonly used security device.) We assume that the key agreement protocol is taking place in the presence of an active computationally unbounded adversary Eve. The adversary may have partial knowledge about w, so we assume only that w has some entropy from Eve's point of view. Thus, the goal of the protocol is to convert this non-uniform secret w into a uniformly distributed string R that is fully secret from Eve. R may then be used as a key for running symmetric cryptographic protocols (such as encryption, authentication, etc.).

Because we make no computational assumptions, the entropy in R can come only from w. Thus such a protocol must minimize the entropy loss during its execution, so that R is as long as possible. The best previous results have entropy loss of $\Theta(\kappa^2)$, where κ is the security parameter, thus requiring the password to be very long even for small values of κ. In this work, we present the first protocol for information-theoretic key agreement that has entropy loss **linear** in the security parameter. The result is optimal up to constant factors. We achieve our improvement through a somewhat surprising application of error-correcting codes for the edit distance.

Categories and Subject Descriptors

E.3 [**Data Encryption**]; E.4 [**Coding and Information Theory**]

General Terms

Theory, Security

Keywords

Privacy amplification, Information-theoretic key agreement, Entropy loss

1. INTRODUCTION

The classical problem of privacy amplification, introduced by Bennett, Brassard, and Robert [1], considers the setting in which two parties, Alice and Bob, start out knowing a common string w that is partially secret. Following [2], we make no assumption on the distribution of w beyond a lower bound on its entropy. The goal of Alice and Bob is to perform key agreement: to agree on a string R that is fully secret. Formally, R should be statistically close to uniform from the point of view of the adversary Eve (we will let $2^{-\kappa}$ be the statistical distance between the distribution of R and the uniform distribution, and call κ the *security parameter*). Such R can then be used as a key for symmetric cryptography.

We make no computational assumptions and therefore model Eve as being computationally unbounded. This requirement implies that all the entropy in R comes from w. Thus, one of the most important requirements of such a protocol is that the output length of R must be as long as possible given the entropy of w. The difference between the entropy of w and the length of R is called the *entropy loss*.

We can model the communication channel between Alice and Bob as authenticated or unsecured. Equivalently, we can model Eve as passive or active. If Eve is passive (i.e.,

*Research supported in part by NSF grants 0716835, 0716389, 0830803, 0916574.

†Research supported in part by National Science Foundation grants CNS-0831281 and CNS-0546614

‡Research supported in part by an IBM Faculty Award, Xerox Innovation Group Award, the Okawa Foundation Award, Intel, Teradata, NSF grants 0716835, 0716389, 0830803, 0916574, BSF grant and U.C. MICRO grant.

merely listens in on the messages between Alice and Bob but cannot modify them), strong extractors [17] provide an optimal solution to this problem. Alice simply sends an extractor seed to Bob, they both extract R from w using the seed, and the entropy loss can be as low as 2κ.

However, if Eve is active (i.e., can modify the messages), the problem becomes considerably harder. In particular, one needs to worry not only about achieving R that is $2^{-\kappa}$-close to uniform, but also about ensuring that Alice and Bob output *the same* R with probability at least $1 - 2^{-\kappa}$. While the specific focus of our paper is to obtain R of maximum length, there are other parameters that one might wish to optimize. For instance, one might wish to minimize the round complexity or to minimize the entropy required in w for the protocol to work. Renner and Wolf [19], building on a series of works by Maurer, Renner and Wolf [14, 15, 22, 16], presented the first protocol that is secure against active Eve and works even when w is less than half-entropic (i.e., $h_W \leq \lambda_w/2$ where h_W and λ_w denote the entropy and the length of w). Moreover, by the use of extractors with asymptotically optimal seed length [8] and through the analysis of Kanukurthi and Reyzin [12], it can be seen that the protocol of [19] achieves entropy loss of $\Theta(\kappa^2)$ and takes $\Theta(\kappa)$ rounds of communication. (The work of [12], which builds upon [19], achieves the same asymptotic parameters but considerably improves the constants hidden inside Θ by eliminating the need for complicated extractors.) Dodis and Wichs [7] reduce the number of messages in the protocol from $\Theta(k)$ to just 2, but do not improve the entropy loss. They also present a two-message non-constructive (in other words, non-polynomial-time) protocol with an entropy loss of $\Theta(\kappa)$. While this result shows the theoretical feasibility of achieving such a low entropy loss, the only efficient solution that matches this entropy loss relies on Random Oracles [3]—i.e., an "assumption" that a publicly known truly random function is available. (It should be noted that single-message protocols for the same problem exist [15, 5, 10]; however, they have entropy loss $\lambda_w - h_W + \Theta(\kappa)$ and require thus require w to be at least half-entropic.)

Achieving a *efficient* privacy amplification protocol with entropy loss $\Theta(\kappa)$ and without resorting to the Random Oracle Model has, until now, been an open question.

Our Contribution.

We construct the first efficient protocol for privacy amplification over unsecured channels whose entropy loss (and number of rounds) is linear in the security parameter κ. This security loss is optimal up to constant factors, because extractor bounds require entropy loss at least $2\kappa - O(1)$ even in the case of authenticated channels [18]. We thus demonstrate that, up to constant factors, privacy amplification over unsecured channels can be as entropy-efficient as over authenticated ones.

Extension to Information Reconciliation/Fuzzy Extractors.

Consider the following generalization: Alice starts out with w, but Bob starts out with w' that is close to w in some metric space. Their goal is still the same: to agree on the same uniform string R. This problem is known as privacy amplification with information reconciliation [1] or as fuzzy extractors [6]. Constructions secure against active Eve appeared in [20, 5, 10, 12].

This setting arises, for example, when Alice and Bob have access to a (possibly) noisy channel that can be partially eavesdropped by Eve; or when a trusted server (Alice) stores the biometric of a user (Bob), and the user subsequently uses his fresh biometric reading to authenticate himself to the server; or when Alice and Bob are mobile nodes wanting to authenticate each other based on the fact that their knowledge of a location is greater than Eve's (e.g., if they are much closer to a particular location than Eve, and thus are able to observe it at higher resolution).

Using the same approach as in [12], our protocol extends to this setting, as well.

A Related Problem.

Ishai, Kushilevitz, Ostrovsky, and Sahai [9] consider the problem of constructing a two-party protocol that extracts m "clean" instances of a joint distribution (X, Y) from $\mathcal{O}(m)$ "dirty" instances. This task can be viewed as a generalization of randomness extraction (the special case is when X and Y are identical bits). However, the techniques of [9] do not directly apply to the case when we have only *one* instance of a distribution. Furthermore, the entropy loss achieved in their work is significantly greater (constant factor times m) than in our case, where we obtain entropy loss independent of the entropy or length of the secret and linear in the security parameter.

Construction Techniques.

Our starting point is the protocol for interactive authentication from [12], which generalizes the authentication protocol of Renner and Wolf [19]. We focus only on the case when Alice and Bob share the same secret w; i.e., when $w = w'$ (as mentioned, the more general case can be addressed in the exact same way as in [12]). Using known techniques from the works of [19] and [12], it suffices to construct a message authentication protocol that can authentically transfer a message m from Alice to Bob using w.

The authentication protocol of [19, 12] works by authenticating bits of m one by one. For each bit of m, Bob sends Alice a random extractor seed, and, if the bit is equal to 1, Alice responds with the output of the extractor on input w using Bob's seed. Alice also sends Bob a random extractor seed of her own, to which he always responds (applying the extractor to w using Alice's seed), regardless of the bit of m. Each extractor output is κ bits long. This results in $\Theta(\kappa)$ entropy loss for every bit authenticated, and $\Theta(\kappa^2)$ entropy loss overall, because the message being authenticated needs to be $\Theta(\kappa)$ bits long (it is, actually, a MAC key in the protocol of [12]). The security proof shows that to succeed in breaking such an authentication protocol, the active adversary Eve must respond with *at least one* extractor output on her own without interacting with either Alice or Bob. Because the extractor output is a nearly-uniform κ-bit string, Eve cannot succeed with probability much higher than $2^{-\kappa}$.

The high level intuition for our protocol is as follows. If we were to shorten the length of the extractor output (in the authentication protocol) to be a constant number of bits, then we only lose $\Theta(1)$ bits of entropy for every bit of m and obtain an $\Theta(\kappa)$ entropy loss overall. On the other hand, the success probability of an adversary is a constant (by the same proof as before). If we could instead now ensure that Eve must respond with *several* (namely, $\Theta(\kappa)$) extractor outputs on her own, then we could show that the success probability is $2^{-\kappa}$. This can be done by encoding m in a special error-detecting code of distance $\Theta(\kappa)$ and ensuring that to introduce $\Theta(\kappa)$ errors required to avoid detection, Eve must come up with $\Theta(\kappa)$ extractor outputs on her own.

It turns out that the code we need is a code for the edit distance [13], for the following reasons. We observe that, since the authentication of m is done bit-by-bit, Eve can change m by inserting individual bits, deleting them, or changing them from 0 to 1 or from 1 to 0. Deletions and changes from 0 to 1 require Eve to guess an extractor output on a fresh random seed. Because in the context of [19, 12] the length of m and the number of 1s in it are known a priori to both Alice and Bob, insertions and changes of 1 to 0 must be accompanied by deletions and changes of 0 to 1. Thus, Eve can create edit errors in the message, but at least a quarter of the errors introduced (namely, deletions and changes of 0 to 1) require her to find an extractor output on her own. So, if instead of authenticating the bits of the m, Alice first encoded m in an error-detecting code for 4κ edit errors, Eve would have to respond with at least κ extractor outputs on her own. Of course, the length of the codeword must still remain linear in the length of m. The codes of Schulman and Zuckerman [21] have this property (though we need to modify them to ensure the number of 1s is the same for every codoword of a givon length).

Proof Techniques.

While using an error-detecting code and shortening the extractor outputs intuitively may seem to work in a straightforward manner, the proofs turn out to be quite tricky. In particular, we will need to use a proof technique that is completely different from the one used in [19] and [12], for the following reason. In the authentication protocols of [19, 12], Alice authenticates bits of the message one at a time. The proofs make use of induction on the length of the message received so far by Bob to show that if Eve was successful in changing any bit(s) of the message, then Eve must have responded to *one* extractor output on a random seed on her own. We, on the other hand, cannot use such an induction argument since we need to precisely characterize *how many* extractor outputs Eve must have given in relation to the number of bits modified. Instead, we use a new proof technique wherein we view the entire protocol transcript from the point of view of Eve as a string of literals, where each literal represent an interaction either with Alice or Bob. Using combinatorial arguments, we show that Eve cannot interleave these literals to her advantage without having to respond to many extractor outputs.

Next, one might like to claim that if Eve were to respond with multiple extractor outputs to random, independent seeds, then since the seeds are independent, her success in giving the right response for each of the seeds is also independent. Unfortunately, this intuition does not quite hold and there are subtleties in proving the theorem in this manner. This is because, while average min-entropy (introduced in [6]) gives us a guarantee that on average the entropy in w does not get reduced by too much, it may be the case that there may be a particular bad run (which occurs with very small probability) in which all information about w is revealed. This, in turn, destroys all independence in the probabilities of Eve's success. To counter this, we take the approach of considering two separate cases — the case when the run does not reveal too much about w and where we can argue "sufficient independence" (which happens with high probability), and the case when the run might reveal too much about w (perhaps all of it) and we cannot argue independence (which happens with low probability). Now, if we make an assumption that w begins with $\Theta(\kappa)$ bits of entropy more than what would be needed otherwise, we can show that the probability with which independence does not hold is low enough for our theorem to be true.

Organization of the paper.

We introduce notation and define our security model in Section 2. In Section 3, we briefly describe some of the existing tools that we require for our construction. Our main construction is given in Section 4. We give the proof of our main theorem in 5, providing complete details in the full version [4].

2. PRELIMINARIES

Notation.

Let U_l denote the uniform distribution on $\{0,1\}^l$. Let X_1, X_2 be two probability distributions over some set S. Their *statistical distance* is

$$\mathbf{SD}(X_1, X_2) \stackrel{\text{def}}{=} \max_{T\subseteq S}\{\Pr[X_1 \in T] - \Pr[X_2 \in T]\}$$

$$= \frac{1}{2}\sum_{s\in S}\left|\Pr_{X_1}[s] - \Pr_{X_2}[s]\right|$$

(they are said to be ε-close if $\mathbf{SD}(X_1, X_2) \leq \varepsilon$). The *min-entropy* of a random variable W is $\mathbf{H}_\infty(W) = -\log(\max_w \Pr[W = w])$. For a joint distribution (W, E), define the (average) conditional min-entropy of W given E [6] as

$$\widetilde{\mathbf{H}}_\infty(W \mid E) = -\log(\mathop{\mathbf{E}}_{e\leftarrow E}(2^{-\mathbf{H}_\infty(W|E=e)}))$$

(here the expectation is taken over e for which $\Pr[E = e]$ is nonzero). A computationally unbounded adversary who receives the value of E cannot give the correct value of W (in a single attempt) with probability greater than $2^{-\widetilde{\mathbf{H}}_\infty(W|E)}$. Throughout this paper, for any string x, we use the notation λ_x to denote its length and h_x to denote its entropy (i.e, $\mathbf{H}_\infty(X)$). We make use of the following lemma [6, Lemma 2.2b], which states that the average min-entropy of a variable from the point of view of an adversary does not decrease by more than the number of bits (correlated with the variable) observed by the adversary.

LEMMA 1. *If B has at most 2^λ possible values, then* $\widetilde{\mathbf{H}}_\infty(A \mid B) \geq \mathbf{H}_\infty(A, B) - \lambda \geq \mathbf{H}_\infty(A) - \lambda$.

We also use the following lemma [6, Lemma 2.2a], which says that min-entropy is t bits less than the average min-entropy with probability at most 2^{-t}.

LEMMA 2. *For any $\delta > 0$, the conditional entropy $\mathbf{H}_\infty(A \mid B = b)$ is at least $\widetilde{\mathbf{H}}_\infty(A \mid B) - \log(\frac{1}{\delta})$ with probability at least $1 - \delta$ over the choice of b.*

Model and Security definition.

We now present the formal definition of a Privacy Amplification Protocol. Our definition is actually a modification of the definition from [12, Definition 1] (which focuses on the case where Alice and Bob have correlated secrets, while we restrict our attention to the case where they have identical secrets). Let $w \in \{0,1\}^n$ be chosen according to distribution W be the secret value held by Alice and Bob respectively. Let Protocol (A, B) be executed in the presence of an active adversary Eve. Let C_a be the random variable describing A's view of the communication when (A, B) is executed in the presence of Eve. Likewise, define C_b. (We will use c_a, c_b to denote specific values of these variables.) We denote the private coins of Alice and Bob by r_a and r_b respectively. Alice's output will be denoted by $\mathsf{k_A} = \mathsf{A}(w, c_a, r_a)$, and Bob's by $\mathsf{k_B} = \mathsf{B}(w, c_b, r_b)$ (if successful, both will be of length λ_k; rejection will be denoted by a special symbol $\perp$). Let $C = C_a \cup C_b$ be Eve's view of the protocol; because Eve is computationally unbounded, we can assume she is deterministic.

DEFINITION 1. *An interactive protocol* (A, B) *played by Alice and Bob on a communication channel fully controlled by an adversary Eve, is a* $(h_W, \lambda_k, \delta, \epsilon)$-privacy amplification protocol *if it satisfies the following properties whenever* $\mathbf{H}_\infty(W) \geq h_W$:

1. *Correctness. If Eve is passive, then* $\Pr[\mathsf{k_A} = \mathsf{k_B}] = 1$.
2. *Robustness. The probability that the following experiment outputs "Eve wins" is at most* $2^{-\delta}$*: sample* w *from* W*; let* c_a, c_b *be the communication upon execution of* (A, B) *with Eve(e) actively controlling the channel, and let* $\mathsf{A}(w, c_a, r_a) = \mathsf{k_A}, \mathsf{B}(w, c_b, r_b) = \mathsf{k_B}$*. Output "Eve wins" if* $(\mathsf{k_A} \neq \mathsf{k_B} \wedge \mathsf{k_A} \neq \perp \wedge \mathsf{k_B} \neq \perp)$.
3. *Extraction. Letting* C *denote an active Eve's view of the protocol,*

$$\mathbf{SD}\left((\mathsf{k_A}, C \mid \mathsf{k_A} \neq \perp), (U_{\lambda_k}, C)\right) \leq \epsilon$$

and

$$\mathbf{SD}\left((\mathsf{k_B}, C \mid \mathsf{k_B} \neq \perp), (U_{\lambda_k}, C)\right) \leq \epsilon.$$

An important building block that we will construct is an interactive authentication protocol. In an authentication protocol, Alice additionally takes as input the message m to be authenticated to Bob. We now present the formal definition. (The definition we use is just an interactive variant of one-time message authentication codes. See [12, Definition 4] for one such definition.)

DEFINITION 2. *An interactive protocol* (A, B) *played by Alice and Bob on a communication channel fully controlled by an adversary Eve, is a* (h_W, κ)-interactive authentication protocol *if it satisfies the following properties whenever* $\mathbf{H}_\infty(W) \geq h_W$:

1. *Correctness. If Eve is passive, then* $\Pr[m_A = m_B = m] = 1$.
2. *Robustness. The probability that the following experiment outputs "Eve wins" is at most* $2^{-\kappa}$*: sample* w *from* W*; let* c_a, c_b *be the communication upon execution of* (A, B) *with Eve actively controlling the channel, and let* $\mathsf{A}(w, c_a, r_a, m) = m_A, \mathsf{B}(w, c_b, r_b) = m_B$*. Output "Eve wins" if* $(m_B \neq m_A \wedge m_A \neq \perp \wedge m_B \neq \perp)$.

3. BUILDING BLOCKS

We begin by presenting the building blocks needed for our main construction of a privacy amplification protocol with optimal entropy loss.

3.1 Extractors

Extractors [17] yield a close-to-uniform string from a random variable with high min-entropy, using a uniformly random seed i as a kind of catalyst. Strong extractors are ones in which the extracted string looks random even in the presence of the seed.

DEFINITION 3. *Let* $\mathsf{Ext} : \{0,1\}^n \to \{0,1\}^l$ *be a polynomial time probabilistic function that uses* r *bits of randomness. We say that* Ext *is an* (n, t, l, ε)-strong extractor *if for all pairs of random variables* W *such that* $w \in W$ *is an* n*-bit string and* $\mathbf{H}_\infty(W) \geq t$*, we have* $\mathbf{SD}\left((\mathsf{Ext}(W; X), X), (U_l, X)\right) \leq \varepsilon$*, where* X *is the uniform distribution over* $\{0,1\}^r$.

For the purposes of this work, we would like to argue that extractor outputs are hard to predict for an adversary even when she has some external information $E = e$. The following lemma [12, Lemma 1] (the proof can be found in the full version [11]) shows that strings extracted by extractors have high average min-entropy, even given the seed (as long the entropy of the secret w is high even when conditioned on the external information e).

LEMMA 3. *Let* Ext *be a* (n, t, l, ε)*-strong extractor. Then if* $\mathbf{H}_\infty(W \mid E = e) \geq t$*, and* W *consists of* n*-bit strings,* $\tilde{\mathbf{H}}_\infty(\mathsf{Ext}(W|e, X) \mid X, E) \geq \min\left(l, \log \frac{1}{\varepsilon}\right) - 1$.

3.2 Edit distance codes

Codes for insertion and deletion errors were first considered in the work of Levenshtein [13]. The first polynomial-time encodable and decodable codes that have constant rate and can correct a constant fraction of errors were given by Schulman and Zuckerman in [21]. For our application, we only require the code to be polynomial-time encodable and not necessarily polynomial-time decodable (this will be sufficient to get polynomial-time error detection, which is all we need). Let m be a message of length λ_m. For any two strings c and c' of length λ_c, let $\mathsf{EditDis}(c, c')$ denote the edit distance between c and c'; i.e., the number of single-bit insert and delete operations required to change string c to c' is $\mathsf{EditDis}(c, c')$.

DEFINITION 4. *Let* $m \in \{0,1\}^{\lambda_m}$*. For some constant* $0 < e_A < 1$*, a function* $\mathsf{Edit}(\cdot) : \{0,1\}^{\lambda_m} \to \{0,1\}^{\lambda_c}$*, is a* (λ_m, e_A, ρ)-error-detecting code *for edit errors, if* $\rho\lambda_c = \lambda_m$ *and satisfies the following properties:*

- $c = \mathsf{Edit}(m)$ *can be computed in polynomial (in* λ_m*) time, given* m*, for all* $m \in \{0,1\}^{\lambda_m}$;
- *For any* $m, m' \in \{0,1\}^{\lambda_m}$ *with* $m \neq m'$, $\mathsf{EditDis}(c', c) > e_A\lambda_c$*, where* $c = \mathsf{Edit}(m)$ *and* $c' = \mathsf{Edit}(m')$.

$\rho = \frac{\lambda_m}{\lambda_c}$*, is called the* rate *of the code.*

The theorem from Schulman and Zuckerman [21] is as follows:

THEOREM 1. *Let $0 < e_A < 1$ be a constant. Then, for some constant ρ, there exists a (λ_m, e_A, ρ)-error-detecting code for edit errors.*

Remark. We actually require an error-detecting code Edit(·) for edit distances, in which the Hamming weight (number of 1s) of every codeword is the same. Such codes can be constructed easily[1] using the same construction of Schulman and Zuckerman [21], without losing out on the constant parameters ρ and e_A.

3.3 Interactive authentication protocol

We use the interactive authentication protocol from [12] that is used by Alice and Bob to send bits authentically to each other. Let the security parameter be κ. Let Alice and Bob share an n-bit secret $w \in W$ with min-entropy h_W. Let the message that Alice wishes to authenticate be $m = m_1 \dots m_{\lambda_m}$. Assume that Bob knows λ_m and the number of ones in m (say wt(m)). Let Ext be a $(\lambda_w, t, \kappa + 1, 2^{-\kappa-1})$-strong extractor with seed length q bits. That is, Ext takes seeds of input q, outputs κ + 1-bit strings that are $2^{-\kappa-1}$-close to uniform, as long as the input has sufficient entropy t. (In particular, if $t \geq 3\kappa + 1$ is sufficient if one is using universal hashing.) The authentication protocol from [12], which is a modification of the scheme from [19], is presented below.

Protocol Auth(w, m):
For $i = 1$ to λ_m

1. Alice sends Bob a fresh random challenge $x_i \in_r \{0,1\}^q$.
2. Bob receives x_i, sends $r_{x_i} = \mathsf{Ext}(w; x_i)$, and a fresh random challenge $y_i \in_r \{0,1\}^q$.
3. Alice receives r_{x_i}, y_i, verifies that $r_{x_i} = \mathsf{Ext}(w; x_i)$ and aborts if not.
   She sends $(1, r_{y_i} = \mathsf{Ext}(w; y_i))$ if $m_i = 1$, and $(0, \perp)$ otherwise.
4. Bob receives m_i, r_{y_i} aborts if $m_i = 1$ and $r_{y_i} \neq \mathsf{Ext}(w; y_i)$ and accepts otherwise.
   If $i = \lambda_m$, Bob verifies that the number of ones in the received string = wt(m); aborts otherwise.

Note that step 3 and 4 of each iteration are combined with steps 1 and 2, respectively, of the next iteration.

We say that Eve *responded to a fresh random challenge* sent by Alice (Bob), if Alice (Bob) sends a challenge and Eve responds to it without having received a response to an extractor challenge (on any, not necessarily the same, seed) in the meantime. (Note that if Eve sends $\perp$ in response to Bob's challenge, thereby authenticating a zero bit, it is not considered as a response to a fresh random challenge.) The intuition for the security of the above protocol is as follows. Note that Eve can insert 0 bits (this does not require a response from Alice) and can change a 1 bit to a 0 bit. Since, Bob knows λ_m as well as wt(m), if Eve were to insert 0 bits or change a 1 bit to a 0, then she must also either remove 0 bits or insert 1 bits. Now, removing 0 bits sent by Alice or inserting 1 bits require answering a random challenge of Alice or Bob. By Lemma 3, we have that the r_{x_i} and r_{y_i} values have entropy κ from Eve's point of view. Since the responses (r_{x_i} and r_{y_i}) have entropy κ bits, Eve cannot respond to a fresh random challenge by Alice or Bob with probability $> 2^{-\kappa}$. Hence, the probability of Eve's success can be shown to be at most $2^{-\kappa}$.

To analyze the entropy loss, we see that every round of interaction reveals $\kappa + 1$ bits of information correlated to w in the case when $m_i = 0$ and $2\kappa+2$ bits of information correlated to w in the case when $m_i = 1$. Therefore, by Lemma 1, as long as $\mathbf{H}_\infty(W) \geq t + (\kappa+1)(\lambda_m + \mathsf{wt(m)})$, (where t is the threshold entropy that is needed by the specific extractor used for the extraction to be secure), the entropy in w is sufficient for the extractor to work until the last round (to be precise, we need here an extractor that works for *average* min-entropy; see [12] for details). This leads to an entropy loss of $\Theta(\lambda_m \kappa)$ in the authentication protocol, which translates to an entropy loss of $\Theta(\kappa^2)$ for the key agreement protocol (because the key agreement protocol of [12] needs to authenticate a message—namely, a MAC key—of length $\Theta(\kappa)$).

4. MAIN CONSTRUCTION

Our main construction of a privacy amplification protocol is obtained by building an improved authentication protocol with low entropy loss.

In particular, our main theorem is:

THEOREM 2. *Let κ be the security parameter. Let Edit(·) be a $(4(\kappa+1), e_A, \rho)$-error-detecting code for constants $0 < e_A, \rho < 1$. Let Ext be a $(h_W, t, \tau, 2^{-\tau})$-strong extractor with $\tau = \frac{\rho}{e_A} + 1$. Then there exists an efficient (h_W, κ)-interactive authentication protocol for messages[2] of length $4(\kappa+1)$ with entropy loss $\frac{8\tau(\kappa+1)}{\rho}$. The protocol works as long $h_W \geq \frac{8\tau(\kappa+1)}{\rho} + t + \kappa + 1$.* [3]

Given that e_A, ρ and τ are constants, using the result of [12] on converting a message authentication protocol to a protocol for privacy amplification, we obtain the following corollary to Theorem 2:

COROLLARY 1. *There exists an efficient $(h_W, \lambda_k, 2^{-\kappa}, \epsilon)$ privacy amplification protocol with entropy loss $\mathcal{O}(\kappa)$. The length of the extracted key $\lambda_k = h_W - 2\log\frac{1}{\epsilon} - \mathcal{O}(\kappa)$.*

The rest of the paper will focus on proving Theorem 2. Below, we present our improved authentication protocol. We present the proof of security and entropy loss for our authentication protocol in Section 5.

Improved Authentication Protocol.

We start with the authentication protocol described in Section 3.3 and decrease the length of the extractor output in each round to be a constant τ (instead of $\kappa+1$). This gives

[1] Schulman and Zuckerman [21] build a two-layered code constructing a greedy code for edit errors on logarithmic size blocks of messages. By considering the space of codewords for this greedy code to be such that the Hamming weight of all codewords is the same, one can get the required construction.

[2] We note that the message length can be $z(\kappa+1)$, for arbitrary constant z. In this case, we require $\tau = \frac{4\rho}{ze_A} - 1$.

[3] It is easy to see that if we universal hashing as our extractor, t can be set to be $3\tau + 1$ thereby giving us a protocol that works as long as $h_W = \Theta(\kappa)$.

us an $\Theta(\lambda_m)$ entropy loss for the authentication protocol as desired. Unfortunately, the security of this protocol no longer holds. The security proof in [12] shows that in order to get Bob to accept any message $m' \neq m$, Eve must respond to at least *one* fresh random challenge from either Alice or Bob. The probability with which Eve could respond to a fresh random challenge from either Alice or Bob is $2^{-\tau+1}$, which not high enough if τ is a constant.

To rectify this problem, we ensure that in order to make Bob accept a different message, Eve must respond to *many* (namely, $\Theta(\kappa)$) fresh random challenges, which translates into a success probability of only $2^{-\kappa}$ as desired. To do so, we have Alice transmit the message $c = \mathsf{Edit}(m)$ (see Definition 4) and Bob verify that c is a valid codeword (or, equivalently, since we do not require that codeword validity be efficiently verifiable, Alice can send m to Bob in the clear and Bob can re-encode it to check if he gets c).

We now describe the authentication protocol precisely. Let the security parameter be κ. Let Alice and Bob share an λ_w-bit secret $w \in W$ with min-entropy h_W. Let the message that Alice wishes to authenticate be $m \in \{0,1\}^{\lambda_m}$. Let Ext be a average-case $(\lambda_w, t, \tau, 2^{-\tau})$-strong extractor with seed length q bits for some constants tand τ. Let $\mathsf{Edit}(\cdot)$ be a (λ_m, e_A, ρ)-error-detecting code for constants $0 < e_A, \rho < 1$, such that the Hamming weight of all codewords is the same (call it $\mathsf{wt(c)}$).

Protocol $\mathsf{NewAuth}(w, m)$:

1. Alice sends Bob the message m. Let the message received by Bob be m'.
2. Alice and Bob execute protocol $\mathsf{Auth}(w, c)$ for $c = \mathsf{Edit}(m)$, using extractor Ext for all the responses.
3. Let the string received by Bob be denoted by c'. Bob computes $\mathsf{Edit}(m')$. If $c' \neq \mathsf{Edit}(m')$, then Bob rejects. Otherwise, Bob accepts m' as the message received.

Intuition.

The key to our improvement is to show that protocol Auth gives Eve an edit channel in the following sense. We will show that the success probability of Eve in changing the message c to a message c' is related by a constant factor to the edit distance between these two messages; since this distance must be greater than $e_A\lambda_c$ for Bob to accept at the end, Eve will fail if $a_A\lambda_c$ is high enough.

Indeed, consider what Eve can do. She can not deliver a message from Alice to Bob (this corresponds to deleting a bit from the c), but then she would have to reply to Alice's challenge contained in that message on her own to avoid detection; the probability of guessing a correct response to such a challenge is at most $2^{-\tau+1}$. She can also try to change a message from Alice from conveying a "0" bit to conveying a "1" bit, but that would require coming up with a response to Bob's challenge, which again can happen with probability at most $2^{-\tau+1}$. If Eve attempts to do these things multiple times, the probabilities are (almost) multiply, because of the freshness of random extractor seeds, which ensures (almost) independence She can also "insert" bits by replying to Bob's challenges on her own or change a "1" to a "0", but since the number of 1s and the total length are fixed, she will have to pay elsewhere with deletions and changes of "0" to "1".

We translate this intuition into a proof in the next section.

5. PROOF OF MAIN THEOREM

In this section, we prove our main theorem. Namely we show that the new authentication protocol we presented in Section 4 is a secure authentication scheme with $\Theta(\lambda_m)$ entropy loss, where λ_m is the length of the message being authenticated. Some proof details are omitted for lack of space and are presented in the full version [4].

We prove this in two broad steps. First we show that the authentication protocol gives Eve an edit distance channel in the following sense – Eve can modify several bits of the message that Alice authenticates to Bob. However, irrespective of what algorithm Eve uses or what modifications she does, the edit distance between the two messages can be bounded in terms of the security parameter.

Technical Challenges.

As mentioned before, the security of [19, 12] rely on showing that for Eve to modify the message that Alice sent, she would have to respond to at least one fresh random challenge on her own. They prove this using induction on the length of the message received by Bob so far and show that at any stage either Eve has responded to a random challenge on her own or the string received by Bob is not non-trivially different from what Alice sent.

We, on the other hand, cannot use such an inductive proof on the length of the message for the following reason. The statement we want to make is not about whether Eve responded to a random challenge on her own or not. Instead, we would want to keep track of how many random challenges Eve responded to **and** precisely study the effects of responding to these challenges on the edit distance of the messages. Since the entire protocol is just an interleaving of challenges and responses sent back and forth, categorizing points in the protocol where Eve responded to a fresh random challenge on her own becomes a delicate task. In fact, it turns out that viewing the protocol in terms of the message received by Bob (or Alice) as was done in [19, 12] does not capture all the information needed to categorize the points where Eve had to respond to a random challenge.

Instead, we need to use a new proof technique in which we view the entire protocol from Eve's perspective. In fact, we represent Eve's view of any valid run of the authentication protocol by a string E. This string will allow us to capture all the information including the order in which Eve interacted with the honest parties. This turns out be crucial in categorizing points in the protocol in which Eve had to respond to a random challenge. Once we do this, we use combinatorial arguments to relate the number of random challenges that Eve responded to on her own to the edit distance between the messages of the honest parties. Finally, we compute the probability with which Eve can respond to all the fresh random challenges.

Organization.

In Section 5.1 we will introduce the notation for the string representation of the protocol. Using that we will characterize precisely (in Section 5.1.1), the points in the protocol (that actually correspond to literals in the string E) where Eve must respond to a fresh random challenge. We call these points as costly literals. Now, if we could compute the probability with which Eve can respond to every fresh random challenge, and relate the number of costly literals in E to the edit distance between the two messages m and m', then we will be done. We do precisely this. In Section 5.2, we present the details of relating the edit distance between m and m' to the number of costly literals in the string E. Finally, we compute the probability with which Eve can respond to fresh random challenge (that correspond to the costly literals in E) in Section 5.3.

Notation.

Let $\mathbb{A}$ be an alphabet. Let $a \in \mathbb{A}$ be a literal from the alphabet. When we write a^*, we mean all strings of the form $\underbrace{aa\cdots a}_{i}$, where $i \geq 0$ is an integer. When $i \geq 1$, we write a^+. Let x_1 and x_2 denote any two strings. We write $x_1||x_2$ to denote the concatenation of the two strings.

5.1 String representation of the authentication protocol

We now present our proof ideas in more detail. As mentioned before, we view the entire protocol as it takes place from Eve's perspective. In any round i, Eve's interaction with Alice will consist of Eve sending a challenge y_i and response $(\mathsf{Ext}(w; x_{i-1}))$ to the challenge issued by Alice in the previous round (x_{i-1}). Alice then sends Eve a challenge x_i and a response to the challenge received by her in the previous round (i.e., $\mathsf{Ext}(w; y_{i-1})$). We will call this two-message interaction that starts with a message from Eve to Alice and then from Alice to Eve as a *roundtrip* between Eve and Alice. To be more concise, we will use the literal a to denote this *roundtrip* that takes place between Eve and Alice. Let us now consider Eve's interaction with Bob. In any round i, Eve's interaction with Bob starts with Eve sending a challenge x_i and response $(\mathsf{Ext}(w; y_{i-1}))$ to the challenge issued by Bob in the previous round (y_{i-1}). Bob then sends Eve a challenge y_i and a response to the challenge received by her in the previous round (i.e., $\mathsf{Ext}(w; x_{i-1})$). We denote this *roundtrip* between Eve and Bob by b.

The notation a and b will be important for our proof. Note that we do not index a or b by the round i. This is because that information will largely be irrelevant to us. However, in any roundtrip with Alice, Alice is authenticating some bit (either 0 or 1) and Bob is receiving some bit (either 0 or 1). This allows us to have two different literals, a_0 and a_1 depending on which bit Alice is authenticating in that roundtrip. Likewise, we will also use b_0 and b_1 to denote Eve's roundtrips with Bob. If we do not subscript the a or b literals, it means that the claim holds irrespective of the bit being authenticated.

In the first interaction between Eve and Bob, he receives just a challenge from Eve and no response to any challenge. So we will distinguish the first interaction between Eve and Bob (from subsequent interactions) by denoting it as b_c. Likewise, in the last interaction between Eve and Alice, Alice receives **only** a response from Eve and no challenge (to which Alice would have had to respond to). So we will denote this last interaction between Eve and Alice by a_r.

Using this notation, we can write out the entire protocol from Eve's point of view by simply creating a string (call it E) denoting Eve's actions. As an example, if Eve is passive and Alice is authenticating $m = m_1, m_2, \cdots, m_{\lambda_m}$ to Bob, then $\mathrm{E} = b_c, a_{m_1}, b_{m_1}, a_{m_2}, b_{m_2}, \cdots, a_{m_{\lambda_m}}, b_{m_{\lambda_m}}, a_r$. Note that since Eve might be active, E will not necessarily take the structure as above. Instead E can be any interleaving of a and b variables.

Let $\alpha(\mathrm{E})$ be a function that outputs the subscripts of the a literals (other than a_r) read out in order. Then it is easy to see that $\alpha(\mathrm{E})$ represents the message authenticated by Alice. Likewise if $\beta(\mathrm{E})$ is a function that outputs the subscripts of the b literals (other than b_c) read out in order, then $\beta(\mathrm{E})$ is nothing but the message received by Bob. Observe that if Eve is passive, E will take the structure described above and $\alpha(\mathrm{E}) = \beta(\mathrm{E})$ (which is consistent with the fact that Alice's and Bob's messages are equal).

(Note that the literals a_r, b_c do not form a part of the messages $\alpha(\mathrm{E}), \beta(\mathrm{E})$. The literal b_c is defined for semantic purposes. The literal a_r, on the other hand, will be needed to make the edit distance bounds go through.)

Recall that we would like to use the string representation E, to categorize those points in the protocol where Eve would have to respond to a fresh random challenge. This brings us to the notion of *costly literals.*

DEFINITION 5. *A literal in E is marked as costly, if in the real run of the protocol (that E represents) Eve would have to respond to a fresh random challenge on her own in the roundtrip corresponding to the costly literal.*

5.1.1 Characterizing costly literals in string E

In this section, we precisely characterize the literals in E that are marked costly. We use the following lemma, the proof of which can be found in the full version of this paper [4].

LEMMA 4. *The following statements about costly literals are true:*

1. *Any $a-$literal is marked as costly if it is not immediately preceded by a $b-$literal in E.*
2. *A b_1 literal is a costly literal if it is not immediately preceded by a $a-$literal.*
3. *In addition, a b_1-literal is also marked as costly literal if all the $a-$ literals contained between this b_1-literal and the previous $b-$literal occurring in E are all a_0-literals. In other words, if the sequence looks like this $b^* a_0^+ \underline{b_1}$ then the underlined b_1 literal is marked as costly.*

5.2 Bounding edit distance in terms of the number of costly literals

We wish to show that a high edit distance between $\alpha(\mathrm{E})$ and $\beta(\mathrm{E})$ cannot be achieved without a lot of costly literals. In other words, we wish to construct a method to convert $\alpha(\mathrm{E})$ into $\beta(\mathrm{E})$ such that the total number of edit operations (insertions and deletions) performed is bounded by a constant times the number of costly literals. We will do this in two steps:

1. First, we will present an algorithm that converts the string E into a new string E′ with the property that Alice and Bob receive the exact same messages in E′ i.e., $\alpha(\mathrm{E}') = \beta(\mathrm{E}')$. Moreover this message is nothing but the message received by Bob in E i.e., $\beta(\mathrm{E}') = \beta(\mathrm{E})$. We will do this in such a manner that the total number of edit operations performed (in order to convert E to E′) will be at most $4\mathsf{L}$, where L is the number of costly literals in E.

2. Next, it will become apparent from the above algorithm description, that the exact edit operations used to convert E to E′ can also be used to convert $\alpha(\mathrm{E})$ into $\beta(\mathrm{E})$ directly. (In that sense, the intermediary step of converting E into E′ is only for clarity of exposition; it does not change the edit distance in any way since the underlying edit operations are the same.)

The rest of this section is devoted to formally stating and proving the relation between the edit distance and the number of costly literals in E. For clarity of exposition, we state our theorems in the case where the string to be authenticated is balanced (i.e., the number of 1s and 0s are equal). The proof trivially extends to the case when this may not be true, but Bob knows the number of 1s in the string (as is the case with the edit distance code Edit(·) used). Let the number of costly literals in E be at most L. Then the following theorem states that the edit distance between the message authenticated by Alice and received by Bob is at most 4L.

THEOREM 3. *Let E be a string consisting of a_0, b_0, a_1, b_1 literals (as well as the special literals a_r, b_c) as defined above. Let it hold that the number of times each literal appears in the string E is the same (excluding the special literals which appear just once). Let the number of costly literals in E be at most* L. *Let E′ be the string as defined above. Then the edit distance between E and E′ is at most* 4L.

PROOF. As mentioned before, we will first focus on converting E that has at most L costly literals into E′ such that $\alpha(\mathrm{E}') = \beta(\mathrm{E}') = \beta(\mathrm{E})$ using at most 4L edit operations. It will be evident after this, that these edit operations can be used to convert $\alpha(\mathrm{E})$ into $\beta(\mathrm{E})$. We first present a sketch of the proof.

1. We first scan E and mark what we call the *edit* literals in E. These edit literals are marked such that the edit distance between E and E′ is precisely the number of edit literals in E.
2. Now, we need to show that if the number of costly literals is L, then the number of edit literals is at most 4L. It will be easier to prove the above statement by categorizing edit literals into (disjoint sets of) *good edit literals* and *bad edit literals*. Our proof will be in three steps:
   (a) Using the notation, *#bad* to denote the number of bad edit literals and *#edit* to denote the number of edit literals, we first show that $\#edit \leq 2\times\#bad$ (Lemma 5).
   (b) Next, letting *#costly* to denote the number of costly literals, we will show that $\#bad \leq 2\times\#costly = 2\mathsf{L}$ (Lemma 6).
   (c) Finally, combining the above two lemmas, we get $\#edit \leq 4\times\ \#costly = 4\mathsf{L}$, which is the required statement.

□

We now proceed to give the details of the above proof. We begin by defining *edit* literals. Next, we show how to mark literals as good edit literals and bad edit literals.

DEFINITION 6. *Edit Literals: An edit literal is any a literal that needs to be deleted from E or any b literal that needs to be inserted into E to obtain E′. (When we say that a b literal is inserted, we actually mean that the "b literal" is inserted as a corresponding "a literal". If a literal b_p, $p \in \{0,1\}$ is marked as an edit literal then an a_p literal is inserted in the appropriate position.)*

Clearly the edit distance between E and E′ is precisely the number of edit literals in E. As we describe next, to mark the edit literals in E, we first split E into disjoint substrings and mark out the edit literals in each substring.

MARKING BAD/GOOD EDIT LITERALS IN E. To do this, let E be written as the concatenation of k strings; i.e., $\mathrm{E} = \mathrm{E}_1||\mathrm{E}_2||\cdots||\mathrm{E}_k$. Each E_i consists of a continuous sequence of one or more a literals followed by one or more b literals (except for the first and last E_i's. E_1 might not have any a literals and E_k might not have any b literals.) As examples, consider $\mathrm{E} = \underbrace{a_1, a_1, a_1, b_c, b_1}_{\mathrm{E}_1}, a_0, \cdots, b_0, \underbrace{a_1, a_r, b_0, b_0}_{\mathrm{E}_k}$ and $\mathrm{E} = \underbrace{b_c}_{\mathrm{E}_1}, \underbrace{a_1, a_1, a_1, b_0, b_1}_{\mathrm{E}_2}, a_0, \cdots, b_0, \underbrace{a_1, a_0, a_r}_{\mathrm{E}_k}$. In the former, all substrings including E_1 and E_k are of the form a^+b^+. In the latter, E_1 is of the form a^*b^+ and E_k is of the form a^+b^*.

We now describe the algorithm to mark literals in each substring E_i as (good/bad) edit literals.

Algorithm MarkEdits

1. If E_i has the form $a^*a_pb_qb^*$ (where $p, q \in \{0,1\}$), call the last a and the first b literal as pivots and proceed as follows:
   (a) if $p = q$, mark every literal in the E_i other than the pivots as a bad edit literal.
   (b) if $p = 1, q = 0$, mark every literal in the E_i other than the $a-$pivot as a bad edit literal. In addition, mark the $a-$pivot as a good edit literal.
   (c) if $p = 0, q = 1$: If E_i is of the form $a^*a_1a^*a_0b_1b^*$, make the a literal subscripted by 1 as the pivot (instead of the original $a-$pivot) and mark all literals other than the pivots as bad edit literals. (There may be many different a_1 literals. Which specific one we chose as the pivot is immaterial.)
   (d) if $p = 0, q = 1$: If E_i is not of the form $a^*a_1a^*a_0b_1b^*$ (i.e., E_i is of the form $a_0^*a_0b_1b^*$), mark every literal in the E_i other than the $a-$pivot as a bad edit literal. In addition, mark the $a-$pivot as a good edit literal.
2. If E_i has the form a^+ mark all but one of the a literals as bad.
3. If E_i has the form b^+ then the first b must be b_c. Mark all but the b_c literal as bad.

We use the following lemmas, the proofs of which can be found in the full version [4].

LEMMA 5. *$\#edit \leq 2 \times \#bad$.*

LEMMA 6. *$\#bad \leq 2 \times \#costly$.*

PROOF. To prove this lemma, we will categorize our bad edit literals into bad_{b_0}, bad_{b_1}, and bad_a disjoint sets of literals (we mostly will not distinguish between the different kinds of bad_a literals.) To show that $\#bad \leq 2 \times \#costly$, we need to show that $bad_{b_0} + bad_{b_1} + bad_a \leq 2 \times \#costly$. We will prove this in two steps. First we will show that $\#bad_{b_1} + \#bad_a \leq \#costly$ (Lemma 7). Next we will show that $\#bad_{b_0} \leq \#bad_{b_1} + \#bad_a$ (Lemma 8). □

LEMMA 7. $\#bad_{b_1} + \#bad_a \leq \#costly$.

LEMMA 8. $\#bad_{b_0} \leq \#bad_{b_1} + \#bad_a$.

Theorem 3 states if E has at most L costly literals, then the edit distance between E and E′ is at most 4L. We will use the contra-positive to this theorem which states that Eve cannot create an E that has just L costly literals such that the edit distance between E and E′ is > 4L.

As we mentioned earlier, the process of converting E to E′ using just edit operations is isomorphic to the process of converting $\alpha(E)$ and $\beta(E)$. Therefore the edit distance between E and E′ is precisely the edit distance between $\alpha(E)$ and $\beta(E)$, which are nothing but the messages sent by Alice call it (m_A)and received by Bob(m_B) respectively.

We use this and the fact that the number costly literals correspond exactly to the number of fresh random challenges that Eve responded to on her own to get the following corollary to Theorem 3.

COROLLARY 2. *Let Alice and Bob execute protocol Auth in the presence of an active adversary Eve. Let m_A denote the message sent by Alice and let m_B denote the message received by Bob. Let the edit distance between m_A and m_B be at least 4L. Then Eve must have responded to at least L fresh random challenges on her own.*

5.3 Relating the number of fresh random challenge responses to the probability of Eve's success

So far we have shown that the edit distance between the message authenticated by Alice and received by Bob gives us a lower bound on the number of fresh random challenges (or extractor seeds) that Eve needs to respond to (with extractor outputs) on her own. In this section, our goal will be to get an upper bound on the probability with which she can succeed in responding to all of those random challenges.

It follows from Lemma 3 that the output of the extractor looks unpredictable to an adversary who has access to some information about the secret W (as long as the seed is a fresh random seed chosen independently of E). This lemma was used in [12] to bound the probability with which Eve succeeds in responding to a *single* fresh random challenge on her own. In this section our goal will be to extend this argument to the case where Eve will have to respond to multiple random challenges. We would expect that if Eve succeeds in responding to a single random challenge with probability at most $2^{-(\lambda_r-1)}$ then the probability that Eve responds to μ fresh random challenges (chosen independently) would be at most $2^{-\mu(\lambda_r-1)}$. Unfortunately, for reasons explained after the proof of the next lemma, that's not quite the case, but we can get something close: we show that the probability that Eve responds to μ fresh random challenges on her own is $2^{-\mu(\lambda_r-1)} + 2^{-\kappa-1}$, if the average min-entropy of w at the last extraction is at least $t+\kappa+1$ (where, recall, t is the entropy needed for the extractor to work).

Consider a run of Protocol Auth where Eve receives (not necessarily at the same time and separated by other protocol message) μ random challenges $x_1, \cdots, x_\mu$, to which Eve needs to respond (with a guess for $\mathsf{Ext}(w, x_i)$ of length λ_r) on her own. Let $S_i = 1$ if Eve's response to the ith challenge is correct, and 0 otherwise. For simplicity of notation, assume that the protocol goes on even if $S_i = 0$ (in reality, Alice or Bob will abort). Let Tr_i denote all the information that Eve has about w just before she responds with $\mathsf{Ext}(w, x_i)$. We will assume that Tr_i includes $S_1, \ldots, S_{i-1}$, but not x_i. (Note that it follows from the authentication protocol that x_i is independent of Tr_i.)

We prove the following lemma (the proof can be found in the full version).

LEMMA 9. *Assume $\widetilde{\mathbf{H}}_\infty(w \mid \mathsf{Tr}_\mu) \geq \kappa + 1 + t$. Then, $\Pr[$Eve successfully responds to μ fresh random challenges$] \leq 2^{-\mu(\lambda_r-1)} + 2^{-\kappa-1}$ (where the probability is taken over the w and randomness of the challenges.)*

5.4 Putting it all together

In this section, we combine our theorems to give the proof of our main result (Theorem 2).

PROOF. In protocol $\mathsf{NewAuth}(w, m)$, Alice first converts the message m to a codeword $c = \mathsf{Edit}(\cdot)$. Next, Alice executes protocol $\mathsf{Auth}(w, c)$ and authenticates the bits of c to Bob. We have λ_m, the length of message m, to be $4(\kappa+1)$ and hence $\lambda_c = \frac{4(\kappa+1)}{\rho}$.

The correctness of the protocol follows from the correctness of $\mathsf{Auth}(w, c)$ and the distance property of the code $\mathsf{Edit}(\cdot)$.

We consider an adversary Eve that succeeds in the security game of the interactive authentication protocol. Now, in order to succeed in the security game, Eve must make Bob accept a message $m' \neq m$. We first note that if $m' \neq m$, then by the property of the edit distance code $\mathsf{Edit}(\cdot)$, $\mathsf{EditDis}(c', c) > e_A\lambda_c$, where $c = \mathsf{Edit}(m), c' = \mathsf{Edit}(m')$. So, now if Eve were to make Bob accept a message $m' \neq m$, she must make Bob accept a message $c' \neq c$ in $\mathsf{Auth}(w, c)$, where the edit distance between c' and c is greater than $e_A\lambda_c = \frac{4e_A(\kappa+1)}{\rho}$. Now, by Corollary 2, this means that Eve must respond to more than $\frac{e_A(\kappa+1)}{\rho}$ fresh random challenges. Next, by Lemma 9, the probability of Eve responding to $\frac{e_A(\kappa+1)}{\rho}$ fresh random challenges is at most $p = 2^{-\frac{e_A(\kappa+1)}{\rho}(\tau-1)} + 2^{-(\kappa+1)}$. Now, we have $\tau = \frac{\rho}{e_A} + 1$ and hence we get $p < 2^{-\kappa}$.

To calculate the entropy loss, first note that we authenticate a message c of length $\frac{4(\kappa+1)}{\rho}$. While authenticating a 0 bit, Eve gets to see 1 extractor response and while authenticating a 1 bit, Eve gets to see 2 extractor responses. Since the length of each extractor response is τ, we get that the entropy loss is at most $2 \times \frac{4(\kappa+1)}{\rho} \times \tau = \frac{8\tau(\kappa+1)}{\rho}$, which proves the theorem.

□

As mentioned before, the above authentication protocol can be used to construct a privacy amplification protocol. Since ρ, e_A and τ are constants, we obtain $\Theta(\kappa)$ entropy loss in all the protocols.

6. CONCLUSIONS

We have presented a protocol that allows two parties sharing a low entropy secret to extract a shared key of optimal length – if the shared secret has entropy m, then the length of the extracted key is $m - \Theta(\kappa)$ where κ is the security parameter. We obtain our result through a somewhat unexpected application of edit distance codes. While our protocol has optimal entropy loss, it has a round complexity of $\Theta(\kappa)$. On the other hand, Dodis and Wichs [7] showed nonconstructively that there exists a protocol with both optimal entropy loss and optimal round complexity (2 rounds). An interesting open problem would be to bring down the round complexity of a protocol with optimal entropy loss (such as ours) to 2 with a polynomial-time protocol.

7. ACKNOWLEDGMENTS

We thank Alexandr Andoni, Yevgeniy Dodis, and Madhu Sudan for helpful discussions. We also thank the anonymous reviewers of STOC 2010 for their detailed comments.

8. REFERENCES

[1] C. Bennett, G. Brassard, and J.-M. Robert. Privacy amplification by public discussion. *SIAM Journal on Computing*, 17(2):210–229, 1988.

[2] C. H. Bennett, G. Brassard, C. Crépeau, and U. M. Maurer. Generalized privacy amplification. *IEEE Transactions on Information Theory*, 41(6):1915–1923, 1995.

[3] X. Boyen, Y. Dodis, J. Katz, R. Ostrovsky, and A. Smith. Secure remote authentication using biometric data. In R. Cramer, editor, *Advances in Cryptology—EUROCRYPT 2005*, volume 3494 of *LNCS*, pages 147–163. Springer-Verlag, 2005.

[4] N. Chandran, B. Kanukurthi, R. Ostrovsky, and L. Reyzin. Privacy amplification with asymptotically optimal entropy loss. Cryptology ePrint Archive, 2010. http://eprint.iacr.org/2010/.

[5] Y. Dodis, J. Katz, L. Reyzin, and A. Smith. Robust fuzzy extractors and authenticated key agreement from close secrets. In C. Dwork, editor, *Advances in Cryptology—CRYPTO 2006*, volume 4117 of *LNCS*, pages 232–250. Springer-Verlag, 20–24 Aug. 2006.

[6] Y. Dodis, R. Ostrovsky, L. Reyzin, and A. Smith. Fuzzy extractors: How to generate strong keys from biometrics and other noisy data. *SIAM Journal on Computing*, 38(1):97–139, 2008. arXiv:cs/0602007.

[7] Y. Dodis and D. Wichs. Non-malleable extractors and symmetric key cryptography from weak secrets. In *Proceedings of the Forty-First Annual ACM Symposium on Theory of Computing*, pages 601–610, Bethesda, Maryland, 31 May–2 June 2009.

[8] V. Guruswami, C. Umans, and S. P. Vadhan. Unbalanced expanders and randomness extractors from Parvaresh-Vardy codes. In *IEEE Conference on Computational Complexity*, pages 96–108, 2007.

[9] Y. Ishai, E. Kushilevitz, R. Ostrovsky, and A. Sahai. Extracting correlations. In *50th Annual Symposium on Foundations of Computer Science*, Atlanta, Georgia, Oct. 2009. IEEE.

[10] B. Kanukurthi and L. Reyzin. An improved robust fuzzy extractor. In R. Ostrovsky, R. D. Prisco, and I. Visconti, editors, *Sixth Conference on Security and Cryptography in Networks SCN '08*, volume 5229 of *LNCS*, pages 206–223, Sept. 2008.

[11] B. Kanukurthi and L. Reyzin. Key agreement from close secrets over unsecured channels. Technical Report 2008/494, Cryptology ePrint archive, `http://eprint.iacr.org`, 2008.

[12] B. Kanukurthi and L. Reyzin. Key agreement from close secrets over unsecured channels. In A. Joux, editor, *Advances in Cryptology—EUROCRYPT 2009*, volume 5479 of *LNCS*. Springer, 2009.

[13] V. I. Levenshtein. Binary codes capable of correcting deletions, insertions and reversals. *Soviet Physics Doklady*, 10:707–710, Feb. 1966.

[14] U. Maurer. Information-theoretically secure secret-key agreement by NOT authenticated public discussion. In W. Fumy, editor, *Advances in Cryptology—EUROCRYPT 97*, volume 1233 of *LNCS*, pages 209–225. Springer-Verlag, 1997.

[15] U. Maurer and S. Wolf. Privacy amplification secure against active adversaries. In B. S. Kaliski, Jr., editor, *Advances in Cryptology—CRYPTO '97*, volume 1294 of *LNCS*, pages 307–321. Springer-Verlag, 1997.

[16] U. Maurer and S. Wolf. Secret-key agreement over unauthenticated public channels — Part III: Privacy amplification. *IEEE Trans. Info. Theory*, 49(4):839–851, 2003.

[17] N. Nisan and D. Zuckerman. Randomness is linear in space. *Journal of Computer and System Sciences*, 52(1):43–53, 1996.

[18] J. Radhakrishnan and A. Ta-Shma. Bounds for dispersers, extractors, and depth-two superconcentrators. *SIAM Journal on Computing*, 13(1):2–24, 2000.

[19] R. Renner and S. Wolf. Unconditional authenticity and privacy from an arbitrarily weak secret. In D. Boneh, editor, *Advances in Cryptology—CRYPTO 2003*, volume 2729 of *LNCS*, pages 78–95. Springer-Verlag, 2003.

[20] R. Renner and S. Wolf. The exact price for unconditionally secure asymmetric cryptography. In C. Cachin and J. Camenisch, editors, *Advances in Cryptology—EUROCRYPT 2004*, volume 3027 of *LNCS*, pages 109–125. Springer-Verlag, 2004.

[21] L. J. Schulman and D. Zuckerman. Asymptotically good codes correcting insertions, deletions, and transpositions. *IEEE Transactions on Information Theory*, 45(7):2552–2557, 1999.

[22] S. Wolf. Strong security against active attacks in information-theoretic secret-key agreement. In K. Ohta and D. Pei, editors, *Advances in Cryptology—ASIACRYPT '98*, volume 1514 of *LNCS*, pages 405–419. Springer-Verlag, 1998.

Erratum for: On Basing One-Way Functions on NP-Hardness

Adi Akavia
Weizmann Institute
Rehovot, Israel
adi.akavia@weizmann.ac.il

Oded Goldreich
Weizmann Institute
Rehovot, Israel
oded.goldreich@weizmann.ac.il

Shafi Goldwasser
MIT and Weizmann Institute
Camridge MA, USA
and Rehovot, Israel
shafi@csail.mit.edu

Dana Moshkovitz
Institute for Advanced Study
Princeton NJ, USA
dana.moshkovitz@gmail.com

ABSTRACT

This is an errata for our STOC'06 paper, "On Basing One-Way Functions on NP-Hardness".

There is a gap in the proof of our results regarding adaptive reductions, and we currently do not know whether Theorem 3 (as stated in Section 2) holds.

Available at: http://doi.acm.org/10.1145/1132516.1132614

Categories and Subject Descriptors

F.0 [**Theory of Computation**]: GENERAL

General Terms

Theory

DETAILS

We elaborate on the gap in our proof of Theorem 3 in our STOC 2006 paper "On Basing One-Way Functions on NP-Hardness".

Before detailing the gap, we note that the "warm-up" case discussed in the beginning of Section 2.1 (i.e., f having polynomially bounded preimage size) remains intact, and so all assertions made with respect to adaptive reductions are valid when applied to this special case. We also note that the said gap does not effect our analysis of non-adaptive reductions (presented in Section 2.2, Theorem 5).

The gap in our proof originates from the implicit assumption that the expected size of $T_i^{(k)} = f^{-1}(y_i^{(k)}) \cap h_{k,i,\ell_i^{(k)}}(0^{\ell_i^{(k)}})$ is $2^{\ell_i^{(k)}} \cdot |f^{-1}(y_i^{(k)})|$ (cf., also Eq (2)). This would have been true if $y_i^{(k)}$ is fixed independently of $h_{k,i,\ell_i^{(k)}}$ (or, in other words, if $h_{k,i,\ell_i^{(k)}}$ is uniformly distributed given $y_i^{(k)}$), and $y_i^{(k)}$ is indeed fixed if the prover did not cheat in prior rounds of copy k (i.e., $A_j^{(k)} = T_j^{(k)}$ for every $j < i$). However, if such a cheating occurs with respect to copy k, then the cheating prover may set $y_i^{(k)}$ (among a few possibilities) based on the value of all h's including $h_{k,i,\ell_i^{(k)}}$. (Specifically, the prover may choose to cheat in round i' of copy k if this allows it to select an answer that both leads the reduction to a wrong answer and allows $T_j^{(k)}$ to be larger than expected.) Consequently, for such k's $T_i^{(k)}$ may be larger than we expect, and this excess may be used to claim smaller sizes for additional k' (i.e., have $A_j^{(k')} \subset T_j^{(k')}$).

STOC'10, June 5–8, 2010, Cambridge, Massachusetts, USA.
ACM 978-1-4503-0050-6/10/06.

Author Index

www.ingramcontent.com/pod-product-compliance
Lightning Source LLC
LaVergne TN
LVHW080104011026
849160LV00013B/1025